GRAPHIC NOVELS
CORE COLLECTION

SECOND EDITION

CORE COLLECTION SERIES

FORMERLY
STANDARD CATALOG SERIES

SHAUNA GRIFFIN, GENERAL EDITOR

CHILDREN'S CORE COLLECTION
MIDDLE & JUNIOR HIGH CORE COLLECTION
SENIOR HIGH CORE COLLECTION
NONFICTION CORE COLLECTION
FICTION CORE COLLECTION
YOUNG ADULT FICTION CORE COLLECTION
GRAPHIC NOVELS CORE COLLECTION

GRAPHIC NOVELS
CORE COLLECTION

SECOND EDITION

EDITED BY

KENDAL SPIRES

H. W. Wilson
A Division of EBSCO Information Services
Ipswich, Massachusetts
2018
GREY HOUSE PUBLISHING

ISBN 978-1-68217-662-7

Abridged Dewey Decimal Classification and Relative Index, Edition 15 is © 2004-2012 OCLC Online Computer Library Center, Inc. Used with Permission. DDC, Dewey, Dewey Decimal Classification, and WebDewey are registered trademarks of OCLC.

Graphic Novels Core Collection, Second Edition, 2018, published by Grey House Publishing, Inc., Amenia, NY, under exclusive license from EBSCO Information Services, Inc.

**Publisher's Cataloging-In-Publication Data
(Prepared by The Donohue Group, Inc.)**

Names: Spires, Kendal, editor.
Title: Graphic novels core collection / edited by Kendal Spires.
Other Titles: Core collection series.
Description: Second edition. | Ipswich, Massachusetts : H. W. Wilson, a division of EBSCO Information Services ; Amenia, NY : Grey House Publishing, 2018. | Includes indexes.
Identifiers: ISBN 9781682176627 (hardcover)
Subjects: LCSH: Graphic novels--Bibliography. | Best books.
Classification: LCC PN6710 .G73 2018 | DDC 016.7415--dc23

PRINTED IN THE UNITED STATES OF AMERICA

CONTENTS

PREFACE

GRAPHIC NOVELS CORE COLLECTION is a selective list of fiction and nonfiction comics and graphic novels for all ages, together with professional aids for librarians and a selection of nonfiction prose materials about comics history and culture. This Core Collection is an abridgement of the database available via EBSCO*host* from EBSCO Information Services which has an additional two recommendation levels, Lexile® measures, book reviews, and expanded metadata, updated weekly. Contact your EBSCO sales rep for a free trial.

What's in this Edition?

This second edition includes nearly 2,500 book titles at the Most Highly Recommended and Core Collection recommendation levels. A star (★) at the start of an entry indicates that a book is a "most highly recommended" title. These titles constitute a shortlist of the essential books in a given category or on a given subject. There are often a number of recommended titles on a single subject, and the star designation helps a user who wants only one or two.

History

The Collection was created as an online database in 2007 at H. W. Wilson, with original curation and annotation by librarian Katharine Kan. The initial incarnation contained 1,000 recommended titles, with more added every month after the collection's launch. After EBSCO acquired H. W. Wilson in 2011, new advisors built out the database further.

Scope

All books listed are published in the United States, or published in Canada or the United Kingdom and distributed in the United States. Some out of print books are included under the consideration that, though they are no longer available for purchase, they should not be weeded by libraries which already own them.

The Core Collection excludes non-English-language materials, with the exception of bilingual materials. It does include English-language translations of international material, including Japanese manga, Korean manhwa, Franco-Belgian comics ("bandes dessinées"), and others.

Preparation

Books included in this edition were selected by experienced collection development librarians representing public, academic, and school libraries across the United States who also act as a committee of advisors on library policy and trends. The names of participating librarians and their affiliations are listed in the Acknowledgments. To offer feedback or suggest improvements for the next edition, please contact corecollections@ebsco.com.

Organization

Organization and indexing of the records was performed by Grey House Publishing. The Core Collection is organized into multiple parts: the List of Works and separate Author, Title, and Subject Indices.

List of Works. This is arranged in groupings according to grade level (PreK through Grade 5, Grades 6 though 8, Grades 9 through 12, Adult) and by main entry (usually writer/creator, sometimes title or editor) within each section.

Author, Title, and Subject Indices. Three separate indices represent the List of Works with entries for creators, titles, and subjects. Some responsible persons (illustrators, translators, editors, etc.) may not appear in the index of this edition.

ACKNOWLEDGMENTS

H. W. Wilson and EBSCO Information Services express special gratitude to the following librarians who both advised the company in editorial matters and assisted in the selection and weeding of titles for this Core Collection:

Advisory Board

Robin Brenner
Teen Librarian
Public Library of Brookline
Brookline, Massachusetts

Julie Corsaro
Library Consultant & Adjunct Professor of
    English, Children's Literature
College of William & Mary
Williamsburg, Virginia

Gail de Vos
Adjunct Associate Professor
University of Alberta
Edmonton, Alberta

Brian Flota
Humanities Librarian
James Madison University
Harrisonburg, VA

Francisca Goldsmith
Consulting Librarian
Worcester, Massachusetts

Steven Jablonski
Collection Development Librarian
Skokie Public Library
Skokie, IL

John Meier
Science Librarian
Penn State University
University Park, PA

Marcela Peres
Library Director
Lewiston Public Library
Lewiston, Maine

James Stubbs
Digital Services Librarian
Florence County Library System
Florence, SC

Rebecca Vargha
Head of Information and Library Science
    Library
University of North Carolina
Chapel Hill, NC

Linda Ward-Callaghan
Youth Services Manager
Joliet Public Library
Joliet, IL

Neal Wyatt
Columnist and Contributing Editor,
    Library Journal
Richmond, VA

The editors also wish to thank EBSCO/NoveList librarians Kaitlin Conner and Suzanne Temple for their help in weeding this collection.

DIRECTIONS FOR USE OF THE
CORE COLLECTION

USES OF THE COLLECTION

GRAPHIC NOVELS CORE COLLECTION is designed to serve a number of purposes:

As an aid in purchasing. The Core Collection is designed to assist in the selection and ordering of titles. Annotations are provided for each title along with information concerning the publisher, ISBN, price, and availability. In evaluating the suitability of a work each library will want to consider the special character of the patron base it serves.

As an aid to the readers' advisor. The work of the reader's advisor is furthered by the information about sequels and companion volumes and the descriptive and critical annotations in the List of Works, and by the subject access in the Index.

As an aid in verification of information. For this purpose full bibliographical data are provided in the List of Works. Entries also include recommended subject headings based upon *Sears List of Subject Headings* and a suggested classification derived from the *Abridged Dewey Decimal Classification and Relative Index*. Notes describe editions available, awards, publication history, and other titles in the series. For the most up-to-date metadata please consult the EBSCO*host* Graphic Novels Core Collection database.

As an aid in curriculum support and following Common Core standards. The subject indexing, grade levels, and annotations are helpful in identifying materials appropriate for lesson planning and classroom use and for following Common Core curricula.

As an aid in collection maintenance. Information about titles available on a subject facilitates decisions to rebind, replace, or discard items. If a book has been demoted to Supplementary or Archival recommendation level (usually because it is no longer in print but sometimes for other reasons), and therefore no longer appears in the print abridgement of the database, that demotion is not intended as a sign that the book is no longer valuable or that it should necessarily be weeded from library collections.

As an instructional aid. The Core Collection is useful in courses that deal with graphic novels & comics as literature and with graphic novel collection development.

ORGANIZATION

The Core Collection consists of two parts: a List of Works, and Author, Title, and Subject indices.

Part 1. List of Works

The List of Works is arranged by four age groups: Pre-Kindergarten to Grade 5, Grades 6 through 8, Grades 9 through 12, and Adult. Titles repeat across sections according to the grade levels listed in their bibliographic data. The information supplied for each book includes bibliographic description, suggested subject headings, an annotation, and frequently an evaluation from a notable source. Librarians should note that many graphic works are not marketed by age as strictly as prose works, and thus, a book's presence in a juvenile age group is not necessarily indicative of a lack of appeal to adults, especially with regard to the High School category.

Within groups, works are arranged alphabetically under main entry, usually the writer and/or creator, and sometimes the title or editor in the case of anthologies with multiple authors. For space considerations, many multi-volume series are condensed into a single entry, with full metadata for the initial volume and a note listing any subsequent volumes.

It should be noted that some titles can be listed under more than one creator. If a particular title is not found where it might be expected, the indexes should be consulted to determine if it is classified elsewhere. Librarians looking for all titles in the collection about a particular character or team (e.g. Superman or the Fantastic Four) are encouraged to consult the index for that particular character's subject heading.

Each listing consists of a full bibliographical description. Prices, which are always subject to change, have been obtained from the publisher, when available, and are as current as possible. Entries include recommended subject headings derived from the *Sears List of Subject Headings*, a suggested classification number from the *Abridged Dewey Decimal Classification and Relative Index*, a brief description of the contents, and, whenever possible, an evaluation from a quoted source. The following is an example of a typical entry and a description of its components:

Keatinge, Joe

    Shutter; Volume 1: Wanderlost. Joe Keatinge; illustrated by Leila Del Duca, Owen Gieni, Ed Brisson. Image Comics 2014 136 p. Color illustration

Grades: 11 12 Adult   **Fic; 741.5**

    1. Explorers ; 2. Family secrets — Fiction

    1632151456; 9781632151452, $9.99

    In this graphic novel by Joe Keatinge, illustrated by Leila Del Duca, Owen Gieni, and Ed Brisson, "Kate Kristopher, once the most famous explorer of an Earth far more fantastic than the one we know, is forced to return to the adventurous life she left behind when a family secret threatens to destroy everything she spent her life protecting." (Publisher's note)

    "Keatinge and Del Duca have created a contemporary world that teems with casual miracles and feels all the more real and lived in for it. Crammed with the elements of children's storybooks, the art offers soft lines and a panoply of almost-recognizable storybook figures that honor those hallowed childhood recollections." Booklist

    Originally published in single magazine form as Shutter #1-6

        Volume 1 of 5

The names of the writer and the artists are given in conformity with *Anglo-American Cataloguing Rules*, 2nd edition, 2002 revision. The title of the book is *Shutter*, the first volume. The book was published by Image Comics in 2014.

The book has 136 pages and colored illustrations. It sells for $9.99. (Prices given were current when the Collection went to press.) The book is recommended for adults and older teens.

At the end of the last line of type in the body entry is **Fic; 741.5** in bold face type. These are classification numbers derived from the fifteenth edition of the *Abridged Dewey Decimal Classification*. Most of the titles in the collection are listed under 741.5, the Dewey number for comic books and graphic novels, and many have additional numbers listed as well: "Fic" for fiction, and additional number classifications for nonfiction (e.g. graphic biographies or memoirs).

The numbered terms "1. Explorers ; 2. Family secrets — Fiction" are recommended subject headings for this book based on *Sears List of Subject Headings*.

The ISBN (International Standard Book Number) is included to facilitate ordering. The Library of Congress control number is provided when available.

Following are four notes supplying additional information about the book. The first is a description of the book's content, in this case, a description from the publisher. The second is a critical note from *Booklist*. Such annotations are useful in evaluating books for selection and in determining which of several books on the same subject is best suited for the individual reader. The third note describes the form in which the book was originally published (in this case, in single comic book issues), and the final notes that it is the first of five volumes. Notes are also made to describe sequels and companion volumes, editions available, and awards.

Part 2. Author, Title, and Subject Indices

The Index is three separate alphabetical lists of all the books entered in the Core Collection. Each book is entered under author, title, and subject. The page number is the key to the location of the main entry for the book in the List of Works.

The following are examples of Index entries for the book cited above:

Author   Keatinge, Joe, 608, 980

Title   Shutter; Volume 1: Wanderlost, 608, 980

Subject   **EXPLORERS**
                      Keatinge, Joe. Shutter; Volume 1: Wanderlost, 608, 980

Standards Used

Anglo-American Cataloguing Rules, 2nd ed., 2002 revision, 2005 update. Chicago: American Library Association, 2005.

Dewey, Melvil. *Abridged Dewey Decimal Classification and Relative Index*. 15th ed. Edited by Joan S. Mitchell, et al. Dublin, Ohio: OCLC, 2012.

Bristow, Barbara A. and Kendal Spires, eds. *Sears List of Subject Headings*. 22nd ed. Ipswich, MA: The H. W. Wilson Company, 2018.

OUTLINE OF CLASSIFICATION

Reproduced below is the Second Summary of the Dewey Decimal Classification.* Please note, however, that the inclusion of this outline is not to be considered a substitute for consulting the Dewey Decimal Classification itself.

000 Computer science, knowledge & systems
010 Bibliographies
020 Library & information sciences
030 Encyclopedias & books of facts
040 [Unassigned]
050 Magazines, journals & serials
060 Associations, organizations & museums
070 News media, journalism & publishing
080 Quotations
090 Manuscripts & rare books

100 Philosophy
110 Metaphysics
120 Epistemology
130 Parapsychology & occultism
140 Philosophical schools of thought
150 Psychology
160 Logic
170 Ethics
180 Ancient, medieval & eastern philosophy
190 Modern western philosophy

200 Religion
210 Philosophy & theory of religion
220 The Bible
230 Christianity & Christian theology
240 Christian practice & observance
250 Christian pastoral practice & religious orders
260 Christian organization, social work & worship
270 History of Christianity
280 Christian denominations
290 Other religions

300 Social sciences, sociology & anthropology
310 Statistics
320 Political science
330 Economics
340 Law
350 Public administration & military science
360 Social problems & social services
370 Education
380 Commerce, communications & transportation
390 Customs, etiquette & folklore

400 Language
410 Linguistics
420 English & Old English languages
430 German & related languages
440 French & related languages
450 Italian, Romanian & related languages
460 Spanish & Portuguese languages
470 Latin & Italic languages
480 Classical & modern Greek languages
490 Other languages

500 Science
510 Mathematics
520 Astronomy
530 Physics
540 Chemistry
550 Earth sciences & geology
560 Fossils & prehistoric life
570 Life sciences; biology
580 Plants (Botany)
590 Animals (Zoology)

600 Technology
610 Medicine & health
620 Engineering
630 Agriculture
640 Home & family management
650 Management & public relations
660 Chemical engineering
670 Manufacturing
680 Manufacture for specific uses
690 Building & construction

700 Arts
710 Landscaping & area planning
720 Architecture
730 Sculpture, ceramics & metalwork
740 Drawing & decorative arts
750 Painting
760 Graphic arts
770 Photography & computer art
780 Music
790 Sports, games & entertainment

800 Literature, rhetoric & criticism
810 American literature in English
820 English & Old English literatures
830 German & related literatures
840 French & related literatures
850 Italian, Romanian & related literatures
860 Spanish & Portuguese literatures
870 Latin & Italian literatures
880 Classical & modern Greek literatures
890 Other literatures

900 History
910 Geography & travel
920 Biography & genealogy
930 History of ancient world (to ca. 499)
940 History of Europe
950 History of Asia
960 History of Africa
970 History of North America
980 History of South America
990 History of other areas

* Reproduced from Edition 15 of the Abridged Dewey Decimal Classification and Relative Index, published in 2012, by permission of OCLC Online Computer Library Center, Inc., owner of copyright.

GRAPHIC NOVELS CORE COLLECTION

SECOND EDITION

CHILDREN: PRE K-5

Abadzis, Nick
★ **Laika**. First Second Books 2007 205p. Illustration
Grades: 5 6 7 8 9 10 11 12 Adult   **741.5; Fic**
1. Graphic novels; 2. Soviet Union — History — 1953-1991 — Graphic novels; 3. Space flight — Graphic novels
1-59643-101-6; 978-1-59643-101-0
LC 2006-51907
Laika was the abandoned puppy destined to become Earth's first space traveler. This is her journey. Along with Laika, there is Korolev, once a political prisoner and now a driven engineer at the top of the Soviet space program, and Yelena, the lab technician responsible for Laika's health and life. The book depicts the dedication and struggles of the scientists and technicians who worked in the Soviet space program, based on research Abadzis did before writing this book. The book includes a bibliography of books and websites.
"Abadzis's tear-inducing and solidly researched graphic novel treatment of Laika's surpassingly tragic story is a standout." Publ Wkly

Abnett, Dan
Abraham Lincoln and the Civil War. Rosen Publishing Group 2007 24p. Illustration
Grades: 1 2 3 4 5
741.5; 973.7; 92
1. Biographical graphic novels; 2. Graphic novels; 3. Lincoln, Abraham, 1809-1865; 4. Lincoln, Abraham, 1809-1865 — graphic novels; 5. United States — History — 1861-1865, Civil War — Graphic novels; 6. Lincoln, Abraham, 1809-1865
978-1-4042-3392-8, $22.50
LC 2005037160
Was honest Abe, the man who ended slavery in the U.S., America's first superhero? Beginning readers can enjoy

Courtesy of Rosen Publishing

learning about Lincoln's life and deeds and the Civil War in this simplified comic format book, which also includes a glossary and a timeline of his life..
Part of the Jr. Graphic Biographies series.

Christopher Columbus and the Voyage of 1492. Rosen Publishing Group 2007 24p. Illustration
Grades: 1 2 3 4 5
741.5; 970.01; 92
1. Biographical graphic novels; 2. Graphic novels; 3. Columbus, Christopher, 1451-1506; 4. America — Exploration
978-1-4042-3390-4, $22.50
LC 2005037161
Readers journey along with Columbus on his history-making 1492 voyage to find a water route to Asia in this simplified graphic

Courtesy of Rosen Publishing

novel for beginning readers. The book includes a glossary and a timeline of his life.
Part of the Jr. Graphic Biographies series.

George Washington and the American Revolution. Rosen Publishing Group 2007 24p. Illustration
Grades: 1 2 3 4 5
741.5; 973.4; 92
1. Biographical graphic novels; 2. Graphic novels; 3. Washington, George, 1732-1799; 4. United States — History — 1775-1783, Revolution — Graphic novels
978-1-4042-3395-9, $22.50
LC 2005037163
If the patriots hadn't won the war, Washington would have been one of the greatest traitors in history. Instead he led the rebels to victory and a great democracy was born. The simplified graphic novel introduces the story to beginning readers and includes a glossary and a timeline of his life.
Part of the Jr. Graphic Biographies series.

Courtesy of Rosen Publishing

Harriet Tubman and the Underground Railroad. Rosen Publishing Group 2007 24p. Illustration
Grades: 1 2 3 4 5
741.5; 973.7; 92
1. Biographical graphic novels; 2. Graphic novels; 3. Slavery — United States — Graphic novels; 4. Underground Railroad — Graphic novels; 5. Tubman, Harriet, 1820?-1913
978-1-4042-3393-5, $22.50
LC 2005037162
Beginning readers can follow Tubman as she risks everything to escape to freedom, and then returns again and again to lead other Africans out of enslavement. This simplified graphic novel includes a glossary and timeline of her life.
Part of the Jr. Graphic Biographies series.

Courtesy of Rosen Publishing

Hernan Cortes and the Fall of the Aztec Empire. Rosen Publishing Group 2007 24p. Illustration
Grades: 1 2 3 4 5
741.5; 972; 92
1. Biographical graphic novels; 2. Graphic novels; 3. Cortes, Hernan, 1485-1547; 4. Mexico — History — Conquest, 1519-1540
978-1-4042-3391-1, $22.50
LC 2006002706

Courtesy of Rosen Publishing

The ruthless explorer Cortes devastated an entire people in his search for fame and gold for himself and for his country. This simplified graphic novel retelling introduces the story for beginning readers, and includes a glossary and a time line.

Part of the Jr. Graphic Biographies series.

Abouet, Marguerite
Akissi: feline invasion. by Marguerite Abouet; illustrated by Mathiew Sapin. Flying Eye Books 2013 48 p. Illustration
Grades: 2 3 4 5   **741.5; Fic**
1. Conduct of life; 2. Siblings
190926301X; 9781909263017, $14.95

This book, by Marguerite Abouet, presents "African vignettes aimed at a younger audience. All seven episodes feature young Akissi and her brother Fofana or her friends getting into trouble for less-than-exemplary...behavior. In 'Good Mums,'...she borrows a neighbor's baby and tenderly feeds it a stew concocted from discarded scraps found in the market. 'Home Cinema' has her playing lookout while Fofana sells spots in front of the television set to neighborhood children." (Kirkus Reviews)

Aguirre, Jorge
★ **Giants** beware!. written by Jorge Aguirre; illustrated by Rafael Rosado. First Second 2012 202 p.
Grades: 3 4 5   **741.5/973**
1. Fairy tales; 2. Graphic novels; 3. Humorous graphic novels; 4. Fairy tales — Graphic novels; 5. Adventure graphic novels
1596435828; 9781596435827
                                                                LC 2011030471
In this children's graphic novel, "spunky Claudette is set on becoming a monster slayer like her father.... When she hears the story of a giant on the loose, she is determined to leave her home — accompanied by her cowardly brother, Gaston, and best friend Marie — in order to set things right.... When Claudette discovers that not all stories are as they seem, she and her friends must fool the adults who have come to bring them home to protect an innocent monster." (Publishers Weekly)

Other titles in this series are: Dragons beware! (2015); Monsters beware! (2018)

Monsters beware!. written by Jorge Aguirre; art by Rafael Rosado; story by Jorge Aguirre & Rafael Rosado; color by John Novak. First Second 2018 176 p. Color; Illustration (The chronicles of Claudette)
Grades: 3 4 5   **741.5; Fic**
1. Wizards; 2. Witchcraft; 3. Monsters
9781626721807, $14.99
                                                                LC 2017941159
This graphic novel for children in the Chronicles of Claudette series, by Jorge Aguirre, "begins when Claudette's town hosts the annual Warrior Games.... Claudette manages to gets herself, Marie, and Gaston chosen as her town's representatives. But none of Claudette's past battles has prepared her for this.... [T]hey must stop the vicious Sea Queen and her evil children from using the Warrior Games to free the dark Wizard Grombach and conquer the world!" (Publisher's note)

"Previous installments put a higher premium on subverting social stereotypes, but the story never loses sight of the fact that friendship trumps winning, intelligence and diplomacy have their place in victory, and that it's not just shape but intention that makes a monster." Booklist

Allan, Von
Stargazer, volume one. Von Allan Studio 2010 115p. Illustration
Grades: 4 5 6 7 8 9   **741.5; Fic**
1. Adventure graphic novels; 2. Friendship — Graphic novels; 3. Graphic novels; 4. Science fiction graphic novels

Courtesy of Von Allan Studio

978-0-9781237-2-7, $14.95

Marni's grandmother has just died, and she left a strange device that the two of them played with whenever Marni had visited. No one knows how Marni's grandmother got it, and it has never done anything. Her best friends, Elora and Sophie, come over for a last backyard campout before the weather turns cold, and when they each put a hand on the device, an extremely bright light nearly blinds them. After things seem to go back to normal, the girls go outside to find Marni's house gone, the device vanished, and none of the stars look familiar. In the morning, they pack up the little food they had brought for their campout, Elora's telescope, and Sophie's pennywhistle, and hike towards a tower Elora had spotted. They know they're in a totally strange place when they come upon a statue of nonhuman, alien creatures. As they continue, they come upon a strange house, where they find food, and then a mute, boy-sized robot. Even though the three friends bicker with each other, they work together to find a way home. Allan includes extensive notes on his writing process, and an excerpt from his script. The cover art shows one interesting looking character who doesn't appear in this volume. While their age isn't specified, the girls look to be tweens, with the slightly awkward, coltish bodies and movements of pre-adolescents. The strongest language used is one instance of the word "damn."

Volume 1 of 2

Allen, Chris
William Shakespeare's Othello. adapted by Vincent Goodwin; illustrated by Chris Allen.. ABDO/Magic Wagon 2008 48p. Illustration
Grades: 5 6 7 8 9 10   **822.3; 741.5**
1. Authors; 2. Dramatists; 3. Graphic novels; 4. Poets; 5. Shakespeare, William, 1564-1616 — Adaptations
978-1-60270-192-2, $28.50
                                                                LC 2008-10743
Othello the Moor is a successful general, married to the beautiful Desdemona. Life should be good, but he's incredibly jealous of anyone who looks at his wife. Iago wants Othello's position and decides that he should destroy Othello by fabricating an affair between Desdemona and Cassio. This graphic novel adaptation keeps some of the original dialog from Shakespeare's play while paring down the action to simplify it for readers who would struggle with the original. The book includes a short biography of Shakespeare, a summary of the plot, a glossary, and a sampling of famous lines and phrases.

Part of the Graphic Shakespeare series

Alley, Zoe B.
★ **There's** a wolf at the door. pictures by R. W. Alley. Roaring Brook Press 2008 40p. Illustration
Grades: K 1 2 3   **398.2; 741.5; Fic**
1. Graphic novels; 2. Humorous graphic novels; 3. Wolves — Folklore — Graphic novels
978-1-59643-275-8, $19.95; 1-59643-275-6
                                                                LC 2007-44025
As his plans are spoiled over and over again, the wolf keeps trying to find his dinner, in this retelling of five well-known stories and fables.

This is a "hilarious romp.... Illustrated with softly colored pen-and-ink drawings, these five stories meld seamlessly together. The text is full of puns, alliteration, and occasional rhymes." SLJ

A Neal Porter book

Alvarez, Lorena

★ **Nightlights**. Lorena Alvarez. Nobrow Press 2017 56 p. Color; Illustration

Grades: 4 5 6 7   **741.5**

1. Girls — Graphic novels; 2. Female friendship — Graphic novels

1910620130; 9781910620137, $18.95

In this graphic novel, written and illustrated by Lorena Alvarez, "every night, tiny stars appear out of the darkness in little Sandy's bedroom. She catches them and creates wonderful creatures to play with until she falls asleep, and in the morning brings them back to life in the whimsical drawings that cover her room." (Publisher's note)

"Alvarez's haunting artwork features coiling plumes of lush colors and Miyazaki-esque beasts that create a sense of brooding melancholy. It's a deliciously hair-raising story that thoughtfully explores themes of isolation, creativity, and how social pressures can encroach on individuality." Pub Wkly

Anderson, Kevin J.

Grumpy old monsters. Kevin J. Anderson, Rebecca Moesta; [art by] Guillermo Mendoza, Paco Cavero. IDW Publishing 2004 96p. Illustration

Grades: 4 5 6 7 8 9   **741.5; Fic**

1. Graphic novels; 2. Humorous graphic novels; 3. Monsters — Graphic novels

1-932382-35-6, $13.99

The old monsters Frankenstein's Monster, Dracula, the Mummy, and the Werewolf, have all retired and moved to the old monsters' home, where Nurse Wrentch terrorizes them and only little Tiffany Frankenstein, granddaughter of old Dr. F., comes to visit. But this time she comes with terrible news the Van Helsing Corporation is about to take possession of Castle Frankenstein, tear it down, and build luxury condominiums. The monsters decide they must come out of retirement and help Tiffany stop the horror if they can escape Nurse Wrentch!

Annable, Graham

Peter & Ernesto: a tale of two sloths. Graham Annable. First Second 2018 128 p. Color; Illustration

Grades: 1 2 3 4   **741.5; Fic**

1. Friendship; 2. Sloths

9781626725614, $17.99

                                                LC 2017941165

"Peter and Ernesto are sloths. Peter and Ernesto are friends.... Peter loves their tree and never wants to leave, while Ernesto loves the sky and wants to see it from every place on Earth. When Ernesto leaves to have a grand adventure, Peter stays behind and frets. The two friends grow even closer in separation, as Peter the homebody expands his horizons and Ernesto the wanderer learns the value of home." (Publisher's note)

"Working in multipanel sequences and individual frames, Annable bounces between the ebullient Ernesto and the worrywart Peter, rendering each with equal affection." Pub Wkly

Aoi, Haruka

A **Little** Snow Fairy Sugar, Volume 1. Haruka Aoi, translated by Kaoru Bertrand. ADV Manga 2006 168p. Illustration

Grades: 3 4 5 6 7 8   **741.5; Fic**

1. Fairies — Graphic novels; 2. Graphic novels; 3. Kodomo manga; 4. Manga; 5. Shonen manga

1-4139-0333-9, $9.99

Eleven-year-old Saga Bergstrom lives with her grandmother and maintains a very tight, controlled schedule; in addition to school, she works part-time in a coffee shop, and every afternoon at 4:00, she goes to the music store to play her dead mother's piano. Then, one day her life becomes chaotic when she encounters Sugar, an apprentice season fairy.

Saga is the only human who can see Sugar, which can be very embarrassing when she screams in frustration at Sugar. Sugar and her fellow apprentice season fairies, Salt and Pepper, need to find twinkles to make their magic seeds grow so they can become full season fairies. The problem is, no one knows what twinkles are. In the meantime, Sugar and Saga need to find a way to get along with each other. The story and the art are very sweet and cute.

Volume 1 of 3

Atangan, Patrick

Songs of our ancestors: The yellow jar: two tales from Japanese tradition. NBM 2003 48p. Illustration (Songs of our ancestors)

Grades: 5 6 7 8 9 10 11 12   **741.5**

1. Folklore — Japan — Graphic novels; 2. Graphic novels

1-56163-331-3, $12.92

                                                LC 2002-32132

"To render two magical Japanese legends, one about a fisherman who discovers a fair maiden in a big pot, the other about a monk whose fastidiously kept garden is invaded by two chrysanthemums, Atangan charmingly adopts the sharp outlines, boldly juxtaposed color fields, and striking compositions of eighteenth-century Japanese woodblock prints." Booklist

Other titles in this series are: Silk tapestry and other Chinese folktales (2004); Tree of love (2005)

Aureliani, Franco

Superman Family Adventures; Volume 1. by Art Baltazar and Franco Aureliani, illustrated by Art Baltazar. DC Comics 2013 128 p. Color; Illustration (Superman Family Adventures)

Grades: 1 2 3   **741.5; Fic**

1. Graphic novels; 2. Superheroes — Comic books, strips, etc.; 3. Superman (Fictitious character) — Comic books, strips, etc.; 4. Superhero graphic novels

140124050X; 9781401240509, $12.99

                                                LC 2013009138

This graphic novel, by Art Baltazar and Franco, features superheroes such as "Superman, Superboy, Supergirl [and] Krypto the Superdog. The entire Superman family is re-imagined here in this energetic all-ages graphic novel. Read on as the heroes of Metropolis fight foes such as Bizarro, Metallo, Lex Luthor and...giant monkeys." (Publisher's note)

"Adult readers will get a kick out of the clever homage to their favorite superhero, and kids will be powerless to resist the silly playfulness; colorful animated characters; and easy-to-follow, superpower-packed stories." Booklist

Followed by: Volume 2 (2014); Originally published in single magazine form in Superman Family Adventures #1-6.

Azuma, Kiyohiko

Yotsuba&!. by Kiyohiko Azuma. Yen Press 2009 224 p. Illustration

Grades: 5 6 7 8   **741.5; Fic**

1. Shonen manga; 2. Moving — Graphic novels; 3. Manga

0316073091; 9780316073875, $13

In this book, by Kiyohiko Azuma, "Yotsuba is the charming new girl in town.... In seven stories, the green-haired four-year-old discovers air conditioners, doorbells, cicadas, swings and more, and does it all with the energy of a small hurricane. Her excitement is contagious and infects her handsome young adoptive father as well as the gaggle of pretty girls next door, all of whom get tangled up in her adventures as they try to keep up with her." (Publisher's note)

"Yotsuba is the charming new girl in town in this all-ages shojo manga by the author of the popular Azumanga Daioh series. In seven stories, the green-haired four-year-old discovers air conditioners, doorbells, cicadas, swings and more, and does it all with the energy of a small hurricane." Pub Wkly

Originally published in the U.S. by ADV; Volume 1 of an ongoing series

Azuma, Naomi

Suihelibe!, vol. 1. Naomi Azuma; translated by Sheldon Drzka. DC Comics/CMX 2008 160p. Illustration

Grades: 3 4 5 6 7 8   **741.5; Fic**

1. Graphic novels; 2. Humorous graphic novels; 3. Manga; 4. Science fiction graphic novels; 5. Shonen manga

978-1-4012-1900-0, $9.99

On the cover of the manga, several chemistry elements are listed: hydrogen, helium, lithium, and belium (which probably should be beryllium). First year junior high school student Tetsu just wants to join the biology club at school, when a small flying saucer crashes into the classroom. Lan, the alien pilot who looks like a cute girl, enlists Tetsu's help to recover some escaped life forms from her planet. In order for them to accomplish this task, they need to keep the biology club going, but the student council president wants to shut down the club, so they have three months to round up three more members, even as they hunt Noids (the life forms). There's a lot of shouting and slapstick humor.

Volume 1 of 2

Bailey, Chris

Major Damage. Sky Dog Press 2004 un Illustration

Grades: 3 4 5 6 7 8   **741.5; Fic**

1. Graphic novels; 2. Humorous graphic novels; 3. Superhero graphic novels

0-9721831-4-0, $14.95

Before The Incredibles, there was Major Damage: the tale of a little boy who is transformed into his favorite super hero, protecting the world from mutants, monsters, and alien scum. Eight-year-old Melvin was trick or treating on Halloween night, dressed as his favorite superhero, Major Damage, when he was abducted by the Mucus Men; the harmless scientists mistook Melvin for the real hero, assumed he'd had an accident, and "restored" his powers and returned him to Earth. Meanwhile, Melvin's mother thinks her son has disappeared.

Baker, Kyle

Through the looking-glass. by Lewis Carroll; adapted by Kyle Baker. Papercutz 2008 un Illustration (Classics illustrated)

Grades: 3 4 5 6 7 8 9

741.5; Fic

1. Fantasy graphic novels; 2. Graphic novels; 3. Carroll, Lewis, 1832-1898 — Adaptations

978-1-59707-115-4, $9.95;
1-59707-115-3

This is Carroll's sequel to Alice's Adventures in Wonderland. This time, Alice climbs through the looking-glass in her house and finds herself in a land with talking flowers and insects, Tweedledee and Tweedledum (who recite "The Walrus and the Carpenter"), the White Queen who needs help pinning her shawl straight, Humpty Dumpty, the Red Queen, and more. The Eisner Award-winning Baker uses a different style from his usual cartoony look here, more reminiscent of Tenniel's classic illustrations of Carroll's books.

Courtesy of NBM Publishing

Baldwin, Christopher

Little Dee and the penguin. by Christopher Baldwin. Dial Books for Young Readers 2016 128 p. Color; Illustration

Grades: 3 4 5 6   **741.5**

1. Animals — Fiction; 2. Graphic novels; 3. Human-animal relationships — Fiction; 4. Humorous stories; 5. Friendship — Graphic novels; 6. Animals — Graphic novels

9781101994290, $17.99; 1101994290; 9780803741089, $10.99

LC 2015010378

In this graphic novel, by Christopher Baldwin, "when Little Dee meets a motley crew of animals deep in the forest, she knows she's found the perfect set of new friends. Between the bossy vulture, the slightly dim dog, the nurturing bear, and the happy-go-lucky penguin,...they're a family. And they're on the run. A pair of hungry polar bears are after the penguin, and the rest of the team are determined to protect her." (Publisher's note)

"Baldwin's full-color illustrations appeal to all of the senses and keep the story moving — through travel by plane, raft, boat, and on foot, ahead of a pair of hungry polar bears all the way. A must-read for all would-be adventurers." Kirkus

Baltazar, Art

Aw yeah comics and...action!; Volume 1. by Art Baltaza & Franco Aureliani. Dark Horse Books 2014 1:00 PM Color; Illustration

Grades: 3 4 5 6   **741.5**

1. Graphic novels; 2. Superheroes; 3. Cats; 4. Insects

1616555580; 9781616555580, $12.99

LC 2014430639

This graphic novel, by Art Baltaza & Franco, is the "comic you've heard so much about! Action Cat! Adventure Bug! And their adventures in the Aw Yeah Comics Universe!...It's up to Action Cat and Adventure Bug to stop the bad guys! Follow these amazing superheroes!" (Publisher's note)

Patrick the Wolf Boy Volume 1. written by Art Baltazar & Franco Aureliani; drawn by Art Baltazar. Devil's Due Publishing 2004 un Illustration

Grades: 2 3 4 5 6 7 8 9 10 11 12 Adult   **741.5; Fic**

1. Graphic novels; 2. Humorous graphic novels

1-932796-27-4, $10.95

Patrick looks at first glance like the other kids in school, but he's a werewolf. A cute werewolf. He resembles Eddie Munster (from the 1960s television comedy series "The Munsters"), and he doesn't speak, although he growls a lot and sometimes howls. He gives his teacher an apple — but with a skull biting the apple. When he goes fishing with his dad, he prefers to scare the bear into giving him his catch. He loves to play tag with the neighborhood squirrel. And when Valentine's Day comes, he makes sure that his babysitter likes him better. His utterly normal parents adore him and understand his growls; so does Neve, his classmate at school.

Volume 1 of 4

Tiny Titans: welcome to the treehouse. Art Baltazar & Franco, writers; Art Baltazar, artist; Nick J. Napolitano, Art Baltazar, letters. DC Comics 2009 144p. Illustration

Grades: K 1 2 3   **741.5; Fic**

1. Graphic novels; 2. Humorous graphic novels; 3. Superhero graphic novels; 4. Teen Titans (Fictional characters); 5. Flash (Fictional character); 6. Robin (Fictional character)

978-1-4012-2078-5, $12.99

Eisner Award: Best Publication for Kids (2009); Eisner Award: Best Publication for Kids (2011)

Here are the Teen Titans as never seen before: as little kids. They all attend Sidekick City Elementary School, where their principal and teachers are supervillains, and they get into playground showdowns with the Fearsome Five. Baltazar and Franco, who have created such characters as

Patrick the Wolf Boy, present a series of short stories, most one or two pages long, featuring little kid versions of Robin, Starfire, Wonder Girl, Cassie, Speedy, Kid Flash, Cyborg, Beast Boy, Raven, and more. While these stories are written for the young readers, the humor may also appeal to teens and adults.

Other titles in this series are: Tiny Titans: adventures in awesomeness (2009); Tiny Titans: sidekickin' it (2010); Tiny Titans: the first rule of pet club (2010); Tiny Titans: field trippin' (2011); Tiny Titans: the treehouse and beyond! (2011); Tiny Titans: growing up tiny! (2012); Tiny Titans: aw yeah Titans! (2013); Tiny Titans: return to the treehouse (2015)

Bar-el, Dan
    That one spooky night. Kids Can Press 2012 80 p.
Grades: 2 3 4 5
741.5
    1. Witches — Juvenile fiction; 2. Halloween; 3. Dracula, Count (Fictional character); 4. Dracula, Count (Fictional character)
    1554537517; 9781554537518, $16.95

Courtesy of Kids Can Press

    This book by Dan Bar-el presents "a graphic novel for the Halloween season.... In 'Broom with a View,' a girl accidentally ends up with a real witch's broom, leading to a magical experience. In '10,000 Tentacles Under the Tub,' two boys find their post-trick-or-treating bath transformed into an undersea world. The final story, 'The Fang Gang,' follows a group of friends as they end up in Dracula's mansion on the scariest night of the year." (School Library Journal)

Barker, Clive
    The **Thief** of Always. IDW Publishing 2005 144p. Illustration
Grades: 4 5 6 7 8 9 10
741.5; Fic
    1. Fantasy graphic novels; 2. Graphic novels; 3. Horror graphic novels
    1-933239-17-4, $35.00; 1-933239-38-7 (pa), $19.99

CLIVE BARKER
THE THIEF OF ALWAYS
Courtesy of IDW Publishing

    Clive Barker's fable for younger readers is adapted here into graphic novel format. Mr. Hood's Holiday House has stood for a thousand years, welcoming countless children to enjoy a blissful round of treats and holidays...for a price. Then bored young Harvey Swick comes, and he notices disquieting little details that make him realize the place is more of a trap. Things are spooky but not terrifying, with little violence.
    Originally published as The Thief of Always issues #1-3.

Beechen, Adam
    Justice League Unlimited Vol. 1: United They Stand. written by Adam Beechen; illustrated by Carlo Barbieri, Ethen Beavers, Walden Wong; colored by Heroic Age; lettered by Phil Balsman, Pat Brosseau, Nick J. Napolitano. DC Comics 2005 104p. Illustration
Grades: 4 5 6 7 8 9
741.5; Fic
    1. Graphic novels; 2. Justice League (Fictional characters); 3. Superhero graphic novels
    1401205127; 9781401205126, $6.99

Leaping straight out of their Cartoon Network show, the Worlds Greatest Heroes have their own comics series. This inaugural collection features these tales: Divide Conquer, Poker Face, Small Time, Local Hero and Monitor Duty.
    Volume 1 of 5

Bell, Cece
    ★ El deafo. Cece Bell; color by David Lasky. Abrams Books 2014 233 p. Color; Illustration
Grades: 3 4 5 6 7
741.5; 92
    1. Friendship; 2. Hearing aids for children; 3. Schools; 4. Deaf children; 5. Autobiographical graphic novels
    1419710206; 9781419710209, $21.95
                    LC 2013955590
    Newbery Honor Book (2015); Eisner Award: Best Publication for Kids (2015)
    "In this...graphic novel memoir, author/illustrator Cece Bell chronicles her hearing loss at a young age and her subsequent experiences with the Phonic Ear, a very powerful — and very awkward — hearing aid. The Phonic Ear gives Cece the ability to hear — sometimes things she shouldn't — but also isolates her from her classmates." (Publisher's note)
    "Bell's bold and blocky full-color cartoons perfectly complement her childhood stories — she often struggles to fit in and sometimes experiences bullying, but the cheerful illustrations promise a sunny future." Booklist

Bertozzi, Nick
    Lewis & Clark. First Second 2011 136p. Illustration
Grades: 5 6 7 8
978; 741.5
    978-1-59643-450-9 (pa), $16.99; 1-59643-450-3 (pa)
                    LC 2010-36255
    "Bertozzi offers an innovative take on Meriwether Lewis and William Clark's epic journey in this oversized graphic offering. Portraying the arduous trek through rough terrain and encounters with often unwelcoming natives, sequential panels transport readers alongside the famous duo and their equally renowned translator, Sacagawea, as they travel from St. Louis to the Pacific coast. Within a fictional framework, the narrative weaves in facets of the characters' personalities, including Lewis's tempestuous melancholy, Charbonneau's inept bumbling and Sacagawea's ability to endure this voyage surrounded by her intensely masculine cohorts." (Kirkus)

    ★ Shackleton: Antarctic odyssey. Nick Bertozzi. First Second 2014 128 p. Illustration; Map
Grades: 5 6 7 8 9 10
741.5; 919.89
    1. Explorers — Great Britain — Biography; 2. Graphic novels; 3. Antarctica — Discovery and exploration — British; 4. Antarctica — Exploration; 5. Shackleton, Ernest Henry, Sir, 1874-1922
    1596434511; 9781596434516, $16.99
    This book by Nick Bertozzi describes how "Ernest Shackleton was one of the last great Antarctic explorers, and he led one of the most ambitious Antarctic expeditions ever undertaken. This is his story, and the story of the dozens of men who threw in their lot with him — many of whom nearly died in the unimaginably harsh conditions of the journey." (Publisher's note)
    "Bertozzi eschews all narrative explanation, relying solely on dialogue among the crew and the detailed black-and-white panels to tell the story. The snow- and ice-bound journey is the perfect match for Bertozzi's minimal style — vast stretches of white become gasp-worthy, desolate vistas." Booklist

Bevard, Robby
    Sir Arthur Conan Doyle's the adventure of the Norwood Builder. ABDO/Magic Wagon 2010 48p. Illustration

Grades: 4 5 6 7 8 9   **741.5; Fic**
1. Graphic novels; 2. Holmes, Sherlock (Fictional character); 3. Mystery graphic novels
978-1-60270-725-2, $28.50; 1-60270-725-1

LC 2009-32459

Young solicitor Mr. McFarlane begs Holmes to clear his name when he's accused of the murder of Jonas Oldacre, the Norwood Builder. Inspector Lestrade thinks he has a solid case, and the evidence seems to implicate McFarlane, especially since Mr. Oldacre's new will made McFarlane his sole heir. Holmes points to the lack of a body, and digs up more clues in his quest to save McFarlane. This graphic novel adaptation of Doyle's short story retains the suspense of the original, but perpetuates the stereotypical portrayals of Holmes in the deerstalker and caped coat which he never wore in the original stories. The book includes a brief drawing lesson, a short glossary, a brief biography of Doyle, and a listing of his other writings.

Part of The Graphic Novel Adventures of Sherlock Holmes

Bliss, Harry

★ **Grace** for Gus. written and illustrated by Harry Bliss. Katherine Tegen Books 2018 40 p. Color; Illustration
Grades: K 1 2 3   **741.5; Fic**
1. Pets; 2. Human-animal relationships; 3. Guinea pigs; 4. Money-making projects for children
9780062644107, $17.99

LC 2016963696

In this children's book, by Harry Bliss, "Grace is the quiet girl in the class. And Gus is the class guinea pig. Grace knows that Gus is lonely, and so she sets off one night to help out her furry friend. Wherever she goes, Grace amazes and delights as she shares her many talents, showing how one person with a little pizzazz can make a difference." (Publisher's note)

"Bliss' graphic novel-like picture book is mostly wordless, with the bulk of the story following Grace on her fund-raising escapades. The intensely detailed scenes are full of clever storytelling, and he fills the crowds with iconic New Yorkers (Spike Lee, Andy Warhol) and cartoonists (Edward Gorey, Shel Silverstein) and cartoon characters (Nancy, Tintin)." Booklist

★ **Luke** on the loose: a Toon Book. TOON Books 2009 32p. Illustration; Map
Grades: PreK K 1 2   **741.5; Fic**
1. Graphic novels; 2. Humorous graphic novels; 3. New York (State) — Graphic novels
978-1-935179-00-9, $12.95; 1-935179-00-4

LC 2008-35699

A young boy's fascination with pigeons soon erupts into a full-blown chase around Central Park, across the Brooklyn Bridge, through a fancy restaurant, and into the sky

"The cartoon panels are so successful at engaging readers that young children do not have to be able to read the text to enjoy the story. Each drawing is filled with humorous details." SLJ

Boldman, Craig

Archie Day by Day Volume 1. Archie Comics 2003 96p. Illustration
Grades: 3 4 5 6 7 8 9 10 11 12 Adult   **741.5; Fic**
1. Andrews, Archie (Fictional character); 2. Graphic novels; 3. Humorous graphic novels
1-879794-16-0, $10.95

Archie and his pals have been comics' most celebrated teenage humor characters for over 60 years, since 1941. Now for the first time, selections from Archie's worldwide syndicated newspaper strip are collected in this volume. This black and white edition includes a selection of daily strips from the mid-1990s, chronicling life in Riverdale, USA.

Bonneval, Gwen de

William and the lost spirit. Gwen de Bonneval; illustrated by Matthieu Bonhomme; colors by Walter; translation, Anne Collins Smith and Owen M. Smith; [lettering by Dennis Pacheco]. Graphic Universe 2013 152 p.
Grades: 4 5 6 7
Fic; 741.5/944
1. Families — Fiction; 2. Folklore — Fiction; 3. Graphic novels; 4. Knights and knighthood — Fiction; 5. Middle Ages — Fiction; 6. Mythology — Fiction; 7. Voyages and travels — Fiction; 8. Fantasy fiction
1467708070; 9780761385677; 9781467708074, $9.95

Courtesy of Lerner Publishing Group

LC 2012008115

In this book, as "William sets out to find his father (who might be dead, or lost, or both), he is joined by a knight, a troubadour, and a very unusual goat. Soon he enters a mysterious world that is populated with an amazing cast of characters, including Prester John, dog-faced men, and headless people whose faces are on their chests." (School Library Journal)

Booth, Jack

Kazuma's Quest. Harcourt Achieve/Steck-Vaughn 2007 48p. Illustration
Grades: 3 4 5 6 7 8   **741.5; Fic**
1. Graphic novels; 2. Samurai — Graphic novels
978-1-4190-3215-8, $8.99

Kazuma is a young samurai who sets out to confront his father's murderer and reclaim his family's sword. The famous swordsman Matayemon offers to help him. Will they be able to outsmart their enemies? This is historical fiction in graphic novel format with facts about the samurai interspersed throughout the story in prose sections.

Part of the Timeline Graphic Novels series.

Nomad King. Harcourt Achieve/Steck-Vaughn 2006 48p. Illustration
Grades: 3 4 5 6 7 8   **741.5; 92; Fic**
1. Graphic novels; 2. Khan, Genghis, ca. 1162-1227; 3. Mongolia — History — Graphic novels
978-1-4190-3201-1, $8.99

In the sparse, windswept land of Mongolia in the late 12th century, Temujin becomes leader of his tribe at the age of nine. Over the years, this ruthless leader battles warring tribes for power then unites them under his rule, becoming Genghis Khan. He gradually extends his empire beyond Mongolia and China; will he be able to take over the world? This historical graphic novel includes prose intervals that provide more information about the Mongols and about Genghis Khan.

Part of the Timeline Graphic Novels series.

Raiders of the Seas. Harcourt Achieve/Steck-Vaughn 2006 48p. Illustration
Grades: 3 4 5 6 7 8   **741.5; Fic**
1. Adventure graphic novels; 2. Graphic novels; 3. Pirates — Graphic novels
978-1-4190-3207-3, $8.99

Nicholas Bloom is a young sailor who lands in bad company when he joins the ship of a pirate named Blackbeard. Together they sail the seas, raiding and plundering. When Nick learns more about Blackbeard's evil ways, he must decide what to do next. This historical graphic novel includes prose intervals that give information about pirates and the differences between them and privateers.

Part of the Timeline Graphic Novels series.

Boothby, Ian

Sparks!. written by Ian Boothby; art by Nina Matsumoto, with color by David Dedrick. Graphix / Scholastic 2018 192 p. Color; Illustration
Grades: 2 3 4 5   **741.5; Fic**
1. Adventure and adventurers; 2. Extraterrestrial beings; 3. Cats
9781338029468, $12.99; 9781338029475; 9781338029482
LC 2017943774

In this book, by Ian Boothby, illustrated by Nina Matsumoto, "August is a brilliant inventor who is afraid of the outside. Charlie is a crack pilot who isn't afraid of anything. Together these pals save lives every day. They also happen to be cats who pilot a powerful, mechanical dog suit! Always eager to leap into danger, this feline duo have their work cut out for them as they try to thwart Princess, an evil alien bent on enslaving mankind." (Publisher's note)

"Boothby's background as a comedy writer shows in the tight timing, clever banter, and over-the-top dialogue, while Matsumoto's archly funny cartoons-buoyant, colorful artwork filled with speedy action, riotous sight gags, and animated character designs-perfectly complement the script." Booklist

Bosma, Sam

Fantasy Sports; 1. Sam Bosma. Nobrow Press 2015 56 p. Color; Illustration
Grades: 5 6 7 8   **741.5; Fic**
1. Mummies — Graphic novels; 2. Basketball — Graphic novels; 3. Adventure graphic novels
1907704809; 9781907704802, $19.95
Ignatz Award Winner: Outstanding Comic (2016)

In this graphic novel, written and illustrated by Sam Bosma, "a young explorer and her musclebound friend go treasure hunting in a mummy's tomb — but if they want to get rich, they're going to have to best the mummy in a game of hoops! Can they trust their bandaged adversary to play by the rules? Or will they be stuck in the tomb...forever?" (Publisher's note)

"Bosma's colorfully jumbled, slanty panels look like the inspired offspring of Spirited Away and Space Jam, capturing magical intrigue, fast-paced basketball action, and the best kind of on-the-court trash talk in one go." Booklist

Other titles in this series are: The Bandit of Barbel Bay (2016); The Green King (2017)

Boyd, David

Napoleon's Last Stand. Harcourt Achieve/Steck-Vaughn 2006 48p. Illustration
Grades: 3 4 5 6 7 8   **741.5; Fic**
1. Adventure graphic novels; 2. Graphic novels; 3. Napoleon I, Emperor of the French
978-1-4190-3208-0, $8.99

Charlotte Bonaparte helps her famous uncle Napoleon escape from the island of Elba. As Napoleon prepares to go to war, Charlotte makes her own plans. This historical fiction graphic novel depicts some of the events of the Battle of Waterloo, so there is some battlefield violence. The book includes prose intervals that provide more information about Napoleon, his English opponent, the Duke of Wellington, the battle, and the death of Napoleon.

Part of the Timeline Graphic Novels series.

Britt, Fanny

★ Jane, the fox & me. [written by] Fanny Britt; [illustrated by] Isabelle Arsenault; translated by Christine Morelli and Susan Ouriou. Pgw 2013 101 p.
Grades: 5 6 7 8 9   **Fic**
1. Teenage girls — Fiction; 2. Alienation (Social psychology) — Fiction
1554983606; 9781554983605, $19.95
Governor General's Award: Children's Illustration (2013); Eisner Nominee: Best Publication for Children (2014)

Written by Fanny Britt, illustrated by Isabelle Arsentault, and translated by Christine Morelli and Susan Ouriou, this "graphic novel reveals the casual brutality of which children are capable, but also assures readers that redemption can be found through connecting with another, whether the other is a friend, a fictional character or even, amazingly, a fox." (Publisher's note) It "centers on Hélène, ostracized by her former friends and now a loner at school." (Horn Book Magazine)

"Britt's well-constructed narrative is achieved sensitively through Arsenault's impressionistic artwork.... An elegant and accessible approach to an important topic." Booklist

Louis undercover. by Fanny Britt; illustrated by Isabelle Arsenault; translated by Christelle Morelli and Susan Ouriou. Groundwood Books 2017 160 p. Color; Illustration
Grades: 5 6 7 8   **741.5**
1. Brothers — Fiction; 2. Father-son relationship — Fiction
9781554988594, $19.95; 9781554988600; 1554988594

In this book, by Fanny Britt, translated by Christelle Morelli and Susan Ouriou, illustrated by Isabelle Arsenault, "Louis's dad cries — Louis knows this because he spies on him. His dad misses the happy times when their family was together, just as Louis does. But as it is, he and his little brother, Truffle, have to travel back and forth between their dad's country house and their mom's city apartment, where she tries to hide her own tears." (Publisher's note)

"Working in moody ink and pencil, Arsenault excels at capturing characters in the grip of powerful emotions they're trying to conceal, and also at conveying a sense of place — both city and country are evocatively drawn." Pub Wkly

Brosgol, Vera

★ Be prepared. Vera Brosgol; color by Alec Longstreth. First Second 2018 256 p. Color; Illustration
Grades: 4 5 6 7 8   **741.5; Fic**
1. Social acceptance — Fiction; 2. Camps — Fiction; 3. Friendship — Fiction
9781626724440, $22.99; 9781626724457
LC 2017946145

In this book, by Vera Brosgol, "all Vera wants to do is fit in — but that's not easy for a Russian girl in the suburbs. Her friends live in fancy houses and their parents can afford to send them to the best summer camps. Vera's single mother can't afford that sort of luxury, but there's one summer camp in her price range — Russian summer camp. Vera is sure she's found the one place she can fit in, but camp is far from what she imagined." (Publisher's note)

"Brosgol's artwork has immense depth, from the facial expressions and gestures to the spot-on visual gags, and she strikes a perfect balance between heartfelt honesty and uproarious, self-deprecating humor." Booklist

Brown, Don

★ The great American dust bowl. by Don Brown. Houghton Mifflin Harcourt 2013 80 p.
Grades: 5 6 7 8 9   **978**
1. Droughts — United States — History; 2. Dust storms — History; 3. Dust Bowl Era, 1931-1939
0547815506; 9780547815503, $18.99

Author Don Brown presents a "graphic novel of one of America's most catastrophic natural events: the Dust Bowl. On a clear, warm Sunday, April 14, 1935, a wild wind whipped up millions upon millions of these specks of dust to form a duster, a savage storm on America's high southern plains." (Publisher's note)

"In this bleak yet compelling graphic-novel-style glimpse at the Dirty Thirties, Brown crisply paces the narrative with fascinating glimpses of the sociological and geological causes of the Dust Bowl. The color brown is a recurring theme here, as Brown relies, aptly, almost entirely on shades of brown throughout. Primary source material is used liberally, as characters speak directly to the reader, documentary-style." (Horn Book)

Brown, Jeffrey

Lucy & Andy Neanderthal. Jeffrey Brown. Crown Publishers 2016 224 p. Color; Illustration

Grades: 2 3 4 5   **741.5; Fic**

1. Brothers and sisters — Fiction; 2. Graphic novels; 3. Humorous stories; 4. Neanderthals — Fiction; 5. Siblings — Graphic novels

9780385388351, $12.99; 9780385388375

LC 2015032399

This first book in the "Lucy and Andy Neanderthal" graphic novel series by Jeffrey Brown "features Lucy and her goofball brother Andy, as the Paleo pair take on a wandering baby sibling, bossy teens, cave paintings, and a mammoth hunt. But what will happen when they encounter a group of humans?" (Publisher's note)

"Kids will learn a great deal about the Neanderthals while laughing their way through the story. Brown demonstrates a depth of knowledge of the subject, with a few winking anachronisms." SLJ

Another title about Lucy and Andy is: The stone cold age (2017)

★ **Star** Wars: Jedi Academy. Jeffrey Brown; [edited by] Rex Ogle. Scholastic, Inc 2013 160 p. Illustration (Star Wars: Jedi Academy)

Grades: 3 4 5 6 7   **741.5; Fic**

1. Star Wars — Comic books, strips, etc.; 2. Middle schools — Fiction; 3. Outer space — Fiction

0545505178; 9780545505178, $12.99; 9780545609999

LC 2013931939

In this book, by Jeffrey Brown, "Roan Novachez thought he was destined to attend Pilot Academy Middle School, just as his older brother and father did. His dreams are crushed when he is rejected by Pilot Academy and accepted into a sketchy new school called Coruscant Jedi Academy.... Confused and struggling to keep up, Roan tries to fly under the radar and passes the time drawing comics of his daily life at his strange boarding school." (Booklist)

"While it might be disappointing for those familiar with this world to see scant representation of beloved characters, it makes the book an easy starting point for new fans. There are plenty of references to other elements (the T-16 Skyhopper and Jedi training remotes, for example) for diehards to get excited about." SLJ

Other titles in this series are: Return of the Padawan (2014);The Phantom Bully (2015)

Star Wars: Jedi academy 2: Return of the Padawan. Jeffrey Brown; [edited by] Rex Ogle. Scholastic 2014 176 p. Illustration (Star Wars: Jedi academy)

Grades: 3 4 5 6 7   **741.5**

1. Caricatures and cartoons — Fiction; 2. Life on other planets — Fiction; 3. Middle schools — Fiction; 4. Star Wars fiction; 5. School stories

0545621259; 9780545621250, $12.99

LC 2014931163

"After surviving his first year at Jedi Academy, Roan Novachez thought his second year would be a breeze. He couldn't have been more wrong. Roan feels like he's drifting apart from his friends, and it's only made worse when Roan discovers he's not the amazing pilot he thought he'd be. When the school bullies take him under their wing, he decides they aren't so bad after all — or are they?" (Publisher's note)

"Roan is a very sympathetic main character, and readers will feel his pain and laugh at his misfortune in equal measure. Roan's hand-lettered journal entries alternate with short paneled sequences and 'screenshots' of academy message boards and other ephemera." Kirkus

Star Wars: Jedi Academy; 3: The Phantom Bully. by Jeffrey Brown. Scholastic Press 2015 176 p. Illustration (Star Wars: Jedi Academy)

Grades: 3 4 5 6 7   **741.5; Fic**

1. School stories; 2. Star Wars films; 3. Middle schools

0545621267; 9780545621267, $12.99

"It's hard to believe this is Roan's last year at Jedi Academy. He's been busier than ever learning to fly (and wash) starships, swimming in the Lake Country on Naboo, studying for the Jedi obstacle course exam, and tracking down dozens of vorpak clones — don't ask. But now, someone is setting him up to get in trouble with everyone at school, including Yoda. If he doesn't find out who it is, and fast, he may get kicked out of school!" (Publisher's note)

"The third graphic novel in the Jedi Academy series turns out to be a love story, although it takes the characters a while to realize it.... [B]y the close of this high jinks-filled year, every student at the academy gets a satisfying ending, even the bullies and troublemakers." Kirkus

Brremaud, Frederic

Little tails in the savannah. by Frederic Brremaud, illustrated by Federico Bertolucci, translated by Mike Kennedy. Lion Forge 2017 32 p. Color; Illustration

Grades: PreK K 1 2   **741.5; Fic**

1. Dogs — Juvenile fiction; 2. Squirrels — Juvenile fiction

1942367384; 9781942367383, $14.99

In this picture book in the Little Tails series, by Frederic Brremaud, illustrated by Federico Bertolucci, translated by Mike Kennedy, "Chipper and Squizzo are a precocious puppy and squirrel who love to explore new and exciting environments, flying their cardboard box airplane to wondrous worlds full of fascinating animals and creatures." (Publisher's note)

Bullock, Mike

Lions, tigers and bears volume 2: betrayal. Image Comics 2008 un Illustration

Grades: 3 4 5 6 7 8 9   **741.5; Fic**

1. Adventure graphic novels; 2. Fantasy graphic novels; 3. Graphic novels

978-1-58240-930-6, $14.99

Joey and Courtney's winter wonderland is shattered when the Big Cats of the Night Pride arrive with terrible news from the Stuffed Animal Kingdom. Now all that stands between the horrible Beasties and children everywhere are Joey, Courtney, and their imaginations. For the evil Valthraax and his minions have taken over the Crystal Castle, imprisoned King Bear, and plot to capture all children who aren't being protected by the Stuffed Animal Militia. There is some fighting violence between the Night Pride and their allies against the Beasties.

Burks, James

Bird & Squirrel on the run. James Burks. Graphix / Scholastic Press 2012 128 p. Illustration

Grades: 2 3 4 5   **741.5**

1. Cats — fiction; 2. Adventure fiction — fiction; 3. Squirrels — fiction

0545312833; 9780545312837, $8.99

LC 2011934532

"Bird and Squirrel outwit Cat and become best friends in this zany adventure. Squirrel is afraid of his own shadow. Bird doesn't have a care in the world. And Cat wants to eat Bird and Squirrel. Of course, he'll have to catch them first, and that's not going to be easy. Join this trio as they head south for the winter in a hilarious road trip. But watch out! Cat is waiting around every bend, and he's one pesky feline." (Publisher's note)

Other titles in this series are: Bird & Squirrel on ice (2014); Bird & Squirrel on the edge! (2015)

Butzer, C. M.

★ **Gettysburg:** the graphic novel. Bowen Books/HarperCollins 2009 80p. Illustration

Grades: 3 4 5 6 7 8 9 10 11 12   **741.5; 973.7**

1. American speeches — Graphic novels; 2. Gettysburg (Pa.), Battle of, 1863; 3. Graphic novels; 4. Lincoln, Abraham, 1809-1865 — Graphic novels; 5. Lincoln, Abraham, 1809-1865 — Work — Gettysburg address; 8. Gettysburg address: Lincoln, Abraham

978-0-06-156176-4, $16.99; 978-0-06-156175-7 (pa), $8.99

LC 2008-10657

In the summer of 1863, everyone knew that the Battle of Gettysburg would be an important battle that could determine the course of the War Between the States, the Civil War. What they didn't know was who would prevail. Butzer uses primary sources to play out the battle that lasted three days and caused tremendous casualties, the aftermath that nearly overwhelmed the town of Gettysburg, and the effort to build the monument to commemorate the fallen. He uses a somber blue and gray wash in his illustrations. Lincoln's famous Gettysburg Address was only 271 words long and appear in their entirety, against images of the nation's past. Some panels depicting the violence of the battles, and particularly the dead on the battlefield, could be disturbing for sensitive younger readers; but this battle was ugly and overwhelming in its violence. Butzer includes extensive end notes to explain what he depicted, and to note the sources of the dialog and narration.

Byrne, Eugene

★ **Darwin:** a graphic biography. by Eugene Byrne; illustrated by Simon Gurr. Smithsonian Books 2013 96 p. Illustration

Grades: 5 6 7 8 9 10 11 12 Adult

576.8/2092; 576.8; 92

1. Evolution (Biology) — Comic books, strips, etc; 2. Graphic novels; 3. Natural selection — Comic books, strips, etc; 4. Darwin, Charles, 1809-1882; 5. Evolution

1588343529; 9781588343529, $9.95

LC 2012951786

This work of graphic nonfiction by Eugene Byrne and Simon Gurr presents a "summary of [Charles] Darwin's life and achievement.... Darwin was an indifferent student...until he received an invitation to

Courtesy of Smithsonian Books

take a voyage that 'would change the course of history.'...The animals he encountered seemed so different...that he theorized that if it weren't a matter of different conditions that resulted in such 'transmutation,' they might well have had a different creator." (Kirkus Reviews)

Includes bibliographical references.

Caldwell, Ben

The **Wizard** of Oz. written by L. Frank Baum; adapted by Ben Caldwell. Sterling Children's Books 2012 32 p. Illustration (All-Action Classics)

Grades: 4 5 6   **741.5**

1. Fantasy graphic novels; 2. Graphic novels; 3. Oz (Imaginary place) — Comic books, strips, etc.; 4. Tornadoes — Fiction; 5. Voyages and travels — Graphic novels; 6. Baum, L. Frank (Lyman Frank), 1856-1919 — Adaptations

1402731531; 9781402731532, $7.95

LC 2013363513

This book is a graphic novel adaptation of L. Frank Baum's classic tale "The Wizard of Oz." Author and illustrator Ben Caldwell "follows Baum's original novel rather than the iconic film. The heroes are pursued by the Kalidah, 'horrific beasts, with heads like tigers and bodies like bears,' and the famous path the four friends follow, as in the original, is called the 'road of golden bricks.'" (Publishers Weekly)

Cammuso, Frank

Knights of the lunch table: the dodgeball chronicles. Graphix 2008 141p.

Grades: 3 4 5 6   **741.5; Fic**

1. Graphic novels; 2. Humorous graphic novels; 3. School stories — Graphic novels

978-0-439-90322-6 (pa), $9.99; 0-439-90322-X (pa)

Artie King's family has moved and now he has to start at a new school, Camelot Middle School. Dodgeball is the big game at Camelot, and the Horde is a champion team; the Horde members are also the worst bullies in the school.... Artie immediately gets into trouble with Joe, the leader of the Horde.... However, he manages to open the broken old locker...[which] provides mysterious, useful stuff, such as a lunch. Joe challenges Artie to a dodgeball game; Artie has new friends Percy and Wayne who'll help him, and then he meets Gwen. And science teacher Mr. Merlyn is also on his side.

"Arthurian legend gets an update for young readers in this outstanding graphic novel.... The funny, fast-paced tale of young Arthur's quest to defeat the bullies stands well on its own. The appealing illustrations are full of color, action, and life." SLJ

Followed by: Knights of the lunch table: the dragon players (2009)

★ **Knights** of the lunch table: the dragon players. Scholastic/Graphix 2009 127p.

Grades: 3 4 5 6   **741.5; Fic**

1. Arthurian romances — Adaptations — Graphic novels; 2. Conduct of life — Graphic novels; 3. Contests — Graphic novels; 4. Graphic novels; 5. Humorous graphic novels; 6. Schools — Graphic novels

978-0-439-90323-3 (pa), $9.99; 0-439-90323-8 (pa)

LC 2008-51463

Artie King may have won the dodgeball game against the school bullies, but life is not easy. The new challenge comes with the dueling robot tournament at school; it's all part of Dragon Day, and The Horde has won every year by cheating — they force the smartest kid in school to design and build their robot. This year, they've done it to Percy. Circumstances force Artie's hand and willy nilly, he has entered the tournament. Seeking an edge, they go to Evo, a mysterious techno wiz kid who can build any gadget; the problem for Artie is, is cheating by getting help from Evo? Cammuso's bright, cartoony art and schoolyard version of Arthurian legend provides lots of fun action as well as making readers think about ethics

Followed by: Knights of the lunch table: the battling bands (2011);

Sequel to: Knights of the lunch table: the dodgeball chronicles (2008)

The **Misadventures** of Salem Hyde; 1: Spelling Trouble. by Frank Cammuso. Harry N Abrams Inc 2013 96 p. Color; Illustration

Grades: 2 3 4   **Fic**

1. School stories; 2. Occult fiction

1419708031; 9781419708039, $14.95

This is the first book in Frank Cammuso's Salem Hyde series. Here, "Salem Hyde just wants a friend. After a misguided attempt to use her magic lands her in the principal's office, Salem's family decides she needs an animal companion. One well-placed call later, she meets knowledgeable and talkative feline Percival J. Whamsford III, otherwise known as Whammy. Whammy isn't just a chatty kitty; he is a Magical Animal

Companion and will help Salem learn how to use her magic properly." (Kirkus Reviews)

Other titles in this series are:Big birthday bash (2014);Cookie camp catastrophe (2014);Dinosaur dilemma (2015);Frozen fiasco (2016)

Otto's backwards day: a Toon book. by Frank Cammuso with Jay Lynch. Toon Books, is an imprint of Candlewick Press 2013 32 p.
Grades: K 1 2   **741.5**
1. Birthdays — Fiction; 2. Cats — Fiction; 3. Graphic novels; 4. Humorous stories; 5. Humorous fiction
1935179330; 9781935179337, $12.95
LC 2012047661
Eisner Nominee: Best Publication for Early Readers (2014)

"Someone stole Otto's birthday! When Otto and his robot sidekick, Toot, follow the crook, they discover a topsy-turvy world where rats chase cats and people wear underpants over their clothes. To get his presents back, Otto needs to solve a slew of backwards puzzles — but his greatest challenge comes at the journey's very end. On this special day, will Otto discover something even better than cake or gifts?" (Publisher's note)

Camper, Cathy
★ **Lowriders** in space; book 1. by Cathy Camper; illustrated by Raul Gonzalez III. Chronicle Books 2014 112 p. Color; Illustration (Lowriders)
Grades: 4 5 6 7 8   **741.5**
1. Competition (Psychology) — Fiction; 2. Friendship — Fiction; 3. Graphic novels; 4. Lowriders — Fiction; 5. Mexican Americans — Fiction; 6. Automobiles — Fiction; 7. Space vehicles; 8. Mechanics (Persons)
9781452121550, $22.99; 1452121559
LC 2013040709
Cathy Camper "introduces readers to Lupe Impala, Flapjack Octopus, and Elirio Malaria, three friends who love working with cars and dream of having their own garage shop. One day they see an opportunity to achieve their goal — a car competition. When they start working on a lowrider to prepare it for the competition, an out-of-this world journey begins." (School Library Journal)

"Raúl's snazzy panels — impressively drawn in only red, blue, and black ballpoint pen on tea-stained paper — resemble an amped-up Mighty Mouse cartoon rendered in anarchic yet skillful doodles. It's a joyfully explosive style, and it perfectly matches the Latino characters and barrio setting." Booklist

Another title in this series is: Lowriders to the center of the Earth (2016)

Lowriders to the center of the Earth. by Cathy Camper; illustrated by Raul the Third. Chronicle Books 2016 128 p. Color; Illustration
Grades: 4 5 6 7 8   **741.5; Fic**
1. Aztec gods — Comic books, strips, etc; 2. Lowriders; 3. Automobiles — Graphic novels; 4. Mexican Americans — Graphic novels; 5. Gods and goddesses — Graphic novels; 6. Cats — Graphic novels
1452138362; 9781452123431, $22.99; 9781452138367; 1452123438
LC 2015021996
Pura Belpré Illustrator Award (2017)

"Lupe Impala, Elirio Malaria, and El Chavo Octopus are living their dream at last. They're the proud owners of their very own garage. But when their beloved cat Genie goes missing, they need to do everything they can to find him. Little do they know the trail will lead them to the realm of Mictlantecuhtli, the Aztec god of the Underworld, who is keeping Genie prisoner!" (Publisher's note)

"Raúl the Third's ultradetailed crosshatched artwork more than meets the demands of this cast-of-thousands comic opus." Kirkus

Carre, Lilli
The **fir-tree**. It Books/HarperCollins 2009 un Illustration
Grades: 3 4 5 6 7 8 9 10 11 12 Adult   **741.5; Fic**
1. Authors; 2. Children's authors; 3. Christmas — Graphic novels; 4. Christmas trees — Graphic novels; 5. Dramatists; 6. Graphic novels; 7. Novelists; 8. Short story writers; 9. Andersen, Hans Christian, 1805-1875 — Adaptations
978-0-06-178236-7, $14.99

A young fir-tree only wants to grow tall; it's never satisfied and doesn't notice the sunlight and clean air. It never rejoices in anything, but grumbles and complains. When it sees some trees being cut down and taken away, it wonders what it's missing. The birds tell of seeing the trees inside homes, beautifully decorated, and it becomes jealous. When it does grow tall and beautiful, a woodsman comes along and cuts it down, hauling it to town to become a Christmas tree in a house. It enjoys the family playing around the tree at Christmas, but after the holiday, the family throws it into a storeroom. Will the tree ever see its forest again? Lilli Carre uses delicate coloring and illustrations to adapt Andersen's sad Christmas story. Although this is suitable for young readers, adults may better appreciate the tragedy and Carre's idiosyncratic illustrations her people have long, loopy arms.

Castellucci, Cecil
Odd Duck. by Cecil Castellucci, illustrated by Sara Varon. First Second 2013 96 p.
Grades: 1 2 3 4 5   **E**
1. Eccentrics and eccentricities — fiction; 2. Friendship — fiction; 3. Ducks — fiction
1596435577; 9781596435575, $15.99

In this book by Cecil Castellucci, illustrated by Sara Varon, "Theodora is a perfectly normal duck. She may swim with a teacup balanced on her head and stay north when the rest of the ducks fly south for the winter, but there's nothing so odd about that. Chad, on the other hand, is one strange bird. Theodora quite likes him, but she can't overlook his odd habits. It's a good thing Chad has a normal friend like Theodora to set a good example for him." (Publisher's note)

Castiglia, Paul
America's 1st Patriotic Comic Book Hero: The Shield Volume 1. Archie Comics 2002 96p. Illustration
Grades: 3 4 5 6 7 8 9 10 11 12 Adult   **741.5; Fic**
1. Adventure graphic novels; 2. Graphic novels; 3. Superhero graphic novels
1-879794-08-X, $12.95

A hero with great power, strength and courage who donned the colors of the American flag. A hero who lived for democracy and protected the world from the foes of freedom! No, it's not who you think... it's THE SHIELD, who predated his well known counterpart by over a year. This historic full color trade paperback reprints his first 8 stories from PEP and SHIELD/WIZARD Comics. It includes his first appearance and origin, along with the covers of the comics they originally appeared in, dating from 1940.

Archie Americana Series: Best of the Forties Book 2. Archie Comics 2002 96p. Illustration
Grades: 3 4 5 6 7 8 9 10 11 12 Adult   **741.5; Fic**
1. Andrews, Archie (Fictional character); 2. Graphic novels; 3. Humorous graphic novels
1-879794-09-8, $10.95

In 1941, Pep Comics introduced Archie Andrews, "America's newest boyfriend." Since then, Archie and his perennial teenage friends have entertained readers with their misadventures. This book includes stories from 1946 through 1949, with more slapstick and screwball comedy from Archie and the gang.

Archie Americana Series: Best of the Eighties. Archie Comics 2001 96p. Illustration
Grades: 3 4 5 6 7 8 9 10 11 12 Adult   **741.5; Fic**
1. Andrews, Archie (Fictional character); 2. Graphic novels; 3. Humorous graphic novels
1-879794-06-3, $10.95

During the 1980s pop culture ruled America; even the President was a former actor. In this volume, Archie and friends experience the punk movement, the "Urban Cowboy" craze, see the rise of MTV, get into the preppie, new wave and "Flashdance" fashions, play Trivial Pursuit, and boogie at the roller disco.
Volume 1 of 2

Best of Josie and the Pussycats Volume 1. Archie Comics 2001 96p. Illustration
Grades: 3 4 5 6 7 8 9 10 11 12 Adult   **741.5; Fic**
1. Adventure graphic novels; 2. Graphic novels; 3. Humorous graphic novels; 4. Rock music — Graphic novels
1-879794-07-1, $10.95

This book reprints a selection of stories about rock group Josie and the Pussycats, from their origin in 1963 to 1988. Josie, Melody, and Valerie are the Pussycats, along with their roadie Alan M., their shifty manager Alex, and his conniving sister, Alexandra. They make music, but along the way they also solve mysteries.

Sonic the Hedgehog: The Beginning. Archie Comics 2003 96p. Illustration
Grades: 3 4 5 6 7 8 9 10 11 12 Adult   **741.5; Fic**
1. Adventure graphic novels; 2. Graphic novels; 3. Humorous graphic novels; 4. Sonic the Hedgehog (Fictional character)
1-879794-12-8, $10.95

In 1993, Sonic the Hedgehog sped his way from video games to comic books, and has been going strong ever since. Now, readers can enjoy his earliest comic book adventures with this edition that reprints the first appearances of Tails, Princess Sally, Antoine, Rotor, Uncle Chuck, and Muttski. Fans can also marvel at Sonic's magic rings, the freedom emeralds, and King Acorn's magic crown; while booing and hissing at the villainous Robotnik, his evil Swat-Bots, and his myriad dastardly devices.

Cauvin, Raoul
The **bluecoats** no. 1: Robertsonville Prison. Cinebook Ltd. 2008 48p. Illustration
Grades: 5 6 7 8 9 10   **741.5; Fic**
1. Adventure graphic novels; 2. Graphic novels; 3. Humorous graphic novels; 4. United States — History — 1861-1865, Civil War — Prisoners and prisons — Graphic novels
978-1-90546-071-7, $11.95

Sergeant Chesterfield and Corporal Blutch are Union soldiers during the Civil War; Blutch tends to be lazy, and Chesterfield always seems to be getting him out of trouble; but after one battle, they're both in trouble when they're captured by Confederate troops and are force-marched to Robertsonville Prison. They constantly get into trouble with a soldier and camp guard named Cockroach, and Chesterfield leads multiple attempts to escape the prison. Then when they succeed, they're wearing stolen Confederate uniforms and ultimately end up in a Union prison camp. Prison camps aren't normally subjects of humor, but the humor in this book is reminiscent of the old television series Hogan's Heroes, which was set in a German prisoner of war camp

Chad, Jon
Leo Geo and his miraculous journey through the center of the earth. Jon Chad. Roaring Brook Press 2012 40 p.
Grades: 2 3 4 5   **FIC**
1. Adventure and adventurers — Fiction; 2. Geology — Fiction; 3. Graphic novels; 4. Kings, queens, rulers, etc. — Fiction; 5. Magic — Fiction; 6. Scientists — Graphic novels; 7. Earth — Internal structure — Graphic novels; 8. Adventure graphic novels; 9. Explorers — Graphic novels
9.7816E+12

LC 2011017353

In this book, "the featureless protagonist, an enthusiastic scientist named Leo, sets off on a journey to the center of the Earth through the book's tall pages, and readers are encouraged to turn the book vertically to follow his trek downward. Leo spouts real science facts, but also encounters fantastic creatures in the Earth's mantle at temperatures where nothing ought to be able to survive. Leo uses some big scientific words and even a few wicked-looking math equations, although he is careful to clarify most of what he says for younger audiences." (Publishers Weekly)

Leo Geo and the cosmic crisis: Matt Data and the cosmic crisis. Jon Chad. Roaring Brook Press 2013 40 p. Color; Illustration
Grades: 2 3 4 5   **741.5**
1. Adventure and adventurers — Fiction; 2. Astronauts — Fiction; 3. Graphic novels; 4. Magic — Fiction; 5. Space flight — Fiction; 6. Astronomy
1596438223; 9781596438224, $16.99

LC 2013001296

In this 2-in-1 book, "[Leo Geo] and his space-based scientist brother Matt Data trace looping paths through crowded spacescapes toward each other. Before they meet in the middle, both encounter black holes, white holes, wormholes, asteroids, space pirates and some distinctly more unusual 'space sights.'" (Kirkus Reviews)

"The bright, detailed, full-page panels are covered with strange creatures and planetary objects that will catch and hold young readers' attention, and the scientific information is simply presented and well-integrated into the dialogue. The varied layout of the pages, vertical and horizontal, and the 'search engine,' a hunt for specific objects throughout the book, encourage engagement with the story." SLJ
Sequel to Leo Geo and His Miraculous Journey through the Center of the Earth (2012)

Volcanoes: fire and life. Jon Chad; with color by Sophie Goldstein. First Second 2016 128 p. Color; Illustration (Science comics)
Grades: 4 5 6 7   **741.5; 551.21**
1. Volcanoes
1626723613; 9781626723610, $19.99

This book in the Science Comics series, by Jon Chad, focuses on volcanoes. "Thanks to magma vents, shifting continental plates, and volcanic eruptions, we know that our planet is alive and in motion. Alongside Aurora, a young explorer, you'll learn that volcanoes are just one of the massively powerful forces at work on our planet. From catastrophic destruction to the creation of new land masses, volcanoes have made their mark on our amazing Earth." (Publisher's note)

"Chad's well-drawn and clearly labeled diagrams in rich, saturated colors concisely explain key concepts, and vocabulary words are defined both in the text and a glossary. While the stylized cartoon figures and adventure narrative are an entertaining framework, the science fittingly occupies the center stage." Booklist

Chanani, Nidhi
Pashmina. Nidhi Chanani. First Second 2017 161 p. Color; Illustration
Grades: 4 5 6 7 8   **741.5**

1. India — Fiction; 2. Mother-daughter relationship — Fiction
1626720886; 9781626720879; 9781626720886, $21.99

LC 2016961589

In this graphic novel, by Nidhi Chanani, "Priyanka Das has so many unanswered questions: Why did her mother abandon her home in India years ago? What was it like there? And most importantly, who is her father, and why did her mom leave him behind? But Pri's mom avoids these questions.... For Pri, her mother's homeland can only exist in her imagination. That is, until she finds a mysterious pashmina tucked away in a forgotten suitcase." (Publisher's note)

"Contemporary reality is shown in grayscale; the past in sepia hues; and Pri's imagined India in rich colors that radiate off the pages. Priyanka is a realistically complex, sometimes moody character, with depth shown through her varied interests and inquisitive musings." Horn Book

Chantler, Scott

The **captive** prince. Scott Chantler. Kids Can Press 2012 116 p. Color illustration
Grades: 4 5 6 7
741.5; 741.5/971; Fic
1. Thieves — Fiction; 2. Graphic novels; 3. Adventure fiction
9781554537778, $8.95; 9781451782806, $17.95 ; 1554537762; 9781554537761, $17.95

Courtesy of Kids Can Press

This children's adventure book by Scott Chantler is the "third title of the...Three Thieves graphic novel series[.] Dessa, Topper and Fisk are still running from the Queen's Dragons and trying to find Dessa's missing twin brother. But when Dessa inadvertently rescues a prince — putting kingdoms at stake and love on the line — the adventure quickly becomes a royal mess!" (Publisher's note)

The **iron** hand. Scott Chantler. Kids Can Press 2016 126 p. Color; Illustration (Three thieves)
Grades: 3 4 5 6
741.5
1. Orphans — Graphic novels; 2. Knights and knighthood — Graphic novels; 3. Adventure fiction
1771380527; 9781771380522, $16.95

LC 2016032329

Courtesy of Kids Can Press

In this conclusion to the Three Thieves series, by Scott Chantler, "now that Dessa has learned the truth about her past, she agrees to form an alliance with the badly injured Captain Drake against Greyfalcon. The pair travel together to the royal city to rescue Dessa's twin brother, Jared, from Greyfalcon's evil clutches and put Jared in his rightful place on the throne. But their plans go awry when they arrive to find Jared already on the throne!" (Publisher's note)

"A well-wrought, well-timed, and satisfying finale to this well-conceived series." Kirkus

The **king's** dragon. Scott Chantler. Kids Can Press 2014 112 p. Illustration; Color (Three Thieves)
Grades: 3 4 5 6
741.5; Fic
1. Fantasy graphic novels; 2. Knights and knighthood — Graphic novels
9781554537792, $8.95; 1554537797

In this graphic novel written and illustrated by Scott Chantler, "royal knight Capt. Drake...briefly catches up with his quarry, Dessa, a young

circus acrobat hobbled (but not much) by a broken leg, and also looks back on his early days as a member of the elite but corrupt Dragons." (Kirkus Reviews)

"Black-and-white art among color signifies the flashback scenes, making the transitions easy to follow. The backstory will be satisfying to fans." Horn Book

Tower of treasure. Kids Can Press 2010 112p. Illustration (Three thieves)
Grades: 3 4 5 6
741.5
1. Acrobats and acrobatics — Fiction; 2. Adventure graphic novels; 3. Circus — Fiction; 4. Graphic novels; 5. Thieves — Fiction
978-1-55453-414-2, $17.99; 1-55453-414-3; 978-1-55453-415-9 (pa), $8.95; 1-55453-415-1 (pa)

Courtesy of Kids Can Press

"As an acrobat in a traveling circus, 14-year-old orphan Dessa Redd flies through the air with ease. Still, she is weighed down by troubling memories. But when her ragtag circus troupe pulls into the city of Kingsbridge, Dessa feels a tickle of hope. Maybe here in the royal city she will finally find her twin brother — or the mysterious man who snatched him away when they were just children. Meanwhile, Topper, the circus juggler, recruits Dessa and the circus strongman, Fisk, for the job of robbing the royal treasury." (Publisher's note)

Other titles in this series are:The sign of the black rock (2011);The captive prince (2012);The king's dragon (2014);Pirates of the silver coast (2014);The dark island (2016);The iron hand (2016)

Chen, Wei Dong

Monkey King: Journey to the West. created by Wei Dong Chen; illustrated by Chao Peng. JR Comics 2012 173 p. Illustration
Grades: 5 6 7 **Fic; 741.5/951**
1. Graphic novels; 2. Chinese mythology
8994208712; 9788994208718, $29.27

This is the third volume in Wei Dong Chen's Monkey King series, a graphic novel series based on the Chinese classical literature novel "Journey to the West." In "the first volume, Sun Wu Kong is born from a stone and goes on a quest of find the secret of eternal life. In succeeding volumes the Monkey King steals the heavenly peaches and is imprisoned by Buddha for 500 years." (Library Media Connection)

Monkey King: The Bane of Heaven. created by Wei Dong Chen; illustrated by Chao Peng. Jr Comics 2012 174 p. Illustration
Grades: 5 6 7 **741.5/951; Fic**
1. Graphic novels; 2. Chinese mythology
8994208704; 9788994208701, $29.27

This is the second volume in Wei Dong Chen's Monkey King series. Here, "Sun Wu Kong is named emperor of heaven, [and] begins to make himself comfortable among the gods, and quickly wears out his welcome." The series is a retelling of the classical Chinese work "Journey to the West." (Booklist)

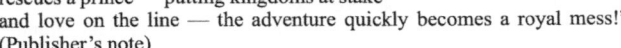

Chmakova, Svetlana

★ **Awkward.** by Svetlana Chmakova. Yen Press 2015 210 p. Illustration; Color

Grades: 5 6 7 8   **741.5**

1. Clubs — Fiction; 2. Graphic novels; 3. Middle schools — Fiction; 4. Popularity — Fiction; 5. Schools — Fiction; 6. School stories — Graphic novels

0316381306; 0316381322; 9780316381307; 9780316381321, $24

LC 2015945195

Eisner Nominee: Best Publication for Teens (2016)

In this middle grade book, by Svetlana Chmakova, "protagonist Peppi is fantastically imperfect.... She is the new girl at Berrybrook Middle School and is having a hard time fitting in because of her struggles with social anxiety. The work opens with the young teen pushing away the first person who tries to help her, Jaime, and it only gets more awkward from there." (School Library Journal)

Brave. Svetlana Chmakova. Yen Press 2017 238 p. Color; Illustration

Grades: 4 5 6 7   **741.5; Fic**

1. Popularity — fiction; 2. Middle schools — fiction

0316363170; 9780316363174, $24; 9780316363181

LC 2017934376

In this book, by Svetlana Chmakova, "in his daydreams, Jensen is the biggest hero that ever was, saving the world and his friends on a daily basis. But his middle school reality is very different — math is hard, getting along with friends is hard.... And the pressure's on even more once the school newspaper's dynamic duo, Jenny and Akilah, draw Jensen into the whirlwind of school news, social-experiment projects, and behind-the-scenes club drama." (Publisher's note)

"This is a subtle, well-observed treatment of a kid who doesn't fit in. The various threads of friendship and belonging are woven masterfully and ring true, with a conclusion that brings everything together." SLJ

CLAMP (Mangaka group)

Angelic Layer. CLAMP. Dark Horse Manga 2012 426 p.

Grades: 5 6 7 8   **741.5; Fic**

1. Games — Fiction; 2. Japan — Fiction; 3. Manga; 4. Shonen manga

161655021X; 9781616550219, $19.99

"Junior high student Misaki Suzuhara has just arrived in Tokyo to live with her glamorous TV news star aunt and to attend the prestigious Eriol Academy. But what excites her above everything is Angelic Layer, the arena game where you control an 'Angel' — a miniature robot fighter whose moves depend on your mind!" (Publisher's note)

Originally published in the U.S. by Tokyopop; Volume 1 of 2

Clanton, Ben

★ **Narwhal:** Unicorn of the Sea. Ben Clanton. McClelland & Stewart Ltd 2016 64 p. Color; Illustration (Narwhal and Jelly)

Grades: 5 6 7 8   **741.5; Fic**

1. Jellyfishes — fiction; 2. Friendship; 3. Narwhal — fiction

1101918268; 9781101918265, $12.99

LC 2016042380

Eisner Award: Best Publication for Early Readers (2017)

"Narwhal is a happy-go-lucky narwhal. Jelly is a no-nonsense jellyfish. The two might not have a lot in common, but they do they love waffles, parties and adventures. Join Narwhal and Jelly as they discover the whole wide ocean together." (Publisher's note)

"The incessant charm and unabashed joy should make this an easy sell. Swimmingly delightful and a guaranteed smile-maker." Kirkus

Another title in this series is: Super Narwhal and Jelly Jolt (2017)

Super Narwhal and Jelly Jolt. Ben Clanton. Tundra Books 2017 64 p. Color; Illustration (Narwhal and Jelly)

Grades: 1 2 3
741.5

1. Superheroes — Fiction; 2. Narwhal — fiction; 3. Friendship; 4. Superhero graphic novels

9781101918296, $12.99; 9781101918302; 9781101919194

LC 2016948348

Courtesy of Tundra Books

In this graphic novel, by Ben Clanton, "happy-go-lucky Narwhal and no-nonsense Jelly find their inner superheroes in three new under-the-sea adventures. In the first story, Narwhal reveals his superhero alter-ego.... Next, Narwhal uses his superpower to help a friend find his way back home. In the third story, Jelly is feeling blue and Narwhal comes to the rescue.... Clanton showcases the joys of friendship and the power of believing in yourself and others...." (Publisher's note)

"The laughs are mighty, but even mightier is Narwhal's anything-is-possible attitude and deep reserves of heart." Pub Wkly

Coelho, Rogério

Boat of dreams. Rogerio Coelho. Tilbury House Publishers 2017 80 p. Color; Illustration

Grades: 1 2 3 4
741.5; E

1. Dreams — Fiction; 2. Boats and boating — Fiction; 3. Stories without words

9780884485285, $22.95; 9780884485346

LC 2016951433

Courtesy of Tilbury House Publishers

This wordless picture book/graphic hybrid by Rogerio Coelho "opens with an elderly man waking up. He goes outside and we discover he lives at the seaside. After a floating bottle beaches, he opens it to find a piece of paper. He begins to draw: a picture of a boat. He places the paper back in the bottle and returns it to the sea. The action then shifts to a city, where a small boy finds an envelope at his doorstep. Inside is the drawing." (Booklist)

"A nuanced physical and emotional landscape aimed to capture experienced readers but likely to snag the occasional neophyte as well." Kirkus

First published in Brazil by Editora Positivo Ltda., in 2015 — Colophon.

Cohn, Ariel

The **Zoo** Box. Ariel Cohn; illustrated by Aron Nels Steinke. First Second 2014 48 p. Color; Illustration

Grades: K 1 2
741.5; Fic

1. Human-animal relationships — Fiction; 2. Zoos — Juvenile fiction

1626720525; 9781626720527, $17.99

Eisner Award: Best Publication for Early Readers (2015)

"When Erika and Patrick's parents leave them home alone for the night, they head straight to the attic to explore. When they open a mysterious box, hundreds of animals come pouring out! Soon the town is awash in more and more zoo animals, until Erika and Patrick discover that...the animals now run a zoo full of humans!" (Publisher's note)

"Simple panel design on picture-book-size pages with bright colors, bold figures, and easy-reading text in the word balloons make this book great fun for new readers." Booklist

Colfer, Eoin

Artemis Fowl: the graphic novel. adapted by Eoin Colfer and Andrew Donkin; art by Giovanni Rigano; color by Paolo Lammana. Hyperion Books for Children 2007 un Illustration

Grades: 4 5 6 7 8 9   **741; 741.5; Fic**

1. Adventure graphic novels; 2. Fantasy graphic novels; 3. Graphic novels

978-0-7868-4881-2, $18.99; 0-7868-4881-2; 978-0-7868-4882-9 (pa), $9.99; 0-7868-4882-0 (pa)

Twelve-year-old genius and criminal mastermind Artemis Fowl runs his missing father's crime empire and gets his hands on a book that will give him access to the underground fairy world. This graphic novel adaptation gives the book a European look and color palette

"Excellent use of color and shading gives the panels a tremendous sense of light with enchanting effect. Characters are expressively brought to life with fun, exaggerated style." SLJ

Other Artemis Fowl graphic novels are: Artemis Fowl: the Arctic incident (2009); Artemis Fowl: the eternity code (2013); Artemis Fowl: the opal deception (2014)

Conner, Daniel

William Shakespeare's A midsummer night's dream. adapted by Daniel Conner; illustrated by Rod Espinosa.. ABDO/Magic Wagon 2008 48p. Illustration

Grades: 5 6 7 8 9 10   **741.5; Fic**

1. Graphic novels.; 2. Youths' writings.; 3. Shakespeare, William — Adaptations

978-1-60270-191-5, $28.50

LC 2008-10745

In Athens, the ruler Theseus prepares to marry Hippolyta. Meanwhile, Hermia and Lysander run away to the forest because Hermia doesn't want to marry Demetrius, who follows them into the forest with Helena, whom he loves. Enter Puck, mischievous fairy who serves Oberon, the King of the Fairies. When he is ordered to find a flower whose nectar acts like a love potion and use it on Queen Titania, Puck also decides to play with the two young couples. And meanwhile again, a group of guildsmen prepare a play for their ruler's wedding. Havoc ensues. This graphic novel adaptation retains some of the original language from Shakespeare's play, while paring down the story to appeal to struggling readers. The book includes a short biography of Shakespeare, a summary of the play, a glossary, and a short selection of famous lines and phrases from the play.

Part of the Graphic Shakespeare series

Cook, Katie

Gronk; Volume 1: a monster's story. by Katie Cook; interior color by Kevin Minor. Action Lab Entertainment 2015 64 p. Color; Illustration

Grades: 2 3 4 5   **741.5; Fic**

1. Friendship — Graphic novels; 2. Monsters — Graphic novels

9781632290885, $9.99; 163229088X

In this graphic novel by Katie Cook, "Gronk is a monster...and not a very good one. 'Gronk' tells the tale of a young monster who has turned her back on monsterdom (mostly because no one found her scary) and has become fascinated with humans. She moves in with her human friend Dale and her pets Kitty and Harli, a 160 lb. Newfoundland Dale wants to declare as a dependent to the IRS." (Publisher's note)

"While the humor centers on the imaginative and curious monster's mischief, there is an underlying message of acceptance and inclusion throughout. Originally published as a black-and-white webcomic, this collection adds vivid colors to Cook's strong line work and sweetly expressive characters." SLJ

Cooper, John

Richard the Lionheart: The Life of a King and Crusader. by David West & Jackie Gaff; illustrated by John Cooper. Rosen Publishing Group 2005 48p. Illustration

Grades: 3 4 5 6 7 8   **942.03; 741.5; 92**

1. Biographical graphic novels; 2. Graphic novels; 3. Richard, I, King of England; 4. Great Britain — History — 1154-1399, Plantagenets — Graphic novels

1-4042-0241-2, $29.25

LC 2004011267

Politician, military leader, crusader, and King of England, Richard the Lionheart has been the subject of Middle Ages' studies for centuries. His early years were marked by bitter rivalry with his father and brothers, but once crowned King in 1189, his primary ambition was to lead a crusade to the Holy Land to recapture the city of Jerusalem. This graphic novel treats readers to a retelling of the King's battle against Saladin for control of the Holy Land, his subsequent imprisonment, and ultimate return to the throne. It includes additional information, a glossary, and a list of books for further reading.

Part of the Graphic Nonfiction series.

Corona, Jorge

Feathers. written & illustrated by Jorge Corona; colors by Jen Hickman; letters by Deron Bennett. Archaia 2015 160 p. Illustration

Grades: 5 6 7 8   **741.5; Fic**

1. Monsters — Graphic novels; 2. Orphans — Graphic novels

9781608867530, $24.99; 1608867536

LC 2015055238

In this graphic novel, written & illustrated by Jorge Corona, "Poe has lived his entire eleven-year-old life hidden away under the protection of his adoptive father, Gabriel. He spends his days secretly helping...bands of orphans who roam the slums.... When Bianca, an over-protected girl from the wealthy City beyond the Wall, escapes into the Maze in search of adventure, their worlds collide." (Publisher's note)

"Poe is a true underdog hero, and Bianca's wish to be set free from her restricting life is something to which middle grades readers can relate. Stunning illustrations contrast the stark white orderly city with the dark and dangerous Maze." SLJ

Cosson, M. J.

Sherlock Holmes and a scandal in Bohemia. based on the stories of Sir Arthur Conan Doyle; adapted by Murray Shaw and M.J. Cosson; illustrated by Sophie Rohrbach.. Lerner Publishing Group/Graphic Universe 2010 48p. Illustration

Grades: 3 4 5 6 7 8

741.5; Fic

1. Authors; 2. Graphic novels; 3. Mystery graphic novels; 4. Mystery writers; 5. Novelists; 6. Doyle, Arthur Conan Sir, 1859-1930 — Adaptations

978-0-7613-6185-5, $26.60; 978-0-7613-6197-8 (pa), $6.95

Courtesy of Lerner Publishing Group

LC 2009-51763

The King of Bohemia comes to Sherlock Holmes and asks him to retrieve a photograph from the king's former lover, Irene Adler. He wants to be married, and Miss Adler is blackmailing him with the incriminating photograph. Holmes dons a disguise in order to steal the photo from Miss Adler's house, but the singer proves to be an intelligent, formidable foe. This book adapts the story written by Sir Arthur Conan Doyle, with sepia-toned art. It includes clues to Holmes' reasoning and a list for further reading.

Coudray, Philippe

Benjamin Bear in Brain storms!. by Philippe Coudray. TOON Books 2015 40 p. Color; Illustration (Benjamin Bear)
Grades: PreK K 1 2   **741.5**
1. Bears — Fiction; 2. Graphic novels; 3. Humorous stories; 4. Humorous fiction; 5. Creative thinking — Graphic novels
1935179829; 9781935179825, $12.95
                                                LC 2014028851
"Benjamin Bear can always surprise his friends, whether it's by walking on his hands during a snowstorm or by using a tree as a parachute. This unassuming bear may at first seem down-to-earth, but his ideas are always out of this world." (Publisher's note)

"Benjamin Bear returns for a third round of humorously bizarre mini-sagas.... Coudray uses visuals effectively to consistently get laughs (many of the strips are completely wordless)." Horn Book

★ **Benjamin** Bear in Bright ideas!: a Toon book. by Philippe Coudray. Toon Books 2013 32 p.
Grades: PreK K 1   **741.5/973**
1. Bears — Fiction; 2. Graphic novels; 3. Humorous stories; 4. Animals — Graphic novels; 5. Picture books for children
1935179225; 9781935179221, $12.95
                                                LC 2012022895
This children's picture book is part of the Benjamin Bear series, where the bear and his animal friends appear in minimalist fables drawn...from French cartoonist [Philippe] Coudray's original series.... In 'Can I Get a Ride?' [Benjamin] picks up one woodland hitchhiker after another until, in the last panel, tables turn and they have to carry him. In 'See-Saw,' he 'helps' a fox carry a log (and demonstrates a principle of physics) not by lifting the long end, but by hopping onto the short end." (Kirkus)

Benjamin Bear in Fuzzy thinking: a Toon book. Toon Books 2011 32p. Illustration
Grades: PreK K 1 2   **741.5; 741**
1. Bears — Graphic novels; 2. Graphic novels; 3. Humorous graphic novels
978-1-935179-12-2, $12.99; 1-935179-12-8
                                                LC 2011000801
"The latest entry in the TOON Books line of emerging-reader comics pushes a whole new sort of envelope: outré humor for the early grade-school set. These single-page strips starring a peculiar bear and his critter pals will feel fresh to young readers not just because the jokes rely on incisive understatement rather than broad-stroke exaggeration but also because the humor requires a bit of work to arrive at the surprising, sometimes sophisticated, and yet rarely out-of-reach punch lines." (Booklist)

Other titles in this series are:Benjamin Bear in Bright Ideas (2013);Benjamin Bear in Brain Storms (2015)

Craddock, Erik

Robot frenzy; 8. Erik Craddock. Random House Books for Young Readers 2013 96 p. (Stone rabbit)
Grades: 2 3 4 5 6   **741.5/973**
1. Animals — Fiction; 2. Chores — Fiction; 3. Graphic novels; 4. Humorous stories; 5. Robots — Graphic novels; 6. Rabbits — Graphic novels
0375869131; 9780375869136, $6.99; 9780375969133
                                                LC 2012049524
In this graphic novel by Erik Craddock "Stone Rabbit and his friends create robots to help out with chores [but] a glitch in the programming

sends the 'bots into a malfunctioning frenzy! Will our long-eared hero be able to shut down these mechanical maniacs before they destroy Happy Glades? Or will his systems crash?" (Publisher's note)

Stone Rabbit: Pirate Palooza. Random House Children's Books 2009 96p.
Grades: 2 3 4 5   **741.5; Fic**
1. Adventure graphic novels; 2. Graphic novels; 3. Humorous graphic novels; 4. Pirates — Graphic novels
978-0-375-95660-7, $11.99; 978-0-375-85660-0 (pa), $5.99
Our unnamed bunny hero plays at pro wrestling with his friend Andy when they break a leg on the coffee table. On their way to buy a replacement leg, Andy gets sidetracked to the local comics store for new comics day; and the rabbit finds a wooden leg. It's the peg leg of Barnacle Bob, a legendary pirate. When the rabbit uses it to fix his coffee table, he releases the ghosts of Barnacle Bob, his crew, and his ship, the Biscotti. Andy becomes the cabin boy while our rabbit hero becomes the first mate, and there's all kinds of trouble.

"This book will give those children who love the ridiculous just what they want: a zany, mile-a-minute graphic novel.... The bold illustrations are bursting at the seams with energy." SLJ
Other titles in this series are: BC Mambo (2009); Deep-Space Disco (2009); Superhero stampede (2009); Ninja slice (2010)

Superhero stampede. Random House 2010 94p. Illustration
Grades: 2 3 4 5   **741; 741.5**
978-0-375-85877-2, $5.99; 0-375-85877-6
"Stone Rabbit and his friends get sucked into the world of Andy's favorite comic book, where they become the superhero characters. The villains tempt Andy to the dark side, appealing to his anger about the teasing and name-calling to which Stone Rabbit and Henri have subjected him." (Booklist)

Crane, Jordan

The **clouds** above. Fantagraphics 2005 216p. Illustration
Grades: 3 4 5 6 7 8   **741.5; Fic**
1. Fantasy graphic novels; 2. Graphic novels
1-560976-27-6, $18.95
Simon and his cat Jack embark on an adventure among the clouds one day when Simon skips school and finds a rickety stairway leading skyward. They find a friendly cloud, flee thunderstorms and trick a flock of belligerent birds, only to find themselves back at school.

"Everything's exciting...and the dialogue is witty and bubbly.... The book is a joy to look at—Crane's loose, gliding lines burst with character, and his compositional gifts make every panel worth contemplating on its own." Publ Wkly

Crilley, Mark

★ **Akiko** pocket-size, vol. 1. Sirius Entertainment 2004 192p. Illustration
Grades: 3 4 5 6 7 8 9 10   **741.5; Fic**
1. Adventure graphic novels; 2. Graphic novels; 3. Science fiction graphic novels
1-579890-67-9, $11.95
Fourth-grader Akiko travels to the planet Smoo, on a mission to rescue King Froptoppit's son from the evil Alia Rellapor. Teamed up with the scruffy adventurer Spuckler, bookish Mr. Beeba, Spuckler's robot Gax, and the floating alien known as Poog, Akiko faces sea monsters, Sky Pirates, Sleeslup worms, and other dangers as they travel around the planet on their quest. This is the first volume in an ongoing series of graphic novels. Crilley also has written a series of prose fiction featuring Akiko and her friends.

Croall, Marie P.

Marwe: into the land of the dead: an East African legend. author, Marie P. Croall; pencils by Ray Lago and inks by Craig Hamilton.. Lerner Publishing Group 2009 48p. Illustration
Grades: 3 4 5 6 7 8 9
741.5; Fic
1. Fantasy graphic novels; 2. Folklore — East Africa — Graphic novels; 3. Graphic novels
978-0-8225-7134-6, $27.93

Courtesy of Lerner Publishing Group

LC 2007-1828

In this story retold from the oral tradition of the Chaga people in East Africa, Marwe lives in a village where times are hard and food is scarce. When she and her brother leave the family's bean fields to cool off at the river, monkeys destroy the entire crop. When her brother goes off to ask the family's forgiveness, Marwe sees something strange in the water and dives down; she passes through a strange doorway and finds herself in another land. Soon she learns she has come to the land of the dead, where an old woman welcomes her. Too scared to go home, Marwe stays there, and despite assurances that she needn't do anything, she works in the fields. When will Marwe think it's time to return home to her anxious and mourning family?
Part of the Graphic Universe Myths and Legends series

Psyche & eros: the lady and the monster: a Greek myth. story by Marie Croall; pencils and inks by Ron Randall. Lerner Publishing Group 2009 48p. Illustration
Grades: 3 4 5 6 7 8 9
741.5; Fic
1. Fantasy graphic novels; 2. Graphic novels; 3. Greek mythology — Graphic novels
978-0-8225-7177-3, $27.93

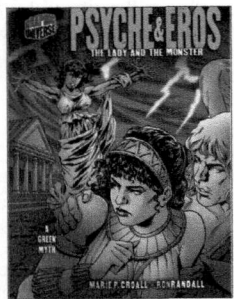

Courtesy of Lerner Publishing Group

LC 2007-43353

Psyche is a beautiful young woman, so beautiful that men start to give her gifts instead of taking them to the temple. This makes Aphrodite jealous, and she sends her son, Eros, to prick Psyche with an arrow so no man will ever fall in love with her. However, Eros falls in love with Psyche. He arranges for the Oracle to tell Psyche's father that his daughter must be taken up on a mountain to marry a monster. He only comes to her at night, and they love each other; but Psyche's sisters convince her that she should see her husband. When hot wax from her candle burns Eros and wakens him, he must leave her. Now Psyche, unable to convince any other god or goddess to help her, must go to Aphrodite, who sets impossible tasks that Psyche manages to accomplish with help from unexpected sources.
Part of the Graphic Universe Myths and Legends series

Cutting, Robert

March of the Dinosaurs. Harcourt Achieve/Steck-Vaughn 2006 48p. Illustration
Grades: 3 4 5 6 7 8
741.5; Fic
1. Dinosaurs — Graphic novels; 2. Graphic novels; 3. Science fiction graphic novels
978-1-4190-3194-6, $8.99

Traveling on a time machine, a scientist from the future goes back to the Cretaceous Age of the Dinosaurs with her niece and nephew. The time machine breaks down just as a giant meteor hurtles toward the Earth. Will they escape or will they share the fate of the dinosaurs? This science fiction graphic novel includes prose intervals that give facts about dinosaurs.
Part of the Timeline Graphic Novels series.

Mars Colony. Harcourt Achieve/Steck-Vaughn 2006 48p. Illustration
Grades: 3 4 5 6 7 8
741.5; Fic
1. Graphic novels; 2. Mystery graphic novels; 3. Science fiction graphic novels
978-1-4190-3213-4, $8.99

In the year 2130, the Chang family is one of 128 families sent to Mars to found the first human colony there. Jenny Chang and her brother Derek eagerly explore their new home; they are in for a big surprise. This science fiction story is interspersed with facts about Mars and space exploration.
Part of the Timeline Graphic Novels series.

Czekaj, Jef

Grampa & Julie: Shark hunters. Top Shelf 2004 un Illustration
Grades: 2 3 4 5 6
741.5; Fic
1. Adventure graphic novels; 2. Graphic novels; 3. Humorous graphic novels
1-891830-52-X, $14.95

"In this full-color graphic novel, Julie and her grampa spend summer vacation looking for the largest shark in the world, Stephen. Meeting Stephen leads to even more exciting adventures, including a quest to find Stephen's mom. The shark hunters meet monkeys at the bottom of the ocean, pirates, and even aliens. Gramma has to rescue them from a couple of scrapes." Booklist

"Taken from the pages of Nickelodeon magazine, this charming children's comic overflows with humor, adventure and whimsy." Publ Wkly

Dahl, Roald

The **Gremlins:** The Lost Walt Disney Production: A Royal Air Force Story. Dark Horse Books 2006 un Illustration
Grades: 4 5 6 7 8 9 10 11 12 Adult
741.5; Fic
1. Graphic novels; 2. Humorous graphic novels; 3. World War, 1939-1945 — Graphic novels
978-1-59307-496-8, $12.95

This is an illustrated novella, the first published work of RAF Flight Lieutenant Roald Dahl in his only collaboration with Walt Disney Studios. Originally published in 1943, the story was supposed to become a film combining live action with animation; the movie was never made, although the studio produced a lot of illustrations and samples. The story tells about one young Royal Air Force pilot named Gus, who first sees the little gremlins that wreak havoc on his plane. While the gremlins first cause lots of trouble, eventually Gus convinces them to work with the RAF.

Daning, Tom

African Mythology: Anansi. Rosen Publishing Group 2007 24p. Illustration
Grades: 1 2 3 4 5
398.2; 741.5
1. African mythology — Graphic novels; 2. Anansi (Legendary character) — Graphic novels; 3. Graphic novels
978-1-4042-3398-0, $22.50

LC 2006002786

Anansi the spider is a trickster. In this graphic novel retelling of a West African myth, Anansi must outsmart the powerful and dangerous creatures of Africa to become the owner of all the stories in the world. Written for beginning readers, this book includes a simple family tree of the gods.
Part of the Jr. Graphic Mythologies series.

Chinese Mythology: The Four Dragons. Rosen Publishing Group 2007 24p. Illustration

Courtesy of Rosen Publishing

Grades: 1 2 3 4 5   **398.2; 741.5**
1. Chinese mythology — Graphic novels; 2. Folklore — China — Graphic novels; 3. Graphic novels
978-1-4042-3400-0, $22.50

LC 2006002787

The origins of the four great rivers of China are revealed in this classic myth. Against the landscapes of China, four dragons struggle against the Jade Emperor to bring water to the people of China in this simplified graphic novel for beginning readers. The book also provides a simple family tree.

Part of the Jr. Graphic Mythologies series.

Egyptian Mythology: Osiris and Isis. Rosen Publishing Group 2007 24p. Illustration
Grades: 1 2 3 4 5
299; 741.5
1. Egyptian mythology — Graphic novels; 2. Graphic novels; 3. Isis (Egyptian deity) — Graphic novels; 4. Osiris (Egyptian deity) — Graphic novels
978-1-4042-3399-7, $22.50

LC 2006003373

Courtesy of Rosen Publishing

Hieroglyphs reveal how Osiris, the King of Egypt, became the King of the Dead. His queen, Isis, restores the body of her murdered husband and helps him become king of the underworld in this simplified graphic novel. It includes a family tree of the gods.

Part of the Jr. Graphic Mythologies series.

Mesoamerican Mythology: Quetzalcoatl. Rosen Publishing Group 2007 24p. Illustration
Grades: 1 2 3 4 5
299.7; 741.5
1. Aztecs — Religion — Graphic novels; 2. Graphic novels; 3. Quetzalcoatl (Aztec deity) — Graphic novels
978-1-4042-3401-7

LC 2006003371

Courtesy of Rosen Publishing

Quetzalcoatl and Tezcatlipoca were never friends. But the two gods unite to defeat Tlatecuhtli, the demon caiman of the sea. The thrilling battle between the gods leads to the creation of the sky and land. This simplified graphic novel also includes a family tree of the gods.

Part of the Jr. Graphic Mythologies series.

Roman Mythology: Romulus and Remus. Rosen Publishing Group 2007 24p. Illustration
Grades: 1 2 3 4 5   **398.2; 292; 741.5**
1. Classical mythology — Graphic novels; 2. Graphic novels; 3. Remus (Legendary character) — Graphic novels; 4. Romulus (Legendary character) — Graphic novels
978-1-4042-3397-3, $22.50

LC 2006003372

Romulus and Remus, raised by wolves, were the twin founders of Rome. This simplified graphic novel for beginning readers recounts how the young bothers came to be cast out in the wilderness and how they avenged themselves upon their evil uncle. The book includes a simple family tree.

Part of the Jr. Graphic Mythologies series.

Dauvillier, Loïc
  Hidden: a child's story of the Holocaust. written by Loic Dauvillier; illustrated by Marc Lizano; color by Greg Salsedo; translated by Alexis Siegel. First Second 2014 80 p. Color; Illustration
Grades: 1 2 3 4 5
741.5
1. Grandmothers — Fiction; 2. Graphic novels; 3. Jews — France — Fiction; 4. France — History — German occupation, 1940-1945 — Fiction; 5. Holocaust, 1939-1945 — Fiction
1596438738; 9781596438736, $16.99

LC 2013023168

Mildred L. Batchelder Honor Book (2015)

"Dounia, a grandmother, tells her granddaughter the story even her son has never heard: how, as a young Jewish girl in Paris, she was hidden away from the Nazis by a series of neighbors and friends who risked their lives to keep her alive when her parents had been taken to concentration camps." (Publisher's note)

"Lizano's stylized illustrations depict characters with oversize heads, reminiscent of 'Peanuts' comics, giving this difficult subject an age-appropriate touch." SLJ

Originally published in 2012 by Le Lombard under the title L'Enfant Caché — Copyright page.

Davis, Eleanor
  ★ The **secret** science alliance and the copycat crook. Bloomsbury 2009 153p. Illustration
Grades: 3 4 5 6 7 8   **741.5; Fic**
1. Adventure graphic novels; 2. Graphic novels; 3. Humorous graphic novels; 4. Inventors — Fiction; 5. School stories
978-1-59990-142-8, $18.99; 1-59990-142-0; 978-1-59990-396-5 (pa), $10.99; 1-59990-396-2 (pa)

LC 2008-45399

Eleven-year-old Julian Calendar thought changing schools would mean leaving his "nerdy" persona behind, but instead he forms an alliance with fellow inventors Greta and Ben and works with them to prevent an adult from using one of their gadgets for nefarious purposes

"With its frenetically eye-catching, full-color panels chock-full of humorous and informative detail, Davis's first (of many, one hopes) graphic adventure of the SSA pumps new life into the kids' secret society formula." Kirkus

Stinky: a Toon Book. RAW Junior 2008 40p. Illustration
Grades: K 1 2 3   **741.5; Fic**
1. Friendship — Graphic novels; 2. Graphic novels; 3. Humorous graphic novels; 4. Monsters — Graphic novels
978-0-9799238-4-5, $12.95; 0-9799238-4-0

LC 2007-94387

A Geisel Award honor book, 2009

Stinky the monster is sort of a young Shrek — a little grumpy, he loves pickles and likes his swamp nicely yucky and mucky, with no kids. Kids are gross, they like to take baths. When a new boy dares to build a treehouse in the middle of his swamp, Stinky takes action with all kinds of crazy plans to scare the boy away. However, every plan backfires, so what's a monster to do?

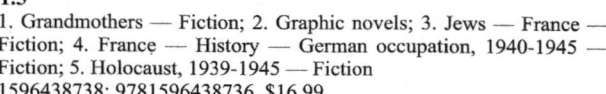

Courtesy of Rosen Publishing

"The charming cartoon artwork, full of humorous details, complements the text, and the muted color scheme makes Stinky endearing rather than scary. The simple vocabulary and repetition of words make the text accessible for emergent readers." SLJ

De Groot, Bob

Clifton Jade. Cinebook 2008 48p.

Grades: 5 6 7 8 9   **741.5; Fic**
1. Adventure graphic novels; 2. Graphic novels; 3. Humorous graphic novels; 4. Spies — Graphic novels
978-1-905460-52-6, $11.95

Sir Harold Wilberforce Clifton, ex-Secret Service and retired Colonel, works as a private detective, as well as leading a troop of young scouts. With the help of his housekeeper, Mrs. Partridge, who's also a dab hand at auto mechanics, he still helps the government. This time, however, he's being tailed by someone and then summoned to a retirement home where he finds his old World War II nemesis, Otto Kartoffeln, who tells him a group of neo-Nazis are searching for a long-lost Nazi treasure in order to bring about the 4th Reich. The mysterious shadow is Jade, a young agent who was trying to complete her training; now she and Clifton must stop the neo-Nazis from finding the treasure.

Part of the Clifton series, originally published in France as Clifton Jade.

Del Rio, Tania

Sabrina the Teenage Witch: The Magic Revisited. Archie Comics 2006 un Illustration

Grades: 4 5 6 7 8 9   **741.5; Fic**
1. Fantasy graphic novels; 2. Graphic novels; 3. Humorous graphic novels; 4. Witches — Graphic novels
1-879794-19-5, $7.49

The first four issues of Sabrina the Teenage Witch's "manga makeover" are collected in this special edition trade paperback. Writer-artist Tania del Rio presents these tales of magical flights of fancy and romantic intrigue... sprinkled with a dash of humor. Sabrina's awakening powers and the various love triangle combinations that have formed since keep her busy at school, on dates, and...everywhere.

Delsante, Vito

Before they were famous: Babe Ruth. Aladdin Paperbacks 2009 121p.

Grades: 3 4 5 6 7 8   **741.5; 920**
1. Baseball players; 2. Baseball players — Graphic novels; 3. Biographical graphic novels; 4. Graphic novels; 5. Ruth, Babe, 1895-1948
978-1-4169-5071-4, $8.99

      LC 2008-929319

Babe Ruth is still considered to be one of the best professional baseball players of all time, and he was the first "home run king" of the sport. This graphic novel, adapted from Babe Ruth by Guernsey Van Riper, Jr., part of the Childhood of Famous Americans series, takes readers back to the troubled childhood of George Ruth. In Baltimore, Maryland in 1902, the Ruth family struggles to keep their restaurant going, and their young son George is a troublemaker; eventually, they send George to St. Mary's Industrial School for Boys. It's a boarding school run by Catholic monks, and George will have to stay there until he's twenty-one. At the school, George discovers baseball, and it transforms his life. When he's asked to sign up with the Baltimore Orioles at the age of nineteen, his new teammates call him Babe. This fictionalized biography will help young readers get a sense of the person behind the legend.

DeMatteis, J. M.

Abadazad: The Dream Thief. by J.M. DeMatteis; drawings by Mike Ploog; colors by Nick Bell. Hyperion Books for Children 2006 un Illustration

Grades: 5 6 7 8 9   **741.5; Fic**
1. Adventure graphic novels; 2. Fantasy graphic novels; 3. Graphic novels
1-4231-00646, $9.99

In the magical land of Abadazad, Kate needs all the help she can get when she encounters the Lanky Man. He's mean and heartless, and he wants to steal children's dreams. Everyone seems to be against her, which only makes her more determined to find her brother. And Matt is getting closer, isn't he? This story is a hybrid, combining prose text with pages of sequential art from the original comic books.

Abadazad: The Road to Inconceivable. Hyperion Books for Children 2006 un Illustration

Grades: 5 6 7 8 9   **741.5; Fic**
1. Adventure graphic novels; 2. Fantasy graphic novels; 3. Graphic novels
1-4231-0062-X, $9.99

Kate's little brother Matt disappeared five years ago, and Kate thinks she will never see him again. But then she finds out that Matt is trapped in the world of Abadazad. Will Kate have the courage to look for her brother? And if she leaves home, will she ever return? This story began as comic books, but the publisher went out of business before the story was completed. Now it's published as a hybrid, combining prose sections with pages of sequential art and spot illustrations.

★ The **stardust** kid. Boom! Studios 2008 un Illustration
Grades: 3 4 5 6 7 8 9 10 11 12 Adult   **741.5; Fic**
1. Adventure graphic novels; 2. Fantasy graphic novels; 3. Graphic novels
978-1-934506-04-2, $14.99

Twelve-year-old Cody's best friend is Paul Brightfield; they share a deep bond that goes far beyond mere friendship. What no one else knows is that Paul isn't human, he's one of the last Old Ones, ancient elemental beings who lived before man existed. One night, Paul disappears, and a hate-filled creature who has existed long buried beneath Wilde Park bursts out with a desire to destroy everything in the world. Only Cody, his little sister K.M., and his friend Alana and her little brother Nathaniel, remain, and somehow they must find The Stardust Kid and discover a way to stop the hate and restore their world. Some creatures might be frightening to younger readers, but anyone who likes the Harry Potter books shouldn't have a problem with this book.

Dembicki, Matt

★ **Trickster:** Native American tales: a graphic collection. edited by Matt Dembicki. Fulcrum 2010 231p. Illustration

Grades: 5 6 7 8
398.2; 398
1. Folklore — Graphic novels; 2. Graphic novels; 3. Native Americans — Folklore
978-1-55591-724-1 (pa), $22.95; 1-55591-724-0 (pa)

      LC 2009-49668

TRICKSTER

Courtesy of Fulcrum Publishing

"More than 40 storytellers and cartoonists have contributed to this original and provocative compendium of traditional folklore presented in authentic, colorful, and engaging sequential art. The stories are drawn from a variety of Native peoples across North America, and so the trickster character appears variously as Rabbit, a raccoon, Coyote, and in other guises; landscapes, clothing and rhythms of speech and action also vary in keeping with distinct traditions. Realistic, impressionistic, painterly, and cartoon styles of art are employed to echo and announce the tone of each tale and telling style, making this a rich visual treasure as well as cultural trove." SLJ

DeMolay, Jack
   Atlantis: The Mystery of the Lost City. Rosen Publishing Group 2007 24p. Illustration
Grades: 1 2 3 4 5
398.2; 741.5
   1. Atlantis — Graphic novels; 2. Graphic novels
   978-1-4042-3407-9
                        LC 2006003854

Courtesy of Rosen Publishing

   According to Plato, eleven thousand years ago a shining city with a marvelous civilization stood on a great island in the ocean. And then, disaster struck. Beginning readers can join the search for the lost city of Atlantis in this simplified graphic novel. The "Did You Know?" section provides more facts.
   Part of the Jr. Graphic Mysteries series.

   The **Bermuda** Triangle: The Disappearance of Flight 19. Rosen Publishing Group 2007 24p. Illustration
Grades: 1 2 3 4 5
741.5; 001.9
   1. Bermuda Triangle — Graphic novels; 2. Graphic novels
   978-1-4042-3404-8, $22.50
                        LC 20050337337

Courtesy of Rosen Publishing

   One day in 1945, five US Air Force bombers flew out to sea on a routine mission — and disappeared without a trace. Were they victims of a supernatural force? Beginning readers explore the mystery of the Bermuda Triangle in this simplified graphic novel. The "Did You Know?" section provides additional facts.
   Part of the Jr. Graphic Mysteries series.

   Bigfoot: A North American Legend. Rosen Publishing Group 2007 24p. Illustration
Grades: 1 2 3 4 5
741.5; 001.9
   1. Graphic novels; 2. Sasquatch — Graphic novels
   978-1-4042-3405-5, $22.50
                        LC 2006003390

Courtesy of Rosen Publishing

   Beginning readers track the sightings of the mysterious creature throughout the Pacific Northwest and uncover the ongoing search for proof of Bigfoot's existence in this simplified graphic novel. The "Did You Know?" section includes more facts.
   Part of the Jr. Graphic Mysteries series.

   The **Loch** Ness Monster: Scotland's Mystery Beast. Rosen Publishing Group 2007 24p. Illustration
Grades: 1 2 3 4 5
741.5; 001.9
   1. Graphic novels; 2. Loch Ness Monster — Graphic novels
   978-1-4042-3406-2, $22.50
                        LC 20050337336

Courtesy of Rosen Publishing

   Beginning readers uncover evidence of Nessie's existence through historical sightings and present-day efforts to locate this mysterious beast in this simplified graphic novel. The "Did You Know?" section provides additional facts.
   Part of the Jr. Graphic Mysteries series.

Demolis, Flo
   Around the world in 80 days. IDW Publishing 2009 60p. Illustration
Grades: 5 6 7 8 9   **741.5; Fic**
   1. Adventure graphic novels; 2. Authors; 3. Children's authors; 4. Graphic novels; 5. Novelists; 6. Science fiction writers; 7. Travel — Graphic novels; 8. Verne, Jules, 1828-1905 — Adaptations/Graphic novels
   978-1-60010-394-0, $14.99
   This graphic novel Verne's globe-trotting adventures of Phileas Fogg, English gentleman, his newly-hired French manservant, Passepartout, and the English detective, Fix, who pursues Fogg, convinced he is a master bank robber. Fogg makes a bet with fellow members of the Reform Club in 1872 that he can travel around the world in eighty days, but his precipitous departure makes Scotland Yard suspect him. The three men travel through India, where Fogg saves a beautiful young Indian woman from being burned alive, to Hong Kong, then Japan and then across the United States and onward. This adaptation was originally published in France. The book includes biographical information about Verne, historical information about what the world was like in the 1870s, and an analysis of the novel.

Despeyroux, Denise
   Dark graphic tales by Edgar Allan Poe. adapted by Denise Despeyroux; illustrations by Miquel Serratosa. Enslow Publishers 2012 96 p.
Grades: 3 4 5   **741.5; 741.5/946**
   1. Children's stories, American; 2. Graphic novels; 3. Horror stories; 4. Horror tales, American; 5. Short stories; 6. Mental illness — Fiction; 7. Horror fiction
   0766040860; 9780766040861, $30.60

                        LC 2011034273
   "This entry in the 'Dark Graphic Novels' series adapts three [Edgar Allan] Poe stories.... In 'The Gold Bug,' a man becomes obsessed with a golden beetle that is the key to an ancient mystery.... 'The System of Doctor Tarr and Professor Fether' chronicles a man's attendance at a banquet in an insane asylum and his dawning realization of what's happened to the patients. 'The Fall of the House of Usher'...tells of a brother's slow decline into insanity." (Booklist)
   Includes bibliographical references.

Deutsch, Barry
   Hereville: how Mirka caught a fish. Barry Deutsch. Amulet Books 2015 140 p. Color; Illustration
Grades: 4 5 6 7   **741.5/973**
   1. Jewish girls — Fiction; 2. Fishes — Fiction; 3. Babysitting — Fiction
   9781419708008, $17.95

In this book, by Barry Deutsch, "Welcome back to Hereville, where Mirka, the world's first time-travelling, monster-fighting Orthodox Jewish girl...[is] stuck babysitting her disapproving little sister, Layele. When Mirka pushes her sister into a stream, they both get in too deep with an angry magic fish.... When the fish kidnaps Layele, Mirka must find a way to save her little sister, and the clues she needs are hidden in her stepmother Fruma's past." (Publisher's note)

★ **Hereville:** how Mirka got her sword. Barry Deutsch; colors by Jake Richmond. Amulet Books 2010 137p. Illustration

Grades: 4 5 6 7   **741.5; Fic**
  1. Dragons — Graphic novels; 2. Fantasy graphic novels; 3. Graphic novels; 4. Jews — Graphic novels
  978-0-8109-8422-6, $15.95; 0-8109-8422-9; 9781419706196

LC 2010-924236

Mirka and her family live in an Orthodox Jewish village called Hereville. All she really wants to do is fight dragons, but what she has to fight is a troublesome pig that talks. Then Mirka meets the witch who lives nearby, and then confronts a troll, and soon she finds she has much more adventure than she knows how to handle.

"Deutsch creates authentic characters spiced with just enough fantasy to surprise.... Details of Orthodox daily life are well blended into the art and given just the right touches of explanation to keep readers on track." Booklist

Other titles in this series are: How Mirka met a meteorite (2012); How Mirka caught a fish (2014)

★ **Hereville:** How Mirka Met a Meteorite. Barry Deutsch; colors by Jake Richmond. Amulet Books 2012 123 p.

Grades: 3 4 5 6 7   **741.5**
  1. Witches — Fiction; 2. Adventure graphic novels; 3. Jews — Graphic novels; 4. Trolls — Fiction
  1419703986; 9781419703980, $16.95

LC 2012947050

This graphic novel by Barry Deutsch features a "wisecracking, adventure-loving, sword-wielding Orthodox Jewish heroine.... She fearlessly stands up to local bullies. She battles a very large, very menacing pig. And she boldly accepts a challenge from a mysterious witch, a challenge that could bring Mirka her heart's desire: a dragon-slaying sword! All she has to do is find — and outwit — the giant troll who's got it!" (Publisher's note)

Di Fiori, Lawrence
  Jackie and the Shadow Snatcher. [by] Lawrence Di Fiori. Alfred A. Knopf for Young Readers 2006 un Illustration

Grades: K 1 2 3 4   **741.5; Fic**
  1. Adventure graphic novels; 2. Graphic novels; 3. Mystery graphic novels
  0-375-87515-8; 0-375-97515-2 (lib bdg), $17.99

LC 2005-18290

"In this picture-book-size graphic novel, Di Fiori uses black-and-white illustrations to tell the story of Jackie, a boy who has lost his lunch pail, his math book, and his shadow. Wise Mr. Socrates tells Jackie that the evil Shadow Snatcher is the thief, and Jackie must confront him to get his shadow back.... The scenery is beautifully detailed without overwhelming the panels. Children will care less about that, however, than about the rollicking, old-fashioned adventure." Booklist

Diamond, Jeremy
  Nascar heroes #2: Who is Jimmy Dash?. 2009 un

Grades: 3 4 5 6 7 8   **741.5; Fic**

  1. Automobile racing — Graphic novels; 2. Graphic novels; 3. NASCAR — Graphic novels; 4. Superhero graphic novels
  978-1-59961-663-6, $22.78

LC 2009-9008

The accident that gave the Flatstock pit crew, plus Dashiell, super powers, also gave them to Jack Diesel; and he doesn't have any good intentions. When Jimmy Dash and Team Flatstock keep winning NASCAR races, Diesel resorts to dirty tricks with his laser heat vision and illegal gadgets on his cars. However, Team Flatstock owner Astor also gained powers in the accident; she sees visions of the near future. Diesel decides the entire Flatstock team would do anything for Astor, so he kidnaps her; Dashiell reveals his identity to the guys, and they go to rescue Astor. However, that's much easier said than done when Diesel will use any dirty trick to win.

Dirge, Roman
  It ate Billy on Christmas. Dark Horse Books 2007 un Illustration
Grades: 4 5 6 7 8 9 10 11 12 Adult   **741.5; Fic**
  1. Graphic novels; 2. Horror graphic novels; 3. Humorous graphic novels
  978-1-59307-853-9, $12.95

Lumi has been bullied by her brother Billy all her life, and this Christmas would have been more of the same, but for the weird, ugly little monster that crawled up from the abandoned well and came into their house. Mistaking it for the stuffed puppy she had requested from her parents, Lumi watches in amazement as it devours the bullying Billy when he shoots it with darts from his new dart gun. She makes a cardboard Billy, which fools her unsuspecting and clueless parents. A few weeks later, back at school, Lumi has to face the bullies who have made her school life miserable, but she has her "puppy" in her backpack and it's hungry.... Dirge wrote the story and drew the black and white illustrations, while Daily provided the color paintings. The story shows the monster eating Billy in one gulp, but there's little actual violence on the pages. The dark humor and twisted story line will appeal to those who enjoy Coraline and The Wolves in the Walls by Neil Gaiman, and the weird humor of Edward Gorey cartoons.

Donkin, Andrew
  ★ **Illegal**. Eoin Colfer, Andrew Donkin; art by Giovanni Rigano; lettering by Chris Dickey. Sourcebooks Inc 2018 144 p. Illustration
Grades: 5 6 7 8 9   **741.5; Fic**
  1. Poor people — Juvenile fiction; 2. Undocumented immigrants — Juvenile fiction; 3. Poor — Fiction; 4. Siblings — Fiction; 5. Undocumented immigrants — Fiction
  1492662143; 9781492662143, $19.99

In this book, by Eoin Colfer and Andrew Donkin, illustrated by Giovanni Rigano, "Ebo is alone. His brother, Kwame, has disappeared, and Ebo knows it can only be to attempt the hazardous journey to Europe, and a better life — the same journey their sister set out on months ago.... He sets out after Kwame and joins him on the quest to reach Europe. Ebo's epic journey takes him across the Sahara Desert to the dangerous streets of Tripoli, and finally out to the merciless sea." (Publisher's note)

"The format allows sensitive and difficult topics such as murder, death, and horrific, traumatizing conditions to unfold for children, Ebo's reactions speaking volumes and dramatic perspectives giving a sense of scope. A creators' note provides factual context, and an appendix offers an Eritrean refugee's minimemoir in graphic form." Kirkus

Dorison, Guillaume
  The **planet** of music. [original screenplay] by Clélia Constantine; adapted by Guillaume Dorison; illustrated by Élyum Studio; based on the

Courtesy of Lerner Publishing Group

masterpiece by Antoine de Saint-Exupéry; translation, Anne Collins Smith and Owen Smith. Graphic Universe 2012 54 p.
Grades: 3 4 5   **Fic; 741.5/944**
1. Snakes — Fiction; 2. Foxes — Fiction; 3. Science fiction — Fiction; 4. Music — Fiction
9780822594246; 0822594242; 9780761387534, $7.95
    LC 2011051352
This children's story, by Clelia Constantine, is book 3 of "The Little Prince" series. "With his wide-eyed innocence and unflappable devotion to helping others, the Little Prince works to save imperiled planets with the help of the Fox. Here, they stop the Snake from creating war between a music-loving populace and a flower-loving citizenry." (Kirkus Reviews)
Based on the animated series and an original story by Clélia Constantine.||An animated series based on the novel Le Petit Prince by Antoine de Saint Exupéry. Developed for television by Matthieu Delaporte, Alexandre de la Patellière, and Bertrand Gatignol. Directed by Pierre-Alain Chartier — Copyright p.

Downey, Glen
Escape from East Berlin. Harcourt Achieve/Steck-Vaughn 2007 48p. Illustration
Grades: 3 4 5 6 7 8   **741.5; Fic**
1. Adventure graphic novels; 2. Graphic novels; 3. Germany (East) — Graphic novels
978-1-4190-3222-6, $8.99
In the summer of 1963, President Kennedy of the United States speaks in West Berlin about liberty. From the other side of the Berlin Wall, the Kappel family listens to his every word. They decide to make a bid for freedom, but at what cost? This historical fiction graphic novel includes prose intervals that describe Berlin as the divided city after World War II, the building of the Wall, the various escape attempts made by East Berliners, part of President Kennedy's speech, and the fall of the Wall in 1989. There is brief violence when a vicious East German soldier is shot.
Part of the Timeline Graphic Novels series.

Fire Mountain. Harcourt Achieve/Steck-Vaughn 2006 48p. Illustration
Grades: 3 4 5 6 7 8   **741.5; Fic**
1. Adventure graphic novels; 2. Graphic novels; 3. Volcanoes — Graphic novels; 4. Pompeii (Extinct city) — Graphic novels
978-1-4190-3198-4, $8.99
Cato is a young slave boy in the bustling Roman city of Pompeii. When Mount Vesuvius erupts without warning, Cato is separated from his mother. Will they survive the terrifying day and be reunited? This historical fiction graphic novel includes prose intervals that provide additional information about what happened at Pompeii and Herculaneum, about Vesuvius and other famous volcanoes, and about the modern excavations.
Part of the Timeline Graphic Novels series.

Ice Journey. Harcourt Achieve/Steck-Vaughn 2007 48p. Illustration
Grades: 3 4 5 6 7 8   **741.5; Fic**
1. Adventure graphic novels; 2. Graphic novels; 3. Ice age — Graphic novels
978-1-4190-3204-2, $8.99
It is the Ice Age in North America, and the land is covered in ice and snow. Bruno, a young giant short-faced bear, is being hunted down by a saber-toothed cat. While his sister, Ursula, looks for him, she meets some interesting creatures of the Ice Age. This graphic novel includes prose

intervals that provide information on the real animals that lived during the Ice Age, the early people who may have lived towards the end of the Ice Age, and on the impact of global warming on the world today.
Part of the Timeline Graphic Novels series.

Rebel Prince. Harcourt Achieve/Steck-Vaughn 2007 48p. Illustration
Grades: 3 4 5 6 7 8   **741.5; Fic**
1. Graphic novels; 2. Henry V, King of England, 1387-1422; 3. Great Britain — Kings and Rulers — Graphic novels
978-1-4190-3217-2, $8.99
In 15th century London, young Will works at a tavern where Prince Hal and his companions hang out. When royal duties call, will Prince Hal be able to rise to the challenge? What is in store for young Will? This historical fiction graphic novel tells the story of how playful Prince Hal became King Henry V of England. It includes prose interludes that provide additional information about his father Henry IV, portrayals of Henry V, and about the famous battle at Agincourt.
Part of the Timeline Graphic Novels series.

Duffy, Chris
★ **Fable** Comics: Classic Tales Told by Extraordinary Cartoonists. edited by Chris Duffy. First Second 2015 128 p. Illustration
Grades: 1 2 3 4 5   **741.5; 398.2**
1. Aesop's fables — Adaptations — Comic books, strips, etc.; 2. Fables — Comic books, strips, etc.; 3. Fairy tales
1626721076; 9781626721074, $19.99
This collection, edited by Chris Duffy, "has something to offer every reader. Seventeen fairy tales are wonderfully adapted and illustrated in comics format by seventeen different cartoonists, including Raina Telgemeier, Brett Helquist, Cherise Harper, and more." (Publisher's note)
"Editor Duffy delivers another knockout collection of comics, this time focusing on fables. Although the majority are interpretations of different Aesop stories, other selections have their roots in Russia, India, and the U.S. Ranging from familiar to obscure, modern to traditional, this vibrant collection boasts an impressive catalog of top-name artists, who interpret the original tales with an astonishing range of creativity and originality." Booklist

Fairy Tale Comics: Classic Tales Told by Extraordinary Cartoonists. compiled by Chris Duffy. First Second 2013 128 p. Illustration
Grades: K 1 2 3 4 5   **741.5; Fic**
1. Fairy tales — Graphic novels; 2. Princesses — Graphic novels; 3. Dogs — Graphic novels
1596438231; 9781596438231, $19.99
In this book, editor Chris Duffy "has assembled a...lineup of comics versions of more than a dozen fairy tales in this...follow-up to 'Nursery Rhyme Comics.' Favorites like 'The Twelve Dancing Princesses' and 'Rapunzel' (whose heroines gain significant agency) join rarities like 'The Small Tooth Dog' and 'The Boy Who Drew Cats.'" (Publishers Weekly)
"Every artist here knows how to turn in an elegant, flowing story, and every tale is pitch-perfect for young readers and intimate read-alouds. Overall, the book is an ideal choice for a child's first comics experience and a new way to enjoy old favorites." Booklist

Dumas, Alexandre
The **three** musketeers. Campfire 2010 104p. Illustration
Grades: 3 4 5 6 7 8 9   **741.5; Fic**
1. Adventure graphic novels; 2. Graphic novels
978-93-80028-57-8, $12.99
Young D'Artagnan comes to Paris, determined to become a king's musketeer, but runs into trouble with three musketeers in one day. When they band together to tight Cardinal Richelieu's forces, they become friends. The friends soon find themselves involved in averting a plot to

discredit Queen Anne, and their efforts to help her cause them to run afoul of Richelieu. D'Artagnan, Athos, Porthos, and Aramis also must deal with Milady de Winter, a beautiful and deadly woman with her own agenda. This graphic novel adaptation features art that emphasizes the humor in the historical adventure. It also puts most of the violence off-panel, so the story is suitable for younger readers.

Dunn, Joeming W.

The **brain**: a graphic novel tour. by Joeming Dunn; illustrated by Rod Espinosa.. Magic Wagon/Graphic Planet 2009 32p. Illustration (Graphic adventures. The human body)

Grades: 2 3 4 5 6

612.8; 741.5

1. Brain — Graphic novels; 2. Graphic novels

978-1-60270-683-5, $27.07

LC 2009-17650

Courtesy of ABDO Publishing.

Teacher Ms Hansen leads her Explorers class on a tour of the human brain. They learn about how the brain's different parts control body functions through the nervous system, and how people should protect their head while participating in certain physical activities, to avoid damaging the brain. The tour is very similar to the Ms Frizzle's Magic School Bus science series by way of The Fantastic Voyage in that Ms Hansen's class shrinks to microscopic size in order to get into the brain. Back matter in the book includes a diagram of the brain, some "fun facts," a brief glossary, and information on how to use ABDO's website to find links to more information on the Internet. The author owns Antarctica Press and is also a physician; artist Espinosa has published such books as The Courageous Princess and Neotopia.

This book is part of the Graphic Adventures: The Human Body series.

The **eyes**: a graphic novel tour. illustrated by Rod Espinosa. Magic Wagon 2009 32p. Illustration (Graphic adventures. The human body)

Grades: 2 3 4 5 6

612.8; 741.5

1. Eye — Graphic novels; 2. Graphic novels

978-1-60270-684-2, $27.07

LC 2009-17651

Courtesy of ABDO Publishing.

Teacher Ms. Hansen leads her Explorers class on a tour of the human eye. They learn about how the eye functions, what purpose blinking serves, how the iris works to control the amount of light that enters the eye, and why tears are important. The tour is very similar to the Ms Frizzle's Magic School Bus science series by way of The Fantastic Voyage, in that Ms Hansen's class shrinks to microscopic size in order to get into the eye. Back matter in the book include a diagram of the eye, fun facts that include information on color blindness and vision problems, a short glossary, and information on how to use ABDO's website to find links for more information on the Internet. The author owns Antarctica Press and is also a physician; artist Espinosa has published such books as The Courageous Princess and Neotopia.

This book is part of the Graphic Adventures: The Human Body series.

H.G. Wells' The time machine. H.G. Wells; adapted by Joeming Dunn; illustrated by Ben Dunn.. ABDO Publishing Group/Magic Wagon 2008 32p. Illustration

Grades: 3 4 5 6 7 8

741.5; Fic

1. Adventure graphic novels; 2. Authors; 3. Graphic novels; 4. Historians; 5. Novelists; 6. Science fiction graphic novels; 7. Science fiction writers; 8. Writers on politics; 9. Writers on science; 10. WWells, H. G. (Herbert George), 1866-1946 — Adaptations

978-1-60270-054-3, $27.07

LC 2007-6447

Courtesy of ABDO Publishing.

A gentleman hosts his friends at dinner one evening in London and then takes their leave in his time machine. When he returns, he tells them of his trip into the future, of the two peoples he encountered, the Eloi and the Morlocks, and what he learned of their relationship. When his friends refuse to believe him, the Traveler sets out again in his machine. This simplified graphic novel adaptation allows younger readers and struggling readers to get the main plot of the classic story. The book includes a brief biography of Wells and list of his other works.

Part of the Graphic Planet Graphic Classics series.

The **heart**: a graphic novel tour. by Joeming Dunn; illustrated by Rod Espinosa.. Magic Wagon/Graphic Planet 2009 32p. Illustration (Graphic adventures. The human body)

Grades: 2 3 4 5 6

612.8; 741.5

1. Graphic novels; 2. Heart — Graphic novels

978-1-60270-685-9, $27.07

LC 2009-17851

Courtesy of ABDO Publishing.

Teacher Ms. Hansen leads her Explorers class on a tour of the human heart. They learn about how the heart functions, how it pumps blood through the circulatory system, and the functions of the major veins and arteries. The tour is very similar to the Ms Frizzle's Magic School Bus science series by way of The Fantastic Voyage, in that Ms Hansen's class shrink to microscopic size in order to get into the bloodstream. Back matter in the book include a diagram of the heart, fun facts, a short glossary, and information on how to use ABDO's website to find links for more information on the Internet. The author owns Antarctica Press and is also a physician; artist Espinosa has published such books as The Courageous Princess and Neotopia.

Includes bibliographical references; This book is part of the Graphic Adventures: The Human Body series.

Journey to the center of the earth. adapted by Joeming Dun; illustrated by Rod Espinosa.. Magic Wagon/Graphic Planet 2009 32p. Illustration

Grades: 3 4 5 6 7

741.5; Fic

1. Adventure graphic novels; 2. Graphic novels; 3. Novelists; 4. Science fiction graphic novels; 5. Verne, Jules, 1828-1905; 6. Verne, Jules, 1828-1905 — Adaptations

978-1-60270678-1, $27.07

LC 2009-8588

Professor Otto Liedenbrock, his nephew Axel, and their guide Hans follow the

Courtesy of ABDO Publishing.

instructions in an old note left by explorer Arne Saknussemm to descend into an old volcano in Iceland, seeking a way to the center of the Earth. This graphic novel provides an easy-reading adaptation of Jules Verne's classic adventure story. Back matter includes a brief biography of Verne, a list of some of his novels, and a short glossary. It is a curious addition to the Graphic Planet series called Graphic Horror, since there is no horror in the book.

This is part of the Graphic Horror Series 2.

The **kidneys:** a graphic novel tour. illustrated by Rod Espinosa.. ABDO/Magic Wagon 2009 32p. (Graphic adventures. The human body)
Grades: 2 3 4 5 6
612.2; 741.5
  1. Graphic novels; 2. Kidneys — Graphic novels
  978-1-60270-686-6, $27.07
             LC 2009-17852

Courtesy of ABDO Publishing.

Ms. Hansen and her Explorers class, including the aliens Xeni and Zeno Zelman, take off on another tour inside the human body, this time into the kidneys, the body's filter to get rid of waste from the blood and to regulate the levels of water, salt, and other minerals. The tour starts in the blood system, into the left renal artery into the left kidney. Young readers might enjoy the fact that the Explorers exit the body through the urinary tract, which is where the kidneys send the waste called urea. This graphic novel series combines aspects of the Magic School Bus series and the movie Fantastic Voyage. The book includes additional facts about the kidneys, a glossary, and a link to find websites for more information. Dunn is a physician and owner of Antarctic Publishing, a comic book publishing house.

Part of the Graphic Adventures: The Human Body series.

The **liver:** a graphic novel tour. illustrated by Rod Espinosa.. ABDO/Magic Wagon 2009 32p. Illustration (Graphic adventures. The human body)
Grades: 2 3 4 5 6
612.2; 741.5
  1. Graphic novels; 2. Liver — Graphic novels
  978-1-60270-687-3, $27.07
             LC 2009-17853

Courtesy of ABDO Publishing.

Ms. Hansen and her Explorers class, including the aliens Xeni and Zeno Zelman, take off on another tour inside the human body, this time into the liver. The tour starts in the mouth, through the esophagus into the stomach, then through the small intestine into the liver. The liver breaks down digested proteins and medicines, and helps to convert carbohydrates to sugars; it also stores vitamins and minerals such as iron. This graphic novel series combines aspects of the Magic School Bus series and the movie Fantastic Voyage. The book includes additional facts about the liver, a glossary, and a link to find websites for more information. Dunn is a physician and owner of Antarctic Publishing, a comic book publishing house.

Part of the Graphic Adventures: The Human Body series.

The **Lungs:** a graphic novel tour. ABDO/Magic Wagon 2009 32p. Illustration
Grades: 2 3 4 5 6
                  612.2; 741.5

  1. Graphic novels; 2. Lungs — Graphic novels; 3. Respiratory system — Graphic novels
  978-1-60270-688-0, $27.07
             LC 2009-17854

Courtesy of ABDO Publishing.

Ms. Hansen and her Explorers class, including the aliens Xeni and Zeno Zelman, take off on another tour inside the human body, this time into the lungs. The tour starts in the nose, through the larynx into the trachea (windpipe), then through the bronchi into the lungs. The lungs do more than help the body breathe and circulate oxygen; they help the body to speak. This graphic novel series combines aspects of the Magic School Bus series and the movie Fantastic Voyage. The book includes additional facts about the lungs, a glossary, and a link to find websites for more information. Dunn is a physician and owner of Antarctic Publishing, a comic book publishing house.

Part of the Graphic Adventures: The Human Body series.

Peter Pan. J.M. Barrie; adapted by Joeming Dunn; illustrated by Ben Dunn. ABDO Publishing/Magic Wagon 2008 32p.
Grades: 2 3 4 5 6
741.5; Fic
  1. Adventure graphic novels; 2. Fantasy graphic novels; 3. Graphic novels; 4. Peter Pan (Fictional character); 5. Barrie, J. M. (James Matthew), 1860-1937 — Adaptations
  978-1-60270-052-9, $27.07
             LC 2007-12070

Courtesy of ABDO Publishing.

John, Michael, and Wendy love hearing their mother's stories, but they don't know that another young boy has been listening to them as well. When their protective dog Nana steals Peter Pan's shadow, the children meet him and Wendy sews his shadow back. Then the children agree to return with Peter to the magical Neverland. Can they survive in a land of pirates, Lost Boys, and Tinker Bell? The book provides a simplified adaptation that introduces young readers to Barrie's classic tale. It includes a brief biography of Barrie.

Part of the Graphic Classics series

Dwinell, Kim
  Surfside girls: the secret of Danger Point. by Kim Dwinell. Top Shelf Productions 2017 235 p. Color; Illustration
Grades: 3 4 5 6
741.5; Fic
  1. Surfing — Fiction; 2. Friendship — Fiction; 3. Summer — Fiction
  9781603094115, $19.99; 1603094113

Courtesy of IDW Publishing

In this book, by Kim Dwinell, "things are getting weird in Surfside. Lately, Samantha's best friend Jade explodes into fits of giggles whenever she sees a boy, and it's throwing a wrench into the kick-back summer of surfing and hanging out that Sam had planned. But after swimming through a secret underwater cave, Sam starts to... see things. Like ghosts. And pirates. And maybe something even scarier! Can she and Jade get to the bottom of this mystery in time to save their town?" (Publisher's note)

"First-time graphic novelist Dwinell creates spacious panels with a less-is-more approach to detail that evokes the wide-open ocean and beach environment, keeps readers focused on the characters and their concerns, and creates a sense of otherness where the pallid ghosts are concerned." Pub Wkly

Eaton, Maxwell

The **flying** beaver brothers and the birds vs bunnies: birds vs. bunnies. by Maxwell Eaton III. Alfred A. Knopf 2013 96 p. Illustration

Grades: 1 2 3 4 5 **Fic; 741.5/973**
1. Beavers — Fiction; 2. Birds — Fiction; 3. Graphic novels; 4. Islands — Fiction; 5. Rabbits — Fiction; 6. Animals — Graphic novels
0449810224; 9780449810224, $6.99; 9780449810231, $12.99; 9780449810248

LC 2012034047

This graphic novel, written and illustrated by Maxwell Eaton III, presents the fourth story of his characters the Flying Beaver Brothers. They "set off in their sailboat to enjoy...rest and relaxation at [a] nearby island. But the birds and bunnies who live on Little Beaver Island have other ideas. Before long, Ace and Bub find themselves embroiled in an all-out war between the feathers and the fuzz [and attempt to] bring peace to Little Beaver Island." (Publisher's note)

Eisenberg, Adam

The **Creation** of Iron Man. Rosen Publishing Group 2006 48p. Illustration

Grades: 4 5 6 7 8 9 10 **741.5**
1. Graphic novels; 2. Iron Man (Fictional character); 3. Superhero graphic novels
978-1-4042-0767-7, $29.25

LC 2006000167

This volume discusses the unique character of Tony Stark, developed by Stan Lee and Jack Kirby, who was unable to live a normal life and invented a special iron suit that gave him superpowers. The book includes information about the times in which Lee and Kirby worked at Marvel Comics.

Part of the Action Heroes series.

Eisner, Will

The **Last** Knight: An Introduction to Don Quixote. NBM Publishing 2000 32p. Illustration

Grades: 3 4 5 6 7 8 9 10 **741.5; Fic**
1. Adventure graphic novels; 2. Graphic novels; 3. Novelists; 4. Poets; 5. Cervantes Saavedra, Miguel de, 1547-1616 — Adaptations
1-56163-251-1; 978-1-56163-251-0, $15.95

LC 2001-265049

This is Eisner's graphic novel remake of Don Quixote. Here are the adventures of a Spanish country gentleman and his companion who set out, like knights of old, to search for adventure. As the subtitle says, this book hits the highlights and serves to introduce the classic tale to younger readers.

Moby Dick. by Herman Melville; adapted by Will Eisner. NBM Publishing 2001 32p. Illustration

Grades: 3 4 5 6 7 8 9 10 **741.5; Fic**
1. Adventure graphic novels; 2. Graphic novels; 3. Whaling — Graphic novels
1-56163-293-7, $15.95; 1-56163-294-5 (pa)

LC 2001-032989

Ishmael, a sailor, recounts the ill-fated voyage of a whaling ship led by the fanatical Captain Ahab in search of the white whale that had crippled him. Eisner's adaptation hits the highlights of the novel.

The **Princess** and the Frog. NBM Publishing 1999 32p. Illustration

Grades: 3 4 5 6 7 8 9 10 **741.5; Fic**
1. Fairy tales — Graphic novels; 2. Fantasy graphic novels; 3. Graphic novels
1-56163-244-9, $15.95; 1-56163-346-1 (pa)

A good prince, turned into a frog by a spiteful wizard, exacts from a princess a promise which she is reluctant to fulfill, despite his kindness and her desire not to hurt him. Comics master Will Eisner adapted the familiar tale by the Brothers Grimm.

Eliopoulos, Chris

Courtesy of Oni Press

Yo Gabba Gabba!: Gabba Ball!. Oni Press 2010 un Illustration

Grades: PreK K
741.5; Fic
1. Games — Graphic novels; 2. Graphic novels; 3. Humorous graphic novels; 4. Yo gabba gabba! (Television program)
978-1-934964-55-2, $7.99

The inhabitants of Gabba Land play Gabba Ball, in which the main idea is to share; each character shares his or her name and one way he or she likes to play with the ball. This brightly colored graphic novel is a board book suitable for very young pre-readers, using the characters from the popular children's television series. Eliopoulos uses a very simple panel design, motion lines so young eyes can follow the action, and simple dialog in word balloons as well as wordless panels.

Ellerton, Sarah

Inverloch, Volume 1. Seven Seas 2006 un Illustration

Grades: 4 5 6 7 8 9 10 11 12 **741.5; Fic**
1. Adventure graphic novels; 2. Fantasy graphic novels; 3. Graphic novels
1-933164-13-1, $14.99

In a world where humans, elves, and other beings coexist, albeit not altogether peacefully, Acheron is a young da'kor, a horned wolf-like race that lives in the forests. He encounters a beautiful elf and takes her quest for his own — to find another elf who went missing twelve years before. Teased by his brothers as a lousy hunter, feared by humans who think da'kor are dangerous beasts, innocent Acheron finds that the world beyond the forest is full of danger, intrigue, and betrayal.

This story began online as a webcomic.

Espinosa, Rod

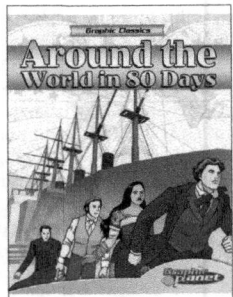
Courtesy of ABDO Publishing.

Around the world in 80 days. adapted and illustrated by Rod Espinosa.. ABDO/Red Wagon 2008 32p. Illustration

Grades: 3 4 5 6 7 8 9
741.5; Fic
1. Adventure graphic novels; 2. Verne, Jules, 1828-1905 — Adaptations
978-1-60270-050-5, $27.07

LC 2007-6444

In 1872, English gentleman Phileas Fogg makes a wager that he can travel around the world in just 80 days. Unfortunately, at the time of his wager, a daring robber has made off with a fortune, and Scotland Yard detective Fix is convinced Fogg is the villain. The chase is on, around the world. This comic book adaptation has been written for younger, reluctant, and struggling readers and provides highlights of the adventures in the original novel by Verne. The book includes a brief biography of Verne, a short list of some of his other works, and a brief glossary.

The **courageous** princess; Volume 3: The Dragon Queen. by Rod Espinosa. Dark Horse Books 2015 180 p. Illustration
Grades: 4 5 6 7 8   **741.5**
1. Graphic novels; 2. Princesses — Fiction; 3. Adventure graphic novels
1616557249; 9781616557249, $19.99
LC 2014037517
In this book, by Rod Espinosa, "Princess Mabelrose has journeyed far and saved herself and others from danger and tyranny, but she has yet to make her way home. In the conclusion to the Courageous Princess trilogy, Mabelrose must use her generous spirit, as well as her brains, to melt the heart of the Dragon Queen and gain her freedom. But she still has to bring her father and her friends back from the queen's unreachable Unremembered Lands." (Publisher's note)
"Espinosa's artwork leaps from the pages with action and vivid colors, with clean and easy-to-follow panels. Animal and human characters are distinctive and diverse." SLJ

★ The **courageous** princess; Volume 1: Beyond the hundred kingdoms. by Rod Espinosa. Dark Horse Books 2015 245 p Color; Illustration
Grades: 3 4 5 6 7 8   **741.5; Fic**
1. Adventure and adventurers — Comic books, strips, etc.; 2. Princesses — Comic books, strips, etc.; 3. Princesses — Juvenile fiction
9781616557225, $19.99
"Princess Mabelrose may not be the fairest of the land, but she has enough brains and bravery to fend for herself in a fantasy world of danger and adventure! From a mighty dragon with an army of trolls to a tyrant tiger king, Mabelrose meets each challenge with pluck and intelligence, winning the help and friendship of the many kindred spirits she encounters in her quest to find her way home." (Publisher's note)
Other volumes in this series are: The unencumbered lands; The dragon queen

The **courageous** princess; Volume 2: The unremembered lands. by Rod Espinosa. Dark Horse Books 2015 237 p Color; Illustration
Grades: 3 4 5 6 7 8   **741.5; Fic**
1. Fantasy; 2. Princesses — Juvenile fiction
9781616557232, $19.99
"The smart and plucky Princess Mabelrose has escaped a dragon and freed the people of Leptia from a tyrant. Journeying home, Mabelrose discovers that her father was coming to her rescue-but now, he and a posse of princes are the ones who need rescuing! So Mabelrose begins a new quest..." (Publisher's note)

Lewis and Clark. ABDO/Magic Wagon 2008 32p. Illustration (Bio-graphics)
Grades: 3 4 5 6 7 8 9
917.8; 92; 741.5; 917
1. Lewis and Clark Expedition (1804-1806) — Graphic novels; 2. Biographical graphic novels; 3. Explorers; 4. Graphic novels; 5. Territorial governors; 6. Clark, William, 1770-1838; 7. Lewis, Meriwether, 1774-1809; 8. West (U.S.) — Exploration — Graphic novels
978-1-60270-069-7, $27.07
LC 2007-5578

Courtesy of ABDO Publishing.

This graphic format book tells the story of the Lewis and Clark Expedition, which explored the land of the Louisiana Purchase, as authorized in 1803 by President Thomas Jefferson. The book includes a timeline of the Expedition, a map of the route, and a list of books for further reading.

Lewis Carroll's Alice in Wonderland. adapted and illustrated by Rod Espinosa. Antarctic Press 2007 un Illustration
Grades: 4 5 6 7 8 9   **741.5**
1. Adventure graphic novels; 2. Fantasy graphic novels; 3. Graphic novels; 4. Humorous graphic novels
978-0-9787725-8-1, $14.95
Espinosa (The Courageous Princess) adapts Lewis Carroll's classic tale into a graphic novel full of pop culture references (check out the Mad Hatter, for instance). It's still the original story, which starts when the daydreaming Alice sees a rabbit checking his pocket watch and runs after him, only to find herself in a strange world with bizarre creatures.

Faller, Regis
Polo: The Runaway Book. Roaring Brook Press 2006 80p. Illustration
Grades: K 1 2 3   **741.5; Fic**
1. Adventure graphic novels; 2. Graphic novels; 3. Stories without words — Graphic novels
1-59643-189-X, $16.95
The little dog Polo receives a book as a gift, but a little round green alien creature steals it, and the chase is on. Polo pursues the thief up a rope into the sky onto a pink cotton candy cloud, through a funhouse mirror, and through other strange and wonderful places, making friends as he goes. The only words uttered are Polo's cry, "My book!" in several places.
Originally published in France as Polo, mon livre.

Farrens, Brian
William Shakespeare's King Lear. adapted by Brian Farrens; illustrated by Ben Dunn.. ABDO/Magic Wagon 2008 48p. Illustration
Grades: 5 6 7 8 9 10   **822.3; 741.5**
1. Authors; 2. Dramatists; 3. Graphic novels; 4. Poets; 5. Shakespeare, William, 1564-1616 — Adaptations
978-1-60270-189-2, $28.50
LC 2008-10739
King Lear divides his kingdom among his three daughters but disowns Cordelia, the youngest, when she refuses to flatter him with insincerity. Then his older daughters renege on their promise to care for him, and he goes mad and roams the countryside. Meanwhile, Edmund, the illegitimate son of the Earl of Gloucester, plays political games in his quest for power. This graphic novel adaptation retains some of the original language from Shakespeare's play, while paring down the story to appeal to struggling readers. The book includes a short biography, a summary of the play, a glossary, and a short selection of famous lines and phrases from the play.
Part of the Graphic Shakespeare series

Fein, Eric
The **Creation** of the Fantastic Four. Rosen Publishing Group 2006 48p. Illustration
Grades: 4 5 6 7 8 9 10   **741.5**
1. Fantastic Four (Fictional character); 2. Graphic novels; 3. Superhero graphic novels
978-1-4042-0765-3, $29.25
LC 2005031170
Describes the history and development of the action heroes called the Fantastic Four and how they got their superpowers. Created in 1961 by the Marvel power team of Jack Kirby and Stan Lee, the Fantastic Four was the first superhero team the men created.
Part of the Action Heroes series.

The **Creation** of the Incredible Hulk. Rosen Publishing Group 2006 48p. Illustration

Grades: 4 5 6 7 8 9 10   **741.5**

1. Graphic novels; 2. Superhero graphic novels; 3. Hulk (Fictional character)

978-1-4042-0764-6, $29.25

LC 2005035267

Discusses the unique character developed in 1962 by Stan Lee and Jack Kirby who was unable to live a normal life after he was affected by a gamma bomb's blast and Dr. Bruce Banner became the huge, inarticulate, super-strong Hulk. The book also includes information on the cultural climate in the U.S. at the time, and on the way the two men worked together at Marvel Comics.

Part of the Action Heroes series.

Fingeroth, Danny

Action Heroes: The Creation of the X-Men. Rosen Publishing Group, Inc. 2007 48p. Illustration

Grades: 3 4 5 6 7 8   **741.5**

1. Graphic novels; 2. X-Men (Fictional characters)

1-4042-0762-7 (lib bdg), $29.25

Veteran Marvel Comics writer Fingeroth gives young readers a brief introduction to the creation of the Marvel superhero team, the X-Men. The book focuses on the two creators, Stan Lee and Jack Kirby, and also discusses the state of the comics industry in the early 1960s, as well as the cultural/social background that led Lee and Kirby to create a team of mutant superheroes. It includes a timeline of the X-Men creators, highlights from the long-running series, a glossary, books for further reading, and a bibliography. Photographs and color reproductions of the art highlight the book. Due to the popular series of X-Men movies, people know the characters, even if they've never read the comics.

Flood, Joe

Sharks: nature's perfect hunter. Joe Flood. First Second 2018 128 p. Color; Illustration (Science comics)

Grades: 3 4 5 6 7   **597.3; 741.5**

1. Animals; 2. Sharks; 3. Marine animals

9781626727878, $19.99; 9781626727885

LC 2017941169

This book, in the Science Comics series, by Joe Flood, looks "at the dynamic hammerhead, infamous great white, primordial megalodon, and the gentle nurse shark, the rare species that will let a scuba diver pet them! This book is filled to the gills with jaw-dropping illustrations and razor-sharp facts that shed light on these fascinating creatures of the deep, including their undersea terrain, cunning adaptability, and staggering variety." (Publisher's note)

"Flood addresses the lore and fear that surrounds these predators, most of it coming from literature and the media. Detailed illustrations complement the text beautifully, with close-ups of the various features of different sharks as well as useful diagrams and charts." SLJ

Flores, Madeleine

Help us! Great Warrior. written and illustrated by Madeleine Flores; colors by Trillian Gunn. Boom! Box 2016 160 p. Color; Illustration

Grades: 5 6 7 8 9 10   **741.5; Fic**

1. Courage — Fiction; 2. Demonology — Fiction; 3. Fantasy fiction — Fiction; 4. Fantasy graphic novels

1608868028; 9781608868025, $19.99

This book "is about a very powerful (but deceptively tiny) Great Warrior who protects her village from evil-doers and looks rad while doing it! Possessing great strength and even greater self-confidence, she's ready to kick some butts and save everyone, especially hunks/pals/handsome

skeletons. But Great Warrior has a secret...and will her friends stand by her side when they find it out?" (Publisher's note)

"The art is clean and colorful and ideal for the tone, which is similar to the TV show Adventure Time but a bit more accessible. The book also carries the same message about friendship and self-esteem." SLJ

Originally published in single magazine form as Help us! Great Warrior No. 1-6

Fontana, Shea

Date with disaster: a graphic novel. Shea Fontana; illustrated by Yancey Labat. Dc Comics 2018 127 p. Color; Illustration (DC Super Hero Girls)

Grades: 3 4 5 6   **741.5; Fic**

1. Teenage girls — Fiction; 2. Superheroes — Fiction; 3. Women superheroes — Fiction

1401278787; 9781401278786, $9.99

"Catwoman is out alone on the prowl one night when KABOOM — an explosion at S.T.A.R. Labs rouses the other girls from their slumber. Star students Batgirl and Lois Lane both know the lab incident is fishy, and they meet later to share clues. But nothing could've prepared Batgirl for what they see next — Batgirl's dad on a date!" (Publisher's note)

Dc Super Hero Girls; Volume 1: Finals Crisis. writer, Shea Fontana; art, Yancey Labat; color, Monica Kubina; lettering, Janice Chiang. DC Comics 2016 128 p. Color; Illustration

Grades: 2 3 4 5   **741.5; Fic**

1. Female superhero graphic novels; 2. School stories — Graphic novels

9781401262471, $9.99; 1401262473

LC 2016032279

"Wonder Woman, Supergirl, Harley Quinn, Batgirl and their friends are learning to become heroes, but no one knew the trials that awaited them. In the first original graphic novel from the DC Super Hero Girls line, meet the students of Superhero High School as they find out that fun, friendship and hard work are all parts of growing up!" (Publisher's note)

Forget, Thomas

The **Creation** of Captain America. Rosen Publishing Group 2006 48p. Illustration

Grades: 4 5 6 7 8 9 10   **741.5**

1. Captain America (Fictional character); 2. Graphic novels; 3. Superhero graphic novels; 4. Captain America (Fictional character)

978-1-4042-0766-0, $29.25

LC 2005032024

Captain America has been a hero since 1940 and saved comic books and Marvel Comic Group. This volume discusses the times during which Cap was created and how the character has changed over the years. In light of the character's death in the aftermath of the Marvel Civil War storyline that played out in comics during 2006 and 2007, this book may have wide appeal.

Part of the Action Heroes series.

Forsythe, Matthew

Jinchalo. Matthew Forsythe. Drawn & Quarterly 2012 120 p. Illustration

Grades: 3 4 5 6 7 8   **Fic; 741.5/971**

1. Fantasy comics books, strips, etc; 2. Fantasy graphic novels; 3. Spirits — Fiction

1770460675; 9781770460676, $17.95

LC 2012379212

This graphic novel, by Matthew Forsythe, is a "companion to...[the author's] 'Ojingogo,'...[staring] the same little girl as its heroine. When the mischievous shape-shifter Jinchalo hatches from a mysterious egg,...magical troubles drag the pair out of the safety of her home, through the small village where she resides, up, up, and away. In the course of their flight, they visit a robot garden, follow a vine into the clouds, and leave the village far behind." (Publisher's note)

Frampton, Otis
Oddly Normal; Volume 1. written and illustrated by Otis Frampton. Image Comics 2015 128 p. Illustration
Grades: 4 5 6 7 8   **741.5; Fic**
1. Fantasy graphic novels; 2. Graphic novels; 3. Humorous graphic novels
9781632152268, $9.99; 1632152266
"Oddly must travel to Fignation to uncover the mystery of her parents' disappearance. Join Oddly as she navigates a strange new school, teenage angst, monstrous bullies, and Evil itself on an unforgettable fantasy adventure through the vibrant world of Fignation in Oddly Normal." (Publisher's note)
First published 2006 by Viper Comics; Volume 1 of 3

Oddly Normal; Volume 2. written & illustrated by Otis Frampton. Image Comics 2015 Color; Illustration
Grades: 4 5 6 7 8   **741.5; Fic**
1. Monsters — Graphic novels; 2. School stories; 3. Witches — Graphic novels
1632154846; 9781632154842, $9.99
"Oddly, the green-haired half witch, is now living with her great-aunt in Fignation after the mysterious disappearance of her parents. After using memory fragments to help reassure Oddly that she was, indeed, wanted and loved by her mom and dad, Auntie Oddly is thrilled when Oddly is invited to a party. Oddly is finally making friends in Fignation! Sure, they may not be the most popular kids in school, but maybe that doesn't matter, especially when they find even the most mundane things, like the hokey pokey, utterly fascinating." (Booklist)
Collects Oddly Normal issues #6-10

Oddly Normal; Volume 3. written & illustrated by Otis Frampton. Image Comics 2016 Color; Illustration
Grades: 4 5 6 7 8   **741.5; Fic**
1. Witches — Graphic novels; 2. School stories; 3. Monsters — Graphic novels
9781632156921, $9.99; 163215692X
Collects Oddly Normal #11-15
"Oddly Normal's adventures in Fignation continue with Rocketball games, broom races and life changing revelations." (Publisher's note)

Fulop, Scott D.
Archie Americana Series: Best of the Forties Volume 1. Archie Comics 1991 128p. Illustration
Grades: 3 4 5 6 7 8 9 10 11 12 Adult   **741.5; Fic**
1. Andrews, Archie (Fictional character); 2. Graphic novels; 3. Humorous graphic novels
1-879794-00-4, $11.95
In 1941, Pep Comics introduced Archie Andrews, "America's newest boyfriend." Since then, Archie and his perennial teenage friends have entertained readers with their misadventures. This book includes the very first Archie story, with the first appearance of Betty and Veronica, Reggie, Jughead, Mr. Weatherbee, Miss Grundy, and the rest of the Archie characters as they originally appeared.

Furse, Sophie
Moby Dick. Barron's Educational Series, Inc. 2007 48p. Illustration
Grades: 3 4 5 6 7 8 9   **741.5**
1. Graphic novels; 2. Melville, Herman — Adaptations
978-0-7641-5977-0; 978-0-7641-3492-0 (pa)

Ishmael's dream of adventure on a whaling ship becomes a nightmare as the voyage turns into a struggle for survival. Captain Ahab, maimed by a monster whale, is obsessed with revenge. As the crew discovers, he is willing to risk everything to destroy that whale. This volume includes a brief biography and timeline of Melville, and information on the legacy of his novel.

Gagne, Michel
The **saga** of Rex. Image 2010 200p. Illustration
Grades: 4 5 6 7 8   **741.5; Fic**
1. Foxes — Graphic novels; 2. Science fiction — Graphic novels
978-1-60706-322-3, $17.99; 1-60706-322-0
"Originally serialized in Kazu Kibuishi's Flight anthologies, the story of the intergalactically adorable fox named Rex is collected here. The tale dispenses with words entirely after the first of six chapters.... Rex gets plucked from his home planet to enter a cosmic ritual in which alien shape-shifters and their chosen companions (e.g., Rex) undergo a series of trials on a constantly morphing world." (Booklist)

Gaiman, Neil
★ The **graveyard** book graphic novel Volume 2. based on the novel by Neil Gaiman; adapted by P. Craig Russell; illustrated by David LaFuente, Scott Hampton, P. Craig Russell, Kevin Nowlan, Galen Showman; colorist, Lovern Kindzierski; letterer, Rick Parker. HarperCollins 2014 188 p. Color; Illustration
Grades: 5 6 7 8 9 10   **741.5; Fic**
1. Cemeteries — Fiction; 2. Dead — Fiction; 3. Graphic novels; 4. Orphans — Fiction; 5. Supernatural — Fiction; 6. Supernatural graphic novels
0062194836; 9780062194831, $19.99

LC 2013497350
"Russell concludes the two-part adaptation of Gaiman's Newbery Medal winner, encompassing the final three chapters of the novel. Bod, raised by the ghostly denizens of a graveyard, is a young adult now, yearning for knowledge of the world of the living. After a showdown with a pair of school bullies...Bod finally confronts the ancient order who murdered his family and overcomes them with his supernatural know-how and his innate courage and cleverness." (Booklist)
"Russell and his team of illustrators continue to do this amazing story justice with images that lead readers down a path into Bod's dark and magical graveyard world. Gaiman has the ability to weave beauty and intrigue into a story that has a strong potential to frighten." VOYA

Gallagher, John
Buzzboy: Trouble in paradise. Sky Dog Press 2002 144p. Illustration
Grades: 5 6 7 8 9 10 11 12   **741.5; Fic**
1. Graphic novels; 2. Humorous graphic novels; 3. Superhero graphic novels
0-8721831-0-8, $11.95
Imagine a superhero who jokes constantly, watches way too many old television shows, and loves junk food, and you have Buzzboy. Years before, he was sidekick to Captain Ultra, but the evil Dr. Schism destroyed all superheroes and their sidekicks, except for Captain Ultra. Now, Ultra has declared martial law in the city of New Paradise, and his police stomp out all rebellions. Then a mysterious superhero stops the Hoppers (police) it's Buzzboy, older and back from the dead! Aided by sarcastic teen sorceress Becca and reformed mad scientist Doc Cyber, Buzzboy is here to save the day.
Another title in this series is: Buzzboy: Monsters, dreams, & milkshakes (2003)

Galligan, Gale

Dawn and the impossible three. a graphic novel by Gale Galligan; with color by Braden Lamb [based on the book by Ann M. Martin]. Graphix 2017 145 p. Color; Illustration

Grades: 3 4 5 6   **741.5; Fic**

1. Girls — Fiction; 2. Female friendship — Fiction; 3. Babysitting — Fiction; 4. Babysitters — Fiction; 5. Girls' clubs — Fiction

9781338067354; 9781338067309, $24.99; 9781338067118

LC 2016960080

"Dawn Schafer is the newest member of The Baby-sitters Club. While she's still adjusting to life in Stoneybrook..., she's eager to accept her first big job. But taking care of the three Barrett kids would be too much for any baby-sitter.... On top of all that, Dawn wants to fit in with the other members of the BSC, but she can't figure out how to get along with Kristy." (Publisher's note)

"Slightly more serious than its predecessors, this offering tackles the weighty issues of divorce and ki dnapping but manages to resolve things tidily in the comfortably episodic manner that fans of the series expect. This volume introduces new artist Galligan, who replaces veteran Raina Telgemeier." Kirkus

Ganeri, Anita

Cleopatra: The Life of an Egyptian Queen. by Gary Jeffrey & Anita Ganeri; illustrated by Ross Watton. Rosen Publishing Group 2005 48p. Illustration

Grades: 3 4 5 6 7 8

92; 741.5; 932

1. Biographical graphic novels; 2. Graphic novels; 3. Cleopatra, Queen of Egypt, d. 30 B.C.; 4. Egypt — History — Graphic novels

1-4042-0242-0, $29.25

LC 2004014162

Courtesy of Rosen Publishing

Queen of Egypt, companion of Julius Caesar, and wife of Mark Antony, Cleopatra lived one of history's most fabled lives. Renowned for her great beauty and intelligence, Cleopatra was a strong ruler determined to restore the glory of Ptolemaic rule to Egypt by using her relationships with Caesar and Antony to achieve her goals. Readers will learn why the events of her life — including her tragic suicide — have inspired writers and artists for centuries. This graphic novel includes additional information and a list of books for further reading.

Part of the Graphic Nonfiction series.

Harriet Tubman: The Life of an African-American Abolitionist. by Rob Shone & Anita Ganeri; illustrated by Rob Shone. Rosen Publishing Group 2005 48p. Illustration

Grades: 3 4 5 6 7 8 9

92; 741.5

1. African American women — Graphic novels; 2. Biographical graphic novels; 3. Graphic novels; 4. Underground Railroad — Graphic novels; 5. Tubman, Harriet, 1819 or 1820-1913

1-4042-0245-5, $29.25

Born a slave in the United States, Harriet Tubman escaped from bondage to risk her life and newfound liberty in becoming a leading abolitionist in the years before the American Civil War. Tubman

Courtesy of Rosen Publishing

surreptitiously led hundreds of escaped Southern slaves to freedom in the North along the Underground Railroad, earning her the nickname as "the Moses of her people." This graphic novel format book tells her story. It includes additional information about the Underground Railroad and her legacy in the civil rights movement, and a list of books for further reading.

Part of the Graphic Nonfiction series.

Ganter, Amy Kim

Goosebumps: Terror Trips. Scholastic/Graphix 2007 137p. Illustration

Grades: 4 5 6 7 8 9   **741.5; Fic**

1. Graphic novels; 2. Horror graphic novels; 3. Stine, R. L.; 4. Stine, R. L. — Adaptations

978-0-439-85780-2, $8.99

Stine's Goosebumps series was very popular years ago, and is enjoying a resurgence of popularity with new editions of the prose books. The graphic novel adaptations, all done by well-known independent comics creators, bring the stories to a new audience. Goosebumps: Creepy Creatures is also available.

This volume adapts three of Stine's Goosebumps novels into graphic novel format. Noted independent comic creator Thompson adapts One Day at Horrorland, about one family's ordeal in a very strange, all-too-realistic amusement park. Canadian artist Tolagson adapts A Shocker on Shock Street, which depicts the horrific adventures of two kids on a movie studio lot where the horror is more than just special effects. Global manga creator Ganter adapts Deep Trouble, in which a brother and sister find a real mermaid.

Garcia, Tracy J.

Eli Whitney. by Tracy J. Garcia. PowerKids Press 2013 24 p. Color illustration

Grades: 3 4 5 6

609.2; 92; 741.5

1. Cotton gins and ginning; 2. Inventors — United States — Biography — Juvenile; 3. Inventors — United States; 4. Whitney, Eli, 1765-1825

1477700757; 1477701354; 1477701362; 9781477700754, $25.25; 9781477701355, $10.60; 9781477701362

LC 2012019319

Courtesy of Rosen Publishing

This graphic novel by Tracy J. Garcia focuses on "Eli Whitney [who] changed manufacturing with the cotton gin and helped make improvements in the area of mass production through interchangeable parts. Readers will [be exposed to] how Whitney also drastically changed farming in America with his inventions." (Publisher's note)

Includes index.

Thomas Edison. by Tracy J. Garcia. PowerKids Press 2013 24 p. (Jr. graphic American inventors)

Grades: 3 4 5 6

621.3092; 92; 621.3

1. Businessmen — United States — Biography — Comic books, strips, etc.; 2. Electrical engineers — United States — Biography — Comic books, strips, etc.; 3. Inventors — United States — Biography — Comic books, strips, etc.; 4. Inventors

Courtesy of Rosen Publishing

— Graphic novels; 5. Edison, Thomas A. (Thomas Alva), 1847-1931
1477700765; 9781477700761, $25.25; 9781477701379; 9781477701386

LC 2012018690

This graphic novel by Tracy J. Garcia focuses on "Thomas Edison [who] was a prolific inventor with nearly 2,000 patents. One of his most noted inventions is the practical electrical light bulb. Readers will be [exposed to] the life of Thomas Edison, one of America's great inventors and businessmen." (Publisher's note)

Includes index.

Garland, Sarah
Azzi in Between. by Sarah Garland. Frances Lincoln Children's Books 2013 40 p.
Grades: 1 2 3 4   **Fic**
1. Immigrants — Fiction; 2. Refugees — Fiction
1847802613; 9781847802613, $17.99

In this book, illustrated by Sarah Garland, "Azzi and her parents...have to leave their home and escape to another country...In the new country they must learn to speak a new language, find a new home and Azzi must start a new school.... Azzi begins to learn English and understand that she is not the only one who has had to flee her home.... But Grandma has been left behind and Azzi misses her more than anything. Will Azzi ever see her grandma again?" (Publisher's note)

"[T]his sensitive tale of a young war refugee slowly adapting to a new life will strike chords of sympathy and recognition almost anywhere." Kirkus

Gay, Marie-Louise
Short stories for little monsters. Marie-Louise Gay. Groundwood Books 2017 48 p. Color; Illustration
Grades: K 1 2 3   **S C; Fic; 741.5**
1. Short stories — Collections; 2. Children's stories; 3. Comic books, strips, etc.
9781554988969, $19.95; 1554988969

This collection of illustrated stories, by Marie-Louise Gay, "gives us a glimpse into the things children wonder about every day. What do cats really see? What do trees talk about? Should you make funny faces on a windy day? Do worms rule the world? Do mothers always tell the truth? Do snails have nightmares?" (Publisher's note)

"In this comic collection disguised as a picture book, each short, highly imaginative story is contained on a spread.... Detailed line and wash illustrations filled with humor depict everyday goings-on and childlike antics and present a multiracial cast of kids and adults (plus even a few nonhuman creatures, such as snails, trees, and worms)." SLJ

Gelatt, Philip
Indiana Jones adventures vol. 1. Dark Horse Comics 2008 un Illustration
Grades: 4 5 6 7 8 9   **741.5; Fic**
1. Adventure graphic novels; 2. Archeology — Graphic novels; 3. Graphic novels; 4. Jones, Indiana (Fictional character)
978-1-59307-905-5, $6.95

It's winter of 1930 in Sweden, and Dr. Henry Jones Jr. (Indiana Jones) finds an ancient pre-Christian temple of a religion devoted to war; he gets a scroll while Dr. Lawrence, the pretty British archeologist with him, runs with a valuable gold ring. When Indy decides to steal the ring back from the British Museum, the unscrupulous French archeologist Belloq, who works for the Nazis, steals the scroll from Marcus Brody, Indy's friend. From London, Indy and Dr. Lawrence pursue Belloq to Egypt to recover the scroll before he can sell it to the Nazis. This original graphic novel story provides adventure suitable for younger readers.

Gelev, Penko
Moby Dick. Barron's Educational Series, Inc. 2007 48p. Illustration
Grades: 3 4 5 6 7 8 9   **741.5**
1. Graphic novels; 2. Melville, Herman — Adaptations
978-0-7641-5977-0; 978-0-7641-3492-0 (pa)

Ishmael's dream of adventure on a whaling ship becomes a nightmare as the voyage turns into a struggle for survival. Captain Ahab, maimed by a monster whale, is obsessed with revenge. As the crew discovers, he is willing to risk everything to destroy that whale. This volume includes a brief biography and timeline of Melville, and information on the legacy of his novel.

Giarrusso, Chris
G-Man, volume 1: learning to fly. Image Comics 2010 un Illustration
Grades: 3 4 5 6   **741.5; Fic**
1. Graphic novels; 2. Humorous graphic novels; 3. Superhero graphic novels
978-1-60706-270-7 (pa), $9.99; 1-60706-270-4 (pa)

Mikey G. is G-Man, the newest superhero on the block, in a town full of superheroes (he made his cape from the family's magic blanket). His friends Billy Demon, Tan Man, Sparky, and the Suntrooper are all ready to help, but G-Man also has to deal with his older brother Great Man (aka Dave) and their superhero dad, Mr. G.

This "hits all the right notes, from its friendly cartoon figures to the occasionally hilarious one-liners." Booklist

This is a new edition, in a larger size and with a new ISBN; Other titles in this series are:Cape crisis (2010);Coming home (2013)

G-Man, volume 2: cape crisis. Image comics 2010 un Illustration
Grades: 3 4 5 6 7 8   **741.5; Fic**
1. Graphic novels; 2. Humorous graphic novels; 3. Superhero graphic novels
978-1-60706-271-4, $9.99

The trouble starts when G-Man (aka Mikey) tells everyone that his magic cape gives him the power to fly; then everyone wants to fly. When he gives them bracelets made from the scraps of the magic blanket, everyone starts flying around and causing trouble. Then, when G-Man rounds up all the bracelets, he finds older brother Great Man (aka Dave) is selling more bracelets for $1,000 apiece. However, dividing up the magic into so many small bits is not only allowing unscrupulous people to commit crimes with their new powers, it is causing instabilities that could backfire disastrously. And that's exactly what happens. Now the brothers have to go on a quest to find the one being who can restore the magic to G-Man's cape.

Gieter, De
Papyrus: the Rameses' revenge. Cinebook 2007 48p. Illustration
Grades: 3 4 5 6 7 8   **741.5; Fic**
1. Adventure graphic novels; 2. Graphic novels; 3. Egypt — History — Graphic novels
978-1-905460-35-9, $11.95

In ancient Egypt, Papyrus is a mischievous boy who has become a friend of the Princess Theti-Cheri, daughter of the Pharaoh, thanks to the magic sword that protects him. When Theti-Cheri insists on traveling down the Nile to see Rameses' Temple with just Papyrus, their friend Imhotep, and just a few guards, Papyrus is sure they will run into trouble. At the temple, they face two rival bands of plunderers who seek the treasure in the temple.

Part of the Papyrus series, originally published in France as Papyrus La Vengeance des Ramses.

Gilson
Melusine: Halloween. Cinebook Ltd 2007 48p. Illustration
Grades: 3 4 5 6 7 8   **741.5; Fic**

1. Graphic novels; 2. Humorous graphic novels; 3. Witches — Graphic novels

978-1-905460-34-2, $11.95

Melusine is a sorcerer's apprentice who wants to become a powerful witch. However, she's not always successful. Her friend Cancrelune can never get her potions right, and cousin Melisande is a fairy who always wants to make everything light, pretty, and fun. This volume collects stories that focus on Halloween, with pumpkin carving, monster calling, and children going trick-or-treating.

First published 2000 in France

Melusine: love potions. Cinebook 2010 48p. Illustration
Grades: 3 4 5 6 7 8   **741.5; Fic**
1. Graphic novels; 2. Humorous graphic novels; 3. Witches — Graphic novels

978-1-84918-005-4, $11.95

Young witch in training Melusine tries to make love potions, in between encounters with her clumsy fellow student Cancrelune and various villagers who want to fall in love (or not). The full-color cartoony art keeps the witches, vampires, ghosts, dragons, and monsters more humorous looking than spooky.

Originally published in France as Melusine 5 Philtres d'amour

Melusine: The vampire's ball. Cinebook Ltd. 2008 48p. Illustration
Grades: 3 4 5 6 7 8   **741.5; Fic**
1. Graphic novels; 2. Humorous graphic novels; 3. Witches — Graphic novels

978-1-905460-69-4, $11.95

The young witch Melusine is back for more fun with all her family, including witches Adrazelle and Cancrelune, the ghostly Madam and vampire Master of the haunted castle, and more. Melusine tries to make different potions, turns toads into dragons and vice versa, tries to avoid too many cleaning chores in the castle, and more. Some of the situations are slightly gruesome, as when a particularly nasty knight ends up eaten by a monstrous tree in the forest, or when the male vampires get too drunk to get under cover before sunrise and turn into piles of ash.

Goodwin, Vincent

Sir Arthur Conan Doyle's The adventure of the speckled band. adapted by, Vincent Goodwin; illustrated by, Ben Dunn. ABDO/Magic Wagon 2010 48p. Illustration
Grades: 4 5 6 7 8 9
741.5; Fic
1. Authors; 2. Graphic novels; 3. Holmes, Sherlock (Fictional character) — Graphic novels; 4. Mystery graphic novels; 5. Doyle, Arthur Conan Sir, 1859-1930 — Adaptations
978-1-60270-727-6, $28.50;
1-60270-727-8

LC 2009-32461   *Courtesy of ABDO Publishing.*

Consulting detective Sherlock Holmes and his partner Dr. John Watson come to the aid of Miss Helen Stoner. After moving back to England from India with their stepfather, Helen's twin sister died under mysterious circumstances. Now, two years later, Helen knows something is terribly wrong in her stepfather's house. Both men suspect the gypsies that Dr. Roylott, the stepfather, has allowed to live on his property, but Holmes soon suspects something else. This graphic novel adaptation has been done by Goodwin and Dunn, who are experienced creators with Antarctic Press (Dunn started the publishing house). The book includes a brief glossary, a short

biography of Doyle, a listing of his published works, and a short sketching lesson by Dunn.

Part of The Graphic Novel Adventures of Sherlock Holmes

Sir Arthur Conan Doyle's The adventure of the Red-Headed League. ABDO/Magic Wagon 2010 48p. Illustration
Grades: 4 5 6 7 8 9
741.5; Fic
1. Authors; 2. Graphic novels; 3. Holmes, Sherlock (Fictional character) — Graphic novels; 4. Mystery graphic novels; 5. Doyle, Arthur Conan Sir, 1859-1930 — Adaptations
978-1-60270-726-9, $28.50;
1-60270-726-X

LC 2009-32460   *Courtesy of ABDO Publishing.*

Consulting detective Sherlock Holmes and his friend Dr. John Watson take the case of Jabez Wilson, an ordinary tradesman with an extraordinary tale. His pawn shop assistant had found an advertisement in the newspaper asking for eligible men to apply for membership in The RedHeaded League, and he helped Mr. Wilson fight through a crowd of redheaded men and to be accepted into the League. Wilson was paid four pounds a week for a few hours' work copying out an encyclopedia; then suddenly, all trace of the League disappeared. He wants Holmes to find out what has happened. This graphic novel adaptation has been done by Goodwin and Dunn, who are experienced creators with Antarctic Press (Dunn started the publishing house). The book includes a brief glossary, a short biography of Doyle, a listing of his published works, and a short sketching lesson by Dunn.

Part of The Graphic Novel Adventures of Sherlock Holmes

Sir Arthur Conan Doyle's The adventure of the blue carbuncle. adapted by Vincent Goodwin; illustrated by Ben Dunn. Magic Wagon 2012 48 p. Color illustration (Graphic novel adventures of Sherlock Holmes)
Grades: 2 3 4
741.5/973; Fic
1. Graphic novels; 2. Holmes, Sherlock (Fictitious character) — Comic books, strips, etc; 3. Mystery and detective stories; 4. Doyle, Arthur Conan, Sir, 1859-1930; 5. Mystery graphic novels; 6. Mystery fiction
1616418915; 9781616418915, $29.93;
9781614788379, $20.95

LC 2011052251   *Courtesy of ABDO Publishing.*

This graphic novel, adapted by Vincent Goodwin, illustrated by Ben Dunn, retells a mystery story featuring Sir Arthur Conan Doyle's detective Sherlock Holmes. "Holmes must discover how the Countess of Morcar's stolen jewel came to be inside a Christmas goose! The mystery begins with a street fight and ends with a full confession. Join the wild goose chase with Sherlock Holmes in the adventure of the blue carbuncle." (Publisher's note)

Includes bibliographical references (p. 47).

Sir Arthur Conan Doyle's, The adventure of the empty house. ABDO/Magic Wagon 2010 48p. Illustration
Grades: 4 5 6 7 8 9
741.5; Fic
1. Authors; 2. Graphic novels; 3. Holmes, Sherlock (Fictional character); 4. Mystery graphic novels; 5. Mystery writers; 6. Novelists; 7. Doyle, Arthur Conan Sir, 1859-1930; 8. Doyle, Arthur Conan Sir, 1859-1930 — Adaptations

Courtesy of ABDO Publishing.

978-1-60270-724-5, $28.50; 1-60270-724-3

Three years before, Dr. Watson witnessed the death of his friend Sherlock Holmes, who plummeted to his death along with archvillain Dr. Moriarty. Now, Inspector Lestrade asks Watson's help in a puzzling murder case, but it stumps Watson as well. Then, to his utter surprise, Holmes comes to him, explaining that he pretended to die. Together again, the two men work on the case, hoping to catch one of Moriarty's dangerous henchmen. This graphic novel adapts Doyle's original story which was the "comeback" after killing Holmes in "The Final Problem." The art depicts Watson as a fairly young man, but persists in putting Holmes into the deerstalker cap and caped overcoat which Doyle's Holmes never wore. The book includes a brief drawing lesson, a short glossary, brief biography of Doyle, and a listing of his other writings.

Part of The Graphic Novel Adventures of Sherlock Holmes

Sir Arthur Conan Doyle's, The adventure of the dancing men. ABDO/Magic Wagon 2010 48p. Illustration
Grades: 4 5 6 7 8 9

1. Authors; 2. Graphic novels; 3. Holmes, Sherlock (Fictional character); 4. Mystery graphic novels; 5. Doyle, Arthur Conan Sir, 1859-1930 — Adaptations
978-1-60270-723-8, $28.50;
1-60270-723-5

When strange writing that looks like dancing men starts appearing around the estate of Mr. Cubitt, he comes to Sherlock Holmes for help. He thinks it's the work of pranksters, but his American wife seems

Courtesy of ABDO Publishing.

frightened. As he brings more of the writing samples to Holmes, the detective works on the case, but he may not be able to solve it before tragedy strikes the Cubitts. This book adapts Doyle's short story; it includes a short glossary, a brief biography of Doyle, a short drawing lesson, and a list of Doyle's other writings. Dunn's art depicts Holmes and Dr. Watson as younger men, but continues the stereotypical portrayal of Holmes with the deerstalker cap and shoulder caped coat which Doyle never had him wear in the original stories.

Part of The Graphic Novel Adventures of Sherlock Holmes series

Sir Arthur Conan Doyle's, The adventure of the Abbey Grange. ABDO/Magic Wagon 2010 48p. Illustration
Grades: 4 5 6 7 8 9
741.5; Fic
1. Authors; 2. Graphic novels; 3. Holmes, Sherlock (Fictional character); 4. Doyle, Arthur Conan Sir, 1859-1930
978-1-60270-722-1, $28.50;
1-60270-722-7

A robbery and murder have occurred, and Sir Eustace Brackenstall is dead. His wife and maid say that a gang of robbers invaded their home, tied up Lady Brackenstall and killed Sir Eustace, but Holmes doesn't believe their story. As he investigates, he learns that Sir Eustace was a cruel man, and even though

Courtesy of ABDO Publishing.

Lady Brackenstall has lied, Holmes sympathizes with her. This book adapts Doyle's short story; it includes a short glossary, a brief biography of Doyle, a short drawing lesson, and a list of Doyle's other writings. Dunn's art depicts Holmes and Dr. Watson as younger men, but continues the stereotypical portrayal of Holmes with the deerstalker cap and shoulder caped coat which Doyle never had him wear in the original stories.

Part of The Graphic Novel Adventures of Sherlock Holmes series.

Goscinny, Rene
Asterix and Caesar's Gift. Orion/Sterling Publishing 2004 48p. Illustration
Grades: 4 5 6 7 8 9 10 11 12 Adult   **741.5; Fic**
1. Asterix (Fictional character); 2. Graphic novels; 3. Humorous graphic novels
0-75286-645-1, $12.95; 0-75286-646-X (pa)

When Legionary Tremensdelirius gets the title deeds to the little Gaulish village as a bonus, he swaps them with tavern landlord Orthopaedix for a drink. Funnily enough, Asterix and his friends aren't keen to hand over their village to anyone else. After a chieftaincy election campaign and a showdown with the Romans, both events fiercely contested, can all still end well?

Asterix and Cleopatra. Orion/Sterling Publishing 2004 48p. Illustration
Grades: 4 5 6 7 8 9 10 11 12 Adult   **741.5; Fic**
1. Asterix (Fictional character); 2. Graphic novels; 3. Humorous graphic novels
0-75286-606-0, $12.95; 0-75286-607-9 (pb)

How can lovely Queen Cleopatra show Julius Caesar that ancient Egypt is still a great nation? Her architect Edifis recruits his Gaulish friends to help him build a magnificent palace within three months. There are villainous saboteurs to be outwitted, but Asterix, Obelix, and Getafix still find time to go sight-seeing, and leave their mark on the Pyramids and the Sphinx's nose.

Asterix and the Banquet. Orion/Sterling Publishing 2004 48p. Illustration
Grades: 4 5 6 7 8 9 10 11 12 Adult   **741.5; Fic**
1. Asterix (Fictional character); 2. Graphic novels; 3. Humorous graphic novels
0-75286-608-0, $12.95; 0-75286-609-5 (pa)

When the Romans try to contain the threat from the Gaulish village by building a stockade around it, Asterix and Obelix lay a bet with them. They will break out and claim their right to travel freely all over Gaul, collecting the local delicacies and bringing them back to prove their point. Ham from Lutetia, fizzy wine from Durocortorum, fish stew from Massilia in the south...soon their shopping bag is full. Outwitting Romans, a couple of treacherous Gauls, and the thieves Villanus and Unscrupulus, they set off for home...but who's that little dog who has been following them all the way from Lutetia?

Asterix and the Cauldron. Orion/Sterling Publishing 2004 48p. Illustration
Grades: 4 5 6 7 8 9 10 11 12 Adult   **741.5; Fic**
1. Asterix (Fictional character); 2. Graphic novels; 3. Humorous graphic novels
0-75286-629-X, $9.95

There's financial skulduggery in ancient Gaul. When local Chief Whosemoralsarelastix wants a cauldron full of money kept out of Roman hands, the cash disappears while Asterix is guarding it. He and Obelix must earn enough to repay it through fairground gladiatorial contests, trendy theatrical performances, even bank robbery — they'll try anything. But whose morals are really elastic? And how to the pirates, just for once, get an unexpected bonus?

Asterix and the Class Act. Orion/Sterling Publishing 2004 56p. Illustration
Grades: 4 5 6 7 8 9 10 11 12 Adult   **741.5; Fic**
  1. Asterix (Fictional character); 2. Graphic novels; 3. Humorous graphic novels
  0-75286-068-2, $12.95; 0-75286-640-0 (pa)
  This volume collects 14 stories, including the day Asterix and Obelix were born (in the middle of a fish fight); how Obelix goes back to school; fashion in ancient Gaul; how Dogmatix helps the village cockerel win a duel, and how he's adopted as a Roman mascot; Obelix's adventures under the mistletoe; the bid for the very first Gaulish Olympics, and more.

★ **Asterix** the Gaul. written by René Goscinny and illustrated by Albert Uderzo; translated by Anthea Bell and Derek Hockridge. Orion Media 2004 48p. Illustration; Map
Grades: 4 5 6 7 8 9 10 11 12   **741.5; Fic**
  1. Graphic novels; 2. Humorous graphic novels; 3. France — History — Graphic novels
  0-7528-6604-4, $12.95; 0-7528-6605-2 (pa), $9.95
  Meet Asterix, a diminutive but extremely strong Gaul living in ancient France during the time of the Roman Republic. Together with his friend Obelix, Asterix continually outwits the Roman Legionnaires sent to conquer Gaul for Julius Caesar. Full of puns and outrageous humor, the books also manage to teach a lot of history. This is the first in a long-running series of graphic novels translated from the original French.
  Translated from the French; Other titles in this series are: Asterix and Caesar's Gift; Asterix and Cleopatra; Asterix and the actress; Asterix and the banquet; Asterix and the big fight; Asterix and the cauldron; Asterix and the Goths; Asterix and the Great Crossing; Asterix and the laurel wreath; Asterix the legionary; Asterix and the Normans; Asterix and the Roman Agent; Asterix and the soothsayer; Asterix at the Olympic Games; Asterix in Belgium; Asterix in Britain; Asterix in Corsica; Asterix in Spain; Asterix in Switzerland; Asterix Obelix and Co.; Asterix the gladiator; Asterix The Mansions of the Gods

Asterix and the Laurel Wreath. Orion/Sterling Publishing 2004 48p. Illustration
Grades: 4 5 6 7 8 9 10 11 12 Adult   **741.5; Fic**
  1. Asterix (Fictional character); 2. Graphic novels; 3. Humorous graphic novels
  0-75286-636-2, $12.95; 0-75286-637-0 (pa)
  Chief Vitalstatistix rashly invites his brother-in-law to dine on a stew seasoned with Caesar's laurel wreath, so Asterix and Obelix must to go Rome to fetch those laurels. Hoping to get access to Caesar, they sell themselves as slaves, but can they do a deal with the corrupt Goldendelicius to swap the laurels for parsley?

Asterix in Britain. Orion/Sterling Publishing 2004 48p. Illustration
Grades: 4 5 6 7 8 9 10 11 12 Adult   **741.5; Fic**
  1. Asterix (Fictional character); 2. Graphic novels; 3. Humorous graphic novels
  0-85286-618-4, $12.95; 0-75286-619-2 (pa)
  The Romans have invaded Britain, but one village still holds out. Asterix and Obelix come to help, with a barrel of magic potion in hand. But to deliver the precious brew, the Gaulish heroes must face fog, rain, bad food, warm beer, and the Romans too.

Asterix the Legionary. Orion/Sterling Publishing 2004 48p. Illustration
Grades: 4 5 6 7 8 9 10 11 12 Adult   **741.5; Fic**
  1. Asterix (Fictional character); 2. Graphic novels; 3. Humorous graphic novels

0-75286-620-6, $12.95; 0-75286-621-4 (pa)
  It's off to the wars for Asterix and Obelix: they've enlisted as legionnaires in order to rescue Tragicomix, whom the Romans forcibly conscripted. The two find Tragicomix and succeed in causing the biggest commotion ever on a battlefield.

The **Caliph's** vacation. Cinebook Ltd 2008 48p. Illustration
Grades: 3 4 5 6 7 8   **741.5; Fic**
  1. Graphic novels; 2. Humorous graphic novels
  978-1-905460-61-8, $11.95
  Iznogoud, the Grand Vizier of Baghdad the Magnificent, wants to be Caliph, and he hatches all kinds of schemes to do in the good, kindhearted, not-too-bright Caliph, Haroun Al Plassid. First, they go to the beach, where Iznogoud and his henchman Wa'at Alahf try to drown him (the Caliph floats), send him into shark-infested waters (his suntan oil reeks), and other attempts that end up nearly doing in Iznogoud. A scheme to use a weather wizard to kill the Caliph with winter snow ends up with everyone enjoying a ski vacation. Then Iznogoud comes up with a poisoned elixir but can't get the Caliph to drink it. Goscinny is best known in the U.S. for his Asterix comics, but Iznogoud is just as filled with puns and humor, with a villain as the main character. Readers will enjoy the Wile E. Coyote type of hijinks.
  First published 2000 in France

Dalton City: a Lucky Luke adventure. Cinebook 2007 48p. Illustration
Grades: 3 4 5 6 7 8   **741.5; Fic**
  1. Graphic novels; 2. Humorous graphic novels; 3. Western stories — Graphic novels
  978-1-905460-13-7, $9.99
  Goscinny, cocreator of Asterix, gives readers his wacky version of the American Old West in the Lucky Luke Adventures. Luke is a traveling good guy, who shoots faster than his shadow. He cleans up Fenton City, a festering sore of depravity in Texas, by capturing Dean Fenton, the boss of the town. Fenton ends up in the same prison as the Dalton brothers, a gang of not-too-smart outlaws that Luke keeps having to put away. They break out of the prison and take over Fenton City, calling it Dalton City. When Lucky Luke shows up, they ask him for advice on how to make the town a haven for outlaws, and Luke sees his chance to round up a whole lot of bad guys.
  Part of the Lucky Luke Adventures series, originally published in France as Lucky Luke Dalton City.

The **tenderfoot:** Lucky Luke adventure, vol. 13. Cinbook Ltd. 2008 48p. Illustration
Grades: 3 4 5 6 7 8   **791.5; Fic**
  1. Graphic novels; 2. Humorous graphic novels; 3. Western stories — Graphic novels
  978-1-905460-65-6, $11.95
  When Rancher Baddy passes away, his heir, an Englishman, comes to town to take over the ranch. Jack Ready wants the ranch, so he plans to give the "tenderfoot" reasons to go away. When Lucky Luke, who can shoot faster than his shadow, helps Waldo get through the "welcoming ceremonies" and the phlegmatic Englishman shows he's more than a match for anything the cowboys can think to do, Jack Ready comes up with the only other plan that might work — frame Waldo for Jack's murder. The book has no real violence, but it does show drinking and gambling in the saloon. While some readers might fret over the stereotyping of the Native American characters, they should note that every single character in the book, including Lucky Luke himself, is a caricature of a "type," from rough cowboy to noble Indian, to Chinese, to hoity-toity Englishmen, to gunfighters. This is translated from the original French stories written by Rene Goscinny, who also wrote Asterix.

Gould, Jane H.

George Washington Carver. by Jane Gould. PowerKids Press 2013 24 p. Color illustration
Grades: 3 4 5 6
630.92; 92

Courtesy of Rosen Publishing

1. African American agriculturists — Biography — Comic books, strips, etc.; 2. African American educators — Biography — Comic books, strips, etc.; 3. African American scientists — Biography — Comic books, strips, etc.; 4. Agriculturists — United States — Biography — Comic books, strips, etc.; 5. Peanuts — United States — History — Comic books, strips, etc.; 6. African American inventors; 7. Carver, George Washington, 1864?-1943
1477700781; 9781477700785, $25.25; 9781477701416, $10.60; 9781477701423

LC 2012018689

In this biography of inventor George Washington Carver, author Jane Gould "provides the requisite biographical details, including Carver's early...separation from his mother, but also traces themes of his career, drawing connections between his kind masters' waste-not values and his future devotion to finding new uses for farm by-products." (Booklist)
Includes index.

Steve Jobs. by Jane Gould. PowerKids Press 2013 24 p.
Grades: 3 4 5 6
338.7; 92

Courtesy of Rosen Publishing

1. Apple Computer, Inc. — History; 2. Businessmen — United States — Biography; 3. Computer engineers — United States — Biography; 4. Jobs, Steve; 5. Inventors; 6. Jobs, Steve, 1955-2011
1477700803; 9781477700808, $25.25; 9781477701454

LC 2012020633

This graphic novel by Jane Gould is a biography of Steven Jobs, "best known for being a co-founder of Apple Inc. Before Apple Inc., he was a brilliant designer and inventor who approached business with an unexpected savvy and joy of discovery. Jobs created gadgets that transformed today's digital era." (Publisher's note)
Includes index.

Gownley, Jimmy

★ **Amelia** Rules! Volume Three: Superheroes. Renaissance Press 2006 174p. Illustration
Grades: 3 4 5 6
741.5; Fic
1. Friendship — Graphic novels; 2. Graphic novels; 3. Humorous graphic novels
9780971216969, $11.99

This third volume of Amelia Rules! contains one storyline, about the summer after fourth grade. First, Amelia faces the possibility of another move (across town); then new friends Trishia and Ninja Joan join Amelia and Rhonda, while Reggie and Pajama Man fight crime — actually, the Legion of Steves. The guys even team up with the Park Terrace Ninjas. In the middle of all the summer fun, Amelia learns Trishia's terrible secret and doesn't know how to help.
Originally published as Amelia Rules! issues #11-16.

Amelia rules! True things (adults don't want kids to know). Atheneum Books for Young Readers 2010 163p.
Grades: 3 4 5 6
741.5; 741
978-1-4169-8609-6 (pa), $10.99; 1-4169-8609-X (pa)

★ **Amelia** rules! when the past is a present. Renaissance Press 2008 168p. Illustration
Grades: 3 4 5 6
741.5; Fic
1. Friendship — Graphic novels; 2. Graphic novels; 3. Humorous graphic novels
978-0-9712169-8-3, $24.95; 978-0-9712169-9-0 (pa), $11.99

The kids are now in fifth grade, and Amelia and Rhonda are officially friends and not enemies any more. Amelia is going to her first dance (with a boy no less — Kyle the ninja), but she's not the only one with a date. Is Amelia's mom seeing someone too? Perhaps Reggie (a.k.a. Captain Amazing) can shed some light on the situation, by spying on their date. But it's not all fun for the 10-year-old spitfire. A good friend " Joan " reveals that her father will be deployed to Iraq with his job in the military, and it gets Amelia thinking about her own family, her past, and what it means for the present.

Amelia rules!: The meaning of life — and other stuff. written and illustrated by Jimmy Gownley. Atheneum Books for Young Readers 2011 147p. Illustration
Grades: 3 4 5 6
741.5; 741
978-1-4169861-3-3, $19.99; 1-4169861-3-8; 978-1-4169861-2-6 (pa), $10.99; 1-4169861-2-X (pa)

LC 2011018407

"Though it is a slender volume, Gownley does not shy away from tough topics, presenting them in a way that is both approachable and understandable to kids.... With all of the tribulations Amelia must deal with, she paints an accurate portrait of what preteens must deal with and how fast they sometimes have to grow up." Kirkus

★ **Amelia** rules!: the whole world's crazy!. Renaissance Press 2003 176p.
Grades: 3 4 5 6
741.5; Fic
1. Family life — Graphic novels; 2. Friendship — Graphic novels; 3. Graphic novels; 4. Humorous graphic novels
0-9712169-3-2, $24.95; 0-9712169-2-4 (pa), $14.95

"Amelia...is getting used to life with her newly divorced mom and her hip, young aunt Tanner; settling in at a strange new school; and finding a group of friends. Amelia is no sweet innocent, nor are her three G.A.S.P (Gathering of Awesome Superpals) buddies: Reggie, superhero in the making; Rhonda, Amelia's tough bete noire with a fourth-grade "thing" for Reggie; and quiet, mysterious Pajamaman. Jealousy, meanness, sadness, and confusion, as well as surprising generosity, and love crisscross the pages in energetic, freewheeling, full-color cartoon art that unwraps a kid's-eye view of life honestly, poignantly, and with a hefty dollop of melodrama." Booklist

Other titles in this series are: Amelia rules!: What makes you happy? (2004); Amelia rules! Superheroes (2005); Amelia rules! a very ninja Christmas (2009); Amelia rules! When the past is a present (2010); Amelia rules! The tweenage guide to not being unpopular (2010); Amelia rules! True things (adults don't want kids to know) (2010); Amelia rules! The meaning of life. . . and other stuff (2011); Amelia rules! Her permanent record (2012)

Amelia rules: The tweenage guide to not being unpopular. Atheneum Books for Young Readers 2010 187p.
Grades: 3 4 5 6
741; 741.5
978-1-4169-8610-2, $18.99; 1-4169-8610-3; 978-1-4169-8608-9 (pa), $10.99; 1-4169-8608-1 (pa)

LC 2009053665

★ **Her** permanent record. written and illustrated by Jimmy Gownley. Atheneum Books for Young Readers 2012 144 p.
Grades: 3 4 5 6   **741.5**
1. Aunts — Fiction; 2. Friendship — Fiction; 3. Graphic novels; 4. Schools — Fiction; 5. Voyages and travels — Fiction; 6. Missing persons — Fiction; 7. School stories
1416986154; 9781416986140; 9781416986157, $19.99
LC 2011053039

This book is the eighth installment of the "Amelia Rules!" series by Jimmy Gownley. "With her new spot on the cheerleading squad, [and] Aunt Tanner's hordes of adoring fans,...Amelia's sailing seems remarkably smooth. Then Tanner disappears...sending Amelia into full panic mode. And when she boards a bus on an epic journey to find Tanner...it quickly becomes clear that if Amelia has learned anything in her eleven years, it's that life is never through with surprises." (Publisher's note)

Grahame, Kenneth
Classics illustrated deluxe # 1: the wind in the willows. NBM/Papercutz 2007 144p. Illustration
Grades: 3 4 5 6 7 8
741.5; Fic
1. Animals — Graphic novels; 2. Fantasy graphic novels; 3. Graphic novels; 4. Humorous graphic novels
978-1-59707-095-9, $19.99;
978-1-59707-096-6 (pa), $13.95

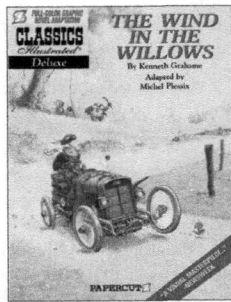
Courtesy of NBM Publishing

Kenneth Grahame's classic story of the wild Mister Toad's misadventures and crazy enthusiasms that get him into great trouble from which his friends Badger, Mole, and Rat must extricate him gets a deluxe, full-color graphic novel treatment with art that looks like classic 1930s-style animation.

Gravel, Elise
The **great** Antonio. by Elise Gravel. TOON Books, an imprint of RAW Junior, LLC 2017 64 p. Color; Illustration
Grades: K 1 2 3   **741.5; 92; 796.41**
1. Actors — Canada — Biography; 2. Strong men — Canada — Biography; 3. Weight lifters — Canada — Biography; 4. Barichievich, Antonio, 1925-2003
9781943145089, $12.95
LC 2016003371

This children's book asks, "what made the Great Antonio so great? He weighed as much as a horse! He once wrestled a bear. He could devour twenty-five roasted chickens at one sitting. In this whimsical book [in the Toon Books series], beloved author and illustrator Elise Gravel tells the true story of Antonio Barichievich, the larger-than-life Montreal strongman who had muscles as big as his heart." (Publisher's note)

"The text is spare and engaging, and the type is set to integrate neatly with the playful art. A tribute as heartfelt as it is joyous and a fitting way to remember this larger-than-life performer." Kirkus

A TOON Book.

Gray, Harold
★**Harold** Gray's Little Orphan Annie; Volume one: the complete daily comics, 1924-27: Will tomorrow ever come? IDW Publishing 2008 385p. Illustration
Grades: 2 3 4 5 6 7 8 9 10 11 12 Adult   **741.5; Fic**
1. Adventure graphic novels; 2. Graphic novels; 3. Little Orphan Annie (Fictional character); 4. Orphans — Graphic novels

978-1-60010-140-3, $39.99

Little Orphan Annie started as a daily newspaper comic strip in one newspaper, the New York Daily News, on August 5, 1924. It became a popular strip, syndicated to newspapers all over the world. It eventually became a Broadway, a hit movie, and Annie became an iconic character. This book is the first comprehensive collection of Gray's comic strip and is the first volume of a series planned to

Courtesy of IDW Publishing

collect all of Gray's Little Orphan Annie strips. She is an orphan girl living in an orphanage, with an unscrupulous director who hires Annie out for work. When wealthy Mrs. Warbucks, trying to prove that she cares for the poor, takes Annie on a "trial" adoption, Annie eventually meets Oliver Warbucks, whom she calls "Daddy." As the strips go on, Annie undergoes many hardships and perils, facing everything with spunk and a positive attitude. She's no wilting girl, though " she can fight (she has a mean right hook) and will take on any bully. She rescues the dog she calls Sandy, who rewards her with a loyal friendship. This volume includes more than 1,000 comic strips, many of which haven't seen publication since their original newspaper appearance. During the first years of the strip's publication, the color Sunday comics had no connection to the weekday storylines, but a few Sunday pages are included in this book. This book may appeal most to adults who remember reading Little Orphan Annie in the "funnies" pages, but the stories will appeal to all ages. Contributing Editor Jeet Heer provides a biography of Harold Gray.

Gray-Wilburn, Renée
Earthquakes!. by Renee Gray-Wilburn; illustrated by Aleksandar Sotirovski. Capstone Press 2012 24 p. Color illustration
Grades: 1 2 3 4
551.22
1. Earthquakes; 2. Graphic novels
1429676051; 1429679506; 9781429676052, $23.32; 9781429679503, $5.95
LC 2011028740

Courtesy of Capstone Press

This graphic novel, written by Renee Gray-Wilburn and illustrated by Aleksandar Sotirovski, is part of the "First Graphics: Wild Earth" series. The book explains the geophysics behind earthquakes, the methods used by earth scientists to measure them, and advice on how to stay safe when experiencing one.

Includes bibliographical references and index

Volcanoes!. by Renée Gray-Wilburn; illustrated by Aleksandar Sotirovski. Capstone Press 2012 24 p. Color illustration
Grades: 1 2 3 4
551.21
1. Volcanoes; 2. Earth sciences
142967606X; 9781429676069, $23.32
LC 2011028742

Courtesy of Capstone Press

This graphic novel, written by Renee Gray-Wilburn and illustrated by Aleksandar Sotirovski, is part of the "First Graphics: Wild Earth" series. The book explains the geophysics behind volcanoes, the methods used by earth scientists to measure them, and advice on how to stay safe when experiencing the eruption from one.

Includes bibliographical references (p. 23) and index

Green, John (John Patrick)
Hippopotamister. by John Patrick Green. First Second 2016 96 p. Color; Illustration
Grades: K 1 2 3   **741.5; Fic**
1. Hippopotamus; 2. Zoos
1626722005; 9781626722002, $17.99
LC 2015944386
In this book, by John Patrick Green, "the zoo isn't what it used to be. It's run down, and Hippo hardly ever gets any visitors. So he decides to set off for the outside with his friend Red Panda. To make it in the human world, Hippo will have to become a Hippopotamister: he'll have to act like a human, get a job, and wear a hat as a disguise." (Publisher's note)

"Using large-scale panels and a crisp drawing style, Green captures the absurdities of each situation with a good-natured cheer in each panel. A cheerfully bright palette and highly expressive characters bring vibrant energy to the pages, echoing the upbeat tone of the story." Booklist

Griffith, Saul
Howtoons: tools of mass construction. Dr. Saul Griffith, co-creator, writer & engineer; Nick Dragotta, co-creator, writer & artist; Ingrid Dragotta, project & book design; Arwen Griffith, editor; Joost Bonsen, co-creator & writer. Image Comics 2014 360 p. Illustration
Grades: 2 3 4 5 6 7   **741.5; 507.8**
1. Self-instruction; 2. Educational games
1632151014; 9781632151018, $17.99
"Follow Celine and Tucker as they learn through play with over 50 DIY projects! This brother-and-sister pair use everyday objects to invent toys that readers can build. Combining comics and real-life science and engineering principles, Howtoons are designed to encourage kids to become active participants in the world around them." (Publisher's note)

"The bright, somewhat chaotic artwork is designed to capture a kid's attention and imagination. The projects are not laid out in a staid, step-by-step manner, and several of them will require extra thought or adult assistance, but the variety is hard to beat, as the creators cover art, math, engineering, science, and more." Booklist

Grine, Chris
Chickenhare. Chris Grine. Graphix / Scholastic 2013 160 p.
Grades: 4 5 6 7 8 9   **741.5**
1. Animals — Graphic novels; 2. Taxidermy — Fiction; 3. Escapes — Fiction
0545485088; 9780545485081, $10.99
LC 2012936214
Author Chris Grine presents a children's comic book. "What's a chickenhare? A cross between a chicken and a rabbit, of course. And that makes Chickenhare the rarest animal around! So when he and his turtle friend Abe are captured and sold to the evil taxidermist Klaus, they've got to find a way to escape before Klaus turns them into stuffed animals. With the help of two other strange creatures, Banjo and Meg, they might even get away. But with Klaus and his thugs hot on their trail, the adventure is only just beginning for this unlikely quartet of friends." (Publisher's note)

Guibert, Emmanuel
Ariol 2: Thunder Horse. by Emmanuel Guibert; illustrated by Marc Boutavant. Papercutz 2013 124 p.
Grades: 2 3 4 5   **741.5/944; Fic**
1. Heroes and heroines — Fiction; 2. Children's literature

1597074128; 9781597074124, $12.99
This book, written by Emmanuel Guibert and illustrated by Marc Boutavant, presents artwork and vignettes featuring the character Ariol. Ariol "[does] everything he can to grow up and become just like [his hero] the guardian of the stars." (Publisher's note) "The author dares to depict the exclusionary, argumentative, self-centered ways children can sometimes behave." (Booklist)
Translated from the French.

Courtesy of NBM Publishing

Ariol: Happy as a pig. by Emmanuel Guibert; illustrated by Marc Boutavant. Papercutz 2013 124 p.
Grades: 2 3 4 5
741.5
1. Donkeys — Comic books, strips, etc.; 2. Friendship — Comic books, strips, etc.; 3. Schools — Comic books, strips, etc.; 4. Swine — Comic books, strips, etc.; 5. Pigs — Juvenile fiction
159707487X; 9781597074872, $12.99
In this book, by Emmanuel Guibert and illustrated by Marc Boutavant, "Ariol's best friend, Ramono, is a pig. He's also loud, impulsive, [and] irresponsible.... Sneaking into a parking garage to play with fuses, carting grandpa's dog around in a wheelbarrow, wrestling matches with his sister; you may have thought Ariol was trouble enough, but you've never seen Ramono on the loose!" (Publisher's note)

Courtesy of NBM Publishing

"Boutavant's bright and buoyant illustrations and Guibert's pitch-perfect dialogue elevate the simple, everyday stories to illuminate something refreshingly honest about being a kid." Booklist

Ariol: Just a Donkey Like You and Me. Papercutz 2013 124 p. Illustration
Grades: 2 3 4 5   **741.5**
1. Animals — Graphic novels; 2. School stories — Graphic novels
1597073997; 9781597073998, $12.99
This book follows Ariol and his ensemble, a "cast of anthropomorphized animal children," in "10 10-page stories, originally from France, which offer...slice-of-life vignettes. Whether Ariol is joining his father for a trip to the ATM, arguing with a friend about sneakers, accompanying his grandmother to the movies, pursuing his great crush, or emulating his favorite superhero, the author dares to depict the exclusionary, argumentative, self-centered ways children can sometimes behave." (Booklist)
Other titles in this series are: Thunder horse (2013); Happy as a pig (2013); A beautiful cow (2014)

Ariol; 4: a beautiful cow. Emmanuel Guibert, illustrated by Marc Boutavant. Papercutz 2014 124 p. Color; Illustration
Grades: 2 3 4 5
741.5
1. Cattle — Fiction; 2. Animals — Fiction
1597075132; 9781597075138, $12.99
In this children's book by Emmanuel Guibert, illustrated by Marc Boutavant, part of the Ariol series, "Petula is a beautiful cow

Courtesy of NBM Publishing

who smells nice, has pretty hair, and makes Ariol tremble when she's around. And even though Ariol's story so far is almost 400 pages long, he still hasn't worked up the courage to tell Petula that he loves her! Instead, he keeps accidentally saying all the wrong things every time she turns around to talk to him in class." (Publisher's note)

"Silly situations and memorable characters make for an enjoyable, quick read. The easy-to-follow panels and colors that seem to pop from the pages make this graphic novel particularly pleasing." SLJ

Translated from the French

Guojing

★ The **only** child. by Guojing. Schwartz & Wade Books 2015 112 p. Illustration
Grades: K 1 2 3 4 5   **741.5; Fic**
1. Adventure and adventurers — Fiction; 2. Graphic novels; 3. Lost children — Fiction; 4. Stories without words; 5. Adventure fiction
9780553497045, $19.99; 9780553497052
LC 2014026977

Eisner Nominee: Best Publication for Early Readers (2016)

In this wordless graphic novel, by Guojing, a "little girl — lost and alone — follows a mysterious stag deep into the woods, and, like Alice down the rabbit hole, she finds herself in a strange and wondrous world. But... home and family are very far away. How will she get back there?" (Publisher's note)

"Each arresting, softly penciled panel is surprisingly luminous in spite of its monochromatic palette, and in those gentle scenes, Guojing evokes a wide range of feeling, especially the lonesomeness of the little girl, who never quite seems at ease alone." Booklist

Hale, Dean

★ **Calamity** Jack. Bloombury 2010 144p. Illustration
Grades: 4 5 6 7 8 9   **741.5; Fic**
1. Adventure graphic novels; 2. Fantasy graphic novels; 3. Folklore — Graphic novels; 4. Graphic novels
9781599903736, $14.99; 9781599900766, $19.99
LC 2008-41332

In this sequel to Rapunzel's Revenge, the reader meets Jack as a child growing up in the city of Shyport; Jack has been a schemer practically since birth, but he hasn't had a whole lot of luck. His schemes usually end in unforeseen consequences. When he goes up against the giant Blunderboar, the magic beanstalk he uses to reach the giant's floating fortress destroys his neighborhood and his mother's bakery, and he just manages to leave town with a certain gold-egg-laying goose under his arm. After the events of the first book, Jack and Rapunzel come to Shyport, where Jack hopes to help his mother rebuild her bakery with the golden eggs he now has. However, they come to a city transformed Blunderboar has taken over, his security company claims to be keeping giant ants at bay, and Jack's mother is being held prisoner. Jack is still wanted for what he had done, and only Prudence, Jack's hat-loving pixie partner-in-crime, is willing to help. Then Jack and Rapunzel meet Freddie Sparksmith, newspaperman and gadget inventor, and they team up for a rescue mission. The book includes a lot of action and some non-gory violence.

Companion to: Rapunzel's Revenge

★ **Rapunzel's** revenge. [by] Shannon and Dean Hale; illustrated by Nathan Hale. Bloomsbury 2008 144p. Illustration; Map
Grades: 5 6 7 8   **741.5; Fic**
1. Fairy tales — Graphic novels; 2. Fantasy graphic novels; 3. Graphic novels; 4. Humorous graphic novels
1-59990-070-X; 1-59990-288-5 (pa); 978-1-59990-070-4, $18.99; 978-1-59990-288-3 (pa), $14.99
LC 2007-37670

In this graphic novel, Rapunzel escapes "from the enchanted tree where Mother Gothel imprisoned her. Rapunzel sets off alone through the ghost towns and Badlands of Gothel's Reach. She is determined to find Gothel's Villa and teach Mother Gothel a long-overdue lesson for her years of treachery and lies, and help her real mother get out of the mine camps where Mother Gothel has kept her enslaved." (Publisher's note)

"The dialogue is witty, the story is an enticing departure from the original, and the illustrations are magically fun and expressive." SLJ

Another title about these characters is: Calamity Jack (2009)

Hale, Nathan

Alamo all-stars. Nathan Hale. Harry N Abrams Inc 2016 122 p. Illustration; Color (Nathan Hale's Hazardous Tales)
Grades: 3 4 5 6   **741.5; 976.4**
1. Texas — History — Revolution, 1835-1836; 2. Alamo (San Antonio, Tex.) — History — Siege, 1836; 3. United States — History — 1815-1861 — Graphic novels
1419719025; 9781419719028, $12.95

This graphic novel, sixth in author Nathan Lane's Hazardous Tales series, "relays the facts, politics, military actions, and prominent personalities that defined the Texas Revolution.... Beginning with the expeditions of the so-called 'Land Pirates,' through the doomed stand at the Alamo, and ending with the victory over Santa Anna at the Battle of San Jacinto, the entire Texas saga is on display." (Publisher's note)

"The irreverent tone, interjections by the narrators, and often humorous backstories of the major players lighten the mood and break up battle scenes in digestible pieces, and Hale's dynamic cartoon art renders each character uniquely enough that they're easy to tell apart — no small feat, given the large cast." Booklist

Includes bibliographical references

Donner dinner party. by Nathan Hale. Harry N Abrams Inc 2013 123 p. (Nathan Hale's Hazardous Tales)
Grades: 5 6 7 8   **979.4; 741.5**
1. Donner party; 2. Sierra Nevada Mountains
1419708562; 9781419708565, $12.95

In this graphic novel, author Nathan Hale "tells the harrowing story of the ill-fated Donner party. Beginning with their departure from Springfield, Illinois, in 1846, Hale depicts the party's progress...and includes lots of factual details, such as a roster of everyone in the party, how they died, and a helpful map showing just how...close they came to California before meeting their grisly end." (Booklist)

"This informative graphic novel capitalizes on enticingly gross history to great effect, balancing raw facts with strong storytelling." Booklist

Nathan Hale's hazardous tales: big bad ironclad!. Nathan Hale. Abrams 2012 118 p.
Grades: 4 5 6   **973.7**
1. Comic books, strips, etc.; 2. United States — History — 1861-1865, Civil War — Naval operations; 3. Cushing, William
1419703951; 9781419703959, $12.95
LC 2012947181

Author Nathan Hale "covers the history of the amazing ironclad steam warships used in the Civil War [in his book 'Big Bad Ironclad!'] From the ship's inventor, who had a history of blowing things up and only 100 days to complete his project, to the mischievous William Cushing, who pranked his way through the whole war, this book is filled with...facts." (Publisher's note)

Includes bibliographical references.; Map on endpapers.

Nathan Hale's hazardous tales: one dead spy. Nathan Hale. Amulet Books 2012 128 p.
Grades: 3 4 5 6 7   **741.5/973**

1. United States — History — Graphic novels; 2. Hale, Nathan, 1755-1776
141970396X; 9781419703966, $12.95

LC 2012947189

In this graphic novel, historical figure "[Nathan] Hale, convicted of espionage, forestalls death by telling stories from American history. In this volume, he's helped by the hangman in telling the story of the early days of the revolution. He takes readers from his college days at Yale to the Boston Massacre, the Boston Tea Party, his joining the 7th Connecticut regiment, the Battle of Bunker Hill and other pivotal scenes in New England and New York City." (Kirkus)

Other titles in this series are: Big bad ironclad! (2012); Donner dinner party (2013); Treaties, trenches, mud, and blood (2014); The underground abductor (2015); Alamo all-stars (2016); Raid of no return (2017)

Nathan Hale's hazardous tales: treaties, trenches, mud, and blood (a World War I tale). by Nathan Hale. Amulet Books 2014 128 p. Color illustration; Color; Map (Nathan Hale's hazardous tales)
Grades: 4 5 6 7 **741.5; 940.3**
1. World War, 1914-1918 — Comic books, strips, etc; 2. World War, 1914-1918
1419708082; 9781419708084, $12.95

LC 2013049048

"Nathan Hale, Revolutionary War hero, continues to distract his executioners in this fourth volume, which tackles WWI's complex events." (Horn Book)

"Per established series formula, a frame tale finds the author's more-renowned namesake holding off the hangman, Scheherazade-like, with tales from our country's future history. In this volume, he covers the war's prelude, precipitation, major campaigns and final winding down in small but reasonably easy-to-follow two-color panels.... Hale cogently conveys the mind-numbing scale of it all as well as the horrors of trench warfare." Kirkus

Includes bibliographical references

The **underground** abductor: an abolitionist tale. Nathan Hale. Harry N Abrams Inc. 2015 125 p. Illustration; Color (Nathan Hale's Hazardous Tales)
Grades: 3 4 5 6 7 **92; 741.5**
1. Fugitive slaves — United States — Comic books, strips, etc.; 2. Underground Railroad — Comic books, strips, etc.; 3. Tubman, Harriet, 1820?-1913; 4. Biographical graphic novels
9781419715365, $12.95; 1419715364
Eisner Nominee: Best Publication for Kids (2016)

In this graphic novel, "a fictionalized Nathan Hale (a patriot from the American Revolutionary War) tells stories about America's most extraordinary heroes and villains. In this installment, Hale tells his British captors about Harriet Tubman, the spy and nurse who helped hundreds of American slaves run away in the 1800s on the Underground Railroad." (School Library Journal)

Includes bibliographical references

Hale, Shannon

Real friends. Shannon Hale; illustrated by LeUyen Pham. First Second 2017 224 p. Color; Illustration
Grades: 3 4 5 6 **92; 741.5**
1. Bullies; 2. Friendship
9781626724167, $21.99; 9781626727854

LC 2016945552

In this graphic memoir, by Shannon Hale, illustrated by LeUyen Pham, "Shannon and Adrienne have been best friends ever since they were little. But one day, Adrienne starts hanging out with Jen, the most popular girl in class and the leader of a circle of friends called The Group. Everyone in The Group wants to be Jen's #1, and some girls would do anything to stay on top...even if it means bullying others." (Publisher's note)

"The author reflects on her life from the vantage point of adulthood, displaying a mature awareness of her own flaws and an understanding of the behavior of unsympathetic kids such as Wendy and Jenny, and her accessible writing and hopeful tone will speak to readers. Pham's gentle cartoon images make effective use of perspective and composition to underscore Shannon's sense of alienation." SLJ

Hama, Larry

The **Battle** of First Bull Run: The Civil War Begins. The Rosen Publishing Group 2007 48p. Illustration
Grades: 3 4 5 6 7 8 9
741.5; 973.7
1. Bull Run. 1st Battle of, 1861 — Graphic novels; 2. Graphic novels; 3. War — Graphic novels; 4. United States — History — 1861-1865, Civil War — Graphic novels
978-1-4042-0776-9, $29.25

Courtesy of Rosen Publishing

Three months after the shelling of Fort Sumter, Union and Confederate forces met for the first time in earnest combat. However, neither side was prepared at this early stage of the war, and confusion reigned on the battlefield. Finally, Confederate reinforcements forced the Union army into a panicked retreat. The intensity — and ill preparedness — of both armies convinced the nation that the conflict between the states would be a long, bloody ordeal. The book includes background information, a glossary, and a list of books for further reading.

Part of the Graphic Battles of the Civil War series. The book is also available in paperback from Osprey Publishing under the title The War is On!: Battle of First Bull Run.

The **battle** of Iwo Jima: guerilla warfare in the Pacific. by Larry Hama; illustrated by Anthony Williams. Rosen Pub. 2007 48p. Illustration; Map (Graphic battles of World War II)
Grades: 5 6 7 8 9
940.54
1. Graphic novels; 2. Iwo Jima, Battle of, 1945 — Graphic novels; 3. World War, 1939-1945 — Graphic novels
978-1-4042-0781-3 (lib bdg), $29.25; 1-4042-0781-3 (lib bdg)

LC 2006007645

Courtesy of Rosen Publishing

"Using a graphic novel to introduce the battle for Iwo Jima makes it very accessible. Before the graphic-novel section of the book begins, Hama provides a short, informative background piece describing the run-up to World War II, the significance of the Japanese war machine, and the importance of the tiny island of Iwo Jima. Then the graphic novel, illustrated by Williams in camouflage colors, does a terrific job of examining the ups and downs of the battle as well as the horror of so many losses — on both sides." Booklist

Includes bibliographical references

The **Battle** of Shiloh: Surprise Attack!. Rosen Publishing Group 2007 48p. Illustration
Grades: 3 4 5 6 7 8 **741.5; 973.7**
1. Graphic novels; 2. Shiloh (Tenn.), Battle of, 1862 — Graphic novels; 3. United States — History — 1861-1865, Civil War — Graphic novels

978-1-4042-0779-0, $29.25;
978-1-84603-050-5 (pb)

LC 2006007309

Courtesy of Rosen Publishing

The first major Civil War battle in the Western theater, Shiloh came as a horrifying shock to both the American public and those in arms. On April 6, 1862, Confederate forces staged a surprise attack on the Union army encamped along the Tennessee River. Fighting was fierce as General Grant struggled to hold off the enemy until his reinforcements arrived the following day so that he could 'Whip 'em tomorrow'. Though nearly driven into the Tennessee River, the Union army could ultimately claim victory — won at a dear cost. With nearly 24,000 total casualties in two days' fighting, 'Bloody Shiloh' served as a wake-up call to the nation, announcing that the continuing fight for the Union would be devastating for both sides. This book brings to life one of the Civil War's bloodiest battles in graphic novel format. It also includes eight pages of background information placing Shiloh in its historical context, detailing the key players, and describing the build-up to the fighting and its aftermath.

Part of the Graphic Battles of the Civil War series; the paperback edition is published by Osprey.

Spider-Girl presents Wild Thing: crash course. Marvel Entertainment 2007 un Illustration

Grades: 5 6 7 8 9 10 **741.5**

1. Adventure graphic novels; 2. Graphic novels; 3. Superhero graphic novels

978-0-7851-2606-5, $7.99

A few years in the future, in the alternate Marvel Universe where Peter Parker and Mary Jane had a daughter who has become Spider-Girl, Wolverine and Elektra got together and they had a daughter, too Rina Logan, also known as Wild Thing. She has psychic claws that work pretty much like Wolverine's claws, and she has his fast healing power. She still has to deal with high school even as she fights against bad guys, demons, evil droids, and more.

Harper, Charise Mericle

Bean Dog and Nugget: the ball. Charise Mericle Harper. Robin Corey Books 2013 48 p. Illustration (Bean Dog and Nugget)

Grades: K 1 2 3 **741.5/973; Fic**

1. Friendship — Fiction; 2. Graphic novels; 3. Humorous stories; 4. Lost and found possessions — Fiction; 5. Friendship; 6. Humorous fiction

0307977072; 9780307977076, $4.99; 9780307977083, $12.99 ; 9780307977090, $14.97

LC 2012029373

This children's story, written and illustrated by Charise Mericle Harper, "introduces young readers to...Bean Dog and Nugget.... In...the first book in this series, Bean Dog and Nugget lose Bean Dog's shiny new ball in a bush. They dream up elaborate and silly ways to get it back while they argue about who is actually going to go and get it. Enter Superdog and Ninja Nugget." (Publisher's note)

Fashion Kitty. Hyperion Books for Children 2005 90p. Illustration

Grades: 3 4 5 6 7 8 9 **741.5; Fic**

1. Cats — Graphic novels; 2. Graphic novels; 3. Humorous graphic novels

0-7868-5134-1, $8.99

Kiki Kittie is a very unusual cat. For one thing, she has a mouse for a pet — and that's kind of like a human having a chocolate cake for a pet. Kiki also has a natural flair for fashion, but up until a recent birthday, she was just an ordinary fashionable kitty. Then, on that day, she discovered that she had special powers: she can turn into Fashion Kitty, able to mix and match hundreds of outfits in a single second. Regular cat by day, Fashion Kitty by night, Kiki is always ready to answer a call of despair and save other cats from making fashion faux pas

Other titles about Fashion Kitty are: Fashion Kitty versus the Fashion Queen (2007); Fashion Kitty and the unlikely hero (2008); Fashion Kitty and the B.O.Y.S. (2011)

Fashion Kitty Versus the Fashion Queen. Hyperion Paperbacks for Children 2007 90p. Illustration

Grades: 3 4 5 6 7 8 9 **741.5; Fic**

1. Cats — Graphic novels; 2. Graphic novels; 3. Humorous graphic novels

978-0-7868-3726-7, $8.99

After her last adventure, Fashion Kitty is truly becoming a hero. At school, she is more popular than ever. She's even been mentioned in several articles in the local newspaper, (which she clips out and saves in a scrapbook, of course). But not everyone is excited about Fashion Kitty's newfound popularity. A spoiled new kitty named Cassandra doesn't like sharing the spotlight. And when Fashion Kitty starts inspiring the other kitties at school to be more independent about their style choices, Cassandra really doesn't like it. So she hatches a plan (evil, of course) that involves lying, conniving, and outlawing bright colors and patterns. Fashion Kitty knows she must put an end to Cassandra's reign of terror. She will use her fashion sense, quick smarts, and the power of friendship to overcome fashion evil.

Harrell, Rob

Monster on the Hill. by Rob Harrell. Top Shelf Productions 2013 192 p. Color; Illustration

Grades: 4 5 6 7 8

741.5

1. Monsters — Graphic novels; 2. Friendship — Graphic novels

1603090754; 9781603090759, $19.95

Courtesy of Rosen Publishing

This graphic novel by Rob Harrell is set in "1860s England [where] every...township is terrorized by a...monster — much to the townsfolk's delight! Each town's...monster is a source of local pride [and] tourism. Unfortunately, for...Stoker-on-Avon, their monster isn't quite as impressive. Can the morose Rayburn get a monstrous makeover and become a proper horror? It's up to the eccentric Dr. Charles Wilkie and plucky street urchin Timothy to get him up to snuff." (Publisher's note)

Hatke, Ben

★ **Legends** of Zita the spacegirl. Ben Hatke. First Second 2012 205 p. Color illustration

Grades: 4 5 6 **741.5**

1. Fame — Fiction; 2. Graphic novels; 3. Heroes — Fiction; 4. Robots — Fiction; 5. Science fiction; 6. Science fiction graphic novels; 7. Adventure fiction

1596434473; 9781596434479, $12.99; 9781596438064, $18.99

LC 2012012748

This graphic novel, by Ben Hatke, is a children's science fiction adventure story. "Zita is determined to find her way home to earth, following the events of the first book.... Zita's exploits from her first adventure have made her an intergalactic megastar! But she's about to find out that fame doesn't come without a price. And who can you trust when your true self is being eclipsed by your public persona, and you've got a robot doppelganger wreaking havoc...while wearing your face?" (Publisher's note)

"Hatke's arrestingly vibrant art commands instant adoration of its reader... Readers would be hard-pressed to not find something to like in these tales; they're a winning formula of eye-catching aesthetics, plot and creativity, adeptly executed. Imaginative and utterly bewitching." Kirkus

★ **Little** Robot. by Ben Hatke. First Second 2015 144 p. Color; Illustration
Grades: K 1 2 3 4 5   **741.5; Fic**
1. Friendship — Comic books, strips, etc.; 2. Girls — Comic books, strips, etc.; 3. Good and evil — Comic books, strips, etc.; 4. Robots
1626720800; 9781626720800, $16.99
Eisner Award: Best Publication for Early Readers (2016)

In this graphic novel, by Ben Hatke, "when a little girl finds an adorable robot in the woods, she presses a button and accidentally activates him for the first time. Now, she finally has a friend. But the big, bad robots are coming to collect the little guy for nefarious purposes, and it's all up to a five-year-old armed only with a wrench and a fierce loyalty to her mechanical friend to save the day!" (Publisher's note)

"Unframed panel illustrations lend an expansive quality to this lively, mostly wordless graphic novel for younger readers. The absence of defined frames allows the watercolor to bleed out into the plentiful white space between panels, giving the girl and the robot space to move and even allowing the characters and dialogue to break the pattern in organic ways." Horn Book

Mighty Jack and the Goblin King. Ben Hatke. First Second 2017 208 p. Color; Illustration
Grades: 4 5 6 7   **741.5**
1. Monsters — Graphic novels; 2. Magic — Fiction; 3. Siblings — Graphic novels
9781626722668, $14.99; 9781626722675, $22.99
LC 2016961549

"In this follow-up to Mighty Jack, the titular character and his friend Lilly travel through a portal in search of Jack's sister, Maddy, who has been kidnapped by an ogre. The duo are separated and must battle their own monsters, helped along the way by even more winsome and fantastical creatures than in the first volume." (School Library Journal)

Mighty Jack; Volume 1. Ben Hatke; color by Alex Campbell and Hilary Sycamore. First Second 2016 203 p. Color; Illustration
Grades: 4 5 6 7   **741.5; Fic**
1. Brothers and sisters — Fiction; 2. Autistic children — Fiction; 3. Fantasy fiction
1626722641; 9781626722644, $14.99
LC 2015951861

In this book, by Ben Hatke, "Jack might be the only kid in the world who's dreading summer. But he's got a good reason: summer is when his single mom takes a second job and leaves him at home to watch his autistic kid sister, Maddy. It's a lot of responsibility, and it's boring, too, because Maddy doesn't talk. Ever. But then, one day at the flea market, Maddy does talk — to tell Jack to trade their mom's car for a box of mysterious seeds. It's the best mistake Jack has ever made." (Publisher's note)
Another title in this series is: Mighty Jack and the goblin king (2017)

★ **Nobody** likes a goblin. by Ben Hatke. First Second 2016 40 p. Color; Illustration
Grades: PreK K 1 2   **E; 741.5**
1. Goblins; 2. Friendship
1626720819; 9781626720817, $17.99
LC 2015944387

In this children's story, by Ben Hatke, "Goblin, a cheerful little homebody, lives in a cosy, rat-infested dungeon, with his only friend, Skeleton. Every day, Goblin and Skeleton play with the treasure in their

dungeon. But one day, a gang of 'heroic' adventurers bursts in. These marauders trash the place, steal all the treasure, and make off with Skeleton — leaving Goblin all alone!" (Publisher's note)

"Hatke (Little Robot) renders the characters' antic facial expressions, their fairy tale costumes, and the fantasy landscape with polished skill, and his story gallops along cheerfully with the clear prospect of a happy ending. Especially gratifying is Hatke's casting of reviled characters as heroes; without moralizing, he makes it clear that sometimes it's the most unassuming creatures who have the warmest hearts." Pub Wkly

★ The **Return** of Zita the Spacegirl. by Ben Hatke. First Second 2014 240 p.
Grades: 3 4 5 6   **741.5**
1. Good and evil — Fiction; 2. Graphic novels; 3. Outer space — Fiction; 4. Science fiction graphic novels; 5. Science fiction; 6. Prisoners — Fiction
1626720584; 9781626720589, $18.99

"Zita the Spacegirl has saved planets, battled monsters, and wrestled with interplanetary fame. But she faces her biggest challenge yet in the third and final installment of the Zita adventures. Wrongfully imprisoned on a penitentiary planet, Zita has to plot the galaxy's greatest jailbreak before the evil prison warden can execute his plan of interstellar domination!" (Publisher's note)

"The art is colorful, detailed, and child-friendly. Readers of all ages can relate to the themes of friendship and loyalty while enjoying the fantasy of a far-out sci-fi adventure." Horn Book

★ **Zita** the spacegirl. First Second 2011 182p. Illustration
Grades: 3 4 5 6   **741.5**
1. Graphic novels; 2. Science fiction graphic novels
1-59643-446-5 (pa); 1-59643-695-6; 978-1-59643-446-2 (pa), $10.99; 978-1-59643-695-4, $17.99

When her best friend is abducted by an alien doomsday cult, Zita leaps to the rescue and finds herself a stranger on a strange planet.

Hayes, Geoffrey
★ **Benny** and Penny in How to say goodbye. Geoffrey Hayes. Toon Books 2016 32 p. Color; Illustration (Benny and Penny)
Grades: PreK K 1 2   **741.5; Fic**
1. Brothers and sisters — Fiction; 2. Death — Fiction; 3. Graphic novels; 4. Mice — Fiction; 5. Loss (Psychology)
9781935179993, $12.95; 1935179993
LC 2016003372

"Penny found a dead salamander, but her brother Benny is refusing to help her bury it. Is it silly to hold a service for Little Sallie, or could this tiny salamander mean something more to the siblings?...Hayes shares this gentle tale of a child's early encounter with death." (Publisher's note)

"With humor, directness, and unfailing honesty, Hayes's sensitive cartooning and sharp dialogue play up the big emotions of these little mice." Pub Wkly

Benny and Penny in just pretend: a Toon Book. [by] Geoffrey Hayes. Toon Books 2008 32p. Illustration
Grades: PreK K 1 2   **741; 741.5**
1. Mice — Graphic novels; 2. Siblings — Graphic novels
978-0-9799238-0-7, $12.95; 0-9799238-0-8

"How can Benny pretend to be a brave pirate when his pesky little sister, Penny, wants to tag along and is always asking for a hug? He tries to lose her, but when he does, he starts to feel a little lost himself. Penny proves her bravery, saves Benny from a bug, and gets the hug she wants." (Publisher's note)
Other titles about Benny and Penny are: Benny and Penny in the big no-no! (2009); Benny and Penny in the toy breaker (2010);Benny and

Penny in Lights out! (2012);Benny and Penny in Lost and found! (2014); Benny and Penny in How to say goodbye (2016)

★ **Benny** and Penny in Lights out!: a Toon book. by Geoffrey Hayes. Toon Books 2012 32 p. Illustration

Grades: K 1 2   **741.5**
1. Bedtime — Fiction; 2. Brothers and sisters — Fiction; 3. Graphic novels; 4. Mice — Fiction; 5. Siblings — Fiction; 6. Picture books for children
1935179209; 9781935179207, $12.95

LC 2011050927

This children's picture book follows mouse brother and sister Benny and Penny. Penny is getting ready for bed, but "her restless big brother interrupts obnoxiously with warnings about the Boogey Mouse, loud belches and other distractions. When Benny realizes that he's left his prized pirate hat in the backyard, though, Penny braves the Boogey Mouse to follow him...and prod him into reclaiming it from the spooky, dark playhouse." (Kirkus)

Benny and Penny in Lost and found: a Toon book. by Geoffrey Hayes. Toon Books 2014 40 p. Color; Illustration

Grades: PreK K 1 2   **741.5; Fic**
1. Brothers and sisters — Fiction; 2. Graphic novels; 3. Lost and found possessions — Fiction; 4. Mice — Fiction
1935179640; 9781935179641, $12.95

LC 2014000649

"Benny's in a foul mood! He can't find his pirate hat, and he's been sent outside to cool his temper. When he and Penny wander away from home and realize they're lost, they must handle their emotions and put their heads together." (Publisher's note)

"The text is easily accessible to emerging readers, with simple, repeating words, while also enforcing ideas about controlling emotions and being responsible for one's actions without being overbearing. Children will easily relate to Penny and Benny as they grapple with sibling issues that are very real to this age group." SLJ

★ **Benny** and Penny in The big no-no!: a Toon Book. RAW Junior 2009 32p. Illustration

Grades: PreK K 1 2   **741; 741.5**
1. Mice — Fiction; 2. Brothers and sisters — Fiction
978-0-9799238-9-0, $12.95; 0-9799238-9-1

LC 2008-36307

Theodor Seuss Geisel Award (2010)

"Benny and his sister Penny know it's wrong to sneak into someone else's backyard but their mysterious new neighbor — or is it a monster? — may be a thief. They go snooping and discover a lot about themselves and...a new friend." (Publisher's note)

★ **Benny** and Penny in the Toy breaker: a Toon Book. TOON Books 2010 32p. Illustration; Map

Grades: PreK K 1   **741.5; Fic**
1. Bullies — Graphic novels; 2. Cousins — Graphic novels; 3. Graphic novels; 4. Humorous graphic novels; 5. Mice — Graphic novels; 6. Siblings — Graphic novels
978-1-935179-07-8, $12.95; 1-935179-07-1

LC 2009-38066

Mouse siblings Benny and Penny unite against their bullying cousin Bo, who breaks just about everything he plays with. When they hear he's coming for a visit, they try to hide all their toys, although Penny doesn't want to give up holding her monkey. Bo wants to join in with their treasure hunt, but Benny and Penny don't want to play with him. The reader sees that much of the trouble stems from the others trying to grab their things away from Bo. Left to themselves, the children eventually work out a peaceful resolution (after poor Monkey's arm gets torn off — but Mommy will fix it).

"Hayes's cartooning is witty, expressing much with the glint of an eye or twitch of a whicker, and the neat cartoon panels carefully allow a good beginning-reader balance between information in the pictures and in the ballooned dialogue." Horn Book

Helfand, Lewis

Conquering Everest: the lives of Edmund Hillary and Tenzing Norgay. Campfire 2011 96p. Illustration

Grades: 10 3 4 5 6 7 8 9   **741.5; 796.522**
1. Mountaineering — Graphic novels; 2. Mountaineers; 3. Nonfiction writers; 4. Hillary, Edmund Sir; 5. Tenzing Norgay, 1914-1986; 6. Mount Everest — Graphic novels
978-93-80741-24-6, $12.99

Tenzing Norgay immigrated to Nepal with his Tibetan family when he was a boy, and he worked hard over the years to become one of the best Sherpas who helped the European, American, and other climbers who journeyed to Nepal to climb Mount Everest. Edmund Hillary was the son of a beekeeper from New Zealand, who became fascinated with mountain climbing during World War II. He came to Nepal in 1953 as part of a British expedition to reach Everest's peak, and Norgay came to be the sirdar, the head Sherpa and organizer of the expedition's support system. These two men became the first to reach Everest's summit at 11:30 a.m. on May 29, 1953. This graphic novel tells the story of the two men from such different backgrounds, and their friendship. The book notes that on May 22, 2010, Californian thirteen-year-old Jordan Romero became the youngest climber to reach Everest's peak. Tayal's panels show some of the massive scale of the mountain.

Henkes, Kevin

★ **Egg**. Kevin Henkes. Greenwillow Books, An Imprint of HarperCollins Publishers 2017 40 p. Color; Illustration

Grades: PreK K 1 2   **E**
1. Animals — Infancy — Fiction; 2. Birth — Fiction; 3. Eggs — Fiction; 4. Friendship — Fiction; 5. Animal reproduction — Fiction; 6. Eggs — Fiction
0062408720; 9780062408723, $17.99; 9780062408730

LC 2016005267

This children's story, by Kevin Henkes, "is a graphic novel for preschoolers about four eggs, one big surprise, and an unlikely friendship.... One is blue, one is pink, one is yellow, and one is green. Three of the eggs hatch, revealing three baby birds who fly away. But the green egg does not hatch. Why not? When the three birds return to investigate, they're in for a big surprise!" (Publisher's note)

"Another stunner from Henkes, who is able to evoke so much with few words and such seemingly simple illustrations. Gorgeous and thought-provoking." Kirkus

Herge

★ The **adventures** of Tintin, vol. 1: Tintin in America, Cigars of the Pharaoh, The Blue Lotus. Little, Brown 1994 192p. Illustration

Grades: 4 5 6 7 8 9   **741.5; Fic**
1. Adventure graphic novels; 2. Graphic novels; 3. Tintin (Fictional character) — Graphic novels
0-316-35940-8, $18.99

Tintin, the heroic boy reporter from France, travels to America where he outwits gangsters in Chicago of the 1930s and adventures in the Wild West; sails the Mediterranean Sea with faithful dog Snowy and finds himself in a mystery involving a movie tycoon, drugs, and cigars in an ancient Egyptian tomb; then he travels to India to finally solve the mystery. This Little, Brown edition reprints some of the early Tintin adventures published in the 1930s in a 3-in-1 volume. This is the first in a series that reprints most of the Tintin stories by Herge. Librarians and teachers should note that the books retain some stereotypical depictions of people of other cultures and remember that these were acceptable and expected at the time of original publication.

Tintin and the Picaros. Little, Brown 1978 62p. Illustration
Grades: 4 5 6 7 8 9   **741.5; Fic**
1. Adventure graphic novels; 2. Graphic novels; 3. Humorous graphic novels; 4. Tintin (Fictional character)
0-316-35849-5, $10.99

LC 77-090973
Tintin and his friends rescue prima donna Bianca Castafiore while trying to help restore their friend Alcazar to power in San Theodoros — but they'll have to defeat General Tapioca and his troops to do it.

Tintin in Tibet. Little, Brown 1978 62p. Illustration
Grades: 4 5 6 7 8 9   **741.5; Fic**
1. Adventure graphic novels; 2. Graphic novels; 3. Humorous graphic novels; 4. Tintin (Fictional character)
0-316-35839-8, $10.99

LC 80-191368
Tintin, Snowy, and Captain Haddock trek through the snow-covered Himalayas to rescue their friend Chang from the hands of an abominable snowman.

Tintin: The Broken Ear. Little, Brown 1978 62p. Illustration
Grades: 4 5 6 7 8 9   **741.5; Fic**
1. Adventure graphic novels; 2. Graphic novels; 3. Humorous graphic novels; 4. Tintin (Fictional character)
0-316-35850-9, $10.99

LC 77-090970
A fetish which originally belonged to the Arumbayas tribe in San Theodoros is stolen from a museum, then returned; soon Tintin discovers that the returned fetish is a forgery. When he follows the trail of the stolen fetish, it leads him and Snowy to South America and to San Theodoros, where he gets caught in the middle of a civil war. Tintin gets into all kinds of trouble even as he tries to find out why so many people want the fetish.

★ **Tintin:** The Calculus Affair. Little, Brown 1976 62p. Illustration
Grades: 4 5 6 7 8 9   **741.5; Fic**
1. Adventure graphic novels; 2. Graphic novels; 3. Humorous graphic novels; 4. Tintin (Fictional character)
0-316-35847-9, $10.99

LC 76-13280
Unscrupulous Bordurians have kidnapped Professor Calculus, and Tintin, Snowy, and Captain Haddock are soon on the trail again, to rescue their friend. It's no easy task to rescue the Professor and save his fantastic invention; spies are everywhere, and Calculus lies deep in the fortress of Bakhine. But the Bordurians now have to deal with Tintin ...

Tintin: Cigars of the Pharaoh. Little, Brown 1975 62p. Illustration
Grades: 4 5 6 7 8 9   **741.5; Fic**
1. Adventure graphic novels; 2. Graphic novels; 3. Humorous graphic novels; 4. Tintin (Fictional character)
0-316-35836-3, $10.99

LC 74-021620
Tintin and Snowy are on a cruise to Egypt when they happen to meet Professor Sophocles Sarcophagus (the first of Tintin's absent-minded professors) and join his expedition. But they become embroiled in a complicated scheme involving a fakir, cigars marked with an unusual brand, and Rajijah, the poison of madness. Tintin meets the detectives Thompson and Thomson as well as the movie mogul Rastapopolous. Herge wrote this book in 1932 then revised it in 1955.

Tintin: Destination Moon. Little, Brown 1976 62p. Illustration
Grades: 4 5 6 7 8 9   **741.5; Fic**

1. Adventure graphic novels; 2. Graphic novels; 3. Humorous graphic novels; 4. Tintin (Fictional character)
0-316-35845-2, $10.99

LC 76-013279
Professor Calculus has designed a rocket for an expedition to the Moon. He summons Tintin and Captain Haddock (along with Snowy) to the country of Syldavia, where he's been working. Despite spies being everywhere and mysterious explosions and other problems, the rocket is soon ready to launch, and Professor Calculus wants Tintin and Captain Haddock to go with him — to the Moon.

Tintin: Explorers On the Moon. Little, Brown 1976 62p. Illustration
Grades: 4 5 6 7 8 9   **741.5; Fic**
1. Adventure graphic novels; 2. Graphic novels; 3. Humorous graphic novels; 4. Tintin (Fictional character)
0-316-35846-0, $10.99

LC 76-013297
Tintin, Captain Haddock, and Prof. Calculus are headed for the Moon when they discover Thompson and Thomson, who had inadvertently stowed away on the rocket. But there's more trouble when they land on the Moon and go exploring, for Colonel Jorgen is there, another stowaway, and he wants revenge on Tintin.

Tintin: Flight 714. Little, Brown 1975 62p. Illustration
Grades: 4 5 6 7 8 9   **741.5; Fic**
1. Adventure graphic novels; 2. Graphic novels; 3. Humorous graphic novels; 4. Tintin (Fictional character)
0-316-35837-1, $10.99

LC 74-021623
Tintin, Snowy, Captain Haddock, and Professor Calculus land in Djakarta and meet millionaire Mr. Carreidas, who invites them to fly to Sydney with him in his prototype jet. They find themselves in the middle of a plot to steal their new friend's fortune, and they decide to stop it.

Tintin: Land of Black Gold. Little, Brown 1975 62p. Illustration
Grades: 4 5 6 7 8 9   **741.5; Fic**
1. Adventure graphic novels; 2. Graphic novels; 3. Humorous graphic novels; 4. Tintin (Fictional character)
0-316-35844-4, $10.99

LC 75-007896
The world is on the brink of a crisis when car engines begin to explode without explanation or warning; someone has been tampering with the oil supply. Tintin travels to the Middle East to investigate, and he helps Sheik Ben Kalish Ezab, whose son is kidnapped by one of Tintin's old enemies.

Tintin: Prisoners of the Sun. Little, Brown 1975 62p. Illustration
Grades: 4 5 6 7 8 9   **741.5; Fic**
1. Adventure graphic novels; 2. Graphic novels; 3. Humorous graphic novels; 4. Tintin (Fictional character)
0-316-35843-6, $10.99

LC 75-007897
Tintin, Snowy, and Captain Haddock travel to Peru to rescue Professor Calculus. They meet Indian boy Zorrino, and they must travel into the jungle to the Andes to find their old friend.

Tintin: Red Rackham's Treasure. Little, Brown 1974 62p. Illustration
Grades: 4 5 6 7 8 9   **741.5; Fic**
1. Adventure graphic novels; 2. Graphic novels; 3. Humorous graphic novels; 4. Tintin (Fictional character)
0-316-35834-7, $10.99

LC 73-021253
Tintin and his friends search for the pirate booty left by Captain Haddock's pirate ancestor. They're aided in their quest by the hard-of-hearing inventor, Professor Calculus.

Tintin: The Castafiore Emerald. Little, Brown 1975 62p. Illustration
Grades: 4 5 6 7 8 9   **741.5; Fic**
1. Adventure graphic novels; 2. Graphic novels; 3. Humorous graphic novels; 4. Tintin (Fictional character)
0-316-35842-8, $10.99

Tintin and Snowy investigate when prima donna Bianca Castafiore's jewels are stolen, in particular, her emerald.

Tintin: The Seven Crystal Balls. Little, Brown 1975 62p. Illustration
Grades: 4 5 6 7 8 9   **741.5; Fic**
1. Adventure graphic novels; 2. Graphic novels; 3. Humorous graphic novels; 4. Tintin (Fictional character)
0-316-35840-1, $10.99

LC 75-007921

Tragedy strikes the members of an expedition which returned after violating Incan burial chambers; the seven men fall into comas, one by one, and fragments of crystal are found by their bodies. Tintin, Professor Calculus, Captain Haddock, and Thompson and Thomson investigate, but then Calculus disappears — he's been kidnapped.

Hernandez, Jaime
The **dragon** slayer: folktales from Latin America. by Jaime Hernandez; with an introduction by F. Isabel Campoy. TOON Graphics 2018 40 p. Color; Illustration
Grades: PreK K 1 2 3 4   **398.2; 741.5**
1. Folklore — Latin America; 2. Graphic novels; 3. Tales — Latin America; 4. Dragons — Juvenile fiction; 5. Giants — Juvenile fiction
1943145296; 9781943145294, $9.99

LC 2017042011

In this book, "a trio of Latin American folktales are given a makeover.... In his six-panel pages, [author Jaime] Hernandez flexes his considerable storytelling skills, his deceptively simple art conveying all the detail, nuance, and expression of character each story needs...In addition to the tales themselves, the book opens with an on-point essay by author F. Isabel Campoy, putting the mix of Spanish and Native American influences in context." (Kirkus Reviews)

"Rousing tales, spirited artwork, and rich backmatter ensure that this slim graphic novel for kids becomes a rich resource for all caregivers, not just those of Latinx children." Kirkus

Includes bibliographical references

Hicks, Faith Erin
★ The **Adventures** of Superhero Girl. written and drawn by Faith Erin Hicks; colors by Cris Peter; introduction by Kurt Busiek. Dark Horse Comics 2013 112 p. Illustration; Color
Grades: 4 5 6 7 8 9 10 11 12 Adult   **741.5; Fic**
1. Female superhero graphic novels
1616550848; 9781616550844, $16.99

Eisner Award: Best Publication for Kids (2014)

This graphic novel features "Superhero Girl [who] has some Superman-like powers, although she can't fly, just leap over tall buildings, and she works to protect the small town where she went to get away from her charismatic superhero brother, Kevin. She fights bad-guy ninjas, bank robbers, even a tentacled space monster, but she also struggles to pay rent...and she has to deal with her future supervillain self." (Voice of Youth Advocates)

"It's superhero as person instead of as corporate symbol or fight machine.... This strip shines because it's fresh and lighthearted without wallowing in angst." Pub Wkly

★ The **Nameless** City. Faith Erin Hicks; color by Jordie Bellaire. First Second 2016 240 p. Color; Illustration
Grades: 5 6 7 8 9 10   **741.5; Fic**

1. Cities and towns — Fiction; 2. Friendship — Fiction; 3. Survival — Fiction; 4. Fantasy graphic novels; 5. Survival skills — Fiction
1626721564; 9781626721562, $14.99; 9781626721579

LC 2015020651

"Every nation that invades the City gives it a new name.... The natives don't let themselves get caught up in the unending wars. To them, their home is the Nameless City.... Kaidu is...a Dao born and bred — a member of the latest occupying nation. Rat is a native of the Nameless City. At first, she hates Kai for everything he stands for, but his love of his new home may be the one thing that can bring these two unlikely friends together." (Publisher's note)

"With comprehensive world building, well-rounded characters, and entertaining action, this expertly executed story will find a home with a wide variety of readers, all of whom will be eagerly awaiting the next installment." Booklist

★ The **stone** heart. Faith Erin Hicks. First Second 2017 256 p. Color; Illustration (The nameless city)
Grades: 5 6 7 8 9 10   **741.5; Fic**
1. Fantasy fiction — Graphic novels; 2. Adventure fiction; 3. Magic — Fiction
1626721599; 9781626721586; 9781626721593, $21.99

LC 2016938731

In this book, by Faith Erin Hicks, "Kaidu and Rat have only just recovered from the assassination attempt on the General of All Blades when more chaos breaks loose in the Nameless City: deep conflicts within the Dao nation are making it impossible to find a political solution for the disputed territory of the City itself." (Publisher's note)

"Flourishing from the strong worldbuilding and characterization of the first installment, this middle volume...provides a vital and enthralling closer look at those readers have already met as well as unfurling more of the Chinese-inspired city's past, as colorist Bellaire brings all to stunning emotional life." Kirkus

Hiiragi, Aoi
Baron: The Cat Returns. story and art by Aoi Hiiragi; translation & English adaptation, Naoko Amemiya. Viz/Studio Ghibli Library 2005 222p. Illustration
Grades: 3 4 5 6 7 8 9   **741.5; Fic**
1. Cats — Graphic novels; 2. Fantasy graphic novels; 3. Graphic novels; 4. Kodomo manga; 5. Manga
1-59116-956-9, $9.99

Awkward teen Haru saves a cat from being run over one afternoon, but she never expected the trouble it would cause. He is a cat prince, and his father wants to bring Haru into the kingdom of the cats to be his son's bride. A mysterious voice sends Haru to the Cat Office, where she meets Baron, a toy cat come to life, the fat cat Muta, and a magical crow. When the cats come and bear Haru to the kingdom of the cats, the three friends follow to help bring Haru back home.

This one-volume manga was the basis for the feature-length anime (Japanese animated film) called "The Cat Returns," which was produced by Studio Ghibli, the animation studio run by famed anime director Hayao Miyazaki and some partners.

Hirsch, Andy
Dogs: from predator to protector. Andy Hirsch. First Second 2017 128 p. Color; Illustration (Science comics)
Grades: 4 5 6 7 8   **741.5; 636.7**
1. Comic books, strips, etc.; 2. Dogs
9781626727670, $19.99; 9781626727687

LC 2016961597

"How well do you know our favorite furry companion? Did they really descend from wolves? What's the difference between a Chihuahua and a

Saint Bernard? And just how smart are they? Join one friendly mutt on a journey to discover the secret origin of dogs, how genetics and evolution shape species, and where in the world his favorite ball bounced off to." (Publisher's note)

"Thorough, clearly presented scientific information is lightened by silly asides from dog-narrator Rudy to keep readers entertained and engaged as they learn a huge amount about the science of dogs." Kirkus

Includes bibliographical references

Holm, Jennifer L.
Babymouse for president. by Jennifer L. Holm & Matthew Holm. Random House 2012 89 p.
Grades: 3 4 5 6   741.5
1. Graphic novels; 2. Mice — Fiction; 3. Schools — Fiction; 4. School stories; 5. Elections — Fiction
0375867805; 9780375867804, $6.99; 9780375967801
                                                    LC 2011024118

In this book by Jennifer L. Holm and Matt, Holm, part of the Babymouse series, "it's election season and if anyone knows what...the student council needs, it's Babymouse. The only trouble is, everyone else is running for President, too — even Babymouse's locker! Will Felicia Furrypaws turn out the meangirl coalition? Does Babymouse have what it takes to become the voice of the people?" (Publisher's note)

Babymouse: cupcake tycoon. by Jennifer L. Holm & Matthew Holm. Random House 2010 89p.
Grades: 3 4 5 6   741.5; 741
1. Mice — Graphic novels; 2. School stories — Graphic novels
978-0-375-86573-2 (pa), $6.99; 0-375-86573-X (pa)

"It's champagne wishes and cupcake dreams for Babymouse! The school library is having a fund-raiser, and Babymouse is determined to raise the most money and WIN the GRAND PRIZE. Or...er, to help the school! The competition is fierce, but Babymouse will stop at nothing to get what she wants, even if it means outselling every last kid in school...including her nefarious nemesis, Felicia Furrypaws." (Publisher's note)

Babymouse: mad scientist. by Jennifer L. Holm & Matthew Holm. Random House 2011 91p. Illustration
Grades: 3 4 5 6   741.5; 741
1. Babymouse (Fictional character); 2. Amoeba — Fiction; 3. Science projects — Fiction
978-0-375-96574-6 (lib bdg), $12.99; 0-375-96574-2 (lib bdg); 978-0-375-86574-9 (pa), $6.99; 0-375-86574-8 (pa)
                                                    LC 2009-47388

"Babymouse decides to enter the science fair. She daydreams about science-fiction movies and television shows (Star Trek, The Attack of the 50-Foot Woman); fantasizes about winning the Nobel Prize; learns about the scientific method in class — and then she discovers an amoeba named Squish." (Booklist)

Babymouse: monster mash. Random House 2008 93p.
Grades: 3 4 5 6   741; 741.5; Fic
1. Graphic novels; 2. Halloween — Graphic novels; 3. Humorous graphic novels; 4. Mice — Graphic novels
978-0-375-93789-7 (lib bdg), $11.99; 978-0-375-84387-7 (pa), $5.99
                                                    LC 2008-08433

It's Halloween, and Babymouse loves dressing up in spooky costumes to go trick-or-treating with best buddy Wilson. Of course, Felicia has to say that girls must be pretty "It's a rule." Then Babymouse's mother tells her she can have a Halloween party, and when Felicia finds out, she bullies Babymouse into inviting her and orders her to go trick-or-treating with them. Felicia is not a nice kid on Halloween; she leads her cronies in teepeeing and egging houses. But at Babymouse's party, she decides to do

things her way after all. For this Halloween volume, the color scheme doesn't include pink, but orange. Babymouse imagines herself in classic horror movie scenarios, but they shouldn't be too scary for most young readers.

Another title in the author's series about Babymouse

Babymouse: puppy love. [by] Jennifer L. Holm and Matthew Holm. Random House 2007 91p. Illustration
Grades: 3 4 5 6   741.5
1. Mice — Graphic novels; 2. Pets — Graphic novels
978-0-375-93990-7 (lib bdg), $12.99; 978-0-375-83990-0 (pa), $5.99
                                                    LC 2007-61012

"Babymouse doesn't exactly have a great history with pets — even her goldfish ran away from home. But all that's about to change. Will Babymouse get the dog of her dreams? Will she ever find her missing fish?" (Publisher's note)

Babymouse: skater girl. [by] Jennifer L. Holm & Matthew Holm. Random House 2007 91p. Illustration
Grades: 3 4 5 6   741.5; 741
Babymouse (Fictional character)
978-0-375-93989-1 (lib bdg); 0-375-93989-X (lib bdg); 978-0-375-83989-4 (pa), $5.99; 0-375-83989-5 (pa)
                                                    LC 2006-50444

"Babymouse daydreams about being a medal-winning figure skater. She can almost hear the roar of the crowd, the fans cheering her name, the sportscasters' excitement. But when she's actually noticed by a professional coach and told she has talent, Babymouse develops a lust for glory...which is greatly tested by the harsh reality of before- and after-school practices, a ban on cupcakes, and no free time for friends." (Horn Book)

Babymouse: the musical. by Jennifer & Matthew Holm. Random House 2009 96p. Illustration
Grades: 3 4 5 6   741.5; Fic
1. Graphic novels; 2. Humorous graphic novels; 3. Mice — Graphic novels; 4. School stories — Graphic novels
978-0-375-93791-0, $11.99; 978-0-375-84388-4 (pa), $5.99
                                                    LC 2008-10891

The school is going to produce a musical, and Babymouse auditions. Unfortunately, she has a tendency to trip over her own two feet, and the lead role demands someone who can sing and dance. Nemesis Felicia wins the lead role, and Babymouse is her understudy, while new transfer student Henry Higgins (a British hedgehog) has the male lead role. As Babymouse gets through school days (complete with the torture of dodgeball) and rehearsals, she daydreams Broadway musicals.

Another title in the author's series about Babymouse

Camp Babymouse. Random House 2007 95p. Illustration
Grades: 2 3 4 5 6   741.5; Fic
1. Babymouse (Fictional character); 2. Graphic novels; 3. Humorous graphic novels
978-0-375-93988-4 (lib bdg), $12.99; 978-0-375-83988-7 (pa), $5.99

Babymouse is looking forward to Camp Wild Whiskers, and two weeks of fresh air, fun, and friendship. She can't wait for the adventures to start. All that she has to do is relax and make sure she doesn't get lost in the wilderness. What could possibly go wrong? Will camp be all that Babymouse dreams of? Problems such as losing points by spilling punch, tipping her canoe during the canoe race, accidentally starting a really big fire, and her cabin mates complaining that she'll put them in last place make her wonder if she should even be there.

Comics Squad: recess!. comics by Jarrett J. Krosoczka, Gene Yang, Eric Wight, Jennifer L. Holm and Matthew Holm, Ursula Vernon, Dan Santat, Raina Telgemeier and Dave Roman, Dav Pilkey; edited by Jennifer

L. Holm, Matthew Holm, and Jarrett J. Krosoczka. Random House Inc. 2014 144 p. Illustration; Color

Grades: 2 3 4 5 6   **741.5**

1. Graphic novels; 2. Humorous stories; 3. Recess — Fiction; 4. Schools — Fiction; 5. Short stories; 6. Comic books, strips, etc.; 7. School stories

0385370032; 9780385370035, $7.99; 9780385370042, $12.99

LC 2013035223

"An all-star lineup of graphic novel notables contributes original works to this anthology, sharing the common thread of recess." (School Library Journal)

"[T]his lively, upbeat and all-around-awesome offering is consistently convivial and laugh-out-loud funny from cover to cover." Kirkus

Another title in this series is: Lunch! (2016)

Extreme Babymouse. by Jennifer L. Holm & Matthew Holm. Random House Inc. 2013 91 p. Color illustration

Grades: 2 3 4   **741.5/973**

1. Graphic novels; 2. Imagination — Fiction; 3. Mice — Fiction; 4. Schools — Fiction; 5. Snowboarding — Fiction; 6. Mice — Juvenile fiction

0307931609, $6.99; 9780307931603

LC 2012022834

Author Matthew Holm presents the seventeenth book in his series on Babymouse, which focuses on snowboarding. "(Uh, snowboarding, Babymouse? Is that really a good idea? You don't exactly have a good history with...er, being outside). Will Babymouse make it off the bunny slope? Will this winter be extreme — or just extremely lame? And does locker really have a cousin? Find out in EXTREME Babymouse! Snowy Mountain will never be the same!" (Publisher's note)

★ **Sunny** side up. Jennifer L. Holm & Matthew Holm; with color by Lark Pien. Graphix 2015 224 p. Illustration

Grades: 3 4 5 6   **741.5; Fic**

1. Summer — Fiction; 2. Friendship — Fiction; 3. Grandfathers — Fiction; 4. Adventure fiction; 5. Florida — Fiction

0545741653; 9780545741651, $23.99

LC 2014957906

Eisner Nominee: Best Publication for Kids (2016)

In this book, by Jennifer L. Holm, illustrated by Matthew Holm, "Sunny Lewin has been packed off to Florida to live with her grandfather for the summer. At first she thought Florida might be fun.... But the place where Gramps lives is no amusement park. It's full of...old people. Really old people. Luckily, Sunny isn't the only kid around. She meets Buzz, a boy who is completely obsessed with comic books, and soon they're having adventures of their own." (Publisher's note)

"Woven into the Florida frolic though, through dated flashback images, is the real reason for Sunny's last-minute visit: her older brother is struggling with addiction, and Sunny thinks she got him in trouble. Though Sunny will appeal to all kinds of readers, an authors' note shares the Holms' hope to let kids in similar situations know that it's OK to feel sad and to talk about it. Clear dialogue bubbles, plenty of wordless spreads, and Matthew's cartoons and beach-umbrella color palette keep Sunny's story an upbeat one that readers will easily stick with." Booklist

Holm, Matthew

Babymouse #11: dragonslayer. [by] Jennifer L. Holm & Matthew Holm. Random House Childrens Books 2009 96p. Illustration

Grades: 3 4 5 6   **741.5; Fic**

1. Babymouse (Fictional character); 2. Graphic novels; 3. Humorous graphic novels; 4. Mathematics — Graphic novels; 5. Mice — Graphic novels

978-0-375-95712-3, $12.99; 978-0-375-85712-6 (pa), $5.99

LC 2008-51110

Babymouse loves to read, and to daydream about the books she reads, but she does NOT do well in math. In fact, she's just received an F on a test, and her teacher decides to have her join the Mathletes in order to make up for it. The Mathletes compete with other school teams in math competitions, and they have wanted to win the Golden Slide Rule for a long time. A competing team called the Owlgarithms have won it year after year. However, Babymouse seems to be more of a liability than a new asset for the team. She suffers through lunchtime practice sessions and much prefers to daydream of adventures with The Lion, the Witch, and the Wardrobe or The Hobbit rather than do math. Then, at the math competition, events conspire to make her the team's only hope in a final round against one of the Owlgorithms. The book is illustrated in the usual black, white and pink, and it might, just might, help some girls think of math as something they can do well (after all, if Babymouse can compete in a math tournament, maybe they can, too).

Cover title: Babymouse Dragonslayer

Babymouse burns rubber!. by Jennifer L. Holm & Matthew Holm. Random House 2010 91p. Illustration

Grades: 3 4 5 6   **741.5; 741**

978-0-375-95713-0 (lib bdg), $12.99; 0-375-95713-8 (lib bdg); 978-0-375-85713-3 (pa), $5.99; 0-375-85713-3 (pa)

LC 2009018819

"Babymouse dreams of glory in the soap box derby but doesn't put much effort into preparation. She sweet-talks best friend and fellow contestant Wilson into building (and re-building) her car, preventing him from being ready on race day." (Horn Book)

Babymouse: heartbreaker. Random House 2006 91p.

Grades: 3 4 5 6   **741; Fic; 741.5**

1. Babymouse (Fictional character); 2. Graphic novels; 3. Humorous graphic novels; 4. Mice — Graphic novels; 5. Valentine's Day — Graphic novels

0-375-93798-6 (lib bdg), $12.99; 0-375-83798-1 (pa), $5.99; 978-0-375-93798-9 (lib bdg); 978-0-375-83798-2 (pa)

LC 2006-45418

"Romantic Babymouse...here finds her confidence shaken by the impending Valentine's Day dance at school.... The text and illustrations successfully differentiate between reality and daydreams, and there's a good amount of humor injected in both." Horn Book

Another title in the author's series about Babymouse

Babymouse: queen of the world. Random House Books for Young Readers 2005 91p. Illustration

Grades: 3 4 5 6   **741.5; Fic**

1. Babymouse (Fictional character); 2. Friendship — Graphic novels; 3. Graphic novels; 4. Humorous graphic novels; 5. Mice — Graphic novels

0-375-93229-1 (lib bdg), $12.99; 0-375-83229-7 (pa), $5.95

LC 2004-51166

"In this energetic comic...Babymouse, a wise-cracking rodent stand-in for your average, adventure-seeking nine-year-old, strives to capture popular Felicia's goodwill, finally achieving her end at the expense of Wilson Weasel, truest of friends. But, wouldn't you know it, Felicia's world has little to offer a smart, fun-loving mouse, after all." Booklist

Other titles in this series are: Our hero (2005); Beach babe (2006); Rock star (2006); Heartbreaker (2006); Camp Babymouse (2007); Skater girl (2007); Puppy love (2007); Monster mash (2008); Babymouse the musical (2009); Dragonslayer (2009); Babymouse burns rubber (2010); Cupcake tycoon (2010); Mad scientist (2011); A very Babymouse Christmas (2011); Babymouse for president (2012); Extreme Babymouse (2012); Happy birthday Babymouse (2014); Bad babysitter (2015); Babymouse goes for the gold (2016)

Comics Squad: recess!. comics by Jarrett J. Krosoczka, Gene Yang, Eric Wight, Jennifer L. Holm and Matthew Holm, Ursula Vernon, Dan

Santat, Raina Telgemeier and Dave Roman, Dav Pilkey; edited by Jennifer L. Holm, Matthew Holm, and Jarrett J. Krosoczka. Random House Inc. 2014 144 p. Illustration; Color

Grades: 2 3 4 5 6 **741.5**

1. Graphic novels; 2. Humorous stories; 3. Recess — Fiction; 4. Schools — Fiction; 5. Short stories; 6. Comic books, strips, etc.; 7. School stories
0385370032; 9780385370035, $7.99; 9780385370042, $12.99

LC 2013035223

"An all-star lineup of graphic novel notables contributes original works to this anthology, sharing the common thread of recess." (School Library Journal)

"[T]his lively, upbeat and all-around-awesome offering is consistently convivial and laugh-out-loud funny from cover to cover." Kirkus

Another title in this series is: Lunch! (2016)

Squish, Super Amoeba. by Jennifer L. Holm & Matthew Holm. Random House 2011 90p. Illustration (Squish)

Grades: 3 4 5 **741.5; Fic**

1. Amebas — Fiction; 2. Bullies — Fiction; 3. Graphic novels; 4. School stories; 5. Superheroes — Fiction
978-0-375-93783-5 (lib bdg), $12.99; 0-375-93783-8 (lib bdg); 978-0-375-84389-1 (pa), $6.99; 0-375-84389-2 (pa)

LC 2010-08004

Other titles in this series are:Brave new pond (2011);The power of the parasite (2012);Captain Disaster (2012);Game on! (2013);Fear the amoeba (2014)

Swing it, Sunny!. Jennifer L. Holm & Matthew Holm; with color by Lark Pien. Scholastic Press 2017 224 p. Color; Illustration

Grades: 3 4 5 6 **741.5**

1. Brothers and sisters; 2. Brothers and sisters — Fiction; 3. Dysfunctional families — Comic books, strips, etc; 4. Family problems — Fiction; 5. Graphic novels; 6. Middle schools — Comic books, strips, etc; 7. Middle schools — Fiction; 8. Schools — Fiction
9780545741705, $24.99; 9780545741729, $12.99; 9780545741767

LC 2016054939

In this book, by Jennifer and Matthew Holm, "Summer's over and it's time for Sunny Lewin to enter the strange and unfriendly hallways of...middle school. When her Gramps calls her from Florida to ask how she's doing, she always tells him she's fine. But the truth? Sunny is NOT having the best time." (Publisher's note)

"Using a combination of short exchanges of dialogue and frequent wordless reaction shots, the Holms again leverage simply drawn scenes colored by Pien into a loosely autobiographical narrative that is poignant and hilarious in turn and emotionally rich throughout." Kirkus

A **very** Babymouse Christmas. by Jennifer L. Holm & Matthew Holm. Random House Childrens Books 2011 89p. Illustration (Babymouse)

Grades: 3 4 5 6 **741.5**

1. Christmas — Fiction; 2. Gifts — Fiction; 3. Graphic novels; 4. Humorous graphic novels; 5. Imagination — Fiction; 6. Mice — Fiction
978-0-375-96779-5, $12.99; 978-0-375-86779-8 (pa), $6.99

LC 2010027988

"Babymouse feels she simply cannot live without the Whiz Bang, this Christmas's must-have gift. This graphic novel's single-minded focus reflects Babymouse's all-consuming obsession, a condition with which readers are likely to be familiar. Her holiday-classic-inspired, pink-hued daydreams allow Babymouse to switch off the mania for a while." (Horn Book)

Horowitz, Anthony

Stormbreaker: the graphic novel. [by] Anthony Horowitz; adapted Antony Johnston; illustrated by Kanako Damerum & Yusuru Takasaki. Philomel Books 2006 un Illustration (Alex Rider)

Grades: 5 6 7 8 **741; 741.5**

1. Graphic novels; 2. Spies — Graphic novels
0-399-24633-9, $14.99

In this graphic novel version on Horowitz's novel, fourteen-year-old Alex Rider is coerced into continuing his uncle's dangerous work for Britain's intelligence agency, MI6.

"If it's possible, this is even more rapidly paced than the novel. Alex remains an appealing hero here, and the idea of a heroic teen up against insidious adults continues to be an extremely powerful draw for readers." Booklist

Other graphic novel adaptations in this series are:Point blank (2007);Skeleton key (2009);Eagle strike (2012)

Hosler, Jay

Clan Apis. Active Synapse 2000 158p. Illustration

Grades: 4 5 6 7 8 9 10 11 12

741.5; Fic

1. Bees — Graphic novels; 2. Graphic novels; 3. Science — Graphic novels
0-9677255-0-X, $15

Courtesy of Active Synapse

"Opening with a creation myth... and working through the biological, sociological, and ecological changes affecting the life of Nyuki the bee, the text is a combination of authoritative science; appealing, detailed black-and-white drawings; and dialogue replete with humor, pubescent angst, political sloganeering, and more. Nyuki's colony undertakes migration to a new hive, is beset by a woodpecker, and hibernates through a winter that yields to a revitalizing spring." Booklist

★ **Last** of the sandwalkers. written and illustrated by Jay Hosler. First Second 2015 312 p. Illustration

Grades: 5 6 7 8 9 10 **741.5; Fic**

1. Beetles — Fiction; 2. Graphic novels; 3. Science fiction; 4. Scientific expeditions — Fiction; 5. Adventure fiction
162672024X; 9781626720244, $16.99

LC 2014045542

This book, by Jay Hosler, is about a "civilization of beetles. In this bug's paradise, beetles write books, run restaurants, and even do scientific research. But not too much scientific research is allowed by the powerful elders, who guard a terrible secret about the world outside.... Lucy is not one to quietly cooperate, however. This tiny field scientist defies the law of her safe but authoritarian home and leads a team of researchers out into the desert." (Publisher's note)

"Hosler's cartooning is no less meticulous than his writing and similarly retains a sense of animated energy and humor, engaging readers with characters that are far from human, but filled with humanity." Booklist

Includes bibliographical references

The **Sandwalk** Adventures: An Adventure in Evolution Told in Five Chapters. Active Synapse 2003 160p. Illustration

Grades: 4 5 6 7 8 9 10 11 12 Adult

576.8; 741.5

1. Evolution — Graphic novels; 2. Graphic novels; 3. Science — Graphic novels; 4. Darwin, Charles; 5. Darwin, Charles — Graphic novels

Courtesy of Active Synapse

0-9677255-1-8, $20

Scientist Hosler explains Darwin's theory of evolution in a whimsical fashion. Follicle mites Mara and Willy live in Darwin's left eyebrow, and by accident they discover that Darwin, whom they call the god Flycatcher, can hear Mara. He thinks he's going crazy, but as he takes his daily walks on the Sandwalk at his home in England, Darwin does his best to convince Mara and Willy that he isn't a god and tells them about evolution. Hosler uses humor and whimsy, but also did a lot of research; the book includes explanatory notes and a long bibliography of sources.

Hotta, Yumi

★ **Hikaru** No Go, Volume 1. [by] Yumi Hotta and Takeshi Obata. Viz Media, LLC 2004 192p. Illustration
Grades: 5 6 7 8 9 10 11 12   **741.5; Fic**
1. Board games — Graphic novels; 2. Graphic novels; 3. Manga; 4. Shonen manga
1-59116-222-X, $7.95
Sixth-grade Hikaru Shindo's discovery of a bloodstained game board leads to an encounter with the ghost of Go master Fujiwara-no-Sai and the formation of an unbeatable Go team.
Volume 1 of 23

Howard, Abby

Dinosaur empire!. by Abby Howard. Amulet Books 2017 128 p. Color illustration; Color; Map (Earth before us)
Grades: 4 5 6   **741.5; 567.91**
1. Paleontology; 2. Dinosaurs
1419723065; 9781683351139; 9781419723063, $15.95
LC 2016056055
Ronnie is just a normal fifth-grader trying to pass her science class's impossible quiz on the history of dinosaurs...until she happens upon her neighbor — Ms. Lernin — a retired paleontologist. With the assistance of Science Magic, Ronnie and Ms. Lernin travel back through time and space to experience the Mesozoic Era firsthand." (Publisher's note)
"An in-depth look at dinosaurs, geography, and evolution, presented through an appealing framing device.... Howard details characteristics of dinosaurs and other prehistoric creatures, covers similarities and differences among different species, and offers information on evolution, convergent evolution, and mutations." SLJ

Hughes, Susan

No girls allowed: tales of daring women dressed as men for love, freedom and adventure. written by Susan Hughes; llustrated by Willow Dawson. Kids Can Press 2008 80p. Illustration
Grades: 3 4 5 6 7 8 9
306.7; 741.5
1. Biographical graphic novels; 2. Graphic novels; 3. Transvestites — Graphic novels
978-1-55453-177-6, $16.95;
978-1-55453-178-3 (pa), $9.95
LC 2007-9060846

Courtesy of Kids Can Press

This book collects short biographies in graphic format of young women who dressed as and pretended to be men in order to do and be what they wanted. The real Mu Lan did pretend to be her father's son in order to serve in the Chinese Emperor's army to protect her father. Hatshepsut was an Egyptian princess who was determined to be pharaoh, although that role could only go to men. Margaret Buckley was a young Englishwoman who became Dr. James Barry in the early nineteenth century. Seven women's stories are told here, and the book includes a short list of books for further reading.

Humphreys, Jessica Dee

Child Soldier: When Boys and Girls Are Used in War. Michel Chikwanine, Jessica Dee Humphreys; illustrated by Claudia Davila. Kids Can Press 2015 48 p. Color; Illustration
Grades: 5 6 7 8
741.5; 355
1. Chikwanine, Michel; 2. Child soldiers
1771381264; 9781771381260, $17.95
Eisner Nominee: Best Publication for Kids (2016)

Courtesy of Kids Can Press

This children's book, written by Michel Chikwanine and Jessica Dee Humphreys, and illustrated by Claudia Davila, describes the experience of a child solder. "Michel Chikwanine was five years old when he was abducted from his schoolyard soccer game in the Democratic Republic of Congo and forced to become a soldier for a brutal rebel militia. Against the odds, Michel managed to escape..., but he was never the same again." (Publisher's note)

"Chikwanine's narration is matter of fact but never didactic, emphasizing less the gruesome details and more young Michel's emotional response and attempts to make sense of the world around him. Earthy hued and gentle, the images make a potentially disturbing topic accessible." SLJ

Hurchalla, Elizabeth

Ben 10 Alien Force: Ben 10 returns. Del Rey 2008 96p. Illustration
Grades: 3 4 5 6 7 8   **741.5; Fic**
1. Adventure graphic novels; 2. Graphic novels; 3. Science fiction graphic novels
978-0-345-51438-7, $7.99
Ben Tennyson had lived as Ben 10, a superhero thanks to the watch-like Omnitrix that could transform him into any of ten superpowered alien life-forms. Five years ago, he put away the Omnitrix in order to live a normal life. However, his Grandpa Max is a Plumber, a member of an intergalactic police force, and he has continued his work. Now fifteen years old and a star soccer player, Ben visits Grandpa Max's trailer only to learn that Max has disappeared, a weird and creepy alien tries to get him, and Max has left a cryptic holographic message. Ben digs out his Omnitrix, seeks out his cousin Gwen, who has super powers of her own, and then they run into another Plumber who has been searching for Max. They team up to find him and to learn why more aliens are coming to Earth and engaging in illegal transactions. This book is illustrated with screen captures from the Cartoon Network program.

Hutchison, David

Oz: The Manga. Antarctic Press 2006 un Illustration
Grades: 4 5 6 7 8 9
741.5; Fic
1. Fantasy graphic novels; 2. Graphic novels; 3. Baum, L. Frank — Adaptations
978-1-932453-69-0, $14.95
This is Baum's classic novel, The Wizard of Oz, adapted into manga format by Hutchison. All the characters are here: Dorothy, Toto, the Cowardly Lion, the Tin

Courtesy of Antarctic Press

Woodsman, the Scarecrow, the Wizard. And all the main plot elements are here, from the cyclone that blows Dorothy and Toto to Oz to the Flying Monkeys to dealing with the Wicked Witch. The art makes this adaptation shine, especially the Tin Woodsman, who is a steampunk wonder.

Ikeda, Akiko

Chibikuro party. Dark Horse Books 2008 un Illustration

Grades: 2 3 4 5 6 7   **741.5; Fic**

1. Adventure graphic novels; 2. Animals — Graphic novels; 3. Graphic novels; 4. Humorous graphic novels

978-1-59582-128-7, $9.95

One night the moon wakes up Dayan's shadow — it's the one night that the shadows are free to move about on their own. Dayan's shadow, Chip (Dayan names him) wakes him up and wants him to go to the shadows' party, called the Chibikuro Party. The Satan of Death Forest sends Noel disguised as a shadow to kidnap all the shadows, and Noel tricks the shadows by saying they can go with him and be free forever. Dayan hears all this, and he rouses his friends to save their shadows from Death Forest.

Part of the Dayan's collection books series

Dayan's birthday. Dark Horse Books 2008 un Illustration

Grades: 2 3 4 5 6 7   **741.5; Fic**

1. Animals — Graphic novels; 2. Graphic novels; 3. Humorous graphic novels

978-1-59582-125-6, $9.95

The cat Dayan learns that he has a birthday, but he doesn't know what it is. He goes to a trio of witches to find out when his birthday will come, and then he throws a big party for everyone. However, he forgot to invite the witches, and they come to take his birthday back. This book is done in a small picture book format and is translated from Japanese. The woodland creatures serve the witches strong liquor to help Dayan

Part of the Dayan's collection book series

Thursday rainy party. Dark Horse Boks 2008 un Illustration

Grades: 2 3 4 5 6 7   **741.5; Fic**

1. Animals — Graphic novels; 2. Graphic novels; 3. Humorous graphic novels

978-1-59582-126-3, $9.95

One day Dayan gets caught in the rain, and he meets a friendly frog. He invites the frog to come to Willie the mouse's next rainy Thursday party, but learns the frog doesn't know anything about days of the week. Dayan creates a special calendar for his new friend, but the next rainy Thursday doesn't happen for several weeks; did the frog keep up with the calendar, and will he come to Willie's party?

Part of the Dayan's collection books series

White Eurocka. Dark Horse Books 2008 un Illustration

Grades: 2 3 4 5 6 7   **741.5; Fic**

1. Animals — Graphic novels; 2. Graphic novels; 3. Humorous graphic novels

978-1-59582-127-0, $9.95

Winter comes to the land of Tachiel along with a strong cold wave, much colder than most winters. As the festival of Eurocka approaches, Dayan and his friends find that many other creatures have come from the North penguins, walruses, and polar bears, to participate in the festival. During the celebrations, a baby polar bear cub magically arrives.

Part of the Dayan's collection books series

Isenberg, Marty

Transformers animated volume 1. IDW Publishing 2008 un Illustration

Grades: 2 3 4 5 6 7 8   **741.5; Fic**

1. Adventure graphic novels; 2. Graphic novels; 3. Robots — Graphic novels; 4. Science fiction graphic novels; 5. Transformers (Fictional characters); 6. Transformers (Fictional characters)

978-1-60010-151-9, $7.99

When Optimus Prime and his team of misfit Autobots accidentally unearth the Allspark, they are attacked by Megatron, leader of the Decepticons. The fight causes the Autobots' ship to travel from deep space to Earth in the twenty-second century, and to New Detroit. Now the fight between the Autobots and the Decepticons will take place on Earth, where humans live, humans who don't know what all these sentient robots are doing. This book adapts stories from the new animated television series and uses screen captures from the programs to illustrate the book.

Ishihara, Yoko

★ The **manga** cookbook. presented by the Manga University Culinary Institute; illustrations by Chihiro Hattori; [with recipes by Yoko Ishihara]. Japanime Co. Ltd. 2007 158p. Illustration

Grades: 4 5 6 7 8 9 10 11 12

641.5; 741.5

1. Graphic novels; 2. Japanese cooking — Graphic novels; 3. Manga

978-4-921205-07-2, $14.95

Courtesy of Japanime Co.

Food appears frequently in manga and in anime, but just what are the characters eating? This book is an illustrated step-by-step guide to preparing some Japanese dishes, from onigiri (rice balls) to yakitori (skewered grilled chicken), oshinko (pickled vegetables), udon (Japanese noodles), to traditional sweets and desserts. Definitions of terms and ingredients used, basic cooking guidelines, and instructions on how to properly use chopsticks are all included. The recipes are authentic but have been simplified somewhat so older children and teens with some basic kitchen skills can prepare the foods. Adult supervision is recommended for younger children and for children who aren't very experienced with using knives, measuring spoons, and cooking on the stove.

Jacques, Brian

Redwall: the graphic novel. by Brian Jacques; illustrated by Bret Blevins; adapted by Stuart Moore; lettering by Richard Starkings. Philomel Books 2007 143p. Illustration

Grades: 4 5 6 7 8 9   **741.5; Fic**

1. Adventure graphic novels; 2. Fantasy graphic novels; 3. Graphic novels; 4. Mice — Graphic novels

978-0-399-24481-0, $12.99; 0-399-24481-6

When Cluny the rat's army attacks Redwall Abbey, young Matthias the mouse follows in the footsteps of the long-ago hero Martin the Warrior to defend his home

"The story is a page-turner, and the detailed black-and-white drawings capture both the passion and the pathos." SLJ

Jakobsen, Lars

The **mysterious** manuscript. Lars Jakobsen. Graphic Universe 2012 48 p.

Grades: 4 5 6 7 8   **741.5/9489; Fic**

1. Crime — Fiction; 2. Graphic novels; 3. Time travel — Fiction; 4. Scotland — Fiction; 5. Mystery comic books, strips, etc.; 6. Mystery fiction; 7. Time travel — Graphic novels

0761378839; 9780761378839, $27.93

LC 2011027146

Courtesy of Lerner Publishing Group

This graphic novel, by Lars Jakobsen, is part of the "Mortensen's Escapades" series. "A book collector shows Mortensen...an illuminated manuscript from 1512. When Mortensen sees a painting of an airplane on one of its pages, he knows he has a mystery to unravel. With a zap from his time gun, he travels back to medieval Scotland to look for clues. A wise scribe and a mute witch help him...[to] answer...how did an airplane crash land in the Middle Ages?" (Publisher's note)

The **Santa** Fe jail. by Lars Jakobsen; illustrated by Lars Jakobsen. Graphic Universe 2012 48 p.

Grades: 4 5 6   **741.5/9489; Fic**

1. Graphic novels; 2. Kidnapping — Fiction; 3. Time travel — Fiction; 4. Time travel — Graphic novels
0822594218; 9780761378860; 9780822594215, $6.95

LC 2011044643

This adventure graphic novel, by Lars Jakobsen, is book 2 of the "Mortensen's Escapades" series. In it "Mortensen is given a special assignment: deliver...[a] ransom to the Santa Fe Jail. But the kidnappers are time travelers, so nothing is as simple as it seems.... Mortensen...is drugged by a mysterious woman. He awakens to find himself packed inside a cargo plane that is about to nose dive into the jungles of Tanzania." (Publisher's note)

Courtesy of Lerner Publishing Group

The **secret** mummy. art by Lars Jakobsen; story by Lars Jakobsen; translation by Lars Jakobsen and Robyn Chapman. Graphic Universe 2013 48 p. (Mortensen's escapades)

Grades: 4 5 6 7 8

741.5/9489

1. Criminals — Fiction; 2. Graphic novels; 3. Time travel — Fiction; 4. Transplantation of organs, tissues, etc. — Fiction; 5. Vampires — Graphic novels
0761379150; 9780761379157, $27.93

LC 2012027015

Courtesy of Lerner Publishing Group

This is the fourth Mortensen adventure from Lars Jakobsen. "Mortensen, an agent dedicated to relentlessly fighting the ever-cresting wave of nefarious time-traveling criminals, now faces vampires in 19th-century Transylvania. Jumping uneasily through time from Prague to Transylvania to Bosnia and Paris, this wayward hero follows a creepy count thought to be a villainous vampire and the shadowy sarcophagus that seems tied to him." (Kirkus)

Originally published in Danish under title: Den falske mumie, in 2012.

Jamieson, Victoria

★ **All's** faire in middle school. Victoria Jamieson.. Dial Books for Young Readers 2017 248 p. Color; Illustration

Grades: 4 5 6 7 8   **741.5; Fic**

1. Middle schools; 2. Friendship; 3. Family life
0525429999; 9780525429982, $20.99; 9780525429999, $12.99

LC 2016044190

In this book, by Victoria Jamieson, "eleven-year-old Imogene (Impy) has grown up with two parents working at the Renaissance Faire, and she's eager to begin her own training as a squire. First, though, she'll need to prove her bravery. Luckily Impy has just the quest in mind — she'll go to public school after a life of being homeschooled! But it's not easy to act like a noble knight-in-training in middle school. Impy falls in with a group of girls who seem really nice (until they don't)." (Publisher's note)

"Jamieson masterfully taps into the voice and concerns of middle-schoolers, and the offbeat setting of the Renaissance faire adds some lively texture." Booklist

The **great** pet escape. Victoria Jamieson. Henry Holt & Co. 2016 64 p. Color; Illustration (Pets on the Loose!)

Grades: 1 2 3 4   **741.5; Fic**

1. Escapes — Fiction; 2. Graphic novels; 3. Humorous stories; 4. Pets — Fiction; 5. Schools — Fiction; 6. Humorous fiction
9781627791052, $15.99; 1627791051; 9781627791069

LC 2015003257

In this book, by Victoria Jamieson, the "class pets at Daisy P. Flugelhorn Elementary School want OUT...and GW (short for George Washington), the deceptively cute hamster in the second-grade classroom, is just the guy to lead the way. But when he finally escapes and goes to find his former partners in crime, Barry and Biter, he finds that they actually LIKE being class pets. Impossible!" (Publisher's note)

"The hilariously expressive rodents guarantee laughs from page one with plenty of slapstick humor and pointed one-liners. Jamieson makes excellent use of a variety of panel sizes to maximize the action." Booklist

Another title in this series is: The great art caper (2017)

★ **Roller** girl. by Victoria Jamieson. Dial Books 2015 240 p. Color; Illustration

Grades: 4 5 6 7 8   **741.5; Fic**

1. Friendship — Fiction; 2. Graphic novels; 3. Roller derby — Fiction; 4. Roller skating — Fiction
0803740166; 9780803740167, $12.99

LC 2014011310

Newbery Honor Book (2016); Eisner Nominee: Best Publication for Kids (2016)

This graphic novel, by Victoria Jamieson, is "about friendship and surviving junior high through the power of roller derby. For most of her twelve years, Astrid has done everything with her best friend Nicole. But after Astrid falls in love with roller derby and signs up for derby camp, Nicole decides to go to dance camp instead. And so begins the most difficult summer of Astrid's life as she struggles to keep up with the older girls at camp." (Publisher's note)

"Jamieson captures this snapshot of preteen angst with a keenly decisive eye, brilliantly juxtaposing the nuances of roller derby with the twists and turns of adolescent girls' friendships." Kirkus

Jeffrey, Gary
Elasmosaurus: the long-necked swimmer. illustrated by Terry Riley. Rosen Publishing Group 2009 32p. Illustration

Grades: 2 3 4 5 6 7

567.9; 741.5

1. Dinosaurs — Graphic novels; 2. Graphic novels
978-1-4358-2505-5, $25.25

LC 2008-3881

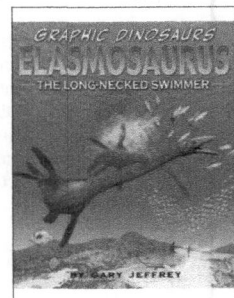

Courtesy of Rosen Publishing

This book uses comic book style art to introduce young readers to the elasmosaurus, which lived in the ancient shallow ocean that used to cover Kansas. The book provides some science-based speculation on what the dinosaur's life might have been like. Additional material includes information on fossil evidence, quick facts about the elasmosaurus, and a glossary.

Part of the Graphic Dinosaurs series.

Stegosaurus: the plated dinosaur. illustrated by James Field.. Rosen Publishing Group 2009 32p. Illustration
Grades: 2 3 4 5 6 7
567.9; 741.5
1. Dinosaurs — Graphic novels; 2. Graphic novels
978-1-4358-2503-1, $25.25
LC 2007-50587

Courtesy of Rosen Publishing

This book uses comic book style art to introduce young readers to the stegosaurus, with some science-based speculation on what the dinosaur's life might have been like. Additional material includes information on fossil evidence, quick facts about the stegosaurus, and a glossary.

Part of the Graphic Dinosaurs series.

Johnson, Joe

Classics illustrated deluxe #2: tales from the Brothers Grimm. Papercutz 2008 144p. Illustration
Grades: 3 4 5 6 7 8
741.5; Fic
1. Fantasy graphic novels; 2. Folklore — Graphic novels; 3. Graphic novels
978-1-59707-101-7, $17.95

This volume of Papercutz's new Classics Illustrated Deluxe series collects French adaptations of four tales from the Brothers Grimm (Wilhelm and Jakob): Hansel and Gretel, Learning to Shudder, The Devil and the Three Golden Hairs, and The Valiant Little Tailor. These comic book adaptations don't shy away from showing scary monsters, saying rude things without using really bad language, and showing some violence.

Part of the Classics Illustrated Deluxe series

Courtesy of NBM Publishing

Johnson, R. Kikuo

The **Shark** King: a Toon book. by R. Kikuo Johnson. TOON Books 2012 39 p. Color illustration
Grades: 2 3 4 5
741.5/973; Fic
1. Folklore — Hawaii; 2. Graphic novels; 3. Sharks — Folklore; 4. Father-son relationship
1935179160; 9781935179160, $12.95
LC 2011026592

This graphic novel written and illustrated by R. Kikuo Johnson re-tells a traditional Hawaiian folktale. "Born to a loving human woman, Nanaue is a happy child (rather than the flesh-eating monster of yore) with a huge appetite and a jagged line on his back that sometimes opens into a snapping, toothy mouth. His mischievous nature soon leads him into trouble, and he dives off a cliff to escape angry villagers from whom he had been stealing fish. This unites him with his father — a huge shark who had

taken human form to marry Nanaue's mother, Kalei, but returned to the sea on the night of his birth." (Kirkus)

Jolley, Dan

Alien Incident on Planet J. by Dan Jolley; illustrated by Matt Wendt; [coloring by Hi-Fi Design; lettering by Marshall Dillon].. Lerner Publishing Group/Graphic Universe 2008 112p. Illustration
Grades: 3 4 5 6 7 8 9
741.5; Fic
1. Adventure graphic novels; 2. Graphic novels; 3. Plot-your-own stories — Graphic novels; 4. Science fiction graphic novels
978-0-8225-6998-5, $27.93;
978-0-8225-8876-4 (pa), $7.93
LC 2007-44116

Courtesy of Lerner Publishing Group

In this new take on the "Choose Your Own Adventure" type of book that combines pages of prose text with pages of comic book sequences, you are a young human stuck on Planet J; your spaceship needs a new part, and you'll never get off this planet if you don't make peace with the Makanuk, the Zirifubi, and the Frongo. Some choices will end badly, others will be better, and the choices are all up to the reader.

This is Volume 8 of the Twisted Journeys series.

Escape from Pyramid X. Lerner Publishing Group/Graphic Universe 2007 112p. Illustration (Twisted Journeys)
Grades: 3 4 5 6 7 8 9
741.5; Fic
1. Adventure graphic novels; 2. Graphic novels; 3. Mummies — Graphic novels
978-0-8225-6777-6, $27.93;
978-0-8225-6779-0 (pa), $7.95
LC 2006-101598

In the series called Twisted Journeys, readers choose how the story will progress. Pages of text alternate with comic book-style pages. In this volume, you the reader are a student who won an essay contest to be part of an archeological dig led by Professor Emil Snackport, at the site of a newly discovered pyramid. In some story lines,

Courtesy of Lerner Publishing Group

you encounter smugglers, in others, a malevolent mummy. Readers will find many scenarios played out, depending on their choices; some end well, others not so well.

Pigling: a Cinderella story: a Korean tale. Graphic Universe 2008 48pp. Illustration (Graphic myths and legends)
Grades: 3 4 5 6 7 8 9
741.5; Fic
1. Fairy tales — Graphic novels; 2. Graphic novels; 3. Korea — Folklore — Graphic novels
978-0-8225-7174-2, $27.93;
0-8225-7174-9
LC 2007-40891

In old Korea, in a time when magic still exists, Pear Blossom lives happily with her parents. But when her mother dies, her father quickly remarries a spiteful woman and her mean daughter, and they turn Pear Blossom's

Courtesy of Lerner Publishing Group

life into misery. They treat her like a servant and call her Pigling. Omoni (mother in Korean) makes impossible demands of Pear Blossom, and each time magical creatures help her achieve the tasks. Then on the day of a festival, a handsome magistrate sees Pear Blossom on the road, and she runs away, frightened, leaving a sandal behind.

The **Smoking** Mountain: The Story of Popocatepetl and Iztaccihuatl: An Aztec Legend. story by Dan Jolley; pencils and inks by David Witt. Lerner Publishing Group 2009 48p. Illustration
Grades: 3 4 5 6 7 8 9
741.5; Fic
1. Aztecs — Folklore — Graphic novels; 2. Fantasy graphic novels; 3. Graphic novels
978-0-8225-7178-0, $27.93; 9781580138260

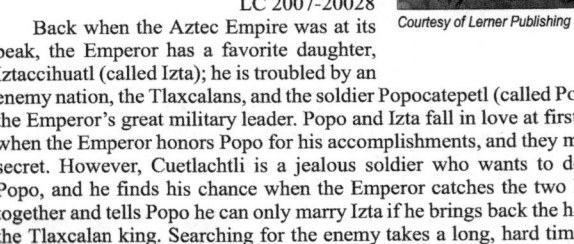

LC 2007-20028
Courtesy of Lerner Publishing Group

Back when the Aztec Empire was at its peak, the Emperor has a favorite daughter, Iztaccihuatl (called Izta); he is troubled by an enemy nation, the Tlaxcalans, and the soldier Popocatepetl (called Popo) is the Emperor's great military leader. Popo and Izta fall in love at first sight when the Emperor honors Popo for his accomplishments, and they meet in secret. However, Cuetlachtli is a jealous soldier who wants to destroy Popo, and he finds his chance when the Emperor catches the two lovers together and tells them the Emperor can only marry Izta if he brings back the head of the Tlaxcalan king. Searching for the enemy takes a long, hard time, and Cuetlachtli sends a messenger back to Tenochtitlan with word that Popo has died, which sends Izta into a decline. When victorious Popo returns, he finds his lover dead, and takes her to the top of a mountain where he stands over her until his death. Now there are two mountains in Mexico, named for the two lovers. Jolley sets the story as one told by a Mexican tour guide, using contemporary language; artist Witt conducted research to make the art look as authentic as possible. The book includes a list of books, websites, and DVDs for more information and entertainment.

Part of the Graphic Universe Myths and Legends series

The **time** travel trap. illustrated by Matt Wendt. Graphic Universe 2008 111p. Illustration (Twisted journeys)
Grades: 3 4 5 6 7 8 9
741.5; Fic
1. Adventure graphic novels; 2. Graphic novels; 3. Plot-your-own stories — Graphic novels; 4. Science fiction graphic novels
978-0-7613-9472-3 (lib bdg), $27.93; 0-7613-9472-9 (lib bdg); 978-0-8225-8874-0 (pa), $7.95; 0-8225-8874-9 (pa)

LC 2007-6101
Courtesy of Lerner Publishing Group

In this new take on the "Choose Your Own Adventure" type of book that combines pages of prose text with pages of comic book sequences, you are caught in a time machine a fellow student built for the school's science fair. Depending on the choices, you could end up at a medieval joust, facing woolly mammoths and "cavemen," or future aliens. Some choices will end badly, others will be better, and the choices are all up to the reader.

This is Volume 7 of the Twisted Journeys series.

Vampire hunt. illustrated by Gregory Titus; [coloring by Hi-Fi Design; lettering by Marshall Dillon]. Lerner Publishing Group/Graphic Universe 2008 112p. Illustration
Grades: 3 4 5 6 7 8 9
741.5; Fic
1. Adventure graphic novels; 2. Graphic novels; 3. Plot-your-own stories — Graphic novels; 4. Science fiction graphic novels; 5. Vampires — Graphic novels
978-0-8225-8877-1, $27.93; 978-0-8225-8879-5 (pa), $7.95

LC 2007-043732
Courtesy of Lerner Publishing Group

In this new take on the "Choose Your Own Adventure" type of book that combines pages of prose text with pages of comic book sequences, you are a vampire, and you must defend yourself and your castle from vampire hunters. Some choices will end badly, others will be better, and the choices are all up to the reader.

This is Volume 7 of the Twisted Journeys series

Kanata, Konami
★ **Chi's** sweet home, volume 1. Vertical, Inc. 2010 166p. Illustration
Grades: 5 6 7 8 9 10 11 12 Adult   **741.5; Fic**
1. Cats — Graphic novels; 2. Graphic novels; 3. Humorous graphic novels; 4. Manga; 5. Seinen manga
9781-934287-81-1

Young kitten Chi gets separated from her family while out on a stroll, then she meets little boy Yohei and his parents. They take her home, even though their apartment building has a strict no pets policy. While they try to find someone to take her in, they feed her, give her a cozy bed, set up a box with shredded newspaper for a litter box, and do their best to help her. Even though readers can read what she's thinking, Chi behaves just like a cat, with cat problems such as thinking the litter box is a wonderful play area instead of the place to do her business, and taking fright at Yohei's "vrooming" as he plays with his toy cars. The book is great for younger readers as well as anyone who likes cats. There is one panel where Yohei is sitting on the toilet while Chi is in her litter box in the bathroom, and a scene at the veterinarian's office where the doctor sticks a thermometer in to take Chi's temperature. And, of course, Chi tends to urinate in inappropriate places.

Also available in 3-in-1 omnibus editions; Volume 1 of 12

Keenan, Sheila
Dogs of war. by Sheila Keenan and illustrated by Nathan Fox. Graphix 2013 208 p.
Grades: 4 5 6 7   **741.5**
1. Dogs — War use — Fiction; 2. Graphic novels; 3. Vietnam War, 1961-1975 — Fiction; 4. World War, 1914-1918 — Fiction; 5. World War, 1939-1945 — Fiction; 6. War — Graphic novels; 7. Dogs — Fiction
0545128870; 9780545128872, $22.99; 9780545128889

LC 2011006735

This graphic novel, by Sheila Keenan, "tells the stories of the canine military heroes of World War I, World War II, and the Vietnam War. This collection of three fictional stories was inspired by historic battles and real military practice. Each story tells the remarkable adventures of a soldier and his service dog...bringing to life the faithful dogs who braved bombs, barrages, and battles to save the lives of countless soldiers." (Publisher's note)

Includes bibliographical references

Kelly, Joe

★ **Captain** Stoneheart and the Truth Fairy. Joe Kelly, story; Chris Bachalo, artwork; Aron Lusen, color; Richard Starkings, lettering & edits. Image Comics 2008 un Illustration

Grades: 5 6 7 8 9 10 11 12 Adult   **741.5; Fic**
  1. Adventure graphic novels; 2. Fairies — Graphic novels; 3. Fantasy graphic novels; 4. Graphic novels; 5. Pirates — Graphic novels
978-1-58240-865-1, $19.99

The story, in rhyming text with lushly drawn and colored art, tells the tale of the pirate named Captain Stoneheart, a fierce and angry pirate who won't let people tell him what to do. After attacking a peaceful ship and killing everyone on it, his crew discovers a caged fairy in the hold, and Stoneheart knows he can wreak havoc and scourge the world with her powers. Somehow they connect even through his anger, and when she finds a way to save Stoneheart and his crew even when she is free to leave the pirates and save herself, Stoneheart starts to change. Alas, the good times can't last, and he commits one final act that destroys everything and everyone around him because he won't let anyone tell him what to do, even if he loves that one person. There is some fighting violence, and there are some monsters, so this is not a story for very young readers. Older elementary school age children who love the old fairy tales with the tragic endings will be able to handle this story.

Douglas Fredericks and the House of They. Image Comics 2009 80p. Illustration

Grades: 3 4 5 6   **741.5; Fic**
  1. Adventure graphic novels; 2. Graphic novels; 3. Humorous graphic novels
978-1-58240-994-8, $17.99

Douglas Fredericks just wants to give his parents a very original, unique anniversary present, but every time he comes up with an idea, someone tells him "They" say it can't happen. After many different attempts, he builds the first self-baking cake, Cake City, that will provide cake for fifteen years, because his parents (especially the Captain, his father) love cake, and then wants to just sample the first piece, people come along and tell him "No, Douglas, don't! You know what They say! You can't have your cake and eat it too!" So, Douglas decides to go find the House of They to confront the people there. After many trials, he can finally ask "WHY?" and he refuses to accept "Because They say so" as an answer. Kelly, Roman, and colorist Molina are part of The Man of Action Studios that has created the television cartoon Ben 10, as well as many comics; they have used the deluxe picture book format for this story, with full-page color art on every other page (with quite a few double-page spreads) it even has a ribbon marker.

Ketcham, Hank

★ **Hank** Ketcham's Complete Dennis the Menace (Volume 1): 1951-1952. Fantagraphics Books 2005 590p. Illustration

Grades: 2 3 4 5 6 7 8 9 10 11 12 Adult   **741.5; Fic**
  1. Dennis the Menace (Fictional character); 2. Graphic novels; 3. Humorous graphic novels
1-56097-680-2, $24.95

This volume is the first of a series that will reprint every Dennis the Menace cartoon. The first cartoon was published in sixteen newspapers on March 12, 1951, and the cartoon was soon picked up by many more newspapers. This volume collects the daily single-panel cartoons from March 1951 through December 1952. In these cartoons, readers meet five-and-a-half-year-old Dennis Mitchell, his parents, retired neighbors George and Martha Wilson, Dennis' dog Ruff, and neighborhood pals Joey and Margaret. Every cartoon hearkens back to the positive aspects of growing up in suburban Middle America and the joys (mostly) of being a child. While older adults will catch all the references to past popular culture (i.e. Hopalong Cassidy), younger readers will enjoy the humor arising from everyday situations.

Kibuishi, Kazu

Amulet book five: prince of the elves. Kazu Kibuishi. Graphix 2012 208 p. (Amulet)

Grades: 3 4 5 6 7 8   **741.5**
  1. Amulets — Comic books, strips, etc; 2. Brothers and sisters — Comic books, strips, etc; 3. Charms — Comic books, strips, etc; 4. Elves — Comic books, strips, etc; 5. Imaginary places — Comic books, strips, etc; 6. Magic — Comic books, strips, etc; 7. Graphic novels; 8. Single-parent families — Juvenile fiction; 9. Magic — Juvenile fiction; 10. Fantasy graphic novels
0545208890; 9780545208895, $12.99

LC 2012935527

Author Kazu Kibuishi presents book five in the graphic novel series. "Emily has survived the chaos of the Guardian Academy, but Max Griffin, who is working for the Elf King, has escaped with the Mother Stone. The Elf King has now forged new amulets, which will allow him the ability to invade Cielis and destroy it once and for all. Emily and her friends desperately make preparations to defend Cielis in what will inevitably be a brutal war, and they can only hope that it will be enough to defeat the Elf King." (Publisher's note)

"Anchored by dazzlingly lush art and a complex, character-laden plot, Kibuishi's Amulet series remains a must-have for all elementary- and middle-school graphic-novel collections. Devoted fans will appreciate that this volume begins to flesh-out the backstory of two characters while starting to tie together a few of the many plot elements." Booklist

Amulet, book four: The Last Council. Graphix 2011 207p.
Grades: 3 4 5 6 7 8   **741.5**
  1. Fantasy graphic novels; 2. Adventure graphic novels
978-0-545-20887-1, $10.99; 0-545-20887-4

"Emily and her friends think they'll find the help they need in Cielis, but something isn't right. Streets that were once busy are deserted, and the townspeople who are left live in crippling fear. Emily is escorted to the Academy where she's expected to compete for a spot on the Guardian Council, the most powerful Stonekeepers. But as the number of competitors gets smaller and smaller, a terrible secret is slowly uncovered — a secret that, if left buried, means certain destruction of everything Emily fights for." (Publisher's note)

Amulet, book one: The Stonekeeper. Graphix 2008 185p.
Grades: 3 4 5 6 7 8   **741; Fic; 741.5**
  1. Adventure graphic novels; 2. Fantasy graphic novels; 3. Graphic novels; 4. Mystery graphic novels
978-0-439-84680-6, $21.99; 0-439-84680-3; 978-0-439-84681-3 (pa), $9.99; 0-439-84681-1 (pa)

After a family tragedy, Emily, Navin, and their mother move to an ancestral home to start a new life. When their mother is kidnapped by a tentacled creature, Em and Navin have to figure out how to set things straight and save their mother's life.

"Filled with excitement, monsters, robots, and mysteries, this fantasy adventure will appeal to many readers." SLJ

Other titles in this series are: The Stonekeeper's curse (2009); The Cloud Searchers (2010); The Last Council (2011); Prince of the elves (2012); Escape from Lucien (2014); Firelight (2016)

Amulet, book three: The Cloud Searchers. Graphix 2010 197p.
Grades: 3 4 5 6 7 8   **741.5; 741**
  1. Fantasy graphic novels; 2. Adventure graphic novels
978-0-545-20885-7 (pa), $10.99; 0-545-20885-8 (pa)

"Emily, Navin, and their crew of resistance fighters charter an airship and set off in search of the lost city of Cielis, which is believed to be located on an island high above the clouds. The mysterious Leon Redbeard is their guide, and there's a surprising new addition to the crew: the Elf King's son, Trellis. But is he ally or enemy? And will Emily ever be able to trust the voice of the Amulet?" (Publisher's note)

Amulet, book two: The Stonekeeper's curse. Graphix 2009 217p.
Grades: 3 4 5 6 7 8   **741.5; 741**
1. Fantasy graphic novels; 2. Adventure graphic novels
978-0-439-84683-7, $10.99; 0-439-84683-8

"Emily and Navin's mother is still in a coma from the arachnopod's poison, and there's only one place to find help: Kanalis, the bustling, beautiful city of waterfalls. But when Em, her brother, and Miskit and the rest of the robotic crew aboard the walking house reach the city, they quickly realize that seeking help is looking for trouble, dangerous trouble." (Publisher's note)

Amulet; Book 6: Firelight. Kazu Kibuishi. Graphix 2016 208 p. Color; Illustration; Map (Amulet)
Grades: 3 4 5 6 7 8   **741.5; Fic**
1. Memory — Graphic novels; 2. Fantasy graphic novels
0545839661; 9780545433167; 9780545678421; 9780545839662, $24.99
LC 2015936071

"Emily, Trellis, and Vigo visit Algos Island, where they can access and enter lost memories. They're hoping to uncover the events of Trellis's mysterious childhood — knowledge they can use against the Elf King.... Meanwhile, the Voice of Emily's Amulet is getting stronger, and threatens to overtake her completely." (Publisher's note)

★ **Copper**. Graphix/Scholastic 2010 94p. Illustration
Grades: 5 6 7 8   **741; 741.5; Fic**
1. Adventure graphic novels; 2. Dogs — Graphic novels; 3. Graphic novels; 4. Science fiction graphic novels
978-0-545-09892-2, $21.99; 0-545-09892-0; 978-0-545-09893-9 (pa), $12.99; 0-545-09893-9 (pa)

A collection of graphic novel adventures about a boy named Copper and his dog, Fred, including "navigating a dangerous forest of giant mushrooms, [and] surviving a crash landing in a homemade airplane — that run from lyrical to the downright apocalyptic. Illustrated in a deceptively simple style, its solemn tenor and deep strangeness...will likely inspire heavy investment from those who prefer a somewhat off-kilter read." Booklist

Escape from Lucien. Kazu Kibuishi. Scholastic / Graphix 2014 256 p. Illustration; Map (Amulet)
Grades: 3 4 5 6 7 8   **741.5; Fic**
1. Kings and rulers — Fiction; 2. Brothers and sisters — Fiction; 3. Elves — Fiction
9780545433150, $12.99
LC 2013957419

"Navin and his classmates journey to Lucien, a city ravaged by war and plagued by mysterious creatures, where they search for a beacon essential to their fight against the Elf King. Meanwhile, Emily heads back into the Void with Max, one of the Elf King's loyal followers, where she learns his darkest secrets. The stakes, for both Emily and Navin, are higher than ever." (Publisher's note)

"Most of the cleanly drawn, lushly backgrounded panels focus on faces, with occasional full-spread scenes adding dramatic visual highlights." Kirkus

Explorer: the hidden doors. edited by Kazu Kibuishi. Abrams Books 2014 128 p. Color; Illustration (Explorer)
Grades: 4 5 6 7 8   **741.5**
1. Bullying — Fiction; 2. Monsters — Fiction; 3. Comic books, strips, etc.; 4. Doors — Fiction

1419708821; 9781419708824, $19.95; 9781419708848
LC 2014938941

In this collection of comics edited by Kazu Kibuishi, "a bullied boy discovers a door guarded by a sly monster...A painting of a door opens in a forgotten Egyptian tomb...A portal in the park promises to turn you into a much cooler version 2.0 — if you can just get the bugs out." (Publisher's note)

"Readers are once again presented with an array of stories created by a cast of comics authors and illustrators smartly assembled by Kibuishi...The range in this slim volume is expansive. From funny to deep and fantastical to refined, all of the stories have a compelling narrative arc. The colors are just as varied, and are universally dynamic and nuanced. Consider this (and previous series installments) as a necessary addition to any graphic novel collection." SLJ

Other titles in the series are: The Mystery Boxes (2012); The Lost Islands (2013)

Explorer: the lost islands. Kazu Kibuishi. Abrams Books 2013 128 p. (Explorer)
Grades: 4 5 6 7 8   **741.5; Fic**
1. Islands; 2. Graphic novels
1419708813; 141970883X; 9781419708817, $19.95; 9781419708831, $10.95
LC 2013935794

In this follow-up to "Explorer: The Mystery Boxes," Kazu Kibuishi and a crew of cartoonists again take turns weaving seven tales based around a loose theme. This time the motif is islands, and the contributors are left to interpret it in illustrated shorts. Some, by using their strange and remote settings as microcosms, underscore the value of hard work...or finding one's niche..., while others examine more abstract concepts such as exploration and isolation." (Publishers Weekly)

Explorer: the mystery boxes. edited by Kazu Kibuishi. Abrams Books 2012 126 p. (Explorer)
Grades: 4 5 6 7 8   **S C; 741.5**
1. Boxes; 2. Boxes — Fiction; 3. Graphic novels; 4. Short stories; 5. Mystery graphic novels
1419700103; 9781419700095, $10.95; 9781419700101, $19.95
LC 2011025343

This collection of short stories offers "[s]even...stories [which] answer one simple question: what's in the box?...[E]ach of these...illustrated short graphic works revolves around a central theme: a mysterious box and the marvels — or mayhem — inside. Artists include...Kazu Kibuishi, Raina Telgemeier ('Smile'), and Dave Roman ('Astronaut Academy'), as well as Jason Caffoe, Stuart Livingston, Johane Matte, Rad Sechrist (all contributors to the...comics anthology series 'Flight'), and...artist Emily Carroll." (Publisher's note)

Seven graphic stories.

Flight explorer. edited by Kazu Kibuiski. Villard 2008 112p. Illustration
Grades: 4 5 6 7   **741.5; Fic**
1. Adventure graphic novels; 2. Fantasy graphic novels; 3. Graphic novels; 4. Humorous graphic novels; 5. Science fiction graphic novels
978-0-345-50313-8 (pa), $10; 0-345-50313-9 (pa)

This anthology includes stories that Kibuishi kept from Flight Volume 4 because they had all-ages appeal, as well as stories submitted especially for this volume. Kibuishi's own Copper and his talking dog cross a deep canyon by leaping onto mushrooms, only to discover the vegetation is intelligent. Kean Soo's Jellaby and his human friends frolic in the snow. Missile Mouse by Jake Parker defends a village on another planet, only to discover his coming was prophesied (this story includes two uses of the word "crap"). The other stories will appeal to younger readers, while some of the humor will also appeal to older readers. Other than the one bad word in "Missile Mouse" (noted above), there shouldn't be any other content that would keep this book out of most elementary and middle schools.

"Every story has a layout that promotes an acute sense of pacing and showcases the crisp, defined, full-color art." SLJ

Kim, Julie J.

★ **Where's** Halmoni?. Julie Kim. Little Bigfoot, an imprint of Sasquatch Books 2017 96 p. Color; Illustration

Grades: 1 2 3 4   741.5
1. Animals — Fiction; 2. Brothers and sisters — Fiction; 3. Folklore — Korea; 4. Goblins — Fiction; 5. Graphic novels; 6. Siblings — Graphic novels; 7. Goblins — Graphic novels; 8. Fantasy graphic novels
9781632170774, $19.99

LC 2016056020

This graphic novel, by Julie Kim, "follows a young Korean girl and boy whose search for their missing grandmother leads them into a world inspired by Korean folklore, complete with mischievous goblins (dokkebi), a greedy tiger, a clever rabbit, and a wily fox.... They discover a window...new to their grandmother's home....They crawl through and discover an unfamiliar fantastical world, and their adventure begins." (Publisher's note)

"The sibling banter is believable and delightful, Kim's panel sequences teem with energy, and her story spotlights comedy over danger." Pub Wkly

Kim, Susan

★ **City** of spies. [by] Susan Kim [and] Laurence Klavan; illustrated by Pascal Dizin. First Second 2010 172p. Illustration

Grades: 4 5 6 7   741.5; Fic
1. Adventure graphic novels; 2. Graphic novels; 3. Spies — Graphic novels; 4. World War, 1939-1945 — Graphic novels
1-59643-262-4 (pa); 978-1-59643-262-8 (pa), $17

"With her mother gone and a father who has better things to do than be bothered raising a daughter, Evelyn is sent to live with her unconventional Aunt Lia in the bohemian art world of 1942 New York City.... Evelyn spends much of her time in the company of imaginary superheroes, fouling up the plans of Nazi spies. Before long she finds an unlikely friend in the building superintendent — s son, Tony. Together, they...stumble upon an actual Nazi plot. With stupefying precision, Dizin — s art channels Hergé — s Tintin in tone, palette, and with the remarkable expressiveness of the clean, flexible figures.... With villains and danger that just border on the genuinely scary, the tale is filled not only with a thrilling sense of excitement but also with a child — s longing for a grown-up to believe in." Booklist

Kitchen, Alexa

★ **Grown-ups** are dumb! (No offense). Hyperion Books 2009 un Illustration

Grades: 3 4 5 6 7 8   741.5; Fic
1. Family life — Graphic novels; 2. Graphic novels; 3. Humorous graphic novels
978-1-4231-1331-7, $8.99

Twelve-year-old Alexa Kitchen wrote the comics collected here when she was ten years old. Her characters Molly, Sharon, and Kathy navigate life in school (and piles of homework), and at home (with pesky younger brothers). In other cartoons, she depicts the frustrations of dealing with incomprehensible paper folding instructions, the joys (and despairs) of messy rooms, and of toddler Hurricane Abby's exploration of her house. Kitchen's art ranges from the heavy pencils in the cartoons about Molly to scratchy ink in most of the other stories, to highly detailed drawings of the incredibly messy bedroom, all on pink pages. She describes herself as the world's youngest professional cartoonist," has been drawing cartoons

since she could hold a pencil, and already has several books published; in 2007, at the age of ten, she was nominated for a Harvey and an Eisner Award for her book Drawing Comics is Easy! (Except When It's Hard).

Kneece, Mark

The **Twilight** Zone: the after hours. adaptation by Mark Kneece; illustrated by Rebekah Isaacs. Walker & Company 2008 un Illustration

Grades: 5 6 7 8 9 10   741.5; Fic
1. Graphic novels; 2. Supernatural graphic novels; 3. Twilight zone (Television program) — Graphic novels
978-0-8027-9716-2, $16.99; 978-0-8027-9717-9 (pa), $9.99

LC 2008-4310

Marsha White visits a department store to buy an advertised gold thimble, is taken by elevator to a floor with empty display cases except for one, which has the thimble, and she deals with an odd saleswoman who knows her name. When Marsha is in the elevator, she discovers the thimble is defective and tries to complain, but the manager insists there is no eighteenth floor, the store has no elevator, and the store has never carried gold thimbles. As she begins to leave, Marsha faints at the sight of a mannequin that looks exactly like the strange saleswoman, and she's put into a back room to recover. When she wakes up, the store has been closed and she's locked in. This is an actual episode of the old Twilight Zone television show.

"Kneece's adaptation is quick and enjoyable and introduces a classic TV series to a new generation of readers. Isaacs's illustrations are clean, distinct and cinematic in scope, employing an interesting variety of angles." Kirkus

The **Twilight** Zone: walking distance. adaptation from Rod Serling's original script by Mark Kneece; illustrated by Dove McHargue. Walker & Company 2008 un Illustration

Grades: 5 6 7 8 9 10   741.5; Fic
1. Graphic novels; 2. Supernatural graphic novels; 3. Twilight zone (Television program) — Graphic novels
978-0-8027-9714-8, $16.99; 978-0-8027-9715-5 (pa), $9.99

LC 2008-4273

Thirty-nine-year-old businessman Martin Sloan's car blows a tire as he's driving, and he realizes he is within walking distance of his hometown. Leaving his car to be repaired, he decides to walk there. However, when he reaches town, he has also gone back in time. Can he find his boyhood self and give his younger self advice? Or will everyone think he's just crazy? This is an actual episode of the old Twilight Zone television show.

The story is "exceptionally well told and...[is] brilliantly adapted to a new medium." SLJ

Koch, Falynn

Plagues: the microscopic battlefield. Falynn Christine Koch. First Second 2017 128 p. Color; Illustration (Science comics)

Grades: 4 5 6 7 8   741.5; 614.5
1. Microorganisms; 2. Plague; 3. Epidemics
9781626727533, $19.99; 9781626727526

LC 2016945566

In this book in the Science Comics series, by Falynn Christine Koch, "we get to know the critters behind history's worst diseases. We delve into the biology and mechanisms of infections, diseases, and immunity, and also the incredible effect that technology and medical science have had on humanity's ability to contain and treat disease." (Publisher's note)

"A reassuring picture of ever more stout defenses ranged against a scary, invisible world." Kirkus

Includes bibliographical references (page 122)

Science comics: bats: learning to fly. Falynn Koch. First Second 2017 128 p. Color; Illustration
Grades: 3 4 5 6   **599.4; 741.5**
1. Bats; 2. Animal flight; 3. Animal rescue
9781626724082; 9781626724099, $19.99

LC 2016938728

This graphic novel in the Science Comics series, by Falynn Koch, follows "a little brown bat whose wing is injured by humans on a nature hike. He is taken to a bat rehabilitation center where he meets many different species of bats. They teach him how they fly, what they eat, and where they like to live." (Publisher's note)

"With plenty of informative back matter, this inviting, engaging nonfiction comic is perfect for kids hungry for science." Booklist

Kochalka, James

Johnny Boo & the happy apples. Top Shelf Productions 2009 42p. Illustration
Grades: K 1 2 3
741.5; Fic
1. Apples — Graphic novels; 2. Ghosts — Graphic novels; 3. Graphic novels; 4. Humorous graphic novels
978-1-60309-041-4, $9.95

Courtesy of IDW Publishing

Little ghost Johnny Boo has floppy, droopy, floopy muscles and wants to make them strong. Then the ice cream monster comes and says he now eats happy apples that make him strong. Johnny Boo wants to eat happy apples and get strong muscles, too, but when he eats a mushy apple he finds on the ground, his arm muscle becomes super floopy, like a long, limp noodle. What's he to do? Squiggle tries to use his squiggle power, but it only ties up Johnny Boo into a knot. Then ice cream monster returns and accidentally eats Johnny Boo and Squiggle, thinking they look like vanilla ice cream. The ghosts get out when he burps. Younger readers who are easily scared might be upset about Johnny Boo and Squiggle getting eaten, although they might think having a television in the stomach is funny.

Johnny Boo and the mean little boy. Top Shelf 2010 Illustration
Grades: K 1 2 3
741; 741.5
978-1-60309-059-9, $9.95

Courtesy of IDW Publishing

"When Johnny Boo announces a play date with his quiet new friend Rocky the Rock, trusty sidekick Squiggle is left to find a new friend of his own. How about this nice fellow named the Mean Little Boy? He sure is fond of his butterfly net, and he's got a great game to play with Squiggle... but, wait a minute, maybe the Mean Little Boy isn't actually so nice!" (Publisher's note)

Johnny Boo zooms to the moon!. James Kochalka. Top Shelf Productions 2014 40 p. Color; Illustration (Johnny Boo)
Grades: K 1 2 3   **741.5**
1. Space flight to the moon; 2. Skateboarding — Fiction
1603093494; 9781603093491, $9.95

In this book by James Kochalka, "Johnny Boo and Squiggle attempt to skateboard to the moon, encountering returning characters such as the friendly but not-so-bright stars and the not-so-scary ice cream monster. They also make a new friend in girl ghost Susie Boom, an enthusiastic moon resident whose powerful 'BOOM!' is equal to Johnny's signature 'BOO!'" (School Library Journal)

Johnny Boo, book two: Twinkle power!. Top Shelf Productions 2008 40p. Illustration
Grades: K 1 2 3
741.5; Fic
1. Friendship — Graphic novels; 2. Ghosts — Graphic novels; 3. Graphic novels; 4. Humorous graphic novels
978-1-60309-015-5, $9.95

Courtesy of IDW Publishing

Courtesy of IDW Publishing

Little ghost Johnny Boo and his pet ghost Squiggle play in the night and wonder what kind of power stars have. Then Squiggle zooms around and messes up Johnny Boo's hair; he thinks it's funny, but Johnny doesn't. Then Ice Cream Monster comes to play and wants Johnny to teach him how to boo, but the monster prefers "EEK!" over the usual "BOO!" So what power is better: Boo Power? Squiggle Power? Twinkle Power? How about Giggle Power, or even Wiggle Power?

Johnny Boo: the best little ghost in the world!. Top Shelf Productions 2008 40p.
Grades: K 1 2 3   **741; 741.5; Fic**
1. Friendship — Graphic novels; 2. Ghosts — Graphic novels; 3. Graphic novels; 4. Humorous graphic novels
978-1-60309-013-1, $9.95

"Johnny Boo may be the best little ghost in the world, with the best little ghost pet, Squiggle, but that doesn — t mean he's ready to face down scary Ice Cream Monster. When the monster turns out not to be scary after all, Johnny and Squiggle take it on as a new, if unpredictable, friend. Kochalka — s simple line drawings and bright crayon colors stand out in this sweet, silly graphic novel.... The dialogue is fairly simple but never simplistic, and the text is printed clearly enough to make the book accessible to children just beginning to pick up chapter books." Booklist

Courtesy of IDW Publishing

Other titles in this series are: Johnny Boo: Twinkle power (2009); Johnny Boo and the happy apples (2009); Johnny Boo and the mean little boy (2010);Johnny Boo does something! (2013);Johnny Boo zooms to the moon! (2014); Johnny Boo goes like this! (2016)

Monkey vs. Robot. Top Shelf Productions 2000 144p. Illustration
Grades: 5 6 7 8 9 10 11 12   **741.5; Fic**
1. Graphic novels
1-891830-15-5, $14.95

The book is almost wordless, allowing the reader to imagine one's own narrative. While there is violence, it's not graphic, and this little fable provides much food for thought.

"A very simply illustrated black and white pictorial narrative about a battle between a monkey community and a self-run robot factory encroaching on the monkeys' unspoiled forest domain." Publ Wkly

Another title in this series is: Monkey vs. Robot and the crystal of power (2003)

Peanutbutter & Jeremy's best book ever. Alternative Comics 2003 280p. Illustration

Grades: 4 5 6 7 8 9 10 11 12
741.5; Fic
1. Friendship — Graphic novels; 2. Graphic novels; 3. Humorous graphic novels
1-891867-46-6, $14.95

Peanutbutter is a sweet cat who acts like a hardworking office cat but usually naps on top of the paperwork, and Jeremy is a troublemaking crow; and they are friends. Jeremy may seem spiteful and sometimes does very mean things to Peanutbutter, such as pretending to threaten the cat with a pistol, but most of the stories are silly and fun.

Courtesy of Alternative Comics

Pinky & Stinky. Top Shelf Productions 2002 208p. Illustration
Grades: 4 5 6 7 8 9 10 11 12 Adult   **741.5; Fic**
1. Adventure graphic novels; 2. Friendship — Graphic novels; 3. Graphic novels; 4. Humorous graphic novels
1-891830-29-7, $17.95

Pinky & Stinky are fat little piglets, but just because they're cuties doesn't mean that they're not brave astronauts! When they embark on a daring mission to be the first pigs on Pluto, things go horribly wrong and they crash land on the moon. There they meet some not-so-friendly moon men, and end up in the middle of a conflict between the American space program and a race of alien ice creatures.

Kondo, Robert
The **dam** keeper; Book 1. Robert Kondo and Daisuke Tsutsumi. First Second 2017 153 p. Color; Illustration
Grades: 3 4 5 6   **741.5**
1. Adventure & adventurers — Comic books, strips, etc.; 2. Animals — Fiction; 3. Dams — Fiction
1626724261; 9781626724266, $19.99
     LC 2016961560

In this book in The Dam Keeper series, by Robert Kondo and Dice Tsutsumi, "Pig is the dam keeper. Except for his best friend, Fox, and the town bully, Hippo, few are aware of his tireless efforts. But a new threat is on the horizon — a tidal wave of black fog is descending on Sunrise Valley. Now Pig, Fox, and Hippo must face the greatest danger imaginable: the world on the other side of the dam." (Publisher's note)

"Kondo and Tsutsuma expand on the world of their Oscar-nominated animated short film of the same name, about a young pig who keeps his town safe from a terrifying black fog.... The tug-of-war between light and dark extends out of the plot and right into the images in a haunting story that contrasts the power of friendship with the weight of responsibility and the capacity for growth." Pub Wkly

Krosoczka, Jarrett J.
Comics Squad: recess!. comics by Jarrett J. Krosoczka, Gene Yang, Eric Wight, Jennifer L. Holm and Matthew Holm, Ursula Vernon, Dan Santat, Raina Telgemeier and Dave Roman, Dav Pilkey; edited by Jennifer L. Holm, Matthew Holm, and Jarrett J. Krosoczka. Random House Inc. 2014 144 p. Illustration; Color

Grades: 2 3 4 5 6   **741.5**
1. Graphic novels; 2. Humorous stories; 3. Recess — Fiction; 4. Schools — Fiction; 5. Short stories; 6. Comic books, strips, etc.; 7. School stories
0385370032; 9780385370035, $7.99; 9780385370042, $12.99
     LC 2013035223

"An all-star lineup of graphic novel notables contributes original works to this anthology, sharing the common thread of recess." (School Library Journal)

"[T]his lively, upbeat and all-around-awesome offering is consistently convivial and laugh-out-loud funny from cover to cover." Kirkus

Another title in this series is: Lunch! (2016)

Lunch Lady and the author visit vendetta. Alfred A. Knopf 2009 un Illustration
Grades: 3 4 5 6 7 8   **741; 741.5**
1. School stories — Graphic novels; 2. Teachers — Graphic novels
978-0-375-96094-9 (lib bdg), $12.99; 978-0-375-86094-2 (pa), $5.99
     LC 2009014886

The school lunch lady, a secret crime fighter, investigates a suspicious author after he visits the school and the gym teacher goes missing.

Lunch Lady and the bake sale bandit. Alfred A. Knopf 2010 un Illustration
Grades: 3 4 5 6 7 8   **741.5; 741**
1. School children — Food — Graphic novels; 2. School stories — Graphic novels
978-0-375-96729-0 (lib bdg), $12.99; 0-375-96729-X (lib bdg);
978-0-375-86729-3 (pa), $6.99; 0-375-86729-5 (pa)
     LC 2010012781

"The Breakfast Bunch is excited for the upcoming bake sale-and the best part is that it's raising money for an awesome field trip. But when all the snacks go missing, it's no laughing matter. Someone is sabotaging the bake sale. But why?" (Publisher's note)

Lunch Lady and the cyborg substitute. Alfred A. Knopf 2009 un Illustration
Grades: 3 4 5 6 7 8   **741.5; Fic**
1. Graphic novels; 2. Humorous graphic novels; 3. Robots — Graphic novels; 4. School children — Food — Graphic novels; 5. School stories — Graphic novels
978-0-375-94683-7 (lib bdg), $11.99; 0-375-94683-7 (lib bdg);
978-0-375-84683-0 (pa), $5.99; 0-375-84683-2 (pa)
     LC 2008-4709

The school lunch lady is a secret crime fighter who uncovers an evil plot to replace all the popular teachers with robots

"Yellow-highlighted pen-and-ink cartoons are as energetic and smile-provoking as Lunch Lady — s epithets of "Cauliflower!" and Betty — s ultimate weapon, the hairnet." Booklist

Other titles in this series are: Lunch Lady and the league of librarians (2009); Lunch Lady and the author visit vendetta (2009); Lunch Lady and the summer camp shakedown (2010); Lunch Lady and the bake sale bandit (2010); Lunch lady and the field trip fiasco (2011); Lunch Lady and the mutant mathletes (2012); Lunch Lady and the picture day peril (2012); Lunch Lady and the video game villain (2013); Lunch Lady and the schoolwide scuffle (2013)

Lunch Lady and the field trip fiasco. Alfred A. Knopf 2011 un Illustration
Grades: 3 4 5 6 7 8   **741.5**
1. Art — Forgeries — Fiction; 2. School stories — Graphic novels
978-0-375-96730-6, $12.99; 978-0-375-86730-9 (pa), $6.99
     LC 2011005907

"Lunch Lady and the Breakfast Bunch are on a school field trip to a famous art museum. But while Lunch Lady is busy taking in all the culture, the kids have caught onto something strange-some of the artwork looks suspiciously fake! Now Dee, Hector, and Terrence are determined to get to the bottom of this conspiracy, but Lunch Lady is too awed to catch on. Will she snap out of it and come to the rescue? Or will the Breakfast Bunch have to handle this operation alone?" (Publisher's note)

Lunch Lady and the League of Librarians. Alfred A. Knopf 2009 un Illustration
Grades: 3 4 5 6 7 8   **741; Fic; 741.5**
1. Games — Graphic novels; 2. Graphic novels; 3. Humorous graphic novels; 4. Librarians — Graphic novels; 5. School children — Food — Graphic novels; 6. School stories — Graphic novels
978-0-375-94684-4 (lib bdg), $11.99; 0-375-94684-5 (lib bdg);
978-0-375-84684-7 (pa), $5.99; 0-375-84684-0 (pa)
                                                      LC 2008043117
The school lunch lady, a secret crime fighter, sets out to stop a group of librarians bent on destroying a shipment of video games, while a group of students known as the Breakfast Bunch provides back-up

"The black-and-white pen-and-ink illustrations have splashes of yellow in nearly every panel. The clean layout, featuring lots of open space, is well suited for the intended audience.... With its appealing mix of action and humor, this clever, entertaining addition to the series should have wide appeal." SLJ
Other titles about the Lunch Lady are: Lunch lady and the cyborg substitute (2009); Lunch lady and the author visit vendetta (2009); Lunch Lady and the summer camp shakedown (2010); Lunch Lady and the bake sale bandit (2010); Lunch Lady and the field trip fiasco (2011);Lunch Lady and the mutant mathletes (2012);Lunch Lady and the picture day peril (2012);Lunch Lady and the video game villain (2013);Lunch Lady and the schoolwide shuffle (2014)

Lunch Lady and the summer camp shakedown. Alfred A. Knopf 2010 un Illustration
Grades: 3 4 5 6 7 8   **741; 741.5**
1. Camps — Graphic novels; 2. Humorous graphic novels
978-0-375-86095-9 (pa), $6.99; 0-375-86095-9 (pa)
Lunch Lady and the Breakfast Bunch kids are looking forward to a relaxing summer vacation with no funny business. What evils could befall them at summer camp?

"The two-color art is loopy and energetic, with varied, easy-to-follow page layouts. Jokes and puns are sprinkled throughout to keep the energy high until the exciting finale." SLJ

Labatt, Mary
★ **Mummy** mayhem: a Sam & Friends mystery, book three. Kids Can Press 2010 96p. Illustration
Grades: 3 4 5 6 7 8
741.5; Fic
1. Dogs — Graphic novels; 2. Graphic novels; 3. Humorous graphic novels; 4. Mummies — Graphic novels; 5. Mystery graphic novels
978-1-55453-470-8, $16.95
                          LC C2010-900107-9
Sam the sheepdog feels left out when her human friends Jennie and Beth go on a school field trip to the museum without her. She experiences her own mystery, though, when she finds dog treats left in the snow,

Courtesy of Kids Can Press

hears mysterious chanting, and sees a shadowy figure following her around. The museum has brought an exhibit of Ancient Egypt to town, including the mummy of the pharaoh Menopharsib — could the mummy be searching Woolford for Sam, who resembles Akasheput, the pharaoh's

pet dog, whose mummy was stolen years ago? This third book in the series has just enough spooky goings-on for younger readers.
Based on the novel The Mummy Lives! by Mary Labatt

Lambert, Joseph
The **Center** for Cartoon Studies presents Annie Sullivan and the trials of Helen Keller. by Joseph Lambert. Disney Hyperion Books 2012 92 p. Color illustration
Grades: 5 6 7   **362.4/1092; 362.4; 92**
1. American women authors — History; 2. People with disabilities — United States — History; 3. Female friendship — United States — History; 4. Graphic novels; 5. Women — United States — Biography; 6. Women — United States — History; 7. Keller, Helen, 1880-1968; 8. Sullivan, Annie, 1866-1936; 9. Female friendship — Graphic novels; 10. Women authors — Biography; 11. People with disabilities — Graphic novels
1423113365; 9781423113362
                                                      LC 2011036324
This nonfiction graphic novel about Annie Sullivan and Helen Keller "focuses on the trials both Annie and Helen struggle with in their lives," particularly the incident when Helen was accused of plagiarism in her story 'The Frost King' and interrogated at the Perkins Institution. "Helen's perspective is...communicated in dialogue-free black panels in which she is represented as only a gray silhouette" by author/illustrator Joseph Lambert. (Kirkus Reviews)

Langridge, Roger
Jim Henson's the Musical Monsters of Turkey Hollow. adapted from Jim Henson's screenplay by Roger Langridge. Simon & Schuster 2014 96 p. Color; Illustration
Grades: 4 5 6 7   **741.5**
1. Music; 2. Monsters
1608864340; 9781608864348, $24.99
"Turkey Hollow is a picturesque town where hundreds of years ago, unbeknownst to the citizens, a meteorite landed nearby a small brook on the outskirts of town. One Thanksgiving, while young Timmy Henderson practices his guitar, he's accompanied by strange, unearthly, musical sounds. That meteorite wasn't a rock at all but an egg holding seven furry, goofy monsters, each with a unique musical sound. After the initial shock, Timmy befriends the lovable creatures following him all around Turkey Hollow." (Publisher's note)

"Based on a never-produced Jim Henson screenplay, this folksy story captures the spirit of Muppet holiday specials like Emmet Otter's Jug-Band Christmas.... Subdued autumnal colors make up most of the palette in Langridge's clean-lined panels, while musical moments are full of big, swirling words in bright colors." Booklist

★ **Snarked!:** Forks and Hope. Roger Langridge. BOOM! Studios 2012 128 p. Illustration
Grades: 5 6 7 8   **741.5/973; Fic**
1. Fantasy fiction; 2. Adventure fiction; 3. Swindlers and swindling — Fiction
1608860957; 9781608860951, $14.99
Eisner Award: Best Publication for Kids (2011)
This graphic novel is the first in Roger Langridge's "Snarked!" series. It presents "an epic adventure featuring the Red Queen's children, Princess Scarlett and her baby brother Rusty, as they set out in search of the missing Red King. And who better to help guide the way than the Walrus and the Carpenter from [Lewis Carroll's] 'Through the Looking Glass'." (Publisher's note)
Volume 1 of 3

Larson, Hope

All summer long. by Hope Larson. Farrar, Straus & Giroux 2018 176 p. Color; Illustration

Grades: 5 6 7 8   **741.5; Fic**

1. Friendship — Juvenile fiction; 2. Bildungsromans; 3. Summer — Juvenile fiction

0374310718; 9780374304850; 9780374310714, $12.99

LC 2017956974

In this book, by Hope Larson, "thirteen-year-old Bina has a long summer ahead of her.... [H]er best friend, Austin...[is] off to soccer camp for a month, and he's been acting kind of weird.... [When] Austin comes home from camp,...he's acting even weirder.... How Bina and Austin rise above their growing pains and reestablish their friendship and respect for their differences makes for a touching and funny coming-of-age story." (Publisher's note)

"Larson's panels are superb at revealing emotional conflict, subtext, and humor within the deceptively simple third-person limited plot, allowing characters to grow and develop emotionally over only a few spreads." Kirkus

★ **Chiggers.** [by] Hope Larson; lettered by Jason Azzopardi. Atheneum Books for Young Readers 2008 170p. Illustration

Grades: 5 6 7 8 9   **741.5; Fic**

1. Camps — Fiction; 2. Friendship — Graphic novels; 3. Graphic novels

978-1-4169-3584-1, $17.99; 978-1-4169-3587-2 (pa), $9.99

LC 2008-09557

When Abby returns to the same summer camp she always goes to, she is dismayed to find that her old friends have changed, and the only person who wants to be her friend is the strange new girl, Shasta.

"Chiggers provides a ticket to summer fun. Larson delicately handles both the usual middle-school angst and the additional pressures that come with being somewhat different.... The content is perfect for upper elementary and middle school students." SLJ

Compass south. Hope Larson; illustrated by Rebecca Mock. Margaret Ferguson Books/Farrar, Straus & Giroux 2016 224 p. Color; Illustration

Grades: 4 5 6 7   **741.5; Fic**

1. Brothers and sisters — Fiction; 2. Buried treasure — Fiction; 3. Graphic novels; 4. Twins — Fiction; 5. Adventure and adventurers — Fiction; 6. Voyages and travels — Fiction; 7. Juvenile delinquents — Fiction; 8. Siblings — Fiction; 9. Gangs — Juvenile fiction; 10. New Orleans (La.) — Juvenile fiction

0374300437; 9780374300432, $17.99

LC 2015039907

"When 12-year-old twins Alexander and Cleopatra's father disappears, they join the Black Hook Gang and are caught by the police pulling off a heist. They agree to reveal the identity of the gang in exchange for tickets to New Orleans.... Neither Alexander nor Cleo realizes the real danger they are in-they are being followed by pirates who think they hold the key to treasure." (Publisher's note)

"A variety of panel sizes keeps the pace brisk while allowing for the occasional pause to set the scene or linger in an emotional moment." Horn Book

Another title in this series is: Knife's edge (2017)

Knife's edge. Hope Larson; illustrated by Rebecca Mock. Farrar, Straus & Giroux 2017 224 p. Color; Illustration; Map

Grades: 4 5 6 7   **741.5; Fic**

1. Sea stories — Graphic novels; 2. Pirates — Graphic novels; 3. Adventure graphic novels

9780374300449, $19.99

LC 2016951407

In this juvenile graphic novel, by Hope Larson, illustrated by Rebecca Mock, book two in the "Four Points" series, "twelve-year-old twin

adventurers Cleopatra and Alexandra Dodge are reunited with their father and realize that two family heirlooms reveal the location of a treasure that is their birthright. When they set sail with Captain Tarboro on the Almira, they know they're heading into danger — the ocean is filled with new and old enemies." (Publisher's note)

"As in its predecessor, every question answered leads the twins to more questions to be asked, and it ends with a breath-catching cliffhanger. An action-packed sophomore volume, with no loss of wind in its sails." Kirkus

A **wrinkle** in time: the graphic novel. Madeleine L'Engle; adapted and illustrated by Hope Larson. Farrar Straus Giroux 2012 392 p.

Grades: 4 5 6 7   **741.5**

1. Graphic novels; 2. Science fiction; 3. L'Engle, Madeleine. Wrinkle in time — Adaptations; 4. Time travel — Fiction; 5. Space and time — Fiction

0374386153; 9780374386153, $19.99

LC 2010044120

Hope Larson presents a graphic novel adaptation of Madeleine L'Engle's "allegorical fantasy in which a group of young people are guided through the universe by Mrs. Who, Mrs. Which and Mrs. What — women who possess supernatural powers. They traverse fictitious regions, meet and face evil and demonstrate courage at the right moment. Religious allusions are secondary to the philosophical struggle designed to yield the meaning of life and one's place on earth." (Kirkus Reviews)

Laudec

Cedric, vol. 1: High-risk class. Cinebook Ltd. 2008 48p. Illustration

Grades: 3 4 5 6 7 8   **741.5; Fic**

1. Graphic novels; 2. Humorous graphic novels; 3. School stories — Graphic novels

978-1-905460-68-7, $11.95

Eight-year-old Cedric is the type of boy who likes to play with his chums, doesn't always get good grades, and has a crush on his teacher, Miss Nelly. Then Chen starts at his school; she's Chinese, she's cute, and Cedric falls head over heels for her. He can't just tell her, of course. Meanwhile, he gets into all kinds of mischief with his friends, including playing with a remote control car, planting stink bombs all over school, drinking champagne when his grandfather says he did so to get the courage to propose to his grandmother. Each time he does something naughty, he does face consequences for his actions. This book is translated from the French.

Lawrence, Mike (Comic book artist)

Star scouts. Mike Lawrence. First Second 2017 192 p. Color; Illustration

Grades: 4 5 6   **741.5; Fic**

1. Human-alien encounters — Juvenile fiction; 2. Alien abduction — Juvenile fiction; 3. Scouts and scouting — Juvenile fiction

9781626722804, $14.99

LC 2016938730

In this book in the Star Scouts series, by Mike Lawrence, "Avani is the new kid in town, and...everyone in school thinks she's weird, especially the girls in her Flower Scouts troop.... But everything changes when Avani is 'accidentally' abducted by a spunky alien named Mabel.... Collecting alien specimens (like Avani) goes with the territory.... Avani might be weird, but in the Star Scouts she fits right in." (Publisher's note)

Another title in this series is: The league of lasers (2018)

Le Gall, Frank

Freedom!. Frank Le Gall; illustrated by Flore Balthazar; coloring by Robin Doo. Graphic Universe 2012 40 p. Color illustration

Grades: 2 3 4   **741.5/973**

1. Graphic novels; 2. Animals — Fiction; 3. Cats — Graphic novels; 4. Freedom — Fiction; 5. Mice — Graphic novels
0761378847; 9780761378846

LC 2011021726

"Miss Annie is a kitten, and she does all of the expected kitten activities — playing with pens and yarn, napping on armchairs, and begging for food. But she does the unexpected, too, like befriending a mouse she knows she's supposed to hunt. On her first adventure outside of the house, she meets two older cats, Zeno and Miss Rostropovna, who guide her through the big, new world. Annie has a wide range of expressions, from her perked ears to the tip of her pert tail." (Publishers Weekly)

"A charming balance of cartoon and natural kitty-ness in full-color, eight-panel pages, this cat's-eye view of life will induce purrs in feline fans everywhere." Kirkus

Leloup, Roger
Yoko Tsuno, bk. 3: the prey and the ghost. Cinebook 2008 48p. Illustration
Grades: 3 4 5 6 7 8   **741.5; Fic**
1. Ghosts — Graphic novels; 2. Graphic novels; 3. Mystery graphic novels
978-1-905460-56-4, $11.95

Young electronics engineer Yoko Tsuno has driven to Scotland to investigate the Loch Ness Monster, when she and her companion Pol find they've taken a wrong turn. Then they encounter a distraught young woman on the road who's being chased by dogs. The young woman is Cecelia, stepdaughter of Sir William, whose parents both died. She's convinced that her mother is haunting their castle, and Yoko finds a way to investigate just what is going on.

Part of the Yoko Tsuno series, originally published in France as Yoko Tsuno 12 La Proie et l'ombre.

Lie, Bjorn Rune
The **wolf's** whistle. by B.R. Lie and S.J. Donaldson.. Nobrow 2012 88 p. Illustration; Color
Grades: 4 5 6 7 8 9 10   **741.5; Fic**
1. Fractured fairy tales; 2. Revenge — Fiction
1907704035; 9781907704031, $18.00

This children's book by Bjorn Rune Lie "digs into the troubled upbringing of one of storydom's most maligned figures: the house-blowing-down wolf. As a wolf cub, little Robert loved superhero comics...which led to much torment at the hands of three piggish brothers. Robert grows up to be not much... when the building owned by the Honeyroasts burns down with three of Robert's best friends trapped inside, the spark of vengeance and justice is kindled in the wolf." (Booklist)

Limke, Jeff
Jason: Quest for the Golden Fleece. Lerner Publishing Group/Graphic Universe 2007 48p. Illustration
Grades: 3 4 5 6 7 8 9
292.1; 741.5
1. Graphic novels; 2. Greek mythology — Graphic novels; 3. Jason (Greek mythology) — Graphic novels
978-0-8225-5967-2, $26.60 lib bdg

Jason's uncle Pelias had stole the throne when Jason was a child; now a young man, Jason must prove himself by retrieving the priceless Golden Fleece from the far-off land of Colchis. He gathers a ship of heroes, the

Courtesy of Lerner Publishing Group

Argonauts, to aid him on his quest; but when they arrive in Colchis, the king insists that Jason prove himself in dangerous trials, and the king's daughter, Medea, has plans for Jason. This retelling is based on the heroic poem by Apollonius of Rhodes. The book includes a glossary and a list of books and websites for further reading.

King Arthur: Excalibur Unsheathed. Lerner Publishing Group/Graphic Universe 2007 48p. Illustration
Grades: 3 4 5 6 7 8 9
398.2; 741.5
1. Arthurian romances — Graphic novels; 2. Graphic novels; 3. Malory, Sir Thomas, 15th c — Adaptations
978-0-8225-3083-1, $26.60 lib. Bdg.

This story is adapted from Sir Thomas Malory's Le Morte D'Arthur. Young squire Arthur's life, and that of England, changes the day he pulls out the mysterious Sword in the Stone. Guided by Merlin the magician, Arthur takes his place as King of England. Can he win peace and freedom for his country? The book includes a glossary and a list of books for further reading.

Courtesy of Lerner Publishing Group

Lin, Yali
Hawthorne's the Scarlet letter: the Manga edition. Wiley Publishing 2009 186p. Illustration
Grades: 5 6 7 8 9 10 11 12   **741.5; Fic**
1. Authors; 2. Graphic novels; 3. Novelists; 4. Short story writers; 5. Hawthorne, Nathaniel, 1804-1864 — Adaptations
978-0-470-14889-1, $9.99

Hester Prynne, a young married woman in puritanical Massachusetts, stands in public shame when she bears a child long after her husband had disappeared. She refuses to identify the father of her child and instead wears the scarlet letter A always. The young minister Arthur Dimmesdale lives with his guilt in secret, but the physician, Roger Chillingworth, is actually Hester's husband, returned for vengeance. He vows to find the man who fathered Pearl, Hester's daughter, and destroy him. Meanwhile, Pearl grows up in a society that shuns her mother, and she comes to see the A as her mother's badge of honor. This book is a manga style adaptation of Hawthorne's novel.

Liniers
★ The **big** wet balloon: a Toon book. by Liniers. Toon Books 2013 32 p. Color; Illustration (Easy-to-read comics. Level 2)
Grades: PreK K 1 2   **741.5; Fic**
1. Balloons — Fiction; 2. Graphic novels; 3. Rain and rainfall — Fiction; 4. Sisters — Fiction; 5. Rain
1935179322; 9781935179320, $12.95

LC 2012047662

Eisner Nominee: Best Publication for Early Readers (2014)

This book by Ricardo Liniers "shows several tableaus of two little girls who wake up in the room they share and spend the day together. The older sister suggests fun things to do, like shouting at the top of their lungs while they run through a rain shower. Though they have one small misunderstanding, these siblings are loving and thoughtful — good companions whatever the weather." (New York Times Book Review)

"An uncommonly family-friendly tale, great for parents to share with their kids." Booklist

★ **Good** night, Planet. by Liniers. TOON Books 2017 36 p. Color; Illustration

Grades: PreK K 1 2 **741.5**
1. Dogs — Fiction; 2. Graphic novels; 3. Mice — Fiction; 4. Toys — Fiction; 5. Moon — Fiction; 6. Night; 7. Friendship
9781943145201, $12.95; 1943145202

LC 2017013136

Eisner Award: Best Publication for Early Readers (2018)

In this graphic novel, by Liniers, "when you go off to sleep, your toys go out to play! After a long day of jumping in leaves and reading her favorite books, this little girl is wornout, but her favorite stuffed animal, Planet, is just getting started. Planet befriends a dog, gobbles a cookie, and takes a leap into the unknown." (Publisher's note)

"Liniers has a gift for wordless storytelling through his art-only panels, using muted tones in watercolor under skillfully drawn pen-and-ink lines that create thin outlines and heavy areas of shading. The lettering is distinct and whimsical, and the lines of dialogue are funny, conveying Planet's personality as patient, kind, and quick-witted." Kirkus

★ **Written** and Drawn by Henrietta. by Liniers. TOON Books 2015 64 p. Color; Illustration
Grades: 1 2 3 4 **741.5**
1. Authorship — Fiction; 2. Drawing — Fiction; 3. Graphic novels
9781935179900, $12.95; 193517990X

LC 2015004010

Mildred L. Batchelder Honor Book (2016); Eisner Nominee: Best Publication for Early Readers (2016)

"Reading books is fun...but what about making them? Armed with new colored pencils, Henrietta's ready to try. Peek over her shoulder as she draws the story of a brave young girl, a three-headed monster, and an impossibly wide world of adventure." (Publisher's note)

"Argentine cartoonist Liniers presents a graphic ode to the pleasures and challenges of composition, starring his recurring character Henrietta, a young bibliophile. The little girl's cat, Fellini, looks on as she writes and illustrates 'The Monster with Three Heads and Two Hats.' Page by page, she narrates her process, her own story appearing in a childlike, colored-pencil scrawl alongside Liniers' polished panels.... Henrietta and her creator are kindred spirits, displaying equal knacks for the surreal and the utterly charming." Kirkus

Liu, Na
★ **Little** White Duck: a childhood in China. Na Liu and Andrés Vera Martínez. Graphic Universe 2012 96 p. Color illustration
Grades: 4 5 6
741.5/973
1. Graphic novels; 2. Biographical graphic novels; 3. China — History — 1976-; 4. Liu, Na, 1973-
0761365877; 9780761365877, $29.27; 9780761381150, $9.95; 0761381155

LC 2011005347

Courtesy of Lerner Publishing Group

This graphic novel provides a "glimpse into Chinese girlhood during the 1970s and '80s." It begins with the 3-year-old narrator trying to understand the death of Chairman Mao. "From there, her life unfolds in short sketches.... She explains about the four pests that plague China...and her stomach-turning school assignment to catch rats and deliver the severed tails to her teacher...[as well as] the origins of Chinese New Year, her favorite holiday." (Kirkus Reviews)

"This picturesque treasure introduces Chinese culture through a personal perspective that is both delightful and thought-provoking." SLJ

Loeb, Jeph
Shazam!: the greatest stories ever told. DC Comics 2008 224p. Illustration
Grades: 4 5 6 7 8 9 10 11 12 Adult **741.5; Fic**
1. Adventure graphic novels; 2. Captain Marvel (Fictional character); 3. Graphic novels; 4. Superhero graphic novels
978-1-4012-1674-0, $24.99

This book collects comics stories about Captain Marvel dating from 1940 to 1998. Captain Marvel predated Superman as a comic book superhero; young newsboy Billy Batson could transform into the flying superhero by shouting the magic word "Shazam!" This gave him the wisdom of Solomon, the strength of Hercules, the stamina of Atlas, the power of Zeus, the courage of Achilles, and the speed of Mercury. In these fourteen stories, he battles against such foes as Dr. Sivana, Mr. Mind, and the Monster Society of Evil.

Loux, Matthew
★ **Salt** water taffy: The legend of Old Salty. Oni Press 2008 un Illustration
Grades: 2 3 4
741.5; Fic
1. Adventure graphic novels; 2. Graphic novels; 3. Humorous graphic novels; 4. Mystery graphic novels
978-1-932664-94-2, $5.95

Courtesy of Oni Press

Eleven-year-old Jack Putnam and his eight-year-old brother Benny aren't very happy with their parents' choice to spend a summer-long vacation in dinky little Chowder Bay, Maine. They cheer up a bit when they taste the delicious salt water taffy candy made in town, then they meet a local fisherman, old Angus O'Neil, who tells terrific stories of fishing adventures at sea. And then Jack and Benny come upon a mystery when all the salt water taffy in the local store disappears, and they try to solve the mystery

Loux "dishes up an entertaining, exciting story for young graphic-novel readers.... The high-contrast black-and-white art, accomplished with bold line work, is used to good effect, displaying fluidity while still remaining quirky and fun." Booklist

Other titles in this series are: A climb up Mt. Barnabas (2008); The truth about Dr. True (2009); Caldera's revenge! Part 1 (2011); Caldera's revenge! Part 2 (2011)

Luciani, Brigitte
★ **Mr.** Badger and Mrs. Fox #1: The meeting. illustrated by Eve Tharlet. Graphic Universe 2010 32p. Illustration (Mr. Badger and Mrs. Fox)
Grades: 1 2 3
741.5
1. Badgers — Graphic novels; 2. Foxes — Graphic novels; 3. Graphic novels; 4. Siblings — Graphic novels
0-7613-5625-8 (lib bdg); 0-7613-5631-2 (pa); 978-0-7613-5625-7 (lib bdg); $25.26; 978-0-7613-5631-8 (pa), $6.95

LC 2009032617

Courtesy of Lerner Publishing Group

Having lost their home, a fox and her daughter move in with a badger and his three children, but when the youngsters throw a big party hoping to prove that they are incompatible, their plan backfires.

Other titles in this series are: A hubbub (2010); What a team! (2011); Peace and quiet (2012); The carnival (2014); The wild cat (2018)

Lucke, Deb

The **Lunch** Witch. by Deb Lucke. Papercutz 2015 180 p. Illustration
Grades: 3 4 5 6
741.5; Fic
1. Witches — Fiction; 2. School children — Fiction; 3. Friendship — Fiction
1629911623; 9781629911625, $14.99

Courtesy of NBM Publishing

In this book, by Deb Lucke, "Grunhilda inherits her famous ancestors' recipes and cauldron, but no one believes in magic anymore. Despite the fact that Grunhilda's only useful skill is cooking up potfuls of foul brew, she finds a job listing that might suit her: lunch lady. She delights in scaring the kids until she meets a timid little girl named Madison with a big set of glasses who becomes an unlikely friend." (Publisher's note)

"Lucke's splotchy, textured, quixotically paced, visual storytelling, with its mixture of crisply defined panels and sprawling full-page spreads, perfectly fits the outsider lives of both protagonists." VOYA

Another title about the Lunch Witch is: Knee-Deep in Niceness (2016)

Lutes, Jason

★ **Houdini**: the handcuff king. Hyperion Books for Children/Jump at the Sun 2007 90p. Illustration (Center for Cartoon Studies presents)
Grades: 4 5 6 7 8 9 10
92; 741.5
1. Biographical graphic novels; 2. Graphic novels; 3. Magicians; 4. Nonfiction writers; 5. Houdini, Harry, 1874-1926
978-0-7868-3902-5, $16.99; 978-0-7868-3903-2 (pa), $9.99

On May 1, 1908, magician Harry Houdini performed one of his famous handcuff escapes, this time in handcuffs and leg irons, while jumping off the Cambridge Bridge in Massachusetts into the frigid Boston River. This graphic novel takes the reader through Houdini's day, from 5:00 a.m. as he makes his preparations, makes a practice jump, coaches his wife Bess on how she's to help him, and then makes the jump.

This is a "fascinating graphic novel.... The format will instantly draw a lot of attention from readers and then hold on to it. Lutes and Bertozzi use grayscale comic panels to share their story about the life of Harry Houdini in a unique way.... The book resembles a hybrid between fiction and nonfiction, and the ingenious choice of format will appeal to a broad age range of readers." Voice Youth Advocates

Lyga, Barry

★ **Wolverine**: worst day ever. by Barry Lyga; artist, Todd Nauck. Marvel Publishing 2009 184p. Illustration
Grades: 5 6 7 8 9
741.5; Fic
1. Graphic novels; 2. Humorous graphic novels; 3. Superhero graphic novels; 4. Wolverine (Fictional character)
978-0-7851-3757-3, $14.99; 0-7851-3757-2

Teenager Eric Mattias has just recently discovered he has mutant powers. Very sucky mutant powers: suddenly no one notices him even when he's in the same room. He's not invisible, but he might as well be, and people don't even notice him when he speaks. Eric decides to follow Wolverine around and see if he can't pick up a few pointers about living a loner-type life, as the adamantium-clawed mutant tends to do. Only when they end up in a remote forested area does Eric realize he may not have

made the smartest move, because someone else has come, someone who is as strong as Wolverine, and maybe meaner: Sabretooth.

"It's a coming-of-age tale with bursts of action that's sure to appeal to its large, built-in audience." Booklist

Lynch, Jay

Mo and Jo: fighting together forever: a toon book. by [illustrator] Dean Haspiel & [writer] Jay Lynch. RAW Junior 2008 40p. Illustration
Grades: K 1 2 3
741.5; Fic
1. Graphic novels; 2. Humorous graphic novels; 3. Siblings — Graphic novels; 4. Superhero graphic novels
978-0-9799238-5-2, $12.95

Mona and Joey are battling twins, and everything they do turns into a fight. They both love the same superhero, the Mighty Mojo. One day he comes to their house and says he needs to retire and gives them his costume, which has all his powers

"The text is peppered with puns and some clever idiom work, reinforced by repetition as well as what's happening in the clean panels and art." Booklist

★ **Otto's** orange day: a Toon Book. by Frank Cammuso [art] & Jay Lynch [story]. TOON Books 2008 40p. Illustration
Grades: K 1 2
741.5; 741
1. Magic — Graphic novels; 2. Cats — Graphic novels
978-0-9799238-2-1, $12.95; 0-9799238-2-4

"When Otto the cat meets a magical genie, he knows just what to wish for: he makes the whole world orange! At first, this new, bright world seems like a lot of fun, but when his mom serves orange spinach for lunch, Otto realizes that his favorite color isn't the best color for everything." Publisher's note

"This is a text-book example of how to use page composition, expanding panel size, color, and stylized figures to make sequential art fresh, energetic, and lively." Booklist

LC 2007040759

MacHale, D. J.

Pendragon book one: the merchant of death graphic novel. adapted and illustrated by Carla Speed McNeil. Aladdin Paperbacks 2008 172p. Illustration
Grades: 5 6 7 8 9 10
741.5; Fic
1. Adventure graphic novels; 2. Fantasy graphic novels; 3. Graphic novels
978-1-4169-5080-6, $9.99; 1-4169-5080-X

LC 2007-937920

Fourteen-year-old Bobby Pendragon has had a good life with a loving family, friends, and sports, but it all changes the night his Uncle Press takes him into New York City, to a deserted subway station that contains a gate that leads them to another world. On Denduron, a peaceful tribe called the Milago face annihilation from the Bedowan, and Uncle Press expects Bobby to help him stop it. Press is what he calls a Traveler, and he says Bobby is one, too, and they have a job to do. Bobby is able to write journals and send them home to his best friends Mark and Courtney. Meanwhile, he needs to learn so much, can he do it in time to help — and stay alive?

"This graphic-format adaptation streamlines the already fast-moving experience, providing satisfying interpretations of favorite characters and situations." Booklist

MacPherson, Dwight L.

Kid Houdini and the silver dollar misfits. Viper Comics 2008 un Illustration
Grades: 3 4 5 6 7 8 9
741.5; Fic

1. Graphic novels; 2. Magicians; 3. Mystery graphic novels; 4. Nonfiction writers; 5. Supernatural graphic novels; 6. Houdini, Harry, 1874-1926
978-0 — 9802385-2-5, $9.95

In 1886, ten-year-old Harry Houdini runs away from home, only to find himself a prisoner in Professor Murat's circus. Harry joins the "freak" children: Lydia the snake girl (and her snake Terra), Hans the legless boy, and Jacques and Joe the Siamese twins and they form a detective agency that will solve mysteries for the fee of a silver dollar. Near Kansas City, a girl named Bea hires them to find her missing father whom she fears was kidnapped. However, when the gang gets to her house, they discover that her mother has now been kidnapped, too. It all has to do with a treasure map that leads to a lost gold mine, and the gang needs to solve that mystery in order to find Bea's parents. A young Harry Houdini and his friends make a fun team and they face some supernatural elements in their cases, much like the old Scooby-Doo cartoons " and with a similar scary-fun factor.

Maeda, Shunshin
Ninja baseball Kyuma!, vol. 1. Udon Entertainment 2009 200p. Illustration
Grades: 2 3 4 5 6   **741.5; Fic**
1. Baseball — Graphic novels; 2. Graphic novels; 3. Humorous graphic novels; 4. Manga; 5. Ninja — Graphic novels; 6. Kodomo
978-1-897376-86-7, $7.99

Young Kyuma Hattori, descendant of famous ninja Hanzo Hattori, is the last ninja left in the ninja compound in the mountains, and he trains with his faithful dog Inui. Kaoru is captain of the Moonstar City Club baseball team, comprised of elementary school students. When teammate Yohko says her crystal ball says they need to look to the mountains to help their team win, Kaoru goes up the mountain and finds Kyuma and asks him to join their team. Kyuma knows nothing about modern society or sports like baseball, and he thinks he's joining an army to go to battle against their enemy. Will his team ever figure out Kyuma is really a ninja, and will Kyuma ever figure out that a baseball game is just a game? The book includes some ninja-style fighting, but no violence or bad language.

Marois, André
The **sandwich** thief. by Andre Marois; illustrated by Patrick Doyon. Chronicle Books 2016 160 p. Color; Illustration
Grades: 2 3 4 5   **Fic**
1. Lost and found possessions — Fiction; 2. Lost articles — Juvenile fiction; 3. Mystery and detective stories; 4. Sandwiches — Fiction; 5. Schools — Fiction; 6. Stealing — Fiction; 7. Thieves — Fiction; 8. Theft — Fiction; 9. Mystery fiction; 10. School stories — Fiction
1452146594; 9781452146591, $14.99
LC 2015045045

In this book, by Andre Marois, illustrated by Patrick Doyon, "Marin loves the sandwiches his parents make for him — every day they're different and more delicious than the last. One morning, someone dares to steal his favorite sandwich: ham-cheddar-kale. Furious, Marin begins a fevered and famished investigation to unmask the thief. The days go by, the suspects multiply, and Marin's sandwiches continue to disappear." (Publisher's note)

Originally published in Canada in 2013 by Les Éditions de la Pastèque under the title Le voleur de sandwichs.

Marsden, Mariah
Anne of Green Gables: a graphic novel. Mariah Marsden, edited by Kendra Phipps and Erika Kuster, illustrated by Brenna Thummler. Andrews McMeel Pub. 2017 232 p. Color; Illustration
Grades: 3 4 5 6 7   **741.5**

1. Country life — Fiction; 2. Orphans — Fiction; 3. Friendship — Fiction
9781449479602, $10.99
LC 2017932307

In this graphic novel, by Mariah Marsden, edited by Kendra Phipps and Erika Kuster, illustrated by Brenna Thummler, "when Matthew and Marilla Cuthbert decide to adopt an orphan who can help manage their family farm, they have no idea what delightful trouble awaits them. With flame-red hair and an unstoppable imagination, 11-year-old Anne Shirley takes Green Gables by storm." (Publisher's note)

"An orphan with "hair as red as carrots" and the mischief she creates come to vivid life in this graphic novel version of Lucy Maud Montgomery's classic novel, a debut for both author and artist. Thummler's crisp illustrations warmly capture pug-nosed Anne's indomitable spirit as she navigates her new life." Pub Wkly

Martz, John
A **Cat** Named Tim and Other Stories. John Martz. Koyama Press 2014 52 p. Color; Illustration
Grades: PreK K 1
741.5
1. Short stories; 2. Animals — Graphic novels
1927668107; 9781927668108, $19.95

This book by John Martz is set "in Tim's world, [where] a cat can paint on the ceiling and a happy pig couple can wait months for the bus. A duck and a mouse love to go flying, in a plane, of course. Every page is an adventure and each character is colorful in this collection of comics." (Publisher's note)

Courtesy of Koyama Press

"In four off-kilter, virtually wordless stories, Martz...sketches out wild journeys, career mishaps, and unpredictable turns of events involving a small cast of amiable animals.... Martz's crisp, graphic forms defy readers' expectations — not to mention logic and the rules of physics — delivering pleasing absurdity with every page turn." Pub Wkly

Matheny, Bill
The **Batman** Strikes! Vol. 1: Crime Time. DC Comics 2005 un Illustration
Grades: 4 5 6 7 8 9   **741.5; Fic**
1. Batman (Fictional characters); 2. Graphic novels; 3. Superhero graphic novels; 4. Joker (Fictional character)
1-4012-0509-7, $6.99

This book boasts five action-packed adventures of the Dark Knight Detective: Penguin Rising, City of Bats, Outlaw and Disorder, Without a Chance and Deadly Partner. Batman goes up against the Penguin, the Joker, Manbat, and other villains.

The **Batman** Strikes!: duty calls. written by Bill Matheny, J. Torres; illustrated by Christopher Jones, Terry Beatty. DC Comics 2007 144p. Illustration
Grades: 3 4 5 6 7 8 9   **741.5; Fic**
1. Adventure graphic novels; 2. Batman (Fictional character); 3. Graphic novels; 4. Superhero graphic novels; 5. Catwoman (Fictional character); 6. Batgirl (Fictional character)
978-1-4012-1548-4, $12.99

This volume of Bat-stories is based on the new WB Kids cartoon series. Batman takes on Clayface, the Penguin, the Riddler, Catwoman, and Poison Ivy; Batgirl steps in because Pamela Isley used to be Barbara

Gordon's friend. The stories have lots of action, fast quips, and no foul language or actual violence.

McCann, Jim

★ **Return** of the Dapper Men. written by Jim McCann; art by Janet Lee; lettered by Dave Lanphear; edited by Stephen Christy. Archaia Comics 2010 un Illustration

Grades: 4 5 6 7 8   **741.5; Fic**
  1. Graphic novels; 2. Robots — Graphic novels; 3. Science fiction graphic novels
  978-1-932386-90-5, $24.95; 1-932386-90-4

"In the dreamy land of Anorev, children, all under age 11, live underground among intricate gear-work mechanisms, while elegant robots live in abandoned houses aboveground.... All are perpetually stuck in the same day, and time has, essentially, ceased to mean anything — until 314 Dapper Men rain from the sky and set in motion the impetus for change.... Where this book truly stands out is how well the story works in concert with Lee's stunning artwork, which employs an art nouveau sheen.... A true dazzler that speaks on multiple levels for both child and adult readers and one that gets richer with each read." Booklist

McCloskey, Kevin

The **real** poop on pigeons!. by Kevin McCloskey. Toon Books 2016 40 p. Color; Illustration

Grades: 1 2 3 4   **741.5; 636.5**
  1. Pigeons
  9781935179931, $12.95
                                                           LC 2015030551

"When a bearded park visitor expresses his dislike for pigeons, a brigade of children dressed in pigeon costumes descend and proceed to explain why pigeons are wonderful." (Publishers Weekly)

"Funny and informative, this attractive work of graphic nonfiction offers emerging comics readers an intriguing look at a commonly dismissed and ignored animal." SLJ

Snails are just my speed!. by Kevin McCloskey. Toon Books 2017 40 p. Color; Illustration

Grades: PreK K 1   **741.5; 594**
  1. Snails — Juvenile literature
  9781943145270, $12.95
                                                           LC 2017044164

This educational comic book in the Giggle and Learn series, by Kevin McCloskey, is about snails. "Did you know snails build roads like engineers and go undercover in camouflage like spies? Did you know they can be smaller than a seed or bigger than a grown-up's hand?...[The author] mixes snail science, art, and hilarity...[in this] book." (Publisher's note)

"This will be a particular joy for the science- minded, but between spotting the snails hidden among rocks and taking a cue from the drawing lesson in back, there's plenty of fun here for casual readers, too." Booklist

We dig worms!. by Kevin McCloskey. TOON Books 2015 40 p. Color; Illustration

Grades: K 1 2   **592.64; 741.5**
  1. Earthworms
  1935179802; 9781935179801, $12.95
                                                           LC 2014028775

This children's book, by Kevin McCloskey, explores "what do worms do all day? How do they see? And why are they so cold and squishy? Find out by going on an underground tour through the hidden world of earthworms. Kevin McCloskey's book even shows readers what's happening inside a worm's body — brain, crop, gizzard, and more." (Publisher's note)

McCoola, Marika

Baba Yaga's assistant. Marika McCoola; illustrated by Emily Carroll. Candlewick Press 2015 136 p. Color; Illustration

Grades: 4 5 6 7
741.5; Fic
  1. Supernatural graphic novels; 2. Fairy tales — Graphic novels; 3. Witches — Graphic novels
  076366961X; 9780763669614, $16.99
                                                           LC 2014951398

Eisner Nominee: Best Publication for Kids (2016)

BABA YAGA'S ASSISTANT. Text copyright © 2015 by Marika McCoola. Illustrations copyright © 2015 by Emily Carroll. Reproduced by permission of the publisher, Candlewick Press, Somerville, MA.

In this graphic novel, by Marika McCoola and Emily Carroll, "Russian folklore icon Baba Yaga mentors a lonely teen.... Most children think twice before braving a haunted wood filled with terrifying beasties to match wits with a witch, but not Masha. Her beloved grandma taught her many things: that stories are useful, that magic is fickle, that nothing is too difficult or too dirty to clean. The fearsome witch of folklore needs an assistant, and Masha needs an adventure." (Publisher's note)

"McCoola's offering is a well-nuanced delight, satisfyingly blending fairy tale, legend, and thrills. As a perfect complement, Carroll's evocative art enthralls, capturing both the emotion and the magic of McCoola's yarn and breathing new life into an old folk tale." Kirkus

McCranie, Stephen

Mal and Chad: the biggest, bestest time ever. Philomel Books 2011 218p. Illustration

Grades: 2 3 4 5   **741; 741.5**
  1. Adventure graphic novels; 2. Dogs — Graphic novels; 3. Graphic novels; 4. Schools — Graphic novels; 5. Time travel — Graphic novels
  978-0-399-25221-1, $9.99; 0-399-25221-5
                                                           LC 2010036904

"Mal is a super kid genius and Chad is a talking dog, but no one knows it. What's it like to be so extraordinary and yet so invisible? Not even Megan, Mal's secret crush, has any idea that Mal is anything more than a dork. Fortunately, Mal and Chad are best friends with a penchant for adventure . . . even if the time-traveling does get them grounded by Mal's mom." (Publisher's note)

McHale, Pat

Over the Garden Wall: Tome of the Unknown. by Pat McHale, illustrated by Jim Campbell. Boom! Studios 2016 144 p. Color; Illustration

Grades: 3 4 5 6   **741.5; Fic**
  1. Fantasy graphic novels; 2. Brothers — Fiction
  1608868362; 9781608868360, $19.99

Eisner Award: Best Publication for Kids (2016)

Short adventures from the world of Campbell's Cartoon Network miniseries. "Wirt and Greg are brothers, lost in a strange and endless wood called the Unknown. To find their way home, they must make it through this eerie place, where their only guides are a sardonic bluebird named Beatrice, and an elderly Woodsman. But as things become stranger and stranger, can they find their way out...alive?" (Publisher's note)

McKeever, Sean

Mary Jane Vol. 1: Circle of Friends. Marvel Entertainment Group 2004 96p. Illustration

Grades: 5 6 7 8 9 10 11 12 **741.5; Fic**
1. Graphic novels; 2. Romance graphic novels; 3. Spider-Man (Fictional character); 4. Superhero graphic novels
0-7851-1467-X, $6.99
High school student Mary Jane Watson hangs out with her friends (including nerdy Peter Parker) and starts dating old friend Harry Osborn even as she fantasizes about the new costumed superhero in town: Spider-Man. In this series, high school romance and friendships take center stage while the superhero action happens off the page and in the sidelines. This is the first of two volumes, then a new ongoing comics series called Spider-Man Loves Mary Jane continues the story.

McLeod, Bob
★ **SuperHero** ABC. HarperCollins Pubs. 2006 40p. Illustration
Grades: PreK K 1 2 **E; 741.5**
1. Alphabet; 2. Graphic novels; 3. Superheroes — Fiction
0-06-074514-2, $15.99; 0-06-074515-0 (lib bdg), $16.89; 0-06-074516-9 (pa), $7.99
LC 2004-22180
Humorous SuperHeroes such as Goo Girl and The Volcano represent the letters of the alphabet from A to Z.
"There's strong appeal here for the youngest comic-book fans, with many doses of humor along the way. Each figure has special powers, of course, which readers learn about through alliterative captions and action-packed illustrations." SLJ

Medley, Linda
★ **Castle** waiting. Fantagraphics 2006 456p. Illustration
Grades: 5 6 7 8 9 10 11 12 **741.5; Fic**
1. Fairy tales — Graphic novels; 2. Fantasy graphic novels; 3. Graphic novels
1-56097-747-7, $29.95
All of Medley's previously self-published comics are collected here in one volume for the first time. The titular castle was the home of Sleeping Beauty, whose story is retold from the viewpoint of the flibbertigibbet ladies in waiting. After the flighty princess awakens with the kiss of a handsome but not too bright prince, the castle becomes a sanctuary for various misfits. Readers will find references to many fairy tales, folk tales, and nursery rhymes in Medley's book, and her clean, clear black-and-white art reflects the works of classic illustrators such as Arthur Rackham.

Castle waiting; Volume II. by Linda Medley; [graphic design by Adam Grano; edited by Kim Thompson]. Fantagraphics Books 2013 464 p. Color; Illustration
Grades: 5 6 7 8 9 10 11 12 **741.5/973**
1. Fairy tales — Graphic novels
1606996339; 9781606996331, $29.99
LC 2014381744
In this graphic novel, by Linda Medley, "Lady Jain settles into her new life.... Unexpected visitors result in the discovery and exploration of a secret passageway, not to mention an epic bowling tournament. A quest for ladies' underpants, the identity of her baby son Pindar's father, the education of Simon, Rackham and Chess arguing about the "manly arts," and an escape-prone goat are just a few of the elements in this...new volume." (Publisher's note)

Meister, Cari
Goalkeeper goof. illustrated by Cori Doerrfeld.. Stone Arch Books 2009 32p. Illustration
Grades: K 1 2 3 **741.5; Fic**
1. Graphic novels; 2. Soccer — Graphic novels
978-1-4342-1292-4, $21.32; 978-1-4342-1409-6 (pa), $4.95
LC 2008-31965

David loves playing soccer, but he doesn't like having to be the goalkeeper, because he can't catch the ball to prevent the other team from scoring; his teammates call him Goalkeeper Goof. But this time, he has a new strategy to help him remember that he can use his hands when he's the goalkeeper. This very simple graphic novel is aimed at new readers; it provides a sample page in the front of the book to show how to read comic book style panels, and it includes a short glossary, discussion questions, and writing prompts.
This is part of the My First Graphic Novel series.

Courtesy of Capstone Press

Mercado, Yehudi
Sci-fu; Book 1: Kick it off. Yehudi Mercado; additional colors by David Wheeler; edited by James Lucas Jones and Desiree Wilson; designed by Kate Z. Stone. Oni Press 2018 144 p. Color; Illustration
Grades: 4 5 6 7 8 **741.5; Fic**
1. Extraterrestrial beings — Fiction; 2. Turntablists — Fiction; 3. Teenage boys — Fiction; 4. Robots — Fiction; 5. Disc jockeys — Fiction
1620104725; 9781620104729, $12.99
LC 2017948857
In this book, author Yehudi Mercado "sets his sights on 1980s Brooklyn and Wax, a young mix-master who scratches the perfect beat and accidentally summons a UFO that transports his family, best friend, and current crush to the robot-dominated planet of Discopia. Now Wax and his crew must master the intergalactic musical martial art of Sci-Fu to fight the power and save Earth. Word to your mother." (Publisher's note)
"Mercado uses onomatopoeia and visualized sound waves to emphasize that this is an aural adventure; color-coded speech balloons help readers keep track of who is spitting rhymes. His caricatured figures and dynamic layouts, coupled with a neon palette and graffiti flourishes, make for an entertaining story with a little something for everyone: hip-hop, tech-driven action, and romance." Pub Wkly

Meyer, Christopher
Adventures of Rabbit and Bear Paws: The voyageurs. Little Spirit Bear Productions 2008 32p. Illustration
Grades: 3 4 5 6 7 **741.5; Fic**
1. Adventure graphic novels; 2. Graphic novels; 3. Humorous graphic novels; 4. Native Americans — Graphic novels
978-0-9739906-2-1, $7.95
Pintsize, twelve-year-old Rabbit and giant, ten-year-old Bear Paws are brothers and members of the Ojibwa in the eighteenth century. Village medicine man Grey Stone and his wife Clover Blossom raise the brothers, who like to play and play pranks that tend to backfire. In this volume, Rabbit proves he's not a good lacrosse player; then Eagle Wing, a voyageur, stops off to visit Grey Stone on his way to this year's journey. Rabbit and Bear Paws travel with him to be carriers as Eagle Wing and the white fur traders make their trade journey. This book uses authentic details about traditions of the Ojibwa, the Mohawk, and other Nations.

Millar, Mark
Superman Adventures Vol. 3: Last Son of Krypton. written by Mark Millar, David Michelinie; illustrated by Aluir Amancio, Ron Boyd, Terry Austin, Mike Manley, Neil Vokes; colored by Marie Severin; lettered by Phil Felix; Superman created by Jerry Siegel and Joe Shuster. DC Comics 2006 112p. Illustration

Grades: 4 5 6 7 8 9   **741.5; Fic**
1. Graphic novels; 2. Superhero graphic novels; 3. Superman (Fictional character)
978-1-4012-1037-3, $6.99

Superman confronts his own past as he encounters survivors from Krypton, including his parents, Jor-El and Lara. Plus, someone wants to expose Clark's secret to Lex Luthor and the world. Will an encounter with Dr. Fate mean the end of Superman?

Millionaire, Tony
Sock Monkey: The Glass Doorknob. Dark Horse Comics 2002 un Illustration
Grades: K 1 2 3   **741.5; Fic**
1. Graphic novels; 2. Humorous graphic novels
1-56971-782-6, $14.95

The Sock Monkey and the other toys in the house marvel at the prismatic spectrum shining on the parlor floor. They notice that the dazzling colors are somehow emanating from the beautiful glass doorknob on the front door. Winter turns to spring and the apple tree at the front of the house sprouts its new leaves, casting a warm green shadow on the door. But something happens to the doorknob, it seems to be broken, the magical light show has come to a disheartening end. As the leaves grow heavier, joy leaves the house, until Mr. Crow comes up with plan: to repair the doorknob using very scientifical techniques. Meanwhile outside, notions of celestial events, planetary rhythm, and farmers' almanacs are discussed by two new characters, a bug and a bird named Rickets and Scurvy.

That Darn Yarn. DH Press/Dark Horse Comics 2005 un Illustration
Grades: K 1 2 3   **741.5; Fic**
1. Graphic novels; 2. Humorous graphic novels; 3. Toys — Graphic novels
1-59582-009-4, $7.95

This book tells two stories. In the black-and-white pages, Ann-Louise decides to make a present for David's birthday; when she finds a basket full of yarn and knitting needles, she starts knitting and creates a sock monkey doll. In the facing color pages, a sock monkey doll sits on the banister at the top of some stairs and starts to slide down the banister, but the yarn at the tip of its tail has caught on a nail, and the sock monkey starts to unravel as he continues his flight down.

Millionaire has written Sock Monkey comics that are rather subversive and fairly mature, but this picture book-format book is one for children to enjoy.

Mizuna, Tomomi
The **big** adventures of Majoko, volume 1. manga, Tomomi Mizuna; original work/supervision, Machiko Fuji; original illustrations, Mieko Yuchi. UDON Entertainment 2009 200p. Illustration
Grades: 3 4 5 6 7 8   **741; 741.5; Fic**
1. Fantasy graphic novels; 2. Graphic novels; 3. Manga; 4. Witches — Graphic novels; 5. Kodomo
978-1-89737-681-2 (pa), $7.99; 1-89737-681-2 (pa)

"Young witch Majoko sends her diary to the human world to find an adventuring partner and through it finds shy, quiet Nana. Together the two girls have a rollicking series of escapades.... Characters are simply drawn, but the backgrounds are nicely detailed and the plot elements are clearly thought out and easy to follow.... The content is very appropriate for the intended audience." Booklist

Volume 1 of a 5-volume series

Morse, Scott
Magic Pickle. with color by Jose Garibaldi. Scholastic/Graphix 2008 un Illustration
Grades: 2 3 4 5   **741.5**

1. Graphic novels; 2. Humorous graphic novels; 3. Superhero graphic novels
978-0-439-87995-8 (pa), $9.99; 0-439-87995-7 (pa)

"When Weapon Kosher, the Magic Pickle, erupts from the bedroom floor of little Jo Jo Wigman, she has to answer a lot of questions! What's the Magic Pickle's connection to the Brotherhood of Evil Produce? What is "Dill Justice?" How did Danny Johnson get to be so cute?" Publisher's note

"Starting with an irresistibly goofy premise, Morse layers on sly humor, astute references, and blazing action, turning in a charming, slam-bang story." Booklist

Other titles in this series are: Magic Pickle and the Planet of the Grapes (2008); Magic Pickle vs. the Egg Poacher (2008); Magic Pickle and the Garden of Evil (2009); Magic Pickle and the Creature from the Black Legume (2009)

Mouly, Françoise
Big fat Little Lit. [edited by] Art Spiegelman and Francoise Mouly. Puffin 2006 144p. Illustration
Grades: 2 3 4 5 6 7 8   **741.5; Fic**
1. Folklore — Graphic novels; 2. Graphic novels
0-14-240706-2, $14.99

This volume collects all three previously published Little Lit books: Little Lit: Once Upon a Time, Little Lit: Strange Stories for Strange Kids, and Little Lit: It Was a Dark and Silly Night. Many comics creators and children's book writers and illustrators contributed stories, including Ian Falconer, Daniel Clowes, Maurice Sendak, David Sedaris, Chris Ware, Jules Feiffer, Barbara McClintock, Crockett Johnson, J. Otto Siebold, Neil Gaiman, Art Spiegelman, and Lemony Snicket.

Naifeh, Ted
★ **Courtney** Crumrin and the night things. Oni Press 2005 128p. Illustration
Grades: 5 6 7 8 9 10 11 12
741.5; Fic
1. Fantasy graphic novels; 2. Graphic novels; 3. Supernatural graphic novels
1-929998-60-0, $11.95

Courtesy of Oni Press

Courtney's social-climber parents take her out of her comfortable city neighborhood and move into an upscale suburb to live with her creepy Great-Uncle Aloysius in her spooky old house. She has to face uppity classmates and things that go bump in the night; but she ends up making friends with the spooks! Courtney deals with magic and the supernatural, but she's no altruistic Harry Potter; in this series, magic sometimes bites hard.

Other titles in this series are: Courtney Crumrin and the coven of Mystics (2003); Courtney Crumrin in the twilight kingdom (2004); Courtney Crumrin's monstrous holiday (2009); Courtney Crumrin: the witch next door (2014); Courtney Crumrin: the final spell (2014)

Neel, Julien
Down in the dumps. written and illustrated by Julien Neel; translation by Carol Klio Burrell. Graphic Universe 2012 48 p. (Lou!)

Courtesy of Lerner Publishing Group

Grades: 4 5 6 **741.5**
1. Best friends — Fiction; 2. Dating (Social customs) — Fiction; 3. Friendship — Fiction; 4. Graphic novels; 5. Junior high schools — Fiction; 6. Mothers and daughters — Fiction; 7. Schools — Fiction; 8. School stories — Graphic novels
076138779X; 9780761387794, $27.93

LC 2012003973

This book is the third in Julien Neel's Lou! series. Here, "Lou is depressed because the boy of her dreams has moved away. To make matters worse, her mother, an aspiring author, has a serious love interest that makes her even more scatterbrained than usual. Lou feels quite left out as she heads off to the first day of school, only to discover that she and her best friend are not in the same class." (School Library Journal)

The **perfect** summer. [story and art by] Julien Neel; [translation by Carol Klio Burrell]. Graphic Universe 2012 48 p. (Lou!) Grades: 4 5 6
741.5
1. Dating (Social customs) — Fiction; 2. Graphic novels; 3. Mothers and daughters — Fiction; 4. Summer — Fiction; 5. Vacations — Fiction; 6. Adolescence — Graphic novels; 7. Vacations — Graphic novels
0761387803; 9780761387800, $27.93

Courtesy of Lerner Publishing Group

LC 2012002988

This book is the fourth in Julien Neel's Lou! series. Here, "she vacations with a friend at an amazing beach house while her mother is on a book tour. The friendship drama [of junior high school] has settled into a nice group of girls she enjoys being with. That just leaves the boy situation, which is complicated, since Tristan is back in her life." (School Library Journal)

Nobleman, Marc Tyler
Boys of steel: the creators of Superman. illustrated by Ross MacDonald. Knopf 2008 un Illustration
Grades: 1 2 3 **92**
1. Shuster, Joe, 1914-1992; 2. Siegel, Jerry, 1914-1996; 3. Superman (Fictional character)
978-0-375-83802-6, $16.99; 0-375-83802-3; 978-0-375-93802-3 (lib bdg), $19.99; 0-375-93802-8 (lib bdg)

LC 2007041606

"This book brings the young men behind the Man of Steel to a picture-book audience. Along with a compressed account of the partnership between nerdy high-school outcasts Joe Shuster and Jerry Siegel, Nobleman includes insights about superheroes' cultural significance and the chord struck by Superman — a hero who would always come home even as World War II loomed on the horizon." Booklist

Nordling, Lee
Chavo the invisible: a graphic novel. Lee Nordling, illustrated by Flavio B. Silva. Graphic Universe 2018 32 p. Color; Illustration
Grades: PreK K 1 2 **741.5; Fic**
1. Ability — Fiction; 2. Games — Fiction; 3. Graphic novels; 4. Stories without words; 5. Tag games — Fiction; 6. Games — Juvenile fiction
1512413321; 9781512413328, $25.32

LC 2017006470

In this graphic novel by Lee Nordling, illustrated by Flavio B. Silva, "Chavo is the last player to get picked for capture the flag. But that's okay. Chavo's small, but he just might surprise people with his quick thinking. Can Chavo protect his flag? Will he outwit the other team? Find out in this

word-free graphic novel, the third installment in the Game for Adventure series." (Publisher's note)

"Vibrant colors in distinct palettes, good comic timing, and engaging facial expressions make it easy to follow the action as well as the ups and downs of Chavo's experience." SLJ

North, Ryan
★ **Adventure** Time. Ryan North; illustrated by Braden Lamb and Shelli Paroline. Simon & Schuster 2012 128 p. Color; Illustration
Grades: 3 4 5 6 7 8 9 10 **741.5**
1. Imaginary places; 2. Adventure fiction
1608862801; 9781608862801, $14.99

"The totally algebraic adventures of Finn and Jake have come to the comic book page! The Lich, a super-lame, SUPER-SCARY skeleton dude, has returned to the the Land of Ooo, and he's bent on total destruction! Luckily, Finn and Jake are on the case...but can they succeed against their most destructive foe yet?" (Publisher's note)

"The comic series has been every bit as good as the show, with epic magic battles with an evil Lich, a multi-part time travel story, and a host of backup strips by some of the best indie cartoonists out there." Comics Alliance
Volume 1 of 17

Nybakken, Scott
Batman Adventures Vol. 2: Shadows & Masks. DC Comics 2004 112p. Illustration
Grades: 4 5 6 7 8 9 **741.5; Fic**
1. Batman (Fictional characters); 2. Graphic novels; 3. Superhero graphic novels
978-1-4012-0330-2, $6.95

A deadly new gang is threatening Gotham City, and it's up to the Dark Knight Detective to take it down, from the inside. He goes on an undercover mission in this volume.

Nykko
The **elsewhere** chronicles book two: the shadow spies. Lerner Publishing Group/Graphic Universe 2009 48p. Illustration
Grades: 4 5 6 7 8
741.5; Fic
1. Adventure graphic novels; 2. Fantasy graphic novels; 3. Graphic novels; 4. Horror graphic novels
978-0-7613-4460-5, $27.93; 978-0-7613-3964-9 (pa), $6.95

Courtesy of Lerner Publishing Group

LC 2008-39443

When the Shadow Door shatters, the passageway closes and Rebecca and Max are trapped in Elsewhere; they set out to find another way home. The problem is that wherever there is darkness, the Shadow Spies hunt them. Back in Grandpa Gabe's house, Noah and Theo work to find a replacement lens for the movie projector so they can get through and rescue their friends. Meanwhile, the police think Max and Rebecca have been kidnapped, and the boys have to work around the investigation. It's clear to the kids that Grandpa Gabe had explored Elsewhere, and his notes have left clues for them; Max and Rebecca also meet people who have been fighting a long war against the Shadows and who know Grandpa Gabe. Whatever else they do, they must keep the Shadow Spies away from Earth.

Originally published in France as Les Enfants d'ailleurs, winner of the 2007 Lyon Festival Youth Prize.

The **elsewhere** chronicles, book three: the master of shadows. Lerner Publishing Group/Graphic Universe 2009 48p. Illustration
Grades: 4 5 6 7 8
741.5; Fic
1. Fantasy graphic novels; 2. Graphic novels; 3. Horror graphic novels
978-0-7613-4461-2, $27.93; 978-0-7613-4744-6 (pa), $6.95
LC 2008-39444

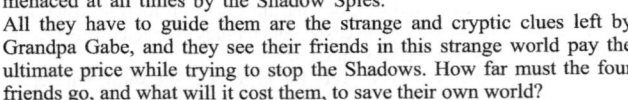
Courtesy of Lerner Publishing Group

Theo and Noah have joined Rebecca and Max in Elsewhere, but they are on the run, pursued by the Master of Shadows and menaced at all times by the Shadow Spies. All they have to guide them are the strange and cryptic clues left by Grandpa Gabe, and they see their friends in this strange world pay the ultimate price while trying to stop the Shadows. How far must the four friends go, and what will it cost them, to save their own world?

Originally published in France as *Les Enfants d'ailleurs*, winner of the 2007 Lyon Festival Youth Prize.

The **tower** of shadows. by Nykko, illustrated by Bannister; translation by Carol Klio Burrell]. Graphic Universe 2013 48 p. (The ElseWhere chronicles)
Grades: 4 5 6 7
741.5; Fic
1. Graphic novels; 2. Horror stories; 3. Grandfathers — Fiction; 4. Magic — Fiction; 5. Imaginary places
1467712337; 9781467712330, $27.93
LC 2013000317

Courtesy of Lerner Publishing Group

In this graphic novel by Nykko, "the time has come to confront the Master of Shadows. Rebecca, Max, and Theo must follow Grandpa Gabe into the heart of the Master's realm, the Tower of Shadows. But can Grandpa Gabe be trusted? There's a reason he's so familiar with the dark powers that rule Elsewhere: he created them. Grandpa Gabe's plan might just be a suicide mission, but it's their last chance to save our world — and Rebecca's life." (Publisher's note)

"Bannister's atmospheric illustrations feature expressive characters placed in finely detailed, eerily organic landscapes or dim subterranean reaches inhabited by menacing swirls of shadow." Kirkus

O'Brien, Patrick
Captain Raptor and the space pirates. [by] Kevin O'Malley and Patrick O'Brien; illustrations by Patrick O'Brien. Walker & Co. 2007 un Illustration
Grades: 1 2 3
E; 741.5
1. Dinosaurs — Fiction; 2. Pirates — Fiction; 3. Life on other planets — Fiction
978-0-8027-9571-7, $16.95; 0-8027-9571-4; 978-0-8027-9572-4 (lib bdg), $17.85; 0-8027-9572-2 (lib bdg)
LC 2006101182

Captain Raptor and the crew of the Megatooth are called back into action to save the planet Jurassica from rogue space pirates who have stolen their sacred jewels.

O'Connor, George
★ **Apollo:** the brilliant one. George O'Connor. First Second 2016 80 p. Color; Illustration

Grades: 5 6 7 8 9 10   **292.2**
1. Gods, Greek; 2. Mythology; 3. Greek mythology; 4. Apollo (Greek deity)
1626720169; 9781626720152, $9.99; 9781626720169
LC 2015014172

O'Connor "continues to turn his extensive knowledge of the original Greek myths into...graphic novel storytelling. Mighty Apollo is known by all as the god of the sun, but there's more to this Olympian than a bright smile and a shining chariot." (Publisher's note)

A Neal Porter Book.

★ **Ares:** bringer of war. George O'Connor. First Second Books 2015 80 p. Color; Illustration (Olympians)
Grades: 4 5 6 7 8 9   **741.5**
1. Ares (Greek deity) — Comic books, strips, etc; 2. Trojan War — Graphic novels; 3. Greek mythology — Graphic novels
1626720134; 1626720142; 9781626720138; 9781626720145, $16.99
LC 2014041225

This graphic novel by George O'Connor "continues in the tenth year of the fabled Trojan War where two infamous gods of war go to battle. The spotlight is thrown on Ares, god of war, and primarily focuses on his battle with the clever and powerful Athena. As the battle culminates and the gods try to one-up each other to win, the human death toll mounts." (Publisher's note)

"In this nuanced, multilayered view of the usually vilified bringer of war, O'Connor continues his exceptional graphic novel series about the Greek gods.... The author's extensive notes amusingly explain connections to The Odyssey, The Aeneid, and the series' previous works." SLJ

A Neal Porter Book.; Other titles in this series are: Athena: Grey-eyed Goddess (2010); Zeus: King of the Gods (2010); Hera: The Goddess and her Glory (2011); Hades: Lord of the Dead (2012); Poseidon: Earth Shaker (2013); Aphrodite: Goddess of Love (2014)

★ **Artemis:** wild goddess of the hunt. George O'Connor. First Second 2017 76 p. Illustration (Olympians)
Grades: 4 5 6 7 8   **292.2/114; 292.2; 741.5**
1. Artemis (Greek deity); 2. Greek mythology
9781626725218, $17.99; 9781626725225
LC 2016938491

In this book, by George O'Connor, "Artemis, Goddess of the Hunt, finds power through her skilled hunting ability and mighty bow. She slays those who wish to do harm to the innocent and takes care of the young and helpless. She protects women and young girls, helps in childbirth, soothes, and is unrivaled in her hunting abilities." (Publisher's note)

"Though the author is true to the original tales...he injects a feminist perspective, emphasizing Artemis's strong relationships with other women." SLJ

Includes bibliographical references.

★ **Athena:** grey-eyed goddess. First Second 2010 76p. Illustration
Grades: 5 6 7 8   **741; 741.5**
1. Athena (Greek deity); 2. Classical mythology
978-1-59643-649-7, $16.99; 1-59643-649-2; 978-1-59643-432-5 (pa), $9.99; 1-59643-432-5 (pa)

This tells "five myths involving Athena, including complementary (or conflicting) stories of how she gained the Pallas moniker along with quick treatments of Perseus and Medusa and the weaver Arachne." Booklist

"O'Connor's drawings, full of energetic diagonals and expressive faces, are nicely balanced by spare settings and minimalistic backgrounds. A sophisticated color palette, full of midtones and subtle contrasts, and panel layouts that vary from page to page further distinguish the art. The author's affection for his subject is evident in a chatty note. Profiles of major characters, notes, and discussion questions appear in addition to the usual back matter. An exceptional graphic novel." SLJ

★ **Hades**. First Second 2012 76p Color illustration (Olympians)
Grades: 5 6 7 8 9   **741.5; 398.2093; 398.2093801**
1. Hades (Greek deity) — Comic books, strips, etc.; 2. Mother-daughter relationship — Fiction; 3. Graphic novels; 4. Greek mythology
9781596437616

LC 2011017563

In this book, a "tempestuous mother-daughter relationship makes up the centerpiece of [author and illustrator George] O'Connor's...Olympian portrait. Snatched down to the Underworld in the wake of a screaming fight with her mother Demeter,...raging adolescent Kore (meaning, generically 'The Maiden') initially gives her quiet, gloomy captor Hades a hard time too. After grabbing the opportunity to give herself a thorough makeover and changing her name to Persephone ('Bringer of Destruction'), though, she takes charge of her life — so surely that, when offered the opportunity to return to her remorseful mom, she lies about having eaten those pomegranate seeds so she can spend half of each year as Queen of the Dead." (Kirkus)
Includes bibliographical references.

★ **Hera**: the goddess and her glory. First Second 2011 76p. Illustration
Grades: 5 6 7 8   **741; 741.5**
978-1-59643-433-2, $9.99; 1-59643-433-3

★ **Hermes:** tales of the trickster. George O'Connor. First Second 2018 76 p. Color; Illustration (Olympians)
Grades: 4 5 6 7 8   **741.5; 292.2**
1. Greek mythology — Fiction; 2. Gods and goddesses — Fiction
9781626725249; 9781626725256, $10.99; 9781626725263

LC 2017941162

In this book in the Olympians series, author "George O'Connor delves into the myth of Hermes, the trickster god. From his infancy, when he bewitches animals and bends them to his will (stealing a herd of Apollo's prize cattle in the bargain), to his adolescence and adulthood when he becomes father to the equally mischievous Pan, Hermes's story is wildly entertaining as he brings a little bit of chaos to everything he touches or creates." (Publisher's note)

"O'Connor illustrates the speedy god's mischievousness with cartoon slapstick flair, playing up his witty repartee and sly, impish appeal. O'Connor's artwork is as solid as ever, with muscle-bound deities and grotesque monsters aplenty." Booklist
Includes bibliographical references

★ **Poseidon:** earth shaker. by George O'Connor. Roaring Brook Press 2012 80 p. (Olympians)
Grades: 4 5 6   **741.5/973**
1. Greek mythology — Graphic novels
1596437383; 1596438282; 9781596437388, $9.99; 9781596438286, $16.99

LC 2011052219

This graphic novel, by George O'Connor, is part of the "Olympians" series, featuring the mythology of the Greco-Roman gods. "The fifth installment of the Olympians series of graphic novels...turns the spotlight on that most mysterious and misunderstood of the Greek gods.... Thrill to such famous myths as Theseus and the Minotaur, Odysseus and Polyphemos, and the founding of Athens — and learn how the tempestuous Poseidon became the King of the Seas." (Publisher's note)
Includes bibliographical references and index; A Neal Porter book.

★ **Zeus:** king of the gods. First Second 2010 76p. Illustration
Grades: 5 6 7 8   **741.5**
978-1-59643-431-8, $16.99; 1-59643-625-5; 978-1-59643-432-5 (pa), $9.99; 1-59643-431-7 (pa)

"O'Connor unveils his new Olympians graphic-novel series with this story of the daddy of Greek gods. Most immediately striking about this,

aside from the exciting artwork, is the care O'Connor takes to visualize the creation myth that begins with Gaea creating and taking as a husband the sky, Ouranos. Their children the Titans and other proto-Olympian entities are often neglected or at best murkily covered, but here they're vividly portrayed with all the magnificence of their beyond-good-and-evil power. After this breathtaking and lengthy sequence, Zeus enters the scene to grow from a feisty nymph-needling youth to a lightning bolt-wielding avenger." (Booklist)

Other titles in this series are:Athena, grey-eyed goddess (2010);Hera, the goddess and her glory (2011);Hades, lord of the dead (2012);Poseidon, earth shaker (2013);Aphrodite, goddess of love (2013);Ares, bringer of war (2015); Apollo, the brilliant one (2016); Artemis, wild goddess of the hunt (2017); Hermes, tales of the trickster (2018)

O'Malley, Kevin

Captain Raptor and the moon mystery. Kevin O'Malley; illustrations by Patrick O'Brien. Walker & Co. 2005 un Illustration
Grades: 1 2 3 4
Fic; 741.5; E
1. Dinosaurs — Graphic novels; 2. Graphic novels; 3. Science fiction graphic novels
0-8027-8935-8, $16.95; 0-8027-8936-6 (lib bdg), $17.85

Courtesy of Bloomsbury Children's

LC 2004-53624

When something lands on one of the moons of the planet Jurassica, Captain Raptor and his spaceship crew go to investigate

"An action-packed science-fiction romp starring a cast of dinosaur characters.... Presented in comic-book style, this story blends an eye-catching layout with a quick-moving plot, tongue-in-cheek humor, and an imaginative setting." SLJ

Other titles about Captain Raptor are: Captain Raptor and the space pirates (2007); Captain Raptor and the perilous planet (2018)

O'Neill, Katie

★ **Princess** princess ever after. Katie O'Neill; [edited by] Ari Yarwood. Oni Press 2016 56 p. Color; Illustration
Grades: 4 5 6 7 8
741.5; Fic
1. Princesses — Juvenile fiction; 2. Fantasy graphic novels; 3. Magic — Fiction; 4. LGBT people — Fiction
1620103400; 9781620103401, $12.99

LC 2016931407

In this book, by Katie O'Neill, "when the heroic princess Amira rescues the kind-hearted princess Sadie from her tower prison, neither expects to find a true friend in the bargain. Yet as they adventure across the kingdom, they discover that they bring out the very best in the other person. They'll need to join forces and use all the know-how, kindness, and bravery they have in order to defeat their greatest foe yet: a jealous sorceress." (Publisher's note)

"The princesses' affection for each other deepens with every challenge — and every round of snappy banter — and when wedding bells ring, they're for a couple who truly know and have freely chosen one another." O'Neill delivers an alternative fairy tale that challenges conventions with

Courtesy of Oni Press

every twist of the plot but doesn't veer into heavy-handed preachiness that pulls readers out of the story." Kirkus

★ The **tea** dragon society. written & illustrated by Katie O'Neill. Oni Press 2017 72 p. Color; Illustration
Grades: 4 5 6 7 8
741.5
1. Blacksmithing — Fiction; 2. Dragons — Fiction; 3. Tea — Fiction
1620104415; 9781620104415, $17.99
LC 2017936880

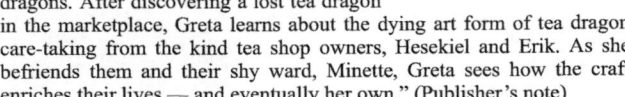
Courtesy of Oni Press

Eisner Award: Best Publication for Kids (2018)

This book, by Katie O'Neill, "follows the story of Greta, a blacksmith apprentice, and the people she meets as she becomes entwined in the enchanting world of tea dragons. After discovering a lost tea dragon in the marketplace, Greta learns about the dying art form of tea dragon care-taking from the kind tea shop owners, Hesekiel and Erik. As she befriends them and their shy ward, Minette, Greta sees how the craft enriches their lives — and eventually her own." (Publisher's note)

"In alluringly hued, manga-inspired illustrations, O'Neill's diverse characters distray an array of different skin colors, orientations, and abilities. Helping to add depth to the worldbuilding is an excerpt from a fictional tome that explains the history of tea dragons and their individual characteristics. Undeniably whimsical and extremely cute." Kirkus

Oakley, Mark

Thieves & kings. [by Mark Oakley]. I Box Pub 1998 154p. Illustration
Grades: 4 5 6 7 8 9 10 11 12
741.5; Fic
1. Adventure graphic novels; 2. Fantasy graphic novels; 3. Graphic novels
0-9681025-0-6, $18.95
LC 2003-446777

In a story that mixes pages of text with pages of comic book art, the reader meets the young thief Rubel, who has returned home from a long voyage to find things no longer as they were. He has to deal with soldiers and pirates, princes and princesses, a strange young wizard, and a mysterious Shadow Lady.

Originally published as individual issues of the Thieves & kings comic series, beginning in 1994; Volume 1 of 5

Ostertag, Molly
The **witch** boy. Molly Knox Ostertag. Scholastic Press 2017 224 p. Color; Illustration
Grades: 3 4 5 6
741.5; Fic
1. Shapeshifting — Fiction; 2. Witches — Graphic novels; 3. Fantasy graphic novels
9781338089523, $24.99; 9781338089530; 9781338089516, $12.99; 1338089528

In this graphic novel, by Molly Knox Ostertag, "in thirteen-year-old Aster's family, all the girls are raised to be witches, while boys grow up to be shapeshifters. Anyone who dares cross those lines is exiled. Unfortunately for Aster, he still hasn't shifted...and he's still fascinated by witchery, no matter how forbidden it might be. When a mysterious danger threatens the other boys, Aster knows he can help — as a witch." (Publisher's note)

Followed by: The hidden witch (2018)

Ottaviani, Jim
Primates: The Fearless Science of Jane Goodall, Dian Fossey, and Biruté Galdikas. Jim Ottaviani; illustrated by Maris Wicks. First Second 2013 133 p. Color; Illustration
Grades: 5 6 7 8 9 10 Adult
741.5; 599.8
1. Primates; 2. Fossey, Dian, 1932-1985; 3. Goodall, Jane, 1934-; 4. Galdikas, Birute, 1946-
1596438657; 9781596438651, $19.99
LC 2013427678

This book presents an "account of the three greatest primatologists of the last century: Jane Goodall, Dian Fossey, and Biruté Galdikas. These three ground-breaking researchers were all students of the great Louis Leakey, and each made profound contributions to primatology — and to our own understanding of ourselves." (Publisher's note)

"More story than study, the book provides an accessible introduction to Goodall's, Fossey's and Galdikas' lives and work." Kirkus

Includes bibliographical references, page 138

★ **T-Minus:** the race to the moon. [illustrated by] Zander Cannon, Kevin Cannon. Aladdin 2009 124p. Illustration
Grades: 4 5 6 7 8 9 10 11 12 Adult
629.45; 741.5
1. Apollo project — Graphic novels; 2. Gemini project — Graphic novels; 3. Graphic novels; 4. Space flight to the moon — Graphic novels
978-1-4169-8682-9, $21.99; 1-4169-8682-0; 978-1-4169-4960-2 (pa), $12.99; 1-4169-4960-7 (pa)
LC 2009-920999

Ottaviani, Zander Cannon, and Kevin Cannon show what happened when the U.S. and the U.S.S.R. started the space race in the 1950s, and how it progressed to the NASA Apollo 11 mission which landed two men on the moon in July of 1969.

"Organized as a countdown, making the outcome seem inevitable, the frequent, prominent sidebars list a type of rocket, the duration of its flight, and whether the mission was a success or a failure. There are more than 30 attempts chronicled, and the shift between Soviet and U.S. successes creates an interesting balance in the narrative.... Ottaviani is particular with facts and eager to inspire readers with regard to the scientific process." SLJ

Pak, Greg
★ **Mech** Cadet Yu; Volume 1. written by Greg Pak; illustrated by Takeshi Miyazawa; colored by Triona Farrell. Simon & Schuster 2018 128 p. Color; Illustration
Grades: 4 5 6 7 8
741.5; Fic
1. Robots — Fiction; 2. Extraterrestrial beings — Fiction; 3. Graphic novels
1684151953; 9781684151950, $14.99

"Every year, giant sentient robots from outer space come to Earth and bond forever with a brand new crop of cadets at Sky Corps Academy to help keep the planet safe. But this year, instead of making a connection with a cadet, one of the mechs bonds with Stanford, a young kid working with his Mom as a janitor at Sky Corps. Stanford has the opportunity of a lifetime but he'll first have to earn the trust of his classmates if he's to defend the planet from the monstrous Sharg." (Publisher's note)

"Set in the near future in Arizona, the tale strikes the perfect balance between action and drama. The battle sequences are thrilling and the characterization, writing, and dialogue strong." SLJ

Volume 1 of 3

Parker, Jake
★ **Missile** Mouse: the star crusher. Graphix 2010 172p. (Missile Mouse)
Grades: 3 4 5 6
741; Fic; 741.5
1. Adventure graphic novels; 2. Graphic novels; 3. Mice — Graphic novels; 4. Science fiction graphic novels

978-0-545-11714-2, $21.99; 0-545-11714-3; 978-0-545-11715-9 (pa), $10.99; 0-545-11715-1 (pa)

"When his mission to recover an ancient star compass goes wrong, intrepid Galactic Security Agent Missile Mouse finds himself saddled with a partner.... The two are to retrieve a missing scientist who holds the key to a horrible weapon, the Star Crusher, in his hereditary memory.... [This is] a gem in story and art. Bright, action-filled, at times wordless panels keep the pages turning. Intelligent space opera and a realistically rounded hero will have young fans of the future demanding the next volume." Kirkus

Pastrovicchio, Lorenzo
   Wizards of Mickey, vol. 1: mouse magic. writer: Stefano Ambrosio; artists: Lorenzo Pastrovicchio ... [et al.]; translation: Saida Temafonte; editor, Aaron Sparrow; letterers Troy Peteri [and] Deron Bennett; designer Erika Terriquez. Boom! Studios 2010 un Illustration
Grades: 3 4 5 6 7 8 9   **741.5; Fic**
   1. Adventure graphic novels; 2. Fantasy graphic novels; 3. Graphic novels; 4. Humorous graphic novels; 5. Mickey Mouse (Fictional character)
978-1-60886-541-3, $9.99
   Wizard's apprentice Mickey loses a magic talisman called the Diamagic when he and the village fall afoul of a con man who steals it from them. Mickey pursues the con man, but he learns he'll have to compete in the Great Wizard's Tournament to win it back if he can father a team to work with him. He ends up with Donald and Goofy, both misfit bunglers, but somehow they'll have to compete against Peg-Leg Pete and the Phantom Blot. This book, originally written and published in Italy, is full of fantasy adventure and fun with recognizable Disney characters.
   Volume 1 of 3

Pearson, Luke
   Hilda and the Bird Parade. by Luke Pearson. Flying Eye Books 2013 44 p. Color illustration (Hildafolk)
Grades: 2 3 4 5   **741.5**
   1. Birds — Fiction; 2. City and town life — Fiction
1909263060; 9781909263062, $24
   This book, by Luke Pearson, follows "Hilda and her mother are settling into the fictional town of Trolberg. It's a far cry from their idyllic mountain home: Hilda's mother is nervous about letting her daughter roam free, and the local kids' idea of a good time is to...throw rocks at birds. When a large, black bird is left injured and amnesiac after being hit by one such rock, Hilda tries to help it remember how to fly as well as find its own way home." (Publishers Weekly)
   "Environment being so crucial to the tale, Pearson's expressive architecture and city design are nothing short of remarkable, giving a personality to neighborhoods and even individuals doorways. His large-headed, stick-legged cartooning employs both humor and empathy and gracefully reflects the book's tone, a perfect pitch between childlike adventure, subtle mystery, and gentle lyricism." Booklist

   Hilda and the Black Hound. by Luke Pearson. Flying Eye Books 2014 64 p. Color; Illustration (Hildafolk)
Grades: 3 4 5 6 7   **741.5**
   1. City and town life — Fiction; 2. Girls — Fiction; 3. Comic books, strips, etc.; 4. Dogs — Fiction
9781909263185, $24; 1909263184
   In this graphic novel by Luke Pearson, "Hilda...meets the Nisse: a mischievous but charismatic bunch of misfits who occupy a world beside — but also somehow within — our own, and where the rules of physics don't quite match up. Meanwhile, on the streets of Trolberg, a dark specter looms." (Publisher's note)
   "The full-size volume offers a minimum of 10 panels of varying sizes per page. Darker shades dominate when the beast lurks, and earth tones and reds and oranges when the characters go about their daily business. Touches of humor abound in both images and dialogue." SLJ

   Hilda and the Midnight Giant. Luke Pearson. Nobrow Press 2012 40p Color illustration
Grades: 4 5 6 7 8   **741.5**
   1. Girls — Fiction; 2. Forests and forestry — Fiction; 3. Giants — Fiction
1907704256; 9781907704253, $24.00
   In this book, the "protagonist finds her world turned upside down as she faces the prospect of leaving her snow-capped birthplace for the hum of the megalopolis, where her mother (an architect) has been offered a prestigious job. During Hilda's daily one-and-a-half hour trek to school she looks for ways to stall her mother's decision. She conspires with the beings of the mystical Blue Forest to delay the inevitable. Will they help or hinder her? More importantly, who is this mysterious Midnight Giant?"

   Hilda and the Stone Forest. by Luke Pearson. Flying Eye Books 2016 64 p. Color; Illustration
Grades: 3 4 5 6   **741.5; Fic**
   1. Trolls — Juvenile fiction; 2. Mother-daughter relationship — Juvenile fiction; 3. Magic — Juvenile fiction
1909263745; 9781909263741, $19.95
   "Hilda is hardly at home anymore, seeking days filled with excitement, and her mother can't help but worry. In a moment of tension, the pair find themselves flung far away into a mysterious, dark forest — the land of the trolls! Can they work together to escape the clutches of these sinister stone creatures?" (Publisher's note)
   "Pearson has perfected Hilda's Scandinavian-style fantasy world, and his artwork is as captivating as ever, but the change in focus from Hilda's derring-do to the realistic consequences of her escapades keeps it from being just another series installment." Booklist

★ **Hilda** and the troll. Luke Pearson. Flying Eye Books 2013 40 p. Color; Illustration (Hildafolk)
Grades: 3 4 5 6   **741.5; Fic**
   1. Adventure fiction; 2. Explorers — Fiction; 3. Trolls — Fiction
1909263141; 9781909263147, $18.95
   This book, by Luke Pearson, is "about an adventurous little girl and her habit of befriending anything, no matter how curious it might seem. While on an expedition to illustrate the magical creatures of the mountains around her home, Hilda spots a mountain troll. As the blue-haired explorer sits and sketches, she slowly starts to nod off. By the time she wakes up, the troll has totally disappeared and, even worse, Hilda is lost in a snowstorm." (Publisher's note)
   "The art is as whimsical as the protagonist, and the bright colors enhance this comic book's magical-realistic effect." Horn Book
   Originally published 2010 as Hildafolk; Other titles about Hilda are:Hilda and the Midnight Giant (2012);Hilda and the Bird Parade (2013);Hilda and the Black Hound (2014);Hilda and the Stone Forest (2016)

Peirce, Lincoln
   Big Nate: game on!. by Lincoln Peirce. Andrews McMeel Pub., LLC 2013 224 p. Color illustration
Grades: 1 2 3 4 5 6   **Fic; 741.5/973**
   1. Comic books, strips, etc.; 2. Sports — Fiction; 3. Games — Fiction
1449427774; 9781449427771, $9.99
                                                   LC 2012952339
   This book, written and illustrated by Lincoln Peirce, features a collection of his "Big Nate" comic strip. "To sixth-grader Nate Wright, life is one big game. From fine-tuning his trash-talking skills on the basketball court to his cocky [attitude] in the soccer goal, Nate can be a bigger

challenge to his teammates than their opponents." The book features "Nate and his friends" mostly hapless sports encounters." (Publisher's note)

Perfit, Michael R.

Older than dirt: a wild but true history of Earth. by Don Brown & Mike Perfit. Houghton Mifflin Harcourt 2017 112 p. Color; Illustration

Grades: 4 5 6 7 8   **741.5; 551.7**

1. Origin of the Earth; 2. Earth sciences; 3. Historical geology; 4. Earth (Planet) — Origin; 5. Historical geology

9781328468277; 9780544805033, $18.99; 0544805038

LC 2016018643

This book, by Don Brown and Mike Perfit, describes how, "almost 14.5 billion years ago, it all started with a BIG BANG and what began as a cloud of gas, dust, and rock eventually took shape and bloomed into a molten sphere. Battered by asteroid collisions, ice ages, and shifting tectonic plates, our fledgling planet finally pushed forth continents.... Geological activity continues to sculpt the earth's landscape, sometimes with terrible consequences for its inhabitants." (Publisher's note)

"In 100 fact-crammed but surprisingly zippy pages, nonfiction graphic novelist extraordinaire Brown covers 14 billion years of Earth's development. From the big bang to our planet's origin to landmass formation to the appearance of life, Brown and scientific consultant Perfit provide an astonishingly comprehensive overview and manage to humanize it with witty asides from the woodchuck and worm who serve as surrogate teacher and student, as well as quick visits with important historical scientists." Booklist

Includes bibliographical references (pages 98-101)

Petersen, David

★ **Mouse** Guard: Fall 1152. Archaia Studios Press 2007 un Illustration

Grades: 5 6 7 8   **741.5; Fic**

1. Fantasy graphic novels; 2. Graphic novels; 3. Mice — Graphic novels

978-1-932386-57-8, $24.95; 1-932386-57-2

Eisner Award: Best Publication for Kids (2008)

In a medieval world populated by animals, mice have their own civilization but live in constant peril from predators. They live in hidden towns protected by the Guard, who also escort travelers between towns. Three young members of the Guard, Lieam, Saxon, and Kenzie, go in search of a missing grain merchant. They find him dead in the belly of a snake who tried to eat them; but they also find evidence that the dead merchant is a traitor. Now they need to find out to whom he was betraying the Guard and why. While this story features animals and is suitable for most readers who can handle some fighting action, there's nothing cute or Disney-esque in the art. Characters die, this is a serious story, but readers who have read Bone or the Harry Potter series can handle the action in this book. This is the first in a series.

Followed by: Mouse Guard: Winter 1152 (2009); Originally published as Mouse Guard issues #1-6.

Mouse Guard: Winter 1152. story & art by David Petersen. Archaia Studios Press 2009 un Illustration

Grades: 5 6 7 8   **741.5; Fic**

978-1-932386-74-5, $24.95; 1-932386-74-2

"In the Winter of 1152, the Mouse Guard face a food and supply shortage threatening the lives of many mouse through a cold and icy season. Some of the Guard's finest — Saxon, Kenzie, Lieam, and Sadie, led by Celanawe, the legendary Black Axe — traverse the snow-blanketed territories acting as diplomats to improve relations between the mouse cities and the Guard, and find themselves on a race against time to deliver crucial medicines." (Publisher's note)

Followed by: Mouse Guard: The black axe (2013)

Mouse Guard; 3: The Black Axe. by David Petersen. Archaia Entertainment, LLC 2013 192 p.

Grades: 5 6 7 8   **741.5; Fic**

1. Mice — Fiction; 2. Adventure fiction; 3. Fantasy fiction

1936393069; 9781936393060, $24.95

Harvey Award: Best Graphic Album of Previously Published Work (2014)

This book, by David Petersen, part of the Eisner Award-winning fantasy comic series, tells "the tale of wise oldfur and longtime Mouse Guard member Celanawe, as he fulfills the promise made to young Lieam to detail the day his paw first touched the legendary weapon, the Black Axe. The arrival of distant kin takes Celanawe on an adventure that will carry him across the sea to uncharted waters and lands, all while unraveling the legend of Farrer, the blacksmith who forged the mythical weapon." (Publisher's note)

"[N]ewcomers and fans alike will find much to explore in Petersen's finely wrought artwork, high-stakes intrigue, and derring-do tale." Booklist

Mouse Guard; volume 1: legends of the guard. Jeremy Bastian, Ted Naifeh, Alex Sheikman, et al. Archaia Entertainment 2010 144 p. Color illustration

Grades: 5 6 7 8   **741.5**

1. Mice — Fiction; 2. Short stories — Collections; 3. Adventure fiction

1932386947 (Vol. 1); 9781932386943 (Vol. 1), $19.95

Eisner Award: Best Anthology (2011)

"Petersen turns to the tested and reliable bar story as a framing device to allow other writers and artists to play in his Mouse Guard universe, where heroic mice heroes are set in a world of epic fantasy.... One night barkeep June...stages a story-telling contest. What follows are thirteen tales of danger and adventure, as protagonists contend against the predators around them and the flaws that divide mouse from mouse." (Publisher's note)

"More than just supplemental material, this book broadens Petersen's magnificently imagined miniature world and is a welcome addition for any collection that values quality, all-ages graphic novels." Booklist

Mouse Guard; volume 2: legends of the guard. Archaia Entertainment 2010 144 p. Color; Illustration

Grades: 5 6 7 8   **741.5**

1. Short stories — Collections; 2. Mice — Fiction; 3. Adventure fiction

9781936393268 (Vol. 2), $19.95; 1936393263 (Vol. 2)

Eisner Nominee: Best Publication for Kids (2014); Harvey Nominee: Best Anthology (2014); Harvey Nominee: Best Continuing or Limited Series (2014)

"Inside the June Alley Inn, located in the western mouse city of Barkstone, mice gather to tell tales, each trying to outdo the other. A competition, of sorts, begins. The rules: Every story must contain one truth, one lie, and have never been told in that tavern before. With the winner getting his bar tab cleared, fantastic stories are spun throughout the evening!" (Publisher's note)

"The art styles of the ensuing stories are all over the map, from the elegant, tapestry-worthy The Battle of the Hawk's Mouse & the Fox's Mouse, by Jeremy Bastian, to the joltingly cartoony A Mouse Named Fox, from Katie Cook. In substance, the stories are equally varied, but all champion the heroism of the noble mouse warriors and even include a couple clever takes on classics." Booklist

Petrucha, Stefan

Nancy Drew, Girl Detective #1: The Demon of River Heights. NBM/Papercutz 2005 un Illustration

Grades: 4 5 6 7 8 9   **741.5; Fic**

1. Adventure graphic novels; 2. Graphic novels; 3. Mystery graphic novels

1-59707-004-1, $12.95; 1-59707-000-9, $7.95

Everyone's favorite girl detective makes her graphic novel debut. Nancy also makes her debut in a horror film concerning a monstrous River Heights urban legend " but is it really an urban legend, or does the River Heights Demon truly exist? And will Nancy, Bess, and George live long enough to find out? This graphic novel series updates Nancy and her friends to the twenty-first century, but she's still a klutz.

Courtesy of NBM Publishing

Peyo

The **purple** smurfs. by Yvan Delporte and Peyo. Papercutz 2010 55p. Color; Illustration
Grades: 1 2 3 4   **741.5**
1. Smurfs (Fictional characters) — Comic books, strips, etc.; 2. Magic — Comic books, strips, etc.
1-59707-206-0; 978-1-59707-206-9, $5.99; 978-1-59707-207-6, $10.99; 1-59707-207-9

"[T]his previously untranslated version of the [Smurfs'] first solo collection (1963) offers three tales: A fly's contagious bite turns nearly all of the Smurfs into aggressive purple grunters...; one Smurf's determination to fly results in multiple crashes and calamities; another's desire to find peace and quiet away from Smurf Village runs afoul of a mosquito and other hazards. Replete with pratfalls, butt-biting and like slapstick, the neatly squared-off comic-strip-style panels look small at first glance, but coated paper and high production values make both the dialogue and the brightly colored art easy to read." (Kirkus Reviews)

Courtesy of NBM Publishing

Translated from the French; Other titles in this series are: The Smurfs and the magic flute (2010); The Smurf king (2010); The Smurfette (2011); The Smurfs and the egg (2011); The Smurfs and the howlibird (2011); Astrosmurf (2011); The smurf apprentice (2011); Gargamel and the Smurfs (2011); The return of the Smurfette (2012); The Smurf Olympics (2012); Smurf vs. Smurf (2012); Smurf soup (2012); The baby Smurf (2013); The Smurflings (2013); The Aerosmurf (2013); The Smurfs Christmas (2013)

The **Smurfs** anthology; Vol. 1. Peyo. Papercutz 2013 190 p. Color illustration (The Smurfs graphic novels)
Grades: 4 5 6 7 8 9 10 11 12 Adult
741.5
1. Comic books, strips, etc.
1597074179; 9781597074179, $19.99

"Newly remastered and presented in original publication order, along with a Smurfy collection of historical notes and photographs, the stories in this volume," by Belgian comics artist Peyo, "introduce us to Papa Smurf, Gargamel, Smurfette, and the rest of the village." (Publisher's note)

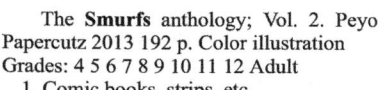
Courtesy of NBM Publishing

The **Smurfs** anthology; Vol. 2. Peyo. Papercutz 2013 192 p. Color illustration
Grades: 4 5 6 7 8 9 10 11 12 Adult   **741.5**
1. Comic books, strips, etc.

1597074454; 9781597074452, $19.99

"Newly remastered and presented in original publication order, along with a Smurfy collection of historical notes and photographs, this volume," by Belgian comics artist Peyo, "introduces us to Smurfette and features a 'Johan and Peewit' story never before seen in the U.S." (Publisher's note)

"[A] delightful and instructive mix of Peyo's colorful tales. A series of essays interspersed throughout the collection provides social and historical context for the cartoons." Booklist

Translated from the French

Courtesy of NBM Publishing

Phelan, Matt

★ **Bluffton:** my summers with Buster Keaton. written and illustrated by Matt Phelan. Candlewick Press 2013 240 p. Color; Illustration
Grades: 3 4 5 6
741.5; Fic
1. Vaudeville — Fiction; 2. Keaton, Buster
076365079X; 9780763650797, $22.99
LC 2012947260

In this graphic novel by Matt Phelan, set "in the summer of 1908, in Muskegon, Michigan, a visiting troupe of vaudeville performers is about the most exciting thing since baseball. Henry has a few months to ogle...a slapstick actor his own age named Buster Keaton. Henry longs to learn to take a fall like Buster...but Buster just wants to play ball with Henry and his friends." (Publisher's note)

BLUFFTON. Copyright © 2013 by Matt Phelan. Reproduced by permission of the publisher, Candlewick Press, Somerville, MA

"Historical detail, a rich sense of place, expert pacing — Phelan...keeps all the plates in the air in this fictionalized recreation of the boyhood summers of Buster Keaton. In lightly sketched, gently tinted watercolor panels, Phelan conveys the excitement a troupe of summering vaudeville actors brings to sleepy Bluffton." Pub Wkly

★ **Snow** White: A Graphic Novel. by Matt Phelan. Candlewick Press 2016 216 p. Illustration; Color
Grades: 4 5 6 7 8
741.5; Fic
1. New York (N.Y.) — Fiction; 2. Depressions — 1929 — Fiction
0763672335; 9780763672331, $19.99

This graphic novel, by Matt Phelan, "delivers a darkly stylized noir Snow White set against the backdrop of Depression-era Manhattan. The scene: New York City.... Enter a cast of familiar characters: a young girl, Samantha White, returning after being sent away by her cruel stepmother, the Queen of the Follies, years earlier; her father, the King of Wall Street, who survives the stock market crash only to suffer a strange and sudden death; [and] seven street urchins." (Publisher's note)

SNOW WHITE. Copyright © 2016 by Matt Phelan. Reproduced by permission of the publisher, Candlewick Press, Somerville, MA.

"With a keen historical slant, a bit of action and intrigue, high visual interest, and the fairy-tale leaning, this will awe a wide readership. Brilliant." Kirkus

★ The **storm** in the barn. Candlewick Press 2009 201p. Illustration
Grades: 4 5 6 7 8 9
741.5; Fic
1. Adventure graphic novels; 2. Dust storms — Graphic novels; 3. Graphic novels; 4. Kansas — Graphic novels; 5. Monsters — Graphic novels; 6. United States — History — 1933-1945 — Graphic novels
978-0-7636-3618-0, $24.99;
0-7636-3618-5; 978-0-7636-5290-6 (pa), $14.99; 0-7636-5290-3 (pa)

THE STORM IN THE BARN.
Copyright © 2009 by Matt Phelan.
Reproduced by permission of the publisher, Candlewick Press, Somerville, MA.

In Kansas of 1937, the land has been in the grip of the Dust Bowl for four years, and eleven-year-old Jack Carter has seen his family worn down by it. But the day Jack outruns a dust storm all the way home from town, he glimpses something odd in the abandoned Talbot barn, and he tries to find the courage to go into the barn and confront what is there.

"Children can read this as a work of historical fiction, a piece of folklore, a scary story, a graphic novel, or all four. Written with simple, direct language, it — s an almost wordless book: the illustrations" shadowy grays and blurry lines eloquently depict the haze of the dust. A complex but accessible and fascinating book." SLJ

Phillips, Craig
Giants, trolls, witches, beasts: ten tales from the deep, dark woods. Craig Phillips, with an introduction by Carole Wilkinson. Allen & Unwin 2018 192 p. Illustration
Grades: 2 3 4 5
741.5; 398.2
1. Folklore; 2. Tall tales — Juvenile literature
1760113263; 9781760113261, $19.99

In this graphic novel, by Craig Phillips, with an introduction by Carole Wilkinson, "a cobbler girl tricks the Wawel Dragon, after all the king's knights fail. The Polar Bear King loses his skin. Momotaro, born from a peach, defies the ogres everyone else is too scared to face. Snow White and Rose Red make friends with a bear. From Poland to Iceland, Japan to Germany, these 10 fairytales from across the globe re-told as comics will have you enthralled." (Publisher's note)

"Phillips retells 10 folktales from Japan, the United States, and several Eastern and Western European countries, with colorful, captivating, and action-packed illustrations. Children whose folktale repertoire is limited only to those depicted on film and screen will find the selections fresh and new." SLJ

Pien, Lark
★ **Long** Tail Kitty. by Lark Pien. Blue Apple Books 2009 51 p. Color illustration
Grades: 1 2 3 4
741.5
1. Cats — Fiction; 2. Neighborhoods — Fiction; 3. Humorous graphic novels
9781934706442, $17.99; 2008042448

"Long Tail Kitty narrates five episodes of his daily life. First he introduces his house and his town, including landmarks from each of his tales. He picks flowers, finds they can talk and plays chase with a bee. In winter he slides on the ice and has cocoa with Good Tall Mouse. He hosts a food fest with friends and refrains from eating all the Choco Crispy Doggy Discs. Finally, he spends an activity-filled day with buddies from outer space." (Kirkus Reviews)

"The volume's appeal lies in the tidy, thoughtfully shaded panels and the cast's playful banter and witty barbs." Horn Book

Pilkey, Dav
★ **Dog** Man. Dav Pilkey. Graphix 2016 240 p. Color; Illustration (Dog Man)
Grades: 2 3 4
741.5; Fic
1. Human-animal relationships — Fiction; 2. Working dogs — Fiction; 3. Dogs — Fiction
9780545581608, $9.99; 9780545581639

LC 2016932063

"George and Harold have created a new hero who digs into deception, claws after crooks, and rolls over robbers. When Greg the police dog and his cop companion are injured on the job, a life-saving surgery changes the course of history.... With the head of a dog and the body of a human, this heroic hound has a real nose for justice. But can he resist the call of the wild to answer the call of duty?" (Publisher's note)

"From the doodle-scratch art and jumbled panel borders to crossed-out words with simulated grammar and spelling lapses to the generous helpings of potty humor, the book feels like a frantic message of delirious imagination from one child to another." Booklist

Other titles about Dog Man are: Dog Man unleashed (2016); A tale of two kittens (2017); Dog Man and Cat King (2017)

Dog Man unleashed. Dav Pilkey. Graphix 2017 224 p. Color; Illustration
Grades: 2 3 4
741.5; Fic
1. Police — Graphic novels; 2. Adventure fiction — Juvenile fiction; 3. Dogs — Graphic novels
9780545935203, $9.99; 9780545935432

LC 2016936340

In this graphic novel in the Dog Man series, by Dav Pilkey, "Dog Man, the newest hero from the creator of Captain Underpants, is still learning a few tricks of the trade. Petey the cat is out of the bag, and his criminal curiosity is taking the city by storm. Something fishy is going on! Can Dog Man unleash justice on this ruffian in time to save the city, or will Petey get away with the purr-fect crime?" (Publisher's note)

"The frenetic plot, full of treasure chests, mountain escapes, jailbreaks, magic ploys, potty humor, and over-the-top reactions, will have magnetic appeal for kids." Booklist

Pittman, Eddie
Red's Planet; Book 1: A World Away from Home. by Eddie Pittman. Amulet Books 2016 192 p. Color; Illustration
Grades: 3 4 5 6
741.5; Fic
1. Extraterrestrial beings — Juvenile fiction; 2. Science fiction — Graphic novels; 3. Kidnapping — Juvenile fiction; 4. Outer space — Juvenile fiction
9781419719080; 1419719076; 9781419719073, $19.95

This book, by Eddie Pittman, is "an intergalactic graphic novel fantasy.... Meet Red, a quirky, headstrong 10-year-old who longs to live in her own perfect paradise far away from her annoying foster family. But when a UFO mistakenly kidnaps her, Red finds herself farther away than she could have possibly imagined — across the galaxy and aboard an enormous spaceship owned by the Aquilari, an ancient creature with a taste for rare and unusual treasures." (Publisher's note)

"Red, a precocious 10-year-old brimming with a likable mix of sass and joie de vivre, is portrayed in exceptionally clear and brightly wrought panels, with a sweeping cinematic lens that lends equal attention to action and expression." Kirkus

Another title in this series is: Friends and Foes (2017)

Plumeri, Arnaud

Dinosaurs 2: Bite of the Allosaurus. Bloz, art; Arnaud Plumeri, story; Maëla Cosson, colorist; Nanette McGuinness, translation. Papercutz 2014 56 p. Color; Illustration
Grades: 2 3 4 5   **567.9; 741.5**
1. Paleontologists — Comic books, strips, etc.; 2. Graphic novels; 3. Dinosaurs — Juvenile literature
1597075159; 9781597075152, $10.99

"When you're a dinosaur, there's only one thing to fear: the dinosaurs that are bigger than YOU! In the latest chapter of this thunderously funny series we find out how the giants among giants lived millions of years ago." (Publisher's note)

"For the sheer number of dinosaur names dropped, Plumeri and Bloz' series is impressive, but they deserve extra kudos for peppering the facts with jokey, sometimes crass visual humor, ensuring that the science goes down easy." Booklist
Translated from the French

Dinosaurs; 1: In the Beginning. Arnaud Plumeri, illustrated by Bloz. Papercutz 2014 56 p. Color; Illustration
Grades: 2 3 4 5   **741.5; 567.9**
1. Paleontology — Juvenile literature; 2. Dinosaurs — Juvenile literature
159707490X; 9781597074902, $10.99

In this book, by Arnaud Plumeri and illustrated by Bloz, "kid dinos show us what their lives were like in short, funny, teeth-gnashing bursts of prehistoric mayhem. DINOSAURS is your guided tour through the rough-and-tumble world of the mightiest beasts to ever walk the earth!" (Publisher's note)

"Each brief vignette is a winning combination of colorful dinosaurs, chuckle-worthy jokes, paleontology facts, and well-explained terminology." Booklist
Originally published in France; Other titles in this series are:Bite of the Albertosaurus;Jurassic smarts

Poe, Marshall

Turning points: a house divided. Aladdin Paperbacks 2008 122p. Illustration
Grades: 3 4 5 6 7 8   **741.5; Fic**
1. Abolitionists — Graphic novels; 2. Graphic novels; 3. United States — History — 1815-1861 — Graphic novels
978-1-4169-5057-8, $8.99

LC 2008-929317
Owen and Amos Bennington's abolitionist parents are killed in 1856, and the brothers vow to continue their parents' quest to end slavery. However, younger brother Amos thinks the abolitionists aren't doing enough, while Owen works for a peaceful, political solution. When they move to Kansas, things don't go as planned, as proslavery people use violence to get their way. When Owen wants to move back East, Amos runs away and joins John Brown's forces, who fight against slavery with force. Owen moves to Illinois and works for Abraham Lincoln. Amos finally realizes that Brown's way is wrong and leaves just before the attempted takeover of Harper's Ferry; he makes his way across the land slowly, hoping against hope that he can find Owen again. This fictional story highlights the years leading up to the Civil War, showing a private, personal side of Lincoln and letting younger readers see the kinds of divisions suffered by many families as they debated and argued the cause of abolition or slavery, and of political action or force to end slavery.

Turning Points: Little Rock nine. Simon & Schuster/Aladdin Paperbacks 2008 122p. Illustration
Grades: 3 4 5 6 7 8 9   **741.5; Fic**

1. African Americans — Civil rights — Graphic novels; 2. African Americans — Education — Graphic novels; 3. Graphic novels; 4. United States — History — 1953-1961 — Graphic novels
978-1-4169-5066-0, $7.99

LC 2007-937918
Sixteen-year-old William McNally and fifteen-year-old Thomas Johnson both live in Little Rock, Arkansas, in the summer of 1957. They both love baseball and teasing their little sisters. There's just one big difference: William is white, and Thomas, the son of the McNally family's maid, is black. After the U.S. Supreme Court rules in favor of desegregating public schools, Little Rock Central High School prepares to enroll its first nine African-American students, and William and Thomas are caught in the middle of a storm. William's family has divided over the issue, and Thomas' parents don't want him to get hurt and forbid him to try to enter the school. The book portrays the issues of the time and the personal beliefs of both sides to let readers see what it was like back then. William, Thomas, and their families are fictional, but what happened at Little Rock Central High School is an important part of American history.

Preciado, Tony

Super grammar: learn grammar with superheroes. written by Tony Preciado; illustrated by Rhode Montijo; colored by Jenny Hansen; inked by Joe To. Scholastic 2012 176 p. Color illustration (Illustrating the point)
Grades: 4 5 6 7 8   **428**
1. English language — Grammar — Juvenile literature; 2. Superheroes — Juvenile fiction; 3. English language — Grammar — Juvenile fiction
0545425158; 9780545425155, $8.99

LC 2012289091
In this book by Tony Preciado, illustrated by Rhode Montijo, "all of the major elements of grammar...[are] personified with superhero or super villain identities.... You'll meet the vibrant super heroine The Adverb, and you'll learn about her awesome ability to modify verbs and other adverbs.... You'll actually meet the sinister twin brothers, Double Negative, and you'll learn how to avoid being tricked into falling for their double talk." (Publisher's note)

Priddy, Joel

The **gift** of the Magi. It Books/HarperCollins 2009 un Illustration
Grades: 5 6 7 8 9 10 11 12 Adult   **741.5; Fic**
1. Authors; 2. Christmas — Graphic novels; 3. Gifts — Graphic novels; 4. Graphic novels; 5. Short story writers; 6. Henry, O., 1862-1910 — Adaptations
978-0-06-178239-8, $14.99

Della and Jim are a young married couple, struggling to make ends meet when Jim's pay has been cut. It's Christmas time, but despite squeezing every penny, Della has managed to save only a little bit of money, and it's not enough to buy Jim a good present. He owns a gold pocket watch, and Della wants to buy him a chain for it. She has only one thing of value that she can sell her beautiful, long, long hair. Out of her love for Jim, Della sacrifices her hair. And, of course, Jim has sacrificed his gold pocket watch in order to buy beautiful hair combs for Della's gorgeous hair. As O. Henry says, they "most unwisely sacrificed for each other the greatest treasures of their house," but also that "of all who give gifts these two were the wisest." Joel Priddy's adaptation of this classic story uses black and white illustrations except when Della lets down her hair to consider her one treasure. He preserves much of O. Henry's original prose, which means that younger readers will have to look up a lot of words to understand the story. This book is suitable for younger readers but will also appeal to teens and adults.

Reed, M. K.

Dinosaurs: fossils and feathers. by MK Reed, illustrated by Joe Flood. First Second 2016 117 p. Color; Illustration

Grades: 4 5 6 7 8   741.5; 567.9

1. Dinosaurs — Juvenile literature; 2. Paleontology — Juvenile literature

9781626727281, $60; 9781626721449, $19.99; 1626721432; 9781626721432, $9.99; 1626721440

LC 2016012765

In this graphic novel by MK Reed, illustrated by Joe Flood, published as part of the Science Comics series, "learn all about the history of paleontology! This fascinating look at dinosaur science covers the last 150 years of dinosaur hunting, and illuminates how our ideas about dinosaurs have changed — and continue to change." (Publisher's note)

"There's some humor along with a solid presentation of facts, and the clean design helps makes the information accessible; the somewhat advanced content makes the book most appropriate for upper-elementary-age readers." Horn Book

Includes bibliographical references.

Renier, Aaron

★ The **unsinkable** Walker Bean. written and illustrated by Aaron Renier; colored by Alec Longstreth. First Second 2010 191p. Illustration

Grades: 5 6 7 8   741.5; Fic

1. Adventure stories; 2. Sea stories

978-1-59643-453-0 (pa), $13.99; 1-59643-453-8 (pa)

"Walker Bean never wanted to be a high-seas pirate waging a pitched battle against the forces of the deep. It just worked out that way. Mild, meek, and a little geeky, Walker is always happiest in his grandfather's workshop, messing around with his inventions. But when his beloved grandfather is struck by an ancient curse, it falls on Walker to return an accursed pearl skull to the witches who created it—and his path will be strewn with pirates, magical machines, ancient lore, and deadly peril." (Publisher's note)

Followed by: The unsinkable Walker Bean and the knights of the waxing moon (2018)

Renner, Benjamin

★ The **big** bad fox. Benjamin Renner; English translation by Joe Johnson. First Second 2017 187 p. Color; Illustration

Grades: 3 4 5 6 7   741.5/973; Fic

1. Foxes — Fiction; 2. Chickens — Comic books, strips, etc.; 3. Chickens — Fiction; 4. Foxes — Comic books, strips, etc.; 5. Foxes — Fiction; 6. Parenting — Fiction

9781626723313, $15.99; 1626723311, $15.99

LC 2016945555

In this book, by Benjamin Renner, "fox dreams of being the terror of the barnyard. But no one is intimidated by him, least of all the hens — when he picks a fight with one, he always ends up on the losing end. Even the wolf, the most fearsome beast of the forest, can't teach him how to be a proper predator. It looks like the fox will have to spend the rest of his life eating turnips." (Publisher's note)

Originally published as Le grand méchant renard by Éditions Delcourt in 2015.

Riess, Natalie

Space battle lunchtime; Volume 1: lights, camera, snacktion!. Natalie Riess; [edited by] Robin Herrera. Oni Press 2016 120 p. Color; Illustration

Grades: 3 4 5 6 7   741.5; Fic

1. Reality television programs — Juvenile fiction

1620103133; 9781620103135, $12.99

LC 2016937918

"Earth baker Peony gets the deal of a lifetime when she agrees to be a contestant on the Universe's hottest reality TV show, Space Battle Lunchtime! But that was before she knew that it shoots on location... on a spaceship... and her alien competitors don't play nice! Does Peony really have what it takes to be the best cook in the Galaxy? Tune in and find out!" (Publisher's note)

Courtesy of Oni Press

"An odd yet well-spun mixture of food fiction and space tales, with a dash of pop culture, this unusual charmer defies genre conventions and seems to revel in its own sheer individuality and campy wonder." Kirkus

Another title in this series is: A recipe for disaster (2017)

Space battle lunchtime; Volume two: A recipe for disaster. by Natalie Riess. Oni Press 2017 120 p. Color; Illustration

Grades: 3 4 5 6 7

741.5; Fic

1. Bakers and bakeries — Comic books, strips, etc.; 2. Extraterrestrial beings — Comic books, strips, etc.

9781620104040, $12.99; 1620104040

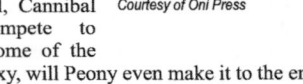

Courtesy of Oni Press

"It's almost time for the season finale of Space Battle Lunchtime, and finalist Peony...is nowhere to be found!...[S]he's been kidnapped and taken to the set of Space Battle Lunchtime's biggest rival, Cannibal Coliseum, where chefs compete to cook...each other. Up against some of the most dangerous aliens in the galaxy, will Peony even make it to the end of the show? Stay tuned!" (Publisher's note)

"Given that there's a relative dearth of LGBTQ characters in kids' comics, this is a welcome addition to a growing wave of better representation. Riess' illustrations are colorful and bubbly, with hints of manga influence that goes well with the lively space adventure." Booklist

Riordan, Rick

Percy Jackson & the Olympians, book one: the lightning thief: the graphic novel. adapted by Robert Venditti; art by Attila Futaki; color by José Villarrubia; layouts by Orpheus Collar; lettering by Chris Dickey. Hyperion Books for Children 2010 un Illustration

Grades: 5 6 7 8 9 10   **741.5; Fic**

1. Adventure graphic novels; 2. Fantasy graphic novels; 3. Graphic novels; 4. Greek mythology — Graphic novels

978-1-4231-1696-7, $19.99; 978-1-4321-1710-0 (pa), $9.99

Twelve-year-old Percy Jackson has had a hard time in school, but when a teacher transforms into a Fury and tries to kill him during a field trip to the museum, his life becomes even more complicated. He learns that he is the son of one of the Greek gods and a human woman, and then he learns that he should never have been born, and that the gods think he has stolen Zeus's master lightning bolt. Percy, his best friend Grover (a satyr), and Annabeth, daughter of Athena, have ten days to recover the lightning bolt and prevent all-out war among the Olympians. This graphic novel adapts Riordan's novel, NOT the movie. Futaki makes the water action look great in an adaptation that should make the book fans happy.

The **red** pyramid: the graphic novel. Rick Riordan; adapted by Orpheus Collar; lettered by Jared Fletcher. Disney/Hyperion Books 2012 un Color; Illustration (The Kane chronicles)

Grades: 4 5 6 7 8 9   741.5

1. Egyptian mythology — Fiction; 2. Magic — Fiction; 3. Brothers and sisters — Fiction
1423150694; 1423150686; 9781423150695, $12.99; 9781423150688, $21.99

LC 2012007905

"Since their mother's death, Sadie and Carter have become near-strangers. While Sadie has lived with her grandparents in London, Carter has traveled the world with their father, the famed Egyptologist Dr. Julius Kane. One night, Dr. Kane brings the siblings to the British Museum, where he hopes to set things right for his family. Instead, he unleashes the Egyptian god Set, who banishes him to oblivion and forces the children to flee for their lives." (Publisher's note)

"Out of necessity, much of the dialogue is dedicated to explaining actions and events, but a constant stream of humor prevents the reader from getting bogged down by logistics. The colorful artwork has an almost painting-like quality,...and some clever visual jokes and thoughtful use of panels make good use of the format." VOYA

Rioux, Jo-Anne

The **golden** twine; Book 1. Jo Rioux. Kids Can Press 2012 111 p. Color illustration

Grades: 5 6 7 8
741.5/971; 741.5; Fic
1. Paranormal fiction; 2. Magic — Fiction; 3. Dragons — Fiction; 4. Monsters — Fiction
1554536367; 9781554536368, $17.95; 9781554536375

Courtesy of Kids Can Press

In this book by author Jo Rioux, "parentless young storyteller Suri [buys a dragon tooth that brings her luck] ...The ball of magical golden string that she finds...belongs to a trio of vicious tiger creatures called 'caitsiths' who use the string to masquerade as humans and...want it back... Suri [also] achieves her ...desire to become a monster tamer when she meets Byron, a humongous if overly friendly dog, and the surly 500-year-old imp Caglio who...created him." (Kirkus)

Robbins, Trina

★ The **drained** brains caper. [by] Trina Robbins and Tyler Page. Graphic Universe 2010 64p. Illustration (Chicagoland Detective Agency)
Grades: 4 5 6 7
Fic; 741; 741.5
1. Brainwashing — Fiction; 2. Graphic novels; 3. Humorous graphic novels; 4. Japanese Americans — Graphic novels; 5. Mystery graphic novels; 6. Schools — Graphic novels
978-0-7613-4601-2 (lib bdg), $27.97; 0-7613-4601-5 (lib bdg);
978-0-7613-5635-6 (pa), $6.95; 0-7613-5635-5 (pa)

Courtesy of Lerner Publishing Group

LC 2009-32620

Required to attend summer school after moving to Chicagoland, thirteen-year-old manga-love Megan Yamamura needs help from twelve-year-old computer genius Raf Hernandez to escape the maniacal principal's mind control experiment.

This tells "an entertaining story.... Page's black-and-white cartooning has a loose manga slant, with peppy goofiness popping out from stippled screen tones." Booklist

Other titles in this series are: The Maltese mummy (2011);Night of the living dogs (2012);The big flush (2012);The bark in space (2013);A midterm night's scheme (2014)

Roberts, Steven

Henry Ford. by Steven Roberts. PowerKids Press 2013 24 p. (Jr. graphic American inventors)
Grades: 3 4 5 6   **338.7/629222092; 92**
1. Automobile industry and trade — United States — Biography; 2. Industrialists — United States — Biography; 3. Ford, Henry, 1863-1947; 4. Inventors
147770079X; 9781477700792, $25.25; 9781477701430; 9781477701447

LC 2012020485

This book, by Steven Roberts, presents a biography of inventor Henry Ford. "It looks at the man who perfected the mass market automobile. From a young age Ford tinkered with farm machines and fixed neighbors' watches. That led to jobs working with steam engines and then, under the employment of Thomas Edison, the internal combustion engine. Inspired by the work flow of other factories, Ford created the Model T,and in just a few years, he was creating a million cars per year." (Booklist)
Includes index.

Robert Fulton. by Steven Roberts. PowerKids Press 2013 24 p.
Grades: 3 4 5 6   **92**
1. Inventors — United States — Biography; 2. Marine engineers — United States — Biography; 3. Steamboats; 4. Fulton, Robert, 1765-1815
1477700773; 9781477700778, $25.25; 9781477701393; 9781477701409

LC 2012020630

In this graphic novel by Steven Roberts "readers will [learn] more about [Robert] Fulton and his contributions to American society through easy to follow text and vibrant illustrations." It notes that "Robert Fulton didn t actually invent what he is most commonly associated with, yet Fulton s innovations on the steamboat changed America s trade and travel in a progressive way." (Publisher's note)
Includes bibliographical references (p. 24) and index

Rodolphe

Scrooge: A Christmas Carol & A Remembrance of Mugby. Adapted by Rodolphe & Estelle Meyrand. Papercutz 2012 96 p. Color illustration
Grades: 3 4 5 6
Fic; 741.5/973
1. Christmas — Fiction; 2. Ghosts — Fiction; 3. England — Fiction; 4. Ghost stories; 5. Supernatural — Fiction
1597073458; 1597073466; 9781597073455, $11.99; 9781597073462, $15.00

Courtesy of NBM Publishing

This book, part of the Classics Illustrated Deluxe series, presents a graphic adaptation of the Charles Dickens stories "A Christmas Carol" and "Mugby Junction." In "A Christmas Carol," miser Ebenezer Scrooge is "visited by three spirits who will show him the way to change" on Christmas Eve. (Masterplots) "Mugby Junction" also features elements of the supernatural and a protagonist to whom his future is revealed." (Publisher's note)

Rogers, Gregory

Midsummer knight. Roaring Brook Press 2007 un Illustration

Grades: K 1 2 3 4 5   **741.5**

1. Bears — Fiction; 2. Fairies — Fiction; 3. Heroes and heroines — Fiction; 4. Stories without words

978-1-59643-183-6, $16.95; 1-59643-183-0

LC 2006-51013

A bear is rescued by a fairy in an enchanted wood and agrees to return the favor by leading the battle against a usurper who has imprisoned the king and queen, along with their loyal subjects, in the dungeon of their castle

"This is another wordless adventure, depicted in colorful, comics-style panels that will delight young readers." Booklist

First published in Australia 2006; Companion volume to: The boy, the bear, the baron, the bard (2004)

Rol, Ruud van der

The **search**. [by] Eric Heuvel, Ruud van der Rol [and] Lies Schippers; [English translation by Lorraine T. Miller]. Farrar, Straus and Giroux 2009 61p. Illustration

Grades: 5 6 7 8 9   **741.5; Fic**

1. Grandmothers — Fiction; 2. Graphic novels; 3. Holocaust survivors — Fiction; 4. Holocaust, 1933-1945 — Graphic novels; 5. Jews — Netherlands — Fiction

978-0-374-36517-2, $18.99; 978-0-374-46455-4 (pa), $9.99

LC 2009-13603

After recounting her experience as a Jewish girl living in Amsterdam during the Holocaust, Esther, helped by her grandson, embarks on a search to discover what happened to her parents before they died in a concentration camp.

Esther, her grandson Daniel, and her friend Helena's grandson Jeroen visit the Dutch farm where Esther hid during the Nazi occupation of the Netherlands during World War II. She tells her story, of how she managed to escape the Nazi roundup of Jews, but how her family died in a concentration camp. Daniel helps her find an old friend from the farm, now living in Israel, and he tells her what happened to her family in Auschwitz. The book depicts some of the horrendous, horrible things that happened but does it without graphic violence or gore.

Roman, Dave

Astronaut Academy: Zero gravity. First Second Books 2011 185p. Illustration

Grades: 4 5 6 7 8   **741; 741.5; Fic**

1. Graphic novels; 2. Humorous graphic novels; 3. School life — Graphic novels; 4. Science fiction graphic novels

9781596436206, $9.99; 9781596437562, $16.99

LC 2010-941434

Hakata Soy has been the leader of a futuristic superhero team, but he has given that up and just wants to be a normal student at Astronaut Academy, a school on a space station, where students take such courses as anti-gravity gymnastics and fire-throwing. Other students include Doug Hiro, who always wears his space helmet, rich girl Maribelle Mellonbelly, Miyumi San (Maribelle's rival), and egotistical Billy Lee. Hakata Soy has some trouble adjusting to school life, and things get much worse when the villainous Gotcha Birds steal a robotic twin to Hakata Soy and reprogram it to kill him. The comics originally appeared as web comics, then as mini comics that Roman took to various comic cons; this is the first trade book collection of the stories. Middle grade students, boys and girls, will enjoy this book, which is full of humor and action with little actual violence.

"Students like the introspective Hakata Soy, the space-gymnastics-obsessed Doug Hiro, and the snooty rich girl Mirabelle Mellonbelly meet up at Astronaut Academy, a middle school where the zany mixes with the postmodern.... Silliness is high on the agenda, aided by minimal, cartoonish art that plays on manga tropes but also manages to build character into the simple lines of a face.... This is one for readers looking for more involved and complex comedy than a cursory glance at the images might lead one to expect." Booklist

Followed by: Astronaut academy: Re-entry (2013)

Roques, Dominique

Anna Banana and the chocolate explosion. by Dominique Roques; illustrated by Alexis Dormal. First Second 2015 28 p. Color; Illustration

Grades: PreK K 1 2   **741.5; E**

1. Baking — Fiction; 2. Toys — Fiction

1626720207; 9781626720206

LC 2014047289

Eisner Nominee: Best Publication for Early Readers (2016)

"Anna and her six extremely animate toy animals are back — this time, for an ultimately collaborative adventure in the kitchen.... When Anna offers a lesson on baking a chocolate cake, everyone's in.... Fuzzball's untutored way with utensils and the batter — 'SPLAT! SPLAT! SPLAT!' — gives rise to a wayward swing, an airborne, ricocheting bowl, and a stupendous detonation of chocolate that spares no critter or surface." (Kirkus Reviews)

Originally published: Paris : Dargaud, 2012 as Déluge de chocolat.

Rosca, Madeleine

Hollow Fields Omnibus collection. Seven Seas Entertainment 2009 un Illustration

Grades: 5 6 7 8 9 10   **741.5; Fic**

1. Adventure graphic novels; 2. Graphic novels; 3. Science fiction graphic novels

978-1-934876-72-5, $14.99

Rosca is an Australian global manga creator who won one of the inaugural International Manga Awards ¿Shorei¿ awards given by the Japanese government in 2007.

Lucy Snow was supposed to start school at a nice elementary school in town, but she manages to lose her way in a forest and finds herself at Miss Weaver's Academy for the Scientifically Gifted and Ethically Unfettered a school for archvillains in training. Lucy's fellow students are all learning how to be mad scientists and evil geniuses, with classes such as Live Taxidermy, Cross-Species Body-Part Transplantation, and Killer Robot Construction. Hollow Fields, as the school is also called, also has a practice guaranteed to make everyone compete to do well: the student with the lowest grades at the end of the week is sent to the windmill for detention, and thus far no student has ever returned. Miss Weaver has experimented on herself, as have all the Engineers who teach; what the reader learns is that they need new, young blood to keep their stitched-together bodies going, for they are all more than a hundred years old. Befriended by a talking box that calls itself Doctor Bleak, Lucy struggles to hold her own in her classes, despite her innate niceness. She decides she needs to discover just what goes on in the windmill, and how she can make things right. The book includes some mild violence.

Rosenstiehl, Agnes

★ **Silly** Lilly and the four seasons. Toon Books 2008 36p. Illustration

Grades: PreK K 1   **741; 741.5**

1. Graphic novels; 2. Humorous graphic novels; 3. Seasons — Graphic novels

978-0-9799238-1-4, $12.95; 0-9799238-1-6

"Rosenstiehl follows Lilly...as she undertakes simple, familiar activities through the seasons.... Lilly is bold and engaging.... The text is very brief,...the colors are warm and bright, and the panels are large enough to draw in children new to books and reading." Booklist

Rubin, Sean
   Bolivar. by Sean Rubin. Archaia, a division of Boom Entertainment 2017 224 p. Color; Illustration
Grades: 3 4 5 6   741.5; Fic
   1. Boys — Fiction; 2. Dinosaurs — Fiction
   1684150698; 9781684150694, $29.99
   In this book, by Sean Rubin, "Sybil knows that there is something off about her next door neighbor, but she can't seem to get anyone to believe her. Everyone is so busy going about their days in the busy streets of New York City that they don't notice Bolivar. They don't notice his odd height, his tiny arms, or his long tail. No one but Sybil sees that Bolivar is a dinosaur." (Publisher's note)
   "The text, delivered in bite-size speech bubbles and compact sentences, crackles with sly humor. And Rubin's sweeping panoramas (from city blocks to the subway) and idiosyncratic details-all rendered in rich hues and lively cross-hatching-never fail to infuse the everyday with a dash of quiet magic." Booklist

Ruiz, Emilio
   Waluk. by Emilio Ruiz; illustrated by Ana Miralles; translated and adapted by Dan Oliverio. Graphic Universe 2013 52 p.
Grades: 3 4 5 6
741.5; Fic
   1. Bears — Fiction; 2. Graphic novels; 3. Polar bear — Fiction; 4. Tundras — Fiction; 5. Friendship — Fiction
   1467715980; 1467716065; 9781467715980, $26.60; 9781467716062, $7.95

Courtesy of Lerner Publishing Group

                                            LC 2012047787
   "Young Waluk is all alone. His mother has abandoned him, as is the way of polar bears, and now he must fend for himself. But he doesn't know much about the world — and unfortunately, his Arctic world is changing quickly. The ice is melting, and food is hard to find." (Publisher's note)
   "Marrying exemplary sequential storytelling, mythology, and science and enhanced through respectful anthropomorphizing, Waluk takes readers into a realistic world of polar bears endangered by climate change." Booklist
   Originally published in Spanish in Bilbao, Spain, by Astiberri, in 2011, under the title: Wáluk.

Runton, Andy
   ★ **Owly** Vol. 2: Just a Little Blue. Top Shelf Productions 2005 127p. Illustration
Grades: K 1 2 3 4 5 6 7 8 9 10 11 12 Adult   741.5; Fic
   1. Friendship — Graphic novels; 2. Graphic novels; 3. Stories without words — Graphic novels
   1-891830-64-3, $10
   Owly is a kind, yet lonely, little owl who's always on the search for new friends and adventure. Owly learns that sometimes you have to make sacrifices and work at things that are important, especially friendship. He and Wormy try to help a stubborn bluebird by building a new home, but the bluebird rejects it and them.

   ★ **Owly** Vol. 3: Flying Lessons. Top Shelf Productions 2005 143p. Illustration
Grades: K 1 2 3 4 5 6 7 8 9 10 11 12 Adult   741.5; Fic
   1. Friendship — Graphic novels; 2. Graphic novels; 3. Stories without words — Graphic novels

1-891830-76-7, $10
   Owly figures out why he can't fly (he failed his childhood flying lessons), and helps another forest creature with his own flying problems. The flying squirrel is frightened by Owly, for he knows owls are hunters, but Owly isn't like that. How can he convince the squirrel he just wants to be friends?

   ★ **Owly** vol. 4: a time to be brave. Top Shelf Productions 2007 132p. Illustration
Grades: K 1 2 3 4 5 6 7 8 9 10 11 12 Adult   741.5; Fic
   1. Fantasy graphic novels; 2. Friendship — Graphic novels; 3. Graphic novels; 4. Owls — Graphic novels; 5. Stories without words — Graphic novels
   978-1-891830-89-1, $10
   A new visitor comes to the forest, but Wormy is scared of him because Owly had just read stories about a scary dragon, and the visitor seems to look scary. The visitor is just as scared of Owly. Things aren't just as they seem, and everyone soon finds out that a little bravery and a lot of friendship can fix just about anything. This is the latest volume in Runton's nearly wordless series about Owly and his friends.

   ★ **Owly** volume five: tiny tales. Top Shelf Productions 2008 175p. Illustration
Grades: K 1 2 3 4 5 6 7 8 9 10 11 12 Adult   741.5; Fic
   1. Friendship — Graphic novels; 2. Graphic novels; 3. Humorous graphic novels
   978-1-60309-019-3, $10
   This volume gathers short stories about Owly and his friends, including stories originally published for Free Comic Book Day issues from Top Shelf Productions, the first Owly mini-comics, drawings of Owly before he met Wormy, and more. Among the stories, Owly saves a friend from drowning in the cold river when the ice cracks, only to get caught in the hole himself; Owly finds a way to keep both the bees and hummingbirds happy when they get into a "turf" battle; Owly helps a friend when she falls and breaks the fancy potted plant she bought for a present; and more.

   ★ **Owly:** The way home and The bittersweet summer. [by] Andy Runton. Top Shelf 2004 160p. Illustration
Grades: K 1 2 3 4 5 6 7 8 9 10 11 12   741.5; Fic
   1. Friendship — Graphic novels; 2. Graphic novels; 3. Owls — Graphic novels
   1-891830-62-7, $10

                                            LC 2005298860
   Rotund little Owly befriends Wormy despite their differences, and together they help a couple of hummingbirds and learn that friendship doesn't end with separation.
   "The whimsical black-and-white art is done with great facility for expressing emotion, and Runton's reliance on icons and pictures in lieu of the usual dialogue makes the story perfect for give-and-take between children and their parents." Booklist
   Other titles in this series are: Owly: Just a little blue (2005); Owly: Flying lessons (2005);Owly: A time to be brave (2007);Owly: Tiny tales (2008)

Russell, P. Craig
   ★ **Coraline**. based on the novel by Neil Gaiman; adapted and illustrated by P. Craig Russell; colorist, Lovern Kindzierski; letterer, Todd Klein. HarperCollins 2008 186p. Illustration
Grades: 4 5 6 7   741; Fic; 741.5
   1. Graphic novels; 2. Horror graphic novels; 3. Gaiman, Neil, 1960- — Adaptations
   978-0-06-082543-0, $18.99; 978-0-06-082544-7 (lib bdg), $19.89
                                            LC 2007-930658

"An adaptation of Gaiman's 2002 novel Coraline,...a tale of childhood nightmares. As in the original story, Coraline wanders around her new house and discovers a door leading into a mirror place, where she finds her button-eyed "other mother," who is determined to secure Coraline's love one way or another. This version is a virtuoso adaptation.... A master of fantastical landscapes, Russell sharpens the realism of his imagery, perserving the humanity of the characters and heightening the horror." Booklist

Fairy Tales of Oscar Wilde Vol. 4: The Devoted Friend & The Nightingale and the Rose. NBM Publishing 2004 un Illustration
Grades: 5 6 7 8 9   **741.5; Fic**
1. Fantasy graphic novels; 2. Graphic novels; 3. Wilde, Oscar, 1854-1900
978-1-56163-391-3, $16.99
This volume adapts The Devoted Friend," on what constitutes real friendship, and The Nightingale and the Rose," a story of sacrifice to love with a cruel twist. In both stories, innocence is sacrificed to cynicism and shallowness.

Fairy tales of Oscar Wilde: 5: The Happy Prince. illustrated by P. Craig Russell. Nantier, Beall, Minoustchine 2012 32 p. Color illustration
Grades: 3 4 5 6 7 8   **741.5/973; Fic**
1. Generosity — Fiction; 2. Fairy tales; 3. Wilde, Oscar, 1854-1900
1561636266; 9781561636266, $16.99
                                                            LC 93229468
For this book, "Eisner Award-winning [P. Craig] Russell has adapted into graphic novel form" the Oscar Wilde fairy tale "The Happy Prince." In the story, "a swallow...befriends the statue of the Happy Prince, who was indeed happy when he lived a sheltered life. Now, however, the prince stands over the city as a statue and sees all the suffering. With the help of the swallow, he breaks down the pieces of himself, his rubies, sapphire, and gold, to feed the starving people." (Publishers Weekly)

★ The **graveyard** book graphic novel Volume 1. based on the novel by Neil Gaiman; adapted by P. Craig Russell; illustrated by Kevin Nowlan, P. Craig Russell, Tony Harris, Scott Hampton, Galen Showman, Jill Thompson, Stephen B. Scott; colorist, Lovern Kindzierski; letterer, Rick Parker. HarperCollins 2014 188 p. Color; Illustration
Grades: 5 6 7 8 9 10   **741.5; Fic**
1. Cemeteries — Fiction; 2. Orphans — Fiction; 3. Graphic novels; 4. Gaiman, Neil — Adaptations
9780062194817, $19.99; 006219481X
                                                            LC 2013953799
This graphic novel is an adaptation of the "Newbery Medal-winning novel, [where] Bod is an unusual boy..., the only living resident of a graveyard. Raised from infancy by the ghosts, werewolves, and other cemetery denizens, Bod has learned the antiquated customs of his guardians' time as well as their ghostly teachings." (Publisher's note)
"Russell brings his decades of comics know-how to this lovely, lyrical adaptation of [Gaiman's] well-loved, Newbery Medal — winning book. Not content to rely exclusively on his own distinctive talents, Russell has enlisted some of the industry's greatest contemporary illustrators as contributors, who fill the panels with appropriately gothic tones. In order to give ample room to the novel's twists and turns, the adaptation has been divided into two parts." Booklist

Ruth, Greg
The **lost** boy. Greg Ruth. GRAPHIX 2013 192 p.
Grades: 3 4 5 6 7   **741.5**
1. Historical fiction — Fiction; 2. Fantasy fiction
0439823323; 9780439823319; 9780439823326, $12.99; 9780545576901
                                                            LC 2013937147

This book by Greg Ruth "opens as a boy named Nate moves to a new town and discovers a tape recorder hidden underneath the floorboards of his bedroom. The action shifts back several decades as Nate listens to recordings left by Walter Pidgen, an outcast boy who disappeared without a trace. Along with a neighbor, Tabitha, Nate is drawn into a supernatural battle involving the denizens of an ancient woodland kingdom, which include talking toys and insects." (Publishers Weekly)

Sava, Scott Christian
Cameron and his dinosaurs. IDW Publishing 2009 174p. Illustration
Grades: 3 4 5 6 7 8   **741.5; Fic**
1. Adventure graphic novels; 2. Dinosaurs — Graphic novels; 3. Graphic novels; 4. Humorous graphic novels; 5. Robots — Graphic novels
978-1-60010-315-5, $12.99
The mad scientist, Professor Poindexter P. Poppycock, uses dinosaur DNA to create living dinosaurs which he plans to use for nefarious purposes. Unfortunately for him, he gave them human intelligence and the ability to speak, and the dinosaurs Charlie the tyrannosaurus rex, Dee Dee the pterodactyl, Lizzy the triceratops, and Vinnie the brachiosaurus decline to be evil and leave him. They befriend young Cameron, who helps to introduce them to the world. Professor Poppycock then creates robotic dinosaurs to do the will of the Brotherhood of Universal Revolution for Political Subterfuge (B.U.R.P.S.) to kidnap the President and take over the country. It will be up to Charlie, Dee Dee, Lizzy, Vinnie, and Cameron in his new souped-up wheelchair (with some awesome top-secret adaptations) to save the President and stop the robot dinosaurs. This book reads like an action-packed cartoon.

Hyperactive. by Scott Christian Sava; artist, Joseph Bergin. IDW Publishing/Worthwhile Children's Books 2009 108p. Illustration
Grades: 3 4 5 6 7 8   **741.5; Fic**
1. Adventure graphic novels; 2. Graphic novels; 3. Humorous graphic novels; 4. Superhero graphic novels
978-1-60010-313-1, $12.99; 1-60010-313-8
"Joey Johnson learns he can move at super speed and puts his power to good use doing household chores. But when word gets out, a shady executive sees the opportunity to make big bucks off of Joey's super DNA.... With its surprise ending, which suggests more to come, a readership of young boys will ensure that this one flies off the shelf at the speed of light." Booklist

The **lab**: hey . . . test this!. Astonish Factory 2004 120p. Illustration
Grades: 5 6 7 8 9   **741.5; Fic**
1. Graphic novels; 2. Humorous graphic novels; 3. Science fiction graphic novels
0-9721259-3-0, $14.95
"A collection of previously published comics and original stories that highlight the working relationship between Livingston, a scientist mole, and his goofball assistant, Esteban, a weasel whose ultrasensitivity to chemicals makes him an excellent test subject for new products. With bright, colorful pictures, the stories usually consist of observing Esteban's outlandish reactions to Livingston's concoctions, such as floating to the ceiling, shrinking to microscopic size, or singing uncontrollably." SLJ

My Grandparents are Secret Agents. IDW Publishing 2009 104p.
Grades: 3 4 5 6   **741.5; Fic**
1. Adventure graphic novels; 2. Graphic novels; 3. Humorous graphic novels; 4. Mystery graphic novels
978-1-60010-314-8, $11.99
Secret agents The Sicilian and the Diva defeat Dr. Dementia, and after the successful mission they want to spend a weekend with their grandchildren, Nicholas and Alyssa, while the kids' parents go on a romantic trip. However, the Social Security Administration (a secret government agency working to keep the U.S. safe) needs their top two

agents to go after a villain named Purple Haze, who intends to use a time machine to make everything go back to the late 1960s. Grandma and Grandpa have to take Nicholas and Alyssa with them, along with the robot security dog named S.N.A.C.K.S., to stop the whacked-out villain. Spanish illustrator Mourgues and the Invasor Creative Art Studio use a very colorful, cartoony style.

Sazaklis, John
DC super heroes storybook collection. Jerry Siegel, Joe Shuster, Bob Kane, and William Moulton Marston. Harper 2012 186 p. Illustration
Grades: 2 3 4 5   **741.5; Fic**
1. Superheroes — Fiction; 2. Wonder Woman (Fictional character); 3. Catwoman (Fictional character); 4. Superman (Fictional character); 5. Batman (Fictional character); 6. Joker (Fictional character)
006212398X; 9780062123985, $11.99

"This...collection features adventures, battles, and more, starring Superman, Batman, and Wonder Woman. These figures are the most widely recognized and, arguably, the most powerful in the DC universe. Many well-known villains are also featured, including Catwoman, The Joker, and Lex Luthor. However, all evil plans are thwarted and justice is served by our heroes, who work together well." (School Library Journal)

Schulz, Charles M.
★ The **Complete** Peanuts: 1950-1952. Fantagraphics Books 2004 330p. Illustration
Grades: 2 3 4 5 6 7 8 9 10 11 12 Adult   **741.5; Fic**
1. Graphic novels; 2. Humorous graphic novels; 3. Peanuts (Comic strip) — Graphic novels
1-56097-589-X, $28.95

This is the first volume of a project to collect all of Schulz's Peanuts comic strips from 1950 to 2000. This volume includes the strips published from October 2, 1950 through all of 1952. These early strips featured characters younger readers may not recognize: Patty (not Peppermint Patty), Violet, Shermy, and a Snoopy who behaves like a normal dog. Schroeder is a baby who's already a whiz at the toy piano; Lucy is a toddler who already causes trouble for Charlie Brown; Linus shows up as a baby in September 1952. Lucy pulls the football trick on Charlie Brown for the first time in November 1952. This volume also includes a biography of Schulz and a long interview with him.
Volume 1 of 26

Schweizer, Chris
The **creeps**; 1: night of the Frankenfrogs. by Chris Schweizer. Abrams Books 2015 128 p. Color; Illustration
Grades: 3 4 5 6   **741.5; Fic**
1. Frogs — fiction; 2. School stories — Fiction; 3. Scientists — Fiction
9781419713798, $17.95; 9781419717666, $9.95
LC 2014955691

In this book, by Chris Schweizer, as "punishment for creating a giant mess in their school, Carol, Jarvis, Mitchell, and Rosario (known to their classmates as the Creeps) are being forced to perform the tasks normally completed by the janitor. When they discover that the frog specimens intended for dissection in their science class are missing, they know that they will be blamed, so they set out to discover who the real culprit might be." (School Library Journal)

"An excellent complement to his prose, Schweizer's cleanly paneled art is bright and busy, ever ready with a gag that helps blend the ghastly with the goofy, making his gang's antics reminiscent of Scooby Doo.... Silly fun with a smattering of science." Kirkus
Another title in this series is: The trolls will feast! (2016)

Scott, Mairghread
The **city** on the other side. Mairghread Scott, illustrated by Robin Robinson. First Second 2018 224 p. Color; Illustration
Grades: 4 5 6 7   **741.5; Fic**
1. Imaginary wars and battles — Comic books, strips, etc.; 2. Fairies — Comic books, strips, etc.; 3. Magic — Comic books, strips, etc.; 4. Missing persons — Comic books, strips, etc.
9781250152558, $23.99; 9781626724570
LC 2017941171

In this book, by Mairghread Scott, illustrated by Robin Robinson, "Isabel plays the part of a perfectly proper little girl.... She's...not the kind of girl who goes on adventures. But that all changes when Isabel breaches an invisible barrier and steps into another world. She discovers a city not unlike her own, but magical and dangerous.... Only Isabel, with the help of a magical necklace,...stands a chance of ending the war before it destroys the fairy world." (Publisher's note)

"Robinson's colorful, dynamic artwork crackles with spirited fun and portrays San Francisco and its fairy-realm equivalent in broad, evocative panels." Kirkus

Seagle, Steven T.
Camp Midnight. written by Steven T. Seagle; drawn by Jason Adam Katzenstein. Image Comics 2016 248 p. Color; Illustration
Grades: 3 4 5 6   **741.5; Fic**
1. Camps — Fiction; 2. Monsters — Fiction
1632155559; 9781632155559, $16.99

In this graphic novel, by Steven T. Seagle, illustrated by Jason Adam Katzenstein, "reluctant Skye is accidentally sent to the wrong summer camp. Not wanting to please her 'step monster,' Skye is dead-set on not fitting in. That won't be a problem, as everyone at Camp Midnight-with the exception of fellow camper and fast-friend Mia-is a full-fledged monster!" (Publisher's note)

"Skye's character is spunky and totally believable, and her facial expressions are priceless. The other campers are weird and funny — hugely exaggerated and drawn with a wild and crazy art style employing just a few lurid colors, which works wonderfully to evoke the mood of every camp situation." SLJ

Sell, Chad
★ The **cardboard** kingdom. by Chad Sell; [with contributions by] Jay Fuller, David Demeo, Katie Schenkel, Manuel Betancourt, Molly Muldoon, Vid Alliger, Cloud Jacobs, Michael Cole, and Barbara Perez Marquez. Alfred A. Knopf 2018 288 p. Color; Illustration
Grades: 4 5 6 7   **741.5; Fic**
1. Friendship — Fiction; 2. Costume — Fiction; 3. Imagination — Comic books, strips, etc.
1524719374; 9781524719371, $20.99

"Welcome to a neighborhood of kids who transform ordinary boxes into colorful costumes, and their ordinary block into cardboard kingdom. This is the summer when sixteen kids encounter knights and rogues, robots and monsters — and their own inner demons — on one last quest before school starts again. In the Cardboard Kingdom, you can be anything you want to be — imagine that!" (Publisher's note)

"Sell's playful, expressive, and boldly colored artwork always keeps the mood fun, quickly shifting between the real world and the kids' imagined scenes in the Cardboard Kingdom. The blocky figures have a great cartoon quality, and, with a wide range of skin tones, genders, and family types, every kid reading will have someone to relate to." Booklist

Sexton, Adam
Hawthorne's the Scarlet letter: the Manga edition. Wiley Publishing 2009 186p. Illustration

Grades: 5 6 7 8 9 10 11 12   **741.5; Fic**
1. Authors; 2. Graphic novels; 3. Novelists; 4. Short story writers; 5. Hawthorne, Nathaniel, 1804-1864; 6. Hawthorne, Nathaniel, 1804-1864 — Adaptations/Graphic novels
978-0-470-14889-1, $9.99

Hester Prynne, a young married woman in puritanical Massachusetts, stands in public shame when she bears a child long after her husband had disappeared. She refuses to identify the father of her child and instead wears the scarlet letter A always. The young minister Arthur Dimmesdale lives with his guilt in secret, but the physician, Roger Chillingworth, is actually Hester's husband, returned for vengeance. He vows to find the man who fathered Pearl, Hester's daughter, and destroy him. Meanwhile, Pearl grows up in a society that shuns her mother, and she comes to see the A as her mother's badge of honor. This book is a manga style adaptation of Hawthorne's novel.

Sfar, Joann

★ The **little** prince. adapted from the book by Antoine de Saint-Exupéry; translated by Sarah Ardizzone; colour by Brigitte Findakly. Houghton Mifflin Harcourt 2010 110p. Illustration
Grades: 5 6 7 8 9   **741; Fic; 741.5**
1. Extraterrestrial beings — Graphic novels; 2. Fantasy graphic novels; 3. Graphic novels; 4. Saint-Exupéry, Antoine de, 1900-1944 — Adaptations
978-0-547-33802-6, $19.99; 0-547-33802-3

"On the surface, this is a straight graphic-novel retelling of the narrator pilot getting stranded in the desert, where he meets a curious little boy who claims to be from a wee planet very far away.... The ultimately tricky task is to honor the source but not sound like an adaptation (otherwise, why not just read the original") and Sfar nails it on both counts.... Everything is handled with both reverence and ingenuity." Booklist

Little Vampire Does Kung Fu!. stories and drawings by Joann Sfar; colors by Walter; translated by Mark and Alexis Siegel. Simon & Schuster Books for Young Readers 2003 un Illustration
Grades: 4 5 6 7 8 9   **741.5; Fic**
1. Fantasy graphic novels; 2. Graphic novels; 3. Humorous graphic novels; 4. Vampires — Graphic novels
0-689-85769-1, $12.95

LC 2003-045770

Jeffrey the jerk is a bully and everyone knows it. Little Vampire isn't about to stand around and watch him pick on his best friend, Michael. There's only one thing to do: travel to the highest mountain and seek kung fu lessons from the master... There's an icky moment when Little Vampire's monster friends spit up bits of Jeffrey (whom they ate) and they try to put him together again.

Little Vampire goes to school. stories and drawings by Joann Sfar; colors by Walter; translated by Mark and Alexis Siegel. Simon & Schuster Bks. for Young Readers 2003 40p. Illustration
Grades: 2 3 4 5   **741.5; Fic**
1. Graphic novels; 2. Vampires — Graphic novels
0-689-85717-9, $12.95

LC 2002-152656

A lonely little vampire, yearning for a friend, gets permission from the other monsters to go to school and makes the acquaintance of a boy who does not believe that vampires are real

Another title about Little Vampire is: Little Vampire does kung fu! (2003)

Shakespeare, William

William Shakespeare's Twelfth night. adapted by Vincent Goodwin illustrated by Cynthia Martin. ABDO/Magic Wagon 2008 48p. Illustration

Grades: 5 6 7 8 9 10
822.3; 741.5
1. Authors; 2. Dramatists; 3. Graphic novels; 4. Poets; 5. Shakespeare, William, 1564-1616 — Adaptations
978-1-60270-195-3, $28.50

LC 2008-10747

Courtesy of ABDO Publishing.

Twins Viola and Sebastian are separated in a shipwreck. Viola decides to disguise herself as a man since she's alone, and this sets the stage for mixed-up identities and a comic love triangle. This graphic novel adaptation retains some of the original language from Shakespeare's play, while paring down the story to appeal to struggling readers. The book includes a short biography, a summary of the play, a glossary, and a short selection of famous lines and phrases from the play.

Part of the Graphic Shakespeare series

Shanower, Eric

★ The **Wonderful** Wizard of Oz. writer, Eric Shanower; artist, Skottie Young; colorist, Jean-Francois Beaulieu; letterer, Jeff Eckleberry; adapted from the novel by L. Frank Baum. Marvel Entertainment 2009 192p. Illustration
Grades: 3 4 5 6 7 8 9 10 11 12 Adult   **741.5; Fic**
1. Adventure graphic novels; 2. Authors; 3. Children's authors; 4. Dramatists; 5. Fantasy graphic novels; 6. Graphic novels; 7. Journalists; 8. Baum, L. Frank, 1856-1919 — Adaptations
978-0-7851-2921-9, $29.99

A twister picks up the house Dorothy and her dog Toto are in and carries them from Kansas to the land of Oz; the house lands on top of the Wicked Witch of the East, and the Munchkins, who were her slaves, hail Dorothy as a great sorceress. All the girl wants is to get back home to Kansas, but all anyone can say is that she must go to the Emerald City and ask the Great Wizard Oz to send her home. As she travels along the Yellow Brick Road, she meets a scarecrow who wants brains so people won't think he's a dummy, a tin man who wants a heart so he can love, and a great cowardly lion who wants courage so he'll truly be king of the beasts. However, once they reach the Emerald City and each see the Wizard Oz, they learn they must do what no one, including the Wizard himself, could ever do kill the Wicked Witch of the West. Shanower's adaptation of L. Frank Baum's novel keeps all the charm of the original, while Skottie Young's art banishes any lingering images of the old Technicolor movie; Beaulieu's muted color palette works with Young's art, while Eckleberry's lettering adds to an overall effect of magic and wonder. This book will appeal to all ages

Other Oz adapations by Shanower and Young are: The Marvelous Land of Oz; Ozma of Oz; Dorothy and the Wizard in Oz; The Road to Oz; The Emerald City of Oz

Shapiro, David

Terra Tempo: the four corners of time. David Shapiro, Christopher Herndon, Erica Melville. Craigmore Creations 2013 272 p. (Terra Tempo)
Grades: 5 6 7   **741.5**
1. Colorado Plateau — Fiction; 2. Time travel — Fiction; 3. Dinosaurs — Fiction
098444226X; 9780984442263, $17.99

LC 2012944924

This book is part of the "Terra Tiempo" series by David R. Shapiro and Erica Melville. "When Ari discovers a time map of the Colorado Plateau, he and the twins find themselves on a fast paced journey from Earth s underwater beginnings to the steamy jungles and huge creatures of the creepy Cretaceous. But this time, there is more at stake than just survival. This time, they are not alone." (Publisher's note)

Shaw, Murray

Sherlock Holmes and the adventure of the blue gem. based on the stories of Sir Arthur Conan Doyle; adapted by Murray Shaw and M.J. Cosson; illustrated by Sophie Rohrbach. Lerner Publishing Group/Graphic Universe 2010 48p. Illustration

Grades: 3 4 5 6 7 8

741.5; Fic

1. Authors; 2. Gems — Graphic novels; 3. Graphic novels; 4. Holmes, Sherlock (Fictional character) — Graphic novels; 5. Mystery graphic novels; 6. Mystery writers; 7. Novelists; 8. Doyle, Arthur Conan Sir, 1859-1930 — Adaptations

978-0-7613-6190-9, $26.60

Courtesy of Lerner Publishing Group

LC 2009-51758

In this graphic adaptation of Doyle's "The Adventure of the Blue Carbuncle," Sherlock Holmes and Dr. Watson work on a Christmas holiday mystery when a train conductor brings them a Christmas goose and a man's hat that he found. They find a large blue gem in the throat of the goose, a famous gem that had been stolen from its owner. Holmes and Watson trace the owner of the hat, who starts them on a path to find out who stole the gem and stuffed it into the goose. This book includes discussion questions and a reading list that includes a mix of age-appropriate mysteries and nonfiction books and websites. Rohrbach's art looks almost like woodcuts; she unfortunately uses the stereotypical (and incorrect) look of the deerstalker cap and caped coat for Holmes. Her muted color palette of mostly browns matches the Victorian time period of the Holmes mysteries.

This is #3 in the On the Case with Holmes and Watson series.

Shiga, Jason

Meanwhile. Abrams/Amulet 2010 un Illustration

Grades: 4 5 6 7 8 9   **741.5**

1. Graphic novels; 2. Science fiction graphic novels

0-8109-8423-7; 978-0-8109-8423-3, $15.95

LC 2009-39844

In this choose-your-own adventure graphic novel, a boy stumbles on the laboratory of a mad scientist who asks him to choose between testing a mind-reading device, a time machine, and a doomsday machine. (Bull Cent Child Books)

Shintani, Kaoru

Young Miss Holmes: casebook 1-2. by Kaoru Shintani. Seven Seas 2012 384 p.

Grades: 4 5 6 7   **741.5; 741.5952/223**

1. Girls — Fiction; 2. Detectives — Fiction

1935934864; 9781935934868, $16.99

In this book by Kaoru Shintani "Christie Holmes is a prodigy. At ten years old, she's as familiar with the sciences and classics as any older student at Cambridge or Oxford. And her facility with logic is reminiscent of her uncle, the eminent Sherlock Holmes himself. Christie's implacable curiosity leads her from one dangerous adventure to another, often joining forces with Uncle Sherlock and Doctor Watson on their famed investigations." (Publisher's note)

Young Miss Holmes: casebook 3-4. by Kaoru Shintani. Seven Seas 2012 384 p.

Grades: 4 5 6 7   **741.5**

1. Family — Fiction; 2. Detectives — Fiction

1935934945; 9781935934943, $16.99

In this graphic novel by Kaoru Shintani readers "experience classic Sherlock Holmes tales from the POV of his...niece. Sherlock Holmes' precocious niece Christie is back, as she helps her famous uncle solve such cases as: The Hound of the Baskervilles, The Adventure of the Six Napoleons, the Red-Headed League, and more!" (Publisher's note)

Shone, Rob

Earthquakes. The Rosen Publishing Group 2007 48p. Illustration

Grades: 3 4 5 6 7 8

551.22; 741.5

1. Earthquakes — Graphic novels; 2. Graphic novels

978-1-4042-1989-2, $26.25

Courtesy of Rosen Publishing

The book describes earthquake zones and how earthquakes happen, then it dramatizes three major disasters: the San Francisco earthquake of 1906, the Great Hanshin Earthquake that devastated Kobe, Japan in 1995, and the South Asia Earthquake that struck Kashmir, Pakistan in 2005. Additional information includes an explanation of the Richter scale, a glossary, and a list of books for further reading.

Part of the Graphic Natural Disasters series.

Giganotosaurus: the giant southern lizard. illustrated by Terry Riley. Rosen Publishing Group 2009 32p. Illustration

Grades: 3 4 5 6 7

668; 741.5

1. Dinosaurs — Graphic novels; 2. Graphic novels

978-1-4358-2502-4, $25.25

Courtesy of Rosen Publishing

LC 2008-3265

This book uses the comic book format to provide information about the Giganotosaurus, a giant meat-eating dinosaur from the Cretaceous Period. Information about its hunting habits and lifestyle are based on research and fossil records.

Part of the Graphic Dinosaur series

Muhammad Ali: The Life of a Boxing Hero. Rosen Publishing Group 2006 48p. Illustration

Grades: 3 4 5 6 7 8 9

741.5; 796.8; 92

1. African American athletes — Graphic novels; 2. Biographical graphic novels; 3. Boxing — Biography — Graphic novels; 4. Graphic novels; 5. Ali, Muhammad, 1942-2016

978-1-4042-0856-8, $29.25

Courtesy of Rosen Publishing

LC 2005035521

This book uses the graphic novel format to tell of the life and career of boxing great Muhammad Ali. He started his career as Cassius Clay but changed his name when he converted to the Nation of Islam. He used his fame as a boxer to advocate against U.S. involvement in Vietnam, and to raise funds for charity. The book includes a list of all his boxing matches, and a list of books for further reading.

Part of the Rosen Graphic Biographies series.

Triceratops: The Three Horned Dinosaur. Rosen Publishing Group 2007 32p. Illustration

Grades: 2 3 4 5 6 7

567.9; 741.5

1. Dinosaurs — Graphic novels; 2. Graphic novels; 3. Triceratops — Graphic novels
978-1-4042-3896-1, $25.25

LC 2007-374

Courtesy of Rosen Publishing

This volume uses colorful comic book style illustrations to explore the habitat, diet, and behavior of the triceratops. At the front of the book, facts about the triceratops are presented, while at the back of the book readers will find a picture gallery of other creatures mentioned in the book.

Part of the Graphic Dinosaurs series.

Tyrannosaurus: The Tyrant Lizard. Rosen Publishing Group 2007 32p. Illustration

Grades: 2 3 4 5 6 7

567.9; 741.5

1. Dinosaurs — Graphic novels; 2. Graphic novels; 3. Tyrannosaurus — Graphic novels
978-1-4042-3897-8, $25.25

LC 2007-0442

This volume uses colorful comic book style illustrations to explore the habitat, diet, and behavior of the tyrannosaurus. At the front of the book, facts about the tyrannosaurus are presented, while at the back of the book readers will find a picture gallery of other creatures mentioned in the book.

Part of the Graphic Dinosaurs series.

Volcanoes. The Rosen Publishing Group 2007 48p. Illustration

Grades: 3 4 5 6 7 8

551.21; 741.5

1. Graphic novels; 2. Volcanoes — Graphic novels
978-1-4042-1988-5, $29.25

The book first describes how volcanoes form, briefly discusses killer volcanoes, then uses comic book-style illustrations to dramatize the eruption of Vesuvius in A.D. 79, which buried Pompeii; Krakatoa, which erupted in 1883 and destroyed the island near Sumatra (a new island started growing in 1967); and Mount St. Helens in Washington, which erupted in 1980. Additional

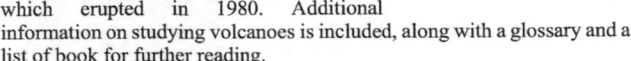

Courtesy of Rosen Publishing

information on studying volcanoes is included, along with a glossary and a list of book for further reading.

Part of the Graphic Natural Disasters series.

Sias, Ryan

Zoe and Robot: let's pretend. Blue Apple 2011 un Illustration (Balloon Toons)

Grades: K 1 2 3

741.5; Fic

1. Graphic novels; 2. Humorous graphic novels; 3. Imagination — Graphic novels; 4. Robots — Graphic novels
978-1-60905-063-4, $10.99; 1-60905-063-0

LC 2010046829

A young girl named Zoe wants Robot to play pretend with her, but she has to teach Robot how to pretend, because "Robots do not know how to pretend." From imagining a pile of pillows is a mountain to feeling the wind from a whirring fan, Zoe tries to help Robot. Finally, she draws mountains on a pair of goggles that she puts on Robot.

"The colorful art and simple panel designs make it easy to follow the story.... Beginning readers can easily catch the visual cues that help them interpret the simple dialogue, and they will enjoy the humor.... This is a fun, easy-to-read graphic novel for beginning readers." Booklist

Siegel, Mark

★ The **sand** warrior. Mark Siegel and Alexis Siegel; illustrated by Xanthe Boume, Matt Rockefeller, and Boya Sun.. Random House 2017 256 p. Color; Illustration; Map (5 worlds)

Grades: 3 4 5 6

741.5; Fic

1. Adventure and adventurers — Fiction; 2. Graphic novels; 3. Heroes — Fiction; 4. Science fiction; 5. Fantasy fiction — Graphic novels
1101935863; 9781101935866, $18.99; 9781101935873; 9781101935880

LC 2016018284

In this book, by Mark Siegel and Alexis Siegel, illustrated by Xanthe Boume, Matt Rockefeller, and Boya Sun, "the Five Worlds are on the brink of extinction unless five ancient and mysterious beacons are lit. When war erupts, three unlikely heroes will discover there's more to themselves — and more to their worlds — than meets the eye." (Publisher's note)

"Explosions, attacks, and evildoing are relieved by neatly timed interludes in tranquil settings. The main characters share an unglamorous, pre- adolescent look, and the authors seize the opportunity to explore issues of race, class, and scarcity." Pub Wkly

Another title in this series is: The cobalt prince (2018)

Siegel, Siena Cherson

To dance: a ballerina's graphic novel. [by] Siena Cherson Siegel; [illustrated by] Mark Siegel. Simon & Schuster 2006 un Illustration

Grades: 4 5 6 7

741.5; 92

1. Autobiographical graphic novels; 2. Ballet; 3. Ballet dancers; 4. Graphic novels; 5. Puerto Ricans — Biography; 6. Siegel, Siena Cherson
1-4169-2687-9 (pa), $9.99

In this memoir of her youth in dance from ages six to eighteen, Siegel tells what it was like to be totally involved in dance, in ballet-all the joys and the physical pain. She worked as a young dancer with George Ballanchine. Her absolute desire to be a dancer took her from her native Puerto Rico to New York City to study. Her simple but heartfelt narration is ably illustrated by her husband Mark Siegel.

Aladdin paperbacks

Simon, Eddy

Pele: the king of soccer. written by Eddy Simon; illustrated by Vincent Brascaglia; English translation by Joe Johnson. First Second 2017 144 p. Color; Illustration

Grades: 4 5 6 7 8 9

92; 741.5

1. Pelé, 1940-; 2. Soccer players — Biography
9781626727557, $15.99; 9781626729797

LC 2016961595

"Edson Arantes do Nascimento, known to his schoolmates as Pelé, grew up in poverty in the Sao Paulo region of Brazil. He was too poor to afford a real soccer ball, so he played with a ball of newspaper.... He dominated the youth leagues and signed his first professional soccer contract at the age of fifteen. Within two years he was celebrated internationally, when he led Brazil to victory at the world cup." (Publisher's note)

"This particularly smart delineation of Pelé has it all: his career, his blunders, decency, and goodness. And his gift." Kirkus

Translation of: Le roi Pelé: l'homme et la légende

Simpson, Dana

Phoebe and Her Unicorn. Dana Simpson. Andrews McMeel 2014 224 p. Color illustration

Grades: 3 4 5   **741.5**

1. Unicorns — Fiction; 2. Girls — Graphic novels

1449446205; 9781449446208, $9.99

LC bl2014039099

In this graphic novel, by Dana Simpson, "Phoebe skipped a rock across a pond and accidentally hit a unicorn in the face. Improbably, this led to Phoebe being granted one wish, and she used it to make the unicorn, Marigold Heavenly Nostrils, her obligational best friend. But can a vain mythical beast and a nine-year-old daydreamer really forge a connection?" (Publisher's note)

"A pink, bubble-gum bonbon of a tale spun of a likable, albeit self-centered, fourth-grader and her magical, self-obsessed, although sometimes-kind, unicorn." Kirkus

Other titles in this series are: Unicorn on a roll (2015); Unicorn vs. Goblins (2016); Razzle Dazzle Unicorn (2016); Unicorn Crossing (2017); The Magic Storm (2017); Unicorn of Many Hats (2018)

Unicorn on a Roll: Another Phoebe and Her Unicorn Adventure. by Dana Simpson. Paw Prints 2015 222 pages Color; Illustration

Grades: 3 4 5   **741.5; Fic**

1. Friendship — Juvenile fiction; 2. Unicorns — Juvenile fiction

9781449470760, $9.99

LC 2014921935

This book, by Dana Simpson, is about the "magical friendship of Phoebe and her best friend, unicorn Marigold Heavenly Nostrils.... [The] reader is invited on a journey into the lives of Phoebe and Marigold as they navigate the difficulties of grade school, celebrate the winter holidays, and explore their super hero/super villain personas together." (Publisher's note)

"Phoebe always has a friend to rely on, and Marigold always has someone to admire her extraordinary beauty, her clever wit, and her exceptional modesty. The character designs for Phoebe and Marigold are charming, and the artwork is admirably consistent." Booklist

Slade, Christian

Korgi, Book 1: Sprouting Wings. Top Shelf Productions 2007 88p. Illustration

Grades: 2 3 4 5 6 7 8 9 10 11 12 Adult

741.5; Fic

1. Dogs — Graphic novels; 2. Fantasy graphic novels; 3. Graphic novels; 4. Stories without words — Graphic novels

978-1-891830-90-7, $10

In this wordless book, a young Mollie (woodland people) named Ivy and her young Korgi companion named Sprout embark on adventures in Korgi Hollow, an enchanted place. When they wander from the Mollie village, the two fall through a hole in the ground and find nasty, monstrous creatures who want to eat them. As they deal with the

Courtesy of IDW Publishing

danger and make their escape, Ivy and Sprout both discover new talents. Slade's extensively cross-hatched yet delicate art is highly expressive, and readers young and old will have no trouble figuring out what is going on.

The Korgi are based on Welsh corgi dogs, of which Slade and his wife have two.

Korgi, book 2. Top Shelf Productions 2008 un Illustration

Grades: 3 4 5 6 7 8 9 10 11 12 Adult

741.5; Fic

1. Adventure graphic novels; 2. Fantasy graphic novels; 3. Graphic novels; 4. Stories without words — Graphic novels

978-1-60309-010-0, $10

In this second wordless volume, the young Mollie named Ivy and her Korgi cub Sprout, experience a harrowing adventure. Someone has been hunting the Mollies and cutting off their wings. Ivy and Sprout rescue one older Mollie named Art and his Korgi when they fall into a deep trap in the woods;

Courtesy of IDW Publishing

then as Ivy flies, a barbed arrow cuts one of her wings off. She and Sprout see a strange creature carrying her wing and they follow him to his place, where he hangs all the Mollie wings like trophies. Ivy decides she wants her wing back, but she and Sprout will have to fight the creature and his automated and nasty bots.

Slavin, Bill

Big star Otto. written by Bill Slavin with Esperança Melo; art by Bill Slavin. Kids Can Press 2015 95 p. (Elephants Never Forget)

Grades: 3 4 5 6   **741.5**

1. Chimpanzees — Juvenile fiction; 2. Elephants — Juvenile fiction; 3. Kidnapping — Juvenile fiction; 4. Graphic novels; 5. Parrots — Juvenile fiction

1894786963; 9781894786966, $16.95

"In this conclusion to the Elephants Never Forget graphic novel trilogy, [by Bill Slavin], big-hearted hero Otto and his parrot pal Crackers have landed in Hollywood, the final stop in their journey across America in search of their good friend Georgie the chimpanzee. They've been hot on Georgie's trail since he was abducted from Africa by the sinister Man with the Wooden Nose, and now they're sure they've finally found his location." (Publisher's note)

Smith, Jeff

★ **Bone** Book Seven: ghost circles. Scholastic/GRAPHIX 2008 152p. Illustration

Courtesy of Kids Can Press

Grades: 3 4 5 6 7 8 9 10 11 12 Adult   **741.5; Fic**

1. Adventure graphic novels; 2. Fantasy graphic novels; 3. Graphic novels

978-0-439-70629-2, $19.99; 978-0-439-70634-6 (pa), $9.99

LC 2007-9568403

The Bone cousins, Gran'ma Ben, Thorn, and their loyal rat creature cub Bartleby venture on a journey through the mysterious ghost circles to Atheia, the old city of the royal family. Meanwhile, the Barrelhaven villagers and the Veni Yan face enemy hordes. Steve Hamaker is the colorist for this full color version of Smith's comic epic.

★ **Bone** vol. 8: treasure hunters. Scholastic/Graphix 2008 138p. Illustration

Grades: 5 6 7 8 9 10 11 12 Adult   **741.5; Fic**

1. Adventure graphic novels; 2. Fantasy graphic novels; 3. Graphic novels
978-0-439-70630-8, $18.95; 978-0-439-70633-9 (pa), $9.99

LC 2008-9568403

The Bone cousins, Gran'ma Ben, and Thorn reach the city of Atheia, where they prepare to battle the Lord of the Locusts. Meanwhile, Thorn's visions are becoming more threatening and Phoney Bone is convinced Atheia is rich in gold, and he is determined to find it. But all is not well in Atheia, and Thorn is in great danger, not only from Briar and the Lord of the Locusts. This edition is in full color, done by Steve Hamaker.

★ **Bone:** out from Boneville. Scholastic Graphix 2005 144p. Illustration

Grades: 4 5 6 7 8 9 10 11 12   **741.5; Fic**
1. Adventure graphic novels; 2. Fantasy graphic novels; 3. Graphic novels
9780439706407, $12.99; 0439706408; 0439706238; 9780439706230, $26.99

"After being run out of Boneville, the three Bone cousins — Fone Bone, Phoney Bone, and Smiley Bone — are separated and lost in a vast, uncharted desert. One by one, they find their way into a deep, forested valley filled with wonderful and terrifying creatures. Eventually, the cousins are reunited at a farmstead run by tough Gran'ma Ben and her spirited granddaughter, Thorn. But little do the Bones know, there are dark forces conspiring against them and their adventures are only just beginning!" (Publisher's note)

"The nine-volume Bone graphic novel series was the toast of the comics world when it was published by Smith's own Cartoon Books beginning in the early 1990s; in this first volume of Scholastic's new edition, the original b&w art has been beautifully converted into color." Pub Wkly

Also available Bone: one volume edition $39.95 from Cartoon Books (ISBN 1-8889-6314-X); Other titles in this series are: Bone: the great cow race (vol. 2); Bone: eyes of the storm (vol. 3); Bone: the dragonslayer (vol. 4); Bone: Rock Jaw: master of the Eastern border (vol. 5); Bone: old man's cave (vol. 6); Bone: ghost circles (vol. 7); Bone: treasure hunters (vol. 8); Bone: crown of horns (vol. 9)

Bone: Rose. by Jeff Smith; with illustrations by Charles Vess. Scholastic Graphix 2009 138p. Illustration

Grades: 4 5 6 7 8   **741.5; Fic**
1. Adventure graphic novels; 2. Fantasy graphic novels; 3. Graphic novels
978-0-545-13542-9, $21.99; 0-545-13542-7; 978-0-545-13543-6 (pa), $10.99; 0-545-13543-5 (pa)

"When a terrifying dragon attacks the small towns of the Northern Valley, a young Princess Rose (known later as Gran'ma Ben) must defeat it. The beast is actually the ancient evil, the Lord of the Locusts, and while Rose faces danger with honor, her elder sister, Princess Briar, follows a more sinister path." (Publisher's note)

Bone: tall tales. by Jeff Smith with Tom Sniegoski; color by Steve Hamaker. Graphix 2010 108p. Illustration

Grades: 4 5 6 7 8   **741; 741.5**
978-0-545-14095-9, $21.99; 0-545-14095-1; 978-0-545-14096-6 (pa), $10.99; 0-545-14096-X (pa)

"Long before the Bone cousins were ever lost in the uncharted desert on the outskirts of the Valley, Big Johnson Bone, the discoverer of the Rolling Bone River, founded Boneville. But little is known of the mighty explorer's adventures before he started his famous trading post. So when Smiley Bone sits down with a group of young campers to retell the legendary stories of Boneville's origin and its tough, no-nonsense founder, what they hear are tall tales in typical BONE fashion." (Publisher's note)

★ **Little** Mouse gets ready. TOON Books 2009 32p. Illustration

Grades: PreK K 1   **741.5; Fic**
1. Clothing and dress — Graphic novels; 2. Graphic novels; 3. Humorous graphic novels; 4. Mice — Graphic novels
978-1-935179-01-6, $12.95; 1-935179-01-2

LC 2008-55403

ALA ALSC Geisel Award Honor Book (2010)

"Little Mouse is eager to go to the barn with his mother. He slowly and methodically gets dressed, which is quite an accomplishment for the little guy, only to be reminded, in classic noodlehead fashion, that mice don't wear clothes.... The cartoon illustrations are large and uncomplicated without being babyish, and the punch line is preceded with places for knowing giggles." SLJ

Soo, Kean
★ **Jellaby:** monster in the city. Hyperion Books 2009 172p. Illustration

Grades: 4 5 6 7 8 9   **741.5; Fic**
1. Fantasy graphic novels; 2. Friendship — Graphic novels; 3. Graphic novels; 4. Monsters — Graphic novels
1-4231-0565-6 (pa); 978-1-4231-0565-7 (pa), $9.99

Beginning right where the first book ended, Portia, Jason, and Jellaby continue on their way to Toronto, walking after Portia panicked and they got off the train. They're searching for a way home for Jellaby, and they think a door somewhere in Exhibition Place, where the Canadian National Exhibition is taking place, holds a clue. Portia feels torn between wanting to help her friend yet not wanting to say goodbye forever, and her ambivalence causes a rift between her and Jason. When she doesn't want to trust a masked magician who seems to know too much about them and Jellaby, Portia leaves Jason. They all end up in the Automotive Building, where the masked man leads Jason and Jellaby down below the building, while Portia seems to find her long lost father. But is he really her father, and just what is waiting for Jason and Jellaby under the Automotive Building? Soo again uses a mostly purple color palette.

Another title in the author's series about Jellaby

★ **Jellaby;** Volume 1: the lost monster. by Kean Soo. Stone Arch Books 2014 160 p. Color; Illustration (Jellaby)

Courtesy of Capstone Press

Grades: 4 5 6 7 8 9
741.5
1. Extraterrestrial beings — Fiction; 2. Human-alien encounters — Comic books, strips, etc; 3. Monsters — Fiction; 4. Friendship — Fiction
1434291952; 9781434264206, $12.95 ; 9781434291950, $19.99

LC 2013037026

"Portia has just moved to a new neighborhood with her mom. Adjusting to life without a father is hard enough, but school is boring and her classmates are standoffish.... But things start to get better when Portia mounts a midnight excursion into the woods behind her house where she discovers a shy and sweet purple monster. Life with Jellaby is exciting, but Portia's purple friend has secrets of his own." (Publisher's note)

"Soo grounds the story in a fairly gritty contemporary reality, where kids deal with bullies and well-meaning adults try to help. Clear, clean lines and easy-to-follow panel layouts round out the package." Booklist

First published 2008; Originally published: New York : Hyperion Books for Children, 2008. A Capstone imprint.

Spender, Nick

Rosa Parks: The Life of a Civil Rights Heroine. Rosen Publishing Group 2006 48p. Illustration

Grades: 3 4 5 6 7 8 9   **741.5; 323.092; 92; 323**

1. African American women — Alabama — Montgomery — Biography — Graphic novels; 2. African Americans — Civil rights — Alabama — Montgomery — History — 20th century — Graphic novels; 3. Biographical graphic novels; 4. Graphic novels; 5. Parks, Rosa, 1913-2005

978-1-4042-0864-3, $29.25

LC 2006002735

This book uses the graphic novel format to tell of the life of Rosa Parks and her act of defiance that inspired the Montgomery Bus Boycott. Additional information explains Jim Crow laws and briefly covers the civil rights movement. The book includes a list of books for further reading.

Part of the Rosen Graphic Biographies series.

Spiegelman, Art

Big fat Little Lit. [edited by] Art Spiegelman and Francoise Mouly. Puffin 2006 144p. Illustration

Grades: 2 3 4 5 6 7 8   **741.5; Fic**

1. Folklore — Graphic novels; 2. Graphic novels

0-14-240706-2, $14.99

This volume collects all three previously published Little Lit books: Little Lit: Once Upon a Time, Little Lit: Strange Stories for Strange Kids, and Little Lit: It Was a Dark and Silly Night. Many comics creators and children's book writers and illustrators contributed stories, including Ian Falconer, Daniel Clowes, Maurice Sendak, David Sedaris, Chris Ware, Jules Feiffer, Barbara McClintock, Crockett Johnson, J. Otto Siebold, Neil Gaiman, Art Spiegelman, and Lemony Snicket.

Spires, Ashley

★ **Binky** takes charge. by Ashley Spires. Kids Can Press 2012 64 p. Color illustration

Grades: 4 5 6   **741.5/971; Fic**

1. Picture books for children; 2. Cats — Fiction; 3. Spy stories

1554537037; 9781554537037, $16.95; 9781554537686, $8.95; 9781451765137, $17.95

"Felines of the Universe Ready for Space Travel (F.U.R.S.T.) and Captain Gracie are pleased to announce that Lt. Binky is about to get his first recruit to train [in this book by Ashley Spires.]...There — s a new diversity program at F.U.R.S.T., and Gordon, a dog, has been assigned to Binky. Binky decides to give it his all. As expected, Gordon falls short. Then Binky discovers the unthinkable: Gordon seems to be leaving coded messages in outer space...If they are to prove Gordon is a double agent, Gracie and Binky will need incontrovertible proof!" (Kirkus)

Courtesy of Kids Can Press

★ **Binky** the space cat. Kids Can Press 2009 64p. Illustration

Grades: 2 3 4 5   **741.5; Fic**

1. Cats — Graphic novels; 2. Graphic novels; 3. Humorous graphic novels; 4. Space flight — Graphic novels

Courtesy of Kids Can Press

978-1-55453-309-1, $16.95; 1-55453-309-0; 978-1-55453-419-7 (pa), $7.95; 1-55453-419-4 (pa)

Binky the cat lives with two humans (an unnamed mother and son) in what he thinks of as a space station. He's determined to become a space cat and venture into outer space with his stuffed mousie Ted, and to that end he gets his space cat kit through the mail, complete with instructions to build a space ship.

"Spires's mix of sly, dry and slapstick humor in her first graphic novel is perfect.... Details in the muted watercolor illustrations, like mousie Ted covering his nose as Binky releases "space gas," will keep readers of all ages giggling, whether they're cat lovers or not." Kirkus

Other titles about Binky are: Binky to the rescue (2010); Binky under pressure (2011);Binky takes charge (2012);License to scratch (2013)

★ **Binky** to the rescue: a Binky adventure. Kids Can Press 2010 64p. Illustration

Grades: 2 3 4 5   **741.5; Fic**

1. Adventure graphic novels; 2. Cats — Graphic novels; 3. Graphic novels; 4. Humorous graphic novels

978-1-55453-502-6, $16.95; 1-55453-502-6; 978-1-55453-597-2 (pa), $8.95; 1-55453-597-2 (pa)

LC 2009-906866-4

While in hot pursuit of an alien invader (a fly) in his space station (house), Binky, a Certified Space Cat, falls out of the space station porthole (bathroom window) and

Courtesy of Kids Can Press

lands in outer space (outside) for the first time. As he starts to explore, Binky finds his copilot Ted (his stuffed mousie), but then comes under attack by aliens (wasps). Rescued by one of his humans (Mom), Binky soon realizes Ted is still in outer space and he must get him back.

"The muted palette and variety of panel shapes, sound effects, expressive characters and deadpan humor work in perfect rib-tickling harmony." Kirkus

Companion to: Binky the Space Cat (2009)

Fluffy strikes back. by Ashley Spires. Kids Can Press 2016 72 p. Color; Illustration

Grades: 2 3 4 5 6   **741.5; Fic**

1. Cats — Fiction; 2. Humorous fiction — Fiction; 3. Insects — Fiction

1771381272; 9781771381277, $15.95

"Fluffy Vandermere, the cat sergeant in charge of P.U.R.S.T. (Pets of the Universe Ready for Space Travel), works tirelessly to protect the world from alien (aka bug) domination.... Now, suddenly and without warning, Fluffy discovers P.U.R.S.T. headquarters, the most secure building in the

Courtesy of Kids Can Press

world, is under attack by an angry swarm of insects, and they're armed with every cat's worst nightmare — - spray bottles! " (Publisher's note)

"Spires' muted Photoshop illustrations clearly and adorably depict the story's action, while the arrangement of panels, which include security footage, schematics, and subterranean cross sections, ramps up the suspense and comedy." Booklist

Gordon: bark to the future!. Ashley Spires. Kids Can Press 2018 72 p. Color; Illustration

Grades: 1 2 3 4   **741.5; Fic**

1. Life on other planets — Juvenile fiction; 2. Pets — Juvenile fiction; 3. Dogs — Juvenile fiction

1771384093; 9781771384094, $15.99

"It's all up to Gordon now. His partner has been captured. His superior officer has been neutralized. And his distress calls to P.U.R.S.T. (Pets of the Universe Ready for Space Travel) have gone unanswered. That means he must fight the aliens alone! But Gordon's not a fighter — his deadliest weapon is his mind. So what's a genius dog to do? Time travel, of course!" (Publisher's note)

"Spires' second post-Binky graphic tale in her ongoing series is wry, dry, and adorable. As always, the animal characters do not speak, but their expressions and body language (and the hilariously deadpan narration) tell the tale across the small panels drawn in muted tones." Kirkus

Stanley, John

★ **Little** Lulu, vol. 1: My dinner with Lulu. [by] John Stanley and Irving Tripp. Dark Horse Comics 2005 200p. Illustration

Grades: 4 5 6 7 8 9 10 11 12 Adult   **741.5; Fic**

1. Friendship — Graphic novels; 2. Graphic novels; 3. Humorous graphic novels

1-59307-318-6, $9.95

Lulu Moppet plays with best friend Tubby, except when he hangs out with the other neighborhood boys and tries to keep girls out of their clubhouse; she deals with terrible toddler Alvin by weaving extravagant tales featuring herself; and other everyday adventures. This is the first volume of a series that will eventually reprint every Little Lulu comic for new young readers.

Volume 1 of 29

★ **Nancy,** volume 1: the Johnny Stanley Library. Drawn & Quarterly 2009 128p. Illustration

Grades: 2 3 4 5 6 7 8 9 10 11 12 Adult   **741.5; Fic**

1. Graphic novels; 2. Humorous graphic novels; 3. Nancy (Fictional character)

978-1-897299-77-7, $24.95

LC c2009-901565-X

The comic book character Nancy was created by Ernie Bushmiller; Dell Comics published the comics scripted by John Stanley with art by Dan Gormley starting with issue 146 in 1957. In these stories, Nancy meets Oona Goosepimple, a spooky girl who lives in a haunted house, has an incredible run of bad luck because of what she thinks is a four-leaf clover, and has all kinds of everyday adventures and misadventures with her friend Sluggo, their nemesis Spike, neighborhood rich kid Rollo, and her Aunt Fritzi. Always short of money yet needing some to buy ice cream sodas and other treats, many of Nancy's adventures with Sluggo involve various moneymaking schemes to get the dime needed (those were the days ...). The kinds of adventures the kids have are somewhat similar to Stanley's other work on Little Lulu, but set in an urban environment rather than the suburban neighborhood of Lulu and her friends. The book, designed by Seth, retains the soft original coloring of the old comics, with the paper even looking like old comics (but much sturdier). This book should have the same all-ages appeal as Little Lulu; the 2009 Free Comic Book Day issue featuring Nancy was a big hit with readers five years old and up to adults who remembered reading Nancy comics when they were kids.

Steinberg, David

The **adventures** of Daniel Boom AKA Loud Boy: game on!. written by D.J. Steinberg; illustrated by Brian Smith. Grosset & Dunlap 2009 96p. Illustration

Grades: 3 4 5 6 7 8   **741.5; Fic**

1. Graphic novels; 2. Humorous graphic novels; 3. Superhero graphic novels

978-0-448-44700-1, $5.99

Loud Boy and the rest of the Freak Five thought they had helped put all the members of Kid Rid behind bars, but now "Old Fogey" Fogelman has broken out of jail. Daniel Boom, AKA Loud Boy, his sister Jeannie S., Sid, Rex, and Violet work together to help Daniel's uncle hide something called a Flooggget from Fogelman it looks like a banana, but it is a device that can digitize three-dimensional objects. Uncle Stanley warns the super powered kids that Fogelman intends to use the device on children, but he has to flee before telling them everything. Then Daniel makes a new friend, J R, who gets him hooked on the new game called Pig Planet. The other Freak Five members try to get Daniel's attention, but succeed only when it's too late, and J R has stolen the Flooggget and given it to Fogelman. It turns out J R is a robot built by Fogelman, and he uses the Flooggget to digitize the 1.7 million children playing Pig Planet. Daniel figures the only way to save the kids and stop Fogelman is to get into the game himself but can he win?

Steinke, Aron Nels

Mr. Wolf's class. Aron Nels Steinke. Scholastic 2018 160 p. Color; Illustration

Grades: 2 3 4 5   **741.5; Fic**

1. First day of school — Fiction; 2. Teachers — Fiction; 3. Animals — Fiction

9781338047684, $9.99; 9781338047691; 9781338047707

LC 2017945601

In this book in the Mr. Wolf's Class series, by Aron Nels Steinke, "Mr. Wolf has just started teaching at Hazelwood Elementary. He wants the first day of school to go well, but he's got his hands full with his new class. Some of his students include: Margot, who is new in town and is trying to make friends.... Aziza, who just wants everyone to be quiet and do their work. And Penny, who is VERY sleepy because she has a new baby brother at home, goes missing!" (Publisher's note)

"With calm intelligence and amusing, accessible realism, Steinke creates a cast in which any young reader will immediately find someone to embrace and a world that's invitingly recognizable. Friendly figures and compositions that favor flow over flash make the cartooning equally inviting." Booklist

Stine, R. L.

Goosebumps Graphix: Scary Summer. Scholastic/Graphix 2007 137p. Illustration

Grades: 4 5 6 7 8 9   **741.5; Fic**

1. Graphic novels; 2. Horror graphic novels

978-0-439-85782-6, $8.99

Someone's creeping through the garden, doing nasty things! Dean Haspiel, a veteran of Batman and Justice League comics, knows just how to portray "The Revenge of the Lawn Gnomes." In his comic series like The Bakers and Plastic Man, Kyle Baker proves he's one funny artist, the perfect guy to draw a story about fun and games at camp — until "The Horror at Camp Jellyjam" is uncovered. And Courtney Crumrin creator Ted Naifeh adapts and illustrates "Ghost Beach," in which Terri and Jerry go on vacation with some of their father's cousins and meet other kids who dress in old-fashioned clothes and caution them about ghosts.

Slappy's tales of horror. adapted and illustrated by Dave Roman, Jamie Tolagson, Gabriel Hernandez, and Ted Naifeh; color by Jose Garibaldi. Graphix / Scholastic 2015 176 p.

Grades: 3 4 5 6   **741.5; Fic**

1. Stine, R. L. — Adaptations.; 2. Horror fiction; 3. Monsters — Graphic novels

9780545835954, $12.99; 9780545836005, $24.99

LC 2014959511

In this book "[f]our Goosebumps Graphix tales by master of horror R. L. Stine are adapted into full-color comics and feature a brand-new Slappy story by bestselling author, Dave Roman.... Roman [also] creates the horrifying drawings for 'The Night of the Living Dummy,' the origin story about that most evil of all ventriloquist dummies, Slappy!" Illustrators Jamie Tolagson, Gabriel Hernandez, and Ted Naifeh are also included. (Publisher's note)

"Each segment has the hallmarks of the individual artist as he balances comedy and horror, childishness and seriousness: Tolagson's deep shadows and brisk pace keep readers guessing at what is actually perilous, and Hernandez's pen and ink scratches help bridge the gap between mundane and dangerous. The more cartoony styles of Naifeh and Roman may reduce the fear factor, but Naifeh's sense of mood remains top-notch." SLJ

Sturm, James

Adventures in cartooning: how to turn your doodles into comics. [by] James Sturm, Andrew Arnold, Alexis Frederick-Frost. First Second 2009 109p. Illustration

Grades: 2 3 4 5   **741.5; Fic**
1. Cartooning — Technique; 2. Comic books, strips, etc. — Technique; 3. Cartooning
978-1-59643-369-4 (pa), $12.95; 1-59643-369-8 (pa)

When a princess wants to draw her own comic book, the magic comic book elf shows her how to do it through the course of a story about a knight, his hungry (and easily scared) horse, and the knight's quest to find a dragon. Young aspiring cartoonists will learn about the importance of panels to convey the passage of time, how to use word balloons and different lettering to convey emotion, how to show motion, create sound effects, and lots more, even as they will giggle over the action in the story. As the magic comic book elf says, anyone who can draw simple shapes and objects can be a cartoonist.

Other titles in this series are:Adventures in cartooning activity book (2010);Christmas special (2012);Characters in action (2013);Sleepless knight (2015);Gryphons aren't so great (2015)

★ **Adventures** in cartooning: Chistmas special. James Sturm, Andrew Arnold, Alexis Frederick-Frost. First Second 2012 64 p. Illustration

Grades: 2 3 4 5   **741.5/973; Fic**
1. Cartooning — Technique; 2. Christmas stories; 3. Comic books, strips, etc. — Technique; 4. Santa Claus; 5. Cartooning; 6. Elves
1596437308; 9781596437302, $9.99; 9781613830741, $17.45
LC 2012011299

Author James Sturm presents a children's holiday story, part of the "Adventures In Cartooning series.... Christmas is coming! The Magic Cartooning Elf and his friend the Knight help Santa make a Christmas comic. But will kids put away their iPads, smart phones, and video games long enough to read a book?...[Sturm] will inspire children to pick up a pencil and draw up a snow storm!" (Publisher's note)

Ape and Armadillo take over the world. by James Sturm. TOON Books 2016 40 p. Color; Illustration

Grades: K 1 2 3   **741.5; Fic**
1. Apes — Fiction; 2. Armadillos — Fiction; 3. Friendship — Fiction; 4. Graphic novels; 5. Imagination — Fiction
1943145091; 9781943145096, $12.95
LC 2016003370

"Armadillo is trying to come up with a plan for global domination...but with every new idea, being a bad guy seems a little less fun — especially if ruling the world means losing your best friend. Readers will delight in...[the] tender and just depiction of a friendship in peril." (Publisher's note)

"Sturm's large, vibrant panels are ideal for engaging young readers, and quirky details (is that an alligator in the sewer") will ensure devoted contemplation." Booklist

A Toon book.

Ogres Awake!. by James Sturm, Alexis Frederick-Frost and Andrew Arnold. First Second 2016 40 p. Color; Illustration (Adventures in cartooning)

Grades: K 1 2 3   **741.5; Fic**
1. Monsters — Graphic novels; 2. Giants — Graphic novels; 3. Drawing — Technique
1596436530; 9781596436534, $14.99

In this graphic novel by James Sturm, Alexis Frederick-Frost and Andrew Arnold, "the knight and her horse, Edward, have made a startling discovery: there are three huge ogres asleep at her doorstep! When they wake up, the kingdom is in big trouble! The knight, Edward, and some garden gnomes fight back, not with swords and shields, but with potato peelers and spoons. It turns out that ogres are pretty friendly when they have full stomachs!" (Publisher's note)

" This fun graphic novel for prereaders and beginning readers is filled with colorful, deceptively simple art and easy-to-read panels. The word balloons and sound effects add to the comical tension in the story, while the structure and panel arrangements lend themselves to teaching early primary students about creating comics." Booklist

★ **Satchel** Paige: striking out Jim Crow. Hyperion Books for Children/Jump at the Sun 2007 90p. Illustration

Grades: 4 5 6 7 8 9 10   **92; 741.5**
1. African Americans — Biography — Graphic novels; 2. Baseball — Graphic novels; 3. Baseball players; 4. Biographical graphic novels; 5. Graphic novels; 6. Paige, Satchel, 1906-1982
978-0-7868-3901-8, $9.99; 978-0-7868-3900-1, $16.99

Narrated by an African American who played in the Negro Leagues for a short time, this book sketches part of the career of Leroy "Satchel" Paige, a star of the Negro Leagues. Young Emmet scored a run off Paige in a game, but suffered a career-ending knee injury. Readers get a sense of the rough life African Americans faced in the south during the 1920s, 1930s, and 1940s. Then Paige and his team come to Tuckwilla, Alabama in 1944 to play an all-White team, and Emmet and his son attend the game and watch how Paige and his team take apart the home boys. There's one panel showing a man who has been lynched and hanged; most of the violence is mentioned but not depicted on the pages.

Part of The Center for Cartoon Studies Presents series

Sumerak, Marc

Franklin Richards, son of a genius: not-so-secret invasion. story, Chris Eliopoulos & Marc Sumerak; script, Marc Sumerak; art & letters Chris Eliopoulos. Marvel Entertainment 2009 un Illustration

Grades: 3 4 5 6 7 8 9   **741.5; Fic**
1. Fantastic Four (Fictional characters); 2. Graphic novels; 3. Humorous graphic novels; 4. Superhero graphic novels
978-0-7851-3369-8, $9.99

This latest volume includes stories featuring Franklin Richards, son of Reed and Sue Richards of the Fantastic Four. Young Franklin, aided and abetted (albeit reluctantly) by his robot companion H.E.R.B.I.E., builds a replica of the first Iron Man robotic armor, drinks one of his dad's formulas and proceeds to belch HUGELY, de-ages his dad so they can play together, and then a multiplicity of Franklin Richards in many different timelines get into similar trouble. There are more stories, lots of silly humor and superhero action, drawn by coauthor Eliopoulos.

Spider-Man and Power Pack: Big-City Super Heroes. Marvel Entertainment 2007 un Illustration

Grades: 3 4 5 6 7 8   **741.5; Fic**

1. Graphic novels; 2. Power Pack (Fictional characters); 3. Spider-Man (Fictional character); 4. Superhero graphic novels
0-7851-2357-1, $6.99

When the Power family moves to New York City, Marvel's youngest superheroes, the Power Pack, have a whole new city to explore. Julie (Lightspeed), Alex (Zero-G), Jack (Mass Master), and little Katie (Energizer) meet and team up with Spider-Man and help him defeat Venom, the Sandman, and the Vulture. Katie also gets infected by the Venom symbiote, and Spidey gets dumped into a vat of liquid that turns him into a kid again.

Originally published as Spider-Man and Power Pack issues #1-4.

Sutherland, Tui
Wings of fire : the graphic novel; Book 1: The dragonet prophecy. by Tui T. Sutherland; adapted by Barry Deutsch; art by Mike Holmes; color by Maarta Laiho. Graphix 2018 224 p. Color; Illustration; Map
Grades: 4 5 6 7   **741.5; Fic**
1. Imaginary wars and battles; 2. Friendship; 3. Dragons — Fiction
9780545942164, $24.99
LC 2017955178

"Clay has grown up under the mountain, chosen along with four other dragonets to fulfill a...prophecy and end the war between the dragon tribes of Pyrrhia.... So when one of the dragonets is threatened, all five spring into action. Together, they will choose freedom over fate, leave the mountain, and fulfill their destiny — on their own terms." (Publisher's note)

"Adapted from Sutherland's middle-grade series, the story is surprisingly riveting; the politics involved between the warring factions and dragon races makes for great world building, and the war-torn world, complete with gladiatorial-style fights and backstabbings, is an intriguing backdrop for the five dragons' development." Booklist

Takamisaki, Ryo
Megaman NT Warrior Vol. 1. Viz/Viz Kids 2004 186p. Illustration
Grades: 4 5 6 7 8 9   **741.5; Fic**
1. Graphic novels; 2. Manga; 3. Science fiction graphic novels; 4. Shonen manga
1-59116-465-6, $7.95

The year is 200X and everyone is now connected to the Cyber Network. People carry their own PET (Personal terminal) and are paired up with an artificial intelligence program called a NetNavi (or NetNavigator). Computers have turned the world into a bright and shiny utopia, but there's always trouble in paradise. While the invention of the PET and NetNavis has brought great benefits to the world, computer hacking, virus spreading, and other high-tech crimes are becoming a major problem. A sinister organization by the name of World Three has appeared, and they've vowed to destroy this technological wonderland. Enter Lan Hikari, an intensely curious and cheerful fifth grader. Synchronized with his NetNavigator, MegaMansupercharged, he becomes a super-charged dynamo. In and out of the Net, Lan and MegaMan do their best to thwart World Three's neverending quest to take over the world. The book includes some raunchy humor and lots of action.

Pokemon: the rise of Darkrai. story & art by Ryo Takamisaki; English translation, Kaori Inoue. Viz Media/VizKids 2008 un Illustration
Grades: 2 3 4 5 6 7 8 9   **741.5; Fic**
1. Adventure graphic novels; 2. Fantasy graphic novels; 3. Graphic novels; 4. Manga; 5. Shonen manga
978-1-4215-2289-0, $7.99

Ash and his friends come to Alamos Town, home of the Space-Time Towers, and while touring the town, they discover that the town's special garden has been ransacked. Some of the townspeople blame Darkrai, a sinister looking Pokemon that said to haunt the garden. However, Alamos Town faces much more peril when two powerful Pokemon that control

time and space battle each other; it should be impossible for them to meet, and unless Ash and the others " and perhaps Darkrai " can stop them, Alamos Town will be destroyed. This book includes a lot of Pokemon fighting action; the panels are so filled with details that very young readers might find it difficult to follow the action.

Takeuchi, Naoko
★ **Sailor** Moon; Volume 1. Naoko Takeuchi; translator/adapter, William Flanagan. Kodansha Comics 2011 240 p. Illustration; Color
Grades: 5 6 7 8 9 10   **741.5; Fic**
1. Teenage girls — Japan — Comic books, strips, etc; 2. Women heroes — Comic books, strips, etc; 3. Shojo manga; 4. Teenage girls — Fiction; 5. Good and evil — Fiction
1935429744; 9781935429746, $10.99
LC 2012374271

"Usagi Tsukino is a normal girl until she meets up with Luna, a talking cat, who tells her that she is Sailor Moon. As Sailor Moon, Usagi must fight evils and enforce justice, in the name of the Moon and the mysterious Moon Princess. She meets other girls destined to be Sailor Senshi (Sailor Scouts), and together, they fight the forces of evil!" (Publisher's note)

First published in Japan in 2003 by Kodansha Ltd., Tokyo, as Bishoujosenshi Sailor Moon Shinsoban; Volume 1 of 12

Telgemeier, Raina
The **Baby-sitter's** Club: Kristy's great idea: a graphic novel. story by Ann M. Martin; adapted by Raina Telgemeier. Scholastic Graphix 2006 192p. Illustration
Grades: 3 4 5 6   **741.5; Fic**
1. Babysitting — Graphic novels; 2. Friendship — Graphic novels; 3. Graphic novels
0-439-80241-5, $16.99; 0-439-73933-0 (pa), $8.99
LC 2005-37749

Follows the adventures of Kristy and the other members of the Baby-sitters Club as they deal with crank calls, uncontrollable two-year-olds, wild pets, and parents who do not always tell the truth. A graphic novel based on the 1988 book by the same name.

"Comics artist Telgemeier's clean-lined, black-and-white art with stark black details nicely differentiates the four personable seventh-graders who parlay their babysitting experience into a business." Booklist

Also available in full color editions; Other titles about the Baby-sitters Club are: The truth about Stacey (2006); Mary Anne saves the day (2007); Claudia and Mean Janine (2008)

The **Baby-Sitters** Club: The Truth About Stacey. Raina Telgemeier; [adapted from the novel by] Ann M. Martin. Scholastic/Graphix 2006 142p. Illustration
Grades: 3 4 5 6 7 8 9   **741.5**
1. Babysitting — Graphic novels; 2. Friendship — Graphic novels; 3. Graphic novels
0-439-73936-5

Poor Stacey. She's moved to a new town. She's still coming to terms with her diabetes. She's facing baby-sitting problems left and right, and her parents are no help. Luckily, Stacey has three new, true friends: Kristy, Claudia, and Mary Anne. Together they're the BSC, and they will deal with whatever is thrown their way, even if it's a rival baby-sitting club.

★ **Drama**. Raina Telgemeier; with color by Gurihiru. Graphix 2012 233 p. Illustration
Grades: 5 6 7 8   **741.5**
1. Graphic novels; 2. Interpersonal relations — Fiction; 3. Middle schools — Fiction; 4. Schools — Fiction; 5. Theater — Fiction; 6. School stories; 7. LGBT youth — Fiction; 8. Children's plays — Fiction
0545326982; 0545326990; 9780545326988, $23.99; 9780545326995

Stonewall Honor Book (2013)

LC 2011040748

Author Raina Telgemeier's book focuses on a middle school drama production. "Callie loves theater...[S]he's the set designer for the stage crew, and this year she's determined to create a set worthy of Broadway on a middle-school budget. But how can she, when she doesn't know much about carpentry, ticket sales are down, and the crew members are having trouble working together?" (Publisher's note)

"In this realistic and sympathetic story, feelings and thoughts leap off the page, revealing Telgemeier's keen eye for young teen life." Booklist

Includes bibliographical references

★ **Ghosts**. Raina Telgemeier; with color by Braden Lamb. Graphix, an imprint of Scholastic 2016 256 p. Color; Illustration

Grades: 3 4 5 6 7   **741.5; Fic**

1. Cystic fibrosis — Fiction; 2. Families — California, Northern — Comic books, strips, etc; 3. Family life — California, Northern — Fiction; 4. Ghost stories; 5. Ghosts — Comic books, strips, etc; 6. Ghosts — Fiction; 7. Graphic novels; 8. Moving, Household — Comic books, strips, etc; 9. Moving, Household — Fiction; 10. Sisters — Comic books, strips, etc; 11. Sisters — Fiction; 12. California, Northern — Comic books, strips, etc; 13. California, Northern — Fiction

0545540623; 9780545540629, $10.99; 9780545540612, $24.99; 0545540615

LC 2016004672

Eisner Award: Best Publication for Kids (2017)

"Catrina and her family have just moved to Northern California. Bahía de la Luna is different from Cat's hometown — for one thing, everyone is obsessed with ghosts — but the sea air makes it easier for Cat's younger sister, Maya, who has cystic fibrosis (CF), to breathe. Carlos, a new friend and neighbor, introduces the girls to a different perspective on the spiritual world." (School Library Journal)

"In her treatment of illness and death, Telgemeier (Sisters) nudges readers toward the edge of their comfort zone, but she never leaves them alone there. The story is consistently engaging, the plot is tightly built, and — as always — Telgemeier excels at capturing facial expressions." Pub Wkly

★ **Sisters**. Raina Telgemeier; with color by Braden Lamb. Graphix 2014 197 p. Color; Illustration

Grades: 5 6 7 8   **741.5; 306.875; 92**

1. Interpersonal relations; 2. Autobiographical graphic novels; 3. Family life; 4. Siblings

9780545540599, $24.99; 9780545540605, $10.99

LC 2013008700

"Raina can't wait to be a big sister. But once Amara is born, things aren't quite how she expected them to be.... They are sisters, after all. Raina uses her signature humor...in both present-day narrative and perfectly placed flashbacks to tell the story of her relationship with her sister, which unfolds during the course of a road trip from their home in San Francisco to a family reunion in Colorado." (Publisher's note)

"The author's narrative style is fresh and sharp, and the combination of well-paced and well-placed flashbacks pull the plot together, moving the story forward and helping readers understand the characters' point of view. The volume captures preadolescence in an effortless and uncanny way and turns tough subjects, such as parental marriage problems, into experiences with which readers can identify." (School Library Journal)

★ **Smile**. Scholastic/Graphix 2010 213p. Illustration

Grades: 5 6 7 8   **741; 741.5**

1. Autobiographical graphic novels; 2. Dentistry — Graphic novels; 3. Friendship — Graphic novels; 4. Graphic novels; 5. Personal appearance — Graphic novels

978-0-545-13205-3, $21.99; 0-545-13205-3; 978-0-545-13206-0 (pa), $10.99; 0-545-13206-1 (pa)

LC 2008-51782

Boston Globe-Horn Book Honor: Nonfiction (2010); Eisner Award: Best Publication for Teens (2011)

"Raina just wants to be a normal sixth grader. But one night after Girl Scouts she trips and falls, severely injuring her two front teeth. What follows is a long and frustrating journey with on-again, off-again braces, surgery, embarrassing headgear, and even a retainer with fake teeth attached. And on top of all that, there's still more to deal with: a major earthquake, boy confusion, and friends who turn out to be not so friendly." (Publisher's note)

"Telgemeier has created an utterly charming graphic memoir of tooth trauma, first crushes and fickle friends, sweetly reminiscent of Judy Blume's work." Kirkus

TenNapel, Doug

Cardboard. Doug TenNapel. Graphix / Scholastic 2012 288 p.

Grades: 5 6 7 8   **741.5**

1. Father-son relationship — Graphic novels; 2. Boxes — Fiction; 3. Gifts — Graphic novels; 4. Bullies — Graphic novels; 5. Magic — Graphic novels

0545418720; 9780545418720, $24.99; 9780545418737

LC 2011934533

In this graphic novel, "Cam Howerton's out-of-work father is so broke, the best he can do for Cam's birthday is an empty cardboard box purchased from a toy seller with two mysterious rules: return every unused scrap of cardboard and don't ask for any more.... [T]he box becomes a project. What should father and son make out of the box? 'A boxer,' Cam suggests.... 'Boxer Bill,' created from inanimate material, comes alive. Unfortunately, Marcus, the neighborhood bully...steals the scrap materials, and begins turning out a whole evil empire of cardboard monsters.... [A]fter losing control of them he must unite with Cam and his father to defeat the massive cardboard army.... [Q]uestions are raised about what it means to be a man, what makes a good man, and what forms people's character." (Horn Book)

Terry, Laura

Graveyard shakes. Laura Terry. Graphix 2017 208 p. Color; Illustration

Grades: 3 4 5 6   **741.5; Fic**

1. Sisters — Graphic novels; 2. Ghosts — Juvenile fiction; 3. Children's stories

9780545889544; 9780545889551, $24.99; 9780545889568

LC 2016960079

In this book, by Laura Terry, "Katia and Victoria are sisters and scholarship students at a private boarding school. While Victoria tries to fit in, Katia is unapologetic about her quirks.... After a big fight, Katia runs away from school. And when Victoria goes looking for her, she accidentally tumbles into the underworld of a nearby graveyard. It is inhabited by ghosts, ghouls, and a man named Nikola, who is preparing a sinister spell that's missing one key ingredient." (Publisher's note)

"That the afterlife can be as complicated as regular life will strike a wryly funny note with young outcasts and loners, but Terry never loses sight of the idea that even misfits can find community by being themselves." Pub Wkly

Tetzner, Lisa

The **Black** Brothers: A Novel in Pictures. Front Street 2004 144p. Illustration

Grades: 4 5 6 7 8 9   **741.5; Fic**

1. Chimney sweeps — Graphic novels; 2. Graphic novels

1-932425-04-7, $16.95

In rural Italy, thirteen-year-old Giorgio is sold to a man who supplies chimney sweeps for Milan. After a treacherous journey in which most of the other boys die, Giorgio goes to work for a man whose wife resents another mouth to feed and starves him. He is sent up into chimneys with no training or guidance for how to do the dangerous work. After nearly dying, he is befriended by a doctor and finds the Black Brothers, a group of chimney sweeps who swear loyalty to each other.

This illustrated novel was originally published in German in 1941, and the translation's tone is similar to other children's books, such as Emil and the Detectives.

Tezuka, Osamu

Astro Boy books 1 and 2. Dark Horse Comics 2008 424p. Illustration
Grades: 3 4 5 6 7 8 9 10 11 12 Adult   **741.5; Fic**
1. Adventure graphic novels; 2. Astro Boy (Fictional character); 3. Graphic novels; 4. Robots — Graphic novels; 5. Science fiction graphic novels
978-1-59582-153-9, $14.95

When a scientist loses his young son, he builds a robot to look exactly like the boy, but when he activates the robot, the scientist becomes repulsed and rejects him. Professor Ochanomizu (gotta love the name, it means tea water and is also a famous Tokyo neighborhood) rescues the boy robot from a circus and names him Astro Boy. He deals with aliens, with people who would use robots to commit crimes, and with adventures in outer space. This new edition collects the first two volumes of the Dark Horse manga editions.

Also available in omnibus editions; Volumes 1 and 2 of a 23 volume series

Thielbar, Melinda

The **secret** ghost: a mystery with distance and measuring (Manga math mysteries #3). story by Melinda Thielbar; art by Yuko Ota.. Graphic Universe/Lerner Publishing Group 2009 48p. Illustration
Grades: 1 2 3 4

741.5; Fic
1. Graphic novels; 2. Mathematics — Graphic novels; 3. Measurement — Graphic novels; 4. Mystery graphic novels; 5. Kodomo
978-0-7613-3855-0, $29.27

LC 2008-53243

After Sifu Faiza's kung fu class, the students help to measure the class room so Sifu can purchase shelving. Then Sam tells

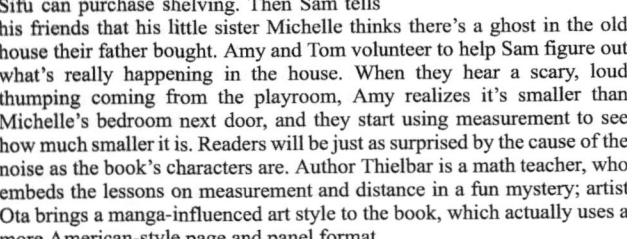

Courtesy of Lerner Publishing Group

his friends that his little sister Michelle thinks there's a ghost in the old house their father bought. Amy and Tom volunteer to help Sam figure out what's really happening in the house. When they hear a scary, loud thumping coming from the playroom, Amy realizes it's smaller than Michelle's bedroom next door, and they start using measurement to see how much smaller it is. Readers will be just as surprised by the cause of the noise as the book's characters are. Author Thielbar is a math teacher, who embeds the lessons on measurement and distance in a fun mystery; artist Ota brings a manga-influenced art style to the book, which actually uses a more American-style page and panel format.

This is the third book in the Manga Math Mysteries series.

Thompson, Jill

Goosebumps: Terror Trips. Scholastic/Graphix 2007 137p. Illustration

Grades: 4 5 6 7 8 9   **741.5; Fic**
1. Graphic novels; 2. Horror graphic novels; 3. Stine, R. L.; 4. Stine, R. L. — Adaptations
978-0-439-85780-2, $8.99

Stine's Goosebumps series was very popular years ago, and is enjoying a resurgence of popularity with new editions of the prose books. The graphic novel adaptations, all done by well-known independent comics creators, bring the stories to a new audience. Goosebumps: Creepy Creatures is also available.

This volume adapts three of Stine's Goosebumps novels into graphic novel format. Noted independent comic creator Thompson adapts One Day at Horrorland, about one family's ordeal in a very strange, all-too-realistic amusement park. Canadian artist Tolagson adapts A Shocker on Shock Street, which depicts the horrific adventures of two kids on a movie studio lot where the horror is more than just special effects. Global manga creator Ganter adapts Deep Trouble, in which a brother and sister find a real mermaid.

★ **Magic** Trixie. written and illustrated by Jill Thompson; lettered by Jason Arthur. Harper Trophy 2008 93p. Illustration
Grades: 3 4 5   **741.5; Fic**
1. Fantasy graphic novels; 2. Graphic novels; 3. Humorous graphic novels; 4. Magic — Graphic novels
978-0-06-117045-4 (pa), $7.99

LC 2007-24298

Magic Trixie is feeling a bit put out; everything in her house seems to revolve around her baby sister, and she doesn't get to do anything fun. If that wasn't bad enough, Show & Tell time is coming up at Monstersorri School, and all her classmates have seen all her tricks too many times. She'll have to come up with a new one that's really special.

"Bright colors and a whimsical style make everything friendly rather than scary. Underneath the supernatural trappings lies a classical story of sibling envy to which every big sister and big brother can relate." Booklist

Other titles in this series are: Magic Trixie sleeps over (2008); Magic Trixie and the dragon (2009)

★ **Magic** Trixie and the dragon. HarperTrophy 2009 94p. Illustration
Grades: 3 4 5   **741.5; Fic**
1. Dragons — Graphic novels; 2. Fantasy graphic novels; 3. Graphic novels; 4. Humorous graphic novels; 5. Magic — Graphic novels; 6. Witches — Graphic novels
978-0-06-117050-8, $7.99

LC 2008-27473

Little witch girl Magic Trixie goes to the circus with Mimi (her grandma), and she gets to see the dragons. Mimi even gives her a real dragon scale as a souvenir, but when she meets up with her friends and shows off the scale, they think she has a pet dragon. Trixie doesn't want them to think she's lying, so she tries her transmogrification skills to make a dragon, but when she gets distracted in the middle of the spell, it changes her baby sister into a dragon. Yikes! Very soon, Trixie learns that taking care of such a pet is a lot of hard work, and she has to try to change the dragon back into her baby sister before her mother finds out. She also has to find a way to get Scratches back when she drives him away by her obsession over having a dragon pet, making him think that being a cat isn't good enough for her.

★ **Scary** Godmother. written and illustrated by Jill Thompson. Dark Horse 2010 207p. Illustration
Grades: 3 4 5   **741; 741.5; Fic**
1. Graphic novels; 2. Halloween — Graphic novels; 3. Supernatural graphic novels
978-1-59582-589-6, $24.99; 1-59582-589-4

It's Halloween night and it's up to Scary Godmother to show one little girl just how much fun spooky can be! Meet Hannah Marie, who, with the help of Scary Godmother, stands up to her mean-spirited cousin Jimmy and her fear of monsters on her first Halloween adventure with the big kids. Later, Hannah joins forces with Orson, the vampire boy, to unravel a mystery near and dear to their hearts.

This is a "collection compiling all four of Thompson's original Scary Godmother stories plus extra goodies. Told in often-rhyming prose and word balloons on vibrant pages that balance a visually lavish picture book aesthetic with sequential-art page composition, the stories burst with complex color tones and creepy cartoon figures." Booklist

Tobin, Paul

I was the cat. written by Paul Tobin; illustrated and colored by Benjamin Dewey; lettered by Jared Jones; edited by Jill Beaton with Robin Herrera; designed by Jason Storey. Oni Press 2014 144 p. Color; Illustration

Grades: 5 6 7 8 9

741.5; Fic

1. Fantasy graphic novels; 2. Cats — Graphic novels
1620101394; 9781620101391, $24.99
LC 2014932452

Eisner Nominee: Best Publication for Kids (2015)

Courtesy of Oni Press

When "Allison Breaking...receives an offer from a mysterious stranger named Burma to write his memoirs, it's an offer she can't refuse, not even with all the red flags popping up. But Burma is quite literally unlike any man Allison's ever known — because he's a cat! And this cat has stories to tell about how he (over the course of a few lifetimes) has shaped the world." (Publisher's note)

Tolagson, Jamie

Goosebumps: Terror Trips. Scholastic/Graphix 2007 137p. Illustration

Grades: 4 5 6 7 8 9

741.5; Fic

1. Graphic novels; 2. Horror graphic novels; 3. Stine, R. L.; 4. Stine, R. L. — Adaptations
978-0-439-85780-2, $8.99

Stine's Goosebumps series was very popular years ago, and is enjoying a resurgence of popularity with new editions of the prose books. The graphic novel adaptations, all done by well-known independent comics creators, bring the stories to a new audience. Goosebumps: Creepy Creatures is also available.

This volume adapts three of Stine's Goosebumps novels into graphic novel format. Noted independent comic creator Thompson adapts One Day at Horrorland, about one family's ordeal in a very strange, all-too-realistic amusement park. Canadian artist Tolagson adapts A Shocker on Shock Street, which depicts the horrific adventures of two kids on a movie studio lot where the horror is more than just special effects. Global manga creator Ganter adapts Deep Trouble, in which a brother and sister find a real mermaid.

Tolstikova, Dasha

A **Year** Without Mom. by Dasha Tolstikova. Groundwood Books 2015 176 p. Color; Illustration

Grades: 5 6 7 8

741.5; 92

1. Tolstikova, Dasha; 2. Mother-daughter relationship; 3. Russia; 4. Refugees
1554986923; 9781554986927, $19.95

This book, by Dasha Tolstikova, "follows 12-year-old Dasha through a year full of turmoil after her mother leaves for America. It is the early 1990s in Moscow, and political change is in the air. But Dasha is more worried about her own challenges as she negotiates family, friendships and school without her mother. Just as she begins to find her own feet, she gets word that she is to join her mother in America — a place that seems impossibly far from everything and everyone she loves." (Publisher's note)

"Scribbly, childlike pencil drawings are filled in with gray wash and accentuated with red and the occasional pop of blue. They are deceptively simple, but with great narrative sophistication, they capture both the specificity of Dasha's experience and the universality of her emotions." Kirkus

Torres, J.

Into the woods. J. Torres; illustrated by Faith Erin Hicks. Kids Can Press 2012 100 p. Color illustration (Bigfoot Boy)

Grades: 3 4 5 6 7

Fic; 741.5; 741.5/971

1. Magic — Graphic novels; 2. Totems and totemism — Graphic novels; 3. Sasquatch — Graphic novels
1554537118; 9781554537112, $17.95

Courtesy of Kids Can Press

In this fantasy graphic novel, "city boy Rufus is staying at his grandmother's house on the edge of a forest for a few days without his parents," and he "decides to explore the woods. He meets a girl named Penny.... When looking for her in the woods, Rufus finds a glowing necklace in a tree. After reading the word on the back, he turns into Bigfoot!...There's danger in the forest as well as magic, and when Penny disappears, Rufus...use[s] the totem to effect a rescue." (Kirkus Reviews)

Followed by: The unkindness of ravens (2013)

★ **Lola:** a ghost story. [by] J. Torres & [illustrated by] Elbert Or. Oni Press 2009 102p. Illustration

Grades: 4 5 6 7 8

741.5; Fic

1. Family life — Graphic novels; 2. Ghosts — Graphic novels; 3. Graphic novels; 4. Philippines — Graphic novels
978-1-934964-33-0, $14.95;
1-934964-33-6

"Lola ("grandmother" in Tagalog) has just died, and Jesse is reluctant to visit her home in the Philippines. He was afraid of her because she was rumored to have magical abilities, and because he thinks she tried to drown him when he was a baby. Jesse listens

Courtesy of Oni Press

to family members tell stories about her as he tries to adjust to their strange mix of superstitions and religion.... Jesse is an unusually nuanced character.... When he sees something extraordinary, it's unclear if he is dreaming, hallucinating, or if he has inherited his grandmother's abilities. Torres's gradual revelation of details will keep readers hanging until they learn the truth. Or's artwork uses sepia tones and smooth lines, and features characters with cute button eyes. But the sweet images can quickly turn horrific when Jesse has his visions. " SLJ

Teen Titans Go! Vol. 1: Truth, Justice, Pizza!. DC Comics 2004 112p. Illustration

Grades: 3 4 5 6 7 8 9

741.5; Fic

1. Graphic novels; 2. Humorous graphic novels; 3. Superhero graphic novels; 4. Teen Titans (Fictional characters)
1-4012-0333-7, $6.95

They're too young to drive, but not too young to save the world. The world's hottest heroes: Robin, Beast Boy, Raven, Cyborg, and Starfire, show how it's done Titan-style, as they go up against teen super villains Gizmo, Jinx, and Mammoth. Things get icky when Raven's bad dad, Trigon, comes out from a huge zit on Raven's forehead (ewwww ...).

Teen Titans Go! Vol. 2: Heroes on Patrol!. J. Torres, Adam Beechen, writers; Todd Nauck, Eric Vedder, pencillers; Lary Stucker, M3th, inkers; Phil Good, Heroic Age, colorists; Phil Balsman, Jared K. Fletcher, letterers; Dave Bullock, collection cover artist. DC Comics 2004 112p. Illustration
Grades: 3 4 5 6 7 8 9   **741.5; Fic**
1. Graphic novels; 2. Humorous graphic novels; 3. Superhero graphic novels; 4. Teen Titans (Fictional characters)
1-4012-0334-5, $6.95

In this volume, the Teen Titans encounter the battling brothers, Thunder and Lightning; Starfire has to deal with her naughty sister Blackfire; they encounter Aqualad; and more.

Teen Titans Go! Vol. 3: Bring It On!. DC Comics 2005 104p. Illustration
Grades: 3 4 5 6 7 8 9   **741.5; Fic**
1. Graphic novels; 2. Humorous graphic novels; 3. Superhero graphic novels; 4. Teen Titans (Fictional characters)
1-4012-0511-9, $6.99

Terra rejoins the Titans to fight Slade's robots; the teen superheroes fight Mumbo; Beast Boy tries to help a man stricken with werewolfism; Speedy joins the Titans to fight Plasmus; and they go up against Kwiz Kid, who's mad at Robin because his ex-girlfriend has a crush on Robin.

Teen Titans Go! Vol. 4: Ready for Action!. DC Comics 2005 104p. Illustration
Grades: 3 4 5 6 7 8 9   **741.5; Fic**
1. Graphic novels; 2. Humorous graphic novels; 3. Superhero graphic novels; 4. Teen Titans (Fictional characters)
978-1-4012-0985-8, $6.99

In this volume, the Titans confront a rampaging Wildebeest, teach the hot-tempered Hotshot the value of patience, battle an army of zombies, find themselves trapped in a deadly video game with the Titans East and more.

Teen Titans Go!: Titans Together!. DC Comics 2007 144p. Illustration
Grades: 3 4 5 6 7 8 9   **741.5**
1. Graphic novels; 2. Superhero graphic novels; 3. Teen Titans (Fictional characters)
978-1-4012-1563-7, $12.99

This volume collects eight adventures of the Teen Titans as seen in the animated series, Teen Titans Go! Robin leads the young team that includes Cyborg, Beast Boy, Raven, and Starfire. The stories have lots of action and bad puns as Beast Boy makes a movie, the Titans find themselves in an alien fighting arena, and Robin's future self, Nightwing, comes when time goes a little haywire and an evil Robin shows up.

Yo Gabba Gabba!: good night, Gabbaland. Oni Press 2010 un Illustration
Grades: PreK K
741.5; Fic

Courtesy of Oni Press

1. Bedtime — Graphic novels; 2. Graphic novels; 3. Humorous graphic novels; 4. Yo Gabba Gabba! (television series)
978-1-934964-56-9, $7.99

DJ Lance announces it's time to get ready for bed, so the inhabitants of Gabbaland clean up and put away their toys, brush their teeth, wash their hands, shake their sillies out, listen to a bedtime story, and go to sleep. Torres and Loux use a different panel arrangement than Eliopoulos did, but this is still a board book that makes it easy for young pre-readers to follow along with the story. Torres uses a lot of repetition, which can encourage young listeners to join in the reading; the routine of getting ready for bed is something most young children will understand and enjoy. Loux makes all the characters recognizable for anyone who watches the series on Nick, Jr., while retaining his individual artistic style, long rubbery arms and all.

Tregonning, Mel

Small things. Mel Tregonning; with an afterword by Barbara Coloroso. Pajama Press 2018 37 p. Illustration
Grades: 3 4 5 6   **741.5; Fic**
1. Anxiety in children — Fiction; 2. Boys — Fiction; 3. Stories without words; 4. Picture books for children; 5. Anxiety — Fiction
1772780421; 9781772780420, $18.95

In author Mel Tregonning's "wordless graphic picture book, a young boy feels alone with his worries. He isn't fitting in well at school. His grades are slipping. He's even lashing out at those who love him.... The boy's worries manifest as tiny beings that crowd around him constantly, overwhelming him and even gnawing away at his very self." (Publisher's note)

"Tregonning creates a visual language for the pain of depression and anxiety, and her story may provide a measure of hope to those who might otherwise have given up in despair." Pub Wkly

Uderzo, Albert

Asterix and Obelix All at Sea. Orion/Sterling Publishing 2002 48p. Illustration
Grades: 4 5 6 7 8 9 10 11 12 Adult   **741.5; Fic**
1. Asterix (Fictional character); 2. Graphic novels; 3. Humorous graphic novels
0-75284-778-3, $9.95

LC 2002-282560

In ancient Rome the slaves are revolting...and not only that, they've stolen Julius Caesar's own galley, the finest warship in the Roman navy. Under their heroic leader Spartakis, the former galley slaves make for the little Gaulish village where Julius Caesar's old enemies Asterix and Obelix live — only to find the place in crisis, for Obelix, after drinking the druid Getafix's magic potions on the sly, is first turned to stone and then reverts to childhood. In search of a cure for him Asterix, Getafix and their new friends the galley slaves sail to the wonderful continent of Atlantis, ruled by its high priest Absolutlifabulos — and the ensuing sea battles against the Roman navy are fast and furious ...

Van Lente, Fred

George Washington. Fred Van Lente, illustrated by Ryan Dunlavey. HarperCollins 2018 128 p. Color; Illustration (Action presidents)
Grades: 4 5 6 7 8   **741.5; 92**
1. Washington, George, 1732-1799; 2. Biography; 3. Presidents — United States
9780062234057, $9.99

LC 2017950229

Includes bibliographical references

In this book in the Action Presidents series, by Fred Van Lente, illustrated by Ryan Dunlavey, "we all know that George Washington was our first president and a hero of the American Revolution, but did you also know that he didn't want to be president and had teeth so bad that he hated to smile?...U.S. history comes to life like never before! Historically accurate and highly entertaining...[w]ith timelines, maps, charts, and more." (Publisher's note)

"Van Lente aims to contextualize historical figures who are often blindly lionized..., a goal that comes through clearly amid a flurry of gags and jokes." Pub Wkly

Howtoons; Volume 1: (re)ignition. writer: Fred Van Lente; artist: Tom Fowler; colors: Jordie Bellaire; letters: Rus Wooton. Image Comics 2015 160 p. Illustration; Color
Grades: 5 6 7 8   **741.5**
1. Science — Experiments — Comic books, strips, etc.; 2. Siblings — Graphic novels; 3. Science fiction graphic novels
9781632150561, $9.99; 1632150565

In this graphic novel by Fred Van Lente and illustrated by Tom Fowler, "Celine and Tuck's parents put them to sleep for centuries to ride out the energy crisis — but when they awake in the far future and Mom and Dad are missing, it's the kids who have to save the day! Celine and Tuck must explore a strange, new Earth using their gadgeteering skills to create projects and experiments to survive hostile tribes and bizarre mechanized threats." (Publisher's note)

"Step-by-step instructions and warnings for each device are included. The materials needed for each project varies. Each example features icons denoting what kind of energy this project represents. An icon glossary provides further explanation." SLJ

Varon, Sara
Robot dreams. First Second 2007 205p. Illustration
Grades: 3 4 5 6 7 8 9 10 11 12 Adult   **741; 741.5; Fic**
1. Dogs — Graphic novels; 2. Graphic novels; 3. Robots — Graphic novels
978-1-59643-108-9 (pa), $16.95; 1-59643-108-3 (pa)
LC 2006-52640

The friendship between a dog and a robot is portrayed in this wordless graphic novel. (Bull Cent Child Books)

"Varon's drawing style is uncomplicated, and her colors are clean and refeshing. Although her story seems equally simple, it is invested with true emotion." Booklist

A Junior Library Guild book

Sweaterweather. Alternative Comics 2006 96p. Illustration
Grades: 3 4 5 6 7 8 9
741.5; Fic
1. Animals — Graphic novels; 2. Friendship — Graphic novels; 3. Graphic novels; 4. Stories without words — Graphic novels
1-891867-93-8, $14.95

A turtle, a rabbit, and other creatures venture out on a wordless snowy journey full of friendship and sweetness. Varon includes interactive bits to the book, such as paper dolls, postcards, and stamps.

First published 2003

Courtesy of Alternative Comics

Venable, Colleen A. F.
And then there were gnomes. illustrated by Stephanie Yue. Graphic Universe 2010 47p. Illustration (Guinea Pig, pet shop private eye)
Grades: 2 3 4   **741; Fic; 741.5**

Courtesy of Lerner Publishing Group

1. Graphic novels; 2. Guinea pigs — Graphic novels; 3. Hamsters — Graphic novels; 4. Humorous graphic novels; 5. Mice — Graphic novels; 6. Mystery graphic novels
978-0-7613-4599-2 (lib bdg), $27.93; 0-7613-4599-X (lib bdg);
978-0-7613-5480-2 (pa), $6.95;
0-7613-5480-8 (pa)
LC 2009-20896

Guinea pig detective Sasspants and her sidekick Hamisher the hamster try to solve a mystery when the mice in Mr. Venezi's pet shop are going missing and all the clues point to a ghost.

"The story is never scary. Everything about it could be described as cute, from the art to the characters' personalities." Publ Wkly

Fish you were here. illustrated by Stephanie Yue. Graphic Universe 2011 46p. Illustration
Grades: 2 3 4
741.5
978-0-7613-5224-2, $27.93;
0-7613-5224-4
LC 2011001079

"Befuddled but lovable Mr. Venez"'s still advertising for an assistant to help him in his pet shop.... When ninth-grader Viola arrives, she seems the perfect employee. She turns a light on the lizards. She gives the ferrets tons of toys and tubes. She even puts the correct

Courtesy of Lerner Publishing Group

animal names on the cages; Mr. Venezi had labeled the chinchillas, 'gorillas,' among other misnomers. She does so well that guinea pig detective Sasspants becomes suspicious, and Mr. Venezi feels unneeded. When Mr. Venezi turns up missing and Viola, without supervision, starts slacking, Detective Sasspants is on the case." (Kirkus)

Hamster and cheese. illustrated by Stephanie Yue. Graphic Universe 45p. Illustration
Grades: 2 3 4
741.5; 741
978-0-7613-4598-5 (lib bdg), $27.93;
0-7613-4598-1 (lib bdg);
978-0-7613-5479-6 (pa), $6.95;
0-7613-5479-4 (pa)

"There is skullduggery afoot at Mr. Venezi's Pets & Stuff: Someone keeps stealing his sandwich, which he puts outside the koala cage every day. No, he doesn't sell koalas; they're really hamsters, but Mr. Venezi is both

Courtesy of Lerner Publishing Group

shortsighted and incompetent (though very kind). The only cage that's correctly labeled is the one holding the guinea pig — but someone has stolen the G, so little Hamisher the koala, er, hamster has decided that guinea pig Sasspants must be a P.I. and therefore can crack the case." (Kirkus)

Other titles in this series are: And then there were gnomes (2010); The ferret's foot (2011); Fish you were here (2011);Raining cats and detectives (2012);Going, going, dragon! (2013)

Raining cats and detectives. Colleen A.F. Venable; illustrated by Stephanie Yue. Graphic Universe 2012 46 p. Color illustration

Grades: 2 3 4

741.5; Fic

1. Animals — Fiction; 2. Graphic novels; 3. Guinea pigs — Fiction; 4. Hamsters — Fiction; 5. Humorous stories; 6. Mystery and detective stories; 7. Pet shops — Fiction; 8. Cats — Fiction; 9. Detectives — Fiction; 10. Missing persons — Fiction
0761360085; 9780761360087, $27.93

Courtesy of Lerner Publishing Group

LC 2011021626

"Guinea pig Sasspants, her faithful, exuberantly enthusiastic sidekick, Hamisher the hamster, and all the denizens of Mr. Venezi's Pets & Stuff are still in the store...Then (human) Detective Pickles arrives and adopts Sasspants, so when Tummytickles, the bookstore cat next door, vanishes, there's no one to find him. Suddenly, everyone from the goldfish...to the snooty chinchillas are donning detective hats and...well, calling themselves detectives. Will Sasspants return to save the day, or can Hamisher detect on his own?" (Kirkus)

Venditti, Robert

The **lost** hero: the graphic novel. by Rick Riordan; adapted by Robert Venditti; art by Nate Powell; color by Orpheus Collar; lettering by Chris Dickey. Disney-Hyperion Books 2014 192 p. Color; Illustration

Grades: 4 5 6 7 8

741.5

1. Camps — Fiction; 2. Gaia (Greek deity) — Fiction; 3. Graphic novels; 4. Hera (Greek deity) — Fiction; 5. Monsters — Fiction; 6. Mythology, Greek — Fiction; 7. Riordan, Rick. Lost hero — Adaptations; 8. Greek mythology
142316279X; 9781423162797, $21.99; 9781423163251

LC 2013013559

"Jason has a problem. He doesn't remember anything before waking up on a school bus holding hands with a girl. Apparently she's his girlfriend Piper, his best friend is a kid named Leo, and they're all students in the Wilderness School, a boarding school for 'bad kids.' What he did to end up here, Jason has no idea — except that everything seems very wrong." (Publisher's note)

"Powell does an excellent job of adapting the original story into pictorial format, hitting all of the high points and representing all of the major details in the drawings, so little is lost." SLJ

Adapted from the novel The Heroes of Olympus, Book One: The Lost Hero — Copyright page.

Vining, James

First in Space. Oni Press 2007 un Illustration

Grades: 3 4 5 6 7 8

629.4; 741.5; 616

1. Animal experimentation — Graphic novels; 2. Graphic novels; 3. Space flight — Graphic novels
978-1-932664-64-5, $9.95

Vining received a 2006 Xeric Grant to help him complete and publish his book.

This book tells young readers about the early years of the U.S. space program, in the late 1950s and early 1960s. After the Russians successfully sent the dog, Laika,

Courtesy of Oni Press

into space in the Sputnik 2 in 1957, the U.S. successfully sent two monkeys into suborbital space and back in 1959. In 1960, NASA began training young chimpanzees to complete certain tasks; young enlisted men under Sergeant Ed Dittmer took care of the chimpanzees, one chimp per man. In 1961, one of the chimpanzees, nicknamed Ham by his young handler, Beach, became the first chimp in space when NASA sent him up in the Mercury MR-2 rocket. Vining researched this extensively, and he provides a bibliography; but for the book, he focuses on the personal interactions between Beach and Ham and on the training that Ham and the other chimpanzees went through.

Viva, Frank

A **trip** to the bottom of the world with Mouse: a Toon Book. Frank Viva. Toon Books 2012 32 p.

Grades: PreK K 1 2

Fic; 741.5/973

1. Animals — Antarctica — Fiction; 2. Graphic novels; 3. Mice — Fiction; 4. Antarctica — Fiction; 5. Mice — Juvenile fiction; 6. Picture books for children; 7. Antarctica — Description and travel; 8. Voyages and travels — Juvenile fiction
1935179195; 9781935179191

LC 2011049499

This book chronicles the journey of a boy and his mouse friend to the Antarctic. The "tour features both large waves and still waters, glimpses of a killer whale and penguins of various identified sorts, and a dip in waters warmed by a half-sunken volcano. It's all in the company of a querulous mouse whose initial 'Are we there yet?' and eight-times-repeated 'Can we go home now?' inevitably turns to 'Can we go back there soon?' by the end." (Kirkus)

Walker, Landry Q.

Supergirl: cosmic adventures in the 8th grade. DC Comics 2009 144p. Illustration

Grades: 3 4 5 6 7 8

741.5; Fic

1. Graphic novels; 2. Humorous graphic novels; 3. School life — Graphic novels; 4. Superhero graphic novels
978-1-4012-2506-3, $12.99

Kara Zor-El is just an average Kryptonian girl who arrives on Earth sort of accidentally when she has an argument with her mother. Here she discovers she has super powers, just like her cousin, Superman. He tells her she can't just go home, so now she's stuck living on Earth, going to middle school, and her powers can't prevent her from being the new kid in school. She makes one friend, but Lena happens to be related to Superman's nemesis Lex Luthor; then she manages to create a mirror-image self who is evil. On top of that, weird things keep happening at school. Kara may be Supergirl, but can she survive 8th grade?

Weigel, Jeff

Dragon Girl: The Secret Valley. Jeff Weigel. Andrews McMeel Pub 2014 192 p. Illustration

Grades: 2 3 4 5 6

741.5; Fic

1. Orphans — Fiction; 2. Dragons — Fiction
1449441831; 9781449441838, $9.99

LC 2013943302

"Eleven-year-old Alanna and her older brother Hamel are orphans and doing their best to take care of each other until one day Alanna stumbles upon a cave full of dragon eggs. When the eggs hatch with no mother dragon in sight, Alanna decides to take care of the babies herself, even creating a clever costume so that the babies think she, too, is a dragon." (Publisher's note)

"Weigel has created a compulsively likable heroine who seamlessly blends her strength and compassion.... With lovable dragons, flying ships and danger around every corner, this delightful fantasy doesn't disappoint." Kirkus

★ **Thunder** from the sea: adventure on board the HMS Defender. G. P. Putnam's Sons 2010 46p. Illustration
Grades: 3 4 5 6   **741.5; Fic**
1. Great Britain — Royal Navy — Graphic novels; 2. Adventure graphic novels; 3. Graphic novels; 4. Naval art and science — Graphic novels; 5. Europe — History — 1789-1815 — Graphic novels
978-0-399-25089-7, $17.99

LC 2009-32801
In 1805, during the Napoleonic Wars, twelve-year-old Jack Hoyton becomes a member of the crew of HMS Defender, a midsize ship in the British Royal Navy. The Defender patrols along a portion of the French coast to block French ships, but a major gun emplacement in Dumont hampers the ship's efforts. When some of the crew land to fill their barrels with fresh water, French gunmen fire upon them, killing an officer and wounding a crewman. The Captain assigns Jack to be part of the crew that will land and take the guns; when the men arrive, they find that there is no small village, but a major shipbuilding facility, and they're captured.
"Weigel's old-fashioned comics art shows lots of authentic details of eighteenth-century shipboard life, and there is some battle violence.... This picture-book-size graphic novel should find a ready audience of young adventure-loving readers." Booklist
Includes bibliographical references

Weing, Drew
The **creepy** case files of Margo Maloo. by Drew Weing. First Second 2016 121 p. Color; Illustration
Grades: 3 4 5 6   **741.5; Fic**
1. Moving — Fiction; 2. Monsters — Fiction; 3. Mystery graphic novels
1626723397; 9781626723399, $15.99
"Charles just moved to Echo City, and some of his new neighbors give him the creeps. They sneak into his room, steal his toys, and occasionally, they try to eat him. The place is teeming with monsters! Lucky for Charles, Echo City has Margo Maloo, monster mediator. No matter who's causing trouble, Margo knows exactly what to do." (Publisher's note)
"Weing's colorful drawings reward extended examination; Echo City is rife with monster life, and creepy crawlies turn up in the most unexpected places, but domestic scenes and the city streets also show the artist's keen eye for details." SLJ
Another title in this series is: The monster mall (2018)

Flop to the Top!. by Eleanor Davis & Drew Weing. TOON Books 2015 40 p. Color; Illustration
Grades: K 1 2 3   **741.5**
1. Dogs — Fiction; 2. Fame — Fiction; 3. Graphic novels; 4. Humorous stories
1935179896; 9781935179894, $12.95

LC 2015003955
In this children's book, by Eleanor Davis and Drew Weing, "Wanda calls her brother and sister 'fans,' keeps up with celebrity news, and never misses a chance to share a selfie. She's ready to show the world how Wanda-ful she really is, but all people are interested in is...her dog!" (Publisher's note)
"Though centered on difficult emotions that will feel familiar to kids, the story is leavened with comedy, allowing readers to navigate comfortably even as the robust sentences and repetition massage new reading skills." Booklist

Weiser, Joey
Mermin; book one: out of water. Joey Weiser; [edited by] Jill Beaton. Oni Press 2013 152 p. (Mermin)

Grades: 4 5 6
741.5; Fic
1. Science fiction comic books, strips, etc.; 2. Graphic novels; 3. Mermaids and mermen — Fiction
1934964980; 9781934964989, $19.99

LC 2012953664
Other titles in this series are: The big catch (2013); Deep dive (2014); Into Atlantis (2015); Making waves (2017)
Author Joey Weiser presents a graphic novel about merpeople. "MERMIN the MERMAN from MER!" That's the question Pete and his friends ask after finding the fish-boy washed up on the beach! Mermin just escaped the undersea kingdome of Mer, and is ready to have some fun on dry land! But why would this aquatic kid be afraid to swim? Perhaps it has something to do with the fishy pursuers who have followed him from the depths below!? (Publisher's note)

Courtesy of Oni Press

Wells, H. G. (Herbert George)
The **Time** Machine. Stone Arch Books 2007 72p. Illustration
Grades: 3 4 5 6 7 8 9   **741.5; Fic**
1. Adventure graphic novels; 2. Graphic novels; 3. Science fiction graphic novels
978-1-59889-833-0, $23.93

LC 2007-6201
A scientist invents a machine that he claims will travel through time, but his friends laugh at the idea. So the Time Traveler climbs aboard his machine and ends up thousands of years in the future. He meets a race of gentle humans called the Eloi, but he is soon swept up in a fight for his life against evil underground creatures known as Morlocks. Even worse, his Time Machine, his only chance to escape, is trapped deep inside the Morlock caverns. This book is written with an easy vocabulary for struggling and reluctant readers, and it includes some scientific speculations about the future.
Part of the Graphic Revolve series

West, David
Hernan Cortes: The Life of a Spanish Conquistador. by David West & Jackie Gaff; illustrated by Jim Eldridge. Rosen Publishing Group 2005 48p. Illustration
Grades: 3 4 5 6 7 8
92; 741.5; 972
1. Biographical graphic novels; 2. Graphic novels; 3. Cortes, Hernan, 1485-1547; 4. Mexico — History — Conquest, 1519-1540 — Graphic novels
1-4042-0244-7, $29.25

LC 2004005938
Adventurous explorer or ruthless imperialist? In 1519, Spanish conquistador Hernan Cortes led a daring expedition to the heart of the Aztec Empire, in what is now central and southern Mexico. Within two

Courtesy of Rosen Publishing

years, this highly advanced civilization had fallen to the might of Cortes's Spanish conquerors, resulting in the deaths of tens of thousands of Aztecs. This graphic novel explores two cultures in conflict — and the personality of a man driven by both insatiable greed and service to his country. The book includes additional information, a glossary, and a list of books for further reading.

Part of the Graphic Nonfiction series.

Pteranodon: The Giant of the Sky. Rosen Publishing Group 2007 32p. Illustration

Grades: 2 3 4 5 6 7

567.9; 741.5

1. Dinosaurs — Graphic novels; 2. Graphic novels; 3. Pteranodon — Graphic novels

978-1-4042-3895-4, $25.25

LC 2007-1792

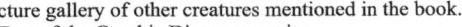

This volume uses colorful comic book style illustrations to explore the habitat, diet, and behavior of the pteranodon. At the front of the book, facts about the pteranodon are presented, while at the back of the book readers will find a picture gallery of other creatures mentioned in the book.

Courtesy of Rosen Publishing

Part of the Graphic Dinosaurs series.

Velociraptor: The Speedy Thief. Rosen Publishing Group 2007 32p. Illustration

Grades: 2 3 4 5 6 7

567.9; 741.5

1. Dinosaurs — Graphic novels; 2. Graphic novels; 3. Velociraptor — Graphic novels

978-1-4042-3898-5, $25.25

LC 2007-873

This volume uses colorful comic book style illustrations to explore the habitat, diet, and behavior of the velociraptor. At the front of the book, facts about the velociraptor are presented, while at the back of the book readers will find a picture gallery of other creatures mentioned in the book.

Courtesy of Rosen Publishing

Part of the Graphic Dinosaurs series.

White, Steve

The **Battle** of Midway: the destruction of the Japanese fleet. The Rosen Publishing Group 2007 48p. Illustration

Grades: 3 4 5 6 7 8 9

741.5; 940.54

1. Graphic novels; 2. Midway, Battle of, 1942 — Graphic novels; 3. War — Graphic novels; 4. World War, 1939-1945 — Graphic novels

978-1-4042-0783-7, $29.25

One of the most important naval battles in history, Midway marked a crucial turning point in the war in the Pacific. With a fleet that had dominated this theater since the attack on Pearl Harbor, the Japanese anticipated certain victory against the US forces, but the attack was not a surprise. The US Navy sank four irreplaceable aircraft carriers, and cleared the way for the island-hopping US counterattack. This book also includes eight pages of authoritative information, placing the battle in its historical context, describing the key players, and its build-up and aftermath.

Part of the Graphic Battles of World War II series. This book is also available in a paperback edition from Osprey Publishing, under the title The Empire Falls: Battle of Midway.

Pearl Harbor: A Day of Infamy. The Rosen Publishing Group 2007 48p. Illustration

Grades: 3 4 5 6 7 8 9

741.5; 940.54

1. Graphic novels; 2. Pearl Harbor (Oahu, Hawaii), Attack on, 1941 — Graphic novels; 3. War — Graphic novels; 4. World War, 1939-1945 — Graphic novels

978-1-4042-0785-1, $29.25

On December 7, 1941, the Japanese Navy launched a surprise attack on American military bases in Pearl Harbor, Hawaii. Masterfully planned and executed, the attack devastated the US Pacific Fleet; in less than two hours, Japanese aircraft had sunk or damaged all eight US battleships anchored in the harbor and had destroyed 151 planes. Thrust into battle, the United States could have only one response: war. This book portrays the attack that drove the United States into World War II in full-color comic book narrative. Featuring the personal stories of front-line heroes like Ken Taylor, George Welch, and mess attendant Dorie Miller, it also provides background material — causes and consequences, key players, and a glossary of terms — as well as a list of additional resources.

Part of the Graphic Battles of World War II series. This book is also available in a paperback edition from Osprey Publishing, under the title Day of Infamy: Attack on Pearl Harbor.

Wicks, Maris

★ **Human** body theater: a nonfiction revue. Maris Wicks. First Second 2015 240 p. Color; Illustration

Grades: 4 5 6 7 8

612; 741.5

1. Human biology; 2. Human anatomy

1626722773; 9781626722774, $19.99; 9781596439290

This book by, Maris Wicks explores human anatomy on a performing stage. In it, "your master of ceremonies is going to lead you through a theatrical revue of each and every biological system of the human body! Starting out as a skeleton, the MC puts on a new layer of her costume (her body) with each 'act.'" (Publisher's note)

"Wicks' playful cartoon artwork in saturated colors makes the potentially daunting and embarrassing subject of anatomy approachable and fun, but never at the expense of accuracy or clarity. This informative, frank exploration of the body perfectly balances science and silliness." Booklist

Includes bibliographical references

Wight, Eric

★ **Frankie** Pickle and the closet of doom. written and illustrated by Eric Wight. Simon & Schuster Books for Young Readers 2009 79p. Illustration

Grades: 2 3 4 5

741.5; Fic

1. Cleanliness — Fiction; 2. Family life — Fiction; 3. Family life — Graphic novels; 4. Graphic novels; 5. Humorous graphic novels; 6. Imagination — Fiction; 7. Orderliness — Graphic novels

978-1-4169-6484-1, $9.99; 1-4169-6484-3

LC 2008-30865

Fourth-grader Frankie Piccolini has a vivid imagination when it comes to cleaning his disastrously messy room, but eventually even he decides that it is just too dirty.

"Wight's hilarious twists of language are matched with a wicked sense of fun in the illustrations and frequent sequential-paneled episodes of pretend play." Kirkus

Other titles about Frankie Pickle are: Frankie Pickle and the Pine Run 3000 (2010); Frankie Pickle and the mathematical menace (2011);Frankie Pickle and the land of the lost recess (2012)

Wilgus, Alison

★ **Flying** machines: how the Wright brothers soared. Alison Wilgus; Molly Brooks. First Second 2017 113 p. Illustration; Color (Science comics)

Grades: 5 6 7 8

629.13; 741.5; 629.130092/273

1. Airplanes — United States — History; 2. Graphic novels; 3. Wright, Orville, 1871-1948; 4. Wright, Wilbur, 1867-1912; 5. Aeronautics
9781626721395; 9781626721401, $19.99

LC 2016945553

In this book, by Alsion Wilgus, illustrated by Molly Brooks, "follow the famous aviators from their bicycle shop in Dayton, Ohio, to the fields of North Carolina where they were to make their famous flights. In an era of dirigibles and hot air balloons, the Wright Brothers were among the first innovators of heavier than air flight. But in the hotly competitive international race toward flight, Orville and Wilbur were up against a lot more than bad weather." (Publisher's note)

"An accessible and engaging introduction to the Wright brothers and how they ushered in the age of flight." Kirkus

Includes bibliographical references.; Book design by John Green; edited by Casey Gonzalez.

Wilson, Britt
Cat Dad, King of the Goblins. Britt Wilson. Koyama Press 2014 48 p. Color; Illustration
Grades: 2 3 4 5
741.5
1. Cats — Fiction; 2. Goblins — Fiction; 3. Fathers — Fiction
1927668115; 9781927668115, $12

Courtesy of Koyama Press

"Miri and Luey have a dilemma. Their dad's been turned into a cat and their closet is a garden full of goblins. There is only one thing for them to do — grab their friend Phil the frog and dive headfirst into a wild, woolly, and wacky adventure." (Publisher's note)

"It's a nonsensical story with an even more nonsensical conclusion, but it's best not to look for logic, since the off-the-wall fun and comical scenes capture kids' imaginative games perfectly." Booklist

Winick, Judd
Hilo: the boy who crashed to Earth. by Judd Winick; with color by Guy Major. Random House Inc 2015 208 p. Color; Illustration (Hilo)
Grades: 2 3 4 5
741.5; Fic
1. Amnesia — Fiction; 2. Extraterrestrial beings — Fiction; 3. Friendship — Fiction; 4. Graphic novels; 5. Identity — Fiction; 6. Robots — Fiction; 7. Science fiction; 8. Extraterrestrial beings — Juvenile fiction
0385386176; 9780385386173, $13.99; 9780385386180

LC 2014030736

"D.J. and his friend Gina are totally normal kids. But that was before a mysterious boy came crashing down from the sky! Hilo doesn't know where he came from, or what he's doing on Earth.... But what if Hilo wasn't the only thing to fall to our planet? Can the trio unlock the secrets of his past? Can Hilo survive a day at school? And are D.J. and Gina ready to save the world?" (Publisher's note)

"Winick has concocted a universally appealing tale with bright, expressive illustrations that gently reminds readers that in this era of overscheduling and insistence on perfection, sometimes just being true to yourself is important enough." Kirkus

Other titles about Hilo are: Saving the whole wide world (2016); The great big boom (2017); Waking the monsters (2018)

Yamamoto, Lun Lun
Swans in space, volume 1. UDON Entertainment 2009 150p. Illustration
Grades: 2 3 4 5 6 7
741.5; Fic
1. Graphic novels; 2. Humorous graphic novels; 3. Manga; 4. Science fiction graphic novels; 5. Kodomo
978-1-897376-93-5, $8.99

Sixth grader Corona is effectively her class's president, representing them on the Cosmos Institute student council. At home, she barely tolerates the obsessive fandom displayed by her father and younger brother for the television show, Space Patrol. Imagine her chagrin when she reaches out to an odd classmate, only to find herself recruited into...the Space Patrol! It's a real organization that works to keep the Earth and other worlds safe, and show's episodes are edited versions of actual missions. Of course, Corona must keep her work in the Space Patrol a secret from anyone who isn't a member; and since she needs to study the old episodes to learn the history, this makes her father and brother think she has become one with them, while her classmates wonder what's wrong with her. Corona must also keep up with not only her school work, which is bad enough, because she's one of the top students, but as class president she has to take responsibility for all kinds of extra activities and work; all this makes her one tired girl. This manga for younger readers is published in full color.

Yang, Gene Luen
Paths & Portals. by Gene Luen Yang; illustrated by Mike Holmes. First Second 2016 96 p. Color; Illustration (Secret Coders)
Grades: 4 5 6 7
741.5; Fic
1. Computer programming — Fiction; 2. School life — Fiction; 3. Schools — Fiction
9781626720763; 1626720762; 1626723400; 9781626723405, $18.99

"There's something lurking beneath the surface of Stately Academy.... In a secret underground classroom Hopper, Eni, and Josh discover that the campus was once home to the Bee School, an institute where teachers, students, and robots worked together to unravel the mysteries of coding. Hopper and her friends are eager to follow in this tradition and become top-rate coders." (Publisher's note)

"Each time the kids write a new program, Holmes breaks down the steps visually, demonstrating each direction with a handy illustration, all in his blocky, expressive, green-hued style." Booklist

Secret coders. Gene Yuen Lang & Mike Holmes. First Second 2015 96 p. Color; Illustration (Secret coders)
Grades: 4 5 6 7
741.5
1. Computer programming — Graphic novels; 2. School stories — Graphic novels
9781626722767, $17.99; 9781626720756; 1626722765

In this graphic novel, by Gene Yuen Lang and Mike Holmes, "Hopper, an enthusiastic 12-year-old girl..., has just started school at the creepy Stately Academy. After getting in a fight...with Eni..., Hopper and Eni become friends while unraveling the secrets of the school. Robotic birds, family troubles, and sinister, child-hating school administrators lead to a story both emotionally rich and rife with learning opportunities." (School Library Journal)

"Holmes' blocky cartoon illustrations, in black, white, and green, clearly depict basic programming concepts with tidy visual cues, such as grids of floor tiles. Yang and Holmes do such a great job explaining the concepts that even programming newbies will be likely to catch on." Booklist

Other titles in this series are: Paths and portals (2016); Secrets and sequences (2017); Robots and repeats (2017); Potions and parameters (2018); Monsters and modules (2018)

Secret coders; 5: potions & parameters. Gene Luen Yang & Mike Holmes. First Second 2018 112 p. Color; Illustration

Grades: 4 5 6 7   **741.5; Fic**
1. Schools — Fiction; 2. Computer programming — Fiction; 3. Gifted children — Fiction
9781626726079, $10.99; 9781626726086
LC 2017941170

In this book in the Secret Coders series, by Gene Luen Yang, illustrated by Mike Holmes, "Dr. One-Zero won't stop until the whole town...embraces the 'true happiness' found in his poisonous potion, Green Pop. And now that he has the Turtle of Light, he's virtually unstoppable. There's one weapon that can defeat him: another Turtle of Light. Unfortunately, they can only be found in another dimension!" (Publisher's note)

"While the coding instruction's as top-notch as ever, in this installment it's interpersonal dynamics and characters that, satisfyingly, take center stage." Kirkus

Yeh, Phil
Dinosaurs Across America. NBM 2007 32p. Illustration
Grades: 2 3 4 5 6   **973; 741.5**
1. Graphic novels; 2. United States — Geography — Graphic novels
978-1-56163-509-2, $12.95

Originally done as a comic book and sold by Cartoonists Across America, a literacy group working for decades to promote the use of comic books to teach literacy to children, this is now a graphic novel. Featuring Yeh's dinosaurs and Patrick Rabbit, the book devotes a half-page to each state in the U.S., packing in basic facts and a simple map along with fun little tidbits (for example, the largest privately owned cattle ranch in the U.S. happens to be in Hawaii, on the island of Hawaii).

YKids
Einstein. Youngjin Singapore 2007 146p. Illustration
Grades: 3 4 5 6 7 8 9   **741.5; 92**
1. Biographical graphic novels; 2. Graphic novels; 3. Einstein, Albert, 1879-1955
978-981-05-4944-2, $14.95

A genius of enormous accomplishment, Albert Einstein overcame numerous hardships-separation from his family, religious discrimination, and the political turmoil of his day-to become one of the greatest minds of the 20th century. As a young boy, Einstein's unending curiosity and constant questioning earned him the reputation of being unfocused and inattentive. This book uses a framing story of a young boy and a robot from the future going back in time to examine the lives of great people and find the one value that will help their situation; from Einstein, they take his insatiable curiosity.
Part of the Great Figures in History series.

Gandhi. Youngjin Singapore 2007 148p. Illustration
Grades: 3 4 5 6 7 8 9   **741.5; 92**
1. Biographical graphic novels; 2. Graphic novels; 3. Gandhi, Mohandas Karamcand, 1869-1948; 4. Gandhi, Mohandas Karamcand, 1869-1948 — graphic novels
978-981-05-4945-9, $14.95

A champion of the poor and lower classes, Mahatma Gandhi helped transform India into the democracy it is today. Young readers of this manga-style biography will learn about the key historical events during this time and how the peaceful efforts of one humble man affected enormous change. This book presents a time line of Gandhi's life-from his roots in a middle-class family in India, to his law-school education in England, his experiences with discrimination, and his key role as a leader in the Indian independence movement. Each volume in the Great Figures in

History series focuses on a key value personified by the biographical subject; in Gandhi's case, it's courage.
Part of the Great Figures in History series.

Little Women: Manga Literary Classics. Youngjin Singapore 2007 145p. Illustration
Grades: 3 4 5 6 7   **741.5; Fic**
1. Graphic novels; 2. Alcott, Louisa May, 1832-1888 — Adaptations
978-981-05-4943-5, $14.95

The story of the March girls-beautiful Meg, tomboy Jo, kind and gentle Beth, and spunky Amy-is retold manga-style and in full color. With their country embroiled in war and their father far from home, the four sisters find themselves thrust into new and trying situations, and with little money and a hard winter ahead, they must learn to adapt. In the year that follows, the girls learn about compassion, sacrifice, love, and more about themselves and each other than they ever imagined.

Treasure Island: Manga Literary Classics. Youngjin Singapore 2007 148p. Illustration
Grades: 3 4 5 6 7   **741.5; Fic**
1. Graphic novels; 2. Stevenson, Robert Louis, 1850-1894 — Adaptations
978-981-05-4942-8, $14.95

Young cabin boy Jim Hawkins throws in his lot with pirates Black Dog, Blind Pew, and the unforgettable Long John Silver in this manga-style retelling of Robert Louis Stevenson's classic adventure story. Jim, overly romantic about life on the high seas, is unprepared for the frightening events ahead, including mutiny and an armed battle that poses a grim dilemma: should his loyalty lie with Captain Smollett or Long John Silver?

Yoon, Salina
Duck, Duck, Porcupine!. Salina Yoon. Bloomsbury Childrens Books 2016 64 p. Color; Illustration
Grades: PreK K 1 2   **741.5; Fic**
1. Porcupines; 2. Brothers and sisters — Fiction; 3. Ducks — Fiction
9781619637238, $9.99; 1619637235
LC 2015022813

In this book, by Salina Yoon, "Big Duck likes to boss around her younger brother, Little Duck, and she fancies herself the leader of their trio — when joined by their gentle friend Porcupine. Little Duck doesn't speak yet, but through his expressions and his actions, he shows that he has a better grasp on any situation than his older sister." (Publisher's note)

"Fresh and funny; a welcome addition to the easy-reader shelf." Horn Book
Another title in this series is: My kite is stuck and other stories (2017)

Yorinks, Arthur
★ **Making** scents. Arthur Yorinks; art by Braden Lamb & Shelli Paroline. First Second 2017 112 p. Illustration; Color
Grades: 2 3 4 5   **741.5; Fic**
1. Dogs; 2. Orphans; 3. Smell
9781596434523, $15.99
LC 2016945550

In this children's story, by Arthur Yorinks, illustrated by Braden Lamb and Shelli Paroline, "Mickey's mom and dad are crazy about canines.... So, naturally, they're raising their son as if he was a dog, and Mickey wants nothing more than to make his parents proud. Just as Mickey is mastering the art of sniffing, a tragic accident forever changes his happy family. Mickey is sent to live with relatives he's never met — relatives who are not fond of kids...and who hate dogs!" (Publisher's note)

"With two dog lovers as parents and the family dogs as siblings, Mickey is raised more like a bloodhound than a child and trained to be a super smeller.... Retro details in the illustrations create a nostalgic feel. Humor stems naturally from the absurdity of the premise, while the heartfelt moments are as tender as they come." — Horn Book Magazine

Yoshizumi, Wataru
   Ultra Maniac Vol. 1. Viz Media/Shojo Beat 2005 184p. Illustration
Grades: 5 6 7 8 9 10   **741.5; Fic**
   1. Graphic novels; 2. Humorous graphic novels; 3. Manga; 4. Romance graphic novels; 5. Shojo manga
   1-59116-917-8, $8.99

Shy Ayu Tateishi has just made a new friend at school. But this new friend, much to her surprise, is no ordinary classmate. Nina Sakura may look like a normal middle school girl, but she's got a big secret. She's a witch. Or, rather, she's studying to be a witch. And, apparently, she's not doing her homework. Her spells are devastating in their ineffectiveness and often result in the most embarrassing situations for poor Ayu. But things wouldn't be so bad if Nina's sorcery didn't make Ayu look silly in front of the one boy she secretly adores. All she wants is a simple love potion. What she gets, however, is a new best friend who almost flunked out of witch school. This is a five-volume manga series.

MIDDLE SCHOOL: 6-8

Aaron, Jason

Star Wars; Volume 1: Skywalker strikes. writers, Jason Aaron; artist, John Cassaday; colorist, Laura Martin; letterer, Chris Eliopoulos. Marvel Enterprises 2015 160 p. Color; Illustration

Grades: 8 9 10 11 12 Adult   **741.5**
1. Star Wars — Graphic novels
0785192131; 9780785192138, $19.99

"Luke Skywalker and the ragtag rebel band opposing the Galactic Empire are fresh off their biggest victory yet — the destruction of the massive Death Star. But the Empire's not toppled yet! Join Luke, Princess Leia, Han Solo, Chewbacca, C-3PO, R2-D2 and the rest of the Rebel Alliance as they fight for freedom against the evil of Darth Vader and his master, the Emperor!" (Publisher's note)

Volume 1 of an ongoing series

Abadzis, Nick

★ **Laika**. First Second Books 2007 205p. Illustration

Grades: 5 6 7 8 9 10 11 12 Adult   **741.5; Fic**
1. Graphic novels; 2. Soviet Union — History — 1953-1991 — Graphic novels; 3. Space flight — Graphic novels
1-59643-101-6; 978-1-59643-101-0

LC 2006-51907

Laika was the abandoned puppy destined to become Earth's first space traveler. This is her journey. Along with Laika, there is Korolev, once a political prisoner and now a driven engineer at the top of the Soviet space program, and Yelena, the lab technician responsible for Laika's health and life. The book depicts the dedication and struggles of the scientists and technicians who worked in the Soviet space program, based on research Abadzis did before writing this book. The book includes a bibliography of books and websites.

"Abadzis's tear-inducing and solidly researched graphic novel treatment of Laika's surpassingly tragic story is a standout." Publ Wkly

Abirached, Zeina

A **game** for swallows: to die, to leave, to return. written by Zeina Abirached; art by Zeina Abirached; translation by Edward Gauvin. Graphic Universe 2012 188 p.

Grades: 7 8 9 10 11 12
741.5
1. Abirached, Zeina, 1981- — Comic books, strips, etc; 2. Beirut (Lebanon) — Comic books, strips, etc; 3. Lebanon — History — Civil War, 1975-1990 — Comic books, strips, etc; 4. Separation; 5. Family — Graphic novels
0761385681; 9780761385684, $29.27

LC 2011038914

Courtesy of Lerner Publishing Group

Mildred L. Batchelder Honor Book (2013)

This graphic novel looks at "the civil war in Lebanon in the 1980s, as seen through the eyes of a child" separated from her parents. "Young Zeina [Abirached] and her brother have been sequestered within the small foyer in their apartment," which "becomes a place for neighbors in the building to congregate and seek asylum. Though war is raging and death always seems to loom near with shells falling and snipers possibly crouching

behind every wall, Zeina and her neighbors try to live the best they can." (Kirkus Reviews)

Translation of Le jeau des hirondelles.

I remember Beirut. Zeina Abirached. Graphic Universe 2014 96 p. Illustration; Map

Grades: 8 9 10 11 12 Adult
741.5; 92
1. Abirached, Zeina, 1981-; 2. Lebanon — History — 20th century; 3. Children and war; 4. War
1467738220; 9781467738224, $29.27

LC 2013047112

Courtesy of Lerner Publishing Group

In this graphic memoir, Zeina Abirached "reveals numerous details from her childhood in Beirut during the war from 1975 to 1990 war. 'I remember' is a recurring phrase and provides a personal frame of reference for the effect of war on kids. Some are simple childhood memories.... Inclusion of...maps and diagrams orient the reader and provide additional perspective." (Kirkus Reviews)

"The blocky, naive-style pictures quietly evoke wartime fears in ways the words simply cannot — bullet holes in the sides of cars, rubble in the streets, her father's eyebrows indicating increasing sadness at the heartbreaking state of a formerly vital market." Booklist

Akamatsu, Ken

Mao-Chan vol. 1. story by Ken Akamatsu; art by Ran. Del Rey Manga 2008 394p. Illustration

Grades: 8 9 10 11 12
741.5; Fic
1. Graphic novels; 2. Humorous graphic novels; 3. Manga; 4. Shonen manga
978-0-345-50181-3, $14.95

When incredibly cute aliens invade Japan and steal its signature landmarks, Japan unleashes the Grade School Defense Corps, made up of second-grade students, such as Mao, Misora, and Sylvie. As their grandfathers, who command Ground, Air, and Marine Defense respectively, plot to make their own granddaughters the big heroes, the girls prefer to work together to defeat the aliens. Readers must love incredible cuteness along with some fan service featuring the older teenage girls. There is very little in this volume other than the mild fan service to indicate reasons for an older teen rating the publisher rates it for ages 16 and up.

Volume 1 of 2

Alice, A. (Alex)

Siegfried 1; 1. written and illustrated by Alex Alice. Archaia Entertainment, LLC 2012 144 p.

Grades: 6 7 8 9 10 11 12
741.5
1. Dragons — Graphic novels; 2. Gods and goddesses — Graphic novels; 3. Orphans — Graphic novels
193639345X; 9781936393459, $24.95

This graphic novel by Alex Alice presents "a three-part story inspired by [Richard] Wagner's classic opera 'The Ring of the Nibelung!' Siegfried, born of the love between a mortal man and a Valkyrie, is a young orphan being raised by Mime, one of the last of the dwarf-goblin Nibelungs. Siegfried yearns to discover who his real parents were..., not knowing that

Odin, father of the Norse gods, has a destiny planned for him: to fight the dragon Fafnir, guardian of the Rheingold!" (Publisher's note)

Volume 1 of 3

Allan, Von

Stargazer, volume one. Von Allan Studio 2010 115p. Illustration

Grades: 4 5 6 7 8 9

741.5; Fic

1. Adventure graphic novels; 2. Friendship — Graphic novels; 3. Graphic novels; 4. Science fiction graphic novels

978-0-9781237-2-7, $14.95

Courtesy of Von Allan Studio

Marni's grandmother has just died, and she left a strange device that the two of them played with whenever Marni had visited. No one knows how Marni's grandmother got it, and it has never done anything. Her best friends, Elora and Sophie, come over for a last backyard campout before the weather turns cold, and when they each put a hand on the device, an extremely bright light nearly blinds them. After things seem to go back to normal, the girls go outside to find Marni's house gone, the device vanished, and none of the stars look familiar. In the morning, they pack up the little food they had brought for their campout, Elora's telescope, and Sophie's pennywhistle, and hike towards a tower Elora had spotted. They know they're in a totally strange place when they come upon a statue of nonhuman, alien creatures. As they continue, they come upon a strange house, where they find food, and then a mute, boy-sized robot. Even though the three friends bicker with each other, they work together to find a way home. Allan includes extensive notes on his writing process, and an excerpt from his script. The cover art shows one interesting looking character who doesn't appear in this volume. While their age isn't specified, the girls look to be tweens, with the slightly awkward, coltish bodies and movements of pre-adolescents. The strongest language used is one instance of the word "damn."

Volume 1 of 2

Allen, Chris

William Shakespeare's Othello. adapted by Vincent Goodwin; illustrated by Chris Allen.. ABDO/Magic Wagon 2008 48p. Illustration

Grades: 5 6 7 8 9 10

822.3; 741.5

1. Authors; 2. Dramatists; 3. Graphic novels; 4. Poets; 5. Shakespeare, William, 1564-1616 — Adaptations

978-1-60270-192-2, $28.50

LC 2008-10743

Othello the Moor is a successful general, married to the beautiful Desdemona. Life should be good, but he's incredibly jealous of anyone who looks at his wife. Iago wants Othello's position and decides that he should destroy Othello by fabricating an affair between Desdemona and Cassio. This graphic novel adaptation keeps some of the original dialog from Shakespeare's play while paring down the action to simplify it for readers who would struggle with the original. The book includes a short biography of Shakespeare, a summary of the plot, a glossary, and a sampling of famous lines and phrases.

Part of the Graphic Shakespeare series

Allison, John

Bad machinery; 1: the case of the team spirit. John Allison; [edited by] James Lucas Jones. Oni Press 2013 112 p. Color; Illustration

Grades: 7 8 9 10 11 12 Adult

741.5

1. Mystery graphic novels; 2. School stories — Graphic novels

1620100843; 9781620100844, $19.99

LC 2012953355

Courtesy of Oni Press

"Shauna. Charlotte. Mildred. Three schoolgirl sleuths. Jack. Linton. Sonny. Three schoolboy investigators. Tackleford. One mid-sized city with a history of countless mysteries. Is there enough room at Griswalds Grammar School for two groups of kid detectives? There better be, because once these kids have set their sights on solving a mystery there's nothing that can derail them. Nothing, except maybe gossip, classwork, new football player cards, torment from siblings, or any number of childhood distractions." (Publisher's note)

"Allison is a triple threat: he plots deftly, draws confidently, and writes dead-on adolescent dialogue. Set in a grammar school in a British working-class community, this first book in his Bad Machinery series — originally published as a webcomic — has three earnest boys vying against three sharp-tongued girls to solve mysteries." Pub Wkly

Other Bad Machinery volumes are: The case of the good boy (2014); The case of the simple soul (2014); The case of the lonely one (2015); The case of the fire inside (2016); The case of the forked road (2017)

Alphona, Adrian

Runaways Vol. 3: The Good Die Young. Marvel Entertainment 2005 un Illustration

Grades: 8 9 10 11 12

741.5; Fic

1. Adventure graphic novels; 2. Graphic novels; 3. Runaways (Fictional characters); 4. Superhero graphic novels

0-7851-1684-2, $7.99

The world as people know it is about to end and the Runaways are the only hope to prevent it. But if the fledgling teenage heroes are going to succeed, they may have to become just as evil as their villainous parents. The Runaways have learned how their parents' criminal organization began, and now they must decide how it should end. As the Runaways' epic battle against their evil parents reaches its shocking conclusion, the team's mole stands revealed, and blood must be shed. Which kids will still be standing when the smoke finally clears?

Runaways Vol. 4: True Believers. Marvel Entertainment 2005 un Illustration

Grades: 8 9 10 11 12

741.5; Fic

1. Adventure graphic novels; 2. Graphic novels; 3. Runaways (Fictional characters); 4. Superhero graphic novels

0-7851-1705-9, $7.99

Now that the evil Pride is gone, nearly every bad guy in the Marvel Universe is trying to fill the power vacuum in Los Angeles, and the Runaways are the only heroes who can stop them. Plus: What does a mysterious new team of young heroes want with the Runaways, and which fan-favorite Marvel characters are part of this group?

Alvarez, Lorena

★ **Nightlights**. Lorena Alvarez. Nobrow Press 2017 56 p. Color; Illustration

Grades: 4 5 6 7

741.5

1. Girls — Graphic novels; 2. Female friendship — Graphic novels

1910620130; 9781910620137, $18.95

In this graphic novel, written and illustrated by Lorena Alvarez, "every night, tiny stars appear out of the darkness in little Sandy's bedroom. She catches them and creates wonderful creatures to play with until she falls asleep, and in the morning brings them back to life in the whimsical drawings that cover her room." (Publisher's note)

"Alvarez's haunting artwork features coiling plumes of lush colors and Miyazaki-esque beasts that create a sense of brooding melancholy. It's a deliciously hair-raising story that thoughtfully explores themes of isolation, creativity, and how social pressures can encroach on individuality." Pub Wkly

Anderson, Kevin J.
Grumpy old monsters. Kevin J. Anderson, Rebecca Moesta; [art by] Guillermo Mendoza, Paco Cavero. IDW Publishing 2004 96p. Illustration
Grades: 4 5 6 7 8 9   **741.5; Fic**
   1. Graphic novels; 2. Humorous graphic novels; 3. Monsters — Graphic novels
1-932382-35-6, $13.99

The old monsters Frankenstein's Monster, Dracula, the Mummy, and the Werewolf, have all retired and moved to the old monsters' home, where Nurse Wrentch terrorizes them and only little Tiffany Frankenstein, granddaughter of old Dr. F., comes to visit. But this time she comes with terrible news the Van Helsing Corporation is about to take possession of Castle Frankenstein, tear it down, and build luxury condominiums. The monsters decide they must come out of retirement and help Tiffany stop the horror if they can escape Nurse Wrentch!

Anderson, Laurie Halse
  ★ **Speak:** the graphic novel. Laurie Halse Anderson, illustrated by Emily Carrol. Farrar, Straus & Giroux 2018 384 p. Illustration
Grades: 7 8 9 10 11 12   **741.5; Fic**
   1. Teenage girls — Comic books, strips, etc.; 2. Loneliness — Comic books, strips, etc.; 3. Rape — Fiction; 4. High schools — Fiction
9780374300289, $19.99
                         LC 2017933387

In this graphic novel, by Laurie Halse Anderson, illustrated by Emily Carrol, Melinda "is friendless — an outcast — because she busted an end-of-summer party by calling the cops, so now nobody will talk to her, let alone listen to her.... Through her work on an art project, she is finally able to face what really happened that night: She was raped by an upperclassman, a guy who still attends Merryweather [High] and is still a threat to her." (Publisher's note)

"This potent retelling of the modern classic Speak blends words and images to create magic: a new representation of a teen whose voice is ripped from her, the battles she must wage to find it again, and the triumph of finally being able to speak out. Carroll's grayscale artwork perfectly depicts the starkness of Melinda's depression through strong ink lines and striking panels that rely on pencil and charcoal textural effects for the backgrounds." SLJ

Anderson, M. T.
  ★ **Yvain:** the Knight of the Lion. M.T. Anderson, illustrated by Andrea Offermann. Candlewick Press 2017 144 p. Color; Illustration
Grades: 7 8 9 10
741.5
   1. Knights and knighthood — Graphic novels
0763659398; 9780763659394, $19.99

In this graphic novel, by M.T. Anderson, illustrated by Andrea Offermann, "sir Yvain sets out from King Arthur's court and defeats a local lord in battle, unknowingly intertwining his future with the lives of two

YVAIN. Text copyright © 2017 by M.T. Anderson. Illustrations copyright © 2017 by Andrea Offermann.

compelling women: Lady Laudine, the beautiful widow of the fallen lord, and her sly maid Lunette." (Publisher's note)

"This adaptation of Chrétien de Troyes' medieval poem beautifully ties together period art and imagery with stylish visual storytelling." Booklist

Aoi, Haruka
A **Little** Snow Fairy Sugar, Volume 1. Haruka Aoi, translated by Kaoru Bertrand. ADV Manga 2006 168p. Illustration
Grades: 3 4 5 6 7 8   **741.5; Fic**
   1. Fairies — Graphic novels; 2. Graphic novels; 3. Kodomo manga; 4. Manga; 5. Shonen manga
1-4139-0333-9, $9.99

Eleven-year-old Saga Bergstrom lives with her grandmother and maintains a very tight, controlled schedule; in addition to school, she works part-time in a coffee shop, and every afternoon at 4:00, she goes to the music store to play her dead mother's piano. Then, one day her life becomes chaotic when she encounters Sugar, an apprentice season fairy. Saga is the only human who can see Sugar, which can be very embarrassing when she screams in frustration at Sugar. Sugar and her fellow apprentice season fairies, Salt and Pepper, need to find twinkles to make their magic seeds grow so they can become full season fairies. The problem is, no one knows what twinkles are. In the meantime, Sugar and Saga need to find a way to get along with each other. The story and the art are very sweet and cute.

Volume 1 of 3

Appignanesi, Richard
Hamlet. [Richard Appignanesi, text adaptor]; illustrated by Emma Vieceli. Harry N. Abrams/Amulet Books 2007 195p. (Manga Shakespeare)
Grades: 8 9 10 11 12 Adult   **822.3; 741.5**
   1. Authors; 2. Dramatists; 3. Graphic novels; 4. Poets; 5. Shakespeare, William, 1564-1616; 6. Shakespeare, William, 1564-1616 — Adaptations
978-0-8109-9324-2, $9.95; 0-8109-9324-4

Shakespeare's classic play of murder and revenge is here adapted into a manga-style graphic novel. It's now set in 2107, after global climate change has devastated the Earth. Appignanesi uses the text of the play and abridges it to fit the pages, while Vieceli's art vigorously carries the story along. The book includes a summary of the plot and a brief biography of Shakespeare.

First published in the United Kingdom

A **midsummer** night's dream. illustrated by Kate Brown. Abrams 2008 207p. (Manga Shakespeare)
Grades: 7 8 9 10   **822.3; 741.5**
   1. Authors; 2. Dramatists; 3. Graphic novels; 4. Poets; 5. Shakespeare, William, 1564-1616 — Adaptations
978-0-8109-9475-1, $9.95; 0-8109-9475-5

Shakespeare's comedy of romance, Faerie, and shenanigans in the forest is adapted into a manga-style graphic novel. Hermia is in love with Lysander, while Demetrius is in love with Hermia, and Helen loves Demetrius. When mischievous fairy Puck decides to have some fun with the powerful love potion he has fetched for Fairy King Oberon, chaos reigns. While the human foursome needs to sort itself out, Oberon seeks revenge against his wife, Queen Titania, by having Puck use the love potion on her so she falls in love with the first creature she sees — who happens to be a yokel to whom Puck gave a donkey's head. The text takes dialog from the original play. The book includes a plot summary and a brief biography of Shakespeare.

Romeo and Juliet. by William Shakespeare; adapted by Richard Appignanesi; illustrated by Sonia Leong. Amulet Books 2007 195p. (Manga Shakespeare)
Grades: 8 9 10 11 12   **822.3; 741.5**
  1. Authors; 2. Dramatists; 3. Graphic novels; 4. Poets; 5. Shakespeare, William, 1564-1616 — Adaptations
978-0-8109-9325-9, $9.95; 0-8109-9325-2

LC 2006-100362

Shakespeare's classic play of star-crossed young lovers gets the manga treatment. The book is set in modern Tokyo with rival yakuza gangs and uses somewhat abridged text from the play for the dialogue.

"Although the richness of the language may be lost, the script keeps the spirit of the story intact, hitting all the major speeches." Booklist
First published in the United Kingdom

The **tempest**. illustrated by Paul Duffield; [adaptor, Richard Appignanesi]. Abrams 2008 207p. Illustration (Manga Shakespeare)
Grades: 7 8 9 10   **822.3; 741.5**
  1. Authors; 2. Dramatists; 3. Graphic novels; 4. Poets; 5. Shakespeare, William, 1564-1616 — Adaptations
978-0-8109-9476-8, $9.95

Prospero and his daughter Miranda have lived on an isolated island for twelve years, after he had been deposed from his rule as Duke of Naples and cast out to sea to die. A powerful magician, Prospero has caused the survivors of a shipwreck to land on his island, in order to get his revenge, for these survivors are his enemies. Problems arise when Miranda falls in love with Ferdinand, the monster Caliban tries to use the survivors to kill Prospero, and Ariel the sprite is trying to set things right while still obeying Shakespeare. The book includes a plot summary and a brief biography of Shakespeare

"This adaptation would be useful both as an introduction to the play and as a companion piece for classroom study of it, using images to illuminate the Bard's eloquent poetry." SLJ

Arai, Kiyoko
  Beauty Pop, Vol. 1. story and art by Kiyoko Arai. Viz Media/Shojo Beat 2006 194p. Illustration
Grades: 7 8 9 10 11 12   **741.5; Fic**
  1. Graphic novels; 2. Hair — Graphic novels; 3. Manga; 4. Shojo manga
978-1-4215-0575-6, $8.99

At Kiri Koshiba's high school, three popular upper classmen do occasional "Scissors Projects," working makeovers on specially selected girls. Narumi Shogo, who cuts hair, wants to become the best beautician in Japan and has won every youth competition — except one, years ago, that a younger girl won. When girls who aren't already pretty ask Narumi for a makeover, he tells them they're too ugly. Kiri helps two of the girls, working a stylist's magic that makes the girls glow; she's not interested in competition, even though her family owns a salon. Narumi wants to know who dares to be the upstart and challenge him, and he sets up the school's cultural festival to be a haircutting duel. Will Kiri even bother to compete?
Volume 1 of 10

Arai, Takahiro
  Cirque du Freak, vol. 1. story, Darren Shan; manga, Takahiro Arai; [translation, Stephen Paul]. Yen Press 2009 un Illustration
Grades: 6 7 8 9 10   **741.5; Fic**
  1. Authors; 2. Graphic novels; 3. Horror graphic novels; 4. Manga; 5. Novelists; 6. Vampires — Graphic novels; 7. Young adult authors; 8. Shan, Darren, 1972- — Adaptations; 9. Shonen manga
978-0-7595-3041-6, $10.99

Middle schoolers Darren and Steve hustle soccer games against older players for money; Steve obsesses over horror movies, while Darren has a huge fascination with spiders. When a mysterious stranger hands Darren a flyer advertising a Cirque du Freak, he and Steve decide they must attend. At the circus, they discover that the freaks in the show are true monsters, not the usual hokey hoaxes, and Darren loves the monstrous spider. Then Steve decides that Mr. Crepsley, the spider handler, is a vampire, and Steve wants more than anything to become a vampire. However, Mr. Crepsley rejects him after tasting his blood Steve is too bloodthirsty. Then Darren steals Madame Octa, the spider, only to lose control of her while she's out of her cage and she bites Steve. Crepsley comes for his pet and tells Darren he'll save Steve, but only if Darren will become his assistant and become a vampire. This book is the English translation of the original Japanese manga that is based on Shan's novel.
Volume 1 of 12

Arakawa, Hiromu
  ★ **Fullmetal** alchemist. by Hiromu Arakawa. Viz 2005 192 p. Illustration
Grades: 8 9 10 11 12   **741.5**
  1. Alchemy — Fiction; 2. Brothers — Fiction; 3. Manga; 4. Shonen manga
1591169208; 9781591169208, $9.99

"Alchemy: the mystical power to alter the natural world.... When two brothers, Edward and Alphonse Elric, dabbled in this power to grant their dearest wish, one of them lost an arm and a leg...and the other became nothing but a soul locked into a body of living steel. Now Edward is an agent of the government, a slave of the military-alchemical complex, using his unique powers to obey orders." (Publisher's note)
Volume 1 of 27; Also available in VIZBIG omnibus editions

Silver spoon; Volume 1. Hiromu Arakawa; translation, Amanda Haley; lettering, Abigail Blackman. Yen Press 2018 192 p. Illustration
Grades: 7 8 9 10 11 12   **741.5; Fic**
  1. Shonen manga; 2. Country life — Fiction; 3. Farm life — Fiction
0316416193; 9780316416191, $15

LC 2017959207

"Yuugo Hachiken chooses to leave the city and enroll at Ooezo Agricultural High School. Having always been at the top of his class, Yuugo assumes a rural school will be a breeze, but mucking out stables, gathering eggs, and chasing errant calves takes a lot out of him—and fills him with something he's never experienced before. Surrounded by endless fields and fresh air, Yuugo discovers a new connection to the land and to life." (Publisher's note)

"Arakawa (Fullmetal Alchemist) takes a personal touch in this fresh take on coming of age.... The simple, character-centered artwork is less arresting than in Arakawa's prior series, but it's bright and funny, littered with unexpected visual gags." Pub Wkly
Volume 1 of an ongoing series

Araki, Hirohiko
  Jojo's Bizarre Adventure: Phantom Blood. Hirohiko Araki; [translation, Evan Galloway; touch-up art & lettering, Mark McMurray]. Viz 2015 255 p. Illustration
Grades: 7 8 9 10 11 12   **741.5; Fic**
  1. Seinen manga; 2. Shonen manga
1421578794; 9781421578798, $19.99

"Young Jonathan Joestar's life is forever changed when he meets his new adopted brother, Dio. For some reason, Dio has a smoldering grudge against him and derives pleasure from seeing him suffer. But every man has his limits, as Dio finds out. This is the beginning of a long and hateful relationship!" (Publisher's note)

"This 1980s manga classic is a cross between 'The Eye of Argon' and glam rock. Muscular bodies that rival Fist of the North Star, dapper fashion, occasional duo-tone, and bold yet intricate pen lines tell a

Victorian tale of manhood, complete with an archeological artifact that demands blood sacrifice." Pub Wkly

Volume 1 of an ongoing series

Atangan, Patrick

Songs of our ancestors: The yellow jar: two tales from Japanese tradition. NBM 2003 48p. Illustration (Songs of our ancestors)

Grades: 5 6 7 8 9 10 11 12   **741.5**

1. Folklore — Japan — Graphic novels; 2. Graphic novels

1-56163-331-3, $12.92

                             LC 2002-32132

"To render two magical Japanese legends, one about a fisherman who discovers a fair maiden in a big pot, the other about a monk whose fastidiously kept garden is invaded by two chrysanthemums, Atangan charmingly adopts the sharp outlines, boldly juxtaposed color fields, and striking compositions of eighteenth-century Japanese woodblock prints." Booklist

Other titles in this series are: Silk tapestry and other Chinese folktales (2004); Tree of love (2005)

Azuma, Kiyohiko

★ **Azumanga** Daioh omnibus. translation, Stephen Paul. Yen Press 2009 675p. Illustration

Grades: 8 9 10 11 12   **741.5; Fic**

1. Graphic novels; 2. High school students — Graphic novels; 3. Humorous graphic novels; 4. Manga; 5. School stories — Graphic novels; 6. Shonen manga

978-0-316-07738-5, $24.99

An omnibus edition of a humorous four-volume manga series featuring a Japanese suburban high school class with a ditzy teacher. The adult teachers go drinking occasionally, and there's one male teacher who ogles the girls in their P.E. uniforms.

First published 2001 in Japan

Yotsuba&!. by Kiyohiko Azuma. Yen Press 2009 224 p. Illustration

Grades: 5 6 7 8   **741.5; Fic**

1. Shonen manga; 2. Moving — Graphic novels; 3. Manga

0316073873; 9780316073875, $13

In this book, by Kiyohiko Azuma, "Yotsuba is the charming new girl in town.... In seven stories, the green-haired four-year-old discovers air conditioners, doorbells, cicadas, swings and more, and does it all with the energy of a small hurricane. Her excitement is contagious and infects her handsome young adoptive father as well as the gaggle of pretty girls next door, all of whom get tangled up in her adventures as they try to keep up with her." (Publisher's note)

"Yotsuba is the charming new girl in town in this all-ages shojo manga by the author of the popular Azumanga Daioh series. In seven stories, the green-haired four-year-old discovers air conditioners, doorbells, cicadas, swings and more, and does it all with the energy of a small hurricane." Pub Wkly

Originally published in the U.S. by ADV; Volume 1 of an ongoing series

Azuma, Naomi

Suihelibe!, vol. 1. Naomi Azuma; translated by Sheldon Drzka. DC Comics/CMX 2008 160p. Illustration

Grades: 3 4 5 6 7 8   **741.5; Fic**

1. Graphic novels; 2. Humorous graphic novels; 3. Manga; 4. Science fiction graphic novels; 5. Shonen manga

978-1-4012-1900-0, $9.99

On the cover of the manga, several chemistry elements are listed: hydrogen, helium, lithium, and belium (which probably should be beryllium). First year junior high school student Tetsu just wants to join the biology club at school, when a small flying saucer crashes into the classroom. Lan, the alien pilot who looks like a cute girl, enlists Tetsu's help to recover some escaped life forms from her planet. In order for them to accomplish this task, they need to keep the biology club going, but the student council president wants to shut down the club, so they have three months to round up three more members, even as they hunt Noids (the life forms). There's a lot of shouting and slapstick humor.

Volume 1 of 2

Bagieu, Pénélope

★ **Brazen:** rebel ladies who rocked the world. Pénélope Bagieu. First Second 2018 304 p. Color; Illustration

Grades: 8 9 10 11 12 Adult   **920; 741.5**

1. Women — Biography; 2. Biography

9781626728684; 9781626728691, $17.99

                           LC 2017941160

"With her characteristic wit and dazzling drawings, celebrated graphic novelist Pénélope Bagieu profiles the lives of...feisty female role models, some world famous, some little known. From Nellie Bly to Mae Jemison or Josephine Baker to Naziq al-Abid, the stories in this comic biography are sure to inspire the next generation of rebel ladies." (Publisher's note)

"Both art and text are clever, smart, and distilled for maximum impact. The women are not idealized, nor are their flaws ignored. Instead, they are treated with wit and empathy.... A fresh and joyous look at women's history that is sure to delight even the most jaded readers." LJ

Originally published in French by Gallimard in 2016 as Culottées: Des femmes qui ne font que ce qu'elles veulent, tome I and in 2017 as Culottées: Des femmes qui ne font que ce qu'elles veulent, tome II

Bailey, Chris

Major Damage. Sky Dog Press 2004 un Illustration

Grades: 3 4 5 6 7 8   **741.5; Fic**

1. Graphic novels; 2. Humorous graphic novels; 3. Superhero graphic novels

0-9721831-4-0, $14.95

Before The Incredibles, there was Major Damage: the tale of a little boy who is transformed into his favorite super hero, protecting the world from mutants, monsters, and alien scum. Eight-year-old Melvin was trick or treating on Halloween night, dressed as his favorite superhero, Major Damage, when he was abducted by the Mucus Men; the harmless scientists mistook Melvin for the real hero, assumed he'd had an accident, and "restored" his powers and returned him to Earth. Meanwhile, Melvin's mother thinks her son has disappeared.

Baker, Kyle

★ **How** to draw stupid and other essentials of cartooning. Watson-Guptill 2008 110p. Illustration

Grades: 8 9 10 11 12 Adult   **741.5**

1. Cartooning — Technique; 2. Graphic novels — Drawing

978-0-8230-0143-9, $16.95

                           LC 2008-922161

"Baker, an award-winning cartoonist and graphic-novel illustrator, gives aspiring cartoonists irreverent advice about how to succeed in their chosen field. He offers instruction in basic drawing techniques such as choosing the right tools and discusses the importance of learning to draw shapes, exaggerating, and using references. But the author's most inspiring advice focuses on how to succeed as a cartoonist." SLJ

Plastic Man: On the Lam!. DC Comics 2004 un Illustration

Grades: 6 7 8 9 10 11 12 Adult   **741.5; Fic**

1. Graphic novels; 2. Humorous graphic novels; 3. Plastic Man (Fictional character); 4. Superhero graphic novels

1-4012-0343-4, $14.95

2005 Eisner Award for Best Publication for a Younger Audience, also 2005 Eisner Award for Best Writer/Artists-Humor for Kyle Baker

Plastic Man has worked as a superhero, but he used to be the criminal Eel O'Brian, a fact he has hidden from the FBI. Now there's been a murder, and Eel O'Brian is the main (and only) suspect. When the FBI learns of his old identity, Plastic Man goes on the lam to clear himself.

Originally published as Plastic Man issues #1-6; this volume is bound in plastic; Volume 1 of 2

Through the looking-glass. by Lewis Carroll; adapted by Kyle Baker. Papercutz 2008 un Illustration (Classics illustrated)

Grades: 3 4 5 6 7 8 9

741.5; Fic

1. Fantasy graphic novels; 2. Graphic novels; 3. Carroll, Lewis, 1832-1898 — Adaptations

978-1-59707-115-4, $9.95;
1-59707-115-3

Courtesy of NBM Publishing

This is Carroll's sequel to Alice's Adventures in Wonderland. This time, Alice climbs through the looking-glass in her house and finds herself in a land with talking flowers and insects, Tweedledee and Tweedledum (who recite "The Walrus and the Carpenter"), the White Queen who needs help pinning her shawl straight, Humpty Dumpty, the Red Queen, and more. The Eisner Award-winning Baker uses a different style from his usual cartoony look here, more reminiscent of Tenniel's classic illustrations of Carroll's books.

Baldwin, Christopher
Little Dee and the penguin. by Christopher Baldwin. Dial Books for Young Readers 2016 128 p. Color; Illustration

Grades: 3 4 5 6 **741.5**

1. Animals — Fiction; 2. Graphic novels; 3. Human-animal relationships — Fiction; 4. Humorous stories; 5. Friendship — Graphic novels; 6. Animals — Graphic novels

9781101994290, $17.99; 1101994290; 9780803741089, $10.99

LC 2015010378

In this graphic novel, by Christopher Baldwin, "when Little Dee meets a motley crew of animals deep in the forest, she knows she's found the perfect set of new friends. Between the bossy vulture, the slightly dim dog, the nurturing bear, and the happy-go-lucky penguin,...they're a family. And they're on the run. A pair of hungry polar bears are after the penguin, and the rest of the team are determined to protect her." (Publisher's note)

"Baldwin's full-color illustrations appeal to all of the senses and keep the story moving — through travel by plane, raft, boat, and on foot, ahead of a pair of hungry polar bears all the way. A must-read for all would-be adventurers." Kirkus

Baltazar, Art
Aw yeah comics and...action!; Volume 1. by Art Baltaza & Franco Aureliani. Dark Horse Books 2014 1:00 PM Color; Illustration

Grades: 3 4 5 6 **741.5**

1. Graphic novels; 2. Superheroes; 3. Cats; 4. Insects
1616555580; 9781616555580, $12.99

LC 2014430639

This graphic novel, by Art Baltaza & Franco, is the "comic you've heard so much about! Action Cat! Adventure Bug! And their adventures in the Aw Yeah Comics Universe!...It's up to Action Cat and Adventure Bug to stop the bad guys! Follow these amazing superheroes!" (Publisher's note)

Patrick the Wolf Boy Volume 1. written by Art Baltazar & Franco Aureliani; drawn by Art Baltazar. Devil's Due Publishing 2004 un Illustration

Grades: 2 3 4 5 6 7 8 9 10 11 12 Adult **741.5; Fic**

1. Graphic novels; 2. Humorous graphic novels
1-932796-27-4, $10.95

Patrick looks at first glance like the other kids in school, but he's a werewolf. A cute werewolf. He resembles Eddie Munster (from the 1960s television comedy series "The Munsters"), and he doesn't speak, although he growls a lot and sometimes howls. He gives his teacher an apple — but with a skull biting the apple. When he goes fishing with his dad, he prefers to scare the bear into giving him his catch. He loves to play tag with the neighborhood squirrel. And when Valentine's Day comes, he makes sure that his babysitter likes him better. His utterly normal parents adore him and understand his growls; so does Neve, his classmate at school.

Volume 1 of 4

Barker, Clive
The **Thief** of Always. IDW Publishing 2005 144p. Illustration

Grades: 4 5 6 7 8 9 10

741.5; Fic

1. Fantasy graphic novels; 2. Graphic novels; 3. Horror graphic novels
1-933239-17-4, $35.00; 1-933239-38-7 (pa), $19.99

Courtesy of IDW Publishing

Clive Barker's fable for younger readers is adapted here into graphic novel format. Mr. Hood's Holiday House has stood for a thousand years, welcoming countless children to enjoy a blissful round of treats and holidays...for a price. Then bored young Harvey Swick comes, and he notices disquieting little details that make him realize the place is more of a trap. Things are spooky but not terrifying, with little violence.

Originally published as The Thief of Always issues #1-3.

Barry, Lynda
★ **What** it is. Drawn & Quarterly 2008 209p. Illustration

Grades: 7 8 9 10 11 12 Adult **818; 741.5**

1. Authorship — Graphic novels; 2. Creative writing — Graphic novels
978-1-897299-35-7, $24.95; 1-897299-35-4

LC c2007-9047319

Independent cartoonist Lynda Barry presents an unconventional book that encourages its readers to write by using her colorful art and asking questions such as "How are monsters different? And how are they the same?" "Can/Do images exist without thinking?" "What is the difference between lying and pretending?" Each question appears with illustrated writing prompts and Barry's own ruminations on the topics. It's a workbook of sorts, but it also exists as a book to be read for itself.

"Every so often a book comes along that surpasses expectations, taking readers on an inspirational voyage that they don't want to leave. This is one such book." SLJ

Beazley, Mark D.
Pet avengers classic. Marvel Entertainment 2009 208p. Illustration

Grades: 7 8 9 10 11 12 Adult **741.5; Fic**

1. Adventure graphic novels; 2. Graphic novels; 3. Pets — Graphic novels; 4. Superhero graphic novels
9780785139669, $24.99

This volume collects the various Marvel Pets stories, from 1960 to 2007, with each story featuring a different pet, from Lockjaw the teleporting dog to Kitty Pryde's dragon Lockheed to Brightwind the winged horse, and many more. Lockjaw, Lockheed, Redwing the falcon, the cat named Niels, and Zabu the saber tooth tiger all starred in th 2009 mini series titled Pet Avengers. Some of the stories in this collection include violence.

Spider-Man: The Birth of Venom. Marvel Entertainment 2007 un Illustration
Grades: 8 9 10 11 12 Adult   **741.5; Fic**
  1. Graphic novels; 2. Spider-Man (Fictional character); 3. Superhero graphic novels; 4. Fantastic Four (Fictional characters)
978-0-7851-2498-6, $29.99
The Beyonder's Battleworld might seem a strange place to get new threads, but it's Spider-Man who becomes unraveled when his new symbiotic, shape-changing costume attempts to darken his life as well as his fashion sense. But ridding himself of his black costume proves an even greater mistake when its alien enmity bonds with mortal madness to form our hero's most dedicated enemy, Venom. Other stories include the first appearances of Puma and the Rose, Mary Jane Watson's startling secret, and the debut of the battling...Bag-Man? The Black Cat, the Fantastic Four and other Marvel characters appear.

Beechen, Adam
Justice League Unlimited Vol. 1: United They Stand. written by Adam Beechen; illustrated by Carlo Barbieri, Ethen Beavers, Walden Wong; colored by Heroic Age; lettered by Phil Balsman, Pat Brosseau, Nick J. Napolitano. DC Comics 2005 104p. Illustration
Grades: 4 5 6 7 8 9   **741.5; Fic**
  1. Graphic novels; 2. Justice League (Fictional characters); 3. Superhero graphic novels
1401205127; 9781401205126, $6.99
Leaping straight out of their Cartoon Network show, the Worlds Greatest Heroes have their own comics series. This inaugural collection features these tales: Divide Conquer, Poker Face, Small Time, Local Hero and Monitor Duty.
Volume 1 of 5

Bell, Cece
  ★ El deafo. Cece Bell; color by David Lasky. Abrams Books 2014 233 p. Color; Illustration
Grades: 3 4 5 6 7   **741.5; 92**
  1. Friendship; 2. Hearing aids for children; 3. Schools; 4. Deaf children; 5. Autobiographical graphic novels
1419710206; 9781419710209, $21.95
LC 2013955590
Newbery Honor Book (2015); Eisner Award: Best Publication for Kids (2015)
"In this...graphic novel memoir, author/illustrator Cece Bell chronicles her hearing loss at a young age and her subsequent experiences with the Phonic Ear, a very powerful — and very awkward — hearing aid. The Phonic Ear gives Cece the ability to hear — sometimes things she shouldn't — but also isolates her from her classmates." (Publisher's note)
"Bell's bold and blocky full-color cartoons perfectly complement her childhood stories — she often struggles to fit in and sometimes experiences bullying, but the cheerful illustrations promise a sunny future." Booklist

Bendis, Brian Michael
Spider-Man; Volume 1: Miles Morales. Brian Michael Bendis, writer; Sarah Pichelli, artist; Gaetano Carlucci, inking assist; Justin Ponsor, colorist; VC's Cory Petit, letterer. Marvel Enterprises 2016 112 p. Color; Illustration (Spider-Man (2016))
Grades: 8 9 10 11 12 Adult   **741.5; Fic**
  0785199616; 9780785199618, $15.99

"Miles Morales is hitting the big time! Not only is he joining the Marvel Universe, but he's also a card-carrying Avenger, rubbing shoulders with the likes of Iron Man, Thor and Captain America! But how have Miles' first eight months been, coming to grips with an All-new, All-Different New York? One thing is the same — nonstop action!" (Publisher's note)
Volume 1 of an ongoing series

Ultimate Fantastic Four Vol. 1: The Fantastic. writers, Brian Michael Bendis & Mark Millar; pencils, Adam Kubert; inks, Danny Miki and John Dell; colors, Dave Stewart; letters, Chris Eliopoulos. Marvel Entertainment 2005 un Illustration
Grades: 8 9 10 11 12 Adult   **741.5; Fic**
  1. Fantastic Four (Fictional characters); 2. Graphic novels; 3. Superhero graphic novels
978-0-7851-1393-5, $12.99
The Ultimate treatment takes the Fantastic Four back to the beginning. High school genius (and bully magnet) Reed Richards suffers at school and also at home with a father who doesn't like his "troublemaking" experiments. When Reed enrolls at a secret government-sponsored school for the most gifted minds in the world, he unwittingly embarks on the journey of a lifetime. This is a story about science, adventure, and above all else, family.
Volume 1 of 15

Ultimate Spider-Man: Power & Responsibility. by Brian Michael Bendis (Author), Mark Bagley (Illustrator). Marvel 2009 200 p. Color illustration
Grades: 7 8 9 10 11 12 Adult   **741.5**
  1. Spider-Man (Fictional character)
0785139400; 9780785139409, $19.99
In this comic book, by Brian Michael Bendis, illustrated by Mark Bagley, "Peter Parker gains super-powers after being bitten by a spider, loses his likable Uncle Ben to violent crime, and learns once again that 'with great power comes great responsibility.'" (Publisher's note)
Collected edition originally published 2001; Volume 1 of 21

Benjamin, Ryan
Star Wars: Empire Volume One: Betrayal. written by Scott Allie, pencilled by Ryan Benjamin, inked by Curtis Arnold. Dark Horse Comics 2003 un Illustration
Grades: 7 8 9 10 11 12 Adult   **741.5; Fic**
  1. Adventure graphic novels; 2. Graphic novels; 3. Science fiction graphic novels; 4. Star Wars — Graphic novels
1-56971-964-0, $12.95
In the weeks before the events in Star Wars: A New Hope, as the Death Star is readied for its fateful first mission, a power-hungry cabal of Grand Moffs and Imperial Officers embark on a dangerous plan to kill Emperor Palpatine and Darth Vader and seize control of the Empire. When word that a Jedi" has made an appearance on a backwater world lures Vader away from his master, the cabal makes its move. But even the galaxy isn't enough of a prize to sate the ambitions of some of the conspirators, and before long the would-be assassins are turning on one another. Their plans are further complicated by the actions of bounty hunter Boba Fett. And, of course, they may have fatally underestimated the cunning of their primary target: Emperor Palpatine.
Volume 1 of 7

Benson, John
Romance Without Tears. Fantagraphics Books 2004 160p. Illustration
Grades: 8 9 10 11 12 Adult   **741.5; Fic**
  1. Graphic novels; 2. Romance graphic novels

1-56097-558-X, $22.95

This revisionist collection of romance comics stories from the '50s challenges the cliché of the "tear-stained face" that later dominated the genre and became widely known and vilified as a tiresome icon of moral uplift. Editor Benson has picked stories that portray stron young women who learn from their mistakes and choose their guys, and get themselves out of trouble. The stories were all originally published by Archer St. John in the late-1940s to mid-1950s.

Bertozzi, Nick
 Lewis & Clark. First Second 2011 136p. Illustration
Grades: 5 6 7 8 **978; 741.5**
 978-1-59643-450-9 (pa), $16.99; 1-59643-450-3 (pa)
 LC 2010-36255
 "Bertozzi offers an innovative take on Meriwether Lewis and William Clark's epic journey in this oversized graphic offering. Portraying the arduous trek through rough terrain and encounters with often unwelcoming natives, sequential panels transport readers alongside the famous duo and their equally renowned translator, Sacagawea, as they travel from St. Louis to the Pacific coast. Within a fictional framework, the narrative weaves in facets of the characters' personalities, including Lewis's tempestuous melancholy, Charbonneau's inept bumbling and Sacagawea's ability to endure this voyage surrounded by her intensely masculine cohorts." (Kirkus)

 ★ **Shackleton**: Antarctic odyssey. Nick Bertozzi. First Second 2014 128 p. Illustration; Map
Grades: 5 6 7 8 9 10 **741.5; 919.89**
 1. Explorers — Great Britain — Biography; 2. Graphic novels; 3. Antarctica — Discovery and exploration — British; 4. Antarctica — Exploration; 5. Shackleton, Ernest Henry, Sir, 1874-1922
 1596434511; 9781596434516, $16.99
 This book by Nick Bertozzi describes how "Ernest Shackleton was one of the last great Antarctic explorers, and he led one of the most ambitious Antarctic expeditions ever undertaken. This is his story, and the story of the dozens of men who threw in their lot with him — many of whom nearly died in the unimaginably harsh conditions of the journey." (Publisher's note)

 "Bertozzi eschews all narrative explanation, relying solely on dialogue among the crew and the detailed black-and-white panels to tell the story. The snow- and ice-bound journey is the perfect match for Bertozzi's minimal style — vast stretches of white become gasp-worthy, desolate vistas." Booklist

Bevard, Robby
 Sir Arthur Conan Doyle's the adventure of the Norwood Builder. ABDO/Magic Wagon 2010 48p. Illustration
Grades: 4 5 6 7 8 9 **741.5; Fic**
 1. Graphic novels; 2. Holmes, Sherlock (Fictional character); 3. Mystery graphic novels
 978-1-60270-725-2, $28.50; 1-60270-725-1
 LC 2009-32459
 Young solicitor Mr. McFarlane begs Holmes to clear his name when he's accused of the murder of Jonas Oldacre, the Norwood Builder. Inspector Lestrade thinks he has a solid case, and the evidence seems to implicate McFarlane, especially since Mr. Oldacre's new will made McFarlane his sole heir. Holmes points to the lack of a body, and digs up more clues in his quest to save McFarlane. This graphic novel adaptation of Doyle's short story retains the suspense of the original, but perpetuates the stereotypical portrayals of Holmes in the deerstalker and caped coat which he never wore in the original stories. The book includes a brief drawing lesson, a short glossary, a brief biography of Doyle, and a listing of his other writings.
 Part of The Graphic Novel Adventures of Sherlock Holmes

Biggs, Gina
 Red String, Vol. 1. Dark Horse Comics 2006 192p. Illustration
Grades: 7 8 9 10 11 12 **741.5; Fic**
 1. Graphic novels; 2. High school life — Graphic novels; 3. Romance graphic novels
 978-1-59307-624-5, $9.95
 First year high school student Miharu Ogawa can't believe it when her parents tell her they've arranged for her to marry the son of their friends, someone she has never met. They won't marry until they finish school, but the whole idea is repugnant. Then Miharu meets a cute guy and knows she has to fight her parents; but the cute guy she likes is Kazuo Fujiwara, the arranged fiance. Now Miharu just has to deal with gossip at school that hurts her friend Reika, and with her manipulative cousin Karen, who wants Kazuo for herself, and other problems and romantic obstacles. Biggs uses the manga format and manga-influenced art to tell her story of high school romance. Other than one panel of tastefully rendered partial nudity, there's no content to keep this from most middle school age readers.
 Volume 1 of 8

Black, Holly
 The Good Neighbors; book one: Kin. Graphix 2008 117p. (The Good Neighbors)
Grades: 7 8 9 10 11 12 **741.5; Fic**
 1. Fairies — Graphic novels; 2. Fantasy graphic novels; 3. Graphic novels
 978-0-439-85562-4, $16.99; 0-439-85562-4
 LC 2007-49008
 Sixteen-year-old Rue has grown up in a world much like ours, except that the human world and the world of faerie have co-existed, as good neighbors, for a long time. When Rue's mother disappears and her professor father becomes the main suspect in the murder of a young woman, Rue's life turns strange. As she digs for information to figure out what is happening in her life, Rue discovers that her mother is a faerie and has returned to that realm because of a broken promise.
 "This sophisticated tale is well served by Naifeh's stylish, angular illustrations." SLJ
 Other titles in this series are: Kith (2009); Kind (2010)

Blackman, Haden
 Star Wars Omnibus: X-Wing Rogue Squadron Volume 1. writers, Haden Blackman ... [et al.]; art, Tomas Giorello ... [et al.]. Dark Horse Comics 2006 un Illustration
Grades: 7 8 9 10 11 12 Adult **741.5; Fic**
 1. Adventure graphic novels; 2. Graphic novels; 3. Science fiction graphic novels; 4. Star Wars — Graphic novels
 978-1-59307-572-9, $24.95
 The greatest star fighters of the Rebel Alliance become the defenders of a New Republic in this massive collection of stories featuring Wedge Antilles, hero of the Battle of Endor, and his team of ace pilots known throughout the galaxy as Rogue Squadron. Meet the Rogues for the first time and learn the fate of the galaxy immediately after the events of Return of the Jedi as the Rebellion's best pilots battle remnants of the Empire wherever its ugly agenda of fear and domination appears. Along with X-Wing Rogue Squadron: The Phantom Affair, this jam-packed volume contains never before collected material, including Star Wars X-Wing Rogue Leader #1-3, Star Wars X-Wing Rogue Squadron: The Rebel

Opposition #1-4, Star Wars X-Wing Rogue Squadron: The Phantom Affair #1-4, and Star Wars Handbook: X-Wing Rogue Squadron.
Volume 1 of 3

Blaylock, Josh
Penguin Bros.. Devil's Due Publishing 2004 un Illustration
Grades: 7 8 9 10 11 12   **741.5; Fic**
1. Graphic novels; 2. Humorous graphic novels; 3. Penguins — Graphic novels; 4. Superhero graphic novels
1-932796-20-7, $10.95
Three teenage penguins living in Chill City, Antarctica are the ones chosen to become their city's heroes, and granted Super Powers. There's only one problem — they'd rather go to concerts, hang with girlfriends, and play video games. It's sleigh cars, super powers and homework in the Penguin Bros. As Blaylock explains at the end of the book, he created the Penguin Bros. when he was six years old — and he has the drawings to prove it.

Bogaert, Harmen Meyndertsz van den
Journey into Mohawk Country. as written by H.M. van den Bogaert, with artwork by George O'Connor and color by Hilary Sycamore. First Second 2006 144p. Illustration
Grades: 8 9 10 11 12   **973.2**
1. Graphic novels; 2. New York (State) — History — 1600-1775, Colonial period — Graphic novels; 3. United States — History — 1600-1775, Colonial period — Graphic novels
1-59643-106-7, $17.95
In 1634, young Dutch trader Harmen Meyndertsz van den Bogaert, several companions, and some native guides traveled deep into what is now New York State, trading tools and weapons and trying to establish new tribal friendships to bolster Dutch trade. van den Bogaert kept a journal throughout his journeys. O'Connor has kept the original text and conducted extensive research in order to make his illustrations as authentic as possible.

Boldman, Craig
Archie Day by Day Volume 1. Archie Comics 2003 96p. Illustration
Grades: 3 4 5 6 7 8 9 10 11 12 Adult   **741.5; Fic**
1. Andrews, Archie (Fictional character); 2. Graphic novels; 3. Humorous graphic novels
1-879794-16-0, $10.95
Archie and his pals have been comics' most celebrated teenage humor characters for over 60 years, since 1941. Now for the first time, selections from Archie's worldwide syndicated newspaper strip are collected in this volume. This black and white edition includes a selection of daily strips from the mid-1990s, chronicling life in Riverdale, USA.

Bonneval, Gwen de
William and the lost spirit. Gwen de Bonneval; illustrated by Matthieu Bonhomme; colors by Walter; translation, Anne Collins Smith and Owen M. Smith; [lettering by Dennis Pacheco]. Graphic Universe 2013 152 p.
Grades: 4 5 6 7
Fic; 741.5/944
1. Families — Fiction; 2. Folklore — Fiction; 3. Graphic novels; 4. Knights and knighthood — Fiction; 5. Middle Ages — Fiction; 6. Mythology — Fiction; 7. Voyages and travels — Fiction; 8. Fantasy fiction; 9. Voyages and travels

Courtesy of Lerner Publishing Group

1467708070; 9780761385677; 9781467708074, $9.95
LC 2012008115
In this book, as "William sets out to find his father (who might be dead, or lost, or both) he is joined by a knight, a troubadour, and a very unusual goat. Soon he enters a mysterious world that is populated with an amazing cast of characters, including Prester John, dog-faced men, and headless people whose faces are on their chests." (School Library Journal)

Booth, Jack
Kazuma's Quest. Harcourt Achieve/Steck-Vaughn 2007 48p. Illustration
Grades: 3 4 5 6 7 8   **741.5; Fic**
1. Graphic novels; 2. Samurai — Graphic novels
978-1-4190-3215-8, $8.99
Kazuma is a young samurai who sets out to confront his father's murderer and reclaim his family's sword. The famous swordsman Matayemon offers to help him. Will they be able to outsmart their enemies? This is historical fiction in graphic novel format with facts about the samurai interspersed throughout the story in prose sections.
Part of the Timeline Graphic Novels series.

Nomad King. Harcourt Achieve/Steck-Vaughn 2006 48p. Illustration
Grades: 3 4 5 6 7 8   **741.5; 92; Fic**
1. Graphic novels; 2. Khan, Genghis, ca. 1162-1227; 3. Mongolia — History — Graphic novels
978-1-4190-3201-1, $8.99
In the sparse, windswept land of Mongolia in the late 12th century, Temujin becomes leader of his tribe at the age of nine. Over the years, this ruthless leader battles warring tribes for power then unites them under his rule, becoming Genghis Khan. He gradually extends his empire beyond Mongolia and China; will he be able to take over the world? This historical graphic novel includes prose intervals that provide more information about the Mongols and about Genghis Khan.
Part of the Timeline Graphic Novels series.

Raiders of the Seas. Harcourt Achieve/Steck-Vaughn 2006 48p. Illustration
Grades: 3 4 5 6 7 8   **741.5; Fic**
1. Adventure graphic novels; 2. Graphic novels; 3. Pirates — Graphic novels
978-1-4190-3207-3, $8.99
Nicholas Bloom is a young sailor who lands in bad company when he joins the ship of a pirate named Blackbeard. Together they sail the seas, raiding and plundering. When Nick learns more about Blackbeard's evil ways, he must decide what to do next. This historical graphic novel includes prose intervals that give information about pirates and the differences between them and privateers.
Part of the Timeline Graphic Novels series.

Bosma, Sam
Fantasy Sports; 1. Sam Bosma. Nobrow Press 2015 56 p. Color; Illustration
Grades: 5 6 7 8   **741.5; Fic**
1. Mummies — Graphic novels; 2. Basketball — Graphic novels; 3. Adventure graphic novels
1907704809; 9781907704802, $19.95
Ignatz Award Winner: Outstanding Comic (2016)
In this graphic novel, written and illustrated by Sam Bosma, "a young explorer and her musclebound friend go treasure hunting in a mummy's tomb — but if they want to get rich, they're going to have to best the mummy in a game of hoops! Can they trust their bandaged adversary to play by the rules? Or will they be stuck in the tomb...forever?" (Publisher's note)

"Bosma's colorfully jumbled, slanty panels look like the inspired offspring of Spirited Away and Space Jam, capturing magical intrigue, fast-paced basketball action, and the best kind of on-the-court trash talk in one go." Booklist

Other titles in this series are: The Bandit of Barbel Bay (2016); The Green King (2017)

Boyd, David
Napoleon's Last Stand. Harcourt Achieve/Steck-Vaughn 2006 48p. Illustration
Grades: 3 4 5 6 7 8   **741.5; Fic**
1. Adventure graphic novels; 2. Graphic novels; 3. Napoleon I, Emperor of the French
978-1-4190-3208-0, $8.99

Charlotte Bonaparte helps her famous uncle Napoleon escape from the island of Elba. As Napoleon prepares to go to war, Charlotte makes her own plans. This historical fiction graphic novel depicts some of the events of the Battle of Waterloo, so there is some battlefield violence. The book includes prose intervals that provide more information about Napoleon, his English opponent, the Duke of Wellington, the battle, and the death of Napoleon.

Part of the Timeline Graphic Novels series.

Braithwaite, Doug
Justice Volume One. Jim Krueger and Alex Ross, story; Doug Braithwaite and Alex Ross, art. DC Comics 2006 160p. Illustration
Grades: 8 9 10 11 12 Adult   **741.5; Fic**
1. Graphic novels; 2. Justice League of America (Fictional characters); 3. Superhero graphic novels
978-1-4012-0969-8, $19.99

The Justice League of America are the World's Greatest Super-Heroes, but now villains — the Riddler, Lex Luthor, Poison Ivy, Captain Cold, and others are banding together and making sweeping, worldwide changes that appear to be noble acts. But, one by one the members of the JLA are being taken down; will anyone be left to truly protect the people of Earth?

Britt, Fanny
★ **Jane,** the fox & me. [written by] Fanny Britt; [illustrated by] Isabelle Arsenault; translated by Christine Morelli and Susan Ouriou. Pgw 2013 101 p.
Grades: 5 6 7 8 9   **Fic**
1. Teenage girls — Fiction; 2. Alienation (Social psychology) — Fiction
1554983606; 9781554983605, $19.95
Governor General's Award: Children's Illustration (2013); Eisner Nominee: Best Publication for Children (2014)

Written by Fanny Britt, illustrated by Isabelle Arsentault, and translated by Christine Morelli and Susan Ouriou, this "graphic novel reveals the casual brutality of which children are capable, but also assures readers that redemption can be found through connecting with another, whether the other is a friend, a fictional character or even, amazingly, a fox." (Publisher's note) It "centers on Hélène, ostracized by her former friends and now a loner at school." (Horn Book Magazine)

"Britt's well-constructed narrative is achieved sensitively through Arsenault's impressionistic artwork.... An elegant and accessible approach to an important topic." Booklist

Louis undercover. by Fanny Britt; illustrated by Isabelle Arsenault; translated by Christelle Morelli and Susan Ouriou. Groundwood Books 2017 160 p. Color; Illustration
Grades: 5 6 7 8   **741.5**
1. Brothers — Fiction; 2. Father-son relationship — Fiction
9781554988594, $19.95; 9781554988600; 1554988594

In this book, by Fanny Britt, translated by Christelle Morelli and Susan Ouriou, illustrated by Isabelle Arsenault, "Louis's dad cries — Louis knows this because he spies on him. His dad misses the happy times when their family was together, just as Louis does. But as it is, he and his little brother, Truffle, have to travel back and forth between their dad's country house and their mom's city apartment, where she tries to hide her own tears." (Publisher's note)

"Working in moody ink and pencil, Arsenault excels at capturing characters in the grip of powerful emotions they're trying to conceal, and also at conveying a sense of place — both city and country are evocatively drawn." Pub Wkly

Brooks, Mark
Arana Vol. 1: The Heart of the Spider. writer, Fiona Avery; pencilers, Mark Brooks & Roger Cruz; inkers, Jaime Mendoza & Victor Olazaba; colorist, UDON's Larry Molinar & Jeannie Lee; letterers, Virtual Calligraphy's Rus Wooton & Chris Eliopoulos. Marvel Entertainment 2005 un Illustration
Grades: 8 9 10 11 12 Adult   **741.5; Fic**
1. Adventure graphic novels; 2. Graphic novels; 3. Superhero graphic novels
0-7851-1506-4, $7.99

She's fierce, she's sassy, she sticks to walls. Anya Corazon, a.k.a. Arana, is a next-generation girl warrior. A scrappy teen from Brooklyn by day, Anya becomes the Hunter of the ancient and mystical Spider Society by night. But first, she must survive her initiation and prove herself on her first mission, all while going to high school and hiding everything from her single-parent dad. Together with her partner, the mysterious mage Miguel, Anya must fight to protect the peace of the world from the sworn enemies of the Spider Society, the evil Sisterhood of the Wasp. There's lots of super hero action here.

Volume 1 of 3

Broome, John
The **Green** Lantern Archives Volume 5. stories by John Broome; art by Gil Kane, Joe Giella. DC Comics 2004 239p. Illustration
Grades: 6 7 8 9 10 11 12 Adult   **741.5; Fic**
1. Graphic novels; 2. Green Lantern (Fictional character); 3. Superhero graphic novels
1-4012-0404-X, $49.95

LC 93-131923

This volume presents the further adventures of Green Lantern Hal Jordan " the Silver Age's science fiction-influenced hero. This time, the Emerald Gladiator squares off against foes such as Dr. Light, Hector Hammond, Evil Star, the Aerialist, and many more. This full-color Archive reprints nine tales from Green Lantern #30-38, originally published in 1964 and 1965.

Showcase Presents: Green Lantern Volume 1. stories by John Broome; art by Gil Kane and Joe Giella. DC Comics 2005 528p. Illustration
Grades: 6 7 8 9 10 11 12 Adult   **741.5; Fic**
1. Graphic novels; 2. Green Lantern (Fictional character); 3. Superhero graphic novels
1-4012-0759-6, $9.99

A dying alien summoned test pilot Hal Jordan and gave him the most powerful weapon in the universe: a power ring. Jordan was inducted into the universe-spanning Green Lantern Corps and assigned to protect a sector of space including Earth. His sheer willpower directs the ring to create fantastic energy constructs and with it, protect the good from evil. In these earliest stories, readers meet the Guardians of the Universe, many of Jordan's intergalactic comrades, and some of his deadliest opponents, including Hector Hammond, Sonar, and Sinestro. The black and white reprints date from 1959 through 1962.

Brosgol, Vera
★ **Anya's** ghost. First Second 2011 221p. Illustration
Grades: 6 7 8 9 10   **741.5; Fic**
1. Friendship — Graphic novels; 2. Ghosts — Graphic novels; 3. Horror graphic novels; 4. School life — Graphic novels
978-1-59643-713-5, $19.99; 1-59643-713-8; 978-1-59643-552-0 (pa), $15.99; 1-59643-552-6 (pa)
              LC 2010036251
"The crisp, sophisticated purple, gray, black, and white palette correlates perfectly with the overall angst of the characters. A juicy mystery, a bit of horror, strong use of the graphic-novel format, and a diverse and unusual cast of characters—that's a pretty impressive achievement in just over two hundred pages." Bulletin of the Center for Children's Books

★ **Be prepared.** Vera Brosgol; color by Alec Longstreth. First Second 2018 256 p. Color; Illustration
Grades: 4 5 6 7 8   **741.5; Fic**
1. Social acceptance — Fiction; 2. Camps — Fiction; 3. Friendship — Fiction
9781626724440, $22.99; 9781626724457
              LC 2017946145
In this book, by Vera Brosgol, "all Vera wants to do is fit in — but that's not easy for a Russian girl in the suburbs. Her friends live in fancy houses and their parents can afford to send them to the best summer camps. Vera's single mother can't afford that sort of luxury, but there's one summer camp in her price range — Russian summer camp. Vera is sure she's found the one place she can fit in, but camp is far from what she imagined." (Publisher's note)
"Brosgol's artwork has immense depth, from the facial expressions and gestures to the spot-on visual gags, and she strikes a perfect balance between heartfelt honesty and uproarious, self-deprecating humor." Booklist

Brown, Don
★ **Drowned** City: Hurricane Katrina and New Orleans. by Don Brown. Houghton Mifflin Harcourt 2015 96 p. Color; Illustration
Grades: 7 8 9 10   **741.5; 363.34**
1. New Orleans (La.) — History — 21st century; 2. Hurricane Katrina, 2005; 3. New Orleans (La.) — History
054415777X, $18.99; 9780544157774, $18.99
              LC 2015458266
Robert F. Sibert Honor Book (2016); Eisner Nominee: Best Publication for Teens (2016)
In this work of graphic nonfiction by Don Brown, "when the calamitous category five Katrina's gusty winds hurl into the city of New Orleans, most people have evacuated the city. The rest of the scared, stubborn, and simply stranded must face the dangers of what is to come — broken levees quickly swelling the city with water. Many families seek safety on their roofs or via floatation devices as a way to row to safety. However, some are not as fortunate." (Children's Literature)
"Brown's narrative is clear and precise, relying exclusively on data and statistics interspersed with quotes from residents, rescue crews, journalists, and news reports. Alone, the text might lack impact, but combined with the haunting imagery, it hits readers like a punch in the gut." Booklist
Includes bibliographical references

★ The **great** American dust bowl. by Don Brown. Houghton Mifflin Harcourt 2013 80 p.

Grades: 5 6 7 8 9   **978**
1. Droughts — United States — History; 2. Dust storms — History; 3. Dust Bowl Era, 1931-1939
0547815506; 9780547815503, $18.99
Author Don Brown presents a "graphic novel of one of America's most catastrophic natural events: the Dust Bowl. On a clear, warm Sunday, April 14, 1935, a wild wind whipped up millions upon millions of these specks of dust to form a duster, a savage storm on America's high southern plains." (Publisher's note)
"In this bleak yet compelling graphic-novel-style glimpse at the Dirty Thirties, Brown crisply paces the narrative with fascinating glimpses of the sociological and geological causes of the Dust Bowl. The color brown is a recurring theme here, as Brown relies, aptly, almost entirely on shades of brown throughout. Primary source material is used liberally, as characters speak directly to the reader, documentary-style." (Horn Book)

Brown, Jeffrey
Incredible Change-Bots. Top Shelf Productions 2007 un Illustration
Grades: 8 9 10 11 12 Adult
741.5; Fic
1. Graphic novels; 2. Humorous graphic novels; 3. Robots — Graphic novels; 4. Science fiction graphic novels
978-1-891830-91-4, $15
Far away in outer space, the Incredible Change-Bots live on the planet Electronocybercircuitron. The Awesomebots and the Fantasticons have lived in relative harmony, until Shootertron, the leader of the Fantasticons, decides to rig the election to rule the planet. The Awesomebots declare war, and over the years the Change-Bots destroy their planet. They then come to Earth, where they continue their fighting, each group gaining their own human allies. Brown has done a fun send-up of the Transformers with this story, and while there is some violence, there is very little in the way of bad language.

Courtesy of IDW Publishing

★ **Star** Wars: Jedi Academy. Jeffrey Brown; [edited by] Rex Ogle. Scholastic, Inc 2013 160 p. Illustration (Star Wars: Jedi Academy)
Grades: 3 4 5 6 7   **741.5; Fic**
1. Star Wars — Comic books, strips, etc.; 2. Middle schools — Fiction; 3. Outer space — Fiction
0545505178; 9780545505178, $12.99; 9780545609999
              LC 2013931939
In this book, by Jeffrey Brown, "Roan Novachez thought he was destined to attend Pilot Academy Middle School, just as his older brother and father did. His dreams are crushed when he is rejected by Pilot Academy and accepted into a sketchy new school called Coruscant Jedi Academy.... Confused and struggling to keep up, Roan tries to fly under the radar and passes the time drawing comics of his daily life at his strange boarding school." (Booklist)
"While it might be disappointing for those familiar with this world to see scant representation of beloved characters, it makes the book an easy starting point for new fans. There are plenty of references to other elements (the T-16 Skyhopper and Jedi training remotes, for example) for diehards to get excited about." SLJ
Other titles in this series are: Return of the Padawan (2014);The Phantom Bully (2015)

Star Wars: Jedi academy 2: Return of the Padawan. Jeffrey Brown; [edited by] Rex Ogle. Scholastic 2014 176 p. Illustration (Star Wars: Jedi academy)
Grades: 3 4 5 6 7   **741.5**

1. Caricatures and cartoons — Fiction; 2. Life on other planets — Fiction; 3. Middle schools — Fiction; 4. Star Wars fiction; 5. Star Wars; 6. School stories
0545621259; 9780545621250, $12.99

LC 2014931163

"After surviving his first year at Jedi Academy, Roan Novachez thought his second year would be a breeze. He couldn't have been more wrong. Roan feels like he's drifting apart from his friends, and it's only made worse when Roan discovers he's not the amazing pilot he thought he'd be. When the school bullies take him under their wing, he decides they aren't so bad after all — or are they?" (Publisher's note)

"Roan is a very sympathetic main character, and readers will feel his pain and laugh at his misfortune in equal measure. Roan's hand-lettered journal entries alternate with short paneled sequences and 'screenshots' of academy message boards and other ephemera." Kirkus

Star Wars: Jedi Academy; 3: The Phantom Bully. by Jeffrey Brown. Scholastic Press 2015 176 p. Illustration (Star Wars: Jedi Academy)
Grades: 3 4 5 6 7   **741.5; Fic**
1. School stories; 2. Star Wars films; 3. Middle schools
0545621267; 9780545621267, $12.99

"It's hard to believe this is Roan's last year at Jedi Academy. He's been busier than ever learning to fly (and wash) starships, swimming in the Lake Country on Naboo, studying for the Jedi obstacle course exam, and tracking down dozens of vorpak clones — don't ask. But now, someone is setting him up to get in trouble with everyone at school, including Yoda. If he doesn't find out who it is, and fast, he may get kicked out of school!" (Publisher's note)

"The third graphic novel in the Jedi Academy series turns out to be a love story, although it takes the characters a while to realize it.... [B]y the close of this high jinks-filled year, every student at the academy gets a satisfying ending, even the bullies and troublemakers." Kirkus

Bullock, Mike
Lions, tigers and bears volume 2: betrayal. Image Comics 2008 un Illustration
Grades: 3 4 5 6 7 8 9   **741.5; Fic**
1. Adventure graphic novels; 2. Fantasy graphic novels; 3. Graphic novels
978-1-58240-930-6, $14.99

Joey and Courtney's winter wonderland is shattered when the Big Cats of the Night Pride arrive with terrible news from the Stuffed Animal Kingdom. Now all that stands between the horrible Beasties and children everywhere are Joey, Courtney, and their imaginations. For the evil Valthraax and his minions have taken over the Crystal Castle, imprisoned King Bear, and plot to capture all children who aren't being protected by the Stuffed Animal Militia. There is some fighting violence between the Night Pride and their allies against the Beasties.

Butzer, C. M.
★ **Gettysburg:** the graphic novel. Bowen Books/HarperCollins 2009 80p. Illustration
Grades: 3 4 5 6 7 8 9 10 11 12   **741.5; 973.7**
1. American speeches — Graphic novels; 2. Gettysburg (Pa.), Battle of, 1863; 3. Graphic novels; 4. Lincoln, Abraham, 1809-1865 — Graphic novels; 5. Lincoln, Abraham, 1809-1865 — Work — Gettysburg address; 8. Gettysburg address: Lincoln, Abraham
978-0-06-156176-4, $16.99; 978-0-06-156175-7 (pa), $8.99

LC 2008-10657

In the summer of 1863, everyone knew that the Battle of Gettysburg would be an important battle that could determine the course of the War Between the States, the Civil War. What they didn't know was who would prevail. Butzer uses primary sources to play out the battle that lasted three days and caused tremendous casualties, the aftermath that nearly overwhelmed the town of Gettysburg, and the effort to build the monument to commemorate the fallen. He uses a somber blue and gray wash in his illustrations. Lincoln's famous Gettysburg Address was only 271 words long and appear in their entirety, against images of the nation's past. Some panels depicting the violence of the battles, and particularly the dead on the battlefield, could be disturbing for sensitive younger readers; but this battle was ugly and overwhelming in its violence. Butzer includes extensive end notes to explain what he depicted, and to note the sources of the dialog and narration.

Byrne, Eugene
★ **Darwin:** a graphic biography. by Eugene Byrne; illustrated by Simon Gurr. Smithsonian Books 2013 96 p. Illustration
Grades: 5 6 7 8 9 10 11 12 Adult
576.8/2092; 576.8; 92
1. Evolution (Biology) — Comic books, strips, etc; 2. Graphic novels; 3. Natural selection — Comic books, strips, etc; 4. Darwin, Charles, 1809-1882; 5. Evolution
1588343529; 9781588343529, $9.95

LC 2012951786

Courtesy of Smithsonian Books

This work of graphic nonfiction by Eugene Byrne and Simon Gurr presents a "summary of [Charles] Darwin's life and achievement.... Darwin was an indifferent student...until he received an invitation to take a voyage that 'would change the course of history.'...The animals he encountered seemed so different...that he theorized that if it weren't a matter of different conditions that resulted in such 'transmutation,' they might well have had a different creator." (Kirkus Reviews)

Includes bibliographical references.

Byrne, John
Superman: The Man of Steel Vol. 1. John Byrne, writer/penciller; Dick Giordano, inker; John Costanza, letterer; Tom Ziuko, colorist; foreword by Ray Bradbury. DC Comics 1991 132p. Illustration
Grades: 8 9 10 11 12 Adult   **741.5; Fic**
1. Graphic novels; 2. Superhero graphic novels; 3. Superman (Fictional character)
978-0930289287, $14.99

This reprint of a 1986 book retells and reinvents the origin and early adventures of the Man of Steel. Superman begins his ascension to iconic hero as he leaves Smallville and becomes Metropolis's revered protector and guardian. Featuring the Man of Steel's legendary first encounters with Lex Luthor, Lois Lane, and Batman, this book also includes a deadly battle with Bizarro, a fateful encounter with Lana Lang, and Superman's astonishing discovery of his Kryptonian heritage.

★ **X-Men:** The Dark Phoenix Saga, 2nd ed.. writer, Chris Claremont; penciler and co-plotter, John Byrne. Marvel Entertainment 2006 200p. Illustration
Grades: 7 8 9 10 11 12 Adult   **741.5; Fic**
1. Graphic novels; 2. Superhero graphic novels; 3. X-Men (Fictional characters)
978-0-7851-2213-5, $24.99

Gathered together by Professor Charles Xavier to protect a world that fears and hates them, the X-Men had fought many battles, been on adventures that spanned galaxies, grappled enemies of limitless might, but none of this could prepare them for the most shocking struggle they would ever face. One of their own members, Jean Grey, has gained power beyond all comprehension, and that power has corrupted her absolutely. Now they must decide if the life of the woman they cherish is worth the existence of the entire universe.

Caldwell, Ben

The **Wizard** of Oz. written by L. Frank Baum; adapted by Ben Caldwell. Sterling Children's Books 2012 32 p. Illustration (All-Action Classics)

Grades: 4 5 6   **741.5**

1. Fantasy graphic novels; 2. Graphic novels; 3. Oz (Imaginary place) — Comic books, strips, etc.; 4. Tornadoes — Fiction; 5. Voyages and travels — Graphic novels

1402731531; 9781402731532, $7.95

LC 2013363513

This book is a graphic novel adaptation of L. Frank Baum's classic tale "The Wizard of Oz." Author and illustrator Ben Caldwell "follows Baum's original novel rather than the iconic film. The heroes are pursued by the Kalidah, 'horrific beasts, with heads like tigers and bodies like bears,' and the famous path the four friends follow, as in the original, is called the 'road of golden bricks.'" (Publishers Weekly)

Callen, Kerry

Halo and Sprocket vol. 2: Natural creatures. SLG Publishing/Amaze Ink 2008 un Illustration

Grades: 8 9 10 11 12 Adult   **741.5; Fic**

1. Angels — Graphic novels; 2. Graphic novels; 3. Humorous graphic novels; 4. Robots — Graphic novels

978-1-59362-131-5, $8.95

Halo the angel and Sprocket the robot live with a young woman named Katie. Their mission: to try to figure out the human race. They are puzzled by Katie's desire for privacy when she's taking a bath; they don't understand why she'll accept being clawed and bitten by a cute little kitten but won't hold a skink; and playing a trivia game causes Halo to show anger. When Halo transforms Sprocket into a human so he can experience what eating food is all about, the temporarily human Sprocket drives Katie crazy with questions about bodily functions such as burping, sneezing, and more.

Halo and Sprocket: Welcome to Humanity. SLG Publishing/Amaze Ink 2003 un Illustration

Grades: 7 8 9 10 11 12   **741.5; Fic**

1. Graphic novels; 2. Humorous graphic novels

0-943151-81-3, $12.95

What do an extremely powerful angel, a socially inexperienced robot, and a young, single woman have in common? Apparently, aside from the house they share, not very much! Logic, metaphysics, and human nature collide as Katie tries to educate both angel and robot about humans, philosophy, and such things as the Tooth Fairy. The book includes some slightly raunchy humor.

Cammuso, Frank

Knights of the lunch table: the dodgeball chronicles. Graphix 2008 141p.

Grades: 3 4 5 6   **741.5; Fic**

1. Graphic novels; 2. Humorous graphic novels; 3. School stories — Graphic novels

978-0-439-90322-6 (pa), $9.99; 0-439-90322-X (pa)

Artie King's family has moved and now he has to start at a new school, Camelot Middle School. Dodgeball is the big game at Camelot, and the Horde is a champion team; the Horde members are also the worst bullies in the school.... Artie immediately gets into trouble with Joe, the leader of the Horde.... However, he manages to open the broken old locker...[which] provides mysterious, useful stuff, such as a lunch. Joe challenges Artie to a dodgeball game; Artie has new friends Percy and Wayne who'll help him,

and then he meets Gwen. And science teacher Mr. Merlyn is also on his side.

"Arthurian legend gets an update for young readers in this outstanding graphic novel.... The funny, fast-paced tale of young Arthur's quest to defeat the bullies stands well on its own. The appealing illustrations are full of color, action, and life." SLJ

Followed by: Knights of the lunch table: the dragon players (2009)

★ **Knights** of the lunch table: the dragon players. Scholastic/Graphix 2009 127p.

Grades: 3 4 5 6   **741.5; Fic**

1. Arthurian romances — Adaptations — Graphic novels; 2. Conduct of life — Graphic novels; 3. Contests — Graphic novels; 4. Graphic novels; 5. Humorous graphic novels; 6. Schools — Graphic novels

978-0-439-90323-3 (pa), $9.99; 0-439-90323-8 (pa)

LC 2008-51463

Artie King may have won the dodgeball game against the school bullies, but life is not easy. The new challenge comes with the dueling robot tournament at school; it's all part of Dragon Day, and The Horde has won every year by cheating — they force the smartest kid in school to design and build their robot. This year, they've done it to Percy. Circumstances force Artie's hand and willy nilly, he has entered the tournament. Seeking an edge, they go to Evo, a mysterious techno wiz kid who can build any gadget; the problem for Artie is, is he cheating by getting help from Evo? Cammuso's bright, cartoony art and schoolyard version of Arthurian legend provides lots of fun action as well as making readers think about ethics

Followed by: Knights of the lunch table: the battling bands (2011); Sequel to: Knights of the lunch table: the dodgeball chronicles (2008)

Camper, Cathy

★ **Lowriders** in space; book 1. by Cathy Camper; illustrated by Raul Gonzalez III. Chronicle Books 2014 112 p. Color; Illustration (Lowriders)

Grades: 4 5 6 7 8   **741.5**

1. Competition (Psychology) — Fiction; 2. Friendship — Fiction; 3. Graphic novels; 4. Lowriders — Fiction; 5. Mexican Americans — Fiction; 6. Automobiles — Fiction; 7. Space vehicles; 8. Mechanics (Persons)

9781452121550, $22.99; 1452121559

LC 2013040709

Cathy Camper "introduces readers to Lupe Impala, Flapjack Octopus, and Elirio Malaria, three friends who love working with cars and dream of having their own garage shop. One day they see an opportunity to achieve their goal — a car competition. When they start working on a lowrider to prepare it for the competition, an out-of-this world journey begins." (School Library Journal)

"Raúl's snazzy panels — impressively drawn in only red, blue, and black ballpoint pen on tea-stained paper — resemble an amped-up Mighty Mouse cartoon rendered in anarchic yet skillful doodles. It's a joyfully explosive style, and it perfectly matches the Latino characters and barrio setting." Booklist

Another title in this series is: Lowriders to the center of the Earth (2016)

Lowriders to the center of the Earth. by Cathy Camper; illustrated by Raul the Third. Chronicle Books 2016 128 p. Color; Illustration

Grades: 4 5 6 7 8   **741.5; Fic**

1. Aztec gods — Comic books, strips, etc; 2. Lowriders; 3. Automobiles — Graphic novels; 4. Mexican Americans — Graphic novels; 5. Gods and goddesses — Graphic novels; 6. Cats — Graphic novels

1452138362; 9781452123431, $22.99; 9781452138367; 1452123438

LC 2015021996

Pura Belpré Illustrator Award (2017)

"Lupe Impala, Elirio Malaria, and El Chavo Octopus are living their dream at last. They're the proud owners of their very own garage. But when their beloved cat Genie goes missing, they need to do everything they can to find him. Little do they know the trail will lead them to the realm of Mictlantecuhtli, the Aztec god of the Underworld, who is keeping Genie prisoner!" (Publisher's note)

"Raúl the Third's ultradetailed crosshatched artwork more than meets the demands of this cast-of-thousands comic opus." Kirkus

Carey, Mike

★ **Re-Gifters**. written by Mike Carey; art by Sonny Liew and Marc Hempel. DC Comics/Minx 2007 148p. Illustration

Grades: 7 8 9 10 11 12   **741.5; Fic**
1. Graphic novels; 2. High school students — Graphic novels; 3. Martial arts — Graphic novels; 4. Romance graphic novels; 5. School stories — Graphic novels
978-1-4012-0371-9 (pa), $9.99; 1-4109-0371-X (pa)

"Jen Dik Seong, or Dixie, is having trouble getting her ki focused. Normally an outstanding hapkido student, she finds that her crush on classmate Adam is affecting her ability to fight. This is not good, as the national competition is fast approaching, and her parents expect her to do well.... Dixie makes a series of poor choices. She decides to spend the entry fee...on an elaborate birthday present for Adam.... This is a terrific read that features complex characters dealing with internal and external conflicts that make them believable and endearing. Lively black-and-white illustrations bring action and emotion to the story." SLJ

Spellbinders: Signs & Wonders. Marvel Entertainment 2005 un Illustration

Grades: 7 8 9 10 11 12 Adult   **741.5; Fic**
1. Graphic novels; 2. Magic — Graphic novels; 3. Mystery graphic novels; 4. Supernatural graphic novels
0-7851-1756-3, $7.99

Getting through high school is hard enough without having to watch your back the whole time, but magic can give you a real edge over the competition. When 15-year-old Kim Vesco moves from Chicago to Salem, MA, she finds that the local student body is divided into rival factions of witches and non-witches, with both sides bidding for her allegiance. And if that weren't enough, an unknown force seems to want her... dead. Between the tribal loyalties of the schoolyard and the brutal, fight-or-die logic of the mage-war, Kim has to steer a course that will keep her alive until she can take the fight back to her enemy and reveal the true identity of someone she thought she already knew: herself.

Carre, Lilli

The **fir-tree**. It Books/HarperCollins 2009 un Illustration

Grades: 3 4 5 6 7 8 9 10 11 12 Adult   **741.5; Fic**
1. Authors; 2. Children's authors; 3. Christmas — Graphic novels; 4. Christmas trees — Graphic novels; 5. Dramatists; 6. Graphic novels; 7. Novelists; 8. Short story writers; 9. Andersen, Hans Christian, 1805-1875 — Adaptations
978-0-06-178236-7, $14.99

A young fir-tree only wants to grow tall; it's never satisfied and doesn't notice the sunlight and clean air. It never rejoices in anything, but grumbles and complains. When it sees some trees being cut down and taken away, it wonders what it's missing. The birds tell of seeing the trees inside homes, beautifully decorated, and it becomes jealous. When it does grow tall and beautiful, a woodsman comes along and cuts it down, hauling it to town to become a Christmas tree in a house. It enjoys the family playing around the tree at Christmas, but after the holiday, the family throws it into a storeroom. Will the tree ever see its forest again? Lilli Carre uses delicate coloring and illustrations to adapt Andersen's sad Christmas story. Although this is suitable for young readers, adults may better

appreciate the tragedy and Carre's idiosyncratic illustrations her people have long, loopy arms.

Carroll, Emily

★ **Through** the woods. Emily Carroll. Margaret K. McElderry Books 2014 208 p. Color; Illustration

Grades: 8 9 10 11 12 Adult   **741.5**
1. Graphic novels; 2. Short stories; 3. Horror fiction; 4. Comic books, strips, etc.
9781442465961, $14.99; 9781442465954, $21.99

                                                          LC 2013030969

Eisner Award: Best Graphic Album — Reprint (2015); Ignatz Award: Outstanding Artist (2015)

In this book, Emily Carroll "crafts five unsettling tales in graphic-novel format inspired by common folkloric themes — from wolves in the woods to peculiar visitors to dark possessions. In 'Our Neighbor's House,' three sisters who find themselves alone in a cabin are taken, one by one, in the middle of the night by a smiling stranger.... 'The Nesting Place' focus on malevolent spirit possession." (Horn Book Magazine)

"All the tales in Carroll's debut graphic novel are fairly standard ghost stories, but it is her eerie illustrations — popping with bold color on black, glossy pages — that masterfully build terrifying tension and a keep-the-lights-on atmosphere." Booklist

Casey, Joe

Godland Volume 1: Hello, Cosmic!. Joe Casey and Tom Scioli. Image Comics 2006 un Illustration

Grades: 8 9 10 11 12 Adult   **741.5; Fic**
1. Adventure graphic novels; 2. Graphic novels; 3. Science fiction graphic novels; 4. Superhero graphic novels
1-58240-712-6, $14.99

The cosmic superhero epic is back and this collection is chock-full of all the "cosmic" one could ask for. Experience the glory of Commander Adam Archer, the enigmatic alien Maxim, the wacky Basil Cronus, the evil Discordia, the confusing Freidrich Nickelhead and that's just scratching the surface. The storytelling and art bring back the kind of story that Stan Lee and Jack Kirby did, with fun superhero action and very little grim, gritty content.

Castellucci, Cecil

The **Plain** Janes. by Cecil Castellucci and Jim Rugg. DC Comics/Minx 2007 un Illustration

Grades: 7 8 9 10 11 12   **741.5; Fic**
1. Art — Graphic novels; 2. Friendship — Graphic novels; 3. Graphic novels; 4. High school students — Graphic novels; 5. School stories — Graphic novels
978-1-4012-1115-8, $9.99

After a bomb attack in Metro City, Jane's parents move to suburban Kent Waters, where Jane feels lost. Then she meets three other Janes at the "reject" table in the high school lunch room, and she convinces them to help her form their own secret club: P.L.A.I.N. — People Loving Art in Neighborhoods. However, their "art attacks" cause the authorities to think that P.L.A.I.N. is a terrorist group.

"The art, inspired by Dan Clowes' work, is absolutely engaging. Packaged like manga this is a fresh, exciting use of the graphic-novel format." Booklist

Another title about the Janes is: Janes in love (2008)

Soupy leaves home. written by Cecil Castellucci; illustrated by Jose Pimienta; lettered by Nate Piekos of Blambot. Dark Horse Books 2017 208 p. Color; Illustration

Grades: 7 8 9 10 11 12   **741.5; Fic**

1. Runaway teenagers — Fiction; 2. Homeless persons — Fiction
9781616554316, $14.99

LC 2016052804

In this book, by Cecil Castellucci, illustrated by Jose Pimienta, "Pearl 'Soupy' Plankette ran away from her abusive father, but has nowhere to go until she stumbles upon a disguise that gives her the key to a new identity. Reborn as a boy named Soupy, she hitches her star to Remy 'Ramshackle' Smith, a hobo who takes her under his wing.... But Ramshackle has his own demons to wrestle with, and he'll need Soupy just as much as she needs him." (Publisher's note)

"A compelling graphic offering that explores relevant gender roles and self-identity through a historical lens." Kirkus

Includes bibliographical references

Castiglia, Paul

America's 1st Patriotic Comic Book Hero: The Shield Volume 1. Archie Comics 2002 96p. Illustration
Grades: 3 4 5 6 7 8 9 10 11 12 Adult   **741.5; Fic**
1. Adventure graphic novels; 2. Graphic novels; 3. Superhero graphic novels
1-879794-08-X, $12.95

A hero with great power, strength and courage who donned the colors of the American flag. A hero who lived for democracy and protected the world from the foes of freedom! No, it's not who you think... it's THE SHIELD, who predated his well known counterpart by over a year. This historic full color trade paperback reprints his first 8 stories from PEP and SHIELD/WIZARD Comics. It includes his first appearance and origin, along with the covers of the comics they originally appeared in, dating from 1940.

Archie Americana Series: Best of the Forties Book 2. Archie Comics 2002 96p. Illustration
Grades: 3 4 5 6 7 8 9 10 11 12 Adult   **741.5; Fic**
1. Andrews, Archie (Fictional character); 2. Graphic novels; 3. Humorous graphic novels
1-879794-09-8, $10.95

In 1941, Pep Comics introduced Archie Andrews, "America's newest boyfriend." Since then, Archie and his perennial teenage friends have entertained readers with their misadventures. This book includes stories from 1946 through 1949, with more slapstick and screwball comedy from Archie and the gang.

Archie Americana Series: Best of the Eighties. Archie Comics 2001 96p. Illustration
Grades: 3 4 5 6 7 8 9 10 11 12 Adult   **741.5; Fic**
1. Andrews, Archie (Fictional character); 2. Graphic novels; 3. Humorous graphic novels
1-879794-06-3, $10.95

During the 1980s pop culture ruled America; even the President was a former actor. In this volume, Archie and friends experience the punk movement, the "Urban Cowboy" craze, see the rise of MTV, get into the preppie, new wave and "Flashdance" fashions, play Trivial Pursuit, and boogie at the roller disco.

Volume 1 of 2

Best of Josie and the Pussycats Volume 1. Archie Comics 2001 96p. Illustration
Grades: 3 4 5 6 7 8 9 10 11 12 Adult   **741.5; Fic**
1. Adventure graphic novels; 2. Graphic novels; 3. Humorous graphic novels; 4. Rock music — Graphic novels
1-879794-07-1, $10.95

This book reprints a selection of stories about rock group Josie and the Pussycats, from their origin in 1963 to 1988. Josie, Melody, and Valerie are the Pussycats, along with their roadie Alan M., their shifty manager Alex,

and his conniving sister, Alexandra. They make music, but along the way they also solve mysteries.

Sonic the Hedgehog: The Beginning. Archie Comics 2003 96p. Illustration
Grades: 3 4 5 6 7 8 9 10 11 12 Adult   **741.5; Fic**
1. Adventure graphic novels; 2. Graphic novels; 3. Humorous graphic novels; 4. Sonic the Hedgehog (Fictional character)
1-879794-12-8, $10.95

In 1993, Sonic the Hedgehog sped his way from video games to comic books, and has been going strong ever since. Now, readers can enjoy his earliest comic book adventures with this edition that reprints the first appearances of Tails, Princess Sally, Antoine, Rotor, Uncle Chuck, and Muttski. Fans can also marvel at Sonic's magic rings, the freedom emeralds, and King Acorn's magic crown; while booing and hissing at the villainous Robotnik, his evil Swat-Bots, and his myriad dastardly devices.

Cauvin, Raoul

The **bluecoats** no. 1: Robertsonville Prison. Cinebook Ltd. 2008 48p. Illustration
Grades: 5 6 7 8 9 10   **741.5; Fic**
1. Adventure graphic novels; 2. Graphic novels; 3. Humorous graphic novels; 4. United States — History — 1861-1865, Civil War — Prisoners and prisons — Graphic novels
978-1-90546-071-7, $11.95

Sergeant Chesterfield and Corporal Blutch are Union soldiers during the Civil War; Blutch tends to be lazy, and Chesterfield always seems to be getting him out of trouble; but after one battle, they're both in trouble when they're captured by Confederate troops and are force-marched to Robertsonville Prison. They constantly get into trouble with a soldier and camp guard named Cockroach, and Chesterfield leads multiple attempts to escape the prison. Then when they succeed, they're wearing stolen Confederate uniforms and ultimately end up in a Union prison camp. Prison camps aren't normally subjects of humor, but the humor in this book is reminiscent of the old television series Hogan's Heroes, which was set in a German prisoner of war camp

Chad, Jon

Volcanoes: fire and life. Jon Chad; with color by Sophie Goldstein. First Second 2016 128 p. Color; Illustration (Science comics)
Grades: 4 5 6 7   **741.5; 551.21**
1. Volcanoes
1626723613; 9781626723610, $19.99

This book in the Science Comics series, by Jon Chad, focuses on volcanoes. "Thanks to magma vents, shifting continental plates, and volcanic eruptions, we know that our planet is alive and in motion. Alongside Aurora, a young explorer, you'll learn that volcanoes are just one of the massively powerful forces at work on our planet. From catastrophic destruction to the creation of new land masses, volcanoes have made their mark on our amazing Earth." (Publisher's note)

"Chad's well-drawn and clearly labeled diagrams in rich, saturated colors concisely explain key concepts, and vocabulary words are defined both in the text and a glossary. While the stylized cartoon figures and adventure narrative are an entertaining framework, the science fittingly occupies the center stage." Booklist

Chanani, Nidhi

Pashmina. Nidhi Chanani. First Second 2017 161 p. Color; Illustration
Grades: 4 5 6 7 8   **741.5**
1. India — Fiction; 2. Mother-daughter relationship — Fiction
1626720886; 9781626720879; 9781626720886, $21.99

LC 2016961589

In this graphic novel, by Nidhi Chanani, "Priyanka Das has so many unanswered questions: Why did her mother abandon her home in India years ago? What was it like there? And most importantly, who is her father, and why did her mom leave him behind? But Pri's mom avoids these questions.... For Pri, her mother's homeland can only exist in her imagination. That is, until she finds a mysterious pashmina tucked away in a forgotten suitcase." (Publisher's note)

"Contemporary reality is shown in grayscale; the past in sepia hues; and Pri's imagined India in rich colors that radiate off the pages. Priyanka is a realistically complex, sometimes moody character, with depth shown through her varied interests and inquisitive musings." Horn Book

Chantler, Scott

The **captive** prince. Scott Chantler. Kids Can Press 2012 116 p. Color illustration
Grades: 4 5 6 7
741.5; 741.5/971; Fic
1. Thieves — Fiction; 2. Graphic novels; 3. Adventure fiction
9781554537778, $8.95; 9781451782806, $17.95 ; 1554537762; 9781554537761, $17.95

Courtesy of Kids Can Press

This children's adventure book by Scott Chantler is the "third title of the...Three Thieves graphic novel series[.] Dessa, Topper and Fisk are still running from the Queen's Dragons and trying to find Dessa's missing twin brother. But when Dessa inadvertently rescues a prince — putting kingdoms at stake and love on the line — the adventure quickly becomes a royal mess!" (Publisher's note)

The **iron** hand. Scott Chantler. Kids Can Press 2016 126 p. Color; Illustration (Three thieves)
Grades: 3 4 5 6
741.5
1. Orphans — Graphic novels; 2. Knights and knighthood — Graphic novels; 3. Adventure fiction
1771380527; 9781771380522, $16.95
LC 2016032329

Courtesy of Kids Can Press

In this conclusion to the Three Thieves series, by Scott Chantler, "now that Dessa has learned the truth about her past, she agrees to form an alliance with the badly injured Captain Drake against Greyfalcon. The pair travel together to the royal city to rescue Dessa's twin brother, Jared, from Greyfalcon's evil clutches and put Jared in his rightful place on the throne. But their plans go awry when they arrive to find Jared already on the throne!" (Publisher's note)

"A well-wrought, well-timed, and satisfying finale to this well-conceived series." Kirkus

The **king's** dragon. Scott Chantler. Kids Can Press 2014 112 p. Illustration; Color (Three Thieves)
Grades: 3 4 5 6
741.5; Fic
1. Fantasy graphic novels; 2. Knights and knighthood — Graphic novels
9781554537792, $8.95; 1554537797

Courtesy of Kids Can Press

In this graphic novel written and illustrated by Scott Chantler, "royal knight Capt. Drake...briefly catches up with his quarry, Dessa, a young circus acrobat hobbled (but not much) by a broken leg, and also looks back on his early days as a member of the elite but corrupt Dragons." (Kirkus Reviews)

"Black-and-white art among color signifies the flashback scenes, making the transitions easy to follow. The backstory will be satisfying to fans." Horn Book

Tower of treasure. Kids Can Press 2010 112p. Illustration (Three thieves)
Grades: 3 4 5 6
741.5
1. Acrobats and acrobatics — Fiction; 2. Adventure graphic novels; 3. Circus — Fiction; 4. Graphic novels; 5. Thieves — Fiction
978-1-55453-414-2, $17.99; 1-55453-414-3; 978-1-55453-415-9 (pa), $8.95; 1-55453-415-1 (pa)

Courtesy of Kids Can Press

"As an acrobat in a traveling circus, 14-year-old orphan Dessa Redd flies through the air with ease. Still, she is weighed down by troubling memories. But when her ragtag circus troupe pulls into the city of Kingsbridge, Dessa feels a tickle of hope. Maybe here in the royal city she will finally find her twin brother — or the mysterious man who snatched him away when they were just children. Meanwhile, Topper, the circus juggler, recruits Dessa and the circus strongman, Fisk, for the job of robbing the royal treasury." (Publisher's note)

Other titles in this series are:The sign of the black rock (2011);The captive prince (2012);The king's dragon (2014);Pirates of the silver coast (2014);The dark island (2016);The iron hand (2016)

Chen, Wei Dong

Monkey King: Journey to the West. created by Wei Dong Chen; illustrated by Chao Peng. JR Comics 2012 173 p. Illustration
Grades: 5 6 7   **Fic; 741.5/951**
1. Graphic novels; 2. Chinese mythology
8994208712; 9788994208718, $29.27

This is the third volume in Wei Dong Chen's Monkey King series, a graphic novel series based on the Chinese classical literature novel "Journey to the West." In "the first volume, Sun Wu Kong is born from a stone and goes on a quest of find the secret of eternal life. In succeeding volumes the Monkey King steals the heavenly peaches and is imprisoned by Buddha for 500 years." (Library Media Connection)

Monkey King: The Bane of Heaven. created by Wei Dong Chen; illustrated by Chao Peng. Jr Comics 2012 174 p. Illustration
Grades: 5 6 7   **741.5/951; Fic**
1. Graphic novels; 2. Chinese mythology
8994208704; 9788994208701, $29.27

This is the second volume in Wei Dong Chen's Monkey King series. Here, "Sun Wu Kong is named emperor of heaven, [and] begins to make himself comfortable among the gods, and quickly wears out his welcome." The series is a retelling of the classical Chinese work "Journey to the West." (Booklist)

Cherrywell, Steph

★ **Pepper** Penwell and the land creature of Monster Lake. [written and drawn by Steph Cherrywell].. SLG Publishing 2011 un Illustration
Grades: 10 11 12 7 8 9 Adult   **741.5; Fic**

1. Graphic novels; 2. Horror graphic novels; 3. Humorous graphic novels; 4. Monsters — Graphic novels; 5. Mystery graphic novels
978-1-59362-205-3, $14.95

British teenager Pepper Penwell prefers solving mysteries over school work and wants to be a detective like her father. When the latest school boots her out, Pepper takes on the case of a missing drum majorette named Lucy. Accompanied by her brother Alex, who inexplicably (it was some kind of accident) has the body of a bird, Pepper travels to Monster Lake, a town trying to establish itself as a tourist attraction based on its local monster, which is a land creature. In the town, Pepper meets strange people, any of whom could be guilty of kidnapping the wealthy and annoying Lucy. However, after Pepper does find Lucy, there's still the matter of the land monster, which is all too real. British slang (arse, bum) provides the mildly harsh language.

Chmakova, Svetlana

★ **Awkward.** by Svetlana Chmakova. Yen Press 2015 210 p. Illustration; Color
Grades: 5 6 7 8   **741.5**
1. Clubs — Fiction; 2. Graphic novels; 3. Middle schools — Fiction; 4. Popularity — Fiction; 5. Schools — Fiction; 6. School stories — Graphic novels
0316381306; 0316381322; 9780316381307; 9780316381321, $24
LC 2015945195
Eisner Nominee: Best Publication for Teens (2016)

In this middle grade book, by Svetlana Chmakova, "protagonist Peppi is fantastically imperfect.... She is the new girl at Berrybrook Middle School and is having a hard time fitting in because of her struggles with social anxiety. The work opens with the young teen pushing away the first person who tries to help her, Jaime, and it only gets more awkward from there." (School Library Journal)

Brave. Svetlana Chmakova. Yen Press 2017 238 p. Color; Illustration
Grades: 4 5 6 7   **741.5; Fic**
1. Popularity — fiction; 2. Middle schools — fiction
0316363170; 9780316363174, $24; 9780316363181
LC 2017934376
In this book, by Svetlana Chmakova, "in his daydreams, Jensen is the biggest hero that ever was, saving the world and his friends on a daily basis. But his middle school reality is very different — math is hard, getting along with friends is hard.... And the pressure's on even more once the school newspaper's dynamic duo, Jenny and Akilah, draw Jensen into the whirlwind of school news, social-experiment projects, and behind-the-scenes club drama." (Publisher's note)

"This is a subtle, well-observed treatment of a kid who doesn't fit in. The various threads of friendship and belonging are woven masterfully and ring true, with a conclusion that brings everything together." SLJ

CLAMP (Mangaka group)

Angelic Layer. CLAMP. Dark Horse Manga 2012 426 p.
Grades: 5 6 7 8   **741.5; Fic**
1. Games — Fiction; 2. Japan — Fiction; 3. Manga; 4. Shonen manga
161655021X; 9781616550219, $19.99

"Junior high student Misaki Suzuhara has just arrived in Tokyo to live with her glamorous TV news star aunt and to attend the prestigious Eriol Academy. But what excites her above everything is Angelic Layer, the arena game where you control an 'Angel' — a miniature robot fighter whose moves depend on your mind!" (Publisher's note)
Originally published in the U.S. by Tokyopop; Volume 1 of 2

★ **Cardcaptor** Sakura: Book 1. story and art by CLAMP. Dark Horse Manga 2010 576 p. Illustration; Color
Grades: 6 7 8 9 10   **741.5; Fic**

1. Magic — Juvenile fiction; 2. Wizards — Fiction; 3. Fantasy fiction — Juvenile fiction; 4. Shojo manga; 5. Manga
1595825223; 9781595825223, $19.99

"Fourth-grader Sakura Kinomoto found a strange book in her father's library — a book made by the wizard Clow to store dangerous spirits sealed within a set of magical cards. But when Sakura opened it up, there was nothing left inside but Kero-chan, the book's cute little guardian beast, who informs Sakura that since the Clow cards seem to have escaped while he was asleep, it's now her job to capture them!" (Publisher's note)

"CLAMP's classic manga series (originally published in the U.S. in a 12-volume, two-series run) is being rereleased in remastered and newly translated omnibus editions that collect three books each." Booklist
Volume 1 of 4

Tsubasa: Reservoir Chronicle Vol. 1. Clamp; translated and adapted by Anthony Gerard; lettered by Dana Hayward. Random House/Del Rey Manga 2004 198p. Illustration
Grades: 8 9 10 11 12   **741.5; Fic**
1. Fantasy graphic novels; 2. Graphic novels; 3. Manga; 4. Shonen manga; 5. Supernatural graphic novels
0-345-47057-5, $10.95
LC 2004-101711
Sakura is the princess of Clow-and possessor of a mysterious, misunderstood power that promises to change the world. Syaoran is her childhood friend and leader of the archaeological dig that took his father's life. They reside in an alternate reality...where whatever you least expect can happen-and does. When Sakura ventures to the dig site to declare her love for Syaoran, a puzzling symbol is uncovered-which triggers a remarkable quest. Now Syaoran embarks upon a desperate journey through other worlds-all in the name of saving Sakura. This series crosses over with xxxHolic, and both of them use characters from past CLAMP manga. The book includes some violence.

XXXHolic Vol. 1. Random House/Del Rey Manga 2004 un Illustration
Grades: 8 9 10 11 12   **741.5; Fic**
1. Fantasy graphic novels; 2. Graphic novels; 3. Manga; 4. Seinen manga; 5. Supernatural graphic novels
0-345-47058-3, $10.95
Watanuki Kimihiro is haunted by visions of ghosts and spirits. Seemingly by chance, he encounters a mysterious witch named Yuuko, who claims she can help. In desperation, he accepts, but realizes that he's just been tricked into working for Yuuko in order to pay off the cost of her services. Soon he's employed in her little shop-a job which turns out to be nothing like his previous work experience. Most of Yuuko's customers live in Japan, but Yuuko and Watanuki are about to have some unusual visitors named Sakura and Syaoran from a land called Clow... The book includes some strong language and graphic violence.

Claremont, Chris

X-Men: The End Book One: Dreamers & Demons. Marvel Entertainment 2005 un Illustration
Grades: 7 8 9 10 11 12 Adult   **741.5; Fic**
1. Graphic novels; 2. Superhero graphic novels; 3. X-Men (Fictional characters)
978-0-7851-1690-5, $14.99
It's the epic finale to the story of the Children of the Atom as X-Men scribe Chris Claremont joins with artist Sean Chen for a trilogy in the style of the Lord of the Rings movies, one that spans the length and breadth of the X-Men canon and brings the saga of Marvel's mutants to a climax. In this volume, the unthinkable happens — attackers succeed in breaching all security at the Xavier School for the Gifted and threaten the lives of all the young mutants living there.

X-Men: The End Book Three: Men & X-Men. writer, Chris Claremont; artist, Sean Chen. Marvel Entertainment 2006 un Illustration
Grades: 7 8 9 10 11 12 Adult　　　　　　**741.5; Fic**
1. Graphic novels; 2. Superhero graphic novels; 3. X-Men (Fictional characters)
978-0-7851-1692-9, $14.99
The endgame of the last tale of Marvel's most popular mutants begins. They've suffered through sneak attacks, betrayals, and fatalities — now, Professor X and Magneto are taking the fight back to the enemy, amidst the stars.

X-Men: The End Book Two: Heroes & Martyrs. Chris Claremont; artist, Sean Chen. Marvel Entertainment 2005 un Illustration
Grades: 7 8 9 10 11 12 Adult　　　　　　**741.5; Fic**
1. Graphic novels; 2. Superhero graphic novels; 3. X-Men (Fictional characters)
978-0-7851-1691-2, $14.99
The Xavier Academy has been reduced to a smoldering crater in a brutal sneak attack, and the casualties number in the hundreds. Now, Cyclops must mobilize the survivors to get to the bottom of who is behind these coordinated strikes on mutants in general and the X-Men in particular.

Cliff, Tony

★ **Delilah** Dirk and the Turkish Lieutenant. by Tony Cliff. First Second 2013 176 p. Illustration
Grades: 7 8 9 10 11 12　　　　　　**741.5; Fic**
1. Women adventurers — Fiction; 2. Historical fiction; 3. Istanbul (Turkey) — Fiction; 4. Adventure fiction
1596438134; 9781596438132, $15.99
LC 2013947230
In this book, "Delilah Dirk has abandoned conventional court life and become a globe-trotting soldier of fortune. She is captured and held prisoner in 1800s Constantinople. Eventually she escapes, taking along the astonished Turkish Lieutenant Erdemogul Selim, whose quiet life centers around a proper cup of tea. This unlikely pair embarks on a wild journey that includes flying a ship, outwitting the Evil Pirate Captain Zakul, and escaping burning buildings." (School Library Journal)
"Plenty of fight scenes will attract male readers, in addition to females looking for strong heroines. All in all, this is a carefree romp across the Ottoman Empire with an upbeat tone that is refreshing." Lib Med Con
Other titles in this series are: Delilah Dirk and the King's Shilling (2016); Delilah Dirk and the Pillars of Hercules (2018)

Cobley, Jason

Frankenstein: the graphic novel. [by] Mary Shelley; script adaptation Jason Cobley; American English adaptation: Joe Sutliff Sanders; linework: Declan Shalvey; coloring: Jason Cardy & Kat Nicholson; lettering: Terry Wiley. Classical Comics 2008 141p. Illustration
Grades: 6 7 8 9 10 11 12 Adult
741.5; Fic
1. Authors; 2. Frankenstein (Fictional character); 3. Graphic novels; 4. Horror graphic novels; 5. Shelley, Mary Wollstonecraft, 1797-1851 — Adaptations; 6. Frankenstein's monster (Fictional character)
978-1-906332-49-5, $16.95
Young scientist Victor Frankenstein becomes obsessed with the idea that technology can create life, and works to prove his theories. However,

© Classical Comics
www.classicalcomics.com

his success doesn't bring him glory, but a living nightmare for himself and everyone around him. This graphic adaptation brings the entire book to the reader, using Shelley's original text for the dialog and narrative. Back matter includes a brief biography of Shelley, her family tree, a description of how she came to write the novel, and information on some of the various adaptations of the story to the stage and to film.
"More than a straightforward retelling, this edition invites readers to explore important social issues such as alienation, the consequences and ethics of scientific studies, as well as the nature of creation and destruction." SLJ
Also available quick text version $16.95 (ISBN: 978-1-906332-50-1); Original text version

Colfer, Eoin

Artemis Fowl: the graphic novel. adapted by Eoin Colfer and Andrew Donkin; art by Giovanni Rigano; color by Paolo Lammana. Hyperion Books for Children 2007 un Illustration
Grades: 4 5 6 7 8 9　　　　　　**741; 741.5; Fic**
1. Adventure graphic novels; 2. Fantasy graphic novels; 3. Graphic novels
978-0-7868-4881-2, $18.99; 0-7868-4881-2; 978-0-7868-4882-9 (pa), $9.99; 0-7868-4882-0 (pa)
Twelve-year-old genius and criminal mastermind Artemis Fowl runs his missing father's crime empire and gets his hands on a book that will give him access to the underground fairy world. This graphic novel adaptation gives the book a European look and color palette
"Excellent use of color and shading gives the panels a tremendous sense of light with enchanting effect. Characters are expressively brought to life with fun, exaggerated style." SLJ
Other Artemis Fowl graphic novels are:Artemis Fowl: the Arctic incident (2009);Artemis Fowl: the eternity code (2013);Artemis Fowl: the opal deception (2014)

Collins, Max Allan

Dick Tracy: The Collins Casefiles Volume 1. Checker Book Publishing Group 2003 164p. Illustration
Grades: 8 9 10 11 12 Adult　　　　　　**741.5; Fic**
1. Dick Tracy (Fictional character); 2. Graphic novels; 3. Mystery graphic novels
0-9741664-2-1, $19.95
LC 2003-23068
This is the first of several volumes collecting Collins' 11-year run on the Dick Tracy comic strips. He took over scripting duties from Chester Gould in 1978, although Gould maintained his byline and consulted with Collins on plot directions. Fletcher, a longtime Gould assistant, took over the drawing and worked with Collins. This volume includes the stories Ängel Top's Last Stand, Return of Haf-and-Haf, and Big Boy's Revenge.

Conner, Daniel

The **picture** of Dorian Gray. adapted by Daniel Conner; illustrated by Chris Allen.. Magic Wagon/Graphic Planet 2009 32p. Illustration
Grades: 6 7 8 9 10
741.5; Fic
1. Authors; 2. Dramatists; 3. Graphic novels; 4. Horror graphic novels; 5. Lecturers; 6. Novelists; 7. Poets; 8. Portraits — Graphic novels; 9. Supernatural graphic novels; 10. Wilde, Oscar, 1854-1900 — Adaptations
978-160270-680-4, $27.07

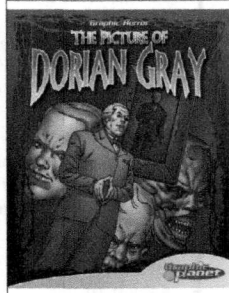

Courtesy of ABDO Publishing.

118

LC 2009-8597

Impossibly handsome, young Dorian Gray sits for a portrait and then impulsively wishes that he could never age and that the portrait should do so in his place. However, as life goes on, he becomes evil; he falls in love with an actress and then spurns her; he murders the portrait artist; and with every act his portrait becomes more and more grotesque while he remains a youthful, handsome fellow. This easy-reading graphic novel adaptation of Oscar Wilde's horror story makes it easier for reluctant and struggling readers to enjoy the story. Back matter includes a brief biography of Wilde, a list of some of his other works, and a short glossary. The question of morality in the story and the violence make this more suitable for somewhat older readers, despite the simplicity of language.

This is part of the Graphic Horror Series 2.

William Shakespeare's A midsummer night's dream. adapted by Daniel Conner; illustrated by Rod Espinosa.. ABDO/Magic Wagon 2008 48p. Illustration
Grades: 5 6 7 8 9 10   **741.5; Fic**
1. Graphic novels.; 2. Youths' writings.; 3. Shakespeare, William — Adaptations
978-1-60270-191-5, $28.50

LC 2008-10745

In Athens, the ruler Theseus prepares to marry Hippolyta. Meanwhile, Hermia and Lysander run away to the forest because Hermia doesn't want to marry Demetrius, who follows them into the forest with Helena, whom he loves. Enter Puck, mischievous fairy who serves Oberon, the King of the Fairies. When he is ordered to find a flower whose nectar acts like a love potion and use it on Queen Titania, Puck also decides to play with the two young couples. And meanwhile again, a group of guildsmen prepare a play for their ruler's wedding. Havoc ensues. This graphic novel adaptation retains some of the original language from Shakespeare's play, while paring down the story to appeal to struggling readers. The book includes a short biography of Shakespeare, a summary of the play, a glossary, and a short selection of famous lines and phrases from the play.

Part of the Graphic Shakespeare series

Cooke, Darwyn
★ The **Spirit** book one. written by Darwyn Cooke and Jeph Loeb; drawn by Darwyn Cooke; inks and finishes by J. Bone; colors by Dave Stewart; letters by Jared K. Fletcher. DC Comics 2007 192p. Illustration
Grades: 8 9 10 11 12 Adult   **741.5; Fic**
1. Batman (Fictional character); 2. Graphic novels; 3. Humorous graphic novels; 4. Superhero graphic novels; 5. The Spirit (Fictional character)
978-1-4012-1461-6; 978-1-4012-1618-4 (pa), $19.99

Will Eisner's character The Spirit was popular for decades. Eisner is gone, but Darwyn Cooke has taken up the pen to update The Spirit while maintaining the action, adventure, and humor of the original stories. Readers will meet Commissioner Dolan and his daughter Ellen, Ebony, bad girl P'Gell, and more. This volume also includes the Eisner Award winning Batman/The Spirit special, written by Jeph Loeb and drawn by Cooke. The upcoming live action movie directed by comics veteran Frank Miller will spark more interest in the comics. The book includes lots of action and some cartoony violence.

"This is fine, entertaining stuff that will satisfy any longtime comics fan; recommended for teens and adults." Libr J

Cooper, John
Richard the Lionheart: The Life of a King and Crusader. by David West & Jackie Gaff; illustrated by John Cooper. Rosen Publishing Group 2005 48p. Illustration
Grades: 3 4 5 6 7 8   **942.03; 741.5; 92**

1. Biographical graphic novels; 2. Graphic novels; 3. Richard, I, King of England; 4. Great Britain — History — 1154-1399, Plantagenets — Graphic novels
1-4042-0241-2, $29.25

LC 2004011267

Politician, military leader, crusader, and King of England, Richard the Lionheart has been the subject of Middle Ages' studies for centuries. His early years were marked by bitter rivalry with his father and brothers, but once crowned King in 1189, his primary ambition was to lead a crusade to the Holy Land to recapture the city of Jerusalem. This graphic novel treats readers to a retelling of the King's battle against Saladin for control of the Holy Land, his subsequent imprisonment, and ultimate return to the throne. It includes additional information, a glossary, and a list of books for further reading.

Part of the Graphic Nonfiction series.

Cooper, Nate
Build your own website: a comic guide to HTML, CSS, and WordPress. Nate Cooper. No Starch Press 2014 250 p. Illustration
Grades: 7 8 9 10 11 12   **006.7**
1. Web site development — Humor; 2. Web sites — Design — Humor; 3. HTML (Document markup language)
1593275226; 9781593275228, $19.95

LC 2014019597

Author Nate Cooper and illustrator Kim Gee present this "illustrated introduction to the basics of creating a website. Join Kim and her little dog Tofu as she learns HTML, the language of web pages, and CSS, the language used to style web pages, from the Web Guru and Glinda, the Good Witch of CSS." (Publisher's note)

"The comic art engages the readers and gives the broad picture of what the reader will learn from Cooper's text which follows. Best suited for beginning self-learning, it is one of the few books on the topic which entertains as well as educates."

Includes index.

Corona, Jorge
Feathers. written & illustrated by Jorge Corona; colors by Jen Hickman; letters by Deron Bennett. Archaia 2015 160 p. Illustration
Grades: 5 6 7 8   **741.5; Fic**
1. Monsters — Graphic novels; 2. Orphans — Graphic novels
9781608867530, $24.99; 1608867536

LC 2015055238

In this graphic novel, written & illustrated by Jorge Corona, "Poe has lived his entire eleven-year-old life hidden away under the protection of his adoptive father, Gabriel. He spends his days secretly helping...bands of orphans who roam the slums.... When Bianca, an over-protected girl from the wealthy City beyond the Wall, escapes into the Maze in search of adventure, their worlds collide." (Publisher's note)

"Poe is a true underdog hero, and Bianca's wish to be set free from her restricting life is something to which middle grades readers can relate. Stunning illustrations contrast the stark white orderly city with the dark and dangerous Maze." SLJ

Cosson, M. J.
Sherlock Holmes and a scandal in Bohemia. based on the stories of Sir Arthur Conan Doyle; adapted by Murray Shaw and M.J. Cosson; illustrated by Sophie Rohrbach.. Lerner Publishing Group/Graphic Universe 2010 48p. Illustration
Grades: 3 4 5 6 7 8   **741.5; Fic**
1. Authors; 2. Graphic novels; 3. Mystery graphic novels; 4. Mystery writers; 5. Novelists; 6. Doyle, Arthur Conan Sir, 1859-1930 — Adaptations

Courtesy of Lerner Publishing Group

978-0-7613-6185-5, $26.60;
978-0-7613-6197-8 (pa), $6.95

LC 2009-51763

The King of Bohemia comes to Sherlock Holmes and asks him to retrieve a photograph from the king's former lover, Irene Adler. He wants to be married, and Miss Adler is blackmailing him with the incriminating photograph. Holmes dons a disguise in order to steal the photo from Miss Adler's house, but the singer proves to be an intelligent, formidable foe. This book adapts the story written by Sir Arthur Conan Doyle, with sepia-toned art. It includes clues to Holmes' reasoning and a list for further reading.

Craddock, Erik

Robot frenzy; 8. Erik Craddock. Random House Books for Young Readers 2013 96 p. (Stone rabbit)

Grades: 2 3 4 5 6   **741.5/973**

1. Animals — Fiction; 2. Chores — Fiction; 3. Graphic novels; 4. Humorous stories; 5. Robots — Graphic novels; 6. Rabbits — Graphic novels

0375869131; 9780375869136, $6.99; 9780375969133

LC 2012049524

In this graphic novel by Erik Craddock "Stone Rabbit and his friends create robots to help out with chores [but] a glitch in the programming sends the 'bots into a malfunctioning frenzy! Will our long-eared hero be able to shut down these mechanical maniacs before they destroy Happy Glades? Or will his systems crash?" (Publisher's note)

Crain, Dale

The **DC** Comics Rarities Archives Volume 1. DC Comics 2004 348p. Illustration

Grades: 7 8 9 10 11 12 Adult   **741.5; Fic**

1. Graphic novels; 2. Superhero graphic novels

1-4012-0007-8, $75

For the first time ever, in one huge collection, three of DC Comics' most hard to find early anthology titles are reprinted in their entirety. This is a 348-page hardcover collecting New York World's Fair 1939, New York World's Fair 1940 and Big All-American Comic Book #1 (1944). The two World's Fair Comics were specially created to be distributed at the legendary New York World's Fair of 1939-40 and feature adventures revolving around the DC heroes' visits there.

The **Seven** Soldiers of Victory Archives Volume 1. DC Comics 2005 237p. Illustration

Grades: 6 7 8 9 10 11 12 Adult   **741.5; Fic**

1. Graphic novels; 2. Superhero graphic novels; 3. Green Arrow (Fictional character)

1-4012-0401-5, $49.95

Collecting Leading Comics #1-4, featuring the adventures of The Seven Soldiers of Victory: The Crimson Avenger, Green Arrow, The Shining Knight, The Vigilante, the Star-Spangled Kid, and their sidekicks Speedy, Stripesy, and Wing (yes, there were eight of them). In 1941, one year after DC Comics launched the Justice Society of America in All-Star Comics, sister company All-American Comics released Leading Comics #1 featuring its very own super-team; in these early stories they take on various criminals and villains who possess super-senses.

Superman Archives Volume 7. DC Comics 2006 237p. Illustration

Grades: 8 9 10 11 12 Adult   **741.5; Fic**

1. Graphic novels; 2. Superhero graphic novels; 3. Superman (Fictional character)

978-1-4012-1051-9, $49.99

This seventh volume of the Superman Archive Editions collects issues 25-29 of Superman, with tales featuring the Man of Steel fighting subversion and sabotage on the home front during World War II, meeting mythic figures like Paul Bunyan and Hercules and foiling villains including the Toyman and the Prankster. This volume also features the first episodes of "Lois Lane, Girl Reporter." These stories were originally published in 1943 and 1944.

Crane, Jordan

The **clouds** above. Fantagraphics 2005 216p. Illustration

Grades: 3 4 5 6 7 8   **741.5; Fic**

1. Fantasy graphic novels; 2. Graphic novels

1-560976-27-6, $18.95

Simon and his cat Jack embark on an adventure among the clouds one day when Simon skips school and finds a rickety stairway leading skyward. They find a friendly cloud, flee thunderstorms and trick a flock of belligerent birds, only to find themselves back at school.

"Everything's exciting...and the dialogue is witty and bubbly.... The book is a joy to look at—Crane's loose, gliding lines burst with character, and his compositional gifts make every panel worth contemplating on its own." Publ Wkly

Crilley, Mark

★ **Akiko** pocket-size, vol. 1. Sirius Entertainment 2004 192p. Illustration

Grades: 3 4 5 6 7 8 9 10   **741.5; Fic**

1. Adventure graphic novels; 2. Graphic novels; 3. Science fiction graphic novels

1-579890-67-9, $11.95

Fourth-grader Akiko travels to the planet Smoo, on a mission to rescue King Froptoppit's son from the evil Alia Rellapor. Teamed up with the scruffy adventurer Spuckler, bookish Mr. Beeba, Spuckler's robot Gax, and the floating alien known as Poog, Akiko faces sea monsters, Sky Pirates, Sleeslup worms, and other dangers as they travel around the planet on their quest. This is the first volume in an ongoing series of graphic novels. Crilley also has written a series of prose fiction featuring Akiko and her friends.

★ **Brody's** ghost: book 1. story and art by Mark Crilley. Dark Horse Books 2010 88p. Illustration

Grades: 8 9 10 11 12 Adult   **741.5; Fic**

1. Adventure graphic novels; 2. Fantasy graphic novels; 3. Ghosts — Graphic novels; 4. Graphic novels; 5. Mystery graphic novels

978-1-59582-521-6, $6.99

In what looks like a near-future city, Brody is down and out, eking out a living by playing guitar on the streets and working part-time as a stock clerk. Then, one day, while playing his guitar, he sees the ghost of a young woman; he thinks he's seeing things, but she won't let him alone until he talks with her. Talia, the ghost, needs to do a great deed before she can get into heaven, and she has decided to solve the mystery of a serial killer called the Penny Murderer, but she needs Brody, who is a ghostseer, to help her. First, though, he needs training to bring out his ghostseer powers, because he doesn't think he has any. Enter Kagemura, the ghost of a samurai, who decides, half-unwillingly, to train Brody. This book is much grittier than Crilley's earlier works, which were more suitable for younger readers; it is aimed more at teen and adult readers and includes some fighting violence but no graphically violent content.

"The setting — an unidentified future city partially in ruins — is a masterpiece of drawing, and Brody and the other characters are equally well crafted.... The story is more than a match for the art: humor, action, and mystery butt up against the reality of Brody's sad life, giving him the opportunity to change who he is." Booklist

Also available in an omnibus edition; Book 1 of 6

Miki Falls Vol. 2: Summer. HarperTeen 2007 178p. Illustration
Grades: 7 8 9 10 11 12 Adult   **741.5; Fic**
1. Graphic novels; 2. Romance graphic novels; 3. Supernatural graphic novels
978-0-06-084617-6, $7.99

Has Miki fallen too hard? It's summer, and Miki Yoshida is learning all about love. Her senior year has blossomed with promise ever since she gained Hiro Sakurai's confidence. Now, she's resolved to keep his trust as he reveals more about his secret mission and warns: "Don't get involved." But Miki fears his work might do more harm than good, and she takes control-with disastrous results. How can trying to make things right turn out so dangerously wrong? Crilley is doing this series in manga style.

Miki Falls, Book One: Spring. HarperCollins/HarperTeen 2007 176p. Illustration
Grades: 7 8 9 10 11 12   **741.5; Fic**
1. Friendship — Graphic novels; 2. Graphic novels; 3. High school students — Graphic novels; 4. School stories — Graphic novels
978-0-06-084616-9, $7.99

"This is Miki Yoshida's final year of high school, and she's determined to make this the best year yet. Miki is in control...until Hiro Sakurai shows up. The tall, handsome new student is hiding something, and Miki wants to know what." Publisher's note

"Crilley uses mystery to drive the narrative and creates characters that the reader will care about. The black-and-white, manga-style art is beautiful." Voice Youth Advocates

Other titles in this series are: Miki Falls, Book Two: Summer; Miki Falls, Book Three: Autumn; Miki Falls, Book Four: Winter

★ **Miki** Falls: Winter. HarperCollins/HarperTeen 2008 176p. Illustration
Grades: 7 8 9 10 11 12   **741.5; Fic**
1. Adventure graphic novels; 2. Fantasy graphic novels; 3. Graphic novels; 4. Romance graphic novels
978-0-06-084619-0, $7.99

LC 2007-931803
Miki and Hiro have been on the run for a while now; it's now winter and they are in the far north of Japan, trying to escape from the Deliverers led by Akuzu who are determined to tear the young couple apart and punish Hiro. Miki is equally determined to stay with Hiro, whom she loves above all else. Can love conquer all? This is the final volume of the series.

Croall, Marie P.

Marwe: into the land of the dead: an East African legend. author, Marie P. Croall; pencils by Ray Lago and inks by Craig Hamilton.. Lerner Publishing Group 2009 48p. Illustration
Grades: 3 4 5 6 7 8 9
741.5; Fic
1. Fantasy graphic novels; 2. Folklore — East Africa — Graphic novels; 3. Graphic novels
978-0-8225-7134-6, $27.93
LC 2007-1828

Courtesy of Lerner Publishing Group

In this story retold from the oral tradition of the Chaga people in East Africa, Marwe lives in a village where times are hard and food is scarce. When she and her brother leave the family's bean fields to cool off at the river, monkeys destroy the entire crop. When her brother goes off to ask the family's forgiveness, Marwe sees something strange in the water and dives down; she passes through a strange doorway and finds herself in another land. Soon she learns she has come to the land of the dead, where an old woman welcomes her. Too scared to go home, Marwe stays there, and despite assurances that she needn't do anything, she works in the fields. When will Marwe think it's time to return home to her anxious and mourning family?

Part of the Graphic Universe Myths and Legends series

Psyche & eros: the lady and the monster: a Greek myth. story by Marie Croall; pencils and inks by Ron Randall. Lerner Publishing Group 2009 48p. Illustration
Grades: 3 4 5 6 7 8 9
741.5; Fic
1. Fantasy graphic novels; 2. Graphic novels; 3. Greek mythology — Graphic novels
978-0-8225-7177-3, $27.93
LC 2007-43353

Courtesy of Lerner Publishing Group

Psyche is a beautiful young woman, so beautiful that men start to give her gifts instead of taking them to the temple. This makes Aphrodite jealous, and she sends her son, Eros, to prick Psyche with an arrow so no man will ever fall in love with her. However, Eros falls in love with Psyche. He arranges for the Oracle to tell Psyche's father that his daughter must be taken up on a mountain to marry a monster. He only comes to her at night, and they love each other; but Psyche's sisters convince her that she should see her husband. When hot wax from her candle burns Eros and wakens him, he must leave her. Now Psyche, unable to convince any other god or goddess to help her, must go to Aphrodite, who sets impossible tasks that Psyche manages to accomplish with help from unexpected sources.

Part of the Graphic Universe Myths and Legends series

Cutting, Robert

March of the Dinosaurs. Harcourt Achieve/Steck-Vaughn 2006 48p. Illustration
Grades: 3 4 5 6 7 8   **741.5; Fic**
1. Dinosaurs — Graphic novels; 2. Graphic novels; 3. Science fiction graphic novels
978-1-4190-3194-6, $8.99

Traveling on a time machine, a scientist from the future goes back to the Cretaceous Age of the Dinosaurs with her niece and nephew. The time machine breaks down just as a giant meteor hurtles toward the Earth. Will they escape or will they share the fate of the dinosaurs? This science fiction graphic novel includes prose intervals that give facts about dinosaurs.

Part of the Timeline Graphic Novels series.

Mars Colony. Harcourt Achieve/Steck-Vaughn 2006 48p. Illustration
Grades: 3 4 5 6 7 8   **741.5; Fic**
1. Graphic novels; 2. Mystery graphic novels; 3. Science fiction graphic novels
978-1-4190-3213-4, $8.99

In the year 2130, the Chang family is one of 128 families sent to Mars to found the first human colony there. Jenny Chang and her brother Derek eagerly explore their new home; they are in for a big surprise. This science fiction story is interspersed with facts about Mars and space exploration.

Part of the Timeline Graphic Novels series.

Czekaj, Jef

Grampa & Julie: Shark hunters. Top Shelf 2004 un Illustration
Grades: 2 3 4 5 6   **741.5; Fic**

1. Adventure graphic novels; 2. Graphic novels; 3. Humorous graphic novels

1-891830-52-X, $14.95

"In this full-color graphic novel, Julie and her grampa spend summer vacation looking for the largest shark in the world, Stephen. Meeting Stephen leads to even more exciting adventures, including a quest to find Stephen's mom. The shark hunters meet monkeys at the bottom of the ocean, pirates, and even aliens. Gramma has to rescue them from a couple of scrapes." Booklist

"Taken from the pages of Nickelodeon magazine, this charming children's comic overflows with humor, adventure and whimsy." Publ Wkly

Dahl, Roald

The **Gremlins:** The Lost Walt Disney Production: A Royal Air Force Story. Dark Horse Books 2006 un Illustration

Grades: 4 5 6 7 8 9 10 11 12 Adult   **741.5; Fic**

1. Graphic novels; 2. Humorous graphic novels; 3. World War, 1939-1945 — Graphic novels

978-1-59307-496-8, $12.95

This is an illustrated novella, the first published work of RAF Flight Lieutenant Roald Dahl in his only collaboration with Walt Disney Studios. Originally published in 1943, the story was supposed to become a film combining live action with animation; the movie was never made, although the studio produced a lot of illustrations and samples. The story tells about one young Royal Air Force pilot named Gus, who first sees the little gremlins that wreak havoc on his plane. While the gremlins first cause lots of trouble, eventually Gus convinces them to work with the RAF.

Dakin, Glenn

Temptation: A Battle of Wits Through All Eternity. Active Images 2004 72p. Illustration

Grades: 8 9 10 11 12 Adult   **741.5**

1. Graphic novels; 2. Humorous graphic novels

0-9740567-5-8, $8.95

It's a constant battle of wits between a hermit who lives out in the wilderness and the devil who wants his soul. While that's the main theme, there are strips in which the devil needs the hermit to babysit his little baby devils so he can see a movie, the devil tries to sell the hermit a set of encyclopedias, and more fun.

Danko, Dan

Leonardo da Vinci: the renaissance man. Dan Danko, illustrated by Lalit Kumar Sharma. Campfire/Kalyani Navyug Media Pvt. Ltd. 2011 68 p.

Grades: 8 9 10   **709.2**

1. Artists — Italy — Biography; 2. Inventors — Italy — Biography; 3. Renaissance — Italy — Biography; 4. Scientists — Italy — Biography; 5. Leonardo, da Vinci, 1452-1519; 6. Biographical graphic novels

9380741014; 9380741200; 9789380741017; 9789380741208, $9.99

LC 2011294404

This graphic novel is a biography of Leonardo da Vinci. It "opens with the theft of the 'Mona Lisa' from the Louvre in 1911, then backtracks to da Vinci's turbulent childhood in Italy during the Renaissance. Throughout the tale, the mind of da Vinci is shown to be always active, always questioning, always seeking ways to create something better." (Voice of Youth Advocates)

David, Peter

Friendly Neighborhood Spider-Man Vol. 1: Derailed. Marvel Entertainment 2006 un Illustration

Grades: 7 8 9 10 11 12 Adult   **741.5; Fic**

1. Graphic novels; 2. Spider-Man (Fictional character); 3. Superhero graphic novels

978-0-7851-2216-6, $14.99

A major character from Peter Parker's past returns, and it looks like Hobgoblin is terrorizing the skies again. Also, a woman chronicles Spider-Man's career on her blog, convinced that he has stalked her for her entire life.

Davis, Eleanor

★ The **secret** science alliance and the copycat crook. Bloomsbury 2009 153p. Illustration

Grades: 3 4 5 6 7 8   **741.5; Fic**

1. Adventure graphic novels; 2. Graphic novels; 3. Humorous graphic novels; 4. Inventors — Fiction; 5. School stories

978-1-59990-142-8, $18.99; 1-59990-142-0; 978-1-59990-396-5 (pa), $10.99; 1-59990-396-2 (pa)

LC 2008-45399

Eleven-year-old Julian Calendar thought changing schools would mean leaving his "nerdy" persona behind, but instead he forms an alliance with fellow inventors Greta and Ben and works with them to prevent an adult from using one of their gadgets for nefarious purposes

"With its frenetically eye-catching, full-color panels chock-full of humorous and informative detail, Davis's first (of many, one hopes) graphic adventure of the SSA pumps new life into the kids' secret society formula." Kirkus

De Groot, Bob

Clifton Jade. Cinebook 2008 48p.

Grades: 5 6 7 8 9   **741.5; Fic**

1. Adventure graphic novels; 2. Graphic novels; 3. Humorous graphic novels; 4. Spies — Graphic novels

978-1-905460-52-6, $11.95

Sir Harold Wilberforce Clifton, ex-Secret Service and retired Colonel, works as a private detective, as well as leading a troop of young scouts. With the help of his housekeeper, Mrs. Partridge, who's also a dab hand at auto mechanics, he still helps the government. This time, however, he's being tailed by someone and then summoned to a retirement home where he finds his old World War II nemesis, Otto Kartoffeln, who tells him a group of neo-Nazis are searching for a long-lost Nazi treasure in order to bring about the 4th Reich. The mysterious shadow is Jade, a young agent who was trying to complete her training; now she and Clifton must stop the neo-Nazis from finding the treasure.

Part of the Clifton series, originally published in France as Clifton Jade.

De Liz, Renae

The **legend** of Wonder Woman. story & pencils by Renae De Liz; inks, colors & letters by Ray Dillon. DC Comics 2016 288 p. Color; Illustration

Grades: 8 9 10 11 12 Adult   **741.5; Fic**

1. Female superhero graphic novels; 2. Superhero graphic novels; 3. Wonder Woman (Fictional character)

1401267289; 9781401267285, $29.99

LC 2016047038

"When a man from the outside world is brought to Themyscira as part of a conspiracy to overthrow its queen, Diana will risk everything to save his innocent life...and lose everything in the process. Soon, the Amazon princess finds herself in a world she never knew existed — America." (Publisher's note)

"Collecting twenty-seven chapters of online material, this spacious, even epic, story affords room for both legend building and healthy doses of action, the supernatural, romance, and humor." Booklist

DeFalco, Tom

The **Amazing** Spider-Girl: Whatever Happened to the Daughter of Spider-Man?. writer, Tom DeFalco; artist, Ron Frenz. Marvel Entertainment 2007 un Illustration

Grades: 7 8 9 10 11 12 Adult   **741.5; Fic**
   1. Graphic novels; 2. Spider-Girl (Fictional character); 3. Superhero graphic novels; 4. Spider-Man (Fictional character)
978-0-7851-2341-5, $14.99

After discovering she had inherited her father's incredible powers, May "Mayday" Parker donned a costume and became the amazing Spider-Girl. Recent events have forced her to hang up her webs and lead a normal life...but how long can May keep from web-slinging when there are villains like Hobgoblin on the loose? This volume begins collecting the second run of Spider-Girl comics; the first 100 issues were published as Spider-Girl and are being collected in digest-sized trade paperbacks. This new series, The Amazing Spider-Girl, features new numbering (from #1 and on) and is being collected in regular comic book-sized trade paperbacks.

Spider-Girl Vol. 2: Like Father, Like Daughter. Marvel Entertainment 2004 un Illustration

Grades: 7 8 9 10 11 12   **741.5; Fic**
   1. Graphic novels; 2. Spider-Girl (Fictional character); 3. Superhero graphic novels
0-7851-1657-5, $7.99

Her name is May Mayday" Parker, and she recently learned her father was the original Spider-Man. The good news is that she's having the time of her life as she hones the amazing spider-like abilities she inherited from him. The bad news is that some of her roughest, toughest battles lie ahead — against the likes of Ladyhawk, the Kingpin of Crime, Mr. Nobody, Crazy Eight...and her own parents. She also learns that it's not easy hiding such a big part of your life from all your friends in school.

Spider-Girl Vol. 4: Turning Point. writer, Tom DeFalco, Ron Frenz; pencils, Pat Olliffe & Ron Frenz; inks, Al Williamson & Sal Buscema. Marvel Entertainment 2005 un Illustration

Grades: 7 8 9 10 11 12   **741.5; Fic**
   1. Graphic novels; 2. Spider-Girl (Fictional character); 3. Superhero graphic novels; 4. Spider-Man (Fictional character)
0-7851-1871-3, $7.99

The adventures of Spider-Man's daughter continue as Mayday once again faces Kaine, Spider-Man swings again, and Darkdevil is...actually nice? Plus: Meet new heroes and villains, take a peek into the fantasies of Mayday's friends, and witness the return of the Green Goblin. In May's life, she's caught between JJ (grandson of J. Jonah Jameson) and Brad; how is a girl to choose?

Spider-Girl Vol. 5: Endgame. Marvel Entertainment 2006 un Illustration

Grades: 7 8 9 10 11 12   **741.5; Fic**
   1. Graphic novels; 2. Spider-Girl (Fictional character); 3. Superhero graphic novels
0-7851-2034-3, $7.99

Spider-Girl faces trouble when her deadliest enemies join forces as the Savage Six (or is it Seven?)! But even with the help of rival/critic heroes like Darkdevil and the Buzz, can she deal with the sudden loss of her super-powers? And, naturally, that's when Normie Osborn escapes from the mental institution, convinced that he, as Green Goblin, must kill Spider-Girl.

Spider-Girl, Vol. 1: Legacy. Marvel Comics 2004 144p. Illustration
Grades: 7 8 9 10 11 12   **741.5; Fic**
   1. Graphic novels; 2. Spider-Girl (Fictional character); 3. Superhero graphic novels; 4. Spider-Man (Fictional character)
0-7851-1441-6, $7.99

In an alternate future in the Marvel Universe, Peter Parker has retired from being Spider-Man after a crippling injury; but he and Mary Jane have a daughter, May. She has just turned sixteen, and suddenly discovers she has superpowers! Soon she finds out who her father used to be, and she decides to be a superhero — but Peter knows the dangers all too well and tries to stop her. Once Mayday decides to be Spider-Girl, though, no one can stop her. This is the first of an ongoing series.

DeFilippis, Nunzio

Play ball. Oni Press, Inc. 2012 144 p.
Grades: 6 7 8 9
741.5/973; Fic
   1. Women athletes — Graphic novels; 2. School stories — Graphic novels; 3. Baseball — Graphic novels
1934964794; 9781934964798, $19.99
          LC 2011933142

This comic "traces a high school girl's struggle to join a boys' baseball team. Freckle-faced Dashiell Brody was good at softball in her private girls' school; now that she's moved to another city with her mother and older sister and they must enroll in public school, she wants to play the real game, despite stereotypical resistance from school administrators and some jocks." (Publishers Weekly)

Courtesy of Oni Press

Del Rio, Tania

Sabrina the Teenage Witch: The Magic Revisited. Archie Comics 2006 un Illustration

Grades: 4 5 6 7 8 9   **741.5; Fic**
   1. Fantasy graphic novels; 2. Graphic novels; 3. Humorous graphic novels; 4. Witches — Graphic novels
1-879794-19-5, $7.49

The first four issues of Sabrina the Teenage Witch's "manga makeover" are collected in this special edition trade paperback. Writer-artist Tania del Rio presents these tales of magical flights of fancy and romantic intrigue... sprinkled with a dash of humor. Sabrina's awakening powers and the various love triangle combinations that have formed since keep her busy at school, on dates, and...everywhere.

Delsante, Vito

Before they were famous: Babe Ruth. Aladdin Paperbacks 2009 121p.

Grades: 3 4 5 6 7 8   **741.5; 920**
   1. Baseball players; 2. Baseball players — Graphic novels; 3. Biographical graphic novels; 4. Graphic novels; 5. Ruth, Babe, 1895-1948
978-1-4169-5071-4, $8.99

          LC 2008-929319

Babe Ruth is still considered to be one of the best professional baseball players of all time, and he was the first "home run king" of the sport. This graphic novel, adapted from Babe Ruth by Guernsey Van Riper, Jr., part of the Childhood of Famous Americans series, takes readers back to the troubled childhood of George Ruth. In Baltimore, Maryland in 1902, the Ruth family struggles to keep their restaurant going, and their young son George is a troublemaker; eventually, they send George to St. Mary's Industrial School for Boys. It's a boarding school run by Catholic monks, and George will have to stay there until he's twenty-one. At the school, George discovers baseball, and it transforms his life. When he's asked to sign up with the Baltimore Orioles at the age of nineteen, his new teammates call him Babe. This fictionalized biography will help young readers get a sense of the person behind the legend.

DeMatteis, J. M.

Abadazad: The Dream Thief. by J.M. DeMatteis; drawings by Mike Ploog; colors by Nick Bell. Hyperion Books for Children 2006 un Illustration

Grades: 5 6 7 8 9   **741.5; Fic**

1. Adventure graphic novels; 2. Fantasy graphic novels; 3. Graphic novels

1-4231-00646, $9.99

In the magical land of Abadazad, Kate needs all the help she can get when she encounters the Lanky Man. He's mean and heartless, and he wants to steal children's dreams. Everyone seems to be against her, which only makes her more determined to find her brother. And Matt is getting closer, isn't he? This story is a hybrid, combining prose text with pages of sequential art from the original comic books.

Abadazad: The Road to Inconceivable. Hyperion Books for Children 2006 un Illustration

Grades: 5 6 7 8 9   **741.5; Fic**

1. Adventure graphic novels; 2. Fantasy graphic novels; 3. Graphic novels

1-4231-0062-X, $9.99

Kate's little brother Matt disappeared five years ago, and Kate thinks she will never see him again. But then she finds out that Matt is trapped in the world of Abadazad. Will Kate have the courage to look for her brother? And if she leaves home, will she ever return? This story began as comic books, but the publisher went out of business before the story was completed. Now it's published as a hybrid, combining prose sections with pages of sequential art and spot illustrations.

★ The **stardust** kid. Boom! Studios 2008 un Illustration

Grades: 3 4 5 6 7 8 9 10 11 12 Adult   **741.5; Fic**

1. Adventure graphic novels; 2. Fantasy graphic novels; 3. Graphic novels

978-1-934506-04-2, $14.99

Twelve-year-old Cody's best friend is Paul Brightfield; they share a deep bond that goes far beyond mere friendship. What no one else knows is that Paul isn't human, he's one of the last Old Ones, ancient elemental beings who lived before man existed. One night, Paul disappears, and a hate-filled creature who has existed long buried beneath Wilde Park bursts out with a desire to destroy everything in the world. Only Cody, his little sister K.M., and his friend Alana and her little brother Nathaniel, remain, and somehow they must find The Stardust Kid and discover a way to stop the hate and restore their world. Some creatures might be frightening to younger readers, but anyone who likes the Harry Potter books shouldn't have a problem with this book.

Dembicki, Matt

★ **Trickster:** Native American tales: a graphic collection. edited by Matt Dembicki. Fulcrum 2010 231p. Illustration

Grades: 5 6 7 8

398.2; 398

1. Folklore — Graphic novels; 2. Graphic novels; 3. Native Americans — Folklore

978-1-55591-724-1 (pa), $22.95; 1-55591-724-0 (pa)

LC 2009-49668

Courtesy of Fulcrum Publishing

"More than 40 storytellers and cartoonists have contributed to this original and provocative compendium of traditional folklore presented in authentic, colorful, and engaging sequential art. The stories are drawn from a variety of Native peoples across North America, and so the trickster character appears variously as Rabbit, a raccoon, Coyote, and in other guises; landscapes, clothing and rhythms of speech and action also vary in keeping with distinct traditions. Realistic, impressionistic, painterly, and cartoon styles of art are employed to echo and announce the tone of each tale and telling style, making this a rich visual treasure as well as cultural trove." SLJ

Demolis, Flo

Around the world in 80 days. IDW Publishing 2009 60p. Illustration

Grades: 5 6 7 8 9   **741.5; Fic**

1. Adventure graphic novels; 2. Authors; 3. Children's authors; 4. Graphic novels; 5. Novelists; 6. Science fiction writers; 7. Travel — Graphic novels; 8. Verne, Jules, 1828-1905 — Adaptations/Graphic novels

978-1-60010-394-0, $14.99

This graphic novel Verne's globe-trotting adventures of Phileas Fogg, English gentleman, his newly-hired French manservant, Passepartout, and the English detective, Fix, who pursues Fogg, convinced he is a master bank robber. Fogg makes a bet with fellow members of the Reform Club in 1872 that he can travel around the world in eighty days, but his precipitous departure makes Scotland Yard suspect him. The three men travel through India, where Fogg saves a beautiful young Indian woman from being burned alive, to Hong Kong, then Japan and then across the United States and onward. This adaptation was originally published in France. The book includes biographical information about Verne, historical information about what the world was like in the 1870s, and an analysis of the novel.

Deutsch, Barry

Hereville: how Mirka caught a fish. Barry Deutsch. Amulet Books 2015 140 p. Color; Illustration

Grades: 4 5 6 7   **741.5/973**

1. Jewish girls — Fiction; 2. Fishes — Fiction; 3. Babysitting — Fiction

9781419708008, $17.95

LC 2015945771

In this book, by Barry Deutsch, "Welcome back to Hereville, where Mirka, the world's first time-travelling, monster-fighting Orthodox Jewish girl...[is] stuck babysitting her disapproving little sister, Layele. When Mirka pushes her sister into a stream, they both get in too deep with an angry magic fish.... When the fish kidnaps Layele, Mirka must find a way to save her little sister, and the clues she needs are hidden in her stepmother Fruma's past." (Publisher's note)

★ **Hereville:** how Mirka got her sword. Barry Deutsch; colors by Jake Richmond. Amulet Books 2010 137p. Illustration

Grades: 4 5 6 7   **741.5; Fic**

1. Dragons — Graphic novels; 2. Fantasy graphic novels; 3. Graphic novels; 4. Jews — Graphic novels

978-0-8109-8422-6, $15.95; 0-8109-8422-9; 9781419706196

LC 2010-924236

Mirka and her family live in an Orthodox Jewish village called Hereville. All she really wants to do is fight dragons, but what she has to fight is a troublesome pig that talks. Then Mirka meets the witch who lives nearby, and then confronts a troll, and soon she finds she has much more adventure than she knows how to handle.

"Deutsch creates authentic characters spiced with just enough fantasy to surprise.... Details of Orthodox daily life are well blended into the art and given just the right touches of explanation to keep readers on track." Booklist

Other titles in this series are: How Mirka met a meteorite (2012); How Mirka caught a fish (2014)

★ **Hereville:** How Mirka Met a Meteorite. Barry Deutsch; colors by Jake Richmond. Amulet Books 2012 123 p.
Grades: 3 4 5 6 7   **741.5**
1. Witches — Fiction; 2. Adventure graphic novels; 3. Jews — Graphic novels; 4. Trolls — Fiction
1419703986; 9781419703980, $16.95

LC 2012947050
This graphic novel by Barry Deutsch features a "wisecracking, adventure-loving, sword-wielding Orthodox Jewish heroine.... She fearlessly stands up to local bullies. She battles a very large, very menacing pig. And she boldly accepts a challenge from a mysterious witch, a challenge that could bring Mirka her heart's desire: a dragon-slaying sword! All she has to do is find — and outwit — the giant troll who's got it!" (Publisher's note)

Diamond, Jeremy
Nascar heroes #2: Who is Jimmy Dash?. 2009 un
Grades: 3 4 5 6 7 8   **741.5; Fic**
1. Automobile racing — Graphic novels; 2. Graphic novels; 3. NASCAR — Graphic novels; 4. Superhero graphic novels
978-1-59961-663-6, $22.78

LC 2009-9008
The accident that gave the Flatstock pit crew, plus Dashiell, super powers, also gave them to Jack Diesel; and he doesn't have any good intentions. When Jimmy Dash and Team Flatstock keep winning NASCAR races, Diesel resorts to dirty tricks with his laser heat vision and illegal gadgets on his cars. However, Team Flatstock owner Astor also gained powers in the accident; she sees visions of the near future. Diesel decides that the entire Flatstock team would do anything for Astor, so he kidnaps her; Dashiell reveals his identity to the guys, and they go to rescue Astor. However, that's much easier said than done when Diesel will use any dirty trick to win.

Dickens, Charles
Classics Illustrated Deluxe #8: Oliver Twist. by Loic Dauvillier; illustrated by Olivier Deloye. Papercutz 2012 238 p.
Grades: 6 7 8 9 10 11 12
741.5
1. London (England) — Fiction; 2. Graphic novels; 3. Orphans — Fiction
9781597073073; 1597073075

Courtesy of NBM Publishing

This graphic novel, by Charles Dickens, adapted by Loic Dauvillier, and illustrated by Olivier Deloye, is part of the "Classic Illustrated Deluxe" series. "The story is about an orphan, Oliver Twist, who endures a miserable existence in a workhouse and then is placed with an undertaker. He escapes and travels to London where he meets...a gang of juvenile pickpockets. Naively unaware of their unlawful activities, Oliver is led to the lair of their elderly criminal trainer Fagin." (Wikipedia)

Dini, Paul
The **World's** Greatest Super-Heroes. Paul Dini; art by Alex Ross. DC Comics 2005 un Illustration
Grades: 6 7 8 9 10 11 12 Adult   **741.5; Fic**

1. Graphic novels; 2. Superhero graphic novels; 3. Justice League (Fictional characters); 4. Wonder Woman (Fictional character); 5. Superman (Fictional character)
1-4012-0254-3, $49.95

LC 2006-159064
This oversize hardcover volume collects the stories that DC originally published separately. Superman tries to singlehandedly end world hunger, only to face suspicion and corruption; Batman tries to stop all criminal activity; and Wonder Woman tries to free oppressed women. They each realize that, despite their super powers, they can't eradicate the problems of the world on their own. The rest of the book portrays the Justice League and highlights each member's super hero origins.

Dirge, Roman
It ate Billy on Christmas. Dark Horse Books 2007 un Illustration
Grades: 4 5 6 7 8 9 10 11 12 Adult   **741.5; Fic**
1. Graphic novels; 2. Horror graphic novels; 3. Humorous graphic novels
978-1-59307-853-9, $12.95

Lumi has been bullied by her brother Billy all her life, and this Christmas would have been more of the same, but for the weird, ugly little monster that crawled up from the abandoned well and came into their house. Mistaking it for the stuffed puppy she had requested from her parents, Lumi watches in amazement as it devours the bullying Billy when he shoots it with darts from his new dart gun. She makes a cardboard Billy, which fools her unsuspecting and clueless parents. A few weeks later, back at school, Lumi has to face the bullies who have made her school life miserable, but she has her "puppy" in her backpack and it's hungry.... Dirge wrote the story and drew the black and white illustrations, while Daily provided the color paintings. The story shows the monster eating Billy in one gulp, but there's little actual violence on the pages. The dark humor and twisted story line will appeal to those who enjoy Coraline and The Wolves in the Walls by Neil Gaiman, and the weird humor of Edward Gorey cartoons.

Dixon, Chuck
Nightwing: Year One. Chuck Dixon and Scott Beatty; penciller Scott McDaniel; inker: Andy Owens. DC Comics 2005 un Illustration
Grades: 7 8 9 10 11 12 Adult   **741.5; Fic**
1. Graphic novels; 2. Nightwing (Fictional character); 3. Superhero graphic novels; 4. Teen Titans (Fictional characters); 5. Robin (Fictional character); 6. Batman (Fictional character)
1-4012-0435-X, $14.99

Dick Grayson was the first Robin, the teen sidekick to the Dark Knight, Batman. Then he became Nightwing and stepped out of Batman's shadow. The story behind that transformation and how it affected Batman, the Teen Titans and Dick himself is explored in this graphic novel. When Batman fires Robin, an angry Dick Grayson is unsure of where to go. On his journey, he receives advice from Superman and aid from Deadman, and makes the decisions that lead him to become a brand new crimefighter.

The **Vanishers.** IDW Publishing 2002 80p. Illustration
Grades: 6 7 8 9 10 11 12 Adult   **741.5; Fic**
1. Adventure graphic novels; 2. Graphic novels; 3. Science fiction graphic novels
0-9712282-6-4, $12.99

From the turn of the 20th century, to medieval England, and into the far-flung future, Andy and Arvis must escape their pursuers, rescue their friends, and return to their own time. Andy's friends begin to disappear and only he remembers that they ever existed. When Andy discovers another student, Arvis Voltoz, has noticed that disappearances, he follows Arvis home and begins an adventure that takes him and Arvis through time.

Doctorow, Cory

In Real Life. Cory Doctorow; illustrated by Jen Wang. First Second Books 2014 192 p. Color; Illustration

Grades: 8 9 10 11 12   **741.5**

1. Computer games — Economic aspects; 2. Video games — Graphic novels; 3. Ethics

1596436581; 9781596436589, $17.99

In this graphic novel, "online gaming and real life collide when a teen discovers the hidden economies and injustices that hide among seemingly innocent pixels.... Anda joins...a group of girls playing the game as girl avatars.... Another guild member named Lucy...asks her if she'd be interested in earning 'real cash.'...She's pulled into a world of real-money economies where workers 'play' the game, garnering items they can then sell for actual money to other players." (Kirkus Reviews)

"Characters come to life through Wang's...fluid forms and emotive faces, and her adroit shift in colors as the story moves between the physical and gaming worlds is subtle and effective." Pub Wkly

Donkin, Andrew

★ **Illegal.** Eoin Colfer, Andrew Donkin; art by Giovanni Rigano; lettering by Chris Dickey. Sourcebooks Inc 2018 144 p. Illustration

Grades: 5 6 7 8 9   **741.5; Fic**

1. Poor people — Juvenile fiction; 2. Undocumented immigrants — Juvenile fiction; 3. Poor — Fiction; 4. Siblings — Fiction; 5. Undocumented immigrants — Fiction

1492662143; 9781492662143, $19.99

In this book, by Eoin Colfer and Andrew Donkin, illustrated by Giovanni Rigano, "Ebo is alone. His brother, Kwame, has disappeared, and Ebo knows it can only be to attempt the hazardous journey to Europe, and a better life — the same journey their sister set out on months ago.... He sets out after Kwame and joins him on the quest to reach Europe. Ebo's epic journey takes him across the Sahara Desert to the dangerous streets of Tripoli, and finally out to the merciless sea." (Publisher's note)

"The format allows sensitive and difficult topics such as murder, death, and horrific, traumatizing conditions to unfold for children, Ebo's reactions speaking volumes and dramatic perspectives giving a sense of scope. A creators' note provides factual context, and an appendix offers an Eritrean refugee's minimemoir in graphic form." Kirkus

Donner, Rebecca

Burnout. written by Rebecca Donner; illustrated by Inaki Miranda. DC Comics/Minx 2008 176p. Illustration

Grades: 7 8 9 10 11 12   **741.5; Fic**

1. Environmental protection — Graphic novels; 2. Graphic novels; 3. Romance graphic novels

978-1-4012-1537-8, $9.99

Danni and her mother have made another in a long series of moves, this time moving in with her mother's boyfriend, lodge owner Hank. Danni can see that Hank is an alcoholic, and he tends to take his anger out on people, including his son Haskell (with whom Danni is forced to share a room for the time being). They live in the Pacific Northwest, in a logging town, and Haskell is a hardcore environmentalist. Danni falls for him despite herself, and she begins to go with him at night to spike trees, which is an act of ecoterrorism. As home life continues to stay rough, Haskell starts to escalate his acts against logging, and Danni has to decide what to do. The book includes scenes of heavy petting.

"Miranda's superb illustrations complement the story well, whether they're showing landscapes of the Pacific Northwest, action sequences, or the eyes of a troubled girl." Publ Wkly

Dorkin, Evan

★ **Beasts** of Burden: animal rites. written by Evan Dorkin; art by Jill Thompson; lettering by Jason Arthur and Jill Thompson. Dark Horse Comics 2010 184p. Illustration

Grades: 8 9 10 11 12 Adult   **741.5; Fic**

1. Cats — Graphic novels; 2. Dogs — Graphic novels; 3. Graphic novels; 4. Mystery graphic novels; 5. Supernatural graphic novels

978-1-59582-513-1, $19.99

2010 Eisner Award for Best Publication for Teens; 2010 Eisner Award to Jill Thompson for Best Painter/Multimedia Artist for Beasts of Burden and Magic Trixie; 2005 Eisner Award for Best Short Story for ¿Unfamiliar;¿ 2004 Eisner Award to Jill Thompson for Best Painter/Multimedia Artist (interior art) for ¿Stray.¿

Burden Hill is just a nice, quiet suburban town full of houses with yards and white picket fences, demonic frogs, zombie roadkill, ghosts, etc. The humans who live in Burden Hill seem to be totally oblivious to the dangers, but the dogs, and one cat, work together to keep their town safe. Jack the beagle, Pugsley (go figure), Ace the husky, Rex the Doberman, Whitey the terrier, and Orphan the cat deal with a haunted dog house, witches, undead dogs, a werewolf, and other monsters. The book includes some mild bad language ("crap" usually from Pugs) and a fair amount of violence. This book includes the four-issue miniseries plus all of the short stories that originally appeared in The Dark Horse Book of Hauntings, The Dark Horse Book of Witchcraft, The Dark Horse Book of the Dead, and The Dark Horse Book of Monsters. Sarah Dyer co-wrote "A Dog and His Boy" with Evan Dorkin.

"Gorgeous artwork and a smart, witty script elevate this tale of household pets who unite to fight occult menaces in idyllic Burden Hill." Publ Wkly

Downey, Glen

Escape from East Berlin. Harcourt Achieve/Steck-Vaughn 2007 48p. Illustration

Grades: 3 4 5 6 7 8   **741.5; Fic**

1. Adventure graphic novels; 2. Graphic novels; 3. Germany (East) — Graphic novels

978-1-4190-3222-6, $8.99

In the summer of 1963, President Kennedy of the United States speaks in West Berlin about liberty. From the other side of the Berlin Wall, the Kappel family listens to his every word. They decide to make a bid for freedom, but at what cost? This historical fiction graphic novel includes prose intervals that describe Berlin as the divided city after World War II, the building of the Wall, the various escape attempts made by East Berliners, part of President Kennedy's speech, and the fall of the Wall in 1989. There is brief violence when a vicious East German soldier is shot.

Part of the Timeline Graphic Novels series.

Fire Mountain. Harcourt Achieve/Steck-Vaughn 2006 48p. Illustration

Grades: 3 4 5 6 7 8   **741.5; Fic**

1. Adventure graphic novels; 2. Graphic novels; 3. Volcanoes — Graphic novels; 4. Pompeii (Extinct city) — Graphic novels

978-1-4190-3198-4, $8.99

Cato is a young slave boy in the bustling Roman city of Pompeii. When Mount Vesuvius erupts without warning, Cato is separated from his mother. Will they survive the terrifying day and be reunited? This historical fiction graphic novel includes prose intervals that provide additional information about what happened at Pompeii and Herculaneum, about Vesuvius and other famous volcanoes, and about the modern excavations.

Part of the Timeline Graphic Novels series.

Ice Journey. Harcourt Achieve/Steck-Vaughn 2007 48p. Illustration

Grades: 3 4 5 6 7 8   **741.5; Fic**

1. Adventure graphic novels; 2. Graphic novels; 3. Ice age — Graphic novels

978-1-4190-3204-2, $8.99

It is the Ice Age in North America, and the land is covered in ice and snow. Bruno, a young giant short-faced bear, is being hunted down by a saber-toothed cat. While his sister, Ursula, looks for him, she meets some interesting creatures of the Ice Age. This graphic novel includes prose intervals that provide information on the real animals that lived during the Ice Age, the early people who may have lived towards the end of the Ice Age, and on the impact of global warming on the world today.

Part of the Timeline Graphic Novels series.

Rebel Prince. Harcourt Achieve/Steck-Vaughn 2007 48p. Illustration Grades: 3 4 5 6 7 8   **741.5; Fic**

1. Graphic novels; 2. Henry V, King of England, 1387-1422; 3. Great Britain — Kings and Rulers — Graphic novels

978-1-4190-3217-2, $8.99

In 15th century London, young Will works at a tavern where Prince Hal and his companions hang out. When royal duties call, will Prince Hal be able to rise to the challenge? What is in store for young Will? This historical fiction graphic novel tells the story of how playful Prince Hal became King Henry V of England. It includes prose interludes that provide additional information about his father Henry IV, portrayals of Henry V, and about the famous battle at Agincourt.

Part of the Timeline Graphic Novels series.

Dumas, Alexandre

The **three** musketeers. Campfire 2010 104p. Illustration Grades: 3 4 5 6 7 8 9   **741.5; Fic**

1. Adventure graphic novels; 2. Graphic novels

978-93-80028-57-6, $12.99

Young D'Artagnan comes to Paris, determined to become a king's musketeer, but runs into trouble with three musketeers in one day. When they band together to tight Cardinal Richelieu's forces, they become friends. The friends soon find themselves involved in averting a plot to discredit Queen Anne, and their efforts to help her cause them to run afoul of Richelieu. D'Artagnan, Athos, Porthos, and Aramis also must deal with Milady de Winter, a beautiful and deadly woman with her own agenda. This graphic novel adaptation features art that emphasizes the humor in the historical adventure. It also puts most of the violence off-panel, so the story is suitable for younger readers.

Dunn, Joeming W.

The **brain**: a graphic novel tour. by Joeming Dunn; illustrated by Rod Espinosa.. Magic Wagon/Graphic Planet 2009 32p. Illustration (Graphic adventures. The human body)

Grades: 2 3 4 5 6

612.8; 741.5

1. Brain — Graphic novels; 2. Graphic novels

978-1-60270-683-5, $27.07

LC 2009-17650

Courtesy of ABDO Publishing.

Teacher Ms Hansen leads her Explorers class on a tour of the human brain. They learn about how the brain's different parts control body functions through the nervous system, and how people should protect their head while participating in certain physical activities, to avoid damaging the brain. The tour is very similar to the Ms Frizzle's Magic School Bus science series by way of The Fantastic Voyage in that Ms Hansen's class shrinks to microscopic size in order to get into the brain. Back matter in the

book includes a diagram of the brain, some "fun facts," a brief glossary, and information on how to use ABDO's website to find links to more information on the Internet. The author owns Antarctica Press and is also a physician; artist Espinosa has published such books as The Courageous Princess and Neotopia.

This book is part of the Graphic Adventures: The Human Body series.

The **eyes**: a graphic novel tour. illustrated by Rod Espinosa. Magic Wagon 2009 32p. Illustration (Graphic adventures. The human body)

Grades: 2 3 4 5 6

612.8; 741.5

1. Eye — Graphic novels; 2. Graphic novels

978-1-60270-684-2, $27.07

Courtesy of ABDO Publishing.

LC 2009-17651

Teacher Ms. Hansen leads her Explorers class on a tour of the human eye. They learn about how the eye functions, what purpose blinking serves, how the iris works to control the amount of light that enters the eye, and why tears are important. The tour is very similar to the Ms Frizzle's Magic School Bus science series by way of The Fantastic Voyage, in that Ms Hansen's class shrinks to microscopic size in order to get into the eye. Back matter in the book include a diagram of the eye, fun facts that include information on color blindness and vision problems, a short glossary, and information on how to use ABDO's website to find links for more information on the Internet. The author owns Antarctica Press and is also a physician; artist Espinosa has published such books as The Courageous Princess and Neotopia.

This book is part of the Graphic Adventures: The Human Body series.

H.G. Wells' The time machine. H.G. Wells; adapted by Joeming Dunn; illustrated by Ben Dunn.. ABDO Publishing Group/Magic Wagon 2008 32p. Illustration Grades: 3 4 5 6 7 8

741.5; Fic

1. Adventure graphic novels; 2. Authors; 3. Graphic novels; 4. Historians; 5. Novelists; 6. Science fiction graphic novels; 7. Science fiction writers; 8. Writers on politics; 9. Writers on science; 10. Wells, H. G. (Herbert George), 1866-1946 — Adaptations

978-1-60270-054-3, $27.07

Courtesy of ABDO Publishing.

LC 2007-6447

A gentleman hosts his friends at dinner one evening in London and then takes their leave in his time machine. When he returns, he tells them of his trip into the future, of the two peoples he encountered, the Eloi and the Morlocks, and what he learned of their relationship. When his friends refuse to believe him, the Traveler sets out again in his machine. This simplified graphic novel adaptation allows younger readers and struggling readers to get the main plot of the classic story. The book includes a brief biography of Wells and list of his other works.

Part of the Graphic Planet Graphic Classics series.

The **heart**: a graphic novel tour. by Joeming Dunn; illustrated by Rod Espinosa.. Magic Wagon/Graphic Planet 2009 32p. Illustration (Graphic adventures. The human body)

Grades: 2 3 4 5 6   **612.8; 741.5**

1. Graphic novels; 2. Heart — Graphic novels

Courtesy of ABDO Publishing.

978-1-60270-685-9, $27.07

LC 2009-17851

Teacher Ms. Hansen leads her Explorers class on a tour of the human heart. They learn about how the heart functions, how it pumps blood through the circulatory system, and the functions of the major veins and arteries. The tour is very similar to the Ms Frizzle's Magic School Bus science series by way of The Fantastic Voyage, in that Ms Hansen's class shrink to microscopic size in order to get into the bloodstream. Back matter in the book include a diagram of the heart, fun facts, a short glossary, and information on how to use ABDO's website to find links for more information on the Internet. The author owns Antarctica Press and is also a physician; artist Espinosa has published such books as The Courageous Princess and Neotopia.

Includes bibliographical references; This book is part of the Graphic Adventures: The Human Body series.

Journey to the center of the earth. adapted by Joeming Dun; illustrated by Rod Espinosa.. Magic Wagon/Graphic Planet 2009 32p. Illustration
Grades: 3 4 5 6 7
741.5; Fic
1. Adventure graphic novels; 2. Graphic novels; 3. Novelists; 4. Science fiction graphic novels; 5. Verne, Jules, 1828-1905; 6. Verne, Jules, 1828-1905 — Adaptations
978-1-60270678-1, $27.07

LC 2009-8588

Professor Otto Liedenbrock, his nephew Axel, and their guide Hans follow the instructions in an old note left by explorer Arne Saknussemm to descend into an old volcano in Iceland, seeking a way to the center of the Earth. This graphic novel provides an easy-reading adaptation of Jules Verne's classic adventure story. Back matter includes a brief biography of Verne, a list of some of his novels, and a short glossary. It is a curious addition to the Graphic Planet series called Graphic Horror, since there is no horror in the book.

This is part of the Graphic Horror Series 2.

Courtesy of ABDO Publishing.

The **kidneys**: a graphic novel tour. illustrated by Rod Espinosa.. ABDO/Magic Wagon 2009 32p. (Graphic adventures. The human body)
Grades: 2 3 4 5 6
612.2; 741.5
1. Graphic novels; 2. Kidneys — Graphic novels
978-1-60270-686-6, $27.07

LC 2009-17852

Ms. Hansen and her Explorers class, including the aliens Xeni and Zeno Zelman, take off on another tour inside the human body, this time into the kidneys, the body's filter to get rid of waste from the blood and to regulate the levels of water, salt, and other minerals. The tour starts in the blood system, into the left renal artery into the left kidney. Young readers might enjoy the fact that the Explorers exit the body through the urinary tract, which is where the kidneys send the waste called urea. This graphic novel series combines aspects of the Magic School Bus series and the movie Fantastic Voyage. The book includes additional facts about the kidneys, a glossary, and a link to find websites for more information. Dunn is a physician and owner of Antarctic Publishing, a comic book publishing house.

Part of the Graphic Adventures: The Human Body series.

The **liver**: a graphic novel tour. illustrated by Rod Espinosa.. ABDO/Magic Wagon 2009 32p. Illustration (Graphic adventures. The human body)
Grades: 2 3 4 5 6
612.2; 741.5
1. Graphic novels; 2. Liver — Graphic novels
978-1-60270-687-3, $27.07

LC 2009-17853

Courtesy of ABDO Publishing.

Ms. Hansen and her Explorers class, including the aliens Xeni and Zeno Zelman, take off on another tour inside the human body, this time into the liver. The tour starts in the mouth, through the esophagus into the stomach, then through the small intestine into the liver. The liver breaks down digested proteins and medicines, and helps to convert carbohydrates to sugars; it also stores vitamins and minerals such as iron. This graphic novel series combines aspects of the Magic School Bus series and the movie Fantastic Voyage. The book includes additional facts about the liver, a glossary, and a link to find websites for more information. Dunn is a physician and owner of Antarctic Publishing, a comic book publishing house.

Part of the Graphic Adventures: The Human Body series.

The **Lungs**: a graphic novel tour. ABDO/Magic Wagon 2009 32p. Illustration
Grades: 2 3 4 5 6
612.2; 741.5
1. Graphic novels; 2. Lungs — Graphic novels; 3. Respiratory system — Graphic novels
978-1-60270-688-0, $27.07

LC 2009-17854

Courtesy of ABDO Publishing.

Ms. Hansen and her Explorers class, including the aliens Xeni and Zeno Zelman, take off on another tour inside the human body, this time into the lungs. The tour starts in the nose, through the larynx into the trachea (windpipe), then through the bronchi into the lungs. The lungs do more than help the body breathe and circulate oxygen; they help the body to speak. This graphic novel series combines aspects of the Magic School Bus series and the movie Fantastic Voyage. The book includes additional facts about the lungs, a glossary, and a link to find websites for more information. Dunn is a physician and owner of Antarctic Publishing, a comic book publishing house.

Part of the Graphic Adventures: The Human Body series.

Peter Pan. J.M. Barrie; adapted by Joeming Dunn; illustrated by Ben Dunn. ABDO Publishing/Magic Wagon 2008 32p.
Grades: 2 3 4 5 6 **741.5; Fic**
1. Adventure graphic novels; 2. Fantasy graphic novels; 3. Graphic novels; 4. Peter Pan (Fictional character); 5. Barrie, J. M. (James Matthew), 1860-1937 — Adaptations
978-1-60270-052-9, $27.07

LC 2007-12070

John, Michael, and Wendy love hearing their mother's stories, but they don't know that another young boy has been listening to them as well. When their protective dog Nana steals Peter Pan's shadow, the children meet him and Wendy sews his shadow back. Then the children agree to return with Peter to the magical Neverland. Can they survive in a land of pirates, Lost Boys, and Tinker Bell? The book provides a simplified adaptation that introduces young readers to Barrie's classic tale. It includes a brief biography of Barrie.

Part of the Graphic Classics series

Courtesy of ABDO Publishing.

The **tell-tale** heart. adapted by Joeming Dunn; illustrated by Rod Espinosa.. Magic Wagon/Graphic Planet 2009 32p. Illustration
Grades: 6 7 8 9 10
741.5; Fic
1. Graphic novels; 2. Guilt — Graphic novels; 3. Homicide — Graphic novels; 4. Horror graphic novels; 5. Poe, Edgar Allan, 1809-1849 — Adaptations
978-1-60270681-1, $27.07

LC 2009-8589

Courtesy of ABDO Publishing.

The young narrator takes care of an old man; he tells the reader he has had no reason to do harm, he never felt any greed for the old man's wealth. However, he hates what he calls the old man's vulture eye, and his hatred of that eye makes him determined to kill the old man so he would never have to look on it again. When he finally murders the old man, however, it's not the eye, but the imagined sound of the old man's beating heart that drives the young killer insane. This easy-reading graphic novel adaptation of Edgar Allan Poe's short story provides a good introduction to Poe's work for reluctant and struggling readers; the emotional intensity of the work makes it more suitable for older readers despite the simplicity of language. Back matter includes a brief biography of Poe, a list of some of his other works, and a short glossary.

This is part of the Graphic Horror Series 2.

Dwinell, Kim
Surfside girls: the secret of Danger Point. by Kim Dwinell. Top Shelf Productions 2017 235 p. Color; Illustration
Grades: 3 4 5 6
741.5; Fic
1. Surfing — Fiction; 2. Friendship — Fiction; 3. Summer — Fiction
9781603094115, $19.99; 1603094113

Courtesy of IDW Publishing

In this book, by Kim Dwinell, "things are getting weird in Surfside. Lately, Samantha's best friend Jade explodes into fits of giggles whenever she sees a boy, and it's throwing a wrench into the kick-back summer of surfing and hanging out that Sam had planned. But after swimming through a secret underwater cave, Sam starts to... see things. Like ghosts. And pirates. And maybe something even scarier! Can she and Jade get to the bottom of this mystery in time to save their town?" (Publisher's note)

"First-time graphic novelist Dwinell creates spacious panels with a less-is-more approach to detail that evokes the wide-open ocean and beach environment, keeps readers focused on the characters and their concerns, and creates a sense of otherness where the pallid ghosts are concerned." Pub Wkly

Dysart, Joshua
★ **Captain** Gravity and the Power of the Vril. Penny-Farthing Press 2006 193p. Illustration
Grades: 8 9 10 11 12
741.5; Fic
1. Adventure graphic novels; 2. Graphic novels; 3. Superhero graphic novels
0-9719012-8-7, $19.95

Courtesy of Penny-Farthing Productions

Some years before, a young African American named Joshua Jones stumbled upon a mysterious stone at an archeological dig and became infused with an element from the stone that gave him power over gravity, including flight. He hid his identity with a helmet and became Captain Gravity. Now it's the 1930s, and Joshua Jones works in Hollywood with the two friends who know his secret. They've been making Captain Gravity movies, and no one else has figured out that the hero is Black. Now, Nazis are searching for the original source of what they call Vril, Joshua's power, and they plan to use it to conquer the Earth. Only Captain Gravity can stop them, and he has to chase them all over the world and to the lost city of Atlantis.

A young, evil Adolf Hitler, an unusual hero for the time, and a story that harks back to the Golden Age of comics storytelling all add up to a great story for this time.

Edginton, Ian
Kingdom of the Wicked. Dark Horse Comics 2004 120p. Illustration
Grades: 8 9 10 11 12 Adult   **741.5; Fic**
1. Adventure graphic novels; 2. Fantasy graphic novels; 3. Graphic novels
1-59307-187-6, $15.95

Christopher Grahame is the premier children's author of the twenty-first century, a publishing phenomenon. With his work translated into everything from Aborigine to Zulu, he is the cornerstone of a multi-million dollar, franchise spewing empire. Is it any surprise then that under all this pressure something has to give? Unfortunately, it's Chris's mind. Stricken by mysterious headaches and blackouts that plagued his childhood, Chris once again finds himself walking the avenues and boulevards of Castrovalva — the fantasy realm he dreamt up as a boy, to while away his recuperation. But like Chris, Castrovalva has also changed. Deluged in mud, blood, and barbed wire, war has come to wonderland. Chris tries to tell himself it's all a bad dream...so why can't he wake up? The book includes violence, strong language, and brief nudity.

Eisenberg, Adam
The **Creation** of Iron Man. Rosen Publishing Group 2006 48p. Illustration
Grades: 4 5 6 7 8 9 10   **741.5**
1. Graphic novels; 2. Iron Man (Fictional character); 3. Superhero graphic novels
978-1-4042-0767-7, $29.25

LC 2006000167

This volume discusses the unique character of Tony Stark, developed by Stan Lee and Jack Kirby, who was unable to live a normal life and invented a special iron suit that gave him superpowers. The book includes information about the times in which Lee and Kirby worked at Marvel Comics.

Part of the Action Heroes series.

Eisinger, Justin

Star Trek: Alien spotlight volume 1. IDW Publishing 2008 152p. Illustration

Grades: 6 7 8 9 10 11 12 Adult   **741.5; Fic**

1. Adventure graphic novels; 2. Graphic novels; 3. Science fiction graphic novels; 4. Star Trek — Graphic novels

978-1-60010-179-3, $19.99

This volume collects a series of one-shots (standalone comics issues), each devoted to one of the alien races featured in the Star Trek series. Readers meet the Gorns, Vulcans, Andorians, Orions, the Borg, and the Romulans in stories that also give the aliens' point of view. The stories are set in the various time periods of the Star Trek universe; for example, Captain Clark Terrell and Pavel Chekov (before they were captured by Khan in "The Wrath of Khan") and their landing party encounter the Gorns on a planet designed to train Gorn warriors, while Captain Picard encounters the Borg.

Eisner, Will

The **Best** of the Spirit. DC Comics 2005 187p. Illustration

Grades: 7 8 9 10 11 12 Adult   **741.5; Fic**

1. Graphic novels; 2. Superhero graphic novels; 3. The Spirit (Fictional character); 4. Spirit (Fictional character)

1-4012-0755-3, $14.99; 9781401207557

Legendary comics creator Will Eisner created The Spirit in 1940, and over the twelve years of its initial publication, he used it to revolutionize the cartooning medium, creating new methods of storytelling, developing new depths of characterization, and inventing such artistic innovations as the splash page. This volume reprints 22 stories from the original run, including the origin story from 1940; the bulk of the stories were initially published in the mid- to late-1940s. These stories allow people to get acquainted with The Spirit, who was a young criminologist named Denny Colt; believed to have been murdered, he was buried in a state of suspended animation and awoke one day in the Wildwood Cemetery. He has since dedicated himself to fighting crime, wearing a suit, fedora, and mask. DC Comics started publishing a new incarnation of The Spirit in 2007, and a motion picture is in the works.

The **Last** Knight: An Introduction to Don Quixote. NBM Publishing 2000 32p. Illustration

Grades: 3 4 5 6 7 8 9 10   **741.5; Fic**

1. Adventure graphic novels; 2. Graphic novels; 3. Novelists; 4. Poets; 5. Cervantes Saavedra, Miguel de, 1547-1616 — Adaptations

1-56163-251-1; 978-1-56163-251-0, $15.95

LC 2001-265049

This is Eisner's graphic novel remake of Don Quixote. Here are the adventures of a Spanish country gentleman and his companion who set out, like knights of old, to search for adventure. As the subtitle says, this book hits the highlights and serves to introduce the classic tale to younger readers.

Moby Dick. by Herman Melville; adapted by Will Eisner. NBM Publishing 2001 32p. Illustration

Grades: 3 4 5 6 7 8 9 10   **741.5; Fic**

1. Adventure graphic novels; 2. Graphic novels; 3. Whaling — Graphic novels

1-56163-293-7, $15.95; 1-56163-294-5 (pa)

LC 2001-032989

Ishmael, a sailor, recounts the ill-fated voyage of a whaling ship led by the fanatical Captain Ahab in search of the white whale that had crippled him. Eisner's adaptation hits the highlights of the novel.

The **Princess** and the Frog. NBM Publishing 1999 32p. Illustration

Grades: 3 4 5 6 7 8 9 10   **741.5; Fic**

1. Fairy tales — Graphic novels; 2. Fantasy graphic novels; 3. Graphic novels

1-56163-244-9, $15.95; 1-56163-346-1 (pa)

A good prince, turned into a frog by a spiteful wizard, exacts from a princess a promise which she is reluctant to fulfill, despite his kindness and her desire not to hurt him. Comics master Will Eisner adapted the familiar tale by the Brothers Grimm.

Ellerton, Sarah

Inverloch, Volume 1. Seven Seas 2006 un Illustration

Grades: 4 5 6 7 8 9 10 11 12   **741.5; Fic**

1. Adventure graphic novels; 2. Fantasy graphic novels; 3. Graphic novels

1-933164-13-1, $14.99

In a world where humans, elves, and other beings coexist, albeit not altogether peacefully, Acheron is a young da'kor, a horned wolf-like race that lives in the forests. He encounters a beautiful elf and takes her quest for his own — to find another elf who went missing twelve years before. Teased by his brothers as a lousy hunter, feared by humans who think da'kor are dangerous beasts, innocent Acheron finds that the world beyond the forest is full of danger, intrigue, and betrayal.

This story began online as a webcomic.

Ellis, Grace

★ **Lumberjanes**; Volume 1: Beware the kitten holy. written by Noelle Stevenson & Grace Ellis; illustrated by Brooke Allen; colors by Maarta Laiho; letters by Aubrey Aiese; created by Shannon Watters, Grace Ellis & Noelle Stevenson. Boom! Studios 2015 128 p. Illustration; Color (Lumberjanes)

Grades: 6 7 8 9 10 11 12 Adult   **741.5; Fic**

1. Female friendship — Graphic novels; 2. Monsters — Fiction; 3. Camps — Fiction; 4. Summer — Fiction; 5. Adventure fiction

1608866874; 9781608866878, $14.99

Eisner Award: Best New Series (2015); Eisner Award: Best Publication for Teens (2015); Harvey Award: Best New Series (2015); Harvey Award: Best Original Graphic Publication For Young Readers (2015)

"[This] graphic novel begins mid-adventure as five campers are out after hours investigating a strange event that they all witnessed: a woman turning into a giant bear. This is just the first of many odd occurrences that Jo, April, Molly, Mal, and Ripley encounter at the summer camp for 'Hardcore Lady Types.' The Lumberjanes, as the scouts are called, band together to solve puzzles, defeat three-eyed creatures, and escape the ire of their watchful counselor Jen." (School Library Journal)

"Humorously riffing on everything from scout badges to the X-Men to feminist heroes…, it's a sharp, smart, and most of all fun celebration of sisterhood." Pub Wkly

Volume 1 of an ongoing series

Lumberjanes; Volume 2: Friendship to the Max. by Noelle Stevenson, Grace Ellis, illustrated by Brooke A Allen, contributed by Shannon Watters. Boom! Studios 2015 112 p. Color; Illustration

Grades: 6 7 8 9 10 11 12 Adult   **741.5; Fic**

1. Fantasy graphic novels; 2. Teenage girls — Fiction; 3. Camping — Fiction

1608867374; 9781608867370, $14.99

"Jo, April, Mal, Molly and Ripley are five best pals determined to have an awesome summer together...and they're not gonna let any insane quest or an array of supernatural critters get in their way! But having stumbled onto a mysterious force wreaking havoc in the camp, it's a race through the woods as the Lumberjanes work together to save not only their friends, but maybe even the whole world!" (Publisher's note)

Enoki, Nobuaki

School Judgment 1: Gakkyu Hotei. story by Nobuaki Enoki; art by Takeshi Obata; translation, Mari Morimoto. Viz 2016 192 p. Illustration
Grades: 7 8 9 10 11 12 **741.5; Fic**
1. Shonen manga; 2. School stories — Graphic novels
1421585669; 9781421585666, $9.99

"In order to curb the crime running rampant in the elementary school system, a new solution has been enacted in the form of the School Judgment System. Now the young students themselves will be responsible for solving the issues that befall them. But are they up for the task?" (Publisher's note)
Volume 1 of 3

Espinosa, Rod

Around the world in 80 days. adapted and illustrated by Rod Espinosa.. ABDO/Red Wagon 2008 32p. Illustration
Grades: 3 4 5 6 7 8 9
741.5; Fic
1. Adventure graphic novels; 2. Verne, Jules, 1828-1905 — Adaptations
978-1-60270-050-5, $27.07

LC 2007-6444

Courtesy of ABDO Publishing.

In 1872, English gentleman Phileas Fogg makes a wager that he can travel around the world in just 80 days. Unfortunately, at the time of his wager, a daring robber has made off with a fortune, and Scotland Yard detective Fix is convinced Fogg is the villain. The chase is on, around the world. This comic book adaptation has been written for younger, reluctant, and struggling readers and provides highlights of the adventures in the original novel by Verne. The book includes a brief biography of Verne, a short list of some of his other works, and a brief glossary.

The **courageous** princess; Volume 3: The Dragon Queen. by Rod Espinosa. Dark Horse Books 2015 180 p. Illustration
Grades: 4 5 6 7 8 **741.5**
1. Graphic novels; 2. Princesses — Fiction; 3. Adventure graphic novels
1616557249; 9781616557249, $19.99

LC 2014037517

In this book, by Rod Espinosa, "Princess Mabelrose has journeyed far and saved herself and others from danger and tyranny, but she has yet to make her way home. In the conclusion to the Courageous Princess trilogy, Mabelrose must use her generous spirit, as well as her brains, to melt the heart of the Dragon Queen and gain her freedom. But she still has to bring her father and her friends back from the queen's unreachable Unremembered Lands." (Publisher's note)

"Espinosa's artwork leaps from the pages with action and vivid colors, with clean and easy-to-follow panels. Animal and human characters are distinctive and diverse." SLJ

★ The **courageous** princess; Volume 1: Beyond the hundred kingdoms. by Rod Espinosa. Dark Horse Books 2015 245 p Color; Illustration
Grades: 3 4 5 6 7 8 **741.5; Fic**

1. Adventure and adventurers — Comic books, strips, etc.; 2. Princesses — Comic books, strips, etc.; 3. Princesses — Juvenile fiction
9781616557225, $19.99

"Princess Mabelrose may not be the fairest of the land, but she has enough brains and bravery to fend for herself in a fantasy world of danger and adventure! From a mighty dragon with an army of trolls to a tyrant tiger king, Mabelrose meets each challenge with pluck and intelligence, winning the help and friendship of the many kindred spirits she encounters in her quest to find her way home." (Publisher's note)
Other volumes in this series are: The unencumbered lands; The dragon queen

The **courageous** princess; Volume 2: The unremembered lands. by Rod Espinosa. Dark Horse Books 2015 237 p Color; Illustration
Grades: 3 4 5 6 7 8 **741.5; Fic**
1. Fantasy; 2. Princesses — Juvenile fiction
9781616557232, $19.99

"The smart and plucky Princess Mabelrose has escaped a dragon and freed the people of Leptia from a tyrant. Journeying home, Mabelrose discovers that her father was coming to her rescue-but now, he and a posse of princes are the ones who need rescuing! So Mabelrose begins a new quest..." (Publisher's note)

Lewis and Clark. ABDO/Magic Wagon 2008 32p. Illustration (Bio-graphics)
Grades: 3 4 5 6 7 8 9
917.8; 92; 741.5; 917
1. Lewis and Clark Expedition (1804-1806) — Graphic novels; 2. Biographical graphic novels; 3. Explorers; 4. Graphic novels; 5. Territorial governors; 6. Clark, William, 1770-1838; 7. Lewis, Meriwether, 1774-1809; 8. West (U.S.) — Exploration — Graphic novels
978-1-60270-069-7, $27.07

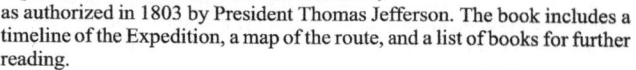

LC 2007-5578

Courtesy of ABDO Publishing.

This graphic format book tells the story of the Lewis and Clark Expedition, which explored the land of the Louisiana Purchase, as authorized in 1803 by President Thomas Jefferson. The book includes a timeline of the Expedition, a map of the route, and a list of books for further reading.

Lewis Carroll's Alice in Wonderland. adapted and illustrated by Rod Espinosa. Antarctic Press 2007 un Illustration
Grades: 4 5 6 7 8 9 **741.5**
1. Adventure graphic novels; 2. Fantasy graphic novels; 3. Graphic novels; 4. Humorous graphic novels
978-0-9787725-8-1, $14.95

Espinosa (The Courageous Princess) adapts Lewis Carroll's classic tale into a graphic novel full of pop culture references (check out the Mad Hatter, for instance). It's still the original story, which starts when the daydreaming Alice sees a rabbit checking his pocket watch and runs after him, only to find herself in a strange world with bizarre creatures.

The **prince** of heroes, chapter I. Antarctic Press 2008 un Illustration
Grades: 8 9 10 11 12
741.5; Fic
1. Adventure graphic novels; 2. Graphic novels; 3. Science fiction graphic novels
978-0-9801255-0-4, $14.95

Courtesy of ABDO Publishing.

Ronen and his mother Aiymie have lived on the planet Irdne for years; now she tells him they must leave and travel to the edge of the universe to meet his father. She refuses to tell Ronen who he is, or to what Darem clan they belong, and this has made them outcasts in Darem society. Then they learn that the Nationalist Armada, a fleet of thousands of ships, is on its way to take over Irdne, and all Darem colonials must leave. Ronen must leave his friends, and his martial arts teacher, behind. During a fight with Baron Ermont Mesozora and Baroness Mazza Mesozora, Ronen strips Mazza's clothing from her; nothing really shows, but it's clear she has lost her pants.

Estes, Max

Coffee and Donuts: A Junkyard Cats Comic. Top Shelf Productions 2006 112p. Illustration

Grades: 6 7 8 9 10 11 12 Adult   **741.5; Fic**

1. Cats — Graphic novels; 2. Graphic novels; 3. Humorous graphic novels

1-891830-80-5, $10

Dwight and Jules live in an unused dumpster and scavenge their food; every morning a mystery person leaves coffee and donuts for them. When, desperate for money, they try (and fail) to rob an armored truck, real crooks Myles and Moose try to force them into real crime.

Farrens, Brian

William Shakespeare's King Lear. adapted by Brian Farrens; illustrated by Ben Dunn.. ABDO/Magic Wagon 2008 48p. Illustration

Grades: 5 6 7 8 9 10   **822.3; 741.5**

1. Authors; 2. Dramatists; 3. Graphic novels; 4. Poets; 5. Shakespeare, William, 1564-1616 — Adaptations

978-1-60270-189-2, $28.50

LC 2008-10739

King Lear divides his kingdom among his three daughters but disowns Cordelia, the youngest, when she refuses to flatter him with insincerity. Then his older daughters renege on their promise to care for him, and he goes mad and roams the countryside. Meanwhile, Edmund, the illegitimate son of the Earl of Gloucester, plays political games in his quest for power. This graphic novel adaptation retains some of the original language from Shakespeare's play, while paring down the story to appeal to struggling readers. The book includes a short biography, a summary of the play, a glossary, and a short selection of famous lines and phrases from the play.

Part of the Graphic Shakespeare series

Fein, Eric

The **Creation** of the Fantastic Four. Rosen Publishing Group 2006 48p. Illustration

Grades: 4 5 6 7 8 9 10   **741.5**

1. Fantastic Four (Fictional character); 2. Graphic novels; 3. Superhero graphic novels

978-1-4042-0765-3, $29.25

LC 2005031170

Describes the history and development of the action heroes called the Fantastic Four and how they got their superpowers. Created in 1961 by the Marvel power team of Jack Kirby and Stan Lee, the Fantastic Four was the first superhero team the men created.

Part of the Action Heroes series.

The **Creation** of the Incredible Hulk. Rosen Publishing Group 2006 48p. Illustration

Grades: 4 5 6 7 8 9 10   **741.5**

1. Graphic novels; 2. Superhero graphic novels; 3. Hulk (Fictional character)

978-1-4042-0764-6, $29.25

LC 2005035267

Discusses the unique character developed in 1962 by Stan Lee and Jack Kirby who was unable to live a normal life after he was affected by a gamma bomb's blast and Dr. Bruce Banner became the huge, inarticulate, super-strong Hulk. The book also includes information on the cultural climate in the U.S. at the time, and on the way the two men worked together at Marvel Comics.

Part of the Action Heroes series.

Fingeroth, Danny

Action Heroes: The Creation of the X-Men. Rosen Publishing Group, Inc. 2007 48p. Illustration

Grades: 3 4 5 6 7 8   **741.5**

1. Graphic novels; 2. X-Men (Fictional characters)

1-4042-0762-7 (lib bdg), $29.25

Veteran Marvel Comics writer Fingeroth gives young readers a brief introduction to the creation of the Marvel superhero team, the X-Men. The book focuses on the two creators, Stan Lee and Jack Kirby, and also discusses the state of the comics industry in the early 1960s, as well as the cultural/social background that led Lee and Kirby to create a team of mutant superheroes. It includes a timeline of the X-Men creators, highlights from the long-running series, a glossary, books for further reading, and a bibliography. Photographs and color reproductions of the art highlight the book. Due to the popular series of X-Men movies, people know the characters, even if they've never read the comics.

Fletcher, Brenden

Gotham Academy; Volume 1: Welcome to Gotham Academy. Becky Cloonan, Brenden Fletcher; illustrated by Karl Kerschl. DC Comics 2015 160 p. Color; Illustration

Grades: 7 8 9 10 11 12   **741.5**

1. Amnesia — Fiction; 2. School stories

9781401254728, $14.99

LC 2015007185

"Gotham Academy [is] the most prestigious school in Gotham City. Only the best and brightest students may enter its halls, study in its classrooms, explore its secret passages, summon its terrifying spirits... Okay, so Gotham Academy isn't like other schools. But Olive Silverlock isn't like other students. After a mysterious incident over summer break, she's back at school with a bad case of amnesia." (Publisher's note)

"Filled with spunky and quirky characters and unexpected plot turns, this work adds an intriguing and fresh layer to the Batman mythos.... Kerschl's campy art is by turns luminous and gloomy, enhancing Cloonan and Fletcher's energetic and sometimes contemplative text." SLJ

Originally published in single magazine form as Gotham Academy #1-6; Other Gotham Academy volumes are: Volume 2, Calamity (2016); Volume 3, Yearbook (2016); Second Semester Volume 1, Welcome Back (2017); Second Semester Volume 2 (2017)

Flood, Joe

Sharks: nature's perfect hunter. Joe Flood. First Second 2018 128 p. Color; Illustration (Science comics)

Grades: 3 4 5 6 7   **597.3; 741.5**

1. Animals; 2. Sharks; 3. Marine animals

9781626727878, $19.99; 9781626727885

LC 2017941169

This book, in the Science Comics series, by Joe Flood, looks "at the dynamic hammerhead, infamous great white, primordial megalodon, and the gentle nurse shark, the rare species that will let a scuba diver pet them! This book is filled to the gills with jaw-dropping illustrations and razor-sharp facts that shed light on these fascinating creatures of the deep, including their undersea terrain, cunning adaptability, and staggering variety." (Publisher's note)

"Flood addresses the lore and fear that surrounds these predators, most of it coming from literature and the media. Detailed illustrations complement the text beautifully, with close-ups of the various features of different sharks as well as useful diagrams and charts." SLJ

Flores, Madeleine
Help us! Great Warrior. written and illustrated by Madeleine Flores; colors by Trillian Gunn. Boom! Box 2016 160 p. Color; Illustration
Grades: 5 6 7 8 9 10   **741.5; Fic**
1. Courage — Fiction; 2. Demonology — Fiction; 3. Fantasy fiction — Fiction; 4. Fantasy graphic novels
1608868028; 9781608868025, $19.99
This book "is about a very powerful (but deceptively tiny) Great Warrior who protects her village from evil-doers and looks rad while doing it! Possessing great strength and even greater self-confidence, she's ready to kick some butts and save everyone, especially hunks/pals/handsome skeletons. But Great Warrior has a secret...and will her friends stand by her side when they find it out?" (Publisher's note)
"The art is clean and colorful and ideal for the tone, which is similar to the TV show Adventure Time but a bit more accessible. The book also carries the same message about friendship and self-esteem." SLJ
Originally published in single magazine form as Help us! Great Warrior No. 1-6

Fontana, Shea
Date with disaster: a graphic novel. Shea Fontana; illustrated by Yancey Labat. Dc Comics 2018 127 p. Color; Illustration (DC Super Hero Girls)
Grades: 3 4 5 6   **741.5; Fic**
1. Teenage girls — Fiction; 2. Superheroes — Fiction; 3. Women superheroes — Fiction
1401278787; 9781401278786, $9.99
"Catwoman is out alone on the prowl one night when KABOOM — an explosion at S.T.A.R. Labs rouses the other girls from their slumber. Star students Batgirl and Lois Lane both know the lab incident is fishy, and they meet later to share clues. But nothing could've prepared Batgirl for what they see next — Batgirl's dad on a date!" (Publisher's note)

Forget, Thomas
The **Creation** of Captain America. Rosen Publishing Group 2006 48p. Illustration
Grades: 4 5 6 7 8 9 10   **741.5**
1. Captain America (Fictional character); 2. Graphic novels; 3. Superhero graphic novels
978-1-4042-0766-0, $29.25
                                              LC 2005032024
Captain America has been a hero since 1940 and saved comic books and Marvel Comic Group. This volume discusses the times during which Cap was created and how the character has changed over the years. In light of the character's death in the aftermath of the Marvel Civil War storyline that played out in comics during 2006 and 2007, this book may have wide appeal.
Part of the Action Heroes series.

Forsythe, Matthew
Jinchalo. Matthew Forsythe. Drawn & Quarterly 2012 120 p. Illustration
Grades: 3 4 5 6 7 8   **Fic; 741.5/971**
1. Fantasy comics books, strips, etc; 2. Fantasy graphic novels; 3. Spirits — Fiction
1770460675; 9781770460676, $17.95
                                              LC 2012379212

This graphic novel, by Matthew Forsythe, is a "companion to...[the author's] 'Ojingogo,'...[staring] the same little girl as its heroine. When the mischievous shape-shifter Jinchalo hatches from a mysterious egg,...magical troubles drag the pair out of the safety of her home, through the small village where she resides, up, up, and away. In the course of their flight, they visit a robot garden, follow a vine into the clouds, and leave the village far behind." (Publisher's note)

Fox, Gardner
The **Atom** Archives Volume 2. DC Comics 2003 215p. Illustration
Grades: 7 8 9 10 11 12 Adult   **741.5; Fic**
1. Atom (Fictional character); 2. Graphic novels; 3. Superhero graphic novels
1-4012-0014-1, $49.95
This volume, reprinting The Atom issues #6-13, originally published in 1963 through 1964, features Mighty Mite's early team-ups with Hawkman and Hawkgirl, the classic villainy of Dr. Light, the return of Chronos, and much more. This Archive Edition reprints the comics in full color in a hardcover edition.

Showcase Presents: Adam Strange Volume One. DC Comics 2007 510p. Illustration
Grades: 6 7 8 9 10 11 12 Adult   **741.5; Fic**
1. Graphic novels; 2. Superhero graphic novels
978-1-4012-1313-8, $16.99
After being mysteriously teleported to a distant world by an alien scientist, Adam Strange went from being an Earth archaeologist to a cosmic adventurer. He soon becomes the hero of the planet Rann, shuttling between his old and new worlds via the Zeta Beam. With the love of his life, Alanna, daughter of Rann's leading scientist, they embark on a series of adventures against all types of space menaces. This black and white volume reprints stories from 1958 through 1963.

Showcase Presents: Hawkman Volume 1. DC Comics 2007 560p. Illustration
Grades: 7 8 9 10 11 12 Adult   **741.5; Fic**
1. Graphic novels; 2. Hawkman (Fictional character); 3. Superhero graphic novels
978-1-4012-1280-3, $16.99
Katar Hol and his wife Shayera, winged law officers from the planet Thanagar, visit Earth to learn about terrestrial police methods. To fit into human society, they adopt the civilian identities of Carter Hall, the curator of the Midway City Museum, and Shiera, his assistant. Dressed in their avian Thanagarian garb, Carter and Shiera patrol the skies of Midway City as Hawkman and Hawkgirl. They plunge headlong into the battle for justice against such villains as the Shadow Thief and Matter Master. With their array of alien weaponry and their scientific skill, this crime-fighting duo continue to defend Earth against nefarious threats. This book collects black and white reprints of thirty-three stories written by Fox, dating from 1961 through 1966 and featuring the work of artists such as Joe Kubert, Murphy Anderson, and Carmine Infantino.

Showcase Presents: Justice League of America Volume 1. all stories written by Gardner Fox; all stories pencilled by Mike Sekowsky ... [et al.]. DC Comics 2005 544p. Illustration
Grades: 6 7 8 9 10 11 12 Adult   **741.5; Fic**
1. Aquaman (Fictitious character); 2. Graphic novels; 3. Justice League of America (Fictional characters); 4. Superhero graphic novels; 5. Green Arrow (Fictional character); 6. Wonder Woman (Fictional character); 7. Superman (Fictional character); 8. Batman (Fictional character); 9. Flash (Fictional character); 10. Green Lantern (Fictional character)
1-4012-0761-8, $16.99
Some of the greatest super heroes in the DC Universe united to form the Justice League of America: Superman, Batman, Wonder Woman, the

Flash, Green Lantern, Martian Manhunter, and Aquaman. Together, they face such foes as Dr. Light, Dr. Destiny, Starro, Felix Faust, Amos Fortune, and the Weapons Master. This volume includes the stories in which the JLS inducts new members to the team: Green Arrow and the Atom. In light of the events in Infinite Crisis, readers might be interested to see how far back the roots of the story went — all the way back to 1960. This black and white reprint volume includes stories published from 1960 through 1962.

Showcase Presents: The Elongated Man Volume 1. writers, John Broome and Gardner Fox; artists, Carmine Infantino [and others]. DC Comics 2006 560p. Illustration
Grades: 6 7 8 9 10 11 12 Adult   **741.5; Fic**
  1. Elongated Man (Fictional characters); 2. Graphic novels; 3. Superhero graphic novels
  978-1-4012-1042-7, $16.99
  Ralph Dibny is the Elongated Man, a self-taught superhero who has harnessed the power of the exotic gingo fruit and attained the ability to stretch himself to fantastic lengths. As the only costumed hero whose identity has been revealed to the world, Elongated Man travels the globe with his adoring wife Sue, solving mysteries and gaining renown for his singular elastic talent. In these stories, originally published from 1960 to 1968 and reprinted here in black and white, Dibny sometimes teams up with the Flash, Batman and Robin, Green Lantern, and Zatanna. Ralph and Sue Dibny were at the heart of the Identity Crisis, so readers might want to see their early adventures.

Frampton, Otis

Oddly Normal; Volume 1. written and illustrated by Otis Frampton. Image Comics 2015 128 p. Illustration
Grades: 4 5 6 7 8   **741.5; Fic**
  1. Fantasy graphic novels; 2. Graphic novels; 3. Humorous graphic novels
  9781632152268, $9.99; 1632152266
  "Oddly must travel to Fignation to uncover the mystery of her parents' disappearance. Join Oddly as she navigates a strange new school, teenage angst, monstrous bullies, and Evil itself on an unforgettable fantasy adventure through the vibrant world of Fignation in Oddly Normal." (Publisher's note)
  First published 2006 by Viper Comics; Volume 1 of 3

Oddly Normal; Volume 2. written & illustrated by Otis Frampton. Image Comics 2015 Color; Illustration
Grades: 4 5 6 7 8   **741.5; Fic**
  1. Monsters — Graphic novels; 2. School stories; 3. Witches — Graphic novels
  1632154846; 9781632154842, $9.99
  "Oddly, the green-haired half witch, is now living with her great-aunt in Fignation after the mysterious disappearance of her parents. After using memory fragments to help reassure Oddly that she was, indeed, wanted and loved by her mom and dad, Auntie Oddly is thrilled when Oddly is invited to a party. Oddly is finally making friends in Fignation! Sure, they may not be the most popular kids in school, but maybe that doesn't matter, especially when they find even the most mundane things, like the hokey pokey, utterly fascinating." (Booklist)
  Collects Oddly Normal issues #6-10

Oddly Normal; Volume 3. written & illustrated by Otis Frampton. Image Comics 2016 Color; Illustration
Grades: 4 5 6 7 8   **741.5; Fic**
  1. Witches — Graphic novels; 2. School stories; 3. Monsters — Graphic novels
  9781632156921, $9.99; 163215692X
  Collects Oddly Normal #11-15

"Oddly Normal's adventures in Fignation continue with Rocketball games, broom races and life changing revelations." (Publisher's note)

Franklin, Tee

★ **Bingo** love. Tee Franklin; illustrated by Jenn St-Onge, Joy San and Genevieve FT. Image Comics 2018 88 p. Color; Illustration
Grades: 8 9 10 11 12 Adult   **741.5**
  1. Lesbians — Fiction; 2. Grandmothers — Fiction
  1534307508; 9781534307506, $9.99
  In this book, by Tee Franklin, illustrated by Jenn St.Onge, Joy San and Genevieve FT, "when Hazel Johnson and Mari McCray met at church bingo in 1963, it was love at first sight. Forced apart by their families and society, Hazel and Mari both married young men and had families.... Now in their mid-'60s,...[they] reunite again at a church bingo hall. Realizing their love for each other is still alive, what these grandmothers do next takes absolute strength and courage." (Publisher's note)
  "Teens and young adults tend to dominate love plots, so it's refreshing to see a romantic tale built around people who age from adolescence through elderhood. Delightful yet realistic, the teen-graded story also works for adults and sophisticated tweens." LJ

Fujimaki, Tadatoshi

Kuroko's Basketball; Volumes 1 & 2. Tadatoshi Fujimaki; translation, Caleb Cook. Viz 2016 384 p. Illustration
Grades: 7 8 9 10 11 12   **741.5; Fic**
  1. Shonen manga; 2. Basketball — Fiction; 3. Manga
  1421587718; 9781421587714, $16.99
  "Kuroko Tetsuya doesn't stand out much.... Though he's just as unremarkable on the basketball court, that's where his plainness gives him an unexpected edge.... And now that he's a high school student, he's on a mission to defeat each member of his legendary middle school team, known as the Miracle Generation, with the help of a new transfer student fresh from the U.S.-Taiga Kagami!" (Publisher's note)
  Volumes 1 and 2 of 30

Fujisaki, Ryu

Hoshin Engi Volume 1. Viz Media/Shonen Jump 2007 192p. Illustration
Grades: 8 9 10 11 12 Adult   **741.5; Fic**
  1. Adventure graphic novels; 2. Fantasy graphic novels; 3. Graphic novels; 4. Manga; 5. Shonen manga
  978-1-4215-1362-1, $7.99
  When his clan is wiped out by a beautiful demon, young Taikobo finds himself in charge of the mysterious Hoshin Project. Its mission: find all immortals living in the human world and seal them away forever. But who do you trust — and whose side are you really on — when you've been trained to hunt demons by a demon. There is demon-fighting action.

Fujishima, Kosuke

Oh My Goddess! Volume 1. story and art by Kosuke Fujishima. Dark Horse Comics 2005 192p. Illustration
Grades: 8 9 10 11 12   **741.5; Fic**
  1. Fantasy graphic novels; 2. Graphic novels; 3. Humorous graphic novels; 4. Manga; 5. Shonen manga
  1593073879; 9781593073879, $10.95
  Alone in his dorm on a Saturday night, Nekomi Tech student Keiichi Morisato dials a wrong number that will change his life forever — reaching the Goddess Technical Help Line. Granted one wish by the charming young goddess Belldandy — a wish for anything in the world — Keiichi wishes she would stay with him always. Complications are bound to ensue from this; the immediate first being the new couple getting tossed out of the dorm — it's males only. As the hapless student and his mysterious "foreign

beauty" ride around looking for a new place to stay — risking the different dangers of seeking shelter with an otaku convinced Belldandy is an imaginary woman, and a Zen priest convinced she's a sinister witch — Keiichi's still got his classes on Monday morning. How is his new "exchange student" companion going to be received on the N.I.T. campus? A little too well for normal life to ever return... This is the beginning of the series in a new edition that restores the original right-to-left page orientation and includes a notes section. This classic "harem" manga has very mild sexual innuendo and focuses more on the comedy.

Volume 1 of 48

Fujiyama, Kairi
Dragon Eye, Volume 1. Ballantine Books/Del Rey Manga 2007 192p. Illustration
Grades: 8 9 10 11 12   **741.5; Fic**
   1. Adventure graphic novels; 2. Graphic novels; 3. Manga; 4. Science fiction graphic novels; 5. Shonen manga
   978-0-345-49665-2, $10.95
   Ten years before, a deadly virus devastated the world, turning its victims into bloodthirsty Dracules; human soon learned that the only cure is death. The people who rose up to fight the Dracules are called VIUS. Now, in the VIUS city Mikuni, a new recruit named Leila Mikami joins VIUS; she's determined to find a Dragon Eye, a powerful magic weapon she plans to use to get revenge for her family's death. To her surprise, bumbling recruit Issa Kazuma is actually a VIUS captain, and when top-level Dracules invade the candidates' final exam, he reveals his Dragon Eye. Leila joins Kazuma's Squad Zero as they work to protect Mikuni from Dracules. This first volume offers lots of action and monster killing.

Fukuchi, Tsubasa
   The **Law** of Ueki Vol. 1. Viz Media 2006 192p. Illustration
Grades: 7 8 9 10 11 12   **741.5; Fic**
   1. Graphic novels; 2. Humorous graphic novels; 3. Manga; 4. Shonen manga
   978-1-4215-0716-3, $9.99
   In a world of powerful celestial beings, an epic contest is being conducted to select the next king. Each Celestial selects a kid in junior high to be his champion and grants him a special power. The kids battle it out, losers are eliminated, and the winners are granted new talents. Seemingly ordinary Kosuke Ueki has been chosen to be a contender in the tournament. Granted the power to change trash into trees, Ueki has two disadvantages to overcome: one, he doesn't know he's a participant in the tournament, and two, how the heck can anyone win a battle with the power to turn trash into trees? Especially when his first opponent has power over fire?

Fulop, Scott D.
   Archie Americana Series: Best of the Forties Volume 1. Archie Comics 1991 128p. Illustration
Grades: 3 4 5 6 7 8 9 10 11 12 Adult   **741.5; Fic**
   1. Andrews, Archie (Fictional character); 2. Graphic novels; 3. Humorous graphic novels
   1-879794-00-4, $11.95
   In 1941, Pep Comics introduced Archie Andrews, "America's newest boyfriend." Since then, Archie and his perennial teenage friends have entertained readers with their misadventures. This book includes the very first Archie story, with the first appearance of Betty and Veronica, Reggie, Jughead, Mr. Weatherbee, Miss Grundy, and the rest of the Archie characters as they originally appeared.

Furse, Sophie
   Moby Dick. Barron's Educational Series, Inc. 2007 48p. Illustration
Grades: 3 4 5 6 7 8 9   **741.5**
   1. Graphic novels; 2. Melville, Herman — Adaptations
   978-0-7641-5977-0; 978-0-7641-3492-0 (pa)
   Ishmael's dream of adventure on a whaling ship becomes a nightmare as the voyage turns into a struggle for survival. Captain Ahab, maimed by a monster whale, is obsessed with revenge. As the crew discovers, he is willing to risk everything to destroy that whale. This volume includes a brief biography and timeline of Melville, and information on the legacy of his novel.

Furudate, Haruichi
   ★ **Haikyu!!**; Volume 1. story and art by Haruichi Furudate; translation, Adrienne Beck. Viz 2016 197 P. Illustration
Grades: 7 8 9 10 11 12   **741.5; Fic**
   1. Shonen manga; 2. Volleyball — Fiction; 3. School stories — Graphic novels
   9781421587660, $9.99; 1421587661
   "Ever since he saw the legendary player known as the 'Little Giant' compete at the national volleyball finals, Shoyo Hinata has been aiming to be the best volleyball player ever! After losing his first and last volleyball match against Tobio Kageyama,...Shoyo Hinata swears to become his rival after graduating middle school. But what happens when the guy he wants to defeat ends up being his teammate?!" (Publisher's note)
   Volume 1 of an ongoing series

Gabrych, Andersen
   DC's Greatest Imaginary Stories. DC Comics 2005 192p. Illustration
Grades: 6 7 8 9 10 11 12 Adult   **741.5; Fic**
   1. Graphic novels; 2. Superhero graphic novels; 3. Flash (Fictional character); 4. Batman (Fictional character); 5. Superman (Fictional character)
   1-4012-0534-8, $19.99
   This volume collects eleven stories that are totally imaginary about many of DC's heroes: Superman marries Lois Lane; in another story, he marries Lana Lang; and in yet another story, he marries Lori Lemaris the mermaid. Batman abandons his millions to drive a taxi. The Flash races into action maskless. Superman and Batman are brothers. In the wedding of the century, it's Super girl and...Jimmy Olsen? And Shazam witnesses atomic bomb and attacks and finds that even he, the World's Mightiest Mortal, can't stop the bombs.

   Will Eisner. Rosen Publishing Group 2005 112p. Illustration
Grades: 8 9 10 11 12 Adult   **741.5; 92**
   1. Cartoonists — Biography; 2. Graphic novels
   1-4042-0286-2, $31.95

                                                  LC 2004016656
   Veteran comics insider Greenberger has written this biography of Eisner, covering his long career in comics, from the 1930s through the early 2000s. Eisner created the groundbreaking comic series The Spirit, and in the 1970s started writing original graphic novels set in New York City. The Eisner Awards for comics are named after him, due to his strong influence on the industry over the decades. This volume includes a list of books for further reading and a bibliography.
   Part of the Library of Graphic Novelists

Gagne, Michel
   The **saga** of Rex. Image 2010 200p. Illustration
Grades: 4 5 6 7 8   **741.5; Fic**
   1. Foxes — Graphic novels; 2. Science fiction — Graphic novels
   978-1-60706-322-3, $17.99; 1-60706-322-0
   "Originally serialized in Kazu Kibuishi's Flight anthologies, the story of the intergalactically adorable fox named Rex is collected here. The tale dispenses with words entirely after the first of six chapters.... Rex gets plucked from his home planet to enter a cosmic ritual in which alien

shape-shifters and their chosen companions (e.g., Rex) undergo a series of trials on a constantly morphing world." (Booklist)

Gaiman, Neil
★ The **graveyard** book graphic novel Volume 2. based on the novel by Neil Gaiman; adapted by P. Craig Russell; illustrated by David LaFuente, Scott Hampton, P. Craig Russell, Kevin Nowlan, Galen Showman; colorist, Lovern Kindzierski; letterer, Rick Parker. HarperCollins 2014 188 p. Color; Illustration
Grades: 5 6 7 8 9 10   **741.5; Fic**
   1. Cemeteries — Fiction; 2. Dead — Fiction; 3. Graphic novels; 4. Orphans — Fiction; 5. Supernatural — Fiction; 6. Supernatural graphic novels
0062194836; 9780062194831, $19.99
                                                      LC 2013497350
"Russell concludes the two-part adaptation of Gaiman's Newbery Medal winner, encompassing the final three chapters of the novel. Bod, raised by the ghostly denizens of a graveyard, is a young adult now, yearning for knowledge of the world of the living. After a showdown with a pair of school bullies...Bod finally confronts the ancient order who murdered his family and overcomes them with his supernatural know-how and his innate courage and cleverness." (Booklist)

"Russell and his team of illustrators continue to do this amazing story justice with images that lead readers down a path into Bod's dark and magical graveyard world. Gaiman has the ability to weave beauty and intrigue into a story that has a strong potential to frighten." VOYA

Gallagher, John
   Buzzboy: Trouble in paradise. Sky Dog Press 2002 144p. Illustration
Grades: 5 6 7 8 9 10 11 12   **741.5; Fic**
   1. Graphic novels; 2. Humorous graphic novels; 3. Superhero graphic novels
0-8721831-0-8, $11.95
Imagine a superhero who jokes constantly, watches way too many old television shows, and loves junk food, and you have Buzzboy. Years before, he was sidekick to Captain Ultra, but the evil Dr. Schism destroyed all superheroes and their sidekicks, except for Captain Ultra. Now, Ultra has declared martial law in the city of New Paradise, and his police stomp out all rebellions. Then a mysterious superhero stops the Hoppers (police) it's Buzzboy, older and back from the dead! Aided by sarcastic teen sorceress Becca and reformed mad scientist Doc Cyber, Buzzboy is here to save the day.

Another title in this series is: Buzzboy: Monsters, dreams, & milkshakes (2003)

Galligan, Gale
   Dawn and the impossible three. a graphic novel by Gale Galligan; with color by Braden Lamb [based on the book by Ann M. Martin]. Graphix 2017 145 p. Color; Illustration
Grades: 3 4 5 6   **741.5; Fic**
   1. Girls — Fiction; 2. Female friendship — Fiction; 3. Babysitting — Fiction; 4. Babysitters — Fiction; 5. Girls' clubs — Fiction
9781338067354; 9781338067309, $24.99; 9781338067118
                                                      LC 2016960080
"Dawn Schafer is the newest member of The Baby-sitters Club. While she's still adjusting to life in Stoneybrook..., she's eager to accept her first big job. But taking care of the three Barrett kids would be too much for any baby-sitter.... On top of all that, Dawn wants to fit in with the other members of the BSC, but she can't figure out how to get along with Kristy." (Publisher's note)

"Slightly more serious than its predecessors, this offering tackles the weighty issues of divorce and ki dnapping but manages to resolve things

tidily in the comfortably episodic manner that fans of the series expect. This volume introduces new artist Galligan, who replaces veteran Raina Telgemeier." Kirkus

Ganeri, Anita
   Cleopatra: The Life of an Egyptian Queen. by Gary Jeffrey & Anita Ganeri; illustrated by Ross Watton. Rosen Publishing Group 2005 48p. Illustration
Grades: 3 4 5 6 7 8
92; 741.5; 932
   1. Biographical graphic novels; 2. Graphic novels; 3. Cleopatra, Queen of Egypt, d. 30 B.C.; 4. Egypt — History — Graphic novels
1-4042-0242-0, $29.25
                                                      LC 2004014162
Queen of Egypt, companion of Julius Caesar, and wife of Mark Antony, Cleopatra lived one of history's most fabled lives. Renowned for her great beauty and intelligence, Cleopatra was a strong ruler determined to restore the glory of Ptolemaic rule to Egypt by using her relationships with Caesar and Antony to achieve her goals. Readers will learn why the events of her life — including her tragic suicide — have inspired writers and artists for centuries. This graphic novel includes additional information and a list of books for further reading.
Part of the Graphic Nonfiction series.

Courtesy of Rosen Publishing

   Harriet Tubman: The Life of an African-American Abolitionist. by Rob Shone & Anita Ganeri; illustrated by Rob Shone. Rosen Publishing Group 2005 48p. Illustration
Grades: 3 4 5 6 7 8 9
92; 741.5
   1. African American women — Graphic novels; 2. Biographical graphic novels; 3. Graphic novels; 4. Underground Railroad — Graphic novels; 5. Tubman, Harriet, 1819 or 1820-1913
1-4042-0245-5, $29.25
Born a slave in the United States, Harriet Tubman escaped from bondage to risk her life and newfound liberty in becoming a leading abolitionist in the years before the American Civil War. Tubman surreptitiously led hundreds of escaped Southern slaves to freedom in the North along the Underground Railroad, earning her the nickname as "the Moses of her people." This graphic novel format book tells her story. It includes additional information about the Underground Railroad and her legacy in the civil rights movement, and a list of books for further reading.
Part of the Graphic Nonfiction series.

Courtesy of Rosen Publishing

Ganter, Amy Kim
   Goosebumps: Terror Trips. Scholastic/Graphix 2007 137p. Illustration
Grades: 4 5 6 7 8 9   **741.5; Fic**
   1. Graphic novels; 2. Horror graphic novels; 3. Stine, R. L.; 4. Stine, R. L. — Adaptations
978-0-439-85780-2, $8.99
Stine's Goosebumps series was very popular years ago, and is enjoying a resurgence of popularity with new editions of the prose books. The graphic novel adaptations, all done by well-known independent

comics creators, bring the stories to a new audience. Goosebumps: Creepy Creatures is also available.

This volume adapts three of Stine's Goosebumps novels into graphic novel format. Noted independent comic creator Thompson adapts One Day at Horrorland, about one family's ordeal in a very strange, all-too-realistic amusement park. Canadian artist Tolagson adapts A Shocker on Shock Street, which depicts the horrific adventures of two kids on a movie studio lot where the horror is more than just special effects. Global manga creator Ganter adapts Deep Trouble, in which a brother and sister find a real mermaid.

Garcia, Tracy J.
Eli Whitney. by Tracy J. Garcia. PowerKids Press 2013 24 p. Color illustration
Grades: 3 4 5 6
609.2; 92; 741.5

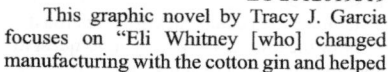

1. Cotton gins and ginning; 2. Inventors — United States — Biography — Juvenile; 3. Inventors — United States; 4. Whitney, Eli, 1765-1825
1477700757; 1477701354; 1477701362; 9781477700754, $25.25; 9781477701355, $10.60; 9781477701362
LC 2012019319

Courtesy of Rosen Publishing

This graphic novel by Tracy J. Garcia focuses on "Eli Whitney [who] changed manufacturing with the cotton gin and helped make improvements in the area of mass production through interchangeable parts. Readers will [be exposed to] how Whitney also drastically changed farming in America with his inventions." (Publisher's note)
Includes index.

Thomas Edison. by Tracy J. Garcia. PowerKids Press 2013 24 p. (Jr. graphic American inventors)
Grades: 3 4 5 6
621.3092; 92; 621.3

1. Businessmen — United States — Biography — Comic books, strips, etc.; 2. Electrical engineers — United States — Biography — Comic books, strips, etc.; 3. Inventors — United States — Biography — Comic books, strips, etc.; 4. Inventors — Graphic novels; 5. Edison, Thomas A. (Thomas Alva), 1847-1931
1477700765; 9781477700761, $25.25; 9781477701379; 9781477701386

Courtesy of Rosen Publishing

LC 2012018690

This graphic novel by Tracy J. Garcia focuses on "Thomas Edison [who] was a prolific inventor with nearly 2,000 patents. One of his most noted inventions is the practical electrical light bulb. Readers will be [exposed to] the life of Thomas Edison, one of America's great inventors and businessmen." (Publisher's note)
Includes index.

Geary, Rick
★ The **Lindbergh** child: America's hero and the crime of the century. written and illustrated by Rick Geary. NBM/ComicsLit 2008 un Illustration; Map (Treasury of XXth century murder)
Grades: 8 9 10 11 12 Adult
364.1; 741.5

1. Air force officers; 2. Air pilots; 3. Generals; 4. Graphic novels; 5. Homicide — Graphic novels; 6. Kidnapping — Graphic novels; 7. Memoirists; 8. Mystery graphic novels; 9. Lindbergh, Charles, 1902-1974
978-1-56163-529-0, $15.95

Courtesy of NBM Publishing

Charles Lindbergh was an American hero following his solo crossing of the Atlantic in an airplane. He married into a wealthy family, he and his wife had a baby, they were building their dream home. Then, one night, the baby was abducted from the house. Geary's account retraces all the highly publicized events, ransom notes (false and otherwise), as well as the string of colorful characters who all claimed they could help but instead snookered the Lindberghs. While Bruno Hauptmann was arrested, tried, convicted, and executed, there remain many questions about what really happened. Geary brings them up for readers to consider.

"A good example of the origins of modern forensics, crime-scene investigation, and celebrity hysteria, this work is an excellent choice for most collections." SLJ

The **murder** of Abraham Lincoln: a chronicle of 62 days in the life of the American Republic, March 4-May 4, 1865. written and illustrated by Rick Geary. NBM ComicsLit 2005 un Illustration; Map (A treasury of Victorian murder)
Grades: 7 8 9 10 11 12
973.7

1. Actors; 2. Graphic novels; 3. Lawyers; 4. Members of Congress; 5. Murderers; 6. Presidents; 7. State legislators; 8. Booth, John Wilkes, 1838-1865; 9.Lincoln, Abraham, 1809-1865 — Assassination
978-1-56163-425-5; 1-56163-425-5, $15.95; 978-1-56163-426-2 (pa); 1-56163-426-3 (pa), $8.95

Courtesy of NBM Publishing

LC 2005-41468

This graphic novel "covers Lincoln's assassination, the events that led up to it, and the aftermath. Geary also makes a point of bringing up still-unanswered questions, like the whereabouts of the missing pages of John Wilkes Booth's journal.... Even teens who know nothing about the tragedy will find their heads chock-full of information when they're finished reading this book." SLJ
Includes bibliographical references

Geissman, Grant
Mad About the Fifties. E.C. Publications/MAD Books 2005 un. Illustration
Grades: 8 9 10 11 12 Adult   **741.5**
1. Graphic novels; 2. Humorous graphic novels; 3. Satire — Graphic novels
1-4012-0753-7, $12.99

MAD Magazine was founded in 1952 as a ten-cent comic book that parodied other comic books; three years later it became a twenty-five cent (cheap!) magazine. This volume collects some of the regular features and parodies of television programs and movies of the decade. Some of the advertising parodies feature tobacco and alcohol products, and some parodies portray the imbibing of alcohol products.

Mad About the Sixties: The Best of the Decade. Mad Books/E.C. Publications 1997 un Illustration

Grades: 7 8 9 10 11 12 Adult   **741.5; Fic**
1. Graphic novels; 2. Humorous graphic novels; 3. Satire — Graphic novels
1-4012-0754-5, $9.99

Alfred E. Newman as a flower child? Ecch! Here is a look back at the Sixties from the satire magazine, full of send-ups, takeoffs, and put-ons from the decade that gave the world Timothy Leary and Tiny Tim. Along with Spy vs. Spy, Sergio Aragones' "Mad Marginals," Don Martin's lunacies, and Snappy Answers to Stupid Questions, this volume includes TV satires such as Star Blecch, Bats-Man, and The Phewgitive, and movie takeoffs 201 Min. of a Space Idiocy, East Side Story, and Flawrence of Arabia. Back in the 1960s, preteens read the magazine and most of them turned out okay ...

Gelatt, Philip
Indiana Jones adventures vol. 1. Dark Horse Comics 2008 un Illustration
Grades: 4 5 6 7 8 9   **741.5; Fic**
1. Adventure graphic novels; 2. Archeology — Graphic novels; 3. Graphic novels; 4. Jones, Indiana (Fictional character)
978-1-59307-905-5, $6.95

It's winter of 1930 in Sweden, and Dr. Henry Jones Jr. (Indiana Jones) finds an ancient pre-Christian temple of a religion devoted to war; he gets a scroll while Dr. Lawrence, the pretty British archeologist with him, runs with a valuable gold ring. When Indy decides to steal the ring back from the British Museum, the unscrupulous French archeologist Belloq, who works for the Nazis, steals the scroll from Marcus Brody, Indy's friend. From London, Indy and Dr. Lawrence pursue Belloq to Egypt to recover the scroll before he can sell it to the Nazis. This original graphic novel story provides adventure suitable for younger readers.

Gelev, Penko
Moby Dick. Barron's Educational Series, Inc. 2007 48p. Illustration
Grades: 3 4 5 6 7 8 9   **741.5**
1. Graphic novels; 2. Melville, Herman — Adaptations
978-0-7641-5977-0; 978-0-7641-3492-0 (pa)

Ishmael's dream of adventure on a whaling ship becomes a nightmare as the voyage turns into a struggle for survival. Captain Ahab, maimed by a monster whale, is obsessed with revenge. As the crew discovers, he is willing to risk everything to destroy that whale. This volume includes a brief biography and timeline of Melville, and information on the legacy of his novel.

Gerber, Steve
Guardians of the Galaxy; Volume 1: Tomorrow's Avengers. by Steve Gerber, Chris Claremont, Gerry Conway, Len Wein, Arnold Drake and Roger Stern and illustrated by Gene Colan, Sal Buscema, Don Heck, and Al Milgrom. Marvel Enterprises 2013 368 p.
Grades: 7 8 9 10 11 12   **741.5**
1. Doctor Strange (Fictitious character); 2. Outer space — Fiction; 3. Superheroes — Fiction; 4. Space warfare — Fiction; 5. Hulk (Fictional character); 6. Captain America (Fictional character)
0785166874; 9780785166870, $39.99

In this graphic novel, written by Steve Gerber, Chris Claremont, Gerry Conway, Len Wien, Arnold Drake and Roger Stern, "Captain America, Doctor Strange, the Thing, the Hulk and other[s]...join the star-spanning heroes in the greatest war the future ever saw! As the Guardians help a planet...rebuild, threats rise from two other worlds: one of them living, the other gone mad!" (Publisher's note)

Giarrusso, Chris
G-Man, volume 1: learning to fly. Image Comics 2010 un Illustration

Grades: 3 4 5 6   **741.5; Fic**
1. Graphic novels; 2. Humorous graphic novels; 3. Superhero graphic novels
978-1-60706-270-7 (pa), $9.99; 1-60706-270-4 (pa)

Mikey G. is G-Man, the newest superhero on the block, in a town full of superheroes (he made his cape from the family's magic blanket). His friends Billy Demon, Tan Man, Sparky, and the Suntrooper are all ready to help, but G-Man also has to deal with his older brother Great Man (aka Dave) and their superhero dad, Mr. G.

This "hits all the right notes, from its friendly cartoon figures to the occasionally hilarious one-liners." Booklist

This is a new edition, in a larger size and with a new ISBN; Other titles in this series are:Cape crisis (2010);Coming home (2013)

G-Man, volume 2: cape crisis. Image comics 2010 un Illustration
Grades: 3 4 5 6 7 8   **741.5; Fic**
1. Graphic novels; 2. Humorous graphic novels; 3. Superhero graphic novels
978-1-60706-271-4, $9.99

The trouble starts when G-Man (aka Mikey) tells everyone that his magic cape gives him the power to fly; then everyone wants to fly. When he gives them bracelets made from the scraps of the magic blanket, everyone starts flying around and causing trouble. Then, when G-Man rounds up all the bracelets, he finds older brother Great Man (aka Dave) is selling more bracelets for $1,000 apiece. However, dividing up the magic into so many small bits is not only allowing unscrupulous people to commit crimes with their new powers, it is causing instabilities that could backfire disastrously. And that's exactly what happens. Now the brothers have to go on a quest to find the one being who can restore the magic to G-Man's cape.

Gieter, De
Papyrus: the Rameses' revenge. Cinebook 2007 48p. Illustration
Grades: 3 4 5 6 7 8   **741.5; Fic**
1. Adventure graphic novels; 2. Graphic novels; 3. Egypt — History — Graphic novels
978-1-905460-35-9, $11.95

In ancient Egypt, Papyrus is a mischievous boy who has become a friend of the Princess Theti-Cheri, daughter of the Pharaoh, thanks to the magic sword that protects him. When Theti-Cheri insists on traveling down the Nile to see Rameses' Temple with just Papyrus, their friend Imhotep, and just a few guards, Papyrus is sure they will run into trouble. At the temple, they face two rival bands of plunderers who seek the treasure in the temple.

Part of the Papyrus series, originally published in France as Papyrus La Vengeance des Ramses.

Gillen, Kieron
Star Wars Darth Vader; Volume 1: Vader. writer, Kieron Gillen; artist, Salvador Larroca; colorist, Edgar Delgado; letterer, VC's Joe Caramagna; cover art, Adi Granov; assistant editors, Charles Beacham & Heather Antos; editor, Jordan D. White. Marvel Enterprises 2015 160 p. Color; Illustration
Grades: 8 9 10 11 12 Adult   **741.5**
1. Star Wars — Graphic novels
0785192557; 9780785192558, $19.99

In this book, by Kieron Gillen, illustrated by Salvador Larocca, "Ever since Darth Vader's first on-screen appearance, he has become one of pop culture's most popular villains. Now, follow Vader straight from the ending of A NEW HOPE into his own solo adventures — showing the Empire's war with the Rebel Alliance from the other side! But when a Dark Lord needs help, who can he turn to?" (Publisher's note)

Contains material originally published in magazine form as Darth Vader #1-6.; Volume 1 of 4

Gillis, Peter B.

The **last** unicorn. original story by Peter S. Beagle; adaptation by Peter B. Gillis; art by Renae De Liz. IDW 2011 167p. Illustration
Grades: 6 7 8 9 10
741.5; Fic
9780451450524 (rpt), $16.00;
978-1-60010-851-8, $24.99;
1-60010-851-2

Courtesy of IDW Publishing

"A beloved story is now a graphic novel in this excellent adaptation.... Much of the original novel's lyrical language has been included, and readers will be eager to find out if the unicorn will give up her quest for love, or if any of Schmendrick's spells will ever turn out right.... The illustrations are graceful and detailed, and inked in warm, glowing colors. This is a worthy successor to the classic novel and film." SLJ

Gillman, Melanie

★ **As** the crow flies. by Melanie Gillman. Iron Circus Comics 2017 272 p Color; Illustration
Grades: 7 8 9 10 11 12
741.5; Fic
1. Gender identity — Fiction; 2. Religious camps — Comic books, strips, etc.; 3. Teenagers — Graphic novels
9781945820069, $30; 1945820063
Stonewall Book Award Honor Book: Children's & Young Adult Literature (2018)

In this book, by Melanie Gillman, "Charlie Lamonte is thirteen years old, queer, black, and questioning what was once a firm belief in God. So naturally, she's spending a week of her summer vacation stuck at an all-white Christian youth backpacking camp. As the journey wears on and the rhetoric wears thin, she can't help but poke holes in the pious obliviousness of this storied sanctuary with little regard for people like herself...or her fellow camper, Sydney." (Publisher's note)

"This contemplative graphic novel, taken from Gillman's ongoing webcomic, perceptively explores race, gender, faith, and friendship. Elegantly composed, richly hued images vividly portray the lush forest setting and shy, thoughtful Charlie's inner turmoil as she yearns to voice her opinions." SLJ

Gilson

Melusine: Halloween. Cinebook Ltd 2007 48p. Illustration
Grades: 3 4 5 6 7 8
741.5; Fic
1. Graphic novels; 2. Humorous graphic novels; 3. Witches — Graphic novels
978-1-905460-34-2, $11.95

Melusine is a sorcerer's apprentice who wants to become a powerful witch. However, she's not always successful. Her friend Cancrelune can never get her potions right, and cousin Melisande is a fairy who always wants to make everything light, pretty, and fun. This volume collects stories that focus on Halloween, with pumpkin carving, monster calling, and children going trick-or-treating.

First published 2000 in France

Melusine: The vampire's ball. Cinebook Ltd. 2008 48p. Illustration
Grades: 3 4 5 6 7 8
741.5; Fic
1. Graphic novels; 2. Humorous graphic novels; 3. Witches — Graphic novels
978-1-905460-69-4, $11.95

The young witch Melusine is back for more fun with all her family, including witches Adrazelle and Cancrelune, the ghostly Madam and vampire Master of the haunted castle, and more. Melusine tries to make different potions, turns toads into dragons and vice versa, tries to avoid too many cleaning chores in the castle, and more. Some of the situations are slightly gruesome, as when a particularly nasty knight ends up eaten by a monstrous tree in the forest, or when the male vampires get too drunk to get under cover before sunrise and turn into piles of ash.

Gilson, Francois

Melusine: love potions. Cinebook 2010 48p. Illustration
Grades: 3 4 5 6 7 8
741.5; Fic
1. Graphic novels; 2. Humorous graphic novels; 3. Witches — Graphic novels
978-1-84918-005-4, $11.95

Young witch in training Melusine tries to make love potions, in between encounters with her clumsy fellow student Cancrelune and various villagers who want to fall in love (or not). The full-color cartoony art keeps the witches, vampires, ghosts, dragons, and monsters more humorous looking than spooky.

Originally published in France as Melusine 5 Philtres d'amour

Goodwin, Vincent

Sir Arthur Conan Doyle's The adventure of the speckled band. adapted by, Vincent Goodwin; illustrated by, Ben Dunn. ABDO/Magic Wagon 2010 48p. Illustration
Grades: 4 5 6 7 8 9
741.5; Fic
1. Authors; 2. Graphic novels; 3. Holmes, Sherlock (Fictional character) — Graphic novels; 4. Mystery graphic novels; 5. Doyle, Arthur Conan Sir, 1859-1930 — Adaptations
978-1-60270-727-6, $28.50;
1-60270-727-8
LC 2009-32461

Courtesy of ABDO Publishing.

Consulting detective Sherlock Holmes and his partner Dr. John Watson come to the aid of Miss Helen Stoner. After moving back to England from India with their stepfather, Helen's twin sister died under mysterious circumstances. Now, two years later, Helen knows something is terribly wrong in her stepfather's house. Both men suspect the gypsies that Dr. Roylott, the stepfather, has allowed to live on his property, but Holmes soon suspects something else. This graphic novel adaptation has been done by Goodwin and Dunn, who are experienced creators with Antarctic Press (Dunn started the publishing house). The book includes a brief glossary, a short biography of Doyle, a listing of his published works, and a short sketching lesson by Dunn.

Part of The Graphic Novel Adventures of Sherlock Holmes

Sir Arthur Conan Doyle's The adventure of the Red-Headed League. ABDO/Magic Wagon 2010 48p. Illustration
Grades: 4 5 6 7 8 9
741.5; Fic
1. Authors; 2. Graphic novels; 3. Holmes, Sherlock (Fictional character) — Graphic novels; 4. Mystery graphic novels; 5. Doyle, Arthur Conan Sir, 1859-1930 — Adaptations
978-1-60270-726-9, $28.50;
1-60270-726-X
LC 2009-32460

Courtesy of ABDO Publishing.

Consulting detective Sherlock Holmes and his friend Dr. John Watson take the case of Jabez Wilson, an ordinary tradesman with an extraordinary tale. His pawn shop assistant had found an advertisement in the newspaper asking for eligible men to apply for membership in The RedHeaded League, and he helped Mr. Wilson fight through a crowd of redheaded men and to be accepted into the League. Wilson was paid four pounds a week for a few hours' work copying out an encyclopedia; then suddenly, all trace of the League disappeared. He wants Holmes to find out what has happened. This graphic novel adaptation has been done by Goodwin and Dunn, who are experienced creators with Antarctic Press (Dunn started the publishing house). The book includes a brief glossary, a short biography of Doyle, a listing of his published works, and a short sketching lesson by Dunn.

Part of The Graphic Novel Adventures of Sherlock Holmes

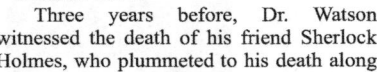

Sir Arthur Conan Doyle's, The adventure of the empty house. ABDO/Magic Wagon 2010 48p. Illustration
Grades: 4 5 6 7 8 9
741.5; Fic
1. Authors; 2. Graphic novels; 3. Holmes, Sherlock (Fictional character); 4. Mystery graphic novels; 5. Mystery writers; 6. Novelists; 7. Doyle, Arthur Conan Sir, 1859-1930; 8. Doyle, Arthur Conan Sir, 1859-1930 — Adaptations
978-1-60270-724-5, $28.50;
1-60270-724-3

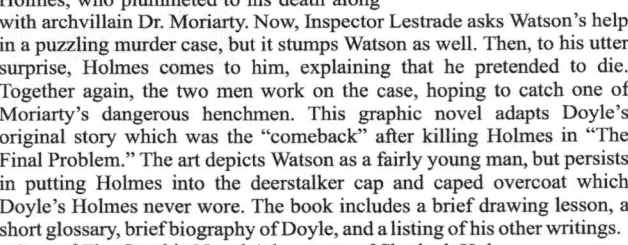

Three years before, Dr. Watson witnessed the death of his friend Sherlock Holmes, who plummeted to his death along with archvillain Dr. Moriarty. Now, Inspector Lestrade asks Watson's help in a puzzling murder case, but it stumps Watson as well. Then, to his utter surprise, Holmes comes to him, explaining that he pretended to die. Together again, the two men work on the case, hoping to catch one of Moriarty's dangerous henchmen. This graphic novel adapts Doyle's original story which was the "comeback" after killing Holmes in "The Final Problem." The art depicts Watson as a fairly young man, but persists in putting Holmes into the deerstalker cap and caped overcoat which Doyle's Holmes never wore. The book includes a brief drawing lesson, a short glossary, brief biography of Doyle, and a listing of his other writings.

Part of The Graphic Novel Adventures of Sherlock Holmes

Sir Arthur Conan Doyle's, The adventure of the dancing men. ABDO/Magic Wagon 2010 48p. Illustration
Grades: 4 5 6 7 8 9

1. Authors; 2. Graphic novels; 3. Holmes, Sherlock (Fictional character); 4. Mystery graphic novels; 5. Doyle, Arthur Conan Sir, 1859-1930 — Adaptations
978-1-60270-723-8, $28.50;
1-60270-723-5

Courtesy of ABDO Publishing.

When strange writing that looks like dancing men starts appearing around the estate of Mr. Cubitt, he comes to Sherlock Holmes for help. He thinks it's the work of pranksters, but his American wife seems frightened. As he brings more of the writing samples to Holmes, the detective works on the case, but he may not be able to solve it before tragedy strikes the Cubitts. This book adapts Doyle's short story; it includes a short glossary, a brief biography of Doyle, a short drawing lesson, and a list of Doyle's other writings. Dunn's art depicts Holmes and

Dr. Watson as younger men, but continues the stereotypical portrayal of Holmes with the deerstalker cap and shoulder caped coat which Doyle never had him wear in the original stories.

Part of The Graphic Novel Adventures of Sherlock Holmes series

Courtesy of ABDO Publishing.

Sir Arthur Conan Doyle's, The adventure of the Abbey Grange. ABDO/Magic Wagon 2010 48p. Illustration
Grades: 4 5 6 7 8 9
741.5; Fic
1. Authors; 2. Graphic novels; 3. Holmes, Sherlock (Fictional character); 4. Doyle, Arthur Conan Sir, 1859-1930
978-1-60270-722-1, $28.50;
1-60270-722-7

A robbery and murder have occurred, and Sir Eustace Brackenstall is dead. His wife and maid say that a gang of robbers invaded their home, tied up Lady Brackenstall and killed Sir Eustace, but Holmes doesn't believe their story. As he investigates, he learns that Sir Eustace was a cruel man, and even though Lady Brackenstall has lied, Holmes sympathizes with her. This book adapts Doyle's short story; it includes a short glossary, a brief biography of Doyle, a short drawing lesson, and a list of Doyle's other writings. Dunn's art depicts Holmes and Dr. Watson as younger men, but continues the stereotypical portrayal of Holmes with the deerstalker cap and shoulder caped coat which Doyle never had him wear in the original stories.

Part of The Graphic Novel Adventures of Sherlock Holmes series.

Goscinny, Rene

Asterix and Caesar's Gift. Orion/Sterling Publishing 2004 48p. Illustration
Grades: 4 5 6 7 8 9 10 11 12 Adult   **741.5; Fic**
1. Asterix (Fictional character); 2. Graphic novels; 3. Humorous graphic novels
0-75286-645-1, $12.95; 0-75286-646-X (pa)

When Legionary Tremensdelirius gets the title deeds to the little Gaulish village as a bonus, he swaps them with tavern landlord Orthopaedix for a drink. Funnily enough, Asterix and his friends aren't keen to hand over their village to anyone else. After a chieftaincy election campaign and a showdown with the Romans, both events fiercely contested, can all still end well?

Asterix and Cleopatra. Orion/Sterling Publishing 2004 48p. Illustration
Grades: 4 5 6 7 8 9 10 11 12 Adult   **741.5; Fic**
1. Asterix (Fictional character); 2. Graphic novels; 3. Humorous graphic novels
0-75286-606-0, $12.95; 0-75286-607-9 (pb)

How can lovely Queen Cleopatra show Julius Caesar that ancient Egypt is still a great nation? Her architect Edifis recruits his Gaulish friends to help him build a magnificent palace within three months. There are villainous saboteurs to be outwitted, but Asterix, Obelix, and Getafix still find time to go sight-seeing, and leave their mark on the Pyramids and the Sphinx's nose.

Asterix and the Banquet. Orion/Sterling Publishing 2004 48p. Illustration
Grades: 4 5 6 7 8 9 10 11 12 Adult   **741.5; Fic**
1. Asterix (Fictional character); 2. Graphic novels; 3. Humorous graphic novels
0-75286-608-0, $12.95; 0-75286-609-5 (pa)

When the Romans try to contain the threat from the Gaulish village by building a stockade around it, Asterix and Obelix lay a bet with them. They will break out and claim their right to travel freely all over Gaul, collecting the local delicacies and bringing them back to prove their point. Ham from Lutetia, fizzy wine from Durocortorum, fish stew from Massilia in the south...soon their shopping bag is full. Outwitting Romans, a couple of treacherous Gauls, and the thieves Villanus and Unscrupulus, they set off for home...but who's that little dog who has been following them all the way from Lutetia?

Asterix and the Cauldron. Orion/Sterling Publishing 2004 48p. Illustration
Grades: 4 5 6 7 8 9 10 11 12 Adult   **741.5; Fic**
   1. Asterix (Fictional character); 2. Graphic novels; 3. Humorous graphic novels
0-75286-629-X, $9.95
   There's financial skulduggery in ancient Gaul. When local Chief Whosemoralsarelastix wants a cauldron full of money kept out of Roman hands, the cash disappears while Asterix is guarding it. He and Obelix must earn enough to repay it through fairground gladiatorial contests, trendy theatrical performances, even bank robbery — they'll try anything. But whose morals are really elastic? And how to the pirates, just for once, get an unexpected bonus?

Asterix and the Class Act. Orion/Sterling Publishing 2004 56p. Illustration
Grades: 4 5 6 7 8 9 10 11 12 Adult   **741.5; Fic**
   1. Asterix (Fictional character); 2. Graphic novels; 3. Humorous graphic novels
0-75286-068-2, $12.95; 0-75286-640-0 (pa)
   This volume collects 14 stories, including the day Asterix and Obelix were born (in the middle of a fish fight); how Obelix goes back to school; fashion in ancient Gaul; how Dogmatix helps the village cockerel win a duel, and how he's adopted as a Roman mascot; Obelix's adventures under the mistletoe; the bid for the very first Gaulish Olympics, and more.

Asterix and the Laurel Wreath. Orion/Sterling Publishing 2004 48p. Illustration
Grades: 4 5 6 7 8 9 10 11 12 Adult   **741.5; Fic**
   1. Asterix (Fictional character); 2. Graphic novels; 3. Humorous graphic novels
0-75286-636-2, $12.95; 0-75286-637-0 (pa)
   Chief Vitalstatistix rashly invites his brother-in-law to dine on a stew seasoned with Caesar's laurel wreath, so Asterix and Obelix must to go Rome to fetch those laurels. Hoping to get access to Caesar, they sell themselves as slaves, but can they do a deal with the corrupt Goldendelicius to swap the laurels for parsley?

Asterix in Britain. Orion/Sterling Publishing 2004 48p. Illustration
Grades: 4 5 6 7 8 9 10 11 12 Adult   **741.5; Fic**
   1. Asterix (Fictional character); 2. Graphic novels; 3. Humorous graphic novels
0-85286-618-4, $12.95; 0-75286-619-2 (pa)
   The Romans have invaded Britain, but one village still holds out. Asterix and Obelix come to help, with a barrel of magic potion in hand. But to deliver the precious brew, the Gaulish heroes must face fog, rain, bad food, warm beer, and the Romans too.

★ **Asterix** the Gaul. written by René Goscinny and illustrated by Albert Uderzo; translated by Anthea Bell and Derek Hockridge. Orion Media 2004 48p. Illustration; Map
Grades: 4 5 6 7 8 9 10 11 12   **741.5; Fic**
   1. Graphic novels; 2. Humorous graphic novels; 3. France — History — Graphic novels
0-7528-6604-4, $12.95; 0-7528-6605-2 (pa), $9.95

   Meet Asterix, a diminutive but extremely strong Gaul living in ancient France during the time of the Roman Republic. Together with his friend Obelix, Asterix continually outwits the Roman Legionnaires sent to conquer Gaul for Julius Caesar. Full of puns and outrageous humor, the books also manage to teach a lot of history. This is the first in a long-running series of graphic novels translated from the original French.
   Translated from the French; Other titles in this series are: Asterix and Caesar's Gift; Asterix and Cleopatra; Asterix and the actress; Asterix and the banquet; Asterix and the big fight; Asterix and the cauldron; Asterix and the Goths; Asterix and the Great Crossing; Asterix and the laurel wreath; Asterix the legionary; Asterix and the Normans; Asterix and the Roman Agent; Asterix and the soothsayer; Asterix at the Olympic Games; Asterix in Belgium; Asterix in Britain; Asterix in Corsica; Asterix in Spain; Asterix in Switzerland; Asterix Obelix and Co.; Asterix the gladiator; Asterix The Mansions of the Gods

Asterix the Legionary. Orion/Sterling Publishing 2004 48p. Illustration
Grades: 4 5 6 7 8 9 10 11 12 Adult   **741.5; Fic**
   1. Asterix (Fictional character); 2. Graphic novels; 3. Humorous graphic novels
0-75286-620-6, $12.95; 0-75286-621-4 (pa)
   It's off to the wars for Asterix and Obelix: they've enlisted as legionnaires in order to rescue Tragicomix, whom the Romans forcibly conscripted. The two find Tragicomix and succeed in causing the biggest commotion ever on a battlefield.

The **Caliph's** vacation. Cinebook Ltd 2008 48p. Illustration
Grades: 3 4 5 6 7 8   **741.5; Fic**
   1. Graphic novels; 2. Humorous graphic novels
978-1-905460-61-8, $11.95
   Iznogoud, the Grand Vizier of Baghdad the Magnificent, wants to be Caliph, and he hatches all kinds of schemes to do in the good, kindhearted, not-too-bright Caliph, Haroun Al Plassid. First, they go to the beach, where Iznogoud and his henchman Wa'at Alahf try to drown him (the Caliph floats), send him into shark-infested waters (his suntan oil reeks), and other attempts that end up nearly doing in Iznogoud. A scheme to use a weather wizard to kill the Caliph with winter snow ends up with everyone enjoying a ski vacation. Then Iznogoud comes up with a poisoned elixir but can't get the Caliph to drink it. Goscinny is best known in the U.S. for his Asterix comics, but Iznogoud is just as filled with puns and humor, with a villain as the main character. Readers will enjoy the Wile E. Coyote type of hijinks.
   First published 2000 in France

Dalton City: a Lucky Luke adventure. Cinebook 2007 48p. Illustration
Grades: 3 4 5 6 7 8   **741.5; Fic**
   1. Graphic novels; 2. Humorous graphic novels; 3. Western stories — Graphic novels
978-1-905460-13-7, $9.99
   Goscinny, cocreator of Asterix, gives readers his wacky version of the American Old West in the Lucky Luke Adventures. Luke is a traveling good guy, who shoots faster than his shadow. He cleans up Fenton City, a festering sore of depravity in Texas, by capturing Dean Fenton, the boss of the town. Fenton ends up in the same prison as the Dalton brothers, a gang of not-too-smart outlaws that Luke keeps having to put away. They break out of the prison and take over Fenton City, calling it Dalton City. When Lucky Luke shows up, they ask him for advice on how to make the town a haven for outlaws, and Luke sees his chance to round up a whole lot of bad guys.
   Part of the Lucky Luke Adventures series, originally published in France as Lucky Luke Dalton City.

The **tenderfoot**: Lucky Luke adventure, vol. 13. Cinbook Ltd. 2008 48p. Illustration

Grades: 3 4 5 6 7 8   **791.5; Fic**
1. Graphic novels; 2. Humorous graphic novels; 3. Western stories — Graphic novels
978-1-905460-65-6, $11.95

When Rancher Baddy passes away, his heir, an Englishman, comes to town to take over the ranch. Jack Ready wants the ranch, so he plans to give the "tenderfoot" reasons to go away. When Lucky Luke, who can shoot faster than his shadow, helps Waldo get through the "welcoming ceremonies" and the phlegmatic Englishman shows he's more than a match for anything the cowboys can think to do, Jack Ready comes up with the only other plan that might work — frame Waldo for Jack's murder. The book has no real violence, but it does show drinking and gambling in the saloon. While some readers might fret over the stereotyping of the Native American characters, they should note that every single character in the book, including Lucky Luke himself, is a caricature of a "type," from rough cowboy to noble Indian, to Chinese, to hoity-toity Englishmen, to gunfighters. This is translated from the original French stories written by Rene Goscinny, who also wrote Asterix.

Gossett, Christian
    King Kong: The 8th Wonder of the World. Dark Horse Books 2006 un Illustration
Grades: 7 8 9 10 11 12 Adult   **741.5; Fic**
1. Graphic novels; 2. King Kong (Fictional character); 3. Science fiction graphic novels
978-1-59307-472-2, $12.95

Director Carl Denham has one chance to make the film of his dreams — hire an unknown actress, kidnap his writer and board a tramp freighter for the mysterious Island of the Skull. But when hostile natives capture actress Ann Darrow, Denham and his crew will face horrors from giant spiders to bloodthirsty dinosaurs to get her back. Yet, nothing can prepare them for the revelation of the mighty wonder in whose clutches Ann truly remains — King Kong. This story adapts the screenplay for the motion picture directed by Peter Jackson, which is based on the original story by Merian C. Cooper and Edgar Wallace.

Gould, Jane H.
    George Washington Carver. by Jane Gould. PowerKids Press 2013 24 p. Color illustration
Grades: 3 4 5 6
630.92; B
1. African American agriculturists — Biography — Comic books, strips, etc.; 2. African American educators — Biography — Comic books, strips, etc.; 3. African American scientists — Biography — Comic books, strips, etc.; 4. Agriculturists — United States — Biography — Comic books, strips, etc.; 5. Peanuts — United States — History — Comic books, strips,

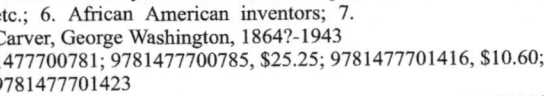
Courtesy of Rosen Publishing

etc.; 6. African American inventors; 7. Carver, George Washington, 1864?-1943
1477700781; 9781477700785, $25.25; 9781477701416, $10.60; 9781477701423
                  LC 2012018689

In this biography of inventor George Washington Carver, author Jane Gould "provides the requisite biographical details, including Carver's early...separation from his mother, but also traces themes of his career, drawing connections between his kind masters' waste-not values and his future devotion to finding new uses for farm by-products." (Booklist)
Includes index.

Steve Jobs. by Jane Gould. PowerKids Press 2013 24 p.
Grades: 3 4 5 6
338.7; 92
1. Apple Computer, Inc. — History; 2. Businessmen — United States — Biography; 3. Computer engineers — United States — Biography; 4. Jobs, Steve; 5. Inventors; 6. Jobs, Steve, 1955-2011
1477700803; 9781477700808, $25.25; 9781477701454
               LC 2012020633

Courtesy of Rosen Publishing

This graphic novel by Jane Gould is a biography of Steven Jobs, "best known for being a co-founder of Apple Inc. Before Apple Inc., he was a brilliant designer and inventor who approached business with an unexpected savvy and joy of discovery. Jobs created gadgets that transformed today's digital era." (Publisher's note)
Includes index.

Gownley, Jimmy
    ★ **Amelia** Rules! Volume Three: Superheroes. Renaissance Press 2006 174p. Illustration
Grades: 3 4 5 6
741.5; Fic
1. Friendship — Graphic novels; 2. Graphic novels; 3. Humorous graphic novels
9780971216969, $11.99

This third volume of Amelia Rules! contains one storyline, about the summer after fourth grade. First, Amelia faces the possibility of another move (across town); then new friends Trishia and Ninja Joan join Amelia and Rhonda, while Reggie and Pajama Man fight crime — actually, the Legion of Steves. The guys even team up with the Park Terrace Ninjas. In the middle of all the summer fun, Amelia learns Trishia's terrible secret and doesn't know how to help.
Originally published as Amelia Rules! issues #11-16.

    Amelia rules! True things (adults don't want kids to know). Atheneum Books for Young Readers 2010 163p.
Grades: 3 4 5 6
741.5; 741
978-1-4169-8609-6 (pa), $10.99; 1-4169-8609-X (pa)

    ★ **Amelia** rules! when the past is a present. Renaissance Press 2008 168p. Illustration
Grades: 3 4 5 6
741.5; Fic
1. Friendship — Graphic novels; 2. Graphic novels; 3. Humorous graphic novels
978-0-9712169-8-3, $24.95; 978-0-9712169-9-0 (pa), $11.99

The kids are now in fifth grade, and Amelia and Rhonda are officially friends and not enemies any more. Amelia is going to her first dance (with a boy no less — Kyle the ninja), but she's not the only one with a date. Is Amelia's mom seeing someone too? Perhaps Reggie (a.k.a. Captain Amazing) can shed some light on the situation, by spying on their date. But it's not all fun for the 10-year-old spitfire. A good friend " Joan " reveals that her father will be deployed to Iraq with his job in the military, and it gets Amelia thinking about her own family, her past, and what it means for the present.

    Amelia rules!: The meaning of life — and other stuff. written and illustrated by Jimmy Gownley. Atheneum Books for Young Readers 2011 147p. Illustration
Grades: 3 4 5 6
741.5; 741
978-1-4169861-3-3, $19.99; 1-4169861-3-8; 978-1-4169861-2-6 (pa), $10.99; 1-4169861-2-X (pa)

LC 2011018407

"Though it is a slender volume, Gownley does not shy away from tough topics, presenting them in a way that is both approachable and understandable to kids.... With all of the tribulations Amelia must deal with, she paints an accurate portrait of what preteens must deal with and how fast they sometimes have to grow up." Kirkus

★ **Amelia** rules!: the whole world's crazy!. Renaissance Press 2003 176p.

Grades: 3 4 5 6   **741.5; Fic**
1. Family life — Graphic novels; 2. Friendship — Graphic novels; 3. Graphic novels; 4. Humorous graphic novels
0-9712169-3-2, $24.95; 0-9712169-2-4 (pa), $14.95

"Amelia...is getting used to life with her newly divorced mom and her hip, young aunt Tanner; settling in at a strange new school; and finding a group of friends. Amelia is no sweet innocent, nor are her three G.A.S.P (Gathering of Awesome Superpals) buddies: Reggie, superhero in the making; Rhonda, Amelia's tough bete noire with a fourth-grade "thing" for Reggie; and quiet, mysterious Pajamaman. Jealousy, meanness, sadness, and confusion, as well as surprising generosity, and love crisscross the pages in energetic, freewheeling, full-color cartoon art that unwraps a kid's-eye view of life honestly, poignantly, and with a hefty dollop of melodrama." Booklist

Other titles in this series are: Amelia rules!: What makes you happy? (2004); Amelia rules! Superheroes (2005); Amelia rules! a very ninja Christmas (2009); Amelia rules! When the past is a present (2010); Amelia rules! The tweenage guide to not being unpopular (2010); Amelia rules! True things (adults don't want kids to know (2010); Amelia rules! The meaning of life. . . and other stuff (2011);Amelia rules! Her permanent record (2012)

Amelia rules: The tweenage guide to not being unpopular. Atheneum Books for Young Readers 2010 187p.

Grades: 3 4 5 6   **741; 741.5**
978-1-4169-8610-2, $18.99; 1-4169-8610-3; 978-1-4169-8608-9 (pa), $10.99; 1-4169-8608-1 (pa)

LC 2009053665

★ **Her** permanent record. written and illustrated by Jimmy Gownley. Atheneum Books for Young Readers 2012 144 p.

Grades: 3 4 5 6   **741.5**
1. Aunts — Fiction; 2. Friendship — Fiction; 3. Graphic novels; 4. Schools — Fiction; 5. Voyages and travels — Fiction; 6. Missing persons — Fiction; 7. School stories
1416986154; 9781416986140; 9781416986157, $19.99

LC 2011053039

This book is the eighth installment of the "Amelia Rules!" series by Jimmy Gownley. "With her new spot on the cheerleading squad, [and] Aunt Tanner's hordes of adoring fans,...Amelia's sailing seems remarkably smooth. Then Tanner disappears...sending Amelia into full panic mode. And when she boards a bus on an epic journey to find Tanner...it quickly becomes clear that if Amelia has learned anything in her eleven years, it's that life is never through with surprises." (Publisher's note)

Grahame, Kenneth
Classics illustrated deluxe # 1: the wind in the willows. NBM/Papercutz 2007 144p. Illustration
Grades: 3 4 5 6 7 8
741.5; Fic

Courtesy of NBM Publishing

1. Animals — Graphic novels; 2. Fantasy graphic novels; 3. Graphic novels; 4. Humorous graphic novels
978-1-59707-095-9, $19.99; 978-1-59707-096-6 (pa), $13.95

Kenneth Grahame's classic story of the wild Mister Toad's misadventures and crazy enthusiasms that get him into great trouble from which his friends Badger, Mole, and Rat must extricate him gets a deluxe, full-color graphic novel treatment with art that looks like classic 1930s-style animation.

Graley, Sarah
Kim Reaper: grim beginnings. by Sarah Graley; lettered by Crank!. Oni Press 2018 112 p. Color; Illustration
Grades: 7 8 9 10 11 12   **741.5; Fic**
1. Infatuation — Fiction; 2. Women college students — Fiction; 3. Lesbians — Fiction
1620104555; 9781620104552, $14.99

LC 2017946413

In this book in the Kim Reaper series, by Sarah Graley, edited by Ari Yarwood, "Kim's job is pretty cool: she's a grim reaper.... Becka's crush is on a beautiful gothic angel that frequents the underworld.... Becka finally...ask[s] Kim on a date! But when she falls into a ghostly portal and interrupts Kim at her job, she sets off a chain of events that will pit the two of them against angry cat-dads, vengeful zombies, and perhaps even the underworld itself." (Publisher's note)

"Graley's adorably goth comic is full of over-the-top slapstick; cute, goggle-eyed characters; a sweet lesbian romance; and, of course, lots of skeletons and trips to hell. The contrast between the macabre plot and bubbly art, in a rich palette of warm jewel tones with pops of fluorescent hues, will be utterly bewitching for the right reader." Booklist

Grant, Alan
Robert Louis Stevenson's Kidnapped. adaptation by Alan Grant; illustrator, Cam Kennedy. Tundra Books 2007 un Illustration
Grades: 6 7 8 9 10   **741.5; Fic**
1. Adventure graphic novels; 2. Graphic novels; 3. Stevenson, Robert Louis, 1850-1894 — Adaptations
978-0-88776-843-9 (pa), $11.95; 0-88776-843-1 (pa)

LC 2007921350

Kidnapped is set in 1751, during the time of the Jacobite rebellion " a tumultuous and tragic period in Scottish history. When David Balfour sets out to find his uncle, he never dreamed that he would be kidnapped " but saved from a life of slavery " and thrown from one escapade to another in the company of the fugitive, masterful swordsman Alan Breck Stewart.

"This is an engaging adaptation, aided by Kennedy's vibrant illustrations in a palette dominated by blues, greens, and sepia tones. The action scenes are exciting." SLJ

Gray, Harold
★ **Harold** Gray's Little Orphan Annie; Volume one: the complete daily comics, 1924-27: Will tomorrow ever come? IDW Publishing 2008 385p. Illustration
Grades: 2 3 4 5 6 7 8 9 10 11 12 Adult
741.5; Fic
1. Adventure graphic novels; 2. Graphic novels; 3. Little Orphan Annie (Fictional character); 4. Orphans — Graphic novels
978-1-60010-140-3, $39.99

Courtesy of IDW Publishing

Little Orphan Annie started as a daily newspaper comic strip in one newspaper, the New York Daily News, on August 5, 1924. It became a popular strip, syndicated to newspapers all over the world. It eventually became a Broadway, a hit movie, and Annie became an iconic character. This book is the first comprehensive collection of Gray's comic strip and is the first volume of a series planned to collect all of Gray's Little Orphan Annie strips. She is an orphan girl living in an orphanage, with an unscrupulous director who hires Annie out for work. When wealthy Mrs. Warbucks, trying to prove that she cares for the poor, takes Annie on a "trial" adoption, Annie eventually meets Oliver Warbucks, whom she calls "Daddy." As the strips go on, Annie undergoes many hardships and perils, facing everything with spunk and a positive attitude. She's no wilting girl, though " she can fight (she has a mean right hook) and will take on any bully. She rescues the dog she calls Sandy, who rewards her with a loyal friendship. This volume includes more than 1,000 comic strips, many of which haven't seen publication since their original newspaper appearance. During the first years of the strip's publication, the color Sunday comics had no connection to the weekday storylines, but a few Sunday pages are included in this book. This book may appeal most to adults who remember reading Little Orphan Annie in the "funnies" pages, but the stories will appeal to all ages. Contributing Editor Jeet Heer provides a biography of Harold Gray.

Griffith, Saul
   Howtoons: tools of mass construction. Dr. Saul Griffith, co-creator, writer & engineer; Nick Dragotta, co-creator, writer & artist; Ingrid Dragotta, project & book design; Arwen Griffith, editor; Joost Bonsen, co-creator & writer. Image Comics 2014 360 p. Illustration
Grades: 2 3 4 5 6 7   **741.5; 507.8**
   1. Self-instruction; 2. Educational games
1632151014; 9781632151018, $17.99
   "Follow Celine and Tucker as they learn through play with over 50 DIY projects! This brother-and-sister pair use everyday objects to invent toys that readers can build. Combining comics and real-life science and engineering principles, Howtoons are designed to encourage kids to become active participants in the world around them." (Publisher's note)
   "The bright, somewhat chaotic artwork is designed to capture a kid's attention and imagination. The projects are not laid out in a staid, step-by-step manner, and several of them will require extra thought or adult assistance, but the variety is hard to beat, as the creators cover art, math, engineering, science, and more." Booklist

Grine, Chris
   Chickenhare. Chris Grine. Graphix / Scholastic 2013 160 p.
Grades: 4 5 6 7 8 9   **741.5**
   1. Animals — Graphic novels; 2. Taxidermy — Fiction; 3. Escapes — Fiction
0545485088; 9780545485081, $10.99
                                                          LC 2012936214
   Author Chris Grine presents a children's comic book. "What's a chickenhare? A cross between a chicken and a rabbit, of course. And that makes Chickenhare the rarest animal around! So when he and his turtle friend Abe are captured and sold to the evil taxidermist Klaus, they've got to find a way to escape before Klaus turns them into stuffed animals. With the help of two other strange creatures, Banjo and Meg, they might even get away. But with Klaus and his thugs hot on their trail, the adventure is only just beginning for this unlikely quartet of friends." (Publisher's note)

   Chickenhare: The House of Klaus. Dark Horse Comics 2006 160p. Illustration
Grades: 7 8 9 10 11 12   **741.5**
   1. Adventure graphic novels; 2. Fantasy graphic novels; 3. Graphic novels

978-1-59307-574-3, $9.95
   Friends Chickenhare (who is exactly that, a cross between a chicken and a hare) and bearded turtle Abe are captives being taken to the mad taxidermist Klaus, who looks like an evil Santa. Chickenhare and Abe escape, along with obnoxious monkey Banjo and horned girl Meg; Chickenhare finds the dead goat Mr. Buttons, and the others encounter the warlike, cave-dwelling Shromph, who have a bone to pick with Klaus. A few harsh words, some violence, and implied cannibalism may be disturbing for younger readers.

   Chickenhare: fire in the hole. Dark Horse Comics 2008 200p. Illustration
Grades: 7 8 9 10 11 12 Adult   **741.5; Fic**
   1. Adventure graphic novels; 2. Fantasy graphic novels; 3. Graphic novels
978-1-59307-907-9, $10.95
   Chickenhare, his friend Abe, and their new friends Scabby, Meg and Banjo managed to escape the evil Taxidermist Klaus, but they have gone from one dangerous situation into...something worse. While at sea in a small boat about to be swamped by rain and waves, Banjo's brother and some warriors from the Underworld pop up, they zap the soul out of Abe and take Banjo and Meg. Chickenhare is left with Scabby and Abe's body. He must venture into the Underworld to recover Abe's soul. Meanwhile, Banjo and Meg face punishment for deserting the Underworld. And just why do the Sea Folk call Chickenhare "Your Majesty"?

Grunwald, Jennifer
   I am Iron Man. edited by Jennifer Grunwald. Marvel Worldwide, Inc. 2010 un Illustration
Grades: 7 8 9 10 11 12 Adult   **741.5; Fic**
   1. Graphic novels; 2. Iron Man (Fictional character); 3. Superhero graphic novels
978-0-7851-4558-5, $16.99
   The first Iron Man movie, released in 2008, was a major hit, but just like the other superhero movies based on Marvel Comics properties, it wasn't based on any particular Iron Man comics. This book collects a two-issue miniseries based on the movie script, written by Peter David with pencils by Sean Chen, a one-shot written by Christos Gage with pencils by Hugo Petrus, and Iron Man #200, which was written by Denny O'Neil with pencils by Mark Bright and originally published in 1985. David and Chen's comic adapts the movie script, hitting all the high points of the action. Gage and Petrus's one-shot, "Security Measures," looks at the action of the movie from the viewpoint of S.H.I.E.L.D. agent Coulson. Iron Man #200 features a battle between Iron Man and Iron Monger, who is Tony Stark's erstwhile partner Obadiah Stane. The book also includes an interview with Kevin Feige, producer of the Iron Man movie, and photos taken on the movie sets. The book actually cuts down on the amount of violence that was shown in the movie.

Gulledge, Laura Lee
   ★ **Page** by Paige. Amulet Books 2011 un Illustration
Grades: 7 8 9 10 11 12   **741.5; Fic**
   1. Artists — Graphic novels; 2. Friendship — Graphic novels; 3. Graphic novels; 4. Humorous graphic novels; 5. New York (N.Y.) — Graphic novels
0-8109-9721-5; 0-8109-9722-3 (pa); 978-0-8109-9721-9, $18.95; 978-0-8109-9722-6 (pa), $9.95
   Teenage Paige Turner (blame her writer parents) moves to New York City from Virginia, and she finds the big city rather overwhelming. She decides to buy a sketchbook and sort out her thoughts and feelings in drawings. Soon she does make some friends, and she explores more of the city, but as she begins to feel happier, she clashes with her parents. All of this goes into her sketchbook journal, which she starts to show to her new

friends — Jules, Longo, and Gabe. The book is organized by Paige's "rules," which she uses to try to change herself, such as "Rule #2: Draw what you know. If you feel it or see it...DRAW IT!"

"Gulledge's b&w illustrations are simple but well-suited to their subject matter; the work as a whole is a good-natured, optimistic portrait of a young woman evolving toward adulthood." Publ Wkly

Hadley, Amy Reeder

Moon Girl and Devil Dinosaur; Volume 1: BFF. by Amy Reeder and Brandon Montclare; illustrated by Natacha Bustos. Marvel Enterprises 2016 136 p. Color; Illustration

Grades: 7 8 9 10 11 12 Adult   **741.5; Fic**

1. Female superhero graphic novels; 2. Dinosaurs — Graphic novels
1302900056; 9781302900052, $17.99

"Lunella LaFayette is a preteen super genius who wants to change the world—but learned the hard way that it takes MORE than just big brains. Fearful of the monstrous INHUMAN genes inside her, life is turned upside down when a savage, red-scaled tyrant is teleported from prehistoric past to a far-flung future we call TODAY. " (Publisher's note)

Contains material originally published in magazine form as MOON GIRL AND DEVIL DINOSAUR #1-6; Volume 1 in an ongoing series

Hale, Dean

★ **Calamity** Jack. Bloombury 2010 144p. Illustration

Grades: 4 5 6 7 8 9   **741.5; Fic**

1. Adventure graphic novels; 2. Fantasy graphic novels; 3. Folklore — Graphic novels; 4. Graphic novels
9781599903736, $14.99; 9781599900766, $19.99

LC 2008-41332

In this sequel to Rapunzel's Revenge, the reader meets Jack as a child growing up in the city of Shyport; Jack has been a schemer practically since birth, but he hasn't had a whole lot of luck. His schemes usually end in unforeseen consequences. When he goes up against the giant Blunderboar, the magic beanstalk he uses to reach the giant's floating fortress destroys his neighborhood and his mother's bakery, and he just manages to leave town with a certain gold-egg-laying goose under his arm. After the events of the first book, Jack and Rapunzel come to Shyport, where Jack hopes to help his mother rebuild her bakery with the golden eggs he now has. However, they come to a city transformed Blunderboar has taken over, his security company claims to be keeping giant ants at bay, and Jack's mother is being held prisoner. Jack is still wanted for what he had done, and only Prudence, Jack's hat-loving pixie partner-in-crime, is willing to help. Then Jack and Rapunzel meet Freddie Sparksmith, newspaperman and gadget inventor, and they team up for a rescue mission. The book includes a lot of action and some non-gory violence.

Companion to: Rapunzel's Revenge

★ **Rapunzel's** revenge. [by] Shannon and Dean Hale; illustrated by Nathan Hale. Bloomsbury 2008 144p. Illustration; Map

Grades: 5 6 7 8   **741.5; Fic**

1. Fairy tales — Graphic novels; 2. Fantasy graphic novels; 3. Graphic novels; 4. Humorous graphic novels
1-59990-070-X; 1-59990-288-5 (pa); 978-1-59990-070-4, $18.99; 978-1-59990-288-3 (pa), $14.99

LC 2007-37670

In this graphic novel, Rapunzel escapes "from the enchanted tree where Mother Gothel imprisoned her. Rapunzel sets off alone through the ghost towns and Badlands of Gothel's Reach. She is determined to find Gothel's Villa and teach Mother Gothel a long-overdue lesson for her years of treachery and lies, and help her real mother get out of the mine camps where Mother Gothel has kept her enslaved." (Publisher's note)

"The dialogue is witty, the story is an enticing departure from the original, and the illustrations are magically fun and expressive." SLJ

Another title about these characters is: Calamity Jack (2009)

Hale, Nathan

Alamo all-stars. Nathan Hale. Harry N Abrams Inc 2016 122 p. Illustration; Color (Nathan Hale's Hazardous Tales)

Grades: 3 4 5 6   **741.5; 976.4**

1. Texas — History — Revolution, 1835-1836; 2. Alamo (San Antonio, Tex.) — History — Siege, 1836; 3. United States — History — 1815-1861 — Graphic novels
1419719025; 9781419719028, $12.95

This graphic novel, sixth in author Nathan Lane's Hazardous Tales series, "relays the facts, politics, military actions, and prominent personalities that defined the Texas Revolution.... Beginning with the expeditions of the so-called 'Land Pirates,' through the doomed stand at the Alamo, and ending with the victory over Santa Anna at the Battle of San Jacinto, the entire Texas saga is on display." (Publisher's note)

"The irreverent tone, interjections by the narrators, and often humorous backstories of the major players lighten the mood and break up battle scenes in digestible pieces, and Hale's dynamic cartoon art renders each character uniquely enough that they're easy to tell apart — no small feat, given the large cast." Booklist

Includes bibliographical references

Donner dinner party. by Nathan Hale. Harry N Abrams Inc 2013 123 p. (Nathan Hale's Hazardous Tales)

Grades: 5 6 7 8   **979.4; 741.5**

1. Donner party; 2. Sierra Nevada Mountains
1419708562; 9781419708565, $12.95

In this graphic novel, author Nathan Hale "tells the harrowing story of the ill-fated Donner party. Beginning with their departure from Springfield, Illinois, in 1846, Hale depicts the party's progress...and includes lots of factual details, such as a roster of everyone in the party, how they died, and a helpful map showing just how...close they came to California before meeting their grisly end." (Booklist)

"This informative graphic novel capitalizes on enticingly gross history to great effect, balancing raw facts with strong storytelling." Booklist

Nathan Hale's hazardous tales: big bad ironclad!. Nathan Hale. Abrams 2012 118 p.

Grades: 4 5 6   **973.7**

1. Comic books, strips, etc.; 2. United States — History — 1861-1865, Civil War — Naval operations; 3. Cushing, William
1419703951; 9781419703959, $12.95

LC 2012947181

Author Nathan Hale "covers the history of the amazing ironclad steam warships used in the Civil War [in his book 'Big Bad Ironclad!'] From the ship's inventor, who had a history of blowing things up and only 100 days to complete his project, to the mischievous William Cushing, who pranked his way through the whole war, this book is filled with...facts." (Publisher's note)

Includes bibliographical references.; Map on endpapers.

Nathan Hale's hazardous tales: one dead spy. Nathan Hale. Amulet Books 2012 128 p.

Grades: 3 4 5 6 7   **741.5/973**

1. United States — History — Graphic novels; 2. Hale, Nathan, 1755-1776
141970396X; 9781419703966, $12.95

LC 2012947189

In this graphic novel, historical figure "[Nathan] Hale, convicted of espionage, forestalls death by telling stories from American history. In this volume, he's helped by the hangman in telling the story of the early days of the revolution. He takes readers from his college days at Yale to the Boston Massacre, the Boston Tea Party, his joining the 7th Connecticut regiment, the Battle of Bunker Hill and other pivotal scenes in New England and New York City." (Kirkus)

Other titles in this series are: Big bad ironclad! (2012); Donner dinner party (2013); Treaties, trenches, mud, and blood (2014); The underground abductor (2015); Alamo all-stars (2016); Raid of no return (2017)

Nathan Hale's hazardous tales: treaties, trenches, mud, and blood (a World War I tale). by Nathan Hale. Amulet Books 2014 128 p. Color illustration; Color; Map (Nathan Hale's hazardous tales)

Grades: 4 5 6 7   **741.5; 940.3**
1. World War, 1914-1918 — Comic books, strips, etc; 2. World War, 1914-1918
1419708082; 9781419708084, $12.95

LC 2013049048

"Nathan Hale, Revolutionary War hero, continues to distract his executioners in this fourth volume, which tackles WWI's complex events." (Horn Book)

"Per established series formula, a frame tale finds the author's more-renowned namesake holding off the hangman, Scheherazade-like, with tales from our country's future history. In this volume, he covers the war's prelude, precipitation, major campaigns and final winding down in small but reasonably easy-to-follow two-color panels.... Hale cogently conveys the mind-numbing scale of it all as well as the horrors of trench warfare." Kirkus

Includes bibliographical references

The **underground** abductor: an abolitionist tale. Nathan Hale. Harry N Abrams Inc. 2015 125 p. Illustration; Color (Nathan Hale's Hazardous Tales)

Grades: 3 4 5 6 7   **92; 741.5**
1. Fugitive slaves — United States — Comic books, strips, etc.; 2. Underground Railroad — Comic books, strips, etc.; 3. Tubman, Harriet, 1820?-1913; 4. Biographical graphic novels
9781419715365, $12.95; 1419715364
Eisner Nominee: Best Publication for Kids (2016)

In this graphic novel, "a fictionalized Nathan Hale (a patriot from the American Revolutionary War) tells stories about America's most extraordinary heroes and villains. In this installment, Hale tells his British captors about Harriet Tubman, the spy and nurse who helped hundreds of American slaves run away in the 1800s on the Underground Railroad." (School Library Journal)

Includes bibliographical references

Hale, Shannon

Real friends. Shannon Hale; illustrated by LeUyen Pham. First Second 2017 224 p. Color; Illustration

Grades: 3 4 5 6   **92; 741.5**
1. Bullies; 2. Friendship
9781626724167, $21.99; 9781626727854

LC 2016945552

In this graphic memoir, by Shannon Hale, illustrated by LeUyen Pham, "Shannon and Adrienne have been best friends ever since they were little. But one day, Adrienne starts hanging out with Jen, the most popular girl in class and the leader of a circle of friends called The Group. Everyone in The Group wants to be Jen's #1, and some girls would do anything to stay on top...even if it means bullying others." (Publisher's note)

"The author reflects on her life from the vantage point of adulthood, displaying a mature awareness of her own flaws and an understanding of the behavior of unsympathetic kids such as Wendy and Jenny, and her accessible writing and hopeful tone will speak to readers. Pham's gentle cartoon images make effective use of perspective and composition to underscore Shannon's sense of alienation." SLJ

Halliday, Ayun

Peanut. Ayun Halliday; illustrated by Paul Hoppe. Schwartz & Wade Books 2012 216 p. Color illustration

Grades: 6 7 8 9 10   **741.5**
1. Food allergy — Fiction; 2. Graphic novels; 3. High schools — Fiction; 4. Mothers and daughters — Fiction; 5. Moving, Household — Fiction; 6. Popularity — Fiction; 7. Schools — Fiction; 8. Moving — Graphic novels; 9. Peanut allergy — Graphic novels; 10. School stories
037586590X, $15.99; 0375965904, $18.99; 9780375865909, $15.99; 9780375965906, $18.99

LC 2009047168

In this graphic novel by Ayun Halliday, illustrated by Paul Hoppe, "Sadie has the perfect plan to snag some friends when she transfers to Plainfield High — pretend to have a peanut allergy. But what happens when you have to hand in that student health form your unsuspecting mom was supposed to fill out? And what if your new friends want to come over and your mom serves them snacks? (Peanut butter sandwich, anyone?)" (Publisher's note)

Hama, Larry

The **Battle** of First Bull Run: The Civil War Begins. The Rosen Publishing Group 2007 48p. Illustration

Grades: 3 4 5 6 7 8 9
741.5; 973.7
1. Bull Run. 1st Battle of, 1861 — Graphic novels; 2. Graphic novels; 3. War — Graphic novels; 4. United States — History — 1861-1865, Civil War — Graphic novels
978-1-4042-0776-9, $29.25

Courtesy of Rosen Publishing

Three months after the shelling of Fort Sumter, Union and Confederate forces met for the first time in earnest combat. However, neither side was prepared at this early stage of the war, and confusion reigned on the battlefield. Finally, Confederate reinforcements forced the Union army into a panicked retreat. The intensity — and ill preparedness — of both armies convinced the nation that the conflict between the states would be a long, bloody ordeal. The book includes background information, a glossary, and a list of books for further reading.

Part of the Graphic Battles of the Civil War series. The book is also available in paperback from Osprey Publishing under the title The War is On!: Battle of First Bull Run.

The **battle** of Iwo Jima: guerilla warfare in the Pacific. by Larry Hama; illustrated by Anthony Williams. Rosen Pub. 2007 48p. Illustration; Map (Graphic battles of World War II)

Grades: 5 6 7 8 9
940.54
1. Graphic novels; 2. Iwo Jima, Battle of, 1945 — Graphic novels; 3. World War, 1939-1945 — Graphic novels
978-1-4042-0781-3 (lib bdg), $29.25; 1-4042-0781-3 (lib bdg)

LC 2006007645

Courtesy of Rosen Publishing

"Using a graphic novel to introduce the battle for Iwo Jima makes it very accessible.

Before the graphic-novel section of the book begins, Hama provides a short, informative background piece describing the run-up to World War II, the significance of the Japanese war machine, and the importance of the tiny island of Iwo Jima. Then the graphic novel, illustrated by Williams in camouflage colors, does a terrific job of examining the ups and downs of the battle as well as the horror of so many losses — on both sides." Booklist
Includes bibliographical references

The **Battle** of Shiloh: Surprise Attack!. Rosen Publishing Group 2007 48p. Illustration
Grades: 3 4 5 6 7 8
741.5; 973.7
1. Graphic novels; 2. Shiloh (Tenn.), Battle of, 1862 — Graphic novels; 3. United States — History — 1861-1865, Civil War — Graphic novels
978-1-4042-0779-0, $29.25;
978-1-84603-050-5 (pb)
LC 2006007309

Courtesy of Rosen Publishing

The first major Civil War battle in the Western theater, Shiloh came as a horrifying shock to both the American public and those in arms. On April 6, 1862, Confederate forces staged a surprise attack on the Union army encamped along the Tennessee River. Fighting was fierce as General Grant struggled to hold off the enemy until his reinforcements arrived the following day so that he could 'Whip 'em tomorrow'. Though nearly driven into the Tennessee River, the Union army could ultimately claim victory — won at a dear cost. With nearly 24,000 total casualties in two days' fighting, 'Bloody Shiloh' served as a wake-up call to the nation, announcing that the continuing fight for the Union would be devastating for both sides. This book brings to life one of the Civil War's bloodiest battles in graphic novel format. It also includes eight pages of background information placing Shiloh in its historical context, detailing the key players, and describing the build-up to the fighting and its aftermath.
Part of the Graphic Battles of the Civil War series; the paperback edition is published by Osprey.

Spider-Girl presents Wild Thing: crash course. Marvel Entertainment 2007 un Illustration
Grades: 5 6 7 8 9 10
741.5
1. Adventure graphic novels; 2. Graphic novels; 3. Superhero graphic novels
978-0-7851-2606-5, $7.99

A few years in the future, in the alternate Marvel Universe where Peter Parker and Mary Jane had a daughter who has become Spider-Girl, Wolverine and Elektra got together and they had a daughter, too Rina Logan, also known as Wild Thing. She has psychic claws that work pretty much like Wolverine's claws, and she has his fast healing power. She still has to deal with high school even as she fights against bad guys, demons, evil droids, and more.

Hamboussi, Peter
Showcase Presents The Flash, Volume One. DC Comics 2007 509p. Illustration
Grades: 7 8 9 10 11 12 Adult
741.5; Fic
1. Graphic novels; 2. Superhero graphic novels; 3. Flash (Fictional character)
978-1-4012-1327-5, $16.99

A freak accident gives Central City police scientist Barry Allen fantastic super-speed abilities. Inspired by his favorite childhood comic book hero, Allen uses the name the Flash and uses his powers to help humanity. He soon finds himself facing such villains as Captain Cold,

Mirror Master, Gorilla Grodd, the Pied Piper, Weather Wizard, and more. This volume collects 39 stories from the 1950s and 1960s in black and white.

Showcase Presents: Legion of Super-Heroes Volume 1. DC Comics 2007 552p. Illustration
Grades: 7 8 9 10 11 12 Adult
741.5; Fic
1. Graphic novels; 2. Legion of Super-Heroes (Fictional characters); 3. Superhero graphic novels
978-1-4012-1382-4, $16.99

The Legion of Super-Heroes, teenagers from across the cosmos, each with a unique ability, are the sworn protectors of the galaxy. Headquartered in their Super-Hero Club House, Lightning Lad, Saturn Girl, and Cosmic Boy have high standards for young hopeful champions wishing to join their ranks. With the largest roster of any super-team of the 2960s, they patrol all sectors of the universe to ensure peace and justice for all sentient beings. This volume collects black and white reprints of stories originally published from 1958 through 1964.

Showcase Presents: Martian Manhunter Volume 1. DC Comics 2007 544p. Illustration
Grades: 7 8 9 10 11 12 Adult
741.5; Fic
1. Graphic novels; 2. Martian Manhunter (Fictional character); 3. Superhero graphic novels
978-1-4012-1368-8, $16.99

After being accidentally teleported to Earth, Martian J'onn J'onzz finds himself stranded in a strange new world, with no way home. Using his powers to disguise his appearance, J'onn J'onzz adopts the name of deceased Denver police detective John Jones. With this new identity, he joins the Middleton Police force, secretly using his powers to help the inhabitants of Earth. Jack Miller and Joe Samachson were principal writers on the series in the early years, and artist Joe Certa did all the pencils; this black and white volume reprints stories originally published from 1953 through 1962.

Haney, Bob
Showcase Presents: Metamorpho, the Element Man Volume 1. DC Comics 2005 560p. Illustration
Grades: 7 8 9 10 11 12 Adult
741.5; Fic
1. Graphic novels; 2. Science fiction graphic novels; 3. Superhero graphic novels
1-4012-0762-6, $16.99

Adventurer Rex Mason would do almost anything for the right price, but he ended up paying with his own humanity for stealing the legendary Orb of Ra for millionaire industrialist Simon Stagg. The mysterious relic transformed Rex into a freakish "element" man, with the ability to transform his body into hundreds of different substances. Calling himself Metamorpho, Rex considered his life cursed and sought a way to reverse the Orb's powers. Along the way, Stagg used Metamorpho's unique skills for his own purposes, and the Element Man would go along, since it meant more time with Stagg's gorgeous daughter Sapphire. The stories in this black and white volume date from 1964 through 1966.

Showcase Presents: Teen Titans Volume 1. stories by Bob Haney; art and covers by Nick Cardy. DC Comics 2006 528p. Illustration
Grades: 6 7 8 9 10 11 12 Adult
741.5; Fic
1. Graphic novels; 2. Superhero graphic novels; 3. Teen Titans (Fictional characters); 4. Robin (Fictional character); 5. Flash (Fictional character)
978-1-4012-0788-5, $16.99

The Teen Titans were all sidekicks to such heroes as Batman, Wonder Woman, Aquaman, and the Flash. When teen heroes Robin, Aqualad, and Kid Flash joined together, they became a forced to be reckoned with. Wonder Girl quickly joined them, and occasionally Speedy would come, and they all proved they were just as capable of defeating the bad guys and saving the world as their mentors, while still being teens and having fun. The black and white reprinted stories originally appeared from 1964 through 1968. Today's teens will get a kick out of what the writers thought was cool "teen speak" back then.

Showcase Presents: Sgt. Rock. DC Comics 2007 543p. Illustration
Grades: 8 9 10 11 12 Adult   **741.5**
1. Adventure graphic novels; 2. Graphic novels; 3. Sgt. Rock (Fictional character); 4. World War, 1939-1945 — Graphic novels
978-1-4012-1713-6, $16.99

Sgt. Rock, created by Robert Kanigher, was an ordinary soldier fighting in World War II. The stories collected in this volume, published from 1959 through 1962, depict Rock and his Easy Company fighting against evil during the war. Even today, Sgt. Rock is a symbol of patriotism and of America's fighting spirit. The stories include battle action.

Hanuka, Tomer
Attack on Titan anthology. Attack on Titan created by Hajime Isayama; edited by Ben Applegate and Jeanine Schaefer; cover, logo, and interior design by Phil Balsman; lettering and interior design by Steve Wands. Kodansha 2016 256 p. Illustration
Grades: 8 9 10 11 12   **741.5**
1. Fantasy fiction — Graphic novels; 2. Horror fiction — Graphic novels; 3. Science fiction graphic novels; 4. Shonen manga
1632362589; 9781632362582, $29.99

This tribute anthology to the manga Attack on Titan features "original stories by a long roster of comic superstars such as Scott Snyder (Batman, American Vampire), Gail Simone (Batgirl), Michael Avon Oeming (Powers), Paolo Rivera (Daredevil, Amazing Spider-Man), Cameron Stewart (Fight Club 2, Batgirl) and Faith Erin Hicks (The Adventures of Superhero Girl)!" (Publisher's note)

"The Victorian-style guide to Titan's walled city by Genevieve Valentine and David López is a standout, as is the contemplative final story by brothers Asaf and Tomer Hanuka." Pub Wkly

Harper, Charise Mericle
Fashion Kitty. Hyperion Books for Children 2005 90p. Illustration
Grades: 3 4 5 6 7 8 9   **741.5; Fic**
1. Cats — Graphic novels; 2. Graphic novels; 3. Humorous graphic novels
0-7868-5134-1, $8.99

Kiki Kittie is a very unusual cat. For one thing, she has a mouse for a pet — and that's kind of like a human having a chocolate cake for a pet. Kiki also has a natural flair for fashion, but up until a recent birthday, she was just an ordinary fashionable kitty. Then, on that day, she discovered that she had special powers: she can turn into Fashion Kitty, able to mix and match hundreds of outfits in a single second. Regular cat by day, Fashion Kitty by night, Kiki is always ready to answer a call of despair and save other cats from making fashion faux pas

Other titles about Fashion Kitty are: Fashion Kitty versus the Fashion Queen (2007); Fashion Kitty and the unlikely hero (2008); Fashion Kitty and the B.O.Y.S. (2011)

Fashion Kitty Versus the Fashion Queen. Hyperion Paperbacks for Children 2007 90p. Illustration
Grades: 3 4 5 6 7 8 9   **741.5; Fic**
1. Cats — Graphic novels; 2. Graphic novels; 3. Humorous graphic novels
978-0-7868-3726-7, $8.99

After her last adventure, Fashion Kitty is truly becoming a hero. At school, she is more popular than ever. She's even been mentioned in several articles in the local newspaper, (which she clips out and saves in a scrapbook, of course). But not everyone is excited about Fashion Kitty's newfound popularity. A spoiled new kitty named Cassandra doesn't like sharing the spotlight. And when Fashion Kitty starts inspiring the other kitties at school to be more independent about their style choices, Cassandra really doesn't like it. So she hatches a plan (evil, of course) that involves lying, conniving, and outlawing bright colors and patterns. Fashion Kitty knows she must put an end to Cassandra's reign of terror. She will use her fashion sense, quick smarts, and the power of friendship to overcome fashion evil.

Harras, Bob
Showcase Presents The Unknown Soldier Volume 1. DC Comics 2006 552p. Illustration
Grades: 8 9 10 11 12 Adult   **741.5; Fic**
1. Adventure graphic novels; 2. Graphic novels; 3. Unknown Soldier (Fictional character)
978-1-4012-1090-8, $16.99

His face hideously disfigured by a grenade explosion in the early days of World War II, the young man who would become the Unknown Soldier was determined to continue fighting for his country. His true identity kept top secret, he became the perfect covert operative, using a multitude of disguises to carry out his exploits against the Axis powers. The first 38 adventures of the Unknown Soldier are collected in this black and white reprint volume, with stories dating from 1970 through 1975.

Showcase Presents: The War That Time Forgot. DC Comics 2007 560p. Illustration
Grades: 6 7 8 9 10 11 12 Adult   **741.5; Fic**
1. Adventure graphic novels; 2. Dinosaurs — Graphic novels; 3. Graphic novels; 4. World War, 1939-1945 — Graphic novels
978-1-4012-1253-7, $16.99

On an unnamed, uncharted Pacific island, dinosaurs continued to thrive while World War II raged across the globe. It is on this island that members of the U.S. Armed Forces found themselves " armed only with standard issue weapons against the deadliest predators ever to roam the Earth. This volume collects Star Spangled War Stories issues #90-128, from 1960 through 1966. There's a lot of war action and dinosaur-fighting action. The stories here have been reprinted in black and white.

Superman: Back in Action. DC Comics 2007 144p. Illustration
Grades: 8 9 10 11 12 Adult   **741.5; Fic**
1. Graphic novels; 2. Superhero graphic novels; 3. Superman (Fictional character)
978-1-4012-1263-6, $14.99

This book collects several stories. When Superman returns after the events of Infinite Crisis, he faces skepticism from the people and then gets kidnapped and put up for an intergalactic auction. In stories from the past, he encounters the Metal Men, Firestorm, and Deadman.

Harrell, Rob
Monster on the Hill. by Rob Harrell. Top Shelf Productions 2013 192 p. Color; Illustration
Grades: 4 5 6 7 8
741.5
1. Monsters — Graphic novels; 2. Friendship — Graphic novels
1603090754; 9781603090759, $19.95

Courtesy of Rosen Publishing

This graphic novel by Rob Harrell is set in "1860s England [where] every...township is terrorized by a...monster — much to the townsfolk's delight! Each town's...monster is a source of local pride [and] tourism. Unfortunately, for...Stoker-on-Avon, their monster isn't quite as impressive. Can the morose Rayburn get a monstrous makeover and become a proper horror? It's up to the eccentric Dr. Charles Wilkie and plucky street urchin Timothy to get him up to snuff." (Publisher's note)

Hashimoto, Kyoko
  Love master A, vol.1. Go! Comi 2008 un Illustration
  Grades: 7 8 9 10 11 12   **741.5; Fic**
  1. Graphic novels; 2. Humorous graphic novels; 3. Manga; 4. Romance graphic novels; 5. Shojo manga
  978-1933617-60-2, $10.99
    Aria starts at a new high school, hoping to have a normal school experience. Since elementary school, when she confessed her love to a classmate and was summarily rejected, she has suffered rejection all through school and earned the ironic nickname "Love Master." Now, she has renounced love. However, on her first day at school, she discovers the school's strange way of selecting Student Council members, and not only is she as a first year student a Student Council member, she is the President! And her reputation has been twisted so everyone thinks she's a real "Love Master" and wants her advice. Tonohashi High School is in for a very interesting year.

Hatke, Ben
  ★ **Legends** of Zita the spacegirl. Ben Hatke. First Second 2012 205 p. Color illustration
  Grades: 4 5 6   **741.5**
  1. Fame — Fiction; 2. Graphic novels; 3. Heroes — Fiction; 4. Robots — Fiction; 5. Science fiction; 6. Science fiction graphic novels; 7. Adventure fiction
  1596434473; 9781596434479, $12.99; 9781596438064, $18.99
                                                             LC 2012012748
    This graphic novel, by Ben Hatke, is a children's science fiction adventure story. "Zita is determined to find her way home to earth, following the events of the first book.... Zita's exploits from her first adventure have made her an intergalactic megastar! But she's about to find out that fame doesn't come without a price. And who can you trust when your true self is being eclipsed by your public persona, and you've got a robot doppelganger wreaking havoc...while wearing your face?" (Publisher's note)
    "Hatke's arrestingly vibrant art commands instant adoration of its reader... Readers would be hard-pressed to not find something to like in these tales; they're a winning formula of eye-catching aesthetics, plot and creativity, adeptly executed. Imaginative and utterly bewitching." Kirkus

  Mighty Jack and the Goblin King. Ben Hatke. First Second 2017 208 p. Color; Illustration
  Grades: 4 5 6 7   **741.5**
  1. Monsters — Graphic novels; 2. Magic — Fiction; 3. Siblings — Graphic novels
  9781626722668, $14.99; 9781626722675, $22.99
                                                             LC 2016961549
    "In this follow-up to Mighty Jack, the titular character and his friend Lilly travel through a portal in search of Jack's sister, Maddy, who has been kidnapped by an ogre. The duo are separated and must battle their own monsters, helped along the way by even more winsome and fantastical creatures than in the first volume." (School Library Journal)

  Mighty Jack; Volume 1. Ben Hatke; color by Alex Campbell and Hilary Sycamore. First Second 2016 203 p. Color; Illustration
  Grades: 4 5 6 7   **741.5; Fic**
  1. Brothers and sisters — Fiction; 2. Autistic children — Fiction; 3. Fantasy fiction
  1626722641; 9781626722644, $14.99

                                                             LC 2015951861
    In this book, by Ben Hatke, "Jack might be the only kid in the world who's dreading summer. But he's got a good reason: summer is when his single mom takes a second job and leaves him at home to watch his autistic kid sister, Maddy. It's a lot of responsibility, and it's boring, too, because Maddy doesn't talk. Ever. But then, one day at the flea market, Maddy does talk — to tell Jack to trade their mom's car for a box of mysterious seeds. It's the best mistake Jack has ever made." (Publisher's note)
    Another title in this series is: Mighty Jack and the goblin king (2017)

  ★ The **Return** of Zita the Spacegirl. by Ben Hatke. First Second 2014 240 p.
  Grades: 3 4 5 6   **741.5**
  1. Good and evil — Fiction; 2. Graphic novels; 3. Outer space — Fiction; 4. Science fiction graphic novels; 5. Science fiction; 6. Prisoners — Fiction
  1626720584; 9781626720589, $18.99
    "Zita the Spacegirl has saved planets, battled monsters, and wrestled with interplanetary fame. But she faces her biggest challenge yet in the third and final installment of the Zita adventures. Wrongfully imprisoned on a penitentiary planet, Zita has to plot the galaxy's greatest jailbreak before the evil prison warden can execute his plan of interstellar domination!" (Publisher's note)
    "The art is colorful, detailed, and child-friendly. Readers of all ages can relate to the themes of friendship and loyalty while enjoying the fantasy of a far-out sci-fi adventure." Horn Book

  ★ **Zita** the spacegirl. First Second 2011 182p. Illustration
  Grades: 3 4 5 6   **741.5**
  1. Graphic novels; 2. Science fiction graphic novels
  1-59643-446-5 (pa); 978-1-59643-695-6; 978-1-59643-446-2 (pa), $10.99; 978-1-59643-695-4, $17.99
    When her best friend is abducted by an alien doomsday cult, Zita leaps to the rescue and finds herself a stranger on a strange planet.

Hayashi, Mikase
  March on earth, volume one. DC Comics/CMX 2009 un Illustration
  Grades: 7 8 9 10 11 12   **741.5; Fic**
  1. Family life — Graphic novels; 2. Graphic novels; 3. Manga; 4. Romance graphic novels; 5. Shojo manga
  978-1-4012-1594-1, $9.99
    When Yuzu was a young girl, her older sister Tsubaki raised her after their parents died. Then a few years ago, Tsubaki got pregnant and decided to have the baby and raise him as a single parent; she would never tell Yuzu who the father was. Just a few months ago, Tsubaki died in a car accident, and Yuzu, now a 10th grader in high school, has decided she will raise her nephew Shou herself. She and Shou live in an apartment in the building owned by Mrs. Kusano, who lives there with her two sons, Seita and Keita. They help her take care of Shou, but even with their help it's difficult to focus on her studies. She reads her sister's picture books to Shou, especially the last one Tsubaki wrote, called March on Earth. Yuzu wants to become a lawyer to help people, but will there be enough money from what her parents left to pay for college, after paying for rent and all the other expenses? Other teens worry about boyfriends, and whether they should go sing karaoke, but Yuzu has to take care of a two-year-old boy and worry about having enough money to buy him one Christmas present. She doesn't seem to see that Seita has fallen for her, and she seems to be oblivious to his efforts to appear before her half naked (wearing only an apron to cook curry, claiming to have just come out of the bath with only a towel around his waist, ...).

Helfand, Lewis

Conquering Everest: the lives of Edmund Hillary and Tenzing Norgay. Campfire 2011 96p. Illustration

Grades: 10 3 4 5 6 7 8 9   **741.5; 796.522**
1. Mountaineering — Graphic novels; 2. Mountaineers; 3. Nonfiction writers; 4. Hillary, Edmund Sir; 5. Tenzing Norgay, 1914-1986; 6. Mount Everest — Graphic novels
978-93-80741-24-6, $12.99

Tenzing Norgay immigrated to Nepal with his Tibetan family when he was a boy, and he worked hard over the years to become one of the best Sherpas who helped the European, American, and other climbers who journeyed to Nepal to climb Mount Everest. Edmund Hillary was the son of a beekeeper from New Zealand, who became fascinated with mountain climbing during World War II. He came to Nepal in 1953 as part of a British expedition to reach Everest's peak, and Norgay came to be the sirdar, the head Sherpa and organizer of the expedition's support system. These two men became the first to reach Everest's summit at 11:30 a.m. on May 29, 1953. This graphic novel tells the story of the two men from such different backgrounds, and their friendship. The book notes that on May 22, 2010, Californian thirteen-year-old Jordan Romero became the youngest climber to reach Everest's peak. Tayal's panels show some of the massive scale of the mountain.

Mother Teresa: Angel of the Slums. by Lewis Helfand and illustrated by Sachin Nagar. Random House Inc 2013 88 p.

Grades: 6 7 8 9   **271.9**
1. Teresa, Mother, 1910-1997
9380028709; 9789380028705, $11.99

This illustrated biography written by Lewis Helfand and illustrated by Sachin Nagar "presents the facts about Mother Teresa, born Agnes Gonxha Bojaxhiu in Macedonia in 1910. The book describes her decision to become a nun, her early work in Europe, and her path to teaching at a convent in India. From there it covers, in greater detail, her life among the poor and sick in Calcutta, and the foundation of Mother Teresa's worldwide charitable order." (Publisher's Weekly)

Nelson Mandela: the unconquerable soul. Lewis Herlfand. Kalyani Navyug Media Pvt LTD 2011 115 p.

Grades: 8 9 10   **741.5; 92**
1. South Africa — History — Graphic novels; 2. Biographical graphic novels; 3. Mandela, Nelson, 1918-
9380741162; 9789380741161, $12.99

LC 2012374765

This book is a graphic novel biography of Nelson Mandela. It "includes a brief history of 20th-century South Africa along with a full account of Mandela's full life.... [B]lack, white, and gray illustrations are" included. "Endnotes include a glossary and additional facts about South Africa." (School Library Journal)

Herge

★ The **adventures** of Tintin, vol. 1: Tintin in America, Cigars of the Pharaoh, The Blue Lotus. Little, Brown 1994 192p. Illustration

Grades: 4 5 6 7 8 9   **741.5; Fic**
1. Adventure graphic novels; 2. Graphic novels; 3. Tintin (Fictional character) — Graphic novels
0-316-35940-8, $18.99

Tintin, the heroic boy reporter from France, travels to America where he outwits gangsters in Chicago of the 1930s and adventures in the Wild West; sails the Mediterranean Sea with faithful dog Snowy and finds himself in a mystery involving a movie tycoon, drugs, and cigars in an ancient Egyptian tomb; then he travels to India to finally solve the mystery. This Little, Brown edition reprints some of the early Tintin adventures published in the 1930s in a 3-in-1 volume. This is the first in a series that reprints most of the Tintin stories by Herge. Librarians and teachers should

note that the books retain some stereotypical depictions of people of other cultures and remember that these were acceptable and expected at the time of original publication.

Tintin and the Picaros. Little, Brown 1978 62p. Illustration

Grades: 4 5 6 7 8 9   **741.5; Fic**
1. Adventure graphic novels; 2. Graphic novels; 3. Humorous graphic novels; 4. Tintin (Fictional character)
0-316-35849-5, $10.99

LC 77-090973

Tintin and his friends rescue prima donna Bianca Castafiore while trying to help restore their friend Alcazar to power in San Theodoros — but they'll have to defeat General Tapioca and his troops to do it.

Tintin in Tibet. Little, Brown 1978 62p. Illustration

Grades: 4 5 6 7 8 9   **741.5; Fic**
1. Adventure graphic novels; 2. Graphic novels; 3. Humorous graphic novels; 4. Tintin (Fictional character)
0-316-35839-8, $10.99

LC 80-191368

Tintin, Snowy, and Captain Haddock trek through the snow-covered Himalayas to rescue their friend Chang from the hands of an abominable snowman.

Tintin: The Broken Ear. Little, Brown 1978 62p. Illustration

Grades: 4 5 6 7 8 9   **741.5; Fic**
1. Adventure graphic novels; 2. Graphic novels; 3. Humorous graphic novels; 4. Tintin (Fictional character)
0-316-35850-9, $10.99

LC 77-090970

A fetish which originally belonged to the Arumbayas tribe in San Theodoros is stolen from a museum, then returned; soon Tintin discovers that the returned fetish is a forgery. When he follows the trail of the stolen fetish, it leads him and Snowy to South America and to San Theodoros, where he gets caught in the middle of a civil war. Tintin gets into all kinds of trouble even as he tries to find out why so many people want the fetish.

★ **Tintin:** The Calculus Affair. Little, Brown 1976 62p. Illustration

Grades: 4 5 6 7 8 9   **741.5; Fic**
1. Adventure graphic novels; 2. Graphic novels; 3. Humorous graphic novels; 4. Tintin (Fictional character)
0-316-35847-9, $10.99

LC 76-13280

Unscrupulous Bordurians have kidnapped Professor Calculus, and Tintin, Snowy, and Captain Haddock are soon on the trail again, to rescue their friend. It's no easy task to rescue the Professor and save his fantastic invention; spies are everywhere, and Calculus lies deep in the fortress of Bakhine. But the Bordurians now have to deal with Tintin ...

Tintin: Cigars of the Pharaoh. Little, Brown 1975 62p. Illustration

Grades: 4 5 6 7 8 9   **741.5; Fic**
1. Adventure graphic novels; 2. Graphic novels; 3. Humorous graphic novels; 4. Tintin (Fictional character)
0-316-35836-3, $10.99

LC 74-021620

Tintin and Snowy are on a cruise to Egypt when they happen to meet Professor Sophocles Sarcophagus (the first of Tintin's absent-minded professors) and join his expedition. But they become embroiled in a complicated scheme involving a fakir, cigars marked with an unusual brand, and Rajijah, the poison of madness. Tintin meets the detectives Thompson and Thomson as well as the movie mogul Rastapopolous. Herge wrote this book in 1932 then revised it in 1955.

Tintin: Destination Moon. Little, Brown 1976 62p. Illustration

Grades: 4 5 6 7 8 9   **741.5; Fic**

1. Adventure graphic novels; 2. Graphic novels; 3. Humorous graphic novels; 4. Tintin (Fictional character)
0-316-35845-2, $10.99

LC 76-013279

Professor Calculus has designed a rocket for an expedition to the Moon. He summons Tintin and Captain Haddock (along with Snowy) to the country of Syldavia, where he's been working. Despite spies being everywhere and mysterious explosions and other problems, the rocket is soon ready to launch, and Professor Calculus wants Tintin and Captain Haddock to go with him — to the Moon.

Tintin: Explorers On the Moon. Little, Brown 1976 62p. Illustration
Grades: 4 5 6 7 8 9 **741.5; Fic**
1. Adventure graphic novels; 2. Graphic novels; 3. Humorous graphic novels; 4. Tintin (Fictional character)
0-316-35846-0, $10.99

LC 76-013297

Tintin, Captain Haddock, and Prof. Calculus are headed for the Moon when they discover Thompson and Thomson, who had inadvertently stowed away on the rocket. But there's more trouble when they land on the Moon and go exploring, for Colonel Jorgen is there, another stowaway, and he wants revenge on Tintin.

Tintin: Flight 714. Little, Brown 1975 62p. Illustration
Grades: 4 5 6 7 8 9 **741.5; Fic**
1. Adventure graphic novels; 2. Graphic novels; 3. Humorous graphic novels; 4. Tintin (Fictional character)
0-316-35837-1, $10.99

LC 74-021623

Tintin, Snowy, Captain Haddock, and Professor Calculus land in Djakarta and meet millionaire Mr. Carreidas, who invites them to fly to Sydney with him in his prototype jet. They find themselves in the middle of a plot to steal their new friend's fortune, and they decide to stop it.

Tintin: Land of Black Gold. Little, Brown 1975 62p. Illustration
Grades: 4 5 6 7 8 9 **741.5; Fic**
1. Adventure graphic novels; 2. Graphic novels; 3. Humorous graphic novels; 4. Tintin (Fictional character)
0-316-35844-4, $10.99

LC 75-007896

The world is on the brink of a crisis when car engines begin to explode without explanation or warning; someone has been tampering with the oil supply. Tintin travels to the Middle East to investigate, and he helps Sheik Ben Kalish Ezab, whose son is kidnapped by one of Tintin's old enemies.

Tintin: Prisoners of the Sun. Little, Brown 1975 62p. Illustration
Grades: 4 5 6 7 8 9 **741.5; Fic**
1. Adventure graphic novels; 2. Graphic novels; 3. Humorous graphic novels; 4. Tintin (Fictional character)
0-316-35843-6, $10.99

LC 75-007897

Tintin, Snowy, and Captain Haddock travel to Peru to rescue Professor Calculus. They meet Indian boy Zorrino, and they must travel into the jungle to the Andes to find their old friend.

Tintin: Red Rackham's Treasure. Little, Brown 1974 62p. Illustration
Grades: 4 5 6 7 8 9 **741.5; Fic**
1. Adventure graphic novels; 2. Graphic novels; 3. Humorous graphic novels; 4. Tintin (Fictional character)
0-316-35834-7, $10.99

LC 73-021253

Tintin and his friends search for the pirate booty left by Captain Haddock's pirate ancestor. They're aided in their quest by the hard-of-hearing inventor, Professor Calculus.

Tintin: The Castafiore Emerald. Little, Brown 1975 62p. Illustration
Grades: 4 5 6 7 8 9 **741.5; Fic**
1. Adventure graphic novels; 2. Graphic novels; 3. Humorous graphic novels; 4. Tintin (Fictional character)
0-316-35842-8, $10.99

Tintin and Snowy investigate when prima donna Bianca Castafiore's jewels are stolen, in particular, her emerald.

Tintin: The Seven Crystal Balls. Little, Brown 1975 62p. Illustration
Grades: 4 5 6 7 8 9 **741.5; Fic**
1. Adventure graphic novels; 2. Graphic novels; 3. Humorous graphic novels; 4. Tintin (Fictional character)
0-316-35840-1, $10.99

LC 75-007921

Tragedy strikes the members of an expedition which returned after violating Incan burial chambers; the seven men fall into comas, one by one, and fragments of crystal are found by their bodies. Tintin, Professor Calculus, Captain Haddock, and Thompson and Thomson investigate, but then Calculus disappears — he's been kidnapped.

Herriman, George
★ **Krazy** & Ignatz, 1937-1938: Shifting Sands Dusts its Cheeks in Powdered Beauty. Fantagraphics Books 2006 176p. Illustration
Grades: 7 8 9 10 11 12 Adult **741.5; Fic**
1. Graphic novels; 2. Humor graphic novels; 3. Krazy Kat (Fictional character)
978-1-56097-734-6, $19.95

Krazy Kat is a love story, focusing on the relationships of its three main characters. Krazy Kat adored Ignatz Mouse. Ignatz Mouse simply tolerated Krazy Kat, except for recurrent onsets of targeted tumescence, which found expression in the fast delivery of bricks to Krazy's cranium. Offisa Pup loved Krazy and sought to protect "her" (Herriman always maintained that Krazy was genderless) by throwing Ignatz in jail. Each of the characters was ignorant of the others' true motivations, and this simple structure allowed Herriman to build entire worlds of meaning into the actions, building thematic depth and sweeping his readers up by the looping verbal rhythms of Krazy & Co.'s unique dialogue. Most of these strips in this volume have not seen print since originally running in Hearst newspapers over 70 years ago. This seventh volume collecting all of the comic strips, is the second one to be published in color; Herriman started doing the strip in color in 1935. Other than the brick-throwing, this book has no violence, foul language, or any other usual objectionable content. Krazy Kat cartoons were made for children in the mid-1930s, and there was a Krazy Kat animated series which aired on television in the mid-1960s.

Heuvel, Eric
A **family** secret. [English translation, Lorraine T. Miller]. Farrar, Straus and Giroux 2009 62p. Illustration
Grades: 7 8 9 10 11 12 **741.5; Fic**
1. Grandmothers — Graphic novels; 2. Graphic novels; 3. Holocaust, 1933-1945 — Graphic novels; 4. Jews — Graphic novels
0-374-32271-6; 978-0-374-42265-3 (pa), $9.99; 0-374-42265-6 (pa); 978-0-374-32271-7, $18.99

LC 2009-13943

While searching his Dutch grandmother's attic for yard sale items, Jeroen finds a scrapbook which leads Gran to tell of her experiences as a girl living in Amsterdam during the Holocaust, when her father was a Nazi sympathizer and Esther, her Jewish best friend, disappeared

This is a "moving graphic novel.... The art is in ink and watercolor, with very clear, highly detailed panels.... [A] gripping story." Booklist

Original Dutch edition, 2003; Anne Frank House

Hickman, Jessica

Womanthology: Heroic. Gail Simone, Camilla D'Errico, Robin Furth, Trina Robbins, Colleen Doran, Fiona Staples, Ming Doyle, Renae De Liz and others. IDW 2012 321 p.

Grades: 8 9 10 11 12   **Fic**

1. Women artists; 2. Comic books, strips, etc. — Authorship
1613771479; 9781613771471, $50

This book is an anthology of comics content from "more than 150 women creators." The book shows "how many diverse styles and subjects can make for great comics. The different portraits and definitions of heroism encompass everything from caped fliers to historical allusions to quiet bravery." (Publishers Weekly)

Hicks, Faith Erin

★ The **Adventures** of Superhero Girl. written and drawn by Faith Erin Hicks; colors by Cris Peter; introduction by Kurt Busiek. Dark Horse Comics 2013 112 p. Illustration; Color

Grades: 4 5 6 7 8 9 10 11 12 Adult   **741.5; Fic**

1. Female superhero graphic novels
1616550848; 9781616550844, $16.99
Eisner Award: Best Publication for Kids (2014)

This graphic novel features "Superhero Girl [who] has some Superman-like powers, although she can't fly, just leap over tall buildings, and she works to protect the small town where she went to get away from her charismatic superhero brother, Kevin. She fights bad-guy ninjas, bank robbers, even a tentacled space monster, but she also struggles to pay rent...and she has to deal with her future supervillain self." (Voice of Youth Advocates)

"It's superhero as person instead of as corporate symbol or fight machine.... This strip shines because it's fresh and lighthearted without wallowing in angst." Pub Wkly

Attack on Titan anthology. Attack on Titan created by Hajime Isayama; edited by Ben Applegate and Jeanine Schaefer; cover, logo, and interior design by Phil Balsman; lettering and interior design by Steve Wands. Kodansha 2016 256 p. Illustration

Grades: 8 9 10 11 12   **741.5**

1. Fantasy fiction — Graphic novels; 2. Horror fiction — Graphic novels; 3. Science fiction graphic novels; 4. Shonen manga
1632362589; 9781632362582, $29.99

This tribute anthology to the manga Attack on Titan features "original stories by a long roster of comic superstars such as Scott Snyder (Batman, American Vampire), Gail Simone (Batgirl), Michael Avon Oeming (Powers), Paolo Rivera (Daredevil, Amazing Spider-Man), Cameron Stewart (Fight Club 2, Batgirl) and Faith Erin Hicks (The Adventures of Superhero Girl)!" (Publisher's note)

"The Victorian-style guide to Titan's walled city by Genevieve Valentine and David López is a standout, as is the contemplative final story by brothers Asaf and Tomer Hanuka." Pub Wkly

Friends with boys. Faith Erin Hicks. First Second 2012 un Illustration

Grades: 6 7 8 9 10   **741.5**

1. Ghost stories; 2. Graphic novels; 3. Teenagers — Fiction
9781596435568, $16.99
LC 2011030470

In this graphic novel, "[the] youngest of four siblings and the only girl, Maggie is both excited and worried about starting high school after being home-schooled her whole life.... As Maggie makes friends with a perky indie girl named Lucy and her mysterious brother, Alistair, she broods over the loss of her mother, who recently left the family without much of an explanation, and tries to figure out what the ghost wants from her." (Bulletin of the Center for Children's Books)

★ The **Nameless** City. Faith Erin Hicks; color by Jordie Bellaire. First Second 2016 240 p. Color; Illustration

Grades: 5 6 7 8 9 10   **741.5; Fic**

1. Cities and towns — Fiction; 2. Friendship — Fiction; 3. Survival — Fiction; 4. Fantasy graphic novels; 5. Survival skills — Fiction
1626721564; 9781626721562, $14.99; 9781626721579
LC 2015020651

"Every nation that invades the City gives it a new name.... The natives don't let themselves get caught up in the unending wars. To them, their home is the Nameless City.... Kaidu is...a Dao born and bred — a member of the latest occupying nation. Rat is a native of the Nameless City. At first, she hates Kai for everything he stands for, but his love of his new home may be the one thing that can bring these two unlikely friends together." (Publisher's note)

"With comprehensive world building, well-rounded characters, and entertaining action, this expertly executed story will find a home with a wide variety of readers, all of whom will be eagerly awaiting the next installment." Booklist

★ The **stone** heart. Faith Erin Hicks. First Second 2017 256 p. Color; Illustration (The nameless city)

Grades: 5 6 7 8 9 10   **741.5; Fic**

1. Fantasy fiction — Graphic novels; 2. Adventure fiction; 3. Magic — Fiction
1626721599; 9781626721586; 9781626721593, $21.99
LC 2016938731

In this book, by Faith Erin Hicks, "Kaidu and Rat have only just recovered from the assassination attempt on the General of All Blades when more chaos breaks loose in the Nameless City: deep conflicts within the Dao nation are making it impossible to find a political solution for the disputed territory of the City itself." (Publisher's note)

"Flourishing from the strong worldbuilding and characterization of the first installment, this middle volume...provides a vital and enthralling closer look at those readers have already met as well as unfurling more of the Chinese-inspired city's past, as colorist Bellaire brings all to stunning emotional life." Kirkus

★ The **war** at Ellsmere. Slave Labor Graphics 2008 156p. Illustration

Grades: 6 7 8 9 10 11   **741.5; Fic**

1. Friendship — Graphic novels; 2. Graphic novels; 3. Humorous graphic novels; 4. School stories — Graphic novels
1-59362-140-X; 978-1-59362-140-7, $12.95

Juniper is the newest scholarship student at the prestigious Ellsmere Academy; she wanted to attend there in order to increase her chances of getting into a good medical school. She's on scholarship because her mom has had to raise her alone since her father died when she was young. Jun makes one friend at Ellsmere, Cassie, who calls herself the cliche of the poor little rich girl. Wealthy Emily calls Cassie "Orphan" because her parents ignore her, and chooses to call Jun "Project," as in Headmistress Ms. Bishop's latest project. Emily is also determined to get rid of Jun, especially when Jun encourages Cassie to work harder and even win the extra credit essay contest. Now it's war, or as Jun puts it, "It's like Upstairs Downstairs meets Lord of the Flies. In plaid skirts. And sweater vests." There's one incident when Jun punches Emily in the face.

"Hicks gives readers enough tension and quirky turns to satisfy and pleasantly surprise." Booklist

Hidaka, Banri

I Hate You More than Anyone! Volume 1. DC Comics/CMX 2007 192p. Illustration

Grades: 7 8 9 10 11 12   **741.5; Fic**

1. Graphic novels; 2. Humorous graphic novels; 3. Manga; 4. Romance graphic novels; 5. Shojo manga
978-1-4012-1310-7, $9.99

Kazuha Akiyoshi is the eldest of six children. She's very responsible and also irresistibly cute, but she is something of a tomboy who has never allowed her romantic side to show throught. Then she meets Mizushima, the first guy to treat her like a girl. He's Kazuha's first crush, but does Mizushima feel the same way about her? And then there's Sugimoto, an older guy who's determined to make himself an important part of her life, only he's the one she hates more than anyone.

Hiiragi, Aoi

Baron: The Cat Returns. story and art by Aoi Hiiragi; translation & English adaptation, Naoko Amemiya. Viz/Studio Ghibli Library 2005 222p. Illustration
Grades: 3 4 5 6 7 8 9   **741.5; Fic**
1. Cats — Graphic novels; 2. Fantasy graphic novels; 3. Graphic novels; 4. Kodomo manga; 5. Manga
1-59116-956-9, $9.99

Awkward teen Haru saves a cat from being run over one afternoon, but she never expected the trouble it would cause. He is a cat prince, and his father wants to bring Haru into the kingdom of the cats to be his son's bride. A mysterious voice sends Haru to the Cat Office, where she meets Baron, a toy cat come to life, the fat cat Muta, and a magical crow. When the cats come and bear Haru to the kingdom of the cats, the three friends follow to help bring Haru back home.

This one-volume manga was the basis for the feature-length anime (Japanese animated film) called "The Cat Returns," which was produced by Studio Ghibli, the animation studio run by famed anime director Hayao Miyazaki and some partners.

Hinds, Gareth

★ **Beowulf**. adapted and illustrated by Gareth Hinds. Candlewick Press 2007 un Illustration
Grades: 8 9 10 11 12 Adult
741.5; Fic
1. Adventure graphic novels; 2. Graphic novels; 3. Monsters — Graphic novels; 4. Beowulf — Graphic novels
978-0-7636-3022-5, $21.99;
0-7636-3022-5; 978-0-7636-3023-2 (pa);
0-7636-3023-3 (pa), $9.99
LC 2006-49023
Graphic novel adaptation of the Old English epic poem, Beowulf

"For fantasy fans both young and old, this makes an ideal introduction to a story without which the entire fantasy genre would look very different; many scenes may be too intense for very young readers." Publ Wkly

BEOWULF. Copyright © 1999, 2000, 2007 by Gareth Hinds. Reproduced by permission of the publisher, Candlewick Press, Somerville, MA.

King Lear. a play by William Shakespeare; adapted and illustrated by Gareth Hinds. Candlewick Press 2009 123p. Illustration
Grades: 7 8 9 10 11 12
741.5; 822.3
1. Shakespeare, William, 1564-1616 — Adaptations
978-0-7636-4343-0, $22.99;
0-7636-4343-2; 978-0-7636-4344-7 (pa), $11.99; 0-7636-4344-0 (pa)
"Employing a range of artistic styles that convey dramatic mood, the artist begins the play almost as a fairy tale, featuring bright,

KING LEAR. Copyright © 2007 by Gareth Hinds. Reproduced by permission of the publisher, Candlewick Press, Somerville, MA.

softly washed drawings. Once Cordelia is cast out and things sour, the images become darker and more compact. As the king descends into madness, the art becomes downright menacing, with Lear appearing as a jagged, ghostly figure drawn with white pencil on a dark background." (Kirkus)

Macbeth. adapted and illustrated by Gareth Hinds. Candlewick Press 2015 152 p. Color illustration; Color; Map
Grades: 8 9 10 11 12
741.5
1. Kings and rulers — Fiction; 2. Scotland — Fiction; 3. Graphic novels; 4. Murder — Fiction; 5. Shakespeare, William, 1564-1616 — Adaptations
0763678023; 9780763669430;
9780763678029, $12.99
LC 2014939338
"Set against the moody backdrop of eleventh-century Scotland, [illustrator] Gareth Hinds's...interpretation takes readers into the claustrophobic mind of a man driven mad by ambition. An evil seed takes root in the mind of Macbeth, a general in the king's army, when three witches tell him he will one day be king." (Publisher's note)

MACBETH. Copyright © 2015 by Gareth Hinds. Reproduced by permission of the publisher, Candlewick Press, Somerville, MA.

"Though many lines of the original are intact, Hinds does undertake some changes to make this version more accessible to contemporary readers, and a closing note addresses those alterations. Students struggling to find an entry point into the Scottish play should look no further than this entertaining and elucidating volume." Booklist

The **merchant** of Venice: a play. by William Shakespeare; adapted and illustrated by Gareth Hinds. Candlewick Press 2008 68p. Illustration
Grades: 8 9 10 11 12 Adult
822.3; 741.5
1. Shakespeare, William, 1564-1616 — Adaptations
978-0-7636-3024-9, $21.99;
978-0-7636-3025-6 (pa), $11.99
LC 2007-938349
Hinds uses a sketchy art style and blue and gray tones to illustrate his graphic adaptation of Shakespeare's controversial play. He sets the play in modern Venice and uses more modern language, including prose, at the beginning of the play and then gradually returns to Shakespeare's original language for the courtroom scenes. The play tells the story of a debt owed to a Jewish merchant of Venice, of a strong-willed young woman who is determined to choose her own husband, and of the quest to save a young man from the fate of having a pound of flesh cut from him.

THE MERCHANT OF VENICE. Copyright © 2008 by Gareth Hinds. Reproduced by permission of the publisher, Candlewick Press, Somerville, MA.

"Fans of the play will find this an intriguing adaptation." Publ Wkly

The **most** excellent and lamentable tragedy of Romeo & Juliet: a play by William Shakespeare, adapted and illustrated by Gareth Hinds. Candlewick Press 2013 128 p.
Grades: 7 8 9 10   **741.5**
1. Graphic novels; 2. Shakespeare, William, 1564-1616 — Tragedies; 3. Shakespeare, William, 1564-1616 — Adaptations

ROMEO AND JULIET. Copyright © 2013 by Gareth Hinds. Reproduced by permission of the publisher, Candlewick Press, Somerville, MA.

0763659487; 0763668079; 9780763659486, $21.99; 9780763668075, $12.99

LC 2012950561

This book by Gareth Hinds presents a graphic novel adaptation of William Shakespeare's play "Romeo and Juliet." "The most notable change between this story and Shakespeare's original is the creative license that Hinds takes with ethnicity — he makes the characters of African, Indian, and Caucasian descent in order to promote the universality of the story. The Shakespearean language is abridged but not adapted into contemporary English." (School Library Journal)

"Cleaving to Shakespeare's words and dramatic arc, Hinds (The Merchant of Venice) creates another splendid graphic novel, tracing each scene in taut, coherent dialogue. The characters, in period dress modified by a few more contemporary touches, are poignantly specific yet universal. Hinds delivers the play's essence and beauty, its glorious language, furious conflict, yearning love, and wrenching tragedy." (Horn Book)

The **Odyssey:** a graphic novel. by Gareth Hinds. Candlewick Press 2010 248 p. Color illustration

Grades: 7 8 9 10 11 12 Adult

741.5

1. Graphic novels; 2. Greek mythology — Graphic novels; 3. Odyssey; 4. Homer

0763642665; 0763642681; 9780763642662, $24.99; 9780763642686

LC 2010007512

"Retells, in graphic novel format, Homer's epic tale of Odysseus, the ancient Greek hero who encounters witches and other obstacles on his journey home after fighting in the Trojan War." (Publisher's note)

Poe: stories and poems: a graphic novel adaptation by Gareth Hinds. Gareth Hinds. Candlewick Press 2017 120 p. Illustration; Color

Grades: 8 9 10 11 12

741.5

1. Literature — Adaptations; 2. Poe, Edgar Allan, 1809-1849

9780763681128, $22; 9780763695095

LC 2017946252

This graphic novel, by Gareth Hinds, is an "adaptation of Edgar Allan Poe's best-known works.... In 'The Cask of Amontillado,' a man exacts revenge on a disloyal friend at carnival.... In 'The Masque of the Red Death,' a prince shielding himself from plague hosts a doomed party inside his abbey stronghold. A prisoner of the Spanish Inquisition, faced with a swinging blade and swarming rats, can't see his tormentors in 'The Pit and the Pendulum.'" (Publisher's note)

" Faithfully preserving the gothic tone of the original texts, from the macabre endpapers filled with symbols of death to the twisted anguished

THE ODYSSEY. Copyright © 2010 by Gareth Hinds. Reproduced by permission of the publisher, Candlewick Press, Somerville, MA.

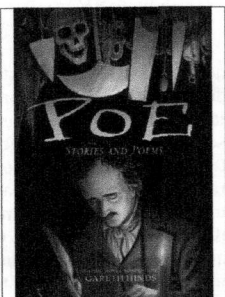

POE: STORIES AND POEMS. Copyright © 2017 by Gareth Hinds. Reproduced by permission of the publisher, Candlewick Press, Somerville, MA.

faces found throughout its pages, the author never shies away from the darkness found there, instead distilling Poe's fascination with madness, death, and terror into single haunting images." Booklist

Hino, Matsuri

Captive hearts, vol. 1. Viz Media/Shojo Beat 2008 200p. Illustration

Grades: 7 8 9 10 11 12   **741.5; Fic**

1. Graphic novels; 2. Manga; 3. Romance graphic novels; 4. Shojo manga

978-1-4215-1932-6, $8.99

Carefree college student Megumi Kuroishi finds his life turned upside down when the last surviving member of the Kogami family, teenage Suzuka, is found in China. That's when Megumi learns of the curse against his family, that they will serve the Kogami family for 100 generations. Whenever he looks into Suzuka's eyes, the curse overwhelms him and he becomes far too subservient; complicating matters is the fact that he does indeed find Suzuka captivating. She likes him, too, but can't trust his feelings because of the curse. The book includes two short romance stories. In "Real Storm," shy high school student Io Ayase has a huge crush on Kuji-sensei, who only wants to help her learn to deal with a pervy stalker. In "Let Time Freeze," Ayu and Yuji are childhood friends now in their senior year of high school, and she doesn't want the year to end; when it does, Yuji will go to university in Tokyo while Ayu must remain behind. Now that she loves him, the impending separation already hurts.

MeruPuri: Marchen Prince Vol. 1. Viz Media/Shojo Beat 2005 un Illustration

Grades: 8 9 10 11 12   **741.5; Fic**

1. Fantasy graphic novels; 2. Graphic novels; 3. Manga; 4. Romance graphic novels; 5. Shojo manga

1-4215-0120-1, $8.99

All high-school freshman Airi Hoshina ever wanted was to someday live in a cozy home with a loving husband, and find joy in the little things in life. As a result, she makes it her daily mission to get to school on time because school legend has it that the longer one's non-tardy streak is, the better boyfriend one will find. But, on the way to school one morning, Airi drops her mirror, one that had been passed down to her through generations, and suddenly finds herself in a bizarre situation. Never in her wildest dreams did she expect to meet Aram, a little boy from a magical kingdom, to have emerged from the mirror in the short time it took her to track it down. The series includes some mild sexual situations.

Hirsch, Andy

Dogs: from predator to protector. Andy Hirsch. First Second 2017 128 p. Color; Illustration (Science comics)

Grades: 4 5 6 7 8   **741.5; 636.7**

1. Comic books, strips, etc.; 2. Dogs

9781626727670, $19.99; 9781626727687

LC 2016961597

"How well do you know our favorite furry companion? Did they really descend from wolves? What's the difference between a Chihuahua and a Saint Bernard? And just how smart are they? Join one friendly mutt on a journey to discover the secret origin of dogs, how genetics and evolution shape species, and where in the world his favorite ball bounced off to." (Publisher's note)

"Thorough, clearly presented scientific information is lightened by silly asides from dog-narrator Rudy to keep readers entertained and engaged as they learn a huge amount about the science of dogs." Kirkus

Includes bibliographical references

Hitch, Bryan

Bryan Hitch's Ultimate Comics Studio. Impact 2010 128p. Illustration

Grades: 7 8 9 10   741.5; 741
1. Fantastic Four (Fictional characters); 2. Captain America (Fictional character)
978-1-6006-1327-2, $24.99; 1-6006-1327-6

"The book is a skillful blend of text, photos of the artist at work, annotated sketches, and finished illustrations. It is a visual treat in its own right, with well-organized subject matter complemented by thoughtful composition and lavish photography and art. Hitch considers himself to be primarily a storyteller, and he delves into the philosophy and technique of visual storytelling. He gives a glimpse into his thought processes, offering 'guided tours' of sketches by walking readers through his work, starting with analyzing script to making decisions regarding action, panels, rhythm, and sample initial sketches." (School Library Journal)

Hiwatari, Saki
Tower of the Future, Vol. 1. DC Comics/CMX 2005 192p. Illustration
Grades: 8 9 10 11 12   741.5; Fic
1. Fantasy graphic novels; 2. Graphic novels; 3. Manga; 4. Romance graphic novels; 5. Shojo manga
978-1-4012-0814-1, $9.99

Takeru's mother has died, and then he finds out that his half-English father has a daughter in England; on her deathbed, Takeru's mother asked that Hyoju be allowed to move to Japan and live with them. Shocked and upset, Takeru's first reaction is anger and disgust. He then meets Ichigo, a girl his age upon whom he immediately has a crush, and a strange little boy named Zen who knows way too much about Takeru. As the series progresses, Takeru learns a little more about Zen and why he knows so much. Also, a fantasy element comes in as Takeru learns about a parasitic being called Noize, and Ichigo's adult older brother has an unhealthy fixation on her.

Holm, Jennifer L.
Babymouse for president. by Jennifer L. Holm & Matthew Holm. Random House 2012 89 p.
Grades: 3 4 5 6   741.5
1. Graphic novels; 2. Mice — Fiction; 3. Schools — Fiction; 4. School stories; 5. Elections — Fiction
0375867805; 9780375867804, $6.99; 9780375967801
                                                LC 2011024118
In this book by Jennifer L. Holm and Matt, Holm, part of the Babymouse series, "it's election season and if anyone knows what...the student council needs, it's Babymouse. The only trouble is, everyone else is running for President, too — even Babymouse's locker! Will Felicia Furrypaws turn out the meangirl coalition? Does Babymouse have what it takes to become the voice of the people?" (Publisher's note)

Babymouse: cupcake tycoon. by Jennifer L. Holm & Matthew Holm. Random House 2010 89p.
Grades: 3 4 5 6   741.5; 741
1. Mice — Graphic novels; 2. School stories — Graphic novels
978-0-375-86573-2 (pa), $6.99; 0-375-86573-X (pa)

"It's champagne wishes and cupcake dreams for Babymouse! The school library is having a fund-raiser, and Babymouse is determined to raise the most money and WIN the GRAND PRIZE. Or...er, to help the school! The competition is fierce, but Babymouse will stop at nothing to get what she wants, even if it means outselling every last kid in school...including her nefarious nemesis, Felicia Furrypaws." (Publisher's note)

Babymouse: mad scientist. by Jennifer L. Holm & Matthew Holm. Random House 2011 91p. Illustration
Grades: 3 4 5 6   741.5; 741

1. Babymouse (Fictional character); 2. Amoeba — Fiction; 3. Science projects — Fiction
978-0-375-96574-6 (lib bdg), $12.99; 0-375-96574-2 (lib bdg); 978-0-375-86574-9 (pa), $6.99; 0-375-86574-8 (pa)
                                                LC 2009-47388
"Babymouse decides to enter the science fair. She daydreams about science-fiction movies and television shows (Star Trek, The Attack of the 50-Foot Woman); fantasizes about winning the Nobel Prize; learns about the scientific method in class — and then she discovers an amoeba named Squish." (Booklist)

Babymouse: monster mash. Random House 2008 93p.
Grades: 3 4 5 6   741; 741.5; Fic
1. Graphic novels; 2. Halloween — Graphic novels; 3. Humorous graphic novels; 4. Mice — Graphic novels
978-0-375-93789-7 (lib bdg), $11.99; 978-0-375-84387-7 (pa), $5.99
                                                LC 2008-08433
It's Halloween, and Babymouse loves dressing up in spooky costumes to go trick-or-treating with best buddy Wilson. Of course, Felicia has to say that girls must be pretty "It's a rule." Then Babymouse's mother tells her she can have a Halloween party, and when Felicia finds out, she bullies Babymouse into inviting her and orders her to go trick-or-treating with them. Felicia is not a nice kid on Halloween; she leads her cronies in teepeeing and egging houses. But at Babymouse's party, she decides to do things her way after all. For this Halloween volume, the color scheme doesn't include pink, but orange. Babymouse imagines herself in classic horror movie scenarios, but they shouldn't be too scary for most young readers.
Another title in the author's series about Babymouse

Babymouse: puppy love. [by] Jennifer L. Holm and Matthew Holm. Random House 2007 91p. Illustration
Grades: 3 4 5 6   741.5
1. Mice — Graphic novels; 2. Pets — Graphic novels
978-0-375-93990-7 (lib bdg), $12.99; 978-0-375-83990-0 (pa), $5.99
                                                LC 2007-61012
"Babymouse doesn't exactly have a great history with pets — even her goldfish ran away from home. But all that's about to change. Will Babymouse get the dog of her dreams? Will she ever find her missing fish?" (Publisher's note)

Babymouse: skater girl. [by] Jennifer L. Holm & Matthew Holm. Random House 2007 91p. Illustration
Grades: 3 4 5 6   741.5; 741
Babymouse (Fictional character)
978-0-375-93989-1 (lib bdg); 0-375-93989-X (lib bdg); 978-0-375-83989-4 (pa), $5.99; 0-375-83989-5 (pa)
                                                LC 2006-50444
"Babymouse daydreams about being a medal-winning figure skater. She can almost hear the roar of the crowd, the fans cheering her name, the sportscasters' excitement. But when she's actually noticed by a professional coach and told she has talent, Babymouse develops a lust for glory...which is greatly tested by the harsh reality of before- and after-school practices, a ban on cupcakes, and no free time for friends." (Horn Book)

Babymouse: the musical. by Jennifer & Matthew Holm. Random House 2009 96p. Illustration
Grades: 3 4 5 6   741.5; Fic
1. Graphic novels; 2. Humorous graphic novels; 3. Mice — Graphic novels; 4. School stories — Graphic novels
978-0-375-93791-0, $11.99; 978-0-375-84388-4 (pa), $5.99
                                                LC 2008-10891
The school is going to produce a musical, and Babymouse auditions. Unfortunately, she has a tendency to trip over her own two feet, and the

lead role demands someone who can sing and dance. Nemesis Felicia wins the lead role, and Babymouse is her understudy, while new transfer student Henry Higgins (a British hedgehog) has the male lead role. As Babymouse gets through school days (complete with the torture of dodgeball) and rehearsals, she daydreams Broadway musicals.

Another title in the author's series about Babymouse

Camp Babymouse. Random House 2007 95p. Illustration
Grades: 2 3 4 5 6   **741.5; Fic**
1. Babymouse (Fictional character); 2. Graphic novels; 3. Humorous graphic novels
978-0-375-93988-4 (lib bdg), $12.99; 978-0-375-83988-7 (pa), $5.99

Babymouse is looking forward to Camp Wild Whiskers, and two weeks of fresh air, fun, and friendship. She can't wait for the adventures to start. All that she has to do is relax and make sure she doesn't get lost in the wilderness. What could possibly go wrong? Will camp be all that Babymouse dreams of? Problems such as losing points by spilling punch, tipping her canoe during the canoe race, accidentally starting a really big fire, and her cabin mates complaining that she'll put them in last place make her wonder if she should even be there.

Comics Squad: recess!. comics by Jarrett J. Krosoczka, Gene Yang, Eric Wight, Jennifer L. Holm and Matthew Holm, Ursula Vernon, Dan Santat, Raina Telgemeier and Dave Roman, Dav Pilkey; edited by Jennifer L. Holm, Matthew Holm, and Jarrett J. Krosoczka. Random House Inc. 2014 144 p. Illustration; Color
Grades: 2 3 4 5 6   **741.5**
1. Graphic novels; 2. Humorous stories; 3. Recess — Fiction; 4. Schools — Fiction; 5. Short stories; 6. Comic books, strips, etc.; 7. School stories
0385370032; 9780385370035, $7.99; 9780385370042, $12.99

LC 2013035223

"An all-star lineup of graphic novel notables contributes original works to this anthology, sharing the common thread of recess." (School Library Journal)

"[T]his lively, upbeat and all-around-awesome offering is consistently convivial and laugh-out-loud funny from cover to cover." Kirkus

Another title in this series is: Lunch! (2016)

★ **Sunny** side up. Jennifer L. Holm & Matthew Holm; with color by Lark Pien. Graphix 2015 224 p. Illustration
Grades: 3 4 5 6   **741.5; Fic**
1. Summer — Fiction; 2. Friendship — Fiction; 3. Grandfathers — Fiction; 4. Adventure fiction; 5. Florida — Fiction
0545741653; 9780545741651, $23.99

LC 2014957906

Eisner Nominee: Best Publication for Kids (2016)

In this book, by Jennifer L. Holm, illustrated by Matthew Holm, "Sunny Lewin has been packed off to Florida to live with her grandfather for the summer. At first she thought Florida might be fun.... But the place where Gramps lives is no amusement park. It's full of...old people. Really old people. Luckily, Sunny isn't the only kid around. She meets Buzz, a boy who is completely obsessed with comic books, and soon they're having adventures of their own." (Publisher's note)

"Woven into the Florida frolic though, through dated flashback images, is the real reason for Sunny's last-minute visit: her older brother is struggling with addiction, and Sunny thinks she got him in trouble. Though Sunny will appeal to all kinds of readers, an authors' note shares the Holms' hope to let kids in similar situations know that it's OK to feel sad and to talk about it. Clear dialogue bubbles, plenty of wordless spreads, and Matthew's cartoons and beach-umbrella color palette keep Sunny's story an upbeat one that readers will easily stick with." Booklist

Holm, Matthew
Babymouse #11: dragonslayer. [by] Jennifer L. Holm & Matthew Holm. Random House Childrens Books 2009 96p. Illustration
Grades: 3 4 5 6   **741.5; Fic**
1. Babymouse (Fictional character); 2. Graphic novels; 3. Humorous graphic novels; 4. Mathematics — Graphic novels; 5. Mice — Graphic novels
978-0-375-95712-3, $12.99; 978-0-375-85712-6 (pa), $5.99

LC 2008-51110

Babymouse loves to read, and to daydream about the books she reads, but she does NOT do well in math. In fact, she's just received an F on a test, and her teacher decides to have her join the Mathletes in order to make up for it. The Mathletes compete with other school teams in math competitions, and they have wanted to win the Golden Slide Rule for a long time. A competing team called the Owlgarithms have won it year after year. However, Babymouse seems to be more of a liability than a new asset for the team. She suffers through lunchtime practice sessions and much prefers to daydream of adventures with The Lion, the Witch, and the Wardrobe or The Hobbit rather than do math. Then, at the math competition, events conspire to make her the team's only hope in a final round against one of the Owlgorithms. The book is illustrated in the usual black, white and pink, and it might, just might, help some girls think of math as something they can do well (after all, if Babymouse can compete in a math tournament, maybe they can, too).

Cover title: Babymouse Dragonslayer

Babymouse burns rubber!. by Jennifer L. Holm & Matthew Holm. Random House 2010 91p. Illustration
Grades: 3 4 5 6   **741.5; 741**
978-0-375-95713-0 (lib bdg), $12.99; 0-375-95713-8 (lib bdg); 978-0-375-85713-3 (pa), $5.99; 0-375-85713-3 (pa)

LC 2009018819

"Babymouse dreams of glory in the soap box derby but doesn't put much effort into preparation. She sweet-talks best friend and fellow contestant Wilson into building (and re-building) her car, preventing him from being ready on race day." (Horn Book)

Babymouse: heartbreaker. Random House 2006 91p.
Grades: 3 4 5 6   **741; Fic; 741.5**
1. Babymouse (Fictional character); 2. Graphic novels; 3. Humorous graphic novels; 4. Mice — Graphic novels; 5. Valentine's Day — Graphic novels
0-375-93798-6 (lib bdg), $12.99; 0-375-83798-1 (pa), $5.99; 978-0-375-93798-9 (lib bdg); 978-0-375-83798-2 (pa)

LC 2006-45418

"Romantic Babymouse...here finds her confidence shaken by the impending Valentine's Day dance at school.... The text and illustrations successfully differentiate between reality and daydreams, and there's a good amount of humor injected in both." Horn Book

Another title in the author's series about Babymouse

Babymouse: queen of the world. Random House Books for Young Readers 2005 91p. Illustration
Grades: 3 4 5 6   **741.5; Fic**
1. Babymouse (Fictional character); 2. Friendship — Graphic novels; 3. Graphic novels; 4. Humorous graphic novels; 5. Mice — Graphic novels
0-375-93229-1 (lib bdg), $12.99; 0-375-83229-7 (pa), $5.95

LC 2004-51166

"In this energetic comic...Babymouse, a wise-cracking rodent stand-in for your average, adventure-seeking nine-year-old, strives to capture popular Felicia's goodwill, finally achieving her end at the expense of

Wilson Weasel, truest of friends. But, wouldn't you know it, Felicia's world has little to offer a smart, fun-loving mouse, after all." Booklist

Other titles in this series are: Our hero (2005); Beach babe (2006); Rock star (2006); Heartbreaker (2006); Camp Babymouse (2007); Skater girl (2007); Puppy love (2007); Monster mash (2008); Babymouse the musical (2009); Dragonslayer (2009); Babymouse burns rubber (2010); Cupcake tycoon (2010); Mad scientist (2011); A very Babymouse Christmas (2011); Babymouse for president (2012); Extreme Babymouse (2012); Happy birthday Babymouse (2014); Bad babysitter (2015); Babymouse goes for the gold (2016)

Comics Squad: recess!. comics by Jarrett J. Krosoczka, Gene Yang, Eric Wight, Jennifer L. Holm and Matthew Holm, Ursula Vernon, Dan Santat, Raina Telgemeier and Dave Roman, Dav Pilkey; edited by Jennifer L. Holm, Matthew Holm, and Jarrett J. Krosoczka. Random House Inc. 2014 144 p. Illustration; Color

Grades: 2 3 4 5 6   **741.5**

1. Graphic novels; 2. Humorous stories; 3. Recess — Fiction; 4. Schools — Fiction; 5. Short stories; 6. Comic books, strips, etc.; 7. School stories

0385370032; 9780385370035, $7.99; 9780385370042, $12.99

LC 2013035223

"An all-star lineup of graphic novel notables contributes original works to this anthology, sharing the common thread of recess." (School Library Journal)

"[T]his lively, upbeat and all-around-awesome offering is consistently convivial and laugh-out-loud funny from cover to cover." Kirkus

Another title in this series is: Lunch! (2016)

Swing it, Sunny!. Jennifer L. Holm & Matthew Holm; with color by Lark Pien. Scholastic Press 2017 224 p. Color; Illustration

Grades: 3 4 5 6   **741.5**

1. Brothers and sisters; 2. Brothers and sisters — Fiction; 3. Dysfunctional families — Comic books, strips, etc; 4. Family problems — Fiction; 5. Graphic novels; 6. Middle schools — Comic books, strips, etc; 7. Middle schools — Fiction; 8. Schools — Fiction

9780545741705, $24.99; 9780545741729, $12.99; 9780545741767

LC 2016054939

In this book, by Jennifer and Matthew Holm, "Summer's over and it's time for Sunny Lewin to enter the strange and unfriendly hallways of...middle school. When her Gramps calls her from Florida to ask how she's doing, she always tells him she's fine. But the truth? Sunny is NOT having the best time." (Publisher's note)

"Using a combination of short exchanges of dialogue and frequent wordless reaction shots, the Holms again leverage simply drawn scenes colored by Pien into a loosely autobiographical narrative that is poignant and hilarious in turn and emotionally rich throughout." Kirkus

A **very** Babymouse Christmas. by Jennifer L. Holm & Matthew Holm. Random House Childrens Books 2011 89p. Illustration (Babymouse)

Grades: 3 4 5 6   **741.5**

1. Christmas — Fiction; 2. Gifts — Fiction; 3. Graphic novels; 4. Humorous graphic novels; 5. Imagination — Fiction; 6. Mice — Fiction

978-0-375-96779-5, $12.99; 978-0-375-86779-8 (pa), $6.99

LC 2010027988

"Babymouse feels she simply cannot live without the Whiz Bang, this Christmas's must-have gift. This graphic novel's single-minded focus reflects Babymouse's all-consuming obsession, a condition with which readers are likely to be familiar. Her holiday-classic-inspired, pink-hued daydreams allow Babymouse to switch off the mania for a while." (Horn Book)

Hopkins, David

Emily Edison. Viper Comics 2006 144p. Illustration

Grades: 7 8 9 10 11 12 Adult   **741.5; Fic**

1. Graphic novels; 2. Humorous graphic novels; 3. Science fiction graphic novels

0-9777883-2-6, $12.95

High schooler Emily has more than her share of problems; along with trying to keep up in school and survive such things as parties and boys, she has to deal with her parents' very mixed marriage. Her father is human, but her mother came from another dimension. Since their divorce, Emily has had to split her time between Earth and elsewhere; and now her grandfather wants her to live permanently in his dimension, and he's prepared to destroy Earth to force her hand. What's a girl to do?

Horikoshi, Kohei

★ **My** Hero Academia; Volume 1. story & art Kohei Horikoshi; translation & English adaptation Caleb Cook. Viz 2015 187 p. Illustration

Grades: 7 8 9 10 11 12   **741.5/952; 741.5**

1. High schools — Fiction; 2. Manga; 3. Shonen manga; 4. High school students — Fiction; 5. Superheroes — Fiction

1421582694; 9781421582696, $9.99

"What would the world be like if 80 percent of the population manifested superpowers called 'Quirks' at age four? Heroes and villains would be battling it out everywhere! Being a hero would mean learning to use your power, but where would you go to study? The Hero Academy of course! But what would you do if you were one of the 20 percent who were born Quirkless? Middle school student Izuku Midoriya wants to be a hero more than anything, but he hasn't got an ounce of power in him. With no chance of ever getting into the prestigious U.A. High School for budding heroes, his life is looking more and more like a dead end. Then an encounter with All Might, the greatest hero of them all, gives him a chance to change his destiny." (Publisher's note)

Volume 1 of an ongoing series

Horowitz, Anthony

Stormbreaker: the graphic novel. [by] Anthony Horowitz; adapted Antony Johnston; illustrated by Kanako Damerum & Yusuru Takasaki. Philomel Books 2006 un Illustration (Alex Rider)

Grades: 5 6 7 8   **741; 741.5**

1. Graphic novels; 2. Spies — Graphic novels

0-399-24633-9, $14.99

In this graphic novel version on Horowitz's novel, fourteen-year-old Alex Rider is coerced into continuing his uncle's dangerous work for Britain's intelligence agency, MI6.

"If it's possible, this is even more rapidly paced than the novel. Alex remains an appealing hero here, and the idea of a heroic teen up against insidious adults continues to be an extremely powerful draw for readers." Booklist

Other graphic novel adaptations in this series are:Point blank (2007);Skeleton key (2009);Eagle strike (2012)

Hosler, Jay

Clan Apis. Active Synapse 2000 158p. Illustration

Grades: 4 5 6 7 8 9 10 11 12

741.5; Fic

1. Bees — Graphic novels; 2. Graphic novels; 3. Science — Graphic novels

0-9677255-0-X, $15

"Opening with a creation myth... and working through the biological, sociological, and ecological changes affecting the life of Nyuki the bee, the text is a combination of authoritative science; appealing, detailed black-and-white drawings; and dialogue

Courtesy of Active Synapse

replete with humor, pubescent angst, political sloganeering, and more. Nyuki's colony undertakes migration to a new hive, is beset by a woodpecker, and hibernates through a winter that yields to a revitalizing spring." Booklist

★ **Last** of the sandwalkers. written and illustrated by Jay Hosler. First Second 2015 312 p. Illustration
Grades: 5 6 7 8 9 10   **741.5; Fic**
1. Beetles — Fiction; 2. Graphic novels; 3. Science fiction; 4. Scientific expeditions — Fiction; 5. Adventure fiction
162672024X; 9781626720244, $16.99
LC 2014045542

This book, by Jay Hosler, is about a "civilization of beetles. In this bug's paradise, beetles write books, run restaurants, and even do scientific research. But not too much scientific research is allowed by the powerful elders, who guard a terrible secret about the world outside.... Lucy is not one to quietly cooperate, however. This tiny field scientist defies the law of her safe but authoritarian home and leads a team of researchers out into the desert." (Publisher's note)

"Hosler's cartooning is no less meticulous than his writing and similarly retains a sense of animated energy and humor, engaging readers with characters that are far from human, but filled with humanity." Booklist
Includes bibliographical references

The **Sandwalk** Adventures: An Adventure in Evolution Told in Five Chapters. Active Synapse 2003 160p. Illustration
Grades: 4 5 6 7 8 9 10 11 12 Adult
576.8; 741.5
1. Evolution — Graphic novels; 2. Graphic novels; 3. Science — Graphic novels; 4. Darwin, Charles; 5. Darwin, Charles — Graphic novels
0-9677255-1-8, $20

Courtesy of Active Synapse

Scientist Hosler explains Darwin's theory of evolution in a whimsical fashion. Follicle mites Mara and Willy live in Darwin's left eyebrow, and by accident they discover that Darwin, whom they call the god Flycatcher, can hear Mara. He thinks he's going crazy, but as he takes his daily walks on the Sandwalk at his home in England, Darwin does his best to convince Mara and Willy that he isn't a god and tells them about evolution. Hosler uses humor and whimsy, but also did a lot of research; the book includes explanatory notes and a long bibliography of sources.

Hotta, Yumi
★ **Hikaru** No Go, Volume 1. [by] Yumi Hotta and Takeshi Obata. Viz Media, LLC 2004 192p. Illustration
Grades: 5 6 7 8 9 10 11 12   **741.5; Fic**
1. Board games — Graphic novels; 2. Graphic novels; 3. Manga; 4. Shonen manga
1-59116-222-X, $7.95

Sixth-grade Hikaru Shindo's discovery of a bloodstained game board leads to an encounter with the ghost of Go master Fujiwara-no-Sai and the formation of an unbeatable Go team.
Volume 1 of 23

Houser, Jody
Faith; Volume 1: Hollywood & Vine. by Jody Houser, illustrated by Marguerite Sauvage and Francis Portela. Valiant Entertainment, LLC 2016 112 p. Color; Illustration
Grades: 8 9 10 11 12 Adult   **741.5; Fic**

1. Female superhero graphic novels; 2. Superheroes
9781682151211, $9.99; 1682151212

"Orphaned at a young age, Faith Herbert — a psionically gifted 'psiot'...is taking control of her destiny and becoming the hard-hitting hero she's always known she can be — complete with a mild-mannered secret identity, unsuspecting colleagues, and a day job as a reporter that routinely throws into her harms way!" (Publisher's note)

Courtesy of Valiant Entertainment

"This is a modern twist on the classic superhero tale. Faith doesn't have the typical superheroine body type, dismantling stereotypes about what it means to be superpowered." SLJ
Originally published in single magazine form as Faith #1-4

Howard, Abby
Dinosaur empire!. by Abby Howard. Amulet Books 2017 128 p. Color illustration; Color; Map (Earth before us)
Grades: 4 5 6   **741.5; 567.91**
1. Paleontology; 2. Dinosaurs
1419723065; 9781683351139; 9781419723063, $15.95
LC 2016056055

Ronnie is just a normal fifth-grader trying to pass her science class's impossible quiz on the history of dinosaurs...until she happens upon her neighbor — Ms. Lernin — a retired paleontologist. With the assistance of Science Magic, Ronnie and Ms. Lernin travel back through time and space to experience the Mesozoic Era firsthand." (Publisher's note)

"An in-depth look at dinosaurs, geography, and evolution, presented through an appealing framing device.... Howard details characteristics of dinosaurs and other prehistoric creatures, covers similarities and differences among different species, and offers information on evolution, convergent evolution, and mutations." SLJ

Hughes, Susan
No girls allowed: tales of daring women dressed as men for love, freedom and adventure. written by Susan Hughes; llustrated by Willow Dawson. Kids Can Press 2008 80p. Illustration
Grades: 3 4 5 6 7 8 9
306.7; 741.5
1. Biographical graphic novels; 2. Graphic novels; 3. Transvestites — Graphic novels
978-1-55453-177-6, $16.95;
978-1-55453-178-3 (pa), $9.95
LC 2007-9060846

Courtesy of Kids Can Press

This book collects short biographies in graphic format of young women who dressed as and pretended to be men in order to do and be what they wanted. The real Mu Lan did pretend to be her father's son in order to serve in the Chinese Emperor's army to protect her father. Hatshepsut was an Egyptian princess who was determined to be pharaoh, although that role could only go to men. Margaret Buckley was a young Englishwoman who became Dr. James Barry in the early nineteenth century. Seven women's stories are told here, and the book includes a short list of books for further reading.

Humphreys, Jessica Dee

Child Soldier: When Boys and Girls Are Used in War. Michel Chikwanine, Jessica Dee Humphreys; illustrated by Claudia Davila. Kids Can Press 2015 48 p. Color; Illustration

Grades: 5 6 7 8

741.5; 355

1. Chikwanine, Michel; 2. Child soldiers

1771381264; 9781771381260, $17.95

Eisner Nominee: Best Publication for Kids (2016)

Courtesy of Kids Can Press

This children's book, written by Michel Chikwanine and Jessica Dee Humphreys, and illustrated by Claudia Davila, describes the experience of a child solder. "Michel Chikwanine was five years old when he was abducted from his schoolyard soccer game in the Democratic Republic of Congo and forced to become a soldier for a brutal rebel militia. Against the odds, Michel managed to escape..., but he was never the same again." (Publisher's note)

"Chikwanine's narration is matter of fact but never didactic, emphasizing less the gruesome details and more young Michel's emotional response and attempts to make sense of the world around him. Earthy hued and gentle, the images make a potentially disturbing topic accessible." SLJ

Humphries, Sam

Jonesy; Volume 1. by Sam Humphries & Caitlin Rose Boyle; colors by Mickey Quinn; letters by Corey Breen; cover by Caitlin Rose Boyle. Boom! Studios 2016 112 p. Color; Illustration

Grades: 7 8 9 10 11 12   741.5; Fic

1. Teenage girls — Fiction; 2. Humorous fiction; 3. Fantasy fiction

1608868834; 9781608868834, $9.99

"Jonesy is a self-described 'cool dork.'...But she has a secret nobody knows. She has the power to make people fall in love!...There's only one catch — it doesn't work on herself. She's gonna have to find love the old-fashioned way, and in the meantime, figure out how to distract herself from the real emotions she inevitably has to face when her powers go wrong." (Publisher's note)

Volume 1 of 3

Hurchalla, Elizabeth

Ben 10 Alien Force: Ben 10 returns. Del Rey 2008 96p. Illustration

Grades: 3 4 5 6 7 8   741.5; Fic

1. Adventure graphic novels; 2. Graphic novels; 3. Science fiction graphic novels

978-0-345-51438-7, $7.99

Ben Tennyson had lived as Ben 10, a superhero thanks to the watch-like Omnitrix that could transform him into any of ten superpowered alien life-forms. Five years ago, he put away the Omnitrix in order to live a normal life. However, his Grandpa Max is a Plumber, a member of an intergalactic police force, and he has continued his work. Now fifteen years old and a star soccer player, Ben visits Grandpa Max's trailer only to learn that Max has disappeared, a weird and creepy alien tries to get him, and Max has left a cryptic holographic message. Ben digs out his Omnitrix, seeks out his cousin Gwen, who has super powers of her own, and then they run into another Plumber who has been searching for Max. They team up to find him and to learn why more aliens are coming to Earth and engaging in illegal transactions. This book is illustrated with screen captures from the Cartoon Network program.

Hutchison, David

Oz: The Manga. Antarctic Press 2006 un Illustration

Grades: 4 5 6 7 8 9

741.5; Fic

1. Fantasy graphic novels; 2. Graphic novels; 3. Baum, L. Frank — Adaptations

978-1-932453-69-0, $14.95

Courtesy of Antarctic Press

This is Baum's classic novel, The Wizard of Oz, adapted into manga format by Hutchison. All the characters are here: Dorothy, Toto, the Cowardly Lion, the Tin Woodsman, the Scarecrow, the Wizard. And all the main plot elements are here, from the cyclone that blows Dorothy and Toto to Oz to the Flying Monkeys to dealing with the Wicked Witch. The art makes this adaptation shine, especially the Tin Woodsman, who is a steampunk wonder.

I-Huan

Real/Fake Princess, Vol. 1. DrMaster Publications 2006 176p. Illustration

Grades: 6 7 8 9 10 11 12

741.5; Fic

1. Adventure graphic novels; 2. Graphic novels; 3. Manhua; 4. Romance graphic novels

978-1-59796-079-3, $9.95

Courtesy of DrMaster Publications

In Tang Dynasty China, the country is in great chaos due to the infamous Jin Kang Rebellion. Fearing the possible destruction that might eventually result, Concubine Liu tearfully entrusts the care of her baby daughter, Princess Yi Fu, to a common citizen named Tang Hui. Tang Hui immediately escapes with the princess to the South. A decade passes, and Emperor Gao Zon of Tang has decided he wants to find all of his long-lost relatives and has appointed Zhong Lu to the task. From there an adventure begins as Zhong Lu discovers and takes a special interest in Princess Yi Fu (renamed Zi Li), who is happily living in a quiet fishing village with her childhood crush and savior — Tang Hui. Returning with Zhong Lu to a life of royalty means leaving behind the humble life she has come to know with the commoners. This is manhua, I-Huan is from Taiwan.

Igarashi, Daisuke

★ **Children** of the sea, vol. 1. Viz Media/Viz Signature 2009 320p. Illustration

Grades: 7 8 9 10 11 12   741; Fic; 741.5

1. Adventure graphic novels; 2. Fantasy graphic novels; 3. Graphic novels; 4. Manga; 5. Mystery graphic novels; 6. Ocean — Graphic novels; 7. Seinen manga

978-1-4215-2914-1, $14.99; 1-4215-2914-9

"As a young girl, Ruka sees a fish turn into light and disappear at the aquarium where her father works, but no one believes her. Years later, the mystery of the ghost of the sea unfolds before Ruka and a pair of mysterious young boys, Umi and Sora." Publ Wkly

"Igarashi's storytelling is quiet, thoughtful, and thought provoking, but it is his drawings that make this manga so amazing. Extremely detailed settings turn panels into mini-masterpieces." Booklist

Volume 1 of 5

Ikeda, Akiko

Chibikuro party. Dark Horse Books 2008 un Illustration
Grades: 2 3 4 5 6 7   **741.5; Fic**
   1. Adventure graphic novels; 2. Animals — Graphic novels; 3. Graphic novels; 4. Humorous graphic novels
978-1-59582-128-7, $9.95
   One night the moon wakes up Dayan's shadow — it's the one night that the shadows are free to move about on their own. Dayan's shadow, Chip (Dayan names him) wakes him up and wants him to go to the shadows' party, called the Chibikuro Party. The Satan of Death Forest sends Noel disguised as a shadow to kidnap all the shadows, and Noel tricks the shadows by saying they can go with him and be free forever. Dayan hears all this, and he rouses his friends to save their shadows from Death Forest.
   Part of the Dayan's collection books series

Dayan's birthday. Dark Horse Books 2008 un Illustration
Grades: 2 3 4 5 6 7   **741.5; Fic**
   1. Animals — Graphic novels; 2. Graphic novels; 3. Humorous graphic novels
978-1-59582-125-6, $9.95
   The cat Dayan learns that he has a birthday, but he doesn't know what it is. He goes to a trio of witches to find out when his birthday will come, and then he throws a big party for everyone. However, he forgot to invite the witches, and they come to take his birthday back. This book is done in a small picture book format and is translated from Japanese. The woodland creatures serve the witches strong liquor to help Dayan
   Part of the Dayan's collection book series

Thursday rainy party. Dark Horse Boks 2008 un Illustration
Grades: 2 3 4 5 6 7   **741.5; Fic**
   1. Animals — Graphic novels; 2. Graphic novels; 3. Humorous graphic novels
978-1-59582-126-3, $9.95
   One day Dayan gets caught in the rain, and he meets a friendly frog. He invites the frog to come to Willie the mouse's next rainy Thursday party, but learns the frog doesn't know anything about days of the week. Dayan creates a special calendar for his new friend, but the next rainy Thursday doesn't happen for several weeks; did the frog keep up with the calendar, and will he come to Willie's party?
   Part of the Dayan's collection books series

White Eurocka. Dark Horse Books 2008 un Illustration
Grades: 2 3 4 5 6 7   **741.5; Fic**
   1. Animals — Graphic novels; 2. Graphic novels; 3. Humorous graphic novels
978-1-59582-127-0, $9.95
   Winter comes to the land of Tachiel along with a strong cold wave, much colder than most winters. As the festival of Eurocka approaches, Dayan and his friends find that many other creatures have come from the North penguins, walruses, and polar bears, to participate in the festival. During the celebrations, a baby polar bear cub magically arrives.
   Part of the Dayan's collection books series

Ikeda, Miyoko

Fairy navigator Runa, vol.1. Del Rey Manga 2010 186p. Illustration
Grades: 7 8 9 10 11 12   **741.5; Fic**
   1. Adventure graphic novels; 2. Fairies — Graphic novels; 3. Fantasy graphic novels; 4. Graphic novels; 5. Magic — Graphic novels; 6. Manga; 7. Shojo manga
978-0-345-52226-9, $10.99
   Fourth grader Runa Rindo has lived in the Children of the Stars School ever since she was very young, it's the only home she has ever really known. All she has from her parents is a ring pendant and a small wooden box. Then two young strangers ask Runa "Are you the Legendary Girl?" And with that, her life changes. Suneri and Mokke are Fairies who can change shape to a cat (Suneri) and an owl (Mokke), and they tell Runa that she is a princess from the Fairy world. When another fairy, Kamachi, kidnaps Runa's best friend, Chae ("my name is Sae!"), Runa finds she must accept her destiny as the one who can control passage between the human and fairy worlds to save Chae.

Inoue, Takehiko

   ★ **Slam** dunk, volume 1: Sakuragi. story and art by Takehiko Inoue; English adaptation Kelly Sue DeConnick. Viz Media/Shonen Jump 2008 197p. Illustration
Grades: 8 9 10 11 12   **741.5; Fic**
   1. Basketball — Graphic novels; 2. Graphic novels; 3. Manga; 4. Shonen manga
978-1-4215-0679-1, $7.99
   Hanamichi Sakuragi is a first year student at Shohoku Prefecture High School; he's got a reputation as a bruising fighter and has suffered 50 rejections from girls who were scared of his fighting. He's looked down on sports all his life, but on this first day of high school, he meets Haruko Akagi; she's not scared of him, and she loves basketball. He falls for her completely, enough to try to play basketball. But, he has competition — Kaeda Rukawa is another first year student; he's a star basketball player, and Haruko has a huge crush on him. Then Sakuragi gets on the bad side of the basketball team captain, who happens to be Haruko's older brother. Sakuragi does everything he can to convince Takenori Akagi to let him join the team. However, he has a long way to go before he can build the fundamental skills to play basketball effectively; will he stick it out? There's some fighting, one male student's buttocks get exposed accidentally, but there's no bad language.
   Original Japanese edition, 1991; Volume 1 of a 31 volume series

Inzana, Ryan

   Ichiro. written & illustrated by Ryan Inzana. Houghton Mifflin/Houghton Mifflin Harcourt 2012 288 p. Illustration; Color
Grades: 7 8 9 10   **741.5/973**
   1. Gods and goddesses — Fiction; 2. Grandfathers — Fiction; 3. Graphic novels; 4. Monsters — Fiction; 5. Supernatural — Fiction; 6. Japan — Fiction; 7. Japan — History — Graphic novels; 8. Fantasy graphic novels; 9. Supernatural graphic novels; 10. Folklore — Japan — Graphic novels; 11. Japanese Americans — Graphic novels
0547252692; 9780547252698

                                LC 2011277558
   This graphic novel depicts the story of Ichiro, "a young American teen, son of a Japanese immigrant and an American soldier killed in combat, [who] goes to Japan with his mother for an extended visit and begins to grapple with sophisticated cultural complexities.... After his mother and Japanese grandfather tell him stories of Japanese history and folklore, Ichiro has a fantastical adventure involving the Japanese myth of the shape-shifting tanuki spirit." (Kirkus Reviews)

Irwin, Jane

   Vogelein: Old Ghosts. Fiery Studios 2007 168p. Illustration
Grades: 7 8 9 10 11 12 Adult
741.5; Fic
   1. Fantasy graphic novels; 2. Graphic novels
0-9743110-1-4, $12.95

Courtesy of Fiery Studios

Though three hundred years have passed since Alexi's death, Vogelein finds herself still haunted by the unkept promise she made to her first Guardian. Now the clockwork faerie must confront her past with the help of Mason, an itinerant musician whose spirit bears a striking resemblance to the one she desperately wants to lay to rest. As she struggles to find peace for both herself and Alexi, Vogelein discovers that centuries-old questions rarely have easy answers, intended paths reveal themselves in mysterious ways, and present-day threats strike just as suddenly as those from long ago.

Isayama, Hajime

★ **Attack** on Titan 1. Hajime Isayama. Kodansha 2012 186 p. Illustration (Attack on Titan)

Grades: 8 9 10 11 12   **741.5**
1. Good and evil — Comic books, strips, etc.; 2. Horror comic books, strips, etc.; 3. Giants — Graphic novels; 4. Shonen manga; 5. Horror graphic novels

1612620248; 9781612620244, $10.99

"Humanity has been devastated by the bizarre, giant humanoids known as the Titans. Little is known about...why they are bent on consuming mankind.... People believe their 100-meter-high walls will protect them from the Titans, but the sudden appearance of an immense Titan is about to change everything." (Publisher's note)

"Along with the setting and intricate, twisting plot, Attack on Titan derives its appeal from its willingness to bend the conventions of shounen manga. Here, friendship and burning spirit do not conquer all, and your favorite character stands a good chance of getting eaten without the opportunity to give a cool speech first." LJ

Volume 1 of an ongoing series

Attack on Titan anthology. Attack on Titan created by Hajime Isayama; edited by Ben Applegate and Jeanine Schaefer; cover, logo, and interior design by Phil Balsman; lettering and interior design by Steve Wands. Kodansha 2016 256 p. Illustration

Grades: 8 9 10 11 12   **741.5**
1. Fantasy fiction — Graphic novels; 2. Horror fiction — Graphic novels; 3. Science fiction graphic novels; 4. Shonen manga

1632362589; 9781632362582, $29.99

This tribute anthology to the manga Attack on Titan features "original stories by a long roster of comic superstars such as Scott Snyder (Batman, American Vampire), Gail Simone (Batgirl), Michael Avon Oeming (Powers), Paolo Rivera (Daredevil, Amazing Spider-Man), Cameron Stewart (Fight Club 2, Batgirl) and Faith Erin Hicks (The Adventures of Superhero Girl)!" (Publisher's note)

"The Victorian-style guide to Titan's walled city by Genevieve Valentine and David López is a standout, as is the contemplative final story by brothers Asaf and Tomer Hanuka." Pub Wkly

Isenberg, Marty

Transformers animated volume 1. IDW Publishing 2008 un Illustration

Grades: 2 3 4 5 6 7 8   **741.5; Fic**
1. Adventure graphic novels; 2. Graphic novels; 3. Robots — Graphic novels; 4. Science fiction graphic novels; 5. Transformers (Fictional characters); 6. Transformers (Fictional characters)

978-1-60010-151-9, $7.99

When Optimus Prime and his team of misfit Autobots accidentally unearth the Allspark, they are attacked by Megatron, leader of the Decepticons. The fight causes the Autobots' ship to travel from deep space to Earth in the twenty-second century, and to New Detroit. Now the fight between the Autobots and the Decepticons will take place on Earth, where humans live, humans who don't know what all these sentient robots are

doing. This book adapts stories from the new animated television series and uses screen captures from the programs to illustrate the book.

Ishihara, Yoko

★ The **manga** cookbook. presented by the Manga University Culinary Institute; illustrations by Chihiro Hattori; [with recipes by Yoko Ishihara]. Japanime Co. Ltd. 2007 158p. Illustration

Courtesy of Japanime Co.

Grades: 4 5 6 7 8 9 10 11 12
641.5; 741.5
1. Graphic novels; 2. Japanese cooking — Graphic novels; 3. Manga

978-4-921205-07-2, $14.95

Food appears frequently in manga and in anime, but just what are the characters eating? This book is an illustrated step-by-step guide to preparing some Japanese dishes, from onigiri (rice balls) to yakitori (skewered grilled chicken), oshinko (pickled vegetables), udon (Japanese noodles), to traditional sweets and desserts. Definitions of terms and ingredients used, basic cooking guidelines, and instructions on how to properly use chopsticks are all included. The recipes are authentic but have been simplified somewhat so older children and teens with some basic kitchen skills can prepare the foods. Adult supervision is recommended for younger children and for children who aren't very experienced with using knives, measuring spoons, and cooking on the stove.

Iwaoka, Hisae

★ **Saturn** apartments, volume 1. [translation, Matt Thorn].. Viz Signature 2010 184p. Illustration

Grades: 7 8 9 10   **741; 741.5; Fic**
1. Graphic novels; 2. Manga; 3. Science fiction graphic novels; 4. Seinen manga

978-1-4215-3364-3, $12.99; 1-4215-3364-2

Far in the future, humankind has left Earth to live in a gigantic ringlike structure that circles the planet. In this structure, humans have developed a class structure based on where one lives: the higher the floor on which you live, the greater your status. Mitsu has just graduated from junior high and is now expected to work as a window washer, just like his father before him. The thing is, his father disappeared while washing windows and is presumed dead. Window washing means one must get into a space suit and go out of the structure into outer space, 35 kilometers above the Earth's surface; space winds and other hazards make the work dangerous and expensive. Even as he wonders still, five years after his father's disappearance, what happened to him, Mitsu finds his job gives him a unique perspective on the lives of those who live in the Saturn Apartments. This is science fiction from the viewpoint of the mundane service work rather than heroics of space action.

"This story of a young teen struggling to live alone will appeal to YAs, and the introspective nature of the narrative will have plenty of crossover appeal for adult readers as well." Booklist

Reads from right to left; Volume 1 of 7

Jablonski, Carla

Defiance. written by Carla Jablonski; art by Leland Purvis; color by Hilary Sycamore. First Second 2011 126p. Illustration

Grades: 7 8 9 10 11 12   **741.5; Fic**
1. World War, 1939-1945 — Fiction; 2. World War, 1939-1945 — Underground movements — Fiction; 3. France — History — 1940-1945, German occupation — Graphic novels

978-1-59643-292-5, $16.99; 1-59643-292-6

LC 2010036253

"World War II has taken its toll on the French countryside. German soldiers patrol the towns, searching for any challenge to their rule. The Tessier siblings, Paul, Marie, and Sophie, keep their noses clean and their faces blank as the French military police tighten their grip on their small country town. But all three are secretly doing their part for the Resistance: the men and women working hard to undermine the Germans and win back France's freedom...even if it ends up costing them their lives." (Publisher's note)

★ **Resistance**, book 1. art by Leland Purvis; color by Hilary Sycamore. First Second Books 2010 121p. Illustration (Resistance)

Grades: 6 7 8 9 10 11 12 **741.5; Fic**

1. Adventure graphic novels; 2. Graphic novels; 3. World War, 1939-1945 — Jews — Rescue — Graphic novels; 4. World War, 1939-1945 — Underground movements — Graphic novels; 5. France — History — 1940-1945, German occupation — Graphic novels

978-1-59643-291-8, $16.99; 1-59643-291-8

Paul and his younger sister Marie live in a small village in Vichy France during World War II. Thus far, the war hasn't really touched them, but now Nazi soldiers come, and Paul's friend, Henri, and his parents are Jews and therefore in danger. When Paul and Marie try to protect Henri, their secret leaks out to members of the Resistance. Although they are young, they soon become recruits in the Resistance. Paul's incessant sketching in his book turns out to be a valuable talent, but he and Marie, and then their older sister, Sylvie, don't quite realize just how dangerous things can get. The cover is very striking, with Paul aiming a slingshot at a Nazi soldier. The Author's Note at the end of the book talks about history, the Resistance, and why the events in France during World War II should not be depicted as black and white, heroic Resistance versus villainous Vichy.

Other titles in this series are: Defiance (2011); Victory (2012)

★ **Victory**. written by Carla Jablonski; art by Leland Purvis; color by Hilary Sycamore.. First Second 2012 123 p. Color illustration

Grades: 6 7 8 9 10 11 12 **741.5/973**

1. Graphic novels; 2. World War, 1939-1945 — France — Fiction; 3. World War, 1939-1945 — France — Juvenile fiction; 4. World War, 1939-1945 — Underground movements — France — Fiction; 5. France — History — German occupation, 1940-1945 — Fiction; 6. Underground movements — Fiction; 7. Resistance to government — Fiction; 8. France — History — Graphic novels; 9. World War, 1939-1945 — Children — Fiction

1596432934; 9781596432932

LC 2011030504

"In this third volume in the graphic novel trilogy about the Tessier family," set during the French Resistance, "Sylvie relays information she gathers from her unwitting German boyfriend, Marie hides a man she discovers after a plane crash in the woods, and Paul is the ears of the Resistance in town.... At the end of the book, Paul travels to Paris to pass along information. He's on the scene for the city's liberation." (Horn Book Magazine)

"The storyline is brisk and edgy, complementing the worn nerves of people who have lived through war... Fans of graphic art and WWII will appreciate this book, as well as reluctant readers who are interested in historical fiction." VOYA

Jacques, Brian

Redwall: the graphic novel. by Brian Jacques; illustrated by Bret Blevins; adapted by Stuart Moore; lettering by Richard Starkings. Philomel Books 2007 143p. Illustration

Grades: 4 5 6 7 8 9 **741.5; Fic**

1. Adventure graphic novels; 2. Fantasy graphic novels; 3. Graphic novels; 4. Mice — Graphic novels

978-0-399-24481-0, $12.99; 0-399-24481-6

When Cluny the rat's army attacks Redwall Abbey, young Matthias the mouse follows in the footsteps of the long-ago hero Martin the Warrior to defend his home

"The story is a page-turner, and the detailed black-and-white drawings capture both the passion and the pathos." SLJ

Jakobsen, Lars

The **mysterious** manuscript. Lars Jakobsen. Graphic Universe 2012 48 p.

Grades: 4 5 6 7 8

741.5/9489; Fic

1. Crime — Fiction; 2. Graphic novels; 3. Time travel — Fiction; 4. Scotland — Fiction; 5. Mystery comic books, strips, etc.; 6. Mystery fiction; 7. Time travel — Graphic novels

0761378839; 9780761378839, $27.93

Courtesy of Lerner Publishing Group

LC 2011027146

This graphic novel, by Lars Jakobsen, is part of the "Mortensen's Escapades" series. "A book collector shows Mortensen...an illuminated manuscript from 1512. When Mortensen sees a painting of an airplane on one of its pages, he knows he has a mystery to unravel. With a zap from his time gun, he travels back to medieval Scotland to look for clues. A wise scribe and a mute witch help him...[to] answer...how did an airplane crash land in the Middle Ages?" (Publisher's note)

The **Santa** Fe jail. by Lars Jakobsen; illustrated by Lars Jakobsen. Graphic Universe 2012 48 p.

Grades: 4 5 6

741.5/9489; Fic

1. Graphic novels; 2. Kidnapping — Fiction; 3. Time travel — Fiction; 4. Time travel — Graphic novels

0822594218; 9780761378860; 9780822594215, $6.95

Courtesy of Lerner Publishing Group

LC 2011044643

This adventure graphic novel, by Lars Jakobsen, is book 2 of the "Mortensen's Escapades" series. In it "Mortensen is given a special assignment: deliver...[a] ransom to the Santa Fe Jail. But the kidnappers are time travelers, so nothing is as simple as it seems.... Mortensen...is drugged by a mysterious woman. He awakens to find himself packed inside a cargo plane that is about to nose dive into the jungles of Tanzania." (Publisher's note)

The **secret** mummy. art by Lars Jakobsen; story by Lars Jakobsen; translation by Lars Jakobsen and Robyn Chapman. Graphic Universe 2013 48 p. (Mortensen's escapades)

Grades: 4 5 6 7 8

741.5/9489

1. Criminals — Fiction; 2. Graphic novels; 3. Time travel — Fiction; 4.

Courtesy of Lerner Publishing Group

Transplantation of organs, tissues, etc. — Fiction; 5. Vampires — Graphic novels

0761379150; 9780761379157, $27.93

LC 2012027015

This is the fourth Mortensen adventure from Lars Jakobsen. "Mortensen, an agent dedicated to relentlessly fighting the ever-cresting wave of nefarious time-traveling criminals, now faces vampires in 19th-century Transylvania. Jumping uneasily through time from Prague to Transylvania to Bosnia and Paris, this wayward hero follows a creepy count thought to be a villainous vampire and the shadowy sarcophagus that seems tied to him." (Kirkus)

Originally published in Danish under title: Den falske mumie, in 2012.

Jamieson, Victoria

★ **All's** faire in middle school. Victoria Jamieson.. Dial Books for Young Readers 2017 248 p. Color; Illustration

Grades: 4 5 6 7 8   **741.5; Fic**

1. Middle schools; 2. Friendship; 3. Family life

0525429999; 9780525429982, $20.99; 9780525429999, $12.99

LC 2016044190

In this book, by Victoria Jamieson, "eleven-year-old Imogene (Impy) has grown up with two parents working at the Renaissance Faire, and she's eager to begin her own training as a squire. First, though, she'll need to prove her bravery. Luckily Impy has just the quest in mind — she'll go to public school after a life of being homeschooled! But it's not easy to act like a noble knight-in-training in middle school. Impy falls in with a group of girls who seem really nice (until they don't)." (Publisher's note)

"Jamieson masterfully taps into the voice and concerns of middle-schoolers, and the offbeat setting of the Renaissance faire adds some lively texture." Booklist

★ **Roller** girl. by Victoria Jamieson. Dial Books 2015 240 p. Color; Illustration

Grades: 4 5 6 7 8   **741.5; Fic**

1. Friendship — Fiction; 2. Graphic novels; 3. Roller derby — Fiction; 4. Roller skating — Fiction

0803740166; 9780803740167, $12.99

LC 2014011310

Newbery Honor Book (2016); Eisner Nominee: Best Publication for Kids (2016)

This graphic novel, by Victoria Jamieson, is "about friendship and surviving junior high through the power of roller derby. For most of her twelve years, Astrid has done everything with her best friend Nicole. But after Astrid falls in love with roller derby and signs up for derby camp, Nicole decides to go to dance camp instead. And so begins the most difficult summer of Astrid's life as she struggles to keep up with the older girls at camp." (Publisher's note)

"Jamieson captures this snapshot of preteen angst with a keenly decisive eye, brilliantly juxtaposing the nuances of roller derby with the twists and turns of adolescent girls' friendships." Kirkus

Jansson, Tove

Moomin Book One. Drawn & Quarterly 2006 96p. Illustration

Grades: 8 9 10 11 12 Adult   **741.5; Fic**

1. Graphic novels; 2. Humorous graphic novels; 3. Moomins (Fictional characters)

1-894937-80-5, $19.95

Jansson is best known in the U.S. for her children's books featuring the Moomins, hippo-shaped creatures. Her comic strips have a more mature outlook. Moomin needs help getting rid of unwanted guests, but the only solution that works costs him his house. Then his scheming friend Sniff involves him in all sorts of shady get-rich-quick schemes. And when Moomin finds his long-lost parents, his father's craving for adventure

causes more trouble. Snorkmaiden, Moomin's girlfriend, is just as bad as Moominpapa, and they spark a boat trip south to a resort, where the naive Moomins think they're houseguests and everyone else, including the hotel staff, assumes they're wealthy eccentrics. The childlike look of the strips belie the goings-on; this book is not really for young readers, although teens and adults will enjoy the whimsy overlaying sharp satire.

Moomin's winter follies. Trove Jansson. Enfant 2012 45 p.

Grades: 8 9 10 11 12 Adult   **741.5**

1. Moomins (Fictional characters); 2. Comic books, strips, etc.

1770460985; 9781770460980, $9.95

Author Tove Jansson presents a graphic novel. "Moomin wakes up one morning to find the pond frozen over, and rather than hibernate, the family decides to brave the winter weather. At first, their wintry adventure seems to be going swimmingly, until Mr. Brisk of the Great Outdoors Club takes over and forces everyone to embrace the winter sports, whether they want to or not." (Comic Vine)

Jeanty, Georges

Buffy the Vampire Slayer season eight; Volume 1: the long way home. Dark Horse Comics 2007 136p. Illustration

Grades: 8 9 10 11 12 Adult   **741.5**

1. Adventure graphic novels; 2. Buffy the Vampire Slayer (Fictional character); 3. Graphic novels; 4. Horror graphic novels

978-1-59307-822-5, $15.95

The television series of Buffy the Vampire Slayer lasted seven seasons; this volume begins the comics-only eighth season. Buffy and her friends may have destroyed the Hellmouth, but all is not fun and games, as an old enemy returns, younger sister Dawn experiences some "growing pains," and a former decoy Slayer has her own troubles. There is a considerable amount of monster fighting.

Volume 1 of 8

Jeffrey, Gary

Elasmosaurus: the long-necked swimmer. illustrated by Terry Riley. Rosen Publishing Group 2009 32p. Illustration

Grades: 2 3 4 5 6 7

567.9; 741.5

1. Dinosaurs — Graphic novels; 2. Graphic novels

978-1-4358-2505-5, $25.25

LC 2008-3881

This book uses comic book style art to introduce young readers to the elasmosaurus, which lived in the ancient shallow ocean that used to cover Kansas. The book provides some science-based speculation on what the dinosaur's life might have been like. Additional material includes information on fossil evidence, quick facts about the elasmosaurus, and a glossary.

Part of the Graphic Dinosaurs series.

Courtesy of Rosen Publishing

Stegosaurus: the plated dinosaur. illustrated by James Field.. Rosen Publishing Group 2009 32p. Illustration

Grades: 2 3 4 5 6 7

567.9; 741.5

1. Dinosaurs — Graphic novels; 2. Graphic novels

978-1-4358-2503-1, $25.25

LC 2007-50587

Courtesy of Rosen Publishing

This book uses comic book style art to introduce young readers to the stegosaurus, with some science-based speculation on what the dinosaur's life might have been like. Additional material includes information on fossil evidence, quick facts about the stegosaurus, and a glossary.

Part of the Graphic Dinosaurs series.

Johns, Geoff

JSA Presents Stars and S.T.R.I.P.E.. DC Comics 2007 192p. Illustration

Grades: 8 9 10 11 12 Adult   **741.5; Fic**
   1. Graphic novels; 2. Superhero graphic novels
   978-1-4012-1390-9, $17.99

Courtney Whitmore is just your typical teenage girl trying to make it through high school, but she's about to stumble upon a secret that will make her life a lot more complicated. Her new stepfather, Pat Dugan, was once Stripesy, sidekick of the Golden Age hero The Star-Spangled Kid. Finding the Kid's old costume, Courtney modifies it for herself and becomes the new Star-Spangled Kid, aiming to fight crime and annoy the heck out of her stepfather. But Dugan isn't about to let his new daughter get into any danger. Putting his mechanical skills to work, he creates a robotic suit called S.T.R.I.P.E., and joins Courtney's battle for justice. They fight side-by-side — and sometimes with each other — taking on aliens, cults, new villains, and more. These stories are the first that Johns wrote in comics, back in 1999.

Showcase Presents Superman Family Volume One. DC Comics 2006 572p. Illustration

Grades: 6 7 8 9 10 11 12 Adult   **741.5; Fic**
   1. Graphic novels; 2. Jimmy Olsen (Fictional character); 3. Lois Lane (Fictional character); 4. Superhero graphic novels; 5. Superman (Fictional character)
   978-1-4012-0787-8, $16.99

This volume spotlights Superman's girlfriend Lois Lane and his pal Jimmy Olsen. Learn more about these two dynamic personalities in their solo stories as each braves danger for the latest scoop. These stories from the 1950s also introduce long-standing elements such as the Daily Planet's Flying Newsroom and Jimmy's penchant for disguises. The Showcase series reprints the older comics stories in black and white collections.

Showcase Presents: Green Arrow Volume 1. DC Comics 2006 528p. Illustration

Grades: 7 8 9 10 11 12 Adult   **741.5; Fic**
   1. Graphic novels; 2. Green Arrow (Fictional character); 3. Superhero graphic novels
   1-4012-0785-5, $16.99

Millionaire Oliver Queen mastered the bow and arrow as a matter of survival when he was trapped on a desert island. Back home in Star City, he chose to use his newfound skills as the costumed champion Green Arrow. With his sidekick, Speedy, he tackled crooks and solved mysteries with energy, style, and the occasional boxing glove arrow. The stories collected in this black and white volume were originally published from 1958 through 1969

Showcase Presents: Superman Volume 1. DC Comics 2005 560p. Illustration

Grades: 6 7 8 9 10 11 12 Adult   **741.5; Fic**
   1. Graphic novels; 2. Superhero graphic novels; 3. Superman (Fictional character)
   1-4012-0758-8, $9.99

This first volume in the Showcase Presents Library of Classics features stories about Superman dating from 1958 through 1959. The adventure collected here have influenced the history of Superman and his extended family. From the introduction of his first love, the mermaid Lori Lemaris, to the introduction of his cousin Supergirl, Superman faces his most dangerous opponents, including Bizarro, Metallo, and Brainiac.

Superman in the Eighties. DC Comics 2006 192p. Illustration

Grades: 8 9 10 11 12 Adult   **741.5; Fic**
   1. Graphic novels; 2. Superhero graphic novels; 3. Superman (Fictional character)
   1-4012-0952-1, $19.99

The '80s were a decade that forever redefined the world's first super-hero. The first half of the decade brought the story of Superman to a close, while the latter half of the decade brought a revamped Man of Steel to an all-new audience. This volume includes ten stories by such creators as John Byrne, Curt Swan, Gil Kane, George Perez, Marv Wolfman, Jim Starlin, and Len Wein. Writer/artist Jerry Ordway provides historical and personal perspectives to these stories.

Superman in the Forties. DC Comics 2005 192p. Illustration

Grades: 6 7 8 9 10 11 12 Adult   **741.5; Fic**
   1. Graphic novels; 2. Superhero graphic novels; 3. Superman (Fictional character)
   1-4012-0457-0, $19.99

At the end of the 1930s, comics saw a new breed of hero. The man could withstand bullets, leap over tall buildings in a single bound, and bend steel in his bare hands. Fighting for the oppressed, this man of steel captured the imagination of the readers. He was, of course, Superman. This volume reprints stories originally published from 1938 through 1949. The reader sees Superman first fighting "regular" criminals, but as the years go by, super-powered villains start to menace Metropolis, along with such villains as Lex Luthor and troublemakers such as the mischievous Mr. Mxyztplk.

Superman: Up, Up and Away!. Kurt Busiek and Geoff Johns, writers; Pete Woods and Renato Guedes, art. DC Comics 2006 192p. Illustration

Grades: 8 9 10 11 12 Adult   **741.5; Fic**
   1. Graphic novels; 2. Superhero graphic novels; 3. Superman (Fictional character); 4. Green Lantern (Fictional character)
   978-1-4012-0954-4, $14.99

In the wake of Infinite Crisis, Superman had lost his powers. For the past year, as Clark Kent he has worked with the help of his super-powered allies, Green Lantern, Supergirl, and Hawkgirl, to keep Metropolis safe. Now, Lex Luthor has been acquitted of his past crimes, and he has managed to get his hands on a powerful and ancient Kryptonian artifact and plans to use it to destroy Superman once and for all. What can a powerless Superman do?

Teen Titans Vol. 4: The Future is Now. DC Comics 2005 un Illustration

Grades: 8 9 10 11 12 Adult   **741.5; Fic**
   1. Graphic novels; 2. Science fiction graphic novels; 3. Superhero graphic novels; 4. Teen Titans (Fictional characters)
   1-4012-0475-9, $9.99

The Titans' weekends are usually a chance to get away from it all, but this time they've gone to the 31st century, where they must help the Legion of Super-Heroes stop a threat known as the Fatal Five Hundred. Their return trip drops them off ten years into their future, and they don't like what they see. And when they finally get back home, they meet Speedy, who has arrived just in time to help them fight Dr. Light.

Johnson, Dan

Sinbad: The legacy. wordsmith, Dan Johnson; illustrator, Naresh Kumar; colorist, Ajo Kurian; letterer, Laxmi Chand Gupta. Campfire 2011 86 p. Color illustration

Grades: 7 8 9 10   **813.6; Fic**

1. Sea stories; 2. Graphic novels; 3. Historical fiction; 4. Sinbad the Sailor (Legendary character)
8190751557; 9788190751551, $12.99

LC 2011287737

In this graphic novel, "[w]hen King Haakim sends his teenage son Habib on a voyage to teach him" maturity, "the spoiled brat makes enemies of Sinbad's crew and is responsible for the ship being blown off course and forced to anchor near islands full of dangerous giant animals, beautiful cannibal women, and [a]...death-obsessed kingdom. Despite this, Sinbad rescues the prince from his blunders, while relating the tale of his own...adventures that helped him grow up." (Publishers Weekly)

Johnson, Joe

Classics illustrated deluxe #2: tales from the Brothers Grimm. Papercutz 2008 144p. Illustration
Grades: 3 4 5 6 7 8

741.5; Fic

1. Fantasy graphic novels; 2. Folklore — Graphic novels; 3. Graphic novels
978-1-59707-101-7, $17.95

Courtesy of NBM Publishing

This volume of Papercutz's new Classics Illustrated Deluxe series collects French adaptations of four tales from the Brothers Grimm (Wilhelm and Jakob): Hansel and Gretel, Learning to Shudder, The Devil and the Three Golden Hairs, and The Valiant Little Tailor. These comic book adaptations don't shy away from showing scary monsters, saying rude things without using really bad language, and showing some violence.

Part of the Classics Illustrated Deluxe series

Jolley, Dan

Alien Incident on Planet J. by Dan Jolley; illustrated by Matt Wendt; [coloring by Hi-Fi Design; lettering by Marshall Dillon].. Lerner Publishing Group/Graphic Universe 2008 112p. Illustration
Grades: 3 4 5 6 7 8 9

741.5; Fic

1. Adventure graphic novels; 2. Graphic novels; 3. Plot-your-own stories — Graphic novels; 4. Science fiction graphic novels
978-0-8225-6998-5, $27.93;
978-0-8225-8876-4 (pa), $7.93

LC 2007-44116

Courtesy of Lerner Publishing Group

In this new take on the "Choose Your Own Adventure" type of book that combines pages of prose text with pages of comic book sequences, you are a young human stuck on Planet J; your spaceship needs a new part, and you'll never get off this planet if you don't make peace with the Makanuk, the Zirifubi, and the Frongo. Some choices will end badly, others will be better, and the choices are all up to the reader.

This is Volume 8 of the Twisted Journeys series.

Escape from Pyramid X. Lerner Publishing Group/Graphic Universe 2007 112p. Illustration (Twisted Journeys)
Grades: 3 4 5 6 7 8 9

741.5; Fic

1. Adventure graphic novels; 2. Graphic novels; 3. Mummies — Graphic novels
978-0-8225-6777-6, $27.93; 978-0-8225-6779-0 (pa), $7.95

LC 2006-101598

In the series called Twisted Journeys, readers choose how the story will progress. Pages of text alternate with comic book-style pages. In this volume, you the reader are a student who won an essay contest to be part of an archeological dig led by Professor Emil Snackport, at the site of a newly discovered pyramid. In some story lines, you encounter smugglers, in others, a malevolent mummy. Readers will find many scenarios played out, depending on their choices; some end well, others not so well.

Courtesy of Lerner Publishing Group

The **girl** who owned a city. by O.T. Nelson; adapted by Dan Jolley; illustrated by Joëlle Jones; coloring by Jenn Manley Lee. Graphic Universe 2012 125 p.
Grades: 6 7 8 9 10

741.5

1. Graphic novels; 2. Science fiction; 3. Survival — Fiction; 4. Children — Graphic novels; 5. Apocalyptic fiction; 6. Adventure graphic novels; 7. Dystopian juvenile fiction
9780761349037; 9780761356349; 0761356347

LC 2009033270

This graphic novel, by Dan Jolley, O.T. Nelson, and illustrated by Joelle Jones, describes a post-apocalyptic world. "A deadly virus killed every adult on Earth, leaving only us kids behind.... I have to make sure we stay alive.... I figured out how to give the kids on Grand Avenue food, homes, and protection against the gangs. But Tom Logan and his army are determined to take away what we've built and rule the streets themselves." (Publisher's note)

Courtesy of Lerner Publishing Group

Pigling: a Cinderella story: a Korean tale. Graphic Universe 2008 48p. Illustration (Graphic myths and legends)
Grades: 3 4 5 6 7 8 9

741.5; Fic

1. Fairy tales — Graphic novels; 2. Graphic novels; 3. Korea — Folklore — Graphic novels
978-0-8225-7174-2, $27.93;
0-8225-7174-9

LC 2007-40891

In old Korea, in a time when magic still exists, Pear Blossom lives happily with her parents. But when her mother dies, her father quickly remarries a spiteful woman and her mean daughter, and they turn Pear Blossom's

Courtesy of Lerner Publishing Group

life into misery. They treat her like a servant and call her Pigling. Omoni (mother in Korean) makes impossible demands of Pear Blossom, and each time magical creatures help her achieve the tasks. Then on the day of a festival, a handsome magistrate sees Pear Blossom on the road, and she runs away, frightened, leaving a sandal behind.

The **Smoking** Mountain: The Story of Popocatepetl and Iztaccihuatl: An Aztec Legend. story by Dan Jolley; pencils and inks by David Witt. Lerner Publishing Group 2009 48p. Illustration
Grades: 3 4 5 6 7 8 9

741.5; Fic

Courtesy of Lerner Publishing Group

1. Aztecs — Folklore — Graphic novels; 2. Fantasy graphic novels; 3. Graphic novels
978-0-8225-7178-0, $27.93;
9781580138260

LC 2007-20028

Back when the Aztec Empire was at its peak, the Emperor has a favorite daughter, Iztaccihuatl (called Izta); he is troubled by an enemy nation, the Tlaxcalans, and the soldier Popocatepetl (called Popo) is the Emperor's great military leader. Popo and Izta fall in love at first sight when the Emperor honors Popo for his accomplishments, and they meet in secret. However, Cuetlachtli is a jealous soldier who wants to destroy Popo, and he finds his chance when the Emperor catches the two lovers together and tells Popo he can only marry Izta if he brings back the head of the Tlaxcalan king. Searching for the enemy takes a long, hard time, and Cuetlachtli sends a messenger back to Tenochtitlan with word that Popo has died, which sends Izta into a decline. When victorious Popo returns, he finds his lover dead, and takes her to the top of a mountain where he stands over her until his death. Now there are two mountains in Mexico, named for the two lovers. Jolley sets the story as one told by a Mexican tour guide, using contemporary language; artist Witt conducted research to make the art look as authentic as possible. The book includes a list of books, websites, and DVDs for more information and entertainment.

Part of the Graphic Universe Myths and Legends series

The **time** travel trap. illustrated by Matt Wendt. Graphic Universe 2008 111p. Illustration (Twisted journeys)
Grades: 3 4 5 6 7 8 9
741.5; Fic
1. Adventure graphic novels; 2. Graphic novels; 3. Plot-your-own stories — Graphic novels; 4. Science fiction graphic novels
978-0-7613-9472-3 (lib bdg), $27.93;
0-7613-9472-9 (lib bdg);
978-0-8225-8874-0 (pa), $7.95;
0-8225-8874-9 (pa)

LC 2007-6101

Courtesy of Lerner Publishing Group

In this new take on the "Choose Your Own Adventure" type of book that combines pages of prose text with pages of comic book sequences, you are caught in a time machine a fellow student built for the school's science fair. Depending on the choices, you could end up at a medieval joust, facing woolly mammoths and "cavemen," or future aliens. Some choices will end badly, others will be better, and the choices are all up to the reader.

This is Volume 7 of the Twisted Journeys series.

Vampire hunt. illustrated by Gregory Titus; [coloring by Hi-Fi Design; lettering by Marshall Dillon]. Lerner Publishing Group/Graphic Universe 2008 112p. Illustration
Grades: 3 4 5 6 7 8 9
741.5; Fic
1. Adventure graphic novels; 2. Graphic novels; 3. Plot-your-own stories — Graphic novels; 4. Science fiction graphic novels; 5. Vampires — Graphic novels
978-0-8225-8877-1, $27.93;
978-0-8225-8879-5 (pa), $7.95

Courtesy of Lerner Publishing Group

LC 2007-043732

In this new take on the "Choose Your Own Adventure" type of book that combines pages of prose text with pages of comic book sequences, you are a vampire, and you must defend yourself and your castle from vampire hunters. Some choices will end badly, others will be better, and the choices are all up to the reader.

This is Volume 7 of the Twisted Journeys series

Wrapped up in you. by Dan Jolley; illustrated by Natalie Nourigat. Graphic Universe 2012 127 p.
Grades: 6 7 8 9 10 11 12
741.5; Fic
1. Graphic novels; 2. Horror stories; 3. Mummies — Fiction; 4. Witches — Fiction; 5. North Carolina — Fiction; 6. Horror graphic novels; 7. Supernatural graphic novels; 8. Mummies — Graphic novels; 9. Romance fiction — Graphic novels
0761368566; 9780761368564, $29.27

LC 2011044655

Courtesy of Lerner Publishing Group

This graphic novel, by Dan Jolley, illustrated by Natalie Nourigat, is book 6 in the "My Boyfriend Is a Monster" series. "Prince Pachacutec — or 'Chuck' — is a man with a past. He died tragically five hundred years ago, but that's all ancient history as far as Staci is concerned. He is everything she could want.... But the witches aren't willing to live and let live. Will Staci fight for Chuck? Or do the witches have a point when they say reanimated corpses make bad boyfriends?" (Publisher's note)

Joy, Bob
Batman: The Greatest Stories Ever Told Volume Two. DC Comics 2007 208p. Illustration
Grades: 7 8 9 10 11 12 Adult   **741.5; Fic**
1. Batman (Fictional characters); 2. Graphic novels; 3. Superhero graphic novels; 4. Batgirl (Fictional character); 5. Joker (Fictional character)
978-1-4012-1214.8, $19.99

This volume includes stories from different periods in the nearly seventy-year career of Batman, from 1940 to 2003. He goes up against classic villains — the Joker, Killer Croc, the Penguin; he meets Batgirl (Barbara Gordon); deals with crooked businessmen and other criminals.

Flash: The Greatest Stories Ever Told. DC Comics 2007 208p. Illustration
Grades: 6 7 8 9 10 11 12 Adult   **741.5; Fic**
1. Flash (Fictional character); 2. Graphic novels; 3. Superhero graphic novels
978-1-4012-1372-5, $19.99

Jay Garrick, Barry Allen, and Wally West are all men who have donned the symbol of the yellow lightning bolt to combat evil as the Flash. Each hero with his own unique style of commanding a mastery over momentum, they have fought separately and together over the years. This volume collects stories that see them pitted against such villains as Gorilla Grodd, the Reverse Flash, the Fiddler, and many others. This volume also includes the story of Barry and Iris' wedding.

Showcase Presents: Batman Vol. 2. DC Comics 2007 510p. Illustration
Grades: 6 7 8 9 10 11 12 Adult   **741.5; Fic**
1. Batman (Fictional character); 2. Graphic novels; 3. Superhero graphic novels; 4. Robin (Fictional character)
978-1-4012-1362-6, $16.99

Over 500 pages of classic adventures are included in this volume collecting Silver Age tales of Batman and Robin as they face their most enduring enemies, including the Joker, Poison Ivy, the Riddler, Blockbuster, and many others. These are the stories that inspired the Dynamic Duo's 1960s TV series, which featured Batman's astonishing detective skills and impressive array of Bat-gadgets. The stories, reprinted in black and white, date from 1965 and 1966.

Kanata, Konami

★ Chi's sweet home, volume 1. Vertical, Inc. 2010 166p. Illustration
Grades: 5 6 7 8 9 10 11 12 Adult   **741.5; Fic**
1. Cats — Graphic novels; 2. Graphic novels; 3. Humorous graphic novels; 4. Manga; 5. Seinen manga
9781-934287-81-1
Young kitten Chi gets separated from her family while out on a stroll, then she meets little boy Yohei and his parents. They take her home, even though their apartment building has a strict no pets policy. While they try to find someone to take her in, they feed her, give her a cozy bed, set up a box with shredded newspaper for a litter box, and do their best to help her. Even though readers can read what she's thinking, Chi behaves just like a cat, with cat problems such as thinking the litter box is a wonderful play area instead of the place to do her business, and taking fright at Yohei's "vrooming" as he plays with his toy cars. The book is great for younger readers as well as anyone who likes cats. There is one panel where Yohei is sitting on the toilet while Chi is in her litter box in the bathroom, and a scene at the veterinarian's office where the doctor sticks a thermometer in to take Chi's temperature. And, of course, Chi tends to urinate in inappropriate places.
Also available in 3-in-1 omnibus editions; Volume 1 of 12

Kanigher, Robert

Showcase Presents: Wonder Woman Vol. 1. DC Comics 2007 528p. Illustration
Grades: 6 7 8 9 10 11 12 Adult   **741.5; Fic**
1. Graphic novels; 2. Superhero graphic novels; 3. Wonder Woman (Fictional character)
978-1-4012-1373-2, $16.99
Wonder Woman faces some of her deadliest challenges as she battles a variety of aliens and robots, and confronts the evil menaces of the Time Master, the Gadget Maker, Dike of Deception, and one of her most incessant foes, the Angle Man. This volume also includes the re-done origin of Wonder Woman, and some of her teenage adventures as Wonder Girl. Created by William Moulton Marston as a strong, liberated warrior in 1941, these adventures published in the late 1950s and early 1960s cast Wonder Woman in a more "traditional" female superhero role.

Kanno, Aya

Otomen; Volume 1. story & art by Aya Kanno. Viz Media 2010 208 p. Illustration
Grades: 8 9 10 11 12   **741.5; Fic**
1. Dating (Social customs) — Fiction; 2. Shojo manga; 3. Teenagers — Fiction
1421521865; 9781421521862, $9.99
"Asuka Masamune is a guy who loves girly things — sewing, knitting, making cute stuffed animals and reading shojo comics. But in a world where boys are expected to act manly, Asuka must hide his beloved hobbies and play the part of a masculine jock instead. Ryo Miyakozuka, on the other hand, is a girl who can't sew or bake a cake to save her life. Asuka finds himself drawn to Ryo, but she likes only the manliest of men! Can Asuka ever show his true self to anyone, much less to the girl that he's falling for?" (Publisher's note)

"Although the art is as sugary and cute as Asuka himself, with lots of sparkling and glitter in the periphery, hidden among all the prettiness are important themes of individuality and being true to yourself, making this an empowering read for teenage girls." Booklist
Volume 1 of 18

Kariya, Tetsu

Oishinbo a la carte: the joy of rice. story by Tetsu Kariya; art by Akira Hanasaki. Viz Signature Edition 2009 268p. Illustration
Grades: 8 9 10 11 12 Adult   **741.5; Fic**
1. Cooking — Graphic novels; 2. Graphic novels; 3. Manga; 4. Rice — Graphic novels; 5. Seinen manga
978-1-4215-2144-2, $12.99
This volume collects the Oishinbo stories centering on rice, the supreme staple of the Japanese diet. As Yamaoka continues, with the help of other Tozai News staffers, to work on the newspaper's Ultimate Menu to celebrate its 100th anniversary, they examine rice. Among other stories, Yamaoka rails against the importing of rice from other countries; he shows that organic rice farming could be unhealthy depending on the farm's location; and he helps the company cafeteria chef attract more business by focusing on homestyle rice dishes. The big competition between the Ultimate Menu and the Supreme Menu is rice balls (omusubi). The stories here may help American readers understand a little more about how important rice is to Japanese culture, and they may want to try some of the dishes. The book includes a recipe for scallop rice, which is published in color with photos. As with the other volumes, this book includes stories that originally appeared throughout the original manga series, so the characters' lives and relationships change abruptly from story to story.

Oishinbo a la carte: vegetables. story by Tetsu Kariya; art by Akira Hanasaki. Viz Media/Viz Signature 2009 268p. Illustration
Grades: 8 9 10 11 12 Adult   **741.5; Fic**
1. Cooking — Vegetables — Graphic novels; 2. Graphic novels; 3. Manga; 4. Seinen manga
978-1-4215-2143-5, $12.99
Tozai News reporter Yamaoka Shiro and his colleagues continue their quest for the Ultimate Menu. In this volume, he competes against his father Kaibara, who represents rival newspaper Teito Times and their Supreme Menu, in a competition involving the vegetables cabbage and turnip. In other stories, Yamaoka and his friends use asparagus as a way to reunite a culinary specialist and a pottery artist who broke up years ago; and they help Tomii's son get over his hatred of eggplant. A number of the stories discuss the debate between organic cultivation and the use of pesticides and imported vegetable types. Since the stories are selected from the Oishinbo series to fit into themes, they skip around in time and lack a real narrative flow. The book is suitable for teens, but the main appeal may be to adults, especially to those who want to read about food. The artist's focus on presenting all the vegetables so realistically and in great detail may just make the reader hungry.

Kawahara, Kazune

High school debut vol. 1. VizMedia/Shojo Beat 2008 184p. Illustration
Grades: 7 8 9 10 11 12   **741.5; Fic**
1. Graphic novels; 2. Manga; 3. Romance graphic novels; 4. Shojo manga
978-1-4215-1481-9, $8.99
Haruna used to be interested only in softball and manga, but now that she's starting in high school, she wants to change her focus, to find a boyfriend and have a fun romance. The problem is, no boy will hit on her. She's done her research in magazines, but nothing is working. Then a friend's comment causes her to decide to find a coach who will help her attract boys. Upperclassman Yoh Komiyama agrees to help her, but only if

Haruna promises to not fall in love with him. It's a struggle, though, for Yoh's sister and his friends decide to tag along for fun. There's one scary moment when a guy tries to abduct Haruna.

Volume 1 of 13

★ **My** Love Story!!; Volume 1. story, Kazune Kawahara; art, Aruko; English adaptations, Ysabet Reinhardt MacFarlane; translation, JN Productions. Viz 2014 184 p. Illustration

Grades: 8 9 10 11 12   **741.5**
   1. Shojo manga; 2. Man-woman relationship — Fiction
1421571447; 9781421571447, $9.99

"Takeo is big and manly in a macho kind of way. His best friend, Sunakawa, is handsome in a pretty/pointy-haired way, which means that girls always find him attractive. One day Takeo rescues a girl named Yamato from a groper on the train, and she starts falling in love with him. Unfortunately for Takeo, he is too dense to realize this and spends most of the story convinced that Yamato is really in love with Sunakawa." (School Library Journal)

"While this cute, romantic comedy is shojo manga, or manga intended for girls, it's unusually and entertainingly told from gruff, clueless, and kindhearted Takeo's perspective." Booklist

Volume 1 of 13

Kawasaki, Anton
   Superman: The Greatest Stories Ever Told Volume Two. DC Comics 2006 192p. Illustration

Grades: 7 8 9 10 11 12 Adult   **741.5; Fic**
   1. Graphic novels; 2. Superhero graphic novels; 3. Superman (Fictional character)
978-1-4012-0956-8, $19.99

This volume includes nine stories from different times in Superman's career. Readers can experience Superman's first meeting with the other dimensional imp Mr. Mxyztplk, his return to Krypton, a deadly battle against the team of Lex Luthor and Braniac, an after-life adventure with Pa Kent, his greatest secret revealed, and more.

Keenan, Sheila
   Dogs of war. by Sheila Keenan and illustrated by Nathan Fox. Graphix 2013 208 p.

Grades: 4 5 6 7   **741.5**
   1. Dogs — War use — Fiction; 2. Graphic novels; 3. Vietnam War, 1961-1975 — Fiction; 4. World War, 1914-1918 — Fiction; 5. World War, 1939-1945 — Fiction; 6. War — Graphic novels; 7. Dogs — Fiction
0545128870; 9780545128872, $22.99; 9780545128889
                 LC 2011006735

This graphic novel, by Sheila Keenan, "tells the stories of the canine military heroes of World War I, World War II, and the Vietnam War. This collection of three fictional stories was inspired by historic battles and real military practice. Each story tells the remarkable adventures of a soldier and his service dog...bringing to life the faithful dogs who braved bombs, barrages, and battles to save the lives of countless soldiers." (Publisher's note)

Includes bibliographical references

Kelly, Joe
   ★ **Captain** Stoneheart and the Truth Fairy. Joe Kelly, story; Chris Bachalo, artwork; Aron Lusen, color; Richard Starkings, lettering & edits. Image Comics 2008 un Illustration

Grades: 5 6 7 8 9 10 11 12 Adult   **741.5; Fic**
   1. Adventure graphic novels; 2. Fairies — Graphic novels; 3. Fantasy graphic novels; 4. Graphic novels; 5. Pirates — Graphic novels
978-1-58240-865-1, $19.99

The story, in rhyming text with lushly drawn and colored art, tells the tale of the pirate named Captain Stoneheart, a fierce and angry pirate who won't let people tell him what to do. After attacking a peaceful ship and killing everyone on it, his crew discovers a caged fairy in the hold, and Stoneheart knows he can wreak havoc and scourge the world with her powers. Somehow they connect even through his anger, and when she finds a way to save Stoneheart and his crew even when she is free to leave the pirates and save herself, Stoneheart starts to change. Alas, the good times can't last, and he commits one final act that destroys everything and everyone around him because he won't let anyone tell him what to do, even if he loves that one person. There is some fighting violence, and there are some monsters, so this is not a story for very young readers. Older elementary school age children who love the old fairy tales with the tragic endings will be able to handle this story.

Douglas Fredericks and the House of They. Image Comics 2009 80p. Illustration

Grades: 3 4 5 6   **741.5; Fic**
   1. Adventure graphic novels; 2. Graphic novels; 3. Humorous graphic novels
978-1-58240-994-8, $17.99

Douglas Fredericks just wants to give his parents a very original, unique anniversary present, but every time he comes up with an idea, someone tells him "They" say it can't happen. After many different attempts, he builds the first self-baking cake, Cake City, that will provide cake for fifteen years, because his parents (especially the Captain, his father) love cake, and then wants to just sample the first piece, people come along and tell him "No, Douglas, don't! You know what They say! You can't have your cake and eat it too!" So, Douglas decides to go find the House of They to confront the people there. After many trials, he can finally ask "WHY?" and he refuses to accept "Because They say so" as an answer. Kelly, Roman, and colorist Molina are part of The Man of Action Studios that has created the television cartoon Ben 10, as well as many comics; they have used the deluxe picture book format for this story, with full-page color art on every other page (with quite a few double-page spreads) it even has a ribbon marker.

★ **I** kill giants. Image Comics 2009 un Illustration

Grades: 8 9 10 11 12   **741.5; Fic**
   1. Family life — Graphic novels; 2. Fantasy graphic novels; 3. Giants — Graphic novels; 4. Graphic novels
978-1-60706-092-5, $15.99

Fifth-grader Barbara Thorson appears to be a smart-aleck troublemaker, and she does get into trouble at school, with great regularity. She has no friends, she has to deal with teachers and a principal who don't understand her, with the bully Taylor, with Sophie, the new girl who wants to be her friend, and now with a school psychologist. She has no time for this nonsense, she is a giant killer, with her mighty weapon she calls Coveleski (after Stanley Coveleski, a baseball player in the early twentieth century). What writer Kelly reveals slowly to the reader is Barbara's real family situation: her mother is dying, her older sister is trying to keep the family together, and Barbara is convinced that if she can slay the Titan, a huge giant, she can keep her mother alive. While Barbara is young, the story has an emotional intensity better suited for older teens.

Space Ghost. DC Comics 2005 un Illustration

Grades: 8 9 10 11 12 Adult   **741.5; Fic**
   1. Graphic novels; 2. Superhero graphic novels
1-4012-0721-9, $14.99

The masked avenger of the cartoon spaceways has been a popular character since his introduction to television in 1966. Since then, people have wondered who he is, how he got those power bands and why he protects the galaxy from evil. Now his story is told for the first time ever, and readers will learn the tragic circumstances that led to his donning a cowl and his first battle with arch nemesis Zorak. This is not the funny character from Cartoon Network.

Kennedy, Mike

Superman: Infinite City. DC Comics 2005 96p. Illustration
Grades: 8 9 10 11 12 Adult   **741.5; Fic**
1. Graphic novels; 2. Superhero graphic novels; 3. Superman (Fictional character)
978-1-4012-0066-4, $17.99

When a villain uses a very powerful weapon in Metropolis, Clark and Lois trace him back to an old town called Infinite City. They find the town abandoned, except for a doorway that leads to another amazing world.... the true Infinite City, where magic and science happily coexist. Superman and Lois step through the magic portal and become embroiled in a war for power on the other side. One faction wants to stay in its dimension, and another wants to branch out to our world. Superman will meet a doppelganger called the Warden, who shares the Kryptonian's might but not his intellect. He will also come across the architect of this world, a robot leader who claims to be what remains of his father Jor-El.

Ketcham, Hank

★ **Hank** Ketcham's Complete Dennis the Menace (Volume 1): 1951-1952. Fantagraphics Books 2005 590p. Illustration
Grades: 2 3 4 5 6 7 8 9 10 11 12 Adult   **741.5; Fic**
1. Dennis the Menace (Fictional character); 2. Graphic novels; 3. Humorous graphic novels
1-56097-680-2, $24.95

This volume is the first of a series that will reprint every Dennis the Menace cartoon. The first cartoon was published in sixteen newspapers on March 12, 1951, and the cartoon was soon picked up by many more newspapers. This volume collects the daily single-panel cartoons from March 1951 through December 1952. In these cartoons, readers meet five-and-a-half-year-old Dennis Mitchell, his parents, retired neighbors George and Martha Wilson, Dennis' dog Ruff, and neighborhood pals Joey and Margaret. Every cartoon hearkens back to the positive aspects of growing up in suburban Middle America and the joys (mostly) of being a child. While older adults will catch all the references to past popular culture (i.e. Hopalong Cassidy), younger readers will enjoy the humor arising from everyday situations.

Kibuishi, Kazu

Amulet book five: prince of the elves. Kazu Kibuishi. Graphix 2012 208 p. (Amulet)
Grades: 3 4 5 6 7 8   **741.5**
1. Amulets — Comic books, strips, etc; 2. Brothers and sisters — Comic books, strips, etc; 3. Charms — Comic books, strips, etc; 4. Elves — Comic books, strips, etc; 5. Imaginary places — Comic books, strips, etc; 6. Magic — Comic books, strips, etc; 7. Graphic novels; 8. Single-parent families — Juvenile fiction; 9. Magic — Juvenile fiction; 10. Fantasy graphic novels
0545208890; 9780545208895, $12.99

LC 2012935527

Author Kazu Kibuishi presents book five in the graphic novel series. "Emily has survived the chaos of the Guardian Academy, but Max Griffin, who is working for the Elf King, has escaped with the Mother Stone. The Elf King has now forged new amulets, which will allow him the ability to invade Cielis and destroy it once and for all. Emily and her friends desperately make preparations to defend Cielis in what will inevitably be a brutal war, and they can only hope that it will be enough to defeat the Elf King." (Publisher's note)

"Anchored by dazzlingly lush art and a complex, character-laden plot, Kibuishi's Amulet series remains a must-have for all elementary- and middle-school graphic-novel collections. Devoted fans will appreciate that this volume begins to flesh-out the backstory of two characters while starting to tie together a few of the many plot elements." Booklist

Amulet, book four: The Last Council. Graphix 2011 207p.
Grades: 3 4 5 6 7 8   **741.5**
1. Fantasy graphic novels; 2. Adventure graphic novels
978-0-545-20887-1, $10.99; 0-545-20887-4

"Emily and her friends think they'll find the help they need in Cielis, but something isn't right. Streets that were once busy are deserted, and the townspeople who are left live in crippling fear. Emily is escorted to the Academy where she's expected to compete for a spot on the Guardian Council, the most powerful Stonekeepers. But as the number of competitors gets smaller and smaller, a terrible secret is slowly uncovered — a secret that, if left buried, means certain destruction of everything Emily fights for." (Publisher's note)

Amulet, book one: The Stonekeeper. Graphix 2008 185p.
Grades: 3 4 5 6 7 8   **741; Fic; 741.5**
1. Adventure graphic novels; 2. Fantasy graphic novels; 3. Graphic novels; 4. Mystery graphic novels
978-0-439-84680-6, $21.99; 0-439-84680-3; 978-0-439-84681-3 (pa), $9.99; 0-439-84681-1 (pa)

After a family tragedy, Emily, Navin, and their mother move to an ancestral home to start a new life. When their mother is kidnapped by a tentacled creature, Em and Navin have to figure out how to set things straight and save their mother's life.

"Filled with excitement, monsters, robots, and mysteries, this fantasy adventure will appeal to many readers." SLJ

Other titles in this series are: The Stonekeeper's curse (2009); The Cloud Searchers (2010); The Last Council (2011); Prince of the elves (2012); Escape from Lucien (2014); Firelight (2016)

Amulet, book three: The Cloud Searchers. Graphix 2010 197p.
Grades: 3 4 5 6 7 8   **741.5; 741**
1. Fantasy graphic novels; 2. Adventure graphic novels
978-0-545-20885-7 (pa), $10.99; 0-545-20885-8 (pa)

"Emily, Navin, and their crew of resistance fighters charter an airship and set off in search of the lost city of Cielis, which is believed to be located on an island high above the clouds. The mysterious Leon Redbeard is their guide, and there's a surprising new addition to the crew: the Elf King's son, Trellis. But is he ally or enemy? And will Emily ever be able to trust the voice of the Amulet?" (Publisher's note)

Amulet, book two: The Stonekeeper's curse. Graphix 2009 217p.
Grades: 3 4 5 6 7 8   **741.5; 741**
1. Fantasy graphic novels; 2. Adventure graphic novels
978-0-439-84683-7, $10.99; 0-439-84683-8

"Emily and Navin's mother is still in a coma from the arachnopod's poison, and there's only one place to find help: Kanalis, the bustling, beautiful city of waterfalls. But when Em, her brother, and Miskit and the rest of the robotic crew aboard the walking house reach the city, they quickly realize that seeking help is looking for trouble, dangerous trouble." (Publisher's note)

Amulet; Book 6: Firelight. Kazu Kibuishi. Graphix 2016 208 p. Color; Illustration; Map (Amulet)
Grades: 3 4 5 6 7 8   **741.5; Fic**
1. Memory — Graphic novels; 2. Fantasy graphic novels
0545839661; 9780545433167; 9780545678421; 9780545839662, $24.99

LC 2015936071

"Emily, Trellis, and Vigo visit Algos Island, where they can access and enter lost memories. They're hoping to uncover the events of Trellis's mysterious childhood — knowledge they can use against the Elf King....

Meanwhile, the Voice of Emily's Amulet is getting stronger, and threatens to overtake her completely." (Publisher's note)

★ **Copper**. Graphix/Scholastic 2010 94p. Illustration

Grades: 5 6 7 8   **741; 741.5; Fic**

1. Adventure graphic novels; 2. Dogs — Graphic novels; 3. Graphic novels; 4. Science fiction graphic novels

978-0-545-09892-2, $21.99; 0-545-09892-0; 978-0-545-09893-9 (pa), $12.99; 0-545-09893-9 (pa)

A collection of graphic novel adventures about a boy named Copper and his dog, Fred, including "navigating a dangerous forest of giant mushrooms, [and] surviving a crash landing in a homemade airplane — that run from lyrical to the downright apocalyptic. Illustrated in a deceptively simple style, its solemn tenor and deep strangeness...will likely inspire heavy investment from those who prefer a somewhat off-kilter read." Booklist

Escape from Lucien. Kazu Kibuishi. Scholastic / Graphix 2014 256 p. Illustration; Map (Amulet)

Grades: 3 4 5 6 7 8   **741.5; Fic**

1. Kings and rulers — Fiction; 2. Brothers and sisters — Fiction; 3. Elves — Fiction

9780545433150, $12.99

LC 2013957419

"Navin and his classmates journey to Lucien, a city ravaged by war and plagued by mysterious creatures, where they search for a beacon essential to their fight against the Elf King. Meanwhile, Emily heads back into the Void with Max, one of the Elf King's loyal followers, where she learns his darkest secrets. The stakes, for both Emily and Navin, are higher than ever." (Publisher's note)

"Most of the cleanly drawn, lushly backgrounded panels focus on faces, with occasional full-spread scenes adding dramatic visual highlights." Kirkus

Explorer: the hidden doors. edited by Kazu Kibuishi. Abrams Books 2014 128 p. Color; Illustration (Explorer)

Grades: 4 5 6 7 8   **741.5**

1. Bullying — Fiction; 2. Monsters — Fiction; 3. Comic books, strips, etc.; 4. Doors — Fiction

1419708821; 9781419708824, $19.95; 9781419708848

LC 2014938941

In this collection of comics edited by Kazu Kibuishi, "a bullied boy discovers a door guarded by a sly monster...A painting of a door opens in a forgotten Egyptian tomb...A portal in the park promises to turn you into a much cooler version 2.0 — if you can just get the bugs out." (Publisher's note)

"Readers are once again presented with an array of stories created by a cast of comics authors and illustrators smartly assembled by Kibuishi...The range in this slim volume is expansive. From funny to deep and fantastical to refined, all of the stories have a compelling narrative arc. The colors are just as varied, and are universally dynamic and nuanced. Consider this (and previous series installments) as a necessary addition to any graphic novel collection." SLJ

Other titles in the series are: The Mystery Boxes (2012); The Lost Islands (2013)

Explorer: the lost islands. Kazu Kibuishi. Abrams Books 2013 128 p. (Explorer)

Grades: 4 5 6 7 8   **741.5; Fic**

1. Islands; 2. Graphic novels

1419708813; 141970883X; 9781419708817, $19.95; 9781419708831, $10.95

LC 2013935794

In this follow-up to "Explorer: The Mystery Boxes," Kazu Kibuishi and a crew of cartoonists again take turns weaving seven tales based

around a loose theme. This time the motif is islands, and the contributors are left to interpret it in illustrated shorts. Some, by using their strange and remote settings as microcosms, underscore the value of hard work...or finding one's niche..., while others examine more abstract concepts such as exploration and isolation." (Publishers Weekly)

Explorer: the mystery boxes. edited by Kazu Kibuishi. Abrams Books 2012 126 p. (Explorer)

Grades: 4 5 6 7 8   **S C; 741.5**

1. Boxes; 2. Boxes — Fiction; 3. Graphic novels; 4. Short stories; 5. Mystery graphic novels

1419700103; 9781419700095, $10.95; 9781419700101, $19.95

LC 2011025343

This collection of short stories offers "[s]even...stories [which] answer one simple question: what's in the box?...[E]ach of these...illustrated short graphic works revolves around a central theme: a mysterious box and the marvels — or mayhem — inside. Artists include...Kazu Kibuishi, Raina Telgemeier ('Smile'), and Dave Roman ('Astronaut Academy'), as well as Jason Caffoe, Stuart Livingston, Johane Matte, Rad Sechrist (all contributors to the...comics anthology series 'Flight'), and...artist Emily Carroll." (Publisher's note)

Seven graphic stories.

Flight explorer. edited by Kazu Kibuiski. Villard 2008 112p. Illustration

Grades: 4 5 6 7   **741.5; Fic**

1. Adventure graphic novels; 2. Fantasy graphic novels; 3. Graphic novels; 4. Humorous graphic novels; 5. Science fiction graphic novels

978-0-345-50313-8 (pa), $10; 0-345-50313-9 (pa)

This anthology includes stories that Kibuishi kept from Flight Volume 4 because they had all-ages appeal, as well as stories submitted especially for this volume. Kibuishi's own Copper and his talking dog cross a deep canyon by leaping onto mushrooms, only to discover the vegetation is intelligent. Kean Soo's Jellaby and his human friends frolic in the snow. Missile Mouse by Jake Parker defends a village on another planet, only to discover his coming was prophesied (this story includes two uses of the word "crap"). The other stories will appeal to younger readers, while some of the humor will also appeal to older readers. Other than the one bad word in "Missile Mouse" (noted above), there shouldn't be any other content that would keep this book out of most elementary and middle schools.

"Every story has a layout that promotes an acute sense of pacing and showcases the crisp, defined, full-color art." SLJ

★ **Flight**, volume six. Villard Books 2009 284p. Illustration

Grades: 8 9 10 11 12 Adult   **741.5; Fic**

1. Fantasy graphic novels; 2. Graphic novels; 3. Short stories — Graphic novels

978-0-345-50590-3, $25

This sixth volume of the graphic anthology series includes stories by fifteen creators: J.P. Ahonen, Graham Annable, Bannister, Phil Craven, Mike Dutton, Michel Gagne, Cory Godbey, Rodolphe Guenoden, Steve Hamaker, Kazu Kibuishi, Andrea Offermann, Richard Pose, Justin Ridge, Rad Sechrist, and Kean Soo. Returning favorite characters includ Jellaby by Soo, Hamaker's Fish N Chips, Kibuishi's Daisy Kutter, and the wordless little fox Rex by Gagne. Bannister's "Cooking Duel" stands out as a lot of fun, as a couple makes a bet about which of them can make the better tasting mushroom quiche; and Justin Ridge's "Dead Bunny" shows that there is a soul mate for just about anyone, including a zombie bunny.

Kick, Russ

The **graphic** canon of children's literature: the world's great kids' lit as comics and visuals. edited by Russ Kick. Seven Stories Press 2014 480 p. Color; Illustration

Grades: 6 7 8 9 10 11 12 Adult   **741.5**

Courtesy of Seven Stories Press

1. Children's literature; 2. Comic books, strips, etc; 3. Graphic novels in education; 4. Literature — Adaptations; 5. Comic books, strips, etc.
1609805305; 9781609805302, $38.95
LC 2014010178

Edited by Russ Kick, "the original three-volume anthology 'The Graphic Canon' presented the world's classic literature — from ancient times to the late twentieth century — as eye-popping comics, illustrations, and other visual forms. In this follow-up volume, young people's literature through the ages is given new life by the best comics artists and illustrators." (Publisher's note)

"These dazzlingly varied renderings run the gamut from haunting to comical while offering visceral reminders that children's stories are often densely layered, infinitely transposable, and peddle in imagery both macabre and whimsical. It is the unfettered imagination of these stories that make them not only wildly entertaining, but also vessels of forgotten truths." Pub Wkly

Kikuta, Michiyo

Mamotte! Lollipop Vol. 1. Random House/Del Rey Manga 2007 224p. Illustration
Grades: 8 9 10 11 12 Adult   741.5; Fic
1. Fantasy graphic novels; 2. Graphic novels; 3. Manga; 4. Shojo manga
978-0-345-49623-2, $10.95

Junior high schooler Nina is ready to fall in love. She's looking for a boy who's cute and sweet-and strong enough to support her when the chips are down. But what happens when Nina's dream comes true...twice? One day, two cute boys literally fall from the sky: they're both wizards and they've come to the Human World to take the Magic Exam. The boys' success on this test depends on protecting Nina from evil, so now Nina has a pair of cute magical boys chasing her everywhere she goes. But, because Nina accidentally swallowed a magic "crystal pearl" that is part of the Magic Exam, Zero and Ichi aren't the only wizards around her, and some are willing to do just about anything to get their hands on the magic pearl.

Kim, Derek Kirk

★ **Good** as Lily. written by Derek Kirk Kim; illustrated by Jesse Hamm; lettering by Jared K. Fletcher. DC Comics/Minx 2007 un Illustration
Grades: 7 8 9 10 11 12   741.5; Fic
1. Fantasy graphic novels; 2. Graphic novels; 3. Humorous graphic novels
978-1-4012-1381-7, $9.99

"On her eighteenth birthday, Korean American Grace suddenly finds herself surrounded by three very corporeal essences of herself: as a small child, as a 30-year-old woman, and as "a cranky old fart." Each of these incarnations is at an emotional precipice, which teenage Grace helps resolve, allowing the other self to quietly disappear.... Kim's pacing and plotting are excellent, and Hamm's black, white, and gray artwork is lively, witty, and full of appropriate comedy and melodrama." Booklist

Kim, Susan

★ **Brain** camp. by Susan Kim and Laurence Klavan; illustrated by Faith Erin Hicks. First Second 2010 151p. Illustration
Grades: 7 8 9 10   741; Fic; 741.5
1. Camps — Graphic novels; 2. Graphic novels; 3. Horror graphic novels; 4. Mystery graphic novels; 5. Science fiction graphic novels

978-1-59643-366-3, $16.99; 1-59643-366-3

Jenna and Lucas are both under-achieving young teens who suddenly receive invitations to join the Fielding Camp for the summer. Pressed by their respective parents to attend, Jenna and Lucas both notice some strange things at the camp, and neither feels like eating the nasty slop served at every meal. The other campers are either intellectually challenged bullies, misfits, or supersmart zombies. At first Dwayne, a self-described spaz, befriends them, but when his cabin "wins" ice cream treats at dinner, Lucas sees the camp counselors sneaking in that night to "inoculate" all his cabin mates. Lucas and Jenna work against time to escape the camp and develop an antidote. Jenna is shown in one panel sitting on a commode when her period comes, and one short sequence shows Lucas having a wet dream and then washing out his stained undies; both situations are nonverbal and drawn with restraint, but school librarians will need to decide whether these two scenes meet their own schools' standards.

The authors present a "well-rounded adventure here, as the far-out (and kind of gross) climax mixes with genuine insight into dealing with parents, fitting into a new crowd, and handling the pressures of performance. Hicks' line work is cool enough to assuage older readers who might be suspicious of the summer-camp setting." Booklist

★ **City** of spies. [by] Susan Kim [and] Laurence Klavan; illustrated by Pascal Dizin. First Second 2010 172p. Illustration
Grades: 4 5 6 7   741.5; Fic
1. Adventure graphic novels; 2. Graphic novels; 3. Spies — Graphic novels; 4. World War, 1939-1945 — Graphic novels
1-59643-262-4 (pa); 978-1-59643-262-8 (pa), $17

"With her mother gone and a father who has better things to do than be bothered raising a daughter, Evelyn is sent to live with her unconventional Aunt Lia in the bohemian art world of 1942 New York City.... Evelyn spends much of her time in the company of imaginary superheroes, fouling up the plans of Nazi spies. Before long she finds an unlikely friend in the building superintendent — s son, Tony. Together, they...stumble upon an actual Nazi plot. With stupefying precision, Dizin — s art channels Hergé — s Tintin in tone, palette, and with the remarkable expressiveness of the clean, flexible figures.... With villains and danger that just border on the genuinely scary, the tale is filled not only with a thrilling sense of excitement but also with a child — s longing for a grown-up to believe in." Booklist

Kirby, Jack

Jack Kirby's Fourth World Omnibus, Volume One. DC Comics 2007 396p. Illustration
Grades: 8 9 10 11 12 Adult   741.5; Fic
1. Graphic novels; 2. Science fiction graphic novels; 3. Superhero graphic novels
978-1-4012-1344-2, $49.99

In the 1970s, legendary comics creator Kirby left Marvel Comics to work for DC Comics, writing and drawing several new series and also taking over Superman's Pal Jimmy Olsen. This volume collects the first three issues of his new series, plus the start of his run on Jimmy Olsen, from issue #133. With the Fourth World storylines in Kirby's New Gods, Forever People, and Mister Miracle, he created new mythologies and epic storylines. This hardcover edition uses a flat paper that shows off the inks and colors brilliantly.

Jack Kirby's Fourth World Omnibus Volume Two. Image Comics 2007 396p. Illustration
Grades: 7 8 9 10 11 12 Adult   741.5; Fic
1. Graphic novels; 2. Superhero graphic novels
978-1-4012-1357-2, $49.99

DC collects four series by Kirby — The New Gods, The Forever People, Mister Miracle, and Superman's Pal Jimmy Olsen — in chronological order as they originally appeared. These comics spanned galaxies, from the streets of Metropolis to the far-flung worlds of New Genesis and Apokolips, as cosmic-powered heroes and villains struggled for supremacy.In this second volume, the evil Darkseid's schemes continue to unfold while the New Gods, the Forever People, Mr. Miracle and other heroes battle his many minions.

Jack Kirby's Omac: one man army corps. DC Comics 2008 176p. Illustration
Grades: 7 8 9 10 11 12 Adult   **741.5; Fic**
   1. Graphic novels; 2. Superhero graphic novels
978-1-4012-1790-7, $24.99

In the 1970s, comics master creator Jack Kirby shocked the comics industry when he left Marvel Comics to work for the opposition DC Comics. He created new characters and new worlds. Among them was an unusual science fiction concept: OMAC, One Man Army Corps. Corporate nobody Buddy Blank is changed by the artificial intelligence "Brother Eye" into a superpowered agent of the Global Peace Agency, fighting bizarre menaces in a disturbing, near-future world. This book collects the complete 8-issue saga as published by DC; readers will note it ends in a cliffhanger that was never resolved.

Silver Star. Image Comics 2007 152p. Illustration
Grades: 8 9 10 11 12 Adult
741.5; Fic
   1. Graphic novels; 2. Superhero graphic novels
978-1-58240-764-7, $34.99

Courtesy of Twomorrows Publishing

Chronicling the rise of Homo-Geneticus, the New Breed of humanity that spawns both Silver Star (Morgan Miller) and the nefarious Darius Brumm. Silver Star was Kirby's final creation and one of only two creator-owned projects published by Pacific Comics in the early '80s. This volume also includes the original screenplay, written by Kirby and Steve Sherman, upon which Kirby based the comic.

Kishimoto, Masashi
   ★ **Naruto.** vol. 1, The tests of the Ninja. story and art by Masashi Kishimoto; [English adaptation by Jo Duffy]. Viz 2003 186p. Illustration
Grades: 7 8 9 10 11 12   **741.5; Fic**
   1. Graphic novels; 2. Manga; 3. Martial arts — Graphic novels; 4. Shonen manga
1-56931-900-6; 978-1-56931-900-0, $7.95

"Teen orphan Naruto wants to become the greatest ninja of all, despite the fact that most people in his village have despised him from birth because a terrible demon has been imprisoned in his body.... Teens love this series." Voice Youth Advocates

First published 1999 in Japan; Volume one of an ongoing series; ?This graphic novel contains material that was originally published in English in Shonen jump #6-10? Verso of title page; Volume 1 of 72

Kitchen, Alexa
   ★ **Grown-ups** are dumb! (No offense). Hyperion Books 2009 un Illustration
Grades: 3 4 5 6 7 8   **741.5; Fic**
   1. Family life — Graphic novels; 2. Graphic novels; 3. Humorous graphic novels
978-1-4231-1331-7, $8.99

Twelve-year-old Alexa Kitchen wrote the comics collected here when she was ten years old. Her characters Molly, Sharon, and Kathy navigate life in school (and piles of homework), and at home (with pesky younger brothers). In other cartoons, she depicts the frustrations of dealing with incomprehensible paper folding instructions, the joys (and despairs) of messy rooms, and of toddler Hurricane Abby's exploration of her house. Kitchen's art ranges from the heavy pencils in the cartoons about Molly to scratchy ink in most of the other stories, to highly detailed drawings of the incredibly messy bedroom, all on pink pages. She describes herself as the world's youngest professional cartoonist," has been drawing cartoons since she could hold a pencil, and already has several books published; in 2007, at the age of ten, she was nominated for a Harvey and an Eisner Award for her book Drawing Comics is Easy! (Except When It's Hard).

Klein, Grady
   The **cartoon** introduction to statistics. by Grady Klein and Alan Dabney, Ph.D. Hill and Wang, a Division of Farrar, Straus and Giroux 2013 240 p.
Grades: 7 8 9 10 11 12   **519.5**
   1. Graphic novels; 2. Mathematical statistics — Comic books, strips, etc; 3. Statistics; 4. Comic books, strips, etc.
0809033593; 9780809033591, $17.95
                                    LC 2012030027

This book, by Grady Klien and Alan Dabney, explores statistics in humorous cartoon illustrations. "Separating the book into two main parts (hunting statistics and gathering parameters) for readers both in and outside the classroom, they explore the key foundational concepts of statistics and the perils of improper methods. They round out the book with the 'Math Cave,' which provides easy access to the formulas every student will want to have close at hand." (Publisher's note)

Kneece, Mark
   The **Twilight** Zone: the after hours. adaptation by Mark Kneece; illustrated by Rebekah Isaacs. Walker & Company 2008 un Illustration
Grades: 5 6 7 8 9 10   **741.5; Fic**
   1. Graphic novels; 2. Supernatural graphic novels; 3. Twilight zone (Television program) — Graphic novels
978-0-8027-9716-2, $16.99; 978-0-8027-9717-9 (pa), $9.99
                                    LC 2008-4310

Marsha White visits a department store to buy an advertised gold thimble, is taken by elevator to a floor with empty display cases except for one, which has the thimble, and she deals with an odd saleswoman who knows her name. When Marsha is in the elevator, she discovers the thimble is defective and tries to complain, but the manager insists there is no eighteenth floor, the store has no elevator, and the store has never carried gold thimbles. As she begins to leave, Marsha faints at the sight of a mannequin that looks exactly like the strange saleswoman, and she's put into a back room to recover. When she wakes up, the store has been closed and she's locked in. This is an actual episode of the old Twilight Zone television show.

"Kneece's adaptation is quick and enjoyable and introduces a classic TV series to a new generation of readers. Isaacs's illustrations are clean, distinct and cinematic in scope, employing an interesting variety of angles." Kirkus

The **Twilight** Zone: walking distance. adaptation from Rod Serling's original script by Mark Kneece; illustrated by Dove McHargue. Walker & Company 2008 un Illustration
Grades: 5 6 7 8 9 10   **741.5; Fic**
   1. Graphic novels; 2. Supernatural graphic novels; 3. Twilight zone (Television program) — Graphic novels
978-0-8027-9714-8, $16.99; 978-0-8027-9715-5 (pa), $9.99
                                    LC 2008-4273

Thirty-nine-year-old businessman Martin Sloan's car blows a tire as he's driving, and he realizes he is within walking distance of his hometown. Leaving his car to be repaired, he decides to walk there. However, when he reaches town, he has also gone back in time. Can he find his boyhood self and give his younger self advice? Or will everyone think he's just crazy? This is an actual episode of the old Twilight Zone television show.

The story is "exceptionally well told and...[is] brilliantly adapted to a new medium." SLJ

Koch, Falynn
Plagues: the microscopic battlefield. Falynn Christine Koch. First Second 2017 128 p. Color; Illustration (Science comics)
Grades: 4 5 6 7 8   **741.5; 614.5**
  1. Microorganisms; 2. Plague; 3. Epidemics
  9781626727533, $19.99; 9781626727526
                                                LC 2016945566
In this book in the Science Comics series, by Falynn Christine Koch, "we get to know the critters behind history's worst diseases. We delve into the biology and mechanisms of infections, diseases, and immunity, and also the incredible effect that technology and medical science have had on humanity's ability to contain and treat disease." (Publisher's note)
"A reassuring picture of ever more stout defenses ranged against a scary, invisible world." Kirkus
Includes bibliographical references (page 122)

  Science comics: bats: learning to fly. Falynn Koch. First Second 2017 128 p. Color; Illustration
Grades: 3 4 5 6   **599.4; 741.5**
  1. Bats; 2. Animal flight; 3. Animal rescue
  9781626724082; 9781626724099, $19.99
                                                LC 2016938728
This graphic novel in the Science Comics series, by Falynn Koch, follows "a little brown bat whose wing is injured by humans on a nature hike. He is taken to a bat rehabilitation center where he meets many different species of bats. They teach him how they fly, what they eat, and where they like to live." (Publisher's note)
"With plenty of informative back matter, this inviting, engaging nonfiction comic is perfect for kids hungry for science." Booklist

Kochalka, James
Monkey vs. Robot. Top Shelf Productions 2000 144p. Illustration
Grades: 5 6 7 8 9 10 11 12   **741.5; Fic**
  1. Graphic novels
  1-891830-15-5, $14.95
The book is almost wordless, allowing the reader to imagine one's own narrative. While there is violence, it's not graphic, and this little fable provides much food for thought.
"A very simply illustrated black and white pictorial narrative about a battle between a monkey community and a self-run robot factory encroaching on the monkeys' unspoiled forest domain." Publ Wkly
Another title in this series is: Monkey vs. Robot and the crystal of power (2003)

  Peanutbutter & Jeremy's best book ever. Alternative Comics 2003 280p. Illustration
Grades: 4 5 6 7 8 9 10 11 12
741.5; Fic
  1. Friendship — Graphic novels; 2. Graphic novels; 3. Humorous graphic novels
  1-891867-46-6, $14.95
  Peanutbutter is a sweet cat who acts like a hardworking office cat but usually naps on

Courtesy of Alternative Comics

top of the paperwork, and Jeremy is a troublemaking crow; and they are friends. Jeremy may seem spiteful and sometimes does very mean things to Peanutbutter, such as pretending to threaten the cat with a pistol, but most of the stories are silly and fun.

  Pinky & Stinky. Top Shelf Productions 2002 208p. Illustration
Grades: 4 5 6 7 8 9 10 11 12 Adult   **741.5; Fic**
  1. Adventure graphic novels; 2. Friendship — Graphic novels; 3. Graphic novels; 4. Humorous graphic novels
  1-891830-29-7, $17.95
  Pinky & Stinky are fat little piglets, but just because they're cuties doesn't mean that they're not brave astronauts! When they embark on a daring mission to be the first pigs on Pluto, things go horribly wrong and they crash land on the moon. There they meet some not-so-friendly moon men, and end up in the middle of a conflict between the American space program and a race of alien ice creatures.

Komura, Ayumi
  Mixed vegetables, vol. 1. story & art by Ayumi Komura; English translation, JN Porductions; English adaptation, Stephanie V.W. Lucianovic. Viz Media/Shojo Beat 2008 un Illustration
Grades: 7 8 9 10 11 12   **741.5; Fic**
  1. Cooking — Graphic novels; 2. Graphic novels; 3. Manga; 4. Romance graphic novels; 5. Shojo manga
  978-1-4215-1967-8, $8.99
  Hanayu Ashitaba is the daughter of the Patisserie Ashitaba, a famous pastry shop, but ever since she was a little girl she has wanted to become a sushi chef. Hayato Hyuga is the son of the famed Sushi Hyuga, but all he's ever wanted to be is a pastry chef, even though he's got mad skills with the knives. Both of them are students at the Oikawa High School Cooking Department, where Hanayu has decided she needs to make Hayato fall for her and marry her. However, Hayato wants Hanayu to teach him more about pastry making.
  Volume 1 of 8

Kondo, Robert
  The **dam** keeper; Book 1. Robert Kondo and Daisuke Tsutsumi. First Second 2017 153 p. Color; Illustration
Grades: 3 4 5 6   **741.5**
  1. Adventure & adventurers — Comic books, strips, etc.; 2. Animals — Fiction; 3. Dams — Fiction
  1626724261; 9781626724266, $19.99
                                                LC 2016961560
In this book in The Dam Keeper series, by Robert Kondo and Dice Tsutsumi, "Pig is the dam keeper. Except for his best friend, Fox, and the town bully, Hippo, few are aware of his tireless efforts. But a new threat is on the horizon — a tidal wave of black fog is descending on Sunrise Valley. Now Pig, Fox, and Hippo must face the greatest danger imaginable: the world on the other side of the dam." (Publisher's note)
"Kondo and Tsutsuma expand on the world of their Oscar-nominated animated short film of the same name, about a young pig who keeps his town safe from a terrifying black fog.... The tug-of-war between light and dark extends out of the plot and right into the images in a haunting story that contrasts the power of friendship with the weight of responsibility and the capacity for growth." Pub Wkly

Konomi, Takeshi
  The **Prince** of Tennis, Vol. 1. Viz Media, LLC 2004 192p. Illustration
Grades: 6 7 8 9 10   **741.5; Fic**
  1. Graphic novels; 2. Manga; 3. Shonen manga; 4. Tennis — Graphic novels
  1-59116-435-4, $7.95

"Ryoma is a former U.S. junior tennis champion who attends a Japanese academy, where his skill and natural talent make him nearly unbeatable. The younger students are inspired by him, but he's ruffling the feathers of the older tennis team members. Then the journalists appear, trying to discover the next champion, adding to the pressure. There's lots of tennis action, dramatically illustrated, and the characters, already pretty boys, are made even more attractive with their intensity." Publ Wkly

This is the first of an ongoing series, up to Volume 9 in September 2005; Volume 1 of 42

Kris

A **bag** of marbles. based on the memoir by Joseph Joffo; adapted by Kris; illustrated by Vincent Bailly; translated by Edward Gauvin. Graphic Universe 2013 126 p. Color; Illustration
Grades: 6 7 8 9 10
940.53; 741.5; B
1. Graphic novels; 2. Holocaust, Jewish (1939-1945) — France — Fiction; 3. Jews — France — Fiction; 4. World War, 1939-1945 — France — Fiction; 5. Joffo, Joseph; 6. Joffo, Maurice; 7. France — History — German occupation, 1940-1945 — Fiction; 8. Children and war — Fiction
1467715166; 9781467707008; 9781467715164, $9.95; 9781467716512

Courtesy of Lerner Publishing Group

LC 2013002284

"Ten years old at the start of the story, Joffo recalls his Jewish family planning their escape from Occupied France during World War II. Tension runs through the story as he and his brother set off on the long journey to the Free Zone, where they plan to meet up with their older brothers. Along the way the boys must hide their Jewish identity, evade train security, and find a passeur, or guide, to take them past guard posts and fences to safe territory." (School Library Journal)

"This graphic-novel adaptation of Joffo's 1973 memoir of the same name succeeds in melding sensitive and accurate imagery with the original narrative flow of a young secular Jewish boy's experiences in occupied France." Booklist

Krosoczka, Jarrett J.

Comics Squad: recess!. comics by Jarrett J. Krosoczka, Gene Yang, Eric Wight, Jennifer L. Holm and Matthew Holm, Ursula Vernon, Dan Santat, Raina Telgemeier and Dave Roman, Dav Pilkey; edited by Jennifer L. Holm, Matthew Holm, and Jarrett J. Krosoczka. Random House Inc. 2014 144 p. Illustration; Color
Grades: 2 3 4 5 6
741.5
1. Graphic novels; 2. Humorous stories; 3. Recess — Fiction; 4. Schools — Fiction; 5. Short stories; 6. Comic books, strips, etc.; 7. School stories
0385370032; 9780385370035, $7.99; 9780385370042, $12.99
LC 2013035223

"An all-star lineup of graphic novel notables contributes original works to this anthology, sharing the common thread of recess." (School Library Journal)

"[T]his lively, upbeat and all-around-awesome offering is consistently convivial and laugh-out-loud funny from cover to cover." Kirkus
Another title in this series is: Lunch! (2016)

Lunch Lady and the author visit vendetta. Alfred A. Knopf 2009 un Illustration
Grades: 3 4 5 6 7 8
741; 741.5
1. School stories — Graphic novels; 2. Teachers — Graphic novels
978-0-375-96094-9 (lib bdg), $12.99; 978-0-375-86094-2 (pa), $5.99

LC 2009014886

The school lunch lady, a secret crime fighter, investigates a suspicious author after he visits the school and the gym teacher goes missing.

Lunch Lady and the bake sale bandit. Alfred A. Knopf 2010 un Illustration
Grades: 3 4 5 6 7 8
741.5; 741
1. School children — Food — Graphic novels; 2. School stories — Graphic novels
978-0-375-96729-0 (lib bdg), $12.99; 0-375-96729-X (lib bdg); 978-0-375-86729-3 (pa), $6.99; 0-375-86729-5 (pa)

LC 2010012781

"The Breakfast Bunch is excited for the upcoming bake sale-and the best part is that it's raising money for an awesome field trip. But when all the snacks go missing, it's no laughing matter. Someone is sabotaging the bake sale. But why?" (Publisher's note)

Lunch Lady and the cyborg substitute. Alfred A. Knopf 2009 un Illustration
Grades: 3 4 5 6 7 8
741.5; Fic
1. Graphic novels; 2. Humorous graphic novels; 3. Robots — Graphic novels; 4. School children — Food — Graphic novels; 5. School stories — Graphic novels
978-0-375-94683-7 (lib bdg), $11.99; 0-375-94683-7 (lib bdg); 978-0-375-84683-0 (pa), $5.99; 0-375-84683-2 (pa)

LC 2008-4709

The school lunch lady is a secret crime fighter who uncovers an evil plot to replace all the popular teachers with robots

"Yellow-highlighted pen-and-ink cartoons are as energetic and smile-provoking as Lunch Lady — s epithets of "Cauliflower!" and Betty — s ultimate weapon, the hairnet." Booklist
Other titles in this series are: Lunch Lady and the league of librarians (2009); Lunch Lady and the author visit vendetta (2009); Lunch Lady and the summer camp shakedown (2010); Lunch Lady and the bake sale bandit (2010); Lunch lady and the field trip fiasco (2011); Lunch Lady and the mutant mathletes (2012); Lunch Lady and the picture day peril (2012); Lunch Lady and the video game villain (2013); Lunch Lady and the schoolwide scuffle (2013)

Lunch Lady and the field trip fiasco. Alfred A. Knopf 2011 un Illustration
Grades: 3 4 5 6 7 8
741.5
1. Art — Forgeries — Fiction; 2. School stories — Graphic novels
978-0-375-96730-6, $12.99; 978-0-375-86730-9 (pa), $6.99

LC 2011005907

"Lunch Lady and the Breakfast Bunch are on a school field trip to a famous art museum. But while Lunch Lady is busy taking in all the culture, the kids have caught onto something strange-some of the artwork looks suspiciously fake! Now Dee, Hector, and Terrence are determined to get to the bottom of this conspiracy, but Lunch Lady is too awed to catch on. Will she snap out of it and come to the rescue? Or will the Breakfast Bunch have to handle this operation alone?" (Publisher's note)

Lunch Lady and the League of Librarians. Alfred A. Knopf 2009 un Illustration
Grades: 3 4 5 6 7 8
741; Fic; 741.5
1. Games — Graphic novels; 2. Graphic novels; 3. Humorous graphic novels; 4. Librarians — Graphic novels; 5. School children — Food — Graphic novels; 6. School stories — Graphic novels
978-0-375-94684-4 (lib bdg), $11.99; 0-375-94684-5 (lib bdg); 978-0-375-84684-7 (pa), $5.99; 0-375-84684-0 (pa)

LC 2008043117

The school lunch lady, a secret crime fighter, sets out to stop a group of librarians bent on destroying a shipment of video games, while a group of students known as the Breakfast Bunch provides back-up

"The black-and-white pen-and-ink illustrations have splashes of yellow in nearly every panel. The clean layout, featuring lots of open space, is well suited for the intended audience.... With its appealing mix of action and humor, this clever, entertaining addition to the series should have wide appeal." SLJ

Other titles about the Lunch Lady are: Lunch lady and the cyborg substitute (2009); Lunch Lady and the author visit vendetta (2009); Lunch Lady and the summer camp shakedown (2010); Lunch Lady and the bake sale bandit (2010); Lunch Lady and the field trip fiasco (2011);Lunch Lady and the mutant mathletes (2012);Lunch Lady and the picture day peril (2012);Lunch Lady and the video game villain (2013);Lunch Lady and the schoolwide shuffle (2014)

Lunch Lady and the summer camp shakedown. Alfred A. Knopf 2010 un Illustration
Grades: 3 4 5 6 7 8   **741; 741.5**
1. Camps — Graphic novels; 2. Humorous graphic novels
978-0-375-86095-9 (pa), $6.99; 0-375-86095-9 (pa)
Lunch Lady and the Breakfast Bunch kids are looking forward to a relaxing summer vacation with no funny business. What evils could befall them at summer camp?

"The two-color art is loopy and energetic, with varied, easy-to-follow page layouts. Jokes and puns are sprinkled throughout to keep the energy high until the exciting finale." SLJ

Kullab, Samya
Escape from Syria. by Samya Kullab; illustrated by Jackie Roche and Mike Freiheit. Firefly Books 2017 96 p. Color; Illustration
Grades: 7 8 9 10 11 12   **741.5**
1. Freiheit, Mike; 2. Refugees — Syria — Fiction; 3. Syria — History — 2011-, Civil War — Refugees — Fiction
1770859829; 9781770859821, $19.95
This "is a fictionalized account that calls on real-life circumstances and true tales of refugee families to serve as a microcosm of the Syrian uprising and the war and refugee crisis that followed. The story spans six years in the lives of Walid, his wife Dalia, and their two children, Amina and Youssef. Forced to flee from Syria, they become asylum-seekers in Lebanon, and finally resettled refugees in the West." (Publisher's note)

"Based on Kullab's extensive experience with refugees, the novel skillfully depicts situations and drastic decisions many Syrian refugees face. The graphic-novel format is perfect for the story, using cinematic techniques to propel the story and adding poignant notes, as when Amina's father reads a text message asking for help and conceals it from her. Extensive endnotes highlight the true events referenced in the book." Kirkus

Kuper, Peter
The **metamorphosis**. [based on the story by] Franz Kafka; adapted by Peter Kuper. Crown 2003 77p. Illustration
Grades: 8 9 10 11 12   **741.5; Fic**
1. Authors; 2. Graphic novels; 3. Novelists; 4. Poets; 5. Short story writers; 6. Kafka, Franz, 1883-1924 — Adaptations
1-4000-4795-1; 1-4000-5299-8 (pa), $10.95; 9781400052998
           LC 2003-273589
"Gregor Samsa wakes up and discovers he has been changed into a giant cockroach. Thus begins "The Metamorphosis," and Kuper translates this story masterfully with his scratchboard illustrations. The text is more spare, but the visuals are so strongly rendered that little of the original is changed or omitted." SLJ

Kurata, Hideyuki
Train + Train, Vol. 1. original story by Hideyuki Kurata; art by Tomomasa Takuma. Go! Comi 2007 196p. Illustration

Grades: 8 9 10 11 12 Adult   **741.5; Fic**
1. Adventure graphic novels; 2. Graphic novels; 3. High school students — Graphic novels; 4. Manga; 5. Shojo manga
978-1-933617-18-3, $10.99
Reiichi and Liae have come to the planet Deloca to board the high school train. On Deloca, different schools run on special trains, with stops where students complete certain assignments; they live in dorms on the trains. Reiichi and Liae are registered to board the "General" school train. Arena Pendleton, on the other hand, has determined to board the Special Train, and she won't let anyone stop her, not even the men her wealthy grandfather has hired to capture her and bring her home. In Ideo City, where the students must board their respective trains, Reiichi accidentally gets involved in a run-in between Arena and Kong Seeval, who intends to take Arena home. Reiichi and Arena become handcuffed together, and he has no choice but to board the Special Train. There's lots of action but little in the way of violence or bad language in this first of a manga series.

Kwitney, Alisa
Token. illustrated by Joelle Jones. DC Comics/Minx 2008 176p. Illustration
Grades: 7 8 9 10 11 12   **741.5; Fic**
1. Graphic novels; 2. Shoplifting — Graphic novels
978-1-4012-1538-5, $9.99
Almost-sixteen Shira lives in Miami's South Beach in the mid-1980s, in a hotel with her attorney father, her grandmother, and elderly friend Minerva. She's sort of a spaz at sports, the popular girls at her Jewish high school think she's weird, and her father has started dating his new secretary. Life isn't good. She impulsively starts shoplifting just to feel something, and then she meets Rafael, a streetwise boy who decides to teach her the finer points of stealing. And more.

Labatt, Mary
★ **Mummy** mayhem: a Sam & Friends mystery, book three. Kids Can Press 2010 96p. Illustration
Grades: 3 4 5 6 7 8
741.5; Fic
1. Dogs — Graphic novels; 2. Graphic novels; 3. Humorous graphic novels; 4. Mummies — Graphic novels; 5. Mystery graphic novels
978-1-55453-470-8, $16.95
         LC C2010-900107-9
Sam the sheepdog feels left out when her human friends Jennie and Beth go on a school field trip to the museum without her. She experiences her own mystery, though, when she finds dog treats left in the snow,

Courtesy of Kids Can Press

hears mysterious chanting, and sees a shadowy figure following her around. The museum has brought an exhibit of Ancient Egypt to town, including the mummy of the pharaoh Menopharsib — could the mummy be searching Woolford for Sam, who resembles Akasheput, the pharaoh's pet dog, whose mummy was stolen years ago? This third book in the series has just enough spooky goings-on for younger readers.

Based on the novel The Mummy Lives! by Mary Labatt

Lagos, Joseph
The **sons** of liberty. created and written by Alexander Lagos and Joseph Lagos; art by Steve Walker; color by Oren Kramek; letters by Chris Dickey. Random House 2010 un Illustration
Grades: 6 7 8 9 10 11 12   **741; 741.5; Fic**

1. Adventure graphic novels; 2. African Americans — Graphic novels; 3. Graphic novels; 4. Superhero graphic novels; 5. United States — History — 1600-1775, Colonial period — Graphic novels
9780375856716, $18.99; 9780375956683, $21.99; 9780375856686, $12.99

In the mid-eighteenth century American colonies, Graham and Brody work as slaves on a tobacco plantation not far from Philadelphia. When they run away after injuring the plantation owner's son for threatening another slave, they seek Benjamin Lay, an eccentric abolitionist who might give them shelter. Instead, William Franklin, son of Benjamin Franklin, finds them and conducts unknown experiments on them.

"History offers few villains as vile as slaveholders, but this graphic novel is far from being a simple revenge thriller. The use of historical figures and well-researched (but embellished) history, and a willingness to flesh out characters and set up situations to pay off in future installments, makes for an uncommonly complex, literate, and satisfying adventure." Booklist

Another title about the Sons of Liberty is: Death and taxes (2011)

Lambert, Joseph

The **Center** for Cartoon Studies presents Annie Sullivan and the trials of Helen Keller. by Joseph Lambert. Disney Hyperion Books 2012 92 p. Color illustration
Grades: 5 6 7   **362.4/1092; 362.4; 92**
1. American women authors — History; 2. People with disabilities — United States — History; 3. Female friendship — United States — History; 4. Graphic novels; 5. Women — United States — Biography; 6. Women — United States — History; 7. Keller, Helen, 1880-1968; 8. Sullivan, Annie, 1866-1936; 9. Female friendship — Graphic novels; 10. Women authors — Biography; 11. People with disabilities — Graphic novels
1423113365; 9781423113362

LC 2011036324

This nonfiction graphic novel about Annie Sullivan and Helen Keller "focuses on the trials both Annie and Helen struggle with in their lives," particularly the incident when Helen was accused of plagiarism in her story 'The Frost King' and interrogated at the Perkins Institution. "Helen's perspective is...communicated in dialogue-free black panels in which she is represented as only a gray silhouette" by author/illustrator Joseph Lambert. (Kirkus Reviews)

Langridge, Roger

Jim Henson's the Musical Monsters of Turkey Hollow. adapted from Jim Henson's screenplay by Roger Langridge. Simon & Schuster 2014 96 p. Color; Illustration
Grades: 4 5 6 7   **741.5**
1. Music; 2. Monsters
1608864340; 9781608864348, $24.99

"Turkey Hollow is a picturesque town where hundreds of years ago, unbeknownst to the citizens, a meteorite landed nearby a small brook on the outskirts of town. One Thanksgiving, while young Timmy Henderson practices his guitar, he's accompanied by strange, unearthly, musical sounds. That meteorite wasn't a rock at all but an egg holding seven furry, goofy monsters, each with a unique musical sound. After the initial shock, Timmy befriends the lovable creatures following him all around Turkey Hollow." (Publisher's note)

"Based on a never-produced Jim Henson screenplay, this folksy story captures the spirit of Muppet holiday specials like Emmet Otter's Jug-Band Christmas.... Subdued autumnal colors make up most of the palette in Langridge's clean-lined panels, while musical moments are full of big, swirling words in bright colors." Booklist

★ **Snarked!:** Forks and Hope. Roger Langridge. BOOM! Studios 2012 128 p. Illustration
Grades: 5 6 7 8   **741.5/973; Fic**
1. Fantasy fiction; 2. Adventure fiction; 3. Swindlers and swindling — Fiction
1608860957; 9781608860951, $14.99
Eisner Award: Best Publication for Kids (2011)

This graphic novel is the first in Roger Langridge's "Snarked!" series. It presents "an epic adventure featuring the Red Queen's children, Princess Scarlett and her baby brother Rusty, as they set out in search of the missing Red King. And who better to help guide the way than the Walrus and the Carpenter from [Lewis Carroll's] 'Through the Looking Glass'." (Publisher's note)
Volume 1 of 3

★ **Thor,** the mighty avenger, v.1.. writer, Roger Langridge; artist, Chris Samnee; colorist, Matthew Wilson. Marvel 2011 un Illustration
Grades: 8 9 10 11 12   **741.5; 741; Fic**
1. Thor (Fictional character)
978-0-7851-4121-1, $14.99; 0-7851-4121-9

"Readers meet the mysterious blond-haired God of Thunder with no memory when historian Jane Foster watches him get tossed out of a Norse exhibition one day. After the gallant fellow helps her out and she takes him in, an utterly charming romance ensues, even as Thor participates in some Norse debauchery and hunts down the secrets of his past." (Booklist)
Volume 1 of 2

Larcenet, Manu

Dungeon: Parade Vol. 1: A Dungeon Too Many. by Joann Sfar, Lewis Trondheim & Manu Larcenet. NBM 2007 un Illustration
Grades: 6 7 8 9 10 11 12 Adult   **741.5; Fic**
1. Adventure graphic novels; 2. Fantasy graphic novels; 3. Graphic novels; 4. Humorous graphic novels
978-1-56163-495-8, $9.95

Marvin the Vegetarian Dragon and Herbert the Duck do battle with the new, rival dungeon next door that is actually a theme park. Then, Herbert finds a magic lamp that has one wish left, and he and Marvin set out on a quest to find a dying sage to get advice on the best wish.

Larson, Hope

All summer long. by Hope Larson. Farrar, Straus & Giroux 2018 176 p. Color; Illustration
Grades: 5 6 7 8   **741.5; Fic**
1. Friendship — Juvenile fiction; 2. Bildungsromans; 3. Summer — Juvenile fiction
0374310718; 9780374304850; 9780374310714, $12.99

LC 2017956974

In this book, by Hope Larson, "thirteen-year-old Bina has a long summer ahead of her.... [H]er best friend, Austin...[is] off to soccer camp for a month, and he's been acting kind of weird.... [When] Austin comes home from camp,...he's acting even weirder.... How Bina and Austin rise above their growing pains and reestablish their friendship and respect for their differences makes for a touching and funny coming-of-age story." (Publisher's note)

"Larson's panels are superb at revealing emotional conflict, subtext, and humor within the deceptively simple third-person limited plot, allowing characters to grow and develop emotionally over only a few spreads." Kirkus

★ **Chiggers.** [by] Hope Larson; lettered by Jason Azzopardi. Atheneum Books for Young Readers 2008 170p. Illustration
Grades: 5 6 7 8 9   **741.5; Fic**
1. Camps — Fiction; 2. Friendship — Graphic novels; 3. Graphic novels

978-1-4169-3584-1, $17.99; 978-1-4169-3587-2 (pa), $9.99

LC 2008-09557

When Abby returns to the same summer camp she always goes to, she is dismayed to find that her old friends have changed, and the only person who wants to be her friend is the strange new girl, Shasta.

"Chiggers provides a ticket to summer fun. Larson delicately handles both the usual middle-school angst and the additional pressures that come with being somewhat different.... The content is perfect for upper elementary and middle school students." SLJ

Compass south. Hope Larson; illustrated by Rebecca Mock. Margaret Ferguson Books/Farrar, Straus & Giroux 2016 224 p. Color; Illustration
Grades: 4 5 6 7 **741.5; Fic**
1. Brothers and sisters — Fiction; 2. Buried treasure — Fiction; 3. Graphic novels; 4. Twins — Fiction; 5. Adventure and adventurers — Fiction; 6. Voyages and travels — Fiction; 7. Juvenile delinquents — Fiction; 8. Siblings — Fiction; 9. Gangs — Juvenile fiction; 10. New Orleans (La.) — Juvenile fiction
0374300437; 9780374300432, $17.99

LC 2015039907

"When 12-year-old twins Alexander and Cleopatra's father disappears, they join the Black Hook Gang and are caught by the police pulling off a heist. They agree to reveal the identity of the gang in exchange for tickets to New Orleans.... Neither Alexander nor Cleo realizes the real danger they are in-they are being followed by pirates who think they hold the key to treasure." (Publisher's note)

"A variety of panel sizes keeps the pace brisk while allowing for the occasional pause to set the scene or linger in an emotional moment." Horn Book

Another title in this series is: Knife's edge (2017)

Goldie Vance; Volume 1. Hope Larson, writer; Brittney Williams, artist; Sarah Stern, color artist. Boom! Studios 2016 112 p. Color; Illustration
Grades: 7 8 9 10 11 12 **741.5; Fic**
1. Mystery fiction; 2. LGBT youth — Fiction; 3. Women detectives — Graphic novels; 4. Hotels — Florida — Graphic novels
1608868982; 9781608868988, $9.99

In this first book in the Goldie Vance series by Hope Larson, illustrated by Brittney Williams, "sixteen-year-old Marigold 'Goldie' Vance lives at a Florida resort with her dad, who manages the place.... Goldie has an insatiable curiosity, which explains her dream to one day become the hotel's in-house detective. When Charles, the current detective, encounters a case he can't crack, he agrees to mentor Goldie in exchange for her help solving the mystery." (Publisher's note)

Volume 1 of an ongoing series

Knife's edge. Hope Larson; illustrated by Rebecca Mock. Farrar, Straus & Giroux 2017 224 p. Color; Illustration; Map
Grades: 4 5 6 7 **741.5; Fic**
1. Sea stories — Graphic novels; 2. Pirates — Graphic novels; 3. Adventure graphic novels
9780374300449, $19.99

LC 2016951407

In this juvenile graphic novel, by Hope Larson, illustrated by Rebecca Mock, book two in the "Four Points" series, "twelve-year-old twin adventurers Cleopatra and Alexandra Dodge are reunited with their father and realize that two family heirlooms reveal the location of a treasure that is their birthright. When they set sail with Captain Tarboro on the Almira, they know they're heading into danger — the ocean is filled with new and old enemies." (Publisher's note)

"As in its predecessor, every question answered leads the twins to more questions to be asked, and it ends with a breath-catching cliffhanger."

An action-packed sophomore volume, with no loss of wind in its sails." Kirkus

Who is AC?. Hope Larson; illustrated by Tintin Pantoja. Atheneum Books for Young Readers 2013 176 p.
Grades: 7 8 9 10 11 12 **741.5/973; Fic**
1. Graphic novels; 2. Superheroes — Fiction; 3. Female superhero graphic novels
1442426500; 9781442426504, $14.99; 9781442465404, $21.99

LC 2011052616

In this book, "Lin, a zine-writing 15-year-old who's just moved to a small town, becomes an unwitting Sailor Moon-style superhero, activated by mysterious cellphone messages and visited by a 'dispatcher' who nags her until she suits up. Her nemesis is a shadowy villain who possesses a glamorous rich girl in order to snare a boy named Trace." (Publishers Weekly)

A **wrinkle** in time: the graphic novel. Madeleine L'Engle; adapted and illustrated by Hope Larson. Farrar Straus Giroux 2012 392 p.
Grades: 4 5 6 7 **741.5**
1. Graphic novels; 2. Science fiction; 3. L'Engle, Madeleine. Wrinkle in time — Adaptations; 4. Time travel — Fiction; 5. Space and time — Fiction
0374386153; 9780374386153, $19.99

LC 2010044120

Hope Larson presents a graphic novel adaptation of Madeleine L'Engle's "allegorical fantasy in which a group of young people are guided through the universe by Mrs. Who, Mrs. Which and Mrs. What — women who possess supernatural powers. They traverse fictitious regions, meet and face evil and demonstrate courage at the right moment. Religious allusions are secondary to the philosophical struggle designed to yield the meaning of life and one's place on earth." (Kirkus Reviews)

Lash, Batton

Mister Negativity and Other Tales of Supernatural Law. Exhibit A Press 2004 170p. Illustration
Grades: 8 9 10 11 12 Adult **741.5; Fic**
1. Graphic novels; 2. Humorous graphic novels; 3. Supernatural graphic novels
0-9633954-8-3, $15.95

LC 2003113227

Attorneys Wolff & Byrd represent clients that include Nagy D'Viti, a fellow with such a negative attitude that he physically repels people, Huberis the Dybbuk, a born again demon seeking church membership, Nicky Gorillo, a gangster who has literally become a gorilla mob boss, Steven Gink, a horror novelist in a coma who summons them through their dreams, Susann, the Muse of Potboilers, who sues the author she has "inspired," and Perry Otter, a boy magician with an unusual affliction.

Lat

Kampung boy. First Second 2006 141p. Illustration
Grades: 7 8 9 10 11 12 Adult **741; 741.5; Fic**
1. Family life — Graphic novels; 2. Graphic novels; 3. Muslims — Graphic novels; 4. Malaysia — Graphic novels
1-59643-121-0, $16.95

LC 2005-34135

"Malaysian cartoonist Lat uses the graphic novel format to share the story of his childhood in a small village, or kampung. From his birth and adventures as a toddler to the enlargement of his world as he attends classes in the village, makes friends, and, finally, departs for a prestigious city boarding school, this autobiography is warm, authentic, and wholly engaging." Booklist

First published 1979 in Malaysia with title: Lat, the kampung boy;
Another title about Lat is: Town boy (2007)

★ **Town** boy. First Second Books 2007 191p. Illustration
Grades: 7 8 9 10 11 12 Adult   **741.5; Fic**
1. Bildungsromans — Graphic novels; 2. Graphic novels; 3. Humorous graphic novels; 4. Malaysia — Graphic novels
978-1-59643-331-1, $16.95; 1-59643-331-0
                                        LC 2006-102857

In this sequel to Kampung Boy, it's the late 1960s and Mat is now a teenager attending a boarding school in the town of Ipoh, far from his kampung. He discovers bustling streets, hip music, heady literature, budding romance, and through it all his growing passion for art.

Laudec
Cedric, vol. 1: High-risk class. Cinebook Ltd. 2008 48p. Illustration
Grades: 3 4 5 6 7 8   **741.5; Fic**
1. Graphic novels; 2. Humorous graphic novels; 3. School stories — Graphic novels
978-1-905460-68-7, $11.95

Eight-year-old Cedric is the type of boy who likes to play with his chums, doesn't always get good grades, and has a crush on his teacher, Miss Nelly. Then Chen starts at his school; she's Chinese, she's cute, and Cedric falls head over heels for her. He can't just tell her, of course. Meanwhile, he gets into all kinds of mischief with his friends, including playing with a remote control car, planting stink bombs all over school, drinking champagne when his grandfather says he did so to get the courage to propose to his grandmother. Each time he does something naughty, he does face consequences for his actions. This book is translated from the French.

Lawrence, Mike (Comic book artist)
Star scouts. Mike Lawrence. First Second 2017 192 p. Color; Illustration
Grades: 4 5 6   **741.5; Fic**
1. Human-alien encounters — Juvenile fiction; 2. Alien abduction — Juvenile fiction; 3. Scouts and scouting — Juvenile fiction
9781626722804, $14.99
                                        LC 2016938730

In this book in the Star Scouts series, by Mike Lawrence, "Avani is the new kid in town, and...everyone in school thinks she's weird, especially the girls in her Flower Scouts troop.... But everything changes when Avani is 'accidentally' abducted by a spunky alien named Mabel.... Collecting alien specimens (like Avani) goes with the territory.... Avani might be weird, but in the Star Scouts she fits right in." (Publisher's note)

Another title in this series is: The league of lasers (2018)

Lee, Jen
★ **Garbage** night. Jen Lee. Nobrow Press 2017 72 p. Color; Illustration
Grades: 7 8 9 10 11 12   **741.5; Fic**
1. Animals — Fiction; 2. Dogs — Fiction; 3. Survival skills — Fiction
1910620211; 9781910620212, $18.95

In this book, by Jen Lee, "in a barren and ransacked backyard, a dog named Simon lives with his two best friends: a raccoon and a deer. The unlikely gang spends their days looting the desolate supermarket and waiting for the return of the hallowed 'garbage night' — but week after week, the bins remain empty. While scavenging one day, the trio meet Barnaby — another abandoned dog who tells them about the 'other town' where humans are still rumored to live." (Publisher's note)

"This follow-up to Lee's previous short story 'Vacancy' (also collected here) tells a simple yet absorbing tale of friendship and survival in a postapocalyptic world.... Lee's expansive universe of anthropomorphic animals comes alive through her spare use of detail: her verbal worldbuilding gives readers just enough information about animal society and what came before to spark the imagination, and vivid, expressive cartooning fills in the gaps." Pub Wkly

Lee, Stan
Essential Fantastic Four Vol. 1, 2nd ed.. Marvel Entertainment 2005 un Illustration
Grades: 7 8 9 10 11 12 Adult   **741.5; Fic**
1. Fantastic Four (Fictional characters); 2. Graphic novels; 3. Superhero graphic novels; 4. Hulk (Fictional character)
978-0-7851-1828-2, $16.99

This massive trade paperback collects the first 20 issues of The Fantastic Four plus the Annual #1. Reprinted in black and white, this volume lets readers get the origin and early stories as originally written by Lee and drawn by Kirby. The Fantastic Four fights against Skrulls, Sub-Mariner, The Impossible Man, The Hulk, the Red Ghost, The Thinker, Doctor Doom (who first appeared in issue #5), the Puppet Master, and many more super villains.

Lee, Tony
★ **Outlaw:** the legend of Robin Hood: a graphic novel. written by Tony Lee; illustrated by Sam Hart; colored by Artur Fujita. Candlewick Press 2009 un Illustration
Grades: 7 8 9 10 11 12
741.5; Fic
1. Adventure graphic novels; 2. Graphic novels; 3. Robin Hood (Fictional character); 4. Great Britain — History — 1154-1399, Plantagenets — Graphic novels; 5. Robin Hood (Legendary character)
978-0-7636-4399-7, $21.99;
0-7636-4399-8; 978-0-7636-4400-0 (pa),
$11.99; 0-7636-4400-5 (pa)
                                        LC 2008-943331

OUTLAW: THE LEGEND OF ROBIN HOOD. Text copyright © 2009 by Tony Lee. Illustrations copyright © 2009 by Sam Hart. Reproduced by permission of the publisher, Candlewick Press, Somerville, MA on behalf of Walker Books, London.

In this retelling of the Robin Hood legend, it's the year 1192, and Robin of Loxley has returned home from the Crusades after receiving news of his father's death. The Sheriff of Nottingham and Sir Guy of Gisburn govern Nottingham at the pleasure of Prince John. When Gisburn treacherously stabs Robin in a murder attempt, Robin escapes to Sherwood Forest, where the outlaws befriend him. With the help of such men as Little John and Friar Tuck, he organizes the outlaws and they start hurting Prince John where it matters — in his moneybags.

"Lee's excellent rendition of the famed selfless hero goes hand-in-hand with Hart's expressive illustrations, featuring lots of closeups and dramatic lighting and a beautiful jewel-toned palette. Teens will get caught up in this exciting page-turner." SLJ

Leloup, Roger
Yoko Tsuno, bk. 3: the prey and the ghost. Cinebook 2008 48p. Illustration
Grades: 3 4 5 6 7 8   **741.5; Fic**
1. Ghosts — Graphic novels; 2. Graphic novels; 3. Mystery graphic novels
978-1-905460-56-4, $11.95

Young electronics engineer Yoko Tsuno has driven to Scotland to investigate the Loch Ness Monster, when she and her companion Pol find they've taken a wrong turn. Then they encounter a distraught young woman on the road who's being chased by dogs. The young woman is Cecelia, stepdaughter of Sir William, whose parents both died. She's convinced that her mother is haunting their castle, and Yoko finds a way to investigate just what is going on.

Part of the Yoko Tsuno series, originally published in France as Yoko Tsuno 12 La Proie et l'ombre.

Levitz, Paul

Justice Society Volume One. writers, Paul Levitz, Gerry Conway; pencillers, Joe Staton, Keith Giffen, Wally Wood, Ric Estrada; inkers, Wally Wood, Bob Layton. DC Comics 2006 224p. Illustration
Grades: 7 8 9 10 11 12 Adult   **741.5; Fic**
1. Graphic novels; 2. Justice Society of America (Fictional characters); 3. Superhero graphic novels; 4. Green Lantern (Fictional character); 5. Flash (Fictional character); 6. Robin (Fictional character)
978-1-4012-0970-4, $14.99

The volume collects stories originally published in the 1970s, when DC revived the very first superhero team that was originally created in 1940: the Justice Society of America. This incarnation of the Justice Society includes the Golden Age Flash and Green Lantern, Hawkman, Dr. Fate, Wildcat, Dr. Mid-Nite, Robin, Power Girl, and the Star-Spangled Kid. Artists on this run include Wally Wood, Joe Staton, Keith Giffen, and Ric Estrada.

Lewis, Corey Sutherland

Sharknife Volume 1. Oni Press 2006 un Illustration
Grades: 8 9 10 11 12 Adult
741.5; Fic
1. Graphic novels; 2. Humorous graphic novels; 3. Martial arts — Graphic novels
1-932664-17-3, $9.95

Courtesy of Oni Press

The Guandong Factory isn't like other restaurants. It's five stories tall, produces more peach dumplings per day than most eateries do in a decade, and it's the home of Sharknife — a mystical protector charged with protecting the establishment from those who would do it harm. But who is this mysterious yet colorful being? Once just a simple busboy, now Caesar Ives is something more — a crazy red rocket hero destined for greatness. But can Caesar juggle both lives — nabbing the girl (the super-sexy Chieko Momuza), and stopping the wide assortment of bizarre baddies that would love to do his precious eatery harm? There's lots of martial arts action.

Lewis, John

★ **March:** Book One. John Lewis; [co-written by] Andrew Aydin; [art by] Nate Powell. Top Shelf Productions 2013 121 p. Illustration
Grades: 8 9 10 11 12 Adult   **741.5; 92**
1. Civil rights movements — United States — Comic books, strips, etc; 2. Lewis, John, 1940 February 21-; 3. African Americans — Civil rights — Graphic novels
9781603093002, $14.95
LC 2013218903
Coretta Scott King (Author) Honor Book (2014)

This graphic novel, by U.S. congressman John Lewis, "in collaboration with co-writer Andrew Aydin and New York Times best-selling artist Nate Powell...spans John Lewis' youth in rural Alabama,

his life-changing meeting with Martin Luther King, Jr., the birth of the Nashville Student Movement, and their battle to tear down segregation through nonviolent lunch counter sit-ins, building to a...climax on the steps of City Hall." (Publisher's note)

"This is superb visual storytelling that establishes a convincing, definitive record of a key eyewitness to significant social change." SLJ

★ **March:** Book Three. by John Lewis and Andrew Aydin; illustrated by Nate Powell. Top Shelf Productions 2016 256 p. Illustration
Grades: 8 9 10 11 12 Adult
328.73; 92
1. Lewis, John, 1940 February 21-; 2. Civil rights — United States
9781603094023, $19.99; 1603094024

Courtesy of IDW Publishing

National Book Award: Young People's Literature (2016); Coretta Scott King (Author) Book Award (2017); Printz Award (2017); Sibert Informational Book Award (2017); YALSA Award for Excellence in Nonfiction for Young Adults (2017); Eisner Award: Best Reality-Based Work (2017)

This book is the "conclusion of the award-winning and best-selling March trilogy. Congressman John Lewis, an American icon and one of the key figures of the civil rights movement, joins co-writer Andrew Aydin and artist Nate Powell to bring the lessons of history to vivid life for a new generation, urgently relevant for today's world." (Publisher's note)

"Though Lewis and Aydin throw a lot at readers in this volume, their message, helped along seamlessly and splendidly by Powell's fantastic, cinematic artwork, is abundantly clear: the victories of the civil rights movement, symbolized in particular by Barack Obama's inauguration, are hard-won and only succeeded through the dogged dedication of a wide variety of people." Booklist

★ **March:** Book Two. by John Lewis and Andrew Aydin; illustrated by Nate Powell. Top Shelf Productions 2015 192 p. Illustration
Grades: 8 9 10 11 12 Adult
741.5; 92
1. African American civil rights workers; 2. African American legislators; 3. African Americans — Civil rights; 4. Autobiographical comic books, strips, etc.; 5. Civil rights movements; 6. Civil rights workers — United States; 7. Legislators — United States; 8. Lewis, John, 1940 February 21-; 9. African Americans — Civil rights — Graphic novels
9781603094009, $19.95; 1603094008

Courtesy of IDW Publishing

LC 2015270634
Eisner Nominee: Best Publication for Teens (2016); Eisner Award: Best Reality-Based Work (2016); Ignatz Nominee: Outstanding Series (2015)

This graphic novel, by John Lewis and Andrew Aydin, illustrated by Nate Powell, "takes us behind the scenes of some of the most pivotal moments of the Civil Rights Movement.... After the success of the Nashville sit-in campaign, John Lewis is more committed than ever to changing the world through nonviolence — but as he and his fellow Freedom Riders board a bus into the vicious heart of the deep south, they will be tested like never before." (Publisher's note)

"Heroism and steadiness of purpose continue to light up Lewis' frank, harrowing account of the civil rights movement's climactic days.... The contrast between the dignified marchers and the vicious, hate-filled actions and expressions of their tormentors will leave a deep impression on readers." Kirkus

Lie, Bjorn Rune

The **wolf's** whistle. by B.R. Lie and S.J. Donaldson.. Nobrow 2012 88 p. Illustration; Color

Grades: 4 5 6 7 8 9 10   **741.5; Fic**

  1. Fractured fairy tales; 2. Revenge — Fiction

1907704035; 9781907704031, $18.00

This children's book by Bjorn Rune Lie "digs into the troubled upbringing of one of storydom's most maligned figures: the house-blowing-down wolf. As a wolf cub, little Robert loved superhero comics...which led to much torment at the hands of three piggish brothers. Robert grows up to be not much... when the building owned by the Honeyroasts burns down with three of Robert's best friends trapped inside, the spark of vengeance and justice is kindled in the wolf." (Booklist)

Limke, Jeff

Jason: Quest for the Golden Fleece. Lerner Publishing Group/Graphic Universe 2007 48p. Illustration

Grades: 3 4 5 6 7 8 9

292.1; 741.5

  1. Graphic novels; 2. Greek mythology — Graphic novels; 3. Jason (Greek mythology) — Graphic novels

978-0-8225-5967-2, $26.60 lib bdg

Courtesy of Lerner Publishing Group

Jason's uncle Pelias had stole the throne when Jason was a child; now a young man, Jason must prove himself by retrieving the priceless Golden Fleece from the far-off land of Colchis. He gathers a ship of heroes, the Argonauts, to aid him on his quest; but when they arrive in Colchis, the king insists that Jason prove himself in dangerous trials, and the king's daughter, Medea, has plans for Jason. This retelling is based on the heroic poem by Apollonius of Rhodes. The book includes a glossary and a list of books and websites for further reading.

King Arthur: Excalibur Unsheathed. Lerner Publishing Group/Graphic Universe 2007 48p. Illustration

Grades: 3 4 5 6 7 8 9

398.2; 741.5

  1. Arthurian romances — Graphic novels; 2. Graphic novels; 3. Malory, Sir Thomas, 15th c — Adaptations

978-0-8225-3083-1, $26.60 lib. Bdg.

Courtesy of Lerner Publishing Group

This story is adapted from Sir Thomas Malory's Le Morte D'Arthur. Young squire Arthur's life, and that of England, changes the day he pulls out the mysterious Sword in the Stone. Guided by Merlin the magician, Arthur takes his place as King of England. Can he win peace and freedom for his country? The book includes a glossary and a list of books for further reading.

Lin, Yali

Hawthorne's the Scarlet letter: the Manga edition. Wiley Publishing 2009 186p. Illustration

Grades: 5 6 7 8 9 10 11 12   **741.5; Fic**

  1. Authors; 2. Graphic novels; 3. Novelists; 4. Short story writers; 5. Hawthorne, Nathaniel, 1804-1864 — Adaptations

978-0-470-14889-1, $9.99

Hester Prynne, a young married woman in puritanical Massachusetts, stands in public shame when she bears a child long after her husband had disappeared. She refuses to identify the father of her child and instead wears the scarlet letter A always. The young minister Arthur Dimmesdale lives with his guilt in secret, but the physician, Roger Chillingworth, is actually Hester's husband, returned for vengeance. He vows to find the man who fathered Pearl, Hester's daughter, and destroy him. Meanwhile, Pearl grows up in a society that shuns her mother, and she comes to see the A as her mother's badge of honor. This book is a manga style adaptation of Hawthorne's novel.

Liu, Na

  ★ **Little** White Duck: a childhood in China. Na Liu and Andrés Vera Martínez. Graphic Universe 2012 96 p. Color illustration

Grades: 4 5 6

741.5/973

  1. Graphic novels; 2. Biographical graphic novels; 3. China — History — 1976-; 4. Liu, Na, 1973-

0761365877; 9780761365877, $29.27; 9780761381150, $9.95; 0761381155

              LC 2011005347

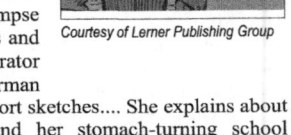

Courtesy of Lerner Publishing Group

This graphic novel provides a "glimpse into Chinese girlhood during the 1970s and '80s." It begins with the 3-year-old narrator trying to understand the death of Chairman Mao. "From there, her life unfolds in short sketches.... She explains about the four pests that plague China...and her stomach-turning school assignment to catch rats and deliver the severed tails to her teacher...[as well as] the origins of Chinese New Year, her favorite holiday." (Kirkus Reviews)

"This picturesque treasure introduces Chinese culture through a personal perspective that is both delightful and thought-provoking." SLJ

Loeb, Jeph

Shazam!: the greatest stories ever told. DC Comics 2008 224p. Illustration

Grades: 4 5 6 7 8 9 10 11 12 Adult   **741.5; Fic**

  1. Adventure graphic novels; 2. Captain Marvel (Fictional character); 3. Graphic novels; 4. Superhero graphic novels

978-1-4012-1674-0, $24.99

This book collects comics stories about Captain Marvel dating from 1940 to 1998. Captain Marvel predated Superman as a comic book superhero; young newsboy Billy Batson could transform into the flying superhero by shouting the magic word "Shazam!" This gave him the wisdom of Solomon, the strength of Hercules, the stamina of Atlas, the power of Zeus, the courage of Achilles, and the speed of Mercury. In these fourteen stories, he battles against such foes as Dr. Sivana, Mr. Mind, and the Monster Society of Evil.

Showcase Presents: Batgirl Volume 1. DC Comics 2007 552p. Illustration

Grades: 6 7 8 9 10 11 12 Adult   **741.5; Fic**

1. Batgirl (Fictional character); 2. Graphic novels; 3. Superhero graphic novels

978-1-4012-1367-1, $16.99

In the late 1960s, DC Comics added a new character to the world of Batman and Robin: Batgirl. Daughter of Commissioner Jim Gordon, Barbara Gordon is a librarian who relocates to Gotham City and soon dons her costume as the crime fighting Batgirl. This volume of black and white reprints includes her early adventures, from 1967 through 1975. The cover art notwithstanding, Batgirl is a woman of action.

Showcase Presents: Batman Vol. 1. DC Comics 2006 552p. Illustration

Grades: 6 7 8 9 10 11 12 Adult   **741.5; Fic**
1. Batman (Fictional character); 2. Graphic novels; 3. Superhero graphic novels

1-4012-1086-4, $16.99

The spotlight's on Batman in this volume featuring Detective Comics #327-342 and Batman #164-174. The Dynamic Duo take on some of their most enduring Rogues Gallery members, including Penguin, the Riddler, and the Outsider in these classic Silver Age stories from the era of famed editor Julius Schwartz. This Showcase edition reprints the comics in black and white."

Superman: The Amazing Transformations of Jimmy Olsen. DC Comics 2007 192p. Illustration

Grades: 6 7 8 9 10 11 12 Adult   **741.5; Fic**
1. Graphic novels; 2. Humorous graphic novels; 3. Superhero graphic novels; 4. Superman (Fictional character)

978-1-4012-1369-5, $14.99

Cub reporter Jimmy Olsen stars in this light-hearted volume collecting some of his most memorable adventures from the late 1950s and 1960s, all of which guest-star Superman. While investigating crime for The Daily Planet, Jimmy undergoes one startling transformation after another, gaining temporary super-powers as Elastic Lad and becoming a Giant Turtle Man, The Wolf-Man of Metropolis, The Human Porcupine and much more. At times like these, Superman finds that he must not only protect Metropolis from Jimmy, but Jimmy from himself.

Lucke, Deb

The **Lunch** Witch. by Deb Lucke. Papercutz 2015 180 p. Illustration

Grades: 3 4 5 6

741.5; Fic
1. Witches — Fiction; 2. School children — Fiction; 3. Friendship — Fiction

1629911623; 9781629911625, $14.99

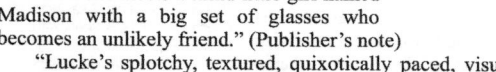

In this book, by Deb Lucke, "Grunhilda inherits her famous ancestors' recipes and cauldron, but no one believes in magic anymore. Despite the fact that Grunhilda's only useful skill is cooking up potfuls of foul brew, she finds a job listing that might suit her: lunch lady. She delights in scaring the kids until she meets a timid little girl named Madison with a big set of glasses who becomes an unlikely friend." (Publisher's note)

Courtesy of NBM Publishing

"Lucke's splotchy, textured, quixotically paced, visual storytelling, with its mixture of crisply defined panels and sprawling full-page spreads, perfectly fits the outsider lives of both protagonists." VOYA

Another title about the Lunch Witch is: Knee-Deep in Niceness (2016)

Lutes, Jason

★ **Houdini:** the handcuff king. Hyperion Books for Children/Jump at the Sun 2007 90p. Illustration (Center for Cartoon Studies presents)

Grades: 4 5 6 7 8 9 10   **92; 741.5**
1. Biographical graphic novels; 2. Graphic novels; 3. Magicians; 4. Nonfiction writers; 5. Houdini, Harry, 1874-1926

978-0-7868-3902-5, $16.99; 978-0-7868-3903-2 (pa), $9.99

On May 1, 1908, magician Harry Houdini performed one of his famous handcuff escapes, this time in handcuffs and leg irons, while jumping off the Cambridge Bridge in Massachusetts into the frigid Boston River. This graphic novel takes the reader through Houdini's day, from 5:00 a.m. as he makes his preparations, makes a practice jump, coaches his wife Bess on how she's to help him, and then makes the jump.

This is a "fascinating graphic novel.... The format will instantly draw a lot of attention from readers and then hold on to it. Lutes and Bertozzi use grayscale comic panels to share their story about the life of Harry Houdini in a unique way.... The book resembles a hybrid between fiction and nonfiction, and the ingenious choice of format will appeal to a broad age range of readers." Voice Youth Advocates

Lyga, Barry

★ **Wolverine:** worst day ever. by Barry Lyga; artist, Todd Nauck. Marvel Publishing 2009 184p. Illustration

Grades: 5 6 7 8 9   **741.5; Fic**
1. Graphic novels; 2. Humorous graphic novels; 3. Superhero graphic novels; 4. Wolverine (Fictional character)

978-0-7851-3757-3, $14.99; 0-7851-3757-2

Teenager Eric Mattias has just recently discovered he has mutant powers. Very sucky mutant powers: suddenly no one notices him even when he's in the same room. He's not invisible, but he might as well be, and people don't even notice him when he speaks. Eric decides to follow Wolverine around and see if he can't pick up a few pointers about living a loner-type life, as the adamantium-clawed mutant tends to do. Only when they end up in a remote forested area does Eric realize he may not have made the smartest move, because someone else has come, someone who is as strong as Wolverine, and maybe meaner: Sabretooth.

"It's a coming-of-age tale with bursts of action that's sure to appeal to its large, built-in audience." Booklist

MacHale, D. J.

Pendragon book one: the merchant of death graphic novel. adapted and illustrated by Carla Speed McNeil. Aladdin Paperbacks 2008 172p. Illustration

Grades: 5 6 7 8 9 10   **741.5; Fic**
1. Adventure graphic novels; 2. Fantasy graphic novels; 3. Graphic novels

978-1-4169-5080-6, $9.99; 1-4169-5080-X

LC 2007-937920

Fourteen-year-old Bobby Pendragon has had a good life with a loving family, friends, and sports, but it all changes the night his Uncle Press takes him into New York City, to a deserted subway station that contains a gate that leads them to another world. On Denduron, a peaceful tribe called the Milago face annihilation from the Bedowan, and Uncle Press expects Bobby to help him stop it. Press is what he calls a Traveler, and he says Bobby is one, too, and they have a job to do. Bobby is able to write journals and send them home to his best friends Mark and Courtney. Meanwhile, he needs to learn so much, can he do it in time to help — and stay alive?

"This graphic-format adaptation streamlines the already fast-moving experience, providing satisfying interpretations of favorite characters and situations." Booklist

Macklin, Ken

The **weasel** patrol. About Comics/About Infinity 2009 104p. Illustration
Grades: 7 8 9 10 11 12 Adult
741.5; Fic
1. Graphic novels; 2. Humorous graphic novels; 3. Science fiction graphic novels; 4. Weasels — Graphic novels
978-0-9790750-8-7, $9.99

Courtesy of About Comics

When criminals strike, the intergalactic troopers called the Weasel Patrol will ferret out the bad guys every time. Despite their utter lack of planning, attentiveness, cohesion, or competence, they always succeed, even if their favorite tactic when faced with danger is to run away. This book includes twelve comedic adventures, in which the weasels face mythical monsters (Big Foot), aliens, kidnapped cattle in disguise, and the ever-ready bad guy Reefer Rick. Willy, Leroy, Biff, Roscoe, and Bob are the genetically uplifted Weasel Patrol. The book includes mild, cartoony violence and no bad language and no nudity. Villainous Reefer Rick smokes. Artist Dowling includes fun little details, such as the Acme name on some of the gadgets.

MacPherson, Dwight L.

Kid Houdini and the silver dollar misfits. Viper Comics 2008 un Illustration
Grades: 3 4 5 6 7 8 9
741.5; Fic
1. Graphic novels; 2. Magicians; 3. Mystery graphic novels; 4. Nonfiction writers; 5. Supernatural graphic novels; 6. Houdini, Harry, 1874-1926
978-0 — 9802385-2-5, $9.95

In 1886, ten-year-old Harry Houdini runs away from home, only to find himself a prisoner in Professor Murat's circus. Harry joins the "freak" children: Lydia the snake girl (and her snake Terra), Hans the legless boy, and Jacques and Joe the Siamese twins and they form a detective agency that will solve mysteries for the fee of a silver dollar. Near Kansas City, a girl named Bea hires them to find her missing father whom she fears was kidnapped. However, when the gang gets to her house, they discover that her mother has now been kidnapped, too. It all has to do with a treasure map that leads to a lost gold mine, and the gang needs to solve that mystery in order to find Bea's parents. A young Harry Houdini and his friends make a fun team and they face some supernatural elements in their cases, much like the old Scooby-Doo cartoons " and with a similar scary-fun factor.

Maeda, Shunshin

Ninja baseball Kyuma!, vol. 1. Udon Entertainment 2009 200p. Illustration
Grades: 2 3 4 5 6
741.5; Fic
1. Baseball — Graphic novels; 2. Graphic novels; 3. Humorous graphic novels; 4. Manga; 5. Ninja — Graphic novels; 6. Kodomo
978-1-897376-86-7, $7.99

Young Kyuma Hattori, descendant of famous ninja Hanzo Hattori, is the last ninja left in the ninja compound in the mountains, and he trains with his faithful dog Inui. Kaoru is captain of the Moonstar City Club baseball team, comprised of elementary school students. When teammate Yohko says her crystal ball says they need to look to the mountains to help their team win, Kaoru goes up the mountain and finds Kyuma and asks him to join their team. Kyuma knows nothing about modern society or sports like baseball, and he thinks he's joining an army to go to battle against their enemy. Will his team ever figure out Kyuma is really a ninja, and will Kyuma ever figure out that a baseball game is just a game? The book includes some ninja-style fighting, but no violence or bad language.

Magruder, Nilah

M.F.K.. Nilah Magruder. Insight Editions 2017 128 p. Color; Illustration
Grades: 7 8 9 10 11 12
741.5
1. Good and evil — Comic books, strips, etc.; 2. Supernatural graphic novels; 3. Voyages and travels — Graphic novels
9781683830047, $24.99; 1683830040

This book, by Nilah Magruder, tells "the story of Abbie, a deaf girl with a mysterious power, who is traveling across a vast desert to scatter her mother's ashes. In a world of sleeping gods, a broken government, and a fragile peace held in the hands of the corrupt, one youth must find the strength to stand up against evil and save humanity." (Publisher's note)

"Magruder's color-saturated, manga-inflected artwork incorporates subtle world building details in the background, and her characters — refreshingly diverse in skin tone and body shape — are deeply expressive and imbued with dynamic movement. With crackling banter, an immersive fantasy, and lots of mysteries still unanswered, this series opener is perfect for fans of both manga and adventure comics." Booklist

Maki, Yoko

Aishiteruze Baby Vol. 1. Viz Media/Shojo Beat 2006 un Illustration
Grades: 8 9 10 11 12 Adult
741.5; Fic
1. Graphic novels; 2. Manga; 3. Shojo manga
978-1-4215-0711-8, $19.95

Kippei Katakura is a 17-year-old playboy who spends his time chasing girls, careless of their feelings. But when his 5-year-old cousin Yuzuyu comes to live with his family after her mother's sudden disappearance, Kippei is put in charge of taking care of her. As Kippei gets to know Yuzuyu and starts to understand how she feels, he also begins to realize that all girls were like Yuzuyu once... Kippei has a lot to figure out, like what to make for Yuzuyu's lunch and how to drop her off at kindergarten while still getting to high school on time. Kippei is enjoying his time with Yuzuyu, but not everyone is happy about it. The girls at school miss their quality time with Kippei, and one decides to play dirty to get him back.

Marcus, Leonard S.

Comics confidential: thirteen graphic novelists talk story, craft, and life outside the box. [edited by] Leonard S. Marcus. Candlewick Press 2016 192 p. Illustration; Color
Grades: 7 8 9 10 11 12
741.5
1. Mystery comic books, strips, etc.; 2. Cartoonists — Biography
076365938X; 9780763659387, $24.99; 9780763692247, $24.99
LC 2016945892

This book by anthologist Leonard S. Marcus features thirteen comic artists and writers. "Here are their moving, funny, inspirational stories: true tales from the crucible of creative struggles that led each to become a master of one of today's most vibrant art forms. The book also contains an original graphic short on the common theme of 'the city' from each of the artists, a mini-comic set in a cityscape of their choosing-present-day, historical, or imaginary." (Publisher's note)

COMICS CONFIDENTIAL. Front jacket illustrations copyright © 2016 by Harry Bliss, Gene Luen Yang, Catia Chien, Dave Roman, Danica Novgorodoff, Hope Larson, Matt Phelan, James Sturm, Sara Varon, Geoffrey Hayes, Mark Siegel, Kazu Kibuishi. Reproduced by permission of the publisher, Candlewick Press, Somerville, MA.

"Marcus's chosen comics creators together represent a nice range of styles, topics, nationalities, backgrounds, and intended audiences, while his insightful questions range from formative childhood influences to various career paths, and from individual creative processes to broader ruminations on the medium of comics. The profiles are concise and informative; taken together as a whole, the book represents a snapshot of the genre as it continues on its upward trajectory." Horn Book

Includes bibliographical references (pages 165-173) and index.

Marsden, Mariah

Anne of Green Gables: a graphic novel. Mariah Marsden, edited by Kendra Phipps and Erika Kuster, illustrated by Brenna Thummler. Andrews McMeel Pub. 2017 232 p. Color; Illustration

Grades: 3 4 5 6 7   **741.5**
1. Country life — Fiction; 2. Orphans — Fiction; 3. Friendship — Fiction
9781449479602, $10.99

         LC 2017932307

In this graphic novel, by Mariah Marsden, edited by Kendra Phipps and Erika Kuster, illustrated by Brenna Thummler, "when Matthew and Marilla Cuthbert decide to adopt an orphan who can help manage their family farm, they have no idea what delightful trouble awaits them. With flame-red hair and an unstoppable imagination, 11-year-old Anne Shirley takes Green Gables by storm." (Publisher's note)

"An orphan with "hair as red as carrots" and the mischief she creates come to vivid life in this graphic novel version of Lucy Maud Montgomery's classic novel, a debut for both author and artist. Thummler's crisp illustrations warmly capture pug-nosed Anne's indomitable spirit as she navigates her new life." Pub Wkly

Mashima, Hiro

Fairy tail vol. 1. translated and adapted by William Flanagan; lettered by North Market Street Graphics. Del Rey Manga 2008 202p. Illustration

Grades: 8 9 10 11 12   **741.5; Fic**
1. Fantasy graphic novels; 2. Graphic novels; 3. Humorous graphic novels; 4. Manga; 5. Shonen manga
978-0-345-50133-2, $10.95

Cute girl wizard Lucy wants to join the Fairy Tail, a club for the most powerful wizards (and the most troublesome " they tend to do stuff such as blow up harbors while fighting the bad guys). However, her ambitions land her in the clutches of a gang of unsavory pirates led by a devious magician, who plan to sell her into slavery. Her only hope is Natsu, a strange boy she has met on her travels. Natsu is not the typical hero: he gets motion sickness, eats like a pig, and his best friend is a talking cat. He is a member of the Fairy Tail, however. The book includes some mild fan service (usually cleavage shots), consumption of alcohol, and lots of magical fighting.

Volume 1 of 63

Matheny, Bill

The **Batman** Strikes! Vol. 1: Crime Time. DC Comics 2005 un Illustration

Grades: 4 5 6 7 8 9   **741.5; Fic**
1. Batman (Fictional characters); 2. Graphic novels; 3. Superhero graphic novels; 4. Joker (Fictional character)
1-4012-0509-7, $6.99

This book boasts five action-packed adventures of the Dark Knight Detective: Penguin Rising, City of Bats, Outlaw and Disorder, Without a Chance and Deadly Partner. Batman goes up against the Penguin, the Joker, Manbat, and other villains.

The **Batman** Strikes!: duty calls. written by Bill Matheny, J. Torres; illustrated by Christopher Jones, Terry Beatty. DC Comics 2007 144p. Illustration

Grades: 3 4 5 6 7 8 9   **741.5; Fic**

1. Adventure graphic novels; 2. Batman (Fictional character); 3. Graphic novels; 4. Superhero graphic novels; 5. Catwoman (Fictional character); 6. Batgirl (Fictional character)
978-1-4012-1548-4, $12.99

This volume of Bat-stories is based on the new WB Kids cartoon series. Batman takes on Clayface, the Penguin, the Riddler, and Poison Ivy; Batgirl steps in because Pamela Isley used to be Barbara Gordon's friend. The stories have lots of action, fast quips, and no foul language or actual violence.

Matsumoto, Natsumi

St. dragon girl, vol. 1. story & art by Natsumi Matsumoto; English adaptation, Heidi Vivolo; translation, Andria Cheng. Viz Media/Shojo Beat 2008 un Illustration

Grades: 7 8 9 10 11 12   **741.5; Fic**
1. Fantasy graphic novels; 2. Graphic novels; 3. Manga; 4. Romance graphic novels; 5. Shojo manga
978-1-4215-2010-0, $8.99

High schooler Momoka Sendou, nicknamed Dragon Girl, is a martial artist; her childhood friend Ryuga Kou is a Chinese sorcerer who banishes demons. They have helped each other over the years, but now the Serpent King has threatened to take Ryuga's cousin Shunran as his bride. Ryuga knows he needs more strength, so he tries to summon the clan's dragon spirit to possess him, but Momoka sees only a threat to her friend and pushes him out of the way; the dragon enters her instead. Ryuga does possess the power to seal or unseal the dragon within Momoka, so now they really have to work together to fight the demons, especially the Serpent King. Complicating matters is the little fact that Momoka loves Ryuga but won't tell him, even though everyone around them knows it.

Volume 1 of 8

Matsumoto, Tomo

Beauty is the Beast Volume 1. Viz Media/Shojo Beat 2005 184p. Illustration

Grades: 7 8 9 10 11 12   **741.5; Fic**
1. Graphic novels; 2. Humorous graphic novels; 3. Manga; 4. Romance graphic novels; 5. Shojo manga
1-4215-0289-5, $8.99

When bubbly eleventh-grader Eimi Yamashita finds out that her parents are relocating for work, she decides to strike out on her own and move into a dormitory for girls. Little does Eimi suspect the exciting romantic adventures that await her there. Eimi's fellow residents are a little bit crazy, but a whole lot of fun. They've got a secret mission planned for Eimi's new resident initiation...and it has something to do with sneaking into the boys dormitory across the street and returning with a special keepsake! Can Eimi pull it off without getting caught by one of the handsomest (and cruelest) boys in the dorm?

Matthews, Brett

The **Lone** Ranger. Dynamite Entertainment 2007 160p. Illustration

Grades: 8 9 10 11 12 Adult   **741.5; Fic**
1. Adventure graphic novels; 2. Graphic novels; 3. Lone Ranger (Fictional character); 4. Western stories — Graphic novels
978-1-933305-39-4, $24.99; 978-1-933305-40-0 (pa), $19.99

"A fiery horse with the speed of light, a cloud of dust, and a hearty 'Hi Yo Silver!' — The Lone Ranger..." A popular radio show starting in the 1930s that became a popular television show that ran from 1949 through 1957, a few film serials (extremely hard to find), some paperback novels, and a movie in 1981, The Lone Ranger became an iconic figure. In March 2008, Disney Studios announced it's planning to make a new Lone Ranger movie. In the meantime, Dynamite Entertainment started publishing Lone Ranger comics in 2006. This Lone Ranger is different from the old radio and television shows, and so is Tonto. These aren't the squeaky clean heroes one might expect, although they are heroic. This volume shows the origin of the Lone Ranger, from a young Texas Ranger who has just joined his father and brother. They are ambushed and all killed, except for John. Tonto, a Native American of unknown tribal nation, takes care of John; he has killed all of the killers. When John recovers from his wounds, they set off to find out who ordered the killing, while the reader knows that another killer is murdering all the dead Rangers' families. This book includes some graphic violence.

Texas Ranger John Reid seeks revenge for the murders of his family and friends, only to find justice...and that he's something greater than he ever thought he could be. Together with Tonto, he rides against rich criminals like Cavendish and the politicians Cavendish backs. This new version of the Lone Ranger includes more violence than some might remember from the old television show and books.

McCann, Jim
★ **Return** of the Dapper Men. written by Jim McCann; art by Janet Lee; lettered by Dave Lanphear; edited by Stephen Christy. Archaia Comics 2010 un Illustration
Grades: 4 5 6 7 8   **741.5; Fic**
1. Graphic novels; 2. Robots — Graphic novels; 3. Science fiction graphic novels
978-1-932386-90-5, $24.95; 1-932386-90-4
"In the dreamy land of Anorev, children, all under age 11, live underground among intricate gear-work mechanisms, while elegant robots live in abandoned houses aboveground.... All are perpetually stuck in the same day, and time has, essentially, ceased to mean anything — until 314 Dapper Men rain from the sky and set in motion the impetus for change.... Where this book truly stands out is how well the story works in concert with Lee's stunning artwork, which employs an art nouveau sheen.... A true dazzler that speaks on multiple levels for both child and adult readers and one that gets richer with each read." Booklist

McClintock, Norah
I, witness. Norah McClintock, Mike Deas. Orca Book Publishers 2012 144 p.
Grades: 6 7 8   **741.5/971; Fic**
1. Witnesses — Graphic novels; 2. Graphic novels; 3. Gangs — Graphic novels
1554697891; 9781459803220; 9781554697892, $16.95; 9781554697908
LC 2012938210
In this book, "teenager David Boone and his friend Robbie witness a brutal murder. Boone talks Robbie out of going to the cops, and a few days later, Robbie's killed in a drive-by.... When Boone is wounded and [his friend] Andre killed at Robbie's funeral, Boone is well and truly scared. Boone's classmates call him coward; his dad sends him to a therapist. Detective Rylander practically begs him for help, but it takes another, unrelated murder to prompt Boone to come forward as a witness." (Kirkus)

McCoola, Marika
Baba Yaga's assistant. Marika McCoola; illustrated by Emily Carroll. Candlewick Press 2015 136 p. Color; Illustration
Grades: 4 5 6 7   **741.5; Fic**
1. Supernatural graphic novels; 2. Fairy tales — Graphic novels; 3. Witches — Graphic novels
076366961X; 9780763669614, $16.99
LC 2014951398
Eisner Nominee: Best Publication for Kids (2016)
In this graphic novel, by Marika McCoola and Emily Carroll, "Russian folklore icon Baba Yaga mentors a lonely teen.... Most children

think twice before braving a haunted wood filled with terrifying beasties to match wits with a witch, but not Masha. Her beloved grandma taught her many things: that stories are useful, that magic is fickle, that nothing is too difficult or too dirty to clean. The fearsome witch of folklore needs an assistant, and Masha needs an adventure." (Publisher's note)
"McCoola's offering is a well-nuanced delight, satisfyingly blending fairy tale, legend, and thrills. As a perfect complement, Carroll's evocative art enthralls, capturing both the emotion and the magic of McCoola's yarn and breathing new life into an old folk tale." Kirkus

BABA YAGA'S ASSISTANT. Text copyright © 2015 by Marika McCoola. Illustrations copyright © 2015 by Emily Carroll. Reproduced by permission of the publisher, Candlewick Press, Somerville, MA.

McHale, Pat
Over the Garden Wall: Tome of the Unknown. by Pat McHale, illustrated by Jim Campbell. Boom! Studios 2016 144 p. Color; Illustration
Grades: 3 4 5 6   **741.5; Fic**
1. Fantasy graphic novels; 2. Brothers — Fiction
1608868362; 9781608868360, $19.99
Eisner Award: Best Publication for Kids (2016)
Short adventures from the world of Campbell's Cartoon Network miniseries. "Wirt and Greg are brothers, lost in a strange and endless wood called the Unknown. To find their way home, they must make it through this eerie place, where their only guides are a sardonic bluebird named Beatrice, and an elderly Woodsman. But as things become stranger and stranger, can they find their way out...alive?" (Publisher's note)

McKay, Sharon E.
War brothers: the graphic novel. Annick Press 2013 176 p. Illustration
Grades: 8 9 10 11 12
741.5; Fic
1. Lord's Resistance Army — Graphic novels; 2. Kidnapping — Graphic novels
1554514894; 9781554514892, $27.95
In this graphic novel, "14-year-old Jacob and his friends are just starting school at George Jones Seminary for Boys. The story tells of their subsequent kidnapping and near induction into the Lord's Resistance Army (LRA). Complete innocents at first, the boys endure near starvation, grueling conditions, and physical violence as they travel out of northern Uganda and into Sudan." (School Library Journal)

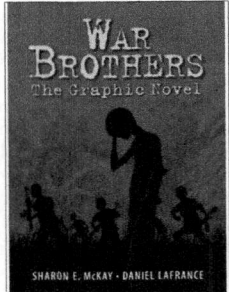

Courtesy of Annick Press

McKeever, Sean
Mary Jane Vol. 1: Circle of Friends. Marvel Entertainment Group 2004 96p. Illustration
Grades: 5 6 7 8 9 10 11 12   **741.5; Fic**
1. Graphic novels; 2. Romance graphic novels; 3. Spider-Man (Fictional character); 4. Superhero graphic novels
0-7851-1467-X, $6.99
High school student Mary Jane Watson hangs out with her friends (including nerdy Peter Parker) and starts dating old friend Harry Osborn even as she fantasizes about the new costumed superhero in town: Spider-Man. In this series, high school romance and friendships take center stage while the superhero action happens off the page and in the sidelines.

This is the first of two volumes, then a new ongoing comics series called Spider-Man Loves Mary Jane continues the story.

McKissack, Fredrick, Jr.
★ **Best** shot in the West: the adventures of Nat Love. by Patricia C. McKissack and Fredrick L. McKissack, Jr.; illustrated by Randy DuBurke. Chronicle Books 2012 129 p. Color illustration; Color; Map
Grades: 7 8 9 10 11 12   978; 92; 741.5
1. African American cowboys — West (U.S.) — Biography — Comic books, strips, etc.; 2. Cowboys — West (U.S.) — Biography — Comic books, strips, etc.; 3. Cowboys — West (U.S.) — Cartoons and comics; 4. Love, Nat, 1854-1921; 5. West (U.S.) — Biography — Comic books, strips, etc.; 6. West (U.S.) — Cartoons and comics; 7. African Americans — Biography — Graphic novels; 8. West (U.S.) — History — Graphic novels; 9. Cowhands — Graphic novels; 10. Railroads — United States
0811857492; 9780811857499, $19.99
LC 2007021419
In this graphic novel, "Nat Love's cattle-driving days are long over and America is a much tamer place when the black cowboy, now a Pullman porter, runs into Bugler, a man he knew back in the day. Bugler's son is a publisher...of...stories from the Wild West, and Love is persuaded to contribute his memoirs. From this...story,...[Patricia C. and Frederick L.] McKissack...segue into Love's adventures, based on his autobiography." (Bulletin of the Center for Children's Books)
Based on: The life and adventures of Nat Love, better known in the cattle country as Deadwood Dick.

Mechner, Jordan
Solomon's thieves. artwork by LeUyen Pham & Alex Puvilland. First Second 2010 139p. Illustration
Grades: 6 7 8 9 10   741.5; Fic
1. Graphic novels; 2. Knights and knighthood — Graphic novels; 3. Middle Ages — Graphic novels; 4. France — History — 0-1328 — Graphic novels
978-1-59643-391-5, $12.99; 1-59643-391-4
LC 2010-282641
Life as a Templar Knight returning from the Crusades is dull" bread, beans, and lots and lots of walking. But after Martin stumbles upon his lost love (now married — to someone else), things begin to get more interesting very quickly. There's a vast conspiracy afoot to destroy the Templar Order and steal their treasure. Soon, Martin finds himself one of the only Templars out of prison — and out for revenge!
"Pham and Puvilland...are again in top form, balancing grainy, hatched textures and clean spaces to lend a weighty historical feel as a vibrant sense of kineticism brings the action sequences to life." Booklist
Includes bibliographical references

Medley, Linda
★ **Castle** waiting. Fantagraphics 2006 456p. Illustration
Grades: 5 6 7 8 9 10 11 12   741.5; Fic
1. Fairy tales — Graphic novels; 2. Fantasy graphic novels; 3. Graphic novels
1-56097-747-7, $29.95
All of Medley's previously self-published comics are collected here in one volume for the first time. The titular castle was the home of Sleeping Beauty, whose story is retold from the viewpoint of the flibbertigibbet ladies in waiting. After the flighty princess awakens with the kiss of a handsome but not too bright prince, the castle becomes a sanctuary for various misfits. Readers will find references to many fairy tales, folk tales, and nursery rhymes in Medley's book, and her clean, clear black-and-white art reflects the works of classic illustrators such as Arthur Rackham.

Castle waiting; Volume II. by Linda Medley; [graphic design by Adam Grano; edited by Kim Thompson]. Fantagraphics Books 2013 464 p. Color; Illustration
Grades: 5 6 7 8 9 10 11 12   741.5/973
1. Fairy tales — Graphic novels
1606996339; 9781606996331, $29.99
LC 2014381744
In this graphic novel, by Linda Medley, "Lady Jain settles into her new life.... Unexpected visitors result in the discovery and exploration of a secret passageway, not to mention an epic bowling tournament. A quest for ladies' underpants, the identity of her baby son Pindar's father, the education of Simon, Rackham and Chess arguing about the "manly arts," and an escape-prone goat are just a few of the elements in this...new volume." (Publisher's note)

Melchior-Durand, Stéphane
The **golden** compass; volume 1: the graphic novel. adapted by Stéphane Melchior, art by Clément Oubrerie; coloring by Clément Oubrerie with Philippe Bruno; translated by Annie Eaton. Alfred A. Knopf 2015 80 p. Color; Illustration
Grades: 6 7 8 9 10   741.5; Fic
1. Fantasy; 2. Graphic novels; 3. Pullman, Philip, 1946- Golden compass — Adaptations; 4. Fantasy graphic novels
9780553523867; 0553523724; 0553523864; 0553523716; 9780553523713, $18.99; 9780553523720
LC 2015005828
In this graphic novel adaptation of the young adult fantasy by Philip Pullman, adapted and illustrated by Stéphane Melchior-Durand and Clément Oubrerie, "Lyra Belacqua is content to run wild among the scholars of Jordan College, with her daemon familiar always by her side. But the arrival of her fearsome uncle, Lord Asriel, draws her to the heart of a terrible struggle-a struggle born of Gobblers and stolen children, and a mysterious substance known as Dust." (Publisher's note)
Originally published by Gallimard Jeunesse, Paris, France, in 2014 — Copyright page.

Mercado, Yehudi
Sci-fu; Book 1: Kick it off. Yehudi Mercado; additional colors by David Wheeler; edited by James Lucas Jones and Desiree Wilson; designed by Kate Z. Stone. Oni Press 2018 144 p. Color; Illustration
Grades: 4 5 6 7 8   741.5; Fic
1. Extraterrestrial beings — Fiction; 2. Turntablists — Fiction; 3. Teenage boys — Fiction; 4. Robots — Fiction; 5. Disc jockeys — Fiction
1620104725; 9781620104729, $12.99
LC 2017948857
In this book, author Yehudi Mercado "sets his sights on 1980s Brooklyn and Wax, a young mix-master who scratches the perfect beat and accidentally summons a UFO that transports his family, best friend, and current crush to the robot-dominated planet of Discopia. Now Wax and his crew must master the intergalactic musical martial art of Sci-Fu to fight the power and save Earth. Word to your mother." (Publisher's note)
"Mercado uses onomatopoeia and visualized sound waves to emphasize that this is an aural adventure; color-coded speech balloons help readers keep track of who is spitting rhymes. His caricatured figures and dynamic layouts, coupled with a neon palette and graffiti flourishes, make for an entertaining story with a little something for everyone: hip-hop, tech-driven action, and romance." Pub Wkly

Meyer, Christopher
Adventures of Rabbit and Bear Paws: The voyageurs. Little Spirit Bear Productions 2008 32p. Illustration

Grades: 3 4 5 6 7   **741.5; Fic**
1. Adventure graphic novels; 2. Graphic novels; 3. Humorous graphic novels; 4. Native Americans — Graphic novels
978-0-9739906-2-1, $7.95

Pintsize, twelve-year-old Rabbit and giant, ten-year-old Bear Paws are brothers and members of the Ojibwa in the eighteenth century. Village medicine man Grey Stone and his wife Clover Blossom raise the brothers, who like to play and play pranks that tend to backfire. In this volume, Rabbit proves he's not a good lacrosse player; then Eagle Wing, a voyageur, stops off to visit Grey Stone on his way to this year's journey. Rabbit and Bear Paws travel with him to be carriers as Eagle Wing and the white fur traders make their trade journey. This book uses authentic details about traditions of the Ojibwa, the Mohawk, and other Nations.

Meyer, Marissa
Wires and nerve; Volume 1. Marissa Meyer; art by Doug Holgate with Stephen Gilpin. Feiwel & Friends 2017 240 p. Color; Illustration
Grades: 7 8 9 10 11 12   **741.5**
1. Cyborgs — Comic books, strips, etc.; 2. Imaginary wars and battles — Comic books, strips, etc.; 3. Androids — Fiction; 4. Imaginary wars and battles — Fiction
9781250078261, $21.99

LC 2016939440

"The 'Lunar Chronicles' continue in this entertaining graphic novel sequel to the existing volumes. This follow-up to the futuristic fairy-tale retellings centers on Iko, cyborg mechanic Cinder's best friend. Acclimating to her human body, the android is trying to help Queen Cinder of Luna ease tensions with Earth by hunting down rogue wolf-hybrid soldiers who were once enslaved by Cinder's evil stepmother and have now been banished to the green planet. Joined by other familiar characters (Cress, Winter, Thorne), loyal Iko defends the new queen against her enemies." (School Library Journal)

"Holgate's dynamic, stylized artwork handily balances the story's action and humor while bringing Meyer's world to vivid life." Pub Wkly
Followed by: Wires and nerve Volume 2, Going rogue

Wires and nerve; Volume 2: gone rogue. Marissa Meyer; illustrated by Stephen Gilpin. Feiwel and Friends 2018 324 p. Illustration
Grades: 7 8 9 10 11 12   **741.5; Fic**
1. Soldiers — Graphic novels; 2. Science fiction comic books, strips, etc.; 3. Imaginary wars and battles — Fiction
1250078288; 9781250078285, $21.99; 9781250078292

LC 2017944825

"Iko — an audacious android and best friend to the Lunar Queen Cinder — has been tasked with hunting down Alpha Lysander Steele, the leader of a rogue band of bioengineered wolf-soldiers who threaten to undo the tenuous peace agreement between Earth and Luna.... Steele and his soldiers plan to satisfy their monstrous appetites with a massacre of the innocent people of Earth." (Publisher's note)

"Iko continues to get more backstory and narrates various parts of the overall story. The pacing of volume two is slightly faster than volume one, as there is no need for introductions and set-up, and it builds to a satisfying ending for all characters involved." VOYA

Millar, Mark
Superman Adventures Vol. 3: Last Son of Krypton. written by Mark Millar, David Michelinie; illustrated by Aluir Amancio, Ron Boyd, Terry Austin, Mike Manley, Neil Vokes; colored by Marie Severin; lettered by Phil Felix; Superman created by Jerry Siegel and Joe Shuster. DC Comics 2006 112p. Illustration
Grades: 4 5 6 7 8 9   **741.5; Fic**
1. Graphic novels; 2. Superhero graphic novels; 3. Superman (Fictional character)

978-1-4012-1037-3, $6.99

Superman confronts his own past as he encounters survivors from Krypton, including his parents, Jor-El and Lara. Plus, someone wants to expose Clark's secret to Lex Luthor and the world. Will an encounter with Dr. Fate mean the end of Superman?

Miller, Frank
Batman: Year One. DC Comics 2005 168p. Illustration
Grades: 8 9 10 11 12 Adult   **741.5; Fic**
1. Batman (Fictional character); 2. Graphic novels; 3. Superhero graphic novels; 4. Catwoman (Fictional character)
978-1-4012-0752-6, $14.99

In the late-1980s, after publishing Miller's Batman: The Dark Knight Returns, DC realized they should remain faithful to the original roots of Batman. Miller then wrote this book, which reinvents the very early years of Batman as a superhero. In this book, Jim Gordon arrives in Gotham City to work in the police department and discovers the high level of corruption there; Batman encounters Selina, who becomes Catwoman, for the first time; and he develops some of the weapons he uses to fight crime. This new edition includes preliminary sketches and other extras.

Miller, John Jackson
Star Wars: Knights of the Old Republic Volume One: Commencement. Dark Horse Comics 2006 un Illustration
Grades: 8 9 10 11 12 Adult   **741.5; Fic**
1. Adventure graphic novels; 2. Graphic novels; 3. Science fiction graphic novels
978-1-59307-640-5, $18.95

Thousands of years before Luke Skywalker would destroy the Death Star in that fateful battle above Yavin 4, one lone Padawan would become a fugitive hunted by his own Masters, charged with murdering every one of his fellow Jedi-in-training. From criminals hiding out in the treacherous under-city of the planet Taris, to a burly, mysterious droid recovered from the desolate landscape of a cratered moon, Padawan Zayne Carrick will find unexpected allies in his desperate race to clear his name before the unmerciful authorities enact swift retribution upon him.

Millionaire, Tony
Sock Monkey: The Inches Incident. Dark Horse Comics 2007 88p. Illustration
Grades: 7 8 9 10 11 12 Adult   **741.5; Fic**
1. Fantasy graphic novels; 2. Graphic novels; 3. Toys — Graphic novels
978-1-59307-842-3, $12.95

Inches the doll was the cutest in the whole house. Loved by everyone, the world was Inches' oyster. Then one day something happened... The Sock Monkey and Mr. Crow became concerned for their diminutive friend, but by then it was too late. The truth sent the terrified Sock Monkey and Crow fleeing for their lives, for Inches had been invaded by a colony of evil ants. The sight of ants swarming over Inches and other things might be too creepy-crawly for some readers; the violence is aimed at toys rather than people, however, this is not a book for younger readers.

Sock Monkey: Uncle Gabby. Dark Horse Comics 2004 un Illustration
Grades: 8 9 10 11 12 Adult   **741.5; Fic**
1. Adventure graphic novels; 2. Graphic novels; 3. Humorous graphic novels
1-59307-026-8, $14.95

Uncle Gabby, the Sock Monkey, and Drinky the crow set off on a journey to solve the mystery of unremembered memories. This looks like a children's book, but the underlying bitter sweetness of a lost past and longing is more suited to teens and adults.

Miyazaki, Hayao
★ **Nausicaa** of the Valley of the Wind, Vol. 1. Viz Media 2004 136p. Illustration
Grades: 7 8 9 10 11 12   **741.5; Fic**
1. Graphic novels; 2. Manga; 3. Science fiction graphic novels; 4. Shonen manga
978-1-59116-408-1, $9.95
In a world devastated by ecological disaster and war, pockets of humanity exist in the vast wastelands. When some begin another war that could totally destroy the world, hope rests upon one young girl, Nausicaa, who can communicate with the strange creatures of the wasteland.
"Miyazaki is best known for his anime features...This tale contains all the classic elements of Miyazaki's films..." (VOYA)
This is a seven-volume series.

Miyazawa, Takeshi
Runaways Vol. 5: Escape to New York. Marvel Entertainment 2006 un Illustration
Grades: 8 9 10 11 12   **741.5; Fic**
1. Adventure graphic novels; 2. Graphic novels; 3. Runaways (Fictional characters); 4. Superhero graphic novels
0-7851-1901-9, $7.99
When a dangerous alien invades Los Angeles, the Runaways' own Karolina Dean may be the only hero in the Marvel Universe who can stop him...but at what cost? Then, the Runaways embark on a coast-to-coast adventure. When Clock is accused of a crime he didn't commit, the vigilante is forced to turn to the teenage Runaways for help. They go on a road trip to New York City. Meanwhile, back in LA, someone is tracking the teens, and it can't be good.

Mizuki, Shigeru
NonNonBa. Shigeru Mizuki; translation by Jocelyne Allen. Drawn & Quarterly 2012 408 p. Illustration; Color
Grades: 7 8 9 10 11 12 Adult   **741.5/952; 741.5**
1. Cartoonists — Japan — Biography — Comic books, strips, etc; 2. Grandmothers — Comic books, strips, etc; 3. Grandparent and child — Comic books, strips, etc; 4. Yokai (Japanese folklore) — Comic books, strips, etc; 5. Mizuki, Shigeru, 1922-2015 — Childhood and youth — Comic books, strips, etc; 6. Shonen manga; 7. Autobiographical graphic novels; 8. Folklore — Japan — Graphic novels; 9. Manga; 10. Grandparent-grandchild relationship — Graphic novels
1770460721; 9781770460720, $26.95
                                        LC 2012427667
This graphic novel, by Shigeru Mizuki, translated by Jocelyne Allen, is "a poetic memoir detailing his interest in yokai (spirit monsters). Mizuki's childhood experiences with yokai influenced the course of his life and oeuvre; he is now known as the forefather of yokai manga.... Mizuki explores the legacy left him by his childhood explorations of the spirit world, explorations encouraged by his grandmother, a grumpy old woman named NonNonBa." (Publisher's note)
Includes bibliographical references; Manga format; reads from back to front, right to left.

Mizuna, Tomomi
The **big** adventures of Majoko, volume 1. manga, Tomomi Mizuna; original work/supervision, Machiko Fuji; original illustrations, Mieko Yuchi. UDON Entertainment 2009 200p. Illustration
Grades: 3 4 5 6 7 8   **741; 741.5; Fic**
1. Fantasy graphic novels; 2. Graphic novels; 3. Manga; 4. Witches — Graphic novels; 5. Kodomo
978-1-89737-681-2 (pa), $7.99; 1-89737-681-2 (pa)

"Young witch Majoko sends her diary to the human world to find an adventuring partner and through it finds shy, quiet Nana. Together the two girls have a rollicking series of escapades.... Characters are simply drawn, but the backgrounds are nicely detailed and the plot elements are clearly thought out and easy to follow.... The content is very appropriate for the intended audience." Booklist
Volume 1 of a 5-volume series

Mizuto, Aqua
Yume Kira Dream Shoppe. Viz Media/Shojo Beat 2007 186p. Illustration
Grades: 7 8 9 10 11 12   **741.5; Fic**
1. Fantasy graphic novels; 2. Graphic novels; 3. Manga; 4. Romance graphic novels; 5. Shojo manga
978-1-4215-1173-3, $8.99
They say that any dream can be made true in exchange for something dear to you. The Yume Kira Dream Shoppe flies through the dusk sky as Rin the shopkeeper listens for wishes that travel on the wind. With the help of his assistant Alpha (a stuffed rabbit), Rin uses the magical wares of the Dream Shoppe to make desires a reality...But it costs the wisher something dear to the person. In the first story, a tree that has never bloomed falls in love with the music played by a young man, then the tree falls in love with the young man; she wishes for a human form so she can tell him how much his music means to her. Then she finds out he suffers from a disease that will take away the use of his hands, and she wants to change her wish...In the second story, Alpha is the one who makes the wish, and at the end of the story, he leaps off a bridge so the young girl who owned him won't be dependent on him; it's so much like a suicide that it might disturb younger readers who might otherwise enjoy this book.

Mochizuki, Jun
Pandora hearts; Volume 1. Jun Mochizuki; [translation, Tomo Kimura; lettering, Tania Biswas]. Yen Press 2013 187 p. Illustration
Grades: 8 9 10 11 12   **741.5; Fic**
1. False imprisonment — Comic books, strips, etc.; 2. Nobility — Fiction
0316076074; 9780316076074, $13
"The air of celebration surrounding fifteen-year-old Oz Vessalius's coming-of-age ceremony quickly turns to horror when he is condemned for a sin about which he knows nothing. He is thrown into an eternal, inescapable prison known as the Abyss from which there is no escape. There, he meets a young girl named Alice, who is not what she seems. Now that the relentless cogs of fate have begun to turn, do they lead only to crushing despair for Oz, or is there some shred of hope for him to grasp on to?" (Publisher's note)
Volume 1 of 24

Morinaga, Ai
My Heavenly Hockey Club Vol. 1. Ballantine Books/Del Rey Manga 2007 212p. Illustration
Grades: 8 9 10 11 12 Adult   **741.5; Fic**
1. Graphic novels; 2. Hockey — Graphic novels; 3. Humorous graphic novels; 4. Manga; 5. Shojo manga
978-0-345-49904-2, $10.95
Hana Suzuki loves only two things in life: eating and sleeping. So when handsome classmate Izumi Oda asks Hana, his major crush, to join the school hockey club, persuading her proves to be a difficult task. True, the Grand Hockey Club is full of boys, and all the boys are super-cute, but given a choice, Hana prefers a sizzling steak to a hot date. Then Izumi mentions the field trips to fancy resorts. Now Hana can't wait for the first away game, with its promise of delicious food and luxurious linens. Of

course there's also the getting up early, working hard, and playing well with others. How will Hana survive?

Morrison, Grant

All-Star Superman, Volume One. written by Grant Morrison; pencilled by Frank Quitely. DC Comics 2007 160p. Illustration

Grades: 8 9 10 11 12 Adult   **741.5; Fic**

1. Graphic novels; 2. Superhero graphic novels; 3. Superman (Fictional character)

978-1-4012-0914-8; 978-1-4012-1102-8 (pa), $12.99

Eisner Award: Best New Series (2006)

Writer Morrison and artist Quitely present several episodes in the life of the iconic superhero, Superman. When he saves a group of scientists from burning up in the sun, what no one realizes is that uber-villain Lex Luthor set up everything in order to kill Superman, who absorbed so much solar radiation that it is now slowly killing him. Once Superman learns that he is dying, he sets out to give Lois Lane a birthday she will never forget, by giving her his powers for one day. Then, when Jimmy Olsen takes charge of the science think tank P.R.O.J.E.C.T. for one day, they discover black kryptonite, which makes Superman turn evil. And, in his guise as Clark Kent, he interviews Lex Luthor in prison, but super-villain Parasite is taken from his shielded cell and begins to absorb Superman's powers, causing chaos.

Also available as a single volume collecting all 12 issues; Originally published as All-Star Superman issues #1-6; Volume 1 of 2

Superman - Action Comics; Volume 1. Grant Morrison, Rags Morales, Andy Kubert. DC Comics 2012 256 p.

Grades: 7 8 9 10 11 12 Adult   **Fic; 741.5/9411**

1. Superhero comic books, strips, etc.; 2. Adventure fiction; 3. Superman (Fictional character)

1401235468; 9781401235468, $24.99

LC 2012010313

This comic book anthology, by Grant Morrison, illustrated by Rags Morales, presents volume one of "The New 52" re-launch of the DC Comics Superman series. This collection includes the first eight issues of the series, depicting "humanity's first encounters with Superman, before he became one of the world's greatest super heroes." (Publisher's note)

Originally published in single magazine form in ACTION COMICS 1-8 — T.p. verso.

Mouly, Françoise

Big fat Little Lit. [edited by] Art Spiegelman and Francoise Mouly. Puffin 2006 144p. Illustration

Grades: 2 3 4 5 6 7 8   **741.5; Fic**

1. Folklore — Graphic novels; 2. Graphic novels

0-14-240706-2, $14.99

This volume collects all three previously published Little Lit books: Little Lit: Once Upon a Time, Little Lit: Strange Stories for Strange Kids, and Little Lit: It Was a Dark and Silly Night. Many comics creators and children's book writers and illustrators contributed stories, including Ian Falconer, Daniel Clowes, Maurice Sendak, David Sedaris, Chris Ware, Jules Feiffer, Barbara McClintock, Crockett Johnson, J. Otto Siebold, Neil Gaiman, Art Spiegelman, and Lemony Snicket.

Myers, Walter Dean

Monster: a graphic novel. by Walter Dean Myers; adapted for graphic novel by Guy A. Sims; illustrated by Dawud Anyabwile. HarperTeen, an imprint of HarperCollinsPublishers 2015 160 p. Illustration

Grades: 8 9 10 11 12   **741.5; Fic**

1. African Americans — Fiction; 2. Graphic novels; 3. Prisons — Fiction; 4. Self-perception — Fiction; 5. Trials (Murder) — Fiction; 6. Myers, Walter Dean, 1937- Monster — Adaptations; 7. Bildungsromans

— Graphic novels; 8. Teenagers — Graphic novels; 9. Trials (Homicide) — Fiction

0062275003; 9780062274991; 9780062275004, $17.99

LC 2013043138

This graphic novel by Guy Sims, illustrated by Dawud Anyabwile, and adapted from the novel by Walter Dean Myers, is a "coming-of-age story about Steve Harmon, a teenager awaiting trial for a murder and robbery. As Steve acclimates to juvenile detention and goes to trial, he envisions the ordeal as a movie." (Publisher's note)

"Using panels like a filmstrip, Sims and Anyabwile achieve several remarkably cinematic effects: alternating grids and splash pages captures the tension between close-up and long shots; the use of jittery lettering and uneven word balloons injects deeper anxiety into the sound design; having a jury view the events recounted in testimony as a movie audience creates incisive visual metaphors." Booklist

Naifeh, Ted

★ **Courtney** Crumrin and the night things. Oni Press 2005 128p. Illustration

Grades: 5 6 7 8 9 10 11 12

741.5; Fic

1. Fantasy graphic novels; 2. Graphic novels; 3. Supernatural graphic novels

1-929998-60-0, $11.95

Courtesy of Oni Press

Courtney's social-climber parents take her out of her comfortable city neighborhood and move into an upscale suburb to live with her creepy Great-Uncle Aloysius in her spooky old house. She has to face uppity classmates and things that go bump in the night; but she ends up making friends with the spooks! Courtney deals with magic and the supernatural, but she's no altruistic Harry Potter; in this series, magic sometimes bites hard.

Other titles in this series are: Courtney Crumrin and the coven of Mystics (2003); Courtney Crumrin in the twilight kingdom (2004); Courtney Crumrin's monstrous holiday (2009); Courtney Crumrin: the witch next door (2014); Courtney Crumrin: the final spell (2014)

Courtney Crumrin and the fire thief's tale. Oni Press 2007 62p. Illustration

Grades: 7 8 9 10 11 12 Adult

741.5; Fic

1. Fantasy graphic novels; 2. Graphic novels; 3. Horror graphic novels; 4. Werewolves — Graphic novels

978-1-932664-85-0, $5.95

Courtney travels with Uncle Aloysius to Romania, where they stay with Alexi Markovic, an old friend of Uncle Aloysius. Things aren't quite right there, though; the townspeople hunt wolves at night unnatural wolves, werewolves. Markovic's daughter has fallen in love with a Romany man even though her father has arranged her betrothal to an influential man in town. Courtney gets involved against Uncle Aloysius' wishes, and learns more than she wanted about werewolf origins and thwarted love.

Courtesy of Oni Press

★ **Courtney** Crumrin in the Twilight Kingdom; 3. Oni Press 2004 un Illustration

Grades: 7 8 9 10 11 12   **741.5; Fic**

1. Fantasy graphic novels; 2. Graphic novels; 3. Magic — Graphic novels; 4. Supernatural graphic novels

Courtesy of Oni Press

1-932664-01-7, $11.95

Courtney has changed schools yet again, but this time she's in the Coven's special class for magical studies. But when a student spell goes wrong and leaves one of her classmates cursed, can Courtney lead the kids into Goblin Town and find a cure, or will misfortune follow the group straight to the Twilight Kingdom? And the law keeper, Templeton, intends to stop Courtney from what he considers her most terrible crime yet.

★ **Courtney** Crumrin's monstrous holiday; 4. Oni Press, Inc. 2009 192p. Illustration
Grades: 7 8 9 10 11 12   **741.5; Fic**
1. Fantasy graphic novels; 2. Graphic novels; 3. Horror graphic novels
978-1-934964-11-8, $11.95

Courtney accompanies Uncle Aloysius on his trip through Europe, and their first stop is in Romania. He has come to visit with an old friend, Professor Alexi Markovic, but they soon find they have stumbled into a family turmoil. Morkovic's daughter Magda loves a young Gypsy, but the local bully and noble (even if he has denounced his title), Petru has claimed Magda as his betrothed. Courtney learns that some of the wolves in the woods surrounding Markovic's house are werewolves, and Petru and his men hunt them, convinced that they are members of the Gypsy group in town. Courtney thinks she's helping a romantic young couple only to be disillusioned by Magda's attitude. Then, in Krumrhein, Germany, she meets a handsome young man named Wolfgang and maybe falls a little in love with him. Which turns out to be a bad thing, for Wolfgang is a vampire. Aloysius had come there for he has learned he has cancer and doesn't want to die; but when he discovers that something is draining the life blood from Courtney, he knows he needs to save her.

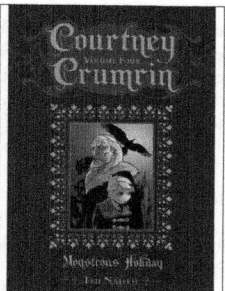

Courtesy of Oni Press

Nakahara, Aya
Love*Com Vol. 1. story and art by Aya Nakahara; [translation & English adaptation, Pookie Rolf]. Viz Media/Shojo Beat 2007 un Illustration
Grades: 8 9 10 11 12   **741.5; Fic**
1. Graphic novels; 2. Humorous graphic novels; 3. Manga; 4. Romance graphic novels; 5. Shojo manga
978-1-4215-1343-0, $8.99

Risa Koizumi is the tallest girl in class, and the last thing she wants is the humiliation of standing next to Atsushi Otoni, the shortest guy. Fate and the whole school have other ideas, and the two find themselves cast as the unwilling stars of a bizarre romantic comedy duo. Rather than bow to the inevitable, Risa and Atsushi join forces to pursue their true objects of affection. But in the quest for love, will their budding friendship become something more complex?
First published 2001 in Japan; Volume 1 of 17

Nakamura, Yoshiki
★ **Skip** Beat! Vol. 1. Viz Media/Shojo Beat 2006 un Illustration
Grades: 8 9 10 11 12   **741.5; Fic**
1. Entertainers — Graphic novels; 2. Graphic novels; 3. Humorous graphic novels; 4. Manga; 5. Shojo manga
978-1-4215-0585-5, $8.99

Kyoko Mogami has followed her true love, Sho, to Tokyo, where he wants to become an idol, a pop star. Idols can be pop singers or actors, and young hopefuls audition at talent agencies hoping to become the next big star. Sho succeeds, then he tosses Kyoko aside, saying that she's boring. Now Kyoko wants revenge, and thinks the best way to get it is to become an idol and eclipse Sho; but the talent agency rejects her audition. Is revenge an appropriate motivation? Kyoko doesn't care.
Nakamura uses different visual techniques to show characters' feelings, and with Kyoko's emotions in particular, especially her anger.
Volume 1 of 36

Naruse, Kaori
Pretear, Volume 1. ADV Manga 2004 188p. Illustration
Grades: 6 7 8 9 10 11 12
741.5; Fic
1. Fantasy graphic novels; 2. Graphic novels; 3. Manga; 4. Shojo manga
1-4139-0144-1, $9.99

Naruse combines elements of fairy tales such as Cinderella and Snow White with fantasy adventure in this four-volume series.

"Himeno's alcoholic novelist father marries a rich businesswoman with two snobby daughters. They treat [Himeno] terribly, of course, but she...is goodhearted, virtuous, and patient. Himeno...[meets] seven knights who use leafe, a substance emitted by everything in the natural world. The Princess of Disaster wants to destroy all the leafe so the world will die. The knights need Himeno to become the Prétear so they can combine with her and combat the princess." SLJ

Courtesy of ADV Manga

Neel, Julien
Down in the dumps. written and illustrated by Julien Neel; translation by Carol Klio Burrell. Graphic Universe 2012 48 p. (Lou!)
Grades: 4 5 6
741.5
1. Best friends — Fiction; 2. Dating (Social customs) — Fiction; 3. Friendship — Fiction; 4. Graphic novels; 5. Junior high schools — Fiction; 6. Mothers and daughters — Fiction; 7. Schools — Fiction; 8. School stories — Graphic novels
076138779X; 9780761387794, $27.93
LC 2012003973

This book is the third in Julien Neel's Lou! series. Here, "Lou is depressed because the boy of her dreams has moved away. To make matters worse, her mother, an aspiring author, has a serious love interest that makes her even more scatterbrained than usual. Lou feels quite left out as she heads off to the first day of school, only to discover that she and her best friend are not in the same class." (School Library Journal)

Courtesy of Lerner Publishing Group

The **perfect** summer. [story and art by] Julien Neel; [translation by Carol Klio Burrell]. Graphic Universe 2012 48 p. (Lou!)

Courtesy of Lerner Publishing Group

Grades: 4 5 6   **741.5**
1. Dating (Social customs) — Fiction; 2. Graphic novels; 3. Mothers and daughters — Fiction; 4. Summer — Fiction; 5. Vacations — Fiction; 6. Adolescence — Graphic novels; 7. Vacations — Graphic novels
0761387803; 9780761387800, $27.93

LC 2012002988

This book is the fourth in Julien Neel's Lou! series. Here, "she vacations with a friend at an amazing beach house while her mother is on a book tour. The friendship drama [of junior high school] has settled into a nice group of girls she enjoys being with. That just leaves the boy situation, which is complicated, since Tristan is back in her life." (School Library Journal)

Neri, G.
★ **Yummy:** the last days of a Southside Shorty. by G. Neri; illustrated by Randy DuBurke. Lee & Low Books 2010 94p. Illustration
Grades: 8 9 10 11 12   **741; 741.5; 92**
978-1-58430-267-4 (pa), $16.95; 1-58430-267-4 (pa)

LC 2006-17771

"In 1994, in the Roseland neighborhood of Chicago's South Side, a 14-year-old girl named Shavon Dean was killed by a stray bullet during a gang shooting. Her killer, Robert "Yummy" Sandifer, was 11 years old. Neri recounts Yummy's three days on the run from police (and, eventually, his own gang) through the eyes of Roger, a fictional classmate of Yummy's. Roger grapples with the unanswerable questions behind Yummy's situation, with the whys and hows of a failed system, a crime-riddled neighborhood, and a neglected community." (Publishers Weekly)

Nicholson, Hope
★ **MOONSHOT:** The Indigenous Comics Collection. edited by Hope Nicholson. Alternate History Comics Inc 2015 176 p. Illustration
Grades: 6 7 8 9 10 11 12 Adult   **741.5**
1. American literature — Native American authors; 2. Graphic novels
0987715259; 9780987715258, $17.99

This comic anthology, edited by Hope Nicholson, "from traditional stories to exciting new visions of the future,...presents some of the finest comic book and graphic novel work in North America. The traditional stories presented in the book are with the permission from the elders in their respective communities, making this a truly genuine, never-before-seen publication." (Publisher's note)

"This collection of folklore from a powerhouse team of Native authors, including Buffy Sainte-Marie and Richard Van Camp, will wow readers with traditional and futuristic tales based on tribal-specific cultural teachings.... The full-page illustrations in some selections and the bright colors in others add depth and understanding to the narratives. The artwork is as diverse as the stories collected." SLJ

Nobleman, Marc Tyler
★ **Bill** the boy wonder: the secret co-creator of Batman. Marc Tyler Nobleman; illustrated by Ty Templeton. Charlesbridge 2012 48 p.
Grades: 6 7 8   **741.5; 741.5/973; 92**
1. Cartoonists — United States — Biography; 2. Batman (Comic strip); 3. Finger, Bill, 1914-1974; 4. Superhero comic books, strips, etc.; 5. Batman (Fictional character)
1580892892; 9781580892896, $17.95

LC 2011025695

Author Marc Tyler Nobleman discusses the creation of Batman, credited to Bob Kane. "A struggling writer named Bill Finger...helped invent Batman, from concept to costume to character. He dreamed up Batman's haunting origins and his colorful nemeses. Despite his brilliance, Bill worked in obscurity. It was only after his death that fans went to bat for

Bill, calling for acknowledgment that he was co-creator of Batman." (Publisher's note)

Nolen-Weathington, Eric
Modern Masters volume twenty-five: Jeff Smith. Twomorrows Publishing 2011 117p. Illustration
Grades: 6 7 8 9 10 11 12 Adult
741.5
1. Artists; 2. Authors; 3. Cartoonists; 4. Comic books, strips, etc. — History and criticism; 5. Graphic novels — History and criticism; 6. Smith, Jeff
978-1-60549-024-3, $15.95

Courtesy of Twomorrows Publishing

This volume in the Modern Masters series focuses on Jeff Smith, creator of Bone. In an interview that covers his childhood, college career, and early work before becoming a cartoonist, Smith talks about how he created Fone Bone when he was just five years old. The artwork in the book includes young Smith's hand-created comics from his childhood. Only a couple of "crap — s slip out. The book includes mostly black and white art and photographs, with a few color illustrations from the Bone comics.

North, Ryan
★ **Adventure** Time. Ryan North; illustrated by Braden Lamb and Shelli Paroline. Simon & Schuster 2012 128 p. Color; Illustration
Grades: 3 4 5 6 7 8 9 10   **741.5**
1. Imaginary places; 2. Adventure fiction
1608862801; 9781608862801, $14.99

"The totally algebraic adventures of Finn and Jake have come to the comic book page! The Lich, a super-lame, SUPER-SCARY skeleton dude, has returned to the the Land of Ooo, and he's bent on total destruction! Luckily, Finn and Jake are on the case...but can they succeed against their most destructive foe yet?" (Publisher's note)

"The comic series has been every bit as good as the show, with epic magic battles with an evil Lich, a multi-part time travel story, and a host of backup strips by some of the best indie cartoonists out there." Comics Alliance

Volume 1 of 17

★ The **unbeatable** Squirrel Girl; Volume 1: Squirrel power!. Ryan North; illustrated by Erica Henderson. Marvel Enterprises 2015 136 p. Color; Illustration
Grades: 7 8 9 10 11 12 Adult   **741.5**
1. Squirrel Girl (Fictional character); 2. Superheroes — Fiction; 3. Female superhero graphic novels; 4. Squirrels — Fiction
0785197028; 9780785197027, $15.99
Eisner Nominee: Best New Series (2016); Eisner Award: Best Publication for Teens (2017)

"Supervillains and criminals meet their match with Tony Stark's friend Squirrel Girl, aka Doreen Green, a college freshman with the appearance, speed, and agility of a squirrel. Fitting in proves to be challenging, as normal girls do not talk to or have a squirrel sidekick, nor do they have super strength. Then there is Squirrel Girl's roommate, who has a tough exterior and is obsessed with knitting and her cat. Luckily, Squirrel Girl has a knack for winning people over. When Galactus threatens Earth, the heroine must rely on more than strength to defeat the Devourer of Worlds. She may have extraordinary strength, an army of squirrels at her disposal, a collection of Deadpool villain trading cards, and nut-inspired catchphrases, but it is her ability to form connections with people that proves to be her most powerful asset.:" (School Library Journal)

Contains material originally published in magazine form as The Unbeatable Squirrel Girl #1-4 and Marvel Super-Heroes #8; Volume 1 of an ongoing series

Nybakken, Scott

Batman Adventures Vol. 2: Shadows & Masks. DC Comics 2004 112p. Illustration

Grades: 4 5 6 7 8 9   **741.5; Fic**

1. Batman (Fictional characters); 2. Graphic novels; 3. Superhero graphic novels

978-1-4012-0330-2, $6.95

A deadly new gang is threatening Gotham City, and it's up to the Dark Knight Detective to take it down, from the inside. He goes on an undercover mission in this volume.

Nykko

The **elsewhere** chronicles book two: the shadow spies. Lerner Publishing Group/Graphic Universe 2009 48p. Illustration

Grades: 4 5 6 7 8

741.5; Fic

1. Adventure graphic novels; 2. Fantasy graphic novels; 3. Graphic novels; 4. Horror graphic novels

978-0-7613-4460-5, $27.93;

978-0-7613-3964-9 (pa) $6.95

LC 2008-39443

Courtesy of Lerner Publishing Group

When the Shadow Door shatters, the passageway closes and Rebecca and Max are trapped in Elsewhere; they set out to find another way home. The problem is that wherever there is darkness, the Shadow Spies hunt them. Back in Grandpa Gabe's house, Noah and Theo work to find a replacement lens for the movie projector so they can get through and rescue their friends. Meanwhile, the police think Max and Rebecca have been kidnapped, and the boys have to work around the investigation. It's clear to the kids that Grandpa Gabe had explored Elsewhere, and his notes have left clues for them; Max and Rebecca also meet people who have been fighting a long war against the Shadows and who know Grandpa Gabe. Whatever else they do, they must keep the Shadow Spies away from Earth.

Originally published in France as Les Enfants d'ailleurs, winner of the 2007 Lyon Festival Youth Prize.

The **elsewhere** chronicles, book three: the master of shadows. Lerner Publishing Group/Graphic Universe 2009 48p. Illustration

Grades: 4 5 6 7 8

741.5; Fic

1. Fantasy graphic novels; 2. Graphic novels; 3. Horror graphic novels

978-0-7613-4461-2, $27.93;

978-0-7613-4744-6 (pa) $6.95

LC 2008-39444

Courtesy of Lerner Publishing Group

Theo and Noah have joined Rebecca and Max in Elsewhere, but they are on the run, pursued by the Master of Shadows and menaced at all times by the Shadow Spies. All they have to guide them are the strange and cryptic clues left by Grandpa Gabe, and they see their friends in this strange world pay the ultimate price while trying to stop the Shadows. How far must the four friends go, and what will it cost them, to save their own world?

Originally published in France as Les Enfants d'ailleurs, winner of the 2007 Lyon Festival Youth Prize.

The **tower** of shadows. by Nykko, illustrated by Bannister; translation by Carol Klio Burrell]. Graphic Universe 2013 48 p. (The ElseWhere chronicles)

Grades: 4 5 6 7

741.5; Fic

1. Graphic novels; 2. Horror stories; 3. Grandfathers — Fiction; 4. Magic — Fiction; 5. Imaginary places

1467712337; 9781467712330, $27.93

LC 2013000317

Courtesy of Lerner Publishing Group

In this graphic novel by Nykko, "the time has come to confront the Master of Shadows. Rebecca, Max, and Theo must follow Grandpa Gabe into the heart of the Master's realm, the Tower of Shadows. But can Grandpa Gabe be trusted? There's a reason he's so familiar with the dark powers that rule Elsewhere: he created them. Grandpa Gabe's plan might just be a suicide mission, but it's their last chance to save our world — and Rebecca's life." (Publisher's note)

"Bannister's atmospheric illustrations feature expressive characters placed in finely detailed, eerily organic landscapes or dim subterranean reaches inhabited by menacing swirls of shadow." Kirkus

O'Connor, George

★ **Aphrodite:** Goddess of love. George O'Connor. First Second 2014 76 p. Color; Illustration (Olympians)

Grades: 6 7 8 9   **741.5**

1. Aphrodite (Greek deity); 2. Graphic novels; 3. Gods and goddesses — Fiction; 4. Aphrodite (Greek deity)

1596437391; 1596439475; 9781596437395, $9.99; 9781596439474, $16.99

This graphic novel, volume six of the Olympians series on Greek mythology, by George O'Connor, "turns the spotlight on Aphrodite, the goddess of love.... O'Connor tackles the story of the Aphrodite from her dramatic birth (emerging from sea-foam) to her role in the Trojan War." (Publisher's note)

"Like the prior volumes, this book injects the mythology with an accessible modern sensibility through its colorful, action-packed graphic storytelling." Horn Book

Includes bibliographical references; Other titles in this series are:Zeus (2010); Athena (2010); Hera (2011); Hades (2012); Poseidon (2013); Ares (2015)

★ **Apollo:** the brilliant one. George O'Connor. First Second 2016 80 p. Color; Illustration

Grades: 5 6 7 8 9 10   **292.2**

1. Gods, Greek; 2. Mythology; 3. Greek mythology; 4. Apollo (Greek deity)

1626720169; 9781626720152, $9.99; 9781626720169

LC 2015014172

O'Connor "continues to turn his extensive knowledge of the original Greek myths into...graphic novel storytelling. Mighty Apollo is known by all as the god of the sun, but there's more to this Olympian than a bright smile and a shining chariot." (Publisher's note)

A Neal Porter Book.

★ **Ares:** bringer of war. George O'Connor. First Second Books 2015 80 p. Color; Illustration (Olympians)

Grades: 4 5 6 7 8 9   **741.5**

   1. Ares (Greek deity) — Comic books, strips, etc; 2. Trojan War — Graphic novels; 3. Greek mythology — Graphic novels

1626720134; 1626720142; 9781626720138; 9781626720145, $16.99

LC 2014041225

This graphic novel by George O'Connor "continues in the tenth year of the fabled Trojan War where two infamous gods of war go to battle. The spotlight is thrown on Ares, god of war, and primarily focuses on his battle with the clever and powerful Athena. As the battle culminates and the gods try to one-up each other to win, the human death toll mounts." (Publisher's note)

"In this nuanced, multilayered view of the usually vilified bringer of war, O'Connor continues his exceptional graphic novel series about the Greek gods.... The author's extensive notes amusingly explain connections to The Odyssey, The Aeneid, and the series' previous works." SLJ

A Neal Porter Book.; Other titles in this series are: Athena: Grey-eyed Goddess (2010); Zeus: King of the Gods (2010); Hera: The Goddess and her Glory (2011); Hades: Lord of the Dead (2012); Poseidon: Earth Shaker (2013); Aphrodite: Goddess of Love (2014)

★ **Artemis:** wild goddess of the hunt. George O'Connor. First Second 2017 76 p. Illustration (Olympians)

Grades: 4 5 6 7 8   **292.2/114; 292.2; 741.5**

   1. Artemis (Greek deity); 2. Greek mythology

9781626725218, $17.99; 9781626725225

LC 2016938491

In this book, by George O'Connor, "Artemis, Goddess of the Hunt, finds power through her skilled hunting ability and mighty bow. She slays those who wish to do harm to the innocent and takes care of the young and helpless. She protects women and young girls, helps in childbirth, soothes, and is unrivaled in her hunting abilities." (Publisher's note)

"Though the author is true to the original tales...he injects a feminist perspective, emphasizing Artemis's strong relationships with other women." SLJ

Includes bibliographical references.

★ **Athena:** grey-eyed goddess. First Second 2010 76p. Illustration

Grades: 5 6 7 8   **741; 741.5**

   1. Athena (Greek deity); 2. Classical mythology

978-1-59643-649-7, $16.99; 1-59643-649-2; 978-1-59643-432-5 (pa), $9.99; 1-59643-432-5 (pa)

This tells "five myths involving Athena, including complementary (or conflicting) stories of how she gained the Pallas moniker along with quick treatments of Perseus and Medusa and the weaver Arachne." Booklist

"O'Connor's drawings, full of energetic diagonals and expressive faces, are nicely balanced by spare settings and minimalistic backgrounds. A sophisticated color palette, full of midtones and subtle contrasts, and panel layouts that vary from page to page further distinguish the art. The author's affection for his subject is evident in a chatty note. Profiles of major characters, notes, and discussion questions appear in addition to the usual back matter. An exceptional graphic novel." SLJ

★ **Hades.** First Second 2012 76p Color illustration (Olympians)

Grades: 5 6 7 8 9   **741.5; 398.2093; 398.2093801**

   1. Hades (Greek deity) — Comic books, strips, etc.; 2. Mother-daughter relationship — Fiction; 3. Graphic novels; 4. Greek mythology

9781596437616

LC 2011017563

In this book, a "tempestuous mother-daughter relationship makes up the centerpiece of [author and illustrator George] O'Connor's...Olympian portrait. Snatched down to the Underworld in the wake of a screaming fight with her mother Demeter,...raging adolescent Kore (meaning, generically

'The Maiden') initially gives her quiet, gloomy captor Hades a hard time too. After grabbing the opportunity to give herself a thorough makeover and changing her name to Persephone ('Bringer of Destruction'), though, she takes charge of her life — so surely that, when offered the opportunity to return to her remorseful mom, she lies about having eaten those pomegranate seeds so she can spend half of each year as Queen of the Dead." (Kirkus)

Includes bibliographical references.

★ **Hera:** the goddess and her glory. First Second 2011 76p. Illustration

Grades: 5 6 7 8   **741; 741.5**

   978-1-59643-433-2, $9.99; 1-59643-433-3

★ **Hermes:** tales of the trickster. George O'Connor. First Second 2018 76 p. Color; Illustration (Olympians)

Grades: 4 5 6 7 8   **741.5; 292.2**

   1. Greek mythology — Fiction; 2. Gods and goddesses — Fiction

9781626725249; 9781626725256, $10.99; 9781626725263

LC 2017941162

In this book in the Olympians series, author "George O'Connor delves into the myth of Hermes, the trickster god. From his infancy, when he bewitches animals and bends them to his will (stealing a herd of Apollo's prize cattle in the bargain), to his adolescence and adulthood when he becomes father to the equally mischievous Pan, Hermes's story is wildly entertaining as he brings a little bit of chaos to everything he touches or creates." (Publisher's note)

"O'Connor illustrates the speedy god's mischievousness with cartoon slapstick flair, playing up his witty repartee and sly, impish appeal. O'Connor's artwork is as solid as ever, with muscle-bound deities and grotesque monsters aplenty." Booklist

Includes bibliographical references

★ **Poseidon:** earth shaker. by George O'Connor. Roaring Brook Press 2012 80 p. (Olympians)

Grades: 4 5 6   **741.5/973**

   1. Greek mythology — Graphic novels

1596437383; 1596438282; 9781596437388, $9.99; 9781596438286, $16.99

LC 2011052219

This graphic novel, by George O'Connor, is part of the "Olympians" series, featuring the mythology of the Greco-Roman gods. "The fifth installment of the Olympians series of graphic novels...turns the spotlight on that most mysterious and misunderstood of the Greek gods.... Thrill to such famous myths as Theseus and the Minotaur, Odysseus and Polyphemos, and the founding of Athens — and learn how the tempestuous Poseidon became the King of the Seas." (Publisher's note)

Includes bibliographical references and index; A Neal Porter book.

★ **Zeus:** king of the gods. First Second 2010 76p. Illustration

Grades: 5 6 7 8   **741.5**

   978-1-59643-431-8, $16.99; 1-59643-625-5; 978-1-59643-432-5 (pa), $9.99; 1-59643-431-7 (pa)

"O'Connor unveils his new Olympians graphic-novel series with this story of the daddy of Greek gods. Most immediately striking about this, aside from the exciting artwork, is the care O'Connor takes to visualize the creation myth that begins with Gaea creating and taking as a husband the sky, Ouranos. Their children the Titans and other proto-Olympian entities are often neglected or at best murkily covered, but here they're vividly portrayed with all the magnificence of their beyond-good-and-evil power. After this breathtaking and lengthy sequence, Zeus enters the scene to grow from a feisty nymph-needling youth to a lightning bolt-wielding avenger." (Booklist)

Other titles in this series are:Athena, grey-eyed goddess (2010);Hera, the goddess and her glory (2011);Hades, lord of the dead

(2012);Poseidon, earth shaker (2013);Aphrodite, goddess of love (2013);Ares, bringer of war (2015); Apollo, the brilliant one (2016); Artemis, wild goddess of the hunt (2017); Hermes, tales of the trickster (2018)

O'Neill, Katie

★ **Princess** princess ever after. Katie O'Neill; [edited by] Ari Yarwood. Oni Press 2016 56 p. Color; Illustration

Grades: 4 5 6 7 8

741.5; Fic

1. Princesses — Juvenile fiction; 2. Fantasy graphic novels; 3. Magic — Fiction; 4. LGBT people — Fiction

1620103400; 9781620103401, $12.99

LC 2016931407

Courtesy of Oni Press

In this book, by Katie O'Neill, "when the heroic princess Amira rescues the kind-hearted princess Sadie from her tower prison, neither expects to find a true friend in the bargain. Yet as they adventure across the kingdom, they discover that they bring out the very best in the other person. They'll need to join forces and use all the know-how, kindness, and bravery they have in order to defeat their greatest foe yet: a jealous sorceress." (Publisher's note)

"The princesses' affection for each other deepens with every challenge — and every round of snappy banter — and when wedding bells ring, they're for a couple who truly know and have freely chosen one another. O'Neill delivers an alternative fairy tale that challenges conventions with every twist of the plot but doesn't veer into heavy-handed preachiness that pulls readers out of the story." Kirkus

★ The **tea** dragon society. written & illustrated by Katie O'Neill. Oni Press 2017 72 p. Color; Illustration

Grades: 4 5 6 7 8

741.5

1. Blacksmithing — Fiction; 2. Dragons — Fiction; 3. Tea — Fiction

1620104415; 9781620104415, $17.99

LC 2017936880

Eisner Award: Best Publication for Kids (2018)

This book, by Katie O'Neill, "follows the story of Greta, a blacksmith apprentice, and the people she meets as she becomes entwined in the enchanting world of tea

Courtesy of Oni Press

dragons. After discovering a lost tea dragon in the marketplace, Greta learns about the dying art form of tea dragon care-taking from the kind tea shop owners, Hesekiel and Erik. As she befriends them and their shy ward, Minette, Greta sees how the craft enriches their lives — and eventually her own." (Publisher's note)

"In alluringly hued, manga-inspired illustrations, O'Neill's diverse characters distray an array of different skin colors, orientations, and abilities. Helping to add depth to the worldbuilding is an excerpt from a fictional tome that explains the history of tea dragons and their individual characteristics. Undeniably whimsical and extremely cute." Kirkus

Oakley, Mark

Thieves & kings. [by Mark Oakley]. I Box Pub 1998 154p. Illustration

Grades: 4 5 6 7 8 9 10 11 12

741.5; Fic

1. Adventure graphic novels; 2. Fantasy graphic novels; 3. Graphic novels

0-9681025-0-6, $18.95

LC 2003-446777

In a story that mixes pages of text with pages of comic book art, the reader meets the young thief Rubel, who has returned home from a long voyage to find things no longer as they were. He has to deal with soldiers and pirates, princes and princesses, a strange young wizard, and a mysterious Shadow Lady.

Originally published as individual issues of the Thieves & kings comic series, beginning in 1994; Volume 1 of 5

Oda, Eiichiro

★ **One** Piece Volume 1. story and art by Eiichiro Oda; [English adaptation by Lance Caselman]. Viz Media/Shonen Jump 2003 216p. Illustration

Grades: 8 9 10 11 12 Adult

741.5; Fic

1. Adventure graphic novels; 2. Fantasy graphic novels; 3. Graphic novels; 4. Manga; 5. Shonen manga

1-56931-901-4, $7.95

Monkey D. Luffy's main ambition is to become a pirate, inspired by listening to the tales of the buccaneer "Red-Haired" Shanks. When he accidentally eats the Gum-Gum Fruit, it gives him strange powers to stretch like rubber, but doing so also invokes the fruit's curse: anybody who consumes it can never learn to swim. Nevertheless, Monkey and his crewmate Roronoa Zoro, master of the three-sword fighting style, sail the Seven Seas of swashbuckling adventure in search of the elusive treasure "One Piece." As the series goes on, Luffy gains more crew and they encounter sea monsters, far away kingdoms, cloud island, and super powered pirates of every shape, size, and description — which means lots of epic and comical fight scenes.

Volume 1 of an ongoing series

Ohba, Tsugumi

Bakuman; Volume 1: Dreams and reality. story by Tsugumi Ohba; art by Takeshi Obata; [translation & adaptation, Tetsuichiro Miyaki]. VIZ Media 2010 194 p. Illustration

Grades: 7 8 9 10 11 12

741.5; Fic

1. Shonen manga; 2. Manga; 3. Cartoonists — Graphic novels

1421535130; 9781421535135, $9.99

"Average student Moritaka Mashiro enjoys drawing for fun. When his classmate and aspiring writer Akito Takagi discovers his talent, he begs Moritaka to team up with him as a manga-creating duo. But what exactly does it take to make it in the manga-publishing world?" (Publisher's note)

Volume 1 of 20

Oima, Yoshitoki

★ A **silent** voice; Volume 1. Yoshitoki Oima; translation, lettering, Steven LeCroy. Kodansha 2015 186 p. Illustration

Grades: 7 8 9 10

741.5; Fic

1. Deaf children; 2. Bullies — Graphic novels; 3. School stories — Graphic novels; 4. Shonen manga

163236056X; 9781632360564, $10.99

Eisner Nominee: Best U.S. Edition of International Material — Asia (2016)

"Shoya is a bully. When Shoko, a girl who can't hear, enters his elementary school class, she becomes their favorite target.... But the children's cruelty goes too far. Shoko is forced to leave the school, and Shoya ends up shouldering all the blame. Six years later, the two meet again. Can Shoya make up for his past mistakes, or is it too late?" (Publisher's note)

Volume 1 of 7

ONE (Manga author)

★ **One-punch** man; Volume 1. story by One; art by Yusuke Murata. Viz 2015 189 p. Illustration

Grades: 8 9 10 11 12 Adult   **741.5; Fic**

1. Seinen manga; 2. Graphic novels; 3. Manga; 4. Superheroes

1421585642; 9781421585642, $9.99

Eisner Nominee: Best U.S. Edition of International Material — Asia (2015)

"Nothing about Saitama passes the eyeball test when it comes to superheroes, from his lifeless expression to his bald head to his unimpressive physique. However, this average-looking guy has a not-so-average problem — he just can't seem to find an opponent strong enough to take on! Every time a promising villain appears, he beats the snot out of 'em with one punch!" (Publisher's note)

"The story is fast-paced, humorous, and entertaining in a way that looks and feels like an action movie." SLJ

Volume 1 of an ongoing series

Osborne, Melissa Jane

The **Wendy** project. written and created by Melissa Jane Osborne; art, colors, and letters by Veronica Fish. Papercutz 2017 96 p. Color; Illustration

Grades: 8 9 10 11 12 Adult

741.5

1. Teenage automobile drivers — Accidents; 2. Graphic novels; 3. Teenage girls — Fiction; 4. Fantasy fiction

1629917699; 9781629917696, $12.99

Courtesy of NBM Publishing

In this graphic novel, by Melissa Jane Osborne, illustrated by Veronica Fish, "Wendy Davies crashes her car into a lake...with her two younger brothers in the backseat. When she wakes in the hospital, she is told that her youngest brother...is dead. Wendy...[insists] that Michael is alive and in the custody of a mysterious flying boy. Placed in a new school, Wendy negotiates fantasy and reality as students and adults around her resemble characters from Neverland." (Publisher's note)

"This unexpected gem stands out among latter-day versions of Peter Pan thanks to its embrace of genuine emotion and psychological gravity." LJ

Osborne, Wayne

FX. story and script by Wayne Osborne; pencils, inks, lettering, colors, by John Byrne. IDW Publishing 2008 160p. Illustration

Grades: 7 8 9 10 11 12 Adult   **741.5; Fic**

1. Adventure graphic novels; 2. Graphic novels; 3. Humorous graphic novels; 4. Superhero graphic novels

978-1-60010-274-5, $19.99

Teenager Tom Talbot was playing with his best friend when Jack accidentally hit Tom so hard he went into a coma. When Tom recovers, he discovers that he's got the power to make what he imagines be real; he discovers this when they're playing around in an alley and Tom imagines he's got a bazooka and really destroys a dumpster. He cobbles together a masked costume, and finds himself fighting superpowered giant talking apes, nasty weapons-bearing lizards, and more. But someone notices him and decides he wants Tom's powers Lord Everos, the Father of Death. And it's not just Tom, either; Vicki, the class weirdo, does really talk with the dead, and Lord Everos wants her, too. And that's not the worst of it, for apparently Tom was never supposed to get the power of the thunderbolt, and a whole pantheon of heroes has just arrived to stop him. Oops again.

Ostertag, Molly

The **witch** boy. Molly Knox Ostertag. Scholastic Press 2017 224 p. Color; Illustration

Grades: 3 4 5 6   **741.5; Fic**

1. Shapeshifting — Fiction; 2. Witches — Graphic novels; 3. Fantasy graphic novels

9781338089523, $24.99; 9781338089530; 9781338089516, $12.99; 1338089528

In this graphic novel, by Molly Knox Ostertag, "in thirteen-year-old Aster's family, all the girls are raised to be witches, while boys grow up to be shapeshifters. Anyone who dares cross those lines is exiled. Unfortunately for Aster, he still hasn't shifted...and he's still fascinated by witchery, no matter how forbidden it might be. When a mysterious danger threatens the other boys, Aster knows he can help — as a witch." (Publisher's note)

Followed by: The hidden witch (2018)

Ostrander, John

Star Wars: Legacy, Volume One: Broken. story, John Ostrander and Jan Duuresma; script, John Ostrander; pencils, Jan Duuresma; inks, Dan Parsons; colors, Brad Anderson; lettering, Michael David Thomas; cover art, Adam Hughes. Dark Horse Comics 2007 un Illustration

Grades: 7 8 9 10 11 12   **741.5; Fic**

1. Adventure graphic novels; 2. Graphic novels; 3. Science fiction graphic novels; 4. Star Wars — Graphic novels

978-1-59307-716-7, $17.95

125 years have passed since the events in Return of the JedI and the days of the New JedI Order. There is a new evil gripping the galaxy, shattering a resurgent Empire and seeking to destroy the last of the JedI. Even as their power is failing, the JedI hold onto one final hope, the last remaining heir to the Skywalker legacy: Cade, who has rejected the way of the JedI. The book's fighting action is at the same level as the motion picture series.

Ottaviani, Jim

Dignifying science: stories about women scientists. written by Jim Ottaviani and illustrated by Donna Barr . . . [et al.]. G.T. Labs 2009 142p. Illustration

Grades: 6 7 8 9 10 11 12

920

Courtesy of G.T. Labs

1. Biographical graphic novels; 2. Graphic novels; 3. Women scientists — Graphic novels

978-0-9788037-3-5, $16.95; 0-9788037-3-5

Ottaviani provides biographical sketches of women scientists such as Lise Meitner, Rosalind Franklin, Barbara McClintock, and Hedy Lamarr (yes, the actress was also an inventor); all the stories are illustrated by women comics artists, including Lea Hernandez, Linda Medley, Anne Timmons, and others.

First published 1999

Primates: The Fearless Science of Jane Goodall, Dian Fossey, and Biruté Galdikas. Jim Ottaviani; illustrated by Maris Wicks. First Second 2013 133 p. Color; Illustration

Grades: 5 6 7 8 9 10 Adult   **741.5; 599.8**

1. Primates; 2. Fossey, Dian, 1932-1985; 3. Goodall, Jane, 1934-; 4. Galdikas, Birute, 1946-

1596438657; 9781596438651, $19.99

LC 2013427678

This book presents an "account of the three greatest primatologists of the last century: Jane Goodall, Dian Fossey, and Biruté Galdikas. These three ground-breaking researchers were all students of the great Louis Leakey, and each made profound contributions to primatology — and to our own understanding of ourselves." (Publisher's note)

"More story than study, the book provides an accessible introduction to Goodall's, Fossey's and Galdikas' lives and work." Kirkus

Includes bibliographical references, page 138

★ **T-Minus:** the race to the moon. [illustrated by] Zander Cannon, Kevin Cannon. Aladdin 2009 124p. Illustration

Grades: 4 5 6 7 8 9 10 11 12 Adult   **629.45; 741.5**

1. Apollo project — Graphic novels; 2. Gemini project — Graphic novels; 3. Graphic novels; 4. Space flight to the moon — Graphic novels
978-1-4169-8682-9, $21.99; 1-4169-8682-0; 978-1-4169-4960-2 (pa), $12.99; 1-4169-4960-7 (pa)

LC 2009-920999

Ottaviani, Zander Cannon, and Kevin Cannon show what happened when the U.S. and the U.S.S.R. started the space race in the 1950s, and how it progressed to the NASA Apollo 11 mission which landed two men on the moon in July of 1969.

"Organized as a countdown, making the outcome seem inevitable, the frequent, prominent sidebars list a type of rocket, the duration of its flight, and whether the mission was a success or a failure. There are more than 30 attempts chronicled, and the shift between Soviet and U.S. successes creates an interesting balance in the narrative.... Ottaviani is particular with facts and eager to inspire readers with regard to the scientific process." SLJ

Pak, Greg

Marvel Nemesis: The Imperfects. writer, Greg Pak; artist, Renato Arlem; colorist, June Chung, Carlos Lopez & William Murai. Marvel Entertainment 2005 un Illustration

Grades: 8 9 10 11 12   **741.5; Fic**

1. Graphic novels; 2. Superhero graphic novels; 3. Wolverine (Fictional character); 4. Spider-Man (Fictional character)
978-0-7851-1778-0, $7.99

An evil scientist sets his cross-hairs on planet Earth, in search of test subjects for his experiments, transforming even the most timid creatures into vicious fighting machines. Thousands of years later, the Thing, Wolverine, Spider-Man, and Elektra all find themselves unwilling participants in the scientist's millennia-old trials...or perhaps not all of them are that unwilling. This book includes some violence and strong language.

★ **Mech** Cadet Yu; Volume 1. written by Greg Pak; illustrated by Takeshi Miyazawa; colored by Triona Farrell. Simon & Schuster 2018 128 p. Color; Illustration

Grades: 4 5 6 7 8   **741.5; Fic**

1. Robots — Fiction; 2. Extraterrestrial beings — Fiction; 3. Graphic novels
1684151953; 9781684151950, $14.99

"Every year, giant sentient robots from outer space come to Earth and bond forever with a brand new crop of cadets at Sky Corps Academy to help keep the planet safe. But this year, instead of making a connection with a cadet, one of the mechs bonds with Stanford, a young kid working with his Mom as a janitor at Sky Corps. Stanford has the opportunity of a lifetime but he'll first have to earn the trust of his classmates if he's to defend the planet from the monstrous Sharg." (Publisher's note)

"Set in the near future in Arizona, the tale strikes the perfect balance between action and drama. The battle sequences are thrilling and the characterization, writing, and dialogue strong." SLJ

Volume 1 of 3

Panetta, Kevin

Zodiac Starforce: By the Power of Astra. script by Kevin Panetta; art, colors, lettering, and cover by Paulina Ganucheau; color flats by Savanna Ganucheau, Kristen Acampora, and Tabby Freeman; chapter break art by Marguerite Sauvage, Kevin Wada, Jacob Wyatt, Babs Tarr. Dark Horse Books 2016 136 p. Color; Illustration

Grades: 8 9 10 11 12 Adult   **741.5**

1. Astrology — Fiction; 2. Friendship — Fiction; 3. Graphic novels; 4. Magic — Fiction; 5. Superheroes — Fiction
1616559136; 9781616559137, $12.99

LC 2015039851

This book, by Kevin Panetta, illustrated by Paulina Ganucheau, focuses on "an elite group of teenage girls with magical powers who have sworn to protect our planet against dark creatures...as long as they can get out of class! Known as the Zodiac Starforce, these high-school girls aren't just combating math tests. They're also battling monsters — not your typical afterschool activity!" (Publisher's note)

Parker, Jake

★ **Missile** Mouse: the star crusher. Graphix 2010 172p. (Missile Mouse)

Grades: 3 4 5 6   **741; Fic; 741.5**

1. Adventure graphic novels; 2. Graphic novels; 3. Mice — Graphic novels; 4. Science fiction graphic novels
978-0-545-11714-2, $21.99; 0-545-11714-3; 978-0-545-11715-9 (pa), $10.99; 0-545-11715-1 (pa)

"When his mission to recover an ancient star compass goes wrong, intrepid Galactic Security Agent Missile Mouse finds himself saddled with a partner.... The two are to retrieve a missing scientist who holds the key to a horrible weapon, the Star Crusher, in his hereditary memory.... [This is] a gem in story and art. Bright, action-filled, at times wordless panels keep the pages turning. Intelligent space opera and a realistically rounded hero will have young fans of the future demanding the next volume." Kirkus

Parker, Jeff

Meteor men. written by Jeff Parker; illustrated by Sandy Jarrell; colored by Kevin Volo; lettered by Crank!. Oni Press 2014 133 p. Color; Illustration

Grades: 8 9 10 11

741.5; Fic

1. Human-alien encounters — Fiction; 2. Science fiction graphic novels; 3. Extraterrestrial beings — Graphic novels
1620101513; 9781620101513, $19.99
Eisner Nominee: Best Publication for Teens (2015)

Courtesy of Oni Press

"On a summer night, Alden Baylor sits in a field watching the largest meteor shower in human history. What begins as teenage adventure becomes something more — the celestial event brings travelers who will change the world completely, and Alden discovers a connection to one of them. How does a young man who had to grow up fast handle the invasion of his planet? Can Alden keep humanity from oblivion?" (Publisher's note)

"Parker combines the familiar concept with gentle domesticity and deliberate humanism, thus circumventing cliché and providing an accessible perspective to the logical and realistic extensions of such an event." SLJ

Pastrovicchio, Lorenzo

Wizards of Mickey, vol. 1: mouse magic. writer: Stefano Ambrosio; artists: Lorenzo Pastrovicchio ... [et al.]; translation: Saida Temafonte; editor, Aaron Sparrow; letterers Troy Peteri [and] Deron Bennett; designer Erika Terriquez. Boom! Studios 2010 un Illustration

Grades: 3 4 5 6 7 8 9   **741.5; Fic**
1. Adventure graphic novels; 2. Fantasy graphic novels; 3. Graphic novels; 4. Humorous graphic novels; 5. Mickey Mouse (Fictional character)
978-1-60886-541-3, $9.99

Wizard's apprentice Mickey loses a magic talisman called the Diamagic when he and the village fall afoul of a con man who steals it from them. Mickey pursues the con man, but he learns he'll have to compete in the Great Wizard's Tournament to win it back if he can father a team to work with him. He ends up with Donald and Goofy, both misfit bunglers, but somehow they'll have to compete against Peg-Leg Pete and the Phantom Blot. This book, originally written and published in Italy, is full of fantasy adventure and fun with recognizable Disney characters.

Volume 1 of 3

Pearson, Luke

Hilda and the Black Hound. by Luke Pearson. Flying Eye Books 2014 64 p. Color; Illustration (Hildafolk)

Grades: 3 4 5 6 7   **741.5**
1. City and town life — Fiction; 2. Girls — Fiction; 3. Comic books, strips, etc.; 4. Dogs — Fiction
9781909263185, $24; 1909263184

In this graphic novel by Luke Pearson, "Hilda...meets the Nisse: a mischievous but charismatic bunch of misfits who occupy a world beside — but also somehow within — our own, and where the rules of physics don't quite match up. Meanwhile, on the streets of Trolberg, a dark specter looms." (Publisher's note)

"The full-size volume offers a minimum of 10 panels of varying sizes per page. Darker shades dominate when the beast lurks, and earth tones and reds and oranges when the characters go about their daily business. Touches of humor abound in both images and dialogue." SLJ

Hilda and the Midnight Giant. Luke Pearson. Nobrow Press 2012 40p Color illustration

Grades: 4 5 6 7 8   **741.5**
1. Girls — Fiction; 2. Forests and forestry — Fiction; 3. Giants — Fiction
1907704256; 9781907704253, $24.00

In this book, the "protagonist finds her world turned upside down as she faces the prospect of leaving her snow-capped birthplace for the hum of the megalopolis, where her mother (an architect) has been offered a prestigious job. During Hilda's daily one-and-a-half hour trek to school she looks for ways to stall her mother's decision. She conspires with the beings of the mystical Blue Forest to delay the inevitable. Will they help or hinder her? More importantly, who is this mysterious Midnight Giant?"

Hilda and the Stone Forest. by Luke Pearson. Flying Eye Books 2016 64 p. Color; Illustration

Grades: 3 4 5 6   **741.5; Fic**
1. Trolls — Juvenile fiction; 2. Mother-daughter relationship — Juvenile fiction; 3. Magic — Juvenile fiction
1909263745; 9781909263741, $19.95

"Hilda is hardly at home anymore, seeking days filled with excitement, and her mother can't help but worry. In a moment of tension, the pair find themselves flung far away into a mysterious, dark forest — the land of the trolls! Can they work together to escape the clutches of these sinister stone creatures?" (Publisher's note)

"Pearson has perfected Hilda's Scandinavian-style fantasy world, and his artwork is as captivating as ever, but the change in focus from Hilda's

derring-do to the realistic consequences of her escapades keeps it from being just another series installment." Booklist

★ **Hilda** and the troll. Luke Pearson. Flying Eye Books 2013 40 p. Color; Illustration (Hildafolk)

Grades: 3 4 5 6   **741.5; Fic**
1. Adventure fiction; 2. Explorers — Fiction; 3. Trolls — Fiction
1909263141; 9781909263147, $18.95

This book, by Luke Pearson, is "about an adventurous little girl and her habit of befriending anything, no matter how curious it might seem. While on an expedition to illustrate the magical creatures of the mountains around her home, Hilda spots a mountain troll. As the blue-haired explorer sits and sketches, she slowly starts to nod off. By the time she wakes up, the troll has totally disappeared and, even worse, Hilda is lost in a snowstorm." (Publisher's note)

"The art is as whimsical as the protagonist, and the bright colors enhance this comic book's magical-realistic effect." Horn Book

Originally published 2010 as Hildafolk; Other titles about Hilda are:Hilda and the Midnight Giant (2012);Hilda and the Bird Parade (2013);Hilda and the Black Hound (2014);Hilda and the Stone Forest (2016)

Peirce, Lincoln

Big Nate: game on!. by Lincoln Peirce. Andrews McMeel Pub., LLC 2013 224 p. Color illustration

Grades: 1 2 3 4 5 6   **Fic; 741.5/973**
1. Comic books, strips, etc.; 2. Sports — Fiction; 3. Games — Fiction
1449427774; 9781449427771, $9.99

LC 2012952339

This book, written and illustrated by Lincoln Peirce, features a collection of his "Big Nate" comic strip. "To sixth-grader Nate Wright, life is one big game. From fine-tuning his trash-talking skills on the basketball court to his cocky [attitude] in the soccer goal, Nate can be a bigger challenge to his teammates than their opponents." The book features "Nate and his friends" mostly hapless sports encounters." (Publisher's note)

Perfit, Michael R.

Older than dirt: a wild but true history of Earth. by Don Brown & Mike Perfit. Houghton Mifflin Harcourt 2017 112 p. Color; Illustration

Grades: 4 5 6 7 8   **741.5; 551.7**
1. Origin of the Earth; 2. Earth sciences; 3. Historical geology; 4. Earth (Planet) — Origin; 5. Historical geology
9781328468277; 9780544805033, $18.99; 0544805038

LC 2016018643

This book, by Don Brown and Mike Perfit, describes how, "almost 14.5 billion years ago, it all started with a BIG BANG and what began as a cloud of gas, dust, and rock eventually took shape and bloomed into a molten sphere. Battered by asteroid collisions, ice ages, and shifting tectonic plates, our fledgling planet finally pushed forth continents.... Geological activity continues to sculpt the earth's landscape, sometimes with terrible consequences for its inhabitants." (Publisher's note)

"In 100 fact-crammed but surprisingly zippy pages, nonfiction graphic novelist extraordinaire Brown covers 14 billion years of Earth's development. From the big bang to our planet's origin to landmass formation to the appearance of life, Brown and scientific consultant Perfit provide an astonishingly comprehensive overview and manage to humanize it with witty asides from the woodchuck and worm who serve as surrogate teacher and student, as well as quick visits with important historical scientists." Booklist

Includes bibliographical references (pages 98-101)

Petersen, David

★ **Mouse** Guard: Fall 1152. Archaia Studios Press 2007 un Illustration

Grades: 5 6 7 8   **741.5; Fic**
1. Fantasy graphic novels; 2. Graphic novels; 3. Mice — Graphic novels
978-1-932386-57-8, $24.95; 1-932386-57-2
Eisner Award: Best Publication for Kids (2008)

In a medieval world populated by animals, mice have their own civilization but live in constant peril from predators. They live in hidden towns protected by the Guard, who also escort travelers between towns. Three young members of the Guard, Lieam, Saxon, and Kenzie, go in search of a missing grain merchant. They find him dead in the belly of a snake who tried to eat them; but they also find evidence that the dead merchant is a traitor. Now they need to find out to whom he was betraying the Guard and why. While this story features animals and is suitable for most readers who can handle some fighting action, there's nothing cute or Disney-esque in the art. Characters die, this is a serious story, but readers who have read Bone or the Harry Potter series can handle the action in this book. This is the first in a series.

Followed by: Mouse Guard: Winter 1152 (2009); Originally published as Mouse Guard issues #1-6.

Mouse Guard: Winter 1152. story & art by David Petersen. Archaia Studios Press 2009 un Illustration

Grades: 5 6 7 8   **741.5; Fic**
978-1-932386-74-5, $24.95; 1-932386-74-2

"In the Winter of 1152, the Mouse Guard face a food and supply shortage threatening the lives of many mouse through a cold and icy season. Some of the Guard's finest — Saxon, Kenzie, Lieam, and Sadie, led by Celanawe, the legendary Black Axe — traverse the snow-blanketed territories acting as diplomats to improve relations between the mouse cities and the Guard, and find themselves on a race against time to deliver crucial medicines." (Publisher's note)

Followed by: Mouse Guard: The black axe (2013)

Mouse Guard; 3: The Black Axe. by David Petersen. Archaia Entertainment, LLC 2013 192 p.

Grades: 5 6 7 8   **741.5; Fic**
1. Mice — Fiction; 2. Adventure fiction; 3. Fantasy fiction
1936393069; 9781936393060, $24.95
Harvey Award: Best Graphic Album of Previously Published Work (2014)

This book, by David Petersen, part of the Eisner Award-winning fantasy comic series, tells "the tale of wise oldfur and longtime Mouse Guard member Celanawe, as he fulfills the promise made to young Lieam to detail the day his paw first touched the legendary weapon, the Black Axe. The arrival of distant kin takes Celanawe on an adventure that will carry him across the sea to uncharted waters and lands, all while unraveling the legend of Farrer, the blacksmith who forged the mythical weapon." (Publisher's note)

"[N]ewcomers and fans alike will find much to explore in Petersen's finely wrought artwork, high-stakes intrigue, and derring-do tale." Booklist

Mouse Guard; volume 1: legends of the guard. Jeremy Bastian, Ted Naifeh, Alex Sheikman, et al. Archaia Entertainment 2010 144 p. Color illustration

Grades: 5 6 7 8   **741.5**
1. Mice — Fiction; 2. Short stories — Collections; 3. Adventure fiction
1932386947 (Vol. 1); 9781932386943 (Vol. 1), $19.95
Eisner Award: Best Anthology (2011)

"Petersen turns to the tested and reliable bar story as a framing device to allow other writers and artists to play in his Mouse Guard universe, where heroic mice heroes are set in a world of epic fantasy.... One night

barkeep June...stages a story-telling contest. What follows are thirteen tales of danger and adventure, as protagonists contend against the predators around them and the flaws that divide mouse from mouse." (Publisher's note)

"More than just supplemental material, this book broadens Petersen's magnificently imagined miniature world and is a welcome addition for any collection that values quality, all-ages graphic novels." Booklist

Mouse Guard; volume 2: legends of the guard. Archaia Entertainment 2010 144 p. Color; Illustration

Grades: 5 6 7 8   **741.5**
1. Short stories — Collections; 2. Mice — Fiction; 3. Adventure fiction
9781936393268 (Vol. 2), $19.95; 1936393263 (Vol. 2)
Eisner Nominee: Best Publication for Kids (2014); Harvey Nominee: Best Anthology (2014); Harvey Nominee: Best Continuing or Limited Series (2014)

"Inside the June Alley Inn, located in the western mouse city of Barkstone, mice gather to tell tales, each trying to outdo the other. A competition, of sorts, begins. The rules: Every story must contain one truth, one lie, and have never been told in that tavern before. With the winner getting his bar tab cleared, fantastic stories are spun throughout the evening!" (Publisher's note)

"The art styles of the ensuing stories are all over the map, from the elegant, tapestry-worthy The Battle of the Hawk's Mouse & the Fox's Mouse, by Jeremy Bastian, to the joltingly cartoony A Mouse Named Fox, from Katie Cook. In substance, the stories are equally varied, but all champion the heroism of the noble mouse warriors and even include a couple clever takes on classics." Booklist

Petrucha, Stefan

Nancy Drew, Girl Detective #1: The Demon of River Heights. NBM/Papercutz 2005 un Illustration

Grades: 4 5 6 7 8 9

741.5; Fic
1. Adventure graphic novels; 2. Graphic novels; 3. Mystery graphic novels
1-59707-004-1, $12.95; 1-59707-000-9, $7.95

Courtesy of NBM Publishing

Everyone's favorite girl detective makes her graphic novel debut. Nancy also makes her debut in a horror film concerning a monstrous River Heights urban legend " but is it really an urban legend, or does the River Heights Demon truly exist? And will Nancy, Bess, and George live long enough to find out? This graphic novel series updates Nancy and her friends to the twenty-first century, but she's still a klutz.

Petty, J. T. (John T.)

The **Fall** of the House of West. by Paul Pope and J. T. Petty; illustrated by David Rubín. First Second 2015 160 p. Illustration (Battling Boy)

Grades: 7 8 9 10 11 12   **741.5; Fic**
1. Gods — Comic books, strips, etc.; 2. Monsters — Comic books, strips, etc.; 3. Graphic novels; 4. Mothers — Fiction; 5. Father-daughter relationship — Fiction; 6. Secrets — Fiction
162672010X; 9781626720107, $9.99

In this graphic novel, by Paul Pope and J. T. Petty, illustrated by David Rubín, "Aurora West is on the verge of solving the mystery of her mother's death, but it's hard keeping her efforts a secret from her grieving father, the legendary monster-hunter Haggard West. Between her school work and her hours training and hunting with her dad, Aurora is hard-pressed to find time to be a secret sleuth. But she's nothing if not persistent." (Publisher's note)

"Rubín's frenetic black-and-white illustrations stylistically complement Pope and Petty's breakneck-paced plotting. True to the genre, the story explores notions of good and evil but provides no easy answers." Kirkus

The **Rise** of Aurora West. by Paul Pope, J. T. Petty, illustrated by David Rubín. First Second Books 2014 160 p. Illustration (Battling Boy)
Grades: 7 8 9 10 11 12   **741.5**
1. Adventure graphic novels; 2. Female superhero graphic novels
1626722684; 9781626722682, $17.99

In this graphic novel, by Paul Pope and J. T. Petty, illustrated by David Rubín, the "world introduced in...'Battling Boy' is rife with monsters and short on heroes.... But in this action-driven extension of the Battling Boy universe, we see it through a new pair of eyes: Aurora West, daughter of Arcopolis's last great hero, Haggard West." (Publisher's note)

"Since Aurora and her father were only briefly mentioned in the previous installment, this volume does a wonderful job of fleshing out their characters further; readers see an Aurora that's not as confident in her abilities, and a slightly jaded and darker side to her heroic father. Pope's gritty, experimental art from the original Battling Boy has been replaced by Rubín's more traditional style, giving a '60s 'Silver Age' appearance to the work." SLJ

Peyo
The **Smurfs** anthology; Vol. 1. Peyo. Papercutz 2013 190 p. Color illustration (The Smurfs graphic novels)
Grades: 4 5 6 7 8 9 10 11 12 Adult
741.5
1. Comic books, strips, etc.
1597074179; 9781597074179, $19.99

"Newly remastered and presented in original publication order, along with a Smurfy collection of historical notes and photographs, the stories in this volume," by Belgian comics artist Peyo, "introduce us to Papa Smurf, Gargamel, Smurfette, and the rest of the village." (Publisher's note)

Courtesy of NBM Publishing

The **Smurfs** anthology; Vol. 2. Peyo. Papercutz 2013 192 p. Color illustration
Grades: 4 5 6 7 8 9 10 11 12 Adult   **741.5**
1. Comic books, strips, etc.
1597074454; 9781597074452, $19.99

"Newly remastered and presented in original publication order, along with a Smurfy collection of historical notes and photographs, this volume," by Belgian comics artist Peyo, "introduces us to Smurfette and features a 'Johan and Peewit' story never before seen in the U.S." (Publisher's note)

"[A] delightful and instructive mix of Peyo's colorful tales. A series of essays interspersed throughout the collection provides social and historical context for the cartoons." Booklist
Translated from the French

Courtesy of NBM Publishing

Phelan, Matt
★ **Bluffton:** my summers with Buster Keaton. written and illustrated by Matt Phelan. Candlewick Press 2013 240 p. Color; Illustration
Grades: 3 4 5 6
741.5; Fic
1. Vaudeville — Fiction; 2. Keaton, Buster
076365079X; 9780763650797, $22.99
LC 2012947260

In this graphic novel by Matt Phelan, set "in the summer of 1908, in Muskegon, Michigan, a visiting troupe of vaudeville performers is about the most exciting thing since baseball. Henry has a few months to ogle...a slapstick actor his own age named Buster Keaton. Henry longs to learn to take a fall like Buster...but Buster just wants to play ball with Henry and his friends." (Publisher's note)

BLUFFTON. Copyright © 2013 by Matt Phelan. Reproduced by permission of the publisher, Candlewick Press, Somerville, MA

"Historical detail, a rich sense of place, expert pacing — Phelan...keeps all the plates in the air in this fictionalized recreation of the boyhood summers of Buster Keaton. In lightly sketched, gently tinted watercolor panels, Phelan conveys the excitement a troupe of summering vaudeville actors brings to sleepy Bluffton." Pub Wkly

★ **Snow** White: A Graphic Novel. by Matt Phelan. Candlewick Press 2016 216 p. Illustration; Color
Grades: 4 5 6 7 8
741.5; Fic
1. New York (N.Y.) — Fiction; 2. Depressions — 1929 — Fiction
0763672335; 9780763672331, $19.99

This graphic novel, by Matt Phelan, "delivers a darkly stylized noir Snow White set against the backdrop of Depression-era Manhattan. The scene: New York City.... Enter a cast of familiar characters: a young girl, Samantha White, returning after being sent away by her cruel stepmother, the Queen of the Follies, years earlier; her father, the King of Wall Street, who survives the stock market crash only to suffer a strange and sudden death; [and] seven street urchins." (Publisher's note)

SNOW WHITE. Copyright © 2016 by Matt Phelan. Reproduced by permission of the publisher, Candlewick Press, Somerville, MA.

"With a keen historical slant, a bit of action and intrigue, high visual interest, and the fairy-tale leaning, this will awe a wide readership. Brilliant." Kirkus

★ The **storm** in the barn. Candlewick Press 2009 201p. Illustration
Grades: 4 5 6 7 8 9
741.5; Fic
1. Adventure graphic novels; 2. Dust storms — Graphic novels; 3. Graphic novels; 4. Kansas — Graphic novels; 5. Monsters — Graphic novels; 6. United States — History — 1933-1945 — Graphic novels
978-0-7636-3618-0, $24.99; 0-7636-3618-5; 978-0-7636-5290-6 (pa), $14.99; 0-7636-5290-3 (pa)

In Kansas of 1937, the land has been in the grip of the Dust Bowl for four years, and

THE STORM IN THE BARN. Copyright © 2009 by Matt Phelan. Reproduced by permission of the publisher, Candlewick Press, Somerville, MA.

eleven-year-old Jack Carter has seen his family worn down by it. But the day Jack outruns a dust storm all the way home from town, he glimpses something odd in the abandoned Talbot barn, and he tries to find the courage to go into the barn and confront what is there.

"Children can read this as a work of historical fiction, a piece of folklore, a scary story, a graphic novel, or all four. Written with simple, direct language, it—s an almost wordless book: the illustrations" shadowy grays and blurry lines eloquently depict the haze of the dust. A complex but accessible and fascinating book." SLJ

Pittman, Eddie

Red's Planet; Book 1: A World Away from Home. by Eddie Pittman. Amulet Books 2016 192 p. Color; Illustration

Grades: 3 4 5 6   **741.5; Fic**

1. Extraterrestrial beings — Juvenile fiction; 2. Science fiction — Graphic novels; 3. Kidnapping — Juvenile fiction; 4. Outer space — Juvenile fiction

9781419719080; 1419719076; 9781419719073, $19.95

This book, by Eddie Pittman, is "an intergalactic graphic novel fantasy.... Meet Red, a quirky, headstrong 10-year-old who longs to live in her own perfect paradise far away from her annoying foster family. But when a UFO mistakenly kidnaps her, Red finds herself farther away than she could have possibly imagined — across the galaxy and aboard an enormous spaceship owned by the Aquilari, an ancient creature with a taste for rare and unusual treasures." (Publisher's note)

"Red, a precocious 10-year-old brimming with a likable mix of sass and joie de vivre, is portrayed in exceptionally clear and brightly wrought panels, with a sweeping cinematic lens that lends equal attention to action and expression." Kirkus

Another title in this series is: Friends and Foes (2017)

Poe, Marshall

Turning points: a house divided. Aladdin Paperbacks 2008 122p. Illustration

Grades: 3 4 5 6 7 8   **741.5; Fic**

1. Abolitionists — Graphic novels; 2. Graphic novels; 3. United States — History — 1815-1861 — Graphic novels

978-1-4169-5057-8, $8.99

LC 2008-929317

Owen and Amos Bennington's abolitionist parents are killed in 1856, and the brothers vow to continue their parents' quest to end slavery. However, younger brother Amos thinks the abolitionists aren't doing enough, while Owen works for a peaceful, political solution. When they move to Kansas, things don't go as planned, as proslavery people use violence to get their way. When Owen wants to move back East, Amos runs away and joins John Brown's forces, who fight against slavery with force. Owen moves to Illinois and works for Abraham Lincoln. Amos finally realizes that Brown's way is wrong and leaves just before the attempted takeover of Harper's Ferry; he makes his way across the land slowly, hoping against hope that he can find Owen again. This fictional story highlights the years leading up to the Civil War, showing a private, personal side of Lincoln and letting younger readers see the kinds of divisions suffered by many families as they debated and argued the cause of abolition or slavery, and of political action or force to end slavery.

Turning Points: Little Rock nine. Simon & Schuster/Aladdin Paperbacks 2008 122p. Illustration

Grades: 3 4 5 6 7 8 9   **741.5; Fic**

1. African Americans — Civil rights — Graphic novels; 2. African Americans — Education — Graphic novels; 3. Graphic novels; 4. United States — History — 1953-1961 — Graphic novels

978-1-4169-5066-0, $7.99

LC 2007-937918

Sixteen-year-old William McNally and fifteen-year-old Thomas Johnson both live in Little Rock, Arkansas, in the summer of 1957. They both love baseball and teasing their little sisters. There's just one big difference: William is white, and Thomas, the son of the McNally family's maid, is black. After the U.S. Supreme Court rules in favor of desegregating public schools, Little Rock Central High School prepares to enroll its first nine African-American students, and William and Thomas are caught in the middle of a storm. William's family has divided over the issue, and Thomas' parents don't want him to get hurt and forbid him to try to enter the school. The book portrays the issues of the time and the personal beliefs of both sides to let readers see what it was like back then. William, Thomas, and their families are fictional, but what happened at Little Rock Central High School is an important part of American history.

Pomplun, Tom

Graphic Classics volume eleven: O. Henry. edited by Tom Pomplun. Eureka Productions 2005 144p. Illustration

Grades: 7 8 9 10 11 12 Adult   **741.5; Fic**

1. Authors; 2. Graphic novels; 3. Short stories — Graphic novels; 4. Short story writers; 5. Henry, O., 1862-1910; 6. Henry, O., 1862-1910 — Adaptations

978-0-9746648-2-0, $11.95

This volume of Graphics Classics adapts some of the short stories by O. Henry, the master of the surprise ending. Stories include "The Ransom of Red Chief," illustrated by Johnny Ryan, "The Gift of the Magi," illustrated by Lisa Weber, "The Caballero's Way" (the original story of the Cisco Kid), illustrated by Mark A. Nelson, and more.

★ **Graphic** Classics volume fourteen: Gothic classics. edited by Tom Pomplun. Eureka Productions 2007 144p. Illustration

Grades: 7 8 9 10 11 12 Adult   **741.5; Fic**

1. Graphic novels; 2. Horror graphic novels; 3. Short stories — Graphic novels

978-0-9787919-0-2, $11.95

This volume includes graphic adaptations of classic novels Carmilla by Joseph Sheridan Le Fanu, The Mysteries of Udolpho by Ann Radcliffe, and Northanger Abbey by Jane Austen, along with shorter works "The Oval Portrait" by Edgar Allan Poe, "At the Gate" by Myla Jo Closser, and "I've a Pain in My Head" by Jane Austen. Radcliffe's novel is one mentioned by Austen in Northanger Abbey and is a famous gothic novel from the late eighteenth century, considered to be the world's first best-seller. Le Fanu's vampire novel was published twenty-five years before Stoker's Dracula. Austen wrote Northanger Abbey as a satire of the popular gothic genre.

Graphic Classics Volume Twelve: Adventure Classics. Eureka Productions 2005 144p. Illustration

Grades: 8 9 10 11 12   **741.5; 808.3**

1. Adventure graphic novels; 2. Graphic novels; 3. Short stories — Graphic novels

978-0-9746648-4-7, $11.95

This volume of the Graphic Classics series includes a selection of poems and short stories that more or less fit the adventure genre. Rudyard Kipling's poem "Gunga Din" is here, as is Robert Service's "The Shooting of Dan McGrew." Short stories include "In the Valley of the Sorceress" by Sax Rohmer, "Tigre" by Zane Grey, "Blood Money" (a Captain Blood story) by Rafael Sabatini, "The Crime of the Brigadier" (a Brigadier Gerard adventure) by Sir Arthur Conan Doyle, "The Roads We Take" by O. Henry, and more. "The Mystery of the Semi-Detached" by Edith Nesbit may surprise readers who only know her as a children's fantasy author.

Pope, Paul
★ **Battling** Boy. Paul Pope; colors by Hilary Sycamore. First Second 2013 208 p. Illustration
Grades: 7 8 9 10 11 12   **741.5; Fic**
1. Superhero graphic novels; 2. Fantasy graphic novels
1596438053; 9781596431454, $15.99; 9781596438057, $24.99
LC 2013030815
Eisner Award: Best Publication for Teens (2014)
In this book, "the hero Haggard West helps battle the evil forces of Sadisto and his hooded ghouls. However, in a shocking turn of events, evil triumphs over good, and the metropolis is left without protection. In a world far, far away, a 13-year-old son of a god has been chosen to help Earth fight the onslaught of monsters as a rite of passage. Sent with only a few possessions, including an array of magical T-shirts, Battling Boy helps the city-but he finds he cannot do it alone." (Kirkus Reviews)
"This is a sophisticated tale for younger readers, but Pope manages to both grant full-scale wish fulfillment and acknowledge the limitations of young boys with equal aplomb. His art, meanwhile, looks like nothing else in comics, with ropy, sinewy figures, dynamic action, and gritty urban design all captured in panels that have the rough, subversive tone of classic punk album covers." Booklist

Porcellino, John
Thoreau at Walden. by John Porcellino, from the writings of Henry David Thoreau; introduction by D.B. Johnson. Hyperion 2008 viii, 99 p. Illustration; Map (Center for Cartoon Studies presents)
Grades: 8 9 10 11 12 Adult   **818/.303; 741.5**
1. Graphic novels; 2. Thoreau, Henry David, 1817-1862; 3. Walden Woods (Mass.) — Social life and customs — Comic books, strips, etc; 4. American authors
1423100387; 1423100395; 9781423100386, $16.99; 9781423100393
LC 2007061358
This graphic novel, by John Porcellino, "introduces ...Henry David Thoreau.... Thoreau's writings, excerpted out of chronological order, are recast into a narrative that moves from the philosopher's self-ostracism from society and his time at Walden and into the feeling of calm reverie he took from his experiences." (Booklist)
"Presents in graphic novel format an account of the two years that Thoreau spent at Walden Pond, excerpted from Thoreau's writings." Publisher's note
Includes bibliographical references (p. 99)

Preciado, Tony
Super grammar: learn grammar with superheroes. written by Tony Preciado; illustrated by Rhode Montijo; colored by Jenny Hansen; inked by Joe To. Scholastic 2012 176 p. Color illustration (Illustrating the point)
Grades: 4 5 6 7 8   **428**
1. English language — Grammar — Juvenile literature; 2. Superheroes — Juvenile fiction; 3. English language — Grammar — Juvenile fiction
0545425158; 9780545425155, $8.99
LC 2012289091
In this book by Tony Preciado, illustrated by Rhode Montijo, "all of the major elements of grammar...[are] personified with superhero or super villain identities.... You'll meet the vibrant super heroine The Adverb, and you'll learn about her awesome ability to modify verbs and other adverbs.... You'll actually meet the sinister twin brothers, Double Negative, and you'll learn how to avoid being tricked into falling for their double talk." (Publisher's note)

Priddy, Joel
The **gift** of the Magi. It Books/HarperCollins 2009 un Illustration
Grades: 5 6 7 8 9 10 11 12 Adult   **741.5; Fic**

1. Authors; 2. Christmas — Graphic novels; 3. Gifts — Graphic novels; 4. Graphic novels; 5. Short story writers; 6. Henry, O., 1862-1910 — Adaptations
978-0-06-178239-8, $14.99
Della and Jim are a young married couple, struggling to make ends meet when Jim's pay has been cut. It's Christmas time, but despite squeezing every penny, Della has managed to save only a little bit of money, and it's not enough to buy Jim a good present. He owns a gold pocket watch, and Della wants to buy him a chain for it. She has only one thing of value that she can sell her beautiful, long, long hair. Out of her love for Jim, Della sacrifices her hair. And, of course, Jim has sacrificed his gold pocket watch in order to buy beautiful hair combs for Della's gorgeous hair. As O. Henry says, they "most unwisely sacrificed for each other the greatest treasures of their house," but also that "of all who give gifts these two were the wisest." Joel Priddy's adaptation of this classic story uses black and white illustrations except when Della lets down her hair to consider her one treasure. He preserves much of O. Henry's original prose, which means that younger readers will have to look up a lot of words to understand the story. This book is suitable for younger readers but will also appeal to teens and adults.

Prince, Liz
★ **Tomboy:** A Graphic Memoir. by Liz Prince. Zest Books 2014 256 p. Illustration
Grades: 7 8 9 10 11 12 Adult
1. Cartoonists — Caricatures and cartoons; 2. Cartoonists — United States — Biography; 3. Gender identity; 4. Graphic novels; 5. Sex role; 6. Prince, Liz; 7. Sex differences (Psychology); 8. Gender role; 9. Stereotype (Social psychology)
9781936976553, $15.99; 1936976552
This memoir, by Liz Prince, "is a graphic novel about refusing gender boundaries, yet unwittingly embracing gender stereotypes at the same time, and realizing later in life that you can be just as much of a girl in jeans and a T-shirt as you can in a pink tutu." (Publisher's note)
"Prince's honest voice and self-deprecating humor help make young Liz a sympathetic and relatable character. The simply rendered black-and-white panel drawings have an unpretentious quality, in keeping with the narrative tone." Horn Book

Pullman, Philip
The **adventures** of John Blake: mystery of the ghost ship. by Philip Pullman; illustrated by Fred Fordham. Graphix 2017 160 p. Color; Illustration
Grades: 8 9 10 11 12   **Fic; 741.5/973; 741.5**
1. Time travel — Graphic novels; 2. Science fiction
1338149121; 9781338149128, $19.99
In this book, by Philip Pullman, illustrated by Fred Fordham, "trapped in the mists of time by a terrible research experiment gone wrong, John Blake and his mysterious ship are doomed to sail between the centuries, searching for a way home. In the ocean of the modern day, John rescues a shipwrecked young girl his own age, Serena, and promises to help. But returning Serena to her own time means traveling to the one place where the ship is in most danger of destruction." (Publisher's note)
"With obvious affection for Tintin, Pullman threads this complicated skein of plot with customary measures of awe and menace...on his first expedition into the graphic novel format, he proves an expert visual storyteller." Booklist

Quinn, Jason
Gandhi: My life is my message. by Jason Quinn; illustrated by Naresh Kumar. Random House Inc 2014 212 p. Color; Illustration
Grades: 8 9 10 11 12 Adult   **741.5; 92**

1. Gandhi, Mahatma, 1869-1948
9380741227; 9789380741222, $16.99

This book by Jason Quinn, illustrated by Naresh Kumar, focuses on the life of "Mohandas Karamchand Gandhi, better known as the Mahatma or Great Soul.... We discover the man behind the legend, following him from his birth in the Indian coastal town of Porbandar in 1869, to the moment of his tragic death at the hands of an assassin in January 1948, just months after the Independence of India." (Publisher's note)

"Just as the writing eloquently intertwines explication with reenactments of dramatic, poignant events, the panels are meticulously arranged to move the reader's attention from broad and busy scenes to intimate close-ups." Booklist

Steve Jobs: genius by design. by Jason Quinn; illustrated by Amit Tayal. Random House Inc 2012 104 p. Illustration; Color
Grades: 7 8 9 10 11 12 Adult   741.5; 92
1. Apple Inc. — Officials & employees; 2. Jobs, Steve, 1955-2011; 3. Computer industry; 4. Biographical graphic novels
9380028768; 9789380028767, $12.99

This graphic novel, by Jason Quinn, illustrated by Amit Tayal, presents a biography of the 20th-century technology entrepreneur and Apple Inc. founder Steve Jobs. "Steve Jobs and his inventions changed the world we live in." The book ranges "from his birth and his adoption, through the advent of the computer age and on into the digital age. Forced out of the company he created, his indomitable vision allowed him to change the world of computers, movies, music and telecommunications." (Publisher's note)

"This cleverly designed volume provides a concise but well-balanced view of Steve Jobs the wunderkind, including his difficult personality and complex genius." Booklist

Raicht, Mike

★ The **Stuff** of Legend; Omnibus one. by Mike Raicht and Brian Smith; illustrated by Charles Paul Wilson III. Th3rd World Studios 2014 284 p. Color illustration (The Stuff of Legend)
Grades: 8 9 10 11 12 Adult   741.5
1. Kidnapping; 2. Rescues; 3. Toys; 4. Graphic novels; 5. Toys — Fiction
9780983216193; 0989574482; 9780989574488, $29.99

"This hardcover collection brings together the first two volumes.... As Allied forces fight the enemy on Europe's war-torn beaches, another battle begins in a child's bedroom in Brooklyn when the nightmarish Boogeyman snatches a boy and takes him to the realm of the Dark. The child's playthings, led by the toy soldier known as the Colonel, band together to stage a daring rescue. On their perilous mission they will confront the boy's bitter and forgotten toys, as well as betrayal in their own ranks." (Publisher's note)

"Wilson renders the harrowing closet netherworld with full-fleshed detailing and sepia tones that nail both the 1940s time frame and the classicism of children's stories. But don't mistake this for a kids' comic-the violence is often explicit, and the Boogeyman creepy enough to slither his way right back onto grownups' most-terrifying lists." Booklist

★ The **stuff** of legend; Omnibus two. by Mike Raicht and Brian Smith; illustrated by Charles Paul Wilson III. Th3rd World Studios 2014 270 p. Color illustration (The Stuff of Legend)
Grades: 8 9 10 11 12 Adult   741.5
1. Horror comic books, strips, etc.; 2. Kidnapping; 3. Toys; 4. Toys — Fiction; 5. Graphic novels
0989574490; 9780989574495, $34.99

The second omnibus edition "finds our toys at a crossroads. Unable to find their boy, our loyal toys' bonds have been tested and broken. Now scattered across The Dark, the toys must decide whether to continue their search or admit defeat and return home." (Publisher's note)

Reed, M. K.

Dinosaurs: fossils and feathers. by MK Reed, illustrated by Joe Flood. First Second 2016 117 p. Color; Illustration
Grades: 4 5 6 7 8   741.5; 567.9
1. Dinosaurs — Juvenile literature; 2. Paleontology — Juvenile literature
9781626727281, $60; 9781626721449, $19.99; 1626721432; 9781626721432, $9.99; 1626721440

LC 2016012765

In this graphic novel by MK Reed, illustrated by Joe Flood, published as part of the Science Comics series, "learn all about the history of paleontology! This fascinating look at dinosaur science covers the last 150 years of dinosaur hunting, and illuminates how our ideas about dinosaurs have changed — and continue to change." (Publisher's note)

"There's some humor along with a solid presentation of facts, and the clean design helps makes the information accessible; the somewhat advanced content makes the book most appropriate for upper-elementary-age readers." Horn Book

Includes bibliographical references.

Regnaud, Jean

★ **My** mommy is in America and she met Buffalo Bill. Jean Regnaud & Émile Bravo; [translation, Vanessa Champion and Elizabeth Tierman]. Fanfare/Ponent Mon 2009 120p. Illustration
Grades: 6 7 8 9 10 11 12 Adult   741.5; Fic
1. Family life — Graphic novels; 2. Graphic novels; 3. Mother — Graphic novels; 4. School life — Graphic novels
978-84-96427-85-3, $25

Essentials Award winner at the 35th Festival of Angouleme,n France, 2008; Tam Tam Literary Award 2009 from Salon du Livres et de la Presse Jeunesse, for Comic Album, age group eight to thirteen years old.

Narrator Jean has just started first grade and has a younger brother, Paul, in kindergarten. They live with their factory boss father and nanny Yvette; Jean says his mother is on a trip. As he talks about his first day at school, meeting a new friend, Alain, and fighting with Paul, he mentions his mother has been away so long he can't quite remember her. Next door neighbor Michelle claims to be receiving postcards from Jean's mother and reads them to him; they come from places such as Switzerland and the United States. As the reader sees Jean and Paul spend a day with their mother's parents and interact with their grandparents' friends, the reader understands what Jean does not: his mother is dead. This book, translated from its original French, won an award for best comic album for ages eight to thirteen; however, with the essential fact never stated and Jean deciding that he's getting to old to believe in his mother, just as he's too old to believe in Father Christmas, makes this more suitable for the upper age range, teens, and adults.

Renier, Aaron

★ The **unsinkable** Walker Bean. written and illustrated by Aaron Renier; colored by Alec Longstreth. First Second 2010 191p. Illustration
Grades: 5 6 7 8   741.5; Fic
978-1-59643-453-0 (pa), $13.99; 1-59643-453-8 (pa)
Followed by: The unsinkable Walker Bean and the knights of the waxing moon (2018)

Renner, Benjamin

★ The **big** bad fox. Benjamin Renner; English translation by Joe Johnson. First Second 2017 187 p. Color; Illustration
Grades: 3 4 5 6 7   741.5/973; Fic

1. Foxes — Fiction; 2. Chickens — Comic books, strips, etc.; 3. Chickens — Fiction; 4. Foxes — Comic books, strips, etc.; 5. Foxes — Fiction; 6. Parenting — Fiction

9781626723313, $15.99; 1626723311, $15.99

LC 2016945555

In this book, by Benjamin Renner, "fox dreams of being the terror of the barnyard. But no one is intimidated by him, least of all the hens — when he picks a fight with one, he always ends up on the losing end. Even the wolf, the most fearsome beast of the forest, can't teach him how to be a proper predator. It looks like the fox will have to spend the rest of his life eating turnips." (Publisher's note)

Originally published as Le grand méchant renard by Éditions Delcourt in 2015.

Riess, Natalie

Space battle lunchtime; Volume 1: lights, camera, snacktion!. Natalie Riess; [edited by] Robin Herrera. Oni Press 2016 120 p. Color; Illustration

Grades: 3 4 5 6 7

741.5; Fic

1. Reality television programs — Juvenile fiction

1620103133; 9781620103135, $12.99

LC 2016937918

Courtesy of Oni Press

"Earth baker Peony gets the deal of a lifetime when she agrees to be a contestant on the Universe's hottest reality TV show, Space Battle Lunchtime! But that was before she knew that it shoots on location... on a spaceship... and her alien competitors don't play nice! Does Peony really have what it takes to be the best cook in the Galaxy? Tune in and find out!" (Publisher's note)

"An odd yet well-spun mixture of food fiction and space tales, with a dash of pop culture, this unusual charmer defies genre conventions and seems to revel in its own sheer individuality and campy wonder." Kirkus

Another title in this series is: A recipe for disaster (2017)

Space battle lunchtime; Volume two: A recipe for disaster. by Natalie Riess. Oni Press 2017 120 p. Color; Illustration

Grades: 3 4 5 6 7

741.5; Fic

1. Bakers and bakeries — Comic books, strips, etc.; 2. Extraterrestrial beings — Comic books, strips, etc.

9781620104040, $12.99; 1620104040

Courtesy of Oni Press

"It's almost time for the season finale of Space Battle Lunchtime, and finalist Peony...is nowhere to be found!...[S]he's been kidnapped and taken to the set of Space Battle Lunchtime's biggest rival, Cannibal Coliseum, where chefs compete to cook...each other. Up against some of the most dangerous aliens in the galaxy, will Peony even make it to the end of the show? Stay tuned!" (Publisher's note)

"Given that there's a relative dearth of LGBTQ characters in kids' comics, this is a welcome addition to a growing wave of better representation. Riess' illustrations are colorful and bubbly, with hints of manga influence that goes well with the lively space adventure." Booklist

Riordan, Rick

Percy Jackson & the Olympians, book one: the lightning thief: the graphic novel. adapted by Robert Venditti; art by Attila Futaki; color by José Villarrubia; layouts by Orpheus Collar; lettering by Chris Dickey. Hyperion Books for Children 2010 un Illustration

Grades: 5 6 7 8 9 10   **741.5; Fic**

1. Adventure graphic novels; 2. Fantasy graphic novels; 3. Graphic novels; 4. Greek mythology — Graphic novels

978-1-4231-1696-7, $19.99; 978-1-4321-1710-0 (pa), $9.99

Twelve-year-old Percy Jackson has had a hard time in school, but when a teacher transforms into a Fury and tries to kill him during a field trip to the museum, his life becomes even more complicated. He learns that he is the son of one of the Greek gods and a human woman, and then he learns that he should never have been born, and that the gods think he has stolen Zeus's master lightning bolt. Percy, his best friend Grover (a satyr), and Annabeth, daughter of Athena, have ten days to recover the lightning bolt and prevent all-out war among the Olympians. This graphic novel adapts Riordan's novel, NOT the movie. Futaki makes the water action look great in an adaptation that should make the book fans happy.

The **red** pyramid: the graphic novel. Rick Riordan; adapted by Orpheus Collar; lettered by Jared Fletcher. Disney/Hyperion Books 2012 un Color; Illustration (The Kane chronicles)

Grades: 4 5 6 7 8 9   **741.5**

1. Egyptian mythology — Fiction; 2. Magic — Fiction; 3. Brothers and sisters — Fiction

1423150694; 1423150686; 9781423150695, $12.99; 9781423150688, $21.99

LC 2012007905

"Since their mother's death, Sadie and Carter have become near-strangers. While Sadie has lived with her grandparents in London, Carter has traveled the world with their father, the famed Egyptologist Dr. Julius Kane. One night, Dr. Kane brings the siblings to the British Museum, where he hopes to set things right for his family. Instead, he unleashes the Egyptian god Set, who banishes him to oblivion and forces the children to flee for their lives." (Publisher's note)

"Out of necessity, much of the dialogue is dedicated to explaining actions and events, but a constant stream of humor prevents the reader from getting bogged down by logistics. The colorful artwork has an almost painting-like quality,...and some clever visual jokes and thoughtful use of panels make good use of the format." VOYA

Rioux, Jo-Anne

The **golden** twine; Book 1. Jo Rioux. Kids Can Press 2012 111 p. Color illustration

Grades: 5 6 7 8

741.5/971; 741.5; Fic

1. Paranormal fiction; 2. Magic — Fiction; 3. Dragons — Fiction; 4. Monsters — Fiction

1554536367; 9781554536368, $17.95; 9781554536375

Courtesy of Kids Can Press

In this book by author Jo Rioux, "parentless young storyteller Suri [buys a dragon tooth that brings her luck]...The ball of magical golden string that she finds...belongs to a trio of vicious tiger creatures called 'caitsiths' who use the string to masquerade as humans and...want it back... Suri [also] achieves her ...desire to become a monster tamer when she meets Byron, a humongous if overly friendly dog, and the surly 500-year-old imp Caglio who...created him." (Kirkus)

Robbins, Trina

★ The **drained** brains caper. [by] Trina Robbins and Tyler Page. Graphic Universe 2010 64p. Illustration (Chicagoland Detective Agency)
Grades: 4 5 6 7
Fic; 741; 741.5
1. Brainwashing — Fiction; 2. Graphic novels; 3. Humorous graphic novels; 4. Japanese Americans — Graphic novels; 5. Mystery graphic novels; 6. Schools — Graphic novels
978-0-7613-4601-2 (lib bdg), $27.97;
0-7613-4601-5 (lib bdg);
978-0-7613-5635-6 (pa), $6.95;
0-7613-5635-5 (pa)

Courtesy of Lerner Publishing Group

LC 2009-32620

Required to attend summer school after moving to Chicagoland, thirteen-year-old manga-love Megan Yamamura needs help from twelve-year-old computer genius Raf Hernandez to escape the maniacal principal's mind control experiment.

This tells "an entertaining story.... Page's black-and-white cartooning has a loose manga slant, with peppy goofiness popping out from stippled screen tones." Booklist

Other titles in this series are: The Maltese mummy (2011);Night of the living dogs (2012);The big flush (2012);The bark in space (2013);A midterm night's scheme (2014)

Roberts, Steven

Henry Ford. by Steven Roberts. PowerKids Press 2013 24 p. (Jr. graphic American inventors)
Grades: 3 4 5 6   **338.7/629222092; 92; B**
1. Automobile industry and trade — United States — Biography; 2. Industrialists — United States — Biography; 3. Ford, Henry, 1863-1947; 4. Inventors
147770079X; 9781477700792, $25.25; 9781477701430;
9781477701447

LC 2012020485

This book, by Steven Roberts, presents a biography of inventor Henry Ford. "It looks at the man who perfected the mass market automobile. From a young age Ford tinkered with farm machines and fixed neighbors' watches. That led to jobs working with steam engines and then, under the employment of Thomas Edison, the internal combustion engine. Inspired by the work flow of other factories, Ford created the Model T,and in just a few years, he was creating a million cars per year." (Booklist)
Includes index.

Robert Fulton. by Steven Roberts. PowerKids Press 2013 24 p.
Grades: 3 4 5 6   **92**
1. Inventors — United States — Biography; 2. Marine engineers — United States — Biography; 3. Steamboats; 4. Fulton, Robert, 1765-1815
1477700773; 9781477700778, $25.25; 9781477701393;
9781477701409

LC 2012020630

In this graphic novel by Steven Roberts "readers will [learn] more about [Robert] Fulton and his contributions to American society through easy to follow text and vibrant illustrations." It notes that "Robert Fulton didn t actually invent what he is most commonly associated with, yet Fulton s innovations on the steamboat changed America s trade and travel in a progressive way." (Publisher's note)
Includes bibliographical references (p. 24) and index

Rodolphe

Scrooge: A Christmas Carol & A Remembrance of Mugby. Adapted by Rodolphe & Estelle Meyrand. Papercutz 2012 96 p. Color illustration
Grades: 3 4 5 6
Fic; 741.5/973
1. Christmas — Fiction; 2. Ghosts — Fiction; 3. England — Fiction; 4. Ghost stories; 5. Supernatural — Fiction
1597073458; 1597073466;
9781597073455, $11.99;
9781597073462, $15.00

Courtesy of NBM Publishing

This book, part of the Classics Illustrated Deluxe series, presents a graphic adaptation of the Charles Dickens stories "A Christmas Carol" and "Mugby Junction." In "A Christmas Carol," miser Ebenezer Scrooge is "visited by three spirits who will show him the way to change" on Christmas Eve. (Masterplots) "Mugby Junction" also features elements of the supernatural and a protagonist to whom his future is revealed." (Publisher's note)

Rol, Ruud van der

The **search**. [by] Eric Heuvel, Ruud van der Rol [and] Lies Schippers; [English translation by Lorraine T. Miller]. Farrar, Straus and Giroux 2009 61p. Illustration
Grades: 5 6 7 8 9   **741.5; Fic**
1. Grandmothers — Fiction; 2. Graphic novels; 3. Holocaust survivors — Fiction; 4. Holocaust, 1933-1945 — Graphic novels; 5. Jews — Netherlands — Fiction
978-0-374-36517-2, $18.99; 978-0-374-46455-4 (pa), $9.99

LC 2009-13603

After recounting her experience as a Jewish girl living in Amsterdam during the Holocaust, Esther, helped by her grandson, embarks on a search to discover what happened to her parents before they died in a concentration camp.

Esther, her grandson Daniel, and her friend Helena's grandson Jeroen visit the Dutch farm where Esther hid during the Nazi occupation of the Netherlands during World War II. She tells her story, of how she managed to escape the Nazi roundup of Jews, but how her family died in a concentration camp. Daniel helps her find an old friend from the farm, now living in Israel, and he tells her what happened to her family in Auschwitz. The book depicts some of the horrendous, horrible things that happened but does it without graphic violence or gore.

Roman, Dave

Agnes Quill: an anthology of mystery. all transcripts written by Dave Roman; illustrated by Jason Ho, Raina Telgemeier, Jeff Zornow and Dave Roman. SLG Publishing 2006 130p. Illustration
Grades: 7 8 9 10 11 12   **741.5**
1. Graphic novels; 2. Horror graphic novels; 3. Mystery graphic novels
978-1-59362-052-3, $10.95

Orphaned teen Agnes Quill lives in the city of Legerdemain and carries on a family tradition; she can see and communicate with ghosts, and she works as a detective to help them. Her cases range from recovering the mummified head of a ghost's old body in order to save the valuable necklace hidden there, to helping a little girl ghost find her doll, to helping a man find his legs, and more. Roman works with artists including Raina Telgemeier, and their styles range from childlike cartoons to gloomy, atmospheric art full of shadows.

"The variety of drawing styles and Agnes' story of being a teenage detective who can see the dead among the living combine in an interesting read that will likely keep readers' attention." Voice Youth Advocates

Astronaut Academy: Zero gravity. First Second Books 2011 185p. Illustration

Grades: 4 5 6 7 8   **741; 741.5; Fic**

1. Graphic novels; 2. Humorous graphic novels; 3. School life — Graphic novels; 4. Science fiction graphic novels
9781596436206, $9.99; 9781596437562, $16.99

LC 2010-941434

Hakata Soy has been the leader of a futuristic superhero team, but he has given that up and just wants to be a normal student at Astronaut Academy, a school on a space station, where students take such courses as anti-gravity gymnastics and fire-throwing. Other students include Doug Hiro, who always wears his space helmet, rich girl Maribelle Mellonbelly, Miyumi San (Maribelle's rival), and egotistical Billy Lee. Hakata Soy has some trouble adjusting to school life, and things get much worse when the villainous Gotcha Birds steal a robotic twin to Hakata Soy and reprogram it to kill him. The comics originally appeared as web comics, then as mini comics that Roman took to various comic cons; this is the first trade book collection of the stories. Middle grade students, boys and girls, will enjoy this book, which is full of humor and action with little actual violence.

"Students like the introspective Hakata Soy, the space-gymnastics-obsessed Doug Hiro, and the snooty rich girl Mirabelle Mellonbelly meet up at Astronaut Academy, a middle school where the zany mixes with the postmodern.... Silliness is high on the agenda, aided by minimal, cartoonish art that plays on manga tropes but also manages to build character into the simple lines of a face.... This is one for readers looking for more involved and complex comedy than a cursory glance at the images might lead one to expect." Booklist

Followed by: Astronaut academy: Re-entry (2013)

Jax Epoch and the Quicken Forbidden: Borrowed Magic. Dave Roman, writer; John Green, artist. AiT/PlanetLar 2003 152p. Illustration

Grades: 7 8 9 10 11 12 Adult   **741.5; Fic**

1. Graphic novels; 2. Science fiction graphic novels
1-932051-11-2, $14.95

When teenager Jax stumbles into an interdimensional portal, she "borrows" several items: an ancient book, a pair of gloves, and a pair of boots. When she returns home through the portal, things are a bit...off. Her little escapade has caused magic to leak into her world, and now she's deep in trouble, unstuck in time and on trial for the crime of crossing dimensions. The story continues in Volume 2: Separation Anxiety.

"Jax is a great character — quite real but with flaws that get her into deep trouble while possessing the aplomb to get herself out." (VOYA)

Followed by Volume 2: Separation Anxiety

Rosa, Don

Walt Disney's Uncle $crooge and Donald Duck: the Son of the sun. [written and drawn by Don Rosa; lettered by John Clark]. Fantagraphics Books 2014 207 p. Color; Illustration

Grades: 7 8 9 10 11 12 Adult   **741.5**

1. Comic books, strips, etc.; 2. Fictional characters; 3. Ducks — Fiction
1606997424; 9781606997420, $29.99

LC 2012287668

This collection by Don Rosa, featuring Disney's Donald Duck and Scrooge McDuck, is "filled with epic adventures, like hunting for buried treasure or recovering stolen money.... At the end of each volume are whole pages of reference notes, explaining each comic in depth and addressing Rosa's process and nods to previous works." (School Library Journal)

"When Rosa began creating Uncle Scrooge comics in 1987, his work instilled childish wonder in readers. Disney comics had entirely disappeared from circulation, and those that had just preceded the fall had

become completely hackneyed-rife with repeating storylines and drab artwork. But under Rosa's creative flair, a zippy, glamorous franchise suddenly appeared, with riveting stories and detailed yet kinetic artwork. While remaining totally true to Scrooge McDuck's ornery persona, Rosa turned the moody miser into a plucky adventurer worthy of Tintin." Pub Wkly

Other titles in this series are: Return to plain awful (2014); Treasure under glass (2015)

Rosca, Madeleine

Hollow Fields Omnibus collection. Seven Seas Entertainment 2009 un Illustration

Grades: 5 6 7 8 9 10   **741.5; Fic**

1. Adventure graphic novels; 2. Graphic novels; 3. Science fiction graphic novels
978-1-934876-72-5, $14.99

Rosca is an Australian global manga creator who won one of the inaugural International Manga Awards ¿Shorei¿ awards given by the Japanese government in 2007.

Lucy Snow was supposed to start school at a nice elementary school in town, but she manages to lose her way in a forest and finds herself at Miss Weaver's Academy for the Scientifically Gifted and Ethically Unfettered a school for archvillains in training. Lucy's fellow students are all learning how to be mad scientists and evil geniuses, with classes such as Live Taxidermy, Cross-Species Body-Part Transplantation, and Killer Robot Construction. Hollow Fields, as the school is also called, also has a practice guaranteed to make everyone compete to do well: the student with the lowest grades at the end of the week is sent to the windmill for detention, and thus far no student has ever returned. Miss Weaver has experimented on herself, as have all the Engineers who teach; what the reader learns is that they need new, young blood to keep their stitched-together bodies going, for they are all more than a hundred years old. Befriended by a talking box that calls itself Doctor Bleak, Lucy struggles to hold her own in her classes, despite her innate niceness. She decides she needs to discover just what goes on in the windmill, and how she can make things right. The book includes some mild violence.

Rubin, Sean

Bolivar. by Sean Rubin. Archaia, a division of Boom Entertainment 2017 224 p. Color; Illustration

Grades: 3 4 5 6   **741.5; Fic**

1. Boys — Fiction; 2. Dinosaurs — Fiction
1684150698; 9781684150694, $29.99

In this book, by Sean Rubin, "Sybil knows that there is something off about her next door neighbor, but she can't seem to get anyone to believe her. Everyone is so busy going about their days in the busy streets of New York City that they don't notice Bolivar. They don't notice his odd height, his tiny arms, or his long tail. No one but Sybil sees that Bolivar is a dinosaur." (Publisher's note)

"The text, delivered in bite-size speech bubbles and compact sentences, crackles with sly humor. And Rubin's sweeping panoramas (from city blocks to the subway) and idiosyncratic details-all rendered in rich hues and lively cross-hatching-never fail to infuse the everyday with a dash of quiet magic." Booklist

Ruiz, Emilio

Waluk. by Emilio Ruiz; illustrated by Ana Miralles; translated and adapted by Dan Oliverio. Graphic Universe 2013 52 p.

Grades: 3 4 5 6   **741.5; Fic**

1. Bears — Fiction; 2. Graphic novels; 3. Polar bear — Fiction; 4. Tundras — Fiction; 5. Friendship — Fiction

Courtesy of Lerner Publishing Group

1467715980; 1467716065;
9781467715980, $26.60;
9781467716062, $7.95

LC 2012047787

"Young Waluk is all alone. His mother has abandoned him, as is the way of polar bears, and now he must fend for himself. But he doesn't know much about the world — and unfortunately, his Arctic world is changing quickly. The ice is melting, and food is hard to find." (Publisher's note)

"Marrying exemplary sequential storytelling, mythology, and science and enhanced through respectful anthropomorphizing, Waluk takes readers into a realistic world of polar bears endangered by climate change." Booklist

Originally published in Spanish in Bilbao, Spain, by Astiberri, in 2011, under the title: Wáluk.

Runton, Andy

★ **Owly** Vol. 2: Just a Little Blue. Top Shelf Productions 2005 127p. Illustration

Grades: K 1 2 3 4 5 6 7 8 9 10 11 12 Adult   **741.5; Fic**

1. Friendship — Graphic novels; 2. Graphic novels; 3. Stories without words — Graphic novels

1-891830-64-3, $10

Owly is a kind, yet lonely, little owl who's always on the search for new friends and adventure. Owly learns that sometimes you have to make sacrifices and work at things that are important, especially friendship. He and Wormy try to help a stubborn bluebird by building a new home, but the bluebird rejects it and them.

★ **Owly** Vol. 3: Flying Lessons. Top Shelf Productions 2005 143p. Illustration

Grades: K 1 2 3 4 5 6 7 8 9 10 11 12 Adult   **741.5; Fic**

1. Friendship — Graphic novels; 2. Graphic novels; 3. Stories without words — Graphic novels

1-891830-76-7, $10

Owly figures out why he can't fly (he failed his childhood flying lessons), and helps another forest creature with his own flying problems. The flying squirrel is frightened by Owly, for he knows owls are hunters, but Owly isn't like that. How can he convince the squirrel he just wants to be friends?

★ **Owly** vol. 4: a time to be brave. Top Shelf Productions 2007 132p. Illustration

Grades: K 1 2 3 4 5 6 7 8 9 10 11 12 Adult   **741.5; Fic**

1. Fantasy graphic novels; 2. Friendship — Graphic novels; 3. Graphic novels; 4. Owls — Graphic novels; 5. Stories without words — Graphic novels

978-1-891830-89-1, $10

A new visitor comes to the forest, but Wormy is scared of him because Owly had just read stories about a scary dragon, and the visitor seems to look scary. The visitor is just as scared of Owly. Things aren't just as they seem, and everyone soon finds out that a little bravery and a lot of friendship can fix just about anything. This is the latest volume in Runton's nearly wordless series about Owly and his friends.

★ **Owly** volume five: tiny tales. Top Shelf Productions 2008 175p. Illustration

Grades: K 1 2 3 4 5 6 7 8 9 10 11 12 Adult   **741.5; Fic**

1. Friendship — Graphic novels; 2. Graphic novels; 3. Humorous graphic novels

978-1-60309-019-3, $10

This volume gathers short stories about Owly and his friends, including stories originally published for Free Comic Book Day issues from Top Shelf Productions, the first Owly mini-comics, drawings of Owly before he met Wormy, and more. Among the stories, Owly saves a friend from drowning in the cold river when the ice cracks, only to get caught in the hole himself; Owly finds a way to keep both the bees and hummingbirds happy when they get into a "turf" battle; Owly helps a friend when she falls and breaks the fancy potted plant she bought for a present; and more.

★ **Owly:** The way home and The bittersweet summer. [by] Andy Runton. Top Shelf 2004 160p. Illustration

Grades: K 1 2 3 4 5 6 7 8 9 10 11 12   **741.5; Fic**

1. Friendship — Graphic novels; 2. Graphic novels; 3. Owls — Graphic novels

1-891830-62-7, $10

LC 2005298860

Rotund little Owly befriends Wormy despite their differences, and together they help a couple of hummingbirds and learn that friendship doesn't end with separation.

"The whimsical black-and-white art is done with great facility for expressing emotion, and Runton's reliance on icons and pictures in lieu of the usual dialogue makes the story perfect for give-and-take between children and their parents." Booklist

Other titles in this series are: Owly: Just a little blue (2005); Owly: Flying lessons (2005);Owly: A time to be brave (2007);Owly: Tiny tales (2008)

Russell, P. Craig

★ **Coraline.** based on the novel by Neil Gaiman; adapted and illustrated by P. Craig Russell; colorist, Lovern Kindzierski; letterer, Todd Klein. HarperCollins 2008 186p. Illustration

Grades: 4 5 6 7   **741; Fic; 741.5**

1. Graphic novels; 2. Horror graphic novels; 3. Gaiman, Neil, 1960- — Adaptations

978-0-06-082543-0, $18.99; 978-0-06-082544-7 (lib bdg), $19.89

LC 2007-930658

"An adaptation of Gaiman's 2002 novel Coraline,...a tale of childhood nightmares. As in the original story, Coraline wanders around her new house and finds a door leading into a mirror place, where she finds her button-eyed "other mother," who is determined to secure Coraline's love one way or another. This version is a virtuoso adaptation.... A master of fantastical landscapes, Russell sharpens the realism of his imagery, perserving the humanity of the characters and heightening the horror." Booklist

Fairy Tales of Oscar Wilde Vol. 4: The Devoted Friend & The Nightingale and the Rose. NBM Publishing 2004 un Illustration

Grades: 5 6 7 8 9

741.5; Fic

1. Fantasy graphic novels; 2. Graphic novels; 3. Wilde, Oscar, 1854-1900

978-1-56163-391-3, $16.99

This volume adapts The Devoted Friend," on what constitutes real friendship, and The Nightingale and the Rose," a story of sacrifice to love with a cruel twist. In both stories, innocence is sacrificed to cynicism and shallowness.

Courtesy of NBM Publishing

Fairy tales of Oscar Wilde: 5: The Happy Prince. illustrated by P. Craig Russell. Nantier, Beall, Minoustchine 2012 32 p. Color illustration
Grades: 3 4 5 6 7 8
741.5/973; Fic
1. Generosity — Fiction; 2. Fairy tales; 3. Wilde, Oscar, 1854-1900
1561636266; 9781561636266, $16.99
LC 93229468

Courtesy of NBM Publishing

For this book, "Eisner Award-winning [P. Craig] Russell has adapted into graphic novel form" the Oscar Wilde fairy tale "The Happy Prince." In the story, "a swallow...befriends the statue of the Happy Prince, who was indeed happy when he lived a sheltered life. Now, however, the prince stands over the city as a statue and sees all the suffering. With the help of the swallow, he breaks down the pieces of himself, his rubies, sapphire, and gold, to feed the starving people." (Publishers Weekly)

★ The **graveyard** book graphic novel Volume 1. based on the novel by Neil Gaiman; adapted by P. Craig Russell; illustrated by Kevin Nowlan, P. Craig Russell, Tony Harris, Scott Hampton, Galen Showman, Jill Thompson, Stephen B. Scott; colorist, Lovern Kindzierski; letterer, Rick Parker. HarperCollins 2014 188 p. Color; Illustration
Grades: 5 6 7 8 9 10
741.5; Fic
1. Cemeteries — Fiction; 2. Orphans — Fiction; 3. Graphic novels; 4. Gaiman, Neil — Adaptations
9780062194817, $19.99; 006219481X
LC 2013953799

This graphic novel is an adaptation of the "Newbery Medal-winning novel, [where] Bod is an unusual boy..., the only living resident of a graveyard. Raised from infancy by the ghosts, werewolves, and other cemetery denizens, Bod has learned the antiquated customs of his guardians' time as well as their ghostly teachings." (Publisher's note)

"Russell brings his decades of comics know-how to this lovely, lyrical adaptation of [Gaiman's] well-loved, Newbery Medal — winning book. Not content to rely exclusively on his own distinctive talents, Russell has enlisted some of the industry's greatest contemporary illustrators as contributors, who fill the panels with appropriately gothic tones. In order to give ample room to the novel's twists and turns, the adaptation has been divided into two parts." Booklist

Ruth, Greg
The **lost** boy. Greg Ruth. GRAPHIX 2013 192 p.
Grades: 3 4 5 6 7
741.5
1. Historical fiction — Fiction; 2. Fantasy fiction
0439823323; 9780439823319, $24.99; 9780439823326, $12.99; 9780545576901
LC 2013937147

This book by Greg Ruth "opens as a boy named Nate moves to a new town and discovers a tape recorder hidden underneath the floorboards of his bedroom. The action shifts back several decades as Nate listens to recordings left by Walter Pidgen, an outcast boy who disappeared without a trace. Along with a neighbor, Tabitha, Nate is drawn into a supernatural battle involving the denizens of an ancient woodland kingdom, which include talking toys and insects." (Publishers Weekly)

Sakai, Stan
★ **Usagi** Yojimbo, book one: The Ronin. Stan Sakai. Fantagraphics Books 1999 144p. Illustration
Grades: 7 8 9 10 11 12
741.5; Fic

1. Adventure graphic novels; 2. Graphic novels; 3. Rabbits — Graphic novels; 4. Samurai — Graphic novels; 5. Usagi Yojimbo (Fictional character); 6. Japan — Graphic novels
0-930193-35-0; 978-0-930193-35-5, $15.95
LC 93-239124

This series contains the adventures of Miyamoto Usagi, a ronin samurai rabbit in 17th-century Japan.
First published 1987; Vol. 1 of an ongoing series; Vols. 1-7 published by Fantagraphics; Vols. 8-25 published by Dark Horse Comics; Volume 1 of an ongoing series

★ **Usagi** Yojimbo: Yokai. created, written, and illustrated by Stan Sakai. Dark Horse Books 2009 62p. Illustration
Grades: 6 7 8 9 10 11 12 Adult
741.5; Fic
1. Adventure graphic novels; 2. Graphic novels; 3. Monsters — Graphic novels; 4. Samurai — Graphic novels; 5. Usagi Yojimbo (Fictional character); 6. Japan — Graphic novels
978-1-59582-362-5, $14.95
LC 2009-20024

As he walks through a spooky forest at night, samurai rabbit Usagi Yojimbo encounters a woman who begs him to find her daughter, who was kidnapped and dragged into the forest. That night, the yokai — monsters, demons, and spirits from Japanese folklore — are amassing for a once-a-century attempt to take over the living world. Armed only with his swords and his wit, Usagi can't hope to win against so many supernatural beings, but luckily Sasuke the Demon Queller has come, knowing about the yokais' plan, and together they fight the gathered monsters. The fighting is not graphic or bloody, and the monsters and demons aren't too scary looking for most younger readers.

"Sakai's art deftly demonstrates that comics can be simultaneously cartoony and scary.... Usagi Yojimbo is a genuine pleasure for readers of all ages." Publ Wkly

Sakurakoji, Kanoko
Backstage Prince, Vol. 1. Viz Media/Shojo Beat 2007 188p. Illustration
Grades: 8 9 10 11 12 Adult
741.5; Fic
1. Graphic novels; 2. Kabuki — Graphic novels; 3. Manga; 4. Romance graphic novels; 5. Shojo manga
978-1-4215-1172-6, $8.99

High school freshman Akari stumbles into hottie Ryusei Horiuchi and hurts him with her school bag. That evening, she stumbles upon the kabuki theater where he, as famous kabuki actor Shonosuke Ichimura, is performing, and becomes his backstage assistant. Ryusei is very shy and aloof, and he's only opened up to his cat, Mr. Ken, and now to Akari; and she, despite herself, has fallen hard for Ryusei. Can an ordinary girl and a handsome, famous actor be together?

Sava, Scott Christian
Cameron and his dinosaurs. IDW Publishing 2009 174p. Illustration
Grades: 3 4 5 6 7 8
741.5; Fic
1. Adventure graphic novels; 2. Dinosaurs — Graphic novels; 3. Graphic novels; 4. Humorous graphic novels; 5. Robots — Graphic novels
978-1-60010-315-5, $12.99

The mad scientist, Professor Poindexter P. Poppycock, uses dinosaur DNA to create living dinosaurs which he plans to use for nefarious purposes. Unfortunately for him, he gave them human intelligence and the ability to speak, and the dinosaurs Charlie the tyrannosaurus rex, Dee Dee the pterodactyl, Lizzy the triceratops, and Vinnie the brachiosaurus decline to be evil and leave him. They befriend young Cameron, who helps to introduce them to the world. Professor Poppycock then creates robotic dinosaurs to do the will of the Brotherhood of Universal Revolution for Political Subterfuge (B.U.R.P.S.) to kidnap the President and take over the country. It will be up to Charlie, Dee Dee, Lizzy, Vinnie, and Cameron in his new souped-up wheelchair (with some awesome top-secret adaptations) to save the President and stop the robot dinosaurs. This book reads like an action-packed cartoon.

Hyperactive. by Scott Christian Sava; artist, Joseph Bergin. IDW Publishing/Worthwhile Children's Books 2009 108p. Illustration
Grades: 3 4 5 6 7 8   741.5; Fic
1. Adventure graphic novels; 2. Graphic novels; 3. Humorous graphic novels; 4. Superhero graphic novels
978-1-60010-313-1, $12.99; 1-60010-313-8

"Joey Johnson learns he can move at super speed and puts his power to good use doing household chores. But when word gets out, a shady executive sees the opportunity to make big bucks off of Joey's super DNA.... With its surprise ending, which suggests more to come, a readership of young boys will ensure that this one flies off the shelf at the speed of light." Booklist

The **lab**: hey . . . test this!. Astonish Factory 2004 120p. Illustration
Grades: 5 6 7 8 9   741.5; Fic
1. Graphic novels; 2. Humorous graphic novels; 3. Science fiction graphic novels
0-9721259-3-0, $14.95

"A collection of previously published comics and original stories that highlight the working relationship between Livingston, a scientist mole, and his goofball assistant, Esteban, a weasel whose ultrasensitivity to chemicals makes him an excellent test subject for new products. With bright, colorful pictures, the stories usually consist of observing Esteban's outlandish reactions to Livingston's concoctions, such as floating to the ceiling, shrinking to microscopic size, or singing uncontrollably." SLJ

My Grandparents are Secret Agents. IDW Publishing 2009 104p.
Grades: 3 4 5 6   741.5; Fic
1. Adventure graphic novels; 2. Graphic novels; 3. Humorous graphic novels; 4. Mystery graphic novels
978-1-60010-314-8, $11.99

Secret agents The Sicilian and the Diva defeat Dr. Dementia, and after the successful mission they want to spend a weekend with their grandchildren, Nicholas and Alyssa, while the kids' parents go on a romantic trip. However, the Social Security Administration (a secret government agency working to keep the U.S. safe) needs their top two agents to go after a villain named Purple Haze, who intends to use a time machine to make everything go back to the late 1960s. Grandma and Grandpa have to take Nicholas and Alyssa with them, along with the robot security dog named S.N.A.C.K.S, to stop the whacked-out villain. Spanish illustrator Mourgues and the Invasor Creative Art Studio use a very colorful, cartoony style.

Schrag, Ariel
Stuck in the middle: seventeen comics from an unpleasant age. edited by Ariel Schrag. Viking 2007 210p. Illustration
Grades: 7 8 9 10 11 12   741.5; Fic
1. Graphic novels; 2. Middle schools — Graphic novels; 3. Teenagers — Graphic novels
978-0-670-06221-8, O.P.

LC 2006-52581
This book collects seventeen short stories about the perils of middle school, each by independent comics creators, including editor Schrag, her younger sister Tania Schrag, Aaron Renier, Daniel Clowes, Gabrielle Bell, and others. Stories include the experience of being the new kid in school, getting betrayed by your best friend, being a Jewish nonathlete at a Christian sports summer camp, finding a creative outlet despite having attention deficit disorder, and more of the everyday bad situations and joys

of being twelve and thirteen years old. Some harsh language (one story is also called "Shit") reflects the reality of young teen life.

Schulz, Charles M.
★ The **Complete** Peanuts: 1950-1952. Fantagraphics Books 2004 330p. Illustration
Grades: 2 3 4 5 6 7 8 9 10 11 12 Adult   741.5; Fic
1. Graphic novels; 2. Humorous graphic novels; 3. Peanuts (Comic strip) — Graphic novels
1-56097-589-X, $28.95

This is the first volume of a project to collect all of Schulz's Peanuts comic strips from 1950 to 2000. This volume includes the strips published from October 2, 1950 through all of 1952. These early strips featured characters younger readers may not recognize: Patty (not Peppermint Patty), Violet, Shermy, and a Snoopy who behaves like a normal dog. Schroeder is a baby who's already a whiz at the toy piano; Lucy is a toddler who already causes trouble for Charlie Brown; Linus shows up as a baby in September 1952. Lucy pulls the football trick on Charlie Brown for the first time in November 1952. This volume also includes a biography of Schulz and a long interview with him.
Volume 1 of 26

Schweizer, Chris
The **creeps**; 1: night of the Frankenfrogs. by Chris Schweizer. Abrams Books 2015 128 p. Color; Illustration
Grades: 3 4 5 6   741.5; Fic
1. Frogs — Fiction; 2. School stories — Fiction; 3. Scientists — Fiction
. 9781419713798, $17.95; 9781419717666, $9.95
LC 2014955691

In this book, by Chris Schweizer, as "punishment for creating a giant mess in their school, Carol, Jarvis, Mitchell, and Rosario (known to their classmates as the Creeps) are being forced to perform the tasks normally completed by the janitor. When they discover that the frog specimens intended for dissection in their science class are missing, they know that they will be blamed, so they set out to discover who the real culprit might be." (School Library Journal)

"An excellent complement to his prose, Schweizer's cleanly paneled art is bright and busy, ever ready with a gag that helps blend the ghastly with the goofy, making his gang's antics reminiscent of Scooby Doo.... Silly fun with a smattering of science." Kirkus
Another title in this series is: The trolls will feast! (2016)

Crogan's loyalty. Chris Schweizer; [edited by] James Lucas Jones. Oni Press, Inc. 2012 150 p. Color; Illustration
Grades: 8 9 10 11 12 Adult
741.5
1. Adventure graphic novels; 2. United States — History — 1775-1783, Revolution — Comic books, strips, etc.
9781934964408, $14.99; 1934964409
LC 2011943514

Courtesy of Oni Press

"Schweizer takes another bite out of history in this story of two brothers divided by the American Revolution. Charlie, the elder Crogan and a Loyalist ranger, is infuriated that his younger brother would turn rebel, stating 'There's a passion that makes most young men wanna tear society down because they ain't in charge of it.' Meanwhile, Will, a colonial scout, is no less incensed that his older brother would stand for a tyrant against his own country." (Booklist)

Crogan's march. Oni Press 2009 212p.
Illustration

Grades: 8 9 10 11 12 Adult

741.5; Fic

1. Adventure graphic novels; 2. Graphic novels; 3. Imperialism — Graphic novels; 4. North Africa — World history — 20th century — Graphic novels

978-1-934964-24-8, $14.95

Courtesy of Oni Press

When brothers Eric and Cory squabble at the dinner table, their father tells them the story of Peter Crogan, one of their ancestors, who fought in the French Foreign Legion in 1912. Crogan's five-year term of service is one month from completion when he's asked to stay and become an officer. His unit is stationed in North Africa, where the French hold territory and depend on the French Foreign Legion to police the territory, putting down the rebellious attacks of the Tuaregs. He finds himself torn between the heroic Captain Poitelet (who tends to be the sole survivor of various battles) and the grizzled sergeant who actually cares about the people the Legion polices. When Crogan's unit escorts a caravan that endures an attack by Tuaregs, the captain's reckless actions endanger everyone, and Crogan must find help. Schweizer's story includes the kind of violence military actions cause, but very little in the way of bad language. Some may wince at the heavily French-accented English of some of the characters ("zee Daughters of France send zem out to all of zee units," etc.). This action-packed historical fiction graphic novel will appeal to teens, but adults who remember such novels as Beau Geste by Percival Christopher Wren (and the movies, of course) will also enjoy reading Schweizer's tale.

This book is part of The Crogan Adventures series; Sequel to:

Crogan's vengeance (2008)

Crogan's vengeance. book design by Keith Wood; edited by James Lucas Jones with Jill Beaton. Oni Press 2008 185p. Illustration

Grades: 8 9 10 11 12 Adult

741.5; Fic

1. Adventure graphic novels; 2. Graphic novels; 3. Pirates — Graphic novels

978-1-934964-06-4, $14.95

Courtesy of Oni Press

Catfoot Crogan serves as an honest and honorable sailor on a ship commanded by an unjust captain when the ship is taken over by pirates. In order to save their lives, the sailors all take the oath to become pirates, but Crogan immediately runs afoul of D'Or, a brutal man who enjoys torturing others. Catfoot is a pirate, but he's determined to remain as honest and honorable as he can be, which continually puts him in danger. This swashbuckling tale shows a less romantic story than Rafael Sabatini's Captain Blood, with more violence, but it is more action-oriented than merely violent.

"Filled with mutiny, ferocious storms, shark-infested waters, commandeering of ships, and — of course — swashbuckling sword fights, this book has high teen appeal." SLJ

Part of the Crogan Adventures series

Scott, Mairghread

The **city** on the other side. Mairghread Scott, illustrated by Robin Robinson. First Second 2018 224 p. Color; Illustration

Grades: 4 5 6 7

741.5; Fic

1. Imaginary wars and battles — Comic books, strips, etc.; 2. Fairies — Comic books, strips, etc.; 3. Magic — Comic books, strips, etc.; 4. Missing persons — Comic books, strips, etc.

9781250152558, $23.99; 9781626724570

LC 2017941171

In this book, by Mairghread Scott, illustrated by Robin Robinson, "Isabel plays the part of a perfectly proper little girl.... She's...not the kind of girl who goes on adventures. But that all changes when Isabel breaches an invisible barrier and steps into another world. She discovers a city not unlike her own, but magical and dangerous.... Only Isabel, with the help of a magical necklace,...stands a chance of ending the war before it destroys the fairy world." (Publisher's note)

"Robinson's colorful, dynamic artwork crackles with spirited fun and portrays San Francisco and its fairy-realm equivalent in broad, evocative panels." Kirkus

Seagle, Steven T.

Camp Midnight. written by Steven T. Seagle; drawn by Jason Adam Katzenstein. Image Comics 2016 248 p. Color; Illustration

Grades: 3 4 5 6

741.5; Fic

1. Camps — Fiction; 2. Monsters — Fiction

1632155559; 9781632155559, $16.99

In this graphic novel, by Steven T. Seagle, illustrated by Jason Adam Katzenstein, "reluctant Skye is accidentally sent to the wrong summer camp. Not wanting to please her 'step monster,' Skye is dead-set on not fitting in. That won't be a problem, as everyone at Camp Midnight-with the exception of fellow camper and fast-friend Mia-is a full-fledged monster!" (Publisher's note)

"Skye's character is spunky and totally believable, and her facial expressions are priceless. The other campers are weird and funny — hugely exaggerated and drawn with a wild and crazy art style employing just a few lurid colors, which works wonderfully to evoke the mood of every camp situation." SLJ

Segami, Akira

Kagetora, volume 1. Akira Segami; translated by Akira Tsubasa; adapted by Nunzuio DeFilippis & Christina Weir; lettered by Ryan & Reilly. Del Rey Manga 2008 202p. Illustration

Grades: 8 9 10 11 12

741.5; Fic

1. Graphic novels; 2. Humorous graphic novels; 3. Manga; 4. Martial arts — Graphic novels; 5. Romance graphic novels; 6. Shonen manga

9780345491411, $10.95

Young ninja Kagetora arrives at the Toudou family dojo on assignment, and he learns that he must teach martial arts to the family hime (princess), Yuki. The problem is, Yuki is a total, absolute klutz; she's also tiny and absolutely cute and charming. As he tries his best to train her, Kagetora finds himself doing the forbidden — he's falling for Yuki. How can he perform his duty? On top of that, Yuki's best friend Aki, one of the Toudou's top students, has been protecting Yuki for years and resents Kagetora's presence. The book includes a lot of fan service, which actually ties into the plot as Kagetora can't help but look at Yuki, even though he knows that his feelings are not appropriate.

Sell, Chad

★ The **cardboard** kingdom. by Chad Sell; [with contributions by] Jay Fuller, David Demeo, Katie Schenkel, Manuel Betancourt, Molly Muldoon, Vid Alliger, Cloud Jacobs, Michael Cole, and Barbara Perez Marquez. Alfred A. Knopf 2018 288 p. Color; Illustration

Grades: 4 5 6 7

741.5; Fic

1. Friendship — Fiction; 2. Costume — Fiction; 3. Imagination — Comic books, strips, etc.

1524719374; 9781524719371, $20.99

"Welcome to a neighborhood of kids who transform ordinary boxes into colorful costumes, and their ordinary block into cardboard kingdom. This is the summer when sixteen kids encounter knights and rogues, robots and monsters — and their own inner demons — on one last quest before school starts again. In the Cardboard Kingdom, you can be anything you want to be — imagine that!" (Publisher's note)

"Sell's playful, expressive, and boldly colored artwork always keeps the mood fun, quickly shifting between the real world and the kids' imagined scenes in the Cardboard Kingdom. The blocky figures have a great cartoon quality, and, with a wide range of skin tones, genders, and family types, every kid reading will have someone to relate to." Booklist

Sexton, Adam
 Hawthorne's the Scarlet letter: the Manga edition. Wiley Publishing 2009 186p. Illustration
 Grades: 5 6 7 8 9 10 11 12   **741.5; Fic**
 1. Authors; 2. Graphic novels; 3. Novelists; 4. Short story writers; 5. Hawthorne, Nathaniel, 1804-1864; 6. Hawthorne, Nathaniel, 1804-1864 — Adaptations/Graphic novels
 978-0-470-14889-1, $9.99
 Hester Prynne, a young married woman in puritanical Massachusetts, stands in public shame when she bears a child long after her husband had disappeared. She refuses to identify the father of her child and instead wears the scarlet letter A always. The young minister Arthur Dimmesdale lives with his guilt in secret, but the physician, Roger Chillingworth, is actually Hester's husband, returned for vengeance. He vows to find the man who fathered Pearl, Hester's daughter, and destroy him. Meanwhile, Pearl grows up in a society that shuns her mother, and she comes to see the A as her mother's badge of honor. This book is a manga style adaptation of Hawthorne's novel.

Sfar, Joann
 Dungeon Vol. 1: Duck Heart. [by] Joann Sfar & Lewis Trondheim. NBM 2003 96p. Illustration
 Grades: 7 8 9 10 11 12
 741.5; Fic
 1. Fantasy graphic novels; 2. Graphic novels; 3. Humorous graphic novels
 1-56163-401-8, $14.95
 "As a result of some unfortunate accidents, Herbert, usually a lowly messenger in the great Dungeon, is called upon to defend it from all manner of beasties. In his endeavors to become a warrior, he is helped by his friend Marvin the vegetarian dragon and by the Dungeon Keeper. *Courtesy of NBM Publishing* Although there's a solid dose of cartoon-style violence and gore, teens will appreciate Herbert's pseudo-slacker attitude, which turns him into an accidental hero time and time again." Booklist
 Other titles in this series are: Dungeon, the early years: the night shirt (2005); Zenith: the barbarian princess (2005)

 ★ The **little** prince. adapted from the book by Antoine de Saint-Exupéry; translated by Sarah Ardizzone; colour by Brigitte Findakly. Houghton Mifflin Harcourt 2010 110p. Illustration
 Grades: 5 6 7 8 9   **741; Fic; 741.5**
 1. Extraterrestrial beings — Graphic novels; 2. Fantasy graphic novels; 3. Graphic novels; 4. Saint-Exupéry, Antoine de, 1900-1944 — Adaptations
 978-0-547-33802-6, $19.99; 0-547-33802-3
 "On the surface, this is a straight graphic-novel retelling of the narrator pilot getting stranded in the desert, where he meets a curious little boy who

claims to be from a wee planet very far away.... The ultimately tricky task is to honor the source but not sound like an adaptation (otherwise, why not just read the original") and Sfar nails it on both counts.... Everything is handled with both reverence and ingenuity." Booklist

 Little Vampire Does Kung Fu!. stories and drawings by Joann Sfar; colors by Walter; translated by Mark and Alexis Siegel. Simon & Schuster Books for Young Readers 2003 un Illustration
 Grades: 4 5 6 7 8 9   **741.5; Fic**
 1. Fantasy graphic novels; 2. Graphic novels; 3. Humorous graphic novels; 4. Vampires — Graphic novels
 0-689-85769-1, $12.95

 LC 2003-045770
 Jeffrey the jerk is a bully and everyone knows it. Little Vampire isn't about to stand around and watch him pick on his best friend, Michael. There's only one thing to do: travel to the highest mountain and seek kung fu lessons from the master... There's an icky moment when Little Vampire's monster friends spit up bits of Jeffrey (whom they ate) and they try to put him together again.

 The **professor's** daughter. [story by] Joann Sfar & [illustrated by] Emmanuel Guibert; translated by Alexis Siegel. First Second Books 2007 63p. Illustration
 Grades: 7 8 9 10 11 12 Adult   **741.5**
 1. Graphic novels; 2. Humorous graphic novels; 3. Mummies — Graphic novels; 4. Romance graphic novels
 978-1-59643-130-0; 1-59643-130-X, $16.95

 LC 2006-22177
 In Victorian London, Lillian, the daughter of a famed archeologist, has fallen in love with the mummy of Imhotep IV; he thinks that Lillian bears a strong resemblance to his long-dead wife. Their love faces many obstacles, from Lillian's father, the police, a pirate who is actually Imhotep III (yes, the father and another mummy), even Queen Victoria herself. Dainty Victorian manners mix with broad farce and black comedy in a beautifully illustrated book with muted colors and sepia tones.

Shakespeare, William
 William Shakespeare's King Lear. Black Dog & Leventhal/Workman Publishing 2006 148p. Illustration
 Grades: 7 8 9 10 11 12 Adult   **741.5; 822.3**
 1. Graphic novels; 2. Tragedy — Graphic novels; 3. Shakespeare, William; 4. Shakespeare, William — Adaptations
 978-1-57912-617-9, $12.95
 This graphic novel adaptation of King Lear, originally published in 1984, uses excerpted text from the play together with full-color illustrations to tell the story of the king whose ill-fated attempts to learn which of his daughters loves him best causes loss and madness.
 Part of the Shakespeare Graphic Library.

 William Shakespeare's Macbeth. Black Dog & Leventhal/Workman Publishing 1982 92p. Illustration
 Grades: 7 8 9 10 11 12 Adult   **822.3; 741.5**
 1. Graphic novels; 2. Tragedy — Graphic novels; 3. Shakespeare, William; 4. Shakespeare, William — Adaptations
 978-1-57912-621-6, $12.95
 This graphic novel adaptation of Macbeth, originally published in 1982, uses excerpted text from the play together with full-color illustrations to tell the story of the Thane of Cawdor who listens to a trio of witches and slays the King of Scotland to take his throne.
 Part of the Shakespeare Graphic Library

 William Shakespeare's Twelfth night. adapted by Vincent Goodwin illustrated by Cynthia Martin. ABDO/Magic Wagon 2008 48p. Illustration
 Grades: 5 6 7 8 9 10   **822.3; 741.5**

1. Authors; 2. Dramatists; 3. Graphic novels; 4. Poets; 5. Shakespeare, William, 1564-1616 — Adaptations
978-1-60270-195-3, $28.50

LC 2008-10747

Twins Viola and Sebastian are separated in a shipwreck. Viola decides to disguise herself as a man since she's alone, and this sets the stage for mixed-up identities and a comic love triangle. This graphic novel adaptation retains some of the original language from Shakespeare's play, while paring down the story to appeal to struggling readers. The book includes a short biography, a summary of the play, a glossary, and a short selection of famous lines and phrases from the play.

Part of the Graphic Shakespeare series

Shanower, Eric

★ The **Wonderful** Wizard of Oz. writer, Eric Shanower; artist, Skottie Young; colorist, Jean-Francois Beaulieu; letterer, Jeff Eckleberry; adapted from the novel by L. Frank Baum. Marvel Entertainment 2009 192p. Illustration

Grades: 3 4 5 6 7 8 9 10 11 12 Adult **741.5; Fic**

1. Adventure graphic novels; 2. Authors; 3. Children's authors; 4. Dramatists; 5. Fantasy graphic novels; 6. Graphic novels; 7. Journalists; 8. Baum, L. Frank, 1856-1919 — Adaptations
978-0-7851-2921-9, $29.99

A twister picks up the house Dorothy and her dog Toto are in and carries them from Kansas to the land of Oz; the house lands on top of the Wicked Witch of the East, and the Munchkins, who were her slaves, hail Dorothy as a great sorceress. All the girl wants is to get back home to Kansas, but all anyone can say is that she must go to the Emerald City and ask the Great Wizard Oz to send her home. As she travels along the Yellow Brick Road, she meets a scarecrow who wants brains so people won't think he's a dummy, a tin man who wants a heart so he can love, and a great cowardly lion who wants courage so he'll truly be king of the beasts. However, once they reach the Emerald City and each see the Wizard Oz, they learn they must do what no one, including the Wizard himself, could ever do kill the Wicked Witch of the West. Shanower's adaptation of L. Frank Baum's novel keeps all the charm of the original, while Skottie Young's art banishes any lingering images of the old Technicolor movie; Beaulieu's muted color palette works with Young's art, while Eckleberry's lettering adds to an overall effect of magic and wonder. This book will appeal to all ages

Other Oz adapations by Shanower and Young are: The Marvelous Land of Oz; Ozma of Oz; Dorothy and the Wizard in Oz; The Road to Oz; The Emerald City of Oz

Shapiro, David

Terra Tempo: the four corners of time. David Shapiro, Christopher Herndon, Erica Melville. Craigmore Creations 2013 272 p. (Terra Tempo)

Grades: 5 6 7 **741.5**

1. Colorado Plateau — Fiction; 2. Time travel — Fiction; 3. Dinosaurs — Fiction
098444226X; 9780984442263, $17.99

LC 2012944924

This book is part of the "Terra Tiempo" series by David R. Shapiro and Erica Melville. "When Ari discovers a time map of the Colorado Plateau, he and the twins find themselves on a fast paced journey from Earth s underwater beginnings to the steamy jungles and huge creatures of the creepy Cretaceous. But this time, there is more at stake than just survival. This time, they are not alone." (Publisher's note)

Shaw, Murray

Sherlock Holmes and the adventure of the blue gem. based on the stories of Sir Arthur Conan Doyle; adapted by Murray Shaw and M.J.

Cosson; illustrated by Sophie Rohrbach. Lerner Publishing Group/Graphic Universe 2010 48p. Illustration

Grades: 3 4 5 6 7 8

741.5; Fic

1. Authors; 2. Gems — Graphic novels; 3. Graphic novels; 4. Holmes, Sherlock (Fictional character) — Graphic novels; 5. Mystery graphic novels; 6. Mystery writers; 7. Novelists; 8. Doyle, Arthur Conan Sir, 1859-1930 — Adaptations
978-0-7613-6190-9, $26.60

LC 2009-51758

Courtesy of Lerner Publishing Group

In this graphic adaptation of Doyle's "The Adventure of the Blue Carbuncle," Sherlock Holmes and Dr. Watson work on a Christmas holiday mystery when a train conductor brings them a Christmas goose and a man's hat that he found. They find a large blue gem in the throat of the goose, a famous gem that had been stolen from its owner. Holmes and Watson trace the owner of the hat, who starts them on a path to find out who stole the gem and stuffed it into the goose. This book includes discussion questions and a reading list that includes a mix of age-appropriate mysteries and nonfiction books and websites. Rohrbach's art looks almost like woodcuts; she unfortunately uses the stereotypical (and incorrect) look of the deerstalker cap and caped coat for Holmes. Her muted color palette of mostly browns matches the Victorian time period of the Holmes mysteries.

This is #3 in the On the Case with Holmes and Watson series.

Shen, Prudence

★ **Nothing** Can Possibly Go Wrong. by Prudence Shen, illustrated by Faith Erin Hicks. First Second 2013 288 p.

Grades: 7 8 9 10 **741.5; Fic**

1. Robots — Juvenile fiction; 2. School stories — Graphic novels; 3. Cheerleading — Juvenile fiction
159643659X; 9781596436596, $16.99

"You wouldn't expect Nate and Charlie to be friends. Charlie's the laid-back captain of the basketball team, and Nate is the neurotic, scheming president of the robotics club. But they are friends, however unlikely — until Nate declares war on the cheerleaders. At stake is funding that will either cover a robotics competition or new cheerleading uniforms — but not both." (Publisher's note)

"Shen's plot ably balances drama, humor, angst, and robotic geekery, giving the book an immediate YA appeal, but one that's broad enough to be enjoyable to older readers, as well. Visually, Hicks's wide-eyed, inky b&w panels infuse the characters with real emotion and personality, capturing the book's heartfelt youthfulness." Pub Wkly

Shiga, Jason

Meanwhile. Abrams/Amulet 2010 un Illustration

Grades: 4 5 6 7 8 9 **741.5**

1. Graphic novels; 2. Science fiction graphic novels
0-8109-8423-7; 978-0-8109-8423-3, $15.95

LC 2009-39844

In this choose-your-own adventure graphic novel, a boy stumbles on the laboratory of a mad scientist who asks him to choose between testing a mind-reading device, a time machine, and a doomsday machine. (Bull Cent Child Books)

Shimabukuro, Mitsutoshi

Toriko, vol. 1. story and art by Mitsutoshi Shimabukuro; [translation, Christine Dashiell; adaptation, Hope Donovan; touch-up art & lettering, Jim Keefe]. Viz Media/Shonen Jump 2010 208p. Illustration

Grades: 8 9 10 11 12 Adult   **741.5; Fic**
1. Adventure graphic novels; 2. Food — Graphic novels; 3. Graphic novels; 4. Humorous graphic novels; 5. Hunting — Graphic novels; 6. Manga; 7. Shonen manga
978-1-4215-3509-8, $9.99

Toriko is a Gourmet Hunter, who earns huge bounties for finding ferocious, delicious foods. We're not talking salmon fishing or deer hunting here, but eight-legged alligators and rare fruit guarded by four-armed, bloodthirsty gorilla-type creatures. Toriko himself has a huge appetite for the rare foods, and sometimes eats most of what he's supposed to bring to the fancy restaurants that hire him. Komatsu, the head chef at Igo, a restaurant that caters to those wealthy enough to afford the rare foods, tags along with Toriko, who is a muscular giant of a man. This odd couple forms a friendship born in their mutual love of fine foods. The book is full of crazy action, lots of bugeyed, drop-jawed, slapstick moments, and some potty humor.

Shimura, Takako
Wandering son: Volume Three. Shimura Takako; translated by Matt Thorn. Fantagraphics Books 2012 200 p.
Grades: 7 8 9 10   **741.5; Fic**
1. Transgender people — Graphic novels; 2. Friendship — Graphic novels; 3. Secrets — Fiction
1606995332; 9781606995334, $19.99

In this graphic novel, by Shimura Takako, "Shuichi and his friend Yoshino have a secret: Shuichi is a boy who wants to be a girl, and Yoshino is a girl who wants to be a boy. But one day...their secret is exposed, and the two find themselves the target of sixth-grade cruelty. Their friendship is strained,...and their mentor, Yuki, reveals the harder reality of being transgendered. Meanwhile, Shuichi's sister, Maho, realizes her dream of becoming a model, and drags Shuichi along." (Publisher's note)

Wandering son: Volume Two. Shimura Takako; translated by Matt Thorn. Fantagraphics Books 2012 200 p.
Grades: 7 8 9 10   **741.5; Fic**
1. Transgender people — Graphic novels; 2. Bildungsromans — Graphic novels; 3. Middle schools — Fiction
1606994565; 9781606994566, $19.99

"In the second volume of Shimura Takako's [Wandering Son series],...transgendered protagonists, Shuichi and Yoshino, have entered the sixth grade. Shuichi spends a precious gift of cash from his grandmother on a special present for himself, a purchase that triggers a chain of events in which his sister Maho learns his secret, and Shuichi inadvertently steals the heart of a boy Maho in interested in." (Publisher's note)

"While the first volume served as an introduction to Shuichi and Yoshino's lives, their stories and identities really begin to evolve in this lovely, exciting, and surprising follow-up." Booklist

Wandering son; Volume four. Shimura Takako; [translation: Matt Thorn]. Fantagraphics Books 2013 219 p.
Grades: 7 8 9 10   **741.5; Fic**
1. Comic books, strips, etc. — Japan — Translations into English; 2. Friendship — Comic books, strips, etc; 3. Gender identity — Comic books, strips, etc; 4. Middle school students — Comic books, strips, etc; 5. Middle schools — Juvenile fiction; 6. Friendship — Graphic novels; 7. Gender role — Graphic novels; 8. Comic books, strips, etc.
1606996053; 9781606996058, $19.99

LC 2013363244

This book, by Shimura Takako, the fourth in the series, "continues the story of Nitori Shuichi, a girl who wants to be a boy named Takatsuki Yoshino.... The story is filled with mixed signals, rumors, unrequited love, boys and girls fighting over one another, and love-hate relationships.... And as the characters get ready to enter middle school, with its gender-specific uniforms, each one is being pushed to conform to society's standards." (School Library Journal)

Reads from right to left.

Wandering son; Volume One. Shimura Takako; translated by Matt Thorn. Fantagraphics 2011 192 p. Illustration
Grades: 7 8 9 10 11 12 Adult   **741.5; Fic**
1. Puberty — Graphic novels; 2. Transgender people — Graphic novels; 3. Manga; 4. Bildungsromans — Graphic novels; 5. Seinen manga
1606994166; 9781606994160, $19.99

This manga "tells the story of a friendship between Shuichi, a young boy who wishes he were a girl, and Yoshino, a young girl who wishes she were a boy.... Shuichi's impulses toward a female identity feel confusing and shameful to him, and it's the girls in his life-first Yoshino, and then Saori-who point out his difference and encourage it.... Both children are teased mercilessly by their classmates, whose sexual development, while perhaps more socially normative, is just as confusing to them." (Publishers Weekly)

Volume 1 of 15 (8 available in English)

Shintani, Kaoru
Young Miss Holmes: casebook 1-2. by Kaoru Shintani. Seven Seas 2012 384 p.
Grades: 4 5 6 7   **741.5; 741.5952/223**
1. Girls — Fiction; 2. Detectives — Fiction
1935934864; 9781935934868, $16.99

In this book by Kaoru Shintani "Christie Holmes is a prodigy. At ten years old, she's as familiar with the sciences and classics as any older student at Cambridge or Oxford. And her facility with logic is reminiscent of her uncle, the eminent Sherlock Holmes himself. Christie's implacable curiosity leads her from one dangerous adventure to another, often joining forces with Uncle Sherlock and Doctor Watson on their famed investigations." (Publisher's note)

Young Miss Holmes: casebook 3-4. by Kaoru Shintani. Seven Seas 2012 384 p.
Grades: 4 5 6 7   **741.5**
1. Family — Fiction; 2. Detectives — Fiction
1935934945; 9781935934943, $16.99

In this graphic novel by Kaoru Shintani readers "experience classic Sherlock Holmes tales from the POV of his...niece. Sherlock Holmes' precocious niece Christie is back, as she helps her famous uncle solve such cases as: The Hound of the Baskervilles, The Adventure of the Six Napoleons, the Red-Headed League, and more!" (Publisher's note)

Shiomi, Chika
Canon Vol. 1. DC Comics/CMX 2007 200p. Illustration
Grades: 8 9 10 11 12 Adult   **741.5; Fic**
1. Graphic novels; 2. Horror graphic novels; 3. Manga; 4. Shojo manga; 5. Vampires — Graphic novels
978-1-4012-1163-9, $9.99

Suspense and the supernatural collide in the tale of Canon — the only student to escape the bloody vampire attack that takes the lives of her fellow classmates. But she doesn't get very far before she is captured, bitten and turned into a vampire herself. Struggling against the terrible needs that compel the undead, Canon commits herself to using her powers for good. She'll do whatever she can to avenge the death of her friends and her own unfortunate fate. Joining forces with Fuui — a talking vampire crow — she begins her quest to find Rodd, Lord of the Vampires. There's some mildly harsh language and lots of fighting vampire attacks, but nothing more than has been seen in most Buffy the Vampire Slayer or Angel episodes on television.

Shivack, Nadia

Inside out: portrait of an eating disorder. written and illustrated by Nadia Shivack. Atheneum Books for Young Readers 2007 un Illustration
Grades: 7 8 9 10 11 12   **741.5; 92**

1. Bulimia — Patients — United States — Biography — Comic books, strips, etc.; 2. Shivack, Nadia — Health — Comic books, strips, etc.
0-689-85216-9, $17.99; 978-0-689-85216-9

LC 2004016096

In this book the author gives readers a harrowing look inside her battle with anorexia and bulimia through pictures and captions.

Shone, Rob

Earthquakes. The Rosen Publishing Group 2007 48p. Illustration
Grades: 3 4 5 6 7 8
551.22; 741.5

1. Earthquakes — Graphic novels; 2. Graphic novels
978-1-4042-1989-2, $26.25

The book describes earthquake zones and how earthquakes happen, then it dramatizes three major disasters: the San Francisco earthquake of 1906, the Great Hanshin Earthquake that devastated Kobe, Japan in 1995, and the South Asia Earthquake that struck Kashmir, Pakistan in 2005. Additional information includes an explanation of the Richter scale, a glossary, and a list of books for further reading.

Courtesy of Rosen Publishing

Part of the Graphic Natural Disasters series.

Giganotosaurus: the giant southern lizard. illustrated by Terry Riley. Rosen Publishing Group 2009 32p. Illustration
Grades: 3 4 5 6 7
668; 741.5

1. Dinosaurs — Graphic novels; 2. Graphic novels
978-1-4358-2502-4, $25.25

LC 2008-3265

This book uses the comic book format to provide information about the Giganotosaurus, a giant meat-eating dinosaur from the Cretaceous Period. Information about its hunting habits and lifestyle are based on research and fossil records.

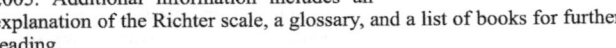

Courtesy of Rosen Publishing

Part of the Graphic Dinosaur series

Muhammad Ali: The Life of a Boxing Hero. Rosen Publishing Group 2006 48p. Illustration
Grades: 3 4 5 6 7 8 9
741.5; 796.8; 92

1. African American athletes — Graphic novels; 2. Biographical graphic novels; 3. Boxing — Biography — Graphic novels; 4. Graphic novels; 5. Ali, Muhammad, 1942-2016
978-1-4042-0856-8, $29.25

LC 2005035521

This book uses the graphic novel format to tell of the life and career of boxing great Muhammad Ali. He started his career as Cassius Clay but changed his name when he

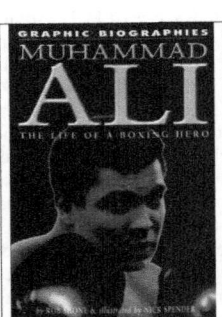

Courtesy of Rosen Publishing

converted to the Nation of Islam. He used his fame as a boxer to advocate against U.S. involvement in Vietnam, and to raise funds for charity. The book includes a list of all his boxing matches, and a list of books for further reading.

Part of the Rosen Graphic Biographies series.

Triceratops: The Three Horned Dinosaur. Rosen Publishing Group 2007 32p. Illustration
Grades: 2 3 4 5 6 7
567.9; 741.5

1. Dinosaurs — Graphic novels; 2. Graphic novels; 3. Triceratops — Graphic novels
978-1-4042-3896-1, $25.25

LC 2007-374

This volume uses colorful comic book style illustrations to explore the habitat, diet, and behavior of the triceratops. At the front of the book, facts about the triceratops are presented, while at the back of the book readers will find a picture gallery of other creatures mentioned in the book.

Courtesy of Rosen Publishing

Part of the Graphic Dinosaurs series.

Tyrannosaurus: The Tyrant Lizard. Rosen Publishing Group 2007 32p. Illustration
Grades: 2 3 4 5 6 7   **567.9; 741.5**

1. Dinosaurs — Graphic novels; 2. Graphic novels; 3. Tyrannosaurus — Graphic novels
978-1-4042-3897-8, $25.25

LC 2007-0442

This volume uses colorful comic book style illustrations to explore the habitat, diet, and behavior of the tyrannosaurus. At the front of the book, facts about the tyrannosaurus are presented, while at the back of the book readers will find a picture gallery of other creatures mentioned in the book.

Part of the Graphic Dinosaurs series.

Volcanoes. The Rosen Publishing Group 2007 48p. Illustration
Grades: 3 4 5 6 7 8
551.21; 741.5

1. Graphic novels; 2. Volcanoes — Graphic novels
978-1-4042-1988-5, $29.25

The book first describes how volcanoes form, briefly discusses killer volcanoes, then uses comic book-style illustrations to dramatize the eruption of Vesuvius in A.D. 79, which buried Pompeii; Krakatoa, which erupted in 1883 and destroyed the island near Sumatra (a new island started growing in 1967); and Mount St. Helens in Washington, which erupted in 1980. Additional

Courtesy of Rosen Publishing

information on studying volcanoes is included, along with a glossary and a list of book for further reading.

Part of the Graphic Natural Disasters series.

Siddell, Thomas

Gunnerkrigg Court: orientation. [by] Tom Siddell. Archaia Studios Press 2009 296p. Illustration
Grades: 6 7 8 9 10 11 12   **741; Fic; 741.5**
978-1-932386-34-9, $26.95; 1-932386-34-3

"Antimony Carver is a precocious and preternaturally self-possessed young girl starting her first year of school at gloomy Gunnerkrigg Court, a very British boarding school that has robots running around along side body-snatching demons, forest gods, and the odd mythical creature. The opening volume in the series follows Antimony through her orientation year: the people she meets, the strange things that happen, and the things she causes to happen as she and her new friend, Kat, unravel the mysteries of the Court and deal with the everyday adventures of growing up." (Publisher's note)

Other titles in this series are: Vol. 2: Research (2009); Vol. 3: Reason (2011); Vol. 4: Materia (2013); Vol. 5: Refine (2015)

Siegel, Mark
★ The **sand** warrior. Mark Siegel and Alexis Siegel; illustrated by Xanthe Boume, Matt Rockefeller, and Boya Sun.. Random House 2017 256 p. Color; Illustration; Map (5 worlds)
Grades: 3 4 5 6   **741.5; Fic**
1. Adventure and adventurers — Fiction; 2. Graphic novels; 3. Heroes — Fiction; 4. Science fiction; 5. Fantasy fiction — Graphic novels
1101935863; 9781101935866, $18.99; 9781101935873; 9781101935880

                                                    LC 2016018284
In this book, by Mark Siegel and Alexis Siegel, illustrated by Xanthe Boume, Matt Rockefeller, and Boya Sun, "the Five Worlds are on the brink of extinction unless five ancient and mysterious beacons are lit. When war erupts, three unlikely heroes will discover there's more to themselves — and more to their worlds — than meets the eye." (Publisher's note)

"Explosions, attacks, and evildoing are relieved by neatly timed interludes in tranquil settings. The main characters share an unglamorous, pre- adolescent look, and the authors seize the opportunity to explore issues of race, class, and scarcity." Pub Wkly

Another title in this series is: The cobalt prince (2018)

Siegel, Siena Cherson
To dance: a ballerina's graphic novel. [by] Siena Cherson Siegel; [illustrated by] Mark Siegel. Simon & Schuster 2006 un Illustration
Grades: 4 5 6 7   **741.5; 92**
1. Autobiographical graphic novels; 2. Ballet; 3. Ballet dancers; 4. Graphic novels; 5. Puerto Ricans — Biography; 6. Siegel, Siena Cherson
1-4169-2687-9 (pa), $9.99
In this memoir of her youth in dance from ages six to eighteen, Siegel tells what it was like to be totally involved in dance, in ballet-all the joys and the physical pain. She worked as a young dancer with George Ballanchine. Her absolute desire to be a dancer took her from her native Puerto Rico to New York City to study. Her simple but heartfelt narration is ably illustrated by her husband Mark Siegel.
Aladdin paperbacks

Sierra, Sergio A.
Frankenstein by Mary Shelley: a Dark graphic novel. adaptation Sergio A. Sierra; illustration Meritxell Ribas. Enslow Publishers 2013 95 p.
Grades: 6 7 8 9 10 11 12 Adult   **741.5**
1. Graphic novels; 2. Horror stories; 3. Monsters — Fiction; 4. Monsters — Graphic novels
0766040844; 9780766040847, $25.26

                                                    LC 2011035826
This book is a black-and-white graphic novel adaptation of Mary Shelley — s 19th-century gothic novel "Frankenstein." The plot tells the "tale of a monster, assembled by a scientist from parts of dead bodies, who develops a mind of his own as he learns to loathe himself and hate his creator." (WorldCat)
Includes bibliographical references.

Silvermoon, Crystal
Les misérables. Victor Hugo; adapted by Crystal Silvermoon; illustrated by SunNeko Lee. Udon Entertainment 2014 337 p. Illustration; Color (Manga Classics)
Grades: 8 9 10 11 12   **741.5; Fic**
1. France — History — 1789-1799, Revolution; 2. Manga
1927925169; 9781927925164, $19.99
In this graphic novel adaptation by Crystal Silvermoon, illustrated by SunNeko Lee, "Victor Hugo's classic novel of love & tragedy during the French Revolution is reborn in this fantastic new manga edition! The gorgeous art of TseMei Lee brings to life the tragic stories of Jean Valjean, Inspector Javert, and the beautiful Fantine, in this epic adaptation of Les Miserables!" (Publisher's note)

"All major plot points and iconic scenes are included in the text and art, and both work seamlessly to tell the story.... The characters, for the most part, are instantly recognizable. It is clear that research has gone into making this adaptation." VOYA

Simon, Eddy
Pele: the king of soccer. written by Eddy Simon; illustrated by Vincent Brascaglia; English translation by Joe Johnson. First Second 2017 144 p. Color; Illustration
Grades: 4 5 6 7 8 9   **92; 741.5**
1. Pelé, 1940-; 2. Soccer players — Biography
9781626727557, $15.99; 9781626729797

                                                    LC 2016961595
"Edson Arantes do Nascimento, known to his schoolmates as Pelé, grew up in poverty in the Sao Paulo region of Brazil. He was too poor to afford a real soccer ball, so he played with a ball of newspaper.... He dominated the youth leagues and signed his first professional soccer contract at the age of fifteen. Within two years he was celebrated internationally, when he led Brazil to victory at the world cup." (Publisher's note)

"This particularly smart delineation of Pelé has it all: his career, his blunders, decency, and goodness. And his gift." Kirkus

Translation of: Le roi Pelé: l'homme et la légende

Simone, Gail
Attack on Titan anthology. Attack on Titan created by Hajime Isayama; edited by Ben Applegate and Jeanine Schaefer; cover, logo, and interior design by Phil Balsman; lettering and interior design by Steve Wands. Kodansha 2016 256 p. Illustration
Grades: 8 9 10 11 12   **741.5**
1. Fantasy fiction — Graphic novels; 2. Horror fiction — Graphic novels; 3. Science fiction graphic novels; 4. Shonen manga
1632362589; 9781632362582, $29.99
This tribute anthology to the manga Attack on Titan features "original stories by a long roster of comic superstars such as Scott Snyder (Batman, American Vampire), Gail Simone (Batgirl), Michael Avon Oeming (Powers), Paolo Rivera (Daredevil, Amazing Spider-Man), Cameron Stewart (Fight Club 2, Batgirl) and Faith Erin Hicks (The Adventures of Superhero Girl)!" (Publisher's note)

"The Victorian-style guide to Titan's walled city by Genevieve Valentine and David López is a standout, as is the contemplative final story by brothers Asaf and Tomer Hanuka." Pub Wkly

Sizer, Paul
Little White Mouse Omnibus Edition. Cafe Digital Studios 2006 447p. Illustration
Grades: 6 7 8 9 10 11 12   **741.5; Fic**
1. Graphic novels; 2. Science fiction graphic novels
978-0-9768565-5-9, $24.95

"In a far future universe, teenaged Loo is the lone survivor of the mysterious destruction of a luxury space liner. She finds an abandoned space mining station, where she must evade a security system that seeks to destroy an intruder such as her, and find a way home before the automated life systems fail. With its strong and appealing young female protagonist, Sizer's story is science fiction that girls will love." (VOYA)

Originally published in serial form, and then as a four-volume series from Blue Line Pro.

Slade, Christian

Korgi, Book 1: Sprouting Wings. Top Shelf Productions 2007 88p. Illustration
Grades: 2 3 4 5 6 7 8 9 10 11 12 Adult
741.5; Fic
1. Dogs — Graphic novels; 2. Fantasy graphic novels; 3. Graphic novels; 4. Stories without words — Graphic novels
978-1-891830-90-7, $10

Courtesy of IDW Publishing

In this wordless book, a young Mollie (woodland people) named Ivy and her young Korgi companion named Sprout embark on adventures in Korgi Hollow, an enchanted place. When they wander from the Mollie village, the two fall through a hole in the ground and find nasty, monstrous creatures who want to eat them. As they deal with the danger and make their escape, Ivy and Sprout both discover new talents. Slade's extensively cross-hatched yet delicate art is highly expressive, and readers young and old will have no trouble figuring out what is going on. The Korgi are based on Welsh corgi dogs, of which Slade and his wife have two.

Korgi, book 2. Top Shelf Productions 2008 un Illustration
Grades: 3 4 5 6 7 8 9 10 11 12 Adult
741.5; Fic
1. Adventure graphic novels; 2. Fantasy graphic novels; 3. Graphic novels; 4. Stories without words — Graphic novels
978-1-60309-010-0, $10

Courtesy of IDW Publishing

In this second wordless volume, the young Mollie named Ivy and her Korgi cub Sprout, experience a harrowing adventure. Someone has been hunting the Mollies and cutting off their wings. Ivy and Sprout rescue one older Mollie named Art and his Korgi when they fall into a deep trap in the woods; then as Ivy flies, a barbed arrow cuts one of her wings off. She and Sprout see a strange creature carrying her wing and they follow him to his place, where he hangs all the Mollie wings like trophies. Ivy decides she wants her wing back, but she and Sprout will have to fight the creature and his automated and nasty bots.

Slavin, Bill

Big star Otto. written by Bill Slavin with Esperança Melo; art by Bill Slavin. Kids Can Press 2015 95 p. (Elephants Never Forget)
Grades: 3 4 5 6
741.5
1. Chimpanzees — Juvenile fiction; 2. Elephants — Juvenile fiction; 3.

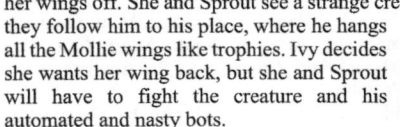
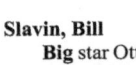
Courtesy of Kids Can Press

Kidnapping — Juvenile fiction; 4. Graphic novels; 5. Parrots — Juvenile fiction
1894786963; 9781894786966, $16.95

"In this conclusion to the Elephants Never Forget graphic novel trilogy, [by Bill Slavin], big-hearted hero Otto and his parrot pal Crackers have landed in Hollywood, the final stop in their journey across America in search of their good friend Georgie the chimpanzee. They've been hot on Georgie's trail since he was abducted from Africa by the sinister Man with the Wooden Nose, and now they're sure they've finally found his location." (Publisher's note)

Smith, Jeff

★ **Bone** Book Seven: ghost circles. Scholastic/GRAPHIX 2008 152p. Illustration
Grades: 3 4 5 6 7 8 9 10 11 12 Adult   **741.5; Fic**
1. Adventure graphic novels; 2. Fantasy graphic novels; 3. Graphic novels
978-0-439-70629-2, $19.99; 978-0-439-70634-6 (pa), $9.99
LC 2007-9568403

The Bone cousins, Gran'ma Ben, Thorn, and their loyal rat creature cub Bartleby venture on a journey through the mysterious ghost circles to Atheia, the old city of the royal family. Meanwhile, the Barrelhaven villagers and the Veni Yan face enemy hordes. Steve Hamaker is the colorist for this full color version of Smith's comic epic.

★ **Bone** vol. 8: treasure hunters. Scholastic/Graphix 2008 138p. Illustration
Grades: 5 6 7 8 9 10 11 12 Adult   **741.5; Fic**
1. Adventure graphic novels; 2. Fantasy graphic novels; 3. Graphic novels
978-0-439-70630-8, $18.95; 978-0-439-70633-9 (pa), $9.99
LC 2008-9568403

The Bone cousins, Gran'ma Ben, and Thorn reach the city of Atheia, where they prepare to battle the Lord of the Locusts. Meanwhile, Thorn's visions are becoming more threatening and Phoney Bone is convinced Atheia is rich in gold, and he is determined to find it. But all is not well in Atheia, and Thorn is in great danger, not only from Briar and the Lord of the Locusts. This edition is in full color, done by Steve Hamaker.

★ **Bone:** out from Boneville. Scholastic Graphix 2005 144p. Illustration
Grades: 4 5 6 7 8 9 10 11 12   **741.5; Fic**
1. Adventure graphic novels; 2. Fantasy graphic novels; 3. Graphic novels
9780439706407, $12.99; 0439706408; 0439706238; 9780439706230, $26.99

"After being run out of Boneville, the three Bone cousins — Fone Bone, Phoney Bone, and Smiley Bone — are separated and lost in a vast, uncharted desert. One by one, they find their way into a deep, forested valley filled with wonderful and terrifying creatures. Eventually, the cousins are reunited at a farmstead run by tough Gran'ma Ben and her spirited granddaughter, Thorn. But little do the Bones know, there are dark forces conspiring against them and their adventures are only just beginning!" (Publisher's note)

"The nine-volume Bone graphic novel series was the toast of the comics world when it was published by Smith's own Cartoon Books beginning in the early 1990s; in this first volume of Scholastic's new edition, the original b&w art has been beautifully converted into color." Pub Wkly

Also available Bone: one volume edition $39.95 from Cartoon Books (ISBN 1-8889-6314-X); Other titles in this series are: Bone: the great cow race (vol. 2); Bone: eyes of the storm (vol. 3); Bone: the dragonslayer (vol. 4); Bone: Rock Jaw: master of the Eastern border (vol. 5); Bone: old man's cave (vol. 6); Bone: ghost circles (vol. 7); Bone: treasure hunters (vol. 8); Bone: crown of horns (vol. 9)

Bone: Rose. by Jeff Smith; with illustrations by Charles Vess. Scholastic Graphix 2009 138p. Illustration

Grades: 4 5 6 7 8   **741.5; Fic**

1. Adventure graphic novels; 2. Fantasy graphic novels; 3. Graphic novels

978-0-545-13542-9, $21.99; 0-545-13542-7; 978-0-545-13543-6 (pa), $10.99; 0-545-13543-5 (pa)

"When a terrifying dragon attacks the small towns of the Northern Valley, a young Princess Rose (known later as Gran'ma Ben) must defeat it. The beast is actually the ancient evil, the Lord of the Locusts, and while Rose faces danger with honor, her elder sister, Princess Briar, follows a more sinister path." (Publisher's note)

Bone: tall tales. by Jeff Smith with Tom Sniegoski; color by Steve Hamaker. Graphix 2010 108p. Illustration

Grades: 4 5 6 7 8   **741; 741.5**

978-0-545-14095-9, $21.99; 0-545-14095-1; 978-0-545-14096-6 (pa), $10.99; 0-545-14096-X (pa)

"Long before the Bone cousins were ever lost in the uncharted desert on the outskirts of the Valley, Big Johnson Bone, the discoverer of the Rolling Bone River, founded Boneville. But little is known of the mighty explorer's adventures before he started his famous trading post. So when Smiley Bone sits down with a group of young campers to retell the legendary stories of Boneville's origin and its tough, no-nonsense founder, what they hear are tall tales in typical BONE fashion." (Publisher's note)

Snyder, Scott

Attack on Titan anthology. Attack on Titan created by Hajime Isayama; edited by Ben Applegate and Jeanine Schaefer; cover, logo, and interior design by Phil Balsman; lettering and interior design by Steve Wands. Kodansha 2016 256 p. Illustration

Grades: 8 9 10 11 12   **741.5**

1. Fantasy fiction — Graphic novels; 2. Horror fiction — Graphic novels; 3. Science fiction graphic novels; 4. Shonen manga

1632362589; 9781632362582, $29.99

This tribute anthology to the manga Attack on Titan features "original stories by a long roster of comic superstars such as Scott Snyder (Batman, American Vampire), Gail Simone (Batgirl), Michael Avon Oeming (Powers), Paolo Rivera (Daredevil, Amazing Spider-Man), Cameron Stewart (Fight Club 2, Batgirl) and Faith Erin Hicks (The Adventures of Superhero Girl)!" (Publisher's note)

"The Victorian-style guide to Titan's walled city by Genevieve Valentine and David López is a standout, as is the contemplative final story by brothers Asaf and Tomer Hanuka." Pub Wkly

Batman; Volume 1: The court of owls. Scott Snyder, writer; Greg Capullo, penciller; Jonathan Glapion, inker. DC Comics 2012 un Color; Illustration (New 52)

Grades: 9 10 11 12 Adult   **741.5**

1. Superhero comic books, strips, etc.; 2. Batman (Fictional character)

1401235425; 9781401235420, $16.99

"After a series of brutal murders rocks Gotham City, Batman begins to realize that perhaps these crimes go far deeper than appearances suggest. As the Caped Crusader begins to unravel this deadly mystery, he discovers a conspiracy going back to his youth and beyond to the origins of the city he's sworn to protect. Could the Court of Owls, once thought to be nothing more than an urban legend, be behind the crime and corruption? Or is Bruce Wayne losing his grip on sanity and falling prey to the pressures of his war on crime?" (Publisher's note)

Soo, Kean

★ **Jellaby:** monster in the city. Hyperion Books 2009 172p. Illustration

Grades: 4 5 6 7 8 9   **741.5; Fic**

1. Fantasy graphic novels; 2. Friendship — Graphic novels; 3. Graphic novels; 4. Monsters — Graphic novels

1-4231-0565-6 (pa); 978-1-4231-0565-7 (pa), $9.99

Beginning right where the first book ended, Portia, Jason, and Jellaby continue on their way to Toronto, walking after Portia panicked and they got off the train. They're searching for a way home for Jellaby, and they think a door somewhere in Exhibition Place, where the Canadian National Exhibition is taking place, holds a clue. Portia feels torn between wanting to help her friend yet not wanting to say goodbye forever, and her ambivalence causes a rift between her and Jason. When she doesn't want to trust a masked magician who seems to know too much about them and Jellaby, Portia leaves Jason. They all end up in the Automotive Building, where the masked man leads Jason and Jellaby down below the building, while Portia seems to find her long lost father. But is he really her father, and just what is waiting for Jason and Jellaby under the Automotive Building? Soo again uses a mostly purple color palette.

Another title in the author's series about Jellaby

★ **Jellaby;** Volume 1: the lost monster. by Kean Soo. Stone Arch Books 2014 160 p. Color; Illustration (Jellaby)

Grades: 4 5 6 7 8 9

741.5

1. Extraterrestrial beings — Fiction; 2. Human-alien encounters — Comic books, strips, etc; 3. Monsters — Fiction; 4. Friendship — Fiction

1434291952; 9781434264206, $12.95 ; 9781434291950, $19.99

                       LC 2013037026

Courtesy of Capstone Press

"Portia has just moved to a new neighborhood with her mom. Adjusting to life without a father is hard enough, but school is boring and her classmates are standoffish.... But things start to get better when Portia mounts a midnight excursion into the woods behind her house where she discovers a shy and sweet purple monster. Life with Jellaby is exciting, but Portia's purple friend has secrets of his own." (Publisher's note)

"Soo grounds the story in a fairly gritty contemporary reality, where kids deal with bullies and well-meaning adults try to help. Clear, clean lines and easy-to-follow panel layouts round out the package." Booklist

First published 2008; Originally published: New York : Hyperion Books for Children, 2008.A Capstone imprint.

Spender, Nick

Rosa Parks: The Life of a Civil Rights Heroine. Rosen Publishing Group 2006 48p. Illustration

Grades: 3 4 5 6 7 8 9   **741.5; 323.092; 92; 323**

1. African American women — Alabama — Montgomery — Biography — Graphic novels; 2. African Americans — Civil rights — Alabama — Montgomery — History — 20th century — Graphic novels; 3. Biographical graphic novels; 4. Graphic novels; 5. Parks, Rosa, 1913-2005

978-1-4042-0864-3, $29.25

                       LC 2006002735

This book uses the graphic novel format to tell of the life of Rosa Parks and her act of defiance that inspired the Montgomery Bus Boycott.

Additional information explains Jim Crow laws and briefly covers the civil rights movement. The book includes a list of books for further reading.

Part of the Rosen Graphic Biographies series.

Spiegelman, Art

Big fat Little Lit. [edited by] Art Spiegelman and Francoise Mouly. Puffin 2006 144p. Illustration

Grades: 2 3 4 5 6 7 8   **741.5; Fic**

1. Folklore — Graphic novels; 2. Graphic novels

0-14-240706-2, $14.99

This volume collects all three previously published Little Lit books: Little Lit: Once Upon a Time, Little Lit: Strange Stories for Strange Kids, and Little Lit: It Was a Dark and Silly Night. Many comics creators and children's book writers and illustrators contributed stories, including Ian Falconer, Daniel Clowes, Maurice Sendak, David Sedaris, Chris Ware, Jules Feiffer, Barbara McClintock, Crockett Johnson, J. Otto Siebold, Neil Gaiman, Art Spiegelman, and Lemony Snicket.

★ **Maus:** a survivor's tale, 2v in 1. Art Spiegelman.. Pantheon Bks. 1996 295 p. Illustration; Map; Color

Grades: 7 8 9 10 11 12 Adult   **741.5; 940.53; 92**

1. Biographical graphic novels; 2. Graphic novels; 3. Holocaust, 1933-1945 — Graphic novels; 4. Spiegelman, Vladek

0-679-40641-7, $35

LC 96-32796

Los Angeles Times Book Prize: Fiction (1992) for Maus II; Pulitzer Prize Special Award (1992); Eisner Award: Best Graphic Album — Reprint for Maus II; Harvey Award: Best Graphic Album of Previously Published Material (1992) for Maus II

"An undisputed classic and award-winning title (including a Pulitzer Prize in 1992) in which renowned cartoonist Spiegelman depicts his father's experiences as a World War II Nazi concentration camp survivor. The memoir is also a chronicle of Spiegelman's relationship with his father as we witness their visits and disagreements. The black-and-white drawings are straightforward, but with an interesting twist: all of the Jews are depicted as mice and the Nazis as cats." LJ

In this work "Spiegelman takes the comic book to a new level of seriousness, portraying Jews as mice and Nazis as cats. Depicting himself being told about the Holocaust by his Polish survivor father, Spiegelman not only explores the concentration-camp experience, but also the guilt, love, and anger between father and son." Rochman. Against borders

Also available: paperback boxed set edition $23.25 (ISBN 0141014083); A combined edition of Maus I : My father bleeds history (1986) and Maus II : And here my troubles began (1991)

Spires, Ashley

★ **Binky** takes charge. by Ashley Spires. Kids Can Press 2012 64 p. Color illustration

Grades: 4 5 6

741.5/971; Fic

1. Picture books for children; 2. Cats — Fiction; 3. Spy stories

1554537037; 9781554537037, $16.95; 9781554537686, $8.95; 9781451765137, $17.95

Courtesy of Kids Can Press

"Felines of the Universe Ready for Space Travel (F.U.R.S.T.) and Captain Gracie are pleased to announce that Lt. Binky is about to get his first recruit to train [in this book by Ashley Spires.]...There — s a new diversity program at F.U.R.S.T., and Gordon, a dog, has been assigned to Binky. Binky decides to give it his all. As expected, Gordon falls short. Then Binky

discovers the unthinkable: Gordon seems to be leaving coded messages in outer space...If they are to prove Gordon is a double agent, Gracie and Binky will need incontrovertible proof!" (Kirkus)

Fluffy strikes back. by Ashley Spires. Kids Can Press 2016 72 p. Color; Illustration

Grades: 2 3 4 5 6

741.5; Fic

1. Cats — Juvenile fiction; 2. Humorous fiction — Fiction; 3. Insects — Fiction

1771381272; 9781771381277, $15.95

Courtesy of Kids Can Press

"Fluffy Vandermere, the cat sergeant in charge of P.U.R.S.T. (Pets of the Universe Ready for Space Travel), works tirelessly to protect the world from alien (aka bug) domination.... Now, suddenly and without warning, Fluffy discovers P.U.R.S.T. headquarters, the most secure building in the world, is under attack by an angry swarm of insects, and they're armed with every cat's worst nightmare — spray bottles! " (Publisher's note)

"Spires' muted Photoshop illustrations clearly and adorably depict the story's action, while the arrangement of panels, which include security footage, schematics, and subterranean cross sections, ramps up the suspense and comedy." Booklist

Stanley, John

★ **Little** Lulu, vol. 1: My dinner with Lulu. [by] John Stanley and Irving Tripp. Dark Horse Comics 2005 200p. Illustration

Grades: 4 5 6 7 8 9 10 11 12 Adult   **741.5; Fic**

1. Friendship — Graphic novels; 2. Graphic novels; 3. Humorous graphic novels

1-59307-318-6, $9.95

Lulu Moppet plays with best friend Tubby, except when he hangs out with the other neighborhood boys and tries to keep girls out of their clubhouse; she deals with terrible toddler Alvin by weaving extravagant tales featuring herself; and other everyday adventures. This is the first volume of a series that will eventually reprint every Little Lulu comic for new young readers.

Volume 1 of 29

★ **Nancy,** volume 1: the Johnny Stanley Library. Drawn & Quarterly 2009 128p. Illustration

Grades: 2 3 4 5 6 7 8 9 10 11 12 Adult   **741.5; Fic**

1. Graphic novels; 2. Humorous graphic novels; 3. Nancy (Fictional character)

978-1-897299-77-7, $24.95

LC c2009-901565-X

The comic book character Nancy was created by Ernie Bushmiller; Dell Comics published the comics scripted by John Stanley with art by Dan Gormley starting with issue 146 in 1957. In these stories, Nancy meets Oona Goosepimple, a spooky girl who lives in a haunted house, has an incredible run of bad luck because of what she thinks is a four-leaf clover, and has all kinds of everyday adventures and misadventures with her friend Sluggo, their nemesis Spike, neighborhood rich kid Rollo, and her Aunt Fritzi. Always short of money yet needing some to buy ice cream sodas and other treats, many of Nancy's adventures with Sluggo involve various moneymaking schemes to get the dime needed (those were the days ...). The kinds of adventures the kids have are somewhat similar to Stanley's other work on Little Lulu, but set in an urban environment rather than the suburban neighborhood of Lulu and her friends. The book, designed by Seth, retains the soft original coloring of the old comics, with the paper even looking like old comics (but much sturdier). This book should have the same all-ages appeal as Little Lulu; the 2009 Free Comic Book Day issue featuring Nancy was a big hit with readers five years old and up to adults who remembered reading Nancy comics when they were kids.

Steele, Hamish

★ **Deadendia:** the watcher's test. Hamish Steele. Nobrow Press 2018 240 p. Color; Illustration
Grades: 7 8 9 10 11 12   741.5; Fic
1. Amusement parks — Fiction; 2. Horror fiction; 3. Transgender people — Fiction; 4. LGBT people — Fiction
1910620475; 9781910620472, $14.95

"Barney and his best friend Norma are just trying to get by and keep their jobs, but working at the Dead End theme park also means battling demonic forces, time traveling wizards, and scariest of all — their love lives! Follow the lives of this diverse group of employees of a haunted house, which may or may not also serve as a portal to hell, in this hilarious and moving graphic novel, complete with talking pugs, vengeful ghosts and LBGTQIA love!" (Publisher's note)

"The art is imaginative and engaging, with rich, evocative color schemes. With time travel, demonic possession, monsters, magic spells, and fights between creatures of pure sadness and pure happiness, there is never a dull moment — but in the realm of human emotion, there are relatable ones." Kirkus

Steinberg, David

The **adventures** of Daniel Boom AKA Loud Boy: game on!. written by D.J. Steinberg; illustrated by Brian Smith. Grosset & Dunlap 2009 96p. Illustration
Grades: 3 4 5 6 7 8   741.5; Fic
1. Graphic novels; 2. Humorous graphic novels; 3. Superhero graphic novels
978-0-448-44700-1, $5.99

Loud Boy and the rest of the Freak Five thought they had helped put all the members of Kid Rid behind bars, but now "Old Fogey" Fogelman has broken out of jail. Daniel Boom, AKA Loud Boy, his sister Jeannie S., Sid, Rex, and Violet work together to help Daniel's uncle hide something called a Floogggget from Fogelman it looks like a banana, but it is a device that can digitize three-dimensional objects. Uncle Stanley warns the super powered kids that Fogelman intends to use the device on children, but he has to flee before telling them everything. Then Daniel makes a new friend, J R, who gets him hooked on the new game called Pig Planet. The other Freak Five members try to get Daniel's attention, but succeed only when it's too late, and J R has stolen the Floogggget and given it to Fogelman. It turns out J R is a robot built by Fogelman, and he uses the Floogggget to digitize the 1.7 million children playing Pig Planet. Daniel figures the only way to save the kids and stop Fogelman is to get into the game himself but can he win?

Stern, Roger

Captain America: War & Remembrance 2nd ed.. writer, Roger Stern; co-plotter & penciler, John Byrne; inker, Joe Rubinstein; colorists, Bob Sharen & George Roussos; letterers, Jim Novak, John Costanza, & Joe Rosen. Marvel Entertainment 2007 207p. Illustration
Grades: 8 9 10 11 12 Adult   741.5; Fic
1. Graphic novels; 2. Superhero graphic novels; 3. Avengers (Fictional characters); 4. Captain America (Fictional character)
978-0-7851-2693-5, $24.99

Captain America's endless war on crime and tyranny sets him against new enemies and old, from an army of robot replicas to the black deeds of Baron Blood. Plus: Cap for president? This book guest-stars the Avengers, S.H.I.E.L.D. and Union Jack, and features Cobra, Mister Hyde and Batroc the Leaper. This is the complete Stern/Byrne run, culminating with the standard-setting version of Cap's origin. Byrne co-scripted as well as pencilled the art.

Spider-Man Visionaries: Roger Stern Vol. 1. Marvel Entertainment 2007 256p. Illustration
Grades: 7 8 9 10 11 12 Adult   741.5; Fic
1. Graphic novels; 2. Spider-Man (Fictional character); 3. Superhero graphic novels
978-0-7851-2710-9, $24.99

Roger Stern sets his stamp on Spider-Man and his supporting cast with a collection of costumed criminals, would-be alien abductors, and gangsters both local and imported. Spidey is up against Belladonna, the Vulture, the Prowler, the Smuggler, Mysterio, a roomful of aliens, and an abundance of gas. These stories were originally published in the 1980s, and Stern worked with a number of different artists, including Steve Leialoha and Marie Severin.

Stevenson, Noelle

Lumberjanes; Volume 3: A Terrible Plan. written by Noelle Stevenson & Shannon Watters; illustrated by Carolyn Nowak [and six others]; colors by Maarta Laiho; cover by Noelle Stevenson. Boom! Studios 2016 112 p. Color; Illustration
Grades: 6 7 8 9 10 11 12 Adult   741.5; Fic
1. Graphic novels; 2. Camps — Fiction; 3. Fantasy fiction; 4. Adventure fiction; 5. Teenage girls — Fiction
1608868036; 9781608868032, $14.99

"Jo, April, Mal, Molly, and Ripley...take on everything that goes bump in the night. From scary stories to magical portals that lead to a land untouched by time, it's definitely not your average summer." (Publisher's note)

"Each camper tells a campfire spine-tingler, ranging from not very scary (the scratching on the side of the car was really...carbon-monoxide-induced hallucinations!) to the shudderworthy. Elsewhere, Mal and Molly are transported to a dangerous, dinosaur-infested alternate universe, and while they are gone, the rest of the Lumberjanes try to earn some piece-of-cake badges, only to fail spectacularly." Booklist

Originally published in single magazine form as Lumberjanes no. 9-12

★ **Nimona.** by Noelle Stevenson. HarperCollins Childrens Books 2015 272 p.
Grades: 7 8 9 10 11 12   741.5
1. Shapeshifting — Comic books, strips, etc.; 2. Fantasy graphic novels; 3. Magic — Graphic novels; 4. Good and evil — Fiction; 5. Heroes and heroines — Graphic novels
0062278231; 9780062278234, $17.99
Eisner Nominee: Best Digital/Web Comic (2015); National Book Award Finalist: Young People's Literature (2015); Eisner Award: Best Graphic Album — Reprint (2016)

In this graphic novel, by Noelle Stevenson, "Nimona is an impulsive young shapeshifter with a knack for villainy. Lord Ballister Blackheart is a villain with a vendetta. As sidekick and supervillain, Nimona and Lord Blackheart are about to wreak some serious havoc. Their mission: prove to the kingdom that Sir Ambrosius Goldenloin and his buddies at the Institution of Law Enforcement and Heroics aren't the heroes everyone thinks they are." (Publisher's note)

"This celebrated webcomic, a mash-up of medieval culture with modern science and technology, is now available in print.... Action scenes dominate as Nimona shifts with Hulk-like ferocity from frightful creatures such as a fire-breathing dragon to a docile cat or a timid child. Dialogue is fresh and witty with an abundance of clever lines." SLJ

Stine, R. L.

Goosebumps Graphix: Scary Summer. Scholastic/Graphix 2007 137p. Illustration

Grades: 4 5 6 7 8 9   **741.5; Fic**

1. Graphic novels; 2. Horror graphic novels

978-0-439-85782-6, $8.99

Someone's creeping through the garden, doing nasty things! Dean Haspiel, a veteran of Batman and Justice League comics, knows just how to portray "The Revenge of the Lawn Gnomes." In his comic series like The Bakers and Plastic Man, Kyle Baker proves he's one funny artist, the perfect guy to draw a story about fun and games at camp — until "The Horror at Camp Jellyjam" is uncovered. And Courtney Crumrin creator Ted Naifeh adapts and illustrates "Ghost Beach," in which Terri and Jerry go on vacation with some of their father's cousins and meet other kids who dress in old-fashioned clothes and caution them about ghosts.

Slappy's tales of horror. adapted and illustrated by Dave Roman, Jamie Tolagson, Gabriel Hernandez, and Ted Naifeh; color by Jose Garibaldi. Graphix / Scholastic 2015 176 p.

Grades: 3 4 5 6   **741.5; Fic**

1. Stine, R. L. — Adaptations.; 2. Horror fiction — Juvenile fiction; 3. Monsters — Graphic novels

9780545835954, $12.99; 9780545836005, $24.99

LC 2014959511

In this book "[f]our Goosebumps Graphix tales by master of horror R. L. Stine are adapted into full-color comics and feature a brand-new Slappy story by bestselling author, Dave Roman.... Roman [also] creates the horrifying drawings for 'The Night of the Living Dummy,' the origin story about that most evil of all ventriloquist dummies, Slappy!" Illustrators Jamie Tolagson, Gabriel Hernandez, and Ted Naifeh are also included. (Publisher's note)

"Each segment has the hallmarks of the individual artist as he balances comedy and horror, childishness and seriousness: Tolagson's deep shadows and brisk pace keep readers guessing at what is actually perilous, and Hernandez's pen and ink scratches help bridge the gap between mundane and dangerous. The more cartoony styles of Naifeh and Roman may reduce the fear factor, but Naifeh's sense of mood remains top-notch." SLJ

Sturm, James

★ **Satchel** Paige: striking out Jim Crow. Hyperion Books for Children/Jump at the Sun 2007 90p. Illustration

Grades: 4 5 6 7 8 9 10   **92; 741.5**

1. African Americans — Biography — Graphic novels; 2. Baseball — Graphic novels; 3. Baseball players; 4. Biographical graphic novels; 5. Graphic novels; 6. Paige, Satchel, 1906-1982

978-0-7868-3901-8, $9.99; 978-0-7868-3900-1, $16.99

Narrated by an African American who played in the Negro Leagues for a short time, this book sketches part of the career of Leroy "Satchel" Paige, a star of the Negro Leagues. Young Emmet scored a run off Paige in a game, but suffered a career-ending knee injury. Readers get a sense of the rough life African Americans faced in the south during the 1920s, 1930s, and 1940s. Then Paige and his team come to Tuckwilla, Alabama in 1944 to play an all-White team, and Emmet and his son attend the game and watch how Paige and his team take apart the home boys. There's one panel showing a man who has been lynched and hanged; most of the violence is mentioned but not depicted on the pages.

Part of The Center for Cartoon Studies Presents series

Sumerak, Marc

Franklin Richards, son of a genius: not-so-secret invasion. story, Chris Eliopoulos & Marc Sumerak; script, Marc Sumerak; art & letters Chris Eliopoulos. Marvel Entertainment 2009 un Illustration

Grades: 3 4 5 6 7 8 9   **741.5; Fic**

1. Fantastic Four (Fictional characters); 2. Graphic novels; 3. Humorous graphic novels; 4. Superhero graphic novels

978-0-7851-3369-8, $9.99

This latest volume includes stories featuring Franklin Richards, son of Reed and Sue Richards of the Fantastic Four. Young Franklin, aided and abetted (albeit reluctantly) by his robot companion H.E.R.B.I.E., builds a replica of the first Iron Man robotic armor, drinks one of his dad's formulas and proceeds to belch HUGELY, de-ages his dad so they can play together, and then a multiplicity of Franklin Richards in many different timelines get into similar trouble. There are more stories, lots of silly humor and superhero action, drawn by coauthor Eliopoulos.

Spider-Man and Power Pack: Big-City Super Heroes. Marvel Entertainment 2007 un Illustration

Grades: 3 4 5 6 7 8   **741.5; Fic**

1. Graphic novels; 2. Power Pack (Fictional characters); 3. Spider-Man (Fictional character); 4. Superhero graphic novels

0-7851-2357-1, $6.99

When the Power family moves to New York City, Marvel's youngest superheroes, the Power Pack, have a whole new city to explore. Julie (Lightspeed), Alex (Zero-G), Jack (Mass Master), and little Katie (Energizer) meet and team up with Spider-Man and help him defeat Venom, the Sandman, and the Vulture. Katie also gets infected by the Venom symbiote, and Spidey gets dumped into a vat of liquid that turns him into a kid again.

Originally published as Spider-Man and Power Pack issues #1-4.

Sutherland, Tui

Wings of fire : the graphic novel; Book 1: The dragonet prophecy. by Tui T. Sutherland; adapted by Barry Deutsch; art by Mike Holmes; color by Maarta Laiho. Graphix 2018 224 p. Color; Illustration; Map

Grades: 4 5 6 7   **741.5; Fic**

1. Imaginary wars and battles; 2. Friendship; 3. Dragons — Fiction

9780545942164, $24.99

LC 2017955178

"Clay has grown up under the mountain, chosen along with four other dragonets to fulfill a...prophecy and end the war between the dragon tribes of Pyrrhia.... So when one of the dragonets is threatened, all five spring into action. Together, they will choose freedom over fate, leave the mountain, and fulfill their destiny — on their own terms." (Publisher's note)

"Adapted from Sutherland's middle-grade series, the story is surprisingly riveting; the politics involved between the warring factions and dragon races makes for great world building, and the war-torn world, complete with gladiatorial-style fights and backstabbings, is an intriguing backdrop for the five dragons' development." Booklist

Suzumi, Atsushi

Haridama magic cram school. Atsushi Suzumi; translated and adapted by Kaya Laterman. Del Rey Manga 2008 202p. Illustration

Grades: 7 8 9 10 11 12   **741.5; Fic**

1. Fantasy graphic novels; 2. Graphic novels; 3. Magic — Graphic novels; 4. Manga; 5. Shonen manga

978-0-345-50136-3, $10.95

LC 2008-299354

Kokuyo and Harika are sorcery students, but they're Obsidians, wizards who must use special stones set in swords to help them cast spells. Other sorcery students think they're inferior because they lack both yin and yang. But Kokuyo and Harika do have something no one else has: the power of friendship. They'll have to figure it out, but when they work together, they don't need their swords. This is a one-volume manga.

Takahashi, Rumiko
★ **InuYasha:** Volume One. by Rumiko Takahashi. Viz 2009 562 p.
Grades: 7 8 9 10 11 12   **741.5; 741.5/952**
  1. Japanese mythology; 2. Shonen manga; 3. Manga
1421532808; 9781421532806, $19.99
                                LC bl2009031710
In this book, by Rumiko Takahashi, "Kagome is a modern Japanese high school girl. Never the type to believe in myths and legends, her world view dramatically changes when, one day, she's pulled out of her own time and into another! There, in Japan's ancient past, Kagome discovers more than a few of those dusty old legends are true, and that her destiny is linked to one legendary creature in particular — the dog like half-demon called Inuyasha!" (Publisher's note)
  Originally published in 56 individual volumes; Volume 1 of 18

Takamisaki, Ryo
  Megaman NT Warrior Vol. 1. Viz/Viz Kids 2004 186p. Illustration
Grades: 4 5 6 7 8 9   **741.5; Fic**
  1. Graphic novels; 2. Manga; 3. Science fiction graphic novels; 4. Shonen manga
1-59116-465-6, $7.95
  The year is 200X and everyone is now connected to the Cyber Network. People carry their own PET (Personal terminal) and are paired up with an artificial intelligence program called a NetNavi (or NetNavigator). Computers have turned the world into a bright and shiny utopia, but there's always trouble in paradise. While the invention of the PET and NetNavis has brought great benefits to the world, computer hacking, virus spreading, and other high-tech crimes are becoming a major problem. A sinister organization by the name of World Three has appeared, and they've vowed to destroy this technological wonderland. Enter Lan Hikari, an intensely curious and cheerful fifth grader. Synchronized with his NetNavigator, MegaMansupercharged, he becomes a super-charged dynamo. In and out of the Net, Lan and MegaMan do their best to thwart World Three's neverending quest to take over the world. The book includes some raunchy humor and lots of action.

  Pokemon: the rise of Darkrai. story & art by Ryo Takamisaki; English translation, Kaori Inoue. Viz Media/VizKids 2008 un Illustration
Grades: 2 3 4 5 6 7 8 9   **741.5; Fic**
  1. Adventure graphic novels; 2. Fantasy graphic novels; 3. Graphic novels; 4. Manga; 5. Shonen manga
978-1-4215-2289-0, $7.99
  Ash and his friends come to Alamos Town, home of the Space-Time Towers, and while touring the town, they discover that the town's special garden has been ransacked. Some of the townspeople blame Darkrai, a sinister looking Pokemon that said to haunt the garden. However, Alamos Town faces much more peril when two powerful Pokemon that control time and space battle each other; it should be impossible for them to meet, and unless Ash and the others " and perhaps Darkrai " can stop them, Alamos Town will be destroyed. This book includes a lot of Pokemon fighting action; the panels are so filled with details that very young readers might find it difficult to follow the action.

Takanashi, Mitsuba
  The **Devil** Does Exist Volume 1. DC Comics/CMX 2005 192p. Illustration
Grades: 7 8 9 10 11 12   **741.5; Fic**
  1. Graphic novels; 2. Manga; 3. Romance graphic novels; 4. Shojo manga
1-4012-0545-3, $9.99
  High school is difficult for most kids. But for Kayano, a shy girl whose single mother seems to work all the time, it's even worse than usual. She's so afraid of drawing attention to herself, in fact, that she can't tell the handsome Kamijo how much she loves him-until one day she finally gets up the courage to write him a letter confessing her feelings. But her plans go awry when the letter falls into the hands of the school's most notorious student, Edogawa Takeru. To Kayano, Takeru seems to be Satan himself. Not only is he devilishly handsome, he is the son of the school's principal. Even the teachers dare not stand up to him. Kayano, appalled by how badly her first attempt at a social life has gone, thinks she can struggle through, and get her letter back. But, Takeru enjoys watching her suffer. Just when she thinks she's solved the problem, her mother comes home to announce she's getting married-to principal Edogawa. Now Kayano will have to live with this devil Takeru 24/7. How will she cope with this literal living hell? The book includes some mild strong language, mild violence, and some brief sexual situations.

Takano, Ichigo
  ★ **Orange;** Volume 1: the complete collection. story and art by Ichigo Takano; translation, Amber Tamosaitis; adaptation, Shannon Fay; lettering and layout, Lys Blakeslee. Seven Seas Entertainment Llc 2016 384 p. Illustration
Grades: 8 9 10 11 12   **741.5; Fic**
  1. High school students — Fiction; 2. Future life — Fiction; 3. Manga; 4. Shojo manga
1626923027; 9781626923027, $19.99
  "On the day that Naho begins 11th grade, she recieves a letter from herself ten years in the future. At first, she writes it off as a prank, but as the letter's predictions come true one by one Naho realizes that the letter might be the real deal. Her future self tells Naho that a new transfer student, a boy named Kakeru, will soon join her class. The letter begs Naho to watch over him, saying that only Naho can save Kakeru from a terrible future." (Publisher's note)
  Volume 1 of 2

  ★ **Orange;** Volume 2: the complete collection. story and art by Ichigo Takano; translation, Amber Tamosaitis; adaptation, Shannon Fay; lettering and layout, Lys Blakeslee. Seven Seas Entertainment Llc 2016 384 p. Illustration
Grades: 8 9 10 11 12   **741.5; Fic**
  1. Shojo manga; 2. Future life — Fiction; 3. High school students — Fiction; 4. Manga
1626922713; 9781626922716, $19.99
  "On the day that Naho begins 11th grade, she recieves a letter from herself ten years in the future. At first, she writes it off as a prank, but as the letter's predictions come true one by one Naho realizes that the letter might be the real deal. Her future self tells Naho that a new transfer student, a boy named Kakeru, will soon join her class. The letter begs Naho to watch over him, saying that only Naho can save Kakeru from a terrible future." (Publisher's note)

Takaya, Natsuki
  ★ **Fruits** Basket Collector's Edition: Volume 1. Natsuki Takaya; translation, Sheldon Drzka; lettering, Lys Blakeslee. Yen Press 2016 400 p. Illustration
Grades: 7 8 9 10 11 12   **741.5; Fic**
  1. Family — Fiction; 2. Secrets — Fiction; 3. Shojo manga
0316360163; 9780316360166, $20
  "After a family tragedy turns her life upside down, plucky high schooler Tohru Honda takes matters into her own hands and moves out...into a tent! Unfortunately for her, she pitches her new home on private land belonging to the mysterious Sohma clan, and it isn't long before the owners discover her secret. But, as Tohru quickly finds out when the family offers to take her in, the Sohmas have a secret of their own — when

touched by the opposite sex, they turn into the animals of the Chinese Zodiac!" (Publisher's note)

Originally published in the U.S. by Tokyopop in 23 volumes; Volume 1 of 12

Twinkle stars; Volume 1. Natsuki Takaya; translation, Sheldon Drzka; lettering, Lys Blakeslee. Yen Press 2016 384 p. Illustration

Grades: 7 8 9 10 11 12   **741.5; Fic**

1. Fantasy fiction; 2. Teenagers — Graphic novels; 3. High school students — Graphic novels; 4. Shojo manga

0316360236; 9780316360234, $20

LC 2016946117

In this book in the Twinke Stars series, by Natsuki Takaya, translated by Sheldon Drzka, "Sakuya Shiina lives with Kanade, her male cousin and foster parent. In times of pain and sadness, she's always taken comfort in looking up at the stars. One day, a mysterious boy suddenly shows up at Sakuya's house for her birthday. He leaves her with kind words, but she has no idea who he is!" (Publisher's note)

Volume 1 of 5

Takeuchi, Naoko

★ **Sailor** Moon; Volume 1. Naoko Takeuchi; translator/adapter, William Flanagan. Kodansha Comics 2011 240 p. Illustration; Color

Grades: 5 6 7 8 9 10   **741.5; Fic**

1. Teenage girls — Japan — Comic books, strips, etc; 2. Women heroes — Comic books, strips, etc; 3. Shojo manga; 4. Teenage girls — Fiction; 5. Good and evil — Fiction

1935429744; 9781935429746, $10.99

LC 2012374271

"Usagi Tsukino is a normal girl until she meets up with Luna, a talking cat, who tells her that she is Sailor Moon. As Sailor Moon, Usagi must fight evils and enforce justice, in the name of the Moon and the mysterious Moon Princess. She meets other girls destined to be Sailor Senshi (Sailor Scouts), and together, they fight the forces of evil!" (Publisher's note)

First published in Japan in 2003 by Kodansha Ltd., Tokyo, as Bishoujosenshi Sailor Moon Shinsoban; Volume 1 of 12

Tamaki, Mariko

★ **Emiko** superstar. written by Mariko Tamaki; illustrated by Steve Rolston. DC Comics/Minx 2008 149p. Illustration

Grades: 7 8 9 10 11 12   **741.5; Fic**

1. Graphic novels; 2. Performance art — Graphic novels; 3. Racially mixed people — Graphic novels

978-1-4012-1536-1, O.P.

"Emiko, a half-Japanese, half-Caucasian Canadian, is a self-described geek facing a summer of babysitting and isolation. Things change when she stumbles upon an underground performing art scene inspired by Andy Warhol's Factory. She eventually takes to the stage...and achieves minor celebrity. Soon, though, Emiko must face the troubling complexities in the lives of her new friends and the consequences of her own questionable actions.... Rolston's playful, vibrant b&w illustrations bring the characters to life." Publ Wkly

★ **Skim**. words by Mariko Tamaki; drawings by Jillian Tamaki. Groundwood Books 2008 144p. Illustration

Grades: 7 8 9 10 11 12   **741; 741.5; Fic**

1. Friendship — Graphic novels; 2. Graphic novels; 3. Humorous graphic novels; 4. School stories — Graphic novels; 5. LGBT youth — Fiction

088899964X; 0-88899-753-1; 9780888999641, 12.95; 978-0-88899-753-1, $18.95

Ignatz Award: Outstanding Graphic Novel (2008)

Skim is Kimberly Keiko Cameron, a not-slim half-Japanese would-be Wiccan goth who attends a private school. When classmate Katie Matthews' ex-boyfriend commits suicide, concerned guidance counselors descend upon the school because so many of the student body goes into mourning overdrive. The popular clique starts a new club, Girls Celebrate Life, and make Katie their project, especially after she falls off her roof and breaks both arms. Kim and her best friend Lisa observe all this, but counselors target Kim for her goth tendencies and are convinced she'll become suicidal any moment. All she is, is in love with her English teacher, Ms. Archer, who seems to reciprocate and then leaves the school. As Lisa starts to get sucked into the GLC, Kim and Katie tentatively begin a new friendship. There is only one rather chaste kiss between Kim and Ms. Archer. Artist Jillian Tamaki draws Kim to look like a classical Heian period Japanese woman.

★ **This** One Summer. Mariko Tamaki, [art by] Jillian Tamaki. First Second 2014 320 p. Illustration

Grades: 7 8 9 10 11 12 Adult   **741.5; Fic**

1. Graphic novels; 2. Friendship — Fiction; 3. Vacations — Fiction

159643774X, 17.99; 9781626720947, $21.99; 9781596437746, 17.99; 1626720940, 21.99

Caldecott Honor Book (2015); Printz Honor Book (2015); Eisner Award: Best Graphic Album — New (2015); Ignatz Award: Outstanding Graphic Novel (2014); Harvey Nominee: Best Artist (2015); Harvey Nominee: Best Graphic Album of Original Work (2015); Harvey Nominee: Best Original Graphic Publication For Young Readers (2015)

"Every summer, Rose goes with her mom and dad to a lake house in Awago Beach.... Rosie's friend Windy is always there, too, like the little sister she never had. But this summer is different.... It's a summer of secrets, and sorrow, and growing up, and it's a good thing Rose and Windy have each other." (Publisher's note)

"This captivating graphic novel presents a fully realized picture of a particular time in a young girl's life, an in-between summer filled with yearning and a sense of ephemerality." SLJ

Tan, Shaun

★ **The arrival**. Arthur A. Levine Books 2007 un Illustration

Grades: 6 7 8 9 10   **741.5; Fic**

1. Graphic novels; 2. Immigrants — Graphic novels; 3. Stories without words

0-439-89529-4, $19.99; 9780439895293

LC 2006-21706

Boston Globe-Horn Book Award special citation (2008)

In this wordless graphic novel, a man leaves his homeland and sets off for a new country, where he must build a new life for himself and his family.

"Young readers will be fascinated by the strange new world the artist creates.... They will linger over the details in the beautiful sepia pictures and will likely pick up the book to pore over it again and again." SLJ

Tanemura, Arina

Full Moon Vol. 1: O Sagashite. Viz Media/Shojo Beat 2005 200p. Illustration

Grades: 7 8 9 10   **741.5; Fic**

1. Fantasy graphic novels; 2. Graphic novels; 3. Manga; 4. Romance graphic novels; 5. Shojo manga

1-59116-928-3, $8.99

Young Mitsuki loves singing and dreams of becoming a pop star. Unfortunately, a malignant tumor in her throat prevents her from pursuing her passion. However, her life turns around when two surprisingly fun-loving harbingers of death appear to grant Mitsuki a temporary reprieve from her illness and give her singing career a magical push start.

They transform her into a 16-year-old, and she becomes a sensation, but when one of the spirits falls in love with Mitsuki, complications abound.

Telgemeier, Raina

The Baby-sitter's Club: Kristy's great idea: a graphic novel. story by Ann M. Martin; adapted by Raina Telgemeier. Scholastic Graphix 2006 192p. Illustration

Grades: 3 4 5 6   **741.5; Fic**
1. Babysitting — Graphic novels; 2. Friendship — Graphic novels; 3. Graphic novels
0-439-80241-5, $16.99; 0-439-73933-0 (pa), $8.99

LC 2005-37749

Follows the adventures of Kristy and the other members of the Baby-sitters Club as they deal with crank calls, uncontrollable two-year-olds, wild pets, and parents who do not always tell the truth. A graphic novel based on the 1988 book by the same name.

"Comics artist Telgemeier's clean-lined, black-and-white art with stark black details nicely differentiates the four personable seventh-graders who parlay their babysitting experience into a business." Booklist

Also available in full color editions; Other titles about the Baby-sitters Club are: The truth about Stacey (2006); Mary Anne saves the day (2007); Claudia and Mean Janine (2008)

The **Baby-Sitters** Club: The Truth About Stacey. Raina Telgemeier; [adapted from the novel by] Ann M. Martin. Scholastic/Graphix 2006 142p. Illustration

Grades: 3 4 5 6 7 8 9   **741.5**
1. Babysitting — Graphic novels; 2. Friendship — Graphic novels; 3. Graphic novels
0-439-73936-5

Poor Stacey. She's moved to a new town. She's still coming to terms with her diabetes. She's facing baby-sitting problems left and right, and her parents are no help. Luckily, Stacey has three new, true friends: Kristy, Claudia, and Mary Anne. Together they're the BSC, and they will deal with whatever is thrown their way, even if it's a rival baby-sitting club.

★ **Drama**. Raina Telgemeier; with color by Gurihiru. Graphix 2012 233 p. Illustration

Grades: 5 6 7 8   **741.5**
1. Graphic novels; 2. Interpersonal relations — Fiction; 3. Middle schools — Fiction; 4. Schools — Fiction; 5. Theater — Fiction; 6. School stories; 7. LGBT youth — Fiction; 8. Children's plays — Fiction
0545326982; 0545326990; 9780545326988, $23.99; 9780545326995

LC 2011040748

Stonewall Honor Book (2013)

Author Raina Telgemeier's book focuses on a middle school drama production. "Callie loves theater...[S]he's the set designer for the stage crew, and this year she's determined to create a set worthy of Broadway on a middle-school budget. But how can she, when she doesn't know much about carpentry, ticket sales are down, and the crew members are having trouble working together?" (Publisher's note)

"In this realistic and sympathetic story, feelings and thoughts leap off the page, revealing Telgemeier's keen eye for young teen life." Booklist
Includes bibliographical references

★ **Ghosts**. Raina Telgemeier; with color by Braden Lamb. Graphix, an imprint of Scholastic 2016 256 p. Color; Illustration

Grades: 3 4 5 6 7   **741.5; Fic**
1. Cystic fibrosis — Fiction; 2. Families — California, Northern — Comic books, strips, etc; 3. Family life — California, Northern — Fiction; 4. Ghost stories; 5. Ghosts — Comic books, strips, etc; 6. Ghosts — Fiction; 7. Graphic novels; 8. Moving, Household — Comic books, strips, etc; 9. Moving, Household — Fiction; 10. Sisters — Comic books, strips, etc; 11. Sisters — Fiction; 12. California, Northern — Comic books, strips, etc; 13. California, Northern — Fiction
0545540623; 9780545540629, $10.99; 9780545540612, $24.99; 0545540615

LC 2016004672

Eisner Award: Best Publication for Kids (2017)

"Catrina and her family have just moved to Northern California. Bahía de la Luna is different from Cat's hometown — for one thing, everyone is obsessed with ghosts — but the sea air makes it easier for Cat's younger sister, Maya, who has cystic fibrosis (CF), to breathe. Carlos, a new friend and neighbor, introduces the girls to a different perspective on the spiritual world." (School Library Journal)

"In her treatment of illness and death, Telgemeier (Sisters) nudges readers toward the edge of their comfort zone, but she never leaves them alone there. The story is consistently engaging, the plot is tightly built, and — as always — Telgemeier excels at capturing facial expressions." Pub Wkly

★ **Sisters**. Raina Telgemeier; with color by Braden Lamb. Graphix 2014 197 p. Color; Illustration

Grades: 5 6 7 8   **741.5; 306.875; 92**
1. Interpersonal relations; 2. Autobiographical graphic novels; 3. Family life; 4. Siblings
9780545540599, $24.99; 9780545540605, $10.99

LC 2013008700

"Raina can't wait to be a big sister. But once Amara is born, things aren't quite how she expected them to be.... They are sisters, after all. Raina uses her signature humor...in both present-day narrative and perfectly placed flashbacks to tell the story of her relationship with her sister, which unfolds during the course of a road trip from their home in San Francisco to a family reunion in Colorado." (Publisher's note)

"The author's narrative style is fresh and sharp, and the combination of well-paced and well-placed flashbacks pull the plot together, moving the story forward and helping readers understand the characters' point of view. The volume captures preadolescence in an effortless and uncanny way and turns tough subjects, such as parental marriage problems, into experiences with which readers can identify." (School Library Journal)

★ **Smile**. Scholastic/Graphix 2010 213p. Illustration

Grades: 5 6 7 8   **741; 741.5**
1. Autobiographical graphic novels; 2. Dentistry — Graphic novels; 3. Friendship — Graphic novels; 4. Graphic novels; 5. Personal appearance — Graphic novels
978-0-545-13205-3, $21.99; 0-545-13205-3; 978-0-545-13206-0 (pa), $10.99; 0-545-13206-1 (pa)

LC 2008-51782

Boston Globe-Horn Book Honor: Nonfiction (2010); Eisner Award: Best Publication for Teens (2011)

"Raina just wants to be a normal sixth grader. But one night after Girl Scouts she trips and falls, severely injuring her two front teeth. What follows is a long and frustrating journey with on-again, off-again braces, surgery, embarrassing headgear, and even a retainer with fake teeth attached. And on top of all that, there's still more to deal with: a major earthquake, boy confusion, and friends who turn out to be not so friendly." (Publisher's note)

"Telgemeier has created an utterly charming graphic memoir of tooth trauma, first crushes and fickle friends, sweetly reminiscent of Judy Blume's work." Kirkus

TenNapel, Doug

Bad Island. created, written, and drawn by Doug TenNapel. Graphix 2011 218p. Illustration

Grades: 6 7 8 9 10   **741.5**

1. Adventure graphic novels; 2. Extraterrestrial beings — Graphic novels; 3. Family life — Graphic novels; 4. Survival after airplane accidents, shipwrecks, etc. — Graphic novels; 5. Father-son relationship — Graphic novels
0545314798; 0545314801 (pa); 9780545314794, $24.99; 9780545314800 (pa)

LC 2011276008

"Dad has decided to take Reese, who is too cool for family outings, and his sister, Janine, on a fishing trip. The vacation takes an unexpected turn when their boat capsizes during a storm and they find themselves marooned on a strange island. To their horror, the family slowly realizes that the island is the submerged body of a giant creature, escaped from another world. The story alternates between the shipwreck survivors and the faraway world that created this "island." Both stories feature conflict between an adolescent son and his father.... Ultimately, both rebellious adolescents grow up and find their place as young men." (School Libr J)

"Though father, mother, teenage son, and tween daughter face the various dangers like a gang of Indiana Joneses, their family stresses are believable.... A clever, old-fashioned adventure with some modern twists and a lighthearted tone." Booklist

Cardboard. Doug TenNapel. Graphix / Scholastic 2012 288 p.
Grades: 5 6 7 8 **741.5**
1. Father-son relationship — Graphic novels; 2. Boxes — Fiction; 3. Gifts — Graphic novels; 4. Bullies — Graphic novels; 5. Magic — Graphic novels
0545418720; 9780545418720, $24.99; 9780545418737

LC 2011934533

In this graphic novel, "Cam Howerton's out-of-work father is so broke, the best he can do for Cam's birthday is an empty cardboard box purchased from a toy seller with two mysterious rules: return every unused scrap of cardboard and don't ask for any more.... [T]he box becomes a project. What should father and son make out of the box? 'A boxer,' Cam suggests.... 'Boxer Bill,' created from inanimate material, comes alive. Unfortunately, Marcus, the neighborhood bully...steals the scrap materials, and begins turning out a whole evil empire of cardboard monsters.... [A]fter losing control of them he must unite with Cam and his father to defeat the massive cardboard army.... [Q]uestions are raised about what it means to be a man, what makes a good man, and what forms people's character." (Horn Book)

Terry, Laura
Graveyard shakes. Laura Terry. Graphix 2017 208 p. Color; Illustration
Grades: 3 4 5 6 **741.5; Fic**
1. Sisters — Graphic novels; 2. Ghosts — Juvenile fiction; 3. Children's stories
9780545889544; 9780545889551, $24.99; 9780545889568

LC 2016960079

In this book, by Laura Terry, "Katia and Victoria are sisters and scholarship students at a private boarding school. While Victoria tries to fit in, Katia is unapologetic about her quirks.... After a big fight, Katia runs away from school. And when Victoria goes looking for her, she accidentally tumbles into the underworld of a nearby graveyard. It is inhabited by ghosts, ghouls, and a man named Nikola, who is preparing a sinister spell that's missing one key ingredient." (Publisher's note)

"That the afterlife can be as complicated as regular life will strike a wryly funny note with young outcasts and loners, but Terry never loses sight of the idea that even misfits can find community by being themselves." Pub Wkly

Tetzner, Lisa
The **Black** Brothers: A Novel in Pictures. Front Street 2004 144p. Illustration
Grades: 4 5 6 7 8 9 **741.5; Fic**
1. Chimney sweeps — Graphic novels; 2. Graphic novels
1-932425-04-7, $16.95

In rural Italy, thirteen-year-old Giorgio is sold to a man who supplies chimney sweeps for Milan. After a treacherous journey in which most of the other boys die, Giorgio goes to work for a man whose wife resents another mouth to feed and starves him. He is sent up into chimneys with no training or guidance for how to do the dangerous work. After nearly dying, he is befriended by a doctor and finds the Black Brothers, a group of chimney sweeps who swear loyalty to each other.

This illustrated novel was originally published in German in 1941, and the translation's tone is similar to other children's books, such as Emil and the Detectives.

Tezuka, Osamu
Astro Boy books 1 and 2. Dark Horse Comics 2008 424p. Illustration
Grades: 3 4 5 6 7 8 9 10 11 12 Adult **741.5; Fic**
1. Adventure graphic novels; 2. Astro Boy (Fictional character); 3. Graphic novels; 4. Robots — Graphic novels; 5. Science fiction graphic novels
978-1-59582-153-9, $14.95

When a scientist loses his young son, he builds a robot to look exactly like the boy, but when he activates the robot, the scientist becomes repulsed and rejects him. Professor Ochanomizu (gotta love the name, it means tea water and is also a famous Tokyo neighborhood) rescues the boy robot from a circus and names him Astro Boy. He deals with aliens, with people who would use robots to commit crimes, and with adventures in outer space. This new edition collects the first two volumes of the Dark Horse manga editions.

Also available in omnibus editions; Volumes 1 and 2 of a 23 volume series

Thompson, Jill
Goosebumps: Terror Trips. Scholastic/Graphix 2007 137p. Illustration
Grades: 4 5 6 7 8 9 **741.5; Fic**
1. Graphic novels; 2. Horror graphic novels; 3. Stine, R. L.; 4. Stine, R. L. — Adaptations
978-0-439-85780-2, $8.99

Stine's Goosebumps series was very popular years ago, and is enjoying a resurgence of popularity with new editions of the prose books. The graphic novel adaptations, all done by well-known independent comics creators, bring the stories to a new audience. Goosebumps: Creepy Creatures is also available.

This volume adapts three of Stine's Goosebumps novels into graphic novel format. Noted independent comic creator Thompson adapts One Day at Horrorland, about one family's ordeal in a very strange, all-too-realistic amusement park. Canadian artist Tolagson adapts A Shocker on Shock Street, which depicts the horrific adventures of two kids on a movie studio lot where the horror is more than just special effects. Global manga creator Ganter adapts Deep Trouble, in which a brother and sister find a real mermaid.

Tobe, Keiko
With the Light: Raising an Autistic Child (Hikari to Tomoni). Yen Press 2007 528p. Illustration
Grades: 8 9 10 11 12 Adult **741.5; Fic**
1. Autism — Graphic novels; 2. Graphic novels; 3. Manga; 4. Josei manga

978-0-7595-2356-2, $14.99

Born during the sunrise — an auspicious beginning — the Azumas' newborn son is named Hikaru, which means "light." But during one play date, his mother notices that her son is slightly different from the other children. In this alternately heartwarming and bittersweet tale, a young mother tries to cope with both the overwhelming discovery of her child's autism and the trials of raising him while keeping her family together. This fictional story is based on true accounts; and the book includes notes about how parents can deal with certain situations depicted in the story.

Volume 1 of 8

Tobin, Paul

I was the cat. written by Paul Tobin; illustrated and colored by Benjamin Dewey; lettered by Jared Jones; edited by Jill Beaton with Robin Herrera; designed by Jason Storey. Oni Press 2014 144 p. Color; Illustration
Grades: 5 6 7 8 9

741.5; Fic
1. Fantasy graphic novels; 2. Cats — Graphic novels
1620101394; 9781620101391, $24.99
LC 2014932452
Eisner Nominee: Best Publication for Kids (2015)

Courtesy of Oni Press

When "Allison Breaking...receives an offer from a mysterious stranger named Burma to write his memoirs, it's an offer she can't refuse, not even with all the red flags popping up. But Burma is quite literally unlike any man Allison's ever known — because he's a cat! And this cat has stories to tell about how he (over the course of a few lifetimes) has shaped the world." (Publisher's note)

Tolagson, Jamie

Goosebumps: Terror Trips. Scholastic/Graphix 2007 137p. Illustration
Grades: 4 5 6 7 8 9

741.5; Fic
1. Graphic novels; 2. Horror graphic novels; 3. Stine, R. L.; 4. Stine, R. L. — Adaptations
978-0-439-85780-2, $8.99

Stine's Goosebumps series was very popular years ago, and is enjoying a resurgence of popularity with new editions of the prose books. The graphic novel adaptations, all done by well-known independent comics creators, bring the stories to a new audience. Goosebumps: Creepy Creatures is also available.

This volume adapts three of Stine's Goosebumps novels into graphic novel format. Noted independent comic creator Thompson adapts One Day at Horrorland, about one family's ordeal in a very strange, all-too-realistic amusement park. Canadian artist Tolagson adapts A Shocker on Shock Street, which depicts the horrific adventures of two kids on a movie studio lot where the horror is more than just special effects. Global manga creator Ganter adapts Deep Trouble, in which a brother and sister find a real mermaid.

Tolstikova, Dasha

A **Year** Without Mom. by Dasha Tolstikova. Groundwood Books 2015 176 p. Color; Illustration
Grades: 5 6 7 8

741.5; 92
1. Tolstikova, Dasha; 2. Mother-daughter relationship; 3. Russia; 4. Refugees
1554986923; 9781554986927, $19.95

This book, by Dasha Tolstikova, "follows 12-year-old Dasha through a year full of turmoil after her mother leaves for America. It is the early 1990s in Moscow, and political change is in the air. But Dasha is more worried about her own challenges as she negotiates family, friendships and school without her mother. Just as she begins to find her own feet, she gets word that she is to join her mother in America — a place that seems impossibly far from everything and everyone she loves." (Publisher's note)

"Scribbly, childlike pencil drawings are filled in with gray wash and accentuated with red and the occasional pop of blue. They are deceptively simple, but with great narrative sophistication, they capture both the specificity of Dasha's experience and the universality of her emotions." Kirkus

Toriyama, Akira

Dragon Ball Full Color 1; 1. tory and art by Akira Toriyama; [translation, Mari Morimoto; English adaptation, Gerard Jones; lettering, John Clark]. Viz 2014 243 p. Color illustration
Grades: 7 8 9 10 11 12   **741.5; Fic**
1. Adventure graphic novels; 2. Extraterrestrial beings — Graphic novels
1421565927; 9781421565927, $19.99

In this graphic novel, by Akira Toriyama, "Son Goku is the greatest hero on Earth. Five years after defeating the demon king Piccolo, he's grown up and had a family — he's married, and he has a child, Son Gohan. But what is the real reason for Goku's incredible strength? A visitor from outer space arrives bearing terrible news — Goku is an alien, and the visitor, Raditz, is Goku's brother! When Raditz turns out to be a ruthless killer, Goku must fight his incredibly strong brother to save his family and the entire human race." (Publisher's note)

"Toriyama's storytelling is beautifully clear and dynamic, showing why he's revered as one of the world's greatest cartoonists.... [His] work is still as humorous and action-packed as when it was created." Pub Wkly

Dragon Ball Z (vizbig edition vol. 1). story & art by Akira Toriyama; [English adaptation, Gerard Jones; translation, Lillian Olsen]. Viz Media/Shonen Jump 2008 528p. Illustration
Grades: 7 8 9 10 11 12   **741.5; Fic**
1. Adventure graphic novels; 2. Graphic novels; 3. Manga; 4. Martial arts — Graphic novels; 5. Shonen manga
978-1-4215-2064-3, $17.99

The first three volumes of DragonBall Z are now collected in a larger size volume. The Saiyans are an alien race of deadly warriors who wipe out entire planets for their own profit and gain. When the Saiyans set their sights on Earth, it's up to Son Goku to fight off the invaders with his superhuman strength. This series is an almost nonstop series of martial arts action scenes, so there's lots of fighting and yelling, but no harsh language.

Also available in 26 individual volumes; Volume 1 of 9

Torres, J.

Days Like This. Oni Press 2003 un Illustration
Grades: 6 7 8 9 10 11 12 Adult

741.5; Fic
1. Graphic novels; 2. Rock music — Graphic novels
1-929998-48-1, $8.95

Courtesy of Oni Press

It's the early 1960s, and rock'n'roll and r&b are ushering in a new golden age of pop music. Tina & the Tiaras, three teenage girl singers, songwriter Karen Prince, and new music mogul Anna Solomon team to create a new girl group sound and move up the charts.

Degrassi the Next Generation Extra Credit Vol. 1: Turning Japanese. Pocket Books 2006 un Illustration
Grades: 8 9 10 11 12   **741.5; Fic**
1. Graphic novels
978-1-4165-3076-3, $9.95

It's the end of Ellie's senior year, and as though final exams aren't enough to worry about, she's been placed in a compromising position by one of her bosses at a comic book company. Is quitting her only option? J.T. turns to the Internet to help cope with the recent troubles in his life. But now he spends most of his time locked in his room, and he can't seem to move on. Is his new habit just making his problems worse? This original story follows the sixth season of the popular television series.

Degrassi the Next Generation Extra Credit Vol. 2: Suddenly Last Summer. Pocket Books 2007 un Illustration
Grades: 8 9 10 11 12   **741.5; Fic**
1. Graphic novels
978-1-4165-3077-0, $9.95

Emma gets her groove back with the help of group therapy and a family trip to New York City. But as she returns to her old self, her relationship with Peter begins to suffer. Is he helping Emma recover, or holding her back? In the meantime, while coaching at basketball camp, Jimmy finds himself dealing with the fallout of a hazing incident. Was the initiation just a prank, or did it cross the line? When the police get involved, Jimmy is faced with a tough decision. This is another original story set during the summer vacation following the sixth season of the popular television series.

Into the woods. J. Torres; illustrated by Faith Erin Hicks. Kids Can Press 2012 100 p. Color illustration (Bigfoot Boy)
Grades: 3 4 5 6 7
Fic; 741.5; 741.5/971
1. Magic — Graphic novels; 2. Totems and totemism — Graphic novels; 3. Sasquatch — Graphic novels
1554537118; 9781554537112, $17.95

In this fantasy graphic novel, "city boy Rufus is staying at his grandmother's house on the edge of a forest for a few days without his parents," and he "decides to explore the woods. He meets a girl named Penny.... When looking for her in the woods, Rufus finds a glowing necklace in a tree. After reading the word on the back, he turns into Bigfoot!...There's danger in the forest as well as magic, and when Penny disappears, Rufus...use[s] the totem to effect a rescue." (Kirkus Reviews)

Followed by: The unkindness of ravens (2013)

Courtesy of Kids Can Press

★ **Lola**: a ghost story. [by] J. Torres & [illustrated by] Elbert Or. Oni Press 2009 102p. Illustration
Grades: 4 5 6 7 8
741.5; Fic
1. Family life — Graphic novels; 2. Ghosts — Graphic novels; 3. Graphic novels; 4. Philippines — Graphic novels
978-1-934964-33-0, $14.95;
1-934964-33-6

"Lola ("grandmother" in Tagalog) has just died, and Jesse is reluctant to visit her home in the Philippines. He was afraid of her

Courtesy of Oni Press

because she was rumored to have magical abilities, and because he thinks she tried to drown him when he was a baby. Jesse listens to family members tell stories about her as he tries to adjust to their strange mix of superstitions and religion.... Jesse is an unusually nuanced character.... When he sees something extraordinary, it's unclear if he is dreaming, hallucinating, or if he has inherited his grandmother's abilities. Torres's gradual revelation of details will keep readers hanging until they learn the truth. Or's artwork uses sepia tones and smooth lines, and features characters with cute button eyes. But the sweet images can quickly turn horrific when Jesse has his visions. " SLJ

Teen Titans Go! Vol. 1: Truth, Justice, Pizza!. DC Comics 2004 112p. Illustration
Grades: 3 4 5 6 7 8 9   **741.5; Fic**
1. Graphic novels; 2. Humorous graphic novels; 3. Superhero graphic novels; 4. Teen Titans (Fictional characters)
1-4012-0333-7, $6.95

They're too young to drive, but not too young to save the world. The world's hottest heroes: Robin, Beast Boy, Raven, Cyborg, and Starfire, show how it's done Titan-style, as they go up against teen super villains Gizmo, Jinx, and Mammoth. Things get icky when Raven's bad dad, Trigon, comes out from a huge zit on Raven's forehead (ewwww ...).

Teen Titans Go! Vol. 2: Heroes on Patrol!. J. Torres, Adam Beechen, writers; Todd Nauck, Eric Vedder, pencillers; Lary Stucker, M3th, inkers; Phil Good, Heroic Age, colorists; Phil Balsman, Jared K. Fletcher, letterers; Dave Bullock, collection cover artist. DC Comics 2004 112p. Illustration
Grades: 3 4 5 6 7 8 9   **741.5; Fic**
1. Graphic novels; 2. Humorous graphic novels; 3. Superhero graphic novels; 4. Teen Titans (Fictional characters)
1-4012-0334-5, $6.95

In this volume, the Teen Titans encounter the battling brothers, Thunder and Lightning; Starfire has to deal with her naughty sister Blackfire; they encounter Aqualad; and more.

Teen Titans Go! Vol. 3: Bring It On!. DC Comics 2005 104p. Illustration
Grades: 3 4 5 6 7 8 9   **741.5; Fic**
1. Graphic novels; 2. Humorous graphic novels; 3. Superhero graphic novels; 4. Teen Titans (Fictional characters)
1-4012-0511-9, $6.99

Terra rejoins the Titans to fight Slade's robots; the teen superheroes fight Mumbo; Beast Boy tries to help a man stricken with werewolfism; Speedy joins the Titans to fight Plasmus; and they go up against Kwiz Kid, who's mad at Robin because his ex-girlfriend has a crush on Robin.

Teen Titans Go! Vol. 4: Ready for Action!. DC Comics 2005 104p. Illustration
Grades: 3 4 5 6 7 8 9   **741.5; Fic**
1. Graphic novels; 2. Humorous graphic novels; 3. Superhero graphic novels; 4. Teen Titans (Fictional characters)
978-1-4012-0985-8, $6.99

In this volume, the Titans confront a rampaging Wildebeest, teach the hot-tempered Hotshot the value of patience, battle an army of zombies, find themselves trapped in a deadly video game with the Titans East and more.

Teen Titans Go!: Titans Together!. DC Comics 2007 144p. Illustration
Grades: 3 4 5 6 7 8 9   **741.5**
1. Graphic novels; 2. Superhero graphic novels; 3. Teen Titans (Fictional characters)
978-1-4012-1563-7, $12.99

This volume collects eight adventures of the Teen Titans as seen in the animated series, Teen Titans Go! Robin leads the young team that includes

Cyborg, Beast Boy, Raven, and Starfire. The stories have lots of action and bad puns as Beast Boy makes a movie, the Titans find themselves in an alien fighting arena, and Robin's future self, Nightwing, comes when time goes a little haywire and an evil Robin shows up.

Tregonning, Mel

Small things. Mel Tregonning; with an afterword by Barbara Coloroso. Pajama Press 2018 37 p. Illustration

Grades: 3 4 5 6   **741.5; Fic**
1. Anxiety in children — Fiction; 2. Boys — Fiction; 3. Stories without words; 4. Picture books for children; 5. Anxiety — Fiction
1772780421; 9781772780420, $18.95

In author Mel Tregonning's "wordless graphic picture book, a young boy feels alone with his worries. He isn't fitting in well at school. His grades are slipping. He's even lashing out at those who love him.... The boy's worries manifest as tiny beings that crowd around him constantly, overwhelming him and even gnawing away at his very self." (Publisher's note)

"Tregonning creates a visual language for the pain of depression and anxiety, and her story may provide a measure of hope to those who might otherwise have given up in despair." Pub Wkly

Tsukuda, Yuto

Food Wars!; Volume 1: endless wilderness. story by Yuto Tsukuda; art by Shun Saeki; translation, Adrienne Beck; touch-up art & lettering, NRP Studios. Viz 2014 208 p. Illustration

Grades: 7 8 9 10 11 12   **741.5**
1. Shonen manga; 2. Manga
1421572540; 9781421572543, $9.99

"Soma Yukihira's old man runs a small family restaurant in the less savory end of town. Aiming to one day surpass his father's culinary prowess, Soma hones his skills day in and day out until one day, out of the blue, his father decides to enroll Soma in a classy culinary school! Can Soma really cut it in a place that prides itself on a 10% graduation rate?" (Publisher's note)

Volume 1 of an ongoing series

Tynion, James, IV

★ The **backstagers**; Volume 1: rebels without applause. created by James Tynion IV and Rian Sygh; written by James Tynion IV; illustrated by Rian Sygh; colors by Walter Baiamonte; letters by Jim Campbell; cover by Veronica Fish. Boom! Studios 2017 112 p. Color; Illustration

Grades: 7 8 9 10 11 12   **741.5**
1. LGBT youth — Fiction; 2. Private schools — Fiction
9781681598796; 1608869938; 9781608869930, $14.99

In this book, by James Tynion IV, illustrated by Rian Sygh, "when Jory transfers to an all-boys private high school, he's taken in by the only ones who don't treat him like a new kid, the lowly stage crew known as the Backstagers. Not only does he gain great, lifetime friends, Jory is also introduced to an entire magical world that lives beyond the curtain. With the unpredictable twists and turns of the underground world, the Backstagers venture into the unknown." (Publisher's note)

"Brimming with feeling and featuring a diverse cast (including a trans character, Beckett), it's an effervescently entertaining story of finding community (and maybe love) in unlikely, even impossible places." Pub Wkly

Volume 1 of an ongoing series

Uderzo, Albert

Asterix and Obelix All at Sea. Orion/Sterling Publishing 2002 48p. Illustration

Grades: 4 5 6 7 8 9 10 11 12 Adult   **741.5; Fic**

1. Asterix (Fictional character); 2. Graphic novels; 3. Humorous graphic novels
0-75284-778-3, $9.95

LC 2002-282560

In ancient Rome the slaves are revolting...and not only that, they've stolen Julius Caesar's own galley, the finest warship in the Roman navy. Under their heroic leader Spartakis, the former galley slaves make for the little Gaulish village where Julius Caesar's old enemies Asterix and Obelix live — only to find the place in crisis, for Obelix, after drinking the druid Getafix's magic potions on the sly, is first turned to stone and then reverts to childhood. In search of a cure for him, Getafix and their new friends the galley slaves sail to the wonderful continent of Atlantis, ruled by its high priest Absolutlifabulos — and the ensuing sea battles against the Roman navy are fast and furious ...

Unita, Yumi

★ **Bunny** drop vol. 1. [translation, Kaori Inoue; lettering, Alexis Eckerman].. Yen Press 2010 196p. Illustration

Grades: 8 9 10 11 12 Adult   **741.5; Fic**
1. Graphic novels; 2. Josei manga; 3. Manga; 4. Unmarried fathers — Graphic novels
978-0-7595-3122-2, $12.99

Thirty-year-old bachelor Daikichi is a salaryman, a junior executive, living on his own in Tokyo. When he goes home for his grandfather's funeral, he discovers that his grandfather had a younger lover who left him with a little girl, Rin (which makes her his aunt). The lover is nowhere to be found, and none of Daikichi's relatives will have anything to do with Rin, who won't talk to anyone but sticks close to Daikichi, who closely resembles his grandfather. When no one will step forward to take care of the six-year-old, Daikichi impulsively decides he will. Once he brings Rin home, the reality of his new situation finally dawns on him; Daikichi is now a single father and has to provide care for Rin. There's one scene with Rin and Daikichi together in their furo bath (a very typical Japanese family scene), and a few panels with Rin and Daikichi in their underwear. In one chapter, Daikichi has to deal with Rin's night time bedwetting, and Rin is shown changing her clothes.

"This sweet-natured manga shows the joys, frustrations, and quirks of family life; and while it is aimed at teens, it would also be more than welcome in the hands of adult readers." Booklist

First published 2006 in Japan; Book reads from right to left in the traditional Japanese format; Volume 1 of 9

Urrea, Luis Alberto

★ **Mr.** Mendoza's paintbrush. artwork by Christopher Cardinale; color masking and compositing, Anthony Cardinale; design, Anne M. Giangiulio. Cinco Puntos Press 2010 un Illustration

Grades: 10 11 12 7 8 9 Adult   **741.5; Fic**
1. Artists — Graphic novels; 2. Graphic novels; 3. Humorous graphic novels; 4. Mexico — Graphic novels
978-1-933693-23-1, $17.95

LC 2008-11636

Rosario is a small town in the Sinaloa region of Mexico, nestled into a wet, green, mango-sweet subtropical landscape. There, Mr. Mendoza wields his paintbrush to write graffiti with a purpose. When Mr. Mendoza catches the young narrator and his best friend Jaime spying on the girls who are swimming, he strips them, writes graffiti all over their bodies, and chases the naked boys down the street through town. He also appoints himself as the town's conscience and angers the authorities with his graffiti on the town's whorehouse, bridge, and other places. Then, one day, he takes his paint and paintbrush to the center square and paints steps into the sky and walks up until he disappears. Women and girls are shown in their underwear, and the naked boys are shown only from the back. The talk of sex, the way the boys sneak peeks at the girls and one of the town's women, make this book suitable for teens even though the format resembles a picture book.

"Not only does the art perfectly capture the mood of the piece — from the blocky woodcuts to the muted earth tones — but it also reinforces the lucid dreamlike quality of its magical realism, serving as an enticing invitation to further explore the genre." Horn Book Guide

Van Lente, Fred
  George Washington. Fred Van Lente, illustrated by Ryan Dunlavey. HarperCollins 2018 128 p. Color; Illustration (Action presidents)
  Grades: 4 5 6 7 8 **741.5; 92**
  1. Washington, George, 1732-1799; 2. Biography; 3. Presidents — United States
  9780062394057, $9.99

  LC 2017950229

Includes bibliographical references

In this book in the Action Presidents series, by Fred Van Lente, illustrated by Ryan Dunlavey, "we all know that George Washington was our first president and a hero of the American Revolution, but did you also know that he didn't want to be president and had teeth so bad that he hated to smile?...U.S. history comes to life like never before! Historically accurate and highly entertaining...[w]ith timelines, maps, charts, and more." (Publisher's note)

"Van Lente aims to contextualize historical figures who are often blindly lionized..., a goal that comes through clearly amid a flurry of gags and jokes." Pub Wkly

  Howtoons; Volume 1: (re)ignition. writer: Fred Van Lente; artist: Tom Fowler; colors: Jordie Bellaire; letters: Rus Wooton. Image Comics 2015 160 p. Illustration; Color
  Grades: 5 6 7 8 **741.5**
  1. Science — Experiments — Comic books, strips, etc.; 2. Siblings — Graphic novels; 3. Science fiction graphic novels
  9781632150561, $9.99; 1632150565

In this graphic novel by Fred Van Lente and illustrated by Tom Fowler, "Celine and Tuck's parents put them to sleep for centuries to ride out the energy crisis — but when they awake in the far future and Mom and Dad are missing, it's the kids who have to save the day! Celine and Tuck must explore a strange, new Earth using their gadgeteering skills to create projects and experiments to survive hostile tribes and bizarre mechanized threats." (Publisher's note)

"Step-by-step instructions and warnings for each device are included. The materials needed for each project varies. Each example features icons denoting what kind of energy this project represents. An icon glossary provides further explanation." SLJ

Van Meter, Jen
  Hopeless Savages. Oni Press 2002 128p. Illustration
  Grades: 7 8 9 10 11 12 Adult
  741.5; Fic
  1. Family — Graphic novels; 2. Graphic novels; 3. Humorous graphic novels; 4. Rock music — Graphic novels
  1-929998-24-4, $13.95

Family ties are the earliest ties that bind, setting the tone for the paths we will take in our future. So what if your father is Dirk Hopeless and your mother Nikki Savage, a superstar couple from the days of punk rock? When you're born a rebel, what can you possibly do to make yourself stand apart? For

Courtesy of Oni Press

Rat Hopeless-Savage, the answer is to leave home and become a normal citizen with a nine-to-five job.

  Hopeless Savages Vol. 2: Ground Zero. Oni Press 2004 128p. Illustration
  Grades: 7 8 9 10 11 12 Adult
  741.5; Fic
  1. Family — Graphic novels; 2. Graphic novels; 3. Humorous graphic novels; 4. Rock music — Graphic novels; 5. Romance graphic novels
  1-929998-99-6, $11.95

Courtesy of Oni Press

When you're sixteen, the world is a different place. When you're Zero Hopeless-Savage, the youngest daughter of rock stars Dirk Hopeless and Nikki Savage, the world is practically unrecognizable. Imagine you're in the midst of high school, you have your first band, and WHAMMO! Some boy comes along who doesn't think you're a total freak, and you think he's pretty swell, too. But before you can do anything about it, there's a TV crew outside your house that wants to chronicle the gossip and scandals of your parents' careers, and a massive misunderstanding has gotten you grounded. How's a self-respecting young lady supposed to handle all that?

  Hopeless Savages Vol. 3: Too Much Hopeless. Oni Press 2004 un Illustration
  Grades: 7 8 9 10 11 12 Adult
  741.5; Fic
  1. Family — Graphic novels; 2. Graphic novels; 3. Humorous graphic novels; 4. Martial arts — Graphic novels; 5. Romance graphic novels
  1-929998-85-6, $11.95

Courtesy of Oni Press

This was supposed to be a leisurely vacation. Arsenal Hopeless-Savage has a rematch with an old high school rival in a kung-fu tournament in Hong Kong. She and her brother Twitch figured they could turn it into a nice jaunt with their boyfriends to meet their aging grandmother, a renowned Chinese fortune teller. Too bad Grandma Shi didn't phone ahead to tell them that it was going to be the trip from Hell. It begins at the airport when a shady character slips something into Arsenal's bag, putting the quartet on the radar of the local bad guys, the British secret service, and the Hong Kong police. It becomes even more complicated when the rest of the Hopeless-Savage clan decides to join the middle children in Asia, getting caught up in the international intrigue themselves. Arsenal is the only person that can get them all out of the jam they're in, and for her it's all too much. Twitch's gay relationship is treated matter-of-factly.

Vance, Steve
  Bad girls. DC Comics 2009 128p. Illustration
  Grades: 8 9 10 11 12 **741.5; Fic**
  1. Graphic novels; 2. Humorous graphic novels; 3. Schools — Graphic novels; 4. Superhero graphic novels
  978-1-4012-2359-5, $14.99

Lauren's first day at San Narciso High becomes a disaster when she collides with the school's uber-nerd Ronald and gets on the wrong side of the school's queen bee cheerleaders led by Tiffany. Things only get worse as the days go by, then Lauren unknowingly helps to create even more trouble when Tiffany, Brittany, Ashley, and Destinee all drink from Ronald's thermos that Lauren had been holding. That thermos held

Ronald's secret science project, a potion that gives the drinker super powers. Oh, and all that stuff about "with great power comes great responsibility?" Pffft! These girls decide to have their own kind of fun at the expense of everyone else. So how is Lauren supposed to stop them? Ronald decides to give her a dose of his potion, and now suddenly she can read minds. How is that supposed to help? Meanwhile, a couple of sinister government agents come to town, and the science teacher wants to find out just what Ronald has been doing ...

Varon, Sara

Robot dreams. First Second 2007 205p. Illustration
Grades: 3 4 5 6 7 8 9 10 11 12 Adult   **741; 741.5; Fic**
1. Dogs — Graphic novels; 2. Graphic novels; 3. Robots — Graphic novels
978-1-59643-108-9 (pa), $16.95; 1-59643-108-3 (pa)

           LC 2006-52640
The friendship between a dog and a robot is portrayed in this wordless graphic novel. (Bull Cent Child Books)
"Varon's drawing style is uncomplicated, and her colors are clean and refeshing. Although her story seems equally simple, it is invested with true emotion." Booklist
A Junior Library Guild book

Sweaterweather. Alternative Comics 2006 96p. Illustration
Grades: 3 4 5 6 7 8 9
741.5; Fic
1. Animals — Graphic novels; 2. Friendship — Graphic novels; 3. Graphic novels; 4. Stories without words — Graphic novels
1-891867-93-8, $14.95
A turtle, a rabbit, and other creatures venture out on a wordless snowy journey full of friendship and sweetness. Varon includes interactive bits to the book, such as paper dolls, postcards, and stamps.
First published 2003

Courtesy of Alternative Comics

Vaughan, Brian K.

★ **Runaways** Vol. 1: Pride & Joy. Marvel Entertainment 2004 un Illustration
Grades: 7 8 9 10 11 12   **741.5; Fic**
1. Graphic novels; 2. Runaways (Fictional characters); 3. Science fiction graphic novels; 4. Superhero graphic novels
0-7851-1379-7, $7.99

All young people believe their parents are evil...but what if they really are? Meet Alex, Karolina, Gert, Chase, Molly and Nico — whose lives are about to take an unexpected turn. When these six young friends discover their parents are all secretly super-powered villains, the shocked teens find strength in one another. Together, they run away from home and straight into the adventure of their lives — vowing to turn the tables on their evil legacy. This is the first volume of an ongoing series.
Originally published as Runaways issues #1-6.; Other Runaways volumes are: 2: Teenage Wasteland; 3: The Good Die Young; 4: True Believers; 5: Escape to New York; 6: Parental Guidance; 7: Live Fast; 8: Dead End Kids; 9: Dead Wrong; 10: Rock Zombies; 11: Homeschooling

Runaways Vol. 2: Teenage Wasteland. Marvel Entertainment 2004 un Illustration
Grades: 8 9 10 11 12   **741.5; Fic**

1. Adventure graphic novels; 2. Graphic novels; 3. Runaways (Fictional characters); 4. Superhero graphic novels
0-7851-1415-7, $7.99
Still on the run from their super-villain parents, the motley crew of super-powered kids finds a kindred spirit in a daring young stranger and welcomes him into their fold. But will this dashing young man help the teens defeat their villainous parents, or tear them apart. Then Marvel's original teen runaway crime fighters, Cloak and Dagger, are sent to catch the runaways.

Runaways Vol. 6: Parental Guidance. Marvel Entertainment 2006 un Illustration
Grades: 8 9 10 11 12   **741.5; Fic**
1. Adventure graphic novels; 2. Graphic novels; 3. Runaways (Fictional characters); 4. Superhero graphic novels
0-7851-1952-3, $7.99
The Pride is back as an all-new group, and they have it in for the Runaways. And when Molly is separated from her teammates, she must survive a night alone on the mean streets of Los Angeles. The eleven-year-old mutant girl soon hooks up with a new group of runaways, but is their mysterious leader a hero or a villain? In this volume, a member of the team dies.

Runaways Vol. 7: Live Fast. Marvel Entertainment 2007 un Illustration
Grades: 8 9 10 11 12   **741.5; Fic**
1. Adventure graphic novels; 2. Graphic novels; 3. Runaways (Fictional characters); 4. Superhero graphic novels
978-0-7851-2267-8, $7.99
The Runaways say good-bye to the past, and make hard decisions about their future. Plus: Still reeling from the events of Young Avengers/Runaways (part of Marvel's Civil War), the teenage heroes must now confront a horrific enemy who threatens to tear the team apart.

Venditti, Robert

Blue Bloods: the graphic novel. by Melissa de la Cruz; adapted by Robert Venditti; art by Alina Urusov; illustrations by Disney Enterprises, Inc.. Hyperion 2013 112 p. Color illustration
Grades: 8 9 10 11 12   **741.5/973; Fic**
1. Graphic novels; 2. Secrets — Fiction; 3. Vampires — Fiction; 4. Wealth — Fiction; 5. New York (N.Y.) — Fiction; 6. Teenagers — Graphic novels; 7. Supernatural graphic novels
9781423134466, $19.99; 9781423134473, $11.99; 142313446X

           LC 2011053237
In this graphic novel, written by Melissa de la Cruz, adapted by Robert Venditti, and illustrated by Alina Urusov, the focus is on a group of New York teenagers. "Schuyler Van Alen is a loner, and happy that way. But when she turns fifteen, her life dramatically changes. A mosaic of blue veins appears on her arms, and she begins to have memories of another time and place. When a classmate is found dead at a night club, the mystery deepens." (Publisher's note)

The **lost** hero: the graphic novel. by Rick Riordan; adapted by Robert Venditti; art by Nate Powell; color by Orpheus Collar; lettering by Chris Dickey. Disney-Hyperion Books 2014 192 p. Color; Illustration
Grades: 4 5 6 7 8   **741.5**
1. Camps — Fiction; 2. Gaia (Greek deity) — Fiction; 3. Graphic novels; 4. Hera (Greek deity) — Fiction; 5. Monsters — Fiction; 6. Mythology, Greek — Fiction; 7. Riordan, Rick. Lost hero — Adaptations; 8. Greek mythology
142316279X; 9781423162797, $21.99; 9781423163251

           LC 2013013559
"Jason has a problem. He doesn't remember anything before waking up on a school bus holding hands with a girl. Apparently she's his

girlfriend Piper, his best friend is a kid named Leo, and they're all students in the Wilderness School, a boarding school for 'bad kids.' What he did to end up here, Jason has no idea — except that everything seems very wrong." (Publisher's note)

"Powell does an excellent job of adapting the original story into pictorial format, hitting all of the high points and representing all of the major details in the drawings, so little is lost." SLJ

Adapted from the novel The Heroes of Olympus, Book One: The Lost Hero — Copyright page.

Viney, Brigit

Great expectations: the graphic novel. Lucent Books 2010 160p. Illustration (Classic graphic novels)

Grades: 7 8 9 10 11 12   **741.5; Fic**

1. Authors; 2. Graphic novels; 3. Novelists; 4. Social classes — Graphic novels; 5. Dickens, Charles, 1812-1870; 6. Dickens, Charles, 1812-1870 — Adaptations/Graphic novels; 7. Great Britain — History — 19th century — Graphic novels

978-1-4205-0372-2, $32.45

LC 2010-924002

In 1812, young orphaned Pip encounters an escaped convict in the graveyard near his home; that encounter changes his life. He had helped the man by stealing food and a file from his older sister's home. When the convict is recaptured, he keeps Pip's secret and claims he was the thief. As time goes by, Pip becomes his brother-inlaw's apprentice as a blacksmith, but then the eccentric Miss Havisham wants Pip to attend to her. Miss Havisham's adopted niece, Estella, calls Pip coarse and rough, which makes him determined to improve himself and become a gentleman. His wish comes true when a mysterious benefactor has Miss Havisham's solicitor, Mr. Jaggers, set Pip up in London, with expenses paid. Pip has only to keep using his nickname, to learn how to be a gentleman, and have "great expectations." Getting his wish doesn't make him happy, however, for he wants Estella, whom he adores, to love him; Miss Havisham has raised Estella to break men's hearts as her heart was once broken by a man. Pip must also learn what is most important to him improving his social standing or standing loyal to family and friends. This graphic novel adaptation includes every chapter in Dickens' original novel; this library bound edition uses a more colloquial American adaptation, which was done by arrangement with Classical Comics, the original publisher. This adaptation is meant for reluctant and struggling readers. The artist, John Stokes, is not credited anywhere in this edition. The back matter includes a biography of Dickens, a glossary, illustrated character summaries, notes on the historical context of the novel, and a brief discussion of the different ending Dickens originally wrote.

Vining, James

First in Space. Oni Press 2007 un Illustration

Grades: 3 4 5 6 7 8

629.4; 741.5; 616

1. Animal experimentation — Graphic novels; 2. Graphic novels; 3. Space flight — Graphic novels

978-1-932664-64-5, $9.95

Vining received a 2006 Xeric Grant to help him complete and publish his book.

This book tells young readers about the early years of the U.S. space program, in the late 1950s and early 1960s. After the Russians successfully sent the dog, Laika, into space in the Sputnik 2 in 1957, the U.S. successfully sent two monkeys into suborbital space and back in 1959. In 1960, NASA began training young

Courtesy of Oni Press

chimpanzees to complete certain tasks; young enlisted men under Sergeant Ed Dittmer took care of the chimpanzees, one chimp per man. In 1961, one of the chimpanzees, nicknamed Ham by his young handler, Beach, became the first chimp in space when NASA sent him up in the Mercury MR-2 rocket. Vining researched this extensively, and he provides a bibliography; but for the book, he focuses on the personal interactions between Beach and Ham and on the training that Ham and the other chimpanzees went through.

Vollmar, Rob

The **castaways**. illustrated by Pablo G. Callejo. NBM/ComicsLit 2007 64p. Illustration

Grades: 6 7 8 9 10 11 12   **Fic; 741.5; 741**

1. Graphic novels; 2. United States — History — 1919-1933 — Graphic novels

978-1-56163-492-7, $17.95

"Afraid that he's just a burden on his family, 13-year-old Tucker Freeman lets himself be driven away from home and jumps on a freight train heading west. His inexperience makes him vulnerable to all the angry, desperate people looking for any way they can survive during America's economic collapse, but fortunately he's taken under the wing of Elijah Hopkins, an elderly colored man who introduces him to the cooperative hobo subculture.... Vollmar's script, based on family reminiscences, rings true; his dialogue has the vocabulary and the rhythms of real people talking.... Callejo's art creates a solid setting in which Tucker's experience can reveal squalor or grace." Publ Wkly

An expanded and newly illustrated edition of the title first published 2002 by Absence of Ink Comic Press

Wagahara, Satoshi

The **devil** is a part-timer!; Volume 1. original story, Satoshi Wagahara; art, Akio Hiiragi; translation, Kevin Gifford; lettering, Lys Blakeslee. Yen Press 2015 240 p. Illustration

Grades: 7 8 9 10   **741.5; Fic**

1. Fantasy; 2. Manga; 3. Shonen manga; 4. Fast food restaurants — Fiction; 5. Devil — Fiction; 6. Demonology — Fiction

0316383139; 9780316383134, $13

LC 2015028390

"It's tough being evil when you have to pay the rent! This comical tale of a demon-lord-turned-fry-slinger follows the daily travails of (former) Devil King Sadao Maou and his general Shiro Ashiya as they navigate the complexities of life in modern-day Tokyo. Having suffered utter defeat at the hands of a plucky hero, they've been banished to earth and stripped of magical power. And if that wasn't enough, that pesky hero is still hell bent on finishing the job." (Publisher's note)

Volume 1 of an ongoing series

Waid, Mark

All-new all-different Avengers; Volume 1: The Magnificent Seven. by Mark Waid; illustrated by Adam Kubert and Mahmud Asrar; color by Sonia Oback. Marvel Enterprises 2016 168 p. Color; Illustration

Grades: 8 9 10 11 12 Adult   **741.5; Fic**

1. Avengers (Fictional characters)

0785199675; 9780785199670, $19.99

In this comic book, by Mark Waid, illustrated by Adam Kubert and Mahmud Asrar, "the Avengers are dead — long live the Avengers! Earth's Mightiest Heroes — Captain America, Thor, Vision and Iron Man — are living separate lives, not tied to any team but when a threat from beyond the stars targets our world, fate draws them together once more, alongside

Nova, Ms. Marvel, and Miles Morales, a.k.a. Spider-Man!" (Publisher's note)

Contains material originally published in magazine form as All-New, All-Different Avengers #1-6, Avengers #0 and Free Comic Book Day 2015 (Avengers) #1

★ **Archie**; Volume 1: The New Riverdale. story by Mark Waid; art by Fiona Staples (issues 1-3), Annie Wu (issue 4), Veronica Fish (issues 5-6); coloring by Andre Szymanowicz with Jen Vaughn; lettering by Jack Morelli. Archie Comics 2016 176 p. Color; Illustration

Grades: 7 8 9 10 11 12 Adult   **741.5; Fic**
1. Teenagers — Graphic novels; 2. Lodge, Veronica (Fictional character); 3. Andrews, Archie (Fictional character); 4. Cooper, Betty (Fictional character)
1627388672; 9781627388672, $19.99

In this first volume of the Archie comic book series by Mark Waid, illustrated by Fiona Staples, Archie Andrews and the Riverdale teens are reimagined "with a fresh, 21st-century spin in time for the franchise's 75th anniversary.... Blonde Betty is a baseball-slugging, down-to-earth car mechanic; Archie is a hapless but cool, guitar-playing teen with a streak of bad luck; and new girl Veronica Lodge is a sleek reality TV alum." (School Library Journal)

"It would seem risky to mess with the tried-and-true Archie formula, but this heartfelt collection is less a tearing-down of the old order than an exuberant exploration of its possibilities. Staples and Waid keep the characters' foundations in place—Archie's still a lovable goof who can't decide between girl-next-door Betty and vampish Veronica — while building a wonderfully new Riverdale for them to explore." Pub Wkly

Collects Archie #1-6; Volume 1 of an ongoing series

Legion of Super-Heroes Vol. 1: Teenage Revolution. DC Comics 2005 un Illustration

Grades: 8 9 10 11 12 Adult   **741.5; Fic**
1. Graphic novels; 2. Science fiction graphic novels; 3. Superhero graphic novels
1-4012-0482-1, $14.99

Poverty, famine, war, and disease have been eliminated in the early days of the 31st century. The Dawning Millenium is utopian: shining, optimistic, hopeful...and deadly dull. Dull, that is, until a team of bright, defiant, super-powered teenagers from different worlds assemble. The come together as activists and fierce dreamers, crusading to make a difference in a society that has forgotten how to change. Cosmic Boy, Lightning Lad, Saturn Girl, and the rest of the Legion of Super-Heroes fight for freedom and justice while learning from, and learning to tolerate, one another.

Walden, Tillie
★ **Spinning**. Tillie Walden. First Second 2017 400 p. Illustration

Grades: 7 8 9 10 11 12   **741.5; 92**
1. Figure skaters — Biography; 2. Graphic memoir; 3. Lesbian teenagers; 4. Walden, Tillie, 1996-
9781626727724, $22.99; 9781626729407, $17.99

                                    LC 2016961586
Eisner Award: Best Reality-Based Work (2018)

This graphic memoir, by Tillie Walden, "captures what it's like to come of age, come out, and come to terms with leaving behind everything you used to know.... For ten years, figure skating was...Walden's life.... But as she switched schools, got into art, and fell in love with her first girlfriend, she began to question how the close-minded world of figure skating fit in with the rest of her life, and whether all the work was worth it." (Publisher's note)

"Walden's cumulative growth and courage to speak up for what she actually wants are unmistakable and deeply satisfying. A stirring,

gorgeously illustrated story of finding the strength to follow one's own path." Booklist

Walker, Landry Q.
Supergirl: cosmic adventures in the 8th grade. DC Comics 2009 144p. Illustration

Grades: 3 4 5 6 7 8   **741.5; Fic**
1. Graphic novels; 2. Humorous graphic novels; 3. School life — Graphic novels; 4. Superhero graphic novels
978-1-4012-2506-3, $12.99

Kara Zor-El is just an average Kryptonian girl who arrives on Earth sort of accidentally when she has an argument with her mother. Here she discovers she has super powers, just like her cousin, Superman. He tells her she can't just go home, so now she's stuck living on Earth, going to middle school, and her powers can't prevent her from being the new kid in school. She makes one friend, but Lena happens to be related to Superman's nemesis Lex Luthor; then she manages to create a mirror-image self who is evil. On top of that, weird things keep happening at school. Kara may be Supergirl, but can she survive 8th grade?

Wallis, Pete
★ **What** does consent really mean?. written by Pete Wallis and Thalia Wallis; illustrated by Joseph Wilkins. Singing Dragon 2017 62 p. Color; Illustration

Grades: 8 9 10 11 12
741.5; 306.70835; 306.7
1. Rape; 2. Sexual harassment; 3. Teenagers — Sexual behavior
1848193300; 9780857012852; 9781848193307, $19.95

Courtesy of Singing Dragon

                                    LC 2017030844
In this book, by Pete Wallis and Thalia Wallis, illustrated by Joseph Wilkins, "following the sexual assault of a classmate, a group of teenage girls find themselves discussing the term consent, what it actually means for them in their current relationships, and how they act and make decisions with peer influence.... This rich graphic novel uncovers the need for more informed conversations with young people around consent and healthy relationships." (Publisher's note)

"Content that could be heavy with pedagogy is instead lightened by informal, occasionally profane language and friendly teasing." SLJ

Includes bibliographical references.

Wang, Jen
★ The **prince** and the dressmaker. Jen Wang. First Second 2018 288 p. Color; Illustration

Grades: 7 8 9 10 11 12   **741.5; Fic**
1. Fashion — Fiction; 2. Princes — Fiction; 3. Romance fiction
9781250159854, $24.99; 9781626723634

                                    LC 2017941173
In this graphic novel, by Jen Wang, "Prince Sebastian is looking for a bride — or rather, his parents are looking for one for him. Sebastian is too busy hiding his secret life from everyone. At night he puts on daring dresses and takes Paris by storm as the fabulous Lady Crystallia — the hottest fashion icon in the world capital of fashion! Sebastian's secret weapon (and best friend) is the brilliant dressmaker Frances — one of only two people who know the truth: sometimes this boy wears dresses." (Publisher's note)

"Frances's daring designs shine in Wang's elegantly drafted and gorgeously colored illustrations, and the irreverently anachronistic approach to the setting provides a lovely and humorous counterbalance to the seriousness of the prince's situation." Pub Wkly

Weigel, Jeff

Dragon Girl: The Secret Valley. Jeff Weigel. Andrews McMeel Pub 2014 192 p. Illustration

Grades: 2 3 4 5 6   **741.5; Fic**

1. Orphans — Fiction; 2. Dragons — Fiction

1449441831; 9781449441838, $9.99

LC 2013943302

"Eleven-year-old Alanna and her older brother Hamel are orphans and doing their best to take care of each other until one day Alanna stumbles upon a cave full of dragon eggs. When the eggs hatch with no mother dragon in sight, Alanna decides to take care of the babies herself, even creating a clever costume so that the babies think she, too, is a dragon." (Publisher's note)

"Weigel has created a compulsively likable heroine who seamlessly blends her strength and compassion.... With lovable dragons, flying ships and danger around every corner, this delightful fantasy doesn't disappoint." Kirkus

★ **Thunder** from the sea: adventure on board the HMS Defender. G. P. Putnam's Sons 2010 46p. Illustration

Grades: 3 4 5 6   **741.5; Fic**

1. Great Britain — Royal Navy — Graphic novels; 2. Adventure graphic novels; 3. Graphic novels; 4. Naval art and science — Graphic novels; 5. Europe — History — 1789-1815 — Graphic novels

978-0-399-25089-7, $17.99

LC 2009-32801

In 1805, during the Napoleonic Wars, twelve-year-old Jack Hoyton becomes a member of the crew of HMS Defender, a midsize ship in the British Royal Navy. The Defender patrols along a portion of the French coast to block French ships, but a major gun emplacement in Dumont hampers the ship's efforts. When some of the crew land to fill their barrels with fresh water, French gunmen fire upon them, killing an officer and wounding a crewman. The Captain assigns Jack to be part of the crew that will land and take the guns; when the men arrive, they find that there is no small village, but a major shipbuilding facility, and they're captured.

"Weigel's old-fashioned comics art shows lots of authentic details of eighteenth-century shipboard life, and there is some battle violence.... This picture-book-size graphic novel should find a ready audience of young adventure-loving readers." Booklist

Includes bibliographical references

Weing, Drew

The **creepy** case files of Margo Maloo. by Drew Weing. First Second 2016 121 p. Color; Illustration

Grades: 3 4 5 6   **741.5; Fic**

1. Moving — Fiction; 2. Monsters — Fiction; 3. Mystery graphic novels

1626723397; 9781626723399, $15.99

"Charles just moved to Echo City, and some of his new neighbors give him the creeps. They sneak into his room, steal his toys, and occasionally, they try to eat him. The place is teeming with monsters! Lucky for Charles, Echo City has Margo Maloo, monster mediator. No matter who's causing trouble, Margo knows exactly what to do." (Publisher's note)

"Weing's colorful drawings reward extended examination; Echo City is rife with monster life, and creepy crawlies turn up in the most unexpected places, but domestic scenes and the city streets also show the artist's keen eye for details." SLJ

Another title in this series is: The monster mall (2018)

Weinstein, Lauren

Girl stories. by Lauren R. Weinstein. Henry Holt 2006 237p. Illustration

Grades: 7 8 9 10 11 12 Adult   **741.5; Fic**

1. Friendship — Graphic novels; 2. Girls — Graphic novels; 3. Graphic novels; 4. Humorous graphic novels

978-0-8050-7863-3, $16.95; 0-8050-7863-0

LC 2005-46205

"Smart, creative Lauren sheds her geeky rep in high school in Weinstein's collection of comic strips, which have to intimacy of a teen's diary. The color-washed sketches have an edgy quality." Booklist

Weiser, Joey

Mermin; book one: out of water. Joey Weiser; [edited by] Jill Beaton. Oni Press 2013 152 p. (Mermin)

Grades: 4 5 6

741.5; Fic

1. Science fiction comic books, strips, etc.; 2. Graphic novels; 3. Mermaids and mermen — Fiction

1934964980; 9781934964989, $19.99

LC 2012953664

Other titles in this series are: The big catch (2013); Deep dive (2014); Into Atlantis (2015); Making waves (2017)

Courtesy of Oni Press

Author Joey Weiser presents a graphic novel about merpeople. "MERMIN the MERMAN from MER!" That's the question Pete and his friends ask after finding the fish-boy washed up on the beach! Mermin just escaped the undersea kingdome of Mer, and is ready to have some fun on dry land! But why would this aquatic kid be afraid to swim? Perhaps it has something to do with the fishy pursuers who have followed him from the depths below!" (Publisher's note)

Wells, H. G. (Herbert George)

Classics illustrated #12: The Island of Dr. Moreau. Papercutz 2011 un Illustration

Grades: 7 8 9 10 11 12 Adult

741.5; Fic

1. Authors; 2. Graphic novels; 3. Historians; 4. Horror graphic novels; 5. Novelists; 6. Science fiction writers; 7. Writers on politics; 8. Writers on science; 9. Wells, H. G. (Herbert George), 1866-1946 — Adaptations

978-1-59707-235-9, $9.99

Courtesy of NBM Publishing

Edward Prendick is the sole survivor of a shipwreck when a passing ship picks him up. It carries a strange cargo of animals, a doctor, who takes care of Prendick, and an odd man who looks more like an ape. Montgomery, the doctor, is taking the animals to a small island he won't name, and Prendick ends up with them when the drunken ship's captain casts him off. On that island, Prendick discovers half-human, half-beast creatures, all created by the arrogant Dr. Moreau. This book adapts Wells' classic story; it was originally published in 1990 as part of the Classics Illustrated line published by First Comics. This edition includes an interview with Steven Grant, who wrote the adaptation.

The **Time** Machine. Stone Arch Books 2007 72p. Illustration

Grades: 3 4 5 6 7 8 9   **741.5; Fic**

1. Adventure graphic novels; 2. Graphic novels; 3. Science fiction graphic novels
978-1-59889-833-0, $23.93

LC 2007-6201

A scientist invents a machine that he claims will travel through time, but his friends laugh at the idea. So the Time Traveler climbs aboard his machine and ends up thousands of years in the future. He meets a race of gentle humans called the Eloi, but he is soon swept up in a fight for his life against evil underground creatures known as Morlocks. Even worse, his Time Machine, his only chance to escape, is trapped deep inside the Morlock caverns. This book is written with an easy vocabulary for struggling and reluctant readers, and it includes some scientific speculations about the future.

Part of the Graphic Revolve series

West, David

Hernan Cortes: The Life of a Spanish Conquistador. by David West & Jackie Gaff; illustrated by Jim Eldridge. Rosen Publishing Group 2005 48p. Illustration
Grades: 3 4 5 6 7 8
92; 741.5; 972

1. Biographical graphic novels; 2. Graphic novels; 3. Cortes, Hernan, 1485-1547; 4. Mexico — History — Conquest, 1519-1540 — Graphic novels
1-4042-0244-7, $29.25

LC 2004005938

Adventurous explorer or ruthless imperialist? In 1519, Spanish conquistador Hernan Cortes led a daring expedition to the heart of the Aztec Empire, in what is now central and southern Mexico. Within two

Courtesy of Rosen Publishing

years, this highly advanced civilization had fallen to the might of Cortes's Spanish conquerors, resulting in the deaths of tens of thousands of Aztecs. This graphic novel explores two cultures in conflict — and the personality of a man driven by both insatiable greed and service to his country. The book includes additional information, a glossary, and a list of books for further reading.

Part of the Graphic Nonfiction series.

Pteranodon: The Giant of the Sky. Rosen Publishing Group 2007 32p. Illustration
Grades: 2 3 4 5 6 7
567.9; 741.5

1. Dinosaurs — Graphic novels; 2. Graphic novels; 3. Pteranodon — Graphic novels
978-1-4042-3895-4, $25.25

LC 2007-1792

This volume uses colorful comic book style illustrations to explore the habitat, diet, and behavior of the pteranodon. At the front of the book, facts about the pteranodon are presented, while at the back of the book readers will find a picture gallery of other creatures mentioned in the book.

Courtesy of Rosen Publishing

Part of the Graphic Dinosaurs series.

Velociraptor: The Speedy Thief. Rosen Publishing Group 2007 32p. Illustration
Grades: 2 3 4 5 6 7

567.9; 741.5

1. Dinosaurs — Graphic novels; 2. Graphic novels; 3. Velociraptor — Graphic novels
978-1-4042-3898-5, $25.25

LC 2007-873

This volume uses colorful comic book style illustrations to explore the habitat, diet, and behavior of the velociraptor. At the front of the book, facts about the velociraptor are presented, while at the back of the book readers will find a picture gallery of other creatures mentioned in the book.

Courtesy of Rosen Publishing

Part of the Graphic Dinosaurs series.

Westerfeld, Scott

Uglies: Shay's story. created by Scott Westerfeld; written by Scott Westerfeld and Devin Grayson; illustrations by Steven Cummings. Del Rey 2012 160 p. Illustration
Grades: 7 8 9 10

741.5

1. Beauty, Personal — Fiction; 2. Friendship — Fiction; 3. Science fiction; 4. Dystopian graphic novels; 5. Conformity — Graphic novels; 6. Plastic surgery — Graphic novels
9780606264754, $22.10; 0345527224; 9780345527226, $10.99

LC 2012374898

This young adult graphic novel retells the story of author Scott Westerfeld's dystopia "Uglies" from "the point of view of recurring frenemy Shay." It is "set in a...future time when discord is suppressed through ruthlessly enforced conformity and obligatory plastic surgery at age 16.... Shay yearns for freedom. An encounter with the flawed and alluring David, a covert envoy from the Smoke, a secret community of nonconformists, may offer Shay the escape she craves." (Publishers Weekly)

Followed by:Uglies: Cutters (2012)

Wheeler, Andrew

Another castle: Grimoire. Andrew Wheeler, Paulina Ganucheau, edited by Ari Yarwood. Oni Press 2017 152 p. Color; Illustration
Grades: 7 8 9 10 11 12 Adult
741.5; Fic

1. Friendship — Fiction; 2. Good and evil — Fiction; 3. Heroes and heroines — Fiction; 4. Princesses — Fiction
1620103117; 9781620103111, $15.99

LC 2016950325

This book, by Andrew Wheeler and Paulina Ganucheau, edited by Ari Yarwood, "begins when Princess Misty of Beldora,...[was] captured by Lord Badlug, the ruler of the neighboring kingdom of

Courtesy of Oni Press

Grimoire. He intends to marry her and conquer Beldora.... The people of Grimoire already suffer under his rule and desperately need a hero.... Together with the citizens of Grimoire,...Misty must fight to protect her kingdom and free both realms from Badlug's tyrannical rule." (Publisher's note)

"Ganucheau contributes some thrilling and bloody action sequences, and her candy-colored palette, suffused with bright pinks and purples, is an inspired touch, just one more way this story subverts expectations." Pub Wkly

White, Steve

The **Battle** of Midway: the destruction of the Japanese fleet. The Rosen Publishing Group 2007 48p. Illustration

Grades: 3 4 5 6 7 8 9   **741.5; 940.54**

1. Graphic novels; 2. Midway, Battle of, 1942 — Graphic novels; 3. War — Graphic novels; 4. World War, 1939-1945 — Graphic novels

978-1-4042-0783-7, $29.25

One of the most important naval battles in history, Midway marked a crucial turning point in the war in the Pacific. With a fleet that had dominated this theater since the attack on Pearl Harbor, the Japanese anticipated certain victory against the US forces, but the attack was not a surprise. The US Navy sank four irreplaceable aircraft carriers, and cleared the way for the island-hopping US counterattack. This book also includes eight pages of authoritative information, placing the battle in its historical context, describing the key players, and its build-up and aftermath.

Part of the Graphic Battles of World War II series. This book is also available in a paperback edition from Osprey Publishing, under the title The Empire Falls: Battle of Midway.

Pearl Harbor: A Day of Infamy. The Rosen Publishing Group 2007 48p. Illustration

Grades: 3 4 5 6 7 8 9   **741.5; 940.54**

1. Graphic novels; 2. Pearl Harbor (Oahu, Hawaii), Attack on, 1941 — Graphic novels; 3. War — Graphic novels; 4. World War, 1939-1945 — Graphic novels

978-1-4042-0785-1, $29.25

On December 7, 1941, the Japanese Navy launched a surprise attack on American military bases in Pearl Harbor, Hawaii. Masterfully planned and executed, the attack devastated the US Pacific Fleet; in less than two hours, Japanese aircraft had sunk or damaged all eight US battleships anchored in the harbor and had destroyed 151 planes. Thrust into battle, the United States could have only one response: war. This book portrays the attack that drove the United States into World War II in full-color comic book narrative. Featuring the personal stories of front-line heroes like Ken Taylor, George Welch, and mess attendant Dorie Miller, it also provides background material — causes and consequences, key players, and a glossary of terms — as well as a list of additional resources.

Part of the Graphic Battles of World War II series. This book is also available in a paperback edition from Osprey Publishing, under the title Day of Infamy: Attack on Pearl Harbor.

Whyte, Campbell

Home time; book one: under the river. Campbell Whyte. Top Shelf Productions 2017 228 p. Illustration

Grades: 7 8 9 10 11 12

741.5; Fic

1. Summer; 2. Mythical animals — Fiction; 3. Fantasy fiction

1603094121; 9781603094122, $24.99

In this book in the Home Time series, by Campbell Whyte, "the last school bell has rung and it's finally HOME TIME! Even though they're twins, Lilly and David don't agree on much... except that the last summer

Courtesy of IDW Publishing

before high school is the perfect time for relaxing with friends. But their plans for sleepovers, fantasy games, and romance are thrown out the window when the whole gang falls into a river and wakes up in a village of fantastic creatures." (Publisher's note)

"Australian comics creator Whyte shifts artistic style with each chapter, moving from pencil sketches to bright, borderline psychedelic

cartoons and even a chapter with a pixelated motif à la vintage arcade games. It's both alienating and engaging, keeping readers as off-balance as the children, who are trapped in an alien landscape they don't quite understand." Pub Wkly

Wicks, Maris

★ **Human** body theater: a nonfiction revue. Maris Wicks. First Second 2015 240 p. Color; Illustration

Grades: 4 5 6 7 8   **612; 741.5**

1. Human biology; 2. Human anatomy

1626722773; 9781626722774, $19.99; 9781596439290

This book by, Maris Wicks explores human anatomy on a performing stage. In it, "your master of ceremonies is going to lead you through a theatrical revue of each and every biological system of the human body! Starting out as a skeleton, the MC puts on a new layer of her costume (her body) with each 'act.'" (Publisher's note)

"Wicks' playful cartoon artwork in saturated colors makes the potentially daunting and embarrassing subject of anatomy approachable and fun, but never at the expense of accuracy or clarity. This informative, frank exploration of the body perfectly balances science and silliness." Booklist

Includes bibliographical references

Wilgus, Alison

★ **Flying** machines: how the Wright brothers soared. Alison Wilgus; Molly Brooks. First Second 2017 113 p. Illustration; Color (Science comics)

Grades: 5 6 7 8   **629.13; 741.5; 629.130092/273**

1. Airplanes — United States — History; 2. Graphic novels; 3. Wright, Orville, 1871-1948; 4. Wright, Wilbur, 1867-1912; 5. Aeronautics

9781626721395; 9781626721401, $19.99

LC 2016945553

In this book, by Alsion Wilgus, illustrated by Molly Brooks, "follow the famous aviators from their bicycle shop in Dayton, Ohio, to the fields of North Carolina where they were to make their famous flights. In an era of dirigibles and hot air balloons, the Wright Brothers were among the first innovators of heavier than air flight. But in the hotly competitive international race toward flight, Orville and Wilbur were up against a lot more than bad weather." (Publisher's note)

"An accessible and engaging introduction to the Wright brothers and how they ushered in the age of flight." Kirkus

Includes bibliographical references.; Book design by John Green; edited by Casey Gonzalez.

Williams, Rob

Star Wars: Rebellion Volume 1: My Brother, My Enemy. script, Rob Williams; Crossroads script, Thomas Andrews; art, Brandon Badeaux and Michel Lacombe; colors, Wil Glass; lettering, Michael Heisler; front cover art, Brandon Badeaux and Brad Anderson; back cover art, Brandon Badeaux and Wil Glass. Dark Horse Comics 2007 un Illustration

Grades: 8 9 10 11 12 Adult   **741.5; Fic**

1. Adventure graphic novels; 2. Graphic novels; 3. Science fiction graphic novels

9781593077112, $14.95; 1593077114

Having rescued Rebel strategist Jorin Sol from the Empire, Luke Skywalker now leads X-Wing attack runs on Imperial convoys to rustle up much needed supplies for the Rebel fleet. Little does he know that within Sol lies a secret that will put the entire Alliance in danger. What's worse, when Luke receives a coded message from Lt. Sunber, who wants to defect to the Rebel Alliance, he must decide whether to trust his old friend or obey the orders of Princess Leia who believes Tank may be part of an Imperial plot to capture the Rebellion's greatest hero.

Volume 1 of 3

Willingham, Bill
Robin: To Kill a Bird. DC Comics 2006 un Illustration
Grades: 8 9 10 11 12 Adult   **741.5; Fic**
1. Graphic novels; 2. Robin (Fictional character); 3. Superhero graphic novels; 4. Robin (Fictional character)
978-1-4012-0909-4, $14.99

It's a brand-new start for Batman's sidekick, Robin: a new town (Bludhaven), a new school, new adventures and new problems.Before our hero can fully recover from the recent deaths of his father and girlfriend Spoiler, he must come face to face with his enemies: the Penguin, the Dark Rider, the Veteran, and a mysterious archer who seems to want the Boy Wonder dead. There's lots of superhero fighting action.

Winick, Judd
★ **Pedro** & me: friendship, loss, & what I learned. Henry Holt and Co. 2009 187p. Illustration
Grades: 7 8 9 10 11 12   **362.1**
1. AIDS (Disease) — Graphic novels; 2. AIDS activists; 3. AIDS patients; 4. Biographical graphic novels; 5. Friendship — Graphic novels; 6. Graphic novels; 7. Television personalities; 8. Real world (Television program) — Graphic novels; 9. Zamora, Pedro, 1972-1994
978-0-8050-8964-6, $16.99
2001 Robert F. Sibert Honor Book for informational books for youth

In this "volume — part graphic novel, part memoir — professional cartoonist Winick pays tribute to his Real World housemate and friend Pedro Zamora, an AIDS activist who died of the disease in 1994." Publ Wkly

First published 2000

Superman/Shazam/First Thunder. DC Comics 2006 128p. Illustration
Grades: 8 9 10 11 12 Adult   **741.5; Fic**
1. Graphic novels; 2. Shazam (Fictional character); 3. Superhero graphic novels; 4. Superman (Fictional character)
978-1-4012-0923-0, $12.99

With one word, young orphan Billy Batson transforms into a man imbued with the powers of the gods, but even one gifted with the Wisdom of Solomon can learn from a Superman. While Superman must stop members of a cult from stealing ancient artifacts from the Metropolis Natural History Museum, Billy must battle giant robots rampaging through Fawcett City. These separate events lead the heroes to cross paths, and a mighty friendship is formed as Earth's most powerful defenders team up to stop such menaces as Lex Luthor, Dr. Sivana, Eclipso, and the monstrous Lord Sabbac. There's some violence, and the climax is heartbreaking.

Wolfram, Amy
Teen Titans year one. written by Amy Wolfram; penciled by Karl Kerschl; inked by Serge Lapointe; colored by Steph Peru, John Rauch; lettered by Nick J. Napolitano; series & collection cover art by Karl Kerschl & Serge Lapointe. DC Comics 2008 144p. Illustration
Grades: 7 8 9 10 11 12   **741.5; Fic**
1. Aquaman (Fictitious character); 2. Graphic novels; 3. Superhero graphic novels; 4. Teen Titans (Fictional characters); 5. Wonder Woman (Fictional character); 6. Green Arrow (Fictional character); 7. Flash (Fictional character); 8. Robin (Fictional character); 9. Batman (Fictional character); 10. Justice League (Fictional characters)
978-1-4012-1927-7, $14.99

Suddenly, the members of the Justice League of America are acting crazy, becoming bullies, breaking the law — what has happened to Batman, Aquaman, the Flash, Green Arrow, and Wonder Woman? Their young partners, Robin, Aqualad, Kid Flash, Speedy, and Wonder Girl, decide to team up together and put things right. They're teens, they're superheroes, they're the Teen Titans. And being teens, they still do teenage things, like overindulge in pizza and soda, go out on dates and mess things up with each other, and deal with celebrity. That last is not typical of teens, but they have to learn to deal with it. This book, written by Wolfram, who wrote for the Teen Titans animated series on television, reimagines the early days of the team. The book includes some violence.

Wood, Brian
The **New** York Four. written by Brian Wood; illustrated by Kelly Ryan; lettering by Jared K. Fletcher. DC Comics/Minx 2008 176p. Illustration
Grades: 8 9 10 11 12   **741.5; Fic**
1. Friendship — Graphic novels; 2. Graphic novels
978-1-4012-1154-7, $9.99

Riley is a college freshman who has grown up so sheltered, protected, and disciplined by her parents that she finds it difficult to make friends. She starts seeing her older sister Angie on the sly; Angie was kicked out of the house years ago for an offense no one will tell Riley. Other than that, Riley almost lives her life through her smart phone, constantly texting to people she's never met in person. Then, just as she opens up to make friends with three fellow freshmen and helps them find work with the same research group for which she works, she "meets" someone she knows only by his user name, "sneakerfreak." Balancing classes, friends, her over-protective parents, her sister, and now this secret online romance is becoming more difficult than Riley ever thought it could be. Each of her friends also has a secret that could have consequences.

Yakin, Boaz
★ **Marathon**. by Boaz Yakin; [illustrations by Joe Infurnari]. First Second 2012 186 p.
Grades: 8 9 10 11 12   **741.5/973**
1. Graphic novels; 2. Greece — History — Persian Wars, 500-449 B.C. — Fiction; 3. Adventure graphic novels; 4. Marathon, Battle of, 490 B.C. — Graphic novels
9781596436800, $16.99; 1596436808

LC 2011030472
This book is a graphical "account of the battle of Marathon" in which "Hippias, former king of Athens, is on his way back with a huge army of Persians to reclaim the throne and crush Athenian democracy.... Eucles, Athens' best runner, is charged to race the 153 miles to Sparta in hopes of finding an ally,... [returning] with the dismaying news that the Spartans will not be coming in time. He joins the savage fight and then runs 26 more miles over rugged mountains to Athens...warning of an impending surprise attack by sea." (Kirkus Reviews)

Yamamoto, Lun Lun
Swans in space, volume 1. UDON Entertainment 2009 150p. Illustration
Grades: 2 3 4 5 6 7   **741.5; Fic**
1. Graphic novels; 2. Humorous graphic novels; 3. Manga; 4. Science fiction graphic novels; 5. Kodomo
978-1-897376-93-5, $8.99

Sixth grader Corona is effectively her class's president, representing them on the Cosmos Institute student council. At home, she barely tolerates the obsessive fandom displayed by her father and younger brother for the television show, Space Patrol. Imagine her chagrin when she reaches out to an odd classmate, only to find herself recruited into...the Space Patrol! It's a real organization that works to keep the Earth and other worlds safe, and show's episodes are edited versions of actual missions. Of course, Corona must keep her work in the Space Patrol a secret from anyone who isn't a member; and since she needs to study the old episodes to learn the history, this makes her father and brother think she has become one with them, while her classmates wonder what's wrong with her. Corona must also keep up with not only her school work, which is bad enough, because she's one of the top students, but as class president she has to take responsibility for all kinds of extra activities and work; all this makes her one tired girl. This manga for younger readers is published in full color.

Yang, Gene Luen

★ **American** born Chinese. by Gene Luen Yang; color by Lark Pien. First Second 2006 233p. Illustration

Grades: 7 8 9 10 11 12   **741.5; Fic**

1. Chinese Americans — Graphic novels; 2. Graphic novels
1-59643-152-0, $16.95; 978-1-59643-152-2

LC 2005-58105

Printz Award (2007); National Book Award Finalist: Young People's Literature (2006); Eisner Award: Best Graphic Album — New (2007)

"Jin Wang is the only Asian American boy in his new school; Danny is a young man deeply embarrassed by his visiting Chinese cousin, portrayed deliberately by the author as an ethnic cliché; and the Monkey King, a figure from Chinese lore, is desperate to be treated like a god. This...story relates how three characters overcome hurdles to find satisfaction within themselves." (Library Journal)

"True to its origin as a Web comic, this story's clear, concise lines and expert coloring are deceptively simple yet expressive. Even when Yang slips in an occasional Chinese ideogram or myth, the sentiments he's depicting need no translation. Yang accomplishes the remarkable feat of practicing what he preaches with this book: accept who you are and you'll already have reached out to others." Publ Wkly

★ **Boxers**. Gene Luen Yang; color by Lark Pien. First Second 2013 328 p.

Grades: 7 8 9 10 11 12 Adult   **741.5**

1. China — History — Boxer Rebellion, 1899-1901 — Graphic novels; 2. Historical fiction
1596433590; 9781596433595, $18.99

LC 2013947229

National Book Award for Young People's Literature: Finalist (2013); Boston Globe-Horn Book Honor: Fiction (2014); Ignatz Nominee: Outstanding Graphic Novel (2014)

"Life in Little Bao's peaceful rural village is disrupted when...a priest and his phalanx of soldiers...arrive." They start "smashing the village god, appropriating property, and administering vicious beatings for no reason. Little Bao and his older brothers train in kung fu and swordplay."...Little Bao "becomes the leader of a peasant army, eventually marching to Beijing." (School Library Journal)

"China's Boxer Rebellion is the unlikely backdrop for this graphic treatment of young villagers on the opposite sides of history. Bao wants to drive out the white devils that poison his country with opium and Christianity. Four-Girl is an unwanted daughter who finds purpose in the missionary life. Their stories collide in a moment of grace that could only be penned by the Printz Award-winning author of 'American Born Chinese.'" LJ

Paths & Portals. by Gene Luen Yang; illustrated by Mike Holmes. First Second 2016 96 p. Color; Illustration (Secret Coders)

Grades: 4 5 6 7   **741.5; Fic**

1. Computer programming — Fiction; 2. School life — Fiction; 3. Schools — Fiction
9781626720763; 1626720762; 1626723400; 9781626723405, $18.99

"There's something lurking beneath the surface of Stately Academy.... In a secret underground classroom Hopper, Eni, and Josh discover that the campus was once home to the Bee School, an institute where teachers, students, and robots worked together to unravel the mysteries of coding. Hopper and her friends are eager to follow in this tradition and become top-rate coders." (Publisher's note)

"Each time the kids write a new program, Holmes breaks down the steps visually, demonstrating each direction with a handy illustration, all in his blocky, expressive, green-hued style." Booklist

★ **Prime** baby. [by] Gene Luen Yang, colors by Derek Kirk Kim. First Second Books 2010 56p. Illustration

Grades: 6 7 8 9 10 11 12   **741.5; Fic**

1. Extraterrestrial beings — Graphic novels; 2. Graphic novels; 3. Humorous graphic novels; 4. Science fiction graphic novels; 5. Siblings — Graphic novels
978-1-59643-612-1, $6.99

Thaddeus K. Fong always preferred to be the center of his family's attention, so the birth of his little sister Maddie has really bothered him. When she's eighteen months old, he notices something about the sounds she makes; her "gaga's" come out in prime numbers. Then his math teacher says that if aliens were ever to try to make contact with humans, it would be through prime numbers. Oh no, Maddie is an intergalactic conduit for invading aliens! Except no one believes Thaddeus. Until Maddie starts burping up strange things that turn out to be little ships for sluglike aliens. They're peaceful missionary types, but that doesn't stop Thaddeus from making them seem hostile. When their parents finally believe Thaddeus, Maddie gets locked up in a research facility. Thaddeus should be ecstatic, his dumb little sister has been put away. So why is he feeling sad? This story was originally serialized in the New York Times magazine and has been printed to preserve the original comic strip format.

"Sf readers who value humor and humanity (not just slam-bang action), Christians, newcomers to graphic novels, and fans of Yang's simultaneously childlike and sophisticated ability to create and maintain tension should all be satisfied by his new book." Booklist

★ **Saints**. by Gene Luen Yang; color by Lark Pien. First Second 2013 170 p.

Grades: 7 8 9 10 11 12 Adult   **741.5**

1. Historical fiction; 2. China — History — Boxer Rebellion, 1899-1901 — Graphic novels
1596436891; 9781596436893, $15.99

LC 2013947228

National Book Award for Young People's Literature: Finalist (2013); Boston Globe-Horn Book Honor: Fiction (2014); Ignatz Nominee: Outstanding Graphic Novel (2014)

This graphic novel, by Gene Luen Yang and Lark Pien, "follows a lonely girl .... Unwanted by her family, Four-Girl isn't even given a proper name until she converts to Catholicism and is baptized by the very same priest who bullies Little Bao's village. Four-Girl, now known as Vibiana, leaves home and finds fulfillment in service to the Church, while Little Bao roams the countryside committing acts of increasing violence as his army grows." (School Library Journal)

"Yang presents a 'diptych' of graphic novels set during China's Boxer Rebellion. Boxers follows Little Bao, who learns to harness the power of ancient gods to fight the spread of Christianity; Saints centers on Four-Girl, who sits squarely on the other side of the rebellion. Yang's characteristic infusions of magical realism, bursts of humor, and distinctively drawn characters make for a compelling read." (Horn Book)

Secret coders. Gene Yuen Lang & Mike Holmes. First Second 2015 96 p. Color; Illustration (Secret coders)

Grades: 4 5 6 7   **741.5**

1. Computer programming — Graphic novels; 2. School stories — Graphic novels
9781626722767, $17.99; 9781626720756; 1626722765

In this graphic novel, by Gene Yuen Lang and Mike Holmes, "Hopper, an enthusiastic 12-year-old girl..., has just started school at the creepy Stately Academy. After getting in a fight...with Eni..., Hopper and Eni become friends while unraveling the secrets of the school. Robotic birds, family troubles, and sinister, child-hating school administrators lead to a story both emotionally rich and rife with learning opportunities." (School Library Journal)

"Holmes' blocky cartoon illustrations, in black, white, and green, clearly depict basic programming concepts with tidy visual cues, such as grids of floor tiles. Yang and Holmes do such a great job explaining the concepts that even programming newbies will be likely to catch on." Booklist

Other titles in this series are: Paths and portals (2016); Secrets and sequences (2017); Robots and repeats (2017); Potions and parameters (2018); Monsters and modules (2018)

Secret coders; 5: potions & parameters. Gene Luen Yang & Mike Holmes. First Second 2018 112 p. Color; Illustration
Grades: 4 5 6 7   **741.5; Fic**
   1. Schools — Fiction; 2. Computer programming — Fiction; 3. Gifted children — Fiction
9781626726079, $10.99; 9781626726086

LC 2017941170
In this book in the Secret Coders series, by Gene Luen Yang, illustrated by Mike Holmes, "Dr. One-Zero won't stop until the whole town...embraces the 'true happiness' found in his poisonous potion, Green Pop. And now that he has the Turtle of Light, he's virtually unstoppable. There's one weapon that can defeat him: another Turtle of Light. Unfortunately, they can only be found in another dimension!" (Publisher's note)

"While the coding instruction's as top-notch as ever, in this installment it's interpersonal dynamics and characters that, satisfyingly, take center stage." Kirkus

The **Shadow** Hero. story by Gene Luen Yang; art by Sonny Liew; lettering by Janice Chiang. First Second 2014 176 p. Color; Illustration
Grades: 6 7 8 9 10   **741.5**
   1. Superheroes — Fiction; 2. Chinese Americans — Fiction; 3. Comic books, strips, etc.
1596436972; 9781596436978, $17.99

This book, by Gene Luen Yang, is about "Green Turtle, a 1940s comic book hero.... The Green Turtle is cast as an unlikely 19-year-old young man, Hank, the son of Chinese immigrants who own a grocery store in 1940s America. When his mother is rescued by a superhero, the loving but overbearing woman decides that it's Hank's fate to become a hero himself, and she does everything in her power to push her son in that direction." (School Library Journal)

"Yang and Liew have crafted an origin story for the Green Turtle, a little-known...World War II-era comic superhero created by cartoonist Chu Hing in 1944. Much about the series remains a mystery, as Yang shares in an author's note, but according to rumors Hing wanted his star to be Chinese, and, not surprisingly for the era, his publishers balked at the idea. Now seventy years later, Yang and Liew vindicate the cartoonist by imagining the Green Turtle as 'perhaps...the first Asian American superhero.'" Horn Book

Yeh, Phil
   Dinosaurs Across America. NBM 2007 32p. Illustration
Grades: 2 3 4 5 6   **973; 741.5**
   1. Graphic novels; 2. United States — Geography — Graphic novels
978-1-56163-509-2, $12.95
Originally done as a comic book and sold by Cartoonists Across America, a literacy group working for decades to promote the use of comic books to teach literacy to children, this is now a graphic novel. Featuring

Yeh's dinosaurs and Patrick Rabbit, the book devotes a half-page to each state in the U.S., packing in basic facts and a simple map along with fun little tidbits (for example, the largest privately owned cattle ranch in the U.S. happens to be in Hawaii, on the island of Hawaii).

YKids
   Einstein. Youngjin Singapore 2007 146p. Illustration
Grades: 3 4 5 6 7 8 9   **741.5; 92**
   1. Biographical graphic novels; 2. Graphic novels; 3. Einstein, Albert, 1879-1955
978-981-05-4944-2, $14.95
A genius of enormous accomplishment, Albert Einstein overcame numerous hardships-separation from his family, religious discrimination, and the political turmoil of his day-to become one of the greatest minds of the 20th century. As a young boy, Einstein's unending curiosity and constant questioning earned him the reputation of being unfocused and inattentive. This book uses a framing story of a young boy and a robot from the future going back in time to examine the lives of great people and find the one value that will help their situation; from Einstein, they take his insatiable curiosity.
Part of the Great Figures in History series.

   Gandhi. Youngjin Singapore 2007 148p. Illustration
Grades: 3 4 5 6 7 8 9   **741.5; 92**
   1. Biographical graphic novels; 2. Graphic novels; 3. Gandhi, Mohandas Karamcand, 1869-1948; 4. Gandhi, Mohandas Karamcand, 1869-1948 — graphic novels
978-981-05-4945-9, $14.95
A champion of the poor and lower classes, Mahatma Gandhi helped transform India into the democracy it is today. Young readers of this manga-style biography will learn about the key historical events during this time and how the peaceful efforts of one humble man affected enormous change. This book presents a time line of Gandhi's life-from his roots in a middle-class family in India, to his law-school education in England, his experiences with discrimination, and his key role as a leader in the Indian independence movement. Each volume in the Great Figures in History series focuses on a key value personified by the biographical subject; in Gandhi's case, it's courage.
Part of the Great Figures in History series.

   Little Women: Manga Literary Classics. Youngjin Singapore 2007 145p. Illustration
Grades: 3 4 5 6 7   **741.5; Fic**
   1. Graphic novels; 2. Alcott, Louisa May, 1832-1888 — Adaptations
978-981-05-4943-5, $14.95
The story of the March girls-beautiful Meg, tomboy Jo, kind and gentle Beth, and spunky Amy-is retold manga-style and in full color. With their country embroiled in war and their father far from home, the four sisters find themselves thrust into new and trying situations, and with little money and a hard winter ahead, they must learn to adapt. In the year that follows, the girls learn about compassion, sacrifice, love, and more about themselves and each other than they ever imagined.

   Treasure Island: Manga Literary Classics. Youngjin Singapore 2007 148p. Illustration
Grades: 3 4 5 6 7   **741.5; Fic**
   1. Graphic novels; 2. Stevenson, Robert Louis, 1850-1894 — Adaptations
978-981-05-4942-8, $14.95
Young cabin boy Jim Hawkins throws in his lot with pirates Black Dog, Blind Pew, and the unforgettable Long John Silver in this manga-style retelling of Robert Louis Stevenson's classic adventure story. Jim, overly romantic about life on the high seas, is unprepared for the frightening events ahead, including mutiny and an armed battle that poses a

grim dilemma: should his loyalty lie with Captain Smollett or Long John Silver?

Yoshida, Tatsuo

Speed Racer: Mach go go go vol. 1 & 2, 2v. by Tatsuo Yoshida; [translation: Joyce Aurino]. Digital Manga Publishing 2008 Illustration
Grades: 7 8 9 10 11 12 Adult   **741.5; Fic**
1. Adventure graphic novels; 2. Automobile racing — Graphic novels; 3. Graphic novels; 4. Manga; 5. Shonen manga
978-1-56970-731-9, set $39.95

This two-volume set reprints the original Speed Racer manga in its entirety, released for the 40th anniversary of Speed Racer. All the characters are here: Speed, Pops, Sparky, Mom, Trixie, Spritle, Chim Chim, and the mysterious Racer X. Readers will learn how Pops had to set out on his own, how Speed became a professional racecar driver in order to help finance Pops design the special, 12 cylinder Mach 5 engine. In addition to racing, Speed has to deal with people who try to steal Pops' engine plans, rival racers who'll try any cheating tactic to win, and try to figure out who Racer X is. While the animated television series was fine for children to watch, this manga includes violent action that makes it more suitable for teen readers. A note about the title: in Japanese, "go" means "5."

Yoshizumi, Wataru

Ultra Maniac Vol. 1. Viz Media/Shojo Beat 2005 184p. Illustration
Grades: 5 6 7 8 9 10   **741.5; Fic**
1. Graphic novels; 2. Humorous graphic novels; 3. Manga; 4. Romance graphic novels; 5. Shojo manga
1-59116-917-8, $8.99

Shy Ayu Tateishi has just made a new friend at school. But this new friend, much to her surprise, is no ordinary classmate. Nina Sakura may look like a normal middle school girl, but she's got a big secret. She's a witch. Or, rather, she's studying to be a witch. And, apparently, she's not doing her homework. Her spells are devastating in their ineffectiveness and often result in the most embarrassing situations for poor Ayu. But things wouldn't be so bad if Nina's sorcery didn't make Ayu look silly in front of the one boy she secretly adores. All she wants is a simple love potion. What she gets, however, is a new best friend who almost flunked out of witch school. This is a five-volume manga series.

Youngquist, Jeff

Spider-Man: Saga of the Sandman. Marvel Entertainment 2007 176p. Illustration
Grades: 7 8 9 10 11 12 Adult   **741.5; Fic**
1. Graphic novels; 2. Spider-Man (Fictional character); 3. Superhero graphic novels; 4. Fantastic Four (Fictional characters); 5. Hulk (Fictional character)
978-0-7851-2497-9, $19.99

It was no day at the beach when criminal Flint Marko was mutated into one of Marveldom's most versatile villains. This book recounts his origins and some of the best battles between Sandman, Spider-Man, the Fantastic Four and the Hulk.

Yun, Mi-Kyung

Bride of the water god, vol. 1. Dark Horse Comics 2007 186p. Illustration
Grades: 8 9 10 11 12 Adult   **741.5**
1. Fantasy graphic novels; 2. Graphic novels; 3. Romance graphic novels
978-1-59307-849-2, $9.95

Soah's impoverished, drought-stricken village sacrifices her to the Water God Habaek in hopes of getting rain. Instead of dying, Soah finds herself in the land of the gods, and she meets Habaek, who is a young boy.

What she doesn't know (but the reader does) is that he takes the form of an adult man at night. She's supposed to be Habaek's bride, but so far she's just an outsider who doesn't belong anywhere. This is sunjeong manwha the Korean equivalent of shojo manga.

Yune, Tommy

Speed Racer & Racer X: the origins collection. IDW Publishing 2008 un Illustration
Grades: 8 9 10 11 12 Adult   **741.5; Fic**
1. Adventure graphic novels; 2. Automobile racing — Graphic novels; 3. Graphic novels; 4. Racer, Speed (Fictional character)
978-1-60010-211-0, $19.99

In 1999, Wildstorm Productions relaunched Speed Racer with a three-part origins story; it was successful enough to launch another three-part story telling the origins of Speed's brother, Racer X (come on, it's not a spoiler, everyone but the Racer family knows this). IDW Publishing has collected the stories into this volume. Here is the story of how Speed becomes the driver of the Mach 5, designed by Pops Racer, and here is the story of why Rex Racer left the family, how he "died," and Racer X was born from the wreckage. There is a lot of racing action, some violence, and some mild fan service.

Zahler, Thomas F.

★ **Love** and capes, vol. 1: do you want to know a secret?. story and art by Thomas F. Zahler. IDW Publishing 2008 160p. Illustration
Grades: 8 9 10 11 12 Adult
741.5; Fic
1. Graphic novels; 2. Humorous graphic novels; 3. Romance graphic novels; 4. Superhero graphic novels
978-1-60010-275-2, $19.99

Independent bookseller Abby falls in love with her accountant, Mark; then he confesses to her that he's the superpowered crime-fighter, the Crusader. How does one have a romantic relationship with a superhero? Even without meaning to do it,

Courtesy of IDW Publishing

Abby gives away Mark's secret to her sister Charlotte. Oops. So begins a "heroically super situation comedy" in which Abby feels she's competing against the beautiful Amazonia (Mark's superpowered ex-girlfriend), not to mention Mark's over-protective mother, and Mark has to deal with Abby's obnoxious brother Quincy, who thinks Mark is a wimp.

Volume 1 of 4

★ **Love** and capes, vol. 2: going to the chapel. IDW Publishing 2010 192p. Illustration
Grades: 8 9 10 11 12 Adult   **741.5; Fic**
1. Graphic novels; 2. Humorous graphic novels; 3. Romance graphic novels; 4. Superhero graphic novels
978-1-60010-680-4, $19.99

Independent bookstore owner Abby and accountant Mark Spencer, who is also the superhero called the Crusader, have fallen deeply and completely in love. Which is wonderful, except Mark can't quite seem to figure out how to propose to Abby and almost blows it. When he gets over that hurdle, more problems crop up. For one thing, Abby wants the PERFECT wedding dress. Then, a super villain impersonates Mark and almost destroys their relationship. Abby has to find a new bookstore employee when her sister Charlotte gets the chance to go back to college in Paris. France. Abby decides she needs to understand what Mark goes through as a superhero, and she gets superpowers, and a new identity, only to learn that it's far more difficult, and tragic, than she ever imagined. And then, on the eve of the wedding, another super villain strikes, this time changing history, and only Abby has the power to put things right again, which she'll have to do if she wants to marry Mark. This story has superhero action, romance, comedy, drama, romance...the only content that might bother some people happens when Abby and Amazonia, Mark's superhero ex-girlfriend, get drunk and bond together.

Zdarsky, Chip

Jughead; Volume 1. story by Chip Zdarsky; art by Erica Henderson; coloring by Andre Szymanowicz; lettering by Jack Morelli; editor, Mike Pellerito. Archie Comics 2016 168 p. Color; Illustration

Grades: 7 8 9 10 11 12 Adult **741.5; Fic**

1. School stories — Graphic novels; 2. Andrews, Archie (Fictional character); 3. Jones, Jughead (Fictional character)

1627388931; 9781627388931, $19.99

Eisner Award: Best Humor Publication (2017)

"Riverdale High provides a quality education and quality hot lunches, but when one of those is tampered with, JUGHEAD JONES swears vengeance! Well, I mean, he doesn't 'swear.' This is still Archie Comics after all." (Publisher's note)

"Zdarsky captures the spirit of the well-known cast while injecting modern sensibilities through dialogue and attitude. Henderson's energetic and dynamic art connects brilliantly with the humor and pace of each chapter. The far-fetched plot befits Jughead's personality, complete with robots, pirates, and lots of food." SLJ

Volume 1 of 2

Aaron, Jason

The **Other** Side. writer, Jason Aaron; artist, Cameron Stewart; colorist, David McCaig; letterer, Pat Brosseau; introduction by Dale Dye. DC Comics/Vertigo 2007 144p. Illustration
Grades: 12 Adult   **741.5; Fic**
  1. Graphic novels; 2. Vietnam War, 1961-1975 — Graphic novels
9781534302228; 978-1-4012-1350-3, $12.99

Billy Everette from Alabama gets drafted into the Marines in 1967; in North Vietnam, Vo Binh Dai volunteers to serve in the People's Army of Vietnam. The book follows these two young men through their training and their journey towards an inevitable confrontation. Billy starts seeing horrifying ghost images of dead soldiers in various stages of decay, and he hears his rifle telling him to kill. Vo maintains a strong sense of patriotism despite the hardships of the march south to find the war. They both end up at Khe Sanh just after the Tet Offensive in February 1968.

Anyone who has seen such movies as "Full Metal Jacket" or "We Were Soldiers Once" will know what to expect in this book; the language is full of expletives and the battle scenes are brutal. Aaron and Stewart bring the harsh reality of war to readers 40 years after the fact.

Originally published as The Other Side issues #1-5.

Star Wars; Volume 1: Skywalker strikes. writers, Jason Aaron; artist, John Cassaday; colorist, Laura Martin; letterer, Chris Eliopoulos. Marvel Enterprises 2015 160 p. Color; Illustration
Grades: 8 9 10 11 12 Adult   **741.5**
  1. Star Wars — Graphic novels
0785192131; 9780785192138, $19.99

"Luke Skywalker and the ragtag rebel band opposing the Galactic Empire are fresh off their biggest victory yet — the destruction of the massive Death Star. But the Empire's not toppled yet! Join Luke, Princess Leia, Han Solo, Chewbacca, C-3PO, R2-D2 and the rest of the Rebel Alliance as they fight for freedom against the evil of Darth Vader and his master, the Emperor!" (Publisher's note)

Volume 1 of an ongoing series

Thor; Volume 1: the goddess of thunder. writer, Jason Aaron; artists, Russell Dauterman (#1-4) & Jorge Molina (#5); color artists, Matthew Wilson (#1-4) & Jorge Molina (#5); letterer, VC's Joe Sabino; cover art, Russell Dauterman & Frank Martin. Marvel Enterprises 2015 136 p. Color; Illustration
Grades: 9 10 11 12 Adult   **741.5**
  1. Women superheroes; 2. Thor (Fictional character)
0785192387; 9780785192381, $24.99

In this book, by Jason Aaron, illustrated by Russell Dauterman, "Mjolnir lies on the moon, unable to be lifted! Something dark has befallen the God of Thunder, leaving him unworthy for the first time ever! But when Frost Giants invade Earth, the hammer will be lifted — and a mysterious woman...the mighty Thor! Who is this new Goddess of Thunder? Not even Odin knows...but she may be Earth's only hope against the Frost Giants!" (Publisher's note)

"When the classic Thor is no longer righteous enough to wield his hero-making mallet, the only person worthy enough to take up the mantle is...well, you don't find out in this volume. But the point is that it's a lady, and she's every bit up to the task, as she proves by taking on bloodthirsty Frost Giants, the Minotaur CEO of megacorporation Roxxon, and the Dark Elf Malekith." Booklist

Contains material originally published in magazine form as Thor #1-5.; Volume 1 of 2

Abadzis, Nick

★ **Laika**. First Second Books 2007 205p. Illustration
Grades: 5 6 7 8 9 10 11 12 Adult   **741.5; Fic**
  1. Graphic novels; 2. Soviet Union — History — 1953-1991 — Graphic novels; 3. Space flight — Graphic novels
1-59643-101-6; 978-1-59643-101-0

LC 2006-51907

Laika was the abandoned puppy destined to become Earth's first space traveler. This is her journey. Along with Laika, there is Korolev, once a political prisoner and now a driven engineer at the top of the Soviet space program, and Yelena, the lab technician responsible for Laika's health and life. The book depicts the dedication and struggles of the scientists and technicians who worked in the Soviet space program, based on research Abadzis did before writing this book. The book includes a bibliography of books and websites.

"Abadzis's tear-inducing and solidly researched graphic novel treatment of Laika's surpassingly tragic story is a standout." Publ Wkly

Abel, Jessica

★ **Drawing** words & writing pictures: making comics: from manga, graphic novels, and beyond. [by] Jessica Abel & Matt Madden. First Second Books 2008 xxi, 282 p. Illustration
Grades: 9 10 11 12 Adult   **741.5**
  1. Cartooning — Technique; 2. Comic books, strips, etc. — Authorship; 3. Drawing — Technique; 4. Graphic novels — Authorship
1596431318; 9781596431317, $34.99

LC 2007044125

Authors Jessica Abel and Matt Madden present "a course on comic creation — for college classes or for independent study — that centers on storytelling and concludes with making a finished comic. With chapters on lettering, story structure, and panel layout, the fifteen lessons offered — each complete with homework, extra credit activities and supplementary reading suggestions — provide a solid introduction for people interested in making their own comics." (Publisher's note)

This "book offers step-by-step entry into a complicated series of skills in a nonscary and approachable way." Libr J

Includes bibliographical references (p. 261-265) and index

La Perdida. Jessica Abel. Pantheon 2006 272p. Illustration
Grades: 11 12 Adult   **741.5; Fic**
  9780375714719; 9781594973673; 0-375-42365-6, 34.95

"Carla, an American estranged from her Mexican father, heads to Mexico City to 'find herself.' She crashes with a former fling, Harry, who has been drinking his way through the capital in the great tradition of his heroes, William S. Burroughs and Jack Kerouac. Harry is good-humored about Carla's reappearance on his doorstep — until he realizes that Carla, who spends her days soaking in the city, exploring Frida Kahlo's house, and learning Spanish, has no intention of leaving." (Publisher's note)

★ **Life** sucks. [text by] Jessica Abel, Gabe Soria; [art by] Warren Pleece; coloring by Hilary Sycamore. First Second Books 2008 186p. Illustration
Grades: 10 11 12 Adult   **741.5; Fic**
  1. Graphic novels; 2. Horror graphic novels; 3. Humorous graphic novels; 4. Romance graphic novels; 5. Vampires — Graphic novels
978-1-59643-107-2, $19.95; 1-59643-107-5

Anyone who thinks the vampire life is all romantic and ethereal better have another think. Dave can tell them, it sucks. He's the night manager for a convenience store, and he's a vampire, "made" by his boss (master), Radu. He's not the only one; in their neighborhood, most of the shops are owned by vampires who make their night managers vampires. Dave can't make himself drink from humans, so he drinks bottled blood. His roommate is human but tolerant. Then Dave sees the perfect girl, Rosa, one of the goth vampire groupies who hangs out in the neighborhood. However, surfer/slacker Wes, whom Dave replaced as the night manager, also has his eye on Rosa, and Wes isn't above killing to get his way. The book includes some violence (including the tearing off of one girl's head), and some harsh language.

"Warren Pleece's art marvelously captures the humor of the mundane that lends the book's crew of late-night wage-slave vamps believability and energy. A really fun read!? Booklist

Mastering comics: drawing words & writing pictures continued. by Jessica Abel and Matt Madden. First Second 2012 xvii, 318 p. Illustration; Color

Grades: 9 10 11 12 Adult   **741.5**
   1. Cartooning — Technique; 2. Comic books, strips, etc. — Technique; 3. Drawing; 4. Cartoonists
1596436174; 9781596436176, $34.99

                       LC 2011037023
Jessica Abel's book "Mastering Comics," written with her husband Matt Madden, is a "course of study for the budding cartoonist. Covering advanced topics such as story composition, coloring, and file formatting, [the book] is a vital companion to the introductory content of the first volume" entitled "Drawing Words & Writing Pictures." (Publisher's note)

Abirached, Zeina

A **game** for swallows: to die, to leave, to return. written by Zeina Abirached; art by Zeina Abirached; translation by Edward Gauvin. Graphic Universe 2012 188 p.

Grades: 7 8 9 10 11 12
741.5
   1. Abirached, Zeina, 1981- — Comic books, strips, etc; 2. Beirut (Lebanon) — Comic books, strips, etc; 3. Lebanon — History — Civil War, 1975-1990 — Comic books, strips, etc; 4. Separation; 5. Family — Graphic novels
0761385681; 9780761385684, $29.27

          LC 2011038914
Mildred L. Batchelder Honor Book (2013)

This graphic novel looks at "the civil war in Lebanon in the 1980s, as seen through the eyes of a child" separated from her parents. "Young Zeina [Abirached] and her brother have been sequestered within the small foyer in their apartment," which "becomes a place for neighbors in the building to congregate and seek asylum. Though war is raging and death always seems to loom near with shells falling and snipers possibly crouching behind every wall, Zeina and her neighbors try to live the best they can." (Kirkus Reviews)

Translation of Le jeau des hirondelles.

I remember Beirut. Zeina Abirached. Graphic Universe 2014 96 p. Illustration; Map

Grades: 8 9 10 11 12 Adult   **741.5; 92**
   1. Abirached, Zeina, 1981-; 2. Beirut (Lebanon) — Biography — Comic books, strips, etc; 3. Beirut (Lebanon) — Biography — Juvenile literature; 4. Lebanon — History — 20th century — Comic books, strips, etc; 5. Lebanon — History — 20th century — Juvenile literature; 6. Children and war; 7. War — Graphic novels
1467738220; 9781467738224, $29.27

          LC 2013047112

Courtesy of Lerner Publishing Group

In this graphic memoir, Zeina Abirached "reveals numerous details from her childhood in Beirut during the war from 1975 to 1990 war. 'I remember' is a recurring phrase and provides a personal frame of reference for the effect of war on kids. Some are simple childhood memories.... Inclusion of...maps and diagrams orient the reader and provide additional perspective." (Kirkus Reviews)

"The blocky, naive-style pictures quietly evoke wartime fears in ways the words simply cannot — bullet holes in the sides of cars, rubble in the streets, her father's eyebrows indicating increasing sadness at the heartbreaking state of a formerly vital market." Booklist

Abouet, Marguerite

★ **Aya:** life in Yop City. by Marguerite Abouet and Clément Oubrerie; translated by Helge Dascher. Drawn & Quarterly 2012 96 p. Color; Illustration

Grades: 10 11 12 Adult   **741.5/944; 741.5**
   1. Africa; 2. Friendship
1770460829; 9781770460829, $24.95

This book, by Marguerite Abouet and Clément Oubrerie, "is the story of the studious and clear-sighted nineteen-year-old Aya, her easygoing friends Adjoua and Bintou, and their meddling relatives and neighbors. It's...[an] account of the simple pleasures and private troubles of everyday life in Yop City." (Publisher's note)

Followed by Aya: Love in Yop City

Aya: love in Yop City. by Marguerite Abouet and Clement Oubrerie; translatied by Helge Dascher. Drawn & Quarterly 2013 328 p. Color illustration

Grades: 10 11 12 Adult   **741.5; Fic**
   1. Graphic novels — Côte d'Ivoire; 2. Teenage girls — Côte d'Ivoire — Comic books, strips, etc; 3. Côte d'Ivoire — Comic books, strips, etc; 4. Ivory Coast — Graphic novels; 5. Nineteen seventies
1770460926; 9781770460928, $24.95

          LC 2012545664
This graphic novel, written by Marguerite Abouet and Clément Oubrerie, comprises the final three chapters of the 'Aya' story,...a lighthearted story about life in the Ivory Coast during the 1970s, a particularly thriving and wealthy time in the country's history. When a professor tries to take advantage of Aya, her plans to become a doctor are...shaken, and she vows to take revenge on [him]." The book includes "recipes, guides to understanding Ivorian slang, street sketches, and concluding remarks from Abouet explaining...social milieu." (Publisher's note)

Aguirre-Sacasa, Roberto

★ **Afterlife** with Archie: Escape from Riverdale. story by Roberto Aguirre-Sacasa; artwork by Francesco Francavilla; lettering by Jack Morelli. Archie Comic Publications 2014 160 p. Color; Illustration (Afterlife with Archie)

Grades: 10 11 12 Adult   **741.5; Fic**
   1. Dogs — Fiction; 2. Zombies — Fiction; 3. Witches — Fiction; 4. Andrews, Archie (Fictional character)
1619889080; 9781619889088, $17.99

          LC 2014430277
In this book, by Roberto Aguirre-Sacasa, "[w]hen Jughead's beloved pet Hot Dog is killed in a hit and run, Jughead turns to the only person he knows who can help bring back his furry best friend-Sabrina the Teenage

Witch. Using dark, forbidden magic, Sabrina is successful and Hot Dog returns to the land of the living. But he's not the same... and soon, the darkness he brings back with him from beyond the grave begins to spread." (Publisher's note)

"Not parody but serious drama, this graphic novel casts off the typical Archie comic lightheartedness and goes deep into the gut.... Paired with Francavilla's dead-on illustrations, the excellent writing from Aguirre-Sacasa...brings constant surprises while confronting the dilemma of remaining humane through crisis." LJ

Volume 1 of an ongoing series

Chilling adventures of Sabrina; Book one: The crucible. story by Roberto Aguirre-Sacasa; artwork by Robert Hack; lettering by Jack Morelli. Archie Comic Publications, Inc. 2016 160 p. Color; Illustration

Grades: 10 11 12 Adult   **741.5; Fic**
1. Comic books, strips, etc. — United States; 2. Sabrina the Teenage Witch (Fictitious character) — Comic books, strips, etc; 3. Witches — Comic books, strips, etc

1627389873; 9781627389877, $17.99

     LC 2016288136

"On the eve of her sixteenth birthday, the young sorceress Sabrina Spellman finds herself at a crossroads, having to choose between an unearthly destiny and her mortal boyfriend, Harvey. But a foe from her family's past has arrived in Greendale, Madame Satan, and she has her own deadly agenda." (Publisher's note)

Volume 1 of an ongoing series

Civil War: Peter Parker, Spider-Man. Marvel Entertainment 2007 un Illustration

Grades: 9 10 11 12 Adult   **741.5; Fic**
1. Graphic novels; 2. Spider-Man (Fictional character); 3. Superhero graphic novels

0-7851-2189-7, $17.99

The Civil War has begun, sides have been chosen. Spider-Man chose to unmask himself to the whole world, and now everyone knows he's Peter Parker. Every action has consequences, but for Peter, will he pay, or will his loved ones pay?

Ahmed, Saladin

Black Bolt; Volume 1: hard time. Saladin Ahmed, writer; Christian Ward with Frazer Irving (#5), artists; VC's Clayton Cowles, letterer. Marvel Enterprises 2017 136 p. Color; Illustration

Grades: 10 11 12 Adult   **741.5; Fic**
1. Superheroes — Fiction; 2. Good and evil — Fiction; 3. Prisons — Fiction

1302907328; 9781302907327, $17.99

Hugo Finalist: Best Graphic Story (2018); Eisner Award: Best New Series (2018)

This first volume in the Black Bolt series "begins with Black Bolt...imprisoned?! Where exactly is he? Why has he been jailed? And who could be powerful enough to hold the uncanny Black Bolt? The answers to both will shock you — and Black Bolt as well! For if he is to learn the truth, he must first win a fight to the death with a fellow inmate — the Absorbing Man!" (Publisher's note)

Aihara, Miki

Tokyo Boys & Girls Volume 1. story and art by Miki Aihara; [English adaptation, Shaenon Garrity; translation, JN Productions]. Viz Media/Shojo Beat 2005 200p. Illustration

Grades: 10 11 12 Adult   **741.5; Fic**
1. Graphic novels; 2. Manga; 3. Romance graphic novels; 4. Shojo manga

1-4215-0020-5, $8.99

Mimori Kosaka's dream comes true when she's accepted to the Meidai Attached High School and gets to wear their super-fashionable uniform. The school year starts off well when Mimori befriends the beautiful Nana, but things quickly turn sour for her when she is chosen to be the class representative. Through a series of unfortunate events, she finds herself the focus of attention by three boys and her teachers, for all the wrong reasons. Mimori is reunited with Atsushi, a boy she knew in elementary school — and it turns out he despises her for allegedly bullying him in their grade school days. In fact, he plans to exact a little revenge. The series includes sexual innuendo, brief sexual situations, and some strong language.

Volume 1 of 5

Akamatsu, Ken

Love Hina: Omnibus 1. by Ken Akamatsu; translated by Satsuki Yamashita; lettered by Hope Donovan. Kodansha Comics 2011 542 p. Illustration

Grades: 11 12 Adult   **741.5**
1. Manga; 2. Shonen manga; 3. Japan — Fiction; 4. Young men — Fiction; 5. Grandmothers — Fiction

1935429477; 9781935429470, $19.99

     LC 2011517873

In this book, by Ken Akamatsu, "Keitaro Urashima fails his entrance exams to get into Tokyo University for the second time.... To make things worse, his parents have kicked him out of his house. Fortunately, his grandmother owns the fabulous Hinata Lodge and has agreed to take Keitaro in as caretaker. What he doesn't know is that the lodge is actually a girl's dorm and he's the only guy around!" (Publisher's note)

Originally published in the U.S. by Tokyopop in 14 volumes; First published in 1999 by Kodansha Ltd., Tokyo as: Love Hina vol. 1-3 — Vol. 1, t.p. verso.; Volume 1 of 5

Mao-Chan vol. 1. story by Ken Akamatsu; art by Ran. Del Rey Manga 2008 394p. Illustration

Grades: 8 9 10 11 12   **741.5; Fic**
1. Graphic novels; 2. Humorous graphic novels; 3. Manga; 4. Shonen manga

978-0-345-50181-3, $14.95

When incredibly cute aliens invade Japan and steal its signature landmarks, Japan unleashes the Grade School Defense Corps, made up of second-grade students, such as Mao, Misora, and Sylvie. As their grandfathers, who command Ground, Air, and Marine Defense respectively, plot to make their own granddaughters the big heroes, the girls prefer to work together to defeat the aliens. Readers must love incredible cuteness along with some fan service featuring the older teenage girls. There is very little in this volume other than the mild fan service to indicate reasons for an older teen rating the publisher rates it for ages 16 and up.

Volume 1 of 2

Alice, A. (Alex)

Siegfried 1; 1. written and illustrated by Alex Alice. Archaia Entertainment, LLC 2012 144 p.

Grades: 6 7 8 9 10 11 12   **741.5**
1. Dragons — Graphic novels; 2. Gods and goddesses — Graphic novels; 3. Orphans — Graphic novels

193639345X; 9781936393459, $24.95

This graphic novel by Alex Alice presents "a three-part story inspired by [Richard] Wagner's classic opera 'The Ring of the Nibelung!' Siegfried, born of the love between a mortal man and a Valkyrie, is a young orphan being raised by Mime, one of the last of the dwarf-goblin Nibelungs. Siegfried yearns to discover who his real parents were..., not knowing that

Odin, father of the Norse gods, has a destiny planned for him: to fight the dragon Fafnir, guardian of the Rheingold!" (Publisher's note)

Volume 1 of 3

Allan, Von

Stargazer, volume one. Von Allan Studio 2010 115p. Illustration

Grades: 4 5 6 7 8 9

741.5; Fic

1. Adventure graphic novels; 2. Friendship — Graphic novels; 3. Graphic novels; 4. Science fiction graphic novels

978-0-9781237-2-7, $14.95

Courtesy of Von Allan Studio

Marni's grandmother has just died, and she left a strange device that the two of them played with whenever Marni had visited. No one knows how Marni's grandmother got it, and it has never done anything. Her best friends, Elora and Sophie, come over for a last backyard campout before the weather turns cold, and when they each put a hand on the device, an extremely bright light nearly blinds them. After things seem to go back to normal, the girls go outside to find Marni's house gone, the device vanished, and none of the stars look familiar. In the morning, they pack up the little food they had brought for their campout, Elora's telescope, and Sophie's pennywhistle, and hike towards a tower Elora had spotted. They know they're in a totally strange place when they come upon a statue of nonhuman, alien creatures. As they continue, they come upon a strange house, where they find food, and then a mute, boy-sized robot. Even though the three friends bicker with each other, they work together to find a way home. Allan includes extensive notes on his writing process, and an excerpt from his script. The cover art shows one interesting looking character who doesn't appear in this volume. While their age isn't specified, the girls look to be tweens, with the slightly awkward, coltish bodies and movements of pre-adolescents. The strongest language used is one instance of the word "damn."

Volume 1 of 2

Allen, Chris

William Shakespeare's Othello. adapted by Vincent Goodwin; illustrated by Chris Allen.. ABDO/Magic Wagon 2008 48p. Illustration

Grades: 5 6 7 8 9 10

822.3; 741.5

1. Authors; 2. Dramatists; 3. Graphic novels; 4. Poets; 5. Shakespeare, William, 1564-1616 — Adaptations

978-1-60270-192-2, $28.50

LC 2008-10743

Othello the Moor is a successful general, married to the beautiful Desdemona. Life should be good, but he's incredibly jealous of anyone who looks at his wife. Iago wants Othello's position and decides that he should destroy Othello by fabricating an affair between Desdemona and Cassio. This graphic novel adaptation keeps some of the original dialog from Shakespeare's play while paring down the action to simplify it for readers who would struggle with the original. The book includes a short biography of Shakespeare, a summary of the plot, a glossary, and a sampling of famous lines and phrases.

Part of the Graphic Shakespeare series

Allison, John

Bad machinery; 1: the case of the team spirit. John Allison; [edited by] James Lucas Jones. Oni Press 2013 112 p. Color; Illustration

Grades: 7 8 9 10 11 12 Adult

741.5

1. Mystery graphic novels; 2. School stories — Graphic novels

1620100843; 9781620100844, $19.99

LC 2012953355

Courtesy of Oni Press

"Shauna. Charlotte. Mildred. Three schoolgirl sleuths. Jack. Linton. Sonny. Three schoolboy investigators. Tackleford. One mid-sized city with a history of countless mysteries. Is there enough room at Griswalds Grammar School for two groups of kid detectives? There better be, because once these kids have set their sights on solving a mystery there's nothing that can derail them. Nothing, except maybe gossip, classwork, new football player cards, torment from siblings, or any number of childhood distractions." (Publisher's note)

"Allison is a triple threat: he plots deftly, draws confidently, and writes dead-on adolescent dialogue. Set in a grammar school in a British working-class community, this first book in his Bad Machinery series — originally published as a webcomic — has three earnest boys vying against three sharp-tongued girls to solve mysteries." Pub Wkly

Other Bad Machinery volumes are: The case of the good boy (2014); The case of the simple soul (2014); The case of the lonely one (2015); The case of the fire inside (2016); The case of the forked road (2017)

★ **Giant** Days; Volume 1. created & written by John Allison; illustrated by Lissa Treiman; colors by Whitney Cogar; letters by Jim Campbell. Boom! Studios 2015 128 p. Color; Illustration

Grades: 10 11 12 Adult

741.5; Fic

1. Women — Fiction; 2. College students — Fiction

1608867897; 9781608867899, $9.99

Eisner Nominee: Best Continuing Series (2016)

"Susan, Esther, and Daisy started at university three weeks ago and became fast friends. But, now away from home for the first time, all three want to reinvent themselves. But in the face of hand-wringing boys, 'personal experimentation,' influenza, mystery-mold, nu-chauvinism, and the willful, unwanted intrusion of 'academia,' they may be lucky just to make it to spring alive." (Publisher's note)

"Allison's pitch-perfect teenage snark is the ideal match for Treiman and Cogar's lush, candy-colored scenes full of rich, character-building detail and marvelous background action. With a masterful hand, they telegraph hilarious visual jokes with the subtlest of cues, like a raised eyebrow or flop of hair, and their figures are full of motion and vitality." Booklist

Volume 1 of an ongoing series

Allred, Mike

Madman; Volume 1. created, written and illustrated by Michael Allred; colors by Laura Allred. Image Comics 2007 268 p. Color; Illustration

Grades: 11 12 Adult

741.5

1. Science fiction graphic novels

1582408106; 9781582408101, $24.99

"This volume introduces Madman and the rest of the eccentric citizens of Snap City: mad genius Dr. Flem, the evil Mr. Mondstadt, and Joe, the love of Frank Einstein's life." (Publisher's note)

Volume 1 of 3

Madman atomic comics, vol. 1. created, written and illustrated by Michael Allred; colors by Laura Allred. Image Comics 2008 un

Grades: 10 11 12 Adult

741.5; Fic

1. Graphic novels; 2. Madman (Fictional character); 3. Science fiction graphic novels

978-1-58240-916-0, $19.99

Frank Einstein, Madman, undergoes a bizarre, phantasmagorical, existential journey that turns out to be something going on in his subconscious self while he's in a coma. His friends Dr. Flem, Joe (Josephine), and the Atomics hook up Astroman, Frank's robotic "clone," as a technological rescue beacon to lead him through his myriad of fictional personae to his true self, but when they think both Frank and Astroman are dead, they send them up into space in a rocket. Astroman tries to go for help, but his batteries run out, then Frank is rescued by Haley FouFou, who proclaims that he is "one of the Four" who must save the universe. He sends for the Atomics to help him defeat the Crimson King, who has been infected with a cosmic virus and will turn the universe inside out if not stopped. The book is not for casual comics readers, although familiarity with previous Madman comics aren't really necessary to understand this new series. Allred challenges readers with existential discussions and elliptical plotting, and he has fun drawing in the style of many different cartoonists and artists. There's some violence and a little partial nudity, but little in the way of harsh language ("monkey spit" is the strongest epithet Frank utters).
Volume 1 of 3

Red rocket 7. Image Comics 2008 un Illustration
Grades: 9 10 11 12 Adult   **741.5; Fic**
1. Graphic novels; 2. Rock music — Graphic novels; 3. Science fiction graphic novels
978-1-58240-998-6, $16.99
In a wild science fiction adventure that spans the history of American rock and roll, the humanoid alien known as Red Rocket is left for dead by the villainous Enfinites, but a robotic guardian creates seven clones, each with their own ability. Seven goes on a world-spanning tour of pop music, working with such artists as Little Richard, Elvis Presley, the Beatles, and David Bowie. On his last tour, rock music journalist Lynn Hayes gets mixed up with Seven, his brother clones, and the evil Enfinites who seek to destroy all the clones and Earth, while they're at it. This book was originally published in 1998 by Dark Horse Comics in an 11x11 album size. This new edition is in the vinyl single size and includes bonus material, including an essay from Allred's editor Jamie S. Rich, an introduction by Robert Rodriguez, and an outro by Gerard Way of Chemical Romance. Allred's book predates all the rock 'n' roll graphic novels that have come out in recent years. The book includes some violence and mild language.

Alphona, Adrian
Runaways Vol. 3: The Good Die Young. Marvel Entertainment 2005 un Illustration
Grades: 8 9 10 11 12   **741.5; Fic**
1. Adventure graphic novels; 2. Graphic novels; 3. Runaways (Fictional characters); 4. Superhero graphic novels
0-7851-1684-2, $7.99
The world as people know it is about to end and the Runaways are the only hope to prevent it. But if the fledgling teenage heroes are going to succeed, they may have to become just as evil as their villainous parents. The Runaways have learned how their parents' criminal organization began, and now they must decide how it should end. As the Runaways' epic battle against their evil parents reaches its shocking conclusion, the team's mole stands revealed, and blood must be shed. Which kids will still be standing when the smoke finally clears?

Runaways Vol. 4: True Believers. Marvel Entertainment 2005 un Illustration
Grades: 8 9 10 11 12   **741.5; Fic**
1. Adventure graphic novels; 2. Graphic novels; 3. Runaways (Fictional characters); 4. Superhero graphic novels
0-7851-1705-9, $7.99

Now that the evil Pride is gone, nearly every bad guy in the Marvel Universe is trying to fill the power vacuum in Los Angeles, and the Runaways are the only heroes who can stop them. Plus: What does a mysterious new team of young heroes want with the Runaways, and which fan-favorite Marvel characters are part of this group?

Altman, Steven-Elliot
The **Irregulars** ... In the Service of Sherlock Holmes. written by Steven-Elliot Altman & Michael Reaves; illustrated by Bong Dazo; lettered by Simon Bowland; cover by Ben Templesmith. Dark Horse Comics 2005 un Illustration
Grades: 9 10 11 12 Adult   **741.5; Fic**
1. Graphic novels; 2. Horror graphic novels; 3. Mystery graphic novels
1-59307-303-8, $12.95
A madman stalks the streets of London's Whitechapel slum, leaving a trail of grisly murders in his wake. The police have only one suspect: a prominent and respected physician named John Watson. The master detective Sherlock Holmes, in order to solve the most fantastic mystery of his career and save his greatest friend from the gallows, employs a band of young street urchins to infiltrate the alleys of Whitechapel. They can go everywhere, see everything, overhear everyone. They are the Baker Street Irregulars, and this is the most fantastic and terrifying adventure of their lives, as they uncover an evil unlike anything Sherlock Holmes has ever faced, and end up in a nightmare future. Grisly murders and horrific sights along with some strong language occur.

Amir
★ **Zahra's** paradise. stories by Amir & Khalil; written by Amir; artwork by Khalil. First Second 2011 255 p. Illustration
Grades: 10 11 12 Adult   **741.5**
1. Missing persons — Fiction; 2. Graphic novels; 3. Iran — History — 1979-; 4. Iran — Politics and government
9781596436428 (pa); 1596436425
                                                    LC 2011017564
This book is "[s]et in the aftermath of Iran's fraudulent elections of 2009...[and] is the fictional story of the search for Mehdi, a young protestor who has vanished into an extrajudicial twilight zone. What's keeping his memory from being obliterated is not the law. It is the grit and guts of his mother, who refuses to surrender her son to fate, and the tenacity of his brother, a blogger, who fuses tradition and technology to explore and explode the void in which Mehdi has vanished." (Publisher's note)

Andelman, Bob
Will Eisner: A Spirited Life. M Presss 2005 375p. Illustration
Grades: 9 10 11 12 Adult   **92; 741.5**
1. Cartoonists — United States — Biography; 2. Graphic novels; 3. Eisner, Will, 1917-2005; 4. Arts — Biography; 5. Artists — Biography; 6. Cartoonists — Biography; 7. Authors — Biography; 8. Literature — Biography
1-59582-011-6, $14.95
                                                    LC 2005026326
Internationally recognized for his genre-busting 1940s art and storytelling style on The Spirit, Will Eisner's greatest legacy may be the graphic novels he championed and created. He was an American master whose work in comics permanently altered the face of global pop culture. This biography explores Eisner's life, detailing a career that spanned 70 years and saw him educate several generations of Army soldiers in the innovative PS Magazine and create the first widely known graphic novel, A Contract with God. Eisner also introduced some of the world's greatest comics art talent: Bob Kane (Batman), Jack Kirby (Fantastic Four), Jules Feiffer, Dave Berg (MAD) and Joe Kubert (Tarzan). And he inspired generations of modern artists and writers, including Frank Miller (Sin

City), Robert Crumb, Harlan Ellison, Neil Gaiman (Sandman, American Gods), Brad Bird (The Incredibles), Patrick McDonnell (Mutts) and Art Spiegelman (Maus). A Spirited Life also includes interviews with many of Eisner's contemporaries, such as Alan Moore, Dave Gibbons, Neil Gaiman, Denis Kitchen, Jim Warren, Dave Sim, Denny O'Neil and Stan Lee.

"Michael Chabon contributes a heartfelt introduction to Andelman's first-ever biography of Will Eisner (1917-2005)...Eisner revolutionized the field...from his 1940s stories featuring masked crime fighter the Spirit to his later, pioneering graphic novels but also as businessman and entrepreneur, teacher, mentor, and the inspiration of countless young artists [like Art Spiegelman].... Besides verifying Eisner's impact on nearly every artist who drew comics in his wake, Andelman shows that Eisner's influence extends to such film directors as Spielberg and Tarantino." Booklist

Andersen, Sarah (Sarah C.)

Adulthood is a myth: A 'Sarah's scribbles' collection. Sarah Andersen. Andrews McMeel Pub 2016 112 p. Illustration
Grades: 10 11 12 Adult   **741.5**
1. Youth; 2. Millennials (Persons) — Comic books, strips, etc.; 3. Comic books, strips, etc.
1449474195; 9781449474195, $14.99

This collection of Sarah's Scribbles comics, by Sarah Andersen, "presents many fan favorites plus dozens of all-new comics.... Like the work of fellow Millennial authors Allie Brosh, Grace Helbig, and Gemma Correll, Sarah's frankness on personal issues like body image, self-consciousness, introversion, relationships, and the frequency of bra-washing makes her comics highly relatable and deeply hilarious." (Publisher's note)

"Andersen is an excellent caricaturist — some of her funniest punch lines are panels of wordless, wide-eyed faces. Like so many talented comedians before her, much of her best material comes from the uncomfortable and even embarrassing aspects of life." Pub Wkly

Anderson, Ho Che

King: a comics biography. Fantagraphics 2010 312p. Illustration
Grades: 10 11 12 Adult   **741.5; 92**
1. African Americans — Biography — Graphic novels; 2. African Americans — Civil rights — Graphic novels; 3. Biographical graphic novels; 4. Civil rights activists; 5. Clergy; 6. Graphic novels; 7. Nobel laureates for peace; 8. Nonfiction writers; 9. King, Martin Luther, Jr., 1929-1968
978-1-60699-310-1, $34.99

"Much of the book (packaged nicely with previously unprinted material, sketches, and a somewhat beside-the-point modern-day "prelude" titled Black Dogs) tracks King from his college days in the 1950s to his death, jamming each page with noirishly drawn frames and tightly packed political debates. Though all the great moments of his civil rights battle are here (from the March on Washington to his less-successful housing campaign in Chicago), Anderson doesn't resort to the cheap cinematic trick of success and fadeout. There is more disappointment here than celebration, suffused with the sorrowful sense of a long, long battle just barely begun. A crowning achievement, like the man it portrays." Publ Wkly

First published 2005

Anderson, Kevin J.

Grumpy old monsters. Kevin J. Anderson, Rebecca Moesta; [art by] Guillermo Mendoza, Paco Cavero. IDW Publishing 2004 96p. Illustration
Grades: 4 5 6 7 8 9   **741.5; Fic**

1. Graphic novels; 2. Humorous graphic novels; 3. Monsters — Graphic novels
1-932382-35-6, $13.99

The old monsters Frankenstein's Monster, Dracula, the Mummy, and the Werewolf, have all retired and moved to the old monsters' home, where Nurse Wrentch terrorizes them and only little Tiffany Frankenstein, granddaughter of old Dr. F., comes to visit. But this time she comes with terrible news the Van Helsing Corporation is about to take possession of Castle Frankenstein, tear it down, and build luxury condominiums. The monsters decide they must come out of retirement and help Tiffany stop the horror if they can escape Nurse Wrentch!

Anderson, Laurie Halse

★ **Speak**: the graphic novel. Laurie Halse Anderson, illustrated by Emily Carrol. Farrar, Straus & Giroux 2018 384 p. Illustration
Grades: 7 8 9 10 11 12   **741.5; Fic**
1. Teenage girls — Comic books, strips, etc.; 2. Loneliness — Comic books, strips, etc.; 3. Rape — Fiction; 4. High schools — Fiction
9780374300289, $19.99

LC 2017933387

In this graphic novel, by Laurie Halse Anderson, illustrated by Emily Carrol, Melinda "is friendless — an outcast — because she busted an end-of-summer party by calling the cops, so now nobody will talk to her, let alone listen to her.... Through her work on an art project, she is finally able to face what really happened that night: She was raped by an upperclassman, a guy who still attends Merryweather [High] and is still a threat to her." (Publisher's note)

"This potent retelling of the modern classic Speak blends words and images to create magic: a new representation of a teen whose voice is ripped from her, the battles she must wage to find it again, and the triumph of finally being able to speak out. Carroll's grayscale artwork perfectly depicts the starkness of Melinda's depression through strong ink lines and striking panels that rely on pencil and charcoal textural effects for the backgrounds." SLJ

Anderson, M. T.

★ **Yvain**: the Knight of the Lion. M.T. Anderson, illustrated by Andrea Offermann. Candlewick Press 2017 144 p. Color; Illustration
Grades: 7 8 9 10
741.5
1. Knights and knighthood — Graphic novels
0763659398; 9780763659394, $19.99

In this graphic novel, by M.T. Anderson, illustrated by Andrea Offermann, "sir Yvain sets out from King Arthur's court and defeats a local lord in battle, unknowingly intertwining his future with the lives of two compelling women: Lady Laudine, the beautiful widow of the fallen lord, and her sly maid Lunette." (Publisher's note)

YVAIN. Text copyright © 2017 by M.T. Anderson. Illustrations copyright © 2017 by Andrea Offermann.

"This adaptation of Chrétien de Troyes' medieval poem beautifully ties together period art and imagery with stylish visual storytelling." Booklist

Andrews, Mark

Tales of Colossus. Image Comics 2006 un Illustration
Grades: 10 11 12 Adult   **741.5; Fic**
1. Adventure graphic novels; 2. Fantasy graphic novels; 3. Graphic novels

1-58240-591-3, $17.99

A knight, whose soul is trapped inside a metal monster called Colossus, lives out an immortal existence slaying evil creatures. Until one day a twisted, evil paladin wielding enchanted weapons arrives in the Kingdom with his own agenda. Their paths cross in a steel pounding, armor glinting no holds barred battle that will change a Kingdom forever. Set during the times of the Crusades, this book is filled with battles and bloodshed, with some nudity and sexual situations.

Anzai, Nobuyuki
Flame of Recca Volume 1. Viz Media 2003 184p. Illustration
Grades: 10 11 12 Adult   **741.5; Fic**
1. Fantasy graphic novels; 2. Graphic novels; 3. Manga; 4. Martial arts — Graphic novels; 5. Ninja — Graphic novels; 6. Shonen manga
1-59116-066-9, $9.95

Teenager Recca Hanabishi is always up for a good-natured tussle with his friends. That's because he's famous at school and around town for being a super ninja geek. Armed with the power to control flame, Recca suddenly finds himself in an awkward situation. On the day he pledges his undying ninja allegiance to a pretty classmate named Yanagi Sakoshita, a mysterious older woman pops into his life. Is she good? Is she evil? What exactly does she want? And what's the deal with tomboy, Fuko Kirisawa? She's got the power of wind at her command. Does she want to smash Recca to smithereens, or does she simply want to kiss him? The series includes strong language, nudity, sexual innuendo, and graphic violence.
Volume 1 of 33

Aoyama, Gosho
Case Closed Volume 1. Viz Media 2004 192p. Illustration
Grades: 9 10 11 12 Adult   **741.5; Fic**
1. Graphic novels; 2. Manga; 3. Mystery graphic novels; 4. Shonen manga
1-59116-327-7, $9.95

Precocious high school student Jimmy Kudo used his keen powers of observation and astute intuition to solve mysteries that have left law enforcement officials baffled. Hot on the trail of a suspect, Jimmy is accosted from behind and fed a strange chemical which physically transforms him into a first-grader. Taking on the pseudonym Conan Edogawa (from favorite mystery writers Arthur Conan Doyle and Edgar Allan Poe), he attempts to track down the people who did this to him. But until he finds a cure for his bizarre condition, Jimmy continues to help the police solve their toughest cases, and he lives with his best friend Rachel, who thinks he's Jimmy's cousin, and her private detective father (who gets credit for cracking all the cases). The murder cases are violent and there's a little sexual innuendo; despite Jimmy's little-kid appearance, the stories are not for younger readers.

Appignanesi, Richard
Hamlet. [Richard Appignanesi, text adaptor]; illustrated by Emma Vieceli. Harry N. Abrams/Amulet Books 2007 195p. (Manga Shakespeare)
Grades: 8 9 10 11 12 Adult   **822.3; 741.5**
1. Authors; 2. Dramatists; 3. Graphic novels; 4. Poets; 5. Shakespeare, William, 1564-1616; 6. Shakespeare, William, 1564-1616 — Adaptations
978-0-8109-9324-2, $9.95; 0-8109-9324-4

Shakespeare's classic play of murder and revenge is here adapted into a manga-style graphic novel. It's now set in 2107, after global climate change has devastated the Earth. Appignanesi uses the text of the play and abridges it to fit the pages, while Vieceli's art vigorously carries the story along. The book includes a summary of the plot and a brief biography of Shakespeare.
First published in the United Kingdom

A **midsummer** night's dream. illustrated by Kate Brown. Abrams 2008 207p. (Manga Shakespeare)
Grades: 7 8 9 10   **822.3; 741.5**
1. Authors; 2. Dramatists; 3. Graphic novels; 4. Poets; 5. Shakespeare, William — Adaptations
978-0-8109-9475-1, $9.95; 0-8109-9475-5

Shakespeare's comedy of romance, Faerie, and shenanigans in the forest is adapted into a manga-style graphic novel. Hermia is in love with Lysander, while Demetrius is in love with Hermia, and Helen loves Demetrius. When mischievous fairy Puck decides to have some fun with the powerful love potion he has fetched for Fairy King Oberon, chaos reigns. While the human foursome needs to sort itself out, Oberon seeks revenge against his wife, Queen Titania, by having Puck use the love potion on her so she falls in love with the first creature she sees — who happens to be a yokel to whom Puck gave a donkey's head. The text takes dialog from the original play. The book includes a plot summary and a brief biography of Shakespeare.

Romeo and Juliet. by William Shakespeare; adapted by Richard Appignanesi; illustrated by Sonia Leong. Amulet Books 2007 195p. (Manga Shakespeare)
Grades: 8 9 10 11 12   **822.3; 741.5**
1. Authors; 2. Dramatists; 3. Graphic novels; 4. Poets; 5. Shakespeare, William, 1564-1616 — Adaptations
978-0-8109-9325-9, $9.95; 0-8109-9325-2

LC 2006-100362

Shakespeare's classic play of star-crossed young lovers gets the manga treatment. The book is set in modern Tokyo with rival yakuza gangs and uses somewhat abridged text from the play for the dialogue.

"Although the richness of the language may be lost, the script keeps the spirit of the story intact, hitting all the major speeches." Booklist
First published in the United Kingdom

The **tempest**. illustrated by Paul Duffield; [adaptor, Richard Appignanesi]. Abrams 2008 207p. Illustration (Manga Shakespeare)
Grades: 7 8 9 10   **822.3; 741.5**
1. Authors; 2. Dramatists; 3. Graphic novels; 4. Poets; 5. Shakespeare, William, 1564-1616 — Adaptations
978-0-8109-9476-8, $9.95

Prospero and his daughter Miranda have lived on an isolated island for twelve years, after he had been deposed from his rule as Duke of Naples and cast out to sea to die. A powerful magician, Prospero has caused the survivors of a shipwreck to land on his island, in order to get his revenge, for these survivors are his enemies. Problems arise when Miranda falls in love with Ferdinand, the monster Caliban tries to use the survivors to kill Prospero, and Ariel the sprite is trying to set things right while still obeying Prospero. The book includes a plot summary and a brief biography of Shakespeare

"This adaptation would be useful both as an introduction to the play and as a companion piece for classroom study of it, using images to illuminate the Bard's eloquent poetry." SLJ

Appollo
★ **Bourbon** Island 1730. by Appollo & Lewis Trondheim; art by Lewis Trondheim; translated by Alexis Siegel. First Second Books 2008 278p. Illustration
Grades: 9 10 11 12 Adult   **741.5; Fic**
1. Adventure graphic novels; 2. Graphic novels; 3. Pirates — Graphic novels; 4. Slavery — Graphic novels
978-1-59643-258-1, $17.95; 1-59643-258-6

LC 2007-46138

On Bourbon Island off the coast of Madagascar, a French ornithologist and his assistant are caught up in an adventure involving slavery, colonialism, and the last days of the great pirates.

"This eccentric but illuminating historical drama...[is] a compelling, engrossing story of people considering whether their cause is worth more to them than their lives." Publ Wkly

Arai, Kiyoko

Beauty Pop, Vol. 1. story and art by Kiyoko Arai. Viz Media/Shojo Beat 2006 194p. Illustration

Grades: 7 8 9 10 11 12   741.5; Fic
1. Graphic novels; 2. Hair — Graphic novels; 3. Manga; 4. Shojo manga
978-1-4215-0575-6, $8.99

At Kiri Koshiba's high school, three popular upper classmen do occasional "Scissors Projects," working makeovers on specially selected girls. Narumi Shogo, who cuts hair, wants to become the best beautician in Japan and has won every youth competition — except one, years ago, that a younger girl won. When girls who aren't already pretty ask Narumi for a makeover, he tells them they're too ugly. Kiri helps two of the girls, working a stylist's magic that makes the girls glow; she's not interested in competition, even though her family owns a salon. Narumi wants to know who dares to be the upstart and challenge him, and he sets up the school's cultural festival to be a haircutting duel. Will Kiri even bother to compete?

Volume 1 of 10

Arai, Takahiro

Cirque du Freak, vol. 1. story, Darren Shan; manga, Takahiro Arai; [translation, Stephen Paul]. Yen Press 2009 un Illustration

Grades: 6 7 8 9 10   741.5; Fic
1. Authors; 2. Graphic novels; 3. Horror graphic novels; 4. Manga; 5. Novelists; 6. Vampires — Graphic novels; 7. Young adult authors; 8. Shan, Darren, 1972- — Adaptations; 9. Shonen manga
978-0-7595-3041-6, $10.99

Middle schoolers Darren and Steve hustle soccer games against older players for money; Steve obsesses over horror movies, while Darren has a huge fascination with spiders. When a mysterious stranger hands Darren a flyer advertising a Cirque du Freak, he and Steve decide they must attend. At the circus, they discover that the freaks in the show are true monsters, not the usual hokey hoaxes, and Darren loves the monstrous spider. Then Steve decides that Mr. Crepsley, the spider handler, is a vampire, and Steve wants more than anything to become a vampire. However, Mr. Crepsley rejects him after tasting his blood Steve is too bloodthirsty. Then Darren steals Madame Octa, the spider, only to lose control of her while she's out of her cage and she bites Steve. Crepsley comes for his pet and tells Darren he'll save Steve, but only if Darren will become his assistant and become a vampire. This book is the English translation of the original Japanese manga that is based on Shan's novel.

Volume 1 of 12

Arakawa, Hiromu

★ **Fullmetal** alchemist. by Hiromu Arakawa. Viz 2005 192 p. Illustration

Grades: 8 9 10 11 12   741.5
1. Alchemy — Fiction; 2. Brothers — Fiction; 3. Manga; 4. Shonen manga
1591169208; 9781591169208, $9.99

"Alchemy: the mystical power to alter the natural world.... When two brothers, Edward and Alphonse Elric, dabbled in this power to grant their dearest wish, one of them lost an arm and a leg...and the other became nothing but a soul locked into a body of living steel. Now Edward is an agent of the government, a slave of the military-alchemical complex, using his unique powers to obey orders." (Publisher's note)

Volume 1 of 27; Also available in VIZBIG omnibus editions

Silver spoon; Volume 1. Hiromu Arakawa; translation, Amanda Haley; lettering, Abigail Blackman. Yen Press 2018 192 p. Illustration

Grades: 7 8 9 10 11 12   741.5; Fic
1. Shonen manga; 2. Country life — Fiction; 3. Farm life — Fiction
0316416193; 9780316416191, $15

LC 2017959207

"Yuugo Hachiken chooses to leave the city and enroll at Ooezo Agricultural High School. Having always been at the top of his class, Yuugo assumes a rural school will be a breeze, but mucking out stables, gathering eggs, and chasing errant calves takes a lot out of him—and fills him with something he's never experienced before. Surrounded by endless fields and fresh air, Yuugo discovers a new connection to the land and to life." (Publisher's note)

"Arakawa (Fullmetal Alchemist) takes a personal touch in this fresh take on coming of age.... The simple, character-centered artwork is less arresting than in Arakawa's prior series, but it's bright and funny, littered with unexpected visual gags." Pub Wkly

Volume 1 of an ongoing series

Araki, Hirohiko

Jojo's Bizarre Adventure: Phantom Blood. Hirohiko Araki; [translation, Evan Galloway; touch-up art & lettering, Mark McMurray.]. Viz 2015 255 p. Illustration

Grades: 7 8 9 10 11 12   741.5; Fic
1. Seinen manga; 2. Shonen manga
1421578794; 9781421578798, $19.99

"Young Jonathan Joestar's life is forever changed when he meets his new adopted brother, Dio. For some reason, Dio has a smoldering grudge against him and derives pleasure from seeing him suffer. But every man has his limits, as Dio finds out. This is the beginning of a long and hateful relationship!" (Publisher's note)

"This 1980s manga classic is a cross between 'The Eye of Argon' and glam rock. Muscular bodies that rival Fist of the North Star, dapper fashion, occasional duo-tone, and bold yet intricate pen lines tell a Victorian tale of manhood, complete with an archeological artifact that demands blood sacrifice." Pub Wkly

Volume 1 of an ongoing series

Asami, Yuu

A.I. revolution volume 1. Go! Comi 2007 216p. Illustration

Grades: 10 11 12 Adult

741.5; Fic
1. Graphic novels; 2. Manga; 3. Robots — Graphic novels; 4. Science fiction graphic novels; 5. Shojo manga
978-1-933617-64-0, $10.99

Courtesy of Go! Comi

In the middle of the twenty-first century, household robots are everywhere. Teenage Sui's father runs MG Company, and he develops a very human-looking robot and wants Sui to "educate" it to act human. Naturally, Sui names the robot Vermillion. He has a special ability to communicate with computers without needing a physical connection, and it is this ability that makes Vermillion a target for the unscrupulous Dr. Sasaki. When Sui and Vermillion foil him, there's still trouble to come. Soon, another human-looking robot comes from another company; but this robot, whom Sui names Kira, has a secret mission and Vermillion is the target. The series includes some boy love elements, sexual innuendo, and mild violence.

Volume 1 of 14

Asamiya, Kia

Junk: Record of the Last Hero Vol. 1. author, Kia Asamyia; translator, Yoshihiro Watanabe. DrMaster Publications 2006 200p. Illustration
Grades: 10 11 12 Adult
741.5; Fic
    1. Graphic novels; 2. Manga; 3. Science fiction graphic novels; 4. Shonen manga
9781597961073, $9.95
    Volume 1 of 7

Courtesy of DrMaster Publications

    High school student Hiro hasn't gone back to school ever since a traumatic run-in with local bullies. Then he applies online for a new gadget, and when it arrives and he activates it, he finds himself encased within a powered armor JUNK suit. He starts going after the bullies in nightly rampages, but then he meets someone else with a JUNK suit who doesn't like the way Hiro is abusing his power. When he accidentally destroys his own home and kills his parents, he must learn to fend for himself and to choose to use his power for good or for evil. The legendary manga-ka (manga creator) Kia Asamiya has written this manga, which includes considerable violence.

Ashby, Ruth

    The **great** American documents: Volume 1, 1620-1830. Ruth Ashby; illustrated by Ernie Colón; editorial consultant Russell Motter. Hill and Wang 2014 160 p. Color illustration
Grades: 9 10 11 12 Adult
973; 741.5
    1. United States — Politics and government — Sources; 2. United States — History — Sources
0809094606; 9780809094608, $40

LC 2013956401
    Written by Ruth Ashby and illustrated by Ernie Colón, "'The Great American Documents: Volume 1' introduces as series narrator none other than Uncle Sam, who walks us through twenty essential documents. Each document gets a chapter, in which Uncle Sam explains its key passages, its origins, how it came to be written, and its impact. This graphic primer is an indispensable resource for students and anyone else who wants the facts of American history close at hand." (Publisher's note)
    "Colon uses well-designed, full-color panel layouts to eloquently blend charts and other informative graphics with straightforward images of events, clothing, and customs as well as clear, concise metaphors, all with an eye toward promoting a solid understanding of the basic facts and their impact." Booklist
    Includes bibliographical references

Askwith, Mark

    Silencers. Image Comics 2007 un Illustration
Grades: 11 12 Adult
741.5; Fic
    1. Graphic novels; 2. Spies — Graphic novels
978-1-58240-728-9, $14.99
    Silencers is a compelling look at spies coming to terms with the changing face of espionage in the new world order. When the newest recruit to the Silencers is murdered, his death triggers a mission of betrayal and revenge. Violence and strong language figure in this story that invokes the themes of John LeCarre's books.

Atangan, Patrick

    Songs of our ancestors: The yellow jar: two tales from Japanese tradition. NBM 2003 48p. Illustration (Songs of our ancestors)
Grades: 5 6 7 8 9 10 11 12
741.5
    1. Folklore — Japan — Graphic novels; 2. Graphic novels

1-56163-331-3, $12.92

LC 2002-32132
    "To render two magical Japanese legends, one about a fisherman who discovers a fair maiden in a big pot, the other about a monk whose fastidiously kept garden is invaded by two chrysanthemums, Atangan charmingly adopts the sharp outlines, boldly juxtaposed color fields, and striking compositions of eighteenth-century Japanese woodblock prints." Booklist
    Other titles in this series are: Silk tapestry and other Chinese folktales (2004); Tree of love (2005)

Auster, Paul

    Paul Auster's City of Glass. Paul Auster; script adaptation, Paul Karasik and David Mazzucchelli; art, David Mazzucchelli. Avon Bks. 1994 129p. Illustration
Grades: 9 10 11 12 Adult
741; 741.5
    1. Private investigators — Fiction; 2. Auster, Paul — Adaptations
0-380-77108-X; 9780380771080, $12

LC 93-91005
    "Auster's acclaimed novel City of Glass, a dreamlike meditation on language and fiction in the form of a detective novel, has been translated into comics form to stunning effect.... This combination story, lecture and literary deconstruction begins when New York City detective novelist Daniel Quinn answers a wrong number. Donning the personas of both the detective he created and his own creator, Auster himself, Quinn attempts to protect a young man, who as a child was kept without light or language for nine years as his lunatic academic father tried to discover 'God's Language.'" (Publishers Weekly)

Azuma, Kiyohiko

    ★ **Azumanga** Daioh omnibus. translation, Stephen Paul. Yen Press 2009 675p. Illustration
Grades: 8 9 10 11 12
741.5; Fic
    1. Graphic novels; 2. High school students — Graphic novels; 3. Humorous graphic novels; 4. Manga; 5. School stories — Graphic novels; 6. Shonen manga
978-0-316-07738-5, $24.99
    An omnibus edition of a humorous four-volume manga series featuring a Japanese suburban high school class with a ditzy teacher. The adult teachers go drinking occasionally, and there's one male teacher who ogles the girls in their P.E. uniforms.
    First published 2001 in Japan

Azzarello, Brian

    Doctor 13: architecture & mortality. DC Comics 2007 un Illustration
Grades: 9 10 11 12 Adult
741.5
    1. Graphic novels; 2. Humorous graphic novels; 3. Superhero graphic novels
978-1-4012-1552-1, $14.99
    Doctor 13, the world's greatest skeptic, sets out with his daughter Tracy to investigate strange doings in the French Alps. The two encounter in short order a vampire, a pirate with a flying ship, a caveman who had been frozen in ice, a mysterious boy who can answer any question for the price of a dime, a talking Nazi gorilla, a cosmic heroine with a constant runny nose, and the ghost of a Confederate general taking time off from haunting a US Army tank. Doctor 13 doesn't believe in any of them, but he works with them when they have to go up against the Architects, the shapers of the universe. The Architects have decided that Doctor 13 and his team of misfits don't belong in the world, and they beg to differ. The book includes some violence.

    Lex Luthor: Man of Steel. DC Comics 2005 Illustration
Grades: 10 11 12 Adult
741.5; Fic

1. Graphic novels; 2. Lex Luthor (Fictional character); 3. Superhero graphic novels; 4. Superman (Fictional character)
1-4012-0454-6, $12.99

Superman has been called many things since becoming a superhero, from the defender of Truth, Justice and the American Way to the Big Blue Boy Scout. Lex Luthor calls him a dangerous threat to all humanity. This book is narrated by Luthor, so the reader sees Superman from his point of view; and to Luthor, Superman is an alien being who can't be trusted. Therefore, Luthor tries to create a superhero of his own, in the form of a beautiful young woman, named Hope. The book includes some violence and sexual situations.

Superman: For Tomorrow Volume One. writer, Brian Azzarello; Penciller, Jim Lee; inker, Scott Williams; colorist, Alex Sinclair; created by Jerry Siegel & Joe Shuster. DC Comics 2005 un Illustration
Grades: 10 11 12 Adult   741.5; Fic
1. Graphic novels; 2. Superhero graphic novels; 3. Superman (Fictional character)
1-4012-0352-3, $14.99

A cataclysmic event has struck the Earth. Millions of people have vanished without a trace. No one is left unaffected — not even Superman. A year has passed, and Superman is left with many questions and very few answers. For a hero who tries to have all the answers, it's torture. And, just as the action heats up and the stakes are raised, one huge question emerges: just how far is Superman willing to go "For Tomorrow"?

Volume 1 of 2

Wonder Woman; Volume 1: Blood. Brian Azzarello, Cliff Chiang, Tony Akins. DC Comics 2012 160 p.
Grades: 11 12 Adult   741.5
1. Superhero comic books, strips, etc.; 2. Greek mythology — Fiction; 3. Wonder Woman (Fictional character)
1401235638; 9781401235635, $22.99
                                        LC 2011051798

In this comic book, author Brian Azzarello "gives Diana (Wonder Woman) a new origin, not as a baby her mother, Hippolyta, molded out of clay but as the illegitimate daughter of Zeus. As such, she's a target for the jealous rage of Hera, Zeus' wife, but she finds a new role as protector of a waifish young woman who's currently carrying Zeus' baby. The king of the gods, meanwhile, has vanished." (Publishers Weekly)

Originally published in single magazine form in WONDER WOMAN 1-6 — T.p. verso.; Other Wonder Woman volumes by Azzarello and Chiang are: 2: Guts; 3: Iron; 4: War

B., David
★ **Epileptic.** Pantheon Books 2005 361p. Illustration
Grades: 11 12 Adult   741.5; 616.8
1. Autobiographical graphic novels; 2. Epilepsy — Graphic novels; 3. Graphic novels
0-375-42318-4, $25; 0-375-71468-5 (pa), $18.95; 9780375423185
                                        LC 2004-53419

"Growing up in the 1960s and 1970s in France's Loire Valley, Jean-Christophe developed grand mal epilepsy around the age of 11. Pierre-Francois, nine, observes his brother's battle with the physical and social implications of the disease; their parents' efforts to find management of it through medical, macrobiotic, and even psychic interventions; and the author's own development in this milieu as a boy obsessed with history and warfare and as a dedicated artist." SLJ

The author's "artwork is magnificent — gorgeously bold, impressionistic representations of the world not as it is but as he's taught himself to perceive it.... B.'s illustrations constantly underscore his writing's wrenching psychological depth; readers can literally see how the chaos of his childhood shaped his vision and mind." Publ Wkly

Original French edition, 2002

Backderf, Derf
Trashed: a graphic novel. by Derf Backderf. Abrams ComicArts 2015 256 p. Illustration
Grades: 10 11 12 Adult   741.5
1. Refuse and refuse disposal — Fiction; 2. Sanitation workers — Fiction
9781419714535, $24.95; 9781419714542
                                        LC 2015011115

Ignatz Award: Outstanding Graphic Novel (2016)

This graphic novel, by Derf Backderf, "is an ode to the crap job of all crap jobs — garbage collector.... [It] follows the raucous escapades of three 20-something friends as they clean the streets of pile after pile of stinking garbage, while battling annoying small-town bureaucrats, bizarre townfolk, sweltering summer heat, and frigid winter storms." (Publisher's note)

"The blocky grotesquerie of Backderf's art is well-suited to the material, and the episodic, slackerish narrative is spiked here and there by brief lessons on the history of the garbage truck, the ecology of the landfill, and an answer to the question of whether rich or poor neighborhoods generate the most trash (hint: it's not the poor). A downbeat but entertaining ode to the odiferous realities of getting by." Pub Wkly

Includes bibliographical references

Bagge, Peter
Apocalypse nerd. Dark Horse Comics 2008 120p. Illustration
Grades: 11 12 Adult   741.5; Fic
1. Adventure graphic novels; 2. End of the world — Graphic novels; 3. Graphic novels
978-1-59307-9024, $13.95

Software engineer Perry and his friend Gordo are just two average suburban guys (okay, maybe not Gordo, since he deals drugs) who have gone on a camping trip in the North Cascade Mountains near Seattle; but on their way up, North Korea nukes Seattle, and the two friends must find a way to survive in the mountain. They become looters, deal with others out to survive any way possible, and do things they never dreamed they would do — including killing others. The book includes lots of harsh language (including s-bombs and f-bombs), partial nudity, and violence.

Bagieu, Pénélope
★ **Brazen:** rebel ladies who rocked the world. Pénélope Bagieu. First Second 2018 304 p. Color; Illustration
Grades: 8 9 10 11 12 Adult   920; 741.5
1. Women — Biography; 2. Biography
9781626728684; 9781626728691, $17.99
                                        LC 2017941160

"With her characteristic wit and dazzling drawings, celebrated graphic novelist Pénélope Bagieu profiles the lives of...feisty female role models, some world famous, some little known. From Nellie Bly to Mae Jemison or Josephine Baker to Naziq al-Abid, the stories in this comic biography are sure to inspire the next generation of rebel ladies." (Publisher's note)

"Both art and text are clever, smart, and distilled for maximum impact. The women are not idealized, nor are their flaws ignored. Instead, they are treated with wit and empathy.... A fresh and joyous look at women's history that is sure to delight even the most jaded readers." LJ

Originally published in French by Gallimard in 2016 as Culottées: Des femmes qui ne font que ce qu?elles veulent, tome I and in 2017 as Culottées: Des femmes qui ne font que ce qu?elles veulent, tome II

Baillie, Liz
My brain hurts volume one. Microcosm Publishing 2008 un Illustration
Grades: 11 12 Adult   741.5; Fic

Courtesy of Microcosm Publishing

1. Friendship — Graphic novels; 2. Graphic novels; 3. Homosexuality — Graphic novels
978-1-934620-03-8, $6

Best friends Kate and Joey are gay and trying to find some happiness with their relationships. They're also thirteen years old, love punk music, dress punk, and get into all kinds of trouble. Joey's father is in denial, Kate doesn't know how to tell her mother. Then one night, a gang of skinheads beat Joey around the head with a chain; he collapses during an interview at a Catholic school and goes into a coma. Meanwhile, one of the skinheads keeps trying to get Kate to go with him; and Kate joins a gay student club at school. The book shows kissing but no other sexual activity, there's no nudity, but there's a lot of strong language, especially the f-bomb.

Volume 1 of 2

Baker, Kyle

★ **How** to draw stupid and other essentials of cartooning. Watson-Guptill 2008 110p. Illustration

Grades: 8 9 10 11 12 Adult   **741.5**

1. Cartooning — Technique; 2. Graphic novels — Drawing
978-0-8230-0143-9, $16.95

         LC 2008-922161

"Baker, an award-winning cartoonist and graphic-novel illustrator, gives aspiring cartoonists irreverent advice about how to succeed in their chosen field. He offers instruction in basic drawing techniques such as choosing the right tools and discusses the importance of learning to draw shapes, exaggerating, and using references. But the author's most inspiring advice focuses on how to succeed as a cartoonist." SLJ

King David. DC Comics/Vertigo 2002 104p. Illustration

Grades: 9 10 11 12 Adult   **741.5; 221**

1. Bible. O.T. — Adaptations; 2. Graphic novels
978-1-56389-866-2, $19.95

Baker retells the Old Testament story of David, the shepherd boy who slew the giant Goliath and later became the King of Israel, after years of dodging King Saul's attempts to kill him. Using a hip, freewheeling style full of irreverent humor, Baker also renders the battles as the bloody messes they were.

Nat Turner. Abrams 2008 207p. Illustration

Grades: 10 11 12 Adult   **741.5; 92**

1. Biographical graphic novels; 2. Graphic novels; 3. Revolutionaries; 4. Slavery — Graphic novels; 5. Slaves; 6. Turner, Nat, 1800?-1831; 7. Turner, Nat, 1800?-1831 — Graphic novels
978-0-8109-9535-2; 0-8109-9535-2, $14.95

         LC 2008-6911

This book "follows the dark legacy of the Virginia slave rebellion and subsequent murders of at least 55 white slave owners and their families in 1831.... Turner is presented as a fiercely intelligent, angry, yet steadfast individual whose potential was dashed in an era of hate and inhumanity. Those characteristics are mirrored in the actions of the slaves' rebellion, in illustrations that are not for the faint of heart or the weak of stomach. The ideas brought forth here are sure to ignite debate and discussion." SLJ

Includes bibliographical references; Originally published 2006 in four volumes; Volume 1 of 2

Plastic Man: On the Lam!. DC Comics 2004 un Illustration

Grades: 6 7 8 9 10 11 12 Adult   **741.5; Fic**

1. Graphic novels; 2. Humorous graphic novels; 3. Plastic Man (Fictional character); 4. Superhero graphic novels

1-4012-0343-4, $14.95
2005 Eisner Award for Best Publication for a Younger Audience, also 2005 Eisner Award for Best Writer/Artists-Humor for Kyle Baker

Plastic Man has worked as a superhero, but he used to be the criminal Eel O'Brian, a fact he has hidden from the FBI. Now there's a murder, and Eel O'Brian is the main (and only) suspect. When the FBI learns of his old identity, Plastic Man goes on the lam to clear himself.

Originally published as Plastic Man issues #1-6; this volume is bound in plastic; Volume 1 of 2

Through the looking-glass. by Lewis Carroll; adapted by Kyle Baker. Papercutz 2008 un Illustration (Classics illustrated)

Grades: 3 4 5 6 7 8 9

741.5; Fic

1. Fantasy graphic novels; 2. Graphic novels; 3. Carroll, Lewis, 1832-1898 — Adaptations
978-1-59707-115-4, $9.95;
1-59707-115-3

Courtesy of NBM Publishing

This is Carroll's sequel to Alice's Adventures in Wonderland. This time, Alice climbs through the looking-glass in her house and finds herself in a land with talking flowers and insects, Tweedledee and Tweedledum (who recite "The Walrus and the Carpenter"), the White Queen who needs help pinning her shawl straight, Humpty Dumpty, the Red Queen, and more. The Eisner Award-winning Baker uses a different style from his usual cartoony look here, more reminiscent of Tenniel's classic illustrations of Carroll's books.

Balak

Last man; 1: The stranger. Bastien Vivés, Michaël Sanlaville, Balak; English translation by Alexis Siegel. First Second 2015 207 p. Illustration

Grades: 9 10 11 12   **741.5; Fic**

1. Martial arts — Comic books, strips, etc; 2. Magic — Fiction
1626720460; 9781626720466, $9.99

         LC 2014045696

In this book, "Adrian has been preparing for the annual Games for years, and he's crushed when his assigned partner manages to get sick right before the event. Richard Aldana arrives late at the Games, and he's...clearly from another world.... Aldana is also seeking a partner in order to compete, and thus magically trained boy Adrian and brutish man Aldana team up and eventually become friends." (Bulletin of the Center for Children's Books)

"Recommend to graphic novel fans looking for something new-they will not be disappointed." SLJ

Originally published: Tournai, Belgium : Casterman, 2013.; Other volumes in this series are: 2, The royal cup; 3, The chase; 4, The show; 5, The order; 6, The rescue

Balce, Nicc

Random Encounter Volume 1. Viper Comics 2006 un Illustration

Grades: 9 10 11 12 Adult   **741.5; Fic**

1. Adventure graphic novels; 2. Graphic novels; 3. Science fiction graphic novels
0-9754193-8-2, $9.95

Strange things are afoot at the...Kwik Mart. With their eerie tromp through the latest Silent Kill game interrupted by a strange sound, Migo, Mica, and Mona begin a journey into the perplexing and uncharted. The discovery of a dead girl in a pool of blood on the roof of Migo's parents' Kwik Mart sends the kids' lives into a maelstrom of confusion, freakish aliens, precipitous resurrection, and enigmatic secrets. It's a wild ride into the unimaginable and astonishing, a...random encounter. There are lots of fighting scenes and some monsters.

Baltazar, Art

Patrick the Wolf Boy Volume 1. written by Art Baltazar & Franco Aureliani; drawn by Art Baltazar. Devil's Due Publishing 2004 un Illustration

Grades: 2 3 4 5 6 7 8 9 10 11 12 Adult   **741.5; Fic**
   1. Graphic novels; 2. Humorous graphic novels
   1-932796-27-4, $10.95

   Patrick looks at first glance like the other kids in school, but he's a werewolf. A cute werewolf. He resembles Eddie Munster (from the 1960s television comedy series "The Munsters"), and he doesn't speak, although he growls a lot and sometimes howls. He gives his teacher an apple — but with a skull biting the apple. When he goes fishing with his dad, he prefers to scare the bear into giving him his catch. He loves to play tag with the neighborhood squirrel. And when Valentine's Day comes, he makes sure that his babysitter likes him better. His utterly normal parents adore him and understand his growls; so does Neve, his classmate at school.

   Volume 1 of 4

Barker, Clive

   The **Thief** of Always. IDW Publishing 2005 144p. Illustration
Grades: 4 5 6 7 8 9 10
741.5; Fic
   1. Fantasy graphic novels; 2. Graphic novels; 3. Horror graphic novels
   1-933239-17-4, $35.00; 1-933239-38-7 (pa), $19.99

   Clive Barker's fable for younger readers is adapted here into graphic novel format. Mr. Hood's Holiday House has stood for a thousand years, welcoming countless children to enjoy a blissful round of treats and holidays...for a price. Then bored young Harvey Swick comes, and he notices disquieting little details that make him realize the place is more of a trap. Things are spooky but not terrifying, with little violence.

   Originally published as The Thief of Always issues #1-3.

Courtesy of IDW Publishing

Barry, Lynda

   The **greatest** of Marlys!. Lynda Barry. Drawn & Quarterly 2016 248 p. Illustration
Grades: 10 11 12 Adult   **741.5; Fic**
   1. Humorous graphic novels; 2. Girls
   1770462643; 9781770462649, $22.95

   In this graphic novel by Lynda Barry, "eight-year-old Marlys Mullen...shines in all her freckled and pig-tailed groovy glory. The trailer park where she and her family live is the grand stage for her dramas big and small. Joining Marlys are her teenaged sister Maybonne, her younger brother Freddie, their mother, and an offbeat array of family members, neighbors, and classmates. Marlys's enthusiasm for life knows no bounds." (Publisher's note)

   "Marlys is bizarre but lovable, and Barry does an excellent job of entertaining readers with her exploits through captivating dialog, varying points of view, and drawings that depict a child's world." LJ

   One hundred demons. Sasquatch Bks. 2002 216p. Illustration
Grades: 10 11 12 Adult   **741.5**
   1. Autobiographical graphic novels; 2. Graphic novels
   1-57061-337-0; 1-57061-459-8 (pa), $17.95

                LC 2002-21657

"Whether she's talking about head lice, old boyfriends, or hippies who 'forgot' to pay her wages, Barry playfully explores, in 'autobifictionalographical' text and art, those demons common to teens — and to us all." Booklist

   ★ **Picture** this: the near-sighted monkey book. with guest watercolorist Kevin Kawula. Drawn and Quarterly 2010 224 p. Color illustration
Grades: 9 10 11 12 Adult   **741.5**
   1. American wit and humor, Pictorial; 2. Graphic novels; 3. Humorous graphic novels
   1897299648; 9781897299647, $29.95

                LC 2010399443

   In author Lynda Barry's book, she "asks 'Why do we stop drawing?' and 'Why do we start?' It features the return of" the character "Marlys, and introduces a new one, the Nearsighted Monkey." The book is a "graphic-memoir-how-to" and a "take home extension of Barry's traveling" writing workshop which focuses on literature illustration. (Publisher's note)

   ★ **What** it is. Drawn & Quarterly 2008 209p. Illustration
Grades: 7 8 9 10 11 12 Adult   **818; 741.5**
   1. Authorship — Graphic novels; 2. Creative writing — Graphic novels
   978-1-897299-35-7, $24.95; 1-897299-35-4

               LC c2007-9047319

   Independent cartoonist Lynda Barry presents an unconventional book that encourages its readers to write by using her colorful art and asking questions such as "How are monsters different? And how are they the same?" "Can/Do images exist without thinking?" "What is the difference between lying and pretending?" Each question appears with illustrated writing prompts and Barry's own ruminations on the topics. It's a workbook of sorts, but it also exists as a book to be read for itself.

   "Every so often a book comes along that surpasses expectations, taking readers on an inspirational voyage that they don't want to leave. This is one such book." SLJ

Beazley, Mark D.

   Pet avengers classic. Marvel Entertainment 2009 208p. Illustration
Grades: 7 8 9 10 11 12 Adult   **741.5; Fic**
   1. Adventure graphic novels; 2. Graphic novels; 3. Pets — Graphic novels; 4. Superhero graphic novels
   9780785139669, $24.99

   This volume collects the various Marvel Pets stories, from 1960 to 2007, with each story featuring a different pet, from Lockjaw the teleporting dog to Kitty Pryde's dragon Lockheed to Brightwind the winged horse, and many more. Lockjaw, Lockheed, Redwing the falcon, the cat named Niels, and Zabu the saber tooth tiger all starred in th 2009 mini series titled Pet Avengers. Some of the stories in this collection include violence.

   Spider-Man: The Birth of Venom. Marvel Entertainment 2007 un Illustration
Grades: 8 9 10 11 12 Adult   **741.5; Fic**
   1. Graphic novels; 2. Spider-Man (Fictional character); 3. Superhero graphic novels; 4. Fantastic Four (Fictional characters)
   978-0-7851-2498-6, $29.99

   The Beyonder's Battleworld might seem a strange place to get new threads, but it's Spider-Man who becomes unraveled when his new symbiotic, shape-changing costume attempts to darken his life as well as his fashion sense. But ridding himself of his black costume proves an even greater mistake when its alien enmity bonds with mortal madness to form our hero's most dedicated enemy, Venom. Other stories include the first appearances of Puma and the Rose, Mary Jane Watson's startling secret, and the debut of the battling...Bag-Man? The Black Cat, the Fantastic Four and other Marvel characters appear.

Bechdel, Alison

★ **Fun** home: a family tragicomic. Houghton Mifflin 2006 232p. Illustration
Grades: 11 12 Adult   **741.5; 92**
1. Artists; 2. Authors; 3. Autobiographical graphic novels; 4. Biography, Individual; 5. Cartoonists; 6. Comic book writers; 7. Essayists; 8. Graphic novels; 9. Novelists; 10. Bechdel, Alison, 1960-
0-618-47794-2, $19.95; 978-0-618-47794-4

LC 2005-30304

This is a memoir in graphic novel format about the author's "childhood, her father's death and their shared homosexuality.... The death was deemed an accident-a truck hit [Mr. Bechdel] as he crossed a road with an armful of garden brush-but Ms. Bechdel suspects suicide." (N Y Times (Late N Y Ed))

This "is one of the very best graphic novels ever." Booklist

Beechen, Adam

Hench. AiT/Planet Lar 2004 un Illustration
Grades: 10 11 12 Adult
741.5; Fic
1. Graphic novels; 2. Superhero graphic novels
1-932051-17-1, $12.95

The fine line between hero and villain is just another of longtime super-villain henchman Mike Fulton's many scars. Now, faced with a terrible choice that could mean life and death for heroes, villains, his family, and himself, Mike ponders just how his normal life went so crazy. There's a little violence but mostly fighting action, and a little bit of strong language.

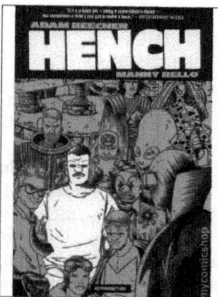
Courtesy of AiT/Planet Lar

Justice League Unlimited Vol. 1: United They Stand. written by Adam Beechen; illustrated by Carlo Barbieri, Ethen Beavers, Walden Wong; colored by Heroic Age; lettered by Phil Balsman, Pat Brosseau, Nick J. Napolitano. DC Comics 2005 104p. Illustration
Grades: 4 5 6 7 8 9   **741.5; Fic**
1. Graphic novels; 2. Justice League (Fictional characters); 3. Superhero graphic novels; 4. Justice League (Fictional characters)
1401205127; 9781401205126, $6.99

Leaping straight out of their Cartoon Network show, the Worlds Greatest Heroes have their own comics series. This inaugural collection features these tales: Divide Conquer, Poker Face, Small Time, Local Hero and Monitor Duty.

Volume 1 of 5

Robin: Wanted. Adam Beechen, writer; Freddie Williams II, artist; Karl Kerschl with Wayne Faucher & Prentis Rollins, artists, pages 6-27; Guy major, Nathan Eyring, colorists; Jared K. Fletcher, Travis Lanham, Phil Balsman, letterers. DC Comics 2007 144p. Illustration
Grades: 9 10 11 12 Adult   **741.5; Fic**
1. Graphic novels; 2. Mystery graphic novels; 3. Robin (Fictional character); 4. Superhero graphic novels; 5. Batgirl (Fictional character)
978-1-4012-1225-4, $12.99

Batgirl — Cassandra Cain — is dead...and the evidence shows that Robin is the killer. Every cop in Gotham City is looking for him now, so he has to find the real killer and clear his name. Someone keeps sending Robin clues that only he can find, and they seem to be leading to a shadowy player

who is making a grab for power in the deadly League of Assassins. Solving this mystery will lead Robin to a confrontation with the new leader of the League of Assassins...and the killer's identity will change Robin's world forever. This book has lots of fighting action.

Beland, Tom

★ **True** story swear to God archives, vol. 1. Image Comics 2008 528p. Illustration
Grades: 10 11 12 Adult   **92; 741.5**
1. Autobiographical graphic novels; 2. Cartoonists; 3. Graphic novels; 4. Romance graphic novels; 5. Beland, Tom, 1962-
978-1-58240-881-1, $19.99

They met at a bus stop at Disneyworld, by chance: he was a cartoonist from Napa, California, and she was a radio personality from Puerto Rico. Their chance meeting blossomed into a romance that survived a long-distance separation, a Category 5 hurricane, his leaving home to move to a new world. Tom Beland writes candidly about the ups and downs of his relationship with Lily, with his family, and all the slings and arrows of life one has to deal with daily. He originally self-published these comics, and they were collected in several trade paperbacks from AiT/PlanetLar. The book includes occasional harsh language (including s-bombs and f-bombs), sexual situations, and frank talk about sex.

Bell, Blake

★ **Strange** & stranger: the world of Steve Ditko. Fantagraphics Books 2008 220p. Illustration
Grades: 10 11 12 Adult   **92; 741.5**
1. Comic books, strips, etc. — History and criticism; 2. Graphic designers; 3. Ditko, Steve; 4. Graphic novels; 5. Spider-Man (Fictional character)
978-1-56097-921-0, $39.99

Steve Ditko may be best known as the cocreator and first artist for Marvel's Spider-Man comics, but he has done much more. Bell tells Ditko's life story and covers his career which has spanned more than 50 years. He also gives Ditko's side of the story in explaining his split with Stan Lee and why he walked away from Spider-Man back in 1966. Ditko's work has been strongly influenced by author/philosopher Ayn Rand, and her Objectivist philosophy has informed his work. The book includes lots of Ditko's art, including many unpublished pieces. Bell doesn't romanticize Ditko, but provides ample reason for the artist's place in comic book history.

Bellstorf, Arne

Baby's in black: Astrid Kirchherr, Stuart Sutcliffe, and the Beatles. Arne Bellstorf. First Second 2012 196 p. Illustration
Grades: 10 11 12 Adult   **782.421; 782.42166092/2**
1. Beatles — Comic books, strips, etc; 2. Rock musicians — England — Comic books, strips, etc; 3. Graphic novels; 4. Romance fiction; 5. Sutcliffe, Stuart, 1940-1962; 6. Kirchherr, Astrid
1596437715; 9781596437715, $24.99

LC 2011049680

This graphic novel tells the love story of "Stuart Sutcliffe, one of the original Beatles," and "German photographer Astrid Kirchherr." The "story offers insight into the time the Beatles spent performing together in Germany before they made it big." Despite the couple's "different languages and worlds, the pair fall into a happy, and seemingly easy, romance. But their happiness is short-lived: the Beatles are being forced to leave the country, and Stuart's health is failing." (Publishers Weekly)

Translated from the German by Michael Waaler.

Bendis, Brian Michael

Jinx: The Definitive Collection. Image Comics 2001 480p. Illustration

Grades: 11 12 Adult   **741.5; Fic**

1. Graphic novels; 2. Mystery graphic novels

978-1-58240-179-9, $24.95

This is a graphic crime noir novel about a bounty hunter, two grifters, and a treasure hunt that propels the character driven story. This extra large edition carries with it the entire epic story, behind the scenes/making of, script excerpts, and an art gallery. The story includes harsh language, nudity, sexual situations, and violence.

Miles Morales; Volume 1: the ultimate Spider-Man : revival. Brian Michael Bendis; illustrated by Dave Marquez, Mark Bagley, Mark Brook, Stuart Immonen, and David Laufente. Marvel Enterprises 2014 144 p. Color; Illustration

Grades: 9 10 11 12   **741.5**

1. Superhero graphic novels; 2. Spider-Man (Fictional character)

0785154175; 9780785154174, $17.99

This Spider-Man comic book was written by Brian Michael Bendis and illustrated by David Marquez. "Here we find Miles back in the red and black and still fighting in the long shadow of the late Peter Parker. Little does Miles know that lurking in that shadow is Norman Osborn and...Peter Parker? On the anniversary of Peter's death, is he really alive and well?" (Booklist)

Contains material originally published in single magazine form as Ultimate Spider-Man #200 and Miles Morales: ultimate Spider-Man #1-5; Volume 1 of 2

★ **Powers:** The Definitive Hardcover Collection Vol. 1. created and produced by Brian Michael Bendis and Mike Avon Oeming; colored by Pat Garrahy with Brian Michael Bendis; lettered by Pat Garrahy with Brian Michael Bendis. Marvel Comics 2006 456p. Illustration

Grades: 11 12 Adult   **741.5; Fic**

1. Graphic novels; 2. Mystery graphic novels; 3. Superhero graphic novels

978-0-7851-1805-3, $29.99

Homicide detectives Christian Walker and Deena Pilgrim investigate homicides in a city where super-powered heroes and villains live, fight, and die. Sometimes the heroes are just as flawed as the villains. And Walker has a secret of his own that gives him special insight in his investigations. The first three storylines have been remastered, reformatted, and collected in this edition which is replete with violence, harsh language, nudity, and sexual situations.

Also available in 16 paperback volumes; Volume 1 of 6

The **Pulse** Vol. 1: Thin Air. Marvel Entertainment 2004 un Illustration

Grades: 10 11 12 Adult   **741.5; Fic**

1. Graphic novels; 2. Superhero graphic novels

0-7851-1332-0, $13.99

Former super hero and current private investigator Jessica Jones has just been offered a new job: a position with the Bugle's new super-hero section, The Pulse. Jessica's first assignment: to uncover the true identity of a former Bugle reporter's super-powered murderer. How is millionaire industrialist Norman Osborn involved in the case? And how will Jessica's discovery affect the entire Marvel Universe? The book includes some violence and strong language.

Spider-Man; Volume 1: Miles Morales. Brian Michael Bendis, writer; Sarah Pichelli, artist; Gaetano Carlucci, inking assist; Justin Ponsor, colorist; VC's Cory Petit, letterer. Marvel Enterprises 2016 112 p. Color; Illustration (Spider-Man (2016))

Grades: 8 9 10 11 12 Adult   **741.5; Fic**

0785199616; 9780785199618, $15.99

"Miles Morales is hitting the big time! Not only is he joining the Marvel Universe, but he's also a card-carrying Avenger, rubbing shoulders with the likes of Iron Man, Thor and Captain America! But how have Miles' first eight months been, coming to grips with an All-new, All-Different New York? One thing is the same — nonstop action!" (Publisher's note)

Volume 1 of an ongoing series

Ultimate Fantastic Four Vol. 1: The Fantastic. writers, Brian Michael Bendis & Mark Millar; pencils, Adam Kubert; inks, Danny Miki and John Dell; colors, Dave Stewart; letters, Chris Eliopoulos. Marvel Entertainment 2005 un Illustration

Grades: 8 9 10 11 12 Adult   **741.5; Fic**

1. Fantastic Four (Fictional characters); 2. Graphic novels; 3. Superhero graphic novels

978-0-7851-1393-5, $12.99

The Ultimate treatment takes the Fantastic Four back to the beginning. High school genius (and bully magnet) Reed Richards suffers at school and also at home with a father who doesn't like his "troublemaking" experiments. When Reed enrolls at a secret government-sponsored school for the most gifted minds in the world, he unwittingly embarks on the journey of a lifetime. This is a story about science, adventure, and above all else, family.

Volume 1 of 15

Ultimate Spider-Man: Power & Responsibility. by Brian Michael Bendis (Author), Mark Bagley (Illustrator). Marvel 2009 200 p. Color illustration

Grades: 7 8 9 10 11 12 Adult   **741.5**

1. Spider-Man (Fictional character)

0785139400; 9780785139409, $19.99

In this comic book, by Brian Michael Bendis, illustrated by Mark Bagley, "Peter Parker gains super-powers after being bitten by a spider, loses his likable Uncle Ben to violent crime, and learns once again that 'with great power comes great responsibility.'" (Publisher's note)

Collected edition originally published 2001; Volume 1 of 21

Benjamin, Ryan

Star Wars: Empire Volume One: Betrayal. written by Scott Allie, pencilled by Ryan Benjamin, inked by Curtis Arnold. Dark Horse Comics 2003 un Illustration

Grades: 7 8 9 10 11 12 Adult   **741.5; Fic**

1. Adventure graphic novels; 2. Graphic novels; 3. Science fiction graphic novels; 4. Star Wars — Graphic novels

1-56971-964-0, $12.95

In the weeks before the events in Star Wars: A New Hope, as the Death Star is readied for its fateful first mission, a power-hungry cabal of Grand Moffs and Imperial Officers embark on a dangerous plan to kill Emperor Palpatine and Darth Vader and seize control of the Empire. When word that a Jedi has made an appearance on a backwater world lures Vader away from his master, the cabal makes its move. But even the galaxy isn't enough of a prize to sate the ambitions of some of the conspirators, and before long the would-be assassins are turning on one another. Their plans are further complicated by the actions of bounty hunter Boba Fett. And, of course, they may have fatally underestimated the cunning of their primary target: Emperor Palpatine.

Volume 1 of 7

Bennett, Joe

Nightwing: the lost year. Marv Wolfman, Marc Andreyko, writers; Jamal Igle, Jon Bosco, Joe Bennett, pencillers; Keith Champagne, Alex Silva, Jack Jadson, inkers; Jason Wright, Edgar Delgado, colorists; Phil

Balsman, Jared K. Fletcher, Travis Lanham, letterers. DC Comics 2008 un Illustration

Grades: 10 11 12 Adult   **741.5; Fic**
  1. Adventure graphic novels; 2. Graphic novels; 3. Nightwing (Fictional character); 4. Superhero graphic novels
978-1-4012-1671-9, $14.99

  Nightwing interrupts a kidnapping attempt only to realize the victim is someone from his past, Liu, his first lover. She says she works for Eddie Hwang, who used to be Metal Eddie, a criminal mastermind who tried to use a teenage Dick Grayson. Liu says Eddie has gone straight. However, the Vigilante, a ruthless killer, is hunting Eddie. Nightwing needs to find out what Eddie really wants, while trying to prevent Vigilante from killing anyone. The book includes some sexual scenes without nudity, and lots of fighting violence.

Bennett, Marguerite
  Batwoman; Volume 1: The many arms of death. Marguerite Bennett, James Tynion IV, writers;Steve Epting, Stephanie Hans, Renato Arlem,artists; Jeromy Cox, Adriano Lucas, colorists;Deron Bennett, letterer; Steve Epting, collectioncover art; Steve Epting, Eddy Barrows, EberFerreira and A. DC Comics 2017 168 p. Color; Illustration

Grades: 9 10 11 12 Adult   **741.5; Fic**
  1. Science fiction; 2. Superheroes — Fiction; 3. Batwoman (Fictional character)
9781401274306, $16.99

          LC 2017051287

  "Someone is selling cutting-edge weaponry on the black market, and their aim is to kill as many people...as possible. With help from her intrepid assistant, Julia Pennyworth, and their high-tech mobile command center, the yacht Sequoia, Batwoman quickly tracks the weapons to their source: a small, lawless island known as Coryana, home to pirates, outlaws...and a year of Batwoman's life." (Publisher's note)

Originally published in single magazine form in BATWOMAN: REBIRTH 1 and BATWOMAN 1-6 — Title page verso.; Volume 1 of an ongoing series

  DC Comics: Bombshells; Volume 2: Allies. written by Marguerite Bennett; art by MirkaAndolfo, Laura Braga, Sandy Jarrell, M. L. Sanapo,Juan Albarran, Marguerite Sauvage; colors by J.Nanjan, Kelly Fitzpatrick, Wendy Broome, JeremyLawson; letters by Wes Abbott; series andcollection co. DC Comics 2016 144 p. Color; Illustration

Grades: 9 10 11 12 Adult   **741.5; Fic**
  1. Women superheroes — Comic books, strips, etc; 2. World War, 1939-1945 — Comic books, strips, etc
1401264484; 9781401264482, $16.99

          LC 2016018856

In this comic book, by Marguerite Bennett, "as World War II rages across Europe, the Allied forces issue a call to arms for the greatest heroines the world has ever known! With an old villain arising from beyond the grave, Wonder Woman, Batwoman, Kara Starikov, Kortni Duginova and Mera must aid the Allied forces while at home, a brave group of Batgirls must defend the homeland!" (Publisher's note)

Benson, John
  Romance Without Tears. Fantagraphics Books 2004 160p. Illustration

Grades: 8 9 10 11 12 Adult   **741.5; Fic**
  1. Graphic novels; 2. Romance graphic novels
1-56097-558-X, $22.95

  This revisionist collection of romance comics stories from the '50s challenges the cliché of the "tear-stained face" that later dominated the genre and became widely known and vilified as a tiresome icon of moral uplift. Editor Benson has picked stories that portray stron young women

who learn from their mistakes and choose their guys, and get themselves out of trouble. The stories were all originally published by Archer St. John in the late-1940s to mid-1950s.

Bertozzi, Nick
  ★ **Shackleton:** Antarctic odyssey. Nick Bertozzi. First Second 2014 128 p. Illustration; Map

Grades: 5 6 7 8 9 10   **741.5; 919.89**
  1. Explorers — Great Britain — Biography; 2. Graphic novels; 3. Antarctica — Discovery and exploration — British; 4. Antarctica — Exploration; 5. Shackleton, Ernest Henry, Sir, 1874-1922
1596434511; 9781596434516, $16.99

  This book by Nick Bertozzi describes how "Ernest Shackleton was one of the last great Antarctic explorers, and he led one of the most ambitious Antarctic expeditions ever undertaken. This is his story, and the story of the dozens of men who threw in their lot with him — many of whom nearly died in the unimaginably harsh conditions of the journey." (Publisher's note)

  "Bertozzi eschews all narrative explanation, relying solely on dialogue among the crew and the detailed black-and-white panels to tell the story. The snow- and ice-bound journey is the perfect match for Bertozzi's minimal style — vast stretches of white become gasp-worthy, desolate vistas." Booklist

Bevard, Robby
  Sir Arthur Conan Doyle's the adventure of the Norwood Builder. ABDO/Magic Wagon 2010 48p. Illustration

Grades: 4 5 6 7 8 9   **741.5; Fic**
  1. Graphic novels; 2. Holmes, Sherlock (Fictional character); 3. Mystery graphic novels
978-1-60270-725-2, $28.50; 1-60270-725-1

          LC 2009-32459

  Young solicitor Mr. McFarlane begs Holmes to clear his name when he's accused of the murder of Jonas Oldacre, the Norwood Builder. Inspector Lestrade thinks he has a solid case, and the evidence seems to implicate McFarlane, especially since Mr. Oldacre's new will made McFarlane his sole heir. Holmes points to the lack of a body, and digs up more clues in his quest to save McFarlane. This graphic novel adaptation of Doyle's short story retains the suspense of the original, but perpetuates the stereotypical portrayals of Holmes in the deerstalker and caped coat which he never wore in the original stories. The book includes a brief drawing lesson, a short glossary, a brief biography of Doyle, and a listing of his other writings.

Part of The Graphic Novel Adventures of Sherlock Holmes

Biggs, Gina
  Red String, Vol. 1. Dark Horse Comics 2006 192p. Illustration

Grades: 7 8 9 10 11 12   **741.5; Fic**
  1. Graphic novels; 2. High school life — Graphic novels; 3. Romance graphic novels
978-1-59307-624-5, $9.95

  First year high school student Miharu Ogawa can't believe it when her parents tell her they've arranged for her to marry the son of their friends, someone she has never met. They won't marry until they finish school, but the whole idea is repugnant. Then Miharu meets a cute guy and knows she has to fight her parents; but the cute guy she likes is Kazuo Fujiwara, the arranged fiance. Now Miharu just has to deal with gossip at school that hurts her friend Reika, and with her manipulative cousin Karen, who wants Kazuo for herself, and other problems and romantic obstacles. Biggs uses the manga format and manga-influenced art to tell her story of high school romance. Other than one panel of tastefully rendered partial nudity, there's no content to keep this from most middle school age readers.

Volume 1 of 8

Bilson, Danny

The **Flash**: Lightning in a Bottle. written by Danny Bilson, Paul Demeo; pencils, Ken Lashley [and others]; inks, Ken Rapmund [and others]. DC Comics 2007 144p. Illustration
Grades: 9 10 11 12 Adult   **741.5; Fic**
1. Graphic novels; 2. Superhero graphic novels; 3. Flash (Fictional character)
978-1-4012-1229-2, $12.99

Bart Allen returned from fighting Superboy Prime inside the Speed Force at the end of the Infinite Crisis with no speed and aged four years into an adult, and also no memory of how he spent the time. One year later, he's a factory worker in Keystone City, when an accident at the factory reconnects him to the Speed Force. That same accident causes Bart's best friend Griffin Gray to gain powers, too, but they drain his life force and cause him to rapidly age. His solution — he siphons off the energy from the slowly aging original Flash, Jay Garrick; but it might kill Garrick. And Griffin's brand of justice is too harsh.

Volume 1 of 2

Black, Holly

The **Good** Neighbors; book one: Kin. Graphix 2008 117p. (The Good Neighbors)
Grades: 7 8 9 10 11 12   **741.5; Fic**
1. Fairies — Graphic novels; 2. Fantasy graphic novels; 3. Graphic novels
978-0-439-85562-4, $16.99; 0-439-85562-4

LC 2007-49008

Sixteen-year-old Rue has grown up in a world much like ours, except that the human world and the world of faerie have co-existed, as good neighbors, for a long time. When Rue's mother disappears and her professor father becomes the main suspect in the murder of a young woman, Rue's life turns strange. As she digs for information to figure out what is happening in her life, Rue discovers that her mother is a faerie and has returned to that realm because of a broken promise.

"This sophisticated tale is well served by Naifeh's stylish, angular illustrations." SLJ

Other titles in this series are: Kith (2009); Kind (2010)

Blackman, Haden

Star Wars Omnibus: X-Wing Rogue Squadron Volume 1. writers, Haden Blackman ... [et al.]; art, Tomas Giorello ... [et al.]. Dark Horse Comics 2006 un Illustration
Grades: 7 8 9 10 11 12 Adult   **741.5; Fic**
1. Adventure graphic novels; 2. Graphic novels; 3. Science fiction graphic novels; 4. Star Wars — Graphic novels
978-1-59307-572-9, $24.95

The greatest star fighters of the Rebel Alliance become the defenders of a New Republic in this massive collection of stories featuring Wedge Antilles, hero of the Battle of Endor, and his team of ace pilots known throughout the galaxy as Rogue Squadron. Meet the Rogues for the first time and learn the fate of the galaxy immediately after the events of Return of the Jedi as the Rebellion's best pilots battle remnants of the Empire wherever its ugly agenda of fear and domination appears. Along with X-Wing Rogue Squadron: The Phantom Affair, this jam-packed volume contains never before collected material, including Star Wars X-Wing Rogue Leader #1-3, Star Wars X-Wing Rogue Squadron: The Rebel Opposition #1-4, Star Wars X-Wing Rogue Squadron: The Phantom Affair #1-4, and Star Wars Handbook: X-Wing Rogue Squadron.

Volume 1 of 3

Blain, Christophe

Gus and his gang. First Second Books 2008 164p. Illustration
Grades: 10 11 12 Adult   **741.5; Fic**
1. Graphic novels; 2. Humorous graphic novels; 3. Western stories — Graphic novels
978-1-59643-170-6, $16.95; 1-59643-170-9

LC 2008-23541

Gus, Gratt, and Clem are three outlaws in this French version of the Old West. Gus much prefers to rob trains, banks are too still for him. What all three of them prefer is to be with women; Gus and Gratt go girl-hunting together in towns such as El Dorado, but Clem doesn't go with them. He has a family, with Ava and their daughter Jamie; but he does have a passionate affair with a free-spirited, red-haired photographer. Everything the three men do is financed by robbing banks, trains...when Gus tries to case a bank, he falls for a woman who works there and ends up pretending to be a writer in order to woo her. The book doesn't follow a straightforward narrative, and the French idea of how the Old West "worked" is more than a bit eccentric. The book also includes lots of sexual content and partial nudity.

Isaac the Pirate 1. To Exotic Lands. NBM 2003 un Illustration
Grades: 10 11 12 Adult   **741.5; Fic**
1. Adventure graphic novels; 2. Graphic novels; 3. Pirates — Graphic novels
1-56163-366-6, $14.95

LC 2003-59288

Isaac is a talented artist with no money but with a wonderful lover back in Paris of the 18th century. He runs into a rich Captain who is taken by his abilities and hires him with a handsome stipend to come along in his voyages. It turns out he's a pirate. Isaac went to make some quick money and come back and marry the love of his life, but he has embarked upon a series of adventures on the high seas from the Caribbean to the icy North, with apparently no end in sight. Meanwhile, his girlfriend is getting attention from another...The book includes some harsh language and violence.

Volume 1 of 2

Blaylock, Josh

How to self-publish comics: not just create them. Josh Blaylock and Tim Seeley; forward by Art Baltazar. Devil's Due Publishing 2015 144 p.
Grades: 10 11 12 Adult   **741.5**
1. Comic books, strips, etc. — Publishing — United States
0991001044; 9780991001040, $19.99

"Josh Blaylock's now classic How-To prose book about the business of comics publishing, after selling out of its updated 2012 edition, is now being re-released to include Tim Seeley's companion writings on the behind-the-scenes realities of being a comic book artist, originally released in pamphlet form." (Publisher's note)

Penguin Bros.. Devil's Due Publishing 2004 un Illustration
Grades: 7 8 9 10 11 12   **741.5; Fic**
1. Graphic novels; 2. Humorous graphic novels; 3. Penguins — Graphic novels; 4. Superhero graphic novels
1-932796-20-7, $10.95

Three teenage penguins living in Chill City, Antarctica are the ones chosen to become their city's heroes, and granted Super Powers. There's only one problem — they'd rather go to concerts, hang with girlfriends, and play video games. It's sleigh cars, super powers and homework in the Penguin Bros. As Blaylock explains at the end of the book, he created the

Penguin Bros. when he was six years old — and he has the drawings to prove it.

Bocquet, José-Louis

Josephine Baker. art by Catel Muller; written by José-Louis Bocquet; historical consultant, Jean-Claude Bouillon-Baker. Harry N Abrams Inc 2017 496 p.

Grades: 11 12 Adult   **741.5; 92**
1. Baker, Josephine, 1906-1975; 2. African American dancers — Biography; 3. Biography
191059329X; 9781910593295, $22.95

LC 2017385203

"Known to many only in the iconic banana costume that made her famous in the 1920s, singer and dancer Josephine Baker lived an incredibly rich life beyond the theater. She was a tireless activist for civil rights and leveraged her status whenever possible to break down racial barriers in the U.S. and around the world. This book follows Baker from her birth in 1906, touching on the many significant events in her life, from her spy work in the French Resistance to adopting the 12 children that made up her Rainbow Tribe." (Booklist)

Bocquet "does Baker's complicated life justice in both appeal and detail. A lengthy chronology anchors key milestones and a massive biographical appendix provides background about important people in the entertainer's life. Muller's high-contrast, black-and-white inks finesse a mostly realistic whimsy and is especially good at rendering people recognizably in few lines." LJ

Originally published in French by Casterman in 2016

Bogaert, Harmen Meyndertsz van den

Journey into Mohawk Country. as written by H.M. van den Bogaert, with artwork by George O'Connor and color by Hilary Sycamore. First Second 2006 144p. Illustration

Grades: 8 9 10 11 12   **973.2**
1. Graphic novels; 2. New York (State) — History — 1600-1775, Colonial period — Graphic novels; 3. United States — History — 1600-1775, Colonial period — Graphic novels
1-59643-106-7, $17.95

In 1634, young Dutch trader Harmen Meyndertsz van den Bogaert, several companions, and some native guides traveled deep into what is now New York State, trading tools and weapons and trying to establish new tribal friendships to bolster Dutch trade. van den Bogaert kept a journal throughout his journeys. O'Connor has kept the original text and conducted extensive research in order to make his illustrations as authentic as possible.

Boldman, Craig

Archie Day by Day Volume 1. Archie Comics 2003 96p. Illustration
Grades: 3 4 5 6 7 8 9 10 11 12 Adult   **741.5; Fic**
1. Andrews, Archie (Fictional character); 2. Graphic novels; 3. Humorous graphic novels
1-879794-16-0, $10.95

Archie and his pals have been comics' most celebrated teenage humor characters for over 60 years, since 1941. Now for the first time, selections from Archie's worldwide syndicated newspaper strip are collected in this volume. This black and white edition includes a selection of daily strips from the mid-1990s, chronicling life in Riverdale, USA.

Braithwaite, Doug

Justice Volume One. Jim Krueger and Alex Ross, story; Doug Braithwaite and Alex Ross, art. DC Comics 2006 160p. Illustration
Grades: 8 9 10 11 12 Adult   **741.5; Fic**

1. Graphic novels; 2. Justice League of America (Fictional characters); 3. Superhero graphic novels
978-1-4012-0969-8, $19.99

The Justice League of America are the World's Greatest Super-Heroes, but now villains — the Riddler, Lex Luthor, Poison Ivy, Captain Cold, and others are banding together and making sweeping, worldwide changes that appear to be noble acts. But, one by one the members of the JLA are being taken down; will anyone be left to truly protect the people of Earth?

Britt, Fanny

★ **Jane,** the fox & me. [written by] Fanny Britt; [illustrated by] Isabelle Arsenault; translated by Christine Morelli and Susan Ouriou. Pgw 2013 101 p.

Grades: 5 6 7 8 9   **Fic**
1. Teenage girls — Fiction; 2. Alienation (Social psychology) — Fiction
1554983606; 9781554983605, $19.95

Governor General's Award: Children's Illustration (2013); Eisner Nominee: Best Publication for Children (2014)

Written by Fanny Britt, illustrated by Isabelle Arsentault, and translated by Christine Morelli and Susan Ouriou, this "graphic novel reveals the casual brutality of which children are capable, but also assures readers that redemption can be found through connecting with another, whether the other is a friend, a fictional character or even, amazingly, a fox." (Publisher's note) It "centers on Hélène, ostracized by her former friends and now a loner at school." (Horn Book Magazine)

"Britt's well-constructed narrative is achieved sensitively through Arsenault's impressionistic artwork.... An elegant and accessible approach to an important topic." Booklist

Britt, Mark Haven

Full-Color. Image Comics 2007 175p. Illustration
Grades: 11 12 Adult   **741.5; Fic**
1. Graphic novels; 2. Revenge — Graphic novels
978-1-58240-840-8, $15.99

A lifetime marked with Napoleonic bosses has generated a rage in Boom that she can't contain anymore — only aim. Her target? Her boss. She's given herself one day to make it all right now that she's quit her job. That same day, Boom comes home to find an old friend standing on her fire escape. David's double-crossed a drug dealer and he's looking for help. She'll help him if he'll help her; but things don't go according to plan. The book has lots of violence, harsh language, and some partial nudity.

Brooks, Mark

Arana Vol. 1: The Heart of the Spider. writer, Fiona Avery; pencilers, Mark Brooks & Roger Cruz; inkers, Jaime Mendoza & Victor Olazaba; colorist, UDON's Larry Molinar & Jeannie Lee; letterers, Virtual Calligraphy's Rus Wooton & Chris Eliopoulos. Marvel Entertainment 2005 un Illustration

Grades: 8 9 10 11 12 Adult   **741.5; Fic**
1. Adventure graphic novels; 2. Graphic novels; 3. Superhero graphic novels
0-7851-1506-4, $7.99

She's fierce, she's sassy, she sticks to walls. Anya Corazon, a.k.a. Arana, is a next-generation girl warrior. A scrappy teen from Brooklyn by day, Anya becomes the Hunter of the ancient and mystical Spider Society by night. But first, she must survive her initiation and prove herself on her first mission, all while going to high school and hiding everything from her single-parent dad. Together with her partner, the mysterious mage Miguel, Anya must fight to protect the peace of the world from the sworn enemies of the Spider Society, the evil Sisterhood of the Wasp. There's lots of super hero action here.

Volume 1 of 3

Broome, John

The **Green** Lantern Archives Volume 5. stories by John Broome; art by Gil Kane, Joe Giella. DC Comics 2004 239p. Illustration

Grades: 6 7 8 9 10 11 12 Adult　　　　　　　　**741.5; Fic**

1. Graphic novels; 2. Green Lantern (Fictional character); 3. Superhero graphic novels

1-4012-0404-X, $49.95

LC 93-131923

This volume presents the further adventures of Green Lantern Hal Jordan " the Silver Age's science fiction-influenced hero. This time, the Emerald Gladiator squares off against foes such as Dr. Light, Hector Hammond, Evil Star, the Aerialist, and many more. This full-color Archive reprints nine tales from Green Lantern #30-38, originally published in 1964 and 1965.

Showcase Presents: Green Lantern Volume 1. stories by John Broome; art by Gil Kane and Joe Giella. DC Comics 2005 528p. Illustration

Grades: 6 7 8 9 10 11 12 Adult　　　　　　　　**741.5; Fic**

1. Graphic novels; 2. Green Lantern (Fictional character); 3. Superhero graphic novels

1-4012-0759-6, $9.99

A dying alien summoned test pilot Hal Jordan and gave him the most powerful weapon in the universe: a power ring. Jordan was inducted into the universe-spanning Green Lantern Corps and assigned to protect a sector of space including Earth. His sheer willpower directs the ring to create fantastic energy constructs and with it, protect the good from evil. In these earliest stories, readers meet the Guardians of the Universe, many of Jordan's intergalactic comrades, and some of his deadliest opponents, including Hector Hammond, Sonar, and Sinestro. The black and white reprints date from 1959 through 1962.

Brosgol, Vera

★ **Anya's** ghost. First Second 2011 221p. Illustration

Grades: 6 7 8 9 10　　　　　　　　**741.5; Fic**

1. Friendship — Graphic novels; 2. Ghosts — Graphic novels; 3. Horror graphic novels; 4. School life — Graphic novels

978-1-59643-713-5, $19.99; 1-59643-713-8; 978-1-59643-552-0 (pa), $15.99; 1-59643-552-6 (pa)

LC 2010036251

"The crisp, sophisticated purple, gray, black, and white palette correlates perfectly with the overall angst of the characters. A juicy mystery, a bit of horror, strong use of the graphic-novel format, and a diverse and unusual cast of characters—that's a pretty impressive achievement in just over two hundred pages." Bulletin of the Center for Children's Books

Brown, Box

Andre the Giant: Life and Legend. by Box Brown. First Second 2014 240 p. Illustration

Grades: 9 10 11 12 Adult　　　　　　　　**741.5; 92**

1. Andre, the Giant, 1946-1993; 2. Wrestling; 3. Actors

1596438517; 9781596438514, $17.99

LC 2014466607

This book, by Box Brown, is a graphic novel biography of Andre Roussimoff. "At his peak, he weighed 500 pounds and stood nearly seven and a half feet tall. But the huge stature that made his fame also signed his death warrant.... [Brown draws] from historical records about Andre's life

as well as a wealth of anecdotes from his colleagues in the wrestling world." (Publisher's note)

Brown "uses professional wrestling's complex narrative devices in this biography, which pulls back the curtain on Andre the Giant (Andre Rousimoff), one of the industry's most well-known figures.... Brown's simple, blocky art keeps the story front and center, and the down-to-earth tone allows him to avoid demonizing or lionizing his subject." Pub Wkly

Includes bibliographical references

Tetris: the games people play. Box Brown. First Second 2016 256 p. Color; Illustration

Grades: 10 11 12 Adult　　　　　　　　**749.8; 741.5**

1. Video games

9781626723153, $19.99; 162672315X

This book, by Box Brown, describes how the video game "Tetris delivers an irresistible, unending puzzle that has players hooked.... Alexey Pajitnov had big ideas about games. In 1984, he created Tetris in his spare time while developing software for the Soviet government. Once Tetris emerged from behind the Iron Curtain, it was an instant hit. Nintendo, Atari, Sega — game developers big and small all wanted Tetris." (Publisher's note)

"A graphic narrative that clarifies a complicated series of international negotiations, making the story interesting even for those who don't care about video games." Kirkus

Brown, Don

★ **Drowned** City: Hurricane Katrina and New Orleans. by Don Brown. Houghton Mifflin Harcourt 2015 96 p. Color; Illustration

Grades: 7 8 9 10　　　　　　　　**741.5; 363.34**

1. New Orleans (La.) — History — 21st century; 2. Hurricane Katrina, 2005; 3. New Orleans (La.) — History

054415777X, $18.99; 9780544157774, $18.99

LC 2015458266

Robert F. Sibert Honor Book (2016); Eisner Nominee: Best Publication for Teens (2016)

In this work of graphic nonfiction by Don Brown, "when the calamitous category five Katrina's gusty winds hurl into the city of New Orleans, most people have evacuated the city. The rest of the scared, stubborn, and simply stranded must face the dangers of what is to come — broken levees quickly swelling the city with water. Many families seek safety on their roofs or via floatation devices as a way to row to safety. However, some are not as fortunate." (Children's Literature)

"Brown's narrative is clear and precise, relying exclusively on data and statistics interspersed with quotes from residents, rescue crews, journalists, and news reports. Alone, the text might lack impact, but combined with the haunting imagery, it hits readers like a punch in the gut." Booklist

Includes bibliographical references

★ The **great** American dust bowl. by Don Brown. Houghton Mifflin Harcourt 2013 80 p.

Grades: 5 6 7 8 9　　　　　　　　**978**

1. Droughts — United States — History; 2. Dust storms — History; 3. Dust Bowl Era, 1931-1939

0547815506; 9780547815503, $18.99

Author Don Brown presents a "graphic novel of one of America's most catastrophic natural events: the Dust Bowl. On a clear, warm Sunday, April 14, 1935, a wild wind whipped up millions upon millions of these specks of dust to form a duster, a savage storm on America's high southern plains." (Publisher's note)

"In this bleak yet compelling graphic-novel-style glimpse at the Dirty Thirties, Brown crisply paces the narrative with fascinating glimpses of the sociological and geological causes of the Dust Bowl. The color brown is a recurring theme here, as Brown relies, aptly, almost entirely on shades of brown throughout. Primary source material is used liberally, as characters speak directly to the reader, documentary-style." (Horn Book)

Brown, Jeffrey

Incredible Change-Bots. Top Shelf Productions 2007 un Illustration
Grades: 8 9 10 11 12 Adult
741.5; Fic
1. Graphic novels; 2. Humorous graphic novels; 3. Robots — Graphic novels; 4. Science fiction graphic novels
978-1-891830-91-4, $15

Courtesy of IDW Publishing

Far away in outer space, the Incredible Change-Bots live on the planet Electronocybercircuitron. The Awesomebots and the Fantasticons have lived in relative harmony, until Shootertron, the leader of the Fantasticons, decides to rig the election to rule the planet. The Awesomebots declare war, and over the years the Change-Bots destroy their planet. They then come to Earth, where they continue their fighting, each group gaining their own human allies. Brown has done a fun send-up of the Transformers with this story, and while there is some violence, there is very little in the way of bad language.

Brubaker, Ed

Criminal, Vol. 1: Coward. writer, Ed Brubaker; art, Sean Phillips; colors by Val Staples. Marvel Entertainment/Icon 2007 un Illustration
Grades: 12 Adult   **741.5; Fic**
1. Criminals — Graphic novels; 2. Graphic novels; 3. Mystery graphic novels
0-7851-2439-X, $14.99

Leo plans heists; he's been a criminal since he was a young kid picking pockets. He lives by rules that keep him alive, rules that make others call him a coward. When old friend Seymour comes to him, along with crooked cop Jeff, and asks him to plan a heist of evidence (blood diamonds) from an evidence transport van, Leo doesn't want it. But when Greta, widow of a dead partner, tells him she needs the money to take care of her sick daughter, Leo takes the job. He plans everything, plans for every possible problem, except one. The target of the heist isn't diamonds, it's pure heroin. And crooked cop Jeff is ready to betray everyone. This is dark crime noir, with lots of harsh language, violence, and a little sex.

Originally published as Criminal issues #1-5.; Other volumes in this series are:Vol. 2: Lawless (2007);Vol. 3: The Dead and the dying (2008);Vol. 4: Bad night (2009);Vol. 5: The sinners (2010);Vol. 6: The last of the innocent (2011)

★ **Gotham** Central; Book One. Ed Brubaker, Greg Rucka; With Michael Lark. DC Comics 2013 235 p. Color illustration
Grades: 11 12 Adult   **741.5**
1. Good and evil — Comic books, strips, etc.; 2. Police — Comic books, strips, etc.; 3. Superheroes — Comic books, strips, etc.; 4. Batman (Fictional character)
1401220371; 9781401220372, $19.99

LC 2012046720
This graphic novel, by Ed Brubaker and Greg Rucka, takes place in "Gotham City: a town teeming with corrupt cops, ruthless crime lords, petty thieves...and just a small handful that would oppose them. Grizzled veteran Harvey Bullock, Captain Maggie Sawyer, detective Renee Montoya and the GCPD are the law force that stands between order and complete anarchy." (Publisher's note)

Series originally collected in five volumes; Originally published in single magazine form in Gotham Central #1-10.; In the Line of Duty;

Other Gotham Central collections are: Book two: Jokers and madmen; Book three: On the freak beat; Book four: Corrigan

The **Sandman** presents: the dead boy detectives. DC Comics/Vertigo 2008 104p. Illustration
Grades: 10 11 12 Adult   **741.5; Fic**
1. Fantasy graphic novels; 2. Ghosts — Graphic novels; 3. Graphic novels; 4. Mystery graphic novels; 5. Supernatural graphic novels
978-1-4012-1855-3, $12.99

Charles Rowland and Edwin Paine spend all their time reading detective stories, watching thrillers at the movie theaters, or just hanging out in their treehouse, and no one cares. Charles and Edwin are ghosts from different times in the past, who have become friends in their new existence. Now, inspired by the stories and movies, they decide to become private detectives, and they take a case from a runaway girl. Someone is killing the runaway children who live in the Underground of London, and that someone is capable of hurting even ghosts like Charles and Edwin. They encounter a man who says his family has hunted the killer for centuries and enlists their help, but is he telling the truth, or are Charles and Edwin in very deep trouble? The book includes some violence.

Brunetti, Ivan

★ An **Anthology** of graphic fiction, cartoons, and true stories. edited by Ivan Brunetti. Yale University Press 2006 400p. Illustration
Grades: 11 12 Adult
741.5
1. American wit and humor, Pictorial; 2. Cartooning — United States — History — 20th century; 3. Comic books, strips, etc. — United States — History — 20th century
978-0-300-11170-5; 0-300-11170-3, $28
LC 2006-14095

Courtesy of Yale University Press

This is an "anthology of contemporary art comics, along with some classic comic strips and other historical materials. . . . Included here are works from such . . . artists as Robert Crumb, Kim Deitch, Art Spiegelman, Chris Ware, Ben Katchor, Charles Burns, Gary Panter, Seth, Phoebe Gloeckner, Daniel Clowes, Lynda Barry, Joe Sacco, and Jaime and Gilbert Hernandez." (Publisher's note)

Brunswick, Glen

The **Gray** Area Vol. 1: All of This Can be Yours. written by Glen Brunswick; pencils by John Romita, Jr.; inks by Klaus Janson; letters by John Workman; colors by Bill Crabtree. Image Comics 2005 un Illustration
Grades: 11 12 Adult   **741.5; Fic**
1. Graphic novels; 2. Superhero graphic novels; 3. Supernatural graphic novels
1-58240-485-2, $14.95

After his execution for double-crossing a drug cartel, Rudy Chance — a brutal, corrupt cop and womanizer — expects he'll wind up in Hell. Instead, he finds himself in the Gray Area, where he is forced to combat evil for an afterlife police force in order to gain a shot at redemption. Given extraordinary powers, Chance hunts down the wicked to condemn and the worthy to heal. But can he control his own dark side, or will it lead him to eternal damnation? The book has foul language and considerable violence.

★ **Jersey** Gods, vol.1: I'd live and I'd die for you. Image Comics 2009 un Illustration
Grades: 10 11 12 Adult   **741.5; Fic**

1. Graphic novels; 2. Humorous graphic novels; 3. Romance graphic novels; 4. Superhero graphic novels
978-1-60706-063-5, $14.99

Jersey Girl Zoe works as an assistant to the fashion editor of her local newspaper in Cherry Hill, New Jersey. She has bad luck with boyfriends who always dump her. Then she meets Barock, a god from another planet (Cumulus), when one of his fights leads him to Earth. She has to deal with her boss stealing her idea of an article series on fashion, while Barock has to deal with betrayals and infighting among the gods of his world. But they're in love; what is a Jersey mall princess to do with a planetary god? And what happens when they both get entangled with a scheme to flood the New Jersey malls with fake designer fashions? The art takes classic Jack Kirby style (big, muscular, square-jawed, clean-cut heroes) and gives it just enough of a twist to be humorous without being satirical. The book includes a lot of action and some violence; there's no nudity, but Zoe is shown in her underwear in one panel.

Buhle, Paul

A **dangerous** woman: the graphic biography of Emma Goldman. The New Press 2007 115p. Illustration

Grades: 10 11 12 Adult   **335; 741.5; 92**

1. Anarchism and anarchists — Graphic novels; 2. Anarchists; 3. Biographical graphic novels; 4. Essayists; 5. Family planning advocates; 6. Graphic novels; 7. Goldman, Emma, 1869-1940
978-1-59558-064-1, $17.95

LC 2007-15415

Emma Goldman was a revolutionary activist, speaker, writer, and feminist and anarchist. An immigrant to the U.S., she spoke out against inhumane working conditions, taught contraception, and opposed conscription for World War I. She founded the Free Speech League (a precursor to the ACLU), and the magazine Mother Earth. When she was deported to Russia just after the Bolshevik Revolution, she became disillusioned with the authoritarianism she found there, and she ended up supporting the fight against fascism in the Spanish Civil War. Rudahl based her graphic novel on Goldman's autobiography. The book includes nudity, sexual situations, and some violence.

Bui, Thi

★ The **best** we could do: an illustrated memoir. Thi Bui. Abrams ComicArts 2017 327 p. Color; Illustration

Grades: 11 12 Adult   **92; 741.5; 973/.0495920092**

1. Autobiographical comics; 2. Graphic novels; 3. Refugees — United States — Biography — Comic books, strips, etc.; 4. Vietnam War, 1961-1975 — Personal narratives, Vietnamese — Comic books, strips, etc.; 5. Bui, Thi; 6. Vietnam War, 1961-1975 — Personal narratives, Vietnamese; 7. Vietnamese Americans — Biography; 8. Bui, Thi
9781613129302; 9781419718779, $24.95

LC 2016940170

National Book Critics Circle Award Finalist: Autobiography (2017)

In this memoir, author Thi Bui "documents the story of her family's daring escape after the fall of South Vietnam in the 1970s, and the difficulties they faced building new lives for themselves. At the heart of Bui's story is a universal struggle: While adjusting to life as a first-time mother, she ultimately discovers what it means to be a parent — the endless sacrifices, the unnoticed gestures, and the depths of unspoken love." (Publisher's note)

"In creatively telling a complicated story with the kind of feeling words alone rarely relay, The Best We Could Do does the very best that comics can do." Booklist

Bullock, Mike

Lions, tigers and bears volume 2: betrayal. Image Comics 2008 un Illustration

Grades: 3 4 5 6 7 8 9   **741.5; Fic**

1. Adventure graphic novels; 2. Fantasy graphic novels; 3. Graphic novels
978-1-58240-930-6, $14.99

Joey and Courtney's winter wonderland is shattered when the Big Cats of the Night Pride arrive with terrible news from the Stuffed Animal Kingdom. Now all that stands between the horrible Beasties and children everywhere are Joey, Courtney, and their imaginations. For the evil Valthraax and his minions have taken over the Crystal Castle, imprisoned King Bear, and plot to capture all children who aren't being protected by the Stuffed Animal Militia. There is some fighting violence between the Night Pride and their allies against the Beasties.

Bunn, Cullen

The **damned** volume one: Three days dead. written by Cullen Bunn; illustrated by Brian Hurtt; colored by Bill Crabtree; lettered by Crank!. Oni Press 2008 un Illustration

Grades: 11 12 Adult   **741.5; Fic**

1. Graphic novels; 2. Humorous graphic novels; 3. Mafia — Graphic novels; 4. Mystery graphic novels; 5. Supernatural graphic novels
978-1-932664-63-8, $14.95

In an alternate world prohibition era, gangsters still grow rich on catering to people's vices, but a more sinister power controls the crime cartels and uses human greed, gluttony, lust, and other mortal sins to fuel a much more lucrative trade: mortal souls. When a feud between two Families is supposed to end with a brokered deal, the bookkeeper brokering the deal is kidnapped. Big Al pulls gumshoe Eddie's corpse out of a ditch and puts him on the case to find the missing bookkeeper. Poor Eddie, he's already dead, but people keep killing him over and over again. The book includes considerable violence, some bad language, and occasional nudity.

Burns, Charles

★ **Black** hole. Charles Burns.. Pantheon Books 2005 1 v. Illustration

Grades: 10 11 12 Adult   **741.5/973**

1. Communicable diseases — Fiction; 2. Teenagers — Fiction; 3. High school students — Fiction; 4. Homicide — Fiction
9780375714726; 9780375423802; 037542380X, $29.95

LC 2005046431

Eisner Awards: Best Graphic Album — Reprint (2006); Harvey Awards: Best Graphic Album — Previously Published (2006); Ignatz Awards: Outstanding Anthology or Collection (2006)

This book takes place in "[s]uburban Seattle, [in] the mid-1970s. We learn from the out-set that a strange plague has descended upon the area's teenagers, transmitted by sexual contact. The disease is manifested in any number of ways — from the hideously grotesque to the subtle (and concealable) — but once you've got it, that's it. There's no turning back. As we inhabit the heads of several key characters — some kids who have it, some who don't, some who are about to get it — what unfolds isn't the expected battle to fight the plague, or bring heightened awareness to it, or even to treat it. What we become witness to instead is a fascinating and eerie portrait of the nature of high school alienation itself — the savagery, the cruelty, the relentless anxiety and ennui, the longing for escape. And then the murders start." (Publisher's note)

Burns, Jason M.

A **Dummy's** Guide to Danger. Viper Comics 2007 un Illustration

Grades: 11 12 Adult   **741.5; Fic**

1. Graphic novels; 2. Mystery graphic novels

978-0-9793680-0-4, $11.95

Private investigator Alan Sirois and his partner Mr. Bloomberg, a paraplegic ventriloquist dummy that Alan believes was shot in the back by an assailant and became crippled when the bullet lodged in his spine, track down a gruesome killer known only as the Flesh Collector. The book includes violence and harsh language.

The **Underworld** Railroad. Viper Comics 2007 112p. Illustration
Grades: 10 11 12 Adult **741.5**
1. Fantasy graphic novels; 2. Graphic novels
978-0-9793680-3-5, $11.95

This book postulates that when a person dies while still wrongly accused, that person's spirit doesn't immediately go to Heaven or to Hell, but must wait to be cleared. In the meantime, the spirit is vulnerable and can be taken by the devil. For these spirits, a system of safe houses offers refuge. In one such safe house, Bruce welcomes the spirit of a man who was falsely accused of murdering his wife. The devil takes the form of a sexy woman who doesn't want to take no for an answer, and she tries to take the spirit by force. The book includes violence, some harsh language, and supernatural action.

Busiek, Kurt
★ **Astro** City: life in the big city. by Kurt Busiek, Brent Anderson, and Alex Ross. DC Comics 2011 192 p. Color illustration
Grades: 11 12 Adult **741.5; Fic**
1. Superhero graphic novels
1401232612; 1401232620; 9781401232610; 9781401232627, $17.99
LC 2012376788

This graphic novel, by Kurt Busiek, Brent Anderson, and Alex Ross, is set in "Astro City, a shining city on a hill where super heroes patrol the skies.... The city's leading super hero tries to be everywhere at once, and berates himself for every wasted second as he longs for just a moment of his own. A smalltime hood learns a hero's secret identity, and tries to figure out how to profit from the knowledge. A beat reporter gets some advice from his editor on his first day on the job." (Publisher's note)

"These heroes are intentionally written to resemble classic superheroes like Superman, Wonder Woman, and the Fantastic Four. The Astro City heroes, however, aren't derivative; the authors introduce well-developed, original characters and use them to delve into the unexplored possibilities and unanswered questions of classic superheroes as well as their relationships with the world around them." LJ

Collected volume originally published 1997; Originally published as Kurt Busiek's Astro city v. 1 #1-6.; Other Astro City volumes are: Confession (1997); Family album (1998); The tarnished angel (2000); Local heroes (2005); The dark age 1: Brothers & other strangers (2008); The dark age 2: Brothers in arms (2010); Shining stars (2011); Through open doors (2014); Victory (2014); Private lives (2015); Lovers quarrel (2015); Honor guard (2016); Reflections (2017)

Astro City: the dark age 1: brothers & other strangers. DC Comics/Wildstorm 2009 256p. Illustration
Grades: 10 11 12 Adult **741.5; Fic**
1. Crime — Graphic novels; 2. Gangs — Graphic novels; 3. Graphic novels; 4. Superhero graphic novels
978-1-4012-2077-8, $19.99

In Astro City of the 1970s, estranged brothers Charles and Royal Williams are still trying to cope with the tragedy that ripped their family apart back in 1959. Charles is an honest cop stuck with a crooked partner who keeps trying to get him to accept graft payments, while Royal has been living the life of a smalltime crook. Their lives keep intersecting with those of the superpowered, heroes and criminals alike. Throughout the book, readers piece together the bits of flashbacks to that pivotal tragedy in 1959; when the only black superhero treats the young brothers with respect, but a battle between superhero Silver Agent and super criminals erupts into the

Williams family's apartment and kills the parents. When Silver Agent walked through the apartment in pursuit of the villains and ignored the dead and surviving civilians, it crushed the boys' spirits, leaving one distrustful of all super powered beings and the other without hope of any good in life. Now, with Silver Agent convicted of murder, an impending war between super powered gangs, and the vengeful Black Velvet and Blue Knight slaughtering criminals even smalltime grifters such as Royal, it's truly a Dark Age in Astro City. The book includes some violence and some harsh language.

Conan Volume 1: The Frost-Giant's Daughter and Other Stories. Dark Horse Comics 2005 un Illustration
Grades: 10 11 12 Adult **741.5; Fic**
1. Adventure graphic novels; 2. Conan the Barbarian (Fictional character); 3. Fantasy graphic novels; 4. Graphic novels
1-59307-301-1, $15.95

Conan the Barbarian wars with the murderous Vanir, meets the Frost Giant's Daughter, and is taken as a slave by the ancient sorcerers of Hyperborea in this volume of new Conan adventures. Busiek and Nord adapt some of Robert E. Howard's original Conan stories and create some original stories, just as Roy Thomas and Barry Windsor-Smith had done in the 1970s. Conan prefers action to thought, and the stories are full of fighting, some nudity and sexual situations.

JLA: Syndicate Rules. DC Comics 2005 un Illustration
Grades: 10 11 12 Adult **741.5; Fic**
1. Adventure graphic novels; 2. Graphic novels; 3. Justice League of America (Fictional characters); 4. Superhero graphic novels
1-4012-0477-5, $17.99

Cosmic upheavals destroyed and rebuilt the antimatter universe, with their super-powered conquerors blaming the JLA. Seeking revenge against their positive matter universe counterparts, the JLA, the Crime Syndicate of Amerika breaches the barrier between universes and brings chaos to Earth. The antimatter universe's Weaponers of Qward tip the balance of power as they employ a new super-weapon that can wipe out both super-teams, and Earth's inhabitants, in a heartbeat.

★ **Marvels**. by Kurt Busiek; illustrated by Alex Ross. Marvel 2010 248 p.
Grades: 10 11 12 Adult **741.5**
1. Marvel Comics Group; 2. Superhero comic books, strips, etc.
078514286X; 9780785142867, $24.99

In this comic book, by Kurt Busiek, illustrated by Alex Ross, "Welcome to New York. Here, burning figures roam the streets, men in brightly colored costumes scale the glass and concrete walls, and creatures from space threaten to devour our world. This is the Marvel Universe, where the ordinary and fantastic interact daily." (Publisher's note)

Followed by Marvels: Eye of the camera

Butler, Octavia
Kindred: a graphic novel adaptation. by Octavia E. Butler, adapted by Damian Duffy, illustrated by John Jennings. Abrams ComicArts 2017 240 p. Illustration
Grades: 10 11 12 Adult **741.5**
1. Time travel — Comic books, strips, etc.; 2. Slavery; 3. Slaves — Comic books, strips, etc.
9781419709470, $24.95; 9780807083703, $16
LC 2016940630

Eisner Award: Best Adaptation from Another Medium (2018)

This graphic novel adaptation, by Octavia E. Butler, adapted by Damian Duffy and illustrated by John Jennings, "tells the story of Dana, a young black woman who is suddenly and inexplicably transported from her home in 1970s California to the pre-Civil War South. As she time-travels between worlds,...she becomes frighteningly entangled in the lives of Rufus, a conflicted white slaveholder and one of Dana's own ancestors, and the many people who are enslaved by him." (Publisher's note)

Butzer, C. M.
★ **Gettysburg:** the graphic novel. Bowen Books/HarperCollins 2009 80p. Illustration
Grades: 3 4 5 6 7 8 9 10 11 12   **741.5; 973.7**
 1. American speeches — Graphic novels; 2. Gettysburg (Pa.), Battle of, 1863; 3. Graphic novels; 4. Lincoln, Abraham, 1809-1865 — Graphic novels; 5. Lincoln, Abraham, 1809-1865 — Work — Gettysburg address; 8. Gettysburg address: Lincoln, Abraham
 978-0-06-156176-4, $16.99; 978-0-06-156175-7 (pa), $8.99
LC 2008-10657
 In the summer of 1863, everyone knew that the Battle of Gettysburg would be an important battle that could determine the course of the War Between the States, the Civil War. What they didn't know was who would prevail. Butzer uses primary sources to play out the battle that lasted three days and caused tremendous casualties, the aftermath that nearly overwhelmed the town of Gettysburg, and the effort to build the monument to commemorate the fallen. He uses a somber blue and gray wash in his illustrations. Lincoln's famous Gettysburg Address was only 271 words long and appear in their entirety, against images of the nation's past. Some panels depicting the violence of the battles, and particularly the dead on the battlefield, could be disturbing for sensitive younger readers; but this battle was ugly and overwhelming in its violence. Butzer includes extensive end notes to explain what he depicted, and to note the sources of the dialog and narration.

Byrne, Eugene
★ **Darwin:** a graphic biography. by Eugene Byrne; illustrated by Simon Gurr. Smithsonian Books 2013 96 p. Illustration
Grades: 5 6 7 8 9 10 11 12 Adult
576.8/2092; 576.8; 92
 1. Evolution (Biology) — Comic books, strips, etc; 2. Graphic novels; 3. Natural selection — Comic books, strips, etc; 4. Darwin, Charles, 1809-1882; 5. Evolution
 1588343529; 9781588343529, $9.95
LC 2012951786

Courtesy of Smithsonian Books

 This work of graphic nonfiction by Eugene Byrne and Simon Gurr presents a "summary of [Charles] Darwin's life and achievement.... Darwin was an indifferent student...until he received an invitation to take a voyage that 'would change the course of history.'...The animals he encountered seemed so different...that he theorized that if it weren't a matter of different conditions that resulted in such 'transmutation,' they might well have had a different creator." (Kirkus Reviews)
 Includes bibliographical references.

Byrne, John
 Superman: The Man of Steel Vol. 1. John Byrne, writer/penciller; Dick Giordano, inker; John Costanza, letterer; Tom Ziuko, colorist; foreword by Ray Bradbury. DC Comics 1991 132p. Illustration
Grades: 8 9 10 11 12 Adult   **741.5; Fic**
 1. Graphic novels; 2. Superhero graphic novels; 3. Superman (Fictional character)
 978-0930289287, $14.99
 This reprint of a 1986 book retells and reinvents the origin and early adventures of the Man of Steel. Superman begins his ascension to iconic hero as he leaves Smallville and becomes Metropolis's revered protector and guardian. Featuring the Man of Steel's legendary first encounters with Lex Luthor, Lois Lane, and Batman, this book also includes a deadly battle with Bizarro, a fateful encounter with Lana Lang, and Superman's astonishing discovery of his Kryptonian heritage.

 Superman: The Man of Steel Vol. 5. John Byrne, Marv Wolfman, writers; John Byrne, Jerry Ordway, pencillers. DC Comics 2006 210p. Illustration
Grades: 9 10 11 12 Adult   **741.5; Fic**
 1. Graphic novels; 2. Superhero graphic novels; 3. Superman (Fictional character); 4. Joker (Fictional character)
 978-1-4012-0948-3, $19.99
 Superman and the staff of the Daily Planet uncover a gang war raging in the city's notorious "Suicide Slum." Journalistic integrity is put to the test when it is revealed that Perry White's son is involved. Will the Daily Planet run a story that will ruin the life of one of their own? And what is the identity of the new protector of the streets, who emerges amid the havoc? Also, love is in the air, as Superman finds himself romantically involved with Big Barda, the amazon from the planet Apokolips, and with Cat Grant. Along with his ever-present nemesis Lex Luthor, Superman faces the evil of Sleez, the Joker, and that fiendish magical imp from the Fifth Dimension, Mr. Mxyzptlk. These stories were originally published in 1987.

★ **X-Men:** The Dark Phoenix Saga, 2nd ed.. writer, Chris Claremont; penciler and co-plotter, John Byrne. Marvel Entertainment 2006 200p. Illustration
Grades: 7 8 9 10 11 12 Adult   **741.5; Fic**
 1. Graphic novels; 2. Superhero graphic novels; 3. X-Men (Fictional characters)
 978-0-7851-2213-5, $24.99
 Gathered together by Professor Charles Xavier to protect a world that fears and hates them, the X-Men had fought many battles, been on adventures that spanned galaxies, grappled enemies of limitless might, but none of this could prepare them for the most shocking struggle they would ever face. One of their own members, Jean Grey, has gained power beyond all comprehension, and that power has corrupted her absolutely. Now they must decide if the life of the woman they cherish is worth the existence of the entire universe.

Cain, Chelsea
 Mockingbird; Volume 1: I can explain. Chelsea Cain, writer; Kate Niemczyk & Ibrahim Moustafa, artists. Marvel Enterprises 2016 136 p. Color; Illustration
Grades: 9 10 11 12 Adult   **741.5**
 1. Spy stories; 2. Women superheroes — Comic books, strips, etc.
 1302901222; 9781302901226, $17.99
 "Agent of S.H.I.E.L.D. Bobbi Morse, the former Avenger known as Mockingbird, goes solo. With a scientific mind and a lethal mastery of martial arts, she's one of the most versatile, in-demand assets at Maria Hill's disposal. And when Lance Hunter's undercover gig at the London Hellfire Club goes south, Mockingbird sets off, battle staves at the ready, to save him." (Publisher's note)
 "Novelist Cain's first foray into comics is rousing fun. Bobbi may be beautiful and skilled at combat, but her real weapon is her brain.... Niemczyk's art perfectly complements Cain's writing." Booklist
 Contains material originally published in single magazine form as Mockingbird: S.H.I.E.L.D. 50th anniversary #1 and Mockingbird #1-5; Volume 1 of 2

 Mockingbird; Volume 2: my feminist agenda. Chelsea Cain, writer; Kate Niemczyk, penciler; Sean Parsons, inker; Rachelle Rosenberg, color artist; VC's Joe Caramagna, letterer. Marvel Enterprises 2017 120 p. Color; Illustration

Grades: 9 10 11 12 Adult   **741.5**
1. Murder — Investigation — Graphic novels; 2. Ocean travel — Fiction; 3. Women superheroes — Comic books, strips, etc.
1302901230; 9781302901233, $15.99

"A top secret mission on behalf of an old friend, a tropical cruise. What could go wrong? Turns out it's a theme cruise — super-hero themed. Bobbi is trapped on a boat with a thousand cosplayers, caped colleagues she was trying to avoid, an ex-boyfriend who keeps showing up at inopportune times. When a passenger is murdered, Bobbi must...find the killer." (Publisher's note)

Contains material originally published in single magazine form as Mockingbird #6-8 and New Avengers #13-14

Callen, Kerry
    Halo and Sprocket vol. 2: Natural creatures. SLG Publishing/Amaze Ink 2008 un Illustration

Grades: 8 9 10 11 12 Adult   **741.5; Fic**
1. Angels — Graphic novels; 2. Graphic novels; 3. Humorous graphic novels; 4. Robots — Graphic novels
978-1-59362-131-5, $8.95

Halo the angel and Sprocket the robot live with a young woman named Katie. Their mission: to try to figure out the human race. They are puzzled by Katie's desire for privacy when she's taking a bath; they don't understand why she'll accept being clawed and bitten by a cute little kitten but won't hold a skink; and playing a trivia game causes Halo to show anger. When Halo transforms Sprocket into a human so he can experience what eating food is all about, the temporarily human Sprocket drives Katie crazy with questions about bodily functions such as burping, sneezing, and more.

Halo and Sprocket: Welcome to Humanity. SLG Publishing/Amaze Ink 2003 un Illustration

Grades: 7 8 9 10 11 12   **741.5; Fic**
1. Graphic novels; 2. Humorous graphic novels
0-943151-81-3, $12.95

What do an extremely powerful angel, a socially inexperienced robot, and a young, single woman have in common? Apparently, aside from the house they share, not very much! Logic, metaphysics, and human nature collide as Katie tries to educate both angel and robot about humans, philosophy, and such things as the Tooth Fairy. The book includes some slightly raunchy humor.

Cannon, Kevin
    The **cartoon** introduction to philosophy. Michael F. Patton and Kevin Cannon; Illustrated by Kevin Cannon. Hill & Wang 2015 176 p. Illustration

Grades: 11 12 Adult   **100; 741.5**
1. Philosophy — Introductions — Comic books, strips, etc; 2. Cartoons and caricatures; 3. Graphic novels
0809033623; 9780809033621, $17.95

LC 2014029343

In this book, authors "Michael F. Patton and Kevin Cannon introduce us to the grand tradition of examined living. With the wisecracking Heraclitus as our guide, we travel down the winding river of philosophy, meeting influential thinkers from nearly three millennia of Western thought and witnessing great debates over everything from ethics to the concept of the self to the nature of reality." (Publisher's note)

"The dynamic, cartoony illustrations might lead some to assume that this title is a little more accessible than it actually is, but anyone with an interest in learning about the philosophers and philosophical concepts that have shaped 21st-century life without having to plow their way through a dry textbook will find this title a stimulating delight." LJ

Includes bibliographical references

Crater XV. by Kevin Cannon. Top Shelf Productions 2013 496 p.

Grades: 10 11 12 Adult
741; Fic
1. Adventure graphic novels; 2. Science fiction graphic novels
1603091009; 9781603091008, $19.95

Courtesy of IDW Publishing

This graphic novel, by Kevin Cannon, "weaves together...swashbuckling adventure, abandoned moon bases, bloodthirsty walruses, rogue astronauts, two-faced femme fatales, sailboat chases, Siberian pirates, international Arctic politics, and a gaggle of horny orphans. Mixed up in all of this are Army Shanks, our salty sea dog still reeling from a devastating loss, and Wendy Byrd, a plucky teenager who wants nothing more than a one-way ticket off the face of the Earth." (Publisher's note)

Far Arden. Kevin Cannon. Top Shelf Productions 2009 400p. Illustration

Grades: 10 11 12 Adult
Fic; 741.5/973
1. Adventure graphic novels; 2. Arctic regions — Graphic novels
9781603090360, $19.95; 1603090363

Courtesy of IDW Publishing

In this graphic novel, by Kevin Cannon, "Army Shanks — crusty old sea dog and legendary brawler of the high Arctic seas...[has] one mission: to find the mythical island paradise known as Far Arden, which lies hidden...in the wintry oceans of the far North. But...he'll have to contend with circus performers, adorable orphans, heinous villains, bitter ex-lovers, well-meaning undergraduates, and the full might of the Royal Canadian Arctic Navy!" (Publisher's note)

Card, Orson Scott
    Ultimate Iron Man Vol. 1. writer: Orson Scott Card; pencils: Andy Kubert and Mark Bagley; inks: Danny Miki ... [et al.]; colors: Richard Isanove; letters: Chris Eliopoulos. Marvel Entertainment 2006 un Illustration

Grades: 10 11 12 Adult   **741.5; Fic**
1. Graphic novels; 2. Iron Man (Fictional character); 3. Superhero graphic novels
9780785121510, $14.99

Iron Man has been part of the Ultimates, but this volume gives his Ultimate origin. Due to an accident that happened before Tony Stark was born, he has grown up to be a super genius, but always in great physical pain. It's the main reason he becomes an alcoholic as an adult.

Carey, Mike
    Crossing Midnight: Cut Here. DC Comics/Vertigo 2007 124p. Illustration

Grades: 11 12 Adult   **741.5; Fic**
1. Fantasy graphic novels; 2. Graphic novels; 3. Horror graphic novels; 4. Mystery graphic novels
978-1-4012-1341-1, $9.99

In present-day Nagasaki, Japan, a set of twins are born — one just before midnight and the other just after. They discover the huge impact this small difference has on their destinies when the after-midnight twin is inducted into a world of supernatural beings and events that intersects with our own world. Together, they will desperately try to stay one step ahead of their terrifying fates while they learn how far the curse afflicting them really stretches. As their father gets mixed up with Yakuza, the story builds with violence, partial nudity, and harsh language.

Neil Gaiman's Neverwhere. DC Comics/Vertigo 2007 un Illustration
Grades: 11 12 Adult   **741.5; Fic**
1. Fantasy graphic novels; 2. Graphic novels; 3. Gaiman, Neil — Adaptations
978-1-4012-1007-6, $19.99

Ordinary Richard Mayhew lives an ordinary life in London, in an ordinary corporate job, with a domineering fiancee. Then one day he does one extraordinary thing: he defies his fiancee to help an injured young woman, and his life changes. That young woman, Door, comes from London Below, a fantastical world made up of the bits and pieces of forgotten city and life from above. Her family has been slaughtered, she's being hunted by a pair of extremely nasty, sadistic, violent assassins, and after Richard helps her he has no choice but to go to London Below, for his entire existence in ordinary London has been wiped out, as though he has never...been.

Neverwhere was first a script for a BBC miniseries written by Neil Gaiman; he then adapted his script into a novel, which is now adapted into graphic novel format.

Originally published as Neverwhere issues #1-9.

★ **Re-Gifters.** written by Mike Carey; art by Sonny Liew and Marc Hempel. DC Comics/Minx 2007 148p. Illustration
Grades: 7 8 9 10 11 12   **741.5; Fic**
1. Graphic novels; 2. High school students — Graphic novels; 3. Martial arts — Graphic novels; 4. Romance graphic novels; 5. School stories — Graphic novels
978-1-4012-0371-9 (pa), $9.99; 1-4109-0371-X (pa)

"Jen Dik Seong, or Dixie, is having trouble getting her ki focused. Normally an outstanding hapkido student, she finds that her crush on classmate Adam is affecting her ability to fight. This is not good, as the national competition is fast approaching, and her parents expect her to do well.... Dixie makes a series of poor choices. She decides to spend the entry fee...on an elaborate birthday present for Adam.... This is a terrific read that features complex characters dealing with internal and external conflicts that make them believable and endearing. Lively black-and-white illustrations bring action and emotion to the story." SLJ

Spellbinders: Signs & Wonders. Marvel Entertainment 2005 un Illustration
Grades: 7 8 9 10 11 12 Adult   **741.5; Fic**
1. Graphic novels; 2. Magic — Graphic novels; 3. Mystery graphic novels; 4. Supernatural graphic novels
0-7851-1756-3, $7.99

Getting through high school is hard enough without having to watch your back the whole time, but magic can give you a real edge over the competition. When 15-year-old Kim Vesco moves from Chicago to Salem, MA, she finds that the local student body is divided into rival factions of witches and non-witches, with both sides bidding for her allegiance. And if that weren't enough, an unknown force seems to want her... dead. Between the tribal loyalties of the schoolyard and the brutal, fight-or-die logic of the mage-war, Kim has to steer a course that will keep her alive until she can take the fight back to her enemy and reveal the true identity of someone she thought she already knew: herself.

★ The **Unwritten:** Tommy Taylor and the ship that sank twice. Mike Carey, illustrated by Peter Gross. Vertigo 2013 160 p. Color; Illustration

Grades: 11 12 Adult   **741.5; Fic**
1. Characters and characteristics in literature; 2. Identity (Philosophical concept) — Comic books, strips, etc; 3. Father-son relationship — Fiction; 4. Characters and characteristics in literature
140122976X; 9781401229764, $22.99

LC 2013020333

In this graphic novel by Mike Carey, "Tom Taylor has lived his life being mistaken for Tommy Taylor, the boy wizard from the world-famous series of novels penned by Tom's long-lost father Wilson. However, after a series of strange events start to parallel the lives of both Taylors — fictional and real — Tom realizes that he might be the character on page made flesh." (Publisher's note)

-"This title can serve as an entry point to the author's 'Unwritten' series, or as a standalone prequel.... The fictional Tommy receives his magical powers in this volume, and in a parallel narrative, Wilson crafts his first book, and orchestrates a twisted publicity stunt to make his son and his book character the same person in the eyes of the public.... Both story lines are equally compelling and balance each other out wonderfully-." SLJ

Carey, Percy
Sentences: the life of M F Grimm. DC Comics/Vertigo 2007 128p. Illustration
Grades: 11 12 Adult   **741.5; 92**
1. Autobiographical graphic novels; 2. Gangs — Graphic novels; 3. Graphic novels; 4. Rap music — Graphic novels; 5. Carey, Percy; 6. Carey, Percy — Graphic novels
978-1-4012-1046-5, $19.99

Percy Carey, known in the Hip Hop world as M.F. Grimm, tells his story, from his escape from poverty on the streets to his rise in the world of Hip Hop music. Life in this world involves cutthroat competition and sometimes violence; Carey lost the use of his legs in gang violence, he has spent time in prison, and he re-invented himself. This is his story, complete with the extremely foul language of the streets, and the violence of the life he led.

Carre, Lilli
The **fir-tree.** It Books/HarperCollins 2009 un Illustration
Grades: 3 4 5 6 7 8 9 10 11 12 Adult   **741.5; Fic**
1. Authors; 2. Children's authors; 3. Christmas — Graphic novels; 4. Christmas trees — Graphic novels; 5. Dramatists; 6. Graphic novels; 7. Novelists; 8. Short story writers; 9. Andersen, Hans Christian, 1805-1875 — Adaptations
978-0-06-178236-7, $14.99

A young fir-tree only wants to grow tall; it's never satisfied and doesn't notice the sunlight and clean air. It never rejoices in anything, but grumbles and complains. When it sees some trees being cut down and taken away, it wonders what it's missing. The birds tell of seeing the trees inside homes, beautifully decorated, and it becomes jealous. When it does grow tall and beautiful, a woodsman comes along and cuts it down, hauling it to town to become a Christmas tree in a house. It enjoys the family playing around the tree at Christmas, but after the holiday, the family throws it into a storeroom. Will the tree ever see its forest again? Lilli Carre uses delicate coloring and illustrations to adapt Andersen's sad Christmas story. Although this is suitable for young readers, adults may better appreciate the tragedy and Carre's idiosyncratic illustrations her people have long, loopy arms.

Carroll, Emily
★ **Through** the woods. Emily Carroll. Margaret K. McElderry Books 2014 208 p. Color; Illustration
Grades: 8 9 10 11 12 Adult   **741.5**

1. Graphic novels; 2. Short stories; 3. Horror fiction; 4. Comic books, strips, etc.
9781442465961, $14.99; 9781442465954, $21.99

LC 2013030969

Eisner Award: Best Graphic Album — Reprint (2015); Ignatz Award: Outstanding Artist (2015)

In this book, Emily Carroll "crafts five unsettling tales in graphic-novel format inspired by common folkloric themes — from wolves in the woods to peculiar visitors to dark possessions. In 'Our Neighbor's House,' three sisters who find themselves alone in a cabin are taken, one by one, in the middle of the night by a smiling stranger.... 'The Nesting Place' focus on malevolent spirit possession." (Horn Book Magazine)

"All the tales in Carroll's debut graphic novel are fairly standard ghost stories, but it is her eerie illustrations — popping with bold color on black, glossy pages — that masterfully build terrifying tension and a keep-the-lights-on atmosphere." Booklist

Casey, Joe
Godland Volume 1: Hello, Cosmic!. Joe Casey and Tom Scioli. Image Comics 2006 un Illustration
Grades: 8 9 10 11 12 Adult   **741.5; Fic**
1. Adventure graphic novels; 2. Graphic novels; 3. Science fiction graphic novels; 4. Superhero graphic novels
1-58240-712-6, $14.99

The cosmic superhero epic is back and this collection is chock-full of all the "cosmic" one could ask for. Experience the glory of Commander Adam Archer, the enigmatic alien Maxim, the wacky Basil Cronus, the evil Discordia, the confusing Freidrich Nickelhead and that's just scratching the surface. The storytelling and art bring back the kind of story that Stan Lee and Jack Kirby did, with fun superhero action and very little grim, gritty content.

Castellucci, Cecil
The **Plain** Janes. by Cecil Castellucci and Jim Rugg. DC Comics/Minx 2007 un Illustration
Grades: 7 8 9 10 11 12   **741.5; Fic**
1. Art — Graphic novels; 2. Friendship — Graphic novels; 3. Graphic novels; 4. High school students — Graphic novels; 5. School stories — Graphic novels
978-1-4012-1115-8, $9.99

After a bomb attack in Metro City, Jane's parents move to suburban Kent Waters, where Jane feels lost. Then she meets three other Janes at the "reject" table in the high school lunch room, and she convinces them to help her form their own secret club: P.L.A.I.N. — People Loving Art in Neighborhoods. However, their "art attacks" cause the authorities to think that P.L.A.I.N. is a terrorist group.

"The art, inspired by Dan Clowes' work, is absolutely engaging. Packaged like manga this is a fresh, exciting use of the graphic-novel format." Booklist

Another title about the Janes is: Janes in love (2008)

Soupy leaves home. written by Cecil Castellucci; illustrated by Jose Pimienta; lettered by Nate Piekos of Blambot. Dark Horse Books 2017 208 p. Color; Illustration
Grades: 7 8 9 10 11 12   **741.5; Fic**
1. Runaway teenagers — Fiction; 2. Homeless persons — Fiction
9781616554316, $14.99

LC 2016052804

In this book, by Cecil Castellucci, illustrated by Jose Pimienta, "Pearl 'Soupy' Plankette ran away from her abusive father, but has nowhere to go until she stumbles upon a disguise that gives her the key to a new identity. Reborn as a boy named Soupy, she hitches her star to Remy 'Ramshackle'

Smith, a hobo who takes her under his wing.... But Ramshackle has his own demons to wrestle with, and he'll need Soupy just as much as she needs him." (Publisher's note)

"A compelling graphic offering that explores relevant gender roles and self-identity through a historical lens." Kirkus

Includes bibliographical references

Castiglia, Paul
America's 1st Patriotic Comic Book Hero: The Shield Volume 1. Archie Comics 2002 96p. Illustration
Grades: 3 4 5 6 7 8 9 10 11 12 Adult   **741.5; Fic**
1. Adventure graphic novels; 2. Graphic novels; 3. Superhero graphic novels
1-879794-08-X, $12.95

A hero with great power, strength and courage who donned the colors of the American flag. A hero who lived for democracy and protected the world from the foes of freedom! No, it's not who you think... it's THE SHIELD, who predated his well known counterpart by over a year. This historic full color trade paperback reprints his first 8 stories from PEP and SHIELD/WIZARD Comics. It includes his first appearance and origin, along with the covers of the comics they originally appeared in, dating from 1940.

Archie Americana Series: Best of the Forties Book 2. Archie Comics 2002 96p. Illustration
Grades: 3 4 5 6 7 8 9 10 11 12 Adult   **741.5; Fic**
1. Andrews, Archie (Fictional character); 2. Graphic novels; 3. Humorous graphic novels
1-879794-09-8, $10.95

In 1941, Pep Comics introduced Archie Andrews, "America's newest boyfriend." Since then, Archie and his perennial teenage friends have entertained readers with their misadventures. This book includes stories from 1946 through 1949, with more slapstick and screwball comedy from Archie and the gang.

Archie Americana Series: Best of the Eighties. Archie Comics 2001 96p. Illustration
Grades: 3 4 5 6 7 8 9 10 11 12 Adult   **741.5; Fic**
1. Andrews, Archie (Fictional character); 2. Graphic novels; 3. Humorous graphic novels
1-879794-06-3, $10.95

During the 1980s pop culture ruled America; even the President was a former actor. In this volume, Archie and friends experience the punk movement, the "Urban Cowboy" craze, see the rise of MTV, get into the preppie, new wave and "Flashdance" fashions, play Trivial Pursuit, and boogie at the roller disco.

Volume 1 of 2

Best of Josie and the Pussycats Volume 1. Archie Comics 2001 96p. Illustration
Grades: 3 4 5 6 7 8 9 10 11 12 Adult   **741.5; Fic**
1. Adventure graphic novels; 2. Graphic novels; 3. Humorous graphic novels; 4. Rock music — Graphic novels
1-879794-07-1, $10.95

This book reprints a selection of stories about rock group Josie and the Pussycats, from their origin in 1963 to 1988. Josie, Melody, and Valerie are the Pussycats, along with their roadie Alan M., their shifty manager Alex, and his conniving sister, Alexandra. They make music, but along the way they also solve mysteries.

Sonic the Hedgehog: The Beginning. Archie Comics 2003 96p. Illustration
Grades: 3 4 5 6 7 8 9 10 11 12 Adult   **741.5; Fic**

1. Adventure graphic novels; 2. Graphic novels; 3. Humorous graphic novels; 4. Sonic the Hedgehog (Fictional character)
1-879794-12-8, $10.95

In 1993, Sonic the Hedgehog sped his way from video games to comic books, and has been going strong ever since. Now, readers can enjoy his earliest comic book adventures with this edition that reprints the first appearances of Tails, Princess Sally, Antoine, Rotor, Uncle Chuck, and Muttski. Fans can also marvel at Sonic's magic rings, the freedom emeralds, and King Acorn's magic crown; while booing and hissing at the villainous Robotnik, his evil Swat-Bots, and his myriad dastardly devices.

Castrée, Geneviève
Susceptible. Geneviève Castrée. Drawn & Quarterly 2012 75 p.
Grades: 9 10 11 12   **741.5; 741.5/971**
1. Graphic novels; 2. Identity (Psychology) — Graphic novels; 3. Family — Graphic novels; 4. Young women — Fiction
1770460888; 9781770460881, $19.95
                                            LC 2013375302
Ignatz Nominee: Outstanding Graphic Novel (2013)
In this graphic novel by Geneviève Castrée "Goglu is a daydreamer with a young working mother, a disengaged stepfather, and a father who lives five thousand miles away. Drawing, punk rock, and the promise of true independence guide Goglu to adulthood while her home — s daily chaos inevitably shapes her identity. It's a testament to the heartbreaking loss of innocence when a child is forced to be the adult amongst grownups." (Publisher's note)

Cauvin, Raoul
The **bluecoats** no. 1: Robertsonville Prison. Cinebook Ltd. 2008 48p. Illustration
Grades: 5 6 7 8 9 10   **741.5; Fic**
1. Adventure graphic novels; 2. Graphic novels; 3. Humorous graphic novels; 4. United States — History — 1861-1865, Civil War — Prisoners and prisons — Graphic novels
978-1-90546-071-7, $11.95
Sergeant Chesterfield and Corporal Blutch are Union soldiers during the Civil War; Blutch tends to be lazy, and Chesterfield always seems to be getting him out of trouble; but after one battle, they're both in trouble when they're captured by Confederate troops and are force-marched to Robertsonville Prison. They constantly get into trouble with a soldier and camp guard named Cockroach, and Chesterfield leads multiple attempts to escape the prison. Then when they succeed, they're wearing stolen Confederate uniforms and ultimately end up in a Union prison camp. Prison camps aren't normally subjects of humor, but the humor in this book is reminiscent of the old television series Hogan's Heroes, which was set in a German prisoner of war camp

Cavallaro, Mike
★ **Parade** (with fireworks). Image Comics/Shadowlands Books 2008 70p. Illustration
Grades: 10 11 12 Adult   **741.5; Fic**
1. Graphic novels; 2. Italy — History — 1914-1945 — Graphic novels
978-1-58240-995-5, $12.99
In 1923, Italy was recovering from the Great War; the fascists were already starting to come into power and battling the socialists. In Maropati, one family gets caught up in the political infighting. Paolo, whose father owns a large olive farm, has come back from living in Chicago, where he learned all about fighting feuds and settling disagreements with guns. On the evening of the Feast of the Epiphany, things in Maropati come to a head, local fascists attack and kill Paolo's brother and cousin, and he chooses to fight back. Despite the fact that the fascists had attacked first, he's the one who is hunted, tried, and convicted, and this shatters his

family. Cavallaro has based this story on what really happened to his family in Italy. This story first appeared as a webcomic, part of ACT-I-VATE, and was nominated for an Eisner Award, for Best Limited Series, in 2008. The book includes violence.

Chadwick, Paul
Concrete Vol. 1: Depths. Dark Horse Comics 2005 208p. Illustration
Grades: 10 11 12 Adult   **741.5; Fic**
1. Adventure graphic novels; 2. Concrete (Fictional character); 3. Graphic novels
1-59307-343-7, $12.95
Part man, part...rock? Over seven feet tall and weighing over a thousand pounds, he is known as Concrete but is in reality the mind of one Ronald Lithgow, trapped inside a shell of stone, a body that allows him to walk unaided on the ocean's floor or survive the crush of a thousand tons of rubble in a collapsed mineshaft...but prevents him from feeling the touch of a human hand. Depths, the first in a series of new collections reprinting the classic early Concrete stories along with never-before-collected short stories, includes the Eisner-nominated "Orange Glow" and "Vagabond," Paul Chadwick's autobiographical account of a cross-country hitchiking trip. Further volumes in the series show that Concrete collects nude paintings.
Volume 1 of 7

Chaykin, Howard
Fritz Leiber's Fafhrd and the Gray Mouser. adaptation and script, Howard Chaykin; pencils, Mike Mignola; inks, Al Williamson; colors, Sherlyn van Valkenburgh; letters, Michael Heisler. Dark Horse Comics 2007 un Illustration
Grades: 11 12 Adult   **741.5; Fic**
1. Adventure graphic novels; 2. Fantasy graphic novels; 3. Graphic novels; 4. Leiber, Fritz; 5. Leiber, Fritz — Adaptations
978-1-59307-713-6, $19.95
This volume, which was first published as a four-issue miniseries by Marvel Comics in 2001, adapts several of Leiber's stories about the huge northern barbarian Fafhrd and the conniving Gray Mouser. "Ill Met in Lankhmar" describes how the two meet; in "The Circle Curse" the two leave Lankhmar only to return because they're bored when away from the city; "The Bazaar of the Bizarre" offers trinkets and treasures which are really enchanted trash. In "Lean Times of Lankhmar," the two friends fall out and the Mouser works for a major thug while Fafhrd becomes a devotee of the god Issek of the Jug.
Leiber poked fun at the "sword and sorcery" type of fantasy adventure, but ended up crafting classic stories in the subgenre. Readers will find humor, swordfights, thievery, sex, and more.

Cherniss, Matt
Powerless. writers, Matt Cherniss & Peter Johnson; artist, Michael Gaydos. Marvel Entertainment 2005 un Illustration
Grades: 9 10 11 12 Adult   **741.5; Fic**
1. Graphic novels; 2. Superhero graphic novels; 3. Wolverine (Fictional character); 4. Spider-Man (Fictional character); 5. Daredevil (Fictional character)
07851-1511-0, $14.99
What makes a hero? Is it his actions, or is it the results of those actions? Powerless explores what it means to be a hero in very human terms. By re-imagining Marvel's most popular characters without superhuman powers, this story strips down to the core heroes readers have all come to know and love. These characters — including Peter Parker, Matt Murdock and Logan — were fated to be heroes. Just because Peter Parker wasn't bitten by a radioactive spider doesn't mean he didn't do battle with a madman named Norman Osborn. Matt Murdock? Blinded,

yes — but with no heightened senses. However, he did become a legal champion of the poor in Hell's Kitchen, and he did cross paths with Wilson Fisk, the Kingpin. And Logan is, of course, the enigmatic — and amnesiac — drifter on the run from his past. Psychiatrist Dr. Watts suffers strange dreams and visions even as he tries to help his three patients. The book includes some violence.

Cherrywell, Steph

★ **Pepper** Penwell and the land creature of Monster Lake. [written and drawn by Steph Cherrywell].. SLG Publishing 2011 un Illustration

Grades: 10 11 12 7 8 9 Adult   741.5; Fic
    1. Graphic novels; 2. Horror graphic novels; 3. Humorous graphic novels; 4. Monsters — Graphic novels; 5. Mystery graphic novels
978-1-59362-205-3, $14.95

British teenager Pepper Penwell prefers solving mysteries over school work and wants to be a detective like her father. When the latest school boots her out, Pepper takes on the case of a missing drum majorette named Lucy. Accompanied by her brother Alex, who inexplicably (it was some kind of accident) has the body of a bird, Pepper travels to Monster Lake, a town trying to establish itself as a tourist attraction based on its local monster, which is a land creature. In the town, Pepper meets strange people, any of whom could be guilty of kidnapping the wealthy and annoying Lucy. However, after Pepper does find Lucy, there's still the matter of the land monster, which is all too real. British slang (arse, bum) provides the mildly harsh language.

Chii

★ The **bride** was a boy. (true) story and art by Chii. Seven Seas Entertainment 2018 158 p. Illustration

Grades: 9 10 11 12 Adult   92; 741.5
    1. Gender identity; 2. Transgender people — Japan — Biography; 3. Manga — Graphic novels — Japan
1626928886; 9781626928886, $13.99

This book, by Chii, is "a diary comic with an upbeat, adorable flair that tells the charming tale of Chii, a woman assigned male at birth. Her story starts with her childhood and follows the ups and downs of exploring her sexuality, gender, and transition-as well as falling in love with a man who's head over heels for her. Now, Chii is about to embark on a new adventure: becoming a bride!" (Publisher's note)

"Equal parts Trans 101 and tear-jerking rom-com, there's no other manga quite like this fun (and revolutionary) book." Pub Wkly

Originally published in Japan in 2016 by Asukashinsha, Tokyo

Church, Kevin

Cover girl. Andrew Cosby & Kevin Church, writers; Mateus Santolouco, pencils; R.M. Yankovicz, inker (chapter one-two); Andre Coelho, inker (chapter three-four); Ed Dukeshire, letterer; Pablo Quiligotti & Brian Miroglio, colorists. Boom! Studios 2008 un Illustration

Grades: 9 10 11 12 Adult   741.5; Fic
    1. Adventure graphic novels; 2. Graphic novels; 3. Mystery graphic novels
978-1-934506-27-1, $14.99

Young struggling actor Alex Martin saves a woman whose car crashes off the road, and the videotape of his rescue helps his fortunes rise, and he snags the lead role in a high-budget action film. However, mysterious black SUVs seem to be following him, and then someone (or several someones) attempt several times to kill him. The studio hires a bodyguard, but Rachel Dodd isn't the usual type. She has to play the part of Alex's girlfriend in order to be by his side. When she and her partner Dwight manage to foil several more attempts to kill Alex, they decide they need to find out who's trying to kill Alex, and why. They soon discover it all comes back to Alex's roadside rescue of the woman, who has since disappeared from public

view. This story is full of action and includes some violence and mildly bad language. Anyone who enjoys fast-paced action films with witty dialog will enjoy this. Teen girls and women may delight in the fact that the action hero is a no-nonsense woman who can shoot and fight as well as any male action movie hero.

Chwast, Seymour

★ The **odyssey**. Homer; adapted by Seymour Chwast. Bloomsbury 2012 128 p. Color; Illustration

Grades: 9 10 11 12 Adult   398.2; 741.5
    1. Graphic novels; 2. Greek mythology — Graphic novels; 3. Homer; 4. Odysseus (Greek mythology); 5. Adventure graphic novels; 6. Epic literature
1608194868; 9781608194865, $

LC 2012010047

"The latest in an unofficial series of graphic novels based on the classics (The Canterbury Tales; The Divine Comedy), veteran illustrator and graphic designer Chwast interprets the Greek epic in straightforward but whimsical line drawings that invest the familiar tale with droll energy.... Our hero is cast as a Buck Rogers-like space traveler, bouncing from planet to planet (instead of island to island) in Deco-inspired rocket ships." (Publishers Weekly)

"While the subjects of his previous comics adaptations had a higher component of moral or philosophical instruction, The Odyssey — particularly in Chwast's hands — is more of a rousing adventure tale, making this imaginative interpretation a genuinely fun read." Booklist

CLAMP (Mangaka group)

★ **Cardcaptor** Sakura: Book 1. story and art by CLAMP. Dark Horse Manga 2010 576 p. Illustration; Color

Grades: 6 7 8 9 10   741.5; Fic
    1. Magic — Juvenile fiction; 2. Wizards — Fiction; 3. Fantasy fiction — Juvenile fiction; 4. Shojo manga; 5. Manga
1595825223; 9781595825223, $19.99

"Fourth-grader Sakura Kinomoto found a strange book in her father's library — a book made by the wizard Clow to store dangerous spirits sealed within a set of magical cards. But when Sakura opened it up, there was nothing left inside but Kero-chan, the book's cute little guardian beast, who informs Sakura that since the Clow cards seem to have escaped while he was asleep, it's now her job to capture them!" (Publisher's note)

"CLAMP's classic manga series (originally published in the U.S. in a 12-volume, two-series run) is being rereleased in remastered and newly translated omnibus editions that collect three books each." Booklist

Volume 1 of 4

Tsubasa: Reservoir Chronicle Vol. 1. Clamp; translated and adapted by Anthony Gerard; lettered by Dana Hayward. Random House/Del Rey Manga 2004 198p. Illustration

Grades: 8 9 10 11 12   741.5; Fic
    1. Fantasy graphic novels; 2. Graphic novels; 3. Manga; 4. Shonen manga; 5. Supernatural graphic novels
0-345-47057-5, $10.95

LC 2004-101711

Sakura is the princess of Clow-and possessor of a mysterious, misunderstood power that promises to change the world. Syaoran is her childhood friend and leader of the archaeological dig that took his father's life. They reside in an alternate reality...where whatever you least expect can happen-and does. When Sakura ventures to the dig site to declare her love for Syaoran, a puzzling symbol is uncovered-which triggers a remarkable quest. Now Syaoran embarks upon a desperate journey through other worlds-all in the name of saving Sakura. This series crosses over with xxxHolic, and both of them use characters from past CLAMP manga. The book includes some violence.

XXXHolic Vol. 1. Random House/Del Rey Manga 2004 un Illustration
Grades: 8 9 10 11 12   **741.5; Fic**
1. Fantasy graphic novels; 2. Graphic novels; 3. Manga; 4. Seinen manga; 5. Supernatural graphic novels
0-345-47058-3, $10.95
Watanuki Kimihiro is haunted by visions of ghosts and spirits. Seemingly by chance, he encounters a mysterious witch named Yuuko, who claims she can help. In desperation, he accepts, but realizes that he's just been tricked into working for Yuuko in order to pay off the cost of her services. Soon he's employed in her little shop-a job which turns out to be nothing like his previous work experience. Most of Yuuko's customers live in Japan, but Yuuko and Watanuki are about to have some unusual visitors named Sakura and Syaoran from a land called Clow... The book includes some strong language and graphic violence.

Claremont, Chris
★ **Wolverine**. Marvel Entertainment 2007 un Illustration
Grades: 9 10 11 12 Adult   **741.5; Fic**
1. Graphic novels; 2. Superhero graphic novels; 3. Wolverine (Fictional character)
978-0-7851-2329-3, $19.99
Originally published in the early 1980s, this was the first miniseries to delve into the character of the berserker mutant, Wolverine, and shape him into something more than a snarling fighting beast. Wolverine loves Mariko, but she is a yakuza boss's daughter; and when he follows her back to Japan, the Hand hires the ninja Yukio to kill Logan. Instead, she falls in love with him. Wolverine fights gangsters and ninja in his bid to win Mariko's heart.

X-Men: The End Book One: Dreamers & Demons. Marvel Entertainment 2005 un Illustration
Grades: 7 8 9 10 11 12 Adult   **741.5; Fic**
1. Graphic novels; 2. Superhero graphic novels; 3. X-Men (Fictional characters)
978-0-7851-1690-5, $14.99
It's the epic finale to the story of the Children of the Atom as X-Men scribe Chris Claremont joins with artist Sean Chen for a trilogy in the style of the Lord of the Rings movies, one that spans the length and breadth of the X-Men canon and brings the saga of Marvel's mutants to a climax. In this volume, the unthinkable happens — attackers succeed in breaching all security at the Xavier School for the Gifted and threaten the lives of all the young mutants living there.

X-Men: The End Book Three: Men & X-Men. writer, Chris Claremont; artist, Sean Chen. Marvel Entertainment 2006 un Illustration
Grades: 7 8 9 10 11 12 Adult   **741.5; Fic**
1. Graphic novels; 2. Superhero graphic novels; 3. X-Men (Fictional characters)
978-0-7851-1692-9, $14.99
The endgame of the last tale of Marvel's most popular mutants begins. They've suffered through sneak attacks, betrayals, and fatalities — now, Professor X and Magneto are taking the fight back to the enemy, amidst the stars.

X-Men: The End Book Two: Heroes & Martyrs. Chris Claremont; artist, Sean Chen. Marvel Entertainment 2005 un Illustration
Grades: 7 8 9 10 11 12 Adult   **741.5; Fic**
1. Graphic novels; 2. Superhero graphic novels; 3. X-Men (Fictional characters)
978-0-7851-1691-2, $14.99

The Xavier Academy has been reduced to a smoldering crater in a brutal sneak attack, and the casualties number in the hundreds. Now, Cyclops must mobilize the survivors to get to the bottom of who is behind these coordinated strikes on mutants in general and the X-Men in particular.

★ **X-Men:** days of future past. Chris Claremont, art by John Byrne. Marvel Worldwide 2011 176 p.
Grades: 9 10 11 12 Adult   **741.5**
1. X-Men (Fictional characters)
0785164537; 9780785164531, $19.99
     LC bl2011037630
"Relive the legendary first journey into the dystopian future of 2013 — where Sentinels stalk the Earth, and the X-Men are humanity's only hope...until they die! Also featuring the first appearance of Alpha Flight, the return of the Wendigo, the history of the X-Men from Cyclops himself...and a demon for Christmas!?" (Publisher's note)

Clevinger, Brian
Atomic Robo; Volume one: Atomic Robo and the Fightin' Scientists of Tesladyne. words, Brian Clevinger; art and cover, Scott Wegener; colors, Ronda Pattison; letters, Jeff Powell. Red 5 Comics 2008 180 p. Color illustration (Atomic Robo)
Grades: 9 10 11 12 Adult   **741.5**
1. Robots — Graphic novels; 2. Science fiction graphic novels; 3. Superhero comic books, strips, etc.
0980930200; 9780980930207, $18.95
This graphic novel, by Brian Clevinger, illustrated by Scott Wegener and Ronda Pattison, collects the first six issues of the action comic series "Atomic Robo." "Atomic Robo and the so-called Action Scientists of Tesladyne become the go-to defense force against the unexplained! See ROBO take on Nazis, giant ants, clockwork mummies, walking pyramids, Mars, cyborgs, and his nemesis, Baron von Helsingard." (Publisher's note)
"[This] series about a scientific adventure robot created by Nikola Tesla has been...funny and yet surprisingly touching at times, a book that features car chases, gun fights and robots punching other robots but never uses them as an excuse to give up on being smart." ComicsAlliance
Volume 1 of an ongoing series

Cliff, Tony
★ **Delilah** Dirk and the king's shilling. Tony Cliff. First Second 2016 272 p.
Grades: 9 10 11 12   **741.5/973**
1. Adventure and adventurers — Fiction; 2. Graphic novels; 3. Espionage — Fiction; 4. Adventure graphic novels; 5. Fantasy graphic novels
1626721556; 9781626721555, $17.99
     LC 2015020653
In this graphic novel, by Tony Cliff, "globetrotting troublemaker Delilah Dirk and her loyal friend Selim are just minding their own business, peacefully raiding castles and and traipsing across enemy lines, when they attract the unwanted attention of the English Army. Before they know it, Delilah and Selim have gotten themselves accused of espionage against the British crown!" (Publisher's note)

★ **Delilah** Dirk and the Turkish Lieutenant. by Tony Cliff. First Second 2013 176 p. Illustration
Grades: 7 8 9 10 11 12   **741.5; Fic**
1. Women adventurers — Fiction; 2. Historical fiction; 3. Istanbul (Turkey) — Fiction; 4. Adventure fiction
1596438134; 9781596438132, $15.99
     LC 2013947230

In this book, "Delilah Dirk has abandoned conventional court life and become a globe-trotting soldier of fortune. She is captured and held prisoner in 1800s Constantinople. Eventually she escapes, taking along the astonished Turkish Lieutenant Erdemogul Selim, whose quiet life centers around a proper cup of tea. This unlikely pair embarks on a wild journey that includes flying a ship, outwitting the Evil Pirate Captain Zakul, and escaping burning buildings." (School Library Journal)

"Plenty of fight scenes will attract male readers, in addition to females looking for strong heroines. All in all, this is a carefree romp across the Ottoman Empire with an upbeat tone that is refreshing." Lib Med Con

Other titles in this series are: Delilah Dirk and the King's Shilling (2016); Delilah Dirk and the Pillars of Hercules (2018)

Clowes, Daniel
★ **Ghost** world. Daniel Clowes. Fantagraphics Bks. 1997 80p. Illustration
Grades: 11 12 Adult   **741.5**
1. Female friendship — Graphic novels; 2. Teenage girls — Fiction
1-56097-280-7 (pa), $19.95; 9781560974277
Ignatz Award: Outstanding Story (1998); Ignatz Award: Outstanding Graphic Novel or Collection (1998)

"Eight interconnected stories about two teens. Enid and Rebecca have been friends for so long that it's difficult for either of them to let the other grow or change. Now Enid will probably leave their working-class neighborhood and go away to college and Rebecca cannot accept this change in their relationship." (School Library Journal)

Clugston-Flores, Chynna
Blue Monday; Volume 1: The Kids Are Alright. writer & illustrator, Chynna Clugston Flores. Image Comics 2016 136 p. Color; Illustration
Grades: 9 10 11 12   **741.5; Fic**
1. Punk rock music — Fiction; 2. Friendship — Graphic novels; 3. Teenagers — Graphic novels; 4. Rock music — Graphic novels
1632157047; 9781632157041, $9.99

"Adolescence is tough, especially when teens are still trying to discover who they are. Part of a group of misfits, high schooler Bleu figures out how to score tickets to see her favorite band, deals with a crush on her new substitute teacher, daydreams in class, takes part in prank wars gone wrong, and takes a stand against sexism. Originally published in the 2000s by Oni Press, this series is available now for the first time in color." (School Library Journal)

Originally published 2003 by Oni Press; Contains material originally published in single magazine form as Blue Monday #1-3 and collected short stories; Other volumes in this series are: Volume 2, Absolute Beginners; Volume 3, Inbetween Days; Volume 4, Painted Moon

Coates, Ta-Nehisi
★ **Black** Panther; Book 1: a nation under our feet. by Ta-Nehisi Coates; illustrated by Brian Stelfreeze; color by Laura Martin. Marvel Enterprises 2016 144 p. Color; Illustration
Grades: 11 12 Adult   **741.5; Fic**
1. Superhero graphic novels; 2. Black Panther (Fictional character)
9781302900533, $16.99; 1302900536

"When a superhuman terrorist group that calls itself The People sparks a violent uprising, the land famed for its incredible technology and proud warrior traditions will be thrown into turmoil. If Wakanda is to survive, it must adapt — but can its monarch, one in a long line of Black Panthers, survive the necessary change?" (Publisher's note)

Originally published in single issues as Black Panther #1-4; Other Black Panther volumes by Coates are: A nation under our feet, book two (2017); A nation under our feet, book three (2017); Avengers of

the new world, part one (2017); Avengers of the new world, part two (2018)

Cobley, Jason
Frankenstein: the graphic novel. [by] Mary Shelley; script adaptation Jason Cobley; American English adaptation: Joe Sutliff Sanders; linework: Declan Shalvey; coloring: Jason Cardy & Kat Nicholson; lettering: Terry Wiley. Classical Comics 2008 141p. Illustration
Grades: 6 7 8 9 10 11 12 Adult
741.5; Fic
1. Authors; 2. Frankenstein (Fictional character); 3. Graphic novels; 4. Horror graphic novels; 5. Shelley, Mary Wollstonecraft, 1797-1851 — Adaptations; 6. Frankenstein's monster (Fictional character)
978-1-906332-49-5, $16.95

© Classical Comics
www.classicalcomics.com

Young scientist Victor Frankenstein becomes obsessed with the idea that technology can create life, and works to prove his theories. However, his success doesn't bring him glory, but a living nightmare for himself and everyone around him. This graphic adaptation brings the entire book to the reader, using Shelley's original text for the dialog and narrative. Back matter includes a brief biography of Shelley, her family tree, a description of how she came to write the novel, and information on some of the various adaptations of the story to the stage and to film.

"More than a straightforward retelling, this edition invites readers to explore important social issues such as alienation, the consequences and ethics of scientific studies, as well as the nature of creation and destruction." SLJ

Also available quick text version $16.95 (ISBN: 978-1-906332-50-1); Original text version

Cole, Allison
Never Ending Summer. Alternative Comics 2004 128p. Illustration
Grades: 10 11 12 Adult
741.5; Fic
1. Autobiographical graphic novels; 2. Cole, Allison
1-891867-66-0, $11.95

Courtesy of Alternative Comics

This story is an autobiographical account that follows a group of friends through a summer filled with uncertainty and confusion. Relationships break down between boyfriends, friends, and family, throughout which the author must discover how to maintain a sense of balance. Parties, excessive drinking, and financial instability add to the commotion. The book reflects upon the immediacy of the present and the potential of events to come. There's very little in the way of strong language or sexual situations.

Colfer, Eoin
Artemis Fowl: the graphic novel. adapted by Eoin Colfer and Andrew Donkin; art by Giovanni Rigano; color by Paolo Lammana. Hyperion Books for Children 2007 un Illustration
Grades: 4 5 6 7 8 9   **741; 741.5; Fic**
1. Adventure graphic novels; 2. Fantasy graphic novels; 3. Graphic novels

978-0-7868-4881-2, $18.99; 0-7868-4881-2; 978-0-7868-4882-9 (pa), $9.99; 0-7868-4882-0 (pa)

Twelve-year-old genius and criminal mastermind Artemis Fowl runs his missing father's crime empire and gets his hands on a book that will give him access to the underground fairy world. This graphic novel adaptation gives the book a European look and color palette

"Excellent use of color and shading gives the panels a tremendous sense of light with enchanting effect. Characters are expressively brought to life with fun, exaggerated style." SLJ

Other Artemis Fowl graphic novels are:Artemis Fowl: the Arctic incident (2009);Artemis Fowl: the eternity code (2013);Artemis Fowl: the opal deception (2014)

Collins, Max Allan

Dick Tracy: The Collins Casefiles Volume 1. Checker Book Publishing Group 2003 164p. Illustration
Grades: 8 9 10 11 12 Adult   **741.5; Fic**
   1. Dick Tracy (Fictional character); 2. Graphic novels; 3. Mystery graphic novels
0-9741664-2-1, $19.95

LC 2003-23068

This is the first of several volumes collecting Collins' 11-year run on the Dick Tracy comic strips. He took over scripting duties from Chester Gould in 1978, although Gould maintained his byline and consulted with Collins on plot directions. Fletcher, a longtime Gould assistant, took over the drawing and worked with Collins. This volume includes the stories Ängel Top's Last Stand, Return of Haf-and Haf, and Big Boy's Revenge.

Johnny Dynamite: Underworld. AiT/Planet Lar 2003 un Illustration
Grades: 10 11 12 Adult
741.5; Fic
   1. Graphic novels; 2. Horror graphic novels; 3. Mystery graphic novels
1-932051-10-4, $12.95

1950s tough-guy private detective Johnny Dynamite goes up against zombies in Las Vegas as well as the mob, and the zombies also have crime on their undead minds. Mob-style violence, with beatings and hits, combines with zombie killings and horror action.

Courtesy of AiT/Planet Lar

Conley, Steve

Astounding space thrills: Argosy Smith and the codex reckoning. IDW Publishing 2008 192p. Illustration
Grades: 9 10 11 12 Adult   **741.5; Fic**
   1. Adventure graphic novels; 2. Graphic novels; 3. Science fiction graphic novels
978-1-60010-320-9, $19.99

Adventurer Argosy Smith lives on an Earth that has changed drastically due to its move thanks to some aliens time flows differently, space folds weirdly, and the Earth has basically become the library of the universe. Smith races against time (he's supposed to die on his 25th birthday, which is tomorrow) to steal a lost manuscript by Leonardo Da Vinci, discover the secret of Split-Space travel, keep two alien races from all-out war, avoid certain death at the hands of little green mercenaries hired by a several-brained-corporate head, and keep the universe from breaking apart. Oh yeah, and celebrate his birthday. The action harkens back to the kind of cosmic science fiction adventure written by E. E. "Doc" Smith, with lots of action.

Conner, Amanda

Harley Quinn; Volume 1. Amanda Conner, Jimmy Palmiotti, writers; Chad Hardin, Stéphane Roux, artists. DC Comics 2014 224 p. Color; Illustration
Grades: 11 12 Adult   **741.5**
   1. Superhero comic books, strips, etc.
1401248926; 9781401248925, $24.99

LC 2014034093

In this comic book, writers Amanda Conner and Jimmy Palmiotti "unleashed Harley [Quinn] on an unsuspecting DC Universe, as she encounters various heroes and villains...and leaves no one unscathed in her wake! With art by Chad Hardin and a slew of comics' best artists including Darwyn Cooke, Sam Kieth, Tony S. Daniel, Paul Pope, Walter Simonson and Art Baltazar!" (Publisher's note)

Harley Quinn; Volume 1: die laughing. Amanda Conner, Jimmy Palmiotti, writers; JohnTimms, Chad Hardin, Bret Blevins, Joseph MichaelLinsner, Jill Thompson, artists; Alex Sinclair,Hi-Fi, Jill Thompson, colorists; Dave Sharpe,letterer; Amanda Conner and Alex Sinclair,original serie. DC Comics 2017 un Color; Illustration
Grades: 11 12 Adult   **741.5; Fic**
   1. Supervillains — Comic books, strips, etc.; 2. Harley Quinn (Fictitious character) — Comic books, strips, etc.
9781401268312, $16.99

"Her name is Dr. Harleen Quinzel, better known to her friends and enemies as playful-but-deadly Harley Quinn. Her ex-boyfriend, the Joker, may be the Clown Prince of Crime, but Harley's the Queen of Coney Island! So when a zombie apocalypse threatens her li'l seaside stretch of paradise, who else would ya call to save your butt? In these action-packed pages, the baddest bad girl in the entire DC Universe joins forces with everyone from her gal-pal Poison Ivy to the leading lights of the New York City punk scene to take down anyone who stands between her and a good time — living, dead or undead." (Publisher's note)

Originally published in single magazine form in HARLEY QUINN 1-7

Conner, Daniel

The **picture** of Dorian Gray. adapted by Daniel Conner; illustrated by Chris Allen.. Magic Wagon/Graphic Planet 2009 32p. Illustration
Grades: 6 7 8 9 10
741.5; Fic
   1. Authors; 2. Dramatists; 3. Graphic novels; 4. Horror graphic novels; 5. Lecturers; 6. Novelists; 7. Poets; 8. Portraits — Graphic novels; 9. Supernatural graphic novels; 10. Wilde, Oscar, 1854-1900 — Adaptations
978-160270-680-4, $27.07

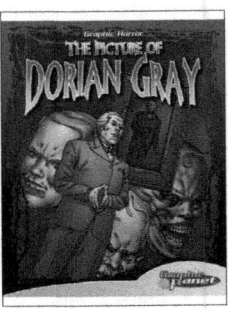

LC 2009-8597   *Courtesy of ABDO Publishing.*

Impossibly handsome, young Dorian Gray sits for a portrait and then impulsively wishes that he could never age and that the portrait should do so in his place. However, as life goes on, he becomes evil; he falls in love with an actress and then spurns her; he murders the portrait artist; and with every act his portrait becomes more and more grotesque while he remains a youthful, handsome fellow. This easy-reading graphic novel adaptation of Oscar Wilde's horror story makes it easier for reluctant and struggling readers to enjoy the story. Back matter includes a brief biography of Wilde, a list of some of his other works, and a short glossary. The question of morality in the story and the violence make this more suitable for somewhat older readers, despite the simplicity of language.

This is part of the Graphic Horror Series 2.

William Shakespeare's A midsummer night's dream. adapted by Daniel Conner; illustrated by Rod Espinosa.. ABDO/Magic Wagon 2008 48p. Illustration
Grades: 5 6 7 8 9 10   **741.5; Fic**
1. Graphic novels.; 2. Youths' writings.; 3. Shakespeare, William; 4. Shakespeare, William — Adaptations.
978-1-60270-191-5, $28.50

LC 2008-10745

In Athens, the ruler Theseus prepares to marry Hippolyta. Meanwhile, Hermia and Lysander run away to the forest because Hermia doesn't want to marry Demetrius, who follows them into the forest with Helena, whom he loves. Enter Puck, mischievous fairy who serves Oberon, the King of the Fairies. When he is ordered to find a flower whose nectar acts like a love potion and use it on Queen Titania, Puck also decides to play with the two young couples. And meanwhile again, a group of guildsmen prepare a play for their ruler's wedding. Havoc ensues. This graphic novel adaptation retains some of the original language from Shakespeare's play, while paring down the story to appeal to struggling readers. The book includes a short biography of Shakespeare, a summary of the play, a glossary, and a short selection of famous lines and phrases from the play.
Part of the Graphic Shakespeare series

Cooke, Darwyn
Batman: Ego and Other Tails. DC Comics 2007 200p. Illustration
Grades: 10 11 12 Adult   **741.5; Fic**
1. Batman (Fictional character); 2. Catwoman (Fictional character); 3. Graphic novels; 4. Mystery graphic novels; 5. Superhero graphic novels
978-1-4012-1529-3, $24.99

This volume collects Cooke's work for DC that focus on Batman and Catwoman. In Ego, after suffering physical and psychological trauma, Batman confronts himself in his mind. The book also includes Catwoman: Selina's Big Score, in which the perfect heist...isn't. The book includes some violence and strong language.

★ **DC:** The New Frontier Vol. 1. DC Comics 2004 un Illustration
Grades: 9 10 11 12 Adult   **741.5; Fic**
1. Graphic novels; 2. Superhero graphic novels; 3. Batman (Fictional character); 4. Superman (Fictional character); 5. Wonder Woman (Fictional character)
1-4012-0350-7, $19.99; 9781401203504
2005 Eisner Award for Best Limited Series.

World War II is over. The Cold War has begun. The Age of the Superhero is in decline. But where are the heroes of tomorrow? This book recounts the dawning of the DC Universe's Silver Age from the perspective of those brave individuals who made it happen. Encounter "keepers of the flame" including Superman, Wonder Woman and Batman, who survived the anti-hero sentiment of the Cold War, as well as eager newcomers like test pilot Hal Jordan and scientist Barry Allen, poised to become the next generation of crime fighters. The book includes some strong language and violence.

★ **DC:** The New Frontier Vol. 2. DC Comics 2005 un Illustration
Grades: 9 10 11 12 Adult   **741.5; Fic**
1. Aquaman (Fictitious character); 2. Graphic novels; 3. Superhero graphic novels; 4. Wonder Woman (Fictional character); 5. Superman (Fictional character); 6. Batman (Fictional character); 7. Flash (Fictional character)
1-4012-0461-9, $19.99
2005 Eisner Award for Best Limited Series.

It's a mystery in space as Superman, the Suicide Squad, and the Challengers of the Unknown encounter a frightening extraterrestrial life form. Could this hideous creature have anything to do with the sense of impending doom all the heroes are experiencing? Meanwhile, pilot Hal Jordan is grounded, while post-war America faces a monstrous threat older than time. Will this challenge bring America and its heroes back together or tear them apart? The book features Green Lantern, the Flash, Martian Manhunter, Aquaman, Wonder Woman, Batman, and more heroes. It includes some strong language and some violence.

★ The **Spirit** book one. written by Darwyn Cooke and Jeph Loeb; drawn by Darwyn Cooke; inks and finishes by J. Bone; colors by Dave Stewart; letters by Jared K. Fletcher. DC Comics 2007 192p. Illustration
Grades: 8 9 10 11 12 Adult   **741.5; Fic**
1. Batman (Fictional character); 2. Graphic novels; 3. Humorous graphic novels; 4. Superhero graphic novels; 5. The Spirit (Fictional character)
978-1-4012-1461-6; 978-1-4012-1618-4 (pa), $19.99

Will Eisner's character The Spirit was popular for decades. Eisner is gone, but Darwyn Cooke has taken up the pen to update The Spirit while maintaining the action, adventure, and humor of the original stories. Readers will meet Commissioner Dolan and his daughter Ellen, Ebony, bad girl P'Gell, and more. This volume also includes the Eisner Award winning Batman/The Spirit special, written by Jeph Loeb and drawn by Cooke. The upcoming live action movie directed by comics veteran Frank Miller will spark more interest in the comics. The book includes lots of action and some cartoony violence.

"This is fine, entertaining stuff that will satisfy any longtime comics fan; recommended for teens and adults." Libr J

The **Spirit** book two. writers, Darwyn Cooke [and others]; artists, J. Bone [and others]; colors by Dave Stewart, Alex Sinclair and Jim Charalampidis; letters by Jared K. Fletcher. DC Comics 2008 un Illustration
Grades: 10 11 12 Adult   **741.5; Fic**
1. Graphic novels; 2. Mystery graphic novels; 3. The Spirit (Fictional character); 4. Spirit (Fictional character)
978-1-4012-1920-8, $24.99

In this second volume of Darwyn Cooke's take on Will Eisner's iconic character, The Spirit, readers meet Silk Satin, a sultry and sexy CIA agent, the villainous Octopus, and El Morte, the criminal who died with Denny Colt only to be raised as a zombie by his mother's supernatural rites. Along the way, the Spirit also works (sort of) with cable crime reporter Ginger Coffee to find out who is killing all the cable news pundits. The book includes violence and some bloodshed.

Cooper, Nate
Build your own website: a comic guide to HTML, CSS, and WordPress. Nate Cooper. No Starch Press 2014 250 p. Illustration
Grades: 7 8 9 10 11 12   **006.7**
1. Web site development — Humor; 2. Web sites — Design — Humor; 3. HTML (Document markup language)
1593275226; 9781593275228, $19.95

LC 2014019597

Author Nate Cooper and illustrator Kim Gee present this "illustrated introduction to the basics of creating a website. Join Kim and her little dog Tofu as she learns HTML, the language of web pages, and CSS, the language used to style web pages, from the Web Guru and Glinda, the Good Witch of CSS." (Publisher's note)

"The comic art engages the readers and gives the broad picture of what the reader will learn from Cooper's text which follows. Best suited for beginning self-learning, it is one of the few books on the topic which entertains as well as educates."
Includes index.

Crain, Dale
The **DC** Comics Rarities Archives Volume 1. DC Comics 2004 348p. Illustration
Grades: 7 8 9 10 11 12 Adult   **741.5; Fic**

1. Graphic novels; 2. Superhero graphic novels
1-4012-0007-8, $75

For the first time ever, in one huge collection, three of DC Comics' most hard to find early anthology titles are reprinted in their entirety. This is a 348-page hardcover collecting New York World's Fair 1939, New York World's Fair 1940 and Big All-American Comic Book #1 (1944). The two World's Fair Comics were specially created to be distributed at the legendary New York World's Fair of 1939-40 and feature adventures revolving around the DC heroes' visits there.

The **Seven** Soldiers of Victory Archives Volume 1. DC Comics 2005 237p. Illustration
Grades: 6 7 8 9 10 11 12 Adult   **741.5; Fic**
1. Graphic novels; 2. Superhero graphic novels; 3. Green Arrow (Fictional character)
1-4012-0401-5, $49.95

Collecting Leading Comics #1-4, featuring the adventures of The Seven Soldiers of Victory: The Crimson Avenger, Green Arrow, the Shining Knight, The Vigilante, the Star-Spangled Kid, and their sidekicks Speedy, Stripesy, and Wing (yes, there were eight of them). In 1941, one year after DC Comics launched the Justice Society of America in All-Star Comics, sister company All-American Comics released Leading Comics #1 featuring its very own super-team; in these early stories they take on various criminals and villains who possess super-senses.

Superman Archives Volume 7. DC Comics 2006 237p. Illustration
Grades: 8 9 10 11 12 Adult   **741.5; Fic**
1. Graphic novels; 2. Superhero graphic novels; 3. Superman (Fictional character)
978-1-4012-1051-9, $49.99

This seventh volume of the Superman Archive Editions collects issues 25-29 of Superman, with tales featuring the Man of Steel fighting subversion and sabotage on the home front during World War II, meeting mythic figures like Paul Bunyan and Hercules and foiling villains including the Toyman and the Prankster. This volume also features the first episodes of "Lois Lane, Girl Reporter." These stories were originally published in 1943 and 1944.

Crane, Jordan
The **Last** Lonely Saturday. Fantagraphics Books 2007 un Illustration
Grades: 10 11 12 Adult   **741.5; Fic**
1. Ghosts — Graphic novels; 2. Graphic novels; 3. Romance graphic novels
978-1-56097-743-8, $8

Using a deep yellow and brown palette, this almost wordless little story follows the day of an older man who gathers his letters addressed to Elinore, sets off to buy flowers, and drives out to the cemetery to visit Elinore's grave. As he sits and hugs the gravestone, the spirit of Elinore comes out and starts to kiss him. In a macabre twist that is portrayed in a sweet, gentle manner, Elinore's spirit finds a way for the two of them to be together.

Crilley, Mark
★ Akiko pocket-size, vol. 1. Sirius Entertainment 2004 192p. Illustration
Grades: 3 4 5 6 7 8 9 10   **741.5; Fic**
1. Adventure graphic novels; 2. Graphic novels; 3. Science fiction graphic novels
1-579890-67-9, $11.95

Fourth-grader Akiko travels to the planet Smoo, on a mission to rescue King Froptoppit's son from the evil Alia Rellapor. Teamed up with the scruffy adventurer Spuckler, bookish Mr. Beeba, Spuckler's robot Gax, and the floating alien known as Poog, Akiko faces sea monsters, Sky Pirates, Sleeslup worms, and other dangers as they travel around the planet on their quest. This is the first volume in an ongoing series of graphic novels. Crilley also has written a series of prose fiction featuring Akiko and her friends.

★ **Brody's** ghost: book 1. story and art by Mark Crilley. Dark Horse Books 2010 88p. Illustration
Grades: 8 9 10 11 12 Adult   **741.5; Fic**
1. Adventure graphic novels; 2. Fantasy graphic novels; 3. Ghosts — Graphic novels; 4. Graphic novels; 5. Mystery graphic novels
978-1-59582-521-6, $6.99

In what looks like a near-future city, Brody is down and out, eking out a living by playing guitar on the streets and working part-time as a stock clerk. Then, one day, while playing his guitar, he sees the ghost of a young woman; he thinks he's seeing things, but she won't let him alone until he talks with her. Talia, the ghost, needs to do a great deed before she can get into heaven, and she has decided to solve the mystery of a serial killer called the Penny Murderer, but she needs Brody, who is a ghostseer, to help her. First, though, he needs training to bring out his ghostseer powers, because he doesn't think he has any. Enter Kagemura, the ghost of a samurai, who decides, half-unwillingly, to train Brody. This book is much grittier than Crilley's earlier works, which were more suitable for younger readers; it is aimed more at teen and adult readers and includes some fighting violence but no graphically violent content.

"The setting — an unidentified future city partially in ruins — is a masterpiece of drawing, and Brody and the other characters are equally well crafted.... The story is more than a match for the art: humor, action, and mystery butt up against the reality of Brody's sad life, giving him the opportunity to change who he is." Booklist

Also available in an omnibus edition; ?The first in a six-volume limited series? Page 4 of cover; Book 1 of 6

Miki Falls Vol. 2: Summer. HarperTeen 2007 178p. Illustration
Grades: 7 8 9 10 11 12 Adult   **741.5; Fic**
1. Graphic novels; 2. Romance graphic novels; 3. Supernatural graphic novels
978-0-06-084617-6, $7.99

Has Miki fallen too hard? It's summer, and Miki Yoshida is learning all about love. Her senior year has blossomed with promise ever since she gained Hiro Sakurai's confidence. Now, she's resolved to keep his trust as he reveals more about his secret mission and warns: "Don't get involved." But Miki fears his work might do more harm than good, and she takes control-with disastrous results. How can trying to make things right turn out so dangerously wrong? Crilley is doing this series in manga style.

Miki Falls, Book One: Spring. HarperCollins/HarperTeen 2007 176p. Illustration
Grades: 7 8 9 10 11 12   **741.5; Fic**
1. Friendship — Graphic novels; 2. Graphic novels; 3. High school students — Graphic novels; 4. School stories — Graphic novels
978-0-06-084616-9, $7.99

"This is Miki Yoshida's final year of high school, and she's determined to make this the best year yet. Miki is in control...until Hiro Sakurai shows up. The tall, handsome new student is hiding something, and Miki wants to know what." Publisher's note

"Crilley uses mystery to drive the narrative and creates characters that the reader will care about. The black-and-white, manga-style art is beautiful." Voice Youth Advocates

Other titles in this series are: Miki Falls, Book Two: Summer; Miki Falls, Book Three: Autumn; Miki Falls, Book Four: Winter

★ **Miki** Falls: Winter. HarperCollins/HarperTeen 2008 176p. Illustration
Grades: 7 8 9 10 11 12   **741.5; Fic**

1. Adventure graphic novels; 2. Fantasy graphic novels; 3. Graphic novels; 4. Romance graphic novels
978-0-06-084619-0, $7.99

LC 2007-931803

Miki and Hiro have been on the run for a while now; it's now winter and they are in the far north of Japan, trying to escape from the Deliverers led by Akuzu who are determined to tear the young couple apart and punish Hiro. Miki is equally determined to stay with Hiro, whom she loves above all else. Can love conquer all? This is the final volume of the series.

Croall, Marie P.

Marwe: into the land of the dead: an East African legend. author, Marie P. Croall; pencils by Ray Lago and inks by Craig Hamilton.. Lerner Publishing Group 2009 48p. Illustration
Grades: 3 4 5 6 7 8 9
741.5; Fic
1. Fantasy graphic novels; 2. Folklore — East Africa — Graphic novels; 3. Graphic novels
978-0-8225-7134-6, $27.93

Courtesy of Lerner Publishing Group

LC 2007-1828

In this story retold from the oral tradition of the Chaga people in East Africa, Marwe lives in a village where times are hard and food is scarce. When she and her brother leave the family's bean fields to cool off at the river, monkeys destroy the entire crop. When her brother goes off to ask the family's forgiveness, Marwe sees something strange in the water and dives down; she passes through a strange doorway and finds herself in another land. Soon she learns she has come to the land of the dead, where an old woman welcomes her. Too scared to go home, Marwe stays there, and despite assurances that she needn't do anything, she works in the fields. When will Marwe think it's time to return home to her anxious and mourning family?

Part of the Graphic Universe Myths and Legends series

Psyche & eros: the lady and the monster: a Greek myth. story by Marie Croall; pencils and inks by Ron Randall. Lerner Publishing Group 2009 48p. Illustration
Grades: 3 4 5 6 7 8 9
741.5; Fic
1. Fantasy graphic novels; 2. Graphic novels; 3. Greek mythology — Graphic novels
978-0-8225-7177-3, $27.93

Courtesy of Lerner Publishing Group

LC 2007-43353

Psyche is a beautiful young woman, so beautiful that men start to give her gifts instead of taking them to the temple. This makes Aphrodite jealous, and she sends her son, Eros, to prick Psyche with an arrow so no man will ever fall in love with her. However, Eros falls in love with Psyche. He arranges for the Oracle to tell Psyche's father that his daughter must be taken up on a mountain to marry a monster. He only comes to her at night, and they love each other; but Psyche's sisters convince her that she should see her husband. When hot wax from her candle burns Eros and wakens him, he must leave her. Now Psyche, unable to convince any other god or goddess to help her, must go to Aphrodite, who sets impossible tasks that Psyche manages to accomplish with help from unexpected sources.

Part of the Graphic Universe Myths and Legends series

Crosby, Andrew

Damn Nation. Dark Horse Comics 2005 un Illustration
Grades: 10 11 12 Adult
741.5; Fic
1. Graphic novels; 2. Horror graphic novels; 3. Vampires — Graphic novels
1-59307-389-5, $12.95

The United States has been shut off from the world by concrete barricades and barbed wire — not because of what might get in, but what might get out. A vampire plague has spread from sea to shining sea, and when a small holdout of scientists trapped outside of Buffalo, N.Y. discover a cure, it's up to a Special Ops team from the President's current offices in London to go in and get it. Yet, not everyone in the world wants to see America back in the saddle again...This story includes some incidental nudity, strong language, and considerable violence.

Cryptic Magazine

Horror book volume 1. Image Comics 2008 un Illustration
Grades: 10 11 12 Adult
741.5; Fic
1. Graphic novels; 2. Horror graphic novels; 3. Short stories — Graphic novels
978-1-58240-956-6, $14.99

This volume collects stories originally published in Cryptic Magazine. Each story reworks a classic horror tale. In the first, readers will find zombies in Vietnam in the year 1968, as an American patrol finds horror in the jungle. "Creature of the Depths" takes on The Creature from the Black Lagoon, as a small troop from a struggling sideshow is hired to help trap a marauding sea creature. In "Frankenstein," years after the monster was killed, the doctor is now an opium addict, but now someone is robbing graves and kidnapping people such as the blacksmith and some prostitutes; the monster isn't dead, but he wants more creatures like himself. And in "Full Moon," a nameless man agrees to help the village priest rescue a couple of kidnapped children who were taken by a vengeful vampire; it is the night of the full moon, and the young man becomes a ravening werewolf. The stories include graphic violence and gore, some partial nudity, and some rough language.

D'Salete, Marcelo

★ **Run** for it: stories of slaves who fought for their freedom. Marcelo D'Salete. Fantagraphics Books 2017 180 p. Illustration
Grades: 9 10 11 12 Adult
741.5
1. Slaves — Fiction; 2. Slavery — Fiction; 3. Fugitive slaves — Fiction
9781683960492, $24.99

LC 2017938231

Eisner Award: Best U.S. Edition of International Material (2018)

This graphic novel, by Marcelo D'Salete, "tells unforgettable stories about Afro-Brazilian slaves who rebelled against oppression.... 'Run For It'...is one of the first literary and artistic efforts to face up to Brazil's hidden history of slavery. These intense tales offer a tragic and gripping portrait of one of history's darkest corners." (Publisher's note)

"First published in 2015 in D'Salete's native Brazil, this striking graphic novel exposes the brutality of slavery on that country's sugarcane plantations via five stories of slaves who attempted escape. With a dry-brush effect, the art conveys the dark, foreboding danger of the jungles surrounding the plantations and the energy and moods of the men and women who react to their enslavement in various ways." Pub Wkly"

Includes bibliographical references (page 174)

Dahl, Roald

The **Gremlins:** The Lost Walt Disney Production: A Royal Air Force Story. Dark Horse Books 2006 un Illustration
Grades: 4 5 6 7 8 9 10 11 12 Adult
741.5; Fic

1. Graphic novels; 2. Humorous graphic novels; 3. World War, 1939-1945 — Graphic novels
978-1-59307-496-8, $12.95

This is an illustrated novella, the first published work of RAF Flight Lieutenant Roald Dahl in his only collaboration with Walt Disney Studios. Originally published in 1943, the story was supposed to become a film combining live action with animation; the movie was never made, although the studio produced a lot of illustrations and samples. The story tells about one young Royal Air Force pilot named Gus, who first sees the little gremlins that wreak havoc on his plane. While the gremlins first cause lots of trouble, eventually Gus convinces them to work with the RAF.

Dakin, Glenn
Temptation: A Battle of Wits Through All Eternity. Active Images 2004 72p. Illustration
Grades: 8 9 10 11 12 Adult **741.5**
1. Graphic novels; 2. Humorous graphic novels
0-9740567-5-8, $8.95

It's a constant battle of wits between a hermit who lives out in the wilderness and the devil who wants his soul. While that's the main theme, there are strips in which the devil needs the hermit to babysit his little baby devils so he can see a movie, the devil tries to sell the hermit a set of encyclopedias, and more fun.

Dalrymple, Farel
The **Wrenchies.** Farel Dalrymple. First Second 2014 304 p. Color; Illustration
Grades: 10 11 12 Adult **741.5**
1. Imaginary places; 2. Science fiction
159643421X; 9781596434219, $19.99

In this book by Farel Dalrymple, "whatever life remains on earth is oppressed by the evil shadowsmen. Only a gang of ruthless and powerful children called the Wrenchies can hope to stand against them. When Hollis, a lonely boy from our world, is magically given access to the future world of the Wrenchies, he finally finds a place he belongs. But it is not an easy world to live in, and Hollis's quest is bigger than he ever dreamed of." (Publisher's note)

"Clearly, it doesn't pay to demand sheer narrative coherence here, but the raw emotional weight of Dalrymple's anger forcibly tows readers through the obfuscating narrative, and the intricate, gritty, and rivetingly grotesque art, in sickly greens and browns peppered with bloody red, plays no small part in that." Booklist

Daly, Paul
Athena Voltaire: the collected webcomics. APE Entertainment 2006 un Illustration
Grades: 9 10 11 12 Adult **741.5; Fic**
1. Adventure graphic novels; 2. Fantasy graphic novels; 3. Graphic novels
978-0-9741398-9-0, $13.95

In "The Terror in Tibet," adventurous pilot (and widow) Athena Voltaire agrees to guide a group of British gentlemen on an expedition into the Himalayas. The time is the 1930s, and Nazis are on the rise in Germany. Athena soon finds out that the British are up to no good, nor are the Germans pursuing them. They're all after something in a remote monastery halfway up Mount Everest, and she decides to prevent anyone from succeeding. In "The Wrath from the Tomb," Dracula's daughter seeks revenge against the men who killed her father; she makes a mistake when she sends men to attack Athena's Arizona ranch. Teens who love the Indiana Jones and Mummy movies will enjoy Athena's adventures. The violence level is about the same as those movies, although the scene in which the vampire is run through with a spear might bother more sensitive readers.

The stories originally appeared as webcomics, and the series was nominated for the first Eisner Award for Best Digital Comic in 2005

Danko, Dan
Leonardo da Vinci: the renaissance man. Dan Danko, illustrated by Lalit Kumar Sharma. Campfire/Kalyani Navyug Media Pvt. Ltd. 2011 68 p.
Grades: 8 9 10 **709.2**
1. Artists — Italy — Biography; 2. Inventors — Italy — Biography; 3. Renaissance — Italy — Biography; 4. Scientists — Italy — Biography; 5. Leonardo, da Vinci, 1452-1519; 6. Biographical graphic novels
9380741014; 9380741200; 9789380741017; 9789380741208, $9.99
LC 2011294404

This graphic novel is a biography of Leonardo da Vinci. It "opens with the theft of the 'Mona Lisa' from the Louvre in 1911, then backtracks to da Vinci's turbulent childhood in Italy during the Renaissance. Throughout the tale, the mind of da Vinci is shown to be always active, always questioning, always seeking ways to create something better." (Voice of Youth Advocates)

David, Peter
Fallen Angel: Down to Earth. DC Comics 2007 136p. Illustration
Grades: 12 Adult **741.5; Fic**
1. Graphic novels; 2. Superhero graphic novels; 3. Supernatural graphic novels
978-1-4012-1268-1, $14.99

Bete Noir is a quiet, almost mundane city by day; but by night it becomes a haven for crime, corruption, and the supernatural. Enter the Fallen Angel, a mysterious and powerful woman who aids people in need when they find themselves at a crossroads in their lives. If she deems a person worthy, she can be a savior; if she doesn't, that person won't live to tell the tale. In this volume, the Angel's nemesis, Black Mariah, has returned to town, and this time she's hunting the Angel. The book includes nudity, sexual situations, foul language, and violence.

Friendly Neighborhood Spider-Man Vol. 1: Derailed. Marvel Entertainment 2006 un Illustration
Grades: 7 8 9 10 11 12 Adult **741.5; Fic**
1. Graphic novels; 2. Spider-Man (Fictional character); 3. Superhero graphic novels
978-0-7851-2216-6, $14.99

A major character from Peter Parker's past returns, and it looks like Hobgoblin is terrorizing the skies again. Also, a woman chronicles Spider-Man's career on her blog, convinced that he has stalked her for her entire life.

Marvel 1602: Fantastick Four. Marvel Entertainment 2007 un Illustration
Grades: 9 10 11 12 Adult **741.5; Fic**
1. Fantastic Four (Fictional characters); 2. Graphic novels; 3. Superhero graphic novels
978-0-7851-2293-7, $14.99

In the year 1602, Count Otto von Doom has an insidious plan that takes him — and the Four of the Fantastick — to the ends of the Earth. What does Doom want? Why doesn't Invisible Woman want to fight him? And what does Shakespeare have to do with it? This book spins off from Marvel 1602 written by Neil Gaiman.

Sachs & Violens. DC Comics 2006 126p. Illustration
Grades: 12 Adult **741.5; Fic**
1. Graphic novels; 2. Mystery graphic novels
978-1-4012-1050-2, $7.99

The brutal killing of a young actress during the shooting of a snuff film sets soft core model Juanita Jean Sachs and photographer Ernie Schultz on a quest to discover those responsible. Their journey takes them from the mean streets of New York City to the back alleys of New Orleans, where they confront the utter depravity and corruption that defines the dark underbelly of American society. But they discover something else as well; something unexpected. Their destiny. This book includes considerable partial nudity, strong language, and graphic violence.

Davis, Rob
The **Motherless** Oven. by Rob Davis. SelfMadeHero 2014 160 p. Illustration
Grades: 9 10 11 12 Adult   **741.5; Fic**
1. Fantasy fiction; 2. Death — Fiction; 3. Parent-child relationship — Fiction; 4. Graphic novels
190683881X; 9781906838812, $19.95
LC 2015296214
In this graphic novel, by Rob Davis, "parents don't make children — children make parents. Scarper's father is his pride and joy, a wind-powered brass construction with a billowing sail. His mother is a Bakelite hairdryer. In this world it rains knives, and household appliances have souls. There are also no birthdays — only deathdays. Scarper's deathday is just three weeks away, and he clings to the mundane repetition of his life at home and high school for comfort." (Publisher's note)
"Davis's dark and shadow-filled art appropriately mindbends and illuminates the text. The variation in panels quickens and pulls back the pace in this enigmatic tale, with the right amount of imagery left open for interpretation." SLJ

Davison, Al
The **Spiral** Cage: An Autobiography. DC Comics 2003 141p. Illustration
Grades: 11 12 Adult   **741.5; 92**
1. Autobiographical graphic novels; 2. Graphic novels; 3. Spina bifida — Graphic novels; 4. Davison, Al, 1960-
0-9740567-1-5, $12.95
Born with severe spina bifida, doctors considered Al Davison a hopeless case, condemned to the 'spiral cage' of his own DNA. In Al's own words and pictures, this book portrays his struggle to overcome 'disability' and the prejudice that surrounds it. The book includes lots of full frontal nudity, but it's not sexual, as Davison shows how he has to struggle physically every single day. The book also includes some strong language.

Dawson, Mike
Troop 142. Mike Dawson.. Secret Acres 2011 1 v. (unpaged) Illustration
Grades: 9 10 11 12   **741.5**
1. Boy Scouts — Comic books, strips, etc; 2. Comic books, strips, etc.; 3. Men — Attitudes; 4. Scouts and scouting — Graphic novels; 5. Camping — Graphic novels
9780979960994, $20
LC 2011924536
This graphic novel, originally published online where it won the 2010 Ignatz Award for Outstanding Online Comic, "follows a group of campers and counselors at a week-long scout retreat in the woods of New Jersey. It is a story as much about adults as it is adolescents, the blurred line between childhood and manhood, and the consequences of authoritative posturing. Dispensing with idyllic notions, [author Mike] Dawson describes...truths about boys and men, the hypocrisy of institutional morality and the resilience of Spam and the human spirit." (Publisher's note)

De Crecy, Nicolas
Glacial Period: A Graphic Novel. NBM/ComicsLit 2006 80p. Illustration
Grades: 10 11 12   **741.5; Fic**
1. Art — Graphic novels; 2. Graphic novels; 3. Museums — France — Graphic novels; 4. Science fiction graphic novels
1-56163-483-2, $14.95; 9781561634835
Thousands of years in the future, the world is in the midst of a glacial period, an Ice Age. All human history has been forgotten, and mankind coexists with genetically-engineered dogs who are intelligent and can speak. A small group of archeologists literally fall upon the Louvre, the great French museum, buried in snow. Their wild misinterpretations of the art works they find have a sharp, satirical bite. One of the dogs, named Hulk, encounters sculptures and statues who want to escape.
This book is a co-edition with the Musee du Louvre and is part of a series of graphic novels that impart the artists' visions of the museum. Crecy reproduces some famous works that are all listed in the back of the book. Many of the paintings and statures are nudes.
Originally published in France in 2005 by Musee du Louvre Editions.

De Groot, Bob
Clifton Jade. Cinebook 2008 48p.
Grades: 5 6 7 8 9   **741.5; Fic**
1. Adventure graphic novels; 2. Graphic novels; 3. Humorous graphic novels; 4. Spies — Graphic novels
978-1-905460-52-6, $11.95
Sir Harold Wilberforce Clifton, ex-Secret Service and retired Colonel, works as a private detective, as well as leading a troop of young scouts. With the help of his housekeeper, Mrs. Partridge, who's also a dab hand at auto mechanics, he still helps the government. This time, however, he's being tailed by someone and then summoned to a retirement home where he finds his old World War II nemesis, Otto Kartoffeln, who tells him a group of neo-Nazis are searching for a long-lost Nazi treasure in order to bring about the 4th Reich. The mysterious shadow is Jade, a young agent who was trying to complete her training; now she and Clifton must stop the neo-Nazis from finding the treasure.
Part of the Clifton series, originally published in France as Clifton Jade.

De Heer, Margreet
Philosophy- a discovery in comics: A discovery in comics. Margreet de Heer. NBM Pub. 2012 120 p.
Grades: 11 12 Adult
100.022/2; 100.022; 741.5
1. Philosophy — Graphic novels; 2. Philosophy — History; 3. Comic books, strips, etc.
1561636983; 9781561636983, $16.99
LC 2012938931

Courtesy of NBM Publishing

This book, by Margreet de Heer, offers an "illustrated primer on philosophy.... Margreet de Heer visualizes the history of Western philosophy and makes it approachable for those with little knowledge of the subject. The book explains the thoughts of philosophers such as Socrates, Plato, Aristotle, Descartes, Spinoza, and Nietzsche, and ponders questions such as 'What is thinking?' 'What is reality?' 'Is there free will?' and 'Why are these ideas still important?'" (Publisher's note)

De Liz, Renae

The **legend** of Wonder Woman. story & pencils by Renae De Liz; inks, colors & letters by Ray Dillon. DC Comics 2016 288 p. Color; Illustration

Grades: 8 9 10 11 12 Adult **741.5; Fic**

1. Female superhero graphic novels; 2. Superhero graphic novels; 3. Wonder Woman (Fictional character)

1401267289; 9781401267285, $29.99

LC 2016047038

"When a man from the outside world is brought to Themyscira as part of a conspiracy to overthrow its queen, Diana will risk everything to save his innocent life...and lose everything in the process. Soon, the Amazon princess finds herself in a world she never knew existed — America." (Publisher's note)

"Collecting twenty-seven chapters of online material, this spacious, even epic, story affords room for both legend building and healthy doses of action, the supernatural, romance, and humor." Booklist

De Radiguès, Max

Moose. Max de Radiguès. Conundrum International 2015 160 p. Illustration

Grades: 10 11 12 Adult **741.5; Fic**

1. Children of gay parents — Fiction; 2. Bullies — Graphic novels

1894994930; 9781894994934, $17

Eisner Nominee: Best Publication for Teens (2016)

"Meet Joe, an average, quiet high school student who is being bullied relentlessly by classmate Jason. No longer able to ride the bus, Joe walks to school every day through the woods finding comfort in Mother Nature. On his way to school, Joe sees a moose, a poignant encounter that helps distract him from the daily indignities. The story continues through many days of continual abuse, slowly revealing more about Joe's life." (Library Journal)

Joe's "beaten-down quietude is reflected in de Radiguès' spare, wintry drawings, which look like a cleaned-up version of Jeffrey Brown. The artist always keeps one eye cocked on the natural world, which is far less sentimental about Joe's position in the predator-prey power structure." Pub Wkly

DeConnick, Kelly Sue

Captain Marvel; 1: in pursuit of flight. by Kelly Sue Deconnick; illustrated by Dexter Soy and Emma Rios. Marvel Worldwide 2013 136 p. Color; Illustration

Grades: 10 11 12 Adult **741.5**

1. Superheroes — Fiction; 2. Female superhero graphic novels

0785165495; 9780785165491, $14.99

In this graphic novel by Kelly Sue Deconnick, illustrated by Dexter Soy and Emma Rios, "Carol Danvers has a new name, a new mission — and all the power she needs to make her own life a living hell. As the new Captain Marvel, Carol is forging from a challenge from her past! It's a firefight in the sky as the Banshee Squadron debut — but who are the Prowlers, and where has Carol seen them before? And how does secret NASA training program Mercury 13 fit in?" (Publisher's note)

Captain Marvel; Volume 2: Down. by Kelly Sue Deconnick and Christopher Sebela; illustrated by Dexter Soy and Filipe Andrade. Marvel Worldwide 2013 136 p. Color; Illustration

Grades: 10 11 12 Adult **741.5**

1. Superhero graphic novels; 2. Captain Marvel (Fictional character)

0785165509; 9780785165507, $14.99

In this graphic novel, by Kelly Sue Deconnick and Christopher Sebela, illustrated by Dexter Soy and Filipe Andrade, "Captain Marvel goes head to head with...Captain Marvel? Former Captain Monica Rambeau returns, but what's her problem with Earth's new Mightiest Hero? What threat is lurking below the ocean's surface? And can both Captain Marvels stop it before they get ship wrecked?" (Publisher's note)

Contains material originally published in magazine form as Captain Marvel #7-12 — T.p. verso.

Pretty deadly; Vol. 1: The shrike. Kelly Sue Deconnick; illustrated by Emma Rios, Jordie Bellaire, Clayton Cowles. Image Comics 2014 120 p. Color; Illustration

Grades: 9 10 11 12 Adult **741.5**

1. Women — Fiction; 2. Death — Graphic novels

1607069628; 9781607069621, $9.99

In this graphic novel by Kelly Sue Deconnick, "Death's daughter rides the wind on a horse made of smoke and her face bears the skull marks of her father. Her origin story is a tale of retribution as beautifully lush as it is unflinchingly savage." (Publisher's note)

Volume 1 of an ongoing series

DeFalco, Tom

The **Amazing** Spider-Girl: Whatever Happened to the Daughter of Spider-Man?. writer, Tom DeFalco; artist, Ron Frenz. Marvel Entertainment 2007 un Illustration

Grades: 7 8 9 10 11 12 Adult **741.5; Fic**

1. Graphic novels; 2. Spider-Girl (Fictional character); 3. Superhero graphic novels; 4. Spider-Man (Fictional character)

978-0-7851-2341-5, $14.99

After discovering she had inherited her father's incredible powers, May "Mayday" Parker donned a costume and became the amazing Spider-Girl. Recent events have forced her to hang up her webs and lead a normal life...but how long can May keep from web-slinging when there are villains like Hobgoblin on the loose? This volume begins collecting the second run of Spider-Girl comics; the first 100 issues were published as Spider-Girl and are being collected in digest-sized trade paperbacks. This new series, The Amazing Spider-Girl, features new numbering (from #1 and on) and is being collected in regular comic book-sized trade paperbacks.

Spider-Girl Vol. 2: Like Father, Like Daughter. Marvel Entertainment 2004 un Illustration

Grades: 7 8 9 10 11 12 **741.5; Fic**

1. Graphic novels; 2. Spider-Girl (Fictional character); 3. Superhero graphic novels

0-7851-1657-5, $7.99

Her name is May Mayday" Parker, and she recently learned her father was the original Spider-Man. The good news is that she's having the time of her life as she hones the amazing spider-like abilities she inherited from him. The bad news is that some of her roughest, toughest battles lie ahead — against the likes of Ladyhawk, the Kingpin of Crime, Mr. Nobody, Crazy Eight...and her own parents. She also learns that it's not easy hiding such a big part of your life from all your friends in school.

Spider-Girl Vol. 4: Turning Point. writer, Tom DeFalco, Ron Frenz; pencils, Pat Olliffe & Ron Frenz; inks, Al Williamson & Sal Buscema. Marvel Entertainment 2005 un Illustration

Grades: 7 8 9 10 11 12 **741.5; Fic**

1. Graphic novels; 2. Spider-Girl (Fictional character); 3. Superhero graphic novels; 4. Spider-Man (Fictional character)

0-7851-1871-3, $7.99

The adventures of Spider-Man's daughter continue as Mayday once again faces Kaine, Spider-Man swings again, and Darkdevil is...actually nice? Plus: Meet new heroes and villains, take a peek into the fantasies of Mayday's friends, and witness the return of the Green Goblin. In May's life, she's caught between JJ (grandson of J. Jonah Jameson) and Brad; how is a girl to choose?

Spider-Girl Vol. 5: Endgame. Marvel Entertainment 2006 un Illustration
Grades: 7 8 9 10 11 12   **741.5; Fic**
1. Graphic novels; 2. Spider-Girl (Fictional character); 3. Superhero graphic novels
0-7851-2034-3, $7.99

Spider-Girl faces trouble when her deadliest enemies join forces as the Savage Six (or is it Seven?)! But even with the help of rival/critic heroes like Darkdevil and the Buzz, can she deal with the sudden loss of her super-powers? And, naturally, that's when Normie Osborn escapes from the mental institution, convinced that he, as Green Goblin, must kill Spider-Girl.

Spider-Girl, Vol. 1: Legacy. Marvel Comics 2004 144p. Illustration
Grades: 7 8 9 10 11 12   **741.5; Fic**
1. Graphic novels; 2. Spider-Girl (Fictional character); 3. Superhero graphic novels; 4. Spider-Man (Fictional character)
0-7851-1441-6, $7.99

In an alternate future in the Marvel Universe, Peter Parker has retired from being Spider-Man after a crippling injury; but he and Mary Jane have a daughter, May. She has just turned sixteen, and suddenly discovers she has superpowers! Soon she finds out who her father used to be, and she decides to be a superhero — but Peter knows the dangers all too well and tries to stop her. Once Mayday decides to be Spider-Girl, though, no one can stop her. This is the first of an ongoing series.

DeFilippis, Nunzio
Play ball. Oni Press, Inc. 2012 144 p.
Grades: 6 7 8 9
741.5/973; Fic
1. Women athletes — Graphic novels; 2. School stories — Graphic novels; 3. Baseball — Graphic novels
1934964794; 9781934964798, $19.99
LC 2011933142

Courtesy of Oni Press

This comic "traces a high school girl's struggle to join a boys' baseball team. Freckle-faced Dashiell Brody was good at softball in her private girls' school; now that she's moved to another city with her mother and older sister and they must enroll in public school, she wants to play the real game, despite stereotypical resistance from school administrators and some jocks." (Publishers Weekly)

Del Col, Anthony
Kill Shakespeare 3: The Tide of Blood. Conor McCreery and Anthony Del Col, illustrated by Andy Belanger. IDW Publishing 2013 140 p. Color; Illustration
Grades: 10 11 12 Adult
741.5
1. Graphic novels; 2. Shakespeare, William, 1564-1616 — Adaptations
1613777329; 9781613777329, $19.99

Courtesy of IDW Publishing

"With Richard III and Lady Macbeth defeated, Hamlet, Juliet, Othello, and Romeo face an even greater danger — Prospero, a rogue wizard who plans to destroy all of creation! Hamlet must embark on a perilous journey to a remote island whose inhabitants have gone mad and want the Dane's blood...if

they aren't beaten to the chase by one of Hamlet's allies." (Publisher's note)

"There's more action, wizardry, and gore than the Bard himself was apt to include, but clever echoes of dialogue, intense emotional turnabouts, and imaginatively theatrical art recall the plays in satisfying ways." Booklist

Originally published as Kill Shakespeare: The Tide of Blood issues #1-5

★ **Kill** Shakespeare, vol. 1: a sea of troubles. created and written by Conor McCreery and Anthony Del Col; art by Andy Belanger; colors by Ian Herring; lettering by Chris Mowry, Robbie Robbins, and Neil Uyetake. IDW Publishing 2010 un Illustration
Grades: 10 11 12 Adult   **741.5; Fic**
1. Adventure graphic novels; 2. Authors; 3. Dramatists; 4. Fantasy graphic novels; 5. Graphic novels; 6. Poets; 7. Shakespeare, William, 1564-1616
978-1-60010-781-8, $19.99

A shipwrecked Hamlet finds himself in England with Richard III, who wants his help to find and kill the wizard, Will Shakespeare, so that Richard can rule with impunity. Haunted by his father's ghost, who tells Hamlet that killing Shakespeare will let him live again, Hamlet agrees to help the English king. Then he discovers that the Lady Juliet Capulet leads an army of rebellion, aided by Othello and Falstaff. They fight against the corrupt Richard, who consults the witch Hecate (who has her own agenda). Falstaff says that Hamlet is the prophesied Shadow King, who will aid the rebellion, while Richard and his allies only want to use Hamlet to destroy Shakespeare, but all agree that only Hamlet can lead them to the wizard. The book includes bloody action and sexual situations, making this more suited to older teens.

"McCreery and Del Col spin an engrossing action-adventure tale of satisfying complexity, full of mystery, deceit, and gory violence, starring a hero who once again must marshal his determination and decide his path." Libr J

Volume 1 of 4

Kill Shakespeare; Volume 2: the blast of war. created and written by Conor McCreery and Anthony Del Col; art by Andy Belanger; colors by Ian Herring; lettering by Chris Mowry, Neil Uyetake, and Shawn Lee; original series edits by Tom Waltz.. IDW 2011 148 p.
Grades: 10 11 12 Adult
741.5
1. Comic books, strips, etc.; 2. Shakespeare, William, 1564-1616 — Fiction; 3. Shakespeare, William, 1564-1616 — Characters
1613770251; 9781613770252, $19.99

Courtesy of IDW Publishing

This book, the second volume of the comic book series, presents a "sweeping fantasy of magic, war, betrayal, and love [which] is set in a world where Shakespeare's characters dwell and Shakespeare himself is an absent god struggling with a heavy conscience. The second volume builds to the climactic finale of Hamlet's quest to find the creatorgod Shakespeare and return peace to a land torn apart by an evil army led by Richard III and Lady Macbeth. Joined by love interest Juliet, the warrior Othello, the wise fool Falstaff, and the spy Iago, Hamlet has built an army of rebels, the prodigals, who hold off their enemies while he searches for their creator. But even victory comes at a cost as friends and foes die in a great final battle." (Publishers Wkly)

"[A]n appropriate air of grandeur and theatricality is much on display, brought forth all the more in Belanger's spectacular and inventive page compositions." Booklist

Del Duca, Leila

Afar. written by Leila Del Duca; art by Kit Seaton; edited by Taneka Stotts. Image Comics 2017 168 p. Illustration; Color

Grades: 9 10 11 12   **741.5973; Fic; 741.5**

1. Astral projection — Fiction; 2. Fantasy fiction; 3. Science fiction graphic novels

1632159414; 9781632159410, $14.99

"Boetema suddenly develops the ability to astrally project to other worlds, unintentionally possessing the bodies of people light years away. Inotu, her inquisitive brother with a pension for trouble, finds himself on the run after he's caught eavesdropping on an illegal business deal between small town business tycoons and their cyborg bodyguard. When Boetema accidentally gets someone hurt while in another girl's body, the siblings are forced to work together." (Publisher's note)

"With little direct exposition, the story depends on Seaton to illustrate the complexity of a setting that features advanced technology, new or mutated animals, and the wildly diverse planets Boetema explores while engaged in what she eventually learns to be astral projection. It's a rousing adventure set in a world that would seem to have many more tales to tell." Pub Wkly

Del Rio, Tania

Sabrina the Teenage Witch: The Magic Revisited. Archie Comics 2006 un Illustration

Grades: 4 5 6 7 8 9   **741.5; Fic**

1. Fantasy graphic novels; 2. Graphic novels; 3. Humorous graphic novels; 4. Witches — Graphic novels

1-879794-19-5, $7.49

The first four issues of Sabrina the Teenage Witch's "manga makeover" are collected in this special edition trade paperback. Writer-artist Tania del Rio presents these tales of magical flights of fancy and romantic intrigue... sprinkled with a dash of humor. Sabrina's awakening powers and the various love triangle combinations that have formed since keep her busy at school, on dates, and...everywhere.

Delano, Jamie

Outlaw Nation. Image Comics 2006 458p. Illustration

Grades: 12 Adult   **741.5; Fic**

1. Adventure graphic novels; 2. Graphic novels; 3. Revenge — Graphic novels

978-1-58240-707-4, $15.99

Story Johnson, a hundred-year-old semi-deranged amnesiac pulp fiction-writer returns home from 25 years MIA in Vietnam. All Story wants is to recover his missing time and catch up with some legendary, larger-than-life Johnson Family members. Trouble is, a lot of cousins have "disappeared," and those that are left have put the blame on him. This story is full of graphic violence, very strong language, nudity, and sexual situations.

Delisle, Guy

★ **Pyongyang:** a journey in North Korea. translated by Helge Dascher. Drawn & Quarterly 2005 176p. Illustration; Map

Grades: 11 12 Adult   **951.93; 741; 741.5**

1. Graphic novels; 2. Korea (North) — Graphic novels

1-896597-89-0; 1-897299-21-4 (pa), $14.95

This book "documents the two months French animator Delisle spent overseeing cartoon production in North Korea.... He records everything

from the omnipresent statues and portraits of dictators Kim Il-Sung and Kim Jong-Il to the brainwashed obedience of the citizens." Booklist

"Pyongyang will appeal to multiple audiences: current events buffs, Persepolis fans and those who just love a good yarn." Publ Wkly

Shenzhen: A Travelogue from China. Drawn & Quarterly 2006 148p. Illustration

Grades: 10 11 12 Adult   **741.5**

1. Autobiographical graphic novels; 2. Graphic novels

1-896597-79-1, $19.95

Shenzhen details Guy Delisle's observations of life in a cold urban city in southern China in 1997 that is sealed off from the rest of the country by electric fences and armed guards. With a dry wit and a clean line, Delisle makes the most of his time spent in Asia overseeing outsourced production for a French animation company. By translating his fish-out-of-water experiences into graphic novels, Delisle is quick to find the humor and point out the differences between Western and Eastern cultures. Yet he never forgets to relay his compassion for the simple freedoms that escape his colleagues by virtue of living in a Communist state. Delisle uses the occasional "s-word."

DeMatteis, J. M.

Abadazad: The Dream Thief. by J.M. DeMatteis; drawings by Mike Ploog; colors by Nick Bell. Hyperion Books for Children 2006 un Illustration

Grades: 5 6 7 8 9   **741.5; Fic**

1. Adventure graphic novels; 2. Fantasy graphic novels; 3. Graphic novels

1-4231-00646, $9.99

In the magical land of Abadazad, Kate needs all the help she can get when she encounters the Lanky Man. He's mean and heartless, and he wants to steal children's dreams. Everyone seems to be against her, which only makes her more determined to find her brother. And Matt is getting closer, isn't he? This story is a hybrid, combining prose text with pages of sequential art from the original comic books.

Abadazad: The Road to Inconceivable. Hyperion Books for Children 2006 un Illustration

Grades: 5 6 7 8 9   **741.5; Fic**

1. Adventure graphic novels; 2. Fantasy graphic novels; 3. Graphic novels

1-4231-0062-X, $9.99

Kate's little brother Matt disappeared five years ago, and Kate thinks she will never see him again. But then she finds out that Matt is trapped in the world of Abadazad. Will Kate have the courage to look for her brother? And if she leaves home, will she ever return? This story began as comic books, but the publisher went out of business before the story was completed. Now it's published as a hybrid, combining prose sections with pages of sequential art and spot illustrations.

★ The **stardust** kid. Boom! Studios 2008 un Illustration

Grades: 3 4 5 6 7 8 9 10 11 12 Adult   **741.5; Fic**

1. Adventure graphic novels; 2. Fantasy graphic novels; 3. Graphic novels

978-1-934506-04-2, $14.99

Twelve-year-old Cody's best friend is Paul Brightfield; they share a deep bond that goes far beyond mere friendship. What no one else knows is that Paul isn't human, he's one of the last Old Ones, ancient elemental beings who lived before man existed. One night, Paul disappears, and a hate-filled creature who has existed long buried beneath Wilde Park bursts out with a desire to destroy everything in the world. Only Cody, his little sister K.M., and his friend Alana and her little brother Nathaniel, remain, and somehow they must find The Stardust Kid and discover a way to stop the hate and restore their world. Some creatures might be frightening to younger readers, but anyone who likes the Harry Potter books shouldn't have a problem with this book.

Demolis, Flo

Around the world in 80 days. IDW Publishing 2009 60p. Illustration
Grades: 5 6 7 8 9   **741.5; Fic**
1. Adventure graphic novels; 2. Authors; 3. Children's authors; 4. Graphic novels; 5. Novelists; 6. Science fiction writers; 7. Travel — Graphic novels; 8. Verne, Jules, 1828-1905 — Adaptations/Graphic novels
978-1-60010-394-0, $14.99

This graphic novel Verne's globe-trotting adventures of Phileas Fogg, English gentleman, his newly-hired French manservant, Passepartout, and the English detective, Fix, who pursues Fogg, convinced he is a master bank robber. Fogg makes a bet with fellow members of the Reform Club in 1872 that he can travel around the world in eighty days, but his precipitous departure makes Scotland Yard suspect him. The three men travel through India, where Fogg saves a beautiful young Indian woman from being burned alive, to Hong Kong, then Japan and then across the United States and onward. This adaptation was originally published in France. The book includes biographical information about Verne, historical information about what the world was like in the 1870s, and an analysis of the novel.

Desberg, Stephen

The **Scorpion:** the devil's mark. Cinebook Ltd. 2008 96p. Illustration
Grades: 10 11 12 Adult   **741.5; Fic**
1. Adventure graphic novels; 2. Graphic novels; 3. Rome — History — Graphic novels
978-1-905460-62-5, $19.95

In Rome of the Renaissance, a young thief called the Scorpion makes a living by unearthing relics in the depths of the Roman Catacombs, which he then sells at high prices to princes, nobles, and bishops. Then Cardinal Trebaldi declares the Scorpion must die. Trebaldi is part of a group called the Nine Families, who made a pact to rule the world back in the time of the Caesars; he has now organized an army of warrior monks to carry out his will, and he has gained the approval of the Nine Families to assassinate the Pope so he can take over and rule Rome. Somehow, the Scorpion threatens that plan. Trebaldi sets a beautiful Egyptian poisoner on the Scorpion's trail, but they will both face betrayal and confront amazing truths. The book includes lots of blade fighting and sexual innuendo without any overt nudity or sexual content.

Dezuniga, Tony

Jonah Hex: Face Full of Violence. Justin Gray, Jimmy Palmiotti, writers; Luke Ross, Tony Dezuniga, artists; Jason Keith, Rob Schwager, colorists; Rob Leigh, letterer. DC Comics/Vertigo 2006 144p. Illustration
Grades: 10 11 12 Adult   **741.5; Fic**
1. Graphic novels; 2. Jonah Hex (Fictional characters); 3. Western graphic novels
978-1-4012-1095-3, $12.99

This book collects the new stories of Jonah Hex, the former Confederate soldier turned bounty hunter, the man with the scarred face. He doles out his brand of justice with his guns, taking vengeance upon murderers, thieves, and others who victimize the weak. The book has foul language and lots of violence.

Di Filippo, Paul

Top 10: Beyond the Farthest Precinct. DC Comics/America's Best Comics 2006 un Illustration
Grades: 10 11 12 Adult   **741.5; Fic**
1. Graphic novels; 2. Mystery graphic novels; 3. Superhero graphic novels

978-1-4012-0991-9, $14.99

In Neopolis, a modern city populated exclusively by super beings, it takes a unique and powerful police force to protect and serve. The officers of Precinct 10, also known as Top Ten, encounter all manner of the super powered and the supernatural on a routine basis. It doesn't help matters when Captain Traynor (Jetman) is unceremoniously replaced. Now the officers must band together, overcome their personal squabbles, and get their city back on track, before it all comes tumbling down on their heads. The book includes some sexual situations.

Dickens, Charles

Classics Illustrated Deluxe #8: Oliver Twist. by Loic Dauvillier; illustrated by Olivier Deloye. Papercutz 2012 238 p.
Grades: 6 7 8 9 10 11 12
741.5
1. London (England) — Fiction; 2. Graphic novels; 3. Orphans — Fiction
9781597073073; 1597073075

Courtesy of NBM Publishing

This graphic novel, by Charles Dickens, adapted by Loic Dauvillier, and illustrated by Olivier Deloye, is part of the "Classic Illustrated Deluxe" series. "The story is about an orphan, Oliver Twist, who endures a miserable existence in a workhouse and then is placed with an undertaker. He escapes and travels to London where he meets...a gang of juvenile pickpockets. Naively unaware of their unlawful activities, Oliver is led to the lair of their elderly criminal trainer Fagin." (Wikipedia)

Diggle, Andy

The **Losers:** Ante Up. DC Comics/Vertigo 2004 160p. Illustration
Grades: 10 11 12 Adult   **741.5; Fic**
1. Adventure graphic novels; 2. Graphic novels
1-4012-0198-9, $9.95

An elite U.S. Special Forces unit is targeted for assassination when they unintentionally uncover the illegal and immoral practices of the C.I.A. Believed dead and with nothing to lose, the team of wet works operatives regroup and begin a mission of revenge against the organization that betrayed them. Only as the team goes after a corrupt oil conglomerate with ties to the C.I.A., do they truly begin to realize the depths of the conspiracy they have discovered and the impossible odds of survival that they face. The book includes lots of foul language and some fairly graphic violence.

Other volumes in this series are: Double down (2004); Trifecta (2005); Close quarters (2006); Endgame (2006)

Silent Dragon. DC Comics/Wildstorm 2006 un Illustration
Grades: 10 11 12 Adult   **741.5; Fic**
1. Adventure graphic novels; 2. Graphic novels; 3. Science fiction graphic novels
978-1-4012-1104-2, $19.99

Tokyo, A.D. 2063: the Yakuza warlord Hideaki has seized total control of Honshu's underworld while ruthlessly crushing all opposition. But his true dream is the overthrow of the government itself. Japan's hard-line military junta will do anything to stop him and they have found the ultimate pawn to set their plan in motion: Renjiro, the chief advisor to the notorious gangster. Caught between a lifetime of honor and loyalty to his Yakuza clan and the iron-fisted might of the military elite, Renjiro will find that the only way to stop a civil war and avoid total annihilation is to play both sides against the middle. The book includes partial nudity, strong language, and lots of bloody violence.

Dini, Paul

Batman: Detective. Paul Dini; Royal McGraw. DC Comics 2007 144p. Illustration

Grades: 9 10 11 12 Adult   **741.5; Fic**
1. Batman (Fictional character); 2. Graphic novels; 3. Superhero graphic novels; 4. Joker (Fictional character)
978-1-4012-1239-1, $14.99

He is in peak physical condition, with a high-tech arsenal at his disposal, but it is perhaps his exceptional detective skills that make Batman the most formidable opponent of the countless deadly villains of Gotham City. In this volume, the Dark Knight faces the Joker, the Riddler, the Penguin, and Poison Ivy, as well as some brand-new villains, while pushing himself to the limit to solve crimes. But can even the most powerful mind outthink unpredictable and crazy foes?

Dark Knight: A True Batman Story. writer, Paul Dini; artist and cover art, Eduardo Risso; letterer, Todd Klein. DC Comics 2016 128 p. Color; Illustration

Grades: 11 12 Adult   **92; 741.5**
1. Dini, Paul; 2. Graphic memoir; 3. Authors
1401241433; 9781401241438, $22.99

In this graphic memoir author Paul Dini shares his traumatic experience and his deep connection with his creative material. "Walking home one evening, he was...viciously beaten within an inch of his life. His recovery process was arduous, hampered by the imagined antics of the villains he was writing...including the Joker, Harley Quinn and the Penguin.... [He] always imagined the Batman at his side...during his darkest moments." (Publisher's note)

"As potent metaphors for the ability to overcome trauma, superheroes perhaps more than any other fantasy figures engender deep, personal connections among their followers. Dini explores the notion that, in real life, Batman can't swing in to save you, though, as it turns out, sometimes he does." Booklist

The **World's** Greatest Super-Heroes. Paul Dini; art by Alex Ross. DC Comics 2005 un Illustration

Grades: 6 7 8 9 10 11 12 Adult   **741.5; Fic**
1. Graphic novels; 2. Superhero graphic novels; 3. Justice League (Fictional characters); 4. Wonder Woman (Fictional character); 5. Batman (Fictional character); 6. Superman (Fictional character)
1-4012-0254-3, $49.95

LC 2006-159064

This oversize hardcover volume collects the stories that DC originally published separately. Superman tries to singlehandedly end world hunger, only to face suspicion and corruption; Batman tries to stop all criminal activity; and Wonder Woman tries to free oppressed women. They each realize that, despite their super powers, they can't eradicate the problems of the world on their own. The rest of the book portrays the Justice League and highlights each member's super hero origins.

Dirge, Roman

It ate Billy on Christmas. Dark Horse Books 2007 un Illustration

Grades: 4 5 6 7 8 9 10 11 12 Adult   **741.5; Fic**
1. Graphic novels; 2. Horror graphic novels; 3. Humorous graphic novels
978-1-59307-853-9, $12.95

Lumi has been bullied by her brother Billy all her life, and this Christmas would have been more of the same, but for the weird, ugly little monster that crawled up from the abandoned well and came into their house. Mistaking it for the stuffed puppy she had requested from her parents, Lumi watches in amazement as it devours the bullying Billy when he shoots it with darts from his new dart gun. She makes a cardboard Billy, which fools her unsuspecting and clueless parents. A few weeks later, back at school, Lumi has to face the bullies who have made her school life

miserable, but she has her "puppy" in her backpack and it's hungry.... Dirge wrote the story and drew the black and white illustrations, while Daily provided the color paintings. The story shows the monster eating Billy in one gulp, but there's little actual violence on the pages. The dark humor and twisted story line will appeal to those who enjoy Coraline and The Wolves in the Walls by Neil Gaiman, and the weird humor of Edward Gorey cartoons.

Lenore: Noogies. Slave Labor Graphics 1999 un Illustration

Grades: 9 10 11 12 Adult   **741.5; Fic**
1. Graphic novels; 2. Horror graphic novels; 3. Humorous graphic novels
0-943151-03-1, $11.95

This book collects the first four issues of the Lenore comic book series. It ventures into the dark, surreal world of a little dead girl and features stories about limbless cannibals, clock monsters, cursed vampire dolls, taxidermied friends, an obsessed would be lover, and more fuzzy animal mutilations than should be legal. The book includes some disturbing images and macabre humor.

Other Lenore books are: Wedgies (2000); Cooties (2005); Swirlies (2012); Purple Nurples (2013)

Something at the Window is Scratching: Children's Tales for Disturbed Children. SLG Publishing 1998 120p. Illustration

Grades: 9 10 11 12 Adult   **741.5; Fic**
1. Graphic novels; 2. Horror graphic novels; 3. Humorous graphic novels
0-943151-09-0, $9.95

Chilling, disturbing, sickly amusing poems accompanied by equally chilling, disturbing, and sickly amusing illustrations bring to mind a very morbid Shel Silverstein with more of a horror twist. In the title tale, what's scratching at the boy's window that night is the son of the Sandman, who died after sending the boy to sleep; in order to give the creature a home, the boy tapes a tail to the creature and presents his parents with their new cat. Despite the moody, dark tone, there is no violence or bad language.

Dixon, Chuck

The **Iron** Ghost. Image Comics 2007 un Illustration

Grades: 10 11 12 Adult   **741.5; Fic**
1. Graphic novels; 2. Mystery graphic novels; 3. World War, 1939-1945 — Graphic novels
978-1-58240-727-2, $15.99

Berlin, Germany, 1945: The tide of the war has turned in favor of the Allies. The fall of the Nazi empire is inevitable, but there is still something even more dangerous than the ever approaching Allies to the Third Reich: The Iron Ghost, who is murdering officials in the Nazi regime. It's up to two non-Nazi German police officers to capture the Ghost. But once they discover the truth will they want to — or even be able to — stop him? The story includes harsh language and considerable violence.

Nightwing: On the Razor's Edge. DC Comics 2005 192p. Illustration

Grades: 9 10 11 12 Adult   **741.5; Fic**
1. Graphic novels; 2. Mystery graphic novels; 3. Nightwing (Fictional character); 4. Superhero graphic novels
1-4012-0437-6, $14.99

Bludhaven has seen its share of battles between its costumed protector, Nightwing, and various criminals. But when an army of ninjas arrives, it's only a harbinger of the deadliest threat yet. Shrike, long thought dead, is back, and he wants revenge on his childhood pal, Nightwing. Shrike's current master, Blockbuster, would be only too happy to see the vigilante destroyed, but Shrike wants to see to Nightwing's destruction personally.

Nightwing: Year One. Chuck Dixon and Scott Beatty; penciller Scott McDaniel; inker: Andy Owens. DC Comics 2005 un Illustration

Grades: 7 8 9 10 11 12 Adult   **741.5; Fic**
1. Graphic novels; 2. Nightwing (Fictional character); 3. Superhero graphic novels; 4. Teen Titans (Fictional characters); 5. Robin (Fictional character); 6. Batman (Fictional character)
1-4012-0435-X, $14.99

Dick Grayson was the first Robin, the teen sidekick to the Dark Knight, Batman. Then he became Nightwing and stepped out of Batman's shadow. The story behind that transformation and how it affected Batman, the Teen Titans and Dick himself is explored in this graphic novel. When Batman fires Robin, an angry Dick Grayson is unsure of where to go. On his journey, he receives advice from Superman and aid from Deadman, and makes the decisions that lead him to become a brand new crimefighter.

Robin, year one. Chuck Dixon, Scott Beatty, writers; Javier Pulido, Marcos Martin, pencillers; Robert Campanella, inker; Lee Loughridge, colorist; Sean Konot, letterer; Javier Pulido, Robert Campanella, original covers; Batman created by Bob Kane. DC Comics 2008 200p. Illustration
Grades: 9 10 11 12 Adult   **741.5; Fic**
1. Batman (Fictional character); 2. Graphic novels; 3. Robin (Fictional character); 4. Superhero graphic novels
978-1-563-89805-1, $14.99

This book takes readers back to Dick Grayson's first year working as Robin, sidekick of the Batman. After his family of aerialists was murdered, Bruce Wayne took in young Dick Grayson, who helped Wayne as Batman solve the murders. Adopted by Wayne, Dick starts training to become his partner in solving crimes on the streets of Gotham City; but not everyone likes it. Captain James Gordon of the Gotham City Police thinks Dick is much too young, and he puts Batman on notice that if anything happens to hurt or kill Robin, Batman will pay. At first, Dick/Robin can easily handle the bad guys. Then he ends up working solo on a case of girls who disappear when one of his friends from school goes missing, and he goes up against the Mad Hatter. Unknown to Robin, or Batman, Two-Face is watching the young crime-fighter's progress, and he decides to test the boy — brutally. When Two-Face beats Robin badly enough to put him into a hospital, Batman "retires" Robin; but when Dick is strong enough, he runs away to live on the streets. There, he encounters Shrike, a contract killer who trains teen boys in ninja-style fighting, and joins his "school," an organization that Dick realizes Batman doesn't know exists. The book includes strong violence.

The **Vanishers.** IDW Publishing 2002 80p. Illustration
Grades: 6 7 8 9 10 11 12 Adult   **741.5; Fic**
1. Adventure graphic novels; 2. Graphic novels; 3. Science fiction graphic novels
0-9712282-6-4, $12.99

From the turn of the 20th century, to medieval England, and into the far-flung future, Andy and Arvis must escape their pursuers, rescue their friends, and return to their own time. Andy's friends begin to disappear and only he remembers that they ever existed. When Andy discovers another student, Arvis Voltoz, has noticed that disappearances, he follows Arvis home and begins an adventure that takes him and Arvis through time.

Doctorow, Cory
★ **Cory** Doctorow's futuristic tales of the here and now. IDW Publishing 2008 152p. Illustration
Grades: 10 11 12 Adult   **741.5; Fic**
1. Graphic novels; 2. Science fiction graphic novels; 3. Short stories — Graphic novels
978-1-60010-172-4, $24.99

Six short stories by noted young science fiction writer and BoingBoing.net coeditor Doctorow are adapted into the graphic format by various comics creators, including Dara Naraghi, Dan Taylor, J. C. Vaughn, James Anthony Kuhoric, Esteve Polls, Daniel Warner, Paul McCaffrey, Dustin Evans, Erich Owen, Robbie Robbins, Chris Mowry,

and more. The stories include "Anda's Game," in which a twelve-year-old girl gets involved in a multi-player game in which she kills enemies and someone starts paying cash for her kills; "Craphound," in which a professional yard sale picker makes friends with one of the aliens who had come to Earth and wants to learn how to be a picker at yard sales; "After the Siege," in which Valentine and her family struggle to survive the disease turning the city's people into zombies as they try to get by during a siege; and "When Sysadmins Ruled the Earth," in which a global catastrophe destroys almost everything, except the computer techs holed up in various company buildings around the world. The stories include violence and some strong language.

In Real Life. Cory Doctorow; illustrated by Jen Wang. First Second Books 2014 192 p. Color; Illustration
Grades: 8 9 10 11 12   **741.5**
1. Computer games — Economic aspects; 2. Video games — Graphic novels; 3. Ethics
1596436581; 9781596436589, $17.99

In this graphic novel, "online gaming and real life collide when a teen discovers the hidden economies and injustices that hide among seemingly innocent pixels.... Anda joins...a group of girls playing the game as girl avatars.... Another guild member named Lucy...asks her if she'd be interested in earning 'real cash.'...She's pulled into a world of real-money economies where workers 'play' the game, garnering items they can then sell for actual money to other players." (Kirkus Reviews)

"Characters come to life through Wang's...fluid forms and emotive faces, and her adroit shift in colors as the story moves between the physical and gaming worlds is subtle and effective." Pub Wkly

Donkin, Andrew
★ **Illegal.** Eoin Colfer, Andrew Donkin; art by Giovanni Rigano; lettering by Chris Dickey. Sourcebooks Inc 2018 144 p. Illustration
Grades: 5 6 7 8 9   **741.5; Fic**
1. Poor people — Juvenile fiction; 2. Undocumented immigrants — Juvenile fiction; 3. Poor — Fiction; 4. Siblings — Fiction; 5. Undocumented immigrants — Fiction
1492662143; 9781492662143, $19.99

In this book, by Eoin Colfer and Andrew Donkin, illustrated by Giovanni Rigano, "Ebo is alone. His brother, Kwame, has disappeared, and Ebo knows it can only be to attempt the hazardous journey to Europe, and a better life — the same journey their sister set out on months ago.... He sets out after Kwame and joins him on the quest to reach Europe. Ebo's epic journey takes him across the Sahara Desert to the dangerous streets of Tripoli, and finally out to the merciless sea." (Publisher's note)

"The format allows sensitive and difficult topics such as murder, death, and horrific, traumatizing conditions to unfold for children, Ebo's reactions speaking volumes and dramatic perspectives giving a sense of scope. A creators' note provides factual context, and an appendix offers an Eritrean refugee's minimemoir in graphic form." Kirkus

Donner, Rebecca
Burnout. written by Rebecca Donner; illustrated by Inaki Miranda. DC Comics/Minx 2008 176p. Illustration
Grades: 7 8 9 10 11 12   **741.5; Fic**
1. Environmental protection — Graphic novels; 2. Graphic novels; 3. Romance graphic novels
978-1-4012-1537-8, $9.99

Danni and her mother have made another in a long series of moves, this time moving in with her mother's boyfriend, lodge owner Hank. Danni can see that Hank is an alcoholic, and he tends to take his anger out on people, including his son Haskell (with whom Danni is forced to share a room for the time being). They live in the Pacific Northwest, in a logging town, and Haskell is a hardcore environmentalist. Danni falls for him despite herself, and she begins to go with him at night to spike trees, which is an act of ecoterrorism. As home life continues to stay rough, Haskell starts to escalate his acts against logging, and Danni has to decide what to do. The book includes scenes of heavy petting.

"Miranda's superb illustrations complement the story well, whether they're showing landscapes of the Pacific Northwest, action sequences, or the eyes of a troubled girl." Publ Wkly

Doran, Colleen

A **Distant** Soil Vol. 1: The Gathering. Image Comics 1997 un Illustration

Grades: 10 11 12 Adult   **741.5; Fic**
1. Adventure graphic novels; 2. Fantasy graphic novels; 3. Graphic novels
1-887279-51-2, $19.95

This is the story of a young girl who is born the heir to an alien religious dynasty, one of comics' most lavish and romantic sagas. Liana and her brother Jason are orphaned and live in a research institution; they get caught up in interplanetary politics and magic. The book includes fantasy, epic scope, psychics, Arthurian legend, smart-mouthed punks, adorable gay couples, bizarre clothing, aliens, death, love, and heavy doses of humor.

A **Distant** Soil Vol. 2: The Ascendant. Image Comics 2000 un Illustration

Grades: 10 11 12 Adult   **741.5; Fic**
1. Adventure graphic novels; 2. Fantasy graphic novels; 3. Graphic novels
1-58240-018-0, $18.95

Liana was born the heir to an alien religious dynasty, then hidden on Earth until Rieken found her and brought her back. But the galaxy's most powerful psionic, the Avatar, already sits on the throne. Revolutionary forces on the planet have taken Jason, however, and intend to turn him into one of their weapons against the throne. Things continue to become more complicated when Jason learns his father started the Resistance movement on Ovanan, and Liana learns that Rieken is actually Seren, the Avatar, and she's a danger to him. Dangerous politics swirl around everyone. The book includes sexual suggestiveness and violence.

A **Distant** Soil Vol. 3: Aria. Image Comics 2001 un Illustration
Grades: 11 12 Adult   **741.5; Fic**
1. Adventure graphic novels; 2. Fantasy graphic novels; 3. Graphic novels
1-58240-201-9, $16.95

Rieken/Seren is the target of assassins, a pawn in a dangerous game of powerful psionics, and he makes a desperate play for freedom. But his ploy threatens to capture him in his own web of deceit, as his darkest secrets are revealed to allies and enemies alike, leading to a showdown with deadly consequences. And Liana, with powers of the Avatar, and Jason, are caught in the middle. The book includes lots of sexual situations, including same-sex relations, harsh language (including f-bombs), and violence.

A **Distant** Soil Vol. 4: Coda. Image Comics 2005 un Illustration
Grades: 11 12 Adult   **741.5; Fic**
1. Adventure graphic novels; 2. Fantasy graphic novels; 3. Graphic novels
1-58240-478-X, $17.99

Liana is born the heir to an alien religious dynasty. Possessing the power to destroy worlds with her mind, Liana is under an assassination order from the government of her father's home world. A foiled coup attempt results in a power vacuum that leaves the alien world without its treasure weapon. The aliens have no choice but to take Liana as their reluctant new Avatar. Only an angry slave and a small group of resistance

fighters can free her — and the universe — from the dangers of her power. The book includes some strong language, nudity, and violence.

Dori, Fabrizio

Gauguin: The Other World. Fabrizio Dori; translation from the French by Edward Gauvin. Harry N Abrams Inc 2017 144 p. Color; Illustration

Grades: 10 11 12 Adult   **759.4; 741.5; 92**
1. Gauguin, Paul, 1848-1903; 2. Artists — Biography
1910593273; 9781910593271, $19.95

LC 2017303720

This book on Paul Gauguin, by Fabrizio Dori, "is a revelatory biography of an artist whose qualities as a man won him few admirers in his own lifetime, but whose talents as a painter would have an enormous influence on the art of Picasso, Matisse, and many more." (Publisher's note)

"The dreamlike nature of the story line is gorgeously borne out in Dori's painted panels — he brilliantly echoes Gauguin's iconic style, from the stylized figures and imagery to the rich, saturated color. Art lovers will appreciate this enigmatic, unsparing foray into the beleaguered painter's psyche." Booklist

Dorkin, Evan

★ **Beasts** of Burden: animal rites. written by Evan Dorkin; art by Jill Thompson; lettering by Jason Arthur and Jill Thompson. Dark Horse Comics 2010 184p. Illustration

Grades: 8 9 10 11 12 Adult   **741.5; Fic**
1. Cats — Graphic novels; 2. Dogs — Graphic novels; 3. Graphic novels; 4. Mystery graphic novels; 5. Supernatural graphic novels
978-1-59582-513-1, $19.99

2010 Eisner Award for Best Publication for Teens; 2010 Eisner Award to Jill Thompson for Best Painter/Multimedia Artist for Beasts of Burden and Magic Trixie; 2005 Eisner Award for Best Short Story for ¿Unfamiliar;¿ 2004 Eisner Award to Jill Thompson for Best Painter/Multimedia Artist (interior art) for ¿Stray.¿

Burden Hill is just a nice, quiet suburban town full of houses with yards and white picket fences, demonic frogs, zombie roadkill, ghosts, etc. The humans who live in Burden Hill seem to be totally oblivious to the dangers, but the dogs, and one cat, work together to keep their town safe. Jack the beagle, Pugsley (go figure), Ace the husky, Rex the Doberman, Whitey the terrier, and Orphan the cat deal with a haunted dog house, witches, undead dogs, a werewolf, and other monsters. The book includes some mild bad language ("crap" usually from Pugs) and a fair amount of violence. This book includes the four-issue miniseries plus all of the short stories that originally appeared in The Dark Horse Book of Hauntings, The Dark Horse Book of Witchcraft, The Dark Horse Book of the Dead, and The Dark Horse Book of Monsters. Sarah Dyer co-wrote "A Dog and His Boy" with Evan Dorkin.

"Gorgeous artwork and a smart, witty script elevate this tale of household pets who unite to fight occult menaces in idyllic Burden Hill." Publ Wkly

Bill & Ted's Most Excellent Adventures Volume Two. Amaze Ink/SLG Publishing 2005 un Illustration
Grades: 9 10 11 12 Adult   **741.5; Fic**
1. Graphic novels; 2. Humorous graphic novels
1-59362-002-0, $13.95

The silly and fun movies "Bill and Ted's Excellent Adventure" and its sequel, "Bill and Ted's Bogus Journey" inspired a Marvel Comics series in the early 1990s. Written by Evan Dorkin, it was nominated for an Eisner Award. This second volume finds the two time-hopping headbangers on the run from a gang from Hell, on trial for tampering with time, and stuck on a planet of superheroes. There's also an invasion of inter-dimensional

Bills and Teds, a pink-slipped Death, and a bogus attempt to prevent Lincoln's assassination.

Doucet, Julie

365 days: a diary by Julie Doucet. Drawn & Quarterly 2008 360p. Illustration

Grades: 12 Adult   **741.5**

1. Art — Graphic novels; 2. Autobiographical graphic novels; 3. Graphic novels

978-1-89729-915-9; 1-89729-915-X

Doucet renounced her comics-centric lifestyle five years ago and focused on art, but the journal she started in late 2002 combines comics with art with text. Her personal narrative combines with collage, doodles, and comics panels to chronicle her life as she became part of a broader arts community. The book includes some harsh language, and one panel towards the end depicts an image combining nudity with a disturbing sexual situation.

Drooker, Eric

Blood song: a silent ballad. introduction by Joe Sacco. Dark Horse 2009 un Illustration

Grades: 11 12 Adult   **741.5**

1. Graphic novels; 2. Stories without words

978-1-59582-389-2, $19.95

"Driven by war from their rural home in Southeast Asia, a young woman and her dog ride the ocean currents to a city in the West. A deeply moving graphic novel, masterfully done." SLJ

First published 2002 by Harcourt

Dryer, Matt

Dwight T. Albatross's The Goon Noir. Dark Horse Comics 2007 Illustration

Grades: 11 12 Adult   **741.5; Fic**

1. Graphic novels; 2. Horror graphic novels; 3. Humorous graphic novels

978-1-59307-785-3, $12.95

The horror comedy series has been described as "EC by way of Looney Tunes," so it seems fitting that comedians and horror creators put their own spin on the Goon characters. Among the distinguished creators featured in this, the very first Goon anthology, are comedians Patton Oswalt and Brian Posehn (both of Comedy Central's Comedians of Comedy and Mr. Show), Reno: 911 co-creator Thomas Lennon, B.P.R.D. scribe John Arcudi, comics great Kevin Nowlan (Tomorrow Stories, Sandman, Superman), fan-favorite Humberto Ramos (Revelations, Spider-Man), Steve Niles, Ryan Sook, Mike Ploog, Bill Morrison, Arvid Nelson, Tony Moore, Hilary Barta, Roger Langridge, Scott Allie and Todd Herman. Powell himself and frequent co-conspirators Tom Sniegoski and Mark Farmer also present the three-part "Peg Leg Full of Heaven," featuring the Little Unholy Bastards, and erstwhile publisher Dwight T. Albatross contributes a little somethin' for the ladies. Readers can expect to find zombies, monster-smashing, some gore, a little harsh language, quite a bit of sexual suggestiveness, and lots of slightly sick humor.

Duffy, Chris

★ **Above** the Dreamless Dead: World War I in Poetry and Comics. edited by Chris Duffy. First Second 2014 144 p. Illustration

Grades: 9 10 11 12 Adult   **741.5**

1. World War, 1914-1918 — Comic books, strips, etc.; 2. World War, 1914-1918 — Poetry

1626720657; 9781626720657, $24.99

In this book edited by Chris Duffy, "various artists adapt the works of some of the most famous WWI poets, including Wilfred Owen, Siegfried Sassoon, and Isaac Rosenberg. The...cartoonists, including Hunt Emerson, Sarah Glidden, and Stuart Immomen, use different approaches to illuminate poems known for its bitter irony and brutal honesty." (Publishers Weekly)

"The work of 'Trench Poets' from WWI is brought vividly to life by accomplished cartoonists. This stunningly effective presentation does much to inform readers of the emotional and physical horrors of war. The volume's small format renders some of the detail difficult to decipher, but anything larger might be overwhelming. There's very mature content, especially in lyrics of soldiers' songs. Reading list." Horn Book

Includes bibliographical references and index

Duggan, Gerry

The **Last** Christmas. Image Comics 2006 un Illustration

Grades: 11 12 Adult   **741.5; Fic**

1. Adventure graphic novels; 2. Graphic novels; 3. Horror graphic novels; 4. Humorous graphic novels; 5. Santa Claus — Graphic novels

978-1-58240-676-3, $14.99

After the apocalypse, no one is safe; not even at the North Pole. After marauders kill Mrs. Claus, Santa withdraws from life and turns his back on Christmas. When he finally emerges from seclusion, the old world is gone forever, and as Santa struggles to find his way in a post-apocalyptic world, can he find a way to save Christmas too? This Christmas story is for all those who love horror movies (especially with killer zombies) and action movies with lots of shooting and killing of bad guys while yelling curses.

Dumas, Alexandre

The **three** musketeers. Campfire 2010 104p. Illustration

Grades: 3 4 5 6 7 8 9   **741.5; Fic**

1. Adventure graphic novels; 2. Graphic novels

978-93-80028-57-6, $12.99

Young D'Artagnan comes to Paris, determined to become a king's musketeer, but runs into trouble with three musketeers in one day. When they band together to tight Cardinal Richelieu's forces, they become friends. The friends soon find themselves involved in averting a plot to discredit Queen Anne, and their efforts to help her cause them to run afoul of Richelieu. D'Artagnan, Athos, Porthos, and Aramis also must deal with Milady de Winter, a beautiful and deadly woman with her own agenda. This graphic novel adaptation features art that emphasizes the humor in the historical adventure. It also puts most of the violence off-panel, so the story is suitable for younger readers.

Dunn, Joeming W.

The **tell-tale** heart. adapted by Joeming Dunn; illustrated by Rod Espinosa.. Magic Wagon/Graphic Planet 2009 32p. Illustration

Grades: 6 7 8 9 10

741.5; Fic

1. Graphic novels; 2. Guilt — Graphic novels; 3. Homicide — Graphic novels; 4. Horror graphic novels; 5. Poe, Edgar Allan, 1809-1849 — Adaptations

978-1-60270681-1, $27.07

LC 2009-8589

Courtesy of ABDO Publishing.

The young narrator takes care of an old man; he tells the reader he has had no reason to do harm, he never felt any greed for the old man's wealth. However, he hates what he calls the old man's vulture eye, and his hatred of that eye makes him determined to kill the old man so he would never have to look on it again. When he finally murders the old man, however, it's not the eye, but the imagined sound of the old man's beating heart that drives the young killer insane. This easy-reading graphic novel adaptation of Edgar Allan Poe's short story provides a good introduction to Poe's work for reluctant and struggling readers; the emotional intensity of the work makes it more suitable for older readers despite the simplicity of language. Back matter includes a brief biography of Poe, a list of some of his other works, and a short glossary.

This is part of the Graphic Horror Series 2.

Dyer, Jamaica
★ **Weird** fishes. SLG Publishing 2009 112p. Illustration
Grades: 10 11 12 Adult   **741.5; Fic**
1. Friendship — Graphic novels; 2. Graphic novels
978-1-59362-177-3, $9.95

Dee sees giant talking ducks and her main confidant is Bones, a talking goldfish. Bunny Boy always wears a bunny suit. The two misfits have been friends for years, but now things are starting to change. Bunny Boy falls for a goth girl and actually wears a mod suit. Dee, however, has problems when her visions begin to darken, ducks become monsters, and bad things hang out in storm clouds. She needs Bunny Boy, but he seems to want more normalcy in his personal relationships. The two teens smoke cigarettes, cut school, and Bunny Boy goes to a party where people are drinking alcohol.

Dysart, Joshua
★ **Captain** Gravity and the Power of the Vril. Penny-Farthing Press 2006 193p. Illustration
Grades: 8 9 10 11 12
741.5; Fic
1. Adventure graphic novels; 2. Graphic novels; 3. Superhero graphic novels
0-9719012-8-7, $19.95

Courtesy of Penny-Farthing Productions

Some years before, a young African American named Joshua Jones stumbled upon a mysterious stone at an archeological dig and became infused with an element from the stone that gave him power over gravity, including flight. He hid his identity with a helmet and became Captain Gravity. Now it's the 1930s, and Joshua Jones works in Hollywood with the two friends who know his secret. They've been making Captain Gravity, and no one else has figured out that the hero is Black. Now, Nazis are searching for the original source of what they call Vril, Joshua's power, and they plan to use it to conquer the Earth. Only Captain Gravity can stop them, and he has to chase them all over the world and to the lost city of Atlantis.

A young, evil Adolf Hitler, an unusual hero for the time, and a story that harks back to the Golden Age of comics storytelling all add up to a great story for this time.

Swamp Thing Vol. 2: Love in Vain. DC Comics/Vertigo 2005 144p. Illustration
Grades: 11 12 Adult   **741.5; Fic**
1. Graphic novels; 2. Horror graphic novels; 3. Science fiction graphic novels
1-4012-0493-7, $14.99

Though he once wielded the combined power of all the Earth's elemental forces, the creature known as Swamp Thing has renounced his omnipotence and returned to his original status as the avatar of the Green, the web of energy connecting all of the world's plant life. But he is now vulnerable, and Arcane is about to break out of his eternal damnation into the world of the living. His designs for revenge threaten to sink not only the Swamp Thing and his family, but everything else under the sun into a never-ending nightmare of corruption and despair. The book includes lots of harsh language, graphic violence, nudity, and sexual situations.

Swamp Thing: Healing the Breach. DC Comics/Vertigo 2006 144p. Illustration
Grades: 10 11 12 Adult   **741.5; Fic**
1. Fantasy graphic novels; 2. Graphic novels; 3. Superhero graphic novels; 4. Swamp Thing (Fictional character)
1-4012-0934-3, $17.99

With the consciousness of Alec Holland still separated from its former host and scattered throughout the world, the Swamp Thing must face a new threat which is manifesting itself inside a growing dead zone in the Gulf of Mexico and contend with the gradual reassembly of the Holland mind and the pain of reintegration that its completion promises. In the meantime, a hurricane threatens the Gulf Coast area where Swamp Thing, and crippled Jordin are staying. The book includes strong language, some nudity and sexual situations, and some violence.

★ **Unknown** soldier: haunted house. DC Comics/Vertigo 2009 144p. Illustration
Grades: 11 12 Adult   **741.5; Fic**
1. Graphic novels; 2. Terrorism — Graphic novels; 3. Uganda — Graphic novels
978-1-4012-2311-3, $9.99

In 2002, Northern Uganda is a beautiful country racked by horrible brutality and war, as an insane extremist Christian rebel and his army of children terrorize their own people. Dr. Lwanga Moses had fled Uganda with his family when he was a child and Idi Amin was in power; now, he has returned to Uganda with his Ugandan wife, full of pacifist ideals and plans to bring hope and healing to his home country. Then he falls prey to the child soldiers and something deep within him erupts, and Dr. Moses becomes an unstoppable killing machine. His face disfigured, he covers it in bandages and becomes an unknown soldier, determined to do whatever it takes, however much violence and killing he must do, to stop the war. Meanwhile, his wife keeps up their medical mission, always wondering what happened to make her husband disappear. This book is full of horrific, gory violence, but with this update of the classic Unknown Soldier character, Dysart also carefully researched into Ugandan politics and conflicts to make his story as authentic as possible.

Edginton, Ian
Kingdom of the Wicked. Dark Horse Comics 2004 120p. Illustration
Grades: 8 9 10 11 12 Adult   **741.5; Fic**
1. Adventure graphic novels; 2. Fantasy graphic novels; 3. Graphic novels
1-59307-187-6, $15.95

Christopher Grahame is the premier children's author of the twenty-first century, a publishing phenomenon. With his work translated into everything from Aborigine to Zulu, he is the cornerstone of a multi-million dollar, franchise spewing empire. Is it any surprise then that under all this pressure something has to give? Unfortunately, it's Chris's mind. Stricken by mysterious headaches and blackouts that plagued his childhood, Chris once again finds himself walking the avenues and boulevards of Castrovalva — the fantasy realm he dreamt up as a boy, to while away his recuperation. But like Chris, Castrovalva has also changed. Deluged in mud, blood, and barbed wire, war has come to wonderland. Chris tries to tell himself it's all a bad dream...so why can't he wake up? The book includes violence, strong language, and brief nudity.

Scarlet Traces. Dark Horse Comics 2003 88p. Illustration
Grades: 9 10 11 12 Adult   **741.5; Fic**
1. Graphic novels; 2. Mystery graphic novels; 3. Science fiction graphic novels
1-56971-940-3, $14.95

A decade after the Martians' abortive assault on the Earth and their attempt to establish an invasion bridgehead on the British Isles, the industrious Victorians have assimilated the Martian technologies into their everyday lives. Hansom cabs now scuttle along the Capital's streets on multi-limbed crab legs and the terrible monopoly of the Martian heat-ray has assured the dominance of the British Empire over two thirds of the Earth's surface. However, there is something rotten at the heart of empire. When the bodies of several young women are found washed up on the Thames, drained of blood, enter Captain Robert Autumn (retired soldier turned gentleman-adventurer) and his former Sergeant Major, now manservant, Archie Currie. Together they are drawn into the mystery which leads them from the gin palaces of the East End, and the grinding poverty of the North, to Whitehall's corridors of power and the very Hall of the Martian King. The book includes violence and some strong language.

Edmondson, Nathan

Black Widow; Volume 1: the finely woven thread. Nathan Edmondson; illustrated by Phil Noto. Marvel Enterprises 2014 144 p. Color; Illustration

Grades: 11 12 Adult   **741.5**

1. Superheroes — Fiction; 2. Undercover operations — Fiction; 3. Black Widow (Fictional character)

0785188193; 9780785188193, $17.99

"The Black Widow goes undercover in Russia, but from its cold streets, the Hand of God reaches out to crush her...and it is as merciless as its name implies. Outmatched by the brute force of a powerful new villain, Natasha faces her deadliest test, and discovers a deadly plot unfolding that spans the entire globe." (Publisher's note)

"Edmondson's fast-paced and action-packed espionage story does an excellent job playing to the character's strengths, using her cunning to assess each situation and her agility and reflexes when it all goes to hell. Noto's luminous watercolorlike panels — a welcome departure from more traditional superhero comics artwork — create a soft atmosphere." Booklist

Contains material originally published in magazine form as Black Widow #1-6 and All new Marvel now! point one #1 — Tp verso.; Volume 1 of 3

Olympus. written by Nathan Edmonson; art by Christian Ward; letters by Jeff Powell. Image Comics 2009 un Illustration

Grades: 10 11 12 Adult   **741.5; Fic**

1. Fantasy graphic novels; 2. Graphic novels; 3. Greek mythology — Graphic novels

978-0-60706-178-6, $14.99

In Ancient Greece, Zeus granted immortality to two brothers, Castor and Pollux (most people might know them as the Gemini twins), then bound them to his service. Three thousand years later, they still serve him on Earth by hunting fugitives from Olympus and maintaining order between the human realm and the divine. This means they have to catch Hermes and cast him off Earth; when they do that, they accidentally leave an opening between the realms for Pelops, son of Tantalus, who has no love for the gods. Ward saturates his sketchy, scratchy lines with wild colors. The book includes violence and some harsh language.

Eisenberg, Adam

The **Creation** of Iron Man. Rosen Publishing Group 2006 48p. Illustration

Grades: 4 5 6 7 8 9 10   **741.5**

1. Graphic novels; 2. Iron Man (Fictional character); 3. Superhero graphic novels

978-1-4042-0767-7, $29.25

                              LC 2006000167

This volume discusses the unique character of Tony Stark, developed by Stan Lee and Jack Kirby, who was unable to live a normal life and invented a special iron suit that gave him superpowers. The book includes information about the times in which Lee and Kirby worked at Marvel Comics.

Part of the Action Heroes series.

Eisinger, Justin

Angel: Spotlight. IDW Publishing 2006 120p. Illustration

Grades: 10 11 12 Adult   **741.5; Fic**

1. Fantasy graphic novels; 2. Graphic novels; 3. Horror graphic novels

978-1-600100-023-6, $19.99

This collection compiles five one-shots focusing on different members of Angel's supporting cast, each from a different creative team. Peter David and Nicola Scott focus on Illyria. Dan Jolly and Mark Pennington handle Gunn, Scott Tipton and Mike Norton feature Wesley. Jeff Mariotte and David Messina present Doyle. And Jay Faerber and Bob Gill offer up a tale of Conner. Monster fighting, demons, and internal organs are on display in the stories.

Star Trek: Alien spotlight volume 1. IDW Publishing 2008 152p. Illustration

Grades: 6 7 8 9 10 11 12 Adult   **741.5; Fic**

1. Adventure graphic novels; 2. Graphic novels; 3. Science fiction graphic novels; 4. Star Trek — Graphic novels

978-1-60010-179-3, $19.99

This volume collects a series of one-shots (standalone comics issues), each devoted to one of the alien races featured in the Star Trek series. Readers meet the Gorns, Vulcans, Andorians, Orions, the Borg, and the Romulans in stories that also give the aliens' point of view. The stories are set in the various time periods of the Star Trek universe; for example, Captain Clark Terrell and Pavel Chekov (before they were captured by Khan in "The Wrath of Khan") and their landing party encounter the Gorns on a planet designed to train Gorn warriors, while Captain Picard encounters the Borg.

Eisner, Will

The **Best** of the Spirit. DC Comics 2005 187p. Illustration

Grades: 7 8 9 10 11 12 Adult   **741.5; Fic**

1. Graphic novels; 2. Superhero graphic novels; 3. The Spirit (Fictional character); 4. Spirit (Fictional character)

1-4012-0755-3, $14.99; 9781401207557

Legendary comics creator Will Eisner created The Spirit in 1940, and over the twelve years of its initial publication, he used it to revolutionize the cartooning medium, creating new methods of storytelling, developing new depths of characterization, and inventing such artistic innovations as the splash page. This volume reprints 22 stories from the original run, including the origin story from 1940; the bulk of the stories were initially published in the mid- to late-1940s. These stories allow people to get acquainted with The Spirit, who was a young criminologist named Denny Colt; believed to have been murdered, he was buried in a state of suspended animation and awoke one day in the Wildwood Cemetery. He has since dedicated himself to fighting crime, wearing a suit, fedora, and mask. DC Comics started publishing a new incarnation of The Spirit in 2007, and a motion picture is in the works.

★ **Comics** and sequential art: principles and practices from the legendary cartoonist. W.W. Norton 2008 175p. Illustration (The Will Eisner library)

Grades: 9 10 11 12 Adult   **741.5**

1. Comic books, strips, etc. — Authorship; 2. Drawing — Technique; 3. Graphic novels — Authorship

978-0-393-33126-4; 0-393-33126-1, $22.95

LC 2008-20042

This book offers the author's ideas, theories, and advice about graphic storytelling and the uses to which the comic book art form can be applied.
First published 1985 by Poorhouse Press

Fagin the Jew. by Will Eisner; foreword by Michael Bendis. Dark Horse 2013 136 p. Illustration
Grades: 11 12 Adult   **741.5**
1. Jews — Great Britain — Fiction
1616551267; 9781616551261, $19.99
This book is author and illustrator Will Eisner's reimagination of author Charles Dickens' character Fagin from the book "Oliver Twist." "Imagining Fagin's impoverished childhood in the slums of London and his initiation into the criminal underworld, Eisner's story counters the anti-Semitism of Victorian literature as his...brushwork creates...[a] portrait of the era." (Publisher's note)
"[T]his compelling counternarrative is framed as Fagin's apologia to Dickens and folds in plenty of historical background about Jews in Europe and England during the late 19th century." LJ
Includes bibliographical references; First published 2003

The **Last** Knight: An Introduction to Don Quixote. NBM Publishing 2000 32p. Illustration
Grades: 3 4 5 6 7 8 9 10   **741.5; Fic**
1. Adventure graphic novels; 2. Graphic novels; 3. Novelists; 4. Poets; 5. Cervantes Saavedra, Miguel de, 1547-1616 — Adaptations
1-56163-251-1; 978-1-56163-251-0, $15.95

LC 2001-265049

This is Eisner's graphic novel remake of Don Quixote. Here are the adventures of a Spanish country gentleman and his companion who set out, like knights of old, to search for adventure. As the subtitle says, this book hits the highlights and serves to introduce the classic tale to younger readers.

Moby Dick. by Herman Melville; adapted by Will Eisner. NBM Publishing 2001 32p. Illustration
Grades: 3 4 5 6 7 8 9 10   **741.5; Fic**
1. Adventure graphic novels; 2. Graphic novels; 3. Whaling — Graphic novels
1-56163-293-7, $15.95; 1-56163-294-5 (pa)

LC 2001-032989

Ishmael, a sailor, recounts the ill-fated voyage of a whaling ship led by the fanatical Captain Ahab in search of the white whale that had crippled him. Eisner's adaptation hits the highlights of the novel.

The **plot:** the secret story of the Protocols of the Elders of Zion. by Will Eisner, with an introduction by Umberto Eco. Norton 2005 vii, 148 p. Illustration (Will Eisner library.)
Grades: 9 10 11 12 Adult   **741.5; 305.892**
1. Antisemitism; 2. Protocols of the wise men of Zion
0393060454; 0393328600; 9780393060454, $19.95

LC 2005040527

This book, by Will Eisner, "examines the astonishing conspiracy and the fabrication of The Protocols of the Elders of Zion.... Purported to be the actual blueprints by Jewish leaders to take over the world, the Protocols, first published in 1902, have become gospel truth to international millions. Presenting a pageant of historical figures,...Eisner unravels and dispels one of the most devastating hoaxes of the twentieth century." (Publisher's note)

The **Princess** and the Frog. NBM Publishing 1999 32p. Illustration
Grades: 3 4 5 6 7 8 9 10   **741.5; Fic**
1. Fairy tales — Graphic novels; 2. Fantasy graphic novels; 3. Graphic novels
1-56163-244-9, $15.95; 1-56163-346-1 (pa)

A good prince, turned into a frog by a spiteful wizard, exacts from a princess a promise which she is reluctant to fulfill, despite his kindness and her desire not to hurt him. Comics master Will Eisner adapted the familiar tale by the Brothers Grimm.

The **Spirit** Archives Volume 14. DC Comics 2004 192p. Illustration
Grades: 9 10 11 12 Adult   **741.5; Fic**
1. Graphic novels; 2. Superhero graphic novels; 3. The Spirit (Fictional character); 4. Spirit (Fictional character)
1-4012-0158-X, $49.95

LC 2001-274103

The adventures of Will Eisner's most famous creation continue in this volume reprinting the Spirit newspaper sections from 1/5/47 to 6/29/47. It features appearances by Ebony, Dolan and Ellen, the seductive P'Gell, Hoagy the Yogi, Silken Floss, Saree and more. Today's readers should understand that Eisner's depiction of Ebony, who is the Spirit's sidekick, was not considered out of place in 1947, even though many might take offense now. Eisner started developing new methods of telling a story and revolutionizing comics along the way.

The **Spirit** Archives Volume 15. DC Comics 2004 192p. Illustration
Grades: 9 10 11 12 Adult   **741.5; Fic**
1. Graphic novels; 2. Superhero graphic novels; 3. The Spirit (Fictional character); 4. Spirit (Fictional character)
1-4012-0162-8, $49.95

LC 2001-274103

Volume 15 reprints The Spirit newspaper sections published from July 6, 1947 to December 28, 1947, featuring the seductive P'Gell, The Octopus, a send up of Li'l Abner, and more. The stories range from broad comedy to crime noir, with plenty of comic violence.

★ The **Spirit:** Femmes fatales. DC Comics 2008 192p. Illustration
Grades: 9 10 11 12   **741.5; Fic**
1. Adventure graphic novels; 2. Graphic novels; 3. Mystery graphic novels; 4. Superhero graphic novels; 5. The Spirit (Fictional character); 6. Spirit (Fictional character)
978-1-4012-1973-4, $19.99

Will Eisner's The Spirit is a classic comic book hero Denny Colt, a young policeman who was killed on the job and has come back from the dead to become a masked, suited crime fighter. And while he fought crime, he also dealt with women, lots of women, some good, some bad, some plain evil, and all beautiful. This book collects 23 stories from the original twelve-year run of The Spirit that feature some of the gorgeous but deadly villainesses who made the Spirit's life...interesting. Readers will meet Silk Satin, P'Gell, Silken Floss, Madam Minx, and true-blue, courageous Ellen Dolan. The stories include some violence and the same kind of sexual tension found in such classic movies as The Maltese Falcon.

El Rassi, Toufic
Arab in America. Last Gasp 2008 118p. Illustration
Grades: 10 11 12 Adult   **92; 741.5**
1. Biographical graphic novels; 2. Graphic novels; 3. Muslims — United States — Graphic novels
978-0-86719-673-3, $14.95

Toufic El Rassi combines a memoir of his life in America with commentary on how Muslims and Arabs have been treated in the U.S. Born in Beirut but living in the U.S. since he was a young boy, El Rassi faced ignorant prejudice and discrimination ever since his family immigrated to this country. In this book he shows how hard it is to maintain an Arab identity in a country saturated with anti-Arab propaganda, examining the roles of media and pop culture in a world with 9/11, two Gulf Wars, and other U.S. involvement in the Middle East. Readers will confront uncomfortable ideas about just what unthinking patriotism and ignorance about the real culture of the Middle East countries do to harm many who are innocent. The book includes some strong language and a few isolated panels with partial nudity.

Eldred, Tim
★ **Grease** monkey. written and drawn by Tim Eldred; [edited by Teresa Nielsen Hayden]. Tor 2006 352p. Illustration
Grades: 9 10 11 12 Adult   741.5; Fic
   1. Graphic novels; 2. Science fiction graphic novels
0-7653-1325-1; 0-7653-1326-X (pa), $19.95

When hostile aliens attacked Earth and left it after killing most of the humans, another group of aliens came and offered to "uplift" one of the animal species to human intelligence so that Earth could rebuild. The dolphins turned them down, but the gorillas went for it. Some generations later, new mechanic Robin Plotnik comes to the space station called Fist of Earth, where he's assigned to work with Chief Mac Gimbensky. Mac is a no-nonsense gorilla who works on the ships of the all-woman Barbarian Squadron. He and Robin work together well, but they each have their romantic problems. This is science fiction from a viewpoint not always seen in most stories.

Ellerton, Sarah
Inverloch, Volume 1. Seven Seas 2006 un Illustration
Grades: 4 5 6 7 8 9 10 11 12   741.5; Fic
   1. Adventure graphic novels; 2. Fantasy graphic novels; 3. Graphic novels
1-933164-13-1, $14.99

In a world where humans, elves, and other beings coexist, albeit not altogether peacefully, Acheron is a young da'kor, a horned wolf-like race that lives in the forests. He encounters a beautiful elf and takes her quest for his own — to find another elf who went missing twelve years before. Teased by his brothers as a lousy hunter, feared by humans who think da'kor are dangerous beasts, innocent Acheron finds that the world beyond the forest is full of danger, intrigue, and betrayal.

This story began online as a webcomic.

Ellis, Grace
★ **Lumberjanes**; Volume 1: Beware the kitten holy. written by Noelle Stevenson & Grace Ellis; illustrated by Brooke Allen; colors by Maarta Laiho; letters by Aubrey Aiese; created by Shannon Watters, Grace Ellis & Noelle Stevenson. Boom! Studios 2015 128 p. Illustration; Color (Lumberjanes)
Grades: 6 7 8 9 10 11 12 Adult   741.5; Fic
   1. Female friendship — Graphic novels; 2. Monsters — Fiction; 3. Camps — Fiction; 4. Summer — Fiction; 5. Adventure fiction
1608866874; 9781608866878, $14.99
Eisner Award: Best New Series (2015); Eisner Award: Best Publication for Teens (2015); Harvey Award: Best New Series (2015); Harvey Award: Best Original Graphic Publication For Young Readers (2015)

"[This] graphic novel begins mid-adventure as five campers are out after hours investigating a strange event that they all witnessed: a woman turning into a giant bear. This is just the first of many odd occurrences that Jo, April, Molly, Mal, and Ripley encounter at the summer camp for 'Hardcore Lady Types.' The Lumberjanes, as the scouts are called, band together to solve puzzles, defeat three-eyed creatures, and escape the ire of their watchful counselor Jen." (School Library Journal)

"Humorously riffing on everything from scout badges to the X-Men to feminist heroes…, it's a sharp, smart, and most of all fun celebration of sisterhood." Pub Wkly

Volume 1 of an ongoing series

Lumberjanes; Volume 2: Friendship to the Max. by Noelle Stevenson, Grace Ellis, illustrated by Brooke A Allen, contributed by Shannon Watters. Boom! Studios 2015 112 p. Color; Illustration
Grades: 6 7 8 9 10 11 12 Adult   741.5; Fic
   1. Fantasy graphic novels; 2. Teenage girls — Fiction; 3. Camping — Fiction
1608867374; 9781608867370, $14.99

"Jo, April, Mal, Molly and Ripley are five best pals determined to have an awesome summer together…and they're not gonna let any insane quest or an array of supernatural critters get in their way! But having stumbled onto a mysterious force wreaking havoc in the camp, it's a race through the woods as the Lumberjanes work together to save not only their friends, but maybe even the whole world!" (Publisher's note)

Moonstruck; Volume 1: Magic to brew. writer, Grace Ellis; artists, Shae Beagle and Kate Leth; colors, Caitlin Quirk; lettering, Clayton Cowles. Image Comics 2018 120 p. Color; Illustration
Grades: 9 10 11 12 Adult   741.5; Fic
   1. Magic — Fiction; 2. Werewolves — Fiction
1534304770; 9781534304772, $9.99

"Werewolf barista Julie and her new girlfriend go on a date to a close-up magic show, but all heck breaks loose when the magician casts a horrible spell on their friend Chet. Now it's up to the team of mythical pals to stop the illicit illusionist before it's too late." (Publisher's note)

"Beagle's art, awash in dreamy pastels and moody lighting, perfectly complements the dialogue and plot, and clever, dynamic panel layouts give the pages lots of compelling visual interest. The refreshing variety of skin tones, gender presentations, and body shapes and sizes (monster and otherwise) emphasizes the overall message of body positivity and an atmosphere of inclusion." Booklist

Volume 1 of an ongoing series

Ellis, Warren
Crecy. Avatar Press 2007 un Illustration
Grades: 10 11 12 Adult   741.5; Fic
   1. Crecy (France), Battle of, 1346 — Graphic novels; 2. Graphic novels; 3. Hundred Years' War, 1339-1453 — Graphic novels; 4. War — Graphic novels
978-1-59291-040-3, $6.99

A highly trained but under equipped army invades another country due to that country's perceived threat to home security. The army conducts shock-and-awe raids designed to terrify the populace. This army is soon driven to ground, and vastly outnumbered. The English army has to stand and fight, under the command of King Edward III, in Crecy, France. On 26 August 1346, modern warfare changed forever. This is the story of England's greatest battle, narrated by a fictional English longbowman. The book is full of battlefield violence and lots of very harsh language, including the f-bomb.

Desolation Jones. DC Comics/Wildstorm 2006 142p. Illustration
Grades: 12 Adult   741.5; Fic
   1. Graphic novels; 2. Mystery graphic novels
978-1-4012-1150-9, $14.99

Michael Jones used to be an MI6 field agent, and he is the first surviving victim of the Desolation Test, a radically dangerous procedure cooked up by the British government. He was kept alive intravenously while being force-fed a steady diet of horrific data and images non-stop as stimulants were continuously pumped into him, for an entire year. Now he lives in Los Angeles, where all the ex-spooks like him have been sent and kept; he works as a private investigator to their secret underground community. Colonel Nigh, who lives for his pornography collection, needs Jones' help to recover a special piece of film — pornography starring Adolf Hitler; Nigh's troublesome daughters all play into the equation. Mature readers who enjoy such titles as Preacher and aren't troubled by nudity, violence, and considerable use of harsh language, will want to read this.

Fell Volume 1: Feral City. Image Comics 2007 un Illustration
Grades: 11 12 Adult   **741.5; Fic**
1. Graphic novels; 2. Mystery graphic novels
978-1-58240-693-0, $14.99
Detective Richard Fell is transferred over the bridge from the big city to Snowtown, a feral district whose police investigations department numbers three and a half people (one detective has no legs). Dumped in this collapsing urban trashzone, Richard Fell is starting all over again. In a place where nothing seems to make any sense, Fell clings to the one thing he knows to be true: everybody's hiding something. Considerable violence and strong language mix with a strong noir-ish mystery.

Freakangels; Volume 1. story Warren Ellis; artwork Paul Duffield. Avatar Press 2008 144 p. Illustration
Grades: 10 11 12 Adult   **741.5; Fic**
1. Psychic ability — Comic books, strips, etc.; 2. Youth — England — London — Comic books, strips, etc.; 3. Apocalyptic fiction; 4. Science fiction graphic novels; 5. Dystopian fiction
1592910564; 9781592910564, $19.99
"Twenty-three years ago, twelve strange children were born in England at exactly the same moment. Six years ago, the world ended. Today, eleven strange 23-year-olds live in and defend Whitechapel, maybe the last real settlement in flooded London. When a dazed, gun-toting girl appears on the outskirts with a deadly grudge against the self-proclaimed Freakangels, the kids realize that an old enemy is still alive beyond the safety of their borders... a twelfth psychic child, evil and exiled, who can program human minds to hate, and send his private, pirate armies into Whitechapel for revenge." (Publisher's note)
Volume 1 of 6

Nextwave: Agents of H.A.T.E. Vol. 1: This is What They Want. Marvel Entertainment 2006 un Illustration
Grades: 10 11 12 Adult   **741.5; Fic**
1. Adventure graphic novels; 2. Graphic novels; 3. Satire — Graphic novels; 4. Superhero graphic novels
0-7851-2278-8, $19.99
H.A.T.E. (The Highest Anti-Terrorism Effort) put together a team of superheroes they call Nextwave: Monica Rambeau (formerly Captain Marvel and Photon), Aaron Stack (the robotic Machine Man), Tabitha Smith (X-Force's Meltdown), monster-hunter Elsa Bloodstone, and The Captain. The team was told they were supposed to fight Bizarre Weapons of Mass Destruction; however, Tabitha lifted some papers that reveal the truth: H.A.T.E. is part of the Beyond Corporation, which is the new version of the terrorist organization formerly known as Silent. The Corporation plans to test its weapons on unsuspecting American towns, so Nextwave goes rogue to stop the weapons and be the good guys. They face an awakened Fin Fang Foom (giant monster lizard), a bad cop turned robotic monster, and their former boss, Dirk Anger. There's lots of action, bad words show as a series of death's heads, and the whole thing is written as a biting satire of superheroes.

Nextwave: Agents of H.A.T.E. Vol. 2: I Kick Your Face. Marvel Entertainment 2007 un Illustration
Grades: 10 11 12 Adult   **741.5; Fic**
1. Graphic novels; 2. Humorous graphic novels; 3. Superhero graphic novels
0-7851-2855-7, $19.99
In this second and final volume of the series, former Captain Marvel Monica Rambeau and the Nextwave team continue their quest to shut down H.A.T.E.'s network of Unusual Weapons of Mass Destruction. They destroy the Mindless Ones, the bizarre Broccoli Men who have been created to look like various superhero teams, and then decide to finish off

S.I.L.E.N.T. itself, the uber-terrorist network that has been funding H.A.T.E. It's a full-on superhero satire with lots of comic book action, and all the bad words appear as skulls.

Orbiter. DC Comics/Vertigo 2004 104p. Illustration
Grades: 10 11 12 Adult   **741.5; Fic**
1. Graphic novels; 2. Mystery graphic novels; 3. Science fiction graphic novels
1-4012-0056-7, $17.95
In the early 21st century, the space shuttle Venture has suddenly returned to Earth after disappearing ten years ago; its crew is missing, except for the catatonic pilot, and the ship is outfitted with new instrumentation, new engines, and is covered in something very much like skin, while its landing gear has Martian sand. Now a team of three specialists must discover where the Venture went, what happened to it, and what happened to the crew. Unfortunately, most of the answers are locked up in the seemingly twisted mind of the pilot. Does he really know the truth or is he simply a demented casualty of a space mission gone wrong? The book includes some foul language.

★ **Planetary**; 2, Vol. 2. Warren Ellis, writer; John Cassaday, artist; Laura DePuy and David Baron, colorists; Ryan Cline, Bill O'Neil and Mike Heisler, letterers. DC Comics 2013 144 p. Color; Illustration
Grades: 11 12 Adult   **741.5**
1. Adventure graphic novels; 2. Parapsychology — Fiction; 3. Superhero comic books, strips, etc.
1563897644; 9781563897641, $14.99
                                        LC 2012046722
This graphic novel, written by Warren Ellis and illustrated by John Cassady, the second in the "Planetary" series, "focuses on the team's mysterious benefactor, the 'Fourth Man.' After paying their final respects to a British occultist with ties to their group, Elijah Snow, Jakita Wagner, and The Drummer continue their super-human archeological studies as they visit a hidden government compound full of radioactive human guinea pigs." (Publisher's note)
Originally published by WildStorm in single magazine form as Planetary #7-#12.

★ **Planetary**; 3: leaving the 20th century, 3. Warren Ellis & John Cassaday, writer, co-creators, artist; Laura Martin, colorist. DC Comics 2005 144 p. Color; Illustration
Grades: 11 12 Adult   **741.5**
1. Science fiction graphic novels; 2. Superhero comic books, strips, etc.; 3. Adventure graphic novels; 4. Mystery graphic novels
1401202942; 9781401202941, $14.99
In this graphic novel, written by Warren Ellis and illustrated by John Cassaday, the third in the "Planetary" series, "Elijah takes a look at his past, making startling revelations and recounting his participation in the first moon shot...in 1851!" (Publisher's note)
Originally published in single magazine form as Planetary #13-18

★ **Planetary**; 4: spacetime archaeology. writer, Warren Ellis; artist, John Cassaday; colorist, Laura Martin; letterer, Comicraft. WildStorm Productions 2010 224 p. Color; Illustration
Grades: 11 12 Adult   **741.5**
1. Graphic novels; 2. Fantasy fiction; 3. Adventure fiction; 4. Superhero comic books, strips, etc.
1401223451; 9781401223458, $17.99
                                        LC 2010294189
This book, by Warren Ellis, is the "fourth and final graphic novel collecting the adventures of Elijah Snow, a powerful, hundred year old man, Jakita Wagner, an extremely powerful but bored woman, and The Drummer, a man with the ability to communicate with machines. Infatuated with tracking down evidence of super-human activity, these

mystery archaeologists of the late 20th Century uncover unknown paranormal secrets and histories." (Publisher's note)

"Engaging as the story itself may be, Planetary's brilliance lies more in the rich history of comics and comic lore that Ellis draws from and cleverly weaves into the narrative from beginning to end." SLJ

Originally published in single magazine form as Planetary #19-27.

★ **Planetary;** vol 1: all over the world and other stories. Warren Ellis, John Cassaday, Laura DePuy. Wildstorm 2012 160 p. Color; Illustration
Grades: 11 12 Adult   **741.5**
1. Science fiction comic books, strips, etc.; 2. Adventure graphic novels; 3. Mystery graphic novels; 4. Parapsychology — Fiction; 5. Archaeologists — Fiction
1563896486; 9781563896484, $14.99

LC 2012024915
Written by Warren Ellis with art by John Cassaday, "this graphic novel features the adventures of Elijah Snow, a hundred year old man, Jakita Wagner, an extremely powerful and bored woman, and The Drummer, a man with the ability to communicate with machines. Infatuated with tracking down evidence of super-human activity, these mystery archaeologists of the late 20th Century uncover unknown paranormal secrets and histories." (Publisher's note)

Also available in an omnibus edition; Originally published by WildStorm Productions in single magazine form as Planetary #1-6 And Planetary Preview.; Other volumes in this series are: Vol. 2: The fourth man; Vol. 3: Leaving the 20th century; Vol. 4: Spacetime archaeology

Ellison, Harlan
Harlan Ellison's Dream Corridor, Vol. 2. Dark Horse Comics 2007 168p. Illustration
Grades: 11 12 Adult   **741.5; Fic**
1. Fantasy graphic novels; 2. Graphic novels
978-1-59307-494-4, $19.95

The words of world-renowned science-fiction author Harlan Ellison are translated onto the page by top comics creators, including Paul Chadwick, Neal Adams, Steve Rude, Gene Colan, Steve Niles, Gerard Jones, Richard Corben and the legendary Oz illustrator Eric Shanower. Most of these stories have never before seen print. Ellison uses strong language and violence a lot in his stories, which include "Opposites Attract," "One Life, Furnished in Early Poverty," "The Discarded", "Moonlighting," and more.

Endo, Hiroki
Tanpenshu Vol. 1. Dark Horse Comics 2007 230p. Illustration
Grades: 11 12 Adult   **741.5; Fic**
1. Graphic novels; 2. Manga; 3. Seinen manga
978-1-59307-637-5, $12.95

The three stories in this first volume are mature explorations of humanity's constant, fumbling attempts to find hope and meaning in a confusing, violent world. A disfigured misfit befriends a doomed yakuza outcast, a group a school kids fail to see the anger that's about to boil over from one of their own and members of an experimental theatre troupe embark on a project that will test both their friendships and the group's grasp on reality. The stories include strong language, nudity and graphic violence, and the cover may disturb some readers.

Englehart, Steve
Batman: Dark Detective. Steve Englehart, writer; Marshall Rogers, penciller; Terry Austin, inker; John Workman, letterer; Chris Chuckry, colorist. DC Comics 2005 144p. Illustration
Grades: 9 10 11 12 Adult   **741.5; Fic**
1. Batman (Fictional character); 2. Graphic novels; 3. Superhero graphic novels; 4. Joker (Fictional character)

1-4012-0898-3, $14.99
When the maniacal Joker enters a gubernatorial election, the Dark Knight takes action. But Batman discovers he's in way over his head when the unexpected return of former girlfriend Silver St. Cloud leaves him torn between love and duty. With adversaries like the Joker, Two-Face, Scarecrow, and others to contend with, Batman must make a choice between his quest for justice and his affections for Silver. And his indecision could cost him everything. The story evokes the style and content of 1970s comics.

Ennis, Garth
Britton, Battler. DC Comics/Wildstorm 2007 un Illustration
Grades: 10 11 12 Adult   **741.5; Fic**
1. Adventure graphic novels; 2. Graphic novels; 3. War — Graphic novels; 4. World War, 1939-1945 — Graphic novels
978-1-4012-1378-7, $19.99

In October, 1942, Allied forces are on the run from the unrelenting forces of the Nazis in North Africa. Wing Commander Robert "Battler" Britton of the Royal Air Force and his squadron are dispatched to an American airstrip to spearhead a joint action against Hitler's war machine. Now they must survive taunts, threats, and assaults...and that's just from the Yanks. There's plenty of war action in the air and on the ground.

War Stories Vol. 2. DC Comics/Vertigo 2006 240p. Illustration
Grades: 10 11 12 Adult   **741.5; Fic**
1. Graphic novels; 2. World War, 1939-1945 — Graphic novels; 3. Spain — History — 1936-1939, Civil War — Graphic novels
978-1-4012-1039-7, $19.99

The brutality and bravery of those who served in history's greatest conflict is brought to life in this book. From the saturation bombing of the Ruhr Valley to the birth of the SAS in the deserts of North Africa, from the blasted wreckage of Guernica to the tracer-filled skies over the North Atlantic, these tales will land the reader in some of the worst combat zones the world has ever seen. Author Ennis includes historical notes at the end of the book. Readers will find strong language and wartime violence in the stories.

Enoki, Nobuaki
School Judgment 1: Gakkyu Hotei. story by Nobuaki Enoki; art by Takeshi Obata; translation, Mari Morimoto. Viz 2016 192 p. Illustration
Grades: 7 8 9 10 11 12   **741.5; Fic**
1. Shonen manga; 2. School stories — Graphic novels
1421585669; 9781421585666, $9.99

"In order to curb the crime running rampant in the elementary school system, a new solution has been enacted in the form of the School Judgment System. Now the young students themselves will be responsible for solving the issues that befall them. But are they up for the task?" (Publisher's note)

Volume 1 of 3

Espinosa, Rod
Around the world in 80 days. adapted and illustrated by Rod Espinosa. ABDO/Red Wagon 2008 32p. Illustration
Grades: 3 4 5 6 7 8 9
741.5; Fic
1. Adventure graphic novels; 2. Verne, Jules, 1828-1905 — Adaptations
978-1-60270-050-5, $27.07

LC 2007-6444
In 1872, English gentleman Phileas Fogg makes a wager that he can travel around the world in just 80 days. Unfortunately, at

Courtesy of ABDO Publishing.

the time of his wager, a daring robber has made off with a fortune, and Scotland Yard detective Fix is convinced Fogg is the villain. The chase is on, around the world. This comic book adaptation has been written for younger, reluctant, and struggling readers and provides highlights of the adventures in the original novel by Verne. The book includes a brief biography of Verne, a short list of some of his other works, and a brief glossary.

Lewis and Clark. ABDO/Magic Wagon 2008 32p. Illustration (Bio-graphics)
Grades: 3 4 5 6 7 8 9
917.8; 92; 741.5; 917
1. Lewis and Clark Expedition (1804-1806) — Graphic novels; 2. Biographical graphic novels; 3. Explorers; 4. Graphic novels; 5. Territorial governors; 6. Clark, William, 1770-1838; 7. Lewis, Meriwether, 1774-1809; 8. West (U.S.) — Exploration — Graphic novels
978-1-60270-069-7, $27.07
LC 2007-5578

Courtesy of ABDO Publishing.

This graphic format book tells the story of the Lewis and Clark Expedition, which explored the land of the Louisiana Purchase, as authorized in 1803 by President Thomas Jefferson. The book includes a timeline of the Expedition, a map of the route, and a list of books for further reading.

Lewis Carroll's Alice in Wonderland. adapted and illustrated by Rod Espinosa. Antarctic Press 2007 un Illustration
Grades: 4 5 6 7 8 9
741.5
1. Adventure graphic novels; 2. Fantasy graphic novels; 3. Graphic novels; 4. Humorous graphic novels
978-0-9787725-8-1, $14.95

Espinosa (The Courageous Princess) adapts Lewis Carroll's classic tale into a graphic novel full of pop culture references (check out the Mad Hatter, for instance). It's still the original story, which starts when the daydreaming Alice sees a rabbit checking his pocket watch and runs after him, only to find herself in a strange world with bizarre creatures.

The **prince** of heroes, chapter I. Antarctic Press 2008 un Illustration
Grades: 8 9 10 11 12
741.5; Fic
1. Adventure graphic novels; 2. Graphic novels; 3. Science fiction graphic novels
978-0-9801255-0-4, $14.95

Courtesy of ABDO Publishing.

Ronen and his mother Aiymie have lived on the planet Irdne for years; now she tells him they must leave and travel to the edge of the universe to meet his father. She refuses to tell Ronen who he is, or to what Darem clan they belong, and this has made them outcasts in Darem society. Then they learn that the Nationalist Armada, a fleet of thousands of ships, is on its way to take over Irdne, and all Darem colonials must leave. Ronen must leave his friends, and his martial arts teacher, behind. During a fight with Baron Ermont Mesozora and Baroness Mazza Mesozora, Ronen strips Mazza's clothing from her; nothing really shows, but it's clear she has lost her pants.

Estes, Max
Coffee and Donuts: A Junkyard Cats Comic. Top Shelf Productions 2006 112p. Illustration

Grades: 6 7 8 9 10 11 12 Adult   **741.5; Fic**
1. Cats — Graphic novels; 2. Graphic novels; 3. Humorous graphic novels
1-891830-80-5, $10

Dwight and Jules live in an unused dumpster and scavenge their food; every morning a mystery person leaves coffee and donuts for them. When, desperate for money, they try (and fail) to rob an armored truck, real crooks Myles and Moose try to force them into real crime.

Hello, Again. Top Shelf Productions 2005 156p. Illustration
Grades: 11 12 Adult   **741.5; Fic**
1. Graphic novels
1-891830-63-5, $10.00

William is finding out that his past may not be buried as deep as he once thought. In fact, a colorful character from his past has just crawled out of the ground and is refusing to leave until William changes his ways. This is the tale of a drunken fisherman, an unfaithful fiancee, and a guilt ridden apartment manager, whose lives intersect with unsuspecting and dangerous consequences. The book includes some strong language and sexual situations (without any nudity).

Eto, Miyuki
Hell girl. Miyuki Eto; created by the Jigoku Shoujo Project; translated and adapted by Gemma Collings; lettered by North Market Street Graphics. Del Rey Manja 2008 un Illustration
Grades: 10 11 12 Adult   **741.5; Fic**
1. Graphic novels; 2. Horror graphic novels; 3. Manga; 4. Shojo manga
978-0-345-50669-6, $10.99

In this volume, Ai Enma, Hell Girl, offers help to a beautiful teen idol who's being stalked by a long-ago costar of a failed children's television show; to a teenage girl who has become the victim of an obsessively possessive boyfriend who threatens the life of her childhood buddy, and to a girl with a sickly younger brother whose parents were killed by a hit-and-run driver and whose aunt and uncle take care of them only because of the money. A young girl discovers her grandmother isn't dead, but when she goes to visit her, she learns that her grandmother had used help from Hell Girl to protect her newborn daughter from a predatory landlord, and the village hates her for it. The horror is mostly psychological, but there is some violence.

Hell girl vol. 2. Del Rey Manga 2008 202p. Illustration
Grades: 10 11 12 Adult   **741.5; Fic**
1. Graphic novels; 2. Horror graphic novels; 3. Manga; 4. Shojo manga
978-0-345-50416-6, $10.95

Hell Girl is the ultimate avenger for those who have no one else to whom they can turn for help. If one goes to her website at midnight and enters the name of one's tormentor, Hell Girl will destroy that person. However, everyone who completes the contract with Hell Girl must also look forward to eternal torment in hell after death. In this volume, a spiteful figure skater tries to turn the two girls who beat her in competition against each other; a teenager only wants to save her younger sister from an abusive nanny; a boy in fragile health discovers who is stalking his best friend; the student class president can find no other way to save her friend from a vengeful new teacher. While there is no really graphic violence or bad language, the intensity of the stories make this series more appropriate for older teens.

Eury, Michael
The **Krypton** Companion. Twomorrows Publishing 2006 240p. Illustration
Grades: 9 10 11 12 Adult   **741.5**
1. Graphic novels; 2. Superhero graphic novels; 3. Superman (Fictional character)

1-893905-61-6, $24.95

This book examines the "Superman mythology" that grew out of Superman comic books published by DC Comics from 1958 through 1986, under the direction of editors Mort Weisinger and Julius Schwartz. It includes interviews with a number of writers and artists who worked on Superman, including Neal Adams, Murphy Anderson, Steve Gerber, Jerry Siegel, Curt Swan, and many others, along with lots of art, photos, and behind-the-scenes stories.

Courtesy of Twomorrows Publishing

Fabry, Glenn
   Neil Gaiman's Neverwhere. DC Comics/Vertigo 2007 un Illustration
Grades: 11 12 Adult   **741.5; Fic**
   1. Fantasy graphic novels; 2. Graphic novels; 3. Gaiman, Neil — Adaptations
978-1-4012-1007-6, $19.99

Ordinary Richard Mayhew lives an ordinary life in London, in an ordinary corporate job, with a domineering fiancee. Then one day he does one extraordinary thing: he defies his fiancee to help an injured young woman, and his life changes. That young woman, Door, comes from London Below, a fantastical world made up of the bits and pieces of forgotten city and life from above. Her family has been slaughtered, she's being hunted by a pair of extremely nasty, sadistic, violent assassins, and after Richard helps her he has no choice but to go to London Below, for his entire existence in ordinary London has been wiped out, as though he has never...been.

Neverwhere was first a script for a BBC miniseries written by Neil Gaiman; he then adapted his script into a novel, which is now adapted into graphic novel format.

Originally published as Neverwhere issues #1-9.

Faerber, Jay
   Noble causes archives volume one. Image Comics 2008 598p. Illustration
Grades: 10 11 12 Adult   **741.5; Fic**
   1. Family life — Graphic novels; 2. Graphic novels; 3. Science fiction graphic novels; 4. Superhero graphic novels
978-1-58240-896-5, $19.99

Normal young woman Liz Donnelly marries superhero Race Noble and gets a firsthand look at the inner workings of the celebrity superhero Noble family. Race is murdered while they're on their honeymoon, but the Nobles keep Liz with them. She finds that she has landed among some of the most dysfunctional people living a soap opera life. She has one brother-in-law who is now housed in a robotic body, another who is sort of immaterial, a sister-in-law who is pregnant and the father is one of the Noble family's greatest enemies, and the media keeps wanting to dig up as much dirt as they can, because gossip makes for high ratings. This volume reprints the early miniseries and the first twelve issues of the ongoing comics series in an economical black and white edition. The book includes violence, partial nudity, and sexual situations.

Volume 1 of 2

Farrens, Brian
   William Shakespeare's King Lear. adapted by Brian Farrens; illustrated by Ben Dunn.. ABDO/Magic Wagon 2008 48p. Illustration
Grades: 5 6 7 8 9 10   **822.3; 741.5**
   1. Authors; 2. Dramatists; 3. Graphic novels; 4. Poets; 5. Shakespeare, William, 1564-1616 — Adaptations

978-1-60270-189-2, $28.50

LC 2008-10739

King Lear divides his kingdom among his three daughters but disowns Cordelia, the youngest, when she refuses to flatter him with insincerity. Then his older daughters renege on their promise to care for him, and he goes mad and roams the countryside. Meanwhile, Edmund, the illegitimate son of the Earl of Gloucester, plays political games in his quest for power. This graphic novel adaptation retains some of the original language from Shakespeare's play, while paring down the story to appeal to struggling readers. The book includes a short biography, a summary of the play, a glossary, and a short selection of famous lines and phrases from the play.

Part of the Graphic Shakespeare series

Fawkes, Ray
   One Soul. Ray Fawkes; [edited by] James Lucas Jones.. Oni Press 2011 176 p. Illustration
Grades: 11 12 Adult
741.5
   1. Identity (Philosophical concept) — Comic books, strips, etc.; 2. Reincarnation — Graphic novels; 3. Identity (Psychology) — Graphic novels; 4. Graphic novels
9781934964668, $24.99

LC 2011922803

Harvey Nominee: Best Graphic Novel (2012); Eisner Nominee: Best Graphic Album — New (2012)

Courtesy of Oni Press

This graphic novel "follows a single soul as it's reincarnated through human history.... Each two-page spread is divided evenly into two three-by-three grids. Each of its 18 individual stories takes place in a single panel in that grid through the book's 88 spreads, so that to follow, say, the life of a silk heiress in Imperial China, the reader fastens the eye to a single spot in the book and then turns the pages quickly.... [Author Ray] Fawkes creates black-and-white tableaux of action, grief, sex and death spanning centuries. Individual spreads allow 18 characters to speak in unison, as when we see every subject's eyes widen simultaneously. When a character dies, his panel goes black for the rest of the book, and we meet the soul itself in cryptic narration." (Publishers Weekly)

Feiffer, Jules
   Explainers. Fantagraphics Books 2008 546p. Illustration
Grades: 9 10 11 12 Adult   **741.5**
   1. Graphic novels; 2. Humorous graphic novels
978-1-56097-835-0, $28.99; 1-56097-835-X

This book collects the comic strips done by Jules Feiffer for the Village Voice, from 1956 through 1966. The alternative weekly newspaper, the only one of its kind back then, provided the then-unknown Feiffer with a forum to tackle all kinds of issues, ranging from relationships, sexuality, love, family, neuroses, politicians and politics, media, race, class, labor, religion, foreign policy, and war, among others. This is the first of four volumes planned to collect Feiffer's entire run of more than 2,000 strips. Older teen readers may be surprised to see just how timely and relevant these strips are, forty and fifty years after their original publication.

   ★ **Kill** My Mother: a graphic novel. Jules Feiffer. Liveright Publishing Corporation 2014 160 p. Illustration
Grades: 11 12 Adult   **741.5**
   1. Graphic novels; 2. Noir fiction; 3. Violence — Fiction
0871403145; 9780871403148, $27.95

LC 2014005844

"Along with three femme fatales, an obsessed daughter, and a loner heroine, 'Kill My Mother' features a fighter turned tap dancer, a small-time thug who dreams of being a hit man, a name-dropping cab driver, a communist liquor store owner, and a hunky movie star with a mind-boggling secret. Culminating in a U.S.O. tour on a war-torn Pacific island, this disparate band of old enemies congregate to settle scores." (Publisher's note)

"The entire work feels pulled from an earlier time yet explosively modern, a madcap relic animated by an outrageous mind. An unusual, unforgettable, incomparable pulpy punch." Kirkus

Passionella and Other Stories. Fantagraphics Books 2006 un Illustration
Grades: 10 11 12 Adult   **741.5; Fic**
1. Graphic novels
978-1-56097-097-2, $19.95

This book collects Feiffer's extended graphic narratives of the late '50s and early '60s. "Excalibur and Rose" is the fable of a village comedian who embarks on a crusade in search of his serious side, which he finds in spades when he encounters his true love, the pathologically depressed Rose. "Passionella" retells Cinderella, seting it in modern Hollywood with a chimney sweep whose fairy godmother transforms her into the "mysterious exotic bewitching temptress" — and movie star — Passionella. "The Lonely Machine" is an account of one man's attempt to find the perfect relationship through robot love, and "Harold Swerg" recounts the predicament of the world's greatest athlete who'd rather stay at his mundane job than compete against others, despite his country's desperate pleas to enter the Olympics. Three more graphic tales and several one-act plays round out this edition. There are some sexual situations.

Fein, Eric
The **Creation** of the Fantastic Four. Rosen Publishing Group 2006 48p. Illustration
Grades: 4 5 6 7 8 9 10   **741.5**
1. Fantastic Four (Fictional character); 2. Graphic novels; 3. Superhero graphic novels
978-1-4042-0765-3, $29.25

LC 2005031170

Describes the history and development of the action heroes called the Fantastic Four and how they got their superpowers. Created in 1961 by the Marvel power team of Jack Kirby and Stan Lee, the Fantastic Four was the first superhero team the men created.

Part of the Action Heroes series.

The **Creation** of the Incredible Hulk. Rosen Publishing Group 2006 48p. Illustration
Grades: 4 5 6 7 8 9 10   **741.5**
1. Graphic novels; 2. Superhero graphic novels; 3. Hulk (Fictional character)
978-1-4042-0764-6, $29.25

LC 2005035267

Discusses the unique character developed in 1962 by Stan Lee and Jack Kirby who was unable to live a normal life after he was affected by a gamma bomb's blast and Dr. Bruce Banner became the huge, inarticulate, super-strong Hulk. The book also includes information on the cultural climate in the U.S. at the time, and on the way the two men worked together at Marvel Comics.

Part of the Action Heroes series.

Ferris, Emil
★ **My** favorite thing is monsters. Emil Ferris. Fantagraphics Books, Inc. 2016 386 p. Color; Illustration
Grades: 11 12 Adult   **741.5; Fic**

1. Girls — Graphic novels; 2. Chicago (Ill.) — Graphic novels; 3. Murder — Investigation — Graphic novels
1606999591; 9781606999592, $39.99

LC 2016946097

Hugo Finalist: Best Graphic Story (2018); Eisner Award: Best Graphic Album — New (2018)

This book, by Emil Ferris, "is the fictional graphic diary of 10-year-old Karen Reyes, filled with B-movie horror and pulp monster magazines iconography. Karen...tries to solve the murder of her enigmatic upstairs neighbor, Anka Silverberg, a holocaust survivor, while the interconnected stories of those around her unfold." (Publisher's note)

"This stunningly ambitious and assured graphic novel, the creator's first, slides gracefully between past and present, reality and imagination, and the shifting kingdom of children and the hard-concrete world of adults. Ferris's writing, full of wordplay, elisions, and unpredictable revelations, suggests the cockeyed genius of Lynda Barry.... But her art, presented on lined notebook paper in the form of Karen's own ballpoint-and-pencil sketches...is entirely her own." Pub Wkly

Fessenden, Larry
The **last** winter. writers, Larry Fessenden and Robert Leaver; art, Brahm Revel; layout, James Felix McKenney. Image Comics 2008 128p. Illustration
Grades: 10 11 12 Adult   **741.5; Fic**
1. Graphic novels; 2. Horror graphic novels; 3. Science fiction graphic novels; 4. Arctic regions — Graphic novels
978-1-58240-936-8, $12.99

Oil company troubleshooter Pollack arrives at the base of the company's advance team in the Arctic National Wildlife Refuge to find out what's holding up the team's reports. Hoffman, who is working on the environmental impact statements, says there's something wrong, the permafrost is melting, and the whole area is unsafe for building any ice roads. Then one of the team dies, and the others begin to succumb to mysterious fears. When Hoffman is recalled to corporate headquarters, the plane crashes, and there's no way out except to find help from other remote stations; there's only one skidoo left, and Pollack and Hoffman head out. Will they find help before everyone dies? The book includes some violence, partial nudity, and some harsh language. This book adapts the script for the 2006 motion picture starring Ron Perlman, which is being released on DVD in September 2008.

Fetter-Vorm, Jonathan
Trinity: a graphic history of the first atomic bomb. Jonathan Fetter-Vorm. Hill and Wang 2012 154 p. Illustration
Grades: 9 10 11 12   **741.5; 623.4**
1. Manhattan Project (U.S.) — History — Comic books, strips, etc; 2. Atomic bomb — United States — History — Comic books, strips, etc; 3. Atomic bomb — History
9780809094684, $22; 9780809093557, $14.95; 0809094681

LC 2011036622

This graphic novel, by Jonathan Fetter-Vorm, presents "the dramatic history of the race to build and the decision to drop the first atomic bomb. This sweeping historical narrative traces the spark of invention from the laboratories of nineteenth-century Europe to the massive industrial and scientific efforts of the Manhattan Project." (Publisher's note)

"Powerfully understated in both text and art, this matter-of-fact account of the atom bomb's development renders scientific complexity intelligible. There is no preaching here, so readers must ponder the illustrations of apocalyptic devastation in order to process the full implications of nuclear warfare." Kirkus

Fies, Brian

Mom's cancer. Abrams ComicArts 2008 115p. Illustration
Grades: 9 10 11 12 Adult **616.99; 741.5**
1. Biographical graphic novels; 2. Cancer — Graphic novels; 3. Graphic novels
978-0-8109-7107-3, $14.95

When writer/cartoonist Fies learned his mother had cancer and that it had already spread from her lungs, he used webcomics to depict what was happening to his mother and the rest of the family as Mom fought the cancer. All the pain, the heartache, the little battles won, the effects on Fies' relationships with his sisters, the ultimate hope are all on the page. In the end, Mom beat the cancer. In an afterword, Fies tells the reader that some of the medications just wore down his mother's body, and she died shortly before the book was published.

First published 2006

Fiffe, Michel

All-new ultimates: power for power. writer: Michel Fiffe; artist: Amilcar Pinna; color artist, Nolan Woodard; letterer, VC's Clayton Cowles; cover artist, David Nakayama; assistant editor, Emily Shaw; editor, Mark Paniccia. Marvel Enterprises 2014 136 p. Color; Illustration
Grades: 9 10 11 12 **741.5**
1. Superheroes — Fiction; 2. Crime — Fiction; 3. Youth — Fiction; 4. Spider-Man (Fictional character)
0785154272; 9780785154273, $17.99

In this graphic novel by Michael Fiffe, illustrated by Amilcar Pinna, "Spider-Man, Black Widow, Kitty Pryde, Bombshell, Cloak and Dagger unite to tackle the vicious, rampant crime wave overtaking Hell's Kitchen! But the young Ultimates are put to the test as they try to survive their first mission: going head to head with the city's most ruthless gang, the Serpent Skulls, led by Diamondback." (Publisher's note)

"Led by Jessica Drew, aka Spider-Woman (later Black Widow), the Ultimates include Spider-Man (Miles Morales, not Peter Parker), the romantic duo Cloak and Dagger, the volatile Bombshell, and the famous Kitty Pryde.... What they lack in experience, they make up for in enthusiasm and loyalty." SLJ

Contains material originally published in magazine form as All-new Ultimates #1-6 — Title page verso.

Filiu, Jean-Pierre

Best of Enemies: A History of US and Middle East Relations: 1783-1953. Jean-Pierre Filiu, David B.. Harry N Abrams Inc. 2012 114 p. Illustration
Grades: 10 11 12 Adult **327.73056022/2; 327.730**
1. Christianity and other religions; 2. Graphic novels; 3. United States — Foreign relations — Middle East
1906838453; 9781906838454, $24.95

This graphic novel looks at "the history of U.S. and Middle East relations." It starts with "the murderous aggression of Gilgamesh-as-avatar .... [The] focus then moves to 1780s skirmishes with Muslim city-states over maritime piracy, shifting priorities of Christian and Muslim nations over oil and anti-Semitism, and the subsequent ousting by the Americans and the British of Iran's Mohammad Mossadegh." (Library Journal)

Fingeroth, Danny

The **Best** of write now!. Twomorrows Publishing 2008 160p. Illustration
Grades: 11 12 Adult **741.5**
1. Comic books, strips, etc. — Authorship; 2. Drawing — Technique; 3. Graphic novels — Authorship
978-1-893905-924, $19.95

Courtesy of Twomorrows Publishing

This collection of articles from Write Now! Magazine features interviews with comics writers such as Brian Michael Bendis, Jeff Loeb, Todd McFarlane, and Paul Levitz, focusing on the art, craft, and business of writing comics. Other articles look at the comics writing and drawing processes, with such professionals as Mark Millar, Bendis, and J. Michael Straczynski; and other articles cover such topics as breaking into comics publishing, dealing with writer's block, and surviving in the comics industry. Comics titans Stan Lee and Will Eisner are also profiled.

Fisher, Bud

Forever Nuts: Classic Screwball Strips: The Early Years of Mutt & Jeff. NBM 2007 192 Illustration
Grades: 10 11 12 Adult **741.5**
1. Graphic novels; 2. Mutt & Jeff (Fictional characters)
978-1-56163-502-3, $24.95

One of the most long lasting and popular humor strips in history, Mutt and Jeff had many memorable moments of serious goofiness and irreverence. Here's a rediscovery of a true oddball classic maybe only outdone by the antic high living of its own creator. 2007 is the one hundredth anniversary of its start. In these early strips, alcohol consumption, smoking, gambling, and various other pursuits considered to be vices are portrayed.

Fleming, Ann Marie

The **Magical** Life of Long Tack Sam: An Illustrated Memoir. Ann Marie Fleming.. Riverhead Books 2007 170 p. Illustration; Color
Grades: 11 12 Adult **741.5; 92; 793.8092**
1. Biographical graphic novels; 2. Graphic novels; 3. Magicians — Graphic novels; 4. Long Tack Sam
1594482640; 9781594482649, $20

LC 2007060352

This graphic memoir, by Ann Marie Fleming, was "inspired by the award-winning documentary-and the life and mystery of China's greatest magician. Who was Long Tack Sam? He was born in 1885. He ran away from Shangdung Province to join the circus. He was an acrobat. A magician. A comic. An impresario. A restaurateur. A theater owner. A world traveler. An East-West ambassador. A mentor to Orson Welles. He was considered the greatest act in the history of vaudeville." (Publisher's note)

Includes bibliographical references (p. 168-169)

Fletcher, Brenden

Batgirl; Volume 2: Family Business. written by Cameron Stewart, Brenden Fletcher; artby Babs Tarr, Bengal; additional art by JoelGomez, Jake Wyatt [and five others]; colors bySerge Lapointe, Babs Tarr [and four others;letters by Steve Wands; collection cover art byCameron Ste. DC Comics 2016 176 p. Color; Illustration
Grades: 10 11 12 Adult **741.5; Fic**
1. Female superhero graphic novels; 2. Batgirl (Fictional character)
1401259669; 9781401259662, $16.99

LC 2015037665

"Barbara Gordon has made some big changes to her Batgirl alter ego. She has a new look, new support team and new home base in Burnside-Gotham's trendiest neighborhood. But [then]...her father drops a bombshell: Babs isn't the only masked crime-fighter in the family anymore. Jim Gordon is the new Batman." (Publisher's note)

Gotham Academy; Volume 1: Welcome to Gotham Academy. Becky Cloonan, Brenden Fletcher; illustrated by Karl Kerschl. DC Comics 2015 160 p. Color; Illustration
Grades: 7 8 9 10 11 12   **741.5**
1. Amnesia — Fiction; 2. School stories
9781401254728, $14.99

LC 2015007185

"Gotham Academy [is] the most prestigious school in Gotham City. Only the best and brightest students may enter its halls, study in its classrooms, explore its secret passages, summon its terrifying spirits... Okay, so Gotham Academy isn't like other schools. But Olive Silverlock isn't like other students. After a mysterious incident over summer break, she's back at school with a bad case of amnesia." (Publisher's note)

"Filled with spunky and quirky characters and unexpected plot turns, this work adds an intriguing and fresh layer to the Batman mythos.... Kerschl's campy art is by turns luminous and gloomy, enhancing Cloonan and Fletcher's energetic and sometimes contemplative text." SLJ

Originally published in single magazine form as Gotham Academy #1-6; Other Gotham Academy volumes are: Volume 2, Calamity (2016); Volume 3, Yearbook (2016); Second Semester Volume 1, Welcome Back (2017); Second Semester Volume 2 (2017)

Flores, Madeleine
Help us! Great Warrior. written and illustrated by Madeleine Flores; colors by Trillian Gunn. Boom! Box 2016 160 p. Color; Illustration
Grades: 5 6 7 8 9 10   **741.5; Fic**
1. Courage — Fiction; 2. Demonology — Fiction; 3. Fantasy fiction — Fiction; 4. Fantasy graphic novels
1608868028; 9781608868025, $19.99

This book "is about a very powerful (but deceptively tiny) Great Warrior who protects her village from evil-doers and looks rad while doing it! Possessing great strength and even greater self-confidence, she's ready to kick some butts and save everyone, especially hunks/pals/handsome skeletons. But Great Warrior has a secret...and will her friends stand by her side when they find it out?" (Publisher's note)

"The art is clean and colorful and ideal for the tone, which is similar to the TV show Adventure Time but a bit more accessible. The book also carries the same message about friendship and self-esteem." SLJ

Originally published in single magazine form as Help us! Great Warrior No. 1-6

Foglio, Kaja
Girl Genius Omnibus Edition #1. story by Kaja & Phil Foglio; art by Phil Foglio. Airship Entertainment 2006 312p. Illustration
Grades: 9 10 11 12 Adult   **741.5; Fic**
1. Adventure graphic novels; 2. Graphic novels; 3. Science fiction graphic novels
978-1-890856-40-3, $14.95

In a time when the Industrial Revolution has become an all-out war, Mad Science rules the world. Agatha Clay is a student at Transylvania Polygnostic University, a complete klutz with rotten luck. But when the University is overthrown and a mechanical monster stalks the streets, it begins to look as though Agatha may carry a spark of Mad Science after all. She ends up aboard the giant airship Castle Wulfenbach, and finds an ally in Krosp the Cat (a genetic experiment with a smattering of Napoleon's brain cells); she also becomes friends with Gilgamesh, Baron Wulfenbach's son. When the Monster Engine is activated, Agatha and Gil battle it, then Agatha and Krosp make their escape. This black and white edition contains the first three volumes of the Girl Genius collection: Agatha Heterodyne & the Beetleburg Clank, Agatha Heterodyne & the Airship City, and Agatha Heterodyne & the Monster Engine. Agatha tends to do a lot of her best tech work while wearing pajamas.

Forget, Thomas
The **Creation** of Captain America. Rosen Publishing Group 2006 48p. Illustration
Grades: 4 5 6 7 8 9 10   **741.5**
1. Captain America (Fictional character); 2. Graphic novels; 3. Superhero graphic novels
978-1-4042-0766-0, $29.25

LC 2005032024

Captain America has been a hero since 1940 and saved comic books and Marvel Comic Group. This volume discusses the times during which Cap was created and how the character has changed over the years. In light of the character's death in the aftermath of the Marvel Civil War storyline that played out in comics during 2006 and 2007, this book may have wide appeal.

Part of the Action Heroes series.

Fox, Gardner
The **Atom** Archives Volume 2. DC Comics 2003 215p. Illustration
Grades: 7 8 9 10 11 12 Adult   **741.5; Fic**
1. Atom (Fictional character); 2. Graphic novels; 3. Superhero graphic novels
1-4012-0014-1, $49.95

This volume, reprinting The Atom issues #6-13, originally published in 1963 through 1964, features Mighty Mite's early team-ups with Hawkman and Hawkgirl, the classic villainy of Dr. Light, the return of Chronos, and much more. This Archive Edition reprints the comics in full color in a hardcover edition.

Showcase Presents: Adam Strange Volume One. DC Comics 2007 510p. Illustration
Grades: 6 7 8 9 10 11 12 Adult   **741.5; Fic**
1. Graphic novels; 2. Superhero graphic novels
978-1-4012-1313-8, $16.99

After being mysteriously teleported to a distant world by an alien scientist, Adam Strange went from being an Earth archaeologist to a cosmic adventurer. He soon becomes the hero of the planet Rann, shuttling between his old and new worlds via the Zeta Beam. With the love of his life, Alanna, daughter of Rann's leading scientist, they embark on a series of adventures against all types of space menaces. This black and white volume reprints stories from 1958 through 1963.

Showcase Presents: Hawkman Volume 1. DC Comics 2007 560p. Illustration
Grades: 7 8 9 10 11 12 Adult   **741.5; Fic**
1. Graphic novels; 2. Hawkman (Fictional character); 3. Superhero graphic novels
978-1-4012-1280-3, $16.99

Katar Hol and his wife Shayera, winged law officers from the planet Thanagar, visit Earth to learn about terrestrial police methods. To fit into human society, they adopt the civilian identities of Carter Hall, the curator of the Midway City Museum, and Shiera, his assistant. Dressed in their avian Thanagarian garb, Carter and Shiera patrol the skies of Midway City as Hawkman and Hawkgirl. They plunge headlong into the battle for justice against such villains as the Shadow Thief and Matter Master. With their array of alien weaponry and their scientific skill, this crime-fighting duo continue to defend Earth against nefarious threats. This book collects black and white reprints of thirty-three stories written by Fox, dating from 1961 through 1966 and featuring the work of artists such as Joe Kubert, Murphy Anderson, and Carmine Infantino.

Showcase Presents: Justice League of America Volume 1. all stories written by Gardner Fox; all stories pencilled by Mike Sekowsky ... [et al.]. DC Comics 2005 544p. Illustration
Grades: 6 7 8 9 10 11 12 Adult   **741.5; Fic**

1. Aquaman (Fictitious character); 2. Graphic novels; 3. Justice League of America (Fictional characters); 4. Superhero graphic novels; 5. Green Arrow (Fictional character); 6. Wonder Woman (Fictional character); 7. Superman (Fictional character); 8. Batman (Fictional character); 9. Flash (Fictional character); 10. Green Lantern (Fictional character)
1-4012-0761-8, $16.99

Some of the greatest super heroes in the DC Universe united to form the Justice League of America: Superman, Batman, Wonder Woman, the Flash, Green Lantern, Martian Manhunter, and Aquaman. Together, they face such foes as Dr. Light, Dr. Destiny, Starro, Felix Faust, Amos Fortune, and the Weapons Master. This volume includes the stories in which the JLS inducts new members to the team: Green Arrow and the Atom. In light of the events in Infinite Crisis, readers might be interested to see how far back the roots of the story went — all the way back to 1960. This black and white reprint volume includes stories published from 1960 through 1962.

Showcase Presents: The Elongated Man Volume 1. writers, John Broome and Gardner Fox; artists, Carmine Infantino [and others]. DC Comics 2006 560p. Illustration
Grades: 6 7 8 9 10 11 12 Adult   **741.5; Fic**
1. Elongated Man (Fictional characters); 2. Graphic novels; 3. Superhero graphic novels
978-1-4012-1042-7, $16.99

Ralph Dibny is the Elongated Man, a self-taught superhero who has harnessed the power of the exotic gingo fruit and attained the ability to stretch himself to fantastic lengths. As the only costumed hero whose identity has been revealed to the world, Elongated Man travels the globe with his adoring wife Sue, solving mysteries and gaining renown for his singular elastic talent. In these stories, originally published from 1960 to 1968 and reprinted here in black and white, Dibny sometimes teams up with the Flash, Batman and Robin, Green Lantern, and Zatanna. Ralph and Sue Dibny were at the heart of the Identity Crisis, so readers might want to see their early adventures.

Fraction, Matt
Casanova; Volume 1: Luxuria. Matt Fraction and Gabriel Bá; colors by Cris Pete; letters by Dustin Harbin. Image Comics 2007 un Illustration
Grades: 11 12 Adult   **741.5; Fic**
1. Adventure graphic novels; 2. Graphic novels; 3. Science fiction graphic novels; 4. Spies — Graphic novels
9781582408972; 978-1-58240-689-3, $24.99

Meet Casanova Quinn: prodigal son of a law-and-order family hell-bent on keeping the world safe and sound through its organization, E.M.P.I.R.E,; now blackmailed into betraying his father and E.M.P.I.R.E. Luxuria collects the first volume of Casanova as its titular star transforms from devil-may-care thrill-seeker into the most dangerous man in the world. What happens when the ultimate player gets played? Find out in this genre-bending story that combines spy action with science fiction. Frequent use of harsh language combines with sexual situations and violence to make this more appropriate for older teens and adults.

Also available in a deluxe hardcover edition; Other Casanova volumes are: 2: Gula; 3: Avaritia; 4: Acedia

The **Five** Fists of Science. Image Comics 2006 un Illustration
Grades: 9 10 11 12 Adult   **741.5; Fic**
1. Adventure graphic novels; 2. Graphic novels; 3. Science fiction graphic novels
1-58240-605-7, $12.99

At the beginning of the twentieth century, Mark Twain and Nicola Tesla work to save the world from the menace of war. J.P. Morgan, Andrew Carnegie, Thomas Edison, and Guillermo Marconi are having the Innsmouth Tower built; what the world doesn't know is that they intend to summon some monstrous old gods (anyone familiar with H.P. Lovecraft and his Cthulhu Mythos will catch on immediately). Meanwhile, Twain

and Tesla have been trying to interest world leaders in technology that will end all war, only to find that no one is interested. When Marconi realizes what Morgan is really planning, he tells Tesla and Twain, in hopes that their robotic machine can stop Morgan. Some harsh language and violence pepper the story.

Hawkeye: Little Hits. by Matt Fraction (Author), David Aja (Illustrator), Javier Pulido (Illustrator), Steve Lieber (Illustrator), Francesco Francavilla (Illustrator), Jesse Hamm (Illustrator). Marvel Worldwide 2013 136 p.
Grades: 11 12 Adult   **741.5; Fic**
1. Avengers (Fictional characters); 2. Superheroes — Fiction; 3. Graphic novels
0785165630; 9780785165637, $16.99

In this graphic novel, by Matt Fraction, "ace archer Clint Barton faces the digital doomsday of-DVR-Mageddon! Then: Cherry's got a gun. And she looks good in it. And Hawkeye gets very, very distracted. Plus: Valentine's Day with the heartthrob of the Marvel Universe? This will be...confusing." (Publisher's note)

"Fraction's writing is superb, but it's Eisner-winning Aja's wildly creative page layouts that have matured into something truly unique and demanding of critical attention." Booklist

Hawkeye: my life as a weapon. by Matt Fraction (Author), David Aja (Illustrator), Javier Pulido (Illustrator). Marvel Worldwide 2013 136 p.
Grades: 11 12 Adult   **741.5; Fic**
1. Avengers (Fictional characters); 2. Graphic novels; 3. Superheroes — Fiction
0785165622; 9780785165620, $16.99

In this book, by Matt Fraction, "Clint Barton-aka the self-made hero Hawkeye-fights for justice! With ex-Young Avenger Kate Bishop by his side, he's out to prove himself as one of Earth's Mightiest Heroes! SHIELD recruits Clint to intercept a packet of incriminating evidence-before he becomes the most wanted man in the world." (Publisher's note)

Hawkeye: Rio Bravo. by Matt Fraction; illustrated by Francesco Francavilla, David Aja and Annie Wu. Marvel Enterprises 2015 160 p. Color; Illustration
Grades: 10 11 12 Adult   **741.5973; 741.5**
1. Superhero comic books, strips, etc.
0785185313; 9780785185314, $17.99

In this comic book, by Matt Fraction, "Reeling from recent events, even Hawkeye wants to know what his new status quo is. Who's with him? Who's against him? Who's trying to kill him and why? So many dang questions! And just when Clint's rock bottom couldn't arrive fast enough...his brother shows up. After a lifetime of decisions both good and bad, Clint and Barney Barton have to realize that they are brothers and ultimately, they're the only ones who can save one another." (Publisher's note)

Hawkeye; Volume 3: L.A. Woman. by Matt Fraction; illustrated by Annie Wu and Javier Pulido. Marvel Worldwide 2014 144 p. Color; Illustration
Grades: 11 12 Adult   **741.5**
1. Assassins — Fiction; 2. Musicians — Fiction; 3. Criminals — Fiction; 4. Los Angeles (Calif.) — Fiction
0785183906; 9780785183907, $15.99

In this book, by Matt Fraction, illustrated by Annie Wu and Javier Pulido, "Kate Bishop heads to Los Angeles to get away from New York, life, and Clint Barton — but not away from trouble! Because Madame Masque is hanging out at poolside with the rich and famous as well! As Kate helps a reclusive and Sixties-damaged pop music genius find his lost masterpiece, Madame Masque finds Kate. By which we mean starts trying to kill her again." (Publisher's note)

"Fraction's unique brand of storytelling is both light with humor and deep with meaning, and he keeps it fresh by constantly bringing in new characters." Booklist

Contains material originally published in magazine form as Hawkeye #14, #16, #18, #20 and Annual #1 — Title page verso.

Frakes, Colleen

Prison island: a graphic memoir. by Colleen Frakes. Houghton Mifflin Harcourt 2015 187 p. Illustration

Grades: 9 10 11 12 Adult   **741.5; 92**

1. Washington (State); 2. Prisons — United States

1942186029; 9781942186021, $16.99

In this graphic memoir, by Colleen Frake, "McNeil Island in Washington state was the home of the last prison island in the United States, accessible only by air or sea. It was also home to about fifty families, including...Frake's. Her parents-like nearly everyone else on the island-both worked in the prison, where her father was the prison's captain and her mother worked in security." (Publisher's note)

Franklin, Tee

★ **Bingo** love. Tee Franklin; illustrated by Jenn St-Onge, Joy San and Genevieve FT. Image Comics 2018 88 p. Color; Illustration

Grades: 8 9 10 11 12 Adult   **741.5**

1. Lesbians — Fiction; 2. Grandmothers — Fiction

1534307508; 9781534307506, $9.99

In this book, by Tee Franklin, illustrated by Jenn St.Onge, Joy San and Genevieve FT, "when Hazel Johnson and Mari McCray met at church bingo in 1963, it was love at first sight. Forced apart by their families and society, Hazel and Mari both married young men and had families.... Now in their mid-'60s,...[they] reunite again at a church bingo hall. Realizing their love for each other is still alive, what these grandmothers do next takes absolute strength and courage." (Publisher's note)

"Teens and young adults tend to dominate love plots, so it's refreshing to see a romantic tale built around people who age from adolescence through elderhood. Delightful yet realistic, the teen-graded story also works for adults and sophisticated tweens." LJ

Frusin, Marcello

Loveless Vol. 1: A Kin of Homecoming. Brian Azzarello; Marcelo Frusin; Patricia Mulvihill, colorist; Clem Robins, letterer; Marcelo Frusin, covers. DC Comics/Vertigo 2006 128p. Illustration

Grades: 12 Adult   **741.5; Fic**

1. Graphic novels; 2. Western graphic novel

978-1-4012-1061-8, $9.99

Wes Cutter is a wanted man running from a violent past — the horrors of the Civil War, a brutal stint in a Union prison camp, and the savage fallout of Reconstruction. Now he's on a quest for the one thing in short supply: peace. Joining Wes is his beautiful wife Ruth, a woman who has been to hell and back herself — and hides dark secrets of her own. The road they travel will be a bloody one, leaving a trail of bodies stretching from Missouri to the Pacific Ocean. The book contains graphic violence, copious use of foul language, nudity, and sexual situations.

Volume 1 of 3

Fujimaki, Tadatoshi

Kuroko's Basketball; Volumes 1 & 2. Tadatoshi Fujimaki; translation, Caleb Cook. Viz 2016 384 p. Illustration

Grades: 7 8 9 10 11 12   **741.5; Fic**

1. Shonen manga; 2. Basketball — Fiction; 3. Manga

1421587718; 9781421587714, $16.99

"Kuroko Tetsuya doesn't stand out much.... Though he's just as unremarkable on the basketball court, that's where his plainness gives him

an unexpected edge.... And now that he's a high school student, he's on a mission to defeat each member of his legendary middle school team, known as the Miracle Generation, with the help of a new transfer student fresh from the U.S.-Taiga Kagami!" (Publisher's note)

Volumes 1 and 2 of 30

Fujisaki, Ryu

Hoshin Engi Volume 1. Viz Media/Shonen Jump 2007 192p. Illustration

Grades: 8 9 10 11 12 Adult   **741.5; Fic**

1. Adventure graphic novels; 2. Fantasy graphic novels; 3. Graphic novels; 4. Manga; 5. Shonen manga

978-1-4215-1362-1, $7.99

When his clan is wiped out by a beautiful demon, young Taikobo finds himself in charge of the mysterious Hoshin Project. Its mission: find all immortals living in the human world and seal them away forever. But who do you trust — and whose side are you really on — when you've been trained to hunt demons by a demon. There is demon-fighting action.

Fujishima, Kosuke

Oh My Goddess! Volume 1. story and art by Kosuke Fujishima. Dark Horse Comics 2005 192p. Illustration

Grades: 8 9 10 11 12   **741.5; Fic**

1. Fantasy graphic novels; 2. Graphic novels; 3. Humorous graphic novels; 4. Manga; 5. Shonen manga

1593073879; 9781593073879, $10.95

Alone in his dorm on a Saturday night, Nekomi Tech student Keiichi Morisato dials a wrong number that will change his life forever — reaching the Goddess Technical Help Line. Granted one wish by the charming young goddess Belldandy — a wish for anything in the world — Keiichi wishes she would stay with him always. Complications are bound to ensue from this; the immediate first being the new couple getting tossed out of the dorm — it's males only. As the hapless student and his mysterious "foreign beauty" ride around looking for a new place to stay — risking the different dangers of seeking shelter with an otaku convinced Belldandy is an imaginary woman, and a Zen priest convinced she's a sinister witch — Keiichi's still got his classes on Monday morning. How is his new "exchange student" companion going to be received on the N.I.T. campus? A little too well for normal life to ever return... This is the beginning of the series in a new edition that restores the original right-to-left page orientation and includes a notes section. This classic "harem" manga has very mild sexual innuendo and focuses more on the comedy.

Volume 1 of 48

Fujiyama, Kairi

Dragon Eye, Volume 1. Ballantine Books/Del Rey Manga 2007 192p. Illustration

Grades: 8 9 10 11 12   **741.5; Fic**

1. Adventure graphic novels; 2. Graphic novels; 3. Manga; 4. Science fiction graphic novels; 5. Shonen manga

978-0-345-49665-2, $10.95

Ten years before, a deadly virus devastated the world, turning its victims into bloodthirsty Dracules; human soon learned that the only cure is death. The people who rose up to fight the Dracules are called VIUS. Now, in the VIUS city Mikuni, a new recruit named Leila Mikami joins VIUS; she's determined to find a Dragon Eye, a powerful magic weapon she plans to use to get revenge for her family's death. To her surprise, bumbling recruit Issa Kazuma is actually a VIUS captain, and when top-level Dracules invade the candidates' final exam, he reveals his Dragon Eye. Leila joins Kazuma's Squad Zero as they work to protect Mikuni from Dracules. This first volume offers lots of action and monster killing.

Fukuchi, Tsubasa

The **Law** of Ueki Vol. 1. Viz Media 2006 192p. Illustration
Grades: 7 8 9 10 11 12   **741.5; Fic**
1. Graphic novels; 2. Humorous graphic novels; 3. Manga; 4. Shonen manga
978-1-4215-0716-3, $9.99

In a world of powerful celestial beings, an epic contest is being conducted to select the next king. Each Celestial selects a kid in junior high to be his champion and grants him a special power. The kids battle it out, losers are eliminated, and the winners are granted new talents. Seemingly ordinary Kosuke Ueki has been chosen to be a contender in the tournament. Granted the power to change trash into trees, Ueki has two disadvantages to overcome: one, he doesn't know he's a participant in the tournament, and two, how the heck can anyone win a battle with the power to turn trash into trees? Especially when his first opponent has power over fire?

Fulop, Scott D.

Archie Americana Series: Best of the Forties Volume 1. Archie Comics 1991 128p. Illustration
Grades: 3 4 5 6 7 8 9 10 11 12 Adult   **741.5; Fic**
1. Andrews, Archie (Fictional character); 2. Graphic novels; 3. Humorous graphic novels
1-879794-00-4, $11.95

In 1941, Pep Comics introduced Archie Andrews, "America's newest boyfriend." Since then, Archie and his perennial teenage friends have entertained readers with their misadventures. This book includes the very first Archie story, with the first appearance of Betty and Veronica, Reggie, Jughead, Mr. Weatherbee, Miss Grundy, and the rest of the Archie characters as they originally appeared.

Fumino, Yuki

I hear the sunspot. by Yuki Fumino. One Peace Books 2017 200 p. Illustration
Grades: 10 11 12 Adult
741.5; Fic
1. Manga; 2. Gay teenagers — Fiction; 3. Male friendship — Fiction; 4. Teenage boys — Fiction
1944937307; 9781944937300, $12.95

Courtesy of One Peace Books

In this book, by Yuki Fumino, "because of a hearing disability, Kohei is often misunderstood and has trouble integrating into life on campus, so he learns to keep his distance. That is until he meets the outspoken and cheerful Taichi. He tells Kohei that his hearing loss is not his fault. Taichia's words cut through Kohei's usual defense mechanisms and open his heart. More than friends, less than lovers, their relationship changes Kohei forever." (Publisher's note)

"Fumino's debut manga is a simultaneously heartwarming and heartbreaking story about the chance meeting and budding romance between two awkward yet lovable male college students." LJ

Furse, Sophie

Moby Dick. Barron's Educational Series, Inc. 2007 48p. Illustration
Grades: 3 4 5 6 7 8 9   **741.5**
1. Graphic novels; 2. Melville, Herman — Adaptations
978-0-7641-5977-0; 978-0-7641-3492-0 (pa)

Ishmael's dream of adventure on a whaling ship becomes a nightmare as the voyage turns into a struggle for survival. Captain Ahab, maimed by a monster whale, is obsessed with revenge. As the crew discovers, he is willing to risk everything to destroy that whale. This volume includes a brief biography and timeline of Melville, and information on the legacy of his novel.

Furudate, Haruichi

★ **Haikyu!!**; Volume 1. story and art by Haruichi Furudate; translation, Adrienne Beck. Viz 2016 197 P. Illustration
Grades: 7 8 9 10 11 12   **741.5; Fic**
1. Shonen manga; 2. Volleyball — Fiction; 3. School stories — Graphic novels
9781421587660, $9.99; 1421587661

"Ever since he saw the legendary player known as the 'Little Giant' compete at the national volleyball finals, Shoyo Hinata has been aiming to be the best volleyball player ever! After losing his first and last volleyball match against Tobio Kageyama,...Shoyo Hinata swears to become his rival after graduating middle school. But what happens when the guy he wants to defeat ends up being his teammate?!" (Publisher's note)

Volume 1 of an ongoing series

Gabrych, Andersen

Batgirl : Destruction's Daughter. DC Comics 2006 un Illustration
Grades: 10 11 12 Adult   **741.5; Fic**
1. Adventure graphic novels; 2. Batgirl (Fictional characters); 3. Graphic novels; 4. Superhero graphic novels
978-1-4012-0896-7, $19.99

Cassandra Cain was quickly accepted as the new Batgirl after helping Batman during Gotham's darkest hours. Trained in deadly martial arts from early childhood by a notorious assassin, Batgirl developed the uncanny ability to anticipate her opponents' movements to make her unbeatable in combat. Now, the Dark Knight's young protégé is determined to discover who her true mother is, and her quest, brings her face-to-face with the League of Assassins and into mortal combat with the deadliest woman alive, Lady Shiva. It all ends in a life or death battle at the edge of Lazarus Pit, and only one person will survive. There's a fair amount of blood shed in the many fights.

Batgirl: Kicking Assassins. DC Comics 2005 un Illustration
Grades: 9 10 11 12 Adult   **741.5; Fic**
1. Batgirl (Fictional character); 2. Graphic novels; 3. Superhero graphic novels
1-4012-0439-2, $14.99

It's a fresh start for Batgirl as Cassandra Cain is building a new life for herself in Bludhaven. But with the Penguin also moving to town and setting up a criminal empire, can Batgirl keep the streets safe, or will she face something more sinister and vile than before? With the Brotherhood of Evil, Deathstroke, and the Ravager coming at her one after the other, Batgirl barely has the chance to settle into her new neighborhood before the fists start to fly. The book includes lots of fighting.

DC's Greatest Imaginary Stories. DC Comics 2005 192p. Illustration
Grades: 6 7 8 9 10 11 12 Adult   **741.5; Fic**
1. Graphic novels; 2. Superhero graphic novels; 3. Flash (Fictional character); 4. Batman (Fictional character); 5. Superman (Fictional character)
1-4012-0534-8, $19.99

This volume collects eleven stories that are totally imaginary about many of DC's heroes: Superman marries Lois Lane; in another story, he marries Lana Lang; and in yet another story, he marries Lori Lemaris the mermaid. Batman abandons his millions to drive a taxi. The Flash races into action maskless. Superman and Batman are brothers. In the wedding of the century, it's Super girl and...Jimmy Olsen? And Shazam witnesses atomic bomb and attacks and finds that even he, the World's Mightiest Mortal, can't stop the bombs.

Will Eisner. Rosen Publishing Group 2005 112p. Illustration

Grades: 8 9 10 11 12 Adult   **741.5; 92**
1. Cartoonists — Biography; 2. Graphic novels
1-4042-0286-2, $31.95

LC 2004016656

Veteran comics insider Greenberger has written this biography of Eisner, covering his long career in comics, from the 1930s through the early 2000s. Eisner created the groundbreaking comic series The Spirit, and in the 1970s started writing original graphic novels set in New York City. The Eisner Awards for comics are named after him, due to his strong influence on the industry over the decades. This volume includes a list of books for further reading and a bibliography.

Part of the Library of Graphic Novelists

Gaiman, Neil

The **Books** of Magic. writer, Neil Gaiman; illustrators, John Bolton, Charles Vess [and others]; letterer, Todd Klein; [introduction by Roger Zelazny]. DC Comics/Vertigo 1993 un Illustration
Grades: 10 11 12 Adult   **741.5; Fic**
1. Fantasy graphic novels; 2. Graphic novels; 3. Magic — Graphic novels; 4. Supernatural graphic novels
1-56389-082-8, $19.99

A quartet of fallen mystics dubbed the "Trench Coat Brigade "is introduced in this first collection of the adventures of Timothy Hunter. John Constantine, the Phantom Stranger, Dr. Occult, and Mister E take Hunter on a tour of the magical realms. Along the way he's introduced to Vertigo's greatest practitioners of magic and must choose whether or not to join their ranks. And they must decide if he should live...or die. While the publisher rates it for mature readers, there's little in the way of strong language or overt violence, and no nudity.

Creatures of the Night. Dark Horse Comics 2004 46p. Illustration
Grades: 10 11 12 Adult   **741.5; Fic**
1. Fantasy graphic novels; 2. Graphic novels; 3. Supernatural graphic novels
1-56971-936-5, $12.95

Artist Zulli has adapted two of Gaiman's prose short stories into comic book form. In "The Price," a mysterious black cat comes to a family living in the English countryside. Soon after he arrives, the father notices that in the mornings, the cat is scratched and bleeding. Each morning after that, the cat suffers more injuries; maybe the family isn't quite so safe in the countryside after all. "The Daughter of Owls" is a baby girl abandoned on the steps of the Dymton Church in the late 1800s. Sequestered in the convent, the girl lives in solitary silence for fourteen years, cared for after a fashion by a nun, and then by a woman in Dymton. When the woman gossips about the silent girl's beauty, the men of Dymton hatch a dastardly plot which ends in tragedy.

★ **Death:** The High Cost of Living. DC Comics/Vertigo 1994 104p. Illustration
Grades: 10 11 12 Adult   **741.5; Fic**
1. Adventure graphic novels; 2. Fantasy graphic novels; 3. Graphic novels
1-56389-133-6, $12.95

A member of the Endless, a family of beings who have existed longer than the gods, Death enjoys manifesting herself in the persona of a Goth girl. She is taking her one-day-a-century holiday in New York City, where she meets suicidal teen Sexton, and they end up searching the city for the witch Mad Hettie's heart, which she has hidden away...somewhere. Then the Eremite hunts her, to steal Death's ankh and therefore her power. The book includes some violence and some strong language.

Death: The Time of Your Life. DC Comics/Vertigo 1997 96p. Illustration
Grades: 10 11 12 Adult   **741.5; Fic**

1. Adventure graphic novels; 2. Fantasy graphic novels; 3. Graphic novels; 4. Horror graphic novels
1-56389-333-9, $12.99

This is the story of Foxglove, a rising star of the music world who must wrestle with revealing her true sexual orientation as her companion, Hazel, is lured into the realm of Death. As one of the Endless, Death met the two young women on her latest once a century holiday, so it's only natural that she would appear now. The book includes some strong language, sexual situations, and some violence.

★ The **graveyard** book graphic novel Volume 2. based on the novel by Neil Gaiman; adapted by P. Craig Russell; illustrated by David LaFuente, Scott Hampton, P. Craig Russell, Kevin Nowlan, Galen Showman; colorist, Lovern Kindzierski; letterer, Rick Parker. HarperCollins 2014 188 p. Color; Illustration
Grades: 5 6 7 8 9 10   **741.5; Fic**
1. Cemeteries — Fiction; 2. Dead — Fiction; 3. Graphic novels; 4. Orphans — Fiction; 5. Supernatural — Fiction; 6. Supernatural graphic novels
0062194836; 9780062194831, $19.99

LC 2013497350

"Russell concludes the two-part adaptation of Gaiman's Newbery Medal winner, encompassing the final three chapters of the novel. Bod, raised by the ghostly denizens of a graveyard, is a young adult now, yearning for knowledge of the world of the living. After a showdown with a pair of school bullies...Bod finally confronts the ancient order who murdered his family and overcomes them with his supernatural know-how and his innate courage and cleverness." (Booklist)

"Russell and his team of illustrators continue to do this amazing story justice with images that lead readers down a path into Bod's dark and magical graveyard world. Gaiman has the ability to weave beauty and intrigue into a story that has a strong potential to frighten." VOYA

How to talk to girls at parties. by Neil Gaiman; adaptation, art, & lettering by Fabio Moon and Gabriel Ba. Dark Horse Books 2016 61 p. Color; Illustration
Grades: 11 12 Adult   **741.5; Fic**
1. Teenagers — Graphic novels; 2. Teenage boys — Graphic novels
9781616559557, $17.99

LC 2015050695

In this graphic novel, by Neil Gaiman, illustrated by Fábio Moon and Gabriel Bá, "Enn is a sixteen-year-old boy who just doesn't understand girls, while his friend Vic seems to have them all figured out. Both teenagers are in for the shock of their young lives, however, when they crash a local party only to discover that the girls there are far, far more than they appear!" (Publisher's note)

Marvel 1602. [Neil Gaiman, writer; Andy Kubert, illustrator; Richard Isanove, digital painting; Todd Klein, lettering]. Marvel Comics 2005 un Illustration
Grades: 10 11 12 Adult   **741.5; 741; Fic**
1. Doctor Doom (Fictitious character); 2. Graphic novels; 3. Superhero graphic novels; 4. X-Men (Fictional characters); 5. Daredevil (Fictional character)
0-7851-1073-9, $24.99; 0-7851-1073-9 (pa), $19.99

This book "takes the Marvel superheroes and villains of the 1960s — the original X-Men, Daredevil, Dr. Doom, and many others — and places them in the early 17th century." Libr J

"The improbable combination works remarkably well, as the superheroes' strange abilities adapt to Elizabethan culture. This glorious adventure is peppered with Scott McKowen's gorgeous, moody cover-art woodcuts." Publ Wkly

First published in magazine form as Marvel 1602 #1-8

★ **Neil** Gaiman and Charles Vess' Stardust: being a romance within the realms of Faerie. DC Comics/Vertigo 2007 213p. Illustration
Grades: 10 11 12 Adult 741.5; Fic
1. Fantasy graphic novels; 2. Graphic novels
978-1-4012-1190-5, $39.95

In the sleepy English countryside at the dawn of the Victorian Era, young Tristran Thorn has lost his heart to beautiful Victoria Forester. But Victoria is cold and distant — as distant, in fact, as the star she and Tristran see fall from the sky on a crisp October evening. For the coveted prize of Victoria's hand, Tristran vows to retrieve the fallen star and deliver it to his beloved. It is an oath that sends the lovelorn swain into a world that is strange beyond imagining, a world populated by evil old witches, deadly clutching trees, and goblin press-gangs — a world redeemed only by true love. The story includes some sexual situations and partial nudity. This deluxe hardcover edition includes bonus material such as Gaiman's initial proposal and a number of preliminary sketches and new artwork from Vess. This illustrated novel is published by a comic book publisher and can go in either fiction or in the graphic novel section.

Neil Gaiman's Midnight Days. DC Comics/Vertigo 2000 un Illustration
Grades: 10 11 12 Adult 741.5; Fic
1. Fantasy graphic novels; 2. Graphic novels; 3. Horror graphic novels
1-56389-517-X, $17.99

This book collects some of Gaiman's earliest work for Vertigo. Included in these never-before-reprinted and original publications are tales featuring the Golden Age Sandman, Morpheus, the Swamp Thing, and John Constantine. Some of the stories include strong language, violence, and nudity.

★ The **Sandman** Volume 10: The Wake. DC Comics/Vertigo 1997 un Illustration
Grades: 10 11 12 Adult 741.5; Fic
1. Adventure graphic novels; 2. Fantasy graphic novels; 3. Graphic novels; 4. Sandman (Fictional character)
1-56389-279-0, $19.99

In the last chapter of the Sandman saga, the Endless and all the dreamers come to celebrate the life and mourn the passing of the King of Dreams. Meanwhile, the new Dream, who was once the boy Daniel Hall, waits for the others to come and meet him. The King is dead, long live the King. The book includes some nudity and violence.

Sandman Volume 2: The Doll's House. DC Comics/Vertigo 1991 255p. Illustration
Grades: 10 11 12 Adult 741.5; Fic
1. Fantasy graphic novels; 2. Graphic novels; 3. Horror graphic novels; 4. Sandman (Fictional character)
0-930289-59-5, $19.99

LC 92-159876

In this second volume, Rose Walker is the dream vortex who must be killed to save the Dreaming. In the meantime, she wanders the world hunting for her younger brother, and along the way she attends a "Cereal" convention, which is actually a serial killers' convention. Morpheus must track down four of his major arcana dreams that were lost during his long imprisonment. And Morpheus meets once a century with Hob, a man who had wished to never die. The book includes graphic violence, some partial nudity, and strong language.

★ **Sandman** Volume 3: Dream Country. DC Comics/Vertigo 1991 un Illustration
Grades: 10 11 12 Adult 741.5; Fic
1. Fantasy graphic novels; 2. Graphic novels; 3. Horror graphic novels; 4. Sandman (Fictional character)
1-56389-016-X, $14.99

LC 92-159876

This third volume collects four stories; the two standouts are "A Dream of a Thousand Cats," in which a purebred Siamese remembers her first litter of mixed-breed cats that her owners killed and ventures into the cat version of the dreaming in which Morpheus is a huge black cat and discovers her mission in life — cat owners may never look at their sleeping cats the same way again; and "A Midsummer Night's Dream" recounts the adventures of William Shakespeare and his company of players as they are summoned to perform their play to a highly select audience — King Oberon and Queen Titania of Faerie. This story won the World Fantasy Award for Best Short Story when it was first published. The book includes nudity, sexual situations, and some violence.

Sandman Volume 4: The Season of Mists. DC Comics/Vertigo 1994 un Illustration
Grades: 10 11 12 Adult 741.5; Fic
1. Fantasy graphic novels; 2. Graphic novels; 3. Horror graphic novels; 4. Sandman (Fictional character)
1-56389-041-0, $19.99

LC 92-159876

Lucifer has grown tired of being the lord of Hell. He kicks out the demons and the damned alike, closes up shop, and gives the key to Hell to Morpheus. Beings from all the world's mythologies converge on the lord of Dream to seize this instrument of power. All Morpheus wants is to search for the soul of his first love, Nada, whom he had consigned to Hell long ago. The book includes violence, strong language, and nudity.

Sandman Volume 5: A Game of You. DC Comics/Vertigo 1993 un Illustration
Grades: 10 11 12 Adult 741.5; Fic
1. Fantasy graphic novels; 2. Graphic novels; 3. Horror graphic novels; 4. Sandman (Fictional character)
1-56389-089-5, $19.99

Take an apartment house, mix in a drag queen, a lesbian couple, some talking animals, a talking severed head, a confused heroine, and the deadly Cuckoo. Stir vigorously with a hurricane and Morpheus himself and you get this fifth installment of the Sandman series. This story stars Barbie, who first makes an appearance in The Doll's House, who here finds herself a princess in a vivid dreamworld. The book includes violence, partial nudity, and strong language.

Sandman Volume 6: Fables & Reflections. DC Comics/Vertigo 1994 un Illustration
Grades: 10 11 12 Adult 741.5; Fic
1. Fantasy graphic novels; 2. Graphic novels; 3. Horror graphic novels; 4. Sandman (Fictional character)
9781563891052, $19.99; 1563891050

Morpheus, the King of Dreams, observes and interacts with an odd assortment of historical and fictional characters throughout time. Featuring tales of kings, explorers, spies, and werewolves, this book of myth and imagination delves into the dark dreams of Augustus Caesar, Haroun Al Raschid, Marco Polo, Cain and Abel, Emperor Joshua Norton I, and Orpheus to illustrate the effects that these subconscious musings have had on the course of history and mankind. The book includes some violence, nudity, and strong language.

Sandman Volume 7: Brief Lives. DC Comics/Vertigo 1995 un Illustration
Grades: 10 11 12 Adult 741.5; Fic
1. Fantasy graphic novels; 2. Graphic novels; 3. Horror graphic novels; 4. Sandman (Fictional character)
1-56389-138-7, $19.99

LC 92-159876

Delirium, youngest sister of the Endless, prevails upon her brother, Dream, to help her find their missing sibling, Destruction, who disappeared several centuries ago. Their travels take them through the world of the waking until a final confrontation with the missing member of the Endless and the resolution of Dream's relationship with his son change the endless forever. The book includes violence, nudity, sexual situations, and strong language.

★ The **Sandman** Volume 8: World's End. DC Comics/Vertigo 1995 un Illustration
Grades: 10 11 12 Adult   **741.5; Fic**
1. Adventure graphic novels; 2. Fantasy graphic novels; 3. Graphic novels; 4. Sandman (Fictional character)
1-56389-171-9, $19.99
A "reality storm" draws an unusual cast of characters together. They take shelter in a tavern, where they amuse each other with their life stories. Although Morpheus is never a focus in these stories, each has something to say about the nature of stories and dreams. The book includes some violence, some strong language, and brief partial nudity and sexual situations.

★ The **Sandman** Volume 9: The Kindly Ones. DC Comics/Vertigo 1996 un Illustration
Grades: 10 11 12 Adult   **741.5; Fic**
1. Adventure graphic novels; 2. Fantasy graphic novels; 3. Graphic novels; 4. Sandman (Fictional character)
1-56389-205-7, $19.99
Distraught by the kidnapping and presumed death of her son Daniel, and believing Morpheus to be responsible, Lyta Hall calls the ancient wrath of the Furies down upon him. A former super heroine blames Morpheus for the death of her child and summons an ancient curse of vengeance against the Lord of Dream. The kindly ones" enter his realm and force a sacrifice that will change the Dreaming forever. The book includes violence, strong language, and partial nudity.

★ The **Sandman**, Vol. 1: Preludes and Nocturnes. DC Comics/Vertigo 1991 236p. Illustration
Grades: 10 11 12 Adult   **741.5; Fic**
1. Fantasy — Graphic novels; 2. Graphic novels; 3. Mythology — Graphic novels
978-1-56389-011-6, $19.95
"Gaiman's stories of Morpheus, the Lord of Dream, his Endless siblings (Death, Destruction, Delirium, Desire, Destiny, and Despair), his enemies, and many figures who spring from various mythologies and folklore have changed many readers' ideas about comics and graphic novels." (VOYA)
Various artists worked with Gaiman to illustrate his stories, which include some strong depictions of violence and occasional nudity.
Other Sandman volumes are: 2: A Doll's House; 3: Dream Country; 4: Season of Mists; 5: A Game of You; 6: Fables and Reflections; 7: Brief Lives; 8: World's End; 9: The Kindly Ones;10: The Wake

The **Sandman**: Endless Nights. DC Comics/Vertigo 2004 un Illustration
Grades: 11 12 Adult   **741.5; Fic**
1. Fantasy graphic novels; 2. Graphic novels; 3. Sandman (Fictional character)
1-4012-0113-X, $19.99
This volume reveals the legend of the Endless, a family of magical and mythical beings who exist and interact in the real world. Born at the beginning of time, Destiny, Death, Dream, Desire, Despair, Delirium and Destruction are seven brothers and sisters who each lord over their respective realms. These seven peculiar and powerful siblings each reveal more about their true-being as they star in their own tales of curiosity and wonder. A different artist interprets each story by Gaiman. The book includes considerable nudity and sexual situations, and some violence.

★ The **Sandman**: the dream hunters. D.C. Comics/Vertigo 2009 144p. Illustration
Grades: 10 11 12 Adult   **741.5; Fic**
1. Dreams — Graphic novels; 2. Graphic novels; 3. Love — Graphic novels; 4. Supernatural graphic novels
978-1-4012-2424-0, $24.99
In old Japan, creatures of myth and legend live among the people. Two such creatures, a badger and a fox, make a wager to force a humble monk to leave the temple he tends alone up in the mountains. Because the young monk can see through their disguises to their true nature, both badger and fox lose the wager, and the fox falls in love with the handsome young man and remains nearby. Meanwhile, a wealthy man who has mastered demons yet cannot find peace in his soul decides to steal the young monk's inner strength for his own. The fox tries to protect the monk, and even makes a bargain with the great black fox in her dreams, to sacrifice her life for the man she loves. Then, when she suffers the consequences of the evil dreams sent by the wealthy man through his demons, the monk ventures into the Dreaming in a quest to save the fox, whom he finally realizes he loves. When he makes the decision to take back the dream that will kill him, the fox decides to take revenge on the wealthy man, the onmyoji, and comes to him as a beautiful young woman to destroy him. Russell has adapted the novella written by Gaiman and illustrated by Yoshitaka Amano. It includes some nudity.

Gallagher, John
Buzzboy: Trouble in paradise. Sky Dog Press 2002 144p. Illustration
Grades: 5 6 7 8 9 10 11 12   **741.5; Fic**
1. Graphic novels; 2. Humorous graphic novels; 3. Superhero graphic novels
0-8721831-0-8, $11.95
Imagine a superhero who jokes constantly, watches way too many old television shows, and loves junk food, and you have Buzzboy. Years before, he was sidekick to Captain Ultra, but the evil Dr. Schism destroyed all superheroes and their sidekicks, except for Captain Ultra. Now, Ultra has declared martial law in the city of New Paradise, and his police stomp out all rebellions. Then a mysterious superhero stops the Hoppers (police) it's Buzzboy, older and back from the dead! Aided by sarcastic teen sorceress Becca and reformed mad scientist Doc Cyber, Buzzboy is here to save the day.
Another title in this series is: Buzzboy: Monsters, dreams, & milkshakes (2003)

Gallagher, Monica
Gods & undergrads, Book 1. Lipstick Press 2007 un Illustration
Grades: 10 11 12 Adult   **741.5; Fic**
1. College students — Graphic novels; 2. Graphic novels; 3. Greek mythology — Graphic novels; 4. School stories — Graphic novels
978-0-9794589-0-3, $10
College sophomore Lelaina Pentheus has decided to move on campus at Troy University, and by some chance meetings and good luck joins several juniors in an apartment. Her new friends quickly learn that Lelaina has some strange quirks, like fainting a lot, and hands that can suddenly turn hot and blister. She doesn't know why, nor why she has strange markings on her face; she was adopted as an infant. Then she gets strange messages that "they're coming" — from a talking frog, from her roommate's brother, and then from a stranger who claims he's Hermes, the Greek messenger god. This book collects the first three chapters of Gallagher's story, which first appeared as webcomics at www.eatyourlipstick.com.
Also available online as webcomic

Gallaher, David

High moon. DC Comics 2009 un Illustration
Grades: 10 11 12 Adult   **741.5; Fic**
1. Graphic novels; 2. Horror graphic novels; 3. Werewolves — Graphic novels; 4. Western stories — Graphic novels
978-1-4012-2462-2, $14.99
2009 Harvey Award for Best OnLine Comics Work.

It starts in a small town in Texas, with mysterious happenings and then the disappearance of a girl. Ex-Pinkerton detective McGregor comes to town hunting a criminal named Conroy and gets involved in the town's problems. Mr. Hunter, father of the missing girl, doesn't know the half of it; the town is filled with werewolves resentful of human progress. Conroy is a werewolf, and so is McGregor. When McGregor dies fighting the werewolves from the mines, Conroy takes his identity and continues his travels. In Ragged Rock, he finds more trouble stemming from an old hate, and the real McGregor's brother, Tristan, has come to find his brother's killer. Conroy soon learns that he can be killed, but he won't stay dead. The book includes considerable violence.

Originally published online at www.zudacomics.com.

Ganeri, Anita

Harriet Tubman: The Life of an African-American Abolitionist. by Rob Shone & Anita Ganeri; illustrated by Rob Shone. Rosen Publishing Group 2005 48p. Illustration
Grades: 3 4 5 6 7 8 9

Courtesy of Rosen Publishing

92; 741.5
1. African American women — Graphic novels; 2. Biographical graphic novels; 3. Graphic novels; 4. Underground Railroad — Graphic novels; 5. Tubman, Harriet, 1819 or 1820-1913
1-4042-0245-5, $29.25
Born a slave in the United States, Harriet Tubman escaped from bondage to risk her life and newfound liberty in becoming a leading abolitionist in the years before the American Civil War. Tubman surreptitiously led hundreds of escaped Southern slaves to freedom in the North along the Underground Railroad, earning her the nickname as "the Moses of her people." This graphic novel format book tells her story. It includes additional information about the Underground Railroad and her legacy in the civil rights movement, and a list of books for further reading.

Part of the Graphic Nonfiction series.

Ganter, Amy Kim

Goosebumps: Terror Trips. Scholastic/Graphix 2007 137p. Illustration
Grades: 4 5 6 7 8 9   **741.5; Fic**
1. Graphic novels; 2. Horror graphic novels; 3. Stine, R. L.; 4. Stine, R. L. — Adaptations
978-0-439-85780-2, $8.99
Stine's Goosebumps series was very popular years ago, and is enjoying a resurgence of popularity with new editions of the prose books. The graphic novel adaptations, all done by well-known independent comics creators, bring the stories to a new audience. Goosebumps: Creepy Creatures is also available.

This volume adapts three of Stine's Goosebumps novels into graphic novel format. Noted independent comic creator Thompson adapts One Day at Horrorland, about one family's ordeal in a very strange, all-too-realistic amusement park. Canadian artist Tolagson adapts A Shocker on Shock Street, which depicts the horrific adventures of two kids on a movie studio lot where the horror is more than just special effects. Global manga creator

Ganter adapts Deep Trouble, in which a brother and sister find a real mermaid.

Gay, Roxane

Black Panther: world of Wakanda. written by Roxane Gay, Ta-Nehisi Coates, RembertBrowne, Yona Harvey; pencilled by Alitha E.Martinez, Afua N. Richardson, Joe Bennett; inkedby Alitha E. Martinez, Roberto Poggi, Afua N.Richardson; colored by Tamra Bonvillain, RachelleRosenberg. Marvel Enterprises 2017 144 p. Color; Illustration
Grades: 10 11 12 Adult   **741.5; Fic**
1. Graphic novels; 2. Superheroes; 3. Black Panther (Fictional character)
130290650X; 9781302906504, $17.99
Eisner Award: Best Limited Series (2018)

This book, by Ta-Nehisi Coates, Roxane Gay and Yona Harvey, presents the story of "Ayo and Aneka, young women recruited to become Dora Milaje, an elite task force trained to protect the crown of Wakanda at all costs. Their first assignment will be to protect Queen Shuri... but what happens when your nation needs your hearts and minds, but you already gave them to each other? Meanwhile, former king T'Challa lies with bedfellows so dark, disgrace is inevitable." (Publisher's note)

Contains materials originally published in magazine form as Black Panther: world of Wakanda #1-6

Geary, Rick

The **Beast** of Chicago: An Account of the Life and Crimes of Herman W. Mudgett, Known to the World as H. H. Holmes. NBM 2003 un Illustration
Grades: 9 10 11 12 Adult   **364.152; 741.5**
1. Graphic novels; 2. Homicide — Graphic novels; 3. Mystery graphic novels
1-56163-362-3, $8.95
He was the world's first serial killer and he existed in the late 19th century, operating around the Chicago World's Fair, building a literal house of horrors, replete with chutes for dead bodies, gas chambers, surgical rooms. He methodically murdered up to 200 people, mostly young women. Geary steers away from gore to focus on such things as Holmes' "lab" in his castle. The book is still not for the squeamish, but the art is restrained.

Part of the A Treasury of Victorian Murder series.

The **Borden** Tragedy: A Memoir of the Infamous Double Murder at Fall River, Mass., 1892. NBM 1997 80p. Illustration
Grades: 9 10 11 12 Adult   **364.152; 741.5**
1. Graphic novels; 2. Homicide — Graphic novels; 3. Mystery graphic novels
1-56163-189-2, $8.95; 9781561631896
Including such details as maps of Fall River, Massachusetts as it was in 1892, Geary presents the facts and documented speculations about the case of Lizzie Borden, a thirty-year-old spinster accused and tried for murdering her parents. The popular rhyme "Lizzie Borden took an axe, gave her mother forty whacks, when she saw what she had done, she gave her father forty-one" was apparently sung to the tune of "Tararaboomdeeay." Geary leaves it to the reader to decide if Lizzie was guilty or not.

Part of the A Treasury of Victorian Murder series.

Famous players: the mysterious death of William Desmond Taylor. NBM/ComicsLit 2009 un Illustration
Grades: 9 10 11 12 Adult   **364.152; 741.5**
1. Graphic novels; 2. Homicide — Graphic novels; 3. Motion picture directors; 4. Motion picture producers and directors — Graphic novels; 5. Murder victims; 6. Mystery graphic novels; 7. Taylor, William Desmond, 1877-1922

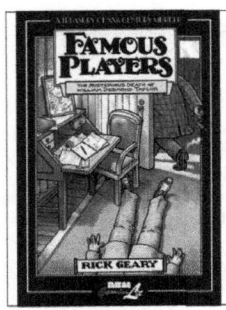

Courtesy of NBM Publishing

978-1-56163-555-9, $15.95; 978-1-56163-559-7 (pa), $9.95

Hollywood in 1922 was just coming into its own as a mecca for filmmakers as the silent films became more and more popular. One of the new studios was Famous Players Studio, and William Desmond Taylor was one of its successful directors, along with Cecil B. DeMille. Then, on the morning of February 2, 1922, Taylor's cook/valet/general house servant Henry Peavey arrived at 7:30 and found Taylor's body on the floor of the living room. He'd been shot, but by whom? As the investigation progresses, several prominent actresses come under suspicion, along with a former cook and house servant; and his own mysterious past starts to come to light. However, the police are never able to solve the case. Geary provides a list of his sources for anyone who would like to know more about this Twentieth-Century Murder mystery. He depicts the crime with little gore or violence.

This is part of the Treasury of XXth Century Murder series.

J. Edgar Hoover: a graphic biography. Hill and Wang 2008 102p. Illustration
Grades: 9 10 11 12 Adult   **363.2; 92; 741.5**
1. United States — Federal Bureau of Investigation — Graphic novels; 2. Biographical graphic novels; 3. FBI officials; 4. Graphic novels; 5. Hoover, J. Edgar (John Edgar), 1895-1972
978-0-8090-9503-2; 0-8090-9503-3, $16.95

LC 2007-25193

Rick Geary has written a biography of J. Edgar Hoover, who served in the federal government for 55 years and under eight presidents, most notably as director of the Federal Bureau of Investigation. He was appointed to that position on May 10, 1924. Geary covers Hoover's sometimes controversial career, including his refusal to involve the FBI directly into investigations of crimes against civil rights workers and the 1963 bombing in Birmingham, Alabama, and the bureau's investigation of Martin Luther King, Jr. He tastefully discusses Hoover's undercover sexual life.

"As solid, thrilling and informative a guide to the life of the America's most powerful authoritarian as one could ask for." Kirkus

★ The **Lindbergh** child: America's hero and the crime of the century. written and illustrated by Rick Geary. NBM/ComicsLit 2008 un Illustration; Map (Treasury of XXth century murder)
Grades: 8 9 10 11 12 Adult
364.1; 741.5
1. Air force officers; 2. Air pilots; 3. Generals; 4. Graphic novels; 5. Homicide — Graphic novels; 6. Kidnapping — Graphic novels; 7. Memoirists; 8. Mystery graphic novels; 9. Lindbergh, Charles, 1902-1974
978-1-56163-529-0, $15.95

Courtesy of NBM Publishing

Charles Lindbergh was an American hero following his solo crossing of the Atlantic in an airplane. He married into a wealthy family, he and his wife had a baby, they were building their dream home. Then, one night, the baby was abducted from the house. Geary's account retraces all the highly publicized events, ransom notes (false and otherwise), as well as the string of colorful characters who all claimed they could help but instead snookered the Lindberghs. While Bruno Hauptmann was arrested, tried,

convicted, and executed, there remain many questions about what really happened. Geary brings them up for readers to consider.

"A good example of the origins of modern forensics, crime-scene investigation, and celebrity hysteria, this work is an excellent choice for most collections." SLJ

The **lives** of Sacco and Vanzetti. Rick Geary.. NBM Comics Lit 2011 80 p. Illustration
Grades: 9 10 11 12 Adult
345; 741.5; 345.73
1. Sacco-Vanzetti Trial, Dedham, Mass., 1921 — Comic books, strips, etc.; 2. Trials (Murder) — Massachusetts — Dedham — Comic books, strips, etc.; 3. Sacco, Nicola, 1891-1927 — Trials, litigation, etc. — Comic books, strips, etc.; 4. Vanzetti, Bartolomeo, 1888-1927 — Trials, litigation, etc. — Comic books, strips, etc.; 5. Anarchism and anarchists — Graphic novels; 6. Sacco-Vanzetti case; 7. United States — History — 1919-1933 — Graphic novels
1561636053; 9781561636051, $15.99

Courtesy of NBM Publishing

LC 2011927818

"Geary lays out what is known and not known about the case, in which two Italian anarchist immigrants were put to death after being found guilty of robbery and murder. The...narrative not only details the events of the crime, manhunt, and trial but also includes information about the lives of Sacco and Vanzetti and their families." (Publishers Weekly)

Includes bibliographical references.

Madison square tragedy: the murder of Stanford White : 25 June, 1906. written and illustrated by Rick Geary. NBM Pub. 2013 80 p. Illustration (Treasury of xxth century murder)
Grades: 9 10 11 12 Adult
741.5; 364.152
1. Mystery graphic novels; 2. Murder — Graphic novels
1561637629; 9781561637621, $15.99

LC 2013947335

Courtesy of NBM Publishing

In this graphic novel, by Rick Geary, as architect Stanford White "became popular and in demand, he also became quite self-indulgent: he had a taste for budding young showgirls on Broadway, even setting up a private apartment to entertain them in.... When he met Evelyn Nesbit...he knew he was on to something special. However, Evelyn eventually married a young Pittsburgh decadent heir with a dark side who developed a deep hatred for White and what he may or may not have done to her." (Publisher's note)

"In this entry in his series recounting historical murder cases, Geary tackles an infamous crime that scandalized New York City in 1901.... Geary's old-fashioned black-and-white line drawings, vividly evoking the turn-of-the-century milieu, and his reliance on text-heavy captions as a sort of voice-over impart a documentary air to his thoroughly researched account." Booklist

Includes bibliographical references

The **murder** of Abraham Lincoln: a chronicle of 62 days in the life of the American Republic, March 4-May 4, 1865. written and illustrated by

Courtesy of NBM Publishing

Rick Geary. NBM ComicsLit 2005 un Illustration; Map (A treasury of Victorian murder)

Grades: 7 8 9 10 11 12   **973.7**

1. Actors; 2. Graphic novels; 3. Lawyers; 4. Members of Congress; 5. Murderers; 6. Presidents; 7. State legislators; 8. Booth, John Wilkes, 1838-1865; 9. Lincoln, Abraham, 1809-1865 — Assassination

978-1-56163-425-5; 1-56163-425-5, $15.95; 978-1-56163-426-2 (pa); 1-56163-426-3 (pa), $8.95

LC 2005-41468

This graphic novel "covers Lincoln's assassination, the events that led up to it, and the aftermath. Geary also makes a point of bringing up still-unanswered questions, like the whereabouts of the missing pages of John Wilkes Booth's journal.... Even teens who know nothing about the tragedy will find their heads chock-full of information when they're finished reading this book." SLJ

Includes bibliographical references

The **Mystery** of Mary Rogers: A Chronicle of the Disappearance and Murder of The Beautiful Segar Girl in July, 1841 - A Crime Which was Never Solved - And Which Inspired the Sensational Tale by Edgar A. Poe. NBM 2001 un Illustration

Grades: 9 10 11 12 Adult

364.152; 741.5

1. Graphic novels; 2. Homicide — Graphic novels; 3. Mystery graphic novels

1-56163-274-0, $15.95

Courtesy of NBM Publishing

Mary Rogers was a compellingly beautiful lass employed in a cigar store in New York City in the mid-nineteenth century. She had a few suitors. Then, she suddenly disappeared, her body recovered in the Hudson off the Jersey side. The press had a field day with all the possible shocking possibilities. Rape... her "fooling around" between lovers...even gang rape. Never was this case solved. The hypotheses remain many. Even Edgar Allen Poe thought to have solved the case and presented that in his tale "The Mystery of Mary Roget."

Part of the A Treasury of Victorian Murder series.

The **saga** of the bloody Benders: the infamous homicidal family of Labette County, Kansas. NBM/ComicsLit 2007 un Illustration

Grades: 9 10 11 12 Adult

364.152; 741.5

1. Graphic novels; 2. Homicide — Graphic novels; 3. Mystery graphic novels

978-1-56163-498-9, $15.95

Courtesy of NBM Publishing

In Kansas, around the year 1870, the Bender family ran the Bender Inn and grocery store in Labette County, Kansas. Soon after they open their inn to travelers, people start to disappear, usually people with a fair amount of money with them. When the authorities investigate, the family disappears, and the people of Labette County make grisly discoveries in the Bender Inn's cellar. Geary includes just enough gory details for readers to comprehend the Benders' crimes. Earlier volumes in this series focused on famous nineteenth century murders and criminals, but the crimes of this more obscure family are just as dastardly for true crime aficionados.

Part of the series, A Treasury of Victorian Murders

★ The **terrible** Axe-Man of New Orleans. music and lyrics by Rick Geary. NBM Publishing/ComicsLit 2010 un Illustration; Map (Treasury of XXth century murder)

Grades: 9 10 11 12 Adult

364.152; 741.5

1. Graphic novels; 2. Homicide — Graphic novels; 3. Mystery graphic novels; 4. New Orleans (La.) — History — Graphic novels

978-1-56163-581-8, $15.99

LC 2010-926782

Geary tells the story of the Terrible Axe-Man, who murdered grocers in New Orleans right after World War I. In each case,

Courtesy of NBM Publishing

the murderer removed a piece of the door to the house, borrowed an axe found at the property, then aimed straight for the head of his victim. From May 23, 1918 to October 27, 1919, the Axe-Man killed six people and badly wounded six more, then disappeared. Geary lays out the known facts, then shows some of the speculation. The black and white art helps to mitigate the violence and gore, so the book is suitable for teens who enjoy true-life mysteries.

"Geary's exacting, historically accurate approach makes this...a natural for true-crime fans as well as comics lovers." Booklist

Includes bibliographical references; Nights of terror! A city awash in blood!

★ **Trotsky:** a graphic biography. Hill and Wang 2009 103p. Illustration; Map

Grades: 9 10 11 12 Adult   **92; 741.5**

1. Biographical graphic novels; 2. Communism — Soviet Union — Graphic novels; 3. Communist leaders; 4. Graphic novels; 5. Nonfiction writers; 6. Political leaders; 7. Revolutionaries; 8. Trotsky, Leon, 1879-1940; 9. Russia — Politics and government — 1894-1917 — Graphic novels; 10. Soviet Union — Politics and government — Graphic novels

978-0-8090-9508-7, $16.95; 0-8090-9508-4

LC 2008-50235

Geary provides a graphic biography of Leon Trotsky, the "brain" behind the Russian Revolution of 1917. The book, with its black and white panel art, chronicles Trotsky's tumultuous relationships with Lenin and Stalin, the contentious debates within the revolutionary movement, Trotsky's many exiles, and his murder in Mexico in 1940.

"Geary's familiar cartoonlike drawing style and factual presentation make this title an accessible and concise introduction to Trotsky's life." SLJ

Includes bibliographical references; A novel graphic from Hill and Wang

Geissman, Grant

Mad About the Fifties. E.C. Publications/MAD Books 2005 un. Illustration

Grades: 8 9 10 11 12 Adult   **741.5**

1. Graphic novels; 2. Humorous graphic novels; 3. Satire — Graphic novels

1-4012-0753-7, $12.99

MAD Magazine was founded in 1952 as a ten-cent comic book that parodied other comic books; three years later it became a twenty-five cent (cheap!) magazine. This volume collects some of the regular features and parodies of television programs and movies of the decade. Some of the advertising parodies feature tobacco and alcohol products, and some parodies portray the imbibing of alcohol products.

Mad About the Sixties: The Best of the Decade. Mad Books/E.C. Publications 1997 un Illustration
Grades: 7 8 9 10 11 12 Adult   **741.5; Fic**
1. Graphic novels; 2. Humorous graphic novels; 3. Satire — Graphic novels
1-4012-0754-5, $9.99

Alfred E. Newman as a flower child? Ecch! Here is a look back at the Sixties from the satire magazine, full of send-ups, takeoffs, and put-ons from the decade that gave the world Timothy Leary and Tiny Tim. Along with Spy vs. Spy, Sergio Aragones' "Mad Marginals," Don Martin's lunacies, and Snappy Answers to Stupid Questions, this volume includes TV satires such as Star Blecch, Bats-Man, and The Phewgitive, and movie takeoffs 201 Min. of a Space Idiocy, East Side Story, and Flawrence of Arabia. Back in the 1960s, preteens read the magazine and most of them turned out okay ...

Gelatt, Philip
Indiana Jones adventures vol. 1. Dark Horse Comics 2008 un Illustration
Grades: 4 5 6 7 8 9   **741.5; Fic**
1. Adventure graphic novels; 2. Archeology — Graphic novels; 3. Graphic novels; 4. Jones, Indiana (Fictional character)
978-1-59307-905-5, $6.95

It's winter of 1930 in Sweden, and Dr. Henry Jones Jr. (Indiana Jones) finds an ancient pre-Christian temple of a religion devoted to war; he gets a scroll while Dr. Lawrence, the pretty British archeologist with him, runs with a valuable gold ring. When Indy decides to steal the ring back from the British Museum, the unscrupulous French archeologist Belloq, who works for the Nazis, steals the scroll from Marcus Brody, Indy's friend. From London, Indy and Dr. Lawrence pursue Belloq to Egypt to recover the scroll before he can sell it to the Nazis. This original graphic novel story provides adventure suitable for younger readers.

Gelev, Penko
Moby Dick. Barron's Educational Series, Inc. 2007 48p. Illustration
Grades: 3 4 5 6 7 8 9   **741.5**
1. Graphic novels; 2. Melville, Herman — Adaptations
978-0-7641-5977-0; 978-0-7641-3492-0 (pa)

Ishmael's dream of adventure on a whaling ship becomes a nightmare as the voyage turns into a struggle for survival. Captain Ahab, maimed by a monster whale, is obsessed with revenge. As the crew discovers, he is willing to risk everything to destroy that whale. This volume includes a brief biography and timeline of Melville, and information on the legacy of his novel.

Georges, Nicole J.
Fetch: How a Bad Dog Brought Me Home. Nicole J. Georges. Mariner Books/Houghton Mifflin Harcourt 2017 328 p. Illustration
Grades: 11 12 Adult   **92; 741.5**
1. Human-animal relationships; 2. Dogs; 3. Autobiographical graphic novels
9780544577831, $17.95; 0544577833

In this illustrated memoir, author Nicole J. Georges reflects how when she "was sixteen she adopted Beija, a dysfunctional shar-pei/corgi mix — a troublesome combination of tiny and attack, just like teenaged Nicole herself. For the next fifteen years, Beija would be the one constant in her life. Through depression, relationships gone awry, and an unmoored young adulthood played out against the backdrop of the Portland punk scene, Beija was there." (Publisher's note)

"Drawn in black and white with watercolor washes and elegant hand lettering, this book is an homage to classic zine aesthetics that captures an incomparable friendship. An honest, moving portrayal of the essential bond between humans and animals." Pub Wkly

Gerber, Steve
Guardians of the Galaxy; Volume 1: Tomorrow's Avengers. by Steve Gerber, Chris Claremont, Gerry Conway, Len Wein, Arnold Drake and Roger Stern and illustrated by Gene Colan, Sal Buscema, Don Heck, and Al Milgrom. Marvel Enterprises 2013 368 p.
Grades: 7 8 9 10 11 12   **741.5**
1. Doctor Strange (Fictitious character); 2. Outer space — Fiction; 3. Superheroes — Fiction; 4. Space warfare — Fiction; 5. Hulk (Fictional character); 6. Captain America (Fictional character)
0785166874; 9780785166870, $39.99

In this graphic novel, written by Steve Gerber, Chris Claremont, Gerry Conway, Len Wien, Arnold Drake and Roger Stern, "Captain America, Doctor Strange, the Thing, the Hulk and other[s]...join the star-spanning heroes in the greatest war the future ever saw! As the Guardians help a planet...rebuild, threats rise from two other worlds: one of them living, the other gone mad!" (Publisher's note)

Gibbons, Dave
★ The **Originals**. DC Comics/Vertigo 2004 un Illustration
Grades: 10 11 12 Adult   **741.5; Fic**
1. Gangs — Graphic novels; 2. Graphic novels; 3. Science fiction graphic novels
1-4012-0355-8, $24.95
2005 Eisner Award for Best Graphic Album — New.

In a retro-futuristic city of industrial gray where hover scooters, music, and drugs rule the street, the Originals are the toughest, most stylish gang around. For two childhood friends, Lel and Bok, nothing is more important than being one of them. But being part of the crowd will bring its own deadly consequences. Gibbons draws upon the world of the Mods in 1960s England and sets it in an alternate world. Violence, harsh language, and sexual situations are part of this world.

Giffen, Keith
52 aftermath: The Four Horsemen. DC Comics 2008 144p. Illustration
Grades: 10 11 12 Adult   **741.5; Fic**
1. Batman (Fictional character); 2. Graphic novels; 3. Superhero graphic novels; 4. Superman (Fictional character); 5. Wonder Woman (Fictional character)
978-1-4012-1781-5, $19.99

During the event of 52 weeks, a cadre of scientists created the Four Horsemen of Apokolips, creatures of destructive power that killed Black Adam's family and pretty much destroyed his nation, Bialya. Black Adam destroyed the Horsemen; but, he only destroyed their physical forms. Now, War, Famine, Pestilence, and Death have returned, taking over new human hosts. Superman, Batman, and Wonder Woman are on the scene, but they might not be enough to destroy the Horsemen. Their best hope may be Dr. Cale, who helped create the Horsemen in the first place. Can she be trusted? The book includes violence.

52 Volume Two. Geoff Johns, Grant Morrison, Greg Rucka, Mark Waid, Keith Giffen. DC Comics 2007 304p. Illustration
Grades: 10 11 12 Adult   **741.5; Fic**
1. Adventure graphic novels; 2. Graphic novels; 3. Superhero graphic novels
978-1-4012-1364-0, $19.99

Lex Luthor's created meta humans become Infinity, Inc. even as John Steel finds out that Luthor can control the power within them — including removing them. Ralph Dibny takes up the helmet of Dr. Fate. The Question and Renee Montoya travel to Kahndaq, on the trail of Intergang's weapons. Black Adam and Isis get married. Booster Gold's dubious heroism ends badly. Supernova bothers Luthor. Adam Strange, Animal Man, and Starfire escape from the planet where they had been trapped, with help from...Lobo? The year without Superman, Batman, and Wonder Woman continues. The book includes some sexually suggestive scenes, violence, and some strong language.

Gill, Joel

Strange fruit; Volume 1: Uncelebrated narratives from Black history. words and pictures by Joel Christian Gill; foreword by Henry Louis Gates, Jr. Fulcrum Publishing 2014 176 p. Color; Illustration
Grades: 9 10 11 12 Adult
973.04960730092/2; 741.5; 92

1. African Americans — Biography — Comic books, strips, etc; 2. African Americans — Biography; 3. African Americans — History — Anecdotes — Comic books, strips, etc; 4. African Americans — History — Anecdotes — Juvenile literature; 5. Graphic novels; 6. Heroes — United States — Biography — Comic books, strips, etc; 7. Heroes — United States — Biography; 8. Success
1938486293; 9781938486296, $23.95

Courtesy of Fulcrum Publishing

LC 2014010803

This book, illustrated by Joel Christian Gill, "is a collection of stories from African American history that exemplifies success in the face of great adversity. This unique graphic anthology offers historical and cultural commentary on nine uncelebrated heroes [such as escaped slave] Henry 'Box' Brown,...Alexander Crummel and the Noyes Academy [and] Marshall 'Major' Taylor...the first black champion in any sport." (Publisher's note)

"The short narratives are conversational in tone and the accompanying detailed images convey tragic beauty. Gil doesn't shy away from portraying brutal scenes, but does so without sensationalism. The panels vary in size and orientation, pushing the momentum of each vignette forward with great success." SLJ

Gillen, Kieron

Star Wars Darth Vader; Volume 1: Vader. writer, Kieron Gillen; artist, Salvador Larroca; colorist, Edgar Delgado; letterer, VC's Joe Caramagna; cover art, Adi Granov; assistant editors, Charles Beacham & Heather Antos; editor, Jordan D. White. Marvel Enterprises 2015 160 p. Color; Illustration
Grades: 8 9 10 11 12 Adult 741.5
1. Star Wars — Graphic novels
0785192557; 9780785192558, $19.99

In this book, by Kieron Gillen, illustrated by Salvador Larocca, "Ever since Darth Vader's first on-screen appearance, he has become one of pop culture's most popular villains. Now, follow Vader straight from the ending of A NEW HOPE into his own solo adventures — showing the Empire's war with the Rebel Alliance from the other side! But when a Dark Lord needs help, who can he turn to?" (Publisher's note)
Contains material originally published in magazine form as Darth Vader #1-6.; Volume 1 of 4

★ **Young** Avengers: mic-drop at the edge of time and space. by Kieron Gillen; illustrated by Jamie McKelvie. Marvel Enterprises 2014 112 p. Color illustration
Grades: 10 11 12 Adult 741.5; Fic

1. Graphic novels; 2. Heroes — Fiction — Comic books, strips, etc.; 3. Science fiction comic books, strips, etc.; 4. Loki (Norse Deity) — Comic books, strips, etc.; 5. Superheroes — Fiction; 6. Captain America (Fictional character)
9780785185307, $15.99; 0785185305

"They say you can never go home. For the Young Avengers, that's not true. They can go home — it's just that if they do, the universe may end. Better not go home then, eh? (Wait, what are you doing, Young Avengers? You've decided to go home?!") The team takes on the gig to save reality, but is Kate Bishop an enemy in waiting? Is this the last we see of the loveable/strangle-able Kid Loki?" (Publisher's note)

"Gillen is an intelligent, savvy writer who gives more space to the battle's buildup and after-party than to the battle itself and even in the midst of the fight relies more on intimate character conflict than epic fisticuffs.... The overt focus on fluid sexuality...and smart teen dialogue that rings familiar and true give this series high appeal for new adults in particular." Booklist

★ **Young** avengers: style substance. Kieron Gillen, writer; Jamie McKelvie, Mike Norton, artist; Matthew Wilson, color artist; VC's Clayton Cowles, letterer. Marvel Enterprises 2013 128 p. Illustration
Grades: 10 11 12 Adult 741.5; Fic
1. Superhero graphic novels; 2. Teenagers — Fiction
9780785167082, $15.99; 0785167080

Author Kieron Gillen and illustrator Jamie McKelvie tell the story of "Wiccan, Hulkling and Kate 'Hawkeye' Bishop with Kid Loki, Marvel Boy and Ms. America.... As a figure from Loki's past emerges, Wiccan makes a horrible mistake that comes back to bite everyone on their communal posteriors. Fight scenes! Fake IDs! And plentiful feels! (aka 'meaningful emotional character beats'...)" (Publisher's note)

"The story...flies by, thanks to clever banter and lightning pacing.... McKelvie turns in clean, polished pages with eye-popping character work and shows some real and very welcome imagination with action sequences." Booklist
Contains material originally published in magazine form Young Avengers #1-5 and Marvel now! point one #1 — Tp verso

★ **Young** Avengers; Volume 2: alternative cultures. Kieron Gillen, illustrated by Kate Brown and Jamie McKelvie. Marvel Enterprises 2014 112 p. Color illustration (Young Avengers)
Grades: 9 10 11 12 Adult 741.5
1. Comic books, strips, etc.; 2. Graphic novels; 3. Heroes; 4. Science fiction comic books, strips, etc.; 5. Superhero comic books, strips, etc.; 6. Fantasy fiction
0785167099; 9780785167099, $15.99

"Existential horror turns cosmic horror as something emerges from the shadows of the past...and it seems that the Young Avengers have one more thing to worry about. The team races desperately across the multi-verse in pursuit of their missing friend, but their road trip goes crazy as it reaches its destination." (Publisher's note)

"As with the previous one, this slim volume is a quick read with snappy dialogue and fast, cleanly depicted action that pops with cinematic digital coloring effects." Booklist
Contains material originally published as Young Avengers (2013) #6-10

Gillis, Peter B.

The **last** unicorn. original story by Peter S. Beagle; adaptation by Peter B. Gillis; art by Renae De Liz. IDW 2011 167p. Illustration

Courtesy of IDW Publishing

Grades: 6 7 8 9 10   **741.5; Fic**
9780451450524 (rpt), $16.00; 978-1-60010-851-8, $24.99;
1-60010-851-2

"A beloved story is now a graphic novel in this excellent adaptation.... Much of the original novel's lyrical language has been included, and readers will be eager to find out if the unicorn will give up her quest for love, or if any of Schmendrick's spells will ever turn out right.... The illustrations are graceful and detailed, and inked in warm, glowing colors. This is a worthy successor to the classic novel and film." SLJ

Gillman, Melanie
    ★ **As** the crow flies. by Melanie Gillman. Iron Circus Comics 2017 272 p Color; Illustration
Grades: 7 8 9 10 11 12   **741.5; Fic**
1. Gender identity — Fiction; 2. Religious camps — Comic books, strips, etc.; 3. Teenagers — Graphic novels
9781945820069, $30; 1945820063
Stonewall Book Award Honor Book: Children's & Young Adult Literature (2018)
In this book, by Melanie Gillman, "Charlie Lamonte is thirteen years old, queer, black, and questioning what was once a firm belief in God. So naturally, she's spending a week of her summer vacation stuck at an all-white Christian youth backpacking camp. As the journey wears on and the rhetoric wears thin, she can't help but poke holes in the pious obliviousness of this storied sanctuary with little regard for people like herself...or her fellow camper, Sydney." (Publisher's note)
"This contemplative graphic novel, taken from Gillman's ongoing webcomic, perceptively explores race, gender, faith, and friendship. Elegantly composed, richly hued images vividly portray the lush forest setting and shy, thoughtful Charlie's inner turmoil as she yearns to voice her opinions." SLJ

Gilson, Che
    Avigon: Gods & Demons. writer, Che Gilson; artist, Jimmie Robinson. Image Comics 2005 un Illustration
Grades: 10 11 12 Adult   **741.5; Fic**
1. Fantasy graphic novels; 2. Graphic novels
1-58240-503-4, $19.95
Avigon, a clockwork creation, has to escape, her mechanical world is killing her very soul. The sky is black with acrid smoke, the rivers run slick with oil, and bizarre clockwork creatures roam the streets. Above it all, eccentric and power-hungry politicians and egomaniacal clockwork masters govern with stone cold hearts. But how can Avigon escape a surreal world of machines where she herself is one? Her desperate search will lead her to the darkest regions of humanity and to the arms of her destiny. The book includes some violence.

Gipi
    Notes for a war story. translated by Spectrum. First Second Books 2007 126p. Illustration
Grades: 10 11 12 Adult   **741.5; Fic**
1. Crime — Graphic novels; 2. Graphic novels; 3. War — Graphic novels
978-1-59643-261-1, $16.95
                     LC 2006-49716
Giuliano, a loner among outsiders, is one of three young drifters caught up in the whirlwind of a war in the Balkans. The three boys are like passing shadows; they live in abandoned houses, dodge the occasional bomb, and steal car parts for money. Meeting Felix — a powerful, fast-talking mercenary — changes everything for them. Felix is an expert manipulator; he speaks to their ambition and to their desires for power, wealth, and purpose. They're instantly hooked, especially the trio's unofficial leader, Stefano, and they soon escalate from petty crime to

working on behalf of a mafia-style militia, bullying and extorting money in Felix's name. But as Giuliano comes to realize, they don't know what they're fighting for — if they're even fighting for anything. There's some naturally occurring violence and harsh language.
Original Italian edition, 2004

Glidden, Sarah
    How to understand Israel in 60 days or less. writer & artist, Sarah Glidden; letterer Clem Robins. Vertigo/DC Comics 2010 206p. Illustration; Map
Grades: 11 12 Adult   **915.694; 741.5**
1. Glidden, Sarah — Travel — Comic books, strips, etc.; 2. Taglit—Birthright Israel (Organization) — Comic books, strips, etc.; 3. Americans — Israel — Comic books, strips, etc.; 4. Israel — Description and travel — Comic books, strips, etc.; 5. Israel — History — Comic books, strips, etc.; 6. Graphic novels
978-1-4012-2233-8, $24.99; 9781401222345, $19.99
This book "is Sarah [Glidden]'s memoir not only of her Israeli government-sponsored trip through Tel Aviv, Jerusalem, the Golan Heights, Masada and other famous locations, but of the emotional journey she never expected to take while she was there. Her experience clashes with her preconceived notions again and again, particularly when she tries to take a non-chaperoned trip into the West Bank. Sarah is forced to question first her political beliefs and, ultimately, her own sense of identity." (Publisher's note)

Goetzinger, Annie
    Girl in dior. Annie Goetzinger; translation by Joe Johnson; lettering by Ortho. NBM Pub. 2015 128 p. Color; Illustration
Grades: 9 10 11 12 Adult
741.5
1. Fashion designers; 2. Fashion design; 3. Dior, Christian, 1905-1957
1561639141; 9781561639144, $27.99
                   LC 2014956278

Courtesy of NBM Publishing

This book, by Annie Goetzinger, "covers the 1947 groundbreaking first fashion show put on by designer Christian Dior.... We watch the magic happen through the eyes of Clara Nohant, a young 'fashion chronicler,' a fictional character injected into the story amid real-life modistes, drapers, pattern makers, muses, magazine editors, and movie stars who surrounded the designer." (School Library Journal)
"Goetzinger's detailed, expressive faces and figures seem to be illuminated from within, and the garments themselves are a great tribute to the author's background in fashion illustration." Booklist
Initially published in French as Jeune fille en Dior

Goldstein, Nancy
    ★ **Jackie** Ormes: the first African American woman cartoonist. University of Michigan Press 2008 225p. Illustration
Grades: 10 11 12 Adult   **92; 741.5**
1. African American women — Biography; 2. Cartoonists; 3. Ormes, Jackie, 1911-1985
978-0-472-11624-9, $35; 0-472-11624-X
                   LC 2007-35395
This book covers the life and career of Jackie Ormes, who was the first African American woman cartoonist. She wrote and drew comic strips that ran in Black newspapers such as the Pittsburgh Courier and the Chicago Defender. She was part of the Black elite in Chicago and knew other

luminaries such as singer Eartha Kitt and musician/composer/conductor Duke Ellington. She was also investigated by the FBI because of her Leftist political ideas and activities. While she did such things as create Torchy paper dolls, based on her beautiful and sexy cartoon character, and cute Patty-Jo dolls, Ormes also used her comic strips to put forth her political views. This book reproduces some of her cartoons and comic strips, in both black and white and in color.

Includes bibliographical references

Gonick, Larry
★ The **cartoon** history of the modern world: Part 1: from Columbus to the U.S. Constitution. Collins 2007 259p. Illustration
Grades: 9 10 11 12 Adult   **741.5; 909.08**
    1. Graphic novels; 2. Modern history — Graphic novels
    978-0-06-076004-5; 0-06-076004-4, $17.95
                                                        LC 2006-49146
The book begins with a "15-page distillation of pre-Columbian America; and while Europe and North America receive most of the attention, Gonick does include at least some highlights from other parts of the world. Covering such topics as the Protestant Reformation, the British defeat of the Spanish Armada, the Copernican model of the universe, and the American Revolution, he writes and draws with considerable wit and authority, and is obviously well versed in his subject." SLJ
Followed by:The Cartoon History of the Modern World Part 2: From the Bastille to Baghdad (2009)

★ The **Cartoon** History of the Universe Volumes 1-7: From the Big Bang to Alexander the Great. Main Street Books/Doubleday & Co. 1990 368p. Illustration
Grades: 9 10 11 12 Adult   **741.5; 902.07**
    1. Graphic novels; 2. World history — Graphic novels
    0-385-26520-4, $22.95; 9780385265201
                                                        LC 02-288002
Gonick presents a quick tour of world history, starting from the Big Bang through the life of Alexander the Great. He presents facts in the text, while his illustrations provide an irreverently humorous counterpoint. There's partial nudity with some of the ancient people.

★ The **Cartoon** History of the Universe Volumes 8-13: From the Springtime of China to the Fall of Rome. Main Street Books/Doubleday & Co. 1994 305p. Illustration
Grades: 9 10 11 12 Adult   **741.5; 902.07; 902**
    1. Graphic novels; 2. World history — Graphic novels
    0-385-42093-5, $22.95
                                                        LC 02-288002
Gonick presents a quick tour of world history, continuing with Alexander the Great's march to India (and his about-face), focusing on India and China, then going back to Rome and covering the Western World through the end of Justinian's reign, around 564 A.D. He also tells the story of Jeshua ben Joseph (Jesus). He presents facts in the text, while his illustrations provide an irreverently humorous counterpoint. There's partial nudity and some violence with the depictions of wars and battles.

★ The **Cartoon** History of the Universe III: From the Rise of Arabia to the Renaissance. W. W. Norton 2002 300p. Illustration
Grades: 9 10 11 12 Adult   **741.5; 909.07**
    1. Graphic novels; 2. World history — Graphic novels
    0-393-32403-6, $21.95
                                                        LC 02-288002
This volume begins in the year 395, covers the birth of Islam, the Crusades, the Asian and African nations, the Mongol conquests, the Ottoman Empire, the Black Death, the Italian Renaissance, the rise of Spain, and culminates in the year 1492. The facts in the text are accompanied again by his irreverently humorous illustrations.

Goodwin, Michael
Economix: how and why our economy works (and doesn't work) in words and pictures. Michael Goodwin. Harry N. Abrams Inc. 2012 304 p. Illustration
Grades: 11 12 Adult   **330**
    1. Economics — Comic books, strips, etc; 2. Economic development; 3. Cost and standard of living
    9780810988392, $19.95
                                                        LC 2011052119
Author Michael Goodwin discusses the economy, "human nature and our attempts to make the most of what we've got...and sometimes what our neighbors have got...[The book explains concepts from] the beginning of Western economic thought, to markets free and otherwise, to economic failures, successes, limitations, and future possibilities." (Publisher's note)

"This dense yet readable exegesis makes economics entertaining despite current financial shenanigans worldwide. Goodwin takes a chronological approach, starting with the history of banking in the 17th century. As he marches through four centuries of economic theories and theorists, he attempts to show what happened, what succeeded, and what went wrong in terms of both public and private good, with a focus on the reasons particular theories didn't pan out in real life." LJ
Includes bibliographical references and index

Goodwin, Vincent
Sir Arthur Conan Doyle's The adventure of the speckled band. adapted by, Vincent Goodwin; illustrated by, Ben Dunn. ABDO/Magic Wagon 2010 48p. Illustration
Grades: 4 5 6 7 8 9
741.5; Fic
    1. Authors; 2. Graphic novels; 3. Holmes, Sherlock (Fictional character) — Graphic novels; 4. Mystery graphic novels; 5. Doyle, Arthur Conan Sir, 1859-1930 — Adaptations
    978-1-60270-727-6, $28.50; 1-60270-727-8
                                        LC 2009-32461

Courtesy of ABDO Publishing.

Consulting detective Sherlock Holmes and his partner Dr. John Watson come to the aid of Miss Helen Stoner. After moving back to England from India with their stepfather, Helen's twin sister died under mysterious circumstances. Now, two years later, Helen knows something is terribly wrong in her stepfather's house. Both men suspect the gypsies that Dr. Roylott, the stepfather, has allowed to live on his property, but Holmes soon suspects something else. This graphic novel adaptation has been done by Goodwin and Dunn, who are experienced creators with Antarctic Press (Dunn started the publishing house). The book includes a brief glossary, a short biography of Doyle, a listing of his published works, and a short sketching lesson by Dunn.
Part of The Graphic Novel Adventures of Sherlock Holmes

Sir Arthur Conan Doyle's The adventure of the Red-Headed League. ABDO/Magic Wagon 2010 48p. Illustration
Grades: 4 5 6 7 8 9   **741.5; Fic**
    1. Authors; 2. Graphic novels; 3. Holmes, Sherlock (Fictional character) — Graphic novels; 4. Mystery graphic novels; 5. Doyle, Arthur Conan Sir, 1859-1930 — Adaptations
    978-1-60270-726-9, $28.50; 1-60270-726-X
                                        LC 2009-32460
Consulting detective Sherlock Holmes and his friend Dr. John Watson take the case of Jabez Wilson, an ordinary tradesman with an extraordinary

Courtesy of ABDO Publishing.

tale. His pawn shop assistant had found an advertisement in the newspaper asking for eligible men to apply for membership in The RedHeaded League, and he helped Mr. Wilson fight through a crowd of redheaded men and to be accepted into the League. Wilson was paid four pounds a week for a few hours' work copying out of an encyclopedia; then suddenly, all trace of the League disappeared. He wants Holmes to find out what has happened. This graphic novel adaptation has been done by Goodwin and Dunn, who are experienced creators with Antarctic Press (Dunn started the publishing house). The book includes a brief glossary, a short biography of Doyle, a listing of his published works, and a short sketching lesson by Dunn.

Part of The Graphic Novel Adventures of Sherlock Holmes

Sir Arthur Conan Doyle's, The adventure of the empty house. ABDO/Magic Wagon 2010 48p. Illustration
Grades: 4 5 6 7 8 9
741.5; Fic
1. Authors; 2. Graphic novels; 3. Holmes, Sherlock (Fictional character); 4. Mystery graphic novels; 5. Mystery writers; 6. Novelists; 7. Doyle, Arthur Conan Sir, 1859-1930; 8. Doyle, Arthur Conan Sir, 1859-1930 — Adaptations
978-1-60270-724-5, $28.50;
1-60270-724-3

Courtesy of ABDO Publishing.

Three years before, Dr. Watson witnessed the death of his friend Sherlock Holmes, who plummeted to his death along with archvillain Dr. Moriarty. Now, Inspector Lestrade asks Watson's help in a puzzling murder case, but it stumps Watson as well. Then, to his utter surprise, Holmes comes to him, explaining that he pretended to die. Together again, the two men work on the case, hoping to catch one of Moriarty's dangerous henchmen. This graphic novel adapts Doyle's original story which was the "comeback" after killing Holmes in "The Final Problem." The art depicts Watson as a fairly young man, but persists in putting Holmes into the deerstalker cap and caped overcoat which Doyle's Holmes never wore. The book includes a brief drawing lesson, a short glossary, brief biography of Doyle, and a listing of his other writings.

Part of The Graphic Novel Adventures of Sherlock Holmes

Sir Arthur Conan Doyle's, The adventure of the dancing men. ABDO/Magic Wagon 2010 48p. Illustration
Grades: 4 5 6 7 8 9

1. Authors; 2. Graphic novels; 3. Holmes, Sherlock (Fictional character); 4. Mystery graphic novels; 5. Mystery writers; 6. Novelists; 7. Doyle, Arthur Conan Sir, 1859-1930; 8. Doyle, Arthur Conan Sir, 1859-1930 — Adaptations/Graphic novels; 9. Holmes, Sherlock (Fictional character)
978-1-60270-723-8, $28.50;
1-60270-723-5

Courtesy of ABDO Publishing.

When strange writing that looks like dancing men starts appearing around the estate of Mr. Cubitt, he comes to Sherlock

Holmes for help. He thinks it's the work of pranksters, but his American wife seems frightened. As he brings more of the writing samples to Holmes, the detective works on the case, but he may not be able to solve it before tragedy strikes the Cubitts. This book adapts Doyle's short story; it includes a short glossary, a brief biography of Doyle, a short drawing lesson, and a list of Doyle's other writings. Dunn's art depicts Holmes and Dr. Watson as younger men, but continues the stereotypical portrayal of Holmes with the deerstalker cap and shoulder caped coat which Doyle never had him wear in the original stories.

Part of The Graphic Novel Adventures of Sherlock Holmes series

Sir Arthur Conan Doyle's, The adventure of the Abbey Grange. ABDO/Magic Wagon 2010 48p. Illustration
Grades: 4 5 6 7 8 9
741.5; Fic
1. Authors; 2. Graphic novels; 3. Holmes, Sherlock (Fictional character); 4. Doyle, Arthur Conan Sir, 1859-1930
978-1-60270-722-1, $28.50;
1-60270-722-7

A robbery and murder have occurred, and Sir Eustace Brackenstall is dead. His wife and maid say that a gang of robbers invaded their home, tied up Lady Brackenstall and killed Sir Eustace, but Holmes doesn't believe their story. As he

Courtesy of ABDO Publishing.

investigates, he learns that Sir Eustace was a cruel man, and even though Lady Brackenstall has lied, Holmes sympathizes with her. This book adapts Doyle's short story; it includes a short glossary, a brief biography of Doyle, a short drawing lesson, and a list of Doyle's other writings. Dunn's art depicts Holmes and Dr. Watson as younger men, but continues the stereotypical portrayal of Holmes with the deerstalker cap and shoulder caped coat which Doyle never had him wear in the original stories.

Part of The Graphic Novel Adventures of Sherlock Holmes series.

Goscinny, Rene
Asterix and Caesar's Gift. Orion/Sterling Publishing 2004 48p. Illustration
Grades: 4 5 6 7 8 9 10 11 12 Adult   **741.5; Fic**
1. Asterix (Fictional character); 2. Graphic novels; 3. Humorous graphic novels
0-75286-645-1, $12.95; 0-75286-646-X (pa)
When Legionary Tremensdelirius gets the title deeds to the little Gaulish village as a bonus, he swaps them with tavern landlord Orthopaedix for a drink. Funnily enough, Asterix and his friends aren't keen to hand over their village to anyone else. After a chieftaincy election campaign and a showdown with the Romans, both events fiercely contested, can all still end well?

Asterix and Cleopatra. Orion/Sterling Publishing 2004 48p. Illustration
Grades: 4 5 6 7 8 9 10 11 12 Adult   **741.5; Fic**
1. Asterix (Fictional character); 2. Graphic novels; 3. Humorous graphic novels
0-75286-606-0, $12.95; 0-75286-607-9 (pb)
How can lovely Queen Cleopatra show Julius Caesar that ancient Egypt is still a great nation? Her architect Edifis recruits his Gaulish friends to help him build a magnificent palace within three months. There are villainous saboteurs to be outwitted, but Asterix, Obelix, and Getafix still find time to go sight-seeing, and leave their mark on the Pyramids and the Sphinx's nose.

Asterix and the Banquet. Orion/Sterling Publishing 2004 48p. Illustration

Grades: 4 5 6 7 8 9 10 11 12 Adult   **741.5; Fic**

1. Asterix (Fictional character); 2. Graphic novels; 3. Humorous graphic novels

0-75286-608-0, $12.95; 0-75286-609-5 (pa)

When the Romans try to contain the threat from the Gaulish village by building a stockade around it, Asterix and Obelix lay a bet with them. They will break out and claim their right to travel freely all over Gaul, collecting the local delicacies and bringing them back to prove their point. Ham from Lutetia, fizzy wine from Durocortorum, fish stew from Massilia in the south...soon their shopping bag is full. Outwitting Romans, a couple of treacherous Gauls, and the thieves Villanus and Unscrupulus, they set off for home...but who's that little dog who has been following them all the way from Lutetia?

Asterix and the Cauldron. Orion/Sterling Publishing 2004 48p. Illustration

Grades: 4 5 6 7 8 9 10 11 12 Adult   **741.5; Fic**

1. Asterix (Fictional character); 2. Graphic novels; 3. Humorous graphic novels

0-75286-629-X, $9.95

There's financial skulduggery in ancient Gaul. When local Chief Whosemoralsarelastix wants a cauldron full of money kept out of Roman hands, the cash disappears while Asterix is guarding it. He and Obelix must earn enough to repay it through fairground gladiatorial contests, trendy theatrical performances, even bank robbery — they'll try anything. But whose morals are really elastic? And how to the pirates, just for once, get an unexpected bonus?

Asterix and the Class Act. Orion/Sterling Publishing 2004 56p. Illustration

Grades: 4 5 6 7 8 9 10 11 12 Adult   **741.5; Fic**

1. Asterix (Fictional character); 2. Graphic novels; 3. Humorous graphic novels

0-75286-068-2, $12.95; 0-75286-640-0 (pa)

This volume collects 14 stories, including the day Asterix and Obelix were born (in the middle of a fish fight); how Obelix goes back to school; fashion in ancient Gaul; how Dogmatix helps the village cockerel win a duel, and how he's adopted as a Roman mascot; Obelix's adventures under the mistletoe; the bid for the very first Gaulish Olympics, and more.

★ **Asterix** the Gaul. written by René Goscinny and illustrated by Albert Uderzo; translated by Anthea Bell and Derek Hockridge. Orion Media 2004 48p. Illustration; Map

Grades: 4 5 6 7 8 9 10 11 12   **741.5; Fic**

1. Graphic novels; 2. Humorous graphic novels; 3. France — History — Graphic novels

0-7528-6604-4, $12.95; 0-7528-6605-2 (pa), $9.95

Meet Asterix, a diminutive but extremely strong Gaul living in ancient France during the time of the Roman Republic. Together with his friend Obelix, Asterix continually outwits the Roman Legionnaires sent to conquer Gaul for Julius Caesar. Full of puns and outrageous humor, the books also manage to teach a lot of history. This is the first in a long-running series of graphic novels translated from the original French.

Translated from the French; Other titles in this series are: Asterix and Caesar's Gift; Asterix and Cleopatra; Asterix and the actress; Asterix and the banquet; Asterix and the big fight; Asterix and the cauldron; Asterix and the Goths; Asterix and the Great Crossing; Asterix and the laurel wreath; Asterix the legionary; Asterix and the Normans; Asterix and the Roman Agent; Asterix and the soothsayer; Asterix at the Olympic Games; Asterix in Belgium; Asterix in Britain; Asterix in Corsica; Asterix in Spain; Asterix in Switzerland; Asterix Obelix and Co.; Asterix the gladiator; Asterix The Mansions of the Gods

Asterix and the Laurel Wreath. Orion/Sterling Publishing 2004 48p. Illustration

Grades: 4 5 6 7 8 9 10 11 12 Adult   **741.5; Fic**

1. Asterix (Fictional character); 2. Graphic novels; 3. Humorous graphic novels

0-75286-636-2, $12.95; 0-75286-637-0 (pa)

Chief Vitalstatistix rashly invites his brother-in-law to dine on a stew seasoned with Caesar's laurel wreath, so Asterix and Obelix must to go Rome to fetch those laurels. Hoping to get access to Caesar, they sell themselves as slaves, but can they do a deal with the corrupt Goldendelicius to swap the laurels for parsley?

Asterix in Britain. Orion/Sterling Publishing 2004 48p. Illustration

Grades: 4 5 6 7 8 9 10 11 12 Adult   **741.5; Fic**

1. Asterix (Fictional character); 2. Graphic novels; 3. Humorous graphic novels

0-85286-618-4, $12.95; 0-75286-619-2 (pa)

The Romans have invaded Britain, but one village still holds out. Asterix and Obelix come to help, with a barrel of magic potion in hand. But to deliver the precious brew, the Gaulish heroes must face fog, rain, bad food, warm beer, and the Romans too.

Asterix the Legionary. Orion/Sterling Publishing 2004 48p. Illustration

Grades: 4 5 6 7 8 9 10 11 12 Adult   **741.5; Fic**

1. Asterix (Fictional character); 2. Graphic novels; 3. Humorous graphic novels

0-75286-620-6, $12.95; 0-75286-621-4 (pa)

It's off to the wars for Asterix and Obelix: they've enlisted as legionnaires in order to rescue Tragicomix, whom the Romans forcibly conscripted. The two find Tragicomix and succeed in causing the biggest commotion ever on a battlefield.

Gossett, Christian

King Kong: The 8th Wonder of the World. Dark Horse Books 2006 un Illustration

Grades: 7 8 9 10 11 12 Adult   **741.5; Fic**

1. Graphic novels; 2. King Kong (Fictional character); 3. Science fiction graphic novels

978-1-59307-472-2, $12.95

Director Carl Denham has one chance to make the film of his dreams — hire an unknown actress, kidnap his writer and board a tramp freighter for the mysterious Island of the Skull. But when hostile natives capture actress Ann Darrow, Denham and his crew will face horrors from giant spiders to bloodthirsty dinosaurs to get her back. Yet, nothing can prepare them for the revelation of the mighty wonder in whose clutches Ann truly remains — King Kong. This story adapts the screenplay for the motion picture directed by Peter Jackson, which is based on the original story by Merian C. Cooper and Edgar Wallace.

Graley, Sarah

Kim Reaper: grim beginnings. by Sarah Graley; lettered by Crank!. Oni Press 2018 112 p. Color; Illustration

Grades: 7 8 9 10 11 12   **741.5; Fic**

1. Infatuation — Fiction; 2. Women college students — Fiction; 3. Lesbians — Fiction

1620104555; 9781620104552, $14.99

LC 2017946413

In this book in the Kim Reaper series, by Sarah Graley, edited by Ari Yarwood, "Kim's job is pretty cool: she's a grim reaper.... Becka's crush is on a beautiful gothic angel that frequents the underworld.... Becka finally...ask[s] Kim on a date! But when she falls into a ghostly portal and interrupts Kim at her job, she sets off a chain of events that will pit the two of them against angry cat-dads, vengeful zombies, and perhaps even the underworld itself." (Publisher's note)

"Graley's adorably goth comic is full of over-the-top slapstick; cute, goggle-eyed characters; a sweet lesbian romance; and, of course, lots of skeletons and trips to hell. The contrast between the macabre plot and bubbly art, in a rich palette of warm jewel tones with pops of fluorescent hues, will be utterly bewitching for the right reader." Booklist

Gran, Meredith
Octopus Pie 1. by Meredith Gran. Image Comics 2016 200 p.
Grades: 11 12 Adult   **741.5**
  1. Brooklyn (New York, N.Y.) — Fiction; 2. Roommates — Fiction; 3. College graduates — Fiction
1632156326; 9781632156327, $14.99

In this graphic novel, by Meredith Gran, collecting part of her long-running webcomic, "we follow grumpy twenty-something Eve and her stoner roommate Hanna as they navigate post-college life. They'll take on crazed childhood rivals, troubling art scenes, the discomfort of exes, and maybe even... friendship? All this and more in the fictional, totally made-up city of Brooklyn." (Publisher's note)

Volume 1 of 5

Grant, Alan
Robert Louis Stevenson's Kidnapped. adaptation by Alan Grant; illustrator, Cam Kennedy. Tundra Books 2007 un Illustration
Grades: 6 7 8 9 10   **741.5; Fic**
  1. Adventure graphic novels; 2. Graphic novels; 3. Stevenson, Robert Louis, 1850-1894 — Adaptations
978-0-88776-843-9 (pa), $11.95; 0-88776-843-1 (pa)
                           LC 2007921350

Kidnapped is set in 1751, during the time of the Jacobite rebellion " a tumultuous and tragic period in Scottish history. When David Balfour sets out to find his uncle, he never dreamed that he would be kidnapped " but saved from a life of slavery " and thrown from one escapade to another in the company of the fugitive, masterful swordsman Alan Breck Stewart.

"This is an engaging adaptation, aided by Kennedy's vibrant illustrations in a palette dominated by blues, greens, and sepia tones. The action scenes are exciting." SLJ

Gray, Harold
  ★**Harold** Gray's Little Orphan Annie; Volume one: the complete daily comics, 1924-27: Will tomorrow ever come? IDW Publishing 2008 385p. Illustration
Grades: 2 3 4 5 6 7 8 9 10 11 12 Adult
741.5; Fic
  1. Adventure graphic novels; 2. Graphic novels; 3. Little Orphan Annie (Fictional character); 4. Orphans — Graphic novels
978-1-60010-140-3, $39.99

Courtesy of IDW Publishing

Little Orphan Annie started as a daily newspaper comic strip in one newspaper, the New York Daily News, on August 5, 1924. It became a popular strip, syndicated to newspapers all over the world. It eventually became a Broadway, a hit movie, and Annie became an iconic character. This book is the first comprehensive collection of Gray's comic strip and is the first volume of a series planned to collect all of Gray's Little Orphan Annie strips. She is an orphan girl living in an orphanage, with an unscrupulous director who hires Annie out for work. When wealthy Mrs. Warbucks, trying to prove that she cares for the poor, takes Annie on a "trial" adoption, Annie eventually meets Oliver Warbucks, whom she calls "Daddy." As the strips go on, Annie undergoes many hardships and perils, facing everything with spunk and a positive attitude. She's no wilting girl, though " she can fight (she has a mean right hook) and will take on any bully. She rescues the dog she calls Sandy, who rewards her with a loyal friendship. This volume includes more than 1,000 comic strips, many of which haven't seen publication since their original newspaper appearance. During the first years of the strip's publication, the color Sunday comics had no connection to the weekday storylines, but a few Sunday pages are included in this book. This book may appeal most to adults who remember reading Little Orphan Annie in the "funnies" pages, but the stories will appeal to all ages. Contributing Editor Jeet Heer provides a biography of Harold Gray.

Gray, Justin
  Jonah Hex: Guns of Vengeance. writers Justin Gray and Jimmy Palmiotti; art Luke Ross. DC Comics 2007 144p. Illustration
Grades: 11 12 Adult   **741.5; Fic**
  1. Adventure graphic novels; 2. Graphic novels; 3. Supernatural graphic novels; 4. Western graphic novels
978-1-4012-1249-0, $12.99

Jonah Hex, a mysterious bounty hunter and thinking man's killer, was a hero to some and a villain to others — and his name was spoken in whispers. He had no friends, but he did have two companions: one was death and the other... the smell of gun smoke. Haunted by the ghosts of his past, present, and future, the bullets fly as Jonah Hex battles bounty hunters, vengeful spirits, alligators, and sideshow freaks. This Western is full of graphic violence, harsh language, and some sexual situations and nudity.

  ★ **Power** girl: a new beginning. Justin Gray & Jimmy Palmiotti, writers; Amanda Conner, artist and covers; Paul Mounts, colorist; John J. Hill, letterer. DC Comics 2010 un Illustration
Grades: 9 10 11 12 Adult   **741.5; Fic**
  1. Graphic novels; 2. Superhero graphic novels
978-1-4012-2618-3, $17.99

Kara Zor-L came from Krypton, just like her very famous cousin Kal-L, who became Superman, but she had lived in a parallel universe, known as Earth 2. Since then, she has come to this world's New York City and started all over again as Karen Starr and reopening her business, a progressive technology company called Starrware Labs. She's also Power Girl, since she has many of Superman's superpowers. Before she can get Starrware Labs fully up and running with all essential positions filled, she has to deal with a horde of fear-inducing robots sent by the Ultra-Humanite to destroy Manhattan. Then, a trio of party-crashing aliens and their pursuer start wrecking the rest of Manhattan as they fight in the streets. The book has lots of action but no really graphic violence, and some "fan service" as it's called in manga there are some panty shots, and Karen/Power Girl deals with men staring at her bust. Her costume has a cutout design on the chest, which the writers and artist treat with some great humor. Co-writer Palmiotti and artist Conner are a couple themselves, and their close work shows in sheer fun of this book.

Grayson, Devin
  Nightwing: Mobbed Up. DC Comics 2006 128p. Illustration
Grades: 10 11 12 Adult   **741.5; Fic**
  1. Graphic novels; 2. Nightwing (Fictional character); 3. Superhero graphic novels
978-1-4012-0907-0, $12.99

Injured and dejected, cut off from all allegiances, Dick Grayson decides to turn his misery into an advantage and a new purpose. He arranges to be adopted into one of New York City's crime families. In doing so he begins a new odyssey, one that sweeps him into the depths of the criminal underworld. Try as he may, however, he can't put his crime-fighting alter ego behind him forever, so Nightwing returns. But which side is he on? There's some violence, but despite the mob, little in the way of harsh language.

Nightwing: Renegade. DC Comics 2006 144p. Illustration
Grades: 9 10 11 12 Adult   **741.5; Fic**
1. Graphic novels; 2. Nightwing (Fictional character); 3. Superhero graphic novels; 4. Robin (Fictional character)
978-1-4012-0908-7, $14.99

Once he was Robin, but Dick Grayson stepped out from the shadow of the Bat to become his own hero, Nightwing. Now the events of the past year have taken a heavy toll on Dick, and he's seemingly embraced the darkness within himself. He's got a new costume, a new name — Renegade — and he serves a new master. But could Nightwing really be working for Deathstroke, the deadly assassin and his longtime nemesis? As Renegade takes Deathstroke's daughter Ravager under his wing, the two old enemies will play a dangerous game of cat and mouse. But who's manipulating whom, and what do these two brilliant minds really want from each other? Just when Nightwing thinks he has it all figured out, Deathstroke makes a move so shocking, Nightwing's world will never be the same. There's plenty of action, but little overt violence or harsh language.

Green, Katie
Lighter than my shadow. Katie Green. Lion Forge 2017 505 p. Illustration
Grades: 9 10 11 12 Adult   **92; 741.5**
1. Eating disorders; 2. Graphic novels; 3. Autobiographical graphic novels; 4. Eating disorders — Graphic novels
1941302416; 9781941302415, $19.99
           LC 2013432027

This book, by Katie Green, is "a graphic memoir of eating disorders, abuse and recovery. Like most kids, Katie was a picky eater. She'd sit at the table in silent protest, hide uneaten toast in her bedroom, listen to parental threats that she'd have to eat it for breakfast. But in any life a set of circumstance can collide, and normal behavior might soon shade into something sinister, something deadly. One day you can find yourself being told you have two weeks to live." (Publisher's note)

"Minimal dialogue and narration keep the focus on Green's grayscale artwork, which viscerally reflects how Green saw herself while in the grips of her eating disorder.... As the story moves into Green's college years and beyond, she finds balance amid many setbacks but never sugarcoats the difficult and ongoing nature of recovery." Pub Wkly

First published in 2013 by Jonathan Cape, an imprint of Vintage

Greenberg, Isabel
The **encyclopedia** of early earth: a novel. Isabel Greenberg. Little, Brown and Co. 2013 176 p.
Grades: 10 11 12 Adult   **741.5; Fic**
1. Earth — Fiction; 2. Fables; 3. Travel — Fiction
0316225819; 9780316225816, $23
           LC 2013939419

Author Isabel Greenberg presents a "series of illustrated and linked tales [which] chronicles the explorations of a young man as he paddles from his home in the North Pole to the South Pole. There, he meets his true love, but their romance is ill-fated. Early Earth's unusual and finicky polarity means the lovers can never touch." (Publisher's note)

"Greenberg deeply immerses readers in the themes and lessons of world mythology, but she remarkably never merely apes classic myths-the way each of Early Earth's cultures tweaks the same ideas and characters for their own myths is a veritable lesson in comparative theology." Booklist

Grell, Mike
The **Complete** Jon Sable, Freelance Volume 1. IDW Publishing 2005 180p. Illustration
Grades: 10 11 12 Adult   **741.5; Fic**
1. Adventure graphic novels; 2. Graphic novels
1-932382-77-1, $24.99

The initial 54-page story guest-stars Ronald Reagan, and the second is Sable's famous 108-page origin saga. Sable is a mercenary willing to act as a private eye or bodyguard if the money is right and the job promises excitement. The origin story depicts how he became that way after his family was massacred. There's lots of fighting action and bloodshed in this story, originally published by First Comics in the early 1980s.

Grillo-Marxuach, Javier
★ The **Middleman:** the collected series indispensability. Viper Comics 2008 336p. Illustration
Grades: 9 10 11 12 Adult   **741.5; Fic**
1. Adventure graphic novels; 2. Graphic novels; 3. Humorous graphic novels; 4. Science fiction graphic novels
978-0-9802385-4-9, $19.95

This book collects all three volumes of The Middleman comics series. Art student Wendy Watson works as a temp agency hire, when one day she's working at a scientific laboratory where things go totally wrong and a mysterious guy who calls himself The Middleman takes care of the monsters. Unfortunately for Wendy, the cover story that a gas main explosion caused all the mess also indicates that her lucky Zippo lighter, the only thing she has from her long-missing father, ignited the gas leak. Unemployed Wendy soon finds herself recruited by the Jolly Fats Wehawkin Temp Agency, which is actually the cover for The Middleman and his henchperson, robotic Ida. Wendy soon finds herself battling intelligent apes out to rule the criminal underworld, crazy Lucha Libre wrestlers, and more "exotic problems," at the side of the enigmatic, super-good guy, The Middleman. The book includes some violence, some nudity, and some sexual innuendo. The series was adapted into a television series on ABC Family which ran for one season; the DVD boxed set is scheduled for a summer 2009 release.

Grine, Chris
Chickenhare. Chris Grine. Graphix / Scholastic 2013 160 p.
Grades: 4 5 6 7 8 9   **741.5**
1. Animals — Graphic novels; 2. Taxidermy — Fiction; 3. Escapes — Juvenile fiction
0545485088; 9780545485081, $10.99
           LC 2012936214

Author Chris Grine presents a children's comic book. "What's a chickenhare? A cross between a chicken and a rabbit, of course. And that makes Chickenhare the rarest animal around! So when he and his turtle friend Abe are captured and sold to the evil taxidermist Klaus, they've got to find a way to escape before Klaus turns them into stuffed animals. With the help of two other strange creatures, Banjo and Meg, they might even get away. But with Klaus and his thugs hot on their trail, the adventure is only just beginning for this unlikely quartet of friends." (Publisher's note)

Chickenhare: The House of Klaus. Dark Horse Comics 2006 160p. Illustration
Grades: 7 8 9 10 11 12   **741.5**
1. Adventure graphic novels; 2. Fantasy graphic novels; 3. Graphic novels
978-1-59307-574-3, $9.95

Friends Chickenhare (who is exactly that, a cross between a chicken and a hare) and bearded turtle Abe are captives being taken to the mad taxidermist Klaus, who looks like an evil Santa. Chickenhare and Abe escape, along with obnoxious monkey Banjo and horned girl Meg;

Chickenhare finds the dead goat Mr. Buttons, and the others encounter the warlike, cave-dwelling Shromph, who have a bone to pick with Klaus. A few harsh words, some violence, and implied cannibalism may be disturbing for younger readers.

Chickenhare: fire in the hole. Dark Horse Comics 2008 200p. Illustration
Grades: 7 8 9 10 11 12 Adult   741.5; Fic
1. Adventure graphic novels; 2. Fantasy graphic novels; 3. Graphic novels
978-1-59307-907-9, $10.95

Chickenhare, his friend Abe, and their new friends Scabby, Meg and Banjo managed to escape the evil Taxidermist Klaus, but they have gone from one dangerous situation into...something worse. While at sea in a small boat about to be swamped by rain and waves, Banjo's brother and some warriors from the Underworld pop up, they zap the soul out of Abe and take Banjo and Meg. Chickenhare is left with Scabby and Abe's body. He must venture into the Underworld to recover Abe's soul. Meanwhile, Banjo and Meg face punishment for deserting the Underworld. And just why do the Sea Folk call Chickenhare "Your Majesty"?

Grist, Paul
Kane Vol. 1: Greetings from New Eden. Image Comics 2004 127p. Illustration
Grades: 10 11 12 Adult   741.5; Fic
1. Graphic novels; 2. Mystery graphic novels
1-58240-340-6, $11.95

Detective Kane returns to active duty with the New Eden Police Dept. following a six month suspension after he shot and killed his partner Dennis Harvey. His fellow police officers give Kane a welcome back gift — a couple of bullets with his name engraved on them. Partnered with a new detective, Kate Felix, Kane soon finds out nothing has changed in the city of New Eden. In his first two days back, Kane has to deal with a siege, a kidnapping and a bomb attack. And then there's the Crime Boss of New Eden, Oscar Darke... The book includes some harsh language and violence.

Kane Vol. 2: Rabbit Hunt. Image Comics 2004 un Illustration
Grades: 10 11 12 Adult   741.5; Fic
1. Graphic novels; 2. Mystery graphic novels
1-58240-355-4, $12.95

It's a bad day for Mister Floppsie Whoppsie, New Eden's self-styled Rabbit for Hire. The freelance rabbit business isn't going as well as it should. He's hung over. The rent's due. There's a knock at the door and a gun-wielding homicidal maniac barges into the room. That's when things start to go downhill. And Detective Kane still can't trust anyone in the New Eden Police Department. The book includes some strong language and violence.

Kane Vol. 4: Thirty-Ninth. Image Comics 2005 un Illustration
Grades: 10 11 12 Adult   741.5; Fic
1. Graphic novels; 2. Mystery graphic novels
1-58240-468-2, $16.95

When Detective Kane returned to active duty with the New Eden Police Dept. following a six-month suspension in the wake of shooting and killing his partner, his fellow police officers gave him a welcome back gift: a couple of bullets with his name on them. Now, a sniper is taking pot shots at the police. An ex-cop is looking to take revenge on the cop who turned him in. There's rioting in the streets and the Mayor's been kidnapped again. It's another typical week for the police in New Eden's Precinct 39. The book has some strong language and violence.

Grunwald, Jennifer
Civil War: Marvel Universe. Marvel Entertainment 2007 un Illustration
Grades: 9 10 11 12 Adult   741.5; Fic
1. Graphic novels; 2. Superhero graphic novels; 3. Daredevil (Fictional character)
978-0-7851-2470-2, $11.99

Civil War is encompassing the entire Marvel Universe, and the effects of the war are being felt by every hero, villain and civilian. In Civil War: Choosing Sides, five stories shine a spotlight on the wildcards and impact players whose part in the Civil War has yet to be told — including Daredevil/Iron Fist, U.S.Agent, the Irredeemable Ant-Man, Venom and even...Howard the Duck? On Earth, the Sentry confronts his inner demons as the shadows of past and future battles tear him apart. Within The Negative Zone, the walls of 42 are pulled back to reveal the return of one of the Marvel's greatest heroes. And in She-Hulk, Civil War threatens the rights of every American super hero. So whose side will Marvel's top superhuman lawyer fight for? And how can she possibly choose, when she feels one way as She-Hulk, and another as Jen Walters?

I am Iron Man. edited by Jennifer Grunwald. Marvel Worldwide, Inc. 2010 un Illustration
Grades: 7 8 9 10 11 12 Adult   741.5; Fic
1. Graphic novels; 2. Iron Man (Fictional character); 3. Superhero graphic novels
978-0-7851-4558-5, $16.99

The first Iron Man movie, released in 2008, was a major hit, but just like the other superhero movies based on Marvel Comics properties, it wasn't based on any particular Iron Man comics. This book collects a two-issue miniseries based on the movie script, written by Peter David with pencils by Sean Chen, a one-shot written by Christos Gage with pencils by Hugo Petrus, and Iron Man #200, which was written by Denny O'Neil with pencils by Mark Bright and originally published in 1985. David and Chen's comic adapts the movie script, hitting all the high points of the action. Gage and Petrus's one-shot, "Security Measures," looks at the action of the movie from the viewpoint of S.H.I.E.L.D. agent Coulson. Iron Man #200 features a battle between Iron Man and Iron Monger, who is Tony Stark's erstwhile partner Obadiah Stane. The book also includes an interview with Kevin Feige, producer of the Iron Man movie, and photos taken on the movie sets. The book actually cuts down on the amount of violence that was shown in the movie.

Guera, R. M.
Scalped: Indian Country. DC Comics/Vertigo 2007 128p. Illustration
Grades: 12 Adult   741.5; Fic
1. Graphic novels; 2. Mystery graphic novels
978-1-4012-1317-6, $9.99

Fifteen years ago, Dashiell "Dash? Bad Horse ran away from a life of abject poverty and utter hopelessness on the Prairie Rose Indian Reservation in hopes of finding something better. Now he's come back home armed with nothing but a set of nunchucks, a hell-bent-for-leather attitude and one dark secret, to find nothing much has changed on "The Rez" — short of a glimmering new casino, and a once-proud people overcome by drugs and organized crime. Is he here to set things right or just get a piece of the action? This book has lots of graphic violence, harsh language, nudity, and sexual situations.
Volume 1 of 10

Guggenheim, Marc
Civil War: Wolverine. Marvel Entertainment 2007 un Illustration
Grades: 10 11 12 Adult   741.5; Fic
1. Graphic novels; 2. Superhero graphic novels; 3. Wolverine (Fictional character)

978-0-7851-1980-7, $17.99

In the aftermath of the Stamford tragedy, Logan makes it his personal mission to take down the man responsible. No sooner does he begin his hunt, however, than he discovers someone else is stalking the same prey: a mysterious trio whose identity, and disturbing mission, unsettles him. This book includes some bloody violence and some strong language.

Guibert, Emmanuel
★ **Alan's** war. First Second 2008 304p. Illustration
Grades: 10 11 12 Adult   **92; 940.54; 741.5**
1. Biographical graphic novels; 2. Graphic novels; 3. Soldiers; 4. Veterans; 5. World War, 1939-1945 — Graphic novels; 6. Cope, Alan Ingram, 1925-1999 — Graphic novels
978-1-59643-096-9; 1-59643-096-6, $24

                                         LC 2007-46190

French cartoonist Guibert met and became friends with Alan Cope and interviewed him at length to create this book. It recreates Cope's memories of being an eighteen-year-old G.I. during World War II. Unlike the war movies that focus on battles, this book focuses on more everyday, mundane memories of the day-to-day life of a soldier. Cope frankly describes a bout with crabs (genital lice), matter-of-factly tells of casual man-to-man sexual encounters among the soldiers, and gives the reader a feel for what happened back then. He also talks about postwar relationships and travels.

This is a "poignant and frank graphic memoir of young soldier who was told to serve his country in WWII and how it changed him forever.... Cope and Guibert forge a story that resonates with humanity." Publ Wkly

★ The **photographer**. [by] Emmanuel Guibert, Didier Lefèvre and Frédéric Lemercier; translated by Alexis Siegel. First Second 2009 267p. Illustration; Map
Grades: 11 12 Adult   **92; 741.5; 958.1**
978-1-59643-375-5; 1-59643-375-2, $29.95

"In 1986, photographer Didier Lefèvre documented a seasoned Médecins sans Frontières (Doctors without Borders) team en route to a region in the way of the insurgents' war with the Soviet army supporting Afghanistan's then-Marxist government. This wedding of his photos and Guibert's European-realist comics records his arduous, frightening round trip from Normandy, where his mother lived." (Booklist)

Gulledge, Laura Lee
★ **Page** by Paige. Amulet Books 2011 un Illustration
Grades: 7 8 9 10 11 12   **741.5; Fic**
1. Artists — Graphic novels; 2. Friendship — Graphic novels; 3. Graphic novels; 4. Humorous graphic novels; 5. New York (N.Y.) — Graphic novels
0-8109-9721-5; 0-8109-9722-3 (pa); 978-0-8109-9721-9, $18.95; 978-0-8109-9722-6 (pa), $9.95

Teenage Paige Turner (blame her writer parents) moves to New York City from Virginia, and she finds the big city rather overwhelming. She decides to buy a sketchbook and sort out her thoughts and feelings in drawings. Soon she does make some friends, and she explores more of the city, but as she begins to feel happier, she clashes with her parents. All of this goes into her sketchbook journal, which she starts to show to her new friends — Jules, Longo, and Gabe. The book is organized by Paige's "rules," which she uses to try to change herself, such as "Rule #2: Draw what you know. If you feel it or see it...DRAW IT!"

"Gulledge's b&w illustrations are simple but well-suited to their subject matter; the work as a whole is a good-natured, optimistic portrait of a young woman evolving toward adulthood." Publ Wkly

Gunter, Miles
Zombee. Image Comics 2006 un Illustration
Grades: 10 11 12 Adult   **741.5; Fic**

1. Graphic novels; 2. Horror graphic novels; 3. Humorous graphic novels
978-1-58240-662-6, $12.99

A dutiful Samurai, a madcap Ninja and a bizarro Zen Monk team up to battle the undead in Feudal Japan. Can these unlikely allies stay friends long enough to stop the zombees from taking over their homeland? Gory and violent zombie-destroying action combines with comedy and foul language (most of it very anachronistic); the cover image, with the zombie head flying amongst sprays of blood while a samurai holds his sword, lets the reader know exactly what to expect.

Gurewich, Nicholas
The **Trial** of Colonel Sweeto and other stories: a collection of the comic strips. Dark Horse Comics 2007 96p. Illustration
Grades: 11 12 Adult   **741.5**
1. Graphic novels; 2. Humorous graphic novels
978-1-59307-844-7, $14.95

Gurewich's Perry Bible Fellowship is a popular webcomic; now they're collected into this hardcover volume. The full-color strips betray a twisted sense of humor with a strong bias for the bizarre, and some strips use nudity and violence.

Hadley, Amy Reeder
Moon Girl and Devil Dinosaur; Volume 1: BFF. by Amy Reeder and Brandon Montclare; illustrated by Natacha Bustos. Marvel Enterprises 2016 136 p. Color; Illustration
Grades: 7 8 9 10 11 12 Adult   **741.5; Fic**
1. Female superhero graphic novels; 2. Dinosaurs — Graphic novels
1302900056; 9781302900052, $17.99

"Lunella LaFayette is a preteen super genius who wants to change the world—but learned the hard way that it takes MORE than just big brains. Fearful of the monstrous INHUMAN genes inside her, life is turned upside down when a savage, red-scaled tyrant is teleported from prehistoric past to a far-flung future we call TODAY. " (Publisher's note)

Contains material originally published in magazine form as MOON GIRL AND DEVIL DINOSAUR #1-6; Volume 1 in an ongoing series

Hale, Dean
★ **Calamity** Jack. Bloombury 2010 144p. Illustration
Grades: 4 5 6 7 8 9   **741.5; Fic**
1. Adventure graphic novels; 2. Fantasy graphic novels; 3. Folklore — Graphic novels; 4. Graphic novels
9781599903736, $14.99; 9781599900766, $19.99

                                          LC 2008-41332

In this sequel to Rapunzel's Revenge, the reader meets Jack as a child growing up in the city of Shyport; Jack has been a schemer practically since birth, but he hasn't had a whole lot of luck. His schemes usually end in unforeseen consequences. When he goes up against the giant Blunderboar, the magic beanstalk he uses to reach the giant's floating fortress destroys his neighborhood and his mother's bakery, and he just manages to leave town with a certain gold-egg-laying goose under his arm. After the events of the first book, Jack and Rapunzel come to Shyport, where Jack hopes to help his mother rebuild her bakery with the golden eggs he now has. However, they come to a city transformed Blunderboar has taken over, his security company claims to be keeping giant ants at bay, and Jack's mother is being held prisoner. Jack is still wanted for what he had done, and only Prudence, Jack's hat-loving pixie partner-in-crime, is willing to help. Then Jack and Rapunzel meet Freddie Sparksmith, newspaperman and gadget inventor, and they team up for a rescue mission. The book includes a lot of action and some non-gory violence.

Companion to: Rapunzel's Revenge

Halliday, Ayun

Peanut. Ayun Halliday; illustrated by Paul Hoppe. Schwartz & Wade Books 2012 216 p. Color illustration

Grades: 6 7 8 9 10   **741.5**

1. Food allergy — Fiction; 2. Graphic novels; 3. High schools — Fiction; 4. Mothers and daughters — Fiction; 5. Moving, Household — Fiction; 6. Popularity — Fiction; 7. Schools — Fiction; 8. Moving — Graphic novels; 9. Peanut allergy — Graphic novels; 10. School stories

037586590X, $15.99; 0375965904, $18.99; 9780375865909, $15.99; 9780375965906, $18.99

LC 2009047168

In this graphic novel by Ayun Halliday, illustrated by Paul Hoppe, "Sadie has the perfect plan to snag some friends when she transfers to Plainfield High — pretend to have a peanut allergy. But what happens when you have to hand in that student health form your unsuspecting mom was supposed to fill out? And what if your new friends want to come over and your mom serves them snacks? (Peanut butter sandwich, anyone?)" (Publisher's note)

Hama, Larry

The **Battle** of First Bull Run: The Civil War Begins. The Rosen Publishing Group 2007 48p. Illustration

Grades: 3 4 5 6 7 8 9   **741.5; 973.7**

1. Bull Run. 1st Battle of, 1861 — Graphic novels; 2. Graphic novels; 3. War — Graphic novels; 4. United States — History — 1861-1865, Civil War — Graphic novels

978-1-4042-0776-9, $29.25

Three months after the shelling of Fort Sumter, Union and Confederate forces met for the first time in earnest combat. However, neither side was prepared at this early stage of the war, and confusion reigned on the battlefield. Finally, Confederate reinforcements forced the Union army into a panicked retreat. The intensity — and ill preparedness — of both armies convinced the nation that the conflict between the states would be a long, bloody ordeal. The book includes background information, a glossary, and a list of books for further reading.

Part of the Graphic Battles of the Civil War series. The book is also available in paperback from Osprey Publishing under the title The War is On!: Battle of First Bull Run.

The **battle** of Iwo Jima: guerilla warfare in the Pacific. by Larry Hama; illustrated by Anthony Williams. Rosen Pub. 2007 48p. Illustration; Map (Graphic battles of World War II)

Grades: 5 6 7 8 9   **940.54**

1. Graphic novels; 2. Iwo Jima, Battle of, 1945 — Graphic novels; 3. World War, 1939-1945 — Graphic novels

978-1-4042-0781-3 (lib bdg), $29.25; 1-4042-0781-3 (lib bdg)

LC 2006007645

"Using a graphic novel to introduce the battle for Iwo Jima makes it very accessible. Before the graphic-novel section of the book begins, Hama provides a short, informative background piece describing the run-up to World War II, the significance of the Japanese war machine, and the importance of the tiny island of Iwo Jima. Then the graphic novel, illustrated by Williams in camouflage colors, does a terrific job of examining the ups and downs of the battle as well as the horror of so many losses — on both sides." Booklist

Includes bibliographical references

Spider-Girl presents Wild Thing: crash course. Marvel Entertainment 2007 un Illustration

Grades: 5 6 7 8 9 10   **741.5**

1. Adventure graphic novels; 2. Graphic novels; 3. Superhero graphic novels

978-0-7851-2606-5, $7.99

A few years in the future, in the alternate Marvel Universe where Peter Parker and Mary Jane had a daughter who has become Spider-Girl, Wolverine and Elektra got together and they had a daughter, too Rina Logan, also known as Wild Thing. She has psychic claws that work pretty much like Wolverine's claws, and she has his fast healing power. She still has to deal with high school even as she fights against bad guys, demons, evil droids, and more.

Hamboussi, Peter

Showcase Presents The Flash, Volume One. DC Comics 2007 509p. Illustration

Grades: 7 8 9 10 11 12 Adult   **741.5; Fic**

1. Graphic novels; 2. Superhero graphic novels; 3. Flash (Fictional character)

978-1-4012-1327-5, $16.99

A freak accident gives Central City police scientist Barry Allen fantastic super-speed abilities. Inspired by his favorite childhood comic book hero, Allen uses the name the Flash and uses his powers to help humanity. He soon finds himself facing such villains as Captain Cold, Mirror Master, Gorilla Grodd, the Pied Piper, Weather Wizard, and more. This volume collects 39 stories from the 1950s and 1960s in black and white.

Showcase Presents: Legion of Super-Heroes Volume 1. DC Comics 2007 552p. Illustration

Grades: 7 8 9 10 11 12 Adult   **741.5; Fic**

1. Graphic novels; 2. Legion of Super-Heroes (Fictional characters); 3. Superhero graphic novels

978-1-4012-1382-4, $16.99

The Legion of Super-Heroes, teenagers from across the cosmos, each with a unique ability, are the sworn protectors of the galaxy. Headquartered in their Super-Hero Club House, Lightning Lad, Saturn Girl, and Cosmic Boy have high standards for young hopeful champions wishing to join their ranks. With the largest roster of any super-team of the 2960s, they patrol all sectors of the universe to ensure peace and justice for all sentient beings. This volume collects black and white reprints of stories originally published from 1958 through 1964.

Showcase Presents: Martian Manhunter Volume 1. DC Comics 2007 544p. Illustration

Grades: 7 8 9 10 11 12 Adult   **741.5; Fic**

1. Graphic novels; 2. Martian Manhunter (Fictional character); 3. Superhero graphic novels

978-1-4012-1368-8, $16.99

After being accidentally teleported to Earth, Martian J'onn J'onzz finds himself stranded in a strange new world, with no way home. Using his powers to disguise his appearance, J'onn J'onzz adopts the name of deceased Denver police detective John Jones. With this new identity, he joins the Middleton Police force, secretly using his powers to help the inhabitants of Earth. Jack Miller and Joe Samachson were principal writers on the series in the early years, and artist Joe Certa did all the pencils; this black and white volume reprints stories originally published from 1953 through 1962.

Tangent Comics, volume one. Edited by Peter Hamboussi. DC Comics 2007 206p. Illustration

Grades: 9 10 11 12 Adult   **741.5**

1. Graphic novels; 2. Superhero graphic novels; 3. Flash (Fictional character); 4. Green Lantern (Fictional character)

978-1-4012-1530-9, $19.99

In 1997, DC published a series of comics featuring familiar character names, but they were all...different. The Atom had atomic powers, the Flash (a woman) was made of light, the Metal Men weren't robots but soldiers, the Green Lantern was a woman and used an artifact to raise the dead for one final mission, and so on. Now, DC has collected some of the stories into this trade paperback collection.

Haney, Bob

Showcase Presents: Metamorpho, the Element Man Volume 1. DC Comics 2005 560p. Illustration
Grades: 7 8 9 10 11 12 Adult   **741.5; Fic**
  1. Graphic novels; 2. Science fiction graphic novels; 3. Superhero graphic novels
1-4012-0762-6, $16.99
Adventurer Rex Mason would do almost anything for the right price, but he ended up paying with his own humanity for stealing the legendary Orb of Ra for millionaire industrialist Simon Stagg. The mysterious relic transformed Rex into a freakish "element" man, with the ability to transform his body into hundreds of different substances. Calling himself Metamorpho, Rex considered his life cursed and sought a way to reverse the Orb's powers. Along the way, Stagg used Metamorpho's unique skills for his own purposes, and the Element Man would go along, since it meant more time with Stagg's gorgeous daughter Sapphire. The stories in this black and white volume date from 1964 through 1966.

Showcase Presents: Teen Titans Volume 1. stories by Bob Haney; art and covers by Nick Cardy. DC Comics 2006 528p. Illustration
Grades: 6 7 8 9 10 11 12 Adult   **741.5; Fic**
  1. Graphic novels; 2. Superhero graphic novels; 3. Teen Titans (Fictional characters); 4. Robin (Fictional character); 5. Flash (Fictional character)
978-1-4012-0788-5, $16.99
The Teen Titans were all sidekicks to such heroes as Batman, Wonder Woman, Aquaman, and the Flash. When teen heroes Robin, Aqualad, and Kid Flash joined together, they became a forced to be reckoned with. Wonder Girl quickly joined them, and occasionally Speedy would come, and they all proved they were just as capable of defeating the bad guys and saving the world as their mentors, while still being teens and having fun. The black and white reprinted stories originally appeared from 1964 through 1968. Today's teens will get a kick out of what the writers thought was cool "teen speak" back then.

Showcase Presents: Sgt. Rock. DC Comics 2007 543p. Illustration
Grades: 8 9 10 11 12 Adult   **741.5**
  1. Adventure graphic novels; 2. Graphic novels; 3. Sgt. Rock (Fictional character); 4. World War, 1939-1945 — Graphic novels
978-1-4012-1713-6, $16.99
Sgt. Rock, created by Robert Kanigher, was an ordinary soldier fighting in World War II. The stories collected in this volume, published from 1959 through 1962, depict Rock and his Easy Company fighting against evil during the war. Even today, Sgt. Rock is a symbol of patriotism and of America's fighting spirit. The stories include battle action.

Hanuka, Tomer

Attack on Titan anthology. Attack on Titan created by Hajime Isayama; edited by Ben Applegate and Jeanine Schaefer; cover, logo, and interior design by Phil Balsman; lettering and interior design by Steve Wands. Kodansha 2016 256 p. Illustration
Grades: 8 9 10 11 12   **741.5**
  1. Fantasy fiction — Graphic novels; 2. Horror fiction — Graphic novels; 3. Science fiction graphic novels; 4. Shonen manga
1632362589; 9781632362582, $29.99
This tribute anthology to the manga Attack on Titan features "original stories by a long roster of comic superstars such as Scott Snyder (Batman, American Vampire), Gail Simone (Batgirl), Michael Avon Oeming (Powers), Paolo Rivera (Daredevil, Amazing Spider-Man), Cameron Stewart (Fight Club 2, Batgirl) and Faith Erin Hicks (The Adventures of Superhero Girl)!" (Publisher's note)

"The Victorian-style guide to Titan's walled city by Genevieve Valentine and David López is a standout, as is the contemplative final story by brothers Asaf and Tomer Hanuka." Pub Wkly

Hara, Hidenori

Train_Man: Densha Otoko, Vol. 1. Viz Media 2006 208p. Illustration
Grades: 9 10 11 12   **741.5; Fic**
  1. Graphic novels; 2. Romance graphic novels; 3. Seinen manga
978-1-4215-0848-1, $9.99
This is another manga version of the Train Man story from Japan, which tells the story of how a young anime fanatic uses advice from an online forum (2channel) to date and then pursue a romantic relationship with a young woman he saved from a harasser. This version utilizes most of the Japanese emoticons used by the forum members. It's written for a slightly older audience than Densha Otoko; on one page, Train_Man imagines Hermess (the young woman) in the shower.

Harper, Charise Mericle

Fashion Kitty. Hyperion Books for Children 2005 90p. Illustration
Grades: 3 4 5 6 7 8 9   **741.5; Fic**
  1. Cats — Graphic novels; 2. Graphic novels; 3. Humorous graphic novels
0-7868-5134-1, $8.99
Kiki Kittie is a very unusual cat. For one thing, she has a mouse for a pet — and that's kind of like a human having a chocolate cake for a pet. Kiki also has a natural flair for fashion, but up until a recent birthday, she was just an ordinary fashionable kitty. Then, on that day, she discovered that she had special powers: she can turn into Fashion Kitty, able to mix and match hundreds of outfits in a single second. Regular cat by day, Fashion Kitty by night, Kiki is always ready to answer a call of despair and save other cats from making fashion faux pas
Other titles about Fashion Kitty are: Fashion Kitty versus the Fashion Queen (2007); Fashion Kitty and the unlikely hero (2008); Fashion Kitty and the B.O.Y.S. (2011)

Fashion Kitty Versus the Fashion Queen. Hyperion Paperbacks for Children 2007 90p. Illustration
Grades: 3 4 5 6 7 8 9   **741.5; Fic**
  1. Cats — Graphic novels; 2. Graphic novels; 3. Humorous graphic novels
978-0-7868-3726-7, $8.99
After her last adventure, Fashion Kitty is truly becoming a hero. At school, she is more popular than ever. She's even been mentioned in several articles in the local newspaper, (which she clips out and saves in a scrapbook, of course). But not everyone is excited about Fashion Kitty's newfound popularity. A spoiled new kitty named Cassandra doesn't like sharing the spotlight. And when Fashion Kitty starts inspiring the other kitties at school to be more independent about their style choices, Cassandra really doesn't like it. So she hatches a plan (evil, of course) that involves lying, conniving, and outlawing bright colors and patterns. Fashion Kitty knows she must put an end to Cassandra's reign of terror. She will use her fashion sense, quick smarts, and the power of friendship to overcome fashion evil.

Harras, Bob

Showcase Presents The Unknown Soldier Volume 1. DC Comics 2006 552p. Illustration
Grades: 8 9 10 11 12 Adult   **741.5; Fic**
  1. Adventure graphic novels; 2. Graphic novels; 3. Unknown Soldier (Fictional character)
978-1-4012-1090-8, $16.99
His face hideously disfigured by a grenade explosion in the early days of World War II, the young man who would become the Unknown Soldier

was determined to continue fighting for his country. His true identity kept top secret, he became the perfect covert operative, using a multitude of disguises to carry out his exploits against the Axis powers. The first 38 adventures of the Unknown Soldier are collected in this black and white reprint volume, with stories dating from 1970 through 1975.

Showcase Presents: The War That Time Forgot. DC Comics 2007 560p. Illustration
Grades: 6 7 8 9 10 11 12 Adult   **741.5; Fic**
1. Adventure graphic novels; 2. Dinosaurs — Graphic novels; 3. Graphic novels; 4. World War, 1939-1945 — Graphic novels
978-1-4012-1253-7, $16.99
On an unnamed, uncharted Pacific island, dinosaurs continued to thrive while World War II raged across the globe. It is on this island that members of the U.S. Armed Forces found themselves " armed only with standard issue weapons against the deadliest predators ever to roam the Earth. This volume collects Star Spangled War Stories issues #90-128, from 1960 through 1966. There's a lot of war action and dinosaur-fighting action. The stories here have been reprinted in black and white.

Superman: Back in Action. DC Comics 2007 144p. Illustration
Grades: 8 9 10 11 12 Adult   **741.5; Fic**
1. Graphic novels; 2. Superhero graphic novels; 3. Superman (Fictional character)
978-1-4012-1263-6, $14.99
This book collects several stories. When Superman returns after the events of Infinite Crisis, he faces skepticism from the people and then gets kidnapped and put up for an intergalactic auction. In stories from the past, he encounters the Metal Men, Firestorm, and Deadman.

Harris, Micah
Heaven's War. Micah Harris, writer; Michael Gaydos, artist. Image Comics 2003 118p. Illustration
Grades: 9 10 11 12 Adult   **741.5**
1. Adventure graphic novels; 2. Fantasy graphic novels; 3. Graphic novels
1-58240-330-9, $12.95
In this graphic novel, "J.R.R. Tolkien and C.S. Lewis are called upon by eccentric fellow fantasist Charles Williams to join him against occultist Aleister Crowley. Crowley seeks an entrance into the Heavenly realms with the intent of manipulating the angelic battles that shape human history and thus mold the world according to his will. Their conflict with Crowley will take this trio of authors...to the very edge of Heaven." (Publisher's note)

Hart, Christopher
The **reformed.** Del Rey Manga 2008 170p. Illustration
Grades: 10 11 12 Adult   **741.5; Fic**
1. Fantasy graphic novels; 2. Graphic novels; 3. Horror graphic novels; 4. Mystery graphic novels; 5. Vampires — Graphic novels
978-0-345-49663-8, $10.95
Handsome, wealthy Giancarlo is a vampire who has lived for hundreds of years and is lonely. Then he meets Jenny, a beautiful young woman who stirs feelings he hasn't known for centuries; he's willing to become mortal again to be with her. However, brutal, ghoulish murders plaguing the city have made him the target of a relentless homicide cop. And the real killer, a dangerous vampire, also wants to destroy Giancarlo. The book includes graphic, bloody violence.

Hartland, Jessie
Steve Jobs: insanely great. Jessie Hartland. Schwartz & Wade Books 2015 272 p. Illustration
Grades: 9 10 11 12 Adult   **338.761; 92**

1. Computer engineers — United States — Biography; 2. Graphic novels; 3. Jobs, Steve, 1955-2011; 4. Computer programming
0307982955; 9780307982957, $22.95; 9780307982964
LC 2014005768
Author Jessie Hartland presents this "biography in graphic format [as a] complement to more text-heavy books on Steve Jobs like Walter Isaacson's biography. Presenting the story of the ultimate American entrepreneur, who brought us Apple Computer, Pixar, Macs, iPods, iPhones and more, this unique and stylish book is sure to appeal to the legions of readers who live and breathe the techno-centric world Jobs created." (Publisher's note)
"Luddites and iFans alike should find this volume an illuminating introduction to Jobs's life and the recent history of consumer electronics." SLJ
Includes bibliographical references and index

Hartzell, Andy
★ **Fox** bunny funny. Top Shelf Productions 2007 102p. Illustration
Grades: 9 10 11 12 Adult   **741.5; Fic**
1. Animals — Graphic novels; 2. Fantasy graphic novels; 3. Graphic novels; 4. Stories without words — Graphic novels
978-1-891830-97-6, $10
The rules are simple: you're either a fox or a bunny. Foxes oppress and devour, bunnies suffer and die. Everyone knows their place. Everyone's satisfied. So what happens when a secret desire puts you at odds with your society? Starting from a simple premise — and without using a single word — this book leads the reader on a zigzag chase in and out of rabbit holes, and through increasingly strange landscapes where funny animals have serious identity problems. The tale swerves from slapstick to horror and back again before landing at the inevitable climax, in which all the old rules are shattered. Some moments of violence and dismemberment might be disturbing for some readers.
"Deftly presented in crisp black-and-white, block-print-like panels, this is a must for libraries supporting LGBT collections." Booklist

Hashiguchi, Takashi
Yakitate!! Japan, Vol. 1. Viz Media 2006 196p. Illustration
Grades: 10 11 12 Adult   **741.5; Fic**
1. Baking — Graphic novels; 2. Bread — Graphic novels; 3. Graphic novels; 4. Manga; 5. Shonen manga
978-1-4215-0719-4, $9.99
When still a little boy, Kazuma Azuma became fascinated with bread after meeting a baker who taught him how to bake it. He begins to experiment with baking different types of bread to find the one he can call "Ja-pan," the national bread of Japan ("pan" is Japanese for bread). At sixteen, Kazuma is almost totally self-taught, but he gets accepted as a candidate for employment at Pantasia, a bakery chain. Only one person can become the new baker at Pantasia, and Kazuma intends to win,...but he is totally ignorant of European bread names (such as croissants). This series is an example of a genre unique to manga, a story focused on food. Most of the action takes place in kitchens, but there's some crude humor.
Volume 1 of 26

Hashimoto, Kyoko
Love master A, vol.1. Go! Comi 2008 un Illustration
Grades: 7 8 9 10 11 12   **741.5; Fic**
1. Graphic novels; 2. Humorous graphic novels; 3. Manga; 4. Romance graphic novels; 5. Shojo manga
978-1933617-60-2, $10.99
Aria starts at a new high school, hoping to have a normal school experience. Since elementary school, when she confessed her love to a classmate and was summarily rejected, she has suffered rejection all

through school and earned the ironic nickname "Love Master." Now, she has renounced love. However, on her first day at school, she discovers the school's strange way of selecting Student Council members, and not only is she as a first year student a Student Council member, she is the President! And her reputation has been twisted so everyone thinks she's a real "Love Master" and wants her advice. Tonohashi High School is in for a very interesting year.

Hata, Kenjiro
Hayate the Combat Butler Volume 1. Viz Media 2006 182p. Illustration
Grades: 10 11 12 Adult   **741.5; Fic**
1. Graphic novels; 2. Humorous graphic novels; 3. Manga; 4. Romance graphic novels; 5. Shonen manga
978-1-4215-0851-1, $9.99
Hardworking teenager Hayate has a plan to pay back the yakuza — who are now the legal owners of his vital organs (thanks to his deadbeat parents): he'll kidnap someone and ransom them for a mountain of money. But things get tricky when his would-be kidnappee — who as luck would have it is the daughter of a mind-bogglingly wealthy family — mistakes Hayate's actions for a confession of love, and hires him to be her personal servant. At least his employment future is secure, or so he thinks... The book includes some strong language and mild sexual situations.

Hatori, Bisco
Ouran High School Host Club Volume 1. Viz Media/Shojo Beat 2005 184p. Illustration
Grades: 9 10 11 12 Adult   **741.5; Fic**
1. Graphic novels; 2. Humorous graphic novels; 3. Manga; 4. Shojo manga
1-59116-915-1, $8.99
Haruhi is a scholarship student at an exclusive private school: Ouran High School, where it turns out the bespectacled, short-haired Haruhi is the only student from a lower-middle class family in attendance. Then, to make matters worse, one day she breaks an $80,000 vase that belongs to one of the campus clubs, a mysterious outfit called the "Host Club," consisting of six superrich (and gorgeous) guys. Haruhi can't afford to pay back the cost of the vase, of course, so she's forced to work for the Host Club. And it's there that she discovers just how rich all the boys are and how different the rich are from "regular" folks...And meanwhile, the eccentric but good-hearted rich boys are shocked to find out how life is on the other side...
Volume 1 of 18

Hayakawa, Tomoko
The **Wallflower** 1: Yamatonadeshiko Shichihenge. Random House/Del Rey Manga 2004 224p. Illustration
Grades: 10 11 12 Adult   **741.5; Fic**
1. Graphic novels; 2. Humorous graphic novels; 3. Manga; 4. Shojo manga
0-345-47912-2, $10.95
It's a gorgeous, spacious mansion, and four handsome, fifteen-year-old friends are allowed to live in it for free. There's only one condition — that within three years the guys must transform the owner's wallflower niece into a lady befitting the palace in which they all live. How hard can it be? Enter Sunako Nakahara, the agoraphobic, horror-movie-loving, pockmark-faced, frizzy-haired, fashion-illiterate recluse who tends to break into explosive nosebleeds whenever she sees anyone attractive. This project is going to take more than the four heroes ever expected: it needs a miracle. The series includes some mildly harsh language, some mild sexual situations, and mild violence.

Hayashi, Fumino
Neon Genesis Evangelion: Angelic Days Vol. 1. ADV Manga 2006 184p. Illustration
Grades: 10 11 12 Adult
741.5; Fic
1. Graphic novels; 2. Manga; 3. Romance graphic novels; 4. Science fiction graphic novels; 5. Shojo manga
978-1-4139-0344-7, $9.99
This manga series is set in the world of Neon Genesis Evangelion, but in this series, life isn't quite so angst-ridden. Choosing the right girl is more important than saving the world. The book includes some mild sexual situations.

Courtesy of ADV Manga

Hayashi, Mikase
March on earth, volume one. DC Comics/CMX 2009 un Illustration
Grades: 7 8 9 10 11 12   **741.5; Fic**
1. Family life — Graphic novels; 2. Graphic novels; 3. Manga; 4. Romance graphic novels; 5. Shojo manga
978-1-4012-1594-1, $9.99
When Yuzu was a young girl, her older sister Tsubaki raised her after their parents died. Then a few years ago, Tsubaki got pregnant and decided to have the baby and raise him as a single parent; she would never tell Yuzu who the father was. Just a few months ago, Tsubaki died in a car accident, and Yuzu, now a 10th grader in high school, has decided she will raise her nephew Shou herself. She and Shou live in an apartment in the building owned by Mrs. Kusano, who lives there with her two sons, Seita and Keita. They help her take care of Shou, but even with their help it's difficult to focus on her studies. She reads her sister's picture books to Shou, especially the last one Tsubaki wrote, called March on Earth. Yuzu wants to become a lawyer to help people, but will there be enough money from what her parents left to pay for college, after paying for rent and all the other expenses? Other teens worry about boyfriends, and whether they should go sing karaoke, but Yuzu has to take care of a two-year-old boy and worry about having enough money to buy him one Christmas present. She doesn't seem to see that Seita has fallen for her, and she seems to be oblivious to his efforts to appear before her half naked (wearing only an apron to cook curry, claiming to have just come out of the bath with only a towel around his waist, ...).

Heer, Margreet de
Science, a discovery in comics. Margreet de Heer. NBM Publishing 2013 192 p. (A discovery in comics)
Grades: 9 10 11 12 Adult
500
1. Scientists — History; 2. Science
1561637505; 9781561637508, $19.99
          LC 2013939851
"This history of scientific discovery, [by Margreet de Heer] is presented as a series of conversations about understanding the laws that govern the universe.... Beginning with the ideals of scientific observation and inquiry, the book moves to detailed chronologies of the evolutions of biology, physics, geology, etc. Much of the

Courtesy of NBM Publishing

information is organized in time-line form, which is used to depict the gradual accumulation and transformation of concepts." (School Library Journal)

"Although the information on any one topic is very basic, a great many topics are treated, thanks to the economy of de Heer's visual presentation, and they are all handled very well, thanks to the energy of her drawing style and the vividness of Kohl's coloring." Booklist

Heinberg, Allan

Avengers: the children's crusade. Allan Heinberg, writer; Jim Cheung, penciler; Mark Morales, et al., inkers; Justin Ponsor, Paul Mounts, colorists; VC's Cory Petit, letterer. Marvel Worldwide 2012 248 p.

Grades: 9 10 11 12   **741.5/973; Fic**
1. Voyages and travels — Graphic novels; 2. Superhero comic books, strips, etc.
0785135499; 9780785135494, $29.99

In this comic book, "the Young Avengers are the heroes of tomorrow. But two of their members-twin brothers Wiccan and Speed-are boys without a past. When Wiccan's powers begin spiraling out of control, the team sets out to find the one person who might be able to help: the Scarlet Witch, who may be the twins' mother, and whose own uncontrollable powers once almost destroyed the Avengers and nearly wiped out the mutant race." (Publisher's note)

Young Avengers Vol. 1: Sidekicks. writer, Allan Heinberg; pencils, Jim Cheung; inks, John Dell, Mark Morales & Drew Geraci; colors, Justin Ponsor; letters, Virtual Calligraphy's Cory Petit. Marvel Entertainment 2006 un Illustration

Grades: 9 10 11 12 Adult   **741.5; Fic**
1. Graphic novels; 2. Superhero graphic novels
978-0-7851-2018-6, $14.99

"In the wake of Avengers Disassembled, a mysterious new group of teen super heroes appears. But who are they? Where did they come from? And what right do they have to call themselves the Young Avengers?" (Publisher's note)

Helfand, Lewis

Conquering Everest: the lives of Edmund Hillary and Tenzing Norgay. Campfire 2011 96p. Illustration

Grades: 10 3 4 5 6 7 8 9   **741.5; 796.522**
1. Mountaineering — Graphic novels; 2. Mountaineers; 3. Nonfiction writers; 4. Hillary, Edmund Sir; 5. Tenzing Norgay, 1914-1986; 6. Mount Everest — Graphic novels
978-93-80741-24-6, $12.99

Tenzing Norgay immigrated to Nepal with his Tibetan family when he was a boy, and he worked hard over the years to become one of the best Sherpas who helped the European, American, and other climbers who journeyed to Nepal to climb Mount Everest. Edmund Hillary was the son of a beekeeper from New Zealand, who became fascinated with mountain climbing during World War II. He came to Nepal in 1953 as part of a British expedition to reach Everest's peak, and Norgay came to be the sirdar, the head Sherpa and organizer of the expedition's support system. These two men became the first to reach Everest's summit at 11:30 a.m. on May 29, 1953. This graphic novel tells the story of the two men from such different backgrounds, and their friendship. The book notes that on May 22, 2010, Californian thirteen-year-old Jordan Romero became the youngest climber to reach Everest's peak. Tayal's panels show some of the massive scale of the mountain.

Mother Teresa: Angel of the Slums. by Lewis Helfand and illustrated by Sachin Nagar. Random House Inc 2013 88 p.

Grades: 6 7 8 9   **271.9**
1. Teresa, Mother, 1910-1997
9380028709; 9789380028705, $11.99

This illustrated biography written by Lewis Helfand and illustrated by Sachin Nagar "presents the facts about Mother Teresa, born Agnes Gonxha

Bojaxhiu in Macedonia in 1910. The book describes her decision to become a nun, her early work in Europe, and her path to teaching at a convent in India. From there it covers, in greater detail, her life among the poor and sick in Calcutta, and the foundation of Mother Teresa's worldwide charitable order." (Publisher's Weekly)

Nelson Mandela: the unconquerable soul. Lewis Herlfand. Kalyani Navyug Media Pvt LTD 2011 115 p.

Grades: 8 9 10   **741.5; 92**
1. South Africa — History — Graphic novels; 2. Biographical graphic novels; 3. Mandela, Nelson, 1918-
9380741162; 9789380741161, $12.99

LC 2012374765

This book is a graphic novel biography of Nelson Mandela. It "includes a brief history of 20th-century South Africa along with a full account of Mandela's full life.... [B]lack, white, and gray illustrations are" included. "Endnotes include a glossary and additional facts about South Africa." (School Library Journal)

Helfer, Andrew

Malcolm X: a graphic biography. written by Andrew Helfer; art by Randy DuBurke. Hill and Wang 2006 102p. Illustration

Grades: 10 11 12 Adult   **92; 741.5**
1. African Americans — Biography — Graphic novels; 2. Biographical graphic novels; 3. Black Muslim leaders; 4. Black Muslims — Graphic novels; 5. Civil rights activists; 6. Graphic novels; 7. Malcolm X, 1925-1965
978-0-8090-9504-9; 0-8090-9504-1, $15.95

LC 2006-13743

The authors "tell the story of Malcolm X's short life — his meeting with Dr. Martin Luther King Jr., the two leaders describing the opposite ideological ends of the fight for civil rights; and his eventual assassination by other members of the Nation of Islam (NOI) — in narration and detailed b&white drawings, sharp as photographs in a newspaper.... Helfer and DuBurke have created an evocative and studied look at not only Malcolm X but the racial conflict that defined and shaped him." Publ Wkly

Ronald Reagan: a graphic biography. written by Andrew Helfer; art by Steve Buccellato and Joe Staton. Hill and Wang 2007 102p. Illustration

Grades: 9 10 11 12 Adult   **92; 741.5**
1. Actors; 2. Biographical graphic novels; 3. Governors; 4. Graphic novels; 5. Presidents; 6. Presidents — United States — Graphic novels; 7. Reagan, Ronald, 1911-2004
978-0-8090-9507-0, $16.95

LC 2006-16437

This graphic novel biography covers the life of Ronald Reagan, who began as an actor and ended his career as the fortieth president of the U.S. The book discusses Reagan's work as a union president (Screen Actor's Guild), a General Motors pitchman on television, Governor of California, and his terms as President. It also covers some of the scandals that occurred during his gubernatorial and presidential terms, including the Iran/Contra arms-for-hostages deal, and the assassination attempt by John Hinkley.

Includes bibliographical references; A novel graphic from Hill and Wang

Hennessey, Jonathan

★ The Gettysburg Address: A Graphic Adaptation. by Jonathan Hennessey and illustrated by Aaron McConnell. HarperCollins 2013 224 p.

Grades: 9 10 11 12 Adult   **973.7**
1. Gettysburg (Pa.), Battle of, 1863; 2. Speeches; 3. Lincoln, Abraham, 1809-1865
0061969761; 9780061969768, $15.99

This graphic novel by Jonathan Hennessey and illustrated by Aaron McConnell "is a full-color illustrated look at Abraham Lincoln — s most famous speech, the bloody battle of the Civil War that prompted it, and how they led to a defining point in the history of America. Using Lincoln — s words as a keystone, and drawing from first-person accounts, 'The Gettysburg Address' shows us the events through the eyes of those who lived through the events of the War, from soldiers to slaves." (Publisher's note)

★ The **United** States Constitution: a graphic adaptation. written by Jonathan Hennessey; art by Aaron McConnell. Hill and Wang 2008 149p. Illustration
Grades: 9 10 11 12 Adult   **342; 741.5**
1. Constitutional history — United States — Graphic novels; 2. Graphic novels; 3. United States — Constitution — Graphic novels
978-0-8090-9487-5; 0-8090-9487-8, $35; 978-0-8090-9470-7 (pa); 0-8090-9470-3 (pa), $16.95

LC 2008-17927

The author and illustrator go "through the entire U. S. Constitution, article by article, amendment by amendment, explaining their meaning and implications — in comics format. Avoiding the didactic, the book succeeds in being both consistently entertaining and illuminating." Publ Wkly
Includes bibliographical references

Herge
★ The **adventures** of Tintin, vol. 1: Tintin in America, Cigars of the Pharaoh, The Blue Lotus. Little, Brown 1994 192p. Illustration
Grades: 4 5 6 7 8 9   **741.5; Fic**
1. Adventure graphic novels; 2. Graphic novels; 3. Tintin (Fictional character) — Graphic novels
0-316-35940-8, $18.99

Tintin, the heroic boy reporter from France, travels to America where he outwits gangsters in Chicago of the 1930s and adventures in the Wild West; sails the Mediterranean Sea with faithful dog Snowy and finds himself in a mystery involving a movie tycoon, drugs, and cigars in an ancient Egyptian tomb; then he travels to India to finally solve the mystery. This Little, Brown edition reprints some of the early Tintin adventures published in the 1930s in a 3-in-1 volume. This is the first in a series that reprints most of the Tintin stories by Herge. Librarians and teachers should note that the books retain some stereotypical depictions of people of other cultures and remember that these were acceptable and expected at the time of original publication.

Tintin and the Picaros. Little, Brown 1978 62p. Illustration
Grades: 4 5 6 7 8 9   **741.5; Fic**
1. Adventure graphic novels; 2. Graphic novels; 3. Humorous graphic novels; 4. Tintin (Fictional character)
0-316-35849-5, $10.99

LC 77-090973

Tintin and his friends rescue prima donna Bianca Castafiore while trying to help restore their friend Alcazar to power in San Theodoros — but they'll have to defeat General Tapioca and his troops to do it.

Tintin in Tibet. Little, Brown 1978 62p. Illustration
Grades: 4 5 6 7 8 9   **741.5; Fic**
1. Adventure graphic novels; 2. Graphic novels; 3. Humorous graphic novels; 4. Tintin (Fictional character)
0-316-35839-8, $10.99

LC 80-191368

Tintin, Snowy, and Captain Haddock trek through the snow-covered Himalayas to rescue their friend Chang from the hands of an abominable snowman.

Tintin: The Broken Ear. Little, Brown 1978 62p. Illustration

Grades: 4 5 6 7 8 9   **741.5; Fic**
1. Adventure graphic novels; 2. Graphic novels; 3. Humorous graphic novels; 4. Tintin (Fictional character)
0-316-35850-9, $10.99

LC 77-090970

A fetish which originally belonged to the Arumbayas tribe in San Theodoros is stolen from a museum, then returned; soon Tintin discovers that the returned fetish is a forgery. When he follows the trail of the stolen fetish, it leads him and Snowy to South America and to San Theodoros, where he gets caught in the middle of a civil war. Tintin gets into all kinds of trouble even as he tries to find out why so many people want the fetish.

★ **Tintin:** The Calculus Affair. Little, Brown 1976 62p. Illustration
Grades: 4 5 6 7 8 9   **741.5; Fic**
1. Adventure graphic novels; 2. Graphic novels; 3. Humorous graphic novels; 4. Tintin (Fictional character)
0-316-35847-9, $10.99

LC 76-13280

Unscrupulous Bordurians have kidnapped Professor Calculus, and Tintin, Snowy, and Captain Haddock are soon on the trail again, to rescue their friend. It's no easy task to rescue the Professor and save his fantastic invention; spies are everywhere, and Calculus lies deep in the fortress of Bakhine. But the Bordurians now have to deal with Tintin ...

Tintin: Cigars of the Pharaoh. Little, Brown 1975 62p. Illustration
Grades: 4 5 6 7 8 9   **741.5; Fic**
1. Adventure graphic novels; 2. Graphic novels; 3. Humorous graphic novels; 4. Tintin (Fictional character)
0-316-35836-3, $10.99

LC 74-021620

Tintin and Snowy are on a cruise to Egypt when they happen to meet Professor Sophocles Sarcophagus (the first of Tintin's absent-minded professors) and join his expedition. But they become embroiled in a complicated scheme involving a fakir, cigars marked with an unusual brand, and Rajijah, the poison of madness. Tintin meets the detectives Thompson and Thomson as well as the movie mogul Rastapopolous. Herge wrote this book in 1932 then revised it in 1955.

Tintin: Destination Moon. Little, Brown 1976 62p. Illustration
Grades: 4 5 6 7 8 9   **741.5; Fic**
1. Adventure graphic novels; 2. Graphic novels; 3. Humorous graphic novels; 4. Tintin (Fictional character)
0-316-35845-2, $10.99

LC 76-013279

Professor Calculus has designed a rocket for an expedition to the Moon. He summons Tintin and Captain Haddock (along with Snowy) to the country of Syldavia, where he's been working. Despite spies being everywhere and mysterious explosions and other problems, the rocket is soon ready to launch, and Professor Calculus wants Tintin and Captain Haddock to go with him — to the Moon.

Tintin: Explorers On the Moon. Little, Brown 1976 62p. Illustration
Grades: 4 5 6 7 8 9   **741.5; Fic**
1. Adventure graphic novels; 2. Graphic novels; 3. Humorous graphic novels; 4. Tintin (Fictional character)
0-316-35846-0, $10.99

LC 76-013297

Tintin, Captain Haddock, and Prof. Calculus are headed for the Moon when they discover Thompson and Thomson, who had inadvertently stowed away on the rocket. But there's more trouble when they land on the Moon and go exploring, for Colonel Jorgen is there, another stowaway, and he wants revenge on Tintin.

Tintin: Flight 714. Little, Brown 1975 62p. Illustration
Grades: 4 5 6 7 8 9   **741.5; Fic**

1. Adventure graphic novels; 2. Graphic novels; 3. Humorous graphic novels; 4. Tintin (Fictional character)
0-316-35837-1, $10.99

LC 74-021623

Tintin, Snowy, Captain Haddock, and Professor Calculus land in Djakarta and meet millionaire Mr. Carreidas, who invites them to fly to Sydney with him in his prototype jet. They find themselves in the middle of a plot to steal their new friend's fortune, and they decide to stop it.

Tintin: Land of Black Gold. Little, Brown 1975 62p. Illustration
Grades: 4 5 6 7 8 9 **741.5; Fic**
1. Adventure graphic novels; 2. Graphic novels; 3. Humorous graphic novels; 4. Tintin (Fictional character)
0-316-35844-4, $10.99

LC 75-007896

The world is on the brink of a crisis when car engines begin to explode without explanation or warning; someone has been tampering with the oil supply. Tintin travels to the Middle East to investigate, and he helps Sheik Ben Kalish Ezab, whose son is kidnapped by one of Tintin's old enemies.

Tintin: Prisoners of the Sun. Little, Brown 1975 62p. Illustration
Grades: 4 5 6 7 8 9 **741.5; Fic**
1. Adventure graphic novels; 2. Graphic novels; 3. Humorous graphic novels; 4. Tintin (Fictional character)
0-316-35843-6, $10.99

LC 75-007897

Tintin, Snowy, and Captain Haddock travel to Peru to rescue Professor Calculus. They meet Indian boy Zorrino, and they must travel into the jungle to the Andes to find their old friend.

Tintin: Red Rackham's Treasure. Little, Brown 1974 62p. Illustration
Grades: 4 5 6 7 8 9 **741.5; Fic**
1. Adventure graphic novels; 2. Graphic novels; 3. Humorous graphic novels; 4. Tintin (Fictional character)
0-316-35834-7, $10.99

LC 73-021253

Tintin and his friends search for the pirate booty left by Captain Haddock's pirate ancestor. They're aided in their quest by the hard-of-hearing inventor, Professor Calculus.

Tintin: The Castafiore Emerald. Little, Brown 1975 62p. Illustration
Grades: 4 5 6 7 8 9 **741.5; Fic**
1. Adventure graphic novels; 2. Graphic novels; 3. Humorous graphic novels; 4. Tintin (Fictional character)
0-316-35842-8, $10.99

Tintin and Snowy investigate when prima donna Bianca Castafiore's jewels are stolen, in particular, her emerald.

Tintin: The Seven Crystal Balls. Little, Brown 1975 62p. Illustration
Grades: 4 5 6 7 8 9 **741.5; Fic**
1. Adventure graphic novels; 2. Graphic novels; 3. Humorous graphic novels; 4. Tintin (Fictional character)
0-316-35840-1, $10.99

LC 75-007921

Tragedy strikes the members of an expedition which returned after violating Incan burial chambers; the seven men fall into comas, one by one, and fragments of crystal are found by their bodies. Tintin, Professor Calculus, Captain Haddock, and Thompson and Thomson investigate, but then Calculus disappears — he's been kidnapped.

Hernandez, Gilbert
Chance in hell. Fantagraphics Books 2007 120p. Illustration
Grades: 11 12 Adult **741.5**
1. Graphic novels
978-1-56097-833-6, $16.95

This book tells the story about a little orphan girl who lives in the slum of slums. Nobody knows who she is or where she's from, but her fellow shantytown inhabitants collectively look over her. The three-act story follows the heroine as she is adopted by a decent man who raises her well, and she eventually marries a kind, well-to-do man, only to discover that she can't relate to the good life and the comforts it provides. The book includes sexual situations and lots of foul language, but little nudity.

★ **Heartbreak** Soup: A Love and Rockets Book. Fantagraphics Books 2007 288p. Illustration
Grades: 12 Adult **741.5; Fic**
1. Graphic novels
978-1-56097-783-4, $14.95

This volume collects the first half of Gilbert Hernandez's acclaimed magical-realist tales of "Palomar," the small Central American town, beginning with the groundbreaking "Sopa de Gran Pena" (which introduces most of his main cast of characters as children, plus the imposing newcomer Luba), and continuing on through such modern-day classics as "Ecce Homo," "Act of Contrition," "Duck Feet," and the great love story "For the Love of Carmen." His stories include lots of sexual situations, full nudity, and strong language.

Other Love and Rockets collections by Gilbert Hernandez are: Human Diastrophism; Beyond Palomar; Luba and Her Family; Ofelia

★ **Human** Diastrophism. Fantagraphics Books 2007 256p. Illustration (Love and Rockets)
Grades: 12 Adult **741.5; Fic**
1. Graphic novels
9781560978480, $14.95; 1560978481

This volume collects the second half of Gilbert Hernandez's acclaimed magical-realist tales of "Palomar," the small Central American town, beginning with the landmark "Human Diastrophism," the only full graphic novel length "Palomar" story ever created by Gilbert. In it, a serial killer stalks Palomar-but his depredations, hideous as they are, only serve to exacerbate the cracks in the idyllic Central American town as the modern world begins to intrude. "Diastrophism" concludes with the death (suicide) of one of Palomar's most beloved characters, and a postscript that provides one of the most hauntingly magical moments of the entire series as a rain of ashes drifts down upon Palomar. Also included are all the post — "Diastrophism" stories, in which Luba's past comes back to haunt her, and the seeds are sown for the "Palomar diaspora" that ends this book. Hernandez uses a lot of nudity, sexual situations, strong language, and violence in these stories.

Marble Season. By Gilbert Hernandez. Drawn & Quarterly 2013 128 p. Illustration
Grades: 11 12 Adult **741.5**
1. Graphic novels; 2. Autobiographies
1770460861; 9781770460867, $21.95

LC 2013375524

Written by Gilbert Hernandez, this autobiographical novel "portrays the reality of life in a large family in suburban 1960s California. Pop-culture references — TV shows, comic books, and music — saturate this evocative story of a young family navigating cultural and neighborhood norms set against the golden age of the American dream and the silver age of comics." (Publisher's note)

"Neither overly rosy and romantic nor dark and dramatic, the book focuses on the real bulk of a child's daily life: the long summer months in which nothing eventful happens, the neighborhood kids who come and go, the tomboys and bullies, the temptation of small-time crime, and the confusion and innocence of early sexuality." LJ

Sloth. DC Comics/Vertigo 2006 un Illustration
Grades: 11 12 Adult **741.5; Fic**
1. Graphic novels; 2. Teenagers — Graphic novels

978-1-4012-0366-5, $19.99

Teenager Miguel Serra had suddenly fallen into a coma; a year later he wakes up, back to normal except he moves at a very slow pace; some people call him Sloth Boy. He reconnects with his girlfriend Lita and best friend Romeo and they try to find evidence of an urban legend in the lemon orchards that surround their sleepy town. One encounter causes a change, as suddenly it was Lita who'd been in the year-long coma. She tries to catch the attention of the handsome, popular Miguel and tries to score tickets to the Romeo X concert. Soon she's having intimate relations with both Miguel and Romeo, and when they fight over her, she falls and slips into another coma. Romeo throws himself off a bridge, and Lita wakes up...

This is the first original graphic novel by Hernandez, who co-created Love and Rockets with his brother. Adult language and sexual situations make this more appropriate for older teens.

Hernandez, Jaime

★ The **Girl** from H.O.P.P.E.R.S.: A Love and Rockets Book. Fantagraphics Books 2007 288p. Illustration
Grades: 12 Adult   741.5; Fic
1. Graphic novels; 2. Mexican Americans — California — Los Angeles — Fiction; 3. Punk culture — Fiction
978-1-56097-851-0, $14.95

In this second volume, having abandoned the sci-fi trappings of the earliest Love & Rockets stories, Hernandez refined his approach, settling on the more naturalistic environment of the fictional Los Angeles barrio, Hoppers, and the lives of the young Mexican-Americans and punk rockers who live there. A central story is "The Death of Speedy." In this volume, Maggie also begins her on-again and off-again romance with Ray D., leading to friction and an eventual separation from Hopey. Hernandez uses nudity, sexual situations, and strong language in these stories.

★ **Maggie** the Mechanic: a love and rockets book. Fantagraphics Books 2007 276p. Illustration
Grades: 12 Adult   741.5; Fic
1. Graphic novels
978-1-56097-784-1, $14.95

This is the first of three volumes by Jaime Hernandez, collecting the adventures of the spunky Maggie, her annoying best friend and sometime lover Hopey, and their circle of friends, including their bombshell friend Penny Century, Maggie's weirdo mentor Izzy — as well as the wrestler Rena Titanon and Maggie's handsome love interest, Rand Race. Maggie the Mechanic collects the earliest, punkiest, most heavily sci-fi stories of Maggie and her circle of friends. Hernandez uses some nudity, sexual situations, and some harsh language in these stories.

Other Love and Rockets collections by Jaime Hernandez are: The Girl from H.O.P.P.E.R.S.; Perla La Loca; Penny Century; Esperanza

Hernandez, Lea

Rumble Girls: Silky Warrior Tansie. NBM 2003 un Illustration
Grades: 10 11 12 Adult   741.5; Fic
1. Graphic novels; 2. Martial arts — Graphic novels; 3. Science fiction graphic novels
1-56163-370-4, $9.95

In a future world where media is run by suits (literally, they have no bodies) and everyone watches battles between warriors in battlesuits called hardskins, orphaned Raven Tansania Ransom trains to be a hardskin pilot at the girls' school academie Juliet. When a relationship gone sour causes Raven to sign with super media corporation Enteco to become a Rumble Girl, school rival Carmen signs on, too, for she wants to destroy Raven by any means possible. The book includes lots of fighting action and some sexual activity.

Hernandez worked with the Japanese anime/manga group known as Gainax and developed her manga-esque style from her experience there.

Rumble Girls originally appeared in comics issues published by Image Comics and then online as webcomics.

Herriman, George

★ **Krazy** & Ignatz, 1937-1938: Shifting Sands Dusts its Cheeks in Powdered Beauty. Fantagraphics Books 2006 176p. Illustration
Grades: 7 8 9 10 11 12 Adult   741.5; Fic
1. Graphic novels; 2. Humor graphic novels; 3. Krazy Kat (Fictional character)
978-1-56097-734-6, $19.95

Krazy Kat is a love story, focusing on the relationships of its three main characters. Krazy Kat adored Ignatz Mouse. Ignatz Mouse simply tolerated Krazy Kat, except for recurrent onsets of targeted tumescence, which found expression in the fast delivery of bricks to Krazy's cranium. Offisa Pup loved Krazy and sought to protect "her" (Herriman always maintained that Krazy was genderless) by throwing Ignatz in jail. Each of the characters was ignorant of the others' true motivations, and this simple structure allowed Herriman to build entire worlds of meaning into the actions, building thematic depth and sweeping his readers up by the looping verbal rhythms of Krazy & Co.'s unique dialogue. Most of these strips in this volume have not seen print since originally running in Hearst newspapers over 70 years ago. This seventh volume collecting all of the comic strips, is the second one to be published in color; Herriman started doing the strip in color in 1935. Other than the brick-throwing, this book has no violence, foul language, or any other usual objectionable content. Krazy Kat cartoons were made for children in the mid-1930s, and there was a Krazy Kat animated series which aired on television in the mid-1960s.

Heuvel, Eric

A **family** secret. [English translation, Lorraine T. Miller]. Farrar, Straus and Giroux 2009 62p. Illustration
Grades: 7 8 9 10 11 12   741.5; Fic
1. Grandmothers — Graphic novels; 2. Graphic novels; 3. Holocaust, 1933-1945 — Graphic novels; 4. Jews — Graphic novels
0-374-32271-6; 978-0-374-42265-3 (pa), $9.99; 0-374-42265-6 (pa); 978-0-374-32271-7, $18.99

LC 2009-13943

While searching his Dutch grandmother's attic for yard sale items, Jeroen finds a scrapbook which leads Gran to tell of her experiences as a girl living in Amsterdam during the Holocaust, when her father was a Nazi sympathizer and Esther, her Jewish best friend, disappeared

This is a "moving graphic novel.... The art is in ink and watercolor, with very clear, highly detailed panels.... [A] gripping story." Booklist

Original Dutch edition, 2003; Anne Frank House

Hickman, Jessica

Womanthology: Heroic. Gail Simone, Camilla D'Errico, Robin Furth, Trina Robbins, Colleen Doran, Fiona Staples, Ming Doyle, Renae De Liz and others. IDW 2012 321 p.
Grades: 8 9 10 11 12   Fic
1. Women artists; 2. Comic books, strips, etc. — Authorship
1613771479; 9781613771471, $50

This book is an anthology of comics content from "more than 150 women creators." The book shows "how many diverse styles and subjects can make for great comics. The different portraits and definitions of heroism encompass everything from caped fliers to historical allusions to quiet bravery." (Publishers Weekly)

Hickman, Jonathan

The **nighty** news. Image Comics 2007 184p.
Grades: 11 12 Adult   741.5

1. Crime — Graphic novels; 2. Graphic novels; 3. Mass media — Graphic novels
978-1-58240-766-1, $16.99

As an act of violence spirals out of control to encompass the entirety of the news media, a cult has emerged from the errors and retractions that have ruined careers, marriages and even lives. Under direction from his cult master The Voice, The Hand leads an army of followers committed to revolution, willing to die for their cause. Targeting journalists of all kinds, they launch a campaign of terror and violence that plays out in the media. The story includes considerable violence and foul language with page design that is very different from the usual comics panels.

Hickman, Troy
Common Grounds: Baker's dozen. Image Comics/Top Cow Productions 2004 144p. Illustration
Grades: 9 10 11 12 Adult   **741.5; Fic**
1. Graphic novels; 2. Superhero graphic novels
978-1-58240-841-5, $14.99

Superheroes and supervillains need a place where they can relax, unwind, and not worry about the next battle. Common Grounds is just such a place — a chain of coffee shops with bakery counters, totally neutral ground. Here, hero and villain can relax and take a break in the restroom ("Head Games"), a teenage superhero who doubts herself and an older superpowered religious Jew can encourage each other ("Sanctuary"), a group of overweight heroes can meet ("Fat Chance"), or formerly evil monsters can get custom takeout and shoot the breeze ("Where Monsters Dine"). The book includes a baker's dozen (thirteen) stories.

Hicks, Faith Erin
★ The **Adventures** of Superhero Girl. written and drawn by Faith Erin Hicks; colors by Cris Peter; introduction by Kurt Busiek. Dark Horse Comics 2013 112 p. Illustration; Color
Grades: 4 5 6 7 8 9 10 11 12 Adult   **741.5; Fic**
1. Female superhero graphic novels
1616550848; 9781616550844, $16.99
Eisner Award: Best Publication for Kids (2014)

This graphic novel features "Superhero Girl [who] has some Superman-like powers, although she can't fly, just leap over tall buildings, and she works to protect the small town where she went to get away from her charismatic superhero brother, Kevin. She fights bad-guy ninjas, bank robbers, even a tentacled space monster, but she also struggles to pay rent...and she has to deal with her future supervillain self." (Voice of Youth Advocates)

"It's superhero as person instead of as corporate symbol or fight machine.... This strip shines because it's fresh and lighthearted without wallowing in angst." Pub Wkly

Attack on Titan anthology. Attack on Titan created by Hajime Isayama; edited by Ben Applegate and Jeanine Schaefer; cover, logo, and interior design by Phil Balsman; lettering and interior design by Steve Wands. Kodansha 2016 256 p. Illustration
Grades: 8 9 10 11 12   **741.5**
1. Fantasy fiction — Graphic novels; 2. Horror fiction — Graphic novels; 3. Science fiction graphic novels; 4. Shonen manga
1632362589; 9781632362582, $29.99

This tribute anthology to the manga Attack on Titan features "original stories by a long roster of comic superstars such as Scott Snyder (Batman, American Vampire), Gail Simone (Batgirl), Michael Avon Oeming (Powers), Paolo Rivera (Daredevil, Amazing Spider-Man), Cameron Stewart (Fight Club 2, Batgirl) and Faith Erin Hicks (The Adventures of Superhero Girl)!" (Publisher's note)

"The Victorian-style guide to Titan's walled city by Genevieve Valentine and David López is a standout, as is the contemplative final story by brothers Asaf and Tomer Hanuka." Pub Wkly

Friends with boys. Faith Erin Hicks. First Second 2012 un Illustration
Grades: 6 7 8 9 10   **741.5**
1. Ghost stories; 2. Graphic novels; 3. Teenagers — Fiction
9781596435568, $16.99
LC 2011030470

In this graphic novel, "[the] youngest of four siblings and the only girl, Maggie is both excited and worried about starting high school after being home-schooled her whole life.... As Maggie makes friends with a perky indie girl named Lucy and her mysterious brother, Alistair, she broods over the loss of her mother, who recently left the family without much of an explanation, and tries to figure out what the ghost wants from her." (Bulletin of the Center for Children's Books)

★ The **Nameless** City. Faith Erin Hicks; color by Jordie Bellaire. First Second 2016 240 p. Color; Illustration
Grades: 5 6 7 8 9 10   **741.5; Fic**
1. Cities and towns — Fiction; 2. Friendship — Fiction; 3. Survival — Fiction; 4. Fantasy graphic novels; 5. Survival skills — Fiction
1626721564; 9781626721562, $14.99; 9781626721579
LC 2015020651

"Every nation that invades the City gives it a new name.... The natives don't let themselves get caught up in the unending wars. To them, their home is the Nameless City.... Kaidu is...a Dao born and bred — a member of the latest occupying nation. Rat is a native of the Nameless City. At first, she hates Kai for everything he stands for, but his love of his new home may be the one thing that can bring these two unlikely friends together." (Publisher's note)

"With comprehensive world building, well-rounded characters, and entertaining action, this expertly executed story will find a home with a wide variety of readers, all of whom will be eagerly awaiting the next installment." Booklist

★ The **stone** heart. Faith Erin Hicks. First Second 2017 256 p. Color; Illustration (The nameless city)
Grades: 5 6 7 8 9 10   **741.5; Fic**
1. Fantasy fiction — Graphic novels; 2. Adventure fiction; 3. Magic — Fiction
1626721599; 9781626721586; 9781626721593, $21.99
LC 2016938731

In this book, by Faith Erin Hicks, "Kaidu and Rat have only just recovered from the assassination attempt on the General of All Blades when more chaos breaks loose in the Nameless City: deep conflicts within the Dao nation are making it impossible to find a political solution for the disputed territory of the City itself." (Publisher's note)

"Flourishing from the strong worldbuilding and characterization of the first installment, this middle volume...provides a vital and enthralling closer look at those readers have already met as well as unfurling more of the Chinese-inspired city's past, as colorist Bellaire brings all to stunning emotional life." Kirkus

★ The **war** at Ellsmere. Slave Labor Graphics 2008 156p. Illustration
Grades: 6 7 8 9 10 11   **741.5; Fic**
1. Friendship — Graphic novels; 2. Graphic novels; 3. Humorous graphic novels; 4. School stories — Graphic novels
1-59362-140-X; 978-1-59362-140-7, $12.95

Juniper is the newest scholarship student at the prestigious Ellsmere Academy; she wanted to attend there in order to increase her chances of getting into a good medical school. She's on scholarship because her mom has had to raise her alone since her father died when she was young. Jun makes one friend at Ellsmere, Cassie, who calls herself the cliche of the poor little rich girl. Wealthy Emily calls Cassie "Orphan" because her parents ignore her, and chooses to call Jun "Project," as in Headmistress Ms. Bishop's latest project. Emily is also determined to get rid of Jun, especially when Jun encourages Cassie to work harder and even win the extra credit essay contest. Now it's war, or as Jun puts it, "It's like Upstairs Downstairs meets Lord of the Flies. In plaid skirts. And sweater vests." There's one incident when Jun punches Emily in the face.

"Hicks gives readers enough tension and quirky turns to satisfy and pleasantly surprise." Booklist

Hidaka, Banri
I Hate You More than Anyone! Volume 1. DC Comics/CMX 2007 192p. Illustration
Grades: 7 8 9 10 11 12   **741.5; Fic**
1. Graphic novels; 2. Humorous graphic novels; 3. Manga; 4. Romance graphic novels; 5. Shojo manga
978-1-4012-1310-7, $9.99
Kazuha Akiyoshi is the eldest of six children. She's very responsible and also irresistibly cute, but she is something of a tomboy who has never allowed her romantic side to show throught. Then she meets Mizushima, the first guy to treat her like a girl. He's Kazuha's first crush, but does Mizushima feel the same way about her? And then there's Sugimoto, an older guy who's determined to make himself an important part of her life, only he's the one she hates more than anyone.

Higashimura, Akiko
Princess Jellyfish 1. by Akiko Higashimura. Random House Inc 2016 400 p.
Grades: 10 11 12 Adult   **741.5**
1. Tokyo (Japan) — Fiction; 2. Young women — Fiction; 3. Manga; 4. Josei manga
1632362287; 9781632362285, $19.99
In this book, by Akiko Higashimura, "Tsukimi Kurashita has a strange fascination with jellyfish. She's loved them from a young age and has carried that love with her to her new life in the big city of Tokyo. There, she resides in Amamizukan.... However, a chance meeting at a pet shop has Tsukimi crossing paths with one of the things that the residents of Amamizukan have been desperately trying to avoid-a beautiful and fashionable woman!" (Publisher's note)
Volume 1 of 9

Hiiragi, Aoi
Baron: The Cat Returns. story and art by Aoi Hiiragi; translation & English adaptation, Naoko Amemiya. Viz/Studio Ghibli Library 2005 222p. Illustration
Grades: 3 4 5 6 7 8 9   **741.5; Fic**
1. Cats — Graphic novels; 2. Fantasy graphic novels; 3. Graphic novels; 4. Kodomo manga; 5. Manga
1-59116-956-9, $9.99
Awkward teen Haru saves a cat from being run over one afternoon, but she never expected the trouble it would cause. He is a cat prince, and his father wants to bring Haru into the kingdom of the cats to be his son's bride. A mysterious voice sends Haru to the Cat Office, where she meets Baron, a toy cat come to life, the fat cat Muta, and a magical crow. When the cats come and bear Haru to the kingdom of the cats, the three friends follow to help bring Haru back home.

This one-volume manga was the basis for the feature-length anime (Japanese animated film) called "The Cat Returns," which was produced by Studio Ghibli, the animation studio run by famed anime director Hayao Miyazaki and some partners.

Hill, Joe
★ **Locke** & key: welcome to Lovecraft. written by Joe Hill; art by Gabriel Rodriguez. IDW Publishing 2008 158p. Illustration
Grades: 10 11 12 Adult
741.5; Fic
1. Graphic novels; 2. Horror graphic novels; 3. Mystery graphic novels
978-1-60010-237-0, $24.99;
978-1-60010-384-1 (pa), $19.99

Courtesy of IDW Publishing

After Rendell Locke is murdered by a former student, Sam Lesser, who then tried to find and kill the rest of the family, Nina Locke takes her children, Tyler, Kinsey, and Bode to Lovecraft, Massachusetts, to live with Rendell's brother Duncan in Keyhouse. Tyler needs to deal with the guilt he feels because of a conversation with Sam Lesser, in which he said Sam should kill his dad. Kinsey had taken Bode and hidden from Sam, keeping them both safe, but she feels as though she'll never be safe again. Bode finds a door at Keyhouse, and when he goes through it, he dies and his ghost wanders around. There's definitely something weird at Keyhouse, and something is living at the bottom of the well in the well house — something that uses both Bode and Sam Lesser — and wants revenge. The book includes bloody violence. Joe Hill is the son of Stephen King.

"This first of...several volumes delivers on all counts, boasting a solid story bolstered by exceptional work from Chilean artist Rodriguez...that resembles a fusion of Rick Geary and Cully Hamner with just a dash of Frank Quitely." Publ Wkly
Other titles in this series are:Vol 2: Head Games (2009);Vol 3: Crown of Shadows (2010);Vol 4: Keys to the Kingdom (2011);Vol 5: Clockworks (2012);Vol 6: Alpha & Omega (2014)

Hinds, Gareth
★ **Beowulf**. adapted and illustrated by Gareth Hinds. Candlewick Press 2007 un Illustration
Grades: 8 9 10 11 12 Adult
741.5; Fic
1. Adventure graphic novels; 2. Graphic novels; 3. Monsters — Graphic novels; 4. Beowulf — Graphic novels
978-0-7636-3022-5, $21.99;
0-7636-3022-5; 978-0-7636-3023-2 (pa);
0-7636-3023-3 (pa), $9.99
LC 2006-49023
Graphic novel adaptation of the Old English epic poem, Beowulf

"For fantasy fans both young and old, this makes an ideal introduction to a story without which the entire fantasy genre would look very different; many scenes may be too intense for very young readers." Publ Wkly

BEOWULF. Copyright © 1999, 2000, 2007 by Gareth Hinds. Reproduced by permission of the publisher, Candlewick Press, Somerville, MA.

King Lear. a play by William Shakespeare; adapted and illustrated by Gareth Hinds. Candlewick Press 2009 123p. Illustration
Grades: 7 8 9 10 11 12   **741.5; 822.3**
1. Shakespeare, William, 1564-1616 — Adaptations
978-0-7636-4343-0, $22.99; 0-7636-4343-2; 978-0-7636-4344-7 (pa), $11.99; 0-7636-4344-0 (pa)
"Employing a range of artistic styles that convey dramatic mood, the artist begins the play almost as a fairy tale, featuring bright, softly washed drawings. Once Cordelia is cast out and things sour, the images become

KING LEAR. Copyright © 2007 by Gareth Hinds. Reproduced by permission of the publisher, Candlewick Press, Somerville, MA.

darker and more compact. As the king descends into madness, the art becomes downright menacing, with Lear appearing as a jagged, ghostly figure drawn with white pencil on a dark background." (Kirkus)

Macbeth. adapted and illustrated by Gareth Hinds. Candlewick Press 2015 152 p. Color illustration; Color; Map
Grades: 8 9 10 11 12   741.5
1. Kings and rulers — Fiction; 2. Scotland — Fiction; 3. Graphic novels; 4. Murder — Fiction; 5. Shakespeare, William, 1564-1616 — Adaptations
0763678023; 9780763669430; 978076367802 9, \$12.99
LC 2014939338

"Set against the moody backdrop of eleventh-century Scotland, [illustrator] Gareth Hinds's...interpretation takes readers into the claustrophobic mind of a man driven mad by ambition. An evil seed takes root in the mind of Macbeth, a general in the king's army, when three witches tell him he will one day be king." (Publisher's note)

"Though many lines of the original are intact, Hinds does undertake some changes to make this version more accessible to contemporary readers, and a closing note addresses those alterations. Students struggling to find an entry point into the Scottish play should look no further than this entertaining and elucidating volume." Booklist

The **merchant** of Venice: a play. by William Shakespeare; adapted and illustrated by Gareth Hinds. Candlewick Press 2008 68p. Illustration
Grades: 8 9 10 11 12 Adult
822.3; 741.5
1. Shakespeare, William, 1564-1616 — Adaptations
978-0-7636-3024-9, \$21.99; 978-0-7636-3025-6 (pa), \$11.99
LC 2007-938349

Hinds uses a sketchy art style and blue and gray tones to illustrate his graphic adaptation of Shakespeare's controversial play. He sets the play in modern Venice and uses more modern language, including prose, at the beginning of the play and then gradually returns to Shakespeare's original language for the courtroom scenes. The play tells the story of a debt owed to a Jewish merchant of Venice, of a strong-willed young woman who is determined to choose her own husband, and of the quest to save a young man from the fate of having a pound of flesh cut from him.

"Fans of the play will find this an intriguing adaptation." Publ Wkly

The **most** excellent and lamentable tragedy of Romeo & Juliet: a play by William Shakespeare. by William Shakespeare, adapted and illustrated by Gareth Hinds. Candlewick Press 2013 128 p.

MACBETH. Copyright © 2015 by Gareth Hinds. Reproduced by permission of the publisher, Candlewick Press, Somerville, MA.

THE MERCHANT OF VENICE. Copyright © 2008 by Gareth Hinds. Reproduced by permission of the publisher, Candlewick Press, Somerville, MA.

Grades: 7 8 9 10
741.5
1. Graphic novels; 2. Shakespeare, William, 1564-1616 — Tragedies; 3. Shakespeare, William, 1564-1616 — Adaptations
0763659487; 0763668079; 9780763659486, \$21.99; 9780763668075, \$12.99
LC 2012950561

This book by Gareth Hinds presents a graphic novel adaptation of William Shakespeare's play "Romeo and Juliet." "The most notable change between this story and Shakespeare's original is the creative license that Hinds takes with ethnicity — he makes the characters of African, Indian, and Caucasian descent in order to promote the universality of the story. The Shakespearean language is abridged but not adapted into contemporary English." (School Library Journal)

"Cleaving to Shakespeare's words and dramatic arc, Hinds (The Merchant of Venice) creates another splendid graphic novel, tracing each scene in taut, coherent dialogue. The characters, in period dress modified by a few more contemporary touches, are poignantly specific yet universal. Hinds delivers the play's essence and beauty, its glorious language, furious conflict, yearning love, and wrenching tragedy." (Horn Book)

The **Odyssey**: a graphic novel. by Gareth Hinds. Candlewick Press 2010 248 p. Color illustration
Grades: 7 8 9 10 11 12 Adult
741.5
1. Graphic novels; 2. Greek mythology — Graphic novels; 3. Odyssey; 4. Homer
0763642665; 0763642681; 9780763642662, \$24.99; 9780763642686
LC 2010007512

"Retells, in graphic novel format, Homer's epic tale of Odysseus, the ancient Greek hero who encounters witches and other obstacles on his journey home after fighting in the Trojan War." (Publisher's note)

Poe: stories and poems: a graphic novel adaptation by Gareth Hinds. Gareth Hinds. Candlewick Press 2017 120 p. Illustration; Color
Grades: 8 9 10 11 12
741.5
1. Literature — Adaptations; 2. Poe, Edgar Allan, 1809-1849
9780763681128, \$22; 9780763695095
LC 2017946252

This graphic novel, by Gareth Hinds, is an "adaptation of Edgar Allan Poe's best-known works.... In 'The Cask of Amontillado,' a man exacts revenge on a disloyal friend at carnival.... In 'The Masque of the Red Death,' a prince shielding himself from plague hosts a doomed party inside his abbey stronghold. A prisoner of the Spanish Inquisition, faced with a swinging blade and swarming rats, can't see his tormentors in 'The Pit and the Pendulum.'" (Publisher's note)

ROMEO AND JULIET. Copyright © 2013 by Gareth Hinds. Reproduced by permission of the publisher, Candlewick Press, Somerville, MA.

THE ODYSSEY. Copyright © 2010 by Gareth Hinds. Reproduced by permission of the publisher, Candlewick Press, Somerville, MA.

POE: STORIES AND POEMS. Copyright © 2017 by Gareth Hinds. Reproduced by permission of the publisher, Candlewick Press, Somerville, MA.

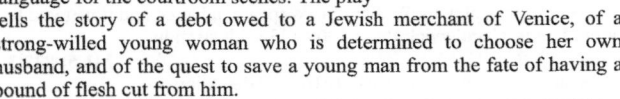

" Faithfully preserving the gothic tone of the original texts, from the macabre endpapers filled with symbols of death to the twisted anguished faces found throughout its pages, the author never shies away from the darkness found there, instead distilling Poe's fascination with madness, death, and terror into single haunting images." Booklist

Hino, Matsuri

Captive hearts, vol. 1. Viz Media/Shojo Beat 2008 200p. Illustration
Grades: 7 8 9 10 11 12   **741.5; Fic**
1. Graphic novels; 2. Manga; 3. Romance graphic novels; 4. Shojo manga
978-1-4215-1932-6, $8.99

Carefree college student Megumi Kuroishi finds his life turned upside down when the last surviving member of the Kogami family, teenage Suzuka, is found in China. That's when Megumi learns of the curse against his family, that they will serve the Kogami family for 100 generations. Whenever he looks into Suzuka's eyes, the curse overwhelms him and he becomes far too subservient; complicating matters is the fact that he does indeed find Suzuka captivating. She likes him, too, but can't trust his feelings because of the curse. The book includes two short romance stories. In "Real Storm," shy high school student Io Ayase has a huge crush on Kuji-sensei, who only wants to help her learn to deal with a pervy stalker. In "Let Time Freeze," Ayu and Yuji are childhood friends now in their senior year of high school, and she doesn't want the year to end; when it does, Yuji will go to university in Tokyo while Ayu must remain behind. Now that she loves him, the impending separation already hurts.

MeruPuri: Marchen Prince Vol. 1. Viz Media/Shojo Beat 2005 un Illustration
Grades: 8 9 10 11 12   **741.5; Fic**
1. Fantasy graphic novels; 2. Graphic novels; 3. Manga; 4. Romance graphic novels; 5. Shojo manga
1-4215-0120-1, $8.99

All high-school freshman Airi Hoshina ever wanted was to someday live in a cozy home with a loving husband, and find joy in the little things in life. As a result, she makes it her daily mission to get to school on time because school legend has it that the longer one's non-tardy streak is, the better boyfriend one will find. But, on the way to school one morning, Airi drops her mirror, one that had been passed down to her through generations, and suddenly finds herself in a bizarre situation. Never in her wildest dreams did she expect to meet Aram, a little boy from a magical kingdom, to have emerged from the mirror in the short time it took her to track it down. The series includes some mild sexual situations.

Vampire Knight, Vol. 1. story & art by Matsuri Hino. Viz Media/Shojo Beat 2007 un Illustration
Grades: 10 11 12   **741.5; Fic**
1. Fantasy graphic novels; 2. Graphic novels; 3. Manga; 4. Shojo manga; 5. Vampires — Graphic novels
978-1-4215-0822-1, $8.99

Ten years ago, little Yuki was saved from a vampire attack that killed her family, and the headmaster of Cross Academy adopted her. Cross Academy has two groups of students: the normal human Day Class and the vampires of the Night Class. Yuki and Zero, a fellow Day Class student, work as guardians to keep the Academy's secret and ensure that there is only limited contact between the Classes. Vampires may not be evil, but their very appearance is extremely seductive, and Yuki and Zero have their hands full trying to maintain order. Trouble starts when some of the Night Class try to push the rules, and Zero's attitude towards them becomes even more hostile.

Volume 1 of 19

Hirano, Kohta

Hellsing Volume 1. Dark Horse Comics 2003 208p. Illustration
Grades: 11 12 Adult   **741.5; Fic**
1. Graphic novels; 2. Horror graphic novels; 3. Manga; 4. Seinen manga
1-59307-056-X, $13.95

There's a secret organization somewhere in England created to defend the Queen and country from monsters of all sorts. Enter Hellsing, an agency, long in tooth, with the experience, know-how, and... special equipment to handle the problems that arise when vampires, ghouls, and the like take on these dark forces. The special "equipment" is another vampire, and a big pistol loaded with special silver bullets. This series focuses on the violence of destroying vampires who love to slaughter people. Some might be offended by the portrayal of the Roman Catholic Church as insanely fundamentalist and using inquisitors and brainwashed killer nuns. The series includes lots of graphic violence and harsh language.

Hiroumi, Aoi

Shibuya goldfish; 1. Hiroumi Aoi; translation by Ko Ransom; lettering by Abigail Blackman. Yen Press 2018 240 p. Illustration
Grades: 10 11 12 Adult   **741.5; Fic**
1. Teenagers — Fiction; 2. Goldfish — Graphic novels; 3. Goldfish — Fiction
1975327446; 9781975327446, $15

LC 2018935616

"High schooler Hajime Tsukiyoda went to Shibuya that day hoping only to find inspiration for his next film. He never expected to find himself smack-dab in the middle of a real-life horror movie. Without warning, schools of massive goldfish descend upon the crowded streets, and the mystified onlookers' confusion quickly turns to terror as the fish begin to feed." (Publisher's note)

Hirsh, Ananth

Lucky Penny. Ananth Hirsh, Yuko Ota. Oni Press 2016 199 p. Illustration
Grades: 10 11 12 Adult
741.5; Fic
1. Fortune — Comic books, strips, etc; 2. Success — Fiction
1620102870; 9781620102879, $19.99
LC 2015948229

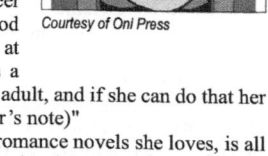
Courtesy of Oni Press

In this book, by Ananth Hirsh and Yuko Ota, "Penny Brighton...lost her job. And her apartment. In the same day. But it's okay, her friend has a cozy storage unit she can crash in. And there's bound to be career opportunities at the neighborhood laundromat.... Plus, there's this sweet guy at the community center.... Surely Penny is a capable of becoming an actual responsible adult, and if she can do that her luck's bound to change! Right?" (Publisher's note)"

"Quirky Penny, like characters in the romance novels she loves, is all heart, and she'll easily charm readers with her smoking, drinking, train-wreck style." Booklist

Hitch, Bryan

Bryan Hitch's Ultimate Comics Studio. Impact 2010 128p. Illustration
Grades: 7 8 9 10   **741.5; 741**
1. Fantastic Four (Fictional characters); 2. Captain America (Fictional character)
978-1-6006-1327-2, $24.99; 1-6006-1327-6

"The book is a skillful blend of text, photos of the artist at work, annotated sketches, and finished illustrations. It is a visual treat in its own right, with well-organized subject matter complemented by thoughtful composition and lavish photography and art. Hitch considers himself to be primarily a storyteller, and he delves into the philosophy and technique of visual storytelling. He gives a glimpse into his thought processes, offering 'guided tours' of sketches by walking readers through his work, starting with analyzing script to making decisions regarding action, panels, rhythm, and sample initial sketches." (School Library Journal)

Hiwatari, Saki

Tower of the Future, Vol. 1. DC Comics/CMX 2005 192p. Illustration
Grades: 8 9 10 11 12   **741.5; Fic**
    1. Fantasy graphic novels; 2. Graphic novels; 3. Manga; 4. Romance graphic novels; 5. Shojo manga
978-1-4012-0814-1, $9.99

Takeru's mother has died, and then he finds out that his half-English father has a daughter in England; on her deathbed, Takeru's mother asked that Hyoju be allowed to move to Japan and live with them. Shocked and upset, Takeru's first reaction is anger and disgust. He then meets Ichigo, a girl his age upon whom he immediately has a crush, and a strange little boy named Zen who knows way too much about Takeru. As the series progresses, Takeru learns a little more about Zen and why he knows so much. Also, a fantasy element comes in as Takeru learns about a parasitic being called Noize, and Ichigo's adult older brother has an unhealthy fixation on her.

Hodgson, William Hope

The **House** on the Borderland. BiblioBazaar 2006 88p. Illustration
Grades: 10 11 12 Adult   **741.5; Fic**
    1. Graphic novels; 2. Horror graphic novels
978-1-4264-3828-8, $11.99

This book adapts Hodgson's horror novel. It sits astride two worlds, the bleak world of colorless normality, and the realms of cosmic horror where reason my yet have a last chance to conquer fear. To this ancient dwelling a challenger comes, to exorcise its shadowed curse, to plumb its pits of ultimate perversity and, perhaps, to prevent evil's emergence into the present. This book includes strong language, violence, and brief nudity.

Hogan, James P.

The **Two** Faces of Tomorrow. story by James P. Hogan; art and adaptation by Yukinobu Hoshino; translation, Frederik L. Schodt and Toren Smith; lettering and retouch, Tomoko Saito. Dark Horse Comics 2006 576p. Illustration
Grades: 9 10 11 12 Adult   **741.5**
    1. Computers — Graphic novels; 2. Graphic novels; 3. Manga; 4. Science fiction graphic novels; 5. Seinen manga
978-1-59307-563-7

Midway through the 21st century, an integrated global computer network manages much of the world's affairs. A proposed major software upgrade — an artificial intelligence — will give the system an unprecedented degree of independent decision-making, but serious questions are raised in regard to how much control can safely be given to a non-human intelligence. In order to more fully assess the system, a new space-station habitat — a world in miniature — is developed for deployment of the fully operational system, named Spartacus. This mini-world can then be "attacked" in a series of escalating tests to assess the system's responses and capabilities. If Spartacus gets out of hand, the system can be shut down and the station destroyed... unless Spartacus decides to take matters into its own hands and take the fight to Earth. This

manga adaptation of Hogan's novel includes some harsh language and brief incidental nudity.

Hope, Jane

Introducing Buddha, New Ed.. Totem Books 2005 176p. Illustration
Grades: 10 11 12 Adult
294.3; 741.5
    1. Buddhism — Graphic novels; 2. Graphic novels
978-1-84046-633-1, $12.95
    LC 95-060973

Courtesy of Icon Books

This book uses cartoons and a spare text to describe the life and teachings of the Buddha. Author Jane Hope shows that enlightenment is a matter of experiencing the truth individually and by inspiration which is passed from teacher to student. The book explains the practices of meditation, Taoism and Zen. It goes on to describe the role of Buddhism in modern Asia and its growing influence on Western thought. The book includes a list of books for further reading.

Hopkins, David

Emily Edison. Viper Comics 2006 144p. Illustration
Grades: 7 8 9 10 11 12 Adult   **741.5; Fic**
    1. Graphic novels; 2. Humorous graphic novels; 3. Science fiction graphic novels
0-9777883-2-6, $12.95

High schooler Emily has more than her share of problems; along with trying to keep up in school and survive such things as parties and boys, she has to deal with her parents' very mixed marriage. Her father is human, but her mother came from another dimension. Since their divorce, Emily has had to split her time between Earth and elsewhere; and now her grandfather wants her to live permanently in his dimension, and he's prepared to destroy Earth to force her hand. What's a girl to do?

Horikoshi, Kohei

★ **My** Hero Academia; Volume 1. story & art Kohei Horikoshi; translation & English adaptation Caleb Cook. Viz 2015 187 p. Illustration
Grades: 7 8 9 10 11 12   **741.5/952; 741.5**
    1. High schools — Fiction; 2. Manga; 3. Shonen manga; 4. High school students — Fiction; 5. Superheroes — Fiction
1421582694; 9781421582696, $9.99

"What would the world be like if 80 percent of the population manifested superpowers called 'Quirks' at age four? Heroes and villains would be battling it out everywhere! Being a hero would mean learning to use your power, but where would you go to study? The Hero Academy of course! But what would you do if you were one of the 20 percent who were born Quirkless? Middle school student Izuku Midoriya wants to be a hero more than anything, but he hasn't got an ounce of power in him. With no chance of ever getting into the prestigious U.A. High School for budding heroes, his life is looking more and more like a dead end. Then an encounter with All Might, the greatest hero of them all, gives him a chance to change his destiny." (Publisher's note)

Volume 1 of an ongoing series

Hornschemeier, Paul

Let Us Be Perfectly Clear. Fantagraphics Books 2006 136p. Illustration
Grades: 11 12 Adult   **741.5; Fic**
    1. Graphic novels; 2. Short stories — Graphic novels

978-1-56097-752-0, $19.95

This is a collection of Paul Hornschemeier's full-color short stories from a variety of sources, none of which has been available to the book trade. The book is designed as a "flip book" in the tradition of the old Ace paperbacks, with one side featuring comedic work (or as comedic as Hornschemeier's mind allows), and the other decidedly more morose. On the "funny" menu, we are treated to Dr. Rodentia (an unfortunate-looking fellow with only apathy as his weapon), a detailed artist's catalogue exploring such modern masterpieces as "Accidental Late-Night Sex With a Radiator," musings on the cancerous nature of civilization as observed by a deceased cat and a cotton-based airbus, the scatological "Feelings Check," the ever pathetic Vanderbilt Millions and his fantasies of self-worth, and the multi-narrative story that started the Forlorn Funnies comics series: "The Men and Women of the Television." On the "forlorn" plate is the cold examination of the dyslexic narcoleptic and his bungled plans of murder, a sea creature's balancing of morality and sustenance, the Western romance "Wanted," a metal man's self-destructive search for meaning, and the story of two men meeting; it may disgust readers, without a single visually objectionable panel. The other stories do include strong language and some violence.

Mother, come home. with an introduction by Thomas Tennant. Fantagraphics 2004 128p. Illustration
Grades: 11 12 Adult   **741.5; Fic**
  1. Graphic novels; 2. Mental illness — Graphic novels
  978-1-56097-973-9 (pa)
  In this "story, a young child struggles with the death of his mother and his father's collapse. Clean-lined artwork leaves plenty of room for strong emotional content linked to themes of euthanasia, suicide, and depression." Booklist

Hoshino, Katsura
  D.Gray-Man Volume 1. story and art by Katsura Hoshino; translation and English adaptation, Mayumi Kobayashi. Viz Media/Shonen Jump Advanced 2006 192p. Illustration
Grades: 10 11 12 Adult   **741.5; Fic**
  1. Adventure graphic novels; 2. Fantasy graphic novels; 3. Graphic novels; 4. Manga; 5. Supernatural graphic novels; 6. Shonen manga
  978-1-4215-0623-4, $7.99
  Set in a fictional end of the 19th century England, the story revolves around a teenage boy named Allen Walker who is cursed with a cross mark on his hand that turns his arm into an enormous weapon, which he uses to hunt down and kill akumas. An akuma, generated by The Millenium Earl, a 1,000-year-old phantom, is implanted into a human's soul during a moment of devastation and despair. The phantom uses the demons to then carry out his goal: destroy all humankind. Allen, a 15-year-old boy, roams the Earth in search of Innocence. Washed away to unknown parts of the world after The Great Flood, Innocence is the mysterious substance used to create weapons that obliterate the akumas. The action is over-the-top in style, with lots of demon-fighting action.

Hosler, Jay
  Clan Apis. Active Synapse 2000 158p. Illustration
Grades: 4 5 6 7 8 9 10 11 12   **741.5; Fic**
  1. Bees — Graphic novels; 2. Graphic novels; 3. Science — Graphic novels
  0-9677255-0-X, $15
  "Opening with a creation myth... and working through the biological, sociological, and ecological changes affecting the life of Nyuki the bee, the text is a combination of authoritative science; appealing, detailed black-and-white drawings; and dialogue replete with humor, pubescent angst, political sloganeering, and more. Nyuki's colony undertakes

Courtesy of Active Synapse

migration to a new hive, is beset by a woodpecker, and hibernates through a winter that yields to a revitalizing spring." Booklist

  ★ **Evolution:** the story of life on Earth. written by Jay Hosler; art by Zander Cannon and Kevin Cannon. Hill and Wang 2011 150p. Illustration
Grades: 9 10 11 12 Adult
741.5; 576.8
  1. Evolution (Biology); 2. Graphic novels
  0809094762; 9780809094769
                                    LC 2010-05777
  Alien scientist Bloort-183 takes King Floorsh-727 and Prince Floorsh-418 on a tour of Earth's history, explaining the theory of evolution. These are the same aliens who explored human genetics in The Stuff of Life. The illustrations by Kevin Cannon and Zander Cannon (no relation to each other) help human readers see how the theory of evolution explains the beginnings of life on Earth, the four conditions needed for natural selection, the Cambrian explosion, the Permian extinction, sexual selection, the evolution of modern humans, and the Earth scientists who studied the life forms and made the scientific discoveries. The book includes an illustrated glossary, a list of further reading, and endpapers filled with all kinds of dinosaurs.
  "This delightful book seems ideal for nonscientists who want to entertainingly brush up their knowledge of evolution as well as for students from middle school on up." Booklist

  ★ **Last** of the sandwalkers. written and illustrated by Jay Hosler. First Second 2015 312 p. Illustration
Grades: 5 6 7 8 9 10   **741.5; Fic**
  1. Beetles — Fiction; 2. Graphic novels; 3. Science fiction; 4. Scientific expeditions — Fiction; 5. Adventure fiction
  162672024X; 9781626720244, $16.99
                                    LC 2014045542
  This book, by Jay Hosler, is about a "civilization of beetles. In this bug's paradise, beetles write books, run restaurants, and even do scientific research. But not too much scientific research is allowed by the powerful elders, who guard a terrible secret about the world outside.... Lucy is not one to quietly cooperate, however. This tiny field scientist defies the law of her safe but authoritarian home and leads a team of researchers out into the desert." (Publisher's note)
  "Hosler's cartooning is no less meticulous than his writing and similarly retains a sense of animated energy and humor, engaging readers with characters that are far from human, but filled with humanity." Booklist
  Includes bibliographical references

  The **Sandwalk** Adventures: An Adventure in Evolution Told in Five Chapters. Active Synapse 2003 160p. Illustration
Grades: 4 5 6 7 8 9 10 11 12 Adult
576.8; 741.5
  1. Evolution — Graphic novels; 2. Graphic novels; 3. Science — Graphic novels; 4. Darwin, Charles; 5. Darwin, Charles — Graphic novels
  0-9677255-1-8, $20
  Scientist Hosler explains Darwin's theory of evolution in a whimsical fashion. Follicle mites Mara and Willy live in Darwin's left eyebrow, and by accident they discover that Darwin, whom they call the god

Courtesy of Active Synapse

Flycatcher, can hear Mara. He thinks he's going crazy, but as he takes his daily walks on the Sandwalk at his home in England, Darwin does his best to convince Mara and Willy that he isn't a god and tells them about evolution. Hosler uses humor and whimsy, but also did a lot of research; the book includes explanatory notes and a long bibliography of sources.

Hosoda, Mamoru
Wolf children Ame & Yuki. original story: Mamoru Hosoda; art: Yu; character design: Yoshiyuki Sadamoto; translation: Jocelyne Allen; lettering: Tania Biswas, Lys Blakeslee. Yen Press 2014 538 p. Color; Illustration
Grades: 10 11 12 Adult   **741.5**
1. Widows — Fiction; 2. Seinen manga; 3. Werewolves — Fiction; 4. Manga
031640165X; 9780316401654, $26
"When Hana falls in love with a young interloper she encounters in her college class, the last thing she expects to learn is that he is part wolf. Instead of rejecting her lover upon learning his secret, she accepts him with open arms.... But after what seems like a mere moment of bliss to Hana, the father of her children is tragically taken from her." (Publisher's note)
"This emotion-laden work focuses on family and community issues.... The soft color palette of these watercolors complements the tender emotion of the plot." Lib Med Con

Hotta, Yumi
★ **Hikaru** No Go, Volume 1. [by] Yumi Hotta and Takeshi Obata. Viz Media, LLC 2004 192p. Illustration
Grades: 5 6 7 8 9 10 11 12   **741.5; Fic**
1. Board games — Graphic novels; 2. Graphic novels; 3. Manga; 4. Shonen manga
1-59116-222-X, $7.95
Sixth-grade Hikaru Shindo's discovery of a bloodstained game board leads to an encounter with the ghost of Go master Fujiwara-no-Sai and the formation of an unbeatable Go team.
Volume 1 of 23

Houck, Janet
Kashimashi: Girl Meets Girl Vol. 1. story by Satoru Akahori; art by Yukimaru Katsura; [translation, Adrienne Beck; adaptation, Janet Houck]. Seven Seas Entertainment 2006 un Illustration
Grades: 10 11 12 Adult   **741.5; Fic**
1. Fantasy graphic novels; 2. Graphic novels; 3. Manga; 4. Romance graphic novels; 5. Yuri manga
978-1-933164-34-2, $10.99
Being a girl is harder than it looks. For Hazumu, this couldn't be truer, because just the other day, she... was a he. Shunned by the girl of his dreams, Hazumu loses himself in the mountains and is promptly squashed by an oncoming space ship. The alien inside, feeling guilty, rebuilds Hazumu's body... but as the wrong gender! Now Hazumu must learn how to be the girl his parents always wanted while dealing with the trials and tribulations of being caught in a love triangle between two girls — his childhood friend, Tomari, and Yasuna, the girl who rejected him but is now strangely attracted to him/her. This yuri (girl-girl romance) manga was published in a shonen magazine in Japan. The book includes partial nudity and sexual situations.
Volume 1 of 5

Houser, Jody
Faith; Volume 1: Hollywood & Vine. by Jody Houser, illustrated by Marguerite Sauvage and Francis Portela. Valiant Entertainment, LLC 2016 112 p. Color; Illustration
Grades: 8 9 10 11 12 Adult   **741.5; Fic**

1. Female superhero graphic novels; 2. Superheroes
9781682151211, $9.99; 1682151212
"Orphaned at a young age, Faith Herbert — a psionically gifted 'psiot'...is taking control of her destiny and becoming the hard-hitting hero she's always known she can be — complete with a mild-mannered secret identity, unsuspecting colleagues, and a day job as a reporter that routinely throws into her harms way!" (Publisher's note)
"This is a modern twist on the classic superhero tale. Faith doesn't have the typical superheroine body type, dismantling stereotypes about what it means to be superpowered." SLJ
Originally published in single magazine form as Faith #1-4

Courtesy of Valiant Entertainment

Howard, Josh
Dead @17: compendium edition. Viper Comics 2008 336p. Illustration
Grades: 10 11 12 Adult   **741.5; Fic**
1. Adventure graphic novels; 2. Graphic novels; 3. Horror graphic novels
978-0-9793680-3, $24.95
Seventeen-year-old Nara Kilday's murder is the start of a new battle between good and evil. Her best friend Hazy investigates Nara's death and uncovers a dark side that he hadn't known. Meanwhile, an evil has raised an army of the undead, intending to reshape the world in its image. Among the undead is Nara, however, and she may just be the only thing standing in the way of Armageddon. Well, Nara, Hazy and Noel, that is. This book collects the original trilogy; Howard has revised and expanded it, and this book also includes cover and pinup galleries as well as a section of fan-produced arts and photographs. The book includes nudity and bloody violence.

Dead@17: Revolution. Viper Comics 2005 un Illustration
Grades: 10 11 12 Adult   **741.5; Fic**
1. Graphic novels; 2. Horror graphic novels; 3. Mystery graphic novels
0-9754193-3-1, $14.95
A political assassination plot by a mysterious group called Heaven's Militia unravels a government conspiracy with ties to Nara's past and future. She's forced to make a choice that could expose her secret to the world and puts her at odds with Noel Raddemer, her one ally. But somehow she has to stop the demon Bolabogg from achieving his goal, or the world will not survive. The book includes violence, strong language, and nudity.

Dead@17: The Complete First Series, Special Edition. Viper Comics 2006 un Illustration
Grades: 10 11 12   **741.5; Fic**
1. Graphic novels; 2. Horror graphic novels; 3. Mystery graphic novels
0-9754193-6-6, $14.95
Seventeen-year-old Nara has a pretty good life, but it ends suddenly when she's stabbed to death. An investigator gives best friend Hazy Nara's diary, and she finds it filled with weird, arcane symbols and writing. Then zombies rise up all over town and some attack Hazy; she's saved by — Nara. It turns out Nara is one of the Resurrected," and the person who has raised the zombies wants Nara for his own evil purposes. The book includes bloody violence and some strong language.

Hudlin, Reginald
Black Panther: Civil War. Marvel Entertainment 2007 un Illustration
Grades: 9 10 11 12 Adult   **741.5; Fic**

1. Black Panther (Fictional character); 2. Graphic novels; 3. Superhero graphic novels

978-0-7851-2235-7, $17.99

King T'Challa and Queen Ororo, Black Panther and Storm, embark on a diplomatic tour that will have them spanning the globe and beyond. Stops include Latveria (Dr. Doom), the Moon (Black Bolt and the Inhumans), Atlantis (Namor the Sub-Mariner) and the Civil War-ravaged United States, for a meeting with none other than the point man for the U.S. government's implementation of the Superhuman Registration Act: Tony Stark, T'Challa's former Avengers teammate. Will the Black Panther and Storm decide to step off the sidelines of the Civil War and get involved?

Black Panther: The Bride. Marvel Entertainment 2006 un Illustration
Grades: 9 10 11 12 Adult   **741.5; Fic**
1. Black Panther (Fictional character); 2. Graphic novels; 3. Superhero graphic novels

978-0-7851-2107-7, $14.99

Every king needs a queen, and the Black Panther, who is also the King of Wakanda, sets out on an epic quest to find a wife. His heart is Storm's if she'll accept his hand in marriage. The question is, does she want it? With a super hero civil war ready to explode in the U.S., and snakes in the Wakanda court preparing to make their moves, the road to the altar could not be more complicated.

Hughes, Susan

No girls allowed: tales of daring women dressed as men for love, freedom and adventure. written by Susan Hughes; Ilustrated by Willow Dawson. Kids Can Press 2008 80p. Illustration
Grades: 3 4 5 6 7 8 9

306.7; 741.5
1. Biographical graphic novels; 2. Graphic novels; 3. Transvestites — Graphic novels
978-1-55453-177-6, $16.95;
978-1-55453-178-3 (pa), $9.95
LC 2007-9060846

Courtesy of Kids Can Press

This book collects short biographies in graphic format of young women who dressed as and pretended to be men in order to do and be what they wanted. The real Mu Lan did pretend to be her father's son in order to serve in the Chinese Emperor's army to protect her father. Hatshepsut was an Egyptian princess who was determined to be pharaoh, although that role could only go to men. Margaret Buckley was a young Englishwoman who became Dr. James Barry in the early nineteenth century. Seven women's stories are told here, and the book includes a short list of books for further reading.

Huizenga, Kevin

★ **Curses**. Drawn & Quarterly 2006 145p. Illustration
Grades: 11 12 Adult   **741.5; Fic**
1. Graphic novels
978-1-894937-86-3, $21.95

Huizenga's central character in his comics is Glenn Ganges, a seemingly middle-class man living in the suburbs whose blank-eyed wonderment at everyday experiences brings together such diverse aspects of the world as golf, theology, late-night diners, parenthood, politics, Sudanese refugees, and hallucinatory vision, into a complete experience as multifaceted as our own lives. There is some use of strong language.

Humphries, Sam

Jonesy; Volume 1. by Sam Humphries & Caitlin Rose Boyle; colors by Mickey Quinn; letters by Corey Breen; cover by Caitlin Rose Boyle. Boom! Studios 2016 112 p. Color; Illustration
Grades: 7 8 9 10 11 12   **741.5; Fic**
1. Teenage girls — Fiction; 2. Humorous fiction; 3. Fantasy fiction
1608868834; 9781608868834, $9.99

"Jonesy is a self-described 'cool dork.'...But she has a secret nobody knows. She has the power to make people fall in love!...There's only one catch — it doesn't work on herself. She's gonna have to find love the old-fashioned way, and in the meantime, figure out how to distract herself from the real emotions she inevitably has to face when her powers go wrong." (Publisher's note)
Volume 1 of 3

Hutchison, David

Biowulf Volume 1. Antarctic Press 2007 un Illustration
Grades: 10 11 12 Adult   **741.5; Fic**
1. Adventure graphic novels; 2. Beowulf — Adaptations — Graphic novels; 3. Graphic novels; 4. Horror graphic novels; 5. Science fiction graphic novels
978-0-9787725-2-9, $14.95

In the staggering wreckage of Earth's future, the great King Hrothgar and his armies have known only victory after bloody victory. Now, on the brink of uniting the battling lands and bringing the long wars to an end, Hrothgar's rule is threatened. His actions have awakened the ancient evil of the Grendel, and his men are powerless to defend themselves against the demon's wrath. Only with the aid of the young hero Beowulf and a cunning trap can they hope to kill Grendel and finally know peace. In this cyberpunk adaptation, Beowulf is an Advance, a genetically engineered, cybernetically enhanced human warrior; and Grendel is a monster, but he's not the real villain. The book includes a lot of graphic, bloody violence.

Oz: The Manga. Antarctic Press 2006 un Illustration
Grades: 4 5 6 7 8 9

741.5; Fic
1. Fantasy graphic novels; 2. Graphic novels; 3. Baum, L. Frank — Adaptations
978-1-932453-69-0, $14.95

Courtesy of Antarctic Press

This is Baum's classic novel, The Wizard of Oz, adapted into manga format by Hutchison. All the characters are here: Dorothy, Toto, the Cowardly Lion, the Tin Woodsman, the Scarecrow, the Wizard. And all the main plot elements are here, from the cyclone that blows Dorothy and Toto to Oz to the Flying Monkeys to dealing with the Wicked Witch. The art makes this adaptation shine, especially the Tin Woodsman, who is a steampunk wonder.

Hyde, Laurence

Southern Cross. Drawn & Quarterly 2007 256p. Illustration
Grades: 10 11 12 Adult   **741.5**
1. Atomic bomb — Testing — Graphic novels; 2. Stories without words — Graphic novels; 3. Graphic novels
978-1-897299-10-4, $24.95

This is a wordless novel, told in 118 wood engravings, about the atomic bomb testing performed by the United States in the South Pacific following World War II. This new hardcover edition is a facsimile of the original edition, published in 1951. Laurence Hyde was infuriated with the United States' continued testing in the Bikini Atoll, following the mass destruction and unthinkable horrors resulting from the atomic bombs dropped on Hiroshima and Nagasaki in August 1945. The story depicts the evacuation of the Polynesian islander from their homes; during the evacuation, a fisherman kills a sailor who attempts to rape his wife. The couple flees with their child into the jungle to avoid capture. After the other islanders have evacuated, the Americans detonate an atom bomb on the ocean floor, and the fisherman and his family suffer horribly from the effects. The book includes nudity and depiction of the attempted rape.

Miles, Hyman

Shirley Jackson's The Lottery: The Authorized Graphic Adaptation. Miles Hyman. Hill & Wang 2016 160 p. Illustration

Grades: 10 11 12 Adult   **741.5**

1. Lotteries — Comic books, strips, etc.; 2. Rites and ceremonies — Comic books, strips, etc.; 3. Villages — Comic books, strips, etc.
9780809066490, $30; 9780809066506; 9780809066513

LC 2016007147

This graphic adaptation by Miles Hyman allows readers to experience Shirley Jackson's short story "The Lottery" "as never before, or to discover it anew. He has crafted an eerie vision of the hamlet where the tale unfolds and the unforgettable ritual its inhabitants set into motion. Hyman's full-color, meticulously detailed panels create a noirish atmosphere that adds a new dimension of dread to the original story." (Publisher's note)

"Hyman, Jackson's grandson, imbues realistic characters with a blocky stoicism in full-color panels flooded with sun-parched orange light. Much of the rendition is wordless, the art carrying this tale of quiet horror." LJ

I-Huan

Real/Fake Princess, Vol. 1. DrMaster Publications 2006 176p. Illustration
Grades: 6 7 8 9 10 11 12

741.5; Fic

1. Adventure graphic novels; 2. Graphic novels; 3. Manhua; 4. Romance graphic novels
978-1-59796-079-3, $9.95

Courtesy of DrMaster Publications

In Tang Dynasty China, the country is in great chaos due to the infamous Jin Kang Rebellion. Fearing the possible destruction that might eventually result, Concubine Liu tearfully entrusts the care of her baby daughter, Princess Yi Fu, to a common citizen named Tang Hui. Tang Hui immediately escapes with the princess to the South. A decade passes, and Emperor Gao Zon of Tang has decided he wants to find all of his long-lost relatives and has appointed Zhong Lu to the task. From there an adventure begins as Zhong Lu discovers and takes a special interest in Princess Yi Fu (renamed Zi Li), who is happily living in a quiet fishing village with her childhood crush and savior — Tang Hui. Returning with Zhong Lu to a life of royalty means leaving behind the humble life she has come to know with the commoners. This is manhua, I-Huan is from Taiwan.

Igarashi, Daisuke

★ **Children** of the sea, vol. 1. Viz Media/Viz Signature 2009 320p. Illustration
Grades: 7 8 9 10 11 12   **741; Fic; 741.5**

1. Adventure graphic novels; 2. Fantasy graphic novels; 3. Graphic novels; 4. Manga; 5. Mystery graphic novels; 6. Ocean — Graphic novels; 7. Seinen manga
978-1-4215-2914-1, $14.99; 1-4215-2914-9

"As a young girl, Ruka sees a fish turn into light and disappear at the aquarium where her father works, but no one believes her. Years later, the mystery of the ghost of the sea unfolds before Ruka and a pair of mysterious young boys, Umi and Sora." Publ Wkly

"Igarashi's storytelling is quiet, thoughtful, and thought provoking, but it is his drawings that make this manga so amazing. Extremely detailed settings turn panels into mini-masterpieces." Booklist

Volume 1 of 5

Ikeda, Miyoko

Fairy navigator Runa, vol.1. Del Rey Manga 2010 186p. Illustration
Grades: 7 8 9 10 11 12   **741.5; Fic**

1. Adventure graphic novels; 2. Fairies — Graphic novels; 3. Fantasy graphic novels; 4. Graphic novels; 5. Magic — Graphic novels; 6. Manga; 7. Shojo manga
978-0-345-52226-9, $10.99

Fourth grader Runa Rindo has lived in the Children of the Stars School ever since she was very young, it's the only home she has ever really known. All she has from her parents is a ring pendant and a small wooden box. Then two young strangers ask Runa "Are you the Legendary Girl?" And with that, her life changes. Suneri and Mokke are Fairies who can change shape to a cat (Suneri) and an owl (Mokke), and they tell Runa that she is a princess from the Fairy world. When another fairy, Kamachi, kidnaps Runa's best friend, Chae ("my name is Sae!"), Runa finds she must accept her destiny as the one who can control passage between the human and fairy worlds to save Chae.

Ikeda, Riyoko

Claudine. story and art by Riyoko Ikeda; translation by Jocelyne Allen; lettering and retouch by CK Russell. Seven Seas Entertainment 2018 104 p. Illustration
Grades: 9 10 11 12 Adult   **741.5; Fic**

1. Gender identity — Fiction; 2. LGBT people — Fiction
1626928916; 9781626928916, $13.99

This book, by Riyoko Ikeda, tells the story of Claudine, who was "born...in a female-assigned body that doesn't reflect the man inside. [T]his heart-wrenching story follows Claudine through life, pain, and the love of several women... Ikeda explores gender and sexuality in early twentieth century France in this powerful tale about identity, culture, and self-acceptance." (Publisher's note)

"Featuring flowing layouts and glamorously stylized, statuesque figures, the first English translation of this novella, originally published in 1978, from the creator of The Rose of Versailles is well-timed to spark conversation around transgender representation in literary history." Pub Wkly

Inagaki, Riichiro

Eyeshield 21 Volume 1. Viz Media/Shonen Jump Advanced 2005 208p. Illustration
Grades: 10 11 12 Adult   **741.5; Fic**

1. Football — Graphic novels; 2. Graphic novels; 3. Humorous graphic novels; 4. Manga; 5. Shonen manga
1-59116-752-3, $7.99

What does a wimpy kid who's been bullied all his life have to depend on but his own two feet? Sena Kobayakawa is about to start his first year in high school and he's vowed not to get picked on anymore. Unfortunately, the sadistic captain of the football team already has his eye on Sena and his lightning-fast speed. As the Devil Bats' "secret weapon," Sena uses a superhero-like secret identity, Eyeshield 21, to protect himself from other teams. This is a football story for people who don't know or like American football. The series includes crude humor, strong language, and some playing field violence.

Inoue, Takehiko

★ **Real,** volume 1. story & art by Takehiko Inoue. Viz Media 2008 222p. Illustration

Grades: 10 11 12 Adult　　　　**741; Fic; 741.5**

1. Basketball — Graphic novels; 2. Graphic novels; 3. Manga; 4. Sports — Graphic novels; 5. Wheelchair basketball — Graphic novels; 6. Seinen manga

978-1-4215-1989-0, $12.99

Nomiya was the controlling rider on a motorcycle when he got into an accident that paralyzed the young woman riding with him; now he has dropped out of high school in his senior year and feels guilty. Togawa is stuck in a wheelchair but still plays basketball, which was the only thing Nomiya was good at in school. Togawa has quit the wheelchair basketball team, but he still plays. Nomiya starts playing while in a wheelchair, and they soon start a bit of a scam against regular players. They each have their own goals, but can they work together and find a better life for themselves? The book includes some harsh language, partial nudity, and Nomiya commits a bodily act against his school when he leaves.

"A compelling story of tragedy and struggle, Real is sure to appeal to teens — especially to male readers." SLJ

Original Japanese edition, 2001; Volume 1 of an ongoing series

★ **Slam** dunk, volume 1: Sakuragi. story and art by Takehiko Inoue; English adaptation Kelly Sue DeConnick. Viz Media/Shonen Jump 2008 197p. Illustration

Grades: 8 9 10 11 12　　　　**741.5; Fic**

1. Basketball — Graphic novels; 2. Graphic novels; 3. Manga; 4. Shonen manga

978-1-4215-0679-1, $7.99

Hanamichi Sakuragi is a first year student at Shohoku Prefecture High School; he's got a reputation as a bruising fighter and has suffered 50 rejections from girls who were scared of his fighting. He's looked down on sports all his life, but on this first day of high school, he meets Haruko Akagi; she's not scared of him, and she loves basketball. He falls for her completely, enough to try to play basketball. But, he has competition — Kaeda Rukawa is another first year student; he's a star basketball player, and Haruko has a huge crush on him. Then Sakuragi gets on the bad side of the basketball team captain, who happens to be Haruko's older brother. Sakuragi does everything he can to convince Takenori Akagi to let him join the team. However, he has a long way to go before he can build the fundamental skills to play basketball effectively; will he stick it out? There's some fighting, one male student's buttocks get exposed accidentally, but there's no bad language.

Original Japanese edition, 1991; Volume 1 of a 31 volume series

★ **Vagabond,** Vol. 1. by Takehiko Inoue; [English adaptation by Yuji Oniki]. Viz 2002 un Illustration

Grades: 11 12 Adult　　　　**741.5; Fic**

1. Graphic novels; 2. Manga; 3. Samurai — Graphic novels; 4. Seinen manga; 5. Musashi, Miyamoto, c. 1584-1645

1-59116-034-0, $12.95

Based on the novel Musashi by Eiji Yoshikawa, this is the story of Shinmen Takezo, a young foot soldier who survived the Battle of Sekigahara, which marked the beginning of the Tokugawa Era in Japan. Destined to become the legendary sword saint Miyamoto Musashi, Takezo is a wild young brute, a cold-hearted killer who wants to make a name for himself. This first volume in the ongoing series includes sword fights, some nudity, and sexual situations.

Also available as 12 VIZBIG volumes; Volume 1 of 37

Inzana, Ryan

Ichiro. written & illustrated by Ryan Inzana. Houghton Mifflin/Houghton Mifflin Harcourt 2012 288 p. Illustration; Color

Grades: 7 8 9 10　　　　**741.5/973**

1. Gods and goddesses — Fiction; 2. Grandfathers — Fiction; 3. Graphic novels; 4. Monsters — Fiction; 5. Supernatural — Fiction; 6. Japan — Fiction; 7. Japan — History — Graphic novels; 8. Fantasy graphic novels; 9. Supernatural graphic novels; 10. Folklore — Japan — Graphic novels; 11. Japanese Americans — Graphic novels

0547252692; 9780547252698

LC 2011277558

This graphic novel depicts the story of Ichiro, "a young American teen, son of a Japanese immigrant and an American soldier killed in combat, [who] goes to Japan with his mother for an extended visit and begins to grapple with sophisticated cultural complexities.... After his mother and Japanese grandfather tell him stories of Japanese history and folklore, Ichiro has a fantastical adventure involving the Japanese myth of the shape-shifting tanuki spirit." (Kirkus Reviews)

Irwin, Jane

Vogelein: Old Ghosts. Fiery Studios 2007 168p. Illustration

Grades: 7 8 9 10 11 12 Adult

741.5; Fic

1. Fantasy graphic novels; 2. Graphic novels

0-9743110-1-4, $12.95

Courtesy of Fiery Studios

Though three hundred years have passed since Alexi's death, Vogelein finds herself still haunted by the unkept promise she made to her first Guardian. Now the clockwork faerie must confront her past with the help of Mason, an itinerant musician whose spirit bears a striking resemblance to the one she desperately wants to lay to rest. As she struggles to find peace for both herself and Alexi, Vogelein discovers that centuries-old questions rarely have easy answers, intended paths reveal themselves in mysterious ways, and present-day threats strike just as suddenly as those from long ago.

Isayama, Hajime

★ **Attack** on Titan 1. Hajime Isayama. Kodansha 2012 186 p. Illustration (Attack on Titan)

Grades: 8 9 10 11 12　　　　**741.5**

1. Good and evil — Comic books, strips, etc.; 2. Horror comic books, strips, etc.; 3. Giants — Graphic novels; 4. Shonen manga; 5. Horror graphic novels

1612620248; 9781612620244, $10.99

"Humanity has been devastated by the bizarre, giant humanoids known as the Titans. Little is known about...why they are bent on consuming mankind.... People believe their 100-meter-high walls will protect them from the Titans, but the sudden appearance of an immense Titan is about to change everything." (Publisher's note)

"Along with the setting and intricate, twisting plot, Attack on Titan derives its appeal from its willingness to bend the conventions of shounen manga. Here, friendship and burning spirit do not conquer all, and your favorite character stands a good chance of getting eaten without the opportunity to give a cool speech first." LJ

Volume 1 of an ongoing series

Attack on Titan anthology. Attack on Titan created by Hajime Isayama; edited by Ben Applegate and Jeanine Schaefer; cover, logo, and interior design by Phil Balsman; lettering and interior design by Steve Wands. Kodansha 2016 256 p. Illustration

Grades: 8 9 10 11 12　　　　**741.5**

1. Fantasy fiction — Graphic novels; 2. Horror fiction — Graphic novels; 3. Science fiction graphic novels; 4. Shonen manga

1632362589; 9781632362582, $29.99

This tribute anthology to the manga Attack on Titan features "original stories by a long roster of comic superstars such as Scott Snyder (Batman, American Vampire), Gail Simone (Batgirl), Michael Avon Oeming (Powers), Paolo Rivera (Daredevil, Amazing Spider-Man), Cameron Stewart (Fight Club 2, Batgirl) and Faith Erin Hicks (The Adventures of Superhero Girl)!" (Publisher's note)

"The Victorian-style guide to Titan's walled city by Genevieve Valentine and David López is a standout, as is the contemplative final story by brothers Asaf and Tomer Hanuka." Pub Wkly

Ishida, Sui

Tokyo Ghoul: Re; Volume 1. by Sui Ishida. Viz 2017 224 p. Illustration

Grades: 10 11 12 Adult   **741.5**

1. Horror fiction — Graphic novels; 2. Seinen manga

142159496X; 9781421594965, $12.99

In this book, by Sui Ishida, "Haise Sasaki has been tasked with teaching Qs Squad how to be outstanding investigators, but his assignment is complicated by the troublesome personalities of his students and his own uncertain grasp of his Ghoul powers. Can he pull them together as a team, or will Qs Squad first assignment be their last?" (Publisher's note)

Volume 1 of an ongoing series

Tokyo Ghoul; Volume 1. by Sui Ishida; translation, Joe Yamazaki. Viz 2015 224 p. Illustration

Grades: 10 11 12 Adult   **741.5**

1. Seinen manga; 2. Horror fiction; 3. Manga; 4. College students — Fiction

1421580365; 9781421580364, $12.99

"Ghouls live among us, the same as normal people in every way-except their craving for human flesh. Ken Kaneki is an ordinary college student until a violent encounter turns him into the first half-human half-ghoul hybrid. Trapped between two worlds, he must survive Ghoul turf wars, learn more about Ghoul society and master his new powers." (Publisher's note)

Volume 1 of 14

Ishihara, Yoko

★ The **manga** cookbook. presented by the Manga University Culinary Institute; illustrations by Chihiro Hattori; [with recipes by Yoko Ishihara]. Japanime Co. Ltd. 2007 158p. Illustration

Grades: 4 5 6 7 8 9 10 11 12

641.5; 741.5

1. Graphic novels; 2. Japanese cooking — Graphic novels; 3. Manga

978-4-921205-07-2, $14.95

Courtesy of Japanime Co.

Food appears frequently in manga and in anime, but just what are the characters eating? This book is an illustrated step-by-step guide to preparing some Japanese dishes, from onigiri (rice balls) to yakitori (skewered grilled chicken), oshinko (pickled vegetables), udon (Japanese noodles), to traditional sweets and desserts. Definitions of terms and ingredients used, basic cooking guidelines, and instructions on how to properly use chopsticks are all included. The recipes are authentic but have been simplified somewhat so older children and teens with some basic kitchen skills can prepare the foods. Adult supervision is recommended for younger children and for children who aren't very experienced with using knives, measuring spoons, and cooking on the stove.

Iwaaki, Hitoshi

Parasyte vol. 3. Del Rey Manga 2008 284p. Illustration

Grades: 10 11 12 Adult   **741.5; Fic**

1. Graphic novels; 2. Horror graphic novels; 3. Manga; 4. Science fiction graphic novels; 5. Seinen manga

978-0-345-49825-0, $12.95

Alien parasites have invaded Earth and taken over the minds and bodies of ordinary people, in order to be able to feed on humans. Shin has been invaded by a parasite, but he stopped the invasion of his body and limited it to one arm. He can communicate with the parasite, whom he has named Migi (Japanese for right), and he can sense who is actually a parasite masquerading as a human. Now he's been approached by two mysterious victims of the invasion: Tamiya, a beautiful school teacher, and Shimada, another student. What do they really want? The book includes gory violence.

Parasyte vol.4. Del Rey Manga 2008 296p. Illustration

Grades: 10 11 12 Adult   **741.5; Fic**

1. Graphic novels; 2. Horror graphic novels; 3. Manga; 4. Seinen manga

978-0-345-49826-7, $14.95

Shinichi and Migi, the Parasyte that merged with him, continue their search for the Parasytes who kill humans, even as Shinichi tries to be a "normal" high school student. Then he meets Kana, a classmate who seems to have a knack for sensing the killer aliens. The fact that the aliens are getting into politics in order to gain positions of power disturbs Shinichi, but he also suspects that Migi may be infiltrating his brain, too. The book includes violence and bloodshed, and brief partial nudity.

Parasyte, Vol. 1. Ballantine Books/Del Rey Manga 2007 282p. Illustration

Grades: 11 12 Adult   **741.5; Fic**

1. Graphic novels; 2. Horror graphic novels; 3. Manga; 4. Science fiction graphic novels; 5. Seinen manga

978-0-345-49624-9, $12.95

Aliens come to Earth in a silent invasion, taking over human bodies; their plan is to kill and eat humans. One ordinary high school student, Shin, fights off an alien and it only manages to get into his right hand. Once the parasitic alien has matured while still stuck in Shin's right hand, it can't get to his brain. They settle into an uneasy relationship, as Migi (Japanese for "right") tries to learn everything and Shin just tries to keep up a normal appearance. Soon, though, they find other aliens, and Shin can't let the parasites take over without trying to fight back.

Iwaaki alleviates the horror with plenty of dark humor; he also uses harsh language, including f-bombs and s-bombs, and some sexual innuendo.

Originally published in a flipped (American style) manga series by Tokyopop from 1997 to 2002; this edition retains the right-to-left orientation, Japanese sound effects, and other original elements.

Iwanaga, Ryoutaro

Pumpkin scissors vol. 1. translated by Ikoi Hiroe. Del Rey Manga 2007 218p. Illustration

Grades: 10 11 12 Adult   **Fic; 741; 741.5**

1. Adventure graphic novels; 2. Graphic novels; 3. Manga; 4. Shonen manga

978-0-345-50119-6, $10.95

The bitter war between the Empire and the Republic of Frost has ended, but three years after the cease-fire, the Empire is still ravaged by starvation and disease, and bandits terrorize the people. Can the Imperial Army State Section III, aka Pumpkin Scissors, stop a renegade force bent on destruction? And who is the mysterious stranger helping Pumpkin Scissors? The book includes some violence and mildly harsh language.

Iwaoka, Hisae

★ **Saturn** apartments, volume 1. [translation, Matt Thorn].. Viz Signature 2010 184p. Illustration

Grades: 7 8 9 10   **741; 741.5; Fic**

1. Graphic novels; 2. Manga; 3. Science fiction graphic novels; 4. Seinen manga

978-1-4215-3364-3, $12.99; 1-4215-3364-2

Far in the future, humankind has left Earth to live in a gigantic ringlike structure that circles the planet. In this structure, humans have developed a class structure based on where one lives: the higher the floor on which you live, the greater your status. Mitsu has just graduated from junior high and is now expected to work as a window washer, just like his father before him. The thing is, his father disappeared while washing windows and is presumed dead. Window washing means one must get into a space suit and go out of the structure into outer space, 35 kilometers above the Earth's surface; space winds and other hazards make the work dangerous and expensive. Even as he wonders still, five years after his father's disappearance, what happened to him, Mitsu finds his job gives him a unique perspective on the lives of those who live in the Saturn Apartments. This is science fiction from the viewpoint of the mundane service work rather than heroics of space action.

"This story of a young teen struggling to live alone will appeal to YAs, and the introspective nature of the narrative will have plenty of crossover appeal for adult readers as well." Booklist

Reads from right to left; Volume 1 of 7

Jablonski, Carla

Defiance. written by Carla Jablonski; art by Leland Purvis; color by Hilary Sycamore. First Second 2011 126p. Illustration

Grades: 7 8 9 10 11 12   **741.5; Fic**

1. World War, 1939-1945 — Fiction; 2. World War, 1939-1945 — Underground movements — Fiction; 3. France — History — 1940-1945, German occupation — Graphic novels

978-1-59643-292-5, $16.99; 1-59643-292-6

LC 2010036253

"World War II has taken its toll on the French countryside. German soldiers patrol the towns, searching for any challenge to their rule. The Tessier siblings, Paul, Marie, and Sophie, keep their noses clean and their faces blank as the French military police tighten their grip on their small country town. But all three are secretly doing their part for the Resistance: the men and women working hard to undermine the Germans and win back France's freedom...even if it ends up costing them their lives." (Publisher's note)

★ **Resistance,** book 1. art by Leland Purvis; color by Hilary Sycamore. First Second Books 2010 121p. Illustration (Resistance)

Grades: 6 7 8 9 10 11 12   **741.5; Fic**

1. Adventure graphic novels; 2. Graphic novels; 3. World War, 1939-1945 — Jews — Rescue — Graphic novels; 4. World War, 1939-1945 — Underground movements — Graphic novels; 5. France — History — 1940-1945, German occupation — Graphic novels

978-1-59643-291-8, $16.99; 1-59643-291-8

Paul and his younger sister Marie live in a small village in Vichy France during World War II. Thus far, the war hasn't really touched them, but now Nazi soldiers come, and Paul's friend, Henri, and his parents are Jews and therefore in danger. When Paul and Marie try to protect Henri, their secret leaks out to members of the Resistance. Although they are young, they soon become recruits in the Resistance. Paul's incessant sketching in his book turns out to be a valuable talent, but he and Marie, and then their older sister, Sylvie, don't quite realize just how dangerous things can get. The cover is very striking, with Paul aiming a slingshot at a Nazi soldier. The Author's Note at the end of the book talks about history, the Resistance, and why the events in France during World War II should not be depicted as black and white, heroic Resistance versus villainous Vichy.

Other titles in this series are: Defiance (2011); Victory (2012)

★ **Victory.** written by Carla Jablonski; art by Leland Purvis; color by Hilary Sycamore.. First Second 2012 123 p. Color illustration

Grades: 6 7 8 9 10 11 12   **741.5/973**

1. Graphic novels; 2. World War, 1939-1945 — France — Fiction; 3. World War, 1939-1945 — France — Juvenile fiction; 4. World War, 1939-1945 — Underground movements — France — Fiction; 5. France — History — German occupation, 1940-1945 — Fiction; 6. Underground movements — Fiction; 7. Resistance to government — Fiction; 8. France — History — Graphic novels; 9. World War, 1939-1945 — Children — Fiction

1596432934; 9781596432932

LC 2011030504

"In this third volume in the graphic novel trilogy about the Tessier family," set during the French Resistance, "Sylvie relays information she gathers from her unwitting German boyfriend, Marie hides a man she discovers after a plane crash in the woods, and Paul is the ears of the Resistance in town.... At the end of the book, Paul travels to Paris to pass along information. He's on the scene for the city's liberation." (Horn Book Magazine)

"The storyline is brisk and edgy, complementing the worn nerves of people who have lived through war... Fans of graphic art and WWII will appreciate this book, as well as reluctant readers who are interested in historical fiction." VOYA

Jackson, Sherard

Assembly. Antarctic Press 2003

Grades: 9 10 11 12

741.5; Fic

1. Graphic novels; 2. Science fiction graphic novels

1-932453-51-2; 978-1-932453-51-5, $9.99

In a future world in which war is a constant, a young woman enters the military as a doctor, only to find she must pilot a battle suit. In one pitched battle full of violence and casualties, she makes a devastating discovery about her pacifist older sister.

Courtesy of Antarctic Press

"In our time of violence all over the world, this slim book examines one teenage girl's motivation for becoming a soldier in a world consumed by war." Voice Youth Advocates

Jacobson, Sidney

The **9/11 report**: a graphic adaptation. by Sid Jacobson and Ernie Colón; [with a foreword by Thomas H. Kean and Lee H. Hamilton]. Hill and Wang 2006 133p. Illustration

Grades: 9 10 11 12 Adult   **973.931; 741.5**

1. Graphic novels; 2. September 11 terrorist attacks, 2001 — Graphic novels

0-8090-5738-7; 978-0-8090-5738-2, $30; 0-8090-5739-5 (pa); 978-0-8090-5739-9 (pa), $16.95

"The book aims to make...[The 9/11 Commission Report] more accessible to all readers and draw in young adults.... This graphic adaptation is an important and necessary part of any collection." Libr J

On cover: Based on the final report of the National Commission on Terrorist Attacks upon the United States

Anne Frank: the Anne Frank House authorized graphic biography. [by] Sid Jacobson and Ernie Colón. Hill and Wang 2010 152p. Illustration
Grades: 9 10 11 12 Adult **92; 741.5**
  1. Holocaust, 1933-1945 — Graphic novels; 2. Jews — Netherlands — Graphic novels
  978-0-8090-2684-5, $30; 978-0-8090-2685-2 (pa), $16.95
LC 2010-5776
Draws on the archives of the Anne Frank House to relate the short but inspiring life of the Jewish teen memoirist, from the lives of her parents to Anne's years keeping her private diary while hidden from the Nazis to her untimely death in a concentration camp.

Jacques, Brian
  Redwall: the graphic novel. by Brian Jacques; illustrated by Bret Blevins; adapted by Stuart Moore; lettering by Richard Starkings. Philomel Books 2007 143p. Illustration
Grades: 4 5 6 7 8 9 **741.5; Fic**
  1. Adventure graphic novels; 2. Fantasy graphic novels; 3. Graphic novels; 4. Mice — Graphic novels
  978-0-399-24481-0, $12.99; 0-399-24481-6
When Cluny the rat's army attacks Redwall Abbey, young Matthias the mouse follows in the footsteps of the long-ago hero Martin the Warrior to defend his home
"The story is a page-turner, and the detailed black-and-white drawings capture both the passion and the pathos." SLJ

Jansson, Tove
  Moomin Book One. Drawn & Quarterly 2006 96p. Illustration
Grades: 8 9 10 11 12 Adult **741.5; Fic**
  1. Graphic novels; 2. Humorous graphic novels; 3. Moomins (Fictional characters)
  1-894937-80-5, $19.95
Jansson is best known in the U.S. for her children's books featuring the Moomins, hippo-shaped creatures. Her comic strips have a more mature outlook. Moomin needs help getting rid of unwanted guests, but the only solution that works costs him his house. Then his scheming friend Sniff involves him in all sorts of shady get-rich-quick schemes. And when Moomin finds his long-lost parents, his father's craving for adventure causes more trouble. Snorkmaiden, Moomin's girlfriend, is just as bad as Moominpapa, and they spark a boat trip south to a resort, where the naive Moomins think they're houseguests and everyone else, including the hotel staff, assumes they're wealthy eccentrics. The childlike look of the strips belie the goings-on; this book is not really for young readers, although teens and adults will enjoy the whimsy overlaying sharp satire.

  Moomin's winter follies. Trove Jansson. Enfant 2012 45 p.
Grades: 8 9 10 11 12 Adult **741.5**
  1. Moomins (Fictional characters); 2. Comic books, strips, etc.
  1770460985; 9781770460980, $9.95
Author Tove Jansson presents a graphic novel. "Moomin wakes up one morning to find the pond frozen over, and rather than hibernate, the family decides to brave the winter weather. At first, their wintry adventure seems to be going swimmingly, until Mr. Brisk of the Great Outdoors Club takes over and forces everyone to embrace the winter sports, whether they want to or not." (Comic Vine)

Jason
  The **Left** Bank Gang. Fantagraphics Books 2006 46p. Illustration
Grades: 10 11 12 Adult **741.5; Fic**
  1. Graphic novels; 2. Mystery graphic novels
  978-1-56097-742-1, $12.95
Double-crosses, violence, and harsh language pepper this little noir story that depicts Ernest Hemingway, F. Scott Fitzgerald, Ezra Pound, and

James Joyce as struggling cartoonists in 1920s Paris. Zelda Fitzgerald and Gertrude Stein are there, as well. Everyone is portrayed as dog-headed people, in Jason's signature art style.

  Meow, Baby!. Fantagraphics Books 2005 un Illustration
Grades: 10 11 12 Adult **741.5; Fic**
  1. Graphic novels; 2. Humorous graphic novels
  1-56097-695-0, $16.95
Jason unleashes his inner Scandinavian goofball with this big collection of hilarious shorter pieces. God, the Devil, mummies, vampires, zombies, werewolves, reanimated skeletons, space invaders, Death, cavemen, Godzilla and Elvis populate these most often wordless blackout gags, side by side with Jason's usual Little-Orphan-Annie-eyed, rabbit-and-bird-head protagonists — a "lighter side" of one of the best cartoonists of the new millennium. Some nudity and sexual situations, and a little violence, plus seeing what zombies eat are subtly present.

Jeanty, Georges
  Buffy the Vampire Slayer season eight; Volume 1: the long way home. Dark Horse Comics 2007 136p. Illustration
Grades: 8 9 10 11 12 Adult **741.5**
  1. Adventure graphic novels; 2. Buffy the Vampire Slayer (Fictional character); 3. Graphic novels; 4. Horror graphic novels
  978-1-59307-822-5, $15.95
The television series of Buffy the Vampire Slayer lasted seven seasons; this volume begins the comics-only eighth season. Buffy and her friends may have destroyed the Hellmouth, but all is not fun and games, as an old enemy returns, younger sister Dawn experiences some "growing pains," and a former decoy Slayer has her own troubles. There is a considerable amount of monster fighting.
  Volume 1 of 8

Jenkins, Paul
  Civil War: Front Line Book 1. Marvel Entertainment 2007 un Illustration
Grades: 9 10 11 12 Adult **741.5; Fic**
  1. Graphic novels; 2. Superhero graphic novels
  978-0-7851-2312-5, $14.99
In "Embedded," reporters Sally Floyd and Ben Urich seek the truth at the heart of the war. In "The Accused," the lone survivor of the team that caused the Stamford tragedy has been found, and this vilified hero is placed under arrest for the deaths of an entire town. And his trouble is just beginning. This volume includes other stories, including the mystery of the Atlanteans.

  Civil War: Front Line Book 2. Marvel Entertainment 2007 un Illustration
Grades: 9 10 11 12 Adult **741.5; Fic**
  1. Graphic novels; 2. Superhero graphic novels
  978-0-7851-2469-6, $14.99
In "Embedded," hot on the trail of a revelation that could explode the rift between the pro-registration and anti-registration heroes and forever change the nature of the Registration Act, the Daily Bugle's Ben Urich and Sally Floyd have the story. Can they bring the power to the people? In "The Accused," his powers are gone, he's been held culpable for the worst super-human disaster in history, and every super-villain in prison is looking to take a piece of Speedball. Will he make it out alive, and with hundreds of deaths on his conscience, does he want to? In the meantime, Norman Osborn shoots an Atlantean ambassador, bringing the U.S. to the brink of war; and there's a traitor in Stark's group. This volume includes some violence.

  Revelations. created by Paul Jenkins and Humberto Ramos; story by Paul Jenkins; art by Humberto Ramos; colors by Leonardo Olea and Edgar

Delgado; letters by Richard Starkings and Comicraft. Dark Horse Comics 2006 un Illustration
Grades: 11 12 Adult   **741.5; Fic**
  1. Catholic church — Graphic novels; 2. Graphic novels; 3. Mystery graphic novels
978-1-59307-239-1, $17.95

When a Cardinal in line to succeed the dying Pope falls from a high window in the Vatican, a priest calls on his friend, tough London cop Charlie Northern, to investigate. Once in Rome, Northern confronts coverups and secrets as he tries to find out what happened. What he learns will shake him to his atheistic core. This violent murder mystery will appeal to fans of The Da Vinci Code and other works depicting religious conspiracies.

Originally published as Revelations issues #1-6.

Johns, Geoff

52, Volume One. Geoff Johns, Grant Morrison, Greg Rucka, Mark Waid, Keith Giffen. DC Comics 2007 304p. Illustration
Grades: 10 11 12 Adult   **741.5; Fic**
  1. Adventure graphic novels; 2. Graphic novels; 3. Mystery graphic novels; 4. Science fiction graphic novels; 5. Superhero graphic novels; 6. Superman (Fictional character)
978-1-4012-1353-4, $19.99

The events of Infinite Crisis have left Superman, Batman and Wonder Woman missing, many other superheroes dead or injured. Black Adam, the long-time nemesis of Shazam, seeks to gain allies to form a group to go up against the U.S. Ralph Dibny investigates a cult built around the idea of resurrecting Superboy. The Blue Beetle tries to use information from the 25th century to gain wealth and become the next big superhero. John Steel tries to go up against ex-President Lex Luthor, who has developed a drug that can "create" superheroes. DC Comics gathered four writers, a breakdown artist (Giffen), and a host of pencillers and inkers to create a year-long weekly comic book that plays out the action in real time. Johns, Morrison, Rucka, and Waid also worked together on every issue.

Originally published as 52 issues #1-13.; Volume 1 of 4

Batman: War Games Act Three: Endgame. DC Comics 2005 un Illustration
Grades: 10 11 12 Adult   **741.5; Fic**
  1. Batman (Fictional character); 2. Graphic novels; 3. Mystery graphic novels; 4. Superhero graphic novels
1-4012-0431-7, $14.99

Black Mask has made Batman's training scenario a chilling reality. The various crime families are leaderless, and the soldiers run for their lives while trying to grab a piece of the underworld pie for themselves. Batman and his allies have failed to contain the chaos threatening the lives of Gotham City's people. The media have exploited the situation so people think Batman is acting against their best interests. Worse, he has lost the trust and support of Commissioner Akins, just when he needs it the most. Before the day is over, a friend and ally will be dead, familial ties will be broken, and the balance of power in the city will be forever altered.

The **Flash:** The Secret of Barry Allen. DC Comics 2005 un Illustration
Grades: 9 10 11 12 Adult   **741.5; Fic**
  1. Flash (Fictional character); 2. Graphic novels; 3. Superhero graphic novels
1-4012-0723-5, $19.99

This volume details the events in Wally West's life as he regains his memory of being the Flash. He carefully chooses which friends and allies to whom he will again reveal his identity. Then, he and his pal Nightwing are confronted with the return of Gorilla Grodd, more savage than ever. But the biggest shock in the Fastest Man Alive's life comes when he reads a letter from his mentor and predecessor, Barry Allen, revealing a dark decision that haunted him to the day he died. And after reading it, Wally needs to reassess what it means to be a hero in a world growing ever darker.

The **Flash:** crossfire. [by] Geoff Johns, writer; Scott Kolins, Rich Burchett, Justiniano, pencillers; Doug Hazlewood, Dan Panosian, Walden Wong, inkers; James Sinclair, colorist; Gaspar Saladino, Bill Oakley, letterers; Brian Bolland, Scott Kolins, original covers. DC Comics 2004 212p. Illustration
Grades: 10 11 12 Adult   **741.5; Fic**
  1. Graphic novels; 2. Superhero graphic novels; 3. Flash (Fictional character)
1-4012-0195-4, $17.95

                                                    LC 2004-555611
"Eight...rogues have joined forces to take over Flash's town of Keystone City. As if that weren't enough, the Thinker, an artificial intelligence with a personality — a walking computer virus of sorts — is attempting to absorb the minds of the city's inhabitants, including Flash's. Writer Johns demonstrates his ability to reinvigorate the series' classic elements.... Teens will appreciate it as mainstream superhero fare, executed with complexity and flair." Booklist

The **Flash:** Wonderland. DC Comics 2007 144p. Illustration
Grades: 9 10 11 12 Adult   **741.5; Fic**
  1. Graphic novels; 2. Superhero graphic novels; 3. Flash (Fictional character)
978-1-4012-1489-0, $12.99

The Flash, Wally West, finds himself on a parallel Earth in which there's no Speed Force, and without that energy source, he has no power. The cops think he's a murderer, and the only one who can help him is one of his enemies, Captain Cold, who's also in the same world. They join forces to try to get back to their Earth, but they've got to find out who brought them here.

Green Lantern Corps: Recharge. Geoff Johns, Dave Gibbons, writers; Patrick Gleason, penciller; Prentis Rollins, Christian Alamy, inkers; Phil Balsman, Pat Brosseau, Travis Lanham, letterers; Moose Baumann, colorist. DC Comics 2006 un Illustration
Grades: 9 10 11 12 Adult   **741.5; Fic**
  1. Graphic novels; 2. Superhero graphic novels; 3. Green Lantern (Fictional character)
978-1-4012-0962-9, $12.99

After the return of Hal Jordan, the Guardians of the Universe have re-formed the Green Lantern Corps. The best and the brightest from across the universe find themselves chosen as members of the new Corps and summoned to the planet Oa, given power rings that turn strength of will into reality, and for training. While veteran ring-bearers gladly return to duty, some new recruits resent being drafted into the Corps against their will. Kyle Rayner, Guy Gardner, and Kilowog set out to train the new Green Lanterns, but something is making its way to Oa, something that threatens the very existence of the planet and the Guardians; can the new Corps stop it?

Green Lantern: No Fear. DC Comics 2006 un Illustration
Grades: 10 11 12 Adult   **741.5; Fic**
  1. Graphic novels; 2. Green Lantern (Fictional character); 3. Superhero graphic novels
978-14012-0466-2, $24.99

Hal Jordan has been resurrected and redeemed. Now it's tie to get on with his life as Green Lantern, protector of space sector 2814. But even as he returns to the skies as an Air Force pilot, Jordan faces new threats from his old foes. The deadly Manhunter androids and the mutated Shark return with shocking violence...yet they are just precursors to even greater dangers. A maddened Black Hand embarks on a murderous rampage just as the Lantern finds himself the object of an alien race's insidious plan to harvest humans as living weapons of war. Johns works with artists Carlos

Pacheco, Ethan Van Sciver, Darwyn Cooke, and Simone Bianchi in the stories collected here. There is some strong language, and violence, some graphic.

Green Lantern: Rebirth. DC Comics 2005 un Illustration
Grades: 9 10 11 12 Adult **741.5; Fic**
1. Graphic novels; 2. Green Lantern (Fictional character); 3. Superhero graphic novels
9781401204655, $14.99
He was the greatest Green Lantern of them all. Then Hal Jordan went mad and ultimately died in an attempt to redeem himself. But fate was not done with him. Kyle Rayner, the sole Green Lantern, crashes back to Earth with a coffin bearing Hal Jordan's body, saying feverishly, "Parallax is coming." And Hal Jordan has returned. And so has Parallax, and the Spectre. Will one of them win and possess Jordan forever? Or can he become the Green Lantern once again?

Infinite Crisis. DC Comics 2006 262p. Illustration
Grades: 9 10 11 12 Adult **741.5; Fic**
1. Graphic novels; 2. Superhero graphic novels
978-1-4012-0959-9, $24.99
Four heroes, trapped in limbo since the original Crisis on Infinite Earths, are about to reveal themselves: one is dying, one wants to save her and restore an entire world that vanished and the other two seek unrivaled power. The plan they concoct is literally earth-shattering, and the world's greatest superheroes may not be enough to stop their attempt to alter the very nature of reality.

JSA Presents Stars and S.T.R.I.P.E.. DC Comics 2007 192p. Illustration
Grades: 8 9 10 11 12 Adult **741.5; Fic**
1. Graphic novels; 2. Superhero graphic novels
978-1-4012-1390-9, $17.99
Courtney Whitmore is just your typical teenage girl trying to make it through high school, but she's about to stumble upon a secret that will make her life a lot more complicated. Her new stepfather, Pat Dugan, was once Stripesy, sidekick of the Golden Age hero The Star-Spangled Kid. Finding the Kid's old costume, Courtney modifies it for herself and becomes the new Star-Spangled Kid, aiming to fight crime and annoy the heck out of her stepfather. But Dugan isn't about to let his new daughter get into any danger. Putting his mechanical skills to work, he creates a robotic suit called S.T.R.I.P.E., and joins Courtney's battle for justice. They fight side-by-side — and sometimes with each other — taking on aliens, cults, new villains, and more. These stories are the first that Johns wrote in comics, back in 1999.

JSA: Black Vengeance. DC Comics 2006 208p. Illustration
Grades: 10 11 12 Adult **741.5; Fic**
1. Graphic novels; 2. Justice Society of America (Fictional characters); 3. Superhero graphic novels
978-1-4012-0966-7, $19.99
The JSA's former comrade, the Spectre, is now without a human host and running rampant, dealing out a brutal form of justice, encouraged by the new Eclipso. Atom-Smasher, also a former JSA member, seeks forgiveness for his actions in Kahndaq. Before the JSA decides whether or not to readmit him, Khandaq's ruler, Black Adam, summons the atomic hero back to the Middle East. When the JSA follow, all are forced to re-examine what it means to be a hero.

JSA: Lost. DC Comics 2005 208p. Illustration
Grades: 9 10 11 12 Adult **741.5; Fic**
1. Graphic novels; 2. Science fiction graphic novels; 3. Superhero graphic novels
1-4012-0722-7, $19.99

The first Hourman sits alone at the end of time, having given his life to protect humanity. Sand, former chairman of the JSA, became one with the planet Earth to keep it whole. Hal Jordan sacrificed himself to become the new Spectre and keep the world safe. Now the JSA find themselves visiting old friends and new, rectifying injustices, aware that as they fix one problem, an even larger one is brewing in the time stream. The end of this volume contains spoilers about the killer's identity in the Identity Crisis. The book includes lots of superhero action and some violence.

Power Girl. Geoff Johns, Paul Levitz, Paul Kupperberg, writers; Amanda Conner ... [et al.], pencillers; Jimmy Palmiotti ... [et al.], inkers; Paul Mounts ... [et al.], colorists; Rob Leigh ... [et al.], letterers. DC Comics 2006 176p. Illustration
Grades: 9 10 11 12 Adult **741.5; Fic**
1. Adventure graphic novels; 2. Graphic novels; 3. Superhero graphic novels
978-1-4012-0968-1, $14.99
Who is Power Girl? Is she Superman's cousin from a parallel world? Is she the granddaughter of an ancient Atlantean sorcerer? Is she a pawn in a game of cosmic chess that threatens the known universe? Whoever she is, she's playing a major role in recent DC Universe titles. In these stories, some dating back to 1975, her reality keeps changing. The more recent stories include a little bit of suggestiveness.

Showcase Presents Superman Family Volume One. DC Comics 2006 572p. Illustration
Grades: 6 7 8 9 10 11 12 Adult **741.5; Fic**
1. Graphic novels; 2. Jimmy Olsen (Fictional character); 3. Lois Lane (Fictional character); 4. Superhero graphic novels; 5. Superman (Fictional character)
978-1-4012-0787-8, $16.99
This volume spotlights Superman's girlfriend Lois Lane and his pal Jimmy Olsen. Learn more about these two dynamic personalities in their solo stories as each braves danger for the latest scoop. These stories from the 1950s also introduce long-standing elements such as the Daily Planet's Flying Newsroom and Jimmy's penchant for disguises. The Showcase series reprints the older comics stories in black and white collections.

Showcase Presents: Green Arrow Volume 1. DC Comics 2006 528p. Illustration
Grades: 7 8 9 10 11 12 Adult **741.5; Fic**
1. Graphic novels; 2. Green Arrow (Fictional character); 3. Superhero graphic novels; 4. Green Arrow (Fictional character)
1-4012-0785-5, $16.99
Millionaire Oliver Queen mastered the bow and arrow as a matter of survival when he was trapped on a desert island. Back home in Star City, he chose to use his newfound skills as the costumed champion Green Arrow. With his sidekick, Speedy, he tackled crooks and solved mysteries with energy, style, and the occasional boxing glove arrow. The stories collected in this black and white volume were originally published from 1958 through 1969

Showcase Presents: Jonah Hex Volume 1. DC Comics 2005 528p. Illustration
Grades: 10 11 12 Adult **741.5; Fic**
1. Graphic novels; 2. Jonah Hex (Fictional character); 3. Western graphic novels
1-4012-0760-X, $16.99
He was a hero to some, a villain to others; and wherever he rode, people spoke his name in whispers. He had no friends, this Jonah Hex, but he did have two companions: one was death itself, the other — the acrid smell of gun smoke. These are the earliest adventures of the gunslinger, which were first published in the early 1970s, at a time when the spaghetti westerns of Sergio Leone and others had introduced tough, violent antiheroes to the American fiction staple. The stories include a

considerable amount of violence, but it's not too graphic, and very little strong language.

Showcase Presents: Superman Volume 1. DC Comics 2005 560p. Illustration
Grades: 6 7 8 9 10 11 12 Adult   **741.5; Fic**
   1. Graphic novels; 2. Superhero graphic novels; 3. Superman (Fictional character)
1-4012-0758-8, $9.99
   This first volume in the Showcase Presents Library of Classics features stories about Superman dating from 1958 through 1959. The adventure collected here have influenced the history of Superman and his extended family. From the introduction of his first love, the mermaid Lori Lemaris, to the introduction of his cousin Supergirl, Superman faces his most dangerous opponents, including Bizarro, Metallo, and Brainiac.

Superman in the Eighties. DC Comics 2006 192p. Illustration
Grades: 8 9 10 11 12 Adult   **741.5; Fic**
   1. Graphic novels; 2. Superhero graphic novels; 3. Superman (Fictional character)
1-4012-0952-1, $19.99
   The '80s were a decade that forever redefined the world's first super-hero. The first half of the decade brought the story of Superman to a close, while the latter half of the decade brought a revamped Man of Steel to an all-new audience. This volume includes ten stories by such creators as John Byrne, Curt Swan, Gil Kane, George Perez, Marv Wolfman, Jim Starlin, and Len Wein. Writer/artist Jerry Ordway provides historical and personal perspectives to these stories.

Superman in the Forties. DC Comics 2005 192p. Illustration
Grades: 6 7 8 9 10 11 12 Adult   **741.5; Fic**
   1. Graphic novels; 2. Superhero graphic novels; 3. Superman (Fictional character)
1-4012-0457-0, $19.99
   At the end of the 1930s, comics saw a new breed of hero. The man could withstand bullets, leap over tall buildings in a single bound, and bend steel in his bare hands. Fighting for the oppressed, this man of steel captured the imagination of the readers. He was, of course, Superman. This volume reprints stories originally published from 1938 through 1949. The reader sees Superman first fighting "regular" criminals, but as the years go by, super-powered villains start to menace Metropolis, along with such villains as Lex Luthor and troublemakers such as the mischievous Mr. Mxyztplk.

Superman: Up, Up and Away!. Kurt Busiek and Geoff Johns, writers; Pete Woods and Renato Guedes, art. DC Comics 2006 192p. Illustration
Grades: 8 9 10 11 12 Adult   **741.5; Fic**
   1. Graphic novels; 2. Superhero graphic novels; 3. Superman (Fictional character); 4. Green Lantern (Fictional character)
978-1-4012-0954-4, $14.99
   In the wake of Infinite Crisis, Superman had lost his powers. For the past year, as Clark Kent he has worked with the help of his super-powered allies, Green Lantern, Supergirl, and Hawkgirl, to keep Metropolis safe. Now, Lex Luthor has been acquitted of his past crimes, and he has managed to get his hands on a powerful and ancient Kryptonian artifact and plans to use it to destroy Superman once and for all. What can a powerless Superman do?

Superman; Volume 6: the men of tomorrow. Geoff Johns, writer; John Romita Jr, Klaus Janson, artists. DC Comics 2015 256 p. Color; Illustration
Grades: 10 11 12 Adult   **741.5; Fic**
   1. Superhero graphic novels; 2. Superman (Fictional character)
1401252397; 9781401252397, $24.99

LC 2015008050

"Enter Ulysses, the Man of Tomorrow, into the Man of Steel's life. This strange visitor shares many of Kal-El's experiences, including having been rocketed from a world with no future. New and exciting mysteries and adventures await. Plus, Perry White offers Clark a chance to return to The Daily Planet!" (Publisher's note)
   Collects Superman #32-39 (New 52 relaunch)

Teen Titans Vol. 1: A Kid's Game. Geoff Johns, writer; Mike McKone & Tom Grummett, pencillers; Marlo Alquiza & Nelson, inkers; Jeromy Cox, colorist; Comicraft, letterer. DC Comics 2004 un Illustration
Grades: 9 10 11 12 Adult   **741.5; Fic**
   1. Graphic novels; 2. Superhero graphic novels; 3. Teen Titans (Fictional characters); 4. Flash (Fictional character); 5. Robin (Fictional character); 6. Batman (Fictional character); 7. Superman (Fictional character)
1-4012-0308-6, $9.95
   As the adolescent sidekicks of the world's most powerful heroes, Robin, Superboy, Wonder Girl, and Impulse have fought alongside their mentors in many battles. But when Cyborg, a former teen hero, realizes that this new generation of super-heroes needs to be guided and trained, he recruits the young adventurers into the new Teen Titans. Now as Earth's future champions begin working together as a unified team, they quickly learn the true consequences of the path they have chosen. Featuring Batman, Superman, Wonder Woman and the Flash, this action-packed volume includes the Teen Titans' inaugural adventures as they face off against the deadly mercenary Deathstroke, contend with the fanatical villainy of Brother Blood and take on the heroes of the Justice League. The level of action and some violence puts this beyond most young fans of the Cartoon Network series, "Teen Titans Go."

Teen Titans Vol. 4: The Future is Now. DC Comics 2005 un Illustration
Grades: 8 9 10 11 12 Adult   **741.5; Fic**
   1. Graphic novels; 2. Science fiction graphic novels; 3. Superhero graphic novels; 4. Teen Titans (Fictional characters)
1-4012-0475-9, $9.99
   The Titans' weekends are usually a chance to get away from it all, but this time they've gone to the 31st century, where they must help the Legion of Super-Heroes stop a threat known as the Fatal Five Hundred. Their return trip drops them off ten years into their future, and they don't like what they see. And when they finally get back home, they meet Speedy, who has arrived just in time to help them fight Dr. Light.

Teen Titans Vol. 5: Life and Death. Geoff Johns [and others], writers; Tony S. Daniel ... [et a], pencillers; Marlo Alquiza [and others], inkers; Jeromy Cox [and others], colorists; Phil Balsman [and others], letterers. DC Comics 2006 210p. Illustration
Grades: 10 11 12 Adult   **741.5; Fic**
   1. Graphic novels; 2. Superhero graphic novels; 3. Teen Titans (Fictional characters); 4. Robin (Fictional character)
978-1-4012-0978-0, $14.99
   The line between life and death is crossed as the Teen Titans must confront the deceased members of the team that have seemingly returned from the dead. As Donna Troy recruits the mightiest members of the team to battle in the Infinite Crisis, Robin is confronted by his predecessor, the bygone Boy Wonder, Jason Todd. The remaining Titans face the onslaught of Brother Blood and his army of followers which include the deceased Titans Aquagirl, Omen, Hawk, and Dove. As the Crisis hits, Superboy teams up with all of the reserve members of the team to battle his evil counterpart from another dimension. There is considerable violence in the personal battles.

Teen Titans Vol. 6: Titans Around the World. Geoff Johns, writer; Tony Daniel, art. DC Comics 2007 192p. Illustration
Grades: 9 10 11 12 Adult   **741.5; Fic**

1. Graphic novels; 2. Superhero graphic novels; 3. Teen Titans (Fictional characters); 4. Robin (Fictional character)
978-1-4012-1217-9, $14.99

The tragic events of Infinite Crisis tore apart the Teen Titans. It's one year later, and the core members of the Titans return to re-form the team. Robin, Wonder Girl, and Cyborg go with interim members Kid Devil and Ravager on a journey to find their former colleagues, but they discover there had been a traitor in their ranks. With the identity and intent of the saboteur unknown, the team must be ready at all times for an assault. They meet with the Doom Patrol and fight the Brotherhood of Evil.

Johnson, Crockett
Barnaby; Volume 1: 1942-1943, 1. by Crockett Johnson. Fantagraphics 2012 318 p. Illustration; Color
Grades: 10 11 12 Adult   **741.5**
1. Boys — Comic books, strips, etc; 2. Fairies — Comic books, strips, etc; 3. Children — Comic books, strips, etc.
9781606995228, $35; 1606995227
LC 2013363489

This volume, by Crockett Johnson, presents the collected comic strips of "Barnaby" from 1942-1943, which "revolved around a precocious five-year-old named Barnaby Baxter and his fairly godfather Jackeen J. O'Malley. Yet O'Malley, a cigar-chomping, bumbling con-artist and fast-talker, was not your typical protector." (Publisher's note)
Volume 1 of 5

Johnson, Dan
Sinbad: The legacy. wordsmith, Dan Johnson; illustrator, Naresh Kumar; colorist, Ajo Kurian; letterer, Laxmi Chand Gupta. Campfire 2011 86 p. Color illustration
Grades: 7 8 9 10   **813.6; Fic**
1. Sea stories; 2. Graphic novels; 3. Historical fiction; 4. Sinbad the Sailor (Legendary character)
8190751557; 9788190751551, $12.99
LC 2011287737

In this graphic novel, "[w]hen King Haakim sends his teenage son Habib on a voyage to teach him" maturity, "the spoiled brat makes enemies of Sinbad's crew and is responsible for the ship being blown off course and forced to anchor near islands full of dangerous giant animals, beautiful cannibal women, and [a]...death-obsessed kingdom. Despite this, Sinbad rescues the prince from his blunders, while relating the tale of his own...adventures that helped him grow up." (Publishers Weekly)

Johnson, Mat
★ **Incognegro.** art by Warren Pleece. DC Comics/Vertigo 2008 136p. Illustration
Grades: 10 11 12 Adult   **741.5; Fic**
1. African Americans — Southern states — Graphic novels; 2. Graphic novels; 3. Mystery graphic novels
9781401210977, $19.99

In the early 20th century, light-skinned African American reporters risked their lives to cover the lynching murders of African Americans in the South; this process of "passing" was called "going incognegro." Zane Pinchback is a reporter from Harlem who has just narrowly escaped from one such reporting assignment when his editor sends him back down to Mississippi; this time, the man charged with murdering a white woman is Pinchback's own twin brother. He decides to investigate and find the real murderer in order to free his brother, but a Ku Klux Klansman has also come to town hunting the "Incognegro" reporter. This book portrays hangings and mutilations and uses the "n" word as it was used during the time period.

Johnson, R. Kikuo
Night Fisher. Fantagraphics Books 2005 144 Illustration
Grades: 11 12 Adult   **741.5; Fic**
1. Bildungsromans — Graphic novels; 2. Graphic novels
1-56097-719-1, $12.95

Loren Foster was handed an island paradise when he moved to the island of Maui in Hawaii with his dentist father six years ago. But, with the end of high school just around the corner, his best friend Shane has grown distant. Their friendship is put to the test when they get mixed up in a frivolous crime that leads to an arrest. Some drug use, strong language, and a sexual situation occur.

Jolley, Dan
Alien Incident on Planet J. by Dan Jolley; illustrated by Matt Wendt; [coloring by Hi-Fi Design; lettering by Marshall Dillon].. Lerner Publishing Group/Graphic Universe 2008 112p. Illustration
Grades: 3 4 5 6 7 8 9
741.5; Fic
1. Adventure graphic novels; 2. Graphic novels; 3. Plot-your-own stories — Graphic novels; 4. Science fiction graphic novels
978-0-8225-6998-5, $27.93;
978-0-8225-8876-4 (pa), $7.93
LC 2007-44116

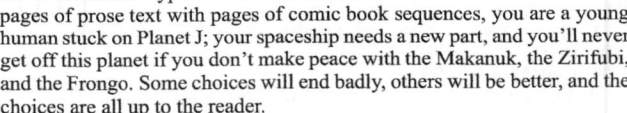
Courtesy of Lerner Publishing Group

In this new take on the "Choose Your Own Adventure" type of book that combines pages of prose text with pages of comic book sequences, you are a young human stuck on Planet J; your spaceship needs a new part, and you'll never get off this planet if you don't make peace with the Makanuk, the Zirifubi, and the Frongo. Some choices will end badly, others will be better, and the choices are all up to the reader.

This is Volume 8 of the Twisted Journeys series.

Escape from Pyramid X. Lerner Publishing Group/Graphic Universe 2007 112p. Illustration (Twisted Journeys)
Grades: 3 4 5 6 7 8 9
741.5; Fic
1. Adventure graphic novels; 2. Graphic novels; 3. Mummies — Graphic novels
978-0-8225-6777-6, $27.93;
978-0-8225-6779-0 (pa), $7.95
LC 2006-101598

Courtesy of Lerner Publishing Group

In the series called Twisted Journeys, readers choose how the story will progress. Pages of text alternate with comic book-style pages. In this volume, you the reader are a student who won an essay contest to be part of an archeological dig led by Professor Emil Snackport, at the site of a newly discovered pyramid. In some story lines, you encounter smugglers, in others, a malevolent mummy. Readers will find many scenarios played out, depending on their choices; some end well, others not so well.

The **girl** who owned a city. by O.T. Nelson; adapted by Dan Jolley; illustrated by Joëlle Jones; coloring by Jenn Manley Lee. Graphic Universe 2012 125 p.
Grades: 6 7 8 9 10   **741.5**
1. Graphic novels; 2. Science fiction; 3. Survival — Fiction; 4. Children — Graphic novels; 5. Apocalyptic fiction; 6. Adventure graphic novels; 7. Dystopian juvenile fiction

9780761349037; 9780761356349; 0761356347

LC 2009033270

This graphic novel, by Dan Jolley, O.T. Nelson, and illustrated by Joelle Jones, describes a post-apocalyptic world. "A deadly virus killed every adult on Earth, leaving only us kids behind.... I have to make sure we stay alive.... I figured out how to give the kids on Grand Avenue food, homes, and protection against the gangs. But Tom Logan and his army are determined to take away what we've built and rule the streets themselves." (Publisher's note)

Courtesy of Lerner Publishing Group

Pigling: a Cinderella story: a Korean tale. Graphic Universe 2008 48p. Illustration (Graphic myths and legends)
Grades: 3 4 5 6 7 8 9   **741.5; Fic**
1. Fairy tales — Graphic novels; 2. Graphic novels; 3. Korea — Folklore — Graphic novels
978-0-8225-7174-2, $27.93;
0-8225-7174-9

LC 2007-40891

In old Korea, in a time when magic still exists, Pear Blossom lives happily with her parents. But when her mother dies, her father quickly remarries a spiteful woman and her mean daughter, and they turn Pear Blossom's life into misery. They treat her like a servant and call her Pigling. Omoni (mother in Korean) makes impossible demands of Pear Blossom, and each time magical creatures help her achieve the tasks. Then on the day of a festival, a handsome magistrate sees Pear Blossom on the road, and she runs away, frightened, leaving a sandal behind.

Courtesy of Lerner Publishing Group

The **Smoking** Mountain: The Story of Popocatepetl and Iztaccihuatl: An Aztec Legend. story by Dan Jolley; pencils and inks by David Witt. Lerner Publishing Group 2009 48p. Illustration
Grades: 3 4 5 6 7 8 9
741.5; Fic
1. Aztecs — Folklore — Graphic novels; 2. Fantasy graphic novels; 3. Graphic novels
978-0-8225-7178-0, $27.93;
9781580138260

LC 2007-20028

Back when the Aztec Empire was at its peak, the Emperor has a favorite daughter, Iztaccihuatl (called Izta); he is troubled by an enemy nation, the Tlaxcalans, and the soldier

Courtesy of Lerner Publishing Group

Popocatepetl (called Popo) is the Emperor's great military leader. Popo and Izta fall in love at first sight when the Emperor honors Popo for his accomplishments, and they meet in secret. However, Cuetlachtli is a jealous soldier who wants to destroy Popo, and he finds his chance when the Emperor catches the two lovers together and tells Popo he can only marry Izta if he brings back the head of the Tlaxcalan king. Searching for the enemy takes a long, hard time, and Cuetlachtli sends a messenger back to Tenochtitlan with word that Popo has died, which sends Izta into a decline. When victorious Popo returns, he finds his lover dead, and takes her to the top of a mountain where he stands over her until his death. Now there are two mountains in Mexico, named for the two lovers. Jolley sets

the story as one told by a Mexican tour guide, using contemporary language; artist Witt conducted research to make the art look as authentic as possible. The book includes a list of books, websites, and DVDs for more information and entertainment.

Part of the Graphic Universe Myths and Legends series

The **time** travel trap. illustrated by Matt Wendt. Graphic Universe 2008 111p. Illustration (Twisted journeys)
Grades: 3 4 5 6 7 8 9
741.5; Fic
1. Adventure graphic novels; 2. Graphic novels; 3. Plot-your-own stories — Graphic novels; 4. Science fiction graphic novels
978-0-7613-9472-3 (lib bdg), $27.93;
0-7613-9472-9 (lib bdg);
978-0-8225-8874-0 (pa), $7.95;
0-8225-8874-9 (pa)

LC 2007-6101

Courtesy of Lerner Publishing Group

In this new take on the "Choose Your Own Adventure" type of book that combines pages of prose text with pages of comic book sequences, you are caught in a time machine a fellow student built for the school's science fair. Depending on the choices, you could end up at a medieval joust, facing woolly mammoths and "cavemen," or future aliens. Some choices will end badly, others will be better, and the choices are all up to the reader.

This is Volume 7 of the Twisted Journeys series.

Vampire hunt. illustrated by Gregory Titus; [coloring by Hi-Fi Design; lettering by Marshall Dillon]. Lerner Publishing Group/Graphic Universe 2008 112p. Illustration
Grades: 3 4 5 6 7 8 9
741.5; Fic
1. Adventure graphic novels; 2. Graphic novels; 3. Plot-your-own stories — Graphic novels; 4. Science fiction graphic novels; 5. Vampires — Graphic novels
978-0-8225-8877-1, $27.93;
978-0-8225-8879-5 (pa), $7.95

LC 2007-043732

Courtesy of Lerner Publishing Group

In this new take on the "Choose Your Own Adventure" type of book that combines pages of prose text with pages of comic book sequences, you are a vampire, and you must defend yourself and your castle from vampire hunters. Some choices will end badly, others will be better, and the choices are all up to the reader.

This is Volume 7 of the Twisted Journeys series

Wrapped up in you. by Dan Jolley; illustrated by Natalie Nourigat. Graphic Universe 2012 127 p.
Grades: 6 7 8 9 10 11 12
741.5; Fic
1. Graphic novels; 2. Horror stories; 3. Mummies — Fiction; 4. Witches — Fiction; 5. North Carolina — Fiction; 6. Horror graphic novels; 7. Supernatural graphic novels; 8. Mummies — Graphic novels; 9. Romance fiction — Graphic novels
0761368566; 9780761368564, $29.27

Courtesy of Lerner Publishing Group

LC 2011044655

This graphic novel, by Dan Jolley, illustrated by Natalie Nourigat, is book 6 in the "My Boyfriend Is a Monster" series. "Prince Pachacutec — or 'Chuck' — is a man with a past. He died tragically five hundred years ago, but that's all ancient history as far as Staci is concerned. He is everything she could want.... But the witches aren't willing to live and let live. Will Staci fight for Chuck? Or do the witches have a point when they say reanimated corpses make bad boyfriends?" (Publisher's note)

Jones, Bruce

Deadman: Deadman Walking. DC Comics 2007 128p. Illustration

Grades: 11 12 Adult   **741.5; Fic**

1. Graphic novels; 2. Mystery graphic novels; 3. Superhero graphic novels; 4. Supernatural graphic novels

978-1-4012-1236-0, $12.99

Brandon Cayce is about to find out the answers to the question of what happens after we die; unfortunately, he's going to find out by becoming a dead man himself. Now come new questions. Why did his brother crash an airliner, killing everyone aboard—including Brandon? Why does Brandon find himself drawn to Sarah, his sister-in-law and onetime love? Who are those men trying to kill him...and can you even kill a Deadman? The book includes a lot of violence, some nudity and sexual situations.

Nightwing: Brothers in Blood. Bruce Jones, writer; Joe Dodd, Paco Diaz, Robert Teranishi, pencillers; Bit, Nathan Massengill, Wes Craig, inkers; Javier Rodriguez Studio, Guy Major, colorists; Pat Brosseau [and others], letterers. DC Comics 2007 168p. Illustration

Grades: 10 11 12 Adult   **741.5; Fic**

1. Graphic novels; 2. Nightwing (Fictional character); 3. Superhero graphic novels; 4. Robin (Fictional character)

978-1-4012-1224-7, $14.99

After Bludhaven was destroyed in the Infinite Crisis, Dick Grayson relocated to New York City. It's a year later, and he has new friends, a new flame, and new criminal masterminds to fight. But, there's also another Nightwing, one who kills criminals without mercy — it's Jason Todd, the former Robin who succeeded Dick but was then killed by the Joker. He's been resurrected, but his idea of justice is twisted. And New York City has meta-human criminal kingpins, the Pierce brothers, who want both Nightwings dead. The book includes some sexual situations along with superhero violence.

Jones, Sabrina

★ **Isadora** Duncan: a graphic biography. Hill & Wang 2008 129p. Illustration

Grades: 9 10 11 12 Adult   **92; 792.8; 741.5**

1. Biographical graphic novels; 2. Dancers; 3. Dancers — Graphic novels; 4. Graphic novels; 5. Duncan, Isadora, 1878-1927

978-0-8090-9497-4, $18.95

LC 2008-17928

Dancer Isadora Duncan thrilled and appalled her audiences at the turn of the twentieth century and beyond; she chose to wear freeflowing costumes with no corsets or other confining undergarments, and she danced barefoot. She used choreographic elements from the ancient Greeks, with flowing movements as free as her garments. Jones sifts through the various books about Duncan, from the autobiography and others, with all their contradictory information, to depict a unique and contradictory woman who deeply influenced modern dance well beyond her death. The black and white art shows Duncan always in Greek-styled gowns. There are two panels which show nudity in the context of Duncan's dance performances.

Includes bibliographical references.

Race to incarcerate: a graphic retelling. Sabrina Jones and Marc Mauer. The New Press 2013 128 p. Illustration

Grades: 9 10 11 12 Adult   **364.6; 364.6\0973**

1. Crime prevention — United States — Comic books, strips, etc; 2. Criminal justice, Administration of — United States — Comic books, strips, etc; 3. Discrimination in criminal justice administration — United States — Comic books, strips, etc; 4. Graphic novels; 5. Imprisonment — United States — Comic books, strips, etc; 6. Prison sentences — United States — Comic books, strrips, etc; 7. Administration of criminal justice — United States; 8. Prisons — United States; 9. Crime prevention

1595585419; 9781595585417, $17.95

LC 2012049688

"Jones channels the tradition of liberal-Left political cartooning to give this graphic documentary a dynamic, woodcut-like look that galvanizes its adaptation of Mauer's tract of the same name. Its subject is imprisonment in the U.S., especially, since the war on drugs was launched in the 1980s, the push to jail as many as possible (as it sometimes seems). Since the opening of the first 'penitentiary' in 1829 and preceded by 'getting tough on crime' policies, the war on drugs has reversed the emphasis on rehabilitation in U.S. prisons." (Booklist)

Includes bibliographical references and index; Based on Race to Incarcerate by Marc Mauer.

Joong-Ki, Park

Shaman Warrior, Volume One. Dark Horse Comics 2006 214p. Illustration

Grades: 11 12 Adult   **741.5; Fic**

1. Adventure graphic novels; 2. Fantasy graphic novels; 3. Graphic novels; 4. Manwha

978-1-59307-638-2, $12.95

Warrior Wizard Yarong and his faithful servant Batu travel to the desert wastelands of Kugai on a mission for their king. However, they find only an overwhelming force of fighters led by a warrior who seeks to kill Yarong. The two warriors face on attack after the other, until Yarong realizes he is going to die; he sends Batu away, to find Yarong's baby daughter Yaki. They have been betrayed by their General for political expediency. This was a top-selling manwha in Korea; the kinetic, violent story will appeal to older readers who enjoy Lone Wolf & Cub, Blade of the Immortal, and other warrior epics.

Joy, Bob

Batman: The Greatest Stories Ever Told Volume Two. DC Comics 2007 208p. Illustration

Grades: 7 8 9 10 11 12 Adult   **741.5; Fic**

1. Batman (Fictional characters); 2. Graphic novels; 3. Superhero graphic novels; 4. Batgirl (Fictional character); 5. Joker (Fictional character)

978-1-4012-1214.8, $19.99

This volume includes stories from different periods in the nearly seventy-year career of Batman, from 1940 to 2003. He goes up against classic villains — the Joker, Killer Croc, the Penguin; he meets Batgirl (Barbara Gordon); deals with crooked businessmen and other criminals.

Flash: The Greatest Stories Ever Told. DC Comics 2007 208p. Illustration

Grades: 6 7 8 9 10 11 12 Adult   **741.5; Fic**

1. Flash (Fictional character); 2. Graphic novels; 3. Superhero graphic novels

978-1-4012-1372-5, $19.99

Jay Garrick, Barry Allen, and Wally West are all men who have donned the symbol of the yellow lightning bolt to combat evil as the Flash. Each hero with his own unique style of commanding a mastery over momentum, they have fought separately and together over the years. This volume collects stories that see them pitted against such villains as Gorilla Grodd, the Reverse Flash, the Fiddler, and many others. This volume also includes the story of Barry and Iris' wedding.

Showcase Presents: Batman Vol. 2. DC Comics 2007 510p. Illustration
Grades: 6 7 8 9 10 11 12 Adult   **741.5; Fic**
 1. Batman (Fictional character); 2. Graphic novels; 3. Superhero graphic novels; 4. Robin (Fictional character)
978-1-4012-1362-6, $16.99
 Over 500 pages of classic adventures are included in this volume collecting Silver Age tales of Batman and Robin as they face their most enduring enemies, including the Joker, Poison Ivy, the Riddler, Blockbuster, and many others. These are the stories that inspired the Dynamic Duo's 1960s TV series, which featured Batman's astonishing detective skills and impressive array of Bat-gadgets. The stories, reprinted in black and white, date from 1965 and 1966.

Ka, Olivier
 ★ **Why** I killed Peter. NBM 2008 112p. Illustration
Grades: 10 11 12 Adult   **741.5**
 1. Biographical graphic novels; 2. Catholic church — Clergy — Graphic novels; 3. Child sexual abuse — Graphic novels; 4. Graphic novels
978-1-56163-543-6, $18.95
 Olivier Ka writes of his life and of the lifelong effect of one particular act. He grows up in France, the child of what he describes as hippie parents. Their lifestyle is very open, and young Olivier sees adults naked a lot, and his parents sleep with other partners quite often. Into this comes young priest Peter, a liberal type of cleric who wears shirts and jeans rather than cassocks and other vestments, who plays the guitar during services. Olivier likes him a lot, because Peter really talks with him and listens, more like a fun uncle than a priest. Over the years, Peter remains a part of the family, and Olivier goes to his summer camps. Then the summer Olivier is twelve, Peter asks him to do something that makes Olivier uncomfortable. They will sleep side by side in their own sleeping bags, but completely naked "to be equal," and they will massage each other's belly. It starts out like that, but ends...well. Olivier continues to go to the summer camps until he's fifteen, but he and Peter never do anything like that again. Years later, as an adult, Olivier suffers emotional problems, and attending services in a Catholic church makes him physically ill. Eventually, when his own daughter is twelve years old, Olivier writes this story, makes a friend who is an artist, and they create the graphic novel. And Olivier confronts Peter after so many years. The act Peter committed with Olivier is not depicted on the page, but there is nudity and some sexual situations, along with strong language.

Kagami, Takaya
 Seraph of the end; Vol 1: vampire reign. by Takaya Kagami, Daisuke Furuya, illustrated by Yamato Yamamoto. Viz 2014 197 p. Illustration
Grades: 9 10 11 12   **741.5**
 1. Shonen manga; 2. Manga; 3. Vampires — Graphic novels
1421571501; 9781421571508, $9.99
 "After a catastrophic epidemic kills every adult on earth, vampires arise from the shadows to enslave the remaining human population. Yuichiro escapes from captivity and joins the Japanese Imperial Demon Army. But before he's allowed to fight..., he has to...make new friends with his fellow aspiring monster slayers!" (Publisher's note)
 "Yamamoto's black-and-white illustrations are eye-catching and powerful, capturing architectural details of crumbling cities, extreme close-ups of conflicted characters, explosions, and fight scenes with equal skill." SLJ
 Volume 1 of an ongoing series

Kakalios, James
 The **Physics** of Superheroes. James Kakalios.. Gotham Books 2009 424 p.
Grades: 11 12 Adult   **530**
 1. Comic books, strips, etc.; 2. Heroes and heroines; 3. Physics — Study and teaching; 4. Superman (Fictional character); 5. Batman (Fictional character); 6. Spider-Man (Fictional character)
1592405088; 9781592405084, $18
                    LC 2009028814
 "With The Physics of Superheroes, named one of the best science books of 2005 by Discover, he introduced his colorful approach to an even wider audience. Now Kakalios presents a totally updated, expanded edition that features even more superheroes and findings from the cutting edge of science. With three new chapters and completely revised throughout with a splashy, redesigned package, the book that explains why Spider-Man's webbing failed his girlfriend, the probable cause of Krypton's explosion, and the Newtonian physics at work in Gotham City is electrifying from cover to cover." (Publisher's note)
 "By combining his love for physics with his love of comic books,...Kakalios has written a book for the general reader [that covers] all of the basic points in a first-level college physics course and is difficult to put down.... That all of this is accomplished with enough humor to make you laugh aloud is an added bonus." Pub Wkly
 Includes bibliographical references and index

Kamio, Yoko
 Boys Over Flowers (Hana Yori Dango) Volume 1. Viz Media/Shojo 2003 208p. Illustration
Grades: 9 10 11 12 Adult   **741.5; Fic**
 1. Graphic novels; 2. Manga; 3. Romance graphic novels; 4. Shojo manga
1-56931-996-0, $9.99
 When her only friend, Makiko, accidentally offends F4 leader Tsukasa, Tsukushi boldly defends her. Enraged, Tsukasa puts the dreaded red tag in Tsukushi's locker — a sign that she is now a target for the abuse of the F4 gang and the entire school. But when Tsukushi fights the gang with their own weapon, Tsukasa finds himself falling for her. Tsukushi comes from a poor family but attends a prestigious school ruled by the rich students; she manages to hold her own against any bullying. There's some violence in the bullying, and some sexual situations.
 Volume 1 of 37

Kanata, Konami
 ★ **Chi's** sweet home, volume 1. Vertical, Inc. 2010 166p. Illustration
Grades: 5 6 7 8 9 10 11 12 Adult   **741.5; Fic**
 1. Cats — Graphic novels; 2. Graphic novels; 3. Humorous graphic novels; 4. Manga; 5. Seinen manga
9781-934287-81-1
 Young kitten Chi gets separated from her family while out on a stroll, then she meets little boy Yohei and his parents. They take her home, even though their apartment building has a strict no pets policy. While they try to find someone to take her in, they feed her, give her a cozy bed, set up a box with shredded newspaper for a litter box, and do their best to help her. Even though readers can read what she's thinking, Chi behaves just like a cat, with cat problems such as thinking the litter box is a wonderful play area instead of the place to do her business, and taking fright at Yohei's "vrooming" as he plays with his toy cars. The book is great for younger readers as well as anyone who likes cats. There is one panel where Yohei is sitting on the toilet while Chi is in her litter box in the bathroom, and a scene at the veterinarian's office where the doctor sticks a thermometer in to take Chi's temperature. And, of course, Chi tends to urinate in inappropriate places.
 Also available in 3-in-1 omnibus editions; Volume 1 of 12

Kane, Bob

Batman in the forties. Batman created by Bob Kane; [introduction by Bill Schelly]. DC Comics 2004 192p. Illustration

Grades: 9 10 11 12 Adult   **741; 741.5; Fic**

1. Batman (Fictional character); 2. Graphic novels; 3. Superhero graphic novels; 4. Catwoman (Fictional character); 5. Robin (Fictional character); 6. Joker (Fictional character)

1-4012-0206-3, $19.95

"The 17 selections include such milestones as Batman's first appearance in May 1939, the two-page story of his origins from November 1939, and the 1940 introduction of his young partner, Robin.... Other stories feature early appearances by some of Batman's most renowned arch-enemies: the Joker, Catwoman, and Two-Face.... Most compelling are the earliest stories; crude as they are, their naive verve and raw directness remain effective." Booklist

Originally published (1939-1949) in single magazine form as Batman 7, 15, 20, 31, 37, 47, 48, 49, Detective Comics 27, 33, 38, 49, 80, Real Fact Comics 5, Star-Spangled Comics 70, World's Finest Comics 30

Kanigher, Robert

Showcase Presents: Wonder Woman Vol. 1. DC Comics 2007 528p. Illustration

Grades: 6 7 8 9 10 11 12 Adult   **741.5; Fic**

1. Graphic novels; 2. Superhero graphic novels; 3. Wonder Woman (Fictional character)

978-1-4012-1373-2, $16.99

Wonder Woman faces some of her deadliest challenges as she battles a variety of aliens and robots, and confronts the evil menaces of the Time Master, the Gadget Maker, Dike of Deception, and one of her most incessant foes, the Angle Man. This volume also includes the re-done origin of Wonder Woman, and some of her teenage adventures as Wonder Girl. Created by William Moulton Marston as a strong, liberated warrior in 1941, these adventures published in the late 1950s and early 1960s cast Wonder Woman in a more "traditional" female superhero role.

Kanno, Aya

Blank slate volume 1. Viz Media/Shojo Beat 2008 un Illustration

Grades: 10 11 12 Adult   **741.5; Fic**

1. Adventure graphic novels; 2. Graphic novels; 3. Manga; 4. Mystery graphic novels; 5. Shojo manga

978-1-4215-1924-1, $8.99

Zen is a beautiful young man with no memory of who or what he was, all he knows is that he gets urges to kill and he does so. The nation of Amata had been taken over by the Galayans twenty years ago, and Zen inadvertently gets involved with the resistance when he kidnaps the Galay general's daughter Rian. He ends up with Hakka, an unlicensed doctor who helps the Amatans. But what does Hakka know about Zen? This book includes considerable violence.

Otomen; Volume 1. story & art by Aya Kanno. Viz Media 2010 208 p. Illustration

Grades: 8 9 10 11 12   **741.5; Fic**

1. Dating (Social customs) — Fiction; 2. Shojo manga; 3. Teenagers — Fiction

1421521865; 9781421521862, $9.99

"Asuka Masamune is a guy who loves girly things — sewing, knitting, making cute stuffed animals and reading shojo comics. But in a world where boys are expected to act manly, Asuka must hide his beloved hobbies and play the part of a masculine jock instead. Ryo Miyakozuka, on the other hand, is a girl who can't sew or bake a cake to save her life. Asuka finds himself drawn to Ryo, but she likes only the manliest of men! Can Asuka ever show his true self to anyone, much less to the girl that he's falling for?" (Publisher's note)

"Although the art is as sugary and cute as Asuka himself, with lots of sparkling and glitter in the periphery, hidden among all the prettiness are important themes of individuality and being true to yourself, making this an empowering read for teenage girls." Booklist

Volume 1 of 18

Kariya, Tetsu

Oishinbo a la carte: the joy of rice. story by Tetsu Kariya; art by Akira Hanasaki. Viz Signature Edition 2009 268p. Illustration

Grades: 8 9 10 11 12 Adult   **741.5; Fic**

1. Cooking — Graphic novels; 2. Graphic novels; 3. Manga; 4. Rice — Graphic novels; 5. Seinen manga

978-1-4215-2144-2, $12.99

This volume collects the Oishinbo stories centering on rice, the supreme staple of the Japanese diet. As Yamaoka continues, with the help of other Tozai News staffers, to work on the newspaper's Ultimate Menu to celebrate its 100th anniversary, they examine rice. Among other stories, Yamaoka rails against the importing of rice from other countries; he shows that organic rice farming could be unhealthy depending on the farm's location; and he helps the company cafeteria chef attract more business by focusing on homestyle rice dishes. The big competition between the Ultimate Menu and the Supreme Menu is rice balls (omusubi). The stories here may help American readers understand a little more about how important rice is to Japanese culture, and they may want to try some of the dishes. The book includes a recipe for scallop rice, which is published in color with photos. As with the other volumes, this book includes stories that originally appeared throughout the original manga series, so the characters' lives and relationships change abruptly from story to story.

Oishinbo a la carte: vegetables. story by Tetsu Kariya; art by Akira Hanasaki. Viz Media/Viz Signature 2009 268p. Illustration

Grades: 8 9 10 11 12 Adult   **741.5; Fic**

1. Cooking — Vegetables — Graphic novels; 2. Graphic novels; 3. Manga; 4. Seinen manga

978-1-4215-2143-5, $12.99

Tozai News reporter Yamaoka Shiro and his colleagues continue their quest for the Ultimate Menu. In this volume, he competes against his father Kaibara, who represents rival newspaper Teito Times and their Supreme Menu, in a competition involving the vegetables cabbage and turnip. In other stories, Yamaoka and his friends use asparagus as a way to reunite a culinary specialist and a pottery artist who broke up years ago; and they help Tomii's son get over his hatred of eggplant. A number of the stories discuss the debate between organic cultivation and the use of pesticides and imported vegetable types. Since the stories are selected from the Oishinbo series to fit into themes, they skip around in time and lack a real narrative flow. The book is suitable for teens, but the main appeal may be to adults, especially to those who want to read about food. The artist's focus on presenting all the vegetables so realistically and in great detail may just make the reader hungry.

Kashyap, Keshni

Tina's mouth. Keshni Kashyap; illustrated by Mari Araki.. Houghton Mifflin Harcourt 2011 242 p. Illustration

Grades: 9 10 11 12   **741.5; Fic**

1. East Indian Americans — Fiction; 2. Graphic novels; 3. High schools — Fiction; 4. Individuality — Fiction; 5. Schools — Fiction; 6. California, Southern — Fiction; 7. Teenagers — Graphic novels; 8. Girls — Graphic novels

9780618945191, $18.95; 0618945199

LC 2011030439

"Tina, an Indian-American living in San Francisco, writes an illustrated diary to Jean-Paul Sartre as part of a semesterlong existentialism class.... Tina's best friend ditches her for a boy and Tina has a crush on someone but has trouble making it work. All the while, Tina observes her older siblings' love anxiety, her sister's move back home after a broken heart, and her brother's disastrous exploration of Indian dating sites.." (Publishers Weekly)

Katin, Miriam

We are on our own: a memoir. Drawn & Quarterly 2006 122p. Illustration

Grades: 9 10 11 12 Adult   **92; 741; 741.5**
1. Animators; 2. Artists; 3. Autobiographical graphic novels; 4. Cartoonists; 5. Holocaust, 1933-1945 — Graphic novels; 6. Illustrators; 7. World War, 1939-1945 — Graphic novels; 8. Katin, Miriam
1-896597-20-3, $19.95

LC 2005-9063602

In this WWII memoir, the author recounts "how she and her mother faked their deaths and fled Budapest after the Nazis occupied the city. With forged papers obtained from a black marketer, they escaped to the countryside in the guise of a servant girl and her illegitimate child. Katin relates their harrowing lives there and her mother's desperate search for her missing husband after the war.... This impressive book belongs in all serious graphic novel collections and is also a natural for Jewish studies." Booklist

Kawahara, Kazune

High school debut vol. 1. VizMedia/Shojo Beat 2008 184p. Illustration

Grades: 7 8 9 10 11 12   **741.5; Fic**
1. Graphic novels; 2. Manga; 3. Romance graphic novels; 4. Shojo manga
978-1-4215-1481-9, $8.99

Haruna used to be interested only in softball and manga, but now that she's starting in high school, she wants to change her focus, to find a boyfriend and have a fun romance. The problem is, no boy will hit on her. She's done her research in magazines, but nothing is working. Then a friend's comment causes her to decide to find a coach who will help her attract boys. Upperclassman Yoh Komiyama agrees to help her, but only if Haruna promises to not fall in love with him. It's a struggle, though, for Yoh's sister and his friends decide to tag along for fun. There's one scary moment when a guy tries to abduct Haruna.

Volume 1 of 13

★ **My** Love Story!!; Volume 1. story, Kazune Kawahara; art, Aruko; English adaptations, Ysabet Reinhardt MacFarlane; translation, JN Productions. Viz 2014 184 p. Illustration

Grades: 8 9 10 11 12   **741.5**
1. Shojo manga; 2. Man-woman relationship — Fiction
1421571447; 9781421571447, $9.99

"Takeo is big and manly in a macho kind of way. His best friend, Sunakawa, is handsome in a pretty/pointy-haired way, which means that girls always find him attractive. One day Takeo rescues a girl named Yamato from a groper on the train, and she starts falling in love with him. Unfortunately for Takeo, he is too dense to realize this and spends most of the story convinced that Yamato is really in love with Sunakawa." (School Library Journal)

"While this cute, romantic comedy is shojo manga, or manga intended for girls, it's unusually and entertainingly told from gruff, clueless, and kindhearted Takeo's perspective." Booklist

Volume 1 of 13

Kawasaki, Anton

JLA: The Greatest Stories Ever Told. DC Comics 2006 192p. Illustration

Grades: 9 10 11 12 Adult   **741.5; Fic**

1. Aquaman (Fictitious character); 2. Justice League of America (Fictional characters); 3. Superhero graphic novels; 4. Batman (Fictional character); 5. Flash (Fictional character); 6. Green Lantern (Fictional character); 7. Green Arrow (Fictional character); 8. Superman (Fictional character); 9. Wonder Woman (Fictional character)
978-1-4012-0932-2, $19.99

Superman. Batman. Wonder Woman. Green Lantern. The Flash. Aquaman. Martian Manhunter. Green Arrow. Black Canary. They are the World's Greatest Super-Heroes, and they compose the Justice League of America. For over 45 years, this all-star team of DC's greatest characters has entertained generations of comics fans. And now, this new collection reprints eight of their greatest tales in one volume, covering nearly every era and incarnation of the League, from classic adventures of the Silver Age, to stories that formed the basis of the best-selling Identity Crisis, to newer tales featuring a humorous League and the return of the classic lineup.

Superman/Batman: The Greatest Stories Ever Told. DC Comics 2007 192p. Illustration

Grades: 9 10 11 12 Adult   **741.5; Fic**
1. Batman (Fictional character); 2. Graphic novels; 3. Superhero graphic novels; 4. Superman (Fictional character)
978-1-4012-1227-8, $19.99

They are two of the world's biggest icons, and they couldn't be more different. One is the most powerful being on the planet with an array of superpowers, a shining symbol of hope embodying truth, justice, and the American way. The other has no powers, but has trained his mind and body to the peak of perfection, a dark vigilante determined to strike fear into evildoers' hearts. Together, this popular and unlikely pair starred in numerous team-ups over several decades; this book collects ten of those stories, from 1952 to the 2000s.

Superman: The Greatest Stories Ever Told Volume Two. DC Comics 2006 192p. Illustration

Grades: 7 8 9 10 11 12 Adult   **741.5; Fic**
1. Graphic novels; 2. Superhero graphic novels; 3. Superman (Fictional character)
978-1-4012-0956-8, $19.99

This volume includes nine stories from different times in Superman's career. Readers can experience Superman's first meeting with the other dimensional imp Mr. Mxyztplk, his return to Krypton, a deadly battle against the team of Lex Luthor and Brainiac, an after-life adventure with Pa Kent, his greatest secret revealed, and more.

Keatinge, Joe

Shutter; Volume 1: Wanderlost. Joe Keatinge; illustrated by Leila Del Duca, Owen Gieni, Ed Brisson. Image Comics 2014 136 p. Color illustration

Grades: 11 12 Adult   **741.5; Fic**
1. Explorers — Graphic novels; 2. Family secrets — Fiction
1632151456; 9781632151452, $9.99

In this graphic novel by Joe Keatinge, illustrated by Leila Del Duca, Owen Gieni, and Ed Brisson, "Kate Kristopher, once the most famous explorer of an Earth far more fantastic than the one we know, is forced to return to the adventurous life she left behind when a family secret threatens to destroy everything she spent her life protecting." (Publisher's note)

"Keatinge and Del Duca have created a contemporary world that teems with casual miracles and feels all the more real and lived in for it. Crammed with the elements of children's storybooks, the art offers soft lines and a panoply of almost-recognizable storybook figures that honor those hallowed childhood recollections." Booklist

Originally published in single magazine form as Shutter #1-6; Volume 1 of 5

Keller, Michael

Charles Darwin's On the Origin of Species: a graphic adaptation. [by] Michael Keller; art by Nicolle Rager Fuller. Rodale 2009 192p. Illustration

Grades: 9 10 11 12 Adult   **576.8; 741.5**

1. Darwin, Charles, 1809-1882 — Adaptations; 2. Heredity — Graphic novels; 3. Evolution — Graphic novels; 4. Natural selection — Graphic novels

978-1-60529-697-5; 1-60529-697-X, $19.99; 978-1-60529-948-8 (pa); 1-60529-948-0 (pa), $14.99

        LC 2009-11387

"The first part of this book gives the background and context in which Darwin developed his theory of natural selection. Arriving home in 1836 after five years of exploration aboard the Beagle, he is asked to explain what he learned. Thus the structure of this graphic novel is established. Through his voice, readers learn about his discoveries and observations, his correspondence with other scientists who helped him formulate his theories, as well as his personal life. The second section highlights the salient points of the original On the Origin of Species." (School Library Journal)

Kelly, Joe

★ **Captain** Stoneheart and the Truth Fairy. Joe Kelly, story; Chris Bachalo, artwork; Aron Lusen, color; Richard Starkings, lettering & edits. Image Comics 2008 un Illustration

Grades: 5 6 7 8 9 10 11 12 Adult   **741.5; Fic**

1. Adventure graphic novels; 2. Fairies — Graphic novels; 3. Fantasy graphic novels; 4. Graphic novels; 5. Pirates — Graphic novels

978-1-58240-865-1, $19.99

The story, in rhyming text with lushly drawn and colored art, tells the tale of the pirate named Captain Stoneheart, a fierce and angry pirate who won't let people tell him what to do. After attacking a peaceful ship and killing everyone on it, his crew discovers a caged fairy in the hold, and Stoneheart knows he can wreak havoc and scourge the world with her powers. Somehow they connect even through his anger, and when she finds a way to save Stoneheart and his crew even when she is free to leave the pirates and save herself, Stoneheart starts to change. Alas, the good times can't last, and he commits one final act that destroys everything and everyone around him because he won't let anyone tell him what to do, even if he loves that one person. There is some fighting violence, and there are some monsters, so this is not a story for very young readers. Older elementary school age children who love the old fairy tales with the tragic endings will be able to handle this story.

★ **Deadpool**. by Joe Kelly, pencilled by Ed McGuinness, Aaron Lopresti, Bernard Chang, Shannon Denton, Pete Woods, Rob Liefield. Marvel Enterprises 2014 1160 p. Color; Illustration

Grades: 10 11 12 Adult   **741.5; Fic**

1. Superhero graphic novels; 2. Deadpool (Fictional character)

9780785185598, $125; 0785185593

This collects multiple Marvel Comics runs featuring the character of Deadpool. "Wade Wilson is a self-loathing killer for hire...but he dreams of being a hero. So when an interdimensional organization reveals that his destiny is to save the world, is it the chance for redemption Deadpool has longed for — or is it too good to be true?" (Publisher's note)

Collects Deadpool (1997) 1-33, -1, 0; Daredevil/Deadpool Annual '97; Deadpool/Death Annual '98; Baby's first Deadpool Book; Amazing Spider-Man (1963) 47, 611; and Deadpool 900

★ **I** kill giants. Image Comics 2009 un Illustration

Grades: 8 9 10 11 12   **741.5; Fic**

1. Family life — Graphic novels; 2. Fantasy graphic novels; 3. Giants — Graphic novels; 4. Graphic novels

978-1-60706-092-5, $15.99

Fifth-grader Barbara Thorson appears to be a smart-aleck troublemaker, and she does get into trouble at school, with great regularity. She has no friends, she has to deal with teachers and a principal who don't understand her, with the bully Taylor, with Sophie, the new girl who wants to be her friend, and now with a school psychologist. She has no time for this nonsense, she is a giant killer, with her mighty weapon she calls Coveleski (after Stanley Coveleski, a baseball player in the early twentieth century). What writer Kelly reveals slowly to the reader is Barbara's real family situation: her mother is dying, her older sister is trying to keep the family together, and Barbara is convinced that if she can slay the Titan, a huge giant, she can keep her mother alive. While Barbara is young, the story has an emotional intensity better suited for older teens.

Space Ghost. DC Comics 2005 un Illustration

Grades: 8 9 10 11 12 Adult   **741.5; Fic**

1. Graphic novels; 2. Superhero graphic novels

1-4012-0721-9, $14.99

The masked avenger of the cartoon spaceways has been a popular character since his introduction to television in 1966. Since then, people have wondered who he is, how he got those power bands and why he protects the galaxy from evil. Now his story is told for the first time ever, and readers will learn the tragic circumstances that led to his donning a cowl and his first battle with arch nemesis Zorak. This is not the funny character from Cartoon Network.

Kelso, Megan

The **Squirrel** Mother: Stories. Fantagraphics Books 2006 147p. Illustration

Grades: 10 11 12 Adult   **741.5; Fic**

1. Graphic novels

978-1-56097-746-9, $16.95

Kelso's work is characterized by subject matter that fits roughly into two disparate camps: personal and semi-autobiographical stories that draw heavily on the details of her childhood and adolescence, and stories about the idea of America and American history, such as a trilogy of short pieces about Alexander Hamilton. This book features 15 stories, including two stories, "Meow Face" and "Aide de Camp," done especially for this volume. The personal stories are each self-contained but in a sense take place in the same world where similar characters inhabit different stories. The "America" stories are broader in subject matter, taking on events of political and historical significance and wrestling with ideas having to do with the American experience.

Kennedy, Mike

Alien vs. Predator: Thrill of the Hunt. Dark Horse Comics 2004 un Illustration

Grades: 10 11 12 Adult   **741.5; Fic**

1. Graphic novels; 2. Horror graphic novels; 3. Science fiction graphic novels

1-59307-257-0, $6.95

In the future, after a technological catastrophe that started a second dark age, all memory of vicious bug-like aliens and brutal predatory aliens that hunted humans has been forgotten. Now, mankind has reached out to space again, and humans are once again caught in the middle of a deadly struggle between the two most lethal species ever encountered. And once again, whoever wins...humans lose. The book includes some bloody violence.

Aliens vs. Predator: civilized beasts. Dark Horse Comics 2008 un Illustration

Grades: 9 10 11 12 Adult   **741.5; Fic**

1. Graphic novels; 2. Horror graphic novels; 3. Science fiction graphic novels

978-1-59307-342-8, $6.95

It was supposed to have been a short business tour, but the group has been stranded on the remote planet for eight months. The humans have been aided by a Predator they've named Smiley, and occasionally they have to hunt an alien out to kill them. When a rescue ship arrives, however, it is crewed by illegal synthetic humans, then everyone gets mixed into the Predators' new hunt of Aliens. Whoever wins, the humans will lose. The book includes considerable violence, including the tearing off of limbs.

Superman: Infinite City. DC Comics 2005 96p. Illustration
Grades: 8 9 10 11 12 Adult   **741.5; Fic**
1. Graphic novels; 2. Superhero graphic novels; 3. Superman (Fictional character)
978-1-4012-0066-4, $17.99

When a villain uses a very powerful weapon in Metropolis, Clark and Lois trace him back to an old town called Infinite City. They find the town abandoned, except for a doorway that leads to another amazing world.... the true Infinite City, where magic and science happily coexist. Superman and Lois step through the magic portal and become embroiled in a war for power on the other side. One faction wants to stay in its dimension, and another wants to branch out to our world. Superman will meet a doppelganger called the Warden, who shares the Kryptonian's might but not his intellect. He will also come across the architect of this world, a robot leader who claims to be what remains of his father Jor-El.

Ketcham, Hank
★ **Hank** Ketcham's Complete Dennis the Menace (Volume 1): 1951-1952. Fantagraphics Books 2005 590p. Illustration
Grades: 2 3 4 5 6 7 8 9 10 11 12 Adult   **741.5; Fic**
1. Dennis the Menace (Fictional character); 2. Graphic novels; 3. Humorous graphic novels
1-56097-680-2, $24.95

This volume is the first of a series that will reprint every Dennis the Menace cartoon. The first cartoon was published in sixteen newspapers on March 12, 1951, and the cartoon was soon picked up by many more newspapers. This volume collects the daily single-panel cartoons from March 1951 through December 1952. In these cartoons, readers meet five-and-a-half-year-old Dennis Mitchell, his parents, retired neighbors George and Martha Wilson, Dennis' dog Ruff, and neighborhood pals Joey and Margaret. Every cartoon hearkens back to the positive aspects of growing up in suburban Middle America and the joys (mostly) of being a child. While older adults will catch all the references to past popular culture (i.e. Hopalong Cassidy), younger readers will enjoy the humor arising from everyday situations.

Kibuishi, Kazu
Flight v2. [editor/art director, Kazu Kibuishi]. Villard 2007 432p. Illustration
Grades: 10 11 12 Adult   **741.5**
1. Fantasy graphic novels; 2. Graphic novels; 3. Short stories — Graphic novels
978-0-345-49637-9, $24.95

In this themed story collection, "more than 30 accomplished young artists take off on the theme, sometimes loosely construed, of flight.... At more than 400 pages, there is something in this elegantly produced collection for everyone, including readers who usually snub comics." Booklist

Stories are by various authors; previously published by Image Comics; v1 published 2004 by Image Comics; Villard edition published 2007

★ **Flight** v3. [editor/art director, Kazu Kibuishi].. Ballantine Books 2006 351p. Illustration
Grades: 9 10 11 12 Adult   **741.5**

1. Fantasy graphic novels; 2. Graphic novels; 3. Short stories — Graphic novels
978-0-345-49039-1; 0-345-49039-8, $24.95

LC 2006-45883

This third volume of Flight includes 26 short stories by mostly young writers, many of whom have webcomics. Some, such as Michael Gagne and Becky Cloonan, have published a number of books. The stories range from whimsical interludes to ironic fables to mini-epics of derring-do; ironically, most of the stories have only a tangential connection to the theme of flight.
Sequel to Flight v2 (2005)

Flight volume five. Villard Books 2008 364p. Illustration
Grades: 9 10 11 12 Adult   **741.5; Fic**
1. Graphic novels; 2. Short stories — Graphic novels
978-0-345-50589-7, $25

This latest volume contains twenty-one stories from creators such as Svetlana Chmakova, Dave Roman, Phil Craven, Kean Soo, Scott Campbell, Graham Annable, editor Kibuishi, and others. The stories include another episode in the adventures of Jellaby, the true meaning of baseball and what it is to be a true professional player ("Beisbol 2"), another episode in Michael Gagne's "The Saga of Rex," and a tale of what happens when a trio of high-tech "Worry Dolls" goes to work to help an unemployed actor. In this volume, the stories are somewhat longer than in previous volumes and most have actual plots to go with the artwork. Stories range from realistic to the fantastic, from whimsical to dramatic to tragic.

★ **Flight,** volume six. Villard Books 2009 284p. Illustration
Grades: 8 9 10 11 12 Adult   **741.5; Fic**
1. Fantasy graphic novels; 2. Graphic novels; 3. Short stories — Graphic novels
978-0-345-50590-3, $25

This sixth volume of the graphic anthology series includes stories by fifteen creators: J.P. Ahonen, Graham Annable, Bannister, Phil Craven, Mike Dutton, Michel Gagne, Cory Godbey, Rodolphe Guenoden, Steve Hamaker, Kazu Kibuishi, Andrea Offermann, Richard Pose, Justin Ridge, Rad Sechrist, and Kean Soo. Returning favorite characters include Jellaby by Soo, Hamaker's Fish N Chips, Kibuishi's Daisy Kutter, and the wordless little fox Rex by Gagne. Bannister's "Cooking Duel" stands out as a lot of fun, as a couple makes a bet about which of them can make the better tasting mushroom quiche; and Justin Ridge's "Dead Bunny" shows that there is a soul mate for just about anyone, including a zombie bunny.

Flight: Volume Four. Random House/Villard 2007 344p. Illustration
Grades: 9 10 11 12 Adult   **741.5; Fic**
1. Fantasy graphic novels; 2. Graphic novels; 3. Short stories — Graphic novels
978-0-345-49040-7, $24.95

This fourth volume of the graphic novel anthology series includes 25 stories by creators ranging from veterans such as Michel Gagne and Graham Annable to newer creators such as Clio Chiang and Neil Babra. Most of the artists have webcomics; a number of them work in animation (Gagne most recently worked on the motion picture Ratatouille); some have worked on major graphic novel projects — Lark Pien colored Gene Yang's American Born Chinese, and Raina Telgemeier works on the graphic novel adaptations of The Baby-Sitters Club. While there is little harsh language and no nudity, some of the stories have more mature themes.

★ **Flight:** Volume One. edited by Kazu Kibuishi. Villard 2007 207 p.
Grades: 9 10 11 12 Adult   **741.5**
1. Comic books, strips, etc.
0345496361; 9780345496362, $27

This comic book, edited by Kazu Kibuishi, includes work from "Bengal, Bill Mudron, Catia Chien, Chris Appelhans, Clio Chiang, Derek

Kirk Kim, Dylan Meconis, Enrico Casarosa, Erika Moen, Hope Larson, Jacob Magraw-Mickelson, Jake Parker, Jen Wang, Joel Carroll, Kazu Kibuishi, Khang Le, Neil Babra, Philip Craven, Rad Sechrist, and Vera Brosgol." (Publisher's note)

Volume 1 of 8

Kick, Russ

The **graphic** canon of children's literature: the world's great kids' lit as comics and visuals. edited by Russ Kick. Seven Stories Press 2014 480 p. Color; Illustration
Grades: 6 7 8 9 10 11 12 Adult
741.5

1. Children's literature; 2. Comic books, strips, etc; 3. Graphic novels in education; 4. Literature — Adaptations; 5. Comic books, strips, etc.
1609805305; 9781609805302, $38.95

LC 2014010178

Courtesy of Seven Stories Press

Edited by Russ Kick, "the original three-volume anthology 'The Graphic Canon' presented the world's classic literature — from ancient times to the late twentieth century — as eye-popping comics, illustrations, and other visual forms. In this follow-up volume, young people's literature through the ages is given new life by the best comics artists and illustrators." (Publisher's note)

"These dazzlingly varied renderings run the gamut from haunting to comical while offering visceral reminders that children's stories are often densely layered, infinitely transposable, and peddle in imagery both macabre and whimsical. It is the unfettered imagination of these stories that make them not only wildly entertaining, but also vessels of forgotten truths." Pub Wkly

The **graphic** canon, volume 2: from Kubla Khan to the Bronte sisters to The picture of Dorian Gray. edited by Russ Kick. Seven Stories Press 2012 499 p.
Grades: 11 12 Adult
741.5

1. Comic books, strips, etc. — History and criticism; 2. Graphic novels in education; 3. Literature — Adaptations; 4. Graphic novels; 5. Literature — Collections
1609803787; 9781609803780, $34.95

LC 2012013176

Courtesy of Seven Stories Press

This book, edited by Russ Kick, collects "original graphic versions of [19th-century] classic literature, from [Samuel Taylor] Coleridge's 'Kubla Khan' to Wilde's 'The Picture of Dorian Gray'.... Contributors include Maxon Crumb, John Porcellino, and Megan Kelso. Each selection is prefaced with a short introduction to provide context, and a rationale is included for the marriage of a particular writer with a particular artist." (Publishers Weekly)

Includes index.

Kidd, Chip

Mythology: the DC Comics art of Alex Ross. text by Chip Kidd; introduction by M. Night Shymalan; photography by Geoff Spear. Pantheon Bks. 2003 un Illustration; Color
Grades: 9 10 11 12 Adult   **741.5\092; 741; 741.5**
0-375-42240-4, $35

LC 2003-46740

"Ross's gouache painted art glows on the pages. Interspersed with quotations by the artist and those who know him, Kidd's sparse text takes readers on a brief tour of Ross's childhood to his early days in advertising and comic books, finally ending with the limited series "Kingdom Come" (Warner, 1998), which combined hyper-realistic artwork with unusually complex storytelling. The book not only displays samples of finished works but also includes sketches, photographs of live models, and comic art dating back to the 1930s." SLJ

Kieth, Sam

The **Maxx** Volume 1. DC Comics/Wildstorm 2003 unp. Illustration
Grades: 10 11 12 Adult   **741.5; Fic**

1. Adventure graphic novels; 2. Fantasy graphic novels; 3. Graphic novels
1-4012-0124-5, $17.95

Thinking himself a typical superhero, Maxx is a homeless bum living in a cardboard box, aided by freelance social worker Julie Winters. Maxx travels to another world, "The Outback," where he's a hero and saves Julie from strange imaginary creatures and from his ultimate enemy, Mr. Gone. The reader also meets Sarah, who wants to be a writer, is mad at her mom, and is too chicken to kill herself. People who like their superhero comics very postmodern, existential, and very strange will like this. The book has some violence.

Zero Girl. DC Comics/Wildstorm 2001 114p. Illustration
Grades: 9 10 11 12 Adult   **741.5; Fic**

1. Fantasy graphic novels; 2. Graphic novels
1-56389-851-9, $14.95

Amy Smootster is a high school social outcast who lives her life content in her own world. But it seems that Amy's world is full of strange happenings such as the spontaneous appearances of puddles of water around her and two-sided conversations with insects. And there's something weird with her and circles and the fact that squares are inimical to her. With the help of her guidance counselor (upon whom she has a crush), Amy eventually accepts and embraces her abnormal abilities and discovers her place in the world.

Zero Girl: Full Circle. DC Comics/Wildstorm 2003 110p. Illustration
Grades: 9 10 11 12 Adult   **741.5; Fic**

1. Fantasy graphic novels; 2. Graphic novels
1-4012-0170-9, $17.95

Amy Smootster's now an adult, working as a guidance counselor. Her former crush, Tim Foster, is now a single parent with a troubled daughter. Tim enlists Amy's aid in helping her adjust, but the young girl, Nikki, has plans — and abilities — of her own. The book includes some strong language.

Kikuta, Michiyo

Mamotte! Lollipop Vol. 1. Random House/Del Rey Manga 2007 224p. Illustration
Grades: 8 9 10 11 12 Adult   **741.5; Fic**

1. Fantasy graphic novels; 2. Graphic novels; 3. Manga; 4. Shojo manga
978-0-345-49623-2, $10.95

Junior high schooler Nina is ready to fall in love. She's looking for a boy who's cute and sweet-and strong enough to support her when the chips are down. But what happens when Nina's dream comes true...twice? One day, two cute boys literally fall from the sky: they're both wizards and they've come to the Human World to take the Magic Exam. The boys' success on this test depends on protecting Nina from evil, so now Nina has a pair of cute magical boys chasing her everywhere she goes. But, because Nina accidentally swallowed a magic "crystal pearl" that is part of the Magic Exam, Zero and Ichi aren't the only wizards around her, and some are willing to do just about anything to get their hands on the magic pearl.

Kim, Derek Kirk

★ **Good** as Lily. written by Derek Kirk Kim; illustrated by Jesse Hamm; lettering by Jared K. Fletcher. DC Comics/Minx 2007 un Illustration

Grades: 7 8 9 10 11 12   **741.5; Fic**
1. Fantasy graphic novels; 2. Graphic novels; 3. Humorous graphic novels

978-1-4012-1381-7, $9.99

"On her eighteenth birthday, Korean American Grace suddenly finds herself surrounded by three very corporeal essences of herself: as a small child, as a 30-year-old woman, and as "a cranky old fart." Each of these incarnations is at an emotional precipice, which teenage Grace helps resolve, allowing the other self to quietly disappear.... Kim's pacing and plotting are excellent, and Hamm's black, white, and gray artwork is lively, witty, and full of appropriate comedy and melodrama." Booklist

Same difference. Derek Kirk Kim.. First Second 2011 90p. Illustration

Grades: 9 10 11 12 Adult   **741.5**
1. Graphic novels; 2. Family — Fiction; 3. Youth — Fiction; 4. Love — Fiction; 5. Short stories

9781596436572; 1596436573

LC 2010052663

This collection of short stories is concerned with young people, and gives particular focus to romantic and familial relationships. "The title story focuses on 20-somethings Nancy and Simon, who are racked with guilt. Why? Simon has turned down a date with a friend because she is blind, and Nancy has read love letters meant for someone else-and answered them, giving the jilted ex-boyfriend false hope. Through a series of credible coincidences, both eventually make amends. ...[The] collection also includes stories about high school track, weed wacking, familial relationships, celebrity interviews, and autobiographical tales." (School Libr J)

Kim, Susan

★ **Brain** camp. by Susan Kim and Laurence Klavan; illustrated by Faith Erin Hicks. First Second 2010 151p. Illustration

Grades: 7 8 9 10   **741; Fic; 741.5**
1. Camps — Graphic novels; 2. Graphic novels; 3. Horror graphic novels; 4. Mystery graphic novels; 5. Science fiction graphic novels
978-1-59643-366-3, $16.99; 1-59643-366-3

Jenna and Lucas are both under-achieving young teens who suddenly receive invitations to join the Fielding Camp for the summer. Pressed by their respective parents to attend, Jenna and Lucas both notice some strange things at the camp, and neither feels like eating the nasty slop served at every meal. The other campers are either intellectually challenged bullies, misfits, or supersmart zombies. At first Dwayne, a self-described spaz, befriends them, but when his cabin "wins" ice cream treats at dinner, Lucas sees the camp counselors sneaking in that night to "inoculate" all his cabin mates. Lucas and Jenna work against time to escape the camp and develop an antidote. Jenna is shown in one panel sitting on a commode when her period comes, and one short sequence shows Lucas having a wet dream and then washing out his stained undies; both situations are nonverbal and drawn with restraint, but school librarians will need to decide whether these two scenes meet their own schools' standards.

The authors present a "well-rounded adventure here, as the far-out (and kind of gross) climax mixes with genuine insight into dealing with parents, fitting into a new crowd, and handling the pressures of performance. Hicks' line work is cool enough to assuage older readers who might be suspicious of the summer-camp setting." Booklist

Kindt, Matt

2 Sisters: A Super-Spy Graphic Novel. Top Shelf Productions 2004 334p. Illustration

Grades: 9 10 11 12 Adult   **741.5; Fic**
1. Adventure graphic novels; 2. Graphic novels; 3. Spies — Graphic novels

1-891830-58-9, $19.95

This World War II era spy thriller spans not only the globe, but time as well — from England to Spain and from ancient Roman times through the era of Pirates and Buccaneers. This spy story is the backdrop for the unique tale of two sisters, their relationship and the secrets they share. Readers will find a world of shady gypsies, mysterious rockets, buried treasure, pen-guns, cyanide teeth, and romance. The book includes violence.

Pistolwhip. Matt Kindt, writing and art; Jason Hall, writing and layout assist. Top Shelf Productions 2001 120p. Illustration

Grades: 10 11 12 Adult   **741.5; Fic**
1. Adventure graphic novels; 2. Graphic novels; 3. Mystery graphic novels

1-891830-23-6, $14.95

LC 2002-280685

Readers will find a naïve bellhop's struggle towards a life's ambition, an expatriate musician on the run, a young woman's battle with her paranoia and her past, and the mysterious figure who wants to control their lives. Set in an exotic atmosphere of a by-gone era, this is a tale crafted with a crime noir feel. The book includes violence and some strong language.

Super Spy. Top Shelf Productions 2007 336p. Illustration

Grades: 9 10 11 12 Adult

741.5; S C
1. Adventure graphic novels; 2. Graphic novels; 3. Spies — Graphic novels; 4. World War, 1939-1945 — Graphic novels
978-1-891830-96-9, $19.95

Courtesy of IDW Publishing

Set during World War II, the book follows the everyday life of several spies as they go about their work. A writer hides secret messages in the text of the children's picture book he's writing; the wife of a German officer desperately needs to escape with her child; a female German master assassin encounters several of the Allied spies, with mostly fatal results. As the stories go on, the reader starts to see the interweaving connections between them. Some violence is depicted on the pages, but there's no nudity and little in the way of harsh language.

King, Stacy

Pride and prejudice. adapted by Stacy King; illustrated by Po Tse. Udon Entertainment 2014 369 p. Illustration

Grades: 9 10 11 12 Adult   **741.5**
1. Manga; 2. Austen, Jane, 1775-1817 — Adaptations

1927925177; 9781927925171, $24.99

In this manga adaption by Stacy King, "Pride & Prejudice is delightfully transformed.... All of the joy, heartache, and romance of Jane Austen's original [is] perfectly illuminated by the sumptuous art of manga-ka Po Tse." (Publisher's note)

King, Tom

Batman; Volume 1: I am Gotham. Tom King, Scott Snyder, writers; David Finch,Mikel Janín, Ivan Reis [and six others], artists;Jordie Bellaire, June Chung, Marcelo Maiolo,colorists; John Workman, Deron Bennett, letterers; David Finch with Jordie Bellaire, collection cover art. DC Comics 2017 192 p. Color; Illustration (DC Rebirth)

Grades: 9 10 11 12 Adult   **741.5; Fic**

1. Superheroes — Fiction; 2. Graphic novels; 3. Batman (Fictional character)

9781401267773, $16.99

LC 2016047042

"He is Gotham City's hero.... He is Batman. And he is not alone. There are two new heroes in town — a pair of masked metahumans.... Calling themselves Gotham and Gotham Girl, they've saved Batman's life, fought by his side and learned from his example. But what happens if Gotham's new guardians go bad? What if they blame the Dark Knight for the darkness that threatens to drown their city?" (Publisher's note)

King "employs a deep understanding of what makes a character tick, what makes him distinct, and what makes him appealing, here teaming Batman with a pair of superpowered amateur heroes who he at first tries to shepherd and then, when things go dark, he must bring to justice. Finch is an ideal partner: his Jim Lee-style figures, embellished with a darker line and more substantial detail, capture the humanity amid all the crunching action." Booklist

Originally published in single magazine form in BATMAN 1-6, BATMAN: REBIRTH 1; Volume 1 of an ongoing series

★ The **Vision**; Volume 1: Little Worse Than a Man. Tom King, writer; Gabriel Hernandez Walta, artist; Jordie Bellaire, color artist; VC's Clayton Cowles, letterer. Marvel Enterprises 2016 136 p. Color; Illustration

Grades: 11 12 Adult   **741.5; Fic**

1. Vision (Fictional character); 2. Superhero graphic novels

0785196579; 9780785196570, $17.99

Eisner Award: Best Limited Series (2017)

"The Vision wants to be human, and what's more human than family? So...he builds them. A wife, Virginia. Two teenage twins, Viv and Vin. They look like him. They have his powers. They share his grandest ambition — or is that obsession? — the unrelenting need to be ordinary. Behold the Visions!" (Publisher's note)

Contains material originally published in magazine form as Vision #1-6; Volume 1 of 2

★ The **Vision**; Volume 2: Little Better Than a Beast. Tom King, writer; Michael Walsh (#7) & Gabriel Hernandez Walta (#8-12), artists; Jordie Bellaire, color artist; VC's Clayton Cowles, letterer; Mike Del Mundo, cover artist. Marvel Enterprises 2016 136 p. Color; Illustration

Grades: 11 12 Adult   **741.5; Fic**

1. Superhero graphic novels; 2. Vision (Fictional character)

0785196587; 9780785196587, $19.99

Eisner Award: Best Limited Series (2017)

"Once upon a time a robot and a witch fell in love. What followed was a tale of the dead and the dying, of the hopeful and the lost, of the wronged and the avenged. And in the end, after both had fallen, the witch and the robot rose from their dirt and eyed each other across a field of blood and bone." (Publisher's note)

Originally published in single issue form as Vision #7-12

Kirby, Jack

Jack Kirby's Fourth World Omnibus, Volume One. DC Comics 2007 396p. Illustration

Grades: 8 9 10 11 12 Adult   **741.5; Fic**

1. Graphic novels; 2. Science fiction graphic novels; 3. Superhero graphic novels

978-1-4012-1344-2, $49.99

In the 1970s, legendary comics creator Kirby left Marvel Comics to work for DC Comics, writing and drawing several new series and also taking over Superman's Pal Jimmy Olsen. This volume collects the first three issues of his new series, plus the start of his run on Jimmy Olsen, from

issue #133. With the Fourth World storylines in Kirby's New Gods, Forever People, and Mister Miracle, he created new mythologies and epic storylines. This hardcover edition uses a flat paper that shows off the inks and colors brilliantly.

Jack Kirby's Fourth World Omnibus Volume Two. Image Comics 2007 396p. Illustration

Grades: 7 8 9 10 11 12 Adult   **741.5; Fic**

1. Graphic novels; 2. Superhero graphic novels

978-1-4012-1357-2, $49.99

DC collects four series by Kirby — The New Gods, The Forever People, Mister Miracle, and Superman's Pal Jimmy Olsen — in chronological order as they originally appeared. These comics spanned galaxies, from the streets of Metropolis to the far-flung worlds of New Genesis and Apokolips, as cosmic-powered heroes and villains struggled for supremacy. In this second volume, the evil Darkseid's schemes continue to unfold while the New Gods, the Forever People, Mr. Miracle and other heroes battle his many minions.

Jack Kirby's Omac: one man army corps. DC Comics 2008 176p. Illustration

Grades: 7 8 9 10 11 12 Adult   **741.5; Fic**

1. Graphic novels; 2. Superhero graphic novels

978-1-4012-1790-7, $24.99

In the 1970s, comics master creator Jack Kirby shocked the comics industry when he left Marvel Comics to work for the opposition DC Comics. He created new characters and new worlds. Among them was an unusual science fiction concept: OMAC, One Man Army Corps. Corporate nobody Buddy Blank is changed by the artificial intelligence "Brother Eye" into a superpowered agent of the Global Peace Agency, fighting bizarre menaces in a disturbing, near-future world. This book collects the complete 8-issue saga as published by DC; readers will note it ends in a cliffhanger that was never resolved.

Silver Star. Image Comics 2007 152p. Illustration

Grades: 8 9 10 11 12 Adult

741.5; Fic

1. Graphic novels; 2. Superhero graphic novels

978-1-58240-764-7, $34.99

Chronicling the rise of Homo-Geneticus, the New Breed of humanity that spawns both Silver Star (Morgan Miller) and the nefarious Darius Brumm. Silver Star was Kirby's final creation and one of only two creator-owned projects published by Pacific Comics in the early '80s. This volume also includes the original screenplay, written by Kirby and Steve Sherman, upon which Kirby based the comic.

Courtesy of Twomorrows Publishing

Kirkman, Robert

Invincible: ultimate collection, Vol. 1. written by Robert Kirkman; pencilled by Cory Walker and Ryan Ottley. Image Comics 2005 400p. Illustration

Grades: 9 10 11 12   **741.5; Fic**

1. Graphic novels; 2. Superhero graphic novels

1-58240-500-X, $34.95

Eisner Nominee: Best Continuing Series (2016)

High school senior Mark Grayson develops super powers, but it's only logical because his father is superhero Omni-Man. Soon enough Mark gets a costume, a mask, and a name — Invincible. He also joins a team of teenage superheroes as they track down the person who is turning fellow students into walking bombs. Then Mark learns that evil sometimes wears the face of someone familiar, someone respected, and loved. And he'll need all the power he can muster to save himself — and Earth. This edition includes extra features, including a sketchbook section.

"The story is compelling, presenting teenage melodrama without a trace of condescension, and even the inevitable superhero-crush-on-a-girl-he-can-never-have subplot receives a fresh spin." Voice Youth Advocates

Also available in individual trade paperback editions; Originally published as Invincible, issues #1-13; Volume 1 of 12

★ The **Walking** Dead. Robert Kirkman, creator, writer, letterer; Tony Moore, penciler, inker, gray tones; Charlie Adlard, penciler, inker; Cliff Rathburn, gray tones; Rus Wooten, letterer. Image Comics 2006 un Illustration
Grades: 10 11 12 Adult   **741.5; Fic**
   1. Graphic novels; 2. Horror graphic novels
   978-1-58240-619-0, $29.99

This hardcover features the first 12 issues of the hit series along with the covers for the issues in one oversized hardcover volume. An epidemic of apocalyptic proportions has swept the globe, causing the dead to rise and feed on the living. In a matter of months, society has crumbled. Rick Grimes finds himself one of the few survivors in this terrifying future. A couple months ago he was a small town cop who had never fired a shot and only ever saw one dead body. Separated from his family, he must now sort through all the death and confusion to try and find his wife and son. And when he finds them, along with a few other survivors, they must try to find a place of safety, for the walking dead are everywhere. The book includes lots of zombie violence, strong language, and some sexual situations.

Also available in trade paperback, omnibus, and compendium editions; Previously published as The Walking Dead issues #1-12.; Book 1 of an ongoing series

Kishimoto, Masashi
★ **Naruto**. vol. 1, The tests of the Ninja. story and art by Masashi Kishimoto; [English adaptation by Jo Duffy]. Viz 2003 186p. Illustration
Grades: 7 8 9 10 11 12   **741.5; Fic**
   1. Graphic novels; 2. Manga; 3. Martial arts — Graphic novels; 4. Shonen manga
   1-56931-900-6; 978-1-56931-900-0, $7.95

"Teen orphan Naruto wants to become the greatest ninja of all, despite the fact that most people in his village have despised him from birth because a terrible demon has been imprisoned in his body.... Teens love this series." Voice Youth Advocates

First published 1999 in Japan; Volume one of an ongoing series; ?This graphic novel contains material that was originally published in English in Shonen jump #6-10? Verso of title page; Volume 1 of 72

Kishimoto, Seishi
O-Parts Hunter Vol. 1. Viz Media 2006 185p. Illustration
Grades: 10 11 12 Adult   **741.5; Fic**
   1. Adventure graphic novels; 2. Fantasy graphic novels; 3. Graphic novels; 4. Manga; 5. Shonen manga
   978-1-4215-0855-9, $9.99

In the not too distant future, mankind fights over relics from an ancient civilization called O-Parts, each of which contain incredible powers. Some people with special abilities to use the O-Parts to their full potential are known as O.P.T.s (or O-Parts Tacticians). Jio is a young boy with a tragic past who only trusts one thing in the world: money. He is actually a very powerful O.P.T., and inside him sleeps a demon of incredible ferocity. He meets up with a girl named Ruby who, like her famous father before her, wants to become a treasure hunter. Though Jio doesn't believe in friendship, he agrees to be Ruby's bodyguard, and together they go on a

dangerous quest to discover as many O-Parts as they can. The story uses some harsh language and violence, occasionally graphic. Mangaka Kishimoto is twin brother to Masashi Kishimoto, mangaka of Naruto.

Kishiro, Yukito
Battle Angel Alita Vol. 1: Rusty Angel. Viz Media 2003 un Illustration
Grades: 10 11 12 Adult   **741.5; Fic**
   1. Graphic novels; 2. Manga; 3. Science fiction graphic novels; 4. Seinen manga
   1-56931-945-6, $9.95

When Doc Ido, a talented cyberphysician, finds cyborg Alita's head in a junk heap, she has lost all memory of her past life. But when he reconstructs her, she discovers her body still instinctively remembers the Panzer Kunst, the most powerful cyborg fighting technique ever known. In the post-apocalyptic world of the Scrapyard, as the secrets of Alita's past unfold, each day is a struggle for survival. The book includes graphic violence and strong language.

Volume 1 of 9

Kleid, Neil
Brownsville. NBM 2006 208p. Illustration
Grades: 10 11 12 Adult
741.5; 973.9
   1. Gangs — Graphic novels; 2. Graphic novels; 3. United States — History — 20th century — Graphic novels
   1-56163-458-1, $18.95

Courtesy of NBM Publishing

Brownsville, in Brooklyn, New York, was an impoverished part of the city in the early twentieth century. Filled with tenements and poor Jews, it became the breeding ground for criminals. This book follows the lives of Allie Tanennbaum, Abe Reles, and other young hoods organized by Louis Lepke Buchalter into the deadly "Murder, Inc." in the 1930s.

"The history of Jewish gangsters is often overshadowed by images of The Godfather and stories of the Italian mafia, but the events and players come to life in the stark images of this historical overview." (VOYA)

Klein, Grady
The **cartoon** introduction to statistics. by Grady Klein and Alan Dabney, Ph.D. Hill and Wang, a Division of Farrar, Straus and Giroux 2013 240 p.
Grades: 7 8 9 10 11 12   **519.5**
   1. Graphic novels; 2. Mathematical statistics — Comic books, strips, etc; 3. Statistics; 4. Comic books, strips, etc.
   0809033593; 9780809033591, $17.95

LC 2012030027

This book, by Grady Klien and Alan Dabney, explores statistics in humorous cartoon illustrations. "Separating the book into two main parts (hunting statistics and gathering parameters) for readers both in and outside the classroom, they explore the key foundational concepts of statistics and the perils of improper methods. They round out the book with the 'Math Cave,' which provides easy access to the formulas every student will want to have close at hand." (Publisher's note)

Kleist, Reinhard

Johnny Cash: I see a darkness: a graphic novel. [translated from the German edition by Michael Waaler]. Abrams ComicArts 2009 221p. Illustration

Grades: 11 12 Adult   **741.5; 92**

1. Cash, Johnny; 2. Country musicians — Graphic novels

978-0-8109-8463-9, $17.95

         LC 2010-279149

The author "presents a biography (with seemingly invented dialog that stays true to the facts) focusing on Cash's turning points: from his poor family's 1935 relocation to a New Deal-created cotton farming community, through his troubled first marriage, endless touring, the amphetamine abuse of his early musical career, and climaxing with a famous, highly charged 1968 concert at California's Folsom Prison. Kleist also dramatizes several of Cash's songs and relates the tragic story of Glen Sherley, a Folsom inmate who sent Cash a song he had written hoping Cash would play it in the show. The ruggedness of Kleist's black-and-white illustrations suits their subject, as the stark portrayal of Cash's withdrawal from drugs is inventive and harrowing.... This thoughtful and compelling portrait of a towering talent with a tortured soul is recommended for all teen and adult music fans." Libr J

Knapp, Michael

Out of picture: art from the outside looking in volume 2. Villard Books 2008 238p. Illustration

Grades: 10 11 12 Adult   **741.5; Fic**

1. Graphic novels; 2. Short stories — Graphic novels

978-0-345-49873-1, $30

Animation production artists who have worked together at Blue Sky Studios have put together another volume of short stories in comics form. In one story, a giant of a man wants only to become a farmer, but the military has hunted him down because he was a biological weapon used by them to win a war; now, he can't be allowed to live. In another story, a young boy takes his first airplane ride and sees a strange being riding on the wing, fly-fishing in the sky. In another story, three friends " a cat, a pigeon, and a grumpy gargoyle " need to find a new home when their antique shop home is destroyed. None of the stories uses graphic violence or much in the way of harsh language, but the moods and intensity of emotion make the book more suitable for older teens and adults.

Kneece, Mark

The **Twilight** Zone: the after hours. adaptation by Mark Kneece; illustrated by Rebekah Isaacs. Walker & Company 2008 un Illustration

Grades: 5 6 7 8 9 10   **741.5; Fic**

1. Graphic novels; 2. Supernatural graphic novels; 3. Twilight zone (Television program) — Graphic novels

978-0-8027-9716-2, $16.99; 978-0-8027-9717-9 (pa), $9.99

         LC 2008-4310

Marsha White visits a department store to buy an advertised gold thimble, is taken by elevator to a floor with empty display cases except for one, which has the thimble, and she deals with an odd saleswoman who knows her name. When Marsha is in the elevator, she discovers the thimble is defective and tries to complain, but the manager insists there is no eighteenth floor, the store has no elevator, and the store has never carried gold thimbles. As she begins to leave, Marsha faints at the sight of a mannequin that looks exactly like the strange saleswoman, and she's put into a back room to recover. When she wakes up, the store has been closed and she's locked in. This is an actual episode of the old Twilight Zone television show.

"Kneece's adaptation is quick and enjoyable and introduces a classic TV series to a new generation of readers. Isaacs's illustrations are clean,

distinct and cinematic in scope, employing an interesting variety of angles." Kirkus

The **Twilight** Zone: walking distance. adaptation from Rod Serling's original script by Mark Kneece; illustrated by Dove McHargue. Walker & Company 2008 un Illustration

Grades: 5 6 7 8 9 10   **741.5; Fic**

1. Graphic novels; 2. Supernatural graphic novels; 3. Twilight zone (Television program) — Graphic novels

978-0-8027-9714-8, $16.99; 978-0-8027-9715-5 (pa), $9.99

         LC 2008-4273

Thirty-nine-year-old businessman Martin Sloan's car blows a tire as he's driving, and he realizes he is within walking distance of his hometown. Leaving his car to be repaired, he decides to walk there. However, when he reaches town, he has also gone back in time. Can he find his boyhood self and give his younger self advice? Or will everyone think he's just crazy? This is an actual episode of the old Twilight Zone television show.

The story is "exceptionally well told and...[is] brilliantly adapted to a new medium." SLJ

Knisley, Lucy

An **Age** of License. Lucy Knisley. Fantagraphics 2014 208 p. Illustration; Color; Map

Grades: 11 12 Adult   **741.5; 92**

1. Autobiographical graphic novels; 2. Europe — Description and travel

1606997688; 9781606997680, $19.99

"'An Age of License' is [author Lucy] Knisley's comics travel memoir recounting her charming (and romantic!) adventures. It's punctuated by whimsical visual devices (such as a 'new experiences' funnel); peppered with the cute cats she meets along the way; and, of course, features her hallmark — drawings and descriptions of food that will make your mouth water." (Publisher's note)

"Knisley makes memoir comics seem both sophisticated and approachable-and beyond these, useful in helping an individual delve into and communicate personal issues." LJ

★ **Relish:** My Life in the Kitchen. by Lucy Knisley. First Second 2013 192 p.

Grades: 9 10 11 12 Adult   **741.5; 92**

1. Food; 2. Cooking

1596436239; 9781596436237, $17.99

Alex Award (2014)

This book is a memoir from food-lover Lucy Knisley. "Having grown up surrounded by delicious food, thanks to her gourmand father and earthy superchef mother, Knisley looks back on her childhood and adolescence through her roving palette and voracious appetite for new tastes and experiences. With each memory Knisley shares, she shows that life, like a good meal, should be savored and that all food — even junk food — is more than 'just fuel.'" (Publishers Weekly)

"Knisley tempers any navel-gazing impulses with humor, humility, and honesty.... Just about everything in this rambling memoir is handled with good cheer." Booklist

Kochalka, James

Monkey vs. Robot. Top Shelf Productions 2000 144p. Illustration

Grades: 5 6 7 8 9 10 11 12   **741.5; Fic**

1. Graphic novels

1-891830-15-5, $14.95

The book is almost wordless, allowing the reader to imagine one's own narrative. While there is violence, it's not graphic, and this little fable provides much food for thought.

"A very simply illustrated black and white pictorial narrative about a battle between a monkey community and a self-run robot factory encroaching on the monkeys' unspoiled forest domain." Publ Wkly

Another title in this series is: Monkey vs. Robot and the crystal of power (2003)

Peanutbutter & Jeremy's best book ever. Alternative Comics 2003 280p. Illustration
Grades: 4 5 6 7 8 9 10 11 12
741.5; Fic
1. Friendship — Graphic novels; 2. Graphic novels; 3. Humorous graphic novels
1-891867-46-6, $14.95

Courtesy of Alternative Comics

Peanutbutter is a sweet cat who acts like a hardworking office cat but usually naps on top of the paperwork, and Jeremy is a troublemaking crow; and they are friends. Jeremy may seem spiteful and sometimes does very mean things to Peanutbutter, such as pretending to threaten the cat with a pistol, but most of the stories are silly and fun.

Pinky & Stinky. Top Shelf Productions 2002 208p. Illustration
Grades: 4 5 6 7 8 9 10 11 12 Adult **741.5; Fic**
1. Adventure graphic novels; 2. Friendship — Graphic novels; 3. Graphic novels; 4. Humorous graphic novels
1-891830-29-7, $17.95

Pinky & Stinky are fat little piglets, but just because they're cuties doesn't mean that they're not brave astronauts! When they embark on a daring mission to be the first pigs on Pluto, things go horribly wrong and they crash land on the moon. There they meet some not-so-friendly moon men, and end up in the middle of a conflict between the American space program and a race of alien ice creatures.

Koga, Yun
Loveless; Volume 1 and 2. story and art by Yun Kouga; translation Ray Yoshimoto; English adaptation Lillian Diaz-Przybyl. VIZ Media 2012 376 p. Illustration
Grades: 11 12 Adult **741.5; Fic**
1. Fantasy graphic novels; 2. Josei manga; 3. Magic — Graphic novels
1421549905; 9781421549903, $14.99

"When his beloved older brother is brutally murdered, Ritsuka is heartbroken but determined to search for answers. His only lead is Soubi, a mysterious, handsome college student who offers him an intimate link to his brother's other life: a dark and vibrant world of spell battles and secret names. Will Ritsuka's relationship with Soubi ultimately lead to the truth or further down the rabbit hole than he imagined possible?" (Publisher's note)

Originally published in the U.S. by Tokyopop; Volumes 1-2 of an ongoing series

Koike, Kazuo
Lone wolf and cub omnibus. 1. by Kazuo Koike; illustrated by Goseki Kojima. Dark Horse Manga 2013 706 p. Illustration
Grades: 9 10 11 12 Adult **741.5; 741.5952**
1. Seinen manga; 2. Samurai — Graphic novels; 3. Manga
1616551348; 9781616551346, $19.99

This graphic novel, by Kazuo Koike, illustrated by Goseki Kojima, is a "samurai epic.... [It] begins its second life at Dark Horse Manga with new, larger editions of over 700 pages." (Publisher's note)

Also available in 28 single volumes; Volume 1 of 12

Path of the Assassin Vol. 1: Serving in the Dark. Dark Horse Manga 2006 314p. Illustration
Grades: 11 12 Adult **741.5; Fic**
1. Adventure graphic novels; 2. Graphic novels; 3. Manga; 4. Samurai — Graphic novels; 5. Seinen manga
978-1-59307-502-6, $9.95

This is the story of Hattori Hanzo, the fabled master ninja whose duty was to protect Tokugawa Ieyasu. Ieyasu was the shogun who would unite Japan into one great nation. But before he could do that, he had to grow up and learn how to love the ladies. As the secret caretaker of such an influential future leader, not only does Hanzo use vast and varied ninja talents, but in living closely with Ieyasu, he forms a close friendship with the young shogun. The two men get into bawdy escapades, the book includes nudity, strong language, and graphic violence."

Kominsky-Crumb, Aline
Need More Love: A Graphic Memoir. MQ Publications Ltd 2007 383p. Illustration
Grades: 11 12 Adult **741.5; Fic**
1. Autobiographical graphic novels; 2. Graphic novels; 3. Kominsky-Crumb, Aline, 1948-
978-1-84601-133-7, $30

Crumb was one of the pioneers of women's comics and became well-known during the Sixties and Seventies, along with her husband R. Crumb. This is her memoir of her life, taken from her comics published over the past four decades, incorporating photos and short prose text pieces along with memorabilia. She covers not only her life, but of her family, her husband, and other movers and shakers of the art and music worlds from the Sixties into the 21st century. The book includes considerable nudity, sexual situations, and harsh language.

Komura, Ayumi
Mixed vegetables, vol. 1. story & art by Ayumi Komura; English translation, JN Porductions; English adaptation, Stephanie V.W. Lucianovic. Viz Media/Shojo Beat 2008 un Illustration
Grades: 7 8 9 10 11 12 **741.5; Fic**
1. Cooking — Graphic novels; 2. Graphic novels; 3. Manga; 4. Romance graphic novels; 5. Shojo manga
978-1-4215-1967-8, $8.99

Hanayu Ashitaba is the daughter of the Patisserie Ashitaba, a famous pastry shop, but ever since she was a little girl she has wanted to become a sushi chef. Hayato Hyuga is the son of the famed Sushi Hyuga, but all he's ever wanted to be is a pastry chef, even though he's got mad skills with the knives. Both of them are students at the Oikawa High School Cooking Department, where Hanayu has decided she needs to make Hayato fall for her and marry her. However, Hayato wants Hanayu to teach him more about pastry making.

Volume 1 of 8

Konomi, Takeshi
The **Prince** of Tennis, Vol. 1. Viz Media, LLC 2004 192p. Illustration
Grades: 6 7 8 9 10 **741.5; Fic**
1. Graphic novels; 2. Manga; 3. Shonen manga; 4. Tennis — Graphic novels
1-59116-435-4, $7.95

"Ryoma is a former U.S. junior tennis champion who attends a Japanese academy, where his skill and natural talent make him nearly unbeatable. The younger students are inspired by him, but he's ruffling the feathers of the older tennis team members. Then the journalists appear, trying to discover the next champion, adding to the pressure. There's lots of tennis action, dramatically illustrated, and the characters, already pretty boys, are made even more attractive with their intensity." Publ Wkly

This is the first of an ongoing series, up to Volume 9 in September 2005; Volume 1 of 42

Kouno, Fumiyo

Town of evening calm, Country of cherry blossoms. Last Gasp 2006 104p. Illustration
Grades: 9 10 11 12 Adult   **741.5; Fic**
1. Atomic bomb victims — Graphic novels; 2. Graphic novels; 3. Manga; 4. Japan — History — 1952- — Graphic novels; 5. Seinen manga
978-0-86719-665-8, $9.99

In 1955, Hiroshima has been recovering from the devastation of the Atom Bomb in August 1945. Minami is one of the survivors of the bomb, and she tries not to remember the events of that day when most of her family died. She even pushes away Uchikoshi, a co-worker who likes her, feeling guilty that she survived when so many didn't; but when she finally comes to terms with her past and allows Uchikoshi in, radiation sickness manifests. Fifty years later, old school friends Nanami and Toko run into each other as Nanami follows her father who has been behaving oddly; he goes to Hiroshima, for he is Minami's younger brother. This quiet, one-volume manga uses gentle, sweet art to bring home to readers the lingering after-effects of the bombing of Hiroshima.

Kris

A **bag** of marbles. based on the memoir by Joseph Joffo; adapted by Kris; illustrated by Vincent Bailly; translated by Edward Gauvin. Graphic Universe 2013 126 p. Color; Illustration
Grades: 6 7 8 9 10
940.53; 741.5; B
1. Graphic novels; 2. Holocaust, Jewish (1939-1945) — France — Fiction; 3. Jews — France — Fiction; 4. World War, 1939-1945 — France — Fiction; 5. Joffo, Joseph; 6. Joffo, Maurice; 7. France — History — German occupation, 1940-1945 — Fiction; 8. Children and war — Fiction
1467715166; 9781467707008; 9781467715164, $9.95; 9781467716512

Courtesy of Lerner Publishing Group

LC 2013002284

"Ten years old at the start of the story, Joffo recalls his Jewish family planning their escape from Occupied France during World War II. Tension runs through the story as he and his brother set off on the long journey to the Free Zone, where they plan to meet up with their older brothers. Along the way the boys must hide their Jewish identity, evade train security, and find a passeur, or guide, to take them past guard posts and fences to safe territory." (School Library Journal)

"This graphic-novel adaptation of Joffo's 1973 memoir of the same name succeeds in melding sensitive and accurate imagery with the original narrative flow of a young secular Jewish boy's experiences in occupied France." Booklist

Kubert, Joe

Yossel: April 19, 1943: a story of the Warsaw Ghetto Uprising. Ibooks; Simon & Schuster 2003 121p. Illustration
Grades: 9 10 11 12 Adult   **940.53; Fic**
1. Graphic novels; 2. Holocaust, 1933-1945 — Comic books, strips, etc.; 3. Holocaust, 1933-1945 — Graphic novels; 4. Warsaw (Poland) — History — Uprising of 1943 — Comic books, strips, etc.

0-7434-7516-X, $24.95

"Imagining his life as it might have been had his parents not left for America in 1926, Kubert portrays himself as a ghetto youngster whose drawing ability ingratiates him with the Nazis, allowing him to overhear their plans and aid the underground resistance. Besides depicting life in the ghetto with shocking vividness, Kubert shows the barbarism of the concentration camps through the eyes of an escapee. In a striking departure from standard comics presentation, the artwork is printed in rough, penciled form rather than as finished ink drawings. The visual looseness this gives to work that is stylized by mainstream-comics standards conjures a potent intimacy that adds to the story's impact." Booklist

Kubo, Tite

★ **Bleach,** Vol. 1. [story and art by Tite Kubo; English adaptation, Lance Caselman; translation, Joe Yamazaki]. Viz Shonen Jump 2004 190p. Illustration
Grades: 9 10 11 12   **741.5; Fic**
1. Adventure graphic novels; 2. Graphic novels; 3. Manga; 4. Shonen manga; 5. Supernatural graphic novels
1-59116-441-9, $7.95

Teenage Ichigo Kurasaki has always been able to see ghosts, but that never really affected his life, until the night a Hollow, an evil spirit that preys on humans, attacks him. Soul Reaper Rukia Kuchiki tries to help Ichigo save himself and his family, but somehow he manages to absorb all her powers. Now he's a Soul Reaper, and he must work to protect the innocent from the Hollows. This is the first volume of an ongoing manga series that is full of fighting action and irreverent humor.

Volume 1 of 74

Kullab, Samya

Escape from Syria. by Samya Kullab; illustrated by Jackie Roche and Mike Freiheit. Firefly Books 2017 96 p. Color; Illustration
Grades: 7 8 9 10 11 12   **741.5**
1. Freiheit, Mike; 2. Refugees — Syria — Fiction; 3. Syria — History — 2011-, Civil War — Refugees — Fiction
1770859829; 9781770859821, $19.95

This "is a fictionalized account that calls on real-life circumstances and true tales of refugee families to serve as a microcosm of the Syrian uprising and the war and refugee crisis that followed. The story spans six years in the lives of Walid, his wife Dalia, and their two children, Amina and Youssef. Forced to flee from Syria, they become asylum-seekers in Lebanon, and finally resettled refugees in the West." (Publisher's note)

"Based on Kullab's extensive experience with refugees, the novel skillfully depicts situations and drastic decisions many Syrian refugees face. The graphic-novel format is perfect for the story, using cinematic techniques to propel the story and adding poignant notes, as when Amina's father reads a text message asking for help and conceals it from her. Extensive endnotes highlight the true events referenced in the book." Kirkus

Kuper, Peter

The **jungle**. [based on the story by] Upton Sinclair; adapted by Peter Kuper. Papercutz 2010 un Illustration (Classics Illustrated)
Grades: 9 10 11 12 Adult   **741.5; Fic**
1. Authors; 2. Biographers; 3. Graphic novels; 4. Immigrants — Graphic novels; 5. Meat industry — Graphic novels; 6. Novelists; 7. Socialist leaders; 8. Sinclair, Upton, 1878-1968 — Adaptations; 9. Chicago (Ill.) — Graphic novels
978-1-59707-192-5, $9.99

"Jurgis and his family have immigrated to America from Lithuania, settled in Chicago, and found jobs in the meatpacking plant. The family seems to be living the American dream: having their own home, and a means of support, even if the work is hard and disgusting. Peter Kuper's dark, colored, cartoon-style illustrations, framed in black, bring to life Sinclair's original work and highlight the atrocities perpetuated upon the Rudkus family." Libr Media Connect

First published 1991 by First Publishing

The **metamorphosis**. [based on the story by] Franz Kafka; adapted by Peter Kuper. Crown 2003 77p. Illustration
Grades: 8 9 10 11 12   **741.5; Fic**
   1. Authors; 2. Graphic novels; 3. Novelists; 4. Poets; 5. Short story writers; 6. Kafka, Franz, 1883-1924 — Adaptations
1-4000-4795-1; 1-4000-5299-8 (pa), $10.95; 9781400052998
LC 2003-273589

"Gregor Samsa wakes up and discovers he has been changed into a giant cockroach. Thus begins "The Metamorphosis," and Kuper translates this story masterfully with his scratchboard illustrations. The text is more spare, but the visuals are so strongly rendered that little of the original is changed or omitted." SLJ

Sticks and stones: an epic in pictures. Three Rivers Press 2004 un Illustration
Grades: 10 11 12 Adult   **741.5; Fic**
   1. Graphic novels; 2. Stories without words
1-4000-5257-2, $13.95
LC 2004-45969

"A stone giant is born from a volcano and demands the fealty of the people around him. He makes them build him a stone castle; then he discovers a nearby peaceful village made entirely of wood and sets about conquering it and plundering its resources. Meanwhile, a small resistance front develops, led by a woman from the stone tribe and a boy from the wood tribe, and eventually the stone empire and its despot meet a grim fate. Kuper's narrative is beautifully constructed, from its grand sweep to its minute details." Publ Wkly

Kupperberg, Paul

Archie; 3: the married life : two worlds, two loves, two destinies. written by Paul Kupperberg; pencils by Fernando Ruiz, Pat & Tim Kennedy; inking by Al Milgrom and Bob Smith; letters by Janice Chiang and Jack Moretti; coloring by Glenn Whitmore. Archie Comic Publications 2013 320 p. Color illustration
Grades: 9 10 11 12 Adult   **741.5/973; Fic**
   1. Comic books, strips, etc.; 2. Marriage — Fiction; 3. Andrews, Archie (Fictional character)
1936975351; 9781936975358, $19.99
LC 2013409812

This graphic novel by Paul Kupperberg "explores Archie Andrews' life down two paths — if he had married girl-next-door Betty Cooper or wealthy socialite Veronica Lodge. In this volume, things really start getting interesting, as the mysterious Dilton Doiley subplots that have been bubbling just below the surface since the series' beginning start to affect... well, everything!" (Publisher's note)

"Eye-opening for longtime fanatics and an invigorating soap opera for newcomers." Booklist

Kurata, Hideyuki

Train + Train, Vol. 1. original story by Hideyuki Kurata; art by Tomomasa Takuma. Go! Comi 2007 196p. Illustration
Grades: 8 9 10 11 12 Adult   **741.5; Fic**
   1. Adventure graphic novels; 2. Graphic novels; 3. High school students — Graphic novels; 4. Manga; 5. Shojo manga
978-1-933617-18-3, $10.99

Reiichi and Liae have come to the planet Deloca to board the high school train. On Deloca, different schools run on special trains, with stops where students complete certain assignments; they live in dorms on the trains. Reiichi and Liae are registered to board the "General" school train. Arena Pendleton, on the other hand, has determined to board the Special Train, and she won't let anyone stop her, not even the men her wealthy grandfather has hired to capture her and bring her home. In Ideo City, where the students must board their respective trains, Reiichi accidentally gets involved in a run-in between Arena and Kong Seeval, who intends to take Arena home. Reiichi and Arena become handcuffed together, and he has no choice but to board the Special Train. There's lots of action but little in the way of violence or bad language in this first of a manga series.

Kverneland, Steffen

Munch. Steffen Kverneland; translated from Norwegian by Francesca M. Nichols. SelfMadeHero 2016 280 p. Illustration
Grades: 10 11 12 Adult   **92; 741.5**
   1. Munch, Edvard, 1863-1944; 2. Painters — Biography; 3. Biographical graphic novels
1910593125; 9781910593127, $24.95

This book in the Art Masters series by Steffen Kverneland "uses text drawn exclusively from the quotes of Edvard Munch and his contemporaries. Filled with authenticity and life, Munch debunks the familiar myth of the half-mad expressionist painter-anguished, starving, and ill-treated-and draws out his neglected sense of humor and optimism." (Publisher's note)

"Kverneland's skill at infusing Munch's own techniques and imagery into the biography is extraordinary, and the stories behind the controversial paintings are fascinating and wryly funny." LJ

Includes bibliographical references (pages 278-279)

Kwitney, Alisa

Token. illustrated by Joelle Jones. DC Comics/Minx 2008 176p. Illustration
Grades: 7 8 9 10 11 12   **741.5; Fic**
   1. Graphic novels; 2. Shoplifting — Graphic novels
978-1-4012-1538-5, $9.99

Almost-sixteen Shira lives in Miami's South Beach in the mid-1980s, in a hotel where her attorney father, her grandmother, and elderly friend Minerva. She's sort of a spaz at sports, the popular girls at her Jewish high school think she's weird, and her father has started dating his new secretary. Life isn't good. She impulsively starts shoplifting just to feel something, and then she meets Rafael, a streetwise boy who decides to teach her the finer points of stealing. And more.

Lagos, Joseph

The **sons** of liberty. created and written by Alexander Lagos and Joseph Lagos; art by Steve Walker; color by Oren Kramek; letters by Chris Dickey. Random House 2010 un Illustration
Grades: 6 7 8 9 10 11 12   **741; 741.5; Fic**
   1. Adventure graphic novels; 2. African Americans — Graphic novels; 3. Graphic novels; 4. Superhero graphic novels; 5. United States — History — 1600-1775, Colonial period — Graphic novels
9780375856716, $18.99; 9780375956683, $21.99; 9780375856686, $12.99

In the mid-eighteenth century American colonies, Graham and Brody work as slaves on a tobacco plantation not far from Philadelphia. When they run away after injuring the plantation owner's son for threatening another slave, they seek Benjamin Lay, an eccentric abolitionist who might give them shelter. Instead, William Franklin, son of Benjamin Franklin, finds them and conducts unknown experiments on them.

"History offers few villains as vile as slaveholders, but this graphic novel is far from being a simple revenge thriller. The use of historical figures and well-researched (but embellished) history, and a willingness to flesh out characters and set up situations to pay off in future installments, makes for an uncommonly complex, literate, and satisfying adventure." Booklist

Another title about the Sons of Liberty is: Death and taxes (2011)

Landis, Max

Superman: American alien. Max Landis, writer; Nick Dragotta, Tommy LeeEdwards, Joëlle Jones, Jae Lee, Francis Manapul,Jonathan Case, artists; Alex Guimarães, Tommy LeeEdwards, Rico Renzi, June Chung, Francis Manapul,Jonathan Case, Lee Loughridge, colorists; JohnWorkma. DC Comics 2016 224 p. Color; Illustration

Grades: 9 10 11 12 Adult   **741.5; Fic**

1. Superhero comic books, strips, etc.; 2. Superheroes; 3. Superman (Fictional character)

9781401262563, $24.99

LC 2016032268

This book, by Max Landis, "presents seven stories from the life of the man who will be the Man of Steel, seven pivotal moments that turned a sometimes good, sometimes angry, sometimes funny, always human, all-American alien into the world's first superhero.... This is the story of Clark Kent, a Kansas farm boy who happens to be from another planet. It's the story of a...reporter with a nose for the truth who's keeping the biggest secret the world has ever known." (Publisher's note)

"Landis brings a fresh and lively humanism to each of these tales, tangling throughout with Clark's uncertain feelings about his powers." Pub Wkly

Originally published in single magazine form as Superman: American Alien 1-7

Langridge, Roger

★ **Thor,** the mighty avenger, v.1.. writer, Roger Langridge; artist, Chris Samnee; colorist, Matthew Wilson. Marvel 2011 un Illustration

Grades: 8 9 10 11 12   **741.5; 741; Fic**

1. Thor (Fictional character)

978-0-7851-4121-1, $14.99; 0-7851-4121-9

"Readers meet the mysterious blond-haired God of Thunder with no memory when historian Jane Foster watches him get tossed out of a Norse exhibition one day. After the gallant fellow helps her out and she takes him in, an utterly charming romance ensues, even as Thor participates in some Norse debauchery and hunts down the secrets of his past." (Booklist)

Volume 1 of 2

Lapham, David

Batman: City of Crime. David Lapham, writer; Ramon Bachs, penciler; Nathan Massengill, inker; Jason Wright, colorist; Jared K. Fletcher, letterer. DC Comics 2006 288p. Illustration

Grades: 10 11 12 Adult   **741.5; Fic**

1. Batman (Fictional character); 2. Graphic novels; 3. Mystery graphic novels; 4. Superhero graphic novels

978-1-4012-0897-4, $19.99

Dave Lapham, the creator of the ultra-gritty noir series Stray Bullets, weaves a story of the Dark Knight facing an unspeakable crime. Batman first investigates the deaths of six teenage girls, then he learns of even worse crimes. As he tries to shut down a drug ring that's turned deadly, Bruce Wayne must contend with a wayward 14-year-old who's getting dangerously close to Gotham's underworld. In Gotham City, not every villain wears a mask; not every hero wears a cape; not every victim is innocent; and some secrets should remain buried. This volume includes violence.

Silverfish. DC Comics/Vertigo 2007 un Illustration

Grades: 11 12 Adult   **741.5; Fic**

1. Graphic novels; 2. Mystery graphic novels

978-1-4012-1048-9, $24.99

What starts as a childish bid for her father's affections turns into nail-biting suspense when teenaged Mia searches her new stepmother's purse, only to find a secret stash of money, a bloody knife and a mysterious address book. In the meantime, Daniel is on the trail of the woman who betrayed him; and the silverfish he keeps seeing in his mind's eye are telling him to kill again.

Larcenet, Manu

Dungeon: Parade Vol. 1: A Dungeon Too Many. by Joann Sfar, Lewis Trondheim & Manu Larcenet. NBM 2007 un Illustration

Grades: 6 7 8 9 10 11 12 Adult   **741.5; Fic**

1. Adventure graphic novels; 2. Fantasy graphic novels; 3. Graphic novels; 4. Humorous graphic novels

978-1-56163-495-8, $9.95

Marvin the Vegetarian Dragon and Herbert the Duck do battle with the new, rival dungeon next door that is actually a theme park. Then, Herbert finds a magic lamp that has one wish left, and he and Marvin set out on a quest to find a dying sage to get advice on the best wish.

Larsen, Erik

Savage Dragon Archives Volume 1. Image Comics 2006 616p. Illustration

Grades: 10 11 12 Adult   **741.5; Fic**

1. Graphic novels; 2. Mystery graphic novels; 3. Superhero graphic novels; 4. Hellboy (Fictional character)

978-1-58240-723-4, $19.99

The earliest adventures are collected for the first time in one volume as Savage Dragon defends Chicago from Overlord and the Vicious Circle. Savage Dragon, a big, green, fin-headed alien with no memory of his early life before being found in an empty field in Chicago, is a superhero who actually works as a police officer with the Chicago Police Department. This is the complete Overlord epic from start to finish, culminating in a battle that can only end one way. Guest-starring the WildC.A.T.S and the Teenage Mutant Ninja Turtles. This black and white reprint volume includes a lot of fighting violence, some strong language, and some skimpy women's costumes.

Larson, Hope

★ **Chiggers**. [by] Hope Larson; lettered by Jason Azzopardi. Atheneum Books for Young Readers 2008 170p. Illustration

Grades: 5 6 7 8 9   **741.5; Fic**

1. Camps — Fiction; 2. Friendship — Graphic novels; 3. Graphic novels

978-1-4169-3584-1, $17.99; 978-1-4169-3587-2 (pa), $9.99

LC 2008-09557

When Abby returns to the same summer camp she always goes to, she is dismayed to find that her old friends have changed, and the only person who wants to be her friend is the strange new girl, Shasta.

"Chiggers provides a ticket to summer fun. Larson delicately handles both the usual middle-school angst and the additional pressures that come with being somewhat different.... The content is perfect for upper elementary and middle school students." SLJ

Goldie Vance; Volume 1. Hope Larson, writer; Brittney Williams, artist; Sarah Stern, color artist. Boom! Studios 2016 112 p. Color; Illustration

Grades: 7 8 9 10 11 12   **741.5; Fic**

1. Mystery fiction; 2. LGBT youth — Fiction; 3. Women detectives — Graphic novels; 4. Hotels — Florida — Graphic novels

1608868982; 9781608868988, $9.99

In this first book in the Goldie Vance series by Hope Larson, illustrated by Brittney Williams, "sixteen-year-old Marigold 'Goldie' Vance lives at a Florida resort with her dad, who manages the place.... Goldie has an insatiable curiosity, which explains her dream to one day become the hotel's in-house detective. When Charles, the current detective, encounters a case he can't crack, he agrees to mentor Goldie in exchange for her help solving the mystery." (Publisher's note)

Volume 1 of an ongoing series

Gray horses. Oni Press 2006 un Illustration
Grades: 9 10 11 12 Adult
741.5; Fic
  1. Dreams — Graphic novels; 2. Graphic novels
  1-932664-36-X, 14.95

Courtesy of Oni Press

LC 2006-280748
French exchange student Noemie has traveled to Onion City on her own, where she makes friends with free-spirited Anna, a neighbor and baker's daughter who sculpts in bread. As she walks around the city, she finds herself the target of a mysterious young photographer. However, it's in her dreams that things are weird. Every night she dreams of a girl named Marcy who finds help from a talking horse to get away from her mother; she must find a place to hide a photograph before her mother burns everything "contaminated" from illness. As the dreams progress every night, Noemie is more able to live in the moment. Much of the text is bilingual.

Who is AC?. Hope Larson; illustrated by Tintin Pantoja. Atheneum Books for Young Readers 2013 176 p.
Grades: 7 8 9 10 11 12
741.5/973; Fic
  1. Graphic novels; 2. Superheroes — Fiction; 3. Female superhero graphic novels
  1442426500; 9781442426504, $14.99; 9781442465404, $21.99

LC 2011052616
In this book, "Lin, a zine-writing 15-year-old who's just moved to a small town, becomes an unwitting Sailor Moon-style superhero, activated by mysterious cellphone messages and visited by a 'dispatcher' who nags her until she suits up. Her nemesis is a shadowy villain who possesses a glamorous rich girl in order to snare a boy named Trace." (Publishers Weekly)

Lash, Batton
Mister Negativity and Other Tales of Supernatural Law. Exhibit A Press 2004 170p. Illustration
Grades: 8 9 10 11 12 Adult
741.5; Fic
  1. Graphic novels; 2. Humorous graphic novels; 3. Supernatural graphic novels
  0-9633954-8-3, $15.95

LC 2003113227
Attorneys Wolff & Byrd represent clients that include Nagy D'Viti, a fellow with such a negative attitude that he physically repels people, Huberis the Dybbuk, a born again demon seeking church membership, Nicky Gorillo, a gangster who has literally become a gorilla mob boss, Steven Gink, a horror novelist in a coma who summons them through their dreams, Susann, the Muse of Potboilers, who sues the author she has "inspired," and Perry Otter, a boy magician with an unusual affliction.

Sonovawitch! And Other tales of Supernatural Law. Exhibit A Press 2000 166p. Illustration
Grades: 9 10 11 12 Adult
741.5; Fic
  1. Graphic novels; 2. Horror graphic novels; 3. Humorous graphic novels; 4. Law — Graphic novels
  0-9633954-6-7, $14.95

Alanna Wolff and Jeff Byrd are attorneys who represent the supernatural and the supernaturally afflicted. In this volume, their clients include "Dr. Life," a physician dedicated to reviving the dead; "Bugsy" Renfield, a vampire member of the Nosferatu crime cartel; Ygor, a hunchback charged with teaching Satanism to preschool children; Martin Woodhull, accused of "hexual harassment" when his mother, a witch, puts a love spell on one of his co-workers; Dekoo Kei, a Japanese holy man who guards a jewel that can unleash the power of the giant reptilian monster, the Gormagon; and Barry Hopper, a nice guy whose soul has accidentally possessed the body of the demon Wasistlos, who is not too happy to deal with its "inner human." And their secretary, Mavis, has an adventure all her own.

Tales of supernatural law. Exhibit A Press 2005 184p. Illustration
Grades: 9 10 11 12 Adult
741.5; Fic
  1. Graphic novels; 2. Humorous graphic novels; 3. Lawyers — Graphic novels; 4. Supernatural graphic novels
  0-9633954-9-1, $16.95

This volume reprints the first eight issues of the ongoing comics series that used to be called Wolff & Byrd, Counselors of the Macabre and is now called Supernatural Law. Alanna Wolff and Jeff Byrd provide legal services for monsters, vampires, zombies, ghosts, and other things that go bump in the night. In these stories, they help a couple who foolishly used a monkey's paw to make wishes, another couple whose house becomes haunted every full moon, a supermodel seeking redress for a curse, a horror television host accused of exposing children to violence, a swamp monster who would like his fifteen minutes of fame, and the interdimensional being Th'Lulu.

Lasko-Gross, Miss
Escape from Special. Fantagraphics Books 2006 un Illustration
Grades: 10 11 12 Adult
741.5; Fic
  1. Autobiographical graphic novels; 2. Girls — Graphic novels; 3. Graphic novels
  978-1-56097-804-6, $16.95

This semi-autobiographical graphic novel uses short episodes to depict the childhood and teen years of Melissa. Sometimes willful, she gets into trouble at school, is branded "special" (as in special education), has very few friends, and has to see a therapist. With biting honesty, Melissa endures the casual cruelty of so-called friends, mis-uses bad words to comic effect, and questions why she should do things like attend Jewish school when her parents don't go to Temple. Occasional nudity and harsh language occur throughout the book.

Lat
Kampung boy. First Second 2006 141p. Illustration
Grades: 7 8 9 10 11 12 Adult
741; 741.5; Fic
  1. Family life — Graphic novels; 2. Graphic novels; 3. Muslims — Graphic novels; 4. Malaysia — Graphic novels
  1-59643-121-0, $16.95

LC 2005-34135
"Malaysian cartoonist Lat uses the graphic novel format to share the story of his childhood in a small village, or kampung. From his birth and adventures as a toddler to the enlargement of his world as he attends classes in the village, makes friends, and, finally, departs for a prestigious city boarding school, this autobiography is warm, authentic, and wholly engaging." Booklist

First published 1979 in Malaysia with title: Lat, the kampung boy; Another title about Lat is: Town boy (2007)

★ **Town** boy. First Second Books 2007 191p. Illustration
Grades: 7 8 9 10 11 12 Adult
741.5; Fic

1. Bildungsromans — Graphic novels; 2. Graphic novels; 3. Humorous graphic novels; 4. Malaysia — Graphic novels
978-1-59643-331-1, $16.95; 1-59643-331-0

LC 2006-102857

In this sequel to Kampung Boy, it's the late 1960s and Mat is now a teenager attending a boarding school in the town of Ipoh, far from his kampung. He discovers bustling streets, hip music, heady literature, budding romance, and through it all his growing passion for art.

Latour, Jason

Spider-Gwen; Volume 0: Most Wanted?. written by Jason Latour, art by Robbi Rodriguez. Marvel Enterprises 2015 112 p.

Grades: 9 10 11 12 Adult   741.5
1. Female superhero comic books, strips, etc.; 2. Superhero comic books, strips, etc.; 3. Spider-Woman (Fictional character)
0785197737; 9780785197737, $16.99

"Gwen Stacy is Spider-Woman, but you knew that already. What you DON'T know is what friends and foes are waiting for her in the aftermath of Spider-Verse! From the fan-favorite creative team that brought you Spider-Gwen's origin story in EDGE OF SPIDER-VERSE, Jason Latour and Robbie Rodriguez!" (Publisher's note)
Originally published in single issue form as Spider-Gwen #1-5; First volume of an ongoing series

Layman, John

★ **Chew,** volume one: taster's choice. written & lettered by John Layman; drawn & coloured by Rob Guillory. Image Comics 2009 un Illustration

Grades: 10 11 12 Adult   741.5; Fic
1. Cannibalism — Graphic novels; 2. Graphic novels; 3. Mystery graphic novels; 4. Science fiction graphic novels
978-1-60706-159-5, $9.99

Police detective Tony Chu is a good detective with a weird secret: he's Cibopathic he gets psychic impressions from whatever he eats. It means he is a vegetarian, but it also means he can learn important facts about a case by nibbling on the corpse of a murder victim. Aside from the "ewwww" factor, he tends to have a high success rate in solving his cases. In his world, the FDA (yes, Food and Drug Administration) has become the most powerful law enforcement agency on the planet, and chicken is a forbidden food because of the avian flu. The FDA's Special Crimes Division makes Tony one of their agents and gives him their strangest, sickest, most bizarre unsolved cases, hoping to use his Cibopathic abilities to close them. This story includes cannibalism, violence, some gore, and some bad language. It has also been cited by many comics reviewers as one of the top comics series of 2009.
Volume 1 of 12

Lee, Jen

★ **Garbage** night. Jen Lee. Nobrow Press 2017 72 p. Color; Illustration

Grades: 7 8 9 10 11 12   741.5; Fic
1. Animals — Fiction; 2. Dogs — Fiction; 3. Survival skills — Fiction
1910620211; 9781910620212, $18.95

In this book, by Jen Lee, "in a barren and ransacked backyard, a dog named Simon lives with his two best friends: a raccoon and a deer. The unlikely gang spends their days looting the desolate supermarket and waiting for the return of the hallowed 'garbage night' — but week after week, the bins remain empty. While scavenging one day, the trio meet Barnaby — another abandoned dog who tells them about the 'other town' where humans are still rumored to live." (Publisher's note)
"This follow-up to Lee's previous short story 'Vacancy' (also collected here) tells a simple yet absorbing tale of friendship and survival

in a postapocalyptic world.... Lee's expansive universe of anthropomorphic animals comes alive through her spare use of detail: her verbal worldbuilding gives readers just enough information about animal society and what came before to spark the imagination, and vivid, expressive cartooning fills in the gaps." Pub Wkly

Lee, Stan

Essential Fantastic Four Vol. 1, 2nd ed.. Marvel Entertainment 2005 un Illustration

Grades: 7 8 9 10 11 12 Adult   741.5; Fic
1. Fantastic Four (Fictional characters); 2. Graphic novels; 3. Superhero graphic novels; 4. Hulk (Fictional character)
978-0-7851-1828-2, $16.99

This massive trade paperback collects the first 20 issues of The Fantastic Four plus the Annual #1. Reprinted in black and white, this volume lets readers get the origin and early stories as originally written by Lee and drawn by Kirby. The Fantastic Four fights against Skrulls, Sub-Mariner, The Impossible Man, The Hulk, the Red Ghost, The Thinker, Doctor Doom (who first appeared in issue #5), the Puppet Master, and many more super villains.

★ **Stan** Lee's How to draw comics: from the legendary co-creator of Spider-Man, the Incredible Hulk, Fantastic Four, X-Men, and Iron Man. Watson-Guptill Publication 2010 224p. Illustration

Grades: 9 10 11 12 Adult   741.5
1. Comic books, strips, etc. — Authorship; 2. Drawing — Technique; 3. X-Men (Fictional characters); 4. Fantastic Four (Fictional characters); 5. Graphic novels; 6. Hulk (Fictional character); 7. Iron Man (Fictional character); 8. Spider-Man (Fictional character)
978-0-8230-0083-8, $24.99

LC 2010-5781

Includes bibliographical references

Stan's soapbox: The collection. Marvel Entertainment 2008 144p. Illustration

Grades: 9 10 11 12 Adult   741.5; 814
1. Fantastic Four (Fictional characters); 2. X-Men (Fictional characters); 3. Graphic novels; 4. Spider-Man (Fictional character)
978-0-9797602-9-7, $14.99

Stan Lee is probably one of the best-known faces of American comics, he helped to create many of the iconic superhero characters published by Marvel Comics, including the Fantastic Four, Spider-Man, and the X-Men. As an editor for Marvel, he wrote editorials that ran in every Marvel comic published from 1967-1980; these were called "Stan's Soapbox." This book, published as a co-venture with the Hero Initiative as a fundraiser to help comic creators in financial need, collects all of the Stan's Soapbox editorials from those Marvel comics. Readers can go back in time as they read what Lee wrote; the book also includes the major events happening in the U.S. and the world during those years

Lee, Tony

★ **Outlaw:** the legend of Robin Hood: a graphic novel. written by Tony Lee; illustrated by Sam Hart; colored by Artur Fujita. Candlewick Press 2009 un Illustration

Grades: 7 8 9 10 11 12   741.5; Fic
1. Adventure graphic novels; 2. Graphic novels; 3. Robin Hood (Fictional character); 4. Great Britain — History — 1154-1399, Plantagenets — Graphic novels; 5. Robin Hood (Legendary character)
978-0-7636-4399-7, $21.99; 0-7636-4399-8; 978-0-7636-4400-0 (pa), $11.99; 0-7636-4400-5 (pa)

LC 2008-943331

In this retelling of the Robin Hood legend, it's the year 1192, and Robin of Loxley has returned home from the Crusades after receiving news of his father's death. The Sheriff of Nottingham and Sir Guy of Gisburn govern Nottingham at the pleasure of Prince John. When Gisburn treacherously stabs Robin in a murder attempt, Robin escapes to Sherwood Forest, where the outlaws befriend him. With the help of such men as Little John and Friar Tuck, he organizes the outlaws and they start hurting Prince John where it matters — in his moneybags.

"Lee's excellent rendition of the famed selfless hero goes hand-in-hand with Hart's expressive illustrations, featuring lots of closeups and dramatic lighting and a beautiful jewel-toned palette. Teens will get caught up in this exciting page-turner." SLJ

OUTLAW: THE LEGEND OF ROBIN HOOD. Text copyright © 2009 by Tony Lee. Illustrations copyright © 2009 by Sam Hart. Reproduced by permission of the publisher, Candlewick Press, Somerville, MA on behalf of Walker Books, London.

Lehmann, Matthias

Hwy 115. Fantagraphics Books 2006 un Illustration

Grades: 12 Adult   **741.5; Fic**
1. Graphic novels; 2. Mystery graphic novels
978-1-56097-733-9, $19.95

Two detectives, René and Agatha, are on the tracks of Robert Illot, a serial killer whose modus operandi is to suffocate his victim with various objects (including chickens and lightbulbs) along the highways and byways of France. As they get closer and closer to catching up with him, seeking out and interrogating men and women from his past life at the insane asylum, he always stays one step ahead and the row of corpses grows longer and longer... In this lengthy original graphic novel by Matthias Lehmann, dreams and flashbacks converge with the ongoing narrative, with graphically depicted sex and lots of murders.

Lemire, Jeff

★ **Black** hammer; Volume 1: Secret origins. script by Jeff Lemire; art by Dean Ormston; colors by Dave Stewart; letters by Todd Klein; cover by Dean Ormston with Dave Stewart; chapter breaks by Dean Ormston, Jeff Lemire, and Dave Stewart. Dark Horse Books 2017 152 p. Color; Illustration

Grades: 11 12 Adult   **741.5; Fic**
1. Superheroes — Fiction; 2. Adventure graphic novels
9781616557867, $14.99; 1616557869

LC 2016045234

Eisner Award: Best New Series (2017)

In this graphic novel, by Jeff Lemire, illustrated by Dean Ormston, "the old champions of Spiral City — Abraham Slam, Golden Gail, Colonel Weird, Madame Dragonfly, and Barbalien — now lead simple lives in an idyllic, timeless farming village from which there is no escape! But as they employ all of their super abilities to free themselves from this strange purgatory, a mysterious stranger works to bring them back into action for one last adventure!" (Publisher's note)

"As the narrative unfolds, the haunting backstories add greater context and intrigue to the mysteries of the present. There's an astonishing clarity to the characters and their motivations amid what could easily become a convoluted backstory filled with interstellar exploration, multiverse travelling, alien diplomacy, and quiet farm life." Pub Wkly

This volume collects issues #1-#6 of the Dark Horse Comics series Black Hammer — Title page verso.

★ **Descender:** Tin Stars Book one. by Jeff Lemire; illustrated by Dustin Nguyen. Image Comics 2015 160 p.
Grades: 9 10 11 12 Adult   **741.5**

1. Science fiction comic books, strips, etc.; 2. Androids — Fiction; 3. Robots — Fiction
1632154269; 9781632154262, $9.99

LC bl2015040509

In this science fiction comic book, by Jeff Lemire, illustrated by Dustin Nguyen, "Young Robot boy TIM-21 and his companions struggle to stay alive in a universe where all androids have been outlawed and bounty hunters lurk on every planet." (Publisher's note)

Volume 1 of an ongoing series

★ **Essex** County, Vol. 1: Tales from the Farm. Top Shelf Productions 2007 un Illustration
Grades: 10 11 12 Adult   **741.5; Fic**
1. Farm life — Graphic novels; 2. Friendship — Graphic novels; 3. Graphic novels; 4. Orphans — Graphic novels
978-1-891830-88-4, $9.95

Orphaned ten-year-old Lester lives with his bachelor uncle Ken on a southwestern Ontario farm. He constantly wears a mask and cape, imagining that he's protecting the place from invading space aliens. Uncle Ken doesn't know how to deal with Lester, and their relationship becomes strained. Only one grown-up, Jimmy, who runs the gas station and convenience store, can connect with Lester on his level.

"Lemire enriches this rather familiar scenario with telling, particularizing detail, ensuring that this time the old heartwarming routine is unforgettably special." Booklist

Volume 1 of 3

★ **Essex** County, vol. 2: Ghost stories. Top Shelf Productions 2007 224p. Illustration
Grades: 10 11 12 Adult   **741.5; Fic**
1. Brothers — Graphic novels; 2. Graphic novels; 3. Hockey — Graphic novels
978-1-891830-94-5, $14.95

Ghost Story follows the lives and relationship of brothers Lou and Vince Lebeuf over the course of nearly seven decades. Elder brother Lou, now a deaf and lonely man, lives out his final days on his farm full of guilt and regret for the decisions he made that tore his family apart. From their childhood on the farm, to Toronto in the 1950s (where they both played professional hockey), Lou is left to revisit his life, his decisions and his regrets. This is the second volume of Lemire's stories of Essex County.

★ **Essex** County, vol. 3: The country nurse. Top Shelf Productions 2008 127p. Illustration
Grades: 10 11 12 Adult   **741.5; Fic**
1. Family life — Graphic novels; 2. Graphic novels
978-1-891830-95-2, $9.95

In this third and final volume in the Essex County trilogy, the story follows country nurse Anne Morgan through one day as she drives around the county to visit patients. In between her meetings with Jimmy at the gas station, Ken and his nephew Lester at the farm, and learning that elderly Mr. LeBeuf, Jimmy's father, had died the previous night, readers see the story of an orphanage that existed almost a century ago. When it burned down one night and the caretaker died getting all the children out, the nun in charge led them on a cold winter hike to find shelter and help in Essex County. Anne is a descendant of the nun, while Jimmy, Ken, and Lester are all descendants of one orphan. And all their stories come together as Anne makes her rounds of the day.

"Well written and beautifully drawn, this wonderful close to a powerful trilogy is ideal for fans of realistic stories in comics." SLJ

Green Arrow. written by Jeff Lemire; art by Andrea Sorrentino; color by Marcelo Maiolo with Andrea Sorrentino,Matt Hollingsworth & Hi-Fi; additional art byDenys Cowan & Bill Sienkiewicz (New tricks &Secret origin); letters by Rob Leigh, Dezi Sienty& Taylo. DC Comics 2016 464 p. Color; Illustration

Grades: 9 10 11 12 Adult **741.5**
1. Superhero graphic novels; 2. Green Arrow (Fictional character)
1401257615; 9781401257613, $49.99

LC 2015034646

"Oliver Queen is on the run and being hunted by the greatest enemy he never knew he had — Komodo, a mysterious archer who is the Green Arrow's better in every way. But this new villain is just one piece of the puzzle of Green Arrow's past. Komodo has thrown Oliver's life into disarray, making Oliver question the details of his time on the island — and his long-dead father's involvement. Once the murky secrets of Green Arrow's past surface, things will never be the same again. When Oliver finally discovers the truth about himself, can he use it to become the Green Arrow that he needs to be?" (Publisher's note)

Hawkeye: all-new Hawkeye. by Jeff Lemire; illustrated by Ramon Perez. Marvel Enterprises 2015 112 p. Color; Illustration
Grades: 11 12 Adult **741.5**
1. Superhero comic books, strips, etc.
0785194037; 9780785194033, $15.99

In this comic book, by Jeff Lemire, illustrated by Ramon Perez, "Hawkeye returns.... With Kate Bishop, his trusted ward and protégé (not titles she would use) back at his side, Team Hawkeye is thrown into an all new adventure spanning two generations of avenging archers. Past and present lives collide as Kate and Clint face a threat that will challenge everything they know about what it means to be Hawkeye." (Publisher's note)

Old man Logan; Volume 1: berzerker. writer, Jeff Lemire; artist, Andrea Sorrentino; colorist, Marcelo Maiolo; letterer, VC's Cory Petit. Marvel Enterprises 2016 128 p. Color; Illustration
Grades: 11 12 Adult **741.5**
1. Superheroes comic books, strips, etc.; 2. Wolverine (Fictional character)
078519620X; 9780785196204, $16.99

"Logan — the man who no longer calls himself Wolverine — will have endured many atrocities: The Marvel Universe's villains will have banded together and rid the world of its heroes. Logan's closest friend, Hawkeye, will have been murdered in cold blood right before his eyes. And driven mad by the same radiation that gave him his superhuman strength, Bruce Banner will have fathered a family of hillbilly Hulks..." (Publisher's note)

Contains material originally published in magazine form as Old Man Logan #1-4 and Wolverine: Old Man Logan Giant-Size; Volume 1 of an ongoing series

Plutona. script: Jeff Lemire; art: Emi Lenox; letters: Steve Wands; story: Emi Lenox & Jeff Lemire; colors: Jordie Bellaire; book design: Sasha Head; Plutona created by Emi Lenox; Plutona's last adventure by Jeff Lemire. Image Comics 2016 128 p. Color; Illustration
Grades: 10 11 12 Adult **741.5; Fic**
1. Mystery graphic novels; 2. Superhero graphic novels; 3. Children — Graphic novels
1632156016; 9781534300132; 9781632156013, $16.99

In this graphic novel, by Jeff Lemire, illustrated by Emi Lenox, "five kids discover the body of the world's greatest super hero, Plutona, in the woods after school one day. This discovery sends them on a dark journey that will threaten to tear apart their friendship and their lives." (Publisher's note)

"The wary tone of adolescent alliances and small thoughtless cruelties is captured perfectly. Colorist Bellaire works magic, contrasting the muted primaries of the school scenes against the cool shadows of the forest." Pub Wkly

Originally published in single magazine form as Plutona #1-5

Roughneck. Jeff Lemire. Gallery 13, an imprint of Simon & Schuster Inc. 2017 272 p. Color; Illustration
Grades: 11 12 Adult **741.5; Fic**
1. Brothers and sisters — Fiction
1501160990; 9781501160998, $29.99; 9781476774008; 9781476773995, $19.99
Alex Award (2018)

"Derek Ouellette's glory days in the NHL are far behind-now, he's known mostly for alcoholism, public urination, and bar fights. When his younger sister, Beth, arrives in town, addicted to Oxycontin and fleeing an abusive boyfriend, he finds he can no longer hide at the bottom of a bottle. The siblings take to the wilderness, in search of sobriety, solitude, and, possibly, a second chance." (Publishers Weekly)

Lemire "exhibits deep empathy for his characters, a keen understanding of difficult family dynamics, and an eye for the way that moments of grace can emerge in the midst of brutality. Full-color flashback sequences interrupt the main story, which is presented in washes of black and blue that highlight the sad state of the characters' lives as well as the barren Canadian wilderness." LJ

Teen Titans; Volume 1: Earth One. written by Jeff Lemire; pencils by Terry Dodson. DC Comics 2014 144 p. Color; Illustration
Grades: 10 11 12 Adult **741.5**
1. Teen Titans (Fictional characters); 2. Teenagers — Comic books, strips, etc.; 3. Superhero comic books, strips, etc.
1401245560; 9781401245566, $22.99

LC 2014032609

This book, by Jeff Lemire and Terry Dodson, is a "new original graphic novel in DC's popular 'Earth One' series.... The Teen Titans never felt like normal kids... but they had no idea how right they were. Their seemingly idyllic Oregon upbringing hides a secret — one that will bring killers, shamans, and extraterrestrials down on their heads, and force them into an alliance that could shake the planet to its foundations!" (Publisher's note)

"Rather than more minor tinkering with the teenaged super-hero team, this graphic novel is a full-scale reboot: what if, in an alternative world, circumstances brought together young people who echo the regular Teen Titans but are totally different people?...Lemire's (Essex County) script exploits teen angst efficiently and with some fresh imagination, while the Dodsons (Wonder Woman) produce lovely art, especially in panels showing Navajo seer Raven." Pub Wkly

Trillium. Jeff Lemire, writer & artist; Jeff Lemire, Jose Villarrubia, colorists; Carlos M. Mangual, letterer. DC Comics/Vertigo 2014 192 p. Color; Illustration
Grades: 11 12 Adult **741.5**
1. Science fiction graphic novels; 2. Time travel — Graphic novels; 3. Romance fiction
1401249000; 9781401249007, $16.99

LC 2014011939

Eisner Nominee: Best Limited Series (2014)

This graphic novel, by Jeff Lemire, with color by Jose Villarrubia and lettering by Carlos M. Mangual, "spins the tale of two star-crossed loved through space in time.... [In] the year 3797,...botanist Nika Temsmith is researching a strange species on a remote science station near the outermost rim of colonized space.... [In] 1921,...English explorer William Pike leads an expedition into the dense jungles of Peru in search of the fabled 'Lost Temple of the Incas.'" (Publisher's note)

"Lemire's art excels, combining his trademark sketchiness with gorgeous watercolors. But it's the layouts that take the book to new heights of creativity. Lemire tells two stories at once by turning the panels upside down, disorienting the reader as much as his heroes." Pub Wkly

Leth, Kate

Patsy Walker, A.K.A. Hellcat!; Volume 1: Hooked on a Feline. Kate Leth, writer; Brittney L. Williams (#1-5) & Natasha Allegri (#6), artists; Megan Wilson (#1-5) & Natasha Allegri (#6), color artists. Marvel Enterprises 2016 136 p. Color; Illustration

Grades: 9 10 11 12 Adult   **741.5; Fic**
1. Female superhero graphic novels; 2. Mother-daughter relationship — Fiction; 3. New York (N.Y.) — Fiction
1302900358; 9781302900359, $17.99

"Patsy Walker has managed to escape her past, her enemies and Hell itself (literally) — but nothing compares to job hunting in New York City! Between trying to make rent and dodging bullets, Patsy barely has time to deal with her mother.... As she goes from living a double life to a triple, what the hell is Patsy Walker supposed to do?" (Publisher's note)

Volume 1 of 3

Levitz, Paul

Justice Society Volume One. writers, Paul Levitz, Gerry Conway; pencillers, Joe Staton, Keith Giffen, Wally Wood, Ric Estrada; inkers, Wally Wood, Bob Layton. DC Comics 2006 224p. Illustration

Grades: 7 8 9 10 11 12 Adult   **741.5; Fic**
1. Graphic novels; 2. Justice Society of America (Fictional characters); 3. Superhero graphic novels; 4. Green Lantern (Fictional character); 5. Flash (Fictional character); 6. Robin (Fictional character)
978-1-4012-0970-4, $14.99

The volume collects stories originally published in the 1970s, when DC revived the very first superhero team that was originally created in 1940: the Justice Society of America. This incarnation of the Justice Society includes the Golden Age Flash and Green Lantern, Hawkman, Dr. Fate, Wildcat, Dr. Mid-Nite, Robin, Power Girl, and the Star-Spangled Kid. Artists on this run include Wally Wood, Joe Staton, Keith Giffen, and Ric Estrada.

Lewis, Corey Sutherland

Sharknife Volume 1. Oni Press 2006 un Illustration

Grades: 8 9 10 11 12 Adult

741.5; Fic
1. Graphic novels; 2. Humorous graphic novels; 3. Martial arts — Graphic novels
1-932664-17-3, $9.95

Courtesy of Oni Press

The Guandong Factory isn't like other restaurants. It's five stories tall, produces more peach dumplings per day than most eateries do in a decade, and it's the home of Sharknife — a mystical protector charged with protecting the establishment from those who would do it harm. But who is this mysterious yet colorful being? Once just a simple busboy, now Caesar Ives is something more — a crazy red rocket hero destined for greatness. But can Caesar juggle both lives — nabbing the girl (the super-sexy Chieko Momuza), and stopping the wide assortment of bizarre baddies that would love to do his precious eatery harm? There's lots of martial arts action.

Lewis, Edith Patton

The **claws** come out: astounding tales of broads and monsters. IDW Publishing 2007 152p. Illustration

Grades: 10 11 12 Adult   **741.5**
1. Fantasy graphic novels; 2. Graphic novels; 3. Horror graphic novels; 4. Humorous graphic novels
978-160010-120-5, $19.99

The subtitle may sound rude (come on, calling women broads?), but all the women in the stories are strong, capable, willing to fight off monsters, vampires, and zombies. A young woman goes on a date for the first time in years, not knowing her ideal guy is a vampire. A teenage girl walking home after a date has a close encounter of the strange kind, but the aliens end up in trouble. An apathetic scientist/aspiring rock star works late at the lab defrosting the Abominable Snowman and finds trouble when a power outage allows the creature to get free. A fortune teller accidentally starts a zombie epidemic with a very powerful love potion. Lewis plays horror for laughs, with some violence and sexual innuendo.

Lewis, John

★ **March:** Book One. John Lewis; [co-written by] Andrew Aydin; [art by] Nate Powell. Top Shelf Productions 2013 121 p. Illustration

Grades: 8 9 10 11 12 Adult   **741.5; 92**
1. Civil rights movements — United States — Comic books, strips, etc; 2. Lewis, John, 1940 February 21-; 3. African Americans — Civil rights — Graphic novels
9781603093002, $14.95

LC 2013218903

Coretta Scott King (Author) Honor Book (2014)

This graphic novel, by U.S. congressman John Lewis, "in collaboration with co-writer Andrew Aydin and New York Times best-selling artist Nate Powell...spans John Lewis' youth in rural Alabama, his life-changing meeting with Martin Luther King, Jr., the birth of the Nashville Student Movement, and their battle to tear down segregation through nonviolent lunch counter sit-ins, building to a...climax on the steps of City Hall." (Publisher's note)

"This is superb visual storytelling that establishes a convincing, definitive record of a key eyewitness to significant social change." SLJ

★ **March:** Book Three. by John Lewis and Andrew Aydin; illustrated by Nate Powell. Top Shelf Productions 2016 256 p. Illustration

Grades: 8 9 10 11 12 Adult

328.73; 92
1. Lewis, John, 1940 February 21-; 2. Civil rights — United States
9781603094023, $19.99; 1603094024

National Book Award: Young People's Literature (2016); Coretta Scott King (Author) Book Award (2017); Printz Award (2017); Sibert Informational Book Award (2017); YALSA Award for Excellence in Nonfiction for Young Adults (2017); Eisner Award: Best Reality-Based Work (2017)

Courtesy of IDW Publishing

This book is the "conclusion of the award-winning and best-selling March trilogy. Congressman John Lewis, an American icon and one of the key figures of the civil rights movement, joins co-writer Andrew Aydin and artist Nate Powell to bring the lessons of history to vivid life for a new generation, urgently relevant for today's world." (Publisher's note)

"Though Lewis and Aydin throw a lot at readers in this volume, their message, helped along seamlessly and splendidly by Powell's fantastic, cinematic artwork, is abundantly clear: the victories of the civil rights movement, symbolized in particular by Barack Obama's inauguration, are hard-won and only succeeded through the dogged dedication of a wide variety of people." Booklist

★ **March:** Book Two. by John Lewis and Andrew Aydin; illustrated by Nate Powell. Top Shelf Productions 2015 192 p. Illustration

Grades: 8 9 10 11 12 Adult   **741.5; 92**

1. African American civil rights workers; 2. African American legislators; 3. African Americans — Civil rights; 4. Autobiographical comic books, strips, etc.; 5. Civil rights movements; 6. Civil rights workers — United States; 7. Legislators — United States; 8. Lewis, John, 1940 February 21-; 9. African Americans — Civil rights — Graphic novels
9781603094009, $19.95; 1603094008
LC 2015270634

Eisner Nominee: Best Publication for Teens (2016); Eisner Award: Best Reality-Based Work (2016); Ignatz Nominee: Outstanding Series (2015)

Courtesy of IDW Publishing

This graphic novel, by John Lewis and Andrew Aydin, illustrated by Nate Powell, "takes us behind the scenes of some of the most pivotal moments of the Civil Rights Movement.... After the success of the Nashville sit-in campaign, John Lewis is more committed than ever to changing the world through nonviolence — but as he and his fellow Freedom Riders board a bus into the vicious heart of the deep south, they will be tested like never before." (Publisher's note)

"Heroism and steadiness of purpose continue to light up Lewis' frank, harrowing account of the civil rights movement's climactic days.... The contrast between the dignified marchers and the vicious, hate-filled actions and expressions of their tormentors will leave a deep impression on readers." Kirkus

Lie, Bjorn Rune

The **wolf's** whistle. by B.R. Lie and S.J. Donaldson.. Nobrow 2012 88 p. Illustration; Color
Grades: 4 5 6 7 8 9 10   **741.5; Fic**
1. Fractured fairy tales; 2. Revenge — Fiction
1907704035; 9781907704031, $18.00

This children's book by Bjorn Rune Lie "digs into the troubled upbringing of one of storydom's most maligned figures: the house-blowing-down wolf. As a wolf cub, little Robert loved superhero comics...which led to much torment at the hands of three piggish brothers. Robert grows up to be not much... when the building owned by the Honeyroasts burns down with three of Robert's best friends trapped inside, the spark of vengeance and justice is kindled in the wolf." (Booklist)

Lieberman, A. J..

Martian Manhunter: The Others Among Us. A.J. Lieberman, writer; Al Barrionuevo, penciller; Bit, inker; Marta Martinez, colorist; Rob Leigh, Travis Lanham, John J. Hill, letterers. DC Comics 2007 208p. Illustration
Grades: 10 11 12 Adult   **741.5; Fic**
1. Graphic novels; 2. Martian Manhunter (Fictional character); 3. Superhero graphic novels; 4. Justice League (Fictional characters)
978-1-4012-1335-0, $19.99

J'onn J'onzz, the Martian Manhunter, came to Earth years ago to warn all of humanity of an impending invasion. He believed himself to be the sole surviving member of his race and thus decided to use his incredible super-powers to help safeguard the people of his adopted world as a member of the Justice League of America. His discovery of a Martian artifact on Earth sets him on a quest to discover the origin of the relic which leads to a stunning discovery, the ramifications of which will forever change the way he sees himself, humanity and his destiny. He discovers that a shadowy branch of the U.S. government has imprisoned and experimented upon a group of Green Martians. Why were they being held captive, and what mysterious predator still stalks the survivors of Mars? His quest for truth will bring J'onn into conflict with humans, with every friend he has made on this planet. This book includes violence.

Liew, Sonny

★ The **art** of Charlie Chan Hock Chye. Sonny Liew. Pantheon Books 2016 320 p. Color; Illustration
Grades: 11 12 Adult   **741.5; Fic**
1. Singapore — Economic conditions — Comic books, strips, etc; 2. Singapore — Politics and government — Comic books, strips, etc; 3. Comic books, strips, etc.; 4. Illustrators
9781101870693, $30; 1101870699
LC 2015023576

Eisner Award: Best U.S. Edition of International Material — Asia (2017)

"In this graphic novel, [Sonny] Liew presents the life and work of an obscure comic-book creator in tandem with the turbulent modern history of Singapore.... [It] opens with his two-page comic juxtaposing a pair of prominent Singaporean leaders–Lee Kuan Yew, the long-standing prime minister who shrewdly if brutally oversaw the country's rise as an economic power; and Lim Chin Siong, a charismatic, populist orator who was outmaneuvered by political rivals, jailed as a dissident, and exiled." (Kirkus Reviews)

Originally published 2015 in Singapore

Limke, Jeff

Jason: Quest for the Golden Fleece. Lerner Publishing Group/Graphic Universe 2007 48p. Illustration
Grades: 3 4 5 6 7 8 9
292.1; 741.5
1. Graphic novels; 2. Greek mythology — Graphic novels; 3. Jason (Greek mythology) — Graphic novels
978-0-8225-5967-2, $26.60 lib bdg

Courtesy of Lerner Publishing Group

Jason's uncle Pelias had stole the throne when Jason was a child; now a young man, Jason must prove himself by retrieving the priceless Golden Fleece from the far-off land of Colchis. He gathers a ship of heroes, the Argonauts, to aid him on his quest; but when they arrive in Colchis, the king insists that Jason prove himself in dangerous trials, and the king's daughter, Medea, has plans for Jason. This retelling is based on the heroic poem by Apollonius of Rhodes. The book includes a glossary and a list of books and websites for further reading.

King Arthur: Excalibur Unsheathed. Lerner Publishing Group/Graphic Universe 2007 48p. Illustration
Grades: 3 4 5 6 7 8 9
398.2; 741.5
1. Arthurian romances — Graphic novels; 2. Graphic novels; 3. Malory, Sir Thomas, 15th c — Adaptations
978-0-8225-3083-1, $26.60 lib. Bdg.

Courtesy of Lerner Publishing Group

This story is adapted from Sir Thomas Malory's Le Morte D'Arthur. Young squire Arthur's life, and that of England, changes the day he pulls out the mysterious Sword in the Stone. Guided by Merlin the magician, Arthur takes his place as King of England. Can he win peace and freedom for his country? The book includes a glossary and a list of books for further reading.

Lin, Yali

Hawthorne's the Scarlet letter: the Manga edition. Wiley Publishing 2009 186p. Illustration

Grades: 5 6 7 8 9 10 11 12   **741.5; Fic**

1. Authors; 2. Graphic novels; 3. Novelists; 4. Short story writers; 5. Hawthorne, Nathaniel, 1804-1864 — Adaptations

978-0-470-14889-1, $9.99

Hester Prynne, a young married woman in puritanical Massachusetts, stands in public shame when she bears a child long after her husband had disappeared. She refuses to identify the father of her child and instead wears the scarlet letter A always. The young minister Arthur Dimmesdale lives with his guilt in secret, but the physician, Roger Chillingworth, is actually Hester's husband, returned for vengeance. He vows to find the man who fathered Pearl, Hester's daughter, and destroy him. Meanwhile, Pearl grows up in a society that shuns her mother, and she comes to see the A as her mother's badge of honor. This book is a manga style adaptation of Hawthorne's novel.

Little, Jason

Shutterbug follies. Doubleday Graphic Novels 2002 153p. Illustration

Grades: 10 11 12 Adult   **741.5**

1. Graphic novels; 2. Mystery graphic novels

0-385-50346-6, $24.95

LC 2002-727189

This novel was "originally serialized as both a weekly newspaper comic strip and a web comics serial.... Scrappy 18-year-old Bee is working in a New York photo lab when a picture of a naked female corpse that's not quite what it appears to be piques her interest. Her amateur investigation of its photographer leads her to an ever-deepening mystery, a friendly cab driver, a cute but nervous photo assistant, some scary doings with the Russian mob and finally, into deadly danger." Publ Wkly

"With nearly implausible coincidences, a dash of slapstick humor, and a few red herrings, this is a detective romp, and the ending panel leaves readers breathlessly awaiting a sequel." SLJ

Liu, Marjorie M.

★ **Monstress;** Volume 1: Awakening. Marjorie Liu, writer; Sana Takeda, artist; Rus Wooton, lettering & design. Image Comics 2016 192 p. Color; Illustration

Grades: 11 12 Adult   **741.5; Fic**

1. Steampunk fiction; 2. Fantasy graphic novels; 3. Monsters — Graphic novels

1632157098; 9781632157096, $9.99

Eisner Nominee: Best New Series (2016); Hugo Award: Best Graphic Story (2017)

"Set in an alternate matriarchal 1900s Asia, in a richly imagined world of art deco-inflected steampunk, 'Monstress' tells the story of a teenage girl who is struggling to survive the trauma of war, and who shares a mysterious psychic link with a monster of tremendous power, a connection that will transform them both and make them the target of both human and otherworldly powers." (Publisher's note)

"Takeda's artwork creates a lush and dangerous world for Liu's equally dangerous characters. The work is infused with feminist themes; almost all of the characters are strong — and deadly — women." SLJ

Volume 1 of an ongoing series

★ **Monstress;** Volume 2: the blood. Marjorie Liu; Sana Takeda, artist; Rus Wooton, lettering & design. Image Comics 2017 144 p. Color; Illustration

Grades: 11 12 Adult   **741.5; Fic**

1. Steampunk fiction; 2. Monsters — Fiction; 3. Adventure fiction

1534300414; 9781534300415, $16.99

Hugo Award: Best Graphic Story (2018); Eisner Award: Best Publication for Teens (2018); Eisner Award: Best Continuing Series (2018)

"Maika, Kippa, and Ren journey to Thyria in search of answers to her past... and discover a new, terrible, threat." (Publisher's note)

Loeb, Jeph

Batman: The Long Halloween. Jeph Loeb, writer; Tim Sale, artist; Gregory Wright, colors; Richard Starkings & Comicraft, letters. DC Comics 1999 375p. Illustration

Grades: 9 10 11 12 Adult   **741.5; Fic**

1. Batman (Fictional character); 2. Graphic novels; 3. Mystery graphic novels; 4. Superhero graphic novels

1563894270; 9781563894275, $19.99

LC 99-218572

Taking place during Batman's early days of crime fighting, this collection tells the story of a mysterious killer who murders his prey only on holidays. Working with District Attorney Harvey Dent and Lieutenant James Gordon, Batman races against the calendar as he tries to discover who Holiday is before he claims his next victim each month. This story also ties into the events that transform Harvey Dent into Batman's deadly enemy, Two-Face. The book includes some violence

Batman: Dark Victory. written by Jeph Loeb; art by Tim Sale. DC Comics 2014 400 p. Color; Illustration

Grades: 9 10 11 12 Adult   **741.5; Fic**

1. Serial killers — Graphic novels; 2. Crime — Graphic novels; 3. Batman (Fictional character)

1401244017; 9781401244019, $24.99

LC 2013041357

This collection "continues the story of 'The Long Halloween.' It is early in Batman's crimefighting career, when James Gordon, Harvey Dent, and the vigilante himself were all just beginning their roles as Gotham's protectors. Once a town controlled by organized crime, Gotham City suddenly finds itself being run by lawless freaks, such as Poison Ivy, Mr. Freeze, and the Joker. Witnessing his city's dark evolution, the Dark Knight completes his transformation into the city's greatest defender." (Publisher's note)

Collected edition originally published 2001

Batman: Hush. Jeph Loeb, writer; Jim Lee, penciller; Scott Williams, inker; Richard Starkings, letterer; Alex Sinclair, colorist; Jim Lee & Scott Williams, original series covers; Batman created by Bob Kane. DC Comics 2009 320 p. Illustration; Color

Grades: 9 10 11 12 Adult   **741.5/973**

1. Batman (Fictitious character) — Comic books, strips, etc; 2. Batman (Fictional character)

1401223176; 9781401223175, $24.99

LC 2009502034

This comic book, by Jeph Loeb, "is a thrilling mystery of action, intrigue, and deception,...in which Batman sets out to discover the identity of a mysterious mastermind using the Joker, Riddler, Ra's al Ghul and the Dark Knight's other enemies — and allies — as pawns in a plan to wreak havoc." (Publisher's note)

Originally published in single magazine form in Batman 608-619, Wizard 0 — T.p. verso.

Catwoman: When in Rome. Jeph Loeb, writer; Tim Sale, artist; Dave Stewart, colorist; Richard Starkings, lettering. DC Comics 2005 un Illustration

Grades: 10 11 12 Adult   **741.5; Fic**

1. Catwoman (Fictional character); 2. Graphic novels; 3. Mystery graphic novels; 4. Superhero graphic novels; 5. Joker (Fictional character)

1-4012-0432-5, $19.99; 1-4012-0717-0 (pa), $12.99

Catwoman travels to Rome with some unfinished business with the Falcone crime family. Accompanied by the Riddler, she dreams almost nightly about Batman, which annoys her to no end; she has gone to see Don Verinni, but even as she's talking to him, he dies from the Joker's poison. With help from local Sicilian hitman Christopher Castillo, Catwoman and Riddler get away, but when more mobsters come after her with Mr. Freeze's ice gun, Catwoman knows something is definitely wrong in Rome.

With frequent flashes of partial nudity and considerable violence, this title is more appropriate for older teens and adults.

Originally published as Catwoman: When in Rome issues #1-6 and Batman: Dark Victory issue #13.

Shazam!: the greatest stories ever told. DC Comics 2008 224p. Illustration
Grades: 4 5 6 7 8 9 10 11 12 Adult   **741.5; Fic**
  1. Adventure graphic novels; 2. Captain Marvel (Fictional character); 3. Graphic novels; 4. Superhero graphic novels
978-1-4012-1674-0, $24.99

This book collects comics stories about Captain Marvel dating from 1940 to 1998. Captain Marvel predated Superman as a comic book superhero; young newsboy Billy Batson could transform into the flying superhero by shouting the magic word "Shazam!" This gave him the wisdom of Solomon, the strength of Hercules, the stamina of Atlas, the power of Zeus, the courage of Achilles, and the speed of Mercury. In these fourteen stories, he battles against such foes as Dr. Sivana, Mr. Mind, and the Monster Society of Evil.

Showcase Presents: Batgirl Volume 1. DC Comics 2007 552p. Illustration
Grades: 6 7 8 9 10 11 12 Adult   **741.5; Fic**
  1. Batgirl (Fictional character); 2. Graphic novels; 3. Superhero graphic novels
978-1-4012-1367-1, $16.99

In the late 1960s, DC Comics added a new character to the world of Batman and Robin: Batgirl. Daughter of Commissioner Jim Gordon, Barbara Gordon is a librarian who relocates to Gotham City and soon dons her costume as the crime fighting Batgirl. This volume of black and white reprints includes her early adventures, from 1967 through 1975. The cover art notwithstanding, Batgirl is a woman of action.

Showcase Presents: Batman Vol. 1. DC Comics 2006 552p. Illustration
Grades: 6 7 8 9 10 11 12 Adult   **741.5; Fic**
  1. Batman (Fictional character); 2. Graphic novels; 3. Superhero graphic novels
1-4012-1086-4, $16.99

The spotlight's on Batman in this volume featuring Detective Comics #327-342 and Batman #164-174. The Dynamic Duo take on some of their most enduring Rogues Gallery members, including Penguin, the Riddler, and the Outsider in these classic Silver Age stories from the era of famed editor Julius Schwartz. This Showcase edition reprints the comics in black and white."

Superman/Batman: Supergirl. Jeph Loeb, writer; Michael Turner, artist; Peter Steigerwald, colorist; Richard Starkings, letterer. DC Comics 2005 un Illustration
Grades: 10 11 12 Adult   **741.5; Fic**
  1. Batman (Fictional character); 2. Graphic novels; 3. Superhero graphic novels; 4. Superman (Fictional character); 5. Wonder Woman (Fictional character)
1-4012-0250-0, $12.99

Batman has discovered something strange on the bottom of Gotham Bay which leads him to a mysterious and powerful teenaged girl who's bent on destroying Gotham City. What's her connection to Superman? Why does Wonder Woman want to hide her from the outside world? Will Darkseid succeed in recruiting her into doing his bidding? Who is she?

Superman/Doomsday: The Collected Edition. DC Comics 2006 412p. Illustration
Grades: 10 11 12 Adult   **741.5; Fic**
  1. Graphic novels; 2. Superhero graphic novels; 3. Superman (Fictional character)
978-1-4012-1107-3, $19.99

Doomsday killed Superman. Now the Man of Steel wants payback. Superman travesl to the nightmare world of Apokolips for a confrontation with Doomsday, the creature who cost the Man of Steel his life. With the help of the mysterious, time-traveling Waverider, superman at last discovers the shocking truth of his greatest enemy's origin. And just when he thinks the terror is finally over, the murderous juggernaut returns to Earth more powerful than ever.

Superman: Our Worlds at War. DC Comics 2006 512p. Illustration
Grades: 9 10 11 12 Adult   **741.5; Fic**
  1. Graphic novels; 2. Superhero graphic novels; 3. Superman (Fictional character); 4. Wonder Woman (Fictional character); 5. Green Lantern (Fictional character)
978-1-4012-1129-5, $24.99

Imperiex has been unleashed. As planets are destroyed in its mighty wake and with Earth in its path as it seeks to remake the universe in its twisted image, Superman is forced to form alliances with President Lex Luthor and Darkseid, even as he also joins with such heroes as Wonder Woman, Green Lantern, and many others. For once, this looks like a job that not even Superman can handle.

Superman: The Amazing Transformations of Jimmy Olsen. DC Comics 2007 192p. Illustration
Grades: 6 7 8 9 10 11 12 Adult   **741.5; Fic**
  1. Graphic novels; 2. Humorous graphic novels; 3. Superhero graphic novels; 4. Superman (Fictional character)
978-1-4012-1369-5, $14.99

Cub reporter Jimmy Olsen stars in this light-hearted volume collecting some of his most memorable adventures from the late 1950s and 1960s, all of which guest-star Superman. While investigating crime for The Daily Planet, Jimmy undergoes one startling transformation after another, gaining temporary super-powers as Elastic Lad and becoming a Giant Turtle Man, The Wolf-Man of Metropolis, The Human Porcupine and much more. At times like these, Superman finds that he must not only protect Metropolis from Jimmy, but Jimmy from himself.

Lolos, Vasilis

The **last** call volume 1. Oni Press 2007 un Illustration
Grades: 10 11 12 Adult
741.5; Fic
  1. Graphic novels; 2. Mystery graphic novels; 3. Supernatural graphic novels
978-1-932664-69-0, $11.95

Courtesy of Oni Press

Teenagers Sam and Alec have gone joyriding in Alec's mother's car, jamming to heavy metal rock, when the car dies, and something hits them. They awaken to find themselves on a strange train with very odd people. The conductor throws Alec off the train, and Sam meets some of the other passengers on the train. When he goes back to the compartment where he and Alec woke up on the train, he witnesses the murder of the ticketed passenger who had the compartment. Now Sam works with Mr. S, the shadow person who existed in dead Benny's body, to try to find out who murdered him. The book includes some harsh language, including occasional use of the f-bomb, and some violence.

Lott, Renee

Festering romance. Oni Press 2009 184p.
Grades: 9 10 11 12 Adult
741.5; Fic
   1. Ghosts — Graphic novels; 2. Graphic novels; 3. Romance graphic novels
978-1-934964-18-7, $11.95

Courtesy of Oni Press

College student Janet prefers to spend her time in her apartment, playing video games with her roommate and best friend Paul who happens to be a ghost. However, her friends keep setting her up on blind dates, and then one of them, Derek, turns out to be a nice guy. Subsequent dates don't go so well, though, because Derek also has a ghostly roommate Carol, who in life was his girlfriend. Janet and Derek blame each other for not telling the truth about their ghostly companions, but they each need to face the truth of why Paul and Carol are still with them. The book includes only some mildly bad language (crap, pissed off).

Loux, Matthew

Sidescrollers. Oni Press 2006 un Illustration
Grades: 10 11 12 Adult
741.5; Fic
   1. Friendship — Graphic novels; 2. Graphic novels; 3. Humorous graphic novels
1-932664-50-5, $11.95

Courtesy of Oni Press

Brian, Brad, and Matt are the kind of young man who works just enough to get by and be able to play video games, eat junk food, and hang around. Things change when their neighbor Amber, who works with them at the local McGreggor's, is going to the big local rock show where Brian's brother's band will be playing. Unfortunately for the guys, she's going with Dick (he'd rather be called Richard), the bully football player. Since Matt is sweet on Amber, the guys decide they have to save her from Dick, and their quest gets them out of the house, on the road, and in a whole lot of trouble. The book includes strong language, including the s-bomb and f-bomb, some sexual innuendo, and some fistfight violence.

Love, Jeremy

★ **Bayou,** volume one. created by Jeremy Love; colors by Patrick Morgan. Zuda Comics/DC Comics 2009 un Illustration
Grades: 9 10 11 12 Adult
741.5; Fic
   1. African Americans — Graphic novels; 2. Fantasy graphic novels; 3. Graphic novels; 4. Monsters — Graphic novels
978-1-4012-2382-3, $14.99
2009 Glyph Comics Awards: Story of the Year, Best Writer, Best Artist, Best Female Character (Lee), Best Comic Strip
In a little southern town called Charon in 1933, Lee Wagstaff lives the kind of precarious life that African Americans under Jim Crow laws had to live. She's friends with white Lily Westmoreland, but that friendship doesn't protect her when Lily's mother accuses Lee of theft. Then Lily

disappears, victim of a swamp monster, and the town's white men haul her father off to jail, most likely to face a lynching. Lee has to find Lily to save her father, but when she goes to the swamp where Lily disappeared, she falls into a strange land of monsters. There she meets Bayou, a blues-singing swamp monster who helps her, and Lee faces the evil in the strange land to find and save her friend. This book collects the first four chapters of the webcomic by Love, which was one of the first webcomics from Zuda, run by DC Comics. The book includes disturbing images of hanged people, and a white man hits Lee so hard she flies through the air and lands on her back with her face torn up. The "n" word is represented by "n*****" while other harsh language is plainly written. The book contains enough violence to bother squeamish and sensitive readers.
   "Extremely beautiful, scary and wonderful, this...comic takes readers to a pair of almost familiar, frequently threatening worlds." Publ Wkly
   Volume 1 of 2

Lovecraft, H. P. (Howard Phillips)

The **Lovecraft** Anthology 2: A Graphic Collection of H.P. Lovecrafts Short Stories. H. P. Lovecraft; edited by Dan Lockwood; illustrated by Alice Duke.. Harry N Abrams Inc 2012 128 p.
Grades: 11 12 Adult   **741.5/942; 741.5; S C**
   1. Short stories; 2. Horror fiction
1906838437; 9781906838430, $19.95
   This book presents "a graphic anthology of tales" by horror fiction author H. P. Lovecraft. "From the insidious mutations of 'The Shadow over Innsmouth' to the mindbending threat of 'The Call of Cthulhu,' this collection explores themes of insanity, inherited guilt, and arcane ritual." (Publisher's note)

Lutes, Jason

★ **Houdini:** the handcuff king. Hyperion Books for Children/Jump at the Sun 2007 90p. Illustration (Center for Cartoon Studies presents)
Grades: 4 5 6 7 8 9 10   **92; 741.5**
   1. Biographical graphic novels; 2. Graphic novels; 3. Magicians; 4. Nonfiction writers; 5. Houdini, Harry, 1874-1926
978-0-7868-3902-5, $16.99; 978-0-7868-3903-2 (pa), $9.99
   On May 1, 1908, magician Harry Houdini performed one of his famous handcuff escapes, this time in handcuffs and leg irons, while jumping off the Cambridge Bridge in Massachusetts into the frigid Boston River. This graphic novel takes the reader through Houdini's day, from 5:00 a.m. as he makes his preparations, makes a practice jump, coaches his wife Bess on how she's to help him, and then makes the jump.
   This is a "fascinating graphic novel.... The format will instantly draw a lot of attention from readers and then hold on to it. Lutes and Bertozzi use grayscale comic panels to share their story about the life of Harry Houdini in a unique way.... The book resembles a hybrid between fiction and nonfiction, and the ingenious choice of format will appeal to a broad age range of readers." Voice Youth Advocates

Jar of Fools. Drawn & Quarterly 2003 152p. Illustration
Grades: 10 11 12 Adult   **741.5; Fic**
   1. Graphic novels
1-896597-72-6, $16.95
   Haunted by the death of his escape-artist brother and a failed romance, the remaining hope of washed-up stage magician Ernie Weiss lies in his aging mentor, Al Flosso. But Al is slipping further into senility with each passing day. Meanwhile, Esther O'Dea, Ernie's ex-love, struggles to find peace in her own life, and a con man named Nathan Lender sets some mysterious plans for Ernie's future in motion in his efforts to make things right for his twelve-year-old daughter Claire.

Lyga, Barry

★ **Wolverine:** worst day ever. by Barry Lyga; artist, Todd Nauck. Marvel Publishing 2009 184p. Illustration

Grades: 5 6 7 8 9   741.5; Fic

1. Graphic novels; 2. Humorous graphic novels; 3. Superhero graphic novels; 4. Wolverine (Fictional character)

978-0-7851-3757-3, $14.99; 0-7851-3757-2

Teenager Eric Mattias has just recently discovered he has mutant powers. Very sucky mutant powers: suddenly no one notices him even when he's in the same room. He's not invisible, but he might as well be, and people don't even notice him when he speaks. Eric decides to follow Wolverine around and see if he can't pick up a few pointers about living a loner-type life, as the adamantium-clawed mutant tends to do. Only when they end up in a remote forested area does Eric realize he may not have made the smartest move, because someone else has come, someone who is as strong as Wolverine, and maybe meaner: Sabretooth.

"It's a coming-of-age tale with bursts of action that's sure to appeal to its large, built-in audience." Booklist

MacDonald, Heidi

The **Nightmare** factory: based on the stories of Thomas Ligotti. HarperCollins/Fox Atomic Comics 2007 Illustration

Grades: 10 11 12 Adult   741.5

1. Graphic novels; 2. Horror graphic novels

978-0-06-124353-0, $17.99

In the universe of horror master Thomas Ligotti, clowns take part in a sinister winter festival, a scheming girlfriend makes reality itself come unraveled, a crumbling asylum's destruction unleashes a greater horror, and a mysterious Teatro comes and goes, leaving only shattered dreams in its wake. Ligotti's tales of terror take the reader to places few would suspect exist, where madness is only a thought away. This book adapts four of Ligotti's chilling tales by writers and artists Stuart Moore, Joe Harris, Colleen Doran (The Sandman), Ben Templesmith (30 Days of Night), Ted McKeever (Batman), and Michael Gaydos (Alias). Ligotti provides introductions to each story. Violence, some harsh language, and some nudity appear in some of the stories.

MacHale, D. J.

Pendragon book one: the merchant of death graphic novel. adapted and illustrated by Carla Speed McNeil. Aladdin Paperbacks 2008 172p. Illustration

Grades: 5 6 7 8 9 10   741.5; Fic

1. Adventure graphic novels; 2. Fantasy graphic novels; 3. Graphic novels

978-1-4169-5080-6, $9.99; 1-4169-5080-X

LC 2007-937920

Fourteen-year-old Bobby Pendragon has had a good life with a loving family, friends, and sports, but it all changes the night his Uncle Press takes him into New York City, to a deserted subway station that contains a gate that leads them to another world. On Denduron, a peaceful tribe called the Milago face annihilation from the Bedowan, and Uncle Press expects Bobby to help him stop it. Press is what he calls a Traveler, and he says Bobby is one, too, and they have a job to do. Bobby is able to write journals and send them home to his best friends Mark and Courtney. Meanwhile, he needs to learn so much, can he do it in time to help — and stay alive?

"This graphic-format adaptation streamlines the already fast-moving experience, providing satisfying interpretations of favorite characters and situations." Booklist

Mack, Stan

★ **Taxes,** the tea party, and those revolting rebels: a comics history of the American revolution. Stan Mack. NBM Pub. 2012 166 p.

Grades: 9 10 11 12 Adult
741.5

1. United States — History — 1775-1783, Revolution — Comic books, strips, etc.; 2. United States — Politics and government — 1775-1783, Revolution — Comic books, strips, etc.; 3. United States — History — 1600-1775, Colonial period — Comic books, strips, etc.; 4. Wit and humor

1561636975; 9781561636976, $14.99

LC 2012938930

Courtesy of NBM Publishing

This historical comic book, by Stan Mack, is a humorous narrative overview of the U.S. Revolutionary War. "This graphic account of the birth of the United States stars a chubby, insecure King George III, rebellious and misunderstood colonists, and loudmouthed and insensitive aristocrats, providing information about the Boston Tea Party and the revolt against the status quo." (Publisher's note)

Macklin, Ken

The **weasel** patrol. About Comics/About Infinity 2009 104p. Illustration

Grades: 7 8 9 10 11 12 Adult

741.5; Fic

1. Graphic novels; 2. Humorous graphic novels; 3. Science fiction graphic novels; 4. Weasels — Graphic novels

978-0-9790750-8-7, $9.99

When criminals strike, the intergalactic troopers called the Weasel Patrol will ferret out the bad guys every time. Despite their utter lack of planning, attentiveness, cohesion, or competence, they always succeed, even if their favorite tactic when faced with danger is to run away. This book includes twelve comedic adventures, in which the weasels face mythical monsters (Big Foot), aliens, kidnapped cattle in disguise, and the ever-ready bad guy Reefer Rick. Willy, Leroy, Biff, Roscoe, and Bob are the genetically uplifted Weasel Patrol. The book includes mild, cartoony violence and no bad language and no nudity. Villainous Reefer Rick smokes. Artist Dowling includes fun little details, such as the Acme name on some of the gadgets.

MacPherson, Dwight L.

Kid Houdini and the silver dollar misfits. Viper Comics 2008 un Illustration

Grades: 3 4 5 6 7 8 9

741.5; Fic

1. Graphic novels; 2. Magicians; 3. Mystery graphic novels; 4. Nonfiction writers; 5. Supernatural graphic novels; 6. Houdini, Harry, 1874-1926

978-0 — 9802385-2-5, $9.95

In 1886, ten-year-old Harry Houdini runs away from home, only to find himself a prisoner in Professor Murat's circus. Harry joins the "freak" children: Lydia the snake girl (and her snake Terra), Hans the legless boy, and Jacques and Joe the Siamese twins and they form a detective agency that will solve mysteries for the fee of a silver dollar. Near Kansas City, a girl named Bea hires them to find her missing father whom she fears was kidnapped. However, when the gang gets to her house, they discover that her mother has now been kidnapped, too. It all has to do with a treasure map that leads to a lost gold mine, and the gang needs to solve that mystery in order to find Bea's parents. A young Harry Houdini and his friends make a fun team and they face some supernatural elements in their cases, much like the old Scooby-Doo cartoons " and with a similar scary-fun factor.

Magruder, Nilah
M.F.K.. Nilah Magruder. Insight Editions 2017 128 p. Color; Illustration
Grades: 7 8 9 10 11 12   **741.5**
1. Good and evil — Comic books, strips, etc.; 2. Supernatural graphic novels; 3. Voyages and travels — Graphic novels
9781683830047, $24.99; 1683830040

This book, by Nilah Magruder, tells "the story of Abbie, a deaf girl with a mysterious power, who is traveling across a vast desert to scatter her mother's ashes. In a world of sleeping gods, a broken government, and a fragile peace held in the hands of the corrupt, one youth must find the strength to stand up against evil and save humanity." (Publisher's note)

"Magruder's color-saturated, manga-inflected artwork incorporates subtle world building details in the background, and her characters — refreshingly diverse in skin tone and body shape — are deeply expressive and imbued with dynamic movement. With crackling banter, an immersive fantasy, and lots of mysteries still unanswered, this series opener is perfect for fans of both manga and adventure comics." Booklist

Mahler, Nicolas
Lone Racer. Top Shelf Productions 2007 92p. Illustration
Grades: 11 12 Adult   **741.5; Fic**
1. Graphic novels; 2. Humorous graphic novels; 3. Racing — Graphic novels
978-1-891830-69-3, $12.95

Years before, Lone Racer was a champion; now, he keeps plugging away despite taunts from the younger racers. He does it for his hospitalized wife. When he's not at the track or the hospital, he's at Bar Juanjo with old racing pal Rubber. When mechanic-turned-cop Irksome talks Lone Racer into a bank robbery and then chickens out, things get dire, and Racer decides he has to win a race to regain his self-respect. His "middling love-affair," which he breaks off because he can't stop thinking about his wife, adds more adult content to the book, along with the bar scenes. Mahler's art style is different — bodies curve oddly and heads are nothing but hats and noses; he also uses black, white and dull brick red for color.

"...this corny-old-movie scenario is, thanks largely to its looks, delightfully ludicrous." (Booklist)

Maier, Corinne
Einstein. Corinne Maier; art by Anne Simon. Nobrow Press 2016 72 p. Color; Illustration
Grades: 9 10 11 12   **92; 530.092; 741.5**
1. Einstein, Albert, 1879-1955; 2. Biographical graphic novels; 3. Physicists — Biography; 4. Einstein, Albert, 1879-1955
9781910620014, $19.95; 1910620017

This graphic biography of physicist Albert Einstein by Corinne Maier, illustrated by Anne Simon, offers "a caricature version of Einstein, a rumpled and mustachioed older man, with a nimbus of hair.... The cartoon style and conventions are well suited to expressing what Einstein calls the 'universe of my thoughts.'...The book succeeds as a creative exploration of Einstein's genius and the factors and forces that may have influenced him." (School Library Journal)

"The savvy script and illustration celebrate Einstein's life and work in a memorably imaginative visual saga." Pub Wkly
First published in French: Dargaud, 2015.

Mairowitz, David Zane
Kafka. [by] David Zane Mairowitz and Robert Crumb; edited by Richard Appignanesi. Fantagraphics Books 2007 176p. Illustration

Grades: 10 11 12 Adult   **92; 741.5**
1. Authors; 2. Biographical graphic novels; 3. Graphic novels; 4. Novelists; 5. Poets; 6. Short story writers; 7. Kafka, Franz, 1883-1924
978-1-56097-806-0, $14.95

This book combines a biography of Kafka with illustrated plot descriptions of many of his works, including The Metamorphosis. Crumb renders the stories in comic book form, while the biographical information is presented mostly in text.
Authors names reversed on cover

Maki, Yoko
Aishiteruze Baby Vol. 1. Viz Media/Shojo Beat 2006 un Illustration
Grades: 8 9 10 11 12 Adult   **741.5; Fic**
1. Graphic novels; 2. Manga; 3. Shojo manga
978-1-4215-0711-8, $19.95

Kippei Katakura is a 17-year-old playboy who spends his time chasing girls, careless of their feelings. But when his 5-year-old cousin Yuzuyu comes to live with his family after her mother's sudden disappearance, Kippei is put in charge of taking care of her. As Kippei gets to know Yuzuyu and starts to understand how she feels, he also begins to realize that all girls were like Yuzuyu once... Kippei has a lot to figure out, like what to make for Yuzuyu's lunch and how to drop her off at kindergarten while still getting to high school on time. Kippei is enjoying his time with Yuzuyu, but not everyone is happy about it. The girls at school miss their quality time with Kippei, and one decides to play dirty to get him back.

Mapa, Lorina
★ **Duran** Duran, Imelda Marcos, and me: a graphic memoir. by Lorina Mapa. Conundrum Press 2017 131 p. Illustration
Grades: 11 12 Adult   **741.597**
1. Cartoonists — Canada — Biography; 2. Mapa, Lorina — Childhood and youth — Comic books, strips, etc.; 3. Philippines; 4. Women cartoonists; 5. Women illustrators; 6. Autobiographies
1772620114; 9781772620115, $18

This book, by Lorina Mapa, is "a graphic memoir about growing up in the Philippines in the 1980s with Duran Duran, Imelda Marcos, and the EDSA Revolution. Mapa returns to Manila as an adult for the funeral of her father and come to terms with her past. A graphic love letter to her parents, family, friends, country of birth, and perhaps even to herself." (Publisher's note)

"[Mapa's] memoir of life in the Philippines is both touching and joyous, with vivid recollections of food, matriarchy, family, and politics told in an Hergé-inspired style that's deceptively simple but apt for its subject." — Publishers Weekly
Includes discography.

Marchetto, Marisa Acocella
Cancer Vixen: A True Story. by Marisa Acocella Marchetto. Pantheon Books 2009 211 p. Color; Illustration
Grades: 11 12 Adult   **741.5; 92**
1. Autobiographical graphic novels; 2. Breast — Cancer; 3. Graphic novels; 4. Marchetto, Marisa Acocella
037571474X; 9780375714740, $16.95

LC 200640967
In this graphic memoir, "Marisa Acocella Marchetto tells the story of her eleven-month, ultimately triumphant bout with breast cancer — from diagnosis to cure." (Publisher's note)

The author "tells the story of her eleven-month, ultimately triumphant bout with breast cancer — from diagnosis to cure, and every challenging step in between." Publisher's note

"The fashion details are great fun, drawn in a spare loose style, but it's the heart of her story, the support and love she gets from her family and friends, that make Cancer Vixen a universal story that's hard to put down." Publ Wkly

Marcus, Ken

Super human resources season one. Ape Entertainment 2009 un Illustration

Grades: 9 10 11 12 Adult   741.5; Fic

1. Graphic novels; 2. Humorous graphic novels; 3. Superhero graphic novels

978-1-934944-68-4, $12.95

Super Crises International hires out super heroes people with capes, claws, radioactive half-lives,...And, like any business, it has a human resources office that keeps up with expense reports, payroll, cleaning up the conference rooms after crossovers gone wrong...Tim from Temps-RUs comes to SCI to work in accounts receivable, and he soon learns that running a super hero business is definitely not fun. Something is not right with the bills, and Gordon from the corporate office threatens to shut down the office. On top of that, the office copier has attained sentience and decides to destroy all organic life, and his boss in Accounts plans to destroy SCI. Just another day at the office...The book includes some superhero fighting violence with no bloodshed.

Marcus, Leonard S.

Comics confidential: thirteen graphic novelists talk story, craft, and life outside the box. [edited by] Leonard S. Marcus. Candlewick Press 2016 192 p. Illustration; Color

Grades: 7 8 9 10 11 12

741.5

1. Mystery comic books, strips, etc.; 2. Cartoonists — Biography

076365938X; 9780763659387, $24.99; 9780763692247, $24.99

LC 2016945892

This book by anthologist Leonard S. Marcus features thirteen comic artists and writers. "Here are their moving, funny, inspirational stories: true tales from the crucible of creative struggles that led each to become a master of one of today's most vibrant art forms. The book also contains an original graphic short on the common theme of 'the city' from each of the artists, a mini-comic set in a cityscape of their choosing-present-day, historical, or imaginary." (Publisher's note)

COMICS CONFIDENTIAL. Front jacket illustrations copyright © 2016 by Harry Bliss, Gene Luen Yang, Catia Chien, Dave Roman, Danica Novgorodoff, Hope Larson, Matt Phelan, James Sturm, Sara Varon, Geoffrey Hayes, Mark Siegel, Kazu Kibuishi. Reproduced by permission of the publisher, Candlewick Press, Somerville, MA.

"Marcus's chosen comics creators together represent a nice range of styles, topics, nationalities, backgrounds, and intended audiences, while his insightful questions range from formative childhood influences to various career paths, and from individual creative processes to broader ruminations on the medium of comics. The profiles are concise and informative; taken together as a whole, the book represents a snapshot of the genre as it continues on its upward trajectory." Horn Book

Includes bibliographical references (pages 165-173) and index.

Marshall, Gary

Studio space: the world's greatest comic illustrators at work. interviews & edited by Joel Meadows & Gary Marshall. Image Comics 2008 318p. Illustration

Grades: 10 11 12 Adult   741.5

1. Cartoonists; 2. Comic books, strips, etc.; 3. Graphic novels

978-1-58240-909-2, $49.99; 978-1-58240-908-5 (pa), $29.99

Twenty modern comics artists talk about their careers, their work, and their working methods. Each of them is photographed in his studio, and samples of their artwork are included. The artists are: Brian Bolland, Tim Bradstreet, Howard Chaykin, Steve Dillon, Tommy Lee Edwards, Duncan Fegredo, Dave Gibbons, Adam Hughes, Joe Kubert, Jim Lee, Mike Mignola, Frank Miller, Sean Phillips, George Pratt, Alex Ross, Tim Sale, Walt Simonson, Bryan Talbot, Dave Taylor, and Sergio Toppi.

Martinson, Lars

Tonoharu: part one. Pliant Press/Top Shelp Productions 2008 128p. Illustration

Grades: 11 12 Adult

741.5; Fic

1. Graphic novels; 2. Teachers — Graphic novels; 3. Japan — Graphic novels

9780980102369, $14.95; 9780980102321, $19.95; 0980102367; 0980102324

LC 2007-940522

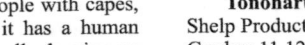

Courtesy of IDW Publishing

Daniel Wells looks back at his first year working as an assistant junior high school teacher in rural Japan as he must make a decision whether to renew his contract or leave Japan. In Tonoharu, he leads an isolated, almost monastic life, hampered by his lack of Japanese language skills and ignorance of Japanese culture. He wonders why his predecessor lasted only one year, and whether he will last beyond that as well. Meanwhile, he tries to work with the teachers at school and tries to pursue a relationship with another American teacher who lives a few towns away by train. This volume includes some harsh language, including the s-bomb, and some partial nudity.

Volume 1 of 3

Marz, Ron

Samurai: Heaven and Earth. Dark Horse Comics 2006 un Illustration

Grades: 11 12 Adult   741.5; Fic

1. Adventure graphic novels; 2. Graphic novels; 3. Samurai — Graphic novels

1-59307-388-7, $14.95

How far will a man travel for love? What battles will he fight? Will he cross heaven and earth to be by the side of the woman he loves? Beginning in feudal Japan of 1704, Samurai: Heaven & Earth follows Shiro, a lone samurai warrior sworn to be reunited with the love of his life who has been spirited away by his enemies. His pursuit of Yoshiko will carry him farther than he could have imagined — from his native Japan to the sprawling empire of China, across Europe, and finally to Paris itself. There, in the fabled halls of King Louis XIV's Versailles, he must cross blades with the greatest swordsmen ever known if he is to reclaim his love. Readers will find nudity, sexual situations, and violence (including beheadings).

Masamune, Shirow

Black magic. Shirow Masamune. Dark Horse Manga 2008 200p. Illustration

Grades: 10 11 12 Adult   741.5; Fic

1. Graphic novels; 2. Manga; 3. Science fiction graphic novels; 4. Seinen manga

978-1-59307-696-2, $14.95

Millions of years ago, the planet Venus teemed with life and an advanced civilization. In this past, the Nemesis supercomputer controls government functions, with bioroid "executors" created to carry out the system's utopian edicts. But trouble brews, even in good times, as different executors vie for control of Nemesis; these struggles force the governing system to secretly create Duna Typhon, a super-bioroid "sleeper." Raised among humans, she possesses awesome magical powers to be used to protect Nemesis. That time has now come. This was Masamune's first published manga series. The book includes some violence and harsh language.

Mashiba, Shin

Yumekui Kenbun: Nightmare Inspector volume 1. story and art by Shin Mashiba; translation, Gemma Collinge; adaptation, Kelly Sue DeConnick. Viz Media 2008 184p. Illustration
Grades: 9 10 11 12 Adult   **741.5; Fic**
1. Dreams — Graphic novels; 2. Fantasy graphic novels; 3. Graphic novels; 4. Manga; 5. Shonen manga
978-1-4215-1758-2, $9.99

In Japan, during the Taisho Era (1920s), there is a special place where people who suffer nightmares can go for help. At the Silver Star Tea House, Hiruko is a special kind of private investigator who can rid people of their darkest visions, for the price of eating their nightmares. In this first volume, Hiruko helps a young gatekeeper who suffers nightmares about his beautiful master, but when Hiruko enters the nightmare, he learns the gatekeeper's secret and true nature. He also helps a young woman who suffers nightmares of losing pieces of herself (her eyes, her hand, etc.), a young fan who dreams that his favorite movie star commits suicide, an unforgiving son whose father haunts his dreams, a young man who can never see the face of the ideal woman in his dreams. Some stories end in O. Henry-type twists; some stories include some violence.

Mashima, Hiro

Fairy tail vol. 1. translated and adapted by William Flanagan; lettered by North Market Street Graphics. Del Rey Manga 2008 202p. Illustration
Grades: 8 9 10 11 12   **741.5; Fic**
1. Fantasy graphic novels; 2. Graphic novels; 3. Humorous graphic novels; 4. Manga; 5. Shonen manga
978-0-345-50133-2, $10.95

Cute girl wizard Lucy wants to join the Fairy Tail, a club for the most powerful wizards (and the most troublesome " they tend to do stuff such as blow up harbors while fighting the bad guys). However, her ambitions land her in the clutches of a gang of unsavory pirates led by a devious magician, who plan to sell her into slavery. Her only hope is Natsu, a strange boy she has met on her travels. Natsu is not the typical hero: he gets motion sickness, eats like a pig, and his best friend is a talking cat. He is a member of the Fairy Tail, however. The book includes some mild fan service (usually cleavage shots), consumption of alcohol, and lots of magical fighting.

Volume 1 of 63

Massey, Jim

Maintenance volume 1: it's a dirty job . . .. written by Jim Massey; illustrated by Robbi Rodriguez. Oni Press 2007 88p. Illustration
Grades: 10 11 12 Adult
741.5; Fic
1. Graphic novels; 2. Humorous graphic novels; 3. Science fiction graphic novels
978-1-932664-62-1, $9.95

Doug and Manny work as custodians at TerroMax Inc., the world's biggest and best evil science think tank. The messes they have to clean up include toxic spill monsters and a talking manshark who wants to go out on the town. They also have to worry about the mad

Courtesy of Oni Press

scientists, would-be dictators, and the cute young woman who works at reception. The book includes some harsh language, including the s-bomb, and some violence.

Matheny, Bill

The **Batman** Strikes! Vol. 1: Crime Time. DC Comics 2005 un Illustration
Grades: 4 5 6 7 8 9   **741.5; Fic**
1. Batman (Fictional characters); 2. Graphic novels; 3. Superhero graphic novels; 4. Joker (Fictional character)
1-4012-0509-7, $6.99

This book boasts five action-packed adventures of the Dark Knight Detective: Penguin Rising, City of Bats, Outlaw and Disorder, Without a Chance and Deadly Partner. Batman goes up against the Penguin, the Joker, Manbat, and other villains.

The **Batman** Strikes!: duty calls. written by Bill Matheny, J. Torres; illustrated by Christopher Jones, Terry Beatty. DC Comics 2007 144p. Illustration
Grades: 3 4 5 6 7 8 9   **741.5; Fic**
1. Adventure graphic novels; 2. Batman (Fictional character); 3. Graphic novels; 4. Superhero graphic novels; 5. Catwoman (Fictional character); 6. Batgirl (Fictional character)
978-1-4012-1548-4, $12.99

This volume of Bat-stories is based on the new WB Kids cartoon series. Batman takes on Clayface, the Penguin, the Riddler, Catwoman, and Poison Ivy; Batgirl steps in because Pamela Isley used to be Barbara Gordon's friend. The stories have lots of action, fast quips, and no foul language or actual violence.

Matsui, Yusei

★ **Assassination** classroom 1: Time for assassination. Yusei Matsui. Viz 2014 192 p. Illustration
Grades: 9 10 11 12   **741.5**
1. Shonen manga; 2. Manga; 3. School stories — Graphic novels; 4. Assassination — Fiction
1421576074; 9781421576077, $9.99
Eisner Nominee: Best U.S. Edition of International Material — Asia (2016) [for volumes 2-7]

In this graphic novel, by Yusei Matsui, "the students in Class 3-E of Kunugigaoka Junior High have a new teacher: an alien octopus with bizarre powers and unlimited strength, who's just destroyed the moon and is threatening to destroy the earth — unless they can kill him first!...Will the deed be accomplished through pity, brute force or poison..." And what chance does their teacher have of repairing his students' tattered self-esteem?" (Publisher's note)

"This book begins as a simple adventure story, but the further teens get into the story, the more they will see the subtext of 'bad' students becoming empowered to find their real talents. Matsui's artwork is filled with action and humor, capturing the realistic aspects of the human characters and the smiley face and tentacles of the alien." SLJ

Volume 1 of 21

Matsumoto, Natsumi

St. dragon girl, vol. 1. story & art by Natsumi Matsumoto; English adaptation, Heidi Vivolo; translation, Andria Cheng. Viz Media/Shojo Beat 2008 un Illustration
Grades: 7 8 9 10 11 12   **741.5; Fic**
1. Fantasy graphic novels; 2. Graphic novels; 3. Manga; 4. Romance graphic novels; 5. Shojo manga
978-1-4215-2010-0, $8.99

High schooler Momoka Sendou, nicknamed Dragon Girl, is a martial artist; her childhood friend Ryuga Kou is a Chinese sorcerer who banishes demons. They have helped each other over the years, but now the Serpent King has threatened to take Ryuga's cousin Shunran as his bride. Ryuga knows he needs more strength, so he tries to summon the clan's dragon spirit to possess him, but Momoka sees only a threat to her friend and pushes him out of the way; the dragon enters her instead. Ryuga does possess the power to seal or unseal the dragon within Momoka, so now they really have to work together to fight the demons, especially the Serpent King. Complicating matters is the little fact that Momoka loves Ryuga but won't tell him, even though everyone around them knows it.

Volume 1 of 8

Matsumoto, Taiyo
  Sunny; Volume 1. Taiyo Matsumoto; translation by Michael Arias; lettering by Deron Bennett; book design by Fawn Lau. Viz 2013 224 p.
Grades: 9 10 11 12 Adult   **741.5; Fic**
  1. Orphans — Graphic novels; 2. Automobiles — Fiction
1421555255; 9781421555256, $22.99
  Eisner Nominee: Best U.S. Edition of International Material — Asia (2016) [for volume 5]; Cartoonist Studio Prize (2014)
  In this graphic novel by Taiyo Matsumoto, a "Nissan Sunny 1200 may look like a broken-down old car in front of a Japanese home for orphans. To the children and teens of the orphanage, though, the Sunny is a clubhouse, a spaceship, a getaway vehicle, and one of the few places that is truly theirs after they are abandoned by their parents. Readers catch glimpses of each of the orphans' lives, both the imaginary adventures they devise while in the Sunny and the sometimes heartbreaking ones outside of it." (Publisher's note)
  Volume 1 of 6

Matsumoto, Tomo
  Beauty is the Beast Volume 1. Viz Media/Shojo Beat 2005 184p. Illustration
Grades: 7 8 9 10 11 12   **741.5; Fic**
  1. Graphic novels; 2. Humorous graphic novels; 3. Manga; 4. Romance graphic novels; 5. Shojo manga
1-4215-0289-5, $8.99
  When bubbly eleventh-grader Eimi Yamashita finds out that her parents are relocating for work, she decides to strike out on her own and move into a dormitory for girls. Little does Eimi suspect the exciting romantic adventures that await her there. Eimi's fellow residents are a little bit crazy, but a whole lot of fun. They've got a secret mission planned for Eimi's new resident initiation...and it has something to do with sneaking into the boys dormitory across the street and returning with a special keepsake! Can Eimi pull it off without getting caught by one of the handsomest (and cruelest) boys in the dorm?

Matsushita, Yoko
  Descendants of Darkness Vol. 1. Viz Media/Shojo 2004 200p. Illustration
Grades: 10 11 12 Adult   **741.5; Fic**
  1. Fantasy graphic novels; 2. Graphic novels; 3. Humorous graphic novels; 4. Manga; 5. Shojo manga
1-59116-507-5, $9.99
  As a Shinigami, a Guardian of Death, Asato Tsuzuki has a lot to think about. First of all, there are all those dead people. Someone's got to escort them safely to the afterlife. Then there's all that bureaucracy. The affairs of death come with a lot of paperwork, budgetary concerns and endless arcana. Combining supernatural action with heavy dollops of romance, sex and humor, this book proves one thing: Death is big business...and business is good. The book includes graphic violence, some strong language, and some sexual situations.

Matthews, Brett
  The **Lone** Ranger. Dynamite Entertainment 2007 160p. Illustration
Grades: 8 9 10 11 12 Adult   **741.5; Fic**
  1. Adventure graphic novels; 2. Graphic novels; 3. Lone Ranger (Fictional character); 4. Western stories — Graphic novels
978-1-933305-39-4, $24.99; 978-1-933305-40-0 (pa), $19.99
  "A fiery horse with the speed of light, a cloud of dust, and a hearty 'Hi Yo Silver!' — The Lone Ranger..." A popular radio show starting in the 1930s that became a popular television show that ran from 1949 through 1957, a few film serials (extremely hard to find), some paperback novels, and a movie in 1981, The Lone Ranger became an iconic figure. In March 2008, Disney Studios announced it's planning to make a new Lone Ranger movie. In the meantime, Dynamite Entertainment started publishing Lone Ranger comics in 2006. This Lone Ranger is different from the old radio and television shows, and so is Tonto. These aren't the squeaky clean heroes one might expect, although they are heroic. This volume shows the origin of the Lone Ranger, from a young Texas Ranger who has just joined his father and brother. They are ambushed and all killed, except for John. Tonto, a Native American of unknown tribal nation, takes care of John; he has killed all of the killers. When John recovers from his wounds, they set off to find out who ordered the killing, while the reader knows that another killer is murdering all the dead Rangers' families. This book includes some graphic violence.
  Texas Ranger John Reid seeks revenge for the murders of his family and friends, only to find justice...and that he's something greater than he ever thought he could be. Together with Tonto, he rides against rich criminals like Cavendish and the politicians Cavendish backs. This new version of the Lone Ranger includes more violence than some might remember from the old television show and books.

Max
  Bardín the Superrealist. Fantagraphics Books 2006 82p. Illustration
Grades: 10 11 12 Adult   **741.5; Fic**
  1. Graphic novels; 2. Humorous graphic novels
978-1-56097-759-9, $19.95
  Everyman Bardín finds himself suddenly transported (well, at least his upper half) to another dimension, where an "Andalusian Dog" (a reference to Buñuel's Un Chien Andalou) serves as his ill-tempered guide. In a series of vignettes, gags, illustrations, text pieces, and dream stories, ping-ponging back between the surrealist world and the "real" world, Bardín examines, questions, and defends his own beliefs, convictions and philosophies while tangling with the Dog and the Holy Trinity in a variety of guises (including a familiar-looking mouse with red shorts and white gloves). In other stories, he imagines himself in a painting by Brueghel the Elder, tries to deal with his onanism in a productive way, is enlightened, dodges his real "creator" Max in the street, has several nightmares and hallucinations, and, in the book's climactic episode, "The Sound and the Fury," battles a bona fide dragon. There are some sexual situations and some other adult situations regarding the male's gender-defining organs.

Maxwell, Matt
  Strangeways: murder moon. Highway 62 Press 2008 144p. Illustration
Grades: 10 11 12 Adult   **741.5; Fic**
  1. Fantasy graphic novels; 2. Graphic novels; 3. Horror graphic novels; 4. Werewolves — Graphic novels; 5. Western stories — Graphic novels
978-0-9796957-0-4, $13.95
  In the year 1868, ex-Army officer Seth Collins works as a stagecoach guard and tries to forget the horrors of the Civil War. However, he now faces a different kind of horror: something hunts the people of Silver Branch, including Collins' estranged sister; a strange, seemingly unkillable wolf prowls the wilderness, stalking and killing people from the town. The people have their own secrets, and soon Collins finds himself trapped

between the obligations of family and friendship, between the secretive townspeople and the killing beast. The book includes violence and some strong language.

Mazzotta, Antony

Bombaby: The Screen Goddess. SLG Publishing/AmazeInk Comics 2004 un Illustration

Grades: 10 11 12 Adult   **741.5; Fic**

1. Fantasy graphic novels; 2. Graphic novels

1-59362-003-9, $13.95

Sangeeta Mukherjee is the daughter of well-to-do, traditional parents, dealing with a bratty little sister and an arranged marriage when an out-of-body experience reveals that she is not an ordinary young woman. Sangeeta is, in fact, the reincarnation of India's ancient protector, the Goddess of Mumbai. But how will Sangeeta use this new-found power? Can she make a difference in a male-dominated society? Sangeeta must defy traditional expectations to choose what kind of life she wants and discover her true self. There is some violence in the story.

McCay, Winsor

Winsor McCay: Early Works Volume 1. Checker Book Publishing Group 2003 201p. Illustration

Grades: 10 11 12 Adult   **741.5; Fic**

1. Graphic novels; 2. Humorous graphic novels

0-9741664-0-5, $19.95

LC 2003-12920

This volume is a collection of turn-of-the-century rarities from cartooning and animation pioneer, Winsor McCay: Tales of the Jungle Imps," Little Sammy Sneeze," Dreams of a Rarebit Fiend," and Pilgrim's Progress." Best known for Little Nemo in Slumberland, and the seminal animated feature Gertie the Dinosaur, McCay puts his artistic talent and whimsical humor on full display here. Readers should note that when these stories were first published in the early 1900s (Tales of the Jungle Imps" was published in 1903), McCay's artistic vision of the jungle imps" wasn't considered racist.

McCloud, Scott

Reinventing comics: how imagination and technology are revolutionizing an art form. Paradox Press 2000 237p. Illustration

Grades: 11 12 Adult   **741; 741.5**

1. Cartoons and caricatures; 2. Comic books, strips, etc.

0-06-095350-0, $22.95

LC 00-710457

The author maps out "'12 revolutions', which, he believes, need to take place for comics to survive and finally be recognized as a legitimate art form. The topics progress from the oldest of comic-related arguments (seeking respect) to the use of computer technology to renew and expand its audience. These brilliantly presented discussions concern comics as literature, comics as art, creators' rights, industry innovation, and public perception, among other topics." Libr J

★ **Understanding** comics: the invisible art. HarperPerennial 1994 215p. Illustration

Grades: 9 10 11 12 Adult   **741.5**

1. Comic books, strips, etc. — History and criticism; 2. Cartooning — Technique

0-06-097625-X, $22.95; 9780060976255

McCloud "conducts a genial, well-researched and funny tour of virtually every historical and perceptual aspect of comics, which he calls 'sequential art,' that is, art that consists of sequences of words and pictures. Beginning in the 11th century with the Bayeux tapestry, he examines pre-Columbian picture languages and the printing press, presenting a quick survey of the historical development of early sequential pictures into the

specialized visual language of comics.... He dissects the vocabulary of the medium, cheerfully analyzing the psychological power of comics and their central role in our ultra-visual culture." (Publishers Weekly)

Includes bibliographical references; First published 1993 by Kitchen Sink Press

McCulloch, Derek

★ **Stagger** Lee. Image Comics 2006 232p. Illustration

Grades: 10 11 12 Adult   **741.5; Fic**

1. Folk songs — United States — Graphic novels; 2. Graphic novels

1-58240-607-3, $17.99

What is known: On Christmas of 1895, in Bill Curtis' saloon in St. Louis, "Stag" Lee Shelton shot Billy Lyons. There have been many songs written about this incident, using some version or another of his name: Stacker Lee, Stack-A-Lee, Stack O'Lee, and more. This graphic novel, part historical fiction, part historical essay, examines the legend that grew in the many songs written and sung about the incident. The book contains some sexual situations and some strong language along with some violence.

McDuffie, Dwayne

Static shock: rebirth of the cool. writers, Dwayne McDuffie, Robert L. Washington III; artist, John Paul Leon; pencilers, John Paul Leon, Denys Cowan. DC Comics 2009 192p. Illustration

Grades: 9 10 11 12 Adult   **741.5; Fic**

1. African Americans — Graphic novels; 2. Graphic novels; 3. Science fiction graphic novels; 4. Superhero graphic novels

978-1-4012-2262-8, $19.99

In 1993, Milestone Comics published superhero comics written for African American readers, featuring African American superheroes. One of those heroes was Static, an inner city teenager imbued with the power of lightning and electricity. DC Comics has brought back Static by reprinting the two Milestone Comics miniseries. High school teen Virgil Hawkins is just trying to survive high school, getting by without joining gangs, and trying to get a date with the girl he really likes. He's also Static, with electromagnetic powers he gained on a night the city calls "The Big Bang." The problem is, he's not the only one who gained super powers of one kind or another that night, and most of those who did are using their powers to help them commit more crimes. Static wants to be a hero, but he faces incredible odds, including his own family's situation. The book includes some harsh language, at least one usage of the one-fingered salute, and violence.

McElroy, Clint, (podcaster)

The **adventure** zone: here there be gerblins. based on the podcast by Griffin McElroy, Clint McElroy, Travis McElroy, Justin McElory; adaptation by Clint McElroy, Carey Pietsch; art by Carey Pietsch. First Second 2018 256 p. Color; Illustration

Grades: 10 11 12 Adult

1. Elves — Fiction; 2. Warriors — Fiction; 3. Magic — Comic books, strips, etc.; 4. Fantasy graphic novels

9781250153708, $19.99

LC 2017946143

In this graphic novel, by Clint McElroy, Griffin McElroy, illustrated by Carey Pietsch, "join Taako the elf wizard, Merle the dwarf cleric, and Magnus the human warrior for an adventure they are poorly equipped to handle AT BEST, guided ('guided') by their snarky DM.... Like the smash-hit podcast it's based on, [this] will tickle your funny bone, tug your heartstrings, and probably pants you if you give it half a chance." (Publisher's note)

"Readers familiar with tabletop gaming or the McElroys' podcast will appreciate the snarky dialogue, the rampant geekiness, and the critical fail rolls that result in comic injury and mayhem." SLJ

McFarlane, Todd

Spawn Collection Volume 1. Image Comics 2005 un Illustration
Grades: 11 12 Adult   **741.5; Fic**
1. Fantasy graphic novels; 2. Graphic novels; 3. Horror graphic novels;
4. Mystery graphic novels
1-58240-563-8, $19.95

Al Simmons, formerly a soldier, was resurrected from the ashes of his own grave. Reborn as a creature from the depths of Hell, disfigured, homeless, and alone, this new warrior known as Spawn now wanders the shadowy alleys of New York City in search of his past life. Robbed of his memories and identity, this freshly created man whose body is nothing more than scars and torn flesh becomes a protector of the weak, the poor, the downtrodden, and other victims of circumstance. While Spawn tries to piece together his confusing existence, an unwelcome mentor reveals the purpose of his abrupt return to earth. But since this guide comes from the dark side, can he be trusted to tell the truth? And just what is the truth? In this twisted world of shadow players, nothing is as it appears. The book includes graphic violence and harsh language.

McGruder, Aaron

Birth of a nation: a comic novel. Aaron McGruder and Reginald Hudlin; illustrated by Kyle Baker. Three Rivers Press 2005 144p. Illustration
Grades: 10 11 12 Adult   **741.5; Fic**
1. Graphic novels; 2. Humorous graphic novels; 3. Political satire — Graphic novels
978-1-4000-8316-9, $14.95

LC 2004047838

East St. Louis, Illinois ("the inner city without an outer city"), is an impoverished town, but Fred Fredericks, its idealistic mayor, rallies his fellow citizens to the polls for the presidential election, only to find hundreds of them turned away for trumped-up reasons. As a result of the mass disenfranchisement of East St. Louis, a radical right-wing junta led by a dim-witted Texas governor seizes the Oval Office. Prodded by shady black billionaire and old friend John Roberts, Fredericks devises a radical plan of protest: East St. Louis will secede from the Union. Roberts' financial dealings result in East St. Louis becoming flush with money. Problems set in almost immediately: controversies rage over the name and national anthem of the new country (they decide on the Republic of Blackland with an anthem sung to the tune of the theme from Good Times), and local thug Roscoe becomes a warlord and turns his gang into a paramilitary force. When the U.S. military begins to move in, Fredericks is forced to decide whether his protest is worth taking all the way. The book includes some strong language, partial nudity, and sexual situations.

McKay, Sharon E.

War brothers: the graphic novel. Annick Press 2013 176 p. Illustration
Grades: 8 9 10 11 12
741.5; Fic
1. Lord's Resistance Army — Graphic novels; 2. Kidnapping — Graphic novels
1554514894; 9781554514892, $27.95

In this graphic novel, "14-year-old Jacob and his friends are just starting school at George Jones Seminary for Boys. The story tells of their subsequent kidnapping and near induction into the Lord's Resistance Army (LRA). Complete innocents at first, the boys endure near starvation, grueling conditions, and physical violence as they travel out of northern Uganda and into Sudan." (School Library Journal)

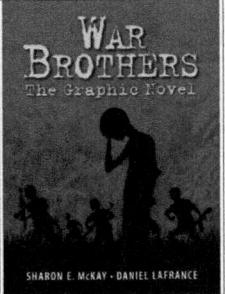
Courtesy of Annick Press

McKeever, Sean

Mary Jane Vol. 1: Circle of Friends. Marvel Entertainment Group 2004 96p. Illustration
Grades: 5 6 7 8 9 10 11 12   **741.5; Fic**
1. Graphic novels; 2. Romance graphic novels; 3. Spider-Man (Fictional character); 4. Superhero graphic novels
0-7851-1467-X, $6.99

High school student Mary Jane Watson hangs out with her friends (including nerdy Peter Parker) and starts dating old friend Harry Osborn even as she fantasizes about the new costumed superhero in town: Spider-Man. In this series, high school romance and friendships take center stage while the superhero action happens off the page and in the sidelines. This is the first of two volumes, then a new ongoing comics series called Spider-Man Loves Mary Jane continues the story.

McKenna, Aline Brosh

Jane. written by Aline Brosh McKenna; illustrated by Ramón K. Pérez; colored by Irma Kniivila with Ramón K. Pérez; lettered by Deron Bennett. Simon & Schuster 2017 224 p. Color; Illustration
Grades: 11 12 Adult   **741.5; Fic**
1. Young women — Fiction; 2. Man-woman relationship — Fiction; 3. Graphic novels
1608869814; 9781608869817, $24.99

This graphic novel, by Aline McKenna, illustrated by Ramon K. Perez, presents "a reimagining of Charlotte Brontë's classic novel Jane Eyre set in present day.... Growing up in a broken home in a small fishing town, Jane dreamed of escaping to art school and following the allure of New York City. When that dream becomes a reality however, it's not long before she feels out of place by the size of the city and the talent of her peers." (Publisher's note)

"With his stylish and realistic art, Eisner Award winner Pérez...gives Jane a pretty and capable look, resembling an older Nancy Drew, while the tortured billionaire Rochester appears grim and craggily swoonworthy. Kniivila and Pérez use vivid colors counterpointed with soft pencils and black and white inks to change scenes and convey emotions beautifully." LJ

McKissack, Fredrick, Jr.

★ **Best** shot in the West: the adventures of Nat Love. by Patricia C. McKissack and Fredrick L. McKissack, Jr.; illustrated by Randy DuBurke. Chronicle Books 2012 129 p. Color illustration; Color; Map
Grades: 7 8 9 10 11 12   **B; 978; 92; 741.5**
1. African American cowboys — West (U.S.) — Comic books, strips, etc.; 2. Cowboys — West (U.S.) — Biography — Comic books, strips, etc.; 3. Cowboys — West (U.S.) — Cartoons and comics; 4. Love, Nat, 1854-1921; 5. West (U.S.) — Biography — Comic books, strips, etc.; 6. West (U.S.) — Cartoons and comics; 7. African Americans — Biography — Graphic novels; 8. West (U.S.) — History — Graphic novels; 9. Cowhands — Graphic novels; 10. Railroads — United States
0811857492; 9780811857499, $19.99

LC 2007021419

In this graphic novel, "Nat Love's cattle-driving days are long over and America is a much tamer place when the black cowboy, now a Pullman porter, runs into Bugler, a man he knew back in the day. Bugler's son is a publisher...of...stories from the Wild West, and Love is persuaded to contribute his memoirs. From this...story,...[Patricia C. and Frederick L.] McKissack...segue into Love's adventures, based on his autobiography." (Bulletin of the Center for Children's Books)

Based on: The life and adventures of Nat Love, better known in the cattle country as Deadwood Dick.

McNamara, Jason

   Continuity. AiT/Planet Lar 2006 un
Illustration
Grades: 11 12 Adult
741.5; Fic
   1. Dreams — Graphic novels; 2. Graphic
novels
978-1-932051-43-8, $12.95

Courtesy of AiT/Planet Lar

   Alicia's life as a typical suburban misfit
takes a horrific turn as her dreams begin to
alter reality. She quickly finds herself
orphaned, pregnant, and on the run from a
pharmaceutical police state. Now she's
fighting to stay awake and restore the world
she once knew. But when a lonely doctor
offers Alicia redemption, will she accept? Or
will her dreams tear reality apart? Harsh
language and some violence make this more appropriate for older teens and
adult readers.

   The **Martian** confederacy, volume 1. Girl Twirl Comics 2008 143p.
Illustration
Grades: 10 11 12 Adult
741.5; Fic
   1. Graphic novels; 2. Humorous graphic novels; 3. Mystery graphic
novels; 4. Science fiction graphic novels; 5. Mars (Planet) — Graphic
novels
978-0-9794207-1-9, $15

   Mars in the year 3535 is pretty much a dump, with toxic air and
stripped of its natural resources by the corporations that run the planet.
Boone, Spinner (a bear) and Lou (a female android) are smalltime outlaws
who take on the crooked Alcalde when he steals a professor's cure for the
toxic air. As illustrator Braddock says, the story is basically The Dukes of
Hazzard on Mars, with redneck good ol' boy outlaws doing the right thing
against the corrupt government. However, Lou is no Daisy Duke, but a
tough fighter. There is some violence, mostly fist fights, and some brief
sexual situations and partial nudity.

McNeil, Carla Speed

   The **Finder** library; Volume 2. by Carla Speed McNeil. Dark Horse
Books 2012 636 p. Illustration
Grades: 11 12 Adult
741.5
   1. Science fiction graphic novels
159582653X; 9781595826534, $24.99

   "Since 1996, Finder has set the bar for science-fiction storytelling,
with a lush, intricate world and compelling characters. Now, Dark Horse is
proud to present four more story arcs of Carla Speed McNeil's
groundbreaking series in a single, affordably priced volume!" (Publisher's
note)

   The **Finder** Library; Volume one. illustrated by the author. Dark Horse
2011 630 p. Illustration
Grades: 11 12 Adult
741.5/973
   1. Science fiction graphic novels
1595826521; 9781595826527, $24.99
   This science fiction graphic novel anthology, by Carla Speed McNeil,
collects and reprints several of the author's Eisner Award-winning graphic
novels within the "Finder" series. This volume includes the novels
"Sin-Eater," "Talisman," and "King of the Cats," along with commentary
and footnotes from the author. (Publisher's note)

Meadows, Joel

   Studio space: the world's greatest comic illustrators at work.
interviews & edited by Joel Meadows & Gary Marshall. Image Comics
2008 318p. Illustration
Grades: 10 11 12 Adult
741.5
   1. Cartoonists; 2. Comic books, strips, etc.; 3. Graphic novels
978-1-58240-909-2, $49.99; 978-1-58240-908-5 (pa), $29.99

   Twenty modern comics artists talk about their careers, their work, and
their working methods. Each of them is photographed in his studio, and
samples of their artwork are included. The artists are: Brian Bolland, Tim
Bradstreet, Howard Chaykin, Steve Dillon, Tommy Lee Edwards, Duncan
Fegredo, Dave Gibbons, Adam Hughes, Joe Kubert, Jim Lee, Mike
Mignola, Frank Miller, Sean Phillips, George Pratt, Alex Ross, Tim Sale,
Walt Simonson, Bryan Talbot, Dave Taylor, and Sergio Toppi.

Mechner, Jordan

   Solomon's thieves. artwork by LeUyen Pham & Alex Puvilland. First
Second 2010 139p. Illustration
Grades: 6 7 8 9 10
741.5; Fic
   1. Graphic novels; 2. Knights and knighthood — Graphic novels; 3.
Middle Ages — Graphic novels; 4. France — History — 0-1328 —
Graphic novels
978-1-59643-391-5, $12.99; 1-59643-391-4

              LC 2010-282641
   Life as a Templar Knight returning from the Crusades is dull" bread,
beans, and lots and lots of walking. But after Martin stumbles upon his lost
love (now married — to someone else), things begin to get more interesting
very quickly. There's a vast conspiracy afoot to destroy the Templar Order
and steal their treasure. Soon, Martin finds himself one of the only
Templars out of prison — and out for revenge!

   "Pham and Puvilland...are again in top form, balancing grainy,
hatched textures and clean spaces to lend a weighty historical feel as a
vibrant sense of kineticism brings the action sequences to life." Booklist
   Includes bibliographical references

Medina, Tony

   ★ **I** am Alfonso Jones. Tony Medina; illustrated by Stacey Robinson
and John Jennings. Tu Books, an imprint of Lee & Low Books Inc. 2017
176 p. Illustration
Grades: 9 10 11 12
741.5; Fic
   1. Police shootings — Fiction; 2. Death — Fiction
9781620142639, $18.95

              LC 2017014950
   In this graphic novel, by Tony Medina, illustrated by Stacey Robinson
and John Jennings, "Alfonso Jones can't wait to play the role of Hamlet in
his school's hip-hop rendition of the classic Shakespearean play.... But as
he is buying his first suit, an off-duty police officer mistakes a clothes
hanger for a gun, and he shoots Alfonso. When Alfonso wakes up in the
afterlife, he's on a ghost train guided by well-known victims of police
shootings." (Publisher's note)

   "Medina's textual narrative starts tightly with black-and-white visuals
that follow suit, zoomed in closely on a single spiraling bullet. And from
there it expands, exploring Alfonso's bright, short life and bringing his
death and those that survive him steadily into view to confront the
repercussions of white supremacy." Horn Book

Medley, Linda

   ★ **Castle** waiting. Fantagraphics 2006 456p. Illustration
Grades: 5 6 7 8 9 10 11 12
741.5; Fic
   1. Fairy tales — Graphic novels; 2. Fantasy graphic novels; 3. Graphic
novels
1-56097-747-7, $29.95

All of Medley's previously self-published comics are collected here in one volume for the first time. The titular castle was the home of Sleeping Beauty, whose story is retold from the viewpoint of the flibbertigibbet ladies in waiting. After the flighty princess awakens with the kiss of a handsome but not too bright prince, the castle becomes a sanctuary for various misfits. Readers will find references to many fairy tales, folk tales, and nursery rhymes in Medley's book, and her clean, clear black-and-white art reflects the works of classic illustrators such as Arthur Rackham.

Castle waiting; Volume II. by Linda Medley; [graphic design by Adam Grano; edited by Kim Thompson]. Fantagraphics Books 2013 464 p. Color; Illustration
Grades: 5 6 7 8 9 10 11 12   **741.5/973**
1. Fairy tales — Graphic novels
1606996339; 9781606996331, $29.99
LC 2014381744
In this graphic novel, by Linda Medley, "Lady Jain settles into her new life.... Unexpected visitors result in the discovery and exploration of a secret passageway, not to mention an epic bowling tournament. A quest for ladies' underpants, the identity of her baby son Pindar's father, the education of Simon, Rackham and Chess arguing about the "manly arts," and an escape-prone goat are just a few of the elements in this...new volume." (Publisher's note)

Melchior-Durand, Stéphane
The **golden** compass; volume 1: the graphic novel. adapted by Stéphane Melchior, art by Clément Oubrerie; coloring by Clément Oubrerie with Philippe Bruno; translated by Annie Eaton. Alfred A. Knopf 2015 80 p. Color; Illustration
Grades: 6 7 8 9 10   **741.5; Fic**
1. Fantasy; 2. Graphic novels; 3. Pullman, Philip, 1946- Golden compass — Adaptations; 4. Fantasy graphic novels
9780553523867; 0553523724; 0553523864; 0553523716; 9780553523713, $18.99; 9780553523720
LC 2015005828
In this graphic novel adaptation of the young adult fantasy by Philip Pullman, adapted and illustrated by Stéphane Melchior-Durand and Clément Oubrerie, "Lyra Belacqua is content to run wild among the scholars of Jordan College, with her daemon familiar always by her side. But the arrival of her fearsome uncle, Lord Asriel, draws her to the heart of a terrible struggle-a struggle born of Gobblers and stolen children, and a mysterious substance known as Dust." (Publisher's note)
Originally published by Gallimard Jeunesse, Paris, France, in 2014 — Copyright page.

Meltzer, Brad
Green Arrow: The Archer's Quest. DC Comics 2003 176p. Illustration
Grades: 9 10 11 12 Adult   **741.5; Fic**
1. Adventure graphic novels; 2. Graphic novels; 3. Green Arrow (Fictional character); 4. Superhero graphic novels; 5. Green Arrow (Fictional character)
1-4012-0044-3, $14.95
Oliver Queen, the Green Arrow, has come back from the dead; certain items were supposed to have been destroyed once he was dead, but it never happened. Now, he and his former sidekick now known as Arsenal travel around, seeking those legendary artifacts in order to protect those people Oliver loves. The book includes some violence.

★ **Identity** Crisis. DC Comics 2005 un Illustration
Grades: 9 10 11 12 Adult   **741.5; Fic**
1. Green Arrow (Fictional character)
978-1-4012-0688-8, $24.99; 978-1-4012-0458-7 (pa)

It's been said that super-heroes keep secret identities to protect their loved ones. Elongated Man (Ralph Dibny) is one of the few without a confidential alter ego. So when his wife, Sue, is murdered in her own home, the tragedy hits the crime fighting community like a sledgehammer. As the fraternity of champions begins scouring the country for clues and suspects, Green Arrow, Hawkman, Black Canary, the Atom, and Zatanna stay behind, with a powerful secret to protect. Things get worse when other superheroes' family members receive threatening notes. And when the secret is discovered, the ramifications will forever change the world of super-powered heroes and villains.

Justice League of America: The Tornado's Path. Brad Meltzer, writer; Ed Benes, penciller; Sandra Hope, inker; Rob Leigh, letterer; Alex Sinclair, colorist. DC Comics 2007 228p. Illustration
Grades: 9 10 11 12 Adult   **741.5; Fic**
1. Graphic novels; 2. Justice League of America (Fictional characters); 3. Superhero graphic novels; 4. Superman (Fictional character); 5. Batman (Fictional character); 6. Wonder Woman (Fictional character)
978-1-4012-1349-7, $24.99
After traumatic events shattered the Justice League, trust was in short supply, but after it's all over, Superman, Batman, and Wonder Woman meet to choose who will become members of the new Justice League; but while they meet in secret, dark forces move against their friends and allies. A mysterious organization has helped the android Justice Leaguer known as Red Tornado to transfer his consciousness into the human body he's always wanted. But their motives may not have Red Tornado's best interests in mind. Instead, this is only the first step in a sinister conspiracy of super villains. The Justice League will have to rise again to save Red Tornado, and the world. But who will answer the call? The violence and fighting result in bloodshed.

Meyer, Marissa
Wires and nerve; Volume 1. Marissa Meyer; art by Doug Holgate with Stephen Gilpin. Feiwel & Friends 2017 240 p. Color; Illustration
Grades: 7 8 9 10 11 12   **741.5**
1. Cyborgs — Comic books, strips, etc.; 2. Imaginary wars and battles — Comic books, strips, etc.; 3. Androids — Fiction; 4. Imaginary wars and battles — Fiction
9781250078261, $21.99
LC 2016939440
"The 'Lunar Chronicles' continue in this entertaining graphic novel sequel to the existing volumes. This follow-up to the futuristic fairy-tale retellings centers on Iko, cyborg mechanic Cinder's best friend. Acclimating to her human body, the android is trying to help Queen Cinder of Luna ease tensions with Earth by hunting down rogue wolf-hybrid soldiers who were once enslaved by Cinder's evil stepmother and have now been banished to the green planet. Joined by other familiar characters (Cress, Winter, Thorne), loyal Iko defends the new queen against her enemies." (School Library Journal)
"Holgate's dynamic, stylized artwork handily balances the story's action and humor while bringing Meyer's world to vivid life." Pub Wkly
Followed by: Wires and nerve Volume 2, Going rogue

Wires and nerve; Volume 2: gone rogue. Marissa Meyer; illustrated by Stephen Gilpin. Feiwel and Friends 2018 324 p. Illustration
Grades: 7 8 9 10 11 12   **741.5; Fic**
1. Soldiers — Graphic novels; 2. Science fiction comic books, strips, etc.; 3. Imaginary wars and battles — Fiction
1250078288; 9781250078285, $21.99; 9781250078292
LC 2017944825
"Iko — an audacious android and best friend to the Lunar Queen Cinder — has been tasked with hunting down Alpha Lysander Steele, the leader of a rogue band of bioengineered wolf-soldiers who threaten to undo the tenuous peace agreement between Earth and Luna.... Steele and his

soldiers plan to satisfy their monstrous appetites with a massacre of the innocent people of Earth." (Publisher's note)

"Iko continues to get more backstory and narrates various parts of the overall story. The pacing of volume two is slightly faster than volume one, as there is no need for introductions and set-up, and it builds to a satisfying ending for all characters involved." VOYA

Meyer, Scott

Help is on the way: a collection of basic instructions. Dark Horse Books 2008 120p. Illustration
Grades: 10 11 12 Adult   741.5; Fic
1. Graphic novels; 2. Humorous graphic novels
978-1-59307-995-6, $9.95

This book collects Meyer's web comic called Basic Instructions. Using a four-panel format, he covers a variety of situations with wry humor, from How to Win an Argument to How to Pick a Password to How to Disguise a Yawn, and many more. The black and white art is fairly static, with a cast of characters Meyer uses and reuses. The humor is in the text, with a lot of fast-looking dialog. Many of the situations deal with marriage and with the workplace, while a number of them will resonate with those in the "nerd culture;" language is only mildly harsh (calling someone an "ass").

Mignola, Mike

The **Dark** Horse Book of Witchcraft. edited by Scott Allie. Dark Horse Comics 2004 96p. Illustration
Grades: 9 10 11 12 Adult   741.5; Fic
1. Graphic novels; 2. Horror graphic novels; 3. Witchcraft — Graphic novels; 4. Hellboy (Fictional character)
1-59307-108-6, $14.95

This anthology conjures up eight tales of horror and magic. Mignola presents a Hellboy story; Thompson and Dorkin return to the dog characters they created in "Stray" from a previous anthology volumes. Morse presents an evocative and carefully researched tale of old Salem, digging into the madness of the accusations leveled there, which ended more than thirty lives in a few short months. The book reprints a classic Clark Ashton Smith story, "Mother of Toads," illustrated by Gary Gianni, and more. There's some strong language and some graphic images of horror and violence.

Hellboy: into the silent sea. story by Mike Mignola and Gary Gianni; art by Gary Gianni; colors by Dave Stewart; letters by Clem Robins; cover art by Mike Mignola with Dave Stewart. Dark Horse Books 2017 56 p. Color; Illustration
Grades: 11 12 Adult   741.5; Fic
1. Hellboy (Fictional character)
9781506701431, $14.99

LC 2016049406

In this graphic novel, by Mike Mignola, Gary Gianni, and Dave Stewart, "Hellboy sets sail from the wreckage of a deserted island only to cross paths with a ghost ship. Taken captive by the phantom crew that plans to sell him to the circus, Hellboy is dragged along by a captain who will stop at nothing in pursuit of a powerful sea creature." (Publisher's note)

Hellboy in hell; Volume 2. story and art by Mike Mignola; colored by Dave Stewart; lettered by Clem Robins; cover art by Mike Mignola & Dave Stewart. Dark Horse Books 2016 96 p.
Grades: 10 11 12 Adult   741.5
1. Hell — Comic books, strips, etc.; 2. Damned — Comic books, strips, etc.; 3. Hellboy (Fictional character)
9781506701134, $17.99

LC 2016015900

"After facing off for a second time against the Vampire of Prague, Hellboy...comes down with a fatal illness, and seeks the help of an incompetent team of doctors. As he explores the geography of Hell,...Hellboy gets a glimpse of the new World Tree that he helped to create, stands accused of murder by his own sister and, in a way, brings about the destruction of Pandemonium." (Publisher's note)

"The acclaimed saga comes to an end with this story arc in which Hellboy dies and returns to his infernal birthplace, where he continues his work of punching out supernatural baddies." Pub Wkly

This volume collects Hellboy in Hell #6-#10 and Hellboy: The Exorcist of Vorsk from Dark Horse Presents Volume 3 #16, all originally published by Dark Horse Comics.; Death card

★ **Hellboy** Volume 1: Seed of Destruction. by Mike Mignola; script by John Byrne; miniseries colors by Mark Chiarello; cover colors by Dave Stewart; short-story colors by Matthew Hollingsworth. Dark Horse Comics 2003 un Illustration
Grades: 9 10 11 12 Adult   741.5; Fic
1. Fantasy graphic novels; 2. Graphic novels; 3. Hellboy (Fictional character); 4. Horror graphic novels; 5. Mystery graphic novels
9781593070946; 1-59307-094-2, $17.95
Eisner Award: Best Graphic Album — Reprint (1995); Eisner Award: Best Writer/Artist (1995)

When strangeness threatens to engulf the world, a strange man will come to save it. Sent to investigate a mystery with supernatural overtones, the good-guy big red demon, Hellboy, discovers the secrets of his own origins, and his link to the Nazi occultists who promised Hitler a final solution in the form of a demonic avatar. The book includes some violence and horror.

Other Hellboy volumes are: 2: Wake the Devil; 3: The Chained Coffin and Others; 4: The Right Hand of Doom; 5: Conqueror Worm; 6: Strange Places; 7: The Troll Witch and Others; 8: Darkness Calls; 9: The Wild Hunt; 10: The Crooked Man and Others; 11: The Bride of Hell and Others; 12: The Storm and the Fury; 13: Hellboy in Mexico

Hellboy Volume 2: Wake the Devil, 2nd ed.. Dark Horse Comics 2003 un Illustration
Grades: 9 10 11 12 Adult   741.5; Fic
1. Fantasy graphic novels; 2. Graphic novels; 3. Hellboy (Fictional character); 4. Horror graphic novels; 5. Mystery graphic novels
1-59307-095-0, $17.95

A murder in a New York wax museum and a missing corpse lead Hellboy into ancient Romanian castles on the trail of a sleeping legend: the original nobleman vampire. Nazi scientists prepare for the return of their occult master and the end of the world, and Hellboy confronts his purpose on earth. The book includes some violence, strong language and some nonsexual partial nudity.

Hellboy Volume 3: The Chained Coffin and Others 2nd ed.. Dark Horse Comics 2004 un Illustration
Grades: 9 10 11 12 Adult   741.5; Fic
1. Fantasy graphic novels; 2. Graphic novels; 3. Hellboy (Fictional character); 4. Horror graphic novels; 5. Mystery graphic novels
1-59307-091-8, $17.95

This volume collects short stories Mignola wrote for various other publications; it includes The Corpse," which some critics think is the best Hellboy story he has written. Mignola provides notes before each story. The book includes some violence, strong language, and nonsexual partial nudity.

Hellboy Volume 4: The Right Hand of Doom 2nd ed.. Dark Horse Comics 2004 un Illustration
Grades: 9 10 11 12 Adult   741.5; Fic
1. Fantasy graphic novels; 2. Graphic novels; 3. Hellboy (Fictional character); 4. Horror graphic novels; 5. Mystery graphic novels

1-59307-093-4, $17.95

This volume collects more Hellboy short stories Mignola wrote for various other publications; it includes Pancakes," a cute two-page story set when he was a young demon. The Right Hand of Doom" is a long story that takes up most of the volume. The book includes some violence and strong language.

Hellboy Volume 5: Conqueror Worm 2nd ed.. Dark Horse Comics 2004 un Illustration
Grades: 9 10 11 12 Adult   741.5; Fic
1. Fantasy graphic novels; 2. Graphic novels; 3. Hellboy (Fictional character); 4. Horror graphic novels; 5. Mystery graphic novels
1-59307-092-6, $17.95
2002 Eisner Award for Best Limited Series.

At the end of World War II, American costumed-adventurer Lobster Johnson led an Allied attack on Hitler's space program, but not before the Nazis were able to launch the first man into space. Now, after sixty years, Hellboy is partnered with an artifical man — a Frankenstein's monster implanted by Bureau scientists with a bomb — to travel to the ruined castle in Norway to intercept the returning capsule, and its single passenger...the conqueror worm. The book includes violence, strong language, and partial nudity.

Hellboy Volume 6: Strange Places. Dark Horse Comics 2006 un Illustration
Grades: 9 10 11 12 Adult   741.5; Fic
1. Fantasy graphic novels; 2. Graphic novels; 3. Hellboy (Fictional character); 4. Horror graphic novels; 5. Mystery graphic novels
978-1-59307-475-3, $17.95

After leaving the Bureau for Paranormal Research and Defense, Hellboy's travels take him briefly to Africa, then for a two-year stint at the bottom of the ocean. An ancient witch doctor, a giant fish woman and keeper of the secret history of the universe force Hellboy to either accept his role in the coming apocalypse, or have that role stolen from him. Weird undersea creatures and talking lions populate this turning-point adventure, which reveals secrets buried since Hellboy's very creation. The book includes some violence and strong language.

Hellboy volume 8: Darkness calls. Dark Horse Comics 2008 un Illustration
Grades: 10 11 12 Adult   741.5; Fic
1. Fantasy graphic novels; 2. Graphic novels; 3. Hellboy (Fictional character); 4. Horror graphic novels
978-1-59307-896-6, $19.95

Hellboy has finally returned from his adventures at sea, but no sooner has he settled on land than a conclave of witches drags him from his respite and into the heart of Russian folklore, where he becomes the quarry of the powerful and bloodthirsty witch Baba Yaga. Bent on revenge for the eye she had lost to Hellboy, Baba Yaga has enlisted the aid of Koshchei, a deathless warrior who will stop at nothing to destroy Hellboy. Meanwhile, in England, the Gruagach and his minions seek to regain the powers they once had over the world. The book includes brief partial nudity and a lot of bloodshed.

Jenny Finn: doom messiah. Boom! Studios 2008 un Illustration
Grades: 11 12 Adult   741.5; Fic
1. Fantasy graphic novels; 2. Graphic novels; 3. Horror graphic novels
978-1-934506-14-1, $14.99

In Victorian London, wherever the mysterious Jenny Finn goes, death and destruction follow in her wake as a plague sweeps through the city, affecting men. Meanwhile, someone is murdering and eviscerating whores. Goodhearted butcher Joe thinks Jenny Finn is an innocent girl who doesn't belong in the bad part of the city, and in his efforts to help her, he becomes embroiled in a battle between good and evil, with secret societies, an invasion of monstrous sea creatures, and a murderous artist. The book includes nudity, scenes in a whorehouse, harsh language, and violence.

Millar, Mark
Chosen. Dark Horse Comics 2005 un Illustration
Grades: 10 11 12 Adult   741.5; Fic
1. Graphic novels; 2. Supernatural graphic novels
1-59307-213-9, $17.95

Imagine you're twelve years old and suddenly discover that you are the returned Jesus Christ. You can turn water into wine, make the crippled walk and perhaps even raise the dead. What do you and your family do, and how does it affect you knowing that you're destined to grow up and take part in a conflict that people have been waiting almost two thousand years for? The book contains strong language, including the f-bomb.

Civil War. writer, Mark Millar; penciler, Steve McNiven. Marvel Entertainment 2007 un Illustration
Grades: 9 10 11 12 Adult   741.5; Fic
1. Graphic novels; 2. Superhero graphic novels; 3. Iron Man (Fictional character); 4. Captain America (Fictional character)
0-7851-2179-X, $24.99

The landscape of the Marvel Universe is changing, and it's time to choose: Whose side are you on? A conflict has been brewing for more than a year, and a single misstep by a costumed superhero costs thousands of lives and ignites the fuse of a superhero civil war. Teams, friendships, and families begin to fall apart as they must choose. What is the choice? The government wants to register all super powered individuals. Iron Man agrees and takes the government's side. Captain America sees registration as a step down the slippery slope towards the abolishment of civil rights for superheroes.

Superman Adventures Vol. 3: Last Son of Krypton. written by Mark Millar, David Michelinie; illustrated by Aluir Amancio, Ron Boyd, Terry Austin, Mike Manley, Neil Vokes; colored by Marie Severin; lettered by Phil Felix; Superman created by Jerry Siegel and Joe Shuster. DC Comics 2006 112p. Illustration
Grades: 4 5 6 7 8 9   741.5; Fic
1. Graphic novels; 2. Superhero graphic novels; 3. Superman (Fictional character)
978-1-4012-1037-3, $6.99

Superman confronts his own past as he encounters survivors from Krypton, including his parents, Jor-El and Lara. Plus, someone wants to expose Clark's secret to Lex Luthor and the world. Will an encounter with Dr. Fate mean the end of Superman?

Superman: Red Son. Mark Millar, Dave Johnson, Kilian Plunkett, Andrew Robinson, Walden Wong. DC Comics 2014 168 p. Color; Illustration
Grades: 11 12 Adult   741.5
1. Superman (Fictional character)
1401247113; 9781401247119, $17.99

LC 2013049659

Eisner Nominee: Best Limited Series (2004)

This comic book, by Mark Millar, illustrated by Dave Johnson, Kilian Plunkett, Andrew Robinson, and Walden Wong, "is a vivid tale of Cold War paranoia, that reveals how the ship carrying the infant who would later be known as Superman lands in the midst of the 1950s Soviet Union. Raised on a collective, the infant grows up and becomes a symbol to the Soviet people, and the world changes drastically from what we know." (Publisher's note)

Red Son

Wanted. Top Cow 2008 208p. Illustration
Grades: 11 12 Adult   741.5; Fic

1. Graphic novels; 2. Mystery graphic novels; 3. Superhero graphic novels
978-1-58240-497-4, $19.99

Wesley Gibson is a typical office worker, a nobody with a boring life...until he discovers that he is the son of "The Killer," a member of an underground fraternity of supervillains who've been running the world since 1986. After his father is killed, Wesley becomes the new Killer and he joins the villains while trying to unravel the mystery of his father's murder. This book is the basis for the motion picture starring Jamie MacElvoy and Angelina Jolie that was released during the summer of 2008. The book includes lots of graphic violence, very harsh language (with lots of f-bombs), and nudity.

Miller, Frank
   300. Dark Horse Comics 1999 88p. Illustration
Grades: 10 11 12 Adult   **741.5; Fic**
   1. Graphic novels; 2. Thermopylae, Battle of, 480 B.C. — Graphic novels
978-1-56971-402-7, $30

Miller paints a highly fictionalized, stylized account of the Battle of Thermopylae, where the Spartan King Leonidas and a relatively small band of Spartans held off the massive army of Emperor Xerxes of Persia long enough for Athens to gather its troops for the final showdown. The Spartans all died, but their sacrifice saved Greece in the end. Watercolor paintings by artist Varley use an earthy palette to depict the stark landscape and violent battles. This book is the basis for the hit motion picture released in March 2007.

   ★ **Batman,** the Dark Knight returns. Frank Miller; with Klaus Janson and Lynn Varley. DC Comics 2013 198 p.
Grades: 11 12 Adult   **741.5**
   1. Superheroes — Comic books, strips, etc.; 2. Batman (Fictional character); 3. Robin (Fictional character)
1563893428; 9781563893421, $19.99
                                    LC 2013008716
This graphic novel, by Frank Miller, "completely reinvents the legend of Batman.... The Dark Knight returns in a blaze of fury, taking on a whole new generation of criminals and matching their level of violence. He is soon joined by a new Robin — a girl named Carrie Kelley, who proves to be just as invaluable as her predecessors. But can Batman and Robin deal with the threat posed by their deadliest enemies, after years of incarceration have made them into perfect psychopaths?" (Publisher's note)
Originally published in single magazine form as Batman, the Dark Knight returns 1-4.

   Batman: Year One. DC Comics 2005 168p. Illustration
Grades: 8 9 10 11 12 Adult   **741.5; Fic**
   1. Batman (Fictional character); 2. Graphic novels; 3. Superhero graphic novels; 4. Catwoman (Fictional character)
978-1-4012-0752-6, $14.99
In the late-1980s, after publishing Miller's Batman: The Dark Knight Returns, DC realized they should remain faithful to the original roots of Batman. Miller then wrote this book, which reinvents the very early years of Batman as a superhero. In this book, Jim Gordon arrives in Gotham City to work in the police department and discovers the high level of corruption there; Batman encounters Selina, who becomes Catwoman, for the first time; and he develops some of the weapons he uses to fight crime. This new edition includes preliminary sketches and other extras.

   Batman: the Dark Knight strikes again. [by] Frank Miller, Lynn Varley, Todd Klein, Batman created by Bob Kane. DC Comics 2002 247p. Illustration
Grades: 10 11 12 Adult   **741.5; Fic**

1. Graphic novels; 2. Superhero graphic novels; 3. Batman (Comic strip); 4. Batman (Fictional character)
1-56389-844-6; 1-56389-929-9 (pa), $19.99
                                    LC 2003-544916
"Batman leads the opposition in a dystopian near-future when security concerns have spurred a repressive crackdown. Other costumed heroes side with either the government or Batman.... The book's authoritarian society resonates with the post-9/11 environment, though Miller's cheekiness dispels notions that this is serious commentary." Booklist
Originally published in single magazine form as Batman: the Dark Knight strikes again 1-3; Based on Batman comic strip; Sequel to Batman: the Dark Knight returns (1986)

   ★ **Sin** City Vol. 1: The Hard Goodbye. Dark Horse Comics 2005 208p. Illustration
Grades: 11 12 Adult   **741.5; Fic**
   1. Graphic novels; 2. Mystery graphic novels
1-59307-293-7, $17

Sin City is the place — tough as leather and dry as tinder. Love is the fuel, and Marv has the match...not to mention a condition." He's gunning after Goldie's killer, so it's time to watch this town burn. Frank Miller is one of modern comic's first talents to publish a comic book that he created, crafted, and owned. That book is Sin City, which grew from the wellspring of Miller's passionate desire to create a comic book with two distinct qualities — it wouldn't be a superhero comic, and it had to be a crime comic. Enter Marv and Goldie. And a psychotic killer. And a crime-drenched town. And a corrupted diocese. The stark black and white art includes nudity and graphic violence, along with lots of harsh language.

   Sin City Vol. 2: A Dame to Kill For. Dark Horse Comics 2005 208p. Illustration
Grades: 11 12 Adult   **741.5; Fic**
   1. Graphic novels; 2. Mystery graphic novels
1-59307-294-5, $17

It's one of those hot nights, dry and windless. The kind that makes people do sweaty, secret things. Dwight's thinking of all the ways he's screwed up and what he'd give for one clear chance to wipe the slate clean, to dig his way out of the numb gray hell that is his life. And he'd give anything. Just to cut loose. Just to feel the fire. One more time. And then Ava calls. Dwight thinks it's love, but Ava just needs him to kill her rich husband and she betrays him. No one does that to Dwight and gets away with it. This book includes lots of harsh language, graphic violence, nudity, and sexual situations.

Miller, John Jackson
   Star Wars: Knights of the Old Republic Volume One: Commencement. Dark Horse Comics 2006 un Illustration
Grades: 8 9 10 11 12 Adult   **741.5; Fic**
   1. Adventure graphic novels; 2. Graphic novels; 3. Science fiction graphic novels
978-1-59307-640-5, $18.95

Thousands of years before Luke Skywalker would destroy the Death Star in that fateful battle above Yavin 4, one lone Padawan would become a fugitive hunted by his own Masters, charged with murdering every one of his fellow Jedi-in-training. From criminals hiding out in the treacherous under-city of the planet Taris, to a burly, mysterious droid recovered from the desolate landscape of a cratered moon, Padawan Zayne Carrick will find unexpected allies in his desperate race to clear his name before the unmerciful authorities enact swift retribution upon him.

Millionaire, Tony
   Billy Hazelnuts. Fantagraphics Books 2005 111 Illustration
Grades: 9 10 11 12 Adult   **741.5; Fic**

1. Adventure graphic novels; 2. Graphic novels; 3. Humorous graphic novels

1-56097-701-9, $19.95

This book transmutes nursery rhymes and the golem myth into a storybook about Becky, girl scientist, her friend Billy Hazelnuts (who was created from cooking ingredients by tailless mice), and their journey to find the missing moon while battling an evil steam-driven alligator with a seeing-eye skunk. Millionaire fuses the darker spirit of older fairy tales with an adventure story, throws gender politics into the mix, and uses his highly detailed, old-fashioned looking art to pull it all together.

Sock Monkey: The Inches Incident. Dark Horse Comics 2007 88p. Illustration

Grades: 7 8 9 10 11 12 Adult   **741.5; Fic**

1. Fantasy graphic novels; 2. Graphic novels; 3. Toys — Graphic novels

978-1-59307-842-3, $12.95

Inches the doll was the cutest in the whole house. Loved by everyone, the world was Inches' oyster. Then one day something happened... The Sock Monkey and Mr. Crow became concerned for their diminutive friend, but by then it was too late. The truth sent the terrified Sock Monkey and Crow fleeing for their lives, for Inches had been invaded by a colony of evil ants. The sight of ants swarming over Inches and other things might be too creepy-crawly for some readers; the violence is aimed at toys rather than people, however, this is not a book for younger readers.

Sock Monkey: Uncle Gabby. Dark Horse Comics 2004 un Illustration

Grades: 8 9 10 11 12 Adult   **741.5; Fic**

1. Adventure graphic novels; 2. Graphic novels; 3. Humorous graphic novels

1-59307-026-8, $14.95

Uncle Gabby, the Sock Monkey, and Drinky the crow set off on a journey to solve the mystery of unremembered memories. This looks like a children's book, but the underlying bitter sweetness of a lost past and longing is more suited to teens and adults.

Miyazaki, Hayao

★ **Nausicaa** of the Valley of the Wind, Vol. 1. Viz Media 2004 136p. Illustration

Grades: 7 8 9 10 11 12   **741.5; Fic**

1. Graphic novels; 2. Manga; 3. Science fiction graphic novels; 4. Shonen manga

978-1-59116-408-1, $9.95

In a world devastated by ecological disaster and war, pockets of humanity exist in the vast wastelands. When some begin another war that could totally destroy the world, hope rests upon one young girl, Nausicaa, who can communicate with the strange creatures of the wasteland.

"Miyazaki is best known for his anime features...This tale contains all the classic elements of Miyazaki's films..." (VOYA)

This is a seven-volume series.

Miyazawa, Takeshi

Runaways Vol. 5: Escape to New York. Marvel Entertainment 2006 un Illustration

Grades: 8 9 10 11 12   **741.5; Fic**

1. Adventure graphic novels; 2. Graphic novels; 3. Runaways (Fictional characters); 4. Superhero graphic novels

0-7851-1901-9, $7.99

When a dangerous alien invades Los Angeles, the Runaways' own Karolina Dean may be the only hero in the Marvel Universe who can stop him...but at what cost? Then, the Runaways embark on a coast-to-coast adventure. When Clock is accused of a crime he didn't commit, the vigilante is forced to turn to the teenage Runaways for help. They go on a road trip to New York City. Meanwhile, back in LA, someone is tracking the teens, and it can't be good.

Mizuki, Shigeru

NonNonBa. Shigeru Mizuki; translation by Jocelyne Allen. Drawn & Quarterly 2012 408 p. Illustration; Color

Grades: 7 8 9 10 11 12 Adult   **741.5/952; 741.5**

1. Cartoonists — Japan — Biography — Comic books, strips, etc; 2. Grandmothers — Comic books, strips, etc; 3. Grandparent and child — Comic books, strips, etc; 4. Yokai (Japanese folklore) — Comic books, strips, etc; 5. Mizuki, Shigeru, 1922-2015 — Childhood and youth — Comic books, strips, etc; 6. Shonen manga; 7. Autobiographical graphic novels; 8. Folklore — Japan — Graphic novels; 9. Manga; 10. Grandparent-grandchild relationship — Graphic novels

1770460721; 9781770460720, $26.95

LC 2012427667

This graphic novel, by Shigeru Mizuki, translated by Jocelyne Allen, is "a poetic memoir detailing his interest in yokai (spirit monsters). Mizuki's childhood experiences with yokai influenced the course of his life and oeuvre; he is now known as the forefather of yokai manga.... Mizuki explores the legacy left him by his childhood explorations of the spirit world, explorations encouraged by his grandmother, a grumpy old woman named NonNonBa." (Publisher's note)

Includes bibliographical references; Manga format; reads from back to front, right to left.

Mizushiro, Setona

After School Nightmare Volume 1. Go! Comi 2006 200p. Illustration

Grades: 10 11 12 Adult

741.5; Fic

1. Graphic novels; 2. Horror graphic novels; 3. Manga; 4. Shojo manga; 5. Supernatural graphic novels

978-1-933617-16-9, $10.99

You have just awakened to find your darkest, ugliest secret revealed to classmates who would do anything to destroy you. This is what's happened to Ichijou Mashiro, whose elite school education turns into the most horrifying experience of his life when he's enlisted by a mysterious school nurse to take an after-hours class. Only those who

Courtesy of Go! Comi

pass the class will graduate, and the only way for Mashiro to pass is to enter into a nightmare world... where his body and soul will be at the mercy of his worst enemies. Can Mashiro keep his life-long secret — that he is not truly a he" nor entirely a she" — or will he finally be öutted" in the most humiliating way possible? The book includes graphic violence, strong language, and sexual situations.

Mizuto, Aqua

Yume Kira Dream Shoppe. Viz Media/Shojo Beat 2007 186p. Illustration

Grades: 7 8 9 10 11 12   **741.5; Fic**

1. Fantasy graphic novels; 2. Graphic novels; 3. Manga; 4. Romance graphic novels; 5. Shojo manga

978-1-4215-1173-3, $8.99

They say that any dream can be made true in exchange for something dear to you. The Yume Kira Dream Shoppe flies through the dusk sky as Rin the shopkeeper listens for wishes that travel on the wind. With the help of his assistant Alpha (a stuffed rabbit), Rin uses the magical wares of the Dream Shoppe to make desires a reality...But it costs the wisher something dear to the person. In the first story, a tree that has never bloomed falls in love with the music played by a young man, then the tree falls in love with the young man; she wishes for a human form so she can tell him how much his music means to her. Then she finds out he suffers from a disease that will take away the use of his hands, and she wants to change her wish...In the second story, Alpha is the one who makes the wish, and at the end of the story, he leaps off a bridge so the young girl who owned him won't be dependent on him; it's so much like a suicide that it might disturb younger readers who might otherwise enjoy this book.

Mochizuki, Jun

Pandora hearts; Volume 1. Jun Mochizuki; [translation, Tomo Kimura; lettering, Tania Biswas]. Yen Press 2013 187 p. Illustration
Grades: 8 9 10 11 12   741.5; Fic
1. False imprisonment — Comic books, strips, etc.; 2. Nobility — Fiction
0316076074; 9780316076074, $13

"The air of celebration surrounding fifteen-year-old Oz Vessalius's coming-of-age ceremony quickly turns to horror when he is condemned for a sin about which he knows nothing. He is thrown into an eternal, inescapable prison known as the Abyss from which there is no escape. There, he meets a young girl named Alice, who is not what she seems. Now that the relentless cogs of fate have begun to turn, do they lead only to crushing despair for Oz, or is there some shred of hope for him to grasp on to?" (Publisher's note)
Volume 1 of 24

Mochizuki, Minetaro

Dragon Head Vol. 1. Tokyopop 2006 223p. Illustration
Grades: 11 12 Adult   741.5; Fic
1. Apocalyptic fiction — Graphic novels; 2. Graphic novels; 3. Manga; 4. Science fiction graphic novels; 5. Seinen manga
1-59532-914-5, $9.99

The end of everyone was just the beginning...Returning home by train after a class trip, Teru Aoki takes a most frightening ride inside a mountain tunnel. When the train derails, nearly everyone aboard is killed. Amidst the bloody carnage, Teru discovers two survivors — but salvation is far from their grasp. As they try to dig out from the wreck in order to come up with a plan to stay alive, the lack of light and food, combined with the stench of death and decay, will lead one member of the group down a dark and demented path. And with sudden, violent earthquakes shaking the tunnel, escaping to the outside world may lead them to an even greater danger... Violence, strong language, partial nudity, and sexual situations occur in the series.

Modan, Rutu

Exit Wounds. Drawn & Quarterly 2007 160p. Illustration
Grades: 12 Adult   741.5; Fic
1. Graphic novels; 2. Israelis — Graphic novels; 3. Mystery graphic novels
1-897299-06-0, $19.95

Israeli taxi driver Koby Franco lives and works in Tel Aviv; he lives with his Aunt Ruby and Uncle Aryeh, and he hasn't seen his father in a long time. One evening he gets a fare; Numi is a soldier, and she tells Koby she thinks his father may have been killed in a terrorist bombing in Hadera. He reluctantly helps her, against the advice of his family, and he and Numi try to trace his father's last few months and see whether he died or not. As they do this, Koby must deal with his feelings about a father who never really connected with his own family. Angry with Numi because she'd had an affair with his father, Koby eventually becomes her friend, and then her lover. The book includes one fairly graphic sex scene without any nudity.

Moeller, Christopher

Iron Empires: Faith Conquers. Dark Horse Comics 2004 un Illustration
Grades: 9 10 11 12 Adult   741.5; Fic
1. Graphic novels; 2. Science fiction graphic novels
1-59307-015-2, $17.95

In the far future, eight weary nations are scattered among three million light years of the Milky Way Galaxy, all that is left of a once vast human civilization. The Vaylen Terror has ravaged humanity through the years, seizing a thousand worlds in a bloody rush, then pausing for decades of consolidation During these intervals of calm, the empires rebuild, rearm, then wage war on their neighbors. In this volume, readers will meet tough, uncompromising warrior-priest Trevor Faith, battling for his life and conscience on a border world. The book includes some strong language and lots of fighting violence.

Iron Empires: Sheva's War. Dark Horse Comics 2004 un Illustration
Grades: 9 10 11 12 Adult   741.5; Fic
1. Graphic novels; 2. Science fiction graphic novels
1-59307-110-8, $17.95

In the far future, eight weary nations are scattered among three million light years of the Milky Way Galaxy, all that is left of a once vast human civilization. The Vaylen Terror has ravaged humanity through the years, seizing a thousand worlds in a bloody rush, then pausing for decades of consolidation During these intervals of calm, the empires rebuild, rearm, then wage war on their neighbors. In this volume, readers will meet the beautiful Karsan noblewoman, Ahmi Sheva. As the planet she despises but is duty-bound to defend is caught up in an empire-wide catastrophe, Sheva finds herself fighting, not just for survival, but for her humanity. The book includes strong language and violence.

Moon, Fábio

De: Tales: Stories from Urban Brazil. Fábio Moon, Gabriel Bá. Dark Horse Comics 2006 112p. Illustration
Grades: 10 11 12 Adult   741.5; Fic
1. Graphic novels
1593074859, $14.95

This collection of short stories features Moon and Ba, who are twins, working together, in tandem, or separately — trading off on the roles of writing and illustrating, sharing those roles or flying solo. Brimming with all the details of human life, their tales move from the urban reality of their home in Sao Paulo to the magical realism of their Latin American background. Some stories feature brief partial nudity and sexual situations and some mild harsh language.

Moore, Alan

★ **Batman:** the killing joke: the deluxe edition. written by Alan Moore; illustrated by Brian Bolland. DC Comics 2008 un Illustration
Grades: 10 11 12 Adult   741.5; Fic
1. Batman (Fictional character); 2. Graphic novels; 3. Joker (Fictional character); 4. Superhero graphic novels; 5. Batgirl (Fictional character)
978-1-4012-1667-2, $17.99

This story was originally published in 1988, and it set Barbara Gordon on the path to become Oracle. The Joker says one bad day is all that separates the sane from the psychotic, and he sets out to prove it by driving Commissioner Jim Gordon insane by hurting his daughter Barbara. She has been Batgirl, but all her training and skills can't stop the Joker from shooting her in the spine. Then he takes Commissioner Gordon. Batman has to find the Joker and stop him. This story also reveals the origin of the Joker. This book includes violence and nonsexual partial nudity.

★ **From** Hell. Top Shelf Productions 2000 un Illustration
Grades: 11 12 Adult   741.5; Fic

1. Graphic novels; 2. Jack the Ripper murders, London (England), 1888 — Graphic novels; 3. Mystery graphic novels
0-9585783-4-6, $35

Legendary comics writer Alan Moore and artist Eddie Campbell have created a hallucinatory piece of crime fiction about Jack the Ripper. Detailing the events that led up to the Whitechapel murders and the cover-up that followed, Moore posits the theory that a Masonic conspiracy covered up the involvement of Queen Victoria's grandson. He tells the story from the viewpoint of the victims, of the police investigating the case, and of the killer. The book includes graphic violence and depiction of the murder victims, harsh language, and nudity.

Courtesy of IDW Publishing

The **League** of Extraordinary Gentlemen: Black Dossier. DC Comics/America's Best Comics 2007 208p. Illustration
Grades: 12 Adult   **741.5**
1. Adventure graphic novels; 2. Graphic novels; 3. Spies — Graphic novels
978-1-4012-0306-1, $29.99

Britain in 1958 is not the world we knew; the country is still at war with Germany (led by Hynkel). The League of Extraordinary Gentlemen had been disbanded after the last world war, and the members of the Murray Group" were labelled impersons." But now, the ever-youthful Mina Murray and a rejuvenated Allan Quatermain return to London and retrieve the Black Dossier, a legendary volume that details all the known facts about the league, going back centuries. Government spies pursue them, including one rather smarmy young agent called Jimmie (who likes his martinis stirred not shaken), Bulldog Drummond, and others. The book includes lots of full-frontal nudity, sexual situations, foul language, and violence.

Promethea Book Five. DC Comics/America's Best Comics 2005 160p. Illustration
Grades: 10 11 12 Adult   **741.5; Fic**
1. Adventure graphic novels; 2. Fantasy graphic novels; 3. Graphic novels
1-4012-0620-4, $14.99

Sophie, the new personification of the goddess Promethea, went into hiding after government agents destroyed her world. As the years have passed, Sophie has suppressed the goddess within her, but now, with the help of Tom Strong, the government is closing in on her again, and she has no choice but to release the mystic power of Promethea, thereby unleashing an apocalypse upon the world and everyone in it, both foe and friend. This is the final volume of the series. The book includes nudity, sexual situations, harsh language, and violence.

Promethea Book One. Alan Moore, writer; J.H. Williams III, penciller; Mick Gray, inker; additional art by Charles Vess. DC Comics/America's Best Comics 2001 160p. Illustration
Grades: 10 11 12 Adult   **741.5; Fic**
1. Adventure graphic novels; 2. Fantasy graphic novels; 3. Graphic novels
1-56389-667-2, $14.99

Sophie Bangs was a just an ordinary college student in a futuristic New York when a simple assignment changed her life forever. While researching Promethea, a mythical warrior woman, Sophie receives a cryptic warning to cease her investigations. Ignoring the cautionary notice, she continues her studies and is almost killed by a shadowy creature when she learns the secret of Promethea. Surviving the encounter, Sophie soon finds herself transformed into Promethea, the living embodiment of the imagination. Her trials have only begun as she must master the secrets of her predecessors before she is destroyed by Promethea's ancient enemy. The book includes some strong language, partial nudity, and violence.
Volume 1 of 5

Smax Collected Edition. DC Comics/America's Best Comics 2004 un Illustration
Grades: 10 11 12 Adult   **741.5; Fic**
1. Adventure graphic novels; 2. Graphic novels; 3. Humorous graphic novels; 4. Science fiction graphic novels
1-4012-0290-X, $12.99

Jeff Smax, a major character in Alan Moore's Top 10 series, must return to his home world after many years on Earth. Accompanied by his fellow Neopolis Precinct Ten police officer Robin Toybox Slinger, he must face a myriad of challenges ranging from cutting through mountainous red tape to go on a quest, doing battle with the most monstrous of all dragons, and adapting to a world where the laws of physics are not only unheard of, they just plain don't work. And then there's Jeff's sister...While there's little in the way of bad language and the violence is mostly against fantasy monsters, the book does include some sexual suggestiveness. And in Jeff's world, sex with one's sister is normal.

Top 10 Book Two. DC Comics/Wildstorm 2002 un Illustration
Grades: 10 11 12 Adult   **741.5; Fic**
1. Fantasy graphic novels; 2. Graphic novels; 3. Superhero graphic novels
1-56389-966-3, $14.95

Imagine a city where every citizen, from poorest slum-dweller to corporate honcho, has unusual powers and abilities — not to mention an alter ego and costume. How would you police such a city? Neopolis is the city of super powered citizens, and the police officers of Precinct Ten are also super powered. In this volume, they investigate the murder of an ex-sidekick rock star, deal with a murderous police commissioner who kills one of their own, and just try to get by each day. The book includes violence, nudity, and sexual situations.

Top 10: Book One. DC Comics/America's Best Comics 2000 un Illustration
Grades: 9 10 11 12 Adult   **741.5; Fic**
1. Graphic novels; 2. Mystery graphic novels; 3. Superhero graphic novels
1-56389-668-0, $17.95

Imagine a city where every citizen, from poorest slum-dweller to corporate honcho, has unusual powers and abilities, not to mention an alter ego and a costume. How does one police such a city? Rookie cop Robyn Singer is about to find out in her first day as part of Precinct 10 in Neopolis.

Top 10: The Forty-Niners. DC Comics/America's Best Comics 2005 un Illustration
Grades: 10 11 12 Adult   **741.5; Fic**
1. Graphic novels; 2. Superhero graphic novels
1-4012-0573-9, $17.99

This is the tale of Neopolis, a modern metropolis with a citizenry made up exclusively of super beings. In this city where everyone is blessed with powers, it takes a unique and powerful police force to protect and serve. The officers of Precinct 10 encounter all manner of the super powered and the supernatural on a routine basis. The TOP 10 team of writer Alan Moore and artist Gene Ha reunites for a graphic novel that delves into the past, revealing the origins of Neopolis and the first officers of Top Ten, from 1949. Discover the original Top 10 officers who blazed the trail and made Neopolis the city it is today. Some sexual situations and superhero violence occur in the book.

★ **V for vendetta.** written by Alan Moore; art by David Lloyd; coloring by David Lloyd, Steve Whitaker, Siobhan Dodds; lettering by Jenny O'Connor, Steve Craddock, Elitta Fell. DC Comics 2008 288p. Illustration

Grades: 10 11 12 Adult   **741.5; Fic**
    1. Graphic novels; 2. Science fiction graphic novels
    978-1-4012-0841-7; 1-4012-0841-X, $19.99

The book is set in an alternate world in which England has embraced fascism after a devastating war has destroyed a lot of the world; it's 1997, and a young woman named Eve tries prostitution, only to be caught by the police on her first night. A man wearing a Guy Fawkes mask saves her, and thus begins his campaign to restore human spirit by rebelling against the oppressive government. Known only as V, he uses terror tactics and murder to dismantle the government. Occasional nudity, some violence, and harsh language along with a complex plot make this a book for mature-minded readers.

?Originally published in single magazine form in the United States as V for Vendetta 1-10? Title page

★ **Watchmen.** Alan Moore, writer; Dave Gibbons, illustrator/letterer; John Higgins, colorist. DC Comics 2005 Illustration

Grades: 11 12 Adult   **741.5; Fic**
    1. Comic books, strips, etc.; 2. Graphic novels; 3. Superhero graphic novels
    1-4012-0713-8; 978-0-930289-23-2 (pa)
    Hugo Award: Other Forms (1988); Eisner Award: Best Finite Series (1988); Eisner Award: Best Graphic Album (1988)

"It all begins with the paranoid delusions of a half-insane hero called Rorschach. But is Rorschach really insane or has he infact uncovered a plot to murder super-heroes and, even worse, millions of innocent civilians? On the run from the law, Rorschach reunites with his former teammates in a desperate attempt to save the world and their lives, but what they uncover will shock them to their very core and change the face of the planet!" (Publisher's note)

"Nearly 20 years after the original publication, "Watchmen" shows an eerie prescience: the symmetry between current events and the conclusion of its story, concerning a villain who believes he can stave off real war by distracting the populace with a trumped-up one, and an act of mass murder perpetrated in the heart of New York City, is almost too fearful to bear." N Y Times Book Rev

Originally published in single magazine form as Watchmen 1-12; trade paperback edition still available; Issued in slipcase. Awards: 1988 Eisner Award for Best Finite Series, Best Graphic Album, Best Writer, Best Writer/Artist; 1988 Hugo Award for Other Forms; 2005 listed in Time Magazine's 100 Greatest English Language Novels; 2006 Eisner Award to Watchmen Absolute Edition for Best Archival Collection, Comic Books

Moore, Richard

Boneyard Volume 1. NBM 2005 96p. Illustration

Grades: 9 10 11 12 Adult

741.5; Fic
    1. Graphic novels; 2. Humorous graphic novels; 3. Supernatural graphic novels
    978-1-56163-427-9, $10.95

Michael Paris has inherited a plot in the remote town of Raven Hollow. As he arrives, he gets to find out what a doozie that is: he's inherited a cemetery that the villagers want razed. Why? It's haunted with apparently frightening creatures putting a curse on the whole town. But when Paris actually gets to

Courtesy of NBM Publishing

meet some of the denizens of his inherited headache, it turns out they aren't all that bad (Abbey the vampire, in fact, is quite cute) and maybe the evil is not where it may seem... This book was originally published in black and white; this edition is in full color.

Boneyard Volume 2. NBM 2006 96p. Illustration

Grades: 9 10 11 12 Adult

741.5; Fic
    1. Graphic novels; 2. Humorous graphic novels; 3. Supernatural graphic novels
    978-1-56163-487-3, $11.95

Courtesy of NBM Publishing

Now that Beelzebub has been dealt a blow, it's the turn of the IRS to make Paris' life hell. But then, a certain beauteous Roxanna miraculously appears looking to solve all monetary problems. Paris resists as best he can, even putting on a monsters boxing contest to raise money, but the lures and the pressures... how strong can he stay? And as if that's not enough, Nessie the sexy gill girl (think of a female Creature from the Black Lagoon) and Abbey the vampire contend for Paris' affections. This book was originally published in black and white; this edition is in full color. The book includes some sexual innuendo.

Boneyard Volume 3. NBM 2008 96p. Illustration

Grades: 10 11 12 Adult

741.5; Fic
    1. Graphic novels; 2. Humorous graphic novels; 3. Supernatural graphic novels
    978-1-56163-515-3, $12.95

Courtesy of NBM Publishing

Glump devises a wondrous scheme to do a Monsters on the Beach special swimsuit issue to help the cash-strapped Michael Paris. Never mind that Glump is hiding a much worse scheme within the scheme. On a darker note, Roxanne shows her true powerful demonic self, resulting in a potentially deadly showdown with Abbey. With this volume, Moore kicks the sensual sexiness of the female characters up a notch. This is the color edition; the black and white edition, published in 2004, seems to be unavailable.

Boneyard Volume 4. NBM 2005 un Illustration

Grades: 10 11 12 Adult   **741.5; Fic**
    1. Graphic novels; 2. Humorous graphic novels; 3. Supernatural graphic novels
    978-1-56163-424-8, $9.95

As Abbey recovers from her showdown with the much more powerful Lilith (who had disguised herself as Roxanna), swamp girl Nessie starts taking the upper hand in her pursuit of Michael (never mind she's married to Frankenstein monster-like Brutus). Meanwhile, Glump continues his schemes to rule the world, this time launching the "Doomsday Frog.DD However, everyone comes together to face a new threat: zombies sprouting up from the cemetery. And Michael discovers that not all monsters are...nice. The book includes some partial nudity and sexual situations, and violence. This is the original black and white edition.

Boneyard Volume 5. NBM 2006 un Illustration

Grades: 10 11 12 Adult   **741.5; Fic**
    1. Graphic novels; 2. Humorous graphic novels; 3. Supernatural graphic novels
    978-1-56163-479-8, $9.95

After dealing with the zombie mess from the previous volume, Abbey, Michael and the Boneyard gang have to confront a two-pronged threat: a huge, masked,chainsaw-wielding serial killer in a girl's summer camp and the Pumpkinhead, whose very presence puts all in the 'yard into fevered sleep. Abbey barely survives the confrontation with the chainsaw brute, now it's up to Michael to face the worst threat, with Nodoze and a baseball bat. This book includes violence and some sexual innuendo.

Moore, Terry
★ **Strangers** in Paradise Pocket Book 1. Abstract Studio 2003 360p.
Illustration
Grades: 11 12 Adult   **741.5; Fic**
   1. Graphic novels; 2. Mystery graphic novels
   1-892597-26-8, $17.95
   Katchoo is a beautiful young woman living a quiet life with everything going for her. She's smart, independent and very much in love with her best friend, Francine. Then Katchoo meets David, a gentle but persistent young man who is determined to win Katchoo's heart. The resulting love triangle is a touching comedy of romantic errors until Katchoo's former employer comes looking for her and $850,000 in missing mob money. As her idyllic life begins to fall apart, Katchoo discovers no one can be trusted and that the past she thought she left behind now threatens to destroy her and everything she loves, including Francine. This thick pocket book edition collects several of the original trade paperback volumes. The story includes strong language, sexual situations, nudity, and some violence.

★ **Strangers** in Paradise Pocket Book 2. Abstract Studio 2004 344p.
Illustration
Grades: 10 11 12 Adult   **741.5; Fic**
   1. Friendship — Graphic novels; 2. Graphic novels
   1-892597-29-8, $17.95
   The second Strangers In Paradise pocket book finds Katchoo following David to California where she comes face to face with Darcy Parker. When Darcy makes Katchoo an offer she can't refuse, Katchoo transforms from prey to predator and begins to spin a web of her own. This book features 5 pages of Jim Lee art to open the story, hero-style. Also included is the most popular Strangers in Paradise short story ever — the Xena parody, "Warrior Princess." This volume collects several of the original trade paperback collections, including Vol. 6, High School. This volume includes violence, strong language, nudity, and sexual situations.

★ **Strangers** in Paradise Pocket Book 3. Abstract Studio 2004 372p.
Illustration
Grades: 10 11 12 Adult   **741.5; Fic**
   1-892597-30-4, $17.95
   In this third pocket book volume, Francine is stuck in a bad marriage and Katchoo is a successful artist but keeps everyone at a distance. David's mysterious past links him even closer to Katchoo, who still can't escape the Mafia life she had led with Darcy Parker. There are more friendships, breakups, makeups, and action. Readers should expect to find strong language, nudity, and sexual situations along with a little violence.

★ **Strangers** in Paradise Pocket Book 4. Abstract Studio 2005 360p.
Illustration
Grades: 10 11 12 Adult   **741.5; Fic**
   1. Friendship — Graphic novels; 2. Graphic novels
   1-892597-31-1, $17.95
   Katchoo still loves Francine, but her wild past and dangerous enemies, such as Mafia types, prove to be more than Francine can handle. Meanwhile, David wants more than friendship with Katchoo. And then Francine, on the verge of another marriage, calls it off and decides to return to Houston and see what will happen with Katchoo. This fourth pocket book volume collects three of the original trade paperback collections.

★ **Strangers** in Paradise Pocket Book 5. Abstract Studio 2005 376p.
Illustration
Grades: 10 11 12 Adult   **741.5; Fic**
   1. Friendship — Graphic novels; 2. Graphic novels
   1-892597-38-1, $17.95
   While David finds solace with Katchoo, Francine can think of nothing but her past relationship with her former best friend and brings home a tattoo to prove it. It seems that Katchoo is destined to move on without Francine into the world of glitz, glamour, and art showings with her stunning display of 100 nudes. As Katchoo becomes the toast of the town, Francine finds herself looking for peace in the Caribbean. Our unlikely friends seem to be drifting apart until they are set on a collision course back to Houston. This pocket book volume also includes the Molly & Poo stories, which are illustrated prose stories set in Victorian England. Strong language, nudity, sexual situations, and violence punctuate the stories.

★ **Strangers** in Paradise Pocket Book 6. Abstract Studio 2007 272p.
Illustration
Grades: 10 11 12 Adult   **741.5; Fic**
   1. Friendship — Graphic novels; 2. Graphic novels
   1-892597-39-X, $17.95
   Brad and Francine prepare to move to Houston, while free spirit Casey gets involved in the lives of her new roommates in Las Vegas and discovers a stalker. Back in Houston, Casey and David get Katchoo and Francine together again. Then David has to tell Casey and Katchoo his secret, a medical condition that may kill him. And in the final story, Francine leaves the cheating Brad and tries to reconnect with Katchoo, but she learns she's going to have to fight for her. This series lasted 90 issues and has ended the way Moore wanted it to. The stories include strong language, nudity, sexual situations, and violence.

Mori, Kaoru
★ A **bride's** story, v1. Kaoru Mori. Yen Press 2011 192 p. Illustration
Grades: 11 12 Adult   **741.5**
   1. Arranged marriage — Comic books, strips, etc; 2. Man-woman relationships — Comic books, strips, etc; 3. Asia, Central — History — 19th century — Comic books, strips, etc; 4. Arranged marriage — Fiction; 5. Women — China; 6. Silk Road
   0316180998; 9780316180993, $17
                                              LC 2012450076
   Eisner Nominee: Best U.S. Edition of International Material — Asia (2016) [for volume 7]
   In this graphic novel, author "Kaoru Mori brings the nineteenth-century Silk Road to lavish life, chronicling the story of Amir Halgal, a young woman from a nomadic tribe betrothed to a twelve-year-old boy eight years her junior. Coping with cultural differences, blossoming feelings for her new husband, and expectations from both her adoptive and birth families, Amir strives to find her role as she settles into a new life and a new home in a society quick to define that role for her." (Publisher's note)
   "By the end of this first volume, the plot is only beginning to bloom, but there is ample enjoyment in watching the small, everyday activities that make up the family's life — laundry, hunting, raising children. Amir's cheerfulness is infectious, both to her new family and to readers." Booklist
   Volume 1 of an ongoing series

Emma 1. Kaori Mori; translation, Sheldon Drzka; lettering, Abigail Blackman. Yen Press 2015 386 p. Illustration
Grades: 10 11 12 Adult   **741.5**
   1. Great Britain — History — Victoria, 1837-1901 — Fiction; 2. Shojo manga; 3. Household employees — Graphic novels
   0316302236; 9780316302234, $35
   In this manga by Kaoru Mori, translated by Sheldon Drzka, "calling upon his former governess, William Jones, gentleman, is startled when his

knock is answered by an uncommonly beautiful servant, the soft-spoken Emma. Throughout his visit, William's eyes drift to the maid whenever she enters the room, and he contrives to meet Emma socially as she goes about her errands. But London society is a web of strict codes and divisions." (Publisher's note)

Originally published in Japan; Previously published in the U.S. by CMX in 10 volumes; Volume 1 of 4

Emma, Vol. 3. DC Comics/CMX 2007 188p. Illustration
Grades: 9 10 11 12 Adult   **741.5**
1. Graphic novels; 2. Household employees — Graphic novels; 3. Manga; 4. Romance graphic novels; 5. Shojo manga
978-1-4012-1134-9, $9.99

In 1885 England, Emma works as a maid for a widow; she meets William, son of a wealthy merchant. Since they each belong to a different social class, they shouldn't fall in love, but they do. In this third volume, Emma's employer has died and Emma leaves, while William throws himself into the family business. On the train, Emma meets a maid who works in a fairly large household that needs another maid, and she decides to apply there. The family, immigrants from Germany, insists on formality; Emma feels a bit lost but works well and makes a good impression. Warnings on the book tell of suggestive situations, but there has been nothing objectionable in the first four volumes.

Emma, vol. 8. DC Comics/CMX 2009 208p. Illustration
Grades: 10 11 12 Adult   **741.5; Fic**
1. Graphic novels; 2. Manga; 3. Great Britain — History — 19th century — Graphic novels
978-1-4012-2070-9, $9.99

This eighth volume collects short stories focusing on some of the supporting characters who have appeared throughout the course of the seven-volume series. One story features a young Kelly Stowner and her husband Doug, who struggle to save up the two shillings needed for them to visit the Great Exhibition. Eleanor Campbell, whose engagement to William Jones has just ended, spends a vacation at Brighton trying to get over his rejection of her, and meets a surprising young man. One story is a series of vignettes of different characters reading the newspaper. And klutzy housemaid Natasha returns home for a visit. One of the story vignettes features a conversation between an older gentleman and his mistress, who is nude throughout the story.

Morinaga, Ai
My Heavenly Hockey Club Vol. 1. Ballantine Books/Del Rey Manga 2007 212p. Illustration
Grades: 8 9 10 11 12 Adult   **741.5; Fic**
1. Graphic novels; 2. Hockey — Graphic novels; 3. Humorous graphic novels; 4. Manga; 5. Shojo manga
978-0-345-49904-2, $10.95

Hana Suzuki loves only two things in life: eating and sleeping. So when handsome classmate Izumi Oda asks Hana, his major crush, to join the school hockey club, persuading her proves to be a difficult task. True, the Grand Hockey Club is full of boys, and all the boys are super-cute, but given a choice, Hana prefers a sizzling steak to a hot date. Then Izumi mentions the field trips to fancy resorts. Now Hana can't wait for the first away game, with its promise of delicious food and luxurious linens. Of course there's also the getting up early, working hard, and playing well with others. How will Hana survive?

Morrison, Grant
All-Star Superman, Volume One. written by Grant Morrison; pencilled by Frank Quitely. DC Comics 2007 160p. Illustration
Grades: 8 9 10 11 12 Adult   **741.5; Fic**

1. Graphic novels; 2. Superhero graphic novels; 3. Superman (Fictional character)
978-1-4012-0914-8; 978-1-4012-1102-8 (pa), $12.99
Eisner Award: Best New Series (2006)

Writer Morrison and artist Quitely present several episodes in the life of the iconic superhero, Superman. When he saves a group of scientists from burning up in the sun, what no one realizes is that uber-villain Lex Luthor set up everything in order to kill Superman, who absorbed so much solar radiation that it is now slowly killing him. Once Superman learns that he is dying, he sets out to give Lois Lane a birthday she will never forget, by giving her his powers for one day. Then, when Jimmy Olsen takes charge of the science think tank P.R.O.J.E.C.T. for one day, they discover black kryptonite, which makes Superman turn evil. And, in his guise as Clark Kent, he interviews Lex Luthor in prison, but super-villain Parasite is taken from his shielded cell and begins to absorb Superman's powers, causing chaos.

Also available as a single volume collecting all 12 issues; Originally published as All-Star Superman issues #1-6; Volume 1 of 2

Batman and son. Grant Morrison, writer; Andy Kubert, penciller; Jesse Delperdang, inker; Guy Major, Dave Stewart, colorists; Jared K. Fletcher, Rob Leigh, Nick J. Napolitano, letterers. DC Comics 2007 200p. Illustration
Grades: 9 10 11 12 Adult   **741.5; Fic**
1. Batman (Fictional character); 2. Graphic novels; 3. Superhero graphic novels; 4. Joker (Fictional character)
978-1-4012-1240-7, $24.99

Talia, daughter of archvillain Ra's al Ghul and Batman's onetime love, returns with a teenage boy she claims is Batman's son. She leaves Damian with Batman, but while the boy has Batman's skills, he was raised among the League of Assassins and doesn't share his father's morals. Soon, both Tim Drake, Bruce Wayne's newly adopted heir, and the faithful Alfred, become Damian's targets. The book also includes an interlude about the Joker, and a story set in the future, when Damian becomes Batman. The book includes some gory violence.

★ **Batman:** Arkham Asylum: A Serious House on Serious Earth. written by Grant Morrison; illustrated by Dave McKean; lettered by Gaspar Saladino; Batman created by Bob Kane. DC Comics 2004 un Illustration
Grades: 11 12 Adult   **741.5; Fic**
1. Batman (Fictional character); 2. Graphic novels; 3. Horror graphic novels; 4. Superhero graphic novels; 5. Joker (Fictional character)
1-4012-0425-2, $17.99

LC 2006-276659

In this painted graphic novel, the inmates of Arkham Asylum have taken over Gotham's detention center for the criminally insane on April Fools Day, demanding Batman in exchange for their hostages. Accepting their challenge, Batman is forced to live and endure the personal hells of the Joker, Scarecrow, Poison Ivy, Two-Face and many other sworn enemies in order to save the innocents and retake the prison. During his run through this gauntlet, the Dark Knight's own sanity is placed in jeopardy. This edition also reproduces the original script with annotations by Morrison and editor Karen Berger. The book includes violence and some disturbing images.

★ **Doom** Patrol; Volume 1: Crawling from the Wreckage. written by Grant Morrison; pencillers, Richard Case, Doug Braithwaite; inkers, Scott Hanna, Carlos Garzon, John Nyberg; colorists, Daniel Vozza and Michele Wolfman; letterer, John Workman. DC Comics 2004 190 p. Color; Illustration
Grades: 10 11 12 Adult   **741.5; Fic**
1. Superhero comic books, strips, etc.
9781563890345, $19.99; 1563890348

"The new Doom Patrol puts itself back together after nearly being destroyed, and things start to get a lot weirder for everybody. The Chief leads Robotman, the recently formed Rebis and new member Crazy Jane against the Scissormen, part of a dangerous philosophical location that has escaped into our world and is threatening to engulf reality itself." (Publisher's note)

Other Doom Patrol volumes by Morrison are: 2, The Painting That Ate Paris; 3, Down Paradise Way; 4, Musclebound; 5, Magic Bus; 6, Planet Love

Joe the Barbarian. by Grant Morrison and illustrated by Sean Murphy. Vertigo 2013 224 p.
Grades: 10 11 12 Adult   **741.5**
1. Graphic novels; 2. Hallucinations and illusions — Fiction; 3. Diabetes — Fiction
1401237479; 9781401237479, $19.99
                                                            LC 2012047802
In this graphic novel by Grant Morrison "Joe is an imaginative young kid of 11 who happens to suffer from type 1 diabetes. Without supervision and insulin, he can easily slip into a delirious, disassociative state that presages coma and death. One fateful day, his condition causes him to believe he has entered a vivid fantasy world in which he is the lost savior — a fantastic land based on the layout and contents of his home." (Publisher's note)

Originally published in a single magazine form in Joe the Barbarian 1-8.

Kid Eternity. DC Comics/Vertigo 2006 un Illustration
Grades: 10 11 12 Adult   **741.5; Fic**
1. Fantasy graphic novels; 2. Graphic novels; 3. Horror graphic novels
1-4012-0933-5, $14.99
Comics visionary Grant Morrison re-imagines the character of Kid Eternity, a young man who died before his true time and returns to Earth as a ghostly spirit, along with his guardian Mister Keeper. This book follows the terrifying night of aspiring stand-up comedian Jerry Sullivan as he joins Kid Eternity, who just escaped from Hell, on a quest back there to free Mister Keeper. Then the Kid learns he's been used as a pawn in the struggle between Order and Chaos. The book includes considerable violence and harsh language (f-bombs and s-bombs included).

The **Multiversity** deluxe edition. Grant Morrison, Frank Quitely, Ivan Reis. DC Comics 2015 448 p. Color; Illustration
Grades: 9 10 11 12 Adult   **741.5/973**
1. Superhero comic books, strips, etc.
1401256821; 9781401256821, $49.99
                                                            LC 2015014166
This comic book, by Grant Morrison, presents "a cast of unforgettable heroes from 52 alternative Earths of the DC Multiverse! Prepare to meet the Vampire League of Earth-43, the Justice Riders of Earth-18, Superdemon, Doc Fate, the super-sons of Superman and Batman, the rampaging Retaliators of Earth-8, the Atomic Knights of Justice, Dino-Cop, Sister Miracle, Lady Quark and the latest, greatest Super Hero of Earth-Prime: YOU!" (Publisher's note)

Supergods: what masked vigilantes,miraculous mutants, and a sun god from Smallvillecan teach us about being human. Spiegel & Grau 2011 444p. Illustration
Grades: 11 12 Adult   **741.5**
1. Comic books, strips, etc.; 2. Comic books, strips, etc. — United States; 3. Heroes; 4. Superheroes; 5. Wolverine (Fictional character); 6. Superman (Fictional character)
1-4000-6912-2; 978-1-4000-6912-5
                                                            LC 2010053712

A graphic novelist presents a history of the superhero in American comic books and movies. Index.
Includes bibliographical references

Superman - Action Comics; Volume 1. Grant Morrison, Rags Morales, Andy Kubert. DC Comics 2012 256 p.
Grades: 7 8 9 10 11 12 Adult   **Fic; 741.5/9411**
1. Superhero comic books, strips, etc.; 2. Adventure fiction; 3. Superman (Fictional character)
1401235468; 9781401235468, $24.99
                                                            LC 2012010313
This comic book anthology, by Grant Morrison, illustrated by Rags Morales, presents volume one of "The New 52" re-launch of the DC Comics Superman series. This collection includes the first eight issues of the series, depicting "humanity's first encounters with Superman, before he became one of the world's greatest super heroes." (Publisher's note)

Originally published in single magazine form in ACTION COMICS 1-8 — T.p. verso.

WE 3. DC Comics/Vertigo 2005 un Illustration
Grades: 10 11 12 Adult   **741.5; Fic**
1. Animal experimentation — Graphic novels; 2. Graphic novels; 3. Science fiction graphic novels
1-4012-0495-3, $12.99
2005 Eisner Award for Best Artist for Frank Quitely; this series was cited.

A top-secret research facility has taken a dog, a cat, and a rabbit and used cybernetics to transform the pets into armored smart weapons. The WE 3 are very successful; their enhanced intelligence allows them to communicate verbally with each other and adapt to any situation to carry out their mission. However, they're only prototypes, and when the project scientists advance to the next stage, the WE 3 are to be terminated. What the scientists and military brass haven't counted on is that their smart weapons possess enough reasoning to escape. Now Bandit the dog, Tinker the cat, and Pirate the rabbit are loose, and they want to find "Home." And they're ready to kill to find it.

Originally published as WE 3 issues #1-3.

Wonder Woman, earth one; Volume 1. written by Grant Morrison; art by Yanick Paquette; colors by Nathan Fairbairn; letters by Todd Klein. DC Comics 2016 144 p. Color; Illustration
Grades: 11 12 Adult   **741.5; Fic**
1. Female superhero graphic novels; 2. Superhero graphic novels; 3. Wonder Woman (Fictional character)
1401229786; 9781401229788, $22.99
                                                            LC 2016006066
This comic book, written by Grant Morrison, with art by Yanick Paquette, presents the "origin of Wonder Woman.... For millennia, the Amazons of Paradise Island have created a thriving society away from the blight of man. One resident, however, is not satisfied with this secluded life-Diana, Princess of the Amazons, knows there is more in this world and wants to explore, only to be frustrated by her protective mother, Hippolyta." (Publisher's note)

"Both novices and the initiated will find great fun in this flawlessly streamlined remolding, and, in his inimitable style, Morrison offers a fiercer, stranger, more epic, more textured, and, incidentally, more diverse interpretation." Booklist

Mulligan, Brennan Lee
★ **Strong** Female Protagonist; Book one. Brennan Lee Mulligan and Molly Ostertag. Top Shelf Productions 2014 220 p. Illustration
Grades: 11 12 Adult   **741.5**
1. College students — Fiction; 2. Superheroes — Fiction
0692246185; 9780692246184, $19.95

"Alison Green, aka Mega Girl, lives in a dark world fraught with difficult relationships. She is a biodynamic, who, along with other young people who possess special capabilities, rejects her role as a superhero and attempts to revert to the life of a 'normal' college freshman. However,...she encounters situations that test her resolve to no longer use her powers." (School Library Journal)

Originally appeared as a webcomic

Courtesy of IDW Publishing

Myers, Walter Dean

Monster: a graphic novel. by Walter Dean Myers; adapted for graphic novel by Guy A. Sims; illustrated by Dawud Anyabwile. HarperTeen, an imprint of HarperCollinsPublishers 2015 160 p. Illustration

Grades: 8 9 10 11 12   **741.5; Fic**

1. African Americans — Fiction; 2. Graphic novels; 3. Prisons — Fiction; 4. Self-perception — Fiction; 5. Trials (Murder) — Fiction; 6. Myers, Walter Dean, 1937- Monster — Adaptations; 7. Bildungsromans — Graphic novels; 8. Teenagers — Graphic novels; 9. Trials (Homicide) — Fiction

0062275003; 9780062274991; 9780062275004, $17.99

LC 2013043138

This graphic novel by Guy Sims, illustrated by Dawud Anyabwile, and adapted from the novel by Walter Dean Myers, is a "coming-of-age story about Steve Harmon, a teenager awaiting trial for a murder and robbery. As Steve acclimates to juvenile detention and goes to trial, he envisions the ordeal as a movie." (Publisher's note)

"Using panels like a filmstrip, Sims and Anyabwile achieve several remarkably cinematic effects: alternating grids and splash pages captures the tension between close-up and long shots; the use of jittery lettering and uneven word balloons injects deeper anxiety into the sound design; having a jury view the events recounted in testimony as a movie audience creates incisive visual metaphors." Booklist

Naifeh, Ted

★ **Courtney** Crumrin and the night things. Oni Press 2005 128p. Illustration

Grades: 5 6 7 8 9 10 11 12

741.5; Fic

1. Fantasy graphic novels; 2. Graphic novels; 3. Supernatural graphic novels

1-929998-60-0, $11.95

Courtesy of Oni Press

Courtney's social-climber parents take her out of her comfortable city neighborhood and move into an upscale suburb to live with her creepy Great-Uncle Aloysius in her spooky old house. She has to face uppity classmates and things that go bump in the night; but she ends up making friends with the spooks! Courtney deals with magic and the supernatural, but she's no altruistic Harry Potter; in this series, magic sometimes bites hard.

Other titles in this series are: Courtney Crumrin and the coven of Mystics (2003); Courtney Crumrin in the twilight kingdom (2004); Courtney Crumrin's monstrous holiday (2009); Courtney Crumrin: the witch next door (2014); Courtney Crumrin: the final spell (2014)

Courtney Crumrin and the fire thief's tale. Oni Press 2007 62p. Illustration

Grades: 7 8 9 10 11 12 Adult

741.5; Fic

1. Fantasy graphic novels; 2. Graphic novels; 3. Horror graphic novels; 4. Werewolves — Graphic novels

978-1-932664-85-0, $5.95

Courtney travels with Uncle Aloysius to Romania, where they stay with Alexi Markovic, an old friend of Uncle Aloysius. Things aren't quite right there, though; the townspeople hunt wolves at night unnatural wolves, werewolves. Markovic's daughter has fallen in love with a Romany man even though her father has arranged her betrothal to an influential man in town. Courtney gets involved against Uncle Aloysius' wishes, and learns more than she wanted about werewolf origins and thwarted love.

Courtesy of Oni Press

★ **Courtney** Crumrin in the Twilight Kingdom; 3. Oni Press 2004 un Illustration

Grades: 7 8 9 10 11 12

741.5; Fic

1. Fantasy graphic novels; 2. Graphic novels; 3. Magic — Graphic novels; 4. Supernatural graphic novels

1-932664-01-7, $11.95

Courtney has changed schools yet again, but this time she's in the Coven's special class for magical studies. But when a student spell goes wrong and leaves one of her classmates cursed, can Courtney lead the kids into Goblin Town and find a cure, or will misfortune follow the group straight to the Twilight Kingdom? And the law keeper, Templeton, intends to stop Courtney from what he considers her most terrible crime yet.

Courtesy of Oni Press

★ **Courtney** Crumrin's monstrous holiday; 4. Oni Press, Inc. 2009 192p. Illustration

Grades: 7 8 9 10 11 12

741.5; Fic

1. Fantasy graphic novels; 2. Graphic novels; 3. Horror graphic novels

978-1-934964-11-8, $11.95

Courtney accompanies Uncle Aloysius on his trip through Europe, and their first stop is in Romania. He has come to visit with an old friend, Professor Alexi Markovic, but they soon find they have stumbled into a family turmoil. Morkovic's daughter Magda loves a young Gypsy, but the local bully and noble (even if he has denounced his title), Petru has claimed Magda as his betrothed. Courtney learns that some of the wolves in the woods surrounding Markovic's house are werewolves, and Petru and his men hunt them, convinced that they are members of the Gypsy group in town. Courtney thinks she's helping a romantic young couple only to be disillusioned by Magda's attitude. Then, in Krumrhein, Germany, she meets a handsome young man named Wolfgang and maybe falls a little in love with him. Which turns out to be a bad thing, for Wolfgang is a vampire. Aloysius had come there for he has learned he has cancer and doesn't want to die; but when he discovers that something is draining the life blood from Courtney, he knows he needs to save her.

Nakahara, Aya

Love*Com Vol. 1. story and art by Aya Nakahara; [translation & English adaptation, Pookie Rolf]. Viz Media/Shojo Beat 2007 un Illustration

Grades: 8 9 10 11 12   741.5; Fic

1. Graphic novels; 2. Humorous graphic novels; 3. Manga; 4. Romance graphic novels; 5. Shojo manga

978-1-4215-1343-0, $8.99

Risa Koizumi is the tallest girl in class, and the last thing she wants is the humiliation of standing next to Atsushi Otoni, the shortest guy. Fate and the whole school have other ideas, and the two find themselves cast as the unwilling stars of a bizarre romantic comedy duo. Rather than bow to the inevitable, Risa and Atsushi join forces to pursue their true objects of affection. But in the quest for love, will their budding friendship become something more complex?

First published 2001 in Japan; Volume 1 of 17

Nakajo, Hisaya

★ Hana-Kimi: For You in Full Bloom Volume 1. Viz Media/Shojo 2004 184p. Illustration

Grades: 10 11 12 Adult   741.5; Fic

1. Graphic novels; 2. Humorous graphic novels; 3. Manga; 4. Romance graphic novels; 5. Shojo manga

1-59116-329-3, $9.95

Japanese-American track-and-field star Mizuki has transferred to a high school in Japan...but not just any school. To be close to her idol, high jumper Izumi Sano, she's going to an all-guys' high school...and disguising herself as a boy. But as fate would have it, they're more than classmates...they're roommates. Now, Mizuki must keep her secret in the classroom, the locker room, and her own bedroom. And her classmates — and the school nurse — must cope with a new transfer student who may make them question their own orientation... The book includes some strong language, brief nudity, and sexual situations.

Nakamura, Yoshiki

★ Skip Beat! Vol. 1. Viz Media/Shojo Beat 2006 un Illustration

Grades: 8 9 10 11 12   741.5; Fic

1. Entertainers — Graphic novels; 2. Graphic novels; 3. Humorous graphic novels; 4. Manga; 5. Shojo manga

978-1-4215-0585-5, $8.99

Kyoko Mogami has followed her true love, Sho, to Tokyo, where he wants to become an idol, a pop star. Idols can be pop singers or actors, and young hopefuls audition at talent agencies hoping to become the next big star. Sho succeeds, then he tosses Kyoko aside, saying that she's boring. Now Kyoko wants revenge, and thinks the best way to get it is to become an idol and eclipse Sho; but the talent agency rejects her audition. Is revenge an appropriate motivation? Kyoko doesn't care.

Nakamura uses different visual techniques to show characters' feelings, and with Kyoko's emotions in particular, especially her anger.

Volume 1 of 36

Nakazawa, Keiji

★ Barefoot Gen: Hadashi no Gen : a cartoon story of Hiroshima. by Keiji Nakazawa; translated by Project Gen. New Society Publishers 1987 284 p. Illustration

Grades: 10 11 12 Adult   741.5; 741.5/952

1. Hiroshima-shi (Japan) — History — Bombardment, 1945 — Comic books, strips, etc; 2. Hiroshima (Japan) — Bombardment, 1945

0865710945; 0865710953; 0867196025; 9780867196023, $14.95

LC 88187202

This book, by Keiji Nakazawa, is "an all-new translation of the author's first-person experiences of Hiroshima and its aftermath. [It] is a reminder of the suffering war brings to innocent people.... Volume one of this ten-part series details the events leading up to and immediately following the atomic bombing of Hiroshima." (Publisher's note)

Volume 1 of 10

Naruse, Kaori

Pretear, Volume 1. ADV Manga 2004 188p. Illustration

Grades: 6 7 8 9 10 11 12

741.5; Fic

1. Fantasy graphic novels; 2. Graphic novels; 3. Manga; 4. Shojo manga

1-4139-0144-1, $9.99

Courtesy of ADV Manga

Naruse combines elements of fairy tales such as Cinderella and Snow White with fantasy adventure in this four-volume series.

"Himeno's alcoholic novelist father marries a rich businesswoman with two snobby daughters. They treat [Himeno] terribly, of course, but she...is goodhearted, virtuous, and patient. Himeno...[meets] seven knights who use leafe, a substance emitted by everything in the natural world. The Princess of Disaster wants to destroy all the leafe so the world will die. The knights need Himeno to become the Pretear so they can combine with her and combat the princess." SLJ

Neri, G.

★ Yummy: the last days of a Southside Shorty. by G. Neri; illustrated by Randy DuBurke. Lee & Low Books 2010 94p. Illustration

Grades: 8 9 10 11 12   741; 741.5; 92

978-1-58430-267-4 (pa), $16.95; 1-58430-267-4 (pa)

LC 2006-17771

"In 1994, in the Roseland neighborhood of Chicago's South Side, a 14-year-old girl named Shavon Dean was killed by a stray bullet during a gang shooting. Her killer, Robert "Yummy" Sandifer, was 11 years old. Neri recounts Yummy's three days on the run from police (and, eventually, his own gang) through the eyes of Roger, a fictional classmate of Yummy's. Roger grapples with the unanswerable questions behind Yummy's situation, with the whys and hows of a failed system, a crime-riddled neighborhood, and a neglected community." (Publishers Weekly)

Newlevant, Hazel

Chainmail Bikini: The Anthology of Women Gamers. edited by Hazel Newlevant. Alternative Comics 2016 204 p. Illustration

Grades: 9 10 11 12 Adult   741.5

1. Games; 2. Women — Recreation; 3. Anthologies; 4. Comic books, strips, etc.

1513600125; 9781513600123, $20

This anthology, edited by Hazel Newlevant, with a cover illustration by Hellen Jo and comics by Annie Mok, Jane Mai, Molly Ostertag, MK Reed, and Sophie Yanow, "explore[s] the real-life impact of entering a fantasy world, and how games can connect us with each other and teach us about ourselves.... [It] shows that while women are not always the target market for gaming, they are a vital and thoroughly engaged part of it." (Publisher's note)

'A cavalcade of talent tackles the intersection of gaming and womanhood in this heartfelt anthology of short, largely autobiographical comics. With pieces on the Sims, Darkstalkers, and live-action roleplaying, no corner of gaming (video or otherwise) is left unexplored — and no aspect of gender, either." Pub Wkly

Nicholson, Hope

★ **MOONSHOT:** The Indigenous Comics Collection. edited by Hope Nicholson. Alternate History Comics Inc 2015 176 p. Illustration

Grades: 6 7 8 9 10 11 12 Adult   **741.5**

1. American literature — Native American authors; 2. Graphic novels

0987715259; 9780987715258, $17.99

This comic anthology, edited by Hope Nicholson, "from traditional stories to exciting new visions of the future,...presents some of the finest comic book and graphic novel work in North America. The traditional stories presented in the book are with the permission from the elders in their respective communities, making this a truly genuine, never-before-seen publication." (Publisher's note)

"This collection of folklore from a powerhouse team of Native authors, including Buffy Sainte-Marie and Richard Van Camp, will wow readers with traditional and futuristic tales based on tribal-specific cultural teachings.... The full-page illustrations in some selections and the bright colors in others add depth and understanding to the narratives. The artwork is as diverse as the stories collected." SLJ

Nicieza, Fabian

Civil War: Thunderbolts. Marvel Entertainment 2007 un Illustration

Grades: 9 10 11 12 Adult   **741.5; Fic**

1. Graphic novels; 2. Superhero graphic novels

0-7851-1947-7, $13.99

The Super Human Registration Act has been signed into law, sides are being chosen, but what side do the former villains called the Thunderbolts fall on? Well, their identities are already public knowledge, and they sure can get good publicity by hunting down renegade heroes, so...it's time for the Thunderbolts to, err, kick some spandex butt. Except, they also wear spandex, so ...

Civil War: X-Men Universe. Peter David, Fabian Nicieza; artists, Dennis Carlo, Barry Windsor-Smith. Marvel Entertainment 2007 un Illustration

Grades: 9 10 11 12 Adult   **741.5; Fic**

1. Deadpool (Fictional character); 2. Graphic novels; 3. Superhero graphic novels; 4. X-Men (Fictional characters)

978-0-7851-2243-2, $13.99

The divisiveness of Civil War has spread to X-Factor: half of them want to cooperate with the government; the other half wants to take a stand against it. Quicksilver's return to the team may well decide whether X-Factor stays together or cracks apart. Plus: Cable and Deadpool find themselves on opposite sides of the fence, and both refuse to budge. It's going to lead to a fight, but this one may change both their lives.

Deadpool & Cable. written by Fabian Nicieza, Dan Slott, Reilly Brown; pencilled by Reilly Brown, Mark Brooks, Patrick Zircher, Lan Medina, Ron Lim, Staz Johnson. Marvel Enterprises 2014 1272 p. Color; Illustration

Grades: 10 11 12 Adult   **741.5; Fic**

1. Deadpool (Fictional character); 2. Superhero graphic novels; 3. Cable (Fictional character)

9780785192763, $125; 078519276X

This collects issues 1-50 of the comic book series of the same name. "Wade Wilson is Deadpool, the mentally disturbed merc with a mouth and a healing factor that just won't quit! Nathan Summers is Cable, the messianic mutant from the future who plans to save us all — whether we want him to or not!" (Publisher's note)

Contains material originally published in magazine form as Cable & Deadpool #1-50, Deadpool/GLI summer fun spectacular and Deadpool #27

Nightow, Yasuhiro

★ **Trigun** Maximum Volume 1: The Hero Returns. Dark Horse Comics 2004 192p. Illustration

Grades: 10 11 12 Adult   **741.5; Fic**

1. Adventure graphic novels; 2. Graphic novels; 3. Manga; 4. Science fiction graphic novels; 5. Seinen manga

1-59307-196-5, $9.95

Vash the Stampede disappeared for two years after blasting a crater onto the moon orbiting the desert planet he saved from annihilation. But, with good and bad people alike trying to track him down he won't stay lost for long. He teams up again with Wolfwood, and learns of a new villain named Knives. As with the original manga series, humor combines with lots of fighting action; this time there's more violence, and some nudity and harsh language.

★ **Trigun** Volume 1. Dark Horse Comics 2003 360p. Illustration

Grades: 9 10 11 12 Adult   **741.5; Fic**

1. Adventure graphic novels; 2. Graphic novels; 3. Manga; 4. Science fiction graphic novels; 5. Shonen manga

1-59307-052-7, $14.95

Somehow, the past has placed a sixty billion double dollar bounty on Vash's head and the gunslinging pacifist can't seem to get away from money grubbing, itchy-trigger-finger citizenry. Find out why Vash is worth so much money dead. Feel the clumsy worry of the unfortunate citizens of the pulverous planet. Follow the follies of an unlikely hero in a forbidding world. Join Vash the Stampede " with his troubled past and uncanny ability to dodge a gazillion bullets " and a cavalcade of unlucky characters on a dusty, desert planet in the distant future. This series combines Old West action with high-tech weaponry and some crazy humor as bounty hunters and a couple of insurance investigators hunt for Vash. The series includes some harsh language, violence, partial nudity, and brief mild sexual innuendo.

Niles, Steve

30 Days of Night. IDW Publishing 2003 104p. Illustration

Grades: 10 11 12 Adult

741.5; Fic

1. Graphic novels; 2. Horror graphic novels; 3. Vampires — Graphic novels

0-9719775-5-0, $17.99

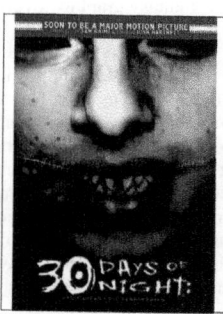

Courtesy of IDW Publishing

The long night of winter is coming to Barrow, Alaska; it's normal, and the people living in this isolated town don't mind. However, this particular winter, a band of vampires has decided to come up to Barrow for the month-long night and play. Sheriff Eben Olemaun and his deputy, wife Stella, and the people of Barrow have no idea of the terror and death they face when vampires can roam freely all night, all thirty days of it.

This is pure, raw horror with monstrous vampires; these are not the romantic, sexy vampires of so many supernatural romances, but nasty, ugly, blood-sucking monsters. Templesmith's art and the technique of setting his panels on black pages adds a claustrophobic element that adds to the horror.

30 Days of Night: Dark Days. IDW Publishing 2004 144p. Illustration

Grades: 10 11 12 Adult

741.5; Fic

Courtesy of IDW Publishing

1. Graphic novels; 2. Horror graphic novels; 3. Vampires — Graphic novels

1-932382-16-X, $19.99

In this sequel, the action shifts from Barrow, Alaska to Los Angeles, as Stella Olemaun, her life forever altered by the vampires' assault and her husband's death, rededicates herself to wiping out vampires and alerting the world to their shadowed existence. Along the way, she meets new allies and new foes — lots and lots of enemies. The book includes lots of graphic violence and harsh language.

30 Days of Night: Return to Barrow. IDW Publishing 2004 144p. Illustration
Grades: 11 12 Adult
741.5; Fic
1. Graphic novels; 2. Horror graphic novels; 3. Vampires — Graphic novels
1-932382-36-4, $19.99

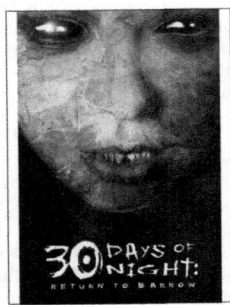

Courtesy of IDW Publishing

Three years before, vampires came to Barrow, Alaska at the beginning of the long winter night and slaughtered most of the town's inhabitants. Sheriff Olemaun died saving the town and his deputy wife died fighting vampires elsewhere. Now a new sheriff has come to town four days before the winter night, and the vampires are returning to destroy Barrow for good. Monstrous, evil creatures who slaughter viciously with lots of bloodshed combine with Templesmith's art that promotes a claustrophobic feeling of terror in this sequel to 30 Days of Night.

Originally published as 30 Days of Night: Return to Barrow issues #1-6.

Freaks of the Heartland. Dark Horse Comics 2005 un Illustration
Grades: 10 11 12 Adult
741.5; Fic
1. Fantasy graphic novels; 2. Graphic novels; 3. Horror graphic novels
1-59307-029-2, $17.95

Some folks would call Trevor's brother a monster. But to Trevor, Will is just another kid trapped in a dark reality he can't comprehend. When the situation moves from bad to worse, and their father threatens to do away with Will, Trevor learns that they're not alone — that "freak" children were born to other families in Gristlewood Valley. And just as they were all born at the same time, it seems their sad, frustrated, and emotionally spent parents seem to be hatching a plan to see that they disappear at the same time. Against all odds, and with nothing but love for his brother in his heart, Trevor is going to do whatever he can to get Will, and the other freak children, out of harm's way, if it's not already too late. The book includes fairly graphic violence and harsh language.

Nilsen, Anders
Dogs & Water. Drawn & Quarterly 2007 96p. Illustration
Grades: 10 11 12 Adult
741.5
1. Graphic novels
978-1-897299-08-1

A young man wandering a nameless path has only a stuffed bear as a companion, which inertly endures his desperation, anger, and musings along the way. The landscape is cold and bleak with few landmarks, and offers only precarious encounters with animals and armed men. These interactions are rife with instinct, the drive for survival, and human ethics concerning the killed and injured. He finds acceptance with a pack of dogs, though their nature is wild and their potential threat is as unsettling as the sudden presence of a massive pipeline on the horizon. The road disappears and only blind circumstance remains. All is uncertain and all can be lost, but he continues on regardless. This is for the thoughtful reader who doesn't mind a little bit of harsh language and some violence.

Ninomiya, Tomoko
★ **Nodame** Cantabile, Vol. 1. Ballantine Books/Del Rey Manga 2005 188p. Illustration
Grades: 10 11 12 Adult
741.5; Fic
1. Graphic novels; 2. Manga; 3. Music — Graphic novels; 4. Romance graphic novels; 5. Shojo manga
0-345-48172-0, $10.95
2004 Kodansha Manga Award for Shojo Manga.

Music student Shinichi Chiaki dreams of becoming a conductor, but his fear of flying and arrogant attitude hold him back. Then he meets Megumi Noda, who has a natural talent for piano, but she can't read a music score, she's a slovenly mess, and her apartment is a disaster area. Shinichi starts working with her, and Megumi falls for him. Romantic complications, new friendships, and music ensue. There are some mild sex scenes.

Nishino, Jyutaroh
Steel fist Riku vol. 1. Jyutaroh Nishino; [Sheldon Drzka, translation and adaptation]. DC Comics/CMX 2008 162p. Illustration
Grades: 9 10 11 12 Adult
741.5; Fic
1. Graphic novels; 2. Humorous graphic novels; 3. Manga; 4. Martial arts — Graphic novels; 5. Shonen manga
978-1-4012-1752-5, $9.99

Teenage Riku lives with Rocky, her gruff, adopted dad ("Call me Sensei!" he roars when she calls him Pops), who trained her in martial arts. In their world, semi-humans are common, such as a Pig Man, or the fact that Riku has a fist of steel. Rocky now runs a shop selling celebrity photos, but he used to be a professional martial artist. When the daughter of his old master ventures into the shop, Rocky kidnaps her in order to demand a rematch, 20 years after the fact, with his old rival Utsugizaki. This doesn't sit well with Riku, and she decides to take matters into her own hands. The book includes some raunchy humor and fan service (Riku's powers become even stronger when her breasts are unbound); Rocky is obsessed with women's breasts and suffers many nosebleeds (manga symbol for sexual arousal) while watching his DVDs, and characters declare that they're pissed off or that someone is a pain in the butt.

Nolen-Weathington, Eric
Modern Masters volume twenty-five: Jeff Smith. Twomorrows Publishing 2011 117p. Illustration
Grades: 6 7 8 9 10 11 12 Adult
741.5
1. Artists; 2. Authors; 3. Cartoonists; 4. Comic books, strips, etc. — History and criticism; 5. Graphic novels — History and criticism; 6. Smith, Jeff
978-1-60549-024-3, $15.95

Courtesy of Twomorrows Publishing

This volume in the Modern Masters series focuses on Jeff Smith, creator of Bone. In an interview that covers his childhood, college career, and early work before becoming a cartoonist, Smith talks about how he created Fone Bone when he was just five years old. The artwork in the book includes young Smith's hand-created comics from his childhood. Only a couple of "crap — s slip out. The book includes mostly black and white art and photographs, with a few color illustrations from the Bone comics.

Nonaka, Eiji
Cromartie High School, Vol. 1. [translated by Brendan Frayne]. ADV Manga 2005 158p. Illustration

Grades: 10 11 12 Adult   **741.5; Fic**
1. Graphic novels; 2. High school students — Graphic novels; 3. Humorous graphic novels; 4. Manga; 5. School stories — Graphic novels; 6. Shonen manga
1-4139-0257-X, $10.95
Takashi Kamiyama enrolled at Cromartie High School, the worst high school in Tokyo, to help a friend, who then flunked the entrance exam. Now he's stuck in a school filled with juvenile delinquents, street toughs, and some very strange characters. They include a shirtless guy who looks like Freddy Mercury and never says anything, a gorilla who is smarter than everyone else, and Mechazawa, who looks like a canister-shaped robot. American readers may not be aware that, in Japan, students must pass entrance exams to get into the high school of their choice. It doesn't matter how rich your family is if you can't pass an entrance exam with a high enough score to get into a top school. This is the first volume of an ongoing manga full of wacky and sometimes deadpan humor.

North, Ryan
★ **Adventure** Time. Ryan North; illustrated by Braden Lamb and Shelli Paroline. Simon & Schuster 2012 128 p. Color; Illustration
Grades: 3 4 5 6 7 8 9 10   **741.5**
1. Imaginary places; 2. Adventure fiction
1608862801; 9781608862801, $14.99
"The totally algebraic adventures of Finn and Jake have come to the comic book page! The Lich, a super-lame, SUPER-SCARY skeleton dude, has returned to the the Land of Ooo, and he's bent on total destruction! Luckily, Finn and Jake are on the case...but can they succeed against their most destructive foe yet?" (Publisher's note)
"The comic series has been every bit as good as the show, with epic magic battles with an evil Lich, a multi-part time travel story, and a host of backup strips by some of the best indie cartoonists out there." Comics Alliance
Volume 1 of 17

★ The **unbeatable** Squirrel Girl; Volume 1: Squirrel power!. Ryan North; illustrated by Erica Henderson. Marvel Enterprises 2015 136 p. Color; Illustration
Grades: 7 8 9 10 11 12 Adult   **741.5**
1. Squirrel Girl (Fictional character); 2. Superheroes — Fiction; 3. Female superhero graphic novels; 4. Squirrels — Fiction
0785197028; 9780785197027, $15.99
Eisner Nominee: Best New Series (2016); Eisner Award: Best Publication for Teens (2017)
"Supervillains and criminals meet their match with Tony Stark's friend Squirrel Girl, aka Doreen Green, a college freshman with the appearance, speed, and agility of a squirrel. Fitting in proves to be challenging, as normal girls do not talk to or have a squirrel sidekick, nor do they have super strength. Then there is Squirrel Girl's roommate, who has a tough exterior and is obsessed with knitting and her cat. Luckily, Squirrel Girl has a knack for winning people over. When Galactus threatens Earth, the heroine must rely on more than strength to defeat the Devourer of Worlds. She may have extraordinary strength, an army of squirrels at her disposal, a collection of Deadpool villain trading cards, and nut-inspired catchphrases, but it is her ability to form connections with people that proves to be her most powerful asset.:" (School Library Journal)
Contains material originally published in magazine form as The Unbeatable Squirrel Girl #1-4 and Marvel Super-Heroes #8; Volume 1 of an ongoing series

Nybakken, Scott
Batman Adventures Vol. 2: Shadows & Masks. DC Comics 2004 112p. Illustration
Grades: 4 5 6 7 8 9   **741.5; Fic**

1. Batman (Fictional characters); 2. Graphic novels; 3. Superhero graphic novels
978-1-4012-0330-2, $6.95
A deadly new gang is threatening Gotham City, and it's up to the Dark Knight Detective to take it down, from the inside. He goes on an undercover mission in this volume.

O'Connor, George
★ **Aphrodite:** Goddess of love. George O'Connor. First Second 2014 76 p. Color; Illustration (Olympians)
Grades: 6 7 8 9   **741.5**
1. Aphrodite (Greek deity); 2. Graphic novels; 3. Gods and goddesses — Fiction; 4. Aphrodite (Greek deity)
1596437391; 1596439475; 9781596437395, $9.99; 9781596439474, $16.99
This graphic novel, volume six of the Olympians series on Greek mythology, by George O'Connor, "turns the spotlight on Aphrodite, the goddess of love.... O'Connor tackles the story of the Aphrodite from her dramatic birth (emerging from sea-foam) to her role in the Trojan War." (Publisher's note)
"Like the prior volumes, this book injects the mythology with an accessible modern sensibility through its colorful, action-packed graphic storytelling." Horn Book
Includes bibliographical references; Other titles in this series are:Zeus (2010); Athena (2010); Hera (2011); Hades (2012); Poseidon (2013); Ares (2015)

★ **Apollo:** the brilliant one. George O'Connor. First Second 2016 80 p. Color; Illustration
Grades: 5 6 7 8 9 10   **292.2**
1. Gods, Greek; 2. Mythology; 3. Greek mythology; 4. Apollo (Greek deity)
1626720169; 9781626720152, $9.99; 9781626720169
                                      LC 2015014172
O'Connor "continues to turn his extensive knowledge of the original Greek myths into...graphic novel storytelling. Mighty Apollo is known by all as the god of the sun, but there's more to this Olympian than a bright smile and a shining chariot." (Publisher's note)
A Neal Porter Book.

★ **Ares:** bringer of war. George O'Connor. First Second Books 2015 80 p. Color; Illustration (Olympians)
Grades: 4 5 6 7 8 9   **741.5**
1. Ares (Greek deity) — Comic books, strips, etc; 2. Trojan War — Graphic novels; 3. Greek mythology — Graphic novels
1626720134; 1626720142; 9781626720138; 9781626720145, $16.99
                                      LC 2014041225
This graphic novel by George O'Connor "continues in the tenth year of the fabled Trojan War where two infamous gods of war go to battle. The spotlight is thrown on Ares, god of war, and primarily focuses on his battle with the clever and powerful Athena. As the battle culminates and the gods try to one-up each other to win, the human death toll mounts." (Publisher's note)
"In this nuanced, multilayered view of the usually vilified bringer of war, O'Connor continues his exceptional graphic novel series about the Greek gods.... The author's extensive notes amusingly explain connections to The Odyssey, The Aeneid, and the series' previous works." SLJ
A Neal Porter Book.; Other titles in this series are: Athena: Grey-eyed Goddess (2010); Zeus: King of the Gods (2010); Hera: The Goddess and her Glory (2011); Hades: Lord of the Dead (2012); Poseidon: Earth Shaker (2013); Aphrodite: Goddess of Love (2014)

★ **Hades**. First Second 2012 76p Color illustration (Olympians)
Grades: 5 6 7 8 9   **741.5; 398.2093; 398.2093801**

1. Hades (Greek deity) — Comic books, strips, etc.; 2. Mother-daughter relationship — Fiction; 3. Graphic novels; 4. Greek mythology
9781596437616

LC 2011017563

In this book, a "tempestuous mother-daughter relationship makes up the centerpiece of [author and illustrator George] O'Connor's...Olympian portrait. Snatched down to the Underworld in the wake of a screaming fight with her mother Demeter,...raging adolescent Kore (meaning, generically 'The Maiden') initially gives her quiet, gloomy captor Hades a hard time too. After grabbing the opportunity to give herself a thorough makeover and changing her name to Persephone ('Bringer of Destruction'), though, she takes charge of her life — so surely that, when offered the opportunity to return to her remorseful mom, she lies about having eaten those pomegranate seeds so she can spend half of each year as Queen of the Dead." (Kirkus)
Includes bibliographical references.

O'Malley, Bryan Lee
★ **Scott** Pilgrim's Precious Little Life, Vol. 1. Oni Press 2004 un Illustration
Grades: 10 11 12 Adult
741.5; Fic
1. Graphic novels; 2. Humorous graphic novels; 3. Martial arts — Graphic novels; 4. Romance graphic novels
1-932664-08-4, $11.95

Courtesy of Oni Press

"Scott Pilgrim's life is totally sweet. He's 23 years old, he's in a rock band, he's 'between jobs,' and he's dating a cute high school girl. Nothing could possibly go wrong, unless a seriously mind-blowing, dangerously fashionable, rollerblading delivery girl named Ramona Flowers starts cruising through his dreams and sailing by him at parties. Will Scott's awesome life get turned upside-down? Will he have to face Ramona's seven sexy evil ex-boyfriends in battle? The short answer is yes." (Publisher's note)

Also available in full-color hardcover editions; Other titles in this series are: Scott Pilgrim vs. the World (2005); Scott Pilgrim & the Infinite Sadness (2006); Scott Pilgrim Gets It Together (2007); Scott Pilgrim vs. the Universe (2009); Scott Pilgrim's Finest Hour (2010)

★ **Seconds**. Bryan Lee O'Malley. Ballantine Books 2014 336 p. Color; Illustration
Grades: 10 11 12 Adult
741.5
1. Restaurants — Fiction; 2. Graphic novels
0345529375; 9780345529374, $25

LC 2013456979

In this graphic novel by Bryan Lee O'Malley, "Katie's got it pretty good. She's a talented young chef, she runs a successful restaurant, and she has big plans to open an even better one. Then, all at once, progress on the new location bogs down, her charming ex-boyfriend pops up, her fling with another chef goes sour, and her best waitress gets badly hurt. And just like that, Katie's life goes from pretty good to not so much." (Publisher's note)

"O'Malley's engaging narrative voice hasn't diminished — -even the self-absorbed Katie is likeable enough to root for, although it's obvious that she's making things worse for herself. O'Malley's sweet, nimble art, now in color, has acquired more confidence: the plot unfolds cinematically, and his character designs are more appealing than ever." Pub Wkly

O'Neil, Dennis
The **DC** comics guide to writing comics. introduction by Stan Lee. Watson-Guptill 2001 128p. Illustration
Grades: 11 12 Adult
808; 741.5
1. Comic books, strips, etc. — Authorship
0-8230-1027-9, $19.95

LC 2001-26101

"In this valuable guide, Dennis O'Neil, a living legend in the comics industry, reveals his insider tricks and no-fail techniques for comic storytelling. Readers will discover the various methods of writing scripts (full script vs. plot first), as well as procedures for developing a story structure, building subplots, creating well-rounded characters, and much more." (Publisher's note)

★ **Green** Lantern, Green Arrow. Dennis O'Neil, Elliot Maggin, writers; Neal Adams, penciller; Neal Adams, Dick Giordano, Frank Giacoia, Dan Adkins, Berni Wrightson, inkers; Cory Adams, Jack Adler, colorists; John Costanza, Joe Letterese, letterers. DC Comics 2012 361 p. Color illustration
Grades: 10 11 12 Adult
741.5
1. Superheroes — Comic books, strips, etc.; 2. Green Lantern (Fictional character); 3. Green Arrow (Fictional character)
1401235174; 9781401235178, $29.99

LC 2013363523

In this comic book collection, "Green Lantern Hal Jordan continued his usual cosmic-spanning adventures, as he used his amazing Power Ring to police Sector 2814 against universe-threatening menaces. Meanwhile, on Earth, the archer known as Green Arrow, was confronting menaces of a different kind: racism, poverty, drugs, and other social ills!" (Publisher's note)

Originally published in single magazine form in Green Lantern 76-87, 89; Flash 217-219, 226. Green Lantern/Green Arrow 1-7.

The **Question**: Zen and violence. DC Comics 2007 174p. Illustration
Grades: 11 12 Adult
741.5; Fic
1. Crime — Graphic novels; 2. Graphic novels; 3. Superhero graphic novels
978-1-4012-1579-8, $19.99

Investigative reporter Vic Sage, who is also the faceless, morally conflicted avenger known as The Question, works to bring down the politically corrupted mayor of Hub City and his advisers, but they have hired the mercenary Lady Shiva, who defeats him in combat and the henchmen of the crooked Rev. Hatch throw him into the river. But, Sage is not dead, he's rescued and healed, and told to find Richard Dragon. He stays with Dragon for a year, training in martial arts and disciplining himself. When he returns to Hub City, he now has the focus to go after the criminals and politicians mucking up the city. The book includes lots of violence and some harsh language.

Oakley, Mark
Thieves & kings. [by Mark Oakley]. I Box Pub 1998 154p. Illustration
Grades: 4 5 6 7 8 9 10 11 12
741.5; Fic
1. Adventure graphic novels; 2. Fantasy graphic novels; 3. Graphic novels
0-9681025-0-6, $18.95

LC 2003-446777

In a story that mixes pages of text with pages of comic book art, the reader meets the young thief Rubel, who has returned home from a long voyage to find things no longer as they were. He has to deal with soldiers and pirates, princes and princesses, a strange young wizard, and a mysterious Shadow Lady.

Originally published as individual issues of the Thieves & kings comic series, beginning in 1994; Volume 1 of 5

Obata, Yuki

★ **We** were there, vol. 1. story & art by Yuki Obata. Viz Media/Shojo Beat 2008 un Illustration

Grades: 10 11 12   **741.5; Fic**

1. Graphic novels; 2. Manga; 3. Romance graphic novels; 4. Shojo manga

978-1-4215-2018-6, $8.99

Fifteen-year-old Nanami Takahashi has just started high school, with high hopes for making friends and doing well, but things don't go as smoothly as she had hoped. She struggles with math, then she gets sort of railroaded into being the class president. She also falls for Motoharu Yano, an irresponsible boy who somehow is the most popular person in the class. His carefree attitude covers his grief for the death of his girlfriend, an older girl whose younger sister is their classmate, Yuri Yamamoto. Nanami struggles with classwork, with the responsibilities of being class president, and with her conflicting feelings about Motoharu. Some of the black and white art looks airbrushed; these pages occur at the beginning of each chapter. Viz has rated this series for older teens due to sexual themes, but they don't occur in this first volume.

Original Japanese edition, 2002; Volume 1 of 18

Oda, Eiichiro

★ **One** Piece Volume 1. story and art by Eiichiro Oda; [English adaptation by Lance Caselman]. Viz Media/Shonen Jump 2003 216p. Illustration

Grades: 8 9 10 11 12 Adult   **741.5; Fic**

1. Adventure graphic novels; 2. Fantasy graphic novels; 3. Graphic novels; 4. Manga; 5. Shonen manga

1-56931-901-4, $7.95

Monkey D. Luffy's main ambition is to become a pirate, inspired by listening to the tales of the buccaneer "Red-Haired" Shanks. When he accidentally eats the Gum-Gum Fruit, it gives him strange powers to stretch like rubber, but doing so also invokes the fruit's curse: anybody who consumes it can never learn to swim. Nevertheless, Monkey and his crewmate Roronoa Zoro, master of the three-sword fighting style, sail the Seven Seas of swashbuckling adventure in search of the elusive treasure "One Piece." As the series goes on, Luffy gains more crew and they encounter sea monsters, far away kingdoms, cloud island, and super powered pirates of every shape, size, and description — which means lots of epic and comical fight scenes.

Volume 1 of an ongoing series

Oh! Great

Air Gear Vol. 1. Random House/Del Rey Manga 2006 un Illustration

Grades: 10 11 12 Adult   **741.5; Fic**

1. Adventure graphic novels; 2. Graphic novels; 3. Manga; 4. Shonen manga

978-0-345-49278-4, $10.95

LC bd 06-250081

Itsuki Minami is the toughest kid at Higashi Junior High School, plus he lives with the mysterious and sexy Noyamano sisters. Life is never dull, but it becomes dangerous when Itsuki leads his school to victory over some vindictive Westside punks with gangster connections. Now he stands to lose his school, his friends, and everything he cares about. But in his darkest hour, the Noyamano girls come to Itsuki's aid. They can teach him a powerful skill that will save their school from the gangsters' siege-and introduce Itsuki to a thrilling and terrifying new world. The series includes crude humor, violence, partial nudity, sexual situations (including hints at sexual violence), and harsh language.

Ohba, Tsugumi

Bakuman; Volume 1: Dreams and reality. story by Tsugumi Ohba; art by Takeshi Obata; [translation & adaptation, Tetsuichiro Miyaki]. VIZ Media 2010 194 p. Illustration

Grades: 7 8 9 10 11 12   **741.5; Fic**

1. Shonen manga; 2. Manga; 3. Cartoonists — Graphic novels

1421535130; 9781421535135, $9.99

"Average student Moritaka Mashiro enjoys drawing for fun. When his classmate and aspiring writer Akito Takagi discovers his talent, he begs Moritaka to team up with him as a manga-creating duo. But what exactly does it take to make it in the manga-publishing world?" (Publisher's note)

Volume 1 of 20

★ **Death** Note, Vol. 1. story by Tsugumi Ohba; art by Takeshi Obata; [translation & adaptation, Pookie Rolf]. Viz Shonen Jump Advanced 2005 196p. Illustration

Grades: 10 11 12   **741.5; Fic**

1. Graphic novels; 2. Manga; 3. Suspense graphic novels; 4. Shonen manga

1-4215-0168-6, $7.99

When brilliant, bored high school student Light Kagami finds a Death Note, a notebook that belongs to a shinigami (Japanese death god), he decides to improve the world by ridding it of criminals. The police frown upon the murders and investigate, and the brilliant and eccentric young detective known only as L joins the police in Japan to hunt the killer. Light has Ryuk, the shinigami whose Death Note he's using, so the game is on.

"It is a fascinating exploration of two brilliant young men and their intricate relationship even as the story explores the idea of 'the ends justify the means.'" (VOYA)

Also available in 2-in-1 editions; Volume 1 of a 12 volume series

Oima, Yoshitoki

★ **A silent** voice; Volume 1. Yoshitoki Oima; translation, lettering, Steven LeCroy. Kodansha 2015 186 p. Illustration

Grades: 7 8 9 10   **741.5; Fic**

1. Deaf children; 2. Bullies — Graphic novels; 3. School stories — Graphic novels; 4. Shonen manga

163236056X; 9781632360564, $10.99

Eisner Nominee: Best U.S. Edition of International Material — Asia (2016)

"Shoya is a bully. When Shoko, a girl who can't hear, enters his elementary school class, she becomes their favorite target.... But the children's cruelty goes too far. Shoko is forced to leave the school, and Shoya ends up shouldering all the blame. Six years later, the two meet again. Can Shoya make up for his past mistakes, or is it too late?" (Publisher's note)

Volume 1 of 7

Oliver, Simon

The **Exterminators** Vol. 1: The Bug Brothers. DC Comics/Vertigo 2006 128p. Illustration

Grades: 11 12 Adult   **741.5; Fic**

1. Graphic novels; 2. Horror graphic novels

978-1-4012-1064-9, $9.99

This book focuses on a dysfunctional group of bug killers prowling the barrios and bungalows of Los Angeles. Henry James, the newest exterminator, sees the job as a way to cleanse the sins of his dark past; he has a hard time getting his view across to his careerist girlfriend, sociopathic partner and the general bunch of freaks he calls co-workers. Meanwhile, what Henry and the "bug brothers" of Bug-Bee-Gone Co. don't understand is that human beings may be the true pests — and bugs could be the real exterminator. This book has graphic violence, some nudity and sexual situations, and lots and lots of nasty bugs, rats, and other pests.

ONE (Manga author)
★ **One-punch** man; Volume 1. story by One; art by Yusuke Murata. Viz 2015 189 p. Illustration
Grades: 8 9 10 11 12 Adult   **741.5; Fic**
1. Seinen manga; 2. Graphic novels; 3. Manga; 4. Superheroes
1421585642; 9781421585642, $9.99
Eisner Nominee: Best U.S. Edition of International Material — Asia (2015)

"Nothing about Saitama passes the eyeball test when it comes to superheroes, from his lifeless expression to his bald head to his unimpressive physique. However, this average-looking guy has a not-so-average problem — he just can't seem to find an opponent strong enough to take on! Every time a promising villain appears, he beats the snot out of 'em with one punch!" (Publisher's note)

"The story is fast-paced, humorous, and entertaining in a way that looks and feels like an action movie." SLJ

Volume 1 of an ongoing series

Osajyefo, Kwanza
Black; Volume 1. Kwanza Osajyefo, creator/writer; Tim Smith 3, creator/designer; Jamal Igle, illustrator; Khary Randolph, cover artist; Sarah Litt, editor; Robin Riggs, inks; Derwin Roberson, tones; David Sharpe, letters; Matt Pizzolo, publisher. Black Mask Comics 2017 208 p. Color; Illustration
Grades: 11 12 Adult   **741.5; Fic**
1. Superheroes — Fiction; 2. African Americans — Fiction
9781628751864, $19.99; 162875186X

In this graphic novel, by Kwanza Osajyefo, illustrated by Jamal Igle, Robin Riggs, Tim Smith III, and Derwin Roberson, "in a world that already hates and fears them — what if only Black people had superpowers. After miraculously surviving being gunned down by police, a young man learns that he is part of the biggest lie in history. Now he must decide whether it's safer to keep it a secret or if the truth will set him free." (Publisher's note)

Osborne, Melissa Jane
The **Wendy** project. written and created by Melissa Jane Osborne; art, colors, and letters by Veronica Fish. Papercutz 2017 96 p. Color; Illustration
Grades: 8 9 10 11 12 Adult
741.5
1. Teenage automobile drivers — Accidents; 2. Graphic novels; 3. Teenage girls — Fiction; 4. Fantasy fiction
1629917699; 9781629917696, $12.99

Courtesy of NBM Publishing

In this graphic novel, by Melissa Jane Osborne, illustrated by Veronica Fish, "Wendy Davies crashes her car into a lake...with her two younger brothers in the backseat. When she wakes in the hospital, she is told that her youngest brother...is dead. Wendy...[insists] that Michael is alive and in the custody of a mysterious flying boy. Placed in a new school, Wendy negotiates fantasy and reality as students and adults around her resemble characters from Neverland." (Publisher's note)

"This unexpected gem stands out among latter-day versions of Peter Pan thanks to its embrace of genuine emotion and psychological gravity." LJ

Osborne, Rob
Sunset City, For Active Senior Living. AiT/Planet Lar 2005 un Illustration
Grades: 12 Adult
741.5; Fic
1. Graphic novels; 2. Retirement communities — Graphic novels
1-932051-41-4, $9.95

Courtesy of AiT/Planet Lar

Sunset City is a typical retirement community. Its residents enjoy golf and gossip and they all seem content to fritter away their golden years. Except Frank McDonald. A retired widower, he wrestles with the question: why am I here? Reading the newspaper, Frank keeps up on the minutia of the day; it provides a buzz to an otherwise humdrum life. One morning, Frank is overcome by a startling story, and he does something extraordinary: he takes life by the balls. The story includes some harsh language and violence, and the climactic scene may bother some readers.

Osborne, Wayne
FX. story and script by Wayne Osborne; pencils, inks, lettering, colors, by John Byrne. IDW Publishing 2008 160p. Illustration
Grades: 7 8 9 10 11 12 Adult   **741.5; Fic**
1. Adventure graphic novels; 2. Graphic novels; 3. Humorous graphic novels; 4. Superhero graphic novels
978-1-60010-274-5, $19.99

Teenager Tom Talbot was playing with his best friend when Jack accidentally hit Tom so hard he went into a coma. When Tom recovers, he discovers that he's got the power to make what he imagines be real; he discovers this when they're playing around in an alley and Tom imagines he's got a bazooka and really destroys a dumpster. He cobbles together a masked costume, and finds himself fighting superpowered giant talking apes, nasty weapons-bearing lizards, and more. But someone notices him and decides he wants Tom's powers Lord Everos, the Father of Death. And it's not just Tom, either; Vicki, the class weirdo, does really talk with the dead, and Lord Everos wants her, too. And that's not the worst of it, for apparently Tom was never supposed to get the power of the thunderbolt, and a whole pantheon of heroes has just arrived to stop him. Oops again.

Ostrander, John
The **Legend** of Grimjack, Volume 1. IDW Publishing 2005 125p. Illustration
Grades: 10 11 12 Adult   **741.5; Fic**
1. Adventure graphic novels; 2. Fantasy graphic novels; 3. Graphic novels
1-932382-51-8, $19.99

Gathering all of the earliest GrimJack stories from the comic book series of the 1980s in one tome for the first time, The Legend of GrimJack, Volume One introduces the major characters and origin stories and also includes the GrimJack/Starslayer crossover saga. This volume also includes a brand new story and art as well as critical background information heretofore unrevealed. The book is full of grim, gritty action with considerable violence; the comics were originally published by First Comics in 1983 and 1984.

Star Wars: Legacy, Volume One: Broken. story, John Ostrander and Jan Duuresma; script, John Ostrander; pencils, Jan Duuresma; inks, Dan Parsons; colors, Brad Anderson; lettering, Michael David Thomas; cover art, Adam Hughes. Dark Horse Comics 2007 un Illustration
Grades: 7 8 9 10 11 12   **741.5; Fic**

1. Adventure graphic novels; 2. Graphic novels; 3. Science fiction graphic novels; 4. Star Wars — Graphic novels
978-1-59307-716-7, $17.95

125 years have passed since the events in Return of the JedI and the days of the New JedI Order. There is a new evil gripping the galaxy, shattering a resurgent Empire and seeking to destroy the last of the JedI. Even as their power is failing, the JedI hold onto one final hope, the last remaining heir to the Skywalker legacy: Cade, who has rejected the way of the JedI. The book's fighting action is at the same level as the motion picture series.

Ota, Yuko

Our cats are more famous than us: a Johnny Wander collection. Ananth Hirsh & Yuko Ota. Oni Press 2017 411 p. Illustration
Grades: 9 10 11 12 Adult
741.5

Courtesy of Oni Press

1. Graphic novels; 2. Humorous stories — Comic books, strips, etc.; 3. American wit and humor; 4. Comic books, strips, etc. — United States
9780998099507; 9781620103845; 1620103834; 9781620103838, $39.99
LC 2016952156

"Cartoonist and writer duo Ananth Hirsh and [Yuko] Ota present the first full collection of their webcomic Johnny Wander. This beautifully told volume spans eight years, four cats, and three moves. The telling, often revealing illustrations are supported by funny text when necessary but are allowed to stand alone and breathe. From life after college to growing up to dealing with friends, and cats, all of life's ups and downs are deftly addressed in this...work." (School Library Journal)

Otsuka, Eiji

MPD-Psycho No. 1. original story and script, Eiji Otsuka; art, Sho-u Tajima; translation, Kumar Sivasubramanian; English adaptation, Philip R. Simon; lettering, Steve Dutro. Dark Horse Comics 2007 186p. Illustration
Grades: 12 Adult   **741.5; Fic**
1. Graphic novels; 2. Horror graphic novels; 3. Manga; 4. Mystery graphic novels; 5. Seinen manga
978-1-59307-770-9, $10.95

Tokyo police detective Kobayashi Yousuke's life is changed forever after a serial killer notices something "special" about him. That same killer mutilates Kobayashi's girlfriend and kick-starts a "multiple personality battle" within Kobayashi that pushes him into a complex tempest of interconnected deviants and evil forces. After prison he works for a private detective organization, and the cases are all bloody and weird. The book shows lots of graphic violence and nudity, along with strong language. This series is very popular in Japan.

Ottaviani, Jim

Bone sharps, cowboys, and thunder lizards: a tale of Edwin Drinker Cope, Othniel Charles Marsh, and the gilded age of paleontology. by Jim Ottaviani & Big Time Attic. G.T. Labs 2005 165p. Illustration
Grades: 9 10 11 12 Adult   **560**
1. Biographical graphic novels; 2. Fossils — Graphic novels; 3. Graphic novels; 4. Paleontologists; 5. Zoologists; 6. Cope, E. D. (Edward Drinker), 1840-1897; 7. Marsh, Othniel Charles, 1831-1899
0-9660106-6-3; 978-0-9660106-6-4, $22.95

LC 2005-920326

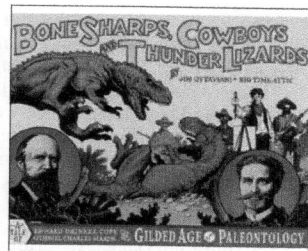

Courtesy of G.T. Labs

"Ottaviani portrays the heyday of American dinosaur hunting with a ripsnorting Western feel. Rival scientist/dinosaur hunters Marsh and Cope play out their real-life drama in a mostly accurate historical telling. Copious notes at the back of the book point out where Ottaviani departs from the facts; science and history become fun in his hands." Voice Youth Advocates

Includes bibliographical references; Title from cover

Dignifying science: stories about women scientists. written by Jim Ottaviani and illustrated by Donna Barr . . . [et al.]. G.T. Labs 2009 142p. Illustration
Grades: 6 7 8 9 10 11 12
920
1. Biographical graphic novels; 2. Graphic novels; 3. Women scientists — Graphic novels
978-0-9788037-3-5, $16.95; 0-9788037-3-5

Ottaviani provides biographical sketches of women scientists such as Lise Meitner, Rosalind Franklin, Barbara McClintock, and Hedy Lamarr (yes, the actress was also an inventor); all the stories are illustrated by women comics artists, including Lea Hernandez, Linda Medley, Anne Timmons, and others.

Courtesy of G.T. Labs

First published 1999

Fallout. written by Jim Ottaviani, with art by various artists. G.T. Labs 2001 239 p. Illustration
Grades: 11 12 Adult
355.8; 741.5
1. Atomic bomb; 2. Nuclear energy; 3. Nuclear weapons
0966010639; 9780966010633, $24.95
LC 2001091068

In this nonfiction graphic novel about atomic bombs, by Jim Ottaviani, "the focus...is on the scientists themselves — in particular J. Robert Oppenheimer and Leo Szilard, whose lives offer a cautionary tale about the uneasy alliance between the military, the government, and the beginnings of 'big science.'" (Publisher's note)

Courtesy of G.T. Labs

★ **Feynman**. written by Jim Ottaviani; art by Leland Myrick; coloring by Hilary Sycamore. First Second 2011 262 p. Illustration; Color
Grades: 9 10 11 12 Adult   **92; 530.092**
1. Biography, Individual; 2. Physicists — Graphic novels; 3. Feynman, Richard Phillips, 1918-1988; 4. Musicians — Biography; 5. Atomic bomb; 6. Nobel Prizes
1596432594; 9781596432598, $29.99; 9781596438279, $19.99; 9781451722406, $33.99

LC 2010036260

Author Jim Ottaviani presents a "graphic novel biography...[of] Nobel-winning quantum physicist, adventurer, musician, world-class raconteur, and one of the greatest minds of the twentieth century: Richard

Feynman...[The book] tells the story of the great man's life from his childhood in Long Island to his work on the Manhattan Project and the Challenger disaster." (Publisher's note)

"This is a fascinating look at the life of an eccentric genius, a man who worked on the Manhattan Project, won a Nobel Prize, was the first great physicist to teach freshmen classes, and was the investigator into the cause of the Challenger explosion who discovered the problem was the 0-rings. This work was so entertaining it was difficult to put down." Voice Youth Advocates

The **Imitation** Game: Alan Turing Decoded. Jim Ottaviani; illustrated by Leland Purvis. Harry N Abrams Inc 2016 240 p. Illustration
Grades: 9 10 11 12 Adult   **92; 741.5**
1. Turing, Alan Mathison, 1912-1954; 2. Mathematicians — Biography; 3. Turing, Alan Mathison, 1912-1954; 4. Biographical graphic novels
9781613129319; 9781419718939, $24.95; 1419718932

This book, by Jim Ottaviani and illustrated by Leland Purvis, "present[s] a historically accurate graphic novel biography of English mathematician and scientist Alan Turing. [It covers] Turing's life and groundbreaking research — as an unconventional genius who was arrested, tried, convicted, and punished for being openly gay, and whose innovative work still fuels the computing and communication systems that define our modern world." (Publisher's note)

"This adaptation uses a pastel palette of watercolors, strong black lines, and dynamic storytelling devices to bring Turing's tale to life. Multiple narratives, including those of Turing, his mother, and several of his colleagues and friends, weave in and out, following Turing from adolescence to the end of his short life." SLJ

Includes bibliographical references

Primates: The Fearless Science of Jane Goodall, Dian Fossey, and Biruté Galdikas. Jim Ottaviani; illustrated by Maris Wicks. First Second 2013 133 p. Color; Illustration
Grades: 5 6 7 8 9 10 Adult   **741.5; 599.8**
1. Primates; 2. Fossey, Dian, 1932-1985; 3. Goodall, Jane, 1934-; 4. Galdikas, Birute, 1946-
1596438657; 9781596438651, $19.99
LC 2013427678

This book presents an "account of the three greatest primatologists of the last century: Jane Goodall, Dian Fossey, and Biruté Galdikas. These three ground-breaking researchers were all students of the great Louis Leakey, and each made profound contributions to primatology — and to our own understanding of ourselves." (Publisher's note)

"More story than study, the book provides an accessible introduction to Goodall's, Fossey's and Galdikas' lives and work." Kirkus
Includes bibliographical references, page 138

Suspended in language: Niels Bohr's life, discoveries, and the century he shaped. written by Jim Ottaviani; illustrated and lettered by Leland Purvis. G.T. Labs 2009 318p. Illustration
Grades: 10 11 12 Adult
92
1. Biographical graphic novels; 2. Graphic novels; 3. Nobel laureates for physics; 4. Physicists — Graphic novels; 5. Quantum theory — Graphic novels; 6. Bohr, Niels Henrik David, 1885-1962
978-0-9788037-2-8, $24.95

"Quantum physics gets an accessible yet substantive introduction through art that

Courtesy of G.T. Labs

mixes fantasy and realism. Great for teens who like science." Booklist
Includes bibliographical references; First published 2004; ?Additional art by Jay Hosler, Roger Langridge, Steve Leialoha, Linda Medley, and Jeff Parker.?

★ **T-Minus**: the race to the moon. [illustrated by] Zander Cannon, Kevin Cannon. Aladdin 2009 124p. Illustration
Grades: 4 5 6 7 8 9 10 11 12 Adult   **629.45; 741.5**
1. Apollo project — Graphic novels; 2. Gemini project — Graphic novels; 3. Graphic novels; 4. Space flight to the moon — Graphic novels
978-1-4169-8682-9, $21.99; 1-4169-8682-0; 978-1-4169-4960-2 (pa), $12.99; 1-4169-4960-7 (pa)
LC 2009-920999

Ottaviani, Zander Cannon, and Kevin Cannon show what happened when the U.S. and the U.S.S.R. started the space race in the 1950s, and how it progressed to the NASA Apollo 11 mission which landed two men on the moon in July of 1969.

"Organized as a countdown, making the outcome seem inevitable, the frequent, prominent sidebars list a type of rocket, the duration of its flight, and whether the mission was a success or a failure. There are more than 30 attempts chronicled, and the shift between Soviet and U.S. successes creates an interesting balance in the narrative.... Ottaviani is particular with facts and eager to inspire readers with regard to the scientific process." SLJ

Wire mothers: Harry Harlow and the science of love. [by] Jim Ottaviani [and] Dylan Meconis. G. T. Labs 2007 84p. Illustration
Grades: 9 10 11 12 Adult
152.4; 741.5
1. Graphic novels; 2. Love — Graphic novels; 3. Psychologists; 4. Harlow, Harry F., 1905-1981
978-0-9788037-1-1, $12.95; 0-9788037-1-X
LC 2007-900136

In the 1950s, psychologists warned parents about the dangers of too much love; in fact, they denied love was anything more than a base instinct based on the need for food. When scientist Harry Harlow began his experiments on mother love, was more than just an outsider trying to make his name. He was also an unhappy man who knew in his gut the truth about what love, and its absence, meant, and he set about to prove it. His experiments on monkeys and their stark results shocked the world. The emotional intensity of his experiments might be overwhelming for younger readers.

"This nonfiction graphic novel retelling psychologist Harry Harlow's famous experiments is as disturbing as it is excellent." Publ Wkly
Includes bibliographical references; A General Tektronics Labs book

Pak, Greg

Marvel Nemesis: The Imperfects. writer, Greg Pak; artist, Renato Arlem; colorist, June Chung, Carlos Lopez & William Murai. Marvel Entertainment 2005 un Illustration
Grades: 8 9 10 11 12   **741.5; Fic**
1. Graphic novels; 2. Superhero graphic novels; 3. Wolverine (Fictional character); 4. Spider-Man (Fictional character)
978-0-7851-1778-0, $7.99

An evil scientist sets his cross-hairs on planet Earth, in search of test subjects for his experiments, transforming even the most timid creatures into vicious fighting machines. Thousands of years later, the Thing, Wolverine, Spider-Man, and Elektra all find themselves unwilling participants in the scientist's millennia-old trials...or perhaps not all of them are that unwilling. This book includes some violence and strong language.

X-Men: Phoenix: Endsong. Marvel Entertainment 2005 un Illustration
Grades: 9 10 11 12 Adult   **741.5; Fic**
  1. Graphic novels; 2. Superhero graphic novels; 3. X-Men (Fictional characters)
978-0-7851-1924-1, $14.99
  The mysterious and powerful Phoenix Force is life incarnate, and yet it consumes whole worlds in a moment. Its long history with the X-Men is fraught with tragedy... especially concerning one of the most beloved of their number, Jean Grey. What will happen when the Phoenix returns to Earth in search of the one mortal who could ever contain its power... only to find her dead?

Palmiotti, Jimmy
  Manhunter: Street Justice. Marc Andreyko, writer; Jesus Saiz, penciller; Jimmy Palmiotti, inker; Steve Buccellato, colorist; Phil Balsman, Jared K. Fletcher, Pat Brosseau, letterers. DC Comics 2005 un Illustration
Grades: 10 11 12 Adult   **741.5; Fic**
  1. Graphic novels; 2. Superhero graphic novels
1-4012-0728-6, $12.99
  When top federal prosecutor Kate Spencer loses a case against a super-villain, setting him free to kill again, she breaks the laws she has long upheld to become Los Angeles' newest crime fighting vigilante. Prosecuting super-villains has been her life's work But these criminals never stay locked up for good. Now, using confiscated met human weaponry she raided from an evidence locker, Kate tracks the perps who have eluded justice in the courts and delivers a long-overdue eye for an eye. She's found her true calling. She is the Manhunte. And she likes it. Plenty of violence, an anti-heroine who smokes and is willing to kill the criminals she hunts, make this superhero title one for older readers.
  Volume 1 of 6

  Uncle Sam and the Freedom Fighters. written by Justin Gray and Jimmy Palmiotti; art by Daniel Acuna. DC Comics 2007 208p. Illustration
Grades: 10 11 12 Adult   **741.5; Fic**
  1. Graphic novels; 2. Superhero graphic novels
978-1-4012-1336-7, $14.99
  Meet the all-new Phantom Lady, Doll Man, Human Bomb and the Ray — members of the government task force known as SHADE, the country's first line of defense against super-powered threats and terrorists in the wake of the Infinite Crisis. When the resurrected Uncle Sam makes them realize that Father Time has used them to further his own interests that will harm the United States, they work with Uncle Sam as the new Freedom Fighters. There is considerable violence in this superhero title.

Panetta, Kevin
  Zodiac Starforce: By the Power of Astra. script by Kevin Panetta; art, colors, lettering, and cover by Paulina Ganucheau; color flats by Savanna Ganucheau, Kristen Acampora, and Tabby Freeman; chapter break art by Marguerite Sauvage, Kevin Wada, Jacob Wyatt, Babs Tarr. Dark Horse Books 2016 136 p. Color; Illustration
Grades: 8 9 10 11 12 Adult   **741.5**
  1. Astrology — Fiction; 2. Friendship — Fiction; 3. Graphic novels; 4. Magic — Fiction; 5. Superheroes — Fiction
1616559136; 9781616559137, $12.99
                                                              LC 2015039851
  This book, by Kevin Panetta, illustrated by Paulina Ganucheau, focuses on "an elite group of teenage girls with magical powers who have sworn to protect our planet against dark creatures...as long as they can get

out of class! Known as the Zodiac Starforce, these high-school girls aren't just combating math tests. They're also battling monsters — not your typical afterschool activity!" (Publisher's note)

Papadatos, Alekos
  Democracy. concept, Alecos Papadatos; story, Alecos Papadatos & Abraham Kawa; script, Abraham Kawa; art direction & drawings, Alecos Papdatos; colouring, Annie Di Donna. Bloomsbury 2015 236 p. Color; Illustration
Grades: 11 12 Adult   **741.5**
  1. Athens (Greece) — Fiction; 2. War stories; 3. Democracy
1608197190; 9781608197194, $27
  This book by Alecos Papadatos, Abraham Kawa, and Annie Di Donna "opens in 490 B.C., with Athens at war. The hero of the story, Leander, is trying to rouse his comrades for the morrow's battle against a far mightier enemy, and begins to recount his own life, having borne direct witness to the evils of the old tyrannical regimes and to the emergence of a new political system. The tale that emerges is one of daring, danger, and big ideas, of the death of the gods and the tortuous birth of democracy." (Publisher's note)
  "Papadatos's lively and energetic art illuminates battles, alliances, political machinations, and vivid personalities, and Di Donna's intense coloring is gloriously rich without a touch of gaudiness. For those interested in further background, the extensive back matter features useful commentary on both legendary and historical figures and concepts." Pub Wkly

Papadimitriou, Christos H.
  ★ **Logicomix.** [written by] Apostolos Doxiadis, Christos H. Papadimitriou; art, Alecos Papadatos; color, Annie Di Donna. Bloomsbury 2009 347p. Illustration
Grades: 11 12 Adult   **741.5; Fic**
  1. Biographical graphic novels; 2. Comic books, strips, etc.; 3. Essayists; 4. Graphic novels; 5. Logicians; 6. Mathematicians; 7. Mathematics — Graphic novels; 8. Nobel laureates for literature; 9. Nonfiction writers; 10. Philosophers; 11. Philosophy — Graphic novels; 12. Russell, Bertrand, 1872-1970; 13. Russell, Bertrand, 1872-1970 — Fiction
0-7475-9720-0, $22.95; 978-0-7475-9720-9
  This is a "graphic novel based on the life of the philosopher and mathematician Bertrand Russell." (Publisher's note)

Parker, Jeff
  Meteor men. written by Jeff Parker; illustrated by Sandy Jarrell; colored by Kevin Volo; lettered by Crank!. Oni Press 2014 133 p. Color; Illustration
Grades: 8 9 10 11   **741.5; Fic**
  1. Human-alien encounters — Fiction; 2. Science fiction graphic novels; 3. Extraterrestrial beings — Graphic novels
1620101513; 9781620101513, $19.99
  Eisner Nominee: Best Publication for Teens (2015)
  "On a summer night, Alden Baylor sits in a field watching the largest meteor shower in human history. What begins as teenage adventure becomes something more — the celestial event brings travelers who will change the world completely, and Alden discovers a connection to one of them. How does a young man who had to grow up fast handle the invasion of his planet? Can Alden keep humanity from oblivion?" (Publisher's note)
  "Parker combines the familiar concept with gentle domesticity and deliberate humanism, thus circumventing cliché and providing an accessible perspective to the logical and realistic extensions of such an event." SLJ

Parks, Ande

Capote in Kansas. Oni Press 2005 121p. Illustration

Grades: 10 11 12

741.5; 92; Fic

1. Biographical graphic novels; 2. Graphic novels; 3. Capote, Truman

1-932664-29-7, $11.95

Courtesy of Oni Press

This book is Parks' fictional account of what Truman Capote might have done during his time in Kansas as he researched the story that became his bestselling book, In Cold Blood. As Capote begins to connect with Perry Smith, one of the killers, and with investigators and others, he also meets the ghost of teenage Nancy Mae Clutter, one of the victims. This book predated the movie Capote, starring Philip Seymour Hoffman, but it might appeal to the movie's fans. A few harsh words and Capote's open homosexuality should not deter most libraries from getting this book.

Union Station. Oni Press 2003 116p. Illustration

Grades: 11 12 Adult

364.1; 741.5

1. Crimes — United States — Graphic novels; 2. FBI — Graphic novels; 3. Graphic novels

1-929998-69-4, $11.95

Kansas City, 1933. Frank Nash is a petty criminal who has been pinched by the Feds and is being brought back into town by train. When FBI agent Reed Vetterli heads down to Union Station to meet Nash and his uniformed escort, he has no reason to suspect that there will be any action. Neither does Charles Thompson, a reporter sent down to the station just to see what the fuss is for. Little do they know that Frank's buddy, Vern Miller, is going to bust him out. Nash may not be a big time player, but he's still earned some loyalty. The resulting clash ends in a massacre, with no one knowing who pulled the trigger first — or even who pulled it at all. Rumor has it that Pretty Boy Floyd was on the scene, but no one knows for sure, and J. Edgar Hoover

Courtesy of Oni Press

doesn't particularly care. He just wants Floyd's butt in an electric chair, and when Vetterli, Miller, and Thompson find themselves in the way of Hoover's justice, they can't duck for cover fast enough. This graphic novel is based on a true incident. The book includes violence and strong language.

Pastrovicchio, Lorenzo

Wizards of Mickey, vol. 1: mouse magic. writer: Stefano Ambrosio; artists: Lorenzo Pastrovicchio ... [et al.]; translation: Saida Temafonte; editor, Aaron Sparrow; letterers Troy Peteri [and] Deron Bennett; designer Erika Terriquez. Boom! Studios 2010 un Illustration

Grades: 3 4 5 6 7 8 9

741.5; Fic

1. Adventure graphic novels; 2. Fantasy graphic novels; 3. Graphic novels; 4. Humorous graphic novels; 5. Mickey Mouse (Fictional character)

Courtesy of Oni Press

978-1-60886-541-3, $9.99

Wizard's apprentice Mickey loses a magic talisman called the Diamagic when he and the village fall afoul of a con man who steals it from them. Mickey pursues the con man, but he learns he'll have to compete in the Great Wizard's Tournament to win it back if he can father a team to work with him. He ends up with Donald and Goofy, both misfit bunglers, but somehow they'll have to compete against Peg-Leg Pete and the Phantom Blot. This book, originally written and published in Italy, is full of fantasy adventure and fun with recognizable Disney characters.

Volume 1 of 3

Pekar, Harvey, 1939-2010

Quitter. DC Comics/Vertigo 2005 un Illustration

Grades: 10 11 12 Adult

741.5; 92

1. Autobiographical graphic novels; 2. Graphic novels; 3. Monsters — Graphic novels; 4. Pekar, Harvey, 1939-2010

1-4012-0399-X, $19.95

Harvey Pekar is now a famed independent comics creator, whose series American Splendor was adapted into a hit motion picture. In this book, he recounts his childhood, teen years, and early adulthood and examines the experiences that shaped his life. He gives an unflinchingly honest portrait of a boy who used fighting to get a tough reputation, who needed to excel in sports and academics and would quit if he felt he couldn't achieve what he wanted. He allows the reader to see into his soul.

Students for a Democratic Society: a graphic history. written by Harvey Pekar; art by Gary Dumm; edited by Paul Buhle. Hill & Wang 2008 214p. Illustration

Grades: 10 11 12 Adult

378.1; 741.5

1. Students for a Democratic Society — Graphic novels — History; 2. College students — Political activity — Graphic novels; 3. Graphic novels

978-0-8090-8939-0 (pa), $16; 978-0-8090-9539-1, $22

LC 2007-40641

Students for a Democratic Society formed as an organization in 1960, but had its roots as a New Left group in the League for Industrial Democracy, founded in 1905 with members such as Jack London and Upton Sinclair. The members in 1960 included Al Haber and Tom Hayden, and one of their most famous documents is the Port Huron Statement of 1962. By the late 1960s, with opposition to the Vietnam War in full swing, a radical subgroup called the Weathermen became more violent. Graphic novelist Pekar is joined by members of the SDS in telling the story of the organization, which dissolved soon after its 1969 convention. The book includes some harsh language and violence.

"The book acts like a sophisticated handbook on an often misunderstood organization. It's good comics and excellent history." Publ Wkly

Percy, Benjamin

Green Arrow; Volume 1: the death & life of Oliver Queen. Benjamin Percy, writer; Otto Schmidt, Juan Ferreyra, artists & colorists; Nate Piekos of Blambot, letterer; Juan Ferreyra, series & collection cover artist. DC Comics 2017 160 p. Color; Illustration

Grades: 11 12 Adult

741.5

1. Superheroes comic books, strips, etc.; 2. Green Arrow (Fictional character)

1401267815; 9781401267810, $16.99

LC 2016039348

"Oliver Queen, playboy socialite, CEO of Queen Industries and philanthropic do-gooder...patrols the streets of Seattle, where he champions the oppressed as a true social justice warrior. He is Green Arrow. But how can you fight the man when you are the man? That's the question left with Oliver after an electric, love-at-first-sight encounter with Black Canary, the superhero rock star." (Publisher's note)

Originally published in single magazine form in GREEN ARROW: REBIRTH 1, GREEN ARROW 1-5; Volume 1 of an ongoing series

Pérez, Ramón

Jim Henson's tale of sand. written by Jim Henson and Jerry Juhl; as realized by Ramón K. Pérez; colors by Ian Herring with Ramón K. Pérez; lettering and font design by Deron Bennett based on the handwriting of Jim Henson; edited by Stephen Christy.. Archaia Entertainment 2012 152 p.

Grades: 10 11 12 Adult   **741.5**

1. Fantasy graphic novels; 2. Adventure graphic novels; 3. Deserts — Graphic novels; 4. Southwestern States — Graphic novels

1936393093; 9781936393091

This graphic novel "follows its hapless protagonist as he is cast out into the desert by the cheerful Sheriff Tate.... The scruffy hero is a pawn in a game whose rules are concealed from him, pursued across a surrealistic southwest U.S. by an implacable hunter and hindered by the eccentric, bizarre inhabitants of the great desolation. The prize waiting for him at the end of the chase, should he survive to reach the end, is one he will never guess at." (Publishers Weekly)

Petrucha, Stefan

Nancy Drew, Girl Detective #1: The Demon of River Heights. NBM/Papercutz 2005 un Illustration

Grades: 4 5 6 7 8 9   **741.5; Fic**

1. Adventure graphic novels; 2. Graphic novels; 3. Mystery graphic novels

1-59707-004-1, $12.95; 1-59707-000-9, $7.95

Everyone's favorite girl detective makes her graphic novel debut. Nancy also makes her debut in a horror film concerning a monstrous River Heights urban legend " but is it really an urban legend, or does the River Heights Demon truly exist? And will Nancy, Bess, and George live long enough to find out? This graphic novel series updates Nancy and her friends to the twenty-first century, but she's still a klutz.

Petty, J. T. (John T.)

The Fall of the House of West. by Paul Pope and J. T. Petty; illustrated by David Rubín. First Second 2015 160 p. Illustration (Battling Boy)

Grades: 7 8 9 10 11 12   **741.5; Fic**

1. Gods — Comic books, strips, etc.; 2. Monsters — Comic books, strips, etc.; 3. Graphic novels; 4. Mothers — Fiction; 5. Father-daughter relationship — Fiction; 6. Secrets — Fiction

162672010X; 9781626720107, $9.99

In this graphic novel, by Paul Pope and J. T. Petty, illustrated by David Rubín, "Aurora West is on the verge of solving the mystery of her mother's death, but it's hard keeping her efforts a secret from her grieving father, the legendary monster-hunter Haggard West. Between her school work and her hours training and hunting with her dad, Aurora is hard-pressed to find time to be a secret sleuth. But she's nothing if not persistent." (Publisher's note)

Courtesy of NBM Publishing

"Rubín's frenetic black-and-white illustrations stylistically complement Pope and Petty's breakneck-paced plotting. True to the genre, the story explores notions of good and evil but provides no easy answers." Kirkus

The **Rise** of Aurora West. by Paul Pope, J. T. Petty, illustrated by David Rubín. First Second Books 2014 160 p. Illustration (Battling Boy)

Grades: 7 8 9 10 11 12   **741.5**

1. Adventure graphic novels; 2. Female superhero graphic novels

1626722684; 9781626722682, $17.99

In this graphic novel, by Paul Pope and J. T. Petty, illustrated by David Rubín, the "world introduced in...'Battling Boy' is rife with monsters and short on heroes.... But in this action-driven extension of the Battling Boy universe, we see it through a new pair of eyes: Aurora West, daughter of Arcopolis's last great hero, Haggard West." (Publisher's note)

"Since Aurora and her father were only briefly mentioned in the previous installment, this volume does a wonderful job of fleshing out their characters further; readers see an Aurora that's not as confident in her abilities, and a slightly jaded and darker side to her heroic father. Pope's gritty, experimental art from the original Battling Boy has been replaced by Rubín's more traditional style, giving a '60s 'Silver Age' appearance to the work." SLJ

Peyo

The Smurfs anthology; Vol. 1. Peyo. Papercutz 2013 190 p. Color illustration (The Smurfs graphic novels)

Grades: 4 5 6 7 8 9 10 11 12 Adult   **741.5**

1. Comic books, strips, etc.

1597074179; 9781597074179, $19.99

"Newly remastered and presented in original publication order, along with a Smurfy collection of historical notes and photographs, the stories in this volume," by Belgian comics artist Peyo, "introduce us to Papa Smurf, Gargamel, Smurfette, and the rest of the village." (Publisher's note)

The Smurfs anthology; Vol. 2. Peyo. Papercutz 2013 192 p. Color illustration

Grades: 4 5 6 7 8 9 10 11 12 Adult   **741.5**

1. Comic books, strips, etc.

1597074454; 9781597074452, $19.99

"Newly remastered and presented in original publication order, along with a Smurfy collection of historical notes and photographs, this volume," by Belgian comics artist Peyo, "introduces us to Smurfette and features a 'Johan and Peewit' story never before seen in the U.S." (Publisher's note)

"[A] delightful and instructive mix of Peyo's colorful tales. A series of essays interspersed throughout the collection provides social and historical context for the cartoons." Booklist

Translated from the French

Courtesy of NBM Publishing

Phelan, Matt

★ **The** storm in the barn. Candlewick Press 2009 201p. Illustration

Grades: 4 5 6 7 8 9

741.5; Fic

1. Adventure graphic novels; 2. Dust storms — Graphic novels; 3. Graphic novels; 4. Kansas — Graphic novels; 5. Monsters — Graphic novels; 6. United States — History — 1933-1945 — Graphic novels

978-0-7636-3618-0, $24.99; 0-7636-3618-5; 978-0-7636-5290-6 (pa), $14.99; 0-7636-5290-3 (pa)

In Kansas of 1937, the land has been in the grip of the Dust Bowl for four years, and eleven-year-old Jack Carter has seen his family worn down by it. But the day Jack outruns a dust storm all the way home from town, he glimpses something odd in the abandoned Talbot barn, and he tries to find the courage to go into the barn and confront what is there.

"Children can read this as a work of historical fiction, a piece of folklore, a scary story, a graphic novel, or all four. Written with simple, direct language, it's an almost wordless book: the illustrations" shadowy grays and blurry lines eloquently depict the haze of the dust. A complex but accessible and fascinating book." SLJ

Pini, Wendy

ElfQuest Archives Vol. 1. DC Comics 2003 216p. Illustration
Grades: 9 10 11 12 Adult

741.5; Fic

1. Adventure graphic novels; 2. Elves — Graphic novels; 3. Fantasy graphic novels; 4. Graphic novels
1-4012-0128-8, $49.99

Existing on a prehistoric world, the World of Two Moons, in which humans and elves are bitter enemies, the Wolfriders live a dangerous life of fatal battles, deadly hunts, and tribal traditions. Proud of their history but unaware of their origin, the Wolfriders are on an eternal quest to learn the mysteries of their past. This hardcover edition includes the Wolfriders' fateful battle with a band of humans, their surprising discovery of another clan of elves, and Cutter's first meeting with the enchanting healer, Leetah. The Pinis started publishing the ElfQuest stories as black and white comics in the mid-1970s; this is a full-color deluxe hardcover edition of the first five issues. The book includes partial nudity, brief sexual situations, and violence.

ElfQuest Archives Vol. 3. DC Comics 2005 224p. Illustration
Grades: 9 10 11 12 Adult

741.5; Fic

1. Adventure graphic novels; 2. Elves — Graphic novels; 3. Fantasy graphic novels; 4. Graphic novels
1-4012-0412-0, $49.99

This third volume collects ElfQuest #11-15. When Leetah and some of the others try to catch up to Cutter to warn him of danger, they are taken as slaves into the towering and mysterious Blue Mountain, stronghold of the ancient elves called the Gliders. There Cutter and the Wolfriders must face the evil Winnowill, who wields strong magic, to save family and friends. The book includes violence, partial nudity, and sexual situations.

ElfQuest; Volume 1: the final quest. by Wendy and Richard Pini; colors by Sonny Strait; letters by Nate Piekos of Blambot. Dark Horse Books 2015 192 p. Illustration
Grades: 9 10 11 12 Adult

741.5

1. Elves — Comic books, strips, etc; 2. Fantasy graphic novels; 3. Elves — Fiction
1616554096; 9781616554095, $17.99

LC 2014046866

In this book, by by Wendy and Richard Pini, "the elves sought a safe haven against all who would do them harm. But the dream that Chief Cutter and his Wolfriders fought and died for, the Palace of the High Ones, may be the very thing destroying them. The skills that helped them survive the harsh world are fading, and there is a growing threat from a tyrant obsessed with exterminating all elves — creating a disastrous brew that must surely boil over." (Publisher's note)

Courtesy of NBM Publishing

THE STORM IN THE BARN.
Copyright © 2009 by Matt Phelan.
Reproduced by permission of the publisher, Candlewick Press, Somerville, MA.

"For more than 30 years, the Pinis' ElfQuest saga has satisfied readers with tales of the glamorous but fierce elves who share an alien planet with nonmagical, often hostile humans. New readers may feel baffled at this point, but they can catch on soon." Pub Wkly

ElfQuest Archives Vol. 2. DC Comics 2005 226p. Illustration
Grades: 9 10 11 12 Adult

741.5; Fic

1. Adventure graphic novels; 2. Elves — Graphic novels; 3. Fantasy graphic novels; 4. Graphic novels
1-4012-0129-6, $49.99

The Wolfriders have found sanctuary, and Cutter and Leetah become lifemates. But their peace is threatened once more by men, and the trolls, and by the twin mysteries of the Forbidden Grove and Blue Mountain. The book includes some violence and brief partial nudity.

ElfQuest; Volume 2: the final quest. by Wendy and Richard Pini; colors by Sonny Strait; letters by Nate Piekos of Blambot. Dark Horse Books 2016 136 p. Color; Illustration
Grades: 9 10 11 12 Adult

741.5; Fic

1. Elves — Comic books, strips, etc; 2. Fantasy graphic novels; 3. Elves — Fiction
161655410X; 9781616554101, $17.99

LC 2015045160

In this book, by Wendy and Richard Pini, "Sunstream, son of Wolfrider chief Cutter Kinseeker, finally fulfills his destiny and becomes the psychic link among all the elfin tribes scattered across the World of Two Moons.... But a devastating secret, long hidden in plain sight, is also moving into the light. When the full impact of this revelation becomes known, it will affect the entire elfin race forever." (Publisher's note)

This volume collects and reprints the comic books ElfQuest: The Final Quest #7-#12.

Piskor, Ed

Wizzywig. Ed Piskor. Top Shelf Productions 2012 288 p. Illustration
Grades: 11 12 Adult

741.5

1. Telephones — Fiction; 2. Computer hackers — Fiction
1603090975; 9781603090971, $19.95

This graphic novel, "inspired by tales of real-life hackers...follows the story of Kevin 'Boingthump' Phenicle, who gets his start tapping into telephone lines as a teenager and works his way up to infiltrating the phone company and its database. At his side is his best (and indeed only) friend, Winston, who goes from helping Kevin with his hacking to defending him on the radio when Kevin is eventually caught and incarcerated." (Publishers Weekly)

"With heavy technology content and social-issue relevance, plus hacker and comics industry in-jokes, this is a techie's dream read, enhanced by Piskor's thorough research and judiciously unpretty black-and-white art." LJ

X-men; 1: grand design. Ed Piskor. Marvel Enterprises 2018 120 p. Color; Illustration
Grades: 10 11 12 Adult

741.5; Fic

1. X-Men (Fictional characters); 2. Comic books, strips, etc.; 3. Superheroes
1302904892; 9781302904890, $29.99

In this book, author Ed Piskor, "takes you on a pulse-pounding tour of X-Men history unlike anything you've ever experienced before, an intricate labor of love that stitches together hundreds of classic and obscure stories into one seamless masterpiece of X-Men lore. This volume collects

Courtesy of IDW Publishing

X-MEN: GRAND DESIGN and includes X-MEN #1 from 1963, masterfully recolored by Ed, along with other extras including recolored classic pinups." (Publisher's note)

"Much as Piskor masterfully took on the scope of rap music in his acclaimed Hip Hop Family Tree series, he synthesizes hundreds of (sometimes contradictory) tales and specific details generated by their hundreds of past creators, faithfully integrating it all into one entertaining story line." Pub Wkly

Poe, Marshall
   Turning Points: Little Rock nine. Simon & Schuster/Aladdin Paperbacks 2008 122p. Illustration
Grades: 3 4 5 6 7 8 9   **741.5; Fic**
   1. African Americans — Civil rights — Graphic novels; 2. African Americans — Education — Graphic novels; 3. Graphic novels; 4. United States — History — 1953-1961 — Graphic novels
978-1-4169-5066-0, $7.99
                                                      LC 2007-937918
   Sixteen-year-old William McNally and fifteen-year-old Thomas Johnson both live in Little Rock, Arkansas, in the summer of 1957. They both love baseball and teasing their little sisters. There's just one big difference: William is white, and Thomas, the son of the McNally family's maid, is black. After the U.S. Supreme Court rules in favor of desegregating public schools, Little Rock Central High School prepares to enroll its first nine African-American students, and William and Thomas are caught in the middle of a storm. William's family has divided over the issue, and Thomas' parents don't want him to get hurt and forbid him to try to enter the school. The book portrays the issues of the time and the personal beliefs of both sides to let readers see what it was like back then. William, Thomas, and their families are fictional, but what happened at Little Rock Central High School is an important part of American history.

Pomplun, Tom
   Graphic Classics volume eleven: O. Henry. edited by Tom Pomplun. Eureka Productions 2005 144p. Illustration
Grades: 7 8 9 10 11 12 Adult   **741.5; Fic**
   1. Authors; 2. Graphic novels; 3. Short stories — Graphic novels; 4. Short story writers; 5. Henry, O., 1862-1910; 6. Henry, O., 1862-1910 — Adaptations
978-0-9746648-2-0, $11.95
   This volume of Graphics Classics adapts some of the short stories by O. Henry, the master of the surprise ending. Stories include "The Ransom of Red Chief," illustrated by Johnny Ryan, "The Gift of the Magi," illustrated by Lisa Weber, "The Caballero's Way" (the original story of the Cisco Kid), illustrated by Mark A. Nelson, and more.

   Graphic Classics volume eight: Mark Twain. edited by Tom Pomplun. Eureka Productions 2007 144p. Illustration
Grades: 9 10 11 12 Adult   **741.5; 818**
   1. Adventure graphic novels; 2. Authors; 3. Essayists; 4. Graphic novels; 5. Humorists; 6. Humorous graphic novels; 7. Memoirists; 8. Novelists; 9. Satirists; 10. Short stories — Graphic novels; 11. Short story writers; 12. Travel writers; 13. Twain, Mark, 1835-1910 — Adaptations
978-0-9787919-2-6, $11.95
   This book includes an adaptation of "Tom Sawyer Abroad" by Tom Pomplun and George Sellas, "The Mysterious Stranger" by Rick Geary, "A Dog's Tale" by Lance Tooks, "The Celebrated Jumping Frog of Calaveras County" by Kevin Atkinson, and "The Carnival of Crime in Connecticut" by Antonella Caputo and Nick Miller. Also in this volume are "Is He Living or Is He Dead?," "A Curious Pleasure Excursion," and eight women artists interpret Mark Twain's "Advice to Little Girls."

   "With a terrific lineup of artists and unbeatable material, Pomplun has assembled a collection of Mark Twain's work that should delight graphic

novel fans and anyone seeking to boost their general cultural knowledge." Publ Wkly [review of 2004 edition]
   First published 2004

   ★ **Graphic** Classics volume fourteen: Gothic classics. edited by Tom Pomplun. Eureka Productions 2007 144p. Illustration
Grades: 7 8 9 10 11 12 Adult   **741.5; Fic**
   1. Graphic novels; 2. Horror graphic novels; 3. Short stories — Graphic novels
978-0-9787919-0-2, $11.95
   This volume includes graphic adaptations of classic novels Carmilla by Joseph Sheridan Le Fanu, The Mysteries of Udolpho by Ann Radcliffe, and Northanger Abbey by Jane Austen, along with shorter works "The Oval Portrait" by Edgar Allan Poe, "At the Gate" by Myla Jo Closser, and "I've a Pain in My Head" by Jane Austen. Radcliffe's novel is one mentioned by Austen in Northanger Abbey and is a famous gothic novel from the late eighteenth century, considered to be the world's first best-seller. Le Fanu's vampire novel was published twenty-five years before Stoker's Dracula. Austen wrote Northanger Abbey as a satire of the popular gothic genre.

   Graphic Classics Volume Twelve: Adventure Classics. Eureka Productions 2005 144p. Illustration
Grades: 8 9 10 11 12   **741.5; 808.3**
   1. Adventure graphic novels; 2. Graphic novels; 3. Short stories — Graphic novels
978-0-9746648-4-7, $11.95
   This volume of the Graphic Classics series includes a selection of poems and short stories that more or less fit the adventure genre. Rudyard Kipling's poem "Gunga Din" is here, as is Robert Service's "The Shooting of Dan McGrew." Short stories include "In the Valley of the Sorceress" by Sax Rohmer, "Tigre" by Zane Grey, "Blood Money" (a Captain Blood story) by Rafael Sabatini, "The Crime of the Brigadier" (a Brigadier Gerard adventure) by Sir Arthur Conan Doyle, "The Roads We Take" by O. Henry, and more. "The Mystery of the Semi-Detached" by Edith Nesbit may surprise readers who only know her as a children's fantasy author.

Pope, Paul
   Batman: Year 100. DC Comics 2007 232p. Illustration
Grades: 10 11 12 Adult   **741.5; Fic**
   1. Batman (Fictional character); 2. Graphic novels; 3. Science fiction graphic novels; 4. Superhero graphic novels
978-1-4012-1192-9, $19.99
   This is a futuristic mystery of epic proportions set in a dark, dystopian world devoid of privacy and filled with government conspiracies, psychic police, holographic caller ID and absolutely no room for "secret identities." In Gotham City, 2039, a federal agent is murdered and a contingent of Washington's top agents is hot on the suspect's trail. The Batman, a forgotten icon from the past, is wanted for the murder. Amid the chaos Gotham City Police Detective Gordon, grandson of the former commissioner, discovers that the man they are chasing shouldn't exist at all. The book has some bloody violence and some strong language.

   ★ **Battling** Boy. Paul Pope; colors by Hilary Sycamore. First Second 2013 208 p. Illustration
Grades: 7 8 9 10 11 12   **741.5; Fic**
   1. Superhero graphic novels; 2. Fantasy graphic novels
1596438053; 9781596431454, $15.99; 9781596438057, $24.99
                                                      LC 2013030815
Eisner Award: Best Publication for Teens (2014)
   In this book, "the hero Haggard West helps battle the evil forces of Sadisto and his hooded ghouls. However, in a shocking turn of events, evil triumphs over good, and the metropolis is left without protection. In a world far, far away, a 13-year-old son of a god has been chosen to help

Earth fight the onslaught of monsters as a rite of passage. Sent with only a few possessions, including an array of magical T-shirts, Battling Boy helps the city-but he finds he cannot do it alone." (Kirkus Reviews)

"This is a sophisticated tale for younger readers, but Pope manages to both grant full-scale wish fulfillment and acknowledge the limitations of young boys with equal aplomb. His art, meanwhile, looks like nothing else in comics, with ropy, sinewy figures, dynamic action, and gritty urban design all captured in panels that have the rough, subversive tone of classic punk album covers." Booklist

Porcellino, John

King-Cat Classics. Drawn & Quarterly 2007 384p. Illustration
Grades: 10 11 12 Adult   741.5
1. Autobiographical graphic novels; 2. Graphic novels
978-1-894937-91-7, $29.95

This large collection focuses on the first fifty issues of Porcellino's autobiographical comics, with extensive endnotes and an index, along with selections of all the extra ephemera that makes an individual issue of King-Cat a unique experience-essays, articles, stories, and letters from friends. Included are more than two hundred and fifty pages of comics, ranging from Porcellino's earliest scrawls to his later, minimalist delineations. The comics range through all of his concerns-family, family pets, the natural world, work, music, romance. He uses some strong language and some sexual situations.

Thoreau at Walden. by John Porcellino, from the writings of Henry David Thoreau; introduction by D.B. Johnson. Hyperion 2008 viii, 99 p. Illustration; Map (Center for Cartoon Studies presents)
Grades: 8 9 10 11 12 Adult   818/.303; 741.5
1. Graphic novels; 2. Thoreau, Henry David, 1817-1862; 3. Walden Woods (Mass.) — Social life and customs — Comic books, strips, etc; 4. American authors
1423100387; 1423100395; 9781423100386, $16.99; 9781423100393
LC 2007061358

This graphic novel, by John Porcellino, "introduces ...Henry David Thoreau.... Thoreau's writings, excerpted out of chronological order, are recast into a narrative that moves from the philosopher's self-ostracism from society and his time at Walden and into the feeling of calm reverie he took from his experiences." (Booklist)

"Presents in graphic novel format an account of the two years that Thoreau spent at Walden Pond, excerpted from Thoreau's writings." Publisher's note

Includes bibliographical references (p. 99)

Powell, Eric

Billy the Kid's Old Timey Oddities. Dark Horse Comics 2006 un Illustration
Grades: 10 11 12 Adult   741.5; Fic
1. Graphic novels; 2. Horror graphic novels; 3. Monsters — Graphic novels
1-59307-448-4, $13.95

Notorious outlaw and gunslinger William Henry McCarty — known as Billy the Kid — faked his death and is alive and well when Fineas Sproule, the four-armed owner of a sideshow called Sproule's Biological Curiosities, identifies him and then makes an offer the Kid can't refuse. They seek a mystical gem called the Golem's Heart, and they must travel from the U.S. to Europe, to an isolated castle that is home to Victor Frankenstein. They need Billy's prowess with guns to protect them on their journey. When they arrive in the village near the castle, however, everyone is captured by the mad scientist, who plans to conduct horrible and nasty experiments on everyone. Billy has thought of his companions as freaks,

but they're nothing like the pitiable monsters created by Frankenstein. This will appeal to horror movie fans who love monsters.

Originally published as Billy the Kid's Old Timey Oddities issues #1-4.

The **Goon** Vol. 1: Nothin' But Misery. Dark Horse Comics 2003 un Illustration
Grades: 9 10 11 12 Adult   741.5; Fic
1. Graphic novels; 2. Horror graphic novels; 3. Humorous graphic novels
1-56971-998-5, $15.95

Bones will be broken and heads will roll! An insane priest is building himself an army of the undead and filling the town with zombies, and there's only one man who can put them in their place: the man they call Goon. This volume collects The Goon series and The Goon Color Special, originally published by Albatross Exploding Funny Books, presented here for the first time in full color. Readers meet Goon, his pal Frankie, and lots of weird monsters in a story that mixes crime noir, horror, and slapstick comedy. The monsters and zombies look like they just came out of an old EC horror comic; they look icky but funny at the same time.

Powell, Nate

★ **Swallow** me whole. Top Shelf Productions 2008 un Illustration
Grades: 10 11 12 Adult   741.5; Fic
1. Graphic novels; 2. Mental illness — Graphic novels
978-1-60309-033-9, $20.95

Stepsiblings Ruth and Perry share their secrets with each other; Ruth hears insects talking to her, and Perry has to deal with a tiny wizard who forces him to draw all the time. In high school, Ruth is diagnosed as an obsessive compulsive with schizophrenic tendencies, while Perry manages to hide his wizard. Ruth sees cicadas and other insects always surrounding her, to the point that she thinks she's completely covered with them and she can fly. Her Memaw (grandmother) warns her that what she sees can swallow her whole. This book includes considerable use of foul language, especially the f-bomb, and the story takes a very thoughtful, mature reader to comprehend what is happening.

Priddy, Joel

The **gift** of the Magi. It Books/HarperCollins 2009 un Illustration
Grades: 5 6 7 8 9 10 11 12 Adult
741.5; Fic
1. Authors; 2. Christmas — Graphic novels; 3. Gifts — Graphic novels; 4. Graphic novels; 5. Short story writers; 6. Henry, O., 1862-1910 — Adaptations
978-0-06-178239-8, $14.99

Della and Jim are a young married couple, struggling to make ends meet when Jim's pay has been cut. It's Christmas time, but despite squeezing every penny, Della has managed to save only a little bit of money, and it's not enough to buy Jim a good present. He owns a gold pocket watch, and Della

Courtesy of IDW Publishing

wants to buy him a chain for it. She has only one thing of value that she can sell her beautiful, long, long hair. Out of her love for Jim, Della sacrifices her hair. And, of course, Jim has sacrificed his gold pocket watch in order to buy beautiful hair combs for Della's gorgeous hair. As O. Henry says, they "most unwisely sacrificed for each other the greatest treasures of their house," but also that "of all who give gifts these two were the wisest." Joel Priddy's adaptation of this classic story uses black and white illustrations except when Della lets down her hair to consider her one treasure. He preserves much of O. Henry's original prose, which means that younger readers will have to look up a lot of words to understand the story. This book is suitable for younger readers but will also appeal to teens and adults.

Prince, Liz

★ **Tomboy:** A Graphic Memoir. by Liz Prince. Zest Books 2014 256 p. Illustration

Grades: 7 8 9 10 11 12 Adult

1. Cartoonists — Caricatures and cartoons; 2. Cartoonists — United States — Biography; 3. Gender identity; 4. Graphic novels; 5. Sex role; 6. Prince, Liz; 7. Sex differences (Psychology); 8. Gender role; 9. Stereotype (Social psychology)

9781936976553, $15.99; 1936976552

This memoir, by Liz Prince, "is a graphic novel about refusing gender boundaries, yet unwittingly embracing gender stereotypes at the same time, and realizing later in life that you can be just as much of a girl in jeans and a T-shirt as you can in a pink tutu." (Publisher's note)

"Prince's honest voice and self-deprecating humor help make young Liz a sympathetic and relatable character. The simply rendered black-and-white panel drawings have an unpretentious quality, in keeping with the narrative tone." Horn Book

Pullman, Philip

The **adventures** of John Blake: mystery of the ghost ship. by Philip Pullman; illustrated by Fred Fordham. Graphix 2017 160 p. Color; Illustration

Grades: 8 9 10 11 12   Fic; 741.5/973; 741.5

1. Time travel — Graphic novels; 2. Science fiction

1338149121; 9781338149128, $19.99

In this book, by Philip Pullman, illustrated by Fred Fordham, "trapped in the mists of time by a terrible research experiment gone wrong, John Blake and his mysterious ship are doomed to sail between the centuries, searching for a way home. In the ocean of the modern day, John rescues a shipwrecked young girl his own age, Serena, and promises to help. But returning Serena to her own time means traveling to the one place where the ship is in most danger of destruction." (Publisher's note)

"With obvious affection for Tintin, Pullman threads this complicated skein of plot with customary measures of awe and menace...on his first expedition into the graphic novel format, he proves an expert visual storyteller." Booklist.

Quinn, Jason

Gandhi: My life is my message. by Jason Quinn; illustrated by Naresh Kumar. Random House Inc 2014 212 p. Color; Illustration

Grades: 8 9 10 11 12 Adult   741.5; 92

1. Gandhi, Mahatma, 1869-1948

9380741227; 9789380741222, $16.99

This book by Jason Quinn, illustrated by Naresh Kumar, focuses on the life of "Mohandas Karamchand Gandhi, better known as the Mahatma or Great Soul.... We discover the man behind the legend, following him from his birth in the Indian coastal town of Porbandar in 1869, to the moment of his tragic death at the hands of an assassin in January 1948, just months after the Independence of India." (Publisher's note)

"Just as the writing eloquently intertwines explication with reenactments of dramatic, poignant events, the panels are meticulously arranged to move the reader's attention from broad and busy scenes to intimate close-ups." Booklist

Steve Jobs: genius by design. by Jason Quinn; illustrated by Amit Tayal. Random House Inc 2012 104 p. Illustration; Color

Grades: 7 8 9 10 11 12 Adult   741.5; 92

1. Apple Inc. — Officials & employees; 2. Jobs, Steve, 1955-2011; 3. Computer industry; 4. Biographical graphic novels

9380028768; 9789380028767, $12.99

This graphic novel, by Jason Quinn, illustrated by Amit Tayal, presents a biography of the 20th-century technology entrepreneur and Apple Inc. founder Steve Jobs. "Steve Jobs and his inventions changed the world we live in." The book ranges "from his birth and his adoption, through the advent of the computer age and on into the digital age. Forced out of the company he created, his indomitable vision allowed him to change the world of computers, movies, music and telecommunications." (Publisher's note)

"This cleverly designed volume provides a concise but well-balanced view of Steve Jobs the wunderkind, including his difficult personality and complex genius." Booklist

Rabagliati, Michel

Paul Has a Summer Job. Drawn & Quarterly 2003 un Illustration

Grades: 10 11 12 Adult   741.5; Fic

1. Graphic novels

1-896597-54-8, $16.95

Paul is outraged that he is forced to stop his high school art training, but he's been asked to put art aside because his other grades are so terribly low. Defiant, he quits school and anticipates a summer of leisure. But instead Paul follows the path of so many Quebecois teenagers: he lands a job as a counselor at one of the many summer camps in the mountains outside the city. There he finds himself guiding a motley band of kids, misfits and troublemakers, much like himself. The book includes some nudity, sexual situations, and strong language.

Raicht, Mike

★ The **Stuff** of Legend; Omnibus one. by Mike Raicht and Brian Smith; illustrated by Charles Paul Wilson III. Th3rd World Studios 2014 284 p. Color illustration (The Stuff of Legend)

Grades: 8 9 10 11 12 Adult   741.5

1. Kidnapping; 2. Rescues; 3. Toys; 4. Graphic novels; 5. Toys — Fiction

9780983216193; 0989574482; 9780989574488, $29.99

"This hardcover collection brings together the first two volumes.... As Allied forces fight the enemy on Europe's war-torn beaches, another battle begins in a child's bedroom in Brooklyn when the nightmarish Boogeyman snatches a boy and takes him to the realm of the Dark. The child's playthings, led by the toy soldier known as the Colonel, band together to stage a daring rescue. On their perilous mission they will confront the boy's bitter and forgotten toys, as well as betrayal in their own ranks." (Publisher's note)

"Wilson renders the harrowing closet netherworld with full-fleshed detailing and sepia tones that nail both the 1940s time frame and the classicism of children's stories. But don't mistake this for a kids' comic-the violence is often explicit, and the Boogeyman creepy enough to slither his way right back onto grownups' most-terrifying lists." Booklist

★ The **stuff** of legend; Omnibus two. by Mike Raicht and Brian Smith; illustrated by Charles Paul Wilson III. Th3rd World Studios 2014 270 p. Color illustration (The Stuff of Legend)

Grades: 8 9 10 11 12 Adult   741.5

1. Horror comic books, strips, etc.; 2. Kidnapping; 3. Toys; 4. Toys — Fiction; 5. Graphic novels

0989574490; 9780989574495, $34.99

The second omnibus edition "finds our toys at a crossroads. Unable to find their boy, our loyal toys' bonds have been tested and broken. Now scattered across The Dark, the toys must decide whether to continue their search or admit defeat and return home." (Publisher's note)

Rall, Ted

2024. NBM/ComicsLit 2001 96p. Illustration

Grades: 10 11 12 Adult   741.5; Fic

1. Graphic novels; 2. Satire — Graphic novels; 3. Science fiction graphic novels

1-56163-279-1, $16.95

Move forward two decades. The giant media moguls and software companies have become the new big brothers. They want the best for everyone. They know what's best for everyone. And society has chosen to be consumer heaven with no questions asked. A terrifying future where the past doesn't matter and no one cares. The motto to live by: "yes, no, whatever." Ted Rall updates and spoofs 1984 in a look at where the U.S. could be headed. Rall uses harsh language and some sexual situations.

Reed, Gary
Renfield: A Tale of Madness. Image Comics 2006 192p. Illustration
Grades: 9 10 11 12 Adult   **741.5; Fic**
1. Graphic novels; 2. Horror graphic novels; 3. Vampires — Graphic novels

978-1-58240-674-9, $19.99

This book delves into the story of the bug-eating asylum inmate Renfield, from Bram Stoker's Dracula. Renfield foretold the coming of the vampire to England. Possessed by almost demonic forces and impassioned with the zeal of a religious fanatic, Renfield must struggle to grasp the overwhelming need to serve the darkness against his own humanity. There is some violence in this story that retells part of the story of Dracula, and particularly of Mina Harker, from Renfield's viewpoint.

Courtesy of NBM Publishing

Regnaud, Jean
★ **My** mommy is in America and she met Buffalo Bill. Jean Regnaud & Émile Bravo; [translation, Vanessa Champion and Elizabeth Tierman]. Fanfare/Ponent Mon 2009 120p. Illustration
Grades: 6 7 8 9 10 11 12 Adult   **741.5; Fic**
1. Family life — Graphic novels; 2. Graphic novels; 3. Mother — Graphic novels; 4. School life — Graphic novels

978-84-96427-85-3, $25

Essentials Award winner at the 35th Festival of Angouleme,n France, 2008; Tam Tam Literary Award 2009 from Salon du Livres et de la Presse Jeunesse, for Comic Album, age group eight to thirteen years old.

Narrator Jean has just started first grade and has a younger brother, Paul, in kindergarten. They live with their factory boss father and nanny Yvette; Jean says his mother is on a trip. As he talks about his first day at school, meeting a new friend, Alain, and fighting with Paul, he mentions his mother has been away so long he can't quite remember her. Next door neighbor Michelle claims to be receiving postcards from Jean's mother and reads them to him; they come from places such as Switzerland and the United States. As the reader sees Jean and Paul spend a day with their mother's parents and interact with their grandparents' friends, the reader understands what Jean does not: his mother is dead. This book, translated from its original French, won an award for best comic album for ages eight to thirteen; however, with the essential fact never stated and Jean deciding that he's getting to old to believe in his mother, just as he's too old to believe in Father Christmas, makes this more suitable for the upper age range, teens, and adults.

Remender, Rick
Deadly Class; Volume 1: Reagan Youth. Rick Remender, writer, co-creator; Wes Craig, artist, co-creator; Lee Loughridge, colorist; Rus

Wooton, letterer; Sebastian Girner, editor. Image Comics 2014 160 p. Color; Illustration
Grades: 11 12 Adult   **741.5; Fic**
1. Assassins — Fiction; 2. School stories — Graphic novels

1632150034; 9781632150035, $9.99

"It's 1987. Marcus Lopez hates school.... The jocks are hassling his friends. He can't focus in class. But...the teachers are members of an ancient league of assassins, the class he's failing is 'Dismemberment 101,' and his crush has a double-digit body count. Welcome to the most brutal high school on earth." (Publisher's note)

Originally published in single magazine form as Deadly class #1-6; Volume 1 of an ongoing series

Fear Agent Volume One: Re-Ignition. story, Rick Remender; pencils, Tony Moore. Dark Horse Comics 2007 un Illustration
Grades: 9 10 11 12 Adult   **741.5; Fic**
1. Adventure graphic novels; 2. Graphic novels; 3. Science fiction graphic novels

978-1-59307-764-8, $13.95

Heath Huston, an alien exterminator, stumbles upon a plot by a race called the Dressites to send feeders to Earth. The feeders are a life-form that consumes all organic matter until a planet is destroyed. When Huston and the human scientist, Mara, try to go in Huston's AI ship to Earth, they discover that the ship has taken on a type of hyper-fuel it can't handle, and they crashland on a planet in its distant past, whose dominant race invaded Earth. Huston is the last of the Fear Agents, elite soldiers of Earth, and he thinks he can prevent the invasion by changing the past.

Originally published by Image Comics as Fear Agent issues #1-4.; Volume 1 of 6

Fear Agent Volume Two: My Way. Dark Horse Comics 2007 un Illustration
Grades: 11 12 Adult   **741.5; Fic**
1. Adventure graphic novels; 2. Graphic novels; 3. Science fiction graphic novels

978-1-59307-766-2, $14.95

Lost, beaten and trapped in the past, Heath Huston must face the demons of his inevitable future when he finds himself face to face with the automaton regime responsible for robbing him of all he loves. With the knowledge that the Feeders are progressing ever closer to Earth, will Heath be able to get payback from the automaton empire in time to save his home planet from the scourge of an alien infestation? This volume has nudity, sexual situations, harsh language, and violence.

Strange Girl Vol. 1: Girl Afraid. Image Comics 2005 un Illustration
Grades: 11 12 Adult   **741.5; Fic**
1. Graphic novels; 2. Horror graphic novels; 3. Supernatural graphic novels

978-1-58240-543-8, $12.99

Ten years after the Rapture, beautiful occultist Bethany Black and her pet runt demon Bloato embark on a road trip to the last open gateway to heaven, in hopes of befriending God and escaping hell on earth. The book includes considerable graphic violence, harsh language, and some nudity.

Strange Girl Vol. 2: Heaven Knows I'm Miserable Now. Image Comics 2006 un Illustration
Grades: 11 12 Adult   **741.5; Fic**
1. Graphic novels; 2. Horror graphic novels; 3. Supernatural graphic novels

978-1-58240-642-8, $14.99

There's a point in every journey where there seems to be no light — no hope. After returning to the human stronghold, Dead Western, Bethany Black learns there is little hope she'll ever find respite from hell on Earth.

The book includes considerable graphic violence, harsh language, and some nudity.

Uncanny Avengers: the red shadow. Rick Remender, illustrated by John Cassaday. Marvel Worldwide 2013 136 p.
Grades: 10 11 12 Adult   **741.5; Fic**
1. Avengers (Fictional characters); 2. X-Men (Fictional characters); 3. Thor (Fictional character); 4. Wolverine (Fictional character); 5. Captain America (Fictional character)
0785168443; 9780785168447, $24.99

In this graphic novel by Rick Remender, "Captain America creates a sanctioned Avengers unit comprised of Avengers and X-Men, humans and mutants working together...so why is Professor Xavier's dream more at risk than ever? The Red Skull has returned — straight out of the 1940s and full of hatred — and his rebirth will alter the Marvel Universe forever!" (Publisher's note)

"[D]ense, intelligent writing that asks significant questions; a battle not only of arms but of ideologies; and a cast of characters that gives movie stars like Captain America, Thor, and Wolverine their due without ignoring the rich personalities of lesser-known players.... Cassaday's art, the most purely gorgeous in contemporary superhero comics [is] so clean and clear the pages practically glow with life." Booklist

Revel, Brahm
Guerillas Volume 2: Volume 2. Brahm Revel; [edited by] Charlie Chu. Oni Press, Inc 2012 120 p.
Grades: 11 12 Adult   **741; Fic**
1. Monkeys — Graphic novels; 2. Vietnam War, 1961-1975 — Graphic novels; 3. Military personnel — United States — Graphic novels
1934964999; 9781934964996, $17.99
LC 2012930679

In this book by Brahm revel "Private John Francis Clayton's strange tour of duty in Vietnam gets stranger as he struggles with the unbelievable facts he is faced with. The elite platoon of simian soldiers he's encountered don't make any more sense to him than the war he's been sent to fight, but is this squad of chain-smoking chimps the most dangerous force in the jungle, or are they merely a distraction from the larger evil growing in the wild?" (Publisher's note)

Rhoades, Shirrel
Comic books: how the industry works. afterword by Stan Lee. Peter Lang Publishing, Inc. 2008 406p. Illustration
Grades: 11 12 Adult
741.5
1. Comic books, strips, etc. — History and criticism; 2. Graphic novels — History and criticism; 3. Publishers and publishing
978-0-8204-8892-9, $32.95
LC 2007-32719

Rhoades, who was publisher of Marvel Comics after Stan Lee and has worked in publishing for more than forty years, gives an insider's look at how the comic book industry works. He discusses how superhero characters are created, how comic books are put together, how they're sold, how comics' intellectual property is licensed to other industries, adapting comics to television and movies, what manga is all about, and the move of graphic novels into bookstores. The chapters are broken down into subsections, and there are frequent sidebars with labels such as "speak up," "flashback,"

Courtesy of Oni Press

"comics trivia!" and others that provide even more tidbits of information in a highly readable format.

★ A **complete** history of American comic books. afterword by Steve Geppi. Peter Lang Publishing Inc. 2008 353p. Illustration
Grades: 9 10 11 12 Adult
741.5
1. Comic books, strips, etc. — History and criticism; 2. Graphic novels — History and criticism
978-1-4331-0110-6; 1-4331-0110-6, $119.95; 978-1-4331-0107-6 (pa); 1-4331-0107-6 (pa), $39.95
LC 2007-43460

Rhoades, former publisher of Marvel Comics (after Stan Lee stepped down to move to Hollywood and focus on Marvel Comics in the movies), dates the beginning of the American comic book to the 1930s, when the format was first used. He covers the history of comics from that time to the present, covering all the big names (Will Eisner, Jack Kirby, Stan Lee, etc.). The book is peppered with fun sidebars with such labels as "flashback," "comics trivia," "looking back," "true facts," and so one. These help to make the book fun to read. Rhoades doesn't employ a straight narrative, but includes interviews, the side bars, comics milestones, a list of fanboys who have and had careers in comics, and a comic book quiz.

Includes bibliographical references

Richardson, Mike
47 Ronin. writer, Mike Richardson; artist, Stan Sakai. Dark Horse 2014 151 p. Color; Illustration
Grades: 11 12 Adult
741.5
1. Comic books, strips, etc.; 2. Samurai — Graphic novels
1595829547; 9781595829542, $19.99

Written by Mike Richardson and illustrated by Stan Sakai, "this collection of the acclaimed [comic book] mini-series recounts this sweeping saga of honor and violence in all its grandeur. Opening with the tragic incident that sealed the fate of Lord Asano, 47 Ronin follows a dedicated group of Asano's vassals on their years-long path of vengeance!" (Publisher's note)

"Richardson, founder of Dark Horse Comics, and Sakai, creator of the long-running and award-laden Usagi Yojimbo samurai series, combine talents to produce this terrific graphic interpretation of one of Japan's most important sagas.... The level of talent, the research, and the attention to both narrative and artistic detail shine through in this volume." LJ

Ricketts, Mark
Night Trippers. Image Comics 2006 184p. Illustration
Grades: 10 11 12 Adult   **741.5; Fic**
1. Graphic novels; 2. Horror graphic novels; 3. Vampires — Graphic novels
978-1-58240-606-0, $16.99

Once upon a time in swinging London, around 1966, there was a serial killer who loved Elvis, a fab foursome that worshipped Satan, trendy vampires looking for kicks, an ancient and hungry evil, young and hungry love... and there was revolution in the air. Get your trip together, baby. Tune in, turn on and fang out. The book includes some strong language and violence (especially vampire killing).

Ridley, John
The **American** Way. DC Comics/Wildstorm 2007 192p. Illustration
Grades: 10 11 12 Adult   **741.5; Fic**
1. Graphic novels; 2. Science fiction graphic novels; 3. Superhero graphic novels
978-1-4012-1256-8, $19.99

The 1960s were a decade of incredible change for America. It was a time of innocence. It was a time of optimism. It was a time of heroes. In the early '40s, the United States government hatched a plan to create the Civil

Defense Corps: a group of "super-heroes" who could fight alien invasions, evil super-powered beings and communism, all in front of an adoring public, courtesy of television. But that dream was far from reality by the 60s, as new C.D.C. Marketing Director Wesley Catham is about to discover. How far will America go to protect its dream of a better tomorrow? White racists use the n-word, plus there's violence, and other foul language.

Another volume in this series is: Those Above and Those Below (2018)

Riordan, Rick

Percy Jackson & the Olympians, book one: the lightning thief: the graphic novel. adapted by Robert Venditti; art by Attila Futaki; color by José Villarrubia; layouts by Orpheus Collar; lettering by Chris Dickey. Hyperion Books for Children 2010 un Illustration

Grades: 5 6 7 8 9 10   **741.5; Fic**
    1. Adventure graphic novels; 2. Fantasy graphic novels; 3. Graphic novels; 4. Greek mythology — Graphic novels
978-1-4231-1696-7, $19.99; 978-1-4321-1710-0 (pa), $9.99

Twelve-year-old Percy Jackson has had a hard time in school, but when a teacher transforms into a Fury and tries to kill him during a field trip to the museum, his life becomes even more complicated. He learns that he is the son of one of the Greek gods and a human woman, and then he learns that he should never have been born, and that the gods think he has stolen Zeus's master lightning bolt. Percy, his best friend Grover (a satyr), and Annabeth, daughter of Athena, have ten days to recover the lightning bolt and prevent all-out war among the Olympians. This graphic novel adapts Riordan's novel, NOT the movie. Futaki makes the water action look great in an adaptation that should make the book fans happy.

The **red** pyramid: the graphic novel. Rick Riordan; adapted by Orpheus Collar; lettered by Jared Fletcher. Disney/Hyperion Books 2012 un Color; Illustration (The Kane chronicles)

Grades: 4 5 6 7 8 9   **741.5**
    1. Egyptian mythology — Fiction; 2. Magic — Fiction; 3. Brothers and sisters — Fiction
1423150694; 1423150686; 9781423150695, $12.99; 9781423150688, $21.99

                                                        LC 2012007905
"Since their mother's death, Sadie and Carter have become near-strangers. While Sadie has lived with her grandparents in London, Carter has traveled the world with their father, the famed Egyptologist Dr. Julius Kane. One night, Dr. Kane brings the siblings to the British Museum, where he hopes to set things right for his family. Instead, he unleashes the Egyptian god Set, who banishes him to oblivion and forces the children to flee for their lives." (Publisher's note)

"Out of necessity, much of the dialogue is dedicated to explaining actions and events, but a constant stream of humor prevents the reader from getting bogged down by logistics. The colorful artwork has an almost painting-like quality,...and some clever visual jokes and thoughtful use of panels make good use of the format." VOYA

Robinson, Alex

Too cool to be forgotten. Top Shelf Productions 2008 128p. Illustration

Grades: 11 12 Adult   **741.5; Fic**
    1. Graphic novels; 2. Humorous graphic novels; 3. School stories — Graphic novels; 4. Time travel — Graphic novels
978-1-891830-98-3, $14.95

Andy Wicks is in his forties and a longtime smoker who has tried just about everything to quit smoking. Now he's going to try hypnosis, what's the worst thing that could happen? Well, when he wakes up, he finds himself back in high school, in 1985, as his high school sophomore self. Is

he doomed to relive all his mistakes, or can he use his return as a second chance to get things right? Things like asking out that girl from math class.... Then he finds himself reliving time with his father, who died of Lou Gehrig's disease in 1985 after a sudden decline. Is this, after all, what he really needs to do? The book includes quite a bit of harsh language and lots of drinking and smoking at a party.

Robinson, Dave

Introducing Ethics. Totem Books 2005 176p. Illustration

Grades: 10 11 12 Adult
170; 741.5
    1. Ethics — Graphic novels; 2. Graphic novels
1-84046-580-8, $12.95

What are the acceptable limits of scientific investigation and genetic engineering, the rights and wrongs of animal rights, euthanasia and civil disobedience? This book confronts these dilemmas, tracing arguments of moral thinkers, including Socrates, Plato, Aristotle, and brings us up to date with postmodern critics. Using cartoons and a spare text, this book provides an introductory look at ethics; it includes a list of books for further reading.

Courtesy of IDW Publishing

Introducing Kierkegaard, Rev. ed.. Totem Books 2007 176p. Illustration

Grades: 10 11 12 Adult   **142; 741.5**
    1. Existentialism — Graphic novels; 2. Graphic novels; 3. Philosophy — Graphic novels; 4. Kierkegaard, Soren, 1813-1855
978-1-84046-758-1, $12.95

Soren Kierkegaard is regarded as the founder of Existentialism and the first modern theologian. Philosophy, in Kierkegaard's radical view, was of no use unless it permanently changed people's lives. His distrust of grand abstract schemes, particularly Hegel's, and his insistence that philosophy is essentially writing also identify him as a forerunner of postmodernism. This book uses cartoons and a spare text to introduce readers to the ideas and life of Kierkegaard; it includes a list of books for further reading.

Courtesy of Icon Books

Introducing Philosophy. Totem Books 2004 176p. Illustration

Grades: 10 11 12 Adult
100; 741.5
    1. Graphic novels; 2. Philosophy — Graphic novels
1-84046-576-X, $12.95

This volume uses cartoons and a spare text to provide an introductory guide to the thinking of all the significant philosophers of the Western world, from Heraclitus to Derrida. It examines and explains their key arguments and ideas. The book includes a list of books for further reading.

Courtesy of Icon Books

Robinson, James Dale

Batman: Face the Face. James Robinson, writer; Leonard Kirk, Don Kramer, pencillers. DC Comics 2006 192p. Illustration

Grades: 10 11 12 Adult   741.5; Fic
    1. Batman (Fictional character); 2. Graphic
novels; 3. Mystery graphic novels; 4.
Superhero graphic novels; 5. Robin
(Fictional character)
978-1-4012-0910-0, $14.99

Courtesy of Icon Books

One year ago, Batman and Robin disappeared from Gotham City. Before his departure, Batman chose a guardian to protect Gotham's citizens from the city's usual predators. Now, the Dynamic Duo return to find that some of their most notorious foes are being brutally murdered, leaving Batman to wonder if the man he entrusted to carry on in his place has confused justice with vengeance. With James Gordon back as Commissioner and Harvey Bullock back on the Gotham police force, it's almost like old times. But Bruce Wayne also has a decision to make about Tim Drake. The book includes some graphic violence.

Earth 2; Volume 1. James Robinson, writer; Nicola Scott, Eduardo Pansica, pencillers; Trevor Scott, Sean Parsons, inkers.. DC Comics 2013 160 p.

Grades: 9 10 11 12   741.5; Fic
    1. Superheroes — Fiction; 2. Flash (Fictional character); 3. Justice League (Fictional characters); 4. Green Lantern (Fictional character)
1401237746; 9781401237745, $22.99

LC 2012046491

This graphic novel, by James Robinson, Nicola Scott, and Trevor Scott "reimagine[s] the classic Justice Society of America. Earth's greatest heroes have defeated grave threats from Apokolips. Left in their stead is a group of young, untrained heroes who pick up the pieces in the...aftermath. The Flash, Green Lantern, Hawkgirl and the Atom are humanity's...guardians, but not the ones we've all known. These are different heroes, in a strange and foreign world with dangerous new villains." (Publisher's note)

Originally published in single magazine form in Earth 2 1-6.; Volume 1 of 6

Rodriguez, Jason

Postcards: True Stories That Never Happened. Random House/Villard 2007 152p. Illustration

Grades: 10 11 12 Adult   741.5
    1. Graphic novels; 2. Short stories — Graphic novels
978-0-345-49850-2

Sixteen short stories inspired by antique postcards are in this anthology. Writers and artists include Tom Beland, Harvey Pekar, Stuart Moore, Neil Kleid, A. David Lewis, Ande Parks, and others. Stories range from the elegeiac (Beland's "Time") to ironic ("Best Side Out" by Antony Johnston) to dark horror ("Send Louis His Underwear" by Matt Dembicki) to heroic (Robert Tinnell's "The Midnight Caller's Holiday in Hades").

Rol, Ruud van der

The **search**. [by] Eric Heuvel, Ruud van der Rol [and] Lies Schippers; [English translation by Lorraine T. Miller]. Farrar, Straus and Giroux 2009 61p. Illustration

Grades: 5 6 7 8 9   741.5; Fic

1. Grandmothers — Fiction; 2. Graphic novels; 3. Holocaust survivors — Fiction; 4. Holocaust, 1933-1945 — Graphic novels; 5. Jews — Netherlands — Fiction
978-0-374-36517-2, $18.99; 978-0-374-46455-4 (pa), $9.99

LC 2009-13603

After recounting her experience as a Jewish girl living in Amsterdam during the Holocaust, Esther, helped by her grandson, embarks on a search to discover what happened to her parents before they died in a concentration camp.

Esther, her grandson Daniel, and her friend Helena's grandson Jeroen visit the Dutch farm where Esther hid during the Nazi occupation of the Netherlands during World War II. She tells her story, of how she managed to escape the Nazi roundup of Jews, but how her family died in a concentration camp. Daniel helps her find an old friend from the farm, now living in Israel, and he tells her what happened to her family in Auschwitz. The book depicts some of the horrendous, horrible things that happened but does it without graphic violence or gore.

Roman, Dave

Agnes Quill: an anthology of mystery. all transcripts written by Dave Roman; illustrated by Jason Ho, Raina Telgemeier, Jeff Zornow and Dave Roman. SLG Publishing 2006 130p. Illustration

Grades: 7 8 9 10 11 12   741.5
    1. Graphic novels; 2. Horror graphic novels; 3. Mystery graphic novels
978-1-59362-052-3, $10.95

Orphaned teen Agnes Quill lives in the city of Legerdemain and carries on a family tradition; she can see and communicate with ghosts, and she works as a detective to help them. Her cases range from recovering the mummified head of a ghost's old body in order to save the valuable necklace hidden there, to helping a little girl ghost find her doll, to helping a man find his legs, and more. Roman works with artists including Raina Telgemeier, and their styles range from childlike cartoons to gloomy, atmospheric art full of shadows.

"The variety of drawing styles and Agnes' story of being a teenage detective who can see the dead among the living combine in an interesting read that will likely keep readers' attention." Voice Youth Advocates

Jax Epoch and the Quicken Forbidden: Borrowed Magic. Dave Roman, writer; John Green, artist. AiT/PlanetLar 2003 152p. Illustration

Grades: 7 8 9 10 11 12 Adult   741.5; Fic
    1. Graphic novels; 2. Science fiction graphic novels
1-932051-11-2, $14.95

When teenager Jax stumbles into an interdimensional portal, she "borrows" several items: an ancient book, a pair of gloves, and a pair of boots. When she returns home through the portal, things are a bit...off. Her little escapade has caused magic to leak into her world, and now she's deep in trouble, unstuck in time and on trial for the crime of crossing dimensions. The story continues in Volume 2: Separation Anxiety.

"Jax is a great character — quite real but with flaws that get her into deep trouble while possessing the aplomb to get herself out." (VOYA)

Followed by Volume 2: Separation Anxiety

Rosa, Don

Walt Disney's Uncle $crooge and Donald Duck: the Son of the sun. [written and drawn by Don Rosa; lettered by John Clark]. Fantagraphics Books 2014 207 p. Color; Illustration

Grades: 7 8 9 10 11 12 Adult   741.5
    1. Comic books, strips, etc.; 2. Fictional characters; 3. Ducks — Fiction
1606997424; 9781606997420, $29.99

LC 2012287668

This collection by Don Rosa, featuring Disney's Donald Duck and Scrooge McDuck, is "filled with epic adventures, like hunting for buried treasure or recovering stolen money.... At the end of each volume are whole pages of reference notes, explaining each comic in depth and addressing Rosa's process and nods to previous works." (School Library Journal)

"When Rosa began creating Uncle Scrooge comics in 1987, his work instilled childish wonder in readers. Disney comics had entirely disappeared from circulation, and those that had just preceded the fall had become completely hackneyed-rife with repeating storylines and drab artwork. But under Rosa's creative flair, a zippy, glamorous franchise suddenly appeared, with riveting stories and detailed yet kinetic artwork. While remaining totally true to Scrooge McDuck's ornery persona, Rosa turned the moody miser into a plucky adventurer worthy of Tintin." Pub Wkly

Other titles in this series are: Return to plain awful (2014); Treasure under glass (2015)

Rosca, Madeleine
Hollow Fields Omnibus collection. Seven Seas Entertainment 2009 un Illustration
Grades: 5 6 7 8 9 10   **741.5; Fic**
1. Adventure graphic novels; 2. Graphic novels; 3. Science fiction graphic novels
978-1-934876-72-5, $14.99
Rosca is an Australian global manga creator who won one of the inaugural International Manga Awards ¿Shorei¿ awards given by the Japanese government in 2007.

Lucy Snow was supposed to start school at a nice elementary school in town, but she manages to lose her way in a forest and finds herself at Miss Weaver's Academy for the Scientifically Gifted and Ethically Unfettered a school for archvillains in training. Lucy's fellow students are all learning how to be mad scientists and evil geniuses, with classes such as Live Taxidermy, Cross-Species Body-Part Transplantation, and Killer Robot Construction. Hollow Fields, as the school is also called, also has a practice guaranteed to make everyone compete to do well: the student with the lowest grades at the end of the week is sent to the windmill for detention, and thus far no student has ever returned. Miss Weaver has experimented on herself, as have all the Engineers who teach; what the reader learns is that they need new, young blood to keep their stitched-together bodies going, for they are all more than a hundred years old. Befriended by a talking box that calls itself Doctor Bleak, Lucy struggles to hold her own in her classes, despite her innate niceness. She decides she needs to discover just what goes on in the windmill, and how she can make things right. The book includes some mild violence.

Ross, Edward (Comic book artist)
★ **Filmish:** A Graphic Journey Through Film. Edward Ross. Harry N Abrams Inc 2015 199 p. Illustration
Grades: 11 12 Adult   **741.5; 791.43**
1. Motion pictures — Production and direction — Graphic novels; 2. Motion pictures — History and criticism
1910593036; 9781910593035, $24.95

In this nonfiction graphic novel, by Edward Ross, "Ross's cartoon alter ego guides readers through the annals of cinematic history, introducing some of the strange and fascinating concepts at work in the movies. Each chapter focuses on a particular theme-the body, architecture, language-and explores an eclectic mix of cinematic triumphs, from 'A Trip to the Moon' to 'Top Gun.'" (Publisher's note)

Includes bibliographical references (pages 196-199) and filmography (pages 194-195).

Ross, Steve
Marked. Seabury Books 2005 un Illustration
Grades: 9 10 11 12 Adult   **741.5; 225**
1. Bible. N.T. Mark — Adaptations; 2. Graphic novels

1-59627-002-0, $20

An occupied country. A people infested with demons. A time of revolution. A liberator rises. One of the oldest stories in human history comes alive in this telling of the Gospel of Mark. Join a carpenter as he changes the world. This is a human story of passion and murder. Of a compassionate man brutally killed and yet alive. Ross has set the story in a futuristic, urban world.

Rubio, Salva
Monet: itinerant of light. Salva Rubio, writer; Efa, art; lettering by Ortho; translation by Montana Kane. NBM Graphic Novels 2017 112 p. Color; Illustration
Grades: 9 10 11 12 Adult   **92; 741.5**
1. Monet, Claude, 1840-1926; 2. Painters — France — Biography; 3. Impressionism (Art)
9781681121390, $24.99

LC 2017910452

This book, by Salva Rubio, illustrated by Efa, narrates "the life of...French painter, [Claude Monet], one of the founders of Impressionism.... From the Salon des Refuses ('Salon of the Rejected') and many struggling years without recognition, money, and yet a family to raise, all the way to great success, critically and financially, Monet pursued insistently one vision: catching the light in painting, refusing to compromise on this ethereal pursuit." (Publisher's note)

Courtesy of NBM Publishing

"Monet himself narrates, and most of the text focuses on that narration, which allows the imagery to open and explore much of the same visual landscape that occupies his paintings. Efa's illustrations are stunning; full of strong, lush color and bold impressionistic brush strokes that call forth Monet's style but never imitate." LJ

Rucka, Greg
Batwoman: elegy. Greg Rucka, writer; J.H. Williams III, artist; Dave Stewart, colorist; Todd Klein, letters.. DC Comics 2010 1 v. Color illustration
Grades: 11 12 Adult   **741.5**
1. Batwoman (Fictitious character) — Comic books, strips, etc.; 2. Superheroes — Fiction; 3. Graphic novels; 4. Mentally ill — Fiction
9781401226923, $24.99; 1401226922

LC 2010283560

"Batwoman battles a madwoman known only as Alice, inspired by Alice in Wonderland, who sees her life as a fairy tale and everyone around her as expendable! Batwoman must stop Alice from unleashing a toxic death cloud over all of Gotham City — but Alice has more up her sleeve than just poison, and Batwoman's life will never ever be the same." (Publisher's note)

"[A] nuanced, literary, and culturally charged story, but the real knockout element is Williams' art nouveau inspired compositions." Booklist

Superman: That Healing Touch. writer[s], Greg Rucka, Geoff Johns & Jeremy Johns; pencillers, Matthew Clark [and others]; inkers, John Dell [and others]; colorists, Sno Cone, Tanya & Richard Horie; letterers, Jared K. Fletcher, Rob Leigh. DC Comics 2005 168p. Illustration
Grades: 9 10 11 12 Adult   **741.5; Fic**
1. Graphic novels; 2. Superhero graphic novels; 3. Superman (Fictional character)

1-4012-0453-8, $14.99

Ruin is out to kill Superman and those closest to him. He has unleashed Replikon and his son to soften up the Man of Steel, but now he unleashes his deadliest attack yet, twin Parasites who can sap the life from even a Kryptonian. Lois Lane, still recovering from a gunshot wound, Lana Lang, and Jimmy Olsen are all threatened. And each time, Superman insists that no one will die on his watch.

Whiteout Volume 1: The Definitive Edition. Oni Press 2007 128p. Illustration
Grades: 11 12 Adult   **741.5; Fic**
  1. Graphic novels; 2. Mystery graphic novels
978-1-932664-70-6, $13.95

One of Oni Press' earliest and most acclaimed books returns in a brand new re-mastered and re-formatted edition. U.S. Marshal Carrie Stetko has made Antarctica her home. In the vastness of The Ice, she found peace...Or at least that's what she thought, until someone commits a murder in her jurisdiction and the lawwoman is forced to use her detective skills once more or become another victim to this mysterious killer. The book includes violence and harsh language, including copious use of the f-bomb.

Whiteout Volume 2: Melt, The Definitive Edition. Oni Press 2007 120p. Illustration
Grades: 11 12 Adult
741.5; Fic
  1. Graphic novels; 2. Mystery graphic novels
978-1-932664-71-3, $13.95
2000 Eisner Award for Best Finite Series/Limited Series.

Courtesy of Oni Press

One of Oni Press' earliest and most acclaimed books returns in a brand new re-mastered and re-formatted edition. U.S. Marshal Carrie Stetko investigates the explosion that destroyed a Russian science station that may have been a cache for weapons. The book includes violence, copious harsh language, nudity and sexual situations.

Wonder Woman: Land of the Dead. Greg Rucka, Geoff Johns, writers; Drew Johnson ... [et al.], pencillers; Michael Bair ... [et al.], inkers; Richard & Tanya Horie, James Sinclair, colorists; Todd Klein, Pat Brosseau, letterers. DC Comics 2006 128p. Illustration
Grades: 9 10 11 12 Adult
741.5; Fic
  1. Graphic novels; 2. Superhero graphic novels; 3. Wonder Woman (Fictional character); 4. Flash (Fictional character)
1-4012-0938-6, $12.99

Courtesy of Oni Press

Just as Wonder Woman is starting to deal with her blindness (self-inflicted, in order to defeat Medusa), the Cheetah returns and teams up with another villain known for speed: The Reverse Flash. Wally West, the real Flash, joins forces with Wonder Woman to stop the villainous duo from causing untold havoc. Then, the goddess Athena sends Wonder Woman on a journey to retrieve Hermes from the Underworld. Joined by Wonder Girl and Ferdinand the Minotaur, Wonder Woman must face unimagined peril to complete her mission. But should she succeed, what will Diana ask in return from the all-seeing Goddess of Wisdom?

Wonder Woman; Volume 1: The lies. Greg Rucka, writer; Liam Sharp, artist; MatthewClark, penciller (pages 7-26); Sean Parsons,inker (pages 7-26); Laura Martin, Jeremy Colwell,colorists; Jodi Wynne, letterer; Liam Sharp &Laura Martin, collection and original series coverarti. DC Comics 2017 176 p. Color; Illustration
Grades: 9 10 11 12 Adult   **741.5; Fic**
  1. Comic books, strips, etc.; 2. Female superhero comic books, strips, etc.; 3. Wonder Woman (Fictional character)
1401267785; 9781401267780, $16.99

LC 2017001077

"Princess Diana of Themyscira — known to the world as Wonder Woman — is one of the greatest superheroes in history.... To solve the riddle of her origin, she must...[find] a way back to her vanished home. To get there, she must team up with her greatest enemy, the feral beast-woman, Cheetah. Will this unlikely alliance shine the light of truth on Diana's darkest secrets, or bury them — and her — forever?" (Publisher's note)
Originally published in single magazine form in WONDER WOMAN: REBIRTH 1, WONDER WOMAN 1, 3, 5, 7, 9, 11; Other volumes in this series are: 2, Year one; 3, The truth; 4, Godwatch

Wonder Woman; Volume 2: Year One. Greg Rucka, writer; Nicola Scott, artist; Bilquis Evely, artist (Interlude); Romulo Fajardo Jr., colorist; Jodi Wynne, letterer; Nicola Scott & Romulo Fajardo Jr., collection cover artists.. DC Comics 2017 168 p. Color; Illustration
Grades: 9 10 11 12 Adult   **741.5**
  1. Female superhero graphic novels; 2. Wonder Woman (Fictional character)
1401268803; 9781401268800, $16.99

LC 2017015508

"The team of [Greg] Rucka and artist Nicola Scott weave the definitive and shocking tale of Diana's first year as Earth's protector. Paradise has been breached, Ares stirs, and the Amazons must answer with a champion of their own...one who is willing to sacrifice her home amongst her sisters to save a world she has never seen. Wonder Woman's journey begins in this epic origin story!" (Publisher's note)
Originally published in single magazine form in WONDER WOMAN 2, 4, 6, 8, 10, 12, 14

Rugg, Jim
  Street Angel. SLG Publishing 2005 208p. Illustration
Grades: 10 11 12 Adult   **741.5; Fic**
  1. Adventure graphic novels; 2. Graphic novels; 3. Homeless persons — Graphic novels
1-59362-012-8, $14.95

Homeless, orphaned, rarely in school, twelve-year-old skateboarder Jesse "Street Angel" Sanchez uses her board skills and kung fu to fight crime on the streets of Wilkesborough, the worst ghetto in Angel City. She has to fight Dr. Pangaea and his ninja forces, deal with time-warping pirates and Inca warriors, go dumpster-diving to find food...Jesse does a lot of slicing and dicing with her handy sword and knows how to handle automatic weapons as well in the many graphically depicted fight scenes.
Originally published as Street Angel issues #1-5.

Runton, Andy
  ★ **Owly** Vol. 2: Just a Little Blue. Top Shelf Productions 2005 127p. Illustration
Grades: K 1 2 3 4 5 6 7 8 9 10 11 12 Adult   **741.5; Fic**
  1. Friendship — Graphic novels; 2. Graphic novels; 3. Stories without words — Graphic novels
1-891830-64-3, $10

Owly is a kind, yet lonely, little owl who's always on the search for new friends and adventure. Owly learns that sometimes you have to make sacrifices and work at things that are important, especially friendship. He and Wormy try to help a stubborn bluebird by building a new home, but the bluebird rejects it and them.

★ **Owly** Vol. 3: Flying Lessons. Top Shelf Productions 2005 143p. Illustration
Grades: K 1 2 3 4 5 6 7 8 9 10 11 12 Adult   741.5; Fic
1. Friendship — Graphic novels; 2. Graphic novels; 3. Stories without words — Graphic novels
1-891830-76-7, $10

Owly figures out why he can't fly (he failed his childhood flying lessons), and helps another forest creature with his own flying problems. The flying squirrel is frightened by Owly, for he knows owls are hunters, but Owly isn't like that. How can he convince the squirrel he just wants to be friends?

★ **Owly** vol. 4: a time to be brave. Top Shelf Productions 2007 132p. Illustration
Grades: K 1 2 3 4 5 6 7 8 9 10 11 12 Adult   741.5; Fic
1. Fantasy graphic novels; 2. Friendship — Graphic novels; 3. Graphic novels; 4. Owls — Graphic novels; 5. Stories without words — Graphic novels
978-1-891830-89-1, $10

A new visitor comes to the forest, but Wormy is scared of him because Owly had just read stories about a scary dragon, and the visitor seems to look scary. The visitor is just as scared of Owly. Things aren't just as they seem, and everyone soon finds out that a little bravery and a lot of friendship can fix just about anything. This is the latest volume in Runton's nearly wordless series about Owly and his friends.

★ **Owly** volume five: tiny tales. Top Shelf Productions 2008 175p. Illustration
Grades: K 1 2 3 4 5 6 7 8 9 10 11 12 Adult   741.5; Fic
1. Friendship — Graphic novels; 2. Graphic novels; 3. Humorous graphic novels
978-1-60309-019-3, $10

This volume gathers short stories about Owly and his friends, including stories originally published for Free Comic Book Day issues from Top Shelf Productions, the first Owly mini-comics, drawings of Owly before he met Wormy, and more. Among the stories, Owly saves a friend from drowning in the cold river when the ice cracks, only to get caught in the hole himself; Owly finds a way to keep both the bees and hummingbirds happy when they get into a "turf" battle; Owly helps a friend when she falls and breaks the fancy potted plant she bought for a present; and more.

★ **Owly**: The way home and The bittersweet summer. [by] Andy Runton. Top Shelf 2004 160p. Illustration
Grades: K 1 2 3 4 5 6 7 8 9 10 11 12   741.5; Fic
1. Friendship — Graphic novels; 2. Graphic novels; 3. Owls — Graphic novels
1-891830-62-7, $10
LC 2005298860

Rotund little Owly befriends Wormy despite their differences, and together they help a couple of hummingbirds and learn that friendship doesn't end with separation.

"The whimsical black-and-white art is done with great facility for expressing emotion, and Runton's reliance on icons and pictures in lieu of the usual dialogue makes the story perfect for give-and-take between children and their parents." Booklist

Other titles in this series are: Owly: Just a little blue (2005); Owly: Flying lessons (2005);Owly: A time to be brave (2007);Owly: Tiny tales (2008)

Russell, Mark
Prez; Volume 1: Corndog-in-chief. written by Mark Russell; pencils by Ben Caldwell, Dominike Domo Stanton; inks by Mark Morales, Sean Parsons, John Lucas; color by Jeremy Lawson; letters by Travis Lanham, Marilyn Patrizio, Sal Cipriano; covers by Ben Caldwell. DC Comics 2016 144 p. Color; Illustration
Grades: 10 11 12 Adult   741.5; Fic
1. Women presidents — Comic books, strips, etc; 2. Presidents — United States — Fiction; 3. Graphic novels
1401259790; 9781401259792, $14.99
LC 2015038025

"Oregon teen Beth Ross has just been elected President of the United States of America.... Now the eyes of the nation are on Beth. But in a world so out of control that the poor are willing to shoot themselves on TV for a chance at a better life, will even the new president have the power needed to overthrow the nation's true leaders — Boss Smiley and his corporate shadow government?" (Publisher's note)

"Caldwell brightens the mood with crazy character design, particularly the special interest representatives hiding behind holographic masks and bloated walking tanks manned by unapologetic gamers. Trenchant political satire for the millennial set." Booklist

Russell, P. Craig
Fairy Tales of Oscar Wilde Vol. 4: The Devoted Friend & The Nightingale and the Rose. NBM Publishing 2004 un Illustration
Grades: 5 6 7 8 9   741.5; Fic
1. Fantasy graphic novels; 2. Graphic novels; 3. Wilde, Oscar, 1854-1900
978-1-56163-391-3, $16.99

This volume adapts The Devoted Friend," on what constitutes real friendship, and The Nightingale and the Rose," a story of sacrifice to love with a cruel twist. In both stories, innocence is sacrificed to cynicism and shallowness.

★ The **graveyard** book graphic novel Volume 1. based on the novel by Neil Gaiman; adapted by P. Craig Russell; illustrated by Kevin Nowlan, P. Craig Russell, Tony Harris, Scott Hampton, Galen Showman, Jill Thompson, Stephen B. Scott; colorist, Lovern Kindzierski; letterer, Rick Parker. HarperCollins 2014 188 p. Color; Illustration
Grades: 5 6 7 8 9 10

Courtesy of NBM Publishing

741.5; Fic
1. Cemeteries — Fiction; 2. Orphans — Fiction; 3. Graphic novels; 4. Gaiman, Neil — Adaptations
9780062194817, $19.99; 006219481X
LC 2013953799

This graphic novel is an adaptation of the "Newbery Medal-winning novel, [where] Bod is an unusual boy..., the only living resident of a graveyard. Raised from infancy by the ghosts, werewolves, and other cemetery denizens, Bod has learned the antiquated customs of his guardians' time as well as their ghostly teachings." (Publisher's note)

"Russell brings his decades of comics know-how to this lovely, lyrical adaptation of [Gaiman's] well-loved, Newbery Medal — winning book. Not content to rely exclusively on his own distinctive talents, Russell has enlisted some of the industry's greatest contemporary illustrators as contributors, who fill the panels with appropriately gothic tones. In order to give ample room to the novel's twists and turns, the adaptation has been divided into two parts." Booklist

Ryall, Chris

Beowulf. writer, Chris Ryall; artist, Gabriel Rodriguez, Mark A. Nelson. IDW Publishing 2007 104p. Illustration
Grades: 10 11 12 Adult   741.5; Fic
1. Fantasy graphic novels; 2. Graphic novels; 3. Beowulf — Adaptation — Graphic novels
978-1-60010-128-1, $17.99

This graphic novel adaptation of the motion picture screenplay written by Neil Gaiman and Roger Avary takes liberties with the original epic. In this version, the warrior Beowulf slays the monster Grendel who has slain many of King Hrothgar's warriors, but is seduced by Grendel's demon mother. This story states that Grendel is Hrothgar's son. It basically turns the epic saga upside down, showing that the heroes bring about the monsters. The book includes harsh language, nudity, and graphic violence.

Sacco, Joe

The **fixer**: a story from Sarajevo. Joe Sacco. Drawn and Quarterly 2003 105p. Illustration
Grades: 9 10 11 12 Adult   741; 741.5
1. Yugoslav War, 1991-1995 — Journalists — Comic books, strips, etc.; 2. Sarajevo (Bosnia and Hercegovina) — History — Siege, 1992-1996 — Comic books, strips, etc.
9781896597607, $24.95

"Joe Sacco goes behind the scene of war correspondence to reveal the anatomy of the big scoop. He begins by returning us to the dying days of Balkan conflict and introduces us to his own fixer; a man looking to squeeze the last bit of profit from Bosnia before the reconstruction begins. Thanks to a complex relationship with the fixer Joe discovers the crimes of opportunistic warlords and gangsters who run the countryside in times of war. But the west is interested in a different spin on the stories coming out of Bosnia. Almost ten years later, Joe meets up with his fixer and sees how the new Bosnian government has 'dealt' with these criminals and Joe ponders who is holding the reins of power these days." (Publisher's note)

Safe area Gorazde. Fantagraphics Bks. 2000 227p. Illustration
Grades: 10 11 12 Adult   949.7; 741.5; 949.702
1. Yugoslav War, 1991-1995 — Bosnia and Herzegovina — Gorazde — Comic books, strips, etc.; 2. Gorazde (Bosnia and Herzegovina) — History — 1992- — Comic books, strips, etc.
1-56097-392-7, $28.95; 1-56097-470-2 (pa), $19.95

Sacco "spent five months in Bosnia in 1996, immersing himself in the human side of life during wartime, researching stories that are rarely found in conventional news coverage. The book focuses on the Muslim-held enclave of Gorazde, which was besieged by Bosnian Serbs during the war. Sacco lived for a month in Gorazde, entering before the Muslims trapped inside had access to the outside world, electricity or running water." (Publisher's note)

Sadamoto, Yoshiyuki

★ **Neon** Genesis Evangelion Vol. 1 2nd ed.. Viz Media 2004 184p. Illustration
Grades: 10 11 12 Adult   741.5; Fic
1. Graphic novels; 2. Manga; 3. Mecha manga; 4. Science fiction graphic novels; 5. Shonen manga
978-1-4139-0344-7, $9.95

A handful of teenagers must pilot huge biomechanical robots — the Evangelion combat units — against monstrous Ängels" bent on destroying humanity. Among them is Shin, a very reluctant recruit whose scientist father is commander of the secret organization NERV and who has ignored his son all his life. The book includes violence, strong language, nudity, and sexual situations.

Said, Fehed

The **Clarence** Principle. SLG Publishing 2007 un Illustration
Grades: 11 12 Adult   741.5; Fic
1. Death — Graphic novels; 2. Fantasy graphic novels; 3. Graphic novels
978-1-59362-064-6, $12.95

After Clarence commits suicide, he wakes up to find a message written on the bathroom mirror; he opens the door and finds himself in a bizarre afterlife where he meets whimsical and strange people. Some images may be disturbing for more sensitive readers (such as the people with vacant holes instead of eyes, complete with zippers, and some dismemberments).

Sakai, Stan

★ **Usagi** Yojimbo, book one: The Ronin. Stan Sakai. Fantagraphics Books 1999 144p. Illustration
Grades: 7 8 9 10 11 12   741.5; Fic
1. Adventure graphic novels; 2. Graphic novels; 3. Rabbits — Graphic novels; 4. Samurai — Graphic novels; 5. Usagi Yojimbo (Fictional character); 6. Japan — Graphic novels
0-930193-35-0; 978-0-930193-35-5, $15.95

LC 93-239124

This series contains the adventures of Miyamoto Usagi, a ronin samurai rabbit in 17th-century Japan.

First published 1987; Vol. 1 of an ongoing series; Vols. 1-7 published by Fantagraphics; Vols. 8-25 published by Dark Horse Comics; Volume 1 of an ongoing series

★ **Usagi** Yojimbo: Yokai. created, written, and illustrated by Stan Sakai. Dark Horse Books 2009 62p. Illustration
Grades: 6 7 8 9 10 11 12 Adult   741.5; Fic
1. Adventure graphic novels; 2. Graphic novels; 3. Monsters — Graphic novels; 4. Samurai — Graphic novels; 5. Usagi Yojimbo (Fictional character); 6. Japan — Graphic novels
978-1-59582-362-5, $14.95

LC 2009-20024

As he walks through a spooky forest at night, samurai rabbit Usagi Yojimbo encounters a woman who begs him to find her daughter, who was kidnapped and dragged into the forest. That night, the yokai — monsters, demons, and spirits from Japanese folklore — are amassing for a once-a-century attempt to take over the living world. Armed only with his swords and his wit, Usagi can't hope to win against so many supernatural beings, but luckily Sasuke the Demon Queller has come, knowing about the yokais' plan, and together they fight the gathered monsters. The fighting is not graphic or bloody, and the monsters and demons aren't too scary looking for most younger readers.

"Sakai's art deftly demonstrates that comics can be simultaneously cartoony and scary.... Usagi Yojimbo is a genuine pleasure for readers of all ages." Publ Wkly

Sakuragi, Yukiya

Inubaka: Crazy for Dogs, Vol. 1. Viz Media 2007 210p. Illustration
Grades: 10 11 12 Adult   741.5; Fic
1. Dogs — Graphic novels; 2. Graphic novels; 3. Manga; 4. Seinen manga
978-1-4215-1149-8, $9.99

Naive Suguri wants to move to Tokyo and pursue a career now that she's finished high school. Teppei owns Woofles, a new pet store, and desperately needs someone to help take care of the dogs in his store. When Suguri's dog Lupin scores sexually with a purebred Labrador Retriever that Teppei wants to breed to get puppies to sell, Suguri ends up working at Woofles to make up for it. A fair amount of fan service (mostly panty shots), a little sexual innuendo, and lots of dog pee and poop make this title more appropriate for older teens who love dogs.

Sakurakoji, Kanoko

Backstage Prince, Vol. 1. Viz Media/Shojo Beat 2007 188p. Illustration

Grades: 8 9 10 11 12 Adult **741.5; Fic**
1. Graphic novels; 2. Kabuki — Graphic novels; 3. Manga; 4. Romance graphic novels; 5. Shojo manga
978-1-4215-1172-6, $8.99

High school freshman Akari stumbles into hottie Ryusei Horiuchi and hurts him with her school bag. That evening, she stumbles upon the kabuki theater where he, as famous kabuki actor Shonosuke Ichimura, is performing, and becomes his backstage assistant. Ryusei is very shy and aloof, and he's only opened up to his cat, Mr. Ken, and now to Akari; and she, despite herself, has fallen hard for Ryusei. Can an ordinary girl and a handsome, famous actor be together?

Sala, Richard

Mad Night. Fantagraphics Books 2005 231p. Illustration

Grades: 9 10 11 12 Adult **741.5; Fic**
1. Graphic novels; 2. Humorous graphic novels; 3. Mystery graphic novels
1-56097-681-0, $18.95

Judy Drood, girl detective, along with her friend and reluctant aide, Kasper Keene, investigate a series of murders at Lone Mountain College. Imagine Nancy Drew in a noir mystery, mixed in with macabre and humorous elements from Lemony Snicket books and Charles Addams cartoons.

"Reading a Sala comic is a unique experience, both jarring and fun, good for a rainy day or a stormy night." (PW)

Samura, Hiroaki

★ **Blade** of the Immortal Book 1: Blood of a Thousand. art and story by Hiroaki Samura; translation, Dana Lewis & Toren Smith; lettering and retouch, Wayne Truman. Dark Horse Manga 1997 136p. Illustration

Grades: 11 12 Adult **741.5; Fic**
1. Adventure graphic novels; 2. Graphic novels; 3. Manga; 4. Samurai — Graphic novels; 5. Seinen manga
1-56971-239-5, $14.95

1998 winner of Japan's Media Arts Award; 2000 Eisner Award for Best U.S. Edition of Foreign Material

"To end his eternal suffering, he must slay one thousand enemies!" Manji, a ronin warrior of feudal Japan, has been cursed with immortality. To rid himself of this curse and end his life of misery, he must slay one thousand evil men. His quest begins when a young girl named Rin seeks his help in taking revenge on her parents' killers...and his quest won't end until the blood of a thousand has spilled. The problem comes in judging who is truly evil. This series includes lots of graphic violence, much harsh language, partial nudity, sexual situations, and anachronistic situations and dialog.

Volume 1 of 30

Sandoval, Tony

Doomboy. Tony Sandoval; translated by Mike Kennedy. Magnetic Press 2014 136 p. Illustration

Grades: 10 11 12 Adult **741.5; Fic**
1. Teenagers — Fiction; 2. Rock musicians — Fiction
0991332474; 9780991332472, $24.99

Eisner Nominee: Best Publication for Teens (2014)

This graphic novel, by Tony Sandoval, "tells the story of an ordinary, lonely teenager with an active imagination and a love of metal music. When his girlfriend passes away suddenly, he decides to broadcast songs to her beyond the grave, playing his heart out under the secret name 'Doomboy'. What he doesn't realize, however, is that those broadcasts are

picked up all across town... and beyond. Soon the music of Doomboy becomes legendary, and his innocent private life quickly turns inside out." (Publisher's note)

"Sandoval...places cartoon artwork — featuring a wan color palette and oddly large heads on slender bodies — and a well-detailed social scene replete with bands, friendships, breakups and jealousies against the familiar context of adolescent loss and longing to produce a story that is intimate in scale yet epic in emotional terms." LJ

Santiago, Wilfred

★ **21:** the story of Roberto Clemente : a graphic novel. Wilfred Santiago.. Fantagraphics 2011 148p. Illustration

Grades: 11 12 Adult **741.5; 92**
1. Baseball — Graphic novels; 2. Graphic novels; 3. Clemente, Roberto, 1934-1972; 4. Baseball players — Graphic novels
978-1-56097-892-3, $22.99

Presents the story of baseball star Roberto Clemente and his journey from an impoverished childhood to fame and fortune, as he strives to go the distance for respect.

Includes bibliographic references.

Satrapi, Marjane

Chicken with plums. Pantheon Books 2006 84p. Illustration

Grades: 11 12 Adult **92; 741.5**
1. Biographical graphic novels; 2. Graphic novels; 3. Lute players; 4. Khan, Nasser Ali, d. 1958
0-375-42415-6; 978-0-375-42415-1, $16.95

LC 2006-43156

In graphic novel format, the author chronicles "the life of her great-uncle Nasser Ali Khan. A revered musician, he takes to his bed and refuses sustenance after his frustrated wife breaks his tar — an Iranian lute — over her knee. It takes him eight days to die, and in that time Satrapi reveals the futures of his children and unearths his past.... Satrapi's deceptively simple, remarkably powerful drawings match the precise but flexible prose she employs in adapting to her multiple roles as educator, folklorist, and grand-niece." New Yorker

★ The **complete** Persepolis. Pantheon Books 2007 341p. Illustration

Grades: 11 12 Adult **92; 741.5**
1. Artists; 2. Authors; 3. Autobiographical graphic novels; 4. Cartoonists; 5. Graphic novels; 6. Memoirists; 7. Novelists; 8. Satrapi, Marjane, 1969-; 9. Iran — Graphic novels
978-0-375-71483-2, $24.95

LC 2007-60106

Ignatz Award: Outstanding Graphic Novel (2005)

Originally published in two separate volumes 2003-2004

Embroideries. Pantheon Books 2005 134p. Illustration

Grades: 11 12 Adult **741.5; 955**
1. Graphic novels; 2. Women — Iran — Graphic novels; 3. Iran — Graphic novels
0-375-42305-2, $16.95

LC 2004-58660

This book "explores the lives of Iranian women young and old. The book begins with Satrapi arriving for afternoon tea at her grandmother's house. There, her mother, aunt and their group of friends tell stories about their lives as women, and, more specifically, the men they've lived with and through." Publ Wkly

"Discussions of sex are frank and explicit and laced with high humor.... Satrapi's simple black-and-white cartooning style is tremendously effective, expertly portraying emotional nuances with just a few lines." Libr J

Sava, Scott Christian

The **lab:** hey . . . test this!. Astonish Factory 2004 120p. Illustration

Grades: 5 6 7 8 9   **741.5; Fic**

1. Graphic novels; 2. Humorous graphic novels; 3. Science fiction graphic novels

0-9721259-3-0, $14.95

"A collection of previously published comics and original stories that highlight the working relationship between Livingston, a scientist mole, and his goofball assistant, Esteban, a weasel whose ultrasensitivity to chemicals makes him an excellent test subject for new products. With bright, colorful pictures, the stories usually consist of observing Esteban's outlandish reactions to Livingston's concoctions, such as floating to the ceiling, shrinking to microscopic size, or singing uncontrollably." SLJ

Schrag, Ariel

Stuck in the middle: seventeen comics from an unpleasant age. edited by Ariel Schrag. Viking 2007 210p. Illustration

Grades: 7 8 9 10 11 12   **741.5; Fic**

1. Graphic novels; 2. Middle schools — Graphic novels; 3. Teenagers — Graphic novels

978-0-670-06221-8, O.P.

LC 2006-52581

This book collects seventeen short stories about the perils of middle school, each by independent comics creators, including editor Schrag, her younger sister Tania Schrag, Aaron Renier, Daniel Clowes, Gabrielle Bell, and others. Stories include the experience of being the new kid in school, getting betrayed by your best friend, being a Jewish nonathlete at a Christian sports summer camp, finding a creative outlet despite having attention deficit disorder, and more of the everyday bad situations and joys of being twelve and thirteen years old. Some harsh language (one story is also called "Shit") reflects the reality of young teen life.

Schultz, Mark

The **stuff** of life: a graphic guide to genetics and DNA. written by Mark Schultz; art by Zander Cannon and Kevin Cannon. Hill and Wang 2009 150p. Illustration

Grades: 9 10 11 12 Adult   **576.5; 741.5**

1. Genetics — Graphic novels; 2. Graphic novels

978-0-8090-8946-8, $30; 978-0-8090-8947-5 (pa), $14.95

Eisner and Harvey Award winning writer Schultz uses the device of an alien writing a report to describe genetics and DNA in five chapters, from molecular structure of Earth organisms to sexual reproduction to genetic inheritance to genetic counseling and the genome Project and beyond. The black and white cartoons add some humor to the sound information, and the book includes a list of suggested reading ranging from magazines and books to websites, along with a glossary of terms.

Includes bibliographical references

Schulz, Charles M.

★ The **Complete** Peanuts: 1950-1952. Fantagraphics Books 2004 330p. Illustration

Grades: 2 3 4 5 6 7 8 9 10 11 12 Adult   **741.5; Fic**

1. Graphic novels; 2. Humorous graphic novels; 3. Peanuts (Comic strip) — Graphic novels

1-56097-589-X, $28.95

This is the first volume of a project to collect all of Schulz's Peanuts comic strips from 1950 to 2000. This volume includes the strips published from October 2, 1950 through all of 1952. These early strips featured characters younger readers may not recognize: Patty (not Peppermint Patty), Violet, Shermy, and a Snoopy who behaves like a normal dog. Schroeder is a baby who's already a whiz at the toy piano; Lucy is a toddler who already causes trouble for Charlie Brown; Linus shows up as a baby in September 1952. Lucy pulls the football trick on Charlie Brown for the first time in November 1952. This volume also includes a biography of Schulz and a long interview with him.

Volume 1 of 26

Schutz, Diana

Sexy Chix: Anthology of Women Cartoonists. Dark Horse Comics 2006 104p. Illustration

Grades: 10 11 12 Adult   **741.5; Fic**

1. Graphic novels; 2. Short stories — Graphic novels; 3. Women — Graphic novels

1-59307-238-4, $12.95

Don't let the title fool you — this isn't the average collection of comics featuring impossibly proportioned vixens in spandex. This time around the sexy chix in question are the writers and artists behind the comics, representing some of the best and brightest talent contributing to the medium of comics and graphic novels today. With stories ranging from mainstream adventures to comic shorts to autobiography, Sexy Chix is devoted to the under-recognized contingent of female cartoonists in an overwhelmingly male-oriented industry. It's about time these creators get to tell the stories they want to, and the result is a variety of artistic visions and styles. Among the sexy chicks are New York Times best-selling author Joyce Carol Oates, Eisner Award-winning illustrator Jill Thompson (Scary Godmother), A Distant Soil writer/artist Colleen Doran, Bitchy Bitch creator Roberta Gregory, DC Comics writer Gail Simone, novelist Sarah Grace McCandless (Grosse Pointe Girl) and many, many more. Some stories include nudity, sexual situations, harsh language, and violence.

Schweizer, Chris

Crogan's loyalty. Chris Schweizer; [edited by] James Lucas Jones. Oni Press, Inc. 2012 150 p. Color; Illustration

Grades: 8 9 10 11 12 Adult   **741.5**

1. Adventure graphic novels; 2. United States — History — 1775-1783, Revolution — Comic books, strips, etc.

9781934964408, $14.99; 1934964409

LC 2011943514

Courtesy of Oni Press

"Schweizer takes another bite out of history in this story of two brothers divided by the American Revolution. Charlie, the elder Crogan and a Loyalist ranger, is infuriated that his younger brother would turn rebel, stating 'There's a passion that makes most young men wanna tear society down because they ain't in charge of it.' Meanwhile, Will, a colonial scout, is no less incensed that his older brother would stand for a tyrant against his own country." (Booklist)

Crogan's march. Oni Press 2009 212p. Illustration

Grades: 8 9 10 11 12 Adult

741.5; Fic

1. Adventure graphic novels; 2. Graphic novels; 3. Imperialism — Graphic novels; 4. North Africa — World history — 20th century — Graphic novels

978-1-934964-24-8, $14.95

When brothers Eric and Cory squabble at the dinner table, their father tells them the story of Peter Crogan, one of their ancestors, who fought in the French Foreign Legion in 1912. Crogan's five-year term of service is one month from completion when he's asked to stay and become an officer. His unit is stationed in North Africa, where the French hold territory and depend on the French Foreign Legion to police the territory, putting down

Courtesy of Oni Press

the rebellious attacks of the Tuaregs. He finds himself torn between the heroic Captain Poitelet (who tends to be the sole survivor of various battles) and the grizzled sergeant who actually cares about the people the Legion polices. When Crogan's unit escorts a caravan that endures an attack by Tuaregs, the captain's reckless actions endanger everyone, and Crogan must find help. Schweizer's story includes the kind of violence military actions cause, but very little in the way of bad language. Some may wince at the heavily French-accented English of some of the characters ("zee Daughters of France send zem out to all of zee units," etc.). This action-packed historical fiction graphic novel will appeal to teens, but adults who remember such novels as Beau Geste by Percival Christopher Wren (and the movies, of course) will also enjoy reading Schweizer's tale.

This book is part of The Crogan Adventures series; Sequel to: Crogan's vengeance (2008)

Crogan's vengeance. book design by Keith Wood; edited by James Lucas Jones with Jill Beaton. Oni Press 2008 185p. Illustration
Grades: 8 9 10 11 12 Adult　　　　**741.5; Fic**
  1. Adventure graphic novels; 2. Graphic novels; 3. Pirates — Graphic novels
978-1-934964-06-4, $14.95

Catfoot Crogan serves as an honest and honorable sailor on a ship commanded by an unjust captain when the ship is taken over by pirates. In order to save their lives, the sailors all take the oath to become pirates, but Crogan immediately runs afoul of D'Or, a brutal man who enjoys torturing others. Catfoot is a pirate, but he's determined to remain as honest and honorable as he can be, which continually puts him in danger. This swashbuckling tale shows a less romantic story than Rafael Sabatini's Captain Blood, with more violence, but it is more action-oriented than merely violent.

Courtesy of Oni Press

"Filled with mutiny, ferocious storms, shark-infested waters, commandeering of ships, and — of course — swashbuckling sword fights, this book has high teen appeal." SLJ

Part of the Crogan Adventures series

Seagle, Steven T.
  American Virgin: Head. DC Comics/Vertigo 2006 112p. Illustration
Grades: 11 12 Adult　　　　**741.5; Fic**
  1. Graphic novels; 2. Mystery graphic novels; 3. Revenge — Graphic novels
978-1-4012-1065-6, $9.99

Adam Chamberlain is a youth minister and author, head of a national virginity movement. When his fiancee, Cassie, is brutally murdered in Africa, Adam travels there with his black-sheep stepsister Cyndi, trying to discover meaning in Cassie's death. Confronted by hit men, paparazzi, pornography, and even the voice of God, Adam finds himself lost in a vortex of spiritually uncharted territory. This series has nudity, strong language, and violence.

  Kafka. Active Images 2006 un Illustration
Grades: 10 11 12 Adult　　　　**741.5; Fic**

1. Adventure graphic novels; 2. Graphic novels; 3. Mystery graphic novels
0-9766761-5-X, $14.99

Dan Hutton lost everything...his name, his past, his wife, his life. Having lived in a witness relocation program for years, Dan is told his new identity has been compromised, by two different groups who each claim to be CIA operatives. Unable to trust anyone, Dan runs back to the world that took everything he loved, hoping he can reclaim his past. The book is filled with suspense and action with very little violence.

Segami, Akira
  Kagetora, volume 1. Akira Segami; translated by Akira Tsubasa; adapted by Nunziuo DeFilippis & Christina Weir; lettered by Ryan & Reilly. Del Rey Manga 2008 202p. Illustration
Grades: 8 9 10 11 12　　　　**741.5; Fic**
  1. Graphic novels; 2. Humorous graphic novels; 3. Manga; 4. Martial arts — Graphic novels; 5. Romance graphic novels; 6. Shonen manga
9780345491411, $10.95

Young ninja Kagetora arrives at the Toudou family dojo on assignment, and he learns that he must teach martial arts to the family hime (princess), Yuki. The problem is, Yuki is a total, absolute klutz; she's also tiny and absolutely cute and charming. As he tries his best to train her, Kagetora finds himself doing the forbidden — he's falling for Yuki. How can he perform his duty? On top of that, Yuki's best friend Aki, one of the Toudou's top students, has been protecting Yuki for years and resents Kagetora's presence. The book includes a lot of fan service, which actually ties into the plot as Kagetora can't help but look at Yuki, even though he knows that his feelings are not appropriate.

Sen, Jai
  Garlands of Moonlight. Shoto Press 2002 86p. Illustration
Grades: 9 10 11 12 Adult　　　　**741.5; Fic**
  1. Graphic novels; 2. Horror graphic novels; 3. Vampires — Graphic novels
0-9717564-0-6, $4.59

　　　　　　　　　　　　LC 03-311055

Silent and merciless, a creature of darkness has come to prey on an island village. Babies vanish, mothers are murdered, and the threat of evil grows with each night. The village becomes a battleground as the onrush of the twentieth century clashes with tradition — and the restless spirits of the island's mythical past... Set in late colonial Indonesia, this book relates a Malay vampire legend in graphic novel format. Printed in a black and silver duotone, the book captures the feel of turn-of-the-century daguerreotype photographs. There is some violence.

Malay Mysteries Book 1

Seth
  Clyde Fans Book 1. Drawn & Quarterly 2004 156p. Illustration
Grades: 11 12 Adult　　　　**741.5; Fic**
  1. Graphic novels
1-896597-84-X, $19.95

This book focuses on the lives of two brothers and their fan manufacturing company. After one more disastrous attempt at selling, Simon returns to the office defeated and unsure of what he'll do next. Even after studying manuals on the art of selling, he still can't seem to clinch that final deal. In the eyes of his brother Abraham, he is a failure. Simon's plight is reminiscent of Arthur Miller's play, "Death of a Salesman." Here, Seth explores the complex and fascinating relationship of the two brothers behind Clyde Fans. There's one brief scene of incidental nudity.

  Wimbledon Green: The Greatest Comic Book Collector in the World. Drawn & Quarterly 2005 un Illustration
Grades: 11 12 Adult　　　　**741.5; Fic**

1. Collectors and collecting — Graphic novels; 2. Graphic novels
1-896597-93-9, $19.95

Meet Wimbledon Green, the self-proclaimed world's greatest comic-book collector who brokered the world's best comic-book deal in the history of collecting. Comic-book retailers, auctioneers, and conventioneers from around North America, as well as Green's collecting rivals, weigh in on the man and his vast collection of comic books. Are Green's intentions honorable? Does he truly love comics or is he driven by the need to conquer? Lastly, is he really even Wimbledon Green?

Sexton, Adam
Hawthorne's the Scarlet letter: the Manga edition. Wiley Publishing 2009 186p. Illustration
Grades: 5 6 7 8 9 10 11 12   **741.5; Fic**
1. Authors; 2. Graphic novels; 3. Novelists; 4. Short story writers; 5. Hawthorne, Nathaniel, 1804-1864; 6. Hawthorne, Nathaniel, 1804-1864 — Adaptations/Graphic novels
978-0-470-14889-1, $9.99

Hester Prynne, a young married woman in puritanical Massachusetts, stands in public shame when she bears a child long after her husband had disappeared. She refuses to identify the father of her child and instead wears the scarlet letter A always. The young minister Arthur Dimmesdale lives with his guilt in secret, but the physician, Roger Chillingworth, is actually Hester's husband, returned for vengeance. He vows to find the man who fathered Pearl, Hester's daughter, and destroy him. Meanwhile, Pearl grows up in a society that shuns her mother, and she comes to see the A as her mother's badge of honor. This book is a manga style adaptation of Hawthorne's novel.

Sfar, Joann
Dungeon Vol. 1: Duck Heart. [by] Joann Sfar & Lewis Trondheim. NBM 2003 96p. Illustration
Grades: 7 8 9 10 11 12   **741.5; Fic**
1. Fantasy graphic novels; 2. Graphic novels; 3. Humorous graphic novels
1-56163-401-8, $14.95

"As a result of some unfortunate accidents, Herbert, usually a lowly messenger in the great Dungeon, is called upon to defend it from all manner of beasties. In his endeavors to become a warrior, he is helped by his friend Marvin the vegetarian dragon and by the Dungeon Keeper. Although there's a solid dose of cartoon-style violence and gore, teens will appreciate Herbert's pseudo-slacker attitude, which turns him into an accidental hero time and time again." Booklist

Courtesy of NBM Publishing

Other titles in this series are: Dungeon, the early years: the night shirt (2005); Zenith: the barbarian princess (2005)

Klezmer, Book One: Tales of the Wild East. First Second Books 2006 140p. Illustration
Grades: 11 12 Adult   **741.5**
1. Graphic novels; 2. Jews — Graphic novels; 3. Musicians — Graphic novels
1-59643-198-9

Klezmer tells a tale of love, friendship, survival, and the joy of making music in pre-World War II Eastern Europe. Noah is perfectly content as the leader of a traveling klezmer band, until his bandmates are brutally murdered by rival musicians. He sets out for Odessa alone, but is joined by Chava, a beautiful girl with a voice like an angel. Meanwhile, Yaacov is

expelled from his yeshiva for stealing; he too makes his way to Odessa along with Vincenzo, a violinist, and Tshokola, a gypsy entertainer. When these five misfits finally come together, they must set aside their differences and learn to work together (and rock a crowd) through their music. Some nudity and a fair amount of violence make this better for older readers.

★ The **little** prince. adapted from the book by Antoine de Saint-Exupéry; translated by Sarah Ardizzone; colour by Brigitte Findakly. Houghton Mifflin Harcourt 2010 110p. Illustration
Grades: 5 6 7 8 9   **741; Fic; 741.5**
1. Extraterrestrial beings — Graphic novels; 2. Fantasy graphic novels; 3. Graphic novels; 4. Saint-Exupéry, Antoine de, 1900-1944 — Adaptations
978-0-547-33802-6, $19.99; 0-547-33802-3

"On the surface, this is a straight graphic-novel retelling of the narrator pilot getting stranded in the desert, where he meets a curious little boy who claims to be from a wee planet very far away.... The ultimately tricky task is to honor the source but not sound like an adaptation (otherwise, why not just read the original") and Sfar nails it on both counts.... Everything is handled with both reverence and ingenuity." Booklist

Little Vampire Does Kung Fu!. stories and drawings by Joann Sfar; colors by Walter; translated by Mark and Alexis Siegel. Simon & Schuster Books for Young Readers 2003 un Illustration
Grades: 4 5 6 7 8 9   **741.5; Fic**
1. Fantasy graphic novels; 2. Graphic novels; 3. Humorous graphic novels; 4. Vampires — Graphic novels
0-689-85769-1, $12.95

LC 2003-045770
Jeffrey the jerk is a bully and everyone knows it. Little Vampire isn't about to stand around and watch him pick on his best friend, Michael. There's only one thing to do: travel to the highest mountain and seek kung fu lessons from the master... There's an icky moment when Little Vampire's monster friends spit up bits of Jeffrey (whom they ate) and they try to put him together again.

The **professor's** daughter. [story by] Joann Sfar & [illustrated by] Emmanuel Guibert; translated by Alexis Siegel. First Second Books 2007 63p. Illustration
Grades: 7 8 9 10 11 12 Adult   **741.5**
1. Graphic novels; 2. Humorous graphic novels; 3. Mummies — Graphic novels; 4. Romance graphic novels
978-1-59643-130-0; 1-59643-130-X, $16.95

LC 2006-22177
In Victorian London, Lillian, the daughter of a famed archeologist, has fallen in love with the mummy of Imhotep IV; he thinks that Lillian bears a strong resemblance to this long-dead wife. Their love faces many obstacles, from Lillian's father, the police, a pirate who is actually Imhotep III (yes, the father and another mummy), even Queen Victoria herself. Dainty Victorian manners mix with broad farce and black comedy in a beautifully illustrated book with muted colors and sepia tones.

★ The **rabbi's** cat. Pantheon Books 2005 142p. Illustration
Grades: 11 12 Adult   **741.5; Fic**
1. Graphic novels; 2. Jews — Graphic novels; 3. Rabbis — Graphic novels; 4. France — History — 1914-1940 — Graphic novels; 5. North Africa — Graphic novels
0-375-42281-1, $21.95; 0-375-71464-2 (pa), $16.95

LC 2004-61406
"A slinky gray cat lives with a rabbi and his beautiful young daughter. One day, the feline eats their parrot, only to find that he has gained the bird's ability to talk. Witty and highly intelligent, the cat immediately decides that he wants to learn more about Judaism, from the Kabbalah to the Torah.... There is plenty for teens to like — humor, romance, and

theological questioning combined with a folkloric quality to bring to life a multifaceted work." SLJ

Vampire loves. color by Audré Jardel; translation by Alexis Siegel. First Second Books 2006 187p. Illustration

Grades: 9 10 11 12 Adult   **741.5; Fic**

1. Graphic novels; 2. Romance graphic novels; 3. Vampires — Graphic novels

978-1-59643-093-8; 1-59643-093-1, $16.95

LC 2005-21498

When the vampire Ferdinand breaks up with Lani, his cheating girlfriend, he starts looking for love and romance. In the process he meets the vampire sisters Ritaline and Aspirine, tries his hand at detective work, goes on a cruise and meets the ghost, Sigh, and gets mixed up in a fight between mummy pirates and Professor Joseph Bell.

"Edgy and creepy but at the same time universal and normal, Vampire Loves is a unique study in contrasts that will be a pleasurable discovery for graphic novel enthusiasts." Voice Youth Advocates

First published in four volumes in France with title: Grand vampire

Shaffer, Neal

The **Awakening**. Oni Press 2004 104p. Illustration

Grades: 10 11 12 Adult   **741.5; Fic**

1. Graphic novels; 2. Horror graphic novels; 3. Mystery graphic novels

1-932664-00-9, $9.95

Francesca, the only child of an affluent family, is excited to be attending one of the most prestigious boarding schools in New England. Unfortunately, things go horribly wrong when, shortly after her arrival, she finds one of her classmates brutally murdered, sending her into a deep shock, putting her into a coma. Even worse, immediately following the tragic incident, Francesca begins to have visions of which girl will be slain next, and even though she has awakened, she's unable to tell anyone about it. Is this a new horror being visited on the longstanding institution, or is it something much more, going to the core of the school itself, to an evil that defies description? The book includes strong language, violence, and some nudity.

Courtesy of Oni Press

Shakespeare, William

William Shakespeare's King Lear. Black Dog & Leventhal/Workman Publishing 2006 148p. Illustration

Grades: 7 8 9 10 11 12 Adult   **741.5; 822.3**

1. Graphic novels; 2. Tragedy — Graphic novels; 3. Shakespeare, William; 4. Shakespeare, William — Adaptations

978-1-57912-617-9, $12.95

This graphic novel adaptation of King Lear, originally published in 1984, uses excerpted text from the play together with full-color illustrations to tell the story of the king whose ill-fated attempts to learn which of his daughters loves him best causes loss and madness.

Part of the Shakespeare Graphic Library.

Courtesy of ABDO Publishing.

William Shakespeare's Macbeth. Black Dog & Leventhal/Workman Publishing 1982 92p. Illustration

Grades: 7 8 9 10 11 12 Adult   **822.3; 741.5**

1. Graphic novels; 2. Tragedy — Graphic novels; 3. Shakespeare, William; 4. Shakespeare, William — Adaptations

978-1-57912-621-6, $12.95

This graphic novel adaptation of Macbeth, originally published in 1982, uses excerpted text from the play together with full-color illustrations to tell the story of the Thane of Cawdor who listens to a trio of witches and slays the King of Scotland to take his throne.

Part of the Shakespeare Graphic Library

William Shakespeare's Twelfth night. adapted by Vincent Goodwin illustrated by Cynthia Martin. ABDO/Magic Wagon 2008 48p. Illustration

Grades: 5 6 7 8 9 10   **822.3; 741.5**

1. Authors; 2. Dramatists; 3. Graphic novels; 4. Poets; 5. Shakespeare, William, 1564-1616 — Adaptations

978-1-60270-195-3, $28.50

LC 2008-10747

Twins Viola and Sebastian are separated in a shipwreck. Viola decides to disguise herself as a man since she's alone, and this sets the stage for mixed-up identities and a comic love triangle. This graphic novel adaptation retains some of the original language from Shakespeare's play, while paring down the story to appeal to struggling readers. The book includes a short biography, a summary of the play, a glossary, and a short selection of famous lines and phrases from the play.

Part of the Graphic Shakespeare series

Courtesy of ABDO Publishing.

Shanower, Eric

★ **Age** of Bronze vol. 1: A Thousand Ships. Image Comics 2001 223p. Illustration (Age of bronze)

Grades: 10 11 12   **741.5; Fic**

1. Graphic novels; 2. Greek mythology — Graphic novels; 3. Trojan War — Graphic novels

1-58240-212-4; 1-58240-200-0 (pa), $19.95

Shanower includes frank sex scenes and doesn't shy away from the brutal violence of war.

This is "the first part of a seven-volume graphic novel about the Trojan War.... The book begins with the story of Paris, the milk-white bull and the kidnapping of Helen, and goes up to the start of the war." Publ Wkly

"This series retells the story of the Trojan War, going back to the young Trojan prince Paris and the petty rivalry of several goddesses that set the events into motion. Shanower conducted extensive reasearch of the world of that time — its technology, architecture, clothing, armor, and weapons. His books are more "real" than any Hollywood movie depiction." Voice Youth Advocates

Includes bibliographical references; Other books in the Age of Bronze series include: Betrayal (2008); Sacrifice (2004)

★ **Age** of bronze volume 3A: Betrayal part one. Image Comics 2007 176p. Illustration

Grades: 10 11 12 Adult   **741.5; Fic**

1. Adventure graphic novels; 2. Graphic novels; 3. Greek mythology — Graphic novels; 4. Troy (Extinct city) — Graphic novels

978-1-58240-755-5, $17.99

The graphic novel retelling of the story of the Trojan War continues, as High King Agamemnon's army passes the island of Tenedos on its journey to conquer Troy. When a snake bites Philoktetes on the foot, his cries of pain bother the army so much that Odysseus must find a solution. Then, the Achaeans send an embassy to Troy in hopes of preventing a war. This book includes some nudity and sexual situations as well as some violence. Shanower includes a lengthy bibliography of historical sources.

Sequel to Sacrifice (2004)

★ **Age** of Bronze: Betrayal part 2. by Eric Shanower. Image Comics 2013 176 p. Illustration
Grades: 10 11 12 Adult   **741.5**
1. Trojan War — Fiction; 2. Greece — Fiction; 3. Graphic novels
1607067579; 9781607067573

In this graphic novel, written and illustrated by Eric Shanower, "the Trojan plain fills with death as Achaean forces clash in blood with the Trojan army. In the city of Troy, Pandarus pulls the strings to put Troilus in Cressida's bed. But when Cressida is ripped away to the enemy camp, how far will Troilus fight? (Publisher's note)

"Shanower's graphic-novel retelling of the Trojan War is one of the great artistic visions of the comics medium. Where both mythology and heroic-adventure comics typically lean toward vast spectacle and archetypal characters, Shanower is uncompromising in his sharp, humanizing focus. Betrayal, Part 2, the second part of the third part of Shanower's projected seven-part series, begins with Achilles and his Myrmidons invading the beach of Troy and ends with Troilus' breakdown during a bloody skirmish with a squad of Achaeans.... Seldom has a work shined so brightly on every page." Booklist

★ **Age** of Bronze: Sacrifice. Image Comics 2004 223p. Illustration; Map (Age of bronze)
Grades: 10 11 12 Adult   **741; 741.5; Fic**
1. Graphic novels; 2. Greek mythology — Graphic novels; 3. Trojan War — Graphic novels
1-58240-360-0; 1-58240-399-6 (pa), $19.95

"Sacrifice begins by recapitulating the story thus far. Paris sails back to Troy, just as self-regarding and shortsighted as when he left. Thrilled with his own prize (Helen), he has no understanding of the political complications. Priam does, but he is swayed by the machinations of Helen and by Hecuba's generosity. Not only are the major characters (Achilles, Klytemnestra, Odysseus) complex, but even a minor player like Telephus is carefully developed." SLJ

Includes bibliographical references; Followed by Betrayal (2008); This is the second book in the author's projected seven-volume graphic novel about the Trojan War. The first volume, A thousand ships, was published in 2001

Little Nemo: Return to Slumberland. written by Eric Shanower; illustrated by Gabriel Rodriguez. IDW Publishing 2015 120 p. Color; Illustration
Grades: 10 11 12 Adult
741.5
1. Friendship — Graphic novels; 2. Dreaming — Graphic novels
1631400592; 9781631400599, $21.99
Eisner Award: Best Limited Series (2015)

This graphic novel, by Eric Shanower, illustrated by Gabriel Rodriguez, "sees King Morpheus' daughter, in the Royal Palace of Slumberland, selecting her next-playmate — Nemo! Only Nemo has no interest in being anyone's playmate, dream or no dream!" (Publisher's note)

Originally published as: Little Nemo: Return to Slumberland, issues #1-4

Courtesy of IDW Publishing

★ The **Wonderful** Wizard of Oz. writer, Eric Shanower; artist, Skottie Young; colorist, Jean-Francois Beaulieu;

letterer, Jeff Eckleberry; adapted from the novel by L. Frank Baum. Marvel Entertainment 2009 192p. Illustration
Grades: 3 4 5 6 7 8 9 10 11 12 Adult   **741.5; Fic**
1. Adventure graphic novels; 2. Authors; 3. Children's authors; 4. Dramatists; 5. Fantasy graphic novels; 6. Graphic novels; 7. Journalists; 8. Baum, L. Frank, 1856-1919 — Adaptations
978-0-7851-2921-9, $29.99

A twister picks up the house Dorothy and her dog Toto are in and carries them from Kansas to the land of Oz; the house lands on top of the Wicked Witch of the East, and the Munchkins, who were her slaves, hail Dorothy as a great sorceress. All the girl wants is to get back home to Kansas, but all anyone can say is that she must go to the Emerald City and ask the Great Wizard Oz to send her home. As she travels along the Yellow Brick Road, she meets a scarecrow who wants brains so people won't think he's a dummy, a tin man who wants a heart so he can love, and a great cowardly lion who wants courage so he'll truly be king of the beasts. However, once they reach the Emerald City and each see the Wizard Oz, they learn they must do what no one, including the Wizard himself, could ever do kill the Wicked Witch of the West. Shanower's adaptation of L. Frank Baum's novel keeps all the charm of the original, while Skottie Young's art banishes any lingering images of the old Technicolor movie; Beaulieu's muted color palette works with Young's art, while Eckleberry's lettering adds to an overall effect of magic and wonder. This book will appeal to all ages

Other Oz adapations by Shanower and Young are: The Marvelous Land of Oz; Ozma of Oz; Dorothy and the Wizard in Oz; The Road to Oz; The Emerald City of Oz

Sheikman, Alex
Robotika. Archaia Studios Press 2006 128p. Illustration
Grades: 11 12 Adult   **741.5; Fic**
1. Adventure graphic novels; 2. Graphic novels; 3. Science fiction graphic novels
978-1-932386-21-9, $19.95

In a future world full of human/machine hybrids and organic technology, a samurai named Niko serves the Queen. When a new piece of technology that can revolutionize the world and render cyborgs obsolete is stolen and its inventor killed, the Queen sends Niko to retrieve it. He must fight and kill many warriors along the way and succeeds, only to see the Queen destroy the object to create a hair ornament. He gives up the sword, but still joins yojimbo (wandering masterless samurai bodyguards) Cherokee Geisha and Uri Bronski to protect a caravan of pilgrims seeking their god's temple.

Sheikman uses color, differing visual styles, even vertical lettering (for Cherokee Geisha's speech), and combines genre elements of the Western, samurai action, and science fiction to create a story set in a well-realized world. Two short stories give background on Cherokee Geisha and Bronski.

Originally published as Robotika issues #1-4.

Shen, Prudence
★ **Nothing** Can Possibly Go Wrong. by Prudence Shen, illustrated by Faith Erin Hicks. First Second 2013 288 p.
Grades: 7 8 9 10   **741.5; Fic**
1. Robots — Juvenile fiction; 2. School stories — Graphic novels; 3. Cheerleading — Juvenile fiction
159643659X; 9781596436596, $16.99

"You wouldn't expect Nate and Charlie to be friends. Charlie's the laid-back captain of the basketball team, and Nate is the neurotic, scheming president of the robotics club. But they are friends, however unlikely — until Nate declares war on the cheerleaders. At stake is funding that will either cover a robotics competition or new cheerleading uniforms — but not both." (Publisher's note)

"Shen's plot ably balances drama, humor, angst, and robotic geekery, giving the book an immediate YA appeal, but one that's broad enough to be enjoyable to older readers, as well. Visually, Hicks's wide-eyed, inky b&w panels infuse the characters with real emotion and personality, capturing the book's heartfelt youthfulness." Pub Wkly

Shiga, Jason

Bookhunter. Sparkplug Comics 2007 un Illustration

Grades: 10 11 12 Adult   **741.5; Fic**
1. Graphic novels; 2. Humorous graphic novels; 3. Librarians — Graphic novels; 4. Mystery graphic novels
978-0-9742715-6-9, $15

When a rare Caxton Bible is stolen from the Oakland Public Library in 1973, Agent Bay of the Library Police is on the case. Reading very much like a police procedural mystery, but set in the library, Bookhunter combines humor, library technology of the early 1970s, and lots of action movie tropes. The book includes a few harsh words and some violence.

★ **Demon;** Volume 1. Jason Shiga; [edited by] Calista Brill. First Second 2016 176 p. Color; Illustration

Grades: 11 12 Adult   **741.5; Fic**
1. Mystery fiction
1626724520; 9781626724525, $19.99

LC 2015958711

Eisner Award: Best Graphic Album — Reprint (2017)

In this book, by Jason Shiga, "Jimmy Yee cannot die. A noose around his neck, a razor across his wrist, and even a bullet to his head all yield the same results: he awakes from each suicide attempt, miraculously unharmed, in his shabby room at the Sunbeam Motel. Has he gone mad? Or has he truly died and found himself in hell?" (Publisher's note)

"As with Shiga's other books, there are puzzles aplenty to solve, with an added layer of urgent narrative drive. Originally serialized as a webcomic, the story will prove just as addictive for readers finding it in print." Pub Wkly

Volume 1 of 4

Meanwhile. Abrams/Amulet 2010 un Illustration

Grades: 4 5 6 7 8 9   **741.5**
1. Graphic novels; 2. Science fiction graphic novels
0-8109-8423-7; 978-0-8109-8423-3, $15.95

LC 2009-39844

In this choose-your-own adventure graphic novel, a boy stumbles on the laboratory of a mad scientist who asks him to choose between testing a mind-reading device, a time machine, and a doomsday machine. (Bull Cent Child Books)

Shimabukuro, Mitsutoshi

Toriko, vol. 1. story and art by Mitsutoshi Shimabukuro; [translation, Christine Dashiell; adaptation, Hope Donovan; touch-up art & lettering, Jim Keefe]. Viz Media/Shonen Jump 2010 208p. Illustration

Grades: 8 9 10 11 12 Adult   **741.5; Fic**
1. Adventure graphic novels; 2. Food — Graphic novels; 3. Graphic novels; 4. Humorous graphic novels; 5. Hunting — Graphic novels; 6. Manga; 7. Shonen manga
978-1-4215-3509-8, $9.99

Toriko is a Gourmet Hunter, who earns huge bounties for finding ferocious, delicious foods. We're not talking salmon fishing or deer hunting here, but eight-legged alligators and rare fruit guarded by four-armed, bloodthirsty gorilla-type creatures. Toriko himself has a huge appetite for the rare foods, and sometimes eats most of what he's supposed to bring to the fancy restaurants that hire him. Komatsu, the head chef at Igo, a restaurant that caters to those wealthy enough to afford the rare foods, tags along with Toriko, who is a muscular giant of a man. This odd

couple forms a friendship born in their mutual love of fine foods. The book is full of crazy action, lots of bugeyed, drop-jawed, slapstick moments, and some potty humor.

Shimura, Takako

Sweet Blue Flowers; Volume 1. story and art by Takako Shimura; translation & adaptation, John Werry; touch-up art & lettering, Monalisa De Asis. Viz 2017 400 p. Illustration

Grades: 10 11 12 Adult   **741.5; Fic**
1. High school students — Fiction; 2. Shojo-ai; 3. Manga; 4. Lesbians — Fiction; 5. Friendship — Fiction
1421592983; 9781421592985, $24.99

"Akira Okudaira is starting high school and is ready for exciting new experiences. And on the first day of school, she runs into her best friend from kindergarten at the train station! Now Akira and Fumi have the chance to rekindle their friendship, but life has gotten a lot more complicated since they were kids... Fumi is glad Akira is back in her life. Even in kindergarten, Akira knew how to stand up for herself, and she was always willing to stand up for Fumi too. But Fumi's first love recently got married, and Fumi is grappling with a broken heart and the fact that her sweetheart was another woman... Can Akira's open heart help dispel the gloom Fumi has been caught up in?" (Publisher's note)

"Through the continuous theme of the school's performance of Wuthering Heights, Shimura's manga explores love, loss, and the importance of friendship, while the cutesy artwork nicely balances the somewhat heavy material." Booklist

Volume 1 of 4

Wandering son: Volume Three. Shimura Takako; translated by Matt Thorn. Fantagraphics Books 2012 200 p.

Grades: 7 8 9 10   **741.5; Fic**
1. Transgender people — Graphic novels; 2. Friendship — Graphic novels; 3. Secrets — Fiction
1606995332; 9781606995334, $19.99

In this graphic novel, by Shimura Takako, "Shuichi and his friend Yoshino have a secret: Shuichi is a boy who wants to be a girl, and Yoshino is a girl who wants to be a boy. But one day...their secret is exposed, and the two find themselves the target of sixth-grade cruelty. Their friendship is strained,...and their mentor, Yuki, reveals the harder reality of being transgendered. Meanwhile, Shuichi's sister, Maho, realizes her dream of becoming a model, and drags Shuichi along." (Publisher's note)

Wandering son: Volume Two. Shimura Takako; translated by Matt Thorn. Fantagraphics Books 2012 200 p.

Grades: 7 8 9 10   **741.5; Fic**
1. Transgender people — Graphic novels; 2. Bildungsromans — Graphic novels; 3. Middle schools — Fiction
1606994565; 9781606994566, $19.99

"In the second volume of Shimura Takako's [Wandering Son series],...transgendered protagonists, Shuichi and Yoshino, have entered the sixth grade. Shuichi spends a precious gift of cash from his grandmother on a special present for himself, a purchase that triggers a chain of events in which his sister Maho learns his secret, and Shuichi inadvertently steals the heart of a boy Maho in interested in." (Publisher's note)

"While the first volume served as an introduction to Shuichi and Yoshino's lives, their stories and identities really begin to evolve in this lovely, exciting, and surprising follow-up." Booklist

Wandering son; Volume four. Shimura Takako; [translation: Matt Thorn]. Fantagraphics Books 2013 219 p.

Grades: 7 8 9 10   **741.5; Fic**
1. Comic books, strips, etc. — Japan — Translations into English; 2. Friendship — Comic books, strips, etc; 3. Gender identity — Comic

books, strips, etc; 4. Middle school students — Comic books, strips, etc;
5. Middle schools — Juvenile fiction; 6. Friendship — Graphic novels;
7. Gender role — Graphic novels; 8. Comic books, strips, etc.
1606996053; 9781606996058, $19.99

LC 2013363244

This book, by Shimura Takako, the fourth in the series, "continues the story of Nitori Shuichi, a girl who wants to be a boy named Takatsuki Yoshino.... The story is filled with mixed signals, rumors, unrequited love, boys and girls fighting over one another, and love-hate relationships.... And as the characters get ready to enter middle school, with its gender-specific uniforms, each one is being pushed to conform to society's standards." (School Library Journal)

Reads from right to left.

Wandering son; Volume One. Shimura Takako; translated by Matt Thorn. Fantagraphics 2011 192 p. Illustration
Grades: 7 8 9 10 11 12 Adult   **741.5; Fic**
1. Puberty — Graphic novels; 2. Transgender people — Graphic novels;
3. Manga; 4. Bildungsromans — Graphic novels; 5. Seinen manga
1606994166; 9781606994160, $19.99

This manga "tells the story of a friendship between Shuichi, a young boy who wishes he were a girl, and Yoshino, a young girl who wishes she were a boy.... Shuichi's impulses toward a female identity feel confusing and shameful to him, and it's the girls in his life-first Yoshino, and then Saori-who point out his difference and encourage it.... Both children are teased mercilessly by their classmates, whose sexual development, while perhaps more socially normative, is just as confusing to them." (Publishers Weekly)

Volume 1 of 15 (8 available in English)

Shiomi, Chika

Canon Vol. 1. DC Comics/CMX 2007 200p. Illustration
Grades: 8 9 10 11 12 Adult   **741.5; Fic**
1. Graphic novels; 2. Horror graphic novels; 3. Manga; 4. Shojo manga;
5. Vampires — Graphic novels
978-1-4012-1163-9, $9.99

Suspense and the supernatural collide in the tale of Canon — the only student to escape the bloody vampire attack that takes the lives of her fellow classmates. But she doesn't get very far before she is captured, bitten and turned into a vampire herself. Struggling against the terrible needs that compel the undead, Canon commits herself to using her powers for good. She'll do whatever she can to avenge the death of her friends and her own unfortunate fate. Joining forces with Fuui — a talking vampire crow — she begins her quest to find Rodd, Lord of the Vampires. There's some mildly harsh language and lots of fighting vampire attacks, but nothing more than has been seen in most Buffy the Vampire Slayer or Angel episodes on television.

Night of the Beasts Volume 1. Go! Comi 2006 200p. Illustration
Grades: 10 11 12 Adult   **741.5; Fic**
1. Graphic novels; 2. Horror graphic novels; 3. Manga; 4. Shojo manga;
5. Supernatural graphic novels
978-1-933617-14-5, $10.99

Aria's got a reputation as the toughest girl in school because she can't resist taking on bullies — especially guys who aggressively hit on innocent girls. Which is why she's taken by surprise when her first kiss is stolen by a complete stranger. Not only does he keep making moves on her, but it seems like every time they meet, it's at the latest crime scene of a murder spree that's plaguing Aria's neighborhood. How is it that he seems to know all about the supernatural murderer of these innocent girls? And how will Aria react to his claim only she can save him from a destiny so bloody that even the violent deeds of black demon slaughtering victims all over town

will pale in comparison? The book includes mildly strong language, some bloody violence, and mild sexual situations.

Yurara, Vol. 1. Viz Media/Shojo Beat 2007 192p. Illustration
Grades: 10 11 12 Adult   **741.5; Fic**
1. Fantasy graphic novels; 2. Ghosts — Graphic novels; 3. Graphic novels; 4. Manga; 5. Shojo manga
978-1-4215-1350-8, $8.99

Translated by JN Productions. First year high school student Yurara Tsukinowa is a quiet girl; she has seen ghosts most of her life, but has kept it a secret from anyone outside her family. Since she reacts emotionally in the presence of ghosts, she has a reputation for being weird. At school, she meets Mei Tendo and Yako Hoshino, two handsome boys who have powers to ward off vengeful spirits. When she's threatened by the ghost of a girl at her classroom desk, Yurara's guardian spirit manifests herself; this dark-haired, bold girl has the power to release souls. Yurara has to fend off Mei's teasing advances and her female classmates' jealousy while trying to figure out just what she can now do. The story features some supernatural violence and sexual innuendo.

Shirai, Kaiu

The **promised** Neverland; Volume 1. story by Kaiu Shirai; art by Posuka Demizu; translation, Satsuki Yamashita; touch-up art & lettering, Mark McMurray; design, Julian (JR) Robinson; editor, Alexis Kirsch. Viz 2017 183 p. Illustration
Grades: 9 10 11 12   **741.5; Fic**
1. Orphans — Graphic novels; 2. Demonology — Fiction; 3. Orphanages — Fiction; 4. Shonen manga
1421597128; 9781421597126, $9.99

"The children of the Grace Field House orphanage have their happy lives upended when they find out they're being raised to be fed to demons. Can they escape their fate before it's too late?...Emma, Norman and Ray are the brightest kids at the...orphanage.... One day, though, Emma and Norman uncover the dark truth of the outside world they are forbidden from seeing." (Publisher's note)

Volume 1 of an ongoing series

Shirow, Masamune

The **ghost** in the shell. story and art by Shirow Masamune; translation and English adaptation, Frederik L. Schodt and Toren Smith. Kodansha Comics 2009 348 p. Illustration; Color
Grades: 11 12 Adult   **741.5; 741.5/952**
1. Cyborgs — Comic books, strips, etc; 2. Androids — Fiction
9781935429012, $26.99

LC 2010292697

In this book, by Shirow Masamune, "the line between man and machine has been inexorably blurred.... In this rapidly converging landscape, cyborg superagent Major Motoko Kusanagi is charged to track down the craftiest and most dangerous terrorists and cybercriminals.... When Major Kusanagi tracks the cybertrail of one such master hacker, the Puppeteer, her quest leads her into a world beyond information and technology." (Publisher's note)

Translated and adapted from the Japanese.; Other titles in this series are: Ghost in the Shell 2: Man-Machine Interface; Ghost in the Shell 1.5: Human-Error Processor

Shivack, Nadia

Inside out: portrait of an eating disorder. written and illustrated by Nadia Shivack. Atheneum Books for Young Readers 2007 un Illustration
Grades: 7 8 9 10 11 12   **741.5; 92**
1. Bulimia — Patients — United States — Biography — Comic books, strips, etc.; 2. Shivack, Nadia — Health — Comic books, strips, etc.
0-689-85216-9, $17.99; 978-0-689-85216-9

LC 2004016096

In this book the author gives readers a harrowing look inside her battle with anorexia and bulimia through pictures and captions.

Shone, Rob

Muhammad Ali: The Life of a Boxing Hero. Rosen Publishing Group 2006 48p. Illustration
Grades: 3 4 5 6 7 8 9   741.5; 796.8; 92
1. African American athletes — Graphic novels; 2. Biographical graphic novels; 3. Boxing — Biography — Graphic novels; 4. Graphic novels; 5. Ali, Muhammad, 1942-; 6. Ali, Muhammad, 1942- — graphic novels
978-1-4042-0856-8, $29.25

LC 2005035521

This book uses the graphic novel format to tell of the life and career of boxing great Muhammad Ali. He started his career as Cassius Clay but changed his name when he converted to the Nation of Islam. He used his fame as a boxer to advocate against U.S. involvement in Vietnam, and to raise funds for charity. The book includes a list of all his boxing matches, and a list of books for further reading.

Part of the Rosen Graphic Biographies series.

Courtesy of Rosen Publishing

Siddell, Thomas

Gunnerkrigg Court: orientation. [by] Tom Siddell. Archaia Studios Press 2009 296p. Illustration
Grades: 6 7 8 9 10 11 12   741; Fic; 741.5
978-1-932386-34-9, $26.95; 1-932386-34-3
"Antimony Carver is a precocious and preternaturally self-possessed young girl starting her first year of school at gloomy Gunnerkrigg Court, a very British boarding school that has robots running around along side body-snatching demons, forest gods, and the odd mythical creature. The opening volume in the series follows Antimony through her orientation year: the people she meets, the strange things that happen, and the things she causes to happen as she and her new friend, Kat, unravel the mysteries of the Court and deal with the everyday adventures of growing up." (Publisher's note)

Other titles in this series are: Vol. 2: Research (2009); Vol. 3: Reason (2011); Vol. 4: Materia (2013); Vol. 5: Refine (2015)

Sierra, Sergio A.

Frankenstein by Mary Shelley: a Dark graphic novel. adaptation Sergio A. Sierra; illustration Meritxell Ribas. Enslow Publishers 2013 95 p.
Grades: 6 7 8 9 10 11 12 Adult   741.5
1. Graphic novels; 2. Horror stories; 3. Monsters — Fiction; 4. Monsters — Graphic novels
0766040844; 9780766040847, $25.26

LC 2011035826

This book is a black-and-white graphic novel adaptation of Mary Shelley — s 19th-century gothic novel "Frankenstein." The plot tells the "tale of a monster, assembled by a scientist from parts of dead bodies, who develops a mind of his own as he learns to loathe himself and hate his creator." (WorldCat)

Includes bibliographical references.

Sievert, Tim

That salty air. Top Shelf Productions 2008 116p. Illustration
Grades: 10 11 12 Adult   741.5; Fic

1. Bereavement — Graphic novels; 2. Fishing — Graphic novels; 3. Graphic novels; 4. Ocean — Graphic novels
978-1-60309-005-6, $10

Fisherman Hugh has treated the ocean and its inhabitants with respect and reverence, but when he receives word that his mother died by drowning at sea, he acts as though the ocean itself has betrayed him. His loyal wife MaryAnne has just learned that she's pregnant, and she tries to help her husband. But he returns to fishing with a vengeful attitude that nearly destroys him. A mystical giant squid figures in Hugh's struggles deal with his grief and with the world.

Silvermoon, Crystal

Les misérables. Victor Hugo; adapted by Crystal Silvermoon; illustrated by SunNeko Lee. Udon Entertainment 2014 337 p. Illustration; Color (Manga Classics)
Grades: 8 9 10 11 12   741.5; Fic
1. France — History — 1789-1799, Revolution; 2. Manga
1927925169; 9781927925164, $19.99

In this graphic novel adaptation by Crystal Silvermoon, illustrated by SunNeko Lee, "Victor Hugo's classic novel of love & tragedy during the French Revolution is reborn in this fantastic new manga edition! The gorgeous art of TseMei Lee brings to life the tragic stories of Jean Valjean, Inspector Javert, and the beautiful Fantine, in this epic adaptation of Les Miserables!" (Publisher's note)

"All major plot points and iconic scenes are included in the text and art, and both work seamlessly to tell the story.... The characters, for the most part, are instantly recognizable. It is clear that research has gone into making this adaptation." VOYA

Simmons, Josh

House. Fantagraphics Books 2007 un Illustration
Grades: 11 12 Adult   741.5; Fic
1. Graphic novels; 2. Horror graphic novels
978-1-56097-855-8, $12.95

In the thick of a dense wood, a young man comes upon a decrepit house and two teen-aged girls, who quickly decide to explore the abandoned house together. Simmons captures the aloof ennui and deep curiosity of being a teenager-that is, until events force them to confront their own mortality. One of the girls takes a horrible fall, and her clothes are torn; for the rest of the book she is partially nude because of it.

Simon, Eddy

Pele: the king of soccer. written by Eddy Simon; illustrated by Vincent Brascaglia; English translation by Joe Johnson. First Second 2017 144 p. Color; Illustration
Grades: 4 5 6 7 8 9   92; 741.5
1. Pelé, 1940-; 2. Soccer players — Biography
9781626727557, $15.99; 9781626729797

LC 2016961595

"Edson Arantes do Nascimento, known to his schoolmates as Pelé, grew up in poverty in the Sao Paulo region of Brazil. He was too poor to afford a real soccer ball, so he played with a ball of newspaper.... He dominated the youth leagues and signed his first professional soccer contract at the age of fifteen. Within two years he was celebrated internationally, when he led Brazil to victory at the world cup." (Publisher's note)

"This particularly smart delineation of Pelé has it all: his career, his blunders, decency, and goodness. And his gift." Kirkus

Translation of: Le roi Pelé: l'homme et la légende

Simone, Gail

Attack on Titan anthology. Attack on Titan created by Hajime Isayama; edited by Ben Applegate and Jeanine Schaefer; cover, logo, and interior design by Phil Balsman; lettering and interior design by Steve Wands. Kodansha 2016 256 p. Illustration

Grades: 8 9 10 11 12   **741.5**

1. Fantasy fiction — Graphic novels; 2. Horror fiction — Graphic novels; 3. Science fiction graphic novels; 4. Shonen manga

1632362589; 9781632362582, $29.99

This tribute anthology to the manga Attack on Titan features "original stories by a long roster of comic superstars such as Scott Snyder (Batman, American Vampire), Gail Simone (Batgirl), Michael Avon Oeming (Powers), Paolo Rivera (Daredevil, Amazing Spider-Man), Cameron Stewart (Fight Club 2, Batgirl) and Faith Erin Hicks (The Adventures of Superhero Girl)!" (Publisher's note)

"The Victorian-style guide to Titan's walled city by Genevieve Valentine and David López is a standout, as is the contemplative final story by brothers Asaf and Tomer Hanuka." Pub Wkly

Birds of Prey Vol. 4: The Battle Within. DC Comics 2006 240p. Illustration

Grades: 9 10 11 12 Adult   **741.5**

1. Adventure graphic novels; 2. Birds of Prey (Fictional characters); 3. Graphic novels; 4. Superhero graphic novels

978-1-4012-1096-0

Oracle and the others have left Gotham after their headquarters was destroyed but continue their work, stopping a young witch with a split personality, then taking on a met human vigilante who calls herself Harvest and kills unpunished killers. However, Oracle's controlling ways have caused Huntress to remove herself and go after Gotham mobsters on her own. Black Canary enlists the help of Wildcat in Singapore to go after drug dealers, while back home Oracle is overcome by the techno-virus left in her body after she had defeated Brainiac. There's lots of fighting action, but little graphic violence.

Birds of Prey Vol. 5: Perfect Pitch. DC Comics 2007 Illustration

Grades: 10 11 12 Adult   **741.5; Fic**

1. Birds of Prey (Fictional characters); 2. Graphic novels; 3. Superhero graphic novels; 4. Batgirl (Fictional character); 5. Joker (Fictional character)

978-1-4012-1191-2, $17.99

After being paralyzed by the Joker, former Batgirl Barbara Gordon became Oracle and formed a crime-fighting team with other female heroes including the martial artist with a devastating sonic scream, Black Canary, the vigilante known as the Huntress and the mysterious Lady Blackhawk. In this collection, the team is shaken up as members depart and new teammates are added to the roster. Who will be asked to join Oracle in her all-new Birds Of Prey? Who will refuse, and who will fly the coop for good? There's lots of hand-to-hand fighting in this book.

Birds of Prey: Between Dark & Dawn. DC Comics 2006 un Illustration

Grades: 9 10 11 12 Adult   **741.5; Fic**

1. Birds of Prey (Fictional characters); 2. Graphic novels; 3. Superhero graphic novels; 4. Justice League (Fictional characters)

978-1-4012-0940-7, $14.99

Huntress goes undercover to infiltrate a religious cult with a dangerous secret and a hidden operative, while Black Canary and Oracle uncover the true nature of Sovereign Brusaw's organization. It all leads to the Huntress's battle against former Justice League member Vixen. Oracle wages a private, internal battle against Brainiac, who has infected her with a techno-organic virus. Finally, the Birds must face the aftermath of the Gotham Gang War, leading to a decision that changes the team's fate forever.

Birds of Prey: Of Like Minds. Gail Simone, writer; Ed Benes, penciller; Alex Lei with Rob Lea, inkers; Hi-Fi, colorist; John E. Workman, Rob Leigh, Jared K. Fletcher, letterers; Ed Benes, Alex Lei with Rob Lei, original series covers. DC Comics 2004 143 p. Color; Illustration

Grades: 9 10 11 12 Adult   **741.5**

1. Female superhero graphic novels; 2. Catwoman (Fictional character); 3. Black Canary (Fictional character)

9781401201920, $14.99; 140120192X

LC 2005295809

"The wheelchair-bound Oracle (Barbara Gordon, formerly Batgirl) now fights crime as a superhacker and cyberspy. Her field agent, Dinah Lance, is the Black Canary, a tough martial artist. When a case goes wrong, and a blackmailer called Savant captures the Canary, he threatens to kill her unless Oracle can supply him with a choice piece of information: the secret identity of Batman." (Library Journal)

Originally published in single magazine form in Birds of prey #56-61

Birds of Prey: Sensei & Student. [Gail Simone, writer; Ed Benes ... [et al.], pencillers; Alex Lei ... [et al.], inkers; Hi-Fi, colorist; Jared K. Fletcher, Rob Leigh, Nick Napolitano, letterers]. DC Comics 2005 un Color; Illustration

Grades: 9 10 11 12 Adult   **741.5**

1. Huntress (Fictional character); 2. Oracle (Fictional character); 3. Female superhero comic books, strips, etc.; 4. Black Canary (Fictional character)

9781401204341, $17.99; 1401204341

"Black Canary goes to China on a mission of mercy and runs into the DC Universe's most deadly combatant; Lady Shiva! Shiva is acting with a hidden agenda, making Canary an offer that could change the course of her life. Meanwhile, Oracle's life is tearing at the seams as the information she feeds out to aid her various heroes starts going strangely and dangerously awry! Not to mention Huntress stumbling upon some of her secrets!" (Publisher's note)

Originally published in single magazine form in Birds of Prey #62-68 — T.p. verso.

Superman: Strange Attractors. written by Gail Simone; pencilled by John Byrne. DC Comics 2006 un Illustration

Grades: 9 10 11 12 Adult   **741.5; Fic**

1. Graphic novels; 2. Superhero graphic novels; 3. Superman (Fictional character)

1401209173; 9781401209179, $14.99

First, Superman must contend with Dr. Polaris, but something's just not right with the good doctor.... Then, Dr. Psycho comes to Metropolis to mess with Superman's head. And with his Secret Society comrade Black Adam not far behind, a throw down between Adam and Superman is a certainty. Plus, Satanus, the Queen of Fables, and Livewire make Superman's life a living nightmare.

Welcome to Tranquility volume 2. DC Comics/Wildstorm 2008 144p. Illustration

Grades: 10 11 12 Adult   **741.5; Fic**

1. Graphic novels; 2. Horror graphic novels; 3. Superhero graphic novels; 4. Zombies — Graphic novels

978-1-4012-1773-0, $19.99

Tranquility, the town where retired superheroes and villains live side-by-side, was rocked by violence and murders, but has been recovering. Now, zombies keep coming back from the dead. It's up to Sheriff Tommy Lindo to find out what's happening, but it's going to take all the retired heroes and villains, and some thought long dead, to fight the powerful demon who wants the human infestation gone from the city. The book includes some partial nudity and lots of violence, especially zombie fighting.

Welcome to Tranquility, book one. Gail Simone, writer; Neil Googe, artist. DC Comics/Wildstorm 2007 144p. Illustration
Grades: 10 11 12 Adult   **741.5; Fic**
  1. Crime — Graphic novels; 2. Graphic novels; 3. Superhero graphic novels
978-1-4012-1516-3, $19.99

    Tranquility is like any other small town in America, except for one thing — it's the town where superpowered beings go when they want to retire and raise families. From the Golden Age to the Modern Age, heroes and villains alike live in Tranquility, and the unique blend of personalities and conflicts causes headaches for local law enforcement. When a camera crew comes with a reporter to film a news segment about the town, things get turned upside down by a murder, and it becomes clear Tranquility isn't...tranquil. The book includes violence and harsh language.

Sizer, Paul
  Little White Mouse Omnibus Edition. Cafe Digital Studios 2006 447p. Illustration
Grades: 6 7 8 9 10 11 12   **741.5; Fic**
  1. Graphic novels; 2. Science fiction graphic novels
978-0-9768565-5-9, $24.95

    "In a far future universe, teenaged Loo is the lone survivor of the mysterious destruction of a luxury space liner. She finds an abandoned space mining station, where she must evade a security system that seeks to destroy an intruder such as her, and find a way home before the automated life systems fail. With its strong and appealing young female protagonist, Sizer's story is science fiction that girls will love." (VOYA)
    Originally published in serial form, and then as a four-volume series from Blue Line Pro.

Slade, Christian
  Korgi, Book 1: Sprouting Wings. Top Shelf Productions 2007 88p. Illustration
Grades: 2 3 4 5 6 7 8 9 10 11 12 Adult   **741.5; Fic**
  1. Dogs — Graphic novels; 2. Fantasy graphic novels; 3. Graphic novels; 4. Stories without words — Graphic novels
978-1-891830-90-7, $10

    In this wordless book, a young Mollie (woodland people) named Ivy and her young Korgi companion named Sprout embark on adventures in Korgi Hollow, an enchanted place. When they wander from the Mollie village, the two fall through a hole in the ground and find nasty, monstrous creatures who want to eat them. As they deal with the danger and make their escape, Ivy and Sprout both discover new talents. Slade's extensively cross-hatched yet delicate art is highly expressive, and readers young and old will have no trouble figuring out what is going on. The Korgi are based on Welsh corgi dogs, of which Slade and his wife have two.

Courtesy of IDW Publishing

  Korgi, book 2. Top Shelf Productions 2008 un Illustration
Grades: 3 4 5 6 7 8 9 10 11 12 Adult   **741.5; Fic**
  1. Adventure graphic novels; 2. Fantasy graphic novels; 3. Graphic novels; 4. Stories without words — Graphic novels
978-1-60309-010-0, $10

    In this second wordless volume, the young Mollie named Ivy and her Korgi cub Sprout, experience a harrowing adventure. Someone has been hunting the Mollies and cutting off their wings. Ivy and Sprout rescue one older Mollie named Art and his Korgi when they fall into a deep trap in the woods; then as Ivy flies, a barbed arrow cuts one of her wings off. She and

Sprout see a strange creature carrying her wing and they follow him to his place, where he hangs all the Mollie wings like trophies. Ivy decides she wants her wing back, but she and Sprout will have to fight the creature and his automated and nasty bots.

Courtesy of IDW Publishing

Slott, Dan
  Silver Surfer; Volume 1: New Dawn. storytellers, Dan Slott & Michael Allred; color artist, Laura Allred; Letterer, VC's Clayton Cowles. Marvel Enterprises 2014 128 p. Color; Illustration
Grades: 9 10 11 12 Adult
741.5; Fic
  1. Superhero graphic novels; 2. Silver Surfer (Fictional character)
0785188789; 9780785188780, $17.99

    "The universe is big. Bigger than you could ever imagine. And the Silver Surfer, lone sentinel of the skyways, is about to discover that the best way to see it...is with someone else. Meet Dawn Greenwood, the Earth girl who's challenged the Surfer to go beyond the boundaries of the known universe." (Publisher's note)

  Silver Surfer; Volume 2: Worlds Apart. storytellers: Dan Slott & Michael Allred; color artist: Laura Allred; letterer: VC's Joe Sabino. Marvel Enterprises 2015 120 p. Color; Illustration
Grades: 9 10 11 12 Adult   **741.5; Fic**
  1. Superhero graphic novels; 2. Silver Surfer (Fictional character)
0785188797; 9780785188797, $15.99
  Eisner Nominee: Best Continuing Series (2016)

    "Dawn has earned her spot on the board, and she and the Surfer are going to explore the universe together.... But can they survive the threats of Warrior One, the Greatest Monster in the Galaxy?...And witness...as the Surfer takes on his former master: Galactus!" (Publisher's note)
    Collects issues #6-10 of Silver Surfer

  Silver Surfer; Volume 3: Last Days. storytellers, Dan Slott & Michael Allred; color artist: Laura Allred; Letterer, VC's Joe Sabino. Marvel Enterprises 2016 120 p. Color; Illustration
Grades: 9 10 11 12 Adult   **741.5; Fic**
  1. Superhero graphic novels; 2. Silver Surfer (Fictional character)
0785197370; 9780785197379, $17.99
  Eisner Nominee: Best Continuing Series (2016)

    "The hurt that Dawn Greenwood felt after learning about the Silver Surfer's history (see the last volume) and is the potential snag along the seem-to-be lovers' fairytale romance. Will it be overcome? Is there love for each other real? How can they really know when all of reality seems to be warping around them?" (Publisher's note)
    Contains material originally published in magazine form as Silver Surfer #11-15

Small, David, 1945-
  ★ **Stitches:** a memoir. W.W. Norton 2009 329p. Illustration
Grades: 10 11 12 Adult   **741.5; 92**
  1. Art teachers; 2. Artists; 3. Authors; 4. Autobiographical graphic novels; 5. Cancer — Graphic novels; 6. Children's authors; 7. Comic books, strips, etc.; 8. Family life — Graphic novels; 9. Graphic novels; 10. Illustrators; 11. Small, David, 1945-
978-0-393-06857-3, $23.95; 0-393-06857-9

    LC 2009-22526
  National Book Award Finalist: Young People's Literature (2009)
    David Small grew up in a dysfunctional family, with a radiologist father who was distant, an angry mother who expressed her anger in

eloquent silences, and an older brother who played drums a lot to express his frustrations. When he was eleven, he had a lump, a growth, on the side of his neck. Nothing was done until he was fourteen. He thought he was going in for a minor surgery to remove the cyst from his neck; instead, there were two surgeries, and when he woke up, he had no voice — a vocal cord was removed. He later learned he had cancer, something his parents refused to discuss. After he finds his mother in bed with another woman and his father confesses that he exposed him to x-rays when he was very young, Small leaves home at age sixteen, with little except his dreams that his art could be his life. In one early scene, Small shows the indignities wrought upon his body by his father, including an enema. In another scene, young Small and his older brother look at their father's medical books and see a woman's breast and a man's penis; towards the end of the book, Small draws his grandmother stripping all her clothes off and dancing wildly after setting her house on fire. Other than these few images, Small's depictions of his horrible childhood and teen years are quiet and low-key.

"Emotionally raw, artistically compelling and psychologically devastating graphic memoir of childhood trauma." Kirkus

Smith, Jeff

★ **Bone** Book Seven: ghost circles. Scholastic/GRAPHIX 2008 152p. Illustration

Grades: 3 4 5 6 7 8 9 10 11 12 Adult   **741.5; Fic**
1. Adventure graphic novels; 2. Fantasy graphic novels; 3. Graphic novels

978-0-439-70629-2, $19.99; 978-0-439-70634-6 (pa), $9.99

LC 2007-9568403

The Bone cousins, Gran'ma Ben, Thorn, and their loyal rat creature cub Bartleby venture on a journey through the mysterious ghost circles to Atheia, the old city of the royal family. Meanwhile, the Barrelhaven villagers and the Veni Yan face enemy hordes. Steve Hamaker is the colorist for this full color version of Smith's comic epic.

★ **Bone** vol. 8: treasure hunters. Scholastic/Graphix 2008 138p. Illustration

Grades: 5 6 7 8 9 10 11 12 Adult   **741.5; Fic**
1. Adventure graphic novels; 2. Fantasy graphic novels; 3. Graphic novels

978-0-439-70630-8, $18.95; 978-0-439-70633-9 (pa), $9.99

LC 2008-9568403

The Bone cousins, Gran'ma Ben, and Thorn reach the city of Atheia, where they prepare to battle the Lord of the Locusts. Meanwhile, Thorn's visions are becoming more threatening and Phoney Bone is convinced Atheia is rich in gold, and he is determined to find it. But all is not well in Atheia, and Thorn is in great danger, not only from Briar and the Lord of the Locusts. This edition is in full color, done by Steve Hamaker.

★ **Bone:** out from Boneville. Scholastic Graphix 2005 144p. Illustration

Grades: 4 5 6 7 8 9 10 11 12   **741.5; Fic**
1. Adventure graphic novels; 2. Fantasy graphic novels; 3. Graphic novels

9780439706407, $12.99; 0439706408; 0439706238; 9780439706230, $26.99

"After being run out of Boneville, the three Bone cousins — Fone Bone, Phoney Bone, and Smiley Bone — are separated and lost in a vast, uncharted desert. One by one, they find their way into a deep, forested valley filled with wonderful and terrifying creatures. Eventually, the cousins are reunited at a farmstead run by tough Gran'ma Ben and her spirited granddaughter, Thorn. But little do the Bones know, there are dark forces conspiring against them and their adventures are only just beginning!" (Publisher's note)

"The nine-volume Bone graphic novel series was the toast of the comics world when it was published by Smith's own Cartoon Books

beginning in the early 1990s; in this first volume of Scholastic's new edition, the original b&w art has been beautifully converted into color." Pub Wkly

Also available Bone: one volume edition $39.95 from Cartoon Books (ISBN 1-8889-6314-X); Other titles in this series are: Bone: the great cow race (vol. 2); Bone: eyes of the storm (vol. 3); Bone: the dragonslayer (vol. 4); Bone: Rock Jaw: master of the Eastern border (vol. 5); Bone: old man's cave (vol. 6); Bone: ghost circles (vol. 7); Bone: treasure hunters (vol. 8); Bone: crown of horns (vol. 9)

Smith, Juliana

★ **(H)afrocentric** comics; Volumes 1-4. illustrator, Ronald Nelson; writer, Juliana Jewels Smith; colorist, Mike Hampton; foreword by Kiese Laymon.. PM Press 2017 136 p. Illustration

Grades: 9 10 11 12 Adult   **741**
1. African American college students — Political activity — Comic books, strips, etc.; 2. African Americans — Political activity — Comic books, strips, etc.; 3. Gentrification — Comic books, strips, etc.; 4. Social reformers — Comic books, strips, etc.

1629634484; 9781629634487, $20

LC 2017942907

This comic book, by Juliana Smith, illustrated by Mike Hampton and Ronald Nelson, foreword by Kiese Laymon, tackles the most pressing issues of the day — including racism,...and the housing crisis — with humor and biting satire. When gentrification strikes the neighborhood surrounding Ronald Reagan University, Naima Pepper recruits a group of disgruntled undergrads of color to launch the first and only anti-gentrification social networking site, mydiaspora.com." (Publisher's note)

Statement of responsibility from cover.

Smith, Mark Andrew

Popgun, volume one: a graphic mixtape. Image Comics 2007 448p. Illustration

Grades: 11 12 Adult   **741.5**
1. Graphic novels; 2. Short stories — Graphic novels

978-1-58240-824-8, $29.99

This anthology of graphic short stories rams through the various genres with stories from comics veterans and newcomers, including Eric Larsen, Mike Allred, Dan Hipp, Rick Remender, Phil Yeh, Richard Starkings, Jamie S. Rich, Jim Mahfood, Leah Moore, and many more. Many of the stories include nudity, sexual situations, harsh language, and violence.

Sniegoski, Tom

Talent. written by Christopher Golden & Tom Sniegoski; art by Paul Azaceta; colors by Ron Riley; letters by Marshall Dillon. Boom! Studios 2007 120p. Illustration

Grades: 10 11 12 Adult   **741.5**
1. Graphic novels; 2. Mystery graphic novels

978-1-934506-05-9, $14.99

When a plane crashes, sole survivor Nicholas Dane discovers he can channel his dead fellow passengers' talents. Chased by the killers who destroyed the plane, Dane stays one step ahead of death, while putting the pieces of the mystery together. Aided by a...spirit...Dane soon learns that some of the passengers on the ill-fated flight were killers working for the organization now hunting him. The book includes violence.

Snyder, Scott

Attack on Titan anthology. Attack on Titan created by Hajime Isayama; edited by Ben Applegate and Jeanine Schaefer; cover, logo, and interior design by Phil Balsman; lettering and interior design by Steve Wands. Kodansha 2016 256 p. Illustration

Grades: 8 9 10 11 12   **741.5**

1. Fantasy fiction — Graphic novels; 2. Horror fiction — Graphic novels; 3. Science fiction graphic novels; 4. Shonen manga

1632362589; 9781632362582, $29.99

This tribute anthology to the manga Attack on Titan features "original stories by a long roster of comic superstars such as Scott Snyder (Batman, American Vampire), Gail Simone (Batgirl), Michael Avon Oeming (Powers), Paolo Rivera (Daredevil, Amazing Spider-Man), Cameron Stewart (Fight Club 2, Batgirl) and Faith Erin Hicks (The Adventures of Superhero Girl)!" (Publisher's note)

"The Victorian-style guide to Titan's walled city by Genevieve Valentine and David López is a standout, as is the contemplative final story by brothers Asaf and Tomer Hanuka." Pub Wkly

Batman: night of the owls. by Scott Snyder and Greg Capullo. DC Comics 2013 368 p. Illustration; Color

Grades: 10 11 12 Adult   **741.5/973; Fic**

1. Graphic novels; 2. Batgirl (Fictional character); 3. Nightwing (Fictional character); 4. Robin (Fictional character); 5. Batman (Fictional character); 6. Catwoman (Fictional character)

1401237738; 9781401237738, $29.99

LC 2012040574

This graphic novel, written by Scott Snyder and Greg Capullo, features the superhero Batman. "As evil spreads across Gotham City, Batman's allies, including Red Robin, Batwing, Robin, Batgirl, the Birds of Prey, Nightwing and even Catwoman find themselves in a battle coming from all sides. The Court of Owls have shown their hand, and it's up to the collective effort of these heroes, some more unlikely than others, in this sprawling tale of corruption and violence."

Originally published in single magazine form in Batman 8-11, Nightwing 8-9, All-Star Western 9, Catwoman 9, Batgirl 9, Batman: The Dark Knight 9, Batman and Robin 9, Batwing 9, Birds Of Prey 9, Red Hood and The Outlaws 9, Batman Annual 1.

Soo, Kean

★ **Jellaby:** monster in the city. Hyperion Books 2009 172p. Illustration

Grades: 4 5 6 7 8 9   **741.5; Fic**

1. Fantasy graphic novels; 2. Friendship — Graphic novels; 3. Graphic novels; 4. Monsters — Graphic novels

1-4231-0565-6 (pa); 978-1-4231-0565-7 (pa), $9.99

Beginning right where the first book ended, Portia, Jason, and Jellaby continue on their way to Toronto, walking after Portia panicked and they got off the train. They're searching for a way home for Jellaby, and they think a door somewhere in Exhibition Place, where the Canadian National Exhibition is taking place, holds a clue. Portia feels torn between wanting to help her friend yet not wanting to say goodbye forever, and her ambivalence causes a rift between her and Jason. When she doesn't want to trust a masked magician who seems to know too much about them and Jellaby, Portia leaves Jason. They all end up in the Automotive Building, where the masked man leads Jason and Jellaby down below the building, while Portia seems to find her long lost father. But is he really her father, and just what is waiting for Jason and Jellaby under the Automotive Building? Soo again uses a mostly purple color palette.

Another title in the author's series about Jellaby

★ **Jellaby;** Volume 1: the lost monster. by Kean Soo. Stone Arch Books 2014 160 p. Color; Illustration (Jellaby)

Grades: 4 5 6 7 8 9   **741.5**

1. Extraterrestrial beings — Fiction; 2. Human-alien encounters — Comic books, strips, etc; 3. Monsters — Fiction; 4. Friendship — Fiction

1434291952; 9781434264206, $12.95 ; 9781434291950, $19.99

LC 2013037026

"Portia has just moved to a new neighborhood with her mom. Adjusting to life without a father is hard enough, but school is boring and her classmates are standoffish.... But things start to get better when Portia mounts a midnight excursion into the woods behind her house where she discovers a shy and sweet purple monster. Life with Jellaby is exciting, but Portia's purple friend has secrets of his own." (Publisher's note)

Courtesy of Capstone Press

"Soo grounds the story in a fairly gritty contemporary reality, where kids deal with bullies and well-meaning adults try to help. Clear, clean lines and easy-to-follow panel layouts round out the package." Booklist

First published 2008; Originally published: New York : Hyperion Books for Children, 2008. A Capstone imprint.

Sorachi, Hideaki

Gin Tama Vol. 1. Viz Media/Shonen Jump Advanced 2007 216p. Illustration

Grades: 10 11 12 Adult   **741.5; Fic**

1. Graphic novels; 2. Humorous graphic novels; 3. Manga; 4. Shonen manga

978-1-4215-1358-4, $7.99

The samurai didn't stand a chance. First, the aliens invaded Japan. Next, they took all the jobs. And then they confiscated everyone's swords. So what does a hotheaded former samurai like Sakata "Gin" Gintoki do to make ends meet? Take any odd job that comes his way, even if it means losing his dignity. Sleazy alien moneylenders, monsters on the rampage, and a ticking time bomb may all be in a day's work for Gin, but a drop in his blood sugar level means trouble for everyone. Some harsh language and lots of fighting action fill this alternate history comedy.

Spencer, Nick

Morning Glories; 1: for a better future. Nick Spencer, words; Joe Eisma, art; Rodin Esquejo, covers; Alex Sollazzo, colors; Johnny Lowe, letters. Image 2011 192 p. Illustration

Grades: 9 10 11 12 Adult   **741.5**

1. Comic books, strips, etc.; 2. Good and evil — Fiction; 3. School stories

1607063077; 9781607063070, $9.99

Originally published in single magazine form as Morning Glories #1-6

"Morning Glory Academy is one of the most prestigious prep schools in the country...but something sinister and deadly lurks behind its walls. When six gifted, but troubled, students arrive, they find themselves trapped and fighting for their lives as the secrets of the academy reveal themselves." (Publisher's note)

"[C]ompelling character studies, mind games, and action-packed sequences [feature] in this gorgeously inked mystery." Booklist

Volume 1 of 10

Morning glories; Volume five: Tests. Nick Spencer, illustrated by Joe Eisma. Image Comics 2013 136 p. Color; Illustration

Grades: 10 11 12 Adult   **741.5**

1. Graphic novels; 2. School stories

1607067749; 9781607067740, $12.99

"The Glories are scattered, The Faculty broken, and The Truants on the attack!" (Publisher's note)

Originally published in single magazine form Morning Glories, #26-29 — T.p. verso

Spender, Nick

Rosa Parks: The Life of a Civil Rights Heroine. Rosen Publishing Group 2006 48p. Illustration

Grades: 3 4 5 6 7 8 9   **741.5; 323.092; 92; 323**

1. African American women — Alabama — Montgomery — Biography — Graphic novels; 2. African Americans — Civil rights — Alabama — Montgomery — History — 20th century — Graphic novels; 3. Biographical graphic novels; 4. Graphic novels; 5. Parks, Rosa, 1913-2005

978-1-4042-0864-3, $29.25

LC 2006002735

This book uses the graphic novel format to tell of the life of Rosa Parks and her act of defiance that inspired the Montgomery Bus Boycott. Additional information explains Jim Crow laws and briefly covers the civil rights movement. The book includes a list of books for further reading.

Part of the Rosen Graphic Biographies series.

Spiegelman, Art

★ In the shadow of no towers. Pantheon Books 2004 Illustration

Grades: 10 11 12 Adult   **741; 973.931; 741.5**

1. Graphic novels; 2. September 11 terrorist attacks, 2001 — Graphic novels

0-375-42307-9, $19.95

LC 2004-43870

This is a "memoir of the attacks on the World Trade Center, which Spiegelman witnessed from close range, a rant on their effects on the world at large and within the author, and a monograph on the Sunday newspaper comic strips of the early 20th century." N Y Times Book Rev

The author "provides a hair-raising and wry account of his family's frantic efforts to locate one another on September 11 as well as a morbidly funny survey of his trademark sense of existential doom.... This is a powerful and quirky work of visual storytelling by a master comics artist." Publ Wkly

★ Maus: a survivor's tale, 2v in 1. Art Spiegelman.. Pantheon Bks. 1996 295 p. Illustration; Map; Color

Grades: 7 8 9 10 11 12 Adult   **741.5; 940.53; 92**

1. Biographical graphic novels; 2. Graphic novels; 3. Holocaust, 1933-1945 — Graphic novels; 4. Spiegelman, Vladek

0-679-40641-7, $35

LC 96-32796

Los Angeles Times Book Prize: Fiction (1992) for Maus II; Pulitzer Prize Special Award (1992); Eisner Award: Best Graphic Album — Reprint for Maus II; Harvey Award: Best Graphic Album of Previously Published Material (1992) for Maus II

"An undisputed classic and award-winning title (including a Pulitzer Prize in 1992) in which renowned cartoonist Spiegelman depicts his father's experiences as a World War II Nazi concentration camp survivor. The memoir is also a chronicle of Spiegelman's relationship with his father as we witness their visits and disagreements. The black-and-white drawings are straightforward, but with an interesting twist: all of the Jews are depicted as mice and the Nazis as cats." LJ

In this work "Spiegelman takes the comic book to a new level of seriousness, portraying Jews as mice and Nazis as cats. Depicting himself being told about the Holocaust by his Polish survivor father, Spiegelman not only explores the concentration-camp experience, but also the guilt, love, and anger between father and son." Rochman. Against borders

Also available: paperback boxed set edition $23.25 (ISBN 0141014083); A combined edition of Maus I : My father bleeds history (1986) and Maus II : And here my troubles began (1991)

★ MetaMaus. Pantheon Books 2011 299p. Illustration

Grades: 11 12 Adult   **92; 741.5; 940.53**

1. Authors; 2. Autobiographical graphic novels; 3. Cartoonists; 4. Cartoonists — Graphic novels; 5. Graphic novels; 6. Holocaust survivors — Graphic novels; 7. Holocaust, 1933-1945 — Graphic novels; 8. Nonfiction writers; 9. Spiegelman, Art

978-0-375-42394-9, $35

LC 2010052045

The New York cartoonist traces the creative process that went into drawing his Pulitzer Prizewinning classic, revealing the sources of his inspiration and describing his parents' emotional struggles as Holocaust survivors after the end of World War II.

Stanley, John

★ Little Lulu, vol. 1: My dinner with Lulu. [by] John Stanley and Irving Tripp. Dark Horse Comics 2005 200p. Illustration

Grades: 4 5 6 7 8 9 10 11 12 Adult   **741.5; Fic**

1. Friendship — Graphic novels; 2. Graphic novels; 3. Humorous graphic novels

1-59307-318-6, $9.95

Lulu Moppet plays with best friend Tubby, except when he hangs out with the other neighborhood boys and tries to keep girls out of their clubhouse; she deals with terrible toddler Alvin by weaving extravagant tales featuring herself; and other everyday adventures. This is the first volume of a series that will eventually reprint every Little Lulu comic for new young readers.

Volume 1 of 29

★ Nancy, volume 1: the Johnny Stanley Library. Drawn & Quarterly 2009 128p. Illustration

Grades: 2 3 4 5 6 7 8 9 10 11 12 Adult   **741.5; Fic**

1. Graphic novels; 2. Humorous graphic novels; 3. Nancy (Fictional character)

978-1-897299-77-7, $24.95

LC c2009-901565-X

The comic book character Nancy was created by Ernie Bushmiller; Dell Comics published the comics scripted by John Stanley with art by Dan Gormley starting with issue 146 in 1957. In these stories, Nancy meets Oona Goosepimple, a spooky girl who lives in a haunted house, has an incredible run of bad luck because of what she thinks is a four-leaf clover, and has all kinds of everyday adventures and misadventures with her friend Sluggo, their nemesis Spike, neighborhood rich kid Rollo, and her Aunt Fritzi. Always short of money yet needing some to buy ice cream sodas and other treats, many of Nancy's adventures with Sluggo involve various moneymaking schemes to get the dime needed (those were the days ...). The kinds of adventures the kids have are somewhat similar to Stanley's other work on Little Lulu, but set in an urban environment rather than the suburban neighborhood of Lulu and her friends. The book, designed by Seth, retains the soft original coloring of the old comics, with the paper even looking like old comics (but much sturdier). This book should have the same all-ages appeal as Little Lulu; the 2009 Free Comic Book Day issue featuring Nancy was a big hit with readers five years old and up to adults who remembered reading Nancy comics when they were kids.

Starkings, Richard

Elephantmen: Wounded Animals. Richard Starkings, story & lettering; Moritat, lead artist; Boo Cook, Ladrönn, covers; J.G. Roshell, design. Image Comics 2007 un Illustration

Grades: 10 11 12 Adult   **741.5; Fic**

1. Graphic novels; 2. Mystery graphic novels; 3. Science fiction graphic novels

978-1-58240-691-6, $24.99

They were genetically engineered to be super-human weapons of mass destruction, but now they must walk amongst the people they were created to destroy and face hatred and fear every day. Ebony Hide is one of them, an Elephantman. Even when he is befriended by a small girl, Hide is still haunted by his past and is forced to recognize that suspicion and contempt will always be his constant companions. The book includes some violence and strong language.

Starlin, Jim

Batman: a death in the family. writers, Jim Starlin, Marv Wolfman; layouts and co-plotter, George Perez; pencillers, Jim Aparo, Tom Grummett; inkers, Mike DeCarlo, Bob McLeod; original series covers, Mike Mignola and George Perez. DC Comics 2011 269 p. Color illustration (Batman)

Grades: 10 11 12 Adult   **741.5**
1. Good and evil — Comic books, strips, etc.; 2. Superheroes — Comic books, strips, etc.; 3. Batman (Fictional character); 4. Joker (Fictional character); 5. Robin (Fictional character)
1401232744; 9781401232740, $24.99

LC 2012376784

In this graphic novel, "Batman readers were allowed to vote on the outcome of the story and they decided that Robin should die! As the second person to assume the role of Batman's sidekick, Jason Todd had a completely different personality than the original Robin. Rash and prone to ignore Batman's instructions, Jason was always quick to act without regard to consequences. In this fatal instance, Robin ignores his mentor's warnings when he attempts to take on the Joker by himself." (Publisher's note)

Batman created by Bob Kane.||Originally published in single magazine form in Batman #426-429, 440-442, The New Titans #60-61 and Batman Annual #25.||Includes a new afterword by writer Marv Wolfman — P. [4] of cover.

Stassen, Jean-Philippe

Deogratias: a tale of Rwanda. [by] Stassen; translated by Alex Siegel. Roaring Brook 2006 79p. Illustration

Grades: 11 12 Adult   **741.5; Fic**
1. Genocide — Graphic novels; 2. Graphic novels; 3. Rwanda — Graphic novels
1-59643-103-2; 978-1-59643-103-4, $17.95

LC 2005-17576

In this "fictionalized account of the Rwandan genocide, readers meet Deogratias, a teenaged Hutu. His friends Benina and Apollinaria are Tutsi — a race that is being ethnically cleansed by Hutu extremists. As the conflict escalates, Deogratias witnesses murders and is forced to become involved in brutal acts of violence. He suffers a mental breakdown. The story is told through a series of flashbacks while he skates the line between rational and insane. Stassen spares his readers none of the brutality and visceral cruelties of this atrocity. Scenes of rape, harsh language, and some sexual content solidly designate this book for a mature audience.... A masterful work with vibrant, confident art, this book will stay with and haunt its readers." SLJ

Steele, Hamish

★ **Deadendia:** the watcher's test. Hamish Steele. Nobrow Press 2018 240 p. Color; Illustration

Grades: 7 8 9 10 11 12   **741.5; Fic**
1. Amusement parks — Fiction; 2. Horror fiction; 3. Transgender people — Fiction; 4. LGBT people — Fiction
1910620475; 9781910620472, $14.95

"Barney and his best friend Norma are just trying to get by and keep their jobs, but working at the Dead End theme park also means battling demonic forces, time traveling wizards, and scariest of all — their love lives! Follow the lives of this diverse group of employees of a haunted house, which may or may not also serve as a portal to hell, in this hilarious

and moving graphic novel, complete with talking pugs, vengeful ghosts and LBGTQIA love!" (Publisher's note)

"The art is imaginative and engaging, with rich, evocative color schemes. With time travel, demonic possession, monsters, magic spells, and fights between creatures of pure sadness and pure happiness, there is never a dull moment — but in the realm of human emotion, there are relatable ones." Kirkus

Stein, Leslie

Present. Leslie Stein. Drawn & Quarterly 2017 168 p. Color; Illustration

Grades: 11 12 Adult   **741.5; Fic**
1. New York (N.Y.) — Fiction; 2. Storytelling — Graphic novels
1770462945; 9781770462946, $21.95
LA Times Book Prize: Graphic Novel/Comics (2017)

In this book, "Leslie Stein takes us on a sinuous urban stroll divorced from destination, glimpsing New York City through her open eyes. While she is closing up a bar late at night, she is also an adolescent at a rave in the mountains, an adult grappling with her grandfather's fading memory or at one of her first waitressing jobs." (Publisher's note)

"Stein's vibrant watercolors are a marvel, especially in the palette: dribbles of cerulean, slashes of black, and dots of deepest crimson are as captivating as any plot twist. Even the lettering tells a story, often exploding on the page in different colors and sizes. It all adds up to a sweet, relatable portrait of the minutiae that make life worth living." Pub Wkly

Stephenson, Eric

Put the Book Back on the Shelf: A Belle & Sebastian Anthology. Image Comics 2006 un Illustration

Grades: 10 11 12 Adult   **741.5; Fic**
1. Graphic novels; 2. Short stories — Graphic novels
1-58240-600-6, $19.99

Belle and Sebastian is a Scottish indie pop band that has gained critical acclaim for its music. In this anthology, independent comic creators and cartoonists put their own spins on a cross section of Belle and Sebastian's songs, crafting narratives inspired by the band's music. Rick Spears, Andi Watson, Jennifer de Guzman, Leela Corman, Rick Remender, Ande Park, ad Mark Ricketts are just a few of the creators who contributed to this collection. Nudity, drug use, and violence occur in some of the stories.

Stern, Roger

Captain America: War & Remembrance 2nd ed.. writer, Roger Stern; co-plotter & penciler, John Byrne; inker, Joe Rubinstein; colorists, Bob Sharen & George Roussos; letterers, Jim Novak, John Costanza, & Joe Rosen. Marvel Entertainment 2007 207p. Illustration

Grades: 8 9 10 11 12 Adult   **741.5; Fic**
1. Graphic novels; 2. Superhero graphic novels; 3. Avengers (Fictional characters); 4. Captain America (Fictional character)
978-0-7851-2693-5, $24.99

Captain America's endless war on crime and tyranny sets him against new enemies and old, from an army of robot replicas to the black deeds of Baron Blood. Plus: Cap for president? This book guest-stars the Avengers, S.H.I.E.L.D. and Union Jack, and features Cobra, Mister Hyde and Batroc the Leaper. This is the complete Stern/Byrne run, culminating with the standard-setting version of Cap's origin. Byrne co-scripted as well as pencilled the art.

Spider-Man Visionaries: Roger Stern Vol. 1. Marvel Entertainment 2007 256p. Illustration

Grades: 7 8 9 10 11 12 Adult   **741.5; Fic**
1. Graphic novels; 2. Spider-Man (Fictional character); 3. Superhero graphic novels
978-0-7851-2710-9, $24.99

Roger Stern sets his stamp on Spider-Man and his supporting cast with a collection of costumed criminals, would-be alien abductors, and gangsters both local and imported. Spidey is up against Belladonna, the Vulture, the Prowler, the Smuggler, Mysterio, a roomful of aliens, and an abundance of gas. These stories were originally published in the 1980s, and Stern worked with a number of different artists, including Steve Leialoha and Marie Severin.

Stevenson, Noelle
Lumberjanes; Volume 3: A Terrible Plan. written by Noelle Stevenson & Shannon Watters; illustrated by Carolyn Nowak [and six others]; colors by Maarta Laiho; cover by Noelle Stevenson. Boom! Studios 2016 112 p. Color; Illustration
Grades: 6 7 8 9 10 11 12 Adult   **741.5; Fic**
  1. Graphic novels; 2. Camps — Fiction; 3. Fantasy fiction; 4. Adventure fiction; 5. Teenage girls — Fiction
  1608868036; 9781608868032, $14.99

"Jo, April, Mal, Molly, and Ripley...take on everything that goes bump in the night. From scary stories to magical portals that lead to a land untouched by time, it's definitely not your average summer." (Publisher's note)

"Each camper tells a campfire spine-tingler, ranging from not very scary (the scratching on the side of the car was really...carbon-monoxide-induced hallucinations!) to the shudderworthy. Elsewhere, Mal and Molly are transported to a dangerous, dinosaur-infested alternate universe, and while they are gone, the rest of the Lumberjanes try to earn some piece-of-cake badges, only to fail spectacularly." Booklist

Originally published in single magazine form as Lumberjanes no. 9-12

★ **Nimona**. by Noelle Stevenson. HarperCollins Childrens Books 2015 272 p.
Grades: 7 8 9 10 11 12   **741.5**
  1. Shapeshifting — Comic books, strips, etc.; 2. Fantasy graphic novels; 3. Magic — Graphic novels; 4. Good and evil — Fiction; 5. Heroes and heroines — Graphic novels
  0062278231; 9780062278234, $17.99
Eisner Nominee: Best Digital/Web Comic (2015); National Book Award Finalist: Young People's Literature (2015); Eisner Award: Best Graphic Album — Reprint (2016)

In this graphic novel, by Noelle Stevenson, "Nimona is an impulsive young shapeshifter with a knack for villainy. Lord Ballister Blackheart is a villain with a vendetta. As sidekick and supervillain, Nimona and Lord Blackheart are about to wreak some serious havoc. Their mission: prove to the kingdom that Sir Ambrosius Goldenloin and his buddies at the Institution of Law Enforcement and Heroics aren't the heroes everyone thinks they are." (Publisher's note)

"This celebrated webcomic, a mash-up of medieval culture with modern science and technology, is now available in print.... Action scenes dominate as Nimona shifts with Hulk-like ferocity from frightful creatures such as a fire-breathing dragon to a docile cat or a timid child. Dialogue is fresh and witty with an abundance of clever lines." SLJ

Stewart, Cameron
★ **Batgirl**; Volume 1: Batgirl of Burnside. written by Cameron Stewart & Brenden Fletcher; art by Babs Tarr; breakdown art by Cameron Stewart. DC Comics 2015 176 p. Color; Illustration
Grades: 10 11 12 Adult   **741.5**
  1. Batgirl (Fictional character)
  9781401253325, $24.99

LC 2015006319

"Barbara Gordon's ready for a fresh start. She's packing her bags, crossing the bridge, and heading to Gotham's coolest neighborhood: Burnside. And when a freak fire burns up her costume and gear, Babs has the chance to become a whole new Batgirl! But she barely slips on her new DIY costume before Batgirl starts trending as Gotham's first viral vigilante — and attracting a new wave of enemies." (Publisher's note)

"While most attempts at updating an established character to tap into the youth culture zeitgeist feel phony and fall flat, this reinvigoration of Batgirl manages to be big fun and actually tuned in to Millennial culture.... The supporting cast is diverse and fully developed, and the action is intense, rendered in a bright, dynamic style that evokes animation with just a hint of Japanese influence." LJ

Stine, R. L.
Goosebumps Graphix: Scary Summer. Scholastic/Graphix 2007 137p. Illustration
Grades: 4 5 6 7 8 9   **741.5; Fic**
  1. Graphic novels; 2. Horror graphic novels
  978-0-439-85782-6, $8.99

Someone's creeping through the garden, doing nasty things! Dean Haspiel, a veteran of Batman and Justice League comics, knows just how to portray "The Revenge of the Lawn Gnomes." In his comic series like The Bakers and Plastic Man, Kyle Baker proves he's one funny artist, the perfect guy to draw a story about fun and games at camp — until "The Horror at Camp Jellyjam" is uncovered. And Courtney Crumrin creator Ted Naifeh adapts and illustrates "Ghost Beach," in which Terri and Jerry go on vacation with some of their father's cousins and meet other kids who dress in old-fashioned clothes and caution them about ghosts.

Stok, Barbara
Vincent. by Barbara Stok; translation by Laura Watkinson. SelfMadeHero 2014 144 p. Color; Illustration
Grades: 9 10 11 12 Adult   **741.5; 92**
  1. Gogh, Vincent van, 1853-1890
  1906838798; 9781906838799, $19.95

LC 2014431349

This biography, by Barbara Stok, "documents the brief and intense period of creativity Vincent van Gogh (1853-1890) spent in Arles, Provence, in southern France. Here van Gogh dreams of setting up an artists' studio-a haven where he and his friends can paint together. But attacks of mental illness leave the painter confused and disoriented.... Throughout this period of intense emotion and hardship, Vincent's brother Theo stands by him." (Publisher's note)

"Stok doesn't try to reproduce van Gogh's visuals; instead, she uses heavy lines, solid colors, and minimal background details to focus attention on characters and history. When she breaks away from this pattern — in jagged panel lines showing van Gogh's slipping sanity, or the brilliance of his paintings exploding behind him — it's emotionally charged and made all the more immediate by the iconography." Pub Wkly

Text in English, translated from the Dutch

Straczynski, J. Michael
Civil War: Fantastic Four. writers, J. Michael Straczynski & Dwayne McDuffie; penciller, Mike McKone; inkers, Andy Lanning, Kris Justice, & Cam Smith; colorist, Paul Mounts. Marvel Entertainment 2007 un Illustration
Grades: 9 10 11 12 Adult   **741.5; Fic**
  1. Fantastic Four (Fictional character); 2. Graphic novels; 3. Superhero graphic novels
  0-7851-2227-3, $17.99

One member of the Fantastic Four lies hospitalized, a casualty of the Civil War that has fragmented the superhuman community. Another member of the team is secretly helping the opposition. Amid the tumult and tensions, the Fantastic Four is breaking up. Who will toe the line with the government, who will join the resistanace, and who will leave the battlefield altogether?

Civil War: The Amazing Spider-Man. Marvel Entertainment 2007 un Illustration
Grades: 9 10 11 12 Adult   **741.5; Fic**
1. Graphic novels; 2. Spider-Man (Fictional character); 3. Superhero graphic novels
0-7851-2237-0, $17.99

Life couldn't be more complicated — or more dangerous — for Peter Parker. After rushing to the aftermath of the Stamford Massacre to offer aid to its victims, Peter travels with Tony Stark to Washington, D.C. and the White House, where the enactment of the Super Human Registration Act appears imminent. As the world braces for the implications of legislation that will forever change the societal status of super heroes, Peter is forced to make an important personal decision, maybe the most important decision of his life. As Civil War tears apart the super hero community, will Spidey stay true to that decision?

Sturm, James
★ **Satchel** Paige: striking out Jim Crow. Hyperion Books for Children/Jump at the Sun 2007 90p. Illustration
Grades: 4 5 6 7 8 9 10   **92; 741.5**
1. African Americans — Biography — Graphic novels; 2. Baseball — Graphic novels; 3. Baseball players; 4. Biographical graphic novels; 5. Graphic novels; 6. Paige, Satchel, 1906-1982
978-0-7868-3901-8, $9.99; 978-0-7868-3900-1, $16.99

Narrated by an African American who played in the Negro Leagues for a short time, this book sketches part of the career of Leroy "Satchel" Paige, a star of the Negro Leagues. Young Emmet scored a run off Paige in a game, but suffered a career-ending knee injury. Readers get a sense of the rough life African Americans faced in the south during the 1920s, 1930s, and 1940s. Then Paige and his team come to Tuckwilla, Alabama in 1944 to play an all-White team, and Emmet and his son attend the game and watch how Paige and his team take apart the home boys. There's one panel showing a man who has been lynched and hanged; most of the violence is mentioned but not depicted on the pages.
Part of The Center for Cartoon Studies Presents series

Suburbia, Liz
★ **Sacred** Heart. Liz Suburbia. Fantagraphics 2015 312 p. Illustration
Grades: 11 12 Adult   **741.5; Fic**
1. Mystery fiction; 2. Teenagers — Graphic novels
1606998412; 9781606998410, $24.99
                                                  LC 2015942121
Alex Award (2016)

In this graphic novel, by Liz Suburbia, "the children of...Alexandria are just trying to live like normal teens until their parents' promised return from a mysterious, four-year religious pilgrimage, and Ben Schiller is no exception. She's just trying to take care of her sister...and get through her teen years. But her relationship with her best friend is changing, her younger sister is hiding a dark secret, and a terrible tragedy is coming for them all." (Publisher's note)

Sumerak, Marc
Franklin Richards, son of a genius: not-so-secret invasion. story, Chris Eliopoulos & Marc Sumerak; script, Marc Sumerak; art & letters Chris Eliopoulos. Marvel Entertainment 2009 un Illustration
Grades: 3 4 5 6 7 8 9   **741.5; Fic**
1. Fantastic Four (Fictional characters); 2. Graphic novels; 3. Humorous graphic novels; 4. Superhero graphic novels

978-0-7851-3369-8, $9.99

This latest volume includes stories featuring Franklin Richards, son of Reed and Sue Richards of the Fantastic Four. Young Franklin, aided and abetted (albeit reluctantly) by his robot companion H.E.R.B.I.E., builds a replica of the first Iron Man robotic armor, drinks one of his dad's formulas and proceeds to belch HUGELY, de-ages his dad so they can play together, and then a multiplicity of Franklin Richards in many different timelines get into similar trouble. There are more stories, lots of silly humor and superhero action, drawn by coauthor Eliopoulos.

Sun Tzu
The **art** of war. Roundtable Press 2011 un Illustration
Grades: 9 10 11 12 Adult   **741.5**
1. Competition — Graphic novels; 2. Graphic novels; 3. Philosophers; 4. Strategy — Graphic novels; 5. Writers on the military; 6. Sun-tzu, 6th cent. B.C.
978-1-61066-010-5, $12.95

Sun Tzu's classic book on strategy has now been adapted into a graphic novel. This adaptation is more a summary of the principles of strategy discussed in The Art of War, illustrated by Clester using modern situations to demonstrate the principles. For example, Sun Tzu's statement that "he who wishes to fight must first count the cost" is depicted with rival gangsters. This short book can't replace the original, but it provides a good summary of the main points and serves as an introduction for high school students and busy adults who may not have the time to read the whole original text.

Suzumi, Atsushi
Haridama magic cram school. Atsushi Suzumi; translated and adapted by Kaya Laterman. Del Rey Manga 2008 202p. Illustration
Grades: 7 8 9 10 11 12   **741.5; Fic**
1. Fantasy graphic novels; 2. Graphic novels; 3. Magic — Graphic novels; 4. Manga; 5. Shonen manga
978-0-345-50136-3, $10.95
                                                  LC 2008-299354

Kokuyo and Harika are sorcery students, but they're Obsidians, wizards who must use special stones set in swords to help them cast spells. Other sorcery students think they're inferior because they lack both yin and yang. But Kokuyo and Harika do have something no one else has: the power of friendship. They'll have to figure it out, but when they work together, they don't need their swords. This is a one-volume manga.

Tagame, Gengoroh
My **brother's** husband. Gengoroh Tagame; translated by Anne Ishii. Pantheon 2017 352 p. Illustration
Grades: 11 12 Adult   **741.5**
1. Gay men — Japan — Comic books, strips, etc; 2. Japan — Fiction; 3. Gay men — Fiction
1101871512; 9781101871515, $24.95
                                                  LC 2016047082
Eisner Award: Best U.S. Edition of International Material — Asia (2018)

In this book, by Gengoroh Tagame, translated by Anne Ishii, "Yaichi is a work-at-home suburban dad in contemporary Tokyo; formerly married to Natsuki, father to their young daughter, Kana. Their lives suddenly change with the arrival at their doorstep of a hulking, affable Canadian named Mike Flanagan, who declares himself the widower of Yaichi's estranged gay twin, Ryoji." (Publisher's note)

"This winsome look at culture clash compares the largely still-closeted Japanese gay culture with the West, underscoring a theme of universal yearning for family." LJ

Originally published as Otouto no Otto by Futabasha Publishers Ltd., Tokyo, in 2014 — Title page verso.; Volume 1 of 2

Takahashi, Rumiko

★ **InuYasha:** Volume One. by Rumiko Takahashi. Viz 2009 562 p.
Grades: 7 8 9 10 11 12   **741.5; 741.5/952**

1. Japanese mythology; 2. Shonen manga; 3. Manga
1421532808; 9781421532806, $19.99

LC bl2009031710

In this book, by Rumiko Takahashi, "Kagome is a modern Japanese high school girl. Never the type to believe in myths and legends, her world view dramatically changes when, one day, she's pulled out of her own time and into another! There, in Japan's ancient past, Kagome discovers more than a few of those dusty old legends are true, and that her destiny is linked to one legendary creature in particular — the dog like half-demon called Inuyasha!" (Publisher's note)

Originally published in 56 individual volumes; Volume 1 of 18

Ranma 1/2. Rumiko Takahashi, translated from Japanese by Gerard Jones & Matt Thorn. Viz Media 2014 359 p. Illustration
Grades: 10 11 12 Adult   **741.5**

1. Shonen manga; 2. Manga; 3. Gender role — Fiction
1421565943; 9781421565941, $14.99

"One day, teenaged martial artist Ranma Saotome went on a training mission with his father and ended up taking a dive into some cursed springs at a legendary training ground in China. Now, every time he's splashed with cold water, he changes into a girl. His father, Genma, changes into a panda! What's a half-guy, half-girl to do?" (Publisher's note)

"One of the bestselling manga from the early '90s, a gender-bending rom-com mixed with copious martial arts action, returns in this rerelease. World-class martial artist Ranma Saotome has been cursed with a special fate: when doused with cold water, he turns into a girl. This oddity is little more than an irritation to him until he becomes engaged to Akane Tendo, a prodigiously strong fighter who also happens to hate men." Pub Wkly

38 volumes originally released in Japan from 1987-1996

Takamisaki, Ryo

Megaman NT Warrior Vol. 1. Viz/Viz Kids 2004 186p. Illustration
Grades: 4 5 6 7 8 9   **741.5; Fic**

1. Graphic novels; 2. Manga; 3. Science fiction graphic novels; 4. Shonen manga
1-59116-465-6, $7.95

The year is 200X and everyone is now connected to the Cyber Network. People carry their own PET (Personal terminal) and are paired up with an artificial intelligence program called a NetNavi (or NetNavigator). Computers have turned the world into a bright and shiny utopia, but there's always trouble in paradise. While the invention of the PET and NetNavis has brought great benefits to the world, computer hacking, virus spreading, and other high-tech crimes are becoming a major problem. A sinister organization by the name of World Three has appeared, and they've vowed to destroy this technological wonderland. Enter Lan Hikari, an intensely curious and cheerful fifth grader. Synchronized with his NetNavigator, MegaMansupercharged, he becomes a super-charged dynamo. In and out of the Net, Lan and MegaMan do their best to thwart World Three's neverending quest to take over the world. The book includes some raunchy humor and lots of action.

Pokemon: the rise of Darkrai. story & art by Ryo Takamisaki; English translation, Kaori Inoue. Viz Media/VizKids 2008 un Illustration
Grades: 2 3 4 5 6 7 8 9   **741.5; Fic**

1. Adventure graphic novels; 2. Fantasy graphic novels; 3. Graphic novels; 4. Manga; 5. Shonen manga
978-1-4215-2289-0, $7.99

Ash and his friends come to Alamos Town, home of the Space-Time Towers, and while touring the town, they discover that the town's special garden has been ransacked. Some of the townspeople blame Darkrai, a sinister looking Pokemon that said to haunt the garden. However, Alamos Town faces much more peril when two powerful Pokemon that control time and space battle each other; it should be impossible for them to meet, and unless Ash and the others " and perhaps Darkrai " can stop them, Alamos Town will be destroyed. This book includes a lot of Pokemon fighting action; the panels are so filled with details that very young readers might find it difficult to follow the action.

Takanashi, Mitsuba

The **Devil** Does Exist Volume 1. DC Comics/CMX 2005 192p. Illustration
Grades: 7 8 9 10 11 12   **741.5; Fic**

1. Graphic novels; 2. Manga; 3. Romance graphic novels; 4. Shojo manga
1-4012-0545-3, $9.99

High school is difficult for most kids. But for Kayano, a shy girl whose single mother seems to work all the time, it's even worse than usual. She's so afraid of drawing attention to herself, in fact, that she can't tell the handsome Kamijo how much she loves him-until one day she finally gets up the courage to write him a letter confessing her feelings. But her plans go awry when the letter falls into the hands of the school's most notorious student, Edogawa Takeru. To Kayano, Takeru seems to be Satan himself. Not only is he devilishly handsome, he is the son of the school's principal. Even the teachers dare not stand up to him. Kayano, appalled by how badly her first attempt at a social life has gone, thinks she can struggle through, and get her letter back. But, Takeru enjoys watching her suffer. Just when she thinks she's solved the problem, her mother comes home to announce she's getting married-to principal Edogawa. Now Kayano will have to live with this devil Takeru 24/7. How will she cope with this literal living hell? The book includes some mild strong language, mild violence, and some brief sexual situations.

Takano, Ichigo

★ **Orange;** Volume 1: the complete collection. story and art by Ichigo Takano; translation, Amber Tamosaitis; adaptation, Shannon Fay; lettering and layout, Lys Blakeslee. Seven Seas Entertainment Llc 2016 384 p. Illustration
Grades: 8 9 10 11 12   **741.5; Fic**

1. High school students — Fiction; 2. Future life — Fiction; 3. Manga; 4. Shojo manga
1626923027; 9781626923027, $19.99

"On the day that Naho begins 11th grade, she recieves a letter from herself ten years in the future. At first, she writes it off as a prank, but as the letter's predictions come true one by one Naho realizes that the letter might be the real deal. Her future self tells Naho that a new transfer student, a boy named Kakeru, will soon join her class. The letter begs Naho to watch over him, saying that only Naho can save Kakeru from a terrible future." (Publisher's note)

Volume 1 of 2

★ **Orange;** Volume 2: the complete collection. story and art by Ichigo Takano; translation, Amber Tamosaitis; adaptation, Shannon Fay; lettering and layout, Lys Blakeslee. Seven Seas Entertainment Llc 2016 384 p. Illustration
Grades: 8 9 10 11 12   **741.5; Fic**

1. Shojo manga; 2. Future life — Fiction; 3. High school students — Fiction; 4. Manga

1626922713; 9781626922716, $19.99

"On the day that Naho begins 11th grade, she recieves a letter from herself ten years in the future. At first, she writes it off as a prank, but as the letter's predictions come true one by one Naho realizes that the letter might be the real deal. Her future self tells Naho that a new transfer student, a boy named Kakeru, will soon join her class. The letter begs Naho to watch over him, saying that only Naho can save Kakeru from a terrible future." (Publisher's note)

Takaya, Natsuki

★ **Fruits** Basket Collector's Edition: Volume 1. Natsuki Takaya; translation, Sheldon Drzka; lettering, Lys Blakeslee. Yen Press 2016 400 p. Illustration

Grades: 7 8 9 10 11 12   **741.5; Fic**
1. Family — Fiction; 2. Secrets — Fiction; 3. Shojo manga
0316360163; 9780316360166, $20

"After a family tragedy turns her life upside down, plucky high schooler Tohru Honda takes matters into her own hands and moves out...into a tent! Unfortunately for her, she pitches her new home on private land belonging to the mysterious Sohma clan, and it isn't long before the owners discover her secret. But, as Tohru quickly finds out when the family offers to take her in, the Sohmas have a secret of their own — when touched by the opposite sex, they turn into the animals of the Chinese Zodiac!" (Publisher's note)

Originally published in the U.S. by Tokyopop in 23 volumes; Volume 1 of 12

Twinkle stars; Volume 1. Natsuki Takaya; translation, Sheldon Drzka; lettering, Lys Blakeslee. Yen Press 2016 384 p. Illustration

Grades: 7 8 9 10 11 12   **741.5; Fic**
1. Fantasy fiction; 2. Teenagers — Graphic novels; 3. High school students — Graphic novels; 4. Shojo manga
0316360236; 9780316360234, $20

LC 2016946117

In this book in the Twinke Stars series, by Natsuki Takaya, translated by Sheldon Drzka, "Sakuya Shiina lives with Kanade, her male cousin and foster parent. In times of pain and sadness, she's always taken comfort in looking up at the stars. One day, a mysterious boy suddenly shows up at Sakuya's house for her birthday. He leaves her with kind words, but she has no idea who he is!" (Publisher's note)

Volume 1 of 5

Takemiya, Keiko

★ **To** Terra Volume One. Keiko Takemiya; [translation, Dawn T. Laabs]. Vertical, Inc. 2007 343p. Illustration

Grades: 9 10 11 12 Adult   **741.5; Fic**
1. Graphic novels; 2. Manga; 3. Psychics — Graphic novels; 4. Science fiction graphic novels; 5. Shojo manga
9781932234671, $13.95; 1932234675

The future. Having driven Terra to the brink of environmental collapse, humanity decides to reform itself by ushering in the age of Superior Domination (S.D.), a system of social control in which children are no longer the offspring of parents but progeny of a universal computer. The new social order, however, results in an unexpected byproduct: the Mu, a mutant race with extrasensory powers who are forced in exile by The System. The saga begins on educational planet Ataraxia, where Jomy Marcus Shin, a brash and unpredictable teenager, is nervously preparing to enter adult society. When his Maturity Check goes wrong, the Mu intervene in the great hope that Jomy, who possesses Mu telepathy and human physical strength, can lead them back home, to Terra...

Volume 1 of 3

Takeuchi, Mick

Her Majesty's Dog, Vol. 1. Go! Comi 2005 200p. Illustration

Grades: 10 11 12 Adult   **741.5; Fic**
1. Graphic novels; 2. Manga; 3. Romance graphic novels; 4. Shojo manga; 5. Supernatural graphic novels
0-9768957-3-0, $10.99

New students Amane and Hyoue cause a stir in their high school because they kiss so much. Amane is a psychic, Hyoue is actually her guardian demon-dog, and he feeds on her life force by their kisses. Together, they hunt demons, but in school they need to learn how to deal with everyday hazards such as bullies, jealousy, and making friends. This series combines teen romance with supernatural horror.

Takeuchi, Naoko

★ **Sailor** Moon; Volume 1. Naoko Takeuchi; translator/adapter, William Flanagan. Kodansha Comics 2011 240 p. Illustration; Color

Grades: 5 6 7 8 9 10   **741.5; Fic**
1. Teenage girls — Japan — Comic books, strips, etc; 2. Women heroes — Comic books, strips, etc; 3. Shojo manga; 4. Teenage girls — Fiction; 5. Good and evil — Fiction
1935429744; 9781935429746, $10.99

LC 2012374271

"Usagi Tsukino is a normal girl until she meets up with Luna, a talking cat, who tells her that she is Sailor Moon. As Sailor Moon, Usagi must fight evils and enforce justice, in the name of the Moon and the mysterious Moon Princess. She meets other girls destined to be Sailor Senshi (Sailor Scouts), and together, they fight the forces of evil!" (Publisher's note)

First published in Japan in 2003 by Kodansha Ltd., Tokyo, as Bishoujosenshi Sailor Moon Shinsoban; Volume 1 of 12

Takizawa, Seiho

Who Fighter with Heart of Darkness. Dark Horse Manga 2006 208p. Illustration

Grades: 10 11 12 Adult   **741.5; Fic**
1. Graphic novels; 2. Manga; 3. Seinen manga; 4. War — Graphic novels
978-1-59307-626-9, $11.95

The first story in this anthology, "Who Fighter," is a play on the legendary "Foo Fighters," the nickname given to the mysterious, UFO-like fireballs that were sighted by World War II pilots. An ace Japanese pilot manages to shoot one of the fireballs down... or does he? As ominous signs and visions begin to follow in his steps, the bewildered pilot wonders if he's lost not only his memory of the incident-but also his very mind. "Heart of Darkness" is Takizawa's take on the Joseph Conrad novel. A Japanese war hero, Colonel Kurutsu, has gone rogue, setting up his own private kingdom deep upriver in the jungles of Burma. A young captain, sent to execute Kurutsu, finds that the true reasons for the Colonel's "desertion" are very different from what he was told. Finally, a short piece, "Tanks," closes out the collection with a surreal voyage through one hundred years of armored vehicle battles. The book includes some violence and some mildly strong language.

Talbot, Bryan

★ **Alice** in Sunderland: An Entertainment. Dark Horse Comics 2007 324p. Illustration

Grades: 10 11 12 Adult   **741.5**
1. Fantasy graphic novels; 2. Graphic novels
978-1-59307-673-3

Sunderland was once the greatest center of learning in Christendom and the birthplace of English consciousness. In the time of Lewis Carroll it was the greatest shipbuilding port in the world, and here are buried the roots of Carroll's surreal masterpiece, Alice in Wonderland. Talbot mixes fact and fiction in his meditation on myth, history, storytelling. The book includes some strong language, particularly Briticisms.

★ **The tale** of one bad rat. Dark Horse 2010 un Illustration
Grades: 9 10 11 12 Adult   **741.5; Fic**
1. Child sexual abuse — Graphic novels; 2. Graphic novels; 3. Runaway teenagers — Graphic novels
978-1-59582-493-6, $19.99

This book's "heroine is teenager Helen Potter, who has run away from an abusive father and whose path to recovery takes her from a squat in London to refuge at an inn in the British countryside. Along the way, she meets characters and situations that Talbot derives from the work of Helen's namesake, Beatrix Potter, whose life he symbolically links to Helen's. Talbot's vivid, realistic full-color illustration brilliantly evokes the story's settings, yet even more effective are his compassionate characterizations." Booklist

First published 1995; ?This volume collects issues one through four of the Dark Horse comic-book series? Verso of title page

Tamaki, Jillian
★ **SuperMutant** Magic Academy. Jillian Tamaki. Drawn & Quarterly 2015 274 p. Illustration
Grades: 10 11 12 Adult   **741.5; Fic**
1. Comic books, strips, etc. — Canada; 2. Private schools — Comic books, strips, etc; 3. Teenagers — Comic books, strips, etc; 4. Teenagers — Fiction; 5. Fantasy graphic novels; 6. School stories
1770461981; 9781770461987, $22.95

LC 2015376543
Eisner Award: Best Publication for Teens (2016); Ignatz Nominee: Outstanding Artist (2015); Ignatz Nominee: Outstanding Anthology or Collection (2015)

In this graphic novel, author Jillian Tamaki "paints a teenaged world filled with just as much ennui and uncertainty, but also with a sharp dose of humor and irreverence.... The SuperMutant Magic Academy is a prep school for mutants and witches, but their paranormal abilities take a backseat to everyday teen concerns. Science experiments go awry, bake sales are upstaged, and the new kid at school is a cat who will determine the course of human destiny." (Publisher's note)

"There are flickering moments of transcendent wisdom and kindness, but the overall tone is one of insouciant, salty resignation to the mundane realities of existence. Simultaneously heartbreaking and hilarious." Booklist

Tamaki, Mariko
★ **Emiko** superstar. written by Mariko Tamaki; illustrated by Steve Rolston. DC Comics/Minx 2008 149p. Illustration
Grades: 7 8 9 10 11 12   **741.5; Fic**
1. Graphic novels; 2. Performance art — Graphic novels; 3. Racially mixed people — Graphic novels
978-1-4012-1536-1, O.P.

"Emiko, a half-Japanese, half-Caucasian Canadian, is a self-described geek facing a summer of babysitting and isolation. Things change when she stumbles upon an underground performing art scene inspired by Andy Warhol's Factory. She eventually takes to the stage...and achieves minor celebrity. Soon, though, Emiko must face the troubling complexities in the lives of her new friends and the consequences of her own questionable actions.... Rolston's playful, vibrant b&w illustrations bring the characters to life." Publ Wkly

★ **Skim**. words by Mariko Tamaki; drawings by Jillian Tamaki. Groundwood Books 2008 144p. Illustration
Grades: 7 8 9 10 11 12   **741; 741.5; Fic**
1. Friendship — Graphic novels; 2. Graphic novels; 3. Humorous graphic novels; 4. School stories — Graphic novels; 5. LGBT youth — Fiction
088899964X; 0-88899-753-1; 9780888999641, 12.95; 978-0-88899-753-1, $18.95
Ignatz Award: Outstanding Graphic Novel (2008)

Skim is Kimberly Keiko Cameron, a not-slim half-Japanese would-be Wiccan goth who attends a private school. When classmate Katie Matthews' ex-boyfriend commits suicide, concerned guidance counselors descend upon the school because so many of the student body goes into mourning overdrive. The popular clique starts a new club, Girls Celebrate Life, and make Katie their project, especially after she falls off her roof and breaks both arms. Kim and her best friend Lisa observe all this, but counselors target Kim for her goth tendencies and are convinced she'll become suicidal any moment. All she is, is in love with her English teacher, Ms. Archer, who seems to reciprocate and then leaves the school. As Lisa starts to get sucked into the GLC, Kim and Katie tentatively begin a new friendship. There is only one rather chaste kiss between Kim and Ms. Archer. Artist Jillian Tamaki draws Kim to look like a classical Heian period Japanese woman.

★ **This** One Summer. Mariko Tamaki, [art by] Jillian Tamaki. First Second 2014 320 p. Illustration
Grades: 7 8 9 10 11 12 Adult   **741.5; Fic**
1. Graphic novels; 2. Friendship — Fiction; 3. Vacations — Fiction
159643774X, 17.99; 9781626720947, $21.99; 9781596437746, 17.99; 1626720940, 21.99
Caldecott Honor Book (2015); Printz Honor Book (2015); Eisner Award: Best Graphic Album — New (2015); Ignatz Award: Outstanding Graphic Novel (2014); Harvey Nominee: Best Artist (2015); Harvey Nominee: Best Graphic Album of Original Work (2015); Harvey Nominee: Best Original Graphic Publication For Young Readers (2015)

"Every summer, Rose goes with her mom and dad to a lake house in Awago Beach.... Rosie's friend Windy is always there, too, like the little sister she never had. But this summer is different.... It's a summer of secrets, and sorrow, and growing up, and it's a good thing Rose and Windy have each other." (Publisher's note)

"This captivating graphic novel presents a fully realized picture of a particular time in a young girl's life, an in-between summer filled with yearning and a sense of ephemerality." SLJ

Tan, Shaun
★ **The arrival**. Arthur A. Levine Books 2007 un Illustration
Grades: 6 7 8 9 10   **741.5; Fic**
1. Graphic novels; 2. Immigrants — Graphic novels; 3. Stories without words
0-439-89529-4, $19.99; 9780439895293

LC 2006-21706
Boston Globe-Horn Book Award special citation (2008)

In this wordless graphic novel, a man leaves his homeland and sets off for a new country, where he must build a new life for himself and his family.

"Young readers will be fascinated by the strange new world the artist creates.... They will linger over the details in the beautiful sepia pictures and will likely pick up the book to pore over it again and again." SLJ

Tanemura, Arina
Full Moon Vol. 1: O Sagashite. Viz Media/Shojo Beat 2005 200p. Illustration
Grades: 7 8 9 10   **741.5; Fic**
1. Fantasy graphic novels; 2. Graphic novels; 3. Manga; 4. Romance graphic novels; 5. Shojo manga

1-59116-928-3, $8.99

Young Mitsuki loves singing and dreams of becoming a pop star. Unfortunately, a malignant tumor in her throat prevents her from pursuing her passion. However, her life turns around when two surprisingly fun-loving harbingers of death appear to grant Mitsuki a temporary reprieve from her illness and give her singing career a magical push start. They transform her into a 16-year-old, and she becomes a sensation, but when one of the spirits falls in love with Mitsuki, complications abound.

Tarr, Babs

Motor crush; Volume 1. creators, Brenden Fletcher, Cameron Stewart, Babs Tarr; colors and production assistant, Heather Danforth; lettering, Aditya Bidikar.. Image Comics 2017 136 p.

Grades: 9 10 11 12 Adult   **741.5**

1. Motorcycle racing — Comic books, strips, etc.; 2. Adventure graphic novels; 3. Women motorcyclists — Comic books, strips, etc.

9781534301894, $9.99

In this graphic novel in the Motor Crush series, by Brenden Fletcher, Cameron Stewart, and Babs Tarr, "by day, Domino Swift competes for fame & fortune in a worldwide motorcycle racing league. By night, she cracks heads of rival gangs in brutal bike wars to gain possession of a rare, valuable contraband: an engine-boosting 'machine narcotic' known as Crush." (Publisher's note)

"This series, a spiritual successor to Speed Racer's rubber-burning mayhem, is packed with fun characters, visceral high-speed action, romance, and a general sense of unbridled action. The whole package is worthy of note, and Stewart and Tarr's art really grabs the reader by the eyeballs. It's heavily animation-influenced and practically leaps off the page." PW.

Originally published as Motor crush #1-5 — Page [2].

Tatsumi, Yoshihiro

★ The **Push** Man and Other Stories. Yoshihiro Tatsumi; [translated by Yuji Oniki]. Drawn & Quarterly 2005 208p. Illustration

Grades: 12 Adult   **741.5; Fic**

1. City and town life — Japan — Graphic novels; 2. Graphic novels; 3. Manga; 4. Seinen manga

1-896597-85-8, $19.95

Tatsumi is considered the grandfather of alternate manga for the adult reader; the stories in this collection date back to the late 1960s and explore the darker aspects of Japanese urban life. The look of his art is very different from most manga, and his stories comment on the interplay between an overwhelming, bustling, crowded, modern society and the troubled emotional and sexual life of the individual. He invented the term "gekiga" ("dramatic pictures") in 1957 to describe his manga Strong sexual overtones, violence, and strong language make Tatsumi's work more suitable for older, mature-minded teens and adults.

Telgemeier, Raina

The **Baby-Sitters** Club: The Truth About Stacey. Raina Telgemeier; [adapted from the novel by] Ann M. Martin. Scholastic/Graphix 2006 142p. Illustration

Grades: 3 4 5 6 7 8 9   **741.5**

1. Babysitting — Graphic novels; 2. Friendship — Graphic novels; 3. Graphic novels

0-439-73936-5

Poor Stacey. She's moved to a new town. She's still coming to terms with her diabetes. She's facing baby-sitting problems left and right, and her parents are no help. Luckily, Stacey has three new, true friends: Kristy, Claudia, and Mary Anne. Together they're the BSC, and they will deal with whatever is thrown their way, even if it's a rival baby-sitting club.

TenNapel, Doug

Bad Island. created, written, and drawn by Doug TenNapel. Graphix 2011 218p. Illustration

Grades: 6 7 8 9 10   **741.5**

1. Adventure graphic novels; 2. Extraterrestrial beings — Graphic novels; 3. Family life — Graphic novels; 4. Survival after airplane accidents, shipwrecks, etc. — Graphic novels; 5. Father-son relationship — Graphic novels

0545314798; 0545314801 (pa); 9780545314794, $24.99; 9780545314800 (pa)

LC 2011276008

"Dad has decided to take Reese, who is too cool for family outings, and his sister, Janine, on a fishing trip. The vacation takes an unexpected turn when their boat capsizes during a storm and they find themselves marooned on a strange island. To their horror, the family slowly realizes that the island is the submerged body of a giant creature, escaped from another world. The story alternates between the shipwreck survivors and the faraway world that created this "island." Both stories feature conflict between an adolescent son and his father.... Ultimately, both rebellious adolescents grow up and find their place as young men." (School Libr J)

"Though father, mother, teenage son, and tween daughter face the various dangers like a gang of Indiana Joneses, their family stresses are believable.... A clever, old-fashioned adventure with some modern twists and a lighthearted tone." Booklist

Black Cherry. Image Comics 2007 un Illustration

Grades: 11 12 Adult   **741.5; Fic**

1. Graphic novels; 2. Horror graphic novels; 3. Mystery graphic novels; 4. Science fiction graphic novels

978-1-58240-830-9, $17.99

Down-on-his-luck Mafioso Eddie Paretti is so desperate for cash he's agreed to steal a dead body from his own mob boss. Things only get worse when he discovers the body isn't human. With few options and fewer people he can trust, Eddie calls on the man who raised him, Father McHugh. The priest tells Eddie that the body was stolen from his monastery by the Mafia. Father McHugh is accompanied by Mary, a beautiful woman Eddie swears looks just like a stripper he once fell in love with named Black Cherry. The book is full of very foul language (f-bombs and s-bombs galore), nudity, sexual situations, and graphic violence. It also has a deeply-felt religious core that may confuse some readers. TenNapel has written a foreword for readers that explains it.

Tetzner, Lisa

The **Black** Brothers: A Novel in Pictures. Front Street 2004 144p. Illustration

Grades: 4 5 6 7 8 9   **741.5; Fic**

1. Chimney sweeps — Graphic novels; 2. Graphic novels

1-932425-04-7, $16.95

In rural Italy, thirteen-year-old Giorgio is sold to a man who supplies chimney sweeps for Milan. After a treacherous journey in which most of the other boys die, Giorgio goes to work for a man whose wife resents another mouth to feed and starves him. He is sent up into chimneys with no training or guidance for how to do the dangerous work. After nearly dying, he is befriended by a doctor and finds the Black Brothers, a group of chimney sweeps who swear loyalty to each other.

This illustrated novel was originally published in German in 1941, and the translation's tone is similar to other children's books, such as Emil and the Detectives.

Tezuka, Osamu

Astro Boy books 1 and 2. Dark Horse Comics 2008 424p. Illustration

Grades: 3 4 5 6 7 8 9 10 11 12 Adult   **741.5; Fic**

1. Adventure graphic novels; 2. Astro Boy (Fictional character); 3. Graphic novels; 4. Robots — Graphic novels; 5. Science fiction graphic novels

978-1-59582-153-9, $14.95

When a scientist loses his young son, he builds a robot to look exactly like the boy, but when he activates the robot, the scientist becomes repulsed and rejects him. Professor Ochanomizu (gotta love the name, it means tea water and is also a famous Tokyo neighborhood) rescues the boy robot from a circus and names him Astro Boy. He deals with aliens, with people who would use robots to commit crimes, and with adventures in outer space. This new edition collects the first two volumes of the Dark Horse manga editions.

Also available in omnibus editions; Volumes 1 and 2 of a 23 volume series

★ **Black** Jack, volume 1. Vertical, Inc. 2008 287p. Illustration
Grades: 9 10 11 12 Adult   **741.5; Fic**
1. Graphic novels; 2. Manga; 3. Medical practice — Graphic novels; 4. Surgeons — Graphic novels; 5. Shonen manga

978-1-934287-27-9, $16.95

Black Jack is the only known name for a mysterious, scarred surgeon from Japan who can perform surgical miracles but is considered to be a creepy mercenary. He will perform highly risky surgeries for an exorbitant price, and he's unlicensed. However, most people don't realize that he actually does a lot for more altruistic reasons as well. In this first volume that reprints the original stories by pioneer mangaka (manga creator) Tezuka, stories include one in which Black Jack operates on a crime boss's son using the body of an unjustly convicted man; and one where he removes a teratoid cystoma from a unidentified wealthy and famous woman, but he refuses to kill the cystoma, which contains the body parts of the woman's unborn twin. While there are some surgical scenes that might not be for the squeamish, the stories offer little in the way of graphic violence or bad language while providing action and some thought about ethics and morals.

"With genre-spanning stories — horror, sci-fi, romance — and Tezuka's signature blend of drama, bathos and extreme broad comedy jammed together on every page, Black Jack is a wild but extravagantly entertaining ride." Publ Wkly

Volume 1 of 17

★ **Buddha** Volume 1: Kapilavastu. Vertical, Inc. 2003 400p. Illustration
Grades: 10 11 12 Adult   **741.5; Fic**
1. Buddhism — Graphic novels; 2. Graphic novels; 3. Manga; 4. Seinen manga

1-932234-56-X (pa); 1-932234-43-8, $24.95; 9781932234565, $14.95

In this first of eight volumes, Tezuka starts the story of Buddha before the birth of the prince Siddhartha. His fictional characters, the slave Chapra, the pariah Tatta, the monk Naradatta, and many others, populate the story and will have an effect on the prince's life. The book includes sexual situations and considerable nudity; the pariahs never wore clothes. Tezuka also throws in a lot of humorous and anachronistic comments; but underlying everything is a profoundly deep understanding of Buddhism. The book also includes some violence.

Thomas, Roy
The **Chronicles** of Conan Volume 1: Tower of the Elephant and Other Stories. Dark Horse Comics 2003 166p. Illustration
Grades: 9 10 11 12 Adult   **741.5; Fic**
1. Adventure graphic novels; 2. Conan the Barbarian (Fictional character); 3. Fantasy graphic novels; 4. Graphic novels

1-59307-016-0, $15.95

In the early 1970s, Robert E. Howard's Conan the Barbarian exploded on to the comics scene. Writer Roy Thomas teamed with a young artist named Barry Smith, and together the two mapped out Conan adventures over the course of their 24-issue run together. Thomas and Smith defined Conan for a generation of comics readers, and now those stories are collected here in a series of trade paperbacks. This series features completely remastered color and text corrections, and contains material not available for nearly thirty years. Some of the stories are original, others adapt the original Howard stories; they all include action and violence and some suggestive scenes, as Conan fights warriors and monsters and encounters beautiful, sexy women.

Thompson, Craig, 1975-
★ **Blankets:** an illustrated novel. Top Shelf 2003 582p. Illustration
Grades: 10 11 12 Adult   **92; 741.5**
1. Artists; 2. Autobiographical graphic novels; 3. Cartoonists; 4. Family life — Graphic novels; 5. Graphic novels; 6. Illustrators; 7. Thompson, Craig, 1975-

1-891830-43-0, $29.95; 9781891830433

LC 2004-297892

This "memoir recreates the confusion, emotional pain and isolation of the author's rigidly fundamentalist Christian upbringing, along with the trepidation of growing into maturity. Skinny, naive and spiritually vulnerable, Thompson and his younger brother manage to survive their parents' overbearing discipline (the brothers are sometimes forced to sleep in "the cubbyhole," a forbidding and claustrophobic storage chamber) through flights of childhood fancy and a mutual love of drawing...Thompson manages to explore adolescent social yearnings, the power of young love and the complexities of sexual attraction with a rare combination of sincerity, pictorial lyricism and taste. His exceptional b&w drawings balance representational precision with a bold and wonderfully expressive line for pages of ingenious, inventively composed and poignant imagery." Publ Wkly

Thompson, Jill
Death: At Death's Door. DC Comics/Vertigo 2003 204p. Illustration
Grades: 10 11 12 Adult   **741.5; Fic**
1. Adventure graphic novels; 2. Fantasy graphic novels; 3. Graphic novels; 4. Horror graphic novels; 5. Humorous graphic novels

1-56389-938-8, $9.95

A member of the Endless, a family of beings who have existed longer than the gods, Death enjoys manifesting herself in the persona of a Goth girl. Along with her siblings, she interacts and influences the lives of humans on a daily basis. In this shojo manga-style adventure, Death's little sisters, Delirium and Despair, have thrown a party at her apartment for hell's escapees. But as the festivities get out of control, it falls on Death's black-clad shoulders to regain order and save the afterlife — not to mention her carpet. Despair is always drawn as nude. The events in this book occur around the time of the Sandman volume, Season of Mists.

Goosebumps: Terror Trips. Scholastic/Graphix 2007 137p. Illustration
Grades: 4 5 6 7 8 9   **741.5; Fic**
1. Graphic novels; 2. Horror graphic novels; 3. Stine, R. L.; 4. Stine, R. L. — Adaptations

978-0-439-85780-2, $8.99

Stine's Goosebumps series was very popular years ago, and is enjoying a resurgence of popularity with new editions of the prose books. The graphic novel adaptations, all done by well-known independent comics creators, bring the stories to a new audience. Goosebumps: Creepy Creatures is also available.

This volume adapts three of Stine's Goosebumps novels into graphic novel format. Noted independent comic creator Thompson adapts One Day at Horrorland, about one family's ordeal in a very strange, all-too-realistic amusement park. Canadian artist Tolagson adapts A Shocker on Shock

Street, which depicts the horrific adventures of two kids on a movie studio lot where the horror is more than just special effects. Global manga creator Ganter adapts Deep Trouble, in which a brother and sister find a real mermaid.

The **Little** Endless Storybook. DC Comics/Vertigo 2004 un Illustration
Grades: 9 10 11 12 Adult   **741.5; Fic**
1. Adventure graphic novels; 2. Fantasy graphic novels; 3. Graphic novels
14012-0428-7, $15.95

Jill Thompson takes Neil Gaiman's the Endless and draws them as little children in this story. Puppy Barnabas has been entrusted with watching and protecting Delirium, who is always easily...distracted. When he leaves her for just a minute or so, she gets lost. He searches the waking world but can't find her. Now, he must travel to the strange and unlikely realms of each of the Endless to see if Delirium's siblings have seen their missing sister. While the pictures are cute and the book resembles a child's picture book, the story has enough of an edge to make it more suitable for older teens. Despair is, as always, drawn as nude.

★ **Wonder** Woman: the true Amazon. Jill Thompson, writer and artist; Jason Arthur, letterer. DC Comics 2016 128 p. Color; Illustration
Grades: 9 10 11 12 Adult   **741.5; Fic**
1. Princesses — Graphic novels; 2. Amazons — Graphic novels; 3. Wonder Woman (Fictional character)
1401249019; 9781401249014, $22.99
Eisner Award: Best Graphic Album — New (2017)

"Young Diana has the fawning attention of her nation, but she soon grows spoiled and ungrateful. When a series of tragic events takes its toll, Diana must learn to grow up, take responsibility, and seize her destiny." (Publisher's note)

"Thompson's art is soft and magical, atypical of superhero comics. In her capable hands, this work provides insight into the early years of the heroine and is a solid addition to the stand-alone stories of her character." LJ

Thompson, Kelly
Hawkeye : Kate Bishop : anchor points. Kelly Thompson, writer; Leonardo Romero (#1-4) & Michael Walsh (#5-6), artists; Jordie Bellaire, color artist; VC's Joe Sabino, letterer; Julian Totino Tedesco, cover art. Marvel Enterprises 2017 136 p. Color; Illustration
Grades: 9 10 11 12 Adult   **741.5; Fic**
1. Private investigators — Fiction; 2. Good and evil — Comic books, strips, etc.; 3. Women superheroes — Comic books, strips, etc.
1302905147; 9781302905149, $17.99

"Kate is heading back out west and returning to Los Angeles, with her bow and arrow and P.I. badge in tow. There are crimes to solve and she's the best archer to handle 'em! The City of Angels has a new guardian angel. This is Kate Bishop like you've never seen her before, in a brand-new saga that really hits the mark!" (Publisher's note)
Volume 1 of 3

Thompson, Kim
Popeye Vol. 1: I Yam What I Yam!. Fantagraphics Books 2006 182p. Illustration
Grades: 10 11 12 Adult   **741.5**
1. Graphic novels; 2. Humorous graphic novels; 3. Popeye (Fictional character)
978-1-56097-779-7, $29.95

This is the first volume in a series that will publish all of Segar's original comic strips featuring Popeye, Olive Oyl, Wimpy, and all the other characters people have known from cartoons and a motion picture. This volume covers the years 1928 through 1930 and feature Popeye's courtship of Olive Oyl, meeting the Sea Hag, and Castor Oyl's attempts to turn Popeye into a boxing champion. With all the fighting going on, this book really isn't meant for children.

Thompson, Robbie
Silk; Volume 0: the life and times of Cindy Moon. by Robbie Thompson; illustrated by Stacey Lee. Marvel Enterprises 2015 160 p. Color; Illustration
Grades: 9 10 11 12 Adult   **741.5; Fic**
1. Women superheroes — Comic books, strips, etc.
0785197044; 9780785197041, $19.99

In this comic book, by Robbie Thompson, illustrated by Stacey Lee, "Cindy Moon...learned that she had been bitten by the same radioactive spider from the first arc of AMAZING SPIDER-MAN. She then went on to save Peter Parker's life (more than once!) and traverse the Spider-Verse alongside Spider-Woman. Now, as SILK, Cindy is on her own in New York City, searching for her past, defining her own future, and webbing up wrong-doers along the way!" (Publisher's note)
Other Silk volumes are: 1, Sinister (2016); 2, The negative (2017)

Thrash, Maggie
★ **Honor** girl: a graphic memoir. Maggie Thrash. Candlewick Press 2015 272 p. Color; Illustration
Grades: 9 10 11 12   **741.5; 92**
1. Thrash, Maggie; 2. Camps; 3. Teenage girls; 4. Lesbians
076367382X; 9780763673826, $19.99
                                                  LC 2014951805
LA Times Book Prize Finalist: Graphic Novel/Comics (2015)

This graphic memoir, by Maggie Thrash, relates how the author "has spent basically every summer of her fifteen-year-old life at the one-hundred-year-old Camp Bellflower for Girls, set deep in the heart of Appalachia.... A split-second of innocent physical contact pulls Maggie into a gut-twisting love for a...female counselor named Erin. But Camp Bellflower is an impossible place for a girl to fall in love with another girl." (Publisher's note)

HONOR GIRL. Copyright © 2015 by Maggie Thrash. Reproduced by permission of the publisher, Candlewick Press, Somerville, MA.

"Thrash finds both heartwarming support from her friends and smarmy disapproval from adults in the southern camp, and although she doesn't deny her burgeoning feelings, her revelation doesn't result in easy confidence, either. Though the understated artwork might not appeal to all readers, this honest, raw, and touching graphic memoir will resonate with teens coming to terms with identities of all stripes." Booklist

Tieri, Frank
Civil War: War Crimes. writer, Frank Tieri; artist, Staz Johnson. Marvel Entertainment 2007 un Illustration
Grades: 10 11 12 Adult   **741.5; Fic**
1. Graphic novels; 2. Superhero graphic novels; 3. Iron Man (Fictional character); 4. Captain America (Fictional character)
0-7851-2652-X, $17.99

Wilson Fisk, the incarcerated ex-Kingpin of Crime, proposes a deal to Iron Man, to use his underworld connections to help track down Captain America and his anti-Registration underground in exchange for consideration on his sentence. But can the Kingpin be trusted, or is he playing a deeper game? In a Civil War prequel story, career criminal Jackie Dio, fresh out of prison, finds the New York underworld has changed, and he finds trouble. If he's going to have a shot at surviving, he may have to find the shadowy figure known only as "The Consultant" — that is, if he even exists. There is more graphic violence in this title, and some strong language.

Tobe, Keiko

With the Light: Raising an Autistic Child (Hikari to Tomoni). Yen Press 2007 528p. Illustration
Grades: 8 9 10 11 12 Adult   741.5; Fic
1. Autism — Graphic novels; 2. Graphic novels; 3. Manga; 4. Josei manga
978-0-7595-2356-2, $14.99

Born during the sunrise — an auspicious beginning — the Azumas' newborn son is named Hikaru, which means "light." But during one play date, his mother notices that her son is slightly different from the other children. In this alternately heartwarming and bittersweet tale, a young mother tries to cope with both the overwhelming discovery of her child's autism and the trials of raising him while keeping her family together. This fictional story is based on true accounts; and the book includes notes about how parents can deal with certain situations depicted in the story.

Volume 1 of 8

Tobin, Paul

I was the cat. written by Paul Tobin; illustrated and colored by Benjamin Dewey; lettered by Jared Jones; edited by Jill Beaton with Robin Herrera; designed by Jason Storey. Oni Press 2014 144 p. Color; Illustration
Grades: 5 6 7 8 9   741.5; Fic
1. Fantasy graphic novels; 2. Cats — Graphic novels
1620101394; 9781620101391, $24.99

LC 2014932452

Eisner Nominee: Best Publication for Kids (2015)

When "Allison Breaking...receives an offer from a mysterious stranger named Burma to write his memoirs, it's an offer she can't refuse, not even with all the red flags popping up. But Burma is quite literally unlike any man Allison's ever known — because he's a cat! And this cat has stories to tell about how he (over the course of a few lifetimes) has shaped the world." (Publisher's note)

Toboso, Yana

Black butler, vol. 1. by Yana Toboso [translation: Tomo Kimura; lettering: Tania Biswas].. Yen Press 2010 184p. Illustration
Grades: 10 11 12 Adult   741.5; Fic
1. Fantasy graphic novels; 2. Graphic novels; 3. Household employees — Graphic novels; 4. Manga; 5. Mystery graphic novels; 6. Shonen manga
978-0-316-08084-2, $10.99

In an alternate England, the young Earl Phantomhive, Ciel, lives just outside London; he's only twelve years old, but he runs a massive toy manufacturing company, aided by his butler Sebastian. In this world, magic coexists with science and technology, cars from the early twentieth century drive the roads and Ciel tests video games. Sebastian commands the other workers: Finnian the Gardener (who tends to kill plants), Mey-Rin the klutzy housemaid, and Baldroy the chef, who always has a cigarette dangling from the corner of his mouth. The dapper butler always finds a way to save the day, whether it's transforming a destroyed courtyard into a Japanese rock garden, teaching his young charge to dance the waltz, or saving him from gangsters. He is too good to be true; he is, as he says, "a

devil of a butler." The book includes some graphic violence and occasional, mildly bad language ("bastard," "damned").

First volume in an ongoing series; Volume 1 of an ongoing series

Tolagson, Jamie

Goosebumps: Terror Trips. Scholastic/Graphix 2007 137p. Illustration
Grades: 4 5 6 7 8 9   741.5; Fic
1. Graphic novels; 2. Horror graphic novels; 3. Stine, R. L.; 4. Stine, R. L. — Adaptations
978-0-439-85780-2, $8.99

Stine's Goosebumps series was very popular years ago, and is enjoying a resurgence of popularity with new editions of the prose books. The graphic novel adaptations, all done by well-known independent comics creators, bring the stories to a new audience. Goosebumps: Creepy Creatures is also available.

This volume adapts three of Stine's Goosebumps novels into graphic novel format. Noted independent comic creator Thompson adapts One Day at Horrorland, about one family's ordeal in a very strange, all-too-realistic amusement park. Canadian artist Tolagson adapts A Shocker on Shock Street, which depicts the horrific adventures of two kids on a movie studio lot where the horror is more than just special effects. Global manga creator Ganter adapts Deep Trouble, in which a brother and sister find a real mermaid.

Tomasi, Peter

The bridge: how the Roeblings connected Brooklyn to New York. Peter J. Tomasi, illustrated by Sara DuVall. Abrams ComicArts 2018 208 p. Color; Illustration
Grades: 11 12 Adult   741.5; 624.2
1. Comic books, strips, etc; 2. Graphic novels; 3. Roebling, Emily Warren, 1843-1903 — Biography — Comic books, strips, etc; 4. Roebling, Washington Augustus, 1837-1926 — Biography — Comic books, strips, etc; 5. Brooklyn Bridge (New York, N.Y.) — History — Comic books, strips, etc; 6. Bridges; 7. Roebling, Washington Augustus, 1837-1926; 8. Roebling, Emily Warren, 1843-1903
9781419728525, $24.99

LC 2017046927

"In this inspiring graphic novel, author Peter J. Tomasi and illustrator Sara Duvall show the building of the Brooklyn Bridge as it has never been seen before, and the marriage of the Roeblings — based on intellectual equality and mutual support — that made the construction of this iconic structure possible." (Publisher's note)

"Rather than being a story of a singular genius overcoming adversity, the book is a paean to collaboration. Iconic structures often have fascinating stories behind them, but rarely do the tellings emphasize the human as this one does." Pub Wkly

Tomine, Adrian

★ **Shortcomings**. Drawn & Quarterly 2007 108p. Illustration
Grades: 10 11 12 Adult   741.5; Fic
1. Graphic novels
978-1-897299-16-6, $19.95; 1-897299-16-8

Ben Tanaka, a Japanese American in his late twenties, has trouble. His girlfriend, Miko, suspects that Ben's wandering eye is doing so in the direction of white women. This accusation, and its various implications, becomes the subject of heated, spiraling debate, setting in motion a story that pits California against New York (they both live in Berkeley), devotion against desire, and truth against truth. The book includes some strong language, nudity, and sexual situations.

Toriyama, Akira

Dragon Ball Full Color 1; 1. tory and art by Akira Toriyama; [translation, Mari Morimoto; English adaptation, Gerard Jones; lettering, John Clark]. Viz 2014 243 p. Color illustration

Grades: 7 8 9 10 11 12   **741.5; Fic**

1. Adventure graphic novels; 2. Extraterrestrial beings — Graphic novels

1421565927; 9781421565927, $19.99

In this graphic novel, by Akira Toriyama, "Son Goku is the greatest hero on Earth. Five years after defeating the demon king Piccolo, he's grown up and had a family — he's married, and he has a child, Son Gohan. But what is the real reason for Goku's incredible strength? A visitor from outer space arrives bearing terrible news — Goku is an alien, and the visitor, Raditz, is Goku's brother! When Raditz turns out to be a ruthless killer, Goku must fight his incredibly strong brother to save his family and the entire human race." (Publisher's note)

"Toriyama's storytelling is beautifully clear and dynamic, showing why he's revered as one of the world's greatest cartoonists.... [His] work is still as humorous and action-packed as when it was created." Pub Wkly

Dragon Ball Z (vizbig edition vol. 1). story & art by Akira Toriyama; [English adaptation, Gerard Jones; translation, Lillian Olsen]. Viz Media/Shonen Jump 2008 528p. Illustration

Grades: 7 8 9 10 11 12   **741.5; Fic**

1. Adventure graphic novels; 2. Graphic novels; 3. Manga; 4. Martial arts — Graphic novels; 5. Shonen manga

978-1-4215-2064-3, $17.99

The first three volumes of DragonBall Z are now collected in a larger size volume. The Saiyans are an alien race of deadly warriors who wipe out entire planets for their own profit and gain. When the Saiyans set their sights on Earth, it's up to Son Goku to fight off the invaders with his superhuman strength. This series is an almost nonstop series of martial arts action scenes, so there's lots of fighting and yelling, but no harsh language.

Also available in 26 individual volumes; Volume 1 of 9

Torres, Alissa

★ **American** widow. illustrated by Sungyoon Choi. Villard Books 2008 209p. Illustration

Grades: 11 12 Adult   **92; 974.7; 741.5**

1. Autobiographical graphic novels; 2. Educators; 3. Graphic novels; 4. Memoirists; 5. September 11 terrorist attacks, 2001 — Graphic novels; 6. Widows — Graphic novels; 7. Torres, Alissa

978-0-345-50069-4, $22

LC 2008-08396

Alissa Torres' husband Luis had just started his new job in the World Trade Center on September 10, 2001. The next day, he died in the terrorist attacks that destroyed the twin towers. Alissa was more than seven months pregnant. In this book, she recounts the personal struggles she suffered as a pregnant "terror widow," first heaped upon with sympathy, then publicly scorned. She describes the tragedies suffered by all the families who lost loved ones on September 11, 2001 and the frustrations they experienced dealing with bureaucrats as they tried to get even the smallest physical trace of their loved ones.

The author's "tragedy of errors inspires anger on her behalf, although the story is calmly and beautifully told. Choi's simple and attractive line art is set off by turquoise wash, yielding to a full-color photo at the end when Alissa embraces her life anew." Libr J

Torres, J.

Days Like This. Oni Press 2003 un Illustration

Grades: 6 7 8 9 10 11 12 Adult   **741.5; Fic**

1. Graphic novels; 2. Rock music — Graphic novels

1-929998-48-1, $8.95

It's the early 1960s, and rock'n'roll and r&b are ushering in a new golden age of pop music. Tina & the Tiaras, three teenage girl singers, songwriter Karen Prince, and new music mogul Anna Solomon team to create a new girl group sound and move up the charts.

Courtesy of Oni Press

Degrassi the Next Generation Extra Credit Vol. 1: Turning Japanese. Pocket Books 2006 un Illustration

Grades: 8 9 10 11 12

741.5; Fic

1. Graphic novels

978-1-4165-3076-3, $9.95

It's the end of Ellie's senior year, and as though final exams aren't enough to worry about, she's been placed in a compromising position by one of her bosses at a comic book company. Is quitting her only option? J.T. turns to the Internet to help cope with the recent troubles in his life. But now he spends most of his time locked in his room, and he can't seem to move on. Is his new habit just making his problems worse? This original story follows the sixth season of the popular television series.

Degrassi the Next Generation Extra Credit Vol. 2: Suddenly Last Summer. Pocket Books 2007 un Illustration

Grades: 8 9 10 11 12   **741.5; Fic**

1. Graphic novels

978-1-4165-3077-0, $9.95

Emma gets her groove back with the help of group therapy and a family trip to New York City. But as she returns to her old self, her relationship with Peter begins to suffer. Is he helping Emma recover, or holding her back? In the meantime, while coaching at basketball camp, Jimmy finds himself dealing with the fallout of a hazing incident. Was the initiation just a prank, or did it cross the line? When the police get involved, Jimmy is faced with a tough decision. This is another original story set during the summer vacation following the sixth season of the popular television series.

Teen Titans Go! Vol. 1: Truth, Justice, Pizza!. DC Comics 2004 112p. Illustration

Grades: 3 4 5 6 7 8 9   **741.5; Fic**

1. Graphic novels; 2. Humorous graphic novels; 3. Superhero graphic novels; 4. Teen Titans (Fictional characters)

1-4012-0333-7, $6.95

They're too young to drive, but not too young to save the world. The world's hottest heroes: Robin, Beast Boy, Raven, Cyborg, and Starfire, show how it's done Titan-style, as they go up against teen super villains Gizmo, Jinx, and Mammoth. Things get icky when Raven's bad dad, Trigon, comes out from a huge zit on Raven's forehead (ewwww ...).

Teen Titans Go! Vol. 2: Heroes on Patrol!. J. Torres, Adam Beechen, writers; Todd Nauck, Eric Vedder, pencillers; Lary Stucker, M3th, inkers; Phil Good, Heroic Age, colorists; Phil Balsman, Jared K. Fletcher, letterers; Dave Bullock, collection cover artist. DC Comics 2004 112p. Illustration

Grades: 3 4 5 6 7 8 9   **741.5; Fic**

1. Graphic novels; 2. Humorous graphic novels; 3. Superhero graphic novels; 4. Teen Titans (Fictional characters)

1-4012-0334-5, $6.95

In this volume, the Teen Titans encounter the battling brothers, Thunder and Lightning; Starfire has to deal with her naughty sister Blackfire; they encounter Aqualad; and more.

Teen Titans Go! Vol. 3: Bring It On!. DC Comics 2005 104p. Illustration
Grades: 3 4 5 6 7 8 9   **741.5; Fic**
1. Graphic novels; 2. Humorous graphic novels; 3. Superhero graphic novels; 4. Teen Titans (Fictional characters)
1-4012-0511-9, $6.99

Terra rejoins the Titans to fight Slade's robots; the teen superheroes fight Mumbo; Beast Boy tries to help a man stricken with werewolfism; Speedy joins the Titans to fight Plasmus; and they go up against Kwiz Kid, who's mad at Robin because his ex-girlfriend has a crush on Robin.

Teen Titans Go! Vol. 4: Ready for Action!. DC Comics 2005 104p. Illustration
Grades: 3 4 5 6 7 8 9   **741.5; Fic**
1. Graphic novels; 2. Humorous graphic novels; 3. Superhero graphic novels; 4. Teen Titans (Fictional characters)
978-1-4012-0985-8, $6.99

In this volume, the Titans confront a rampaging Wildebeest, teach the hot-tempered Hotshot the value of patience, battle an army of zombies, find themselves trapped in a deadly video game with the Titans East and more.

Teen Titans Go!: Titans Together!. DC Comics 2007 144p. Illustration
Grades: 3 4 5 6 7 8 9   **741.5**
1. Graphic novels; 2. Superhero graphic novels; 3. Teen Titans (Fictional characters)
978-1-4012-1563-7, $12.99

This volume collects eight adventures of the Teen Titans as seen in the animated series, Teen Titans Go! Robin leads the young team that includes Cyborg, Beast Boy, Raven, and Starfire. The stories have lots of action and bad puns as Beast Boy makes a movie, the Titans find themselves in an alien fighting arena, and Robin's future self, Nightwing, comes when time goes a little haywire and an evil Robin shows up.

Tran, G. B.
Vietnamerica: a family's journey. written and illustrated by GB Tran.. Villard Books 2010 279 p. Color illustration
Grades: 11 12 Adult   **741.5**
1. Illustrators; 2. Graphic novels; 3. Vietnamese Americans — Biography; 4. Artists
0345508726; 9780345508720, $30

LC 2011283144

"GB Tran is a young Vietnamese American artist who grew up distant from (and largely indifferent to) his family's history. Born and raised in South Carolina as a son of immigrants, he knew that his parents had fled Vietnam during the fall of Saigon. But even as they struggled to adapt to life in America, they preferred to forget the past — and to focus on their children's future. It was only in his late twenties that GB began to learn their extraordinary story. When his last surviving grandparents die within months of each other, GB visits Vietnam for the first time and begins to learn the tragic history of his family, and of the homeland they left behind." (Publisher's note)

"The comic utilizes a dizzying barrage of effects to depict the characters' confusing experience: different lettering styles, realistic action set against full-page government posters, sound effects swirling from panel to panel, action-packed panoramas breaking apart as South Vietnam collapses." Pub Wkly

Trondheim, Lewis
Poppies of Iraq. cowritten by Brigitte Findakly & Lewis Trondheim; drawn by Lewis Trondheim; colored by Brigitte Findakly; translated by Helge Dascher. Drawn & Quarterly 2017 32 p. Color; Illustration
Grades: 9 10 11 12 Adult   **92; 741.5**

1. Women cartoonists — France — Biography — Comic books, strips, etc.; 2. Women cartoonists — Iraq — Biography — Comic books, strips, etc.; 3. Findakly, Brigitte; 4. Iraq — History — 1958-1979 — Comic books, strips, etc.; 5. Iraq — Social conditions — 20th century — Comic books, strips, etc.; 6. Autobiographical graphic novels; 7. Women — Iraq
1770462937; 9781770462939, $21.95

This book, translated by Helge Dascher, "is Brigitte Findakly's nuanced tender chronicle of her relationship with her homeland Iraq, co-written and drawn by her husband, the acclaimed cartoonist Lewis Trondheim. In spare and elegant detail, they share memories of her middle class childhood touching on cultural practices, the education system, Saddam Hussein's state control, and her family's history as Orthodox Christians in the Arab world." (Publisher's note)

"Each story arc is punctuated by family photos and cultural notes that help bring the family to life and make their experiences personal. Findakly is never naive or sentimental, recounting her life in Iraq with the innocence of a child but the cognizance of an adult." Booklist

Truong, Marcelino
Saigon Calling: London 1963-75. by Marcelino Truong; translated by David Homel. Arsenal Pulp Press 2017 280 p. Illustration
Grades: 9 10 11 12 Adult   **92; 741.5; 942.1**
1. London (England); 2. Immigrants
9781551526898, $26.95; 1551526891

In this book, by Marcelino Truong, translated by David Homel, "young Marcelino and his family move from Saigon to London in order to escape the war following the assassination of South Vietnamese President Diem, for whom Marcelino's diplomat father was a personal interpreter. In London, his father struggles to build a new life for his children and his wife, whose bipolar spells are becoming increasingly violent. But for Marco and his siblings, swinging London is an exciting place to be." (Publisher's note)

Courtesy of Arsenal Pulp Press

"The second volume of the author's critically acclaimed graphic memoir of the Vietnam War era.The son of a French mother and a Vietnamese diplomat father, Truong combines powerful visual imagery with deft narrative as he recounts his teenage years in London and France while developing mixed emotions and allegiances about the war tearing his homeland apart." Kirkus

Translated from the French

Tsukuda, Yuto
Food Wars!; Volume 1: endless wilderness. story by Yuto Tsukuda; art by Shun Saeki; translation, Adrienne Beck; touch-up art & lettering, NRP Studios. Viz 2014 208 p. Illustration
Grades: 7 8 9 10 11 12   **741.5**
1. Shonen manga; 2. Manga
1421572540; 9781421572543, $9.99

"Soma Yukihira's old man runs a small family restaurant in the less savory end of town. Aiming to one day surpass his father's culinary prowess, Soma hones his skills day in and day out until one day, out of the blue, his father decides to enroll Soma in a classy culinary school! Can Soma really cut it in a place that prides itself on a 10% graduation rate?" (Publisher's note)

Volume 1 of an ongoing series

Tsutsumi, Daisuke

Out of picture: art from the outside looking in volume 2. Villard Books 2008 238p. Illustration

Grades: 10 11 12 Adult   **741.5; Fic**

1. Graphic novels; 2. Short stories — Graphic novels
978-0-345-49873-1, $30

Animation production artists who have worked together at Blue Sky Studios have put together another volume of short stories in comics form. In one story, a giant of a man wants only to become a farmer, but the military has hunted him down because he was a biological weapon used by them to win a war; now, he can't be allowed to live. In another story, a young boy takes his first airplane ride and sees a strange being riding on the wing, fly-fishing in the sky. In another story, three friends " a cat, a pigeon, and a grumpy gargoyle " need to find a new home when their antique shop home is destroyed. None of the stories uses graphic violence or much in the way of harsh language, but the moods and intensity of emotion make the book more suitable for older teens and adults.

Tynion, James, IV

★ The **backstagers;** Volume 1: rebels without applause. created by James Tynion IV and Rian Sygh; written by James Tynion IV; illustrated by Rian Sygh; colors by Walter Baiamonte; letters by Jim Campbell; cover by Veronica Fish. Boom! Studios 2017 112 p. Color; Illustration

Grades: 7 8 9 10 11 12   **741.5**

1. LGBT youth — Fiction; 2. Private schools — Fiction
9781681598796; 1608869938; 9781608869930, $14.99

In this book, by James Tynion IV, illustrated by Rian Sygh, "when Jory transfers to an all-boys private high school, he's taken in by the only ones who don't treat him like a new kid, the lowly stage crew known as the Backstagers. Not only does he gain great, lifetime friends, Jory is also introduced to an entire magical world that lives beyond the curtain. With the unpredictable twists and turns of the underground world, the Backstagers venture into the unknown." (Publisher's note)

"Brimming with feeling and featuring a diverse cast (including a trans character, Beckett), it's an effervescently entertaining story of finding community (and maybe love) in unlikely, even impossible places." Pub Wkly

Volume 1 of an ongoing series

The **woods;** Volume 1: The arrow. James Tynion IV; illustrated by Michael Dialynas. Boom! Studios 2014 96 p. Color; Illustration

Grades: 11 12 Adult   **741.5**

1. Science fiction graphic novels; 2. Missing persons — Graphic novels; 3. High school students — Fiction
1608864545; 9781608864546, $9.99

"On October 16, 2013, 437 students, 52 teachers, and 24 additional staff from Bay Point Preparatory High School in suburban Milwaukee, WI vanished without a trace. Countless light years away, far outside the bounds of the charted universe, 513 people find themselves in the middle of an ancient, primordial wilderness. Where are they? The answers will prove stranger than anyone could possibly imagine." (Publisher's note)

"Tynion pulls no punches as he puts these kids through hell, and in the few moments they are allowed to stop to take a breath, they reveal very unique and original personalities, making them less like horror stereotypes and more like real, breathing kids." Booklist

Volume 1 of 9

Uderzo, Albert

Asterix and Obelix All at Sea. Orion/Sterling Publishing 2002 48p. Illustration

Grades: 4 5 6 7 8 9 10 11 12 Adult   **741.5; Fic**

1. Asterix (Fictional character); 2. Graphic novels; 3. Humorous graphic novels

0-75284-778-3, $9.95

LC 2002-282560

In ancient Rome the slaves are revolting...and not only that, they've stolen Julius Caesar's own galley, the finest warship in the Roman navy. Under their heroic leader Spartakis, the former galley slaves make for the little Gaulish village where Julius Caesar's old enemies Asterix and Obelix live — only to find the place in crisis, for Obelix, after drinking the druid Getafix's magic potions on the sly, is first turned to stone and then reverts to childhood. In search of a cure for him Asterix, Getafix and their new friends the galley slaves sail to the wonderful continent of Atlantis, ruled by its high priest Absolutlifabulos — and the ensuing sea battles against the Roman navy are fast and furious ...

Ukazu, Ngozi

★ **Check,** please!: #hockey. Ngozi Ukazu. First Second 2018 288 p. Color; Illustration

Grades: 9 10 11 12   **741.5; Fic**

1. Hockey players — Fiction; 2. College sports — Fiction; 3. LGBT people — Fiction
9781250177957; 9781250177964, $16.99

LC 2017957140

In this book, by Ngozi Ukazu, "Eric Bittle may be a former junior figure skating champion, vlogger extraordinaire, and very talented amateur pâtissier, but being a freshman on the Samwell University hockey team is a whole new challenge. It is nothing like co-ed club hockey back in Georgia!...[This book is] a collection of the first half, freshmen and sophmore year, of the megapopular webcomic series of the same name." (Publisher's note)

"Although this appears to be a simple sports comic at first glance, it is far more complex. Through a combination of hilarious team banter, foodie humor, and a lovable main character, Ukazu has crafted a compelling story about acceptance, identity, and confidence." SLJ

Umezu, Kazuo

Scary Book Volume 1: Reflections. Kazuo Umezu; translation, Kumar Sivasubramanian; lettering and retouch, Kathryn Renta. Dark Horse Manga 2006 231p. Illustration

Grades: 10 11 12 Adult   **741.5; Fic**

1. Graphic novels; 2. Horror graphic novels; 3. Manga; 4. Shojo manga
978-1-59307-476-0, $13.95

This book offers two tales: "Mirror," in which a narcissistic girl's reflection begins to take ruthless command of her life; and "Demon of Vengeance," where a sadistic warlord bent on seeking retribution for his selfish and reckless son's injuries finds the tables of revenge turned against him. Umezu is considered a master of horror manga; these stories were originally published in the 1960s and 1970s in Japan. This book includes some violence and some strong language.

Other titles in this series are: Volume 2: Insects; Volume 3: Faces

Unita, Yumi

★ **Bunny** drop vol. 1. [translation, Kaori Inoue; lettering, Alexis Eckerman].. Yen Press 2010 196p. Illustration

Grades: 8 9 10 11 12 Adult   **741.5; Fic**

1. Graphic novels; 2. Josei manga; 3. Manga; 4. Unmarried fathers — Graphic novels
978-0-7595-3122-2, $12.99

Thirty-year-old bachelor Daikichi is a salaryman, a junior executive, living on his own in Tokyo. When he goes home for his grandfather's funeral, he discovers that his grandfather had a younger lover who left him with a little girl, Rin (which makes her his aunt). The lover is nowhere to be found, and none of Daikichi's relatives will have anything to do with Rin, who won't talk to anyone but sticks close to Daikichi, who closely resembles his grandfather. When no one will step forward to take care of the six-year-old, Daikichi impulsively decides he will. Once he brings Rin home, the reality of his new situation finally dawns on him; Daikichi is now a single father and has to provide care for Rin. There's one scene with Rin and Daikichi together in their furo bath (a very typical Japanese family scene), and a few panels with Rin and Daikichi in their underwear. In one chapter, Daikichi has to deal with Rin's night time bedwetting, and Rin is shown changing her clothes.

"This sweet-natured manga shows the joys, frustrations, and quirks of family life; and while it is aimed at teens, it would also be more than welcome in the hands of adult readers." Booklist

First published 2006 in Japan; Book reads from right to left in the traditional Japanese format; Volume 1 of 9

Urasawa, Naoki

★ **Monster;** Volume 1. story & art by Naoki Urasawa; translation & English adaptation, Camellia Nieh; lettering, Steve Dutro; editor, Mike Montesa. Viz Media 2014 418 p. Illustration; Color

Grades: 10 11 12 Adult   741.5
1. Serial killers — Fiction; 2. Physicians — Fiction
142156906X; 9781421569062, $19.99

"Dr. Tenma is the third son in a family of doctors, who left Japan years ago to work under his idol in a hospital in Dusseldorf, Germany.... He's on the fast track to promotion and power, until he refuses the hospital director's order to leave the victim of a brutal crime on the table and go help the mayor instead. Suddenly he goes from the cusp of a bright future to a grunt. His fiancée leaves him, his promotion is given away, and his patients are removed from his care. But when the men who took everything from Tenma wind up suddenly dead, he's set down a path that will change his life forever." (School Library Journal)

Volume 1 of 9

★ **Naoki** Urasawa's 20th century boys, vol. 1. story & art by Naoki Urasawa; with the cooperation of Takashi Nagasaki; [English adaptation, Akemi Wegmüller]. Viz Media 2009 216p.

Grades: 10 11 12 Adult   741.5; Fic
1. Graphic novels; 2. Manga; 3. Mystery graphic novels; 4. Seinen manga
978-1-59116-922-2, $12.99

In 1997, Kenji has given up his dream of being a rock musician and manages his family's convenience store. When one of his childhood friends, a science teacher, commits suicide, Kenji starts to think back to 1969, when he and his friends created a hideaway, swore to do what they could to save the world, and buried a time capsule with a symbol they designed drawn on top. In 1997, that symbol starts showing up as graffiti in Kenji's neighborhood. And a strange cult led by a man who calls himself "Friend" uses that symbol (an eye with a hand pointing upward). As Kenji reunites with his buddies, they talk about what they did in 1969, and they dig up the time capsule. Does it have anything to do with their friend Donkey's death? The book includes graphic violence and partial nudity.

Volume 1 of 22

★ **Pluto.** by Naoki Urasawa & Osamu Tezuka; co-authored with Takashi Nagasaki; translation, Jared Cook & Frederick L. Schodt. Viz Media 2009 200 p. Illustration

Grades: 9 10 11 12 Adult   741.5; Fic
1. Astro Boy (Fictional character); 2. Graphic novels; 3. Manga; 4. Mystery graphic novels; 5. Robots — Graphic novels; 6. Robots — Fiction; 7. Seinen manga
1421519186; 9781421519180, $12.99

"In a distant future where sentient humanoid robots pass for human, someone or some thing is out to destroy the seven great robots of the world. Europol's top detective Gesicht is assigned to investigate these mysterious robot serial murders — the only catch is that he himself is one of the seven targets." (Publisher's note)

"In a tribute to Osamu Tezuka's (the 'God of Manga') classic Astro Boy, Urasawa takes one of Tezuka's story arcs and reimagines it as a noir detective story. Along the way, he brings in themes of racism, war, and what it means to be human." Booklist

Original Japanese edition, 2004; Volume 1 of 8

Urrea, Luis Alberto

★ **Mr.** Mendoza's paintbrush. artwork by Christopher Cardinale; color masking and compositing, Anthony Cardinale; design, Anne M. Giangiulio. Cinco Puntos Press 2010 un Illustration

Grades: 10 11 12 7 8 9 Adult   741.5; Fic
1. Artists — Graphic novels; 2. Graphic novels; 3. Humorous graphic novels; 4. Mexico — Graphic novels
978-1-933693-23-1, $17.95

LC 2008-11636

Rosario is a small town in the Sinaloa region of Mexico, nestled into a wet, green, mango-sweet subtropical landscape. There, Mr. Mendoza wields his paintbrush to write graffiti with a purpose. When Mr. Mendoza catches the young narrator and his best friend Jaime spying on the girls who are swimming, he strips them, writes graffiti all over their bodies, and chases the naked boys down the street through town. He also appoints himself as the town's conscience and angers the authorities with his graffiti on the town's whorehouse, bridge, and other places. Then, one day, he takes his paint and paintbrush to the center square and paints steps into the sky and walks up until he disappears. Women and girls are shown in their underwear, and the naked boys are shown only from the back. The talk of sex, the way the boys sneak peeks at the girls and one of the town's women, make this book suitable for teens even though the format resembles a picture book.

"Not only does the art perfectly capture the mood of the piece — from the blocky woodcuts to the muted earth tones — but it also reinforces the lucid dreamlike quality of its magical realism, serving as an enticing invitation to further explore the genre." Horn Book Guide

Usdin, Carly

Heavy vinyl. created & written by Carly Usdin; penciled by Nina Vakueva, inked by Irene Flores, colored by Rebeca Nalty, with Kieran Quigley & Walter Baiamonte, lettered by Jim Campbell. Boom! Box 2018 112 p. Color; Illustration

Grades: 10 11 12 Adult   741.5; Fic
1. Hand-to-hand fighting — Fiction; 2. Record stores — Fiction; 3. Teenage girls — Comic books, strips, etc.
1684151414; 9781684151417, $14.99

"Starry-eyed Chris has just started the dream job every outcast kid in town wants: working at Vinyl Mayhem. It's as rad as she imagined.... When Rosie Riot, the staff's favorite singer, mysteriously vanishes the night before her band's show, Chris discovers her co-workers are doing more than just sorting vinyl...Her local indie record store is also a front for a teen girl vigilante fight club!" (Publisher's note)

"The time period is reinforced by constant references to late-1990s bands, pop culture, clothing, and cultural subgroups. The illustrations are colorful and refined, and the diverse cast of characters presents a broad range of identities that are all treated matter-of-factly." Booklist

Van Lente, Fred

Action Philosophers Giant-Size Thing Vol. 2. Evil Twin Comics 2007 94p. Illustration

Grades: 9 10 11 12 Adult   180; 741.5
1. Graphic novels; 2. Philosophers — Graphic novels
978-0-9778329-1-0, $8.95

Karl Marx: The People's Hero! Jacques Derrida: The Deconstructonator! St. Thomas Aquinas: The Scholastic Spastic! Isaac ben-Luria: Rabbi of the Mystic Arts! They're not just great thinkers,...They also make great comics. This book collects issues #4-6 of the Action Philosophers series, detailing the lives and thoughts of the men above, plus Machiavelli, Sartre, Descartes, Kierkegaard, Wittgenstein. There's just a little bit of strong language in this volume.

Action philosophers!. Evil Twin Comics 2006 92p. Illustration
Grades: 10 11 12   **100**
1. Graphic novels; 2. Humorous graphic novels; 3. Philosophy — Graphic novels
0-9778329-0-2; 978-0-9778329-0-3, $6.95

This book combines a summary of the basic tenets of philosophers Plato, Bodhidharma, Nietzsche, Thomas Jefferson, St. Augustine, Ayn Rand, Sigmund Freud, Carl Jung, and Joseph Campbell with irreverent artistic portrayals. Imagine Plato as a masked wrestler (shouting "Plato smash!"), or Bodhidharma as a kung fu master. The section on Freud frankly discusses and portrays some of his more controversial psychosexual ideas.

The **comic** book history of comics. by Fred Van Lente and Ryan Dunlavey. IDW Pub. 2012 224 p. Illustration; Map
Grades: 10 11 12
741.5/9; 741.5
1. Comic books, strips, etc. — History
1613771975; 9781613771976, $21.99

Courtesy of Evil Twin Comics

This book by Fred Van Lente and Ryan Dunlavy "trac[es] comics from the late 19th century through the next 100 years, and cover[s] the creative, business, and social factors that shaped them.... It takes...detours that trace the flow of underground comics, explaining the economics of the direct market and the speculative implosion of the 1990s with a clear sense of how these affect content, and delving into the histories of European, English, and Japanese scenes." (Publishers Weekly)

Van Meter, Jen
Hopeless Savages. Oni Press 2002 128p. Illustration
Grades: 7 8 9 10 11 12 Adult
741.5; Fic
1. Family — Graphic novels; 2. Graphic novels; 3. Humorous graphic novels; 4. Rock music — Graphic novels
1-929998-24-4, $13.95

Courtesy of IDW Publishing

Family ties are the earliest ties that bind, setting the tone for the paths we will take in our future. So what if your father is Dirk Hopeless and your mother Nikki Savage, a superstar couple from the days of punk rock? When you're born a rebel, what can you possibly do to make yourself stand apart? For Rat Hopeless-Savage, the answer is to leave home and become a normal citizen with a nine-to-five job.

Hopeless Savages Vol. 2: Ground Zero. Oni Press 2004 128p. Illustration
Grades: 7 8 9 10 11 12 Adult   **741.5; Fic**
1. Family — Graphic novels; 2. Graphic novels; 3. Humorous graphic novels; 4. Rock music — Graphic novels; 5. Romance graphic novels
1-929998-99-6, $11.95

When you're sixteen, the world is a different place. When you're Zero Hopeless-Savage, the youngest daughter of rock stars Dirk Hopeless and Nikki Savage, the world is practically unrecognizable. Imagine you're in the midst of high school, you have your first band, and WHAMMO! Some boy comes along who doesn't think you're a total freak, and you think he's pretty swell, too. But before you can do anything about it, there's a TV crew outside your house that wants to chronicle the gossip and scandals of your parents' careers, and a massive misunderstanding has gotten you grounded. How's a self-respecting young lady supposed to handle all that?

Courtesy of Oni Press

Hopeless Savages Vol. 3: Too Much Hopeless. Oni Press 2004 un Illustration
Grades: 7 8 9 10 11 12 Adult
741.5; Fic
1. Family — Graphic novels; 2. Graphic novels; 3. Humorous graphic novels; 4. Martial arts — Graphic novels; 5. Romance graphic novels
1-929998-85-6, $11.95

Courtesy of Oni Press

This was supposed to be a leisurely vacation. Arsenal Hopeless-Savage has a rematch with an old high school rival in a kung-fu tournament in Hong Kong. She and her brother Twitch figured they could turn it into a nice jaunt with their boyfriends to meet their aging grandmother, a renowned Chinese fortune teller. Too bad Grandma Shi didn't phone ahead to tell them that it was going to be the trip from Hell. It begins at the airport when a shady character slips something into Arsenal's bag, putting the quartet on the radar of the local bad guys, the British secret service, and the Hong Kong police. It becomes even more complicated when the rest of the Hopeless-Savage clan decides to join the middle children in Asia, getting caught up in the international intrigue themselves. Arsenal is the only person that can get them all out of the jam they're in, and for her it's all too much. Twitch's gay relationship is treated matter-of-factly.

Courtesy of Oni Press

Van Sciver, Noah
The **Hypo:** The Melancholic Young Lincoln. Noah Van Sciver. Fantagraphics 2012 192 p. Illustration
Grades: 11 12 Adult   **92; 973.7092; 741.5**
1. Lincoln, Abraham, 1809-1865; 2. Biographical graphic novels; 3. Depression (Psychology)
1606996193; 9781606996195, $24.99

This graphic novel, by Noah Van Sciver, "is based on [Abraham] Lincoln's battle with depression.... [It] follows the twenty-something Abraham Lincoln as...a rising Whig in the state's legislature as he arrives in Springfield, IL to practice law.... But, as time passes and uncertainty creeps in, young Lincoln is forced to battle a dark cloud of depression brought on by a chain of defeats and failures culminating into a nervous breakdown that threatens his life and sanity." (Publisher's note)

"A thoroughly engaging graphic novel that seamlessly balances investigation and imagination." Pub Wkly

Vance, Steve

Bad girls. DC Comics 2009 128p. Illustration
Grades: 8 9 10 11 12   **741.5; Fic**
1. Graphic novels; 2. Humorous graphic novels; 3. Schools — Graphic novels; 4. Superhero graphic novels
978-1-4012-2359-5, $14.99

Lauren's first day at San Narciso High becomes a disaster when she collides with the school's uber-nerd Ronald and gets on the wrong side of the school's queen bee cheerleaders led by Tiffany. Things only get worse as the days go by, then Lauren unknowingly helps to create even more trouble when Tiffany, Brittany, Ashley, and Destinee all drink from Ronald's thermos that Lauren had been holding. That thermos held Ronald's secret science project, a potion that gives the drinker super powers. Oh, and all that stuff about "with great power comes great responsibility?" Pffft! These girls decide to have their own kind of fun at the expense of everyone else. So how is Lauren supposed to stop them? Ronald decides to give her a dose of his potion, and now suddenly she can read minds. How is that supposed to help? Meanwhile, a couple of sinister government agents come to town, and the science teacher wants to find out just what Ronald has been doing ...

Varon, Sara

Robot dreams. First Second 2007 205p. Illustration
Grades: 3 4 5 6 7 8 9 10 11 12 Adult   **741; 741.5; Fic**
1. Dogs — Graphic novels; 2. Graphic novels; 3. Robots — Graphic novels
978-1-59643-108-9 (pa), $16.95; 1-59643-108-3 (pa)
LC 2006-52640

The friendship between a dog and a robot is portrayed in this wordless graphic novel. (Bull Cent Child Books)

"Varon's drawing style is uncomplicated, and her colors are clean and refreshing. Although her story seems equally simple, it is invested with true emotion." Booklist

A Junior Library Guild book

Sweaterweather. Alternative Comics 2006 96p. Illustration
Grades: 3 4 5 6 7 8 9   **741.5; Fic**
1. Animals — Graphic novels; 2. Friendship — Graphic novels; 3. Graphic novels; 4. Stories without words — Graphic novels
1-891867-93-8, $14.95

A turtle, a rabbit, and other creatures venture out on a wordless snowy journey full of friendship and sweetness. Varon includes interactive bits to the book, such as paper dolls, postcards, and stamps.

First published 2003

Vaughan, Brian K.

Batman: false faces. DC Comics 2008 160p. Illustration
Grades: 10 11 12 Adult
741.5; Fic
1. Batman (Fictional character); 2. Graphic novels; 3. Superhero graphic novels; 4. Wonder Woman (Fictional character)
978-1-4012-1640-5, $19.99

Throughout his crimefighting career, the Dark Knight has managed to balance his double life as Batman and billionaire Bruce Wayne. But he has taken on other identities as well, including that of criminal Matches Malone. What happens when leading

Courtesy of Alternative Comics

multiple lives becomes too much to handle? As Batman faces old enemies the Ventriloquist and the Mad Hatter, his greatest adversary may be his own secret lives. And Wonder Woman faces a crisis of her own, when Clayface steals part of the source of her power, and she must enlist the help of Donna Troy. The book includes some violence.

Doctor Strange: The Oath. Marvel Enterprises 2007 un Illustration
Grades: 9 10 11 12 Adult   **741.5; Fic**
1. Doctor Strange (Fictional character); 2. Graphic novels; 3. Superhero graphic novels
0-7851-2211-7, $13.99

Doctor Stephen Strange embarks on the most important paranormal investigation of his career, as he sets out to solve an attempted murder — his own. And with his most trusted friend, Wong, also at death's door, Strange turns to an unexpected corner of the Marvel Universe to recruit a new ally. The Night Nurse runs a clandestine clinic for superheroes, but she insists on accompanying Doctor Strange on his quest to find help for Wong.

The **Escapists**. Dark Horse Books 2009 176p. Illustration
Grades: 10 11 12 Adult   **741.5; Fic**
1. Adventure graphic novels; 2. Comic books, strips, etc. — Graphic novels; 3. Graphic novels
978-1-59582-361-8, $14.95

Inspired by Michael Chabon's Pulitzer Prizewinning novel, The Amazing Adventures of Kavalier and Clay, this story shows what it's like to start with nothing in Cleveland, Ohio, and end up with a comic so hot a major corporation wants to steal it from you. Maxwell Roth spends his inheritance to buy the rights to The Escapist, the comic book character created by Kavalier and Clay decades ago, and he and his high school friend Case Weaver set out to make new comics of The Escapist. Artist Denny Jones joins them, and together the three create a new comic book series that makes a smash debut. Then, Omnigrip Corporation, which long ago sold the rights away, wants it back. When Roth says no, the corporation uses every dirty trick to force him to sell the rights back. The story of Roth, Weaver, and Jones is intermixed with adventures of the Escapist from the old comics. Artists Steve Rolston and Philip Bond illustrate the present-day story of the three independent comics creators, while Jason Shawn Alexander and Eduardo Barreto illustrate the classic Escapist stories. The book includes some violence and some harsh language.

Ex Machina Vol. 1: The First Hundred Days. DC Comics/Wildstorm 2005 un Illustration
Grades: 10 11 12 Adult   **741.5; Fic**
1. Graphic novels; 2. Politics — Graphic novels; 3. Superhero graphic novels
978-1-4012-0612-3, $9.99

This book tells the story of civil engineer Mitchell Hundred, who becomes America's first living, breathing super-hero after a strange accident gives him amazing powers. Eventually Mitchell tires of risking his life merely to maintain the status quo, retires from masked crime fighting, and runs for mayor of New York City, winning by a landslide. But Mayor Hundred has to worry about more than just budget problems and an antagonistic governor, especially when a mysterious hooded figure begins assassinating plow drivers during the worst snowstorm in the city's history. Strong language and some violence figures into this political superhero story."

Volume 1 of 10

★ **Paper** Girls; Volume 1. writer, Brian K. Vaughan; artist, Cliff Chiang; colors, Matt Wilson; letters, Jared K. Fletcher. Image Comics 2016 144 p. Color; Illustration
Grades: 11 12 Adult   **741.5; Fic**
1. Halloween — Fiction; 2. Girls — Fiction; 3. Science fiction graphic novels

1632156741; 9781632156747, $9.99

Eisner Award: Best New Series (2016)

"In the early hours after Halloween of 1988, four 12-year-old newspaper delivery girls uncover the most important story of all time. Suburban drama and otherworldly mysteries collide in this smash-hit series about nostalgia, first jobs, and the last days of childhood." (Publisher's note)

"Vaughan's spiky writing and Chiang's vivid, dramatically skewed art make for a potent mix, particularly in the darkly comic dream sequences that punctuate the action." Pub Wkly

Collects issues #1-5 of Paper Girls; Volume 1 of an ongoing series

★ **Pride** of Baghdad. DC Comics/Vertigo 2006 136p. Illustration

Grades: 10 11 12   **741.5; Fic**

1. Animals — Graphic novels; 2. Graphic novels; 3. War — Graphic novels; 4. Iraq — Graphic novels

1-4012-0314-0, $19.99

Vaughan based his original graphic novel on an incident that occurred in 2003, when the Allied forces began bombing Baghdad. The bombs destroy the wall of the Baghdad Zoo, and a small group of lions escapes into the city, only to encounter death and destruction they can't comprehend. All they want is freedom to live and hunt their prey, but they become the most innocent victims of war. Graphic scenes of violence as bombs kill animals could provoke intense emotional reactions.

★ **Runaways** Vol. 1: Pride & Joy. Marvel Entertainment 2004 un Illustration

Grades: 7 8 9 10 11 12   **741.5; Fic**

1. Graphic novels; 2. Runaways (Fictional characters); 3. Science fiction graphic novels; 4. Superhero graphic novels

0-7851-1379-7, $7.99

All young people believe their parents are evil...but what if they really are? Meet Alex, Karolina, Gert, Chase, Molly and Nico — whose lives are about to take an unexpected turn. When these six young friends discover their parents are all secretly super-powered villains, the shocked teens find strength in one another. Together, they run away from home and straight into the adventure of their lives — vowing to turn the tables on their evil legacy. This is the first volume of an ongoing series.

Originally published as Runaways issues #1-6.; Other Runaways volumes are: 2: Teenage Wasteland; 3: The Good Die Young; 4: True Believers; 5: Escape to New York; 6: Parental Guidance; 7: Live Fast; 8: Dead End Kids; 9: Dead Wrong; 10: Rock Zombies; 11: Homeschooling

Runaways Vol. 2: Teenage Wasteland. Marvel Entertainment 2004 un Illustration

Grades: 8 9 10 11 12   **741.5; Fic**

1. Adventure graphic novels; 2. Graphic novels; 3. Runaways (Fictional characters); 4. Superhero graphic novels

0-7851-1415-7, $7.99

Still on the run from their super-villain parents, the motley crew of super-powered kids finds a kindred spirit in a daring young stranger and welcomes him into their fold. But will this dashing young man help the teens defeat their villainous parents, or tear them apart? Then Marvel's original teen runaway crime fighters, Cloak and Dagger, are sent to catch the runaways.

Runaways Vol. 6: Parental Guidance. Marvel Entertainment 2006 un Illustration

Grades: 8 9 10 11 12   **741.5; Fic**

1. Adventure graphic novels; 2. Graphic novels; 3. Runaways (Fictional characters); 4. Superhero graphic novels

0-7851-1952-3, $7.99

The Pride is back as an all-new group, and they have it in for the Runaways. And when Molly is separated from her teammates, she must survive a night alone on the mean streets of Los Angeles. The eleven-year-old mutant girl soon hooks up with a new group of runaways, but is their mysterious leader a hero or a villain? In this volume, a member of the team dies.

Runaways Vol. 7: Live Fast. Marvel Entertainment 2007 un Illustration

Grades: 8 9 10 11 12   **741.5; Fic**

1. Adventure graphic novels; 2. Graphic novels; 3. Runaways (Fictional characters); 4. Superhero graphic novels

978-0-7851-2267-8, $7.99

The Runaways say good-bye to the past, and make hard decisions about their future. Plus: Still reeling from the events of Young Avengers/Runaways (part of Marvel's Civil War), the teenage heroes must now confront a horrific enemy who threatens to tear the team apart.

Y: The Last Man Vol. 1: Unmanned. Brian K. Vaughan, writer; Pia Guerra, penciller; José Marzán, Jr., inker; Pamela Rambo, colorist; Clem Robins, letterer. DC Comics/Vertigo 2003 128p. Illustration

Grades: 10 11 12 Adult   **741.5; Fic**

1. Graphic novels; 2. Science fiction graphic novels

978-1-56389-980-5, $12.99

Escape artist Yorick Brown and his male pet monkey are the only surviving males left on Earth after a plague instantaneously kills all the other males on the planet. As women take over...everything...latter-day Amazons declare all men must die, Yorick's congresswoman mother arranges protection for him, and mysterious Israeli soldiers seem highly amused. The story includes strong language, nudity, and violence.

Volume 1 of 10

Vaughn, Sarah

Sleepless; Volume 1. Sarah Vaughn, writer; Leila del Duca, artist; Alissa Sallah, editor & colors; Deron Bennett, letters. Image Comics 2018 168 p. Color; Illustration

Grades: 10 11 12 Adult   **741.5; Fic**

1. Fantasy fiction — Graphic novels; 2. Romance fiction — Graphic novels

1534306846; 9781534306844, $16.99

"Lady 'Poppy' Pyppenia is guarded by the Sleepless Knight Cyrenic but becomes endangered when an assassin threatens her life in the new king's reign. As Poppy and Cyrenic try to discover who wants her dead, they must navigate the dangerous waters of life at court and of their growing feelings for one another." (Publisher's note)

Volume 1 of an ongoing series

Venditti, Robert

Blue Bloods: the graphic novel. by Melissa de la Cruz; adapted by Robert Venditti; art by Alina Urusov; illustrations by Disney Enterprises, Inc.. Hyperion 2013 112 p. Color illustration

Grades: 8 9 10 11 12   **741.5/973; Fic**

1. Graphic novels; 2. Secrets — Fiction; 3. Vampires — Fiction; 4. Wealth — Fiction; 5. New York (N.Y.) — Fiction; 6. Teenagers — Graphic novels; 7. Supernatural graphic novels

9781423134466, $19.99; 9781423134473, $11.99; 142313446X

LC 2011053237

In this graphic novel, written by Melissa de la Cruz, adapted by Robert Venditti, and illustrated by Alina Urusov, the focus is on a group of New York teenagers. "Schuyler Van Alen is a loner, and happy that way. But when she turns fifteen, her life dramatically changes. A mosaic of blue veins appears on her arms, and she begins to have memories of another time and place. When a classmate is found dead at a night club, the mystery deepens." (Publisher's note)

The **homeland** directive. created & written by Robert Venditti; illustrated & colored by Mike Huddleston. Top Shelf Productions 2011 148p. Color illustration
Grades: 11 12 Adult   **741.5**
1. Political corruption — Fiction; 2. Suspense fiction; 3. Mystery fiction; 4. Bioterrorism — Fiction
9.7816E+12

This book tells the story of Dr. Laura Regan, head of the U.S. National Center for Infectious Diseases. "When her research partner is murdered and Laura is blamed for the crime, she finds herself at the heart of a vast and deadly conspiracy." (Publisher's note). "A cabinet minister decides to persuade the public that more trackable behavior is in the service of antiterrorist surveillance. But since his incentive involves virally induced 'justified' death for thousands along the way, Regan throws in with the good feds to stop a developing plague and expose the minister. Not that she has much choice: the bad fed operatives are out to kill her since she created the vaccine that could stop their plot cold." (Libr J)

The **Surrogates**. Top Shelf Productions 2006 208p. Illustration
Grades: 10 11 12 Adult
741.5; Fic
1. Graphic novels; 2. Mystery graphic novels; 3. Science fiction graphic novels
1-891830-87-2, $19.95

Courtesy of IDW Publishing

The year is 2054, and life has been reduced to a data feed. The fusing of virtual reality and cybernetics has ushered in the era of the surrogate, a new technology that lets users interact with the world without ever leaving their homes. It's a perfect world, and it's up to Detectives Harvey Greer and Pete Ford of the Metro Police Department to keep it that way. But to do so they'll need to stop a techno-terrorist bent on returning society to a time when people lived their lives instead of merely experiencing them. There's some violence in the story.

Verheiden, Mark
Aliens Omnibus Volume 1. Dark Horse Comics 2007 384p. Illustration
Grades: 10 11 12 Adult
741.5; Fic
1. Adventure graphic novels; 2. Graphic novels; 3. Science fiction graphic novels
978-1-59307-727-3, $24.95

Courtesy of IDW Publishing

The first three Dark Horse Aliens stories based on the movies are collected in this volume: Outbreak, Nightmare Asylum, and Female War. Outbreak starts thirteen years after the events of the movie Aliens; Billie is in a mental institution suffering from nightmares about what happened at the colony outpost of Rim, and Wilks is in prison. They're both offered a chance to return to Rim. In Female War, Ripley must go with another team of Marines to another planet for another "bug hunt." The stories use strong language and show violence as the humans fight the Aliens.

Superman: Sacrifice: Countdown to Infinite Crisis. Greg Rucka, Mark Verheiden, Gail Simone, writers; Ed Benes ... [et al.], pencillers; Alex Lei ... [et al.], inkers; Rod Reis ... [et al.], colorists; Todd Klein ... [et al.], letterers. DC Comics 2005 un Illustration
Grades: 10 11 12 Adult   **741.5; Fic**
1. Graphic novels; 2. Superhero graphic novels; 3. Superman (Fictional character); 4. Wonder Woman (Fictional character)
1-4012-0919-X, $14.99

The pivotal story that forever alters the relationship between Superman and Wonder Woman is collected here for the first time. Max Lord has taken over Superman's mind and has him in his total thrall. With his peers and loved ones threatened, Superman is helpless. But not Wonder Woman, who must battle past the Man of Steel and decisively end the threat. Her actions, and the repercussions, are explored in this story that leads into Infinite Crisis. Some of the fighting in this book is brutal.

Superman: The Journey. DC Comics 2006 144p. Illustration
Grades: 9 10 11 12 Adult   **741.5; Fic**
1. Graphic novels; 2. Superhero graphic novels; 3. Superman (Fictional character); 4. Flash (Fictional character)
1-4012-0918-1, $14.99

Even the Man of Steel needs to get away from it all, and when he tries to relocate his Fortress of Solitude to South America, a chain of events begins that will test his bravery more than ever. After his first contact with an OMAC, a cybernetic being set to destroy all super-heroes, Superman then must contend with the arrival in Metropolis of Bizarro, as well as Zoom, the Reverse-Flash. Then Blackrock returns with more power than ever; and Lex Luthor seeks deadly vengeance, again.

Vernon, Ursula
★ **Digger:** the complete Omnibus edition. by Ursula Vernon. Sofawolf Press, Inc. 2013 850 p.
Grades: 9 10 11 12 Adult   **741.5; Fic**
1. Adventure graphic novels; 2. Wombats — Graphic novels
1936689324; 9781936689323, $29.44
Hugo Award: Best Graphic Story (2012)

This graphic novel, by Ursula Vernon, is "about a particularly no-nonsense wombat who finds herself stuck on the wrong end of a one-way tunnel in a strange land where nonsense seems to be the specialty. Now, with the help of a talking statue of a god, an outcast hyena, a shadow-being of indeterminate origin, and an oracular slug she seeks to find out where she is and how to go about getting back to her Warren." (Publisher's note)

Vess, Charles
The **Book** of Ballads. Tor 2004 192p. Illustration
Grades: 11 12 Adult   **741.5; 808.81**
1. Ballads — Graphic novels; 2. Graphic novels
0-765-31214-X, $24.95

"Vess shows off his ability to use a wide variety of styles and formats.... The ballad from which each story is taken is written in its traditional form at the end of each tale." (VOYA)

Artist Vess works with authors such as Charles de Lint, Neil Gaiman, Jane Yolen, Jeff Smith, and others who adapt ballads from the English, Scottish, and Irish traditions. Moods range from comedic hilarity (such as in "Galtee Farmer") to the somber lover's test ("Sovay"). Many of the stories include nudity and some sexual content.

Viney, Brigit
Great expectations: the graphic novel. Lucent Books 2010 160p. Illustration (Classic graphic novels)
Grades: 7 8 9 10 11 12   **741.5; Fic**
1. Authors; 2. Graphic novels; 3. Novelists; 4. Social classes — Graphic novels; 5. Dickens, Charles, 1812-1870; 6. Dickens, Charles, 1812-1870 — Adaptations/Graphic novels; 7. Great Britain — History — 19th century — Graphic novels
978-1-4205-0372-2, $32.45

LC 2010-924002

In 1812, young orphaned Pip encounters an escaped convict in the graveyard near his home; that encounter changes his life. He had helped the man by stealing food and a file from his older sister's home. When the convict is recaptured, he keeps Pip's secret and claims he was the thief. As time goes by, Pip becomes his brother-inlaw's apprentice as a blacksmith, but then the eccentric Miss Havisham wants Pip to attend to her. Miss Havisham's adopted niece, Estella, calls Pip coarse and rough, which makes him determined to improve himself and become a gentleman. His wish comes true when a mysterious benefactor has Miss Havisham's solicitor, Mr. Jaggers, set Pip up in London, with expenses paid. Pip has only to keep using his nickname, to learn how to be a gentleman, and have "great expectations." Getting his wish doesn't make him happy, however, for he wants Estella, whom he adores, to love him; Miss Havisham has raised Estella to break men's hearts as her heart was once broken by a man. Pip must also learn what is most important to him improving his social standing or standing loyal to family and friends. This graphic novel adaptation includes every chapter in Dickens' original novel; this library bound edition uses a more colloquial American adaptation, which was done by arrangement with Classical Comics, the original publisher. This adaptation is meant for reluctant and struggling readers. The artist, John Stokes, is not credited anywhere in this edition. The back matter includes a biography of Dickens, a glossary, illustrated character summaries, notes on the historical context of the novel, and a brief discussion of the different ending Dickens originally wrote.

Vollmar, Rob

The **castaways**. illustrated by Pablo G. Callejo. NBM/ComicsLit 2007 64p. Illustration

Grades: 6 7 8 9 10 11 12   **Fic; 741.5; 741**

  1. Graphic novels; 2. United States — History — 1919-1933 — Graphic novels

978-1-56163-492-7, $17.95

"Afraid that he's just a burden on his family, 13-year-old Tucker Freeman lets himself be driven away from home and jumps on a freight train heading west. His inexperience makes him vulnerable to all the angry, desperate people looking for any way they can survive during America's economic collapse, but fortunately he's taken under the wing of Elijah Hopkins, an elderly colored man who introduces him to the cooperative hobo subculture.... Vollmer's script, based on family reminiscences, rings true; his dialogue has the vocabulary and the rhythms of real people talking.... Callejo's art creates a solid setting in which Tucker's experience can reveal squalor or grace." Publ Wkly

An expanded and newly illustrated edition of the title first published 2002 by Absence of Ink Comic Press

Voloj, Julian

Ghetto Brother: Warrior to Peacemaker. Julian Voloj; illustrated by Claudia Ahlering. NBM Publishing 2015 128 p. Illustration

Grades: 11 12 Adult   **741.5; 92**

  1. Melendez, Benjy; 2. Peace movements; 3. Gangs — Graphic novels; 4. Puerto Ricans — New York (N.Y.)

1561639486; 9781561639489, $12.99

This graphic novel by Julian Voloj, illustrated by Claudia Ahlering, "tells the true story of Benjy Melendez, a Bronx legend, son of Puerto-Rican immigrants, who founded, at the end of the 1960s, the notorious Ghetto Brothers gang. From the seemingly bombed-out ravages of his neighborhood, wracked by drugs, poverty, and violence, he managed to extract an incredibly positive energy from this riot ridden era: his multiracial gang promoted peace rather than violence." (Publisher's note)

"Using Melendez as narrator-protagonist, Voloj places the seminal events of November and December 1971 in the contexts of post-WWII Puerto Rican immigration and difficult assimilation to New York, and of Melendez's personal development as he learned of and adopted his Jewish heritage. Ahlering bases her artwork partly on news and documentary photography, although she doesn't incorporate or copy photos but draws on them for detail, composition, and tonal variety." Booklist

Wagahara, Satoshi

The **devil** is a part-timer!; Volume 1. original story, Satoshi Wagahara; art, Akio Hiiragi; translation, Kevin Gifford; lettering, Lys Blakeslee. Yen Press 2015 240 p. Illustration

Grades: 7 8 9 10

741.5; Fic

  1. Fantasy; 2. Manga; 3. Shonen manga; 4. Fast food restaurants — Fiction; 5. Devil — Fiction; 6. Demonology — Fiction

0316383139; 9780316383134, $13

LC 2015028390

Courtesy of NBM Publishing

"It's tough being evil when you have to pay the rent! This comical tale of a demon-lord-turned-fry-slinger follows the daily travails of (former) Devil King Sadao Maou and his general Shiro Ashiya as they navigate the complexities of life in modern-day Tokyo. Having suffered utter defeat at the hands of a plucky hero, they've been banished to earth and stripped of magical power. And if that wasn't enough, that pesky hero is still hell bent on finishing the job." (Publisher's note)

Volume 1 of an ongoing series

Wagner, John

A **History** of Violence. DC Comics/Vertigo 2004 286p. Illustration

Grades: 11 12 Adult   **741.5; Fic**

  1. Graphic novels; 2. Mystery graphic novels; 3. Revenge — Graphic novels

978-1-56389-367-4, $9.99

It was just another quiet day at McKenna's Diner — until a couple of wanted killers walked in looking for trouble. Instead, they got bullets, and Tom McKenna got to be an instant media celebrity. That got him a lot of attention from some people he thought he'd escaped long ago. The kind of people who never forget a face — even after twenty years.... Now Tom must confront a group of cold-blooded mobsters intent on settling the score. As much as he tries to deny it, he's a man with a history of violence — and with the lives of his family hanging in the balance, he'll do anything to make sure his secret past stays buried...forever. This story has lots of graphic violence and strong language. This original graphic novel was originally published in 1997.

Wagner, Matt

Batman and the Monster Men: Dark Moon Rising. DC Comics 2006 144p. Illustration

Grades: 10 11 12 Adult   **741.5; Fic**

  1. Batman (Fictional character); 2. Graphic novels; 3. Mystery graphic novels; 4. Superhero graphic novels

978-1-4012-1091-5, $14.99

It has been one year since the mysterious Batman first appeared to protect the people of Gotham. In that time, he has waged war on the common criminals and members of organized crime who have plagued his city. But the brutal massacre of some of the city's most notorious gangsters reveals that a far more dangerous threat is emerging, one for which the young Bruce Wayne is woefully unprepared: genetically engineered, horribly mutated men who have developed a taste for human flesh. They are the stuff of nightmare. And as they wreak havoc on Gotham's criminal community, Batman soon discovers that even the woman he loves may be threatened. Can the Dark Knight stop the carnage, or will he become the next victim of the Monster Men? The book includes violence, some graphic.

Batman/Superman/Wonder Woman: Trinity. DC Comics 2003 208p. Illustration
Grades: 9 10 11 12 Adult   **741.5; Fic**
 1. Batman (Fictional character); 2. Graphic novels; 3. Superhero graphic novels; 4. Superman (Fictional character); 5. Wonder Woman (Fictional character)
1-4012-0187-3, $17.99
 When Batman's greatest nemesis, Ra's al Ghul, recruits Bizarro and an Amazon warrior to aid him in his plan to create global chaos, the Dark Knight Detective suddenly finds himself working with the Man of Steel and the Amazon Princess, Wonder Woman. Looking to thwart the madman's plot to simultaneously destroy all satellite communications as well as all of the world's oil reserves, Earth's greatest heroes reluctantly band together. But if Batman, Superman and Wonder Woman are to have any hope of stopping Ra's nuclear missile assault, they will first need to overcome their own biases and reconcile their differing philosophies. The book includes some violence.

Madame Xanadu: disenchanted. writer, Matt Wagner; penciller, Amy Reeder Hadley; inkers, Amy Reeder Hadley (issues 1-2), Richard Friend (issues 3-10); colorist, Guy Major; letterer, Jared K. Fletcher; introduction, James Robinson. DC Comics/Vertigo 2009 un Illustration
Grades: 10 11 12 Adult   **741.5; Fic**
 1. Fantasy graphic novels; 2. Graphic novels; 3. Magic — Graphic novels
978-1-4012-2291-8, $12.99
 In the days of King Arthur and Camelot, Nimue used woodland magic. Despite her power, the warnings of a stranger with glowing eyes comes too late for her to save the land against the machinations of Merlin and her own sister, Morgana. Using her herb lore to maintain her youth, Nimue next shows up in the court of Kublai Khan, where she is known as the Western Seer. Again, the Phantom Stranger shows up, this time with the party of Marco Polo, who become targets of a plot to discredit the Westerners. Nimue helps, only to learn that it wasn't enough, and the Stranger abandons her in the middle of the Gobi Desert. Then she appears in France, known there as Madame Xanadu, a favorite of Queen Marie Antoinette. This time, Nimue reads the portents for herself and knows that the Revolution will topple the King; the Phantom Stranger appears again, but because she can't trust him, she ends up imprisoned, betrayed by the former Queen whom she believed to be a friend, and Nimue has to trick Death herself. In London of the 1880s, Madame Xanadu tries to help the prostitutes of Whitechapel, but the Phantom Stranger says the murders committed by Jack the Ripper serve a larger purpose and he thwarts her again. In New York City of the 1930s, Nimue has found another magician, John Zatara and they are lovers, but the Phantom Stranger comes again and this time Nimue decides to trap him. What consequences will her actions have upon the people around her, including a heroic policeman named James Corrigan? The book includes some gory violence, some harsh language, some sexual suggestiveness and one not-very-graphic rape scene. This series, in its pamphlet comic issue form, was nominated for four Eisner Awards in 2009: Best Writer, Best Cover Artist, Best New Series, and Best Penciler Inker Team.
 Volume 1 of 4

Wagner, Richard
 Richard Wagner's The Ring of the Nibelung Volume One. Dark Horse Comics 2002 un Illustration
Grades: 9 10 11 12 Adult   **741.5; Fic**
 1. Fantasy graphic novels; 2. Graphic novels; 3. Norse mythology — Graphic novels; 4. Opera — Graphic novels

1-56971-666-8, $21.95
2001 Eisner Award for Best Limited Series; 2001 Eisner Award to P. Craig Russell for Best Penciller/Inker of Penciller/Inker Team.
 The Rhinegold and The Valkyrie comprise the first volume of Russell's adaptation of the Ring cycle by German composer Richard Wagner. Woton has exhausted himself and his godly resources to have a mighty fortress built with the labor of the giants, Fasolt and Fafnir. But in his bargaining with them, he has promised the fair Freia, keeper of the golden apple tree whose fruit gives power and immortality to the gods. The giants come to collect their pay, and only Logé, the trickster god, can find something to offer the giants in exchange: the Rhinegold. The only problem is, Woton doesn't have the Rhinegold yet.

 Richard Wagner's The Ring of the Nibelung Volume Two. Dark Horse Comics 2002 un Illustration
Grades: 9 10 11 12 Adult   **741.5; Fic**
 1. Fantasy graphic novels; 2. Graphic novels; 3. Norse mythology — Graphic novels; 4. Opera — Graphic novels
1-56971-734-6, $21.95
2001 Eisner Award for Best Limited Series; 2001 Eisner Award to P. Craig Russell for Best Penciller/Inker of Penciller/Inker Team.
 This volume adapts Wagner's Siegfried and Gotterdammerung: The Twilight of the Gods. Siegfried is separated from his love, the Valkyrie Brunhilde, and even the All-Father himself cannot make things right. In the conclusion, all of creation hangs in the balance because of gods meddling in the affairs of man — all over the gold of the Rhinemaids.

Waid, Mark
 All-new all-different Avengers; Volume 1: The Magnificent Seven. by Mark Waid; illustrated by Adam Kubert and Mahmud Asrar; color by Sonia Oback. Marvel Enterprises 2016 168 p. Color; Illustration
Grades: 8 9 10 11 12 Adult   **741.5; Fic**
 1. Avengers (Fictional characters)
0785199675; 9780785199670, $19.99
 In this comic book, by Mark Waid, illustrated by Adam Kubert and Mahmud Asrar, "the Avengers are dead — long live the Avengers! Earth's Mightiest Heroes — Captain America, Thor, Vision and Iron Man — are living separate lives, not tied to any team but when a threat from beyond the stars targets our world, fate draws them together once more, alongside Nova, Ms. Marvel, and Miles Morales, a.k.a. Spider-Man!" (Publisher's note)
 Contains material originally published in magazine form as All-New, All-Different Avengers #1-6, Avengers #0 and Free Comic Book Day 2015 (Avengers) #1

 Amazing Spider-Man: family business. by Mark Waid and James Robinson; illustrated by Gabriele Dell'Otto and Werther Dell'Edera. Marvel Enterprises 2014 112 p. Color; Illustration
Grades: 9 10 11 12 Adult   **741.5**
 1. Spider-Man (Fictional character)
0785184406; 9780785184409, $24.99
 In this graphic novel, by Mark Waid and James Robinson, "someone has Spider-Man in their crosshairs and the only person in the Marvel Universe who can save him is...Peter Parker's sister?! As the web-slinger meets family he never knew, will she end up becoming his greatest ally...or the one who damns him? And what does the KINGPIN have to do with it?" (Publisher's note)
 "Waid's story is perfectly blended, with all the one-liners and gags that fans have come to expect as well as a level of mystery and intrigue that's a welcome addition. And with four villains vying for the death of Spider-Man (one literally dug up from the past), this original graphic novel is certainly not short on action." Booklist
 Marvel OGN — Cover page 1.

★ **Archie**; Volume 1: The New Riverdale. story by Mark Waid; art by Fiona Staples (issues 1-3), Annie Wu (issue 4), Veronica Fish (issues 5-6); coloring by Andre Szymanowicz with Jen Vaughn; lettering by Jack Morelli. Archie Comics 2016 176 p. Color; Illustration

Grades: 7 8 9 10 11 12 Adult   **741.5; Fic**

1. Teenagers — Graphic novels; 2. Lodge, Veronica (Fictional character); 3. Andrews, Archie (Fictional character); 4. Cooper, Betty (Fictional character)

1627388672; 9781627388672, $19.99

In this first volume of the Archie comic book series by Mark Waid, illustrated by Fiona Staples, Archie Andrews and the Riverdale teens are reimagined "with a fresh, 21st-century spin in time for the franchise's 75th anniversary.... Blonde Betty is a baseball-slugging, down-to-earth car mechanic; Archie is a hapless but cool, guitar-playing teen with a streak of bad luck; and new girl Veronica Lodge is a sleek reality TV alum." (School Library Journal)

"It would seem risky to mess with the tried-and-true Archie formula, but this heartfelt collection is less a tearing-down of the old order than an exuberant exploration of its possibilities. Staples and Waid keep the characters' foundations in place—Archie's still a lovable goof who can't decide between girl-next-door Betty and vampish Veronica — while building a wonderfully new Riverdale for them to explore." Pub Wkly

Collects Archie #1-6; Volume 1 of an ongoing series

★ **Daredevil**. writer, Mark Waid; artists, Paolo Rivera, Marcos Martin. Marvel 2013 Color illustration (Daredevil (2011-2014))

Grades: 10 11 12 Adult   **741.5**

1. Superhero comic books, strips, etc.; 2. Spider-Man (Fictional character); 3. Daredevil (Fictional character)

0785168060; 9780785168065, $34.99

"Matt Murdock is back in New York and hoping to resuscitate his law practice, but not everyone is happy to see him. And Daredevil hits the streets as Klaw, master of sound, makes his deadly return! Then, a blind client holds the key to a global conspiracy perpetrated by some familiar foes. Can Daredevil protect him long enough to bring down an international criminal organization? And when a piece of cutting-edge technology goes missing, Daredevil and Punisher team up to track it down and clear the Black Cat of the crime. But is Black Cat really innocent?! And after someone exhumes Battlin' Jack Murdock's grave, DD heads underground to find the villain responsible." (Publisher's note)

Collects Daredevil (2011) 1-10, 10.1; Amazing Spider -Man (1963) 677; Volume 1 of 2 (hardcover collection)

Daredevil; Volume 1: Devil at bay. writer, Mark Waid; artists, Chris Samnee and Peter Krause. Marvel Enterprises 2014 un Color; Illustration (Daredevil (2014-2015))

Grades: 9 10 11 12 Adult   **741.5; Fic**

1. Superhero graphic novels; 2. Daredevil (Fictional character)

0785154116; 9780785154112, $17.99

Other titles in this series are: Volume 2, West-case scenario; Volume 3, The Daredevil you know; Volume 4, The autobiography of Matt Murdock

"Daredevil has headed west, and now protects [San Francisco's] streets from evil — both as a costumed hero and as blind lawyer Matt Murdock! But big changes are in store for Matt, as old haunts and familiar faces rise to give the devil his due. The Owl is back, and he isn't working alone...but old enemies are small potatoes compared to Matt 's new "friend": the would-be hero known as the Shroud!" (Publisher's note)

Contains material originally published in single magazine form as Daredevil #1-5 and #0.1

Legion of Super-Heroes Vol. 1: Teenage Revolution. DC Comics 2005 un Illustration

Grades: 8 9 10 11 12 Adult   **741.5; Fic**

1. Graphic novels; 2. Science fiction graphic novels; 3. Superhero graphic novels

1-4012-0482-1, $14.99

Poverty, famine, war, and disease have been eliminated in the early days of the 31st century. The Dawning Millenium is utopian: shining, optimistic, hopeful...and deadly dull. Dull, that is, until a team of bright, defiant, super-powered teenagers from different worlds assemble. The come together as activists and fierce dreamers, crusading to make a difference in a society that has forgotten how to change. Cosmic Boy, Lightning Lad, Saturn Girl, and the rest of the Legion of Super-Heroes fight for freedom and justice while learning from, and learning to tolerate, one another.

Legion of Super-Heroes Vol. 2: Death of a Dream. DC Comics 2006 un Illustration

Grades: 9 10 11 12 Adult   **741.5; Fic**

1. Graphic novels; 2. Legion of Super-Heroes (Fictional characters); 3. Superhero graphic novels

978-1-4012-0971-1, $14.99

A bright, defiant, energized team of super-powered teenagers from different worlds joins forces to form a legion of passionate activists that crusade to leave their mark on a complacent society that has forgotten how to fight for change. A hidden mastermind plans the downfall of the United Planets, and only the Legion has the combined knowledge and power needed to stop him. But a struggle for control of the team has split the Legion into two clashing factions. Can the members put aside their personal differences in time to stop the intergalactic menace?

Supergirl and the Legion of Super-Heroes: Strange Visitor from Another Century. DC Comics 2006 144p. Illustration

Grades: 10 11 12 Adult   **741.5; Fic**

1. Graphic novels; 2. Mystery graphic novels; 3. Superhero graphic novels

978-1-4012-0916-2, $14.99

In the 31st century, the rebel teens of the Legion of Super-Heroes has ended the greatest threat to the peace and stability of the galaxy. The United Planets want to make the Legion an officially sanctioned peace-keeping force. Then, 21st-century hero Supergirl arrives in their time, with no memory of how she got there and no idea how to get back, so she applies for full-time Legionnaire membership. The story includes superhero action, and some violence in a locked-room mystery.

Superman: Birthright. DC Comics 2004 304p. Illustration

Grades: 9 10 11 12 Adult   **741.5; Fic**

1. Graphic novels; 2. Superhero graphic novels; 3. Superman (Fictional character)

1-4012-0252-7, $19.99

LC 2005-284647

The whole world knows that Superman fights for truth and justice...but why does he? What drives a farm boy from Kansas to divide his life between posing as a mild-mannered reporter and embarking on a career as a super hero? This book retells the origin of Superman, from his infancy through his first appearance as Superman, and why Lex Luthor is so obsessed with destroying him.

Walden, Tillie

The **end** of summer. Tillie Walden. Avery Hill Publishing 2016 108 p. Color; Illustration

Grades: 11 12 Adult   **741.5; Fic**

1. Winter — Fiction; 2. Cats — Fiction; 3. Graphic novels

1910395926; 9781910395264, $18

In this graphic novel, by Tillie Walden, "at the beginning of a winter that is predicted to last for three years, Lars is battling illness and boredom. He passes the time with his siblings and his giant cat, Nemo, as secrets are revealed and tensions within the family begin to simmer..." (Publisher's note)

★ **Spinning**. Tillie Walden. First Second 2017 400 p. Illustration
Grades: 7 8 9 10 11 12   **741.5; 92**
1. Figure skaters — Biography; 2. Graphic memoir; 3. Lesbian teenagers; 4. Walden, Tillie, 1996-
9781626727724, $22.99; 9781626729407, $17.99

LC 2016961586

Eisner Award: Best Reality-Based Work (2018)

This graphic memoir, by Tillie Walden, "captures what it's like to come of age, come out, and come to terms with leaving behind everything you used to know.... For ten years, figure skating was...Walden's life.... But as she switched schools, got into art, and fell in love with her first girlfriend, she began to question how the close-minded world of figure skating fit in with the rest of her life, and whether all the work was worth it." (Publisher's note)

"Walden's cumulative growth and courage to speak up for what she actually wants are unmistakable and deeply satisfying. A stirring, gorgeously illustrated story of finding the strength to follow one's own path." Booklist

Wallis, Pete
★ **What** does consent really mean?. written by Pete Wallis and Thalia Wallis; illustrated by Joseph Wilkins. Singing Dragon 2017 62 p. Color; Illustration
Grades: 8 9 10 11 12
741.5; 306.70835; 306.7
1. Rape; 2. Sexual harassment; 3. Teenagers — Sexual behavior
1848193300; 9780857012852; 9781848193307, $19.95

Courtesy of Avery Hill Publishing

LC 2017030844

In this book, by Pete Wallis and Thalia Wallis, illustrated by Joseph Wilkins, "following the sexual assault of a classmate, a group of teenage girls find themselves discussing the term consent, what it actually means for them in their current relationships, and how they act and make decisions with peer influence.... This rich graphic novel uncovers the need for more informed conversations with young people around consent and healthy relationships." (Publisher's note)

"Content that could be heavy with pedagogy is instead lightened by informal, occasionally profane language and friendly teasing." SLJ

Includes bibliographical references.

Wang, Jen
★ The **prince** and the dressmaker. Jen Wang. First Second 2018 288 p. Color; Illustration
Grades: 7 8 9 10 11 12
741.5; Fic
1. Fashion — Fiction; 2. Princes — Fiction; 3. Romance fiction
9781250159854, $24.99; 9781626723634

LC 2017941173

In this graphic novel, by Jen Wang, "Prince Sebastian is looking for a bride — or rather, his parents are looking for one for him. Sebastian is too busy hiding his secret life from everyone. At night he puts on daring dresses and takes Paris by storm as the fabulous Lady Crystallia — the hottest fashion icon in the world capital of fashion!

Courtesy of Singing Dragon

Sebastian's secret weapon (and best friend) is the brilliant dressmaker Frances — one of only two people who know the truth: sometimes this boy wears dresses." (Publisher's note)

"Frances's daring designs shine in Wang's elegantly drafted and gorgeously colored illustrations, and the irreverently anachronistic approach to the setting provides a lovely and humorous counterbalance to the seriousness of the prince's situation." Pub Wkly

Watanabe, Taeko
Kaze Hikaru, Vol. 1. story & art by Taeko Watanabe; [English adaptation, Annette Garcia; translation, Mai Ihara]. Viz Shojo Beat 2005 190p. Illustration
Grades: 10 11 12 Adult   **741.5; Fic**
1. Graphic novels; 2. Japan — History — 0-1868 — Graphic novels; 3. Manga; 4. Shojo manga
9781421501895, $8.99

"The talk of catamites and homosexual sex among the young men of the Mibu-Roshi and the almost perpetually drunken state of their older members make this title more suited to older teens." (VOYA)

In the waning years of the Tokugawa Shogunate, a band of young samurai called the Mibu-Roshi, gathers in Tokyo. They are loyal to the Shogun and will eventually become the Shinsengumi. Fifteen-year-old Seizaburo Kamiya, who has lost his father and brother to murderous supporters of the Emperor, joins the Mibu-Roshi, and young master swordsman Okita Soji befriends him. Soon, though, Soji learns Seizaburo's secret — he's actually a girl. He agrees to keep her secret and Sei becomes a mainstay in the group, but that doesn't end her danger.

Volume 1 of an ongoing series

Watase, Yuu
Ceres: Celestial Legend Vol. 1: Aya. story and art by Yû Watase; [English adaptation, Gary Leach; translation, Lillian Olsen]. Viz Media/Shojo 2003 208p. Illustration
Grades: 10 11 12 Adult   **741.5; Fic**
1. Graphic novels; 2. Horror graphic novels; 3. Manga; 4. Romance graphic novels; 5. Science fiction graphic novels; 6. Shojo manga
1-56931-980-4, $9.95

Aya and her twin brother Aki thought they were going to a celebration of their sixteenth birthday at their grandfather's home, but the funeral-like atmosphere tips them off that something's not right. Their "birthday present" turns out to be a mummified hand — the power of which forces an awakening within Aya, and painful wounds all over Aki's body. Grandfather Mikage announces that Aki will be heir to the Mikage fortune, and Aya must die. Aya has allies in the athletic cook and martial artist Yûhi, and the attractive, mysterious Tôya. But can even two handsome and resourceful guys save Aya when it's her own power that's out of control? The series includes nudity, sexual situations, strong language, and violence.

Volume 1 of 14

Fushigi yugi: the mysterious play. by Yuu Watase. VIZ Media LLC 2009 573 p. Illustration; Color
Grades: 9 10 11 12   **741.5**
1. Quests (Expeditions) — Comic books, strips, etc.; 2. Teenage girls — Comic books, strips, etc.; 3. Women heroes — Comic books, strips, etc.; 4. Fantasy fiction; 5. Graphic novels; 6. Books and reading — Fiction
142152290X; 9781421522906, $17.99

"Miaka Yuki is an ordinary junior-high student who is suddenly whisked away into the world of a book, The Universe Of The Four Gods. There she becomes the priestess of the god Suzaku, and is charged with finding all seven of her Celestial-Warrior protectors." (Publisher's note)

Volume 1 of 6

Watsuki, Nobuhiro

Rurouni Kenshin: Meiji swordsman romantic story [Vol. 1]. story and art by Nobuhiro Watsuki; [English adaptation, Gerard Jones; translation, Kenichiro Yagi; touch-up art & lettering, Steve Dutro].. Viz 2008 576p. Illustration

Grades: 10 11 12   **741.5; Fic**

1. Graphic novels; 2. Manga; 3. Japan — History — 1868-1945 — Graphic novels; 4. Shonen manga

978-1-4215-2073-5, $17.99

"The story of a young wandering samurai — who bears a reverse blade sword and strives not to kill after seeing and committing much bloodshed in the battles to bring the Emperor back to power in 1868"becomes much more than mere historical saga. Kenshin's relationships with new and old friends and enemies makes compelling storytelling." Voice Youth Advocates

This twenty-eight volume series was completed in late 2006

Way, Gerard

★ The **Umbrella** Academy: Apocalypse Suite. Gerard Way; art, Gabriel Ba; colors, Dave Stewart. Dark Horse Books 2008 192 p. Color; Illustration

Grades: 11 12 Adult   **741.5; Fic**

1. Superheroes — Fiction; 2. Brothers and sisters — Fiction

1593079788; 9781593079789, $17.99

Eisner Award: Best Limited Series (2008)

In this graphic novel, by Gerard Way, illustrated by Gabriel Ba, "forty-seven extraordinary children were spontaneously born to women who'd previously shown no signs of pregnancy. Millionaire inventor Reginald Hargreeves adopted seven of the children; when asked why, his only explanation was, 'To save the world.' These seven children form the Umbrella Academy, a dysfunctional family of superheroes with bizarre powers." (Publisher's note)

The **Umbrella** Academy: Dallas. by Gerard Way. Dark Horse 2009 192 p. Color; Illustration

Grades: 11 12 Adult   **741.5; Fic**

1. Dysfunctional families — Fiction; 2. Superheroes — Fiction; 3. Kennedy, John F. (John Fitzgerald), 1917-1963 — Fiction

159582345X; 9781595823458, $17.99

"The Umbrella Academy is a group of superheroes who were mysteriously born at the same time, adopted and raised together as a family and a team.... In this volume, the bizarrely childlike time-traveling team member Number Five recruits his siblings to right a wrong-to save President Kennedy before he is assassinated, possibly saving the world in the bargain." (Publishers Weekly)

"Way has a special affinity for enigmatic plotlines, in which minor details and major occurrences are left unexplained for ages, and he isn't afraid to literally end the world.... Such stuff makes spectacular fodder for Bá's chunky, irresistibly hooky art, bursting with constellations of weird, exciting, and funny touches." Booklist

Weeks, Lee

Civil War: Captain America. writer, Ed Brubaker; art, Mike Perkins ... [et al.]; colorist, Matt Mila; letterer, Virtual calligraphy's Joe Caramagna. Marvel Entertainment 2007 un Illustration

Grades: 9 10 11 12 Adult   **741.5; Fic**

1. Captain America (Fictional character); 2. Graphic novels; 3. Superhero graphic novels

0-7851-2798-4, $11.99

Captain America has clashed with the government and his friends and become a renegade because of his opposition to the Super Human Registration Act. The life of his girlfriend, Agent 13, is torn apart as her superiors use her divided loyalties against her. Elsewhere, the Red Skull

returns, and the Winter Soldier once again comes face-to-face with Cap; but which side will he choose? Winter Soldier, who was once Bucky Barnes, Captain America's partner, faces his first Christmas in the 21st century, and the truth of the terrible things he was forced to do as the Winter Soldier.

Weiner, Stephen

Hellboy: the companion. Stephen Weiner, Jason Hall, Victoria Blake with additional material by Mike Mignola; featuring the art of Mike Mignola, Guy Davis, Ryan Sook, Duncan Fegredo, Jason Shawn Alexander, and Paul Azaceta. Dark Horse Comics 2008 240p. Illustration

Grades: 10 11 12 Adult   **741.5**

1. Graphic novels; 2. Hellboy (Fictional character); 3. Horror graphic novels

978-1-59307-655-9, $14.95

Mike Mignola's Hellboy debuted in 1994 and has built up a growing audience for its world of Victorian occult societies, prehistoric gods, arcane Nazi experiments, and a big red demon for a good guy. Now librarian and comics historian Weiner, comics writer Hall, and journalist Blake put together a guide to Mignola's created world, illustrated with new art by Mignola as well as art from fourteen years of Hellboy from Mignola and the other artists who have worked with him over the years, including Guy Davis, Duncan Fegredo, Paul Azaceta, and others. The book includes character profiles, a timeline, and the literary heritage of Hellboy.

Weinstein, Lauren

Girl stories. by Lauren R. Weinstein. Henry Holt 2006 237p. Illustration

Grades: 7 8 9 10 11 12 Adult   **741.5; Fic**

1. Friendship — Graphic novels; 2. Girls — Graphic novels; 3. Graphic novels; 4. Humorous graphic novels

978-0-8050-7863-3, $16.95; 0-8050-7863-0

LC 2005-46205

"Smart, creative Lauren sheds her geeky rep in high school in Weinstein's collection of comic strips, which have to intimacy of a teen's diary. The color-washed sketches have an edgy quality." Booklist

Weir, Ivy Noelle

Archival quality. written by Ivy Noelle Weir; illustrated and colored by Steenz; lettered by Joamette Gil; edited by Robin Herrera. Oni Press 2018 280 p. Color; Illustration

Grades: 9 10 11 12 Adult   **741.5; Fic**

1. Librarians with disabilities — Fiction; 2. Librarians — Fiction; 3. Mental illness — Fiction; 4. Ghost stories

1620104709; 9781620104705, $19.99

LC 2017948855

In this book by Ivy Noelle Weir, illustrated by Steenz, "after losing her job at the library, Cel Walden starts working at the...Logan Museum as an archivist. But the job may not be the second chance she was hoping for, and she finds herself confronting her mental health, her relationships, and...her grasp on reality as she begins to dream of a young woman she's never met, but feels strangely drawn to." (Publisher's note)

"This horror story is more atmospheric than gory, aside from some bloody noses, and effectively creates an unsettling mood. The rich colors, comic interjections, and expressive features and gestures of Steenz's art add levity." SLJ

Wells, H. G. (Herbert George)

Classics illustrated #12: The Island of Dr. Moreau. Papercutz 2011 un Illustration

Grades: 7 8 9 10 11 12 Adult   **741.5; Fic**

1. Authors; 2. Graphic novels; 3. Historians; 4. Horror graphic novels; 5. Novelists; 6. Science fiction writers; 7. Writers on politics; 8. Writers on science; 9. Wells, H. G. (Herbert George), 1866-1946 — Adaptations
978-1-59707-235-9, $9.99

Edward Prendick is the sole survivor of a shipwreck when a passing ship picks him up. It carries a strange cargo of animals, a doctor, who takes care of Prendick, and an odd man who looks more like an ape. Montgomery, the doctor, is taking the animals to a small island he won't name, and Prendick ends up with them when the drunken ship's captain casts him off. On that island, Prendick discovers half-human, half-beast creatures, all created by the arrogant Dr. Moreau. This book adapts Wells' classic story; it was originally published in 1990 as part of the Classics Illustrated line published by First Comics. This edition includes an interview with Steven Grant, who wrote the adaptation.

The **Time** Machine. Stone Arch Books 2007 72p. Illustration
Grades: 3 4 5 6 7 8 9   **741.5; Fic**
1. Adventure graphic novels; 2. Graphic novels; 3. Science fiction graphic novels
978-1-59889-833-0, $23.93

LC 2007-6201

A scientist invents a machine that he claims will travel through time, but his friends laugh at the idea. So the Time Traveler climbs aboard his machine and ends up thousands of years in the future. He meets a race of gentle humans called the Eloi, but he is soon swept up in a fight for his life against evil underground creatures known as Morlocks. Even worse, his Time Machine, his only chance to escape, is trapped deep inside the Morlock caverns. This book is written with an easy vocabulary for struggling and reluctant readers, and it includes some scientific speculations about the future.

Part of the Graphic Revolve series

Westerfeld, Scott
Spill zone; 1. Scott Westerfeld; illustrated by Alex Puvilland. First Second 2017 211 p. Color; Illustration (Spill zone)
Grades: 10 11 12

Courtesy of NBM Publishing

741.5; Fic
1. Orphans — Fiction; 2. Photographers — Fiction; 3. Sisters — Fiction
9781250164292; 9781596439368, $22.99

LC 2016945565

"Uncanny manifestations and lethal dangers now await anyone who enters the Spill Zone. The Spill claimed Addison's parents and scarred her little sister.... Addison provides for her sister by photographing the Zone's twisted attractions.... Art collectors pay top dollar for these bizarre images, but getting close enough for the perfect shot can mean death — or worse." (Publisher's note)

"This unnerving, gripping title — Westerfeld's first original graphic novel — is bound to entice older comics fans, especially those interested in darker sci-fi and nuanced characterization." School Library Journal.

Another title in this series is: The broken vow (2018)

Uglies: Shay's story. created by Scott Westerfeld; written by Scott Westerfeld and Devin Grayson; illustrations by Steven Cummings. Del Rey 2012 160 p. Illustration
Grades: 7 8 9 10   **741.5**
1. Beauty, Personal — Fiction; 2. Friendship — Fiction; 3. Science fiction; 4. Dystopian graphic novels; 5. Conformity — Graphic novels; 6. Plastic surgery — Graphic novels
9780606264754, $22.10; 0345527224; 9780345527226, $10.99
LC 2012374898

This young adult graphic novel retells the story of author Scott Westerfeld's dystopia "Uglies" from "the point of view of recurring frenemy Shay." It is "set in a...future time when discord is suppressed through ruthlessly enforced conformity and obligatory plastic surgery at age 16.... Shay yearns for freedom. An encounter with the flawed and alluring David, a covert envoy from the Smoke, a secret community of nonconformists, may offer Shay the escape she craves." (Publishers Weekly)

Followed by:Uglies: Cutters (2012)

Whedon, Joss
★ **Astonishing** X-Men Vol. 1: Gifted. writer, Joss Whedon; artist, John Cassaday; colorist, Laura Martin; letterer, Chris Eliopoulos; cover art, John Cassaday. Marvel Entertainment 2004 un Illustration
Grades: 9 10 11 12 Adult   **741.5; Fic**
1. Graphic novels; 2. Superhero graphic novels; 3. X-Men (Fictional characters)
978-0-7851-1531-1, $14.99
Eisner Award: Best Continuing Series (2006); Eisner Award: Best Penciller/Inker (2005); Volume 1 of 12

Cyclops and Emma Frost re-form the X-Men with the express purpose of ästonishing" the world. But when breaking news regarding the mutant gene unexpectedly hits the airwaves, will it derail their new plans before they even get started? As demand for the mutant cure" reaches near-riot levels, the X-Men go head-to-head with the enigmatic Ord, with an unexpected ally — and some unexpected adversaries — tipping the scales.

Other Astonishing X-Men volumes by Whedon and Cassaday are: 2: Dangerous; 3: Torn; 4: Unstoppable

Fray. Dark Horse Comics 2003 un Illustration
Grades: 9 10 11 12 Adult   **741.5; Fic**
1. Adventure graphic novels; 2. Graphic novels; 3. Monsters — Graphic novels
1-56971-751-6, $19.95

Hundreds of years in the future, Manhattan has become a deadly slum, run by mutant crime-lords and disinterested cops. Stuck in the middle is a young girl who thought she had no future, but learns she has a great destiny. In a world so poisoned that it doesn't notice the monsters on its streets, how can a street kid like Fray unite a fallen city against a demonic plot to consume mankind? Creator Whedon set this story in the future of Buffy the Vampire Slayer's world, with Fray a new slayer, aided by a demonic Watcher. The story has some violence and mild harsh language.

Wheeler, Andrew
Another castle: Grimoire. Andrew Wheeler, Paulina Ganucheau, edited by Ari Yarwood. Oni Press 2017 152 p. Color; Illustration
Grades: 7 8 9 10 11 12 Adult   **741.5; Fic**
1. Friendship — Fiction; 2. Good and evil — Fiction; 3. Heroes and heroines — Fiction; 4. Princesses — Fiction
1620103117; 9781620103111, $15.99

LC 2016950325

This book, by Andrew Wheeler and Paulina Ganucheau, edited by Ari Yarwood, "begins when Princess Misty of Beldora,...[was] captured by Lord Badlug, the ruler of the neighboring kingdom of Grimoire. He intends to marry her and conquer Beldora.... The people of Grimoire already suffer under his rule and desperately need a hero.... Together with the citizens of Grimoire,...Misty must fight to protect her kingdom and free both realms from Badlug's tyrannical rule." (Publisher's note)

"Ganucheau contributes some thrilling and bloody action sequences, and her candy-colored palette, suffused with bright pinks and purples, is an inspired touch, just one more way this story subverts expectations." Pub Wkly

White, Steve

The **Battle** of Midway: the destruction of the Japanese fleet. The Rosen Publishing Group 2007 48p. Illustration

Grades: 3 4 5 6 7 8 9   **741.5; 940.54**

1. Graphic novels; 2. Midway, Battle of, 1942 — Graphic novels; 3. War — Graphic novels; 4. World War, 1939-1945 — Graphic novels

978-1-4042-0783-7, $29.25

One of the most important naval battles in history, Midway marked a crucial turning point in the war in the Pacific. With a fleet that had dominated this theater since the attack on Pearl Harbor, the Japanese anticipated certain victory against the US forces, but the attack was not a surprise. The US Navy sank four irreplaceable aircraft carriers, and cleared the way for the island-hopping US counterattack. This book also includes eight pages of authoritative information, placing the battle in its historical context, describing the key players, and its build-up and aftermath.

Part of the Graphic Battles of World War II series. This book is also available in a paperback edition from Osprey Publishing, under the title The Empire Falls: Battle of Midway.

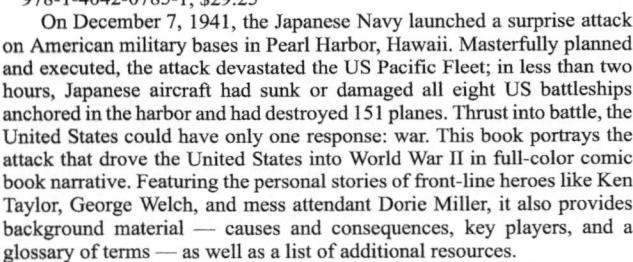

Courtesy of Oni Press

Pearl Harbor: A Day of Infamy. The Rosen Publishing Group 2007 48p. Illustration

Grades: 3 4 5 6 7 8 9

741.5; 940.54

1. Graphic novels; 2. Pearl Harbor (Oahu, Hawaii), Attack on, 1941 — Graphic novels; 3. War — Graphic novels; 4. World War, 1939-1945 — Graphic novels

978-1-4042-0785-1, $29.25

On December 7, 1941, the Japanese Navy launched a surprise attack on American military bases in Pearl Harbor, Hawaii. Masterfully planned and executed, the attack devastated the US Pacific Fleet; in less than two hours, Japanese aircraft had sunk or damaged all eight US battleships anchored in the harbor and had destroyed 151 planes. Thrust into battle, the United States could have only one response: war. This book portrays the attack that drove the United States into World War II in full-color comic book narrative. Featuring the personal stories of front-line heroes like Ken Taylor, George Welch, and mess attendant Dorie Miller, it also provides background material — causes and consequences, key players, and a glossary of terms — as well as a list of additional resources.

Part of the Graphic Battles of World War II series. This book is also available in a paperback edition from Osprey Publishing, under the title Day of Infamy: Attack on Pearl Harbor.

Whyte, Campbell

Home time; book one: under the river. Campbell Whyte. Top Shelf Productions 2017 228 p. Illustration

Grades: 7 8 9 10 11 12   **741.5; Fic**

1. Summer; 2. Mythical animals — Fiction; 3. Fantasy fiction

1603094121; 9781603094122, $24.99

In this book in the Home Time series, by Campbell Whyte, "the last school bell has rung and it's finally HOME TIME! Even though they're twins, Lilly and David don't agree on much... except that the last summer before high school is the perfect time for relaxing with friends. But their plans for sleepovers, fantasy games, and romance are thrown out the window when the whole gang falls into a river and wakes up in a village of fantastic creatures." (Publisher's note)

"Australian comics creator Whyte shifts artistic style with each chapter, moving from pencil sketches to bright, borderline psychedelic cartoons and even a chapter with a pixelated motif à la vintage arcade games. It's both alienating and engaging, keeping readers as off-balance as the children, who are trapped in an alien landscape they don't quite understand." Pub Wkly

Williams, J. H., III

Batman: Snow. story by J.H. Williams, Dan Curtis Johnson; script & dialogue, Dan Curtis Johnson; art and original covers, Seth Fisher; colors Dave Stewart; letterer, Phil Balsman. DC Comics 2007 128p. Illustration

Grades: 9 10 11 12 Adult   **741.5; Fic**

1. Adventure graphic novels; 2. Batman (Fictional character); 3. Graphic novels; 4. Superhero graphic novels

978-1-4012-1265-0, $14.99

At the dawn of his career, Batman recruits allies for his war on crime in order to really protect Gotham City. Everything changes when a brilliant scientist's desperate attempt to save the life of his terminally ill wife goes tragically wrong, and a new type of threat is born. As Batman faces his first super-powered villain, Mr. Freeze, he begins to realize that malfeasance comes in many deadly forms, and some offenders are more powerful than he. How will the crime fighter overcome this new menace while protecting not only his associates, but also the innocent citizens of Gotham? This book has lots of action and some mildly harsh language.

Courtesy of IDW Publishing

Williams, J. H., III.

Batwoman; Volume 1: Hydrology. J.H. Williams III, W. Haden Blackman. DC Comics 2012 160 p. Color; Illustration

Grades: 11 12 Adult

741.5; Fic

1. Women superheroes — Comic books, strips, etc.; 2. Batwoman (Fictional character)

1401234658; 9781401234652, $22.99

LC 2012002252

"Batwoman (a.k.a. Kate Kane) faces deadly new challenges in her war against Gotham City's underworld.... Who or what is stealing children from the barrio, and for what vile purpose? Will Kate train her cousin, Bette Kane (a.k.a. Flamebird), as her new sidekick? How will she handle unsettling revelations about her father, Colonel Jacob Kane? And why is a certain government agency suddenly taking an interest in her?" (Publisher's note)

"Williams and Blackman write a perfect story, and Williams as illustrator offers a flowing, nonlinear style that pulls the reader onward as if through a dream — a dream that is sometimes pleasant, sometimes a nightmare, but always vivid." LJ"

Originally published in single magazine form in Batwoman 0-5 — T.p. verso.

Batwoman; Volume 2: To drown the world. J.H. Williams III, W. Haden Blackman, Amy Reeder, Trevor McCarthy. DC Comics 2012 144 p. Color; Illustration

Grades: 11 12 Adult   **741.5; Fic**

1. Women superheroes — Comic books, strips, etc.; 2. Batwoman (Fictional character)

1401237908; 9781401237905, $22.99

LC 2012032148

"Six lives, inextricably linked in the past and present, each on a collision course with the others: Batwoman, fighting for duty and vengeance against a threat of arcane power. Detective Maggie Sawyer, investigating a case that could end her career. DEO Agent Cameron Chase, commanding a vigilante she despises. Colonel Jacob Kane, clutching at a life that's slipping away. Maro, a new villain corrupting Gotham City. And Kate Kane, wrestling with decisions that will test her loyalties." (Publisher's note)

Originally published in single magazine form in Batwoman 6-11.

Batwoman; Volume 3: World's finest. J.H. Williams III, W. Haden Blackman, writers; J.H. Williams III, artist; Trevor McCarthy, additional art; Todd Klein, letterer. DC Comics 2013 168 p. Color; Illustration

Grades: 11 12 Adult　　　　　　　　　　　**741.5; Fic**
　　1. Women superheroes — Comic books, strips, etc.; 2. Batwoman (Fictional character)

9781401242466, $22.99; 9781401246105; 1401246109; 1401242464
　　　　　　　　　　　　　　　　　　LC 2013016902
　　"Batwoman's search for Medusa brings her together with the Amazing Amazon, Wonder Woman, but even the teaming of the World's Finest might not be enough to bring down the mythological monster — leading Bones, the DEO, Abbot and the Religion of Crime all descend on Gotham City to take part in the fight." (Publisher's note)

Originally published in single magazine form in Batwoman 12-17, 0.

Batwoman; Volume 4: This blood is thick. J.H. Williams III, W. Haden Blackman, writers; Trevor McCarthy, Francesco Francavilla, Walden Wong, Sandu Florea, Derek Fridolfs, artists. DC Comics 2014 160 p. Color; Illustration

Grades: 11 12 Adult　　　　　　　　　　　**741.5; Fic**
　　1. Women superheroes — Comic books, strips, etc.; 2. Batwoman (Fictional character)

1401246214; 9781401246211, $22.99
　　　　　　　　　　　　　　　　　　LC 2013049639
　　"After taking down Medusa, Batwoman expected her life to get easier. Not so much when caught in the crossfire between Batman and the D.E.O., Department of Extranormal Operations. The organization has their sights set on the Dark Knight, and could be using Batwoman to capture him. But is Batman the true threat?" (Publisher's note)

Collects Batwoman #18-24

Williams, Rob

Star Wars: Rebellion Volume 1: My Brother, My Enemy. script, Rob Williams; Crossroads script, Thomas Andrews; art, Brandon Badeaux and Michel Lacombe; colors, Wil Glass; lettering, Michael Heisler; front cover art, Brandon Badeaux and Brad Anderson; back cover art, Brandon Badeaux and Wil Glass. Dark Horse Comics 2007 un Illustration

Grades: 8 9 10 11 12 Adult　　　　　　　**741.5; Fic**
　　1. Adventure graphic novels; 2. Graphic novels; 3. Science fiction graphic novels

9781593077112, $14.95; 1593077114
　　Having rescued Rebel strategist Jorin Sol from the Empire, Luke Skywalker now leads X-Wing attack runs on Imperial convoys to rustle up much needed supplies for the Rebel fleet. Little does he know that within Sol lies a secret that will put the entire Alliance in danger. What's worse, when Luke receives a coded message from Lt. Sunber, who wants to defect to the Rebel Alliance, he must decide whether to trust his old friend or obey the orders of Princess Leia who believes Tank may be part of an Imperial plot to capture the Rebellion's greatest hero.

　　Volume 1 of 3

Willingham, Bill

Day of Vengeance: Countdown to Infinite Crisis. Bill Willingham, Judd Winick; art by various. DC Comics 2005 un Illustration

Grades: 9 10 11 12 Adult　　　　　　　　**741.5; Fic**
　　1. Adventure graphic novels; 2. Graphic novels; 3. Superhero graphic novels; 4. Superman (Fictional character)

1-4012-0840-1, $12.99
　　Eclipso, the original spirit of vengeance, needs a new human host. The Spectre, the current spirit of vengeance, has just lost its human host and is vulnerable. When Eclipso seeks a new body, it first tries to control Superman; it takes Captain Marvel, the World's Mightiest Marvel, to stop him. Inhabiting the body of a familiar, tortured soul, Eclipso sets its sights on seducing the Spectre and destroying Earth's practitioners of magic. Seven heroes stand in their way. All very different. All with different goals at stake. And then they find an eighth, a girl who might be the most powerful teenager in the universe. Can this group, who call themselves Shadowpact, stop the angry spirits of vengeance?

Fables Vol 8: Wolves. DC Comics/Vertigo 2006 160p. Illustration

Grades: 10 11 12 Adult　　　　　　　　　**741.5; Fic**
　　1. Adventure graphic novels; 2. Fantasy graphic novels; 3. Graphic novels

978-1-4012-1001-4, $17.99
　　Fabletown's ex-sheriff Bigby Wolf and ex-deputy mayor (and power behind King Cole's former mayoral throne) Snow White finally tie the knot in this arc from the series about the fairy-tale characters who walk among us (or, at least, New Yorkers). That can't happen before Mowgli finds missing, moping Bigby and the latter undertakes a reprisal mission against the Adversary. This eighth volume includes some violence, strong language, and nudity.

★ **Fables** Vol. 1: Legends in Exile. DC Comics/Vertigo 2002 128p. Illustration

Grades: 10 11 12 Adult　　　　　　　　　**741.5; Fic**
　　1. Fantasy graphic novels; 2. Graphic novels; 3. Mystery graphic novels

1-56389-942-6, $9.99; 9781401237554
　　In Fabletown, where fairy tale legends live alongside regular New Yorkers, the question on everyone's mind is who killed Rose Red? But only the Big Bad Wolf can actually solve the case (since he's the Fabletown sheriff) — and, along with Rose's sister Snow White, keep the Fabletown community from coming apart at the seams. The book includes strong language, violence, nudity, and sexual situations.

　　Also available in deluxe hardcover editions; Volume 1 of a 22 volume series

Fables Vol. 2: Animal Farm. DC Comics/Vertigo 2003 128p. Illustration

Grades: 10 11 12 Adult　　　　　　　　　**741.5; Fic**
　　1. Fantasy graphic novels; 2. Graphic novels

1-4012-0077-X, $12.95
　　In upstate New York, the non-human Fable characters have lived for centuries on a farm, miles from mankind. But all is not well on the farm — and a conspiracy to free them from the shackles of their perceived imprisonment may lead to a war that could wrest control of the Fables community away from Snow White. Goldilocks and the Three Little Pigs inflame the farm's inhabitants with fiery revolutionary rhetoric, and both Snow White and her sister Rose Red face threats to their lives. The book includes violence and some strong language.

Fables Vol. 3: Storybook Love. DC Comics/Vertigo 2004 190p. Illustration

Grades: 10 11 12 Adult　　　　　　　　　**741.5; Fic**
　　1. Fantasy graphic novels; 2. Graphic novels

1-4012-0256-X, $14.99
　　In the Fables' world, there isn't a lot of happily-ever-after to go around. As refugees from the lands of make-believe, the Fables have been driven from their storybook realms and forced to blend into the mundane world. But that doesn't mean they don't have any room for romance, or the pain, betrayal, and jealous rage that go along with it. In fact, love may be blooming between two of the most hard-bitten, no-nonsense Fables around — Snow White and Bigby Wolf. Meanwhile, Bigby teams up with several

other Fables to stop a reporter from publishing a story that exposes the Fables and the lives they've built in New York. The book includes violence.

Fables Vol. 5: The Mean Seasons. DC Comics/Vertigo 2005 168p. Illustration
Grades: 11 12 Adult   **741.5; Fic**
1. Adventure graphic novels; 2. Fantasy graphic novels; 3. Graphic novels
1-4012-0486-4, $14.99
With the Battle of Fabletown won, and the surrounding city of New York none the wiser, the Fables have gained a little time for rebuilding and reflection, in between the interrogation of the Adversary's agent and the anticipation of Snow White's impending motherhood. For Bigby Wolf, the father of the soon-to-be newborns, that means a visit with an old friend, and a reminiscence of another, even deadlier war. For the new Mayor of Fabletown, Prince Charming, it means a rude awakening to the harsh realities of civic administration, and its conflicting demands. And for Snow herself, it means a long, painful labor, and a series of joyful, heart wrenching surprises. The book includes some violence, brief sexual situations, and strong language.

Fables Vol. 6: Homelands. DC Comics/Vertigo 2005 192p. Illustration
Grades: 10 11 12 Adult   **741.5; Fic**
1. Adventure graphic novels; 2. Fantasy graphic novels; 3. Graphic novels
1-4012-0500-3, $14.99
The Fables have beaten back the Adversary's first advance into their world, but now they must prepare themselves for the war that is sure to follow. Jack decides to skip town and heads for Hollywood, where he becomes a sleazy movie mogul. Boy Blue appropriates some weapons and heads back to the Homelands, killing enemies as he makes his way to the heart of enemy territory. The story features some nudity and sexual situations, some strong language, and considerable violence.

Fables: Arabian Nights (And Days); Volume 7. Bill Willingham, writer; Mark Buckingham, Jim Fern, pencillers; Steve Leialoha, Jimmy Palmiotti, Andrew Pepoy, inkers; Daniel Vozzo, colorist; Todd Klein, letterer. DC Comics/Vertigo 2006 un Illustration
Grades: 10 11 12 Adult   **741.5; Fic**
1. Fantasy graphic novels; 2. Graphic novels
978-1-4012-1000-7, $14.99
Now that the Adversary's identity has been revealed, it's time to begin making preparations in earnest for the defense of the Fabletown stronghold. That means forging new alliances with whoever remains unconquered by the Adversary's legions. But the arrival in Fabletown of a delegation from the Arabian Homelands shows just how tricky this kind of coalition-building can be...especially when one side is concealing Weapons of Magical Destruction. This volume includes some strong language and violence.

Robin/Batgirl: Fresh Blood. Bill Willingham, Andersen Gabrych, writers; Damion Scott, Alé Garza & Jesse Delperdang, artists; Guy Major, Wildstorm FX, colorists; Phil Balsman, Rob Leigh, letterers. DC Comics 2005 un Illustration
Grades: 9 10 11 12 Adult   **741.5; Fic**
1. Batgirl (Fictional character); 2. Graphic novels; 3. Robin (Fictional character); 4. Superhero graphic novels; 5. Nightwing (Fictional character)
1-4012-0433-3, $12.99
After the traumatic events of Batman: War Games, two of Gotham's youngest heroes, Robin and Batgirl, relocate to Bludhaven, where they must pick up the pieces of their lives and start anew. But before they can get fully settled in, they discover they have new threats to face, including

Nightwing's enemy Shrike and their old friend the Penguin. In order to save the day, the two heroes realize there's only one thing they can do: battle each other to the death.

Robin: Days of Fire and Madness. DC Comics 2006 144p. Illustration
Grades: 9 10 11 12 Adult   **741.5; Fic**
1. Graphic novels; 2. Mystery graphic novels; 3. Robin (Fictional character); 4. Superhero graphic novels; 5. Robin (Fictional character)
978-1-4012-0911-7, $14.99
Recruited into a covert military team by the mysterious and powerful man known only as the Veteran, Robin realizes that he has entered an entirely new world of danger when his first assignment takes him to the Middle East where he and his new teammates engage an enemy of unimaginable horror, flesh-eating demons. Back home, the battle continues as the Teen Wonder comes face to face with the inexplicable resurrection of his former girlfriend — determined to kill Robin in order to stay with Tim Drake forever — even as the city of Bludhaven suffers an attack by the supremely powerful, supremely deadly OMACs. Can the mystical superheroes of Shadowpact save Robin and his newfound allies? Or will this be his final battle? Lots of superhero fighting and demon fighting.

Robin: To Kill a Bird. DC Comics 2006 un Illustration
Grades: 8 9 10 11 12 Adult   **741.5; Fic**
1. Graphic novels; 2. Robin (Fictional character); 3. Superhero graphic novels; 4. Robin (Fictional character)
978-1-4012-0909-4, $14.99
It's a brand-new start for Batman's sidekick, Robin: a new town (Bludhaven), a new school, new adventures and new problems. Before our hero can fully recover from the recent deaths of his father and girlfriend Spoiler, he must come face to face with his enemies: the Penguin, the Dark Rider, the Veteran, and a mysterious archer who seems to want the Boy Wonder dead. There's lots of superhero fighting action.

Wilson, G. Willow
★ **Cairo**. written by G. Willow Wilson; art by M.K. Perker; lettered by Travis Lanham. DC Comics/Vertigo 2007 160p. Illustration
Grades: 9 10 11 12 Adult   **741.5; Fic**
1. Adventure graphic novels; 2. Fantasy graphic novels; 3. Graphic novels
978-1-4012-1140-0, $24.99
A stolen hookah, a spiritual underworld, and a genie on the run change the lives of five strangers in Cairo. A drug runner, a down-on-his-luck journalist, an American expatriate, a troubled young student, and a female Israeli soldier end up all working together to help the jinn that Lebanese American Shaheed calls Shams to recover a special box from the evil magic-wielding drug lord Nar. The book includes some violence.
"Scripting and art complement each other well in an adventure with lots of appeal for readers willing to try a literary graphic novel and for those simply looking for the next good one." Booklist

★ **Ms.** Marvel; Volume 1: No Normal. writer, G. Willow Wilson; artist, Adrian Alphona. Marvel Enterprises 2014 120 p. Color; Illustration
Grades: 9 10 11 12 Adult   **741.5**
1. Female superhero comic books, strips, etc.; 2. Muslim women — Fiction
078519021X; 9780785190219, $15.99
Hugo Award: Best Graphic Story (2015)
In this comic, written by G. Willow Wilson and illustrated by Adrian Alphona, "Kamala Khan is an ordinary girl from Jersey City — until she is suddenly empowered with extraordinary gifts. But who truly is the all-new Ms. Marvel? Teenager? Muslim? Inhuman? Find out as...Kamala discovers the dangers of her newfound powers [and] she unlocks a secret behind them as well." (Publisher's note)

"Wilson's story touches on many issues bubbling up around comics today — diversity, gender, culture, sexuality — though never with a heavy hand. The story is the focus here, and together with Alphona's playful and stylish artwork, Wilson offers a superhero comic full to bursting with heart and charm." Booklist

Contains material originally published in magazine form as Ms. Marvel #1-5 and All-new Marvel now! point one #1 — Title page; Volume 1 of an ongoing series

Ms. Marvel; Volume 2: Generation Why. by G. Willow Wilson; illustrated by Jacob Wyatt and Adrian Alphona. Marvel Enterprises 2015 136 p. Color; Illustration

Grades: 9 10 11 12 Adult   **741.5**
1. Muslim women — Fiction; 2. Pakistani Americans — Fiction; 3. Teenage girls — Fiction; 4. Women superheroes; 5. Female superhero comic books, strips, etc.; 6. Wolverine (Fictional character)
0785190228; 9780785190226, $15.99

"Who is the Inventor, and what does he want with the all-new Ms. Marvel and all her friends? Maybe Wolverine can help! Kamala may be fan-girling out when her favorite (okay maybe Top Five) super hero shows up, but that won't stop her from protecting her hometown." (Publisher's note)

"Alphona's distinctive panels make great use of exaggerated angles and distorted figures, and his line work, more intricate than most comic-book artists', packs each page with captivating, tongue-in-cheek detail." Booklist

Contains material originally published in magazine form as Ms. Marvel #6-11 — Title page verso.

Ms. Marvel; Volume 3: Crushed. G. Willow Wilson; illustrated by Takeshi Miyazawa and Elmo Bondoc. Marvel Enterprises 2015 112 p. Color; Illustration

Grades: 9 10 11 12 Adult   **741.5**
1. Pakistani Americans — Comic books, strips, etc.; 2. Superhero comic books, strips, etc.; 3. Teenage girls — Comic books, strips, etc.; 4. Female superhero graphic novels; 5. Valentine's Day — Graphic novels
0785192271; 9780785192275, $15.99

"Love is in the air in Jersey City as Valentine's Day arrives! Kamala Khan may not be allowed to go to the school dance...but Ms. Marvel is! Well sort of — by crashing it attempting to capture Asgard's most annoying trickster! Yup, it's a special Valentine's Day story featuring Marvel's favorite charlatan, Loki!" (Publisher's note)

"As always, Wilson's rollicking superhero action is sprinkled with both hilarity and meaningful cultural commentary, and Kamala herself is as appealing as ever." Booklist

Contains material originally published in magazine form as Ms. Marvel #12-15 and S.H.I.E.L.D #2.

Ms. Marvel; Volume 4: Last Days. by G. Willow Wilson; illustrated by Adrian Alphona. Marvel Enterprises 2015 120 p. Color; Illustration

Grades: 9 10 11 12 Adult   **741.5; Fic**
1. Pakistani Americans — Fiction; 2. Teenage girls — Fiction; 3. Women superheroes — Comic books, strips, etc.
0785197362; 9780785197362, $17.99

"When the world is about to end, do you still keep fighting? From the moment, Kamala put on her costume, she's been challenged, but nothing has prepared her for this: the Last Days of the Marvel Universe. Fists up, let's do this, Jersey City. Plus a VERY special guest appearance fans have been clamoring for!" (Publisher's note)

"Alphona's lanky figures, fantastic use of color, and cinematic depiction of movement continue to dazzle, especially the rich diversity of characters that pack the teeming panels." Booklist

Contains material originally published in magazine form as Ms. Marvel #16-19 and Amazing Spider-Man #7-8.

Ms. Marvel; Volume 5: Super Famous. G. Willow Wilson; illustrated by Takeshi Miyazawa, Adrian Alphona, Nico Leon. Marvel Enterprises 2016 144 p. Color; Illustration

Grades: 9 10 11 12 Adult   **741.5; Fic**
1. Teenage girls — Fiction; 2. Female superhero graphic novels; 3. Pakistani Americans — Fiction
0785196110; 9780785196112, $17.99

"Kamala Khan is officially an Avenger! But will being one of Earth's Mightiest Heroes be everything she imagined? Or is life as a celebrity harder than she thought? But while saving the world is important, Jersey City still needs its protector too. A development company that co-opted Ms. Marvel's face for its project might well have more in mind for gentrification than just real estate." (Publisher's note)

Contains material originally published in magazine form as Ms. Marvel (2015) #1-6

Winget, Larry

Shut up, stop whining and get a life: a kick-butt approach to a better life. Smarter Comics 2011 80p. Illustration

Grades: 10 11 12 Adult   **646.7; 741.5**
1. Graphic novels; 2. Self-help techniques — Graphic novels; 3. Self-improvement — Graphic novels
978-1-61066-002-0, $12.95

Larry Winget's bestselling self-help book is now a graphic novel. Self-described "Pitbull of Personal Development" Winget's approach takes aim at the usual advice found in most self-help books; he says that people need to take responsibility for their own lives, acknowledge their mistakes, learn from them, and change what they need to change in order to achieve their goals, whatever they may be. Even if one doesn't agree with everything he says, his approach is refreshing and full of common sense advice. Comics writer Bunn adapts Winget's prose, and comics illustrator Clester uses a lot of humor in the art to make Winget's points. Older teens and college students may discover that this book can truly help them.

Winick, Judd

Green Lantern: New Journey, Old Path. Judd Winick, writer; Darryl Banks, Mark Bright, Dale Eaglesham, pencillers. DC Comics 2001 192p. Illustration

Grades: 9 10 11 12 Adult   **741.5; Fic**
1. Graphic novels; 2. Green Lantern (Fictional character); 3. Superhero graphic novels; 4. Justice League (Fictional characters)
1-56389-729-6, $12.95

Nero, an escaped mental patient, is bequeathed a Yellow Lantern Ring by the Qwardians. Possessing the mind of a demon and the skill of an artist, he wreaks havoc in New York City and could possibly decimate the planet. With the Justice League pushed to the limit trying to contain Nero's hordes, Green Lantern Kyle Rayner stands alone against a maniac whose power could surpass his own.

★ **Pedro** & me: friendship, loss, & what I learned. Henry Holt and Co. 2009 187p. Illustration

Grades: 7 8 9 10 11 12   **362.1**
1. AIDS (Disease) — Graphic novels; 2. AIDS activists; 3. AIDS patients; 4. Biographical graphic novels; 5. Friendship — Graphic novels; 6. Graphic novels; 7. Television personalities; 8. Real world (Television program) — Graphic novels; 9. Zamora, Pedro, 1972-1994
978-0-8050-8964-6, $16.99
2001 Robert F. Sibert Honor Book for informational books for youth

In this "volume — part graphic novel, part memoir — professional cartoonist Winick pays tribute to his Real World housemate and friend

Pedro Zamora, an AIDS activist who died of the disease in 1994." Publ Wkly

First published 2000

Superman/Shazam/First Thunder. DC Comics 2006 128p. Illustration

Grades: 8 9 10 11 12 Adult 741.5; Fic
1. Graphic novels; 2. Shazam (Fictional character); 3. Superhero graphic novels; 4. Superman (Fictional character)
978-1-4012-0923-0, $12.99

With one word, young orphan Billy Batson transforms into a man imbued with the powers of the gods, but even one gifted with the Wisdom of Solomon can learn from a Superman. While Superman must stop members of a cult from stealing ancient artifacts from the Metropolis Natural History Museum, Billy must battle giant robots rampaging through Fawcett City. These separate events lead the heroes to cross paths, and a mighty friendship is formed as Earth's most powerful defenders team up to stop such menaces as Lex Luthor, Dr. Sivana, Eclipso, and the monstrous Lord Sabbac. There's some violence, and the climax is heartbreaking.

Wolfman, Marv
Homeland: The Illustrated History of the State of Israel. Nachschon Press 2007 124p. Illustration

Grades: 9 10 11 12 Adult 305.892; 741.5; 956.94
1. Graphic novels; 2. Israelis — Graphic novels; 3. Jews — Graphic novels; 4. Israel — History — Graphic novels; 5. Palestine — Graphic novels
978-0-9771507-0-0, $19.95

Using the conceit that a university professor is teaching a class, this book covers about 4,000 years of history in the Middle East, focused on Israel. It goes back to the Biblical narrative of Abram's journey from Mesopotamia, quickly progresses to the Middle Ages, explains the complicated circumstances surrounding the Zionist movement and efforts to establish the modern state of Israel, and covers the recent situations there. Readers may not be so familiar with the history of Israel and the Jews beyond the Old Testament narratives, the World War II Holocaust, and the current struggles. This book gives a concise explanation of the history which is valuable whether or not one supports Israel today.

Wolfram, Amy
Teen Titans year one. written by Amy Wolfram; penciled by Karl Kerschl; inked by Serge Lapointe; colored by Steph Peru, John Rauch; lettered by Nick J. Napolitano; series & collection cover art by Karl Kerschl & Serge Lapointe. DC Comics 2008 144p. Illustration

Grades: 7 8 9 10 11 12 741.5; Fic
1. Aquaman (Fictitious character); 2. Graphic novels; 3. Superhero graphic novels; 4. Teen Titans (Fictional characters); 5. Wonder Woman (Fictional character); 6. Green Arrow (Fictional character); 7. Flash (Fictional character); 8. Robin (Fictional character); 9. Batman (Fictional character); 10. Justice League (Fictional characters)
978-1-4012-1927-7, $14.99

Suddenly, the members of the Justice League of America are acting crazy, becoming bullies, breaking the law — what has happened to Batman, Aquaman, the Flash, Green Arrow, and Wonder Woman? Their young partners, Robin, Aqualad, Kid Flash, Speedy, and Wonder Girl, decide to team up together and put things right. They're teens, they're superheroes, they're the Teen Titans. And being teens, they still do teenage things, like overindulge in pizza and soda, go out on dates and mess things up with each other, and deal with celebrity. That last is not typical of teens, but they have to learn to deal with it. This book, written by Wolfram, who wrote for the Teen Titans animated series on television, reimagines the early days of the team. The book includes some violence.

Wood, Brian
DMZ Vol. 1: On the Ground. Brian Wood, writer, artist, creator; Riccardo Burchiell, artist and creator; Jared K. Fletcher, letterer. DC Comics/Vertigo 2006 128p. Illustration

Grades: 11 12 Adult 741.5
1. Adventure graphic novels; 2. Graphic novels
978-1-4012-1062-5

In the near future, America's worst nightmare has come true. With military adventurism overseas bogging down the Army and National Guard, the U.S. government mistakenly neglects the very real threat of anti-establishment militias scattered across the 50 states. Like a sleeping giant, Middle America rises up and violently pushes its way to the shining seas, coming to a standstill at the line in the sand — Manhattan. Or as the world now knows it, the DMZ. Matty Roth, a nave aspiring photojournalist, lands a dream gig following a veteran war correspondent into the heart of the DMZ. Things soon go terribly wrong, and Matty finds himself lost and alone in a world he's only seen on television. This story has lots of harsh language and violence.

Volume 1 of 12

The **New** York Four. written by Brian Wood; illustrated by Kelly Ryan; lettering by Jared K. Fletcher. DC Comics/Minx 2008 176p. Illustration

Grades: 8 9 10 11 12 741.5; Fic
1. Friendship — Graphic novels; 2. Graphic novels
978-1-4012-1154-7, $9.99

Riley is a college freshman who has grown up so sheltered, protected, and disciplined by her parents that she finds it difficult to make friends. She starts seeing her older sister Angie on the sly; Angie was kicked out of the house years ago for an offense no one will tell Riley. Other than that, Riley almost lives her life through her smart phone, constantly texting to people she's never met in person. Then, just as she opens up to make friends with three fellow freshmen and helps them find work with the same research group for which she works, she "meets" someone she knows only by his user name, "sneakerfreak." Balancing classes, friends, her over-protective parents, her sister, and now this secret online romance is becoming more difficult than Riley ever thought it could be. Each of her friends also has a secret that could have consequences.

Woodfin, Rupert
Introducing Aristotle, New Edition. Totem Books 2006 176p. Illustration

Grades: 10 11 12 Adult 100; 741.5
1. Ancient philosophy — Graphic novels; 2. Graphic novels; 3. Aristotle, 384-322 B.C.
978-1-84046-759-8, $12.95

Aristotle was named the "master of those who know." He is a foundational thinker in every field of inquiry. He established logic as a systematic discipline, conceived the earliest rules of science, developed a rational psychology, a political science and an outline of sociology, and gave us a virtue theory of ethics that is still a model today. His contributions to metaphysics continue to permeate modern philosophy. He supplied the first theory of aesthetics, which still provides the basis of debates today. Aristotle's authority extended beyond his time to influence Islamic society and medieval scholasticism. For fifteen hundred years he remained the paradigm of knowledge itself, until scientific empiricism in the 17th century is said to have discredited his methods. Is this true? How 'scientific' is Aristotle? This volume uses cartoons and a spare text to introduce readers to Aristotle's philosophy; it includes a list of books for further reading.

Marxism: a graphic guide. by Rupert Woodfin, illustrated by Oscar Zarate. Pgw 2018 176 p. Illustration

Grades: 10 11 12 Adult 741.5; 335.4

1. Communism; 2. Marxism; 3. Marx, Karl, 1818-1883
1785783068; 9781785783067, $17.95
Includes bibliographical references (pages 180-183) and index

This book, by Rupert Woodfin, illustrated by Oscar Zarate, "traces the story of [Karl] Marx's original philosophy, from its roots in 19th-century European thinkers like [Georg] Hegel, to its influence on modern-day culture. It looks at Marxism's Russian disciples...who forged a ruthless, dogmatic Communism, and the alternative Marxist approaches of [Antonio] Gramsci, the Frankfurt School of critical theory and the structuralist Marxism of Althusser in the 1960s." (Publisher's note)"

Courtesy of Icon Books

"Zarate's skillfully rendered, brushy drawings, often blended with collages of found art, ably support Woodfin's explorations of the various permutations of Marx's teachings. The comics illuminate the intricacies and fluidity of political philosophy, showing how Marx's ideology, originally forged to benefit the lower laboring classes, also provided the framework for the human rights abuses under Stalin's communist dictatorship, as well as for the intellectually rigorous Frankfurt School of critical theory." Pub Wkly

Wyld, Evie
Everything is teeth. Evie Wyld; illustrated by Joe Sumner. Pantheon Books 2016 128 p. Illustration
Grades: 10 11 12 Adult   **B; 92; 741.5; 823/.92**
1. Sharks — Comic books, strips, etc; 2. Women authors, English — Biography; 3. Wyld, Evie; 4. Australia — New South Wales — Comic books, strips, etc; 5. Women authors — Biography
1101870818; 9781101870815, $24.95

        LC 2015023575
This autobiographical graphic novel, by Evie Wyld and illustrated by Joe Sumner, "is a deeply moving graphic memoir about family, love, loss, and the irresistible forces that, like sharks, course through life unseen, ready to emerge at any moment." (Publisher's note)

"A rite-of-passage memoir that has powerful poetry in its ellipses." Kirkus

Yabuki, Kentaro
Black Cat, Volume 1. Viz Media/Shonen Jump 2006 200p. Illustration
Grades: 10 11 12 Adult   **741.5; Fic**
1. Adventure graphic novels; 2. Graphic novels; 3. Manga; 4. Shonen manga
978-1-4215-0605-0, $7.99

Translated by JN Productions. Train Heartnet, known as "Black Cat," worked as a top assassin for a secret organization called Chronos, but quit. Now he's a sweeper, a bounty hunter, partnered with the one-eyed Sven. Even as Train has to deal with assassins from his past, he and Sven go after wanted men for the bounties. Then beautiful thief Rinslet Walker proposes that they partner with her to take down a weapons smuggler who is developing dangerous new weapons. At first glance, Train's world is similar to ours, but science fictional elements such as nanotechnology and mystical elements of chi come into play as well. Sven seems to always have a cigarette in hand, and Train seems to always find someone he has to fight, but in the first four volumes there hasn't been any gratuitous cleavage or panty shots.

Yagi, Norihiro
Claymore Vol. 1. Viz Media/Shonen Jump Advanced 2006 188p. Illustration
Grades: 10 11 12 Adult   **741.5; Fic**
1. Fantasy graphic novels; 2. Graphic novels; 3. Horror graphic novels; 4. Manga; 5. Shonen manga
978-1-4215-0618-0, $7.99

A Claymore — a female warrior named for the sword she carries — travels from medieval village to village to destroy Yoma, monsters who disguise themselves as humans and who are almost impossible to kill. Claymores are half-humans, half-demons who willingly transformed themselves by mixing their blood with monster's blood. Clare, nicknamed silver-eyed killer, is such a powerful Claymore, she can slay a Yoma using only one hand. But she must constantly struggle to keep from becoming a monster herself. The book includes a considerable amount of monster-slaying violence.

Yakin, Boaz
★ **Marathon**. by Boaz Yakin; [illustrations by Joe Infurnari]. First Second 2012 186 p.
Grades: 8 9 10 11 12   **741.5/973**
1. Graphic novels; 2. Greece — History — Persian Wars, 500-449 B.C. — Fiction; 3. Adventure graphic novels; 4. Marathon, Battle of, 490 B.C. — Graphic novels
9781596436800, $16.99 ; 1596436808

        LC 2011030472
This book is a graphical "account of the battle of Marathon" in which "Hippias, former king of Athens, is on his way back with a huge army of Persians to reclaim the throne and crush Athenian democracy.... Eucles, Athens' best runner, is charged to race the 153 miles to Sparta in hopes of finding an ally,... [returning] with the dismaying news that the Spartans will not be coming in time. He joins the savage fight and then runs 26 more miles over rugged mountains to Athens...warning of an impending surprise attack by sea." (Kirkus Reviews)

Yang, Gene Luen
★ **American** born Chinese. by Gene Luen Yang; color by Lark Pien. First Second 2006 233p. Illustration
Grades: 7 8 9 10 11 12   **741.5; Fic**
1. Chinese Americans — Graphic novels; 2. Graphic novels
1-59643-152-0, $16.95; 978-1-59643-152-2

        LC 2005-58105
Printz Award (2007); National Book Award Finalist: Young People's Literature (2006); Eisner Award: Best Graphic Album — New (2007)

"Jin Wang is the only Asian American boy in his new school; Danny is a young man deeply embarrassed by his visiting Chinese cousin, portrayed deliberately by the author as an ethnic cliché; and the Monkey King, a figure from Chinese lore, is desperate to be treated like a god. This...story relates how three characters overcome hurdles to find satisfaction within themselves." (Library Journal)

"True to its origin as a Web comic, this story's clear, concise lines and expert coloring are deceptively simple yet expressive. Even when Yang slips in an occasional Chinese ideogram or myth, the sentiments he's depicting need no translation. Yang accomplishes the remarkable feat of practicing what he preaches with this book: accept who you are and you'll already have reached out to others." Publ Wkly

★ **Boxers**. Gene Luen Yang; color by Lark Pien. First Second 2013 328 p.
Grades: 7 8 9 10 11 12 Adult   **741.5**
1. China — History — Boxer Rebellion, 1899-1901 — Graphic novels; 2. Historical fiction
1596433590; 9781596433595, $18.99

LC 2013947229

National Book Award for Young People's Literature: Finalist (2013); Boston Globe-Horn Book Honor: Fiction (2014); Ignatz Nominee: Outstanding Graphic Novel (2014)

"Life in Little Bao's peaceful rural village is disrupted when...a priest and his phalanx of soldiers...arrive." They start "smashing the village god, appropriating property, and administering vicious beatings for no reason. Little Bao and his older brothers train in kung fu and swordplay."...Little Bao "becomes the leader of a peasant army, eventually marching to Beijing." (School Library Journal)

"China's Boxer Rebellion is the unlikely backdrop for this graphic treatment of young villagers on the opposite sides of history. Bao wants to drive out the white devils that poison his country with opium and Christianity. Four-Girl is an unwanted daughter who finds purpose in the missionary life. Their stories collide in a moment of grace that could only be penned by the Printz Award-winning author of 'American Born Chinese.'" LJ

★ The **eternal** smile: three stories. Gene Luen Yang and Derek Kirk Kim. First Second 2009 170p. Illustration
Grades: 9 10 11 12   **741.5; Fic**
978-1-59643-156-0, $16.95; 1-59643-156-3

"In three graphic novellas, Yang and Kim explore the power of dreams and, more to the point, the power of waking up." (Horn Book)

★ **Level** up. Gene Luen Yang; [illustrated by Thien Pham].. First Second Books 2011 160p. Illustration
Grades: 10 11 12 Adult   **741.5; Fic**
1. Angels — Graphic novels; 2. Bildungsromans — Graphic novels; 3. Chinese Americans — Graphic novels; 4. College students — Graphic novels
978-1-59643-235-2, $15.99

LC 2010-36257

"Pham's watercolor artwork, mostly in muted pallet, is a perfect match for Yang's story. This gentle tale of loss and redemption, family responsibility, and dreams might not be to all teens' tastes (especially by the end), but the mix of fantasy and realism will please the right crowd." Voice Youth Advocates

★ **Prime** baby. [by] Gene Luen Yang, colors by Derek Kirk Kim. First Second Books 2010 56p. Illustration
Grades: 6 7 8 9 10 11 12   **741.5; Fic**
1. Extraterrestrial beings — Graphic novels; 2. Graphic novels; 3. Humorous graphic novels; 4. Science fiction graphic novels; 5. Siblings — Graphic novels
978-1-59643-612-1, $6.99

Thaddeus K. Fong always preferred to be the center of his family's attention, so the birth of his little sister Maddie has really bothered him. When she's eighteen months old, he notices something about the sounds she makes; her "gaga's" come out in prime numbers. Then his math teacher says that if aliens were ever to try to make contact with humans, it would be through prime numbers. Oh no, Maddie is an intergalactic conduit for invading aliens! Except no one believes Thaddeus. Until Maddie starts burping up strange things that turn out to be little ships for sluglike aliens. They're peaceful missionary types, but that doesn't stop Thaddeus from making them seem hostile. When their parents finally believe Thaddeus, Maddie gets locked up in a research facility. Thaddeus should be ecstatic, his dumb little sister has been put away. So why is he feeling sad? This story was originally serialized in the New York Times magazine and has been printed to preserve the original comic strip format.

"Sf readers who value humor and humanity (not just slam-bang action), Christians, newcomers to graphic novels, and fans of Yang's simultaneously childlike and sophisticated ability to create and maintain tension should all be satisfied by his new book." Booklist

★ **Saints**. by Gene Luen Yang; color by Lark Pien. First Second 2013 170 p.
Grades: 7 8 9 10 11 12 Adult   **741.5**
1. Historical fiction; 2. China — History — Boxer Rebellion, 1899-1901 — Graphic novels
1596436891; 9781596436893, $15.99

LC 2013947228

National Book Award for Young People's Literature: Finalist (2013); Boston Globe-Horn Book Honor: Fiction (2014); Ignatz Nominee: Outstanding Graphic Novel (2014)

This graphic novel, by Gene Luen Yang and Lark Pien, "follows a lonely girl .... Unwanted by her family, Four-Girl isn't even given a proper name until she converts to Catholicism and is baptized by the very same priest who bullies Little Bao's village. Four-Girl, now known as Vibiana, leaves home and finds fulfillment in service to the Church, while Little Bao roams the countryside committing acts of increasing violence as his army grows." (School Library Journal)

"Yang presents a 'diptych' of graphic novels set during China's Boxer Rebellion. Boxers follows Little Bao, who learns to harness the power of ancient gods to fight the spread of Christianity; Saints centers on Four-Girl, who sits squarely on the other side of the rebellion. Yang's characteristic infusions of magical realism, bursts of humor, and distinctively drawn characters make for a compelling read." (Horn Book)

The **Shadow** Hero. story by Gene Luen Yang; art by Sonny Liew; lettering by Janice Chiang. First Second 2014 176 p. Color; Illustration
Grades: 6 7 8 9 10   **741.5**
1. Superheroes — Fiction; 2. Chinese Americans — Fiction; 3. Comic books, strips, etc.
1596436972; 9781596436978, $17.99

This book, by Gene Luen Yang, is cast as "Green Turtle, a 1940s comic book hero.... The Green Turtle is cast as an unlikely 19-year-old young man, Hank, the son of Chinese immigrants who own a grocery store in 1940s America. When his mother is rescued by a superhero, the loving but overbearing woman decides that it's Hank's fate to become a hero himself, and she does everything in her power to push her son in that direction." (School Library Journal)

"Yang and Liew have crafted an origin story for the Green Turtle, a little-known...World War II-era comic superhero created by cartoonist Chu Hing in 1944. Much about the series remains a mystery, as Yang shares in an author's note, but according to rumors Hing wanted his star to be Chinese, and, not surprisingly for the era, his publishers balked at the idea. Now seventy years later, Yang and Liew vindicate the cartoonist by imagining the Green Turtle as 'perhaps...the first Asian American superhero.'" Horn Book

Superman; Volume 1: Before truth. written by Gene Luen Yang; art by John Romita Jr., Klaus Janson, Scott Hanna; color by Dean White, Wil Quintana, Tomeu Morey, Leonardo Olea, Blond, Hi-Fi; letters by Rob Leigh, Travis Lanham; collection cover art by John Romita Jr., Klaus Janson,. DC Comics 2016 224 p. Color; Illustration
Grades: 9 10 11 12 Adult   **741.5**
1. Superhero comic books, strips, etc.; 2. Superman (Fictional character)
9781401259815, $22.99

LC 2015049454

"Superman is going through some changes. First, there's his new 'solar flare' power, which releases tremendous amounts of energy but leaves him functionally human...for 24 hours. But an even bigger change is coming. A new company called Hordr has sprung up, and its business is secrets. If you have one that you want to keep hidden, Hordr can control you-and no one has a bigger secret than Clark Kent." (Publisher's note)

"Yang's creative script deftly merges modern technology with super-pseudoscience, and introduces a new, intriguing character of color to the DCU." Pub Wkly

Yang, Jeff

Secret identities: the Asian American superhero anthology. Jeff Yang, Parry Shen, Keith Chow, Jerry Ma. New Press 2009 194p. Illustration

Grades: 9 10 11 12 Adult   741.5; Fic

1. Asian Americans — Graphic novels; 2. Graphic novels; 3. Superhero graphic novels

978-1-59558-398-7, $21.95

LC 2009-1536

Yang, Shen, Chow, and coeditor Jerry Ma have put together a collection of twenty-six stories by Asian American creators about Asian American superheroes. The book is divided into sections: War and Remembrance, Many Masks, When Worlds Collide, Girl Power, Ordinary Heroes, and From Headline to Hero. The Preface, the Prologue, all section introductions, and the Epilogue, are all done in comic book format. Creators include Gene Luen Yang, Greg Pak, Dustin Nguyen, Kazu Kibuishi, Cliff Chiang, Christine Norrie, and many more. Some stories deal with the Nisei soldiers of the 100th Battalion/442nd Regimental Combat Team during World War II, others confront the idea that the Asian character can only be the sidekick, still others explore the stereotypical attitudes of some Americans toward Asian Americans. The book includes some violence and some harsh language.

Yazawa, Ai

Nana, Volume One. story & art by Ai Yazawa; [English adaptation, Allison Wolfe; translation, Koji Goto]. Viz Media/Shojo Beat 2006 un Illustration

Grades: 11 12 Adult   741.5; Fic

1. Graphic novels; 2. Josei manga; 3. Manga; 4. Romance graphic novels; 5. Shojo manga

978-1-4215-0108-6, $8.99

Two young women, both named Nana, both the same age, but different in personalities, each want to move to Tokyo. Nana Komatsu is somewhat immature, and so far her life has revolved around men. Nana Osaki is a punk rock vocalist with an attitude to match; she wants to make her band a success. Nana K wants to be with her friends even if she failed all the college entrance exams; she also wants to become more self-reliant. The two Nanas meet on the train to Tokyo, then meet again when looking for an affordable apartment. The series includes considerable strong language and sexual situations.

Volume 1 of 21

Paradise Kiss; Volume 1. Ai Yazawa. Vertical 2012 258 p. Illustration

Grades: 11 12 Adult   741.5; Fic

1. Josei manga; 2. High school students — Japan — Comic books, strips, etc.; 3. Teenage girls — Comic books, strips, etc.

1935654713; 9781935654711, $19.95

In this book, by Ai Yazawa, "Yukari is a...high school senior...studying for her college entrance exams. Sadly the prospect of subjecting herself to a meaningless dull life leaves her feeling depressed.... Yukari begins to ignore her courses and...hang out with a group of fashion design students. But what Yukari doesn't know is that this circle is known as Paradise Kiss, and they are run by...young designers already making their mark on the Asian scene." (Publisher's note)

Volume 1 of 3

YKids

Einstein. Youngjin Singapore 2007 146p. Illustration

Grades: 3 4 5 6 7 8 9   741.5; 92

1. Biographical graphic novels; 2. Graphic novels; 3. Einstein, Albert, 1879-1955

978-981-05-4944-2, $14.95

A genius of enormous accomplishment, Albert Einstein overcame numerous hardships-separation from his family, religious discrimination, and the political turmoil of his day-to become one of the greatest minds of the 20th century. As a young boy, Einstein's unending curiosity and constant questioning earned him the reputation of being unfocused and inattentive. This book uses a framing story of a young boy and a robot from the future going back in time to examine the lives of great people and find the one value that will help their situation; from Einstein, they take his insatiable curiosity.

Part of the Great Figures in History series.

Gandhi. Youngjin Singapore 2007 148p. Illustration

Grades: 3 4 5 6 7 8 9   741.5; 92

1. Biographical graphic novels; 2. Graphic novels; 3. Gandhi, Mohandas Karamcand, 1869-1948; 4. Gandhi, Mohandas Karamcand, 1869-1948 — graphic novels

978-981-05-4945-9, $14.95

A champion of the poor and lower classes, Mahatma Gandhi helped transform India into the democracy it is today. Young readers of this manga-style biography will learn about the key historical events during this time and how the peaceful efforts of one humble man affected enormous change. This book presents a time line of Gandhi's life-from his roots in a middle-class family in India, to his law-school education in England, his experiences with discrimination, and his key role as a leader in the Indian independence movement. Each volume in the Great Figures in History series focuses on a key value personified by the biographical subject; in Gandhi's case, it's courage.

Part of the Great Figures in History series.

Yoshida, Tatsuo

Speed Racer: Mach go go go vol. 1 & 2, 2v. by Tatsuo Yoshida; [translation: Joyce Aurino]. Digital Manga Publishing 2008 Illustration

Grades: 7 8 9 10 11 12 Adult   741.5; Fic

1. Adventure graphic novels; 2. Automobile racing — Graphic novels; 3. Graphic novels; 4. Manga; 5. Shonen manga

978-1-56970-731-9, set $39.95

This two-volume set reprints the original Speed Racer manga in its entirety, released for the 40th anniversary of Speed Racer. All the characters are here: Speed, Pops, Sparky, Mom, Trixie, Spritle, Chim Chim, and the mysterious Racer X. Readers will learn how Pops had to set out on his own, how Speed became a professional racecar driver in order to help finance Pops design the special, 12 cylinder Mach 5 engine. In addition to racing, Speed has to deal with people who try to steal Pops' engine plans, rival racers who'll try any cheating tactic to win, and try to figure out who Racer X is. While the animated television series was fine for children to watch, this manga includes violent action that makes it more suitable for teen readers. A note about the title: in Japanese, "go" means "5."

Yoshizumi, Wataru

Ultra Maniac Vol. 1. Viz Media/Shojo Beat 2005 184p. Illustration

Grades: 5 6 7 8 9 10   741.5; Fic

1. Graphic novels; 2. Humorous graphic novels; 3. Manga; 4. Romance graphic novels; 5. Shojo manga

1-59116-917-8, $8.99

Shy Ayu Tateishi has just made a new friend at school. But this new friend, much to her surprise, is no ordinary classmate. Nina Sakura may look like a normal middle school girl, but she's got a big secret. She's a witch. Or, rather, she's studying to be a witch. And, apparently, she's not doing her homework. Her spells are devastating in their ineffectiveness and often result in the most embarrassing situations for poor Ayu. But things wouldn't be so bad if Nina's sorcery didn't make Ayu look silly in front of the one boy she secretly adores. All she wants is a simple love potion. What she gets, however, is a new best friend who almost flunked out of witch school. This is a five-volume manga series.

Young, Keezy
  Taproot: A Story About a Gardener and a Ghost. story and art by Keezy Young; letterer: AW's Tom Napolitano; assistant editor: Hazel Newlevant; editor: Andrea Colvin. Lion Forge 2017 128 p. Illustration
Grades: 10 11 12 Adult   **741.5**
  1. Ghost stories; 2. Future life — Fiction; 3. Gay men — Fiction
1941302467; 9781941302460, $10.99

  In this book, by Keezy Young, "Blue is having a hard time moving on. He's in love with his best friend. He's also dead. Luckily, Hamal can see ghosts, leaving Blue free to haunt him to his heart's content. But something eerie is happening in town, leaving the local afterlife unsettled, and when Blue realizes Hamal's strange ability may be putting him in danger, Blue has to find a way to protect him, even if it means... leaving him." (Publisher's note)

  "There's enough gentle spookiness to give this some edge, but at its heart, it's a beautifully illustrated love story between two brown young men, and that's a refreshing change of pace." Booklist

Youngquist, Jeff
  Spider-Man: Saga of the Sandman. Marvel Entertainment 2007 176p. Illustration
Grades: 7 8 9 10 11 12 Adult   **741.5; Fic**
  1. Graphic novels; 2. Spider-Man (Fictional character); 3. Superhero graphic novels; 4. Fantastic Four (Fictional characters); 5. Hulk (Fictional character)
978-0-7851-2497-9, $19.99

  It was no day at the beach when criminal Flint Marko was mutated into one of Marveldom's most versatile villains. This book recounts his origins and some of the best battles between Sandman, Spider-Man, the Fantastic Four and the Hulk.

Yukimura, Makoto
  Planetes Omnibus 1. by Makoto Yukimura. Random House Inc 2015 528 p.
Grades: 10 11 12 Adult
  1. Space colonies — Fiction; 2. Outer space — Exploration — Fiction; 3. Science fiction graphic novels; 4. Space debris — Fiction
1616559217; 9781616559212, $19.99

  In this book, by Makoto Yukimura, "It's the 2070s, and mankind has conquered space, making interplanetary travel possible and igniting the imaginations of the world. It's also vastly increased the amount of dangerous space debris, and someone has to clean it up. Hachimaki, Yuri, and Fee are a crew on that beat, each with their own goals, tendencies, and personal problems." (Publisher's note)
  Originally published in the U.S. by Tokyopop in 4 volumes; Volume 1 of 2

Yumi, Kiiro
  ★ **Library** wars, vol. 1: love & war. story and art by Kiiro Yumi; original concept by Hiro Arikawa; [English translation & adaptation, Kinami Watabe]. Viz Media/Shojo Beat 2010 166p. Illustration
Grades: 9 10 11 12 Adult   **741.5; Fic**
  1. Censorship — Graphic novels; 2. Graphic novels; 3. Librarians — Graphic novels; 4. Manga; 5. Shojo manga
978-1-4215-3488-6, $9.99

  In Japan of the near future, the federal government passes the Media Betterment Act, and the Media Betterment Committee goes on book hunts to destroy any "unsuitable" book. The libraries strike back with the Library Defense Force, a paramilitary organization dedicated to protecting the freedom to read. Iku Kasahara started to work for libraries and wants more than anything to join the Library Defense Force; she's physically very capable, but drill instructor Sergeant Dojo doesn't seem to like her very much and pushes her very hard. Iku must improve her library skills as well as her physical skills if she's to work effectively as a soldier librarian.

  This book "delivers an appealing, determined female lead in the midst of an intriguing war on censorship being waged in bookstores and libraries." SLJ
  First published 2008 in Japan; Volume 1 of 14

Yun, Mi-Kyung
  Bride of the water god, vol. 1. Dark Horse Comics 2007 186p. Illustration
Grades: 8 9 10 11 12 Adult   **741.5**
  1. Fantasy graphic novels; 2. Graphic novels; 3. Romance graphic novels
978-1-59307-849-2, $9.95

  Soah's impoverished, drought-stricken village sacrifices her to the Water God Habaek in hopes of getting rain. Instead of dying, Soah finds herself in the land of the gods, and she meets Habaek, who is a young boy. What she doesn't know (but the reader does) is that he takes the form of an adult man at night. She's supposed to be Habaek's bride, but so far she's just an outsider who doesn't belong anywhere. This is sunjeong manwha the Korean equivalent of shojo manga.

Yune, Tommy
  Speed Racer & Racer X: the origins collection. IDW Publishing 2008 un Illustration
Grades: 8 9 10 11 12 Adult   **741.5; Fic**
  1. Adventure graphic novels; 2. Automobile racing — Graphic novels; 3. Graphic novels; 4. Racer, Speed (Fictional character)
978-1-60010-211-0, $19.99

  In 1999, Wildstorm Productions relaunched Speed Racer with a three-part origins story; it was successful enough to launch another three-part story telling the origins of Speed's brother, Racer X (come on, it's not a spoiler, everyone but the Racer family knows this). IDW Publishing has collected the stories into this volume. Here is the story of how Speed becomes the driver of the Mach 5, designed by Pops Racer, and here is the story of why Rex Racer left the family, how he "died," and Racer X was born from the wreckage. There is a lot of racing action, some violence, and some mild fan service.

Zahler, Thomas F.
  ★ **Love** and capes, vol. 1: do you want to know a secret?. story and art by Thomas F. Zahler. IDW Publishing 2008 160p. Illustration
Grades: 8 9 10 11 12 Adult   **741.5; Fic**
  1. Graphic novels; 2. Humorous graphic novels; 3. Romance graphic novels; 4. Superhero graphic novels
978-1-60010-275-2, $19.99

  Independent bookseller Abby falls in love with her accountant, Mark; then he confesses to her that he's the superpowered crime-fighter, the Crusader. How does one have a romantic relationship with a superhero? Even without meaning to do it, Abby gives away Mark's secret to her sister Charlotte. Oops. So begins a "heroically super situation comedy" in which Abby feels she's competing against the beautiful Amazonia (Mark's superpowered ex-girlfriend), not to mention Mark's over-protective mother, and Mark has to deal with Abby's obnoxious brother Quincy, who thinks Mark is a wimp.
  Volume 1 of 4

  ★ **Love** and capes, vol. 2: going to the chapel. IDW Publishing 2010 192p. Illustration
Grades: 8 9 10 11 12 Adult   **741.5; Fic**

1. Graphic novels; 2. Humorous graphic novels; 3. Romance graphic novels; 4. Superhero graphic novels
978-1-60010-680-4, $19.99

Independent bookstore owner Abby and accountant Mark Spencer, who is also the superhero called the Crusader, have fallen deeply and completely in love. Which is wonderful, except Mark can't quite seem to figure out how to propose to Abby and almost blows it. When he gets over that hurdle, more problems crop up. For one thing, Abby wants the PERFECT wedding dress. Then, a super villain impersonates Mark and almost destroys their relationship. Abby has to find a new bookstore employee when her sister Charlotte gets the chance to go back to college in Paris. France. Abby decides she needs to understand what Mark goes through as a superhero, and she gets superpowers, and a new identity, only to learn that it's far more difficult, and tragic, than she ever imagined. And then, on the eve of the wedding, another super villain strikes, this time changing history, and only Abby has the power to put things right again, which she'll have to do if she wants to marry Mark. This story has superhero action, romance, comedy, drama, romance...the only content that might bother some people happens when Abby and Amazonia, Mark's superhero ex-girlfriend, get drunk and bond together.

Courtesy of IDW Publishing

Zdarsky, Chip
   Jughead; Volume 1. story by Chip Zdarsky; art by Erica Henderson; coloring by Andre Szymanowicz; lettering by Jack Morelli; editor, Mike Pellerito. Archie Comics 2016 168 p. Color; Illustration
Grades: 7 8 9 10 11 12 Adult   741.5; Fic
   1. School stories — Graphic novels; 2. Andrews, Archie (Fictional character); 3. Jones, Jughead (Fictional character)
1627388931; 9781627388931, $19.99
Eisner Award: Best Humor Publication (2017)
   "Riverdale High provides a quality education and quality hot lunches, but when one of those is tampered with, JUGHEAD JONES swears vengeance! Well, I mean, he doesn't 'swear.' This is still Archie Comics after all." (Publisher's note)
   "Zdarsky captures the spirit of the well-known cast while injecting modern sensibilities through dialogue and attitude. Henderson's energetic and dynamic art connects brilliantly with the humor and pace of each chapter. The far-fetched plot befits Jughead's personality, complete with robots, pirates, and lots of food." SLJ
   Volume 1 of 2

Zimmerman, Dwight Jon
   The **hammer** and the anvil: Frederick Douglass, Abraham Lincoln, and the end of slavery in America. Dwight Jon Zimmerman; illustrated by Wayne Vansant; foreword by James M. McPherson; editorial consultant, Craig Symonds. Hill and Wang 2012 ix, 150 p. Color illustration; Color; Map
Grades: 10 11 12 Adult   973.7092; 92; 741.5
   1. African American abolitionists — Biography — Comic books, strips, etc; 2. Antislavery movements — United States — History — 19th century — Comic books, strips, etc; 3. Presidents — United States — Biography — Comic books, strips, etc; 4. Douglass, Frederick, 1818-1895 — Comic books, strips, etc; 5. Lincoln, Abraham, 1809-1865 — Comic books, strips, etc; 6. Presidents — United States — Biography; 7. Abolitionists — Biography
0809053586; 9780809053582, $24.95; 9780809053599, $15.95; 0809053594

LC 2011032361
   This book presents a "graphic biography" of "Abraham Lincoln and Frederick Douglass. For both men, the book...show[s] the challenges that they faced as children, their efforts to overcome difficult circumstances, and the very real impact both men had on shaping the social and political consciousness of their times. It draws parallels between the humble circumstances of their early years...[and] look[s] at the difficulties both men faced and what motivated them." (Publishers Weekly)
   Includes bibliographical references.; A novel graphic from Hill and Wang.

Zubkavich, Jim
   Skullkickers: 1000 Opas and a dead body. writer/creator, Jim Zub; line art, Edwin Huang and Chris Stevens; colors, Misty Coates and Chris Stevens. Image Comics 2011 un Illustration
Grades: 9 10 11 12 Adult   741.5; Fic
   1. Adventure graphic novels; 2. Fantasy graphic novels; 3. Graphic novels; 4. Humorous graphic novels
978-1-60706-366-7, $9.99
   "Over here you've got an axe-wielding dwarf brawler, and over there you've got a gun-slinging giant, who's clearly the brains of the operation. These two nameless mercenaries witness an assassination, then take the job of recovering the royal victim's stolen corpse. An escape from town guards, a poisoning, one dream prophecy, a demon-possessed leg, and dozens of splattery battles later, and volume 1 ends with both a hard-won ale and a tantalizing cliff-hanger." (Booklist)
   First published in magazine form as Skullkickers #1-5; Volume 1 of 6

Aaron, Jason

The **Other** Side. writer, Jason Aaron; artist, Cameron Stewart; colorist, David McCaig; letterer, Pat Brosseau; introduction by Dale Dye. DC Comics/Vertigo 2007 144p. Illustration
Grades: 12 Adult   **741.5; Fic**
  1. Graphic novels; 2. Vietnam War, 1961-1975 — Graphic novels
9781534302228; 978-1-4012-1350-3, $12.99

Billy Everette from Alabama gets drafted into the Marines in 1967; in North Vietnam, Vo Binh Dai volunteers to serve in the People's Army of Vietnam. The book follows these two young men through their training and their journey towards an inevitable confrontation. Billy starts seeing horrifying ghost images of dead soldiers in various stages of decay, and he hears his rifle telling him to kill. Vo maintains a strong sense of patriotism despite the hardships of the march south to find the war. They both end up at Khe Sanh just after the Tet Offensive in February 1968.

Anyone who has seen such movies as "Full Metal Jacket" or "We Were Soldiers Once" will know what to expect in this book; the language is full of expletives and the battle scenes are brutal. Aaron and Stewart bring the harsh reality of war to readers 40 years after the fact.

Originally published as The Other Side issues #1-5.

Southern Bastards; Volume 1: here was a man. by Jason Aaron, illustrated by Jason LaTour. Image Comics 2014 128 p. Color; Illustration
Grades: Adult   **741.5; Fic**
  1. Vigilantes — Graphic novels; 2. Alabama — Fiction; 3. Crime — Graphic novels
1632150166; 9781632150165, $9.99
Eisner Award: Best Continuing Series (2016)

"What does old Earl Tubb do when he returns home to Craw County, Ala., only to find the place a veritable criminal fiefdom run by Euless Boss, the local high school football coach? Why, pick up the stick helpfully cleaved by lightning from a tree growing out of his daddy's grave and start meting out justice just like his father, the old sheriff, did." (Publishers Weekly)

Volume 1 of an ongoing series

Star Wars; Volume 1: Skywalker strikes. writers, Jason Aaron; artist, John Cassaday; colorist, Laura Martin; letterer, Chris Eliopoulos. Marvel Enterprises 2015 160 p. Color; Illustration
Grades: 8 9 10 11 12 Adult   **741.5**
  1. Star Wars — Graphic novels
0785192131; 9780785192138, $19.99

"Luke Skywalker and the ragtag rebel band opposing the Galactic Empire are fresh off their biggest victory yet — the destruction of the massive Death Star. But the Empire's not toppled yet! Join Luke, Princess Leia, Han Solo, Chewbacca, C-3PO, R2-D2 and the rest of the Rebel Alliance as they fight for freedom against the evil of Darth Vader and his master, the Emperor!" (Publisher's note)

Volume 1 of an ongoing series

Thor; Volume 1: the goddess of thunder. writer, Jason Aaron; artists, Russell Dauterman (#1-4) & Jorge Molina (#5); color artists, Matthew Wilson (#1-4) & Jorge Molina (#5); letterer, VC's Joe Sabino; cover art, Russell Dauterman & Frank Martin. Marvel Enterprises 2015 136 p. Color; Illustration
Grades: 9 10 11 12 Adult   **741.5**
  1. Women superheroes; 2. Thor (Fictional character)
0785192387; 9780785192381, $24.99

In this book, by Jason Aaron, illustrated by Russell Dauterman, "Mjolnir lies on the moon, unable to be lifted! Something dark has befallen the God of Thunder, leaving him unworthy for the first time ever! But when Frost Giants invade Earth, the hammer will be lifted — and a mysterious woman...the mighty Thor! Who is this new Goddess of Thunder? Not even Odin knows...but she may be Earth's only hope against the Frost Giants!" (Publisher's note)

"When the classic Thor is no longer righteous enough to wield his hero-making mallet, the only person worthy enough to take up the mantle is...well, you don't find out in this volume. But the point is that it's a lady, and she's every bit up to the task, as she proves by taking on bloodthirsty Frost Giants, the Minotaur CEO of megacorporation Roxxon, and the Dark Elf Malekith." Booklist

Contains material originally published in magazine form as Thor #1-5.; Volume 1 of 2

Abadzis, Nick

★ **Laika**. First Second Books 2007 205p. Illustration
Grades: 5 6 7 8 9 10 11 12 Adult   **741.5; Fic**
  1. Graphic novels; 2. Soviet Union — History — 1953-1991 — Graphic novels; 3. Space flight — Graphic novels
1-59643-101-6; 978-1-59643-101-0

LC 2006-51907

Laika was the abandoned puppy destined to become Earth's first space traveler. This is her journey. Along with Laika, there is Korolev, once a political prisoner and now a driven engineer at the top of the Soviet space program, and Yelena, the lab technician responsible for Laika's health and life. The book depicts the dedication and struggles of the scientists and technicians who worked in the Soviet space program, based on research Abadzis did before writing this book. The book includes a bibliography of books and websites.

"Abadzis's tear-inducing and solidly researched graphic novel treatment of Laika's surpassingly tragic story is a standout." Publ Wkly

Abel, Jessica

★ **Drawing** words & writing pictures: making comics: from manga, graphic novels, and beyond. [by] Jessica Abel & Matt Madden. First Second Books 2008 xxi, 282 p. Illustration
Grades: 9 10 11 12 Adult   **741.5**
  1. Cartooning — Technique; 2. Comic books, strips, etc. — Authorship; 3. Drawing — Technique; 4. Graphic novels — Authorship
1596431318; 9781596431317, $34.99

LC 2007044125

Authors Jessica Abel and Matt Madden present "a course on comic creation — for college classes or for independent study — that centers on storytelling and concludes with making a finished comic. With chapters on lettering, story structure, and panel layout, the fifteen lessons offered — each complete with homework, extra credit activities and supplementary reading suggestions — provide a solid introduction for people interested in making their own comics." (Publisher's note)

This "book offers step-by-step entry into a complicated series of skills in a nonscary and approachable way." Libr J

Includes bibliographical references (p. 261-265) and index

La Perdida. Jessica Abel. Pantheon 2006 272p. Illustration
Grades: 11 12 Adult   **741.5; Fic**
  9780375714719; 9781594973673; 0-375-42365-6, 34.95

"Carla, an American estranged from her Mexican father, heads to Mexico City to 'find herself.' She crashes with a former fling, Harry, who has been drinking his way through the capital in the great tradition of his heroes, William S. Burroughs and Jack Kerouac. Harry is good-humored about Carla's reappearance on his doorstep — until he realizes that Carla, who spends her days soaking in the city, exploring Frida Kahlo's house, and learning Spanish, has no intention of leaving." (Publisher's note)

★ **Life** sucks. [text by] Jessica Abel, Gabe Soria; [art by] Warren Pleece; coloring by Hilary Sycamore. First Second Books 2008 186p. Illustration

Grades: 10 11 12 Adult   **741.5; Fic**
   1. Graphic novels; 2. Horror graphic novels; 3. Humorous graphic novels; 4. Romance graphic novels; 5. Vampires — Graphic novels
978-1-59643-107-2, $19.95; 1-59643-107-5

Anyone who thinks the vampire life is all romantic and ethereal better have another think. Dave can tell them, it sucks. He's the night manager for a convenience store, and he's a vampire, "made" by his boss (master), Radu. He's not the only one; in their neighborhood, most of the shops are owned by vampires who make their night managers vampires. Dave can't make himself drink from humans, so he drinks bottled blood. His roommate is human but tolerant. Then Dave sees the perfect girl, Rosa, one of the goth vampire groupies who hangs out in the neighborhood. However, surfer/slacker Wes, whom Dave replaced as the night manager, also has his eye on Rosa, and Wes isn't above killing to get his way. The book includes some violence (including the tearing off of one girl's head), and some harsh language.

"Warren Pleece's art marvelously captures the humor of the mundane that lends the book's crew of late-night wage-slave vamps believability and energy. A really fun read!? Booklist

Mastering comics: drawing words & writing pictures continued. by Jessica Abel and Matt Madden. First Second 2012 xvii, 318 p. Illustration; Color

Grades: 9 10 11 12 Adult   **741.5**
   1. Cartooning — Technique; 2. Comic books, strips, etc. — Technique; 3. Drawing; 4. Cartoonists
1596436174; 9781596436176, $34.99

                              LC 2011037023

Jessica Abel's book "Mastering Comics," written with her husband Matt Madden, is a "course of study for the budding cartoonist. Covering advanced topics such as page composition, coloring, and file formatting, [the book] is a vital companion to the introductory content of the first volume" entitled "Drawing Words & Writing Pictures." (Publisher's note)

Abirached, Zeina
   I remember Beirut. Zeina Abirached. Graphic Universe 2014 96 p. Illustration; Map

Grades: 8 9 10 11 12 Adult
741.5; 92
   1. Abirached, Zeina, 1981-; 2. Lebanon — History — 20th century; 3. Children and war; 4. War
1467738220; 9781467738224, $29.27
                LC 2013047112

In this graphic memoir, Zeina Abirached "reveals numerous details from her childhood in Beirut during the war from 1975 to 1990 war. 'I remember' is a recurring phrase and provides a personal frame of reference for the effect of war on kids. Some are simple childhood memories.... Inclusion of...maps and diagrams orient the reader and provide additional perspective." (Kirkus Reviews)

Courtesy of Lerner Publishing Group

"The blocky, naive-style pictures quietly evoke wartime fears in ways the words simply cannot — bullet holes in the sides of cars, rubble in the streets, her father's eyebrows indicating increasing sadness at the heartbreaking state of a formerly vital market." Booklist

Abouet, Marguerite
   ★ **Aya:** life in Yop City. by Marguerite Abouet and Clément Oubrerie; translated by Helge Dascher. Drawn & Quarterly 2012 96 p. Color; Illustration

Grades: 10 11 12 Adult   **741.5/944; 741.5**
   1. Africa — Fiction; 2. Friendship — Fiction
1770460829; 9781770460829, $24.95

This book, by Marguerite Abouet and Clément Oubrerie, "is the story of the studious and clear-sighted nineteen-year-old Aya, her easygoing friends Adjoua and Bintou, and their meddling relatives and neighbors. It's...[an] account of the simple pleasures and private troubles of everyday life in Yop City." (Publisher's note)
   Followed by Aya: Love in Yop City

   Aya: love in Yop City. by Marguerite Abouet and Clement Oubrerie; translatied by Helge Dascher. Drawn & Quarterly 2013 328 p. Color illustration

Grades: 10 11 12 Adult   **741.5; Fic**
   1. Graphic novels — Côte d'Ivoire; 2. Teenage girls — Côte d'Ivoire — Comic books, strips, etc; 3. Côte d'Ivoire — Comic books, strips, etc; 4. Ivory Coast — Graphic novels; 5. Nineteen seventies
1770460926; 9781770460928, $24.95
                LC 2012545664

This graphic novel, written by Marguerite Abouet and Clément Oubrerie, comprises the final three chapters of the 'Aya' story,...a lighthearted story about life in the Ivory Coast during the 1970s, a particularly thriving and wealthy time in the country's history. When a professor tries to take advantage of Aya, her plans to become a doctor are...shaken, and she vows to take revenge on [him]." The book includes "recipes, guides to understanding Ivorian slang, street sketches, and concluding remarks from Abouet explaining...social milieu." (Publisher's note)

Aguirre-Sacasa, Roberto
   ★ **Afterlife** with Archie: Escape from Riverdale. story by Roberto Aguirre-Sacasa; artwork by Francesco Francavilla; lettering by Jack Morelli. Archie Comic Publications 2014 160 p. Color; Illustration (Afterlife with Archie)

Grades: 10 11 12 Adult   **741.5; Fic**
   1. Dogs — Fiction; 2. Zombies — Fiction; 3. Witches — Fiction; 4. Andrews, Archie (Fictional character)
1619889080; 9781619889088, $17.99
                LC 2014430277

In this book, by Roberto Aguirre-Sacasa, "[w]hen Jughead's beloved pet Hot Dog is killed in a hit and run, Jughead turns to the only person he knows who can help bring back his furry best friend-Sabrina the Teenage Witch. Using dark, forbidden magic, Sabrina is successful and Hot Dog returns to the land of the living. But he's not the same... and soon, the darkness he brings back with him from beyond the grave begins to spread." (Publisher's note)

"Not parody but serious drama, this graphic novel casts off the typical Archie comic lightheartedness and goes deep into the gut.... Paired with Francavilla's dead-on illustrations, the excellent writing from Aguirre-Sacasa...brings constant surprises while confronting the dilemma of remaining humane through crisis." LJ
   Volume 1 of an ongoing series

   Chilling adventures of Sabrina; Book one: The crucible. story by Roberto Aguirre-Sacasa; artwork by Robert Hack; lettering by Jack Morelli. Archie Comic Publications, Inc. 2016 160 p. Color; Illustration

Grades: 10 11 12 Adult   **741.5; Fic**
   1. Comic books, strips, etc. — United States; 2. Sabrina the Teenage Witch (Fictitious character) — Comic books, strips, etc; 3. Witches — Comic books, strips, etc

1627389873; 9781627389877, $17.99

LC 2016288136

"On the eve of her sixteenth birthday, the young sorceress Sabrina Spellman finds herself at a crossroads, having to choose between an unearthly destiny and her mortal boyfriend, Harvey. But a foe from her family's past has arrived in Greendale, Madame Satan, and she has her own deadly agenda." (Publisher's note)

Volume 1 of an ongoing series

Civil War: Peter Parker, Spider-Man. Marvel Entertainment 2007 un Illustration

Grades: 9 10 11 12 Adult   **741.5; Fic**

1. Graphic novels; 2. Spider-Man (Fictional character); 3. Superhero graphic novels

0-7851-2189-7, $17.99

The Civil War has begun, sides have been chosen. Spider-Man chose to unmask himself to the whole world, and now everyone knows he's Peter Parker. Every action has consequences, but for Peter, will he pay, or will his loved ones pay?

Ahmed, Saladin

Black Bolt; Volume 1: hard time. Saladin Ahmed, writer; Christian Ward with Frazer Irving (#5), artists; VC's Clayton Cowles, letterer. Marvel Enterprises 2017 136 p. Color; Illustration

Grades: 10 11 12 Adult   **741.5; Fic**

1. Superheroes — Fiction; 2. Good and evil — Fiction; 3. Prisons — Fiction

1302907328; 9781302907327, $17.99

Hugo Finalist: Best Graphic Story (2018); Eisner Award: Best New Series (2018)

This first volume in the Black Bolt series "begins with Black Bolt...imprisoned?! Where exactly is he? Why has he been jailed? And who could be powerful enough to hold the uncanny Black Bolt? The answers to both will shock you — and Black Bolt as well! For if he is to learn the truth, he must first win a fight to the death with a fellow inmate — the Absorbing Man!" (Publisher's note)

Ahrens, Lois

The **Real** cost of prisons comix. [edited by] Lois Ahrens. PM Press 2008 72 p. Illustration

Grades: Adult

365; 741.5

1. Prisoners — Social aspects — United States — Comic books, strips, etc; 2. Prisoners — United States — Comic books, strips, etc; 3. Prisons — Social aspects — United States — Comic books, strips, etc; 4. Prisons — United States — Comic books, strips, etc

1604860340; 9781604860344, $14.95; 9781604861747; 9781604861761

Courtesy of PM Press

LC 2008929092

This nonfiction graphic novel, edited by Lois Ahrens, "provides a crash course in what drives mass incarceration, the human and community costs, and how to stop the numbers from going even higher. This volume collects the three comic books published by the Real Cost of Prisons Project." (Publisher's note)

Includes bibliographical references

Aihara, Miki

Tokyo Boys & Girls Volume 1. story and art by Miki Aihara; [English adaptation, Shaenon Garrity; translation, JN Productions]. Viz Media/Shojo Beat 2005 200p. Illustration

Grades: 10 11 12 Adult   **741.5; Fic**

1. Graphic novels; 2. Manga; 3. Romance graphic novels; 4. Shojo manga

1-4215-0020-5, $8.99

Mimori Kosaka's dream comes true when she's accepted to the Meidai Attached High School and gets to wear their super-fashionable uniform. The school year starts off well when Mimori befriends the beautiful Nana, but things quickly turn sour for her when she is chosen to be the class representative. Through a series of unfortunate events, she finds herself the focus of attention by three boys and her teachers, for all the wrong reasons. Mimori is reunited with Atsushi, a boy she knew in elementary school — and it turns out he despises her for allegedly bullying him in their grade school days. In fact, he plans to exact a little revenge. The series includes sexual innuendo, brief sexual situations, and some strong language.

Volume 1 of 5

Akamatsu, Ken

Love Hina: Omnibus 1. by Ken Akamatsu; translated by Satsuki Yamashita; lettered by Hope Donovan. Kodansha Comics 2011 542 p. Illustration

Grades: 11 12 Adult   **741.5**

1. Manga; 2. Shonen manga; 3. Japan — Fiction; 4. Young men — Fiction; 5. Grandmothers — Fiction

1935429477; 9781935429470, $19.99

LC 2011517873

In this book, by Ken Akamatsu, "Keitaro Urashima fails his entrance exams to get into Tokyo University for the second time.... To make things worse, his parents have kicked him out of his house. Fortunately, his grandmother owns the fabulous Hinata Lodge and has agreed to take Keitaro in as caretaker. What he doesn't know is that the lodge is actually a girl's dorm and he's the only guy around!" (Publisher's note)

Originally published in the U.S. by Tokyopop in 14 volumes; First published in 1999 by Kodansha Ltd., Tokyo as: Love Hina vol. 1-3 — Vol. 1, t.p. verso.; Volume 1 of 5

Allison, John

Bad machinery; 1: the case of the team spirit. John Allison; [edited by] James Lucas Jones. Oni Press 2013 112 p. Color; Illustration

Grades: 7 8 9 10 11 12 Adult

741.5

1. Mystery graphic novels; 2. School stories — Graphic novels

1620100843; 9781620100844, $19.99

LC 2012953355

Courtesy of Oni Press

"Shauna. Charlotte. Mildred. Three schoolgirl sleuths. Jack. Linton. Sonny. Three schoolboy investigators. Tackleford. One mid-sized city with a history of countless mysteries. Is there enough room at Griswalds Grammar School for two groups of kid detectives? There better be, because once these kids have set their sights on solving a mystery there's nothing that can derail them. Nothing, except maybe gossip, classwork, new football player cards, torment from siblings, or any number of childhood distractions." (Publisher's note)

"Allison is a triple threat: he plots deftly, draws confidently, and writes dead-on adolescent dialogue. Set in a grammar school in a British working-class community, this first book in his Bad Machinery series —

originally published as a webcomic — has three earnest boys vying against three sharp-tongued girls to solve mysteries." Pub Wkly

Other Bad Machinery volumes are: The case of the good boy (2014); The case of the simple soul (2014); The case of the lonely one (2015); The case of the fire inside (2016); The case of the forked road (2017)

★ **Giant** Days; Volume 1. created & written by John Allison; illustrated by Lissa Treiman; colors by Whitney Cogar; letters by Jim Campbell. Boom! Studios 2015 128 p. Color; Illustration
Grades: 10 11 12 Adult   **741.5; Fic**
1. Women — Fiction; 2. College students — Fiction
1608867897; 9781608867899, $9.99
Eisner Nominee: Best Continuing Series (2016)

"Susan, Esther, and Daisy started at university three weeks ago and became fast friends. Now, away from home for the first time, all three want to reinvent themselves. But in the face of hand-wringing boys, 'personal experimentation,' influenza, mystery-mold, nu-chauvinism, and the willful, unwanted intrusion of 'academia,' they may be lucky just to make it to spring alive." (Publisher's note)

"Allison's pitch-perfect teenage snark is the ideal match for Treiman and Cogar's lush, candy-colored scenes full of rich, character-building detail and marvelous background action. With a masterful hand, they telegraph hilarious visual jokes with the subtlest of cues, like a raised eyebrow or flop of hair, and their figures are full of motion and vitality." Booklist

Volume 1 of an ongoing series

Allred, Mike

Madman; Volume 1. created, written and illustrated by Michael Allred; colors by Laura Allred. Image Comics 2007 268 p. Color; Illustration
Grades: 11 12 Adult   **741.5**
1. Science fiction graphic novels
1582408106; 9781582408101, $24.99

"This volume introduces Madman and the rest of the eccentric citizens of Snap City: mad genius Dr. Flem, the evil Mr. Mondstadt, and Joe, the love of Frank Einstein's life." (Publisher's note)

Volume 1 of 3

Madman atomic comics, vol. 1. created, written and illustrated by Michael Allred; colors by Laura Allred. Image Comics 2008 un
Grades: 10 11 12 Adult   **741.5; Fic**
1. Graphic novels; 2. Madman (Fictional character); 3. Science fiction graphic novels
978-1-58240-916-0, $19.99

Frank Einstein, Madman, undergoes a bizarre, phantasmagorical, existential journey that turns out to be something going on in his subconscious self while he's in a coma. His friends Dr. Flem, Joe (Josephine), and the Atomics hook up Astroman, Frank's robotic "clone," as a technological rescue beacon to lead him through his myriad of fictional personae to his true self, but when they think both Frank and Astroman are dead, they send them up into space in a rocket. Astroman tries to go for help, but his batteries run out, then Frank is rescued by Haley FouFou, who proclaims that he is "one of the Four" who must save the universe. He sends for the Atomics to help him defeat the Crimson King, who has been infected with a cosmic virus and will turn the universe inside out if not stopped. The book is not for casual comics readers, although familiarity with previous Madman comics aren't really necessary to understand this new series. Allred challenges readers with existential discussions and elliptical plotting, and he has fun drawing in the style of many different cartoonists and artists. There's some violence and a little partial nudity, but

little in the way of harsh language ("monkey spit" is the strongest epithet Frank utters).

Volume 1 of 3

Red rocket 7. Image Comics 2008 un Illustration
Grades: 9 10 11 12 Adult   **741.5; Fic**
1. Graphic novels; 2. Rock music — Graphic novels; 3. Science fiction graphic novels
978-1-58240-998-6, $16.99

In a wild science fiction adventure that spans the history of American rock and roll, the humanoid alien known as Red Rocket is left for dead by the villainous Enfinites, but a robotic guardian creates seven clones, each with their own ability. Seven goes on a world-spanning tour of pop music, working with such artists as Little Richard, Elvis Presley, the Beatles, and David Bowie. On his last tour, rock music journalist Lynn Hayes gets mixed up with Seven, his brother clones, and the evil Enfinites who seek to destroy all the clones and Earth, while they're at it. This book was originally published in 1998 by Dark Horse Comics in an 11x11 album size. This new edition is in the vinyl single size and includes bonus material, including an essay from Allred's editor Jamie S. Rich, an introduction by Robert Rodriguez, and an outro by Gerard Way of Chemical Romance. Allred's book predates all the rock 'n' roll graphic novels that have come out in recent years. The book includes some violence and mild language.

Alpert, Abby

Read on — graphic novels: reading lists for every taste. Abby Alpert. Libraries Unlimited 2012 xxi, 177 p.
Grades: Adult   **016**
1. Graphic novels — Bibliography; 2. Libraries — Special collections — Graphic novels; 3. Public libraries — United States — Book lists; 4. Readers' advisory services — United States; 5. Best books
1591588251; 1610691555; 9781591588252, $40; 9781610691550
LC 2011039792

This book on graphic novels by Abby Alpert, part of the Read On series, offers "more than 500 original annotations organized within 70 thematic lists. The broad selection of titles is further categorized by key appeal elements, including story, character, setting, language, and mood, providing unique access points that allow discovery of interests to transcend subject headings in catalogs." (Publisher's note)

"This accessible guide is equally effective for collection building, readers' advisory, or individual perusal, and most public collections will find it perceptive and helpful. Recommended." Booklist

Includes index.

Altman, Steven-Elliot

The **Irregulars** ... In the Service of Sherlock Holmes. written by Steven-Elliot Altman & Michael Reaves; illustrated by Bong Dazo; lettered by Simon Bowland; cover by Ben Templesmith. Dark Horse Comics 2005 un Illustration
Grades: 9 10 11 12 Adult   **741.5; Fic**
1. Graphic novels; 2. Horror graphic novels; 3. Mystery graphic novels
1-59307-303-8, $12.95

A madman stalks the streets of London's Whitechapel slum, leaving a trail of grisly murders in his wake. The police have only one suspect: a prominent and respected physician named John Watson. The master detective Sherlock Holmes, in order to solve the most fantastic mystery of his career and save his greatest friend from the gallows, employs a band of young street urchins to infiltrate the alleys of Whitechapel. They can go everywhere, see everything, overhear everyone. They are the Baker Street Irregulars, and this is the most fantastic and terrifying adventure of their lives, as they uncover an evil unlike anything Sherlock Holmes has ever faced, and end up in a nightmare future. Grisly murders and horrific sights along with some strong language occur.

Amir
★ **Zahra's** paradise. stories by Amir & Khalil; written by Amir; artwork by Khalil. First Second 2011 255 p. Illustration
Grades: 10 11 12 Adult   **741.5**
1. Missing persons — Fiction; 2. Graphic novels; 3. Iran — History — 1979-; 4. Iran — Politics and government
9781596436428 (pa); 1596436425

LC 2011017564
This book is "[s]et in the aftermath of Iran's fraudulent elections of 2009...[and] is the fictional story of the search for Mehdi, a young protestor who has vanished into an extrajudicial twilight zone. What's keeping his memory from being obliterated is not the law. It is the grit and guts of his mother, who refuses to surrender her son to fate, and the tenacity of his brother, a blogger, who fuses tradition and technology to explore and explode the void in which Mehdi has vanished." (Publisher's note)

Andelman, Bob
Will Eisner: A Spirited Life. M Presss 2005 375p. Illustration
Grades: 9 10 11 12 Adult   **92; 741.5**
1. Cartoonists — United States — Biography; 2. Graphic novels; 3. Eisner, Will, 1917-2005; 4. Arts — Biography; 5. Artists — Biography; 6. Cartoonists — Biography; 7. Authors — Biography; 8. Literature — Biography
1-59582-011-6, $14.95

LC 2005026326
Internationally recognized for his genre-busting 1940s art and storytelling style on The Spirit, Will Eisner's greatest legacy may be the graphic novels he championed and created. He was an American master whose work in comics permanently altered the face of global pop culture. This biography explores Eisner's life, detailing a career that spanned 70 years and saw him educate several generations of Army soldiers in the innovative PS Magazine and create the first widely known graphic novel, A Contract with God. Eisner also introduced some of the world's greatest comics art talent: Bob Kane (Batman), Jack Kirby (Fantastic Four), Jules Feiffer, Dave Berg (MAD) and Joe Kubert (Tarzan). And he inspired generations of modern artists and writers, including Frank Miller (Sin City), Robert Crumb, Harlan Ellison, Neil Gaiman (Sandman, American Gods), Brad Bird (The Incredibles), Patrick McDonnell (Mutts) and Art Spiegelman (Maus). A Spirited Life also includes interviews with many of Eisner's contemporaries, such as Alan Moore, Dave Gibbons, Neil Gaiman, Denis Kitchen, Jim Warren, Dave Sim, Denny O'Neil and Stan Lee.

"Michael Chabon contributes a heartfelt introduction to Andelman's first-ever biography of Will Eisner (1917-2005)...Eisner revolutionized the field...from his 1940s stories featuring masked crime fighter the Spirit to his later, pioneering graphic novels but also as businessman and entrepreneur, teacher, mentor, and the inspiration of countless young artists [like Art Spiegelman].... Besides verifying Eisner's impact on nearly every artist who drew comics in his wake, Andelman shows that Eisner's influence extends to such film directors as Spielberg and Tarantino." Booklist

Andersen, Sarah (Sarah C.)
Adulthood is a myth: A 'Sarah's scribbles' collection. Sarah Andersen. Andrews McMeel Pub 2016 112 p. Illustration
Grades: 10 11 12 Adult   **741.5**
1. Youth; 2. Millennials (Persons) — Comic books, strips, etc.; 3. Comic books, strips, etc.
1449474195; 9781449474195, $14.99

This collection of Sarah's Scribbles comics, by Sarah Andersen, "presents many fan favorites plus dozens of all-new comics.... Like the work of fellow Millennial authors Allie Brosh, Grace Helbig, and Gemma Correll, Sarah's frankness on personal issues like body image, self-consciousness, introversion, relationships, and the frequency of bra-washing makes her comics highly relatable and deeply hilarious." (Publisher's note)

"Andersen is an excellent caricaturist — some of her funniest punch lines are panels of wordless, wide-eyed faces. Like so many talented comedians before her, much of her best material comes from the uncomfortable and even embarrassing aspects of life." Pub Wkly

Anderson, Ho Che
King: a comics biography. Fantagraphics 2010 312p. Illustration
Grades: 10 11 12 Adult   **741.5; 92**
1. African Americans — Biography — Graphic novels; 2. African Americans — Civil rights — Graphic novels; 3. Biographical graphic novels; 4. Civil rights activists; 5. Clergy; 6. Graphic novels; 7. Nobel laureates for peace; 8. Nonfiction writers; 9. King, Martin Luther, Jr., 1929-1968
978-1-60699-310-1, $34.99

"Much of the book (packaged nicely with previously unprinted material, sketches, and a somewhat beside-the-point modern-day "prelude" titled Black Dogs) tracks King from his college days in the 1950s to his death, jamming each page with noirishly drawn frames and tightly packed political debates. Though all the great moments of his civil rights battle are here (from the March on Washington to his less-successful housing campaign in Chicago), Anderson doesn't resort to the cheap cinematic trick of success and fadeout. There is more disappointment here than celebration, suffused with the sorrowful sense of a long, long battle just barely begun. A crowning achievement, like the man it portrays." Publ Wkly

First published 2005

Andrews, Mark
Tales of Colossus. Image Comics 2006 un Illustration
Grades: 10 11 12 Adult   **741.5; Fic**
1. Adventure graphic novels; 2. Fantasy graphic novels; 3. Graphic novels
1-58240-591-3, $17.99

A knight, whose soul is trapped inside a metal monster called Colossus, lives out an immortal existence slaying evil creatures. Until one day a twisted, evil paladin wielding enchanted weapons arrives in the Kingdom with his own agenda. Their paths cross in a steel pounding, armor glinting no holds barred battle that will change a Kingdom forever. Set during the times of the Crusades, this book is filled with battles and bloodshed, with some nudity and sexual situations.

Anzai, Nobuyuki
Flame of Recca Volume 1. Viz Media 2003 184p. Illustration
Grades: 10 11 12 Adult   **741.5; Fic**
1. Fantasy graphic novels; 2. Graphic novels; 3. Manga; 4. Martial arts — Graphic novels; 5. Ninja — Graphic novels; 6. Shonen manga
1-59116-066-9, $9.95

Teenager Recca Hanabishi is always up for a good-natured tussle with his friends. That's because he's famous at school and around town for being a super ninja geek. Armed with the power to control flame, Recca suddenly finds himself in an awkward situation. On the day he pledges his undying ninja allegiance to a pretty classmate named Yanagi Sakoshita, a mysterious older woman pops into his life. Is she good? Is she evil? What exactly does she want? And what's the deal with tomboy, Fuko Kirisawa? She's got the power of wind at her command. Does she want to smash

Recca to smithereens, or does she simply want to kiss him? The series includes strong language, nudity, sexual innuendo, and graphic violence.

Volume 1 of 33

Aoyama, Gosho

Case Closed Volume 1. Viz Media 2004 192p. Illustration

Grades: 9 10 11 12 Adult   **741.5; Fic**

1. Graphic novels; 2. Manga; 3. Mystery graphic novels; 4. Shonen manga

1-59116-327-7, $9.95

Precocious high school student Jimmy Kudo used his keen powers of observation and astute intuition to solve mysteries that have left law enforcement officials baffled. Hot on the trail of a suspect, Jimmy is accosted from behind and fed a strange chemical which physically transforms him into a first-grader. Taking on the pseudonym Conan Edogawa (from favorite mystery writers Arthur Conan Doyle and Edgar Allan Poe), he attempts to track down the people who did this to him. But until he finds a cure for his bizarre condition, Jimmy continues to help the police solve their toughest cases, and he lives with his best friend Rachel, who thinks he's Jimmy's cousin, and her private detective father (who gets credit for cracking all the cases). The murder cases are violent and there's a little sexual innuendo; despite Jimmy's little-kid appearance, the stories are not for younger readers.

Appignanesi, Richard

Hamlet. [Richard Appignanesi, text adaptor]; illustrated by Emma Vieceli. Harry N. Abrams/Amulet Books 2007 195p. (Manga Shakespeare)

Grades: 8 9 10 11 12 Adult   **822.3; 741.5**

1. Authors; 2. Dramatists; 3. Graphic novels; 4. Poets; 5. Shakespeare, William, 1564-1616; 6. Shakespeare, William, 1564-1616 — Adaptations

978-0-8109-9324-2, $9.95; 0-8109-9324-4

Shakespeare's classic play of murder and revenge is here adapted into a manga-style graphic novel. It's now set in 2107, after global climate change has devastated the Earth. Appignanesi uses the text of the play and abridges it to fit the pages, while Vieceli's art vigorously carries the story along. The book includes a summary of the plot and a brief biography of Shakespeare.

First published in the United Kingdom

Appollo

★ **Bourbon** Island 1730. by Appollo & Lewis Trondheim; art by Lewis Trondheim; translated by Alexis Siegel. First Second Books 2008 278p. Illustration

Grades: 9 10 11 12 Adult   **741.5; Fic**

1. Adventure graphic novels; 2. Graphic novels; 3. Pirates — Graphic novels; 4. Slavery — Graphic novels

978-1-59643-258-1, $17.95; 1-59643-258-6

LC 2007-46138

On Bourbon Island off the coast of Madagascar, a French ornithologist and his assistant are caught up in an adventure involving slavery, colonialism, and the last days of the great pirates.

"This eccentric but illuminating historical drama...[is] a compelling, engrossing story of people considering whether their cause is worth more to them than their lives." Publ Wkly

Araki, Hirohiko

Rohan at the Louvre. Hirohiko Araki. NBM Pub. 2012 128 p. Color illustration

Grades: Adult   **Fic; 741.5/952; 741.5**

1. Fantasy fiction; 2. Adolescence — Graphic novels; 3. Supernatural graphic novels; 4. Artists — Graphic novels; 5. Seinen manga; 6. Manga

1561636150; 9781561636150, $19.99

LC 2011944475

This fantasy graphic novel "tells of a young man's encounter with a mysterious divorcée who moves into his grandmother's boarding house." As a teen, Rohan's manga art "attract[s] the attention of the beautiful, apparently emotionally disturbed boarder, who tells him of the darkest, most evil painting ever crafted." She disappears after destroying his work. "Ten years later, Rohan...discovers the mysterious evil painting is housed in one of the [Louvre] museum's closed wings." (Publishers Weekly)

Courtesy of NBM Publishing

Asami, Yuu

A.I. revolution volume 1. Go! Comi 2007 216p. Illustration

Grades: 10 11 12 Adult

741.5; Fic

1. Graphic novels; 2. Manga; 3. Robots — Graphic novels; 4. Science fiction graphic novels; 5. Shojo manga

978-1-933617-64-0, $10.99

In the middle of the twenty-first century, household robots are everywhere. Teenage Sui's father runs MG Company, and he develops a very human-looking robot and wants Sui to "educate" it to act human. Naturally, Sui names the robot Vermillion. He has a special ability to communicate with

Courtesy of Go! Comi

computers without needing a physical connection, and it is this ability that makes Vermillion a target for the unscrupulous Dr. Sasaki. When Sui and Vermillion foil him, there's still trouble to come. Soon, another human-looking robot comes from another company; but this robot, whom Sui names Kira, has a secret mission and Vermillion is the target. The series includes some boy love elements, sexual innuendo, and mild violence.

Volume 1 of 14

Asamiya, Kia

Junk: Record of the Last Hero Vol. 1. author, Kia Asamyia; translator, Yoshihiro Watanabe. DrMaster Publications 2006 200p. Illustration

Grades: 10 11 12 Adult

741.5; Fic

1. Graphic novels; 2. Manga; 3. Science fiction graphic novels; 4. Shonen manga

9781597961073, $9.95

Volume 1 of 7

High school student Hiro hasn't

Courtesy of DrMaster Publications

gone back to school ever since a traumatic run-in with local bullies. Then he applies online for a new gadget, and when it arrives and he activates it, he finds himself encased within a powered armor JUNK suit. He starts going after the bullies in nightly rampages, but then he meets someone else with a JUNK suit who doesn't like the way Hiro is abusing his power. When he accidentally destroys his own home and kills his parents, he must learn to fend for himself and to choose to use his power for good or for evil. The legendary manga-ka (manga creator) Kia Asamiya has written this manga, which includes considerable violence.

Asano, Inio

Goodnight Punpun; Volume 1. story and art by Inio Asano. Viz 2016 408 p. Illustration

Grades: Adult   **741.5; Fic**

1. Boys — Graphic novels; 2. Bildungsromans — Graphic novels; 3. Seinen manga

1421586207; 9781421586205, $24.99

"This is Punpun Onodera's coming-of-age story. His parents' marriage is falling apart. His dad goes to jail, and his mom goes to the hospital.... He has a crush on a girl who lives in a weird cult.... Punpun keeps hoping things will get better, but they really, really don't. Meet Punpun Punyama. He's an average kid.... He wants to find some porn. That's what he wants, but what does he get...?" (Publisher's note)

"This coming-of-age story blends fantasy and reality into a strangely compelling tale. Punpun and his family are drawn as birdlike stick figures rather than humans, though no one notices. The humans are all caricatures, which makes their happy smiles and their painful grimaces even more poignant." Booklist

Originally published in Japan in 13 volumes; Volume 1 of 7

Nijigahara Holograph. by Inio Asano; translated by Matt Thorn. Fantagraphics 2014 200 p. Illustration

Grades: Adult   **741.5**

1. Mystery fiction; 2. School children — Fiction; 3. Curses — Fiction; 4. Murder — Fiction

1606995839; 9781606995839, $29.99

In this magna, by Inio Asano, "as butterflies ominously proliferate in town, the rumor of a mysterious creature lurking in the tunnel behind the school spreads among the children. When the body of Arié Kimura's mother is found by this tunnel's entrance,...the legend seems to be confirmed.... In order to appease the wrath of the beast, the children decide to offer it a sacrifice: The unfortunate Arié, whom they believe to be the cause of the curse." (Publisher's note)

"Asano...delivers a dark and twisted psychological horror story that links together a series of characters and tragic events in one timeline that have devastating ramifications for a second timeline. Equal parts beautiful and highly disturbing, this story of love and loss, obsession and vengeance, is sometimes too opaque to be easily understood, but it has the kind of depth and layers that encourage multiple readings." Pub Wkly

Ashby, Ruth

The **great** American documents: Volume 1, 1620-1830. Ruth Ashby; illustrated by Ernie Colón; editorial consultant Russell Motter. Hill and Wang 2014 160 p. Color illustration

Grades: 9 10 11 12 Adult   **973; 741.5**

1. United States — Politics and government — Sources; 2. United States — History — Sources

0809094606; 9780809094608, $40

LC 2013956401

Written by Ruth Ashby and illustrated by Ernie Colón, "'The Great American Documents: Volume 1' introduces as series narrator none other than Uncle Sam, who walks us through twenty essential documents. Each document gets a chapter, in which Uncle Sam explains its key passages, its origins, how it came to be written, and its impact. This graphic primer is an indispensable resource for students and anyone else who wants the facts of American history close at hand." (Publisher's note)

"Colon uses well-designed, full-color panel layouts to eloquently blend charts and other informative graphics with straightforward images of events, clothing, and customs as well as clear, concise metaphors, all with an eye toward promoting a solid understanding of the basic facts and their impact." Booklist

Includes bibliographical references

Askwith, Mark

Silencers. Image Comics 2007 un Illustration

Grades: 11 12 Adult   **741.5; Fic**

1. Graphic novels; 2. Spies — Graphic novels

978-1-58240-728-9, $14.99

Silencers is a compelling look at spies coming to terms with the changing face of espionage in the new world order. When the newest recruit to the Silencers is murdered, his death triggers a mission of betrayal and revenge. Violence and strong language figure in this story that invokes the themes of John LeCarre's books.

Auster, Paul

Paul Auster's City of Glass. Paul Auster; script adaptation, Paul Karasik and David Mazzucchelli; art, David Mazzucchelli. Avon Bks. 1994 129p. Illustration

Grades: 9 10 11 12 Adult   **741; 741.5**

1. Private investigators — Fiction; 2. Auster, Paul — Adaptations

0-380-77108-X; 9780380771080, $12

LC 93-91005

"Auster's acclaimed novel City of Glass, a dreamlike meditation on language and fiction in the form of a detective novel, has been translated into comics form to stunning effect.... This combination story, lecture and literary deconstruction begins when New York City detective novelist Daniel Quinn answers a wrong number. Donning the personas of both the detective he created and his own creator, Auster himself, Quinn attempts to protect a young man, who as a child was kept without light or language for nine years as his lunatic academic father tried to discover 'God's Language.'" (Publishers Weekly)

Axe, David

War is boring: bored stiff, scared to death in the world's worst war zones. David Axe and Matt Bors. New American Library 2010 124p. Illustration

Grades: Adult   **92; 741.5**

1. Journalists — Graphic novels; 2. War — Graphic novels

978-0-451-23011-9, $12.95

"As a correspondent for The Washington Times, C-SPAN and BBC Radio, Axe flew from conflict to conflict, reveling in death, danger, and destruction abroad while, back in D.C., his apartment gathered dust, his plants died, and his relationships withered. War reporting was physically, emotionally, and financially draining-and disillusioning. Loosely based on the web comic of the same name, with extensive new material, War Is Boring takes us to Lebanon and Somalia; to arms bazaars across the United States; to Detroit, as David tries to reconnect with his family-and to Chad, as David attempts to bring attention to the Darfur genocide." (Publisher's note)

Azzarello, Brian

100 bullets: the deluxe edition. Brian Azzarello, writer; Eduardo Risso, artist. DC Comics 2011 456 p. Color illustration

Grades: Adult   **741.5/973**

1. Crime — Comic books, strips, etc

1401232019; 1401250564; 9781401232016, $49.99; 9781401250560, $24.99

LC 2011534002

This graphic novel, by Brian Azzarello, illustrated by Eduardo Risso, "features a mysterious agent named Graves who approaches ordinary citizens and gives them an opportunity to exact revenge on a person who has wronged them. Offering his clients an attaché case containing proof of the deed and a gun, he guarantees his 'clients' full immunity for all of their actions, including murder. This volume collects 100 Bullets #1-19." (Publisher's note)

Originally collected in 13 volumes; Originally published in single magazine form.; Volume 1 of 5

Doctor 13: architecture & mortality. DC Comics 2007 un Illustration
Grades: 9 10 11 12 Adult   **741.5**
1. Graphic novels; 2. Humorous graphic novels; 3. Superhero graphic novels
978-1-4012-1552-1, $14.99

Doctor 13, the world's greatest skeptic, sets out with his daughter Tracy to investigate strange doings in the French Alps. The two encounter in short order a vampire, a pirate with a flying ship, a caveman who had been frozen in ice, a mysterious boy who can answer any question for the price of a dime, a talking Nazi gorilla, a cosmic heroine with a constant runny nose, and the ghost of a Confederate general taking time off from haunting a US Army tank. Doctor 13 doesn't believe in any of them, but he works with them when they have to go up against the Architects, the shapers of the universe. The Architects have decided that Doctor 13 and his team of misfits don't belong in the world, and they beg to differ. The book includes some violence.

Lex Luthor: Man of Steel. DC Comics 2005 Illustration
Grades: 10 11 12 Adult   **741.5; Fic**
1. Graphic novels; 2. Lex Luthor (Fictional character); 3. Superhero graphic novels; 4. Superman (Fictional character)
1-4012-0454-6, $12.99

Superman has been called many things since becoming a superhero, from the defender of Truth, Justice and the American Way to the Big Blue Boy Scout. Lex Luthor calls him a dangerous threat to all humanity. This book is narrated by Luthor, so the reader sees Superman from his point of view; and to Luthor, Superman is an alien being who can't be trusted. Therefore, Luthor tries to create a superhero of his own, in the form of a beautiful young woman, named Hope. The book includes some violence and sexual situations.

Superman: For Tomorrow Volume One. writer, Brian Azzarello; Penciller, Jim Lee; inker, Scott Williams; colorist, Alex Sinclair; created by Jerry Siegel & Joe Shuster. DC Comics 2005 un Illustration
Grades: 10 11 12 Adult   **741.5; Fic**
1. Graphic novels; 2. Superhero graphic novels; 3. Superman (Fictional character)
1-4012-0352-3, $14.99

A cataclysmic event has struck the Earth. Millions of people have vanished without a trace. No one is left unaffected — not even Superman. A year has passed, and Superman is left with many questions and very few answers. For a hero who tries to have all the answers, it's torture. And, just as the action heats up and the stakes are raised, one huge question emerges: just how far is Superman willing to go "For Tomorrow"?

Volume 1 of 2

Wonder Woman; Volume 1: Blood. Brian Azzarello, Cliff Chiang, Tony Akins. DC Comics 2012 160 p.
Grades: 11 12 Adult   **741.5**
1. Superhero comic books, strips, etc.; 2. Greek mythology — Fiction; 3. Wonder Woman (Fictional character)
1401235638; 9781401235635, $22.99
LC 2011051798

In this comic book, author Brian Azzarello "gives Diana (Wonder Woman) a new origin, not as a baby her mother, Hippolyta, molded out of clay but as the illegitimate daughter of Zeus. As such, she's a target for the jealous rage of Hera, Zeus' wife, but she finds a new role as protector of a

waifish young woman who's currently carrying Zeus' baby. The king of the gods, meanwhile, has vanished." (Publishers Weekly)

Originally published in single magazine form in WONDER WOMAN 1-6 — T.p. verso.; Other Wonder Woman volumes by Azzarello and Chiang are: 2: Guts; 3: Iron; 4: War

B., David

Black paths. David B. SelfMadeHero 2011 128 p. Color illustration
Grades: Adult   **741.5; Fic**
1. Fascism — Italy; 2. Historical fiction; 3. Graphic novels
190683833X; 9781906838331, $24.95
LC 2011507750

This graphic novel, by David B., takes place during the Interwar period. "When the Austro-Hungarian Empire disintegrated after World War I,...Gabriele d'Annunzio...stormed the city [of Fiume] with 3,000 Italian nationalists. D'Annunzio declared Fiume a free republic and himself commander.... David B. uses this real event as a backdrop...[for] the tragic love story of a beautiful torch singer and a young soldier haunted by the horrors of trench warfare." (Publisher's note)

★ **Epileptic**. Pantheon Books 2005 361p. Illustration
Grades: 11 12 Adult   **741.5; 616.8**
1. Autobiographical graphic novels; 2. Epilepsy — Graphic novels; 3. Graphic novels
0-375-42318-4, $25; 0-375-71468-5 (pa), $18.95; 9780375423185
LC 2004-53419

"Growing up in the 1960s and 1970s in France's Loire Valley, Jean-Christophe developed grand mal epilepsy around the age of 11. Pierre-Francois, nine, observes his brother's battle with the physical and social implications of the disease; their parents' efforts to find management of it through medical, macrobiotic, and even psychic interventions; and the author's own development in this milieu as a boy obsessed with history and warfare and as a dedicated artist." SLJ

The author's "artwork is magnificent — gorgeously bold, impressionistic representations of the world not as it is but as he's taught himself to perceive it.... B.'s illustrations constantly underscore his writing's wrenching psychological depth; readers can literally see how the chaos of his childhood shaped his vision and mind." Publ Wkly

Original French edition, 2002

Backderf, Derf

My friend Dahmer. written & illustrated by Derf Backderf. Abrams ComicArts 2012 221 p.
Grades: Adult   **741.5**
1. Dahmer, Jeffrey — Comic books, strips, etc.; 2. Friendship — Graphic novels; 3. High school — Graphic novels; 4. Autobiographical graphic novels; 5. Comic books, strips, etc.
9.78142E+12
LC 2011285306

Alex Award (2013)

This book is an "exploration of notorious serial killer Jeffrey Dahmer by his high-school classmate.... In this graphic novel, [Derf] Backderf interweaves his memories of Dahmer with additional information gleaned from news reports, public interviews, and the memories of other classmates and community members. The book traces Dahmer's progression from experimenting with roadkill to...his first human victim just post-high school." (Bulletin of the Center for Children's Books)

Trashed: a graphic novel. by Derf Backderf. Abrams ComicArts 2015 256 p. Illustration
Grades: 10 11 12 Adult   **741.5**
1. Refuse and refuse disposal — Fiction; 2. Sanitation workers — Fiction

9781419714535, $24.95; 9781419714542

LC 2015011115

Ignatz Award: Outstanding Graphic Novel (2016)

This graphic novel, by Derf Backderf, "is an ode to the crap job of all crap jobs — garbage collector.... [It] follows the raucous escapades of three 20-something friends as they clean the streets of pile after pile of stinking garbage, while battling annoying small-town bureaucrats, bizarre townfolk, sweltering summer heat, and frigid winter storms." (Publisher's note)

"The blocky grotesquerie of Backderf's art is well-suited to the material, and the episodic, slackerish narrative is spiked here and there by brief lessons on the history of the garbage truck, the ecology of the landfill, and an answer to the question of whether rich or poor neighborhoods generate the most trash (hint: it's not the poor). A downbeat but entertaining ode to the odiferous realities of getting by." Pub Wkly

Includes bibliographical references

Bagge, Peter

Apocalypse nerd. Dark Horse Comics 2008 120p. Illustration

Grades: 11 12 Adult   **741.5; Fic**

1. Adventure graphic novels; 2. End of the world — Graphic novels; 3. Graphic novels

978-1-59307-9024, $13.95

Software engineer Perry and his friend Gordo are just two average suburban guys (okay, maybe not Gordo, since he deals drugs) who have gone on a camping trip in the North Cascade Mountains near Seattle; but on their way up, North Korea nukes Seattle, and the two friends must find a way to survive in the mountain. They become looters, deal with others out to survive any way possible, and do things they never dreamed they would do — including killing others. The book includes lots of harsh language (including s-bombs and f-bombs), partial nudity, and violence.

Woman Rebel: The Margaret Sanger Story. Peter Bagge. Drawn and Quarterly 2013 104 p. Illustration

Grades: Adult   **741.5; 92**

1. Sanger, Margaret, 1879-1966; 2. Birth control; 3. Women political activists

1770461264; 9781770461260, $21.95

Author Peter Bagge presents a "biography of [Margaret Sanger,] the social and political maverick, jam-packed with fact and fun. In his signature cartoony, rubbery style, Bagge presents the life of the birth-control activist, educator, nurse, mother, and protofeminist from her birth in the late nineteenth century to her death after the invention of the birth control pill." (Publisher's note)

Sanger "bursts into life on the page, via Bagge's wonderful facial expressions and exuberant line work, in a manner that no historical text can match. Bagge has conducted meticulous research to separate the truth about Sanger from the fiction, and he documents his work with extensive notes." Pub Wkly

Bagieu, Pénélope

★ **Brazen:** rebel ladies who rocked the world. Pénélope Bagieu. First Second 2018 304 p. Color; Illustration

Grades: 8 9 10 11 12 Adult   **920; 741.5**

1. Women — Biography; 2. Biography

9781626728684; 9781626728691, $17.99

LC 2017941160

"With her characteristic wit and dazzling drawings, celebrated graphic novelist Pénélope Bagieu profiles the lives of...feisty female role models, some world famous, some little known. From Nellie Bly to Mae Jemison or Josephine Baker to Naziq al-Abid, the stories in this comic biography are sure to inspire the next generation of rebel ladies." (Publisher's note)

"Both art and text are clever, smart, and distilled for maximum impact. The women are not idealized, nor are their flaws ignored. Instead, they are treated with wit and empathy.... A fresh and joyous look at women's history that is sure to delight even the most jaded readers." LJ

Originally published in French by Gallimard in 2016 as Culottées: Des femmes qui ne font que ce qu?elles veulent, tome I and in 2017 as Culottées: Des femmes qui ne font que ce qu?elles veulent, tome II

Baillie, Liz

My brain hurts volume one. Microcosm Publishing 2008 un Illustration

Grades: 11 12 Adult

741.5; Fic

1. Friendship — Graphic novels; 2. Graphic novels; 3. Homosexuality — Graphic novels

978-1-934620-03-8, $6

Courtesy of Microcosm Publishing

Best friends Kate and Joey are gay and trying to find some happiness with their relationships. They're also thirteen years old, love punk music, dress punk, and get into all kinds of trouble. Joey's father is in denial, Kate doesn't know how to tell her mother. Then one night, a gang of skinheads beat Joey around the head with a chain; he collapses during an interview at a Catholic school and goes into a coma. Meanwhile, one of the skinheads keeps trying to get Kate to go with him; and Kate joins a gay student club at school. The book shows kissing but no other sexual activity, there's no nudity, but there's a lot of strong language, especially the f-bomb.

Volume 1 of 2

Baker, Kyle

★ **How** to draw stupid and other essentials of cartooning. Watson-Guptill 2008 110p. Illustration

Grades: 8 9 10 11 12 Adult   **741.5**

1. Cartooning — Technique; 2. Graphic novels — Drawing

978-0-8230-0143-9, $16.95

LC 2008-922161

"Baker, an award-winning cartoonist and graphic-novel illustrator, gives aspiring cartoonists irreverent advice about how to succeed in their chosen field. He offers instruction in basic drawing techniques such as choosing the right tools and discusses the importance of learning to draw shapes, exaggerating, and using references. But the author's most inspiring advice focuses on how to succeed as a cartoonist." SLJ

King David. DC Comics/Vertigo 2002 104p. Illustration

Grades: 9 10 11 12 Adult   **741.5; 221**

1. Bible. O.T. — Adaptations; 2. Graphic novels

978-1-56389-866-2, $19.95

Baker retells the Old Testament story of David, the shepherd boy who slew the giant Goliath and later became the King of Israel, after years of dodging King Saul's attempts to kill him. Using a hip, freewheeling style full of irreverent humor, Baker also renders the battles as the bloody messes they were.

Nat Turner. Abrams 2008 207p. Illustration

Grades: 10 11 12 Adult   **741.5; 92**

1. Biographical graphic novels; 2. Graphic novels; 3. Revolutionaries; 4. Slavery — Graphic novels; 5. Slaves; 6. Turner, Nat, 1800?-1831; 7. Turner, Nat, 1800?-1831 — Graphic novels

978-0-8109-9535-2; 0-8109-9535-2, $14.95

LC 2008-6911

This book "follows the dark legacy of the Virginia slave rebellion and subsequent murders of at least 55 white slave owners and their families in 1831.... Turner is presented as a fiercely intelligent, angry, yet steadfast individual whose potential was dashed in an era of hate and inhumanity. Those characteristics are mirrored in the actions of the slaves' rebellion, in illustrations that are not for the faint of heart or the weak of stomach. The ideas brought forth here are sure to ignite debate and discussion." SLJ

Includes bibliographical references; Originally published 2006 in four volumes; Volume 1 of 2

Plastic Man: On the Lam!. DC Comics 2004 un Illustration
Grades: 6 7 8 9 10 11 12 Adult   741.5; Fic
   1. Graphic novels; 2. Humorous graphic novels; 3. Plastic Man (Fictional character); 4. Superhero graphic novels
   1-4012-0343-4, $14.95
2005 Eisner Award for Best Publication for a Younger Audience, also 2005 Eisner Award for Best Writer/Artists-Humor for Kyle Baker

Plastic Man has worked as a superhero, but he used to be the criminal Eel O'Brian, a fact he has hidden from the FBI. Now there's been a murder, and Eel O'Brian is the main (and only) suspect. When the FBI learns of his old identity, Plastic Man goes on the lam to clear himself.

Originally published as Plastic Man issues #1-6; this volume is bound in plastic; Volume 1 of 2

Balce, Nicc
   Random Encounter Volume 1. Viper Comics 2006 un Illustration
Grades: 9 10 11 12 Adult   741.5; Fic
   1. Adventure graphic novels; 2. Graphic novels; 3. Science fiction graphic novels
   0-9754193-8-2, $9.95

Strange things are afoot at the...Kwik Mart. With their eerie tromp through the latest Silent Kill game interrupted by a strange sound, Migo, Mica, and Mona begin a journey into the perplexing and uncharted. The discovery of a dead girl in a pool of blood on the roof of Migo's parents' Kwik Mart sends the kids' lives into a maelstrom of confusion, freakish aliens, precipitous resurrection, and enigmatic secrets. It's a wild ride into the unimaginable and astonishing, a...random encounter. There are lots of fighting scenes and some monsters.

Baltazar, Art
   Patrick the Wolf Boy Volume 1. written by Art Baltazar & Franco Aureliani; drawn by Art Baltazar. Devil's Due Publishing 2004 un Illustration
Grades: 2 3 4 5 6 7 8 9 10 11 12 Adult   741.5; Fic
   1. Graphic novels; 2. Humorous graphic novels
   1-932796-27-4, $10.95

Patrick looks at first glance like the other kids in school, but he's a werewolf. A cute werewolf. He resembles Eddie Munster (from the 1960s television comedy series "The Munsters"), and he doesn't speak, although he growls a lot and sometimes howls. He gives his teacher an apple — but with a skull biting the apple. When he goes fishing with his dad, he prefers to scare the bear into giving him his catch. He loves to play tag with the neighborhood squirrel. And when Valentine's Day comes, he makes sure that his babysitter likes him better. His utterly normal parents adore him and understand his growls; so does Neve, his classmate at school.

Volume 1 of 4

Barker, Meg-John
   ★ **Queer:** a graphic history. Meg-John Barker; Julia Scheele. Icon Books 2016 176 p. Illustration
Grades: Adult   306.76; 741.5
   1. LGBT people; 2. Queer theory
   1785780719; 9781785780714, $17.95

This book, by Meg-John Barker and Julia Scheele, presents "the histories of queer thought and LGBTQ+ action.... A kaleidoscope of characters from the diverse worlds of pop-culture, film, activism and academia guide us on a journey through the ideas, people and events that have shaped 'queer theory'." (Publisher's note)

Courtesy of Icon Books

"Here, sequential art is used to delineate and untangle the sticky webs of queer theory discourse, past to present. In a style similar to that of Scott McCloud's seminal Understanding Comics-albeit richer with text-author Barker...describes the contributions of pertinent scholars, as well as the landmark developments in this school of thought and those that led up to it, in accessible prose." LJ

Barry, Lynda
   The **greatest** of Marlys!. Lynda Barry. Drawn & Quarterly 2016 248 p. Illustration
Grades: 10 11 12 Adult   741.5; Fic
   1. Humorous graphic novels; 2. Girls
   1770462643; 9781770462649, $22.95

In this graphic novel by Lynda Barry, "eight-year-old Marlys Mullen...shines in all her freckled and pig-tailed groovy glory. The trailer park where she and her family live is the grand stage for her dramas big and small. Joining Marlys are her teenaged sister Maybonne, her younger brother Freddie, their mother, and an offbeat array of family members, neighbors, and classmates. Marlys's enthusiasm for life knows no bounds." (Publisher's note)

"Marlys is bizarre but lovable, and Barry does an excellent job of entertaining readers with her exploits through captivating dialog, varying points of view, and drawings that depict a child's world." LJ

   One hundred demons. Sasquatch Bks. 2002 216p. Illustration
Grades: 10 11 12 Adult   741.5
   1. Autobiographical graphic novels; 2. Graphic novels
   1-57061-337-0; 1-57061-459-8 (pa), $17.95

                                                    LC 2002-21657
"Whether she's talking about head lice, old boyfriends, or hippies who 'forgot' to pay her wages, Barry playfully explores, in 'autobifictionalographical' text and art, those demons common to teens — and to us all." Booklist

   ★ **Picture** this: the near-sighted monkey book. with guest watercolorist Kevin Kawula. Drawn and Quarterly 2010 224 p. Color illustration
Grades: 9 10 11 12 Adult   741.5
   1. American wit and humor, Pictorial; 2. Graphic novels; 3. Humorous graphic novels; 4. Animals — Graphic novels
   1897299648; 9781897299647, $29.95

                                                    LC 2010399443
In author Lynda Barry's book, she "asks 'Why do we stop drawing?' and 'Why do we start?' It features the return of" the character "Marlys, and introduces a new one, the Nearsighted Monkey." The book is a "graphic-memoir-how-to" and a "take home extension of Barry's traveling" writing workshop which focuses on literature illustration. (Publisher's note)

   Syllabus: Notes from an accidental professor. Lynda Barry. Farrar Straus & Giroux 2014 200 p. Illustration; Color
Grades: Adult   741.5
   1. Creative writing; 2. Authorship — Study and teaching

1770461612; 9781770461611, $19.95

LC bl2014044622

Lynda Barry "believes that anyone can be a writer and she has set out to prove it.... [This volume] will make her...lesson plans and writing exercises available to the public for home or classroom use.... Collaged texts, ballpoint pen doodles, and watercolour washes adorn...yellow lined pages, which offer advice on finding a creative voice and using memories to inspire the writing process." (Publisher's note)

★ **What** it is. Drawn & Quarterly 2008 209p. Illustration
Grades: 7 8 9 10 11 12 Adult   **818; 741.5**
  1. Authorship — Graphic novels; 2. Creative writing — Graphic novels
978-1-897299-35-7, $24.95; 1-897299-35-4

LC c2007-9047319

Independent cartoonist Lynda Barry presents an unconventional book that encourages its readers to write by using her colorful art and asking questions such as "How are monsters different? And how are they the same?" "Can/Do images exist without thinking?" "What is the difference between lying and pretending?" Each question appears with illustrated writing prompts and Barry's own ruminations on the topics. It's a workbook of sorts, but it also exists as a book to be read for itself.

"Every so often a book comes along that surpasses expectations, taking readers on an inspirational voyage that they don't want to leave. This is one such book." SLJ

Beaton, Kate

Hark! A vagrant. Drawn and Quarterly 2011 168p. Illustration
Grades: Adult   **741.5**
  1. Comic books, strips, etc.
1770460608; 9781770460607

LC 2011505458

The book offers a collection of comic strips by author Kate Beaton, "a series of short gag cartoons, primarily about history and literature, with a particularly Canadian bent.... Comics about long-suffering heroines like Jane Eyre, Laura Secord, and 'Every Lady Scientist in History Who Ever Did Anything Until Now' highlight the absurdities of gender disparity.... A number of these comics are driven simply by absurdity itself: a kingdom whose royal mascot is a fat pony; a sexy Batman; and teens who solve crimes in a real-life fashion: by hiding behind the school, smoking weed, and lying about it later." (Quill & Quire)
Includes index.

★ **Step** Aside, Pops: A Hark! a Vagrant Collection. Kate Beaton. Drawn & Quarterly 2015 160 p. Illustration
Grades: Adult   **741.5**
  1. World history — Comic books, strips, etc.; 2. Cartoons and caricatures; 3. Wit and humor
1770462082; 9781770462083, $19.95
Eisner Award: Best Humor Publication (2016); Ignatz Award Winner: Outstanding Anthology or Collection (2016)

In this collection of comics by Kate Beaton, "Ida B. Wells, the Black Prince, and Benito Juárez burst off the pages...armed with modern-sounding quips and amusingly on-point repartee. Kate Beaton's second [Drawn and Quarterly] book brings her hysterically funny gaze to bear on these and even more historical, literary, and contemporary figures." (Publisher's note)

"The widely lauded Beaton has created a tidy niche for herself in gag strips that deflate history and literature's more grandiose personalities with highbrow intellectualism and lowbrow barbs." Booklist
Includes index

Beazley, Mark D.

Pet avengers classic. Marvel Entertainment 2009 208p. Illustration

Grades: 7 8 9 10 11 12 Adult   **741.5; Fic**
  1. Adventure graphic novels; 2. Graphic novels; 3. Pets — Graphic novels; 4. Superhero graphic novels
9780785139669, $24.99

This volume collects the various Marvel Pets stories, from 1960 to 2007, with each story featuring a different pet, from Lockjaw the teleporting dog to Kitty Pryde's dragon Lockheed to Brightwind the winged horse, and many more. Lockjaw, Lockheed, Redwing the falcon, the cat named Niels, and Zabu the saber tooth tiger all starred in th 2009 mini series titled Pet Avengers. Some of the stories in this collection include violence.

Spider-Man: The Birth of Venom. Marvel Entertainment 2007 un Illustration
Grades: 8 9 10 11 12 Adult   **741.5; Fic**
  1. Graphic novels; 2. Spider-Man (Fictional character); 3. Superhero graphic novels; 4. Fantastic Four (Fictional characters)
978-0-7851-2498-6, $29.99

The Beyonder's Battleworld might seem a strange place to get new threads, but it's Spider-Man who becomes unraveled when his new symbiotic, shape-changing costume attempts to darken his life as well as his fashion sense. But ridding himself of his black costume proves an even greater mistake when its alien enmity bonds with mortal madness to form our hero's most dedicated enemy, Venom. Other stories include the first appearances of Puma and the Rose, Mary Jane Watson's startling secret, and the debut of the battling...Bag-Man? The Black Cat, the Fantastic Four and other Marvel characters appear.

Bechdel, Alison

★ **Are** you my mother?: a comic drama. Alison Bechdel. Houghton Mifflin Harcourt 2012 286 p.
Grades: Adult   **741.5/973; 741.5; B**
  1. Cartoonists — United States — Comic books, strips, etc; 2. Bechdel, Alison, 1960- — Comic books, strips, etc; 3. Autobiographical graphic novels; 4. Mother-daughter relationship — Graphic novels; 5. Cartoonists — Biography
0618982507; 9780618982509

LC 2012010582

In this book, "[Alison] Bechdel not only searches for keys to [her relationship with her mother] but perhaps even for surrogate mothers, through therapy, girlfriends and the writing of Virginia Woolf, Adrienne Rich, Alice Miller and others. Yet the primary inspiration in this literary memoir is psychoanalyst Donald Winnicott, whose life and work Bechdel explores along with her own." (Kirkus Reviews)

★ **The essential** Dykes to watch out for. Alison Bechdel. Houghton Mifflin Harcourt 2008 xviii, 392 p. Illustration
Grades: Adult   **741.5; Fic**
  1. Comic books, strips, etc.; 2. Lesbians — Fiction; 3. LGBT comic books, strips, etc.
0618968806; 9780618968800, $25

LC 2008036784

This book, by Alison Bechdel, gathers a "selection from all eleven ['Dykes to Watch Out For'] volumes. Here too are sixty of the newest strips, never before published in book form.... Bechdel fuses high and low culture — from foreign policy to domestic routine, hot sex to postmodern theory — in a serial graphic narrative 'suitable for humanists of all persuasions.'" (Publisher's note)

"This ongoing comic strip chronicles the lives of a tight-knit group of lesbian friends over an astounding 21 years of life, work, love, boredom, political activism and countless reversals of fortune. At its heart are six women: the promiscuous Lois, a feminist bookstore clerk with a penchant for gender-bending; her two roommates, the overworked academic Ginger and self-identified 'bisexual lesbian' Sparrow; their domestically partnered friends Clarice and Toni; and Mo, who despite (or perhaps because of) her frequent politically charged outbursts of neurosis is the hub of her circle." Pub Wkly

Includes index.

★ **Fun** home: a family tragicomic. Houghton Mifflin 2006 232p. Illustration

Grades: 11 12 Adult   **741.5; 92**

1. Artists; 2. Authors; 3. Autobiographical graphic novels; 4. Biography, Individual; 5. Cartoonists; 6. Comic book writers; 7. Essayists; 8. Graphic novels; 9. Novelists; 10. Bechdel, Alison, 1960-
0-618-47794-2, $19.95; 978-0-618-47794-4

          LC 2005-30304

This is a memoir in graphic novel format about the author's "childhood, her father's death and their shared homosexuality.... The death was deemed an accident-a truck hit [Mr. Bechdel] as he crossed a road with an armful of garden brush-but Ms. Bechdel suspects suicide." (N Y Times (Late N Y Ed))

This "is one of the very best graphic novels ever." Booklist

Beechen, Adam

Hench. AiT/Planet Lar 2004 un Illustration

Grades: 10 11 12 Adult

741.5; Fic

1. Graphic novels; 2. Superhero graphic novels
1-932051-17-1, $12.95

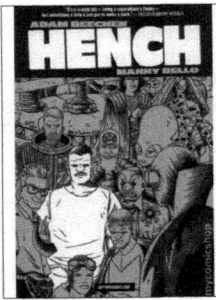

Courtesy of AiT/Planet Lar

The fine line between hero and villain is just another of longtime super-villain henchman Mike Fulton's many scars. Now, faced with a terrible choice that could mean life and death for heroes, villains, his family, and himself, Mike ponders just how his normal life went so crazy. There's a little violence but mostly fighting action, and a little bit of strong language.

Robin: Wanted. Adam Beechen, writer; Freddie Williams II, artist; Karl Kerschl with Wayne Faucher & Prentis Rollins, artists, pages 6-27; Guy major, Nathan Eyring, colorists; Jared K. Fletcher, Travis Lanham, Phil Balsman, letterers. DC Comics 2007 144p. Illustration

Grades: 9 10 11 12 Adult   **741.5; Fic**

1. Graphic novels; 2. Mystery graphic novels; 3. Robin (Fictional character); 4. Superhero graphic novels; 5. Batgirl (Fictional character)
978-1-4012-1225-4, $12.99

Batgirl — Cassandra Cain — is dead...and the evidence shows that Robin is the killer. Every cop in Gotham City is looking for him now, so he has to find the real killer and clear his name. Someone keeps sending Robin clues that only he can find, and they seem to be leading to a shadowy player who is making a grab for power in the deadly League of Assassins. Solving this mystery will lead Robin to a confrontation with the new leader of the League of Assassins...and the killer's identity will change Robin's world forever. This book has lots of fighting action.

Beland, Tom

★ **True** story swear to God archives, vol. 1. Image Comics 2008 528p. Illustration

Grades: 10 11 12 Adult   **92; 741.5**

1. Autobiographical graphic novels; 2. Cartoonists; 3. Graphic novels; 4. Romance graphic novels; 5. Beland, Tom, 1962-
978-1-58240-881-1, $19.99

They met at a bus stop at Disneyworld, by chance: he was a cartoonist from Napa, California, and she was a radio personality from Puerto Rico. Their chance meeting blossomed into a romance that survived a long-distance separation, a Category 5 hurricane, his leaving home to move to a new world. Tom Beland writes candidly about the ups and downs of his relationship with Lily, with his family, and all the slings and arrows of life one has to deal with daily. He originally self-published these comics, and they were collected in several trade paperbacks from AiT/PlanetLar. The book includes occasional harsh language (including s-bombs and f-bombs), sexual situations, and frank talk about sex.

Bell, Blake

★ **Strange** & stranger: the world of Steve Ditko. Fantagraphics Books 2008 220p. Illustration

Grades: 10 11 12 Adult   **92; 741.5**

1. Comic books, strips, etc. — History and criticism; 2. Graphic designers; 3. Ditko, Steve; 4. Graphic novels; 5. Spider-Man (Fictional character)
978-1-56097-921-0, $39.99

Steve Ditko may be best known as the cocreator and first artist for Marvel's Spider-Man comics, but he has done much more. Bell tells Ditko's life story and covers his career which has spanned more than 50 years. He also gives Ditko's side of the story in explaining his split with Stan Lee and why he walked away from Spider-Man back in 1966. Ditko's work has been strongly influenced by author/philosopher Ayn Rand, and her Objectivist philosophy has informed his work. The book includes lots of Ditko's art, including many unpublished pieces. Bell doesn't romanticize Ditko, but provides ample reason for the artist's place in comic book history.

Bell, Gabrielle

Everything is flammable. Gabrielle Bell. Uncivilized Books 2017 160 p. Color; Illustration

Grades: Adult

92; 741.5

1. Bell, Gabrielle; 2. Cartoonists — United States — Biography; 3. Mother-daughter relationship; 4. Autobiographical graphic novels
1941250181; 9781941250181, $25.95

Courtesy of Uncivilized Books

In this graphic memoir, author Gabrielle Bell "returns from New York to her childhood town in rural Northern California after her mother's home is destroyed by a fire. Acknowledging her issues with anxiety, financial hardships, memories of a semi-feral childhood, and a tenuous relationship with her mother, Bell helps her mother put together a new home on top of the ashes." (Publisher's note)

"Bell's vignettes peel back the layers of the mother-daughter relationship with self-deprecating comedy, displaying irritation but also patient forbearance." Pub Wkly

The **Voyeurs**. Gabrielle Bell. Consortium Book Sales & Dist 2012 160 p. Grades: Adult

741.5

1. Cartoonists — Biography; 2. Bell, Gabrielle, 1976-
098468140X; 9780984681402, $24.95

Courtesy of Uncivilized Books

This book by "autobiographical cartoonist [Gabrielle] Bell" presents a "series of full-color vignettes that document her life as part of a free-floating community of indie comics artists drifting between the neighborhood bars of Brooklyn and L.A. and an international and domestic circuit of comics conventions." It includes "drawings of her life, lovers, friends and neurotic obsessions." (Publishers Weekly)

Bell, Marc
Stroppy. by Marc Bell. Farrar Straus & Giroux 2015 64 p. Color illustration
Grades: Adult   **741.5/971; 741.5**
1. Contests — Fiction; 2. Graphic novels; 3. Factories — Fiction
1770462058; 9781770462052, $21.95
LC 2014481388
In this graphic novel, by Marc Bel, "Our hapless hero, Stroppy, is minding his business, working a menial job in one of Monsieur Moustache's factories, when a muscular fellah named Sean blocks up the assembly line. Sean's there to promote an All-Star Schnauzer Band-organized songwriting contest, which he does enthusiastically and at the expense of Stroppy's livelihood, home, and face. Hoping for a cash prize, Stroppy submits a work by his friend Clancy the Poet." (Publisher's note)

Bellstorf, Arne
Baby's in black: Astrid Kirchherr, Stuart Sutcliffe, and the Beatles. Arne Bellstorf. First Second 2012 196 p. Illustration
Grades: 10 11 12 Adult   **782.421; 782.42166092/2**
1. Beatles — Comic books, strips, etc; 2. Rock musicians — England — Comic books, strips, etc; 3. Graphic novels; 4. Romance fiction; 5. Sutcliffe, Stuart, 1940-1962; 6. Kirchherr, Astrid
1596437715; 9781596437715, $24.99
LC 2011049680
This graphic novel tells the love story of "Stuart Sutcliffe, one of the original Beatles," and "German photographer Astrid Kirchherr." The "story offers insight into the time the Beatles spent performing together in Germany before they made it big." Despite the couple's "different languages and worlds, the pair fall into a happy, and seemingly easy, romance. But their happiness is short-lived: the Beatles are being forced to leave the country, and Stuart's health is failing." (Publishers Weekly)
Translated from the German by Michael Waaler.

Bendis, Brian Michael
★ **Jessica** Jones; Volume 1: Alias. Brian Michael Bendis, writer; Michael Gaydos, artist; Matt Hollingsworth, colorist. Marvel Enterprises 2015 216 p. Color; Illustration
Grades: Adult   **741.5; Fic**
1. Superhero comic books, strips, etc.; 2. Private investigators — Fiction
0785198555; 9780785198550, $24.99
"Meet Jessica Jones. Once upon a time, she was a costumed super hero — but not a very good one.... The self-destructive would-be Avenger is now the owner and sole employee of Alias Investigations — a small, private-investigative firm specializing in superhuman cases. When she uncovers the potentially explosive secret of one hero's true identity, Jessica's life immediately becomes expendable." (Publisher's note)
Collected edition originally published 2002 as Alias; Volume 1 of 4

Jessica Jones; Volume 1: uncaged!. writer, Brian Michael Bendis; artist, Michael Gaydos; color artist, Matt Hollingsworth; letterer, VC's Cory Petit; cover art, David Mack. Marvel Enterprises 2017 136 p. Color; Illustration (Jessica Jones (2016))
Grades: Adult   **741.5; Fic**
1. Superheroes — Fiction; 2. Women private investigators — Fiction
1302906356; 9781302906351, $17.99

In this book in the Jessica Jones series, by Brian Michael Bendis, illustrated by Michael Gaydos, "Alias Investigations is open for business, and of all the many mysteries to discover,...[Jessica Jones'] new case may be the most dangerous one! This blistering new series is filled with haunting revelations from Jessica's past, and answers to some of the biggest questions about the new Marvel NOW! universe!" (Publisher's note)
Volume 1 of 3

Jinx: The Definitive Collection. Image Comics 2001 480p. Illustration
Grades: 11 12 Adult   **741.5; Fic**
1. Graphic novels; 2. Mystery graphic novels
978-1-58240-179-9, $24.95
This is a graphic crime noir novel about a bounty hunter, two grifters, and a treasure hunt that propels the character driven story. This extra large edition carries with it the entire epic story, behind the scenes/making of, script excerpts, and an art gallery. The story includes harsh language, nudity, sexual situations, and violence.

★ **Powers:** The Definitive Hardcover Collection Vol. 1. created and produced by Brian Michael Bendis and Mike Avon Oeming; colored by Pat Garrahy with Brian Michael Bendis; lettered by Pat Garrahy with Brian Michael Bendis. Marvel Comics 2006 456p. Illustration
Grades: 11 12 Adult   **741.5; Fic**
1. Graphic novels; 2. Mystery graphic novels; 3. Superhero graphic novels
978-0-7851-1805-3, $29.99
Homicide detectives Christian Walker and Deena Pilgrim investigate homicides in a city where super-powered heroes and villains live, fight, and die. Sometimes the heroes are just as flawed as the villains. And Walker has a secret of his own that gives him special insight in his investigations. The first three storylines have been remastered, reformatted, and collected in this edition which is replete with violence, harsh language, nudity, and sexual situations.
Also available in 16 paperback volumes; Volume 1 of 6

The **Pulse** Vol. 1: Thin Air. Marvel Entertainment 2004 un Illustration
Grades: 10 11 12 Adult   **741.5; Fic**
1. Graphic novels; 2. Superhero graphic novels
0-7851-1332-0, $13.99
Former super hero and current private investigator Jessica Jones has just been offered a new job: a position with the Bugle's new super-hero section, The Pulse. Jessica's first assignment: to uncover the true identity of a former Bugle reporter's super-powered murderer. How is millionaire industrialist Norman Osborn involved in the case? And how will Jessica's discovery affect the entire Marvel Universe? The book includes some violence and strong language.

Spider-Man; Volume 1: Miles Morales. Brian Michael Bendis, writer; Sarah Pichelli, artist; Gaetano Carlucci, inking assist; Justin Ponsor, colorist; VC's Cory Petit, letterer. Marvel Enterprises 2016 112 p. Color; Illustration (Spider-Man (2016))
Grades: 8 9 10 11 12 Adult   **741.5; Fic**
0785199616; 9780785199618, $15.99
"Miles Morales is hitting the big time! Not only is he joining the Marvel Universe, but he's also a card-carrying Avenger, rubbing shoulders with the likes of Iron Man, Thor and Captain America! But how have Miles' first eight months been, coming to grips with an All-new, All-Different New York? One thing is the same — nonstop action!" (Publisher's note)
Volume 1 of an ongoing series

Torso. created and written by Brian Michael Bendis and Mark Andreyko; illustrated and lettered by Brian Michael Bendis. Marvel 2012 un Illustration

Grades: Adult   **364.152; 741.5**
1. Mystery graphic novels; 2. Serial killers — Graphic novels
078515356X; 9780785153566, $24.99

This graphic novel collects issues 1-5 of the comic book series "Torso." This volume tells "the gripping tale of Eliot Ness' chase of America's first serial killer: the mysterious torso killer!" (Publisher's note)
Collected edition originally published 2001

★ **Ultimate** comics Spider-Man; Volume 1. by Brian Michael Bendis, illustrated by Sara Pichelli. Marvel 2012 136 p.

Grades: Adult   **Fic; 741.5/973**
1. Superhero graphic novels; 2. Spider-Man (Fictional character)
0785157123; 9780785157120, $24.99

In this graphic novel by Brian Michael Bendis, illustrated by Sara Pichelli, "Miles Morales IS the new Spider-Man! What's the secret behind his powers, and how will he master them? What new and familiar enemies will rise to challenge this all-new Spider-Man? And will Miles live up to Peter Parker's legacy?" (Publisher's note)
Volume 1 of 5

Ultimate Fantastic Four Vol. 1: The Fantastic. writers, Brian Michael Bendis & Mark Millar; pencils, Adam Kubert; inks, Danny Miki and John Dell; colors, Dave Stewart; letters, Chris Eliopoulos. Marvel Entertainment 2005 un Illustration

Grades: 8 9 10 11 12 Adult   **741.5; Fic**
1. Fantastic Four (Fictional characters); 2. Graphic novels; 3. Superhero graphic novels
978-0-7851-1393-5, $12.99

The Ultimate treatment takes the Fantastic Four back to the beginning. High school genius (and bully magnet) Reed Richards suffers at school and also at home with a father who doesn't like his "troublemaking" experiments. When Reed enrolls at a secret government-sponsored school for the most gifted minds in the world, he unwittingly embarks on the journey of a lifetime. This is a story about science, adventure, and above all else, family.
Volume 1 of 15

Ultimate Spider-Man: Power & Responsibility. by Brian Michael Bendis (Author), Mark Bagley (Illustrator). Marvel 2009 200 p. Color illustration

Grades: 7 8 9 10 11 12 Adult   **741.5**
1. Spider-Man (Fictional character)
0785139400; 9780785139409, $19.99

In this comic book, by Brian Michael Bendis, illustrated by Mark Bagley, "Peter Parker gains super-powers after being bitten by a spider, loses his likable Uncle Ben to violent crime, and learns once again that 'with great power comes great responsibility.'" (Publisher's note)
Collected edition originally published 2001; Volume 1 of 21

Benjamin, Ryan
Star Wars: Empire Volume One: Betrayal. written by Scott Allie, penciled by Ryan Benjamin, inked by Curtis Arnold. Dark Horse Comics 2003 un Illustration

Grades: 7 8 9 10 11 12 Adult   **741.5; Fic**
1. Adventure graphic novels; 2. Graphic novels; 3. Science fiction graphic novels; 4. Star Wars — Graphic novels
1-56971-964-0, $12.95

In the weeks before the events in Star Wars: A New Hope, as the Death Star is readied for its fateful first mission, a power-hungry cabal of Grand Moffs and Imperial Officers embark on a dangerous plan to kill Emperor Palpatine and Darth Vader and seize control of the Empire. When word that a Jedi has made an appearance on a backwater world lures Vader away from his master, the cabal makes its move. But even the galaxy isn't enough of a prize to sate the ambitions of some of the conspirators, and before long the would-be assassins are turning on one another. Their plans are further complicated by the actions of bounty hunter Boba Fett. And, of course, they may have fatally underestimated the cunning of their primary target: Emperor Palpatine.
Volume 1 of 7

Bennett, Joe
Nightwing: the lost year. Marv Wolfman, Marc Andreyko, writers; Jamal Igle, Jon Bosco, Joe Bennett, pencillers; Keith Champagne, Alex Silva, Jack Jadson, inkers; Jason Wright, Edgar Delgado, colorists; Phil Balsman, Jared K. Fletcher, Travis Lanham, letterers. DC Comics 2008 un Illustration

Grades: 10 11 12 Adult   **741.5; Fic**
1. Adventure graphic novels; 2. Graphic novels; 3. Nightwing (Fictional character); 4. Superhero graphic novels
978-1-4012-1671-9, $14.99

Nightwing interrupts a kidnapping attempt only to realize the victim is someone from his past, Liu, his first lover. She says she works for Eddie Hwang, who used to be Metal Eddie, a criminal mastermind who tried to use a teenage Dick Grayson. Liu says Eddie has gone straight. However, the Vigilante, a ruthless killer, is hunting Eddie. Nightwing needs to find out what Eddie really wants, while trying to prevent Vigilante from killing anyone. The book includes some sexual scenes without nudity, and lots of fighting violence.

Bennett, Marguerite
Batwoman; Volume 1: The many arms of death. Marguerite Bennett, James Tynion IV, writers;Steve Epting, Stephanie Hans, Renato Arlem,artists; Jeromy Cox, Adriano Lucas, colorists;Deron Bennett, letterer; Steve Epting, collectioncover art; Steve Epting, Eddy Barrows, EberFerreira and A. DC Comics 2017 168 p. Color; Illustration

Grades: 9 10 11 12 Adult   **741.5; Fic**
1. Science fiction; 2. Superheroes — Fiction; 3. Batwoman (Fictional character)
9781401274306, $16.99

LC 2017051287
"Someone is selling cutting-edge weaponry on the black market, and their aim is to kill as many people...as possible. With help from her intrepid assistant, Julia Pennyworth, and their high-tech mobile command center, the yacht Sequoia, Batwoman quickly tracks the weapons to their source: a small, lawless island known as Coryana, home to pirates, outlaws...and a year of Batwoman's life." (Publisher's note)
Originally published in single magazine form in BATWOMAN: REBIRTH 1 and BATWOMAN 1-6 — Title page verso.; Volume 1 of an ongoing series

DC Comics: Bombshells; Volume 2: Allies. written by Marguerite Bennett; art by MirkaAndolfo, Laura Braga, Sandy Jarrell, M. L. Sanapo, Juan Albarran, Marguerite Sauvage; colors by J.Nanjan, Kelly Fitzpatrick, Wendy Broome, JeremyLawson; letters by Wes Abbott; series andcollection co. DC Comics 2016 144 p. Color; Illustration

Grades: 9 10 11 12 Adult   **741.5; Fic**
1. Women superheroes — Comic books, strips, etc; 2. World War, 1939-1945 — Comic books, strips, etc
1401264484; 9781401264482, $16.99

LC 2016018856
In this comic book, by Marguerite Bennett, "as World War II rages across Europe, the Allied forces issue a call to arms for the greatest heroines the world has ever known! With an old villain arising from beyond the grave, Wonder Woman, Batwoman, Kara Starikov, Kortni

Duginova and Mera must aid the Allied forces while at home, a brave group of Batgirls must defend the homeland!" (Publisher's note)

Benson, John
  Romance Without Tears. Fantagraphics Books 2004 160p. Illustration
Grades: 8 9 10 11 12 Adult   741.5; Fic
  1. Graphic novels; 2. Romance graphic novels
  1-56097-558-X, $22.95

This revisionist collection of romance comics stories from the '50s challenges the cliché of the "tear-stained face" that later dominated the genre and became widely known and vilified as a tiresome icon of moral uplift. Editor Benson has picked stories that portray stron young women who learn from their mistakes and choose their guys, and get themselves out of trouble. The stories were all originally published by Archer St. John in the late-1940s to mid-1950s.

Bertin, Kris
  The **case** of the missing men. Kris Bertin; illustrated by Alexander Forbes. Conundrum Press 2017 224 p. Illustration (Hobtown mystery stories)
Grades: Adult   741.5; Fic
  1. Secret societies — Fiction; 2. Missing persons — Fiction; 3. Teenagers — Fiction
  1772620165; 9781772620160, $20

This graphic novel in the Hobtown Mystery Stories series, by Kris Bertin, illustrated by Alexander Forbes, focuses on "a gang of young teens who have made it their business to investigate each and every one of their town's bizarre occurrences.... Their small world of missing pets and shed-fires is turned upside down when real-life kid adventurer and globetrotter Sam Finch comes to town and enlists them in their first real case — the search for his missing father." (Publisher's note)

"Soaking earnest Nancy Drew-style gumshoeing inside a David Lynch-brand brine, Bertin and Forbes have concocted a true mystery, the kind that does eventually supply some answers, while chalking up copious other moment-by-moment mysteries to the inherent, inexplicable strangeness of life." Booklist

Bertozzi, Nick
  The **Good** Earth. by Pearl S. Buck; graphic adaptation by Nick Bertozzi. Simon & Schuster 2017 144 p. Color; Illustration
Grades: Adult   741.5; Fic
  1. China — Fiction
  1501132768; 9781501132773, $19.99; 9781501132780; 9781501132766, $26.99

"Award-winner Bertozzi turns his attention to Pearl Buck's Pulitzer Prize-winning modern classic. Set in China during the early twentieth century, Buck's cautionary tale follows the life of Wang Lung, a poor farmer who uses a small plot of land to slowly build a massive amount of wealth, property, and power during his lifetime. His happiness and gratitude, so abundant in his early life, is lost in direct proportion to gains in power as he becomes increasingly dissatisfied with his lot. It is not until Wang Lung nears the end of his life that he remembers the simple times of his youth, when the earth provided him with everything he needed." (Booklist)

"Bertozzi's scratchy realism spotlights the characters and their emotions, with just enough scene-setting for context. The limited colors-putty-pinkish and blue with red accents-give surprising scope for emphasis." LJ

Beyer, Mark
  Agony. by Mark Beyer; illustrated by Mark Beyer; introduced by Colson Whitehead. New York Review Comics 2016 192 p. Illustration
Grades: Adult   741.5; Fic
  1. Couples — Comic books, strips, etc.
  1590179811; 9781590179819, $15.95

LC 2015035656
"Amy and Jordan are just like us: hoping for the best, even when things go from bad to worse. They are menaced by bears, beheaded by ghosts, and hunted by the cops, but still they struggle on, bickering and reconciling, scraping together the rent and trying to find a decent movie." (Publisher's note)

"Originally a one-shot from Raw Books in 1987, complete with Spiegelman and Mouly design work, Beyer's calamitous comedy has aged well, its geometric, densely patterned imagery recalling fine art as much as comics and still packing a punch among today's alternative cartoonists." Pub Wkly

Bilson, Danny
  The **Flash:** Lightning in a Bottle. written by Danny Bilson, Paul Demeo; pencils, Ken Lashley [and others]; inks, Ken Rapmund [and others]. DC Comics 2007 144p. Illustration
Grades: 9 10 11 12 Adult   741.5; Fic
  1. Graphic novels; 2. Superhero graphic novels; 3. Flash (Fictional character)
  978-1-4012-1229-2, $12.99

Bart Allen returned from fighting Superboy Prime inside the Speed Force at the end of the Infinite Crisis with no speed and aged four years into an adult, and also no memory of how he spent the time. One year later, he's a factory worker in Keystone City, when an accident at the factory reconnects him to the Speed Force. That same accident causes Bart's best friend Griffin Gray to gain powers, too, but they drain his life force and cause him to rapidly age. His solution — he siphons off the energy from the slowly aging original Flash, Jay Garrick; but it might kill Garrick. And Griffin's brand of justice is too harsh.
  Volume 1 of 2

Blackman, Haden
  Star Wars Omnibus: X-Wing Rogue Squadron Volume 1. writers, Haden Blackman ... [et al.]; art, Tomas Giorello ... [et al.]. Dark Horse Comics 2006 un Illustration
Grades: 7 8 9 10 11 12 Adult   741.5; Fic
  1. Adventure graphic novels; 2. Graphic novels; 3. Science fiction graphic novels; 4. Star Wars — Graphic novels
  978-1-59307-572-9, $24.95

The greatest star fighters of the Rebel Alliance become the defenders of a New Republic in this massive collection of stories featuring Wedge Antilles, hero of the Battle of Endor, and his team of ace pilots known throughout the galaxy as Rogue Squadron. Meet the Rogues for the first time and learn the fate of the galaxy immediately after the events of Return of the Jedi as the Rebellion's best pilots battle remnants of the Empire wherever its ugly agenda of fear and domination appears. Along with X-Wing Rogue Squadron: The Phantom Affair, this jam-packed volume contains never before collected material, including Star Wars X-Wing Rogue Leader #1-3, Star Wars X-Wing Rogue Squadron: The Rebel Opposition #1-4, Star Wars X-Wing Rogue Squadron: The Phantom Affair #1-4, and Star Wars Handbook: X-Wing Rogue Squadron.
  Volume 1 of 3

Blain, Christophe
  Gus and his gang. First Second Books 2008 164p. Illustration
Grades: 10 11 12 Adult   741.5; Fic

1. Graphic novels; 2. Humorous graphic novels; 3. Western stories — Graphic novels
978-1-59643-170-6, $16.95; 1-59643-170-9

LC 2008-23541

Gus, Gratt, and Clem are three outlaws in this French version of the Old West. Gus much prefers to rob trains, banks are too still for him. What all three of them prefer is to be with women; Gus and Gratt go girl-hunting together in towns such as El Dorado, but Clem doesn't go with them. He has a family, with Ava and their daughter Jamie; but he does have a passionate affair with a free-spirited, red-haired photographer. Everything the three men do is financed by robbing banks, trains...when Gus tries to case a bank, he falls for a woman who works there and ends up pretending to be a writer in order to woo her. The book doesn't follow a straightforward narrative, and the French idea of how the Old West "worked" is more than a bit eccentric. The book also includes lots of sexual content and partial nudity.

Isaac the Pirate 1. To Exotic Lands. NBM 2003 un Illustration
Grades: 10 11 12 Adult   **741.5; Fic**
1. Adventure graphic novels; 2. Graphic novels; 3. Pirates — Graphic novels
1-56163-366-6, $14.95

LC 2003-59288

Isaac is a talented artist with no money but with a wonderful lover back in Paris of the 18th century. He runs into a rich Captain who is taken by his abilities and hires him with a handsome stipend to come along in his voyages. It turns out he's a pirate. Isaac went to make some quick money and come back and marry the love of his life, but he has embarked upon a series of adventures on the high seas from the Caribbean to the icy North, with apparently no end in sight. Meanwhile, his girlfriend is getting attention from another...The book includes some harsh language and violence.

Volume 1 of 2

Blaylock, Josh
   How to self-publish comics: not just create them. Josh Blaylock and Tim Seeley; forward by Art Baltazar. Devil's Due Publishing 2015 144 p.
Grades: 10 11 12 Adult   **741.5**
1. Comic books, strips, etc. — Publishing — United States
0991001044; 9780991001040, $19.99

"Josh Blaylock's now classic How-To prose book about the business of comics publishing, after selling out of its updated 2012 edition, is now being re-released to include Tim Seeley's companion writings on the behind-the-scenes realities of being a comic book artist, originally released in pamphlet form." (Publisher's note)

Bocquet, José-Louis
   Josephine Baker. art by Catel Muller; written by José-Louis Bocquet; historical consultant, Jean-Claude Bouillon-Baker. Harry N Abrams Inc 2017 496 p.
Grades: 11 12 Adult   **741.5; 92**
1. Baker, Josephine, 1906-1975; 2. African American dancers — Biography; 3. Biography
191059329X; 9781910593295, $22.95

LC 2017385203

"Known to many only in the iconic banana costume that made her famous in the 1920s, singer and dancer Josephine Baker lived an incredibly rich life beyond the theater. She was a tireless activist for civil rights and leveraged her status whenever possible to break down racial barriers in the U.S. and around the world. This book follows Baker from her birth in 1906, touching on the many significant events in her life, from her spy work in the French Resistance to adopting the 12 children that made up her Rainbow Tribe." (Booklist)

Bocquet "does Baker's complicated life justice in both appeal and detail. A lengthy chronology anchors key milestones and a massive biographical appendix provides background about important people in the entertainer's life. Muller's high-contrast, black-and-white inks finesse a mostly realistic whimsy and is especially good at rendering people recognizably in few lines." LJ
Originally published in French by Casterman in 2016

Kiki de Montparnasse. illustrated by Catel; written by José-Louis Bocquet; translated from the Belgian edition by Nora Mahony. SelfMadeHero 2011 416 p. Illustration
Grades: Adult   **759.4; 741.5**
1. Artists' models — France — Biography — Comic books, strips, etc; 2. Kiki, 1901-1953 — Comic books, strips, etc; 3. Artists' models; 4. Painters; 5. Women — France — History
9781906838256, $24.95

LC 2011431146

This book offers a graphic biography of artist model and actress Alice Prin, better known as Kiki de Montparnasse. In "bohemian Montparnasse [in Paris, France] of the 1920s, Kiki escaped poverty to become one of the most charismatic figures of the avant-garde years between the wars. Partner to [artist] Man Ray, and one of the first emancipated women of the 20th century, Kiki made her mark with her freedom of style, word, and thought that could be learned from only one school-the school of life." (Amazon.com)
Includes bibliographical references (p. 413-415)

Boldman, Craig
   Archie Day by Day Volume 1. Archie Comics 2003 96p. Illustration
Grades: 3 4 5 6 7 8 9 10 11 12 Adult   **741.5; Fic**
1. Andrews, Archie (Fictional character); 2. Graphic novels; 3. Humorous graphic novels
1-879794-16-0, $10.95

Archie and his pals have been comics' most celebrated teenage humor characters for over 60 years, since 1941. Now for the first time, selections from Archie's worldwide syndicated newspaper strip are collected in this volume. This black and white edition includes a selection of daily strips from the mid-1990s, chronicling life in Riverdale, USA.

Bourdain, Anthony
   Get Jiro!. Anthony Bourdain, Joel Rose, Langdon Foss. DC Comics 2012 160 p.
Grades: Adult   **741.5**
1. Cooks — Comic books, strips, etc; 2. Sushi — Graphic novels; 3. Japanese cooking — Graphic novels; 4. Food — Social aspects — Graphic novels
1401228275; 9781401228279, $24.99

LC 2011052113

This graphic novel is set in "futuristic Los Angeles," where "food culture rules all social life, copping to corporate honchos. People even sing about food at karaoke bars. Two reigning culinary empires control the town like mafia, and both want new-in-town sushi chef Jiro on their team. But Jiro has his own plans and prevails by cleverly pitting both sides against each other, snotty international omnivores vs. holistic purists." (Library Journal)

Brabner, Joyce
   Our cancer year. by Joyce Brabner and Harvey Pekar; illustrations by Frank Stack.

Courtesy of Four Walls Eight Windows

Four Walls Eight Windows 1994 252 p. Illustration
Grades: Adult   **741.5; 362.1**
1. Cancer — Personal narratives; 2. Comic books, strips, etc.; 3. Pekar, Harvey, 1939-2010
1568580118; 9781568580111, $19.95

LC 94010523

This graphic novel, by Joyce Brabner and Harvey Pekar, with illustrations by Frank Stack, "center[s] on the year that they found out that Pekar had cancer; the year that also saw Operation Desert Shield turn into Operation Desert Storm. Drawing upon the many personal trials they faced, Pekar and Brabner create a portrait of a man beset with fears both real and imagined." (Amazon)

Braithwaite, Doug
     Justice Volume One. Jim Krueger and Alex Ross, story; Doug Braithwaite and Alex Ross, art. DC Comics 2006 160p. Illustration
Grades: 8 9 10 11 12 Adult   **741.5; Fic**
1. Graphic novels; 2. Justice League of America (Fictional characters); 3. Superhero graphic novels
978-1-4012-0969-8, $19.99

The Justice League of America are the World's Greatest Super-Heroes, but now villains — the Riddler, Lex Luthor, Poison Ivy, Captain Cold, and others are banding together and making sweeping, worldwide changes that appear to be noble acts. But, one by one the members of the JLA are being taken down; will anyone be left to truly protect the people of Earth?

Breathed, Berke
     Bloom County: A New Hope. Berkeley Breathed. IDW Publishing 2016 144 p. Illustration
Grades: Adult
741.5; Fic
1. American wit and humor; 2. Comic books, strips, etc. — United States
9781631406997, $17.99;
163140699X

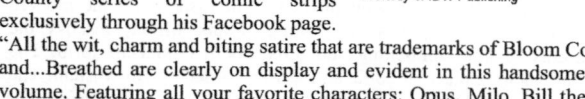

Courtesy of IDW Publishing

Cartoonist Berkeley Breathed previously released the new Bloom County series of comic strips exclusively through his Facebook page.
"All the wit, charm and biting satire that are trademarks of Bloom County and...Breathed are clearly on display and evident in this handsome new volume. Featuring all your favorite characters: Opus, Milo, Bill the Cat, Steve Dallas, Cutter John, and many more." (Publisher's note)
"Breathed returns to Bloom County after a 26-year hiatus. The glorious revisiting of the comic's old visual and sardonic stomping grounds, first seen from 1980 to 1989, is infused with a delightful freshness....The style, though much aligned with the original strip, has a lively, new, energized vitality." LJ

Brenner, Robin E.
     ★ **Understanding** manga and anime. Libraries Unlimited 2007 335p. Illustration
Grades: Adult Professional   **025.2; 741.5**
1. Anime; 2. Libraries — Collection development; 3. Libraries — Special collections — Graphic novels; 4. Manga — Study and teaching
978-1-59158-332-5, $40; 1-59158-332-2

LC 2007-9773

The author "provides thorough explanations of manga and anime vocabulary, potential censorship issues because of cultural disparities, and typical Manga conventions.... No professional collection could possibly be complete without this all-inclusive and exceptional work." Voice Youth Advocates

Britt, Mark Haven
     Full-Color. Image Comics 2007 175p. Illustration
Grades: 11 12 Adult   **741.5; Fic**
1. Graphic novels; 2. Revenge — Graphic novels
978-1-58240-840-8, $15.99

A lifetime marked with Napoleonic bosses has generated a rage in Boom that she can't contain anymore — only aim. Her target? Her boss. She's given herself one day to make it all right now that she's quit her job. That same day, Boom comes home to find an old friend standing on her fire escape. David's double-crossed a drug dealer and he's looking for help. She'll help him if he'll help her; but things don't go according to plan. The book has lots of violence, harsh language, and some partial nudity.

Brooks, Mark
     Arana Vol. 1: The Heart of the Spider. writer, Fiona Avery; pencilers, Mark Brooks & Roger Cruz; inkers, Jaime Mendoza & Victor Olazaba; colorist, UDON's Larry Molinar & Jeannie Lee; letterers, Virtual Calligraphy's Rus Wooton & Chris Eliopoulos. Marvel Entertainment 2005 un Illustration
Grades: 8 9 10 11 12 Adult   **741.5; Fic**
1. Adventure graphic novels; 2. Graphic novels; 3. Superhero graphic novels
0-7851-1506-4, $7.99

She's fierce, she's sassy, she sticks to walls. Anya Corazon, a.k.a. Arana, is a next-generation girl warrior. A scrappy teen from Brooklyn by day, Anya becomes the Hunter of the ancient and mystical Spider Society by night. But first, she must survive her initiation and prove herself on her first mission, all while going to high school and hiding everything from her single-parent dad. Together with her partner, the mysterious mage Miguel, Anya must fight to protect the peace of the world from the sworn enemies of the Spider Society, the evil Sisterhood of the Wasp. There's lots of super hero action here.
     Volume 1 of 3

Broome, John
     The **Green** Lantern Archives Volume 5. stories by John Broome; art by Gil Kane, Joe Giella. DC Comics 2004 239p. Illustration
Grades: 6 7 8 9 10 11 12 Adult   **741.5; Fic**
1. Graphic novels; 2. Green Lantern (Fictional character); 3. Superhero graphic novels
1-4012-0404-X, $49.95

LC 93-131923

This volume presents the further adventures of Green Lantern Hal Jordan " the Silver Age's science fiction-influenced hero. This time, the Emerald Gladiator squares off against foes such as Dr. Light, Hector Hammond, Evil Star, the Aerialist, and many more. This full-color Archive reprints nine tales from Green Lantern #30-38, originally published in 1964 and 1965.

     Showcase Presents: Green Lantern Volume 1. stories by John Broome; art by Gil Kane and Joe Giella. DC Comics 2005 528p. Illustration
Grades: 6 7 8 9 10 11 12 Adult   **741.5; Fic**
1. Graphic novels; 2. Green Lantern (Fictional character); 3. Superhero graphic novels
1-4012-0759-6, $9.99

A dying alien summoned test pilot Hal Jordan and gave him the most powerful weapon in the universe: a power ring. Jordan was inducted into the universe-spanning Green Lantern Corps and assigned to protect a sector of space including Earth. His sheer willpower directs the ring to create fantastic energy constructs and with it, protect the good from evil. In these earliest stories, readers meet the Guardians of the Universe, many of Jordan's intergalactic comrades, and some of his deadliest opponents, including Hector Hammond, Sonar, and Sinestro. The black and white reprints date from 1959 through 1962.

Brown, Box

Andre the Giant: Life and Legend. by Box Brown. First Second 2014 240 p. Illustration

Grades: 9 10 11 12 Adult   **741.5; 92**

1. Andre, the Giant, 1946-1993; 2. Wrestling; 3. Actors

1596438517; 9781596438514, $17.99

LC 2014466607

This book, by Box Brown, is a graphic novel biography of Andre Roussimoff. "At his peak, he weighed 500 pounds and stood nearly seven and a half feet tall. But the huge stature that made his fame also signed his death warrant.... [Brown draws] from historical records about Andre's life as well as a wealth of anecdotes from his colleagues in the wrestling world." (Publisher's note)

Brown "uses professional wrestling's complex narrative devices in this biography, which pulls back the curtain on Andre the Giant (Andre Rousimoff), one of the industry's most well-known figures.... Brown's simple, blocky art keeps the story front and center, and the down-to-earth tone allows him to avoid demonizing or lionizing his subject." Pub Wkly

Includes bibliographical references

Tetris: the games people play. Box Brown. First Second 2016 256 p. Color; Illustration

Grades: 10 11 12 Adult   **749.8; 741.5**

1. Video games

9781626723153, $19.99; 162672315X

This book, by Box Brown, describes how the video game "Tetris delivers an irresistible, unending puzzle that has players hooked.... Alexey Pajitnov had big ideas about games. In 1984, he created Tetris in his spare time while developing software for the Soviet government. Once Tetris emerged from behind the Iron Curtain, it was an instant hit. Nintendo, Atari, Sega — game developers big and small all wanted Tetris." (Publisher's note)

"A graphic narrative that clarifies a complicated series of international negotiations, making the story interesting even for those who don't care about video games." Kirkus

Brown, Chester

Louis Riel: a comic-strip biography. Chester Brown.. Drawn and Quarterly 2003 272 p. Illustration

Grades: Adult   **741.5/971; 741.5**

1. Riel, Louis, 1844-1885 — Comic books, strips, etc.

1896597637; 9781896597638, $24.95

LC 2004396047

"Chester Brown reveals in the dusty closet of Canadian history there are some skeletons that won't stop rattling. To some Louis Riel was one of the founding fathers of a nation but to others he was a murderer who nearly tore a country apart. A man so charismatic he was elected to government twice while in exile with a prize on his head — but so impassioned his dramatic behavior cast serious doubts on his sanity. Riel took on the army, the government, the Queen, and even the Church in the name of freedom." (Publisher's note)

Includes bibliographical references (p. 269) and index

Brown, Jeffrey

Incredible Change-Bots. Top Shelf Productions 2007 un Illustration

Grades: 8 9 10 11 12 Adult   **741.5; Fic**

1. Graphic novels; 2. Humorous graphic novels; 3. Robots — Graphic novels; 4. Science fiction graphic novels

978-1-891830-91-4, $15

Courtesy of IDW Publishing

Far away in outer space, the Incredible Change-Bots live on the planet Electronocybercircuitron. The Awesomebots and the Fantasticons have lived in relative harmony, until Shootertron, the leader of the Fantasticons, decides to rig the election to rule the planet. The Awesomebots declare war, and over the years the Change-Bots destroy their planet. They then come to Earth, where they continue their fighting, each group gaining their own human allies. Brown has done a fun send-up of the Transformers with this story, and while there is some violence, there is very little in the way of bad language.

A **Matter** of Life. written and illustrated by Jeffrey Brown. Top Shelf Productions 2013 96 p. Illustration

Grades: Adult   **741.5/973; Fic**

1. Graphic novels; 2. Family

1603092668, $14.95; 9781603092661

In this graphic novel, author and illustrator Jeffrey Brown "draws upon memories of three generations of Brown men: himself, his minister father, and his preschooler son Oscar. Weaving through time, passing through the quiet suburbs and colorful cities of the midwest, their stories slowly assemble into [an] answer to the big questions: matters of life and death, family and faith, and the search for something beyond oneself." (Publisher's note)

Brownstein, Charles

Eisner/Miller. Dark Horse Books 2005 352p. Illustration

Grades: Adult Professional   **741.5**

1. Graphic novels; 2. Graphic novels — History and criticism; 3. Eisner, Will, 1917-2005; 4. Miller, Frank, 1957-

1-56971-755-9, $19.95

Culture-curious readers and life-long fans of comics are invited to read along as two of the medium's greatest contributors — legendary innovator and godfather of sequential art Will Eisner, and the modern master of cinematic comics storytelling, Frank Miller, discuss the ins-and-outs of this compelling and often controversial art form. The conversations took place in 2002, and were recorded by Brownstein. The book features rare, behind-the-scenes photos of Eisner, Miller, and other notable creators. Some of the reproduced art includes nudity and violence.

Brubaker, Ed

Criminal, Vol. 1: Coward. writer, Ed Brubaker; art, Sean Phillips; colors by Val Staples. Marvel Entertainment/Icon 2007 un Illustration

Grades: 12 Adult   **741.5; Fic**

1. Criminals — Graphic novels; 2. Graphic novels; 3. Mystery graphic novels

0-7851-2439-X, $14.99

Leo plans heists; he's been a criminal since he was a young kid picking pockets. He lives by rules that keep him alive, rules that make others call him a coward. When old friend Seymour comes to him, along with crooked cop Jeff, and asks him to plan a heist of evidence (blood diamonds) from an evidence transport van, Leo doesn't want it. But when Greta, widow of a dead partner, tells him she needs the money to take care of her sick daughter, Leo takes the job. He plans everything, plans for every possible problem, except one. The target of the heist isn't diamonds, it's pure heroin.

And crooked cop Jeff is ready to betray everyone. This is dark crime noir, with lots of harsh language, violence, and a little sex.

Originally published as Criminal issues #1-5.; Other volumes in this series are: Vol. 2: Lawless (2007); Vol. 3: The Dead and the dying (2008); Vol. 4: Bad night (2009); Vol. 5: The sinners (2010); Vol. 6: The last of the innocent (2011)

The **Fade** Out; Act one. by Ed Brubaker; illustrated by Sean Phillips; colors by Elizabeth Breitweiser. Image Comics 2015 120 p. Color; Illustration

Grades: Adult   **741.5; Fic**
1. Actresses — Fiction; 2. Hollywood (Calif.) — Fiction; 3. Noir fiction; 4. Motion pictures — Fiction
1632151715; 9781632151711, $9.99
Eisner Award: Best Limited Series (2016)

This book, by Ed Brubaker, "is an epic noir set in the world of noir itself, the backlots and bars of Hollywood at the end of its Golden Era. A movie stuck in endless reshoots, a writer damaged from the war and lost in the bottle, a dead movie star and the lookalike hired to replace her. Nothing is what it seems in the place where only lies are true." (Publisher's note)

"Waking up from a complete blackout, screenwriter Charlie Parish finds himself half drunk next to the dead body of Valeria Sommers, the starlet of his latest film. As Parish struggles to cover his tracks and uncover details about her death, the studio and its players attempt to distance themselves from Sommers and finish the picture without her. Similar to Brubaker's Fatale series, this is noir at its finest, filled with gritty, deeply flawed characters with twisted motivations, trying to stay one step ahead of each other." Booklist

Originally published in magazine form as The Fade Out #1-4; Volume 1 of 3

Fatale: Death Chases Me. Ed Brubaker and Sean Phillips. Image Comics 2012 144 p.

Grades: Adult   **741.5**
1. Romance fiction; 2. Historical fiction; 3. Paranormal fiction
1607065630; 9781607065630, $14.99

In this book, "[o]ccult forces and gut-wrenching horror collide in 1950s San Francisco, as a corrupt cop and a smitten reporter go toe-to-toe over Jo, an ageless beauty with the looks of a Vargas girl and the heart of a rattle snake, who is desperate to escape the grasp of a satanic cult and their demonic, shape-shifting leader." (Publishers Weekly)

Contains material originally published in magazine form as Fatale #1-5.; Volume 1 of 5

Fatale: West of Hell. by Ed Brubaker and illustrated by Sean Phillips, Dave Stewart, and Bettie Breitweiser. Image comics 2013 128 p.

Grades: Adult   **741.5; Fic**
1. Immortality; 2. Historical fiction
1607067439; 9781607067436, $14.99

In this graphic novel, by Ed Brubaker and illustrated by Sean Phillips, Dave Stewart, and Bettie Breitweiser, "four stories here focus on the antiheroine's search for self-knowledge as we follow her and her predecessors through Dust Bowl Texas, medieval France, the Wild West, and WWII Europe. Tantalizing hints about the forces that spawned her and the unseen, Lovecraftian world that surrounds her are planted throughout the pages." (Booklist)

★ **Gotham** Central; Book One. Ed Brubaker, Greg Rucka; With Michael Lark. DC Comics 2013 235 p. Color illustration

Grades: 11 12 Adult   **741.5**
1. Good and evil — Comic books, strips, etc.; 2. Police — Comic books, strips, etc.; 3. Superheroes — Comic books, strips, etc.; 4. Batman (Fictional character)
1401220371; 9781401220372, $19.99

LC 2012046720

This graphic novel, by Ed Brubaker and Greg Rucka, takes place in "Gotham City: a town teeming with corrupt cops, ruthless crime lords, petty thieves...and just a small handful that would oppose them. Grizzled veteran Harvey Bullock, Captain Maggie Sawyer, detective Renee Montoya and the GCPD are the law force that stands between order and complete anarchy." (Publisher's note)

Series originally collected in five volumes; Originally published in single magazine form in Gotham Central #1-10.; In the Line of Duty; Other Gotham Central collections are: Book two: Jokers and madmen; Book three: On the freak beat; Book four: Corrigan

Kill or be killed; Volume One. by Ed Brubaker; art by Sean Phillips; color by Elizabeth Breitweiser. Image Comics 2017 128 p. Color; Illustration

Grades: Adult   **741.5; Fic**
1. Adventure graphic novels; 2. Murder — Graphic novels
9781534300286, $9.99; 1534300287

"Depressed college student Dylan attempts suicide only to be spared by a demon with the offer of a bargain — kill someone once a month or face death yourself. Dylan soon decides to start targeting criminals overlooked by the system and becomes strangely successful in his violent endeavors. His personal affairs improve, and it seems for the first time he's living the life he's always wanted — which is exactly when the repercussions of his actions start catching up to him." (Library Journal)

Contains material originally published in magazine form as Kill Or Be Killed #1-4; Volume 1 of an ongoing series

The **Sandman** presents: the dead boy detectives. DC Comics/Vertigo 2008 104p. Illustration

Grades: 10 11 12 Adult   **741.5; Fic**
1. Fantasy graphic novels; 2. Ghosts — Graphic novels; 3. Graphic novels; 4. Mystery graphic novels; 5. Supernatural graphic novels
978-1-4012-1855-3, $12.99

Charles Rowland and Edwin Paine spend all their time reading detective stories, watching thrillers at the movie theaters, or just hanging out in their treehouse, and no one cares. Charles and Edwin are ghosts from different times in the past, who have become friends in their new existence. Now, inspired by the stories and movies, they decide to become private detectives, and they take a case from a runaway girl. Someone is killing the runaway children who live in the Underground of London, and that someone is capable of hurting even ghosts like Charles and Edwin. They encounter a man who says his family has hunted the killer for centuries and enlists their help, but is he telling the truth, or are Charles and Edwin in very deep trouble? The book includes some violence.

★ **Scene** of the crime. by Ed Brubaker and illustrated by Michael Lark and Sean Phillips. Image Comics 2012 128 p.

Grades: Adult   **741.5**
1. Noir fiction; 2. Crime — Graphic novels; 3. Mystery graphic novels
1607066327; 9781607066323, $24.99

This graphic novel by Ed Brubaker presents "a hard-hitting mystery story set in a modern-day "Chinatown" that garnered nominations for Best Mini-series and Best Writer in the 2000 Eisner Awards. Also included in this new collection are behind-the-scenes art and stories, a new foreword by Brubaker, and many other extras." (Publisher's note)

Brunetti, Ivan
★ **Aesthetics:** a memoir. by Ivan Brunetti. Yale University Press 2013 120 p. Illustration

Grades: Adult   **759.13**
1. Artists — Biography; 2. Cartoonists — Biography
0300184409; 9780300184402, $25

LC 2012950659

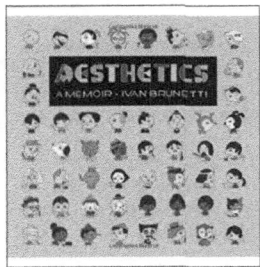

Courtesy of Yale University Press

This autobiography, written by cartoonist and illustrator Ivan Brunetti, traces his artistic trajectory and output, from youthful doodles to his latest cover illustrations and comic strips. It includes "previously unpublished materials, including working drawings, sketches for cartoons, book covers, personal photographs, and items from the artist — s collection of toys and handmade objects. In an introductory essay and captions, Brunetti explains...his creative process and aesthetic sensibility." (Publisher's note)

★ An **Anthology** of graphic fiction, cartoons, and true stories. edited by Ivan Brunetti. Yale University Press 2006 400p. Illustration
Grades: 11 12 Adult
741.5
1. American wit and humor, Pictorial; 2. Cartooning — United States — History — 20th century; 3. Comic books, strips, etc. — United States — History — 20th century
978-0-300-11170-5; 0-300-11170-3, $28
LC 2006-14095

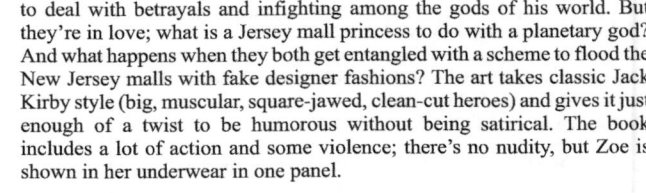

Courtesy of Yale University Press

This is an "anthology of contemporary art comics, along with some classic comic strips and other historical materials. . . . Included here are works from such . . . artists as Robert Crumb, Kim Deitch, Art Spiegelman, Chris Ware, Ben Katchor, Charles Burns, Gary Panter, Seth, Phoebe Gloeckner, Daniel Clowes, Lynda Barry, Joe Sacco, and Jaime and Gilbert Hernandez." (Publisher's note)

Brunswick, Glen
The **Gray** Area Vol. 1: All of This Can be Yours. written by Glen Brunswick; pencils by John Romita, Jr.; inks by Klaus Janson; letters by John Workman; colors by Bill Crabtree. Image Comics 2005 un Illustration

Grades: 11 12 Adult　　　　**741.5; Fic**
1. Graphic novels; 2. Superhero graphic novels; 3. Supernatural graphic novels
1-58240-485-2, $14.95
After his execution for double-crossing a drug cartel, Rudy Chance — a brutal, corrupt cop and womanizer — expects he'll wind up in Hell. Instead, he finds himself in the Gray Area, where he is forced to combat evil for an afterlife police force in order to gain a shot at redemption. Given extraordinary powers, Chance hunts down the wicked to condemn and the worthy to heal. But can he control his own dark side, or will it lead him to eternal damnation? The book has foul language and considerable violence.

★ **Jersey** Gods, vol.1: I'd live and I'd die for you. Image Comics 2009 un Illustration
Grades: 10 11 12 Adult　　　　**741.5; Fic**
1. Graphic novels; 2. Humorous graphic novels; 3. Romance graphic novels; 4. Superhero graphic novels
978-1-60706-063-5, $14.99
Jersey Girl Zoe works as an assistant to the fashion editor of her local newspaper in Cherry Hill, New Jersey. She has bad luck with boyfriends who always dump her. Then she meets Barock, a god from another planet (Cumulus), when one of his fights leads him to Earth. She has to deal with her boss stealing her idea of an article series on fashion, while Barock has

to deal with betrayals and infighting among the gods of his world. But they're in love; what is a Jersey mall princess to do with a planetary god? And what happens when they both get entangled with a scheme to flood the New Jersey malls with fake designer fashions? The art takes classic Jack Kirby style (big, muscular, square-jawed, clean-cut heroes) and gives it just enough of a twist to be humorous without being satirical. The book includes a lot of action and some violence; there's no nudity, but Zoe is shown in her underwear in one panel.

Buhle, Paul
A **dangerous** woman: the graphic biography of Emma Goldman. The New Press 2007 115p. Illustration
Grades: 10 11 12 Adult　　　　**335; 741.5; 92**
1. Anarchism and anarchists — Graphic novels; 2. Anarchists; 3. Biographical graphic novels; 4. Essayists; 5. Family planning advocates; 6. Graphic novels; 7. Goldman, Emma, 1869-1940
978-1-59558-064-1, $17.95
LC 2007-15415
Emma Goldman was a revolutionary activist, speaker, writer, and feminist and anarchist. An immigrant to the U.S., she spoke out against inhumane working conditions, taught contraception, and opposed conscription for World War I. She founded the Free Speech League (a precursor to the ACLU), and the magazine Mother Earth. When she was deported to Russia just after the Bolshevik Revolution, she became disillusioned with the authoritarianism she found there, and she ended up supporting the fight against fascism in the Spanish Civil War. Rudahl based her graphic novel on Goldman's autobiography. The book includes nudity, sexual situations, and some violence.

Bui, Thi
★ The **best** we could do: an illustrated memoir. Thi Bui. Abrams ComicArts 2017 327 p. Color; Illustration
Grades: 11 12 Adult　　　　**92; 741.5; 973/.0495920092**
1. Autobiographical comics; 2. Graphic novels; 3. Refugees — United States — Biography — Comic books, strips, etc.; 4. Vietnam War, 1961-1975 — Personal narratives, Vietnamese — Comic books, strips, etc.; 5. Bui, Thi; 6. Vietnam War, 1961-1975 — Personal narratives, Vietnamese; 7. Vietnamese Americans — Biography; 8. Bui, Thi
9781613129302; 9781419718779, $24.95
LC 2016940170
National Book Critics Circle Award Finalist: Autobiography (2017)
In this memoir, author Thi Bui "documents the story of her family's daring escape after the fall of South Vietnam in the 1970s, and the difficulties they faced building new lives for themselves. At the heart of Bui's story is a universal struggle: While adjusting to life as a first-time mother, she ultimately discovers what it means to be a parent — the endless sacrifices, the unnoticed gestures, and the depths of unspoken love." (Publisher's note)
"In creatively telling a complicated story with the kind of feeling words alone rarely relay, The Best We Could Do does the very best that comics can do." Booklist

Bunn, Cullen
The **damned** volume one: Three days dead. written by Cullen Bunn; illustrated by Brian Hurtt; colored by Bill Crabtree; lettered by Crank!. Oni Press 2008 un Illustration
Grades: 11 12 Adult　　　　**741.5; Fic**
1. Graphic novels; 2. Humorous graphic novels; 3. Mafia — Graphic novels; 4. Mystery graphic novels; 5. Supernatural graphic novels
978-1-932664-63-8, $14.95
In an alternate world prohibition era, gangsters still grow rich on catering to people's vices, but a more sinister power controls the crime

cartels and uses human greed, gluttony, lust, and other mortal sins to fuel a much more lucrative trade: mortal souls. When a feud between two Families is supposed to end with a brokered deal, the bookkeeper brokering the deal is kidnapped. Big Al pulls gumshoe Eddie's corpse out of a ditch and puts him on the case to find the missing bookkeeper. Poor Eddie, he's already dead, but people keep killing him over and over again. The book includes considerable violence, some bad language, and occasional nudity.

Harrow County; Volume 1: countless haints. script, Cullen Bunn; art and lettering, Tyler Crook. Dark Horse 2015 152 p. Color; Illustration
Grades: Adult **741.5**
1. Horror fiction; 2. Ghost stories; 3. Monsters — Fiction
161655780X; 9781616557805, $14.99
Eisner Nominee: Best New Series (2016)
"Emmy always knew that the woods surrounding her home crawled with ghosts and monsters. But on the eve of her eighteenth birthday, she learns that she is connected to these creatures — and to the land itself — in a way she never imagined." (Publisher's note)
"With its heavy narration and sparing dialogue, this feels more like an old fairy tale than a modern horror comic. Although low in traditional scares, it creates a haunting mood rich with an eerie nostalgia that begs to be fleshed out further in future volumes." Booklist
This volume collects Harrow County #1-#4 — Cover

Burns, Charles
★ **Black** hole. Charles Burns.. Pantheon Books 2005 1 v. Illustration
Grades: 10 11 12 Adult **741.5/973**
1. Communicable diseases — Fiction; 2. Teenagers — Fiction; 3. High school students — Fiction; 4. Homicide — Fiction
9780375714726; 9780375423802; 037542380X, $29.95
LC 2005046431
Eisner Awards: Best Graphic Album — Reprint (2006); Harvey Awards: Best Graphic Album — Previously Published (2006); Ignatz Awards: Outstanding Anthology or Collection (2006)
This book takes place in "[s]uburban Seattle, [in] the mid-1970s. We learn from the out-set that a strange plague has descended upon the area's teenagers, transmitted by sexual contact. The disease is manifested in any number of ways — from the hideously grotesque to the subtle (and concealable) — but once you've got it, that's it. There's no turning back. As we inhabit the heads of several key characters — some kids who have it, some who don't, some who are about to get it — what unfolds isn't the expected battle to fight the plague, or bring heightened awareness to it, or even to treat it. What we become witness to instead is a fascinating and eerie portrait of the nature of high school alienation itself — the savagery, the cruelty, the relentless anxiety and ennui, the longing for escape. And then the murders start." (Publisher's note)

The **hive**. Charles Burns. Pantheon Books 2012 56 p.
Grades: Adult **741.5/973**
1. Man-woman relationship — Fiction; 2. Monsters — Fiction; 3. Graphic novels
0307907880; 9780307907882, $21.95
LC 2012002185
Ignatz Nominee: Outstanding Series (2013)
This graphic novel by Charles Burns is "the second volume of a trilogy begun in 'X'ed Out'.... We return to Doug, the protagonist, whose recounting of his relationship with a young woman shifts back and forth between the less surreal of the book's two environments and another where his apparent alter ego works in a dreary factory/ hospital providing books to its monster patients." (Publishers Week)

★ **Sugar** Skull. Charles Burns. Pantheon Books 2014 64 p. Illustration

Grades: Adult **741.5; Fic**
1. Hallucinations and illusions — Graphic novels; 2. Fantasy graphic novels
9780307907905, $23; 0307907902
LC 2014000699
This graphic novel, by Charles Burns, "the third volume in a trilogy concludes a renowned graphic artist's hallucinatory descent into comic-book hell — and it doesn't end prettily.... Without ever resorting to a linear narrative, he concludes the story of Doug that began in 'X'ed Out' and continued with 'The Hive.' Sober for more than a year, he suffers a massive relapse when he returns to his former punk-rock haunts and sees some people who would rather not see him. Yet his dream life and waking life aren't clearly delineated, for Doug or for the reader" (Kirkus Reviews)
"Burns demands and rewards attentive reading, letting the novel unfold in a fractured chronology and employing patterns of repeated imagery and color to draw connections between the two narratives. He brings them together into something altogether new that blends bildungsroman with visceral horror to elucidate the mental state of his protagonist." LJ
Sequel to: The Hive (2012)

★ **X'ed** out. Charles Burns.. Pantheon Books 2010 56 p. Color illustration
Grades: Adult **741.5; Fic**
1. Dreams — Graphic novels; 2. Graphic novels
9780307379139, $21.95; 0307379132
LC 2010005394
In this fantasy graphic novel, by Charles Burns, "Doug is having a strange night. A weird buzzing noise on the other side of the wall has woken him up, and there, across the room, next to a huge hole torn out of the bricks, sits his beloved cat, Inky. Who died years ago. But who's nonetheless slinking out through the hole, beckoning Doug to follow." (Publisher's note)
"Burns's control of the story is masterful — the recurring imagery make it unclear just which is the reality and which is the dream. His sharply delineated art captures a grotesque yet sympathetic view of kids thrust far beyond a world that they can control or even understand." Pub Wkly
Followed by: The Hive (2012)

Burns, Jason M.
A **Dummy's** Guide to Danger. Viper Comics 2007 un Illustration
Grades: 11 12 Adult **741.5; Fic**
1. Graphic novels; 2. Mystery graphic novels
978-0-9793680-0-4, $11.95
Private investigator Alan Sirois and his partner Mr. Bloomberg, a paraplegic ventriloquist dummy that Alan believes was shot in the back by an assailant and became crippled when the bullet lodged in his spine, track down a gruesome killer known only as the Flesh Collector. The book includes violence and harsh language.

The **Underworld** Railroad. Viper Comics 2007 112p. Illustration
Grades: 10 11 12 Adult **741.5**
1. Fantasy graphic novels; 2. Graphic novels
978-0-9793680-3-5, $11.95
This book postulates that when a person dies while still wrongly accused, that person's spirit doesn't immediately go to Heaven or to Hell, but must wait to be cleared. In the meantime, the spirit is vulnerable and can be taken by the devil. For these spirits, a system of safe houses offers refuge. In one such safe house, Bruce welcomes the spirit of a man who was falsely accused of murdering his wife. The devil takes the form of a sexy woman who doesn't want to take no for an answer, and she tries to take the spirit by force. The book includes violence, some harsh language, and supernatural action.

Busiek, Kurt

★ **Astro** City: life in the big city. by Kurt Busiek, Brent Anderson, and Alex Ross. DC Comics 2011 192 p. Color illustration

Grades: 11 12 Adult   **741.5; Fic**

1. Superhero graphic novels

1401232612; 1401232620; 9781401232610; 9781401232627, $17.99

LC 2012376788

This graphic novel, by Kurt Busiek, Brent Anderson, and Alex Ross, is set in "Astro City, a shining city on a hill where super heroes patrol the skies.... The city's leading super hero tries to be everywhere at once, and berates himself for every wasted second as he longs for just a moment of his own. A smalltime hood learns a hero's secret identity, and tries to figure out how to profit from the knowledge. A beat reporter gets some advice from his editor on his first day on the job." (Publisher's note)

"These heroes are intentionally written to resemble classic superheroes like Superman, Wonder Woman, and the Fantastic Four. The Astro City heroes, however, aren't derivative; the authors introduce well-developed, original characters and use them to delve into the unexplored possibilities and unanswered questions of classic superheroes as well as their relationships with the world around them." LJ

Collected volume originally published 1997; Originally published as Kurt Busiek's Astro city v. 1 #1-6.; Other Astro City volumes are: Confession (1997); Family album (1998); The tarnished angel (2000); Local heroes (2005); The dark age 1: Brothers & other strangers (2008); The dark age 2: Brothers in arms (2010); Shining stars (2011); Through open doors (2014); Victory (2014); Private lives (2015); Lovers quarrel (2015); Honor guard (2016); Reflections (2017)

Astro City: the dark age 1: brothers & other strangers. DC Comics/Wildstorm 2009 256p. Illustration

Grades: 10 11 12 Adult   **741.5; Fic**

1. Crime — Graphic novels; 2. Gangs — Graphic novels; 3. Graphic novels; 4. Superhero graphic novels

978-1-4012-2077-8, $19.99

In Astro City of the 1970s, estranged brothers Charles and Royal Williams are still trying to cope with the tragedy that ripped their family apart back in 1959. Charles is an honest cop stuck with a crooked partner who keeps trying to get him to accept graft payments, while Royal has been living the life of a smalltime crook. Their lives keep intersecting with those of the superpowered, heroes and criminals alike. Throughout the book, the readers piece together the bits of flashbacks to that pivotal tragedy in 1959; when the only black superhero treats the young brothers with respect, but a battle between superhero Silver Agent and super criminals erupts into the Williams family's apartment and kills the parents. When Silver Agent walked through the apartment in pursuit of the villains and ignored the dead and surviving civilians, it crushed the boys' spirits, leaving one distrustful of all super powered beings and the other without hope of any good in life. Now, with Silver Agent convicted of murder, an impending war between super powered gangs, and the vengeful Black Velvet and Blue Knight slaughtering criminals even smalltime grifters such as Royal, it's truly a Dark Age in Astro City. The book includes some violence and some harsh language.

Astro City: Through Open Doors. Kurt Busiek; [illustrated by] Brent Anderson. DC Comics/Vertigo 2014 161 p. Color; Illustration (Astro City)

Grades: Adult   **741.5**

1. Imaginary places; 2. Superhero comic books, strips, etc.

1401247520; 9781401247522, $24.99

LC 2013049638

Author and illustrator "Kurt Busiek and Brent Anderson launch their next epic in the world of Astro City when a mysterious door appears, heralding the arrival of the Ambassador. But when an ordinary man is caught in a cosmic conflict, it is up to favorites like Samaritan and Honor Guard, as well as new heroes, to rise to the occasion and save the world!" (Publisher's note)

"When this Eisner and Harvey Award-winning series returned after a hiatus, it relaunched with four excellent stories of the human side of superheroes, collected in Shining Stars. In this succeeding volume, preeminent comics scribe Busiek...reveals the reverse: the extraordinary side of more ordinary folk living among superpowered movers and shakers." LJ

Conan Volume 1: The Frost-Giant's Daughter and Other Stories. Dark Horse Comics 2005 un Illustration

Grades: 10 11 12 Adult   **741.5; Fic**

1. Adventure graphic novels; 2. Conan the Barbarian (Fictional character); 3. Fantasy graphic novels; 4. Graphic novels

1-59307-301-1, $15.95

Conan the Barbarian wars with the murderous Vanir, meets the Frost Giant's Daughter, and is taken as a slave by the ancient sorcerers of Hyperborea in this volume of new Conan adventures. Busiek and Nord adapt some of Robert E. Howard's original Conan stories and create some original stories, just as Roy Thomas and Barry Windsor-Smith had done in the 1970s. Conan prefers action to thought, and the stories are full of fighting, some nudity and sexual situations.

JLA: Syndicate Rules. DC Comics 2005 un Illustration

Grades: 10 11 12 Adult   **741.5; Fic**

1. Adventure graphic novels; 2. Graphic novels; 3. Justice League of America (Fictional characters); 4. Superhero graphic novels

1-4012-0477-5, $17.99

Cosmic upheavals destroyed and rebuilt the antimatter universe, with their super-powered conquerors blaming the JLA. Seeking revenge against their positive matter universe counterparts, the JLA, the Crime Syndicate of Amerika breaches the barrier between universes and brings chaos to Earth. The antimatter universe's Weaponers of Qward tip the balance of power as they employ a new super-weapon that can wipe out both super-teams, and Earth's inhabitants, in a heartbeat.

★ **Marvels**. by Kurt Busiek; illustrated by Alex Ross. Marvel 2010 248 p.

Grades: 10 11 12 Adult   **741.5**

1. Marvel Comics Group; 2. Superhero comic books, strips, etc.

078514286X; 9780785142867, $24.99

In this comic book, by Kurt Busiek, illustrated by Alex Ross, "Welcome to New York. Here, burning figures roam the streets, men in brightly colored costumes scale the glass and concrete walls, and creatures from space threaten to devour our world. This is the Marvel Universe, where the ordinary and fantastic interact daily." (Publisher's note)

Followed by Marvels: Eye of the camera

Butler, Blair

Heart. Blair Butler. Image Comics 2012 120 p. Illustration

Grades: Adult   **741.5; 741**

1. Mixed martial arts — Graphic novels

1607065789; 9781607065784, $12.99

This graphic novel tells the story of "Oren 'Rooster' Redmond, who is looking for more than what his desk job affords him. With a brother already" a mixed martial artist, "Oren trades in watching the sport for an opportunity of self-exploration to find out exactly what he's made of — and what he discovers about himself makes for a story that is, at its heart, eminently human." (Publishers Weekly)

Butler, Octavia

Kindred: a graphic novel adaptation. by Octavia E. Butler, adapted by Damian Duffy, illustrated by John Jennings. Abrams ComicArts 2017 240 p. Illustration

Grades: 10 11 12 Adult   741.5
1. Time travel — Comic books, strips, etc.; 2. Slavery; 3. Slaves — Comic books, strips, etc.
9781419709470, $24.95; 9780807083703, $16

LC 2016940630

Eisner Award: Best Adaptation from Another Medium (2018)

This graphic novel adaptation, by Octavia E. Butler, adapted by Damian Duffy and illustrated by John Jennings, "tells the story of Dana, a young black woman who is suddenly and inexplicably transported from her home in 1970s California to the pre-Civil War South. As she time-travels between worlds,...she becomes frighteningly entangled in the lives of Rufus, a conflicted white slaveholder and one of Dana's own ancestors, and the many people who are enslaved by him." (Publisher's note)

Byrne, Eugene
★ **Darwin:** a graphic biography. by Eugene Byrne; illustrated by Simon Gurr. Smithsonian Books 2013 96 p. Illustration
Grades: 5 6 7 8 9 10 11 12 Adult
576.8/2092; 576.8; 92
1. Evolution (Biology) — Comic books, strips, etc; 2. Graphic novels; 3. Natural selection — Comic books, strips, etc; 4. Darwin, Charles, 1809-1882; 5. Evolution; 6. Darwin, Charles, 1809-1882
1588343529; 9781588343529, $9.95

LC 2012951786

Courtesy of Smithsonian Books

This work of graphic nonfiction by Eugene Byrne and Simon Gurr presents a "summary of [Charles] Darwin's life and achievement.... Darwin was an indifferent student...until he received an invitation to take a voyage that 'would change the course of history.'...The animals he encountered seemed so different...that he theorized that if it weren't a matter of different conditions that resulted in such 'transmutation,' they might well have had a different creator." (Kirkus Reviews)

Includes bibliographical references.

Byrne, John
Superman: The Man of Steel Vol. 1. John Byrne, writer/penciller; Dick Giordano, inker; John Costanza, letterer; Tom Ziuko, colorist; foreword by Ray Bradbury. DC Comics 1991 132p. Illustration
Grades: 8 9 10 11 12 Adult   741.5; Fic
1. Graphic novels; 2. Superhero graphic novels; 3. Superman (Fictional character)
978-0930289287, $14.99

This reprint of a 1986 book retells and reinvents the origin and early adventures of the Man of Steel. Superman begins his ascension to iconic hero as he leaves Smallville and becomes Metropolis's revered protector and guardian. Featuring the Man of Steel's legendary first encounters with Lex Luthor, Lois Lane, and Batman, this book also includes a deadly battle with Bizarro, a fateful encounter with Lana Lang, and Superman's astonishing discovery of his Kryptonian heritage.

Superman: The Man of Steel Vol. 5. John Byrne, Marv Wolfman, writers; John Byrne, Jerry Ordway, pencillers. DC Comics 2006 210p. Illustration
Grades: 9 10 11 12 Adult   741.5; Fic
1. Graphic novels; 2. Superhero graphic novels; 3. Superman (Fictional character); 4. Joker (Fictional character)
978-1-4012-0948-3, $19.99

Superman and the staff of the Daily Planet uncover a gang war raging in the city's notorious "Suicide Slum." Journalistic integrity is put to the test when it is revealed that Perry White's son is involved. Will the Daily Planet run a story that will ruin the life of one of their own? And what is the identity of the new protector of the streets, who emerges amid the havoc? Also, love is in the air, as Superman finds himself romantically involved with Big Barda, the amazon from the planet Apokolips, and with Cat Grant. Along with his ever-present nemesis Lex Luthor, Superman faces the evil of Sleez, the Joker, and that fiendish magical imp from the Fifth Dimension, Mr. Mxyzptlk. These stories were originally published in 1987.

★ **X-Men:** The Dark Phoenix Saga, 2nd ed.. writer, Chris Claremont; penciler and co-plotter, John Byrne. Marvel Entertainment 2006 200p. Illustration
Grades: 7 8 9 10 11 12 Adult   741.5; Fic
1. Graphic novels; 2. Superhero graphic novels; 3. X-Men (Fictional characters)
978-0-7851-2213-5, $24.99

Gathered together by Professor Charles Xavier to protect a world that fears and hates them, the X-Men had fought many battles, been on adventures that spanned galaxies, grappled enemies of limitless might, but none of this could prepare them for the most shocking struggle they would ever face. One of their own members, Jean Grey, has gained power beyond all comprehension, and that power has corrupted her absolutely. Now they must decide if the life of the woman they cherish is worth the existence of the entire universe.

Cain, Chelsea
Mockingbird; Volume 1: I can explain. Chelsea Cain, writer; Kate Niemczyk & Ibrahim Moustafa, artists. Marvel Enterprises 2016 136 p. Color; Illustration
Grades: 9 10 11 12 Adult   741.5
1. Spy stories; 2. Women superheroes — Comic books, strips, etc.
1302901222; 9781302901226, $17.99

"Agent of S.H.I.E.L.D. Bobbi Morse, the former Avenger known as Mockingbird, goes solo. With a scientific mind and a lethal mastery of martial arts, she's one of the most versatile, in-demand assets at Maria Hill's disposal. And when Lance Hunter's undercover gig at the London Hellfire Club goes south, Mockingbird sets off, battle staves at the ready, to save him." (Publisher's note)

"Novelist Cain's first foray into comics is rousing fun. Bobbi may be beautiful and skilled at combat, but her real weapon is her brain.... Niemczyk's art perfectly complements Cain's writing." Booklist

Contains material originally published in single magazine form as Mockingbird: S.H.I.E.L.D. 50th anniversary #1 and Mockingbird #1-5; Volume 1 of 2

Mockingbird; Volume 2: my feminist agenda. Chelsea Cain, writer; Kate Niemczyk, penciler; Sean Parsons, inker; Rachelle Rosenberg, color artist; VC's Joe Caramagna, letterer. Marvel Enterprises 2017 120 p. Color; Illustration
Grades: 9 10 11 12 Adult   741.5
1. Murder — Investigation — Graphic novels; 2. Ocean travel — Fiction; 3. Women superheroes — Comic books, strips, etc.
1302901230; 9781302901233, $15.99

"A top secret mission on behalf of an old friend, a tropical cruise. What could go wrong? Turns out it's a theme cruise — super-hero themed. Bobbi is trapped on a boat with a thousand cosplayers, caped colleagues she was trying to avoid, an ex-boyfriend who keeps showing up at inopportune times. When a passenger is murdered, Bobbi must...find the killer." (Publisher's note)

Contains material originally published in single magazine form as Mockingbird #6-8 and New Avengers #13-14

Callen, Kerry

Halo and Sprocket vol. 2: Natural creatures. SLG Publishing/Amaze Ink 2008 un Illustration

Grades: 8 9 10 11 12 Adult   **741.5; Fic**

1. Angels — Graphic novels; 2. Graphic novels; 3. Humorous graphic novels; 4. Robots — Graphic novels

978-1-59362-131-5, $8.95

Halo the angel and Sprocket the robot live with a young woman named Katie. Their mission: to try to figure out the human race. They are puzzled by Katie's desire for privacy when she's taking a bath; they don't understand why she'll accept being clawed and bitten by a cute little kitten but won't hold a skink; and playing a trivia game causes Halo to show anger. When Halo transforms Sprocket into a human so he can experience what eating food is all about, the temporarily human Sprocket drives Katie crazy with questions about bodily functions such as burping, sneezing, and more.

Campbell, Eddie

ALEC: 'the years have pants'; a life-sized Omnibus. Eddie Campbell. Top Shelf 2009 638 p. Illustration

Grades: Adult

741.5

1. Graphic novels; 2. Campbell, Eddie; 3. Autobiographical graphic novels

1603090479; 9781603090476, $49.95; 9781603090254, $35; 1603090258

Courtesy of IDW Publishing

This book, by Eddie Campbell, collects the author's "autobiographical comics.... The ALEC stories present a version of Campbell's own life, filtered through the alter ego of 'Alec MacGarry.' Over many years, we witness Alec's (and Eddie's) progression 'from beer to wine' — wild nights at the pub, existential despair, the hunt for love, the quest for art, becoming a 'responsible breadwinner,' feeling lost at his own movie premiere, and much more!" (Publisher's note)

"Though best known for his Alan Moore collaboration From Hell, Campbell shows in his MacGarry stories a breezy comic touch that can still flirt with darker topics of artistic responsibility and mortality without weighing down the narrative." Pub Wkly

Bacchus 1. by Eddie Campbell. IDW 2015 560 p.

Grades: Adult

741

1. Comic books, strips, etc.

1603090266; 9781603090261, $39.99

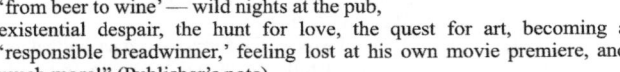

Courtesy of IDW Publishing

This book, by Eddie Campbell, "collects the first half of the Bacchus saga (including Immortality Isn't Forever, The Gods of Business, Doing the Islands with Bacchus, The Eyeball Kid: One Man Show, and Earth, Water, Air & Fire) with new notes and commentary by the author." (Publisher's note)

The **lovely** horrible stuff. Eddie Campbell. Top Shelf Productions 2012 95 p. Illustration

Grades: Adult   **332.4/0222; 332.4; 741.5**

1. Money; 2. Personal finance

1603091521; 9781603091527, $14.95

In this work of graphic nonfiction, "Eddie Campbell...presents a...journey into the wilderness of personal finance. With his trademark blend of research, anecdote, autobiography, and fantasy, Campbell explores how money underwrites human relationships.... The result is a...graphic essay...ranging from the imaginary wealth of Ponzi schemes and television pilots to the all-too-tangible stone currency of the Micronesian island of Yap." (Publisher's note)

Courtesy of IDW Publishing

Cannon, Kevin

The **cartoon** introduction to philosophy. Michael F. Patton and Kevin Cannon; Illustrated by Kevin Cannon. Hill & Wang 2015 176 p. Illustration

Grades: 11 12 Adult   **100; 741.5**

1. Philosophy — Introductions — Comic books, strips, etc; 2. Cartoons and caricatures; 3. Graphic novels

0809033623; 9780809033621, $17.95

LC 2014029343

In this book, authors "Michael F. Patton and Kevin Cannon introduce us to the grand tradition of examined living. With the wisecracking Heraclitus as our guide, we travel down the winding river of philosophy, meeting influential thinkers from nearly three millennia of Western thought and witnessing great debates over everything from ethics to the concept of the self to the nature of reality." (Publisher's note)

"The dynamic, cartoony illustrations might lead some to assume that this title is a little more accessible than it actually is, but anyone with an interest in learning about the philosophers and philosophical concepts that have shaped 21st-century life without having to plow their way through a dry textbook will find this title a stimulating delight." LJ

Includes bibliographical references

Crater XV. by Kevin Cannon. Top Shelf Productions 2013 496 p.

Grades: 10 11 12 Adult

741; Fic

1. Adventure graphic novels; 2. Science fiction graphic novels

1603091009; 9781603091008, $19.95

Courtesy of IDW Publishing

This graphic novel, by Kevin Cannon, "weaves together...swashbuckling adventure, abandoned moon bases, bloodthirsty walruses, rogue astronauts, two-faced femme fatales, sailboat chases, Siberian pirates, international Arctic politics, and a gaggle of horny orphans. Mixed up in all of this are Army Shanks, our salty sea dog still reeling from a devastating loss, and Wendy Byrd, a plucky teenager who wants nothing more than a one-way ticket off the face of the Earth." (Publisher's note)

Far Arden. Kevin Cannon. Top Shelf Productions 2009 400p. Illustration

Grades: 10 11 12 Adult

Fic; 741.5/973

1. Adventure graphic novels; 2. Arctic regions — Graphic novels

9781603090360, $19.95; 1603090363

In this graphic novel, by Kevin Cannon, "Army Shanks — crusty old sea dog and

Courtesy of IDW Publishing

legendary brawler of the high Arctic seas...[has] one mission: to find the mythical island paradise known as Far Arden, which lies hidden...in the wintry oceans of the far North. But...he'll have to contend with circus performers, adorable orphans, heinous villains, bitter ex-lovers, well-meaning undergraduates, and the full might of the Royal Canadian Arctic Navy!" (Publisher's note)

Cannon, Zander

Kaijumax; Volume 1. Zander Cannon; color flatting by Jason Fischer; designed by Fred Chao. Oni Press 2016 168 p. Color; Illustration
Grades: Adult
741.5; Fic
1. Prisons — Fiction; 2. Science fiction; 3. Monsters — Fiction
1620102706; 9781620102701, $9.99
Eisner Nominee: Best New Series (2016)

Courtesy of Oni Press

"On a remote island in the South Pacific lies KAIJUMAX, a maximum security prison for giant monsters. Follow doting father Electrogor as he stands up to the cruel space-superhero warden! See corrupt guard Gupta manage his illicit uranium-dealing empire and pay off his gambling debts to the Queen of the Moon! Watch Mecha-Zon battle his own programming when the monster he was created to destroy shows up on the pound!" (Publisher's note)

"Godzilla meets Oz in this clever exploration of prison life.... Cannon does a wonderful job of exploring both the serious and comic aspects of his high concept, such as the monsters' specialized slang and their frustration in a world not built to their size." Pub Wkly

This volume collects issues #1-6 of the Oni Press series Kaijumax — Title page verso; Volume 1 of an ongoing series

Card, Orson Scott

Ultimate Iron Man Vol. 1. writer: Orson Scott Card; pencils: Andy Kubert and Mark Bagley; inks: Danny Miki ... [et al.]; colors: Richard Isanove; letters: Chris Eliopoulos. Marvel Entertainment 2006 un Illustration
Grades: 10 11 12 Adult
741.5; Fic
1. Graphic novels; 2. Iron Man (Fictional character); 3. Superhero graphic novels
9780785121510, $14.99

Iron Man has been part of the Ultimates, but this volume gives his Ultimate origin. Due to an accident that happened before Tony Stark was born, he has grown up to be a super genius, but always in great physical pain. It's the main reason he becomes an alcoholic as an adult.

Carey, Mike

Crossing Midnight: Cut Here. DC Comics/Vertigo 2007 124p. Illustration
Grades: 11 12 Adult
741.5; Fic
1. Fantasy graphic novels; 2. Graphic novels; 3. Horror graphic novels; 4. Mystery graphic novels
978-1-4012-1341-1, $9.99

In present-day Nagasaki, Japan, a set of twins are born — one just before midnight and the other just after. They discover the huge impact this small difference has on their destinies when the after-midnight twin is inducted into a world of supernatural beings and events that intersects with our own world. Together, they will desperately try to stay one step ahead of their terrifying fates while they learn how far the curse afflicting them

really stretches. As their father gets mixed up with Yakuza, the story builds with violence, partial nudity, and harsh language.

★ **Lucifer;** Book 1. Mike Carey, writer; Scott Hampton ... [et al.], artists; Daniel Vozzo, colorist; Todd Klein, Ellie de Ville, letterers; Neil Gaiman, consultant. Vertigo 2013 381 p. Color; Illustration
Grades: Adult
741.5; Fic
1. Devil — Graphic novels; 2. Angels — Graphic novels; 3. Fantasy fiction
9781401240264, $29.99; 1401240267

"Cast out of Heaven, thrown down to rule in Hell, Lucifer Morningstar has resigned his post and abandoned his kingdom for the mortal city of Los Angles. Emerging from the pages of writer Neil Gaiman's award-winning seriesThe Sandman, the former Lord of Hell is now enjoying a quiet retirement as the propretor of Lux, L.A.'s most elite piano bar. But now an assignment from the Creator Himself is going to change all that." (Publisher's note)

Also available as 11 volumes; Book 1 of 5

Neil Gaiman's Neverwhere. DC Comics/Vertigo 2007 un Illustration
Grades: 11 12 Adult
741.5; Fic
1. Fantasy graphic novels; 2. Graphic novels; 3. Gaiman, Neil; 4. Gaiman, Neil — Adaptations
978-1-4012-1007-6, $19.99

Ordinary Richard Mayhew lives an ordinary life in London, in an ordinary corporate job, with a domineering fiancee. Then one day he does one extraordinary thing: he defies his fiancee to help an injured young woman, and his life changes. That young woman, Door, comes from London Below, a fantastical world made up of the bits and pieces of forgotten city and life from above. Her family has been slaughtered, she's being hunted by a pair of extremely nasty, sadistic, violent assassins, and after Richard helps her he has no choice but to go to London Below, for his entire existence in ordinary London has been wiped out, as though he has never...been.

Neverwhere was first a script for a BBC miniseries written by Neil Gaiman; he then adapted his script into a novel, which is now adapted into graphic novel format.

Originally published as Neverwhere issues #1-9.

Spellbinders: Signs & Wonders. Marvel Entertainment 2005 un Illustration
Grades: 7 8 9 10 11 12 Adult
741.5; Fic
1. Graphic novels; 2. Magic — Graphic novels; 3. Mystery graphic novels; 4. Supernatural graphic novels
0-7851-1756-3, $7.99

Getting through high school is hard enough without having to watch your back the whole time, but magic can give you a real edge over the competition. When 15-year-old Kim Vesco moves from Chicago to Salem, MA, she finds that the local student body is divided into rival factions of witches and non-witches, with both sides bidding for her allegiance. And if that weren't enough, an unknown force seems to want her... dead. Between the tribal loyalties of the schoolyard and the brutal, fight-or-die logic of the mage-war, Kim has to steer a course that will keep her alive until she can take the fight back to her enemy and reveal the true identity of someone she thought she already knew: herself.

The **unwritten:** dead man's knock. Mike Carey & Peter Gross, script, story, art; Ryan Kelly, finishes; Chris Chuckry, Jeanne McGee, colorists; Todd Klein, letterer. DC Comics/Vertigo 2011 160 p.
Grades: Adult
741.5
1. Identity (Philosophical concept) — Comic books, strips, etc; 2. Magicians — Comic books, strips, etc; 3. Secret societies — Graphic novels; 4. Fantasy graphic novels
1401230466; 9781401230463, $14.99

LC 2012376086

This is the third graphic novel in Mike Carey's Unwritten series. Here, a "malevolent, ancient secret society that twists stories to its will becomes the clarified antagonist of Tommy [Taylor] and pals, but its ultimate intentions remain foggy.... Our heroes are left on the verge of chasing down a certain great white whale." (Booklist)

The unwritten created by Gross and Carey.||Originally published in single magazine form as The unwritten 13-18 — T.p. verso.

The **unwritten**: leviathan. Mike Carey & Peter Gross, script, story, art; Vince Locke, Al Davison, finishes; Chris Chuckry, colorist; Todd Klein, letterer; Yuko Shimizu, cover artist. Vertigo/DC Comics 2011 144 p.

Grades: Adult   **741.5**
1. Identity (Philosophical concept) — Comic books, strips, etc; 2. Magicians — Comic books, strips, etc; 3. Fantasy graphic novels
1401232922; 9781401232924, $14.99
                LC 2011275327

This is the fourth graphic novel in Mike Carey's Unwritten series featuring Tom Taylor. Here, Tom "gets sucked into the narrative of 'Moby-Dick.' But the walls between stories are porous, and Tom soon rubs elbows with Sinbad, Baron Münchhausen, Pinocchio, and Frankenstein's monster, who knows way more about what's going on than any stitched-together lug ought to." (Booklist)

The unwritten created by Gross and Carey.||4 — Spine.||Vertigo — Cover.||Originally published in single magazine form as The unwritten 19-24 — T.p. verso.

The **unwritten**: on to genesis. Mike Carey & Peter Gross, script, story, art; Vince Locke, finishes, 1930 sequences; Christ Chuckry, colorist; Todd Klein, letter; Yuko Shimizu, covers. DC Comics 2012 144 p.

Grades: Adult   **741.5**
1. Identity (Philosophical concept) — Comic books, strips, etc; 2. Magicians — Comic books, strips, etc; 3. Fantasy graphic novels; 4. Father-son relationship — Graphic novels
1401233597; 9781401233594, $14.99
                LC 2012372869

This is the fifth graphic novel in Mike Carey's Unwritten series featuring Tom Taylor. Here, Tom "gradually chips away at his origin by learning about his father's history. The gang discovers that Tom's father once worked for the very cartel that killed him and was instrumental in creating another living fictional character, the Tinker, predating Tom by decades." (Booklist)

Originally published in single magazine form as The unwritten 25-30.||The unwritten created by Gross and Carey.||5 — Spine.

The **unwritten**: Tommy Taylor and the war of words. Mike Carey & Peter Gross, script, story, art; M.K. Perker, Dean Ormston, Vince Locke, finishes. DC Comics 2012 240 p.

Grades: Adult   **741.5/973**
1. Characters and characteristics in literature — Comic books, strips, etc; 2. Fame — Psychological aspects — Comic books, strips, etc; 3. Fiction — Comic books, strips, etc; 4. Identity (Philosophical concept) — Comic books, strips, etc; 5. Fantasy graphic novels; 6. Comic books, strips, etc.
1401235603; 9781401235604, $16.99
                LC 2012022581

This comic book is the sixth volume in Mike Carey's "Unwritten" series. "Before his mysterious disappearance and untimely death, the world-famous fantasy author Wilson Taylor helped bring two enduring creations into the world: Tommy Taylor, the fictional boy wizard who starred in his best selling book...and Tom Taylor, his real-life son. Armed

with his father's journals, Tom Taylor begins a journey to uncover the truth behind how he came into this world." (Publisher's note)

Originally published in single magazine form in The Unwritten 31-35, 31.5-35.5.

The **unwritten**: Tommy Taylor and the bogus identity. by Mike Carey and illustrated by Peter Gross. Vertigo 2010 144 p.

Grades: Adult   **741.5/973**
1. Characters and characteristics in literature — Comic books, strips, etc; 2. Identity (Philosophical concept) — Comic books, strips, etc; 3. Magicians — Comic books, strips, etc; 4. Characters and characteristics in literature; 5. Conspiracies — Fiction; 6. Magicians — Graphic novels
1401225659; 9781401225650, $14.99
                LC 2010292145

In this graphic novel by Mike Carey a "scandal reveals that Tom might really be a boy-wizard. Tom comes into contact with a very mysterious, very deadly group that's secretly kept tabs on him. To protect his own life and discover the truth behind his origins, Tom will travel the world, eventually finding himself at locations all featured on a very special map — one kept by the deadly group that charts places throughout world history where fictions have impacted...reality." (Publisher's note)

The unwritten created by Gross and Carey. ||Originally published in single magazine form as The unwritten 1-5 — T.p. verso.; Volume 1 of 11

★ The **Unwritten**: Tommy Taylor and the ship that sank twice. Mike Carey, illustrated by Peter Gross. Vertigo 2013 160 p. Color; Illustration

Grades: 11 12 Adult   **741.5; Fic**
1. Characters and characteristics in literature; 2. Identity (Philosophical concept) — Comic books, strips, etc; 3. Father-son relationship — Fiction; 4. Characters and characteristics in literature
140122976X; 9781401229764, $22.99
                LC 2013020333

In this graphic novel by Mike Carey, "Tom Taylor has lived his life being mistaken for Tommy Taylor, the boy wizard from the world-famous series of novels penned by Tom's long-lost father Wilson. However, after a series of strange events start to parallel the lives of both Taylors — fictional and real — Tom realizes that he might be the character on page made flesh." (Publisher's note)

-"This title can serve as an entry point to the author's 'Unwritten' series, or as a standalone prequel.... The fictional Tommy receives his magical powers in this volume, and in a parallel narrative, Wilson crafts his first book, and orchestrates a twisted publicity stunt to make his son and his book character the same person in the eyes of the public.... Both story lines are equally compelling and balance each other out wonderfully-." SLJ

The **unwritten**; 2: inside man. by Mike Carey and illustrated by Peter Gross. Vertigo 2010 168 p.

Grades: Adult   **741.5/973**
1. Graphic novels; 2. Identity (Philosophical concept) — Comic books, strips, etc; 3. Magicians — Comic books, strips, etc; 4. Time travel — Graphic novels; 5. Magic — Graphic novels; 6. Escapes — Fiction
1401228739; 9781401228736, $12.99
                LC 2010526112

In this graphic novel by Mike Carey "when an enormous scandal reveals that Tom might really be a boy-wizard made flesh, Tom comes into contact with a very mysterious, very deadly group that's secretly kept tabs on him. In this volume, Tom arrives at Donostia prison in Southern France and falls into the orbit of another story: The Song of Roland. His escape from Donostia jail takes him to Stuttgart in 1940, a ghost city inhabited by...Josef Goebbels, and a tortured soul who's crying out for rescue." (Publisher's note)

2 — Spine. Originally published in single magazine form as The unwritten 6-12 — T.p. verso.

The **Unwritten**; Volume 10. Mike Carey, writer; Peter Gross, Al Davison, artists. DC Comics/Vertigo 2014 128 p. Color; Illustration
Grades: Adult   **741.5**
1. Characters and characteristics in literature; 2. Magicians — Graphic novels; 3. Conspiracies — Fiction; 4. Fantasy fiction
1401250556; 9781401250553, $14.99

LC 2014014691

In this book, by Mike Carey and Peter Gross, "Tom Taylor is stranded at the beginning of all creation! Lost in the unwritten scenes of all the world's stories, Tom Taylor is headed back to reality — and all the gods and beasts and monsters ever imagined can't stop him. But there's a toll on the road that may be too high for him or anyone to pay." (Publisher's note)

Originally published in single magazine form in The Unwritten: Apocalypse #1-5.

The **unwritten**; Volume 11: apocalypse. Mike Carey; illustrated by Peter Gross. DC Comics/Vertigo 2015 176 p. Color; Illustration
Grades: Adult   **741.5; Fic**
1. Fantasy comic books, strips, etc.; 2. Storytelling — Fiction; 3. Adventure fiction
1401253482; 9781401253486, $16.99

"Tom Taylor — the real-life counterpart of his father's famous fictional boy-wizard creation, a living bridge between our reality and the realities of every tale ever told — knows the power of stories only too well. Now he's the star of his most important story yet. It's a quest straight out of King Arthur, filled with black knights, ensorcelled swords, and maidens who are fair to a fault." (Publisher's note)

Originally published in single magazine form in THE UNWRITTEN: APOCALYPSE #6-12

The **Unwritten**; volume 7. Mike Carey, Peter Gross. DC Comics/Vertigo 2013 144 p. Color; Illustration
Grades: Adult   **741.5**
1. Comic books, strips, etc.; 2. Characters and characteristics in literature; 3. Identity — Fiction
1401238068; 9781401238063, $14.99

LC 2012047806

"Tom Taylor made big strides in his battle against the cabal in the last volume, but after that victory, his world is starting to unravel. His friends are questioning him and people are beginning to notice the slow apocalypse of disappearing stories. Tom can only do so much to stave it off, but luckily there are a few new characters in the mix, including a unicorn who provides rhyming, enigmatic prophesies at inopportune moments." Booklist

Originally published in single magazine form in The Unwritten 36-41

The **Unwritten**; volume 8, Mike Carey; [illustrated by] Peter Gross. DC Comics/Vertigo 2014 176 p. Color; Illustration
Grades: Adult   **741.5; Fic**
1. Dead — Fiction; 2. Fantasy fiction; 3. Comic books, strips, etc.
1401243010; 9781401243012, $16.99

LC 2013040735

"Tommy ventures into the land of the dead to find and rescue Lizzie. But the journey through Hades pits Tommy against all kinds of enemies of undead. But none of these encounters prepare him for his meeting with the king — or for the responsibilities he has to take on for some very familiar damned souls." (Publisher's note)

Carey, Percy
Sentences: the life of M F Grimm. DC Comics/Vertigo 2007 128p. Illustration
Grades: 11 12 Adult   **741.5; 92**

1. Autobiographical graphic novels; 2. Gangs — Graphic novels; 3. Graphic novels; 4. Rap music — Graphic novels; 5. Carey, Percy; 6. Carey, Percy — Graphic novels
978-1-4012-1046-5, $19.99

Percy Carey, known in the Hip Hop world as M.F. Grimm, tells his story, from his escape from poverty on the streets to his rise in the world of Hip Hop music. Life in this world involves cutthroat competition and sometimes violence; Carey lost the use of his legs in gang violence, he has spent time in prison, and he re-invented himself. This is his story, complete with the extremely foul language of the streets, and the violence of the life he led.

Carlson, David L.
The **hunting** accident: a true story of crime and poetry. David Carlson; [art by] Landis Blair. First Second 2017 464 p. Illustration; Color
Grades: Adult   **741.5; 92**
1. Rizzo, Matt, 1913-1987; 2. Blind; 3. Father-son relationship
9781626726765, $34.99

LC 2016961544

In this book, by David Carlson, illustrated by Landis Blair, "it was a hunting accident — that much Charlie is sure of. That's how his father, Matt Rizzo — a gentle intellectual who writes epic poems in Braille — had lost his vision. It's not until Charlie's troubled teenage years, when he's facing time for his petty crimes, that he learns the truth. Matt Rizzo was blinded by a shotgun blast to the face — but it was while participating in an armed robbery." (Publisher's note)

"This account of two youthful offenders, father and son, at either end of the 1930s-1960s heyday of Chicago's Little Italy brilliantly merges novelistic character development and expressionistic visual presentation." Booklist

Carre, Lilli
The **fir-tree**. It Books/HarperCollins 2009 un Illustration
Grades: 3 4 5 6 7 8 9 10 11 12 Adult   **741.5; Fic**
1. Authors; 2. Children's authors; 3. Christmas — Graphic novels; 4. Christmas trees — Graphic novels; 5. Dramatists; 6. Graphic novels; 7. Novelists; 8. Short story writers; 9. Andersen, Hans Christian, 1805-1875 — Adaptations
978-0-06-178236-7, $14.99

A young fir-tree only wants to grow tall; it's never satisfied and doesn't notice the sunlight and clean air. It never rejoices in anything, but grumbles and complains. When it sees some trees being cut down and taken away, it wonders what it's missing. The birds tell of seeing the trees inside homes, beautifully decorated, and it becomes jealous. When it does grow tall and beautiful, a woodsman comes along and cuts it down, hauling it to town to become a Christmas tree in a house. It enjoys the family playing around the tree at Christmas, but after the holiday, the family throws it into a storeroom. Will the tree ever see its forest again? Lilli Carre uses delicate coloring and illustrations to adapt Andersen's sad Christmas story. Although this is suitable for young readers, adults may better appreciate the tragedy and Carre's idiosyncratic illustrations her people have long, loopy arms.

Carroll, Emily
★ **Through** the woods. Emily Carroll. Margaret K. McElderry Books 2014 208 p. Color; Illustration
Grades: 8 9 10 11 12 Adult   **741.5**
1. Graphic novels; 2. Short stories; 3. Horror fiction; 4. Comic books, strips, etc.
9781442465961, $14.99; 9781442465954, $21.99

LC 2013030969

Eisner Award: Best Graphic Album — Reprint (2015); Ignatz Award: Outstanding Artist (2015)

In this book, Emily Carroll "crafts five unsettling tales in graphic-novel format inspired by common folkloric themes — from wolves in the woods to peculiar visitors to dark possessions. In 'Our Neighbor's House,' three sisters who find themselves alone in a cabin are taken, one by one, in the middle of the night by a smiling stranger.... 'The Nesting Place' focus on malevolent spirit possession." (Horn Book Magazine)

"All the tales in Carroll's debut graphic novel are fairly standard ghost stories, but it is her eerie illustrations — popping with bold color on black, glossy pages — that masterfully build terrifying tension and a keep-the-lights-on atmosphere." Booklist

Carter, James Bucky

Building literacy connections with graphic novels: page by page, panel by panel. edited by James Bucky Carter.. National Council of Teachers of English 2007 164p. Illustration
Grades: Adult Professional   **428; 741.5**
1. Graphic novels — History and criticism; 2. Language arts; 3. Literacy; 4.Teaching
978-0-8141-0392-0; 0-8141-0392-8, $30.95
LC 2007-2806

Each chapter presents practical suggestions for the classroom as it pairs a graphic novel with a more traditional text or examines connections between multiple sources. Some of the pairings include The Scarlet Letter and Katherine Arnoldi's The Amazing True" Story of a Teenage Single Mom; Oliver Twist and Will Eisner's Fagin the Jew; Young adult literature and Marjane Satrapi's Persepolis; Dante's Inferno and an X-Men story; classic fantasies (Peter Pan, The Wizard of Oz, and Alice in Wonderland) and Farel Dalrymple's Pop Gun War; traditional and graphic novel versions of Beowulf. These pairings open up a double world of possibilities-in words and images-to all kinds of learners, from reluctant readers and English language learners to gifted students and those who are critically exploring relevant social issues. An appendix recommends additional graphic novels for use in middle and high school classrooms.

Includes bibliographical references (p. 157-160).

Casey, Joe

Godland Volume 1: Hello, Cosmic!. Joe Casey and Tom Scioli. Image Comics 2006 un Illustration
Grades: 8 9 10 11 12 Adult   **741.5; Fic**
1. Adventure graphic novels; 2. Graphic novels; 3. Science fiction graphic novels; 4. Superhero graphic novels
1-58240-712-6, $14.99

The cosmic superhero epic is back and this collection is chock-full of all the "cosmic" one could ask for. Experience the glory of Commander Adam Archer, the enigmatic alien Maxim, the wacky Basil Cronus, the evil Discordia, the confusing Freidrich Nickelhead and that's just scratching the surface. The storytelling and art bring back the kind of story that Stan Lee and Jack Kirby did, with fun superhero action and very little grim, gritty content.

Castiglia, Paul

America's 1st Patriotic Comic Book Hero: The Shield Volume 1. Archie Comics 2002 96p. Illustration
Grades: 3 4 5 6 7 8 9 10 11 12 Adult   **741.5; Fic**
1. Adventure graphic novels; 2. Graphic novels; 3. Superhero graphic novels
1-879794-08-X, $12.95

A hero with great power, strength and courage who donned the colors of the American flag. A hero who lived for democracy and protected the world from the foes of freedom! No, it's not who you think... it's THE SHIELD, who predated his well known counterpart by over a year. This historic full color trade paperback reprints his first 8 stories from PEP and SHIELD/WIZARD Comics. It includes his first appearance and origin, along with the covers of the comics they originally appeared in, dating from 1940.

Archie Americana Series: Best of the Forties Book 2. Archie Comics 2002 96p. Illustration
Grades: 3 4 5 6 7 8 9 10 11 12 Adult   **741.5; Fic**
1. Andrews, Archie (Fictional character); 2. Graphic novels; 3. Humorous graphic novels
1-879794-09-8, $10.95

In 1941, Pep Comics introduced Archie Andrews, "America's newest boyfriend." Since then, Archie and his perennial teenage friends have entertained readers with their misadventures. This book includes stories from 1946 through 1949, with more slapstick and screwball comedy from Archie and the gang.

Archie Americana Series: Best of the Eighties. Archie Comics 2001 96p. Illustration
Grades: 3 4 5 6 7 8 9 10 11 12 Adult   **741.5; Fic**
1. Andrews, Archie (Fictional character); 2. Graphic novels; 3. Humorous graphic novels
1-879794-06-3, $10.95

During the 1980s pop culture ruled America; even the President was a former actor. In this volume, Archie and friends experience the punk movement, the "Urban Cowboy" craze, see the rise of MTV, get into the preppie, new wave and "Flashdance" fashions, play Trivial Pursuit, and boogie at the roller disco.

Volume 1 of 2

Best of Josie and the Pussycats Volume 1. Archie Comics 2001 96p. Illustration
Grades: 3 4 5 6 7 8 9 10 11 12 Adult   **741.5; Fic**
1. Adventure graphic novels; 2. Graphic novels; 3. Humorous graphic novels; 4. Rock music — Graphic novels
1-879794-07-1, $10.95

This book reprints a selection of stories about rock group Josie and the Pussycats, from their origin in 1963 to 1988. Josie, Melody, and Valerie are the Pussycats, along with their roadie Alan M., their shifty manager Alex, and his conniving sister, Alexandra. They make music, but along the way they also solve mysteries.

Sonic the Hedgehog: The Beginning. Archie Comics 2003 96p. Illustration
Grades: 3 4 5 6 7 8 9 10 11 12 Adult   **741.5; Fic**
1. Adventure graphic novels; 2. Graphic novels; 3. Humorous graphic novels; 4. Sonic the Hedgehog (Fictional character)
1-879794-12-8, $10.95

In 1993, Sonic the Hedgehog sped his way from video games to comic books, and has been going strong ever since. Now, readers can enjoy his earliest comic book adventures with this edition that reprints the first appearances of Tails, Princess Sally, Antoine, Rotor, Uncle Chuck, and Muttski. Fans can also marvel at Sonic's magic rings, the freedom emeralds, and King Acorn's magic crown; while booing and hissing at the villainous Robotnik, his evil Swat-Bots, and his myriad dastardly devices.

Cavallaro, Mike

★ **Parade** (with fireworks). Image Comics/Shadowlands Books 2008 70p. Illustration
Grades: 10 11 12 Adult   **741.5; Fic**
1. Graphic novels; 2. Italy — History — 1914-1945 — Graphic novels
978-1-58240-995-5, $12.99

In 1923, Italy was recovering from the Great War; the fascists were already starting to come into power and battling the socialists. In Maropati, one family gets caught up in the political infighting. Paolo, whose father owns a large olive farm, has come back from living in Chicago, where he learned all about fighting feuds and settling disagreements with guns. On the evening of the Feast of the Epiphany, things in Maropati come to a head, local fascists attack and kill Paolo's brother and cousin, and he chooses to fight back. Despite the fact that the fascists had attacked first, he's the one who is hunted, tried, and convicted, and this shatters his family. Cavallaro has based this story on what really happened to his family in Italy. This story first appeared as a webcomic, part of ACT-I-VATE, and was nominated for an Eisner Award, for Best Limited Series, in 2008. The book includes violence.

Chabouté
Alone. Chabouté; translation by Ivanka Hahnenberger. Gallery 13 2017 496 p. Illustration
Grades: Adult   **741.5; Fic**
1. Lighthouses — Fiction; 2. Sea stories; 3. Hermits — Fiction
9781501153327, $25; 1501153323

"On a tiny lighthouse island far from the rest of the world, a lonely hermit lives out his existence. Every week a supply boat leaves provisions, its occupants never meeting him, never asking the obvious questions. But one day, as a new boatman starts asking the questions all others have avoided, a chain of events unfolds that will irrevocably upend the hermit's solitary life." (Publisher's note)

"This small, graceful story becomes a lush fairy tale through Chabouté's stunning black-and-white art; he lavishes loving detail on the hermit's fantastic inner life and his daily routines on the starkly beautiful island." Pub Wkly

Originally published in French in 2008 by Editions Glénat SA as Tout Seul — Title page verso

Chadwick, Paul
Concrete Vol. 1: Depths. Dark Horse Comics 2005 208p. Illustration
Grades: 10 11 12 Adult   **741.5; Fic**
1. Adventure graphic novels; 2. Concrete (Fictional character); 3. Graphic novels
1-59307-343-7, $12.95

Part man, part...rock? Over seven feet tall and weighing over a thousand pounds, he is known as Concrete but is in reality the mind of one Ronald Lithgow, trapped inside a shell of stone, a body that allows him to walk unaided on the ocean's floor or survive the crush of a thousand tons of rubble in a collapsed mineshaft...but prevents him from feeling the touch of a human hand. Depths, the first in a series of new collections reprinting the classic early Concrete stories along with never-before-collected short stories, includes the Eisner-nominated "Orange Glow" and "Vagabond," Paul Chadwick's autobiographical account of a cross-country hitchhiking trip. Further volumes in the series show that Concrete collects nude paintings.

Volume 1 of 7

Charlesworth, Kate
The **cartoon** history of time. Kate Charlesworth and John Gribbin. Dover Publications 2013 64 p.
Grades: Adult   **530.11; 741.5**
1. Time — History — Caricatures and cartoons; 2. Space and time — Juvenile literature
0486490971; 9780486490977, $19.95
LC 2012049026

This graphic novel, by Kate Charlesworth and John Gribbin, focuses on the history of time. "What is time? How did it begin, and where will it end? Is time travel possible? How does the universe expand, and where do black holes come from? Junior Chicken and Alexis, the Quantum Cat, examine these and other extraordinary concepts, explaining the substance of Stephen Hawking's A Brief History of Time." (Publisher's note)

Reprint of: Cartoon history of time / Kate Charlesworth, John Gribbin. — London : McDonald & Co., Ltd, 1990.

Chast, Roz
★ **Can't** We Talk About Something More Pleasant?: A Memoir. Roz Chast. St. Martin's Press 2014 240 p. Color; Illustration
Grades: Adult   **741.5; 818.6**
1. Aging parents
9781608198061, $28; 1608198065
National Book Critics Circle Award: Autobiography (2014); Kirkus Prize: Nonfiction (2014); National Book Award Finalist: Nonfiction (2014)

In this memoir, author Roz Chast "brings her signature wit to the topic of aging parents. Spanning the last several years of their lives and told through four-color cartoons, family photos, and documents, and a narrative as rife with laughs as it is with tears, Chast's memoir is both comfort and comic relief for anyone experiencing the life-altering loss of elderly parents." (Publisher's note)

Chast "brings her parents and herself to life in the form of her characteristic scratchy-lined, emotionally expressive characters, making the story both more personal and universal." Pub Wkly

Going into town: a love letter to New York. Roz Chast. St. Martin's Press 2017 176 p. Color; Illustration
Grades: Adult   **741.5**
1. New York (N.Y.) — Comic books, strips, etc.; 2. Autobiographies; 3. Graphic memoir; 4. Comic books, strips, etc.
9781633869784; 9781620403211, $28; 1620403218

In this graphic memoir, author Roz Chast thought that "adjusting to life in the suburbs...was surreal. But she recognized that for her kids, the reverse was true. On trips into town, they would marvel at the strange world of Manhattan.... Their wonder inspired 'Going into Town,' part playful guide, part New York stories, and part love letter to the city, told through Chast's laugh-out-loud, touching, and true cartoons." (Publisher's note)

"Observations and advice on making one's way through the city's diversions are mixed with the quirky character that oozes from the metropolis's every concrete pore. It's all delivered with obvious and knowing affection and captured with a keenly observant pen." Pub Wkly

Chatterjee, Pratap
Verax: the true history of whistleblowers, drone warfare, and mass surveillance. Pratap Chatterjee, illustrated by Khalil. Metropolitan Books/Henry Holt & Co. 2017 240 p. Illustration
Grades: Adult   **741.5; 327.12**
1. Mass surveillance; 2. Intelligence service — United States; 3. Whistle blowing
9781627793568; 9781250196323; 9781627793551, $25; 1627793550
LC 2017039292

In this book, illustrated by Khalil, author Pratap Chatterjee "dives deep into the world of electronic surveillance and introduces its cast of characters: developers,...whistleblowers, journalists, and...the devices themselves. He explains the complex ways governments follow the movements and interactions of individuals and countries.... He chronicles the complicity of corporations...and the daring of the journalists and whistleblowers." (Publisher's note)

"Khalil's (Zahra's Paradise) illustrations render real people recognizable in clean black-and-white line art; he does a fantastic job with the numerous charts, diagrams, and visual metaphors." LJ

Chaykin, Howard

Fritz Leiber's Fafhrd and the Gray Mouser. adaptation and script, Howard Chaykin; pencils, Mike Mignola; inks, Al Williamson; colors, Sherlyn van Valkenburgh; letters, Michael Heisler. Dark Horse Comics 2007 un Illustration

Grades: 11 12 Adult   **741.5; Fic**

1. Adventure graphic novels; 2. Fantasy graphic novels; 3. Graphic novels; 4. Leiber, Fritz; 5. Leiber, Fritz — Adaptations
978-1-59307-713-6, $19.95

This volume, which was first published as a four-issue miniseries by Marvel Comics in 2001, adapts several of Leiber's stories about the huge northern barbarian Fafhrd and the conniving Gray Mouser. "Ill Met in Lankhmar" describes how the two meet; in "The Circle Curse" the two leave Lankhmar only to return because they're bored when away from the city; "The Bazaar of the Bizarre" offers trinkets and treasures which are really enchanted trash. In "Lean Times of Lankhmar," the two friends fall out and the Mouser works for a major thug while Fafhrd becomes a devotee of the god Issek of the Jug.

Leiber poked fun at the "sword and sorcery" type of fantasy adventure, but ended up crafting classic stories in the subgenre. Readers will find humor, swordfights, thievery, sex, and more.

Cherniss, Matt

Powerless. writers, Matt Cherniss & Peter Johnson; artist, Michael Gaydos. Marvel Entertainment 2005 un Illustration

Grades: 9 10 11 12 Adult   **741.5; Fic**

1. Graphic novels; 2. Superhero graphic novels; 3. Wolverine (Fictional character); 4. Spider-Man (Fictional character); 5. Daredevil (Fictional character)
07851-1511-0, $14.99

What makes a hero? Is it his actions, or is it the results of those actions? Powerless explores what it means to be a hero in very human terms. By re-imagining Marvel's most popular characters without superhuman powers, this story strips down to the core heroes readers have all come to know and love. These characters — including Peter Parker, Matt Murdock and Logan — were fated to be heroes. Just because Peter Parker wasn't bitten by a radioactive spider doesn't mean he didn't do battle with a madman named Norman Osborn. Matt Murdock? Blinded, yes — but with no heightened senses. However, he did become a legal champion of the poor in Hell's Kitchen, and he did cross paths with Wilson Fisk, the Kingpin. And Logan is, of course, the enigmatic — and amnesiac — drifter on the run from his past. Psychiatrist Dr. Watts suffers strange dreams and visions even as he tries to help his three patients. The book includes some violence.

Cherrywell, Steph

★ **Pepper** Penwell and the land creature of Monster Lake. [written and drawn by Steph Cherrywell].. SLG Publishing 2011 un Illustration

Grades: 10 11 12 7 8 9 Adult   **741.5; Fic**

1. Graphic novels; 2. Horror graphic novels; 3. Humorous graphic novels; 4. Monsters — Graphic novels; 5. Mystery graphic novels
978-1-59362-205-3, $14.95

British teenager Pepper Penwell prefers solving mysteries over school work and wants to be a detective like her father. When the latest school boots her out, Pepper takes on the case of a missing drum majorette named Lucy. Accompanied by her brother Alex, who inexplicably (it was some kind of accident) has the body of a bird, Pepper travels to Monster Lake, a town trying to establish itself as a tourist attraction based on its local monster, which is a land creature. In the town, Pepper meets strange people, any of whom could be guilty of kidnapping the wealthy and annoying Lucy. However, after Pepper does find Lucy, there's still the matter of the land monster, which is all too real. British slang (arse, bum) provides the mildly harsh language.

Chii

★ The **bride** was a boy. (true) story and art by Chii. Seven Seas Entertainment 2018 158 p. Illustration

Grades: 9 10 11 12 Adult   **92; 741.5**

1. Gender identity; 2. Transgender people — Japan — Biography; 3. Manga — Graphic novels — Japan
1626928886; 9781626928886, $13.99

This book, by Chii, is "a diary comic with an upbeat, adorable flair that tells the charming tale of Chii, a woman assigned male at birth. Her story starts with her childhood and follows the ups and downs of exploring her sexuality, gender, and transition-as well as falling in love with a man who's head over heels for her. Now, Chii is about to embark on a new adventure: becoming a bride!" (Publisher's note)

"Equal parts Trans 101 and tear-jerking rom-com, there's no other manga quite like this fun (and revolutionary) book." Pub Wkly

Originally published in Japan in 2016 by Asukashinsha, Tokyo

Church, Kevin

Cover girl. Andrew Cosby & Kevin Church, writers; Mateus Santolouco, pencils; R.M. Yankovicz, inker (chapter one-two); Andre Coelho, inker (chapter three-four); Ed Dukeshire, letterer; Pablo Quiligotti & Brian Miroglio, colorists. Boom! Studios 2008 un Illustration

Grades: 9 10 11 12 Adult   **741.5; Fic**

1. Adventure graphic novels; 2. Graphic novels; 3. Mystery graphic novels
978-1-934506-27-1, $14.99

Young struggling actor Alex Martin saves a woman whose car crashes off the road, and the videotape of his rescue helps his fortunes rise, and he snags the lead role in a high-budget action film. However, mysterious black SUVs seem to be following him, and then someone (or several someones) attempt several times to kill him. The studio hires a bodyguard, but Rachel Dodd isn't the usual type. She has to play the part of Alex's girlfriend in order to be by his side. When she and her partner Dwight manage to foil several more attempts to kill Alex, they decide they need to find out who's trying to kill Alex, and why. They soon discover it all comes back to Alex's roadside rescue of the woman, who has since disappeared from public view. This story is full of action and includes some violence and mildly bad language. Anyone who enjoys fast-paced action films with witty dialog will enjoy this. Teen girls and women may delight in the fact that the action hero is a no-nonsense woman who can shoot and fight as well as any male action movie hero.

Chute, Hillary L.

Why comics?: from underground to everywhere. Hillary L. Chute. Harper 2017 464 p. Illustration

Grades: Adult   **741.5**

1. Cartooning; 2. Comic books, strips, etc. — History and criticism; 3. Comic books, strips, etc. — Influence on mass media; 4. Graphic novels — History and criticism; 5. Superheroes in literature
9780062476807, $40

LC 2017020053

In this book, "comics scholar Hillary Chute reveals the history of comics, underground comics (or comix), and graphic novels, through deep thematic analysis, and fascinating portraits of the fearless men and women behind them. As Scott McCloud revealed the methods behind comics and the way they worked in his classic 'Understanding Comics,' Chute will reveal the themes that Comics handle best, and how the form is uniquely equipped to explore them." (Publisher's note)

Chute "serves up an accessible introduction to the major themes and literary achievements of comics. Arranged topically-disaster, sex, queerness, etc.-the survey offers in-depth analysis of famous works including Fun Home, Jimmy Corrigan, Maus, and Persepolis, and also some lesser-known but key works such as Lynda Barry's One! Hundred!

Demons! Chute's enthusiastic account is accompanied by analysis of the storytelling language of comics (aided by full-color reproduction of the pages in question) and a smattering of biographical analysis." Pub Wkly
Includes bibliographical references and index

Chwast, Seymour
Dante's Divine comedy: a graphic adaptation. adapted by Seymour Chwast. Bloomsbury 2010 127 p. Illustration
Grades: Adult   **741.5**
  1. Future life; 2. Dante Alighieri, 1265-1321
1608190846; 9781608190843, $20

LC 2009044551
In this version of "Dante's Divine Comedy", by Seymour, "Dante and his guide Virgil don fedoras and wander through noirish realms of Hell, Purgatory, and Paradise in this classic satire of human foibles." (Publisher's note)
Chwast "meets his match in one of the cornerstones of Western literature. Distilling Dante's three volumes into little more than 100 pages of large panels (many of them page-sized), he adheres to the tri-partite structure of the original without overburdening the spirit with reverence." Kirkus

★ The **odyssey**. Homer; adapted by Seymour Chwast. Bloomsbury 2012 128 p. Color; Illustration
Grades: 9 10 11 12 Adult   **398.2; 741.5**
  1. Graphic novels; 2. Greek mythology — Graphic novels; 3. Homer; 4. Odysseus (Greek mythology); 5. Adventure graphic novels; 6. Epic literature
1608194868; 9781608194865, $

LC 2012010047
"The latest in an unofficial series of graphic novels based on the classics (The Canterbury Tales; The Divine Comedy), veteran illustrator and graphic designer Chwast interprets the Greek epic in straightforward but whimsical line drawings that invest the familiar tale with droll energy.... Our hero is cast as a Buck Rogers-like space traveler, bouncing from planet to planet (instead of island to island) in Deco-inspired rocket ships." (Publishers Weekly)
"While the subjects of his previous comics adaptations had a higher component of moral or philosophical instruction, The Odyssey — particularly in Chwast's hands — is more of a rousing adventure tale, making this imaginative interpretation a genuinely fun read." Booklist

Claremont, Chris
★ **Wolverine**. Marvel Entertainment 2007 un Illustration
Grades: 9 10 11 12 Adult   **741.5; Fic**
  1. Graphic novels; 2. Superhero graphic novels; 3. Wolverine (Fictional character)
978-0-7851-2329-3, $19.99
Originally published in the early 1980s, this was the first miniseries to delve into the character of the berserker mutant, Wolverine, and shape him into something more than a snarling fighting beast. Wolverine loves Mariko, but she is a yakuza boss's daughter; and when he follows her back to Japan, the Hand hires the ninja Yukio to kill Logan. Instead, she falls in love with him. Wolverine fights gangsters and ninja in his bid to win Mariko's heart.

X-Men: The End Book One: Dreamers & Demons. Marvel Entertainment 2005 un Illustration
Grades: 7 8 9 10 11 12 Adult   **741.5; Fic**
  1. Graphic novels; 2. Superhero graphic novels; 3. X-Men (Fictional characters)
978-0-7851-1690-5, $14.99

It's the epic finale to the story of the Children of the Atom as X-Men scribe Chris Claremont joins with artist Sean Chen for a trilogy in the style of the Lord of the Rings movies, one that spans the length and breadth of the X-Men canon and brings the saga of Marvel's mutants to a climax. In this volume, the unthinkable happens — attackers succeed in breaching all security at the Xavier School for the Gifted and threaten the lives of all the young mutants living there.

X-Men: The End Book Three: Men & X-Men. writer, Chris Claremont; artist, Sean Chen. Marvel Entertainment 2006 un Illustration
Grades: 7 8 9 10 11 12 Adult   **741.5; Fic**
  1. Graphic novels; 2. Superhero graphic novels; 3. X-Men (Fictional characters)
978-0-7851-1692-9, $14.99
The endgame of the last tale of Marvel's most popular mutants begins. They've suffered through sneak attacks, betrayals, and fatalities — now, Professor X and Magneto are taking the fight back to the enemy, amidst the stars.

X-Men: The End Book Two: Heroes & Martyrs. Chris Claremont; artist, Sean Chen. Marvel Entertainment 2005 un Illustration
Grades: 7 8 9 10 11 12 Adult   **741.5; Fic**
  1. Graphic novels; 2. Superhero graphic novels; 3. X-Men (Fictional characters)
978-0-7851-1691-2, $14.99
The Xavier Academy has been reduced to a smoldering crater in a brutal sneak attack, and the casualties number in the hundreds. Now, Cyclops must mobilize the survivors to get to the bottom of who is behind these coordinated strikes on mutants in general and the X-Men in particular.

★ **X-Men:** days of future past. Chris Claremont, art by John Byrne. Marvel Worldwide 2011 176 p.
Grades: 9 10 11 12 Adult   **741.5**
  1. X-Men (Fictional characters)
0785164537; 9780785164531, $19.99

LC bl2011037630
"Relive the legendary first journey into the dystopian future of 2013 — where Sentinels stalk the Earth, and the X-Men are humanity's only hope...until they die! Also featuring the first appearance of Alpha Flight, the return of the Wendigo, the history of the X-Men from Cyclops himself...and a demon for Christmas!?" (Publisher's note)

Clevinger, Brian
Atomic Robo; Volume one: Atomic Robo and the Fightin' Scientists of Tesladyne. words, Brian Clevinger; art and cover, Scott Wegener; colors, Ronda Pattison; letters, Jeff Powell. Red 5 Comics 2008 180 p. Color illustration (Atomic Robo)
Grades: 9 10 11 12 Adult   **741.5**
  1. Robots — Graphic novels; 2. Science fiction graphic novels; 3. Superhero comic books, strips, etc.
0980930200; 9780980930207, $18.95
This graphic novel, by Brian Clevinger, illustrated by Scott Wegener and Ronda Pattison, collects the first six issues of the action comic series "Atomic Robo." "Atomic Robo and the so-called Action Scientists of Tesladyne become the go-to defense force against the unexplained! See ROBO take on Nazis, giant ants, clockwork mummies, walking pyramids, Mars, cyborgs, and his nemesis, Baron von Helsingard." (Publisher's note)
"[This] series about a scientific adventure robot created by Nikola Tesla has been...funny and yet surprisingly touching at times, a book that features car chases, gun fights and robots punching other robots but never uses them as an excuse to give up on being smart." ComicsAlliance
Volume 1 of an ongoing series

Clowes, Daniel

The **complete** eightball. by Daniel Clowes; [edited by] Eric Reynolds. Fantagraphics Books, Inc. 2015 454 p. Color; Illustration
Grades: Adult   **741.5**
1. Underground comic books, strips, etc.; 2. Anthologies; 3. Comic books, strips, etc.
9781606997574, $119.99; 1606997572
LC 2014951638
"This is a two-volume, slipcased facsimile edition of the Daniel Clowes comics anthology; it contains the original installments of Ghost World, the short that the film Art School Confidential was based on, and much more." (Publisher's note)
Originally published as Eightball issues #1-18

★ **Ghost** world. Daniel Clowes. Fantagraphics Bks. 1997 80p. Illustration
Grades: 11 12 Adult   **741.5**
1. Female friendship — Graphic novels; 2. Teenage girls — Fiction
1-56097-280-7 (pa), $19.95; 9781560974277
Ignatz Award: Outstanding Story (1998); Ignatz Award: Outstanding Graphic Novel or Collection (1998)
"Eight interconnected stories about two teens. Enid and Rebecca have been friends for so long that it's difficult for either of them to let the other grow or change. Now Enid will probably leave their working-class neighborhood and go away to college and Rebecca cannot accept this change in their relationship." (School Library Journal)

Mister wonderful. by Daniel Clowes. Pantheon Books 2011 77 p. Color; Illustration
Grades: Adult   **741.5**
1. Man-woman relationships — Fiction; 2. Dating (Social customs) — Fiction
0307378136; 9780307378132, $19.95
LC 2010035354
In this graphic novel, by Daniel Clowes, "meet Marshall. Sitting alone in the local coffee place. He's been set up by his friend Tim on a blind date with someone named Natalie, and now he's just feeling set up. She's nine minutes late and counting. Who was he kidding anyway? Divorced, middle-aged, newly unem ployed, with next to no prospects, Marshall isn't ex actly what you'd call a catch." (Publisher's note)
"Expanded from a serial that ran in the New York Times Magazine, this is a gorgeously staged graphic novella consistently playful and funny on a formal level — there's a running joke involving Marshall's interior monologue covering up images or dialogue, and constant fantasy sequences signaled by drawing-style shifts." Pub Wkly

Wilson. by Daniel Clowes. Drawn and Quarterly 2010 77 p. Color; Illustration
Grades: Adult   **741.5**
1. Graphic novels; 2. Middle aged men — Fiction
1770460071; 9781770460072, $21.95
LC 2010444753
In this graphic novel, after his father dies, Wilson "sets out to find his ex-wife with the hope of rekindling their long-dead relationship, and discovers he has a teenage daughter, born after the marriage ended and given up for adoption. Wilson eventually forces all three to reconnect as a family." (Publisher's note)

Clowes, Daniel Gillespie

★ **Patience**. Daniel Clowes; [edited by] Eric Reynolds. Fantagraphics Books 2016 180 p. Color; Illustration
Grades: Adult   **741.5; Fic**
1. Romance fiction — Graphic novels; 2. Time travel — Graphic novels; 3. Science fiction graphic novels

1606999052; 9781606999059, $29.99
LC 2015953161
Ignatz Award: Outstanding Artist (2016); Ignatz Award: Outstanding Comic (2016)
This graphic novel, by Daniel Clowes, edited by Eric Reynolds, "is a psychedelic science-fiction love story, veering with uncanny precision from violent destruction to deeply personal tenderness in a way that is both quintessentially 'Clowesian' and utterly unique in the author's body of work....Full-color illustrations throughout." (Publisher's note)
"This is a fascinating collage, repurposing elements from action thrillers, psychological horror, and romantic drama. Clowes skillfully anchors each psychedelic turn in human emotion." Pub Wkly

Coates, Ta-Nehisi

★ **Black** Panther; Book 1: a nation under our feet. by Ta-Nehisi Coates; illustrated by Brian Stelfreeze; color by Laura Martin. Marvel Enterprises 2016 144 p. Color; Illustration
Grades: 11 12 Adult   **741.5; Fic**
1. Superhero graphic novels; 2. Black Panther (Fictional character)
9781302900533, $16.99; 1302900536
"When a superhuman terrorist group that calls itself The People sparks a violent uprising, the land famed for its incredible technology and proud warrior traditions will be thrown into turmoil. If Wakanda is to survive, it must adapt — but can its monarch, one in a long line of Black Panthers, survive the necessary change?" (Publisher's note)
Originally published in single issues as Black Panther #1-4; Other Black Panther volumes by Coates are: A nation under our feet, book two (2017); A nation under our feet, book three (2017); Avengers of the new world, part one (2017); Avengers of the new world, part two (2018)

Cobley, Jason

Frankenstein: the graphic novel. [by] Mary Shelley; script adaptation Jason Cobley; American English adaptation: Joe Sutliff Sanders; linework: Declan Shalvey; coloring: Jason Cardy & Kat Nicholson; lettering: Terry Wiley. Classical Comics 2008 141p. Illustration
Grades: 6 7 8 9 10 11 12 Adult
741.5; Fic
1. Authors; 2. Frankenstein (Fictional character); 3. Graphic novels; 4. Horror graphic novels; 5. Shelley, Mary Wollstonecraft, 1797-1851 — Adaptations; 6. Frankenstein's monster (Fictional character)
978-1-906332-49-5, $16.95

© Classical Comics
www.classicalcomics.com

Young scientist Victor Frankenstein becomes obsessed with the idea that technology can create life, and works to prove his theories. However, his success doesn't bring him glory, but a living nightmare for himself and everyone around him. This graphic adaptation brings the entire book to the reader, using Shelley's original text for the dialog and narrative. Back matter includes a brief biography of Shelley, her family tree, a description of how she came to write the novel, and information on some of the various adaptations of the story to the stage and to film.
"More than a straightforward retelling, this edition invites readers to explore important social issues such as alienation, the consequences and ethics of scientific studies, as well as the nature of creation and destruction." SLJ
Also available quick text version $16.95 (ISBN: 978-1-906332-50-1); Original text version

Cole, Allison

Never Ending Summer. Alternative Comics 2004 128p. Illustration
Grades: 10 11 12 Adult
741.5; Fic
1. Autobiographical graphic novels; 2. Cole, Allison
1-891867-66-0, $11.95

Courtesy of Alternative Comics

This story is an autobiographical account that follows a group of friends through a summer filled with uncertainty and confusion. Relationships break down between boyfriends, friends, and family, throughout which the author must discover how to maintain a sense of balance. Parties, excessive drinking, and financial instability add to the commotion. The book reflects upon the immediacy of the present and the potential of events to come. There's very little in the way of strong language or sexual situations.

Collins, Max Allan

Dick Tracy: The Collins Casefiles Volume 1. Checker Book Publishing Group 2003 164p. Illustration
Grades: 8 9 10 11 12 Adult   **741.5; Fic**
1. Dick Tracy (Fictional character); 2. Graphic novels; 3. Mystery graphic novels
0-9741664-2-1, $19.95

LC 2003-23068

This is the first of several volumes collecting Collins' 11-year run on the Dick Tracy comic strips. He took over scripting duties from Chester Gould in 1978, although Gould maintained his byline and consulted with Collins on plot directions. Fletcher, a longtime Gould assistant, took over the drawing and worked with Collins. This volume includes the stories Ängel Top's Last Stand, Return of Haf-and Haf, and Big Boy's Revenge.

Johnny Dynamite: Underworld. AiT/Planet Lar 2003 un Illustration
Grades: 10 11 12 Adult
741.5; Fic
1. Graphic novels; 2. Horror graphic novels; 3. Mystery graphic novels
1-932051-10-4, $12.95

Courtesy of AiT/Planet Lar

1950s tough-guy private detective Johnny Dynamite goes up against zombies in Las Vegas as well as the mob, and the zombies also have crime on their undead minds. Mob-style violence, with beatings and hits, combines with zombie killings and horror action.

Road to Perdition. written by Max Allan Collins; art by Richard Piers Rayner; lettering by Bob Lappan. Pocket Books 2002 302 p.
Grades: Adult   **741.5**
1. Mafia — Graphic novels; 2. Father-son relationship — Graphic novels; 3. Revenge — Graphic novels
0743442245; 9780743442244, $14

LC 2002510761

In this book, by Max Allan Collins, illustrated by Richard Piers Rayner, "Michael O'Sullivan is a deeply religious family man who works as the chief enforcer for an Irish mob family. But after O'Sullivan's eldest son witnesses one of his father's hits, the godfather orders the death of his entire family. Barely surviving an encounter that takes his wife and youngest son, O'Sullivan and his only remaining child embark on a dark

and violent mission of retribution against his former boss." (Publisher's note)

Published by arrangement with DC Comics. — P. 2.||Pocket books graphic novel — Spine.

Collins, Stephen

The **Gigantic** Beard That Was Evil. by Stephen Collins. St. Martin's Press 2014 240 p. Illustration
Grades: Adult   **741.5; Fic**
1. Beards — Fiction; 2. Fables
1250050391; 9781250050397, $20

In this fable tale, by Stephen Collins, "on the island of Here, livin's easy. Conduct is orderly. Lawns are neat. Citizens are clean shaven — and Dave is the most fastidious of them all. Dave is bald, but for a single hair. He loves drawing, his desk job, and the Bangles. But on one fateful day, his life is upended...by an unstoppable (yet pretty impressive) beard." (Publisher's note)

"Collins' illustrations are lush, rounded affairs with voluptuous shading across oblong planes.... With its archetypical conflict and deliberate dissection of language, the story seems aimed at delivering a moral, but the tale ultimately throws its aesthetics into abstraction rather than didacticism." Kirkus

Conley, Steve

Astounding space thrills: Argosy Smith and the codex reckoning. IDW Publishing 2008 192p. Illustration
Grades: 9 10 11 12 Adult   **741.5; Fic**
1. Adventure graphic novels; 2. Graphic novels; 3. Science fiction graphic novels
978-1-60010-320-9, $19.99

Adventurer Argosy Smith lives on an Earth that has changed drastically due to its move thanks to some aliens time flows differently, space folds weirdly, and the Earth has basically become the library of the universe. Smith races against time (he's supposed to die on his 25th birthday, which is tomorrow) to steal a lost manuscript by Leonardo Da Vinci, discover the secret of Split-Space travel, keep two alien races from all-out war, avoid certain death at the hands of little green mercenaries hired by a several-brained-corporate head, and keep the universe from breaking apart. Oh yeah, and celebrate his birthday. The action harkens back to the kind of cosmic science fiction adventure written by E. E. "Doc" Smith, with lots of action.

Conner, Amanda

Harley Quinn; Volume 1. Amanda Conner, Jimmy Palmiotti, writers; Chad Hardin, Stéphane Roux, artists. DC Comics 2014 224 p. Color; Illustration
Grades: 11 12 Adult   **741.5**
1. Superhero comic books, strips, etc.
1401248926; 9781401248925, $24.99

LC 2014034093

In this comic book, writers Amanda Conner and Jimmy Palmiotti "unleashed Harley [Quinn] on an unsuspecting DC Universe, as she encounters various heroes and villains...and leaves no one unscathed in her wake! With art by Chad Hardin and a slew of comics' best artists including Darwyn Cooke, Sam Kieth, Tony S. Daniel, Paul Pope, Walter Simonson and Art Baltazar!" (Publisher's note)

Harley Quinn; Volume 1: die laughing. Amanda Conner, Jimmy Palmiotti, writers; JohnTimms, Chad Hardin, Bret Blevins, Joseph MichaelLinsner, Jill Thompson, artists; Alex Sinclair,Hi-Fi, Jill Thompson, colorists; Dave Sharpe,letterer; Amanda Conner and Alex Sinclair,original serie. DC Comics 2017 un Color; Illustration
Grades: 11 12 Adult   **741.5; Fic**

1. Supervillains — Comic books, strips, etc.; 2. Harley Quinn (Fictitious character) — Comic books, strips, etc.
9781401268312, $16.99

"Her name is Dr. Harleen Quinzel, better known to her friends and enemies as playful-but-deadly Harley Quinn. Her ex-boyfriend, the Joker, may be the Clown Prince of Crime, but Harley's the Queen of Coney Island! So when a zombie apocalypse threatens her li'l seaside stretch of paradise, who else would ya call to save your butt? In these action-packed pages, the baddest bad girl in the entire DC Universe joins forces with everyone from her gal-pal Poison Ivy to the leading lights of the New York City punk scene to take down anyone who stands between her and a good time — living, dead or undead." (Publisher's note)

Originally published in single magazine form in HARLEY QUINN 1-7

Cooke, Darwyn
Batman: Ego and Other Tails. DC Comics 2007 200p. Illustration
Grades: 10 11 12 Adult   **741.5; Fic**
1. Batman (Fictional character); 2. Catwoman (Fictional character); 3. Graphic novels; 4. Mystery graphic novels; 5. Superhero graphic novels
978-1-4012-1529-3, $24.99

This volume collects Cooke's work for DC that focus on Batman and Catwoman. In Ego, after suffering physical and psychological trauma, Batman confronts himself in his mind. The book also includes Catwoman: Selina's Big Score, in which the perfect heist...isn't. The book includes some violence and strong language.

★ **DC:** The New Frontier Vol. 1. DC Comics 2004 un Illustration
Grades: 9 10 11 12 Adult   **741.5; Fic**
1. Graphic novels; 2. Superhero graphic novels; 3. Batman (Fictional character); 4. Superman (Fictional character); 5. Wonder Woman (Fictional character)
1-4012-0350-7, $19.99; 9781401203504
2005 Eisner Award for Best Limited Series.

World War II is over. The Cold War has begun. The Age of the Superhero is in decline. But where are the heroes of tomorrow? This book recounts the dawning of the DC Universe's Silver Age from the perspective of those brave individuals who made it happen. Encounter "keepers of the flame" including Superman, Wonder Woman and Batman, who survived the anti-hero sentiment of the Cold War, as well as eager newcomers like test pilot Hal Jordan and scientist Barry Allen, poised to become the next generation of crime fighters. The book includes some strong language and violence.

★ **DC:** The New Frontier Vol. 2. DC Comics 2005 un Illustration
Grades: 9 10 11 12 Adult   **741.5; Fic**
1. Aquaman (Fictitious character); 2. Graphic novels; 3. Superhero graphic novels; 4. Wonder Woman (Fictional character); 5. Superman (Fictional character); 6. Batman (Fictional character); 7. Flash (Fictional character)
1-4012-0461-9, $19.99
2005 Eisner Award for Best Limited Series.

It's a mystery in space as Superman, the Suicide Squad, and the Challengers of the Unknown encounter a frightening extraterrestrial life form. Could this hideous creature have anything to do with the sense of impending doom all the heroes are experiencing? Meanwhile, pilot Hal Jordan is grounded, while post-war America faces a monstrous threat older than time. Will this challenge bring America and its heroes back together or tear them apart? The book features Green Lantern, the Flash, Martian Manhunter, Aquaman, Wonder Woman, Batman, and more heroes. It includes some strong language and some violence.

Parker: The hunter. Darwyn Cooke. IDW Pub. 2009 140 p.
Grades: Adult   **741.5/973; Fic**

1. Criminals — Graphic novels; 2. Revenge — Graphic novels; 3. Crime — Graphic novels; 4. Adventure graphic novels
1600104932; 9781600104930, $24.99

This graphic novel, illustrated by Darwyn Cooke, is an adaptation of the 1962 crime novel "The Hunter," by Richard Stark. "Betrayed by the woman he loved and double-crossed by his partner in crime, Parker makes his way cross-country with only one thought burning in his mind — to coldly exact his revenge and reclaim what was taken from him!" (Publisher's note)

Courtesy of IDW Publishing

Parker: the score. Darwyn Cooke. IDW Pub. 2012 144 p.
Grades: Adult
Fic; 741.5/971
1. Mystery fiction; 2. Adventure graphic novels; 3. Theft — Fiction; 4. Crime — Graphic novels
1613772084; 9781613772089, $24.99
Harvey Award: Best Graphic Album of Original Work (2013)

This graphic novel, illustrated by Darwyn Cooke, is an adaptation of the 1964 crime novel "The Score," by Richard Stark. "Parker becomes embroiled in a plot with a dozen partners in crime to pull off what might be the ultimate heist — robbing an entire town. Everything was going fine for a while, and then things got bad." (Publisher's note)

Courtesy of IDW Publishing

Richard Stark's Parker: The outfit. illustrated by the author. IDW 2010 160 p. Illustration
Grades: Adult
741.5/973; Fic
1. Suspense fiction; 2. Criminals — Graphic novels; 3. Stark, Richard — Adaptations
1600107621; 9781600107627, $24.99

In this graphic novel, by Darwyn Cooke, "after he evens the score with those who betrayed him and recovers the money he was cheated out of from the syndicate, Parker is riding high, living in swank hotels and enjoying the finer things in life again. Until, that is, he's fingered by a squealer who rats him out to The Outfit for the price they put on his head." (Publisher's note)

Courtesy of IDW Publishing

★ The **Spirit** book one. written by Darwyn Cooke and Jeph Loeb; drawn by Darwyn Cooke; inks and finishes by J. Bone; colors by Dave Stewart; letters by Jared K. Fletcher. DC Comics 2007 192p. Illustration
Grades: 8 9 10 11 12 Adult   **741.5; Fic**
1. Batman (Fictional character); 2. Graphic novels; 3. Humorous graphic novels; 4. Superhero graphic novels; 5. The Spirit (Fictional character)
978-1-4012-1461-6; 978-1-4012-1618-4 (pa), $19.99

Will Eisner's character The Spirit was popular for decades. Eisner is gone, but Darwyn Cooke has taken up the pen to update The Spirit while maintaining the action, adventure, and humor of the original stories. Readers will meet Commissioner Dolan and his daughter Ellen, Ebony, bad girl P'Gell, and more. This volume also includes the Eisner Award winning Batman/The Spirit special, written by Jeph Loeb and drawn by Cooke. The upcoming live action movie directed by comics veteran Frank Miller will spark more interest in the comics. The book includes lots of action and some cartoony violence.

"This is fine, entertaining stuff that will satisfy any longtime comics fan; recommended for teens and adults." Libr J

The **Spirit** book two. writers, Darwyn Cooke [and others]; artists, J. Bone [and others]; colors by Dave Stewart, Alex Sinclair and Jim Charalampidis; letters by Jared K. Fletcher. DC Comics 2008 un Illustration

Grades: 10 11 12 Adult   **741.5; Fic**
1. Graphic novels; 2. Mystery graphic novels; 3. The Spirit (Fictional character); 4. Spirit (Fictional character)
978-1-4012-1920-8, $24.99

In this second volume of Darwyn Cooke's take on Will Eisner's iconic character, The Spirit, readers meet Silk Satin, a sultry and sexy CIA agent, the villainous Octopus, and El Morte, the criminal who died with Denny Colt only to be raised as a zombie by his mother's supernatural rites. Along the way, the Spirit also works (sort of) with cable crime reporter Ginger Coffee to find out who is killing all the cable news pundits. The book includes violence and some bloodshed.

Corman, Leela
Unterzakhn. Leela Corman. Schocken Books 2012 203 p. Illustration
Grades: Adult   **741.5/973**
1. Immigrants — New York (State) — New York — Comic books, strips, etc; 2. Twin sisters — Comic books, strips, etc; 3. Lower East Side (New York, N.Y.) — Comic books, strips, etc
9780805242591, $24.95; 0805242597

LC 2011043769
"For six-year-old Esther and Fanya, the teeming streets of New York's Lower East Side circa 1910 are both a fascinating playground and a place where life's lessons are learned quickly and often cruelly. In drawings that capture both the tumult and the telling details of that street life, Unterzakhn (Yiddish for 'Underthings') tells the story of these sisters." (Publisher's note)

Crain, Dale
The **DC** Comics Rarities Archives Volume 1. DC Comics 2004 348p. Illustration
Grades: 7 8 9 10 11 12 Adult   **741.5; Fic**
1. Graphic novels; 2. Superhero graphic novels
1-4012-0007-8, $75

For the first time ever, in one huge collection, three of DC Comics' most hard to find early anthology titles are reprinted in their entirety. This is a 348-page hardcover collecting New York World's Fair 1939, New York World's Fair 1940 and Big All-American Comic Book #1 (1944). The two World's Fair Comics were specially created to be distributed at the legendary New York World's Fair of 1939-40 and feature adventures revolving around the DC heroes' visits there.

The **Seven** Soldiers of Victory Archives Volume 1. DC Comics 2005 237p. Illustration
Grades: 6 7 8 9 10 11 12 Adult   **741.5; Fic**
1. Graphic novels; 2. Superhero graphic novels; 3. Green Arrow (Fictional character)
1-4012-0401-5, $49.95
Collecting Leading Comics #1-4, featuring the adventures of The Seven Soldiers of Victory: The Crimson Avenger, Green Arrow, the Shining Knight, The Vigilante, the Star-Spangled Kid, and their sidekicks Speedy, Stripesy, and Wing (yes, there were eight of them). In 1941, one year after DC Comics launched the Justice Society of America in All-Star Comics, sister company All-American Comics released Leading Comics #1 featuring its very own super-team; in these early stories they take on various criminals and villains who possess super-senses.

Superman Archives Volume 7. DC Comics 2006 237p. Illustration
Grades: 8 9 10 11 12 Adult   **741.5; Fic**
1. Graphic novels; 2. Superhero graphic novels; 3. Superman (Fictional character)
978-1-4012-1051-9, $49.99

This seventh volume of the Superman Archive Editions collects issues 25-29 of Superman, with tales featuring the Man of Steel fighting subversion and sabotage on the home front during World War II, meeting mythic figures like Paul Bunyan and Hercules and foiling villains including the Toyman and the Prankster. This volume also features the first episodes of "Lois Lane, Girl Reporter." These stories were originally published in 1943 and 1944.

Crane, Jordan
The **Last** Lonely Saturday. Fantagraphics Books 2007 un Illustration
Grades: 10 11 12 Adult   **741.5; Fic**
1. Ghosts — Graphic novels; 2. Graphic novels; 3. Romance graphic novels
978-1-56097-743-8, $8

Using a deep yellow and brown palette, this almost wordless little story follows the day of an older man who gathers his letters addressed to Elinore, sets off to buy flowers, and drives out to the cemetery to visit Elinore's grave. As he sits and hugs the gravestone, the spirit of Elinore comes out and starts to kiss him. In a macabre twist that is portrayed in a sweet, gentle manner, Elinore's spirit finds a way for the two of them to be together.

Crilley, Mark
★ **Brody's** ghost: book 1. story and art by Mark Crilley. Dark Horse Books 2010 88p. Illustration
Grades: 8 9 10 11 12 Adult   **741.5; Fic**
1. Adventure graphic novels; 2. Fantasy graphic novels; 3. Ghosts — Graphic novels; 4. Graphic novels; 5. Mystery graphic novels
978-1-59582-521-6, $6.99

In what looks like a near-future city, Brody is down and out, eking out a living by playing guitar on the streets and working part-time as a stock clerk. Then, one day, while playing his guitar, he sees the ghost of a young woman; he thinks he's seeing things, but she won't let him alone until he talks with her. Talia, the ghost, needs to do a great deed before she can get into heaven, and she has decided to solve the mystery of a serial killer called the Penny Murderer, but she needs Brody, who is a ghostseer, to help her. First, though, he needs training to bring out his ghostseer powers, because he doesn't think he has any. Enter Kagemura, the ghost of a samurai, who decides, half-unwillingly, to train Brody. This book is much grittier than Crilley's earlier works, which were more suitable for younger readers; it is aimed more at teen and adult readers and includes some fighting violence but no graphically violent content.

"The setting — an unidentified future city partially in ruins — is a masterpiece of drawing, and Brody and the other characters are equally well crafted.... The story is more than a match for the art: humor, action, and mystery butt up against the reality of Brody's sad life, giving him the opportunity to change who he is." Booklist

Also available in an omnibus edition; ?The first in a six-volume limited series? Page 4 of cover; Book 1 of 6

Miki Falls Vol. 2: Summer. HarperTeen 2007 178p. Illustration
Grades: 7 8 9 10 11 12 Adult   **741.5; Fic**

1. Graphic novels; 2. Romance graphic novels; 3. Supernatural graphic novels

978-0-06-084617-6, $7.99

Has Miki fallen too hard? It's summer, and Miki Yoshida is learning all about love. Her senior year has blossomed with promise ever since she gained Hiro Sakurai's confidence. Now, she's resolved to keep his trust as he reveals more about his secret mission and warns: "Don't get involved." But Miki fears his work might do more harm than good, and she takes control-with disastrous results. How can trying to make things right turn out so dangerously wrong? Crilley is doing this series in manga style.

Crosby, Andrew
Damn Nation. Dark Horse Comics 2005 un Illustration
Grades: 10 11 12 Adult   741.5; Fic
1. Graphic novels; 2. Horror graphic novels; 3. Vampires — Graphic novels

1-59307-389-5, $12.95

The United States has been shut off from the world by concrete barricades and barbed wire — not because of what might get in, but what might get out. A vampire plague has spread from sea to shining sea, and when a small holdout of scientists trapped outside of Buffalo, N.Y. discover a cure, it's up to a Special Ops team from the President's current offices in London to go in and get it. Yet, not everyone in the world wants to see America back in the saddle again...This story includes some incidental nudity, strong language, and considerable violence.

Crumb, Aline
Drawn together: the collected works of R. and A. Crumb. Aline & R. Crumb. Liveright 2012 272 p. Illustration; Color
Grades: Adult   741.5/973; 741.5
1. Cartoonists — United States — Biography; 2. Crumb, Aline, 1948-; 3. Crumb, R; 4. Comic books, strips, etc.; 5. Cartoons and caricatures; 6. Married people

087140429X; 9780871404299, $29.95

LC 2012013566

In this book by R. and Aline Crumb, a "[s]emi-autobiographical [account], the stories reveal sordid details about the romantic relationship of the Crumbs, from their active (and somewhat violent) sex life in their youth to their still deviant sexual life in their sixties. Plagued by self-hatred, the creators spend most of each panel in dialogue with each other about how awful the world is, how self-deprecating they are, or how much they want to have sex." (Publishers Weekly)

Crumb, R.
The **book** of Genesis. illustrated by R. Crumb. W.W. Norton 2009 un Illustration; Map
Grades: Adult   741.5; 222
978-0-393-06102-4; 0-393-06102-7, $24.95

LC 2009-14303

"Originally thinking that we would do a take off of Adam and Eve, Crumb became so fascinated by the Bible's language, 'a text so great and so strange that it lends itself readily to graphic depictions,' that he decided instead to do a literal interpretation using the text word for word in a version primarily assembled from the translations of Robert Alter and the King James bible." (Publisher's note)

The **Life** and death of Fritz the cat. by R. Crumb. Fantagraphics Books 2012 92 p. Illustration
Grades: Adult   741.5
1. American wit and humor, Pictorial; 2. Caricatures and cartoons — United States; 3. Graphic novels; 4. Underground comic books, strips, etc; 5. Cats — Fiction

1606994808; 9781606994801, $19.99

LC 2012289388

This comic book, by R. Crumb, "contains all the Fritz [the Cat] stories from the earliest sketchbook-drawn tales...to the wild adventure stories...all the way to the despairing 'Fritz the Cat, Superstar' with its infamous ice-pick ending. Plus an introduction by Crumb, sketchbook pages, and more." (Publisher's note)

First paperback edition, May 1993.

R. Crumb Draws the Blues. by Robert Crumb. Last Gasp 1993 100 p. Illustration
Grades: Adult   741.5
1. Comic books, strips, etc.; 2. Short stories — Collections

0867194014; 9780867194012, $16.95

This book, by Robert Crumb, includes comic strips and stories. "Brought together for the first time from all stages of his career these strips range from the silly to the serious. Real people and real problems are the substance of stories like Jelly Roll Morton's Voodoo Curse and Patton while Crumb's celebrated light-hearted zaniness can be seen in Cubist Be-Bop Comics, The Old Songs are The Best Songs and Sunny side up." (Publisher's note)

Crumb, Sophie
Sophie crumb: evolution of a crazy artist. edited by S., A., & R. Crumb.. W.W. Norton & Co. 2011 271 p. Illustration; Color
Grades: Adult   741.092; 741.5
1. Crumb, Sophie — Themes, motives

0393079961; 9780393079968, $27.95

LC 2010020364

This book, by Sophie Crumb, edited by Aline Kominsky-Crumb and R. Crumb, "charts a young artist's life through her own drawings-from toddlerhood to motherhood.... Revealing how an original artistic sensibility is both innate and nurtured, the book features six separate developmental stages, including Sophie's earliest drawings, the elaborate fantasy world of her childhood, her late adolescent rebellion, and her coming of age." (Publisher's note)

Evolution of a crazy artist

Cruse, Howard
The **complete** Wendel. by Howard Cruse. Universe Pub. 2011 288 p. Illustration
Grades: Adult   741.5; Fic
1. Gay men — Comic books, strips, etc; 2. Comic books, strips, etc.; 3. Gay youth — Fiction

0789322161; 9780789322166

LC 2010934608

This book is a compilation of Howard Cruse's comic strip "Wendel," which was published in the newspaper "The Advocate" in the 1980s. "Cruse's feature was an episodic chronicle of life as experienced by young Wendel Trupstock, his lover Ollie and their friends, who collectively represented a particular slice of the American LGBT demographic during a particularly stressful period in recent history, when the afterglow of gay liberation collided with the AIDS epidemic and the ascendancy of Moral Majority-fueled homophobia. Simultaneously a mirror of the days' new events and a comedic portrayal of everyday queer life, drawing Wendel required...what the cartoonist calls an "elasticity of tone," balancing lightheartedness with pain, erotic mischief with mundane follies." (Kirkus

Cryptic Magazine
Horror book volume 1. Image Comics 2008 un Illustration
Grades: 10 11 12 Adult   741.5; Fic
1. Graphic novels; 2. Horror graphic novels; 3. Short stories — Graphic novels

978-1-58240-956-6, $14.99

This volume collects stories originally published in Cryptic Magazine. Each story reworks a classic horror tale. In the first, readers will find zombies in Vietnam in the year 1968, as an American patrol finds horror in the jungle. "Creature of the Depths" takes on The Creature from the Black Lagoon, as a small troop from a struggling sideshow is hired to help trap a marauding sea creature. In "Frankenstein," years after the monster was killed, the doctor is now an opium addict, but now someone is robbing graves and kidnapping people such as the blacksmith and some prostitutes; the monster isn't dead, but he wants more creatures like himself. And in "Full Moon," a nameless man agrees to help the village priest rescue a couple of kidnapped children who were taken by a vengeful vampire; it is the night of the full moon, and the young man becomes a ravening werewolf. The stories include graphic violence and gore, some partial nudity, and some rough language.

Cunningham, Darryl
How to fake a moon landing: exposing the myths of science denial. Darryl Cunningham. Abrams ComicArts 2013 176 p.
Grades: Adult   **001.9**
1. Pseudoscience — Comic books, strips, etc; 2. Science — Graphic novels; 3. Debates and debating
1419706896; 9781419706899, $16.95
LC 2012042210
In this book author-illustrator Darryl Cunningham looks at...hot-button science topics and presents a fact-based, visual assessment of current thinking and research on eight different issues. [He] incorporates comics, photographs, and diagrams to create substantive but easily accessible reportage. Cunningham's distinctive illustrative style shows how information is manipulated by all sides; his easy-to-follow narratives allow readers to draw their own fact-based conclusions." (Publisher's note)

Includes bibliographical references

Psychiatric tales: 11 graphic stories about mental illness. Darryl Cunningham. Bloomsbury 2010 139 p. Illustration
Grades: Adult
1. Mental illness; 2. Psychiatric hospital care; 3. Cunningham, Darryl; 4. Mental health services — Fiction; 5. Graphic medicine
1608192784; 9781608192786, $17; 9781906653088
This graphic novel, by Darryl Cunningham, presents the author's depiction of mental illness and its care. "Having worked for years as a health care assistant in a hospital's psychiatric ward, he states his intent to counter the stigma surrounding mental illness and to represent the patients who suffer from 'this most mysterious group of illnesses.'" (Publishers Weekly)

D'Salete, Marcelo
★ **Run** for it: stories of slaves who fought for their freedom. Marcelo D'Salete. Fantagraphics Books 2017 180 p. Illustration
Grades: 9 10 11 12 Adult   **741.5**
1. Slaves — Fiction; 2. Slavery — Fiction; 3. Fugitive slaves — Fiction
9781683960492, $24.99
LC 2017938231
Eisner Award: Best U.S. Edition of International Material (2018)
This graphic novel, by Marcelo D'Salete, "tells unforgettable stories about Afro-Brazilian slaves who rebelled against oppression.... 'Run For It'...is one of the first literary and artistic efforts to face up to Brazil's hidden history of slavery. These intense tales offer a tragic and gripping portrait of one of history's darkest corners." (Publisher's note)
"First published in 2015 in D'Salete's native Brazil, this striking graphic novel exposes the brutality of slavery on that country's sugarcane plantations via five stories of slaves who attempted escape. With a dry-brush effect, the art conveys the dark, foreboding danger of the jungles

surrounding the plantations and the energy and moods of the men and women who react to their enslavement in various ways." Pub Wkly"
Includes bibliographical references (page 174)

Dahl, Roald
The **Gremlins:** The Lost Walt Disney Production: A Royal Air Force Story. Dark Horse Books 2006 un Illustration
Grades: 4 5 6 7 8 9 10 11 12 Adult   **741.5; Fic**
1. Graphic novels; 2. Humorous graphic novels; 3. World War, 1939-1945 — Graphic novels
978-1-59307-496-8, $12.95
This is an illustrated novella, the first published work of RAF Flight Lieutenant Roald Dahl in his only collaboration with Walt Disney Studios. Originally published in 1943, the story was supposed to become a film combining live action with animation; the movie was never made, although the studio produced a lot of illustrations and samples. The story tells about one young Royal Air Force pilot named Gus, who first sees the little gremlins that wreak havoc on his plane. While the gremlins first cause lots of trouble, eventually Gus convinces them to work with the RAF.

Dakin, Glenn
Temptation: A Battle of Wits Through All Eternity. Active Images 2004 72p. Illustration
Grades: 8 9 10 11 12 Adult   **741.5**
1. Graphic novels; 2. Humorous graphic novels
0-9740567-5-8, $8.95
It's a constant battle of wits between a hermit who lives out in the wilderness and the devil who wants his soul. While that's the main theme, there are strips in which the devil needs the hermit to babysit his little baby devils so he can see a movie, the devil tries to sell the hermit a set of encyclopedias, and more fun.

Dalrymple, Farel
The **Wrenchies**. Farel Dalrymple. First Second 2014 304 p. Color; Illustration
Grades: 10 11 12 Adult   **741.5**
1. Imaginary places; 2. Science fiction
159643421X; 9781596434219, $19.99
In this book by Farel Dalrymple, "whatever life remains on earth is oppressed by the evil shadowsmen. Only a gang of ruthless and powerful children called the Wrenchies can hope to stand against them. When Hollis, a lonely boy from our world, is magically given access to the future world of the Wrenchies, he finally finds a place he belongs. But it is not an easy world to live in, and Hollis's quest is bigger than he ever dreamed of." (Publisher's note)
"Clearly, it doesn't pay to demand sheer narrative coherence here, but the raw emotional weight of Dalrymple's anger forcibly tows readers through the obfuscating narrative, and the intricate, gritty, and rivetingly grotesque art, in sickly greens and browns peppered with bloody red, plays no small part in that." Booklist

Daly, Paul
Athena Voltaire: the collected webcomics. APE Entertainment 2006 un Illustration
Grades: 9 10 11 12 Adult   **741.5; Fic**
1. Adventure graphic novels; 2. Fantasy graphic novels; 3. Graphic novels
978-0-9741398-9-0, $13.95
In "The Terror in Tibet," adventurous pilot (and widow) Athena Voltaire agrees to guide a group of British gentlemen on an expedition into the Himalayas. The time is the 1930s, and Nazis are on the rise in Germany. Athena soon finds out that the British are up to no good, nor are the

Germans pursuing them. They're all after something in a remote monastery halfway up Mount Everest, and she decides to prevent anyone from succeeding. In "The Wrath from the Tomb," Dracula's daughter seeks revenge against the men who killed her father; she makes a mistake when she sends men to attack Athena's Arizona ranch. Teens who love the Indiana Jones and Mummy movies will enjoy Athena's adventures. The violence level is about the same as those movies, although the scene in which the vampire is run through with a spear might bother more sensitive readers.

The stories originally appeared as webcomics, and the series was nominated for the first Eisner Award for Best Digital Comic in 2005

David, Peter
Fallen Angel: Down to Earth. DC Comics 2007 136p. Illustration
Grades: 12 Adult   **741.5; Fic**
1. Graphic novels; 2. Superhero graphic novels; 3. Supernatural graphic novels
978-1-4012-1268-1, $14.99
Bete Noir is a quiet, almost mundane city by day; but by night it becomes a haven for crime, corruption, and the supernatural. Enter the Fallen Angel, a mysterious and powerful woman who aids people in need when they find themselves at a crossroads in their lives. If she deems a person worthy, she can be a savior; if she doesn't, that person won't live to tell the tale. In this volume, the Angel's nemesis, Black Mariah, has returned to town, and this time she's hunting the Angel. The book includes nudity, sexual situations, foul language, and violence.

Friendly Neighborhood Spider-Man Vol. 1: Derailed. Marvel Entertainment 2006 un Illustration
Grades: 7 8 9 10 11 12 Adult   **741.5; Fic**
1. Graphic novels; 2. Spider-Man (Fictional character); 3. Superhero graphic novels
978-0-7851-2216-6, $14.99
A major character from Peter Parker's past returns, and it looks like Hobgoblin is terrorizing the skies again. Also, a woman chronicles Spider-Man's career on her blog, convinced that he has stalked her for her entire life.

Marvel 1602: Fantastick Four. Marvel Entertainment 2007 un Illustration
Grades: 9 10 11 12 Adult   **741.5; Fic**
1. Fantastic Four (Fictional characters); 2. Graphic novels; 3. Superhero graphic novels
978-0-7851-2293-7, $14.99
In the year 1602, Count Otto von Doom has an insidious plan that takes him — and the Four of the Fantastick — to the ends of the Earth. What does Doom want? Why doesn't Invisible Woman want to fight him? And what does Shakespeare have to do with it? This book spins off from Marvel 1602 written by Neil Gaiman.

Sachs & Violens. DC Comics 2006 126p. Illustration
Grades: 12 Adult   **741.5; Fic**
1. Graphic novels; 2. Mystery graphic novels
978-1-4012-1050-2, $7.99
The brutal killing of a young actress during the shooting of a snuff film sets soft core model Juanita Jean Sachs and photographer Ernie Schultz on a quest to discover those responsible. Their journey takes them from the mean streets of New York City to the back alleys of New Orleans, where they confront the utter depravity and corruption that defines the dark underbelly of American society. But they discover something else as well; something unexpected. Their destiny. This book includes considerable partial nudity, strong language, and graphic violence.

Davis, Eleanor
How to be happy. Eleanor Davis. Fantagraphics Books 2014 145 p. Illustration; Color
Grades: Adult   **741.5**
1. Comic books, strips, etc. — United States; 2. Emotions — Comic books, strips, etc; 3. Happiness
1606997408; 9781606997406, $24.99
LC 2013497415
Ignatz Award: Outstanding Anthology or Collection (2015)
This book by Eleanor Davis "is the artist's first collection of graphic/literary short stories. [H]er narratives...are at once compelling and elusive, pregnant with mystery and a deeply satisfying emotional resonance." (Publisher's note)
"What's most noticeable when the stories are laid up against one another is her varied visual approach, adapting her style to best fit the material.... The stories' subjects are equally diverse: a back-to-the-land cult falls apart under a despotic leader; a future dystopia lies on the verge of ecological collapse; a pair of youngsters explores an abandoned house; participants in an 'emotional boot camp' learn how to express grief." Booklist

Davis, Rob
The **Motherless** Oven. by Rob Davis. SelfMadeHero 2014 160 p. Illustration
Grades: 9 10 11 12 Adult   **741.5; Fic**
1. Fantasy fiction; 2. Death — Fiction; 3. Parent-child relationship — Fiction; 4. Graphic novels
190683881X; 9781906838812, $19.95
LC 2015296214
In this graphic novel, by Rob Davis, "parents don't make children — children make parents. Scarper's father is his pride and joy, a wind-powered brass construction with a billowing sail. His mother is a Bakelite hairdryer. In this world it rains knives, and household appliances have souls. There are also no birthdays — only deathdays. Scarper's deathday is just three weeks away, and he clings to the mundane repetition of his life at home and high school for comfort." (Publisher's note)
"Davis's dark and shadow-filled art appropriately mindbends and illuminates the text. The variation in panels quickens and pulls back the pace in this enigmatic tale, with the right amount of imagery left open for interpretation." SLJ

Davison, Al
The **Spiral** Cage: An Autobiography. DC Comics 2003 141p. Illustration
Grades: 11 12 Adult   **741.5; 92**
1. Autobiographical graphic novels; 2. Graphic novels; 3. Spina bifida — Graphic novels; 4. Davison, Al, 1960-
0-9740567-1-5, $12.95
Born with severe spina bifida, doctors considered Al Davison a hopeless case, condemned to the 'spiral cage' of his own DNA. In Al's own words and pictures, this book portrays his struggle to overcome 'disability' and the prejudice that surrounds it. The book includes lots of full frontal nudity, but it's not sexual, as Davison shows how he has to struggle physically every single day. The book also includes some strong language.

Davodeau, Etienne
★ The **initiates:** a comic artist and a wine artisan exchange jobs. Etienne Davodeau. NBM Pub. 2013 272 p.
Grades: Adult   **741.5/944; 741.5**
1. Wine and wine making; 2. Comic books, strips, etc.; 3. Work
1561637033; 9781561637034, $29.99
LC 2012953818

Courtesy of NBM Publishing

This graphic novel, by Étienne Davodeau, "offers a look at the daily devotion to craft in two dissimilar professions. Étienne Davodeau is a comic artist..., Richard Leroy is a winemaker.... But filled with good will and curiosity, the two men exchange professions, and Étienne goes to work in Richard's vineyards and cellar, while Richard, in return, leaps into the world of comics..., ultimately revealing that their endeavors and aspirations are not much different." (Publisher's note)

"The excellent writing, characterizations, and tranquil-yet-stimulating vibe make this a treat to savor slowly, like wine. Davodeau's smoky realism, though black-and-white, manages to suggest the full range of wine-growing climate shifts....Unfortunately, Davodeau is not as forthcoming about how he personally creates comics as Leroy is about the vintner's craft." LJ

Lulu anew. Étienne Davodeau; translation by Joe Johnson; lettering by Ortho. NBM Pub. 2015 160 p. Illustration
Grades: Adult
741.5; Fic
1. Unemployment — Fiction; 2. Life change events — Fiction
1561639729; 9781561639724, $27.99
LC 2014956688

Courtesy of NBM Publishing

In this novel by Etienne Davodeau "at the end of yet another unproductive job interview, Lulu, on a whim, takes off for the shore just to get away from it all. She's got a husband and kids left bewildered but it's nothing against them. This is just her time, getting away from the grind and with no other plan than savoring it. Surprised at her own temerity, she meets other people on the edge of the world. " (Publisher's note)

"Using a cinematic panel structure, Davodeau tightens or spreads out the width of each tier's panels to accommodate pauses, reflection, conflict, and action. A raucous party's kinetic action rat-a-tat-tats through smaller panels; wider panels are used to show wandering through the night, and the occasional full-page single panel drops the tempo to slow reflection and contemplation." Pub Wkly

De Heer, Margreet
Philosophy- a discovery in comics: A discovery in comics. Margreet de Heer. NBM Pub. 2012 120 p.
Grades: 11 12 Adult
100.022/2; 100.022; 741.5
1. Philosophy — Graphic novels; 2. Philosophy — History; 3. Comic books, strips, etc.
1561636983; 9781561636983, $16.99
LC 2012938931

This book, by Margreet de Heer, offers an "illustrated primer on philosophy.... Margreet de Heer visualizes the history of Western philosophy and makes it approachable for those with little knowledge of the subject. The book explains the

Courtesy of NBM Publishing

thoughts of philosophers such as Socrates, Plato, Aristotle, Descartes, Spinoza, and Nietzsche, and ponders questions such as 'What is thinking?' 'What is reality?' 'Is there free will?' and 'Why are these ideas still important?'" (Publisher's note)

De Liz, Renae
The **legend** of Wonder Woman. story & pencils by Renae De Liz; inks, colors & letters by Ray Dillon. DC Comics 2016 288 p. Color; Illustration
Grades: 8 9 10 11 12 Adult **741.5; Fic**
1. Female superhero graphic novels; 2. Superhero graphic novels; 3. Wonder Woman (Fictional character)
1401267289; 9781401267285, $29.99
LC 2016047038

"When a man from the outside world is brought to Themyscira as part of a conspiracy to overthrow its queen, Diana will risk everything to save his innocent life...and lose everything in the process. Soon, the Amazon princess finds herself in a world she never knew existed — America." (Publisher's note)

"Collecting twenty-seven chapters of online material, this spacious, even epic, story affords room for both legend building and healthy doses of action, the supernatural, romance, and humor." Booklist

De Radiguès, Max
Moose. Max de Radiguès. Conundrum International 2015 160 p. Illustration
Grades: 10 11 12 Adult **741.5; Fic**
1. Children of gay parents — Fiction; 2. Bullies — Graphic novels
1894994930; 9781894994934, $17
Eisner Nominee: Best Publication for Teens (2016)

"Meet Joe, an average, quiet high school student who is being bullied relentlessly by classmate Jason. No longer able to ride the bus, Joe walks to school every day through the woods finding comfort in Mother Nature. On his way to school, Joe sees a moose, a poignant encounter that helps distract him from the daily indignities. The story continues through many days of continual abuse, slowly revealing more about Joe's life." (Library Journal)

Joe's "beaten-down quietude is reflected in de Radigues' spare, wintry drawings, which look like a cleaned-up version of Jeffrey Brown. The artist always keeps one eye cocked on the natural world, which is far less sentimental about Joe's position in the predator-prey power structure." Pub Wkly

Dean, Michael
We told you so: comics as art. Tom Spurgeon and Michael Dean, editors. Fantagraphics Books, Inc. 2016 576 p. Illustration; Color
Grades: Adult **741.5**
1. Publishers and publishing — United States — History; 2. Cartooning — United States; 3. Cartoonists — United States
1606999338; 9781606999332, $49.99
LC 2016953075

This book, by Tom Spurgeon and Michael Dean, "tells of Fantagraphics Books' key role in helping build and shape an art movement around a discredited, ignored and fading expression of Americana,...in anecdotal form, in the words of the people who lived it and saw it happen.... [Spurgeon and] Dean assembled an all-star cast of industry figures, critics, cartoonists,...and groundbreaking publications to bring...a detailed account of Fantagraphics' first 40 years." (Publisher's note)

"Fantagraphics' history is also a history of the art form and industry, and the personal touches from candid interviews provide a fascinating insider's perspective." Pub Wkly

DeConnick, Kelly Sue

Bitch planet; Book 2: President Bitch. Kelly Sue DeConnick, script/co-creator; Valentine De Landro, art & covers/co-creator; Taki Soma, art (issue #6); with Kelly Fitzpatrick, colors; Clayton Cowles, letters. Image Comics 2017 144 p. Color; Illustration

Grades: Adult   **741.5; Fic**

  1. Penal colonies — Fiction; 2. Women prisoners — Fiction; 3. Science fiction

1632157179; 9781632157171, $14.99

Hugo Finalist: Best Graphic Story (2018)

"A few years down the road in the wrong direction, a woman's failure to comply with her patriarchal overlords results in exile to the meanest penal planet in the galaxy. But what happened on Earth that this new world order came to pass in the first place? Return to the grim corridors of Auxiliary Compliance Outpost #2, to uncover the first clues to the history of the world as we know it...and meet PRESIDENT BITCH." (Publisher's note)

Bitch Planet; Volume 1: Extraordinary Machine. by Kelly Sue DeConnick and Valentine De Landro. Image Comics 2015 136 p. Color; Illustration

Grades: Adult   **741.5; Fic**

  1. Prisoners — Fiction; 2. Women — Fiction; 3. Science fiction graphic novels

1632153661; 9781632153661, $9.99; 9780606378147; 0606378146

Eisner Nominee: Best New Series (2016)

This comic by Kelly Sue DeConnick and Valentine De Landro is a "riff on women-in-prison sci-fi exploitation. In a future just a few years down the road in the wrong direction, a woman's failure to comply with her patriarchal overlords will result in exile to the meanest penal planet in the galaxy. When the newest crop of fresh femmes arrive, can they work together to stay alive or will hidden agendas, crooked guards, and the deadliest sport on (or off!) Earth take them to their maker?" (Publisher's note)

"Though this sounds like it could get exploitative, DeConnick and De Landro never miss an opportunity to shine a light on sexism, revealing tender backstories for the characters and showcasing the ugly language of the men in power. De Landro expertly uses color to heighten the mood — noxious greens and yellows subtly highlight moments of sexist rhetoric, while the prisoners are rendered in warmer, more realistic tones." Booklist

Originally published in magazine form as Bitch Planet #1-5; Volume 1 of an ongoing series

Captain Marvel; 1: in pursuit of flight. by Kelly Sue DeConnick; illustrated by Dexter Soy and Emma Rios. Marvel Worldwide 2013 136 p. Color; Illustration

Grades: 10 11 12 Adult   **741.5**

  1. Superheroes — Fiction; 2. Female superhero graphic novels

0785165495; 9780785165491, $14.99

In this graphic novel by Kelly Sue DeConnick, illustrated by Dexter Soy and Emma Rios, "Carol Danvers has a new name, a new mission — and all the power she needs to make her own life a living hell. As the new Captain Marvel, Carol is forging from a challenge from her past! It's a firefight in the sky as the Banshee Squadron debut — but who are the Prowlers, and where has Carol seen them before? And how does secret NASA training program Mercury 13 fit in?" (Publisher's note)

Captain Marvel; Volume 2: Down. by Kelly Sue DeConnick and Christopher Sebela; illustrated by Dexter Soy and Filipe Andrade. Marvel Worldwide 2013 136 p. Color; Illustration

Grades: 10 11 12 Adult   **741.5**

  1. Superhero graphic novels; 2. Captain Marvel (Fictional character)

0785165509; 9780785165507, $14.99

In this graphic novel, by Kelly Sue Deconnick and Christopher Sebela, illustrated by Dexter Soy and Filipe Andrade, "Captain Marvel goes head to head with...Captain Marvel? Former Captain Monica Rambeau returns, but what's her problem with Earth's new Mightiest Hero? What threat is lurking below the ocean's surface? And can both Captain Marvels stop it before they get ship wrecked?" (Publisher's note)

Contains material originally published in magazine form as Captain Marvel #7-12 — T.p. verso.

Pretty deadly; Vol. 1: The shrike. Kelly Sue Deconnick; illustrated by Emma Rios, Jordie Bellaire, Clayton Cowles. Image Comics 2014 120 p. Color; Illustration

Grades: 9 10 11 12 Adult   **741.5**

  1. Women — Fiction; 2. Death — Graphic novels

1607069628; 9781607069621, $9.99

In this graphic novel by Kelly Sue Deconnick, "Death's daughter rides the wind on a horse made of smoke and her face bears the skull marks of her father. Her origin story is a tale of retribution as beautifully lush as it is unflinchingly savage." (Publisher's note)

Volume 1 of an ongoing series

DeFalco, Tom

The **Amazing** Spider-Girl: Whatever Happened to the Daughter of Spider-Man?. writer, Tom DeFalco; artist, Ron Frenz. Marvel Entertainment 2007 un Illustration

Grades: 7 8 9 10 11 12 Adult   **741.5; Fic**

  1. Graphic novels; 2. Spider-Girl (Fictional character); 3. Superhero graphic novels; 4. Spider-Man (Fictional character)

978-0-7851-2341-5, $14.99

After discovering she had inherited her father's incredible powers, May "Mayday" Parker donned a costume and became the amazing Spider-Girl. Recent events have forced her to hang up her webs and lead a normal life...but how long can May keep from web-slinging when there are villains like Hobgoblin on the loose? This volume begins collecting the second run of Spider-Girl comics; the first 100 issues were published as Spider-Girl and are being collected in digest-sized trade paperbacks. This new series, The Amazing Spider-Girl, features new numbering (from #1 and on) and is being collected in regular comic book-sized trade paperbacks.

DeForge, Michael

Sticks Angelica, folk hero. Michael DeForge. Drawn & Quarterly 2017 96 p. Color; Illustration

Grades: Adult   **741.5; Fic**

  1. Human-animal relationships — Comic books, strips, etc.; 2. Middle aged women — Comic books, strips, etc.; 3. Forest animals — Comic books, strips, etc.

1770462708; 9781770462700, $21.95

DeForge "follows the titular celebrity hero — 'former: Olympian, poet, scholar, sculptor, minister, activist,' among other things — through a series of one-page adventures. In the first we're told that after a scandal, Sticks has decided to live in the forest with a group of talking animals, and the rest of the book explores the dynamic between hero and fans in surreal episodes." (Publishers Weekly)

"DeForge crafts a work that is equal parts funny, sweet, sentimental, and scathing in its depiction of his main character's narcissism." LJ

Very Casual. Michael DeForge. Koyama Press 2013 152 p. Illustration; Color

Grades: Adult   **741.5**

  1. Comic books, strips, etc. — Canada; 2. Fantasy graphic novels

0987963074; 9780987963079, $15

LC 2013464167

Courtesy of Koyama Press

Ignatz Award: Outstanding Anthology or Collection (2013)

This comic collection, by Michael DeForge, is "culled from mini comics, online comics and anthology contributions.... Included are stories about litter gangs, meat-filled snowmen, righteous cops, beagle/human hybrids, and forest-bound drag queens.... [It also] collects 'Spotting Deer,' which won the Pigskin Peters Award for best non-traditional, non-narrative or avant-garde work at the 2011 Doug Wright Awards." (Publisher's note)

"While often willfully unsettling, DeForge's work resonates on many levels." Pub Wkly

Del Col, Anthony

Kill Shakespeare 3: The Tide of Blood. Conor McCreery and Anthony Del Col, illustrated by Andy Belanger. IDW Publishing 2013 140 p. Color; Illustration
Grades: 10 11 12 Adult
741.5
1. Graphic novels; 2. Shakespeare, William, 1564-1616 — Adaptations
1613777329; 9781613777329, $19.99

Courtesy of IDW Publishing

"With Richard III and Lady Macbeth defeated, Hamlet, Juliet, Othello, and Romeo face an even greater danger — Prospero, a rogue wizard who plans to destroy all of creation! Hamlet must embark on a perilous journey to a remote island whose inhabitants have gone mad and want the Dane's blood...if they aren't beaten to the chase by one of Hamlet's allies." (Publisher's note)

"There's more action, wizardry, and gore than the Bard himself was apt to include, but clever echoes of dialogue, intense emotional turnabouts, and imaginatively theatrical art recall the plays in satisfying ways." Booklist

Originally published as Kill Shakespeare: The Tide of Blood issues #1-5

★ **Kill** Shakespeare, vol. 1: a sea of troubles. created and written by Conor McCreery and Anthony Del Col; art by Andy Belanger; colors by Ian Herring; lettering by Chris Mowry, Robbie Robbins, and Neil Uyetake. IDW Publishing 2010 un Illustration
Grades: 10 11 12 Adult   **741.5; Fic**
1. Adventure graphic novels; 2. Authors; 3. Dramatists; 4. Fantasy graphic novels; 5. Graphic novels; 6. Poets; 7. Shakespeare, William, 1564-1616
978-1-60010-781-8, $19.99

A shipwrecked Hamlet finds himself in England with Richard III, who wants his help to find and kill the wizard, Will Shakespeare, so that Richard can rule with impunity. Haunted by his father's ghost, who tells Hamlet that killing Shakespeare will let him live again, Hamlet agrees to help the English king. Then he discovers that the Lady Juliet Capulet leads an army of rebellion, aided by Othello and Falstaff. They fight against the corrupt Richard, who consults the witch Hecate (who has her own agenda). Falstaff says that Hamlet is the prophesied Shadow King, who will aid the rebellion, while Richard and his allies only want to use Hamlet to destroy Shakespeare, but all agree that only Hamlet can lead them to the wizard.

The book includes bloody action and sexual situations, making this more suited to older teens.

"McCreery and Del Col spin an engrossing action-adventure tale of satisfying complexity, full of mystery, deceit, and gory violence, starring a hero who once again must marshal his determination and decide his path." Libr J

Volume 1 of 4

Kill Shakespeare; Volume 2: the blast of war. created and written by Conor McCreery and Anthony Del Col; art by Andy Belanger; colors by Ian Herring; lettering by Chris Mowry, Neil Uyetake, and Shawn Lee; original series edits by Tom Waltz.. IDW 2011 148 p.
Grades: 10 11 12 Adult
741.5
1. Comic books, strips, etc.; 2. Shakespeare, William, 1564-1616 — Fiction; 3. Shakespeare, William, 1564-1616 — Characters
1613770251; 9781613770252, $19.99

Courtesy of IDW Publishing

This book, the second volume of the comic book series, presents a "sweeping fantasy of magic, war, betrayal, and love [which] is set in a world where Shakespeare's characters dwell and Shakespeare himself is an absent god struggling with a heavy conscience. The second volume builds to the climactic finale of Hamlet's quest to find the creatorgod Shakespeare and return peace to a land torn apart by an evil army led by Richard III and Lady Macbeth. Joined by love interest Juliet, the warrior Othello, the wise fool Falstaff, and the spy Iago, Hamlet has built an army of rebels, the prodigals, who hold off their enemies while he searches for their creator. But even victory comes at a cost as friends and foes die in a great final battle." (Publishers Wkly)

"[A]n appropriate air of grandeur and theatricality is much on display, brought forth all the more in Belanger's spectacular and inventive page compositions." Booklist

Delano, Jamie

★ **John** Constantine, Hellblazer: original sins. Jamie Delano, Rick Veitch, writers; John Ridgway ... [et al.], artists; Lovern Kindzierski, Tatjana Wood, colorists; Annie Halfacree, Todd Klein, John Costanza, letterers. DC Comics 2012 287 p. Color illustration
Grades: Adult   **741.5/973**
1. Superhero comic books, strips, etc.
1401230067; 9781401230067, $19.99

LC 2012021662

This comic book, by Jamie Delano, John Ridgway, Alfredo Alcala, Rick Veitch, and Tom Mandrake, "is the first of a series of new HELLBLAZER editions starring Vertigo's longest running antihero, John Constantine, England's chain-smoking, low-rent magus. This first collection is a loosely connected series of tales of John's early years where Constantine was at his best and at his worst, all at the same time." (Publisher's note)

Originally published in single magazine form as John Constantine, Hellblazer 1-9 and Swamp Thing 76-77.; Volume 1 of an ongoing series

Outlaw Nation. Image Comics 2006 458p. Illustration
Grades: 12 Adult   **741.5; Fic**
1. Adventure graphic novels; 2. Graphic novels; 3. Revenge — Graphic novels
978-1-58240-707-4, $15.99

Story Johnson, a hundred-year-old semi-deranged amnesiac pulp fiction-writer returns home from 25 years MIA in Vietnam. All Story wants is to recover his missing time and catch up with some legendary, larger-than-life Johnson Family members. Trouble is, a lot of cousins have "disappeared," and those that are left have put the blame on him. This story is full of graphic violence, very strong language, nudity, and sexual situations.

Delisle, Guy

Burma chronicles. Drawn & Quarterly 2008 262p. Illustration
Grades: Adult   **741.5; 959.1**
1. Myanmar — Politics and government; 2. Myanmar — Social conditions
978-1-897299-50-0, $19.95
"Delisle follows accounts of sojourns in North Korea (Pyongyang, 2005) and China (Shenzhen, 2006) by chronicling a stint in yet another authoritarian society, Burma, to which he accompanied his wife, a Doctors without Borders administrator, to care for their infant son. He again uses wryly simple cartooning to amusingly recount his culture shock, much of which again stemmed from the host society's repressiveness, replete with censorship, Internet surveillance, and travel restrictions." (Booklist)

Hostage. Guy Delisle; translated by Helge Dascher. Drawn & Quarterly 2017 436 p. Color illustration; Color; Map
Grades: Adult   **92; 364.15; 741.5**
1. André, Christophe; 2. Hostages
1770462791; 9781770462793, $29.95
"In the middle of the night in 1997, Doctors Without Borders administrator Christophe André was kidnapped by armed men and taken away to an unknown destination in the Caucasus region. For three months, André was kept handcuffed in solitary confinement, with little to survive on and almost no contact with the outside world." (Publisher's note)
"Delisle brings the reader so fully into André's world that a simple change in his routine becomes either harrowing or hopeful, and the mundane details of his daily existence, saving a piece of bread from his morning meal for a snack, enjoying some music drifting through the wall into his cell, become heroic acts of defiance." LJ

Jerusalem: chronicles from the Holy City. Guy Delisle; coloured by Lucie Firoud and Guy Delisle; translated from the French by Helge Dascher. Drawn & Quarterly 2012 336 p. Illustration; Color
Grades: Adult   **915.694/4204540207; 915.694**
1. Muslims — Israel; 2. Israel — Social conditions; 3. Jerusalem — Description and travel; 4. Graphic novels; 5. Israel-Arab conflicts
1770460713; 9781770460713, $24.95
In this graphic novel, "Guy Delisle...lays...a cultural road map of contemporary Jerusalem, utilizing the...stranger in a strange land point of view.... He...examines the impact of the conflict on the lives of people on both sides of the wall while...recounting the quotidian: checkpoints, traffic jams, and holidays,...observing the Christian, Jewish, and Muslim populations that call Jerusalem home." (Publisher's note)

★ **Pyongyang:** a journey in North Korea. translated by Helge Dascher. Drawn & Quarterly 2005 176p. Illustration; Map
Grades: 11 12 Adult   **951.93; 741; 741.5**
1. Graphic novels; 2. Korea (North) — Graphic novels
1-896597-89-0; 1-897299-21-4 (pa), $14.95
This book "documents the two months French animator Delisle spent overseeing cartoon production in North Korea.... He records everything from the omnipresent statues and portraits of dictators Kim Il-Sung and Kim Jong-Il to the brainwashed obedience of the citizens." Booklist
"Pyongyang will appeal to multiple audiences: current events buffs, Persepolis fans and those who just love a good yarn." Publ Wkly

Shenzhen: A Travelogue from China. Drawn & Quarterly 2006 148p. Illustration
Grades: 10 11 12 Adult   **741.5**
1. Autobiographical graphic novels; 2. Graphic novels
1-896597-79-1, $19.95
Shenzhen details Guy Delisle's observations of life in a cold urban city in southern China in 1997 that is sealed off from the rest of the country by electric fences and armed guards. With a dry wit and a clean line, Delisle makes the most of his time spent in Asia overseeing outsourced production for a French animation company. By translating his fish-out-of-water experiences into graphic novels, Delisle is quick to find the humor and point out the differences between Western and Eastern cultures. Yet he never forgets to relay his compassion for the simple freedoms that escape his colleagues by virtue of living in a Communist state. Delisle uses the occasional "s-word."

User's guide to neglectful parenting. Guy Delisle; translation by Helge Dascher. Drawn & Quarterly 2013 190 p. Illustration
Grades: Adult   **306.874/2; 306.874**
1. Fatherhood — Comic books, strips, etc; 2. Graphic novels; 3. Parenting — Comic books, strips, etc
1770461175; 9781770461178, $12.95

LC 2013414780
"Quick, light vignettes play on the worries and cares any young parent might have, and offer wry solutions to the petty frustrations of being a dad who works from home." (Publisher's note)
Other titles in this series are: Even more bad parenting advice (2014); The owner's manual to terrible parenting (2015)

DeMatteis, J. M.

★ The **stardust** kid. Boom! Studios 2008 un Illustration
Grades: 3 4 5 6 7 8 9 10 11 12 Adult   **741.5; Fic**
1. Adventure graphic novels; 2. Fantasy graphic novels; 3. Graphic novels
978-1-934506-04-2, $14.99
Twelve-year-old Cody's best friend is Paul Brightfield; they share a deep bond that goes far beyond mere friendship. What no one else knows is that Paul isn't human, he's one of the last Old Ones, ancient elemental beings who lived before man existed. One night, Paul disappears, and a hate-filled creature who has existed long buried beneath Wilde Park bursts out with a desire to destroy everything in the world. Only Cody, his little sister K.M., and his friend Alana and her little brother Nathaniel, remain, and somehow they must find The Stardust Kid and discover a way to stop the hate and restore their world. Some creatures might be frightening to younger readers, but anyone who likes the Harry Potter books shouldn't have a problem with this book.

Desberg, Stephen

The **Scorpion:** the devil's mark. Cinebook Ltd. 2008 96p. Illustration
Grades: 10 11 12 Adult   **741.5; Fic**
1. Adventure graphic novels; 2. Graphic novels; 3. Rome — History — Graphic novels
978-1-905460-62-5, $19.95
In Rome of the Renaissance, a young thief called the Scorpion makes a living by unearthing relics in the depths of the Roman Catacombs, which he then sells at high prices to princes, nobles, and bishops. Then Cardinal Trebaldi declares the Scorpion must die. Trebaldi is part of a group called the Nine Families, who made a pact to rule the world back in the time of the Caesars; he has now organized an army of warrior monks to carry out his will, and he has gained the approval of the Nine Families to assassinate the Pope so he can take over and rule Rome. Somehow, the Scorpion threatens that plan. Trebaldi sets a beautiful Egyptian poisoner on the Scorpion's trail, but they will both face betrayal and confront amazing truths. The

book includes lots of blade fighting and sexual innuendo without any overt nudity or sexual content.

Devlin, Tom

★ **Drawn** & Quarterly: Twenty-five Years of Contemporary Cartooning, Comics, and Graphic Novels. edited by Tom Devlin [with 4 others]; designed by Tracy Hurren and Tom Devlin; translations by Helge Dascher. Farrar, Straus & Giroux 2015 512 p. Illustration; Color
Grades: Adult   741.5
1. Drawn & Quarterly (Firm); 2. Graphic novels; 3. Publishers and publishing
177046199X; 9781770461994, $49.95
Eisner Award: Best Anthology (2016); Ignatz Nominee: Outstanding Anthology or Collection (2015)

"For over two decades, Drawn & Quarterly (D&Q) has been a discerning publisher of graphic novels and a major force in the growth and diversification of the format. This quarter-century compendium...begins with a detailed history of D&Q's humble beginnings in a Montreal apartment with a small stable of artists and very little money. Excerpts from works by D&Q pioneers such as Seth, Chester Brown, Julie Doucet, and Adrian Tomine, as well as relative newcomers such as Michael DeForge and Rutu Modan are interspersed with interviews, photographs, reminisces, and essays of mutual appreciation." (Library Journal)

"This is a magnificent monument to the diversity of aesthetic philosophies and personal styles, and if there's a prevalent theme, it's everyday indignities and how real people face them, even if these real people are occasionally zombies or superheroes." Booklist
Contains stories translated from various languages.; Includes index

Dezuniga, Tony

Jonah Hex: Face Full of Violence. Justin Gray, Jimmy Palmiotti, writers; Luke Ross, Tony Dezuniga, artists; Jason Keith, Rob Schwager, colorists; Rob Leigh, letterer. DC Comics/Vertigo 2006 144p. Illustration
Grades: 10 11 12 Adult   741.5; Fic
1. Graphic novels; 2. Jonah Hex (Fictional characters); 3. Western graphic novels
978-1-4012-1095-3, $12.99

This book collects the new stories of Jonah Hex, the former Confederate soldier turned bounty hunter, the man with the scarred face. He doles out his brand of justice with his guns, taking vengeance upon murderers, thieves, and others who victimize the weak. The book has foul language and lots of violence.

Di Filippo, Paul

Top 10: Beyond the Farthest Precinct. DC Comics/America's Best Comics 2006 un Illustration
Grades: 10 11 12 Adult   741.5; Fic
1. Graphic novels; 2. Mystery graphic novels; 3. Superhero graphic novels
978-1-4012-0991-9, $14.99

In Neopolis, a modern city populated exclusively by super beings, it takes a unique and powerful police force to protect and serve. The officers of Precinct 10, also known as Top Ten, encounter all manner of the super powered and the supernatural on a routine basis. It doesn't help matters when Captain Traynor (Jetman) is unceremoniously replaced. Now the officers must band together, overcome their personal squabbles, and get their city back on track, before it all comes tumbling down on their heads. The book includes some sexual situations.

Diaz Canales, Juan

★ **Blacksad**. text [by] Juan Canales Díaz; illustrated [by] Juanjo Guarnido. Dark Horse 2010 184p. Color; Illustration

Grades: Adult   741.5
1. Private investigators — Fiction; 2. Mystery graphic novels; 3. Noir fiction
9781595823939, $29.99
Harvey Award: Best American Edition of Foreign Material (2011)

"This noir thriller set in 1950s America stars a cast of anthropomorphic animals, with the dirty-handed hero an impeccably trenchcoated black cat. John Blacksad is a sort of private investigator, and these three stories visit territory both familiar and unusual. Our hero's lost love is inexplicably murdered, a misinterpreted killing rocks a white supremacist movement, and a coterie of radical intelligentsia crosses agendas with a version of Commie-hunter Joe McCarthy." (Library Journal)

"All of this material is riveting, and Guarnido's artwork is atmospheric and full of indelibly captured characters — he's a true master of the form. Blacksad is a comics classic, and American readers are fortunate to have these first three in one volume." Pub Wkly

Blacksad: A Silent Hell. writer, Juan Diaz Canales; artist, Juanjo Guarnido. Dark Horse 2012 108 p. Color illustration
Grades: Adult   741.5; Fic
1. Private investigators — Fiction; 2. Noir fiction; 3. Mystery graphic novels
1595829318; 9781595829313, $19.99

"Detective John Blacksad returns, with a new case that takes him to a 1950s New Orleans filled with hot jazz and cold-blooded murder! Hired to discover the fate of a celebrated pianist, Blacksad finds his most dangerous mystery yet in the midst of drugs, voodoo, the rollicking atmosphere of Mardi Gras, and the dark underbelly that it hides!" (Publisher's note)

"If Walt Disney ever made an adult-themed, anthropomorphic Philip Marlowe movie, it might resemble this popular series.... Canales's plot is populated by a colorful mixture of Americana: burlesque houses, snake-oil merchants, Mardi Gras, and the haunted soul of the blues are all key elements in this vibrant, atmospheric noir mystery. The authentic local details of Guarnido's art are balanced by whimsical character design and humor." Pub Wkly

Blacksad: Amarillo. written by Juan Díaz Canales; illustrated by Juanjo Guarnido; translation by Katie LaBarbera and Neal Adams; lettering by Tom Orzechowski and Lois Buhalis. Dark Horse Books 2014 63 p. Color; Illustration
Grades: Adult   741.5
1. Nineteen fifties — Comic books, strips, etc; 2. Detectives — Fiction; 3. Murder — Fiction; 4. Nineteen fifties — Fiction
1616555254; 9781616555252, $17.99

LC 2015295612

In this book, written by Juan Díaz Canales and illustrated by Juanjo Guarnido, "[detective John] Blacksad lands a side job driving a rich Texan's prized yellow Cadillac Eldorado across 1950s America, hitting the back roads from New Orleans to Tulsa. But before long, the car is stolen and Blacksad finds himself mixed up in another murder, with roughneck bikers, a shifty lawyer, one down-and-out Beat generation writer, and some sinister circus folk!" (Publisher's note)

"[W]hile the script is a solid Chandler-esque thriller, it's Guarnido's animation-influenced artwork that's the true draw here, with each panel rife with detail, color, and unforgettable character designs." Pub Wkly

Diggle, Andy

The **Losers:** Ante Up. DC Comics/Vertigo 2004 160p. Illustration
Grades: 10 11 12 Adult   741.5; Fic
1. Adventure graphic novels; 2. Graphic novels
1-4012-0198-9, $9.95

An elite U.S. Special Forces unit is targeted for assassination when they unintentionally uncover the illegal and immoral practices of the C.I.A.

Believed dead and with nothing to lose, the team of wet works operatives regroup and begin a mission of revenge against the organization that betrayed them. Only as the team goes after a corrupt oil conglomerate with ties to the C.I.A., do they truly begin to realize the depths of the conspiracy they have discovered and the impossible odds of survival that they face. The book includes lots of foul language and some fairly graphic violence.

Other volumes in this series are: Double down (2004); Trifecta (2005); Close quarters (2006); Endgame (2006)

Silent Dragon. DC Comics/Wildstorm 2006 un Illustration
Grades: 10 11 12 Adult   **741.5; Fic**
1. Adventure graphic novels; 2. Graphic novels; 3. Science fiction graphic novels
978-1-4012-1104-2, $19.99
Tokyo, A.D. 2063: the Yakuza warlord Hideaki has seized total control of Honshu's underworld while ruthlessly crushing all opposition. But his true dream is the overthrow of the government itself. Japan's hard-line military junta will do anything to stop him and they have found the ultimate pawn to set their plan in motion: Renjiro, the chief advisor to the notorious gangster. Caught between a lifetime of honor and loyalty to his Yakuza clan and the iron-fisted might of the military elite, Renjiro will find that the only way to stop a civil war and avoid total annihilation is to play both sides against the middle. The book includes partial nudity, strong language, and lots of bloody violence.

Dillon, Glyn
The **Nao** of Brown. Glyn Dillon. Self Made Hero 2012 206 p.
Grades: Adult   **741.5**
1. Obsessive-compulsive disorder — Fiction; 2. Meditation — Fiction; 3. Art — Fiction; 4. Japanese Americans — Fiction
1906838429; 9781906838423, $24.95
In this novel by Glyn Dillon "Nao Brown, who's 'hafu' (half Japanese, half English), is...suffering from obsessive-compulsive disorder (OCD) and fighting violent urges to harm other people.... [But] she wants to get her design and illustration career off the ground; and she wants to find love, perfect love.... She also meets Gregory, an interesting washing-machine repairman, and Ray, an art teacher at the Buddhist Center. She begins to draw and meditate to ease her mind and open her heart." (Publisher's note)

Dini, Paul
Batman: Detective. Paul Dini; Royal McGraw. DC Comics 2007 144p. Illustration
Grades: 9 10 11 12 Adult   **741.5; Fic**
1. Batman (Fictional character); 2. Graphic novels; 3. Superhero graphic novels; 4. Joker (Fictional character)
978-1-4012-1239-1, $14.99
He is in peak physical condition, with a high-tech arsenal at his disposal, but it is perhaps his exceptional detective skills that make Batman the most formidable opponent of the countless deadly villains of Gotham City. In this volume, the Dark Knight faces the Joker, the Riddler, the Penguin, and Poison Ivy, as well as some brand-new villains, while pushing himself to the limit to solve crimes. But can even the most powerful mind outthink unpredictable and crazy foes?

Dark Knight: A True Batman Story. writer, Paul Dini; artist and cover art, Eduardo Risso; letterer, Todd Klein. DC Comics 2016 128 p. Color; Illustration
Grades: 11 12 Adult   **92; 741.5**
1. Dini, Paul; 2. Graphic memoir; 3. Authors
1401241433; 9781401241438, $22.99
In this graphic memoir author Paul Dini shares his traumatic experience and his deep connection with his creative material. "Walking home one evening, he was...viciously beaten within an inch of his life. His

recovery process was arduous, hampered by the imagined antics of the villains he was writing...including the Joker, Harley Quinn and the Penguin.... [He] always imagined the Batman at his side...during his darkest moments." (Publisher's note)

"As potent metaphors for the ability to overcome trauma, superheroes perhaps more than any other fantasy figures engender deep, personal connections among their followers. Dini explores the notion that, in real life, Batman can't swing in to save you, though, as it turns out, sometimes he does." Booklist

The **World's** Greatest Super-Heroes. Paul Dini; art by Alex Ross. DC Comics 2005 un Illustration
Grades: 6 7 8 9 10 11 12 Adult   **741.5; Fic**
1. Graphic novels; 2. Superhero graphic novels; 3. Justice League (Fictional characters); 4. Wonder Woman (Fictional character); 5. Batman (Fictional character); 6. Superman (Fictional character)
1-4012-0254-3, $49.95
LC 2006-159064
This oversize hardcover volume collects the stories that DC originally published separately. Superman tries to singlehandedly end world hunger, only to face suspicion and corruption; Batman tries to stop all criminal activity; and Wonder Woman tries to free oppressed women. They each realize that, despite their super powers, they can't eradicate the problems of the world on their own. The rest of the book portrays the Justice League and highlights each member's super hero origins.

Dirge, Roman
It ate Billy on Christmas. Dark Horse Books 2007 un Illustration
Grades: 4 5 6 7 8 9 10 11 12 Adult   **741.5; Fic**
1. Graphic novels; 2. Horror graphic novels; 3. Humorous graphic novels
978-1-59307-853-9, $12.95
Lumi has been bullied by her brother Billy all her life, and this Christmas would have been more of the same, but for the weird, ugly little monster that crawled up from the abandoned well and came into their house. Mistaking it for the stuffed puppy she had requested from her parents, Lumi watches in amazement as it devours the bullying Billy when he shoots it with darts from his new dart gun. She makes a cardboard Billy, which fools her unsuspecting and clueless parents. A few weeks later, back at school, Lumi has to face the bullies who have made her school life miserable, but she has her "puppy" in her backpack and it's hungry.... Dirge wrote the story and drew the black and white illustrations, while Daily provided the color paintings. The story shows the monster eating Billy in one gulp, but there's little actual violence on the pages. The dark humor and twisted story line will appeal to those who enjoy Coraline and The Wolves in the Walls by Neil Gaiman, and the weird humor of Edward Gorey cartoons.

Lenore: Noogies. Slave Labor Graphics 1999 un Illustration
Grades: 9 10 11 12 Adult   **741.5; Fic**
1. Graphic novels; 2. Horror graphic novels; 3. Humorous graphic novels
0-943151-03-1, $11.95
This book collects the first four issues of the Lenore comic book series. It ventures into the dark, surreal world of a little dead girl and features stories about limbless cannibals, clock monsters, cursed vampire dolls, taxidermied friends, an obsessed would be lover, and more fuzzy animal mutilations than should be legal. The book includes some disturbing images and macabre humor.

Other Lenore books are: Wedgies (2000); Cooties (2005); Swirlies (2012); Purple Nurples (2013)

Something at the Window is Scratching: Children's Tales for Disturbed Children. SLG Publishing 1998 120p. Illustration

Grades: 9 10 11 12 Adult 741.5; Fic
1. Graphic novels; 2. Horror graphic novels; 3. Humorous graphic novels
0-943151-09-0, $9.95

Chilling, disturbing, sickly amusing poems accompanied by equally chilling, disturbing, and sickly amusing illustrations bring to mind a very morbid Shel Silverstein with more of a horror twist. In the title tale, what's scratching at the boy's window that night is the son of the Sandman, who died after sending the boy to sleep; in order to give the creature a home, the boy tapes a tail to the creature and presents his parents with their new cat. Despite the moody, dark tone, there is no violence or bad language.

Dixon, Chuck

The **Iron** Ghost. Image Comics 2007 un Illustration
Grades: 10 11 12 Adult 741.5; Fic
1. Graphic novels; 2. Mystery graphic novels; 3. World War, 1939-1945 — Graphic novels
978-1-58240-727-2, $15.99

Berlin, Germany, 1945: The tide of the war has turned in favor of the Allies. The fall of the Nazi empire is inevitable, but there is still something even more dangerous than the ever approaching Allies to the Third Reich: The Iron Ghost, who is murdering officials in the Nazi regime. It's up to two non-Nazi German police officers to capture the Ghost. But once they discover the truth will they want to — or even be able to — stop him? The story includes harsh language and considerable violence.

Nightwing: On the Razor's Edge. DC Comics 2005 192p. Illustration
Grades: 9 10 11 12 Adult 741.5; Fic
1. Graphic novels; 2. Mystery graphic novels; 3. Nightwing (Fictional character); 4. Superhero graphic novels
1-4012-0437-6, $14.99

Bludhaven has seen its share of battles between its costumed protector, Nightwing, and various criminals. But when an army of ninjas arrives, it's only a harbinger of the deadliest threat yet. Shrike, long thought dead, is back, and he wants revenge on his childhood pal, Nightwing. Shrike's current master, Blockbuster, would be only too happy to see the vigilante destroyed, but Shrike wants to see to Nightwing's destruction personally.

Nightwing: Year One. Chuck Dixon and Scott Beatty; penciller Scott McDaniel; inker: Andy Owens. DC Comics 2005 un Illustration
Grades: 7 8 9 10 11 12 Adult 741.5; Fic
1. Graphic novels; 2. Nightwing (Fictional character); 3. Superhero graphic novels; 4. Teen Titans (Fictional characters); 5. Robin (Fictional character); 6. Batman (Fictional character)
1-4012-0435-X, $14.99

Dick Grayson was the first Robin, the teen sidekick to the Dark Knight, Batman. Then he became Nightwing and stepped out of Batman's shadow. The story behind that transformation and how it affected Batman, the Teen Titans and Dick himself is explored in this graphic novel. When Batman fires Robin, an angry Dick Grayson is unsure of where to go. On his journey, he receives advice from Superman and aid from Deadman, and makes the decisions that lead him to become a brand new crimefighter.

Robin, year one. Chuck Dixon, Scott Beatty, writers; Javier Pulido, Marcos Martin, pencillers; Robert Campanella, inker; Lee Loughridge, colorist; Sean Konot, letterer; Javier Pulido, Robert Campanella, original covers; Batman created by Bob Kane. DC Comics 2008 200p. Illustration
Grades: 9 10 11 12 Adult 741.5; Fic
1. Batman (Fictional character); 2. Graphic novels; 3. Robin (Fictional character); 4. Superhero graphic novels
978-1-563-89805-1, $14.99

This book takes readers back to Dick Grayson's first year working as Robin, sidekick of the Batman. After his family of aerialists was murdered, Bruce Wayne took in young Dick Grayson, who helped Wayne as Batman

solve the murders. Adopted by Wayne, Dick starts training to become his partner in solving crimes on the streets of Gotham City; but not everyone likes it. Captain James Gordon of the Gotham City Police thinks Dick is much too young, and he puts Batman on notice that if anything happens to hurt or kill Robin, Batman will pay. At first, Dick/Robin can easily handle the bad guys. Then he ends up working solo on a case of girls who disappear when one of his friends from school goes missing, and he goes up against the Mad Hatter. Unknown to Robin, or Batman, Two-Face is watching the young crime-fighter's progress, and he decides to test the boy — brutally. When Two-Face beats Robin badly enough to put him into a hospital, Batman "retires" Robin; but when Dick is strong enough, he runs away to live on the streets. There, he encounters Shrike, a contract killer who trains teen boys in ninja-style fighting, and joins his "school," an organization that Dick realizes Batman doesn't know exists. The book includes strong violence.

The **Vanishers**. IDW Publishing 2002 80p. Illustration
Grades: 6 7 8 9 10 11 12 Adult 741.5; Fic
1. Adventure graphic novels; 2. Graphic novels; 3. Science fiction graphic novels
0-9712282-6-4, $12.99

From the turn of the 20th century, to medieval England, and into the far-flung future, Andy and Arvis must escape their pursuers, rescue their friends, and return to their own time. Andy's friends begin to disappear and only he remembers that they ever existed. When Andy discovers another student, Arvis Voltoz, has noticed that disappearances, he follows Arvis home and begins an adventure that takes him and Arvis through time.

Doctorow, Cory

★ **Cory** Doctorow's futuristic tales of the here and now. IDW Publishing 2008 152p. Illustration
Grades: 10 11 12 Adult 741.5; Fic
1. Graphic novels; 2. Science fiction graphic novels; 3. Short stories — Graphic novels
978-1-60010-172-4, $24.99

Six short stories by noted young science fiction writer and BoingBoing.net coeditor Doctorow are adapted into the graphic format by various comics creators, including Dara Naraghi, Dan Taylor, J. C. Vaughn, James Anthony Kuhoric, Esteve Polls, Daniel Warner, Paul McCaffrey, Dustin Evans, Erich Owen, Robbie Robbins, Chris Mowry, and more. The stories include "Anda's Game," in which a twelve-year-old girl gets involved in a multi-player game in which she kills enemies and someone starts paying cash for her kills; "Craphound," in which a professional yard sale picker makes friends with one of the aliens who had come to Earth and wants to learn how to be a picker at yard sales; "After the Siege," in which Valentine and her family struggle to survive the disease turning the city's people into zombies as they try to get by during a siege; and "When Sysadmins Ruled the Earth," in which a global catastrophe destroys almost everything, except the computer techs holed up in various company buildings around the world. The stories include violence and some strong language.

Doran, Colleen

A **Distant** Soil Vol. 1: The Gathering. Image Comics 1997 un Illustration
Grades: 10 11 12 Adult 741.5; Fic
1. Adventure graphic novels; 2. Fantasy graphic novels; 3. Graphic novels
1-887279-51-2, $19.95

This is the story of a young girl who is born the heir to an alien religious dynasty, one of comics' most lavish and romantic sagas. Liana and her brother Jason are orphaned and live in a research institution; they get caught up in interplanetary politics and magic. The book includes fantasy, epic scope, psychics, Arthurian legend, smart-mouthed punks, adorable gay couples, bizarre clothing, aliens, death, love, and heavy doses of humor.

A **Distant** Soil Vol. 2: The Ascendant. Image Comics 2000 un Illustration

Grades: 10 11 12 Adult — 741.5; Fic
1. Adventure graphic novels; 2. Fantasy graphic novels; 3. Graphic novels
1-58240-018-0, $18.95

Liana was born the heir to an alien religious dynasty, then hidden on Earth until Rieken found her and brought her back. But the galaxy's most powerful psionic, the Avatar, already sits on the throne. Revolutionary forces on the planet have taken Jason, however, and intend to turn him into one of their weapons against the throne. Things continue to become more complicated when Jason learns his father started the Resistance movement on Ovanan, and Liana learns that Rieken is actually Seren, the Avatar, and she's a danger to him. Dangerous politics swirl around everyone. The book includes sexual suggestiveness and violence.

A **Distant** Soil Vol. 3: Aria. Image Comics 2001 un Illustration
Grades: 11 12 Adult — 741.5; Fic
1. Adventure graphic novels; 2. Fantasy graphic novels; 3. Graphic novels
1-58240-201-9, $16.95

Rieken/Seren is the target of assassins, a pawn in a dangerous game of powerful psionics, and he makes a desperate play for freedom. But his ploy threatens to capture him in his own web of deceit, as his darkest secrets are revealed to allies and enemies alike, leading to a showdown with deadly consequences. And Liana, with powers of the Avatar, and Jason, are caught in the middle. The book includes lots of sexual situations, including same-sex relations, harsh language (including f-bombs), and violence.

A **Distant** Soil Vol. 4: Coda. Image Comics 2005 un Illustration
Grades: 11 12 Adult — 741.5; Fic
1. Adventure graphic novels; 2. Fantasy graphic novels; 3. Graphic novels
1-58240-478-X, $17.99

Liana is born the heir to an alien religious dynasty. Possessing the power to destroy worlds with her mind, Liana is under an assassination order from the government of her father's home world. A foiled coup attempt results in a power vacuum that leaves the alien world without its treasure weapon. The aliens have no choice but to take Liana as their reluctant new Avatar. Only an angry slave and a small group of resistance fighters can free her — and the universe — from the dangers of her power. The book includes some strong language, nudity, and violence.

Dorff, Matt

The **Book** of revelation. Matt Dorff; illustrated by Chris Koelle. Zondervan 2013 187 p. Illustration
Grades: Adult — 228.0022
1. Good and evil; 2. Bible — N.T. Revelation; 3. Bible stories
0310421403; 9780310421405, $19.99

LC 2012941745

This book is a graphic novel adaptation of the Bible's book of Revelation translated by Mark B. Arey and Philemon D. Sevastiades, adapted by Matt Dorff, and illustrated by Chirs Koelle. "Stand in the Apostle John's sandals and watch the New Testament's climactic war between good and evil unfold.... See the Lamb, the Seven-Headed Dragon, and the Beast...Discover anew the story of the ultimate fulfillment of John's faith as the final battle is fought between God and Satan." (Publisher's note)

Translated from the Greek by Fr. Mark Abey and Fr. Philemon Sevastiades.

Dori, Fabrizio

Gauguin: The Other World. Fabrizio Dori; translation from the French by Edward Gauvin. Harry N Abrams Inc 2017 144 p. Color; Illustration
Grades: 10 11 12 Adult — 759.4; 741.5; 92
1. Gauguin, Paul, 1848-1903; 2. Artists — Biography
1910593273; 9781910593271, $19.95

LC 2017303720

This book on Paul Gauguin, by Fabrizio Dori, "is a revelatory biography of an artist whose qualities as a man won him few admirers in his own lifetime, but whose talents as a painter would have an enormous influence on the art of Picasso, Matisse, and many more." (Publisher's note)

"The dreamlike nature of the story line is gorgeously borne out in Dori's painted panels — he brilliantly echoes Gauguin's iconic style, from the stylized figures and imagery to the rich, saturated color. Art lovers will appreciate this enigmatic, unsparing foray into the beleaguered painter's psyche." Booklist

Dorkin, Evan

★ **Beasts** of Burden: animal rites. written by Evan Dorkin; art by Jill Thompson; lettering by Jason Arthur and Jill Thompson. Dark Horse Comics 2010 184p. Illustration
Grades: 8 9 10 11 12 Adult — 741.5; Fic
1. Cats — Graphic novels; 2. Dogs — Graphic novels; 3. Graphic novels; 4. Mystery graphic novels; 5. Supernatural graphic novels
978-1-59582-513-1, $19.99
2010 Eisner Award for Best Publication for Teens; 2010 Eisner Award to Jill Thompson for Best Painter/Multimedia Artist for Beasts of Burden and Magic Trixie; 2005 Eisner Award for Best Short Story for ¿Unfamiliar;¿ 2004 Eisner Award to Jill Thompson for Best Painter/Multimedia Artist (interior art) for ¿Stray.¿

Burden Hill is just a nice, quiet suburban town full of houses with yards and white picket fences, demonic frogs, zombie roadkill, ghosts, etc. The humans who live in Burden Hill seem to be totally oblivious to the dangers, but the dogs, and one cat, work together to keep their town safe. Jack the beagle, Pugsley (go figure), Ace the husky, Rex the Doberman, Whitey the terrier, and Orphan the cat deal with a haunted dog house, witches, undead dogs, a werewolf, and other monsters. The book includes some mild bad language ("crap" usually from Pugs) and a fair amount of violence. This book includes the four-issue miniseries plus all of the short stories that originally appeared in The Dark Horse Book of Hauntings, The Dark Horse Book of Witchcraft, The Dark Horse Book of the Dead, and The Dark Horse Book of Monsters. Sarah Dyer co-wrote "A Dog and His Boy" with Evan Dorkin.

"Gorgeous artwork and a smart, witty script elevate this tale of household pets who unite to fight occult menaces in idyllic Burden Hill." Publ Wkly

Bill & Ted's Most Excellent Adventures Volume Two. Amaze Ink/SLG Publishing 2005 un Illustration
Grades: 9 10 11 12 Adult — 741.5; Fic
1. Graphic novels; 2. Humorous graphic novels
1-59362-002-0, $13.95

The silly and fun movies "Bill and Ted's Excellent Adventure" and its sequel, "Bill and Ted's Bogus Journey" inspired a Marvel Comics series in the early 1990s. Written by Evan Dorkin, it was nominated for an Eisner Award. This second volume finds the two time-hopping headbangers on the run from a gang from Hell, on trial for tampering with time, and stuck on a planet of superheroes. There's also an invasion of inter-dimensional Bills and Teds, a pink-slipped Death, and a bogus attempt to prevent Lincoln's assassination.

Doucet, Julie
  365 days: a diary by Julie Doucet. Drawn & Quarterly 2008 360p. Illustration
  Grades: 12 Adult   **741.5**
  1. Art — Graphic novels; 2. Autobiographical graphic novels; 3. Graphic novels
  978-1-89729-915-9; 1-89729-915-X
  Doucet renounced her comics-centric lifestyle five years ago and focused on art, but the journal she started in late 2002 combines comics with art with text. Her personal narrative combines with collage, doodles, and comics panels to chronicle her life as she became part of a broader arts community. The book includes some harsh language, and one panel towards the end depicts an image combining nudity with a disturbing sexual situation.

Drnaso, Nick
  ★ **Sabrina**. Nick Drnaso. Drawn & Quarterly 2018 204 p. Illustration
  Grades: Adult   **741.5; Fic**
  1. Airmen — Fiction; 2. Conspiracy theories — Fiction; 3. Air forces — Comic books, strips, etc.; 4. Fake news — Comic books, strips, etc.; 5. Missing persons — Comic books, strips, etc.
  177046316X; 9781770463165
  In this graphic novel, by Nick Drnaso, "when Sabrina disappears, an airman in the U.S. Air Force is drawn into a web of suppositions, wild theories, and outright lies. He reports to work every night in a bare, sterile fortress that serves as no protection from a situation that threatens the sanity of Teddy, his childhood friend and the boyfriend of the missing woman. Sabrina's grieving sister, Sandra, struggles to fill her days as she waits in purgatory." (Publisher's note)
  "Cinematic and deeply timely, this tale is torn from today's darkest headlines of fake news, terrorism, and the ultimately dehumanizing effect of the Internet. Drnaso's artwork seems basic at a glance, but page to page, panel to panel it reveals depths of emotion that culminate in a reading experience guaranteed to linger." LJ

Drooker, Eric
  Blood song: a silent ballad. introduction by Joe Sacco. Dark Horse 2009 un Illustration
  Grades: 11 12 Adult   **741.5**
  1. Graphic novels; 2. Stories without words
  978-1-59582-389-2, $19.95
  "Driven by war from their rural home in Southeast Asia, a young woman and her dog ride the ocean currents to a city in the West. A deeply moving graphic novel, masterfully done." SLJ
  First published 2002 by Harcourt

Dryer, Matt
  Dwight T. Albatross's The Goon Noir. Dark Horse Comics 2007 Illustration
  Grades: 11 12 Adult   **741.5; Fic**
  1. Graphic novels; 2. Horror graphic novels; 3. Humorous graphic novels
  978-1-59307-785-3, $12.95
  The horror comedy series has been described as "EC by way of Looney Tunes," so it seems fitting that comedians and horror creators put their own spin on the Goon characters. Among the distinguished creators featured in this, the very first Goon anthology, are comedians Patton Oswalt and Brian Posehn (both of Comedy Central's Comedians of Comedy and Mr. Show), Reno: 911 co-creator Thomas Lennon, B.P.R.D. scribe John Arcudi, comics great Kevin Nowlan (Tomorrow Stories, Sandman, Superman), fan-favorite Humberto Ramos (Revelations, Spider-Man), Steve Niles, Ryan Sook, Mike Ploog, Bill Morrison, Arvid

Nelson, Tony Moore, Hilary Barta, Roger Langridge, Scott Allie and Todd Herman. Powell himself and frequent co-conspirators Tom Sniegoski and Mark Farmer also present the three-part "Peg Leg Full of Heaven," featuring the Little Unholy Bastards, and erstwhile publisher Dwight T. Albatross contributes a little somethin' for the ladies. Readers can expect to find zombies, monster-smashing, some gore, a little harsh language, quite a bit of sexual suggestiveness, and lots of slightly sick humor.

Duffy, Chris
  ★ **Above** the Dreamless Dead: World War I in Poetry and Comics. edited by Chris Duffy. First Second 2014 144 p. Illustration
  Grades: 9 10 11 12 Adult   **741.5**
  1. World War, 1914-1918 — Comic books, strips, etc.; 2. World War, 1914-1918 — Poetry
  1626720657; 9781626720657, $24.99
  In this book edited by Chris Duffy, "various artists adapt the works of some of the most famous WWI poets, including Wilfred Owen, Siegfried Sassoon, and Isaac Rosenberg. The...cartoonists, including Hunt Emerson, Sarah Glidden, and Stuart Immomen, use different approaches to illuminate poems known for its bitter irony and brutal honesty." (Publishers Weekly)
  "The work of 'Trench Poets' from WWI is brought vividly to life by accomplished cartoonists. This stunningly effective presentation does much to inform readers of the emotional and physical horrors of war. The volume's small format renders some of the detail difficult to decipher, but anything larger might be overwhelming. There's very mature content, especially in lyrics of soldiers' songs. Reading list." Horn Book
  Includes bibliographical references and index

Duggan, Gerry
  The **Last** Christmas. Image Comics 2006 un Illustration
  Grades: 11 12 Adult   **741.5; Fic**
  1. Adventure graphic novels; 2. Graphic novels; 3. Horror graphic novels; 4. Humorous graphic novels; 5. Santa Claus — Graphic novels
  978-1-58240-676-3, $14.99
  After the apocalypse, no one is safe; not even at the North Pole. After marauders kill Mrs. Claus, Santa withdraws from life and turns his back on Christmas. When he finally emerges from seclusion, the old world is gone forever, and as Santa struggles to find his way in a post-apocalyptic world, can he find a way to save Christmas too? This Christmas story is for all those who love horror movies (especially with killer zombies) and action movies with lots of shooting and killing of bad guys while yelling curses.

Durieux, Christian
  An **enchantment**. Christian Durieux. NBM Pub. 2013 72 p.
  Grades: Adult
  741.5/9493; 741.5
  1. Fantasy graphic novels; 2. Louvre (Paris, France) — Graphic novels
  9781561637058, $19.99
                              LC 2012950214
  This graphic novel is part of the ComicsLit Louvre series, a series of graphic novels commissioned by the Louvre art museum. In this entry, Belgian artist Christian Durieux "imagines the director of the museum as a faded grey bureaucrat on the verge of

Courtesy of NBM Publishing

retirement, who is swept away into the building's nighttime vastness by a mysterious and pixieish muse. As they playfully romp beneath the ancient works of art,...the aged and cynical director muses on literature and politics." (Publishers Weekly)

Dyer, Jamaica
★ **Weird** fishes. SLG Publishing 2009 112p. Illustration
Grades: 10 11 12 Adult   **741.5; Fic**
1. Friendship — Graphic novels; 2. Graphic novels
978-1-59362-177-3, $9.95

Dee sees giant talking ducks and her main confidant is Bones, a talking goldfish. Bunny Boy always wears a bunny suit. The two misfits have been friends for years, but now things are starting to change. Bunny Boy falls for a goth girl and actually wears a mod suit. Dee, however, has problems when her visions begin to darken, ducks become monsters, and bad things hang out in storm clouds. She needs Bunny Boy, but he seems to want more normalcy in his personal relationships. The two teens smoke cigarettes, cut school, and Bunny Boy goes to a party where people are drinking alcohol.

Dysart, Joshua
Swamp Thing Vol. 2: Love in Vain. DC Comics/Vertigo 2005 144p. Illustration
Grades: 11 12 Adult   **741.5; Fic**
1. Graphic novels; 2. Horror graphic novels; 3. Science fiction graphic novels
1-4012-0493-7, $14.99

Though he once wielded the combined power of all the Earth's elemental forces, the creature known as Swamp Thing has renounced his omnipotence and returned to his original status as the avatar of the Green, the web of energy connecting all of the world's plant life. But he is now vulnerable, and Arcane is about to break out of his eternal damnation into the world of the living. His designs for revenge threaten to sink not only the Swamp Thing and his family, but everything else under the sun into a never-ending nightmare of corruption and despair. The book includes lots of harsh language, graphic violence, nudity, and sexual situations.

Swamp Thing: Healing the Breach. DC Comics/Vertigo 2006 144p. Illustration
Grades: 10 11 12 Adult   **741.5; Fic**
1. Fantasy graphic novels; 2. Graphic novels; 3. Superhero graphic novels; 4. Swamp Thing (Fictional character)
1-4012-0934-3, $17.99

With the consciousness of Alec Holland still separated from its former host and scattered throughout the world, the Swamp Thing must face a new threat which is manifesting itself inside a growing dead zone in the Gulf of Mexico and contend with the gradual reassembly of the Holland mind and the pain of reintegration that its completion promises. In the meantime, a hurricane threatens the Gulf Coast area where Swamp Thing, and crippled Jordin are staying. The book includes strong language, some nudity and sexual situations, and some violence.

★ **Unknown** soldier: haunted house. DC Comics/Vertigo 2009 144p. Illustration
Grades: 11 12 Adult   **741.5; Fic**
1. Graphic novels; 2. Terrorism — Graphic novels; 3. Uganda — Graphic novels
978-1-4012-2311-3, $9.99

In 2002, Northern Uganda is a beautiful country racked by horrible brutality and war, as an insane extremist Christian rebel and his army of children terrorize their own people. Dr. Lwanga Moses had fled Uganda with his family when he was a child and Idi Amin was in power; now, he has returned to Uganda with his Ugandan wife, full of pacifist ideals and plans to bring hope and healing to his home country. Then he falls prey to the child soldiers and something deep within him erupts, and Dr. Moses

becomes an unstoppable killing machine. His face disfigured, he covers it in bandages and becomes an unknown soldier, determined to do whatever it takes, however much violence and killing he must do, to stop the war. Meanwhile, his wife keeps up their medical mission, always wondering what happened to make her husband disappear. This book is full of horrific, gory violence, but with this update of the classic Unknown Soldier character, Dysart also carefully researched into Ugandan politics and conflicts to make his story as authentic as possible.

Edginton, Ian
Kingdom of the Wicked. Dark Horse Comics 2004 120p. Illustration
Grades: 8 9 10 11 12 Adult   **741.5; Fic**
1. Adventure graphic novels; 2. Fantasy graphic novels; 3. Graphic novels
1-59307-187-6, $15.95

Christopher Grahame is the premier children's author of the twenty-first century, a publishing phenomenon. With his work translated into everything from Aborigine to Zulu, he is the cornerstone of a multi-million dollar, franchise spewing empire. Is it any surprise then that under all this pressure something has to give? Unfortunately, it's Chris's mind. Stricken by mysterious headaches and blackouts that plagued his childhood, Chris once again finds himself walking the avenues and boulevards of Castrovalva — the fantasy realm he dreamt up as a boy, to while away his recuperation. But like Chris, Castrovalva has also changed. Deluged in mud, blood, and barbed wire, war has come to wonderland. Chris tries to tell himself it's all a bad dream...so why can't he wake up? The book includes violence, strong language, and brief nudity.

Scarlet Traces. Dark Horse Comics 2003 88p. Illustration
Grades: 9 10 11 12 Adult   **741.5; Fic**
1. Graphic novels; 2. Mystery graphic novels; 3. Science fiction graphic novels
1-56971-940-3, $14.95

A decade after the Martians' abortive assault on the Earth and their attempt to establish an invasion bridgehead on the British Isles, the industrious Victorians have assimilated the Martian technologies into their everyday lives. Hansom cabs now scuttle along the Capital's streets on multi-limbed crab legs and the terrible monopoly of the Martian heat-ray has assured the dominance of the British Empire over two thirds of the Earth's surface. However, there is something rotten at the heart of empire. When the bodies of several young women are found washed up on the Thames, drained of blood, enter Captain Robert Autumn (retired soldier turned gentleman-adventurer) and his former Sergeant Major, now manservant, Archie Currie. Together they are drawn into the mystery which leads them from the gin palaces of the East End, and the grinding poverty of the North, to Whitehall's corridors of power and the very Hall of the Martian King. The book includes violence and some strong language.

Edmondson, Nathan
Black Widow; Volume 1: the finely woven thread. Nathan Edmondson; illustrated by Phil Noto. Marvel Enterprises 2014 144 p. Color; Illustration
Grades: 11 12 Adult   **741.5**
1. Superheroes — Fiction; 2. Undercover operations — Fiction; 3. Black Widow (Fictional character)
0785188193; 9780785188193, $17.99

"The Black Widow goes undercover in Russia, but from its cold streets, the Hand of God reaches out to crush her...and it is as merciless as its name implies. Outmatched by the brute force of a powerful new villain, Natasha faces her deadliest test, and discovers a deadly plot unfolding that spans the entire globe." (Publisher's note)

"Edmondson's fast-paced and action-packed espionage story does an excellent job playing to the character's strengths, using her cunning to assess each situation and her agility and reflexes when it all goes to hell. Noto's luminous watercolorlike panels — a welcome departure from more traditional superhero comics artwork — create a soft atmosphere." Booklist

Contains material originally published in magazine form as Black Widow #1-6 and All new Marvel now! point one #1 — Tp verso.; Volume 1 of 3

Olympus. written by Nathan Edmonson; art by Christian Ward; letters by Jeff Powell. Image Comics 2009 un Illustration

Grades: 10 11 12 Adult   **741.5; Fic**

1. Fantasy graphic novels; 2. Graphic novels; 3. Greek mythology — Graphic novels
978-1-60706-178-6, $14.99

In Ancient Greece, Zeus granted immortality to two brothers, Castor and Pollux (most people might know them as the Gemini twins), then bound them to his service. Three thousand years later, they still serve him on Earth by hunting fugitives from Olympus and maintaining order between the human realm and the divine. This means they have to catch Hermes and cast him off Earth; when they do that, they accidentally leave an opening between the realms for Pelops, son of Tantalus, who has no love for the gods. Ward saturates his sketchy, scratchy lines with wild colors. The book includes violence and some harsh language.

Eisinger, Justin

Angel: Spotlight. IDW Publishing 2006 120p. Illustration

Grades: 10 11 12 Adult   **741.5; Fic**

1. Fantasy graphic novels; 2. Graphic novels; 3. Horror graphic novels
978-1-600100-023-6, $19.99

This collection compiles five one-shots focusing on different members of Angel's supporting cast, each from a different creative team. Peter David and Nicola Scott focus on Illyria. Dan Jolly and Mark Pennington handle Gunn, Scott Tipton and Mike Norton feature Wesley. Jeff Mariotte and David Messina present Doyle. And Jay Faerber and Bob Gill offer up a tale of Conner. Monster fighting, demons, and internal organs are on display in the stories.

Star Trek: Alien spotlight volume 1. IDW Publishing 2008 152p. Illustration

Grades: 6 7 8 9 10 11 12 Adult   **741.5; Fic**

1. Adventure graphic novels; 2. Graphic novels; 3. Science fiction graphic novels; 4. Star Trek — Graphic novels
978-1-60010-179-3, $19.99

This volume collects a series of one-shots (standalone comics issues), each devoted to one of the alien races featured in the Star Trek series. Readers meet the Gorns, Vulcans, Andorians, Orions, the Borg, and the Romulans in stories that also give the aliens' point of view. The stories are set in the various time periods of the Star Trek universe; for example, Captain Clark Terrell and Pavel Chekov (before they were captured by Khan in "The Wrath of Khan") and their landing party encounter the Gorns on a planet designed to train Gorn warriors, while Captain Picard encounters the Borg.

Eisner, Will

The **Best** of the Spirit. DC Comics 2005 187p. Illustration

Grades: 7 8 9 10 11 12 Adult   **741.5; Fic**

1. Graphic novels; 2. Superhero graphic novels; 3. The Spirit (Fictional character); 4. Spirit (Fictional character)
1-4012-0755-3, $14.99; 9781401207557

Legendary comics creator Will Eisner created The Spirit in 1940, and over the twelve years of its initial publication, he used it to revolutionize the cartooning medium, creating new methods of storytelling, developing new depths of characterization, and inventing such artistic innovations as

the splash page. This volume reprints 22 stories from the original run, including the origin story from 1940; the bulk of the stories were initially published in the mid- to late-1940s. These stories allow people to get acquainted with The Spirit, who was a young criminologist named Denny Colt; believed to have been murdered, he was buried in a state of suspended animation and awoke one day in the Wildwood Cemetery. He has since dedicated himself to fighting crime, wearing a suit, fedora, and mask. DC Comics started publishing a new incarnation of The Spirit in 2007, and a motion picture is in the works.

★ **Comics** and sequential art: principles and practices from the legendary cartoonist. W.W. Norton 2008 175p. Illustration (The Will Eisner library)

Grades: 9 10 11 12 Adult   **741.5**

1. Comic books, strips, etc. — Authorship; 2. Drawing — Technique; 3. Graphic novels — Authorship
978-0-393-33126-4; 0-393-33126-1, $22.95

LC 2008-20042

This book offers the author's ideas, theories, and advice about graphic storytelling and the uses to which the comic book art form can be applied.

First published 1985 by Poorhouse Press; ?A Will Eisner instructional book? Cover

★ The **contract** with God trilogy: life on Dropsie Avenue. Will Eisner. W.W. Norton 2005 498 p. Illustration

Grades: Adult   **741.5; Fic**

1. Bronx (New York, N.Y.) — Graphic novels
0393061051; 9780393061055, $35

LC 2005053944

"Comics veteran [Will] Eisner launched a second career with 'A Contract with God' (1978), one that...led the way for the contemporary graphic novel. Two further Depression-era books set on the same fictitious street in the Bronx followed. In the wake of Eisner's...death [in 2005], the three are here gathered into a single volume." (Booklist)

Life on Dropsie Avenue

Fagin the Jew. by Will Eisner; foreword by Michael Bendis. Dark Horse 2013 136 p. Illustration

Grades: 11 12 Adult   **741.5**

1. Jews — Great Britain — Fiction
1616551267; 9781616551261, $19.99

This book is author and illustrator Will Eisner's reimagination of author Charles Dickens' character Fagin from the book "Oliver Twist." "Imagining Fagin's impoverished childhood in the slums of London and his initiation into the criminal underworld, Eisner's story counters the anti-Semitism of Victorian literature as his...brushwork creates...[a] portrait of the era." (Publisher's note)

"[T]his compelling counternarrative is framed as Fagin's apologia to Dickens and folds in plenty of historical background about Jews in Europe and England during the late 19th century." LJ

Includes bibliographical references; First published 2003

★ **Graphic** Storytelling and Visual Narrative. Poorhouse Press 1996 164p. Illustration

Grades: Adult Professional   **741.5**

1. Graphic novels; 2. Graphic novels — Teaching — Aids and devices
0-9614728-2-0, $22.99

A companion to Comics & Sequential Art, this book takes the principles examined in that title and applies them to the process of graphic storytelling. Eisner shows comic artists, filmmakers and graphic designers how to craft stories in a visual medium. Readers will learn everything from the fine points of graphic storytelling to the big picture of the comics medium, including how to: Use art that enhances your story, rather than obscuring it; wield images like narrative tools; write and illustrate effective dialogue; and develop ideas that can be turned into dynamic stories. These lessons and more are illustrated with storytelling samples from Eisner himself along with other comic book favorites, including Pulitzer Prize-winner Art Spiegelman, Robert Crumb, Milton Caniff and Al Capp.

★ **Last** day in Vietnam: a memory. written and illustrated by Will Eisner and edited by Diana Schutz. Dark Horse Comics 2000 79 p.
Grades: Adult   **741.5**
1. Vietnam War, 1961-1975 — Graphic novels; 2. Soldiers — Graphic novels
1569715009; 1616551208; 9781616551209, $17.99
LC 710474
This graphic novel by Will Eisner "recounts the artist's own experiences with soldiers engaged not only in the daily hostilities of war but also in larger, more personal combat. Some of the stories in this novel are comical, some heartrending, some frightening, yet all display the incredible insight into humanity characteristic of Eisner's entire oeuvre." Cover title.

Life, in pictures: autobiographical stories. Will Eisner.. W.W. Norton & Co. 2007 493 p. (Will Eisner library.)
Grades: Adult   **741.5; 92**
1. Cartoonists — United States — Biography — Comic books, strips, etc; 2. Eisner, Will
0393061078; 9780393061079, $29.95
LC 2007032339
This graphic novel, by Will Eisner, offers "an intimate self-portrait of the American icon Will Eisner, and a chronicle of the career that launched a new art form.... 'The Dreamer' and 'To the Heart of the Storm' describe Eisner's gritty early life and career, while 'The Name of the Game' chronicles a personal history of his wife's family. Finally, two shorter pieces illuminate the bookends of a legendary career." (Publisher's note)

The **plot:** the secret story of the Protocols of the Elders of Zion. by Will Eisner, with an introduction by Umberto Eco. Norton 2005 vii, 148 p. Illustration (Will Eisner library.)
Grades: 9 10 11 12 Adult   **741.5; 305.892**
1. Antisemitism; 2. Protocols of the wise men of Zion
0393060454; 0393328600; 9780393060454, $19.95
LC 2005040527
This book, by Will Eisner, "examines the astonishing conspiracy and the fabrication of The Protocols of the Elders of Zion.... Purported to be the actual blueprints by Jewish leaders to take over the world, the Protocols, first published in 1902, have become gospel truth to international millions. Presenting a pageant of historical figures,...Eisner unravels and dispels one of the most devastating hoaxes of the twentieth century." (Publisher's note)

PS magazine: the best of the Preventive maintenance monthly. [by] Will Eisner; introduction by Peter J. Schoomaker; preface by Ann Eisner; selected and with commentary by Eddie Campbell. Abrams ComicArts 2011 272p. Illustration
Grades: Adult   **741.5**
1. United States — Army — Graphic novels; 2. Graphic novels; 3. Repairing — Graphic novels
978-0-8109-9748-6, $21.95
LC 2011012342
"From 1951 to 1971, between The Spirit and A Contract with God, Eisner produced PS Magazine for the army in order to teach the common soldier how best to use, maintain, repair, and requisition their equipment. From explaining how to load a truck correctly to why it won't start, Eisner used a combination of humor, sound technical writing, and graphic storytelling to educate the soldiers.... With Eisner's wonderful artwork and clarity of style making sometimes difficult concepts easy to understand, it's no wonder PS Magazine was so popular with military personnel. A

fascinating document for both fans of Eisner and military history buffs." Publ Wkly

The **Spirit** Archives Volume 14. DC Comics 2004 192p. Illustration
Grades: 9 10 11 12 Adult   **741.5; Fic**
1. Graphic novels; 2. Superhero graphic novels; 3. The Spirit (Fictional character); 4. Spirit (Fictional character)
1-4012-0158-X, $49.95
LC 2001-274103
The adventures of Will Eisner's most famous creation continue in this volume reprinting the Spirit newspaper sections from 1/5/47 to 6/29/47. It features appearances by Ebony, Dolan and Ellen, the seductive P'Gell, Hoagy the Yogi, Silken Floss, Saree and more. Today's readers should understand that Eisner's depiction of Ebony, who is the Spirit's sidekick, was not considered out of place in 1947, even though many might take offense now. Eisner started developing new methods of telling a story and revolutionizing comics along the way.

The **Spirit** Archives Volume 15. DC Comics 2004 192p. Illustration
Grades: 9 10 11 12 Adult   **741.5; Fic**
1. Graphic novels; 2. Superhero graphic novels; 3. The Spirit (Fictional character); 4. Spirit (Fictional character)
1-4012-0162-8, $49.95
LC 2001-274103
Volume 15 reprints The Spirit newspaper sections published from July 6, 1947 to December 28, 1947, featuring the seductive P'Gell, The Octopus, a send up of Li'l Abner, and more. The stories range from broad comedy to crime noir, with plenty of comic violence.

El Rassi, Toufic
Arab in America. Last Gasp 2008 118p. Illustration
Grades: 10 11 12 Adult   **92; 741.5**
1. Biographical graphic novels; 2. Graphic novels; 3. Muslims — United States — Graphic novels
978-0-86719-673-3, $14.95
Toufic El Rassi combines a memoir of his life in America with commentary on how Muslims and Arabs have been treated in the U.S. Born in Beirut but living in the U.S. since he was a young boy, El Rassi faced ignorant prejudice and discrimination ever since his family immigrated to this country. In this book he shows how hard it is to maintain an Arab identity in a country saturated with anti-Arab propaganda, examining the roles of media and pop culture in a world with 9/11, two Gulf Wars, and other U.S. involvement in the Middle East. Readers will confront uncomfortable ideas about just what unthinking patriotism and ignorance about the real culture of the Middle East countries do to harm many who are innocent. The book includes some strong language and a few isolated panels with partial nudity.

Eldred, Tim
★ **Grease** monkey. written and drawn by Tim Eldred; [edited by Teresa Nielsen Hayden]. Tor 2006 352p. Illustration
Grades: 9 10 11 12 Adult   **741.5; Fic**
1. Graphic novels; 2. Science fiction graphic novels
0-7653-1325-1; 0-7653-1326-X (pa), $19.95
When hostile aliens attacked Earth and left it after killing most of the humans, another group of aliens came and offered to "uplift" one of the animal species to human intelligence so that Earth could rebuild. The dolphins turned them down, but the gorillas went for it. Some generations later, new mechanic Robin Plotnik comes to the space station called Fist of Earth, where he's assigned to work with Chief Mac Gimbensky. Mac is a no-nonsense gorilla who works on the ships of the all-woman Barbarian Squadron. He and Robin work together well, but they each have their

romantic problems. This is science fiction from a viewpoint not always seen in most stories.

Ellis, Grace

★ **Lumberjanes;** Volume 1: Beware the kitten holy. written by Noelle Stevenson & Grace Ellis; illustrated by Brooke Allen; colors by Maarta Laiho; letters by Aubrey Aiese; created by Shannon Watters, Grace Ellis & Noelle Stevenson. Boom! Studios 2015 128 p. Illustration; Color (Lumberjanes)

Grades: 6 7 8 9 10 11 12 Adult   741.5; Fic
1. Female friendship — Graphic novels; 2. Monsters — Fiction; 3. Camps — Fiction; 4. Summer — Fiction; 5. Adventure fiction
1608866874; 9781608866878, $14.99
Eisner Award: Best New Series (2015); Eisner Award: Best Publication for Teens (2015); Harvey Award: Best New Series (2015); Harvey Award: Best Original Graphic Publication For Young Readers (2015)

"[This] graphic novel begins mid-adventure as five campers are out after hours investigating a strange event that they all witnessed: a woman turning into a giant bear. This is just the first of many odd occurrences that Jo, April, Molly, Mal, and Ripley encounter at the summer camp for 'Hardcore Lady Types.' The Lumberjanes, as the scouts are called, band together to solve puzzles, defeat three-eyed creatures, and escape the ire of their watchful counselor Jen." (School Library Journal)

"Humorously riffing on everything from scout badges to the X-Men to feminist heroes..., it's a sharp, smart, and most of all fun celebration of sisterhood." Pub Wkly

Volume 1 of an ongoing series

Lumberjanes; Volume 2: Friendship to the Max. by Noelle Stevenson, Grace Ellis, illustrated by Brooke A Allen, contributed by Shannon Watters. Boom! Studios 2015 112 p. Color; Illustration

Grades: 6 7 8 9 10 11 12 Adult   741.5; Fic
1. Fantasy graphic novels; 2. Teenage girls — Fiction; 3. Camping — Fiction
1608867374; 9781608867370, $14.99

"Jo, April, Mal, Molly and Ripley are five best pals determined to have an awesome summer together...and they're not gonna let any insane quest or an array of supernatural critters get in their way! But having stumbled onto a mysterious force wreaking havoc in the camp, it's a race through the woods as the Lumberjanes work together to save not only their friends, but maybe even the whole world!" (Publisher's note)

Moonstruck; Volume 1: Magic to brew. writer, Grace Ellis; artists, Shae Beagle and Kate Leth; colors, Caitlin Quirk; lettering, Clayton Cowles. Image Comics 2018 120 p. Color; Illustration

Grades: 9 10 11 12 Adult   741.5; Fic
1. Magic — Fiction; 2. Werewolves — Fiction
1534304770; 9781534304772, $9.99

"Werewolf barista Julie and her new girlfriend go on a date to a close-up magic show, but all heck breaks loose when the magician casts a horrible spell on their friend Chet. Now it's up to the team of mythical pals to stop the illicit illusionist before it's too late." (Publisher's note)

"Beagle's art, awash in dreamy pastels and moody lighting, perfectly complements the dialogue and plot, and clever, dynamic panel layouts give the pages lots of compelling visual interest. The refreshing variety of skin tones, gender presentations, and body shapes and sizes (monster and otherwise) emphasizes the overall message of body positivity and an atmosphere of inclusion." Booklist

Volume 1 of an ongoing series

Ellis, Warren

The **Authority:** relentless. by Warren Ellis. WildStorm/DC Comics 2000 192 p. Color illustration

Grades: Adult
1. Superhero comic books, strips, etc.
1563896613; 9781563896613, $17.99

This comic book, by Warren Ellis, focuses on "superheroes with believable personalities and community spirit. Two story arcs, each encompassing terror and evil on a global scale, pit the group of seven against armies of superhumans dispatched in scenes reminiscent of the best action movies." (Publisher's note)

Volume 1 of 4

Crecy. Avatar Press 2007 un Illustration

Grades: 10 11 12 Adult   741.5; Fic
1. Crecy (France), Battle of, 1346 — Graphic novels; 2. Graphic novels; 3. Hundred Years' War, 1339-1453 — Graphic novels; 4. War — Graphic novels
978-1-59291-040-3, $6.99

A highly trained but under equipped army invades another country due to that country's perceived threat to home security. The army conducts shock-and-awe raids designed to terrify the populace. This army is soon driven to ground, and vastly outnumbered. The English army has to stand and fight, under the command of King Edward III, in Crecy, France. On 26 August 1346, modern warfare changed forever. This is the story of England's greatest battle, narrated by a fictional English longbowman. The book is full of battlefield violence and lots of very harsh language, including the f-bomb.

Desolation Jones. DC Comics/Wildstorm 2006 142p. Illustration

Grades: 12 Adult   741.5; Fic
1. Graphic novels; 2. Mystery graphic novels
978-1-4012-1150-9, $14.99

Michael Jones used to be an MI6 field agent, and he is the first surviving victim of the Desolation Test, a radically dangerous procedure cooked up by the British government. He was kept alive intravenously while being force-fed a steady diet of horrific data and images non-stop as stimulants were continuously pumped into him, for an entire year. Now he lives in Los Angeles, where all the ex-spooks like him have been sent and kept; he works as a private investigator to their secret underground community. Colonel Nigh, who lives for his pornography collection, needs Jones' help to recover a special piece of film — pornography starring Adolf Hitler; Nigh's troublesome daughters all play into the equation. Mature readers who enjoy such titles as Preacher and aren't troubled by nudity, violence, and considerable use of harsh language, will want to read this.

Fell Volume 1: Feral City. Image Comics 2007 un Illustration

Grades: 11 12 Adult   741.5; Fic
1. Graphic novels; 2. Mystery graphic novels
978-1-58240-693-0, $14.99

Detective Richard Fell is transferred over the bridge from the big city to Snowtown, a feral district whose police investigations department numbers three and a half people (one detective has no legs). Dumped in this collapsing urban trashzone, Richard Fell is starting all over again. In a place where nothing seems to make any sense, Fell clings to the one thing he knows to be true: everybody's hiding something. Considerable violence and strong language mix with a strong noir-ish mystery.

Freakangels; Volume 1. story Warren Ellis; artwork Paul Duffield. Avatar Press 2008 144 p. Illustration

Grades: 10 11 12 Adult   741.5; Fic
1. Psychic ability — Comic books, strips, etc.; 2. Youth — England — London — Comic books, strips, etc.; 3. Apocalyptic fiction; 4. Science fiction graphic novels; 5. Dystopian fiction
1592910564; 9781592910564, $19.99

"Twenty-three years ago, twelve strange children were born in England at exactly the same moment. Six years ago, the world ended. Today, eleven strange 23-year-olds live in and defend Whitechapel, maybe the last real settlement in flooded London. When a dazed, gun-toting girl appears on the outskirts with a deadly grudge against the self-proclaimed Freakangels, the kids realize that an old enemy is still alive beyond the safety of their borders... a twelfth psychic child, evil and exiled, who can program human minds to hate, and send his private, pirate armies into Whitechapel for revenge." (Publisher's note)

Volume 1 of 6

Global frequency. written by Warren Ellis; illustrated by Garry Leach ... [et al.]; David Baron, Art Lyon, colorists; Michael Heisler, letterer.. DC Comics 2013 288 p. Color illustration

Grades: Adult   **Fic; 741.5/973**
  1. Graphic novels; 2. Rescue work — Fiction
1401237975; 9781401237974, $19.99

LC 2012040864

This graphic novel, written by Warren Ellis, "collects the entire 12 issue Global Frequency storyline in one trade paperback. Global Frequency is a worldwide rescue organization. Manned by 1001 operatives, the Frequency is made up of experts in fields as diverse as bio-weapon engineering and Le Parkour Running. Each agent-equipped with a special mobile vid-phone-is specifically chosen by Miranda Zero, enigmatic leader of the Global Frequency, based on proximity [and] expertise." (Publisher's note)

Originally published in single magazine form in Global Frequency 1-12.

Nextwave: Agents of H.A.T.E. Vol. 1: This is What They Want. Marvel Entertainment 2006 un Illustration

Grades: 10 11 12 Adult   **741.5; Fic**
  1. Adventure graphic novels; 2. Graphic novels; 3. Satire — Graphic novels; 4. Superhero graphic novels
0-7851-2278-8, $19.99

H.A.T.E. (The Highest Anti-Terrorism Effort) put together a team of superheroes they call Nextwave: Monica Rambeau (formerly Captain Marvel and Photon), Aaron Stack (the robotic Machine Man), Tabitha Smith (X-Force's Meltdown), monster-hunter Elsa Bloodstone, and The Captain. The team was told they were supposed to fight Bizarre Weapons of Mass Destruction; however, Tabitha lifted some papers that reveal the truth: H.A.T.E. is part of the Beyond Corporation, which is the new version of the terrorist organization formerly known as Silent. The Corporation plans to test its weapons on unsuspecting American towns, so Nextwave goes rogue to stop the weapons and be the good guys. They face an awakened Fin Fang Foom (giant monster lizard), a bad cop turned robotic monster, and their former boss, Dirk Anger. There's lots of action, bad words show as a series of death's heads, and the whole thing is written as a biting satire of superheroes.

Nextwave: Agents of H.A.T.E. Vol. 2: I Kick Your Face. Marvel Entertainment 2007 un Illustration

Grades: 10 11 12 Adult   **741.5; Fic**
  1. Graphic novels; 2. Humorous graphic novels; 3. Superhero graphic novels
0-7851-2855-7, $19.99

In this second and final volume of the series, former Captain Marvel Monica Rambeau and the Nextwave team continue their quest to shut down H.A.T.E.'s network of Unusual Weapons of Mass Destruction. They destroy the Mindless Ones, the bizarre Broccoli Men who have been created to look like various superhero teams, and then decide to finish off S.I.L.E.N.T. itself, the uber-terrorist network that has been funding H.A.T.E. It's a full-on superhero satire with lots of comic book action, and all the bad words appear as skulls.

Orbiter. DC Comics/Vertigo 2004 104p. Illustration

Grades: 10 11 12 Adult   **741.5; Fic**
  1. Graphic novels; 2. Mystery graphic novels; 3. Science fiction graphic novels
1-4012-0056-7, $17.95

In the early 21st century, the space shuttle Venture has suddenly returned to Earth after disappearing ten years ago; its crew is missing, except for the catatonic pilot, and the ship is outfitted with new instrumentation, new engines, and is covered in something very much like skin, while its landing gear has Martian sand. Now a team of three specialists must discover where the Venture went, what's been done to it, and what happened to the crew. Unfortunately, most of the answers are locked up in the seemingly twisted mind of the pilot. Does he really know the truth or is he simply a demented casualty of a space mission gone wrong? The book includes some foul language.

★ **Planetary;** 2, Vol. 2. Warren Ellis, writer; John Cassaday, artist; Laura DePuy and David Baron, colorists; Ryan Cline, Bill O'Neil and Mike Heisler, letterers. DC Comics 2013 144 p. Color; Illustration

Grades: 11 12 Adult   **741.5**
  1. Adventure graphic novels; 2. Parapsychology — Fiction; 3. Superhero comic books, strips, etc.
1563897644; 9781563897641, $14.99

LC 2012046722

This graphic novel, written by Warren Ellis and illustrated by John Cassady, the second in the "Planetary" series, "focuses on the team's mysterious benefactor, the 'Fourth Man.' After paying their final respects to a British occultist with ties to their group, Elijah Snow, Jakita Wagner, and The Drummer continue their super-human archeological studies as they visit a hidden government compound full of radioactive human guinea pigs." (Publisher's note)

Originally published by WildStorm in single magazine form as Planetary #7-#12.

★ **Planetary;** 3: leaving the 20th century, 3. Warren Ellis & John Cassaday, writer, co-creators, artist; Laura Martin, colorist. DC Comics 2005 144 p. Color; Illustration

Grades: 11 12 Adult   **741.5**
  1. Science fiction graphic novels; 2. Superhero comic books, strips, etc.; 3. Adventure graphic novels; 4. Mystery graphic novels
1401202942; 9781401202941, $14.99

In this graphic novel, written by Warren Ellis and illustrated by John Cassaday, the third in the "Planetary" series, "Elijah takes a look at his past, making startling revelations and recounting his participation in the first moon shot...in 1851!" (Publisher's note)

Originally published in single magazine form as Planetary #13-18

★ **Planetary;** 4: spacetime archaeology. writer, Warren Ellis; artist, John Cassaday; colorist, Laura Martin; letterer, Comicraft. WildStorm Productions 2010 224 p. Color; Illustration

Grades: 11 12 Adult   **741.5**
  1. Graphic novels; 2. Fantasy fiction; 3. Adventure fiction; 4. Superhero comic books, strips, etc.
1401223451; 9781401223458, $17.99

LC 2010294189

This book, by Warren Ellis, is the "fourth and final graphic novel collecting the adventures of Elijah Snow, a powerful, hundred year old man, Jakita Wagner, an extremely powerful but bored woman, and The Drummer, a man with the ability to communicate with machines. Infatuated with tracking down evidence of super-human activity, these mystery archaeologists of the late 20th Century uncover unknown paranormal secrets and histories." (Publisher's note)

"Engaging as the story itself may be, Planetary's brilliance lies more in the rich history of comics and comic lore that Ellis draws from and cleverly weaves into the narrative from beginning to end." SLJ
Originally published in single magazine form as Planetary #19-27.

★ **Planetary;** vol 1: all over the world and other stories. Warren Ellis, John Cassaday, Laura DePuy. Wildstorm 2012 160 p. Color; Illustration
Grades: 11 12 Adult   **741.5**
1. Science fiction comic books, strips, etc.; 2. Adventure graphic novels; 3. Mystery graphic novels; 4. Parapsychology — Fiction; 5. Archaeologists — Fiction
1563896486; 9781563896484, $14.99

LC 2012024915
Written by Warren Ellis with art by John Cassaday, "this graphic novel features the adventures of Elijah Snow, a hundred year old man, Jakita Wagner, an extremely powerful and bored woman, and The Drummer, a man with the ability to communicate with machines. Infatuated with tracking down evidence of super-human activity, these mystery archaeologists of the late 20th Century uncover unknown paranormal secrets and histories." (Publisher's note)
Also available in an omnibus edition; Originally published by WildStorm Productions in single magazine form as Planetary #1-6 And Planetary Preview.; Other volumes in this series are: Vol. 2: The fourth man; Vol. 3: Leaving the 20th century; Vol. 4: Spacetime archaeology

StormWatch; Volume one. Warren Ellis, story; Tom Raney ... [et al.], pencils; Randy Elliott, Richard Bennett, inks; Gina Going, colors. DC Comics 2012 296 p. Color illustration
Grades: Adult   **741.5/973; 741.5; Fic**
1. Superhero graphic novels; 2. Adventure fiction; 3. Superhero comic books, strips, etc.
1401234208; 9781401234201, $29.99

LC 2012374614
This comic book anthology, written by Warren Ellis and illustrated by Tom Raney, collects in hardcover graphic novel format volume 1 of the DC Comics series following the adventures of the United Nations-sponsored superhero team Stormwatch, originally created by Jim Lee as part of the Wildstorm Universe. (Wikipedia)
StormWatch created by Jim Lee and Brandon Choi.; Originally published by WildStorm in single magazine form in Stormwatch 37-47. — T.p. verso.

★ **Transmetropolitan:** back on the street. Warren Ellis, writer; Darick Robertson, penciller. DC Comics 2012 142 p.
Grades: Adult   **741.5/973**
1. Journalists — Comic books, strips, etc; 2. Journalists — Comic books, strips, etc.
1401220843; 9781401220846, $14.99

LC 2012017896
In this comic book, by Warren Ellis, illustrated by Darick Robertson, "After years of selfimposed exile from a civilization rife with degradation and indecency, cynical journalist Spider Jerusalem is forced to return to a job he hates and a city he loathes. Working as an investigative reporter for the newspaper The Word, Spider attacks the injustices of his surreal 23rd century surroundings." (Publisher's note)
Originally published in single magazine form as TRANSMETROPOLITAN 1-6.; Volume 1 of 10

Ellison, Harlan
    Harlan Ellison's Dream Corridor, Vol. 2. Dark Horse Comics 2007 168p. Illustration
Grades: 11 12 Adult   **741.5; Fic**
1. Fantasy graphic novels; 2. Graphic novels
978-1-59307-494-4, $19.95

The words of world-renowned science-fiction author Harlan Ellison are translated onto the page by top comics creators, including Paul Chadwick, Neal Adams, Steve Rude, Gene Colan, Steve Niles, Gerard Jones, Richard Corben and the legendary Oz illustrator Eric Shanower. Most of these stories have never before seen print. Ellison uses strong language and violence a lot in his stories, which include "Opposites Attract," "One Life, Furnished in Early Poverty," "The Discarded", "Moonlighting," and more.

Endo, Hiroki
    Tanpenshu Vol. 1. Dark Horse Comics 2007 230p. Illustration
Grades: 11 12 Adult   **741.5; Fic**
1. Graphic novels; 2. Manga; 3. Seinen manga
978-1-59307-637-5, $12.95
The three stories in this first volume are mature explorations of humanity's constant, fumbling attempts to find hope and meaning in a confusing, violent world. A disfigured misfit befriends a doomed yakuza outcast, a group a school kids fail to see the anger that's about to boil over from one of their own and members of an experimental theatre troupe embark on a project that will test both their friendships and the group's grasp on reality. The stories include strong language, nudity and graphic violence, and the cover may disturb some readers.

Englehart, Steve
    Batman: Dark Detective. Steve Englehart, writer; Marshall Rogers, penciller; Terry Austin, inker; John Workman, letterer; Chris Chuckry, colorist. DC Comics 2005 144p. Illustration
Grades: 9 10 11 12 Adult   **741.5; Fic**
1. Batman (Fictional character); 2. Graphic novels; 3. Superhero graphic novels; 4. Joker (Fictional character)
1-4012-0898-3, $14.99
When the maniacal Joker enters a gubernatorial election, the Dark Knight takes action. But Batman discovers he's in way over his head when the unexpected return of former girlfriend Silver St. Cloud leaves him torn between love and duty. With adversaries like the Joker, Two-Face, Scarecrow, and others to contend with, Batman must make a choice between his quest for justice and his affections for Silver. And his indecision could cost him everything. The story evokes the style and content of 1970s comics.

Ennis, Garth
    Britton, Battler. DC Comics/Wildstorm 2007 un Illustration
Grades: 10 11 12 Adult   **741.5; Fic**
1. Adventure graphic novels; 2. Graphic novels; 3. War — Graphic novels; 4. World War, 1939-1945 — Graphic novels
978-1-4012-1378-7, $19.99
In October, 1942, Allied forces are on the run from the unrelenting forces of the Nazis in North Africa. Wing Commander Robert "Battler" Britton of the Royal Air Force and his squadron are dispatched to an American airstrip to spearhead a joint action against Hitler's war machine. Now they must survive taunts, threats, and assaults...and that's just from the Yanks. There's plenty of war action in the air and on the ground.

★ **Preacher;** Book One: Gone to Texas. Garth Ennis, writer; Steve Dillon, artist; Matt Hollingsworth and Pamela Rambo, colorists; Clem Robins, letterer. Vertigo 2009 352 p. Illustration
Grades: Adult   **741.5**
1. Supernatural graphic novels; 2. Horror graphic novels; 3. Western stories — Graphic novels
140122279X; 1401240453, $19.99; 9781401222796, $39.99; 9781401240455
"Merging with a bizarre spiritual force called Genesis, Texan Preacher Jesse Custer becomes completely disillusioned with the beliefs that he had

dedicated his entire life to. Now possessing the power of 'the word,' an ability to make people do whatever he utters, Custer begins a violent and riotous journey across the country. Joined by his gun-toting girlfriend Tulip and the hard drinking Irish vampire Cassidy, the Preacher loses faith in both man and God as he witnesses dark atrocities and improbable calamities during his exploration of America." (Publisher's note)

Originally collected in 9 volumes; Book 1 of 6

The **Punisher;** Volume 1: The Complete Collection. written by Garth Ennis; illustrated by Darick Robertson, Lewis LaRosa and Leandro Fernandez. Marvel Enterprises 2016 424 p. Color; Illustration (Max comics)

Grades: Adult   **741.5; Fic**
1. Punisher (Fictitious character); 2. Superhero graphic novels
1302900153; 9781302900151, $34.99

"Experience the gritty and uncompromising Punisher MAX from the very beginning! When a mob hit killed his beloved wife and children, Frank Castle became the Punisher — an unstoppable one-man army waging war on every piece of criminal scum plaguing New York's streets. But do the Punisher's origins trace back even further?" (Publisher's note)

Collects Born #1-4, Punisher (2004) #1-12; Volume 1 of 7

War Stories Vol. 2. DC Comics/Vertigo 2006 240p. Illustration
Grades: 10 11 12 Adult   **741.5; Fic**
1. Graphic novels; 2. World War, 1939-1945 — Graphic novels; 3. Spain — History — 1936-1939, Civil War — Graphic novels
978-1-4012-1039-7, $19.99

The brutality and bravery of those who served in history's greatest conflict is brought to life in this book. From the saturation bombing of the Ruhr Valley to the birth of the SAS in the deserts of North Africa, from the blasted wreckage of Guernica to the tracer-filled skies over the North Atlantic, these tales will land the reader in some of the worst combat zones the world has ever seen. Author Ennis includes historical notes at the end of the book. Readers will find strong language and wartime violence in the stories.

Estes, Max
Coffee and Donuts: A Junkyard Cats Comic. Top Shelf Productions 2006 112p. Illustration
Grades: 6 7 8 9 10 11 12 Adult   **741.5; Fic**
1. Cats — Graphic novels; 2. Graphic novels; 3. Humorous graphic novels
1-891830-80-5, $10

Dwight and Jules live in an unused dumpster and scavenge their food; every morning a mystery person leaves coffee and donuts for them. When, desperate for money, they try (and fail) to rob an armored truck, real crooks Myles and Moose try to force them into real crime.

Hello, Again. Top Shelf Productions 2005 156p. Illustration
Grades: 11 12 Adult   **741.5; Fic**
1. Graphic novels
1-891830-63-5, $10.00

William is finding out that his past may not be buried as deep as he once thought. In fact, a colorful character from his past has just crawled out of the ground and is refusing to leave until William changes his ways. This is the tale of a drunken fisherman, an unfaithful fiancee, and a guilt ridden apartment manager, whose lives intersect with unsuspecting and dangerous consequences. The book includes some strong language and sexual situations (without any nudity).

Eto, Miyuki
Hell girl. Miyuki Eto; created by the Jigoku Shoujo Project; translated and adapted by Gemma Collings; lettered by North Market Street Graphics. Del Rey Manja 2008 un Illustration

Grades: 10 11 12 Adult   **741.5; Fic**
1. Graphic novels; 2. Horror graphic novels; 3. Manga; 4. Shojo manga
978-0-345-50669-6, $10.99

In this volume, Ai Enma, Hell Girl, offers help to a beautiful teen idol who's being stalked by a long-ago costar of a failed children's television show; to a teenage girl who has become the victim of an obsessively possessive boyfriend who threatens the life of her childhood buddy, and to a girl with a sickly younger brother whose parents were killed by a hit-and-run driver and whose aunt and uncle take care of them only because of the money. A young girl discovers her grandmother isn't dead, but when she goes to visit her, she learns that her grandmother had used help from Hell Girl to protect her newborn daughter from a predatory landlord, and the village hates her for it. The horror is mostly psychological, but there is some violence.

Hell girl vol. 2. Del Rey Manga 2008 202p. Illustration
Grades: 10 11 12 Adult   **741.5; Fic**
1. Graphic novels; 2. Horror graphic novels; 3. Manga; 4. Shojo manga
978-0-345-50416-6, $10.95

Hell Girl is the ultimate avenger for those who have no one else to whom they can turn for help. If one goes to her website at midnight and enters the name of one's tormentor, Hell Girl will destroy that person. However, everyone who completes the contract with Hell Girl must also look forward to eternal torment in hell after death. In this volume, a spiteful figure skater tries to turn the two girls who beat her in competition against each other; a teenager only wants to save her younger sister from an abusive nanny; a boy in fragile health discovers who is stalking his best friend; the student class president can find no other way to save her friend from a vengeful new teacher. While there is no really graphic violence or bad language, the intensity of the stories make this series more appropriate for older teens.

Eury, Michael
Comics Gone Ape!: The Missing Link to Primates in Comics. Twomorrows Publishing 2007 144p. Illustration
Grades: Adult Professional
741.5
1. Comic books, strips, etc. — History; 2. Gorillas — Graphic novels; 3. Graphic novels; 4. Monkeys — Graphic novels; 5. Orangutans — Graphic novels; 6. Primates — Graphic novels
978-1-893905-62-7, $16.95

Courtesy of Twomorrows Publishing

This is a fairly lighthearted look at a fun topic in comics, apes. From King Kong to Banana Sunday, this book looks at the use of apes as characters in comics, ranging from the mainstream comics (Marvel and DC) to independent titles. Chapters discuss the various portrayals of King Kong in films and comics, and Planet of the Apes. The book also includes interviews with comics creators who have done major works featuring apes, including Arthur Adams, Tim Eldred, Joe Kubert, Tony Millionaire, and Anne Timmons. Lots of comics covers, some interior art, and previously unseen sketches are reproduced in black and white.

The **Krypton** Companion. Twomorrows Publishing 2006 240p. Illustration
Grades: 9 10 11 12 Adult
741.5

Courtesy of Twomorrows Publishing

1. Graphic novels; 2. Superhero graphic novels; 3. Superman (Fictional character)
1-893905-61-6, $24.95

This book examines the "Superman mythology" that grew out of Superman comic books published by DC Comics from 1958 through 1986, under the direction of editors Mort Weisinger and Julius Schwartz. It includes interviews with a number of writers and artists who worked on Superman, including Neal Adams, Murphy Anderson, Steve Gerber, Jerry Siegel, Curt Swan, and many others, along with lots of art, photos, and behind-the-scenes stories.

Evanier, Mark

Kirby: king of comics. Mark Evanier; introduction by Neil Gaiman. Abrams 2008 224p. Illustration

Grades: Adult   **92; 741.5**
1. Cartoonists — United States; 2. Kirby, Jack, 1917-1994
9780810994478, $45; 0-8109-9447-X

                                   LC 2007016321

"As a teenager, future television and comics writer Evanier became an assistant to Jack Kirby, one of the foremost artists in the history of American comics. Kirby played a major role in shaping the superhero genre, not only through his innovative, dynamic artwork but through collaborating with Stan Lee to create classic Marvel characters like the Fantastic Four, the Hulk and the X-Men. Evanier has now written this magnificently illustrated biography of his mentor. Rather than employing the academic prose that one might expect from an art book, Evanier, a talented raconteur, tells Kirby's life story in an informal, entertaining manner." (Publishers Weekly)

Fabry, Glenn

Neil Gaiman's Neverwhere. DC Comics/Vertigo 2007 un Illustration
Grades: 11 12 Adult   **741.5; Fic**
1. Fantasy graphic novels; 2. Graphic novels; 3. Gaiman, Neil — Adaptations
978-1-4012-1007-6, $19.99

Ordinary Richard Mayhew lives an ordinary life in London, in an ordinary corporate job, with a domineering fiancee. Then one day he does one extraordinary thing: he defies his fiancee to help an injured young woman, and his life changes. That young woman, Door, comes from London Below, a fantastical world made up of the bits and pieces of forgotten city and life from above. Her family has been slaughtered, she's being hunted by a pair of extremely nasty, sadistic, violent assassins, and after Richard helps her he has no choice but to go to London Below, for his entire existence in ordinary London has been wiped out, as though he has never...been.

Neverwhere was first a script for a BBC miniseries written by Neil Gaiman; he then adapted his script into a novel, which is now adapted into graphic novel format.

Originally published as Neverwhere issues #1-9.

Faerber, Jay

Noble causes archives volume one. Image Comics 2008 598p. Illustration
Grades: 10 11 12 Adult   **741.5; Fic**
1. Family life — Graphic novels; 2. Graphic novels; 3. Science fiction graphic novels; 4. Superhero graphic novels
978-1-58240-896-5, $19.99

Normal young woman Liz Donnelly marries superhero Race Noble and gets a firsthand look at the inner workings of the celebrity superhero Noble family. Race is murdered while they're on their honeymoon, but the Nobles keep Liz with them. She finds that she has landed among some of the most dysfunctional people living a soap opera life. She has one

brother-in-law who is now housed in a robotic body, another who is sort of immaterial, a sister-in-law who is pregnant and the father is one of the Noble family's greatest enemies, and the media keeps wanting to dig up as much dirt as they can, because gossip makes for high ratings. This volume reprints the early miniseries and the first twelve issues of the ongoing comics series in an economical black and white edition. The book includes violence, partial nudity, and sexual situations.

Volume 1 of 2

Farmer, Joyce

Special Exits: a graphic memoir. illustrated by the author. Fantagraphics 2010 208p. Illustration
Grades: Adult   **741.5; 92**
1. Autobiographical graphic novels; 2. Aging parents
9781606993811, $26.99; 160699381X; 1606997602; 9781606997604, $22.99

"Joyce Farmer's memoir chronicles the decline of the author's parents' health, their relationship with one another and with their their daughter, and how they cope with the day-to-day emotional fragility of the most taxing time of their lives." (Publisher's note)

Fawkes, Ray

One Soul. Ray Fawkes; [edited by] James Lucas Jones.. Oni Press 2011 176 p. Illustration
Grades: 11 12 Adult
741.5
1. Identity (Philosophical concept) — Comic books, strips, etc.; 2. Reincarnation — Graphic novels; 3. Identity (Psychology) — Graphic novels; 4. Graphic novels
9781934964668, $24.99

                    LC 2011922803
Harvey Nominee: Best Graphic Novel (2012); Eisner Nominee: Best Graphic Album — New (2012)

Courtesy of Oni Press

This graphic novel "follows a single soul as it's reincarnated through human history.... Each two-page spread is divided evenly into two three-by-three grids. Each of its 18 individual stories takes place in a single panel in that grid through the book's 88 spreads, so that to follow, say, the life of a silk heiress in Imperial China, the reader fastens the eye to a single spot in the book and then turns the pages quickly.... [Author Ray] Fawkes creates black-and-white tableaux of action, grief, sex and death spanning centuries. Individual spreads allow 18 characters to speak in unison, as when we see every subject's eyes widen simultaneously. When a character dies, his panel goes black for the rest of the book, and we meet the soul itself in cryptic narration." (Publishers Weekly)

Feiffer, Jules

Cousin Joseph: a graphic novel. Jules Feiffer. Liveright Publishing Corporation 2016 128 p. Illustration
Grades: Adult   **741.5; Fic**
1. Private investigators — Comic books, strips, etc.; 2. Great Depression, 1929-1939 — Comic books, strips, etc.; 3. Depressions — 1929 — Fiction; 4. Noir fiction
9781631490651, $25.95; 1631490656

                    LC 2016003857
"Meet Big Sam Hannigan. Tough, righteous, a man on a mission. Only problem is, it's the wrong mission.... Our story opens in Bay City in 1931 in the midst of the Great Depression. Big Sam sees himself as a righteous,

truth-seeking patriot, defending the American way, as his Irish immigrant father would have wanted, against a rising tide of left-wing unionism, strikes, and disruption that plague his home town." (Publisher's note)

"n this prequel to his graphic novel, Kill My Mother (2014), Feiffer delivers another noir fever dream, sending America right to the top of the flagpole with a hard-boiled, lyrical punch of immigrant stories, labor relations, and the almighty dollar." Kirkus

Explainers. Fantagraphics Books 2008 546p. Illustration
Grades: 9 10 11 12 Adult   **741.5**
1. Graphic novels; 2. Humorous graphic novels
978-1-56097-835-0, $28.99; 1-56097-835-X

This book collects the comic strips done by Jules Feiffer for the Village Voice, from 1956 through 1966. The alternative weekly newspaper, the only one of its kind back then, provided the then-unknown Feiffer with a forum to tackle all kinds of issues, ranging from relationships, sexuality, love, family, neuroses, politicians and politics, media, race, class, labor, religion, foreign policy, and war, among others. This is the first of four volumes planned to collect Feiffer's entire run of more than 2,000 strips. Older teen readers may be surprised to see just how timely and relevant these strips are, forty and fifty years after their original publication.

★ The **ghost** script: a graphic novel. Jules Feiffer. Liveright Publishing Corp. 2018 160 p. Illustration
Grades: Adult   **741.5; Fic**
1. Ghosts — Comic books, strips, etc.; 2. Mystery comic books, strips, etc.; 3. Graphic novels
9781631493133, $26.95

LC 2018009886

In this book, author Jules Feiffer "closes out his 'Kill My Mother' graphic-novel trilogy by weaving the Hollywood blacklist into his noir quilt of sex, violence, labor, and media.... Once again, Feiffer has delivered a madcap meditation on love, loyalty, identity, and America that is by turns funny, tragic, and triumphant — and thoroughly weird." (Kirkus Reviews)

"This doesn't have quite as many twists and turns as the earlier books, but Feiffer's fractured funhouse mirror of a plot features plenty of surprises (despite frequent flashbacks, readers new to the series should definitely start at the beginning), and his themes of gender fluidity, doubles and disguise, and divided loyalties are as engrossing as ever." Booklist

★ **Kill** My Mother: a graphic novel. Jules Feiffer. Liveright Publishing Corporation 2014 160 p. Illustration
Grades: 11 12 Adult   **741.5**
1. Graphic novels; 2. Noir fiction; 3. Violence — Fiction
0871403145; 9780871403148, $27.95

LC 2014005844

"Along with three femme fatales, an obsessed daughter, and a loner heroine, 'Kill My Mother' features a fighter turned tap dancer, a small-time thug who dreams of being a hit man, a name-dropping cab driver, a communist liquor store owner, and a hunky movie star with a mind-boggling secret. Culminating in a U.S.O. tour on a war-torn Pacific island, this disparate band of old enemies congregate to settle scores." (Publisher's note)

"The entire work feels pulled from an earlier time yet explosively modern, a madcap relic animated by an outrageous mind. An unusual, unforgettable, incomparable pulpy punch." Kirkus

Passionella and Other Stories. Fantagraphics Books 2006 un Illustration
Grades: 10 11 12 Adult   **741.5; Fic**
1. Graphic novels
978-1-56097-097-2, $19.95

This book collects Feiffer's extended graphic narratives of the late '50s and early '60s. "Excalibur and Rose" is the fable of a village comedian who embarks on a crusade in search of his serious side, which he finds in spades when he encounters his true love, the pathologically depressed Rose. "Passionella" retells Cinderella, seting it in modern Hollywood with a chimney sweep whose fairy godmother transforms her into the "mysterious exotic bewitching temptress" — and movie star — Passionella. "The Lonely Machine" is an account of one man's attempt to find the perfect relationship through robot love, and "Harold Swerg" recounts the predicament of the world's greatest athlete who'd rather stay at his mundane job than compete against others, despite his country's desperate pleas to enter the Olympics. Three more graphic tales and several one-act plays round out this edition. There are some sexual situations.

Ferris, Emil
★ **My** favorite thing is monsters. Emil Ferris. Fantagraphics Books, Inc. 2016 386 p. Color; Illustration
Grades: 11 12 Adult   **741.5; Fic**
1. Girls — Graphic novels; 2. Chicago (Ill.) — Graphic novels; 3. Murder — Investigation — Graphic novels
1606999591; 9781606999592, $39.99

LC 2016946097

Hugo Finalist: Best Graphic Story (2018); Eisner Award: Best Graphic Album — New (2018)

This book, by Emil Ferris, "is the fictional graphic diary of 10-year-old Karen Reyes, filled with B-movie horror and pulp monster magazines iconography. Karen...tries to solve the murder of her enigmatic upstairs neighbor, Anka Silverberg, a holocaust survivor, while the interconnected stories of those around her unfold." (Publisher's note)

"This stunningly ambitious and assured graphic novel, the creator's first, slides gracefully between past and present, reality and imagination, and the shifting kingdom of children and the hard-concrete world of adults. Ferris's writing, full of wordplay, elisions, and unpredictable revelations, suggests the cockeyed genius of Lynda Barry.... But her art, presented on lined notebook paper in the form of Karen's own ballpoint-and-pencil sketches...is entirely her own." Pub Wkly

Fessenden, Larry
The **last** winter. writers, Larry Fessenden and Robert Leaver; art, Brahm Revel; layout, James Felix McKenney. Image Comics 2008 128p. Illustration
Grades: 10 11 12 Adult   **741.5; Fic**
1. Graphic novels; 2. Horror graphic novels; 3. Science fiction graphic novels; 4. Arctic regions — Graphic novels
978-1-58240-936-8, $12.99

Oil company troubleshooter Pollack arrives at the base of the company's advance team in the Arctic National Wildlife Refuge to find out what's holding up the team's reports. Hoffman, who is working on the environmental impact statements, says there's something wrong, the permafrost is melting, and the whole area is unsafe for building any ice roads. Then one of the team dies, and the others begin to succumb to mysterious fears. When Hoffman is recalled to corporate headquarters, the plane crashes, and there's no way out except to find help from other remote stations; there's only one skidoo left, and Pollack and Hoffman head out. Will they find help before everyone dies? The book includes some violence, partial nudity, and some harsh language. This book adapts the script for the 2006 motion picture starring Ron Perlman, which is being released on DVD in September 2008.

Fies, Brian
Mom's cancer. Abrams ComicArts 2008 115p. Illustration
Grades: 9 10 11 12 Adult   **616.99; 741.5**
1. Biographical graphic novels; 2. Cancer — Graphic novels; 3. Graphic novels
978-0-8109-7107-3, $14.95

When writer/cartoonist Fies learned his mother had cancer and that it had already spread from her lungs, he used webcomics to depict what was happening to his mother and the rest of the family as Mom fought the cancer. All the pain, the heartache, the little battles won, the effects on Fies' relationships with his sisters, the ultimate hope are all on the page. In the end, Mom beat the cancer. In an afterword, Fies tells the reader that some of the medications just wore down his mother's body, and she died shortly before the book was published.
First published 2006

Filiu, Jean-Pierre
Best of Enemies: A History of US and Middle East Relations: 1783-1953. Jean-Pierre Filiu, David B.. Harry N Abrams Inc. 2012 114 p. Illustration
Grades: 10 11 12 Adult   **327.73056022/2; 327.730**
1. Christianity and other religions; 2. Graphic novels; 3. United States — Foreign relations — Middle East
1906838453; 9781906838454, $24.95
This graphic novel looks at "the history of U.S. and Middle East relations." It starts with "the murderous aggression of Gilgamesh-as-avatar .... [The] focus then moves to 1780s skirmishes with Muslim city-states over maritime piracy, shifting priorities of Christian and Muslim nations over oil and anti-Semitism, and the subsequent ousting by the Americans and the British of Iran's Mohammad Mossadegh." (Library Journal)

Fingerman, Bob
Maximum Minimum Wage. by Bob Fingerman. Image Comics 2013 360 p.
Grades: Adult   **741.5**
1. Cities and towns — Fiction; 2. Cartoonists
1607066742; 9781607066743, $34.99
This collection of comic strips by Bob Fingerman "is the workaday saga of cartoonist Rob Hoffman and his...girlfriend, Sylvia. With their colorful crew of friends, they forge ahead against the brutal indifference of their hometown. This definitive edition includes the original 72-page "pilot" episode (Minimum Wage Book One) and the revised "director's cut" of the main storyline. Plus, a bonus color section featuring original cover paintings and guest pin-ups." (Publisher's note)

Minimum Wage; Book 2: So Many Bad Decisions. by Bob Fingerman. Image Comics 2016 152 p. Illustration
Grades: Adult   **741.5; Fic**
1. Divorced people — Fiction; 2. Cartoonists — Graphic novels
1632157373; 9781632157379, $14.99
Eisner Nominee: Best Limited Series (2016)
In this graphic novel, by Bob Fingerman, "post-divorce Rob continues struggles both romantic and careerist, divvying up time between dating an Ayn Rand-worshipping, Goth wannabe standup comedian, depicting curious sagacious mutant crustaceans, and landing in the not-so-healthy but all-too-familiar embrace of his ex. Can so many bad decisions lead to enlightenment?" (Publisher's note)
"Fingerman remains very skilled in capturing the art of casual conversation, and his depiction of the social spaces of New York City is flawless, with a gallery of vivid urban bystanders who could all be going through their own crises of self-doubt." Pub Wkly

Fingeroth, Danny
The **Best** of write now!. Twomorrows Publishing 2008 160p. Illustration
Grades: 11 12 Adult   **741.5**
1. Comic books, strips, etc. — Authorship; 2. Drawing — Technique; 3. Graphic novels — Authorship
978-1-893905-924, $19.95

This collection of articles from Write Now! Magazine features interviews with comics writers such as Brian Michael Bendis, Jeff Loeb, Todd McFarlane, and Paul Levitz, focusing on the art, craft, and business of writing comics. Other articles look at the comics writing and drawing processes, with such professionals as Mark Millar, Bendis, and J. Michael Straczynski; and other articles cover such topics as breaking into comics publishing, dealing with writer's block, and surviving in the comics industry. Comics titans Stan Lee and Will Eisner are also profiled.

Courtesy of Twomorrows Publishing

Fisher, Bud
Forever Nuts: Classic Screwball Strips: The Early Years of Mutt & Jeff. NBM 2007 192 Illustration
Grades: 10 11 12 Adult   **741.5**
1. Graphic novels; 2. Mutt & Jeff (Fictional characters)
978-1-56163-502-3, $24.95
One of the most long lasting and popular humor strips in history, Mutt and Jeff had many memorable moments of serious goofiness and irreverence. Here's a rediscovery of a true oddball classic maybe only outdone by the antic high living of its own creator. 2007 is the one hundredth anniversary of its start. In these early strips, alcohol consumption, smoking, gambling, and various other pursuits considered to be vices are portrayed.

Fleming, Ann Marie
The **Magical** Life of Long Tack Sam: An Illustrated Memoir. Ann Marie Fleming.. Riverhead Books 2007 170 p. Illustration; Color
Grades: 11 12 Adult   **741.5; 92; 793.8092**
1. Biographical graphic novels; 2. Graphic novels; 3. Magicians — Graphic novels; 4. Long Tack Sam
1594482640; 9781594482649, $20
          LC 2007060352
This graphic memoir, by Ann Marie Fleming, was "inspired by the award-winning documentary-and the life and mystery of China's greatest magician. Who was Long Tack Sam? He was born in 1885. He ran away from Shangdung Province to join the circus. He was an acrobat. A magician. A comic. An impresario. A restaurateur. A theater owner. A world traveler. An East-West ambassador. A mentor to Orson Welles. He was considered the greatest act in the history of vaudeville." (Publisher's note)
Includes bibliographical references (p. 168-169)

Fletcher, Brenden
Batgirl; Volume 2: Family Business. written by Cameron Stewart, Brenden Fletcher; artby Babs Tarr, Bengal; additional art by JoelGomez, Jake Wyatt [and five others]; colors bySerge Lapointe, Babs Tarr [and four others;letters by Steve Wands; collection cover art byCameron Ste. DC Comics 2016 176 p. Color; Illustration
Grades: 10 11 12 Adult   **741.5; Fic**
1. Female superhero graphic novels; 2. Batgirl (Fictional character)
1401259669; 9781401259662, $16.99
          LC 2015037665
"Barbara Gordon has made some big changes to her Batgirl alter ego. She has a new look, new support team and new home base in Burnside-Gotham's trendiest neighborhood. But [then]...her father drops a bombshell: Babs isn't the only masked crime-fighter in the family anymore. Jim Gordon is the new Batman." (Publisher's note)

Foglio, Kaja

Girl Genius Omnibus Edition #1. story by Kaja & Phil Foglio; art by Phil Foglio. Airship Entertainment 2006 312p. Illustration

Grades: 9 10 11 12 Adult   **741.5; Fic**

1. Adventure graphic novels; 2. Graphic novels; 3. Science fiction graphic novels

978-1-890856-40-3, $14.95

In a time when the Industrial Revolution has become an all-out war, Mad Science rules the world. Agatha Clay is a student at Transylvania Polygnostic University, a complete klutz with rotten luck. But when the University is overthrown and a mechanical monster stalks the streets, it begins to look as though Agatha may carry a spark of Mad Science after all. She ends up aboard the giant airship Castle Wulfenbach, and finds an ally in Krosp the Cat (a genetic experiment with a smattering of Napoleon's brain cells); she also becomes friends with Gilgamesh, Baron Wulfenbach's son. When the Monster Engine is activated, Agatha and Gil battle it, then Agatha and Krosp make their escape. This black and white edition contains the first three volumes of the Girl Genius collection: Agatha Heterodyne & the Beetleburg Clank, Agatha Heterodyne & the Airship City, and Agatha Heterodyne & the Monster Engine. Agatha tends to do a lot of her best tech work while wearing pajamas.

Forney, Ellen

★ **Marbles:** mania, depression, Michelangelo, and me : a graphic memoir. by Ellen Forney. Gotham Books 2012 248 p.

Grades: Adult   **741.5/973; 741.5; 92**

1. Manic-depressive illness — Comic books, strips, etc; 2. Forney, Ellen — Comic books, strips, etc; 3. Graphic novels; 4. Cartoonists; 5. Manic-depressive illness

1592407323; 9781592407323, $20

LC 2012014588

"Eisner nominee [Ellen] Forney confesses her struggles with being diagnosed as bipolar in this...memoir. Beginning with the manic episode that led to her diagnosis, Forney chronicles her journey toward reconciling the dual natures of bipolar disorder: a dangerous disease, but also a source of inspiration for many artists." She uses cartoons, realistic illustrations, and photographs "to chronicle her outer life while revealing her inner state of mind." (Publishers Weekly)

Rock steady: brilliant advice from my bipolar life. Ellen Forney. Fantagraphics Books 2018 200 p. Illustration

Grades: Adult   **741.5; 616.895; 92**

1. Autobiographical comics; 2. Manic-depressive illness — Comic books, strips, etc.; 3. Forney, Ellen

9781683961017, $19.99

LC 2017957014

"Forney was diagnosed with bipolar disorder shortly before her thirtieth birthday. She struggled to find effective coping methods and decided to use her talents as an illustrator to share her experience. Her first graphic novel, Marbles: Mania, Depression, Michelangelo & Me (2012), let readers take a peek into her journey into treating and coming to terms with her diagnosis. Rock Steady goes a step beyond, giving readers a first-hand glance into various coping methods for the disorder." (Booklist)

"Forney effortlessly conveys her message in clear, succinct writing combined with energetic but simple visuals to illustrate difficult concepts. What results is a balanced, uncluttered resource, infused with empathy, humor, and encouragement." Pub Wkly

Fox, Gardner

The **Atom** Archives Volume 2. DC Comics 2003 215p. Illustration

Grades: 7 8 9 10 11 12 Adult   **741.5; Fic**

1. Atom (Fictional character); 2. Graphic novels; 3. Superhero graphic novels

1-4012-0014-1, $49.95

This volume, reprinting The Atom issues #6-13, originally published in 1963 through 1964, features Mighty Mite's early team-ups with Hawkman and Hawkgirl, the classic villainy of Dr. Light, the return of Chronos, and much more. This Archive Edition reprints the comics in full color in a hardcover edition.

Showcase Presents: Adam Strange Volume One. DC Comics 2007 510p. Illustration

Grades: 6 7 8 9 10 11 12 Adult   **741.5; Fic**

1. Graphic novels; 2. Superhero graphic novels

978-1-4012-1313-8, $16.99

After being mysteriously teleported to a distant world by an alien scientist, Adam Strange went from being an Earth archaeologist to a cosmic adventurer. He soon becomes the hero of the planet Rann, shuttling between his old and new worlds via the Zeta Beam. With the love of his life, Alanna, daughter of Rann's leading scientist, they embark on a series of adventures against all types of space menaces. This black and white volume reprints stories from 1958 through 1963.

Showcase Presents: Hawkman Volume 1. DC Comics 2007 560p. Illustration

Grades: 7 8 9 10 11 12 Adult   **741.5; Fic**

1. Graphic novels; 2. Hawkman (Fictional character); 3. Superhero graphic novels

978-1-4012-1280-3, $16.99

Katar Hol and his wife Shayera, winged law officers from the planet Thanagar, visit Earth to learn about terrestrial police methods. To fit into human society, they adopt the civilian identities of Carter Hall, the curator of the Midway City Museum, and Shiera, his assistant. Dressed in their avian Thanagarian garb, Carter and Shiera patrol the skies of Midway City as Hawkman and Hawkgirl. They plunge headlong into the battle for justice against such villains as the Shadow Thief and Matter Master. With their array of alien weaponry and their scientific skill, this crime-fighting duo continue to defend Earth against nefarious threats. This book collects black and white reprints of thirty-three stories written by Fox, dating from 1961 through 1966 and featuring the work of artists such as Joe Kubert, Murphy Anderson, and Carmine Infantino.

Showcase Presents: Justice League of America Volume 1. all stories written by Gardner Fox; all stories pencilled by Mike Sekowsky ... [et al.]. DC Comics 2005 544p. Illustration

Grades: 6 7 8 9 10 11 12 Adult   **741.5; Fic**

1. Aquaman (Fictitious character); 2. Graphic novels; 3. Justice League of America (Fictional characters); 4. Superhero graphic novels; 5. Green Arrow (Fictional character); 6. Wonder Woman (Fictional character); 7. Superman (Fictional character); 8. Batman (Fictional character); 9. Flash (Fictional character); 10. Green Lantern (Fictional character)

1-4012-0761-8, $16.99

Some of the greatest super heroes in the DC Universe united to form the Justice League of America: Superman, Batman, Wonder Woman, the Flash, Green Lantern, Martian Manhunter, and Aquaman. Together, they face such foes as Dr. Light, Dr. Destiny, Starro, Felix Faust, Amos Fortune, and the Weapons Master. This volume includes the stories in which the JLS inducts new members to the team: Green Arrow and the Atom. In light of the events in Infinite Crisis, readers might be interested to see how far back the roots of the story went — all the way back to 1960. This black and white reprint volume includes stories published from 1960 through 1962.

Showcase Presents: The Elongated Man Volume 1. writers, John Broome and Gardner Fox; artists, Carmine Infantino [and others]. DC Comics 2006 560p. Illustration

Grades: 6 7 8 9 10 11 12 Adult   **741.5; Fic**

1. Elongated Man (Fictional characters); 2. Graphic novels; 3. Superhero graphic novels

978-1-4012-1042-7, $16.99

Ralph Dibny is the Elongated Man, a self-taught superhero who has harnessed the power of the exotic gingo fruit and attained the ability to stretch himself to fantastic lengths. As the only costumed hero whose identity has been revealed to the world, Elongated Man travels the globe with his adoring wife Sue, solving mysteries and gaining renown for his singular elastic talent. In these stories, originally published from 1960 to 1968 and reprinted here in black and white, Dibny sometimes teams up with the Flash, Batman and Robin, Green Lantern, and Zatanna. Ralph and Sue Dibny were at the heart of the Identity Crisis, so readers might want to see their early adventures.

Fraction, Matt
Casanova; Volume 1: Luxuria. Matt Fraction and Gabriel Bá; colors by Cris Pete; letters by Dustin Harbin. Image Comics 2007 un Illustration
Grades: 11 12 Adult   741.5; Fic
  1. Adventure graphic novels; 2. Graphic novels; 3. Science fiction graphic novels; 4. Spies — Graphic novels
9781582408972; 978-1-58240-689-3, $24.99

Meet Casanova Quinn: prodigal son of a law-and-order family hell-bent on keeping the world safe and sound through its organization, E.M.P.I.R.E.,; now blackmailed into betraying his father and E.M.P.I.R.E. Luxuria collects the first volume of Casanova as its titular star transforms from devil-may-care thrill-seeker into the most dangerous man in the world. What happens when the ultimate player gets played? Find out in this genre-bending story that combines spy action with science fiction. Frequent use of harsh language combines with sexual situations and violence to make this more appropriate for older teens and adults.

Also available in a deluxe hardcover edition; Other Casanova volumes are: 2: Gula; 3: Avaritia; 4: Acedia

The **Five** Fists of Science. Image Comics 2006 un Illustration
Grades: 9 10 11 12 Adult   741.5; Fic
  1. Adventure graphic novels; 2. Graphic novels; 3. Science fiction graphic novels
1-58240-605-7, $12.99

At the beginning of the twentieth century, Mark Twain and Nicola Tesla work to save the world from the menace of war. J.P. Morgan, Andrew Carnegie, Thomas Edison, and Guillermo Marconi are having the Innsmouth Tower built; what the world doesn't know is that they intend to summon some monstrous old gods (anyone familiar with H.P. Lovecraft and his Cthulhu Mythos will catch on immediately). Meanwhile, Twain and Tesla have been trying to interest world leaders in technology that will end all war, only to find that no one is interested. When Marconi realizes what Morgan is really planning, he tells Tesla and Twain, in hopes that their robotic machine can stop Morgan. Some harsh language and violence pepper the story.

Hawkeye: Little Hits. by Matt Fraction (Author), David Aja (Illustrator), Javier Pulido (Illustrator), Steve Lieber (Illustrator), Francesco Francavilla (Illustrator), Jesse Hamm (Illustrator). Marvel Worldwide 2013 136 p.
Grades: 11 12 Adult   741.5; Fic
  1. Avengers (Fictional characters); 2. Superheroes — Fiction; 3. Graphic novels
0785165630; 9780785165637, $16.99

In this graphic novel, by Matt Fraction, "ace archer Clint Barton faces the digital doomsday of-DVR-Mageddon! Then: Cherry's got a gun. And she looks good in it. And Hawkeye gets very, very distracted. Plus: Valentine's Day with the heartthrob of the Marvel Universe? This will be...confusing." (Publisher's note)

"Fraction's writing is superb, but it's Eisner-winning Aja's wildly creative page layouts that have matured into something truly unique and demanding of critical attention." Booklist

Hawkeye: my life as a weapon. by Matt Fraction (Author), David Aja (Illustrator), Javier Pulido (Illustrator). Marvel Worldwide 2013 136 p.
Grades: 11 12 Adult   741.5; Fic
  1. Avengers (Fictional characters); 2. Graphic novels; 3. Superheroes — Fiction
0785165622; 9780785165620, $16.99

In this book, by Matt Fraction, "Clint Barton-aka the self-made hero Hawkeye-fights for justice! With ex-Young Avenger Kate Bishop by his side, he's out to prove himself as one of Earth's Mightiest Heroes! SHIELD recruits Clint to intercept a packet of incriminating evidence-before he becomes the most wanted man in the world." (Publisher's note)

Hawkeye: Rio Bravo. by Matt Fraction; illustrated by Francesco Francavilla, David Aja and Annie Wu. Marvel Enterprises 2015 160 p. Color; Illustration
Grades: 10 11 12 Adult   741.5973; 741.5
  1. Superhero comic books, strips, etc.
0785185313; 9780785185314, $17.99

In this comic book, by Matt Fraction, "Reeling from recent events, even Hawkeye wants to know what his new status quo is. Who's with him? Who's against him? Who's trying to kill him and why? So many dang questions! And just when Clint's rock bottom couldn't arrive fast enough...his brother shows up. After a lifetime of decisions both good and bad, Clint and Barney Barton have to realize that they are brothers and ultimately, they're the only ones who can save one another." (Publisher's note)

Hawkeye; Volume 3: L.A. Woman. by Matt Fraction; illustrated by Annie Wu and Javier Pulido. Marvel Worldwide 2014 144 p. Color; Illustration
Grades: 11 12 Adult   741.5
  1. Assassins — Fiction; 2. Musicians — Fiction; 3. Criminals — Fiction; 4. Los Angeles (Calif.) — Fiction
0785183906; 9780785183907, $15.99

In this book, by Matt Fraction, illustrated by Annie Wu and Javier Pulido, "Kate Bishop heads to Los Angeles to get away from New York, life, and Clint Barton — but not away from trouble! Because Madame Masque is hanging out at poolside with the rich and famous as well! As Kate helps a reclusive and Sixties-damaged pop music genius find his lost masterpiece, Madame Masque finds Kate. By which we mean starts trying to kill her again." (Publisher's note)

"Fraction's unique brand of storytelling is both light with humor and deep with meaning, and he keeps it fresh by constantly bringing in new characters." Booklist

Contains material originally published in magazine form as Hawkeye #14, #16, #18, #20 and Annual #1 — Title page verso.

ODY-C; Volume 1: Off to far Ithicaa. Matt Fraction, Christian Ward. Image Comics 2015 136 p. Illustration
Grades: Adult   741.5; Fic
  1. Science fiction; 2. Epic literature
1632153769; 9781632153760, $9.99

This book, by Matt Fraction, illustrated by Christian Ward, is a "mind-bending, gender-shattering epic science fiction retelling of Homer's Odyssey starting with the end of a great war in the stars and the beginning of a very long journey home for Odyssia and her crew of warriors." (Publisher's note)

This hallucinatory sf recasting of Homer's Odyssey doesn't simply swap the gender of its protagonist — it takes place in a universe where men have suffered genocide at the hands of a paranoid Zeus.... Ward fills the pages to bursting with incredible varicolored psychedelic imagery, bringing extraordinary vividness to scenes of space travel, grotesqueries such as the multibreasted Cyclops, and depictions of nudity, sex, and copious gore." LJ

Volume 1 of an ongoing series

Sex Criminals; 1: one weird trick. Matt Fraction, illustrated by Chip Zdarsky. Image Comics 2014 128 p. Color; Illustration

Grades: Adult   741.5

1. Graphic novels; 2. Bank robberies — Fiction

1607069466; 9781607069461, $9.99

Eisner Award: Best New Series (2014); Harvey Award: Best New Series (2014)

In this comic book series by Matt Fraction, illustrated by Chip Zdarsky, "Suzie's just a regular gal with an irregular gift: when she has sex, she stops time. One day she meets Jon and it turns out he has the same ability. And sooner or later they get around to using their gifts to do what we'd ALL do: rob a couple banks." (Publisher's note)

A "funny, engaging, and inventive new comic book about sex, love, and fighting the man, with a clever sci-fi twist." Comics Alliance

Volume 1 of an ongoing series

Sex Criminals; 2: Two Worlds, One Cop. by Matt Fraction; illustrated by Chip Zdarsky. Image Comics 2015 128 p. Color; Illustration

Grades: Adult   741.5

1. Sex — Fiction; 2. Romance fiction — Graphic novels; 3. Man-woman relationship — Fiction

1632151936; 9781632151933, $14.99

This graphic novel, by Matt Fraction and illustrated by Chip Zdarsky, "finds the honeymoon to be over for Jon and Suzie. Once the thrill of new lust fades, where do you go? Come along and laff and love with Matt and Chip as they brimp back ceaselessly against the past." (Publisher's note)

"At times, Jon and Suzie break the fourth wall, revealing their hookups and complicated feelings they have for themselves and for each other. Even with all the sex in this book — and there's a lot of frank, candid sex — it's at these moments that we truly see them naked, and it's their emotional chemistry that's at the heart of this intimate narrative." Booklist

Frakes, Colleen

Prison island: a graphic memoir. by Colleen Frakes. Houghton Mifflin Harcourt 2015 187 p. Illustration

Grades: 9 10 11 12 Adult   741.5; 92

1. Washington (State); 2. Prisons — United States

1942186029; 9781942186021, $16.99

In this graphic memoir, by Colleen Frake, "McNeil Island in Washington state was the home of the last prison island in the United States, accessible only by air or sea. It was also home to about fifty families, including...Frake's. Her parents-like nearly everyone else on the island-both worked in the prison, where her father was the prison's captain and her mother worked in security." (Publisher's note)

Francavilla, Francesco

The **Black** Beetle: No Way Out. by Francesco Francavilla and edited by Jim Gibbons. Dark Horse 2013 152 p. Illustration

Grades: Adult   741.5

1. Superheroes — Fiction; 2. Organized crime

1616552026; 9781616552022, $19.99

In this comic by Francesco Francavilla, "the Black Beetle...witnesses an explosion that decimates the city's organized crime community, killing dozens. No one gets away with mass murder when the Black Beetle's on the case. When Colt City cries out for justice, there's one man who will answer!" (Publisher's note)

Franklin, Tee

★ **Bingo** love. Tee Franklin; illustrated by Jenn St-Onge, Joy San and Genevieve FT. Image Comics 2018 88 p. Color; Illustration

Grades: 8 9 10 11 12 Adult   741.5

1. Lesbians — Fiction; 2. Grandmothers — Fiction

1534307508; 9781534307506, $9.99

In this book, by Tee Franklin, illustrated by Jenn St.Onge, Joy San and Genevieve FT, "when Hazel Johnson and Mari McCray met at church bingo in 1963, it was love-at first sight. Forced apart by their families and society, Hazel and Mari both married young men and had families.... Now in their mid-'60s,...[they] reunite again at a church bingo hall. Realizing their love for each other is still alive, what these grandmothers do next takes absolute strength and courage." (Publisher's note)

"Teens and young adults tend to dominate love plots, so it's refreshing to see a romantic tale built around people who age from adolescence through elderhood. Delightful yet realistic, the teen-graded story also works for adults and sophisticated tweens." LJ

Frusin, Marcello

Loveless Vol. 1: A Kin of Homecoming. Brian Azzarello; Marcelo Frusin; Patricia Mulvihill, colorist; Clem Robins, letterer; Marcelo Frusin, covers. DC Comics/Vertigo 2006 128p. Illustration

Grades: 12 Adult   741.5; Fic

1. Graphic novels; 2. Western graphic novel

978-1-4012-1061-8, $9.99

Wes Cutter is a wanted man running from a violent past — the horrors of the Civil War, a brutal stint in a Union prison camp, and the savage fallout of Reconstruction. Now he's on a quest for the one thing in short supply: peace. Joining Wes is his beautiful wife Ruth, a woman who has been to hell and back herself — and hides dark secrets of her own. The road they travel will be a bloody one, leaving a trail of bodies stretching from Missouri to the Pacific Ocean. The book contains graphic violence, copious use of foul language, nudity, and sexual situations.

Volume 1 of 3

Fujisaki, Ryu

Hoshin Engi Volume 1. Viz Media/Shonen Jump 2007 192p. Illustration

Grades: 8 9 10 11 12 Adult   741.5; Fic

1. Adventure graphic novels; 2. Fantasy graphic novels; 3. Graphic novels; 4. Manga; 5. Shonen manga

978-1-4215-1362-1, $7.99

When his clan is wiped out by a beautiful demon, young Taikobo finds himself in charge of the mysterious Hoshin Project. Its mission: find all immortals living in the human world and seal them away forever. But who do you trust — and whose side are you really on — when you've been trained to hunt demons by a demon. There is demon-fighting action.

Fulop, Scott D.

Archie Americana Series: Best of the Forties Volume 1. Archie Comics 1991 128p. Illustration

Grades: 3 4 5 6 7 8 9 10 11 12 Adult   741.5; Fic

1. Andrews, Archie (Fictional character); 2. Graphic novels; 3. Humorous graphic novels

1-879794-00-4, $11.95

In 1941, Pep Comics introduced Archie Andrews, "America's newest boyfriend." Since then, Archie and his perennial teenage friends have entertained readers with their misadventures. This book includes the very first Archie story, with the first appearance of Betty and Veronica, Reggie, Jughead, Mr. Weatherbee, Miss Grundy, and the rest of the Archie characters as they originally appeared.

Fumino, Yuki

I hear the sunspot. by Yuki Fumino. One Peace Books 2017 200 p. Illustration

Grades: 10 11 12 Adult

741.5; Fic

1. Manga; 2. Gay teenagers — Fiction; 3. Male friendship — Fiction; 4. Teenage boys — Fiction

1944937307; 9781944937300, $12.95

Courtesy of One Peace Books

In this book, by Yuki Fumino, "because of a hearing disability, Kohei is often misunderstood and has trouble integrating into life on campus, so he learns to keep his distance. That is until he meets the outspoken and cheerful Taichi. He tells Kohei that his hearing loss is not his fault. Taichia's words cut through Kohei's usual defense mechanisms and open his heart. More than friends, less than lovers, their relationship changes Kohei forever." (Publisher's note)

"Fumino's debut manga is a simultaneously heartwarming and heartbreaking story about the chance meeting and budding romance between two awkward yet lovable male college students." LJ

Gabrych, Andersen

Batgirl : Destruction's Daughter. DC Comics 2006 un Illustration

Grades: 10 11 12 Adult

741.5; Fic

1. Adventure graphic novels; 2. Batgirl (Fictional characters); 3. Graphic novels; 4. Superhero graphic novels

978-1-4012-0896-7, $19.99

Cassandra Cain was quickly accepted as the new Batgirl after helping Batman during Gotham's darkest hours. Trained in deadly martial arts from early childhood by a notorious assassin, Batgirl developed the uncanny ability to anticipate her opponents' movements to make her unbeatable in combat. Now, the Dark Knight's young protégé is determined to discover who her true mother is, and her quest, brings her face-to-face with the League of Assassins and into mortal combat with the deadliest woman alive, Lady Shiva. It all ends in a life or death battle at the edge of Lazarus Pit, and only one person will survive. There's a fair amount of blood shed in the many fights.

Batgirl: Kicking Assassins. DC Comics 2005 un Illustration

Grades: 9 10 11 12 Adult

741.5; Fic

1. Batgirl (Fictional character); 2. Graphic novels; 3. Superhero graphic novels

1-4012-0439-2, $14.99

It's a fresh start for Batgirl as Cassandra Cain is building a new life for herself in Bludhaven. But with the Penguin also moving to town and setting up a criminal empire, can Batgirl keep the streets safe, or will she face something more sinister and vile than before? With the Brotherhood of Evil, Deathstroke, and the Ravager coming at her one after the other, Batgirl barely has the chance to settle into her new neighborhood before the fists start to fly. The book includes lots of fighting.

DC's Greatest Imaginary Stories. DC Comics 2005 192p. Illustration

Grades: 6 7 8 9 10 11 12 Adult

741.5; Fic

1. Graphic novels; 2. Superhero graphic novels; 3. Flash (Fictional character); 4. Batman (Fictional character); 5. Superman (Fictional character)

1-4012-0534-8, $19.99

This volume collects eleven stories that are totally imaginary about many of DC's heroes: Superman marries Lois Lane; in another story, he marries Lana Lang; and in yet another story, he marries Lori Lemaris the mermaid. Batman abandons his millions to drive a taxi. The Flash races into action maskless. Superman and Batman are brothers. In the wedding of the century, it's Super girl and...Jimmy Olsen? And Shazam witnesses atomic bomb and attacks and finds that even he, the World's Mightiest Mortal, can't stop the bombs.

Will Eisner. Rosen Publishing Group 2005 112p. Illustration

Grades: 8 9 10 11 12 Adult

741.5; 92

1. Cartoonists — Biography; 2. Graphic novels

1-4042-0286-2, $31.95

LC 2004016656

Veteran comics insider Greenberger has written this biography of Eisner, covering his long career in comics, from the 1930s through the early 2000s. Eisner created the groundbreaking comic series The Spirit, and in the 1970s started writing original graphic novels set in New York City. The Eisner Awards for comics are named after him, due to his strong influence on the industry over the decades. This volume includes a list of books for further reading and a bibliography.

Part of the Library of Graphic Novelists

Gaiman, Neil

The **Books** of Magic. writer, Neil Gaiman; illustrators, John Bolton, Charles Vess [and others]; letterer, Todd Klein; [introduction by Roger Zelazny]. DC Comics/Vertigo 1993 un Illustration

Grades: 10 11 12 Adult

741.5; Fic

1. Fantasy graphic novels; 2. Graphic novels; 3. Magic — Graphic novels; 4. Supernatural graphic novels

1-56389-082-8, $19.99

A quartet of fallen mystics dubbed the "Trench Coat Brigade "is introduced in this first collection of the adventures of Timothy Hunter. John Constantine, the Phantom Stranger, Dr. Occult, and Mister E take Hunter on a tour of the magical realms. Along the way he's introduced to Vertigo's greatest practitioners of magic and must choose whether or not to join their ranks. And they must decide if he should live...or die. While the publisher rates it for mature readers, there's little in the way of strong language or overt violence, and no nudity.

Creatures of the Night. Dark Horse Comics 2004 46p. Illustration

Grades: 10 11 12 Adult

741.5; Fic

1. Fantasy graphic novels; 2. Graphic novels; 3. Supernatural graphic novels

1-56971-936-5, $12.95

Artist Zulli has adapted two of Gaiman's prose short stories into comic book form. In "The Price," a mysterious black cat comes to a family living in the English countryside. Soon after he arrives, the father notices that in the mornings, the cat is scratched and bleeding. Each morning after that, the cat suffers more injuries; maybe the family isn't quite so safe in the countryside after all. "The Daughter of Owls" is a baby girl abandoned on the steps of the Dymton Church in the late 1800s. Sequestered in the convent, the girl lives in solitary silence for fourteen years, cared for after a fashion by a nun, and then by a woman in Dymton. When the woman gossips about the silent girl's beauty, the men of Dymton hatch a dastardly plot which ends in tragedy.

★ **Death:** The High Cost of Living. DC Comics/Vertigo 1994 104p. Illustration

Grades: 10 11 12 Adult

741.5; Fic

1. Adventure graphic novels; 2. Fantasy graphic novels; 3. Graphic novels

1-56389-133-6, $12.95

A member of the Endless, a family of beings who have existed longer than the gods, Death enjoys manifesting herself in the persona of a Goth girl. She is taking her one-day-a-century holiday in New York City, where she meets suicidal teen Sexton, and they end up searching the city for the witch Mad Hettie's heart, which she has hidden away...somewhere. Then the Eremite hunts her, to steal Death's ankh and therefore her power. The book includes some violence and some strong language.

Death: The Time of Your Life. DC Comics/Vertigo 1997 96p. Illustration
Grades: 10 11 12 Adult   **741.5; Fic**
1. Adventure graphic novels; 2. Fantasy graphic novels; 3. Graphic novels; 4. Horror graphic novels
1-56389-333-9, $12.99

This is the story of Foxglove, a rising star of the music world who must wrestle with revealing her true sexual orientation as her companion, Hazel, is lured into the realm of Death. As one of the Endless, Death met the two young women on her latest once a century holiday, so it's only natural that she would appear now. The book includes some strong language, sexual situations, and some violence.

How to talk to girls at parties. by Neil Gaiman; adaptation, art, & lettering by Fabio Moon and Gabriel Ba. Dark Horse Books 2016 61 p. Color; Illustration
Grades: 11 12 Adult   **741.5; Fic**
1. Teenagers — Graphic novels; 2. Teenage boys — Graphic novels
9781616559557, $17.99
LC 2015050695

In this graphic novel, by Neil Gaiman, illustrated by Fábio Moon and Gabriel Bá, "Enn is a sixteen-year-old boy who just doesn't understand girls, while his friend Vic seems to have them all figured out. Both teenagers are in for the shock of their young lives, however, when they crash a local party only to discover that the girls there are far, far more than they appear!" (Publisher's note)

Marvel 1602. [Neil Gaiman, writer; Andy Kubert, illustrator; Richard Isanove, digital painting; Todd Klein, lettering]. Marvel Comics 2005 un Illustration
Grades: 10 11 12 Adult   **741.5; 741; Fic**
1. Doctor Doom (Fictitious character); 2. Graphic novels; 3. Superhero graphic novels; 4. X-Men (Fictional characters); 5. Daredevil (Fictional character)
0-7851-1073-9, $24.99; 0-7851-1073-9 (pa), $19.99

This book "takes the Marvel superheroes and villains of the 1960s — the original X-Men, Daredevil, Dr. Doom, and many others — and places them in the early 17th century." Libr J

"The improbable combination works remarkably well, as the superheroes' strange abilities adapt to Elizabethan culture. This glorious adventure is peppered with Scott McKowen's gorgeous, moody cover-art woodcuts." Publ Wkly

First published in magazine form as Marvel 1602 #1-8

★ **Neil** Gaiman and Charles Vess' Stardust: being a romance within the realms of Faerie. DC Comics/Vertigo 2007 213p. Illustration
Grades: 10 11 12 Adult   **741.5; Fic**
1. Fantasy graphic novels; 2. Graphic novels
978-1-4012-1190-5, $39.95

In the sleepy English countryside at the dawn of the Victorian Era, young Tristran Thorn has lost his heart to beautiful Victoria Forester. But Victoria is cold and distant — as distant, in fact, as the star she and Tristran see fall from the sky on a crisp October evening. For the coveted prize of Victoria's hand, Tristran vows to retrieve the fallen star and deliver it to his beloved. It is an oath that sends the lovelorn swain into a world that is strange beyond imagining, a world populated by evil old witches, deadly clutching trees, and goblin press-gangs — a world redeemed only by true love. The story includes some sexual situations and partial nudity. This deluxe hardcover edition includes bonus material such as Gaiman's initial proposal and a number of preliminary sketches and new artwork from Vess.

This illustrated novel is published by a comic book publisher and can go in either fiction or in the graphic novel section.

Neil Gaiman's Midnight Days. DC Comics/Vertigo 2000 un Illustration
Grades: 10 11 12 Adult   **741.5; Fic**
1. Fantasy graphic novels; 2. Graphic novels; 3. Horror graphic novels
1-56389-517-X, $17.99

This book collects some of Gaiman's earliest work for Vertigo. Included in these never-before-reprinted and original publications are tales featuring the Golden Age Sandman, Morpheus, the Swamp Thing, and John Constantine. Some of the stories include strong language, violence, and nudity.

★ The **Sandman** Volume 10: The Wake. DC Comics/Vertigo 1997 un Illustration
Grades: 10 11 12 Adult   **741.5; Fic**
1. Adventure graphic novels; 2. Fantasy graphic novels; 3. Graphic novels; 4. Sandman (Fictional character)
1-56389-279-0, $19.99

In the last chapter of the Sandman saga, the Endless and all the dreamers come to celebrate the life and mourn the passing of the King of Dreams. Meanwhile, the new Dream, who was once the boy Daniel Hall, waits for the others to come and meet him. The King is dead, long live the King. The book includes some nudity and violence.

Sandman Volume 2: The Doll's House. DC Comics/Vertigo 1991 255p. Illustration
Grades: 10 11 12 Adult   **741.5; Fic**
1. Fantasy graphic novels; 2. Graphic novels; 3. Horror graphic novels; 4. Sandman (Fictional character)
0-930289-59-5, $19.99
LC 92-159876

In this second volume, Rose Walker is the dream vortex who must be killed to save the Dreaming. In the meantime, she wanders the world hunting for her younger brother, and along the way she attends a "Cereal" convention, which is actually a serial killers' convention. Morpheus must track down four of his major arcana dreams that were lost during his long imprisonment. And Morpheus meets once a century with Hob, a man who had wished to never die. The book includes graphic violence, some partial nudity, and strong language.

★ **Sandman** Volume 3: Dream Country. DC Comics/Vertigo 1991 un Illustration
Grades: 10 11 12 Adult   **741.5; Fic**
1. Fantasy graphic novels; 2. Graphic novels; 3. Horror graphic novels; 4. Sandman (Fictional character)
1-56389-016-X, $14.99
LC 92-159876

This third volume collects four stories; the two standouts are "A Dream of a Thousand Cats," in which a purebred Siamese remembers her first litter of mixed-breed cats that her owners killed and ventures into the cat version of the dreaming in which Morpheus is a huge black cat and discovers her mission in life — cat owners may never look at their sleeping cats the same way again; and "A Midsummer Night's Dream" recounts the adventures of William Shakespeare and his company of players as they are summoned to perform their play to a highly select audience — King Oberon and Queen Titania of Faerie. This story won the World Fantasy Award for Best Short Story when it was first published. The book includes nudity, sexual situations, and some violence.

Sandman Volume 4: The Season of Mists. DC Comics/Vertigo 1994 un Illustration
Grades: 10 11 12 Adult   **741.5; Fic**

1. Fantasy graphic novels; 2. Graphic novels; 3. Horror graphic novels; 4. Sandman (Fictional character)
1-56389-041-0, $19.99

LC 92-159876

Lucifer has grown tired of being the lord of Hell. He kicks out the demons and the damned alike, closes up shop, and gives the key to Hell to Morpheus. Beings from all the world's mythologies converge on the lord of Dream to seize this instrument of power. All Morpheus wants is to search for the soul of his first love, Nada, whom he had consigned to Hell long ago. The book includes violence, strong language, and nudity.

Sandman Volume 5: A Game of You. DC Comics/Vertigo 1993 un Illustration
Grades: 10 11 12 Adult   **741.5; Fic**
1. Fantasy graphic novels; 2. Graphic novels; 3. Horror graphic novels; 4. Sandman (Fictional character)
1-56389-089-5, $19.99

Take an apartment house, mix in a drag queen, a lesbian couple, some talking animals, a talking severed head, a confused heroine, and the deadly Cuckoo. Stir vigorously with a hurricane and Morpheus himself and you get this fifth installment of the Sandman series. This story stars Barbie, who first makes an appearance in The Doll's House, who here finds herself a princess in a vivid dreamworld. The book includes violence, partial nudity, and strong language.

Sandman Volume 6: Fables & Reflections. DC Comics/Vertigo 1994 un Illustration
Grades: 10 11 12 Adult   **741.5; Fic**
1. Fantasy graphic novels; 2. Graphic novels; 3. Horror graphic novels; 4. Sandman (Fictional character)
9781563891052, $19.99; 1563891050

Morpheus, the King of Dreams, observes and interacts with an odd assortment of historical and fictional characters throughout time. Featuring tales of kings, explorers, spies, and werewolves, this book of myth and imagination delves into the dark dreams of Augustus Caesar, Haroun Al Raschid, Marco Polo, Cain and Abel, Emperor Joshua Norton I, and Orpheus to illustrate the effects that these subconscious musings have had on the course of history and mankind. The book includes some violence, nudity, and strong language.

Sandman Volume 7: Brief Lives. DC Comics/Vertigo 1995 un Illustration
Grades: 10 11 12 Adult   **741.5; Fic**
1. Fantasy graphic novels; 2. Graphic novels; 3. Horror graphic novels; 4. Sandman (Fictional character)
1-56389-138-7, $19.99

LC 92-159876

Delirium, youngest sister of the Endless, prevails upon her brother, Dream, to help her find their missing sibling, Destruction, who disappeared several centuries ago. Their travels take them through the world of the waking until a final confrontation with the missing member of the Endless and the resolution of Dream's relationship with his son change the endless forever. The book includes violence, nudity, sexual situations, and strong language.

★ The **Sandman** Volume 8: World's End. DC Comics/Vertigo 1995 un Illustration
Grades: 10 11 12 Adult   **741.5; Fic**
1. Adventure graphic novels; 2. Fantasy graphic novels; 3. Graphic novels; 4. Sandman (Fictional character)
1-56389-171-9, $19.99

A "reality storm" draws an unusual cast of characters together. They take shelter in a tavern, where they amuse each other with their life stories. Although Morpheus is never a focus in these stories, each has something to say about the nature of stories and dreams. The book includes some

violence, some strong language, and brief partial nudity and sexual situations.

★ The **Sandman** Volume 9: The Kindly Ones. DC Comics/Vertigo 1996 un Illustration
Grades: 10 11 12 Adult   **741.5; Fic**
1. Adventure graphic novels; 2. Fantasy graphic novels; 3. Graphic novels; 4. Sandman (Fictional character)
1-56389-205-7, $19.99

Distraught by the kidnapping and presumed death of her son Daniel, and believing Morpheus to be responsible, Lyta Hall calls the ancient wrath of the Furies down upon him. A former super heroine blames Morpheus for the death of her child and summons an ancient curse of vengeance against the Lord of Dream. The kindly ones" enter his realm and force a sacrifice that will change the Dreaming forever. The book includes violence, strong language, and partial nudity.

★ The **Sandman**, Vol. 1: Preludes and Nocturnes. DC Comics/Vertigo 1991 236p. Illustration
Grades: 10 11 12 Adult   **741.5; Fic**
1. Fantasy — Graphic novels; 2. Graphic novels; 3. Mythology — Graphic novels
978-1-56389-011-6, $19.95

"Gaiman's stories of Morpheus, the Lord of Dream, his Endless siblings (Death, Destruction, Delirium, Desire, Destiny, and Despair), his enemies, and many figures who spring from various mythologies and folklore have changed many readers' ideas about comics and graphic novels." (VOYA)

Various artists worked with Gaiman to illustrate his stories, which include some strong depictions of violence and occasional nudity.

Other Sandman volumes are: 2: A Doll's House; 3: Dream Country; 4: Season of Mists; 5: A Game of You; 6: Fables and Reflections; 7: Brief Lives; 8: World's End; 9: The Kindly Ones;10: The Wake

The **Sandman**: Endless Nights. DC Comics/Vertigo 2004 un Illustration
Grades: 11 12 Adult   **741.5; Fic**
1. Fantasy graphic novels; 2. Graphic novels; 3. Sandman (Fictional character)
1-4012-0113-X, $19.99

This volume reveals the legend of the Endless, a family of magical and mythical beings who exist and interact in the real world. Born at the beginning of time, Destiny, Death, Dream, Desire, Despair, Delirium and Destruction are seven brothers and sisters who each lord over their respective realms. These seven peculiar and powerful siblings each reveal more about their true-being as they star in their own tales of curiosity and wonder. A different artist interprets each story by Gaiman. The book includes considerable nudity and sexual situations, and some violence.

★ The **Sandman**: Overture. written by Neil Gaiman; art by J.H. Williams III; colors by Dave Stewart; letters by Todd Klein. DC Comics/Vertigo 2015 224 p. Color; Illustration
Grades: Adult   **741.5; Fic**
1. Death — Graphic novels; 2. Fantasy graphic novels; 3. Metaphysics — Fiction
1401248969; 9781401248963, $24.99

LC 2015028077

Hugo Award: Best Graphic Story (2016)

This graphic novel is author "Neil Gaiman's return to the art form that made him famous, ably abetted by artistic luminary JH Williams III whose...images provide an epic scope to The Sandman's origin story. From the birth of a galaxy to the moment that Morpheus is captured, THE SANDMAN: OVERTURE will feature cameo appearances by fan-favorite characters such as The Corinthian, Merv Pumpkinhead and, of course, the

Dream King's siblings: Death, Desire, Despair, Delirium, Destruction and Destiny." (Publisher's note)

"Infinitely adaptable, Williams's dazzling art recalls everyone from Alphonse Mucha to Jack Kirby. Gaiman is in fine form as well — it is a true pleasure to watch him plumb the depths of weirdness that made Sandman a classic." Pub Wkly

Originally published in single magazine form in THE SANDMAN: OVERTURE 1-6

★ The **Sandman**: the dream hunters. D.C. Comics/Vertigo 2009 144p. Illustration
Grades: 10 11 12 Adult   **741.5; Fic**
1. Dreams — Graphic novels; 2. Graphic novels; 3. Love — Graphic novels; 4. Supernatural graphic novels
978-1-4012-2424-0, $24.99

In old Japan, creatures of myth and legend live among the people. Two such creatures, a badger and a fox, make a wager to force a humble monk to leave the temple he tends alone up in the mountains. Because the young monk can see through their disguises to their true nature, both badger and fox lose the wager, and the fox falls in love with the handsome young man and remains nearby. Meanwhile, a wealthy man who has mastered demons yet cannot find peace in his soul decides to steal the young monk's inner strength for his own. The fox tries to protect the monk, and even makes a bargain with the great black fox in her dreams, to sacrifice her life for the man she loves. Then, when she suffers the consequences of the evil dreams sent by the wealthy man through his demons, the monk ventures into the Dreaming in a quest to save the fox, whom he finally realizes he loves. When he makes the decision to take back the dream that will kill him, the fox decides to take revenge on the wealthy man, the onmyoji, and comes to him as a beautiful young woman to destroy him. Russell has adapted the novella written by Gaiman and illustrated by Yoshitaka Amano. It includes some nudity.

Violent cases: words & pictures. Neil Gaiman, Dave McKean. Kitchen Sink Press 1997 64 p. Color illustration
Grades: Adult   **741.5/973**
1. Memory — Fiction; 2. Imagination — Fiction
0878165371; 0878165576; 1616552107; 9781616552107, $19.99
LC 99183676

This novel, by Neil Gaiman and Dave McKean, "presents the often murky nexus between memory and imagination, revealed through the narrator's cloudy childhood remembrance of a visit to Al Capone's osteopath and the impact of his seedy stories on an impressionable youth." (Publisher's note)

Words & pictures; Words and pictures

Gallagher, Monica
Gods & undergrads, Book 1. Lipstick Press 2007 un Illustration
Grades: 10 11 12 Adult   **741.5; Fic**
1. College students — Graphic novels; 2. Graphic novels; 3. Greek mythology — Graphic novels; 4. School stories — Graphic novels
978-0-9794589-0-3, $10

College sophomore Lelaina Pentheus has decided to move on campus at Troy University, and by some chance meetings and good luck joins several juniors in an apartment. Her new friends quickly learn that Lelaina has some strange quirks, like fainting a lot, and hands that can suddenly turn hot and blister. She doesn't know why, nor why she has strange markings on her face; she was adopted as an infant. Then she gets strange messages that "they're coming" — from a talking frog, from her roommate's brother, and then from a stranger who claims he's Hermes, the Greek messenger god. This book collects the first three chapters of Gallagher's story, which first appeared as webcomics at www.eatyourlipstick.com.

Also available online as webcomic

Gallaher, David
High moon. DC Comics 2009 un Illustration
Grades: 10 11 12 Adult   **741.5; Fic**
1. Graphic novels; 2. Horror graphic novels; 3. Werewolves — Graphic novels; 4. Western stories — Graphic novels
978-1-4012-2462-2, $14.99
2009 Harvey Award for Best OnLine Comics Work.

It starts in a small town in Texas, with mysterious happenings and then the disappearance of a girl. Ex-Pinkerton detective McGregor comes to town hunting a criminal named Conroy and gets involved in the town's problems. Mr. Hunter, father of the missing girl, doesn't know the half of it; the town is filled with werewolves resentful of human progress. Conroy is a werewolf, and so is McGregor. When McGregor dies fighting the werewolves from the mines, Conroy takes his identity and continues his travels. In Ragged Rock, he finds more trouble stemming from an old hate, and the real McGregor's brother, Tristan, has come to find his brother's killer. Conroy soon learns that he can be killed, but he won't stay dead. The book includes considerable violence.

Originally published online at www.zudacomics.com.

Gauld, Tom
Baking with Kafka: comics. Tom Gauld. Drawn & Quarterly 2017 160 p. Color; Illustration
Grades: Adult   **741.5**
1. Comic books, strips, etc.; 2. Literature; 3. Wit and humor
1770462961; 9781770462960, $19.95
Eisner Award: Best Humor Publication (2018)

This book, by Tom Gauld, presents a "collection of literary humour cartoons.... [Gauld] stitch[es] together the worlds of literary criticism and pop culture to create brilliantly executed, concise comics. Simultaneously silly and serious, Gauld adds an undeniable lightness to traditionally highbrow themes. From sarcastic panels about the health hazards of being a best-selling writer to a list of magical items for fantasy writers." (Publisher's note)

Goliath. Tom Gauld. Drawn & Quarterly 2012 96 p. Illustration
Grades: Adult   **741.5/9411; 741.5**
1. Goliath (Biblical giant) — Comic books, strips, etc; 2. Battles — Fiction
1770460659; 9781770460652, $19.95
LC 2012397951

This graphic novel by Tom Gauld is a retelling of the Biblical story of David and Goliath. "Gauld turns the brute into a hapless lug doomed by his own meekness.... With the armies of the the Philistines and the Israelites at an impasse, a Philistine captain concocts a crazy scheme to flaunt Goliath's intimidating size and wage psychological warfare on the enemy. He ignores Goliath's objections... reasoning that no one would be nutty enough to take on such a mountain of a man." (Booklist)

Mooncop. Tom Gauld. Farrar, Straus & Giroux 2016 96 p. Color; Illustration
Grades: Adult   **741.5**
1. Space colonies — Comic books, strips, etc.; 2. Police — Comic books, strips, etc.; 3. Moon — Comic books, strips, etc.
1770462546; 9781770462540, $19.95
LC 2016042120

In this graphic novel, by Tom Gauld, "the lunar colony is slowly winding down, like a small town circumvented by a new super highway. As our hero, the Mooncop, makes his daily rounds, his beat grows ever smaller, the population dwindles. A young girl runs away, a dog breaks off his leash, an automaton wanders off from the Museum of the Moon." (Publisher's note)

"A drolly melancholic tale that's more an exploration of inner than of outer space." Booklist

You're All Just Jealous of My Jetpack: Cartoons. by Tom Gauld. Farrar Straus & Giroux 2013 160 p.

Grades: Adult **741.5**
1. Cartoons and caricatures
1770461043; 9781770461048, $19.95

LC 2013375548

This book by Tom Gauld is "a collection of cartoons made for [newspaper] 'The Guardian.' [It] distills perfectly Gauld — s dark humor, impeccable timing, and distinctive style. Arrests by the fiction police and imaginary towns designed by Tom Waits intermingle hilariously with piercing observations about human behavior and whimsical imaginings of the future. Gauld [creates] work infused with a deep understanding of both literary and cartoon history." (Publisher's note)

Gay, Roxane

Black Panther: world of Wakanda. written by Roxane Gay, Ta-Nehisi Coates, RembertBrowne, Yona Harvey; pencilled by Alitha E.Martinez, Afua N. Richardson, Joe Bennett; inkedby Alitha E. Martinez, Roberto Poggi, Afua N.Richardson; colored by Tamra Bonvillain, RachelleRosenberg. Marvel Enterprises 2017 144 p. Color; Illustration

Grades: 10 11 12 Adult **741.5; Fic**
1. Graphic novels; 2. Superheroes; 3. Black Panther (Fictional character)
130290650X; 9781302906504, $17.99

Eisner Award: Best Limited Series (2018)

This book, by Ta-Nehisi Coates, Roxane Gay and Yona Harvey, presents the story of "Ayo and Aneka, young women recruited to become Dora Milaje, an elite task force trained to protect the crown of Wakanda at all costs. Their first assignment will be to protect Queen Shuri... but what happens when your nation needs your hearts and minds, but you already gave them to each other? Meanwhile, former king T'Challa lies with bedfellows so dark, disgrace is inevitable." (Publisher's note)

Contains materials originally published in magazine form as Black Panther: world of Wakanda #1-6

Geary, Rick

The **Beast** of Chicago: An Account of the Life and Crimes of Herman W. Mudgett, Known to the World as H. H. Holmes. NBM 2003 un Illustration

Grades: 9 10 11 12 Adult **364.152; 741.5**
1. Graphic novels; 2. Homicide — Graphic novels; 3. Mystery graphic novels
1-56163-362-3, $8.95

He was the world's first serial killer and he existed in the late 19th century, operating around the Chicago World's Fair, building a literal house of horrors, replete with chutes for dead bodies, gas chambers, surgical rooms. He methodically murdered up to 200 people, mostly young women. Geary steers away from gore to focus on such things as Holmes' "lab" in his castle. The book is still not for the squeamish, but the art is restrained.

Part of the A Treasury of Victorian Murder series.

The **Borden** Tragedy: A Memoir of the Infamous Double Murder at Fall River, Mass., 1892. NBM 1997 80p. Illustration

Grades: 9 10 11 12 Adult **364.152; 741.5**
1. Graphic novels; 2. Homicide — Graphic novels; 3. Mystery graphic novels
1-56163-189-2, $8.95; 9781561631896

Including such details as maps of Fall River, Massachusetts as it was in 1892, Geary presents the facts and documented speculations about the case of Lizzie Borden, a thirty-year-old spinster accused and tried for murdering her parents. The popular rhyme "Lizzie Borden took an axe, gave her mother forty whacks, when she saw what she had done, she gave her father forty-one" was apparently sung to the tune of "Tararaboomdeeay." Geary leaves it to the reader to decide if Lizzie was guilty or not.

Part of the A Treasury of Victorian Murder series.

Famous players: the mysterious death of William Desmond Taylor. NBM/ComicsLit 2009 un Illustration

Grades: 9 10 11 12 Adult
364.152; 741.5
1. Graphic novels; 2. Homicide — Graphic novels; 3. Motion picture directors; 4. Motion picture producers and directors — Graphic novels; 5. Murder victims; 6. Mystery graphic novels; 7. Taylor, William Desmond, 1877-1922
978-1-56163-555-9, $15.95;
978-1-56163-559-7 (pa), $9.95

Courtesy of NBM Publishing

Hollywood in 1922 was just coming into its own as a mecca for filmmakers as the silent films became more and more popular. One of the new studios was Famous Players Studio, and William Desmond Taylor was one of its successful directors, along with Cecil B. DeMille. Then, on the morning of February 2, 1922, Taylor's cook/valet/general house servant Henry Peavey arrived at 7:30 and found Taylor's body on the floor of the living room. He'd been shot, but by whom? As the investigation progresses, several prominent actresses come under suspicion, along with a former cook and house servant; and his own mysterious past starts to come to light. However, the police are never able to solve the case. Geary provides a list of his sources for anyone who would like to know more about this Twentieth-Century Murder mystery. He depicts the crime with little gore or violence.

This is part of the Treasury of XXth Century Murder series.

J. Edgar Hoover: a graphic biography. Hill and Wang 2008 102p. Illustration

Grades: 9 10 11 12 Adult **363.2; 92; 741.5**
1. United States — Federal Bureau of Investigation — Graphic novels; 2. Biographical graphic novels; 3. FBI officials; 4. Graphic novels; 5. Hoover, J. Edgar (John Edgar), 1895-1972
978-0-8090-9503-2; 0-8090-9503-3, $16.95

LC 2007-25193

Rick Geary has written a biography of J. Edgar Hoover, who served in the federal government for 55 years and under eight presidents, most notably as director of the Federal Bureau of Investigation. He was appointed to that position on May 10, 1924. Geary covers Hoover's sometimes controversial career, including his refusal to involve the FBI directly into investigations of crimes against civil rights workers and the 1963 bombing in Birmingham, Alabama, and the bureau's investigation of Martin Luther King, Jr. He tastefully discusses Hoover's undercover sexual life.

"As solid, thrilling and informative a guide to the life of the America's most powerful authoritarian as one could ask for." Kirkus

★ The **Lindbergh** child: America's hero and the crime of the century. written and illustrated by Rick Geary. NBM/ComicsLit 2008 un Illustration; Map (Treasury of XXth century murder)

Grades: 8 9 10 11 12 Adult **364.1; 741.5**
1. Air force officers; 2. Air pilots; 3. Generals; 4. Graphic novels; 5. Homicide — Graphic novels; 6. Kidnapping — Graphic novels; 7. Memoirists; 8. Mystery graphic novels; 9. Lindbergh, Charles, 1902-1974

Courtesy of NBM Publishing

978-1-56163-529-0, $15.95

Charles Lindbergh was an American hero following his solo crossing of the Atlantic in an airplane. He married into a wealthy family, he and his wife had a baby, they were building their dream home. Then, one night, the baby was abducted from the house. Geary's account retraces all the highly publicized events, ransom notes (false and otherwise), as well as the string of colorful characters who all claimed they could help but instead snookered the Lindberghs. While Bruno Hauptmann was arrested, tried, convicted, and executed, there remain many questions about what really happened. Geary brings them up for readers to consider.

"A good example of the origins of modern forensics, crime-scene investigation, and celebrity hysteria, this work is an excellent choice for most collections." SLJ

The **lives** of Sacco and Vanzetti. Rick Geary.. NBM Comics Lit 2011 80 p. Illustration
Grades: 9 10 11 12 Adult
345; 741.5; 345.73
1. Sacco-Vanzetti Trial, Dedham, Mass., 1921 — Comic books, strips, etc.; 2. Trials (Murder) — Massachusetts — Dedham — Comic books, strips, etc.; 3. Sacco, Nicola, 1891-1927 — Trials, litigation, etc. — Comic books, strips, etc.; 4. Vanzetti, Bartolomeo, 1888-1927 — Trials, litigation, etc. — Comic books, strips, etc.; 5. Anarchism and anarchists — Graphic novels; 6. Sacco-Vanzetti case; 7. United States — History — 1919-1933 — Graphic novels
1561636053; 9781561636051, $15.99

Courtesy of NBM Publishing

LC 2011927818

"Geary lays out what is known and not known about the case, in which two Italian anarchist immigrants were put to death after being found guilty of robbery and murder. The...narrative not only details the events of the crime, manhunt, and trial but also includes information about the lives of Sacco and Vanzetti and their families." (Publishers Weekly)
Includes bibliographical references

Madison square tragedy: the murder of Stanford White : 25 June, 1906. written and illustrated by Rick Geary. NBM Pub. 2013 80 p. Illustration (Treasury of xxth century murder)
Grades: 9 10 11 12 Adult
741.5; 364.152
1. Mystery graphic novels; 2. Murder — Graphic novels
1561637629; 9781561637621, $15.99
LC 2013947335

In this graphic novel, by Rick Geary, as architect Stanford White "became popular and in demand, he also became quite self-indulgent: he had a taste for budding young showgirls on Broadway, even setting up a private apartment to entertain them in.... When he met Evelyn Nesbit...he knew he was on to something special. However, Evelyn eventually married a young

Courtesy of NBM Publishing

Pittsburgh decadent heir with a dark side who developed a deep hatred for White and what he may or may not have done to her." (Publisher's note)

"In this entry in his series recounting historical murder cases, Geary tackles an infamous crime that scandalized New York City in 1901.... Geary's old-fashioned black-and-white line drawings, vividly evoking the turn-of-the-century milieu, and his reliance on text-heavy captions as a sort of voice-over impart a documentary air to his thoroughly researched account." Booklist
Includes bibliographical references

The **Mystery** of Mary Rogers: A Chronicle of the Disappearance and Murder of The Beautiful Segar Girl in July, 1841 - A Crime Which was Never Solved - And Which Inspired the Sensational Tale by Edgar A. Poe. NBM 2001 un Illustration
Grades: 9 10 11 12 Adult
364.152; 741.5
1. Graphic novels; 2. Homicide — Graphic novels; 3. Mystery graphic novels
1-56163-274-0, $15.95

Courtesy of NBM Publishing

Mary Rogers was a compellingly beautiful lass employed in a cigar store in New York City in the mid-nineteenth century. She had a few suitors. Then, she suddenly disappeared, her body recovered in the Hudson off the Jersey side. The press had a field day with all the possible shocking possibilities. Rape... her "fooling around" between lovers...even gang rape. Never was this case solved. The hypotheses remain many. Even Edgar Allen Poe thought to have solved the case and presented that in his tale "The Mystery of Mary Roget."

Part of the A Treasury of Victorian Murder series.

The **saga** of the bloody Benders: the infamous homicidal family of Labette County, Kansas. NBM/ComicsLit 2007 un Illustration
Grades: 9 10 11 12 Adult
364.152; 741.5
1. Graphic novels; 2. Homicide — Graphic novels; 3. Mystery graphic novels
978-1-56163-498-9, $15.95

In Kansas, around the year 1870, the Bender family ran the Bender Inn and grocery store in Labette County, Kansas. Soon after they open their inn to travelers, people start to disappear, usually people with a fair amount of money with them. When the authorities investigate, the family disappears,

Courtesy of NBM Publishing

and the people of Labette County make grisly discoveries in the Bender Inn's cellar. Geary includes just enough gory details for readers to comprehend the Benders' crimes. Earlier volumes in this series focused on famous nineteenth century murders and criminals, but the crimes of this more obscure family are just as dastardly for true crime aficionados.

Part of the series, A Treasury of Victorian Murders

★ The **terrible** Axe-Man of New Orleans. music and lyrics by Rick Geary. NBM Publishing/ComicsLit 2010 un Illustration; Map (Treasury of XXth century murder)
Grades: 9 10 11 12 Adult   **364.152; 741.5**
1. Graphic novels; 2. Homicide — Graphic novels; 3. Mystery graphic novels; 4. New Orleans (La.) — History — Graphic novels
978-1-56163-581-8, $15.99

LC 2010-926782

Courtesy of NBM Publishing

Geary tells the story of the Terrible Axe-Man, who murdered grocers in New Orleans right after World War I. In each case, the murderer removed a piece of the door to the house, borrowed an axe found at the property, then aimed straight for the head of his victim. From May 23, 1918 to October 27, 1919, the Axe-Man killed six people and badly wounded six more, then disappeared. Geary lays out the known facts, then shows some of the speculation. The black and white art helps to mitigate the violence and gore, so the book is suitable for teens who enjoy true-life mysteries.

"Geary's exacting, historically accurate approach makes this...a natural for true-crime fans as well as comics lovers." Booklist

Includes bibliographical references; Nights of terror! A city awash in blood!

★ **Trotsky:** a graphic biography. Hill and Wang 2009 103p. Illustration; Map
Grades: 9 10 11 12 Adult   **92; 741.5**
1. Biographical graphic novels; 2. Communism — Soviet Union — Graphic novels; 3. Communist leaders; 4. Graphic novels; 5. Nonfiction writers; 6. Political leaders; 7. Revolutionaries; 8. Trotsky, Leon, 1879-1940; 9. Russia — Politics and government — 1894-1917 — Graphic novels; 10. Soviet Union — Politics and government — Graphic novels
978-0-8090-9508-7, $16.95; 0-8090-9508-4

LC 2008-50235

Geary provides a graphic biography of Leon Trotsky, the "brain" behind the Russian Revolution of 1917. The book, with its black and white panel art, chronicles Trotsky's tumultuous relationships with Lenin and Stalin, the contentious debates within the revolutionary movement, Trotsky's many exiles, and his murder in Mexico in 1940.

"Geary's familiar cartoonlike drawing style and factual presentation make this title an accessible and concise introduction to Trotsky's life." SLJ

Includes bibliographical references; A novel graphic from Hill and Wang

Geissman, Grant
Mad About the Fifties. E.C. Publications/MAD Books 2005 un. Illustration
Grades: 8 9 10 11 12 Adult   **741.5**
1. Graphic novels; 2. Humorous graphic novels; 3. Satire — Graphic novels
1-4012-0753-7, $12.99

MAD Magazine was founded in 1952 as a ten-cent comic book that parodied other comic books; three years later it became a twenty-five cent (cheap!) magazine. This volume collects some of the regular features and parodies of television programs and movies of the decade. Some of the advertising parodies feature tobacco and alcohol products, and some parodies portray the imbibing of alcohol products.

Mad About the Sixties: The Best of the Decade. Mad Books/E.C. Publications 1997 un Illustration
Grades: 7 8 9 10 11 12 Adult   **741.5; Fic**
1. Graphic novels; 2. Humorous graphic novels; 3. Satire — Graphic novels
1-4012-0754-5, $9.99

Alfred E. Newman as a flower child? Ecch! Here is a look back at the Sixties from the satire magazine, full of send-ups, takeoffs, and put-ons

from the decade that gave the world Timothy Leary and Tiny Tim. Along with Spy vs. Spy, Sergio Aragones' "Mad Marginals," Don Martin's lunacies, and Snappy Answers to Stupid Questions, this volume includes TV satires such as Star Blecch, Bats-Man, and The Phewgitive, and movie takeoffs 201 Min. of a Space Idiocy, East Side Story, and Flawrence of Arabia. Back in the 1960s, preteens read the magazine and most of them turned out okay ...

Georges, Nicole J.
Calling Dr. Laura: a graphic memoir. Nicole J. Georges. Houghton Mifflin Harcourt 2013 260 p. Illustration
Grades: Adult   **741.5; 92**
1. Family secrets — Comic books, strips, etc; 2. Identity (Psychology) — Comic books, strips, etc; 3. Georges, Nicole J.; 4. Lesbians' writings; 5. Autobiographical graphic novels
0547615590; 9780547615592, $16.95

LC 2012022389

Lambda Award: Graphic Novel (2014)

This graphic novel by Nicole J. Georges tells how when she "was two years old, her family told her that her father was dead. When she was twenty-three, a psychic told her he was alive. Her sister, saddled with guilt, admits that the psychic is right and that the whole family has conspired to keep him a secret. Sent into a tailspin about her identity, Nicole turns to radio talk-show host Dr. Laura Schlessinger for advice." (Publisher's note)

"Georges' quirky, big-faced, and evocative drawings, tempered by a variety of panel sizes, show the bespectacled author as she comes to terms with her mother's lies to her as a child about her father being dead.... An excellent graphic memoir offering engaging insights for those who share — or don't share any of Georges' worries and traits." Booklist

Fetch: How a Bad Dog Brought Me Home. Nicole J. Georges. Mariner Books/Houghton Mifflin Harcourt 2017 328 p. Illustration
Grades: 11 12 Adult   **92; 741.5**
1. Human-animal relationships; 2. Dogs; 3. Autobiographical graphic novels
9780544577831, $17.95; 0544577833

In this illustrated memoir, author Nicole J. Georges reflects how when she "was sixteen she adopted Beija, a dysfunctional shar-pei/corgi mix — a troublesome combination of tiny and attack, just like teenaged Nicole herself. For the next fifteen years, Beija would be the one constant in her life. Through depression, relationships gone awry, and an unmoored young adulthood played out against the backdrop of the Portland punk scene, Beija was there." (Publisher's note)

"Drawn in black and white with watercolor washes and elegant hand lettering, this book is an homage to classic zine aesthetics that captures an incomparable friendship. An honest, moving portrayal of the essential bond between humans and animals." Pub Wkly

Getz, Trevor R.,
Abina and the important men: a graphic history. Trevor R. Getz, Liz Clarke. Oxford University Press 2012 xix, 179 p. Color; Illustration
Grades: Adult
306.3; 306.3/62092; 741.5
1. Slavery — Law and legislation — Ghana — History — 19th century — Comic books, strips, etc; 2. Women slaves — Ghana — History — 19th century — Comic books, strips, etc; 3. Mansah, Abina — Trials, litigation, etc. — Comic books, strips, etc
0199844399; 9780199844395, $15.95

By permission of Oxford University Press, USA

LC 2011031033

"The story of Abina Mansah — a woman 'without history' who was wrongfully enslaved, escaped to British-controlled territory, and then took her former master to court — takes place in the complex world of the Gold Coast at the onset of late nineteenth-century colonialism. Slavery becomes a contested ground, as cultural practices collide with an emerging wage economy and British officials turn a blind eye to the presence of underpaid domestic workers in the households of African merchants. The main scenes of the story take place in the courtroom, where Abina strives to convince a series of 'important men' — a British judge, two Euro-African attorneys, a wealthy African country 'gentleman,' and a jury of local leaders — that her rights matter." (Publisher's note)

"Oxford heavily promotes this book as a near-revolution in the pedagogy of African history. While it is not quite that innovative, it is an excellent teaching tool on Africa, slavery, women's and legal history, and historical methodology." Choice

Includes bibliographical references

Gibbons, Dave

★ The **Originals**. DC Comics/Vertigo 2004 un Illustration
Grades: 10 11 12 Adult   **741.5; Fic**
1. Gangs — Graphic novels; 2. Graphic novels; 3. Science fiction graphic novels
1-4012-0355-8, $24.95
2005 Eisner Award for Best Graphic Album — New.

In a retro-futuristic city of industrial gray where hover scooters, music, and drugs rule the street, the Originals are the toughest, most stylish gang around. For two childhood friends, Lel and Bok, nothing is more important than being one of them. But being part of the crowd will bring its own deadly consequences. Gibbons draws upon the world of the Mods in 1960s England and sets it in an alternate world. Violence, harsh language, and sexual situations are part of this world.

Giffen, Keith

52 aftermath: The Four Horsemen. DC Comics 2008 144p. Illustration

Grades: 10 11 12 Adult   **741.5; Fic**
1. Batman (Fictional character); 2. Graphic novels; 3. Superhero graphic novels; 4. Superman (Fictional character); 5. Wonder Woman (Fictional character)
978-1-4012-1781-5, $19.99

During the event of 52 weeks, a cadre of scientists created the Four Horsemen of Apokolips, creatures of destructive power that killed Black Adam's family and pretty much destroyed his nation, Bialya. Black Adam destroyed the Horsemen; but, he only destroyed their physical forms. Now, War, Famine, Pestilence, and Death have returned, taking over new human hosts. Superman, Batman, and Wonder Woman are on the scene, but they might not be enough to destroy the Horsemen. Their best hope may be Dr. Cale, who helped create the Horsemen in the first place. Can she be trusted? The book includes violence.

52 Volume Two. Geoff Johns, Grant Morrison, Greg Rucka, Mark Waid, Keith Giffen. DC Comics 2007 304p. Illustration
Grades: 10 11 12 Adult   **741.5; Fic**
1. Adventure graphic novels; 2. Graphic novels; 3. Superhero graphic novels
978-1-4012-1364-0, $19.99

Lex Luthor's created meta humans become Infinity, Inc. even as John Steel finds out that Luthor can control the power within them — including removing them. Ralph Dibny takes up the helmet of Dr. Fate. The Question and Renee Montoya travel to Kahndaq, on the trail of Intergang's weapons. Black Adam and Isis get married. Booster Gold's dubious heroism ends badly. Supernova bothers Luthor. Adam Strange, Animal Man, and Starfire

escape from the planet where they had been trapped, with help from...Lobo? The year without Superman, Batman, and Wonder Woman continues. The book includes some sexually suggestive scenes, violence, and some strong language.

Gill, Joel

Strange fruit; Volume 1: Uncelebrated narratives from Black history. words and pictures by Joel Christian Gill; foreword by Henry Louis Gates, Jr. Fulcrum Publishing 2014 176 p. Color; Illustration
Grades: 9 10 11 12 Adult
973.04960730092/2; 741.5; 92
1. African Americans — Biography — Comic books, strips, etc; 2. African Americans — Biography; 3. African Americans — History — Anecdotes — Comic books, strips, etc; 4. African Americans — History — Anecdotes — Juvenile literature; 5. Graphic novels; 6. Heroes — United States — Biography — Comic books, strips, etc; 7. Heroes — United States — Biography; 8. Success
1938486293; 9781938486296, $23.95

Courtesy of Fulcrum Publishing

LC 2014010803

This book, illustrated by Joel Christian Gill, "is a collection of stories from African American history that exemplifies success in the face of great adversity. This unique graphic anthology offers historical and cultural commentary on nine uncelebrated heroes [such as escaped slave] Henry 'Box' Brown,...Alexander Crummel and the Noyes Academy [and] Marshall 'Major' Taylor...the first black champion in any sport." (Publisher's note)

"The short narratives are conversational in tone and the accompanying detailed images convey tragic beauty. Gil doesn't shy away from portraying brutal scenes, but does so without sensationalism. The panels vary in size and orientation, pushing the momentum of each vignette forward with great success." SLJ

Gillen, Kieron

Star Wars Darth Vader; Volume 1: Vader. writer, Kieron Gillen; artist, Salvador Larroca; colorist, Edgar Delgado; letterer, VC's Joe Caramagna; cover art, Adi Granov; assistant editors, Charles Beacham & Heather Antos; editor, Jordan D. White. Marvel Enterprises 2015 160 p. Color; Illustration
Grades: 8 9 10 11 12 Adult   **741.5**
1. Star Wars — Graphic novels
0785192557; 9780785192558, $19.99

In this book, by Kieron Gillen, illustrated by Salvador Larocca, "Ever since Darth Vader's first on-screen appearance, he has become one of pop culture's most popular villains. Now, follow Vader straight from the ending of A NEW HOPE into his own solo adventures — showing the Empire's war with the Rebel Alliance from the other side! But when a Dark Lord needs help, who can he turn to?" (Publisher's note)

Contains material originally published in magazine form as Darth Vader #1-6.; Volume 1 of 4

The **wicked** + the divine; Volume 1: The Faust act. by Kieron Gillen; illustrated by Jamie McKelvie. Image Comics 2014 144 p. Color; Illustration
Grades: Adult   **741.5**
1. Immortality — Fiction; 2. Gods and goddesses — Fiction
1632150190; 9781632150196, $9.99

LC 2014501185

Eisner Nominee: Best New Series (2015)

"Every ninety years, twelve gods incarnate as humans. They are loved. They are hated. In two years, they are dead.... [G]ods are the ultimate pop stars and pop stars are the ultimate gods. But remember: just because you're immortal, doesn't mean you're going to live forever." (Publisher's note)

"A series of horrifying events backstage after the goddess Amaterasu's latest concert thrusts a mortal woman named Laura into a quest to help clear the reincarnated-as-female Lucifer of a murder she did not commit.... Little is revealed at this stage of the narrative, but the solid storytelling and clean, gorgeous artwork will keep readers engrossed and eager for more." Pub Wkly

Originally published in single magazine form as The wicked + the divine #1-5; Volume 1 of an ongoing series

The **Wicked** + the Divine; Volume 2: Fandemonium. Kieron Gillen; illustrated by Jamie McKelvie and Matt Wilson. Image Comics 2015 168 p. Color illustration

Grades: Adult   741.5; Fic
1. Gods and goddesses — Graphic novels; 2. Conspiracies — Fiction
1632153270; 9781632153272, $14.99

Eisner Nominee: Best New Series (2015)

This is the second volume of an "urban fantasy series where gods are the ultimate pop stars and pop stars are the ultimate gods. Following the tragic and unjust death of Lucifer, it takes a revelation from Inanna to draw Laura back into the worlds of Gods and Superstardom to try and discover the truth behind a conspiracy to subvert divinity." (Publisher's note)

"As Laura does, we delve more deeply into the Pantheon's origins and the book's motivating theme — namely how a search for identity can lead us to define ourselves through celebrity and pop culture. This all makes for a script that satisfyingly favors exploration over sheer thrills, with art providing masterful support. While the keen linework and psychedelic colors counterpoint this complexity, looking deeper reveals delightful and subtle playfulness with form." Booklist

★ **Young** Avengers: mic-drop at the edge of time and space. by Kieron Gillen; illustrated by Jamie McKelvie. Marvel Enterprises 2014 112 p. Color illustration

Grades: 10 11 12 Adult   741.5; Fic
1. Captain America (Fictional character) — Comic books, strips, etc.; 2. Graphic novels; 3. Heroes — Fiction — Comic books, strips, etc.; 4. Science fiction comic books, strips, etc.; 5. Loki (Norse Deity) — Comic books, strips, etc.; 6. Superheroes — Fiction
9780785185307, $15.99; 0785185305

"They say you can never go home. For the Young Avengers, that's not true. They can go home — it's just that if they do, the universe may end. Better not go home then, eh? (Wait, what are you doing, Young Avengers? You've decided to go home?!") The team takes on the gig to save reality, but is Kate Bishop an enemy in waiting? Is this the last we see of the loveable/strangle-able Kid Loki?" (Publisher's note)

"Gillen is an intelligent, savvy writer who gives more space to the battle's buildup and after-party than to the battle itself and even in the midst of the fight relies more on intimate character conflict than epic fisticuffs.... The overt focus on fluid sexuality...and smart teen dialogue that rings familiar and true give this series high appeal for new adults in particular." Booklist

★ **Young** avengers: style substance. Kieron Gillen, writer; Jamie McKelvie, Mike Norton, artist; Matthew Wilson, color artist; VC's Clayton Cowles, letterer. Marvel Enterprises 2013 128 p. Illustration

Grades: 10 11 12 Adult   741.5; Fic
1. Superhero graphic novels; 2. Teenagers — Fiction
9780785167082, $15.99; 0785167080

Author Kieron Gillen and illustrator Jamie McKelvie tell the story of "Wiccan, Hulkling and Kate 'Hawkeye' Bishop with Kid Loki, Marvel Boy and Ms. America.... As a figure from Loki's past emerges, Wiccan makes a horrible mistake that comes back to bite everyone on their communal posteriors. Fight scenes! Fake IDs! And plentiful feels! (aka 'meaningful emotional character beats'...)" (Publisher's note)

"The story...flies by, thanks to clever banter and lightning pacing.... McKelvie turns in clean, polished pages with eye-popping character work and shows some real and very welcome imagination with action sequences." Booklist

Contains material originally published in magazine form Young Avengers #1-5 and Marvel now! point one #1 — Tp verso

★ **Young** Avengers; Volume 2: alternative cultures. Kieron Gillen, illustrated by Kate Brown and Jamie McKelvie. Marvel Enterprises 2014 112 p. Color illustration (Young Avengers)

Grades: 9 10 11 12 Adult   741.5
1. Comic books, strips, etc.; 2. Graphic novels; 3. Heroes; 4. Science fiction comic books, strips, etc.; 5. Superhero comic books, strips, etc.; 6. Fantasy fiction
0785167099; 9780785167099, $15.99

"Existential horror turns cosmic horror as something emerges from the shadows of the past...and it seems that the Young Avengers have one more thing to worry about. The team races desperately across the multi-verse in pursuit of their missing friend, but their road trip goes crazy as it reaches its destination." (Publisher's note)

"As with the previous one, this slim volume is a quick read with snappy dialogue and fast, cleanly depicted action that pops with cinematic digital coloring effects." Booklist

Contains material originally published as Young Avengers (2013) #6-10

Gilson, Che

Avigon: Gods & Demons. writer, Che Gilson; artist, Jimmie Robinson. Image Comics 2005 un Illustration

Grades: 10 11 12 Adult   741.5; Fic
1. Fantasy graphic novels; 2. Graphic novels
1-58240-503-4, $19.95

Avigon, a clockwork creation, has to escape, her mechanical world is killing her very soul. The sky is black with acrid smoke, the rivers run slick with oil, and bizarre clockwork creatures roam the streets. Above it all, eccentric and power-hungry politicians and egomaniacal clockwork masters govern with stone cold hearts. But how can Avigon escape a surreal world of machines where she herself is one? Her desperate search will lead her to the darkest regions of humanity and to the arms of her destiny. The book includes some violence.

Gipi

Notes for a war story. translated by Spectrum. First Second Books 2007 126p. Illustration

Grades: 10 11 12 Adult   741.5; Fic
1. Crime — Graphic novels; 2. Graphic novels; 3. War — Graphic novels
978-1-59643-261-1, $16.95

LC 2006-49716

Giuliano, a loner among outsiders, is one of three young drifters caught up in the whirlwind of a war in the Balkans. The three boys are like passing shadows; they live in abandoned houses, dodge the occasional bomb, and steal car parts for money. Meeting Felix — a powerful, fast-talking mercenary — changes everything for them. Felix is an expert manipulator; he speaks to their ambition and to their desires for power, wealth, and purpose. They're instantly hooked, especially the trio's unofficial leader, Stefano, and they soon escalate from petty crime to working on behalf of a mafia-style militia, bullying and extorting money in

Felix's name. But as Giuliano comes to realize, they don't know what they're fighting for — if they're even fighting for anything. There's some naturally occurring violence and harsh language.

Original Italian edition, 2004

Gladstone, Brooke

★ The **influencing** machine: Brooke Gladstone on the media. illustrated by Josh Neufeld; with additional penciling by Randy Jones and Susann Ferris-Jones.. W. W. Norton 2011 xxii, 170p Illustration; Color
Grades: Adult   302.23
1. Gladstone, Brooke — Comic books, strips, etc.; 2. Mass media; 3. Journalism; 4. Broadcast journalism
0393077799, $23.95; 9780393077797, $16.95

LC 2011009820

This work of graphic nonfiction explores the "history of media's influence.... [F]rom the 'Acta Diurna' posted in ancient Rome to the outcries over President Adams's Alien and Sedition Acts and McCarthy's Red Scare, [Brooke] Gladstone traces not only the birth of the press, but also its various muzzles. The press will not always stay silent, as she illustrates with Daniel Ellsberg and the Pentagon Papers.... Yet government opacity still abounds, and Gladstone pointedly wonders if secrecy really makes us safer.... Gladstone points to seven key biases that cognizant media consumers should worry about: commercial, bad news, status quo, access, visual, narrative, and fairness. These dovetail...into a...discussion of war journalism." (Publishers Weekly)

Includes bibliographical references (p. 163-170).

Glidden, Sarah

How to understand Israel in 60 days or less. writer & artist, Sarah Glidden; letterer Clem Robins. Vertigo/DC Comics 2010 206p. Illustration; Map
Grades: 11 12 Adult   915.694; 741.5
1. Glidden, Sarah — Travel — Comic books, strips, etc.; 2. Taglit—Birthright Israel (Organization) — Comic books, strips, etc.; 3. Americans — Israel — Comic books, strips, etc.; 4. Israel — Description and travel — Comic books, strips, etc.; 5. Israel — History — Comic books, strips, etc.; 6. Graphic novels
978-1-4012-2233-8, $24.99; 9781401222345, $19.99

This book "is Sarah [Glidden]'s memoir not only of her Israeli governmentsponsored trip through Tel Aviv, Jerusalem, the Golan Heights, Masada and other famous locations, but of the emotional journey she never expected to take while she was there. Her experience clashes with her preconceived notions again and again, particularly when she tries to take a non-chaperoned trip into the West Bank. Sarah is forced to question first her political beliefs and, ultimately, her own sense of identity." (Publisher's note)

Rolling Blackouts: Dispatches From Turkey, Syria and Iraq. Sarah Glidden. Drawn & Quarterly 2016 304 p. Color illustration; Color; Map
Grades: Adult   070.4; Fic
1. Foreign news — Comic books, strips, etc.; 2. Journalism — Comic books, strips, etc.; 3. Glidden, Sarah — Travel — Middle East — Comic books, strips, etc.
1770462554; 9781770462557, $24.95

For this graphic novel, author "Sarah Glidden accompanies her two friends — reporters and founders of a journalism non-profit — as they research potential stories on the effects of the Iraq War on the Middle East and, specifically, the war's refugees. Joining the trio is a childhood friend and former Marine whose past service in Iraq adds an unexpected and sometimes unwelcome viewpoint, both to the people they come across and perhaps even themselves." (Publisher's note)

Goetzinger, Annie

Girl in dior. Annie Goetzinger; translation by Joe Johnson; lettering by Ortho. NBM Pub. 2015 128 p. Color; Illustration
Grades: 9 10 11 12 Adult
741.5
1. Fashion designers; 2. Fashion design; 3. Dior, Christian, 1905-1957
1561639141; 9781561639144, $27.99

LC 2014956278

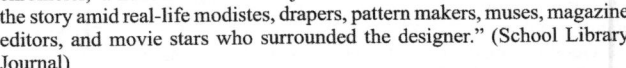

This book, by Annie Goetzinger, "covers the 1947 groundbreaking first fashion show put on by designer Christian Dior.... We watch the magic happen through the eyes of Clara Nohant, a young 'fashion chronicler,' a fictional character injected into

Courtesy of NBM Publishing

the story amid real-life modistes, drapers, pattern makers, muses, magazine editors, and movie stars who surrounded the designer." (School Library Journal)

"Goetzinger's detailed, expressive faces and figures seem to be illuminated from within, and the garments themselves are a great tribute to the author's background in fashion illustration." Booklist

Initially published in French as Jeune fille en Dior

Goldsmith, Francisca

★ The **readers'** advisory guide to graphic novels. Francisca Goldsmith. ALA Editions, an imprint of the American Library Association 2017 xvi, 215 p.
Grades: Adult Professional
025.2
1. Graphic novels — Bibliography; 2. Libraries — Special collections — Graphic novels; 3. Readers' advisory services — United States
0838915094; 9780838915097, $54

LC 2016042034

Goldsmith "presents a readers' advisory guide to graphic novels. She discusses the key qualities of graphic novels and the characteristics of its readers; basic readers'

Courtesy of the American Library Association

advisory methods, with reference to the graphic novel format; tips for working with adults and teens experienced or not experienced with the format; working with teens who are becoming self-aware; reading development, interests, and advisory methods for children; materials by interest, topic, and age group; multimedia aspects; and professional tools." (Publisher's note)

"This is a book to spend time with, not flip through, although a strong index and table of contents make it easily consultable for patron interactions as well." VOYA

Includes bibliographical references and index

Goldstein, Nancy

★ **Jackie** Ormes: the first African American woman cartoonist. University of Michigan Press 2008 225p. Illustration
Grades: 10 11 12 Adult   92; 741.5
1. African American women — Biography; 2. Cartoonists; 3. Ormes, Jackie, 1911-1985
978-0-472-11624-9, $35; 0-472-11624-X

LC 2007-35395

This book covers the life and career of Jackie Ormes, who was the first African American woman cartoonist. She wrote and drew comic strips that ran in Black newspapers such as the Pittsburgh Courier and the Chicago Defender. She was part of the Black elite in Chicago and knew other luminaries such as singer Eartha Kitt and musician/composer/conductor Duke Ellington. She was also investigated by the FBI because of her Leftist political ideas and activities. While she did such things as create Torchy paper dolls, based on her beautiful and sexy cartoon character, and cute Patty-Jo dolls, Ormes also used her comic strips to put forth her political views. This book reproduces some of her cartoons and comic strips, in both black and white and in color.

Includes bibliographical references

Goldstein, Sophie

House of women. Sophie Goldstein. Fantagraphics Books, Inc. 2017 200 p. Illustration
Grades: Adult   **741.5; Fic**
1. Women — Fiction; 2. Science fiction graphic novels
9781683960515, $29.99
                                    LC 2017938233

In this graphic novel, by Sophie Goldstein, "science fiction meets psychosexual drama when four women try to bring 'civilization' to the natives of a remote planet on the fringes of the known universe. Something dark is growing in Mopu. The only question is whether the danger that will undo the women's delicate camaraderie is outside the gates? Or within." (Publisher's note)

"Goldstein's fluid black-and-white art, echoing illustration styles from European woodcuts to Japanese hell scrolls, is a far cry from the attempted realism of most science fiction comics. It gives the story a fairy tale's sublimated horrors and unpredictable psychic depths." Pub Wkly

The **oven**. by Sophie Goldstein. Adhouse Books 2015 80 p. Color; Illustration
Grades: Adult
741.5
1. Dystopias — Comic books, strips, etc; 2. Dystopian fiction
1935233335; 9781935233336, $12.95
                                    LC 2015270630
Ignatz Award: Outstanding Graphic Novel (2015)

Courtesy of AdHouse Books

In this book, by Sophie Goldstein, "Ozone depletion and dwindling resources have driven the human race into domed cities where population controls are strictly enforced. When a young couple goes looking for an anti-government paradise in the desert they may have found more than they bargained for." (Publisher's note)

Gonick, Larry

The **cartoon** guide to statistics. {by} Larry Gonick & Woollcott Smith; {il. by Larry Gonick}. HarperPerennial 1993 230 p. Illustration
Grades: Adult   **741.5; 519.5**
1. Statistics
0062731025; 9780062731029, $17.99
                                    LC 92054683
This book, by Larry Gonick and Woollcott Smith, "covers all the central ideas of modern statistics: the summary and display of data, probability in gambling and medicine, random variables, Bernoulli Trials, the Central Limit Theorem, hypothesis testing, confidence interval estimation, and much more — all explained in simple, clear, and yes, funny illustrations." (Publisher's note)
Includes bibliographical references (p. 221-223) and index

★ The **cartoon** history of the modern world: Part 1: from Columbus to the U.S. Constitution. Collins 2007 259p. Illustration
Grades: 9 10 11 12 Adult   **741.5; 909.08**
1. Graphic novels; 2. Modern history — Graphic novels
978-0-06-076004-5; 0-06-076004-4, $17.95
                                    LC 2006-49146
The book begins with a "15-page distillation of pre-Columbian America; and while Europe and North America receive most of the attention, Gonick does include at least some highlights from other parts of the world. Covering such topics as the Protestant Reformation, the British defeat of the Spanish Armada, the Copernican model of the universe, and the American Revolution, he writes and draws with considerable wit and authority, and is obviously well versed in his subject." SLJ
Followed by:The Cartoon History of the Modern World Part 2: From the Bastille to Baghdad (2009)

★ The **cartoon** history of the modern world. Part II: From the Bastille to Baghdad. Larry Gonick. Harper 2009 260 p.
Grades: Adult   **909.080; 909.0802/07**
1. Modern history — Graphic novels
0060760087; 9780060760083, $23.99
                                    LC 2006049146
This graphic novel, by Larry Gonick, part of the "Cartoon History" series, "opens with the Enlightenment and rolls across Napoleon, the fall of the Ottoman Empire, World War I and II, and all the way to our recent imbroglios in Iraq and Afghanistan." (Publisher's note)
Includes bibliographical references and indexes

★ The **Cartoon** History of the Universe Volumes 1-7: From the Big Bang to Alexander the Great. Main Street Books/Doubleday & Co. 1990 368p. Illustration
Grades: 9 10 11 12 Adult   **741.5; 902.07**
1. Graphic novels; 2. World history — Graphic novels
0-385-26520-4, $22.95; 9780385265201
                                    LC 02-288002
Gonick presents a quick tour of world history, starting from the Big Bang through the life of Alexander the Great. He presents facts in the text, while his illustrations provide an irreverently humorous counterpoint. There's partial nudity with some of the ancient people.

★ The **Cartoon** History of the Universe Volumes 8-13: From the Springtime of China to the Fall of Rome. Main Street Books/Doubleday & Co. 1994 305p. Illustration
Grades: 9 10 11 12 Adult   **741.5; 902.07; 902**
1. Graphic novels; 2. World history — Graphic novels
0-385-42093-5, $22.95
                                    LC 02-288002
Gonick presents a quick tour of world history, continuing with Alexander the Great's march to India (and his about-face), focusing on India and China, then going back to Rome and covering the Western World through the end of Justinian's reign, around 564 A.D. He also tells the story of Jeshua ben Joseph (Jesus). He presents facts in the text, while his illustrations provide an irreverently humorous counterpoint. There's partial nudity and some violence with the depictions of wars and battles.

★ The **Cartoon** History of the Universe III: From the Rise of Arabia to the Renaissance. W. W. Norton 2002 300p. Illustration
Grades: 9 10 11 12 Adult   **741.5; 909.07**
1. Graphic novels; 2. World history — Graphic novels
0-393-32403-6, $21.95
                                    LC 02-288002
This volume begins in the year 395, covers the birth of Islam, the Crusades, the Asian and African nations, the Mongol conquests, the Ottoman Empire, the Black Death, the Italian Renaissance, the rise of

Spain, and culminates in the year 1492. The facts in the text are accompanied again by his irreverently humorous illustrations.

★ The **cartoon** history of the United States. Larry Gonick. HarperPerennial 1991 392 p.

Grades: Adult   **973/.0207; 973.020**

1. United States — History — Comic books, strips, etc; 2. United States — History — Graphic novels

0062730983 ($9.95); 9780062730985, $17.99

LC 91055037

This graphic novel about the history of the United States, by Larry Gonick, is part of the "Cartoon Guide" series. "From the first English colonies to the Gulf War and the S&L debacle, Larry Gonick spells it all out from his unique cartoon perspective." (Publisher's note)

Includes index.

Goodwin, Michael

Economix: how and why our economy works (and doesn't work) in words and pictures. Michael Goodwin. Harry N. Abrams Inc. 2012 304 p. Illustration

Grades: 11 12 Adult   **330**

1. Economics — Comic books, strips, etc; 2. Economic development; 3. Cost and standard of living

9780810988392, $19.95

LC 2011052119

Author Michael Goodwin discusses the economy, "human nature and our attempts to make the most of what we've got...and sometimes what our neighbors have got...[The book explains concepts from] the beginning of Western economic thought, to markets free and otherwise, to economic failures, successes, limitations, and future possibilities." (Publisher's note)

"This dense yet readable exegesis makes economics entertaining despite current financial shenanigans worldwide. Goodwin takes a chronological approach, starting with the history of banking in the 17th century. As he marches through four centuries of economic theories and theorists, he attempts to show what happened, what succeeded, and what went wrong in terms of both public and private good, with a focus on the reasons particular theories didn't pan out in real life." LJ

Includes bibliographical references and index

Gorman, Michele

Getting graphic!: comics for kids. with a foreword by Jeff Smith; and original comic art by Jimmy Gownley. Linworth Books 2007 84p. Illustration

Grades: Adult Professional   **741.5**

1. Graphic novels — Bibliography; 2. Graphic novels — History and criticism

978-1-58683-327-5, $24.95

LC 2007-35033

Gorman presents annotated bibliographies of recommended graphic novels for children ages 6-12 to help librarians develop a quality, age-appropriate graphic novel collection that includes fiction, nonfiction, and manga. Amelia Rules! creator Jimmy Gownley created a comic story featuring his characters, just for this book. The book entries include the title, author, year of publication, publisher, ISBNs (both 10-digit and 13-digit), an annotation, and an age range recommendation. Gorman provides series annotations for series published by Capstone, Stone Arch, Rosen, Lerner, and other educational publishers.

Includes glossary and bibliographical references

Goscinny, Rene

Asterix and Caesar's Gift. Orion/Sterling Publishing 2004 48p. Illustration

Grades: 4 5 6 7 8 9 10 11 12 Adult   **741.5; Fic**

1. Asterix (Fictional character); 2. Graphic novels; 3. Humorous graphic novels

0-75286-645-1, $12.95; 0-75286-646-X (pa)

When Legionary Tremensdelirius gets the title deeds to the little Gaulish village as a bonus, he swaps them with tavern landlord Orthopaedix for a drink. Funnily enough, Asterix and his friends aren't keen to hand over their village to anyone else. After a chieftaincy election campaign and a showdown with the Romans, both events fiercely contested, can all still end well?

Asterix and Cleopatra. Orion/Sterling Publishing 2004 48p. Illustration

Grades: 4 5 6 7 8 9 10 11 12 Adult   **741.5; Fic**

1. Asterix (Fictional character); 2. Graphic novels; 3. Humorous graphic novels

0-75286-606-0, $12.95; 0-75286-607-9 (pb)

How can lovely Queen Cleopatra show Julius Caesar that ancient Egypt is still a great nation? Her architect Edifis recruits his Gaulish friends to help him build a magnificent palace within three months. There are villainous saboteurs to be outwitted, but Asterix, Obelix, and Getafix still find time to go sight-seeing, and leave their mark on the Pyramids and the Sphinx's nose.

Asterix and the Banquet. Orion/Sterling Publishing 2004 48p. Illustration

Grades: 4 5 6 7 8 9 10 11 12 Adult   **741.5; Fic**

1. Asterix (Fictional character); 2. Graphic novels; 3. Humorous graphic novels

0-75286-608-0, $12.95; 0-75286-609-5 (pa)

When the Romans try to contain the threat from the Gaulish village by building a stockade around it, Asterix and Obelix lay a bet with them. They will break out and claim their right to travel freely all over Gaul, collecting the local delicacies and bringing them back to prove their point. Ham from Lutetia, fizzy wine from Durocortorum, fish stew from Massilia in the south...soon their shopping bag is full. Outwitting Romans, a couple of treacherous Gauls, and the thieves Villanus and Unscrupulus, they set off for home...but who's that little dog who has been following them all the way from Lutetia?

Asterix and the Cauldron. Orion/Sterling Publishing 2004 48p. Illustration

Grades: 4 5 6 7 8 9 10 11 12 Adult   **741.5; Fic**

1. Asterix (Fictional character); 2. Graphic novels; 3. Humorous graphic novels

0-75286-629-X, $9.95

There's financial skulduggery in ancient Gaul. When local Chief Whosemoralsarelastix wants a cauldron full of money kept out of Roman hands, the cash disappears while Asterix is guarding it. He and Obelix must earn enough to repay it through fairground gladiatorial contests, trendy theatrical performances, even bank robbery — they'll try anything. But whose morals are really elastic? And how to the pirates, just for once, get an unexpected bonus?

Asterix and the Class Act. Orion/Sterling Publishing 2004 56p. Illustration

Grades: 4 5 6 7 8 9 10 11 12 Adult   **741.5; Fic**

1. Asterix (Fictional character); 2. Graphic novels; 3. Humorous graphic novels

0-75286-068-2, $12.95; 0-75286-640-0 (pa)

This volume collects 14 stories, including the day Asterix and Obelix were born (in the middle of a fish fight); how Obelix goes back to school; fashion in ancient Gaul; how Dogmatix helps the village cockerel win a duel, and how he's adopted as a Roman mascot; Obelix's adventures under the mistletoe; the bid for the very first Gaulish Olympics, and more.

Asterix and the Laurel Wreath. Orion/Sterling Publishing 2004 48p. Illustration

Grades: 4 5 6 7 8 9 10 11 12 Adult   **741.5; Fic**
1. Asterix (Fictional character); 2. Graphic novels; 3. Humorous graphic novels
0-75286-636-2, $12.95; 0-75286-637-0 (pa)

Chief Vitalstatistix rashly invites his brother-in-law to dine on a stew seasoned with Caesar's laurel wreath, so Asterix and Obelix must to go Rome to fetch those laurels. Hoping to get access to Caesar, they sell themselves as slaves, but can they do a deal with the corrupt Goldendelicius to swap the laurels for parsley?

Asterix in Britain. Orion/Sterling Publishing 2004 48p. Illustration
Grades: 4 5 6 7 8 9 10 11 12 Adult   **741.5; Fic**
1. Asterix (Fictional character); 2. Graphic novels; 3. Humorous graphic novels
0-85286-618-4, $12.95; 0-75286-619-2 (pa)

The Romans have invaded Britain, but one village still holds out. Asterix and Obelix come to help, with a barrel of magic potion in hand. But to deliver the precious brew, the Gaulish heroes must face fog, rain, bad food, warm beer, and the Romans too.

Asterix the Legionary. Orion/Sterling Publishing 2004 48p. Illustration

Grades: 4 5 6 7 8 9 10 11 12 Adult   **741.5; Fic**
1. Asterix (Fictional character); 2. Graphic novels; 3. Humorous graphic novels
0-75286-620-6, $12.95; 0-75286-621-4 (pa)

It's off to the wars for Asterix and Obelix: they've enlisted as legionnaires in order to rescue Tragicomix, whom the Romans forcibly conscripted. The two find Tragicomix and succeed in causing the biggest commotion ever on a battlefield.

Gossett, Christian

King Kong: The 8th Wonder of the World. Dark Horse Books 2006 un Illustration

Grades: 7 8 9 10 11 12 Adult   **741.5; Fic**
1. Graphic novels; 2. King Kong (Fictional character); 3. Science fiction graphic novels
978-1-59307-472-2, $12.95

Director Carl Denham has one chance to make the film of his dreams — hire an unknown actress, kidnap his writer and board a tramp freighter for the mysterious Island of the Skull. But when hostile natives capture actress Ann Darrow, Denham and his crew will face horrors from giant spiders to bloodthirsty dinosaurs to get her back. Yet, nothing can prepare them for the revelation of the mighty wonder in whose clutches Ann truly remains — King Kong. This story adapts the screenplay for the motion picture directed by Peter Jackson, which is based on the original story by Merian C. Cooper and Edgar Wallace.

Grace, Sina

Not My Bag. written and illustrated by Sina Grace; design, S. Steven Struble. Image Comics 2012 96 p. Illustration
Grades: Adult   **741.5**
1. Fashion — Fiction; 2. Gay men — Fiction; 3. Retail trade — Fiction; 4. Identity (Psychology) — Fiction
1607065975; 9781607065975, $12.99

"[Sina] Grace draws upon his experience in retail to craft a graphic novel that gives us a window into the life of an artist who is forced to take a job he doesn't really want in order to pay the bills." It presents both a "celebration of fashion...and the introspection of the artist as he looks back

on the relationships that have served to define him.... The protagonist's reliance on his partner's understanding and support gets him through the retail ordeal." (Publishers Weekly)

Graham, Brandon

★ **Prophet** 1. story, Brandon Graham [et al.]; art, Simon Roy [et al.]; colors, Richard Ballermann [et al.]; letters, Ed Brisson.. Image Comics 2012 136 p.
Grades: Adult   **741.5**
1. Adventure fiction; 2. Extraterrestrial beings — Fiction; 3. Soldiers — Fiction
1607066114; 9781607066118, $9.99

"John Prophet, a super soldier who awakes in the future's future after being kept in cryo-sleep beneath the Earth's surface, is ready for his mission. Prophet makes his way through an Earth that has been overrun by squabbling alien tribes living among the rusted debris of Earth's past." (Publishers Weekly)

Originally published in single magazine form as Prophet #21-26.; Volume 1 of 4

★ **Prophet** 3: Empire. by Brandon Graham; illustrated by Simon Roy; Giannis Milonogiannis, Malachi Ward, Matt Sheean. Image Comics 2014 128 p. Color; Illustration
Grades: Adult   **741.5**
1. Science fiction comic books, strips, etc.; 2. Science fiction
1607068583; 9781607068587, $14.99

"The Earth Empire is now rebuilt and gaining a stronger grasp on Earthspace. Facing an even more menacing new threat, Old Man Prophet and his team look for the help of an old ally." (Publisher's note)

"Prophet was originally created by Rob Liefeld in 1992 for Image's 'Youngblood' series, and far-future versions of other Image characters from that time appear here — but no knowledge of them is necessary to appreciate the worldbuilding present. Each artist on the series follows a different set of characters, illustrating only scenes featuring them, and each one renders amazing scientific visions — living starships, grotesque genetically engineered posthumans, truly alien aliens, and all manner of organic technology — with exceptional vividness." LJ

Collects PROPHET #32 & 34-38

★ **Prophet**; 2: Brothers. story by Brandon Graham and Simon Roy; art by Simon Roy, Farel Dalrymple, Giannis Milonogiannis, and Brandom Graham. Image Comics 2013 172 p. Color; Illustration
Grades: Adult   **741.5**
1. Graphic novels; 2. Prophecies — Fiction; 3. War stories
1607067498; 9781607067498, $14.99

"The distant future war continues! Old man Prophet is awake now and searching across the universe for old allies that have survived the centuries since the last war." (Publisher's note)

Collects PROPHET #27-31 and 33

Gran, Meredith

Octopus Pie 1. by Meredith Gran. Image Comics 2016 200 p.
Grades: 11 12 Adult   **741.5**
1. Brooklyn (New York, N.Y.) — Fiction; 2. Roommates — Fiction; 3. College graduates — Fiction
1632156326; 9781632156327, $14.99

In this graphic novel, by Meredith Gran, collecting part of her long-running webcomic, "we follow grumpy twenty-something Eve and her stoner roommate Hanna as they navigate post-college life. They'll take on crazed childhood rivals, troubling art scenes, the discomfort of exes, and maybe even... friendship? All this and more in the fictional, totally made-up city of Brooklyn." (Publisher's note)

Volume 1 of 5

Gravett, Paul

Graphic novels: everything you need to know. Collins Design 2005 192p. Illustration

Grades: Adult Professional   **741.5**

1. Graphic novels — History and criticism

0-06-082425-5; 978-0-06-082425-9, $24.95

"Selecting 30 highly recommended works from many countries...[the author] groups them in separate chapters by theme (childhood, fantasy, crime, sex, superheroes) and devotes a two-page spread to each work, presenting sample pages and discussing them in annotations.... This is a genuinely substantial contribution to the growing literature on graphic novels." Libr J

Includes bibliographical references

Manga: Sixty Years of Japanese Comics. Harper Design International/HarperCollins 2004 176p. Illustration

Grades: Adult Professional   **741.5**

1. Graphic novels; 2. Manga

1-85669-391-0, $24.95

This book presents an accessible and highly-illustrated introduction to the development and diversity of Japanese comics from 1945 to the present. Featuring graphics and extracts from a wide range of manga, the book covers such themes as the specific attributes of manga in contrast to American and European comics; the life and career of Osamu Tezuka, creator of Astro Boy and originator of story manga; boys' comics from the 1960s to the present; the genres and genders of girls' and women's comics; the darker, more realistic themes of gekiga " violent samurai, disturbing horror and apocalyptic science fiction; issues of censorship and protest; and manga's role as a major Japanese export and global influence. Some illustrations from the more adult manga show nudity and sexual situations, as well as violence.

Gray, Harold

★**Harold** Gray's Little Orphan Annie; Volume one: the complete daily comics, 1924-27: Will tomorrow ever come? IDW Publishing 2008 385p. Illustration

Grades: 2 3 4 5 6 7 8 9 10 11 12 Adult

741.5; Fic

1. Adventure graphic novels; 2. Graphic novels; 3. Little Orphan Annie (Fictional character); 4. Orphans — Graphic novels

978-1-60010-140-3, $39.99

Courtesy of IDW Publishing

Little Orphan Annie started as a daily newspaper comic strip in one newspaper, the New York Daily News, on August 5, 1924. It became a popular strip, syndicated to newspapers all over the world. It eventually became a Broadway, a hit movie, and Annie became an iconic character. This book is the first comprehensive collection of Gray's comic strip and is the first volume of a series planned to collect all of Gray's Little Orphan Annie strips. She is an orphan girl living in an orphanage, with an unscrupulous director who hires Annie out for work. When wealthy Mrs. Warbucks, trying to prove that she cares for the poor, takes Annie on a "trial" adoption, Annie eventually meets Oliver Warbucks, whom she calls "Daddy." As the strips go on, Annie undergoes many hardships and perils, facing everything with spunk and a positive attitude. She's no wilting girl, though " she can fight (she has a mean right hook) and will take on any bully. She rescues the dog she calls Sandy, who rewards her with a loyal friendship. This volume includes more than 1,000 comic strips, many of which haven't seen publication since their original newspaper appearance. During the first years of the strip's publication, the color Sunday comics

had no connection to the weekday storylines, but a few Sunday pages are included in this book. This book may appeal most to adults who remember reading Little Orphan Annie in the "funnies" pages, but the stories will appeal to all ages. Contributing Editor Jeet Heer provides a biography of Harold Gray.

Gray, Justin

Jonah Hex: Guns of Vengeance. writers Justin Gray and Jimmy Palmiotti; art Luke Ross. DC Comics 2007 144p. Illustration

Grades: 11 12 Adult   **741.5; Fic**

1. Adventure graphic novels; 2. Graphic novels; 3. Supernatural graphic novels; 4. Western graphic novels

978-1-4012-1249-0, $12.99

Jonah Hex, a mysterious bounty hunter and thinking man's killer, was a hero to some and a villain to others — and his name was spoken in whispers. He had no friends, but he did have two companions: one was death and the other... the smell of gun smoke. Haunted by the ghosts of his past, present, and future, the bullets fly as Jonah Hex battles bounty hunters, vengeful spirits, alligators, and sideshow freaks. This Western is full of graphic violence, harsh language, and some sexual situations and nudity.

★ **Power** girl: a new beginning. Justin Gray & Jimmy Palmiotti, writers; Amanda Conner, artist and covers; Paul Mounts, colorist; John J. Hill, letterer. DC Comics 2010 un Illustration

Grades: 9 10 11 12 Adult   **741.5; Fic**

1. Graphic novels; 2. Superhero graphic novels

978-1-4012-2618-3, $17.99

Kara Zor-L came from Krypton, just like her very famous cousin Kal-L, who became Superman, but she had lived in a parallel universe, known as Earth 2. Since then, she has come to this world's New York City and started all over again as Karen Starr and reopening her business, a progressive technology company called Starrware Labs. She's also Power Girl, since she has many of Superman's superpowers. Before she can get Starrware Labs fully up and running with all essential positions filled, she has to deal with a horde of fear-inducing robots sent by the Ultra-Humanite to destroy Manhattan. Then, a trio of party-crashing aliens and their pursuer start wrecking the rest of Manhattan as they fight in the streets. The book has lots of action but no really graphic violence, and some "fan service" as it's called in manga there are some panty shots, and Karen/Power Girl deals with men staring at her bust. Her costume has a cutout design on the chest, which the writers and artist treat with some great humor. Co-writer Palmiotti and artist Conner are a couple themselves, and their close work shows in sheer fun of this book.

Grayson, Devin

Nightwing: Mobbed Up. DC Comics 2006 128p. Illustration

Grades: 10 11 12 Adult   **741.5; Fic**

1. Graphic novels; 2. Nightwing (Fictional character); 3. Superhero graphic novels

978-1-4012-0907-0, $12.99

Injured and dejected, cut off from all allegiances, Dick Grayson decides to turn his misery into an advantage and a new purpose. He arranges to be adopted into one of New York City's crime families. In doing so he begins a new odyssey, one that sweeps him into the depths of the criminal underworld. Try as he may, however, he can't put his crime-fighting alter ego behind him forever, so Nightwing returns. But which side is he on? There's some violence, but despite the mob, little in the way of harsh language.

Nightwing: Renegade. DC Comics 2006 144p. Illustration

Grades: 9 10 11 12 Adult   **741.5; Fic**

1. Graphic novels; 2. Nightwing (Fictional character); 3. Superhero graphic novels; 4. Robin (Fictional character)
978-1-4012-0908-7, $14.99

Once he was Robin, but Dick Grayson stepped out from the shadow of the Bat to become his own hero, Nightwing. Now the events of the past year have taken a heavy toll on Dick, and he's seemingly embraced the darkness within himself. He's got a new costume, a new name — Renegade — and he serves a new master. But could Nightwing really be working for Deathstroke, the deadly assassin and his longtime nemesis? As Renegade takes Deathstroke's daughter Ravager under his wing, the two old enemies will play a dangerous game of cat and mouse. But who's manipulating whom, and what do these two brilliant minds really want from each other? Just when Nightwing thinks he has it all figured out, Deathstroke makes a move so shocking, Nightwing's world will never be the same. There's plenty of action, but little overt violence or harsh language.

Green, Justin
Binky Brown meets the holy Virgin Mary. Justin Green. McSweeney's Books 2009 63 p. Illustration
Grades: Adult   **741.5**
1. Underground comic books, strips, etc.; 2. Catholic Church
9781934781555, $29; 193478155X

LC 2014427888

"A lost classic of underground cartooning, Binky Brown Meets the Holy Virgin Mary is Justin Green's autobiographical portrayal of his struggle with religion and his own neuroses. Binky Brown is a young Catholic battling all the usual problems of adolescence, puberty, parents, and the fear that the strange ray of energy emanating from his private parts will strike a picture of the Virgin Mary." (Publisher's note)

"This Rosetta Stone of autobiographical comics — or perhaps more appropriately, in this case, 'confessional' comics — receives the deluxe treatment it so richly deserves with this beautiful over-sized edition featuring art reproduced directly from the original pages." Pub Wkly

Green, Katie
Lighter than my shadow. Katie Green. Lion Forge 2017 505 p. Illustration
Grades: 9 10 11 12 Adult   **92; 741.5**
1. Eating disorders; 2. Graphic novels; 3. Autobiographical graphic novels; 4. Eating disorders — Graphic novels
1941302416; 9781941302415, $19.99

LC 2013432027

This book, by Katie Green, is "a graphic memoir of eating disorders, abuse and recovery. Like most kids, Katie was a picky eater. She'd sit at the table in silent protest, hide uneaten toast in her bedroom, listen to parental threats that she'd have to eat it for breakfast. But in any life a set of circumstance can collide, and normal behavior might soon shade into something sinister, something deadly. One day you can find yourself being told you have two weeks to live." (Publisher's note)

"Minimal dialogue and narration keep the focus on Green's grayscale artwork, which viscerally reflects how Green saw herself while in the grips of her eating disorder.... As the story moves into Green's college years and beyond, she finds balance amid many setbacks but never sugarcoats the difficult and ongoing nature of recovery." Pub Wkly

First published in 2013 by Jonathan Cape, an imprint of Vintage

Greenberg, Isabel
The **encyclopedia** of early earth: a novel. Isabel Greenberg. Little, Brown and Co. 2013 176 p.
Grades: 10 11 12 Adult   **741.5; Fic**
1. Earth — Fiction; 2. Fables; 3. Travel — Fiction
0316225819; 9780316225816, $23

LC 2013939419

Author Isabel Greenberg presents a "series of illustrated and linked tales [which] chronicles the explorations of a young man as he paddles from his home in the North Pole to the South Pole. There, he meets his true love, but their romance is ill-fated. Early Earth's unusual and finicky polarity means the lovers can never touch." (Publisher's note)

"Greenberg deeply immerses readers in the themes and lessons of world mythology, but she remarkably never merely apes classic myths-the way each of Early Earth's cultures tweaks the same ideas and characters for their own myths is a veritable lesson in comparative theology." Booklist

★ The **one** hundred nights of hero: a graphic novel. Isabel Greenberg. Little, Brown & Co. 2016 224 p. Color; Illustration
Grades: Adult   **741.5**
1. Storytelling — Graphic novels; 2. Lesbians — Comic books, strips, etc.; 3. Imaginary places — Comic books, strips, etc.
0316259179; 9780316259170, $25

LC 2016948560

In this book, by Isabel Greenberg, "Jerome, a wicked man..., makes a diabolical wager with his friend Manfred: if Manfred can seduce Cherry in one hundred nights, he can have his castle — and Cherry. But what Jerome doesn't know is that Cherry is in love with her maid Hero. The two women hatch a plan: Hero, a member of the League of Secret Story Tellers, will distract Manfred by regaling him with a mesmerizing tale each night for 100 nights, keeping him at bay." (Publisher's note)

"Greenberg combines elements from fairy tales, children's books, and folklore from around the world to create an original but teasingly familiar mythos. Above all, it's a book about the power of storytelling, populating Early Earth with a secret society of storytellers, a grove of memory trees, and women treasuring literacy in defiance of a stern bird god." Pub Wkly

Grell, Mike
The **Complete** Jon Sable, Freelance Volume 1. IDW Publishing 2005 180p. Illustration
Grades: 10 11 12 Adult   **741.5; Fic**
1. Adventure graphic novels; 2. Graphic novels
1-932382-77-1, $24.99

The initial 54-page story guest-stars Ronald Reagan, and the second is Sable's famous 108-page origin saga. Sable is a mercenary willing to act as a private eye or bodyguard if the money is right and the job promises excitement. The origin story depicts how he became that way after his family was massacred. There's lots of fighting action and bloodshed in this story, originally published by First Comics in the early 1980s.

Griffith, Bill
Invisible Ink: My Mother's Love Affair With a Famous Cartoonist. by Bill Griffith. W W Norton & Co Inc 2015 208 p. Illustration
Grades: Adult   **741.5973; 741.5**
1. Mother-son relationship; 2. Parent-child relationship; 3. Cartoonists — Graphic novels
1606998951; 9781606998953, $29.99

LC 2015937719

Eisner Nominee: Best Reality-Based Work (2016)

This book, a memoir by Bill Griffith, "uncovers his mother's secret life which included an affair with a cartoonist and crime novelist in the 1950s and '60s.... Alternating between past and present,...Griffith recreates the quotidian habits of suburban Levittown and the professional and cultural life of mid-century Manhattan in the 1950s and '60s as seen through his mother's and his own teenage eyes." (Publisher's note)

Grillo-Marxuach, Javier
★ The **Middleman:** the collected series indispensability. Viper Comics 2008 336p. Illustration

Grades: 9 10 11 12 Adult   **741.5; Fic**
  1. Adventure graphic novels; 2. Graphic novels; 3. Humorous graphic novels; 4. Science fiction graphic novels
  978-0-9802385-4-9, $19.95

    This book collects all three volumes of The Middleman comics series. Art student Wendy Watson works as a temp agency hire, when one day she's working at a scientific laboratory where things go totally wrong and a mysterious guy who calls himself The Middleman takes care of the monsters. Unfortunately for Wendy, the cover story that a gas main explosion caused all the mess also indicates that her lucky Zippo lighter, the only thing she has from her long-missing father, ignited the gas leak. Unemployed Wendy soon finds herself recruited by the Jolly Fats Wehawkin Temp Agency, which is actually the cover for The Middleman and his henchperson, robotic Ida. Wendy soon finds herself battling intelligent apes out to rule the criminal underworld, crazy Lucha Libre wrestlers, and more "exotic problems," at the side of the enigmatic, super-good guy, The Middleman. The book includes some violence, some nudity, and some sexual innuendo. The series was adapted into a television series on ABC Family which ran for one season; the DVD boxed set is scheduled for a summer 2009 release.

Grine, Chris
  Chickenhare: fire in the hole. Dark Horse Comics 2008 200p. Illustration
Grades: 7 8 9 10 11 12 Adult   **741.5; Fic**
  1. Adventure graphic novels; 2. Fantasy graphic novels; 3. Graphic novels
  978-1-59307-907-9, $10.95

    Chickenhare, his friend Abe, and their new friends Scabby, Meg and Banjo managed to escape the evil Taxidermist Klaus, but they have gone from one dangerous situation into...something worse. While at sea in a small boat about to be swamped by rain and waves, Banjo's brother and some warriors from the Underworld pop up, they zap the soul out of Abe and take Banjo and Meg. Chickenhare is left with Scabby and Abe's body. He must venture into the Underworld to recover Abe's soul. Meanwhile, Banjo and Meg face punishment for deserting the Underworld. And just why do the Sea Folk call Chickenhare "Your Majesty"?

Grist, Paul
  Kane Vol. 1: Greetings from New Eden. Image Comics 2004 127p. Illustration
Grades: 10 11 12 Adult   **741.5; Fic**
  1. Graphic novels; 2. Mystery graphic novels
  1-58240-340-6, $11.95

    Detective Kane returns to active duty with the New Eden Police Dept. following a six month suspension after he shot and killed his partner Dennis Harvey. His fellow police officers give Kane a welcome back gift — a couple of bullets with his name engraved on them. Partnered with a new detective, Kate Felix, Kane soon finds out nothing has changed in the city of New Eden. In his first two days back, Kane has to deal with a siege, a kidnapping and a bomb attack. And then there's the Crime Boss of New Eden, Oscar Darke... The book includes some harsh language and violence.

  Kane Vol. 2: Rabbit Hunt. Image Comics 2004 un Illustration
Grades: 10 11 12 Adult   **741.5; Fic**
  1. Graphic novels; 2. Mystery graphic novels
  1-58240-355-4, $12.95

    It's a bad day for Mister Floppsie Whoppsie, New Eden's self-styled Rabbit for Hire. The freelance rabbit business isn't going as well as it should. He's hung over. The rent's due. There's a knock at the door and a gun-wielding homicidal maniac barges into the room. That's when things start to go downhill. And Detective Kane still can't trust anyone in the New

Eden Police Department. The book includes some strong language and violence.

  Kane Vol. 4: Thirty-Ninth. Image Comics 2005 un Illustration
Grades: 10 11 12 Adult   **741.5; Fic**
  1. Graphic novels; 2. Mystery graphic novels
  1-58240-468-2, $16.95

    When Detective Kane returned to active duty with the New Eden Police Dept. following a six-month suspension in the wake of shooting and killing his partner, his fellow police officers gave him a welcome back gift: a couple of bullets with his name on them. Now, a sniper is taking pot shots at the police. An ex-cop is looking to take revenge on the cop who turned him in. There's rioting in the streets and the Mayor's been kidnapped again. It's another typical week for the police in New Eden's Precinct 39. The book has some strong language and violence.

Groth, Gary
  The **complete** wimmen's comix. edited by Trina Robbins, Gary Groth, and J. Michael Catron. Fantagraphics Books 2015 728 p. Illustration
Grades: Adult   **741.5**
  1. Women cartoonists — History
  9781606998984, $100

                  LC 2015943981
Ignatz Award: Outstanding Anthology or Collection (2016); Eisner Award: Best Archival/Collection Project — Comic Books (2017)

    This book "collects two decades of the groundbreaking underground/alternative anthology Wimmen's Comix. In the late '60s, underground comix changed the way comics readers saw the medium " but there was an important pronoun missing from the revolution. In 1972, ten women cartoonists got together in San Francisco to rectify the situation and produce the first and longest-lasting all-woman comics anthology, Wimmen's Comix." (Publisher's note)

Grunwald, Jennifer
  Civil War: Marvel Universe. Marvel Entertainment 2007 un Illustration
Grades: 9 10 11 12 Adult   **741.5; Fic**
  1. Graphic novels; 2. Superhero graphic novels; 3. Daredevil (Fictional character)
  978-0-7851-2470-2, $11.99

    Civil War is encompassing the entire Marvel Universe, and the effects of the war are being felt by every hero, villain and civilian. In Civil War: Choosing Sides, five stories shine a spotlight on the wildcards and impact players whose part in the Civil War has yet to be told — including Daredevil/Iron Fist, U.S.Agent, the Irredeemable Ant-Man, Venom and even...Howard the Duck? On Earth, the Sentry confronts his inner demons as the shadows of past and future battles tear him apart. Within The Negative Zone, the walls of 42 are pulled back to reveal the return of one of the Marvel's greatest heroes. And in She-Hulk, Civil War threatens the rights of every American super hero. So whose side will Marvel's top superhuman lawyer fight for? And how can she possibly choose, when she feels one way as She-Hulk, and another as Jen Walters?

  I am Iron Man. edited by Jennifer Grunwald. Marvel Worldwide, Inc. 2010 un Illustration
Grades: 7 8 9 10 11 12 Adult   **741.5; Fic**
  1. Graphic novels; 2. Iron Man (Fictional character); 3. Superhero graphic novels
  978-0-7851-4558-5, $16.99

    The first Iron Man movie, released in 2008, was a major hit, but just like the other superhero movies based on Marvel Comics properties, it wasn't based on any particular Iron Man comics. This book collects a two-issue miniseries based on the movie script, written by Peter David with pencils by Sean Chen, a one-shot written by Christos Gage with pencils by Hugo Petrus, and Iron Man #200, which was written by Denny O'Neil with pencils by Mark Bright and originally published in 1985. David and Chen's comic adapts the movie script, hitting all the high points of the action. Gage and Petrus's one-shot, "Security Measures," looks at the action of the movie from the viewpoint of S.H.I.E.L.D. agent Coulson. Iron Man #200 features a battle between Iron Man and Iron Monger, who is Tony Stark's erstwhile partner Obadiah Stane. The book also includes an interview with Kevin Feige, producer of the Iron Man movie, and photos taken on the movie sets. The book actually cuts down on the amount of violence that was shown in the movie.

Guera, R. M.
Scalped: Indian Country. DC Comics/Vertigo 2007 128p. Illustration
Grades: 12 Adult   **741.5; Fic**
1. Graphic novels; 2. Mystery graphic novels
978-1-4012-1317-6, $9.99
Fifteen years ago, Dashiell "Dash? Bad Horse ran away from a life of abject poverty and utter hopelessness on the Prairie Rose Indian Reservation in hopes of finding something better. Now he's come back home armed with nothing but a set of nunchucks, a hell-bent-for-leather attitude and one dark secret, to find nothing much has changed on "The Rez" — short of a glimmering new casino, and a once-proud people overcome by drugs and organized crime. Is he here to set things right or just get a piece of the action? This book has lots of graphic violence, harsh language, nudity, and sexual situations.
Volume 1 of 10

Guggenheim, Marc
Civil War: Wolverine. Marvel Entertainment 2007 un Illustration
Grades: 10 11 12 Adult   **741.5; Fic**
1. Graphic novels; 2. Superhero graphic novels; 3. Wolverine (Fictional character)
978-0-7851-1980-7, $17.99
In the aftermath of the Stamford tragedy, Logan makes it his personal mission to take down the man responsible. No sooner does he begin his hunt, however, than he discovers someone else is stalking the same prey: a mysterious trio whose identity, and disturbing mission, unsettles him. This book includes some bloody violence and some strong language.

Rocketeer adventures: Vol. 2. Peter David, Marc Guggenheim, Stan Sakai, illustrated by Bill Sienkiewicz, Sandy Plunkett. IDW Pub. 2012 136 p. Illustration
Grades: Adult
Fic; 741.5/973
1. Superhero comic books, strips, etc.; 2. Rocketeer (Fictional character)
161377401X; 9781613774014, $24.99
This graphic novel anthology, featuring authors Marc Guggenheim, Sandy Plunkett, Peter David, and others, presents a second volume of adventures of the 1930s hero, the Rocketeer. "Dave Stevens'...distinctive artwork and...story was inspired by the adventure pulp novels of the era The Rocketeer was set in.... Now,...[this book] present[s] new interpretations of The Rocketeer by some of today's finest talents." (Publisher's note)

Courtesy of IDW Publishing

Guibert, Emmanuel
★ **Alan's** war. First Second 2008 304p. Illustration
Grades: 10 11 12 Adult   **92; 940.54; 741.5**

1. Biographical graphic novels; 2. Graphic novels; 3. Soldiers; 4. Veterans; 5. World War, 1939-1945 — Graphic novels; 6. Cope, Alan Ingram, 1925-1999 — Graphic novels
978-1-59643-096-9; 1-59643-096-6, $24
LC 2007-46190
French cartoonist Guibert met and became friends with Alan Cope and interviewed him at length to create this book. It recreates Cope's memories of being an eighteen-year-old G.I. during World War II. Unlike the war movies that focus on battles, this book focuses on more everyday, mundane memories of the day-to-day life of a soldier. Cope frankly describes a bout with crabs (genital lice), matter-of-factly tells of casual man-to-man sexual encounters among the soldiers, and gives the reader a feel for what happened back then. He also talks about postwar relationships and travels.
This is a "poignant and frank graphic memoir of young soldier who was told to serve his country in WWII and how it changed him forever.... Cope and Guibert forge a story that resonates with humanity." Publ Wkly

How the World Was: A California Childhood. Emmanuel Guibert; translated by Kathryn M. Pulver. First Second 2014 160 p. Illustration; Color
Grades: Adult   **741.5; 979.4052092**
1. Friendship; 2. Veterans — United States; 3. Cope, Alan
1596436646; 9781596436640, $19.99
LC 2014434601
This book "is Emmanuel Guibert's moving return to documenting the life of his friend [American veteran named Alan Cope]. Cope grew up in California during the great depression, and this remarkable graphic novel details the little moments that make a young man's life...while capturing the scope of America during the great depression." (Publisher's note)
"Much like sitting at the knee of a favorite grandfather and listening to his gentle musing, right down to an occasionally aimless ramble, this is a gentle, heartfelt, and interesting journey for a lazy afternoon." Booklist

★ The **photographer.** [by] Emmanuel Guibert, Didier Lefèvre and Frédéric Lemercier; translated by Alexis Siegel. First Second 2009 267p. Illustration; Map
Grades: 11 12 Adult   **92; 741.5; 958.1**
978-1-59643-375-5; 1-59643-375-2, $29.95
"In 1986, photographer Didier Lefèvre documented a seasoned Médecins sans Frontières (Doctors without Borders) team en route to a region in the way of the insurgents' war with the Soviet army supporting Afghanistan's then-Marxist government. This wedding of his photos and Guibert's European-realist comics records his arduous, frightening round trip from Normandy, where his mother lived." (Booklist)

Gunter, Miles
Zombee. Image Comics 2006 un Illustration
Grades: 10 11 12 Adult   **741.5; Fic**
1. Graphic novels; 2. Horror graphic novels; 3. Humorous graphic novels
978-1-58240-662-6, $12.99
A dutiful Samurai, a madcap Ninja and a bizarro Zen Monk team up to battle the undead in Feudal Japan. Can these unlikely allies stay friends long enough to stop the zombees from taking over their homeland? Gory and violent zombie-destroying action combines with comedy and foul language (most of it very anachronistic); the cover image, with the zombie head flying amongst sprays of blood while a samurai holds his sword, lets the reader know exactly what to expect.

Gurewich, Nicholas
The **Trial** of Colonel Sweeto and other stories: a collection of the comic strips. Dark Horse Comics 2007 96p. Illustration
Grades: 11 12 Adult   **741.5**

1. Graphic novels; 2. Humorous graphic novels
978-1-59307-844-7, $14.95

Gurewich's Perry Bible Fellowship is a popular webcomic; now they're collected into this hardcover volume. The full-color strips betray a twisted sense of humor with a strong bias for the bizarre, and some strips use nudity and violence.

Ha, Robin

Cook Korean!: a comic book with recipes. Robin Ha. Ten Speed Press 2016 176 p. Color; Illustration

Grades: Adult   **741.5; 641.595**
1. Korean cooking; 2. Cookbooks
9781607748878, $19.99

LC 2015047866

This cookbook and graphic novel by Robin Ha "is the ideal introduction to cooking Korean cuisine at home. Ha's colorful and humorous one- to three-page comics fully illustrate the steps and ingredients needed to bring more than sixty traditional (and some not-so-traditional) dishes to life.... You'll learn how to create everything from easy kimchi (mak kimchi) and soy garlic beef over rice (bulgogi dupbap) to seaweed rice rolls (gimbap) and beyond." (Publisher's note)

"Like Maangchi's Real Korean Cooking, this highly recommended collection is a solid introduction for readers who feel daunted by Korean cooking and ingredients." LJ

Includes bibliographical references and index

Hadley, Amy Reeder

Moon Girl and Devil Dinosaur; Volume 1: BFF. by Amy Reeder and Brandon Montclare; illustrated by Natacha Bustos. Marvel Enterprises 2016 136 p. Color; Illustration

Grades: 7 8 9 10 11 12 Adult   **741.5; Fic**
1. Female superhero graphic novels; 2. Dinosaurs — Graphic novels
1302900056; 9781302900052, $17.99

"Lunella LaFayette is a preteen super genius who wants to change the world—but learned the hard way that it takes MORE than just big brains. Fearful of the monstrous INHUMAN genes inside her, life is turned upside down when a savage, red-scaled tyrant is teleported from prehistoric past to a far-flung future we call TODAY. " (Publisher's note)

Contains material originally published in magazine form as MOON GIRL AND DEVIL DINOSAUR #1-6; Volume 1 in an ongoing series

Hagio, Moto

The **heart** of Thomas. by Moto Hagio, translated by Matt Thorn. Fantagraphics Books 2013 515 p.

Grades: Adult   **741.5; Fic**
1. Shojo manga; 2. School stories — Graphic novels
1606995510; 9781606995518, $39.99

This manga follows the emotional struggles of a high school boy, set in a "boarding school in Germany, sometime in the latter 20th Century. Fourteen year-old Thomas Werner falls from a lonely pedestrian overpass to his death immediately after sending a single, brief letter to a schoolmate." (Publisher's note)

Hall, Justin

No straight lines: four decades of queer comics. Justin Hall. Fantagraphics Books 2012 308 p.

Grades: Adult   **741.5**
1. LGBT comic books, strips, etc.; 2. Comic books, strips, etc. — History and criticism; 3. Homosexuality
1606995065; 9781606995068, $35

This book, edited by Justin Hall, presents an exploration into lesbian, gay, bisexual and transgendered comic books and artists. "The insular nature of the world of queer cartooning...created a fascinating artistic scene. LGBT comics have been an uncensored, internal conversation within the queer community, and thus provide a unique window into the hopes, fears, and fantasies of queer people for the last four decades." (Publisher's note)

Includes bibliographical references.

Hamboussi, Peter

Showcase Presents The Flash, Volume One. DC Comics 2007 509p. Illustration

Grades: 7 8 9 10 11 12 Adult   **741.5; Fic**
1. Graphic novels; 2. Superhero graphic novels; 3. Flash (Fictional character)
978-1-4012-1327-5, $16.99

A freak accident gives Central City police scientist Barry Allen fantastic super-speed abilities. Inspired by his favorite childhood comic book hero, Allen uses the name the Flash and uses his powers to help humanity. He soon finds himself facing such villains as Captain Cold, Mirror Master, Gorilla Grodd, the Pied Piper, Weather Wizard, and more. This volume collects 39 stories from the 1950s and 1960s in black and white.

Showcase Presents: Legion of Super-Heroes Volume 1. DC Comics 2007 552p. Illustration

Grades: 7 8 9 10 11 12 Adult   **741.5; Fic**
1. Graphic novels; 2. Legion of Super-Heroes (Fictional characters); 3. Superhero graphic novels
978-1-4012-1382-4, $16.99

The Legion of Super-Heroes, teenagers from across the cosmos, each with a unique ability, are the sworn protectors of the galaxy. Headquartered in their Super-Hero Club House, Lightning Lad, Saturn Girl, and Cosmic Boy have high standards for young hopeful champions wishing to join their ranks. With the largest roster of any super-team of the 2960s, they patrol all sectors of the universe to ensure peace and justice for all sentient beings. This volume collects black and white reprints of stories originally published from 1958 through 1964.

Showcase Presents: Martian Manhunter Volume 1. DC Comics 2007 544p. Illustration

Grades: 7 8 9 10 11 12 Adult   **741.5; Fic**
1. Graphic novels; 2. Martian Manhunter (Fictional character); 3. Superhero graphic novels
978-1-4012-1368-8, $16.99

After being accidentally teleported to Earth, Martian J'onn J'onzz finds himself stranded in a strange new world, with no way home. Using his powers to disguise his appearance, J'onn J'onzz adopts the name of deceased Denver police detective John Jones. With this new identity, he joins the Middleton Police force, secretly using his powers to help the inhabitants of Earth. Jack Miller and Joe Samachson were principal writers on the series in the early years, and artist Joe Certa did all the pencils; this black and white volume reprints stories originally published from 1953 through 1962.

Tangent Comics, volume one. DC Comics 2007 206p. Illustration

Grades: 9 10 11 12 Adult   **741.5**
1. Graphic novels; 2. Superhero graphic novels; 3. Flash (Fictional character); 4. Green Lantern (Fictional character)
978-1-4012-1530-9, $19.99

In 1997, DC published a series of comics featuring familiar character names, but they were all...different. The Atom had atomic powers, the Flash (a woman) was made of light, the Metal Men weren't robots but soldiers, the Green Lantern was a woman and used an artifact to raise the dead for one final mission, and so on. Now, DC has collected some of the stories into this trade paperback collection.

Hanawalt, Lisa

Hot Dog Taste Test. Lisa Hanawalt. Farrar, Straus & Giroux 2016 176 p. Color; Illustration
Grades: Adult   741.5
1. Wit and humor; 2. Popular culture; 3. Eating customs
1770462376; 9781770462373, $22.95
Ignatz Award Winner: Outstanding Graphic Novel (2016)

This book "serves up Lisa Hanawalt's devastatingly funny comics, saliva-stimulating art, and deliciously screwball lists as she skewers the pomposities of foodie subculture.... [It] dishes out five-star laughs as Hanawalt keenly muses on pop culture, relationships, and the animal in all of us." (Publisher's note)

"Hanawalt has a sharp eye and keen wit and is an incredibly talented illustrator as capable of selling a joke in a pencil sketch as she is at capturing a domestic scene in beautiful watercolors. While the collection might seem scattershot at a glance, the quick skipping among topics and tones puts readers in the mind of the author and is in fact a strength." LJ

Haney, Bob

Showcase Presents: Metamorpho, the Element Man Volume 1. DC Comics 2005 560p. Illustration
Grades: 7 8 9 10 11 12 Adult   741.5; Fic
1. Graphic novels; 2. Science fiction graphic novels; 3. Superhero graphic novels
1-4012-0762-6, $16.99

Adventurer Rex Mason would do almost anything for the right price, but he ended up paying with his own humanity for stealing the legendary Orb of Ra for millionaire industrialist Simon Stagg. The mysterious relic transformed Rex into a freakish "element" man, with the ability to transform his body into hundreds of different substances. Calling himself Metamorpho, Rex considered his life cursed and sought a way to reverse the Orb's powers. Along the way, Stagg used Metamorpho's unique skills for his own purposes, and the Element Man would go along, since it meant more time with Stagg's gorgeous daughter Sapphire. The stories in this black and white volume date from 1964 through 1966.

Showcase Presents: Teen Titans Volume 1. stories by Bob Haney; art and covers by Nick Cardy. DC Comics 2006 528p. Illustration
Grades: 6 7 8 9 10 11 12 Adult   741.5; Fic
1. Graphic novels; 2. Superhero graphic novels; 3. Teen Titans (Fictional characters); 4. Robin (Fictional character); 5. Flash (Fictional character)
978-1-4012-0788-5, $16.99

The Teen Titans were all sidekicks to such heroes as Batman, Wonder Woman, Aquaman, and the Flash. When teen heroes Robin, Aqualad, and Kid Flash joined together, they became a forced to be reckoned with. Wonder Girl quickly joined them, and occasionally Speedy would come, and they all proved they were just as capable of defeating the bad guys and saving the world as their mentors, while still being teens and having fun. The black and white reprinted stories originally appeared from 1964 through 1968. Today's teens will get a kick out of what the writers thought was cool "teen speak" back then.

Showcase Presents: Sgt. Rock. DC Comics 2007 543p. Illustration
Grades: 8 9 10 11 12 Adult   741.5
1. Adventure graphic novels; 2. Graphic novels; 3. Sgt. Rock (Fictional character); 4. World War, 1939-1945 — Graphic novels
978-1-4012-1713-6, $16.99

Sgt. Rock, created by Robert Kanigher, was an ordinary soldier fighting in World War II. The stories collected in this volume, published from 1959 through 1962, depict Rock and his Easy Company fighting against evil during the war. Even today, Sgt. Rock is a symbol of patriotism and of America's fighting spirit. The stories include battle action.

Harkham, Sammy

Everything together: collected stories. Sammy Harkham. Distributed Art Pub Inc 2012
Grades: Adult   741.5
1. Short stories; 2. Graphic novels; 3. Comic books, strips, etc.
0985159502; 9780985159504

Author Sammy Harkham presents a book of "short-story comics, which condense vast amounts of emotion and information into nuanced cartoon narratives...At the center of the book are two vastly different tales: 'Poor Sailor,' a sea-faring myth of a man gone to find wealth for his love; and 'Somersaulting,' a kind of fever dream of teenagers in love, wiling away the summer." (Publisher's note)

These stories originally appeared in different forms in Vice, Mome, Drawn and Quarterly Showcase, Kramers Ergot, Crickets, etc.

Harras, Bob

Showcase Presents The Unknown Soldier Volume 1. DC Comics 2006 552p. Illustration
Grades: 8 9 10 11 12 Adult   741.5; Fic
1. Adventure graphic novels; 2. Graphic novels; 3. Unknown Soldier (Fictional character)
978-1-4012-1090-8, $16.99

His face hideously disfigured by a grenade explosion in the early days of World War II, the young man who would become the Unknown Soldier was determined to continue fighting for his country. His true identity kept top secret, he became the perfect covert operative, using a multitude of disguises to carry out his exploits against the Axis powers. The first 38 adventures of the Unknown Soldier are collected in this black and white reprint volume, with stories dating from 1970 through 1975.

Showcase Presents: The War That Time Forgot. DC Comics 2007 560p. Illustration
Grades: 6 7 8 9 10 11 12 Adult   741.5; Fic
1. Adventure graphic novels; 2. Dinosaurs — Graphic novels; 3. Graphic novels; 4. World War, 1939-1945 — Graphic novels
978-1-4012-1253-7, $16.99

On an unnamed, uncharted Pacific island, dinosaurs continued to thrive while World War II raged across the globe. It is on this island that members of the U.S. Armed Forces found themselves " armed only with standard issue weapons against the deadliest predators ever to roam the Earth. This volume collects Star Spangled War Stories issues #90-128, from 1960 through 1966. There's a lot of war action and dinosaur-fighting action. The stories here have been reprinted in black and white.

Superman: Back in Action. DC Comics 2007 144p. Illustration
Grades: 8 9 10 11 12 Adult   741.5; Fic
1. Graphic novels; 2. Superhero graphic novels; 3. Superman (Fictional character)
978-1-4012-1263-6, $14.99

This book collects several stories. When Superman returns after the events of Infinite Crisis, he faces skepticism from the people and then gets kidnapped and put up for an intergalactic auction. In stories from the past, he encounters the Metal Men, Firestorm, and Deadman.

Harris, Micah

Heaven's War. Micah Harris, writer; Michael Gaydos, artist. Image Comics 2003 118p. Illustration
Grades: 9 10 11 12 Adult   741.5
1. Adventure graphic novels; 2. Fantasy graphic novels; 3. Graphic novels
1-58240-330-9, $12.95

In this graphic novel, "J.R.R. Tolkien and C.S. Lewis are called upon by eccentric fellow fantasist Charles Williams to join him against occultist

Aleister Crowley. Crowley seeks an entrance into the Heavenly realms with the intent of manipulating the angelic battles that shape human history and thus mold the world according to his will. Their conflict with Crowley will take this trio of authors...to the very edge of Heaven." (Publisher's note)

Hart, Christopher

The **reformed**. Del Rey Manga 2008 170p. Illustration

Grades: 10 11 12 Adult   **741.5; Fic**

1. Fantasy graphic novels; 2. Graphic novels; 3. Horror graphic novels; 4. Mystery graphic novels; 5. Vampires — Graphic novels

978-0-345-49663-8, $10.95

Handsome, wealthy Giancarlo is a vampire who has lived for hundreds of years and is lonely. Then he meets Jenny, a beautiful young woman who stirs feelings he hasn't known for centuries; he's willing to become mortal again to be with her. However, brutal, ghoulish murders plaguing the city have made him the target of a relentless homicide cop. And the real killer, a dangerous vampire, also wants to destroy Giancarlo. The book includes graphic, bloody violence.

Hart, Tom

★ **Rosalie** Lightning: a graphic memoir. by Tom Hart and Rosalie Lightning AND Leela Corman and the residents of New York City, Gainesville, Florida, New Mexico, AND Hawaii, as well as various singer-songwriters, film directors, actors, animators, comic artists, donors, lovers and friends. St. Martin's Press 2016 272 p. Illustration

Grades: Adult

92; 741.5

1. Cartoonists — United States — Biography — Comic books, strips, etc; 2. Children — Death — Comic books, strips, etc; 3. Hart, Tom, 1969- — Family — Comic books, strips, etc; 4. Parent-child relationship; 5. Children and death; 6. Father-daughter relationship; 7. Grief — Graphic novels

1250049946; 9781250049940, $19.99

LC 2015039334

Courtesy of Macmillan

This book, a memoir by Tom Hart, is "about the untimely death of his young daughter, Rosalie. His heart-breaking and emotional illustrations strike readers to the core, and take them along his family's journey through loss. Hart uses the graphic form to articulate his and his wife's on-going search for meaning in the aftermath of Rosalie's death, exploring themes of grief, hopelessness, rebirth, and eventually finding hope again." (Publisher's note)

Hartland, Jessie

Steve Jobs: insanely great. Jessie Hartland. Schwartz & Wade Books 2015 272 p. Illustration

Grades: 9 10 11 12 Adult   **338.761; 92**

1. Computer engineers — United States — Biography; 2. Graphic novels; 3. Jobs, Steve, 1955-2011; 4. Computer programming

0307982955; 9780307982957, $22.95; 9780307982964

LC 2014005768

Author Jessie Hartland presents this "biography in graphic format [as a] complement to more text-heavy books on Steve Jobs like Walter Isaacson's biography. Presenting the story of the ultimate American entrepreneur, who brought us Apple Computer, Pixar, Macs, iPods, iPhones and more, this unique and stylish book is sure to appeal to the legions of readers who live and breathe the techno-centric world Jobs created." (Publisher's note)

"Luddites and iFans alike should find this volume an illuminating introduction to Jobs's life and the recent history of consumer electronics." SLJ

Includes bibliographical references and index

Hartzell, Andy

★ **Fox** bunny funny. Top Shelf Productions 2007 102p. Illustration

Grades: 9 10 11 12 Adult   **741.5; Fic**

1. Animals — Graphic novels; 2. Fantasy graphic novels; 3. Graphic novels; 4. Stories without words — Graphic novels

978-1-891830-97-6, $10

The rules are simple: you're either a fox or a bunny. Foxes oppress and devour, bunnies suffer and die. Everyone knows their place. Everyone's satisfied. So what happens when a secret desire puts you at odds with your society? Starting from a simple premise — and without using a single word — this book leads the reader on a zigzag chase in and out of rabbit holes, and through increasingly strange landscapes where funny animals have serious identity problems. The tale swerves from slapstick to horror and back again before landing at the inevitable climax, in which all the old rules are shattered. Some moments of violence and dismemberment might be disturbing for some readers.

"Deftly presented in crisp black-and-white, block-print-like panels, this is a must for libraries supporting LGBT collections." Booklist

Harvey, Robert C.

The **Art** of the Comic Book: An Aesthetic History. University Press of Mississippi 1996 288p. Illustration

Grades: Adult Professional

741.5

1. Comic books, strips, etc. — History and criticism; 2. Graphic novels

0-87805-758-7, $19.95

LC 95-377

Harvey traces the evolution of the comic book as a dynamic narrative art, taking it from its beginnings in the 1930s through the mid-1990s. Enhanced by many illustrations, this examination includes work from both the mainstream and alternative comics creators.

Part of the Studies in Popular Culture series.

Courtesy of University Press of Mississippi

Hashiguchi, Takashi

Yakitate!! Japan, Vol. 1. Viz Media 2006 196p. Illustration

Grades: 10 11 12 Adult   **741.5; Fic**

1. Baking — Graphic novels; 2. Bread — Graphic novels; 3. Graphic novels; 4. Manga; 5. Shonen manga

978-1-4215-0719-4, $9.99

When still a little boy, Kazuma Azuma became fascinated with bread after meeting a baker who taught him how to bake it. He begins to experiment with baking different types of bread to find the one he can call "Ja-pan," the national bread of Japan ("pan" is Japanese for bread). At sixteen, Kazuma is almost totally self-taught, but he gets accepted as a candidate for employment at Pantasia, a bakery chain. Only one person can become the new baker at Pantasia, and Kazuma intends to win,...but he is totally ignorant of European bread names (such as croissants). This series is an example of a genre unique to manga, a story focused on food. Most of the action takes place in kitchens, but there's some crude humor.

Volume 1 of 26

Hata, Kenjiro

Hayate the Combat Butler Volume 1. Viz Media 2006 182p. Illustration

Grades: 10 11 12 Adult   **741.5; Fic**

1. Graphic novels; 2. Humorous graphic novels; 3. Manga; 4. Romance graphic novels; 5. Shonen manga

978-1-4215-0851-1, $9.99

Hardworking teenager Hayate has a plan to pay back the yakuza — who are now the legal owners of his vital organs (thanks to his deadbeat parents): he'll kidnap someone and ransom them for a mountain of money. But things get tricky when his would-be kidnappee — who as luck would have it is the daughter of a mind-bogglingly wealthy family — mistakes Hayate's actions for a confession of love, and hires him to be her personal servant. At least his employment future is secure, or so he thinks... The book includes some strong language and mild sexual situations.

Hatori, Bisco

Ouran High School Host Club Volume 1. Viz Media/Shojo Beat 2005 184p. Illustration

Grades: 9 10 11 12 Adult   **741.5; Fic**

1. Graphic novels; 2. Humorous graphic novels; 3. Manga; 4. Shojo manga

1-59116-915-1, $8.99

Haruhi is a scholarship student at an exclusive private school: Ouran High School, where it turns out the bespectacled, short-haired Haruhi is the only student from a lower-middle class family in attendance. Then, to make matters worse, one day she breaks an $80,000 vase that belongs to one of the campus clubs, a mysterious outfit called the "Host Club," consisting of six superrich (and gorgeous) guys. Haruhi can't afford to pay back the cost of the vase, of course, so she's forced to work for the Host Club. And it's there that she discovers just how rich all the boys are and how different the rich are from "regular" folks...And meanwhile, the eccentric but good-hearted rich boys are shocked to find out how life is on the other side...

Volume 1 of 18

Hayakawa, Tomoko

The **Wallflower** 1: Yamatonadeshiko Shichihenge. Random House/Del Rey Manga 2004 224p. Illustration

Grades: 10 11 12 Adult   **741.5; Fic**

1. Graphic novels; 2. Humorous graphic novels; 3. Manga; 4. Shojo manga

0-345-47912-2, $10.95

It's a gorgeous, spacious mansion, and four handsome, fifteen-year-old friends are allowed to live in it for free. There's only one condition — that within three years the guys must transform the owner's wallflower niece into a lady befitting the palace in which they all live. How hard can it be? Enter Sunako Nakahara, the agoraphobic, horror-movie-loving, pockmark-faced, frizzy-haired, fashion-illiterate recluse who tends to break into explosive nosebleeds whenever she sees anyone attractive. This project is going to take more than the four heroes ever expected: it needs a miracle. The series includes some mildly harsh language, some mild sexual situations, and mild violence.

Hayashi, Fumino

Neon Genesis Evangelion: Angelic Days Vol. 1. ADV Manga 2006 184p. Illustration

Grades: 10 11 12 Adult

741.5; Fic

Courtesy of ADV Manga

1. Graphic novels; 2. Manga; 3. Romance graphic novels; 4. Science fiction graphic novels; 5. Shojo manga

978-1-4139-0344-7, $9.99

This manga series is set in the world of Neon Genesis Evangelion, but in this series, life isn't quite so angst-ridden. Choosing the right girl is more important than saving the world. The book includes some mild sexual situations.

Hayden, Jennifer

★ The **Story** of My Tits. by Jennifer Hayden. Top Shelf Productions 2015 352 p. Illustration

Grades: Adult

92; 362.19; 741.5

1. Breast cancer — Graphic novels

1603090541; 9781603090544, $29.99

Eisner Nominee: Best Reality-Based Work (2016)

Courtesy of IDW Publishing

This book is a "graphic memoir and a cancer narrative.... When Jennifer Hayden was diagnosed with breast cancer at the age of 43, she realized that her tits told a story. Across a lifetime, they'd held so many meanings: hope and fear, pride and embarrassment, life and death. And then they were gone. Now, their story has become a way of understanding her story." (Publisher's note)

"Using famous works of art as metaphors for her own experiences and limiting her drawings to four equally measured panels per page, Hayden's work is matter-of-fact and unsentimental without becoming cold or heartless. The pacing of her storytelling is seamless, as if she were telling the story to the reader across a kitchen table." Booklist

Hayes, Nick

The **rime** of the modern mariner. by Nick Hayes. Penguin Group USA 2011 336 p. Color illustration

Grades: Adult   **745.1; Fic**

1. Marine pollution; 2. Refuse and refuse disposal; 3. Sailors; 4. Sea stories

0670025801; 9780670025800, $32.00

LC 2011459032

This graphic novel by Nick Hayes is an adaptation of Samuel Taylor Coleridge's "The Rime of the Ancient Mariner." "Hayes turns Coleridge's 1797 apocalyptic epic into an ecological warning, wherein a careless litterbug of a businessman is accosted by a sailor with burning eyes and a tale of woe. Part of the story mirrors Coleridge's (a carelessly murdered bird brings damnation upon the crusty mariner's vessel), but the atmospherics are more charged with the dangers of modernity." (Publishers Weekly)

Hedges, Chris

Days of destruction, days of revolt. Chris Hedges and Joe Sacco. Nation Books 2012 xv, 302 p. Illustration

Grades: Adult   **305.5; 305.5/60973; 741.5**

1. Crime — United States; 2. Poor — United States; 3. Social classes — United States; 4. United States — Social conditions — 20th century; 5. Camden (N.J.); 6. Social conflict; 7. Mines and mineral resources — United States; 8. Pine Ridge Indian Reservation (S.D.)

1568586434; 9781568586434, $28; 9781568587103

LC 2012004701

This book by Chris Hedges and Joe Sacco examines the impact of capitalism in America's society through a "tour of some of the worst places in America: the Pine Ridge reservation in South Dakota, which paces the nation in drug abuse, alcoholism, and teen suicide rates; Camden, NJ, one of the country's poorest and most dangerous cities; Welch, WV, where coal companies have relentlessly mined both human and natural resources; and Immokalee, FL, where migrant farm workers toil in virtual slavery." (Columbia Journalism Review)

Includes bibliographical references (p. 287-291) and index

Heer, Margreet de

Science, a discovery in comics. Margreet de Heer. NBM Publishing 2013 192 p. (A discovery in comics)
Grades: 9 10 11 12 Adult
500
1. Scientists — History; 2. Science
1561637505; 9781561637508, $19.99
LC 2013939851

Courtesy of NBM Publishing

"This history of scientific discovery, [by Margreet de Heer] is presented as a series of conversations about understanding the laws that govern the universe.... Beginning with the ideals of scientific observation and inquiry, the book moves to detailed chronologies of the evolutions of biology, physics, geology, etc. Much of the information is organized in time-line form, which is used to depict the gradual accumulation and transformation of concepts." (School Library Journal)

"Although the information on any one topic is very basic, a great many topics are treated, thanks to the economy of de Heer's visual presentation, and they are all handled very well, thanks to the energy of her drawing style and the vividness of Kohl's coloring." Booklist

Heinberg, Allan

Young Avengers Vol. 1: Sidekicks. writer, Allan Heinberg; pencils, Jim Cheung; inks, John Dell, Mark Morales & Drew Geraci; colors, Justin Ponsor; letters, Virtual Calligraphy's Cory Petit. Marvel Entertainment 2006 un Illustration
Grades: 9 10 11 12 Adult　　　　　　　　　　**741.5; Fic**
1. Graphic novels; 2. Superhero graphic novels
978-0-7851-2018-6, $14.99

"In the wake of Avengers Disassembled, a mysterious new group of teen super heroes appears. But who are they? Where did they come from? And what right do they have to call themselves the Young Avengers?" (Publisher's note)

Helfer, Andrew

Malcolm X: a graphic biography. written by Andrew Helfer; art by Randy DuBurke. Hill and Wang 2006 102p. Illustration
Grades: 10 11 12 Adult　　　　　　　　　　**92; 741.5**
1. African Americans — Biography — Graphic novels; 2. Biographical graphic novels; 3. Black Muslim leaders; 4. Black Muslims — Graphic novels; 5. Civil rights activists; 6. Graphic novels; 7. Malcolm X, 1925-1965
978-0-8090-9504-9; 0-8090-9504-1, $15.95
LC 2006-13743

The authors "tell the story of Malcolm X's short life — his meeting with Dr. Martin Luther King Jr., the two leaders describing the opposite ideological ends of the fight for civil rights; and his eventual assassination by other members of the Nation of Islam (NOI) — in narration and detailed b&white drawings, sharp as photographs in a newspaper.... Helfer and DuBurke have created an evocative and studied look at not only Malcolm X but the racial conflict that defined and shaped him." Publ Wkly

Ronald Reagan: a graphic biography. written by Andrew Helfer; art by Steve Buccellato and Joe Staton. Hill and Wang 2007 102p. Illustration
Grades: 9 10 11 12 Adult　　　　　　　　　　**92; 741.5**
1. Actors; 2. Biographical graphic novels; 3. Governors; 4. Graphic novels; 5. Presidents; 6. Presidents — United States — Graphic novels; 7. Reagan, Ronald, 1911-2004
978-0-8090-9507-0, $16.95
LC 2006-16437

This graphic novel biography covers the life of Ronald Reagan, who began as an actor and ended his career as the fortieth president of the U.S. The book discusses Reagan's work as a union president (Screen Actor's Guild), a General Motors pitchman on television, Governor of California, and his terms as President. It also covers some of the scandals that occurred during his gubernatorial and presidential terms, including the Iran/Contra arms-for-hostages deal, and the assassination attempt by John Hinkley.

Includes bibliographical references; A novel graphic from Hill and Wang

Hennessey, Jonathan

The **comic** book story of beer. by Jonathan Hennessey and Mike Smith; artwork by Aaron McConnell. Ten Speed Press 2015 180 p. Color; Illustration
Grades: Adult　　　　　　　　　　**663; 663/.42; 741.5**
1. Beer — History — Comic books, strips, etc; 2. Brewing — History — Comic books, strips, etc.
9781607746355, $18.99
LC 2014044184

This nonfiction graphic novel, by Jonathan Hennessey and Mike Smith, illustrated by Aaron McConnell, "recounts the many-layered past and present of beer through dynamic pairings of pictures and meticulously researched insight into the history of the world's favorite brew." (Publisher's note)

Includes bibliographical references

★ The **Gettysburg** Address: A Graphic Adaptation. by Jonathan Hennessey and illustrated by Aaron McConnell. HarperCollins 2013 224 p.
Grades: 9 10 11 12 Adult　　　　　　　　　　**973.7**
1. Gettysburg (Pa.), Battle of, 1863; 2. Speeches; 3. Lincoln, Abraham, 1809-1865
0061969761; 9780061969768, $15.99

This graphic novel by Jonathan Hennessey and illustrated by Aaron McConnell "is a full-color illustrated look at Abraham Lincoln — s most famous speech, the bloody battle of the Civil War that prompted it, and how they led to a defining point in the history of America. Using Lincoln — s words as a keystone, and drawing from first-person accounts, 'The Gettysburg Address' shows us the events through the eyes of those who lived through the events of the War, from soldiers to slaves." (Publisher's note)

★ The **United** States Constitution: a graphic adaptation. written by Jonathan Hennessey; art by Aaron McConnell. Hill and Wang 2008 149p. Illustration
Grades: 9 10 11 12 Adult　　　　　　　　　　**342; 741.5**
1. Constitutional history — United States — Graphic novels; 2. Graphic novels; 3. United States — Constitution — Graphic novels
978-0-8090-9487-5; 0-8090-9487-8, $35; 978-0-8090-9470-7 (pa); 0-8090-9470-3 (pa), $16.95
LC 2008-17927

The author and illustrator go "through the entire U. S. Constitution, article by article, amendment by amendment, explaining their meaning and implications — in comics format. Avoiding the didactic, the book succeeds in being both consistently entertaining and illuminating." Publ Wkly

Includes bibliographical references

Herald, Nathan

Graphic novels for young readers: a genre guide for ages 4-14. Libraries Unlimited 2011 188p. (Genreflecting advisory series)

Grades: Adult Professional   **025.2**

1. Children's literature; 2. Graphic novels; 3. Graphic novels — Bibliography

1-59884-395-8; 978-1-59884-395-8, $40

LC 2010044947

"The annotated entries are laid out in eight chapters organized by major genre, and from action and adventure to educational. Within chapters, the titles, 600 in all, are arranged alphabetically into popular subgenres such as superheroes, mythology, sports, and many more." (School Library Journal)

Includes bibliographical references

Hernandez, Gilbert

Beyond Palomar: a Love and Rockets book. Gilbert Hernandez. Fantagraphics Books 2007 253 p. Illustration

Grades: Adult   **741.5**

1. Magic — Graphic novels; 2. Science fiction graphic novels

1560978821; 9781560978824, $16.95

LC 2012289993

This book, by Gilbert Hernandez, "collects...two groundbreaking works, together for the first time. 'Poison River'...traces the pre-Palomar childhood of Luba, her teenage marriage to gangster Peter Rio, the secrets behind her mysterious mother, all the way up to her subsequent escape and arrival in Palomar.... 'Love and Rockets X,' set in the early 1990s,...takes us from plush Beverly Hills to the dangerous east side " (Publisher's note)

Chance in hell. Fantagraphics Books 2007 120p. Illustration

Grades: 11 12 Adult   **741.5**

1. Graphic novels

978-1-56097-833-6, $16.95

This book tells the story about a little orphan girl who lives in the slum of slums. Nobody knows who she is or where she's from, but her fellow shantytown inhabitants collectively look over her. The three-act story follows the heroine as she is adopted by a decent man who raises her well, and she eventually marries a kind, well-to-do man, only to discover that she can't relate to the good life and the comforts it provides. The book includes sexual situations and lots of foul language, but little nudity.

★ **Heartbreak** Soup: A Love and Rockets Book. Fantagraphics Books 2007 288p. Illustration

Grades: 12 Adult   **741.5; Fic**

1. Graphic novels

978-1-56097-783-4, $14.95

This volume collects the first half of Gilbert Hernandez's acclaimed magical-realist tales of "Palomar," the small Central American town, beginning with the groundbreaking "Sopa de Gran Pena" (which introduces most of his main cast of characters as children, plus the imposing newcomer Luba), and continuing on through such modern-day classics as "Ecce Homo," "Act of Contrition," "Duck Feet," and the great love story "For the Love of Carmen." His stories include lots of sexual situations, full nudity, and strong language.

Other Love and Rockets collections by Gilbert Hernandez are: Human Diastrophism; Beyond Palomar; Luba and Her Family; Ofelia

★ **Human** Diastrophism. Fantagraphics Books 2007 256p. Illustration (Love and Rockets)

Grades: 12 Adult   **741.5; Fic**

1. Graphic novels

9781560978480, $14.95; 1560978481

This volume collects the second half of Gilbert Hernandez's acclaimed magical-realist tales of "Palomar," the small Central American

town, beginning with the landmark "Human Diastrophism," the only full graphic novel length "Palomar" story ever created by Gilbert. In it, a serial killer stalks Palomar-but his depredations, hideous as they are, only serve to exacerbate the cracks in the idyllic Central American town as the modern world begins to intrude. "Diastrophism" concludes with the death (suicide) of one of Palomar's most beloved characters, and a postscript that provides one of the most hauntingly magical moments of the entire series as a rain of ashes drifts down upon Palomar. Also included are all the post — "Diastrophism" stories, in which Luba's past comes back to haunt her, and the seeds are sown for the "Palomar diaspora" that ends this book. Hernandez uses a lot of nudity, sexual situations, strong language, and violence in these stories.

Julio's Day. Gilbert Hernandez. W W Norton & Co Inc 2013 112 p.

Grades: Adult   **Fic; 741.5/973**

1. Life cycle, Human — Graphic novels; 2. Graphic novels

1606996061; 9781606996065, $19.99

This book, by Gilbert Hernandez, "traces the life of a 100-year-old man from cradle to grave in this fictional graphic novel. It begins in the year 1900, with the scream of a newborn. It ends, 100 pages later, in the year 2000, with the death rattle of a 100-year-old man. The infant and the old man are both Julio, and Gilbert Hernandez's...graphic novel,...traces one life — indeed, one century in a human life — through a series of carefully crafted...vignettes." (Publisher's note)

Luba and her family. Gilbert Hernandez. Fantagraphics Books 2014 228 p. Illustration (The Love & Rockets Library)

Grades: Adult   **741.5; Fic**

1. Immigrants — United States — Fiction; 2. City and town life — Fiction

160699753X; 9781606997536, $18.99

LC 2014430267

This graphic novel, by Gilbert Hernandez, part of the Love and Rocket series, "focuses on the United States, where newly immigrated Luba and her sisters, body-builder Petra and therapist/film star Fritz, find their families' and friends' lives becoming more and more intertwined. As the three sisters have 'memories of sweet youth,' the next generation finds the spotlight." (Publisher's note)

These stories originally appeared in Luba #1-4, Luba's Comics and Stories #1, Measles #1-8, and New Love #1-6 — Title page verso.

Marble Season. By Gilbert Hernandez. Drawn & Quarterly 2013 128 p. Illustration

Grades: 11 12 Adult   **741.5**

1. Graphic novels; 2. Autobiographies

1770460861; 9781770460867, $21.95

LC 2013375524

Written by Gilbert Hernandez, this autobiographical novel "portrays the reality of life in a large family in suburban 1960s California. Pop-culture references — TV shows, comic books, and music — saturate this evocative story of a young family navigating cultural and neighborhood norms set against the golden age of the American dream and the silver age of comics." (Publisher's note)

"Neither overly rosy and romantic nor dark and dramatic, the book focuses on the real bulk of a child's daily life: the long summer months in which nothing eventful happens, the neighborhood kids who come and go, the tomboys and bullies, the temptation of small-time crime, and the confusion and innocence of early sexuality." LJ

Ofelia: a Love and Rockets book. Gilbert Hernandez. Fantagraphics Books 2015 249 p. (Love and Rockets)

Grades: Adult   **741.5; Fic**

1. Families — Comic books, strips, etc; 2. Latin Americans — Comic books, strips, etc; 3. California — Comic books, strips, etc; 4. Graphic novels

1606998064; 9781606998069, $19.99

LC 2014501184

"In Ofelia, the sisters, the kids, and the cousins are all settled comfortably in California after leaving Palomar in Luba and Her Family. Luba and her cousin Ofelia's relationship has always been fraught, but when Ofelia threatens to write a book about Luba, past memories, secrets, resentments, and pain resurface. Meanwhile, Luba's children-genius Socorro, recently out-and-proud Doralis, and prickly Maricela-show that a talent for trouble may be hereditary...." (Publisher's note)

"The latest Complete Love and Rockets Library volume presents content previously collected in Luba: The Book of Ofelia (2006) and Luba (2009) in the sequence of its publication in the serial Love and Rockets. It's the engrossing, sexually explicit, violent, and satirical soap opera (no other term fits) of the incredibly pneumatic Martinez sisters, originally of Palomar, somewhere in Central America, but now long settled and successful in greater L.A." Booklist

These stories originally appeared in Luba #3-9, Luba's comics and stories #2-5, and Measles #3 — Title page verso

★ **Palomar:** the heartbreak soup stories. Gilbert Hernandez. Fantagraphics; Turnaround 2003 522 p. Illustration
Grades: Adult   **741.5; 741.59/73**
1. City and town life — United States; 2. Graphic novels; 3. Latin Americans — Fiction
1560975393; 9781560975397, $39.95

LC 2006355302

This book, by Gilbert Hernandez, "collects every 'Heartbreak Soup' story from 1993 to 2002 in one 500-page deluxe hardcover edition, presenting the epic for the first time as the single novel it was always intended to be. Palomar is the mythical Central American town where the "Heartbreak Soup" stories take place. The stories weave in and out of the town's entire population, crafting an intricate tapestry of Latin American experience." (Publisher's note)

Sloth. DC Comics/Vertigo 2006 un Illustration
Grades: 11 12 Adult   **741.5; Fic**
1. Graphic novels; 2. Teenagers — Graphic novels
978-1-4012-0366-5, $19.99

Teenager Miguel Serra had suddenly fallen into a coma; a year later he wakes up, back to normal except he moves at a very slow pace; some people call him Sloth Boy. He reconnects with his girlfriend Lita and best friend Romeo and they try to find evidence of an urban legend in the lemon orchards that surround their sleepy town. One encounter causes a change, as suddenly it was Lita who'd been in the year-long coma. She tries to catch the attention of the handsome, popular Miguel and tries to score tickets to the Romeo X concert. Soon she's having intimate relations with both Miguel and Romeo, and when they fight over her, she falls and slips into another coma. Romeo throws himself off a bridge, and Lita wakes up...

This is the first original graphic novel by Hernandez, who co-created Love and Rockets with his brother. Adult language and sexual situations make this more appropriate for older teens.

The **Twilight** Children. Gilbert Hernandez, writer; Darwyn Cooke, artist & letterer; Dave Stewart, colorist. DC Comics/Vertigo 2016 144 p. Color; Illustration
Grades: Adult   **741.5; Fic**
1. Latin America — Fiction — Comic books, strips, etc.; 2. Supernatural graphic novels; 3. Science fiction graphic novels
1401262457; 9781401262457, $14.99

LC 2016006071

"When a white orb washes up on the shore of a remote Latin American village, a group of children naturally poke at the strange object to see what it is. The orb explodes, leaving the children completely blind. And when a beautiful young woman who may be an alien is found wandering the seafront, she's taken in by the townspeople, but soon becomes a person of interest to a quirky pair of undercover CIA agents, and the target of affection for a young scientist. Can they come together to prevent an all-out alien invasion and save the souls in this sleepy, seaside town?" (Publisher's note)

"The film noir quality of the narrative brings to mind The Invasion of the Body Snatchers, which plays well to the retro style of Cooke's art and embodies classic elements of early sf's love of minimalism and modernism." LJ

Originally published in single magazine form as THE TWILIGHT CHILDREN 1-4

Hernandez, Jaime
Esperanza: a Love and Rockets book. Jaime Hernandez.. Fantagraphics Books 2011 245 p. Illustration
Grades: Adult   **741.5**
1. Interpersonal relations — Comic books, strips, etc; 2. Mexican Americans — Comic books, strips, etc
1606994492; 9781606994498, $18.99

LC 2012285139

In this book, by Jaime Hernandez, part of the Love and Rockets series, "an older and wiser Maggie faces down her old demons and the 'Ghost of Hoppers' in a full-length graphic novel (which also introduces one of Jaime's greatest recent characters, Vivian the 'Frogmouth,' the near-psychotic bombshell). Meanwhile, the ever-feisty but maturing Hopey (her Spanish birth name giving this collection its title) transitions from tending bar to teaching kindergarten." (Publisher's note)

★ The **Girl** from H.O.P.P.E.R.S.: A Love and Rockets Book. Fantagraphics Books 2007 288p. Illustration
Grades: 12 Adult   **741.5; Fic**
1. Graphic novels; 2. Mexican Americans — California — Los Angeles — Fiction; 3. Punk culture — Fiction
978-1-56097-851-0, $14.95

In this second volume, having abandoned the sci-fi trappings of the earliest Love & Rockets stories, Hernandez refined his approach, settling on the more naturalistic environment of the fictional Los Angeles barrio, Hoppers, and the lives of the young Mexican-Americans and punk rockers who live there. A central story is "The Death of Speedy." In this volume, Maggie also begins her on-again and off-again romance with Ray D., leading to friction and an eventual separation from Hopey. Hernandez uses nudity, sexual situations, and strong language in these stories.

Love and rockets; No. 7: new stories. by Gilbert Hernandez, Jaime Hernandez. Fantagraphics 2015 100 p. Illustration
Grades: Adult   **741.5; Fic**
1. Mexican Americans — Comic books, strips, etc.; 2. Women — Fiction; 3. Graphic novels
160699770X; 9781606997703, $14.99

In this comic, by Gilbert Hernandez and Jaime Hernandez, "Maggie and Hopey take a much-needed break from their humdrum domestic lives and go on a road trip to visit a 'sick friend.' And, when the cat's away, Ray visits some old, sick friends of his own. Plus Tonta's nutty family!" (Publisher's note)

"The latest volume in the current incarnation of Love and Rockets series as an annual trade paperback (it began as a comic book series in 1981) conveys an overall air of regrouping, as Jaime reunites lifelong pals Maggie and Hopey for a road trip, and Gilbert returns briefly to the fictional Latin American village of Palomar and casts his sometimes-actress character Fritz in a goofy costume epic featuring Aladdin and a spaceship." Booklist

The **Love** Bunglers. by Jaime Hernandez. Fantagraphics 2014 104 p. Illustration (Love and Rockets)

Grades: Adult **741.5**
   1. Comic books, strips, etc.; 2. Interpersonal relations
1606997297; 9781606997291, $19.99

This book, by Jaime Hernandez, "[c]ontains the critically acclaimed and award-winning short comic 'Browntown,' as well as other stories chronicling the life and loves of...Hernandez's longtime...heroine Maggie.... After a lifetime of losses, Maggie finds, in the second half, her longtime off and on lover, Ray Dominguez." (Publisher's note)

"Hernandez (Love and Rockets), one of graphic storytelling's modern masters, returns readers to the mundane world of his most lasting creation, Maggie Chascarillo.... This rich tapestry of superb, deceptively minimalist artwork and characterization is rounded out with extended flashbacks to Maggie's adolescence that shed light on how her early experiences affect her actions well into adulthood." Pub Wkly

★ **Maggie** the Mechanic: a love and rockets book. Fantagraphics Books 2007 276p. Illustration
Grades: 12 Adult **741.5; Fic**
   1. Graphic novels
978-1-56097-784-1, $14.95

This is the first of three volumes by Jaime Hernandez, collecting the adventures of the spunky Maggie, her annoying best friend and sometime lover Hopey, and their circle of friends, including their bombshell friend Penny Century, Maggie's weirdo mentor Izzy — as well as the wrestler Rena Titanon and Maggie's handsome love interest, Rand Race. Maggie the Mechanic collects the earliest, punkiest, most heavily sci-fi stories of Maggie and her circle of friends. Hernandez uses some nudity, sexual situations, and some harsh language in these stories.

Other Love and Rockets collections by Jaime Hernandez are: The Girl from H.O.P.P.E.R.S.; Perla La Loca; Penny Century; Esperanza

Penny Century: a Love and Rockets book. Jaime Hernandez. Fantagraphics Books 2010 249 p. Illustration
Grades: Adult **741.5**
   1. Bisexual women — Comic books, strips, etc; 2. Punk culture — Comic books, strips, etc; 3. Women wrestlers — Comic books, strips, etc; 4. Wrestling — Fiction; 5. Bisexuals — Fiction; 6. Punk culture
1606993429; 9781606993422, $18.99

LC 2012289975

This book, by Jaime Hernandez, is "the third volume of the definitive 'Maggie' series.... [It] starts off with a blast with 'Whoa, Nellie!,' a unique graphic novelette in which Maggie, who has settled in with her pro-wrestler aunt for a while, experiences that wild and woolly world first-hand. Then it's back to chills and spills with the old cast of Hopey, Ray Dominguez, and Izzy Ortiz." (Publisher's note)

"What's impressive about Hernandez's work isn't so much each story on its own as it is how all the pieces fit together into a whole world that's almost but not quite like our own. The way one character can shift from being the central protagonist and then a minor character whose existence drives the plot makes the series fascinatingly lifelike." Pub Wkly

Perla la loca: a Love and Rockets book. Jaime Hernandez. Fantagraphics Books 2007 283 p. Illustration
Grades: Adult **741.5**
   1. Bisexuals — Fiction; 2. Punk culture
156097883X; 9781560978831, $18.99

LC 2012289994

In this book, by Jaime Hernandez, "as Maggie, Hopey, and the rest of the Locas prowl Los Angeles, the East Coast, and parts in between trying to recapture the carefree spirit of those early days. "Wigwam Bam" brings us up to date on all the members of Jaime's extensive cast of characters and then drops a narrative bomb on Hopey (and us) in the very last pages." (Publisher's note)

Hernandez, Lea
   Rumble Girls: Silky Warrior Tansie. NBM 2003 un Illustration
Grades: 10 11 12 Adult **741.5; Fic**
   1. Graphic novels; 2. Martial arts — Graphic novels; 3. Science fiction graphic novels
1-56163-370-4, $9.95

In a future world where media is run by suits (literally, they have no bodies) and everyone watches battles between warriors in battlesuits called hardskins, orphaned Raven Tansania Ransom trains to be a hardskin pilot at the girls' school academie Juliet. When a relationship gone sour causes Raven to sign with super media corporation Enteco to become a Rumble Girl, school rival Carmen signs on, too, for she wants to destroy Raven by any means possible. The book includes lots of fighting action and some sexual activity.

Hernandez worked with the Japanese anime/manga group known as Gainax and developed her manga-esque style from her experience there. Rumble Girls originally appeared in comics issues published by Image Comics and then online as webcomics.

Herriman, George
   ★ **Krazy** & Ignatz, 1937-1938: Shifting Sands Dusts its Cheeks in Powdered Beauty. Fantagraphics Books 2006 176p. Illustration
Grades: 7 8 9 10 11 12 Adult **741.5; Fic**
   1. Graphic novels; 2. Humor graphic novels; 3. Krazy Kat (Fictional character)
978-1-56097-734-6, $19.95

Krazy Kat is a love story, focusing on the relationships of its three main characters. Krazy Kat adored Ignatz Mouse. Ignatz Mouse simply tolerated Krazy Kat, except for recurrent onsets of targeted tumescence, which found expression in the fast delivery of bricks to Krazy's cranium. Offisa Pup loved Krazy and sought to protect "her" (Herriman always maintained that Krazy was genderless) by throwing Ignatz in jail. Each of the characters was ignorant of the others' true motivations, and this simple structure allowed Herriman to build entire worlds of meaning into the actions, building thematic depth and sweeping his readers up by the looping verbal rhythms of Krazy & Co.'s unique dialogue. Most of these strips in this volume have not seen print since originally running in Hearst newspapers over 70 years ago. This seventh volume collecting all of the comic strips, is the second one to be published in color; Herriman started doing the strip in color in 1935. Other than the brick-throwing, this book has no violence, foul language, or any other usual objectionable content. Krazy Kat cartoons were made for children in the mid-1930s, and there was a Krazy Kat animated series which aired on television in the mid-1960s.

Heuet, Stéphane
   In Search of Lost Time: Swann's way. Marcel Proust; adaptation and drawings by Stéphane Heuet; translated by Arthur Goldhammer. Liveright Publishing Corporation 2015 224 p. Color illustration; Map
Grades: Adult **741.5**
   1. France — Social life and customs — 19th century — Comic books, strips, etc; 2. France — History — 1815-1914 — Fiction; 3. Memory — Fiction; 4. Graphic novels; 5. Proust, Marcel — Adaptations
1631490354; 9781631490354, $26.95

LC 2014048982

This graphic novel, by Marcel Proust, adapted and illustrated by Stéphane Heuet, and translated by Arthur Goldhammer, "re-presents Proust in graphic form for anyone who has always dreamed of reading him but was put off by the sheer magnitude of the undertaking. This graphic adaptation reveals the fundamental architecture of Proust's work while displaying a remarkable fidelity to his language as well as the novel's themes of time, art, and the elusiveness of memory." (Publisher's note)

Originally published in French as Du côté de chez Swann: Édition Intégrale from À La Recherche du Temps Perdu by Marcel Proust

Hicklenton, John
 100 months: the end of all things. by Johnny Hicklenton; art & words, John Hicklenton; layout, Adam Lavis; foreword, Pat Mills. Cutting Edge Press 2010 170 p. Color illustration
 Grades: Adult   **741.5**
 1. Graphic novels; 2. Capitalism — Fiction; 3. Environmental degradation
 0956544525; 9780956544520, $29.95
                                                  LC 2010467752
 This graphic novel is a parable of environmental devastation, depicting the quest of Mara, Warrior and Earth Goddess, as she seeks revenge against the Longpig: a Satanic personification of capitalism, red in tooth and claw, whose followers, a legion of the damned, look quite a lot like us. The world of the Longpig is rich in killing fields and scenes of mass crucifixion that recall Goya, Blake, and Bacon, and represents a true crossover of the graphic novel form with fine art.... This book was drawn and written in foreknowledge of [Hicklenton — s] imminent death, and its insight into universal themes of life, death, salvation, and damnation seems to come from a place between worlds." (Publisher — s note)

Hickman, Jonathan
 ★ **East** of West; Volume 1: The Promise. Jonathan Hickman, writer; Nick Dragotta, artist; Frank Martin, colors; Rus Wooton, letters. Image Comics 2013 96 p. Color illustration (East of West)
 Grades: Adult   **741.5**
 1. Revenge — Graphic novels; 2. Death — Fiction; 3. Four Horsemen of the Apocalypse — Fiction
 1607067706; 9781607067702, $9.99
 "Hickman starts another high-concept series, this one set in a futuristic Old West and starring none other than the Four Horsemen of the Apocalypse. But there's trouble in the ranks, it seems, between Death and his cohort. What exactly that trouble is, and a swarming host of other tantalizing questions — like what happened between the Civil War and 2066, for instance — are teased out as Death tracks down those who have wronged him." (Booklist)
 First published in single magazine format as East of West #1-5.;
 Volume 1 of an ongoing series

 ★ **East** of West: Volume three: There is no us. by Jonathan Hickman; illustrated by Nick Dragotta. Image Comics 2014 144 p. Color; Illustration
 Grades: Adult   **741.5; Fic**
 1. Graphic novels; 2. Apocalyptic fiction
 9781632151148, $14.99; 1632151146
 The series' third volume, written by Jonathan Hickman and illustrated by Nick Dragotta, "sees the breaking apart of the future-scape of America as the world races forwards towards the apocalypse." (Publisher's note)
 "[T]he already uneasy alliance between the Horsemen's Chosen is destroyed, as a series of betrayals between the different factions marches everyone closer to war and Armageddon. Hickman focuses less on action and more on setup, as many of the characters achieve new positions of power, ready to flex their newfound muscles once the guns are drawn." Booklist

 ★ **East** of West; Volume 2: We Are All One. by Jonathan Hickman; illustrated by Nick Dragotta. Image Comics 2014 144 p. Color; Illustration (East of West)
 Grades: Adult   **741.5**
 1. Comic books, strips, etc.; 2. Four Horsemen of the Apocalypse — Fiction; 3. Death — Fiction
 1607068559; 9781607068556, $14.99
 "In the second volume of this weird western series, the three Horsemen of the Apocalypse continue to manipulate the Chosen, the American leaders sworn to the message, as they plot to bring about the end of the world. Death, the betrayed Horseman, rides out on a quest to locate

his kidnapped son, but a new character, the Ranger, attempts to derail both groups' plans.... Hickman focuses on atmosphere and environment, with slow pacing and sudden quick-on-the-draw action, adding a touch of Lovecraftian horror and epic sci-fi for good measure." Booklist
 Contains material originally published as East of West #6-10.

 Manhattan Projects Volume 1. by Jonathan Hickman, illustrated by Nick Pitarra, Jordie Bellaire. Image Comics 2012 Color illustration
 Grades: Adult   **741.5/973**
 1. Science fiction graphic novels; 2. Scientists — Graphic novels
 1607066084; 9781607066088, $14.99
 This graphic novel, by Jonathan Hickman, illustrated by Nick Pitarra and Jordie Bellaire, images "that the Manhattan Project was really just a front for Oppenheimer, Einstein, Feynman, et al., to get into the really out-there stuff in Los Alamos...while Japanese teleportation machines..., concurrent universes accessed by an enigmatic portal-stone, and shady bargains with warring alien races...[challenge] humanity's fate." (Booklist)

 Volume 1 of an ongoing series

 The **nighty** news. Image Comics 2007 184p.
 Grades: 11 12 Adult   **741.5**
 1. Crime — Graphic novels; 2. Graphic novels; 3. Mass media — Graphic novels
 978-1-58240-766-1, $16.99
 As an act of violence spirals out of control to encompass the entirety of the news media, a cult has emerged from the errors and retractions that have ruined careers, marriages and even lives. Under direction from his cult master The Voice, The Hand leads an army of followers committed to revolution, willing to die for their cause. Targeting journalists of all kinds, they launch a campaign of terror and violence that plays out in the media. The story includes considerable violence and foul language with page design that is very different from the usual comics panels.

Hickman, Troy
 Common Grounds: Baker's dozen. Image Comics/Top Cow Productions 2004 144p. Illustration
 Grades: 9 10 11 12 Adult   **741.5; Fic**
 1. Graphic novels; 2. Superhero graphic novels
 978-1-58240-841-5, $14.99
 Superheroes and supervillains need a place where they can relax, unwind, and not worry about the next battle. Common Grounds is just such a place — a chain of coffee shops with bakery counters, totally neutral ground. Here, hero and villain can relax and take a break in the restroom ("Head Games"), a teenage superhero who doubts herself and an older superpowered religious Jew can encourage each other ("Sanctuary"), a group of overweight heroes can meet ("Fat Chance"), or formerly evil monsters can get custom takeout and shoot the breeze ("Where Monsters Dine"). The book includes a baker's dozen (thirteen) stories.

Hicks, Faith Erin
 ★ The **Adventures** of Superhero Girl. written and drawn by Faith Erin Hicks; colors by Cris Peter; introduction by Kurt Busiek. Dark Horse Comics 2013 112 p. Illustration; Color
 Grades: 4 5 6 7 8 9 10 11 12 Adult   **741.5; Fic**
 1. Female superhero graphic novels
 1616550848; 9781616550844, $16.99
 Eisner Award: Best Publication for Kids (2014)
 This graphic novel features "Superhero Girl [who] has some Superman-like powers, although she can't fly, just leap over tall buildings, and she works to protect the small town where she went to get away from her charismatic superhero brother, Kevin. She fights bad-guy ninjas, bank robbers, even a tentacled space monster, but she also struggles to pay

rent...and she has to deal with her future supervillain self." (Voice of Youth Advocates)

"It's superhero as person instead of as corporate symbol or fight machine.... This strip shines because it's fresh and lighthearted without wallowing in angst." Pub Wkly

Higashimura, Akiko

Princess Jellyfish 1. by Akiko Higashimura. Random House Inc 2016 400 p.

Grades: 10 11 12 Adult   **741.5**

1. Tokyo (Japan) — Fiction; 2. Young women — Fiction; 3. Manga; 4. Josei manga

1632362287; 9781632362285, $19.99

In this book, by Akiko Higashimura, "Tsukimi Kurashita has a strange fascination with jellyfish. She's loved them from a young age and has carried that love with her to her new life in the big city of Tokyo. There, she resides in Amamizukan.... However, a chance meeting at a pet shop has Tsukimi crossing paths with one of the things that the residents of Amamizukan have been desperately trying to avoid-a beautiful and fashionable woman!" (Publisher's note)

Volume 1 of 9

Hill, Joe

★ **Locke** & key: welcome to Lovecraft. written by Joe Hill; art by Gabriel Rodriguez. IDW Publishing 2008 158p. Illustration

Grades: 10 11 12 Adult

741.5; Fic

1. Graphic novels; 2. Horror graphic novels; 3. Mystery graphic novels

978-1-60010-237-0, $24.99;

978-1-60010-384-1 (pa), $19.99

Courtesy of IDW Publishing

After Rendell Locke is murdered by a former student, Sam Lesser, who then tried to find and kill the rest of the family, Nina Locke takes her children, Tyler, Kinsey, and Bode to Lovecraft, Massachusetts, to live with Rendell's brother Duncan in Keyhouse. Tyler needs to deal with the guilt he feels because of a conversation with Sam Lesser, in which he said Sam should kill his dad. Kinsey had taken Bode and hidden from Sam, keeping them both safe, but she feels as though she'll never be safe again. Bode finds a door at Keyhouse, and when he goes through it, he dies and his ghost wanders around. There's definitely something weird at Keyhouse, and something is living at the bottom of the well in the well house — something that uses both Bode and Sam Lesser — and wants revenge. The book includes bloody violence. Joe Hill is the son of Stephen King.

"This first of...several volumes delivers on all counts, boasting a solid story bolstered by exceptional work from Chilean artist Rodriguez...that resembles a fusion of Rick Geary and Cully Hamner with just a dash of Frank Quitely." Publ Wkly

Other titles in this series are:Vol 2: Head Games (2009);Vol 3: Crown of Shadows (2010);Vol 4: Keys to the Kingdom (2011);Vol 5: Clockworks (2012);Vol 6: Alpha & Omega (2014)

Hinds, Gareth

★ **Beowulf**. adapted and illustrated by Gareth Hinds. Candlewick Press 2007 un Illustration

Grades: 8 9 10 11 12 Adult   **741.5; Fic**

1. Adventure graphic novels; 2. Graphic novels; 3. Monsters — Graphic novels; 4. Beowulf — Graphic novels

978-0-7636-3022-5, $21.99;

0-7636-3022-5; 978-0-7636-3023-2 (pa);

0-7636-3023-3 (pa), $9.99

        LC 2006-49023

Graphic novel adaptation of the Old English epic poem, Beowulf

"For fantasy fans both young and old, this makes an ideal introduction to a story without which the entire fantasy genre would look very different; many scenes may be too intense for very young readers." Publ Wkly

BEOWULF. Copyright © 1999, 2000, 2007 by Gareth Hinds. Reproduced by permission of the publisher, Candlewick Press, Somerville, MA.

The **merchant** of Venice: a play. by William Shakespeare; adapted and illustrated by Gareth Hinds. Candlewick Press 2008 68p. Illustration

Grades: 8 9 10 11 12 Adult

822.3; 741.5

1. Shakespeare, William, 1564-1616 — Adaptations

978-0-7636-3024-9, $21.99;

978-0-7636-3025-6 (pa), $11.99

        LC 2007-938349

Hinds uses a sketchy art style and blue and gray tones to illustrate his graphic adaptation of Shakespeare's controversial play. He sets the play in modern Venice and uses more modern language, including prose, at the beginning of the play and then gradually returns to Shakespeare's original language for the courtroom scenes. The play tells the story of a debt owed to a Jewish merchant of Venice, of a strong-willed young woman who is determined to choose her own husband, and of the quest to save a young man from the fate of having a pound of flesh cut from him.

THE MERCHANT OF VENICE. Copyright © 2008 by Gareth Hinds. Reproduced by permission of the publisher, Candlewick Press, Somerville, MA.

"Fans of the play will find this an intriguing adaptation." Publ Wkly

The **Odyssey:** a graphic novel. by Gareth Hinds. Candlewick Press 2010 248 p. Color illustration

Grades: 7 8 9 10 11 12 Adult

741.5

1. Graphic novels; 2. Greek mythology — Graphic novels; 3. Odyssey; 4. Homer

0763642665; 0763642681;

9780763642662, $24.99; 9780763642686

        LC 2010007512

"Retells, in graphic novel format, Homer's epic tale of Odysseus, the ancient Greek hero who encounters witches and other obstacles on his journey home after fighting in the Trojan War." (Publisher's note)

THE ODYSSEY. Copyright © 2010 by Gareth Hinds. Reproduced by permission of the publisher, Candlewick Press, Somerville, MA.

Hirano, Kohta

Hellsing Volume 1. Dark Horse Comics 2003 208p. Illustration

Grades: 11 12 Adult   **741.5; Fic**

1. Graphic novels; 2. Horror graphic novels; 3. Manga; 4. Seinen manga

1-59307-056-X, $13.95

There's a secret organization somewhere in England created to defend the Queen and country from monsters of all sorts. Enter Hellsing, an agency, long in tooth, with the experience, know-how, and... special equipment to handle the problems that arise when vampires, ghouls, and the like take on these dark forces. The special "equipment" is another vampire, and a big pistol loaded with special silver bullets. This series focuses on the violence of destroying vampires who love to slaughter people. Some might be offended by the portrayal of the Roman Catholic Church as insanely fundamentalist and using inquisitors and brainwashed killer nuns. The series includes lots of graphic violence and harsh language.

Hiroumi, Aoi

Shibuya goldfish; 1. Hiroumi Aoi; translation by Ko Ransom; lettering by Abigail Blackman. Yen Press 2018 240 p. Illustration
Grades: 10 11 12 Adult   **741.5; Fic**
   1. Teenagers — Fiction; 2. Goldfish — Graphic novels; 3. Goldfish — Fiction
1975327446; 9781975327446, $15

LC 2018935616

"High schooler Hajime Tsukiyoda went to Shibuya that day hoping only to find inspiration for his next film. He never expected to find himself smack-dab in the middle of a real-life horror movie. Without warning, schools of massive goldfish descend upon the crowded streets, and the mystified onlookers' confusion quickly turns to terror as the fish begin to feed." (Publisher's note)

Hirsh, Ananth

Lucky Penny. Ananth Hirsh, Yuko Ota. Oni Press 2016 199 p. Illustration
Grades: 10 11 12 Adult
741.5; Fic
   1. Fortune — Comic books, strips, etc; 2. Success — Fiction
1620102870; 9781620102879, $19.99

LC 2015948229

Courtesy of Oni Press

In this book, by Ananth Hirsh and Yuko Ota, "Penny Brighton...lost her job. And her apartment. In the same day. But it's okay, her friend has a cozy storage unit she can crash in. And there's bound to be career opportunities at the neighborhood laundromat.... Plus, there's this sweet guy at the community center.... Surely Penny is a capable of becoming an actual responsible adult, and if she can do that her luck's bound to change! Right?" (Publisher's note)"

"Quirky Penny, like characters in the romance novels she loves, is all heart, and she'll easily charm readers with her smoking, drinking, train-wreck style." Booklist

Hodgson, William Hope

The **House** on the Borderland. BiblioBazaar 2006 88p. Illustration
Grades: 10 11 12 Adult   **741.5; Fic**
   1. Graphic novels; 2. Horror graphic novels
978-1-4264-3828-8, $11.99

This book adapts Hodgson's horror novel. It sits astride two worlds, the bleak world of colorless normality, and the realms of cosmic horror where reason my yet have a last chance to conquer fear. To this ancient dwelling a challenger comes, to exorcise its shadowed curse, to plumb its pits of ultimate perversity and, perhaps, to prevent evil's emergence into the present. This book includes strong language, violence, and brief nudity.

Hogan, James P.

The **Two** Faces of Tomorrow. story by James P. Hogan; art and adaptation by Yukinobu Hoshino; translation, Frederik L. Schodt and Toren Smith; lettering and retouch, Tomoko Saito. Dark Horse Comics 2006 576p. Illustration
Grades: 9 10 11 12 Adult   **741.5**
   1. Computers — Graphic novels; 2. Graphic novels; 3. Manga; 4. Science fiction graphic novels; 5. Seinen manga
978-1-59307-563-7

Midway through the 21st century, an integrated global computer network manages much of the world's affairs. A proposed major software upgrade — an artificial intelligence — will give the system an unprecedented degree of independent decision-making, but serious questions are raised in regard to how much control can safely be given to a non-human intelligence. In order to more fully assess the system, a new space-station habitat — a world in miniature — is developed for deployment of the fully operational system, named Spartacus. This mini-world can then be "attacked" in a series of escalating tests to assess the system's responses and capabilities. If Spartacus gets out of hand, the system can be shut down and the station destroyed... unless Spartacus decides to take matters into its own hands and take the fight to Earth. This manga adaptation of Hogan's novel includes some harsh language and brief incidental nudity.

Hogan, Peter

Resident Alien 1: Welcome to Earth!. writer, Peter Hogan; artwork, colors, and letters, Steve Parkhouse. Dark Horse 2013 96 p. Illustration
Grades: Adult   **741.5; Fic**
   1. Science fiction graphic novels; 2. Mystery graphic novels
1616550171; 9781616550172, $14.99

In this graphic novel, "Harry is a space alien who lives as a recluse on Earth. His isolation comes to an end when the town doctor in the rural area he chooses to live in is murdered and the police need another doctor to fill out the death certificate. Harry not only fulfills that request, but ends up subbing for the deceased doctor, navigating human society, and trying to solve the murder." (Publishers Weekly)

Hope, Jane

Introducing Buddha, New Ed.. Totem Books 2005 176p. Illustration
Grades: 10 11 12 Adult
294.3; 741.5
   1. Buddhism — Graphic novels; 2. Graphic novels
978-1-84046-633-1, $12.95

LC 95-060973

Courtesy of Icon Books

This book uses cartoons and a spare text to describe the life and teachings of the Buddha. Author Jane Hope shows that enlightenment is a matter of experiencing the truth individually and by inspiration which is passed from teacher to student. The book explains the practices of meditation, Taoism and Zen. It goes on to describe the role of Buddhism in modern Asia and its growing influence on Western thought. The book includes a list of books for further reading.

Hopkins, David

Emily Edison. Viper Comics 2006 144p. Illustration
Grades: 7 8 9 10 11 12 Adult   **741.5; Fic**
   1. Graphic novels; 2. Humorous graphic novels; 3. Science fiction graphic novels

0-9777883-2-6, $12.95

High schooler Emily has more than her share of problems; along with trying to keep up in school and survive such things as parties and boys, she has to deal with her parents' very mixed marriage. Her father is human, but her mother came from another dimension. Since their divorce, Emily has had to split her time between Earth and elsewhere; and now her grandfather wants her to live permanently in his dimension, and he's prepared to destroy Earth to force her hand. What's a girl to do?

Hornschemeier, Paul

Let Us Be Perfectly Clear. Fantagraphics Books 2006 136p. Illustration

Grades: 11 12 Adult   **741.5; Fic**
1. Graphic novels; 2. Short stories — Graphic novels
978-1-56097-752-0, $19.95

This is a collection of Paul Hornschemeier's full-color short stories from a variety of sources, none of which has been available to the book trade. The book is designed as a "flip book" in the tradition of the old Ace paperbacks, with one side featuring comedic work (or as comedic as Hornschemeier's mind allows), and the other decidedly more morose. On the "funny" menu, we are treated to Dr. Rodentia (an unfortunate-looking fellow with only apathy as his weapon), a detailed artist's catalogue exploring such modern masterpieces as "Accidental Late-Night Sex With a Radiator," musings on the cancerous nature of civilization as observed by a deceased cat and a cotton-based airbus, the scatological "Feelings Check," the ever pathetic Vanderbilt Millions and his fantasies of self-worth, and the multi-narrative story that started the Forlorn Funnies comics series: "The Men and Women of the Television." On the "forlorn" plate is the cold examination of the dyslexic narcoleptic and his bungled plans of murder, a sea creature's balancing of morality and sustenance, the Western romance "Wanted," a metal man's self-destructive search for meaning, and the story of two men meeting; it may disgust readers, without a single visually objectionable panel. The other stories do include strong language and some violence.

Mother, come home. with an introduction by Thomas Tennant. Fantagraphics 2004 128p. Illustration

Grades: 11 12 Adult   **741.5; Fic**
1. Graphic novels; 2. Mental illness — Graphic novels
978-1-56097-973-9 (pa)

In this "story, a young child struggles with the death of his mother and his father's collapse. Clean-lined artwork leaves plenty of room for strong emotional content linked to themes of euthanasia, suicide, and depression." Booklist

Horrocks, Dylan

Sam Zabel and the magic pen. by Dylan Horrocks. Fantagraphics Books 2014 221 p. Color; Illustration

Grades: Adult   **741.5; Fic**
1. Cartoonists — Comic books, strips, etc; 2. Imaginary societies — Comic books, strips, etc; 3. Cartoonists — Graphic novels; 4. Imaginary places
1606997904; 9781606997901, $29.99

LC 2014501149

Eisner Nominee: Best Graphic Album — New (2016)

"Cartoonist Sam Zabel hasn't drawn a comic in years. Stuck in a nightmare of creative block and despair, Sam spends his days writing superhero stories for a large American comics publisher and staring at a blank piece of paper, unable to draw a single line. Then one day he finds a mysterious old comic book set on Mars and is suddenly thrown headlong into a wild, fantastic journey through centuries of comics, stories, and imaginary worlds." (Publisher's note)

Horrocks "presents the various landscapes and characters that Sam encounters in a wonderfully expressive style that subtlety shifts to match the genre represented by each universe he visits, but the author has more lofty aims here than an exploration of the wide world of comics. Instead, the story serves as a meditation on the creative act and raises serious questions about the challenges of building fantasy worlds responsibly, as well as whether individuals are morally accountable for the fantasies running through their heads." LJ

Hoshino, Katsura

D.Gray-Man Volume 1. story and art by Katsura Hoshino; translation and English adaptation, Mayumi Kobayashi. Viz Media/Shonen Jump Advanced 2006 192p. Illustration

Grades: 10 11 12 Adult   **741.5; Fic**
1. Adventure graphic novels; 2. Fantasy graphic novels; 3. Graphic novels; 4. Manga; 5. Supernatural graphic novels; 6. Shonen manga
978-1-4215-0623-4, $7.99

Set in a fictional end of the 19th century England, the story revolves around a teenage boy named Allen Walker who is cursed with a cross mark on his hand that turns his arm into an enormous weapon, which he uses to hunt down and kill akumas. An akuma, generated by The Millenium Earl, a 1,000-year-old phantom, is implanted into a human's soul during a moment of devastation and despair. The phantom uses the demons to then carry out his goal: destroy all humankind. Allen, a 15-year-old boy, roams the Earth in search of Innocence. Washed away to unknown parts of the world after The Great Flood, Innocence is the mysterious substance used to create weapons that obliterate the akumas. The action is over-the-top in style, with lots of demon-fighting action.

Hosler, Jay

★ **Evolution:** the story of life on Earth. written by Jay Hosler; art by Zander Cannon and Kevin Cannon. Hill and Wang 2011 150p. Illustration

Grades: 9 10 11 12 Adult   **741.5; 576.8**
1. Evolution (Biology); 2. Graphic novels
0809094762; 9780809094769

LC 2010-05777

Alien scientist Bloort-183 takes King Floorsh-727 and Prince Floorsh-418 on a tour of Earth's history, explaining the theory of evolution. These are the same aliens who explored human genetics in The Stuff of Life. The illustrations by Kevin Cannon and Zander Cannon (no relation to each other) help human readers see how the theory of evolution explains the beginnings of life on Earth, the four conditions needed for natural selection, the Cambrian explosion, the Permian extinction, sexual selection, the evolution of modern humans, and the Earth scientists who studied the life forms and made the scientific discoveries. The book includes an illustrated glossary, a list of further reading, and endpapers filled with all kinds of dinosaurs.

"This delightful book seems ideal for nonscientists who want to entertainingly brush up their knowledge of evolution as well as for students from middle school on up." Booklist

The **Sandwalk** Adventures: An Adventure in Evolution Told in Five Chapters. Active Synapse 2003 160p. Illustration

Grades: 4 5 6 7 8 9 10 11 12 Adult
576.8; 741.5
1. Evolution — Graphic novels; 2. Graphic novels; 3. Science — Graphic novels; 4. Darwin, Charles; 5. Darwin, Charles — Graphic novels
0-9677255-1-8, $20

Courtesy of Active Synapse

Scientist Hosler explains Darwin's theory of evolution in a whimsical fashion. Follicle mites Mara and Willy live in Darwin's left eyebrow, and by accident they discover that Darwin, whom they call the god Flycatcher, can hear Mara. He thinks he's going crazy, but as he takes his daily walks on the Sandwalk at his home in England, Darwin does his best to convince Mara and Willy that he isn't a god and tells them about evolution. Hosler uses humor and whimsy, but also did a lot of research; the book includes explanatory notes and a long bibliography of sources.

Hosoda, Mamoru
Wolf children Ame & Yuki. original story: Mamoru Hosoda; art: Yu; character design: Yoshiyuki Sadamoto; translation: Jocelyne Allen; lettering: Tania Biswas, Lys Blakeslee. Yen Press 2014 538 p. Color; Illustration
Grades: 10 11 12 Adult   **741.5**
1. Widows — Fiction; 2. Seinen manga; 3. Werewolves — Fiction; 4. Manga
031640165X; 9780316401654, $26
"When Hana falls in love with a young interloper she encounters in her college class, the last thing she expects to learn is that he is part wolf. Instead of rejecting her lover upon learning his secret, she accepts him with open arms.... But after what seems like a mere moment of bliss to Hana, the father of her children is tragically taken from her." (Publisher's note)
"This emotion-laden work focuses on family and community issues.... The soft color palette of these watercolors complements the tender emotion of the plot." Lib Med Con

Houck, Janet
Kashimashi: Girl Meets Girl Vol. 1. story by Satoru Akahori; art by Yukimaru Katsura; [translation, Adrienne Beck; adaptation, Janet Houck]. Seven Seas Entertainment 2006 un Illustration
Grades: 10 11 12 Adult   **741.5; Fic**
1. Fantasy graphic novels; 2. Graphic novels; 3. Manga; 4. Romance graphic novels; 5. Yuri manga
978-1-933164-34-2, $10.99
Being a girl is harder than it looks. For Hazumu, this couldn't be truer, because just the other day, she... was a he. Shunned by the girl of his dreams, Hazumu loses himself in the mountains and is promptly squashed by an oncoming space ship. The alien inside, feeling guilty, rebuilds Hazumu's body... but as the wrong gender! Now Hazumu must learn how to be the girl his parents always wanted while dealing with the trials and tribulations of being caught in a love triangle between two girls — his childhood friend, Tomari, and Yasuna, the girl who rejected him but is now strangely attracted to him/her. This yuri (girl-girl romance) manga was published in a shonen magazine in Japan. The book includes partial nudity and sexual situations.
Volume 1 of 5

Houser, Jody
Faith; Volume 1: Hollywood & Vine. by Jody Houser, illustrated by Marguerite Sauvage and Francis Portela. Valiant Entertainment, LLC 2016 112 p. Color; Illustration
Grades: 8 9 10 11 12 Adult
741.5; Fic
1. Female superhero graphic novels; 2. Superheroes
9781682151211, $9.99; 1682151212
"Orphaned at a young age, Faith Herbert — a psionically gifted 'psiot'...is taking control of her destiny and becoming the

Courtesy of Valiant Entertainment

hard-hitting hero she's always known she can be — complete with a mild-mannered secret identity, unsuspecting colleagues, and a day job as a reporter that routinely throws into her harms way!" (Publisher's note)
"This is a modern twist on the classic superhero tale. Faith doesn't have the typical superheroine body type, dismantling stereotypes about what it means to be superpowered." SLJ
Originally published in single magazine form as Faith #1-4

Howard, Josh
Dead @17: compendium edition. Viper Comics 2008 336p. Illustration
Grades: 10 11 12 Adult   **741.5; Fic**
1. Adventure graphic novels; 2. Graphic novels; 3. Horror graphic novels
978-0-9793680-3, $24.95
Seventeen-year-old Nara Kilday's murder is the start of a new battle between good and evil. Her best friend Hazy investigates Nara's death and uncovers a dark side that he hadn't known. Meanwhile, an evil has raised an army of the undead, intending to reshape the world in its image. Among the undead is Nara, however, and she may just be the only thing standing in the way of Armageddon. Well, Nara, Hazy and Noel, that is. This book collects the original trilogy; Howard has revised and expanded it, and this book also includes cover and pinup galleries as well as a section of fan-produced arts and photographs. The book includes nudity and bloody violence.

Dead@17: Revolution. Viper Comics 2005 un Illustration
Grades: 10 11 12 Adult   **741.5; Fic**
1. Graphic novels; 2. Horror graphic novels; 3. Mystery graphic novels
0-9754193-3-1, $14.95
A political assassination plot by a mysterious group called Heaven's Militia unravels a government conspiracy with ties to Nara's past and future. She's forced to make a choice that could expose her secret to the world and puts her at odds with Noel Raddemer, her one ally. But somehow she has to stop the demon Bolabogg from achieving his goal, or the world will not survive. The book includes violence, strong language, and nudity.

Howe, Sean
Marvel Comics: the untold story. by Sean Howe. Harper 2012 485 p.
Grades: Adult   **741.5/973**
1. Marvel Comics Group; 2. Comic books, strips, etc. — United States — History and criticism; 3. Comic books, strips, etc. — History; 4. Superhero comic books, strips, etc.; 5. United States — History — 20th century
0061992100; 9780061992100, $26.99
                                   LC 2012015058
Author Sean Howe presents a book on the history of Marvel Comics. Howe "reveals the outsized personalities behind the scenes, including Martin Goodman, the self-made publisher who forayed into comics after a get-rich-quick tip in 1939...and Jack Kirby, the World War II veteran who'd co-created Captain America in 1940 and, twenty years later, developed with Lee the bulk of the company's marquee characters in a three-year frenzy of creativity that would be the grounds for future legal battles and endless debates." (Publisher's note)
Includes bibliographical references and index

Hudlin, Reginald
Black Panther: Civil War. Marvel Entertainment 2007 un Illustration
Grades: 9 10 11 12 Adult   **741.5; Fic**
1. Black Panther (Fictional character); 2. Graphic novels; 3. Superhero graphic novels
978-0-7851-2235-7, $17.99

King T'Challa and Queen Ororo, Black Panther and Storm, embark on a diplomatic tour that will have them spanning the globe and beyond. Stops include Latveria (Dr. Doom), the Moon (Black Bolt and the Inhumans), Atlantis (Namor the Sub-Mariner) and the Civil War-ravaged United States, for a meeting with none other than the point man for the U.S. government's implementation of the Superhuman Registration Act: Tony Stark, T'Challa's former Avengers teammate. Will the Black Panther and Storm decide to step off the sidelines of the Civil War and get involved?

Black Panther: The Bride. Marvel Entertainment 2006 un Illustration
Grades: 9 10 11 12 Adult 		**741.5; Fic**
1. Black Panther (Fictional character); 2. Graphic novels; 3. Superhero graphic novels
978-0-7851-2107-7, $14.99
Every king needs a queen, and the Black Panther, who is also the King of Wakanda, sets out on an epic quest to find a wife. His heart is Storm's if she'll accept his hand in marriage. The question is, does she want it? With a super hero civil war ready to explode in the U.S., and snakes in the Wakanda court preparing to make their moves, the road to the altar could not be more complicated.

Huizenga, Kevin
★ **Curses**. Drawn & Quarterly 2006 145p. Illustration
Grades: 11 12 Adult 		**741.5; Fic**
1. Graphic novels
978-1-894937-86-3, $21.95
Huizenga's central character in his comics is Glenn Ganges, a seemingly middle-class man living in the suburbs whose blank-eyed wonderment at everyday experiences brings together such diverse aspects of the world as golf, theology, late-night diners, parenthood, politics, Sudanese refugees, and hallucinatory vision, into a complete experience as multifaceted as our own lives. There is some use of strong language.

Gloriana: Glenn Ganges comics. by Kevin H. Huizenga. Drawn & Quarterly. Distributed in the USA by Farrar, Straus and Giroux 2012 117 p.
Grades: Adult 		**741.5**
1. Comic books, strips, etc; 2. Social interaction — Comic books, strips, etc; 3. Everyday life — Comic books, strips, etc.
1770460616; 9781770460614, $19.95
	LC 2012452358
In this comic book, "Kevin Huizenga exposes the mechanics that underpin everyday life. His protagonist, Glenn Ganges, has conversations about dish soap and library visits that are both faithful depictions of the mundane interactions we all have and so much more: existential dissections of the units that construct our lives." (Publisher's note)

Humphries, Sam
Sacrifice. by Sam Humphries, illustrated by Dalton Rose, edited by Daniel Chabon. Dark Horse 2013 168 p.
Grades: Adult 		**741.5; Fic**
1. Aztecs — Fiction; 2. Time travel — Graphic novels
1595829857; 9781595829856, $19.99
This graphic novel, by Sam Humphries, asks "what happens when a troubled youth is plucked from modern society and thrust though time and space on a psychedelic journey into the heart of the Aztec civilization. [Readers] join Hector on a one-way trip through the past, the present, and the psychedelic into the glory of the Aztec Empire." (Publisher's note)
"Fascinating history combines with fantasy and science fiction...[a]s Hector slides through time." Pub Wkly

Hutchison, David
Biowulf Volume 1. Antarctic Press 2007 un Illustration
Grades: 10 11 12 Adult 		**741.5; Fic**

1. Adventure graphic novels; 2. Beowulf — Adaptations — Graphic novels; 3. Graphic novels; 4. Horror graphic novels; 5. Science fiction graphic novels
978-0-9787725-2-9, $14.95
In the staggering wreckage of Earth's future, the great King Hrothgar and his armies have known only victory after bloody victory. Now, on the brink of uniting the battling lands and bringing the long wars to an end, Hrothgar's rule is threatened. His actions have awakened the ancient evil of the Grendel, and his men are powerless to defend themselves against the demon's wrath. Only with the aid of the young hero Beowulf and a cunning trap can they hope to kill Grendel and finally know peace. In this cyberpunk adaptation, Beowulf is an Advance, a genetically engineered, cybernetically enhanced human warrior; and Grendel is a monster, but he's not the real villain. The book includes a lot of graphic, bloody violence.

Hyde, Laurence
Southern Cross. Drawn & Quarterly 2007 256p. Illustration
Grades: 10 11 12 Adult 		**741.5**
1. Atomic bomb — Testing — Graphic novels; 2. Graphic novels; 3. Stories without words — Graphic novels
978-1-897299-10-4, $24.95
This is a wordless novel, told in 118 wood engravings, about the atomic bomb testing performed by the United States in the South Pacific following World War II. This new hardcover edition is a facsimile of the original edition, published in 1951. Laurence Hyde was infuriated with the United States' continued testing in the Bikini Atoll, following the mass destruction and unthinkable horrors resulting from the atomic bombs dropped on Hiroshima and Nagasaki in August 1945. The story depicts the evacuation of the Polynesian islander from their homes; during the evacuation, a fisherman kills a sailor who attempts to rape his wife. The couple flees with their child into the jungle to avoid capture. After the other islanders have evacuated, the Americans detonate an atom bomb on the ocean floor, and the fisherman and his family suffer horribly from the effects. The book includes nudity and depiction of the attempted rape.

Miles, Hyman
Shirley Jackson's The Lottery: The Authorized Graphic Adaptation. Miles Hyman. Hill & Wang 2016 160 p. Illustration
Grades: 10 11 12 Adult 		**741.5**
1. Lotteries — Comic books, strips, etc.; 2. Rites and ceremonies — Comic books, strips, etc.; 3. Villages — Comic books, strips, etc.
9780809066490, $30; 9780809066506; 9780809066513
	LC 2016007147
This graphic adaptation by Miles Hyman allows readers to experience Shirley Jackson's short story "The Lottery" "as never before, or to discover it anew. He has crafted an eerie vision of the hamlet where the tale unfolds and the unforgettable ritual its inhabitants set into motion. Hyman's full-color, meticulously detailed panels create a noirish atmosphere that adds a new dimension of dread to the original story." (Publisher's note)
"Hyman, Jackson's grandson, imbues realistic characters with a blocky stoicism in full-color panels flooded with sun-parched orange light. Much of the rendition is wordless, the art carrying this tale of quiet horror." LJ

Ikeda, Riyoko
Claudine. story and art by Riyoko Ikeda; translation by Jocelyne Allen; lettering and retouch by CK Russell. Seven Seas Entertainment 2018 104 p. Illustration
Grades: 9 10 11 12 Adult 		**741.5; Fic**
1. Gender identity — Fiction; 2. LGBT people — Fiction
1626928916; 9781626928916, $13.99

This book, by Riyoko Ikeda, tells the story of Claudine, who was "born...in a female-assigned body that doesn't reflect the man inside. [T]his heart-wrenching story follows Claudine through life, pain, and the love of several women.... Ikeda explores gender and sexuality in early twentieth century France in this powerful tale about identity, culture, and self-acceptance." (Publisher's note)

"Featuring flowing layouts and glamorously stylized, statuesque figures, the first English translation of this novella, originally published in 1978, from the creator of The Rose of Versailles is well-timed to spark conversation around transgender representation in literary history." Pub Wkly

Ilya

The **Mammoth** book of cult comics. edited by Ilya. Running Press Book Publishers 2013 448 p. Illustration

Grades: Adult **741.5**
 1. Underground comic books, strips, etc.; 2. Comic books, strips, etc.
 0762454687; 9780762454686, $17.95

LC 2014940740

This book "culls material from rare and lesser-known self-published and small-press comics, some recent but most going back to the 1990s, and many originally published as photocopied minicomics." Included is "'Hummingbird,' Gregory Benton's first issue of an unrealized series about a dysfunctional family reunion." (Publishers Weekly)

"Ilya's selection of comics spanning from 1983 to 2006 — cult comics if in the UK, alternative comics in the U.S. — is altogether outstanding. The variety of style and subject is gratifyingly broad yet exclusive." Booklist

Immonen, Kathryn

Russian Olive to Red King. Kathryn Immonen and Stuart Immonen. AdHouse Books 2015 176 p. Color; Illustration

Grades: Adult

741.5; Fic
 1. Grief — Fiction; 2. Depression (Psychology)
 1935233343; 9781935233343, $24.95

Courtesy of AdHouse Books

"When your lover may be dead, how long can you hold on to what remains? To whatever is left of you? A plane crash, a package, her dog, her voice. A notebook, his writer's block, and heat-distorted summer memories of a search for Jumbo the Elephant and an absent father." (Publisher's note)

Inagaki, Riichiro

Eyeshield 21 Volume 1. Viz Media/Shonen Jump Advanced 2005 208p. Illustration

Grades: 10 11 12 Adult **741.5; Fic**
 1. Football — Graphic novels; 2. Graphic novels; 3. Humorous graphic novels; 4. Manga; 5. Shonen manga
 1-59116-752-3, $7.99

What does a wimpy kid who's been bullied all his life have to depend on but his own two feet? Sena Kobayakawa is about to start his first year in high school and he's vowed not to get picked on anymore. Unfortunately, the sadistic captain of the football team already has his eye on Sena and his lightning-fast speed. As the Devil Bats' "secret weapon," Sena uses a superhero-like secret identity, Eyeshield 21, to protect himself from other teams. This is a football story for people who don't know or like American football. The series includes crude humor, strong language, and some playing field violence.

Inoue, Takehiko

★ **Real,** volume 1. story & art by Takehiko Inoue. Viz Media 2008 222p. Illustration

Grades: 10 11 12 Adult **741; Fic; 741.5**
 1. Basketball — Graphic novels; 2. Graphic novels; 3. Manga; 4. Sports — Graphic novels; 5. Wheelchair basketball — Graphic novels; 6. Seinen manga
 978-1-4215-1989-0, $12.99

Nomiya was the controlling rider on a motorcycle when he got into an accident that paralyzed the young woman riding with him; now he has dropped out of high school in his senior year and feels guilty. Togawa is stuck in a wheelchair but still plays basketball, which was the only thing Nomiya was good at in school. Togawa has quit the wheelchair basketball team, but he still plays. Nomiya starts playing while in a wheelchair, and they soon start a bit of a scam against regular players. They each have their own goals, but can they work together and find a better life for themselves? The book includes some harsh language, partial nudity, and Nomiya commits a bodily act against his school when he leaves.

"A compelling story of tragedy and struggle, Real is sure to appeal to teens — especially to male readers." SLJ

Original Japanese edition, 2001; Volume 1 of an ongoing series

★ **Vagabond,** Vol. 1. by Takehiko Inoue; [English adaptation by Yuji Oniki]. Viz 2002 un Illustration

Grades: 11 12 Adult **741.5; Fic**
 1. Graphic novels; 2. Manga; 3. Samurai — Graphic novels; 4. Seinen manga; 5. Musashi, Miyamoto, c. 1584-1645
 1-59116-034-0, $12.95

Based on the novel Musashi by Eiji Yoshikawa, this is the story of Shinmen Takezo, a young foot soldier who survived the Battle of Sekigahara, which marked the beginning of the Tokugawa Era in Japan. Destined to become the legendary sword saint Miyamoto Musashi, Takezo is a wild young brute, a cold-hearted killer who wants to make a name for himself. This first volume in the ongoing series includes sword fights, some nudity, and sexual situations.

Also available as 12 VIZBIG volumes; Volume 1 of 37

Irving, Christopher

Comics Introspective Volume One: Peter Bagge. Twomorrows Publishing 2007 122p. Illustration

Grades: Adult Professional

741.5
 1. Graphic novels; 2. Bagge, Peter
 978-1-893905-83-2, $16.95

Courtesy of Twomorrows Publishing

Peter Bagge's work runs the gamut from political (his strips for reason.com), to absurdist and satirical (the Batboy strip for Weekly World News), and dramatic (Apocalypse Nerd). From his Seattle studio, Bagge lets journalist Christopher Irving in on everything from just what was on his mind with his long-running Gen X comic Hate!, to what's going on in his head as a political satirist. This volume features an assortment of artwork picked by Bagge himself. The book includes some strong language, and some of the art includes sexual situations.

Irwin, Jane

Vogelein: Old Ghosts. Fiery Studios 2007 168p. Illustration

Grades: 7 8 9 10 11 12 Adult **741.5; Fic**
 1. Fantasy graphic novels; 2. Graphic novels
 0-9743110-1-4, $12.95

Courtesy of Fiery Studios

Though three hundred years have passed since Alexi's death, Vogelein finds herself still haunted by the unkept promise she made to her first Guardian. Now the clockwork faerie must confront her past with the help of Mason, an itinerant musician whose spirit bears a striking resemblance to the one she desperately wants to lay to rest. As she struggles to find peace for both herself and Alexi, Vogelein discovers that centuries-old questions rarely have easy answers, intended paths reveal themselves in mysterious ways, and present-day threats strike just as suddenly as those from long ago.

Ishida, Sui

Tokyo Ghoul: Re; Volume 1. by Sui Ishida. Viz 2017 224 p. Illustration

Grades: 10 11 12 Adult   **741.5**
1. Horror fiction — Graphic novels; 2. Seinen manga
142159496X; 9781421594965, $12.99
In this book, by Sui Ishida, "Haise Sasaki has been tasked with teaching Qs Squad how to be outstanding investigators, but his assignment is complicated by the troublesome personalities of his students and his own uncertain grasp of his Ghoul powers. Can he pull them together as a team, or will Qs Squad first assignment be their last?" (Publisher's note)
Volume 1 of an ongoing series

Tokyo Ghoul; Volume 1. by Sui Ishida; translation, Joe Yamazaki. Viz 2015 224 p. Illustration

Grades: 10 11 12 Adult   **741.5**
1. Seinen manga; 2. Horror fiction; 3. Manga; 4. College students — Fiction
1421580365; 9781421580364, $12.99
"Ghouls live among us, the same as normal people in every way-except their craving for human flesh. Ken Kaneki is an ordinary college student until a violent encounter turns him into the first half-human half-ghoul hybrid. Trapped between two worlds, he must survive Ghoul turf wars, learn more about Ghoul society and master his new powers." (Publisher's note)
Volume 1 of 14

Ito, Junjo

Fragments of Horror. story & art by Junji It?; translation & adaptation, Jocelyn Allen; touch-up art & lettering, Eric Erbes. Viz 2015 224 p. Illustration

Grades: Adult   **741.5**
1. Seinen manga; 2. Horror fiction
1421580799; 9781421580791, $17.99
This book, by Junji Ito is a "collection of delightfully macabre tales from a master of horror manga. An old wooden mansion that turns on its inhabitants. A dissection class with a most unusual subject. A funeral where the dead are definitely not laid to rest. Ranging from the terrifying to the comedic, from the erotic to the loathsome, these stories showcase Junji Ito's long-awaited return to the world of horror." (Publisher's note)
Originally published in Japan in 2014.

GYO 1-2: The Death Stench Creeps. Junji Ito. Viz 2015 400 p. Illustration

Grades: Adult   **741.5**
1. Horror fiction; 2. Manga; 3. Seinen manga
1421579154; 9781421579153, $22.99

In this work graphic novel work of manga by Junji ito "something is rotten in Okinawa... The floating smell of death hangs over the island. What is it? A strange, legged fish appears on the scene. So begins Tadashi and Kaori's spiral into the horror and stench of the sea." (Publisher's note)

Shiver: selected stories. story & art by Junji Ito; translation & adaptation, Jocelyn Allen; touch-up art & lettering, James Dashiell. Viz 2017 392 p. Illustration

Grades: Adult   **741.5; Fic**
1. Manga; 2. Japanese fiction
1421596938; 9781421596938, $22.99
Eisner Nominee: Best U.S. Edition of International Material — Asia (2018)
This horror manga collection "includes nine of Junji Ito's best short stories, as selected by the author himself and presented with accompanying notes and commentary. An arm peppered with tiny holes dangles from a sick girl's window.... After an idol hangs herself, balloons bearing faces appear in the sky, some even featuring your own face.... An offering of nine fresh nightmares for the delectation of horror fans." (Publisher's note)
"Ito switches among Lovecraft-inspired investigations of cosmic menace, body horror in the manner of filmmaker David Cronenberg, and tales of terror emerging from the most mundane sources, reminiscent of Stephen King. But ultimately he's unlike anyone else in his ability to create images that seem drawn from a highly specific, personal, and primordial well of utter darkness." LJ

Uzumaki: spiral into horror. by Junji Ito. Viz 2013 634 p. Illustration; Color

Grades: Adult   **741.5**
1. Horror graphic novels; 2. Manga; 3. Seinen manga
1421561328; 9781421561325, $27.99
In this book, by Junji Ito, "Kurôzu-cho, a small fogbound town on the coast of Japan, is cursed. According to Shuichi Saito...their town is haunted not by a person or being but by a pattern: uzumaki, the spiral, the hypnotic secret shape of the world. It manifests itself in small ways: seashells, ferns, whirlpools in water, whirlwinds in air. And in large ways: the spiral marks on people's bodies, the insane obsessions of Shuichi's father, the voice from the cochlea in your inner ear." (Publisher's note)

Iwaaki, Hitoshi

Parasyte vol. 3. Del Rey Manga 2008 284p. Illustration

Grades: 10 11 12 Adult   **741.5; Fic**
1. Graphic novels; 2. Horror graphic novels; 3. Manga; 4. Science fiction graphic novels; 5. Seinen manga
978-0-345-49825-0, $12.95
Alien parasites have invaded Earth and taken over the minds and bodies of ordinary people, in order to be able to feed on humans. Shin has been invaded by a parasite, but he stopped the invasion of his body and limited it to one arm. He can communicate with the parasite, whom he has named Migi (Japanese for right), and he can sense who is actually a parasite masquerading as a human. Now he's been approached by two mysterious victims of the invasion: Tamiya, a beautiful school teacher, and Shimada, another student. What do they really want? The book includes gory violence.

Parasyte vol.4. Del Rey Manga 2008 296p. Illustration

Grades: 10 11 12 Adult   **741.5; Fic**
1. Graphic novels; 2. Horror graphic novels; 3. Manga; 4. Seinen manga
978-0-345-49826-7, $14.95
Shinichi and Migi, the Parasyte that merged with him, continue their search for the Parasytes who kill humans, even as Shinichi tries to be a "normal" high school student. Then he meets Kana, a classmate who seems to have a knack for sensing the killer aliens. The fact that the aliens are getting into politics in order to gain positions of power disturbs Shinichi,

but he also suspects that Migi may be infiltrating his brain, too. The book includes violence and bloodshed, and brief partial nudity.

Parasyte, Vol. 1. Ballantine Books/Del Rey Manga 2007 282p. Illustration
Grades: 11 12 Adult   741.5; Fic
1. Graphic novels; 2. Horror graphic novels; 3. Manga; 4. Science fiction graphic novels; 5. Seinen manga
978-0-345-49624-9, $12.95

Aliens come to Earth in a silent invasion, taking over human bodies; their plan is to kill and eat humans. One ordinary high school student, Shin, fights off an alien and it only manages to get into his right hand. Once the parasitic alien has matured while still stuck in Shin's right hand, it can't get to his brain. They settle into an uneasy relationship, as Migi (Japanese for "right") tries to learn everything and Shin just tries to keep up a normal appearance. Soon, though, they find other aliens, and Shin can't let the parasites take over without trying to fight back.

Iwaaki alleviates the horror with plenty of dark humor; he also uses harsh language, including f-bombs and s-bombs, and some sexual innuendo.

Originally published in a flipped (American style) manga series by Tokyopop from 1997 to 2002; this edition retains the right-to-left orientation, Japanese sound effects, and other original elements.

Iwanaga, Ryoutaro
Pumpkin scissors vol. 1. translated by Ikoi Hiroe. Del Rey Manga 2007 218p. Illustration
Grades: 10 11 12 Adult   Fic; 741; 741.5
1. Adventure graphic novels; 2. Graphic novels; 3. Manga; 4. Shonen manga
978-0-345-50119-6, $10.95

The bitter war between the Empire and the Republic of Frost has ended, but three years after the cease-fire, the Empire is still ravaged by starvation and disease, and bandits terrorize the people. Can the Imperial Army State Section III, aka Pumpkin Scissors, stop a renegade force bent on destruction? And who is the mysterious stranger helping Pumpkin Scissors? The book includes some violence and mildly harsh language.

Jackson, Jack
Jack Jackson's American History: Los Tejanos & Lost Cause. W W Norton & Co Inc 2013 320 p.
Grades: Adult   976.40022
1. Graphic novels; 2. United States — History
1606995049; 9781606995044, $35

This book is a collection of two historical graphic novels by late artist Jack Jackson. "'Lost Cause'...is a...history of mob violence...that uses the Taylor-Sutton feud in post-Civil War southern Texas" to view "many white Texans' reactions to Reconstruction." The second story is 'Los Tejanos,' which follows the tragic history of Juan Seguin, a heroic tejano who fought brilliantly for Texas's independence." (Publishers Weekly)

Jacobson, Sidney
The **9/11** report: a graphic adaptation. by Sid Jacobson and Ernie Colón; [with a foreword by Thomas H. Kean and Lee H. Hamilton]. Hill and Wang 2006 133p. Illustration
Grades: 9 10 11 12 Adult   973.931; 741.5
1. Graphic novels; 2. September 11 terrorist attacks, 2001 — Graphic novels
0-8090-5738-7; 978-0-8090-5738-2, $30; 0-8090-5739-5 (pa); 978-0-8090-5739-9 (pa), $16.95

"The book aims to make...[The 9/11 Commission Report] more accessible to all readers and draw in young adults.... This graphic adaptation is an important and necessary part of any collection." Libr J
On cover: Based on the final report of the National Commission on Terrorist Attacks upon the United States

Anne Frank: the Anne Frank House authorized graphic biography. [by] Sid Jacobson and Ernie Colón. Hill and Wang 2010 152p. Illustration
Grades: 9 10 11 12 Adult   92; 741.5
1. Holocaust, 1933-1945 — Graphic novels; 2. Jews — Netherlands — Graphic novels
978-0-8090-2684-5, $30; 978-0-8090-2685-2 (pa), $16.95
LC 2010-5776

Draws on the archives of the Anne Frank House to relate the short but inspiring life of the Jewish teen memoirist, from the lives of her parents to Anne's years keeping her private diary while hidden from the Nazis to her untimely death in a concentration camp.

Jansson, Tove
Moomin Book One. Drawn & Quarterly 2006 96p. Illustration
Grades: 8 9 10 11 12 Adult   741.5; Fic
1. Graphic novels; 2. Humorous graphic novels; 3. Moomins (Fictional characters)
1-894937-80-5, $19.95

Jansson is best known in the U.S. for her children's books featuring the Moomins, hippo-shaped creatures. Her comic strips have a more mature outlook. Moomin needs help getting rid of unwanted guests, but the only solution that works costs him his house. Then his scheming friend Sniff involves him in all sorts of shady get-rich-quick schemes. And when Moomin finds his long-lost parents, his father's craving for adventure causes more trouble. Snorkmaiden, Moomin's girlfriend, is just as bad as Moominpapa, and they spark a boat trip south to a resort, where the naive Moomins think they're houseguests and everyone else, including the hotel staff, assumes they're wealthy eccentrics. The childlike look of the strips belie the goings-on; this book is not really for young readers, although teens and adults will enjoy the whimsy overlaying sharp satire.

Moomin's winter follies. Trove Jansson. Enfant 2012 45 p.
Grades: 8 9 10 11 12 Adult   741.5
1. Moomins (Fictional characters); 2. Comic books, strips, etc.
1770460985; 9781770460980, $9.95

Author Tove Jansson presents a graphic novel. "Moomin wakes up one morning to find the pond frozen over, and rather than hibernate, the family decides to brave the winter weather. At first, their wintry adventure seems to be going swimmingly, until Mr. Brisk of the Great Outdoors Club takes over and forces everyone to embrace the winter sports, whether they want to or not." (Comic Vine)

Jason
Hey, wait.... by Jason; [edited and translated from the Norwegian by Kim Thompson]. Fantagraphics 2001 64 p. Illustration
Grades: Adult   741.5
1. Graphic novels — Norway; 2. Autobiographical graphic novels
9781560974635, $12.95; 156097463X
Harvey Award: Best New Talent (2002)

This graphic novel, written and illustrated by the Scandinavian cartoonist Jason, edited and translated from the Norwegian by Kim Thompson, "starts off as a melancholy childhood memoir and then, with a shocking twist midway through, becomes the summary of lives lived, wasted, and lost." (Publisher's note)

The **Left** Bank Gang. Fantagraphics Books 2006 46p. Illustration
Grades: 10 11 12 Adult   741.5; Fic
1. Graphic novels; 2. Mystery graphic novels

978-1-56097-742-1, $12.95

Double-crosses, violence, and harsh language pepper this little noir story that depicts Ernest Hemingway, F. Scott Fitzgerald, Ezra Pound, and James Joyce as struggling cartoonists in 1920s Paris. Zelda Fitzgerald and Gertrude Stein are there, as well. Everyone is portrayed as dog-headed people, in Jason's signature art style.

Meow, Baby!. Fantagraphics Books 2005 un Illustration
Grades: 10 11 12 Adult   741.5; Fic
1. Graphic novels; 2. Humorous graphic novels
1-56097-695-0, $16.95

Jason unleashes his inner Scandinavian goofball with this big collection of hilarious shorter pieces. God, the Devil, mummies, vampires, zombies, werewolves, reanimated skeletons, space invaders, Death, cavemen, Godzilla and Elvis populate these most often wordless blackout gags, side by side with Jason's usual Little-Orphan-Annie-eyed, rabbit-and-bird-head protagonists — a "lighter side" of one of the best cartoonists of the new millennium. Some nudity and sexual situations, and a little violence, plus seeing what zombies eat are subtly present.

On the Camino. Jason. Fantagraphics 2017 192 p. Color; Illustration
Grades: Adult   92; 741.5
1. Spain — Description and travel; 2. Christian pilgrims and pilgrimages; 3. Hiking — Spain; 4. Autobiographical graphic novels
1683960211; 9781683960218, $24.99

This book is "internationally acclaimed cartoonist Jason's first full-length graphic memoir...about his experiences walking a 500-mile pilgrimage for his 50th birthday. Northwestern Spain, observed with the eye of an artist, chronicling both the good (people, conversations) and the bad (blisters, bedbugs) he encountered on his journey." (Publisher's note)

"There are no grand epiphanies in the end, but this intimate travelogue of life's little uncertainties, absurdities, and victories is a revealing addition to the Jason oeuvre." Pub Wkly

Jeanty, Georges
Buffy the Vampire Slayer season eight; Volume 1: the long way home. Dark Horse Comics 2007 136p. Illustration
Grades: 8 9 10 11 12 Adult   741.5
1. Adventure graphic novels; 2. Buffy the Vampire Slayer (Fictional character); 3. Graphic novels; 4. Horror graphic novels
978-1-59307-822-5, $15.95

The television series of Buffy the Vampire Slayer lasted seven seasons; this volume begins the comics-only eighth season. Buffy and her friends may have destroyed the Hellmouth, but all is not fun and games, as an old enemy returns, younger sister Dawn experiences some "growing pains," and a former decoy Slayer has her own troubles. There is a considerable amount of monster fighting.

Volume 1 of 8

Jenkins, Paul
Civil War: Front Line Book 1. Marvel Entertainment 2007 un Illustration
Grades: 9 10 11 12 Adult   741.5; Fic
1. Graphic novels; 2. Superhero graphic novels
978-0-7851-2312-5, $14.99

In "Embedded," reporters Sally Floyd and Ben Urich seek the truth at the heart of the war. In "The Accused," the lone survivor of the team that caused the Stamford tragedy has been found, and this vilified hero is placed under arrest for the deaths of an entire town. And his trouble is just beginning. This volume includes other stories, including the mystery of the Atlanteans.

Civil War: Front Line Book 2. Marvel Entertainment 2007 un Illustration

Grades: 9 10 11 12 Adult   741.5; Fic
1. Graphic novels; 2. Superhero graphic novels
978-0-7851-2469-6, $14.99

In "Embedded," hot on the trail of a revelation that could explode the rift between the pro-registration and anti-registration heroes and forever change the nature of the Registration Act, the Daily Bugle's Ben Urich and Sally Floyd have the story. Can they bring the power to the people? In "The Accused," his powers are gone, he's been held culpable for the worst super-human disaster in history, and every super-villain in prison is looking to take a piece of Speedball. Will he make it out alive, and with hundreds of deaths on his conscience, does he want to? In the meantime, Norman Osborn shoots an Atlantean ambassador, bringing the U.S. to the brink of war; and there's a traitor in Stark's group. This volume includes some violence.

Revelations. created by Paul Jenkins and Humberto Ramos; story by Paul Jenkins; art by Humberto Ramos; colors by Leonardo Olea and Edgar Delgado; letters by Richard Starkings and Comicraft. Dark Horse Comics 2006 un Illustration
Grades: 11 12 Adult   741.5; Fic
1. Catholic church — Graphic novels; 2. Graphic novels; 3. Mystery graphic novels
978-1-59307-239-1, $17.95

When a Cardinal in line to succeed the dying Pope falls from a high window in the Vatican, a priest calls on his friend, tough London cop Charlie Northern, to investigate. Once in Rome, Northern confronts coverups and secrets as he tries to find out what happened. What he learns will shake him to his atheistic core. This violent murder mystery will appeal to fans of The Da Vinci Code and other works depicting religious conspiracies.

Originally published as Revelations issues #1-6.

Jenson-Benjamin, Merideth
Library collections for teens: manga and graphic novels. [by] Kristen Fletcher-Spear and Merideth Jenson-Benjamin. Neal-Schuman Publishers 2010 175p.
Grades: Adult Professional   025.2
1. Comic books, strips, etc.; 2. Graphic novels; 3. Graphic novels — Bibliography; 4. Graphic novels — History and criticism; 5. Libraries — Special collections — Graphic novels; 6. Young adult literature; 7. Young adults' libraries
1-55570-745-9; 978-1-55570-745-3, $55

                                              LC 2010040895

"This practical and accessible manual is a basic primer for librarians who have never picked up a graphic novel — although those with considerable experience may learn a thing or two, too. Chapters cover standard topics, among them the history and evolution of American graphic novels and manga, educational and literacy benefits, collection development and management, selection and review sources, awards, and programming ideas. A detailed glossary and a list of recommended titles are also provided." (Booklist)

Includes glossary and bibliographical references

Johns, Geoff
52, Volume One. Geoff Johns, Grant Morrison, Greg Rucka, Mark Waid, Keith Giffen. DC Comics 2007 304p. Illustration
Grades: 10 11 12 Adult   741.5; Fic
1. Adventure graphic novels; 2. Graphic novels; 3. Mystery graphic novels; 4. Science fiction graphic novels; 5. Superhero graphic novels; 6. Superman (Fictional character)
978-1-4012-1353-4, $19.99

The events of Infinite Crisis have left Superman, Batman and Wonder Woman missing, many other superheroes dead or injured. Black Adam, the long-time nemesis of Shazam, seeks to gain allies to form a group to go up against the U.S. Ralph Dibny investigates a cult built around the idea of resurrecting Superboy. The Blue Beetle tries to use information from the 25th century to gain wealth and become the next big superhero. John Steel tries to go up against ex-President Lex Luthor, who has developed a drug that can "create" superheroes. DC Comics gathered four writers, a breakdown artist (Giffen), and a host of pencillers and inkers to create a year-long weekly comic book that plays out the action in real time. Johns, Morrison, Rucka, and Waid also worked together on every issue.

Originally published as 52 issues #1-13.; Volume 1 of 4

Batman: War Games Act Three: Endgame. DC Comics 2005 un Illustration

Grades: 10 11 12 Adult   **741.5; Fic**
   1. Batman (Fictional character); 2. Graphic novels; 3. Mystery graphic novels; 4. Superhero graphic novels
   1-4012-0431-7, $14.99

Black Mask has made Batman's training scenario a chilling reality. The various crime families are leaderless, and the soldiers run for their lives while trying to grab a piece of the underworld pie for themselves. Batman and his allies have failed to contain the chaos threatening the lives of Gotham City's people. The media have exploited the situation so people think Batman is acting against their best interests. Worse, he has lost the trust and support of Commissioner Akins, just when he needs it the most. Before the day is over, a friend and ally will be dead, familial ties will be broken, and the balance of power in the city will be forever altered.

Batman: earth one. Geoff Johns, Gary Frank. DC Comics 2012 144 p.

Grades: Adult   **741.5**
   1. Superhero graphic novels; 2. Revenge — Graphic novels; 3. Batman (Fictional character)
   1401232086; 9781401232085, $22.99; 9781401232092
                     LC 2012000608

This book is a reimagining of the origin story of the comic book superhero Batman. Here, "Bruce Wayne seeks revenge for his parents" murders against the backdrop of a crime-ridden Gotham City, with a few cosmetic updates, such as Alfred the Butler being portrayed as a grizzled military veteran who trains Bruce Wayne with tough love, and the Penguin as the corrupt mayor of Gotham City." (Publishers Weekly)

★ **DC** Universe Rebirth. Geoff Johns, writer. DC Comics 2016 96 p. Color; Illustration

Grades: Adult   **741.5**
   1. Superhero graphic novels
   1401270727; 9781401270728, $17.99
                     LC 2016042491

This comic, written by Geoff Johns, "heralds in a new era in storytelling and sets the stage for the future of the DC Universe. Wally West is trapped out of time and space, lost in the recesses of dimensional bleed due to the Flashpoint caused by his mentor, Barry Allen. Drifting in this nothingness, only Wally — the man once known as Kid Flash and then the Flash — can see the mystery pervading the universe. Who has stolen 10 years?" (Publisher's note)

Superman created by Jerry Siegel and Joe Shuster, by special arrangement with the Jerry Siegel family

The **Flash:** The Secret of Barry Allen. DC Comics 2005 un Illustration

Grades: 9 10 11 12 Adult   **741.5; Fic**
   1. Flash (Fictional character); 2. Graphic novels; 3. Superhero graphic novels
   1-4012-0723-5, $19.99

This volume details the events in Wally West's life as he regains his memory of being the Flash. He carefully chooses which friends and allies to whom he will again reveal his identity. Then, he and his pal Nightwing

are confronted with the return of Gorilla Grodd, more savage than ever. But the biggest shock in the Fastest Man Alive's life comes when he reads a letter from his mentor and predecessor, Barry Allen, revealing a dark decision that haunted him to the day he died. And after reading it, Wally needs to reassess what it means to be a hero in a world growing ever darker.

The **Flash:** crossfire. [by] Geoff Johns, writer; Scott Kolins, Rich Burchett, Justiniano, pencillers; Doug Hazlewood, Dan Panosian, Walden Wong, inkers; James Sinclair, colorist; Gaspar Saladino, Bill Oakley, letterers; Brian Bolland, Scott Kolins, original covers. DC Comics 2004 212p. Illustration

Grades: 10 11 12 Adult   **741.5; Fic**
   1. Graphic novels; 2. Superhero graphic novels; 3. Flash (Fictional character)
   1-4012-0195-4, $17.95
                     LC 2004-555611

"Eight...rogues have joined forces to take over Flash's town of Keystone City. As if that weren't enough, the Thinker, an artificial intelligence with a personality — a walking computer virus of sorts — is attempting to absorb the minds of the city's inhabitants, including Flash's. Writer Johns demonstrates his ability to reinvigorate the series' classic elements.... Teens will appreciate it as mainstream superhero fare, executed with complexity and flair." Booklist

The **Flash:** Wonderland. DC Comics 2007 144p. Illustration

Grades: 9 10 11 12 Adult   **741.5; Fic**
   1. Graphic novels; 2. Superhero graphic novels; 3. Flash (Fictional character)
   978-1-4012-1489-0, $12.99

The Flash, Wally West, finds himself on a parallel Earth in which there's no Speed Force, and without that energy source, he has no power. The cops think he's a murderer, and the only one who can help him is one of his enemies, Captain Cold, who's also in the same world. They join forces to try to get back to their Earth, but they've got to find out who brought them here.

Green Lantern Corps: Recharge. Geoff Johns, Dave Gibbons, writers; Patrick Gleason, penciller; Prentis Rollins, Christian Alamy, inkers; Phil Balsman, Pat Brosseau, Travis Lanham, letterers; Moose Baumann, colorist. DC Comics 2006 un Illustration

Grades: 9 10 11 12 Adult   **741.5; Fic**
   1. Graphic novels; 2. Superhero graphic novels; 3. Green Lantern (Fictional character)
   978-1-4012-0962-9, $12.99

After the return of Hal Jordan, the Guardians of the Universe have re-formed the Green Lantern Corps. The best and the brightest from across the universe find themselves chosen as members of the new Corps and summoned to the planet Oa, given power rings that turn strength of will into reality, and for training. While veteran ring-bearers gladly return to duty, some new recruits resent being drafted into the Corps against their will. Kyle Rayner, Guy Gardner, and Kilowog set out to train the new Green Lanterns, but something is making its way to Oa, something that threatens the very existence of the planet and the Guardians; can the new Corps stop it?

Green Lantern: No Fear. DC Comics 2006 un Illustration

Grades: 10 11 12 Adult   **741.5; Fic**
   1. Graphic novels; 2. Green Lantern (Fictional character); 3. Superhero graphic novels
   978-14012-0466-2, $24.99

Hal Jordan has been resurrected and redeemed. Now it's tie to get on with his life as Green Lantern, protector of space sector 2814. But even as he returns to the skies as an Air Force pilot, Jordan faces new threats from his old foes. The deadly Manhunter androids and the mutated Shark return with shocking violence...yet they are just precursors to even greater dangers. A maddened Black Hand embarks on a murderous rampage just as the Lantern finds himself the object of an alien race's insidious plan to harvest humans as living weapons of war. Johns works with artists Carlos Pacheco, Ethan Van Sciver, Darwyn Cooke, and Simone Bianchi in the stories collected here. There is some strong language, and violence, some graphic.

Green Lantern: Rebirth. DC Comics 2005 un Illustration
Grades: 9 10 11 12 Adult   **741.5; Fic**
1. Graphic novels; 2. Green Lantern (Fictional character); 3. Superhero graphic novels
9781401204655, $14.99

He was the greatest Green Lantern of them all. Then Hal Jordan went mad and ultimately died in an attempt to redeem himself. But fate was not done with him. Kyle Rayner, the sole Green Lantern, crashes back to Earth with a coffin bearing Hal Jordan's body, saying feverishly, "Parallax is coming." And Hal Jordan has returned. And so has Parallax, and the Spectre. Will one of them win and possess Jordan forever? Or can he become the Green Lantern once again?

Infinite Crisis. DC Comics 2006 262p. Illustration
Grades: 9 10 11 12 Adult   **741.5; Fic**
1. Graphic novels; 2. Superhero graphic novels
978-1-4012-0959-9, $24.99

Four heroes, trapped in limbo since the original Crisis on Infinite Earths, are about to reveal themselves: one is dying, one wants to save her and restore an entire world that vanished and the other two seek unrivaled power. The plan they concoct is literally earth-shattering, and the world's greatest superheroes may not be enough to stop their attempt to alter the very nature of reality.

JSA Presents Stars and S.T.R.I.P.E.. DC Comics 2007 192p. Illustration
Grades: 8 9 10 11 12 Adult   **741.5; Fic**
1. Graphic novels; 2. Superhero graphic novels
978-1-4012-1390-9, $17.99

Courtney Whitmore is just your typical teenage girl trying to make it through high school, but she's about to stumble upon a secret that will make her life a lot more complicated. Her new stepfather, Pat Dugan, was once Stripesy, sidekick of the Golden Age hero The Star-Spangled Kid. Finding the Kid's old costume, Courtney modifies it for herself and becomes the new Star-Spangled Kid, aiming to fight crime and annoy the heck out of her stepfather. But Dugan isn't about to let his new daughter get into any danger. Putting his mechanical skills to work, he creates a robotic suit called S.T.R.I.P.E., and joins Courtney's battle for justice. They fight side-by-side — and sometimes with each other — taking on aliens, cults, new villains, and more. These stories are the first that Johns wrote in comics, back in 1999.

JSA: Black Vengeance. DC Comics 2006 208p. Illustration
Grades: 10 11 12 Adult   **741.5; Fic**
1. Graphic novels; 2. Justice Society of America (Fictional characters); 3. Superhero graphic novels
978-1-4012-0966-7, $19.99

The JSA's former comrade, the Spectre, is now without a human host and running rampant, dealing out a brutal form of justice, encouraged by the new Eclipso. Atom-Smasher, also a former JSA member, seeks forgiveness for his actions in Kahndaq. Before the JSA decides whether or not to readmit him, Khandaq's ruler, Black Adam, summons the atomic hero back to the Middle East. When the JSA follow, all are forced to re-examine what it means to be a hero.

JSA: Lost. DC Comics 2005 208p. Illustration
Grades: 9 10 11 12 Adult   **741.5; Fic**

1. Graphic novels; 2. Science fiction graphic novels; 3. Superhero graphic novels
1-4012-0722-7, $19.99

The first Hourman sits alone at the end of time, having given his life to protect humanity. Sand, former chairman of the JSA, became one with the planet Earth to keep it whole. Hal Jordan sacrificed himself to become the new Spectre and keep the world safe. Now the JSA find themselves visiting old friends and new, rectifying injustices, aware that as they fix one problem, an even larger one is brewing in the time stream. The end of this volume contains spoilers about the killer's identity in the Identity Crisis. The book includes lots of superhero action and some violence.

Justice League; Volume 1. by Geoff Johns and illustrated by Jim Lee and Scott Williams. DC Comics 2013 192 p.
Grades: Adult   **741.5/973**
1. Aquaman (Fictitious character); 2. Superhero graphic novels; 3. Green Lantern (Fictional character); 4. Flash (Fictional character); 5. Batman (Fictional character); 6. Superman (Fictional character); 7. Justice League (Fictional characters); 8. Wonder Woman (Fictional character)
1401237886; 9781401234614; 9781401237882, $16.99
LC 2011051844

This graphic novel by Geoff Johns presents "an all-new origin story for the Justice League! Batman has stumbled upon a dark evil that threatens to destroy the earth.The Dark Knight must trust an alien, a scarlet speedster, an accidental teenage hero, a space cop, an Amazon Princess and an undersea monarch. Will this combination of Superman, The Flash, Cyborg, Green Lantern, Wonder Woman and Aquaman be able to put aside their differences and come together to save the world? (Publisher's note)

Originally published in single magazine form in JUSTICE LEAGUE 1-6 — T.p. verso.

Justice League; Volume 2. Geoff Johns, writer; Jim Lee ... [et .al], pencilers; Alex Sinclair ... [et .al], colorists; Sal Cipriano, Patrick Brosseau, Nick Napolitano, letters. DC Comics 2012 160 p.
Grades: Adult   **741.5**
1. Superheroes — Fiction; 2. Justice League (Fictional characters)
1401237649; 9781401237646, $24.99; 9781401237653
LC 2012040572

This graphic novel, written by Geoff Johns and illustrated by Jim Lee and Scott Williams features the Justice League. "Their never-ending battle against evil results in casualties beyond its super-powered...combatants. Unbeknownst to Earth — s greatest champions, their greatest triumph may contain the seeds of their greatest defeat. For heroes are not the only people who face tragedy and are reborn as something greater than they were before. Villains can take this journey, too." (Publisher's note)

Originally published in single magazine form in Justice League 7-12.

Power Girl. Geoff Johns, Paul Levitz, Paul Kupperberg, writers; Amanda Conner ... [et al.], pencillers; Jimmy Palmiotti ... [et al.], inkers; Paul Mounts ... [et al.], colorists; Rob Leigh ... [et al.], letterers. DC Comics 2006 176p. Illustration
Grades: 9 10 11 12 Adult   **741.5; Fic**
1. Adventure graphic novels; 2. Graphic novels; 3. Superhero graphic novels
978-1-4012-0968-1, $14.99

Who is Power Girl? Is she Superman's cousin from a parallel world? Is she the granddaughter of an ancient Atlantean sorcerer? Is she a pawn in a game of cosmic chess that threatens the known universe? Whoever she is, she's playing a major role in recent DC Universe titles. In these stories, some dating back to 1975, her reality keeps changing. The more recent stories include a little bit of suggestiveness.

Showcase Presents Superman Family Volume One. DC Comics 2006 572p. Illustration
Grades: 6 7 8 9 10 11 12 Adult   **741.5; Fic**

1. Graphic novels; 2. Jimmy Olsen (Fictional character); 3. Lois Lane (Fictional character); 4. Superhero graphic novels; 5. Superman (Fictional character)

978-1-4012-0787-8, $16.99

This volume spotlights Superman's girlfriend Lois Lane and his pal Jimmy Olsen. Learn more about these two dynamic personalities in their solo stories as each braves danger for the latest scoop. These stories from the 1950s also introduce long-standing elements such as the Daily Planet's Flying Newsroom and Jimmy's penchant for disguises. The Showcase series reprints the older comics stories in black and white collections.

Showcase Presents: Green Arrow Volume 1. DC Comics 2006 528p. Illustration

Grades: 7 8 9 10 11 12 Adult   **741.5; Fic**

1. Graphic novels; 2. Green Arrow (Fictional character); 3. Superhero graphic novels; 4. Green Arrow (Fictional character)

1-4012-0785-5, $16.99

Millionaire Oliver Queen mastered the bow and arrow as a matter of survival when he was trapped on a desert island. Back home in Star City, he chose to use his newfound skills as the costumed champion Green Arrow. With his sidekick, Speedy, he tackled crooks and solved mysteries with energy, style, and the occasional boxing glove arrow. The stories collected in this black and white volume were originally published from 1958 through 1969

Showcase Presents: Jonah Hex Volume 1. DC Comics 2005 528p. Illustration

Grades: 10 11 12 Adult   **741.5; Fic**

1. Graphic novels; 2. Jonah Hex (Fictional character); 3. Western graphic novels

1-4012-0760-X, $16.99

He was a hero to some, a villain to others; and wherever he rode, people spoke his name in whispers. He had no friends, this Jonah Hex, but he did have two companions: one was death itself, the other — the acrid smell of gun smoke. These are the earliest adventures of the gunslinger, which were first published in the early 1970s, at a time when the spaghetti westerns of Sergio Leone and others had introduced tough, violent antiheroes to the American fiction staple. The stories include a considerable amount of violence, but it's not too graphic, and very little strong language.

Showcase Presents: Superman Volume 1. DC Comics 2005 560p. Illustration

Grades: 6 7 8 9 10 11 12 Adult   **741.5; Fic**

1. Graphic novels; 2. Superhero graphic novels; 3. Superman (Fictional character)

1-4012-0758-8, $9.99

This first volume in the Showcase Presents Library of Classics features stories about Superman dating from 1958 through 1959. The adventure collected here have influenced the history of Superman and his extended family. From the introduction of his first love, the mermaid Lori Lemaris, to the introduction of his cousin Supergirl, Superman faces his most dangerous opponents, including Bizarro, Metallo, and Brainiac.

Superman in the Eighties. DC Comics 2006 192p. Illustration

Grades: 8 9 10 11 12 Adult   **741.5; Fic**

1. Graphic novels; 2. Superhero graphic novels; 3. Superman (Fictional character)

1-4012-0952-1, $19.99

The '80s were a decade that forever redefined the world's first super-hero. The first half of the decade brought the story of Superman to a close, while the latter half of the decade brought a revamped Man of Steel to an all-new audience. This volume includes ten stories by such creators as John Byrne, Curt Swan, Gil Kane, George Perez, Marv Wolfman, Jim Starlin, and Len Wein. Writer/artist Jerry Ordway provides historical and personal perspectives to these stories.

Superman in the Forties. DC Comics 2005 192p. Illustration

Grades: 6 7 8 9 10 11 12 Adult   **741.5; Fic**

1. Graphic novels; 2. Superhero graphic novels; 3. Superman (Fictional character)

1-4012-0457-0, $19.99

At the end of the 1930s, comics saw a new breed of hero. The man could withstand bullets, leap over tall buildings in a single bound, and bend steel in his bare hands. Fighting for the oppressed, this man of steel captured the imagination of the readers. He was, of course, Superman. This volume reprints stories originally published from 1938 through 1949. The reader sees Superman first fighting "regular" criminals, but as the years go by, super-powered villains start to menace Metropolis, along with such villains as Lex Luthor and troublemakers such as the mischievous Mr. Mxyztplk.

Superman: Up, Up and Away!. Kurt Busiek and Geoff Johns, writers; Pete Woods and Renato Guedes, art. DC Comics 2006 192p. Illustration

Grades: 8 9 10 11 12 Adult   **741.5; Fic**

1. Graphic novels; 2. Superhero graphic novels; 3. Superman (Fictional character); 4. Green Lantern (Fictional character)

978-1-4012-0954-4, $14.99

In the wake of Infinite Crisis, Superman had lost his powers. For the past year, as Clark Kent he has worked with the help of his super-powered allies, Green Lantern, Supergirl, and Hawkgirl, to keep Metropolis safe. Now, Lex Luthor has been acquitted of his past crimes, and he has managed to get his hands on a powerful and ancient Kryptonian artifact and plans to use it to destroy Superman once and for all. What can a powerless Superman do?

Superman; Volume 6: the men of tomorrow. Geoff Johns, writer; John Romita Jr, Klaus Janson, artists. DC Comics 2015 256 p. Color; Illustration

Grades: 10 11 12 Adult   **741.5; Fic**

1. Superhero graphic novels; 2. Superman (Fictional character)

1401252397; 9781401252397, $24.99

                                        LC 2015008050

"Enter Ulysses, the Man of Tomorrow, into the Man of Steel's life. This strange visitor shares many of Kal-El's experiences, including having been rocketed from a world with no future. New and exciting mysteries and adventures await. Plus, Perry White offers Clark a chance to return to The Daily Planet!" (Publisher's note)

Collects Superman #32-39 (New 52 relaunch)

Teen Titans Vol. 1: A Kid's Game. Geoff Johns, writer; Mike McKone & Tom Grummett, pencillers; Marlo Alquiza & Nelson, inkers; Jeromy Cox, colorist; Comicraft, letterer. DC Comics 2004 un Illustration

Grades: 9 10 11 12 Adult   **741.5; Fic**

1. Graphic novels; 2. Superhero graphic novels; 3. Teen Titans (Fictional characters); 4. Flash (Fictional character); 5. Robin (Fictional character); 6. Batman (Fictional character); 7. Superman (Fictional character)

1-4012-0308-6, $9.95

As the adolescent sidekicks of the world's most powerful heroes, Robin, Superboy, Wonder Girl, and Impulse have fought alongside their mentors in many battles. But when Cyborg, a former teen hero, realizes that this new generation of super-heroes needs to be guided and trained, he recruits the young adventurers into the new Teen Titans. Now as Earth's future champions begin working together as a unified team, they quickly learn the true consequences of the path they have chosen. Featuring Batman, Superman, Wonder Woman and the Flash, this action-packed volume includes the Teen Titans' inaugural adventures as they face off against the deadly mercenary Deathstroke, contend with the fanatical villainy of Brother Blood and take on the heroes of the Justice League. The level of action and some violence puts this beyond most young fans of the Cartoon Network series, "Teen Titans Go."

Teen Titans Vol. 4: The Future is Now. DC Comics 2005 un Illustration
Grades: 8 9 10 11 12 Adult   741.5; Fic
1. Graphic novels; 2. Science fiction graphic novels; 3. Superhero graphic novels; 4. Teen Titans (Fictional characters)
1-4012-0475-9, $9.99
The Titans' weekends are usually a chance to get away from it all, but this time they've gone to the 31st century, where they must help the Legion of Super-Heroes stop a threat known as the Fatal Five Hundred. Their return trip drops them off ten years into their future, and they don't like what they see. And when they finally get back home, they meet Speedy, who has arrived just in time to help them fight Dr. Light.

Teen Titans Vol. 5: Life and Death. Geoff Johns [and others], writers; Tony S. Daniel ... [et al], pencillers; Marlo Alquiza [and others], inkers; Jeromy Cox [and others], colorists; Phil Balsman [and others], letterers. DC Comics 2006 210p. Illustration
Grades: 10 11 12 Adult   741.5; Fic
1. Graphic novels; 2. Superhero graphic novels; 3. Teen Titans (Fictional characters); 4. Robin (Fictional character)
978-1-4012-0978-0, $14.99
The line between life and death is crossed as the Teen Titans must confront the deceased members of the team that have seemingly returned from the dead. As Donna Troy recruits the mightiest members of the team to battle in the Infinite Crisis, Robin is confronted by his predecessor, the bygone Boy Wonder, Jason Todd. The remaining Titans face the onslaught of Brother Blood and his army of followers which include the deceased Titans Aquagirl, Omen, Hawk, and Dove. As the Crisis hits, Superboy teams up with all of the reserve members of the team to battle his evil counterpart from another dimension. There is considerable violence in the personal battles.

Teen Titans Vol. 6: Titans Around the World. Geoff Johns, writer; Tony Daniel, art. DC Comics 2007 192p. Illustration
Grades: 9 10 11 12 Adult   741.5; Fic
1. Graphic novels; 2. Superhero graphic novels; 3. Teen Titans (Fictional characters); 4. Robin (Fictional character)
978-1-4012-1217-9, $14.99
The tragic events of Infinite Crisis tore apart the Teen Titans. It's one year later, and the core members of the Titans return to re-form the team. Robin, Wonder Girl, and Cyborg go with interim members Kid Devil and Ravager on a journey to find their former colleagues, but they discover there had been a traitor in their ranks. With the identity and intent of the saboteur unknown, the team must be ready at all times for an assault. They meet with the Doom Patrol and fight the Brotherhood of Evil.

Johnson, Crockett
Barnaby; Volume 1: 1942-1943, 1. by Crockett Johnson. Fantagraphics 2012 318 p. Illustration; Color
Grades: 10 11 12 Adult   741.5
1. Boys — Comic books, strips, etc; 2. Children — Comic books, strips, etc.
9781606995228, $35; 1606995227
                                        LC 2013363489
This volume, by Crockett Johnson, presents the collected comic strips of "Barnaby" from 1942-1943, which "revolved around a precocious five-year-old named Barnaby Baxter and his fairly godfather Jackeen J. O'Malley. Yet O'Malley, a cigar-chomping, bumbling con-artist and fast-talker, was not your typical protector." (Publisher's note)
Volume 1 of 5

Johnson, Mat
★ **Incognegro**. art by Warren Pleece. DC Comics/Vertigo 2008 136p. Illustration
Grades: 10 11 12 Adult   741.5; Fic
1. African Americans — Southern states — Graphic novels; 2. Graphic novels; 3. Mystery graphic novels
9781401210977, $19.99
In the early 20th century, light-skinned African American reporters risked their lives to cover the lynching murders of African Americans in the South; this process of "passing" was called "going incognegro." Zane Pinchback is a reporter from Harlem who has just narrowly escaped from one such reporting assignment when his editor sends him back down to Mississippi; this time, the man charged with murdering a white woman is Pinchback's own twin brother. He decides to investigate and find the real murderer in order to free his brother, but a Ku Klux Klansman has also come to town hunting the "Incognegro" reporter. This book portrays hangings and mutilations and uses the "n" word as it was used during the time period.

Right state. written by Mat Johnson; art by Andrea Mutti; letters by Pat Brosseau. DC Comics 2012 144 p.
Grades: Adult   741.5
1. Militia movements — Comic books, strips, etc; 2. Presidents — Assassination attempts — Comic books, strips, etc; 3. Adventure graphic novels; 4. Presidents — United States — Assassination — Fiction; 5. Militia movements — Fiction
1401229433; 9781401229436, $24.99
                                        LC 2012019780
This graphic novel, by Mat Johnson, illustrated by Andrea Mutti, "follows...a militia group that's plotting to assassinate the...President of the U.S.... [While] ex-Special Forces war hero turned conservative media pundit...Ted Akers'...politics make him a hero to the right-wing fringe and no friend to the current Administration, he takes the assignment...to stop a President from dying and a country from being ripped apart." (Publisher's note)

Johnson, R. Kikuo
Night Fisher. Fantagraphics Books 2005 144 Illustration
Grades: 11 12 Adult   741.5; Fic
1. Bildungsromans — Graphic novels; 2. Graphic novels
1-56097-719-1, $12.95
Loren Foster was handed an island paradise when he moved to the island of Maui in Hawaii with his dentist father six years ago. But, with the end of high school just around the corner, his best friend Shane has grown distant. Their friendship is put to the test when they get mixed up in a frivolous crime that leads to an arrest. Some drug use, strong language, and a sexual situation occur.

Jones, Bruce
Deadman: Deadman Walking. DC Comics 2007 128p. Illustration
Grades: 11 12 Adult   741.5; Fic
1. Graphic novels; 2. Mystery graphic novels; 3. Superhero graphic novels; 4. Supernatural graphic novels
978-1-4012-1236-0, $12.99
Brandon Cayce is about to find out the answers to the question of what happens after we die; unfortunately, he's going to find out by becoming a dead man himself. Now come new questions. Why did his brother crash an airliner, killing everyone aboard—including Brandon? Why does Brandon find himself drawn to Sarah, his sister-in-law and onetime love? Who are those men trying to kill him...and can you even kill a Deadman? The book includes a lot of violence, some nudity and sexual situations.

Nightwing: Brothers in Blood. Bruce Jones, writer; Joe Dodd, Paco Diaz, Robert Teranishi, pencillers; Bit, Nathan Massengill, Wes Craig, inkers; Javier Rodriguez Studio, Guy Major, colorists; Pat Brosseau [and others], letterers. DC Comics 2007 168p. Illustration

Grades: 10 11 12 Adult   **741.5; Fic**
  1. Graphic novels; 2. Nightwing (Fictional character); 3. Superhero graphic novels; 4. Robin (Fictional character)
978-1-4012-1224-7, $14.99

After Bludhaven was destroyed in the Infinite Crisis, Dick Grayson relocated to New York City. It's a year later, and he has new friends, a new flame, and new criminal masterminds to fight. But, there's also another Nightwing, one who kills criminals without mercy — it's Jason Todd, the former Robin who succeeded Dick but was then killed by the Joker. He's been resurrected, but his idea of justice is twisted. And New York City has meta-human criminal kingpins, the Pierce brothers, who want both Nightwings dead. The book includes some sexual situations along with superhero violence.

Jones, Gerard

★ **Men** of Tomorrow: Geeks, Gangsters and the Birth of the Comic Book. Basic Books 2005 384p. Illustration

Grades: Adult Professional   **741.5**
  1. Comic books, strips, etc. — History and criticism; 2. Graphic novels; 3. Popular culture — United States
0-465-03657-0, $15

                         LC 2004009031

Jones chronicles the early history of the comic book, focusing on Jerry Siegel and Joe Schuster, who created Superman, and on Harry Donenfeld, a pornographer and bootlegger looking for a way to beat the censors, and on his partner Jack Liebowitz, who forsook radical socialism for hardcore capitalism. Many of the early leaders in the comics industry were Jewish, and Jewish and Yiddish culture informed many of the comics superheroes.

Jones, Joëlle

Lady killer. story by Joelle Jones & Jamie S. Rich; art by Joëlle Jones; colors by Laura Allred; letters by Crank!. Dark Horse 2015 127 p. Color; Illustration

Grades: Adult   **741.5; Fic**
  1. Mothers — Fiction; 2. Assassins — Fiction
1616557575; 9781616557577, $17.99
Eisner Nominee: Best Limited Series (2016)

"Josie Schuller is a picture-perfect homemaker, wife, and mother — but she's also a ruthless, efficient killer! She's balanced cheerful domestic bliss with coldly performed assassinations, but when Josie finds herself in the crosshairs, her American Dream life is in danger!" (Publisher's note)

Jones, Sabrina

★ **Isadora** Duncan: a graphic biography. Hill & Wang 2008 129p. Illustration

Grades: 9 10 11 12 Adult   **92; 792.8; 741.5**
  1. Biographical graphic novels; 2. Dancers; 3. Dancers — Graphic novels; 4. Graphic novels; 5. Duncan, Isadora, 1878-1927
978-0-8090-9497-4, $18.95

                         LC 2008-17928

Dancer Isadora Duncan thrilled and appalled her audiences at the turn of the twentieth century and beyond; she chose to wear freeflowing costumes with no corsets or other confining undergarments, and she danced barefoot. She used choreographic elements from the ancient Greeks, with flowing movements as free as her garments. Jones sifts through the various books about Duncan, from the autobiography and others, with all their contradictory information, to depict a unique and contradictory woman who deeply influenced modern dance well beyond

her death. The black and white art shows Duncan always in Greek-styled gowns. There are two panels which show nudity in the context of Duncan's dance performances.

Includes bibliographical references.

Race to incarcerate: a graphic retelling. Sabrina Jones and Marc Mauer. The New Press 2013 128 p. Illustration

Grades: 9 10 11 12 Adult   **364.6; 364.6\0973**
  1. Crime prevention — United States — Comic books, strips, etc; 2. Criminal justice, Administration of — United States — Comic books, strips, etc; 3. Discrimination in criminal justice administration — United States — Comic books, strips, etc; 4. Graphic novels; 5. Imprisonment — United States — Comic books, strips, etc; 6. Prison sentences — United States — Comic books, strrips, etc; 7. Administration of criminal justice — United States; 8. Prisons — United States; 9. Crime prevention
1595585419; 9781595585417, $17.95

                         LC 2012049688

"Jones channels the tradition of liberal-Left political cartooning to give this graphic documentary a dynamic, woodcut-like look that galvanizes its adaptation of Mauer's tract of the same name. Its subject is imprisonment in the U.S., especially, since the war on drugs was launched in the 1980s, the push to jail as many as possible (as it sometimes seems). Since the opening of the first 'penitentiary' in 1829 and preceded by 'getting tough on crime' policies, the war on drugs has reversed the emphasis on rehabilitation in U.S. prisons." (Booklist)

Includes bibliographical references and index; Based on Race to Incarcerate by Marc Mauer.

Joong-Ki, Park

Shaman Warrior, Volume One. Dark Horse Comics 2006 214p. Illustration

Grades: 11 12 Adult   **741.5; Fic**
  1. Adventure graphic novels; 2. Fantasy graphic novels; 3. Graphic novels; 4. Manwha
978-1-59307-638-2, $12.95

Warrior Wizard Yarong and his faithful servant Batu travel to the desert wastelands of Kugai on a mission for their king. However, they find only an overwhelming force of fighters led by a warrior who seeks to kill Yarong. The two warriors face on attack after the other, until Yarong realizes he is going to die; he sends Batu away, to find Yarong's baby daughter Yaki. They have been betrayed by their General for political expediency. This was a top-selling manwha in Korea; the kinetic, violent story will appeal to older readers who enjoy Lone Wolf & Cub, Blade of the Immortal, and other warrior epics.

Joy, Bob

Batman: The Greatest Stories Ever Told Volume Two. DC Comics 2007 208p. Illustration

Grades: 7 8 9 10 11 12 Adult   **741.5; Fic**
  1. Batman (Fictional characters); 2. Graphic novels; 3. Superhero graphic novels; 4. Batgirl (Fictional character); 5. Joker (Fictional character)
978-1-4012-1214.8, $19.99

This volume includes stories from different periods in the nearly seventy-year career of Batman, from 1940 to 2003. He goes up against classic villains — the Joker, Killer Croc, the Penguin; he meets Batgirl (Barbara Gordon); deals with crooked businessmen and other criminals.

Flash: The Greatest Stories Ever Told. DC Comics 2007 208p. Illustration

Grades: 6 7 8 9 10 11 12 Adult   **741.5; Fic**
  1. Flash (Fictional character); 2. Graphic novels; 3. Superhero graphic novels

978-1-4012-1372-5, $19.99

Jay Garrick, Barry Allen, and Wally West are all men who have donned the symbol of the yellow lightning bolt to combat evil as the Flash. Each hero with his own unique style of commanding a mastery over momentum, they have fought separately and together over the years. This volume collects stories that see them pitted against such villains as Gorilla Grodd, the Reverse Flash, the Fiddler, and many others. This volume also includes the story of Barry and Iris' wedding.

Showcase Presents: Batman Vol. 2. DC Comics 2007 510p. Illustration
Grades: 6 7 8 9 10 11 12 Adult   **741.5; Fic**
  1. Batman (Fictional character); 2. Graphic novels; 3. Superhero graphic novels; 4. Robin (Fictional character)
978-1-4012-1362-6, $16.99

Over 500 pages of classic adventures are included in this volume collecting Silver Age tales of Batman and Robin as they face their most enduring enemies, including the Joker, Poison Ivy, the Riddler, Blockbuster, and many others. These are the stories that inspired the Dynamic Duo's 1960s TV series, which featured Batman's astonishing detective skills and impressive array of Bat-gadgets. The stories, reprinted in black and white, date from 1965 and 1966.

Ka, Olivier
  ★ **Why** I killed Peter. NBM 2008 112p. Illustration
Grades: 10 11 12 Adult   **741.5**
  1. Biographical graphic novels; 2. Catholic church — Clergy — Graphic novels; 3. Child sexual abuse — Graphic novels; 4. Graphic novels
978-1-56163-543-6, $18.95

Olivier Ka writes of his life and of the lifelong effect of one particular act. He grows up in France, the child of what he describes as hippie parents. Their lifestyle is very open, and young Olivier sees adults naked a lot, and his parents sleep with other partners quite often. Into this comes young priest Peter, a liberal type of cleric who wears shirts and jeans rather than cassocks and other vestments, who plays the guitar during services. Olivier likes him a lot, because Peter really talks with him and listens, more like a fun uncle than a priest. Over the years, Peter remains a part of the family, and Olivier goes to his summer camps. Then the summer Olivier is twelve, Peter asks him to do something that makes Olivier uncomfortable. They will sleep side by side in their own sleeping bags, but completely naked "to be equal," and they will massage each other's belly. It starts out like that, but ends...well. Olivier continues to go to the summer camps until he's fifteen, but he and Peter never do anything like that again. Years later, as an adult, Olivier suffers emotional problems, and attending services in a Catholic church makes him physically ill. Eventually, when his own daughter is twelve years old, Olivier writes this story, makes a friend who is an artist, and they create the graphic novel. And Olivier confronts Peter after so many years. The act Peter committed with Olivier is not depicted on the page, but there is nudity and some sexual situations, along with strong language.

Kakalios, James
  The **Physics** of Superheroes. James Kakalios.. Gotham Books 2009 424 p.
Grades: 11 12 Adult   **530**
  1. Comic books, strips, etc.; 2. Heroes and heroines; 3. Physics — Study and teaching; 4. Superman (Fictional character); 5. Batman (Fictional character); 6. Spider-Man (Fictional character)
1592405088; 9781592405084, $18

LC 2009028814

"With The Physics of Superheroes, named one of the best science books of 2005 by Discover, he introduced his colorful approach to an even wider audience. Now Kakalios presents a totally updated, expanded edition that features even more superheroes and findings from the cutting edge of science. With three new chapters and completely revised throughout with a splashy, redesigned package, the book that explains why Spider-Man's webbing failed his girlfriend, the probable cause of Krypton's explosion, and the Newtonian physics at work in Gotham City is electrifying from cover to cover." (Publisher's note)

"By combining his love for physics with his love of comic books,...Kakalios has written a book for the general reader [that covers] all of the basic points in a first-level college physics course and is difficult to put down.... That all of this is accomplished with enough humor to make you laugh aloud is an added bonus." Pub Wkly
  Includes bibliographical references and index

Kamio, Yoko
  Boys Over Flowers (Hana Yori Dango) Volume 1. Viz Media/Shojo 2003 208p. Illustration
Grades: 9 10 11 12 Adult   **741.5; Fic**
  1. Graphic novels; 2. Manga; 3. Romance graphic novels; 4. Shojo manga
1-56931-996-0, $9.99

When her only friend, Makiko, accidentally offends F4 leader Tsukasa, Tsukushi boldly defends her. Enraged, Tsukasa puts the dreaded red tag in Tsukushi's locker — a sign that she is now a target for the abuse of the F4 gang and the entire school. But when Tsukushi fights the gang with their own weapon, Tsukasa finds himself falling for her. Tsukushi comes from a poor family but attends a prestigious school ruled by the rich students; she manages to hold her own against any bullying. There's some violence in the bullying, and some sexual situations.
  Volume 1 of 37

Kanata, Konami
  ★ **Chi's** sweet home, volume 1. Vertical, Inc. 2010 166p. Illustration
Grades: 5 6 7 8 9 10 11 12 Adult   **741.5; Fic**
  1. Cats — Graphic novels; 2. Graphic novels; 3. Humorous graphic novels; 4. Manga; 5. Seinen manga
9781-934287-81-1

Young kitten Chi gets separated from her family while out on a stroll, then she meets little boy Yohei and his parents. They take her home, even though their apartment building has a strict no pets policy. While they try to find someone to take her in, they feed her, give her a cozy bed, set up a box with shredded newspaper for a litter box, and do their best to help her. Even though readers can read what she's thinking, Chi behaves just like a cat, with cat problems such as thinking the litter box is a wonderful play area instead of the place to do her business, and taking fright at Yohei's "vrooming" as he plays with his toy cars. The book is great for younger readers as well as anyone who likes cats. There is one panel where Yohei is sitting on the toilet while Chi is in her litter box in the bathroom, and a scene at the veterinarian's office where the doctor sticks a thermometer in to take Chi's temperature. And, of course, Chi tends to urinate in inappropriate places.
  Also available in 3-in-1 omnibus editions; Volume 1 of 12

Kane, Bob
  Batman in the forties. Batman created by Bob Kane; [introduction by Bill Schelly]. DC Comics 2004 192p. Illustration
Grades: 9 10 11 12 Adult   **741; 741.5; Fic**
  1. Batman (Fictional character); 2. Graphic novels; 3. Superhero graphic novels; 4. Catwoman (Fictional character); 5. Robin (Fictional character); 6. Joker (Fictional character)
1-4012-0206-3, $19.95

"The 17 selections include such milestones as Batman's first appearance in May 1939, the two-page story of his origins from November

1939, and the 1940 introduction of his young partner, Robin.... Other stories feature early appearances by some of Batman's most renowned arch-enemies: the Joker, Catwoman, and Two-Face.... Most compelling are the earliest stories; crude as they are, their naive verve and raw directness remain effective." Booklist

Originally published (1939-1949) in single magazine form as Batman 7, 15, 20, 31, 37, 47, 48, 49, Detective Comics 27, 33, 38, 49, 80, Real Fact Comics 5, Star-Spangled Comics 70, World's Finest Comics 30

Kanigher, Robert
Showcase Presents: Wonder Woman Vol. 1. DC Comics 2007 528p. Illustration
Grades: 6 7 8 9 10 11 12 Adult   **741.5; Fic**
   1. Graphic novels; 2. Superhero graphic novels; 3. Wonder Woman (Fictional character)
978-1-4012-1373-2, $16.99

Wonder Woman faces some of her deadliest challenges as she battles a variety of aliens and robots, and confronts the evil menaces of the Time Master, the Gadget Maker, Dike of Deception, and one of her most incessant foes, the Angle Man. This volume also includes the re-done origin of Wonder Woman, and some of her teenage adventures as Wonder Girl. Created by William Moulton Marston as a strong, liberated warrior in 1941, these adventures published in the late 1950s and early 1960s cast Wonder Woman in a more "traditional" female superhero role.

Kannenberg, Gene
500 essential graphic novels: the ultimate guide. Collins Design 2008 528p. Illustration
Grades: Adult Professional   **741.5**
   1. Graphic novels — Bibliography
978-0-06-147451-4, $24.95

Divided into ten chapters (Adventure, NonFiction, Crime and Mystery, Fantasy, General Fiction, Horror, Humor, Science Fiction, Superheroes, War), the book lists the Top 10 books in each category and then "the best of the rest." Each entry has a color photo of the cover, a star rating for quality, short plot synopsis, a short critical review (one paragraph long), plus a suggested age rating. Kannenberg includes books that are no longer in print, which may limit this book's usefulness for collection development.

Kanno, Aya
Blank slate volume 1. Viz Media/Shojo Beat 2008 un Illustration
Grades: 10 11 12 Adult   **741.5; Fic**
   1. Adventure graphic novels; 2. Graphic novels; 3. Manga; 4. Mystery graphic novels; 5. Shojo manga
978-1-4215-1924-1, $8.99

Zen is a beautiful young man with no memory of who or what he was, all he knows is that he gets urges to kill and he does so. The nation of Amata had been taken over by the Galayans twenty years ago, and Zen inadvertently gets involved with the resistance when he kidnaps the Galay general's daughter Rian. He ends up with Hakka, an unlicensed doctor who helps the Amatans. But what does Hakka know about Zen? This book includes considerable violence.

Kariya, Tetsu
Oishinbo a la carte: the joy of rice. story by Tetsu Kariya; art by Akira Hanasaki. Viz Signature Edition 2009 268p. Illustration
Grades: 8 9 10 11 12 Adult   **741.5; Fic**
   1. Cooking — Graphic novels; 2. Graphic novels; 3. Manga; 4. Rice — Graphic novels; 5. Seinen manga
978-1-4215-2144-2, $12.99

This volume collects the Oishinbo stories centering on rice, the supreme staple of the Japanese diet. As Yamaoka continues, with the help of other Tozai News staffers, to work on the newspaper's Ultimate Menu to celebrate its 100th anniversary, they examine rice. Among other stories, Yamaoka rails against the importing of rice from other countries; he shows that organic rice farming could be unhealthy depending on the farm's location; and he helps the company cafeteria chef attract more business by focusing on homestyle rice dishes. The big competition between the Ultimate Menu and the Supreme Menu is rice balls (omusubi). The stories here may help American readers understand a little more about how important rice is to Japanese culture, and they may want to try some of the dishes. The book includes a recipe for scallop rice, which is published in color with photos. As with the other volumes, this book includes stories that originally appeared throughout the original manga series, so the characters' lives and relationships change abruptly from story to story.

Oishinbo a la carte: vegetables. story by Tetsu Kariya; art by Akira Hanasaki. Viz Media/Viz Signature 2009 268p. Illustration
Grades: 8 9 10 11 12 Adult   **741.5; Fic**
   1. Cooking — Vegetables — Graphic novels; 2. Graphic novels; 3. Manga; 4. Seinen manga
978-1-4215-2143-5, $12.99

Tozai News reporter Yamaoka Shiro and his colleagues continue their quest for the Ultimate Menu. In this volume, he competes against his father Kaibara, who represents rival newspaper Teito Times and their Supreme Menu, in a competition involving the vegetables cabbage and turnip. In other stories, Yamaoka and his friends use asparagus as a way to reunite a culinary specialist and a pottery artist who broke up years ago; and they help Tomii's son get over his hatred of eggplant. A number of the stories discuss the debate between organic cultivation and the use of pesticides and imported vegetable types. Since the stories are selected from the Oishinbo series to fit into themes, they skip around in time and lack a real narrative flow. The book is suitable for teens, but the main appeal may be to adults, especially to those who want to read about food. The artist's focus on presenting all the vegetables so realistically and in great detail may just make the reader hungry.

Kasser, Tim
Hypercapitalism: the modern economy, its values, and how to change them. Larry Gonick, Timothy Kasser. New Press 2018 224 p. Illustration; Map
Grades: Adult   **330.12; 741.5**
   1. Capitalism; 2. Industries — Middle West; 3. Business ethics
9781620972823, $19.95
                                                               LC 2017030133

This book, by Larry Gonick, Timothy Kasser, "draws from contemporary research on values, well-being, and consumerism to describe concepts (corporate power, free trade, privatization, deregulation) that are critical for understanding the world we live in, and movements (voluntary simplicity, sharing, alternatives to GDP, protests) that have developed in response to the system." (Publisher's note)

"Gonick effortlessly lays out post-1945 capitalism, its evolution, and its application to contemporary business and trade, emphasizing the psychological effect and social cost of commercialism. The second half is prescriptive: a series of proposals for grassroots activism to survive in a world of marketable products and people." Pub Wkly

Includes bibliographical references and index

Katchor, Ben
Hand drying in America. Ben Katchor. Pantheon Books 2013 160 p.
Grades: Adult   **741.5/973; Fic**
   1. Urbanization; 2. Cartoons and caricatures; 3. Graphic novels
0307906906; 9780307906908, $29.95

LC 2012018003

This is a collection of four years' worth of cartoonist Ben Katchor's "cartoons about urban living.... Some of the...stories involve buildings with peculiar characteristics-the shoe-fitting bench in 'The Symbolic Building,' or 'The Souvenir Museum,' where a single souvenir is offered for sale in the gift shop." (Kirkus)

Katin, Miriam

Letting It Go. Miriam Katin. Farrar Straus & Giroux 2013 160 p. Illustration
Grades: Adult   **940.53/18092; 940.53**
1. Berlin (Germany) — Description and travel; 2. Holocaust survivors; 3. Katin, Miriam
1770461035; 9781770461031, $24.95
Ignatz Nominee: Outstanding Artist (2013)

In this memoir graphic novel, by Miriam Katin, "a Holocaust survivor and mother, Katin's world is turned upside down by the news that her adult son is moving to Berlin, a city she's villainized for the past forty years. As she struggles to accept her son's decision, she visits the city twice, first to see her son and then to attend a museum gala featuring her own artwork. What she witnesses firsthand is a city coming to terms with its traumatic past, much as Katin is herself." (Publisher's note)

We are on our own: a memoir. Drawn & Quarterly 2006 122p. Illustration
Grades: 9 10 11 12 Adult   **92; 741; 741.5**
1. Animators; 2. Artists; 3. Autobiographical graphic novels; 4. Cartoonists; 5. Holocaust, 1933-1945 — Graphic novels; 6. Illustrators; 7. World War, 1939-1945 — Graphic novels; 8. Katin, Miriam
1-896597-20-3, $19.95

LC 2005-9063602

In this WWII memoir, the author recounts "how she and her mother faked their deaths and fled Budapest after the Nazis occupied the city. With forged papers obtained from a black marketer, they escaped to the countryside in the guise of a servant girl and her illegitimate child. Katin relates their harrowing lives there and her mother's desperate search for her missing husband after the war.... This impressive book belongs in all serious graphic novel collections and is also a natural for Jewish studies." Booklist

Kawasaki, Anton

JLA: The Greatest Stories Ever Told. DC Comics 2006 192p. Illustration
Grades: 9 10 11 12 Adult   **741.5; Fic**
1. Aquaman (Fictitious character); 2. Justice League of America (Fictional characters); 3. Superhero graphic novels; 4. Batman (Fictional character); 5. Flash (Fictional character); 6. Green Lantern (Fictional character); 7. Green Arrow (Fictional character); 8. Superman (Fictional character); 9. Wonder Woman (Fictional character)
978-1-4012-0932-2, $19.99

Superman. Batman. Wonder Woman. Green Lantern. The Flash. Aquaman. Martian Manhunter. Green Arrow. Black Canary. They are the World's Greatest Super-Heroes, and they compose the Justice League of America. For over 45 years, this all-star team of DC's greatest characters has entertained generations of comics fans. And now, this new collection reprints eight of their greatest tales in one volume, covering nearly every era and incarnation of the League, from classic adventures of the Silver Age, to stories that formed the basis of the best-selling Identity Crisis, to newer tales featuring a humorous League and the return of the classic lineup.

Superman/Batman: The Greatest Stories Ever Told. DC Comics 2007 192p. Illustration

Grades: 9 10 11 12 Adult   **741.5; Fic**
1. Batman (Fictional character); 2. Graphic novels; 3. Superhero graphic novels; 4. Superman (Fictional character)
978-1-4012-1227-8, $19.99

They are two of the world's biggest icons, and they couldn't be more different. One is the most powerful being on the planet with an array of superpowers, a shining symbol of hope embodying truth, justice, and the American way. The other has no powers, but has trained his mind and body to the peak of perfection, a dark vigilante determined to strike fear into evildoers' hearts. Together, this popular and unlikely pair starred in numerous team-ups over several decades; this book collects ten of those stories, from 1952 to the 2000s.

Superman: The Greatest Stories Ever Told Volume Two. DC Comics 2006 192p. Illustration
Grades: 7 8 9 10 11 12 Adult   **741.5; Fic**
1. Graphic novels; 2. Superhero graphic novels; 3. Superman (Fictional character)
978-1-4012-0956-8, $19.99

This volume includes nine stories from different times in Superman's career. Readers can experience Superman's first meeting with the other dimensional imp Mr. Mxyztplk, his return to Krypton, a deadly battle against the team of Lex Luthor and Brainiac, an after-life adventure with Pa Kent, his greatest secret revealed, and more.

Keatinge, Joe

Shutter; Volume 1: Wanderlost. Joe Keatinge; illustrated by Leila Del Duca, Owen Gieni, Ed Brisson. Image Comics 2014 136 p. Color illustration
Grades: 11 12 Adult   **741.5; Fic**
1. Explorers — Graphic novels; 2. Family secrets — Fiction
1632151456; 9781632151452, $9.99

In this graphic novel by Joe Keatinge, illustrated by Leila Del Duca, Owen Gieni, and Ed Brisson, "Kate Kristopher, once the most famous explorer of an Earth far more fantastic than the one we know, is forced to return to the adventurous life she left behind when a family secret threatens to destroy everything she spent her life protecting." (Publisher's note)

"Keatinge and Del Duca have created a contemporary world that teems with casual miracles and feels all the more real and lived in for it. Crammed with the elements of children's storybooks, the art offers soft lines and a panoply of almost-recognizable storybook figures that honor those hallowed childhood recollections." Booklist
Originally published in single magazine form as Shutter #1-6; Volume 1 of 5

Keller, Michael

Charles Darwin's On the Origin of Species: a graphic adaptation. [by] Michael Keller; art by Nicolle Rager Fuller. Rodale 2009 192p. Illustration
Grades: 9 10 11 12 Adult   **576.8; 741.5**
1. Darwin, Charles, 1809-1882 — Adaptations; 2. Heredity — Graphic novels; 3. Evolution — Graphic novels; 4. Natural selection — Graphic novels
978-1-60529-697-5; 1-60529-697-X, $19.99; 978-1-60529-948-8 (pa); 1-60529-948-0 (pa), $14.99

LC 2009-11387

"The first part of this book gives the background and context in which Darwin developed his theory of natural selection. Arriving home in 1836 after five years of exploration aboard the Beagle, he is asked to explain what he learned. Thus the structure of this graphic novel is established. Through his voice, readers learn about his discoveries and observations, his correspondence with other scientists who helped him formulate his theories, as well as his personal life. The second section highlights the salient points of the original On the Origin of Species." (School Library Journal)

Kelly, Joe

★ **Captain** Stoneheart and the Truth Fairy. Joe Kelly, story; Chris Bachalo, artwork; Aron Lusen, color; Richard Starkings, lettering & edits. Image Comics 2008 un Illustration

Grades: 5 6 7 8 9 10 11 12 Adult 741.5; Fic

1. Adventure graphic novels; 2. Fairies — Graphic novels; 3. Fantasy graphic novels; 4. Graphic novels; 5. Pirates — Graphic novels

978-1-58240-865-1, $19.99

The story, in rhyming text with lushly drawn and colored art, tells the tale of the pirate named Captain Stoneheart, a fierce and angry pirate who won't let people tell him what to do. After attacking a peaceful ship and killing everyone on it, his crew discovers a caged fairy in the hold, and Stoneheart knows he can wreak havoc and scourge the world with her powers. Somehow they connect even through his anger, and when she finds a way to save Stoneheart and his crew even when she is free to leave the pirates and save herself, Stoneheart starts to change. Alas, the good times can't last, and he commits one final act that destroys everything and everyone around him because he won't let anyone tell him what to do, even if he loves that one person. There is some fighting violence, and there are some monsters, so this is not a story for very young readers. Older elementary school age children who love the old fairy tales with the tragic endings will be able to handle this story.

★ **Deadpool**. by Joe Kelly, pencilled by Ed McGuinness, Aaron Lopresti, Bernard Chang, Shannon Denton, Pete Woods, Rob Liefield. Marvel Enterprises 2014 1160 p. Color; Illustration

Grades: 10 11 12 Adult 741.5; Fic

1. Superhero graphic novels; 2. Deadpool (Fictional character)

9780785185598, $125; 0785185593

This collects multiple Marvel Comics runs featuring the character of Deadpool. "Wade Wilson is a self-loathing killer for hire...but he dreams of being a hero. So when an interdimensional organization reveals that his destiny is to save the world, is it the chance for redemption Deadpool has longed for — or is it too good to be true?" (Publisher's note)

Collects Deadpool (1997) 1-33, -1, 0; Daredevil/Deadpool Annual '97; Deadpool/Death Annual '98; Baby's first Deadpool Book; Amazing Spider-Man (1963) 47, 611; and Deadpool 900

★ **Deadpool** Classic 1. Fabian Nicieza, Joe Kelly, Mark Waid, and Joe Madureira; illustrated by Rob Liefield, Ian Churchill, Lee Weeks, and Ed McGuinness. Marvel 2008 256 p. Color; Illustration

Grades: Adult 741.5

1. Deadpool (Fictional character); 2. Superhero comic books, strips, etc.

9780785131243, $29.99; 0785131248

"Deadpool, with sidekick Weasel in tow, sets out on a quest for romance, money, and mayhem — not necessarily in that order — only to learn he's being hunted by an enemy he killed years before! As if that isn't enough, the Juggernaut crashes into the action, and it's the unstoppable vs. the un-shut-up-able!" (Publisher's note)

Space Ghost. DC Comics 2005 un Illustration

Grades: 8 9 10 11 12 Adult 741.5; Fic

1. Graphic novels; 2. Superhero graphic novels

1-4012-0721-9, $14.99

The masked avenger of the cartoon spaceways has been a popular character since his introduction to television in 1966. Since then, people have wondered who he is, how he got those power bands and why he protects the galaxy from evil. Now his story is told for the first time ever, and readers will learn the tragic circumstances that led to his donning a cowl and his first battle with arch nemesis Zorak. This is not the funny character from Cartoon Network.

Kelso, Megan

The **Squirrel** Mother: Stories. Fantagraphics Books 2006 147p. Illustration

Grades: 10 11 12 Adult 741.5; Fic

1. Graphic novels

978-1-56097-746-9, $16.95

Kelso's work is characterized by subject matter that fits roughly into two disparate camps: personal and semi-autobiographical stories that draw heavily on the details of her childhood and adolescence, and stories about the idea of America and American history, such as a trilogy of short pieces about Alexander Hamilton. This book features 15 stories, including two stories, "Meow Face" and "Aide de Camp," done especially for this volume. The personal stories are each self-contained but in a sense take place in the same world where similar characters inhabit different stories. The "America" stories are broader in subject matter, taking on events of political and historical significance and wrestling with ideas having to do with the American experience.

Kennedy, Mike

Alien vs. Predator: Thrill of the Hunt. Dark Horse Comics 2004 un Illustration

Grades: 10 11 12 Adult 741.5; Fic

1. Graphic novels; 2. Horror graphic novels; 3. Science fiction graphic novels

1-59307-257-0, $6.95

In the future, after a technological catastrophe that started a second dark age, all memory of vicious bug-like aliens and brutal predatory aliens that hunted humans has been forgotten. Now, mankind has reached out to space again, and humans are once again caught in the middle of a deadly struggle between the two most lethal species ever encountered. And once again, whoever wins...humans lose. The book includes some bloody violence.

Aliens vs. Predator: civilized beasts. Dark Horse Comics 2008 un Illustration

Grades: 9 10 11 12 Adult 741.5; Fic

1. Graphic novels; 2. Horror graphic novels; 3. Science fiction graphic novels

978-1-59307-342-8, $6.95

It was supposed to have been a short business tour, but the group has been stranded on the remote planet for eight months. The humans have been aided by a Predator they've named Smiley, and occasionally they have to hunt an alien out to kill them. When a rescue ship arrives, however, it is crewed by illegal synthetic humans, then everyone gets mixed into the Predators' new hunt of Aliens. Whoever wins, the humans will lose. The book includes considerable violence, including the tearing off of limbs.

Superman: Infinite City. DC Comics 2005 96p. Illustration

Grades: 8 9 10 11 12 Adult 741.5; Fic

1. Graphic novels; 2. Superhero graphic novels; 3. Superman (Fictional character)

978-1-4012-0066-4, $17.99

When a villain uses a very powerful weapon in Metropolis, Clark and Lois trace him back to an old town called Infinite City. They find the town abandoned, except for a doorway that leads to another amazing world.... the true Infinite City, where magic and science happily coexist. Superman and Lois step through the magic portal and become embroiled in a war for power on the other side. One faction wants to stay in its dimension, and another wants to branch out to our world. Superman will meet a doppelganger called the Warden, who shares the Kryptonian's might but not his intellect. He will also come across the architect of this world, a robot leader who claims to be what remains of his father Jor-El.

Ketcham, Hank

★ **Hank** Ketcham's Complete Dennis the Menace (Volume 1): 1951-1952. Fantagraphics Books 2005 590p. Illustration
Grades: 2 3 4 5 6 7 8 9 10 11 12 Adult   **741.5; Fic**
1. Dennis the Menace (Fictional character); 2. Graphic novels; 3. Humorous graphic novels
1-56097-680-2, $24.95

This volume is the first of a series that will reprint every Dennis the Menace cartoon. The first cartoon was published in sixteen newspapers on March 12, 1951, and the cartoon was soon picked up by many more newspapers. This volume collects the daily single-panel cartoons from March 1951 through December 1952. In these cartoons, readers meet five-and-a-half-year-old Dennis Mitchell, his parents, retired neighbors George and Martha Wilson, Dennis' dog Ruff, and neighborhood pals Joey and Margaret. Every cartoon hearkens back to the positive aspects of growing up in suburban Middle America and the joys (mostly) of being a child. While older adults will catch all the references to past popular culture (i.e. Hopalong Cassidy), younger readers will enjoy the humor arising from everyday situations.

Kibuishi, Kazu

Flight v2. [editor/art director, Kazu Kibuishi]. Villard 2007 432p. Illustration
Grades: 10 11 12 Adult   **741.5**
1. Fantasy graphic novels; 2. Graphic novels; 3. Short stories — Graphic novels
978-0-345-49637-9, $24.95

In this themed story collection, "more than 30 accomplished young artists take off on the theme, sometimes loosely construed, of flight.... At more than 400 pages, there is something in this elegantly produced collection for everyone, including readers who usually snub comics." Booklist

Stories are by various authors; previously published by Image Comics; v1 published 2004 by Image Comics; Villard edition published 2007

★ **Flight** v3. [editor/art director, Kazu Kibuishi].. Ballantine Books 2006 351p. Illustration
Grades: 9 10 11 12 Adult   **741.5**
1. Fantasy graphic novels; 2. Graphic novels; 3. Short stories — Graphic novels
978-0-345-49039-1; 0-345-49039-8, $24.95
LC 2006-45883

This third volume of Flight includes 26 short stories by mostly young writers, many of whom have webcomics. Some, such as Michael Gagne and Becky Cloonan, have published a number of books. The stories range from whimsical interludes to ironic fables to mini-epics of derring-do; ironically, most of the stories have only a tangential connection to the theme of flight.

Sequel to Flight v2 (2005)

Flight volume five. Villard Books 2008 364p. Illustration
Grades: 9 10 11 12 Adult   **741.5; Fic**
1. Graphic novels; 2. Short stories — Graphic novels
978-0-345-50589-7, $25

This latest volume contains twenty-one stories from creators such as Svetlana Chmakova, Dave Roman, Phil Craven, Kean Soo, Scott Campbell, Graham Annable, editor Kibuishi, and others. The stories include another episode in the adventures of Jellaby, the true meaning of baseball and what it is to be a true professional player ("Beisbol 2"), another episode in Michael Gagne's "The Saga of Rex," and a tale of what happens when a trio of high-tech "Worry Dolls" goes to work to help an unemployed actor. In this volume, the stories are somewhat longer than in previous volumes and most have actual plots to go with the artwork. Stories range from realistic to the fantastic, from whimsical to dramatic to tragic.

★ **Flight,** volume six. Villard Books 2009 284p. Illustration
Grades: 8 9 10 11 12 Adult   **741.5; Fic**
1. Fantasy graphic novels; 2. Graphic novels; 3. Short stories — Graphic novels
978-0-345-50590-3, $25

This sixth volume of the graphic anthology series includes stories by fifteen creators: J.P. Ahonen, Graham Annable, Bannister, Phil Craven, Mike Dutton, Michel Gagne, Cory Godbey, Rodolphe Guenoden, Steve Hamaker, Kazu Kibuishi, Andrea Offermann, Richard Pose, Justin Ridge, Rad Sechrist, and Kean Soo. Returning favorite characters includ Jellaby by Soo, Hamaker's Fish N Chips, Kibuishi's Daisy Kutter, and the wordless little fox Rex by Gagne. Bannister's "Cooking Duel" stands out as a lot of fun, as a couple makes a bet about which of them can make the better tasting mushroom quiche; and Justin Ridge's "Dead Bunny" shows that there is a soul mate for just about anyone, including a zombie bunny.

Flight: Volume Four. Random House/Villard 2007 344p. Illustration
Grades: 9 10 11 12 Adult   **741.5; Fic**
1. Fantasy graphic novels; 2. Graphic novels; 3. Short stories — Graphic novels
978-0-345-49040-7, $24.95

This fourth volume of the graphic novel anthology series includes 25 stories by creators ranging from veterans such as Michel Gagne and Graham Annable to newer creators such as Clio Chiang and Neil Babra. Most of the artists have webcomics; a number of them work in animation (Gagne most recently worked on the motion picture Ratatouille); some have worked on major graphic novel projects — Lark Pien colored Gene Yang's American Born Chiense, and Raina Telgemeier works on the graphic novel adaptations of The Baby-Sitters Club. While there is little harsh language and no nudity, some of the stories have more mature themes.

★ **Flight:** Volume One. edited by Kazu Kibuishi. Villard 2007 207 p.
Grades: 9 10 11 12 Adult   **741.5**
1. Comic books, strips, etc.
0345496361; 9780345496362, $27

This comic book, edited by Kazu Kibuishi, includes work from "Bengal, Bill Mudron, Catia Chien, Chris Appelhans, Clio Chiang, Derek Kirk Kim, Dylan Meconis, Enrico Casarosa, Erika Moen, Hope Larson, Jacob Magraw-Mickelson, Jake Parker, Jen Wang, Joel Carroll, Kazu Kibuishi, Khang Le, Neil Babra, Philip Craven, Rad Sechrist, and Vera Brosgol." (Publisher's note)

Volume 1 of 8

Kick, Russ

The **graphic** canon of children's literature: the world's great kids' lit as comics and visuals. edited by Russ Kick. Seven Stories Press 2014 480 p. Color; Illustration
Grades: 6 7 8 9 10 11 12 Adult
741.5
1. Children's literature; 2. Comic books, strips, etc; 3. Graphic novels in education; 4. Literature — Adaptations; 5. Comic books, strips, etc.
1609805305; 9781609805302, $38.95
LC 2014010178

Edited by Russ Kick, "the original three-volume anthology 'The Graphic Canon' presented the world's classic literature — from ancient times to the late

Courtesy of Seven Stories Press

twentieth century — as eye-popping comics, illustrations, and other visual forms. In this follow-up volume, young people's literature through the ages is given new life by the best comics artists and illustrators." (Publisher's note)

"These dazzlingly varied renderings run the gamut from haunting to comical while offering visceral reminders that children's stories are often densely layered, infinitely transposable, and peddle in imagery both macabre and whimsical. It is the unfettered imagination of these stories that make them not only wildly entertaining, but also vessels of forgotten truths." Pub Wkly

The **graphic** canon, volume 1: from the epic of Gilgamesh to Shakespeare to Dangerous Liaisons. edited by Russ Kick. Seven Stories Press 2012 501 p.

Grades: Adult
741.5/69; 741.5

Courtesy of Seven Stories Press

1. Comic books, strips, etc. — History and criticism; 2. Graphic novels in education; 3. Literature — Adaptations; 4. Graphic novels; 5. Poetry — Collections; 6. Epic literature; 7. Literature — Collections
1609803760; 9781609803766

LC 2012000276

This anthology edited by Russ Kick "brings classic literatures of the world together with...graphic artists and illustrators.... Volume 1...[spans] the earliest literature through the end of the 1700s.... [including] renditions of "Gilgamesh," "The Iliad,"...the tragedy "Medea" by Euripides...the Books of Daniel and Esther from the Old Testament...Rumi's Sufi poetry...three poems from China's golden age of literature...Plato's "Symposium,"...and "Don Quixote."" (Publisher's note)
Includes index.

The **graphic** canon, volume 2: from Kubla Khan to the Bronte sisters to The picture of Dorian Gray. edited by Russ Kick. Seven Stories Press 2012 499 p.

Grades: 11 12 Adult
741.5

1. Comic books, strips, etc. — History and criticism; 2. Graphic novels in education; 3. Literature — Adaptations; 4. Graphic novels; 5. Literature — Collections
1609803787; 9781609803780, $34.95

LC 2012013176

This book, edited by Russ Kick, collects "original graphic versions of [19th-century] classic literature, from [Samuel Taylor] Coleridge's 'Kubla Khan' to Wilde's 'The Picture of Dorian Gray'.... Contributors include Maxon Crumb, John Porcellino, and Megan Kelso. Each selection is prefaced with a short introduction to provide context, and a rationale is included for the marriage of a particular writer with a particular artist." (Publishers Weekly)
Includes index.

The **Graphic** Canon, volume 3: from Heart of Darkness to Hemingway to Infinite Jest. Edited by Russ Kick. Seven Stories Press 2013 563 p.

Grades: Adult
741.5

1. Graphic novels in education; 2. Literature — Adaptations; 3. Graphic novels; 4. Comic books, strips, etc.
1609803809; 9781609803803, $44.95

LC 2012049460

This collection of comics, edited by Russ Kick, "brings to life the literature of the end of the 20th century and the start of the 21st, including a Sherlock Holmes mystery, an H.G. Wells story, an illustrated guide to the Beat writers, a one-act play from Zora Neale Hurston,...Rilke's...'Letters to a Young Poet,' Anaïs Nin's diaries, the visions of Black Elk, [and] the heroin classic 'The Man With the Golden Arm.'" (Publisher's note)

Courtesy of Seven Stories Press

Here there is less repetition of authors in favor of casting a wider net through the cultural currents that dominated the literary century and a greater use of excerpts and single-image representations of entire works...and the entire project remains an astounding survey of the state of the art form itself." Booklist
Includes index.

Kidd, Chip

Batman: death by design. Chip Kidd, Dave Taylor. DC Comics 2012 104 p.

Grades: Adult
741.5; 741.5/973; Fic

1. Graphic novels; 2. Adventure fiction; 3. Superhero comic books, strips, etc.; 4. Batman (Fictional character)
1401234534; 9781401234539, $24.99

LC 2011051791

This New York Times Bestseller and Amazon Best Book of the Month graphic novel, by Chip Kidd and artist Dave Taylor, follows the DC Comics hero Batman. "As chairman of the Gotham Landmarks Commission, Bruce Wayne has been a key part of [a construction] boom, which signals a golden age of architectural ingenuity for the city. And then, the explosions begin.... Fingers are pointed as Batman must somehow solve the problem and find whoever is behind it all." (Publisher's note)

Mythology: the DC Comics art of Alex Ross. text by Chip Kidd; introduction by M. Night Shymalan; photography by Geoff Spear. Pantheon Bks. 2003 un Illustration; Color

Grades: 9 10 11 12 Adult
741.5\092; 741; 741.5

0-375-42240-4, $35

LC 2003-46740

"Ross's gouache painted art glows on the pages. Interspersed with quotations by the artist and those who know him, Kidd's sparse text takes readers on a brief tour of Ross's childhood to his early days in advertising and comic books, finally ending with the limited series "Kingdom Come" (Warner, 1998), which combined hyper-realistic artwork with unusually complex storytelling. The book not only displays samples of finished works but also includes sketches, photographs of live models, and comic art dating back to the 1930s." SLJ

Kieth, Sam

The **Maxx** Volume 1. DC Comics/Wildstorm 2003 unp. Illustration
Grades: 10 11 12 Adult
741.5; Fic

1. Adventure graphic novels; 2. Fantasy graphic novels; 3. Graphic novels
1-4012-0124-5, $17.95

Thinking himself a typical superhero, Maxx is a homeless bum living in a cardboard box, aided by freelance social worker Julie Winters. Maxx travels to another world, "The Outback," where he's a hero and saves Julie from strange imaginary creatures and from his ultimate enemy, Mr. Gone. The reader also meets Sarah, who wants to be a writer, is mad at her mom, and is too chicken to kill herself. People who like their superhero comics very postmodern, existential, and very strange will like this. The book has some violence.

Zero Girl. DC Comics/Wildstorm 2001 114p. Illustration
Grades: 9 10 11 12 Adult   **741.5; Fic**
  1. Fantasy graphic novels; 2. Graphic novels
  1-56389-851-9, $14.95

Amy Smootster is a high school social outcast who lives her life content in her own world. But it seems that Amy's world is full of strange happenings such as the spontaneous appearances of puddles of water around her and two-sided conversations with insects. And there's something weird with her and circles and the fact that squares are inimical to her. With the help of her guidance counselor (upon whom she has a crush), Amy eventually accepts and embraces her abnormal abilities and discovers her place in the world.

Zero Girl: Full Circle. DC Comics/Wildstorm 2003 110p. Illustration
Grades: 9 10 11 12 Adult   **741.5; Fic**
  1. Fantasy graphic novels; 2. Graphic novels
  1-4012-0170-9, $17.95

Amy Smootster's now an adult, working as a guidance counselor. Her former crush, Tim Foster, is now a single parent with a troubled daughter. Tim enlists Amy's aid in helping her adjust, but the young girl, Nikki, has plans — and abilities — of her own. The book includes some strong language.

Kikuta, Michiyo
  Mamotte! Lollipop Vol. 1. Random House/Del Rey Manga 2007 224p. Illustration
Grades: 8 9 10 11 12 Adult   **741.5; Fic**
  1. Fantasy graphic novels; 2. Graphic novels; 3. Manga; 4. Shojo manga
  978-0-345-49623-2, $10.95

Junior high schooler Nina is ready to fall in love. She's looking for a boy who's cute and sweet-and strong enough to support her when the chips are down. But what happens when Nina's dream comes true...twice? One day, two cute boys literally fall from the sky: they're both wizards and they've come to the Human World to take the Magic Exam. The boys' success on this test depends on protecting Nina from evil, so now Nina has a pair of cute magical boys chasing her everywhere she goes. But, because Nina accidentally swallowed a magic "crystal pearl" that is part of the Magic Exam, Zero and Ichi aren't the only wizards around her, and some are willing to do just about anything to get their hands on the magic pearl.

Kim, Derek Kirk
  Same difference. Derek Kirk Kim.. First Second 2011 90p. Illustration

Grades: 9 10 11 12 Adult   **741.5**
  1. Graphic novels; 2. Family — Fiction; 3. Youth — Fiction; 4. Love — Fiction; 5. Short stories
  9781596436572; 1596436573

LC 2010052663
This collection of short stories is concerned with young people, and gives particular focus to romantic and familial relationships. "The title story focuses on 20-somethings Nancy and Simon, who are racked with guilt. Why? Simon has turned down a date with a friend because she is blind, and Nancy has read love letters meant for someone else-and answered them, giving the jilted ex-boyfriend false hope. Through a series of credible coincidences, both eventually make amends. ...[The] collection also includes stories about high school track, weed wacking, familial relationships, celebrity interviews, and autobiographical tales." (School Libr J)

Kindt, Matt
  2 Sisters: A Super-Spy Graphic Novel. Top Shelf Productions 2004 334p. Illustration
Grades: 9 10 11 12 Adult   **741.5; Fic**
  1. Adventure graphic novels; 2. Graphic novels; 3. Spies — Graphic novels
  1-891830-58-9, $19.95

This World War II era spy thriller spans not only the globe, but time as well — from England to Spain and from ancient Roman times through the era of Pirates and Buccaneers. This spy story is the backdrop for the unique tale of two sisters, their relationship and the secrets they share. Readers will find a world of shady gypsies, mysterious rockets, buried treasure, pen-guns, cyanide teeth, and romance. The book includes violence.

Grass Kings; Volume 1. written by Matt Kindt; illustrated by Tyler Jenkins; lettered by Jim Campbell; cover by Tyler Jenkins. Simon & Schuster 2018 176 p. Color; Illustration
Grades: Adult   **741.5; Fic**
  1. Brothers — Fiction; 2. Mystery fiction; 3. Trailer parks — Fiction
  1684151155; 9781684151158, $29.99

This graphic novel, by Matt Kindt, illustrated by Tyler Jenkins, chronicles "the tragic lives of the Grass Kings, three brothers and rulers of a self-sufficient trailer park kingdom.... The grass kingdom is run by eldest brother Robert.... When a mysterious young woman flees to their community in search of safety, Robert takes her in. As her true identity comes to light, Robert must decide if his chance at atonement is worth risking the entire Kingdom." (Publisher's note)
  Volume 1 of 3

Mind MGMT; Volume one. created, written, and illustrated by Matt Kindt; foreword by Damon Lindelof. Dark Horse 2013 152 p.
Grades: Adult   **741.5/973**
  1. Women journalists — Comic books, strips, etc; 2. Journalists — Graphic novels; 3. Brainwashing — Fiction
  1595827978; 9781595827975, $19.99

LC 2012041667
In this graphic novel by Matt Kindt and edited by Brendan Wright, a young journalist "reporting on a commercial flight where everyone aboard lost their memories...stumbles onto a much bigger story — the top-secret Mind Management program. Her ensuing journey involves weaponized psychics, hypnotic advertising, talking dolphins, and seemingly immortal pursuers, as she attempts to find the flight's missing passenger, the man who was MIND MGMT's greatest success — and its most devastating failure." (Publisher's note)

Pistolwhip. Matt Kindt, writing and art; Jason Hall, writing and layout assist. Top Shelf Productions 2001 120p. Illustration
Grades: 10 11 12 Adult   **741.5; Fic**
  1. Adventure graphic novels; 2. Graphic novels; 3. Mystery graphic novels
  1-891830-23-6, $14.95

LC 2002-280685
Readers will find a naïve bellhop's struggle towards a life's ambition, an expatriate musician on the run, a young woman's battle with her paranoia and her past, and the mysterious figure who wants to control their lives. Set in an exotic atmosphere of a by-gone era, this is a tale crafted with a crime noir feel. The book includes violence and some strong language.

Red Handed: The Fine Art of Strange Crimes. Matt Kindt. First Second 2013 272 p.
Grades: Adult   **Fic; 741.5/973**
  1. Mystery graphic novels; 2. Humorous graphic novels
  159643662X; 9781596436626, $26.99

This graphic novel, by Matt Kindt, is set in "the city of Red Wheelbarrow, where...there has been a rash of crimes so eccentric and random that even Detective Gould is stumped. Will he discover the connection between the compulsive chair thief, the novelist who uses purloined street signs to write her magnum opus, and the photographer who secretly documents peoples' most anguished personal moments?" (Publisher's note)

Super Spy. Top Shelf Productions 2007 336p. Illustration
Grades: 9 10 11 12 Adult
741.5; S C
1. Adventure graphic novels; 2. Graphic novels; 3. Spies — Graphic novels; 4. World War, 1939-1945 — Graphic novels
978-1-891830-96-9, $19.95

Courtesy of IDW Publishing

Set during World War II, the book follows the everyday life of several spies as they go about their work. A writer hides secret messages in the text of the children's picture book he's writing; the wife of a German officer desperately needs to escape with her child; a female German master assassin encounters several of the Allied spies, with mostly fatal results. As the stories go on, the reader starts to see the interweaving connections between them. Some violence is depicted on the pages, but there's no nudity and little in the way of harsh language.

King, Frank
★ **Walt** & Skeezix: 1921 & 1922; Book 1. by Frank O. King; edited by Chris Ware. Drawn & Quarterly 2005 400 p. Illustration; Color
Grades: Adult **741.5**
1. Adoption — Comic books, strips, etc.; 2. Families — Comic books, strips, etc.; 3. Fathers and sons — Comic books, strips, etc.; 4. Father-son relationship — Comic books, strips, etc.; 5. Family life — Comic books, strips, etc.
9781896597645, $29.95; 1896597645
Eisner Nominee: Best Archival Collection (2007); Harvey Nominee: Best Domestic Reprint Project (2006)

This comic strip anthology, by Frank O. King, edited by Chris Ware, "is the first-ever collection of the classic twentieth-century newspaper strip 'Gasoline Alley.'...Not only does this volume reprint the first two years of the strip in which King's friendly and nostalgic imagination took shape but each book in the series features an eighty-page color introduction by Jeet Heer of Canada's 'National Post.'" (Publisher's note)

"Drawn & Quarterly has inaugurated an ambitious series that will eventually reprint the entire Gasoline Alley strip, as written and drawn by the late Frank King.... Gasoline Alley is pure Americana, set in a neighborhood where all the men are infatuated with their automobiles, tinkering with and talking about them endlessly. Disrupting the calm murmur of shoptalk is Skeezix, an orphan left on the doorstep of the chubby and friendly Walt, one of the Alley's only unattached men." Kirkus

Other collections in this series are: Walt & Skeezix: 1923-1924 (2006); Walt & Skeezix: 1925-1926 (2007); Walt & Skeezix: 1927-1928 (2010); Walt & Skeezix: 1929-1930 (2011); Walt Before Skeezix (2014); Walt & Skeezix: 1931-1932 (2015)

King, Stacy
Pride and prejudice. adapted by Stacy King; illustrated by Po Tse. Udon Entertainment 2014 369 p. Illustration
Grades: 9 10 11 12 Adult **741.5**
1. Manga; 2. Austen, Jane, 1775-1817 — Adaptations
1927925177; 9781927925171, $24.99
In this manga adaption by Stacy King, "Pride & Prejudice is delightfully transformed.... All of the joy, heartache, and romance of Jane

Austen's original [is] perfectly illuminated by the sumptuous art of manga-ka Po Tse." (Publisher's note)

King, Stephen
The **dark** man: an illustrated poem. by Stephen King and illustrated by Glenn Chadbourne. Cemetery Dance Publications 2013 88 p.
Grades: Adult
811
1. American poetry — 20th century; 2. Fictional characters
1587674211; 9781587674211, $25

Courtesy of Cemetery Dance Publications

In this book, illustrator Glenn Chadbourne presents an illustrated version of a poem by Stephen King. "Stephen King first wrote about the Dark Man in college after he envisioned a faceless man in cowboy boots and jeans and a denim jacket forever walking the roads. Later this dark man would come to be known around the world as one of King's greatest villains, Randall Flagg." (Publisher's note)

King, Tom
Batman; Volume 1: I am Gotham. Tom King, Scott Snyder, writers; David Finch, Mikel Janín, Ivan Reis [and six others], artists; Jordie Bellaire, June Chung, Marcelo Maiolo, colorists; John Workman, Deron Bennett, letterers; David Finch with Jordie Bellaire, collection cover art. DC Comics 2017 192 p. Color; Illustration (DC Rebirth)
Grades: 9 10 11 12 Adult **741.5; Fic**
1. Superheroes — Fiction; 2. Graphic novels; 3. Batman (Fictional character)
9781401267773, $16.99

LC 2016047042

"He is Gotham City's hero.... He is Batman. And he is not alone. There are two new heroes in town — a pair of masked metahumans.... Calling themselves Gotham and Gotham Girl, they've saved Batman's life, fought by his side and learned from his example. But what happens if Gotham's new guardians go bad? What if they blame the Dark Knight for the darkness that threatens to drown their city?" (Publisher's note)

King "employs a deep understanding of what makes a character tick, what makes him distinct, and what makes him appealing, here teaming Batman with a pair of superpowered amateur heroes who he at first tries to shepherd and then, when things go dark, he must bring to justice. Finch is an ideal partner: his Jim Lee-style figures, embellished with a darker line and more substantial detail, capture the humanity amid all the crunching action." Booklist

Originally published in single magazine form in BATMAN 1-6, BATMAN: REBIRTH 1; Volume 1 of an ongoing series

The **Sheriff** of Babylon; Volume 1. Tom King, writer; Mitch Gerads, art and colors. DC Comics 2016 160 p. Color; Illustration
Grades: Adult **741.5; Fic**
1. War on Terrorism, 2001-2009 — Comic books, strips, etc; 2. Baghdad (Iraq) — Comic books, strips, etc; 3. Murder — Graphic novels
1401264662; 9781401264666, $14.99

LC 2016018384

Former cop turned military contractor Christopher Henry is in Iraq "to train up a new Iraqi police force, and one of his recruits has just been murdered. With civil authority in tatters and dead bodies clogging the streets, Chris is the only person in the Green Zone with any interest in finding out who killed him-and why." (Publisher's note)

Also available in a deluxe hardcover edition; Originally published in single issues as The Sheriff of Babylon #1-4; Volume 1 of 2

Sheriff of Babylon; Volume 2: Pow, pow, pow. Tom King, writer; Mitch Gerads, art and colors; Travis Lanham, lettering; John Paul Leon, cover art and original series covers. DC Comics/Vertigo 2017 144 p. Color; Illustration
Grades: Adult   **741.5**
1. War on Terrorism, 2001-2009 — Comic books, strips, etc; 2. Baghdad (Iraq) — Comic books, strips, etc; 3. Iraq War, 2003-2011 — Veterans — Comic books, strips, etc.
1401267262; 9781401267261, $16.99
                                                    LC 2016050634
"Florida cop turned military consultant, Chris Henry came to Iraq in the aftermath of the 2003 American invasion to train a new generation of post-Saddam police. But the murder of one of his recruits has uncovered a vast web of secrets and lies-one that ties the old regime, the new government, the American military, the criminal underworld and the jihadist network together in a nightmarish tangle of death and deception." (Publisher's note)

Originally published in single magazine form as THE SHERIFF OF BABYLON 7-12

★ The **Vision**; Volume 1: Little Worse Than a Man. Tom King, writer; Gabriel Hernandez Walta, artist; Jordie Bellaire, color artist; VC's Clayton Cowles, letterer. Marvel Enterprises 2016 136 p. Color; Illustration
Grades: 11 12 Adult   **741.5; Fic**
1. Vision (Fictional character); 2. Superhero graphic novels
0785196579; 9780785196570, $17.99
Eisner Award: Best Limited Series (2017)
"The Vision wants to be human, and what's more human than family? So...he builds them. A wife, Virginia. Two teenage twins, Viv and Vin. They look like him. They have his powers. They share his grandest ambition — or is that obsession? — the unrelenting need to be ordinary. Behold the Visions!" (Publisher's note)

Contains material originally published in magazine form as Vision #1-6; Volume 1 of 2

★ The **Vision**; Volume 2: Little Better Than a Beast. Tom King, writer; Michael Walsh (#7) & Gabriel Hernandez Walta (#8-12), artists; Jordie Bellaire, color artist; VC's Clayton Cowles, letterer; Mike Del Mundo, cover artist. Marvel Enterprises 2016 136 p. Color; Illustration
Grades: 11 12 Adult   **741.5; Fic**
1. Superhero graphic novels; 2. Vision (Fictional character)
0785196587; 9780785196587, $19.99
Eisner Award: Best Limited Series (2017)
"Once upon a time a robot and a witch fell in love. What followed was a tale of the dead and the dying, of the hopeful and the lost, of the wronged and the avenged. And in the end, after both had fallen, the witch and the robot rose from their dirt and eyed each other across a field of blood and bone." (Publisher's note)

Originally published in single issue form as Vision #7-12

Kinney, Jay
Anarchy Comics: The Complete Collection. edited by Jay Kinney. Independent Pub Group 2012 224 p.
Grades: Adult
741
1. Anarchism — Comic books, strips, etc.

Courtesy of PM Press

1604865318; 9781604865318, $20
This comic anthology, edited by Jay Kinney, "brings together the legendary four issues of 'Anarchy Comics,' the underground comic that melded anarchist politics with a punk sensibility, producing a...mix of satire, revolt, and artistic experimentation. The anthology [also] features previously unpublished work by Jay Kinney and Sharon Rudahl, along with a detailed introduction by Kinney that traces the history of the comic he founded." (Publisher's note)

Kirby, Jack
Jack Kirby's Fourth World Omnibus, Volume One. DC Comics 2007 396p. Illustration
Grades: 8 9 10 11 12 Adult   **741.5; Fic**
1. Graphic novels; 2. Science fiction graphic novels; 3. Superhero graphic novels
978-1-4012-1344-2, $49.99
In the 1970s, legendary comics creator Kirby left Marvel Comics to work for DC Comics, writing and drawing several new series and also taking over Superman's Pal Jimmy Olsen. This volume collects the first three issues of his new series, plus the start of his run on Jimmy Olsen, from issue #133. With the Fourth World storylines in Kirby's New Gods, Forever People, and Mister Miracle, he created new mythologies and epic storylines. This hardcover edition uses a flat paper that shows off the inks and colors brilliantly.

Jack Kirby's Fourth World Omnibus Volume Two. Image Comics 2007 396p. Illustration
Grades: 7 8 9 10 11 12 Adult   **741.5; Fic**
1. Graphic novels; 2. Superhero graphic novels
978-1-4012-1357-2, $49.99
DC collects four series by Kirby — The New Gods, The Forever People, Mister Miracle, and Superman's Pal Jimmy Olsen — in chronological order as they originally appeared. These comics spanned galaxies, from the streets of Metropolis to the far-flung worlds of New Genesis and Apokolips, as cosmic-powered heroes and villains struggled for supremacy.In this second volume, the evil Darkseid's schemes continue to unfold while the New Gods, the Forever People, Mr. Miracle and other heroes battle his many minions.

Jack Kirby's Omac: one man army corps. DC Comics 2008 176p. Illustration
Grades: 7 8 9 10 11 12 Adult   **741.5; Fic**
1. Graphic novels; 2. Superhero graphic novels
978-1-4012-1790-7, $24.99
In the 1970s, comics master creator Jack Kirby shocked the comics industry when he left Marvel Comics to work for the opposition DC Comics. He created new characters and new worlds. Among them was an unusual science fiction concept: OMAC, One Man Army Corps. Corporate nobody Buddy Blank is changed by the artificial intelligence "Brother Eye" into a superpowered agent of the Global Peace Agency, fighting bizarre menaces in a disturbing, near-future world. This book collects the complete 8-issue saga as published by DC; readers will note it ends in a cliffhanger that was never resolved.

Silver Star. Image Comics 2007 152p. Illustration
Grades: 8 9 10 11 12 Adult
741.5; Fic
1. Graphic novels; 2. Superhero graphic novels
978-1-58240-764-7, $34.99

Courtesy of Twomorrows Publishing

Chronicling the rise of Homo-Geneticus, the New Breed of humanity that spawns both Silver Star (Morgan Miller) and the nefarious Darius Brumm. Silver Star was Kirby's final creation and one of only two creator-owned projects published by Pacific Comics in the early '80s. This volume also includes the original screenplay, written by Kirby and Steve Sherman, upon which Kirby based the comic.

Kirkman, Robert

Outcast; Volume 1: Darkness Surrounds Him Volume 1. Robert Kirkman, creator, writer; Paul Azaceta, artist; Elizabeth Breitweiser, colorist; Rus Wooton, letterer. Image Comics 2015 152 p. Color; Illustration

Grades: Adult   **741.5**
   1. Exorcism — Fiction; 2. Demoniac possession — Fiction
1632150530; 9781632150530, $9.99

LC 2015010536

In this graphic novel by Robert Kirkman and Azaceta "Kyle Barnes has been plagued by demonic possession all his life and now he needs answers. Unfortunately, what he uncovers along the way could bring about the end of life on Earth as we know it! Collects Outcast by Kirkman & Azaceta #1-6." (Publisher's note)

Collects Outcast by Kirkman and Azaceta #1-6.

★ The **Walking** Dead. Robert Kirkman, creator, writer, letterer; Tony Moore, penciler, inker, gray tones; Charlie Adlard, penciler, inker; Cliff Rathburn, gray tones; Rus Wooten, letterer. Image Comics 2006 un Illustration

Grades: 10 11 12 Adult   **741.5; Fic**
   1. Graphic novels; 2. Horror graphic novels
978-1-58240-619-0, $29.99

This hardcover features the first 12 issues of the hit series along with the covers for the issues in one oversized hardcover volume. An epidemic of apocalyptic proportions has swept the globe, causing the dead to rise and feed on the living. In a matter of months, society has crumbled. Rick Grimes finds himself one of the few survivors in this terrifying future. A couple months ago he was a small town cop who had never fired a shot and only ever saw one dead body. Separated from his family, he must now sort through all the death and confusion to try and find his wife and son. And when he finds them, along with a few other survivors, they must try to find a place of safety, for the walking dead are everywhere. The book includes lots of zombie violence, strong language, and some sexual situations.

Also available in trade paperback, omnibus, and compendium editions; Previously published as The Walking Dead issues #1-12.; Book 1 of an ongoing series

Kishimoto, Seishi

O-Parts Hunter Vol. 1. Viz Media 2006 185p. Illustration

Grades: 10 11 12 Adult   **741.5; Fic**
   1. Adventure graphic novels; 2. Fantasy graphic novels; 3. Graphic novels; 4. Manga; 5. Shonen manga
978-1-4215-0855-9, $9.99

In the not too distant future, mankind fights over relics from an ancient civilization called O-Parts, each of which contain incredible powers. Some people with special abilities to use the O-Parts to their full potential are known as O.P.T.s (or O-Parts Tacticians). Jio is a young boy with a tragic past who only trusts one thing in the world: money. He is actually a very powerful O.P.T., and inside him sleeps a demon of incredible ferocity. He meets up with a girl named Ruby who, like her famous father before her, wants to become a treasure hunter. Though Jio doesn't believe in friendship, he agrees to be Ruby's bodyguard, and together they go on a dangerous quest to discover as many O-Parts as they can. The story uses some harsh language and violence, occasionally graphic. Mangaka Kishimoto is twin brother to Masashi Kishimoto, mangaka of Naruto.

Kishiro, Yukito

Battle Angel Alita Vol. 1: Rusty Angel. Viz Media 2003 un Illustration

Grades: 10 11 12 Adult   **741.5; Fic**
   1. Graphic novels; 2. Manga; 3. Science fiction graphic novels; 4. Seinen manga
1-56931-945-6, $9.95

When Doc Ido, a talented cyberphysician, finds cyborg Alita's head in a junk heap, she has lost all memory of her past life. But when he reconstructs her, she discovers her body still instinctively remembers the Panzer Kunst, the most powerful cyborg fighting technique ever known. In the post-apocalyptic world of the Scrapyard, as the secrets of Alita's past unfold, each day is a struggle for survival. The book includes graphic violence and strong language.

Volume 1 of 9

Kitchen, Denis

The **art** of Harvey Kurtzman: the mad genius of comics. by Denis Kitchen and Paul Buhle; introduction by Art Spiegelman; designed by Kitchen, Lind & Associates. Abrams Comicarts 2009 241p. Illustration

Grades: Adult   **741.5**
   1. Kurtzman, Harvey, 1924-1993
978-0-8109-7296-4; 0-8109-7296-4, $40

LC 2008-04809

"Although Kurtzman is best known for — and his greatest cultural impact stems from — his creation of MAD, comics aficionados regard him as one of the medium's most significant and influential talents. The groundbreaking war stories he created for EC Comics in the early 1950s remain unsurpassed in their genre, and while the bulk of his personal work consisted of stories he wrote and designed for other illustrators to complete, his own artwork — brash and energetic, with boldly executed brushwork — is wondrously distinctive.... [T]he volume's main appeal lies in the handsomely displayed wealth of Kurtzman's work, from his most acclaimed stories, reprinted in their entirety, to unpublished strips and rare preparatory drawings." (Booklist)

Kleid, Neil

Brownsville. NBM 2006 208p. Illustration

Grades: 10 11 12 Adult

741.5; 973.9
   1. Gangs — Graphic novels; 2. Graphic novels; 3. United States — History — 20th century — Graphic novels
1-56163-458-1, $18.95

Courtesy of NBM Publishing

Brownsville, in Brooklyn, New York, was an impoverished part of the city in the early twentieth century. Filled with tenements and poor Jews, it became the breeding ground for criminals. This book follows the lives of Allie Tanennbaum, Abe Reles, and other young hoods organized by Louis Lepke Buchalter into the deadly "Murder, Inc." in the 1930s.

"The history of Jewish gangsters is often overshadowed by images of The Godfather and stories of the Italian mafia, but the events and players come to life in the stark images of this historical overview." (VOYA)

Kleist, Reinhard

The **Boxer:** The True Story of Holocaust Survivor Harry Haft. Reinhard Kleist. Harry N Abrams Inc 2014 200 p. Illustration

Grades: Adult   **92; 741.5**

1. Haft, Harry, 1925-2007; 2. Boxers (Sports); 3. Holocaust survivors; 4. Graphic novels
1906838771; 9781906838775, $22.95

LC 2014464671

Ignatz Nominee: Outstanding Graphic Novel (2014)

"Shrimpy but scrappy, teenager Hertzko Haft helps his struggling Jewish family survive Nazi occupation of Poland. But just before he is to marry his love, Leah, Hertzko is sent to a work camp and then to Auschwitz. Over four years, he keeps alive by canny friendships, smuggling, and learning to box in tournaments held to entertain Nazi camp officers. Finally, Hertzko escapes and turns professional boxer, seeking the missing Leah." (Library Journal)

"Drawn in stark black and white panels, characterized by a visceral sharpness of lines and angles, Kleist's narrative is set in a perfect visual landscape." Pub Wkly

Johnny Cash: I see a darkness: a graphic novel. [translated from the German edition by Michael Waaler]. Abrams ComicArts 2009 221p. Illustration
Grades: 11 12 Adult   **741.5; 92**
1. Cash, Johnny; 2. Country musicians — Graphic novels
978-0-8109-8463-9, $17.95

LC 2010-279149

The author "presents a biography (with seemingly invented dialog that stays true to the facts) focusing on Cash's turning points: from his poor family's 1935 relocation to a New Deal-created cotton farming community, through his troubled first marriage, endless touring, the amphetamine abuse of his early musical career, and climaxing with a famous, highly charged 1968 concert at California's Folsom Prison. Kleist also dramatizes several of Cash's songs and relates the tragic story of Glen Sherley, a Folsom inmate who sent Cash a song he had written hoping Cash would play it in the show. The ruggedness of Kleist's black-and-white illustrations suits their subject, as the stark portrayal of Cash's withdrawal from drugs is inventive and harrowing.... This thoughtful and compelling portrait of a towering talent with a tortured soul is recommended for all teen and adult music fans." Libr J

Knapp, Michael
Out of picture: art from the outside looking in volume 2. Villard Books 2008 238p. Illustration
Grades: 10 11 12 Adult   **741.5; Fic**
1. Graphic novels; 2. Short stories — Graphic novels
978-0-345-49873-1, $30

Animation production artists who have worked together at Blue Sky Studios have put together another volume of short stories in comics form. In one story, a giant of a man wants only to become a farmer, but the military has hunted him down because he was a biological weapon used by them to win a war; now, he can't be allowed to live. In another story, a young boy takes his first airplane ride and sees a strange being riding on the wing, fly-fishing in the sky. In another story, three friends " a cat, a pigeon, and a grumpy gargoyle " need to find a new home when their antique shop home is destroyed. None of the stories uses graphic violence or much in the way of harsh language, but the moods and intensity of emotion make the book more suitable for older teens and adults.

Knisley, Lucy
An **Age** of License. Lucy Knisley. Fantagraphics 2014 208 p. Illustration; Color; Map
Grades: 11 12 Adult   **741.5; 92**
1. Autobiographical graphic novels; 2. Europe — Description and travel
1606997688; 9781606997680, $19.99

"'An Age of License' is [author Lucy] Knisley's comics travel memoir recounting her charming (and romantic!) adventures. It's punctuated by

whimsical visual devices (such as a 'new experiences' funnel); peppered with the cute cats she meets along the way; and, of course, features her hallmark — drawings and descriptions of food that will make your mouth water." (Publisher's note)

"Knisley makes memoir comics seem both sophisticated and approachable-and beyond these, useful in helping an individual delve into and communicate personal issues." LJ

Displacement. by Lucy Knisley. Fantagraphics Books, Inc. 2015 156 p. Color; Illustration
Grades: Adult   **741.5**
1. Cartoonists — United States — Biography; 2. Comic books, strips, etc. — United States; 3. Grandparent and child — Comic books, strips, etc; 4. Ocean travel — Comic books, strips, etc; 5. Older people — Travel — Comic books, strips, etc; 6. Knisley, Lucy — Travel — Comic books, strips, etc; 7. Cartoonists — Biography; 8. Grandparent-grandchild relationship; 9. Ocean travel
1606998102; 9781606998106, $19.99

LC 2014501578

Eisner Nominee: Best Reality-Based Work (2016)

"Knisley volunteers to watch over her ailing grandparents on a cruise. (The book's watercolors evoke the ocean that surrounds them.) In a book that is part graphic memoir, part travelogue, and part family history, Knisley not only tries to connect with her grandparents, but to reconcile their younger and older selves." (Publisher's note)

"A moving but also very funny me ditation on time, age and grace." Kirkus

★ **Relish:** My Life in the Kitchen. by Lucy Knisley. First Second 2013 192 p.
Grades: 9 10 11 12 Adult   **741.5; 92**
1. Food; 2. Cooking
1596436239; 9781596436237, $17.99
Alex Award (2014)

This book is a memoir from food-lover Lucy Knisley. "Having grown up surrounded by delicious food, thanks to her gourmand father and earthy superchef mother, Knisley looks back on her childhood and adolescence through her roving palette and voracious appetite for new tastes and experiences. With each memory Knisley shares, she shows that life, like a good meal, should be savored and that all food — even junk food — is more than 'just fuel.'" (Publishers Weekly)

"Knisley tempers any navel-gazing impulses with humor, humility, and honesty.... Just about everything in this rambling memoir is handled with good cheer." Booklist

Something New: Tales from a Makeshift Bride. by Lucy Knisley. First Second 2016 304 p. Color; Illustration
Grades: Adult   **92**
1. Knisley, Lucy; 2. Weddings; 3. Graphic memoir
1626722498; 9781626722491, $19.99

In this graphic novel, by Lucy Knisley, "in 2010, Lucy and her long-term boyfriend John broke up. Three long, lonely years later, John returned to New York, walked into Lucy's apartment, and proposed. This is not that story. It is the story of what came after: The Wedding. DIY maven...Knisley was fascinated by American wedding culture...but also sort of horrified by it. So she set out to plan and execute the adorable DIY wedding to end all adorable DIY weddings." (Publisher's note)

"Whether she's sharing moments that are sensitive, silly, or enraging, Knisley's full-color comics are clever, precise, and appealing as ever." Booklist

Kochalka, James
Pinky & Stinky. Top Shelf Productions 2002 208p. Illustration
Grades: 4 5 6 7 8 9 10 11 12 Adult   **741.5; Fic**

1. Adventure graphic novels; 2. Friendship — Graphic novels; 3. Graphic novels; 4. Humorous graphic novels

1-891830-29-7, $17.95

Pinky & Stinky are fat little piglets, but just because they're cuties doesn't mean that they're not brave astronauts! When they embark on a daring mission to be the first pigs on Pluto, things go horribly wrong and they crash land on the moon. There they meet some not-so-friendly moon men, and end up in the middle of a conflict between the American space program and a race of alien ice creatures.

Koga, Yun

Loveless; Volume 1 and 2. story and art by Yun Kouga; translation Ray Yoshimoto; English adaptation Lillian Diaz-Przybyl. VIZ Media 2012 376 p. Illustration

Grades: 11 12 Adult   **741.5; Fic**

1. Fantasy graphic novels; 2. Josei manga; 3. Magic — Graphic novels

1421549905; 9781421549903, $14.99

"When his beloved older brother is brutally murdered, Ritsuka is heartbroken but determined to search for answers. His only lead is Soubi, a mysterious, handsome college student who offers him an intimate link to his brother's other life: a dark and vibrant world of spell battles and secret names. Will Ritsuka's relationship with Soubi ultimately lead to the truth or further down the rabbit hole than he imagined possible?" (Publisher's note)

Originally published in the U.S. by Tokyopop; Volumes 1-2 of an ongoing series

Koike, Kazuo

Lone wolf and cub omnibus. 1. by Kazuo Koike; illustrated by Goseki Kojima. Dark Horse Manga 2013 706 p. Illustration

Grades: 9 10 11 12 Adult   **741.5; 741.5952**

1. Seinen manga; 2. Samurai — Graphic novels; 3. Manga

1616551348; 9781616551346, $19.99

This graphic novel, by Kazuo Koike, illustrated by Goseki Kojima, is a "samurai epic.... [It] begins its second life at Dark Horse Manga with new, larger editions of over 700 pages." (Publisher's note)

Also available in 28 single volumes; Volume 1 of 12

Path of the Assassin Vol. 1: Serving in the Dark. Dark Horse Manga 2006 314p. Illustration

Grades: 11 12 Adult   **741.5; Fic**

1. Adventure graphic novels; 2. Graphic novels; 3. Manga; 4. Samurai — Graphic novels; 5. Seinen manga

978-1-59307-502-6, $9.95

This is the story of Hattori Hanzo, the fabled master ninja whose duty was to protect Tokugawa Ieyasu. Ieyasu was the shogun who would unite Japan into one great nation. But before he could do that, he had to grow up and learn how to love the ladies. As the secret caretaker of such an influential future leader, not only does Hanzo use vast and varied ninja talents, but in living closely with Ieyasu, he forms a close friendship with the young shogun. The two men get into bawdy escapades, the book includes nudity, strong language, and graphic violence."

Kominsky-Crumb, Aline

Need More Love: A Graphic Memoir. MQ Publications Ltd 2007 383p. Illustration

Grades: 11 12 Adult   **741.5; Fic**

1. Autobiographical graphic novels; 2. Graphic novels; 3. Kominsky-Crumb, Aline, 1948-

978-1-84601-133-7, $30

Crumb was one of the pioneers of women's comics and became well-known during the Sixties and Seventies, along with her husband R. Crumb. This is her memoir of her life, taken from her comics published over the past four decades, incorporating photos and short prose text pieces along with memorabilia. She covers not only her life, but of her family, her husband, and other movers and shakers of the art and music worlds from the Sixties into the 21st century. The book includes considerable nudity, sexual situations, and harsh language.

Kouno, Fumiyo

Town of evening calm, Country of cherry blossoms. Last Gasp 2006 104p. Illustration

Grades: 9 10 11 12 Adult   **741.5; Fic**

1. Atomic bomb victims — Graphic novels; 2. Graphic novels; 3. Manga; 4. Japan — History — 1952- — Graphic novels; 5. Seinen manga

978-0-86719-665-8, $9.99

In 1955, Hiroshima has been recovering from the devastation of the Atom Bomb in August 1945. Minami is one of the survivors of the bomb, and she tries not to remember the events of that day when most of her family died. She even pushes away Uchikoshi, a co-worker who likes her, feeling guilty that she survived when so many didn't; but when she finally comes to terms with her past and allows Uchikoshi in, radiation sickness manifests. Fifty years later, old school friends Nanami and Toko run into each other as Nanami follows her father who has been behaving oddly; he goes to Hiroshima, for he is Minami's younger brother. This quiet, one-volume manga uses gentle, sweet art to bring home to readers the lingering after-effects of the bombing of Hiroshima.

Krigstein, B. (Bernard)

Messages in a Bottle: Comic Book Stories by B. Krigstein. by B. Krigstein; edited and produced by Greg Sadowski. W W Norton & Co Inc 2013 272 p. Illustration; Color

Grades: Adult   **Fic; 741.5/973**

1. Comic books, strips, etc.

1606995804; 9781606995808, $35

LC 2012462153

This anthology, by Marie Severin, edited by Greg Sadowski, features comics by Bernard Krigstein. "Krigstein began his career...during the 1940s and finished it as a respected fine artist and illustrator — but comics historians know him for his explosively creative 1950s.... Greg Sadowski...has assembled the very best of Krigstein's comics work,...running through every genre popular at the time." (Publisher's note)

Kristiansen, Teddy H.

The **Red** Diary: The Re(a)d Diary Flipbook. Steven T. Seagle, Teddy H. Kristiansen. Image Comics 2012 65 p. Color; Illustration

Grades: Adult   **741.5; Fic**

1. War — Graphic novels; 2. Identity — Fiction; 3. Diaries — Graphic novels

1607065606; 9781607065609, $29.99

This book presents a "dual-story graphic novel" by Teddy Kristiansen and Steven T. Seagle. "Published in French, Kristiansen's original story chronicles the search of a biographer for the truth behind the life of an unknown artist who died during WWI. Seagle uses the same images to tell a different tale of war, art, and identity, as an old man searches to connect to the diaries of his youth. Seagle...had not read the original before creating his own story." (Publishers Weekly)

Kubert, Joe

Joe Kubert Presents. Joe Kubert, Sam Glanzman. DC Comics 2013 304 p. Color; Illustration

Grades: Adult   **741.5**

1. Military personnel — Graphic novels; 2. Graphic novels; 3. War — Graphic novels
1401243304; 9781401243302, $19.99

LC 2013026713

This book, by Joe Kubert with illustrations from Brian Buniak and Sam Glanzman, is an "anthology-style graphic novel with original stories with far ranging characters and settings. Included in this new collection are tales featuring heroes from his most famous works, Sgt. Rock and Hawkman, as well as the gritty war epics he is best known for." (Publisher's note)

"The project is a testament not only to Kubert's talent but to the sort of solid, straightforward storytelling largely missing from contemporary mainstream comics; as such, its greatest appeal will be to older readers who prefer his old-school approach." Booklist

Originally published in single magazine form as JOE KUBERT PRESENTS 1-6.

Yossel: April 19, 1943: a story of the Warsaw Ghetto Uprising. Ibooks; Simon & Schuster 2003 121p. Illustration

Grades: 9 10 11 12 Adult   **940.53; Fic**

1. Graphic novels; 2. Holocaust, 1933-1945 — Comic books, strips, etc.; 3. Holocaust, 1933-1945 — Graphic novels; 4. Warsaw (Poland) — History — Uprising of 1943 — Comic books, strips, etc.
0-7434-7516-X, $24.95

"Imagining his life as it might have been had his parents not left for America in 1926, Kubert portrays himself as a ghetto youngster whose drawing ability ingratiates him with the Nazis, allowing him to overhear their plans and aid the underground resistance. Besides depicting life in the ghetto with shocking vividness, Kubert shows the barbarism of the concentration camps through the eyes of an escapee. In a striking departure from standard comics presentation, the artwork is printed in rough, penciled form rather than as finished ink drawings. The visual looseness this gives to work that is stylized by mainstream-comics standards conjures a potent intimacy that adds to the story's impact." Booklist

Kuper, Peter

The **jungle.** [based on the story by] Upton Sinclair; adapted by Peter Kuper. Papercutz 2010 un Illustration (Classics Illustrated)

Grades: 9 10 11 12 Adult   **741.5; Fic**

1. Authors; 2. Biographers; 3. Graphic novels; 4. Immigrants — Graphic novels; 5. Meat industry — Graphic novels; 6. Novelists; 7. Socialist leaders; 8. Sinclair, Upton, 1878-1968 — Adaptations; 9. Chicago (Ill.) — Graphic novels
978-1-59707-192-5, $9.99

"Jurgis and his family have immigrated to America from Lithuania, settled in Chicago, and found jobs in the meatpacking plant. The family seems to be living the American dream: having their own home, and a means of support, even if the work is hard and disgusting. Peter Kuper's dark, colored, cartoon-style illustrations, framed in black, bring to life Sinclair's original work and highlight the atrocities perpetuated upon the Rudkus family." Libr Media Connect

First published 1991 by First Publishing

Ruins. written and illustrated by Peter Kuper; edited by Dan Lockwood. Harry N Abrams Inc 2015 328 p. Color; Illustration

Grades: Adult   **741.5; Fic**

1. Mexican Americans — Fiction; 2. Monarch butterflies; 3. Married people — Fiction; 4. Graphic novels
1906838984; 9781906838980, $29.95

Eisner Award: Best Graphic Album — New (2016)

In this book, by author Peter Kuper, "Samantha and George are a couple heading towards a sabbatical year in the quaint Mexican town of Oaxaca.... For both of them, it will be a collision course with political and personal events that will alter their paths and the town of Oaxaca forever. In

tandem, the remarkable and arduous journey that a Monarch butterfly endures on its annual migration from Canada to Mexico is woven into Ruins." (Publisher's note)

Sticks and stones: an epic in pictures. Three Rivers Press 2004 un Illustration

Grades: 10 11 12 Adult   **741.5; Fic**

1. Graphic novels; 2. Stories without words
1-4000-5257-2, $13.95

LC 2004-45969

"A stone giant is born from a volcano and demands the fealty of the people around him. He makes them build him a stone castle; then he discovers a nearby peaceful village made entirely of wood and sets about conquering it and plundering its resources. Meanwhile, a small resistance front develops, led by a woman from the stone tribe and a boy from the wood tribe, and eventually the stone empire and its despot meet a grim fate. Kuper's narrative is beautifully constructed, from its grand sweep to its minute details." Publ Wkly

Kupperberg, Paul

Archie; 3: the married life : two worlds, two loves, two destinies. written by Paul Kupperberg; pencils by Fernando Ruiz, Pat & Tim Kennedy; inking by Al Milgrom and Bob Smith; letters by Janice Chiang and Jack Moretti; coloring by Glenn Whitmore. Archie Comic Publications 2013 320 p. Color illustration

Grades: 9 10 11 12 Adult   **741.5/973; Fic**

1. Comic books, strips, etc.; 2. Marriage — Fiction; 3. Andrews, Archie (Fictional character)
1936975351; 9781936975358, $19.99

LC 2013409812

This graphic novel by Paul Kupperberg "explores Archie Andrews' life down two paths — if he had married girl-next-door Betty Cooper or wealthy socialite Veronica Lodge. In this volume, things really start getting interesting, as the mysterious Dilton Doiley subplots that have been bubbling just below the surface since the series' beginning start to affect... well, everything!" (Publisher's note)

"Eye-opening for longtime fanatics and an invigorating soap opera for newcomers." Booklist

Kupperman, Michael

All the answers. Michael Kupperman. Simon & Schuster 2018 224 p. Illustration

Grades: Adult   **741.5; 92; 384.54**

1. Fathers and sons — United States — Biography — Comic books, strips, etc.; 2. Gifted children — United States — Biography — Comic books, strips, etc.; 3. Radio personalities — United States — Biography — Comic books, strips, etc.; 4. Radio broadcasting; 5. Kupperman, Joel; 6. Kupperman, Michael
1501166433; 9781501166433, $25

LC 2018080304

"In this moving graphic memoir,...[author] Michael Kupperman traces the life of his reclusive father — the once-world-famous Joel Kupperman, 'Quiz Kid.'... Following a childhood spent in the public eye,...Joel deliberately spent the remainder of his life removed from the world at large.... Kupperman presents a fascinating account of mid-century radio and early television history...and the early age of modern celebrity culture." (Publisher's note)

"Kupperman's solid, line-heavy drawings, which impart credibility to the preposterous concepts of his humorous strips, are equally effective at conveying this real-life drama. His clear-eyed yet touching portrait of his father serves as a a powerful indictment of celebrity culture." Booklist

Kurata, Hideyuki

Train + Train, Vol. 1. original story by Hideyuki Kurata; art by Tomomasa Takuma. Go! Comi 2007 196p. Illustration

Grades: 8 9 10 11 12 Adult   **741.5; Fic**

1. Adventure graphic novels; 2. Graphic novels; 3. High school students — Graphic novels; 4. Manga; 5. Shojo manga

978-1-933617-18-3, $10.99

Reiichi and Liae have come to the planet Deloca to board the high school train. On Deloca, different schools run on special trains, with stops where students complete certain assignments; they live in dorms on the trains. Reiichi and Liae are registered to board the "General" school train. Arena Pendleton, on the other hand, has determined to board the Special Train, and she won't let anyone stop her, not even the men her wealthy grandfather has hired to capture her and bring her home. In Ideo City, where the students must board their respective trains, Reiichi accidentally gets involved in a run-in between Arena and Kong Seeval, who intends to take Arena home. Reiichi and Arena become handcuffed together, and he has no choice but to board the Special Train. There's lots of action but little in the way of violence or bad language in this first of a manga series.

Kurtzman, Harvey

Corpse on the Imjin!: and other stories. Harvey Kurtzman. Fantagraphics Books 2012 227 p.

Grades: Adult   **741.5**

1. Short stories; 2. Comic books, strips, etc.; 3. War — Graphic novels

1606995456; 9781606995457, $28.99

Author Harvey Kurtzman presents a book of short comic stories related to warfare. The book contains stories from cartoonists "including such giants as designer extraordinaire Alex Toth, Marvel comics stalwart Gene Colan, and a pre-Sgt. Rock Joe Kubert... and such unexpected guests as...artist Dave Berg and DC comics veteran Ric Estrada." (Publisher's note)

Kverneland, Steffen

Munch. Steffen Kverneland; translated from Norwegian by Francesca M. Nichols. SelfMadeHero 2016 280 p. Illustration

Grades: 10 11 12 Adult   **92; 741.5**

1. Munch, Edvard, 1863-1944; 2. Painters — Biography; 3. Biographical graphic novels

1910593125; 9781910593127, $24.95

This book in the Art Masters series by Steffen Kverneland "uses text drawn exclusively from the quotes of Edvard Munch and his contemporaries. Filled with authenticity and life, Munch debunks the familiar myth of the half-mad expressionist painter-anguished, starving, and ill-treated-and draws out his neglected sense of humor and optimism." (Publisher's note)

"Kverneland's skill at infusing Munch's own techniques and imagery into the biography is extraordinary, and the stories behind the controversial paintings are fascinating and wryly funny." LJ

Includes bibliographical references (pages 278-279)

Landis, Max

Superman: American alien. Max Landis, writer; Nick Dragotta, Tommy LeeEdwards, Joëlle Jones, Jae Lee, Francis Manapul,Jonathan Case, artists; Alex Guimarães, Tommy LeeEdwards, Rico Renzi, June Chung, Francis Manapul,Jonathan Case, Lee Loughridge, colorists; JohnWorkma. DC Comics 2016 224 p. Color; Illustration

Grades: 9 10 11 12 Adult   **741.5; Fic**

1. Superhero comic books, strips, etc.; 2. Superheroes; 3. Superman (Fictional character)

9781401262563, $24.99

LC 2016032268

This book, by Max Landis, "presents seven stories from the life of the man who will be the Man of Steel, seven pivotal moments that turned a sometimes good, sometimes angry, sometimes funny, always human, all-American alien into the world's first superhero.... This is the story of Clark Kent, a Kansas farm boy who happens to be from another planet. It's the story of a...reporter with a nose for the truth who's keeping the biggest secret the world has ever known." (Publisher's note)

"Landis brings a fresh and lively humanism to each of these tales, tangling throughout with Clark's uncertain feelings about his powers." Pub Wkly

Originally published in single magazine form as Superman: American Alien 1-7

Lanzac, Abel

Weapons of Mass Diplomacy. by Abel Lanzac, illustrated by Christophe Blain, translated by Edward Gauvin. Harry N Abrams Inc 2014 200 p. Color; Illustration

Grades: Adult   **741.5**

1. Graphic novels; 2. United States — Foreign opinion — France; 3. War on Terrorism, 2001-2009 — Influence

190683878X; 9781906838782, $24.95

LC 2014501285

"In 2003, France opposed the U.S. military juggernaut's initiative to chastise Iraq for presumed 'weapons of mass destruction.' With a nail-biting tale conjuring both Dilbert and Franz Kafka's satires, Lanzac (pseudonym of former diplomatic staffer Antonin Baudry) fictionalizes the personalities and power plays leading up to this real and courageous decision.... The hapless Arthur Vlaminck (Baudry's nom-de-toon) signs on as speechwriter for French foreign minister Alexandre Taillard de Vorms. Buffeted by clouds of doublespeak and doublethink as the crisis builds, Arthur gradually realizes that his infuriating boss is actually a gutsy visionary." (Library Journal)

"Besides the Quai d'Orsay, other settings include far-flung embassies and the UN; besides the Minister and Arthur, several other characters are also drolly realized by ace French adventure-comedy cartoonist Blain — all in his characteristic mixture of caricatural figures and highly realistic settings." Booklist

Lapham, David

Batman: City of Crime. David Lapham, writer; Ramon Bachs, penciler; Nathan Massengill, inker; Jason Wright, colorist; Jared K. Fletcher, letterer. DC Comics 2006 288p. Illustration

Grades: 10 11 12 Adult   **741.5; Fic**

1. Batman (Fictional character); 2. Graphic novels; 3. Mystery graphic novels; 4. Superhero graphic novels

978-1-4012-0897-4, $19.99

Dave Lapham, the creator of the ultra-gritty noir series Stray Bullets, weaves a story of the Dark Knight facing an unspeakable crime. Batman first investigates the deaths of six teenage girls, then he learns of even worse crimes. As he tries to shut down a drug ring that's turned deadly, Bruce Wayne must contend with a wayward 14-year-old who's getting dangerously close to Gotham's underworld. In Gotham City, not every villain wears a mask; not every hero wears a cape; not every victim is innocent; and some secrets should remain buried. This volume includes violence.

Silverfish. DC Comics/Vertigo 2007 un Illustration

Grades: 11 12 Adult   **741.5; Fic**

1. Graphic novels; 2. Mystery graphic novels

978-1-4012-1048-9, $24.99

What starts as a childish bid for her father's affections turns into nail-biting suspense when teenaged Mia searches her new stepmother's purse, only to find a secret stash of money, a bloody knife and a mysterious address book. In the meantime, Daniel is on the trail of the woman who betrayed him; and the silverfish he keeps seeing in his mind's eye are telling him to kill again.

Larcenet, Manu

Dungeon: Parade Vol. 1: A Dungeon Too Many. by Joann Sfar, Lewis Trondheim & Manu Larcenet. NBM 2007 un Illustration
Grades: 6 7 8 9 10 11 12 Adult   741.5; Fic
   1. Adventure graphic novels; 2. Fantasy graphic novels; 3. Graphic novels; 4. Humorous graphic novels
   978-1-56163-495-8, $9.95
   Marvin the Vegetarian Dragon and Herbert the Duck do battle with the new, rival dungeon next door that is actually a theme park. Then, Herbert finds a magic lamp that has one wish left, and he and Marvin set out on a quest to find a dying sage to get advice on the best wish.

Larsen, Erik

Savage Dragon Archives Volume 1. Image Comics 2006 616p. Illustration
Grades: 10 11 12 Adult   741.5; Fic
   1. Graphic novels; 2. Mystery graphic novels; 3. Superhero graphic novels; 4. Hellboy (Fictional character)
   978-1-58240-723-4, $19.99
The earliest adventures are collected for the first time in one volume as Savage Dragon defends Chicago from Overlord and the Vicious Circle. Savage Dragon, a big, green, fin-headed alien with no memory of his early life before being found in an empty field in Chicago, is a superhero who actually works as a police officer with the Chicago Police Department. This is the complete Overlord epic from start to finish, culminating in a battle that can only end one way. Guest-starring the WildC.A.T.S and the Teenage Mutant Ninja Turtles. This black and white reprint volume includes a lot of fighting violence, some strong language, and some skimpy women's costumes.

Larson, Hope

Gray horses. Oni Press 2006 un Illustration
Grades: 9 10 11 12 Adult
741.5; Fic
   1. Dreams — Graphic novels; 2. Graphic novels
   1-932664-36-X, 14.95

LC 2006-280748
French exchange student Noemie has traveled to Onion City on her own, where she makes friends with free-spirited Anna, a neighbor and baker's daughter who sculpts in bread. As she walks around the city, she finds herself the target of a mysterious young photographer. However, it's in her dreams that things are weird. Every night she dreams of a girl named Marcy who finds help from a talking horse to get away from her mother; she must find a place to hide a photograph before her mother burns everything "contaminated" from illness. As the dreams progress every night, Noemie is more able to live in the moment. Much of the text is bilingual.

Courtesy of Oni Press

Lash, Batton

Mister Negativity and Other Tales of Supernatural Law. Exhibit A Press 2004 170p. Illustration
Grades: 8 9 10 11 12 Adult   **741.5; Fic**

   1. Graphic novels; 2. Humorous graphic novels; 3. Supernatural graphic novels
   0-9633954-8-3, $15.95

LC 2003113227
Attorneys Wolff & Byrd represent clients that include Nagy D'Viti, a fellow with such a negative attitude that he physically repels people, Huberis the Dybbuk, a born again demon seeking church membership, Nicky Gorillo, a gangster who has literally become a gorilla mob boss, Steven Gink, a horror novelist in a coma who summons them through their dreams, Susann, the Muse of Potboilers, who sues the author she has "inspired," and Perry Otter, a boy magician with an unusual affliction.

Sonovawitch! And Other tales of Supernatural Law. Exhibit A Press 2000 166p. Illustration
Grades: 9 10 11 12 Adult   **741.5; Fic**
   1. Graphic novels; 2. Horror graphic novels; 3. Humorous graphic novels; 4. Law — Graphic novels
   0-9633954-6-7, $14.95
   Alanna Wolff and Jeff Byrd are attorneys who represent the supernatural and the supernaturally afflicted. In this volume, their clients include "Dr. Life," a physician dedicated to reviving the dead; "Bugsy" Renfield, a vampire member of the Nosferatu crime cartel; Ygor, a hunchback charged with teaching Satanism to preschool children; Martin Woodhull, accused of "hexual harassment" when his mother, a witch, puts a love spell on one of his co-workers; Dekoo Kei, a Japanese holy man who guards a jewel that can unleash the power of the giant reptilian monster, the Gormagon; and Barry Hopper, a nice guy whose soul has accidentally possessed the body of the demon Wasistlos, who is not too happy to deal with its "inner human." And their secretary, Mavis, has an adventure all her own.

Tales of supernatural law. Exhibit A Press 2005 184p. Illustration
Grades: 9 10 11 12 Adult   **741.5; Fic**
   1. Graphic novels; 2. Humorous graphic novels; 3. Lawyers — Graphic novels; 4. Supernatural graphic novels
   0-9633954-9-1, $16.95
   This volume reprints the first eight issues of the ongoing comics series that used to be called Wolff & Byrd, Counselors of the Macabre and is now called Supernatural Law. Alanna Wolff and Jeff Byrd provide legal services for monsters, vampires, zombies, ghosts, and other things that go bump in the night. In these stories, they help a couple who foolishly used a monkey's paw to make wishes, another couple whose house becomes haunted every full moon, a supermodel seeking redress for a curse, a horror television host accused of exposing children to violence, a swamp monster who would like his fifteen minutes of fame, and the interdimensional being Th'Lulu.

Lasko-Gross, Miss

Escape from Special. Fantagraphics Books 2006 un Illustration
Grades: 10 11 12 Adult   **741.5; Fic**
   1. Autobiographical graphic novels; 2. Girls — Graphic novels; 3. Graphic novels
   978-1-56097-804-6, $16.95
   This semi-autobiographical graphic novel uses short episodes to depict the childhood and teen years of Melissa. Sometimes willful, she gets into trouble at school, is branded "special" (as in special education), has very few friends, and has to see a therapist. With biting honesty, Melissa endures the casual cruelty of so-called friends, mis-uses bad words to comic effect, and questions why she should do things like attend Jewish school when her parents don't go to Temple. Occasional nudity and harsh language occur throughout the book.

Lat

Kampung boy. First Second 2006 141p. Illustration
Grades: 7 8 9 10 11 12 Adult   **741; 741.5; Fic**
1. Family life — Graphic novels; 2. Graphic novels; 3. Muslims — Graphic novels; 4. Malaysia — Graphic novels
1-59643-121-0, $16.95

LC 2005-34135

"Malaysian cartoonist Lat uses the graphic novel format to share the story of his childhood in a small village, or kampung. From his birth and adventures as a toddler to the enlargement of his world as he attends classes in the village, makes friends, and, finally, departs for a prestigious city boarding school, this autobiography is warm, authentic, and wholly engaging." Booklist

First published 1979 in Malaysia with title: Lat, the kampung boy; Another title about Lat is: Town boy (2007)

★ **Town** boy. First Second Books 2007 191p. Illustration
Grades: 7 8 9 10 11 12 Adult   **741.5; Fic**
1. Bildungsromans — Graphic novels; 2. Graphic novels; 3. Humorous graphic novels; 4. Malaysia — Graphic novels
978-1-59643-331-1, $16.95; 1-59643-331-0

LC 2006-102857

In this sequel to Kampung Boy, it's the late 1960s and Mat is now a teenager attending a boarding school in the town of Ipoh, far from his kampung. He discovers bustling streets, hip music, heady literature, budding romance, and through it all his growing passion for art.

Latour, Jason

Spider-Gwen; Volume 0: Most Wanted?. written by Jason Latour, art by Robbi Rodriguez. Marvel Enterprises 2015 112 p.
Grades: 9 10 11 12 Adult   **741.5**
1. Female superhero comic books, strips, etc.; 2. Superhero comic books, strips, etc.; 3. Spider-Woman (Fictional character)
0785197737; 9780785197737, $16.99

"Gwen Stacy is Spider-Woman, but you knew that already. What you DON'T know is what friends and foes are waiting for her in the aftermath of Spider-Verse! From the fan-favorite creative team that brought you Spider-Gwen's origin story in EDGE OF SPIDER-VERSE, Jason Latour and Robbie Rodriguez!" (Publisher's note)

Originally published in single issue form as Spider-Gwen #1-5; First volume of an ongoing series

Lavie, Boaz

The **Divine**. written by Boaz Lavie; illustrated by Asaf Hanuka, Tomer Hanuka. First Second 2015 160 p. Color; Illustration
Grades: Adult   **741.5; Fic**
1. Fantasy comic books, strips, etc.; 2. Magic — Comic books, strips, etc.; 3. War stories — Graphic novels
9781596436749, $19.99; 1596436743

LC 2014047292

In this graphic novel, written by Boaz Lavie, illustrated by Asaf Hanuka and Tomer Hanuka, "Mark's out of the military...with his boring, safe civilian job doing explosives consulting. But you never really get away from war. So it feels inevitable when his old army buddy Jason comes calling, with a lucrative military contract for a mining job in an obscure South-East Asian country called Quanlom. They'll have to operate under the radar — Quanlom is being torn apart by civil war." (Publisher's note)

"Once in Quanlom the mood pivots from merely ominous to outright wartime nightmare, as Mark is taken prisoner by some particularly vicious preadolescent rebels. The story gets more and more violent and fantasy-like from there. The Hanukas' layered illustrations coat everything with a hyperreal glaze, accentuating the story's dreamlike aspects." Pub Wkly

Layman, John

★ **Chew,** volume one: taster's choice. written & lettered by John Layman; drawn & coloured by Rob Guillory. Image Comics 2009 un Illustration
Grades: 10 11 12 Adult   **741.5; Fic**
1. Cannibalism — Graphic novels; 2. Graphic novels; 3. Mystery graphic novels; 4. Science fiction graphic novels
978-1-60706-159-5, $9.99

Police detective Tony Chu is a good detective with a weird secret: he's Cibopathic he gets psychic impressions from whatever he eats. It means he is a vegetarian, but it also means he can learn important facts about a case by nibbling on the corpse of a murder victim. Aside from the "ewwww" factor, he tends to have a high success rate in solving his cases. In his world, the FDA (yes, Food and Drug Administration) has become the most powerful law enforcement agency on the planet, and chicken is a forbidden food because of the avian flu. The FDA's Special Crimes Division makes Tony one of their agents and gives him their strangest, sickest, most bizarre unsolved cases, hoping to use his Cibopathic abilities to close them. This story includes cannibalism, violence, some gore, and some bad language. It has also been cited by many comics reviewers as one of the top comics series of 2009.

Volume 1 of 12

Leavitt, Sarah

★ **Tangles:** A Story About Alzheimer's, My Mother, and Me. Sarah Leavitt. Skyhorse Pub. 2012 127 p. Illustration; Portrait
Grades: Adult
362.1968; 362.1968/31
1. Family life; 2. Autobiographies; 3. Alzheimer's disease
1616086394; 9781616086398, $14.95

Courtesy of Skyhorse Publishing

"In this...graphic memoir, Sarah Leavitt reveals how Alzheimer's disease transformed her mother Midge — and her family — forever. ...Sarah shares her family's journey...managing to find moments of happiness. Midge, a Harvard-educated intellectual, struggles to comprehend the simplest words; Sarah's father Rob slowly adapts to his new role as full-time caretaker... Sarah and her sister Hannah argue, laugh, and grieve together." (Publisher's note)

Lee, Elaine

Starstruck. Elaine Lee, [writer]; M.W. Kaluta, [artist]; Lee Moyer, [painter]; [Todd Klein, letterer; Charles Vess, Galactic Girl Guides inker; John Workman, G.G.G. letterer; Scott Dunbier, editor]. IDW Publishing 2012 360 p. Illustration; Color
Grades: Adult
741.5
1. Astrology — Fiction; 2. Love — Fiction; 3. Overweight persons — Fiction; 4. Supernatural — Fiction; 5. New Jersey — Fiction; 6. Science fiction comic books, strips, etc.
1613774397; 9781613774397($7.95 Can.), $34.99

Courtesy of IDW Publishing

LC 2010021636

The book presents a collection of "all 13 issues of the completely remastered Starstruck series by Elaine Lee and Michael Wm. Kaluta." The collection presents "360 pages of Starstruck and Galactic Girl Guides adventures, covers, pin-ups, glossary, [and] postcards." The book also introduces new artwork and presents a look into the world of Starstruck. (Comic Vine)

Lee, Stan

Amazing Fantastic Incredible: A Marvelous Memoir. by Stan Lee, Peter David, and Colleen Doran. Simon & Schuster 2015 192 p. Color; Illustration

Grades: Adult **92; 741.5; 741.5973**
1. Lee, Stan, 1922-2018; 2. Comic books, strips, etc. — Authorship
1501107720; 9781501107726, $30

In this graphic novel memoir, "Stan Lee-comic book legend and cocreator of Spider-Man, the X-Men, the Avengers, the Incredible Hulk, and a legion of other Marvel superheroes-shares his iconic legacy and the story of how modern comics came to be." (Publisher's note)

Essential Fantastic Four Vol. 1, 2nd ed.. Marvel Entertainment 2005 un Illustration

Grades: 7 8 9 10 11 12 Adult **741.5; Fic**
1. Fantastic Four (Fictional characters); 2. Graphic novels; 3. Superhero graphic novels; 4. Hulk (Fictional character)
978-0-7851-1828-2, $16.99

This massive trade paperback collects the first 20 issues of The Fantastic Four plus the Annual #1. Reprinted in black and white, this volume lets readers get the origin and early stories as originally written by Lee and drawn by Kirby. The Fantastic Four fights against Skrulls, Sub-Mariner, The Impossible Man, The Hulk, the Red Ghost, The Thinker, Doctor Doom (who first appeared in issue #5), the Puppet Master, and many more super villains.

★ **Stan** Lee's How todraw comics: from the legendary co-creator ofSpider-Man, the Incredible Hulk, Fantastic Four,X-Men, and Iron Man. Watson-Guptill Publication 2010 224p. Illustration

Grades: 9 10 11 12 Adult **741.5**
1. Comic books, strips, etc. — Authorship; 2. Drawing — Technique; 3. X-Men (Fictional characters); 4. Fantastic Four (Fictional characters); 5. Graphic novels; 6. Hulk (Fictional character); 7. Iron Man (Fictional character); 8. Spider-Man (Fictional character)
978-0-8230-0083-8, $24.99

LC 2010-5781

Includes bibliographical references

Stan's soapbox: The collection. Marvel Entertainment 2008 144p. Illustration

Grades: 9 10 11 12 Adult **741.5; 814**
1. Fantastic Four (Fictional characters); 2. X-Men (Fictional characters); 3. Graphic novels; 4. Spider-Man (Fictional character)
978-0-9797602-9-7, $14.99

Stan Lee is probably one of the best-known faces of American comics, he helped to create many of the iconic superhero characters published by Marvel Comics, including the Fantastic Four, Spider-Man, and the X-Men. As an editor for Marvel, he wrote editorials that ran in every Marvel comic published from 1967-1980; these were called "Stan's Soapbox." This book, published as a co-venture with the Hero Initiative as a fundraiser to help comic creators in financial need, collects all of the Stan's Soapbox editorials from those Marvel comics. Readers can go back in time as they read what Lee wrote; the book also includes the major events happening in the U.S. and the world during those years

Lehman, Timothy

Manga: masters of the art. HarperCollins/Collins Design 2005 255p. Illustration

Grades: Adult Professional **741.5**

1. Graphic novels — Authorship; 2. Manga — Authorship
978-0-06-083331-2, $24.95

LC 2005-930652

This is a practical reference book, a look at how this artwork makes it from concept to reality, and a commentary on the format. The artists featured are: Kia Asamiya (Silent Möbius, Batman: Child of Dreams), CLAMP (Chobits, Tsubasa), Takehiko Inoue (Vagabond, Slam Dunk), Erica Sakurazawa (Between the Sheets, The Aromatic Bitters), Jiro Taniguchi (Icaro, The Walking Man), Yuko Tsuno (Swing Shell), Tatsuya Egawa (Golden Boy, Tokyo University Story), Suehiro Maruo (Mr. Arashi's Amazing Freak Show), Reiko Okano (Onmyoji, Fancy Dance), Mafuyu Hiroki (Apples), Miou Takaya (Crazy Heaven, Map of Sacred Pain), and Usamaru Furuya (Short Cuts, Palepoli). They discuss how they became interested in manga, their first published work, where they get their ideas, the creative process, tips and techniques, artistic influences, the genre itself, and much more. Illustrations and photographs of each artist's most seminal works are accompanied by extensive, explanatory captions. Some of the art depicts nudity, sexual situations, and violence.

Fans "will be fascinated by the behind-the-scenes details and the generous samples from stories that prompt seeking out more." Booklist

Lehmann, Matthias

Hwy 115. Fantagraphics Books 2006 un Illustration

Grades: 12 Adult **741.5; Fic**
1. Graphic novels; 2. Mystery graphic novels
978-1-56097-733-9, $19.95

Two detectives, René and Agatha, are on the tracks of Robert Illot, a serial killer whose modus operandi is to suffocate his victim with various objects (including chickens and lightbulbs) along the highways and byways of France. As they get closer and closer to catching up with him, seeking out and interrogating men and women from his past life at the insane asylum, he always stays one step ahead and the row of corpses grows longer and longer... In this lengthy original graphic novel by Matthias Lehmann, dreams and flashbacks converge with the ongoing narrative, with graphically depicted sex and lots of murders.

Lemelman, Gusta

Mendel's daughter: a memoir. Gusta Lemelman, Martin Lemelman. Free Press 2006 217p. Illustration

Grades: Adult **92; 741.5**
074329162X; 9780743291620, $24.99

LC 2006045180

"In 1989 Martin Lemelman videotaped his mother, Gusta, as she opened up about her childhood in 1930s Poland and her eventual escape from Nazi persecution. Mendel's Daughter...is Lemelman's loving transcription of his mother's harrowing testimony, bringing her narrative to life with his own powerful black-and-white drawings, interspersed with reproductions of actual photographs, documents and other relics from that era." (Publisher's note)

Lemire, Jeff

Animal Man; Volume 1: The hunt. Jeff Lemire, writer; Travel Foreman, artist. DC Comics 2012 144 p. Color illustration

Grades: Adult **741.5/973**
1. Superhero comic books, strips, etc.; 2. Family life — Fiction; 3. Superheroes — Fiction
1401235077; 9781401235079, $14.99

LC 2011051856

This comic book by Jeff Lemire, illustrated by Travel Foreman, includes issues 1-6 of "Animal Man." "As a part of the...DC Comics-The New 52 event of September 2011,...Buddy Baker has gone from 'super' man to family man — but is he strong enough...when...his young daughter...manifest[s] her own dangerous powers?...[T]hings take a turn for the worse as Buddy begins a startling transformation of his own that will lead him on a journey into the heart of The Red." (Publisher's note)

"Lemire scripts likable characters and relatable family dynamics, even as he ratchets up the creepiness, ably abetted by Foreman's stark-lined and sinewy art, which basks in the varied ways the human form can be twisted into hideous shapes" Booklist

Originally published in single magazine form in ANIMAL MAN 1-6 — T.p. verso.; Other Animal Man volumes written by Jeff Lemire are: 2: Animal vs. Man (2012); 3: Rotworld: The Red Kingdom (2013); 4: Splinter Species (2014); 5: Evolve or Die! (2014)

★ **Black** hammer; Volume 1: Secret origins. script by Jeff Lemire; art by Dean Ormston; colors by Dave Stewart; letters by Todd Klein; cover by Dean Ormston with Dave Stewart; chapter breaks by Dean Ormston, Jeff Lemire, and Dave Stewart. Dark Horse Books 2017 152 p. Color; Illustration

Grades: 11 12 Adult   **741.5; Fic**
  1. Superheroes — Fiction; 2. Adventure graphic novels
9781616557867, $14.99; 1616557869

LC 2016045234

Eisner Award: Best New Series (2017)

In this graphic novel, by Jeff Lemire, illustrated by Dean Ormston, "the old champions of Spiral City — Abraham Slam, Golden Gail, Colonel Weird, Madame Dragonfly, and Barbalien — now lead simple lives in an idyllic, timeless farming village from which there is no escape! But as they employ all of their super abilities to free themselves from this strange purgatory, a mysterious stranger works to bring them back into action for one last adventure!" (Publisher's note)

"As the narrative unfolds, the haunting backstories add greater context and intrigue to the mysteries of the present. There's an astonishing clarity to the characters and their motivations amid what could easily become a convoluted backstory filled with interstellar exploration, multiverse travelling, alien diplomacy, and quiet farm life." Pub Wkly

This volume collects issues #1-#6 of the Dark Horse Comics series Black Hammer — Title page verso.

★ **Descender:** Tin Stars Book one. by Jeff Lemire; illustrated by Dustin Nguyen. Image Comics 2015 160 p.

Grades: 9 10 11 12 Adult   **741.5**
  1. Science fiction comic books, strips, etc.; 2. Androids — Fiction; 3. Robots — Fiction
1632154269; 9781632154262, $9.99

LC bl2015040509

In this science fiction comic book, by Jeff Lemire, illustrated by Dustin Nguyen, "Young Robot boy TIM-21 and his companions struggle to stay alive in a universe where all androids have been outlawed and bounty hunters lurk on every planet." (Publisher's note)

Volume 1 of an ongoing series

★ **Essex** County, Vol. 1: Tales from the Farm. Top Shelf Productions 2007 un Illustration

Grades: 10 11 12 Adult   **741.5; Fic**
  1. Farm life — Graphic novels; 2. Friendship — Graphic novels; 3. Graphic novels; 4. Orphans — Graphic novels
978-1-891830-88-4, $9.95

Orphaned ten-year-old Lester lives with his bachelor uncle Ken on a southwestern Ontario farm. He constantly wears a mask and cape, imagining that he's protecting the place from invading space aliens. Uncle Ken doesn't know how to deal with Lester, and their relationship becomes strained. Only one grown-up, Jimmy, who runs the gas station and convenience store, can connect with Lester on his level.

"Lemire enriches this rather familiar scenario with telling, particularizing detail, ensuring that this time the old heartwarming routine is unforgettably special." Booklist

Volume 1 of 3

★ **Essex** County, vol. 2: Ghost stories. Top Shelf Productions 2007 224p. Illustration

Grades: 10 11 12 Adult   **741.5; Fic**
  1. Brothers — Graphic novels; 2. Graphic novels; 3. Hockey — Graphic novels
978-1-891830-94-5, $14.95

Ghost Story follows the lives and relationship of brothers Lou and Vince Lebeuf over the course of nearly seven decades. Elder brother Lou, now a deaf and lonely man, lives out his final days on his farm full of guilt and regret for the decisions he made that tore his family apart. From their childhood on the farm, to Toronto in the 1950s (where they both played professional hockey), Lou is left to revisit his life, his decisions and his regrets. This is the second volume of Lemire's stories of Essex County.

★ **Essex** County, vol. 3: The country nurse. Top Shelf Productions 2008 127p. Illustration

Grades: 10 11 12 Adult   **741.5; Fic**
  1. Family life — Graphic novels; 2. Graphic novels
978-1-891830-95-2, $9.95

In this third and final volume in the Essex County trilogy, the story follows country nurse Anne Morgan through one day as she drives around the county to visit patients. In between her meetings with Jimmy at the gas station, Ken and his nephew Lester at the farm, and learning that elderly Mr. LeBeuf, Jimmy's father, had died the previous night, readers see the story of an orphanage that existed almost a century ago. When it burned down one night and the caretaker died getting all the children out, the nun in charge led them on a cold winter hike to find shelter and help in Essex County. Anne is a descendant of the nun, while Jimmy, Ken, and Lester are all descendants of one orphan. And all their stories come together as Anne makes her rounds of the day.

"Well written and beautifully drawn, this wonderful close to a powerful trilogy is ideal for fans of realistic stories in comics." SLJ

Green Arrow. written by Jeff Lemire; art by Andrea Sorrentino; color by Marcelo Maiolo with Andrea Sorrentino,Matt Hollingsworth & Hi-Fi; additional art byDenys Cowan & Bill Sienkiewicz (New tricks &Secret origin); letters by Rob Leigh, Dezi Sienty& Taylo. DC Comics 2016 464 p. Color; Illustration

Grades: 9 10 11 12 Adult   **741.5**
  1. Superhero graphic novels; 2. Green Arrow (Fictional character)
1401257615; 9781401257613, $49.99

LC 2015034646

"Oliver Queen is on the run and being hunted by the greatest enemy he never knew he had — Komodo, a mysterious archer who is the Green Arrow's better in every way. But this new villain is just one piece of the puzzle of Green Arrow's past. Komodo has thrown Oliver's life into disarray, making Oliver question the details of his time on the island — and his long-dead father's involvement. Once the murky secrets of Green Arrow's past surface, things will never be the same again. When Oliver finally discovers the truth about himself, can he use it to become the Green Arrow that he needs to be?" (Publisher's note)

Hawkeye: all-new Hawkeye. by Jeff Lemire; illustrated by Ramon Perez. Marvel Enterprises 2015 112 p. Color; Illustration

Grades: 11 12 Adult   **741.5**
  1. Superhero comic books, strips, etc.
0785194037; 9780785194033, $15.99

In this comic book, by Jeff Lemire, illustrated by Ramon Perez, "Hawkeye returns.... With Kate Bishop, his trusted ward and protégé (not titles she would use) back at his side, Team Hawkeye is thrown into an all new adventure spanning two generations of avenging archers. Past and present lives collide as Kate and Clint face a threat that will challenge everything they know about what it means to be Hawkeye." (Publisher's note)

Old man Logan; Volume 1: berzerker. writer, Jeff Lemire; artist, Andrea Sorrentino; colorist, Marcelo Maiolo; letterer, VC's Cory Petit. Marvel Enterprises 2016 128 p. Color; Illustration

Grades: 11 12 Adult   **741.5**

 1. Superheroes comic books, strips, etc.; 2. Wolverine (Fictional character)

 078519620X; 9780785196204, $16.99

 "Logan — the man who no longer calls himself Wolverine — will have endured many atrocities: The Marvel Universe's villains will have banded together and rid the world of its heroes. Logan's closest friend, Hawkeye, will have been murdered in cold blood right before his eyes. And driven mad by the same radiation that gave him his superhuman strength, Bruce Banner will have fathered a family of hillbilly Hulks..." (Publisher's note)

 Contains material originally published in magazine form as Old Man Logan #1-4 and Wolverine: Old Man Logan Giant-Size; Volume 1 of an ongoing series

Plutona. script: Jeff Lemire; art: Emi Lenox; letters: Steve Wands; story: Emi Lenox & Jeff Lemire; colors: Jordie Bellaire; book design: Sasha Head; Plutona created by Emi Lenox; Plutona's last adventure by Jeff Lemire. Image Comics 2016 128 p. Color; Illustration

Grades: 10 11 12 Adult   **741.5; Fic**

 1. Mystery graphic novels; 2. Superhero graphic novels; 3. Children — Graphic novels

 1632156016; 9781534300132; 9781632156013, $16.99

 In this graphic novel, by Jeff Lemire, illustrated by Emi Lenox, "five kids discover the body of the world's greatest super hero, Plutona, in the woods after school one day. This discovery sends them on a dark journey that will threaten to tear apart their friendship and their lives." (Publisher's note)

 "The wary tone of adolescent alliances and small thoughtless cruelties is captured perfectly. Colorist Bellaire works magic, contrasting the muted primaries of the school scenes against the cool shadows of the forest." Pub Wkly

 Originally published in single magazine form as Plutona #1-5

Roughneck. Jeff Lemire. Gallery 13, an imprint of Simon & Schuster Inc. 2017 272 p. Color; Illustration

Grades: 11 12 Adult   **741.5; Fic**

 1. Brothers and sisters — Fiction

 1501160990; 9781501160998; $29.99; 9781476774008; 9781476773995, $19.99

 Alex Award (2018)

 "Derek Ouellette's glory days in the NHL are far behind-now, he's known mostly for alcoholism, public urination, and bar fights. When his younger sister, Beth, arrives in town, addicted to Oxycontin and fleeing an abusive boyfriend, he finds he can no longer hide at the bottom of a bottle. The siblings take to the wilderness, in search of sobriety, solitude, and, possibly, a second chance." (Publishers Weekly)

 Lemire "exhibits deep empathy for his characters, a keen understanding of difficult family dynamics, and an eye for the way that moments of grace can emerge in the midst of brutality. Full-color flashback sequences interrupt the main story, which is presented in washes of black and blue that highlight the sad state of the characters' lives as well as the barren Canadian wilderness." LJ

Royal City; Volume 1: next of kin. created, written, and illustrated by Jeff Lemire; lettered by Steve Wands. Image Comics 2017 160 p. Color; Illustration

Grades: Adult   **741.5; Fic**

 1. Ghost stories — Comic books, strips, etc.; 2. Family life — Fiction; 3. City and town life — Fiction

 153430262X; 9781534302624, $9.99

 This book, by Jeff Lemire, "follows Patrick Pike, a fading literary star who reluctantly returns to the once-thriving factory town where he grew up. Patrick is quickly drawn back into the dramas of his two adult siblings, his overbearing Mother and his brow beaten Father, all of whom are still haunted by different versions of his youngest brother, Tommy, who drowned decades ago." (Publisher's note)

 "While Lemire's introduction and development of the characters and their backstories are quietly masterful, his wispy graphics-spindly figures, understated staging, and muted colors-are equally intrinsic to the work's potency." Booklist

 Volume 1 of 3

Sweet tooth; 2: in captivity. Jeff Lemire, story & art; Jose Villarrubia, colors; Pat Brosseau, letters. Vertigo/DC Comics 2010 140 p. Color; Illustration (Sweet Tooth)

Grades: Adult   **741.5**

 1. Animal mutation — Comic books, strips, etc; 2. End of the world — Comic books, strips, etc; 3. Plague — Comic books, strips, etc; 4. Survival — Comic books, strips, etc; 5. Mystery graphic novels; 6. Voyages and travels — Graphic novels

 9781401228545 (pa), $14.99; 1401228542

          LC 2010549071

 "Gus thought the man called Jepperd was his protector, his friend. But then Jepperd brought him to a terrible place where half-animal hybrid children like Gus are kept in cages. A place where hard men conduct lethal experiments in a vain attempt to unravel the secret of the plague that has ravaged the world.... Meanwhile, Jepperd himself is a free man, who can roam the wastelands at will. But he can never forget the life he left behind." (Publisher's note)

 "The second arc of Lemire's series continues to wear its influences (The Road, The Stand, Mad Max, Y: The Last Man) proudly on its flanneled sleeve, though Lemire's skillful storytelling ensures that nothing feels derivative." Booklist

Teen Titans; Volume 1: Earth One. written by Jeff Lemire; pencils by Terry Dodson. DC Comics 2014 144 p. Color; Illustration

Grades: 10 11 12 Adult   **741.5**

 1. Teen Titans (Fictional characters); 2. Teenagers — Comic books, strips, etc.; 3. Superhero comic books, strips, etc.

 1401245560; 9781401245566, $22.99

          LC 2014032609

 This book, by Jeff Lemire and Terry Dodson, is a "new original graphic novel in DC's popular 'Earth One' series.... The Teen Titans never felt like normal kids... but they had no idea how right they were. Their seemingly idyllic Oregon upbringing hides a secret — one that will bring killers, shamans, and extraterrestrials down on their heads, and force them into an alliance that could shake the planet to its foundations!" (Publisher's note)

 "Rather than more minor tinkering with the teenaged super-hero team, this graphic novel is a full-scale reboot: what if, in an alternative world, circumstances brought together young people who echo the regular Teen Titans but are totally different people?...Lemire's (Essex County) script exploits teen angst efficiently and with some fresh imagination, while the Dodsons (Wonder Woman) produce lovely art, especially in panels showing Navajo seer Raven." Pub Wkly

Trillium. Jeff Lemire, writer & artist; Jeff Lemire, Jose Villarrubia, colorists; Carlos M. Mangual, letterer. DC Comics/Vertigo 2014 192 p. Color; Illustration

Grades: 11 12 Adult   **741.5**

1. Science fiction graphic novels; 2. Time travel — Graphic novels; 3. Romance fiction
1401249000; 9781401249007, $16.99

LC 2014011939

Eisner Nominee: Best Limited Series (2014)

This graphic novel, by Jeff Lemire, with color by Jose Villarrubia and lettering by Carlos M. Mangual, "spins the tale of two star-crossed loved through space in time.... [In] the year 3797,...botanist Nika Temsmith is researching a strange species on a remote science station near the outermost rim of colonized space.... [In] 1921,...English explorer William Pike leads an expedition into the dense jungles of Peru in search of the fabled 'Lost Temple of the Incas.'" (Publisher's note)

"Lemire's art excels, combining his trademark sketchiness with gorgeous watercolors. But it's the layouts that take the book to new heights of creativity. Lemire tells two stories at once by turning the panels upside down, disorienting the reader as much as his heroes." Pub Wkly

The **underwater** welder. by Jeff Lemire. Top Shelf Productions 2012 220 p.
Grades: Adult
Fic
1. Fatherhood — Graphic novels; 2. Graphic novels; 3. Welders (Persons) — Graphic novels
1603090746; 9781603090742, $19.95

Courtesy of IDW Publishing

This graphic novel by Jeff Lemire follows Jack Joseph, "an underwater welder on an oilrig off the coast of Nova Scotia...[dealing with] the pressures of impending fatherhood. As Jack dives deeper and deeper, he seems to pull further and further away from his young wife and their unborn son. But then, something happens deep on the ocean floor. Jack has a strange and mind-bending encounter that will change the course of his life forever!" (Publisher's note)

Leong, Sonia
101 top tips from professional manga artists. Sonia Leong, Hayden Scott Baron. Barrons Educational Series, Inc. 2013 176 p.
Grades: Adult **741.5**
1. Japanese art; 2. Manga — Study and teaching; 3. Drawing — Technique
1438002068; 9781438002064, $22.99

LC 2012948428

This book, by Sonia Leong and Hayden Scott Baron, focuses on the Japanese drawing known as manga. "With additional insights from a select group of fellow professionals, this illustration-packed book covers all aspects of manga art, presenting advice and instruction on...everything an illustrator needs to know in order to create successful manga art for a variety of media." (Publisher's note)

"Freelance comic artist and illustrator Leong and several contributing artists provide over 100 tips grouped and organized around basic topics, highlighting key aspects of manga such as character design, backgrounds, props, software and media, and even practices of successful professionals." LJ

Lepore, Jill
★ The **Secret** History of Wonder Woman. by Jill Lepore. Alfred A. Knopf 2014 448 p. Plate; Color; Illustration
Grades: Adult **741.5/973**
1. Marston, William Moulton; 2. Feminism in literature; 3. Literature and society — United States; 4. Wonder Woman (Fictitious character)
0385354045; 9780385354042, $29.95

LC 2014011064

This book, by Jill Lepore, is a "work of historical detection revealing that the origin of one of the world's most iconic superheroes hides within it a fascinating family story — and a crucial history of twentieth-century feminism. Wonder Woman, created in 1941, is the most popular female superhero of all time.... Lepore has uncovered an astonishing trove of documents, including the never-before-seen private papers of William Moulton Marston, Wonder Woman's creator." (Publisher's note)

"Lepore demonstrates the power of exploring popular culture as history, and her readable style, as well as the subject matter, allows her to introduce this more nuanced understanding of a complex past to a wide audience." Choice
Includes bibliographical references and index

Leth, Kate
Patsy Walker, A.K.A. Hellcat!; Volume 1: Hooked on a Feline. Kate Leth, writer; Brittney L. Williams (#1-5) & Natasha Allegri (#6), artists; Megan Wilson (#1-5) & Natasha Allegri (#6), color artists. Marvel Enterprises 2016 136 p. Color; Illustration
Grades: 9 10 11 12 Adult **741.5; Fic**
1. Female superhero graphic novels; 2. Mother-daughter relationship — Fiction; 3. New York (N.Y.) — Fiction
1302900358; 9781302900359, $17.99

"Patsy Walker has managed to escape her past, her enemies and Hell itself (literally) — but nothing compares to job hunting in New York City! Between trying to make rent and dodging bullets, Patsy barely has time to deal with her mother.... As she goes from living a double life to a triple, what the hell is Patsy Walker supposed to do?" (Publisher's note)
Volume 1 of 3

Levitz, Paul
Justice Society Volume One. writers, Paul Levitz, Gerry Conway; pencillers, Joe Staton, Keith Giffen, Wally Wood, Ric Estrada; inkers, Wally Wood, Bob Layton. DC Comics 2006 224p. Illustration
Grades: 7 8 9 10 11 12 Adult **741.5; Fic**
1. Graphic novels; 2. Justice Society of America (Fictional characters); 3. Superhero graphic novels; 4. Green Lantern (Fictional character); 5. Flash (Fictional character); 6. Robin (Fictional character)
978-1-4012-0970-4, $14.99

The volume collects stories originally published in the 1970s, when DC revived the very first superhero team that was originally created in 1940: the Justice Society of America. This incarnation of the Justice Society includes the Golden Age Flash and Green Lantern, Hawkman, Dr. Fate, Wildcat, Dr. Mid-Nite, Robin, Power Girl, and the Star-Spangled Kid. Artists on this run include Wally Wood, Joe Staton, Keith Giffen, and Ric Estrada.

Lewis, Corey Sutherland
Sharknife Volume 1. Oni Press 2006 un Illustration
Grades: 8 9 10 11 12 Adult **741.5; Fic**
1. Graphic novels; 2. Humorous graphic novels; 3. Martial arts — Graphic novels
1-932664-17-3, $9.95

The Guandong Factory isn't like other restaurants. It's five stories tall, produces more peach dumplings per day than most eateries do in a decade, and it's the home of Sharknife — a mystical protector charged with protecting the establishment from those who would do it harm. But who is this mysterious yet colorful being? Once just a simple busboy, now Caesar Ives is something more — a crazy red rocket hero destined for greatness. But can Caesar juggle both lives — nabbing the girl (the super-sexy Chieko Momuza), and stopping the wide assortment of bizarre baddies that would love to do his precious eatery harm? There's lots of martial arts action.

Lewis, Edith Patton

The **claws** come out: astounding tales of broads and monsters. IDW Publishing 2007 152p. Illustration

Grades: 10 11 12 Adult   **741.5**

1. Fantasy graphic novels; 2. Graphic novels; 3. Horror graphic novels; 4. Humorous graphic novels

978-160010-120-5, $19.99

The subtitle may sound rude (come on, calling women broads?), but all the women in the stories are strong, capable, willing to fight off monsters, vampires, and zombies. A young woman goes on a date for the first time in years, not knowing her ideal guy is a vampire. A teenage girl walking home after a date has a close encounter of the strange kind, but the aliens end up in trouble. An apathetic scientist/aspiring rock star works late at the lab defrosting the Abominable Snowman and finds trouble when a power outage allows the creature to get free. A fortune teller accidentally starts a zombie epidemic with a very powerful love potion. Lewis plays horror for laughs, with some violence and sexual innuendo.

Lewis, John

★ **March:** Book One. John Lewis; [co-written by] Andrew Aydin; [art by] Nate Powell. Top Shelf Productions 2013 121 p. Illustration

Grades: 8 9 10 11 12 Adult   **741.5; 92**

1. Civil rights movements — United States — Comic books, strips, etc; 2. Lewis, John, 1940 February 21-; 3. African Americans — Civil rights — Graphic novels

9781603093002, $14.95

                 LC 2013218903

Coretta Scott King (Author) Honor Book (2014)

This graphic novel, by U.S. congressman John Lewis, "in collaboration with co-writer Andrew Aydin and New York Times best-selling artist Nate Powell...spans John Lewis' youth in rural Alabama, his life-changing meeting with Martin Luther King, Jr., the birth of the Nashville Student Movement, and their battle to tear down segregation through nonviolent lunch counter sit-ins, building to a...climax on the steps of City Hall." (Publisher's note)

"This is superb visual storytelling that establishes a convincing, definitive record of a key eyewitness to significant social change." SLJ

★ **March:** Book Three. by John Lewis and Andrew Aydin; illustrated by Nate Powell. Top Shelf Productions 2016 256 p. Illustration

Grades: 8 9 10 11 12 Adult

328.73; 92

1. Lewis, John, 1940 February 21-; 2. Civil rights — United States

9781603094023, $19.99; 1603094024

National Book Award: Young People's Literature (2016); Coretta Scott King (Author) Book Award (2017); Printz Award (2017); Sibert Informational Book Award (2017); YALSA Award for Excellence in Nonfiction for Young Adults (2017); Eisner Award: Best Reality-Based Work (2017)

Courtesy of IDW Publishing

This book is the "conclusion of the award-winning and best-selling March trilogy. Congressman John Lewis, an American icon and one of the key figures of the civil rights movement, joins co-writer Andrew Aydin and artist Nate Powell to bring the lessons of history to vivid life for a new generation, urgently relevant for today's world." (Publisher's note)

"Though Lewis and Aydin throw a lot at readers in this volume, their message, helped along seamlessly and splendidly by Powell's fantastic, cinematic artwork, is abundantly clear: the victories of the civil rights movement, symbolized in particular by Barack Obama's inauguration, are hard-won and only succeeded through the dogged dedication of a wide variety of people." Booklist

★ **March:** Book Two. by John Lewis and Andrew Aydin; illustrated by Nate Powell. Top Shelf Productions 2015 192 p. Illustration

Grades: 8 9 10 11 12 Adult

741.5; 92

1. African American civil rights workers; 2. African American legislators; 3. African Americans — Civil rights; 4. Autobiographical comic books, strips, etc.; 5. Civil rights movements; 6. Civil rights workers — United States; 7. Legislators — United States; 8. Lewis, John, 1940 February 21-; 9. African Americans — Civil rights — Graphic novels

9781603094009, $19.95; 1603094008

Courtesy of IDW Publishing

                 LC 2015270634

Eisner Nominee: Best Publication for Teens (2016); Eisner Award: Best Reality-Based Work (2016); Ignatz Nominee: Outstanding Series (2015)

This graphic novel, by John Lewis and Andrew Aydin, illustrated by Nate Powell, "takes us behind the scenes of some of the most pivotal moments of the Civil Rights Movement.... After the success of the Nashville sit-in campaign, John Lewis is more committed than ever to changing the world through nonviolence — but as he and his fellow Freedom Riders board a bus into the vicious heart of the deep south, they will be tested like never before." (Publisher's note)

"Heroism and steadiness of purpose continue to light up Lewis' frank, harrowing account of the civil rights movement's climactic days.... The contrast between the dignified marchers and the vicious, hate-filled actions and expressions of their tormentors will leave a deep impression on readers." Kirkus

Lewis, Jon

True Swamp: choose your poison. Jon Lewis. Uncivilized Books 2012 160 p.

Grades: Adult

741; Fic

1. Frogs — Graphic novels

0984681426; 9780984681426, $19.95

This graphic novel, part of the True Swamp series, focuses on "Lenny the Frog.., an amphibian with a constant inner dialogue of self-doubt, brought on by his interaction with other swamp life. Lenny second-guesses himself at every turn, whether he's facing the swamp fairies, battling for his life against a human, or visiting the creepy resident of a wayward human skull — it's all a catalyst for self-examination, as well as investigation of the big picture." (Publishers weekly)

Courtesy of Uncivilized Books

Li Kunwu

A **Chinese** Life. written by Philippe Ôtié and Li Kunwu; illustrated by Li Kunwu; translated by Edward Gauvin. Harry N Abrams Inc 2012 691p. Illustration; Color

Grades: Adult   **951.05092; 741.5**

1. China — History; 2. Graphic novels; 3. Li Kunwu

1906838550; 9781906838553, $27.50

LC 2012464492

"This distinctively drawn work chronicles the rise and reign of Chairman Mao Zedong, and his sweeping, often cataclysmic vision for the most populated country on the planet. Though the storyline is epic, the storytelling is intimate, reflecting the real life of the book's artist. Li Kunwu spent more than 30 years as a state artist for the Communist Party. He saw firsthand what was happening to his family, his neighbors, and his homeland during this extraordinary time." (Publisher's note)

Translated from the French edition.

Lieberman, A. J..

Martian Manhunter: The Others Among Us. A.J. Lieberman, writer; Al Barrionuevo, penciller; Bit, inker; Marta Martinez, colorist; Rob Leigh, Travis Lanham, John J. Hill, letterers. DC Comics 2007 208p. Illustration
Grades: 10 11 12 Adult   **741.5; Fic**
1. Graphic novels; 2. Martian Manhunter (Fictional character); 3. Superhero graphic novels; 4. Justice League (Fictional characters)
978-1-4012-1335-0, $19.99

J'onn J'onzz, the Martian Manhunter, came to Earth years ago to warn all of humanity of an impending invasion. He believed himself to be the sole surviving member of his race and thus decided to use his incredible super-powers to help safeguard the people of his adopted world as a member of the Justice League of America. His discovery of a Martian artifact on Earth sets him on a quest to discover the origin of the relic which leads to a stunning discovery, the ramifications of which will forever change the way he sees himself, humanity and his destiny. He discovers that a shadowy branch of the U.S. government has imprisoned and experimented upon a group of Green Martians. Why were they being held captive, and what mysterious predator still stalks the survivors of Mars? His quest for truth will bring J'onn into conflict with humans, with every friend he has made on this planet. This book includes violence.

Liew, Sonny

★ The **art** of Charlie Chan Hock Chye. Sonny Liew. Pantheon Books 2016 320 p. Color; Illustration
Grades: 11 12 Adult   **741.5; Fic**
1. Singapore — Economic conditions — Comic books, strips, etc; 2. Singapore — Politics and government — Comic books, strips, etc; 3. Comic books, strips, etc.; 4. Illustrators
9781101870693, $30; 1101870699

LC 2015023576

Eisner Award: Best U.S. Edition of International Material — Asia (2017)

"In this graphic novel, [Sonny] Liew presents the life and work of an obscure comic-book creator in tandem with the turbulent modern history of Singapore.... [It] opens with his two-page comic juxtaposing a pair of prominent Singaporean leaders-Lee Kuan Yew, the long-standing prime minister who shrewdly if brutally oversaw the country's rise as an economic power; and Lim Chin Siong, a charismatic, populist orator who was outmaneuvered by political rivals, jailed as a dissident, and exiled." (Kirkus Reviews)

Originally published 2015 in Singapore

Lin, Hartley

Young Frances. Hartley Lin. AdHouse Books 2018 144 p. Color; Illustration
Grades: Adult   **741.5; Fic**
1. Clerks — Fiction; 2. Corporate culture — Fiction; 3. Office workers — Fiction; 4. Bildungsromans
9781935233428, $19.95

LC 2017957353

In this graphic novel, by Hartley Lin, "after insomniac law clerk Frances Scarland is recruited by her firm's most notorious senior partner, she seems poised for serious advancement-whether she wants it or not. But when her impulsive best friend Vickie decides to move to the opposite coast for an acting role, Frances' confusing existence starts to implode... " (Publisher's note)

"This thoroughly entertaining graphic novel collects the serial comics 'Pope Hats,' which were originally published under the pen name Ethan Rilly. Now published under Lin's real name, the complete arc showcases Lin's disarming brilliance, through skillful comics art and authentic conversational humor." Pub Wkly

Little, Jason

Shutterbug follies. Doubleday Graphic Novels 2002 153p. Illustration
Grades: 10 11 12 Adult   **741.5**
1. Graphic novels; 2. Mystery graphic novels
0-385-50346-6, $24.95

LC 2002-727189

This novel was "originally serialized as both a weekly newspaper comic strip and a web comics serial.... Scrappy 18-year-old Bee is working in a New York photo lab when a picture of a naked female corpse that's not quite what it appears to be piques her interest. Her amateur investigation of its photographer leads her to an ever-deepening mystery, a friendly cab driver, a cute but nervous photo assistant, some scary doings with the Russian mob and finally, into deadly danger." Publ Wkly

"With nearly implausible coincidences, a dash of slapstick humor, and a few red herrings, this is a detective romp, and the ending panel leaves readers breathlessly awaiting a sequel." SLJ

Liu, Marjorie M.

★ **Monstress**; Volume 1: Awakening. Marjorie Liu, writer; Sana Takeda, artist; Rus Wooton, lettering & design. Image Comics 2016 192 p. Color; Illustration
Grades: 11 12 Adult   **741.5; Fic**
1. Steampunk fiction; 2. Fantasy graphic novels; 3. Monsters — Graphic novels
1632157098; 9781632157096, $9.99

Eisner Nominee: Best New Series (2016); Hugo Award: Best Graphic Story (2017)

"Set in an alternate matriarchal 1900s Asia, in a richly imagined world of art deco-inflected steampunk, 'Monstress' tells the story of a teenage girl who is struggling to survive the trauma of war, and who shares a mysterious psychic link with a monster of tremendous power, a connection that will transform them both and make them the target of both human and otherworldly powers." (Publisher's note)

"Takeda's artwork creates a lush and dangerous world for Liu's equally dangerous characters. The work is infused with feminist themes; almost all of the characters are strong — and deadly — women." SLJ

Volume 1 of an ongoing series

★ **Monstress**; Volume 2: the blood. Marjorie Liu; Sana Takeda, artist; Rus Wooton, lettering & design. Image Comics 2017 144 p. Color; Illustration
Grades: 11 12 Adult   **741.5; Fic**
1. Steampunk fiction; 2. Monsters — Fiction; 3. Adventure fiction
1534300414; 9781534300415, $16.99

Hugo Award: Best Graphic Story (2018); Eisner Award: Best Publication for Teens (2018); Eisner Award: Best Continuing Series (2018)

"Maika, Kippa, and Ren journey to Thyria in search of answers to her past... and discover a new, terrible, threat." (Publisher's note)

Lobdell, Scott

Teen Titans; Volume 1. Scott Lobdell, writer; Brett Booth, penciler; Norm Rapmund, inker; Andrew Dalhouse, colorist; Dezi Sienty, Carlos M. Mangual, Travis Lanham, letterers; Brett Booth, Norm Rapmund & Andrew Dalhouse, original series & collection cover artists. DC Comics 2012 168 p.

Grades: Adult   Fic; 741.5/973

1. Teenagers — Comic books, strips, etc.; 2. Superhero comic books, strips, etc.; 3. Robin (Fictional character); 4. Wonder Woman (Fictional character); 5. Flash (Fictional character)

1401236987; 9781401236984, $14.99

LC 2012018770

This comic book anthology, by Scott Lobdell, illustrated by Brett Booth and Norm Rapmund, presents volume 1 of "The New 52" DC Comics series of "Teen Titans." "Batman's former sidekick, is back in action when an international organization called Project N.O.W.H.E.R.E. seeks to capture, kill or co-opt super-powered teenagers. As Red Robin, he's going to have to team up with...Wonder Girl,...Kid Flash and few more all-new teen super-heroes to stand any chance at all." (Publisher's note)

Originally published in single magazine form in TEEN TITANS 1-7.||The new 52! — Cover.

Loeb, Jeph

Batman: The Long Halloween. Jeph Loeb, writer; Tim Sale, artist; Gregory Wright, colors; Richard Starkings & Comicraft, letters. DC Comics 1999 375p. Illustration

Grades: 9 10 11 12 Adult   741.5; Fic

1. Batman (Fictional character); 2. Graphic novels; 3. Mystery graphic novels; 4. Superhero graphic novels

1563894270; 9781563894275, $19.99

LC 99-218572

Taking place during Batman's early days of crime fighting, this collection tells the story of a mysterious killer who murders his prey only on holidays. Working with District Attorney Harvey Dent and Lieutenant James Gordon, Batman races against the calendar as he tries to discover who Holiday is before he claims his next victim each month. This story also ties into the events that transform Harvey Dent into Batman's deadly enemy, Two-Face. The book includes some violence

Batman: Dark Victory. written by Jeph Loeb; art by Tim Sale. DC Comics 2014 400 p. Color; Illustration

Grades: 9 10 11 12 Adult   741.5; Fic

1. Serial killers — Graphic novels; 2. Crime — Graphic novels; 3. Batman (Fictional character)

1401244017; 9781401244019, $24.99

LC 2013041357

This collection "continues the story of 'The Long Halloween.' It is early in Batman's crimefighting career, when James Gordon, Harvey Dent, and the vigilante himself were all just beginning their roles as Gotham's protectors. Once a town controlled by organized crime, Gotham City suddenly finds itself being run by lawless freaks, such as Poison Ivy, Mr. Freeze, and the Joker. Witnessing his city's dark evolution, the Dark Knight completes his transformation into the city's greatest defender." (Publisher's note)

Collected edition originally published 2001

Batman: Hush. Jeph Loeb, writer; Jim Lee, penciller; Scott Williams, inker; Richard Starkings, letterer; Alex Sinclair, colorist; Jim Lee & Scott Williams, original series covers; Batman created by Bob Kane. DC Comics 2009 320 p. Illustration; Color

Grades: 9 10 11 12 Adult   741.5/973

1. Batman (Fictitious character) — Comic books, strips, etc; 2. Batman (Fictional character)

1401223176; 9781401223175, $24.99

LC 2009502034

This comic book, by Jeph Loeb, "is a thrilling mystery of action, intrigue, and deception,...in which Batman sets out to discover the identity of a mysterious mastermind using the Joker, Riddler, Ra's al Ghul and the Dark Knight's other enemies — and allies — as pawns in a plan to wreak havoc." (Publisher's note)

Originally published in single magazine form in Batman 608-619, Wizard 0 — T.p. verso.

Catwoman: When in Rome. Jeph Loeb, writer; Tim Sale, artist; Dave Stewart, colorist; Richard Starkings, lettering. DC Comics 2005 un Illustration

Grades: 10 11 12 Adult   741.5; Fic

1. Catwoman (Fictional character); 2. Graphic novels; 3. Mystery graphic novels; 4. Superhero graphic novels; 5. Joker (Fictional character)

1-4012-0432-5, $19.99; 1-4012-0717-0 (pa), $12.99

Catwoman travels to Rome with some unfinished business with the Falcone crime family. Accompanied by the Riddler, she dreams almost nightly about Batman, which annoys her to no end; she has gone to see Don Verinni, but even as she's talking to him, he dies from the Joker's poison. With help from local Sicilian hitman Christopher Castillo and Riddler get away, but when more mobsters come after her with Mr. Freeze's ice gun, Catwoman knows something is definitely wrong in Rome.

With frequent flashes of partial nudity and considerable violence, this title is more appropriate for older teens and adults.

Originally published as Catwoman: When in Rome issues #1-6 and Batman: Dark Victory issue #13.

Shazam!: the greatest stories ever told. DC Comics 2008 224p. Illustration

Grades: 4 5 6 7 8 9 10 11 12 Adult   741.5; Fic

1. Adventure graphic novels; 2. Captain Marvel (Fictional character); 3. Graphic novels; 4. Superhero graphic novels

978-1-4012-1674-0, $24.99

This book collects comics stories about Captain Marvel dating from 1940 to 1998. Captain Marvel predated Superman as a comic book superhero; young newsboy Billy Batson could transform into the flying superhero by shouting the magic word "Shazam!" This gave him the wisdom of Solomon, the strength of Hercules, the stamina of Atlas, the power of Zeus, the courage of Achilles, and the speed of Mercury. In these fourteen stories, he battles against such foes as Dr. Sivana, Mr. Mind, and the Monster Society of Evil.

Showcase Presents: Batgirl Volume 1. DC Comics 2007 552p. Illustration

Grades: 6 7 8 9 10 11 12 Adult   741.5; Fic

1. Batgirl (Fictional character); 2. Graphic novels; 3. Superhero graphic novels

978-1-4012-1367-1, $16.99

In the late 1960s, DC Comics added a new character to the world of Batman and Robin: Batgirl. Daughter of Commissioner Jim Gordon, Barbara Gordon is a librarian who relocates to Gotham City and soon dons her costume as the crime fighting Batgirl. This volume of black and white reprints includes her early adventures, from 1967 through 1975. The cover art notwithstanding, Batgirl is a woman of action.

Showcase Presents: Batman Vol. 1. DC Comics 2006 552p. Illustration

Grades: 6 7 8 9 10 11 12 Adult   741.5; Fic

1. Batman (Fictional character); 2. Graphic novels; 3. Superhero graphic novels

1-4012-1086-4, $16.99

The spotlight's on Batman in this volume featuring Detective Comics #327-342 and Batman #164-174. The Dynamic Duo take on some of their most enduring Rogues Gallery members, including Penguin, the Riddler, and the Outsider in these classic Silver Age stories from the era of famed editor Julius Schwartz. This Showcase edition reprints the comics in black and white."

Superman/Batman: Supergirl. Jeph Loeb, writer; Michael Turner, artist; Peter Steigerwald, colorist; Richard Starkings, letterer. DC Comics 2005 un Illustration

Grades: 10 11 12 Adult   **741.5; Fic**
1. Batman (Fictional character); 2. Graphic novels; 3. Superhero graphic novels; 4. Superman (Fictional character); 5. Wonder Woman (Fictional character)
1-4012-0250-0, $12.99

Batman has discovered something strange on the bottom of Gotham Bay which leads him to a mysterious and powerful teenaged girl who's bent on destroying Gotham City. What's her connection to Superman? Why does Wonder Woman want to hide her from the outside world? Will Darkseid succeed in recruiting her into doing his bidding? Who is she?

Superman/Doomsday: The Collected Edition. DC Comics 2006 412p. Illustration

Grades: 10 11 12 Adult   **741.5; Fic**
1. Graphic novels; 2. Superhero graphic novels; 3. Superman (Fictional character)
978-1-4012-1107-3, $19.99

Doomsday killed Superman. Now the Man of Steel wants payback. Superman travesl to the nightmare world of Apokolips for a confrontation with Doomsday, the creature who cost the Man of Steel his life. With the help of the mysterious, time-traveling Waverider, superman at last discovers the shocking truth of his greatest enemy's origin. And just when he thinks the terror is finally over, the murderous juggernaut returns to Earth more powerful than ever.

Superman: Our Worlds at War. DC Comics 2006 512p. Illustration

Grades: 9 10 11 12 Adult   **741.5; Fic**
1. Graphic novels; 2. Superhero graphic novels; 3. Superman (Fictional character); 4. Wonder Woman (Fictional character); 5. Green Lantern (Fictional character)
978-1-4012-1129-5, $24.99

Imperiex has been unleashed. As planets are destroyed in its mighty wake and with Earth in its path as it seeks to remake the universe in its twisted image, Superman is forced to form alliances with President Lex Luthor and Darkseid, even as he also joins with such heroes as Wonder Woman, Green Lantern, and many others. For once, this looks like a job that not even Superman can handle.

Superman: The Amazing Transformations of Jimmy Olsen. DC Comics 2007 192p. Illustration

Grades: 6 7 8 9 10 11 12 Adult   **741.5; Fic**
1. Graphic novels; 2. Humorous graphic novels; 3. Superhero graphic novels; 4. Superman (Fictional character)
978-1-4012-1369-5, $14.99

Cub reporter Jimmy Olsen stars in this light-hearted volume collecting some of his most memorable adventures from the late 1950s and 1960s, all of which guest-star Superman. While investigating crime for The Daily Planet, Jimmy undergoes one startling transformation after another, gaining temporary super-powers as Elastic Lad and becoming a Giant Turtle Man, The Wolf-Man of Metropolis, The Human Porcupine and much more. At times like these, Superman finds that he must not only protect Metropolis from Jimmy, but Jimmy from himself.

Lolos, Vasilis
The **last** call volume 1. Oni Press 2007 un Illustration

Grades: 10 11 12 Adult
741.5; Fic
1. Graphic novels; 2. Mystery graphic novels; 3. Supernatural graphic novels
978-1-932664-69-0, $11.95

Courtesy of Oni Press

Teenagers Sam and Alec have gone joyriding in Alec's mother's car, jamming to heavy metal rock, when the car dies, and something hits them. They awaken to find themselves on a strange train with very odd people. The conductor throws Alec off the train, and Sam meets some of the other passengers on the train. When he goes back to the compartment where he and Alec woke up on the train, he witnesses the murder of the ticketed passenger who had the compartment. Now Sam works with Mr. S, the shadow person who existed in dead Benny's body, to try to find out who murdered him. The book includes some harsh language, including occasional use of the f-bomb, and some violence.

Lott, Renee
Festering romance. Oni Press 2009 184p.

Grades: 9 10 11 12 Adult
741.5; Fic
1. Ghosts — Graphic novels; 2. Graphic novels; 3. Romance graphic novels
978-1-934964-18-7, $11.95

Courtesy of Oni Press

College student Janet prefers to spend her time in her apartment, playing video games with her roommate and best friend Paul who happens to be a ghost. However, her friends keep setting her up on blind dates, and then one of them, Derek, turns out to be a nice guy. Subsequent dates don't go so well, though, because Derek also has a ghostly roommate Carol, who in life was his girlfriend. Janet and Derek blame each other for not telling the truth about their ghostly companions, but they each need to face the truth of why Paul and Carol are still with them. The book includes only some mildly bad language (crap, pissed off).

Loux, Matthew
Sidescrollers. Oni Press 2006 un Illustration

Grades: 10 11 12 Adult
741.5; Fic
1. Friendship — Graphic novels; 2. Graphic novels; 3. Humorous graphic novels
1-932664-50-5, $11.95

Courtesy of Oni Press

Brian, Brad, and Matt are the kind of young man who works just enough to get by and be able to play video games, eat junk food, and hang around. Things change when their neighbor Amber, who works with them at the local McGreggor's, is going to the big local rock show where Brian's brother's band will be playing. Unfortunately for the guys, she's going with Dick (he'd rather be called Richard), the bully football player. Since Matt is sweet on Amber, the guys decide they have to save her from Dick, and their quest gets them out of the house, on the road, and in a whole lot of trouble. The book includes strong language, including the s-bomb and f-bomb, some sexual innuendo, and some fistfight violence.

Love, Jeremy

★ **Bayou**, volume one. created by Jeremy Love; colors by Patrick Morgan. Zuda Comics/DC Comics 2009 un Illustration
Grades: 9 10 11 12 Adult   **741.5; Fic**
1. African Americans — Graphic novels; 2. Fantasy graphic novels; 3. Graphic novels; 4. Monsters — Graphic novels
978-1-4012-2382-3, $14.99
2009 Glyph Comics Awards: Story of the Year, Best Writer, Best Artist, Best Female Character (Lee), Best Comic Strip

In a little southern town called Charon in 1933, Lee Wagstaff lives the kind of precarious life that African Americans under Jim Crow laws had to live. She's friends with white Lily Westmoreland, but that friendship doesn't protect her when Lily's mother accuses Lee of theft. Then Lily disappears, victim of a swamp monster, and the town's white men haul her father off to jail, most likely to face a lynching. Lee has to find Lily to save her father, but when she goes to the swamp where Lily disappeared, she falls into a strange land of monsters. There she meets Bayou, a blues-singing swamp monster who helps her, and Lee faces the evil in the strange land to find and save her friend. This book collects the first four chapters of the webcomic by Love, which was one of the first webcomics from Zuda, run by DC Comics. The book includes disturbing images of hanged people, and a white man hits Lee so hard she flies through the air and lands on her back with her face torn up. The "n" word is represented by "n*****" while other harsh language is plainly written. The book contains enough violence to bother squeamish and sensitive readers.

"Extremely beautiful, scary and wonderful, this...comic takes readers to a pair of almost familiar, frequently threatening worlds." Publ Wkly
Volume 1 of 2

Lovecraft, H. P. (Howard Phillips)

The **Lovecraft** Anthology 2: A Graphic Collection of H.P. Lovecrafts Short Stories. H. P. Lovecraft; edited by Dan Lockwood; illustrated by Alice Duke.. Harry N Abrams Inc 2012 128 p.
Grades: 11 12 Adult   **741.5/942; 741.5; S C**
1. Short stories; 2. Horror fiction
1906838437; 9781906838430, $19.95

This book presents "a graphic anthology of tales" by horror fiction author H. P. Lovecraft. "From the insidious mutations of 'The Shadow over Innsmouth' to the mindbending threat of 'The Call of Cthulhu,' this collection explores themes of insanity, inherited guilt, and arcane ritual." (Publisher's note)

Lowe, John

Working Methods: Comic Creators Detail Their Storytelling and Artistic Processes. Twomorrows Publishing 2007 176p. Illustration
Grades: Adult Professional
741.5
1. Comic books, strips, etc. — Technique; 2. Graphic novels
978-1-893905-73-3, $21.95
Professional comic artists interpret scripts every day as they successfully transform the written word into the visual form. This book puts the minds of comic artists under the microscope, highlighting the

Courtesy of Twomorrows Publishing

intricacies of the creative process step by step. For this book, three short scripts are each interpreted in different ways by professional comic artists to illustrate the varied ways in which they "see" and "solve" the problem of making a script succeed in comic form. The book documents the creative and technical choices Mark Schultz, Tim Levins, Jim Mahfood, Scott Hampton, Kelsey Shannon, Chris Brunner, Sean Murphy and Pat Quinn make as they tell a story,. Hundreds of illustrated examples document the artists' processes, and interviews clarify their individual approaches regarding storytelling and layout choices.

Lust, Ulli

★ **Today** Is the Last Day of the Rest of Your Life. by Ulli Lust and translated by Kim Thompson. W W Norton & Co Inc 2012 460 p.
Grades: Adult   **741.5; 741.5/943; 92**
1. Teenage girls — Travel; 2. Summer; 3. Italy — Description and travel
160699557X; 9781606995570, $35
Ignatz Nominee: Outstanding Artist (2013); Ignatz Award: Outstanding Graphic Novel (2013)

This graphic memoir by Ulli Lust, winner of the 2011 Angouleme "Revelation" prize, " recalls when "in 1984, a rebellious,17-year-old, punked-out Ulli Lust set out for a wild hitchhiking trip across Italy, from Naples through Verona and Rome and ending up in Sicily. Lust meticulously shows the who, where, when, and how (specifically, how an often penniless young girl can survive for months on the road) of a sometimes dangerous and sometimes exhilarating journey." (Publisher's note)

★ **Voices** in the dark. by Ulli Lust; translated by John Brownjohn; translation adapted by Nika Knight; English lettering by Kevin Cannon. New York Review Comics 2017 364 p. Color; Illustration
Grades: Adult   **741.5; Fic**
1. Comic books, strips, etc. — Germany — Translations into English; 2. National Socialism — Comic books, strips, etc; 3. World War, 1939-1945 — Comic books, strips, etc; 4. Lust, Ulli, 1967- — Comic books, strips, etc; 5. National socialism — Fiction; 6. World War, 1939-1945 — Graphic novels
1681371057; 9781681371054, $29.95

LC 2017008611
This graphic novel, by Ulli Lust, takes place in "Germany, in the final years of the Third Reich. Hermann Karnau is a sound engineer obsessed with recording the human voice in all its variations — the rantings of leaders, the roar of crowds, the rasp of throats constricted in fear — and indifferent to everything else. Employed by the Nazis, his assignments take him to Party rallies, to the Eastern Front, and into the household of Joseph Goebbels. There he meets Helga, the eldest daughter." (Publisher's note)

"Lust's loose, deceptively simple art, tinted in washes of faded color, creates a mood of deepening claustrophobia as the complicit Karnau and the innocent Helga descend toward the same fate. It's a rare adaptation that, rather than simply transcribing the source material, transcends it." Pub Wkly
Based on a novel by Marcel Beyer; Translated from the German

Lutes, Jason

★ **Berlin**, city of stones: a work of fiction. by Jason Lutes. Drawn & Quarterly 2000 209 p.
Grades: Adult   **741.5**
1. College students — Fiction; 2. Journalists — Fiction; 3. Berlin (Germany) — Fiction
1896597297; 9781896597294, $22.95

LC bl2007002819
This book "presents the first part of Jason Lutes'...trilogy, set in the twilight years of Germany's Weimar Republic. Kurt Severing, a journalist, and Marthe Muller, an art student, are the central figures in a broad cast of

characters intertwined with the historical events unfolding around them. City of Stones covers eight months in Berlin, from September 1928 to May Day, 1929,...documenting the hopes and struggles of its inhabitants." (Publisher's note)

Jar of Fools. Drawn & Quarterly 2003 152p. Illustration
Grades: 10 11 12 Adult   **741.5; Fic**
1. Graphic novels
1-896597-72-6, $16.95

Haunted by the death of his escape-artist brother and a failed romance, the remaining hope of washed-up stage magician Ernie Weiss lies in his aging mentor, Al Flosso. But Al is slipping further into senility with each passing day. Meanwhile, Esther O'Dea, Ernie's ex-love, struggles to find peace in her own life, and a con man named Nathan Lender sets some mysterious plans for Ernie's future in motion in his efforts to make things right for his twelve-year-old daughter Claire.

MacDonald, Heidi
The **Nightmare** factory: based on the stories of Thomas Ligotti. HarperCollins/Fox Atomic Comics 2007 Illustration
Grades: 10 11 12 Adult   **741.5**
1. Graphic novels; 2. Horror graphic novels
978-0-06-124353-0, $17.99

In the universe of horror master Thomas Ligotti, clowns take part in a sinister winter festival, a scheming girlfriend makes reality itself come unraveled, a crumbling asylum's destruction unleashes a greater horror, and a mysterious Teatro comes and goes, leaving only shattered dreams in its wake. Ligotti's tales of terror take the reader to places few would suspect exist, where madness is only a thought away. This book adapts four of Ligotti's chilling tales by writers and artists Stuart Moore, Joe Harris, Colleen Doran (The Sandman), Ben Templesmith (30 Days of Night), Ted McKeever (Batman), and Michael Gaydos (Alias). Ligotti provides introductions to each story. Violence, some harsh language, and some nudity appear in some of the stories.

Mack, Stan
★ **Taxes,** the tea party, and those revolting rebels: a comics history of the American revolution. Stan Mack. NBM Pub. 2012 166 p.
Grades: 9 10 11 12 Adult
741.5
1. United States — History — 1775-1783, Revolution — Comic books, strips, etc.; 2. United States — Politics and government — 1775-1783, Revolution — Comic books, strips, etc.; 3. United States — History — 1600-1775, Colonial period — Comic books, strips, etc.; 4. Wit and humor
1561636975; 9781561636976, $14.99
LC 2012938930

Courtesy of NBM Publishing

This historical comic book, by Stan Mack, is a humorous narrative overview of the U.S. Revolutionary War. "This graphic account of the birth of the United States stars a chubby, insecure King George III, rebellious and misunderstood colonists, and loudmouthed and insensitive aristocrats, providing information about the Boston Tea Party and the revolt against the status quo." (Publisher's note)

Macklin, Ken
The **weasel** patrol. About Comics/About Infinity 2009 104p. Illustration
Grades: 7 8 9 10 11 12 Adult   **741.5; Fic**

1. Graphic novels; 2. Humorous graphic novels; 3. Science fiction graphic novels; 4. Weasels — Graphic novels
978-0-9790750-8-7, $9.99

Courtesy of About Comics

When criminals strike, the intergalactic troopers called the Weasel Patrol will ferret out the bad guys every time. Despite their utter lack of planning, attentiveness, cohesion, or competence, they always succeed, even if their favorite tactic when faced with danger is to run away. This book includes twelve comedic adventures, in which the weasels face mythical monsters (Big Foot), aliens, kidnapped cattle in disguise, and the ever-ready bad guy Reefer Rick. Willy, Leroy, Biff, Roscoe, and Bob are the genetically uplifted Weasel Patrol. The book includes mild, cartoony violence and no bad language and no nudity. Villainous Reefer Rick smokes. Artist Dowling includes fun little details, such as the Acme name on some of the gadgets.

Maclean, Andrew (Andrew Ross)
Apocalyptigirl: an aria for the end times. by Andrew MacLean. Random House Inc 2015 88 p. Color; Illustration
Grades: Adult   **741.5**
1. Apocalyptic fiction; 2. Science fiction
1616555661; 9781616555665, $9.99

This graphic novel, by Andrew MacLean, "is an action-packed sci-fi epic! Alone at the end of the world, Aria is woman with a mission! Traipsing through an overgrown city with her only companion, a cat named Jelly Beans, Aria's search for an ancient relic with immeasurable power has been fruitless so far. But when a run in with a creepy savage sets her on a path to complete her quest, she'll face death head on in the hopes of claiming her prize." (Publisher's note)

Mahler, Nicolas
Lone Racer. Top Shelf Productions 2007 92p. Illustration
Grades: 11 12 Adult   **741.5; Fic**
1. Graphic novels; 2. Humorous graphic novels; 3. Racing — Graphic novels
978-1-891830-69-3, $12.95

Years before, Lone Racer was a champion; now, he keeps plugging away despite taunts from the younger racers. He does it for his hospitalized wife. When he's not at the track or the hospital, he's at Bar Juanjo with old racing pal Rubber. When mechanic-turned-cop Irksome talks Lone Racer into a bank robbery and then chickens out, things get dire, and Racer decides he has to win a race to regain his self-respect. His "middling love-affair," which he breaks off because he can't stop thinking about his wife, adds more adult content to the book, along with the bar scenes. Mahler's art style is different — bodies curve oddly and heads are nothing but hats and noses; he also uses black, white and dull brick red for color.

"...this corny-old-movie scenario is, thanks largely to its looks, delightfully ludicrous." (Booklist)

Mairowitz, David Zane
Kafka. [by] David Zane Mairowitz and Robert Crumb; edited by Richard Appignanesi. Fantagraphics Books 2007 176p. Illustration
Grades: 10 11 12 Adult   **92; 741.5**
1. Authors; 2. Biographical graphic novels; 3. Graphic novels; 4. Novelists; 5. Poets; 6. Short story writers; 7. Kafka, Franz, 1883-1924
978-1-56097-806-0, $14.95

This book combines a biography of Kafka with illustrated plot descriptions of many of his works, including The Metamorphosis. Crumb renders the stories in comic book form, while the biographical information is presented mostly in text.

Authors names reversed on cover

Maki, Yoko
Aishiteruze Baby Vol. 1. Viz Media/Shojo Beat 2006 un Illustration
Grades: 8 9 10 11 12 Adult   741.5; Fic
1. Graphic novels; 2. Manga; 3. Shojo manga
978-1-4215-0711-8, $19.95

Kippei Katakura is a 17-year-old playboy who spends his time chasing girls, careless of their feelings. But when his 5-year-old cousin Yuzuyu comes to live with his family after her mother's sudden disappearance, Kippei is put in charge of taking care of her. As Kippei gets to know Yuzuyu and starts to understand how she feels, he also begins to realize that all girls were like Yuzuyu once... Kippei has a lot to figure out, like what to make for Yuzuyu's lunch and how to drop her off at kindergarten while still getting to high school on time. Kippei is enjoying his time with Yuzuyu, but not everyone is happy about it. The girls at school miss their quality time with Kippei, and one decides to play dirty to get him back.

Mapa, Lorina
★ **Duran** Duran, Imelda Marcos, and me: a graphic memoir. by Lorina Mapa.. Conundrum Press 2017 131 p. Illustration
Grades: 11 12 Adult   741.597
1. Cartoonists — Canada — Biography; 2. Mapa, Lorina — Childhood and youth — Comic books, strips, etc.; 3. Philippines; 4. Women cartoonists; 5. Women illustrators; 6. Autobiographies
1772620114; 9781772620115, $18

This book, by Lorina Mapa, is "a graphic memoir about growing up in the Philippines in the 1980s with Duran Duran, Imelda Marcos, and the EDSA Revolution. Mapa returns to Manilla as an adult for the funeral of her father and come to terms with her past. A graphic love letter to her parents, family, friends, country of birth, and perhaps even to herself." (Publisher's note)

"[Mapa's] memoir of life in the Philippines is both touching and joyous, with vivid recollections of food, matriarchy, family, and politics told in an Hergé-inspired style that's deceptively simple but apt for its subject." — Publishers Weekly

Includes discography.

Marchetto, Marisa Acocella
Cancer Vixen: A True Story. by Marisa Acocella Marchetto. Pantheon Books 2009 211 p. Color; Illustration
Grades: 11 12 Adult   741.5; 92
1. Autobiographical graphic novels; 2. Breast — Cancer; 3. Graphic novels; 4. Marchetto, Marisa Acocella
037571474X; 9780375714740, $16.95

LC 200640967
In this graphic memoir, "Marisa Acocella Marchetto tells the story of her eleven-month, ultimately triumphant bout with breast cancer — from diagnosis to cure." (Publisher's note)

The author "tells the story of her eleven-month, ultimately triumphant bout with breast cancer — from diagnosis to cure, and every challenging step in between." Publisher's note

"The fashion details are great fun, drawn in a spare loose style, but it's the heart of her story, the support and love she gets from her family and friends, that make Cancer Vixen a universal story that's hard to put down." Publ Wkly

Marcus, Ken
Super human resources season one. Ape Entertainment 2009 un Illustration

Grades: 9 10 11 12 Adult   741.5; Fic
1. Graphic novels; 2. Humorous graphic novels; 3. Superhero graphic novels
978-1-934944-68-4, $12.95

Super Crises International hires out super heroes people with capes, claws, radioactive half-lives,...And, like any business, it has a human resources office that keeps up with expense reports, payroll, cleaning up the conference rooms after crossovers gone wrong...Tim from Temps-RUs comes to SCI to work in accounts receivable, and he soon learns that running a super hero business is definitely not fun. Something is not right with the bills, and Gordon from the corporate office threatens to shut down the office. On top of that, the office copier has attained sentience and decides to destroy all organic life, and his boss in Accounts plans to destroy SCI. Just another day at the office...The book includes some superhero fighting violence with no bloodshed.

Maroh, Julie
★ **Blue** Is the Warmest Color. by Julie Maroh. Arsenal Pulp Press 2013 160 p.
Grades: Adult
741.5; Fic
1. Dating (Social customs) — Comic books, strips, etc; 2. Lesbians — Identity; 3. Romance fiction; 4. Lesbians — Fiction
1551525143; 9781551525143, $19.95
LC 2013432454

In this graphic novel by Julie Maroh, "a young woman named Clementine discovers herself and the elusive magic of love when she meets a confident blue-haired girl named Emma: a lesbian love story...that bristles with the energy of youth and rebellion and the eternal light of desire." (Publisher's note)

Courtesy of Arsenal Pulp Press

"Though a bit of a period piece, a lovely and wholehearted coming-out story." Kirkus

Marshall, Gary
Studio space: the world's greatest comic illustrators at work. interviews & edited by Joel Meadows & Gary Marshall. Image Comics 2008 318p. Illustration
Grades: 10 11 12 Adult   741.5
1. Cartoonists; 2. Comic books, strips, etc.; 3. Graphic novels
978-1-58240-909-2, $49.99; 978-1-58240-908-5 (pa), $29.99

Twenty modern comics artists talk about their careers, their work, and their working methods. Each of them is photographed in his studio, and samples of their artwork are included. The artists are: Brian Bolland, Tim Bradstreet, Howard Chaykin, Steve Dillon, Tommy Lee Edwards, Duncan Fegredo, Dave Gibbons, Adam Hughes, Joe Kubert, Jim Lee, Mike Mignola, Frank Miller, Sean Phillips, George Pratt, Alex Ross, Tim Sale, Walt Simonson, Bryan Talbot, Dave Taylor, and Sergio Toppi.

Martinson, Lars
Tonoharu: part one. Pliant Press/Top Shelp Productions 2008 128p. Illustration
Grades: 11 12 Adult
741.5; Fic
1. Graphic novels; 2. Teachers — Graphic novels; 3. Japan — Graphic novels
9780980102369, $14.95;
9780980102321, $19.95; 0980102367;
0980102324

Courtesy of IDW Publishing

LC 2007-940522

Daniel Wells looks back at his first year working as an assistant junior high school teacher in rural Japan as he must make a decision whether to renew his contract or leave Japan. In Tonoharu, he leads an isolated, almost monastic life, hampered by his lack of Japanese language skills and ignorance of Japanese culture. He wonders why his predecessor lasted only one year, and whether he will last beyond that as well. Meanwhile, he tries to work with the teachers at school and tries to pursue a relationship with another American teacher who lives a few towns away by train. This volume includes some harsh language, including the s-bomb, and some partial nudity.

Volume 1 of 3

Marz, Ron

Samurai: Heaven and Earth. Dark Horse Comics 2006 un Illustration
Grades: 11 12 Adult   **741.5; Fic**
1. Adventure graphic novels; 2. Graphic novels; 3. Samurai — Graphic novels
1-59307-388-7, $14.95

How far will a man travel for love? What battles will he fight? Will he cross heaven and earth to be by the side of the woman he loves? Beginning in feudal Japan of 1704, Samurai: Heaven & Earth follows Shiro, a lone samurai warrior sworn to be reunited with the love of his life who has been spirited away by his enemies. His pursuit of Yoshiko will carry him farther than he could have imagined — from his native Japan to the sprawling empire of China, across Europe, and finally to Paris itself. There, in the fabled halls of King Louis XIV's Versailles, he must cross blades with the greatest swordsmen ever known if he is to reclaim his love. Readers will find nudity, sexual situations, and violence (including beheadings).

Masamune, Shirow

Black magic. Shirow Masamune. Dark Horse Manga 2008 200p. Illustration
Grades: 10 11 12 Adult   **741.5; Fic**
1. Graphic novels; 2. Manga; 3. Science fiction graphic novels; 4. Seinen manga
978-1-59307-696-2, $14.95

Millions of years ago, the planet Venus teemed with life and an advanced civilization. In this past, the Nemesis supercomputer controls government functions, with bioroid "executors" created to carry out the system's utopian edicts. But trouble brews, even in good times, as different executors vie for control of Nemesis; these struggles force the governing system to secretly create Duna Typhon, a super-bioroid "sleeper." Raised among humans, she possesses awesome magical powers to be used to protect Nemesis. That time has now come. This was Masamune's first published manga series. The book includes some violence and harsh language.

Mashiba, Shin

Yumekui Kenbun: Nightmare Inspector volume 1. story and art by Shin Mashiba; translation, Gemma Collinge; adaptation, Kelly Sue DeConnick. Viz Media 2008 184p. Illustration
Grades: 9 10 11 12 Adult   **741.5; Fic**
1. Dreams — Graphic novels; 2. Fantasy graphic novels; 3. Graphic novels; 4. Manga; 5. Shonen manga
978-1-4215-1758-2, $9.99

In Japan, during the Taisho Era (1920s), there is a special place where people who suffer nightmares can go for help. At the Silver Star Tea House, Hiruko is a special kind of private investigator who can rid people of their darkest visions, for the price of eating their nightmares. In this first volume, Hiruko helps a young gatekeeper who suffers nightmares about his beautiful master, but when Hiruko enters the nightmare, he learns the gatekeeper's secret and true nature. He also helps a young woman who suffers nightmares of losing pieces of herself (her eyes, her hand, etc.), a young fan who dreams that his favorite movie star commits suicide, an unforgiving son whose father haunts his dreams, a young man who can never see the face of the ideal woman in his dreams. Some stories end in O. Henry-type twists; some stories include some violence.

Massey, Jim

Maintenance volume 1: it's a dirty job . . . . written by Jim Massey; illustrated by Robbi Rodriguez. Oni Press 2007 88p. Illustration
Grades: 10 11 12 Adult
741.5; Fic
1. Graphic novels; 2. Humorous graphic novels; 3. Science fiction graphic novels
978-1-932664-62-1, $9.95

Courtesy of Oni Press

Doug and Manny work as custodians at TerroMax Inc., the world's biggest and best evil science think tank. The messes they have to clean up include toxic spill monsters and a talking manshark who wants to go out on the town. They also have to worry about the mad scientists, would-be dictators, and the cute young woman who works at reception. The book includes some harsh language, including the s-bomb, and some violence.

Matsumoto, Taiyo

Sunny; Volume 1. Taiyo Matsumoto; translation by Michael Arias; lettering by Deron Bennett; book design by Fawn Lau. Viz 2013 224 p.
Grades: 9 10 11 12 Adult   **741.5; Fic**
1. Orphans — Graphic novels; 2. Automobiles — Fiction
1421555255; 9781421555256, $22.99
Eisner Nominee: Best U.S. Edition of International Material — Asia (2016) [for volume 5]; Cartoonist Studio Prize (2014)

In this graphic novel by Taiyo Matsumoto, a "Nissan Sunny 1200 may look like a broken-down old car in front of a Japanese home for orphans. To the children and teens of the orphanage, though, the Sunny is a clubhouse, a spaceship, a getaway vehicle, and one of the few places that is truly theirs after they are abandoned by their parents. Readers catch glimpses of each of the orphans' lives, both the imaginary adventures they devise while in the Sunny and the sometimes heartbreaking ones outside of it." (Publisher's note)

Volume 1 of 6

Matsushita, Yoko

Descendants of Darkness Vol. 1. Viz Media/Shojo 2004 200p. Illustration
Grades: 10 11 12 Adult   **741.5; Fic**
1. Fantasy graphic novels; 2. Graphic novels; 3. Humorous graphic novels; 4. Manga; 5. Shojo manga
1-59116-507-5, $9.99

As a Shinigami, a Guardian of Death, Asato Tsuzuki has a lot to think about. First of all, there are all those dead people. Someone's got to escort them safely to the afterlife. Then there's all that bureaucracy. The affairs of death come with a lot of paperwork, budgetary concerns and endless arcana. Combining supernatural action with heavy dollops of romance, sex and humor, this book proves one thing: Death is big business...and business is good. The book includes graphic violence, some strong language, and some sexual situations.

Matthews, Brett

The **Lone** Ranger. Dynamite Entertainment 2007 160p. Illustration

Grades: 8 9 10 11 12 Adult   **741.5; Fic**

1. Adventure graphic novels; 2. Graphic novels; 3. Lone Ranger (Fictional character); 4. Western stories — Graphic novels

978-1-933305-39-4, $24.99; 978-1-933305-40-0 (pa), $19.99

"A fiery horse with the speed of light, a cloud of dust, and a hearty 'Hi Yo Silver!' — The Lone Ranger..." A popular radio show starting in the 1930s that became a popular television show that ran from 1949 through 1957, a few film serials (extremely hard to find), some paperback novels, and a movie in 1981, The Lone Ranger became an iconic figure. In March 2008, Disney Studios announced it's planning to make a new Lone Ranger movie. In the meantime, Dynamite Entertainment started publishing Lone Ranger comics in 2006. This Lone Ranger is different from the old radio and television shows, and so is Tonto. These aren't the squeaky clean heroes one might expect, although they are heroic. This volume shows the origin of the Lone Ranger, from a young Texas Ranger who has just joined his father and brother. They are ambushed and all killed, except for John. Tonto, a Native American of unknown tribal nation, takes care of John; he has killed all of the killers. When John recovers from his wounds, they set off to find out who ordered the killing, while the reader knows that another killer is murdering all the dead Rangers' families. This book includes some graphic violence.

Texas Ranger John Reid seeks revenge for the murders of his family and friends, only to find justice...and that he's something greater than he ever thought he could be. Together with Tonto, he rides against rich criminals like Cavendish and the politicians Cavendish backs. This new version of the Lone Ranger includes more violence than some might remember from the old television show and books.

Matz

Cyclops. Volume one. [by] Jacomon & Matz; written by Matz; illustrated by Luc Jacamon; translated by Matz and Edward Gauvin. Archaia Entertainment 2011 116p. Illustration

Grades: Adult   **741.5; Fic**

1. Mass media — Graphic novels; 2. Science fiction graphic novels; 3. Soldiers — Graphic novels; 4. War — Graphic novels

978-1-936393-11-4, $19.95

"In the year 2054, the United Nations has outsourced its peacekeeping missions to Multicorp Security. Multicorp pads its bottom line by broadcasting battles live (the camera eye in their helmets leads the troops to be nicknamed Cyclops) and by building story lines around heroes such as Doug Pistoia, a brainy ex-athlete who has a knack for soldiering. But as Pistoia's heroics on the Iran-Turkey border and in Argentina make him a huge star, he begins to question how much of his reality show is actually real. Collecting the first two parts of a four-part series, Cyclops, v.1, asks big questions and sets the stage for further conflict." Booklist

"Sharp art, relevant political commentary, and sexy, action-packed story make this...[a] winner." Publ Wkly

Translated from the French. ?MR, GV, N, SSC: this book contains adult content, graphic violence, nudity and strong sexual content; it is intended for mature readers? Jacket

Max

Bardin the Superrealist. Fantagraphics Books 2006 82p. Illustration

Grades: 10 11 12 Adult   **741.5; Fic**

1. Graphic novels; 2. Humorous graphic novels

978-1-56097-759-9, $19.95

Everyman Bardín finds himself suddenly transported (well, at least his upper half) to another dimension, where an "Andalusian Dog" (a reference to Buñuel's Un Chien Andalou) serves as his ill-tempered guide. In a series of vignettes, gags, illustrations, text pieces, and dream stories, ping-ponging back between the surrealist world and the "real" world,

Bardín examines, questions, and defends his own beliefs, convictions and philosophies while tangling with the Dog and the Holy Trinity in a variety of guises (including a familiar-looking mouse with red shorts and white gloves). In other stories, he imagines himself in a painting by Brueghel the Elder, tries to deal with his onanism in a productive way, is enlightened, dodges his real "creator" Max in the street, has several nightmares and hallucinations, and, in the book's climactic episode, "The Sound and the Fury," battles a bona fide dragon. There are some sexual situations and some other adult situations regarding the male's gender-defining organs.

Maxwell, Matt

Strangeways: murder moon. Highway 62 Press 2008 144p. Illustration

Grades: 10 11 12 Adult   **741.5; Fic**

1. Fantasy graphic novels; 2. Graphic novels; 3. Horror graphic novels; 4. Werewolves — Graphic novels; 5. Western stories — Graphic novels

978-0-9796957-0-4, $13.95

In the year 1868, ex-Army officer Seth Collins works as a stagecoach guard and tries to forget the horrors of the Civil War. However, he now faces a different kind of horror: something hunts the people of Silver Branch, including Collins' estranged sister; a strange, seemingly unkillable wolf prowls the wilderness, stalking and killing people from the town. The people have their own secrets, and soon Collins finds himself trapped between the obligations of family and friendship, between the secretive townspeople and the killing beast. The book includes violence and some strong language.

Mazur, Dan

Comics: the modern history of a global art form. Dan Mazur, Alexander Danner. Thames & Hudson Inc. 2013 319 p. Illustration; Color

Grades: Adult   **741.5**

1. Graphic novels — History and criticism

9780500290965, $39.95

LC 2012954355

"This is the history of comics around the world from the late 1960s to the dawn of the 21st century.Comics is a richly illustrated narrative of extraordinary scope. Examples from all over the world include everything from Crumb and Kirby to RAW; from Metal Hurlant to Marjane Satrapi to nouvelle manga; from both the American mainstream and underground to the evolving and influential British scene." (Publisher's note)

"The topical approach of individual chapters sometimes confuses the overall chronology, but this richly dense treatise will be best read cover-to-cover anyway, as the authors' contextualizing of works and trends builds firmly throughout the text." Choice

Mazzotta, Antony

Bombaby: The Screen Goddess. SLG Publishing/AmazeInk Comics 2004 un Illustration

Grades: 10 11 12 Adult   **741.5; Fic**

1. Fantasy graphic novels; 2. Graphic novels

1-59362-003-9, $13.95

Sangeeta Mukherjee is the daughter of well-to-do, traditional parents, dealing with a bratty little sister and an arranged marriage when an out-of-body experience reveals that she is not an ordinary young woman. Sangeeta is, in fact, the reincarnation of India's ancient protector, the Goddess of Mumbai. But how will Sangeeta use this new-found power? Can she make a difference in a male-dominated society? Sangeeta must defy traditional expectations to choose what kind of life she wants and discover her true self. There is some violence in the story.

Mazzucchelli, David

★ **Asterios** polyp. written and illustrated by David Mazzucchelli. Pantheon 2009 320 p. Illustration

Grades: Adult   **741.5; 741.5973**

1. Comic books, strips, etc.; 2. Graphic novels; 3. Middle aged men — Fiction

0307377326; 9780307377326, $35

LC 2008027859

Eisner Award: Best Graphic Album: New (2010); Eisner Award: Best Writer/Artist (2010)

The protagonist of this graphic novel is Asterios Polyp, a "middle-aged, meagerly successful architect and teacher, aesthete and womanizer, whose life is wholly upended when his New York City apartment goes up in flames." (Publisher's note)

McCay, Winsor

★ **Little** Nemo in Slumberland: So Many Splendid Sundays!. by Winsor McCay. Last Gasp of San Francisco 2006 156 p.

Grades: Adult   **741**

1. Comic books, strips, etc.

0983550409; 9780983550402, $125

This book, by Winsor McCay, is the winner of the "Will Eisner" award and two "Harvey Kurtzman" awards. It is a "reproduction of the...comic strip,...'Little Nemo in Slumberland.' This is the third printing of...a best-of collection from 1905-1910, with 8 pages more than the first two printings and enhanced restoration throughout. Every page is printed in the original size and colors." (Publisher's note)

Winsor McCay: Early Works Volume 1. Checker Book Publishing Group 2003 201p. Illustration

Grades: 10 11 12 Adult   **741.5; Fic**

1. Graphic novels; 2. Humorous graphic novels

0-9741664-0-5, $19.95

LC 2003-12920

This volume is a collection of turn-of-the-century rarities from cartooning and animation pioneer, Winsor McCay: Tales of the Jungle Imps," Little Sammy Sneeze," Dreams of a Rarebit Fiend," and Pilgrim's Progress." Best known for Little Nemo in Slumberland, and the seminal animated feature Gertie the Dinosaur, McCay puts his artistic talent and whimsical humor on full display here. Readers should note that when these stories were first published in the early 1900s (Tales of the Jungle Imps" was published in 1903), McCay's artistic vision of the jungle imps" wasn't considered racist.

McCloud, Scott

★ **Making** Comics: Storytelling Secrets of Comics, Manga and Graphic Novels. HarperCollins 2006 265p. Illustration

Grades: Adult Professional   **741.5**

1. Graphic novels

978-0-06-078094-4, $22.95

In Making Comics, McCloud focuses his analysis on the art form itself, exploring the creation of comics, from the broadest principles to the sharpest details (like how to accentuate a character's facial muscles in order to form the emotion of disgust rather than the emotion of surprise.) And he does all of it through his cartoon stand-in narrator, mixing dry humor and legitimate instruction. McCloud shows his reader how to master the human condition through word and image in a minimalistic way, using the form itself to show how to do it.

Reinventing comics: how imagination and technology are revolutionizing an art form. Paradox Press 2000 237p. Illustration

Grades: 11 12 Adult   **741; 741.5**

1. Cartoons and caricatures; 2. Comic books, strips, etc.

0-06-095350-0, $22.95

LC 00-710457

The author maps out "'12 revolutions', which, he believes, need to take place for comics to survive and finally be recognized as a legitimate art form. The topics progress from the oldest of comic-related arguments (seeking respect) to the use of computer technology to renew and expand its audience. These brilliantly presented discussions concern comics as literature, comics as art, creators' rights, industry innovation, and public perception, among other topics." Libr J

★ The **Sculptor**. by Scott McCloud. First Second 2015 496 p. Illustration

Grades: Adult   **741.5; Fic**

1. Death — Fiction; 2. Sculptors — Fiction; 3. Romance fiction; 4. Graphic novels

9781596435735, $29.99; 1596435739

LC 2014043831

In this graphic novel, by Scott McCloud, "David Smith is giving his life for his art — literally. Thanks to a deal with Death, the young sculptor gets his childhood wish: to sculpt anything he can imagine with his bare hands. But now that he only has 200 days to live, deciding what to create is harder than he thought, and discovering the love of his life at the 11th hour isn't making it any easier!" (Publisher's note)

McCloud "offers exquisite silent passages and modulated panel sizes that guide the reader's emotional journey through powerful shifts and deepen David's compelling character, all while employing a straightforward art style masquerading as simple cartooning shorthand. His brilliant pacing and unobtrusive manipulation of the space between panels creates intimate, intense moments." Booklist

★ **Understanding** comics: the invisible art. HarperPerennial 1994 215p. Illustration

Grades: 9 10 11 12 Adult   **741.5**

1. Comic books, strips, etc. — History and criticism; 2. Cartooning — Technique

0-06-097625-X, $22.95; 9780060976255

McCloud "conducts a genial, well-researched and funny tour of virtually every historical and perceptual aspect of comics, which he calls 'sequential art,' that is, art that consists of sequences of words and pictures. Beginning in the 11th century with the Bayeux tapestry, he examines pre-Columbian picture languages and the printing press, presenting a quick survey of the historical development of early sequential pictures into the specialized visual language of comics.... He dissects the vocabulary of the medium, cheerfully analyzing the psychological power of comics and their central role in our ultra-visual culture." (Publishers Weekly)

Includes bibliographical references; First published 1993 by Kitchen Sink Press

McCulloch, Derek

Gone to Amerikay. written by Derek McCulloch; art by Colleen Doran; colors by José Villarrubia; letters by Jared K. Fletcher. DC Comics 2012 144 p.

Grades: Adult   **741.5**

1. Immigrants — New York (State) — New York — Comic books, strips, etc; 2. Irish Americans — New York (State) — New York — Comic books, strips, etc; 3. Ireland — Emigration and immigration — Comic books, strips, etc; 4. New York (N.Y.) — Social conditions — Comic books, strips, etc; 5. United States — Emigration and immigration — Comic books, strips, etc; 6. Missing persons — Graphic novels; 7. Immigrants — Graphic novels; 8. Irish Americans — Graphic novels

1401223516; 9781401223519, $24.99

LC 2011278790

This graphic novel tells three intertwined stories. "Irish hopeful Ciara O'Dwyer relocates to New York — s notorious slums to await a husband who never arrives; decades later the mystery of what happened to Fintan O'Dwyer remains unsolved until a specter from the past points the way to a resolution. We also meet 1960"s Johnnie McCormack, a roughshod would-be actor who comes to terms with his sexual orientation; and 2010"s euro millionaire Lewis Healy." (Publishers Weekly)

★ **Stagger** Lee. Image Comics 2006 232p. Illustration
Grades: 10 11 12 Adult   **741.5; Fic**
  1. Folk songs — United States — Graphic novels; 2. Graphic novels
1-58240-607-3, $17.99
    What is known: On Christmas of 1895, in Bill Curtis' saloon in St. Louis, "Stag" Lee Shelton shot Billy Lyons. There have been many songs written about this incident, using some version or another of his name: Stacker Lee, Stack-A-Lee, Stack O'Lee, and more. This graphic novel, part historical fiction, part historical essay, examines the legend that grew in the many songs written and sung about the incident. The book contains some sexual situations and some strong language along with some violence.

McDuffie, Dwayne
  Static shock: rebirth of the cool. writers, Dwayne McDuffie, Robert L. Washington III; artist, John Paul Leon; pencilers, John Paul Leon, Denys Cowan. DC Comics 2009 192p. Illustration
Grades: 9 10 11 12 Adult   **741.5; Fic**
  1. African Americans — Graphic novels; 2. Graphic novels; 3. Science fiction graphic novels; 4. Superhero graphic novels
978-1-4012-2262-8, $19.99
    In 1993, Milestone Comics published superhero comics written for African American readers, featuring African American superheroes. One of those heroes was Static, an inner city teenager imbued with the power of lightning and electricity. DC Comics has brought back Static by reprinting the two Milestone Comics miniseries. High school teen Virgil Hawkins is just trying to survive high school, getting by without joining gangs, and trying to get a date with the girl he really likes. He's also Static, with electromagnetic powers he gained on a night the city calls "The Big Bang." The problem is, he's not the only one who gained super powers of one kind or another that night, and most of those who did are using their powers to help them commit more crimes. Static wants to be a hero, but he faces incredible odds, including his own family's situation. The book includes some harsh language, at least one usage of the one-fingered salute, and violence.

McElroy, Clint, (podcaster)
  The **adventure** zone: here there be gerblins. based on the podcast by Griffin McElroy, Clint McElroy, Travis McElroy, Justin McElory; adaptation by Clint McElroy, Carey Pietsch; art by Carey Pietsch. First Second 2018 256 p. Color; Illustration
Grades: 10 11 12 Adult
  1. Elves — Fiction; 2. Warriors — Fiction; 3. Magic — Comic books, strips, etc.; 4. Fantasy graphic novels
9781250153708, $19.99
                        LC 2017946143
    In this graphic novel, by Clint McElroy, Griffin McElroy, illustrated by Carey Pietsch, "join Taako the elf wizard, Merle the dwarf cleric, and Magnus the human warrior for an adventure they are poorly equipped to handle AT BEST, guided ('guided') by their snarky DM.... Like the smash-hit podcast it's based on, [this] will tickle your funny bone, tug your heartstrings, and probably pants you if you give it half a chance." (Publisher's note)
    "Readers familiar with tabletop gaming or the McElroys' podcast will appreciate the snarky dialogue, the rampant geekiness, and the critical fail rolls that result in comic injury and mayhem." SLJ

McFarlane, Todd
  Spawn Collection Volume 1. Image Comics 2005 un Illustration
Grades: 11 12 Adult   **741.5; Fic**
  1. Fantasy graphic novels; 2. Graphic novels; 3. Horror graphic novels; 4. Mystery graphic novels
1-58240-563-8, $19.95
    Al Simmons, formerly a soldier, was resurrected from the ashes of his own grave. Reborn as a creature from the depths of Hell, disfigured, homeless, and alone, this new warrior known as Spawn now wanders the shadowy alleys of New York City in search of his past life. Robbed of his memories and identity, this freshly created man whose body is nothing more than scars and torn flesh becomes a protector of the weak, the poor, the downtrodden, and other victims of circumstance. While Spawn tries to piece together his confusing existence, an unwelcome mentor reveals the purpose of his abrupt return to earth. But since this guide comes from the dark side, can he be trusted to tell the truth? And just what is the truth? In this twisted world of shadow players, nothing is as it appears. The book includes graphic violence and harsh language.

McGruder, Aaron
  Birth of a nation: a comic novel. Aaron McGruder and Reginald Hudlin; illustrated by Kyle Baker. Three Rivers Press 2005 144p. Illustration
Grades: 10 11 12 Adult   **741.5; Fic**
  1. Graphic novels; 2. Humorous graphic novels; 3. Political satire — Graphic novels
978-1-4000-8316-9, $14.95
                        LC 2004047838
    East St. Louis, Illinois ("the inner city without an outer city"), is an impoverished town, but Fred Fredericks, its idealistic mayor, rallies his fellow citizens to the polls for the presidential election, only to find hundreds of them turned away for trumped-up reasons. As a result of the mass disenfranchisement of East St. Louis, a radical right-wing junta led by a dim-witted Texas governor seizes the Oval Office. Prodded by shady black billionaire and old friend John Roberts, Fredericks devises a radical plan of protest: East St. Louis will secede from the Union. Roberts' financial dealings result in East St. Louis becoming flush with money. Problems set in almost immediately: controversies rage over the name and national anthem of the new country (they decide on the Republic of Blackland with an anthem sung to the tune of the theme from Good Times), and local thug Roscoe becomes a warlord and turns his gang into a paramilitary force. When the U.S. military begins to move in, Fredericks is forced to decide whether his protest is worth taking all the way. The book includes some strong language, partial nudity, and sexual situations.

McGuire, Richard
  ★ **Here**. Richard McGuire. Pantheon Books 2014 304 p. Illustration
Grades: Adult   **741.5; Fic**
  1. Future, The — Fiction; 2. Buildings; 3. Rooms
0375406506; 9780375406508, $35
                        LC 2014003489
Cartoonist Studio Prize (2015)
    In this book, author Richard McGuire presents"the long-awaited fulfillment of a pioneering comic vision. 'Here' is the story of a corner of a room and of the events that have occurred in that space over the course of hundreds of thousands of years." (Publisher's note)
    "McGuire's quiet artwork in a subdued full-color palette reveals nuanced gestures beautifully, sometimes with precise lines, others in sketchy sepia tones, all of which emphasize the passage of time. The concept is stunningly simple, and in laying bare the universality of existence-its beauty, ugliness, and mundanity-it is utterly moving." Booklist

McKenna, Aline Brosh

Jane. written by Aline Brosh McKenna; illustrated by Ramón K. Pérez; colored by Irma Kniivila with Ramón K. Pérez; lettered by Deron Bennett. Simon & Schuster 2017 224 p. Color; Illustration

Grades: 11 12 Adult   **741.5; Fic**

1. Young women — Fiction; 2. Man-woman relationship — Fiction; 3. Graphic novels

1608869814; 9781608869817, $24.99

This graphic novel, by Aline McKenna, illustrated by Ramon K. Perez, presents "a reimagining of Charlotte Brontë's classic novel Jane Eyre set in present day.... Growing up in a broken home in a small fishing town, Jane dreamed of escaping to art school and following the allure of New York City. When that dream becomes a reality however, it's not long before she feels out of place by the size of the city and the talent of her peers." (Publisher's note)

"With his stylish and realistic art, Eisner Award winner Pérez...gives Jane a pretty and capable look, resembling an older Nancy Drew, while the tortured billionaire Rochester appears grim and craggily swoonworthy. Kniivila and Pérez use vivid colors counterpointed with soft pencils and black and white inks to change scenes and convey emotions beautifully." LJ

McLeod, Kagan

Infinite kung fu. Top Shelf Productions 2011 464p. Illustration

Grades: Adult

741.5; Fic

1. Graphic novels; 2. Kung fu — Graphic novels; 3. Martial arts — Graphic novels; 4. Superhero graphic novels

978-1-891830-83-9, $24.95

Courtesy of IDW Publishing

"Originally self-published in 2000 and collected here for the first time — and including enough previously unseen pages to nearly double its size — McLeod's genre-blending opus is not merely a kung-fu epic. It's a dystopian, zombie, kung fu epic. Lei Kung is a humble soldier until the eight immortals reveal that his destiny is to defeat their former students so that he may heal a world in which reincarnation has gone horribly wrong, and corpses rise to battle the living. Seldom has a creator's love of a genre been as evident as in McLeod's meticulous homage to the heyday of martial-arts cinema.... Add heaping helpings of zombie gore, a well-imagined future world, and some gritty, street-style line work that suggests the 1970s, and the result is something irresistibly infectious — for those with special tastes." Booklist

McNamara, Jason

Continuity. AiT/Planet Lar 2006 un Illustration

Grades: 11 12 Adult

741.5; Fic

1. Dreams — Graphic novels; 2. Graphic novels

978-1-932051-43-8, $12.95

Alicia's life as a typical suburban misfit takes a horrific turn as her dreams begin to alter reality. She quickly finds herself orphaned, pregnant, and on the run from a pharmaceutical police state. Now she's fighting to stay awake and restore the world she once knew. But when a lonely doctor offers Alicia redemption, will she accept? Or

Courtesy of AiT/Planet Lar

will her dreams tear reality apart? Harsh language and some violence make this more appropriate for older teens and adult readers.

The **Martian** confederacy, volume 1. Girl Twirl Comics 2008 143p. Illustration

Grades: 10 11 12 Adult   **741.5; Fic**

1. Graphic novels; 2. Humorous graphic novels; 3. Mystery graphic novels; 4. Science fiction graphic novels; 5. Mars (Planet) — Graphic novels

978-0-9794207-1-9, $15

Mars in the year 3535 is pretty much a dump, with toxic air and stripped of its natural resources by the corporations that run the planet. Boone, Spinner (a bear) and Lou (a female android) are smalltime outlaws who take on the crooked Alcalde when he steals a professor's cure for the toxic air. As illustrator Braddock says, the story is basically The Dukes of Hazzard on Mars, with redneck good ol' boy outlaws doing the right thing against the corrupt government. However, Lou is no Daisy Duke, but a tough fighter. There is some violence, mostly fist fights, and some brief sexual situations and partial nudity.

McNeil, Carla Speed

The **Finder** library; Volume 2. by Carla Speed McNeil. Dark Horse Books 2012 636 p. Illustration

Grades: 11 12 Adult   **741.5**

1. Science fiction graphic novels

159582653X; 9781595826534, $24.99

"Since 1996, Finder has set the bar for science-fiction storytelling, with a lush, intricate world and compelling characters. Now, Dark Horse is proud to present four more story arcs of Carla Speed McNeil's groundbreaking series in a single, affordably priced volume!" (Publisher's note)

The **Finder** Library; Volume one. illustrated by the author. Dark Horse 2011 630 p. Illustration

Grades: 11 12 Adult   **741.5/973**

1. Science fiction graphic novels

1595826521; 9781595826527, $24.99

This science fiction graphic novel anthology, by Carla Speed McNeil, collects and reprints several of the author's Eisner Award-winning graphic novels within the "Finder" series. This volume includes the novels "Sin-Eater," "Talisman," and "King of the Cats," along with commentary and footnotes from the author. (Publisher's note)

Finder: Third World. story, art, and cover by Carla Speed McNeil; colors by Jenn Manley Lee and Bill Mudron. Random House Inc 2014 169 p. Illustration

Grades: Adult   **741.5**

1. Science fiction graphic novels; 2. Thieves — Graphic novels

1616554673; 9781616554675, $19.99

This graphic novel by Carla Speed McNeil presents a "turning point in the life of Jaeger, a major character in this mysterious, complex, sci-fi flavored world and the intriguing, wily heart of Finder itself! There's never been a metropolis, slum, or building that Jaeger couldn't infiltrate, escape, and/or loot — -until now!" (Publisher's note)

"McNeil's naturalistic dialogue and her lithe, expressively drawn characters highlight her impressive art chops, and the short tales have a kinetic immediacy, while the longer ones have a slow, dreamlike pace." Pub Wkly

Meadows, Joel

Studio space: the world's greatest comic illustrators at work. interviews & edited by Joel Meadows & Gary Marshall. Image Comics 2008 318p. Illustration

Grades: 10 11 12 Adult   **741.5**

1. Cartoonists; 2. Comic books, strips, etc.; 3. Graphic novels
978-1-58240-909-2, $49.99; 978-1-58240-908-5 (pa), $29.99

Twenty modern comics artists talk about their careers, their work, and their working methods. Each of them is photographed in his studio, and samples of their artwork are included. The artists are: Brian Bolland, Tim Bradstreet, Howard Chaykin, Steve Dillon, Tommy Lee Edwards, Duncan Fegredo, Dave Gibbons, Adam Hughes, Joe Kubert, Jim Lee, Mike Mignola, Frank Miller, Sean Phillips, George Pratt, Alex Ross, Tim Sale, Walt Simonson, Bryan Talbot, Dave Taylor, and Sergio Toppi.

Means, Greg

The **Cute** Girl Network. by Greg Means, and MK Reed, illustrated by Joe Flood. First Second 2013 179 p.
Grades: Adult **741.5**
1. Dating (Social customs) — Comic books, strips, etc; 2. Single women — Social networks — Comic books, strips, etc; 3. Dating (Social customs) — Fiction; 4. Romance fiction
1596437510; 9781596437517, $17.99

LC 2013031420

In this graphic novel by MK Reed, Greg Means, and Joe Flood, "Jane's new in town. When she wipes out on her skateboard right in front of Jack's food cart, she finds herself agreeing to go on a date with him. Jane's psyched that her love life is taking a turn for the friskier, but it turns out that Jack has a spotty romantic history. Cue the Cute Girl Network — a phone tree information-pooling group of local single women. Poor Jane is about to learn every detail of Jack's past misadventures." (Publisher's note)

"The snappy dialog is very well matched by Flood's blocky, black-and-white art." LJ

Mechner, Jordan

★ **Templar**. by Jordan Mechner and illustrated by LeUyen Pham and Alex Puvilland. First Second 2013 480 p.
Grades: Adult **741.5**
1. Knights and knighthood — Graphic novels; 2. Popes — Graphic novels; 3. Crusades — Fiction
1596433930; 9781596433939, $39.99

In this graphic novel by Jordan Mechner "Martin is one of a handful of Templar Knights to escape when the king of France and the pope conspire to destroy the noble order. The king aims to frame the Templars for heresy, execute all of them, and make off with their legendary treasure. That's the plan, anyway, but Martin and several other surviving knights mount a counter-campaign to regain the lost treasure of the Knights Templar." (Publisher's note)

Meltzer, Brad

Green Arrow: The Archer's Quest. DC Comics 2003 176p. Illustration
Grades: 9 10 11 12 Adult **741.5; Fic**
1. Adventure graphic novels; 2. Graphic novels; 3. Green Arrow (Fictional character); 4. Superhero graphic novels; 5. Green Arrow (Fictional character)
1-4012-0044-3, $14.95

Oliver Queen, the Green Arrow, has come back from the dead; certain items were supposed to have been destroyed once he was dead, but it never happened. Now, he and his former sidekick now known as Arsenal travel around, seeking those legendary artifacts in order to protect those people Oliver loves. The book includes some violence.

★ **Identity** Crisis. DC Comics 2005 un Illustration
Grades: 9 10 11 12 Adult **741.5; Fic**
1. Green Arrow (Fictional character)
978-1-4012-0688-8, $24.99; 978-1-4012-0458-7 (pa)

It's been said that super-heroes keep secret identities to protect their loved ones. Elongated Man (Ralph Dibny) is one of the few without a confidential alter ego. So when his wife, Sue, is murdered in her own home, the tragedy hits the crime fighting community like a sledgehammer. As the fraternity of champions begins scouring the country for clues and suspects, Green Arrow, Hawkman, Black Canary, the Atom, and Zatanna stay behind, with a powerful secret to protect. Things get worse when other superheroes' family members receive threatening notes. And when the secret is discovered, the ramifications will forever change the world of super-powered heroes and villains.

Justice League of America: The Tornado's Path. Brad Meltzer, writer; Ed Benes, penciller; Sandra Hope, inker; Rob Leigh, letterer; Alex Sinclair, colorist. DC Comics 2007 228p. Illustration
Grades: 9 10 11 12 Adult **741.5; Fic**
1. Graphic novels; 2. Justice League of America (Fictional characters); 3. Superhero graphic novels; 4. Superman (Fictional character); 5. Batman (Fictional character); 6. Wonder Woman (Fictional character)
978-1-4012-1349-7, $24.99

After traumatic events shattered the Justice League, trust was in short supply, but after it's all over, Superman, Batman, and Wonder Woman meet to choose who will become members of the new Justice League; but while they meet in secret, dark forces move against their friends and allies. A mysterious organization has helped the android Justice Leaguer known as Red Tornado to transfer his consciousness into the human body he's always wanted. But their motives may not have Red Tornado's best interests in mind. Instead, this is only the first step in a sinister conspiracy of super villains. The Justice League will have to rise again to save Red Tornado, and the world. But who will answer the call? The violence and fighting result in bloodshed.

Merey, Ilike

a + e 4ever: a graphic novel. Lethe Press 2011 214 p.
Grades: Adult **741.5; Fic**
1. Friendship — Graphic novels; 2. Teenagers — Graphic novels; 3. Love — Graphic novels; 4. Lesbians — Fiction; 5. Androgyny — Fiction
1590213904; 9781590213902

This book tells the story of "Asher Machnik [who] is a teenage boy cursed with a beautiful androgynous face. Guys punch him, girls slag him and by high school he's developed an intense fear of being touched. Art remains his only escape from an otherwise emotionally empty life. Eulalie Mason is the lonely, tough-talking...[lesbian] from school who befriends Ash. The only one to see and accept all of his sides as a loner, a fellow artist and a best friend, she's starting to wonder if ash is ever going to see all of her.... [The book] is a graphic novel set in that ambiguous crossroads where love and friendship, boy and girl, straight and gay meet." (Publisher's note)

Meyer, Scott

Help is on the way: a collection of basic instructions. Dark Horse Books 2008 120p. Illustration
Grades: 10 11 12 Adult **741.5; Fic**
1. Graphic novels; 2. Humorous graphic novels
978-1-59307-995-6, $9.95

This book collects Meyer's web comic called Basic Instructions. Using a four-panel format, he covers a variety of situations with wry humor, from How to Win an Argument to How to Pick a Password to How to Disguise a Yawn, and many more. The black and white art is fairly static, with a cast of characters Meyer uses and reuses. The humor is in the text, with a lot of fast-looking dialog. Many of the situations deal with marriage and with the workplace, while a number of them will resonate with those in the "nerd culture;" language is only mildly harsh (calling someone an "ass").

Mignola, Mike

The **Dark** Horse Book of Witchcraft. edited by Scott Allie. Dark Horse Comics 2004 96p. Illustration

Grades: 9 10 11 12 Adult   **741.5; Fic**

1. Graphic novels; 2. Horror graphic novels; 3. Witchcraft — Graphic novels; 4. Hellboy (Fictional character)

1-59307-108-6, $14.95

This anthology conjures up eight tales of horror and magic. Mignola presents a Hellboy story; Thompson and Dorkin return to the dog characters they created in "Stray" from a previous anthology volumes. Morse presents an evocative and carefully researched tale of old Salem, digging into the madness of the accusations leveled there, which ended more than thirty lives in a few short months. The book reprints a classic Clark Ashton Smith story, "Mother of Toads," illustrated by Gary Gianni, and more. There's some strong language and some graphic images of horror and violence.

Hellboy: into the silent sea. story by Mike Mignola and Gary Gianni; art by Gary Gianni; colors by Dave Stewart; letters by Clem Robins; cover art by Mike Mignola with Dave Stewart. Dark Horse Books 2017 56 p. Color; Illustration

Grades: 11 12 Adult   **741.5; Fic**

1. Hellboy (Fictional character)

9781506701431, $14.99

LC 2016049406

In this graphic novel, by Mike Mignola, Gary Gianni, and Dave Stewart, "Hellboy sets sail from the wreckage of a deserted island only to cross paths with a ghost ship. Taken captive by the phantom crew that plans to sell him to the circus, Hellboy is dragged along by a captain who will stop at nothing in pursuit of a powerful sea creature." (Publisher's note)

Hellboy in Hell: the descent. story and art by Mike Mignola; colored by Dave Stewart; lettered by Clem Robins. Dark Horse 2014 144 p. Illustration; Color

Grades: Adult   **741.5**

1. Comic books, strips, etc.; 2. Hell — Fiction; 3. Hellboy (Fictional character)

1616554444; 9781616554446, $17.99

LC 2012278136

"Hellboy creator...Mike Mignola returns to draw Hellboy's ongoing story for the first time since 'Hellboy: The Conqueror Worm.' It's a story only Mignola could tell, as more of Hellboy's secrets are at last revealed, in the most bizarre depiction of Hell you've ever seen!" (Publisher's note)

"Creator Mignola...celebrates Hellboy's 20th anniversary by killing him off and sending him back from whence he came: Hell.... Despite the grotesquery of his characters, they look believable in their horrific settings, and Mignola's simple but elegant panel design should be studied by everyone who is or who wants to be a cartoonist. The script is a delight, too, as Hellboy's down-to-earth anger and everyman astonishment remains funny and refreshing." Pub Wkly

Volume 1 of 2

Hellboy in hell; Volume 2. story and art by Mike Mignola; colored by Dave Stewart; lettered by Clem Robins; cover art by Mike Mignola & Dave Stewart. Dark Horse Books 2016 96 p.

Grades: 10 11 12 Adult   **741.5**

1. Hell — Comic books, strips, etc.; 2. Damned — Comic books, strips, etc.; 3. Hellboy (Fictional character)

9781506701134, $17.99

LC 2016015900

"After facing off for a second time against the Vampire of Prague, Hellboy...comes down with a fatal illness, and seeks the help of an incompetent team of doctors. As he explores the geography of Hell,...Hellboy gets a glimpse of the new World Tree that he helped to create, stands accused of murder by his own sister and, in a way, brings about the destruction of Pandemonium." (Publisher's note)

"The acclaimed saga comes to an end with this story arc in which Hellboy dies and returns to his infernal birthplace, where he continues his work of punching out supernatural baddies." Pub Wkly

This volume collects Hellboy in Hell #6-#10 and Hellboy: The Exorcist of Vorsk from Dark Horse Presents Volume 3 #16, all originally published by Dark Horse Comics.; Death card

★ **Hellboy** Volume 1: Seed of Destruction. by Mike Mignola; script by John Byrne; miniseries colors by Mark Chiarello; cover colors by Dave Stewart; short-story colors by Matthew Hollingsworth. Dark Horse Comics 2003 un Illustration

Grades: 9 10 11 12 Adult   **741.5; Fic**

1. Fantasy graphic novels; 2. Graphic novels; 3. Hellboy (Fictional character); 4. Horror graphic novels; 5. Mystery graphic novels

9781593070946; 1-59307-094-2, $17.95

Eisner Award: Best Graphic Album — Reprint (1995); Eisner Award: Best Writer/Artist (1995)

When strangeness threatens to engulf the world, a strange man will come to save it. Sent to investigate a mystery with supernatural overtones, the good-guy big red demon, Hellboy, discovers the secrets of his own origins, and his link to the Nazi occultists who promised Hitler a final solution in the form of a demonic avatar. The book includes some violence and horror.

Other Hellboy volumes are: 2: Wake the Devil; 3: The Chained Coffin and Others; 4: The Right Hand of Doom; 5: Conqueror Worm; 6: Strange Places; 7: The Troll Witch and Others; 8: Darkness Calls; 9: The Wild Hunt; 10: The Crooked Man and Others; 11: The Bride of Hell and Others; 12: The Storm and the Fury; 13: Hellboy in Mexico

Hellboy Volume 2: Wake the Devil, 2nd ed.. Dark Horse Comics 2003 un Illustration

Grades: 9 10 11 12 Adult   **741.5; Fic**

1. Fantasy graphic novels; 2. Graphic novels; 3. Hellboy (Fictional character); 4. Horror graphic novels; 5. Mystery graphic novels

1-59307-095-0, $17.95

A murder in a New York wax museum and a missing corpse lead Hellboy into ancient Romanian castles on the trail of a sleeping legend: the original nobleman vampire. Nazi scientists prepare for the return of their occult master and the end of the world, and Hellboy confronts his purpose on earth. The book includes some violence, strong language and some nonsexual partial nudity.

Hellboy Volume 3: The Chained Coffin and Others 2nd ed.. Dark Horse Comics 2004 un Illustration

Grades: 9 10 11 12 Adult   **741.5; Fic**

1. Fantasy graphic novels; 2. Graphic novels; 3. Hellboy (Fictional character); 4. Horror graphic novels; 5. Mystery graphic novels

1-59307-091-8, $17.95

This volume collects short stories Mignola wrote for various other publications; it includes The Corpse," which some critics think is the best Hellboy story he has written. Mignola provides notes before each story. The book includes some violence, strong language, and nonsexual partial nudity.

Hellboy Volume 4: The Right Hand of Doom 2nd ed.. Dark Horse Comics 2004 un Illustration

Grades: 9 10 11 12 Adult   **741.5; Fic**

1. Fantasy graphic novels; 2. Graphic novels; 3. Hellboy (Fictional character); 4. Horror graphic novels; 5. Mystery graphic novels

1-59307-093-4, $17.95

This volume collects more Hellboy short stories Mignola wrote for various other publications; it includes Pancakes," a cute two-page story set when he was a young demon. The Right Hand of Doom" is a long story that takes up most of the volume. The book includes some violence and strong language.

Hellboy Volume 5: Conqueror Worm 2nd ed.. Dark Horse Comics 2004 un Illustration
Grades: 9 10 11 12 Adult   741.5; Fic
1. Fantasy graphic novels; 2. Graphic novels; 3. Hellboy (Fictional character); 4. Horror graphic novels; 5. Mystery graphic novels
1-59307-092-6, $17.95
2002 Eisner Award for Best Limited Series.

At the end of World War II, American costumed-adventurer Lobster Johnson led an Allied attack on Hitler's space program, but not before the Nazis were able to launch the first man into space. Now, after sixty years, Hellboy is partnered with an artifical man — a Frankenstein's monster implanted by Bureau scientists with a bomb — to travel to the ruined castle in Norway to intercept the returning capsule, and its single passenger...the conqueror worm. The book includes violence, strong language, and partial nudity.

Hellboy Volume 6: Strange Places. Dark Horse Comics 2006 un Illustration
Grades: 9 10 11 12 Adult   741.5; Fic
1. Fantasy graphic novels; 2. Graphic novels; 3. Hellboy (Fictional character); 4. Horror graphic novels; 5. Mystery graphic novels
978-1-59307-475-3, $17.95

After leaving the Bureau for Paranormal Research and Defense, Hellboy's travels take him briefly to Africa, then for a two-year stint at the bottom of the ocean. An ancient witch doctor, a giant fish woman and keeper of the secret history of the universe force Hellboy to either accept his role in the coming apocalypse, or have that role stolen from him. Weird undersea creatures and talking lions populate this turning-point adventure, which reveals secrets buried since Hellboy's very creation. The book includes some violence and strong language.

Hellboy volume 8: Darkness calls. Dark Horse Comics 2008 un Illustration
Grades: 10 11 12 Adult   741.5; Fic
1. Fantasy graphic novels; 2. Graphic novels; 3. Hellboy (Fictional character); 4. Horror graphic novels
978-1-59307-896-6, $19.95

Hellboy has finally returned from his adventures at sea, but no sooner has he settled on land than a conclave of witches drags him from his respite and into the heart of Russian folklore, where he becomes the quarry of the powerful and bloodthirsty witch Baba Yaga. Bent on revenge for the eye she had lost to Hellboy, Baba Yaga has enlisted the aid of Koshchei, a deathless warrior who will stop at nothing to destroy Hellboy. Meanwhile, in England, the Gruagach and his minions seek to regain the powers they once had over the world. The book includes brief partial nudity and a lot of bloodshed.

Jenny Finn: doom messiah. Boom! Studios 2008 un Illustration
Grades: 11 12 Adult   741.5; Fic
1. Fantasy graphic novels; 2. Graphic novels; 3. Horror graphic novels
978-1-934506-14-1, $14.99

In Victorian London, wherever the mysterious Jenny Finn goes, death and destruction follow in her wake as a plague sweeps through the city, affecting men. Meanwhile, someone is murdering and eviscerating whores. Goodhearted butcher Joe thinks Jenny Finn is an innocent girl who doesn't belong in the bad part of the city, and in his efforts to help her, he becomes embroiled in a battle between good and evil, with secret societies, an invasion of monstrous sea creatures, and a murderous artist. The book includes nudity, scenes in a whorehouse, harsh language, and violence.

Millar, Mark
Chosen. Dark Horse Comics 2005 un Illustration
Grades: 10 11 12 Adult   741.5; Fic
1. Graphic novels; 2. Supernatural graphic novels
1-59307-213-9, $17.95

Imagine you're twelve years old and suddenly discover that you are the returned Jesus Christ. You can turn water into wine, make the crippled walk and perhaps even raise the dead. What do you and your family do, and how does it affect you knowing that you're destined to grow up and take part in a conflict that people have been waiting almost two thousand years for? The book contains strong language, including the f-bomb.

Chrononauts. Mark Millar, writer & co-creator; Sean Gordon Murphy, artist & co-creator; Matt Hollingsworth, color artist; Chris Eliopoulos, letterer. Image Comics 2015 120 p. Color; Illustration
Grades: Adult   741.5; Fic
1. Science fiction graphic novels; 2. Time travel — Graphic novels
1632154064; 9781632154064, $9.99
Eisner Nominee: Best Limited Series (2016)

"Corbin Quinn and Danny Reilly are two red-blooded American guys who also happen to be scientific geniuses. With the whole world watching, they embark on the world's first time-travel experiment. But when their planned routine goes off-course, they're left to fend for themselves — leading to an era-hopping adventure!" (Publisher's note)

Civil War. writer, Mark Millar; penciler, Steve McNiven. Marvel Entertainment 2007 un Illustration
Grades: 9 10 11 12 Adult   741.5; Fic
1. Graphic novels; 2. Superhero graphic novels; 3. Iron Man (Fictional character); 4. Captain America (Fictional character)
0-7851-2179-X, $24.99

The landscape of the Marvel Universe is changing, and it's time to choose: Whose side are you on? A conflict has been brewing for more than a year, and a single misstep by a costumed superhero costs thousands of lives and ignites the fuse of a superhero civil war. Teams, friendships, and families begin to fall apart as they must choose. What is the choice? The government wants to register all super powered individuals. Iron Man agrees and takes the government's side. Captain America sees registration as a step down the slippery slope towards the abolishment of civil rights for superheroes.

Kick-ass 2. Marvel 2012 208 p.
Grades: Adult   741.5/973; Fic
1. Superhero comic books, strips, etc.
0785152458; 9780785152453, $24.99

This comic book by Mark Millar tells "the tale of a fanboy becoming a homemade superhero.... As Kick-Ass' mission inspires a community of similarly custom-crafted heroes, the Red Mist returns with a hideous revenge and plans to tear down the city." The story includes "the graphic murder of young children and the gang-rape of a teenage girl." (Booklist)

Superior. writer, Mark Millar; penciler, Leinil Yu; Gerry Alanguilan with Jason Paz & Jeff Huet, inkers; Sunny Gho, Javier Tartaglia & Dave McCaig, colorists; Clayton Cowles, letterer. Marvel 2012 200 p. Color illustration
Grades: Adult   Fic; 741.5973
1. Children with physical disabilities — Graphic novels; 2. Superhero graphic novels; 3. Superhero comic books, strips, etc.
0785136185; 9780785136187, $24.99; 9780785153177, $19.99

This comic book anthology, by Mark Millar and illustrated by Leinil Francis Yu, collects the first seven issues of the "Superior" series in graphic novel format. "Simon Pooni had it all going for him...[b]ut that was when he could still move his legs. Now, he's living with multiple sclerosis, missing all the little things he used to take for granted, and escaping into the world of movies and comics with his best friend. Then...SUPERIOR entered his life." (Publisher's note)

Collects Superior # 1-7.

Superman: Red Son. Mark Millar, Dave Johnson, Kilian Plunkett, Andrew Robinson, Walden Wong. DC Comics 2014 168 p. Color; Illustration

Grades: 11 12 Adult **741.5**

1. Superman (Fictional character)

1401247113; 9781401247119, $17.99

LC 2013049659

Eisner Nominee: Best Limited Series (2004)

This comic book, by Mark Millar, illustrated by Dave Johnson, Kilian Plunkett, Andrew Robinson, and Walden Wong, "is a vivid tale of Cold War paranoia, that reveals how the ship carrying the infant who would later be known as Superman lands in the midst of the 1950s Soviet Union. Raised on a collective, the infant grows up and becomes a symbol to the Soviet people, and the world changes drastically from what we know." (Publisher's note)

Red Son

Wanted. Top Cow 2008 208p. Illustration

Grades: 11 12 Adult **741.5; Fic**

1. Graphic novels; 2. Mystery graphic novels; 3. Superhero graphic novels

978-1-58240-497-4, $19.99

Wesley Gibson is a typical office worker, a nobody with a boring life...until he discovers that he is the son of "The Killer," a member of an underground fraternity of supervillains who've been running the world since 1986. After his father is killed, Wesley becomes the new Killer and he joins the villains while trying to unravel the mystery of his father's murder. This book is the basis for the motion picture starring Jamie MacElvoy and Angelina Jolie that was released during the summer of 2008. The book includes lots of graphic violence, very harsh language (with lots of f-bombs), and nudity.

Miller, Frank

300. Dark Horse Comics 1999 88p. Illustration

Grades: 10 11 12 Adult **741.5; Fic**

1. Graphic novels; 2. Thermopylae, Battle of, 480 B.C. — Graphic novels

978-1-56971-402-7, $30

Miller paints a highly fictionalized, stylized account of the Battle of Thermopylae, where the Spartan King Leonidas and a relatively small band of Spartans held off the massive army of Emperor Xerxes of Persia long enough for Athens to gather its troops for the final showdown. The Spartans all died, but their sacrifice saved Greece in the end. Watercolor paintings by artist Varley use an earthy palette to depict the stark landscape and violent battles. This book is the basis for the hit motion picture released in March 2007.

★ **Batman,** the Dark Knight returns. Frank Miller; with Klaus Janson and Lynn Varley. DC Comics 2013 198 p.

Grades: 11 12 Adult **741.5**

1. Superheroes — Comic books, strips, etc.; 2. Batman (Fictional character); 3. Robin (Fictional character)

1563893428; 9781563893421, $19.99

LC 2013008716

This graphic novel, by Frank Miller, "completely reinvents the legend of Batman.... The Dark Knight returns in a blaze of fury, taking on a whole new generation of criminals and matching their level of violence. He is soon joined by a new Robin — a girl named Carrie Kelley, who proves to be just as invaluable as her predecessors. But can Batman and Robin deal with the threat posed by their deadliest enemies, after years of incarceration have made them into perfect psychopaths?" (Publisher's note)

Originally published in single magazine form as Batman, the Dark Knight returns 1-4.

Batman: Year One. DC Comics 2005 168p. Illustration

Grades: 8 9 10 11 12 Adult **741.5; Fic**

1. Batman (Fictional character); 2. Graphic novels; 3. Superhero graphic novels; 4. Catwoman (Fictional character)

978-1-4012-0752-6, $14.99

In the late-1980s, after publishing Miller's Batman: The Dark Knight Returns, DC realized they should remain faithful to the original roots of Batman. Miller then wrote this book, which reinvents the very early years of Batman as a superhero. In this book, Jim Gordon arrives in Gotham City to work in the police department and discovers the high level of corruption there; Batman encounters Selina, who becomes Catwoman, for the first time; and he develops some of the weapons he uses to fight crime. This new edition includes preliminary sketches and other extras.

Batman: the Dark Knight strikes again. [by] Frank Miller, Lynn Varley, Todd Klein, Batman created by Bob Kane. DC Comics 2002 247p. Illustration

Grades: 10 11 12 Adult **741.5; Fic**

1. Graphic novels; 2. Superhero graphic novels; 3. Batman (Comic strip); 4. Batman (Fictional character)

1-56389-844-6; 1-56389-929-9 (pa), $19.99

LC 2003-544916

"Batman leads the opposition in a dystopian near-future when security concerns have spurred a repressive crackdown. Other costumed heroes side with either the government or Batman.... The book's authoritarian society resonates with the post-9/11 environment, though Miller's cheekiness dispels notions that this is serious commentary." Booklist

Originally published in single magazine form as Batman: the Dark Knight strikes again 1-3; Based on Batman comic strip; Sequel to Batman: the Dark Knight returns (1986)

★ **Daredevil** by Frank Miller & Klaus Janson Omnibus. by Frank Miller, Marv Wolfman, Roger McKenzie, David Michelinie; illustrated by Klaus Janson. Marvel Enterprises 2013 840 p.

Grades: Adult **741.5**

1. Science fiction comic books, strips, etc.; 2. Superheroes — Comic books, strips, etc.; 3. Daredevil (Fictional character)

0785185682; 9780785185680, $99.99

This graphic novel, by Frank Miller, Marv Wolfman, Roger McKenzie, and David Michelinie, illustrated by Klaus Janson, "herald one of Daredevil's greatest eras, just in time for the Kingpin and Bullseye's efforts to rob the Man Without Fear of everything he holds dear! Featuring the first appearances of Elektra, Stick and the Hand!" (Publisher's note)

★ **Daredevil:** born again. by Frank Miller; illustrated by David Mazzucchelli. Marvel Worldwide 2010 203 p. Color illustration (Daredevil)

Grades: Adult **741.5**

1. Science fiction comic books, strips, etc.; 2. Superheroes — Comic books, strips, etc.; 3. Daredevil (Fictional character)

0785134816; 9780785134817, $19.99

This graphic novel, by Frank Miller, illustrated by David Mazzucchelli, is the "definitive Daredevil tale! Karen Page, Matt Murdock's former lover, has traded away the Man Without Fear's secret identity for a drug fix. Now, Daredevil must find strength as the Kingpin of

Crime wastes no time taking him down as low as a human can get." (Publisher's note)

Contains material originally published in magazine form as Daredevil #226-233.

Hard boiled. by Frank Miller; illustrated by Geof Darrow. Dark Horse Books 2000 124 p. Color illustration

Grades: Adult   **741.5**

1. Science fiction graphic novels

1878574582; 9781878574589, $16.95

In this graphic novel, by Frank Miller, illustrated by Geof Darrow, "Carl Seltz is a suburban insurance investigator, a loving husband, and devoted father. Nixon is a berserk, homicidal tax collector racking up mind-boggling body counts in a diseased urban slaughterhouse. Unit Four is the ultimate robot killing machine — and the last hope of the future's enslaved mechanical servants. And they're all the same psychotic entity." (Publisher's note)

Ronin. Frank Miller. DC Comics 2014 336 p. Color; Illustration

Grades: Adult   **741.5**

1. Fantasy graphic novels; 2. Samurai — Graphic novels; 3. New York (N.Y.) — Graphic novels

1401248950; 9781401248956, $29.99

LC 2014015203

In this graphic novel, by Frank Miller, "a legendary warrior, the Ronin, a dishonored, masterless 13th Century samurai, is mystically given a second chance to avenge his master's death. Suddenly finding himself reborn in a futuristic and corrupt 21st Century New York City, the samurai discovers he has one last chance to regain his honor: he must defeat the reincarnation of his master's killer, the ancient demon Agat." (Publisher's note)

"Before Miller redefined Batman with a dark, noir look and feel that influenced comics of the 1980s and beyond, his first series followed the adventures of a samurai warrior in a future dystopia.... The over-the-top violence is balanced against nimble and believable human anatomy and motion, and his technique of expressing emotion by showing a single face in multiple panels is especially effective." Pub Wkly"

Original collected edition published 1987; Originally published in single magazine form as Ronin 1-6.

★ **Sin** City Vol. 1: The Hard Goodbye. Dark Horse Comics 2005 208p. Illustration

Grades: 11 12 Adult   **741.5; Fic**

1. Graphic novels; 2. Mystery graphic novels

1-59307-293-7, $17

Sin City is the place — tough as leather and dry as tinder. Love is the fuel, and Marv has the match...not to mention a condition." He's gunning after Goldie's killer, so it's time to watch this town burn. Frank Miller is one of modern comic's first talents to publish a comic book that he created, crafted, and owned. That book is Sin City, which grew from the wellspring of Miller's passionate desire to create a comic book with two distinct qualities — it wouldn't be a superhero comic, and it had to be a crime comic. Enter Marv and Goldie. And a psychotic killer. And a crime-drenched town. And a corrupted diocese. The stark black and white art includes nudity and graphic violence, along with lots of harsh language.

Sin City Vol. 2: A Dame to Kill For. Dark Horse Comics 2005 208p. Illustration

Grades: 11 12 Adult   **741.5; Fic**

1. Graphic novels; 2. Mystery graphic novels

1-59307-294-5, $17

It's one of those hot nights, dry and windless. The kind that makes people do sweaty, secret things. Dwight's thinking of all the ways he's screwed up and what he'd give for one clear chance to wipe the slate clean,

to dig his way out of the numb gray hell that is his life. And he'd give anything. Just to cut loose. Just to feel the fire. One more time. And then Ava calls. Dwight thinks it's love, but Ava just needs him to kill her rich husband and she betrays him. No one does that to Dwight and gets away with it. This book includes lots of harsh language, graphic violence, nudity, and sexual situations.

Miller, John Jackson

Star Wars: Knights of the Old Republic Volume One: Commencement. Dark Horse Comics 2006 un Illustration

Grades: 8 9 10 11 12 Adult   **741.5; Fic**

1. Adventure graphic novels; 2. Graphic novels; 3. Science fiction graphic novels

978-1-59307-640-5, $18.95

Thousands of years before Luke Skywalker would destroy the Death Star in that fateful battle above Yavin 4, one lone Padawan would become a fugitive hunted by his own Masters, charged with murdering every one of his fellow Jedi-in-training. From criminals hiding out in the treacherous under-city of the planet Taris, to a burly, mysterious droid recovered from the desolate landscape of a cratered moon, Padawan Zayne Carrick will find unexpected allies in his desperate race to clear his name before the unmerciful authorities enact swift retribution upon him.

Millionaire, Tony

Billy Hazelnuts. Fantagraphics Books 2005 111 Illustration

Grades: 9 10 11 12 Adult   **741.5; Fic**

1. Adventure graphic novels; 2. Graphic novels; 3. Humorous graphic novels

1-56097-701-9, $19.95

This book transmutes nursery rhymes and the golem myth into a storybook about Becky, girl scientist, her friend Billy Hazelnuts (who was created from cooking ingredients by tailless mice), and their journey to find the missing moon while battling an evil steam-driven alligator with a seeing-eye skunk. Millionaire fuses the darker spirit of older fairy tales with an adventure story, throws gender politics into the mix, and uses his highly detailed, old-fashioned looking art to pull it all together.

Sock Monkey: The Inches Incident. Dark Horse Comics 2007 88p. Illustration

Grades: 7 8 9 10 11 12 Adult   **741.5; Fic**

1. Fantasy graphic novels; 2. Graphic novels; 3. Toys — Graphic novels

978-1-59307-842-3, $12.95

Inches the doll was the cutest in the whole house. Loved by everyone, the world was Inches' oyster. Then one day something happened... The Sock Monkey and Mr. Crow became concerned for their diminutive friend, but by then it was too late. The truth sent the terrified Sock Monkey and Crow fleeing for their lives, for Inches had been invaded by a colony of evil ants. The sight of ants swarming over Inches and other things might be too creepy-crawly for some readers; the violence is aimed at toys rather than people, however, this is not a book for younger readers.

Sock Monkey: Uncle Gabby. Dark Horse Comics 2004 un Illustration

Grades: 8 9 10 11 12 Adult   **741.5; Fic**

1. Adventure graphic novels; 2. Graphic novels; 3. Humorous graphic novels

1-59307-026-8, $14.95

Uncle Gabby, the Sock Monkey, and Drinky the crow set off on a journey to solve the mystery of unremembered memories. This looks like a children's book, but the underlying bitter sweetness of a lost past and longing is more suited to teens and adults.

Mills, Tarpé

Miss Fury: Sensational Sundays 1944-1949. Tarpé Mills.. IDW Publishing 2011 229p Illustration
Grades: Adult   **741.5**
1. Cartoons and caricatures; 2. Superheroes
1600109055; 9781600109058, $49.99

This book offers a collection of the Miss Fury Sunday newspaper adventure comic strip drawn by Tarpé Mills in the 1940s. The adventure comic strip includes "[c]atfights and crossdressers, mad scientists and Gestapo agents with swastika branding irons-it's one...adventure after another in this...collection of the first female superhero created and drawn by a woman. Miss Fury was a sexy adventurer clad in a skin-tight panther costume. By day, she was socialite Marla Drake. By night,...Miss Fury." (Publisher's note)

Miura, Kentaro

Berserk; Volume 1. by Kentaro Miura; translation, Jason DeAngelis ... [et al.]; lettering and retouch, Dan Nakrosis. Dark Horse Manga 2003 224 p. Illustration
Grades: Adult   **741.5**
1. Manga; 2. Seinen manga; 3. Demonology — Fiction
1593070209; 9781593070205, $14.99

LC 2004541107

"Berserk is manga mayhem to the extreme.... His name is Guts, the Black Swordsman, a feared warrior spoken of only in whispers. Bearer of a gigantic sword, an iron hand, and the scars of countless battles and tortures, his flesh is also indelibly marked with The Brand, an unholy symbol that draws the forces of darkness to him and dooms him as their sacrifice." (Publisher's note)

"Published in Japan in 1989, this work has a style characteristic of other 1980s manga, with sparse dialogue, spectacular action sequences and gritty character art. The pencil shading and use of shadows lend an ominous tone, and the frenetic and intense pace make Berserk a strong addition to the fantasy-horror manga genre." Pub Wkly

First published in Japan by Hakusensha, Inc., Tokyo; Volume 1 of an ongoing series

Mizuki, Shigeru

NonNonBa. Shigeru Mizuki; translation by Jocelyne Allen. Drawn & Quarterly 2012 408 p. Illustration; Color
Grades: 7 8 9 10 11 12 Adult   **741.5/952; 741.5**
1. Cartoonists — Japan — Biography — Comic books, strips, etc; 2. Grandmothers — Comic books, strips, etc; 3. Grandparent and child — Comic books, strips, etc; 4. Yokai (Japanese folklore) — Comic books, strips, etc; 5. Mizuki, Shigeru, 1922-2015 — Childhood and youth — Comic books, strips, etc; 6. Shonen manga; 7. Autobiographical graphic novels; 8. Folklore — Japan — Graphic novels; 9. Manga; 10. Grandparent-grandchild relationship — Graphic novels
1770460721; 9781770460720, $26.95

LC 2012427667

This graphic novel, by Shigeru Mizuki, translated by Jocelyne Allen, is "a poetic memoir detailing his interest in yokai (spirit monsters). Mizuki's childhood experiences with yokai influenced the course of his life and oeuvre; he is now known as the forefather of yokai manga.... Mizuki explores the legacy left him by his childhood explorations of the spirit world, explorations encouraged by his grandmother, a grumpy old woman named NonNonBa." (Publisher's note)

Includes bibliographical references; Manga format; reads from back to front, right to left.

Onward towards our noble deaths. translated by Jocelyne Allen. Drawn & Quarterly 2011 372p. Illustration
Grades: Adult   **741.5; 818**

1. Artists; 2. Authors; 3. Biographers; 4. Cartoonists; 5. Comic book writers; 6. Illustrators; 7. Memoirists; 8. Soldiers — Graphic novels; 9. World War, 1939-1945 — Campaigns — New Guinea — Graphic novels; 10. World War, 1939-1945 — Japan — Graphic novels; 11. Mizuki, Shigeru
9781770460416; 978-1-77046-041-6, $24.95

This "English translation of legendary Japanese cartoonist Mizuki's 1973 antiwar screed is a lightly fictionalized account (90 percent fact, he claims in an afterword) of his time in the Imperial Army during WWII. Though some 30 soldiers are introduced in the opening character guide, no more than a few ever really differentiate themselves, a fitting reminder of the low premium that war puts on individual life. What comes through clearly is the litany of indignities the soldiers endure on a daily basis from slap-happy officers, perilously unforgiving conditions, and sudden outbursts of death on the receiving end of the enemy's bombs and bullets.? Booklist

Shigeru Mizuki's Hitler. by Shigeru Mizuki (Author), Zack Davisson (Translator). Farrar, Straus & Giroux 2015 296 p. Illustration
Grades: Adult   **943.086092; 741.5**
1. Germany — Politics and government — 1933-1945; 2. World War, 1939-1945 — Biography; 3. Hitler, Adolf, 1889-1945
1770462104; 9781770462106, $24.95

This graphic novel, by Shigeru Mizuki, translated by Zack Davisson, "delves deep into the history books to create an absorbing and eloquent portrait of [Adolf] Hitler's life. Beginning with Hitler's time in Austria as a starving art student and ending with a Germany in ruins, Shigeru Mizuki's Hitler retraces the path Hitler took in life, coolly examining his charismatic appeal and his calculated political maneuvering." (Publisher's note)

Showa 1944-1953: a history of Japan. Shigeru Mizuki; translated by Zack Davisson. Farrar, Straus & Giroux 2014 540 p. Illustration
Grades: Adult   **952.03/3; 741.5**
1. Japan — History — 1945-1952, Allied Occupation — Graphic novels; 2. World War, 1939-1945 — Japan
1770461620; 9781770461628, $24.95

This graphic novel "continues the award-winning author Shigeru Mizuki's autobiographical and historical account of the Showa period in Japan. This volume recounts the events of the final years of the Pacific War, and the consequences of the war's devastation for Mizuki and the Japanese populace at large." (Publisher's note)

Showa 1953-1989: a history of Japan. Shigeru Mizuki; translation by Zack Davisson. Drawn & Quarterly 2013 552 p. Illustration
Grades: Adult   **952.03/3; 741.5**
1. Comic books, strips, etc. — Japan — Translations into English; 2. Mizuki, Shigeru, 1922-20152015 — Childhood and youth — Comic books, strips, etc; 3. Japan — History — Showa period, 1926-1989 — Comic books, strips, etc; 4. Japan — Social life and customs — Comic books, strips, etc; 5. Japan — Social life and customs; 6. Japan — History — Graphic novels
9781770462014, $24.95; 1770462015

LC 2013464735

Eisner Award: Best U.S. Edition of International Material — Asia (2016)

This graphic novel by Shigeru Mizuki "picks up in the wake of Japan's utter defeat in World War II, as a country reduced to rubble struggles to rise again. The Korean War brings new opportunities to the nation searching for an identity.... Events like the Tokyo Olympiad and the World's Fair introduce a new, friendly Japan to the world, but this period of peace and plenty conceals a populace still struggling to come to terms with the devastation of World War II." (Publisher's note)

"There is more interweaving of Mizuki's life and ruminations in this volume than in the previous three, enriching a historic time line full of political scandals and pop-culture fads and emphasizing Mizuki's study of the yokai, or monsters." Booklist

Translation of: Komikku Showa-shi.

Showa, 1926-1939: a history of Japan. Shigeru Mizuki; translator, Zack Davisson. Drawn & Quarterly 2013 533 p. Illustration
Grades: Adult   **741.5; 952.03**
1. Japan — History — 1926-1945 — Comic books, strips, etc; 2. Japan — Social life and customs — 1912-1945 — Comic books, strips, etc; 3. Japan — History — 1868-1945; 4. Great Depression, 1929-1939
1770461353; 9781770461352, $24.95

LC 2013464735

Translated by Zack Davisson, "'Showa 1926-1939: A History of Japan' is the first volume of Shigeru Mizuki's meticulously researched historical portrait of twentieth-century Japan. This volume deals with the period leading up to World War II, a time of high unemployment and...the Great Depression. Mizuki's photo-realist style effortlessly brings to life the Japan of the 1920s and 1930s, depicting bustling city streets and abandoned graveyards with equal ease." (Publisher's note)

Translation of: Komikku Showa-shi.

Showa, 1939-1944: a history of Japan. Shigeru Mizuki; translation, Zack Davisson. Drawn & Quarterly 2014 548 p. Illustration
Grades: Adult   **952.03; 741.5**
1. Comic books, strips, etc. — Japan — Translations into English; 2. Mizuki, Shigeru, 1922-2015 — Childhood and youth — Comic books, strips, etc; 3. Japan — History — 1926-1945 — Comic books, strips, etc; 4. Japan — Social life and customs — 1912-1945 — Comic books, strips, etc; 5. World War, 1939-1945; 6. Japan — History — 1868-1945
1770461515; 9781770461512, $24.95

LC 2014407869

This book continues "author Shigeru Mizuki's autobiographical and historical account of Showa-era Japan. This volume covers the final moments of the lead-up to World War II and the first few years of the Pacific War, and is a chilling reminder of the harshness of life in Japan during this highly militarized epoch." (Publisher's note)

"As with the first volume, the narrative switches back and forth from a broad historical account of the war to a narrow view seen from the perspective of Mizuki and his family. This restricted view flattens world-changing events and highlights the mundane: the tedium of constant rationing and hunger and, once Mizuki is drafted, the hurry-up-and-wait uncertainty that comes with being a soldier." Booklist

Translation of: Komikku Showa-shi.

Mizushiro, Setona
After School Nightmare Volume 1. Go! Comi 2006 200p. Illustration
Grades: 10 11 12 Adult
741.5; Fic
1. Graphic novels; 2. Horror graphic novels; 3. Manga; 4. Shojo manga; 5. Supernatural graphic novels
978-1-933617-16-9, $10.99

Courtesy of Go! Comi

You have just awakened to find your darkest, ugliest secret revealed to classmates who would do anything to destroy you. This is what's happened to Ichijou Mashiro, whose elite school education turns into the most horrifying experience of his life when he's enlisted by a mysterious school nurse to take an after-hours class. Only those who pass the class will graduate, and the only way for Mashiro to pass is to enter into a nightmare world... where his body and soul will be at the mercy of his worst enemies. Can Mashiro keep his life-long secret — that he is not truly

a he" nor entirely a she" — or will he finally be öutted" in the most humiliating way possible? The book includes graphic violence, strong language, and sexual situations.

Mochizuki, Minetaro
Dragon Head Vol. 1. Tokyopop 2006 223p. Illustration
Grades: 11 12 Adult   **741.5; Fic**
1. Apocalyptic fiction — Graphic novels; 2. Graphic novels; 3. Manga; 4. Science fiction graphic novels; 5. Seinen manga
1-59532-914-5, $9.99

The end of everyone was just the beginning...Returning home by train after a class trip, Teru Aoki takes a most frightening ride inside a mountain tunnel. When the train derails, nearly everyone aboard is killed. Amidst the bloody carnage, Teru discovers two survivors — but salvation is far from their grasp. As they try to dig out from the wreck in order to come up with a plan to stay alive, the lack of light and food, combined with the stench of death and decay, will lead one member of the group down a dark and demented path. And with sudden, violent earthquakes shaking the tunnel, escaping to the outside world may lead them to an even greater danger... Violence, strong language, partial nudity, and sexual situations occur in the series.

Modan, Rutu
Exit Wounds. Drawn & Quarterly 2007 160p. Illustration
Grades: 12 Adult   **741.5; Fic**
1. Graphic novels; 2. Israelis — Graphic novels; 3. Mystery graphic novels
1-897299-06-0, $19.95

Israeli taxi driver Koby Franco lives and works in Tel Aviv; he lives with his Aunt Ruby and Uncle Aryeh, and he hasn't seen his father in a long time. One evening he gets a fare; Numi is a soldier, and she tells Koby she thinks her father may have been killed in a terrorist bombing in Hadera. He reluctantly helps her, against the advice of his family, and he and Numi try to trace his father's last few months and see whether he died or not. As they do this, Koby must deal with his feelings about a father who never really connected with his own family. Angry with Numi because she'd had an affair with his father, Koby eventually becomes her friend, and then her lover. The book includes one fairly graphic sex scene without any nudity.

★ The **Property.** by Rutu Modan and translated by Jessica Cohen. Farrar Straus & Giroux 2013 232 p. Color; Illustration
Grades: Adult   **741.5**
1. Granddaughters — Fiction; 2. Grandmothers — Graphic novels; 3. Memory — Fiction
1770461159; 9781770461154, $24.95

LC 2012517821

Eisner Award: Best Graphic Album — New (2014); Ignatz Nominee: Outstanding Graphic Novel (2013)

In this graphic novel written by Rutu Modan and translated by Jessica Cohen, "Regina Segal takes her granddaughter Mica to Warsaw, hoping to reclaim a family property lost during the Second World War. Regina is forced to recall difficult things about her past. Modan offers up a world populated by prickly seniors, smart-alecky public servants, and stubborn women — a world whose realism is expressed alternately in the absurdity of people's behavior and in the complex consequences of their sacrifices." (Publisher's note)

"Nicely varied panel size and earth-tone coloration further distinguish this gratifying work of comics realism." Booklist

Moebius
★ The **world** of Edena. written and illustrated by Jean Moebius Giraud;color work by Jean Moebius Giraud, incollaboration with Florence Breton, ClaireChampeval [and four others]; translation work byLaure

Dupont for Studio Cutie, Brandon Kander,Diana Schutz, Philip R.. Dark Horse Books 2016 344 p.
Grades: Adult   **741.5**
   1. Utopian fiction; 2. Science fiction graphic novels
9781506702162, $49.99

                              LC 2016025979

Eisner Award: Best U.S. Edition of International Material (2017)

   In this graphic novel, written and illustrated by Moebius, "Stel and Atan are interstellar investigators trying to find a lost space station and its crew. When they discover the mythical paradise planet Edena, their lives are changed forever.... Moebius's 'World of Edena' story arc is comprised of five chapters — Upon a Star, Gardens of Edena, The Goddess, Stel, and Sra — which are all collected here." (Publisher's note)

   "Glowingly illustrated in the elegant clear-line art and rich colors for which Moebius is justly revered, the book careens spectacularly through science fiction, fantasy, allegory, pop psychology, and psychedelia." Pub Wkly

Includes bibliographical references.

Moeller, Christopher

   Iron Empires: Faith Conquers. Dark Horse Comics 2004 un Illustration
Grades: 9 10 11 12 Adult   **741.5; Fic**
   1. Graphic novels; 2. Science fiction graphic novels
1-59307-015-2, $17.95

   In the far future, eight weary nations are scattered among three million light years of the Milky Way Galaxy, all that is left of a once vast human civilization. The Vaylen Terror has ravaged humanity through the years, seizing a thousand worlds in a bloody rush, then pausing for decades of consolidation During these intervals of calm, the empires rebuild, rearm, then wage war on their neighbors. In this volume, readers will meet tough, uncompromising warrior-priest Trevor Faith, battling for his life and conscience on a border world. The book includes some strong language and lots of fighting violence.

   Iron Empires: Sheva's War. Dark Horse Comics 2004 un Illustration
Grades: 9 10 11 12 Adult   **741.5; Fic**
   1. Graphic novels; 2. Science fiction graphic novels
1-59307-110-8, $17.95

   In the far future, eight weary nations are scattered among three million light years of the Milky Way Galaxy, all that is left of a once vast human civilization. The Vaylen Terror has ravaged humanity through the years, seizing a thousand worlds in a bloody rush, then pausing for decades of consolidation During these intervals of calm, the empires rebuild, rearm, then wage war on their neighbors. In this volume, readers will meet the beautiful Karsan noblewoman, Ahmi Sheva. As the planet she despises but is duty-bound to defend is caught up in an empire-wide catastrophe, Sheva finds herself fighting, not just for survival, but for her humanity. The book includes strong language and violence.

Moen, Erika

   Oh joy sex toy; Volume 1. Erika Moen, Matthew Nolan; [edited by] Ari Yarwood. Oni Press 2016 268 p. Color; Illustration
Grades: Adult
306.7; 741.5
   1. Sex; 2. Sex education
1620103621; 9781620103623, $29.99

                      LC 2016940277

   This book "is 268 pages of comics by Erika Moen and Matthew Nolan about sex, sex toy reviews, sexuality, sex education, safer sex practices, interviews with sex

Erika Moen & Matthew Nolan
Courtesy of Oni Press

industry workers, AND MORE. Volume One collects the first year's worth of content from the weekly comic Oh Joy Sex Toy. Combining helpful facts with terrible puns and the occasional Star Trek joke, Volume One is an indispensable resource for fans of sex, fans of comics, and nerds of all stripes." (Publisher's note)

   Oh Joy Sex Toy; Volume 2. by Erika Moen and Matthew Nolan. Oni Press 2016 328 p. Color; Illustration
Grades: Adult
741.5; 306.7
   1. Sex education; 2. Sex
162010363X; 9781620103630, $29.99

   This book "is a hefty 328 pages of comics by Erika Moen and Matthew Nolan. This volume collects the second year's worth of content from the weekly comic Oh Joy Sex Toy, covering all kinds of sex topics in the form of toy reviews, education pieces, interviews and more. With its positivity, terrible puns and diverse cast, Oh Joy Sex Toy is an indispensable resource for anybody exploring comics or their own sexuality." (Publisher's note)

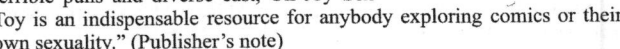

Erika Moen & Matthew Nolan
Courtesy of Oni Press

   Oh joy sex toy; Volume 3. Erika Moen and Matthew Nolan. Oni Press 2016 312 p. Color; Illustration
Grades: Adult
741.5; 306.7
   1. Sex — Comic books, strips, etc.; 2. Sex toys — Comic books, strips, etc.; 3. Sex education — Comic books, strips, etc.
1620103613; 9781620103616, $29.99

   In this third book in the Oh Joy Sex Toy series, authors Erika Moen and Matthew Nolan "review sex toys, share sex education, interview sex workers, and crack horrible, horrible puns, all in the name of promoting sex positivity.... They visit a swingers' house party, a queer porn set and cover all sorts of topics like HPV, foreskins and UTIs, in addition to the newest and oddest sex toys." (Publisher's note)

Moon, Fábio

   De: Tales: Stories from Urban Brazil. Fábio Moon, Gabriel Bá. Dark Horse Comics 2006 112p. Illustration
Grades: 10 11 12 Adult   **741.5; Fic**
   1. Graphic novels
1593074859, $14.95

   This collection of short stories features Moon and Ba, who are twins, working together, in tandem, or separately — trading off on the roles of writing and illustrating, sharing those roles or flying solo. Brimming with all the details of human life, their tales move from the urban reality of their home in Sao Paulo to the magical realism of their Latin American background. Some stories feature brief partial nudity and sexual situations and some mild harsh language.

   Two brothers. Fabio Moon, Gabriel Ba. Dark Horse Books 2015 232 p. Illustration
Grades: Adult   **741.5/981; 741.5**
   1. Brothers — Comic books, strips, etc; 2. Family secrets — Comic books, strips, etc; 3. Brazil — Comic books, strips, etc; 4. Twins — Fiction; 5. Brothers — Fiction; 6. Brazil — Fiction
1616558563; 9781616558567, $24.99

LC 2015018060
Eisner Award: Best Adaptation from Another Medium (2016)

"Twin brothers Omar and Yaqub may share the same features, but they could not be more different from one another. After a brutally violent exchange between the young boys, Yaqub, "the good son," is sent from his home in Brazil to live with relatives in Lebanon, only to return five years later as a virtual stranger to the parents who bore him, his tensions with Omar unchanged." (Publisher's note)

Moore, Alan

★ **Batman:** the killing joke: the deluxe edition. written by Alan Moore; illustrated by Brian Bolland. DC Comics 2008 un Illustration
Grades: 10 11 12 Adult   741.5; Fic
1. Batman (Fictional character); 2. Graphic novels; 3. Joker (Fictional character); 4. Superhero graphic novels; 5. Batgirl (Fictional character)
978-1-4012-1667-2, $17.99

This story was originally published in 1988, and it set Barbara Gordon on the path to become Oracle. The Joker says one bad day is all that separates the sane from the psychotic, and he sets out to prove it by driving Commissioner Jim Gordon insane by hurting his daughter Barbara. She has been Batgirl, but all her training and skills can't stop the Joker from shooting her in the spine. Then he takes Commissioner Gordon. Batman has to find the Joker and stop him. This story also reveals the origin of the Joker. This book includes violence and nonsexual partial nudity.

★ **From** Hell. Top Shelf Productions 2000 un Illustration
Grades: 11 12 Adult
741.5; Fic
1. Graphic novels; 2. Jack the Ripper murders, London (England), 1888 — Graphic novels; 3. Mystery graphic novels
0-9585783-4-6, $35

Legendary comics writer Alan Moore and artist Eddie Campbell have created a hallucinatory piece of crime fiction about Jack the Ripper. Detailing the events that led up to the Whitechapel murders and the cover-up that followed, Moore posits the theory that a Masonic conspiracy covered up the involvement of Queen Victoria's

Courtesy of IDW Publishing

grandson. He tells the story from the viewpoint of the victims, of the police investigating the case, and of the killer. The book includes graphic violence and depiction of the murder victims, harsh language, and nudity.

The **League** of Extraordinary Gentlemen: Black Dossier. DC Comics/America's Best Comics 2007 208p. Illustration
Grades: 12 Adult   **741.5**
1. Adventure graphic novels; 2. Graphic novels; 3. Spies — Graphic novels
978-1-4012-0306-1, $29.99

Britain in 1958 is not the world we knew; the country is still at war with Germany (led by Hynkel). The League of Extraordinary Gentlemen had been disbanded after the last world war, and the members of the Murray Group" were labelled impersons." But now, the ever-youthful Mina Murray and a rejuvenated Allan Quatermain return to London and retrieve the Black Dossier, a legendary volume that details all the known facts about the league, going back centuries. Government spies pursue them, including one rather smarmy young agent called Jimmie (who likes his martinis stirred not shaken), Bulldog Drummond, and others. The book includes lots of full-frontal nudity, sexual situations, foul language, and violence.

★ The **League** of Extraordinary Gentlemen volume 1. Alan Moore, Kevin O'Neill. DC Comics 2012 192 p.
Grades: Adult   **741.5; 741.5/942**
1. Historical fiction
1563898586; 9781563898587, $14.99

LC 2012027560
This book, by Alan Moore and Kevin O'Neill, "features a grand collection of signature 19th-century fictional adventurers, covertly brought together to defend the empire. The League of Extraordinary Gentlemen comprises such characters as Minna Murray (formerly Harker), from Bram Stoker's Dracula; Robert Louis Stevenson's Dr. Jekyll (and his monstrous alter ego, Mr. Hyde); and Jules Verne's Captain Nemo, restored to the dark, grim-visaged Sikh Verne originally intended." (Publisher's note)

Originally published in single magazine form as The League of Extraordinary Gentlemen Vol. 1 #1-6.; Volume 1 of 2

★ **Miracleman;** Book 1: A dream of flying. by Mick Anglo; illustrated by Garry Leach, Alan Davis, Paul Neary, and Steve Dillon. Marvel Enterprises 2014 176 p. Color illustration
Grades: Adult   **741.5**
1. Reporters and reporting — Fiction; 2. Superhero graphic novels
0785154620; 9780785154624, $29.99

"Reporter Michael Moran always knew he was meant for something more-now, an unexpected series of events leads him to reclaim his destiny as Miracleman! After nearly two decades away, Miracleman uncovers his origins and their connection to the British military's 'Project Zarathustra' — while his alter ego, Michael Moran, must reconcile his life as the lesser half of a god." (Publisher's note)

"After two decades out of print, one of the seminal works of modern comics has finally been extricated from legal snarls of incredible complexity and made available again, beautifully recolored. Pre-Swamp Thing, pre-Watchmen, this was the first story by Alan Moore (pseudonymous here) to retool an existing series in a darker, more adult fashion." LJ

Contains material originally published in magazine form as Miracleman #1-4

Nemo: Heart of Ice. by Alan Moore and Kevin O'Neill. Top Shelf Productions 2013 56 p. Illustration
Grades: Adult
Fic; 741
1. Superhero graphic novels; 2. Arctic regions — Graphic novels; 3. Adventure graphic novels
1603092749; 9781603092746, $14.95

Courtesy of IDW Publishing

This graphic novel, by Alan Moore and Kevin O'Neill, begins in "1925, fifteen years after the death of Captain Nemo, when his daughter Janni Dakkar launches a grand Antarctic expedition to lay the old man's burdensome legacy to rest. Accompanied by Nemo's shipmate Ishmael...and her father's log, Janni embarks on a perilous journey to the bottom of the world pursued by employees of an influential publishing tycoon, who seek the return of plundered loot." (Publisher's note)

Promethea Book Five. DC Comics/America's Best Comics 2005 160p. Illustration
Grades: 10 11 12 Adult   **741.5; Fic**
1. Adventure graphic novels; 2. Fantasy graphic novels; 3. Graphic novels
1-4012-0620-4, $14.99

Sophie, the new personification of the goddess Promethea, went into hiding after government agents destroyed her world. As the years have passed, Sophie has suppressed the goddess within her, but now, with the help of Tom Strong, the government is closing in on her again, and she has no choice but to release the mystic power of Promethea, thereby unleashing an apocalypse upon the world and everyone in it, both foe and friend. This is the final volume of the series. The book includes nudity, sexual situations, harsh language, and violence.

Promethea Book One. Alan Moore, writer; J.H. Williams III, penciller; Mick Gray, inker; additional art by Charles Vess. DC Comics/America's Best Comics 2001 160p. Illustration
Grades: 10 11 12 Adult   741.5; Fic
1. Adventure graphic novels; 2. Fantasy graphic novels; 3. Graphic novels
1-56389-667-2, $14.99
Sophie Bangs was a just an ordinary college student in a futuristic New York when a simple assignment changed her life forever. While researching Promethea, a mythical warrior woman, Sophie receives a cryptic warning to cease her investigations. Ignoring the cautionary notice, she continues her studies and is almost killed by a shadowy creature when she learns the secret of Promethea. Surviving the encounter, Sophie soon finds herself transformed into Promethea, the living embodiment of the imagination. Her trials have only begun as she must master the secrets of her predecessors before she is destroyed by Promethea's ancient enemy. The book includes some strong language, partial nudity, and violence.
Volume 1 of 5

★ **Saga** of the Swamp Thing; Book one. written by Alan Moore; art by Stephen Bissette ... [et al.]; colored by Tatjana Wood; lettered by John Costanza, Todd Klein. DC Comics 2012 205 p. Color illustration
Grades: Adult   741.5
1. Swamp Thing (Fictional character)
1401220835; 9781401220839, $19.99
                                          LC 2012374624
This comic book collection, by Alan Moore, "begins with the story "The Anatomy Lesson," a haunting origin story that reshapes SWAMP THING mythology with terrifying revelations that begin a journey of discovery and adventure that will take him across the stars and beyond." (Publisher's note)
Originally published in magazine form as The saga of the Swamp Thing #20-27.; Volumes 2-6 also written by Moore

Smax Collected Edition. DC Comics/America's Best Comics 2004 un Illustration
Grades: 10 11 12 Adult   741.5; Fic
1. Adventure graphic novels; 2. Graphic novels; 3. Humorous graphic novels; 4. Science fiction graphic novels
1-4012-0290-X, $12.99
Jeff Smax, a major character in Alan Moore's Top 10 series, must return to his home world after many years on Earth. Accompanied by his fellow Neopolis Precinct Ten police officer Robin Toybox Slinger, he must face a myriad of challenges ranging from cutting through mountainous red tape to go on a quest, doing battle with the most monstrous of all dragons, and adapting to a world where the laws of physics are not only unheard of, they just plain don't work. And then there's Jeff's sister...While there's little in the way of bad language and the violence is mostly against fantasy monsters, the book does include some sexual suggestiveness. And in Jeff's world, sex with one's sister is normal.

Top 10 Book Two. DC Comics/Wildstorm 2002 un Illustration
Grades: 10 11 12 Adult   741.5; Fic
1. Fantasy graphic novels; 2. Graphic novels; 3. Superhero graphic novels
1-56389-966-3, $14.95

Imagine a city where every citizen, from poorest slum-dweller to corporate honcho, has unusual powers and abilities — not to mention an alter ego and costume. How would you police such a city? Neopolis is the city of super powered citizens, and the police officers of Precinct Ten are also super powered. In this volume, they investigate the murder of an ex-sidekick rock star, deal with a murderous police commissioner who kills one of their own, and just try to get by each day. The book includes violence, nudity, and sexual situations.

Top 10: Book One. DC Comics/America's Best Comics 2000 un Illustration
Grades: 9 10 11 12 Adult   741.5; Fic
1. Graphic novels; 2. Mystery graphic novels; 3. Superhero graphic novels
1-56389-668-0, $17.95
Imagine a city where every citizen, from poorest slum-dweller to corporate honcho, has unusual powers and abilities, not to mention an alter ego and a costume. How does one police such a city? Rookie cop Robyn Singer is about to find out in her first day as part of Precinct 10 in Neopolis.

Top 10: The Forty-Niners. DC Comics/America's Best Comics 2005 un Illustration
Grades: 10 11 12 Adult   741.5; Fic
1. Graphic novels; 2. Superhero graphic novels
1-4012-0573-9, $17.99
This is the tale of Neopolis, a modern metropolis with a citizenry made up exclusively of super beings. In this city where everyone is blessed with powers, it takes a unique and powerful police force to protect and serve. The officers of Precinct 10 encounter all manner of the super powered and the supernatural on a routine basis. The TOP 10 team of writer Alan Moore and artist Gene Ha reunites for a graphic novel that delves into the past, revealing the origins of Neopolis and the first officers of Top Ten, from 1949. Discover the original Top 10 officers who blazed the trail and made Neopolis the city it is today. Some sexual situations and superhero violence occur in the book.

★ **V** for vendetta. written by Alan Moore; art by David Lloyd; coloring by David Lloyd, Steve Whitaker, Siobhan Dodds; lettering by Jenny O'Connor, Steve Craddock, Elitta Fell. DC Comics 2008 288p. Illustration
Grades: 10 11 12 Adult   741.5; Fic
1. Graphic novels; 2. Science fiction graphic novels
978-1-4012-0841-7; 1-4012-0841-X, $19.99
The book is set in an alternate world in which England has embraced fascism after a devastating war has destroyed a lot of the world; it's 1997, and a young woman named Eve tries prostitution, only to be caught by the police on her first night. A man wearing a Guy Fawkes mask saves her, and thus begins his campaign to restore human spirit by rebelling against the oppressive government. Known only as V, he uses terror tactics and murder to dismantle the government. Occasional nudity, some violence, and harsh language along with a complex plot make this a book for mature-minded readers.
?Originally published in single magazine form in the United States as V for Vendetta 1-10? Title page

★ **Watchmen**. Alan Moore, writer; Dave Gibbons, illustrator/letterer; John Higgins, colorist. DC Comics 2005 Illustration
Grades: 11 12 Adult   741.5; Fic
1. Comic books, strips, etc.; 2. Graphic novels; 3. Superhero graphic novels
1-4012-0713-8; 978-0-930289-23-2 (pa)
Hugo Award: Other Forms (1988); Eisner Award: Best Finite Series (1988); Eisner Award: Best Graphic Album (1988)
"It all begins with the paranoid delusions of a half-insane hero called Rorschach. But is Rorschach really insane or has he infact uncovered a plot

to murder super-heroes and, even worse, millions of innocent civilians? On the run from the law, Rorschach reunites with his former teammates in a desperate attempt to save the world and their lives, but what they uncover will shock them to their very core and change the face of the planet!" (Publisher's note)

"Nearly 20 years after the original publication, "Watchmen" shows an eerie prescience: the symmetry between current events and the conclusion of its story, concerning a villain who believes he can stave off real war by distracting the populace with a trumped-up one, and an act of mass murder perpetrated in the heart of New York City, is almost too fearful to bear." N Y Times Book Rev

Originally published in single magazine form as Watchmen 1-12; trade paperback edition still available; Issued in slipcase. Awards: 1988 Eisner Award for Best Finite Series, Best Graphic Album, Best Writer, Best Writer/Artist; 1988 Hugo Award for Other Forms; 2005 listed in Time Magazine's 100 Greatest English Language Novels; 2006 Eisner Award to Watchmen Absolute Edition for Best Archival Collection, Comic Books

Moore, Richard
Boneyard Volume 1. NBM 2005 96p. Illustration
Grades: 9 10 11 12 Adult   **741.5; Fic**
1. Graphic novels; 2. Humorous graphic novels; 3. Supernatural graphic novels
978-1-56163-427-9, $10.95

Michael Paris has inherited a plot in the remote town of Raven Hollow. As he arrives, he gets to find out what a doozie that is: he's inherited a cemetery that the villagers want razed. Why? It's haunted with apparently frightening creatures putting a curse on the whole town. But when Paris actually gets to meet some of the denizens of his inherited headache, it turns out they aren't all that bad (Abbey the vampire, in fact, is quite cute) and maybe the evil is not where it may seem... This book was originally published in black and white; this edition is in full color.

Boneyard Volume 2. NBM 2006 96p. Illustration
Grades: 9 10 11 12 Adult
741.5; Fic
1. Graphic novels; 2. Humorous graphic novels; 3. Supernatural graphic novels
978-1-56163-487-3, $11.95

Now that Beelzebub has been dealt a blow, it's the turn of the IRS to make Paris' life hell. But then, a certain beauteous Roxanna miraculously appears looking to solve all monetary problems. Paris resists as best he can, even putting on a monsters boxing contest to raise money, but the lures and the pressures... how strong can he stay? And as if that's not enough, Nessie the sexy gill girl (think of a female Creature from the Black Lagoon) and Abbey the vampire contend for Paris' affections. This book was originally published in black and white; this edition is in full color. The book includes some sexual innuendo.

Courtesy of NBM Publishing

Boneyard Volume 3. NBM 2008 96p. Illustration
Grades: 10 11 12 Adult
741.5; Fic
1. Graphic novels; 2. Humorous graphic novels; 3. Supernatural graphic novels
978-1-56163-515-3, $12.95

Courtesy of NBM Publishing

Glump devises a wondrous scheme to do a Monsters on the Beach special swimsuit issue to help the cash-strapped Michael Paris. Never mind that Glump is hiding a much worse scheme within the scheme. On a darker note, Roxanne shows her true powerful demonic self, resulting in a potentially deadly showdown with Abbey. With this volume, Moore kicks the sensual sexiness of the female characters up a notch. This is the color edition; the black and white edition, published in 2004, seems to be unavailable.

Boneyard Volume 4. NBM 2005 un Illustration
Grades: 10 11 12 Adult
741.5; Fic
1. Graphic novels; 2. Humorous graphic novels; 3. Supernatural graphic novels
978-1-56163-424-8, $9.95

As Abbey recovers from her showdown with the much more powerful Lilith (who had disguised herself as Roxanne), swamp girl Nessie starts taking the upper hand in her pursuit of Michael (never mind she's married to Frankenstein monster-like Brutus). Meanwhile, Glump continues his schemes to rule the world, this time launching the

Courtesy of NBM Publishing

"Doomsday Frog.DD However, everyone comes together to face a new threat: zombies sprouting up from the cemetery. And Michael discovers that not all monsters are...nice. The book includes some partial nudity and sexual situations, and violence. This is the original black and white edition.

Boneyard Volume 5. NBM 2006 un Illustration
Grades: 10 11 12 Adult   **741.5; Fic**
1. Graphic novels; 2. Humorous graphic novels; 3. Supernatural graphic novels
978-1-56163-479-8, $9.95

After dealing with the zombie mess from the previous volume, Abbey, Michael and the Boneyard gang have to confront a two-pronged threat: a huge, masked,chainsaw-wielding serial killer in a girl's summer camp and the Pumpkinhead, whose very presence puts all in the 'yard into fevered sleep. Abbey barely survives the confrontation with the chainsaw brute, now it's up to Michael to face the worst threat, with Nodoze and a baseball bat. This book includes violence and some sexual innuendo.

Moore, Terry
★ **Strangers** in Paradise Pocket Book 1. Abstract Studio 2003 360p. Illustration
Grades: 11 12 Adult   **741.5; Fic**
1. Graphic novels; 2. Mystery graphic novels
1-892597-26-8, $17.95

Katchoo is a beautiful young woman living a quiet life with everything going for her. She's smart, independent and very much in love with her best friend, Francine. Then Katchoo meets David, a gentle but persistent young man who is determined to win Katchoo's heart. The resulting love triangle is a touching comedy of romantic errors until Katchoo's former employer comes looking for her and $850,000 in missing mob money. As her idyllic life begins to fall apart, Katchoo discovers no one can be trusted and that the past she thought she left behind now threatens to destroy her and everything she loves, including Francine. This thick pocket book edition collects several of the original trade paperback volumes. The story includes strong language, sexual situations, nudity, and some violence.

★ **Strangers** in Paradise Pocket Book 2. Abstract Studio 2004 344p. Illustration
Grades: 10 11 12 Adult   **741.5; Fic**

1. Friendship — Graphic novels; 2. Graphic novels
1-892597-29-8, $17.95

The second Strangers In Paradise pocket book finds Katchoo following David to California where she comes face to face with Darcy Parker. When Darcy makes Katchoo an offer she can't refuse, Katchoo transforms from prey to predator and begins to spin a web of her own. This book features 5 pages of Jim Lee art to open the story, hero-style. Also included is the most popular Strangers in Paradise short story ever — the Xena parody, "Warrior Princess." This volume collects several of the original trade paperback collections, including Vol. 6, High School. This volume includes violence, strong language, nudity, and sexual situations.

★ **Strangers** in Paradise Pocket Book 3. Abstract Studio 2004 372p. Illustration
Grades: 10 11 12 Adult   **741.5; Fic**
1-892597-30-4, $17.95

In this third pocket book volume, Francine is stuck in a bad marriage and Katchoo is a successful artist but keeps everyone at a distance. David's mysterious past links him even closer to Katchoo, who still can't escape the Mafia life she had led with Darcy Parker. There are more friendships, breakups, makeups, and action. Readers should expect to find strong language, nudity, and sexual situations along with a little violence.

★ **Strangers** in Paradise Pocket Book 4. Abstract Studio 2005 360p. Illustration
Grades: 10 11 12 Adult   **741.5; Fic**
1. Friendship — Graphic novels; 2. Graphic novels
1-892597-31-1, $17.95

Katchoo still loves Francine, but her wild past and dangerous enemies, such as Mafia types, prove to be more than Francine can handle. Meanwhile, David wants more than friendship with Katchoo. And then Francine, on the verge of another marriage, calls it off and decides to return to Houston and see what will happen with Katchoo. This fourth pocket book volume collects three of the original trade paperback collections.

★ **Strangers** in Paradise Pocket Book 5. Abstract Studio 2005 376p. Illustration
Grades: 10 11 12 Adult   **741.5; Fic**
1. Friendship — Graphic novels; 2. Graphic novels
1-892597-38-1, $17.95

While David finds solace with Katchoo, Francine can think of nothing but her past relationship with her former best friend and brings home a tattoo to prove it. It seems that Katchoo is destined to move on without Francine into the world of glitz, glamour, and art showings with her stunning display of 100 nudes. As Katchoo becomes the toast of the town, Francine finds herself looking for peace in the Caribbean. Our unlikely friends seem to be drifting apart until they are set on a collision course back to Houston. This pocket book volume also includes the Molly & Poo stories, which are illustrated prose stories set in Victorian England. Strong language, nudity, sexual situations, and violence punctuate the stories.

★ **Strangers** in Paradise Pocket Book 6. Abstract Studio 2007 272p. Illustration
Grades: 10 11 12 Adult   **741.5; Fic**
1. Friendship — Graphic novels; 2. Graphic novels
1-892597-39-X, $17.95

Brad and Francine prepare to move to Houston, while free spirit Casey gets involved in the lives of her new roommates in Las Vegas and discovers a stalker. Back in Houston, Casey and David get Katchoo and Francine together again. Then David has to tell Casey and Katchoo his secret, a medical condition that may kill him. And in the final story, Francine leaves the cheating Brad and tries to reconnect with Katchoo, but she learns she's going to have to fight for her. This series lasted 90 issues and has ended the way Moore wanted it to. The stories include strong language, nudity, sexual situations, and violence.

Mori, Kaoru
★ A **bride's** story, v1. Kaoru Mori. Yen Press 2011 192 p. Illustration
Grades: 11 12 Adult   **741.5**
1. Arranged marriage — Comic books, strips, etc; 2. Man-woman relationships — Comic books, strips, etc; 3. Asia, Central — History — 19th century — Comic books, strips, etc; 4. Arranged marriage — Fiction; 5. Women — China; 6. Silk Road
0316180998; 9780316180993, $17

LC 2012450076

Eisner Nominee: Best U.S. Edition of International Material — Asia (2016) [for volume 7]

In this graphic novel, author "Kaoru Mori brings the nineteenth-century Silk Road to lavish life, chronicling the story of Amir Halgal, a young woman from a nomadic tribe betrothed to a twelve-year-old boy eight years her junior. Coping with cultural differences, blossoming feelings for her new husband, and expectations from both her adoptive and birth families, Amir strives to find her role as she settles into a new life and a new home in a society quick to define that role for her." (Publisher's note)

"By the end of this first volume, the plot is only beginning to bloom, but there is ample enjoyment in watching the small, everyday activities that make up the family's life — laundry, hunting, raising children. Amir's cheerfulness is infectious, both to her new family and to readers." Booklist

Volume 1 of an ongoing series

Emma 1. Kaori Mori; translation, Sheldon Drzka; lettering, Abigail Blackman. Yen Press 2015 386 p. Illustration
Grades: 10 11 12 Adult   **741.5**
1. Great Britain — History — Victoria, 1837-1901 — Fiction; 2. Shojo manga; 3. Household employees — Graphic novels
0316302236; 9780316302234, $35

In this manga by Kaoru Mori, translated by Sheldon Drzka, "calling upon his former governess, William Jones, gentleman, is startled when his knock is answered by an uncommonly beautiful servant, the soft-spoken Emma. Throughout his visit, William's eyes drift to the maid whenever she enters the room, and he contrives to meet Emma socially as she goes about her errands. But London society is a web of strict codes and divisions." (Publisher's note)

Originally published in Japan; Previously published in the U.S. by CMX in 10 volumes; Volume 1 of 4

Emma, Vol. 3. DC Comics/CMX 2007 188p. Illustration
Grades: 9 10 11 12 Adult   **741.5**
1. Graphic novels; 2. Household employees — Graphic novels; 3. Manga; 4. Romance graphic novels; 5. Shojo manga
978-1-4012-1134-9, $9.99

In 1885 England, Emma works as a maid for a widow; she meets William, son of a wealthy merchant. Since they each belong to a different social class, they shouldn't fall in love, but they do. In this third volume, Emma's employer has died and Emma leaves, while William throws himself into the family business. On the train, Emma meets a maid who works in a fairly large household that needs another maid, and she decides to apply there. The family, immigrants from Germany, insists on formality; Emma feels a bit lost but works well and makes a good impression. Warnings on the book tell of suggestive situations, but there has been nothing objectionable in the first four volumes.

Emma, vol. 8. DC Comics/CMX 2009 208p. Illustration
Grades: 10 11 12 Adult   **741.5; Fic**
1. Graphic novels; 2. Manga; 3. Great Britain — History — 19th century — Graphic novels
978-1-4012-2070-9, $9.99

This eighth volume collects short stories focusing on some of the supporting characters who have appeared throughout the course of the seven-volume series. One story features a young Kelly Stowner and her husband Doug, who struggle to save up the two shillings needed for them to visit the Great Exhibition. Eleanor Campbell, whose engagement to William Jones has just ended, spends a vacation at Brighton trying to get over his rejection of her, and meets a surprising young man. One story is a series of vignettes of different characters reading the newspaper. And klutzy housemaid Natasha returns home for a visit. One of the story vignettes features a conversation between an older gentleman and his mistress, who is nude throughout the story.

Morinaga, Ai
My Heavenly Hockey Club Vol. 1. Ballantine Books/Del Rey Manga 2007 212p. Illustration
Grades: 8 9 10 11 12 Adult   **741.5; Fic**
1. Graphic novels; 2. Hockey — Graphic novels; 3. Humorous graphic novels; 4. Manga; 5. Shojo manga
978-0-345-49904-2, $10.95
Hana Suzuki loves only two things in life: eating and sleeping. So when handsome classmate Izumi Oda asks Hana, his major crush, to join the school hockey club, persuading her proves to be a difficult task. True, the Grand Hockey Club is full of boys, and all the boys are super-cute, but given a choice, Hana prefers a sizzling steak to a hot date. Then Izumi mentions the field trips to fancy resorts. Now Hana can't wait for the first away game, with its promise of delicious food and luxurious linens. Of course there's also the getting up early, working hard, and playing well with others. How will Hana survive?

Morrison, Grant
All-Star Superman, Volume One. written by Grant Morrison; pencilled by Frank Quitely. DC Comics 2007 160p. Illustration
Grades: 8 9 10 11 12 Adult   **741.5; Fic**
1. Graphic novels; 2. Superhero graphic novels; 3. Superman (Fictional character)
978-1-4012-0914-8; 978-1-4012-1102-8 (pa), $12.99
Eisner Award: Best New Series (2006)
Writer Morrison and artist Quitely present several episodes in the life of the iconic superhero, Superman. When he saves a group of scientists from burning up in the sun, what no one realizes is that uber-villain Lex Luthor set up everything in order to kill Superman, who absorbed so much solar radiation that it is now slowly killing him. Once Superman learns that he is dying, he sets out to give Lois Lane a birthday she will never forget, by giving her his powers for one day. Then, when Jimmy Olsen takes charge of the science think tank P.R.O.J.E.C.T. for one day, they discover black kryptonite, which makes Superman turn evil. And, in his guise as Clark Kent, he interviews Lex Luthor in prison, but super-villain Parasite is taken from his shielded cell and begins to absorb Superman's powers, causing chaos.
Also available as a single volume collecting all 12 issues; Originally published as All-Star Superman issues #1-6; Volume 1 of 2

Batman and son. Grant Morrison, writer; Andy Kubert, penciller; Jesse Delperdang, inker; Guy Major, Dave Stewart, colorists; Jared K. Fletcher, Rob Leigh, Nick J. Napolitano, letterers. DC Comics 2007 200p. Illustration
Grades: 9 10 11 12 Adult   **741.5; Fic**
1. Batman (Fictional character); 2. Graphic novels; 3. Superhero graphic novels; 4. Joker (Fictional character)
978-1-4012-1240-7, $24.99
Talia, daughter of archvillain Ra's al Ghul and Batman's onetime love, returns with a teenage boy she claims is Batman's son. She leaves Damian with Batman, but while the boy has Batman's skills, he was raised among the League of Assassins and doesn't share his father's morals. Soon, both Tim Drake, Bruce Wayne's newly adopted heir, and the faithful Alfred,

become Damian's targets. The book also includes an interlude about the Joker, and a story set in the future, when Damian becomes Batman. The book includes some gory violence.

★ **Batman:** Arkham Asylum: A Serious House on Serious Earth. written by Grant Morrison; illustrated by Dave McKean; lettered by Gaspar Saladino; Batman created by Bob Kane. DC Comics 2004 un Illustration
Grades: 11 12 Adult   **741.5; Fic**
1. Batman (Fictional character); 2. Graphic novels; 3. Horror graphic novels; 4. Superhero graphic novels; 5. Joker (Fictional character)
1-4012-0425-2, $17.99
LC 2006-276659
In this painted graphic novel, the inmates of Arkham Asylum have taken over Gotham's detention center for the criminally insane on April Fools Day, demanding Batman in exchange for their hostages. Accepting their challenge, Batman is forced to live and endure the personal hells of the Joker, Scarecrow, Poison Ivy, Two-Face and many other sworn enemies in order to save the innocents and retake the prison. During his run through this gauntlet, the Dark Knight's own sanity is placed in jeopardy. This edition also reproduces the original script with annotations by Morrison and editor Karen Berger. The book includes violence and some disturbing images.

★ **Doom** Patrol; Volume 1: Crawling from the Wreckage. written by Grant Morrison; pencillers, Richard Case, Doug Braithwaite; inkers, Scott Hanna, Carlos Garzon, John Nyberg; colorists, Daniel Vozza and Michele Wolfman; letterer, John Workman. DC Comics 2004 190 p. Color; Illustration
Grades: 10 11 12 Adult   **741.5; Fic**
1. Superhero comic books, strips, etc.
9781563890345, $19.99; 1563890348
"The new Doom Patrol puts itself back together after nearly being destroyed, and things start to get a lot weirder for everybody. The Chief leads Robotman, the recently formed Rebis and new member Crazy Jane against the Scissormen, part of a dangerous philosophical location that has escaped into our world and is threatening to engulf reality itself." (Publisher's note)
Other Doom Patrol volumes by Morrison are: 2, The Painting That Ate Paris; 3, Down Paradise Way; 4, Musclebound; 5, Magic Bus; 6, Planet Love

★ **Flex** Mentallo: man of muscle mystery. Grant Morrison, writer; Frank Quitely, artist; Peter Doherty, colorist; Ellie de Ville, letterer. Vertigo/DC Comics 2012 1 v. (unpaged) Color illustration
Grades: Adult   **Fic; 741.5; 741.5/9411**
1. Superheroes — Comic books, strips, etc; 2. Comic books, strips, etc.; 3. Musicians; 4. Mystery fiction
1401232213; 9781401232214, $22.99
LC 2012374596
Author Grant Morrison tells the story of Flex Mentallo, the "Hero of the Beach...and of the Doom Patrol. Now Flex Mentallo, the Man of Muscle Mystery, returns to investigate the sinister dealings of his former comrade, The Fact, and a mysterious rock star whose connection to Flex may hold the key to saving them both.... [The book is] an early collaboration between writer Grant Morrison and artist Frank Quitely." (Publisher's note)
Originally published in single magazine form as Flex Mentallo 1-4.

Joe the Barbarian. by Grant Morrison and illustrated by Sean Murphy. Vertigo 2013 224 p.
Grades: 10 11 12 Adult   **741.5**
1. Graphic novels; 2. Hallucinations and illusions — Fiction; 3. Diabetes — Fiction
1401237479; 9781401237479, $19.99

LC 2012047802

In this graphic novel by Grant Morrison "Joe is an imaginative young kid of 11 who happens to suffer from type 1 diabetes. Without supervision and insulin, he can easily slip into a delirious, disassociative state that presages coma and death. One fateful day, his condition causes him to believe he has entered a vivid fantasy world in which he is the lost savior — a fantastic land based on the layout and contents of his home." (Publisher's note)

Originally published in a single magazine form in Joe the Barbarian 1-8.

Kid Eternity. DC Comics/Vertigo 2006 un Illustration
Grades: 10 11 12 Adult   **741.5; Fic**
1. Fantasy graphic novels; 2. Graphic novels; 3. Horror graphic novels
1-4012-0933-5, $14.99

Comics visionary Grant Morrison re-imagines the character of Kid Eternity, a young man who died before his true time and returns to Earth as a ghostly spirit, along with his guardian Mister Keeper. This book follows the terrifying night of aspiring stand-up comedian Jerry Sullivan as he joins Kid Eternity, who just escaped from Hell, on a quest back there to free Mister Keeper. Then the Kid learns he's been used as a pawn in the struggle between Order and Chaos. The book includes considerable violence and harsh language (f-bombs and s-bombs included).

The **Multiversity** deluxe edition. Grant Morrison, Frank Quitely, Ivan Reis. DC Comics 2015 448 p. Color; Illustration
Grades: 9 10 11 12 Adult   **741.5/973**
1. Superhero comic books, strips, etc.
1401256821; 9781401256821, $49.99

LC 2015014166

This comic book, by Grant Morrison, presents "a cast of unforgettable heroes from 52 alternative Earths of the DC Multiverse! Prepare to meet the Vampire League of Earth-43, the Justice Riders of Earth-18, Superdemon, Doc Fate, the super-sons of Superman and Batman, the rampaging Retaliators of Earth-8, the Atomic Knights of Justice, Dino-Cop, Sister Miracle, Lady Quark and the latest, greatest Super Hero of Earth-Prime: YOU!" (Publisher's note)

Supergods: what masked vigilantes, miraculous mutants, and a sun god from Smallville can teach us about being human. Spiegel & Grau 2011 444p. Illustration
Grades: 11 12 Adult   **741.5**
1. Comic books, strips, etc.; 2. Comic books, strips, etc. — United States; 3. Heroes; 4. Superheroes; 5. Wolverine (Fictional character); 6. Superman (Fictional character)
1-4000-6912-2; 978-1-4000-6912-5

LC 2010053712

A graphic novelist presents a history of the superhero in American comic books and movies. Index.

Includes bibliographical references

Superman - Action Comics; Volume 1. Grant Morrison, Rags Morales, Andy Kubert. DC Comics 2012 256 p.
Grades: 7 8 9 10 11 12 Adult   **Fic; 741.5/9411**
1. Superhero comic books, strips, etc.; 2. Adventure fiction; 3. Superman (Fictional character)
1401235468; 9781401235468, $24.99

LC 2012010313

This comic book anthology, by Grant Morrison, illustrated by Rags Morales, presents volume one of "The New 52" re-launch of the DC Comics Superman series. This collection includes the first eight issues of

the series, depicting "humanity's first encounters with Superman, before he became one of the world's greatest super heroes." (Publisher's note)

Originally published in single magazine form in ACTION COMICS 1-8 — T.p. verso.

WE 3. DC Comics/Vertigo 2005 un Illustration
Grades: 10 11 12 Adult   **741.5; Fic**
1. Animal experimentation — Graphic novels; 2. Graphic novels; 3. Science fiction graphic novels
1-4012-0495-3, $12.99

2005 Eisner Award for Best Artist for Frank Quitely; this series was cited.

A top-secret research facility has taken a dog, a cat, and a rabbit and used cybernetics to transform the pets into armored smart weapons. The WE 3 are very successful; their enhanced intelligence allows them to communicate verbally with each other and adapt to any situation to carry out their mission. However, they're only prototypes, and when the project scientists advance to the next stage, the WE 3 are to be terminated. What the scientists and military brass haven't counted on is that their smart weapons possess enough reasoning to escape. Now Bandit the dog, Tinker the cat, and Pirate the rabbit are loose, and they want to find "Home." And they're ready to kill to find it.

Originally published as WE 3 issues #1-3.

Wonder Woman, earth one; Volume 1. written by Grant Morrison; art by Yanick Paquette; colors by Nathan Fairbairn; letters by Todd Klein. DC Comics 2016 144 p. Color; Illustration
Grades: 11 12 Adult   **741.5; Fic**
1. Female superhero graphic novels; 2. Superhero graphic novels; 3. Wonder Woman (Fictional character)
1401229786; 9781401229788, $22.99

LC 2016006066

This comic book, written by Grant Morrison, with art by Yanick Paquette, presents the "origin of Wonder Woman.... For millennia, the Amazons of Paradise Island have created a thriving society away from the blight of man. One resident, however, is not satisfied with this secluded life-Diana, Princess of the Amazons, knows there is more in this world and wants to explore, only to be frustrated by her protective mother, Hippolyta." (Publisher's note)

"Both novices and the initiated will find great fun in this flawlessly streamlined remolding, and, in his inimitable style, Morrison offers a fiercer, stranger, more epic, more textured, and, incidentally, more diverse interpretation." Booklist

Mulligan, Brennan Lee

★ **Strong** Female Protagonist; Book one. Brennan Lee Mulligan and Molly Ostertag. Top Shelf Productions 2014 220 p. Illustration
Grades: 11 12 Adult
741.5
1. College students — Fiction; 2. Superheroes — Fiction
0692246185; 9780692246184, $19.95

Courtesy of IDW Publishing

"Alison Green, aka Mega Girl, lives in a dark world fraught with difficult relationships. She is a biodynamic, who, along with other young people who possess special capabilities, rejects her role as a superhero and attempts to revert to the life of a 'normal' college freshman. However,...she encounters situations that test her resolve to no longer use her powers." (School Library Journal)

Originally appeared as a webcomic

Murphy, Sean Gordon
Punk Rock Jesus. Sean Murphy. DC Comics 2013 224 p.
Grades: Adult   **745.1; 741.5/973**
  1. Reality television programs — Fiction; 2. Cloning — Fiction
1401237681; 9781401237684, $16.99
                                        LC 2012048551
  In this graphic novel by Sean Murphy "A reality TV show starring a
clone of Jesus Christ causes chaos across the U.S. of the near future. When
falling ratings force the network to cut Jesus's mother from the series the
young star runs away, renounces his religious heritage and forms a punk
rock band. Jesus goes to war against the corporate media complex that
created him." (Publisher's note)
  Originally published in single magazine form in Punk Rock Jesus 1-6.

Nagata, Kabi
  ★ **My** lesbian experience with loneliness. by Kabi Nagata. Seven Seas
Entertainment 2017 152 p. Illustration
Grades: Adult   **741.5; 92**
  1. Autobiographical graphic novels; 2. Lesbians; 3. Lesbianism
1626926034; 9781626926035, $13.99
  This book, by Kabi Nagata, "is an honest and heartfelt look at one
young woman's exploration of her sexuality, mental well-being, and
growing up in our modern age. Told using expressive artwork that invokes
both laughter and tears, this moving and highly entertaining single volume
depicts not only the artist's burgeoning sexuality, but many other personal
aspects of her life that will resonate with readers." (Publisher's note)
  "Nagata draws cute characters in simple, spindly lines tinted with
dollops of pink, making even the lumpiest of her warts-and-all confessions
look adorable. Her strength is in her writing, which mixes shockingly blunt
honesty with humor and small, imaginative observations." Pub Wkly
  Originally published in Japan in 2016 by EAST PRESS, Tokyo

  My solo exchange diary; 1. (true) story & art by Nagata Kabi;
translation, Jocelyne Allen; adaptation, Lianne Sentar. Seven Seas
Entertainment 2018 168 p. Illustration
Grades: Adult   **741.5; 92**
  1. Loneliness; 2. Single women; 3. Lesbians — Sexual behavior
1626928894; 9781626928893, $14.99
  "In this vulnerable autobiographical follow-up to Kabi's surprise-hit
debut manga, My Lesbian Experience with Loneliness, Kabi writes to her
past self: 'Dear Nagata Kabi, hello. This is Nagata Kabi.' She updates
herself on new events, shares deep and not-so-deep thoughts, and
frequently panics over her messy life. Compared to the previous manga,
this sequel is looser, with less of the driving, neurotic urgency that
distinguished Loneliness. Kabi is still struggling to understand sex and
love, still dominated by her disapproving parents, still awkwardly learning
how to be an adult-but circumstances are slowly becoming less dire."
(Publishers Weekly)

Naifeh, Ted
  Courtney Crumrin and the fire thief's
tale. Oni Press 2007 62p. Illustration
Grades: 7 8 9 10 11 12 Adult
741.5; Fic
  1. Fantasy graphic novels; 2. Graphic
novels; 3. Horror graphic novels; 4.
Werewolves — Graphic novels
978-1-932664-85-0, $5.95
  Courtney travels with Uncle Aloysius to
Romania, where they stay with Alexi
Markovic, an old friend of Uncle Aloysius.
Things aren't quite right there, though; the
townspeople hunt wolves at night unnatural

Courtesy of Oni Press

wolves, werewolves. Markovic's daughter has fallen in love with a
Romany man even though her father has arranged her betrothal to an
influential man in town. Courtney gets involved against Uncle Aloysius'
wishes, and learns more than she wanted about werewolf origins and
thwarted love.

Nakajo, Hisaya
  ★ **Hana-Kimi:** For You in Full Bloom Volume 1. Viz Media/Shojo
2004 184p. Illustration
Grades: 10 11 12 Adult   **741.5; Fic**
  1. Graphic novels; 2. Humorous graphic novels; 3. Manga; 4. Romance
graphic novels; 5. Shojo manga
1-59116-329-3, $9.95
  Japanese-American track-and-field star Mizuki has transferred to a
high school in Japan...but not just any school. To be close to her idol, high
jumper Izumi Sano, she's going to an all-guys' high school...and disguising
herself as a boy. But as fate would have it, they're more than
classmates...they're roommates. Now, Mizuki must keep her secret in the
classroom, the locker room, and her own bedroom. And her classmates —
and the school nurse — must cope with a new transfer student who may
make them question their own orientation... The book includes some strong
language, brief nudity, and sexual situations.

Nakazawa, Keiji
  ★ **Barefoot** Gen: Hadashi no Gen : a cartoon story of Hiroshima. by
Keiji Nakazawa; translated by Project Gen. New Society Publishers 1987
284 p. Illustration
Grades: 10 11 12 Adult   **741.5; 741.5/952**
  1. Hiroshima-shi (Japan) — History — Bombardment, 1945 — Comic
books, strips, etc; 2. Hiroshima (Japan) — Bombardment, 1945
0865710945; 0865710953; 0867196025; 9780867196023, $14.95
                                        LC 88187202
  This book, by Keiji Nakazawa, is "an all-new translation of the
author's first-person experiences of Hiroshima and its aftermath. [It] is a
reminder of the suffering war brings to innocent people.... Volume one of
this ten-part series details the events leading up to and immediately
following the atomic bombing of Hiroshima." (Publisher's note)
  Volume 1 of 10

Neufeld, Josh
  A.D.: New Orleans after the deluge. Pantheon Books 2009 193p.
Illustration
Grades: Adult   **741.5; 976.3**
  1. Hurricane Katrina, 2005 — Graphic novels; 2. New Orleans (La.) —
Graphic novels
978-0-307-37814-9, $24.95; 0-307-37814-4
  "Graphic artist Neufeld paints an emotive portrait of New Orleans
during and after Hurricane Katrina, as seen through the eyes of seven of the
city's citizens. The opening panels coalesce into a long cinematic pan, a
thrumming setup for the disaster. The half-page and quarter-page
panels—satellite views of weather patterns and close inspections of
neighborhoods—are crisp, and the two-page spreads are softly focused....
Neufeld's words and images are commensurable and rhythmic, and the
vernacular is sharp. Bristling with attitude and pungent with social
awareness." Kirkus
                                        LC 2008-55687

Newlevant, Hazel
  Chainmail Bikini: The Anthology of Women Gamers. edited by
Hazel Newlevant. Alternative Comics 2016 204 p. Illustration
Grades: 9 10 11 12 Adult   **741.5**

1. Games; 2. Women — Recreation; 3. Anthologies; 4. Comic books, strips, etc.

1513600125; 9781513600123, $20

This anthology, edited by Hazel Newlevant, with a cover illustration by Hellen Jo and comics by Annie Mok, Jane Mai, Molly Ostertag, MK Reed, and Sophie Yanow, "explore[s] the real-life impact of entering a fantasy world, and how games can connect us with each other and teach us about ourselves.... [It] shows that while women are not always the target market for gaming, they are a vital and thoroughly engaged part of it." (Publisher's note)

'A cavalcade of talent tackles the intersection of gaming and womanhood in this heartfelt anthology of short, largely autobiographical comics. With pieces on the Sims, Darkstalkers, and live-action roleplaying, no corner of gaming (video or otherwise) is left unexplored — and no aspect of gender, either." Pub Wkly

★ **Comics** for choice: illustrated abortion stories, history, and politics. edited by Hazel Newlevant and Whit Taylor. Alternative Comics 2018 300 p. Illustration

Grades: Adult   363.4; 741.5

1. Reproduction; 2. Abortion

1681485982; 9781681485980, $25

This book, edited by Hazel Newlevant and Whit Taylor, "is anthology of comics about abortion. As this fundamental reproductive right continues to be stigmatized and jeopardized, over sixty artists and writers have created comics that boldly share their own experiences, and educate readers on the history of abortion, current political struggles, activism, and more." (Publisher's note)

"Abortion is addressed as a political flash point, a personal journey, and a cultural battleground in this powerful anthology. Its diverse nonfiction comics pieces range from the triumphant to the traumatic, and editors Newlevant (No Ivy League) and Taylor (Ghost Stories) ensure no story is dismissed as unworthy." Pub Wkly

Nicholson, Hope

★ **MOONSHOT:** The Indigenous Comics Collection. edited by Hope Nicholson. Alternate History Comics Inc 2015 176 p. Illustration

Grades: 6 7 8 9 10 11 12 Adult   741.5

1. American literature — Native American authors; 2. Graphic novels

0987715259; 9780987715258, $17.99

This comic anthology, edited by Hope Nicholson, "from traditional stories to exciting new visions of the future,...presents some of the finest comic book and graphic novel work in North America. The traditional stories presented in the book are with the permission from the elders in their respective communities, making this a truly genuine, never-before-seen publication." (Publisher's note)

"This collection of folklore from a powerhouse team of Native authors, including Buffy Sainte-Marie and Richard Van Camp, will wow readers with traditional and futuristic tales based on tribal-specific cultural teachings.... The full-page illustrations in some selections and the bright colors in others add depth and understanding to the narratives. The artwork is as diverse as the stories collected." SLJ

Nicieza, Fabian

Civil War: Thunderbolts. Marvel Entertainment 2007 un Illustration

Grades: 9 10 11 12 Adult   741.5; Fic

1. Graphic novels; 2. Superhero graphic novels

0-7851-1947-7, $13.99

The Super Human Registration Act has been signed into law, sides are being chosen, but what side do the former villains called the Thunderbolts fall on? Well, their identities are already public knowledge, and they sure can get good publicity by hunting down renegade heroes, so...it's time for the Thunderbolts to, err, kick some spandex butt. Except, they also wear spandex, so ...

Civil War: X-Men Universe. Peter David, Fabian Nicieza; artists, Dennis Carlo, Barry Windsor-Smith. Marvel Entertainment 2007 un Illustration

Grades: 9 10 11 12 Adult   741.5; Fic

1. Deadpool (Fictional character); 2. Graphic novels; 3. Superhero graphic novels; 4. X-Men (Fictional characters)

978-0-7851-2243-2, $13.99

The divisiveness of Civil War has spread to X-Factor: half of them want to cooperate with the government; the other half wants to take a stand against it. Quicksilver's return to the team may well decide whether X-Factor stays together or cracks apart. Plus: Cable and Deadpool find themselves on opposite sides of the fence, and both refuse to budge. It's going to lead to a fight, but this one may change both their lives.

Deadpool & Cable. written by Fabian Nicieza, Dan Slott, Reilly Brown; pencilled by Reilly Brown, Mark Brooks, Patrick Zircher, Lan Medina, Ron Lim, Staz Johnson. Marvel Enterprises 2014 1272 p. Color; Illustration

Grades: 10 11 12 Adult   741.5; Fic

1. Deadpool (Fictional character); 2. Superhero graphic novels; 3. Cable (Fictional character)

9780785192763, $125; 078519276X

This collects issues 1-50 of the comic book series of the same name. "Wade Wilson is Deadpool, the mentally disturbed merc with a mouth and a healing factor that just won't quit! Nathan Summers is Cable, the messianic mutant from the future who plans to save us all — whether we want him to or not!" (Publisher's note)

Contains material originally published in magazine form as Cable & Deadpool #1-50, Deadpool/GLI summer fun spectacular and Deadpool #27

Niffenegger, Audrey

Raven girl. Audrey Niffenegger. Abrams Comicarts 2013 80 p.

Grades: Adult   398.2; Fic

1. Fairy tales; 2. Raven (Legendary character)

1419707264; 9781419707261, $19.95

LC 2012039266

In this illustrated fairy tale, by Audrey Niffenegger, "a postman...encounters a fledgling raven while on the edge of his route and decides to bring her home. The unlikely couple falls in love and conceives a child — an extraordinary raven girl trapped in a human body. The raven girl feels imprisoned by her arms and legs and covets wings.... She reluctantly grows into a young woman, until one day she meets an unorthodox doctor who is willing to change her." (Publisher's note)

Nightow, Yasuhiro

★ **Trigun** Maximum Volume 1: The Hero Returns. Dark Horse Comics 2004 192p. Illustration

Grades: 10 11 12 Adult   741.5; Fic

1. Adventure graphic novels; 2. Graphic novels; 3. Manga; 4. Science fiction graphic novels; 5. Seinen manga

1-59307-196-5, $9.95

Vash the Stampede disappeared for two years after blasting a crater onto the moon orbiting the desert planet he saved from annihilation. But, with good and bad people alike trying to track him down he won't stay lost for long. He teams up again with Wolfwood, and learns of a new villain named Knives. As with the original manga series, humor combines with lots of fighting action; this time there's more violence, and some nudity and harsh language.

★ **Trigun** Volume 1. Dark Horse Comics 2003 360p. Illustration

Grades: 9 10 11 12 Adult   **741.5; Fic**
  1. Adventure graphic novels; 2. Graphic novels; 3. Manga; 4. Science fiction graphic novels; 5. Shonen manga
1-59307-052-7, $14.95

Somehow, the past has placed a sixty billion double dollar bounty on Vash's head and the gunslinging pacifist can't seem to get away from money grubbing, itchy-trigger-finger citizenry. Find out why Vash is worth so much money dead. Feel the clumsy worry of the unfortunate citizens of the pulverous planet. Follow the follies of an unlikely hero in a forbidding world. Join Vash the Stampede " with his troubled past and uncanny ability to dodge a gazillion bullets " and a cavalcade of unlucky characters on a dusty, desert planet in the distant future. This series combines Old West action with high-tech weaponry and some crazy humor as bounty hunters and a couple of insurance investigators hunt for Vash. The series includes some harsh language, violence, partial nudity, and brief mild sexual innuendo.

Niles, Steve

30 Days of Night. IDW Publishing 2003 104p. Illustration
Grades: 10 11 12 Adult
741.5; Fic
  1. Graphic novels; 2. Horror graphic novels; 3. Vampires — Graphic novels
0-9719775-5-0, $17.99

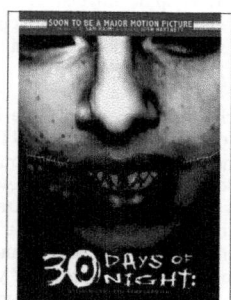

The long night of winter is coming to Barrow, Alaska; it's normal, and the people living in this isolated town don't mind. However, this particular winter, a band of vampires has decided to come up to Barrow for the month-long night and play. Sheriff Eben Olemaun and his deputy, wife Stella, and the people of Barrow have no idea of the

Courtesy of IDW Publishing

terror and death they face when vampires can roam freely all night, all thirty days of it.

This is pure, raw horror with monstrous vampires; these are not the romantic, sexy vampires of so many supernatural romances, but nasty, ugly, blood-sucking monsters. Templesmith's art and the technique of setting his panels on black pages adds a claustrophobic element that adds to the horror.

30 Days of Night: Dark Days. IDW Publishing 2004 144p. Illustration
Grades: 10 11 12 Adult
741.5; Fic
  1. Graphic novels; 2. Horror graphic novels; 3. Vampires — Graphic novels
1-932382-16-X, $19.99

In this sequel, the action shifts from Barrow, Alaska to Los Angeles, as Stella Olemaun, her life forever altered by the vampires' assault and her husband's death, rededicates herself to wiping out vampires and alerting the world to their shadowed existence. Along the way, she meets new allies and new foes — lots and lots of

Courtesy of IDW Publishing

enemies. The book includes lots of graphic violence and harsh language.

30 Days of Night: Return to Barrow. IDW Publishing 2004 144p. Illustration
Grades: 11 12 Adult
741.5; Fic
  1. Graphic novels; 2. Horror graphic novels; 3. Vampires — Graphic novels
1-932382-36-4, $19.99

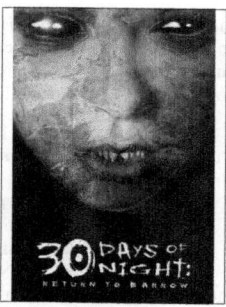

Courtesy of IDW Publishing

Three years before, vampires came to Barrow, Alaska at the beginning of the long winter night and slaughtered most of the town's inhabitants. Sheriff Olemaun died saving the town and his deputy wife died fighting vampires elsewhere. Now a new sheriff has come to town four days before the winter night, and the vampires are returning to destroy Barrow for good. Monstrous, evil creatures who slaughter viciously with lots of bloodshed combine with Templesmith's art that promotes a claustrophobic feeling of terror in this sequel to 30 Days of Night.

Originally published as 30 Days of Night: Return to Barrow issues #1-6.

Freaks of the Heartland. Dark Horse Comics 2005 un Illustration
Grades: 10 11 12 Adult
741.5; Fic
  1. Fantasy graphic novels; 2. Graphic novels; 3. Horror graphic novels
1-59307-029-2, $17.95

Some folks would call Trevor's brother a monster. But to Trevor, Will is just another kid trapped in a dark reality he can't comprehend. When the situation moves from bad to worse, and their father threatens to do away with Will, Trevor learns that they're not alone — that "freak" children were born to other families in Gristlewood Valley. And just as they were all born at the same time, it seems their sad, frustrated, and emotionally spent parents seem to be hatching a plan to see that they disappear at the same time. Against all odds, and with nothing but love for his brother in his heart, Trevor is going to do whatever he can to get Will, and the other freak children, out of harm's way, if it's not already too late. The book includes fairly graphic violence and harsh language.

Nilsen, Anders

  ★ **Big** questions, or, Asomatognosia. Anders Brekhus Nilsen.. Farrar, Straus and Giroux 2011 658p. Illustration
Grades: Adult
741.5
  1. Philosophy; 2. Fables; 3. Graphic novels
9781770460447; 9781770460478; 1770460470

LC 2011488182

Ignatz Award: Outstanding Graphic Novel (2012)

This book is a collection of philosophical comic strips which "is the culmination of ten years and over 600 pages of work that details the metaphysical quandaries of the occupants of an endless plain, existing somewhere between a dream and a Russian steppe. A downed plane is thought to be a bird and the unexploded bomb that came from it is mistaken for a giant egg by the group of birds whose lives the story follows. The indifferent and stranded pilot is of great interest to the birds- some doggedly seek his approval, while others do quite the opposite, leading to tensions in the group.... [The book] has roots in classic fable- the story's birds and snakes have more to say than their human counterparts and there are hints of the classic hero's journey, but the...moral that closes most fables is left here as open and ambiguous." (Publisher's note)

Dogs & Water. Drawn & Quarterly 2007 96p. Illustration
Grades: 10 11 12 Adult
741.5
  1. Graphic novels
978-1-897299-08-1

A young man wandering a nameless path has only a stuffed bear as a companion, which inertly endures his desperation, anger, and musings along the way. The landscape is cold and bleak with few landmarks, and offers only precarious encounters with animals and armed men. These interactions are rife with instinct, the drive for survival, and human ethics concerning the killed and injured. He finds acceptance with a pack of dogs, though their nature is wild and their potential threat is as unsettling as the sudden presence of a massive pipeline on the horizon. The road disappears and only blind circumstance remains. All is uncertain and all can be lost, but he continues on regardless. This is for the thoughtful reader who doesn't mind a little bit of harsh language and some violence.

★ **Don't** Go Where I Can't Follow. by Anders Nilsen. Drawn & Quarterly 2012 90 p. Illustration; Color
Grades: Adult   741.5
1. Terminally ill; 2. Interpersonal relations
1770460918; 9781770460911, $19.95
Ignatz Award: Outstanding Graphic Novel (2007)

This book by Anders Nilsen is an "appreciation of the time the author shared with his fiancée, Cheryl Weaver. The story is told using artifacts of the couple's life together, including early love notes, simple and poetic postcards, tales of their travels in written and comics form, journal entries, and drawings done in the hospital in her final days. It concludes with a beautifully rendered account of Weaver's memorial." (Publisher's note)

Ninomiya, Tomoko
★ **Nodame** Cantabile, Vol. 1. Ballantine Books/Del Rey Manga 2005 188p. Illustration
Grades: 10 11 12 Adult   741.5; Fic
1. Graphic novels; 2. Manga; 3. Music — Graphic novels; 4. Romance graphic novels; 5. Shojo manga
0-345-48172-0, $10.95
2004 Kodansha Manga Award for Shojo Manga.

Music student Shinichi Chiaki dreams of becoming a conductor, but his fear of flying and arrogant attitude hold him back. Then he meets Megumi Noda, who has a natural talent for piano, but she can't read a music score, she's a slovenly mess, and her apartment is a disaster area. Shinichi starts working with her, and Megumi falls for him. Romantic complications, new friendships, and music ensue. There are some mild sex scenes.

Nishino, Jyutaroh
Steel fist Riku vol. 1. Jyutaroh Nishino; [Sheldon Drzka, translation and adaptation]. DC Comics/CMX 2008 162p. Illustration
Grades: 9 10 11 12 Adult   741.5; Fic
1. Graphic novels; 2. Humorous graphic novels; 3. Manga; 4. Martial arts — Graphic novels; 5. Shonen manga
978-1-4012-1752-5, $9.99

Teenage Riku lives with Rocky, her gruff, adopted dad ("Call me Sensei!" he roars when she calls him Pops), who trained her in martial arts. In their world, semi-humans are common, such as a Pig Man, or the fact that Riku has a fist of steel. Rocky now runs a shop selling celebrity photos, but he used to be a professional martial artist. When the daughter of his old master ventures into the shop, Rocky kidnaps her in order to demand a rematch, 20 years after the fact, with his old rival Utsugizaki. This doesn't sit well with Riku, and she decides to take matters into her own hands. The book includes some raunchy humor and fan service (Riku's powers become even stronger when her breasts are unbound); Rocky is obsessed with women's breasts and suffers many nosebleeds (manga symbol for sexual arousal) while watching his DVDs, and characters declare that they're pissed off or that someone is a pain in the butt.

Nolen-Weathington, Eric
Modern Masters volume twenty-five: Jeff Smith. Twomorrows Publishing 2011 117p. Illustration
Grades: 6 7 8 9 10 11 12 Adult   741.5
1. Artists; 2. Authors; 3. Cartoonists; 4. Comic books, strips, etc. — History and criticism; 5. Graphic novels — History and criticism; 6. Smith, Jeff
978-1-60549-024-3, $15.95

This volume in the Modern Masters series focuses on Jeff Smith, creator of Bone. In an interview that covers his childhood, college career, and early work before becoming a cartoonist, Smith talks about how he created Fone Bone when he was just five years old. The artwork in the book includes young Smith's hand-created comics from his childhood. Only a couple of "crap — s slip out. The book includes mostly black and white art and photographs, with a few color illustrations from the Bone comics.

Courtesy of Twomorrows Publishing

Nonaka, Eiji
Cromartie High School, Vol. 1.
[translated by Brendan Frayne]. ADV Manga 2005 158p. Illustration
Grades: 10 11 12 Adult   741.5; Fic
1. Graphic novels; 2. High school students — Graphic novels; 3. Humorous graphic novels; 4. Manga; 5. School stories — Graphic novels; 6. Shonen manga
1-4139-0257-X, $10.95

Takashi Kamiyama enrolled at Cromartie High School, the worst high school in Tokyo, to help a friend, who then flunked the entrance exam. Now he's stuck in a school filled with juvenile delinquents, street toughs, and some very strange characters. They include a shirtless guy who looks like Freddy Mercury and never says anything, a gorilla who is smarter than everyone else, and Mechazawa, who looks like a canister-shaped robot. American readers may not be aware that, in Japan, students must pass entrance exams to get into the high school of their choice. It doesn't matter how rich your family is if you can't pass an entrance exam with a high enough score to get into a top school. This is the first volume of an ongoing manga full of wacky and sometimes deadpan humor.

North, Ryan
★ The **unbeatable** Squirrel Girl; Volume 1: Squirrel power!. Ryan North; illustrated by Erica Henderson. Marvel Enterprises 2015 136 p. Color; Illustration
Grades: 7 8 9 10 11 12 Adult   741.5
1. Squirrel Girl (Fictional character); 2. Superheroes — Fiction; 3. Female superhero graphic novels; 4. Squirrels — Fiction
0785197028; 9780785197027, $15.99
Eisner Nominee: Best New Series (2016); Eisner Award: Best Publication for Teens (2017)

"Supervillains and criminals meet their match with Tony Stark's friend Squirrel Girl, aka Doreen Green, a college freshman with the appearance, speed, and agility of a squirrel. Fitting in proves to be challenging, as normal girls do not talk to or have a squirrel sidekick, nor do they have super strength. Then there is Squirrel Girl's roommate, who has a tough exterior and is obsessed with knitting and her cat. Luckily, Squirrel Girl has a knack for winning people over. When Galactus threatens Earth, the heroine must rely on more than strength to defeat the Devourer of Worlds. She may have extraordinary strength, an army of squirrels at her disposal, a collection of Deadpool villain trading cards, and nut-inspired catchphrases, but it is her ability to form connections with people that proves to be her most powerful asset.:" (School Library Journal)

Contains material originally published in magazine form as The Unbeatable Squirrel Girl #1-4 and Marvel Super-Heroes #8; Volume 1 of an ongoing series

Nury, Fabien

The **death** of Stalin. writer, Fabien Nury; artist, Thierry Robin; colors, Thierry Robin & Lorien Aureyre. Titan Books 2017 119 p. Color; Illustration

Grades: Adult   **741.5; Fic**

1. Soviet Union — Fiction; 2. Stalin, Joseph, 1878-1953 — Death and burial; 3. Soviet Union — History — 1953-1985 — Fiction

1785863401; 9781785863400, $24.99

This graphic novel, by Fabien Nury, illustrated by Thierry Robin, is "set in the aftermath of Stalin's death in the Soviet Union in 1953. When the leader of the Soviet Union, Joseph Stalin, has a stroke — the political gears begin to turn, plunging the super-state into darkness, uncertainty and near civil war. The struggle for supreme power will determine the fate of the nation and of the world. And it all really happened." (Publisher's note)

O'Barr, J.

★ The **Crow**. James O'Barr. Gallery Books 2011 272 p. Illustration; Color

Grades: Adult   **741.5**

1. Crow (Fictitious character) — Comic books, strips, etc; 2. Horror comic books, strips, etc; 3. Angels — Graphic novels; 4. Revenge — Graphic novels

1451627254; 9781451627251, $18.99

LC 2012374273

This graphic novel, by James O'Barr, is the "cathartic story of Eric — who returns from the dead to avenge his and his fiancée's murder at the hands of a street gang...re-released in an expanded version the author originally intended, complete at last with: thirty pages of never-before-seen artwork [and] a new Introduction by... O'Barr." (Publisher's note)

"O'Barr's black-and-white artwork fluctuates wonderfully between brutal, inky darkness and picturesque beauty, mirroring a narrative torn between Eric's memories of his fiancée and the bloody task at hand." LJ

Originally published 1989

O'Malley, Bryan Lee

★ **Scott** Pilgrim's Precious Little Life, Vol. 1. Oni Press 2004 un Illustration

Grades: 10 11 12 Adult

741.5; Fic

1. Graphic novels; 2. Humorous graphic novels; 3. Martial arts — Graphic novels; 4. Romance graphic novels

1-932664-08-4, $11.95

Courtesy of Oni Press

"Scott Pilgrim's life is totally sweet. He's 23 years old, he's in a rock band, he's 'between jobs,' and he's dating a cute high school girl. Nothing could possibly go wrong, unless a seriously mind-blowing, dangerously fashionable, rollerblading delivery girl named Ramona Flowers starts cruising through his dreams and sailing by him at parties. Will Scott's awesome life get turned upside-down? Will he have to face Ramona's seven evil ex-boyfriends in battle? The short answer is yes." (Publisher's note)

Also available in full-color hardcover editions; Other titles in this series are: Scott Pilgrim vs. the World (2005); Scott Pilgrim & the Infinite Sadness (2006); Scott Pilgrim Gets It Together (2007); Scott Pilgrim vs. the Universe (2009); Scott Pilgrim's Finest Hour (2010)

★ **Seconds**. Bryan Lee O'Malley. Ballantine Books 2014 336 p. Color; Illustration

Grades: 10 11 12 Adult   **741.5**

1. Restaurants — Fiction; 2. Graphic novels

0345529375; 9780345529374, $25

LC 2013456979

In this graphic novel by Bryan Lee O'Malley, "Katie's got it pretty good. She's a talented young chef, she runs a successful restaurant, and she has big plans to open an even better one. Then, all at once, progress on the new location bogs down, her charming ex-boyfriend pops up, her fling with another chef goes sour, and her best waitress gets badly hurt. And just like that, Katie's life goes from pretty good to not so much." (Publisher's note)

"O'Malley's engaging narrative voice hasn't diminished — -even the self-absorbed Katie is likeable enough to root for, although it's obvious that she's making things worse for herself. O'Malley's sweet, nimble art, now in color, has acquired more confidence: the plot unfolds cinematically, and his character designs are more appealing than ever." Pub Wkly

O'Neil, Dennis

The **DC** comics guide to writing comics. introduction by Stan Lee. Watson-Guptill 2001 128p. Illustration

Grades: 11 12 Adult   **808; 741.5**

1. Comic books, strips, etc. — Authorship

0-8230-1027-9, $19.95

LC 2001-26101

"In this valuable guide, Dennis O'Neil, a living legend in the comics industry, reveals his insider tricks and no-fail techniques for comic storytelling. Readers will discover the various methods of writing scripts (full script vs. plot first), as well as procedures for developing a story structure, building subplots, creating well-rounded characters, and much more." (Publisher's note)

★ **Green** Lantern, Green Arrow. Dennis O'Neil, Elliot Maggin, writers; Neal Adams, penciller; Neal Adams, Dick Giordano, Frank Giacoia, Dan Adkins, Berni Wrightson, inkers; Cory Adams, Jack Adler, colorists; John Costanza, Joe Letterese, letterers. DC Comics 2012 361 p. Color illustration

Grades: 10 11 12 Adult   **741.5**

1. Superheroes — Comic books, strips, etc.; 2. Green Lantern (Fictional character); 3. Green Arrow (Fictional character)

1401235174; 9781401235178, $29.99

LC 2013363523

In this comic book collection, "Green Lantern Hal Jordan continued his usual cosmic-spanning adventures, as he used his amazing Power Ring to police Sector 2814 against universe-threatening menaces. Meanwhile, on Earth, Oliver Queen, the archer known as Green Arrow, was confronting menaces of a different kind: racism, poverty, drugs, and other social ills!" (Publisher's note)

Originally published in single magazine form in Green Lantern 76-87, 89; Flash 217-219, 226. Green Lantern/Green Arrow 1-7.

The **Question**: Zen and violence. DC Comics 2007 174p. Illustration

Grades: 11 12 Adult   **741.5; Fic**

1. Crime — Graphic novels; 2. Graphic novels; 3. Superhero graphic novels

978-1-4012-1579-8, $19.99

Investigative reporter Vic Sage, who is also the faceless, morally conflicted avenger known as The Question, works to bring down the politically corrupted mayor of Hub City and his advisers, but they have hired the mercenary Lady Shiva, who defeats him in combat and the henchmen of the crooked Rev. Hatch throw him into the river. But, Sage is not dead, he's rescued and healed, and told to find Richard Dragon. He stays with Dragon for a year, training in martial arts and disciplining himself. When he returns to Hub City, he now has the focus to go after the criminals and politicians mucking up the city. The book includes lots of violence and some harsh language.

Oda, Eiichiro

★ **One** Piece Volume 1. story and art by Eiichiro Oda; [English adaptation by Lance Caselman]. Viz Media/Shonen Jump 2003 216p. Illustration
Grades: 8 9 10 11 12 Adult   **741.5; Fic**
  1. Adventure graphic novels; 2. Fantasy graphic novels; 3. Graphic novels; 4. Manga; 5. Shonen manga
1-56931-901-4, $7.95

Monkey D. Luffy's main ambition is to become a pirate, inspired by listening to the tales of the buccaneer "Red-Haired" Shanks. When he accidentally eats the Gum-Gum Fruit, it gives him strange powers to stretch like rubber, but doing so also invokes the fruit's curse: anybody who consumes it can never learn to swim. Nevertheless, Monkey and his crewmate Roronoa Zoro, master of the three-sword fighting style, sail the Seven Seas of swashbuckling adventure in search of the elusive treasure "One Piece." As the series goes on, Luffy gains more crew and they encounter sea monsters, far away kingdoms, cloud island, and super powered pirates of every shape, size, and description — which means lots of epic and comical fight scenes.

Volume 1 of an ongoing series

Oh! Great

Air Gear Vol. 1. Random House/Del Rey Manga 2006 un Illustration
Grades: 10 11 12 Adult   **741.5; Fic**
  1. Adventure graphic novels; 2. Graphic novels; 3. Manga; 4. Shonen manga
978-0-345-49278-4, $10.95
                         LC bd 06-250081

Itsuki Minami is the toughest kid at Higashi Junior High School, plus he lives with the mysterious and sexy Noyamano sisters. Life is never dull, but it becomes dangerous when Itsuki leads his school to victory over some vindictive Westside punks with gangster connections. Now he stands to lose his school, his friends, and everything he cares about. But in his darkest hour, the Noyamano girls come to Itsuki's aid. They can teach him a powerful skill that will save their school from the gangsters' siege-and introduce Itsuki to a thrilling and terrifying new world. The series includes crude humor, violence, partial nudity, sexual situations (including hints at sexual violence), and harsh language.

Oliver, Simon

The **Exterminators** Vol. 1: The Bug Brothers. DC Comics/Vertigo 2006 128p. Illustration
Grades: 11 12 Adult   **741.5; Fic**
  1. Graphic novels; 2. Horror graphic novels
978-1-4012-1064-9, $9.99

This book focuses on a dysfunctional group of bug killers prowling the barrios and bungalows of Los Angeles. Henry James, the newest exterminator, sees the job as a way to cleanse the sins of his dark past; he has a hard time getting his view across to his careerist girlfriend, sociopathic partner and the general bunch of freaks he calls co-workers. Meanwhile, what Henry and the "bug brothers" of Bug-Bee-Gone Co. don't understand is that human beings may be the true pests — and bugs could be the real exterminator. This book has graphic violence, some nudity and sexual situations, and lots and lots of nasty bugs, rats, and other pests.

Ollmann, Joe

The **Abominable** Mr. Seabrook. by Joe Ollmann. Drawn & Quarterly 2017 316 p. Illustration
Grades: Adult   **741.5; 070.92**
  1. Travel writing; 2. Journalists — Biography
1770462678; 9781770462670, $22.95

In this book, by Joe Ollmann, "in the early twentieth century, travel writing represented the desire for the expanding bourgeoisie to experience the exotic cultures of the world past their immediate surroundings. Journalist William Buehler Seabrook was emblematic of this trend — participating in voodoo ceremonies, riding camels cross the Sahara desert, communing with cannibals and most notably, popularizing the term 'zombie' in the West." (Publisher's note)

"Ollmann's illustrations perfectly captures the unease that drives his subject in tight nine-panel grids, and his fascination with his subject is both evident and infectious." LJ

Includes bibliographical references

ONE (Manga author)

★ **One-punch** man; Volume 1. story by One; art by Yusuke Murata. Viz 2015 189 p. Illustration
Grades: 8 9 10 11 12 Adult   **741.5; Fic**
  1. Seinen manga; 2. Graphic novels; 3. Manga; 4. Superheroes
1421585642; 9781421585642, $9.99
Eisner Nominee: Best U.S. Edition of International Material — Asia (2015)

"Nothing about Saitama passes the eyeball test when it comes to superheroes, from his lifeless expression to his bald head to his unimpressive physique. However, this average-looking guy has a not-so-average problem — he just can't seem to find an opponent strong enough to take on! Every time a promising villain appears, he beats the snot out of 'em with one punch!" (Publisher's note)

"The story is fast-paced, humorous, and entertaining in a way that looks and feels like an action movie." SLJ

Volume 1 of an ongoing series

Orlando, Steve

Midnighter; Volume 1: Out. written by Steve Orlando; art by ACO, Stephen Mooney, Alec Morgan, Hugo Petrus; color by Romulo Fajardo, Jr., Allen Passalaqua, Jeromy Cox; letters by Jared K. Fletcher, Tom Napolitano. DC Comics 2016 144 p. Color; Illustration
Grades: Adult   **741.5; Fic**
  1. Midnighter (Fictional character); 2. Superhero graphic novels
1401259782; 9781401259785, $14.99
                       LC 2015044468

"A theft at the God Garden has unleashed a wave of dangerous biotech weapons on the world, and Midnighter intends to put that genie back in the bottle by any means necessary. But something else was stolen from the Garden as well...the secret history of Lucas Trent, the man Midnighter once was!" (Publisher's note)

"Midnighter teleports round the world, experiments with technology and fights off ridiculously high-concept villains.... Orlando carries off the swagger and technique of Midnighter terrifically straight from the start, whilst artist Aco puts together elaborate, distracted, but absorbing page sequences that match the character to a jagged, sharp momentum." (ComicsAlliance)

Collects Midnighter #1-6; Volume 1 of 2

Midnighter; Volume 2: Hard. written by Steve Orlando, Brian K. Vaughan, Christos Gage, Peter Milligan; art by ACO, Hugo Petrus, David Messina, Gaetano Carlucci, Darick Robertson, Karl Story, John Paul Leon, Simon Bisley; color by Romulo Fajardo, Jr., Jeromy Cox, Randy Mayor,. DC Comics 2016 144 p. Color; Illustration
Grades: Adult   **741.5**
  1. Adventure graphic novels; 2. Superhero graphic novels
140126493X; 9781401264932, $14.99
                       LC 2016479890

In this graphic novel, written by Steve Orlando, the second volume of the collected "Midnighter" DC Comics series, "the espionage organization known as Spyral hid...[the Perdition Pistol] beneath as much high-tech security as it could muster-and...someone else just stole it from them. Now only one man can get it back: the human wrecking ball known as the Midnighter. There's only one problem:...[he] must go through the Suicide Squad." (Publisher's note)

Originally published in single magazine form in Midnighter 7-8, Young Romance: the New 52 Valentine's Day special 1, and Midnighter 8-12 — Title page verso.

Osajyefo, Kwanza

Black; Volume 1. Kwanza Osajyefo, creator/writer; Tim Smith 3, creator/designer; Jamal Igle, illustrator; Khary Randolph, cover artist; Sarah Litt, editor; Robin Riggs, inks; Derwin Roberson, tones; David Sharpe, letters; Matt Pizzolo, publisher. Black Mask Comics 2017 208 p. Color; Illustration

Grades: 11 12 Adult   **741.5; Fic**
  1. Superheroes — Fiction; 2. African Americans — Fiction
  9781628751864, $19.99; 162875186X

In this graphic novel, by Kwanza Osajyefo, illustrated by Jamal Igle, Robin Riggs, Tim Smith III, and Derwin Roberson, "in a world that already hates and fears them — what if only Black people had superpowers. After miraculously surviving being gunned down by police, a young man learns that he is part of the biggest lie in history. Now he must decide whether it's safer to keep it a secret or if the truth will set him free." (Publisher's note)

Osborne, Melissa Jane

The **Wendy** project. written and created by Melissa Jane Osborne; art, colors, and letters by Veronica Fish. Papercutz 2017 96 p. Color; Illustration
Grades: 8 9 10 11 12 Adult
741.5
  1. Teenage automobile drivers — Accidents; 2. Graphic novels; 3. Teenage girls — Fiction; 4. Fantasy fiction
  1629917699; 9781629917696, $12.99

In this graphic novel, by Melissa Jane Osborne, illustrated by Veronica Fish, "Wendy Davies crashes her car into a lake...with her two younger brothers in the backseat. When she wakes in the hospital, she is told that her youngest brother...is dead.

Courtesy of NBM Publishing

Wendy...[insists] that Michael is alive and in the custody of a mysterious flying boy. Placed in a new school, Wendy negotiates fantasy and reality as students and adults around her resemble characters from Neverland." (Publisher's note)

"This unexpected gem stands out among latter-day versions of Peter Pan thanks to its embrace of genuine emotion and psychological gravity." LJ

Osborne, Rob

Sunset City, For Active Senior Living. AiT/Planet Lar 2005 un Illustration
Grades: 12 Adult
741.5; Fic
  1. Graphic novels; 2. Retirement communities — Graphic novels
  1-932051-41-4, $9.95

Sunset City is a typical retirement community. Its residents enjoy golf and gossip and they all seem content to fritter away their golden years. Except Frank

Courtesy of AiT/Planet Lar

McDonald. A retired widower, he wrestles with the question: why am I here? Reading the newspaper, Frank keeps up on the minutia of the day; it provides a buzz to an otherwise humdrum life. One morning, Frank is overcome by a startling story, and he does something extraordinary: he takes life by the balls. The story includes some harsh language and violence, and the climactic scene may bother some readers.

Osborne, Wayne

FX. story and script by Wayne Osborne; pencils, inks, lettering, colors, by John Byrne. IDW Publishing 2008 160p. Illustration
Grades: 7 8 9 10 11 12 Adult   **741.5; Fic**
  1. Adventure graphic novels; 2. Graphic novels; 3. Humorous graphic novels; 4. Superhero graphic novels
  978-1-60010-274-5, $19.99

Teenager Tom Talbot was playing with his best friend when Jack accidentally hit Tom so hard he went into a coma. When Tom recovers, he discovers that he's got the power to make what he imagines be real; he discovers this when they're playing around in an alley and Tom imagines he's got a bazooka and really destroys a dumpster. He cobbles together a masked costume, and finds himself fighting superpowered giant talking apes, nasty weapons-bearing lizards, and more. But someone notices him and decides he wants Tom's powers Lord Everos, the Father of Death. And it's not just Tom, either; Vicki, the class weirdo, does really talk with the dead, and Lord Everos wants her, too. And that's not the worst of it, for apparently Tom was never supposed to get the power of the thunderbolt, and a whole pantheon of heroes has just arrived to stop him. Oops again.

Ostrander, John

The **Legend** of Grimjack, Volume 1. IDW Publishing 2005 125p. Illustration
Grades: 10 11 12 Adult   **741.5; Fic**
  1. Adventure graphic novels; 2. Fantasy graphic novels; 3. Graphic novels
  1-932382-51-8, $19.99

Gathering all of the earliest GrimJack stories from the comic book series of the 1980s in one tome for the first time, The Legend of GrimJack, Volume One introduces the major characters and origin stories and also includes the GrimJack/Starslayer crossover saga. This volume also includes a brand new story and art as well as critical background information heretofore unrevealed. The book is full of grim, gritty action with considerable violence; the comics were originally published by First Comics in 1983 and 1984.

Ota, Yuko

Our cats are more famous than us: a Johnny Wander collection. Ananth Hirsh & Yuko Ota. Oni Press 2017 411 p. Illustration
Grades: 9 10 11 12 Adult
741.5
  1. Graphic novels; 2. Humorous stories — Comic books, strips, etc.; 3. American wit and humor; 4. Comic books, strips, etc. — United States
  9780998099507; 9781620103845; 1620103834; 9781620103838, $39.99
          LC 2016952156

"Cartoonist and writer duo Ananth Hirsh and [Yuko] Ota present the first full collection of their webcomic Johnny Wander. This beautifully told volume spans eight

Courtesy of Oni Press

years, four cats, and three moves. The telling, often revealing illustrations are supported by funny text when necessary but are allowed to stand alone and breathe. From life after college to growing up to dealing with friends, and cats, all of life's ups and downs are deftly addressed in this...work." (School Library Journal)

Otomo, Katsuhiro

★ **Akira;** Book five. Katsuhiro Otomo; [translation and English-language adaptation, Yoko Umezawa, Jo Duffy]. Kodansha Comics 2011 413 p.

Grades: Adult   **741.5**

1. Teenagers — Japan — Tokyo — Comic books, strips, etc; 2. Apocalyptic fiction; 3. Supernatural — Fiction; 4. Manga; 5. Seinen manga

1935429078; 9781935429074, $27.99

    LC 2012371500

In this graphic novel, by Katsuhiro Otomo, "Neo-Tokyo lies in ruin, leveled in minutes by the infinite power of the child psychic Akira. From the flooded wasteland of rubble and anarchy rises the Great Tokyo Empire, populated by a ragtag army of zealots and crazies who worship and fear Akira and his mad prime minister, Tetsuo, an angry teen with immense powers of his own- and equally immense, twisted ambitions.... The military strength of the planet is massing to take on the empire." (Publisher's note)

First published in Japan in 1990 by Kodansha Ltd., Tokyo — T.p. verso.; Akira; Akira 5

★ **Akira;** Book four. Katsuhiro Otomo; [translation and English language adaptation, Yoko Umezawa, Jo Duffy]. Kodansha Comics 2010 394 p.

Grades: Adult   **741.5**

1. Parapsychology — Comic books strips, etc; 2. Teenagers — Japan — Tokyo — Comic books strips, etc; 3. Supernatural — Fiction; 4. Seinen manga; 5. Apocalyptic fiction; 6. Manga

193542906X; 9781935429067, $27.99

    LC 2011534775

In this graphic novel, by Katsuhiro Otomo, "Neo-Tokyo lies in ruin. Set off by the bullet of a would-be assassin, the godlike telekinetic fury of the superhuman child Akira has once again demolished [the city].... Now cut off from the rest of the world, the Great Tokyo Empire rises, with Akira its king, the psychic juggernaut Tetsuo its mad prime minister, and a growing army of fanatic acolytes ready to go to any length to please their masters." (Publisher's note)

Translated from the Japanese.First published in Japan in 1987 by Kodansha Ltd., Tokyo — T.p. verso.; Akira

★ **Akira;** Book one. Katsuhiro Otomo; translation and English-language adaptation by Yoko Umezawa, Linda M. York, Jo Duffy. Kodansha Comics 2009 363 p.

Grades: Adult   **741.5; Fic**

1. Teenagers — Japan — Tokyo — Comic books, strips, etc; 2. Seinen manga; 3. Supernatural — Fiction; 4. Apocalyptic fiction; 5. World War III — Fiction; 6. Manga

1935429000; 9781935429005, $24.99

    LC 2010293135

This graphic novel, by Katsuhiro Otomo, is set in "Neo-Tokyo, built on the ashes of a Tokyo annihilated by a blast of unknown origin that triggered World War III. The lives of two streetwise teenage friends, Tetsuo and Kaneda, change forever when paranormal abilities begin to waken in Tetsuo, making him a target for a shadowy agency that will stop at nothing to prevent another catastrophe like the one that leveled Tokyo." (Publisher's note)

First published in Japan in 1984 Kodansha Ltd., Tokyo.

★ **Akira;** Book six. Katsuhiro Otomo; translation and English-language adaptation: Yoko Umezawa, Jo Duffy, Studio Proteus. Kodansha Comics 2011 434 p.

Grades: Adult   **741.5**

1. Teenagers — Japan — Tokyo — Comic books, strips, etc; 2. Apocalyptic fiction; 3. Supernatural — Fiction; 4. Seinen manga; 5. Manga

1935429086; 9781935429081, $29.99

    LC 2011534774

In this graphic novel, by Katsuhiro Otomo, "the armed might of Earth is massed against the godlike powers of two psychic titans, the mute child Akira and the deranged youth Tetsuo. While Akira has unintentionally destoryed the city twice before, Tetsuo has ravaged the surface of the Moon for his sheer amusement, and his madness grows as his abilities expand. But he is gradually losing control of the limitless energies that rage within him." (Publisher's note)

First published in Japan in 1993 by Kodansha Ltd., Tokyo — T.p. verso.; Akira 6

★ **Akira;** Book three. Katsuhiro Otomo; [translation and English-language adaptation, Yoko Umezawa, Linda M. York, Jo Duffy]. Kodansha Comics 2010 282 p.

Grades: Adult   **741.5**

1. Teenagers — Japan — Tokyo — Comic books, strips, etc; 2. Manga; 3. Seinen manga; 4. Supernatural — Fiction; 5. Apocalyptic fiction

1935429043; 9781935429043, $24.99

    LC 2011280454

In this graphic novel, by Katsuhiro Otomo, "Neo-Tokyo has risen from the rubble of a Tokyo destroyed by an apocalyptic telekinetic blast from a young boy called Akira — the subject of a covert government experiment gone wrong now imprisoned for three decades in frozen stasis. But Tetsuo, an unstable youth with immense paranormal abilities of his own, has done the unthinkable: He has released Akira and set into motion a chain of events that could once again destroy the city." (Publisher's note)

First published in 1986 by Kodansha Ltd., Tokyo — T.p. verso.; Akira

★ **Akira;** Book two. Katsuhiro Otomo; [translation and English-language adaptation, Yoko Umezawa, Linda M. York, Jo Duffy]. Kodansha Comics 2010 301 p.

Grades: Adult   **741.5; Fic**

1. Teenagers — Japan — Tokyo — Comic books, strips, etc; 2. Apocalyptic fiction; 3. Manga; 4. Supernatural — Fiction; 5. Seinen manga

1935429027; 9781935429029, $24.99

    LC 2010284394

In this graphic novel, by Katsuhiro Otomo, "Neo-Tokyo has risen from the ashes of a Tokyo obliterated by a monstrous psychokinetic power known only as Akira, a being who yet lives, secretly imprisoned in frozen stasis. Those who stand guard know that Akira's awakening is a terrifying inevitability. Tetsuo, an angry young man with immense — and rapidly growing — psychic abilities, may be their only hope to control Akira when he wakes." (Publisher's note)

First published in 1985 by Kodansha Ltd., Tokyo — T.p. verso.

Otsuka, Eiji

MPD-Psycho No. 1. original story and script, Eiji Otsuka; art, Sho-u Tajima; translation, Kumar Sivasubramanian; English adaptation, Philip R. Simon; lettering, Steve Dutro. Dark Horse Comics 2007 186p. Illustration

Grades: 12 Adult   **741.5; Fic**

1. Graphic novels; 2. Horror graphic novels; 3. Manga; 4. Mystery graphic novels; 5. Seinen manga

978-1-59307-770-9, $10.95

Tokyo police detective Kobayashi Yousuke's life is changed forever after a serial killer notices something "special" about him. That same killer mutilates Kobayashi's girlfriend and kick-starts a "multiple personality battle" within Kobayashi that pushes him into a complex tempest of interconnected deviants and evil forces. After prison he works for a private detective organization, and the cases are all bloody and weird. The book shows lots of graphic violence and nudity, along with strong language. This series is very popular in Japan.

Ottaviani, Jim

Bone sharps, cowboys, andthunder lizards: a tale of Edwin Drinker Cope,Othniel Charles Marsh, and the gilded age ofpaleontology. by Jim Ottaviani & Big Time Attic. G.T. Labs 2005 165p. Illustration
Grades: 9 10 11 12 Adult
560

Courtesy of G.T. Labs

1. Biographical graphic novels; 2. Fossils — Graphic novels; 3. Graphic novels; 4. Paleontologists; 5. Zoologists; 6. Cope, E. D. (Edward Drinker), 1840-1897; 7. Marsh, Othniel Charles, 1831-1899
0-9660106-6-3; 978-0-9660106-6-4, $22.95

LC 2005-920326

"Ottaviani portrays the heyday of American dinosaur hunting with a ripsnorting Western feel. Rival scientist/dinosaur hunters Marsh and Cope play out their real-life drama in a mostly accurate historical telling. Copious notes at the back of the book point out where Ottaviani departs from the facts; science and history become fun in his hands." Voice Youth Advocates

Includes bibliographical references; Title from cover

Fallout. written by Jim Ottaviani, with art by various artists. G.T. Labs 2001 239 p. Illustration
Grades: 11 12 Adult
355.8; 741.5
1. Atomic bomb; 2. Nuclear energy; 3. Nuclear weapons
0966010639; 9780966010633, $24.95

LC 2001091068

In this nonfiction graphic novel about atomic bombs, by Jim Ottaviani, "the focus...is on the scientists themselves — in particular J. Robert Oppenheimer and Leo Szilard, whose lives offer a cautionary tale about the uneasy alliance between the military, the government, and the beginnings of 'big science.'" (Publisher's note)

★ **Feynman**. written by Jim Ottaviani; art by Leland Myrick; coloring by Hilary Sycamore. First Second 2011 262 p. Illustration; Color
Grades: 9 10 11 12 Adult   **92; 530.092**
1. Biography, Individual; 2. Physicists — Graphic novels; 3. Feynman, Richard Phillips, 1918-1988; 4. Musicians — Biography; 5. Atomic bomb; 6. Nobel Prizes
1596432594; 9781596432598, $29.99; 9781596438279, $19.99; 9781451722406, $33.99

LC 2010036260

Author Jim Ottaviani presents a "graphic novel biography...[of] Nobel-winning quantum physicist, adventurer, musician, world-class raconteur, and one of the greatest minds of the twentieth century: Richard Feynman...[The book] tells the story of the great man's life from his childhood in Long Island to his work on the Manhattan Project and the Challenger disaster." (Publisher's note)

"This is a fascinating look at the life of an eccentric genius, a man who worked on the Manhattan Project, won a Nobel Prize, was the first great physicist to teach freshmen classes, and was the investigator into the cause of the Challenger explosion who discovered the problem was the 0-rings. This work was so entertaining it was difficult to put down." Voice Youth Advocates

The **Imitation** Game: Alan Turing Decoded. Jim Ottaviani; illustrated by Leland Purvis. Harry N Abrams Inc 2016 240 p. Illustration
Grades: 9 10 11 12 Adult   **92; 741.5**
1. Turing, Alan Mathison, 1912-1954; 2. Mathematicians — Biography; 3. Turing, Alan Mathison, 1912-1954; 4. Biographical graphic novels
9781613129319; 9781419718939, $24.95; 1419718932

This book, by Jim Ottaviani and illustrated by Leland Purvis, "present[s] a historically accurate graphic novel biography of English mathematician and scientist Alan Turing. [It covers] Turing's life and groundbreaking research — as an unconventional genius who was arrested, tried, convicted, and punished for being openly gay, and whose innovative work still fuels the computing and communication systems that define our modern world." (Publisher's note)

"This adaptation uses a pastel palette of watercolors, strong black lines, and dynamic storytelling devices to bring Turing's tale to life. Multiple narratives, including those of Turing, his mother, and several of his colleagues and friends, weave in and out, following Turing from adolescence to the end of his short life." SLJ

Includes bibliographical references

Primates: The Fearless Science of Jane Goodall, Dian Fossey, and Biruté Galdikas. Jim Ottaviani; illustrated by Maris Wicks. First Second 2013 133 p. Color; Illustration
Grades: 5 6 7 8 9 10 Adult   **741.5; 599.8**
1. Primates; 2. Fossey, Dian, 1932-1985; 3. Goodall, Jane, 1934-; 4. Galdikas, Birute, 1946-
1596438657; 9781596438651, $19.99

LC 2013427678

This book presents an "account of the three greatest primatologists of the last century: Jane Goodall, Dian Fossey, and Biruté Galdikas. These three ground-breaking researchers were all students of the great Louis Leakey, and each made profound contributions to primatology — and to our own understanding of ourselves." (Publisher's note)

"More story than study, the book provides an accessible introduction to Goodall's, Fossey's and Galdikas' lives and work." Kirkus

Includes bibliographical references, page 138

Suspended in language: Niels Bohr's life, discoveries, and the century he shaped. written by Jim Ottaviani; illustrated and lettered by Leland Purvis. G.T. Labs 2009 318p. Illustration
Grades: 10 11 12 Adult
92
1. Biographical graphic novels; 2. Graphic novels; 3. Nobel laureates for physics; 4. Physicists — Graphic novels; 5. Quantum theory — Graphic novels; 6. Bohr, Niels Henrik David, 1885-1962
978-0-9788037-2-8, $24.95

"Quantum physics gets an accessible yet substantive introduction through art that mixes fantasy and realism. Great for teens who like science." Booklist

Courtesy of G.T. Labs

Includes bibliographical references; First published 2004; ?Additional art by Jay Hosler, Roger Langridge, Steve Leialoha, Linda Medley, and Jeff Parker.?

★ **T-Minus:** the race to the moon. [illustrated by] Zander Cannon, Kevin Cannon. Aladdin 2009 124p. Illustration
Grades: 4 5 6 7 8 9 10 11 12 Adult   **629.45; 741.5**
1. Apollo project — Graphic novels; 2. Gemini project — Graphic novels; 3. Graphic novels; 4. Space flight to the moon — Graphic novels
978-1-4169-8682-9, $21.99; 1-4169-8682-0; 978-1-4169-4960-2 (pa), $12.99; 1-4169-4960-7 (pa)
LC 2009-920999
Ottaviani, Zander Cannon, and Kevin Cannon show what happened when the U.S. and the U.S.S.R. started the space race in the 1950s, and how it progressed to the NASA Apollo 11 mission which landed two men on the moon in July of 1969.

"Organized as a countdown, making the outcome seem inevitable, the frequent, prominent sidebars list a type of rocket, the duration of its flight, and whether the mission was a success or a failure. There are more than 30 attempts chronicled, and the shift between Soviet and U.S. successes creates an interesting balance in the narrative.... Ottaviani is particular with facts and eager to inspire readers with regard to the scientific process." SLJ

Wire mothers: Harry Harlow and the science of love. [by] Jim Ottaviani [and] Dylan Meconis. G. T. Labs 2007 84p. Illustration
Grades: 9 10 11 12 Adult
152.4; 741.5
1. Graphic novels; 2. Love — Graphic novels; 3. Psychologists; 4. Harlow, Harry F., 1905-1981
978-0-9788037-1-1, $12.95; 0-9788037-1-X
LC 2007-900136

Courtesy of G.T. Labs

In the 1950s, psychologists warned parents about the dangers of too much love; in fact, they denied love was anything more than a base instinct based on the need for food. When scientist Harry Harlow began his experiments on mother love, was more than just an outsider trying to make his name. He was also an unhappy man who knew in his gut the truth about what love, and its absence, meant, and he set about to prove it. His experiments on monkeys and their stark results shocked the world. The emotional intensity of his experiments might be overwhelming for younger readers.

"This nonfiction graphic novel retelling psychologist Harry Harlow's famous experiments is as disturbing as it is excellent." Publ Wkly
Includes bibliographical references; A General Tektronics Labs book

Padua, Sydney
★ The **Thrilling** Adventures of Lovelace and Babbage: The (Mostly) True Story of the First Computer. Sydney Padua. Pantheon Books 2015 320 p. Illustration
Grades: Adult   **741.5**
1. Inventions — Fiction; 2. Inventors — Fiction; 3. Lovelace, Ada King, Countess of, 1815-1852 — Fiction; 4. Babbage, Charles, 1791-1871 — Fiction
0307908275; 9780307908278, $28.95
LC 2014004455
Eisner Nominee: Best Graphic Album — New (2016)
"Meet Victorian London's most dynamic duo: Charles Babbage, the unrealized inventor of the computer, and his accomplice, Ada, Countess of Lovelace, the peculiar protoprogrammer and daughter of Lord Byron.... [This book] presents a rollicking alternate reality in which Lovelace and Babbage...build the Difference Engine and then use it to build runaway economic models, battle the scourge of spelling errors, [and] explore the wilder realms of mathematics." (Publisher's note)

"A prodigious feat of historically based fantasy that engages on a number of levels." Kirkus

Pak, Greg
X-Men: Phoenix: Endsong. Marvel Entertainment 2005 un Illustration
Grades: 9 10 11 12 Adult   **741.5; Fic**
1. Graphic novels; 2. Superhero graphic novels; 3. X-Men (Fictional characters)
978-0-7851-1924-1, $14.99
The mysterious and powerful Phoenix Force is life incarnate, and yet it consumes whole worlds in a moment. Its long history with the X-Men is fraught with tragedy... especially concerning one of the most beloved of their number, Jean Grey. What will happen when the Phoenix returns to Earth in search of the one mortal who could ever contain its power... only to find her dead?

Palmiotti, Jimmy
Manhunter: Street Justice. Marc Andreyko, writer; Jesus Saiz, penciller; Jimmy Palmiotti, inker; Steve Buccellato, colorist; Phil Balsman, Jared K. Fletcher, Pat Brosseau, letterers. DC Comics 2005 un Illustration
Grades: 10 11 12 Adult   **741.5; Fic**
1. Graphic novels; 2. Superhero graphic novels
1-4012-0728-6, $12.99
When top federal prosecutor Kate Spencer loses a case against a super-villain, setting him free to kill again, she breaks the laws she has long upheld to become Los Angeles' newest crime fighting vigilante. Prosecuting super-villains has been her life's work But these criminals never stay locked up for good. Now, using confiscated met human weaponry she raided from an evidence locker, Kate tracks the perps who have eluded justice in the courts and delivers a long-overdue eye for an eye. She's found her true calling. She is the Manhunte. And she likes it. Plenty of violence, an anti-heroine who smokes and is willing to kill the criminals she hunts, make this superhero title one for older readers.
Volume 1 of 6

Uncle Sam and the Freedom Fighters. written by Justin Gray and Jimmy Palmiotti; art by Daniel Acuna. DC Comics 2007 208p. Illustration
Grades: 10 11 12 Adult   **741.5; Fic**
1. Graphic novels; 2. Superhero graphic novels
978-1-4012-1336-7, $14.99
Meet the all-new Phantom Lady, Doll Man, Human Bomb and the Ray — members of the government task force known as SHADE, the country's first line of defense against super-powered threats and terrorists in the wake of the Infinite Crisis. When the resurrected Uncle Sam makes them realize that Father Time has used them to further his own interests that will harm the United States, they work with Uncle Sam as the new Freedom Fighters. There is considerable violence in this superhero title.

Panetta, Kevin
Zodiac Starforce: By the Power of Astra. script by Kevin Panetta; art, colors, lettering, and cover by Paulina Ganucheau; color flats by Savanna Ganucheau, Kristen Acampora, and Tabby Freeman; chapter break art by Marguerite Sauvage, Kevin Wada, Jacob Wyatt, Babs Tarr. Dark Horse Books 2016 136 p. Color; Illustration
Grades: 8 9 10 11 12 Adult   **741.5**
1. Astrology — Fiction; 2. Friendship — Fiction; 3. Graphic novels; 4. Magic — Fiction; 5. Superheroes — Fiction
1616559136; 9781616559137, $12.99
LC 2015039851
This book, by Kevin Panetta, illustrated by Paulina Ganucheau, focuses on "an elite group of teenage girls with magical powers who have

sworn to protect our planet against dark creatures...as long as they can get out of class! Known as the Zodiac Starforce, these high-school girls aren't just combating math tests. They're also battling monsters — not your typical afterschool activity!" (Publisher's note)

Papadatos, Alekos

Democracy. concept, Alecos Papadatos; story, Alecos Papdatos & Abraham Kawa; script, Abraham Kawa; art direction & drawings, Alecos Papdatos; colouring, Annie Di Donna. Bloomsbury 2015 236 p. Color; Illustration

Grades: 11 12 Adult   **741.5**

1. Athens (Greece) — Fiction; 2. War stories; 3. Democracy
1608197190; 9781608197194, $27

This book by Alecos Papadatos, Abraham Kawa, and Annie Di Donna "opens in 490 B.C., with Athens at war. The hero of the story, Leander, is trying to rouse his comrades for the morrow's battle against a far mightier enemy, and begins to recount his own life, having borne direct witness to the evils of the old tyrannical regimes and to the emergence of a new political system. The tale that emerges is one of daring, danger, and big ideas, of the death of the gods and the tortuous birth of democracy." (Publisher's note)

"Papadatos's lively and energetic art illuminates battles, alliances, political machinations, and vivid personalities, and Di Donna's intense coloring is gloriously rich without a touch of gaudiness. For those interested in further background, the extensive back matter features useful commentary on both legendary and historical figures and concepts." Pub Wkly

Papadimitriou, Christos H.

★ **Logicomix**. [written by] Apostolos Doxiadis, Christos H. Papadimitriou; art, Alecos Papadatos; color, Annie Di Donna. Bloomsbury 2009 347p. Illustration

Grades: 11 12 Adult   **741.5; Fic**

1. Biographical graphic novels; 2. Comic books, strips, etc.; 3. Essayists; 4. Graphic novels; 5. Logicians; 6. Mathematicians; 7. Mathematics — Graphic novels; 8. Nobel laureates for literature; 9. Nonfiction writers; 10. Philosophers; 11. Philosophy — Graphic novels; 12. Russell, Bertrand, 1872-1970; 13. Russell, Bertrand, 1872-1970 — Fiction
0-7475-9720-0, $22.95; 978-0-7475-9720-9

This is a "graphic novel based on the life of the philosopher and mathematician Bertrand Russell." (Publisher's note)

Parks, Ande

Union Station. Oni Press 2003 116p. Illustration

Grades: 11 12 Adult

364.1; 741.5

1. Crimes — United States — Graphic novels; 2. FBI — Graphic novels; 3. Graphic novels
1-929998-69-4, $11.95

Courtesy of Oni Press

Kansas City, 1933. Frank Nash is a petty criminal who has been pinched by the Feds and is being brought back into town by train. When FBI agent Reed Vetterli heads down to Union Station to meet Nash and his uniformed escort, he has no reason to suspect that there will be any action. Neither does Charles Thompson, a reporter sent down to the station just to see what the fuss is for. Little do they know that Frank's buddy, Vern Miller, is going to bust him out. Nash may not be a big time player, but he's still earned some loyalty. The resulting clash ends in a massacre, with no one knowing who

pulled the trigger first — or even who pulled it at all. Rumor has it that Pretty Boy Floyd was on the scene, but no one knows for sure, and J. Edgar Hoover doesn't particularly care. He just wants Floyd's butt in an electric chair, and when Vetterli, Miller, and Thompson find themselves in the way of Hoover's justice, they can't duck for cover fast enough. This graphic novel is based on a true incident. The book includes violence and strong language.

Passmore, Ben

Your black friend and other strangers. by Ben Passmore. Silver Sprocket 2018 112 p.

Grades: Adult   **741.5**

1. Group identity — Comic books, strips, etc.; 2. African Americans — Comic books, strips, etc.; 3. Race relations — Comic books, strips, etc.
1945509201; 9781945509209, $20

This work "is a collection of culturally charged comics by cartoonist Ben Passmore.... [He] masterfully tackles comics about race, gentrification, the prison system, online dating, gross punks, bad street art, kung fu movie references, beating up God, and lots of other grown-up stuff with refreshing doses of humor and lived relatability." (Publisher's note)

"Passmore's intimate and funny style buoys his radical argument, that everyone should work to destroy systemic oppression, in this bracing and eye-opening narrative manifesto." Pub Wkly

Pedrosa, Cyril

Portugal. Cyril Pedrosa; color by Pedrosa and Ruby; translated by Montana Kane; lettering by Calix Ltd. NBM Graphic Novels 2017 264 p. Color; Illustration

Grades: Adult   **741.5**

1. Cartoonists — Fiction; 2. Portugal — Fiction; 3. Families — Fiction
1681121476; 9781681121475, $39.99

LC 2017953030

In this book, by Cyril Pedrosa, "comics artist Simon Muchat is stuck. Suffering writer's block, uninspired, vegetating as a school art teacher, he is losing direction and his taste for life, until one day he is invited to appear at a comics convention in Portugal, the country his family came from.... Meeting its lively citizens and recounting early memories brought by back his distant yet welcoming family all prove reinvigorating." (Publisher's note)

"The emotionally affecting journey hinges on the unique local characters, who immediately call Simon one of their own. Pedrosa's loose, expansive writing style is perfectly complemented by his lush, lightly lined drawings, in which people and their stories overlap each other with discursive enthusiasm." Pub Wkly

Pekar, Harvey, 1939-2010

American splendor: the life and times of Harvey Pekar : stories. by Harvey Pekar; introduction by R. Crumb; art by Kevin Brown ... [et al.]. More American splendor : the life and times of Harvey Pekar : stories / by Harvey Pekar; art by Gregory Budgett ... [et al.].. Ballantine Books 2003 320 p. Color; Illustration

Grades: Adult   **741.5/973**

1. Everyday life — Graphic novels
0345468309; 9780345468307, $24

LC 2003545170

This book, by Harvey Pekar, "is the world's first literary comic book.... Harvey chronicles the ordinary and mundane in stories both funny and touching. His dead-on eye for the frustrations and minutiae of the workaday world mix in a delicate balance with his insight into personal relationships." (Publisher's note)

Other American Splendor books are: More American Splendor (1986); The New American Splendor Anthology (1991); American Splendor

Presents: Bob & Harv's Comics (1996); American Splendor: Unsung Hero (2003); Our Movie Year (2004); Best of American Splendor (2005); Ego & Hubris: The Michael Malice Story (2006); American Splendor: Another Day (2007); American Splendor: Another Dollar (2009)

Harvey Pekar's Cleveland. by Harvey Pekar, illustrated by Joseph Remnant. Top Shelf/Zip 2012 128p Illustration
Grades: Adult   **977.132; 741.5**
1. Autobiographical graphic novels; 2. Cleveland (Ohio); 3. Pekar, Harvey, 1939-2010
1603090916; 9781603090919, $21.99

In this autobiographical graphic novel, by Harvey Pekar, illustrated by Joseph Remnant, "a lifelong Cleveland resident,...combines...autobiographical anecdotes with key moments and characters in the city's history as relayed to us by Our Man and meticulously researched and rendered by artist Joseph Remnant." (Publisher's note)

Not the Israel my parents promised me. Harvey Pekar and JT Waldman. Hill and Wang 2012 172 p.
Grades: Adult   **956.94**
1. Jews — History — Comic books, strips, etc; 2. Jews — United States — Attitudes toward Israel — Comic books, strips, etc; 3. Judaism — History — Comic books, strips, etc; 4. Pekar, Harvey, 1939-2010 — Political and social views — Comic books, strips, etc; 5. Jews — History — Graphic novels; 6. Biographical graphic novels; 7. Zionism — Graphic novels
0809094827; 9780809094820, $24.95

     LC 2011047024

This "posthumous work by [Harvey] Pekar functions as a multipronged exploration of religious, political, and personal histories .... Pekar structures his narrative as a long-running bull session with his collaborator, artist [J.T.] Waldman .... [T]hey explore his parents' very passionate but unusual Zionism..., the history of the Jewish people and the creation of the state of Israel, and Pekar's own evolving feelings about that country." (Publishers Weekly)

Quitter. DC Comics/Vertigo 2005 un Illustration
Grades: 10 11 12 Adult   **741.5; 92**
1. Autobiographical graphic novels; 2. Graphic novels; 3. Monsters — Graphic novels; 4. Pekar, Harvey, 1939-2010
1-4012-0399-X, $19.95

Harvey Pekar is now a famed independent comics creator, whose series American Splendor was adapted into a hit motion picture. In this book, he recounts his childhood, teen years, and early adulthood and examines the experiences that shaped his life. He gives an unflinchingly honest portrait of a boy who used fighting to get a tough reputation, who needed to excel in sports and academics and would quit if he felt he couldn't achieve what he wanted. He allows the reader to see into his soul.

Students for a Democratic Society: a graphic history. written by Harvey Pekar; art by Gary Dumm; edited by Paul Buhle. Hill & Wang 2008 214p. Illustration
Grades: 10 11 12 Adult   **378.1; 741.5**
1. Students for a Democratic Society — Graphic novels — History; 2. College students — Political activity — Graphic novels; 3. Graphic novels
978-0-8090-8939-0 (pa), $16; 978-0-8090-9539-1, $22

     LC 2007-40641

Students for a Democratic Society formed as an organization in 1960, but had its roots as a New Left group in the League for Industrial Democracy, founded in 1905 with members such as Jack London and Upton Sinclair. The members in 1960 included Al Haber and Tom Hayden, and one of their most famous documents is the Port Huron Statement of

1962. By the late 1960s, with opposition to the Vietnam War in full swing, a radical subgroup called the Weathermen became more violent. Graphic novelist Pekar is joined by members of the SDS in telling the story of the organization, which dissolved soon after its 1969 convention. The book includes some harsh language and violence.

"The book acts like a sophisticated handbook on an often misunderstood organization. It's good comics and excellent history." Publ Wkly

Percy, Benjamin
     Green Arrow; Volume 1: the death & life of Oliver Queen. Benjamin Percy, writer; Otto Schmidt, Juan Ferreyra, artists & colorists; Nate Piekos of Blambot, letterer; Juan Ferreyra, series & collection cover artist. DC Comics 2017 160 p. Color; Illustration
Grades: 11 12 Adult   **741.5**
1. Superheroes comic books, strips, etc.; 2. Green Arrow (Fictional character)
1401267815; 9781401267810, $16.99

     LC 2016039348

"Oliver Queen, playboy socialite, CEO of Queen Industries and philanthropic do-gooder...patrols the streets of Seattle, where he champions the oppressed as a true social justice warrior. He is Green Arrow. But how can you fight the man when you are the man? That's the question left with Oliver after an electric, love-at-first-sight encounter with Black Canary, the superhero rock star." (Publisher's note)

Originally published in single magazine form in GREEN ARROW: REBIRTH 1, GREEN ARROW 1-5; Volume 1 of an ongoing series

Pérez, Ramón
     Jim Henson's tale of sand. written by Jim Henson and Jerry Juhl; as realized by Ramón K. Pérez; colors by Ian Herring with Ramón K. Pérez; lettering and font design by Deron Bennett based on the handwriting of Jim Henson; edited by Stephen Christy. Archaia Entertainment 2012 152 p.
Grades: 10 11 12 Adult   **741.5**
1. Fantasy graphic novels; 2. Adventure graphic novels; 3. Deserts — Graphic novels; 4. Southwestern States — Graphic novels
1936393093; 9781936393091

This graphic novel "follows its hapless protagonist as he is cast out into the desert by the cheerful Sheriff Tate.... The scruffy hero is a pawn in a game whose rules are concealed from him, pursued across a surrealistic southwest U.S. by an implacable hunter and hindered by the eccentric, bizarre inhabitants of the great desolation. The prize waiting for him at the end of the chase, should he survive to reach the end, is one he will never guess at." (Publishers Weekly)

Peyo
     The **Smurfs** anthology; Vol. 1. Peyo. Papercutz 2013 190 p. Color illustration (The Smurfs graphic novels)
Grades: 4 5 6 7 8 9 10 11 12 Adult
741.5
1. Comic books, strips, etc.
1597074179; 9781597074179, $19.99

"Newly remastered and presented in original publication order, along with a Smurfy collection of historical notes and photographs, the stories in this volume," by Belgian comics artist Peyo, "introduce us to Papa Smurf, Gargamel, Smurfette, and the rest of the village." (Publisher's note)

Courtesy of NBM Publishing

The **Smurfs** anthology; Vol. 2. Peyo. Papercutz 2013 192 p. Color illustration

Grades: 4 5 6 7 8 9 10 11 12 Adult   **741.5**
1. Comic books, strips, etc.
1597074454; 9781597074452, $19.99

"Newly remastered and presented in original publication order, along with a Smurfy collection of historical notes and photographs, this volume," by Belgian comics artist Peyo, "introduces us to Smurfette and features a 'Johan and Peewit' story never before seen in the U.S." (Publisher's note)

"[A] delightful and instructive mix of Peyo's colorful tales. A series of essays interspersed throughout the collection provides social and historical context for the cartoons." Booklist

Translated from the French

Pini, Wendy

ElfQuest Archives Vol. 1. DC Comics 2003 216p. Illustration
Grades: 9 10 11 12 Adult   **741.5; Fic**
1. Adventure graphic novels; 2. Elves — Graphic novels; 3. Fantasy graphic novels; 4. Graphic novels
1-4012-0128-8, $49.99

Existing on a prehistoric world, the World of Two Moons, in which humans and elves are bitter enemies, the Wolfriders live a dangerous life of fatal battles, deadly hunts, and tribal traditions. Proud of their history but unaware of their origin, the Wolfriders are on an eternal quest to learn the mysteries of their past. This hardcover edition includes the Wolfriders' fateful battle with a band of humans, their surprising discovery of another clan of elves, and Cutter's first meeting with the enchanting healer, Leetah. The Pinis started publishing the ElfQuest stories as black and white comics in the mid-1970s; this is a full-color deluxe hardcover edition of the first five issues. The book includes partial nudity, brief sexual situations, and violence.

ElfQuest Archives Vol. 3. DC Comics 2005 224p. Illustration
Grades: 9 10 11 12 Adult   **741.5; Fic**
1. Adventure graphic novels; 2. Elves — Graphic novels; 3. Fantasy graphic novels; 4. Graphic novels
1-4012-0412-0, $49.99

This third volume collects ElfQuest #11-15. When Leetah and some of the others try to catch up to Cutter to warn him of danger, they are taken as slaves into the towering and mysterious Blue Mountain, stronghold of the ancient elves called the Gliders. There Cutter and the Wolfriders must face the evil Winnowill, who wields strong magic, to save family and friends. The book includes violence, partial nudity, and sexual situations.

ElfQuest; Volume 1: the final quest. by Wendy and Richard Pini; colors by Sonny Strait; letters by Nate Piekos of Blambot. Dark Horse Books 2015 192 p. Illustration
Grades: 9 10 11 12 Adult   **741.5**
1. Elves — Comic books, strips, etc; 2. Fantasy graphic novels; 3. Elves — Fiction
1616554096; 9781616554095, $17.99

LC 2014046866

In this book, by by Wendy and Richard Pini, "the elves sought a safe haven against all who would do them harm. But the dream that Chief Cutter and his Wolfriders fought and died for, the Palace of the High Ones, may be the very thing destroying them. The skills that helped them survive the harsh world are fading, and there is a growing threat from a tyrant obsessed with exterminating all elves — creating a disastrous brew that must surely boil over." (Publisher's note)

"For more than 30 years, the Pinis' ElfQuest saga has satisfied readers with tales of the glamorous but fierce elves who share an alien planet with nonmagical, often hostile humans. New readers may feel baffled at this point, but they can catch on soon." Pub Wkly

ElfQuest Archives Vol. 2. DC Comics 2005 226p. Illustration
Grades: 9 10 11 12 Adult   **741.5; Fic**
1. Adventure graphic novels; 2. Elves — Graphic novels; 3. Fantasy graphic novels; 4. Graphic novels
1-4012-0129-6, $49.99

The Wolfriders have found sanctuary, and Cutter and Leetah become lifemates. But their peace is threatened once more by men, and the trolls, and by the twin mysteries of the Forbidden Grove and Blue Mountain. The book includes some violence and brief partial nudity.

ElfQuest; Volume 2: the final quest. by Wendy and Richard Pini; colors by Sonny Strait; letters by Nate Piekos of Blambot. Dark Horse Books 2016 136 p. Color; Illustration
Grades: 9 10 11 12 Adult   **741.5; Fic**
1. Elves — Comic books, strips, etc; 2. Fantasy graphic novels; 3. Elves — Fiction
161655410X; 9781616554101, $17.99

LC 2015045160

In this book, by Wendy and Richard Pini, "Sunstream, son of Wolfrider chief Cutter Kinseeker, finally fulfills his destiny and becomes the psychic link among all the elfin tribes scattered across the World of Two Moons.... But a devastating secret, long hidden in plain sight, is also moving into the light. When the full impact of this revelation becomes known, it will affect the entire elfin race forever." (Publisher's note)

This volume collects and reprints the comic books ElfQuest: The Final Quest #7-#12.

Piskor, Ed

★ **Hip** Hop Family Tree; Volume 1. By Ed Piskor. Fantagraphics Books 2013 112 p. Color; Illustration
Grades: Adult   **741.5; 782.421649**
1. Graphic novels; 2. Hip-hop — Encyclopedias; 3. Rap music — History and criticism
1606996908; 9781606996904, $24.99
Ignatz Nominee: Outstanding Artist (2014)

Written and illustrated by Ed Piskor in a graphic novel format, "This encyclopedic comics history of the formative years of hip hop captures the vivid personalities and magnetic performances of old-school pioneers and early stars like DJ Kool Herc, Grandmaster Flash and the Furious Five, plus the charismatic players behind the scenes like Russell Simmons; Debbie Harry, Keith Haring and other luminaries make cameos." (Publisher's note)

"Piskor succeeds mightily in chronicling hip-hop's formative years with riveting detail." Pub Wkly

Includes bibliographical references (page 106), discography (page 106) and index.

★ **Hip** hop family tree; volume 2: 1981-1983. by Ed Piskor and Charlie Ahearn. Fantagraphics 2014 112 p. Color; Illustration
Grades: Adult   **741.5; 782.421649**
1. Hip-hop
1606997564; 9781606997567, $27.99
Eisner Award: Best Reality-Based Work (2015)

This graphic novel on the history of hip hop, by Ed Piskor, "covers the years 1981-1983.... Hip Hop has made a big transition from the parks and rec rooms to downtown clubs and vinyl records. The performers make moves to separate themselves from the paying customers by dressing more and more flamboyant until a young group called RUN-DMC comes on the scene to take things back to the streets." (Publisher's note)

"The second collection of Piskor's hip-hop history in comics may be a better place to start reading it than the first. Several longer stories are embedded in it, whereas the first volume was primarily a succession of one-pagers. For instance, the making of the groundbreaking hip-hop movie, Wild Style, occupies several pages, which allows gratifyingly better acquaintance with a handful of players amid the blizzard of faces and names the chronicle throws at us." Booklist

Includes bibliographical references, discographies, and indexes

Hip hop family tree; Volume 3: 1983-1984. by Ed Piskor. W W Norton & Co Inc 2015 110 p. Color; Illustration

Grades: Adult   **782.421649; 741.5**

1. Hip-hop — History and criticism — Comic books, strips, etc.; 2. Rap musicians; 3. Rap music — History and criticism

160699848X; 9781606998489, $27.99

Eisner Nominee: Best Reality-Based Work (2016)

This book, by Ed Piskor, is "the third volume of the popular webcomic.... Book 3 highlights Run DMC's rise to fame and introduces unassailable acts like Whodini, The Fat Boys, Slick Rick, and Doug E Fresh. The Beastie Boys become a rap group. Rick Rubin meets Russell Simmons to form Def Jam." (Publisher's note)

Hip hop family tree; Volume 4. Ed Piskor. Fantagraphics Books 2016 110 p. Color; Illustration

Grades: Adult   **782.421649; 741.5**

1. African American musicians — Comic books, strips, etc; 2. African American youth — Social life and customs — Comic books, strips, etc; 3. Comic books, strips, etc. — United States; 4. Graphic novels — United States; 5. Hip-hop — History and criticism — Comic books, strips, etc; 6. Music — Social aspects — Comic books, strips, etc; 7. Rap (Music) — History and criticism — Comic books, strips, etc; 8. Rap musicians — Comic books, strips, etc; 9. Turntablism — History and criticism — Comic books, strips, etc; 10. Hip-hop; 11. Rap musicians; 12. Rap music — Graphic novels

1606999400; 9781606999400, $27.99

LC 2016561225

This book, by Ed Piskor, presents the "history of hip-hop told in graphic novel form..., [It] charts the rise of Dr. Dre and Def Jam records, and introduces new branches on the 'tree': Will Smith, Salt-N-Pepa, Rakim, and Biz Markie. This volume is also jam-packed with films Hollywood released in an attempt to cash in on the phenomenon, like Breakin', Breakin' 2 Electric Boogaloo, Beat Street, Krush Groove and more." (Publisher's note)

Includes bibliographical references (page 110), discography (page 110) and index

Wizzywig. Ed Piskor. Top Shelf Productions 2012 288 p. Illustration

Grades: 11 12 Adult

741.5

1. Telephones — Fiction; 2. Computer hackers — Fiction

1603090975; 9781603090971, $19.95

Courtesy of IDW Publishing

This graphic novel, "inspired by tales of real-life hackers...follows the story of Kevin 'Boingthump' Phenicle, who gets his start tapping into telephone lines as a teenager and works his way up to infiltrating the phone company and its database. At his side is his best (and indeed only) friend, Winston, who goes from helping Kevin with his hacking to defending him on the radio when Kevin is eventually caught and incarcerated." (Publishers Weekly)

"With heavy technology content and social-issue relevance, plus hacker and comics industry in-jokes, this is a techie's dream read, enhanced by Piskor's thorough research and judiciously unpretty black-and-white art." LJ

X-men; 1: grand design. Ed Piskor. Marvel Enterprises 2018 120 p. Color; Illustration

Grades: 10 11 12 Adult   **741.5; Fic**

1. X-Men (Fictional characters); 2. Comic books, strips, etc.; 3. Superheroes

1302904892; 9781302904890, $29.99

In this book, author Ed Piskor, "takes you on a pulse-pounding tour of X-Men history unlike anything you've ever experienced before, an intricate labor of love that stitches together hundreds of classic and obscure stories into one seamless masterpiece of X-Men lore. This volume collects X-MEN: GRAND DESIGN and includes X-MEN #1 from 1963, masterfully recolored by Ed, along with other extras including recolored classic pinups." (Publisher's note)

"Much as Piskor masterfully took on the scope of rap music in his acclaimed Hip Hop Family Tree series, he synthesizes hundreds of (sometimes contradictory) tales and specific details generated by their hundreds of past creators, faithfully integrating it all into one entertaining story line." Pub Wkly

Pomplun, Tom

Graphic Classics volume eleven: O. Henry. edited by Tom Pomplun. Eureka Productions 2005 144p. Illustration

Grades: 7 8 9 10 11 12 Adult   **741.5; Fic**

1. Authors; 2. Graphic novels; 3. Short stories — Graphic novels; 4. Short story writers; 5. Henry, O., 1862-1910; 6. Henry, O., 1862-1910 — Adaptations

978-0-9746648-2-0, $11.95

This volume of Graphics Classics adapts some of the short stories by O. Henry, the master of the surprise ending. Stories include "The Ransom of Red Chief," illustrated by Johnny Ryan, "The Gift of the Magi," illustrated by Lisa Weber, "The Caballero's Way" (the original story of the Cisco Kid), illustrated by Mark A. Nelson, and more.

Graphic Classics volume eight: Mark Twain. edited by Tom Pomplun. Eureka Productions 2007 144p. Illustration

Grades: 9 10 11 12 Adult   **741.5; 818**

1. Adventure graphic novels; 2. Authors; 3. Essayists; 4. Graphic novels; 5. Humorists; 6. Humorous graphic novels; 7. Memoirists; 8. Novelists; 9. Satirists; 10. Short stories — Graphic novels; 11. Short story writers; 12. Travel writers; 13. Twain, Mark, 1835-1910 — Adaptations

978-0-9787919-2-6, $11.95

This book includes an adaptation of "Tom Sawyer Abroad" by Tom Pomplun and George Sellas, "The Mysterious Stranger" by Rick Geary, "A Dog's Tale" by Lance Tooks, "The Celebrated Jumping Frog of Calaveras County" by Kevin Atkinson, and "The Carnival of Crime in Connecticut" by Antonella Caputo and Nick Miller. Also in this volume are "Is He Living or Is He Dead?," "A Curious Pleasure Excursion," and eight women artists interpret Mark Twain's "Advice to Little Girls."

"With a terrific lineup of artists and unbeatable material, Pomplun has assembled a collection of Mark Twain's work that should delight graphic novel fans and anyone seeking to boost their general cultural knowledge." Publ Wkly [review of 2004 edition]

First published 2004

★ **Graphic** Classics volume fourteen: Gothic classics. edited by Tom Pomplun. Eureka Productions 2007 144p. Illustration

Grades: 7 8 9 10 11 12 Adult   **741.5; Fic**

1. Graphic novels; 2. Horror graphic novels; 3. Short stories — Graphic novels

978-0-9787919-0-2, $11.95

This volume includes graphic adaptations of classic novels Carmilla by Joseph Sheridan Le Fanu, The Mysteries of Udolpho by Ann Radcliffe, and Northanger Abbey by Jane Austen, along with shorter works "The Oval Portrait" by Edgar Allan Poe, "At the Gate" by Myla Jo Closser, and "I've a Pain in My Head" by Jane Austen. Radcliffe's novel is one mentioned by Austen in Northanger Abbey and is a famous gothic novel from the late eighteenth century, considered to be the world's first best-seller. Le Fanu's vampire novel was published twenty-five years before Stoker's Dracula. Austen wrote Northanger Abbey as a satire of the popular gothic genre.

Pond, Mimi

The **customer** is always wrong. Mimi Pond. Drawn & Quarterly 2017 448 p. Illustration
Grades: Adult   92; 741.5
  1. Coffeehouses; 2. Waiters and waitresses
9781770462823; $29.95; 1770462821

This book, by Mimi Pond, "is the saga of a young naïve artist named Madge working in a restaurant of charming drunks, junkies, thieves, and creeps. Oakland in the late seventies is a cheap and quirky haven for eccentrics and Mimi Pond folds the tales of the fascinating sleaze-ball characters that surround young Madge into her workaday waitressing life." (Publisher's note)

"It's a sprawling cast of characters, most of whom appear with little introduction, both because the book is a sequel to Pond's Over Easy and because the story's sense of place is as important as the individual players." Kirkus

Over Easy. Mimi Pond. Farrar Straus & Giroux 2014 272 p. Illustration
Grades: Adult   741.5
  1. Autobiographies; 2. California; 3. Bildungsromans
1770461531; 9781770461536, $24.95

This fictionalized memoir by Mimi Pond "is equal parts time capsule of late 1970s life in California...and bildungsroman of a young woman...from a naïve, sexually inexperienced art-school dropout into a self-aware, self-confident artist.... At first she mimics these new and exotic grown-up friends.... Gradually she realizes that the adults she looks up to are a mess of contradictions, misplaced artistic ambitions, sexual confusion, dependencies, and addictions." (Publisher's note)

Pope, Paul

Batman: Year 100. DC Comics 2007 232p. Illustration
Grades: 10 11 12 Adult   741.5; Fic
  1. Batman (Fictional character); 2. Graphic novels; 3. Science fiction graphic novels; 4. Superhero graphic novels
978-1-4012-1192-9, $19.99

This is a futuristic mystery of epic proportions set in a dark, dystopian world devoid of privacy and filled with government conspiracies, psychic police, holographic caller ID and absolutely no room for "secret identities." In Gotham City, 2039, a federal agent is murdered and a contingent of Washington's top agents is hot on the suspect's trail. The Batman, a forgotten icon from the past, is wanted for the murder. Amid the chaos Gotham City Police Detective Gordon, grandson of the former commissioner, discovers that the man they are chasing shouldn't exist at all. The book has some bloody violence and some strong language.

Porcellino, John

From Lone Mountain. by John Porcellino. Drawn & Quarterly 2018 320 p. Illustration
Grades: Adult   741.5; 92
  1. Porcellino, John; 2. Loss (Psychology); 3. Everyday life; 4. Biography

1770462953; 9781770462953, $22.95

In this book, author John Porcellino "drives through...[Lone Mountain] weaving from small town to small town, experiencing America in slow motion.... 'From Lone Mountain' collects stories from Porcellino's influential zine King-Cat — John enters a new phase of his life, as he remarries and decides to leave his beloved second home Colorado for San Francisco. Grand themes of King-Cat are visited and stated more eloquently than ever before." (Publisher's note)

"Porcellino's minicomic King-Cat, launched in 1989, is the most quietly vital of modern comics, evolving over the years from punk zine to minimalist meditation. This volume, which collects issues 62-68, mixes autobio strips, illustrated memories ('Barbers I Have Known'), confessions, Zen riddles, Top 40 lists, and letters from readers." Pub Wkly

The **Hospital** Suite. John Porcellino. Farrar Straus & Giroux 2014 250 p. Illustration
Grades: Adult   92; 741.5
  1. Porcellino, John; 2. Patients; 3. Obsessive-compulsive disorder; 4. Anxiety
1770461647; 9781770461642, $22.95

Author John Porcellino presents "an autobiographical collection detailing his struggles with illness in the 1990s and early 2000s. In 1997, John began to have severe stomach pain. He soon found out he needed emergency surgery to remove a benign tumor. In the wake of the surgery, he had numerous health complications. The [book] is Porcellino's response to these experiences." (Publisher's note)

Porcellino's "simple, black lines and bare-bones drawings have a powerful economy that present the story cleanly, without flourish, detailing a frightening and inescapable spiral into dysfunction without hyperbole. The result is a clear-eyed, penetrating book about the helplessness of illness." Pub Wkly

King-Cat Classics. Drawn & Quarterly 2007 384p. Illustration
Grades: 10 11 12 Adult   741.5
  1. Autobiographical graphic novels; 2. Graphic novels
978-1-894937-91-7, $29.95

This large collection focuses on the first fifty issues of Porcellino's autobiographical comics, with extensive endnotes and an index, along with selections of all the extra ephemera that makes an individual issue of King-Cat a unique experience-essays, articles, stories, and letters from friends. Included are more than two hundred and fifty pages of comics, ranging from Porcellino's earliest scrawls to his later, minimalist delineations. The comics range through all of his concerns-family, family pets, the natural world, work, music, romance. He uses some strong language and some sexual situations.

Thoreau at Walden. by John Porcellino, from the writings of Henry David Thoreau; introduction by D.B. Johnson. Hyperion 2008 viii, 99 p. Illustration; Map (Center for Cartoon Studies presents)
Grades: 8 9 10 11 12 Adult   818/.303; 741.5
  1. Graphic novels; 2. Thoreau, Henry David, 1817-1862; 3. Walden Woods (Mass.) — Social life and customs — Comic books, strips, etc; 4. American authors
1423100387; 1423100395; 9781423100386, $16.99; 9781423100393
                                                             LC 2007061358

This graphic novel, by John Porcellino, "introduces ...Henry David Thoreau.... Thoreau's writings, excerpted out of chronological order, are recast into a narrative that moves from the philosopher's self-ostracism from society and his time at Walden and into the feeling of calm reverie he took from his experiences." (Booklist)

"Presents in graphic novel format an account of the two years that Thoreau spent at Walden Pond, excerpted from Thoreau's writings." Publisher's note

Includes bibliographical references (p. 99)

Powell, Eric

Billy the Kid's Old Timey Oddities. Dark Horse Comics 2006 un Illustration

Grades: 10 11 12 Adult   **741.5; Fic**

1. Graphic novels; 2. Horror graphic novels; 3. Monsters — Graphic novels

1-59307-448-4, $13.95

Notorious outlaw and gunslinger William Henry McCarty — known as Billy the Kid — faked his death and is alive and well when Fineas Sproule, the four-armed owner of a sideshow called Sproule's Biological Curiosities, identifies him and then makes an offer the Kid can't refuse. They seek a mystical gem called the Golem's Heart, and they must travel from the U.S. to Europe, to an isolated castle that is home to Victor Frankenstein. They need Billy's prowess with guns to protect them on their journey. When they arrive in the village near the castle, however, everyone is captured by the mad scientist, who plans to conduct horrible and nasty experiments on everyone. Billy has thought of his companions as freaks, but they're nothing like the pitiable monsters created by Frankenstein. This will appeal to horror movie fans who love monsters.

Originally published as Billy the Kid's Old Timey Oddities issues #1-4.

The **Goon** Vol. 1: Nothin' But Misery. Dark Horse Comics 2003 un Illustration

Grades: 9 10 11 12 Adult   **741.5; Fic**

1. Graphic novels; 2. Horror graphic novels; 3. Humorous graphic novels

1-56971-998-5, $15.95

Bones will be broken and heads will roll! An insane priest is building himself an army of the undead and filling the town with zombies, and there's only one man who can put them in their place: the man they call Goon. This volume collects The Goon series and The Goon Color Special, originally published by Albatross Exploding Funny Books, presented here for the first time in full color. Readers meet Goon, his pal Frankie, and lots of weird monsters in a story that mixes crime noir, horror, and slapstick comedy. The monsters and zombies look like they just came out of an old EC horror comic; they look icky but funny at the same time.

Powell, Nate

★ **Swallow** me whole. Top Shelf Productions 2008 un Illustration

Grades: 10 11 12 Adult

741.5; Fic

1. Graphic novels; 2. Mental illness — Graphic novels

978-1-60309-033-9, $20.95

Stepsiblings Ruth and Perry share their secrets with each other; Ruth hears insects talking to her, and Perry has to deal with a tiny wizard who forces him to draw all the time. In high school, Ruth is diagnosed as an obsessive compulsive with schizophrenic tendencies, while Perry manages to hide his wizard. Ruth sees cicadas and other insects always surrounding her, to the point that she thinks she's completely covered with them and she can fly. Her Memaw (grandmother) warns her that what she sees can swallow her whole. This book includes considerable use of foul language, especially the f-bomb, and the story takes a very thoughtful, mature reader to comprehend what is happening.

Courtesy of IDW Publishing

Priddy, Joel

The **gift** of the Magi. It Books/HarperCollins 2009 un Illustration

Grades: 5 6 7 8 9 10 11 12 Adult   **741.5; Fic**

1. Authors; 2. Christmas — Graphic novels; 3. Gifts — Graphic novels; 4. Graphic novels; 5. Short story writers; 6. Henry, O., 1862-1910 — Adaptations

978-0-06-178239-8, $14.99

Della and Jim are a young married couple, struggling to make ends meet when Jim's pay has been cut. It's Christmas time, but despite squeezing every penny, Della has managed to save only a little bit of money, and it's not enough to buy Jim a good present. He owns a gold pocket watch, and Della wants to buy him a chain for it. She has only one thing of value that she can sell her beautiful, long, long hair. Out of her love for Jim, Della sacrifices her hair. And, of course, Jim has sacrificed his gold pocket watch in order to buy beautiful hair combs for Della's gorgeous hair. As O. Henry says, they "most unwisely sacrificed for each other the greatest treasures of their house," but also that "of all who give gifts these two were the wisest." Joel Priddy's adaptation of this classic story uses black and white illustrations except when Della lets down her hair to consider her one treasure. He preserves much of O. Henry's original prose, which means that younger readers will have to look up a lot of words to understand the story. This book is suitable for younger readers but will also appeal to teens and adults.

Prince, Liz

★ **Tomboy:** A Graphic Memoir. by Liz Prince. Zest Books 2014 256 p. Illustration

Grades: 7 8 9 10 11 12 Adult

1. Cartoonists — Caricatures and cartoons; 2. Cartoonists — United States — Biography; 3. Gender identity; 4. Graphic novels; 5. Sex role; 6. Prince, Liz; 7. Sex differences (Psychology); 8. Gender role; 9. Stereotype (Social psychology)

9781936976553, $15.99; 1936976552

This memoir, by Liz Prince, "is a graphic novel about refusing gender boundaries, yet unwittingly embracing gender stereotypes at the same time, and realizing later in life that you can be just as much of a girl in jeans and a T-shirt as you can in a pink tutu." (Publisher's note)

"Prince's honest voice and self-deprecating humor help make young Liz a sympathetic and relatable character. The simply rendered black-and-white panel drawings have an unpretentious quality, in keeping with the narrative tone." Horn Book

Quinn, Jason

Gandhi: My life is my message. by Jason Quinn; illustrated by Naresh Kumar. Random House Inc 2014 212 p. Color; Illustration

Grades: 8 9 10 11 12 Adult   **741.5; 92**

1. Gandhi, Mahatma, 1869-1948

9380741227; 9789380741222, $16.99

This book by Jason Quinn, illustrated by Naresh Kumar, focuses on the life of "Mohandas Karamchand Gandhi, better known as the Mahatma or Great Soul.... We discover the man behind the legend, following him from his birth in the Indian coastal town of Porbandar in 1869, to the moment of his tragic death at the hands of an assassin in January 1948, just months after the Independence of India." (Publisher's note)

"Just as the writing eloquently intertwines explication with reenactments of dramatic, poignant events, the panels are meticulously arranged to move the reader's attention from broad and busy scenes to intimate close-ups." Booklist

Steve Jobs: genius by design. by Jason Quinn; illustrated by Amit Tayal. Random House Inc 2012 104 p. Illustration; Color

Grades: 7 8 9 10 11 12 Adult   **741.5; 92**

1. Apple Inc. — Officials & employees; 2. Jobs, Steve, 1955-2011; 3. Computer industry; 4. Biographical graphic novels

9380028768; 9789380028767, $12.99

This graphic novel, by Jason Quinn, illustrated by Amit Tayal, presents a biography of the 20th-century technology entrepreneur and Apple Inc. founder Steve Jobs. "Steve Jobs and his inventions changed the world we live in." The book ranges "from his birth and his adoption, through the advent of the computer age and on into the digital age. Forced out of the company he created, his indomitable vision allowed him to change the world of computers, movies, music and telecommunications." (Publisher's note)

"This cleverly designed volume provides a concise but well-balanced view of Steve Jobs the wunderkind, including his difficult personality and complex genius." Booklist

Rabagliati, Michel
Paul Has a Summer Job. Drawn & Quarterly 2003 un Illustration
Grades: 10 11 12 Adult   **741.5; Fic**
1. Graphic novels
1-896597-54-8, $16.95
Paul is outraged that he is forced to stop his high school art training, but he's been asked to put art aside because his other grades are so terribly low. Defiant, he quits school and anticipates a summer of leisure. But instead Paul follows the path of so many Quebecois teenagers: he lands a job as a counselor at one of the many summer camps in the mountains outside the city. There he finds himself guiding a motley band of kids, misfits and troublemakers, much like himself. The book includes some nudity, sexual situations, and strong language.

Radtke, Kristen
Imagine wanting only this. Kristen Radtke. Pantheon 2017 277 p. Illustration
Grades: Adult   **92; 741.5/973; 741.5**
1. Cartoonists — United States — Biography; 2. Loss (Psychology) — Comic books, strips, etc; 3. Radtke, Kristen; 4. Cartoonists — Graphic novels; 5. Loss (Psychology)
9781101870839, $29.95
                                                LC 2016034575
In this graphic memoir, by Kristen Radtke, "the sudden death of a beloved uncle and the sight of an abandoned mining town after his funeral marked the beginning moments of a lifelong fascination with ruins and with people and places left behind. Over time, this fascination deepened until it triggered a journey around the world in search of ruined places." (Publisher's note)

"A fantastic example of the graphic novel's possibilities as a literary medium, this work is visually imperfect, lyrically beautiful, and unquestionably brave." Library Journal.

Raicht, Mike
★ The **Stuff** of Legend; Omnibus one. by Mike Raicht and Brian Smith; illustrated by Charles Paul Wilson III. Th3rd World Studios 2014 284 p. Color illustration (The Stuff of Legend)
Grades: 8 9 10 11 12 Adult   **741.5**
1. Kidnapping; 2. Rescues; 3. Toys; 4. Graphic novels; 5. Toys — Fiction
9780983216193; 0989574482; 9780989574488, $29.99
"This hardcover collection brings together the first two volumes.... As Allied forces fight the enemy on Europe's war-torn beaches, another battle begins in a child's bedroom in Brooklyn when the nightmarish Boogeyman snatches a boy and takes him to the realm of the Dark. The child's playthings, led by the toy soldier known as the Colonel, band together to stage a daring rescue. On their perilous mission they will confront the boy's bitter and forgotten toys, as well as betrayal in their own ranks." (Publisher's note)

"Wilson renders the harrowing closet netherworld with full-fleshed detailing and sepia tones that nail both the 1940s time frame and the classicism of children's stories. But don't mistake this for a kids' comic-the violence is often explicit, and the Boogeyman creepy enough to slither his way right back onto grownups' most-terrifying lists." Booklist

★ The **stuff** of legend; Omnibus two. by Mike Raicht and Brian Smith; illustrated by Charles Paul Wilson III. Th3rd World Studios 2014 270 p. Color illustration (The Stuff of Legend)
Grades: 8 9 10 11 12 Adult   **741.5**
1. Horror comic books, strips, etc.; 2. Kidnapping; 3. Toys; 4. Toys — Fiction; 5. Graphic novels
0989574490; 9780989574495, $34.99
The second omnibus edition "finds our toys at a crossroads. Unable to find their boy, our loyal toys' bonds have been tested and broken. Now scattered across The Dark, the toys must decide whether to continue their search or admit defeat and return home." (Publisher's note)

Rall, Ted
2024. NBM/ComicsLit 2001 96p. Illustration
Grades: 10 11 12 Adult
741.5; Fic
1. Graphic novels; 2. Satire — Graphic novels; 3. Science fiction graphic novels
1-56163-279-1, $16.95
Move forward two decades. The giant media moguls and software companies have become the new big brothers. They want the best for everyone. They know what's best for everyone. And society has chosen to be consumer heaven with no questions asked. A terrifying future where the past doesn't matter and no one cares. The motto to live by: "yes, no, whatever." Ted Rall updates and spoofs 1984 in a look at where the U.S. could be headed. Rall uses harsh language and some sexual situations.

Courtesy of NBM Publishing

Raymond, Alex
Flash Gordon: On the Planet Mongo: Sundays 1934-37. Alex Raymond, Don Moore; restorations by Peter Maresca. Titan Books 2012 192 p.
Grades: Adult   **Fic**
1. Science fiction comic books, strips, etc.
0857681540; 9780857681546, $39.95
This anthology, by Alex Raymond, collects the comic strips featuring the science fiction hero Flash Gordon published from 1934 to 1937. "Volume One will spotlight the work of Alex Raymond, legendary for some of the finest storytelling of the 20th century.... Introducing Flash Gordon, Dale Arden, Dr. Hans Zarkov, and Ming the Merciless, this volume will catapult readers to the deadly planet Mongo." (Publisher's note)

Redniss, Lauren
Thunder & Lightning: Weather Past, Present, Future. Lauren Redniss. Random House Inc 2015 272 p. Color; Illustration
Grades: Adult   **551.6; 741.5**
1. Meteorology; 2. Weather
0812993179; 9780812993172, $35
This book, by Lauren Redniss, focuses on weather. It "roams from the driest desert on earth to a frigid island in the Arctic, from the Biblical flood to the defeat of the Spanish Armada. Redniss visits the headquarters of the National Weather Service, recounts top-secret rainmaking operations during the Vietnam War, and examines the economic impact of disasters like Hurricane Katrina." (Publisher's note)

"This book is not simply a collection of oddments and odd fellows, but rather a genuine demonstration of weather as a phenomena and how it is fantastical on both the symbolic and systematized levels." Kirkus
Includes bibliographical references

Reed, Gary
Renfield: A Tale of Madness. Image Comics 2006 192p. Illustration
Grades: 9 10 11 12 Adult   **741.5; Fic**
1. Graphic novels; 2. Horror graphic novels; 3. Vampires — Graphic novels
978-1-58240-674-9, $19.99

This book delves into the story of the bug-eating asylum inmate Renfield, from Bram Stoker's Dracula. Renfield foretold the coming of the vampire to England. Possessed by almost demonic forces and impassioned with the zeal of a religious fanatic, Renfield must struggle to grasp the overwhelming need to serve the darkness against his own humanity. There is some violence in this story that retells part of the story of Dracula, and particularly of Mina Harker, from Renfield's viewpoint.

Regnaud, Jean
★ **My** mommy is in America and she met Buffalo Bill. Jean Regnaud & Émile Bravo; [translation, Vanessa Champion and Elizabeth Tierman]. Fanfare/Ponent Mon 2009 120p. Illustration
Grades: 6 7 8 9 10 11 12 Adult   **741.5; Fic**
1. Family life — Graphic novels; 2. Graphic novels; 3. Mother — Graphic novels; 4. School life — Graphic novels
978-84-96427-85-3, $25

Essentials Award winner at the 35th Festival of Angouleme,n France, 2008; Tam Tam Literary Award 2009 from Salon du Livres et de la Presse Jeunesse, for Comic Album, age group eight to thirteen years old.

Narrator Jean has just started first grade and has a younger brother, Paul, in kindergarten. They live with their factory boss father and nanny Yvette; Jean says his mother is on a trip. As he talks about his first day at school, meeting a new friend, Alain, and fighting with Paul, he mentions his mother has been away so long he can't quite remember her. Next door neighbor Michelle claims to be receiving postcards from Jean's mother and reads them to him; they come from places such as Switzerland and the United States. As the reader sees Jean and Paul spend a day with their mother's parents and interact with their grandparents' friends, the reader understands what Jean does not: his mother is dead. This book, translated from its original French, won an award for best comic album for ages eight to thirteen; however, with the essential fact never stated and Jean deciding that he's getting to old to believe in his mother, just as he's too old to believe in Father Christmas, makes this more suitable for the upper age range, teens, and adults.

Remender, Rick
Black Science 1. Rick Remender; illustrated by Matteo Scalera and Dean White. Image Comics 2014 152 p. Illustration
Grades: Adult   **741.5/973**
1. Science — Fiction; 2. Reality
9.78161E+12

LC 2015374544
In this graphic novel by Rick Remender "Grant McKay, former member of The Anarchistic Order of Scientists, has finally done the impossible: He has deciphered Black Science and punched through the barriers of reality. But what lies beyond the veil is...chaos. Grant and his team are lost, living ghosts shipwrecked on an infinite ocean of alien worlds, barreling through the long-forgotten, ancient, and unimaginable dark realms." (Publisher's note)

Deadly Class; Volume 1: Reagan Youth. Rick Remender, writer, co-creator; Wes Craig, artist, co-creator; Lee Loughridge, colorist; Rus Wooton, letterer; Sebastian Girner, editor. Image Comics 2014 160 p. Color; Illustration
Grades: 11 12 Adult   **741.5; Fic**
1. Assassins — Fiction; 2. School stories — Graphic novels
1632150034; 9781632150035, $9.99

"It's 1987. Marcus Lopez hates school.... The jocks are hassling his friends. He can't focus in class. But...the teachers are members of an ancient league of assassins, the class he's failing is 'Dismemberment 101,' and his crush has a double-digit body count. Welcome to the most brutal high school on earth." (Publisher's note)
Originally published in single magazine form as Deadly class #1-6; Volume 1 of an ongoing series

Fear Agent Volume One: Re-Ignition. story, Rick Remender; pencils, Tony Moore. Dark Horse Comics 2007 un Illustration
Grades: 9 10 11 12 Adult   **741.5; Fic**
1. Adventure graphic novels; 2. Graphic novels; 3. Science fiction graphic novels
978-1-59307-764-8, $13.95

Heath Huston, an alien exterminator, stumbles upon a plot by a race called the Dressites to send feeders to Earth. The feeders are a life-form that consumes all organic matter until a planet is destroyed. When Huston and the human scientist, Mara, try to go in Huston's AI ship to Earth, they discover that the ship has taken on a type of hyper-fuel it can't handle, and they crashland on a planet in its distant past, whose dominant race invaded Earth. Huston is the last of the Fear Agents, elite soldiers of Earth, and he thinks he can prevent the invasion by changing the past.
Originally published by Image Comics as Fear Agent issues #1-4.; Volume 1 of 6

Fear Agent Volume Two: My Way. Dark Horse Comics 2007 un Illustration
Grades: 11 12 Adult   **741.5; Fic**
1. Adventure graphic novels; 2. Graphic novels; 3. Science fiction graphic novels
978-1-59307-766-2, $14.95

Lost, beaten and trapped in the past, Heath Huston must face the demons of his inevitable future when he finds himself face to face with the automaton regime responsible for robbing him of all he loves. With the knowledge that the Feeders are progressing ever closer to Earth, will Heath be able to get payback from the automaton empire in time to save his home planet from the scourge of an alien infestation? This volume has nudity, sexual situations, harsh language, and violence.

Strange Girl Vol. 1: Girl Afraid. Image Comics 2005 un Illustration
Grades: 11 12 Adult   **741.5; Fic**
1. Graphic novels; 2. Horror graphic novels; 3. Supernatural graphic novels
978-1-58240-543-8, $12.99

Ten years after the Rapture, beautiful occultist Bethany Black and her pet runt demon Bloato embark on a road trip to the last open gateway to heaven, in hopes of befriending God and escaping hell on earth. The book includes considerable graphic violence, harsh language, and some nudity.

Strange Girl Vol. 2: Heaven Knows I'm Miserable Now. Image Comics 2006 un Illustration
Grades: 11 12 Adult   **741.5; Fic**
1. Graphic novels; 2. Horror graphic novels; 3. Supernatural graphic novels
978-1-58240-642-8, $14.99

There's a point in every journey where there seems to be no light — no hope. After returning to the human stronghold, Dead Western, Bethany Black learns there is little hope she'll ever find respite from hell on Earth.

The book includes considerable graphic violence, harsh language, and some nudity.

Uncanny Avengers: the red shadow. Rick Remender, illustrated by John Cassaday. Marvel Worldwide 2013 136 p.
Grades: 10 11 12 Adult   **741.5; Fic**
1. Avengers (Fictional characters); 2. X-Men (Fictional characters); 3. Thor (Fictional character); 4. Wolverine (Fictional character); 5. Captain America (Fictional character)
0785168443; 9780785168447, $24.99

In this graphic novel by Rick Remender, "Captain America creates a sanctioned Avengers unit comprised of Avengers and X-Men, humans and mutants working together...so why is Professor Xavier's dream more at risk than ever? The Red Skull has returned — straight out of the 1940s and full of hatred — and his rebirth will alter the Marvel Universe forever!" (Publisher's note)

"[D]ense, intelligent writing that asks significant questions; a battle not only of arms but of ideologies; and a cast of characters that gives movie stars like Captain America, Thor, and Wolverine their due without ignoring the rich personalities of lesser-known players.... Cassaday's art, the most purely gorgeous in contemporary superhero comics [is] so clean and clear the pages practically glow with life." Booklist

Revel, Brahm
Guerillas Volume 2: Volume 2. Brahm Revel; [edited by] Charlie Chu. Oni Press, Inc 2012 120 p.
Grades: 11 12 Adult
741; Fic
1. Monkeys — Graphic novels; 2. Vietnam War, 1961-1975 — Graphic novels; 3. Military personnel — United States — Graphic novels
1934964999; 9781934964996, $17.99
                                    LC 2012930679

Courtesy of Oni Press

In this book by Brahm revel "Private John Francis Clayton's strange tour of duty in Vietnam gets stranger as he struggles with the unbelievable facts he is faced with. The elite platoon of simian soldiers he's encountered don't make any more sense to him than the war he's been sent to fight, but is this squad of chain-smoking chimps the most dangerous force in the jungle, or are they merely a distraction from the larger evil growing in the wild?" (Publisher's note)

Rhoades, Shirrel
Comic books: how the industry works. afterword by Stan Lee. Peter Lang Publishing, Inc. 2008 406p. Illustration
Grades: 11 12 Adult   **741.5**
1. Comic books, strips, etc. — History and criticism; 2. Graphic novels — History and criticism; 3. Publishers and publishing
978-0-8204-8892-9, $32.95
                                    LC 2007-32719

Rhoades, who was publisher of Marvel Comics after Stan Lee and has worked in publishing for more than forty years, gives an insider's look at how the comic book industry works. He discusses how superhero characters are created, how comic books are put together, how they're sold, how comics' intellectual property is licensed to other industries, adapting comics to television and movies, what manga is all about, and the move of graphic novels into bookstores. The chapters are broken down into subsections, and there are frequent sidebars with labels such as "speak up,"

"flashback," "comics trivia!" and others that provide even more tidbits of information in a highly readable format.

★ A **complete** history of American comic books. afterword by Steve Geppi. Peter Lang Publishing Inc. 2008 353p. Illustration
Grades: 9 10 11 12 Adult   **741.5**
1. Comic books, strips, etc. — History and criticism; 2. Graphic novels — History and criticism
978-1-4331-0110-6; 1-4331-0110-6, $119.95; 978-1-4331-0107-6 (pa); 1-4331-0107-6 (pa), $39.95
                                    LC 2007-43460

Rhoades, former publisher of Marvel Comics (after Stan Lee stepped down to move to Hollywood and focus on Marvel Comics in the movies), dates the beginning of the American comic book to the 1930s, when the format was first used. He covers the history of comics from that time to the present, covering all the big names (Will Eisner, Jack Kirby, Stan Lee, etc.). The book is peppered with fun sidebars with such labels as "flashback," "comics trivia," "looking back," "true facts," and so one. These help to make the book fun to read. Rhoades doesn't employ a straight narrative, but includes interviews, the side bars, comics milestones, a list of fanboys who have and had careers in comics, and a comic book quiz.

Includes bibliographical references

Ribon, Pamela
My boyfriend is a bear. written by Pamela Ribon; illustrated and colored by Cat Farris; lettered by Saida Temofonte; color assists by Caitlin Like, Gabriel Fischer, Ron Chan, Allyson Willsey & Jon Siruno. Oni Press 2018 176 p. Color; Illustration
Grades: Adult   **741.5; Fic**
1. Bears — Fiction; 2. Dating (Social customs) — Fiction; 3. Human-animal relationships — Fiction
1620104873; 9781620104873, $19.99
                                    LC 2017952716

"Nora has bad luck with men. When she meets an (actual) bear on a hike in the Los Angeles hills, he turns out to be the best romantic partner she's ever had! He's considerate, he's sweet, he takes care of her. But he's a bear, and winning over her friends and family is difficult. Not to mention he has to hibernate all winter. Can true love conquer all?" (Publisher's note)

"Ribon's use of magical realism is a delight from cover to cover, as she cleverly navigates the foibles of millennial dating and friendships. Farris's cartooning is as expressive as it is adorable, inviting the reader to share Nora and the bear's intimacy with every panel." Pub Wkly

Ricca, Brad
Super boys: the amazing adventures of Jerry Siegel and Joe Shuster: the creators of Superman. Brad Ricca. St Martins Pr 2013 432 p.
Grades: Adult
741.5; 92
1. Cartoonists — United States — Biography; 2. Comic books, strips, etc. — United States — History and criticism; 3. Shuster, Joe; 4. Siegel, Jerry, 1914-1996; 5. Superman (Fictional character)
9781250049681; 0312643802; 9780312643805, $27.99
                                    LC 2013004046

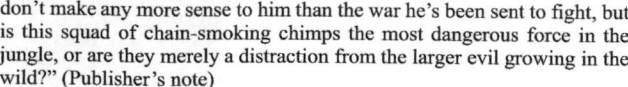
Courtesy of Macmillan

This biography of Superman creators Jerry Siegel and Joe Shuster, by Brad Ricca, "reveals the real-life model for Lois Lane...and the model for Superman himself (Johnny Weissmuller, who played Tarzan). At the center of the story, of course, is Siegel and Shuster's decision to sell the Superman rights to Action Comics for a pittance — a choice they lamented the rest of their lives. The pair endured poverty, bad marriages, bad health, and a lack of recognition for their work." (Publishers Weekly)

"Ricca's comprehensive biography reveals the turmoil and creative genius that led to our most enduring superhero, the Man of Steel." Pub Wkly

Includes bibliographical references (pages 403-406) and index

Richardson, Mike

47 Ronin. writer, Mike Richardson; artist, Stan Sakai. Dark Horse 2014 151 p. Color; Illustration

Grades: 11 12 Adult   **741.5**

1. Comic books, strips, etc.; 2. Samurai — Graphic novels
1595829547; 9781595829542, $19.99

Written by Mike Richardson and illustrated by Stan Sakai, "this collection of the acclaimed [comic book] mini-series recounts this sweeping saga of honor and violence in all its grandeur. Opening with the tragic incident that sealed the fate of Lord Asano, 47 Ronin follows a dedicated group of Asano's vassals on their years-long path of vengeance!" (Publisher's note)

"Richardson, founder of Dark Horse Comics, and Sakai, creator of the long-running and award-laden Usagi Yojimbo samurai series, combine talents to produce this terrific graphic interpretation of one of Japan's most important sagas.... The level of talent, the research, and the attention to both narrative and artistic detail shine through in this volume." LJ

Ricketts, Mark

Night Trippers. Image Comics 2006 184p. Illustration

Grades: 10 11 12 Adult   **741.5; Fic**

1. Graphic novels; 2. Horror graphic novels; 3. Vampires — Graphic novels
978-1-58240-606-0, $16.99

Once upon a time in swinging London, around 1966, there was a serial killer who loved Elvis, a fab foursome that worshipped Satan, trendy vampires looking for kicks, an ancient and hungry evil, young and hungry love... and there was revolution in the air. Get your trip together, baby. Tune in, turn on and fang out. The book includes some strong language and violence (especially vampire killing).

Ridley, John

The **American** Way. DC Comics/Wildstorm 2007 192p. Illustration

Grades: 10 11 12 Adult   **741.5; Fic**

1. Graphic novels; 2. Science fiction graphic novels; 3. Superhero graphic novels
978-1-4012-1256-8, $19.99

The 1960s were a decade of incredible change for America. It was a time of innocence. It was a time of optimism. It was a time of heroes. In the early '40s, the United States government hatched a plan to create the Civil Defense Corps: a group of "super-heroes" who could fight alien invasions, evil super-powered beings and communism, all in front of an adoring public, courtesy of television. But that dream was far from reality by the 60s, as new C.D.C. Marketing Director Wesley Catham is about to discover. How far will America go to protect its dream of a better tomorrow? White racists use the n-word, plus there's violence, and other foul language.

Another volume in this series is: Those Above and Those Below (2018)

Robbins, Trina

The **complete** wimmen's comix. edited by Trina Robbins, Gary Groth, and J. Michael Catron. Fantagraphics Books 2015 728 p. Illustration

Grades: Adult   **741.5**

1. Women cartoonists — History
9781606998984, $100

LC 2015943981

Ignatz Award: Outstanding Anthology or Collection (2016); Eisner Award: Best Archival/Collection Project — Comic Books (2017)

This book "collects two decades of the groundbreaking underground/alternative anthology Wimmen's Comix. In the late '60s, underground comix changed the way comics readers saw the medium " but there was an important pronoun missing from the revolution. In 1972, ten women cartoonists got together in San Francisco to rectify the situation and produce the first and longest-lasting all-woman comics anthology, Wimmen's Comix." (Publisher's note)

Robinson, Alex

Box office poison. by Alex Robinson. Top Shelf Productions 2001 602 p. Illustration

Grades: Adult

741.5

1. Authors — Graphic novels; 2. Brooklyn (New York, N.Y.) — Fiction
1891830198; 9781891830198, $29.95

LC 2009277811

Eisner Nominee: Best Graphic Album — Reprint (2002)

This graphic novel, by Alex Robinson, "is preoccupied with character.... The main personages include Sherman, a wannabe writer stuck in a dead-end bookstore job, and his college pal Ed, a budding comic book

Courtesy of IDW Publishing

artist still looking to get laid for the first time. There are also Jane and Stephen, Sherman's negligent Brooklyn housemates; Dorothy, Sherman's hard-drinking, chain-smoking...girlfriend; and Irving Flavor, a...veteran graphic novelist." (Publishers Weekly)

Our Expanding Universe. Alex Robinson. Top Shelf Productions 2015 256 p. Illustration

Grades: Adult

741.5; 741.5973

1. New York (State) — Graphic novels; 2. Teenagers — Graphic novels; 3. Family — Graphic novels
160309377X; 9781603093774, $19.99

This book, written by Alex Robinson, "returns with a "spiritual sequel" to his Eisner-winning debut Box Office Poison! It's been 15 years since the young cast...has graced the stage. Now, [this book] introduces another Robinson ensemble to explore how time can transform a group of friends.

Courtesy of IDW Publishing

Marriage, children, affairs, divorce and that's just the beginning!" (Publisher's note)

Too cool to be forgotten. Top Shelf Productions 2008 128p. Illustration

Grades: 11 12 Adult   **741.5; Fic**

1. Graphic novels; 2. Humorous graphic novels; 3. School stories — Graphic novels; 4. Time travel — Graphic novels
978-1-891830-98-3, $14.95

Andy Wicks is in his forties and a longtime smoker who has tried just about everything to quit smoking. Now he's going to try hypnosis, what's the worst thing that could happen? Well, when he wakes up, he finds himself back in high school, in 1985, as his high school sophomore self. Is he doomed to relive all his mistakes, or can he use his return as a second chance to get things right? Things like asking out that girl from math class.... Then he finds himself reliving time with his father, who died of Lou Gehrig's disease in 1985 after a sudden decline. Is this, after all, what he really needs to do? The book includes quite a bit of harsh language and lots of drinking and smoking at a party.

Courtesy of IDW Publishing

Robinson, Dave
  Introducing Ethics. Totem Books 2005 176p. Illustration
Grades: 10 11 12 Adult   **170; 741.5**
  1. Ethics — Graphic novels; 2. Graphic novels
  1-84046-580-8, $12.95
  What are the acceptable limits of scientific investigation and genetic engineering, the rights and wrongs of animal rights, euthanasia and civil disobedience? This book confronts these dilemmas, tracing arguments of moral thinkers, including Socrates, Plato, Aristotle, and brings us up to date with postmodern critics. Using cartoons and a spare text, this book provides an introductory look at ethics; it includes a list of books for further reading.

Courtesy of Icon Books

  Introducing Kierkegaard, Rev. ed.. Totem Books 2007 176p. Illustration
Grades: 10 11 12 Adult
142; 741.5
  1. Existentialism — Graphic novels; 2. Graphic novels; 3. Philosophy — Graphic novels; 4. Kierkegaard, Soren, 1813-1855
  978-1-84046-758-1, $12.95
  Soren Kierkegaard is regarded as the founder of Existentialism and the first modern theologian. Philosophy, in Kierkegaard's radical view, was of no use unless it permanently changed people's lives. His distrust of grand abstract schemes, particularly Hegel's, and his insistence that philosophy is essentially writing also identify him as a forerunner of postmodernism. This book uses cartoons and a spare text to introduce readers to the ideas and life of Kierkegaard; it includes a list of books for further reading.

Courtesy of Icon Books

  Introducing Philosophy. Totem Books 2004 176p. Illustration
Grades: 10 11 12 Adult
100; 741.5
  1. Graphic novels; 2. Philosophy — Graphic novels
  1-84046-576-X, $12.95
  This volume uses cartoons and a spare text to provide an introductory guide to the thinking of all the significant philosophers of the Western world, from Heraclitus to

Courtesy of Icon Books

Derrida. It examines and explains their key arguments and ideas. The book includes a list of books for further reading.

Robinson, James Dale
  Batman: Face the Face. James Robinson, writer; Leonard Kirk, Don Kramer, pencillers. DC Comics 2006 192p. Illustration
Grades: 10 11 12 Adult   **741.5; Fic**
  1. Batman (Fictional character); 2. Graphic novels; 3. Mystery graphic novels; 4. Superhero graphic novels; 5. Robin (Fictional character)
  978-1-4012-0910-0, $14.99
  One year ago, Batman and Robin disappeared from Gotham City. Before his departure, Batman chose a guardian to protect Gotham's citizens from the city's usual predators. Now, the Dynamic Duo return to find that some of their most notorious foes are being brutally murdered, leaving Batman to wonder if the man he entrusted to carry on in his place has confused justice with vengeance. With James Gordon back as Commissioner and Harvey Bullock back on the Gotham police force, it's almost like old times. But Bruce Wayne also has a decision to make about Tim Drake. The book includes some graphic violence.

  The **Shade**. James Robinson, Cully Hamner, Frazer Irving, Javier Pulido, Gene Ha, Darwyn Cooke, Jill Thompson. DC Comics 2013 280 p.
Grades: Adult   **741.5**
  1. Adventure graphic novels; 2. Heroes and heroines — Fiction
  1401237827; 9781401237820, $19.99
                    LC 2012046875
  In this graphic novel, author James Robinson "returns to the world of his acclaimed Starman series in this new graphic novel starring the antihero known as The Shade! An attack at the Starman museum kicks off a globe-hopping, centuries spanning quest that will irrevocably change The Shade's life, and ultimately shed light on his true origin!" (Publisher's note)
  Originally published in single magazine form in The Shade 1-12.

  The **Starman** omnibus; Volume one. by James Robinson, illustrated by Tony Harris. DC Comics 2008 448 p. Color illustration
Grades: Adult   **741.5**
  1. Superhero comic books, strips, etc.; 2. Superheroes — Fiction
  1401216994; 9781401216993, $49.99; 9781401219376
                    LC 2011534024
  "Jack Knight — antiques collector and dealer — inherits the name and powers of his father's old Starman identity from his older brother, who has been assassinated. Reluctantly adjusting to his role, Jack reinvents the look of Starman, ditching the traditional red and green in favor of black leather and aviator goggles." (Publisher's note)
  "Of the spate of more-realistic, adult-aimed superhero comics that came in the wake of Alan Moore's genre-defying Watchmen (1987), Starman is arguably the most ambitious and thoughtful." Booklist
  Originally published in single magazine form in Starman #0, 1-16 — T.p. verso.; Volume 1 of 6

Robinson, Jerry
  The **comics:** an illustrated history of comic strip art 1895-2010. Jerry Robinson; illustrated by Walt Kelly. Dark Horse Comics 2011 394 p.
Grades: Adult   **741.5**
  1. Drawing; 2. Comic books, strips, etc. — History and criticism
  1595826572; 9781595826572, $39.99
  This book by Jerry Robinson is a "reworked and updated edition of the 1974 classic that chronicles the origins and evolution of comic strips, from prior to The Yellow Kid through today, and highlights the game-changing contributions of such creative luminaries as Milton Caniff, Walt Kelly, Hal Foster, and Winsor McCay, among countless others." (Publisher's note)

Rodriguez, Jason

Postcards: True Stories That Never Happened. Random House/Villard 2007 152p. Illustration

Grades: 10 11 12 Adult 741.5

1. Graphic novels; 2. Short stories — Graphic novels

978-0-345-49850-2

Sixteen short stories inspired by antique postcards are in this anthology. Writers and artists include Tom Beland, Harvey Pekar, Stuart Moore, Neil Kleid, A. David Lewis, Ande Parks, and others. Stories range from the elegeiac (Beland's "Time") to ironic ("Best Side Out" by Antony Johnston) to dark horror ("Send Louis His Underwear" by Matt Dembicki) to heroic (Robert Tinnell's "The Midnight Caller's Holiday in Hades").

Rokudenashiko

What Is Obscenity?: the story of a good for nothing artist and her pussy. by Rokudenashiko, edited by Graham Kolbeins, translated by Anne Ishii. Koyama Press 2016 168 p. Illustration

Grades: Adult

92; 741.5

1. Igarashi, Megumi, 1972-; 2. Obscenity (Law); 3. Graphic memoir

192766831X; 9781927668313, $20

Courtesy of Koyama Press

"Under the pseudonym Rokudenashiko (good-for-nothing girl), Megumi Igarashi creates cute vulva-imagery art, from cellphone cases to a full-size kayak. But the Japanese police noticed, and when the artist sent a 3-D file of the kayak design to crowdfunding supporters, she was arrested for distributing obscenity." (Library Journal)

Roman, Dave

Jax Epoch and the Quicken Forbidden: Borrowed Magic. Dave Roman, writer; John Green, artist. AiT/PlanetLar 2003 152p. Illustration

Grades: 7 8 9 10 11 12 Adult 741.5; Fic

1. Graphic novels; 2. Science fiction graphic novels

1-932051-11-2, $14.95

When teenager Jax stumbles into an interdimensional portal, she "borrows" several items: an ancient book, a pair of gloves, and a pair of boots. When she returns home through the portal, things are a bit...off. Her little escapade has caused magic to leak into her world, and now she's deep in trouble, unstuck in time and on trial for the crime of crossing dimensions. The story continues in Volume 2: Separation Anxiety.

"Jax is a great character — quite real but with flaws that get her into deep trouble while possessing the aplomb to get herself out." (VOYA)

Followed by Volume 2: Separation Anxiety

Rosa, Don

Walt Disney's Uncle $crooge and Donald Duck: the Son of the sun. [written and drawn by Don Rosa; lettered by John Clark]. Fantagraphics Books 2014 207 p. Color; Illustration

Grades: 7 8 9 10 11 12 Adult 741.5

1. Comic books, strips, etc.; 2. Fictional characters; 3. Ducks — Fiction

1606997424; 9781606997420, $29.99

LC 2012287668

This collection by Don Rosa, featuring Disney's Donald Duck and Scrooge McDuck, is "filled with epic adventures, like hunting for buried treasure or recovering stolen money.... At the end of each volume are whole pages of reference notes, explaining each comic in depth and addressing Rosa's process and nods to previous works." (School Library Journal)

"When Rosa began creating Uncle Scrooge comics in 1987, his work instilled childish wonder in readers. Disney comics had entirely disappeared from circulation, and those that had just preceded the fall had become completely hackneyed-rife with repeating storylines and drab artwork. But under Rosa's creative flair, a zippy, glamorous franchise suddenly appeared, with riveting stories and detailed yet kinetic artwork. While remaining totally true to Scrooge McDuck's ornery persona, Rosa turned the moody miser into a plucky adventurer worthy of Tintin." Pub Wkly

Other titles in this series are: Return to plain awful (2014); Treasure under glass (2015)

Rosenkranz, Patrick

Rebel visions: the underground comix revolution, 1963-1975. Patrick Rosenkranz. Fantagraphics Books 2008 245 p. Illustration; Color

Grades: Adult 741.5

1. American wit and humor, Pictorial — History and criticism; 2. Caricatures and cartoons — United States — History and criticism; 3. Cartoonists — United States — Biography; 4. Erotic comic books, strips, etc. — History and criticism; 5. Underground comic books, strips, etc. — History and criticism; 6. San Francisco (Calif.) — History; 7. Comic books, strips, etc. — History; 8. Cartoonists

156097706X; 9781560977063, $34.99

LC 2013497143

This book, by Patrick Rosenkranz, "is a...chronicle of the guerilla art movement that changed comics and popular culture forever. This comprehensive book follows the movements of about 50 artists from 1963 to 1975, the heyday of the underground comix movement.... The book is centered in San Francisco's Haight-Ashbury district, where Crumb and the rest of his Zap cronies commingled with the rest of the city's countercultural scene." (Publisher's note)

Includes bibliographical references (p. 238) and index

Ross, Edward (Comic book artist)

★ **Filmish:** A Graphic Journey Through Film. Edward Ross. Harry N Abrams Inc 2015 199 p. Illustration

Grades: 11 12 Adult 741.5; 791.43

1. Motion pictures — Production and direction — Graphic novels; 2. Motion pictures — History and criticism

1910593036; 9781910593035, $24.95

In this nonfiction graphic novel, by Edward Ross, "Ross's cartoon alter ego guides readers through the annals of cinematic history, introducing some of the strange and fascinating concepts at work in the movies. Each chapter focuses on a particular theme-the body, architecture, language-and explores an eclectic mix of cinematic triumphs, from 'A Trip to the Moon' to 'Top Gun.'" (Publisher's note)

Includes bibliographical references (pages 196-199) and filmography (pages 194-195).

Ross, Steve

Marked. Seabury Books 2005 un Illustration

Grades: 9 10 11 12 Adult 741.5; 225

1. Bible. N.T. Mark — Adaptations; 2. Graphic novels

1-59627-002-0, $20

An occupied country. A people infested with demons. A time of revolution. A liberator rises. One of the oldest stories in human history comes alive in this telling of the Gospel of Mark. Join a carpenter as he changes the world. This is a human story of passion and murder. Of a compassionate man brutally killed and yet alive. Ross has set the story in a futuristic, urban world.

Rowson, Martin

Gulliver's travels. adapted & updated by Martin Rowson. Atlantic 2012 128 p.

Grades: Adult   **741.5; Fic**

1. Gulliver, Lemuel (Fictitious character) — Comic books, strips, etc. — Fiction; 2. Graphic novels; 3. Voyages and travels — Fiction; 4. Literature — Adaptations; 5. Swift, Jonathan, 1667-1745 — Adaptations

1782390081; 9781782390084, $19.95; 9781848872820

LC 2012397583

This graphic novel, by Martin Rowson, is an adaptation of Jonathan Swift's original story. "After a series of incidents, including being involved in a car crash and being dropped from a helicopter, a man named Gulliver finds himself washed ashore in a land full of tiny people called Lilliputians. This is not the Gulliver of old however; this is his descendant, and he's about to discover an unnerving world." (Publisher's Weekly)

"Rowson revisits Jonathan Swift's classic caustic exploration of human nature in this visceral, contemporary graphic-novel sequel.... A filthy, fantastic and fitting continuation of a misanthropic classic." Kirkus

Rubio, Salva

Monet: itinerant of light. Salva Rubio, writer; Efa, art; lettering by Ortho; translation by Montana Kane. NBM Graphic Novels 2017 112 p. Color; Illustration

Grades: 9 10 11 12 Adult

92; 741.5

1. Monet, Claude, 1840-1926; 2. Painters — France — Biography; 3. Impressionism (Art)

9781681121390, $24.99

LC 2017910452

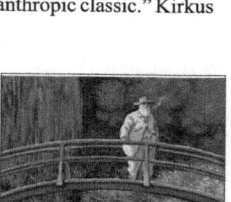

Courtesy of NBM Publishing

This book, by Salva Rubio, illustrated by Efa, narrates "the life of...French painter, [Claude Monet], one of the founders of Impressionism.... From the Salon des Refuses ('Salon of the Rejected') and many struggling years without recognition, money, and yet a family to raise, all the way to great success, critically and financially, Monet pursued insistently one vision: catching the light in painting, refusing to compromise on this ethereal pursuit." (Publisher's note)

"Monet himself narrates, and most of the text focuses on that narration, which allows the imagery to open and explore much of the same visual landscape that occupies his paintings. Efa's illustrations are stunning; full of strong, lush color and bold impressionistic brush strokes that call forth Monet's style but never imitate." LJ

Rucka, Greg

Batwoman: elegy. Greg Rucka, writer; J.H. Williams III, artist; Dave Stewart, colorist; Todd Klein, letters.. DC Comics 2010 1 v. Color illustration

Grades: 11 12 Adult   **741.5**

1. Batwoman (Fictitious character) — Comic books, strips, etc.; 2. Superheroes — Fiction; 3. Graphic novels; 4. Mentally ill — Fiction

9781401226923, $24.99; 1401226922

LC 2010283560

"Batwoman battles a madwoman known only as Alice, inspired by Alice in Wonderland, who sees her life as a fairy tale and everyone around her as expendable! Batwoman must stop Alice from unleashing a toxic death cloud over all of Gotham City — but Alice has more up her sleeve than just poison, and Batwoman's life will never ever be the same." (Publisher's note)

"[A] nuanced, literary, and culturally charged story, but the real knockout element is Williams' art nouveau inspired compositions." Booklist

Lazarus; Book One. By Greg Rucka, illustrated by Michael Lark and Santiago Arcas. Image Comics 2013 96 p. Color; Illustration

Grades: Adult   **741.5**

1. Dystopian fiction; 2. Comic books, strips, etc.

1607068095; 9781607068099, $9.99

"Rucka crafts the story of a world shattered into fiefdoms and controlled by high-tech Mob families. Each family have their very own "Lazarus," a cybernetic warrior pledged to carry out the family's dirty work on their path to control their population.... Lark's sharp yet brooding art manages to be violent without becoming gratuitous, pulling back for the sake of tension and the movement of the story." Booklist

Originally published in single magazine format as Lazarus #1-4.;

Volume 1 of an ongoing series

Queen & Country: the definitive edition, volume 4. by Greg Rucka; illustrated by Anthony Johnston, Brian Hurtt, Scott Morse, Rick Burchett, and Christopher J. Mitten. Oni Press 2009 320 p.

Grades: Adult

741.5

1. Espionage — Graphic novels; 2. Spy stories

1934964131; 9781934964132, $19.95

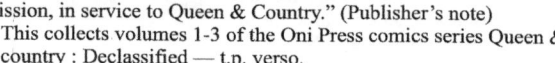

In this graphic novel by Greg Rucka, illustrated by Anthony Johnston, Brian Hurtt, Scott Morse, Rick Burchett, and Christopher J. Mitten, "readers are sucked into the...world of international espionage as SIS field agents are sent all over the world, often on their first mission, in service to Queen & Country." (Publisher's note)

Courtesy of Oni Press

This collects volumes 1-3 of the Oni Press comics series Queen & country : Declassified — t.p. verso.

Queen & country: the definitive edition, volume 1. by Greg Rucka. Oni Press 2008 376 p. Illustration (Queen & country)

Grades: Adult

741.5

1. Spy stories; 2. Espionage — Graphic novels

1932664874; 9781932664874, $19.99

Eisner Award: Best New Series (2002)

In this graphic novel, by Greg Rucka, "readers are introduced to the...world of international espionage as SIS field agent Tara Chase is sent all over the world in service to her Queen & Country all the while Director of Operations Paul Crocker walks a narrow tightrope between his loyalty to his people and the political masters that must be served!" (Publisher's note)

Courtesy of Oni Press

"[T]he work offers the sense that espionage is just another job, exactly as grinding and tedious as any other except that interoffice politics can get people killed. The action sequences are fast-paced and exciting." Pub Wkly

This collects issues 1-12 of the Oni Press comics series Queen & country as well as material from the Oni Press color special 2001 — t.p. verso.; Volume 1 of 4

Queen & country; Volume 03: the definitive edition, volume 3. by Greg Rucka; illustrated by Mike Norton, Steve Rolston, and Chris Samnee. Oni Press 2008 395 p. Illustration (Queen & country)

Grades: Adult

741.5

1. Espionage — Graphic novels; 2. Spy stories

1932664963; 9781932664966, $19.99

LC 2014378005

In this graphic novel by Greg Rucka, illustrated by Mike Norton, Steve Rolston, and Chris Samnee, "readers are sucked into the...world of international espionage as SIS field agent Tara Chase is sent all over the world in service to her Queen & Country all the while Director of Operations Paul Crocker walks a narrow tightrope between his loyalty to his people and the political masters that must be served!" (Publisher's note)

This collects issues 25-32 of the Oni Press comics series Queen & country — t.p. verso.

Courtesy of Oni Press

Queen & country; Volume 02: the definitive edition, volume 2. by Greg Rucka; illustrated by Jason Alexander, Carla Speed McNeil, and Mike Hawthorne. Oni Press 2008 330 p. Illustration (Queen & country)

Grades: Adult

741.5

1. Espionage — Graphic novels; 2. Spy stories

9781932664898, $19.99; 1932664890

LC 2014378787

In this graphic novel by Greg Rucka, illustrated by Jason Alexander, Carla Speed McNeil, and Mike Hawthorne, "SIS field agent Tara Chase is put through the ringer as she must contend with espionage of the industrial kind, ghosts from her director's past, and politicians eager to use the service to their own ends!" (Publisher's note)

This collects issues 13-24 of the Oni Press comics series Queen & country — t.p. verso.

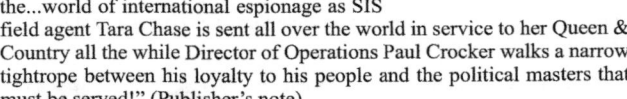

Courtesy of Oni Press

Superman: That Healing Touch. writer[s], Greg Rucka, Geoff Johns & Jeremy Johns; pencillers, Matthew Clark [and others]; inkers, John Dell [and others]; colorists, Sno Cone, Tanya & Richard Horie; letterers, Jared K. Fletcher, Rob Leigh. DC Comics 2005 168p. Illustration

Grades: 9 10 11 12 Adult   **741.5; Fic**

1. Graphic novels; 2. Superhero graphic novels; 3. Superman (Fictional character)

1-4012-0453-8, $14.99

Ruin is out to kill Superman and those closest to him. He has unleashed Replikon and his son to soften up the Man of Steel, but now he unleashes his deadliest attack yet, twin Parasites who can sap the life from even a Kryptonian. Lois Lane, still recovering from a gunshot wound, Lana Lang, and Jimmy Olsen are all threatened. And each time, Superman insists that no one will die on his watch.

Whiteout Volume 1: The Definitive Edition. Oni Press 2007 128p. Illustration

Grades: 11 12 Adult   **741.5; Fic**

1. Graphic novels; 2. Mystery graphic novels

978-1-932664-70-6, $13.95

One of Oni Press' earliest and most acclaimed books returns in a brand new re-mastered and re-formatted edition. U.S. Marshal Carrie Stetko has made Antarctica her home. In the vastness of The Ice, she found peace...Or at least that's what she thought, until someone commits a murder in her jurisdiction and the lawwoman is forced to use her detective skills once more or become another victim to this mysterious killer. The book includes violence and harsh language, including copious use of the f-bomb.

Courtesy of Oni Press

Whiteout Volume 2: Melt, The Definitive Edition. Oni Press 2007 120p. Illustration

Grades: 11 12 Adult   **741.5; Fic**

1. Graphic novels; 2. Mystery graphic novels

978-1-932664-71-3, $13.95

2000 Eisner Award for Best Finite Series/Limited Series.

One of Oni Press' earliest and most acclaimed books returns in a brand new re-mastered and re-formatted edition. U.S. Marshal Carrie Stetko investigates the explosion that destroyed a Russian science station that may have been a cache for weapons. The book includes violence, copious harsh language, nudity and sexual situations.

Courtesy of Oni Press

Wonder Woman: Land of the Dead. Greg Rucka, Geoff Johns, writers; Drew Johnson ... [et al.], pencillers; Michael Bair ... [et al.], inkers; Richard & Tanya Horie, James Sinclair, colorists; Todd Klein, Pat Brosseau, letterers. DC Comics 2006 128p. Illustration

Grades: 9 10 11 12 Adult   **741.5; Fic**

1. Graphic novels; 2. Superhero graphic novels; 3. Wonder Woman (Fictional character); 4. Flash (Fictional character)

1-4012-0938-6, $12.99

Just as Wonder Woman is starting to deal with her blindness (self-inflicted, in order to defeat Medusa), the Cheetah returns and teams up with another villain known for speed: The Reverse Flash. Wally West, the real Flash, joins forces with Wonder Woman to stop the villainous duo from causing untold havoc. Then, the goddess Athena sends Wonder Woman on a journey to retrieve Hermes from the Underworld. Joined by Wonder Girl and Ferdinand the Minotaur, Wonder Woman must face unimagined peril to complete her mission. But should she succeed, what will Diana ask in return from the all-seeing Goddess of Wisdom?

Wonder Woman; Volume 1: The lies. Greg Rucka, writer; Liam Sharp, artist; MatthewClark, penciller (pages 7-26); Sean Parsons,inker (pages 7-26); Laura Martin, Jeremy Colwell,colorists; Jodi Wynne, letterer; Liam Sharp &Laura Martin, collection and original series coverarti. DC Comics 2017 176 p. Color; Illustration

Grades: 9 10 11 12 Adult   **741.5; Fic**

1. Comic books, strips, etc.; 2. Female superhero comic books, strips, etc.; 3. Wonder Woman (Fictional character)

1401267785; 9781401267780, $16.99

LC 2017001077

"Princess Diana of Themyscira — known to the world as Wonder Woman — is one of the greatest superheroes in history.... To solve the

riddle of her origin, she must...[find] a way back to her vanished home. To get there, she must team up with her greatest enemy, the feral beast-woman, Cheetah. Will this unlikely alliance shine the light of truth on Diana's darkest secrets, or bury them — and her — forever?" (Publisher's note)
Originally published in single magazine form in WONDER WOMAN: REBIRTH 1, WONDER WOMAN 1, 3, 5, 7, 9, 11; Other volumes in this series are: 2, Year one; 3, The truth; 4, Godwatch

Wonder Woman; Volume 2: Year One. Greg Rucka, writer; Nicola Scott, artist; Bilquis Evely, artist (Interlude); Romulo Fajardo Jr., colorist; Jodi Wynne, letterer; Nicola Scott & Romulo Fajardo Jr., collection cover artists.. DC Comics 2017 168 p. Color; Illustration
Grades: 9 10 11 12 Adult   **741.5**
  1. Female superhero graphic novels; 2. Wonder Woman (Fictional character)
1401268803; 9781401268800, $16.99

LC 2017015508
"The team of [Greg] Rucka and artist Nicola Scott weave the definitive and shocking tale of Diana's first year as Earth's protector. Paradise has been breached, Ares stirs, and the Amazons must answer with a champion of their own...one who is willing to sacrifice her home amongst her sisters to save a world she has never seen. Wonder Woman's journey begins in this epic origin story!" (Publisher's note)
Originally published in single magazine form in WONDER WOMAN 2, 4, 6, 8, 10, 12, 14

Rugg, Jim
  Street Angel. SLG Publishing 2005 208p. Illustration
Grades: 10 11 12 Adult   **741.5; Fic**
  1. Adventure graphic novels; 2. Graphic novels; 3. Homeless persons — Graphic novels
1-59362-012-8, $14.95
  Homeless, orphaned, rarely in school, twelve-year-old skateboarder Jesse "Street Angel" Sanchez uses her board skills and kung fu to fight crime on the streets of Wilkesborough, the worst ghetto in Angel City. She has to fight Dr. Pangaea and his ninja forces, deal with time-warping pirates and Inca warriors, go dumpster-diving to find food...Jesse does a lot of slicing and dicing with her handy sword and knows how to handle automatic weapons as well in the many graphically depicted fight scenes.
  Originally published as Street Angel issues #1-5.

Runton, Andy
  ★ **Owly** Vol. 2: Just a Little Blue. Top Shelf Productions 2005 127p. Illustration
Grades: K 1 2 3 4 5 6 7 8 9 10 11 12 Adult   **741.5; Fic**
  1. Friendship — Graphic novels; 2. Graphic novels; 3. Stories without words — Graphic novels
1-891830-64-3, $10
  Owly is a kind, yet lonely, little owl who's always on the search for new friends and adventure. Owly learns that sometimes you have to make sacrifices and work at things that are important, especially friendship. He and Wormy try to help a stubborn bluebird by building a new home, but the bluebird rejects it and them.

  ★ **Owly** Vol. 3: Flying Lessons. Top Shelf Productions 2005 143p. Illustration
Grades: K 1 2 3 4 5 6 7 8 9 10 11 12 Adult   **741.5; Fic**
  1. Friendship — Graphic novels; 2. Graphic novels; 3. Stories without words — Graphic novels
1-891830-76-7, $10
  Owly figures out why he can't fly (he failed his childhood flying lessons), and helps another forest creature with his own flying problems. The flying squirrel is frightened by Owly, for he knows owls are hunters,

but Owly isn't like that. How can he convince the squirrel he just wants to be friends?

  ★ **Owly** vol. 4: a time to be brave. Top Shelf Productions 2007 132p. Illustration
Grades: K 1 2 3 4 5 6 7 8 9 10 11 12 Adult   **741.5; Fic**
  1. Fantasy graphic novels; 2. Friendship — Graphic novels; 3. Graphic novels; 4. Owls — Graphic novels; 5. Stories without words — Graphic novels
978-1-891830-89-1, $10
  A new visitor comes to the forest, but Wormy is scared of him because Owly had just read stories about a scary dragon, and the visitor seems to look scary. The visitor is just as scared of Owly. Things aren't just as they seem, and everyone soon finds out that a little bravery and a lot of friendship can fix just about anything. This is the latest volume in Runton's nearly wordless series about Owly and his friends.

  ★ **Owly** volume five: tiny tales. Top Shelf Productions 2008 175p. Illustration
Grades: K 1 2 3 4 5 6 7 8 9 10 11 12 Adult   **741.5; Fic**
  1. Friendship — Graphic novels; 2. Graphic novels; 3. Humorous graphic novels
978-1-60309-019-3, $10
  This volume gathers short stories about Owly and his friends, including stories originally published for Free Comic Book Day issues from Top Shelf Productions, the first Owly mini-comics, drawings of Owly before he met Wormy, and more. Among the stories, Owly saves a friend from drowning in the cold river when the ice cracks, only to get caught in the hole himself; Owly finds a way to keep both the bees and hummingbirds happy when they get into a "turf" battle; Owly helps a friend when she falls and breaks the fancy potted plant she bought for a present; and more.

Russell, Mark
  The **Flintstones**. Mark Russell, writer; Steve Pugh, artist; Chris Chuckry, colorist; Dave Sharpe, letterer; Steve Pugh, collection cover artist. DC Comics 2017 168 p. Color; Illustration
Grades: Adult   **741.5; Fic**
  1. Comic books, strips, etc.; 2. Stone Age — Fiction
9781401268374, $16.99

LC 2016056552
"Welcome to Bedrock, where Paleolithic humans head to dinner for a taste of artisanal mammoth after shopping at Neandertall & Big Men's Clothing, where Wilma shows her modern art, and where, if you take a plane, you could end up sitting on the literal tail section. See Fred, Wilma, Pebbles, Dino, Barney, Betty and Bamm-Bamm as you've never seen them before." (Publisher's note)
"Part of DC's Hanna-Barbera line, The Flintstones is not so much a reimagining of the original concept as a deepening. If the 1960s cartoon plumbed comedy from putting the familiar in an unfamiliar context, the comic thrusts contemporary constructs like politics, consumerism, the military, and TV news into a Stone Age setting to encourage a frank reevaluation of perspective." Booklist
Originally published in single magazine form in THE FLINTSTONES 1-6; Volume 1 of 2

  Prez; Volume 1: Corndog-in-chief. written by Mark Russell; pencils by Ben Caldwell, Dominike Domo Stanton; inks by Mark Morales, Sean Parsons, John Lucas; color by Jeremy Lawson; letters by Travis Lanham, Marilyn Patrizio, Sal Cipriano; covers by Ben Caldwell. DC Comics 2016 144 p. Color; Illustration
Grades: 10 11 12 Adult   **741.5; Fic**
  1. Women presidents — Comic books, strips, etc; 2. Presidents — United States — Fiction; 3. Graphic novels

1401259790; 9781401259792, $14.99

LC 2015038025

"Oregon teen Beth Ross has just been elected President of the United States of America.... Now the eyes of the nation are on Beth. But in a world so out of control that the poor are willing to shoot themselves on TV for a chance at a better life, will even the new president have the power needed to overthrow the nation's true leaders — Boss Smiley and his corporate shadow government?" (Publisher's note)

"Caldwell brightens the mood with crazy character design, particularly the special interest representatives hiding behind holographic masks and bloated walking tanks manned by unapologetic gamers. Trenchant political satire for the millennial set." Booklist

Russell, P. Craig

The **P.** Craig Russell Library of Opera Adaptations; Volume Three: Adaptions of Pelleas & Melisande, Salome, Ein, Heldentraum, Cavalleria Rusticana. P. Craig Russell. NBM Pub. 2004 144 p. Illustration
Grades: Adult

741.5

1. Opera — Graphic novels
1561633895; 9781561633890, $17.95

Courtesy of NBM Publishing

"This collection of [P. Craig] Russell's classic adaptations concludes with Pelleas & Melisande by Maeterlinck and Debussy, Salome by Richard Strauss and the all new The Godfather's Code from Cavalleria Rusticana by Mascagni." (Publisher's note)

The **P.** Craig Russell Library of Opera Adaptations; Volume 1: The Magic Flute. adaptation of Wolfgang Amadeus Mozart, by P. Craig Russell. NBM 2003 138 p. Color; Illustration
Grades: Adult

741.5

1. Opera — Graphic novels
156163350X; 9781561633500, $24.95

LC 2003041218

This book is an adaptation of Wolfgang Amadeus Mozart's "The Magic Flute," by P. Craig Russell. "The story begins as the Queen of the Night sets Prince Tamino on a quest to rescue her daughter, Pamina from the evil Sarastro. On the way, he meets the bird-catcher Papageno, who is 'persuaded' to help Tamino in his quest. Tamino's spiritual quest is counterpoised with Papageno's own earthly search for his one true love, Papagena." (Publisher's note)"

"Sure and confident, Russell's art switches from tense action sequences to slapstick without missing a beat. His sense of physical characterization is also impressive, helping readers keep track of Mozart's often confusing cast of characters.... Much of this graphic novel is told without narration or dialogue (presumably to simulate the longer musical passages Mozart included in the opera), and Russell's selection of sequential images keeps the story moving along without ever losing readers." Pub Wkly

Other titles in this series are: Volume 2: Adaptations of Paprsifal, Ariane and Bluebeard, I Pagliacci; Volume 3: Adaptions of Pelleas & Melisande, Salome, Ein Heldentraum, Cavalleria Rusticana

The **P.** Craig Russell Library of Opera Adaptations; Volume 2: Adaptations of Parsifal, Ariane & Bluebeard, I Pagliacci & Songs By Mahler. art visual direction, P. Craig Russell; story adaptation script, Patrick C. Mason; lettering by, Orzechowski & Kawecki. NBM Pub. 2004 129 p. Illustration
Grades: Adult

741.5

1. Graphic novels; 2. Opera — Stories, plots, etc.
9781561633739; 9781561633722, $24.95

This graphic novel, by P. Craig Russell, presents comic book adaptations of several operas including "Richard Wagner's Parsifal from the legend of the Holy Grail, Ariane & Bluebeard by Maeterlinck and Dukas, 'The Clowns' taken from I Pagliacci by Leoncavallo, as well as two songs by Mahler: 'The Drinking Song of Earth's Sorrow' and 'Unto This World.'" (Publisher's note)

Ryall, Chris

Beowulf. writer, Chris Ryall; artist, Gabriel Rodriguez, Mark A. Nelson. IDW Publishing 2007 104p. Illustration
Grades: 10 11 12 Adult

741.5; Fic

1. Fantasy graphic novels; 2. Graphic novels; 3. Beowulf — Adaptation — Graphic novels
978-1-60010-128-1, $17.99

This graphic novel adaptation of the motion picture screenplay written by Neil Gaiman and Roger Avary takes liberties with the original epic. In this version, the warrior Beowulf slays the monster Grendel who has slain many of King Hrothgar's warriors, but is seduced by Grendel's demon mother. This story states that Grendel is Hrothgar's son. It basically turns the epic saga upside down, showing that the heroes bring about the monsters. The book includes harsh language, nudity, and graphic violence.

Sabin, Roger

Comics, Comix & Graphic Novels: A History of Comic Art. Phaidon Press 1996 240p. Illustration
Grades: Adult Professional

741.5

1. Comic books, strips, etc. — History and criticism; 2. Graphic novels; 3. Graphic novels — History and criticism
0-7148-3993-0 (pa); 0-7148-3008-9, $59.95

Courtesy of Phaidon Press

This fully documented study explores the graphic qualities of the comic book, and the development of the format into a sophisticated and culturally revealing popular art form. The book traces the history of the comic from early cartoon-like woodcuts through to the graphic strips of the nineteenth and twentieth centuries. Organized thematically it explores the various genres of the comic book, including humor, adventure, girls' comics, underground and alternative. The careers of the creators of the best-known characters — from Superman and Tintin to Tank Girl — are revealed, as are the stories behind the much-loved comics such as The Beano (a well-known British comic) and The Incredible Hulk.

Sacco, Joe

The **fixer:** a story from Sarajevo. Joe Sacco. Drawn and Quarterly 2003 105p. Illustration
Grades: 9 10 11 12 Adult

741; 741.5

1. Yugoslav War, 1991-1995 — Journalists — Comic books, strips, etc.; 2. Sarajevo (Bosnia and Hercegovina) — History — Siege, 1992-1996 — Comic books, strips, etc.
9781896597607, $24.95

"Joe Sacco goes behind the scene of war correspondence to reveal the anatomy of the big scoop. He begins by returning us to the dying days of Balkan conflict and introduces us to his own fixer; a man looking to squeeze the last bit of profit from Bosnia before the reconstruction begins. Thanks to a complex relationship with the fixer Joe discovers the crimes of opportunistic warlords and gangsters who run the countryside in times of war. But the west is interested in a different spin on the stories coming out of Bosnia. Almost ten years later, Joe meets up with his fixer and sees how the new Bosnian government has 'dealt' with these criminals and Joe ponders who is holding the reins of power these days." (Publisher's note)

Footnotes in Gaza. Metropolitan Books 2009 418p. Illustration
Grades: Adult   **956.04**
1. Arab-Israeli conflict — 1948-1967 — Comic books, strips, etc.; 2. Violence — Gaza Strip — Rafah — History — 20th century — Comic books, strips, etc.
978-0-8050-7347-8; 0-8050-7347-7, $29.95
LC 2009-28433

★ **Journalism**. Joe Sacco. Metropolitan Books / Henry Holt and Co. 2012 xiv, 191 p. Illustration; Color
Grades: Adult   **355.0209**
1. Military history, Modern — 20th century — Comic books, strips, etc; 2. Military history, Modern — 21st century — Comic books, strips, etc; 3. Society and war — Comic books, strips, etc; 4. War — Comic books, strips, etc; 5. Comic books, strips, etc.; 6. Military history; 7. Journalism
0805094865; 9780805094862, $29.00
LC 2011052079
This book collects multiple short-form journalistic comics by Joe Sacco, depicting major military conflicts of the late 20th and early 21st centuries. Stories include descriptions of "the detention of Saharan refugees who have washed up on the shores of Malta;...the smuggling tunnels of Gaza; the trial of Milan Kovacevic, Bosnian warlord, in The Hague; and...[the U.S. war prison] Abu Ghraib." (Publisher's note)

Palestine. Joe Sacco; [edited by] Kim Thompson. Fantagraphics; Turnaround 2002 120p. Illustration
Grades: Adult   **741.5; 956.9405**
1. Israel-Arab conflicts; 2. Palestine — Graphic novels
9781560974321, $24.99; 1-560-97432-X, £18.99 : CIP entry (Apr.)
LC 2015947334
Sacco's book relates journalism on the life and politics of Palestine under Israeli occupation in graphic form. The work is "based on several months of research and an extended visit to the West Bank and Gaza Strip in the early 1990s (where he conducted over 100 interviews with Palestinians and Jews)." (Publisher's note)

Safe area Gorazde. Fantagraphics Bks. 2000 227p. Illustration
Grades: 10 11 12 Adult   **949.7; 741.5; 949.702**
1. Yugoslav War, 1991-1995 — Bosnia and Herzegovina — Gorazde — Comic books, strips, etc.; 2. Gorazde (Bosnia and Herzegovina) — History — 1992- — Comic books, strips, etc.
1-56097-392-7, $28.95; 1-56097-470-2 (pa), $19.95
Sacco "spent five months in Bosnia in 1996, immersing himself in the human side of life during wartime, researching stories that are rarely found in conventional news coverage. The book focuses on the Muslim-held enclave of Gorazde, which was besieged by Bosnian Serbs during the war. Sacco lived for a month in Gorazde, entering before the Muslims trapped inside had access to the outside world, electricity or running water." (Publisher's note)

War's end: profiles from Bosnia 1995-96. Joe Sacco. Drawn & Quarterly 2005 65 p. Illustration
Grades: Adult   **949.7; 741.5**
1. Yugoslav War, 1991-1995 — Bosnia and Herzegovina — Comic books, strips, etc; 2. Karadzic, Radovan V., 1945- — Comic books, strips, etc; 3. Seric-Shoba, Nebojsa — Comic books, strips, etc; 4. Bosnia and Herzegovina — History — 1992- — Comic books, strips, etc; 5. Bosnia and Hercegovina — Graphic novels; 6. Yugoslav War, 1991-1995 — Graphic novels
9781896597928, $14.95; 1896597920
LC 2005415443

This graphic novel, by Joe Sacco, presents two stories that "visit the Bosnian conflict.... In 'Soba,' Sacco captures the internal torment of the romanticized Sarajevo artist-warrior who captivated the Western media with his guitar and hard-partying ways. In 'Christmas with Karadzic,' Sacco gives the reader an inside peek at the darkly humorous news process that doesn't make the headlines back home as he chases after one of the most hated and sought-after Bosnian Serb leaders." (Publisher's note)
"These two stories by Sacco bookend his definitive works of comics journalism on the Bosnian War, The Fixer and Safe Area Gorazde. Like those books, these stories take readers with Sacco as he searches for some truth in all the conjecture and confronts his own fears and suspicions about the war." Pub Wkly

Sadamoto, Yoshiyuki
★ **Neon** Genesis Evangelion Vol. 1 2nd ed.. Viz Media 2004 184p. Illustration
Grades: 10 11 12 Adult   **741.5; Fic**
1. Graphic novels; 2. Manga; 3. Mecha manga; 4. Science fiction graphic novels; 5. Shonen manga
978-1-4139-0344-7, $9.95
A handful of teenagers must pilot huge biomechanical robots — the Evangelion combat units — against monstrous Angels" bent on destroying humanity. Among them is Shin, a very reluctant recruit whose scientist father is commander of the secret organization NERV and who has ignored his son all his life. The book includes violence, strong language, nudity, and sexual situations.

Said, Fehed
The **Clarence** Principle. SLG Publishing 2007 un Illustration
Grades: 11 12 Adult   **741.5; Fic**
1. Death — Graphic novels; 2. Fantasy graphic novels; 3. Graphic novels
978-1-59362-064-6, $12.95
After Clarence commits suicide, he wakes up to find a message written on the bathroom mirror; he opens the door and finds himself in a bizarre afterlife where he meets whimsical and strange people. Some images may be disturbing for more sensitive readers (such as the people with vacant holes instead of eyes, complete with zippers, and some dismemberments).

Sakai, Stan
★ **Usagi** Yojimbo: Yokai. created, written, and illustrated by Stan Sakai. Dark Horse Books 2009 62p. Illustration
Grades: 6 7 8 9 10 11 12 Adult   **741.5; Fic**
1. Adventure graphic novels; 2. Graphic novels; 3. Monsters — Graphic novels; 4. Samurai — Graphic novels; 5. Usagi Yojimbo (Fictional character); 6. Japan — Graphic novels
978-1-59582-362-5, $14.95
LC 2009-20024
As he walks through a spooky forest at night, samurai rabbit Usagi Yojimbo encounters a woman who begs him to find her daughter, who was kidnapped and dragged into the forest. That night, the yokai — monsters, demons, and spirits from Japanese folklore — are amassing for a once-a-century attempt to take over the living world. Armed only with his swords and his wit, Usagi can't hope to win against so many supernatural beings, but luckily Sasuke the Demon Queller has come, knowing about the yokais' plan, and together they fight the gathered monsters. The fighting is not graphic or bloody, and the monsters and demons aren't too scary looking for most younger readers.
"Sakai's art deftly demonstrates that comics can be simultaneously cartoony and scary.... Usagi Yojimbo is a genuine pleasure for readers of all ages." Publ Wkly

Sakakibara, Mizuki

Tiger & Bunny 1; 1. by Mizuki Sakakibara and illustrated by Masakazu Katsura. Viz 2013 168 p.

Grades: Adult   **741.5**

  1. Television programs — Fiction; 2. Superheroes — Fiction

1421555611; 9781421555614, $9.99

"Superpowered humans known as NEXT...fight crime...while promoting their corporate sponsors on the hit show 'HERO TV.' Hero Wild Tiger['s]...ratings have been slipping. Under orders from his new employer, Wild Tiger finds himself forced to team up with Barnaby Brooks Jr., a rookie with an attitude. Overcoming their differences will be at least as difficult for [them] as taking down...bad guys!" (Publisher's note)

Volume 1 of 9

Sakuragi, Yukiya

Inubaka: Crazy for Dogs, Vol. 1. Viz Media 2007 210p. Illustration

Grades: 10 11 12 Adult   **741.5; Fic**

  1. Dogs — Graphic novels; 2. Graphic novels; 3. Manga; 4. Seinen manga

978-1-4215-1149-8, $9.99

Naive Suguri wants to move to Tokyo and pursue a career now that she's finished high school. Teppei owns Woofles, a new pet store, and desperately needs someone to help take care of the dogs in his store. When Suguri's dog Lupin scores sexually with a purebred Labrador Retriever that Teppei wants to breed to get puppies to sell, Suguri ends up working at Woofles to make up for it. A fair amount of fan service (mostly panty shots), a little sexual innuendo, and lots of dog pee and poop make this title more appropriate for older teens who love dogs.

Sakurakoji, Kanoko

Backstage Prince, Vol. 1. Viz Media/Shojo Beat 2007 188p. Illustration

Grades: 8 9 10 11 12 Adult   **741.5; Fic**

  1. Graphic novels; 2. Kabuki — Graphic novels; 3. Manga; 4. Romance graphic novels; 5. Shojo manga

978-1-4215-1172-6, $8.99

High school freshman Akari stumbles into hottie Ryusei Horiuchi and hurts him with her school bag. That evening, she stumbles upon the kabuki theater where he, as famous kabuki actor Shonosuke Ichimura, is performing, and becomes his backstage assistant. Ryusei is very shy and aloof, and he's only opened up to his cat, Mr. Ken, and now to Akari; and she, despite herself, has fallen hard for Ryusei. Can an ordinary girl and a handsome, famous actor be together?

Sala, Richard

Delphine. Richard Sala. Fantagraphics Books 2013 126 p. Illustration

Grades: Adult   **741.5973**

  1. Fantasy graphic novels; 2. Fairy tales

1606995901; 9781606995907, $24.99

LC 2012289882

This graphic novel, by Richard Sala, darkly retells the fairly tale of Snow White from the perspective of the Prince. "A mysterious traveler gets off the train in a small village surrounded by a thick, sinister forest. He is searching for Delphine, who vanished with only a scrawled-out address on a scrap of paper as a trace." (Publisher's note)

Mad Night. Fantagraphics Books 2005 231p. Illustration

Grades: 9 10 11 12 Adult   **741.5; Fic**

  1. Graphic novels; 2. Humorous graphic novels; 3. Mystery graphic novels

1-56097-681-0, $18.95

Judy Drood, girl detective, along with her friend and reluctant aide, Kasper Keene, investigate a series of murders at Lone Mountain College.

Imagine Nancy Drew in a noir mystery, mixed in with macabre and humorous elements from Lemony Snicket books and Charles Addams cartoons.

"Reading a Sala comic is a unique experience, both jarring and fun, good for a rainy day or a stormy night." (PW)

Samura, Hiroaki

★ **Blade** of the Immortal Book 1: Blood of a Thousand. art and story by Hiroaki Samura; translation, Dana Lewis & Toren Smith; lettering and retouch, Wayne Truman. Dark Horse Manga 1997 136p. Illustration

Grades: 11 12 Adult   **741.5; Fic**

  1. Adventure graphic novels; 2. Graphic novels; 3. Manga; 4. Samurai — Graphic novels; 5. Seinen manga

1-56971-239-5, $14.95

1998 winner of Japan's Media Arts Award; 2000 Eisner Award for Best U.S. Edition of Foreign Material

"To end his eternal suffering, he must slay one thousand enemies!" Manji, a ronin warrior of feudal Japan, has been cursed with immortality. To rid himself of this curse and end his life of misery, he must slay one thousand evil men. His quest begins when a young girl named Rin seeks his help in taking revenge on her parents' killers...and his quest won't end until the blood of a thousand has spilled. The problem comes in judging who is truly evil. This series includes lots of graphic violence, much harsh language, partial nudity, sexual situations, and anachronistic situations and dialog.

Volume 1 of 30

Sanders, Joe

The **Sandman** Papers: An Exploration of the Sandman Mythology. Fantagraphics Books 2006 201p. Illustration

Grades: Adult Professional   **741.5**

  1. Graphic novels; 2. Graphic novels — History and criticism; 3. Gaiman, Neil

978-1-56097-748-3, $18.95

Neil Gaiman's Sandman is a phenomenon-a mass-circulation comic book that caught and held the attention of serious readers. Besides its mass appeal, The Sandman has long interested students and teachers in myriad disciplines, and they have begun sharing their reactions by writing analytical essays. This book gathers some of the best of this criticism, mostly by young scholars. The book contains 12 wide-ranging essays of criticism, exploration, and appreciation. The first half of the book addresses aspects of Sandman more or less in order of publication and the individual essays discuss particular Sandman episodes or story arcs, such as "A Midsummer Night's Dream," "The Kindly Ones," and "Ramadan." The second half examines Gaiman's Sandman stories in relation to his other work and work by other writers-such as Jorge Luis Borges's interest in variable truths or Terry Pratchett's adaptations of ancient myths for modern audiences. Others examine how Gaiman's stories relate to other genres such as horror fiction and to social and cultural concerns about the roles of women. Each grapples with questions of how script and art combine to make The Sandman an especially complex, rewarding comic.

Sandoval, Tony

Doomboy. Tony Sandoval; translated by Mike Kennedy. Magnetic Press 2014 136 p. Illustration

Grades: 10 11 12 Adult   **741.5; Fic**

  1. Teenagers — Fiction; 2. Rock musicians — Fiction

0991332474; 9780991332472, $24.99

Eisner Nominee: Best Publication for Teens (2014)

This graphic novel, by Tony Sandoval, "tells the story of an ordinary, lonely teenager with an active imagination and a love of metal music. When his girlfriend passes away suddenly, he decides to broadcast songs to her beyond the grave, playing his heart out under the secret name 'Doomboy'. What he doesn't realize, however, is that those broadcasts are picked up all across town... and beyond. Soon the music of Doomboy becomes legendary, and his innocent private life quickly turns inside out." (Publisher's note)

"Sandoval...places cartoon artwork — featuring a wan color palette and oddly large heads on slender bodies — and a well-detailed social scene replete with bands, friendships, breakups and jealousies against the familiar context of adolescent loss and longing to produce a story that is intimate in scale yet epic in emotional terms." LJ

Santiago, Wilfred
★ 21: the story of Roberto Clemente : a graphic novel. Wilfred Santiago.. Fantagraphics 2011 148p. Illustration
Grades: 11 12 Adult   **741.5; 92**
1. Baseball — Graphic novels; 2. Graphic novels; 3. Clemente, Roberto, 1934-1972; 4. Baseball players — Graphic novels
978-1-56097-892-3, $22.99
Presents the story of baseball star Roberto Clemente and his journey from an impoverished childhood to fame and fortune, as he strives to go the distance for respect.
Includes bibliographic references.

Satrapi, Marjane
Chicken with plums. Pantheon Books 2006 84p. Illustration
Grades: 11 12 Adult   **92; 741.5**
1. Biographical graphic novels; 2. Graphic novels; 3. Lute players; 4. Khan, Nasser Ali, d. 1958
0-375-42415-6; 978-0-375-42415-1, $16.95
         LC 2006-43156
In graphic novel format, the author chronicles "the life of her great-uncle Nasser Ali Khan. A revered musician, he takes to his bed and refuses sustenance after his frustrated wife breaks his tar — an Iranian lute — over her knee. It takes him eight days to die, and in that time Satrapi reveals the futures of his children and unearths his past.... Satrapi's deceptively simple, remarkably powerful drawings match the precise but flexible prose she employs in adapting to her multiple roles as educator, folklorist, and grand-niece." New Yorker

★ The **complete** Persepolis. Pantheon Books 2007 341p. Illustration
Grades: 11 12 Adult   **92; 741.5**
1. Artists; 2. Authors; 3. Autobiographical graphic novels; 4. Cartoonists; 5. Graphic novels; 6. Memoirists; 7. Novelists; 8. Satrapi, Marjane, 1969-; 9. Iran — Graphic novels
978-0-375-71483-2, $24.95
         LC 2007-60106
Ignatz Award: Outstanding Graphic Novel (2005)
Originally published in two separate volumes 2003-2004

Embroideries. Pantheon Books 2005 134p. Illustration
Grades: 11 12 Adult   **741.5; 955**
1. Graphic novels; 2. Women — Iran — Graphic novels; 3. Iran — Graphic novels
0-375-42305-2, $16.95
         LC 2004-58660
This book "explores the lives of Iranian women young and old. The book begins with Satrapi arriving for afternoon tea at her grandmother's house. There, her mother, aunt and their group of friends tell stories about their lives as women, and, more specifically, the men they've lived with and through." Publ Wkly

"Discussions of sex are frank and explicit and laced with high humor.... Satrapi's simple black-and-white cartooning style is tremendously effective, expertly portraying emotional nuances with just a few lines." Libr J

Sattouf, Riad
★ The **Arab** of the Future 2: A Childhood in the Middle East, 1984-1985: a Graphic Memoir. Riad Sattouf; translated by Sam Taylor. Metropolitan Books 2016 160 p. Illustration
Grades: Adult   **92; 741.5**
1. Sattouf, Riad; 2. Autobiographies; 3. Middle East — Social conditions
1627793518; 9781627793513, $26
The second volume of Riad Sattouf's graphic memoir "takes in the sweep of politics, religion, and poverty, but is steered by acutely observed small moments: the daily sadism of his schoolteacher, the lure of the black market, with its menu of shame and subsistence, and the obsequiousness of his father in the company of those close to the regime." (Publisher's note)
"Rather than being incongruous with the oppressive society and grim events he depicts, Sattouf's broadly cartoonish drawing style imparts a level of attachment that makes his story bearable." Booklist

The **Arab** of the Future 3: A Childhood in the Middle East, 1985-1987: a Graphic Memoir. Riad Sattouf; translated by Sam Taylor. Metropolitan Books 2018 160 p. Illustration
Grades: Adult   **92; 741.5**
1. Cartoonists — France — Biography — Comic books, strips, etc.; 2. Middle East — Biography — Comic books, strips, etc.; 3. Sattouf, Riad
9781627793537, $27; 1627793534
"Further episodes in the author's boyhood as illuminated through this highly praised, multivolume graphic memoir. As the blond-haired son of a French mother and a Syrian Muslim father, Sattouf (The Arab of the Future, Volume 2, 2016, etc.) recounts his years of being shuttled between their homelands and finding ridicule as a foreigner in each." (Kirkus)
"Sattouf's cartoony graphics, rather than being incongruous with the grim reality they depict, accentuate the story's dark humor and make Riad's harrowing tale go down a bit easier." Booklist

★ The **Arab** of the Future: A Graphic Memoir. by Riad Sattouf. Metropolitan Books 2015 160 p. Illustration
Grades: Adult   **741.5; 92**
1. Libya — Social conditions; 2. Arabs — Travel; 3. Sattouf, Riad; 4. Nomads; 5. Arabs
1627793445; 9781627793445, $26
         LC 2014041152
LA Times Book Prize: Graphic Novel/Comics (2015); Eisner Nominee: Best Reality-Based Work (2016)
In this graphic memoir, author Riad Sattouf "recounts his nomadic childhood growing up in rural France, [Muammar] Gaddafi's Libya, and [Hafez] Assad's Syria — but always under the roof of his father, a Syrian Pan-Arabist who drags his family along in his pursuit of grandiose dreams for the Arab nation." (Publisher's note)
"Caught between his parents, Sattouf makes the best of his situation by becoming a master observer and interpreter, his clean, cartoonish art making a social and personal document of wit and understanding." Pub Wkly

Savoia, Sylvain
★ **Marzi:** a memoir. [by] Marzena Sowa with art by Sylvain Savoia; translated by Anjali Singh. DC Comics 2011 230p. Illustration
Grades: Adult   **92; 741.5**
1. Authors; 2. Autobiographical graphic novels; 3. Communism — Poland — Graphic novels; 4. Graphic novels; 5. Novelists; 6. Sowa, Marzena, 1979-
978-1-4012-2959-7, $17.99

LC 2011011160

"Marzena Sowa ("Marzi") shows readers what life was like for her as a young girl growing up in what would soon become post-Communist Poland. While this book starts off with Marzi as a child, the broader political implications presented by the series of vignettes — such as her family's use of ration cards, waiting in long lines for food and petrol, and worrying about her father when he strikes from his factory — are more appropriate for older readers. Savoia's clean and expressive illustrations incorporate the extensive narration nicely and help move the story forward." Booklist

Schodt, Frederik L.

Dreamland Japan: Writings on Modern Manga. Stone Bridge Press 1996 360p. Illustration

Grades: Adult Professional   **741.5**

1. Comic books, strips, etc. — History and criticism; 2. Graphic novels; 3. Manga — History and criticism

0-880656-23-X, $19.95

LC 96-11375

Drawn in styles ranging from the crudely vulgar to the highly refined, and covering every genre from naive romance to high-tech cybervisions, manga (Japanese comics) are a sophisticated narrative art. In Japan, where manga were born, the art is actively evolving, with a whole new generation of younger artists making bold innovations in style and content. Dreamland Japan is a collection of thoughful essays on the state of the manga universe in the mid-1990s. Featured artists include Hinako Sugiura, King Terry, Yoshikazu Ebisu, Kazuichi Hanawa, Murasaki Yamada, Suehiro Maruo, Akira Narita, Shungicu Uchida, Shigeru Mizuki, Reiko Okano, Yuji Aoki, Yoshiharu Tsuge, Milk Morizono, Fujiko F. Fujio, Seiki Tsuchida. There are also discussions of the work of Osamu Tezuka and Hayao Miyazaki, plus features on important magazines of the time, like CoroCoro Comic, Jump, Big Comics, Morning, June, Yan Mama, and the avant-garde Garo, as well as the dojinshi (fan-produced work) phenomenon. Some of the illustrations come from adult titles and portray nudity and sexual situations.

Schrauwen, Olivier

Arsène Schrauwen. drawn by O. Schrauwen. Fantagraphics Books 2014 257 p. Color; Illustration

Grades: Adult   **741.5**

1. Colonists — Comic books, strips, etc; 2. Comic books, strips, etc. — Belgium — Translations into English; 3. Schrauwen, Arsène — Comic books, strips, etc; 4. Utopias — Graphic novels

1606997300; 9781606997307, $34.99

LC 2012285781

"In 1947, the author's grandfather, Arsene Schrauwen, traveled across the ocean to a mysterious, dangerous jungle colony at the behest of his cousin. Together they would build...a modern utopia in the wilderness — but not before Arsene falls in love with his cousin's wife, Marieke." (Publisher's note)

"Arsène's improbable trek through the jungle to achieve a mad dream recalls Fitzcarraldo, and the story's unsettling depiction of the madness underpinning European colonization evokes Conrad, but this is a stunningly unique work." Booklist

This story was first published as a three part series by the author himself — facing title page; The translation and production of this book are funded by the Flemish Literature Fund (Vlaams Fonds boor de Letteren) — end pages.

Schultz, Mark

The **stuff** of life: a graphic guide to genetics and DNA. written by Mark Schultz; art by Zander Cannon and Kevin Cannon. Hill and Wang 2009 150p. Illustration

Grades: 9 10 11 12 Adult   **576.5; 741.5**

1. Genetics — Graphic novels; 2. Graphic novels

978-0-8090-8946-8, $30; 978-0-8090-8947-5 (pa), $14.95

Eisner and Harvey Award winning writer Schultz uses the device of an alien writing a report to describe genetics and DNA in five chapters, from molecular structure of Earth organisms to sexual reproduction to genetic inheritance to genetic counseling and the genome Project and beyond. The black and white cartoons add some humor to the sound information, and the book includes a list of suggested reading ranging from magazines and books to websites, along with a glossary of terms.

Includes bibliographical references

Schulz, Charles M.

★ The **Complete** Peanuts: 1950-1952. Fantagraphics Books 2004 330p. Illustration

Grades: 2 3 4 5 6 7 8 9 10 11 12 Adult   **741.5; Fic**

1. Graphic novels; 2. Humorous graphic novels; 3. Peanuts (Comic strip) — Graphic novels

1-56097-589-X, $28.95

This is the first volume of a project to collect all of Schulz's Peanuts comic strips from 1950 to 2000. This volume includes the strips published from October 2, 1950 through all of 1952. These early strips featured characters younger readers may not recognize: Patty (not Peppermint Patty), Violet, Shermy, and a Snoopy who behaves like a normal dog. Schroeder is a baby who's already a whiz at the toy piano; Lucy is a toddler who already causes trouble for Charlie Brown; Linus shows up as a baby in September 1952. Lucy pulls the football trick on Charlie Brown for the first time in November 1952. This volume also includes a biography of Schulz and a long interview with him.

Volume 1 of 26

Schutz, Diana

Sexy Chix: Anthology of Women Cartoonists. Dark Horse Comics 2006 104p. Illustration

Grades: 10 11 12 Adult   **741.5; Fic**

1. Graphic novels; 2. Short stories — Graphic novels; 3. Women — Graphic novels

1-59307-238-4, $12.95

Don't let the title fool you — this isn't the average collection of comics featuring impossibly proportioned vixens in spandex. This time around the sexy chix in question are the writers and artists behind the comics, representing some of the best and brightest talent contributing to the medium of comics and graphic novels today. With stories ranging from mainstream adventures to comic shorts to autobiography, Sexy Chix is devoted to the under-recognized contingent of female cartoonists in an overwhelmingly male-oriented industry. It's about time these creators get to tell the stories they want to, and the result is a variety of artistic visions and styles. Among the sexy chicks are New York Times best-selling author Joyce Carol Oates, Eisner Award-winning illustrator Jill Thompson (Scary Godmother), A Distant Soil writer/artist Colleen Doran, Bitchy Bitch creator Roberta Gregory, DC Comics writer Gail Simone, novelist Sarah Grace McCandless (Grosse Pointe Girl) and many, many more. Some stories include nudity, sexual situations, harsh language, and violence.

Schweizer, Chris

Crogan's loyalty. Chris Schweizer; [edited by] James Lucas Jones. Oni Press, Inc. 2012 150 p. Color; Illustration

Grades: 8 9 10 11 12 Adult   **741.5**

1. Adventure graphic novels; 2. United States — History — 1775-1783, Revolution — Comic books, strips, etc.
9781934964408, $14.99; 1934964409
LC 2011943514

"Schweizer takes another bite out of history in this story of two brothers divided by the American Revolution. Charlie, the elder Crogan and a Loyalist ranger, is infuriated that his younger brother would turn rebel, stating 'There's a passion that makes most young men wanna tear society down because they ain't in charge of it.' Meanwhile, Will, a colonial scout, is no less incensed that his older brother would stand for a tyrant against his own country." (Booklist)

Courtesy of Oni Press

Crogan's march. Oni Press 2009 212p. Illustration
Grades: 8 9 10 11 12 Adult
741.5; Fic
1. Adventure graphic novels; 2. Graphic novels; 3. Imperialism — Graphic novels; 4. North Africa — World history — 20th century — Graphic novels
978-1-934964-24-8, $14.95

When brothers Eric and Cory squabble at the dinner table, their father tells them the story of Peter Crogan, one of their ancestors, who fought in the French Foreign Legion in 1912. Crogan's five-year term of service is one month from completion when he's asked to stay and become an officer. His unit is stationed in North Africa, where the French hold territory and depend on the French Foreign Legion to police the territory, putting down the rebellious attacks of the Tuaregs. He finds himself torn between the heroic Captain Poitelet (who tends to be the sole survivor of various battles) and the grizzled sergeant who actually cares about the people the Legion polices. When Crogan's unit escorts a caravan that endures an attack by Tuaregs, the captain's reckless actions endanger everyone, and Crogan must find help. Schweizer's story includes the kind of violence military actions cause, but very little in the way of bad language. Some may wince at the heavily French-accented English of some of the characters ("zee Daughters of France send zem out to all of zee units," etc.). This action-packed historical fiction graphic novel will appeal to teens, but adults who remember such novels as Beau Geste by Percival Christopher Wren (and the movies, of course) will also enjoy reading Schweizer's tale.

This book is part of The Crogan Adventures series; Sequel to:
Crogan's vengeance (2008)

Courtesy of Oni Press

Crogan's vengeance. book design by Keith Wood; edited by James Lucas Jones with Jill Beaton. Oni Press 2008 185p. Illustration
Grades: 8 9 10 11 12 Adult
741.5; Fic
1. Adventure graphic novels; 2. Graphic novels; 3. Pirates — Graphic novels
978-1-934964-06-4, $14.95

Catfoot Crogan serves as an honest and honorable sailor on a ship commanded by an unjust captain when the ship is taken over by pirates. In order to save their lives, the sailors all take the oath to become pirates, but

Courtesy of Oni Press

Crogan immediately runs afoul of D'Or, a brutal man who enjoys torturing others. Catfoot is a pirate, but he's determined to remain as honest and honorable as he can be, which continually puts him in danger. This swashbuckling tale shows a less romantic story than Rafael Sabatini's Captain Blood, with more violence, but it is more action-oriented than merely violent.

"Filled with mutiny, ferocious storms, shark-infested waters, commandeering of ships, and — of course — swashbuckling sword fights, this book has high teen appeal." SLJ

Part of the Crogan Adventures series

Seagle, Steven T.
American Virgin: Head. DC Comics/Vertigo 2006 112p. Illustration
Grades: 11 12 Adult
741.5; Fic
1. Graphic novels; 2. Mystery graphic novels; 3. Revenge — Graphic novels
978-1-4012-1065-6, $9.99

Adam Chamberlain is a youth minister and author, head of a national virginity movement. When his fiancee, Cassie, is brutally murdered in Africa, Adam travels there with his black-sheep stepsister Cyndi, trying to discover meaning in Cassie's death. Confronted by hit men, paparazzi, pornography, and even the voice of God, Adam finds himself lost in a vortex of spiritually uncharted territory. This series has nudity, strong language, and violence.

Genius. by Steven T. Seagle, illustrated by Teddy Kristiansen. First Second 2013 128 p.
Grades: Adult
741; Fic
1. Quantum theory — Graphic novels; 2. Physicists — Graphic novels
1596432632; 9781596432635, $17.99

In this graphic novel, by Steven T. Seagle, illustrated by Teddy Kristiansen, "Ted Marx works hard at his career as a quantum physicist. But...then Ted makes a startling discovery: his wife's father once knew Einstein and claims that Einstein entrusted to him a final, devastating secret.... If Ted can convince his father-in-law to tell him what Einstein had to say, his job will be safe. But does he dare reveal Einstein's most dangerous secret to those who might exploit it?" (Publisher's note)

Kafka. Active Images 2006 un Illustration
Grades: 10 11 12 Adult
741.5; Fic
1. Adventure graphic novels; 2. Graphic novels; 3. Mystery graphic novels
0-9766761-5-X, $14.99

Dan Hutton lost everything...his name, his past, his wife, his life. Having lived in a witness relocation program for years, Dan is told his new identity has been compromised, by two different groups who each claim to be CIA operatives. Unable to trust anyone, Dan runs back to the world that took everything he loved, hoping he can reclaim his past. The book is filled with suspense and action with very little violence.

Sen, Jai
Garlands of Moonlight. Shoto Press 2002 86p. Illustration
Grades: 9 10 11 12 Adult
741.5; Fic
1. Graphic novels; 2. Horror graphic novels; 3. Vampires — Graphic novels
0-9717564-0-6, $4.59
LC 03-311055

Silent and merciless, a creature of darkness has come to prey on an island village. Babies vanish, mothers are murdered, and the threat of evil grows with each night. The village becomes a battleground as the onrush of the twentieth century clashes with tradition — and the restless spirits of the island's mythical past... Set in late colonial Indonesia, this book relates a Malay vampire legend in graphic novel format. Printed in a black and silver duotone, the book captures the feel of turn-of-the-century daguerreotype photographs. There is some violence.

Malay Mysteries Book 1

Seth

Clyde Fans Book 1. Drawn & Quarterly 2004 156p. Illustration
Grades: 11 12 Adult   **741.5; Fic**
1. Graphic novels
1-896597-84-X, $19.95

This book focuses on the lives of two brothers and their fan manufacturing company. After one more disastrous attempt at selling, Simon returns to the office defeated and unsure of what he'll do next. Even after studying manuals on the art of selling, he still can't seem to clinch that final deal. In the eyes of his brother Abraham, he is a failure. Simon's plight is reminiscent of Arthur Miller's play, "Death of a Salesman." Here, Seth explores the complex and fascinating relationship of the two brothers behind Clyde Fans. There's one brief scene of incidental nudity.

The **G.N.B.** Double C: the Great Northern Brotherhood of Canadian Cartoonists. Seth. Drawn and Quarterly 2011 133 p. Illustration; Color
Grades: Adult   **741.5/971; 741.5**
1. Cartoonists — Canada — History and criticism — Comic books, strips, etc. — Fiction; 2. Comic books, strips, etc. — Canada — History — Fiction — Pictorial works; 3. Private clubs — Comic books, strips, etc. — Fiction; 4. Cartoonists — Graphic novels; 5. Comic books, strips, etc. — Graphic novels
9781770460539, $24.95; 1770460535

LC 2011505786

This graphic novel, by Seth, is "a sort-of companion piece to 'Wimbledon Green' (2005), in which he limned a fictional history of comic-book collectors, Seth's latest effort postulates an alternate universe set in a Canada where lionized cartoonists were viewed as important cultural figures, with membership in a prestigious guild, the G. N. B. Double C. of the book's title." (Booklist)

Includes index.; Great Northern Brotherhood of Canadian Cartoonists

★ **George** Sprott: 1894-1975 : a picture novella. Seth. Drawn & Quarterly 2009 96p. Illustration
Grades: Adult   **741.5; Fic**
1. Comic books, strips, etc.; 2. Comic books, strips, etc.; 3. Television personalities
9781897299517, $24.95; 1897299516

"Seth weaves the fictional tale of George Sprott, the host of a long-running television program. The events forming the patchwork of George's life are pieced together from the tenuous memories of several informants, who often have contradictory impressions. His estranged daughter describes the man as an unforgivable lout, whereas his niece remembers him fondly. His former assistant recalls a trip to the Arctic during which George abandoned him for two months, while George himself remembers that trip as the time he began writing letters to a former love, from whom he never received replies." (Publisher's note)

It's a good life, if you don't weaken: A Picture Novella. by Seth. Drawn & Quarterly 2001 163, [20] p. Illustration
Grades: Adult   **741.5; 741.5/971**
1. Cartoonists — Canada — Comic books, strips, etc; 2. Seth, 1962- — Comic books, strips, etc; 3. Cartoonists — Graphic novels
1896597319; 1896597327; 1896597335; 189659770X; 9781896597706, $24.95

LC 2005440925

In this picture novella, author Seth "pays homage to the wit and sophistication of the old-fashioned magazine cartoon. While trying to understand his dissatisfaction with the present, Seth discovers the life and work of Kalo, a forgotten New Yorker cartoonist from the 1940s. But his

obsession blinds him to the needs of his lover and the quiet desperation of his family." (Publisher's note)

Originally serialized in issues four thru nine of the comic book series, Palookaville — T.p. verso.; It is a good life, if you do not weaken

Wimbledon Green: The Greatest Comic Book Collector in the World. Drawn & Quarterly 2005 un Illustration
Grades: 11 12 Adult   **741.5; Fic**
1. Collectors and collecting — Graphic novels; 2. Graphic novels
1-896597-93-9, $19.95

Meet Wimbledon Green, the self-proclaimed world's greatest comic-book collector who brokered the world's best comic-book deal in the history of collecting. Comic-book retailers, auctioneers, and conventioneers from around North America, as well as Green's collecting rivals, weigh in on the man and his vast collection of comic books. Are Green's intentions honorable? Does he truly love comics or is he driven by the need to conquer? Lastly, is he really even Wimbledon Green?

Sfar, Joann

Klezmer, Book One: Tales of the Wild East. First Second Books 2006 140p. Illustration
Grades: 11 12 Adult   **741.5**
1. Graphic novels; 2. Jews — Graphic novels; 3. Musicians — Graphic novels
1-59643-198-9

Klezmer tells a tale of love, friendship, survival, and the joy of making music in pre-World War II Eastern Europe. Noah is perfectly content as the leader of a traveling klezmer band, until his bandmates are brutally murdered by rival musicians. He sets out for Odessa alone, but is joined by Chava, a beautiful girl with a voice like an angel. Meanwhile, Yaacov is expelled from his yeshiva for stealing; he too makes his way to Odessa along with Vincenzo, a violinist, and Tshokola, a gypsy entertainer. When these five misfits finally come together, they must set aside their differences and learn to work together (and rock a crowd) through their music. Some nudity and a fair amount of violence make this better for older readers.

The **professor's** daughter. [story by] Joann Sfar & [illustrated by] Emmanuel Guibert; translated by Alexis Siegel. First Second Books 2007 63p. Illustration
Grades: 7 8 9 10 11 12 Adult   **741.5**
1. Graphic novels; 2. Humorous graphic novels; 3. Mummies — Graphic novels; 4. Romance graphic novels
978-1-59643-130-0; 1-59643-130-X, $16.95

LC 2006-22177

In Victorian London, Lillian, the daughter of a famed archeologist, has fallen in love with the mummy of Imhotep IV; he thinks that Lillian bears a strong resemblance to this long-dead wife. Their love faces many obstacles, from Lillian's father, the police, a pirate who is actually Imhotep III (yes, the father and another mummy), even Queen Victoria herself. Dainty Victorian manners mix with broad farce and black comedy in a beautifully illustrated book with muted colors and sepia tones.

★ The **rabbi's** cat. Pantheon Books 2005 142p. Illustration
Grades: 11 12 Adult   **741.5; Fic**
1. Graphic novels; 2. Jews — Graphic novels; 3. Rabbis — Graphic novels; 4. France — History — 1914-1940 — Graphic novels; 5. North Africa — Graphic novels
0-375-42281-1, $21.95; 0-375-71464-2 (pa), $16.95

LC 2004-61406

"A slinky gray cat lives with a rabbi and his beautiful young daughter. One day, the feline eats their parrot, only to find that he has gained the bird's ability to talk. Witty and highly intelligent, the cat immediately decides that he wants to learn more about Judaism, from the Kabbalah to the Torah.... There is plenty for teens to like — humor, romance, and theological questioning combined with a folkloric quality to bring to life a multifaceted work." SLJ

Vampire loves. color by Audré Jardel; translation by Alexis Siegel. First Second Books 2006 187p. Illustration
Grades: 9 10 11 12 Adult   **741.5; Fic**
1. Graphic novels; 2. Romance graphic novels; 3. Vampires — Graphic novels
978-1-59643-093-8; 1-59643-093-1, $16.95

LC 2005-21498
When the vampire Ferdinand breaks up with Lani, his cheating girlfriend, he starts looking for love and romance. In the process he meets the vampire sisters Ritaline and Aspirine, tries his hand at detective work, goes on a cruise and meets the ghost, Sigh, and gets mixed up in a fight between mummy pirates and Professor Joseph Bell.

"Edgy and creepy but at the same time universal and normal, Vampire Loves is a unique study in contrasts that will be a pleasurable discovery for graphic novel enthusiasts." Voice Youth Advocates

First published in four volumes in France with title: Grand vampire

Shaffer, Neal
The **Awakening**. Oni Press 2004 104p. Illustration
Grades: 10 11 12 Adult
741.5; Fic
1. Graphic novels; 2. Horror graphic novels; 3. Mystery graphic novels
1-932664-00-9, $9.95
Francesca, the only child of an affluent family, is excited to be attending one of the most prestigious boarding schools in New England. Unfortunately, things go horribly wrong when, shortly after her arrival, she finds one of her classmates brutally murdered, sending her into a deep shock, putting her into a coma. Even worse,

Courtesy of Oni Press

immediately following the tragic incident, Francesca begins to have visions of which girl will be slain next, and even though she has awakened, she's unable to tell anyone about it. Is this a new horror being visited on the longstanding institution, or is it something much more, going to the core of the school itself, to an evil that defies description? The book includes strong language, violence, and some nudity.

Shakespeare, William
William Shakespeare's King Lear. Black Dog & Leventhal/Workman Publishing 2006 148p. Illustration
Grades: 7 8 9 10 11 12 Adult
741.5; 822.3
1. Graphic novels; 2. Tragedy — Graphic novels; 3. Shakespeare, William; 4. Shakespeare, William — Adaptations
978-1-57912-617-9, $12.95
This graphic novel adaptation of King Lear, originally published in 1984, uses excerpted text from the play together with full-color illustrations to tell the story of the king whose ill-fated attempts to learn which of his daughters loves him best causes loss and madness.

Courtesy of ABDO Publishing.

Part of the Shakespeare Graphic Library.

William Shakespeare's Macbeth. Black Dog & Leventhal/Workman Publishing 1982 92p. Illustration
Grades: 7 8 9 10 11 12 Adult   **822.3; 741.5**
1. Graphic novels; 2. Tragedy — Graphic novels; 3. Shakespeare, William; 4. Shakespeare, William — Adaptations
978-1-57912-621-6, $12.95
This graphic novel adaptation of Macbeth, originally published in 1982, uses excerpted text from the play together with full-color illustrations to tell the story of the Thane of Cawdor who listens to a trio of witches and slays the King of Scotland to take his throne.
Part of the Shakespeare Graphic Library

Shanower, Eric
★ **Age** of bronze volume 3A: Betrayal part one. Image Comics 2007 176p. Illustration
Grades: 10 11 12 Adult   **741.5; Fic**
1. Adventure graphic novels; 2. Graphic novels; 3. Greek mythology — Graphic novels; 4. Troy (Extinct city) — Graphic novels
978-1-58240-755-5, $17.99
The graphic novel retelling of the story of the Trojan War continues, as High King Agamemnon's army passes the island of Tenedos on its journey to conquer Troy. When a snake bites Philoktetes on the foot, his cries of pain bother the army so much that Odysseus must find a solution. Then, the Achaeans send an embassy to Troy in hopes of preventing a war. This book includes some nudity and sexual situations as well as some violence. Shanower includes a lengthy bibliography of historical sources.
Sequel to Sacrifice (2004)

★ **Age** of Bronze: Betrayal part 2. by Eric Shanower. Image Comics 2013 176 p. Illustration
Grades: 10 11 12 Adult   **741.5**
1. Trojan War — Fiction; 2. Greece — Fiction; 3. Graphic novels
1607067579; 9781607067573
In this graphic novel, written and illustrated by Eric Shanower, "the Trojan plain fills with death as Achaean forces clash in blood with the Trojan army. In the city of Troy, Pandarus pulls the strings to put Troilus in Cressida's bed. But when Cressida is ripped away to the enemy camp, how far will Troilus fight? (Publisher's note)

"Shanower's graphic-novel retelling of the Trojan War is one of the great artistic visions of the comics medium. Where both mythology and heroic-adventure comics typically lean toward vast spectacle and archetypal characters, Shanower is uncompromising in his sharp, humanizing focus. Betrayal, Part 2, the second part of the third part of Shanower's projected seven-part series, begins with Achilles and his Myrmidons invading the beach of Troy and ends with Troilus' breakdown during a bloody skirmish with a squad of Achaeans.... Seldom has a work shined so brightly on every page." Booklist

★ **Age** of Bronze: Sacrifice. Image Comics 2004 223p. Illustration; Map (Age of bronze)
Grades: 10 11 12 Adult   **741; 741.5; Fic**
1. Graphic novels; 2. Greek mythology — Graphic novels; 3. Trojan War — Graphic novels
1-58240-360-0; 1-58240-399-6 (pa), $19.95
"Sacrifice begins by recapitulating the story thus far. Paris sails back to Troy, just as self-regarding and shortsighted as when he left. Thrilled with his own prize (Helen), he has no understanding of the political complications. Priam does, but he is swayed by the machinations of Helen and by Hecuba's generosity. Not only are the major characters (Achilles, Klytemnestra, Odysseus) complex, but even a minor player like Telephus is carefully developed." SLJ
Includes bibliographical references; Followed by Betrayal (2008); This is the second book in the author's projected seven-volume graphic

novel about the Trojan War. The first volume, A thousand ships, was published in 2001

Little Nemo: Return to Slumberland. written by Eric Shanower; illustrated by Gabriel Rodriguez. IDW Publishing 2015 120 p. Color; Illustration
Grades: 10 11 12 Adult
741.5
1. Friendship — Graphic novels; 2. Dreaming — Graphic novels
1631400592; 9781631400599, $21.99
Eisner Award: Best Limited Series (2015)

Courtesy of IDW Publishing

This graphic novel, by Eric Shanower, illustrated by Gabriel Rodriguez, "sees King Morpheus' daughter, in the Royal Palace of Slumberland, selecting her next-playmate — Nemo! Only Nemo has no interest in being anyone's playmate, dream or no dream!" (Publisher's note)

Originally published as: Little Nemo: Return to Slumberland, issues #1-4

★ The **Wonderful** Wizard of Oz. writer, Eric Shanower; artist, Skottie Young; colorist, Jean-Francois Beaulieu; letterer, Jeff Eckleberry; adapted from the novel by L. Frank Baum. Marvel Entertainment 2009 192p. Illustration
Grades: 3 4 5 6 7 8 9 10 11 12 Adult **741.5; Fic**
1. Adventure graphic novels; 2. Authors; 3. Children's authors; 4. Dramatists; 5. Fantasy graphic novels; 6. Graphic novels; 7. Journalists; 8. Baum, L. Frank, 1856-1919 — Adaptations
978-0-7851-2921-9, $29.99

A twister picks up the house Dorothy and her dog Toto are in and carries them from Kansas to the land of Oz; the house lands on top of the Wicked Witch of the East, and the Munchkins, who were her slaves, hail Dorothy as a great sorceress. All the girl wants is to get back home to Kansas, but all anyone can say is that she must go to the Emerald City and ask the Great Wizard Oz to send her home. As she travels along the Yellow Brick Road, she meets a scarecrow who wants brains so people won't think he's a dummy, a tin man who wants a heart so he can love, and a great cowardly lion who wants courage so he'll truly be king of the beasts. However, once they reach the Emerald City and each see the Wizard Oz, they learn they must do what no one, including the Wizard himself, could ever do kill the Wicked Witch of the West. Shanower's adaptation of L. Frank Baum's novel keeps all the charm of the original, while Skottie Young's art banishes any lingering images of the old Technicolor movie; Beaulieu's muted color palette works with Young's art, while Eckleberry's lettering adds to an overall effect of magic and wonder. This book will appeal to all ages

Other Oz adapations by Shanower and Young are: The Marvelous Land of Oz; Ozma of Oz; Dorothy and the Wizard in Oz; The Road to Oz; The Emerald City of Oz

Shaw, Dash
Cosplayers: perfect collection. Dash Shaw. Fantagraphics Books 2016 111 p. Color; Illustration
Grades: Adult **741.5; Fic**
1. Cosplay — Comic books, strips, etc; 2. Fans (Persons) — Comic books, strips, etc.
1606999486; 9781606999486, $22.99
LC 2016934405

This graphic novel, by Dash Shaw, "is an ode to the defining element of fandom. It celebrates both the culture's theatricality and D.I.Y. beauty —

as well as its often-awkward conflation of fantasy with reality — in seven interconnected short stories about two young women." (Publisher's note)

New School. by Dash Shaw. W W Norton & Co Inc 2013 340 p.
Grades: Adult **741.5**
1. Brothers — Graphic novels; 2. Amusement parks — Graphic novels
1606996444; 9781606996447, $39.99

In this graphic novel by Dash Shaw "a boy mov[es] to an exotic country and his infatuation with an unfamiliar culture...quickly shifts to disillusionment. Danny — s older brother, Luke, travels to a remote island, [employed by] ClockWorld, an ambitious new amusement park. Danny travels to ClockWorld to convince Luke to return to America. But Luke has made a new life...rendering him almost unrecognizable. Danny...explores the island, ClockWorld, and fights to bring his brother home." (Publisher's note)

Sheikman, Alex
Robotika. Archaia Studios Press 2006 128p. Illustration
Grades: 11 12 Adult **741.5; Fic**
1. Adventure graphic novels; 2. Graphic novels; 3. Science fiction graphic novels
978-1-932386-21-9, $19.95

In a future world full of human/machine hybrids and organic technology, a samurai named Niko serves the Queen. When a new piece of technology that can revolutionize the world and render cyborgs obsolete is stolen and its inventor killed, the Queen sends Niko to retrieve it. He must fight and kill many warriors along the way and succeeds, only to see the Queen destroy the object to create a hair ornament. He gives up the sword, but still joins yojimbo (wandering masterless samurai bodyguards) Cherokee Geisha and Uri Bronski to protect a caravan of pilgrims seeking their god's temple.

Sheikman uses color, differing visual styles, even vertical lettering (for Cherokee Geisha's speech), and combines genre elements of the Western, samurai action, and science fiction to create a story set in a well-realized world. Two short stories give background on Cherokee Geisha and Bronski.

Originally published as Robotika issues #1-4.

Shiga, Jason
Bookhunter. Sparkplug Comics 2007 un Illustration
Grades: 10 11 12 Adult **741.5; Fic**
1. Graphic novels; 2. Humorous graphic novels; 3. Librarians — Graphic novels; 4. Mystery graphic novels
978-0-9742715-6-9, $15

When a rare Caxton Bible is stolen from the Oakland Public Library in 1973, Agent Bay of the Library Police is on the case. Reading very much like a police procedural mystery, but set in the library, Bookhunter combines humor, library technology of the early 1970s, and lots of action movie tropes. The book includes a few harsh words and some violence.

★ **Demon;** Volume 1. Jason Shiga; [edited by] Calista Brill. First Second 2016 176 p. Color; Illustration
Grades: 11 12 Adult **741.5; Fic**
1. Mystery fiction
1626724520; 9781626724525, $19.99
LC 2015958711
Eisner Award: Best Graphic Album — Reprint (2017)

In this book, by Jason Shiga, "Jimmy Yee cannot die. A noose around his neck, a razor across his wrist, and even a bullet to his head all yield the same results: he awakes from each suicide attempt, miraculously unharmed, in his shabby room at the Sunbeam Motel. Has he gone mad? Or has he truly died and found himself in hell?" (Publisher's note)

"As with Shiga's other books, there are puzzles aplenty to solve, with an added layer of urgent narrative drive. Originally serialized as a webcomic, the story will prove just as addictive for readers finding it in print." Pub Wkly

Volume 1 of 4

Shimabukuro, Mitsutoshi

Toriko, vol. 1. story and art by Mitsutoshi Shimabukuro; [translation, Christine Dashiell; adaptation, Hope Donovan; touch-up art & lettering, Jim Keefe]. Viz Media/Shonen Jump 2010 208p. Illustration

Grades: 8 9 10 11 12 Adult   741.5; Fic

1. Adventure graphic novels; 2. Food — Graphic novels; 3. Graphic novels; 4. Humorous graphic novels; 5. Hunting — Graphic novels; 6. Manga; 7. Shonen manga

978-1-4215-3509-8, $9.99

Toriko is a Gourmet Hunter, who earns huge bounties for finding ferocious, delicious foods. We're not talking salmon fishing or deer hunting here, but eight-legged alligators and rare fruit guarded by four-armed, bloodthirsty gorilla-type creatures. Toriko himself has a huge appetite for the rare foods, and sometimes eats most of what he's supposed to bring to the fancy restaurants that hire him. Komatsu, the head chef at Igo, a restaurant that caters to those wealthy enough to afford the rare foods, tags along with Toriko, who is a muscular giant of a man. This odd couple forms a friendship born in their mutual love of fine foods. The book is full of crazy action, lots of bugeyed, drop-jawed, slapstick moments, and some potty humor.

Shimura, Takako

Sweet Blue Flowers; Volume 1. story and art by Takako Shimura; translation & adaptation, John Werry; touch-up art & lettering, Monalisa De Asis. Viz 2017 400 p. Illustration

Grades: 10 11 12 Adult   741.5; Fic

1. High school students — Fiction; 2. Shojo-ai; 3. Manga; 4. Lesbians — Fiction; 5. Friendship — Fiction

1421592983; 9781421592985, $24.99

"Akira Okudaira is starting high school and is ready for exciting new experiences. And on the first day of school, she runs into her best friend from kindergarten at the train station! Now Akira and Fumi have the chance to rekindle their friendship, but life has gotten a lot more complicated since they were kids... Fumi is glad Akira is back in her life. Even in kindergarten, Akira knew how to stand up for herself, and she was always willing to stand up for Fumi too. But Fumi's first love recently got married, and Fumi is grappling with a broken heart and the fact that her sweetheart was another woman... Can Akira's open heart help dispel the gloom Fumi has been caught up in?" (Publisher's note)

"Through the continuous theme of the school's performance of Wuthering Heights, Shimura's manga explores love, loss, and the importance of friendship, while the cutesy artwork nicely balances the somewhat heavy material." Booklist

Volume 1 of 4

Wandering son; Volume One. Shimura Takako; translated by Matt Thorn. Fantagraphics 2011 192 p. Illustration

Grades: 7 8 9 10 11 12 Adult   741.5; Fic

1. Puberty — Graphic novels; 2. Transgender people — Graphic novels; 3. Manga; 4. Bildungsromans — Graphic novels; 5. Seinen manga

1606994166; 9781606994160, $19.99

This manga "tells the story of a friendship between Shuichi, a young boy who wishes he were a girl, and Yoshino, a young girl who wishes she were a boy.... Shuichi's impulses toward a female identity feel confusing and shameful to him, and it's the girls in his life-first Yoshino, and then Saori-who point out his difference and encourage it.... Both children are teased mercilessly by their classmates, whose sexual development, while perhaps more socially normative, is just as confusing to them." (Publishers Weekly)

Volume 1 of 15 (8 available in English)

Shiomi, Chika

Canon Vol. 1. DC Comics/CMX 2007 200p. Illustration

Grades: 8 9 10 11 12 Adult   741.5; Fic

1. Graphic novels; 2. Horror graphic novels; 3. Manga; 4. Shojo manga; 5. Vampires — Graphic novels

978-1-4012-1163-9, $9.99

Suspense and the supernatural collide in the tale of Canon — the only student to escape the bloody vampire attack that takes the lives of her fellow classmates. But she doesn't get very far before she is captured, bitten and turned into a vampire herself. Struggling against the terrible needs that compel the undead, Canon commits herself to using her powers for good. She'll do whatever she can to avenge the death of her friends and her own unfortunate fate. Joining forces with Fuui — a talking vampire crow — she begins her quest to find Rodd, Lord of the Vampires. There's some mildly harsh language and lots of fighting vampire attacks, but nothing more than has been seen in most Buffy the Vampire Slayer or Angel episodes on television.

Night of the Beasts Volume 1. Go! Comi 2006 200p. Illustration

Grades: 10 11 12 Adult   741.5; Fic

1. Graphic novels; 2. Horror graphic novels; 3. Manga; 4. Shojo manga; 5. Supernatural graphic novels

978-1-933617-14-5, $10.99

Aria's got a reputation as the toughest girl in school because she can't resist taking on bullies — especially guys who aggressively hit on innocent girls. Which is why she's taken by surprise when her first kiss is stolen by a complete stranger. Not only does he keep making moves on her, but it seems like every time they meet, it's at the latest crime scene of a murder spree that's plaguing Aria's neighborhood. How is it that he seems to know all about the supernatural murderer of these innocent girls? And how will Aria react to his claim only she can save him from a destiny so bloody that even the violent deeds of black demon slaughtering victims all over town will pale in comparison? The book includes mildly strong language, some bloody violence, and mild sexual situations.

Yurara, Vol. 1. Viz Media/Shojo Beat 2007 192p. Illustration

Grades: 10 11 12 Adult   741.5; Fic

1. Fantasy graphic novels; 2. Ghosts — Graphic novels; 3. Graphic novels; 4. Manga; 5. Shojo manga

978-1-4215-1350-8, $8.99

Translated by JN Productions. First year high school student Yurara Tsukinowa is a quiet girl; she has seen ghosts most of her life, but has kept it a secret from anyone outside her family. Since she reacts emotionally in the presence of ghosts, she has a reputation for being weird. At school, she meets Mei Tendo and Yako Hoshino, two handsome boys who have powers to ward off vengeful spirits. When she's threatened by the ghost of a girl at her classroom desk, Yurara's guardian spirit manifests herself; this dark-haired, bold girl has the power to release souls. Yurara has to fend off Mei's teasing advances and her female classmates' jealousy while trying to figure out just what she can now do. The story features some supernatural violence and sexual innuendo.

Shirow, Masamune

The **ghost** in the shell. story and art by Shirow Masamune; translation and English adaptation, Frederik L. Schodt and Toren Smith. Kodansha Comics 2009 348 p. Illustration; Color

Grades: 11 12 Adult   741.5; 741.5/952

1. Cyborgs — Comic books, strips, etc; 2. Androids — Fiction

9781935429012, $26.99

LC 2010292697

In this book, by Shirow Masamune, "the line between man and machine has been inexorably blurred.... In this rapidly converging landscape, cyborg superagent Major Motoko Kusanagi is charged to track down the craftiest and most dangerous terrorists and cybercriminals.... When Major Kusanagi tracks the cybertrail of one such master hacker, the Puppeteer, her quest leads her into a world beyond information and technology." (Publisher's note)

Translated and adapted from the Japanese.; Other titles in this series are: Ghost in the Shell 2: Man-Machine Interface; Ghost in the Shell 1.5: Human-Error Processor

Siegel, Mark

Sailor Twain: or, The mermaid in the Hudson. Mark Siegel. First Second 2012 399 p.

Grades: Adult   **741.59**

1. Romance fiction — Graphic novels; 2. Fantasy graphic novels; 3. Mermaids and mermen — Fiction; 4. Sailors — Graphic novels
1596436360; 9781596436367, $24.99

LC 2012289260

This historical fantasy graphic novel, by Mark Siegel, is set "one hundred years ago. On the foggy Hudson River, a riverboat captain rescues an injured mermaid from the waters of the busiest port in the United States. A wildly popular — and notoriously reclusive — author makes a public debut. A French nobleman seeks a remedy for a curse. As three lives twine together and race to an unexpected collision, the mystery of the Mermaid of the Hudson deepens." (Publisher's note)

Sierra, Sergio A.

Frankenstein by Mary Shelley: a Dark graphic novel. adaptation Sergio A. Sierra; illustration Meritxell Ribas. Enslow Publishers 2013 95 p.

Grades: 6 7 8 9 10 11 12 Adult   **741.5**

1. Graphic novels; 2. Horror stories; 3. Monsters — Fiction; 4. Monsters — Graphic novels
0766040844; 9780766040847, $25.26

LC 2011035826

This book is a black-and-white graphic novel adaptation of Mary Shelley — s 19th-century gothic novel "Frankenstein." The plot tells the "tale of a monster, assembled by a scientist from parts of dead bodies, who develops a mind of his own as he learns to loathe himself and hate his creator." (WorldCat)

Includes bibliographical references.

Sievert, Tim

That salty air. Top Shelf Productions 2008 116p. Illustration

Grades: 10 11 12 Adult   **741.5; Fic**

1. Bereavement — Graphic novels; 2. Fishing — Graphic novels; 3. Graphic novels; 4. Ocean — Graphic novels
978-1-60309-005-6, $10

Fisherman Hugh has treated the ocean and its inhabitants with respect and reverence, but when he receives word that his mother died by drowning at sea, he acts as though the ocean itself has betrayed him. His loyal wife MaryAnne has just learned that she's pregnant, and she tries to help her husband. But he returns to fishing with a vengeful attitude that nearly destroys him. A mystical giant squid figures in Hugh's struggles deal with his grief and with the world.

Simmonds, Posy

Tamara Drewe. Posy Simmonds. Houghton Mifflin 2008 136 p. Color illustration

Grades: Adult   **741.5/942; 741.5**

1. Graphic novels; 2. Man-woman relationships — Fiction; 3. Villages — Fiction; 4. Man-woman relationship — Fiction
0547154127; 9780547154121, $16.95

LC 2008010924

This graphic novel, by Posy Simmonds, "follows a year at Stonefield, a bucolic writer's retreat run by Beth and Nicholas Hardiman, where Dr. Glen Larson, an American professor and struggling novelist, is staying. The ambitious young Tamara Drewe, mourning the loss of her mother, has returned to her family home nearby. A bookish girl not so long ago, Tamara is now a gossipy columnist at a London paper and undeniably sexy." (Publisher's note)

A Mariner original.||Originally published: London : Random House, 2007.

Simmons, Josh

House. Fantagraphics Books 2007 un Illustration

Grades: 11 12 Adult   **741.5; Fic**

1. Graphic novels; 2. Horror graphic novels
978-1-56097-855-8, $12.95

In the thick of a dense wood, a young man comes upon a decrepit house and two teen-aged girls, who quickly decide to explore the abandoned house together. Simmons captures the aloof ennui and deep curiosity of being a teenager-that is, until events force them to confront their own mortality. One of the girls takes a horrible fall, and her clothes are torn; for the rest of the book she is partially nude because of it.

Simone, Gail

Birds of Prey Vol. 4: The Battle Within. DC Comics 2006 240p. Illustration

Grades: 9 10 11 12 Adult   **741.5**

1. Adventure graphic novels; 2. Birds of Prey (Fictional characters); 3. Graphic novels; 4. Superhero graphic novels
978-1-4012-1096-0

Oracle and the others have left Gotham after their headquarters was destroyed but continue their work, stopping a young witch with a split personality, then taking on a met human vigilante who calls herself Harvest and kills unpunished killers. However, Oracle's controlling ways have caused Huntress to remove herself and go after Gotham mobsters on her own. Black Canary enlists the help of Wildcat in Singapore to go after drug dealers, while back home Oracle is overcome by the techno-virus left in her body after she had defeated Brainiac. There's lots of fighting action, but little graphic violence.

Birds of Prey Vol. 5: Perfect Pitch. DC Comics 2007 Illustration

Grades: 10 11 12 Adult   **741.5; Fic**

1. Birds of Prey (Fictional characters); 2. Graphic novels; 3. Superhero graphic novels; 4. Batgirl (Fictional character); 5. Joker (Fictional character)
978-1-4012-1191-2, $17.99

After being paralyzed by the Joker, former Batgirl Barbara Gordon became Oracle and formed a crime-fighting team with other female heroes including the martial artist with a devastating sonic scream, Black Canary, the vigilante known as the Huntress and the mysterious Lady Blackhawk. In this collection, the team is shaken up as members depart and new teammates are added to the roster. Who will be asked to join Oracle in her all-new Birds Of Prey? Who will refuse, and who will fly the coop for good? There's lots of hand-to-hand fighting in this book.

Birds of Prey: Between Dark & Dawn. DC Comics 2006 un Illustration

Grades: 9 10 11 12 Adult   **741.5; Fic**

1. Birds of Prey (Fictional characters); 2. Graphic novels; 3. Superhero graphic novels; 4. Justice League (Fictional characters)

978-1-4012-0940-7, $14.99

Huntress goes undercover to infiltrate a religious cult with a dangerous secret and a hidden operative, while Black Canary and Oracle uncover the true nature of Sovereign Brusaw's organization. It all leads to the Huntress's battle against former Justice League member Vixen. Oracle wages a private, internal battle against Brainiac, who has infected her with a techno-organic virus. Finally, the Birds must face the aftermath of the Gotham Gang War, leading to a decision that changes the team's fate forever.

Birds of Prey: Of Like Minds. Gail Simone, writer; Ed Benes, penciller; Alex Lei with Rob Lea, inkers; Hi-Fi, colorist; John E. Workman, Rob Leigh, Jared K. Fletcher, letterers; Ed Benes, Alex Lei with Rob Lei, original series covers. DC Comics 2004 143 p. Color; Illustration
Grades: 9 10 11 12 Adult   **741.5**
  1. Female superhero graphic novels; 2. Catwoman (Fictional character); 3. Black Canary (Fictional character)
9781401201920, $14.99; 140120192X

LC 2005295809

"The wheelchair-bound Oracle (Barbara Gordon, formerly Batgirl) now fights crime as a superhacker and cyberspy. Her field agent, Dinah Lance, is the Black Canary, a tough martial artist. When a case goes wrong, and a blackmailer called Savant captures the Canary, he threatens to kill her unless Oracle can supply him with a choice piece of information: the secret identity of Batman." (Library Journal)

Originally published in single magazine form in Birds of prey #56-61

Birds of Prey: Sensei & Student. [Gail Simone, writer; Ed Benes ... [et al.], pencillers; Alex Lei ... [et al.], inkers; Hi-Fi, colorist; Jared K. Fletcher, Rob Leigh, Nick Napolitano, letterers]. DC Comics 2005 un Color; Illustration
Grades: 9 10 11 12 Adult   **741.5**
  1. Huntress (Fictional character); 2. Oracle (Fictional character); 3. Female superhero comic books, strips, etc.; 4. Black Canary (Fictional character)
9781401204341, $17.99; 1401204341

"Black Canary goes to China on a mission of mercy and runs into the DC Universe's most deadly combatant; Lady Shiva! Shiva is acting with a hidden agenda, making Canary an offer that could change the course of her life. Meanwhile, Oracle's life is tearing at the seams as the information she feeds out to aid her various heroes starts going strangely and dangerously awry! Not to mention Huntress stumbling upon some of her secrets!" (Publisher's note)

Originally published in single magazine form in Birds of Prey #62-68 — T.p. verso.

Clean room; Volume 1: Immaculate conception. Gail Simone, writer; Jon Davis-Hunt, artist; Quinton Winter, Jon Davis-Hunt, colorists; Todd Klein, letterer; Jenny Frison, cover art and original series covers. DC Comics/Vertigo 2016 144 p. Color; Illustration
Grades: Adult   **741.5; Fic**
  1. Horror graphic novels; 2. Cults — Graphic novels
9781401262754, $14.99

LC 2016017004

"Somewhere between the realms of self-help and religion lies the Honest World Foundation. Its creator started out as an obscure writer of disposable horror fiction who decided to change the world-one mind at a time.... Is it a cult?...Reporter Chloe Pierce is sure that there's something deeper hiding behind Honest World's facade." (Publisher's note)

Volume 1 of an ongoing series

Superman: Strange Attractors. written by Gail Simone; pencilled by John Byrne. DC Comics 2006 un Illustration
Grades: 9 10 11 12 Adult   **741.5; Fic**

  1. Graphic novels; 2. Superhero graphic novels; 3. Superman (Fictional character)
1401209173; 9781401209179, $14.99

First, Superman must contend with Dr. Polaris, but something's just not right with the good doctor.... Then, Dr. Psycho comes to Metropolis to mess with Superman's head. And with his Secret Society comrade Black Adam not far behind, a throw down between Adam and Superman is a certainty. Plus, Satanus, the Queen of Fables, and Livewire make Superman's life a living nightmare.

Welcome to Tranquility volume 2. DC Comics/Wildstorm 2008 144p. Illustration
Grades: 10 11 12 Adult   **741.5; Fic**
  1. Graphic novels; 2. Horror graphic novels; 3. Superhero graphic novels; 4. Zombies — Graphic novels
978-1-4012-1773-0, $19.99

Tranquility, the town where retired superheroes and villains live side-by-side, was rocked by violence and murders, but has been recovering. Now, zombies keep coming back from the dead. It's up to Sheriff Tommy Lindo to find out what's happening, but it's going to take all the retired heroes and villains, and some thought long dead, to fight the powerful demon who wants the human infestation gone from the city. The book includes some partial nudity and lots of violence, especially zombie fighting.

Welcome to Tranquility, book one. Gail Simone, writer; Neil Googe, artist. DC Comics/Wildstorm 2007 144p. Illustration
Grades: 10 11 12 Adult   **741.5; Fic**
  1. Crime — Graphic novels; 2. Graphic novels; 3. Superhero graphic novels
978-1-4012-1516-3, $19.99

Tranquility is like any other small town in America, except for one thing — it's the town where superpowered beings go when they want to retire and raise families. From the Golden Age to the Modern Age, heroes and villains alike live in Tranquility, and the unique blend of personalities and conflicts causes headaches for local law enforcement. When a camera crew comes with a reporter to film a news segment about the town, things get turned upside down by a murder, and it becomes clear Tranquility isn't...tranquil. The book includes violence and harsh language.

Slade, Christian
  Korgi, Book 1: Sprouting Wings. Top Shelf Productions 2007 88p. Illustration
Grades: 2 3 4 5 6 7 8 9 10 11 12 Adult
741.5; Fic
  1. Dogs — Graphic novels; 2. Fantasy graphic novels; 3. Graphic novels; 4. Stories without words — Graphic novels
978-1-891830-90-7, $10

Courtesy of IDW Publishing

In this wordless book, a young Mollie (woodland people) named Ivy and her young Korgi companion named Sprout embark on adventures in Korgi Hollow, an enchanted place. When they wander from the Mollie village, the two fall through a hole in the ground and find nasty, monstrous creatures who want to eat them. As they deal with the danger and make their escape, Ivy and Sprout both discover new talents. Slade's extensively cross-hatched yet delicate art is highly expressive, and readers young and old will have no trouble figuring out what is going on. The Korgi are based on Welsh corgi dogs, of which Slade and his wife have two.

Korgi, book 2. Top Shelf Productions 2008 un Illustration

Grades: 3 4 5 6 7 8 9 10 11 12 Adult

741.5; Fic

1. Adventure graphic novels; 2. Fantasy graphic novels; 3. Graphic novels; 4. Stories without words — Graphic novels

978-1-60309-010-0, $10

Courtesy of IDW Publishing

In this second wordless volume, the young Mollie named Ivy and her Korgi cub Sprout, experience a harrowing adventure. Someone has been hunting the Mollies and cutting off their wings. Ivy and Sprout rescue one older Mollie named Art and his Korgi when they fall into a deep trap in the woods; then as Ivy flies, a barbed arrow cuts one of her wings off. She and Sprout see a strange creature carrying her wing and they follow him to his place, where he hangs all the Mollie wings like trophies. Ivy decides she wants her wing back, but she and Sprout will have to fight the creature and his automated and nasty bots.

Slott, Dan

Silver Surfer; Volume 1: New Dawn. storytellers, Dan Slott & Michael Allred; color artist; Laura Allred; Letterer, VC's Clayton Cowles. Marvel Enterprises 2014 128 p. Color; Illustration

Grades: 9 10 11 12 Adult

741.5; Fic

1. Superhero graphic novels; 2. Silver Surfer (Fictional character)

0785188789; 9780785188780, $17.99

"The universe is big. Bigger than you could ever imagine. And the Silver Surfer, lone sentinel of the skyways, is about to discover that the best way to see it...is with someone else. Meet Dawn Greenwood, the Earth girl who's challenged the Surfer to go beyond the boundaries of the known universe." (Publisher's note)

Silver Surfer; Volume 2: Worlds Apart. storytellers: Dan Slott & Michael Allred; color artist: Laura Allred; letterer: VC's Joe Sabino. Marvel Enterprises 2015 120 p. Color; Illustration

Grades: 9 10 11 12 Adult

741.5; Fic

1. Superhero graphic novels; 2. Silver Surfer (Fictional character)

0785188797; 9780785188797, $15.99

Eisner Nominee: Best Continuing Series (2016)

"Dawn has earned her spot on the board, and she and the Surfer are going to explore the universe together.... But can they survive the threats of Warrior One, the Greatest Monster in the Galaxy?...And witness...as the Surfer takes on his former master: Galactus!" (Publisher's note)

Collects issues #6-10 of Silver Surfer

Silver Surfer; Volume 3: Last Days. storytellers, Dan Slott & Michael Allred; color artist, Laura Allred; Letterer, VC's Joe Sabino. Marvel Enterprises 2016 120 p. Color; Illustration

Grades: 9 10 11 12 Adult

741.5; Fic

1. Superhero graphic novels; 2. Silver Surfer (Fictional character)

0785197370; 9780785197379, $17.99

Eisner Nominee: Best Continuing Series (2016)

"The hurt that Dawn Greenwood felt after learning about the Silver Surfer's history (see the last volume) and is the potential snag along the seem-to-be lovers' fairytale romance. Will it be overcome? Is there love for each other real? How can they really know when all of reality seems to be warping around them?" (Publisher's note)

Contains material originally published in magazine form as Silver Surfer #11-15

Small, David, 1945-

★ **Stitches:** a memoir. W.W. Norton 2009 329p. Illustration

Grades: 10 11 12 Adult

741.5; 92

1. Art teachers; 2. Artists; 3. Authors; 4. Autobiographical graphic novels; 5. Cancer — Graphic novels; 6. Children's authors; 7. Comic books, strips, etc.; 8. Family life — Graphic novels; 9. Graphic novels; 10. Illustrators; 11. Small, David, 1945-

978-0-393-06857-3, $23.95; 0-393-06857-9

LC 2009-22526

National Book Award Finalist: Young People's Literature (2009)

David Small grew up in a dysfunctional family, with a radiologist father who was distant, an angry mother who expressed her anger in eloquent silences, and an older brother who played drums a lot to express his frustrations. When he was eleven, he had a lump, a growth, on the side of his neck. Nothing was done until he was fourteen. He thought he was going in for a minor surgery to remove the cyst from his neck; instead, there were two surgeries, and when he woke up, he had no voice — a vocal cord was removed. He later learned he had cancer, something his parents refused to discuss. After he finds his mother in bed with another woman and his father confesses that he exposed him to x-rays when he was very young, Small leaves home at age sixteen, with little except his dreams that his art could be his life. In one early scene, Small shows the indignities wrought upon his body by his father, including an enema. In another scene, young Small and his older brother look at their father's medical books and see a woman's breast and a man's penis; towards the end of the book, Small draws his grandmother stripping all her clothes off and dancing wildly after setting her house on fire. Other than these few images, Small's depictions of his horrible childhood and teen years are quiet and low-key.

"Emotionally raw, artistically compelling and psychologically devastating graphic memoir of childhood trauma." Kirkus

Smith, Jeff

★ **Bone** Book Seven: ghost circles. Scholastic/GRAPHIX 2008 152p. Illustration

Grades: 3 4 5 6 7 8 9 10 11 12 Adult

741.5; Fic

1. Adventure graphic novels; 2. Fantasy graphic novels; 3. Graphic novels

978-0-439-70629-2, $19.99; 978-0-439-70634-6 (pa), $9.99

LC 2007-9568403

The Bone cousins, Gran'ma Ben, Thorn, and their loyal rat creature cub Bartleby venture on a journey through the mysterious ghost circles to Atheia, the old city of the royal family. Meanwhile, the Barrelhaven villagers and the Veni Yan face enemy hordes. Steve Hamaker is the colorist for this full color version of Smith's comic epic.

★ **Bone** vol. 8: treasure hunters. Scholastic/Graphix 2008 138p. Illustration

Grades: 5 6 7 8 9 10 11 12 Adult

741.5; Fic

1. Adventure graphic novels; 2. Fantasy graphic novels; 3. Graphic novels

978-0-439-70630-8, $18.95; 978-0-439-70633-9 (pa), $9.99

LC 2008-9568403

The Bone cousins, Gran'ma Ben, and Thorn reach the city of Atheia, where they prepare to battle the Lord of the Locusts. Meanwhile, Thorn's visions are becoming more threatening and Phoney Bone is convinced Atheia is rich in gold, and he is determined to find it. But all is not well in Atheia, and Thorn is in great danger, not only from Briar and the Lord of the Locusts. This edition is in full color, done by Steve Hamaker.

RASL. Jeff Smith. Cartoon Books 2013 472 p. Illustration; Color

Grades: Adult

741.5/973

1. Adventure graphic novels; 2. Thieves — Graphic novels

1888963379; 9781888963373, $39.95

LC 2011277280

In this graphic novel, by Jeff Smith, "when Rasl, a thief and ex-military engineer, discovers the lost journals of Nikola Tesla, he bridges the gap between modern physics and history's most notorious scientist. But his breakthrough comes at a price. In this twisting tale of violence, intrigue, and betrayal, Rasl finds himself in possession of humankind's greatest and most dangerous secret." (Publisher's note)

Also available in four individual volumes

Smith, Juliana

★ **(H)afrocentric** comics; Volumes 1-4. illustrator, Ronald Nelson; writer, Juliana Jewels Smith; colorist, Mike Hampton; foreword by Kiese Laymon.. PM Press 2017 136 p. Illustration

Grades: 9 10 11 12 Adult   **741**

1. African American college students — Political activity — Comic books, strips, etc.; 2. African Americans — Political activity — Comic books, strips, etc.; 3. Gentrification — Comic books, strips, etc.; 4. Social reformers — Comic books, strips, etc.

1629634484; 9781629634487, $20

    LC 2017942907

This comic book, by Juliana Smith, illustrated by Mike Hampton and Ronald Nelson, foreword by Kiese Laymon, tackles the most pressing issues of the day — including racism,...and the housing crisis — with humor and biting satire. When gentrification strikes the neighborhood surrounding Ronald Reagan University, Naima Pepper recruits a group of disgruntled undergrads of color to launch the first and only anti-gentrification social networking site, mydiaspora.com." (Publisher's note)

Statement of responsibility from cover.

Smith, Mark Andrew

Popgun, volume one: a graphic mixtape. Image Comics 2007 448p. Illustration

Grades: 11 12 Adult   **741.5**

1. Graphic novels; 2. Short stories — Graphic novels

978-1-58240-824-8, $29.99

This anthology of graphic short stories rams through the various genres with stories from comics veterans and newcomers, including Eric Larsen, Mike Allred, Dan Hipp, Rick Remender, Phil Yeh, Richard Starkings, Jamie S. Rich, Jim Mahfood, Leah Moore, and many more. Many of the stories include nudity, sexual situations, harsh language, and violence.

Smith, Niki

Crossplay. Niki Smith. Iron Circus Comics 2018 144 p. Illustration

Grades: Adult   **741.5; Fic**

1. Gender identity — Fiction; 2. Friendship — Fiction; 3. Sex — Fiction

1945820144; 9781945820144, $15

"Close friends and new acquaintants at an anime convention confront their crushes, challenge their hang-ups, and question their once-comfortable identities in this [debut] erotic graphic novel [by Niki Smith] about discovering who you're meant to truly be and who you're meant to love." (Publisher's note)

"While appealing as sexually explicit romance, the rather spare story also models kindness and candidness in talking about love and sex." LJ

Sniegoski, Tom

Talent. written by Christopher Golden & Tom Sniegoski; art by Paul Azaceta; colors by Ron Riley; letters by Marshall Dillon. Boom! Studios 2007 120p. Illustration

Grades: 10 11 12 Adult   **741.5**

1. Graphic novels; 2. Mystery graphic novels

978-1-934506-05-9, $14.99

When a plane crashes, sole survivor Nicholas Dane discovers he can channel his dead fellow passengers' talents. Chased by the killers who destroyed the plane, Dane stays one step ahead of death, while putting the pieces of the mystery together. Aided by a...spirit...Dane soon learns that some of the passengers on the ill-fated flight were killers working for the organization now hunting him. The book includes violence.

Snyder, Scott

A. D.: after death. written by Scott Snyder; illustrated by Jeff Lemire; lettered by Steve Wands. Image Comics 2017 224 p. Color; Illustration

Grades: Adult   **741.5**

1. Science fiction graphic novels; 2. Death — Graphic novels

9781632158680, $24.99; 163215868X

This graphic novel by Scott Snyder and illustrated by Jeff Lemire is "set in a future where a genetic cure for death has been found. Years after the discovery, one man starts to question everything, leading him on a mind-bending journey that will bring him face-to-face with his past and his own mortality." (Publisher's note)

"The art elevates this from an exegesis on mortality to a gripping, elegiac illustrated adventure that bedazzles and fascinates. Lemire has a crackerjack sense of storytelling pace and tempo to back up his art chops, and he puts an unearthly spin on fantastic settings and creatures but never forgets that this is a very human story." Pub Wkly

Contains material originally published in single magazine format as A.D.: After Death No. 1-3.

American vampire; Volume 1. Scott Snyder, Stephen King, writers; Rafael Albuquerque, artist; Dave McCaig, colorist; Steve Wands, letterer. Vertigo 2010 un Color; Illustration

Grades: Adult   **741.5**

1. Hollywood (Calif.) — Fiction; 2. Vampires — Fiction; 3. Horror graphic novels

1401229743; 1401228305; 9781401229740, $19.99; 9781401228309, $24.99

    LC 2011453896

Eisner Award: Best New Series (2011)

"This volume follows two stories: one written by Snyder and one written by King. Snyder's story is set in 1920's LA; we follow Pearl, a young woman who is turned into a vampire and sets out on a path of righteous revenge against the European Vampires who tortured and abused her. This story is paired with King's story, a western about Skinner Sweet, the original American Vampire — a stronger, faster creature than any vampire ever seen before, with rattlesnake fangs and powered by the sun." (Publisher's note)

Volume 1 of an ongoing series

Batman: night of the owls. by Scott Snyder and Greg Capullo. DC Comics 2013 368 p. Illustration; Color

Grades: 10 11 12 Adult   **741.5/973; Fic**

1. Graphic novels; 2. Batgirl (Fictional character); 3. Nightwing (Fictional character); 4. Robin (Fictional character); 5. Batman (Fictional character); 6. Catwoman (Fictional character)

1401237738; 9781401237738, $29.99

    LC 2012040574

This graphic novel, written by Scott Snyder and Greg Capullo, features the superhero Batman. "As evil spreads across Gotham City, Batman's allies, including Red Robin, Batwing, Robin, Batgirl, the Birds of Prey, Nightwing and even Catwoman find themselves in a battle coming from all sides. The Court of Owls have shown their hand, and it's up to the collective effort of these heroes, some more unlikely than others, in this sprawling tale of corruption and violence."

Originally published in single magazine form in Batman 8-11, Nightwing 8-9, All-Star Western 9, Catwoman 9, Batgirl 9, Batman:

The Dark Knight 9, Batman and Robin 9, Batwing 9, Birds Of Prey 9, Red Hood and The Outlaws 9, Batman Annual 1.

Batman; Volume 1: The court of owls. Scott Snyder, writer; Greg Capullo, penciller; Jonathan Glapion, inker. DC Comics 2012 un Color; Illustration (New 52)
Grades: 9 10 11 12 Adult   **741.5**
1. Superhero comic books, strips, etc.; 2. Batman (Fictional character)
1401235425; 9781401235420, $16.99
    "After a series of brutal murders rocks Gotham City, Batman begins to realize that perhaps these crimes go far deeper than appearances suggest. As the Caped Crusader begins to unravel this deadly mystery, he discovers a conspiracy going back to his youth and beyond to the origins of the city he's sworn to protect. Could the Court of Owls, once thought to be nothing more than an urban legend, be behind the crime and corruption? Or is Bruce Wayne losing his grip on sanity and falling prey to the pressures of his war on crime?" (Publisher's note)

Batman; Volume 2: The City of Owls. written by Scott Snyderr and James Tynion IV; illustrated by Greg Capullo, Jonathan Glapion, Rafael Albuquerque, Jason Fabok, Becky Cloonan, Andy Clarke, and Sandu Florea; colored by FCO Plascencia Dave McCaig, Peter Steigerwald, Nathan Fairborn;. DC Comics 2013 208 p. Color illustration
Grades: Adult   **Fic; 741.5/973**
1. Graphic novels; 2. Batman (Fictional character)
1401237770; 9781401237776, $24.99; 9781401237783, $16.99
                                    LC 2012045985
    "Batman must stop the Talons that have breeched the Batcave in order to save an innocent life and Gotham City. In the backup story, [readers] learn more about the Pennyworth family and the secrets they've kept from the Wayne family." (Publisher's note)
    Originally published in single magazine form in Batman 8-12, Batman Annual 1 — Title page verso.

Swamp thing volume 1: raise them bones. Scott Snyder, Yanick Paquette, Marco Rudy. DC Comics 2012 168 p. Color illustration
Grades: Adult   **Fic; 741.5/973**
1. Monsters — Graphic novels; 2. Superhero graphic novels; 3. Superhero comic books, strips, etc.
1401234623; 9781401234621, $14.99
                                    LC 2012015245
    This collection, by Scott Snyder, illustrated by Yanick Paquette, presents volume one of "The New 52" re-launch of the DC Comics "Swamp Thing" series. "Alec Holland has his life back...but the 'Green' has plans for it. A monstrous evil is rising in the desert, and it'll take a monster of another kind to defend life as we know it!" (Publisher's note)
    Originally published in single magazine form in SWAMP THING 1-7.; Other Swamp Thing volumes written by Snyder are: 2: Family tree; 3: Rotworld

Sorachi, Hideaki
Gin Tama Vol. 1. Viz Media/Shonen Jump Advanced 2007 216p. Illustration
Grades: 10 11 12 Adult   **741.5; Fic**
1. Graphic novels; 2. Humorous graphic novels; 3. Manga; 4. Shonen manga
978-1-4215-1358-4, $7.99
    The samurai didn't stand a chance. First, the aliens invaded Japan. Next, they took all the jobs. And then they confiscated everyone's swords. So what does a hotheaded former samurai like Sakata "Gin" Gintoki do to make ends meet? Take any odd job that comes his way, even if it means losing his dignity. Sleazy alien moneylenders, monsters on the rampage, and a ticking time bomb may all be in a day's work for Gin, but a drop in his

blood sugar level means trouble for everyone. Some harsh language and lots of fighting action fill this alternate history comedy.

Soule, Charles
She-Hulk; Volume 2: disorderly conduct. Charles Soule; illustrated by Javier Pulido. Marvel Enterprises 2015 136 p. Color; Illustration
Grades: Adult   **741.5**
1. Superheroes; 2. Adventure fiction
0785190201; 9780785190202, $15.99
    "She-Hulk, Hellcat and Giant-Man team up to save one of Jen's officemates...but what else does Hank Pym have at stake, and what isn't he telling them?" (Publisher's note)

Sousanis, Nick
Unflattening. Nick Sousanis. Harvard University Press 2015 208 p. Illustration
Grades: Adult   **741.5; 153.7**
1. Communication — Methodology — Comic books, strips, etc; 2. Graphic novels; 3. Imagery (Psychology) — Comic books, strips, etc; 4. Knowledge, Theory of — Comic books, strips, etc; 5. Visual perception — Comic books, strips, etc; 6. Visual perception; 7. Theory of knowledge
9780674744431, $22.95
                                    LC 2014042019
    This book, by Nick Sousanis, "is an experiment in visual thinking.... Weaving together diverse ways of seeing drawn from science, philosophy, art, literature, and mythology, it uses the collage-like capacity of comics to show that perception is always an active process of incorporating and reevaluating different vantage points." (Publisher's note)
    Includes bibliographical references

Spencer, Nick
Morning Glories; 1: for a better future. Nick Spencer, words; Joe Eisma, art; Rodin Esquejo, covers; Alex Sollazzo, colors; Johnny Lowe, letters. Image 2011 192 p. Illustration
Grades: 9 10 11 12 Adult   **741.5**
1. Comic books, strips, etc.; 2. Good and evil — Fiction; 3. School stories
1607063077; 9781607063070, $9.99
    Originally published in single magazine form as Morning Glories #1-6
    "Morning Glory Academy is one of the most prestigious prep schools in the country...but something sinister and deadly lurks behind its walls. When six gifted, but troubled, students arrive, they find themselves trapped and fighting for their lives as the secrets of the academy reveal themselves." (Publisher's note)
    "[C]ompelling character studies, mind games, and action-packed sequences [feature] in this gorgeously inked mystery." Booklist
    Volume 1 of 10

Morning glories; Volume five: Tests. Nick Spencer, illustrated by Joe Eisma. Image Comics 2013 136 p. Color; Illustration
Grades: 10 11 12 Adult   **741.5**
1. Graphic novels; 2. School stories
1607067749; 9781607067740, $12.99
    "The Glories are scattered, The Faculty broken, and The Truants on the attack!"(Publisher's note)
    Originally published in single magazine form Morning Glories, #26-29 — T.p. verso

Spiegelman, Art
Breakdowns: portrait of the artist as a young @&*!. Art Spiegelman. Pantheon Books 2008 96 p. Illustration; Color

Grades: Adult   **741.5**
1. Comic books, strips, etc.; 2. Spiegelman, Art
0375423958; 9780375423956, $27.50

LC 200860695

This graphic novel, by Art Spiegelman, "traces the artist's evolution from a MAD-comics obsessed boy in Rego Park, Queens, to a neurotic adult examining the effect of his parents' memories of Auschwitz on his own son.... Pulling all this together is an illustrated essay that looks back at the sixties as the artist pushes sixty, and explains the obsessions that brought these works into being." (Publisher's note)

★ **Co-Mix:** A Retrospective of Comics, Graphics, and Scraps. by Art Spiegelman. Farrar Straus & Giroux 2013 120 p.
Grades: Adult   **741.5**
1. Comic books, strips, etc.
1770461140; 9781770461147, $39.95
Harvey Nominee: Best Biographical, Historical, or Journalistic Presentation (2014)

This book, "a companion piece to a retrospective exhibition... collects some of [Art] Spiegelman's best work spanning nearly six decades along with biographical information and critical essays. The editors trace his career from commercial work for Playboy to his underground, experimental work, including the Raw anthology where he first serialized 'Maus'.... The book also features many of Spiegelman's controversial 1990's New Yorker covers and autobiographical comics." (Publishers Weekly)

"Maus did much to 'legitimize' comics to the wider world, but this thoughtfully curated, elegantly presented volume is an even more convincing testament to the potential of the medium." Booklist

★ **In** the shadow of no towers. Pantheon Books 2004 Illustration
Grades: 10 11 12 Adult   **741; 973.931; 741.5**
1. Graphic novels; 2. September 11 terrorist attacks, 2001 — Graphic novels
0-375-42307-9, $19.95

LC 2004-43870

This is a "memoir of the attacks on the World Trade Center, which Spiegelman witnessed from close range, a rant on their effects on the world at large and within the author, and a monograph on the Sunday newspaper comic strips of the early 20th century." N Y Times Book Rev

The author "provides a hair-raising and wry account of his family's frantic efforts to locate one another on September 11 as well as a morbidly funny survey of his trademark sense of existential doom.... This is a powerful and quirky work of visual storytelling by a master comics artist." Publ Wkly

★ **Maus:** a survivor's tale, 2v in 1. Art Spiegelman.. Pantheon Bks. 1996 295 p. Illustration; Map; Color
Grades: 7 8 9 10 11 12 Adult   **741.5; 940.53; 92**
1. Biographical graphic novels; 2. Graphic novels; 3. Holocaust, 1933-1945 — Graphic novels; 4. Spiegelman, Vladek
0-679-40641-7, $35

LC 96-32796

Los Angeles Times Book Prize: Fiction (1992) for Maus II; Pulitzer Prize Special Award (1992); Eisner Award: Best Graphic Album — Reprint for Maus II; Harvey Award: Best Graphic Album of Previously Published Material (1992) for Maus II

"An undisputed classic and award-winning title (including a Pulitzer Prize in 1992) in which renowned cartoonist Spiegelman depicts his father's experiences as a World War II Nazi concentration camp survivor. The memoir is also a chronicle of Spiegelman's relationship with his father as we witness their visits and disagreements. The black-and-white drawings are straightforward, but with an interesting twist: all of the Jews are depicted as mice and the Nazis as cats." LJ

In this work "Spiegelman takes the comic book to a new level of seriousness, portraying Jews as mice and Nazis as cats. Depicting himself being told about the Holocaust by his Polish survivor father, Spiegelman not only explores the concentration-camp experience, but also the guilt, love, and anger between father and son." Rochman. Against borders

Also available: paperback boxed set edition $23.25 (ISBN 0141014083); A combined edition of Maus I : My father bleeds history (1986) and Maus II : And here my troubles began (1991)

★ **MetaMaus.** Pantheon Books 2011 299p. Illustration
Grades: 11 12 Adult   **92; 741.5; 940.53**
1. Authors; 2. Autobiographical graphic novels; 3. Cartoonists; 4. Cartoonists — Graphic novels; 5. Graphic novels; 6. Holocaust survivors — Graphic novels; 7. Holocaust, 1933-1945 — Graphic novels; 8. Nonfiction writers; 9. Spiegelman, Art
978-0-375-42394-9, $35

LC 2010052045

The New York cartoonist traces the creative process that went into drawing his Pulitzer Prizewinning classic, revealing the sources of his inspiration and describing his parents' emotional struggles as Holocaust survivors after the end of World War II.

Spurgeon, Tom
We told you so: comics as art. Tom Spurgeon and Michael Dean, editors. Fantagraphics Books, Inc. 2016 576 p. Illustration; Color
Grades: Adult   **741.5**
1. Publishers and publishing — United States — History; 2. Cartooning — United States; 3. Cartoonists — United States
1606999338; 9781606999332, $49.99

LC 2016953075

This book, by Tom Spurgeon and Michael Dean, "tells of Fantagraphics Books' key role in helping build and shape an art movement around a discredited, ignored and fading expression of Americana,...in anecdotal form, in the words of the people who lived it and saw it happen.... [Spurgeon and] Dean assembled an all-star cast of industry figures, critics, cartoonists,...and groundbreaking publications to bring...a detailed account of Fantagraphics' first 40 years." (Publisher's note)

"Fantagraphics' history is also a history of the art form and industry, and the personal touches from candid interviews provide a fascinating insider's perspective." Pub Wkly

Squarzoni, Philippe
Climate changed: a personal journey through the science. Philippe Squarzoni; translated by Ivanka Hahnenberger. Abrams ComicArts 2014 480 p. Illustration
Grades: Adult   **551.6**
1. Climatic changes — Comic books, strips, etc; 2. Graphic novels; 3. Climate change
1419712551; 9781419712555, $24.95

LC 2014000177

In this book, journalist Philippe Squarzoni "digs deep into the science, economics, politics, international policies, and ethics that together force cataclysmic climate change into our very near global future. While the experts he interviews throughout this volume present accessible yet technically specific details,...it is by inserting himself and his personal exploration of responsibilities and choices that Squarzoni makes the most demanding call to action." (Booklist)

"Squarzoni's text, skillfully translated by Hahnenberger, is supported by his detailed black-and-white art, which conveys the urgency of the situation without falling prey to despair or nihilism." Pub Wkly

Stanley, John

★ **Little** Lulu, vol. 1: My dinner with Lulu. [by] John Stanley and Irving Tripp. Dark Horse Comics 2005 200p. Illustration

Grades: 4 5 6 7 8 9 10 11 12 Adult   **741.5; Fic**
1. Friendship — Graphic novels; 2. Graphic novels; 3. Humorous graphic novels

1-59307-318-6, $9.95

Lulu Moppet plays with best friend Tubby, except when he hangs out with the other neighborhood boys and tries to keep girls out of their clubhouse; she deals with terrible toddler Alvin by weaving extravagant tales featuring herself; and other everyday adventures. This is the first volume of a series that will eventually reprint every Little Lulu comic for new young readers.

Volume 1 of 29

★ **Nancy,** volume 1: the Johnny Stanley Library. Drawn & Quarterly 2009 128p. Illustration

Grades: 2 3 4 5 6 7 8 9 10 11 12 Adult   **741.5; Fic**
1. Graphic novels; 2. Humorous graphic novels; 3. Nancy (Fictional character)

978-1-897299-77-7, $24.95

LC c2009-901565-X

The comic book character Nancy was created by Ernie Bushmiller; Dell Comics published the comics scripted by John Stanley with art by Dan Gormley starting with issue 146 in 1957. In these stories, Nancy meets Oona Goosepimple, a spooky girl who lives in a haunted house, has an incredible run of bad luck because of what she thinks is a four-leaf clover, and has all kinds of everyday adventures and misadventures with her friend Sluggo, their nemesis Spike, neighborhood rich kid Rollo, and her Aunt Fritzi. Always short of money yet needing some to buy ice cream sodas and other treats, many of Nancy's adventures with Sluggo involve various moneymaking schemes to get the dime needed (those were the days ...). The kinds of adventures the kids have are somewhat similar to Stanley's other work on Little Lulu, but set in an urban environment rather than the suburban neighborhood of Lulu and her friends. The book, designed by Seth, retains the soft original coloring of the old comics, with the paper even looking like old comics (but much sturdier). This book should have the same all-ages appeal as Little Lulu; the 2009 Free Comic Book Day issue featuring Nancy was a big hit with readers five years old and up to adults who remembered reading Nancy comics when they were kids.

Starkings, Richard

Elephantmen: Wounded Animals. Richard Starkings, story & lettering; Moritat, lead artist; Boo Cook, Ladrönn, covers; J.G. Roshell, design. Image Comics 2007 un Illustration

Grades: 10 11 12 Adult   **741.5; Fic**
1. Graphic novels; 2. Mystery graphic novels; 3. Science fiction graphic novels

978-1-58240-691-6, $24.99

They were genetically engineered to be super-human weapons of mass destruction, but now they must walk amongst the people they were created to destroy and face hatred and fear every day. Ebony Hide is one of them, an Elephantman. Even when he is befriended by a small girl, Hide is still haunted by his past and is forced to recognize that suspicion and contempt will always be his constant companions. The book includes some violence and strong language.

Starlin, Jim

Batman: a death in the family. writers, Jim Starlin, Marv Wolfman; layouts and co-plotter, George Perez; pencillers, Jim Aparo, Tom Grummett; inkers, Mike DeCarlo, Bob McLeod; original series covers, Mike Mignola and George Perez. DC Comics 2011 269 p. Color illustration (Batman)

Grades: 10 11 12 Adult   **741.5**
1. Good and evil — Comic books, strips, etc.; 2. Superheroes — Comic books, strips, etc.; 3. Batman (Fictional character); 4. Joker (Fictional character); 5. Robin (Fictional character)

1401232744; 9781401232740, $24.99

LC 2012376784

In this graphic novel, "Batman readers were allowed to vote on the outcome of the story and they decided that Robin should die! As the second person to assume the role of Batman's sidekick, Jason Todd had a completely different personality than the original Robin. Rash and prone to ignore Batman's instructions, Jason was always quick to act without regard to consequences. In this fatal instance, Robin ignores his mentor's warnings when he attempts to take on the Joker by himself." (Publisher's note)

Batman created by Bob Kane.||Originally published in single magazine form in Batman #426-429, 440-442, The New Titans #60-61 and Batman Annual #25.||Includes a new afterword by writer Marv Wolfman — P. [4] of cover.

Stassen, Jean-Philippe

Deogratias: a tale of Rwanda. [by] Stassen; translated by Alex Siegel. Roaring Brook 2006 79p. Illustration

Grades: 11 12 Adult   **741.5; Fic**
1. Genocide — Graphic novels; 2. Graphic novels; 3. Rwanda — Graphic novels

1-59643-103-2; 978-1-59643-103-4, $17.95

LC 2005-17576

In this "fictionalized account of the Rwandan genocide, readers meet Deogratias, a teenaged Hutu. His friends Benina and Apollinaria are Tutsi — a race that is being ethnically cleansed by Hutu extremists. As the conflict escalates, Deogratias witnesses murders and is forced to become involved in brutal acts of violence. He suffers a mental breakdown. The story is told through a series of flashbacks while he skates the line between rational and insane. Stassen spares his readers none of the brutality and visceral cruelties of this atrocity. Scenes of rape, harsh language, and some sexual content solidly designate this book for a mature audience.... A masterful work with vibrant, confident art, this book will stay with and haunt its readers." SLJ

Stavans, Ilan

Latino U.S.A.: a cartoon history. by Ilan Stavans; illustrated by Lalo Alcaraz. Basic Books 2012 xxi, 217 p. Illustration

Grades: Adult   **741.5; 973/.0468**
1. Hispanic Americans — Comic books, strips, etc; 2. United States — History — Comic books, strips, etc; 3. Hispanic Americans — History; 4. Latinos (U.S.)

0465082211; 0465082505; 9780465082216, $24.95; 9780465082506

LC 2012429058

This book "represents the culmination of Ilan Stavans' lifelong determination to meet the challenges of capturing the joys, nuances, and multiple dimensions of Latino culture within the context of the English language. In this cartoon history of Latinos, Stavans also seeks to combine the solemnity of so-called 'serious literature' and history with the inherently theatrical and humorous nature of the comics." (Publisher's note)

Includes index.

Steele, Hamish

Pantheon: The True Story of the Egyptian Deities. by Hamish Steele. Nobrow Press 2017 216 p. Color; Illustration

Grades: Adult   **741.5; 299.313**
1. Mythology — Graphic novels; 2. Egyptian mythology

1910620203; 9781910620205, $22.95

In this book, by Hamish Steele, "the most important myth in Ancient Egypt is faithfully retold in glorious color! Horus, son of Isis, vows bloody revenge on his Uncle Set for the murder and usurpation of his Pharaoh father. Based on elements from various versions of the famous Osiris myth, Hamish Steele has resurrected this fantastic story in all its symbolic and humorous glory." (Publisher's note)

"Packed with all the unimaginable violence and sexual impropriety one might expect from mythology, this tale could have been a brutal, heavy read in lesser hands than those of newcomer Steele, whose lively, irreverent sense of humor makes even matricidal duels to the death and multiple poisonings seem like good fun." LJ

Stein, Leslie
Present. Leslie Stein. Drawn & Quarterly 2017 168 p. Color; Illustration
Grades: 11 12 Adult   **741.5; Fic**
1. New York (N.Y.) — Fiction; 2. Storytelling — Graphic novels
1770462945; 9781770462946, $21.95
LA Times Book Prize: Graphic Novel/Comics (2017)

In this book, "Leslie Stein takes us on a sinuous urban stroll divorced from destination, glimpsing New York City through her open eyes. While she is closing up a bar late at night, she is also an adolescent at a rave in the mountains, an adult grappling with her grandfather's fading memory or at one of her first waitressing jobs." (Publisher's note)

"Stein's vibrant watercolors are a marvel, especially in the palette: dribbles of cerulean, slashes of black, and dots of deepest crimson are as captivating as any plot twist. Even the lettering tells a story, often exploding on the page in different colors and sizes. It all adds up to a sweet, relatable portrait of the minutiae that make life worth living." Pub Wkly

Stephenson, Eric
Put the Book Back on the Shelf: A Belle & Sebastian Anthology. Image Comics 2006 un Illustration
Grades: 10 11 12 Adult   **741.5; Fic**
1. Graphic novels; 2. Short stories — Graphic novels
1-58240-600-6, $19.99

Belle and Sebastian is a Scottish indie pop band that has gained critical acclaim for its music. In this anthology, independent comic creators and cartoonists put their own spins on a cross section of Belle and Sebastian's songs, crafting narratives inspired by the band's music. Rick Spears, Andi Watson, Jennifer de Guzman, Leela Corman, Rick Remender, Ande Park, ad Mark Ricketts are just a few of the creators who contributed to this collection. Nudity, drug use, and violence occur in some of the stories.

Stern, Roger
Captain America: War & Remembrance 2nd ed.. writer, Roger Stern; co-plotter & penciler, John Byrne; inker, Joe Rubinstein; colorists, Bob Sharen & George Roussos; letterers, Jim Novak, John Costanza, & Joe Rosen. Marvel Entertainment 2007 207p. Illustration
Grades: 8 9 10 11 12 Adult   **741.5; Fic**
1. Graphic novels; 2. Superhero graphic novels; 3. Avengers (Fictional characters); 4. Captain America (Fictional character)
978-0-7851-2693-5, $24.99

Captain America's endless war on crime and tyranny sets him against new enemies and old, from an army of robot replicas to the black deeds of Baron Blood. Plus: Cap for president? This book guest-stars the Avengers, S.H.I.E.L.D. and Union Jack, and features Cobra, Mister Hyde and Batroc the Leaper. This is the complete Stern/Byrne run, culminating with the standard-setting version of Cap's origin. Byrne co-scripted as well as penciled the art.

Spider-Man Visionaries: Roger Stern Vol. 1. Marvel Entertainment 2007 256p. Illustration
Grades: 7 8 9 10 11 12 Adult   **741.5; Fic**
1. Graphic novels; 2. Spider-Man (Fictional character); 3. Superhero graphic novels
978-0-7851-2710-9, $24.99

Roger Stern sets his stamp on Spider-Man and his supporting cast with a collection of costumed criminals, would-be alien abductors, and gangsters both local and imported. Spidey is up against Belladonna, the Vulture, the Prowler, the Smuggler, Mysterio, a roomful of aliens, and an abundance of gas. These stories were originally published in the 1980s, and Stern worked with a number of different artists, including Steve Leialoha and Marie Severin.

Stevenson, Noelle
Lumberjanes; Volume 3: A Terrible Plan. written by Noelle Stevenson & Shannon Watters; illustrated by Carolyn Nowak [and six others]; colors by Maarta Laiho; cover by Noelle Stevenson. Boom! Studios 2016 112 p. Color; Illustration
Grades: 6 7 8 9 10 11 12 Adult   **741.5; Fic**
1. Graphic novels; 2. Camps — Fiction; 3. Fantasy fiction; 4. Adventure fiction; 5. Teenage girls — Fiction
1608868036; 9781608868032, $14.99

"Jo, April, Mal, Molly, and Ripley...take on everything that goes bump in the night. From scary stories to magical portals that lead to a land untouched by time, it's definitely not your average summer." (Publisher's note)

"Each camper tells a campfire spine-tingler, ranging from not very scary (the scratching on the side of the car was really...carbon-monoxide-induced hallucinations!) to the shudderworthy. Elsewhere, Mal and Molly are transported to a dangerous, dinosaur-infested alternate universe, and while they are gone, the rest of the Lumberjanes try to earn some piece-of-cake badges, only to fail spectacularly." Booklist
Originally published in single magazine form as Lumberjanes no. 9-12

Stewart, Cameron
★ **Batgirl**; Volume 1: Batgirl of Burnside. written by Cameron Stewart & Brenden Fletcher; art by Babs Tarr; breakdown art by Cameron Stewart. DC Comics 2015 176 p. Color; Illustration
Grades: 10 11 12 Adult   **741.5**
1. Batgirl (Fictional character)
9781401253325, $24.99

LC 2015006319

"Barbara Gordon's ready for a fresh start. She's packing her bags, crossing the bridge, and heading to Gotham's coolest neighborhood: Burnside. And when a freak fire burns up her costume and gear, Babs has the chance to become a whole new Batgirl! But she barely slips on her new DIY costume before Batgirl starts trending as Gotham's first viral vigilante — and attracting a new wave of enemies." (Publisher's note)

"While most attempts at updating an established character to tap into the youth culture zeitgeist feel phony and fall flat, this reinvigoration of Batgirl manages to be big fun and actually tuned in to Millennial culture.... The supporting cast is diverse and fully developed, and the action is intense, rendered in a bright, dynamic style that evokes animation with just a hint of Japanese influence." LJ

★ **Sin** titulo. by Cameron Stewart, edited by Sierra Hahn. Dark Horse Books 2013 166 p.
Grades: Adult   **741.5; Fic**
1. Grandfathers — Fiction; 2. Dreams — Fiction; 3. Life change events — Fiction

1616552484; 9781616552480, $19.99

In this Eisner Award-winning book, by Cameron Stewart, "Alex Mackay has no idea that he is letting important relationships slip away, until he drops in on his grandfather, Robert, at his nursing home, only to discover that the old man died a month before. Left pondering the small box of his grandfather's personal effects,...Alex sets out on a journey of discovery that only raises more questions and reveals that his recurring dream of a gnarled tree on a beach is far more important than he previously believed." (Publishers Weekly)

Stok, Barbara

Vincent. by Barbara Stok; translation by Laura Watkinson. SelfMadeHero 2014 144 p. Color; Illustration
Grades: 9 10 11 12 Adult **741.5; 92**
1. Gogh, Vincent van, 1853-1890
1906838798; 9781906838799, $19.95

LC 2014431349

This biography, by Barbara Stok, "documents the brief and intense period of creativity Vincent van Gogh (1853-1890) spent in Arles, Provence, in southern France. Here van Gogh dreams of setting up an artists' studio-a haven where he and his friends can paint together. But attacks of mental illness leave the painter confused and disoriented.... Throughout this period of intense emotion and hardship, Vincent's brother Theo stands by him." (Publisher's note)

"Stok doesn't try to reproduce van Gogh's visuals; instead, she uses heavy lines, solid colors, and minimal background details to focus attention on characters and history. When she breaks away from this pattern — in jagged panel lines showing van Gogh's slipping sanity, or the brilliance of his paintings exploding behind him — it's emotionally charged and made all the more immediate by the iconography." Pub Wkly

Text in English, translated from the Dutch

Straczynski, J. Michael

Civil War: Fantastic Four. writers, J. Michael Straczynski & Dwayne McDuffie; penciller, Mike McKone; inkers, Andy Lanning, Kris Justice, & Cam Smith; colorist, Paul Mounts. Marvel Entertainment 2007 un Illustration
Grades: 9 10 11 12 Adult **741.5; Fic**
1. Fantastic Four (Fictional character); 2. Graphic novels; 3. Superhero graphic novels
0-7851-2227-3, $17.99

One member of the Fantastic Four lies hospitalized, a casualty of the Civil War that has fragmented the superhuman community. Another member of the team is secretly helping the opposition. Amid the tumult and tensions, the Fantastic Four is breaking up. Who will toe the line with the government, who will join the resistance, and who will leave the battlefield altogether?

Civil War: The Amazing Spider-Man. Marvel Entertainment 2007 un Illustration
Grades: 9 10 11 12 Adult **741.5; Fic**
1. Graphic novels; 2. Spider-Man (Fictional character); 3. Superhero graphic novels
0-7851-2237-0, $17.99

Life couldn't be more complicated — or more dangerous — for Peter Parker. After rushing to the aftermath of the Stamford Massacre to offer aid to its victims, Peter travels with Tony Stark to Washington, D.C. and the White House, where the enactment of the Super Human Registration Act appears imminent. As the world braces for the implications of legislation that will forever change the societal status of super heroes, Peter is forced to make an important personal decision, maybe the most important decision of his life. As Civil War tears apart the super hero community, will Spidey stay true to that decision?

Suburbia, Liz

★ **Sacred** Heart. Liz Suburbia. Fantagraphics 2015 312 p. Illustration
Grades: 11 12 Adult **741.5; Fic**
1. Mystery fiction; 2. Teenagers — Graphic novels
1606998412; 9781606998410, $24.99

LC 2015942121

Alex Award (2016)

In this graphic novel, by Liz Suburbia, "the children of...Alexandria are just trying to live like normal teens until their parents' promised return from a mysterious, four-year religious pilgrimage, and Ben Schiller is no exception. She's just trying to take care of her sister...and get through her teen years. But her relationship with her best friend is changing, her younger sister is hiding a dark secret, and a terrible tragedy is coming for them all." (Publisher's note)

Sun Tzu

The **art** of war. Roundtable Press 2011 un Illustration
Grades: 9 10 11 12 Adult **741.5**
1. Competition — Graphic novels; 2. Graphic novels; 3. Philosophers; 4. Strategy — Graphic novels; 5. Writers on the military; 6. Sun-tzu, 6th cent. B.C.
978-1-61066-010-5, $12.95

Sun Tzu's classic book on strategy has now been adapted into a graphic novel. This adaptation is more a summary of the principles of strategy discussed in The Art of War, illustrated by Clester using modern situations to demonstrate the principles. For example, Sun Tzu's statement that "he who wishes to fight must first count the cost" is depicted with rival gangsters. This short book can't replace the original, but it provides a good summary of the main points and serves as an introduction for high school students and busy adults who may not have the time to read the whole original text.

Tagame, Gengoroh

My brother's husband. Gengoroh Tagame; translated by Anne Ishii. Pantheon 2017 352 p. Illustration
Grades: 11 12 Adult **741.5**
1. Gay men — Japan — Comic books, strips, etc; 2. Japan — Fiction; 3. Gay men — Fiction
1101871512; 9781101871515, $24.95

LC 2016047082

Eisner Award: Best U.S. Edition of International Material — Asia (2018)

In this book, by Gengoroh Tagame, translated by Anne Ishii, "Yaichi is a work-at-home suburban dad in contemporary Tokyo; formerly married to Natsuki, father to their young daughter, Kana. Their lives suddenly change with the arrival at their doorstep of a hulking, affable Canadian named Mike Flanagan, who declares himself the widower of Yaichi's estranged gay twin, Ryoji." (Publisher's note)

"This winsome look at culture clash compares the largely still-closeted Japanese gay culture with the West, underscoring a theme of universal yearning for family." LJ

Originally published as Otouto no Otto by Futabasha Publishers Ltd., Tokyo, in 2014 — Title page verso.; Volume 1 of 2

Takahashi, Rumiko

Ranma 1/2. Rumiko Takahashi, translated from Japanese by Gerard Jones & Matt Thorn. Viz Media 2014 359 p. Illustration
Grades: 10 11 12 Adult **741.5**
1. Shonen manga; 2. Manga; 3. Gender role — Fiction
1421565943; 9781421565941, $14.99

"One day, teenaged martial artist Ranma Saotome went on a training mission with his father and ended up taking a dive into some cursed springs at a legendary training ground in China. Now, every time he's splashed with cold water, he changes into a girl. His father, Genma, changes into a panda! What's a half-guy, half-girl to do?" (Publisher's note)

"One of the bestselling manga from the early '90s, a gender-bending rom-com mixed with copious martial arts action, returns in this rerelease. World-class martial artist Ranma Saotome has been cursed with a special fate: when doused with cold water, he turns into a girl. This oddity is little more than an irritation to him until he becomes engaged to Akane Tendo, a prodigiously strong fighter who also happens to hate men." Pub Wkly

38 volumes originally released in Japan from 1987-1996

Takemiya, Keiko

★ **To** Terra Volume One. Keiko Takemiya; [translation, Dawn T. Laabs]. Vertical, Inc. 2007 343p. Illustration

Grades: 9 10 11 12 Adult   **741.5; Fic**
1. Graphic novels; 2. Manga; 3. Psychics — Graphic novels; 4. Science fiction graphic novels; 5. Shojo manga
9781932234671, $13.95; 1932234675

The future. Having driven Terra to the brink of environmental collapse, humanity decides to reform itself by ushering in the age of Superior Domination (S.D.), a system of social control in which children are no longer the offspring of parents but progeny of a universal computer. The new social order, however, results in an unexpected byproduct: the Mu, a mutant race with extrasensory powers who are forced in exile by The System. The saga begins on educational planet Ataraxia, where Jomy Marcus Shin, a brash and unpredictable teenager, is nervously preparing to enter adult society. When his Maturity Check goes wrong, the Mu intervene in the great hope that Jomy, who possesses Mu telepathy and human physical strength, can lead them back home, to Terra...

Volume 1 of 3

Takeuchi, Mick

Her Majesty's Dog, Vol. 1. Go! Comi 2005 200p. Illustration

Grades: 10 11 12 Adult   **741.5; Fic**
1. Graphic novels; 2. Manga; 3. Romance graphic novels; 4. Shojo manga; 5. Supernatural graphic novels
0-9768957-3-0, $10.99

New students Amane and Hyoue cause a stir in their high school because they kiss so much. Amane is a psychic, Hyoue is actually her guardian demon-dog, and he feeds on her life force by their kisses. Together, they hunt demons, but in school they need to learn how to deal with everyday hazards such as bullies, jealousy, and making friends. This series combines teen romance with supernatural horror.

Takizawa, Seiho

Who Fighter with Heart of Darkness. Dark Horse Manga 2006 208p. Illustration

Grades: 10 11 12 Adult   **741.5; Fic**
1. Graphic novels; 2. Manga; 3. Seinen manga; 4. War — Graphic novels
978-1-59307-626-9, $11.95

The first story in this anthology, "Who Fighter," is a play on the legendary "Foo Fighters," the nickname given to the mysterious, UFO-like fireballs that were sighted by World War II pilots. An ace Japanese pilot manages to shoot one of the fireballs down... or does he? As ominous signs and visions begin to follow in his steps, the bewildered pilot wonders if he's lost not only his memory of the incident-but also his very mind. "Heart of Darkness" is Takizawa's take on the Joseph Conrad novel. A Japanese war hero, Colonel Kurutsu, has gone rogue, setting up his own private kingdom deep upriver in the jungles of Burma. A young captain, sent to execute Kurutsu, finds that the true reasons for the Colonel's "desertion" are very different from what he was told. Finally, a short piece, "Tanks," closes out the collection with a surreal voyage through one hundred years

of armored vehicle battles. The book includes some violence and some mildly strong language.

Talbot, Bryan

★ **Alice** in Sunderland: An Entertainment. Dark Horse Comics 2007 324p. Illustration

Grades: 10 11 12 Adult   **741.5**
1. Fantasy graphic novels; 2. Graphic novels
978-1-59307-673-3

Sunderland was once the greatest center of learning in Christendom and the birthplace of English consciousness. In the time of Lewis Carroll it was the greatest shipbuilding port in the world, and here are buried the roots of Carroll's surreal masterpiece, Alice in Wonderland.' Talbot mixes fact and fiction in his meditation on myth, history, storytelling. The book includes some strong language, particularly Briticisms.

★ **The** **tale** of one bad rat. Dark Horse 2010 un Illustration

Grades: 9 10 11 12 Adult   **741.5; Fic**
1. Child sexual abuse — Graphic novels; 2. Graphic novels; 3. Runaway teenagers — Graphic novels
978-1-59582-493-6, $19.99

This book's "heroine is teenager Helen Potter, who has run away from an abusive father and whose path to recovery takes her from a squat in London to refuge at an inn in the British countryside. Along the way, she meets characters and situations that Talbot derives from the work of Helen's namesake, Beatrix Potter, whose life he symbolically links to Helen's. Talbot's vivid, realistic full-color illustration brilliantly evokes the story's settings, yet even more effective are his compassionate characterizations." Booklist

First published 1995; ?This volume collects issues one through four of the Dark Horse comic-book series? Verso of title page

Tamaki, Jillian

★ **Boundless**. Jillian Tamaki. Drawn & Quarterly 2017 248 p. Illustration

Grades: Adult   **741.5; Fic**
1. Women — Fiction; 2. Social media — Fiction; 3. Women — Psychology; 4. Women — Social conditions
1770462872; 9781770462878, $24.95
Eisner Award: Best Graphic Album — Reprint (2018)

This collection of short comics by Jillian Tamaki "explores the virtual and IRL world of contemporary women via a lens both surreal and wry. Jenny becomes obsessed with a strange 'mirror Facebook,' which presents an alternate, possibly better, version of herself. Helen finds her clothes growing baggy, her shoes looser, and as she shrinks away to nothingness, the world around her recedes as well. The animals of the city briefly open their minds to us, and we see the world as they do. A mysterious music file surfaces on the internet and forms the basis of a utopian society-or is it a cult?" (Publisher's note)

"Whether otherworldly or realistic, Tamaki's stories are filled with humor, pathos, and empathy for characters who struggle to transcend their circumstances, histories, and limitations." LJ

★ **SuperMutant** Magic Academy. Jillian Tamaki. Drawn & Quarterly 2015 274 p. Illustration

Grades: 10 11 12 Adult   **741.5; Fic**
1. Comic books, strips, etc. — Canada; 2. Private schools — Comic books, strips, etc; 3. Teenagers — Comic books, strips, etc; 4. Teenagers — Fiction; 5. Fantasy graphic novels; 6. School stories
1770461981; 9781770461987, $22.95

LC 2015376543

Eisner Award: Best Publication for Teens (2016); Ignatz Nominee: Outstanding Artist (2015); Ignatz Nominee: Outstanding Anthology or Collection (2015)

In this graphic novel, author Jillian Tamaki "paints a teenaged world filled with just as much ennui and uncertainty, but also with a sharp dose of humor and irreverence.... The SuperMutant Magic Academy is a prep school for mutants and witches, but their paranormal abilities take a backseat to everyday teen concerns. Science experiments go awry, bake sales are upstaged, and the new kid at school is a cat who will determine the course of human destiny." (Publisher's note)

"There are flickering moments of transcendent wisdom and kindness, but the overall tone is one of insouciant, salty resignation to the mundane realities of existence. Simultaneously heartbreaking and hilarious." Booklist

Tamaki, Mariko

★ **This** One Summer. Mariko Tamaki, [art by] Jillian Tamaki. First Second 2014 320 p. Illustration
Grades: 7 8 9 10 11 12 Adult   **741.5; Fic**
1. Graphic novels; 2. Friendship — Fiction; 3. Vacations — Fiction
159643774X, 17.99; 9781626720947, $21.99; 9781596437746, 17.99; 1626720940, 21.99
Caldecott Honor Book (2015); Printz Honor Book (2015); Eisner Award: Best Graphic Album — New (2015); Ignatz Award: Outstanding Graphic Novel (2014); Harvey Nominee: Best Artist (2015); Harvey Nominee: Best Graphic Album of Original Work (2015); Harvey Nominee: Best Original Graphic Publication For Young Readers (2015)

"Every summer, Rose goes with her mom and dad to a lake house in Awago Beach.... Rosie's friend Windy is always there, too, like the little sister she never had. But this summer is different.... It's a summer of secrets, and sorrow, and growing up, and it's a good thing Rose and Windy have each other." (Publisher's note)

"This captivating graphic novel presents a fully realized picture of a particular time in a young girl's life, an in-between summer filled with yearning and a sense of ephemerality." SLJ

Tardi, Jacques

★ **It** was the war of the trenches. story & art by Jacques Tardi; translated by Kim Thompson. Fantagraphics 2010 118 p. Illustration
Grades: Adult   **741.5**
1. World War, 1914-1918 — Comic books, strips, etc; 2. Military art and science; 3. World War, 1914-1918
1606993534; 9781606993538, $24.99

LC 2014501963

This book, by Jacques Tardi, on World War I "focuses on the day to day of the grunts in the trenches. He also delves deeply into the underlying causes of the war, the madness, the cynical political exploitation of patriotism. Tardi...itemizes the ghastly human cost of the war, and lays out the future 20th century conflicts." (Publisher's note)

"The third Fantagraphics volume bringing the work of eminent French comics creator Tardi to American readers is the first he wrote as well as drew, and it shows that he's as singular a writer as he is an artist. It's a relentlessly grim, ground-level depiction of WWI as seen through the eyes of French soldiers mired in the trenches." Booklist

Includes bibliographical references

New York mon amour. by Jacques Tardi; illustrated by Benjamin Legrand and Dominique Grange.. Fantagraphics Books 2012 82 p. Illustration; Color
Grades: Adult   **741.5/944; Fic; S C**
1. Historical fiction; 2. Crime — Graphic novels; 3. New York (N.Y.) — Graphic novels

1606995243; 9781606995242, $19.99

This graphic novel was "[o]riginally published in the early 1980s" and "captures the then grungy urban sprawl [of New York City], told through four tales of its troubled inhabitants struggling to carve out something resembling a life. The main story [is] about a pitiful exterminator who inadvertently sees too much, thus attracting the worst kind of attention." (Publishers Weekly)

Translated from the French by Kim Thompson.

Tarr, Babs

Motor crush; Volume 1. creators, Brenden Fletcher, Cameron Stewart, Babs Tarr; colors and production assistant, Heather Danforth; lettering, Aditya Bidikar.. Image Comics 2017 136 p.
Grades: 9 10 11 12 Adult   **741.5**
1. Motorcycle racing — Comic books, strips, etc.; 2. Adventure graphic novels; 3. Women motorcyclists — Comic books, strips, etc.
9781534301894, $9.99

In this graphic novel in the Motor Crush series, by Brenden Fletcher, Cameron Stewart, and Babs Tarr, "by day, Domino Swift competes for fame & fortune in a worldwide motorcycle racing league. By night, she cracks heads of rival gangs in brutal bike wars to gain possession of a rare, valuable contraband: an engine-boosting 'machine narcotic' known as Crush." (Publisher's note)

"This series, a spiritual successor to Speed Racer's rubber-burning mayhem, is packed with fun characters, visceral high-speed action, romance, and a general sense of unbridled action. The whole package is worthy of note, and Stewart and Tarr's art really grabs the reader by the eyeballs. It's heavily animation-influenced and practically leaps off the page." PW.

Originally published as Motor crush #1-5 — Page [2].

Tatsumi, Yoshihiro

★ The **Push** Man and Other Stories. Yoshihiro Tatsumi; [translated by Yuji Oniki]. Drawn & Quarterly 2005 208p. Illustration
Grades: 12 Adult   **741.5; Fic**
1. City and town life — Japan — Graphic novels; 2. Graphic novels; 3. Manga; 4. Seinen manga
1-896597-85-8, $19.95

Tatsumi is considered the grandfather of alternate manga for the adult reader; the stories in this collection date back to the late 1960s and explore the darker aspects of Japanese urban life. The look of his art is very different from most manga, and his stories comment on the interplay between an overwhelming, bustling, crowded, modern society and the troubled emotional and sexual life of the individual. He invented the term "gekiga" ("dramatic pictures") in 1957 to describe his manga Strong sexual overtones, violence, and strong language make Tatsumi's work more suitable for older, mature-minded teens and adults.

Taylor, Whit

★ **Comics** for choice: illustrated abortion stories, history, and politics. edited by Hazel Newlevant and Whit Taylor. Alternative Comics 2018 300 p. Illustration
Grades: Adult   **363.4; 741.5**
1. Reproduction; 2. Abortion
1681485982; 9781681485980, $25

This book, edited by Hazel Newlevant and Whit Taylor, "is anthology of comics about abortion. As this fundamental reproductive right continues to be stigmatized and jeopardized, over sixty artists and writers have created comics that boldly share their own experiences, and educate readers on the history of abortion, current political struggles, activism, and more." (Publisher's note)

"Abortion is addressed as a political flash point, a personal journey, and a cultural battleground in this powerful anthology. Its diverse nonfiction comics pieces range from the triumphant to the traumatic, and editors Newlevant (No Ivy League) and Taylor (Ghost Stories) ensure no story is dismissed as unworthy." Pub Wkly

TenNapel, Doug

Black Cherry. Image Comics 2007 un Illustration
Grades: 11 12 Adult   741.5; Fic
1. Graphic novels; 2. Horror graphic novels; 3. Mystery graphic novels; 4. Science fiction graphic novels
978-1-58240-830-9, $17.99

Down-on-his-luck Mafioso Eddie Paretti is so desperate for cash he's agreed to steal a dead body from his own mob boss. Things only get worse when he discovers the body isn't human. With few options and fewer people he can trust, Eddie calls on the man who raised him, Father McHugh. The priest tells Eddie that the body was stolen from his monastery by the Mafia. Father McHugh is accompanied by Mary, a beautiful woman Eddie swears looks just like a stripper he once fell in love with named Black Cherry. The book is full of very foul language (f-bombs and s-bombs galore), nudity, sexual situations, and graphic violence. It also has a deeply-felt religious core that may confuse some readers. TenNapel has written a foreword for readers that explains it.

Tezuka, Osamu

Astro Boy books 1 and 2. Dark Horse Comics 2008 424p. Illustration
Grades: 3 4 5 6 7 8 9 10 11 12 Adult   741.5; Fic
1. Adventure graphic novels; 2. Astro Boy (Fictional character); 3. Graphic novels; 4. Robots — Graphic novels; 5. Science fiction graphic novels
978-1-59582-153-9, $14.95

When a scientist loses his young son, he builds a robot to look exactly like the boy, but when he activates the robot, the scientist becomes repulsed and rejects him. Professor Ochanomizu (gotta love the name, it means tea water and is also a famous Tokyo neighborhood) rescues the boy robot from a circus and names him Astro Boy. He deals with aliens, with people who would use robots to commit crimes, and with adventures in outer space. This new edition collects the first two volumes of the Dark Horse manga editions.

Also available in omnibus editions; Volumes 1 and 2 of a 23 volume series

★ **Black** Jack, volume 1. Vertical, Inc. 2008 287p. Illustration
Grades: 9 10 11 12 Adult   741.5; Fic
1. Graphic novels; 2. Manga; 3. Medical practice — Graphic novels; 4. Surgeons — Graphic novels; 5. Shonen manga
978-1-934287-27-9, $16.95

Black Jack is the only known name for a mysterious, scarred surgeon from Japan who can perform surgical miracles but is considered to be a creepy mercenary. He will perform highly risky surgeries for an exorbitant price, and he's unlicensed. However, most people don't realize that he actually does a lot for more altruistic reasons as well. In this first volume that reprints the original stories by pioneer mangaka (manga creator) Tezuka, stories include one in which Black Jack operates on a crime boss's son using the body of an unjustly convicted man; and one where he removes a teratoid cystoma from a unidentified wealthy and famous woman, but he refuses to kill the cystoma, which contains the body parts of the woman's unborn twin. While there are some surgical scenes that might not be for the squeamish, the stories offer little in the way of graphic violence or bad language while providing action and some thought about ethics and morals.

"With genre-spanning stories — horror, sci-fi, romance — and Tezuka's signature blend of drama, bathos and extreme broad comedy jammed together on every page, Black Jack is a wild but extravagantly entertaining ride." Publ Wkly
Volume 1 of 17

★ **Buddha** Volume 1: Kapilavastu. Vertical, Inc. 2003 400p. Illustration
Grades: 10 11 12 Adult   741.5; Fic
1. Buddhism — Graphic novels; 2. Graphic novels; 3. Manga; 4. Seinen manga
1-932234-56-X (pa); 1-932234-43-8, $24.95; 9781932234565, $14.95

In this first of eight volumes, Tezuka starts the story of Buddha before the birth of the prince Siddhartha. His fictional characters, the slave Chapra, the pariah Tatta, the monk Naradatta, and many others, populate the story and will have an effect on the prince's life. The book includes sexual situations and considerable nudity; the pariahs never wore clothes. Tezuka also throws in a lot of humorous and anachronistic comments; but underlying everything is a profoundly deep understanding of Buddhism. The book also includes some violence.

Thomas, Roy

The **Chronicles** of Conan Volume 1: Tower of the Elephant and Other Stories. Dark Horse Comics 2003 166p. Illustration
Grades: 9 10 11 12 Adult   741.5; Fic
1. Adventure graphic novels; 2. Conan the Barbarian (Fictional character); 3. Fantasy graphic novels; 4. Graphic novels
1-59307-016-0, $15.95

In the early 1970s, Robert E. Howard's Conan the Barbarian exploded on to the comics scene. Writer Roy Thomas teamed with a young artist named Barry Smith, and together the two mapped out Conan adventures over the course of their 24-issue run together. Thomas and Smith defined Conan for a generation of comics readers, and now those stories are collected here in a series of trade paperbacks. This series features completely remastered color and text corrections, and contains material not available for nearly thirty years. Some of the stories are original, others adapt the original Howard stories; they all include action and violence and some suggestive scenes, as Conan fights warriors and monsters and encounters beautiful, sexy women.

Thompson, Craig, 1975-
★ **Blankets:** an illustrated novel. Top Shelf 2003 582p. Illustration
Grades: 10 11 12 Adult   92; 741.5
1. Artists; 2. Autobiographical graphic novels; 3. Cartoonists; 4. Family life — Graphic novels; 5. Graphic novels; 6. Illustrators; 7. Thompson, Craig, 1975-
1-891830-43-0, $29.95; 9781891830433

LC 2004-297892

This "memoir recreates the confusion, emotional pain and isolation of the author's rigidly fundamentalist Christian upbringing, along with the trepidation of growing into maturity. Skinny, naive and spiritually vulnerable, Thompson and his younger brother manage to survive their parents' overbearing discipline (the brothers are sometimes forced to sleep in "the cubbyhole," a forbidding and claustrophobic storage chamber) through flights of childhood fancy and a mutual love of drawing...Thompson manages to explore adolescent social yearnings, the power of young love and the complexities of sexual attraction with a rare combination of sincerity, pictorial lyricism and taste. His exceptional b&w drawings balance representational precision with a bold and wonderfully expressive line for pages of ingenious, inventively composed and poignant imagery." Publ Wkly

★ **Habibi**. Pantheon Books 2011 655p. Illustration
Grades: Adult   741.5; Fic

1. Graphic novels; 2. Refugees — Graphic novels; 3. Slavery — Graphic novels
978-0-375-42414-4, $35

LC 2010050963

"Child bride Dolola is sold by her impoverished parents in the Middle East to a clumsy but well-meaning older man who teaches her to read and write. When slavers kill her husband and kidnap her, she manages to escape carrying the dark-skinned baby of another captive. She finds refuge in an abandoned ship stranded in the desert, where she raises little Zam to adolescence, telling him stories and teaching him literacy. Further adventures separate them but reunite them later. As escaped harem prostitute and escaped eunuch, they forge an intimate bond and move into the future." Libr J"

"Though in the form of a comic book, Thompson's story is decidedly not for youngsters: Rape and murder figure in these pages, as does sex between minors. A mature — in all its meanings — glimpse into a world few Westerners are at home with, and Thompson is respectful throughout." Kirkus

Thompson, Jill

Death: At Death's Door. DC Comics/Vertigo 2003 204p. Illustration
Grades: 10 11 12 Adult   **741.5; Fic**
1. Adventure graphic novels; 2. Fantasy graphic novels; 3. Graphic novels; 4. Horror graphic novels; 5. Humorous graphic novels
1-56389-938-8, $9.95

A member of the Endless, a family of beings who have existed longer than the gods, Death enjoys manifesting herself in the persona of a Goth girl. Along with her siblings, she interacts and influences the lives of humans on a daily basis. In this shojo manga-style adventure, Death's little sisters, Delirium and Despair, have thrown a party at her apartment for hell's escapees. But as the festivities get out of control, it falls on Death's black-clad shoulders to regain order and save the afterlife — not to mention her carpet. Despair is always drawn as nude. The events in this book occur around the time of the Sandman volume, Season of Mists.

The **Little** Endless Storybook. DC Comics/Vertigo 2004 un Illustration
Grades: 9 10 11 12 Adult   **741.5; Fic**
1. Adventure graphic novels; 2. Fantasy graphic novels; 3. Graphic novels
14012-0428-7, $15.95

Jill Thompson takes Neil Gaiman's the Endless and draws them as little children in this story. Puppy Barnabas has been entrusted with watching and protecting Delirium, who is always easily...distracted. When he leaves her for just a minute or so, she gets lost. He searches the waking world but can't find her. Now, he must travel to the strange and unlikely realms of each of the Endless to see if Delirium's siblings have seen their missing sister. While the pictures are cute and the book resembles a child's picture book, the story has enough of an edge to make it more suitable for older teens. Despair is, as always, drawn as nude.

★ **Wonder** Woman: the true Amazon. Jill Thompson, writer and artist; Jason Arthur, letterer. DC Comics 2016 128 p. Color; Illustration
Grades: 9 10 11 12 Adult   **741.5; Fic**
1. Princesses — Graphic novels; 2. Amazons — Graphic novels; 3. Wonder Woman (Fictional character)
1401249019; 9781401249014, $22.99

Eisner Award: Best Graphic Album — New (2017)

"Young Diana has the fawning attention of her nation, but she soon grows spoiled and ungrateful. When a series of tragic events takes its toll, Diana must learn to grow up, take responsibility, and seize her destiny." (Publisher's note)

"Thompson's art is soft and magical, atypical of superhero comics. In her capable hands, this work provides insight into the early years of the

heroine and is a solid addition to the stand-alone stories of her character." LJ

Thompson, Kelly

Hawkeye : Kate Bishop : anchor points. Kelly Thompson, writer; Leonardo Romero (#1-4) & Michael Walsh (#5-6), artists; Jordie Bellaire, color artist; VC's Joe Sabino, letterer; Julian Totino Tedesco, cover art. Marvel Enterprises 2017 136 p. Color; Illustration
Grades: 9 10 11 12 Adult   **741.5; Fic**
1. Private investigators — Fiction; 2. Good and evil — Comic books, strips, etc.; 3. Women superheroes — Comic books, strips, etc.
1302905147; 9781302905149, $17.99

"Kate is heading back out west and returning to Los Angeles, with her bow and arrow and P.I. badge in tow. There are crimes to solve and she's the best archer to handle 'em! The City of Angels has a new guardian angel. This is Kate Bishop like you've never seen her before, in a brand-new saga that really hits the mark!" (Publisher's note)

Volume 1 of 3

Thompson, Kim

Popeye Vol. 1: I Yam What I Yam!. Fantagraphics Books 2006 182p. Illustration
Grades: 10 11 12 Adult   **741.5**
1. Graphic novels; 2. Humorous graphic novels; 3. Popeye (Fictional character)
978-1-56097-779-7, $29.95

This is the first volume in a series that will publish all of Segar's original comic strips featuring Popeye, Olive Oyl, Wimpy, and all the other characters people have known from cartoons and a motion picture. This volume covers the years 1928 through 1930 and feature Popeye's courtship of Olive Oyl, meeting the Sea Hag, and Castor Oyl's attempts to turn Popeye into a boxing champion. With all the fighting going on, this book really isn't meant for children.

Thompson, Robbie

Silk; Volume 0: the life and times of Cindy Moon. by Robbie Thompson; illustrated by Stacey Lee. Marvel Enterprises 2015 160 p. Color; Illustration
Grades: 9 10 11 12 Adult   **741.5; Fic**
1. Women superheroes — Comic books, strips, etc.
0785197044; 9780785197041, $19.99

In this comic book, by Robbie Thompson, illustrated by Stacey Lee, "Cindy Moon...learned that she had been bitten by the same radioactive spider from the first arc of AMAZING SPIDER-MAN. She then went on to save Peter Parker's life (more than once!) and traverse the Spider-Verse alongside Spider-Woman. Now, as SILK, Cindy is on her own in New York City, searching for her past, defining her own future, and webbing up wrong-doers along the way!" (Publisher's note)

Other Silk volumes are: 1, Sinister (2016); 2, The negative (2017)

Tieri, Frank

Civil War: War Crimes. writer, Frank Tieri; artist, Staz Johnson. Marvel Entertainment 2007 un Illustration
Grades: 10 11 12 Adult   **741.5; Fic**
1. Graphic novels; 2. Superhero graphic novels; 3. Iron Man (Fictional character); 4. Captain America (Fictional character)
0-7851-2652-X, $17.99

Wilson Fisk, the incarcerated ex-Kingpin of Crime, proposes a deal to Iron Man, to use his underworld connections to help track down Captain America and his anti-Registration underground in exchange for consideration on his sentence. But can the Kingpin be trusted, or is he playing a deeper game? In a Civil War prequel story, career criminal Jackie

Dio, fresh out of prison, finds the New York underworld has changed, and he finds trouble. If he's going to have a shot at surviving, he may have to find the shadowy figure known only as "The Consultant" — that is, if he even exists. There is more graphic violence in this title, and some strong language.

Tiwary, Vivek J.
The **Fifth** Beatle: The Brian Epstein Story. by Vivek Tiwary; edited by Philip Simon; illustrated by Andrew C. Robinson and Kyle Baker. Dark Horse 2013 144 p. Color; Illustration
Grades: Adult   **92; 741.5**
1. Beatles; 2. Biographical graphic novels; 3. Epstein, Brian, 1934-1967
1616552565; 9781616552565, $19.99
LAMBDA Literary Award Finalist: Graphic Novel (2014); Eisner Award: Best Reality-Based Work (2014); Harvey Award: Best Graphic Album of Original Work (2014); Harvey Award: Best Biographical, Historical, or Journalistic Presentation (2014)
This graphic novel, by Vivek Tiwary, edited by Philip Simon, and illustrated by Andrew C. Robinson and Kyle Baker, "is the untold true story of Brian Epstein, the visionary manager who discovered and guided the Beatles — from their gigs in a tiny cellar in Liverpool to unprecedented international stardom." (Publisher's note)
"Robinson and Baker's artwork is colorful and fluid, and it avoids looking like copies of publicity stills (a cliché of biographical comics), with rich, deep color palettes capturing the mod energy of the '60s." Pub Wkly

Tobe, Keiko
With the Light: Raising an Autistic Child (Hikari to Tomoni). Yen Press 2007 528p. Illustration
Grades: 8 9 10 11 12 Adult   **741.5; Fic**
1. Autism — Graphic novels; 2. Graphic novels; 3. Manga; 4. Josei manga
978-0-7595-2356-2, $14.99
Born during the sunrise — an auspicious beginning — the Azumas' newborn son is named Hikaru, which means "light." But during one play date, his mother notices that her son is slightly different from the other children. In this alternately heartwarming and bittersweet tale, a young mother tries to cope with both the overwhelming discovery of her child's autism and the trials of raising him while keeping her family together. This fictional story is based on true accounts; and the book includes notes about how parents can deal with certain situations depicted in the story.
Volume 1 of 8

Toboso, Yana
Black butler, vol. 1. by Yana Toboso [translation: Tomo Kimura; lettering: Tania Biswas].. Yen Press 2010 184p. Illustration
Grades: 10 11 12 Adult   **741.5; Fic**
1. Fantasy graphic novels; 2. Graphic novels; 3. Household employees — Graphic novels; 4. Manga; 5. Mystery graphic novels; 6. Shonen manga
978-0-316-08084-2, $10.99
In an alternate England, the young Earl Phantomhive, Ciel, lives just outside London; he's only twelve years old, but he runs a massive toy manufacturing company, aided by his butler Sebastian. In this world, magic coexists with science and technology, cars from the early twentieth century drive the roads and Ciel tests video games. Sebastian commands the other workers: Finnian the Gardener (who tends to kill plants), Mey-Rin the klutzy housemaid, and Baldroy the chef, who always has a cigarette dangling from the corner of his mouth. The dapper butler always finds a way to save the day, whether it's transforming a destroyed courtyard into a Japanese rock garden, teaching his young charge to dance the waltz,

or saving him from gangsters. He is too good to be true; he is, as he says, "a devil of a butler." The book includes some graphic violence and occasional, mildly bad language ("bastard," "damned").
First volume in an ongoing series; Volume 1 of an ongoing series

Tomasi, Peter
Batman and Robin; Volume 1. Peter J. Tomasi, writer; Patrick Gleason, penciller; Mick Gray, Guy Major, inkers; John Kalisz, colorist; Patrick Brosseau, letterer.. DC Comics 2012 192 p. Illustration; Color
Grades: Adult   **Fic; 741.5/973**
1. Superhero graphic novels; 2. Fatherhood — Graphic novels; 3. Batman (Fictional character); 4. Robin (Fictional character)
9781401238384, $16.99; 1401234879; 9781401234874, $24.99
LC 2012010314
This graphic novel features a "story arc [that] shows the master crime fighter learning to be a father. Damian Wayne, the latest Robin, spent the first 10 years of his life being trained as an assassin, so he doesn't understand Batman's refusal to kill." Batman has trouble explaining "his rigid code of morality," just as the villain Nobody arrives. He "simply erases the villains he encounters. He is, in short, a dangerously appealing father figure for Batman's alienated son." (Publishers Weekly)
Originally published in single magazine form in BATMAN AND ROBIN 1-8 — T.p. verso.

The **bridge:** how the Roeblings connected Brooklyn to New York. Peter J. Tomasi, illustrated by Sara DuVall. Abrams ComicArts 2018 208 p. Color; Illustration
Grades: 11 12 Adult   **741.5; 624.2**
1. Comic books, strips, etc; 2. Graphic novels; 3. Roebling, Emily Warren, 1843-1903 — Biography — Comic books, strips, etc; 4. Roebling, Washington Augustus, 1837-1926 — Biography — Comic books, strips, etc; 5. Brooklyn Bridge (New York, N.Y.) — History — Comic books, strips, etc; 6. Bridges; 7. Roebling, Washington Augustus, 1837-1926; 8. Roebling, Emily Warren, 1843-1903
9781419728525, $24.99
LC 2017046927
"In this inspiring graphic novel, author Peter J. Tomasi and illustrator Sara Duvall show the building of the Brooklyn Bridge as it has never been seen before, and the marriage of the Roeblings — based on intellectual equality and mutual support — that made the construction of this iconic structure possible." (Publisher's note)
"Rather than being a story of a singular genius overcoming adversity, the book is a paean to collaboration. Iconic structures often have fascinating stories behind them, but rarely do the tellings emphasize the human as this one does." Pub Wkly

Tomine, Adrian
★ **Killing** and Dying. Adrian Tomine. Farrar Straus & Giroux 2015 128 p. Illustration
Grades: Adult   **741.5**
1. Family — Graphic novels; 2. Identity (Psychology) — Graphic novels
1770462090; 9781770462090, $22.95
Ignatz Award: Outstanding Anthology or Collection (2016); Ignatz Award: Outstanding Story (2016)
This graphic novel collection by Adrian Tomine is an "exploration of loss, creative ambition, identity, and family dynamics. 'Amber Sweet' shows the disastrous impact of mistaken identity in a hyper-connected world; 'A Brief History of the Art Form Known as 'Hortisculpture' details the invention and destruction of a vital new art form; the title story, 'Killing and Dying', centers on parenthood, mortality, and stand-up comedy." (Publisher's note)

★ **Shortcomings.** Drawn & Quarterly 2007 108p. Illustration

Grades: 10 11 12 Adult   **741.5; Fic**
1. Graphic novels
978-1-897299-16-6, $19.95; 1-897299-16-8

Ben Tanaka, a Japanese American in his late twenties, has trouble. His girlfriend, Miko, suspects that Ben's wandering eye is doing so in the direction of white women. This accusation, and its various implications, becomes the subject of heated, spiraling debate, setting in motion a story that pits California against New York (they both live in Berkeley), devotion against desire, and truth against truth. The book includes some strong language, nudity, and sexual situations.

Torres, Alissa
★ **American** widow. illustrated by Sungyoon Choi. Villard Books 2008 209p. Illustration
Grades: 11 12 Adult   **92; 974.7; 741.5**
1. Autobiographical graphic novels; 2. Educators; 3. Graphic novels; 4. Memoirists; 5. September 11 terrorist attacks, 2001 — Graphic novels; 6. Widows — Graphic novels; 7. Torres, Alissa
978-0-345-50069-4, $22

LC 2008-08396

Alissa Torres' husband Luis had just started his new job in the World Trade Center on September 10, 2001. The next day, he died in the terrorist attacks that destroyed the twin towers. Alissa was more than seven months pregnant. In this book, she recounts the personal struggles she suffered as a pregnant "terror widow," first heaped upon with sympathy, then publicly scorned. She describes the tragedies suffered by all the families who lost loved ones on September 11, 2001 and the frustrations they experienced dealing with bureaucrats as they tried to get even the smallest physical trace of their loved ones.

The author's "tragedy of errors inspires anger on her behalf, although the story is calmly and beautifully told. Choi's simple and attractive line art is set off by turquoise wash, yielding to a full-color photo at the end when Alissa embraces her life anew." Libr J

Torres, J.
Days Like This. Oni Press 2003 un Illustration
Grades: 6 7 8 9 10 11 12 Adult
741.5; Fic
1. Graphic novels; 2. Rock music — Graphic novels
1-929998-48-1, $8.95

It's the early 1960s, and rock'n'roll and r&b are ushering in a new golden age of pop music. Tina & the Tiaras, three teenage girl singers, songwriter Karen Prince, and new music mogul Anna Solomon team to create a new girl group sound and move up the charts.

Courtesy of Oni Press

Tran, G. B.
Vietnamerica: a family's journey. written and illustrated by GB Tran.. Villard Books 2010 279 p. Color illustration
Grades: 11 12 Adult   **741.5**
1. Illustrators; 2. Graphic novels; 3. Vietnamese Americans — Biography; 4. Artists
0345508726; 9780345508720, $30

LC 2011283144

"GB Tran is a young Vietnamese American artist who grew up distant from (and largely indifferent to) his family's history. Born and raised in South Carolina as a son of immigrants, he knew that his parents had fled Vietnam during the fall of Saigon. But even as they struggled to adapt to life in America, they preferred to forget the past — and to focus on their

children's future. It was only in his late twenties that GB began to learn their extraordinary story. When his last surviving grandparents die within months of each other, GB visits Vietnam for the first time and begins to learn the tragic history of his family, and of the homeland they left behind." (Publisher's note)

"The comic utilizes a dizzying barrage of effects to depict the characters' confusing experience: different lettering styles, realistic action set against full-page government posters, sound effects swirling from panel to panel, action-packed panoramas breaking apart as South Vietnam collapses." Pub Wkly

Trombetta, Jim
The **Horror!** The horror!: comic books the government didn't want you to read!. selected, edited, and with commentary by Jim Trombetta; introduction by R. L. Stine. Abrams ComicArts 2010 304p. Illustration
Grades: Adult   **741.5**
1. Censorship — United States; 2. Comic books, strips, etc.; 3. Horror comic books, strips, etc.; 4. Graphic novels
0810955954; 9780810955950, $29.95

LC 2008-54346

The Horror! The Horror! examines "the pre-Code horror comics of the 1950s." (Publisher's note) Index.
Includes bibliographical references (p. 302) and index.

Trondheim, Lewis
Approximate Continuum Comics. Lewis Trondheim. Fantagraphics Books 2011 144 p. Illustration
Grades: Adult   **92; 741.5**
1. Cartoonists — France — Biography — Comic books, strips, etc; 2. Trondheim, Lewis; 3. Autobiographical graphic novels
1606994107; 9781606994108, $18.99

LC 2013363506

This autobiographical graphic novel, by Lewis Trondheim, depicts the author's life as a cartoon character and "contains the first three chapters serialized in the 'Nimrod' comic book, the last three (never-before-translated) chapters, and a hilarious 'rebuttal' section in which Trondheim's family and cartoonist friends (including Epileptic creator David B. and Trondheim's mom) dispute (or ruefully agree with) Trondheim's depictions." (Publisher's note)

"The simple, unadorned black-and-white line drawings are agreeably loose and deceptively casual, compelling in their humorous expressiveness and economy. Trondheim's autobiographical departure is of a piece with the rest of his sizable body of work, not only in its whimsical intelligence but also in that the characters are portrayed as anthropomorphic animals." Booklist

Poppies of Iraq. cowritten by Brigitte Findakly & Lewis Trondheim; drawn by Lewis Trondheim; colored by Brigitte Findakly; translated by Helge Dascher. Drawn & Quarterly 2017 32 p. Color; Illustration
Grades: 9 10 11 12 Adult   **92; 741.5**
1. Women cartoonists — France — Biography — Comic books, strips, etc.; 2. Women cartoonists — Iraq — Biography — Comic books, strips, etc.; 3. Findakly, Brigitte; 4. Iraq — History — 1958-1979 — Comic books, strips, etc.; 5. Iraq — Social conditions — 20th century — Comic books, strips, etc.; 6. Autobiographical graphic novels; 7. Women — Iraq
1770462937; 9781770462939, $21.95

This book, translated by Helge Dascher, "is Brigitte Findakly's nuanced tender chronicle of her relationship with her homeland Iraq, co-written and drawn by her husband, the acclaimed cartoonist Lewis Trondheim. In spare and elegant detail, they share memories of her middle class childhood touching on cultural practices, the education system,

Saddam Hussein's state control, and her family's history as Orthodox Christians in the Arab world." (Publisher's note)

"Each story arc is punctuated by family photos and cultural notes that help bring the family to life and make their experiences personal. Findakly is never naive or sentimental, recounting her life in Iraq with the innocence of a child but the cognizance of an adult." Booklist

Truong, Marcelino

Saigon Calling: London 1963-75. by Marcelino Truong; translated by David Homel. Arsenal Pulp Press 2017 280 p. Illustration
Grades: 9 10 11 12 Adult
92; 741.5; 942.1
1. London (England); 2. Immigrants
9781551526898, $26.95; 1551526891

Courtesy of Arsenal Pulp Press

In this book, by Marcelino Truong, translated by David Homel, "young Marcelino and his family move from Saigon to London in order to escape the war following the assassination of South Vietnamese President Diem, for whom Marcelino's diplomat father was a personal interpreter. In London, his father struggles to build a new life for his children and his wife, whose bipolar spells are becoming increasingly violent. But for Marco and his siblings, swinging London is an exciting place to be." (Publisher's note)

"The second volume of the author's critically acclaimed graphic memoir of the Vietnam War era. The son of a French mother and a Vietnamese diplomat father, Truong combines powerful visual imagery with deft narrative as he recounts his teenage years in London and France while developing mixed emotions and allegiances about the war tearing his homeland apart." Kirkus
Translated from the French

Such a Lovely Little War: Saigon, 1961-63. by Marcelino Truong, translated by David Homel. Arsenal Pulp Press 2016 272 p. Color; Illustration
Grades: Adult
959.7; 92; 741.5
1. Truong, Marcelino; 2. Vietnam War, 1961-1975
1551526476; 9781551526478, $26.95

Courtesy of Arsenal Pulp Press

This graphic novel, by Marcelino Truong, translated by David Homel, "tells the story of the early years of the Vietnam war as seen through the eyes of a young boy named Marco, the son of a Vietnamese diplomat and his French wife. The book opens in America, where the boy's father works for the South Vietnam embassy.... The family is called back to Saigon in 1961, where the father becomes Prime Minister Ngo Dinh Diem's personal interpreter." (Publisher's note)

"Now a French-based author and artist, Truong forcefully recreates his saga, using a bold, blocky visual style and a muted color palette that deftly renders his family members and vividly captures crowded Saigon cityscapes and besieged countryside." Booklist
Translated from the French

Tsutsumi, Daisuke

Out of picture: art from the outside looking in volume 2. Villard Books 2008 238p. Illustration

Grades: 10 11 12 Adult   **741.5; Fic**
1. Graphic novels; 2. Short stories — Graphic novels
978-0-345-49873-1, $30

Animation production artists who have worked together at Blue Sky Studios have put together another volume of short stories in comics form. In one story, a giant of a man wants only to become a farmer, but the military has hunted him down because he was a biological weapon used by them to win a war; now, he can't be allowed to live. In another story, a young boy takes his first airplane ride and sees a strange being riding on the wing, fly-fishing in the sky. In another story, three friends " a cat, a pigeon, and a grumpy gargoyle " need to find a new home when their antique shop home is destroyed. None of the stories uses graphic violence or much in the way of harsh language, but the moods and intensity of emotion make the book more suitable for older teens and adults.

Tyler, Carol

★ **Soldier's** heart: the campaign to understand my WWII veteran father - a daughter's memoir. by Carol Tyler. Fantagraphics 2015 362 p. Color; Illustration; Map
Grades: Adult   **940.53; 92; 741.5**
1. Tyler, Carol — Family — Comic books, strips, etc.; 2. Father-daughter relationship; 3. World War, 1939-1945 — Biography — Graphic novels
160699896X; 9781606998960, $39.99
Cartoonist Studio Prize (2016); Ignatz Award: Outstanding Graphic Novel (2016)

"The phrase 'soldier's heart' is the predecessor to today's post-traumatic stress disorder (PTSD). This is the underlying theme in Tyler's...biography of her father's life in this book, originally released as the trilogy You'll Never Know, between 2009 and 2012. Tyler tells the story of her father, Charles, his upbringing as a plumber's son in Chicago before he enlists in the army during World War II; his war experience; after the war as he raises his family with his beloved wife, Red; and their lives into the present. The time line jumps between the current day, as Tyler deals with her own troubled marriage and raising her daughter, and the past (her own, her father's, and her mother's)." (Library Journal)
Originally published as three separate volumes

Tynion, James, IV

The **woods**; Volume 1: The arrow. James Tynion IV; illustrated by Michael Dialynas. Boom! Studios 2014 96 p. Color; Illustration
Grades: 11 12 Adult   **741.5**
1. Science fiction graphic novels; 2. Missing persons — Graphic novels; 3. High school students — Fiction
1608864545; 9781608864546, $9.99

"On October 16, 2013, 437 students, 52 teachers, and 24 additional staff from Bay Point Preparatory High School in suburban Milwaukee, WI vanished without a trace. Countless light years away, far outside the bounds of the charted universe, 513 people find themselves in the middle of an ancient, primordial wilderness. Where are they? The answers will prove stranger than anyone could possibly imagine." (Publisher's note)

"Tynion pulls no punches as he puts these kids through hell, and in the few moments they are allowed to stop to take a breath, they reveal very unique and original personalities, making them less like horror stereotypes and more like real, breathing kids." Booklist
Volume 1 of 9

Uderzo, Albert

Asterix and Obelix All at Sea. Orion/Sterling Publishing 2002 48p. Illustration
Grades: 4 5 6 7 8 9 10 11 12 Adult   **741.5; Fic**
1. Asterix (Fictional character); 2. Graphic novels; 3. Humorous graphic novels

0-75284-778-3, $9.95

LC 2002-282560

In ancient Rome the slaves are revolting...and not only that, they've stolen Julius Caesar's own galley, the finest warship in the Roman navy. Under their heroic leader Spartakis, the former galley slaves make for the little Gaulish village where Julius Caesar's old enemies Asterix and Obelix live — only to find the place in crisis, for Obelix, after drinking the druid Getafix's magic potions on the sly, is first turned to stone and then reverts to childhood. In search of a cure for him Asterix, Getafix and their new friends the galley slaves sail to the wonderful continent of Atlantis, ruled by its high priest Absolutlifabulos — and the ensuing sea battles against the Roman navy are fast and furious ...

Umezu, Kazuo

Scary Book Volume 1: Reflections. Kazuo Umezu; translation, Kumar Sivasubramanian; lettering and retouch, Kathryn Renta. Dark Horse Manga 2006 231p. Illustration

Grades: 10 11 12 Adult   **741.5; Fic**

1. Graphic novels; 2. Horror graphic novels; 3. Manga; 4. Shojo manga
978-1-59307-476-0, $13.95

This book offers two tales: "Mirror," in which a narcissistic girl's reflection begins to take ruthless command of her life; and "Demon of Vengeance," where a sadistic warlord bent on seeking retribution for his selfish and reckless son's injuries finds the tables of revenge turned against him. Umezu is considered a master of horror manga; these stories were originally published in the 1960s and 1970s in Japan. This book includes some violence and some strong language.

Other titles in this series are: Volume 2: Insects; Volume 3: Faces

Unita, Yumi

★ **Bunny** drop vol. 1. [translation, Kaori Inoue; lettering, Alexis Eckerman].. Yen Press 2010 196p. Illustration

Grades: 8 9 10 11 12 Adult   **741.5; Fic**

1. Graphic novels; 2. Josei manga; 3. Manga; 4. Unmarried fathers — Graphic novels
978-0-7595-3122-2, $12.99

Thirty-year-old bachelor Daikichi is a salaryman, a junior executive, living on his own in Tokyo. When he goes home for his grandfather's funeral, he discovers that his grandfather had a younger lover who left him with a little girl, Rin (which makes her his aunt). The lover is nowhere to be found, and none of Daikichi's relatives will have anything to do with Rin, who won't talk to anyone but sticks close to Daikichi, who closely resembles his grandfather. When no one will step forward to take care of the six-year-old, Daikichi impulsively decides he will. Once he brings Rin home, the reality of his new situation finally dawns on him; Daikichi is now a single father and has to provide care for Rin. There's one scene with Rin and Daikichi together in their furo bath (a very typical Japanese family scene), and a few panels with Rin and Daikichi in their underwear. In one chapter, Daikichi has to deal with Rin's night time bedwetting, and Rin is shown changing her clothes.

"This sweet-natured manga shows the joys, frustrations, and quirks of family life; and while it is aimed at teens, it would also be more than welcome in the hands of adult readers." Booklist

First published 2006 in Japan; Book reads from right to left in the traditional Japanese format; Volume 1 of 9

Urasawa, Naoki

Master Keaton 1. by Naoki Urasawa, Takashi Nagasaki, and Hokusei Katsushika. Viz 2014 316 p. Illustration

Grades: Adult   **741.5**

1. Insurance investigators — Comic books, strips, etc.; 2. Adventure graphic novels

1421575892; 9781421575896, $19.99

Eisner Nominee: Best U.S. Edition of International Material — Asia (2016) [for volumes 2-4]

"Taichi Hiraga-Keaton, the son of a Japanese zoologist and a noble English woman, is an insurance investigator known for his successful and unorthodox methods of investigation. Educated in archaeology and a former member of the SAS, Master Keaton uses his knowledge and combat training to uncover buried secrets, thwart would-be villains, and pursue the truth." (Publisher's note)

"Though the exotic locales and murder mysteries endemic to this profession are entertaining enough on their own, Keaton's background as an archaeology lecturer and former member of the British Special Air Service is what takes the comic from good to great." Pub Wkly

Volume 1 of 12

★ **Monster;** Volume 1. story & art by Naoki Urasawa; translation & English adaptation, Camellia Nieh; lettering, Steve Dutro; editor, Mike Montesa. Viz Media 2014 418 p. Illustration; Color

Grades: 10 11 12 Adult   **741.5**

1. Serial killers — Fiction; 2. Physicians — Fiction
142156906X; 9781421569062, $19.99

"Dr. Tenma is the third son in a family of doctors, who left Japan years ago to work under his idol in a hospital in Dusseldorf, Germany.... He's on the fast track to promotion and power, until he refuses the hospital director's order to leave the victim of a brutal crime on the table and go help the mayor instead. Suddenly he goes from the cusp of a bright future to a grunt. His fiancée leaves him, his promotion is given away, and his patients are removed from his care. But when the men who took everything from Tenma wind up suddenly dead, he's set down a path that will change his life forever." (School Library Journal)

Volume 1 of 9

★ **Naoki** Urasawa's 20th century boys, vol. 1. story & art by Naoki Urasawa; with the cooperation of Takashi Nagasaki; [English adaptation, Akemi Wegmüller]. Viz Media 2009 216p.

Grades: 10 11 12 Adult   **741.5; Fic**

1. Graphic novels; 2. Manga; 3. Mystery graphic novels; 4. Seinen manga
978-1-59116-922-2, $12.99

In 1997, Kenji has given up his dream of being a rock musician and manages his family's convenience store. When one of his childhood friends, a science teacher, commits suicide, Kenji starts to think back to 1969, when he and his friends created a hideaway, swore to do what they could to save the world, and buried a time capsule with a symbol they designed drawn on top. In 1997, that symbol starts showing up as grafitti in Kenji's neighborhood. And a strange cult led by a man who calls himself "Friend" uses that symbol (an eye with a hand pointing upward). As Kenji reunites with his buddies, they talk about what they did in 1969, and they dig up the time capsule. Does it have anything to do with their friend Donkey's death? The book includes graphic violence and partial nudity.

Volume 1 of 22

Naoki Urasawa's 21st century boys; Volume 1. by Naoki Urasawa. VIZ Media 2013 192 p. Illustration

Grades: Adult   **741.5; Fic**

1. Manga; 2. Science fiction; 3. Mystery fiction; 4. Seinen manga; 5. Tokyo (Japan) — Fiction
1421543265; 9781421543260, $12.99

"War is over. The Friend is dead. Mankind no longer faces the threat of extinction. Peace has finally come to Tokyo... Or has it? The mystery still remains. Nobody knows who the Friend was and where he came from. The only clue is hidden deep within the memories-the memories of the hero

Kenji. It is time to open Pandora's Box to discover what is left at the bottom." (Publisher's note)
Volume 1 of 2

★ **Pluto**. by Naoki Urasawa & Osamu Tezuka; co-authored with Takashi Nagasaki; translation, Jared Cook & Frederick L. Schodt. Viz Media 2009 200 p. Illustration
Grades: 9 10 11 12 Adult 741.5; Fic
1. Astro Boy (Fictional character); 2. Graphic novels; 3. Manga; 4. Mystery graphic novels; 5. Robots — Graphic novels; 6. Robots — Fiction; 7. Seinen manga
1421519186; 9781421519180, $12.99
"In a distant future where sentient humanoid robots pass for human, someone or some thing is out to destroy the seven great robots of the world. Europol's top detective Gesicht is assigned to investigate these mysterious robot serial murders — the only catch is that he himself is one of the seven targets." (Publisher's note)
"In a tribute to Osamu Tezuka's (the 'God of Manga') classic Astro Boy, Urasawa takes one of Tezuka's story arcs and reimagines it as a noir detective story. Along the way, he brings in themes of racism, war, and what it means to be human." Booklist
Original Japanese edition, 2004; Volume 1 of 8

Uriarte, Maximilian
Terminal Lance ultimate omnibus. Maximilian Uriarte. Little, Brown & Co. 2018 352 p. Illustration
Grades: Adult 741.5
1. United States. Marine Corps — Fiction; 2. Biographical fiction; 3. Iraq War, 2003-2011 — Fiction
9780316412247, $30
LC 2017958898
This collection of strips by Maximilian Uriarte covers "a wide range of topics, including the rules governing the wearing of military uniforms, the most popular (and the most disgusting) MREs, the difficulty of keeping a long-distance relationship alive across thousands of miles, and the struggles marines face upon returning home.... [This book] provides a hilarious and deeply intelligent look into every aspect of life for American marines." (Publisher's note)
"Uriarte launched the strip, originally published online and in the Marine Corps Times, while still on active duty. Demonstrating that actual combat takes up a minute portion of a soldier's time, the strips, drawn in a simple, unadorned style, sardonically depict the near-daily tribulations and occasional pleasures of military life." Booklist

The **White** Donkey: Terminal Lance. by Maximilian Uriarte. Little, Brown & Co. 2016 288 p. Illustration
Grades: Adult 741.5; Fic
1. Post-traumatic stress disorder — Fiction; 2. Iraq War, 2003-2011 — Fiction; 3. War stories
0316362832; 9780316362832, $25
This book, by Maximilian Uriarte, "tells the story of Abe, a young Marine recruit who experiences the ugly, pedestrian, and often meaningless side of military service in rural Iraq. He enlists in hopes of finding that missing something in his life but comes to find out that it's not quite what he expected. Abe gets more than he bargained for when his journey takes him to the middle east in war-torn Iraq." (Publisher's note)
"Both respectful to the military and its role and sympathetic to the delicacy of the young soldiers, the story's power lies in a middle-ground view of the ongoing social conflict, seeking to bridge understanding on both sides." Pub Wkly
Originally published in paperback as Terminal lance: the white donley, February 2016 — Title page verso.

Urrea, Luis Alberto
★ **Mr.** Mendoza's paintbrush. artwork by Christopher Cardinale; color masking and compositing, Anthony Cardinale; design, Anne M. Giangiulio. Cinco Puntos Press 2010 un Illustration
Grades: 10 11 12 7 8 9 Adult 741.5; Fic
1. Artists — Graphic novels; 2. Graphic novels; 3. Humorous graphic novels; 4. Mexico — Graphic novels
978-1-933693-23-1, $17.95
LC 2008-11636
Rosario is a small town in the Sinaloa region of Mexico, nestled into a wet, green, mango-sweet subtropical landscape. There, Mr. Mendoza wields his paintbrush to write graffiti with a purpose. When Mr. Mendoza catches the young narrator and his best friend Jaime spying on the girls who are swimming, he strips them, writes graffiti all over their bodies, and chases the naked boys down the street through town. He also appoints himself as the town's conscience and angers the authorities with his graffiti on the town's whorehouse, bridge, and other places. Then, one day, he takes his paint and paintbrush to the center square and paints steps into the sky and walks up until he disappears. Women and girls are shown in their underwear, and the naked boys are shown only from the back. The talk of sex, the way the boys sneak peeks at the girls and one of the town's women, make this book suitable for teens even though the format resembles a picture book.
"Not only does the art perfectly capture the mood of the piece — from the blocky woodcuts to the muted earth tones — but it also reinforces the lucid dreamlike quality of its magical realism, serving as an enticing invitation to further explore the genre." Horn Book Guide

Usdin, Carly
Heavy vinyl. created & written by Carly Usdin; penciled by Nina Vakueva; inked by Irene Flores, colored by Rebeca Nalty, with Kieran Quigley & Walter Baiamonte, lettered by Jim Campbell. Boom! Box 2018 112 p. Color; Illustration
Grades: 10 11 12 Adult 741.5; Fic
1. Hand-to-hand fighting — Fiction; 2. Record stores — Fiction; 3. Teenage girls — Comic books, strips, etc.
1684151414; 9781684151417, $14.99
"Starry-eyed Chris has just started the dream job every outcast kid in town wants: working at Vinyl Mayhem. It's as rad as she imagined.... When Rosie Riot, the staff's favorite singer, mysteriously vanishes the night before her band's show, Chris discovers her co-workers are doing more than just sorting vinyl...Her local indie record store is also a front for a teen girl vigilante fight club!" (Publisher's note)
"The time period is reinforced by constant references to late-1990s bands, pop culture, clothing, and cultural subgroups. The illustrations are colorful and refined, and the diverse cast of characters presents a broad range of identities that are all treated matter-of-factly." Booklist

Van Lente, Fred
Action Philosophers Giant-Size Thing Vol. 2. Evil Twin Comics 2007 94p. Illustration
Grades: 9 10 11 12 Adult
180; 741.5
1. Graphic novels; 2. Philosophers — Graphic novels
978-0-9778329-1-0, $8.95
Karl Marx: The People's Hero! Jacques Derrida: The Deconstructonator! St. Thomas Aquinas: The Scholastic Spastic! Isaac ben-Luria: Rabbi of the Mystic Arts! They're not just great thinkers,...They also make great comics. This book collects issues #4-6 of the

Courtesy of Evil Twin Comics

Action Philosophers series, detailing the lives and thoughts of the men above, plus Machiavelli, Sartre, Descartes, Kierkegaard, Wittgenstein. There's just a little bit of strong language in this volume.

Van Meter, Jen

Hopeless Savages. Oni Press 2002 128p. Illustration
Grades: 7 8 9 10 11 12 Adult
741.5; Fic
1. Family — Graphic novels; 2. Graphic novels; 3. Humorous graphic novels; 4. Rock music — Graphic novels
1-929998-24-4, $13.95

Courtesy of Oni Press

Family ties are the earliest ties that bind, setting the tone for the paths we will take in our future. So what if your father is Dirk Hopeless and your mother Nikki Savage, a superstar couple from the days of punk rock? When you're born a rebel, what can you possibly do to make yourself stand apart? For Rat Hopeless-Savage, the answer is to leave home and become a normal citizen with a nine-to-five job.

Hopeless Savages Vol. 2: Ground Zero. Oni Press 2004 128p. Illustration
Grades: 7 8 9 10 11 12 Adult
741.5; Fic
1. Family — Graphic novels; 2. Graphic novels; 3. Humorous graphic novels; 4. Rock music — Graphic novels; 5. Romance graphic novels
1-929998-99-6, $11.95

Courtesy of Oni Press

When you're sixteen, the world is a different place. When you're Zero Hopeless-Savage, the youngest daughter of rock stars Dirk Hopeless and Nikki Savage, the world is practically unrecognizable. Imagine you're in the midst of high school, you have your first band, and WHAMMO! Some boy comes along who doesn't think you're a total freak, and you think he's pretty swell, too. But before you can do anything about it, there's a TV crew outside your house that wants to chronicle the gossip and scandals of your parents' careers, and a massive misunderstanding has gotten you grounded. How's a self-respecting young lady supposed to handle all that?

Hopeless Savages Vol. 3: Too Much Hopeless. Oni Press 2004 un Illustration
Grades: 7 8 9 10 11 12 Adult
741.5; Fic
1. Family — Graphic novels; 2. Graphic novels; 3. Humorous graphic novels; 4. Martial arts — Graphic novels; 5. Romance graphic novels
1-929998-85-6, $11.95

Courtesy of Oni Press

This was supposed to be a leisurely vacation. Arsenal Hopeless-Savage has a rematch with an old high school rival in a kung-fu tournament in Hong Kong. She and her brother Twitch figured they could turn it into a nice jaunt with their boyfriends to meet their aging grandmother, a renowned Chinese fortune teller. Too bad Grandma Shi didn't phone ahead to tell them that it was going to be the trip from Hell. It begins at the airport when a shady character slips something into Arsenal's bag, putting the quartet on the radar of the local bad guys, the British secret service, and the Hong Kong police. It becomes even more complicated when the rest of the Hopeless-Savage clan decides to join the middle children in Asia, getting caught up in the international intrigue themselves. Arsenal is the only person that can get them all out of the jam they're in, and for her it's all too much. Twitch's gay relationship is treated matter-of-factly.

Van Sciver, Noah

The **Hypo:** The Melancholic Young Lincoln. Noah Van Sciver. Fantagraphics 2012 192 p. Illustration
Grades: 11 12 Adult **92; 973.7092; 741.5**
1. Lincoln, Abraham, 1809-1865; 2. Biographical graphic novels; 3. Depression (Psychology)
1606996193; 9781606996195, $24.99

This graphic novel, by Noah Van Sciver, "is based on [Abraham] Lincoln's battle with depression.... [It] follows the twenty-something Abraham Lincoln as...a rising Whig in the state's legislature as he arrives in Springfield, IL to practice law.... But, as time passes and uncertainty creeps in, young Lincoln is forced to battle a dark cloud of depression brought on by a chain of defeats and failures culminating into a nervous breakdown that threatens his life and sanity." (Publisher's note)

"A thoroughly engaging graphic novel that seamlessly balances investigation and imagination." Pub Wkly

Vance, James

Kings in disguise. James Vance and Dan Burr; introduction by Alan Moore.. W.W. Norton 2006 184 p. Illustration
Grades: Adult **741.5**
1. Great Depression, 1929-1939 — Graphic novels
0393328481(pbk.); 9780393328486(pbk.)
LC 2005058549

Eisner Award: Best Single Issue/Story (1989); Eisner Award: Best New Series (1989); Harvey Award: Best New Series (1989)

"When 12-year-old Freddie's long-out-of-work father leaves home to look for a job, Freddie's older brother Al tries to fill his shoes. But when Al is arrested, Freddie leaves home to look for their father and quickly finds himself living the life of a hobo, riding the rails under the watchful eye of a drifter who calls himself the King of Spain. On his search, Freddie watches and helps as the jobless rally to demand a better life — or try to build that life themselves — all the while dogged by injustice and tragedy in a world that shuns and oppresses them." (Library Journal)

Vanistendael, Judith

When David lost his voice. Judith Vanistendael; [translated from the French edition by: Nora Mahony]. SelfMadeHero 2012 267 p. Color illustration
Grades: Adult **741; Fic**
1. Belgian fiction (French) — 21st century — Comic books, strips, etc; 2. Cancer — Patients — Family relationships — Comic books, strips, etc; 3. Graphic novels — Belgium; 4. Cancer patients — Fiction; 5. Cancer — Graphic novels
1906838542; 9781906838546, $24.95
LC 2012451584

Ignatz Nominee: Outstanding Graphic Novel (2013)

In this graphic novel, by Judith Vanitendael, "David has cancer.... David's wife becomes progressively consumed by the looming shadow of death while his daughters struggle to be as helpful as possible. Meanwhile,

David soldiers on, not wanting the tumor to rob him of everything, including the chance to see his granddaughter grow up." (Publisher's note)

Published in French as David les femmes et la mort, (c) Éditions du Lombard (Dargaud-Lombard S.A.) 2012, by Vanistendael (Judith) — T.p. verso.

Varon, Sara

Robot dreams. First Second 2007 205p. Illustration
Grades: 3 4 5 6 7 8 9 10 11 12 Adult   **741; 741.5; Fic**
1. Dogs — Graphic novels; 2. Graphic novels; 3. Robots — Graphic novels
978-1-59643-108-9 (pa), $16.95; 1-59643-108-3 (pa)

LC 2006-52640

The friendship between a dog and a robot is portrayed in this wordless graphic novel. (Bull Cent Child Books)

"Varon's drawing style is uncomplicated, and her colors are clean and refreshing. Although her story seems equally simple, it is invested with true emotion." Booklist

A Junior Library Guild book

Vaughan, Brian K.

Batman: false faces. DC Comics 2008 160p. Illustration
Grades: 10 11 12 Adult   **741.5; Fic**
1. Batman (Fictional character); 2. Graphic novels; 3. Superhero graphic novels; 4. Wonder Woman (Fictional character)
978-1-4012-1640-5, $19.99

Throughout his crimefighting career, the Dark Knight has managed to balance his double life as Batman and billionaire Bruce Wayne. But he has taken on other identities as well, including that of criminal Matches Malone. What happens when leading multiple lives becomes too much to handle? As Batman faces old enemies the Ventriloquist and the Mad Hatter, his greatest adversary may be his own secret lives. And Wonder Woman faces a crisis of her own, when Clayface steals part of the source of her power, and she must enlist the help of Donna Troy. The book includes some violence.

Doctor Strange: The Oath. Marvel Enterprises 2007 un Illustration
Grades: 9 10 11 12 Adult   **741.5; Fic**
1. Doctor Strange (Fictional character); 2. Graphic novels; 3. Superhero graphic novels
0-7851-2211-7, $13.99

Doctor Stephen Strange embarks on the most important paranormal investigation of his career, as he sets out to solve an attempted murder — his own. And with his most trusted friend, Wong, also at death's door, Strange turns to an unexpected corner of the Marvel Universe to recruit a new ally. The Night Nurse runs a clandestine clinic for superheroes, but she insists on accompanying Doctor Strange on his quest to find help for Wong.

The Escapists. Dark Horse Books 2009 176p. Illustration
Grades: 10 11 12 Adult   **741.5; Fic**
1. Adventure graphic novels; 2. Comic books, strips, etc. — Graphic novels; 3. Graphic novels
978-1-59582-361-8, $14.95

Inspired by Michael Chabon's Pulitzer Prizewinning novel, The Amazing Adventures of Kavalier and Clay, this story shows what it's like to start with nothing in Cleveland, Ohio, and end up with a comic so hot a major corporation wants to steal it from you. Maxwell Roth spends his inheritance to buy the rights to The Escapist, the comic book character created by Kavalier and Clay decades ago, and he and his high school friend Case Weaver set out to make new comics of The Escapist. Artist Denny Jones joins them, and together the three create a new comic book series that makes a smash debut. Then, Omnigrip Corporation, which long

ago sold the rights away, wants it back. When Roth says no, the corporation uses every dirty trick to force him to sell the rights back. The story of Roth, Weaver, and Jones is intermixed with adventures of the Escapist from the old comics. Artists Steve Rolston and Philip Bond illustrate the present-day story of the three independent comics creators, while Jason Shawn Alexander and Eduardo Barreto illustrate the classic Escapist stories. The book includes some violence and some harsh language.

Ex Machina Vol. 1: The First Hundred Days. DC Comics/Wildstorm 2005 un Illustration
Grades: 10 11 12 Adult   **741.5; Fic**
1. Graphic novels; 2. Politics — Graphic novels; 3. Superhero graphic novels
978-1-4012-0612-3, $9.99

This book tells the story of civil engineer Mitchell Hundred, who becomes America's first living, breathing super-hero after a strange accident gives him amazing powers. Eventually Mitchell tires of risking his life merely to maintain the status quo, retires from masked crime fighting, and runs for mayor of New York City, winning by a landslide. But Mayor Hundred has to worry about more than just budget problems and an antagonistic governor, especially when a mysterious hooded figure begins assassinating plow drivers during the worst snowstorm in the city's history. Strong language and some violence figures into this political superhero story.

Volume 1 of 10

★ **Paper** Girls; Volume 1. writer, Brian K. Vaughan; artist, Cliff Chiang; colors, Matt Wilson; letters, Jared K. Fletcher. Image Comics 2016 144 p. Color; Illustration
Grades: 11 12 Adult   **741.5; Fic**
1. Halloween — Fiction; 2. Girls — Fiction; 3. Science fiction graphic novels
1632156741; 9781632156747, $9.99

Eisner Award: Best New Series (2016)

"In the early hours after Halloween of 1988, four 12-year-old newspaper delivery girls uncover the most important story of all time. Suburban drama and otherworldly mysteries collide in this smash-hit series about nostalgia, first jobs, and the last days of childhood." (Publisher's note)

"Vaughan's spiky writing and Chiang's vivid, dramatically skewed art make for a potent mix, particularly in the darkly comic dream sequences that punctuate the action." Pub Wkly

Collects issues #1-5 of Paper Girls; Volume 1 of an ongoing series

★ **The Private** Eye. Brian K. Vaughn; illustrated by Marcos Martin. Image Comics 2015 300 p. Illustration
Grades: Adult   **741.5**
1. Secrets — Fiction; 2. Private investigators — Fiction; 3. Identity — Fiction
1632155729; 9781632155726, $49.99

LC 2016001103

Eisner Award: Best Digital/Online Comic (2015); Harvey Award: Best Online Comics Work (2015)

This graphic novel, by Brian K. Vaughn and illustrated by Marcos Martin, is "about an unlicensed private investigator who stumbles onto the most important case of his life. The series is set in 2076, a time after 'the cloud has burst', revealing everyone's secrets. As a result, there is no more Internet, and people are excessively guarded about their identity, to the point of appearing only masked in public." (Publisher's note)

"Vaughan and Martin's vision of the future is chilling in its realism, but fascinating in its hyperbole. Martin's art — accentuated beautifully by Vicente's colors — handles thrilling action and contemplative scenes equally well, allowing Vaughan's script to dig deep into identity, the balance between liberty and security, the role of technology in our lives, and the implicit trust we place in it." Pub Wkly

★ **Saga** 4. by Brian K. Vaughan; illustrated by Fiona Staples. Image Comics 2014 144 p. Color illustration
Grades: Adult   **741.5**
1. Adventure fiction; 2. Outer space — Fiction; 3. Family — Fiction; 4. Science fiction
1632150778; 9781632150776, $14.99
Eisner Award: Best Continuing Series (2015); Harvey Award: Continuing or Limited Series (2014); Harvey Award: Best Writer (2014); Harvey Award: Best Artist (2014)
"Hazel becomes a toddler, while her family struggles to stay on their feet." (Publisher's note)
Originally published in single issues as Saga #19-24

★ **Saga** [Vol. 3]. Brian K. Vaughan, writer; Fiona Staples, artist. Image Comics 2014 144 p. Color; Illustration
Grades: Adult   **741.5; Fic**
1. Fantasy fiction; 2. Comic books, strips, etc.; 3. Science fiction
1607069318; 9781607069317, $14.99
Eisner Award: Best Continuing Series (2014); Harvey Award: Continuing or Limited Series (2014); Harvey Award: Best Writer (2014; Harvey Award: Best Artist (2014)
In this fantasy comic book by Brian K. Vaughan, illustrated by Fiona Staples, part of a series, "When two soldiers from opposite sides of a never-ending galactic war fall in love, they risk everything to bring a fragile new life into a dangerous old universe.... In volume 3, as new parents Marko and Alana travel to an alien world to visit their hero, the family's pursuers finally close in on their targets." (Publisher's note)
Originally published in single magazine form as Saga #13-18

★ **Saga**. [Vol. 1]. Brian K. Vaughan, illustrated by Fiona Staples. Image Comics 2012 160 p.
Grades: Adult   **741.5; Fic**
1. Adventure graphic novels; 2. Fantasy graphic novels; 3. Family life — Graphic novels; 4. Monsters — Graphic novels
1607066017; 9781607066019, $9.99
Hugo Award: Best Graphic Story (2013); Eisner Award: Best New Series (2013); Eisner Award: Best Continuing Series (2013); Eisner Award: Best Writer (2013)
This fantasy graphic novel, by Brian K. Vaughan, illustrated by Fiona Staples, presents "the sweeping tale of one young family fighting to find their place in the worlds.... Two soldiers from opposite sides of a never-ending galactic war fall in love...[and] risk everything to bring a fragile new life into a dangerous old universe." (Publisher's note)
Rated M / mature.

★ **Saga**. [Vol. 2]. Brian K. Vaughan, illustrated by Fiona Staples. Image Comics 2013 144 p.
Grades: Adult   **741.5; Fic**
1. Adventure graphic novels; 2. Fantasy graphic novels; 3. Monsters — Graphic novels; 4. Family life — Graphic novels
9781607066927, $14.99; 1607066920
TIME Top 10 Comics and Graphic Novels (2013); Washington Post Top 10 Graphic Novels (2013); Eisner Award: Best Continuing Series (2014); Harvey Award: Continuing or Limited Series (2013); Harvey Award: Best Writer (2013); Harvey Award: Best Artist (2013)
"This smash hit continues to be a powerhouse: intergalactic intrigue, truly alien aliens, multifaceted characters, and a universe full of lush environments all wrapped around a compellingly told story of forbidden love in wartime." Booklist
Rated M / mature.

★ **Saga**; Volume 6. Brian K. Vaughan, writer; Fiona Staples, artist; Fonografiks, lettering & design; coordinator, Eric Stephenson. Image Comics 2016 152 p. Color; Illustration
Grades: Adult   **741.5; Fic**
1. Fantasy graphic novels; 2. Science fiction graphic novels
163215711X; 9781632157119, $14.99
Eisner Award: Best Continuing Series (2017)
"After a dramatic time jump, the three-time Eisner Award winner for Best Continuing Series continues to evolve, as Hazel begins the most exciting adventure of her life: kindergarten. Meanwhile, her starcrossed family learns hard lessons of their own." (Publisher's note)
Originally published in single magazine form as Saga #31-36

Saga; Volume Five. by Brian K. Vaughan; illustrated by Fiona Staples. Image Comics 2015 152 p. Color illustration
Grades: Adult   **741.5; 741.5973**
1. Outer space — Fiction; 2. Science fiction
1632154382; 9781632154385, $14.99
"Multiple storylines collide.... While Gwendolyn and Lying Cat risk everything to find a cure for The Will, Marko makes an uneasy alliance with Prince Robot IV to find their missing children, who are trapped on a strange world with terrifying new enemies." (Publisher's note)

Y: The Last Man Vol. 1: Unmanned. Brian K. Vaughan, writer; Pia Guerra, penciller; José Marzán, Jr., inker; Pamela Rambo, colorist; Clem Robins, letterer. DC Comics/Vertigo 2003 128p. Illustration
Grades: 10 11 12 Adult   **741.5; Fic**
1. Graphic novels; 2. Science fiction graphic novels
978-1-56389-980-5, $12.99
Escape artist Yorick Brown and his male pet monkey are the only surviving males left on Earth after a plague instantaneously kills all the other males on the planet. As women take over...everything...latter-day Amazons declare all men must die, Yorick's congresswoman mother arranges protection for him, and mysterious Israeli soldiers seem highly amused. The story includes strong language, nudity, and violence.
Volume 1 of 10

Vaughn, Sarah
Sleepless; Volume 1. Sarah Vaughn, writer; Leila del Duca, artist; Alissa Sallah, editor & colors; Deron Bennett, letters. Image Comics 2018 168 p. Color; Illustration
Grades: 10 11 12 Adult   **741.5; Fic**
1. Fantasy fiction — Graphic novels; 2. Romance fiction — Graphic novels
1534306846; 9781534306844, $16.99
"Lady 'Poppy' Pyppenia is guarded by the Sleepless Knight Cyrenic but becomes endangered when an assassin threatens her life in the new king's reign. As Poppy and Cyrenic try to discover who wants her dead, they must navigate the dangerous waters of life at court and of their growing feelings for one another." (Publisher's note)
Volume 1 of an ongoing series

Vehlmann, Fabien
Beautiful Darkness. by Fabien Vehlmann and Kerascoët and translated by Helge Dascher. Farrar Straus & Giroux 2013 96 p.
Grades: Adult   **741.5**
1. Allegories; 2. Good and evil — Fiction; 3. Princesses — Fiction
1770461299; 9781770461291, $22.95
In this book by Fabien Vehlmann and Kerascoët, readers "join princess Aurora and her friends as they journey to civilization's heart of darkness in a bleak allegory about surviving the human experience. The sweet faces and bright leaves of Kerascoët's delicate watercolors serve to

highlight the evil that dwells beneath Vehlmann's story as pettiness, greed, and jealousy take over." (Publisher's note)

Last Days of an Immortal. Fabien Vehlmann and Gwen de Bonneyal. Pgw 2012 149 p.

Grades: Adult   **Fic; 741.5/944**

1. Death — Graphic novels; 2. Science fiction graphic novels

1936393441; 9781936393442, $24.95

In this science fiction graphic novel, by Fabien Vehlmann, illustrated by Gwen de Bonneyal, "Elijah is a member of the 'Philosophical Police,' who must solve conflicts that arise out of ignorance of the Other. Two species are fighting a war with roots in a crime committed centuries ago, and Elijah must solve the crime and bring peace between their species, while also confronting his own immortality in a world where science provides access to eternal life." (Publisher's note)

Venditti, Robert

The **homeland** directive. created & written by Robert Venditti; illustrated & colored by Mike Huddleston. Top Shelf Productions 2011 148p. Color illustration

Grades: 11 12 Adult

741.5

1. Political corruption — Fiction; 2. Suspense fiction; 3. Mystery fiction; 4. Bioterrorism — Fiction

9.7816E+12

Courtesy of IDW Publishing

This book tells the story of Dr. Laura Regan, head of the U.S. National Center for Infectious Diseases. "When her research partner is murdered and Laura is blamed for the crime, she finds herself at the heart of a vast and deadly conspiracy." (Publisher's note). "A cabinet minister decides to persuade the public that more trackable behavior is in the service of antiterrorist surveillance. But since his incentive involves virally induced 'justified' death for thousands along the way, Regan throws in with the good feds to stop a developing plague and expose the minister. Not that she has much choice: the bad fed operatives are out to kill her since she created the vaccine that could stop their plot cold." (Libr J)

The **Surrogates**. Top Shelf Productions 2006 208p. Illustration

Grades: 10 11 12 Adult

741.5; Fic

1. Graphic novels; 2. Mystery graphic novels; 3. Science fiction graphic novels

1-891830-87-2, $19.95

Courtesy of IDW Publishing

The year is 2054, and life has been reduced to a data feed. The fusing of virtual reality and cybernetics has ushered in the era of the surrogate, a new technology that lets users interact with the world without ever leaving their homes. It's a perfect world, and it's up to Detectives Harvey Greer and Pete Ford of the Metro Police Department to keep it that way. But to do so they'll need to stop a techno-terrorist bent on returning society to a time when people lived their lives instead of merely experiencing them. There's some violence in the story.

Verheiden, Mark

Aliens Omnibus Volume 1. Dark Horse Comics 2007 384p. Illustration

Grades: 10 11 12 Adult   **741.5; Fic**

1. Adventure graphic novels; 2. Graphic novels; 3. Science fiction graphic novels

978-1-59307-727-3, $24.95

The first three Dark Horse Aliens stories based on the movies are collected in this volume: Outbreak, Nightmare Asylum, and Female War. Outbreak starts thirteen years after the events of the movie Aliens; Billie is in a mental institution suffering from nightmares about what happened at the colony outpost of Rim, and Wilks is in prison. They're both offered a chance to return to Rim. In Female War, Ripley must go with another team of Marines to another planet for another "bug hunt." The stories use strong language and show violence as the humans fight the Aliens.

Superman: Sacrifice: Countdown to Infinite Crisis. Greg Rucka, Mark Verheiden, Gail Simone, writers; Ed Benes ... [et al.], pencillers; Alex Lei ... [et al.], inkers; Rod Reis ... [et al.], colorists; Todd Klein ... [et al.], letterers. DC Comics 2005 un Illustration

Grades: 10 11 12 Adult   **741.5; Fic**

1. Graphic novels; 2. Superhero graphic novels; 3. Superman (Fictional character); 4. Wonder Woman (Fictional character)

1-4012-0919-X, $14.99

The pivotal story that forever alters the relationship between Superman and Wonder Woman is collected here for the first time. Max Lord has taken over Superman's mind and has him in his total thrall. With his peers and loved ones threatened, Superman is helpless. But not Wonder Woman, who must battle past the Man of Steel and decisively end the threat. Her actions, and the repercussions, are explored in this story that leads into Infinite Crisis. Some of the fighting in this book is brutal.

Superman: The Journey. DC Comics 2006 144p. Illustration

Grades: 9 10 11 12 Adult   **741.5; Fic**

1. Graphic novels; 2. Superhero graphic novels; 3. Superman (Fictional character); 4. Flash (Fictional character)

1-4012-0918-1, $14.99

Even the Man of Steel needs to get away from it all, and when he tries to relocate his Fortress of Solitude to South America, a chain of events begins that will test his bravery more than ever. After his first contact with an OMAC, a cybernetic being set to destroy all super-heroes, Superman then must contend with the arrival in Metropolis of Bizarro, as well as Zoom, the Reverse-Flash. Then Blackrock returns with more power than ever; and Lex Luthor seeks deadly vengeance, again.

Vernon, Ursula

★ **Digger:** the complete Omnibus edition. by Ursula Vernon. Sofawolf Press, Inc. 2013 850 p.

Grades: 9 10 11 12 Adult   **741.5; Fic**

1. Adventure graphic novels; 2. Wombats — Graphic novels

1936689324; 9781936689323, $29.44

Hugo Award: Best Graphic Story (2012)

This graphic novel, by Ursula Vernon, is "about a particularly no-nonsense wombat who finds herself stuck on the wrong end of a one-way tunnel in a strange land where nonsense seems to be the specialty. Now, with the help of a talking statue of a god, an outcast hyena, a shadow-being of indeterminate origin, and an oracular slug she seeks to find out where she is and how to go about getting back to her Warren." (Publisher's note)

Vess, Charles

The **Book** of Ballads. Tor 2004 192p. Illustration

Grades: 11 12 Adult   **741.5; 808.81**

1. Ballads — Graphic novels; 2. Graphic novels
0-765-31214-X, $24.95

"Vess shows off his ability to use a wide variety of styles and formats.... The ballad from which each story is taken is written in its traditional form at the end of each tale." (VOYA)

Artist Vess works with authors such as Charles de Lint, Neil Gaiman, Jane Yolen, Jeff Smith, and others who adapt ballads from the English, Scottish, and Irish traditions. Moods range from comedic hilarity (such as in "Galtee Farmer") to the somber lover's test ("Sovay"). Many of the stories include nudity and some sexual content.

Vidaurri, S. M.

Iron: Or, The War After. Shane-Michael Vidaurri. Archaia Entertainment 2013 152 p. Illustration
Grades: Adult   **741; Fic**
1. Resistance to government — Graphic novels; 2. Animals — Graphic novels
193639328X; 9781936393282, $24.95

This graphic novel by Shane-Michael Vidaurri, is set in "the aftermath of a long war, in a world of constant winter. An intelligence spy from the Resistance — the rabbit, Hardin — steals secret information from a military base of the Regime. His actions set off a chain of events that reverberates through the ranks of both sides.... When the snow finally settles, who will be the true patriot and who the true traitor?" (Publisher's note)

Voger, Mark

The **Dark** Age: Grim, Great & Gimmicky Post-Modern Comics. Twomorrows Publishing 2006 168p. Illustration
Grades: Adult Professional
741.5
1. Comic books, strips, etc. — History and criticism; 2. Graphic novels; 3. X-Men (Fictional characters); 4. Superman (Fictional character); 5. Hellboy (Fictional character); 6. Batman (Fictional character); 7. Daredevil (Fictional character)
1-893905-53-5, $19.95

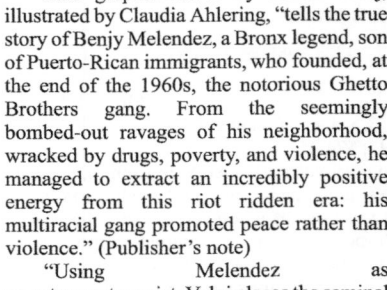
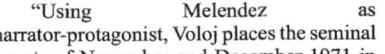
Courtesy of Twomorrows Publishing

Do you remember The Dark Knight Returns and Watchmen? The polybagged premium craze? The death of Superman? Renegade superheroes Spawn, Pitt, Bloodshot and Cyberforce? When vigilantes spilled blood by the gallon — and those were the good guys? Readers can read all about the sometimes glorious, sometimes gory era of comics known as The Dark Age, covering the years from the 1980s into the 2000s. The book features interviews with Dark Age greats Todd McFarlane (Spawn), Dave Gibbons (Watchmen), Jim Lee (X-Men), Kevin Smith (Clerks), Alex Ross (Kingdom Come), Mike Mignola (Hellboy), Erik Larsen (Savage Dragon), J. O'Barr (The Crow), David Lapham (Stray Bullets), Joe Quesada (Daredevil), Mike Allred (Madman), Dennis O'Neil (Batman: Knightfall) and others. It includes a color section spotlighting highlights — and lowlights — of The Dark Age.

Voloj, Julian

Ghetto Brother: Warrior to Peacemaker. Julian Voloj; illustrated by Claudia Ahlering. NBM Publishing 2015 128 p. Illustration
Grades: 11 12 Adult   **741.5; 92**
1. Melendez, Benjy; 2. Peace movements; 3. Gangs — Graphic novels; 4. Puerto Ricans — New York (N.Y.)
1561639486; 9781561639489, $12.99

This graphic novel by Julian Voloj, illustrated by Claudia Ahlering, "tells the true story of Benjy Melendez, a Bronx legend, son of Puerto-Rican immigrants, who founded, at the end of the 1960s, the notorious Ghetto Brothers gang. From the seemingly bombed-out ravages of his neighborhood, wracked by drugs, poverty, and violence, he managed to extract an incredibly positive energy from this riot ridden era: his multiracial gang promoted peace rather than violence." (Publisher's note)

Courtesy of NBM Publishing

"Using Melendez as narrator-protagonist, Voloj places the seminal events of November and December 1971 in the contexts of post-WWII Puerto Rican immigration and difficult assimilation to New York, and of Melendez's personal development as he learned of and adopted his Jewish heritage. Ahlering bases her artwork partly on news and documentary photography, although she doesn't incorporate or copy photos but draws on them for detail, composition, and tonal variety." Booklist

Wagner, John

A **History** of Violence. DC Comics/Vertigo 2004 286p. Illustration
Grades: 11 12 Adult   **741.5; Fic**
1. Graphic novels; 2. Mystery graphic novels; 3. Revenge — Graphic novels
978-1-56389-367-4, $9.99

It was just another quiet day at McKenna's Diner — until a couple of wanted killers walked in looking for trouble. Instead, they got bullets, and Tom McKenna got to be an instant media celebrity. That got him a lot of attention from some people he thought he'd escaped long ago. The kind of people who never forget a face — even after twenty years.... Now Tom must confront a group of cold-blooded mobsters intent on settling the score. As much as he tries to deny it, he's a man with a history of violence — and with the lives of his family hanging in the balance, he'll do anything to make sure his secret past stays buried...forever. This story has lots of graphic violence and strong language. This original graphic novel was originally published in 1997.

Wagner, Matt

Batman and the Monster Men: Dark Moon Rising. DC Comics 2006 144p. Illustration
Grades: 10 11 12 Adult   **741.5; Fic**
1. Batman (Fictional character); 2. Graphic novels; 3. Mystery graphic novels; 4. Superhero graphic novels
978-1-4012-1091-5, $14.99

It has been one year since the mysterious Batman first appeared to protect the people of Gotham. In that time, he has waged war on the common criminals and members of organized crime who have plagued his city. But the brutal massacre of some of the city's most notorious gangsters reveals that a far more dangerous threat is emerging, one for which the young Bruce Wayne is woefully unprepared: genetically engineered, horribly mutated men who have developed a taste for human flesh. They are the stuff of nightmare. And as they wreak havoc on Gotham's criminal community, Batman soon discovers that even the woman he loves may be threatened. Can the Dark Knight stop the carnage, or will he become the next victim of the Monster Men? The book includes violence, some graphic.

Batman/Superman/Wonder Woman: Trinity. DC Comics 2003 208p. Illustration
Grades: 9 10 11 12 Adult   **741.5; Fic**

1. Batman (Fictional character); 2. Graphic novels; 3. Superhero graphic novels; 4. Superman (Fictional character); 5. Wonder Woman (Fictional character)

1-4012-0187-3, $17.99

When Batman's greatest nemesis, Ra's al Ghul, recruits Bizarro and an Amazon warrior to aid him in his plan to create global chaos, the Dark Knight Detective suddenly finds himself working with the Man of Steel and the Amazon Princess, Wonder Woman. Looking to thwart the madman's plot to simultaneously destroy all satellite communications as well as all of the world's oil reserves, Earth's greatest heroes reluctantly band together. But if Batman, Superman and Wonder Woman are to have any hope of stopping Ra's nuclear missile assault, they will first need to overcome their own biases and reconcile their differing philosophies. The book includes some violence.

Madame Xanadu: disenchanted. writer, Matt Wagner; penciller, Amy Reeder Hadley; inkers, Amy Reeder Hadley (issues 1-2), Richard Friend (issues 3-10); colorist, Guy Major; letterer, Jared K. Fletcher; introduction, James Robinson. DC Comics/Vertigo 2009 un Illustration

Grades: 10 11 12 Adult   741.5; Fic

1. Fantasy graphic novels; 2. Graphic novels; 3. Magic — Graphic novels

978-1-4012-2291-8, $12.99

In the days of King Arthur and Camelot, Nimue used woodland magic. Despite her power, the warnings of a stranger with glowing eyes comes too late for her to save the land against the machinations of Merlin and her own sister, Morgana. Using her herb lore to maintain her youth, Nimue next shows up in the court of Kublai Khan, where she is known as the Western Seer. Again, the Phantom Stranger shows up, this time with the party of Marco Polo, who become targets of a plot to discredit the Westerners. Nimue helps, only to learn that it wasn't enough, and the Stranger abandons her in the middle of the Gobi Desert. Then she appears in France, known there as Madame Xanadu, a favorite of Queen Marie Antoinette. This time, Nimue reads the portents for herself and knows that the Revolution will topple the King; the Phantom Stranger appears again, but because she can't trust him, she ends up imprisoned, betrayed by the former Queen whom she believed to be a friend, and Nimue has to trick Death herself. In London of the 1880s, Madame Xanadu tries to help the prostitutes of Whitechapel, but the Phantom Stranger says the murders committed by Jack the Ripper serve a larger purpose and he thwarts her again. In New York City of the 1930s, Nimue has found another magician, John Zatara and they are lovers, but the Phantom Stranger comes again and this time Nimue decides to trap him. What consequences will her actions have upon the people around her, including a heroic policeman named James Corrigan? The book includes some gory violence, some harsh language, some sexual suggestiveness and one not-very-graphic rape scene. This series, in its pamphlet comic issue form, was nominated for four Eisner Awards in 2009: Best Writer, Best Cover Artist, Best New Series, and Best Penciler Inker Team.

Volume 1 of 4

Wagner, Richard

Richard Wagner's The Ring of the Nibelung Volume One. Dark Horse Comics 2002 un Illustration

Grades: 9 10 11 12 Adult   741.5; Fic

1. Fantasy graphic novels; 2. Graphic novels; 3. Norse mythology — Graphic novels; 4. Opera — Graphic novels

1-56971-666-8, $21.95

2001 Eisner Award for Best Limited Series; 2001 Eisner Award to P. Craig Russell for Best Penciller/Inker of Penciller/Inker Team.

The Rhinegold and The Valkyrie comprise the first volume of Russell's adaptation of the Ring cycle by German composer Richard Wagner. Woton has exhausted himself and his godly resources to have a mighty fortress built with the labor of the giants, Fasolt and Fafnir. But in his bargaining with them, he has promised the fair Freia, keeper of the golden apple tree whose fruit gives power and immortality to the gods. The giants come to collect their pay, and only Logé, the trickster god, can find something to offer the giants in exchange: the Rhinegold. The only problem is, Woton doesn't have the Rhinegold yet.

Richard Wagner's The Ring of the Nibelung Volume Two. Dark Horse Comics 2002 un Illustration

Grades: 9 10 11 12 Adult   741.5; Fic

1. Fantasy graphic novels; 2. Graphic novels; 3. Norse mythology — Graphic novels; 4. Opera — Graphic novels

1-56971-734-6, $21.95

2001 Eisner Award for Best Limited Series; 2001 Eisner Award to P. Craig Russell for Best Penciller/Inker of Penciller/Inker Team.

This volume adapts Wagner's Siegfried and Gotterdammerung: The Twilight of the Gods. Siegfried is separated from his love, the Valkyrie Brunhilde, and even the All-Father himself cannot make things right. In the conclusion, all of creation hangs in the balance because of gods meddling in the affairs of man — all over the gold of the Rhinemaids.

Waid, Mark

All-new all-different Avengers; Volume 1: The Magnificent Seven. by Mark Waid; illustrated by Adam Kubert and Mahmud Asrar; color by Sonia Oback. Marvel Enterprises 2016 168 p. Color; Illustration

Grades: 8 9 10 11 12 Adult   741.5; Fic

1. Avengers (Fictional characters)

0785199675; 9780785199670, $19.99

In this comic book, by Mark Waid, illustrated by Adam Kubert and Mahmud Asrar, "the Avengers are dead — long live the Avengers! Earth's Mightiest Heroes — Captain America, Thor, Vision and Iron Man — are living separate lives, not tied to any team but when a threat from beyond the stars targets our world, fate draws them together once more, alongside Nova, Ms. Marvel, and Miles Morales, a.k.a. Spider-Man!" (Publisher's note)

Contains material originally published in magazine form as All-New, All-Different Avengers #1-6, Avengers #0 and Free Comic Book Day 2015 (Avengers) #1

Amazing Spider-Man: family business. by Mark Waid and James Robinson; illustrated by Gabriele Dell'Otto and Werther Dell'Edera. Marvel Enterprises 2014 112 p. Color; Illustration

Grades: 9 10 11 12 Adult   741.5

1. Spider-Man (Fictional character)

0785184406; 9780785184409, $24.99

In this graphic novel, by Mark Waid and James Robinson, "someone has Spider-Man in their crosshairs and the only person in the Marvel Universe who can save him is...Peter Parker's sister?! As the web-slinger meets family he never knew, will she end up becoming his greatest ally...or the one who damns him? And what does the KINGPIN have to do with it?" (Publisher's note)

"Waid's story is perfectly blended, with all the one-liners and gags that fans have come to expect as well as a level of mystery and intrigue that's a welcome addition. And with four villains vying for the death of Spider-Man (one literally dug up from the past), this original graphic novel is certainly not short on action." Booklist

Marvel OGN — Cover page 1.

★ **Archie**; Volume 1: The New Riverdale. story by Mark Waid; art by Fiona Staples (issues 1-3), Annie Wu (issue 4), Veronica Fish (issues 5-6); coloring by Andre Szymanowicz with Jen Vaughn; lettering by Jack Morelli. Archie Comics 2016 176 p. Color; Illustration

Grades: 7 8 9 10 11 12 Adult   741.5; Fic

1. Teenagers — Graphic novels; 2. Lodge, Veronica (Fictional character); 3. Andrews, Archie (Fictional character); 4. Cooper, Betty (Fictional character)

1627388672; 9781627388672, $19.99

In this first volume of the Archie comic book series by Mark Waid, illustrated by Fiona Staples, Archie Andrews and the Riverdale teens are reimagined "with a fresh, 21st-century spin in time for the franchise's 75th anniversary.... Blonde Betty is a baseball-slugging, down-to-earth car mechanic; Archie is a hapless but cool, guitar-playing teen with a streak of bad luck; and new girl Veronica Lodge is a sleek reality TV alum." (School Library Journal)

"It would seem risky to mess with the tried-and-true Archie formula, but this heartfelt collection is less a tearing-down of the old order than an exuberant exploration of its possibilities. Staples and Waid keep the characters' foundations in place—Archie's still a lovable goof who can't decide between girl-next-door Betty and vampish Veronica — while building a wonderfully new Riverdale for them to explore." Pub Wkly

Collects Archie #1-6; Volume 1 of an ongoing series

★ **Daredevil**. writer, Mark Waid; artists, Paolo Rivera, Marcos Martin. Marvel 2013 Color illustration (Daredevil (2011-2014))
Grades: 10 11 12 Adult   741.5
1. Superhero comic books, strips, etc.; 2. Spider-Man (Fictional character); 3. Daredevil (Fictional character)
0785168060; 9780785168065, $34.99

"Matt Murdock is back in New York and hoping to resuscitate his law practice, but not everyone is happy to see him. And Daredevil hits the streets as Klaw, master of sound, makes his deadly return! Then, a blind client holds the key to a global conspiracy perpetrated by some familiar foes. Can Daredevil protect him long enough to bring down an international criminal organization? And when a piece of cutting-edge technology goes missing, Daredevil and Punisher team up to track it down and clear the Black Cat of the crime. But is Black Cat really innocent?! And after someone exhumes Battlin' Jack Murdock's grave, DD heads underground to find the villain responsible." (Publisher's note)

Collects Daredevil (2011) 1-10, 10.1; Amazing Spider -Man (1963) 677; Volume 1 of 2 (hardcover collection)

Daredevil; Volume 1: Devil at bay. writer, Mark Waid; artists, Chris Samnee and Peter Krause. Marvel Enterprises 2014 un Color; Illustration (Daredevil (2014-2015))
Grades: 9 10 11 12 Adult   741.5; Fic
1. Superhero graphic novels; 2. Daredevil (Fictional character)
0785154116; 9780785154112, $17.99

Other titles in this series are: Volume 2, West-case scenario; Volume 3, The Daredevil you know; Volume 4, The autobiography of Matt Murdock

"Daredevil has headed west, and now protects [San Francisco's] streets from evil — both as a costumed hero and as blind lawyer Matt Murdock! But big changes are in store for Matt, as old haunts and familiar faces rise to give the devil his due. The Owl is back, and he isn't working alone...but old enemies are small potatoes compared to Matt 's new "friend": the would-be hero known as the Shroud!" (Publisher's note)

Contains material originally published in single magazine form as Daredevil #1-5 and #0.1

★ **Kingdom** come. Mark Waid, Alex Ross. DC Comics 2012 228 p. Color illustration
Grades: Adult   741.5
1. Heroes — comic books, strips, etc.; 2. Superhero graphic novels; 3. Superman (Fictional character); 4. Batman (Fictional character); 5. Wonder Woman (Fictional character); 6. Justice League (Fictional characters)
1401220347; 9781401220341, $19.99

LC 2012040863

Eisner Award: Best Limited Series (1997)

In this graphic novel, by Mark Waid and Alex Ross, "the DC Universe is spinning inexorably out of control. The new generation of heroes has lost their moral compass, becoming just as reckless and violent as the villains they fight. The previous regime of heroes — the Justice League — returns under the most dire of circumstances, setting up a battle of the old guard against these uncompromising protectors in a battle that will define what heroism truly is." (Publisher's note)

Originally published in single magazine form in Kingdom Come #1-4.

Legion of Super-Heroes Vol. 1: Teenage Revolution. DC Comics 2005 un Illustration
Grades: 8 9 10 11 12 Adult   741.5; Fic
1. Graphic novels; 2. Science fiction graphic novels; 3. Superhero graphic novels
1-4012-0482-1, $14.99

Poverty, famine, war, and disease have been eliminated in the early days of the 31st century. The Dawning Millenium is utopian: shining, optimistic, hopeful...and deadly dull. Dull, that is, until a team of bright, defiant, super-powered teenagers from different worlds assemble. The come together as activists and fierce dreamers, crusading to make a difference in a society that has forgotten how to change. Cosmic Boy, Lightning Lad, Saturn Girl, and the rest of the Legion of Super-Heroes fight for freedom and justice while learning from, and learning to tolerate, one another.

Legion of Super-Heroes Vol. 2: Death of a Dream. DC Comics 2006 un Illustration
Grades: 9 10 11 12 Adult   741.5; Fic
1. Graphic novels; 2. Legion of Super-Heroes (Fictional characters); 3. Superhero graphic novels
978-1-4012-0971-1, $14.99

A bright, defiant, energized team of super-powered teenagers from different worlds joins forces to form a legion of passionate activists that crusade to leave their mark on a complacent society that has forgotten how to fight for change. A hidden mastermind plans the downfall of the United Planets, and only the Legion has the combined knowledge and power needed to stop him. But a struggle for control of the team has split the Legion into two clashing factions. Can the members put aside their personal differences in time to stop the intergalactic menace?

Supergirl and the Legion of Super-Heroes: Strange Visitor from Another Century. DC Comics 2006 144p. Illustration
Grades: 10 11 12 Adult   741.5; Fic
1. Graphic novels; 2. Mystery graphic novels; 3. Superhero graphic novels
978-1-4012-0916-2, $14.99

In the 31st century, the rebel teens of the Legion of Super-Heroes has ended the greatest threat to the peace and stability of the galaxy. The United Planets was to make the Legion an officially sanctioned peace-keeping force. Then, 21st-century hero Supergirl arrives in their time, with no memory of how she got there and no idea how to get back, so she applies for full-time Legionnaire membership. The story includes superhero action, and some violence in a locked-room mystery.

Superman: Birthright. DC Comics 2004 304p. Illustration
Grades: 9 10 11 12 Adult   741.5; Fic
1. Graphic novels; 2. Superhero graphic novels; 3. Superman (Fictional character)
1-4012-0252-7, $19.99

LC 2005-284647

The whole world knows that Superman fights for truth and justice...but why does he? What drives a farm boy from Kansas to divide his life between posing as a mild-mannered reporter and embarking on a career as a super hero? This book retells the origin of Superman, from his infancy through his first appearance as Superman, and why Lex Luthor is so obsessed with destroying him.

Walden, Tillie

The **end** of summer. Tillie Walden. Avery Hill Publishing 2016 108 p. Color; Illustration

Grades: 11 12 Adult

741.5; Fic

1. Winter — Fiction; 2. Cats — Fiction; 3. Graphic novels

1910395269; 9781910395264, $18

Courtesy of Avery Hill Publishing

In this graphic novel, by Tillie Walden, "at the beginning of a winter that is predicted to last for three years, Lars is battling illness and boredom. He passes the time with his siblings and his giant cat, Nemo, as secrets are revealed and tensions within the family begin to simmer..." (Publisher's note)

Walker, Brian

The **comics** before 1945. Brian Walker. H.N. Abrams 2004 p. cm

Grades: Adult

741

1. Comic books, strips, etc. — History and criticism

0-8109-4970-9

LC 2004-9514

"Starting with the late 1800s, the book features informative introductions to US newspaper comic strips, broken down by decade, each placing the funnies in sociocultural/political context and highlighting the roles of important cartoonists and characters. Profiles of comic-strip masters are tucked in between the introductions, and many pages offer brilliant displays of color and black-and-white strips. In his introductory material, Walker does not take the usually cited date of 1895 as the start of comics but goes back to the roots in Europe." (Choice Reviews)

The **comics** since 1945. Brian Walker. H.N. Abrams 2002 p. cm Illustration; Color

Grades: Adult

741.5

1. Comic books, strips, etc. — History and criticism

0-8109-3481-7; 9780810934818, $49.95

LC 2002-8375

"This volume completes Walker's profusely illustrated two-volume history of American newspaper comic strips.... Some 700 illustrations, many in brilliant color, are included. Particularly appealing among them are numerous strips spoofing societal foibles and personalities and others reminiscing about — or humorously reflecting on — their creators or cartooning itself. Walker organizes the content by decade. For each he provides an essay setting strips in historical context, a page each on two or three featured artists, and paragraph-long commentaries on other artists and on genres/themes — all interspersed with scores of images." (Choice)

Ware, Chris

★ **Building** stories. Chris Ware. Pantheon Books 2012 p. cm.

Grades: Adult

741.5/973

1. Buildings; 2. City and town life

9780375424335, $50.00

LC 2012007946

Harvey Nominee: Best Graphic Album of Original Work (2013); Cartoonist Studio Prize (2013)

This graphic novel by Chris Ware, assembled as separate pieces in a box, "imagines the inhabitants of a three-story Chicago apartment building: a 30-something woman who has yet to find someone with whom to spend the rest of her life; a couple, possibly married, who wonder if they can bear each other's company another minute; and the building's landlady, an elderly woman who has lived alone for decades.... 'Building Stories' is a book with no deliberate beginning nor end." (Publisher's note)

★ **Jimmy** Corrigan: the smartest kid on earth. written by F.C. Ware. Pantheon Books 2002 380 p.

Grades: Adult

741.5/973

1. Chicago (Ill.) — Fiction; 2. Men — Fiction; 3. Father-son relationship — Fiction

0375714545; 9780375714542, $19.95

LC 2006272880

Eisner Award: Best Graphic Album: Reprint (2001)

This graphic novel, by F.C. Ware, "is a...view at a lonely and emotionally-impaired 'everyman' (Jimmy Corrigan: The Smartest Kid on Earth), who is provided, at age 36, the opportunity to meet his father for the first time. An improvisatory romance which gingerly deports itself between 1890's Chicago and 1980's small town Michigan, the reader is helped along by thousands of colored illustrations and diagrams." (Publisher's note)

Watanabe, Taeko

Kaze Hikaru, Vol. 1. story & art by Taeko Watanabe; [English adaptation, Annette Garcia; translation, Mai Ihara]. Viz Shojo Beat 2005 190p. Illustration

Grades: 10 11 12 Adult

741.5; Fic

1. Graphic novels; 2. Japan — History — 0-1868 — Graphic novels; 3. Manga; 4. Shojo manga

9781421501895, $8.99

"The talk of catamites and homosexual sex among the young men of the Mibu-Roshi and the almost perpetually drunken state of their older members make this title more suited to older teens." (VOYA)

In the waning years of the Tokugawa Shogunate, a band of young samurai called the Mibu-Roshi, gathers in Tokyo. They are loyal to the Shogun and will eventually become the Shinsengumi. Fifteen-year-old Seizaburo Kamiya, who has lost his father and brother to murderous supporters of the Emperor, joins the Mibu-Roshi, and young master swordsman Okita Soji befriends him. Soon, though, Soji learns Seizaburo's secret — he's actually a girl. He agrees to keep her secret and Sei becomes a mainstay in the group, but that doesn't end her danger.

Volume 1 of an ongoing series

Watase, Yuu

Ceres: Celestial Legend Vol. 1: Aya. story and art by Yû Watase; [English adaptation, Gary Leach; translation, Lillian Olsen]. Viz Media/Shojo 2003 208p. Illustration

Grades: 10 11 12 Adult

741.5; Fic

1. Graphic novels; 2. Horror graphic novels; 3. Manga; 4. Romance graphic novels; 5. Science fiction graphic novels; 6. Shojo manga

1-56931-980-4, $9.95

Aya and her twin brother Aki thought they were going to a celebration of their sixteenth birthday at their grandfather's home, but the funeral-like atmosphere tips them off that something's not right. Their "birthday present" turns out to be a mummified hand — the power of which forces an awakening within Aya, and painful wounds all over Aki's body. Grandfather Mikage announces that Aki will be heir to the Mikage fortune, and Aya must die. Aya has allies in the athletic cook and martial artist Yûhi, and the attractive, mysterious Tôya. But can even two handsome and resourceful guys save Aya when it's her own power that's out of control? The series includes nudity, sexual situations, strong language, and violence.

Volume 1 of 14

Way, Gerard

★ The **Umbrella** Academy: Apocalypse Suite. Gerard Way; art, Gabriel Ba; colors, Dave Stewart. Dark Horse Books 2008 192 p. Color; Illustration

Grades: 11 12 Adult   **741.5; Fic**
  1. Superheroes — Fiction; 2. Brothers and sisters — Fiction
1593079788; 9781593079789, $17.99
Eisner Award: Best Limited Series (2008)

In this graphic novel, by Gerard Way, illustrated by Gabriel Ba, "forty-seven extraordinary children were spontaneously born to women who'd previously shown no signs of pregnancy. Millionaire inventor Reginald Hargreeves adopted seven of the children; when asked why, his only explanation was, 'To save the world.' These seven children form the Umbrella Academy, a dysfunctional family of superheroes with bizarre powers." (Publisher's note)

The **Umbrella** Academy: Dallas. by Gerard Way. Dark Horse 2009 192 p. Color; Illustration

Grades: 11 12 Adult   **741.5; Fic**
  1. Dysfunctional families — Fiction; 2. Superheroes — Fiction; 3. Kennedy, John F. (John Fitzgerald), 1917-1963 — Fiction
159582345X; 9781595823458, $17.99

"The Umbrella Academy is a group of superheroes who were mysteriously born at the same time, adopted and raised together as a family and a team.... In this volume, the bizarrely childlike time-traveling team member Number Five recruits his siblings to right a wrong-to save President Kennedy before he is assassinated, possibly saving the world in the bargain." (Publishers Weekly)

"Way has a special affinity for enigmatic plotlines, in which minor details and major occurrences are left unexplained for ages, and he isn't afraid to literally end the world.... Such stuff makes spectacular fodder for Bá's chunky, irresistibly hooky art, bursting with constellations of weird, exciting, and funny touches." Booklist

Weaver, E. K.

The **Less** Than Epic Adventures of TJ and Amal. by E. K. Weaver. Iron Circus Comics 2015 528 p. Illustration

Grades: Adult
741.5; Fic
  1. Automobile travel — Fiction; 2. Gay men — Fiction
0983875553; 9780983875550, $30
Eisner Nominee: Best Graphic Album — Reprint (2016); Lambda Literary Award: Comics/Graphic (2016)

"Amal Chakravarthy calls off his arranged marriage, comes out to his conservative parents, promptly gets disowned, goes on a bender...and wakes up the next morning to find TJ...in his kitchen. TJ claims that the two have made a drunken pact to drive all the way from Berkeley to Providence. As it happens, Amal promised his sister he'd be there for her graduation from Brown University. And TJ, well...TJ has his own reasons." (Publisher's note)

Courtesy of Iron Circus Comics

Weeks, Lee

Civil War: Captain America. writer, Ed Brubaker; art, Mike Perkins ... [et al.]; colorist, Matt Mila; letterer, Virtual calligraphy's Joe Caramagna. Marvel Entertainment 2007 un Illustration

Grades: 9 10 11 12 Adult   **741.5; Fic**
  1. Captain America (Fictional character); 2. Graphic novels; 3. Superhero graphic novels

0-7851-2798-4, $11.99

Captain America has clashed with the government and his friends and become a renegade because of his opposition to the Super Human Registration Act. The life of his girlfriend, Agent 13, is torn apart as her superiors use her divided loyalties against him. Elsewhere, the Red Skull returns, and the Winter Soldier once again comes face-to-face with Cap; but which side will he choose? Winter Soldier, who was once Bucky Barnes, Captain America's partner, faces his first Christmas in the 21st century, and the truth of the terrible things he was forced to do as the Winter Soldier.

Weiner, Stephen

101 outstanding graphic novels. Stephen Weiner; [edited by] Daniel J. Fingeroth. NBM Pub. 2015 80 p.
Grades: Adult Professional
016.7415; 741.5
  1. Best books — United States.; 2. Graphic novels — Bibliography; 3. Graphic novels
1561639443; 9781561639441, $15.99
LC 2014958652

Courtesy of NBM Publishing

"The popular primer on the best graphic novels, initially called The 101 Best Graphic Novels, is back in its third updated edition. Expert librarian Stephen Weiner — with the crowdsourcing help of professionals in the field, from artists to critics to leading comic store owners — has sifted through the bewildering thousands of graphic novels now available to come up with an outstanding, not-to-be-missed 101." (Publisher's note)

Previously called 101 Best Graphic Novels

Faster Than a Speeding Bullet: The Rise of the Graphic Novel. NBM 2004 64p. Illustration
Grades: Adult Professional   **741.5**
  1. Graphic novels; 2. Graphic novels — History and criticism
1-56163-368-2, $9.95
LC 2003058827

Weiner provides a brief history of graphic novels, from the first comic books in the 1930s to the explosion of publication and mainstream coverage in the early 2000s.

Hellboy: the companion. Stephen Weiner, Jason Hall, Victoria Blake with additional material by Mike Mignola; featuring the art of Mike Mignola, Guy Davis, Ryan Sook, Duncan Fegredo, Jason Shawn Alexander, and Paul Azaceta. Dark Horse Comics 2008 240p. Illustration
Grades: 10 11 12 Adult   **741.5**
  1. Graphic novels; 2. Hellboy (Fictional character); 3. Horror graphic novels
978-1-59307-655-9, $14.95

Mike Mignola's Hellboy debuted in 1994 and has built up a growing audience for its world of Victorian occult societies, prehistoric gods, arcane Nazi experiments, and a big red demon for a good guy. Now librarian and comics historian Weiner, comics writer Hall, and journalist Blake put together a guide to Mignola's created world, illustrated with new art by Mignola as well as art from fourteen years of Hellboy from Mignola and the other artists who have worked with him over the years, including Guy Davis, Duncan Fegredo, Paul Azaceta, and others. The book includes character profiles, a timeline, and the literary heritage of Hellboy.

Weinstein, Lauren

Girl stories. by Lauren R. Weinstein. Henry Holt 2006 237p. Illustration

Grades: 7 8 9 10 11 12 Adult   **741.5; Fic**
1. Friendship — Graphic novels; 2. Girls — Graphic novels; 3. Graphic novels; 4. Humorous graphic novels
978-0-8050-7863-3, $16.95; 0-8050-7863-0

LC 2005-46205

"Smart, creative Lauren sheds her geeky rep in high school in Weinstein's collection of comic strips, which have to intimacy of a teen's diary. The color-washed sketches have an edgy quality." Booklist

Weinstein, Simcha

Up, up, and oy vey!: how Jewish history, culture, and values shaped the comic book superhero. 2006 143p. Illustration
Grades: Adult Professional   **741.5**
1. Comic books, strips, etc. — History — Jewish influences; 2. Graphic novels; 3. X-Men (Fictional characters); 4. Spider-Man (Fictional character); 5. Superman (Fictional character); 6. Captain America (Fictional character); 7. Hulk (Fictional character)
978-1-881927-32-7, $19.95

From the birth of Krypton in Cleveland to the Caped Crusader, Captain America, the Incredible Hulk, Spider-Man, the X-Men, and more, this book chronicles the story behind the story about the origins of the planet's most famous superheroes. While the Jewish contribution to film, theater, music, and comedy has been well-documented, the Jewish role in the creation of the All-American superhero has not been — until now. Rabbi Weinstein explores comics' roots in Jewish values, history, culture, and mysticism.

Weir, Ivy Noelle

Archival quality. written by Ivy Noelle Weir; illustrated and colored by Steenz; lettered by Joamette Gil; edited by Robin Herrera. Oni Press 2018 280 p. Color; Illustration
Grades: 9 10 11 12 Adult   **741.5; Fic**
1. Librarians with disabilities — Fiction; 2. Librarians — Fiction; 3. Mental illness — Fiction; 4. Ghost stories
1620104709; 9781620104705, $19.99

LC 2017948855

In this book by Ivy Noelle Weir, illustrated by Steenz, "after losing her job at the library, Cel Walden starts working at the...Logan Museum as an archivist. But the job may not be the second chance she was hoping for, and she finds herself confronting her mental health, her relationships, and...her grasp on reality as she begins to dream of a young woman she's never met, but feels strangely drawn to." (Publisher's note)

"This horror story is more atmospheric than gory, aside from some bloody noses, and effectively creates an unsettling mood. The rich colors, comic interjections, and expressive features and gestures of Steenz's art add levity." SLJ

Wells, H. G. (Herbert George)

Classics illustrated #12: The Island of Dr. Moreau. Papercutz 2011 un Illustration
Grades: 7 8 9 10 11 12 Adult
741.5; Fic
1. Authors; 2. Graphic novels; 3. Historians; 4. Horror graphic novels; 5. Novelists; 6. Science fiction writers; 7. Writers on politics; 8. Writers on science; 9. Wells, H. G. (Herbert George), 1866-1946 — Adaptations
978-1-59707-235-9, $9.99

Edward Prendick is the sole survivor of a shipwreck when a passing ship picks him up. It carries a strange cargo of animals, a doctor,

Courtesy of NBM Publishing

who takes care of Prendick, and an odd man who looks more like an ape. Montgomery, the doctor, is taking the animals to a small island he won't name, and Prendick ends up with them when the drunken ship's captain casts him off. On that island, Prendick discovers half-human, half-beast creatures, all created by the arrogant Dr. Moreau. This book adapts Wells' classic story; it was originally published in 1990 as part of the Classics Illustrated line published by First Comics. This edition includes an interview with Steven Grant, who wrote the adaptation.

Wertz, Julia

Drinking at the movies. by Julia Wertz; introduction by Janeane Garofalo. Koyama Press 2015 187 p. Illustration
Grades: Adult
741.5
1. Cartoonists — United States — Biography — Comic books, strips, etc; 2. Wertz, Julia — Comic books, strips, etc; 3. Bildungsromans — Graphic novels
1927668263; 9781927668269, $15

LC 2010009234

Courtesy of Koyama Press

This book presents "Julia Wertz's critically acclaimed first graphic memoir in a new format, with a brand new sketchbook from Wertz, and an introduction by Janeane Garofalo. But don't worry; we haven't replaced any of the wrenching and ribald, whiskey-soaked coming-of-age tale." (Publisher's note)

Originally published 2010 by Three Rivers Press

Tenements, towers & trash: an unconventional illustrated history of New York City. Julia Wertz. Black Dog & Leventhal 2017 282 p. Illustration
Grades: Adult   **974.71; 974.7/10222; 741.5**
1. Business enterprises — New York (State) — New York — Pictorial works; 2. New York (N.Y.) — Buildings, structures, etc. — Pictorial works; 3. New York (N.Y.) — History — Pictorial works; 4. New York (N.Y.) — Pictorial works; 5. Historic buildings — New York (N.Y.); 6. Cities and towns — United States; 7. New York (N.Y.) — History
9780316501217, $29.99; 9780316501224

LC 2017933752

In this book, "Julia Wertz takes us behind the New York that you think you know. Not the tourist's New York-the Statue of Liberty makes a brief appearance and the Empire State Building not at all-but the guts, the underbelly, of this city that never sleeps. With drawings and comics in her signature style, Wertz regales us with streetscapes 'Then and Now' and little-known tales." (Publisher's note)

"In presenting the life of the city, Wertz captures change as the most important constant trait of New York City, with a vivid eclecticism that makes this an indispensable guidebook to places lost and found." Pub Wkly

Includes bibliographical references.

Whedon, Joss

★ **Astonishing** X-Men Vol. 1: Gifted. writer, Joss Whedon; artist, John Cassaday; colorist, Laura Martin; letterer, Chris Eliopoulos; cover art, John Cassady. Marvel Entertainment 2004 un Illustration
Grades: 9 10 11 12 Adult   **741.5; Fic**
1. Graphic novels; 2. Superhero graphic novels; 3. X-Men (Fictional characters)
978-0-7851-1531-1, $14.99

Eisner Award: Best Continuing Series (2006); Eisner Award: Best Penciller/Inker (2005); Volume 1 of 12

Cyclops and Emma Frost re-form the X-Men with the express purpose of ästonishing" the world. But when breaking news regarding the mutant gene unexpectedly hits the airwaves, will it derail their new plans before they even get started? As demand for the mutant cure reaches near-riot levels, the X-Men go head-to-head with the enigmatic Ord, with an unexpected ally — and some unexpected adversaries — tipping the scales.

Other Astonishing X-Men volumes by Whedon and Cassaday are: 2: Dangerous; 3: Torn; 4: Unstoppable

Fray. Dark Horse Comics 2003 un Illustration

Grades: 9 10 11 12 Adult   **741.5; Fic**

1. Adventure graphic novels; 2. Graphic novels; 3. Monsters — Graphic novels

1-56971-751-6, $19.95

Hundreds of years in the future, Manhattan has become a deadly slum, run by mutant crime-lords and disinterested cops. Stuck in the middle is a young girl who thought she had no future, but learns she has a great destiny. In a world so poisoned that it doesn't notice the monsters on its streets, how can a street kid like Fray unite a fallen city against a demonic plot to consume mankind? Creator Whedon set this story in the future of Buffy the Vampire Slayer's world, with Fray a new slayer, aided by a demonic Watcher. The story has some violence and mild harsh language.

Wheeler, Andrew

Another castle: Grimoire. Andrew Wheeler, Paulina Ganucheau, edited by Ari Yarwood. Oni Press 2017 152 p. Color; Illustration

Grades: 7 8 9 10 11 12 Adult

741.5; Fic

1. Friendship — Fiction; 2. Good and evil — Fiction; 3. Heroes and heroines — Fiction; 4. Princesses — Fiction

1620103117; 9781620103111, $15.99

LC 2016950325

This book, by Andrew Wheeler and Paulina Ganucheau, edited by Ari Yarwood, "begins when Princess Misty of Beldora,...[was] captured by Lord Badlug, the ruler of the neighboring kingdom of Grimoire. He intends to marry her and conquer Beldora.... The people of Grimoire already suffer under his rule and desperately need a hero.... Together with the citizens of Grimoire,...Misty must fight to protect her kingdom and free both realms from Badlug's tyrannical rule." (Publisher's note)

Courtesy of Oni Press

"Ganucheau contributes some thrilling and bloody action sequences, and her candy-colored palette, suffused with bright pinks and purples, is an inspired touch, just one more way this story subverts expectations." Pub Wkly

Wiebe, Kurtis J.

Rat Queens; 1: Sass & Sorcery. by Kurtis J. Wiebe; edited by Laura Tavishati; illustrated by Roc Upchurch and Ed Brisson. Image Comics 2014 128 p. Color; Illustration (Rat Queens)

Grades: Adult   **741.5**

1. Fantasy fiction; 2. Graphic novels; 3. Gangs — Fiction; 4. Violence — Fiction

1607069458; 9781607069454, $9.99

"The Rat Queens are a tough, insouciant gang of ne'er-do-well girls...who love a good bar brawl. When they are assigned a mission as punishment for their latest recklessness by the mayor of Palisade and it turns out to be a trap, Hannah, Violet, Dee, and Betty come back to the town

to figure out who has it in for them and the other local fighting gangs." (Booklist)

"Possessed of very different body types, personalities, and idiosyncrasies, and not afraid to share exactly what they're feeling, the Rat Queens are refreshing characters whose story will leave readers thirsty for more." Pub Wkly

Originally published in single magazine form as RAT QUEENS #1-5.; Volume 1 of an ongoing series

Williams, Ian (Physician)

The **bad** doctor: the troubled life and times of Dr. Iwan James. by Ian Williams. Pennsylvania State University Press 2015 224 p. Color; Illustration (Graphic medicine)

Grades: Adult   **741.5**

1. Physicians — Fiction; 2. Graphic medicine

0271067543; 9780271067544, $24.95

LC 2015005728

In this graphic novel, by Ian Williams, readers meet "Dr. Iwan James: cyclist, doctor, would-be lover, former heavy metal fan, and, above all, human being. Weighed down by his responsibilities — from diagnosing personality disorders to deciding who can hold a gun license — he doubts his ability to make decisions about the lives of others when he may need more than a little help himself." (Publisher's note)

"The simple black-and-white panels augment the story well enough, but Williams' real strength is using everyday interactions between Dr. James and the people around him to reveal the motives of this complex but relatable character." Booklist

Williams, J. H., III

Batman: Snow. story by J.H. Williams, Dan Curtis Johnson; script & dialogue, Dan Curtis Johnson; art and original covers, Seth Fisher; colors Dave Stewart; letterer, Phil Balsman. DC Comics 2007 128p. Illustration

Grades: 9 10 11 12 Adult   **741.5; Fic**

1. Adventure graphic novels; 2. Batman (Fictional character); 3. Graphic novels; 4. Superhero graphic novels

978-1-4012-1265-0, $14.99

At the dawn of his career, Batman recruits allies for his war on crime in order to really protect Gotham City. Everything changes when a brilliant scientist's desperate attempt to save the life of his terminally ill wife goes tragically wrong, and a new type of threat is born. As Batman faces his first super-powered villain, Mr. Freeze, he begins to realize that malfeasance comes in many deadly forms, and some offenders are more powerful than he. How will the crime fighter overcome this new menace while protecting not only his associates, but also the innocent citizens of Gotham? This book has lots of action and some mildly harsh language.

Williams, J. H., III.

Batwoman; Volume 1: Hydrology. J.H. Williams III, W. Haden Blackman. DC Comics 2012 160 p. Color; Illustration

Grades: 11 12 Adult   **741.5; Fic**

1. Women superheroes — Comic books, strips, etc.; 2. Batwoman (Fictional character)

1401234658; 9781401234652, $22.99

LC 2012002252

"Batwoman (a.ka. Kate Kane) faces deadly new challenges in her war against Gotham City's underworld.... Who or what is stealing children from the barrio, and for what vile purpose? Will Kate train her cousin, Bette Kane (a.k.a. Flamebird), as her new sidekick? How will she handle unsettling revelations about her father, Colonel Jacob Kane? And why is a certain government agency suddenly taking an interest in her?" (Publisher's note)

"Williams and Blackman write a perfect story, and Williams as illustrator offers a flowing, nonlinear style that pulls the reader onward as if through a dream — a dream that is sometimes pleasant, sometimes a nightmare, but always vivid." LJ"

Originally published in single magazine form in Batwoman 0-5 — T.p. verso.

Batwoman; Volume 2: To drown the world. J.H. Williams III, W. Haden Blackman, Amy Reeder, Trevor McCarthy. DC Comics 2012 144 p. Color; Illustration

Grades: 11 12 Adult   **741.5; Fic**
   1. Women superheroes — Comic books, strips, etc.; 2. Batwoman (Fictional character)
1401237908; 9781401237905, $22.99

                           LC 2012032148

"Six lives, inextricably linked in the past and present, each on a collision course with the others: Batwoman, fighting for duty and vengeance against a threat of arcane power. Detective Maggie Sawyer, investigating a case that could end her career. DEO Agent Cameron Chase, commanding a vigilante she despises. Colonel Jacob Kane, clutching at a life that's slipping away. Maro, a new villain corrupting Gotham City. And Kate Kane, wrestling with decisions that will test her loyalties." (Publisher's note)

Originally published in single magazine form in Batwoman 6-11.

Batwoman; Volume 3: World's finest. J.H. Williams III, W. Haden Blackman, writers; J.H. Williams III, artist; Trevor McCarthy, additional art; Todd Klein, letterer. DC Comics 2013 168 p. Color; Illustration

Grades: 11 12 Adult   **741.5; Fic**
   1. Women superheroes — Comic books, strips, etc.; 2. Batwoman (Fictional character)
9781401242466, $22.99; 9781401246105; 1401246109; 1401242464

                           LC 2013016902

"Batwoman's search for Medusa brings her together with the Amazing Amazon, Wonder Woman, but even the teaming of the World's Finest might not be enough to bring down the mythological monster — leading Bones, the DEO, Abbot and the Religion of Crime all descend on Gotham City to take part in the fight." (Publisher's note)

Originally published in single magazine form in Batwoman 12-17, 0.

Batwoman; Volume 4: This blood is thick. J.H. Williams III, W. Haden Blackman, writers; Trevor McCarthy, Francesco Francavilla, Walden Wong, Sandu Florea, Derek Fridolfs, artists. DC Comics 2014 160 p. Color; Illustration

Grades: 11 12 Adult   **741.5; Fic**
   1. Women superheroes — Comic books, strips, etc.; 2. Batwoman (Fictional character)
1401246214; 9781401246211, $22.99

                           LC 2013049639

"After taking down Medusa, Batwoman expected her life to get easier. Not so much when caught in the crossfire between Batman and the D.E.O., Department of Extranormal Operations. The organization has their sights set on the Dark Knight, and could be using Batwoman to capture him. But is Batman the true threat?" (Publisher's note)

Collects Batwoman #18-24

Williams, Rob

Star Wars: Rebellion Volume 1: My Brother, My Enemy. script, Rob Williams; Crossroads script, Thomas Andrews; art, Brandon Badeaux and Michel Lacombe; colors, Wil Glass; lettering, Michael Heisler; front cover art, Brandon Badeaux and Brad Anderson; back cover art, Brandon Badeaux and Wil Glass. Dark Horse Comics 2007 un Illustration

Grades: 8 9 10 11 12 Adult   **741.5; Fic**

1. Adventure graphic novels; 2. Graphic novels; 3. Science fiction graphic novels
9781593077112, $14.95; 1593077114

Having rescued Rebel strategist Jorin Sol from the Empire, Luke Skywalker now leads X-Wing attack runs on Imperial convoys to rustle up much needed supplies for the Rebel fleet. Little does he know that within Sol lies a secret that will put the entire Alliance in danger. What's worse, when Luke receives a coded message from Lt. Sunber, who wants to defect to the Rebel Alliance, he must decide whether to trust his old friend or obey the orders of Princess Leia who believes Tank may be part of an Imperial plot to capture the Rebellion's greatest hero.

Volume 1 of 3

Willingham, Bill

Day of Vengeance: Countdown to Infinite Crisis. Bill Willingham, Judd Winick; art by various. DC Comics 2005 un Illustration

Grades: 9 10 11 12 Adult   **741.5; Fic**
   1. Adventure graphic novels; 2. Graphic novels; 3. Superhero graphic novels; 4. Superman (Fictional character)
1-4012-0840-1, $12.99

Eclipso, the original spirit of vengeance, needs a new human host. The Spectre, the current spirit of vengeance, has just lost its human host and is vulnerable. When Eclipso seeks a new body, it first tries to control Superman; it takes Captain Marvel, the World's Mightiest Marvel, to stop him. Inhabiting the body of a familiar, tortured soul, Eclipso sets its sights on seducing the Spectre and destroying Earth's practitioners of magic. Seven heroes stand in their way. All very different. All with different goals at stake. And then they find an eighth, a girl who might be the most powerful teenager in the universe. Can this group, who call themselves Shadowpact, stop the angry spirits of vengeance?

Fables Vol 8: Wolves. DC Comics/Vertigo 2006 160p. Illustration

Grades: 10 11 12 Adult   **741.5; Fic**
   1. Adventure graphic novels; 2. Fantasy graphic novels; 3. Graphic novels
978-1-4012-1001-4, $17.99

Fabletown's ex-sheriff Bigby Wolf and ex-deputy mayor (and power behind King Cole's former mayoral throne) Snow White finally tie the knot in this arc from the series about the fairy-tale characters who walk among us (or, at least, New Yorkers). That can't happen before Mowgli finds missing, moping Bigby and the latter undertakes a reprisal mission against the Adversary. This eighth volume includes some violence, strong language, and nudity.

Fables Vol. 15: Rose Red. Bill Willingham, writer; Lan Medina, penciller; Steve Leialoha, Craig Hamilton, inkers; Sherilyn van Valkenburgh, colorist; Todd Klein, letterer.. Vertigo 2011 184p Color illustration

Grades: Adult   **741.5**
   1. Folklore; 2. Magic — Fiction; 3. Graphic novels
9.7814E+12

                           LC 2004540381

In this graphic novel, "[t]he next volume in the New York Times best-selling series [written by Mark Buckingham and William Willingham],...Rose Red, sister of Snow White, has finally hit rock bottom. Will she stay there, or is it time to start the long, tortuous climb back up? The Farm is in chaos, as many factions compete to fill the void of her missing leadership. And there's a big magical fight brewing down in the town square." (Publisher's note)

★ **Fables** Vol. 1: Legends in Exile. DC Comics/Vertigo 2002 128p. Illustration

Grades: 10 11 12 Adult   **741.5; Fic**
   1. Fantasy graphic novels; 2. Graphic novels; 3. Mystery graphic novels

1-56389-942-6, $9.99; 9781401237554

In Fabletown, where fairy tale legends live alongside regular New Yorkers, the question on everyone's mind is who killed Rose Red? But only the Big Bad Wolf can actually solve the case (since he's the Fabletown sheriff) — and, along with Rose's sister Snow White, keep the Fabletown community from coming apart at the seams. The book includes strong language, violence, nudity, and sexual situations.

Also available in deluxe hardcover editions; Volume 1 of a 22 volume series

Fables Vol. 2: Animal Farm. DC Comics/Vertigo 2003 128p. Illustration
Grades: 10 11 12 Adult   741.5; Fic
1. Fantasy graphic novels; 2. Graphic novels
1-4012-0077-X, $12.95

In upstate New York, the non-human Fable characters have lived for centuries on a farm, miles from mankind. But all is not well on the farm — and a conspiracy to free them from the shackles of their perceived imprisonment may lead to a war that could wrest control of the Fables community away from Snow White. Goldilocks and the Three Little Pigs inflame the farm's inhabitants with fiery revolutionary rhetoric, and both Snow White and her sister Rose Red face threats to their lives. The book includes violence and some strong language.

Fables Vol. 3: Storybook Love. DC Comics/Vertigo 2004 190p. Illustration
Grades: 10 11 12 Adult   741.5; Fic
1. Fantasy graphic novels; 2. Graphic novels
1-4012-0256-X, $14.99

In the Fables' world, there isn't a lot of happily-ever-after to go around. As refugees from the lands of make-believe, the Fables have been driven from their storybook realms and forced to blend into the mundane world. But that doesn't mean they don't have any room for romance, or the pain, betrayal, and jealous rage that go along with it. In fact, love may be blooming between two of the most hard-bitten, no-nonsense Fables around — Snow White and Bigby Wolf. Meanwhile, Bigby teams up with several other Fables to stop a reporter from publishing a story that exposes the Fables and the lives they've built in New York. The book includes violence.

Fables Vol. 5: The Mean Seasons. DC Comics/Vertigo 2005 168p. Illustration
Grades: 11 12 Adult   741.5; Fic
1. Adventure graphic novels; 2. Fantasy graphic novels; 3. Graphic novels
1-4012-0486-4, $14.99

With the Battle of Fabletown won, and the surrounding city of New York none the wiser, the Fables have gained a little time for rebuilding and reflection, in between the interrogation of the Adversary's agent and the anticipation of Snow White's impending motherhood. For Bigby Wolf, the father of the soon-to-be newborns, that means a visit with an old friend, and a reminiscence of another, even deadlier war. For the new Mayor of Fabletown, Prince Charming, it means a rude awakening to the harsh realities of civic administration, and its conflicting demands. And for Snow herself, it means a long, painful labor, and a series of joyful, heart wrenching surprises. The book includes some violence, brief sexual situations, and strong language.

Fables Vol. 6: Homelands. DC Comics/Vertigo 2005 192p. Illustration
Grades: 10 11 12 Adult   741.5; Fic
1. Adventure graphic novels; 2. Fantasy graphic novels; 3. Graphic novels
1-4012-0500-3, $14.99

The Fables have beaten back the Adversary's first advance into their world, but now they must prepare themselves for the war that is sure to follow. Jack decides to skip town and heads for Hollywood, where he becomes a sleazy movie mogul. Boy Blue appropriates some weapons and heads back to the Homelands, killing enemies as he makes his way to the heart of enemy territory. The story features some nudity and sexual situations, some strong language, and considerable violence.

Fables: Arabian Nights (And Days); Volume 7. Bill Willingham, writer; Mark Buckingham, Jim Fern, pencillers; Steve Leialoha, Jimmy Palmiotti, Andrew Pepoy, inkers; Daniel Vozzo, colorist; Todd Klein, letterer. DC Comics/Vertigo 2006 un Illustration
Grades: 10 11 12 Adult   741.5; Fic
1. Fantasy graphic novels; 2. Graphic novels
978-1-4012-1000-7, $14.99

Now that the Adversary's identity has been revealed, it's time to begin making preparations in earnest for the defense of the Fabletown stronghold. That means forging new alliances with whoever remains unconquered by the Adversary's legions. But the arrival in Fabletown of a delegation from the Arabian Homelands shows just how tricky this kind of coalition-building can be...especially when one side is concealing Weapons of Magical Destruction. This volume includes some strong language and violence.

Fairest. Bill Willingham, Matthew Sturges, writers; Phil Jimenez, Andy Lanning, Steve Sadowski, Mark Farmer, Andrew Pepoy, Shawn McManus, artists. 160 p. Color illustration
Grades: Adult   Fic; 741.5/973
1. Fairy tales — Graphic novels; 2. Comic books, strips, etc.; 3. Legends
9781401235505, $14.99
LC 2012030614

Author Bill Willingham presents a series that "explores the secret histories of Sleeping Beauty, Rapunzel, Cinderella, The Snow Queen, Thumbelina, Snow White, Rose Red and others." The book focuses on "the misadventures of Briar Rose after she is stolen away by the goblin army...And remember: They may be beautiful, but there will be blood." (Vertigo Comics)

Originally published in single magazine form in Fairest 1-7.

Robin/Batgirl: Fresh Blood. Bill Willingham, Andersen Gabrych, writers; Damion Scott, Alé Garza & Jesse Delperdang, artists; Guy Major, Wildstorm FX, colorists; Phil Balsman, Rob Leigh, letterers. DC Comics 2005 un Illustration
Grades: 9 10 11 12 Adult   741.5; Fic
1. Batgirl (Fictional character); 2. Graphic novels; 3. Robin (Fictional character); 4. Superhero graphic novels; 5. Nightwing (Fictional character)
1-4012-0433-3, $12.99

After the traumatic events of Batman: War Games, two of Gotham's youngest heroes, Robin and Batgirl, relocate to Bludhaven, where they must pick up the pieces of their lives and start anew. But before they can get fully settled in, they discover they have new threats to face, including Nightwing's enemy Shrike and their old friend the Penguin. In order to save the day, the two heroes realize there's only one thing they can do: battle each other to the death.

Robin: Days of Fire and Madness. DC Comics 2006 144p. Illustration
Grades: 9 10 11 12 Adult   741.5; Fic
1. Graphic novels; 2. Mystery graphic novels; 3. Robin (Fictional character); 4. Superhero graphic novels; 5. Robin (Fictional character)
978-1-4012-0911-7, $14.99

Recruited into a covert military team by the mysterious and powerful man known only as the Veteran, Robin realizes that he has entered an entirely new world of danger when his first assignment takes him to the Middle East where he and his new teammates engage an enemy of unimaginable horror, flesh-eating demons. Back home, the battle continues as the Teen Wonder comes face to face with the inexplicable resurrection of his former girlfriend — determined to kill Robin in order to stay with Tim Drake forever — even as the city of Bludhaven suffers an attack by the supremely powerful, supremely deadly OMACs. Can the mystical superheroes of Shadowpact save Robin and his newfound allies? Or will this be his final battle? Lots of superhero fighting and demon fighting.

Robin: To Kill a Bird. DC Comics 2006 un Illustration
Grades: 8 9 10 11 12 Adult   **741.5; Fic**
1. Graphic novels; 2. Robin (Fictional character); 3. Superhero graphic novels; 4. Robin (Fictional character)
978-1-4012-0909-4, $14.99
It's a brand-new start for Batman's sidekick, Robin: a new town (Bludhaven), a new school, new adventures and new problems.Before our hero can fully recover from the recent deaths of his father and girlfriend Spoiler, he must come face to face with his enemies: the Penguin, the Dark Rider, the Veteran, and a mysterious archer who seems to want the Boy Wonder dead. There's lots of superhero fighting action.

Wilson, G. Willow
★ **Cairo.** written by G. Willow Wilson; art by M.K. Perker; lettered by Travis Lanham. DC Comics/Vertigo 2007 160p. Illustration
Grades: 9 10 11 12 Adult   **741.5; Fic**
1. Adventure graphic novels; 2. Fantasy graphic novels; 3. Graphic novels
978-1-4012-1140-0, $24.99
A stolen hookah, a spiritual underworld, and a genie on the run change the lives of five strangers in Cairo. A drug runner, a down-on-his-luck journalist, an American expatriate, a troubled young student, and a female Israeli soldier end up all working together to help the jinn that Lebanese American Shaheed calls Shams to recover a special box from the evil magic-wielding drug lord Nar. The book includes some violence.
"Scripting and art complement each other well in an adventure with lots of appeal for readers willing to try a literary graphic novel and for those simply looking for the next good one." Booklist

★ **Ms.** Marvel; Volume 1: No Normal. writer, G. Willow Wilson; artist, Adrian Alphona. Marvel Enterprises 2014 120 p. Color; Illustration
Grades: 9 10 11 12 Adult   **741.5**
1. Female superhero comic books, strips, etc.; 2. Muslim women — Fiction
078519021X; 9780785190219, $15.99
Hugo Award: Best Graphic Story (2015)
In this comic, written by G. Willow Wilson and illustrated by Adrian Alphona, "Kamala Khan is an ordinary girl from Jersey City — until she is suddenly empowered with extraordinary gifts. But who truly is the all-new Ms. Marvel? Teenager? Muslim? Inhuman? Find out as...Kamala discovers the dangers of her newfound powers [and] she unlocks a secret behind them as well." (Publisher's note)
"Wilson's story touches on many issues bubbling up around comics today — diversity, gender, culture, sexuality — though never with a heavy hand. The story is the focus here, and together with Alphona's playful and stylish artwork, Wilson offers a superhero comic full to bursting with heart and charm." Booklist
Contains material originally published in magazine form as Ms. Marvel #1-5 and All-new Marvel now! point one #1 — Title page; Volume 1 of an ongoing series

Ms. Marvel; Volume 2: Generation Why. by G. Willow Wilson; illustrated by Jacob Wyatt and Adrian Alphona. Marvel Enterprises 2015 136 p. Color; Illustration
Grades: 9 10 11 12 Adult   **741.5**

1. Muslim women — Fiction; 2. Pakistani Americans — Fiction; 3. Teenage girls — Fiction; 4. Women superheroes; 5. Female superhero comic books, strips, etc.; 6. Wolverine (Fictional character)
0785190228; 9780785190226, $15.99
"Who is the Inventor, and what does he want with the all-new Ms. Marvel and all her friends? Maybe Wolverine can help! Kamala may be fan-girling out when her favorite (okay maybe Top Five) super hero shows up, but that won't stop her from protecting her hometown." (Publisher's note)
"Alphona's distinctive panels make great use of exaggerated angles and distorted figures, and his line work, more intricate than most comic-book artists', packs each page with captivating, tongue-in-cheek detail." Booklist
Contains material originally published in magazine form as Ms. Marvel #6-11 — Title page verso.

Ms. Marvel; Volume 3: Crushed. G. Willow Wilson; illustrated by Takeshi Miyazawa and Elmo Bondoc. Marvel Enterprises 2015 112 p. Color; Illustration
Grades: 9 10 11 12 Adult   **741.5**
1. Pakistani Americans — Comic books, strips, etc.; 2. Superhero comic books, strips, etc.; 3. Teenage girls — Comic books, strips, etc.; 4. Female superhero graphic novels; 5. Valentine's Day — Graphic novels
0785192271; 9780785192275, $15.99
"Love is in the air in Jersey City as Valentine's Day arrives! Kamala Khan may not be allowed to go to the school dance...but Ms. Marvel is! Well sort of — by crashing it attempting to capture Asgard's most annoying trickster! Yup, it's a special Valentine's Day story featuring Marvel's favorite charlatan, Loki!" (Publisher's note)
"As always, Wilson's rollicking superhero action is sprinkled with both hilarity and meaningful cultural commentary, and Kamala herself is as appealing as ever." Booklist
Contains material originally published in magazine form as Ms. Marvel #12-15 and S.H.I.E.L.D #2.

Ms. Marvel; Volume 4: Last Days. by G. Willow Wilson; illustrated by Adrian Alphona. Marvel Enterprises 2015 120 p. Color; Illustration
Grades: 9 10 11 12 Adult   **741.5; Fic**
1. Pakistani Americans — Fiction; 2. Teenage girls — Fiction; 3. Women superheroes — Comic books, strips, etc.
0785197362; 9780785197362, $17.99
"When the world is about to end, do you still keep fighting? From the moment, Kamala put on her costume, she's been challenged, but nothing has prepared her for this: the Last Days of the Marvel Universe. Fists up, let's do this, Jersey City. Plus a VERY special guest appearance fans have been clamoring for!" (Publisher's note)
"Alphona's lanky figures, fantastic use of color, and cinematic depiction of movement continue to dazzle, especially the rich diversity of characters that pack the teeming panels." Booklist
Contains material originally published in magazine form as Ms. Marvel #16-19 and Amazing Spider-Man #7-8

Ms. Marvel; Volume 5: Super Famous. G. Willow Wilson; illustrated by Takeshi Miyazawa, Adrian Alphona, Nico Leon. Marvel Enterprises 2016 144 p. Color; Illustration
Grades: 9 10 11 12 Adult   **741.5; Fic**
1. Teenage girls — Fiction; 2. Female superhero graphic novels; 3. Pakistani Americans — Fiction
0785196110; 9780785196112, $17.99
"Kamala Khan is officially an Avenger! But will being one of Earth's Mightiest Heroes be everything she imagined? Or is life as a celebrity harder than she thought? But while saving the world is important, Jersey City still needs its protector too. A development company that co-opted

Ms. Marvel's face for its project might well have more in mind for gentrification than just real estate." (Publisher's note)

Contains material originally published in magazine form as Ms. Marvel (2015) #1-6

Wilson, Sean Michael

The **book** of five rings: a graphic novel. from the book by Miyamoto Musashi; based on the translation by William Scott Wilson; adapted by Sean Michael Wilson; illustrated by Chie Kutsuwada; with an afterword by William Scott Wilson;. Shambhala 2012 160 p. Illustration

Grades: Adult

355.5\47; 355.5

Courtesy of Shambhala Publications, Inc.

1. Graphic novels; 2. Military art and science — Early works to 1800 — Comic books, strips, etc; 3. Swordplay — Japan — Early works to 1800 — Comic books, strips, etc; 4. Musashi, Miyamoto, c. 1584-1645 — Adaptations; 5. Martial arts — Graphic novels; 6. Military art and science — Graphic novels

1611800129; 9781611800128, $14.95

LC 2012023362

This "graphic adaptation of [Miyamoto] Musashi's 17th-century treatise on the martial arts makes...use of imagery to emphasize both the narrative and instructional aspects of the original text. Musashi's work is divided into five books, which address each aspect of battle: 'Earth,' 'Fire,' 'Water,' 'Wind,' and 'Emptiness.' That structure is retained here." (Publishers Weekly)

Winget, Larry

Shut up, stop whining and get a life: a kick-butt approach to a better life. Smarter Comics 2011 80p. Illustration

Grades: 10 11 12 Adult

646.7; 741.5

1. Graphic novels; 2. Self-help techniques — Graphic novels; 3. Self-improvement — Graphic novels

978-1-61066-002-0, $12.95

Larry Winget's bestselling self-help book is now a graphic novel. Self-described "Pitbull of Personal Development" Winget's approach takes aim at the usual advice found in most self-help books; he says that people need to take responsibility for their own lives, acknowledge their mistakes, learn from them, and change what they need to change in order to achieve their goals, whatever they may be. Even if one doesn't agree with everything he says, his approach is refreshing and full of common sense advice. Comics writer Bunn adapts Winget's prose, and comics illustrator Clester uses a lot of humor in the art to make Winget's points. Older teens and college students may discover that this book can truly help them.

Winick, Judd

Green Lantern: New Journey, Old Path. Judd Winick, writer; Darryl Banks, Mark Bright, Dale Eaglesham, pencillers. DC Comics 2001 192p. Illustration

Grades: 9 10 11 12 Adult

741.5; Fic

1. Graphic novels; 2. Green Lantern (Fictional character); 3. Superhero graphic novels; 4. Justice League (Fictional characters)

1-56389-729-6, $12.95

Nero, an escaped mental patient, is bequeathed a Yellow Lantern Ring by the Qwardians. Possessing the mind of a demon and the skill of an artist, he wreaks havoc in New York City and could possibly decimate the planet. With the Justice League pushed to the limit trying to contain Nero's hordes, Green Lantern Kyle Rayner stands alone against a maniac whose power could surpass his own.

Superman/Shazam/First Thunder. DC Comics 2006 128p. Illustration

Grades: 8 9 10 11 12 Adult

741.5; Fic

1. Graphic novels; 2. Shazam (Fictional character); 3. Superhero graphic novels; 4. Superman (Fictional character)

978-1-4012-0923-0, $12.99

With one word, young orphan Billy Batson transforms into a man imbued with the powers of the gods, but even one gifted with the Wisdom of Solomon can learn from a Superman. While Superman must stop members of a cult from stealing ancient artifacts from the Metropolis Natural History Museum, Billy must battle giant robots rampaging through Fawcett City. These separate events lead the heroes to cross paths, and a mighty friendship is formed as Earth's most powerful defenders team up to stop such menaces as Lex Luthor, Dr. Sivana, Eclipso, and the monstrous Lord Sabbac. There's some violence, and the climax is heartbreaking.

Winshluss

Pinocchio. Winshluss; colored by Cizo, assisted by Frederic Boniaud, Thomas Bernard, Frederic Felder. Last Gasp 2011 187p Color illustration

Grades: Adult

741.5

1. Graphic novels; 2. Robots — Graphic novels; 3. Pinocchio (Fictional character)

9780867197518; 9780861661725, $23.95

This "graphic novel[, translated from the French,]...begins with a shooting, and then flashes back to Pinocchio's creation (he is now a robot-like android) and adventures. Collodi's original story is also darker than Disney's version. [Author] Winshluss [whose name is Vincent Paronnaud] has injected politics into his story which also played a part in Collodi's original. Monstro the whale is replaced by a toxic, giant mutated fish, and there's even a subplot of a hard-boiled detective woven in.... Pinocchio was awarded the Fauve d'Or at the Festival International de la Bande Dessinée in Angoulême 2009 and best foreign comic book in Germany 2010." (Publisher's note)

Wolfman, Marv

★ **Crisis** on infinite earths. Marv Wolfman, writer; George Perez, penciller; Dick Giordano, Mike DeCarlo, Jerry Ordway, inkers; John Costanza, letterer; original covers by George Perez. DC Comics 2015 364 p. Color; Illustration

Grades: Adult

741.5

1. Science fiction comic books, strips, etc.; 2. Time — Fiction; 3. Superheroes — Fiction

1401258417; 9781401258412, $49.99; 9781563897504

LC 2012032625

This comic book, by Marv Wolfman, illustrated by George Perez, "is the story that changed the DC Universe forever. A mysterious being known as the Anti-Monitor has begun a crusade across time to bring about the end of all existence. As alternate earths are systematically destroyed, the Monitor quickly assembles a team of super-heroes from across time and space to battle his counterpart and stop the destruction." (Publisher's note)

Originally published in single magazine form as Crisis on Infinite Earths 1-12.

Homeland: The Illustrated History of the State of Israel. Nachschon Press 2007 124p. Illustration

Grades: 9 10 11 12 Adult

305.892; 741.5; 956.94

1. Graphic novels; 2. Israelis — Graphic novels; 3. Jews — Graphic novels; 4. Israel — History — Graphic novels; 5. Palestine — Graphic novels

978-0-9771507-0-0, $19.95

Using the conceit that a university professor is teaching a class, this book covers about 4,000 years of history in the Middle East, focused on Israel. It goes back to the Biblical narrative of Abram's journey from Mesopotamia, quickly progresses to the Middle Ages, explains the complicated circumstances surrounding the Zionist movement and efforts to establish the modern state of Israel, and covers the recent situations there. Readers may not be so familiar with the history of Israel and the Jews beyond the Old Testament narratives, the World War II Holocaust, and the current struggles. This book gives a concise explanation of the history which is valuable whether or not one supports Israel today.

Wolk, Douglas
 Reading comics: how graphic novels work and what they mean. Da Capo Press 2007 405p. Illustration
Grades: Adult Professional   **741.5**
 1. Graphic novels — History and criticism
 978-0-306-81509-6; 0-306-81509-5

LC 2007-05232
Suddenly, comics are everywhere: a newly matured art form, filling bookshelves with brilliant, innovative work and shaping the ideas and images of the rest of contemporary culture. In Reading Comics, critic Douglas Wolk shows us why this is and how it came to be. Wolk illuminates the most dazzling creators of modern comics — from Alan Moore to Alison Bechdel to Dave Sim to Chris Ware — and introduces a critical theory that explains where each fits into the pantheon of art. The book is accessible to the hardcore fan and the curious newcomer; it is the first book for people who want to know not just what comics are worth reading, but also the ways to think and talk and argue about them.

Wood, Brian
 Channel zero: the complete collection. Brian Wood. Dark Horse Books 2012 295 p.
Grades: Adult   **741**
 1. Science fiction — Graphic novels; 2. Dystopian graphic novels; 3. Manga
 1595829369; 9781595829368, $19.99
This graphic novel, by Brian Wood, illustrated by Becky Cloonan, collects the 1997 Channel Zero comic book series "that combined art, politics, and graphic design.... Hitting on themes of freedom of expression, hacking, cutting-edge media manipulation, and police surveillance,...[t]he Channel Zero collection contains the original series, the prequel graphic novel Jennie One...and almost fifteen years of extras, rarities, short stories, and unused art." (Publisher's note)

 DMZ Vol. 1: On the Ground. Brian Wood, writer, artist, creator; Riccardo Burchiell, artist and creator; Jared K. Fletcher, letterer. DC Comics/Vertigo 2006 128p. Illustration
Grades: 11 12 Adult   **741.5**
 1. Adventure graphic novels; 2. Graphic novels
 978-1-4012-1062-5
In the near future, America's worst nightmare has come true. With military adventurism overseas bogging down the Army and National Guard, the U.S. government mistakenly neglects the very real threat of anti-establishment militias scattered across the 50 states. Like a sleeping giant, Middle America rises up and violently pushes its way to the shining seas, coming to a standstill at the line in the sand — Manhattan. Or as the world now knows it, the DMZ. Matty Roth, a nave aspiring photojournalist, lands a dream gig following a veteran war correspondent into the heart of the DMZ. Things soon go terribly wrong, and Matty finds himself lost and alone in a world he's only seen on television. This story has lots of harsh language and violence.
 Volume 1 of 12

Woodfin, Rupert
 Introducing Aristotle, New Edition. Totem Books 2006 176p. Illustration
Grades: 10 11 12 Adult
100; 741.5
 1. Ancient philosophy — Graphic novels; 2. Graphic novels; 3. Aristotle, 384-322 B.C.
 978-1-84046-759-8, $12.95
Aristotle was named the "master of those who know." He is a foundational thinker in every field of inquiry. He established logic as a systematic discipline, conceived the earliest rules of science, developed a rational psychology, a political science and an outline of sociology, and gave us a virtue theory of ethics that is still a model today. His

Courtesy of Icon Books

contributions to metaphysics continue to permeate modern philosophy. He supplied the first theory of aesthetics, which still provides the basis of debates today. Aristotle's authority extended beyond his time to influence Islamic society and medieval scholasticism. For fifteen hundred years he remained the paradigm of knowledge itself, until scientific empiricism in the 17th century is said to have discredited his methods. Is this true? How 'scientific' is Aristotle? This volume uses cartoons and a spare text to introduce readers to Aristotle's philosophy; it includes a list of books for further reading.

 Marxism: a graphic guide. by Rupert Woodfin, illustrated by Oscar Zarate. Pgw 2018 176 p. Illustration
Grades: 10 11 12 Adult   **741.5; 335.4**
 1. Communism; 2. Marxism; 3. Marx, Karl, 1818-1883
 1785783068; 9781785783067, $17.95
 Includes bibliographical references (pages 180-183) and index
This book, by Rupert Woodfin, illustrated by Oscar Zarate, "traces the story of [Karl] Marx's original philosophy, from its roots in 19th-century European thinkers like [Georg] Hegel, to its influence on modern-day culture. It looks at Marxism's Russian disciples...who forged a ruthless, dogmatic Communism, and the alternative Marxist approaches of [Antonio] Gramsci, the Frankfurt School of critical theory and the structuralist Marxism of Althusser in the 1960s." (Publisher's note)"
 "Zarate's skillfully rendered, brushy drawings, often blended with collages of found art, ably support Woodfin's explorations of the various permutations of Marx's teachings. The comics illuminate the intricacies and fluidity of political philosophy, showing how Marx's ideology, originally forged to benefit the lower laboring classes, also provided the framework for the human rights abuses under Stalin's communist dictatorship, as well as for the intellectually rigorous Frankfurt School of critical theory." Pub Wkly

Wyld, Evie
 Everything is teeth. Evie Wyld; illustrated by Joe Sumner. Pantheon Books 2016 128 p. Illustration
Grades: 10 11 12 Adult   **B; 92; 741.5; 823/.92**
 1. Sharks — Comic books, strips, etc; 2. Women authors, English — Biography; 3. Wyld, Evie; 4. Australia — New South Wales — Comic books, strips, etc; 5. Women authors — Biography
 1101870818; 9781101870815, $24.95

LC 2015023575
This autobiographical graphic novel, by Evie Wyld and illustrated by Joe Sumner, "is a deeply moving graphic memoir about family, love, loss, and the irresistible forces that, like sharks, course through life unseen, ready to emerge at any moment." (Publisher's note)

"A rite-of-passage memoir that has powerful poetry in its ellipses."
Kirkus

Yabuki, Kentaro
   Black Cat, Volume 1. Viz Media/Shonen Jump 2006 200p. Illustration
Grades: 10 11 12 Adult   **741.5; Fic**
   1. Adventure graphic novels; 2. Graphic novels; 3. Manga; 4. Shonen
manga
978-1-4215-0605-0, $7.99
   Translated by JN Productions. Train Heartnet, known as "Black Cat,"
worked as a top assassin for a secret organization called Chronos, but quit.
Now he's a sweeper, a bounty hunter, partnered with the one-eyed Sven.
Even as Train has to deal with assassins from his past, he and Sven go after
wanted men for the bounties. Then beautiful thief Rinslet Walker proposes
that they partner with her to take down a weapons smuggler who is
developing dangerous new weapons. At first glance, Train's world is
similar to ours, but science fictional elements such as nanotechnology and
mystical elements of chi come into play as well. Sven seems to always have
a cigarette in hand, and Train seems to always find someone he has to fight,
but in the first four volumes there hasn't been any gratuitous cleavage or
panty shots.

Yagi, Norihiro
   Claymore Vol. 1. Viz Media/Shonen Jump Advanced 2006 188p.
Illustration
Grades: 10 11 12 Adult   **741.5; Fic**
   1. Fantasy graphic novels; 2. Graphic novels; 3. Horror graphic novels;
4. Manga; 5. Shonen manga
978-1-4215-0618-0, $7.99
   A Claymore — a female warrior named for the sword she carries —
travels from medieval village to village to destroy Yoma, monsters who
disguise themselves as humans and who are almost impossible to kill.
Claymores are half-humans, half-demons who willingly transformed
themselves by mixing their blood with monster's blood. Clare, nicknamed
silver-eyed killer, is such a powerful Claymore, she can slay a Yoma using
only one hand. But she must constantly struggle to keep from becoming a
monster herself. The book includes a considerable amount of
monster-slaying violence.

Yakin, Boaz
   ★ **Jerusalem:** A Family Portrait. Boaz Yakin; illustrated by Nick
Beretozzi. First Second 2013 400 p.
Grades: Adult   **741.5**
   1. Jerusalem — Graphic novels; 2. Brothers — Graphic novels
1596435755; 9781596435759, $24.99
   This comic "follows the families of two estranged Israeli
brothers-focusing primarily on the sons of those brothers-as the many wars
involving Jerusalem rage around them. They suffer life, death, and
everything in between, all while searching for their own identities within a
passionate love for the place they call home." (Publishers Weekly)

Yang, Gene Luen
   ★ **Boxers**. Gene Luen Yang; color by Lark Pien. First Second 2013
328 p.
Grades: 7 8 9 10 11 12 Adult   **741.5**
   1. China — History — Boxer Rebellion, 1899-1901 — Graphic novels;
2. Historical fiction
1596433590; 9781596433595, $18.99
                    LC 2013947229
National Book Award for Young People's Literature: Finalist (2013);
Boston Globe-Horn Book Honor: Fiction (2014); Ignatz Nominee:
Outstanding Graphic Novel (2014)

"Life in Little Bao's peaceful rural village is disrupted when...a priest
and his phalanx of soldiers...arrive." They start "smashing the village god,
appropriating property, and administering vicious beatings for no reason.
Little Bao and his older brothers train in kung fu and swordplay."...Little
Bao "becomes the leader of a peasant army, eventually marching to
Beijing." (School Library Journal)
   "China's Boxer Rebellion is the unlikely backdrop for this graphic
treatment of young villagers on the opposite sides of history. Bao wants to
drive out the white devils that poison his country with opium and
Christianity. Four-Girl is an unwanted daughter who finds purpose in the
missionary life. Their stories collide in a moment of grace that could only
be penned by the Printz Award-winning author of 'American Born
Chinese.'" LJ

   ★ **Level** up. Gene Luen Yang; [illustrated by Thien Pham].. First
Second Books 2011 160p. Illustration
Grades: 10 11 12 Adult   **741.5; Fic**
   1. Angels — Graphic novels; 2. Bildungsromans — Graphic novels; 3.
Chinese Americans — Graphic novels; 4. College students — Graphic
novels
978-1-59643-235-2, $15.99
                    LC 2010-36257
   "Pham's watercolor artwork, mostly in muted pallet, is a perfect match
for Yang's story. This gentle tale of loss and redemption, family
responsibility, and dreams might not be to all teens' tastes (especially by
the end), but the mix of fantasy and realism will please the right crowd."
Voice Youth Advocates

   ★ **Saints**. by Gene Luen Yang; color by Lark Pien. First Second 2013
170 p.
Grades: 7 8 9 10 11 12 Adult   **741.5**
   1. Historical fiction; 2. China — History — Boxer Rebellion, 1899-1901
— Graphic novels
1596436891; 9781596436893, $15.99
                    LC 2013947228
National Book Award for Young People's Literature: Finalist (2013);
Boston Globe-Horn Book Honor: Fiction (2014); Ignatz Nominee:
Outstanding Graphic Novel (2014)
   This graphic novel, by Gene Luen Yang and Lark Pien, "follows a
lonely girl .... Unwanted by her family, Four-Girl isn't even given a proper
name until she converts to Catholicism and is baptized by the very same
priest who bullies Little Bao's village. Four-Girl, now known as Vibiana,
leaves home and finds fulfillment in service to the Church, while Little Bao
roams the countryside committing acts of increasing violence as his army
grows." (School Library Journal)
   "Yang presents a 'diptych' of graphic novels set during China's Boxer
Rebellion. Boxers follows Little Bao, who learns to harness the power of
ancient gods to fight the spread of Christianity; Saints centers on Four-Girl,
who sits squarely on the other side of the rebellion. Yang's characteristic
infusions of magical realism, bursts of humor, and distinctively drawn
characters make for a compelling read." (Horn Book)

   Superman; Volume 1: Before truth. written by Gene Luen Yang; art
by John RomitaJr., Klaus Janson, Scott Hanna; color by DeanWhite, Wil
Quintana, Tomeu Morey, Leonardo Olea,Blond, Hi-Fi; letters by Rob
Leigh, Travis Lanham; collection cover art by John Romita Jr.,
KlausJanson,. DC Comics 2016 224 p. Color; Illustration
Grades: 9 10 11 12 Adult   **741.5**
   1. Superhero comic books, strips, etc.; 2. Superman (Fictional character)
9781401259815, $22.99
                    LC 2015049454
   "Superman is going through some changes. First, there's his new
'solar flare' power, which releases tremendous amounts of energy but
leaves him functionally human...for 24 hours. But an even bigger change is

coming. A new company called Hordr has sprung up, and its business is secrets. If you have one that you want to keep hidden, Hordr can control you-and no one has a bigger secret than Clark Kent." (Publisher's note)

"Yang's creative script deftly merges modern technology with super-pseudoscience, and introduces a new, intriguing character of color to the DCU." Pub Wkly

Yang, Jeff

Secret identities: the Asian American superhero anthology. Jeff Yang, Parry Shen, Keith Chow, Jerry Ma. New Press 2009 194p. Illustration
Grades: 9 10 11 12 Adult   **741.5; Fic**
  1. Asian Americans — Graphic novels; 2. Graphic novels; 3. Superhero graphic novels
978-1-59558-398-7, $21.95

LC 2009-1536

Yang, Shen, Chow, and coeditor Jerry Ma have put together a collection of twenty-six stories by Asian American creators about Asian American superheroes. The book is divided into sections: War and Remembrance, Many Masks, When Worlds Collide, Girl Power, Ordinary Heroes, and From Headline to Hero. The Preface, the Prologue, all section introductions, and the Epilogue, are all done in comic book format. Creators include Gene Luen Yang, Greg Pak, Dustin Nguyen, Kazu Kibuishi, Cliff Chiang, Christine Norrie, and many more. Some stories deal with the Nisei soldiers of the 100th Battalion/442nd Regimental Combat Team during World War II, others confront the idea that the Asian character can only be the sidekick, still others explore the stereotypical attitudes of some Americans toward Asian Americans. The book includes some violence and some harsh language.

Yazawa, Ai

Nana, Volume One. story & art by Ai Yazawa; [English adaptation, Allison Wolfe; translation, Koji Goto]. Viz Media/Shojo Beat 2006 un Illustration
Grades: 11 12 Adult   **741.5; Fic**
  1. Graphic novels; 2. Josei manga; 3. Manga; 4. Romance graphic novels; 5. Shojo manga
978-1-4215-0108-6, $8.99

Two young women, both named Nana, both the same age, but different in personalities, each want to move to Tokyo. Nana Komatsu is somewhat immature, and so far her life has revolved around men. Nana Osaki is a punk rock vocalist with an attitude to match; she wants to make her band a success. Nana K wants to be with her friends even if she failed all the college entrance exams; she also wants to become more self-reliant. The two Nanas meet on the train to Tokyo, then meet again when looking for an affordable apartment. The series includes considerable strong language and sexual situations.

Volume 1 of 21

Paradise Kiss; Volume 1. Ai Yazawa. Vertical 2012 258 p. Illustration

Grades: 11 12 Adult   **741.5; Fic**
  1. Josei manga; 2. High school students — Japan — Comic books, strips, etc.; 3. Teenage girls — Comic books, strips, etc.
1935654713; 9781935654711, $19.95

In this book, by Ai Yazawa, "Yukari is a...high school senior...studying for her college entrance exams. Sadly the prospect of subjecting herself to a meaningless dull life leaves her feeling depressed.... Yukari begins to ignore her courses and...hang out with a group of fashion design students. But what Yukari doesn't know is that this circle is known as Paradise Kiss, and they are run by...young designers already making their mark on the Asian scene." (Publisher's note)

Volume 1 of 3

Yoshida, Tatsuo

Speed Racer: Mach go go go vol. 1 & 2, 2v. by Tatsuo Yoshida; [translation: Joyce Aurino]. Digital Manga Publishing 2008 Illustration
Grades: 7 8 9 10 11 12 Adult   **741.5; Fic**
  1. Adventure graphic novels; 2. Automobile racing — Graphic novels; 3. Graphic novels; 4. Manga; 5. Shonen manga
978-1-56970-731-9, set $39.95

This two-volume set reprints the original Speed Racer manga in its entirety, released for the 40th anniversary of Speed Racer. All the characters are here: Speed, Pops, Sparky, Mom, Trixie, Spritle, Chim Chim, and the mysterious Racer X. Readers will learn how Pops had to set out on his own, how Speed became a professional racecar driver in order to help finance Pops design the special, 12 cylinder Mach 5 engine. In addition to racing, Speed has to deal with people who try to steal Pops' engine plans, rival racers who'll try any cheating tactic to win, and try to figure out who Racer X is. While the animated television series was fine for children to watch, this manga includes violent action that makes it more suitable for teen readers. A note about the title: in Japanese, "go" means "5."

Yoshinaga, Fumi

★ **Ooku:** the inner chambers. Fumi Yoshinaga. Hakusensha 2005 205 p. Illustration
Grades: Adult   **741.5/952; 741.5**
  1. Japan — History — Graphic novels
1421527472; 9781421527475, $12.99

LC 2009513893

This graphic novel, written and illustrated by Fumi Yoshinaga, is set "in Edo period Japan, [where] a strange new disease called the Red Pox has begun to prey on the country's men.... Women have taken on all the roles traditionally granted to men, even that of the Shogun. The men, precious providers of life, are carefully protected. And the most beautiful of the men are sent to serve in the Shogun's Inner Chamber." (Publisher's note)

Volume 1 of an ongoing series

What did you eat yesterday?; Volume 1. Fumi Yoshinaga. Vertical 2014 153 p. Illustration
Grades: Adult   **741.5**
  1. Cooking, Japanese — Comic books, strips, etc; 2. Gay men — Japan — Tokyo — Comic books, strips, etc; 3. Gourmets — Comic books, strips, etc; 4. Tokyo (Japan) — Fiction; 5. Seinen manga; 6. Gay men — Fiction; 7. Dining — Fiction; 8. Manga
1939130387; 9781939130389, $12.95

LC 2012474656

"A hard-working middle-aged gay couple in Tokyo come to enjoy the finer moments of life through food. After long days at work, either in the law firm or the hair salon, Shiro and Kenji will always have down time together by the dinner table, where they can discuss their troubles, hash out their feelings and enjoy delicately prepared home cooked meals!" (Publisher's note)

"Yoshinaga draws characters with simple, clean realism, exaggerating faces amusingly for emotional moments. Yet the images of food are crafted in fine-line detail, making the ingredients and textures amazingly appetizing. Between episodes, the author provides brief recipes and cooking tips." LJ

Translated from the Japanese; Originally published as: Kinou nani tabeta? in Japan; Volume 1 of an ongoing series

Young, Ethan

Nanjing: the burning city. by Ethan Young. Dark Horse Books 2015 216 p. Plate; Illustration
Grades: Adult   **741.5; 951.04**

1. Nanjing, Battle of, Nanjing, Jiangsu Sheng, China, 1937 — Comic books, strips, etc; 2. Nanking Massacre, Nanjing, Jiangsu Sheng, China, 1937 — Comic books, strips, etc; 3. Nanking Massacre, Nanjing, Jiangsu Sheng, China, 1937; 4. Graphic novels; 5. Sino-Japanese Conflict, 1937-1945; 6. Nanjing (Jiangsu Province, China) massacre, 1937
1616557524; 9781616557522, $24.99

LC 2015008366

Eisner Nominee: Best Graphic Album — New (2016)

Young "has released his most ambitious project yet: an intimate look at what's known as the Rape of Nanjing: six weeks during the Second Sino-Japanese War in 1937-38, in which Japanese troops systematically tortured, sexually assaulted, and executed hundreds of thousands of Chinese soldiers and civilians. Although records of the massacre have largely been destroyed, Young draws on the best information available to tell a fictionalized account of two Chinese soldiers attempting to escape their city. Along the way, they meet several equally desperate refugees, and their destinies become intertwined." (Publishers Weekly)

Young, Keezy
Taproot: A Story About a Gardener and a Ghost. story and art by Keezy Young; letterer: AW's Tom Napolitano; assistant editor: Hazel Newlevant; editor: Andrea Colvin. Lion Forge 2017 128 p. Illustration
Grades: 10 11 12 Adult   **741.5**
1. Ghost stories; 2. Future life — Fiction; 3. Gay men — Fiction
1941302467; 9781941302460, $10.99

In this book, by Keezy Young, "Blue is having a hard time moving on. He's in love with his best friend. He's also dead. Luckily, Hamal can see ghosts, leaving Blue free to haunt him to his heart's content. But something eerie is happening in town, leaving the local afterlife unsettled, and when Blue realizes Hamal's strange ability may be putting him in danger, Blue has to find a way to protect him, even if it means... leaving him." (Publisher's note)

"There's enough gentle spookiness to give this some edge, but at its heart, it's a beautifully illustrated love story between two brown young men, and that's a refreshing change of pace." Booklist

Youngquist, Jeff
Spider-Man: Saga of the Sandman. Marvel Entertainment 2007 176p. Illustration
Grades: 7 8 9 10 11 12 Adult   **741.5; Fic**
1. Graphic novels; 2. Spider-Man (Fictional character); 3. Superhero graphic novels; 4. Fantastic Four (Fictional characters); 5. Hulk (Fictional character)
978-0-7851-2497-9, $19.99

It was no day at the beach when criminal Flint Marko was mutated into one of Marveldom's most versatile villains. This book recounts his origins and some of the best battles between Sandman, Spider-Man, the Fantastic Four and the Hulk.

Yukimura, Makoto
Planetes Omnibus 1. by Makoto Yukimura. Random House Inc 2015 528 p.
Grades: 10 11 12 Adult
1. Space colonies — Fiction; 2. Outer space — Exploration — Fiction; 3. Science fiction graphic novels; 4. Space debris — Fiction
1616559217; 9781616559212, $19.99

In this book, by Makoto Yukimura, "It's the 2070s, and mankind has conquered space, making interplanetary travel possible and igniting the imaginations of the world. It's also vastly increased the amount of dangerous space debris, and someone has to clean it up. Hachimaki, Yuri,

and Fee are a crew on that beat, each with their own goals, tendencies, and personal problems." (Publisher's note)

Originally published in the U.S. by Tokyopop in 4 volumes; Volume 1 of 2

Vinland Saga; Volume 1. Makoto Yukimura; translation, Stephen Paul; lettering, Scott O. Brown; editing, Ben Applegate. Kodansha 2013 467 p. Illustration; Map
Grades: Adult   **741.5; Fic**
1. Revenge — Comic books, strips, etc; 2. Vikings — Comic books, strips, etc; 3. Þorfinnr Karlsefni, active 10th-11th century — Comic books, strips, etc; 4. Canute I, King of England, 995?-1035 — Comic books, strips, etc; 5. Great Britain — History — Anglo-Saxon period, 449-1066 — Comic books, strips, etc; 6. Historical fiction; 7. Vikings — Fiction; 8. Seinen manga
9781612624204, $19.99; 1612624200

LC 2014430279

"As a child, Thorfinn sat at the feet of the great Leif Ericson and thrilled to wild tales of a land far to the west.... Raised by the Vikings who murdered his family, Thorfinn became a terrifying warrior, forever seeking to kill the band's leader, Askeladd, and avenge his father." (Publisher's note)

Volume 1 of an ongoing series

Yumi, Kiiro
★ **Library** wars, vol. 1: love & war. story and art by Kiiro Yumi; original concept by Hiro Arikawa; [English translation & adaptation, Kinami Watabe]. Viz Media/Shojo Beat 2010 166p. Illustration
Grades: 9 10 11 12 Adult   **741.5; Fic**
1. Censorship — Graphic novels; 2. Graphic novels; 3. Librarians — Graphic novels; 4. Manga; 5. Shojo manga
978-1-4215-3488-6, $9.99

In Japan of the near future, the federal government passes the Media Betterment Act, and the Media Betterment Committee goes on book hunts to destroy any "unsuitable" book. The libraries strike back with the Library Defense Force, a paramilitary organization dedicated to protecting the freedom to read. Iku Kasahara started to work for libraries and wants more than anything to join the Library Defense Force; she's physically very capable, but drill instructor Sergeant Dojo doesn't seem to like her very much and pushes her very hard. Iku must improve her library skills as well as her physical skills if she's to work effectively as a soldier librarian.

This book "delivers an appealing, determined female lead in the midst of an intriguing war on censorship being waged in bookstores and libraries." SLJ

First published 2008 in Japan; Volume 1 of 14

Yun, Mi-Kyung
Bride of the water god, vol. 1. Dark Horse Comics 2007 186p. Illustration
Grades: 8 9 10 11 12 Adult   **741.5**
1. Fantasy graphic novels; 2. Graphic novels; 3. Romance graphic novels
978-1-59307-849-2, $9.95

Soah's impoverished, drought-stricken village sacrifices her to the Water God Habaek in hopes of getting rain. Instead of dying, Soah finds herself in the land of the gods, and she meets Habaek, who is a young boy. What she doesn't know (but the reader does) is that he takes the form of an adult man at night. She's supposed to be Habaek's bride, but so far she's just an outsider who doesn't belong anywhere. This is sunjeong manwha the Korean equivalent of shojo manga.

Yune, Tommy
Speed Racer & Racer X: the origins collection. IDW Publishing 2008 un Illustration

Grades: 8 9 10 11 12 Adult   741.5; Fic
1. Adventure graphic novels; 2. Automobile racing — Graphic novels; 3. Graphic novels; 4. Racer, Speed (Fictional character)
978-1-60010-211-0, $19.99

In 1999, Wildstorm Productions relaunched Speed Racer with a three-part origins story; it was successful enough to launch another three-part story telling the origins of Speed's brother, Racer X (come on, it's not a spoiler, everyone but the Racer family knows this). IDW Publishing has collected the stories into this volume. Here is the story of how Speed becomes the driver of the Mach 5, designed by Pops Racer, and here is the story of why Rex Racer left the family, how he "died," and Racer X was born from the wreckage. There is a lot of racing action, some violence, and some mild fan service.

Zahler, Thomas F.

★ **Love** and capes, vol. 1: do you want to know a secret?. story and art by Thomas F. Zahler. IDW Publishing 2008 160p. Illustration
Grades: 8 9 10 11 12 Adult
741.5; Fic
1. Graphic novels; 2. Humorous graphic novels; 3. Romance graphic novels; 4. Superhero graphic novels
978-1-60010-275-2, $19.99

Courtesy of IDW Publishing

Independent bookseller Abby falls in love with her accountant, Mark; then he confesses to her that he's the superpowered crime-fighter, the Crusader. How does one have a romantic relationship with a superhero? Even without meaning to do it, Abby gives away Mark's secret to her sister Charlotte. Oops. So begins a "heroically super situation comedy" in which Abby feels she's competing against the beautiful Amazonia (Mark's superpowered ex-girlfriend), not to mention Mark's over-protective mother, and Mark has to deal with Abby's obnoxious brother Quincy, who thinks Mark is a wimp.

Volume 1 of 4

★ **Love** and capes, vol. 2: going to the chapel. IDW Publishing 2010 192p. Illustration
Grades: 8 9 10 11 12 Adult
741.5; Fic
1. Graphic novels; 2. Humorous graphic novels; 3. Romance graphic novels; 4. Superhero graphic novels
978-1-60010-680-4, $19.99

Independent bookstore owner Abby and accountant Mark Spencer, who is also the superhero called the Crusader, have fallen deeply and completely in love. Which is wonderful, except Mark can't quite seem to figure out how to propose to Abby and almost blows it. When he gets over that hurdle, more problems crop up. For one thing, Abby wants the PERFECT wedding dress. Then, a super villain impersonates Mark and almost destroys their relationship. Abby has to find a new bookstore employee when her sister Charlotte gets the chance to go back to college in Paris, France. Abby decides she needs to understand what Mark goes through as a superhero, and she gets superpowers, and a new identity, only to learn that it's far more difficult, and tragic, than she ever imagined. And then, on the eve of the wedding, another super villain strikes, this time changing history, and only Abby has the power to put things right again, which she'll have to do if she wants to marry Mark. This story has superhero action, romance, comedy, drama, romance...the only content that might bother some people happens when Abby and Amazonia, Mark's superhero ex-girlfriend, get drunk and bond together.

Zapico, Alfonso

James Joyce: portrait of a Dubliner. Alfonso Zapico. Arcade Publishing 2016 231 p. Illustration
Grades: Adult
92; 741.5
1. Novelists, Irish — 20th century — Biography — Comic books, strips, etc; 2. Joyce, James, 1882-1941; 3. Biographical graphic novels
1628726555; 9781628726558, $22.99
LC 2016005080

Courtesy of Skyhorse Publishing

This graphic biography by Alfonso Zapico, translated by David Prendergast, profiles "James Joyce.... With evocative anecdotes and hundreds of ink-wash drawings, Alfonso Zapico invites the reader to share Joyce's journey, from his earliest days in Dublin to his life with his great love, Nora Barnacle, and their children, and his struggles and triumphs as an artist." (Publisher's note)

"Using a traditional sequential panel format, the black-and-white, ink-wash illustrations are surprisingly expressive, capturing Joyce's jocular manner and rabble-rousing with an indulgent yet objective hand. Because it reveals its subject without sensationalizing or glamorizing him, readers will close the book with a better understanding of a complex man and his influential work." Booklist

Includes bibliographical references and index; Translated from the Spanish

Zdarsky, Chip

Jughead; Volume 1. story by Chip Zdarsky; art by Erica Henderson; coloring by Andre Szymanowicz; lettering by Jack Morelli; editor, Mike Pellerito. Archie Comics 2016 168 p. Color; Illustration
Grades: 7 8 9 10 11 12 Adult   741.5; Fic
1. School stories — Graphic novels; 2. Andrews, Archie (Fictional character); 3. Jones, Jughead (Fictional character)
1627388931; 9781627388931, $19.99
Eisner Award: Best Humor Publication (2017)

"Riverdale High provides a quality education and quality hot lunches, but when one of those is tampered with, JUGHEAD JONES swears vengeance! Well, I mean, he doesn't 'swear.' This is still Archie Comics after all." (Publisher's note)

"Zdarsky captures the spirit of the well-known cast while injecting modern sensibilities through dialogue and attitude. Henderson's energetic and dynamic art connects brilliantly with the humor and pace of each chapter. The far-fetched plot befits Jughead's personality, complete with robots, pirates, and lots of food." SLJ

Volume 1 of 2

Zettwoch, Dan

Amazing Facts and Beyond. by Kevin Huizenga and Dan Zettwoch. Uncivilized Books 2013 240 p. Illustration
Grades: Adult
741
1. Curiosities and wonders; 2. Comic books, strips, etc.
0984681469; 9780984681464, $24.95
Ignatz Nominee: Outstanding Anthology or Collection (2014)

Courtesy of Uncivilized Books

This book, written by cartoonists Kevin Huizenga and Dan Zettwoch, features their comic strip character Leon Beyond. It collects the comic-strip's best and most outrageous moments." Topics covered include "the world of optilusors, Robert Skur, dance notation and grooved disc jellyfish, [and] new words and concepts [such as] winkaton or optogenerian." (Publisher's note)

Includes index.

Zimmerman, Dwight Jon

The **hammer** and the anvil: Frederick Douglass, Abraham Lincoln, and the end of slavery in America. Dwight Jon Zimmerman; illustrated by Wayne Vansant; foreword by James M. McPherson; editorial consultant, Craig Symonds. Hill and Wang 2012 ix, 150 p. Color illustration; Color; Map

Grades: 10 11 12 Adult   **973.7092; 92; 741.5**

1. African American abolitionists — Biography — Comic books, strips, etc; 2. Antislavery movements — United States — History — 19th century — Comic books, strips, etc; 3. Presidents — United States — Biography — Comic books, strips, etc; 4. Douglass, Frederick, 1818-1895 — Comic books, strips, etc; 5. Lincoln, Abraham, 1809-1865 — Comic books, strips, etc; 6. Presidents — United States — Biography; 7. Abolitionists — Biography

0809053586; 9780809053582, $24.95; 9780809053599, $15.95; 0809053594

LC 2011032361

This book presents a "graphic biography" of "Abraham Lincoln and Frederick Douglass. For both men, the book...show[s] the challenges that they faced as children, their efforts to overcome difficult circumstances, and the very real impact both men had on shaping the social and political consciousness of their times. It draws parallels between the humble circumstances of their early years...[and] look[s] at the difficulties both men faced and what motivated them." (Publishers Weekly)

Includes bibliographical references.; A novel graphic from Hill and Wang.

Zubkavich, Jim

Skullkickers: 1000 Opas and a dead body. writer/creator, Jim Zub; line art, Edwin Huang and Chris Stevens; colors, Misty Coates and Chris Stevens. Image Comics 2011 un Illustration

Grades: 9 10 11 12 Adult   **741.5; Fic**

1. Adventure graphic novels; 2. Fantasy graphic novels; 3. Graphic novels; 4. Humorous graphic novels

978-1-60706-366-7, $9.99

"Over here you've got an axe-wielding dwarf brawler, and over there you've got a gun-slinging giant, who's clearly the brains of the operation. These two nameless mercenaries witness an assassination, then take the job of recovering the royal victim's stolen corpse. An escape from town guards, a poisoning, one dream prophecy, a demon-possessed leg, and dozens of splattery battles later, and volume 1 ends with both a hard-won ale and a tantalizing cliff-hanger." (Booklist)

First published in magazine form as Skullkickers #1-5; Volume 1 of 6

Author Index

Title Index

Subject Index

AERONAUTICS — JUVENILE LITERATURE

AESOP'S FABLES — ADAPTATIONS — COMIC BOOKS, STRIPS, ETC.

AFRICA — FICTION

AFRICAN AMERICAN ABOLITIONISTS — BIOGRAPHY — COMIC BOOKS, STRIPS, ETC

AFRICAN AMERICAN AGRICULTURISTS — BIOGRAPHY — COMIC BOOKS, STRIPS, ETC. — JUVENILE LITERATURE

AFRICAN AMERICAN CIVIL RIGHTS WORKERS

AFRICAN AMERICAN COLLEGE STUDENTS — POLITICAL ACTIVITY — COMIC BOOKS, STRIPS, ETC.

AFRICAN AMERICAN COWBOYS — WEST (U.S.) — BIOGRAPHY — COMIC BOOKS, STRIPS, ETC. — JUVENILE LITERATURE

AFRICAN AMERICAN COWBOYS — WEST (U.S.) — CARTOONS AND COMICS

AFRICAN AMERICAN DANCERS — BIOGRAPHY

AFRICAN AMERICAN EDUCATORS — BIOGRAPHY — COMIC BOOKS, STRIPS, ETC. — JUVENILE LITERATURE

AFRICAN AMERICAN INVENTORS

AFRICAN AMERICAN LEGISLATORS

AFRICAN AMERICAN MUSICIANS — COMIC BOOKS, STRIPS, ETC

AFRICAN AMERICAN SCIENTISTS — BIOGRAPHY — COMIC BOOKS, STRIPS, ETC. — JUVENILE LITERATURE

AFRICAN AMERICAN WOMEN — BIOGRAPHY

COMIC BOOKS, STRIPS, ETC.

COMIC BOOKS, STRIPS, ETC.

COMIC BOOKS, STRIPS, ETC. — AUTHORSHIP

FARM LIFE — FICTION

FARM LIFE — GRAPHIC NOVELS

FASCISM — ITALY

FASHION — FICTION

FASHION DESIGN

FASHION DESIGNERS

GRAPHIC NOVELS — AUTHORSHIP

GRAPHIC NOVELS — BELGIUM

GRAPHIC NOVELS — BIBLIOGRAPHY

GRAPHIC NOVELS — CÔTE D'IVOIRE

GRAPHIC NOVELS — DRAWING

GRAPHIC NOVELS — HISTORY AND CRITICISM

GRAPHIC NOVELS — JUVENILE LITERATURE

GRAPHIC NOVELS — NORWAY

GRAPHIC NOVELS — TEACHING — AIDS AND DEVICES

GRAPHIC NOVELS — UNITED STATES

GRAPHIC NOVELS IN EDUCATION

GRAPHIC NOVELS.

GREAT BRITAIN — HISTORY — 1154-1399, PLANTAGENETS — GRAPHIC NOVELS

GREAT BRITAIN — HISTORY — 19TH CENTURY — GRAPHIC NOVELS

MANGA — AUTHORSHIP

MANGA — GRAPHIC NOVELS — JAPAN

MANGA — STUDY AND TEACHING

MYSTERY WRITERS

MYTHICAL ANIMALS — JUVENILE FICTION

MYTHOLOGY — FICTION

MYTHOLOGY — GRAPHIC NOVELS

MYTHOLOGY, GREEK — FICTION

MYTHOLOGY, GREEK — JUVENILE LITERATURE

NANCY (FICTIONAL CHARACTER)

NANJING (JIANGSU PROVINCE, CHINA) MASSACRE, 1937

NANJING, BATTLE OF, NANJING, JIANGSU SHENG, CHINA, 1937 — COMIC BOOKS, STRIPS, ETC

NANJING, BATTLE OF, NANJING, JIANGSU SHENG, CHINA, 1937 — JUVENILE LITERATURE

NANKING MASSACRE, NANJING, JIANGSU SHENG, CHINA, 1937 — COMIC BOOKS, STRIPS, ETC

NANKING MASSACRE, NANJING, JIANGSU SHENG, CHINA, 1937 — JUVENILE LITERATURE

SCIENCE FICTION WRITERS

SCIENTIFIC EXPEDITIONS — FICTION

SCIENTISTS — FICTION

SCIENTISTS — GRAPHIC NOVELS

SCIENTISTS — HISTORY

SCIENTISTS — ITALY — BIOGRAPHY

SCOTLAND — FICTION

SCOUTS AND SCOUTING — GRAPHIC NOVELS

SCOUTS AND SCOUTING — JUVENILE FICTION

SCULPTORS — FICTION

SHOPLIFTING — GRAPHIC NOVELS

SHORT STORIES

SHORT STORIES — COLLECTIONS

SHORT STORIES — GRAPHIC NOVELS

SUPERHERO GRAPHIC NOVELS

SUPERMAN (FICTITIOUS CHARACTER)

SUPERMAN (FICTITIOUS CHARACTER) — COMIC BOOKS, STRIPS, ETC.

SUPERNATURAL — FICTION

SUPERNATURAL GRAPHIC NOVELS